U.S. Import Statistics
for
Agricultural Commodities
1981-1986

U.S. Import Statistics
for
Agricultural Commodities
1981-1986

By

Kevin M. Yokoyama
Kulavit Wanitprapha
Stuart T. Nakamoto
PingSun Leung
John C. Roecklein

Transaction Books
New Brunswick (USA) and Oxford (UK)

HD
9004
U18
1988

Library of Congress Catalog Number: 88-15548
ISBN: 0-88738-236-3
Printed in the United States of America

Library of Congress Cataloging-in-Publication Data

U.S. import statistics for agricultural commodities, 1981-1986 / Kevin M. Yokoyama . . . [et al.]. p. cm.
    Includes index.
    ISBN 0-88738-236-3
    1. Produce trade--United States--Statistics. 2. Imports--United States--Statistics. I. Yokoyama, Kevin M.
HD9004.U18 1988
382'.41'097302--dc19

CONTENTS

vi

Acknowledgments

This reference work is a component of a crop-economic database under development for the Sugarlands Project (U.S. Department of Agriculture grant No. 83-CRSR-2152) designed to help identify promising alternative crops for Hawaii agriculture. U.S. Senator Daniel K. Inouye and U.S. Congressman Daniel K. Akaka were instrumental in securing funds for this project administered through the U.S. Department of Agriculture. The Hawaiian Sugar Planters' Association with the support of the Governor's Agriculture Coordinating Committee of the State of Hawaii also provided funds for the project (contract No. 86-1). Without these efforts, this work would not have been possible.

The editors are also grateful to the administration of the College of Tropical Agriculture and Human Resources, University of Hawaii at Manoa and in particular, Dr. Chauncey T.K. Ching, Director of the Hawaii Institute of Tropical Agriculture and Human Resources for assistance and support while this book was being prepared; the State Data Center of the Hawaii State Department of Business and Economic Development, and especially Sharon Nishi for arranging to provide us with U.S. import data tapes which helped make this work possible; to Beth Miller and Adele Furukawa who helped in data processing; and to Helene T. Chun and Janice S. Uehara who spent many long hours in final preparation of this endeavor.

The Editors

Kevin M. Yokoyama is a junior researcher, Department of Agricultural and Resource Economics, College of Tropical Agriculture and Human Resources, University of Hawaii.

Kulavit Wanitprapha is a computer specialist in the same department.

Stuart T. Nakamoto is an assistant professor in the same department.

PingSun Leung is an associate professor in the same department.

John C. Roecklein was a junior researcher in the same department.

Introduction

In Hawaii, as in many other states, the search for alternatives in the agricultural sector is an ongoing process. The U.S. Department of Agriculture has funded a project with the primary objective of identifying potential alternative crops for Hawaii's agricultural industry. As part of the project, a crop-economic database is under development and crops are being evaluated on the basis of the market performance of their related products. To expedite the evaluation of various crops and to enhance the crop-economic database, data tapes were obtained from the Bureau of the Census, U.S. Department of Commerce. This agency collects U.S. import statistics, which importers are required to file with Customs officials.

This reference work is a part of the crop-economic database and contains import statistics over six years (1981-1986) for agriculturally related commodities of non-animal origin. These import statistics generally reflect the flow of commodities into U.S. consumption channels. The framework was initiated by PingSun Leung and John C. Roecklein, but has been significantly modified by the other three editors.

Statistics are provided for the products of over 300 crops. When possible, products are grouped by the crop(s) from which they are known to be derived. A computer procedure was devised to aggregate data based on defined regions of unloading and modes of transportation. For each commodity, annual statistics show the quantity; the f.a.s. (free alongside ship) value; the c.i.f. (cost, insurance, and freight) value; and the import charges. Overall annual summaries are presented; data are also split by the country of origin, region of unloading, and mode of transportation to the United States.

Organization

Imported merchandise is classified as either "agricultural" or "non-agricultural" on the import data tapes and in *U.S. Foreign Trade Statistics Classifications and Cross-Classifications*, a publication of the U.S. Department of Commerce. Incorporated in this publication are statistics for all "agricultural" commodities of non-animal origin and some "non-agricultural" commodities thought to be agriculturally related, such as timber products, textiles, and chemical products.

The U.S. Department of Commerce collects data based on unique commodity descriptions and associated numerical codes as defined in detail in *Tariff Schedules of the United States Annotated (TSUSA)*. This is an official publication of the U.S. International Trade Commission; it is used to classify imported merchandise for assessment of duty and for statistical purposes. The full commodity descriptions can be quite lengthy. For this work, condensed versions of the descriptions, as contained on the import data tapes of the U.S. Department of Commerce, are presented with related statistics. Appendix C contains abbreviations for TSUSA commodities. Occasionally, these short descriptions do not include enough detail to describe the commodity completely. To provide a concise, comprehensible description of imported merchandise, similar TSUSA commodities are grouped into general product name categories in this work.

When TSUSA commodity descriptions provide enough information to identify the crop or crops from which commodities are known to be derived, data are grouped by that crop in Table 1. Reference sources listed in Appendix D were used to help identify the crop from the TSUSA description. Various dictionaries were a major reference in assigning crops to commodities. Statistics are placed in Table 2 when TSUSA commodity descriptions are too general to identify a specific crop. For this table, product name categories are grouped under defined end-use classifications.

Presentation of Data

In Table 1, import statistics are presented as follows:

1. Crop. At the broadest level, crops are listed in alphabetical order.
2. Product. Under each crop, products of that crop are listed alphabetically.
3. TSUSA commodity. Products are grouped by similar TSUSA commodity codes with associated descriptions and units of quantity. Appendix B contains abbreviations for units of quantity.
4. Annual total summaries. Statistics for each TSUSA commodity are presented on a yearly basis showing:

a. The net quantity as reported.

b. The reported f.a.s. value of commodities at the country of origin. Statistics for 1981 reflect the f.a.s. value defined as the transaction value of commodities at the foreign port of exportation. Beginning in 1982, the f.a.s. value represents the value of imports as appraised by the U.S. Customs Service. This value is generally also defined as the transaction value of commodities sold for exportation into the United States, excluding U.S. import duties, freight, insurance, and other charges of transporting the commodities to the United States.

c. The reported c.i.f. value, which consists of the f.a.s. value plus freight, insurance, and other charges, not including import duties, incurred from transporting the commodities from the country of origin to the United States.

d. The reported import charges, or the cost of all freight, insurance, and other charges, not including U.S. import duties, of bringing the agricultural commodities from the country of origin to the United States.

Following the annual total summaries, statistics are further split by:

a. Country of origin. Under each TSUSA commodity, countries where the commodity was grown or manufactured are listed alphabetically. In cases where the country of origin is undetermined, the country of shipment is listed and credited with the transaction. Appendix A lists country abbreviations.

b. Mode of transport. For each country, the reported mode of transportation, denoted as A (air), V (vessel), O (other), or N (non-differentiated), indicates how commodities arrived in the United States. (O) refers to transportation by mail, parcel post, rail, truck, or any other distinct methods of transportation. (O) includes transportation reported as rail or truck but actually sent via air or vessel to Canada or Mexico before being transshipped overland into the United States. In these cases, the country abroad, not Canada or Mexico, is listed as the country of origin. (O) also includes commodities released into U.S. consumption channels from bonded storage warehouses and from U.S. Foreign Trade Zones. In these circumstances, it was not possible to determine the mode of transportation into the United States. (N) denotes cases where statistics could not be separated into (A), (V), and (O) as defined above.

c. Region of unloading. Ports of unloading are grouped into three general regions: E (East), H (Hawaii), or W (West). The ports of unloading are where the commodities arrived in the United States. These may differ from the Customs ports of entry where commodities are cleared for release into U.S. consumption channels. However, in most cases the port of entry is within the denoted region of unloading.
   (W) includes Alaska, Arizona, California, Montana, Oregon, and Washington.
   (E) includes Alabama, Connecticut, District of Columbia, Florida, Georgia, Illinois, Louisiana, Maine, Maryland, Massachusetts, Michigan, Minnesota, Missouri, New York, North Carolina, North Dakota, Ohio, Pennsylvania, Puerto Rico, Rhode Island, South Carolina, Texas, Vermont, Virgin Islands, Virginia, and Wisconsin.

In a few cases, more than one crop is included in the TSUSA commodity description. Thus, statistics may be aggregated for commodities derived from different crops. For example, the description for numerical code **1750300** is **APRICOT AND PEACH, KERNELS**. From this description, two crops--apricot and peach--were identified, and for this work two product names were developed: *Apricot, kernel* and *Peach, kernel*. The same TSUSA commodity number and description will appear under both product names, but the data will be listed only once. To find data under these circumstances, look under the crop that is alphabetically first. Thus, for this example, statistics are located under the product *Apricot, kernel*. Under the crop **Peach** and the product *Peach, kernel*, the message *(See Apricot, kernel under Apricot)* will appear.

When a TSUSA commodity is associated with more than one crop, that TSUSA commodity code will appear under a product for all those crops, but data will be listed only under the crop listed alphabetically first. This was illustrated in the earlier example of apricots and peaches. In these cases, the symbol "**" will appear by those product names. This symbol means that at least one of the TSUSA commodities grouped under the product name is grouped under a product of at least one other crop. To identify those crops, refer to the TSUSA numbers listed in Index D.

In Table 2, general product name categories are placed under end-use classifications. Under each product are the related TSUSA numbers and commodity descriptions. These are followed by annual total summaries and more detailed data following the format in Table 1. No data is listed in either table if there were no imports for that combination of crop/end-use: product: TSUSA commodity: country: mode: region: year.

Four indices were developed to provide more information and to help locate specific statistics. Index A is an alphabetical listing of crops, their related products and the page numbers for Table 1.

Index B is an alphabetical listing of end-use categories, their related non-crop specific products, and the page numbers for Table 2. Index C lists all products defined in Table 1 and Table 2 that were exported to the United States by each country. The page number listed is the first page where the product name appears. Data under each TSUSA commodity grouped under the product must be scanned to find statistics for the country of interest.

Index D is a listing of TSUSA commodity numbers and descriptions extracted from the import data tapes and used for this publication in Table 1 or Table 2. The page number on which the TSUSA commodity and related data appear are indicated along with the crop(s) or end-use category under which each TSUSA commodity is described.

Additional Remarks

The symbols "-" and "*" will occasionally appear where numerical data otherwise would be presented. "-" means that data on the quantity of a given commodity could not be measured; "*" specifies that the quantity of the commodity was less than one but more than zero in relation to the unit of quantity indicated.

When the method of transportation is denoted by (O), the f.a.s. value sometimes equals the c.i.f. value. This occurs when overland transport of commodities originates in Canada or Mexico and when a country abroad sends commodities to Canada or Mexico for transshipment overland into the United States. Under these circumstances, import charges are not required to be reported by those countries bordering the United States.

In cases where Canada is reported as the country of origin, and commodities are sent overland into the United States, the f.a.s. value in 1981 includes costs of transporting commodities from the point of origin to the Canadian border point. Beginning in 1982, this cost of transport within Canada is generally not included in the f.a.s. value when shipment arrives overland into the United States.

Sources of Further Information Relating to Import Statistics

The *Census Catalogue and Guide 1987* lists and describes various import statistical reports published by the U.S. Department of Commerce. Further information about import statistics are available in another publication of the U.S. Department of Commerce, entitled *Guide to Foreign Trade Statistics*, which contains an explanation of how data are collected and describes the coverage of statistics and the sources of errors in compiling data, along with other detailed information relating to imports of merchandise into the United States.

Table 1

U.S. Import Statistics for Crop-Specific Commodities

by

Crop Name

Crop
Product
TSUSA commodity number, description, and unit of quantity

Country	Mode	Reg	Yr	Quantity	F.A.S.	C.I.F.	Charges

A

Abaca

Abaca, fiber, processed
3040400 ABACA FIBERS PROCESSED ETC (LB)

Country	Mode	Reg	Yr	Quantity	F.A.S.	C.I.F.	Charges
TOTAL			81	1,473,459	714,761	798,722	83,961
			82	97,251	68,242	78,936	10,694
			83	228,185	81,533	102,130	20,597
			84	357,644	63,702	86,109	22,407
			85	348,261	132,560	155,180	22,620
			86	12,078	20,457	24,582	4,125
ARGENT	V	E	84	33,069	11,250	13,098	1,848
CHINA M	A	E	85	480	818	1,218	400
	O	E	83	380	354	417	63
ECUADOR	V	E	81	1,401,858	655,224	729,901	74,677
			84	33,069	9,750	11,949	2,199
			85	261,245	100,945	112,649	11,704
JAPAN	V	E	86	1,378	1,732	1,889	157
PHIL R	A	W	85	104	501	590	89
	V	E	81	61,509	53,986	62,301	8,315
			82	97,251	68,242	78,936	10,694
			83	84,184	31,025	38,516	7,491
			85	39,738	11,050	15,550	4,500
			86	10,700	18,725	22,693	3,968
	V	W	81	10,092	5,551	6,520	969
			83	143,621	50,154	63,197	13,043
			84	49,000	14,776	19,836	5,060
			85	44,000	18,430	24,313	5,883
THAILND	V	E	84	242,506	27,926	41,226	13,300
U KING	V	E	85	2,694	816	860	44

Abaca, fiber, raw and waste
3040200 ABACA RAW AND WASTES (LTN)

Country	Mode	Reg	Yr	Quantity	F.A.S.	C.I.F.	Charges
TOTAL			81	20,262	16,866,453	20,289,939	3,423,486
			82	21,698	17,185,213	20,980,650	3,795,437
			83	15,612	11,272,090	13,725,256	2,453,166
			84	15,780	14,112,220	16,715,916	2,603,696
			85	13,916	12,493,252	15,013,118	2,519,866
			86	10,865	7,847,927	9,640,816	1,792,889
BNGLDSH	V	E	82	205	22,200	25,234	3,034
			83	54	7,061	7,141	80
			84	178	45,535	73,383	27,848
BRAZIL	V	E	85	20	6,686	8,477	1,791
CHILE	V	E	85	44	44,337	49,682	5,345
CHINA M	V	E	84	484	225,607	275,467	49,860
CHINA T	V	E	83	97	66,245	86,280	20,035
			84	42	46,334	56,151	9,817
ECUADOR	V	E	81	7,179	7,050,375	7,858,596	808,221
			82	7,650	8,104,524	9,063,643	959,119
			83	6,059	5,076,370	5,759,795	683,425
			84	5,662	4,824,848	5,433,235	608,387
			85	5,304	4,985,531	5,601,261	615,730
			86	3,965	3,807,738	4,298,081	490,343
FRANCE	V	E	84	11	65,036	68,699	3,663
HG KONG	V	E	81	18	18,897	22,342	3,445
			84	63	66,145	84,798	18,653
			85	21	5,554	11,310	5,756
INDNSIA	V	E	84	9	7,920	17,725	9,805
JAPAN	V	E	83	166	130,859	151,783	20,924
			84	21	24,678	29,903	5,225
			85	21	14,269	19,030	4,761
			86	42	19,306	28,413	9,107
KENYA	V	E	84	76	40,646	56,849	16,203
PHIL R	N	E	84	7,460	6,987,726	8,457,665	1,469,939
			85	7,550	6,601,338	8,292,876	1,691,538
	O	E	84	61	60,899	65,324	4,425
	V	E	81	10,911	8,300,567	10,484,004	2,183,437
			82	11,333	7,279,877	9,586,748	2,306,871
			83	7,187	4,694,220	6,036,495	1,342,275
			85	42	40,773	49,193	8,420
			86	5,682	3,145,431	4,226,361	1,080,930
	V	W	81	2,154	1,496,614	1,924,997	428,383
			82	2,510	1,778,612	2,305,025	526,413
			83	2,049	1,297,335	1,683,762	386,427

Country	Mode	Reg	Yr	Quantity	F.A.S.	C.I.F.	Charges
			84	1,438	1,378,898	1,724,595	345,697
			85	789	657,044	824,791	167,747
			86	839	543,076	715,015	171,939
PITCARN	V	E	86	22	13,600	16,800	3,200
SPAIN	V	E	85	79	82,298	91,916	9,618
			86	315	318,776	356,146	37,370
THAILND	V	E	84	65	16,621	24,600	7,979
			85	21	14,102	19,256	5,154
U KING	V	E	84	210	321,327	347,522	26,195
			85	25	41,320	45,326	4,006

Agalloch

Lignaloe, essential oil**
4524000 LIGNALOE OIL OR BOIS DE ROSE (LB)

Country	Mode	Reg	Yr	Quantity	F.A.S.	C.I.F.	Charges
TOTAL			81	217,629	402,663	448,844	46,181
			82	94,248	432,608	470,078	37,470
			83	141,018	1,096,972	1,196,410	99,438
			84	239,984	1,654,909	1,806,560	151,651
			85	146,062	641,110	693,737	52,627
			86	6,441	37,079	37,948	869
BRAZIL	A	E	86	221	1,700	1,711	11
	N	E	84	229,335	1,585,424	1,729,806	144,382
			85	142,827	621,336	673,389	52,053
	V	E	81	209,607	357,671	400,992	43,321
			82	52,592	308,105	339,756	31,651
			83	133,452	1,044,448	1,140,913	96,465
CHINA M	V	W	82	33,334	66,978	72,031	5,053
			84	441	2,935	3,000	65
FR GERM	A	E	84	400	4,712	4,882	170
FRANCE	A	E	82	1,900	20,513	21,267	754
			83	1,507	10,668	11,039	371
			84	2,555	19,131	21,819	2,688
	N	E	85	2,794	17,503	17,972	469
			86	1,820	15,058	15,500	442
INDNSIA	V	E	84	7,143	40,802	45,093	4,291
NETHLDS	V	E	86	4,400	20,321	20,737	416
PERU	O	E	83	6,000	40,827	43,399	2,572
	V	E	81	8,000	44,620	47,472	2,852
			82	6,400	36,640	36,641	1
SPAIN	V	E	85	441	2,271	2,376	105
SWITZLD	A	E	81	22	372	380	8
			82	22	372	383	11
			83	59	1,029	1,059	30
			84	110	1,905	1,960	55

Alfalfa

Alfalfa, seed
1260100 ALFALFA SEEDS (LB)

Country	Mode	Reg	Yr	Quantity	F.A.S.	C.I.F.	Charges
TOTAL			81	425,911	301,793	304,039	2,246
			82	1,198,203	902,358	904,538	2,180
			83	2,045,355	1,489,219	1,521,857	32,638
			84	789,079	688,935	690,791	1,856
			85	592,969	567,926	570,363	2,437
			86	834,615	823,430	840,653	17,223
AFGHAN	O	E	83	308,948	185,368	185,368	
AUSTRAL	A	E	85	26,400	27,513	28,833	1,320
	A	W	83	309	280	820	540
	V	E	86	50,600	48,481	52,623	4,142
	V	H	86	4,409	4,078	4,758	680
	V	W	82	9,200	10,651	12,040	1,389
			86	3,307	3,268	3,572	304
CANADA	N	W	84	6,744	9,388	9,568	180
	O	E	81	399,124	264,245	264,245	
			82	1,167,053	864,781	864,781	
			83	978,510	861,739	861,739	
			84	720,317	620,176	620,176	
			85	402,333	354,513	354,513	
			86	552,181	518,341	518,341	
	O	W	81	13,758	27,393	27,393	
			82	21,509	24,998	24,998	
			83	130,675	127,687	127,687	
			85	154,020	180,502	180,502	
			86	67,396	84,412	84,412	

Crop
Product
TSUSA commodity number, description, and unit of quantity

Country	Mode	Reg	Yr	Quantity	F.A.S.	C.I.F.	Charges
	V	W	84	551	1,018	1,395	377
DENMARK	A	E	83	20	427	471	44
			86	6	34,551	36,624	2,073
	V	E	86	1,271	3,920	4,165	245
FR GERM	O	E	83	22,002	23,495	23,495	
			84	22,046	23,754	23,754	
			86	4,409	5,310	5,310	
FRANCE	O	E	84	24,000	25,111	25,111	
	V	E	83	88,184	68,369	79,366	10,997
	V	W	83	44,092	42,990	47,289	4,299
ITALY	A	W	81	661	1,877	2,915	1,038
			82	440	1,008	1,724	716
			83	550	1,035	1,375	340
	V	E	83	255,365	164,711	179,818	15,107
KOR REP	V	W	85	10,216	5,398	6,515	1,117
N ZEAL	V	W	81	243	1,186	1,337	151
NETHLDS	A	W	82	1	920	995	75
	V	E	83	216,700	13,118	14,429	1,311
PAKISTN	V	E	81	1,102	621	799	178
			86	76,830	44,200	48,400	4,200
	V	W	81	11,023	6,471	7,350	879
			84	15,421	9,488	10,787	1,299
URUGUAY	V	E	86	74,206	76,869	82,448	5,579

Almond

Almond, nut, shelled
1454000 ALMONDS, SHELLED (LB)

Country	Mode	Reg	Yr	Quantity	F.A.S.	C.I.F.	Charges
TOTAL			81	41,848	87,371	92,523	5,152
			82	354,844	361,520	394,571	33,051
			83	210,632	298,244	319,522	21,278
			84	125,111	249,975	266,758	16,783
			85	215,967	226,697	250,562	23,865
			86	405,115	779,528	823,832	44,304
AUSTRAL	V	H	82	146	361	399	38
BRAZIL	V	E	81	10,000	9,200	10,530	1,330
			82	5,000	14,475	15,179	704
			83	40,000	58,000	63,729	5,729
			85	35,000	58,013	62,654	4,641
			86	162,600	403,105	418,641	15,536
CANADA	O	E	81	220	316	316	
			83	212	564	580	16
			84	2,200	2,248	2,248	
			86	10,125	9,315	9,315	
	O	W	85	2,597	2,727	2,727	
CHINA M	O	E	85	500	2,095	2,155	60
	V	E	81	5,146	9,892	10,468	576
			82	2,995	6,474	6,936	462
			83	12,772	16,995	18,327	1,332
			84	17,502	26,050	28,531	2,481
			85	9,636	12,484	13,575	1,091
			86	4,200	2,701	2,978	277
	V	H	81	164	880	954	74
			82	218	320	350	30
			84	576	910	1,027	117
	V	W	81	17,054	54,719	57,051	2,332
			82	16,124	42,727	45,257	2,530
			83	23,759	49,385	51,583	2,198
			84	26,527	48,556	51,080	2,524
			85	10,027	17,368	18,134	766
			86	7,232	14,056	14,693	637
CHINA T	V	E	83	2,359	1,100	1,217	117
	V	W	82	104	393	407	14
DENMARK	V	W	85	4,777	7,280	8,608	1,328
ETHIOP	V	E	86	404	1,157	1,192	35
FR GERM	V	E	85	965	1,177	1,345	168
	V	W	83	1,190	1,380	1,579	199
			85	10,419	23,024	28,111	5,087
			86	40,000	33,818	36,600	2,782
FRANCE	A	E	81	185	593	747	154
	N	W	85	2,205	3,615	4,453	838
	O	E	86	423	1,317	1,415	98
	V	E	81	182	366	390	24
			83	364	513	570	57
			86	9,494	13,858	15,051	1,193
	V	W	82	258	675	713	38
HG KONG	O	E	83	250	843	933	90
	V	E	82	340	1,629	1,680	51
			83	1,574	3,154	3,350	196

Crop
Product
TSUSA commodity number, description, and unit of quantity

Country	Mode	Reg	Yr	Quantity	F.A.S.	C.I.F.	Charges
			84	5,672	7,718	8,820	1,102
	V	W	81	3,160	8,010	8,410	400
			82	3,526	8,031	8,525	494
			83	3,978	9,427	10,022	595
			84	2,330	2,779	2,957	178
			85	2,100	2,514	2,698	184
			86	5,525	6,844	7,211	367
HONDURA	V	E	83	28,000	4,270	5,560	1,290
			85	64,300	9,990	11,821	1,831
			86	20,000	2,135	2,780	645
INDIA	N	E	83	73,175	114,720	120,561	5,841
	V	E	84	30,000	79,409	81,897	2,488
			86	66,300	148,258	153,037	4,779
	V	W	81	100	570	609	39
			83	320	737	823	86
ISRAEL	V	E	84	13,433	34,262	36,898	2,636
			85	1,181	3,196	3,348	152
			86	12,972	38,556	42,119	3,563
ITALY	V	E	84	1,984	4,085	4,360	275
			85	3,600	4,925	5,335	410
			86	2,044	6,170	6,444	274
JAPAN	V	E	84	110	347	376	29
	V	W	83	270	752	788	36
KENYA	O	E	84	1,250	2,824	2,824	
	V	E	82	32,500	69,000	71,500	2,500
MALAYSA	V	E	83	402	764	859	95
MEXICO	O	E	86	2,496	1,560	1,560	
	O	W	81	4,248	1,395	1,395	
			83	3,750	1,800	1,800	
			84	4,000	800	800	
MONGOLA	V	E	85	4,980	7,740	9,159	1,419
NETHLDS	A	W	86	2,205	4,750	7,122	2,372
	V	E	85	40,000	33,248	36,100	2,852
PAKISTN	N	E	82	375	700	800	100
	V	E	81	463	663	830	167
			84	1,764	1,440	1,861	421
	V	W	83	397	360	445	85
PERU	V	W	85	9,900	4,950	6,108	1,158
PORTUGL	V	E	81	926	767	823	56
			84	1,092	1,400	1,860	460
			85	2,000	5,520	5,808	288
SPAIN	A	E	86	1,653	3,848	5,340	1,492
	O	E	86	5,512	12,446	13,180	734
	V	E	82	260,519	170,048	190,519	20,471
			83	17,832	32,753	35,766	3,013
			84	16,671	37,147	41,219	4,072
			85	11,780	26,831	28,423	1,592
			86	13,982	30,834	33,305	2,471
	V	W	86	13,270	37,800	42,460	4,660
SWITZLD	V	E	82	1,000	2,124	2,188	64
TURKEY	O	E	82	21,640	26,560	28,513	1,953
	V	W	82	99	303	351	48
U KING	A	E	83	28	727	1,030	303
	V	E	82	10,000	17,700	21,254	3,554
	V	W	86	1,993	1,800	1,992	192
VENEZ	A	E	86	22,685	5,200	7,397	2,197

Almond, nut, shelled, prepared or preserved
1454100 ALMONDS BLANCHED ROASTED ETC (LB)

Country	Mode	Reg	Yr	Quantity	F.A.S.	C.I.F.	Charges
TOTAL			81	67,403	110,891	118,755	7,864
			82	44,815	74,449	81,088	6,639
			83	99,243	136,341	148,239	11,898
			84	104,128	168,607	·192,959	24,352
			85	245,761	398,005	432,487	34,482
			86	201,926	305,270	324,000	18,730
BELGIUM	V	E	84	340	303	351	48
CANADA	O	E	82	400	320	320	
			83	9,139	12,666	12,666	
			84	14,000	17,619	17,619	
			85	60,456	65,070	65,070	
			86	1,980	2,036	2,036	
CHINA M	V	E	81	2,921	4,221	4,658	437
			82	2,150	5,740	6,203	463
			83	5,350	8,414	9,107	693
			84	2,110	6,002	6,643	641
			86	3,000	4,303	4,639	336
	V	W	81	15,205	14,959	16,310	1,351
			82	1,917	1,532	1,658	126
			83	2,087	1,122	1,191	69
			84	5,328	7,543	8,078	535
			85	5,740	7,047	7,484	437

Crop Product TSUSA commodity number, description, and unit of quantity Country	Mode	Reg	Yr	Quantity	F.A.S.	C.I.F.	Charges
			86	4,770	6,340	6,652	312
CHINA T	O	E	84	300	388	388	
	V	E	84	476	355	437	82
	V	W	84	4,047	2,924	3,317	393
DENMARK	N	E	81	6,746	11,036	11,541	505
	O	E	81	661	1,170	1,291	121
	Q	W	81	12,667	22,133	23,593	1,460
			85	4,890	7,612	7,612	
	V	E	82	6,733	8,582	9,160	578
			83	11,486	13,030	14,136	1,106
			84	6,890	10,287	11,154	867
			85	4,536	5,660	6,388	728
			86	9,038	12,464	14,274	1,810
	V	W	83	2,645	3,208	3,578	370
			84	1,455	1,952	2,244	292
			85	31,360	64,503	73,501	8,998
			86	4,079	4,565	5,365	800
FR GERM	A	E	83	55	300	400	100
	N	E	82	2,222	5,621	6,262	641
	V	E	81	1,453	3,526	3,775	249
			83	12,134	18,832	19,768	936
			84	5,162	9,733	10,201	468
			85	3,336	7,257	7,706	449
			86	4,904	9,638	10,064	426
	V	W	82	1,003	1,953	2,069	116
			83	1,516	1,991	2,237	246
			84	16,403	27,823	33,272	5,449
			85	14,900	22,110	26,893	4,783
			86	4,762	4,122	5,873	1,751
FRANCE	A	E	85	565	2,718	3,257	539
			86	301	1,954	2,195	241
	A	W	86	132	1,284	1,464	180
	N	E	81	200	1,660	1,796	136
			82	1,601	4,186	4,894	708
			83	8,799	15,869	17,338	1,469
			84	778	2,270	2,908	638
	N	W	83	1,344	2,611	2,875	264
			84	4,646	9,060	10,571	1,511
	V	E	83	628	1,121	1,167	46
			84	8,457	6,095	6,630	535
			85	8,451	13,240	15,070	1,830
			86	5,154	8,451	9,315	864
	V	W	82	4,929	10,074	10,412	338
			83	301	798	850	52
			84	229	587	626	39
			85	1,322	1,970	2,113	143
			86	1,325	5,253	5,417	164
GREECE	V	E	86	371	1,161	1,224	63
HG KONG	O	E	86	3,600	3,362	3,691	329
	V	E	81	1,800	2,491	2,793	302
			82	10,506	14,634	16,087	1,453
			83	13,996	15,062	16,750	1,688
			84	1,320	1,762	1,969	207
			85	12,202	13,009	14,550	1,541
			86	11,248	12,077	13,330	1,253
	V	W	81	1,880	5,481	5,738	257
			82	3,023	3,846	4,110	264
			83	6,143	6,869	7,275	406
			84	6,240	7,199	7,721	522
			85	3,600	4,446	4,748	302
			86	26,664	37,414	39,983	2,569
ISRAEL	V	E	84	10,901	29,348	30,990	1,642
			85	11,925	26,511	27,849	1,338
			86	73,262	124,067	129,430	5,363
ITALY	A	E	85	84	1,138	1,521	383
	A	W	84	85	559	696	137
	N	E	85	1,711	5,566	6,311	745
	V	E	82	1,587	2,605	2,725	120
			83	89	262	280	18
			84	1,852	1,171	1,288	117
			85	1,096	1,832	2,080	248
JAPAN	A	W	83	119	728	1,379	651
			84	4,564	10,950	19,065	8,115
			85	2,500	5,352	10,206	4,854
	V	E	84	135	291	346	55
	V	W	85	165	1,847	1,847	
LEBANON	V	E	85	2,149	1,890	2,031	141
MOZAMBQ	V	E	85	35,000	76,776	79,875	3,099
NETHLDS	V	E	81	2,054	1,990	2,273	283
			82	992	1,372	1,503	131
	V	W	81	816	1,025	1,190	165
			82	2,502	2,625	2,915	290
			83	1,177	720	776	56
			85	1,412	1,029	1,150	121
			86	1,102	1,585	1,734	149
PHIL R	V	E	83	2,700	2,812	3,215	403
PORTUGL	A	E	85	558	2,872	2,892	20
	V	E	81	496	675	780	105
			83	13,228	16,400	18,498	2,098
			86	1,653	2,520	2,774	254
SPAIN	V	E	81	16,120	32,400	34,336	1,936
			82	1,590	3,986	4,509	523
			83	2,516	6,598	7,349	751
			84	2,854	5,243	6,765	1,522
			85	19,951	38,392	41,995	3,603
			86	2,412	8,725	9,596	871
	V	W	85	934	1,191	1,371	180
SWITZLD	O	E	81	237	536	581	45
	V	E	81	4,012	7,093	7,549	456
			82	2,593	4,793	5,066	273
			86	2,194	5,029	5,278	249
	V	W	83	2,778	4,814	5,069	255
			84	5,556	9,143	9,680	537
THAILND	V	W	82	516	885	921	36
			83	683	1,155	1,275	120
			86	10,693	17,097	17,843	746
TURKEY	V	W	82	149	399	461	62
U KING	N	E	82	402	1,296	1,813	517
	O	E	85	16,918	18,967	18,967	
			86	29,282	31,823	31,823	
	V	E	81	135	495	551	56
			83	330	959	1,060	101

Almond, nut, unshelled
1451200 ALMONDS NOT SHELLED (LB)

Country	Mode	Reg	Yr	Quantity	F.A.S.	C.I.F.	Charges
TOTAL			81	5,207	16,747	17,751	1,004
			82	558,697	330,765	376,604	45,839
			83	128,992	87,422	97,821	10,399
			84	16,728	17,338	19,108	1,770
			85	5,372	6,057	7,166	1,109
			86	280,024	148,430	173,508	25,078
ARGENT	V	W	86	125,215	91,734	102,982	11,248
BRAZIL	V	E	86	18,580	13,604	13,930	326
CANADA	O	E	81	900	2,084	2,084	
CHINA M	V	E	81	2,000	6,552	7,004	452
			82	1,000	2,146	2,232	86
			83	1,000	2,061	2,275	214
			84	840	1,786	1,998	212
	V	W	81	1,000	2,399	2,553	154
			82	1,750	4,928	5,280	352
			83	5,250	10,790	11,680	890
			84	2,534	4,701	5,016	315
CHINA T	V	W	81	100	608	620	12
			84	4,048	3,195	3,450	255
FR GERM	V	E	81	771	4,111	4,300	189
			82	276	1,188	1,248	60
			83	1,050	809	902	93
			85	331	1,261	1,321	60
FRANCE	V	E	83	528	649	681	32
	V	W	84	328	484	527	43
HG KONG	V	E	83	1,690	1,982	2,176	194
	V	W	84	720	753	809	56
INDIA	O	E	83	425	931	986	55
	V	E	82	165	843	880	37
ISRAEL	A	E	86	97,958	23,775	34,953	11,178
ITALY	V	E	84	612	1,823	2,104	281
			85	3,310	2,614	2,895	281
LEBANON	V	E	86	2,030	2,236	2,477	241
MEXICO	O	W	84	5,520	828	828	
			86	16,148	2,256	2,256	
PAKISTN	V	E	81	276	261	378	117
PORTUGL	V	E	85	1,731	2,182	2,950	768
			86	2,328	1,204	1,317	113
SPAIN	V	E	81	160	732	812	80
			82	555,506	321,660	366,964	45,304
			83	119,049	70,200	79,121	8,921
SWITZLD	V	W	86	594	1,045	1,129	84
THAILND	V	E	84	1,024	1,743	2,007	264
TURKEY	V	W	84	1,102	2,025	2,369	344
U KING	V	E	86	12,328	5,542	7,290	1,748
VENEZ	A	E	86	4,843	7,034	7,174	140

Crop Product TSUSA commodity number, description, and unit of quantity Country	Mode	Reg	Yr	Quantity	F.A.S.	C.I.F.	Charges

Almond, vegetable oil, edible
1765800 SWEET ALMOND OIL (LB)

Country	Mode	Reg	Yr	Quantity	F.A.S.	C.I.F.	Charges
TOTAL			81	12,798	19,438	22,753	3,315
			82	3,182	5,475	5,823	348
			83	3,578	7,851	8,627	776
			84	6,694	10,902	12,070	1,168
			85	3,570	9,172	9,850	678
			86	1,237	8,953	10,144	1,191
CANADA	O	E	82	1,210	402	402	
DOM REP	A	E	83	199	551	568	17
	V	E	84	270	801	864	63
FRANCE	N	E	81	1,439	7,346	7,812	466
			82	858	1,166	1,268	102
			83	743	3,140	3,480	340
	V	E	83	121	332	360	28
			84	741	3,497	3,770	273
			85	843	3,566	3,825	259
			86	270	1,085	1,168	83
	V	W	82	496	2,782	2,916	134
			85	634	1,013	1,013	
INDIA	O	E	84	265	530	577	47
	V	W	82	190	282	319	37
SPAIN	V	E	83	882	1,180	1,340	160
	V	W	81	11,023	11,475	14,254	2,779
U KING	O	E	81	336	617	687	70
			82	428	843	918	75
			83	1,633	2,648	2,879	231
			84	4,864	4,989	5,597	608
			85	888	1,751	1,935	184
			86	967	7,868	8,976	1,108
	V	E	84	254	575	690	115
			85	1,205	2,842	3,077	235
	V	W	84	300	510	572	62

Benzaldehyde
4105200 BENZALDEHYDE (LB)

Country	Mode	Reg	Yr	Quantity	F.A.S.	C.I.F.	Charges
TOTAL			81	1,760	257,620	258,631	1,011
			82	43,210	33,433	36,490	3,057
			83	295,659	142,067	155,011	12,944
			84	1,713,683	809,648	903,669	94,021
			85	468,836	233,760	263,665	29,905
			86	55,560	34,101	40,598	6,497
FR GERM	A	E	81	1,760	257,620	258,631	1,011
	A	W	85	4	2,966	4,538	1,572
	N	E	84	1,486,528	688,555	767,292	78,737
	V	E	82	2,205	3,246	3,308	62
			83	252,448	117,768	129,132	11,364
			84	40,256	18,604	21,335	2,731
			85	441,932	202,394	226,685	24,291
JAPAN	A	E	84	330	4,883	6,200	1,317
			85	1,433	2,777	3,042	265
	A	W	86	4	1,234	1,330	96
NETHLDS	V	E	82	10,141	7,080	7,822	742
			83	43,211	24,299	25,879	1,580
			84	146,885	74,169	81,891	7,722
			85	11,023	5,792	7,687	1,895
			86	55,556	32,867	39,268	6,401
SPAIN	V	E	82	30,864	23,107	25,360	2,253
			84	39,684	23,437	26,951	3,514
			85	13,228	7,981	9,371	1,390
U KING	V	E	85	1,216	11,850	12,342	492

Bitter almond, essential oil
4520200 ALMOND OIL BITTER (LB)

Country	Mode	Reg	Yr	Quantity	F.A.S.	C.I.F.	Charges
TOTAL			81	148,263	271,595	303,120	31,525
			82	157,949	251,317	273,842	22,525
			83	207,491	367,624	398,230	30,606
			84	231,347	433,514	461,334	27,820
			85	112,548	218,700	234,756	16,056
			86	9,854	33,925	35,563	1,638
CANADA	O	E	81	780	1,301	1,483	182
CHINA M	V	E	83	5,644	34,468	35,428	960
	V	W	82	1	515	529	14
DOM REP	A	E	86	614	1,440	1,529	89
FR GERM	A	W	83	90	1,787	1,814	27
	V	E	83	13,228	13,787	18,218	4,431

Country	Mode	Reg	Yr	Quantity	F.A.S.	C.I.F.	Charges
			84	1,323	2,095	2,252	157
FRANCE	N	E	81	106,858	221,324	236,901	15,577
			82	100,823	190,016	199,922	9,906
			83	146,905	251,478	267,873	16,395
			84	189,327	353,770	374,929	21,159
			85	72,437	130,882	140,085	9,203
			86	7,799	18,514	19,634	1,120
	V	E	82	4,189	5,232	5,635	403
GIBRAT	V	E	83	3,180	7,902	8,318	416
HAITI	V	E	81	2,200	2,613	2,783	170
IRELAND	A	E	82	25	700	745	45
JAPAN	A	E	83	481	2,765	4,389	1,624
NETHLDS	V	E	84	4,851	8,455	8,950	495
SPAIN	V	E	81	38,359	45,969	61,554	15,585
			82	52,911	54,854	67,011	12,157
			83	34,834	48,657	55,136	6,479
			84	33,952	67,881	73,082	5,201
			85	38,681	85,790	92,606	6,816
SWITZLD	A	E	81	66	388	399	11
			83	42	1,419	1,457	38
TRINID	A	E	84	1,894	1,313	2,121	808
U KING	A	E	86	1,441	13,971	14,400	429
	O	E	83	3,087	5,361	5,597	236
	V	E	85	1,430	2,028	2,065	37

Aloe

Aloe, natural drug**
4350500 ALOES JALAP MATE ETC, CRUDE (LB)

Country	Mode	Reg	Yr	Quantity	F.A.S.	C.I.F.	Charges
TOTAL			81	1,334,004	1,028,117	1,145,920	117,803
			82	1,473,630	937,220	1,036,533	99,313
			83	1,140,743	1,045,643	1,180,696	135,053
			84	3,324,927	1,435,328	1,717,269	281,941
			85	2,309,755	926,770	1,162,133	235,363
			86	3,173,706	1,826,440	2,202,316	375,876
AUSTRAL	A	E	86	9,279	83,773	90,560	6,787
BELGIUM	V	E	86	1,102	1,678	1,765	87
BRAZIL	V	E	81	220	1,600	1,687	87
			82	231	400	518	118
			83	624	824	1,240	416
			85	1,530	18,459	18,901	442
C RICA	A	E	81	4,671	60,439	62,991	2,552
			82	11,331	187,830	200,492	12,662
			85	5,857	35,249	40,365	5,116
	N	E	83	21,910	355,640	381,666	26,026
			84	3,948	64,483	68,084	3,601
			86	10,882	121,595	133,336	11,741
	V	E	85	1,085	20,770	21,156	386
CHILE	V	W	83	1,118	474	511	37
CHINA M	V	W	82	4,235	2,777	2,952	175
			84	125	577	653	76
DOM REP	V	E	81	92,938	20,818	26,727	5,909
			82	563,413	54,915	68,517	13,602
			83	617,358	116,385	166,792	50,407
			84	1,055,164	163,320	259,429	96,109
			85	1,241,172	135,339	216,018	80,679
			86	1,499,747	147,535	213,618	66,083
DOMINCA	V	E	86	36,444	50,819	55,096	4,277
FR GERM	A	E	82	636	18,805	19,190	385
			86	670	8,736	9,305	569
	V	E	81	3,499	5,138	6,211	1,073
			83	990	1,156	1,248	92
			84	1,091	20,958	21,272	314
			85	842	2,700	2,700	
	V	W	83	1,750	1,612	2,247	635
			84	2,159	1,899	3,291	1,392
			85	4,352	3,722	4,097	375
HAITI	V	E	84	39,783	57,704	71,380	13,676
			85	209,342	176,342	217,702	41,360
			86	162,275	87,861	106,983	19,122
HG KONG	A	W	82	309	901	1,287	386
	V	E	82	255	500	595	95
INDIA	O	E	82	132	376	383	7
			84	661	1,385	1,594	209
	V	W	83	3,296	2,556	2,928	372
INDNSIA	V	W	86	805	1,529	1,720	191
IRAN	V	E	83	661	4,123	4,260	137
			86	11,574	55,699	57,730	2,031
JAMAICA	V	E	84	117,401	45,713	52,421	6,708

Crop Product TSUSA commodity number, description, and unit of quantity Country	Mode	Reg	Yr	Quantity	F.A.S.	C.I.F.	Charges
			85	407,242	121,622	141,507	19,885
			86	372,695	123,502	141,071	17,569
KENYA	V	E	81	43,924	20,032	25,099	5,067
			82	6,637	5,347	6,007	660
			83	10,979	6,158	7,510	1,352
			84	9,605	9,934	11,640	1,706
			85	11,023	6,652	8,292	1,640
			86	11,023	5,186	6,784	1,598
MEXICO	O	E	81	265,422	26,663	26,663	
			82	251,498	22,392	22,392	
			84	935,833	93,251	93,251	
			85	44,000	3,740	3,740	
	V	E	81	4,414	10,740	11,145	405
			84	1,080	4,125	4,234	109
			85	2,204	11,727	11,962	235
N ANTIL	A	E	86	121	1,080	1,276	196
NETHLDS	V	E	81	821,495	784,195	868,545	84,350
			82	539,042	482,650	535,603	52,953
			83	416,402	352,197	397,302	45,105
			84	1,071,329	812,088	952,026	139,938
			85	325,288	269,864	336,852	66,988
			86	934,653	974,549	1,205,675	231,126
NICARAG	A	E	83	4,332	94,889	95,822	933
			84	2,786	57,564	58,834	1,270
	V	E	83	2,124	52,580	53,475	895
REP SAF	A	E	81	49	316	610	294
	O	E	81	3,596	3,691	4,941	1,250
			86	6,614	7,200	7,842	642
	V	E	81	74,132	74,004	85,527	11,523
			82	84,016	80,569	96,665	16,096
			83	58,734	56,658	65,249	8,591
			84	79,724	96,386	111,185	14,799
			85	52,518	81,584	95,743	14,159
			86	105,790	130,605	143,677	13,072
	V	W	81	19,070	20,153	25,412	5,259
S ARAB	A	E	86	12	1,900	2,010	110
SWITZLD	A	E	82	209	5,327	5,548	221
			85	3,300	39,000	43,098	4,098
TURKEY	V	E	84	2,052	856	1,098	242
U KING	A	E	84	2,185	2,085	3,852	1,767
	O	E	84	1	3,000	3,025	25
	V	E	82	2,930	70,440	70,920	480
USSR	O	E	83	465	391	446	55
	V	W	82	2,143	1,889	2,465	576
VENEZ	V	E	86	10,020	23,193	23,868	675
YUGOSLV	V	E	81	574	328	362	34
			82	6,613	2,102	2,999	897

4351000 ALOES,JALAP MANA,ETC ADVANCE (LB)

Country	Mode	Reg	Yr	Quantity	F.A.S.	C.I.F.	Charges
TOTAL			81	24,516	30,054	33,197	3,143
			82	43,115	141,790	145,820	4,030
			83	114,747	97,264	110,159	12,895
			84	813,827	295,345	354,403	59,058
			85	529,979	402,224	451,408	49,184
			86	314,972	423,957	455,641	31,684
AUSTRAL	A	H	86	9,370	51,500	53,301	1,801
BELGIUM	V	E	84	15,395	101,008	101,562	554
BRAZIL	V	E	85	125,187	67,568	79,171	11,603
C RICA	V	E	82	21,790	69,992	70,287	295
CANADA	O	E	85	78,604	183,174	184,749	1,575
	O	W	82	167	1,861	1,861	
			85	24,199	13,488	13,488	
			86	18,318	8,352	8,352	
CHINA M	V	W	84	4,780	17,725	18,974	1,249
CHINA T	V	W	86	4,320	1,692	1,986	294
DOM REP	A	E	86	2,880	1,440	3,128	1,688
	V	E	81	8,865	7,614	8,422	808
			83	33,880	13,764	16,791	3,027
			84	634,147	52,218	98,201	45,983
			85	122,190	20,000	37,272	17,272
			86	5,156	20,113	22,050	1,937
DOMINCA	V	E	84	30,000	2,400	5,002	2,602
			86	52,655	190,242	204,407	14,165
FR GERM	N	E	84	1,378	3,167	3,628	461
	N	W	83	18,319	19,679	25,804	6,125
	O	E	85	985	1,595	1,834	239
	V	E	83	402	572	672	100
			85	537	1,059	1,166	107
	V	W	81	6,966	11,790	12,453	663
			82	529	785	895	110
			86	6,295	24,672	25,750	1,078
FRANCE	A	W	84	1,323	5,179	5,999	820
HAITI	A	E	84	32	320	411	91

Country	Mode	Reg	Yr	Quantity	F.A.S.	C.I.F.	Charges
	V	E	85	72,589	29,430	33,577	4,147
			86	187,578	43,152	52,552	9,400
INDIA	O	E	83	132	325	363	38
	V	E	81	661	1,829	2,158	329
			82	601	2,168	2,424	256
			83	1,755	4,237	4,796	559
			84	860	1,824	2,152	328
			85	2,466	4,931	5,709	778
	V	W	81	1,343	3,748	4,476	728
			82	13,967	10,668	11,842	1,174
			83	1,996	1,816	2,164	348
			84	1,574	1,635	2,017	382
			85	1,981	5,503	6,070	567
			86	2,690	2,787	4,096	1,309
ITALY	A	W	84	4,117	17,900	20,530	2,630
	V	E	84	496	2,529	2,709	180
JAMAICA	V	E	85	92,715	26,262	33,287	7,025
KOR REP	V	W	86	3,800	9,616	9,850	234
MEXICO	O	E	82	1,058	431	431	
			83	42,660	1,451	1,451	
			84	97,691	27,947	27,947	
NETHLDS	A	E	85	120	1,369	1,478	109
	A	W	84	987	1,232	1,325	93
NICARAG	V	E	82	1,087	29,717	30,045	328
PAKISTN	O	E	85	1,124	2,416	2,767	351
REP SAF	A	E	86	22	1,565	1,640	75
	V	E	81	6,681	5,073	5,688	615
			83	222	365	412	47
			84	7,297	13,229	15,719	2,490
			85	3,444	8,630	9,514	884
SWITZLD	A	E	82	772	19,658	20,300	642
			83	5,514	25,319	25,730	411
			84	7,455	22,360	22,477	117
			85	203	15,168	15,514	346
			86	27,603	88,645	89,184	539
	A	W	82	739	4,857	5,609	752
			83	1,558	6,289	7,538	1,249
			85	3,635	21,631	25,812	4,181
U KING	A	E	83	3,900	3,947	4,063	116
	V	E	86	580	4,853	5,095	242
YUGOSLV	V	E	82	2,405	1,653	2,126	473
	V	W	83	4,409	19,500	20,375	875

Anise

Anise, essential oil
4520400 ANISE OIL (LB)

Country	Mode	Reg	Yr	Quantity	F.A.S.	C.I.F.	Charges
TOTAL			81	46,708	311,334	327,362	16,028
			82	77,934	246,812	259,033	12,221
			83	43,789	196,798	204,930	8,132
			84	107,413	533,140	551,757	18,617
			85	41,836	177,357	185,968	8,611
			86	49,581	215,045	222,412	7,367
CANADA	O	E	84	100	745	745	
CHINA M	N	E	83	4,886	32,722	33,785	1,063
			86	10,361	48,904	50,184	1,280
	V	E	81	4,365	49,165	49,873	708
			82	794	7,783	7,901	118
			84	74,106	387,179	399,073	11,894
			85	794	3,764	3,984	220
	V	W	81	2,646	29,061	29,516	455
			82	5,732	49,740	50,555	815
			83	2,822	19,618	20,107	489
FR GERM	V	E	83	441	3,392	3,533	141
FRANCE	N	E	82	37,453	51,418	54,089	2,671
			84	1,984	11,855	12,294	439
			85	8,158	28,247	29,811	1,564
	V	E	81	8,333	80,796	83,727	2,931
			83	4,048	14,290	14,842	552
			86	10,318	42,846	43,699	853
HAITI	V	E	81	2,000	5,088	5,419	331
			85	1,335	2,722	2,940	218
HG KONG	V	E	85	2,381	11,523	11,793	270
IRELAND	V	E	81	1,583	8,526	8,959	433
REP SAF	V	E	86	661	2,400	2,535	135
SPAIN	A	E	84	188	3,834	4,450	616
			85	227	6,838	7,734	896
			86	72	3,294	3,830	536
	A	W	85	220	2,794	3,200	406

Crop
Product
TSUSA commodity number, description, and unit of quantity

Country	Mode	Reg	Yr	Quantity	F.A.S.	C.I.F.	Charges
	N	E	81	27,781	138,698	149,868	11,170
			82	33,955	137,871	146,488	8,617
			84	31,035	129,527	135,195	5,668
			86	28,169	117,601	122,164	4,563
	V	E	83	31,592	126,776	132,663	5,887
			85	28,721	121,469	126,506	5,037

Anise, spice

1610100 ANISE (LB)

Country	Mode	Reg	Yr	Quantity	F.A.S.	C.I.F.	Charges
TOTAL			81	1,155,740	1,267,098	1,389,412	122,314
			82	1,365,808	1,631,242	1,763,177	131,935
			83	1,438,509	1,156,300	1,300,429	144,129
			84	1,895,980	1,318,464	1,526,506	208,042
			85	2,135,178	1,164,872	1,373,544	208,672
			86	1,847,168	1,274,291	1,427,375	153,084
BELGIUM	A	W	84	15,377	12,979	16,980	4,001
CANADA	O	E	81	288	344	344	
			82	660	1,020	1,020	
			83	2,080	3,325	3,325	
			84	1,900	500	500	
CHINA M	O	E	81	911	541	640	99
	O	W	81	1,375	3,057	3,307	250
			86	51	2,295	2,493	198
	V	E	81	203,639	201,510	231,949	30,439
			82	62,778	76,819	84,502	7,683
			83	154,492	152,225	169,557	17,332
			84	162,221	217,323	239,528	22,205
			85	147,672	211,776	227,257	15,481
			86	163,970	154,500	170,806	16,306
	V	H	81	2,800	5,071	5,397	326
			82	2,025	3,815	4,088	273
			83	3,170	5,541	6,091	550
			84	3,110	7,870	8,667	797
			85	1,600	3,502	3,841	339
	V	W	81	16,603	28,034	29,964	1,930
			82	60,700	72,815	81,246	8,431
			83	39,708	57,461	61,557	4,096
			84	68,622	122,690	131,720	9,030
			85	70,474	104,890	113,891	9,001
			86	31,021	36,206	38,678	2,472
CHINA T	V	E	83	11,521	14,033	15,922	1,889
			85	318	2,784	3,094	310
	V	W	82	1,000	2,154	2,354	200
COLOMB	V	E	84	43,292	17,764	24,426	6,662
ECUADOR	V	E	86	33,069	15,391	17,337	1,946
EGYPT	V	E	81	441,412	355,463	390,261	34,798
			82	263,880	252,247	275,376	23,129
			83	44,086	30,860	33,602	2,742
			84	55,112	36,543	40,415	3,872
			85	72,740	43,394	47,776	4,382
			86	279,807	136,486	147,229	10,743
	V	W	82	11,000	11,200	12,565	1,365
			86	11,020	4,740	6,305	1,565
FR GERM	O	E	81	920	1,555	1,753	198
			82	1,846	1,848	2,067	219
			83	5,165	928	960	32
			84	5,502	4,243	5,043	800
	V	E	81	330	960	1,005	45
			82	21,000	41,526	42,982	1,456
			86	2,601	1,915	2,033	118
FRANCE	O	E	83	150	531	551	20
	V	E	83	111	647	681	34
	V	W	81	11,023	14,771	16,090	1,319
			85	133	1,003	1,149	146
GERM DR	V	E	82	12,987	13,440	14,171	731
GREECE	V	E	85	5,412	1,622	2,175	553
HG KONG	V	E	81	6,600	9,697	10,316	619
			82	1,690	1,598	1,774	176
			83	39,878	39,697	45,131	5,434
			84	46,839	62,681	71,128	8,447
			85	4,625	8,838	9,515	677
			86	13,120	16,545	18,808	2,263
	V	H	81	300	598	635	37
			82	1,375	2,532	2,696	164
			83	600	1,003	1,093	90
			84	250	543	629	86
			85	1,000	2,450	2,664	214
			86	794	2,500	2,688	188
	V	W	81	1,650	2,362	2,510	148
			82	6,520	10,611	11,360	749
			83	3,717	4,773	5,150	377
			84	6,531	15,141	16,121	980
			85	4,208	5,769	6,250	481
			86	14,549	18,018	18,955	937
INDIA	V	W	81	992	582	708	126
			82	1,102	887	1,060	173
			83	551	269	329	60
INDNSIA	V	W	83	500	758	802	44
IRELAND	O	E	82	165	488	488	
ITALY	A	E	84	1,192	543	816	273
	A	W	84	551	740	890	150
	V	E	82	92	506	557	51
JAMAICA	V	E	84	22,046	25,486	27,900	2,414
JAPAN	V	W	81	5,774	10,498	11,698	1,200
			84	350	868	904	36
LEBANON	V	E	82	22,040	36,079	38,570	2,491
MALAYSA	V	H	84	600	1,753	1,901	148
MEXICO	O	E	85	9,921	1,890	1,890	
	O	W	82	631	1,566	1,566	
	V	E	82	131,293	117,594	124,221	6,627
			83	11,013	7,192	7,710	518
			84	15,483	7,024	7,915	891
NETHLDS	A	E	83	70	450	655	205
	A	W	84	22,119	15,741	22,290	6,549
	O	E	82	200	454	485	31
	V	E	86	520	1,639	1,653	14
	V	W	81	220	292	319	27
PERU	V	E	81	22,046	28,660	30,001	1,341
PORTUGL	V	E	84	165	270	299	29
SINGAPR	V	E	82	23,942	28,290	30,169	1,879
			83	28,483	28,359	30,059	1,700
SPAIN	N	E	81	395,481	560,639	604,972	44,333
			85	768,203	399,732	505,709	105,977
	O	E	84	13,934	13,910	13,910	
	V	E	81	10,790	11,246	13,185	1,939
			82	286,278	524,167	562,007	37,840
			83	503,609	477,218	543,592	66,374
			84	480,363	357,686	431,321	73,635
			86	994,848	728,733	823,951	95,218
	V	W	81	6,482	8,400	9,372	972
SWITZLD	V	W	86	1,500	1,161	1,339	178
SYRIA	V	E	81	3,307	3,042	3,253	211
			83	441	340	363	23
			84	441	491	519	28
THAILND	O	W	82	278	347	392	45
	V	E	81	375	525	576	51
			84	328	1,050	1,172	122
			86	506	1,220	1,355	135
	V	W	81	776	1,878	2,061	183
			82	2,583	6,206	6,702	496
			83	5,395	11,272	11,991	719
			84	2,984	5,915	6,408	493
			85	4,806	8,437	9,274	837
			86	948	3,078	3,193	115
TURKEY	V	E	81	21,646	17,373	19,096	1,723
			82	449,743	423,033	460,759	37,726
			83	583,769	319,418	361,308	41,890
			84	899,419	376,756	441,250	64,494
			85	1,020,256	357,949	425,439	67,490
			86	287,821	145,000	163,980	18,980
	V	W	84	26,455	10,370	12,170	1,800
			85	23,810	10,836	13,620	2,784
			86	11,023	4,864	6,572	1,708
U KING	A	W	84	794	1,584	1,684	100

Anthurium

Anthurium, fresh

1922140 ANTHURIUMS, FRESH (NO)

Country	Mode	Reg	Yr	Quantity	F.A.S.	C.I.F.	Charges
TOTAL			86	143,450	54,364	62,667	8,303
COLOMB	A	E	86	22	1,093	1,204	111
JAMAICA	A	E	86	98,745	47,949	54,625	6,676
MEXICO	A	E	86	44,000	3,040	3,447	407
THAILND	A	E	86	683	2,282	3,391	1,109

Crop
Product
TSUSA commodity number, description, and unit of quantity

Apple

Apple, dried
1461200 APPLES, DRIED (LB)

Country	Mode	Reg	Yr	Quantity	F.A.S.	C.I.F.	Charges
TOTAL			81	1,571,877	1,074,885	1,268,695	193,810
			82	2,329,307	1,928,784	2,149,745	220,961
			83	3,986,552	4,125,515	4,516,914	391,399
			84	3,303,596	2,861,252	3,194,655	333,403
			85	4,916,670	5,213,549	5,741,994	528,445
			86	4,185,849	4,358,301	4,780,749	422,448
ARGENT	V	E	81	360,002	258,273	289,204	30,931
			82	540,000	429,300	481,151	51,851
			83	373,500	328,750	363,483	34,733
			84	907,825	497,597	554,983	57,386
			85	1,066,905	797,071	894,589	97,518
			86	490,742	389,570	432,303	42,733
	V	W	81	349,238	191,700	220,776	29,076
			82	550,763	370,677	426,710	56,033
			83	1,876,356	1,479,208	1,651,755	172,547
			84	1,326,246	990,907	1,130,263	139,356
			85	1,843,247	1,227,872	1,413,644	185,772
			86	986,359	802,092	896,799	94,707
AUSTRAL	V	E	83	159	309	326	17
			84	785	1,552	1,612	60
			85	4,865	15,188	15,886	698
	V	W	82	595	1,197	1,237	40
			83	397	756	783	27
			84	595	1,171	1,207	36
BELGIUM	O	E	81	4,400	8,043	8,801	758
BRAZIL	V	E	81	80,000	57,335	64,207	6,872
			82	188,000	200,436	211,021	10,585
			83	54,000	43,200	48,379	5,179
	V	W	82	604	2,597	2,864	267
			84	3,400	3,476	3,664	188
CANADA	O	E	81	21,814	4,673	4,673	
			82	50	414	414	
			83	28,660	3,152	3,152	
			84	28,149	10,384	10,384	
			85	7,025	11,687	11,687	
			86	4,555	10,154	10,154	
	O	W	83	174	983	983	
	V	E	86	18,166	12,360	14,428	2,068
CHILE	A	E	86	1,543	1,676	2,725	1,049
	O	E	86	4,408	6,303	6,303	
	V	E	85	303,590	325,355	347,919	22,564
			86	679,784	682,837	737,318	54,481
	V	W	84	24,648	23,855	25,454	1,599
			85	282,223	299,541	346,194	46,653
			86	290,551	318,359	345,271	26,912
CHINA M	O	E	83	500	360	393	33
			84	434	715	732	17
	V	E	81	431,375	267,620	348,739	81,119
			82	254,075	172,558	204,408	31,850
			83	345,873	250,481	299,867	49,386
			84	253,084	220,659	250,621	29,962
			85	40,878	36,472	49,620	13,148
			86	883,824	581,589	638,889	57,300
	V	W	81	198,498	128,596	153,822	25,226
			82	262,153	164,375	202,123	37,748
			83	17,381	14,209	16,701	2,492
			84	74,516	74,609	87,149	12,540
			85	90,984	88,927	101,967	13,040
			86	92,865	93,320	105,235	11,915
CHINA T	N	E	84	116,939	112,619	119,437	6,818
	V	E	83	59,524	51,300	59,760	8,460
	V	W	83	59,524	42,390	51,300	8,910
			86	29,744	32,591	35,249	2,658
FR GERM	V	E	81	111,700	130,183	148,773	18,590
			82	15,157	24,299	24,804	505
			83	2,535	3,719	4,169	450
			84	41,590	70,188	75,543	5,355
			85	26,489	47,308	48,565	1,257
			86	76,058	133,053	140,624	7,571
HG KONG	V	E	83	89,418	72,154	79,719	7,565
			84	89,387	79,612	90,137	10,525
			86	89,366	85,243	98,585	13,342
ISRAEL	O	E	83	220	472	499	27
ITALY	A	E	83	198	252	557	305
			84	29,330	46,897	66,402	19,505
			85	1,609	4,818	7,460	2,642
			86	12,584	24,387	44,665	20,278
	O	E	82	15,885	26,708	29,066	2,358
	V	E	82	320	565	626	61
			83	654,506	1,143,678	1,200,619	56,941
			84	393,235	701,083	749,596	48,513
			85	1,219,311	2,325,538	2,465,591	140,053
			86	501,852	1,153,870	1,234,614	80,744
	V	W	82	268,230	438,566	464,034	25,468
			83	334,530	575,372	611,471	36,099
JAPAN	V	E	83	14,872	12,518	13,083	565
			85	25,872	23,793	28,159	4,366
	V	W	86	445	1,890	2,850	960
KOR REP	N	E	86	3,900	10,552	11,286	734
	V	E	85	3,000	8,760	9,379	619
N ZEAL	A	W	84	343	996	1,320	324
NETHLDS	V	W	83	27,885	58,378	61,347	2,969
PANAMA	A	E	83	1,006	1,360	1,802	442
PHIL R	V	E	83	22,400	9,840	11,499	1,659
REP SAF	V	E	83	8,800	9,094	9,680	586
	V	W	83	5,280	5,109	6,223	1,114
SWITZLD	O	E	81	14,850	28,462	29,700	1,238
			82	231,896	95,464	99,686	4,222
			83	8,250	15,874	16,500	626
			84	9,240	17,619	18,480	861
	V	E	82	2,183	4,225	4,465	240
			84	3,850	7,313	7,671	358
			86	14,903	14,180	18,944	4,764
TURKEY	V	E	85	672	1,219	1,334	115
VENEZ	V	E	86	4,200	4,275	4,507	232

Apple, fresh
1461000 APPLES, FRESH (LB)

Country	Mode	Reg	Yr	Quantity	F.A.S.	C.I.F.	Charges
TOTAL			81	169,076,044	35,141,100	46,247,616	11,106,274
			82	158,444,187	36,483,096	45,426,355	8,943,259
			83	216,486,148	44,261,907	56,727,355	12,465,448
			84	228,460,334	54,974,579	68,918,351	13,943,772
			85	273,601,713	62,640,974	79,156,130	16,515,156
			86	290,197,526	70,373,216	88,396,263	18,023,047
ARGENT	O	E	86	317,660	171,509	171,509	
	V	E	83	2,583,174	353,599	731,847	378,248
			84	323,428	49,705	95,493	45,788
			85	1,845,682	279,414	492,441	213,027
			86	3,985,607	874,147	1,357,935	483,788
AUSTRAL	N	E	81	1,413,472	320,392	640,367	319,975
	V	E	81	267,226	62,822	122,299	59,477
			82	85,470	36,339	53,274	16,935
			83	541,091	127,291	233,869	106,578
			85	1,771,873	522,087	868,033	345,946
			86	414,070	94,768	166,128	71,360
	V	H	84	82,880	21,885	37,814	15,929
			85	20,720	3,730	7,122	3,392
			86	42,248	6,045	12,432	6,387
	V	W	82	143,136	38,375	61,135	22,760
			83	911,101	208,392	357,587	149,195
			84	10,546	5,652	9,582	3,930
			85	1,471,054	342,842	571,917	229,075
			86	1,421,106	273,347	484,232	210,885
AUSTRIA	O	E	84	43,690	2,840	2,840	
BELGIUM	V	E	83	35,000	7,938	11,404	3,466
BERMUDA	V	W	84	155,557	29,366	44,993	15,627
BRAZIL	A	E	86	941	1,881	2,693	812
CANADA	A	H	85	39,275	13,175	18,805	5,630
	A	W	86	5,571	1,728	2,183	455
	N	E	85	10,148,118	635,727	635,727	
	N	W	85	45,156,866	11,099,632	11,099,932	300
	O	E	81	24,688,585	2,374,853	2,375,095	
			82	15,456,204	2,013,613	2,016,568	2,955
			83	28,745,643	2,462,648	2,462,648	
			84	19,185,045	2,581,213	2,581,213	
			85	20,286,756	2,256,405	2,260,958	4,553
			86	56,987,515	5,927,416	5,927,418	2
	O	W	81	58,286,637	13,056,600	13,068,095	11,495
			82	56,809,586	14,337,800	14,337,800	
			83	71,113,241	13,644,079	13,644,079	
			84	52,696,310	12,303,628	12,303,628	
			85	1,361,307	176,711	176,711	
			86	41,255,317	12,283,196	12,283,196	
	V	E	84	40,000	15,500	16,072	572
			85	37,261	9,541	12,933	3,392
CHILE	N	E	82	38,076	11,835	14,693	2,858
			86	51,208,767	8,048,213	12,732,478	4,684,265
	N	W	81	303,217	38,184	80,830	42,646

Crop
Product
TSUSA commodity number, description, and unit of quantity

Country	Mode	Reg	Yr	Quantity	F.A.S.	C.I.F.	Charges
			84	11,177,034	2,180,658	3,362,232	1,181,574
			85	680,136	102,054	182,152	80,098
	O	E	86	132,475	50,188	50,188	
	O	W	82	166,424	70,148	70,148	
			83	85,152	41,748	41,748	
	V	E	81	27,143,030	4,932,407	8,589,090	3,656,683
			82	21,862,643	3,812,310	6,700,474	2,888,164
			83	26,096,180	4,372,345	7,718,732	3,346,387
			84	47,333,920	8,890,208	13,698,903	4,808,695
			85	40,739,740	6,320,568	10,213,092	3,892,524
			86	7,032,871	1,193,520	1,818,640	625,120
	V	W	81	564,483	79,482	159,013	79,531
			82	542,539	114,336	195,361	81,025
			83	6,406,018	974,444	1,746,035	771,591
			85	7,576,295	1,067,211	1,805,848	738,637
			86	10,057,586	1,621,789	2,600,723	978,934
COLOMB	V	E	81	302,600	33,286	46,600	13,314
			82	215,400	26,011	30,608	4,597
			83	215,628	23,048	27,882	4,834
			85	7,137,980	604,527	989,228	384,701
			86	278,040	16,219	26,460	10,241
DOM REP	V	E	81	50,492	34,185	36,984	2,799
			82	944,081	197,253	237,839	40,586
			84	115,500	22,000	28,875	6,875
			86	115,743	83,090	91,180	8,090
ECUADOR	N	E	83	461,379	48,620	75,853	27,233
	V	E	85	45,138	9,935	11,310	1,375
FR GERM	A	E	85	15,828	3,180	16,064	12,884
	O	E	86	44,110	2,646	2,646	
FRANCE	O	E	81	348,200	144,293	144,293	
			82	2,357,317	920,586	920,586	
			83	2,611,250	1,034,593	1,034,593	
			84	765,480	355,410	355,410	
			85	1,626,641	684,290	684,290	
			86	944,174	409,278	409,278	
	V	E	81	6,913,173	2,649,442	3,090,087	440,645
			82	4,811,078	1,528,125	1,765,611	237,486
			83	13,838,177	3,793,957	4,963,443	1,169,486
			84	16,450,826	4,377,564	5,416,581	1,039,017
			85	35,537,567	11,702,421	13,567,919	1,865,498
			86	23,857,438	9,632,932	11,103,616	1,470,684
	V	W	81	39,043	6,186	9,320	3,134
			83	646,212	182,764	215,501	32,737
			85	256,796	115,977	143,022	27,045
GABON	O	W	86	253,194	71,424	71,424	
GUATMAL	V	E	85	30,720	3,840	6,404	2,564
			86	16,800	1,487	1,703	216
ITALY	V	E	82	239,080	119,540	174,998	55,458
			86	39,500	9,296	10,600	1,304
MALAYSA	V	W	81	9,568	7,833	8,655	822
MEXICO	O	E	84	25,344	9,792	9,792	
			85	37,200	7,673	7,673	
	O	W	82	4,320	864	864	
			85	16,128	8,064	8,064	
MOROC	O	E	82	37,800	13,894	13,894	
N ZEAL	A	E	84	2,320	3,832	5,641	1,809
	N	W	82	20,347,384	5,416,078	7,996,196	2,580,118
			83	19,740,763	5,947,717	8,761,850	2,814,133
			84	26,532,687	10,719,450	14,078,605	3,359,155
			85	35,672,536	12,682,904	17,322,730	4,639,826
			86	27,103	15,401	22,121	6,720
	O	E	84	13,524	4,410	4,410	
	V	E	81	14,590,176	3,268,035	5,586,208	2,318,173
			82	2,298,868	387,821	640,505	252,684
			83	15,267,283	4,474,521	6,739,236	2,264,715
			84	10,110,329	3,805,349	5,120,289	1,314,940
			85	24,596,010	5,430,609	7,445,422	2,014,813
			86	15,959,575	6,256,140	8,440,297	2,184,157
	V	H	81	1,403,594	308,027	524,742	216,715
			82	2,107,658	512,059	848,072	336,013
			83	1,848,682	457,578	761,812	304,234
			84	1,433,100	359,286	607,648	248,362
			85	2,266,414	558,092	946,761	388,669
			86	2,625,257	744,605	1,152,715	408,110
	V	W	81	15,734,007	3,762,759	6,112,054	2,349,295
			82	813,827	268,993	380,333	111,340
			83	809,838	250,320	345,534	95,214
			84	115,667	43,095	51,048	7,953
			85	991,980	262,817	403,047	140,230
			86	40,730,384	12,954,181	17,989,380	5,035,199
NAMIBIA	O	E	81	40,500	11,645	11,645	
	V	E	86	2,266,180	1,469,001	2,039,562	570,561
PANAMA	V	W	86	516,850	65,654	93,770	28,116
PERU	V	E	81	588,350	84,274	174,563	90,289

Crop
Product
TSUSA commodity number, description, and unit of quantity

Country	Mode	Reg	Yr	Quantity	F.A.S.	C.I.F.	Charges
REP SAF	O	E	81	2,448,175	930,638	930,729	91
			82	4,629,964	2,192,057	2,192,057	
			83	1,201,113	520,550	520,550	
			85	3,004,640	1,210,018	1,210,018	
			86	1,618,008	688,314	688,314	
	V	E	81	13,941,516	3,035,757	4,536,947	1,501,190
			82	24,533,332	4,465,059	6,775,339	2,310,280
			83	23,329,223	5,335,755	6,333,152	997,397
			84	41,847,147	9,193,736	11,087,282	1,893,546
			85	31,076,171	6,486,727	7,982,720	1,495,993
			86	28,043,436	7,405,801	8,643,442	1,237,641
SPAIN	V	E	85	154,881	40,803	65,787	24,984

Apple, juice**
1651500 APLE A PEAR JC N OV 1 PC AL (GAL)

Country	Mode	Reg	Yr	Quantity	F.A.S.	C.I.F.	Charges
TOTAL			81	81,602,668	60,256,605	68,608,339	8,351,734
			82	103,758,056	92,334,127	103,243,341	10,909,214
			83	149,294,967	112,055,555	126,626,044	14,570,489
			84	167,860,378	122,275,702	138,432,214	16,156,512
			85	214,440,701	136,948,704	157,644,813	20,696,109
			86	227,524,004	192,144,939	211,588,473	19,443,534
ALGERIA	V	E	86	113,680	67,572	76,223	8,651
ANTIGUA	V	E	86	6,840	32,787	38,495	5,708
	V	W	85	23,954	11,064	14,154	3,090
ARGENT	N	E	86	2,103,170	1,739,885	1,974,148	234,263
	N	W	84	9,826,865	5,042,172	5,902,990	860,818
	O	E	83	28,675	40,413	40,413	
			84	10,260	40,799	45,862	5,063
			85	3,190	11,171	11,171	
			86	48,539	39,857	41,868	2,011
	V	E	81	35,096,125	23,290,804	27,179,827	3,889,023
			82	31,204,586	27,896,485	31,892,986	3,996,501
			83	29,473,479	20,658,919	24,521,849	3,862,930
			84	31,673,628	20,228,178	23,931,552	3,703,374
			85	28,073,918	16,548,669	20,125,102	3,576,433
			86	17,941,208	14,678,219	16,798,870	2,120,651
	V	W	81	5,474,074	3,930,416	4,565,531	635,115
			82	10,742,064	8,354,322	9,540,158	1,185,836
			83	7,318,425	4,240,488	5,089,696	849,208
			84	5,602,764	3,307,570	4,003,635	696,065
			85	20,866,998	10,723,455	13,487,626	2,764,171
			86	9,803,868	8,129,508	9,458,828	1,329,320
AUSTRAL	A	H	83	324	463	1,047	584
	N	W	86	106,496	79,213	93,861	14,648
	O	E	84	4,104	17,906	17,906	
	O	W	83	13,200	41,975	48,695	6,720
	V	E	82	132,620	103,134	113,983	10,849
			83	26,460	19,261	20,516	1,255
			84	22,966	14,941	16,903	1,962
			85	2,433,993	1,363,453	1,500,831	137,378
			86	1,120,798	2,460,414	2,710,909	250,495
	V	W	81	52,416	39,387	41,232	1,845
			82	42,900	35,500	41,524	6,024
			83	25,970	16,816	18,837	2,021
			84	258,518	81,558	103,093	21,535
			85	657,335	196,131	237,858	41,727
			86	535,340	574,534	632,618	58,084
AUSTRIA	N	E	83	6,533,971	5,216,304	5,616,225	399,921
			84	2,237,403	1,528,136	1,680,216	152,080
			85	4,053,245	2,451,053	2,703,001	251,948
			86	6,335,979	5,089,382	5,535,706	446,324
	N	W	84	487,229	272,440	319,813	47,373
			86	2,276,099	1,883,560	2,028,552	144,992
	O	E	82	471,551	339,794	375,452	35,658
			83	713,709	961,472	1,074,152	112,680
			84	3,981,991	3,781,550	4,085,849	304,299
			85	4,437,143	3,406,557	3,637,035	230,478
			86	4,193,758	3,730,366	3,977,760	247,394
	V	E	81	535,626	388,994	435,419	46,425
			82	3,166,388	3,066,755	3,348,258	281,503
			83	3,450,069	2,404,537	2,622,979	218,442
			84	9,296,822	8,019,277	8,843,339	824,062
			85	13,280,512	9,835,506	10,864,116	1,028,610
			86	9,243,672	9,107,880	9,986,102	878,222
	V	W	81	334,454	209,454	220,256	10,802
			82	138,750	115,494	123,544	8,050
			83	2,638,308	1,740,252	1,954,937	214,685
			84	1,598,455	1,287,460	1,461,847	174,387
			85	3,945,316	2,347,834	2,678,278	330,444
			86	1,586,535	1,134,829	1,265,681	130,852
BAHRAIN	V	E	85	65,800	39,001	44,659	5,658

Crop
Product
TSUSA commodity number, description, and unit of quantity

Country	Mode	Reg	Yr	Quantity	F.A.S.	C.I.F.	Charges
BELGIUM	N	E	82	44,408	42,541	45,394	2,853
			86	1,961,003	1,782,052	1,948,373	166,321
	N	W	86	3,447,333	3,069,387	3,162,647	93,260
	O	E	83	3,587	20,267	21,522	1,255
			84	780	2,468	2,933	465
			85	697	1,760	1,774	14
			86	3,740,200	2,943,893	3,189,793	245,900
	O	W	86	134,355	133,322	148,322	15,000
	V	E	82	135,542	113,442	121,013	7,571
			83	297,694	385,610	415,892	30,282
			84	248,456	167,422	189,253	21,831
			85	243,691	182,650	204,537	21,887
			86	11,235,931	9,925,886	10,803,059	877,173
	V	W	86	4,051,024	3,330,109	3,624,902	294,793
BRAZIL	O	E	82	7,022	6,682	6,682	
	V	E	81	117,705	65,283	78,112	12,829
			82	213,420	209,402	232,542	23,140
			83	241,740	162,377	174,269	11,892
			84	116,178	72,309	85,370	13,061
			85	561,805	233,836	284,939	51,103
	V	W	84	478,002	187,846	243,493	55,647
BURKINA	V	E	86	107,324	85,861	90,861	5,000
CANADA	A	E	84	110	398	447	49
	A	H	82	314	786	1,127	341
			84	471	1,011	1,511	500
			85	834	2,965	3,702	737
	A	W	81	562	1,728	3,940	2,212
	N	E	81	460	2,196	3,302	1,106
			84	27,188	18,863	21,560	2,697
			86	1,395,981	1,765,888	1,768,288	2,400
	O	E	81	1,331,778	1,161,058	1,162,452	1,394
			82	1,269,715	1,545,858	1,550,140	4,282
			83	1,830,660	2,011,300	2,015,727	4,427
			84	2,267,032	2,438,376	2,449,951	11,575
			85	1,969,492	1,812,260	1,820,462	8,202
			86	2,343,463	2,256,796	2,257,171	375
	O	W	81	85,418	237,870	237,870	
			82	53,220	199,640	199,640	
			83	72,532	224,300	224,300	
			84	58,337	132,129	132,129	
			85	5,029	17,740	17,740	
	V	E	83	22,308	19,871	21,990	2,119
			84	26,950	16,230	19,074	2,844
CHILE	O	E	82	28,050	26,435	26,435	
			85	25,025	16,791	16,791	
	V	E	81	1,575,513	1,174,022	1,283,555	109,533
			82	1,573,500	1,930,301	2,068,709	138,408
			83	3,578,551	2,960,884	3,164,387	203,503
			84	2,483,769	1,987,143	2,165,066	177,923
			85	5,789,132	3,183,087	3,629,493	446,406
			86	7,684,919	7,184,785	7,694,023	509,238
	V	W	81	576,494	331,515	387,471	55,956
			82	21,822	126,047	143,658	17,611
			83	894,082	291,633	332,366	40,733
			84	1,885,936	1,149,920	1,300,444	150,524
			85	621,698	334,553	388,895	54,342
			86	2,897,274	2,613,491	2,869,220	255,729
CHINA M	V	E	84	123,383	67,527	79,681	12,154
			85	392,280	180,226	197,849	17,623
	V	W	84	500	1,292	1,348	56
CHINA T	V	W	85	274,890	115,374	148,832	33,458
DENMARK	O	E	84	3,328	17,425	18,636	1,211
			85	862	2,448	2,826	378
	V	E	82	128,637	134,946	150,560	15,614
			83	527,570	402,248	459,925	57,677
			84	27,757	21,972	23,931	1,959
			85	193,870	105,606	121,310	15,704
			86	266,392	177,911	196,746	18,835
	V	W	83	316,280	211,435	237,438	26,003
			84	150,137	110,352	125,488	15,136
			85	212,330	121,546	135,765	14,219
			86	22,896	102,927	113,794	10,867
ECUADOR	V	E	86	4,414	9,289	11,704	2,415
	V	W	86	7,260	44,387	45,375	988
FR GERM	A	E	81	1,151	5,454	6,313	859
			84	125	406	1,234	828
	N	E	81	2,129,838	1,357,086	1,559,892	202,806
			86	7,336,538	5,189,899	5,869,731	679,832
			84	2,445,866	1,839,627	2,018,909	179,282
			85	5,424,340	3,302,494	3,651,267	348,773
			86	2,467,249	2,987,255	3,362,935	375,680
	N	W	85	4,956,634	2,477,500	2,925,147	447,647
			86	4,434,517	3,286,399	3,656,588	370,189
	O	E	83	3,432	17,482	17,482	
			84	239,198	234,964	257,456	22,492
			85	1,746,283	1,021,997	1,118,444	96,447
			86	1,327,371	1,099,326	1,153,431	54,105
	V	E	81	3,967,576	3,387,807	3,964,597	576,790
			82	13,981,612	12,147,744	13,820,506	1,672,762
			83	24,471,300	18,672,936	21,323,702	2,650,766
			84	30,650,563	23,247,439	25,831,213	2,583,774
			85	38,528,708	26,381,706	29,748,145	3,366,439
			86	42,548,926	35,207,545	38,198,088	2,990,543
	V	H	86	1,490	5,831	7,552	1,721
	V	W	81	602,233	414,164	487,278	73,114
			82	286,784	369,716	417,958	48,242
			83	7,922,278	5,770,941	6,462,638	691,697
			84	1,994,512	1,697,121	1,872,233	175,112
			85	1,089,812	684,104	774,771	90,667
			86	5,890,686	4,802,780	5,306,390	503,610
FRANCE	N	E	83	1,983,948	811,767	872,463	60,696
			84	4,291	12,738	17,794	5,056
			85	2,661,440	1,630,447	1,890,188	259,741
			86	1,068,616	860,029	988,127	128,098
	N	W	86	179,712	149,320	162,640	13,320
	O	E	81	232,978	275,894	294,225	18,331
			84	6,256	21,833	23,485	1,652
			85	78,610	21,132	26,132	5,000
			86	1,261,972	893,495	1,013,353	119,858
	O	W	86	455	2,003	2,120	117
	V	E	81	1,258,673	1,170,484	1,282,670	112,186
			82	1,416,658	1,958,223	2,094,301	136,078
			83	1,862,290	1,414,807	1,551,959	137,152
			84	804,759	840,953	959,515	118,562
			85	505,214	679,666	827,473	147,807
			86	894,643	1,163,352	1,335,405	172,053
	V	W	82	531,724	360,829	401,350	40,521
			83	1,918,654	1,323,360	1,449,190	125,830
			84	27,032	84,882	108,143	23,261
			85	72,668	276,538	350,090	73,552
			86	125,329	225,278	267,400	42,122
GERM DR	V	E	82	15,630	23,728	25,350	1,622
			83	57,334	147,048	158,336	11,288
GREECE	V	E	85	207,877	121,766	140,716	18,950
GUATMAL	V	E	85	825	1,825	2,069	244
			86	1,513	2,470	2,816	346
HAITI	V	E	86	95,480	50,107	57,092	6,985
HG KONG	O	E	84	23,296	17,727	22,034	4,307
	V	E	83	731	1,970	2,071	101
HUNGARY	N	W	85	1,895,716	1,027,583	1,258,218	230,635
	O	E	83	34,552	26,114	26,114	
			85	52,254	37,674	38,066	392
	O	W	82	250,218	75,216	75,216	
	V	E	81	377,022	190,966	240,086	49,120
			82	368,263	406,884	459,485	52,601
			83	1,645,204	2,026,103	2,286,445	260,342
			84	2,819,595	2,518,474	2,843,610	325,136
			85	4,475,050	4,086,855	4,698,356	611,501
			86	5,776,192	7,490,036	8,468,498	978,462
	V	W	83	101,509	116,114	122,037	5,923
			84	119,001	79,422	87,145	7,723
			85	870	1,876	3,507	1,631
			86	145,337	113,140	140,676	27,536
INDIA	V	W	81	278,908	149,574	175,313	25,739
			82	613,452	444,601	570,972	126,371
			83	149,548	93,475	120,797	27,322
			84	345,142	183,020	242,945	59,925
			85	381,970	108,437	184,984	76,547
ISRAEL	N	E	81	1,211,956	867,403	1,024,537	157,134
	O	E	81	157,993	129,305	129,305	
			82	21,336	19,185	19,185	
			83	186,984	116,809	131,439	14,630
			86	81,414	67,676	67,676	
	V	E	81	405,026	295,709	341,937	46,228
			82	2,174,137	2,002,493	2,245,334	242,841
			83	1,400,209	1,125,890	1,238,680	112,790
			84	672,134	710,497	814,629	104,132
			85	1,695,392	943,368	1,064,623	121,255
			86	498,504	285,621	329,416	43,795
	V	W	81	99,712	168,779	182,361	13,582
			82	20,352	124,147	133,476	9,329
			83	77,875	48,356	62,710	14,354
			84	85,451	107,659	124,019	16,360
			85	10,600	35,299	43,612	8,313
ITALY	O	E	83	1,292	3,676	4,297	621
			84	1,997	4,965	7,417	2,452
			85	20,146	69,482	86,089	16,607
			86	52,166	119,248	146,209	26,961

Crop
Product
TSUSA commodity number, description, and unit of quantity

Country	Mode	Reg	Yr	Quantity	F.A.S.	C.I.F.	Charges
	V E		81	18,205	50,487	63,353	12,866
			82	140,185	142,119	166,590	24,471
			83	464,825	300,443	344,120	43,677
			84	1,220,044	778,308	915,212	136,904
			85	510,421	364,665	442,333	77,668
			86	12,459,491	4,910,673	5,405,225	494,552
	V W		84	11,252	33,326	41,811	8,485
			85	113,116	337,557	364,948	27,391
			86	181,162	297,008	347,038	50,030
JAPAN	A E		84	4,800	604	699	95
	V E		84	1,350	1,045	1,159	114
			85	1,235	1,778	1,953	175
	V W		82	234	724	915	191
			83	25,299	17,933	19,687	1,754
			85	247,071	136,404	165,916	29,512
			86	22,540	16,073	18,573	2,500
KOR REP	V E		85	422	1,796	1,970	174
	V W		81	132	1,150	1,299	149
MALI	V E		86	46,711	38,553	42,030	3,477
MAURIT	V E		86	176,528	120,792	136,290	15,498
MEXICO	N E		85	2,140	5,116	5,714	598
	O E		81	2,421,417	2,846,469	2,846,469	
			82	3,002,009	2,767,708	2,767,708	
			83	719,840	704,214	704,214	
			84	351,276	541,375	541,375	
			85	715,571	860,829	860,829	
			86	922,375	2,097,720	2,097,720	
	O W		81	900	2,528	2,528	
			82	22,909	72,221	72,221	
			83	474,942	398,064	398,064	
			84	443,110	296,509	296,509	
			85	216,607	127,933	127,933	
N ANTIL	V E		85	24,980	15,633	17,039	1,406
	V W		85	13,338	44,625	56,843	12,218
N ZEAL	N W		84	58,464	49,007	57,108	8,101
	O E		81	236,168	226,824	226,824	
			82	999,125	976,464	976,464	
			83	392	328	328	
	V E		81	748,832	567,240	685,505	118,265
			82	641,088	1,053,895	1,221,228	167,333
			83	498,624	541,476	638,306	96,830
			84	1,453,137	1,025,253	1,213,947	188,694
			85	177,901	248,428	269,383	20,955
			86	511,030	368,234	434,297	66,063
	V H		84	1,000	5,163	6,947	1,784
	V W		81	1,627,241	1,252,469	1,471,751	219,282
			82	1,293,691	772,113	880,634	108,521
			83	327,488	256,519	301,068	44,549
			84	1,043,560	756,367	885,615	129,248
			85	523,585	303,856	364,294	60,438
			86	3,300,595	2,440,341	2,884,367	444,026
NAMIBIA	V E		81	90,111	55,652	60,078	4,426
			84	133,933	74,222	83,699	9,477
NETHLDS	A E		82	456	1,044	1,864	820
	N E		81	156,236	128,545	137,085	8,540
			82	715,008	584,605	638,881	54,276
			83	272,702	365,656	390,846	25,190
			84	4,459,730	3,692,659	4,159,248	466,589
			85	2,097,433	1,824,854	1,994,670	169,816
			86	7,148,541	4,529,785	4,971,719	441,934
	N W		82	381,872	367,893	393,912	26,019
			84	1,899,220	2,127,633	2,158,045	30,412
			85	3,912,409	2,541,852	2,614,302	72,450
			86	3,586,857	2,779,970	2,900,921	120,951
	O E		81	26,072	131,060	135,784	4,724
			82	112,922	294,193	306,939	12,746
			83	494,027	871,970	944,916	72,946
			84	1,471,825	1,941,179	2,117,581	176,402
			85	2,482,420	2,476,865	2,698,253	221,388
			86	552,220	395,066	444,846	49,780
	V E		81	2,298,872	1,904,559	2,041,692	137,133
			82	6,786,536	5,117,833	5,563,123	445,290
			83	7,653,861	5,713,355	6,188,251	474,896
			84	3,548,332	3,152,961	3,414,796	261,835
			85	9,601,067	5,960,828	6,646,517	685,689
			86	4,598,395	3,546,028	3,879,855	333,827
	V W		81	475,200	344,473	371,184	26,711
			82	25,107	47,365	51,439	4,074
			83	262,723	252,892	270,800	17,908
			84	98,192	412,253	443,443	31,190
			85	557,309	370,408	412,934	42,526
			86	302,282	228,231	251,832	23,601
NORWAY	O E		83	3,600	14,304	17,504	3,200
PERU	V E		83	7,392	36,611	39,129	2,518
	V W		86	13,452	52,157	63,529	11,372
POLAND	V E		83	26,293	18,307	19,469	1,162
			84	102,612	205,185	254,057	48,872
			86	20,869	13,629	16,528	2,899
PORTUGL	V E		81	176,814	160,075	172,138	12,063
			82	1,023,285	934,262	1,004,487	70,225
			83	1,674,358	1,227,944	1,321,046	93,102
			84	3,042,270	2,005,204	2,179,200	173,996
			85	1,782,554	984,398	1,079,108	94,710
			86	3,560,671	2,321,287	2,495,575	174,288
	V W		83	53,295	33,642	38,559	4,917
			85	718,341	379,405	423,947	44,542
			86	459,240	248,639	278,443	29,804
REP SAF	A E		81	60	315	2,597	2,282
	N E		82	4,919,376	3,980,917	4,411,109	430,192
			86	1,274,116	1,750,507	1,867,283	116,776
	O E		81	179,790	181,927	182,658	731
			82	284,557	243,261	251,025	7,764
			83	491,672	441,120	477,688	36,568
			84	54,390	57,866	60,862	2,996
			85	55,440	34,516	34,516	
			86	1,905,860	1,604,425	1,723,912	119,487
	O W		86	79,170	41,366	47,495	6,129
	V E		81	10,758,379	8,074,897	9,110,450	1,035,553
			82	5,453,353	4,727,431	5,180,377	452,946
			83	8,297,851	6,430,727	7,169,028	738,301
			84	9,869,315	7,124,967	7,969,023	844,056
			85	10,230,048	5,998,143	6,854,355	856,212
			86	4,582,006	4,273,462	4,721,812	448,350
	V W		81	1,081,363	849,398	993,868	144,470
			82	248,340	196,581	221,693	25,112
			83	1,641,796	1,123,017	1,271,073	148,056
			84	2,612,685	1,112,076	1,326,921	214,845
			85	3,112,948	1,638,790	1,970,761	331,971
			86	2,497,878	1,569,341	1,787,764	218,423
ROMANIA	V E		85	181,566	79,118	90,730	11,612
S ARAB	V E		86	99,528	68,516	79,358	10,842
SOMALIA	V E		85	221,730	106,104	124,034	17,930
SPAIN	N E		85	1,807,299	896,834	1,053,557	156,723
	O E		81	137,631	133,298	133,298	
			83	226,160	125,977	139,960	13,983
			84	234,176	140,599	157,433	16,834
			85	161,700	78,446	95,816	17,370
	V E		81	3,159,843	2,780,661	3,215,556	434,895
			82	7,675,508	7,213,739	8,120,840	907,101
			83	8,093,309	6,581,149	7,480,696	899,547
			84	14,016,897	10,435,321	12,282,394	1,847,073
			85	12,290,407	8,816,835	10,495,745	1,678,910
			86	10,455,092	9,902,820	11,243,974	1,341,154
	V W		82	263,340	203,585	233,193	29,608
			83	238,735	348,297	363,359	15,062
			84	884,431	468,348	583,758	115,410
			85	5,053,731	2,962,981	3,593,289	630,308
			86	2,343,376	1,760,388	2,006,659	246,271
SWEDEN	O W		81	71	299	299	
	V E		86	550	2,632	3,335	703
SWITZLD	A W		84	31,289	3,683	4,270	587
	N E		82	201,747	108,870	125,310	16,440
			83	366,154	268,849	296,222	27,373
	O E		83	1,019,460	628,010	688,381	60,371
			85	3,816	12,402	12,402	
			86	3,075	11,211	11,411	200
	V E		81	194,733	108,379	124,316	15,937
			83	632,903	446,138	516,570	70,432
			84	1,291,934	864,538	983,200	118,662
			85	479,613	282,103	323,334	41,231
			86	315,706	373,864	426,138	52,274
	V W		83	3,782,731	2,783,038	3,184,844	401,806
			84	1,597,256	795,594	903,320	107,726
			85	752,113	325,381	394,073	68,692
			86	3,170	9,900	11,904	2,004
THAILND	V E		83	176	640	742	102
			84	25,350	12,492	17,358	4,866
TURKEY	O E		81	556,263	483,193	483,193	
			85	24,948	16,394	16,394	
	V E		82	95,606	68,802	77,685	8,883
			83	1,489,943	1,339,248	1,453,256	114,008
			84	2,162,842	1,326,986	1,480,533	153,547
			85	1,998,506	1,084,909	1,234,794	149,885
			86	3,480,526	2,294,685	2,525,823	231,138
	V W		83	551,443	328,721	393,106	64,385
			84	236,600	163,569	178,067	14,498
			85	468,636	205,014	266,446	61,432
			86	127,330	58,245	70,889	12,644

Crop / Product / TSUSA commodity number, description, and unit of quantity — Country	Mode	Reg	Yr	Quantity	F.A.S.	C.I.F.	Charges
U KING	A	E	81	161	336	1,294	958
	A	W	82	38	252	702	450
	N	E	86	2,750	7,049	7,633	584
	O	E	84	29,952	53,642	60,694	7,052
	V	E	81	81,589	75,239	81,722	6,483
			82	44,346	39,043	42,612	3,569
			83	27,352	41,496	44,016	2,520
			84	122,352	101,998	110,052	8,054
			85	142,474	181,713	207,777	26,064
			86	63,190	142,087	159,919	17,832
	V	W	81	188	1,266	1,479	213
			83	690	7,858	9,133	1,275
			84	300	1,766	1,956	190
			85	287,263	198,796	205,008	6,212
URUGUAY	V	E	81	654,066	325,261	382,436	57,175
			86	20,160	11,315	14,920	3,605
YUGOSLV	N	E	83	185,601	208,179	210,620	2,441
			84	52,997	33,987	37,411	3,424
	O	E	82	5,831	5,956	5,956	
			83	135,045	92,856	100,794	7,938
			84	159,186	119,078	124,278	5,200
			85	187,423	143,414	144,709	1,295
	V	E	81	618,640	325,253	392,002	66,749
			82	366,912	232,921	281,496	48,575
			83	1,747,766	1,026,699	1,245,387	218,688
			84	1,970,161	726,523	852,821	126,298
			85	799,923	425,284	499,135	73,851
			86	527,884	691,026	778,448	87,422
	V	W	83	245,247	142,306	167,609	25,303
			84	25,621	18,019	22,311	4,292
			85	545,749	319,812	368,409	48,597
			86	312,355	183,013	220,697	37,684

Apple, paste and pulp**
1524000 APPLE AND QUINCE PASTE AND PULP (LB)

Country	Mode	Reg	Yr	Quantity	F.A.S.	C.I.F.	Charges
TOTAL			83	447,144	305,802	360,595	54,793
			84	941,884	353,495	392,187	38,692
			85	550,450	48,896	55,997	7,101
			86	632,887	161,684	190,241	28,557
ARGENT	V	E	84	22,909	8,474	9,885	1,411
			85	52,941	18,070	21,786	3,716
			86	27,335	13,724	15,702	1,978
AUSTRAL	A	W	83	550	275	1,413	1,138
BRAZIL	V	E	83	8,400	2,300	2,628	328
			84	7,407	1,903	2,445	542
			86	3,920	1,369	1,651	282
	V	W	83	1,800	482	625	143
CANADA	O	E	83	2,447	979	979	
			84	1,257	639	639	
			86	4,733	2,212	2,212	
CHILE	V	E	84	34,128	7,338	8,725	1,387
			86	180,115	40,959	47,959	7,000
FR GERM	V	E	84	25,353	48,783	50,439	1,656
FRANCE	V	E	86	1,102	1,488	1,731	243
MEXICO	O	W	83	61,449	8,185	8,185	
			84	156,640	18,460	18,460	
			85	117,433	14,874	14,874	
			86	152,530	22,692	22,692	
N ZEAL	V	H	83	5,669	1,417	1,820	403
			84	7,084	1,755	2,338	583
NETHLDS	V	E	86	2,778	1,107	1,460	353
PHIL R	V	W	86	3,579	3,986	4,729	743
PORTUGL	V	E	84	6,887	2,507	3,652	1,145
			85	13,228	5,677	6,498	821
REP SAF	O	E	84	4,041	2,503	2,503	
	V	E	83	363,972	291,035	343,366	52,331
			84	674,966	259,855	291,702	31,847
	V	W	85	366,848	10,275	12,839	2,564
			86	256,795	74,147	92,105	17,958
SPAIN	V	E	83	2,857	1,129	1,579	450
			84	882	652	699	47
THAILND	V	E	84	330	626	700	74

Apple, prepared or preserved
1461400 APPLES, PREP OR PRES, NSPF (LB)

Country	Mode	Reg	Yr	Quantity	F.A.S.	C.I.F.	Charges
TOTAL			81	3,695,765	906,536	1,018,293	111,757
			82	2,347,741	670,529	796,475	125,946
			83	2,528,978	609,133	748,746	139,613
			84	8,509,589	1,672,753	2,135,242	462,489
			85	5,938,885	2,009,890	2,314,734	304,844
			86	5,775,176	1,598,344	1,905,233	306,889
AUSTRIA	V	E	84	294	313	352	39
BELGIUM	O	E	85	28,569	7,686	13,486	5,800
	V	E	82	3,119	1,200	1,446	246
			83	25,269	14,231	16,634	2,403
			84	29,462	12,580	14,701	2,121
			85	84,533	59,700	75,251	15,551
			86	61,447	22,756	26,005	3,249
	V	W	83	1,888	821	923	102
			84	1,699	739	868	129
BRAZIL	V	E	85	112,000	59,752	71,021	11,269
C RICA	V	W	84	4,643,870	589,897	842,058	252,161
CANADA	A	H	83	79	436	458	22
			84	1,549	1,171	1,347	176
			86	14,630	6,485	8,443	1,958
	A	W	83	992	397	1,216	819
	O	E	81	1,607,230	442,405	444,405	2,000
			82	452,169	118,040	118,040	
			83	109,987	36,438	36,458	20
			84	484,953	119,642	119,701	59
			85	745,707	197,574	197,574	
			86	1,417,414	365,175	365,175	
	O	W	81	41,800	15,393	15,393	
			82	83,970	38,640	38,640	
			83	41,624	15,228	15,228	
	V	E	81	141,752	41,559	48,802	7,243
			82	35,438	10,358	12,050	1,692
			85	71,442	17,883	20,954	3,071
			86	179,064	46,367	54,090	7,723
CHILE	V	E	83	43,395	9,574	17,762	8,188
			86	247,503	54,167	64,679	10,512
CHINA M	N	E	81	170,710	32,730	39,106	6,376
	O	E	81	30,863	7,577	8,579	1,002
	V	E	81	211,293	48,372	57,060	8,688
			82	671,788	162,789	202,374	39,585
			83	877,137	195,643	253,436	57,793
			84	976,897	227,722	286,741	59,019
			85	216,720	42,028	60,243	18,215
			86	198,411	95,594	115,762	20,168
	V	W	81	813,994	165,721	217,909	52,188
			82	274,940	75,288	93,133	17,845
			83	164,800	46,138	56,365	10,227
			84	184,238	60,994	72,321	11,327
			86	78,641	30,681	37,166	6,485
CHINA T	V	E	81	61,200	13,184	15,895	2,711
			82	30,600	6,430	8,430	2,000
			83	65,145	16,214	19,311	3,097
			84	30,960	6,447	8,428	1,981
	V	W	82	123,923	24,477	34,764	10,287
			83	92,160	17,956	24,403	6,447
DOM REP	V	E	83	31,882	5,503	7,616	2,113
F IND O	V	E	85	39,150	7,082	8,505	1,423
FR GERM	V	E	83	780	674	721	47
			84	106,817	19,669	25,046	5,377
			85	2,100	1,056	1,227	171
			86	82,529	14,541	19,805	5,264
FRANCE	A	E	86	1,311	1,908	2,905	997
	N	E	84	13,417	3,372	3,449	77
	V	E	84	2,656	1,002	1,069	67
			84	10,688	2,656	3,021	365
			85	25	2,535	2,928	393
			86	5,264	10,042	12,064	2,022
	V	W	86	5,244	1,479	1,666	187
GREECE	O	E	83	300	391	706	315
	V	E	85	43,401	8,925	11,238	2,313
GUATMAL	V	E	85	1,848	1,201	1,562	361
HG KONG	V	E	82	40,411	10,457	13,118	2,661
			83	92,605	28,885	35,345	6,460
			84	160,421	34,437	44,462	10,025
	V	W	81	29,880	6,080	7,746	1,666
			82	61,920	11,846	16,967	5,121
			83	32,750	7,292	9,718	2,426
HUNGARY	V	E	83	75,150	14,618	19,541	4,923
			84	1,194,743	208,784	275,337	66,553
			85	3,111,794	523,244	661,665	138,421
			86	2,668,864	446,901	621,199	174,298
INDIA	V	E	81	529	420	441	21
	V	W	83	476	422	479	57
ISRAEL	V	E	84	38,700	6,866	8,590	1,724
			86	85,674	16,476	26,456	9,980
ITALY	A	E	86	440	1,148	2,098	950
	N	W	85	633,700	541,913	586,943	45,030

Crop
Product
TSUSA commodity number, description, and unit of quantity

Country	Mode	Reg	Yr	Quantity	F.A.S.	C.I.F.	Charges
	V	E	81	236,422	54,400	65,178	10,778
			82	75,180	73,936	79,442	5,506
			83	40,992	9,332	11,666	2,334
			84	12,998	5,440	6,341	901
			85	145,520	349,374	369,777	20,403
			86	29,700	65,531	68,300	2,769
	V	W	81	39,683	9,100	10,749	1,649
			83	433,800	71,021	75,605	4,584
			84	206,577	272,918	297,395	24,477
			86	136,412	272,966	291,901	18,935
JAMAICA	A	E	82	13,010	6,355	9,763	3,408
JAPAN	V	E	83	36,592	7,998	9,908	1,910
			84	30,960	6,017	7,998	1,981
	V	W	84	1,032	583	698	115
			85	14,652	14,833	16,650	1,817
MAURIT	V	E	86	223,875	33,461	47,355	13,894
MEXICO	O	E	84	44,000	4,224	4,224	
			86	40,000	3,450	3,450	
N ZEAL	V	H	81	34,000	8,833	11,760	2,927
			82	333,929	85,755	115,502	29,747
			83	300,431	86,580	110,880	24,300
			84	230,106	65,201	85,275	20,074
			85	331,095	96,305	122,700	26,395
			86	232,744	63,903	85,410	21,507
NETHLDS	V	E	82	3,990	1,940	2,129	189
			86	15,649	6,236	7,546	1,310
	V	W	82	3,050	1,803	1,974	171
			83	7,892	4,501	4,899	398
			84	3,133	1,457	1,723	266
			85	11,464	1,726	2,592	866
POLAND	V	E	86	3,704	1,200	1,724	524
REP SAF	V	E	81	276,409	60,762	75,270	14,508
			82	129,777	26,194	33,086	6,892
			85	31,557	6,695	8,463	1,768
			86	33,390	6,434	8,199	1,765
ROMANIA	V	E	85	194,706	31,769	38,864	7,095
SPAIN	V	E	84	16,762	3,332	5,538	2,206
			85	40,500	9,822	12,182	2,360
SWITZLD	O	E	86	2,116	4,649	4,890	241
	V	E	82	6,647	11,952	12,343	391
			83	50,196	17,838	18,399	561
			84	85,313	18,292	19,628	1,336
			85	77,838	27,547	29,580	2,033
			86	9,853	24,406	26,404	1,998
	V	W	85	564	1,240	1,329	89
			86	547	1,188	1,277	89
THAILND	V	W	82	3,880	3,069	3,274	205
			86	750	1,200	1,264	64

Apricot

Apricot, dried

1462200 APRICOTS, DRIED (LB)

Country	Mode	Reg	Yr	Quantity	F.A.S.	C.I.F.	Charges
TOTAL			81	3,868,008	6,740,946	7,051,735	310,789
			82	6,577,004	9,289,789	9,834,120	544,331
			83	11,312,610	11,182,162	11,882,197	700,035
			84	16,791,087	14,605,526	15,629,718	1,024,192
			85	9,922,954	12,132,303	12,715,104	582,801
			86	10,841,649	12,450,423	13,054,922	604,499
AFGHAN	V	W	84	4,405	1,399	1,626	227
ARGENT	O	E	83	37,478	36,402	39,361	2,959
			85	38,052	34,299	34,299	
	V	E	81	56,217	66,188	71,079	4,891
			82	144,666	193,061	206,118	13,057
			83	302,016	334,240	358,156	23,916
			84	300,433	259,723	281,676	21,953
			85	110,386	124,119	133,174	9,055
			86	33,437	62,328	64,781	2,453
	V	W	83	191,989	198,453	213,762	15,309
			84	84,326	95,830	102,061	6,231
AUSTRAL	N	W	86	433,773	781,494	799,393	17,899
	V	E	81	12,125	22,803	23,915	1,112
			82	88,064	162,982	169,365	6,383
			83	44,496	80,910	85,387	4,477
			84	17,747	42,965	44,553	1,588
			85	59,947	96,624	101,469	4,845
			86	94,534	169,552	176,739	7,187
	V	H	82	331	631	661	30
			83	1,102	2,063	2,170	107

Crop
Product
TSUSA commodity number, description, and unit of quantity

Country	Mode	Reg	Yr	Quantity	F.A.S.	C.I.F.	Charges
			85	1,102	1,767	1,908	141
	V	W	81	265,851	585,439	605,956	20,517
			82	789,948	1,770,244	1,823,745	53,501
			83	342,214	726,613	749,567	22,954
			84	71,782	134,102	140,687	6,585
			85	104,938	187,003	193,843	6,840
			86	70,512	97,542	100,862	3,320
CANADA	O	E	81	2,540	2,860	2,860	
			82	266	527	527	
			83	2,276	3,081	3,081	
			84	7,000	9,663	9,663	
			85	37,150	33,712	34,476	764
			86	11,808	13,586	14,204	618
	O	W	86	20,499	29,944	31,576	1,632
CHILE	O	E	86	33,069	31,981	34,125	2,144
	V	E	81	21,826	39,600	41,260	1,660
			82	121,232	188,341	196,572	8,231
			86	62,160	73,818	77,456	3,638
CHINA M	V	E	82	3,655	4,117	4,829	712
			83	75	416	422	6
			84	2,019	1,346	1,565	219
			85	4,070	3,608	4,122	514
	V	H	81	1,102	1,626	1,763	137
	V	W	81	283	286	311	25
			83	1,806	2,603	2,684	81
			84	1,388	2,845	3,023	178
CHINA T	V	E	86	39,200	44,515	46,576	2,061
DENMARK	V	E	84	30,078	36,566	38,912	2,346
FR GERM	V	E	82	44,092	44,000	46,019	2,019
			83	38,581	29,700	31,658	1,958
			86	44,092	40,800	40,939	139
	V	W	86	41,336	39,885	42,385	2,500
FRANCE	V	E	86	39,200	30,253	32,324	2,071
GREECE	O	E	83	392	1,221	1,221	
			85	11,396	10,875	10,875	
	V	E	83	38,080	38,175	40,375	2,200
			86	39,200	33,517	35,293	1,776
HG KONG	V	E	81	2,562	1,673	1,853	180
			82	625	1,804	1,888	84
			83	3,122	3,101	5,413	2,312
	V	H	82	280	483	528	45
			84	350	355	377	22
	V	W	84	2,645	2,185	2,285	100
INDIA	N	E	84	47,470	21,020	24,037	3,017
	V	W	84	106	467	537	70
IRAN	A	W	84	22	320	488	168
	N	E	81	163,582	213,354	230,932	17,578
	V	E	82	39,683	57,690	61,488	3,798
			83	117,947	95,240	104,018	8,778
			84	79,366	52,810	61,270	8,460
			85	38,581	28,550	31,658	3,108
			86	106,350	109,507	114,467	4,960
	V	W	81	60,053	88,396	93,079	4,683
ISRAEL	N	E	86	8,539	26,663	27,600	937
	O	E	83	550	1,062	1,123	61
ITALY	V	E	82	161	354	393	39
			83	7,496	19,584	20,711	1,127
			84	1,499	3,638	3,869	231
			85	44,975	39,950	42,926	2,976
JAPAN	V	E	83	38,499	47,150	47,150	
JORDAN	V	E	86	4,299	2,855	2,998	143
LEBANON	V	E	85	2,024	2,295	2,489	194
			86	11,353	5,502	6,082	580
	V	W	85	5,512	4,687	5,154	467
MEXICO	O	E	82	336	579	579	
			84	30,000	3,750	3,750	
	O	W	81	150	442	442	
	V	W	85	37,423	66,791	68,594	1,803
			86	35,715	76,088	79,629	3,541
NETHLDS	O	E	82	266	486	486	
	V	E	84	39,197	29,088	33,338	4,250
PAKISTN	N	E	82	2,141	2,398	2,861	463
			84	5,122	2,910	3,246	336
	O	E	82	1,146	1,277	1,367	90
			83	4,226	4,363	4,882	519
			84	902	697	774	77
			85	2,260	1,251	1,405	154
	V	E	81	7,025	3,671	4,786	1,115
			83	882	500	559	59
			84	7,417	2,761	3,562	801
			85	4,850	3,720	4,836	1,116
			86	9,921	4,000	4,560	560
	V	W	82	5,019	3,589	4,544	955
			83	12,015	5,333	7,906	2,573

Crop Product TSUSA commodity number, description, and unit of quantity Country	Mode	Reg	Yr	Quantity	F.A.S.	C.I.F.	Charges
			84	3,197	1,710	1,881	171
			86	4,409	2,182	2,500	318
PANAMA	A	E	83	996	2,604	3,450	846
PHIL R	V	E	83	22,400	9,086	10,806	1,720
PITCARN	V	E	86	39,200	40,185	41,994	1,809
REP SAF	V	E	83	36,926	50,116	52,174	2,058
			84	7,289	8,540	9,220	680
			85	77,280	71,826	77,323	5,497
	V	W	82	489,642	520,849	576,204	55,355
			83	450,841	543,872	575,579	31,707
			84	8,800	2,766	3,052	286
			86	110,782	141,203	148,783	7,580
ROMANIA	V	E	82	77,000	103,540	110,250	6,710
SPAIN	O	E	81	53	460	460	
	V	E	81	550,332	780,823	833,182	52,359
			82	451,941	685,596	731,306	45,710
			83	90,000	94,950	100,397	5,447
			84	281,388	169,207	188,606	19,399
			85	203,000	212,780	230,955	18,175
	V	W	84	36,546	30,754	33,174	2,420
			85	87,500	50,999	57,026	6,027
SWITZLD	O	E	84	550	1,582	1,650	68
	V	E	86	78,400	80,069	83,971	3,902
SYRIA	A	W	85	10,751	9,931	11,014	1,083
	O	E	81	6,672	10,593	10,593	
			82	3,559	6,447	6,447	
			83	957	1,394	1,394	
			84	24,685	25,301	26,756	1,455
			86	7,969	6,900	6,900	
	V	E	83	32,142	30,000	31,769	1,769
			84	1,378	1,015	1,360	345
			86	110,109	61,390	68,672	7,282
THAILND	V	H	82	2,204	4,536	4,740	204
TOKELAU	V	E	85	39,200	72,902	73,097	195
TURKEY	N	E	81	2,668,136	4,826,881	5,031,263	204,382
			82	4,132,703	5,313,853	5,647,951	334,098
			83	9,224,135	8,552,220	9,102,830	550,610
			84	14,993,995	13,054,042	13,933,176	879,134
			85	8,821,950	10,875,437	11,385,453	510,016
	O	E	81	11,000	22,070	22,070	
			82	55,708	74,726	77,347	2,621
			83	48,270	55,018	55,371	353
			84	56,506	46,356	48,942	2,586
			85	20,870	30,788	30,788	
			86	2,021	3,958	3,976	18
	O	W	85	2,523	3,410	3,410	
	V	E	81	38,499	73,781	75,931	2,150
			82	120,704	145,814	155,830	10,016
			83	217,949	209,513	225,302	15,789
			84	563,898	491,516	545,853	54,337
			85	152,804	157,889	167,094	9,205
			86	9,288,518	10,379,025	10,898,189	519,164
	V	W	83	441	600	712	112
			84	79,687	68,764	75,286	6,522
			85	2,205	2,100	2,208	108
			86	61,244	61,681	67,948	6,267
U KING	O	E	82	816	918	1,011	93
			83	2,205	2,112	2,270	158
	V	W	82	816	947	1,064	117
YUGOSLV	V	E	85	2,205	4,990	5,508	518

Apricot, fresh or in brine
1462000 APRICOTS, FRESH OR IN BRINE (LB)

Country	Mode	Reg	Yr	Quantity	F.A.S.	C.I.F.	Charges
TOTAL			81	103,580	93,704	127,361	33,657
			82	282,190	269,842	318,862	49,020
			83	1,513,785	305,484	420,688	115,204
			84	639,695	389,727	556,431	166,704
			85	1,444,484	885,648	1,144,126	258,478
			86	3,033,612	1,441,204	1,916,276	475,072
ARGENT	A	E	84	13,549	9,225	21,088	11,863
AUSTRAL	A	W	86	1,829	1,402	2,798	1,396
	V	W	86	37,423	66,274	68,274	2,000
CANADA	O	E	82	33,000	6,601	6,601	
	O	W	82	2,530	801	801	
			83	47,512	24,614	24,614	
			84	116,035	19,023	19,023	
			85	4,056	1,326	1,326	
			86	25,819	16,394	16,394	
CHILE	A	E	83	46,760	23,887	44,863	20,976
			84	109,777	60,379	133,003	72,624
			85	166,873	113,718	213,835	100,117

Country	Mode	Reg	Yr	Quantity	F.A.S.	C.I.F.	Charges
			86	117,818	48,641	135,608	86,967
	N	E	81	25,497	14,016	27,072	13,056
			84	65,597	47,378	56,625	9,247
	N	W	85	40,968	18,440	30,860	12,420
	O	W	84	1,389	630	1,602	972
	V	E	83	3,841	1,192	1,642	450
			85	919,518	393,035	509,464	116,429
			86	2,526,936	1,033,483	1,362,371	328,888
	V	W	84	19,443	11,872	14,984	3,112
			86	88,956	35,598	48,043	12,445
ECUADOR	V	E	83	1,199,058	119,906	182,999	63,093
			84	15,050	16,555	17,515	960
FR GERM	V	E	86	38,580	52,550	54,763	2,213
ITALY	V	E	83	226	332	353	21
IVY CST	V	E	85	79,366	94,139	98,139	4,000
MEXICO	O	E	82	93,500	36,279	36,279	
N ZEAL	A	E	81	1,755	1,831	3,679	1,848
			82	10,187	12,727	20,793	8,066
			84	13,778	18,220	26,035	7,815
	A	H	81	2,189	1,977	3,067	1,090
			82	4,199	3,923	6,023	2,100
			84	7,685	7,656	11,255	3,599
			85	6,457	9,007	11,982	2,975
			86	3,969	6,933	10,180	3,247
	A	W	81	35,529	36,112	50,408	14,296
			82	51,414	63,900	97,607	33,707
			83	17,479	23,307	41,174	17,867
			84	54,436	72,278	117,456	45,178
			85	33,091	27,157	42,738	15,581
			86	27,109	33,380	52,965	19,585
	N	H	86	8,432	7,841	10,757	2,916
	V	E	83	35,379	11,471	15,567	4,096
PAKISTN	O	E	83	550	355	391	36
SPAIN	O	E	84	16,055	3,720	3,720	
	V	E	83	85,980	28,012	31,915	3,903
			84	94,932	23,128	28,211	5,083
			85	14,255	1,203	1,473	270
			86	67,219	20,160	28,512	8,352
	V	W	86	4,125	15,103	17,816	2,713
TURKEY	O	E	84	1,375	1,689	1,689	
	V	E	81	38,610	39,768	43,135	3,367
			82	87,360	145,611	150,758	5,147
			83	77,000	72,408	77,170	4,762
			84	110,594	97,974	104,225	6,251
			85	179,900	227,623	234,309	6,686
			86	85,397	103,445	107,795	4,350

Apricot, kernel**
1750300 APRICOT AND PEACH KERNELS (LB)

Country	Mode	Reg	Yr	Quantity	F.A.S.	C.I.F.	Charges
TOTAL			81	24,080	43,222	47,411	4,189
			82	35,147	56,851	62,206	5,355
			83	76,046	62,186	69,843	7,657
			84	122,897	82,722	91,142	8,420
			85	242,309	145,899	163,956	18,057
			86	411,208	265,232	288,571	23,339
ARGENT	N	E	81	2,193	2,411	2,833	422
AUSTRAL	V	E	82	13,000	10,380	11,397	1,017
			84	121,253	79,873	88,009	8,136
			85	173,349	102,057	114,854	12,797
			86	323,898	198,365	213,584	15,219
	V	W	85	35,891	19,611	22,222	2,611
CHINA M	V	E	81	12,276	25,270	27,827	2,557
			82	8,306	15,779	16,813	1,034
			83	9,749	8,859	10,222	1,363
			84	1,000	1,675	1,828	153
			85	33,069	24,231	26,880	2,649
			86	74,964	54,995	61,420	6,425
	V	H	83	650	1,315	1,466	151
			84	144	284	338	54
	V	W	81	5,409	8,046	8,472	426
			82	3,905	5,977	6,402	425
			83	1,952	3,455	3,599	144
			84	500	890	967	77
FRANCE	A	E	83	1,819	4,485	5,685	1,200
	N	E	82	8,886	22,924	25,661	2,737
HG KONG	V	E	81	3,000	6,110	6,725	615
			82	1,000	1,524	1,660	136
			83	23,740	19,856	21,643	1,787
			86	12,346	11,872	13,567	1,695
	V	W	82	50	267	273	6
			83	250	272	292	20

Crop Product TSUSA commodity number, description, and unit of quantity Country	Mode	Reg	Yr	Quantity	F.A.S.	C.I.F.	Charges
JAPAN	V	E	81	100	731	750	19
N ZEAL	A	E	83	408	569	971	402
REP SAF	V	E	81	1,102	654	804	150
TURKEY	V	E	83	37,478	23,375	25,965	2,590

Apricot, paste and pulp
1524200 APRICOT PASTE AND PULP (LB)

Country	Mode	Reg	Yr	Quantity	F.A.S.	C.I.F.	Charges
TOTAL			81	9,173	3,676	4,569	893
			82	886,814	412,823	472,649	59,826
			83	3,044,572	1,524,931	1,724,444	199,513
			84	3,523,038	1,652,991	1,854,698	201,707
			85	2,404,757	917,682	1,070,886	153,204
			86	1,650,940	572,388	657,382	84,994
ARGENT	O	E	83	85,800	50,052	50,052	
			84	789,701	316,048	365,065	49,017
			85	576,406	178,284	220,731	42,447
			86	173,712	54,293	62,151	7,858
	V	E	82	546,460	231,037	268,839	37,802
			83	1,165,167	446,321	531,360	85,039
			84	635,403	240,390	287,333	46,943
			85	691,813	223,892	273,082	49,190
			86	505,352	160,524	190,126	29,602
	V	W	82	36,000	15,156	18,237	3,081
			83	522,827	207,038	251,331	44,293
			84	150,518	58,716	63,816	5,100
			85	75,201	22,005	28,418	6,413
			86	39,431	15,203	18,811	3,608
AUSTRAL	A	E	82	510	383	938	555
	A	W	83	550	385	1,978	1,593
			85	36,834	16,240	19,488	3,248
BELGIUM	V	E	85	1,519	1,043	1,262	219
			86	2,531	1,871	2,176	305
CANADA	A	E	83	642	460	490	30
	A	W	85	15,444	10,480	11,345	865
	O	E	82	3,919	1,869	1,898	29
			85	5,500	4,000	4,000	
CHILE	V	E	83	35,901	18,677	20,908	2,231
			86	108,674	42,613	46,953	4,340
CHINA M	V	E	81	2,200	918	989	71
			82	600	664	763	99
FRANCE	A	E	84	53	319	379	60
	O	E	82	396	277	302	25
			85	3,559	3,218	3,451	233
	V	E	84	8,936	3,365	3,793	428
			86	1,190	1,549	1,795	246
ITALY	V	E	83	205	425	455	30
			84	45	717	751	34
LEBANON	O	E	85	2,200	1,600	1,600	
	V	E	86	11,023	2,000	2,538	538
MEXICO	O	W	82	1,702	267	267	
NETHLDS	V	W	84	2,442	1,776	2,866	1,090
REP SAF	O	E	82	1,200	554	554	
			83	573	430	430	
	V	E	81	6,173	2,101	2,923	822
			82	295,675	162,115	180,350	18,235
			83	1,194,858	769,423	831,989	62,566
			84	1,935,743	1,030,520	1,128,771	98,251
			85	920,683	427,880	474,072	46,192
			86	733,632	256,060	289,810	33,750
SPAIN	V	E	83	3,840	1,682	2,101	419
			85	49,207	8,771	11,639	2,868
SYRIA	A	W	85	1,500	2,250	2,386	136
			86	3,100	2,000	2,234	234
	O	E	85	7,700	7,220	7,220	
			86	7,800	9,825	9,825	
	V	E	83	34,209	30,038	33,350	3,312
			85	12,401	5,625	6,534	909
			86	62,280	22,365	26,385	4,020
TURKEY	O	E	85	2,000	1,600	1,600	
	V	E	84	197	1,140	1,924	784
	V	W	85	1,102	1,075	1,131	56
			86	2,205	2,900	3,288	388
U KING	O	W	81	800	657	657	
			82	352	501	501	
	V	E	85	1,688	2,499	2,927	428
			86	10	1,185	1,290	105

Apricot, prepared or preserved
1462400 APRICOTS, PREP OR PRES, NSPF (LB)

Country	Mode	Reg	Yr	Quantity	F.A.S.	C.I.F.	Charges
TOTAL			81	427,327	230,654	271,256	40,602
			82	1,423,433	491,857	595,824	103,967
			83	7,960,904	2,034,552	2,454,571	420,019
			84	12,728,017	3,360,192	4,140,199	780,007
			85	10,165,170	2,453,647	3,112,751	659,104
			86	10,158,798	3,917,470	4,571,054	653,584
ARGENT	O	E	86	101,250	13,787	21,256	7,469
	V	E	84	186,676	74,915	99,656	24,741
AUSTRAL	V	E	85	1,200	3,961	4,120	159
	V	H	86	750	1,210	1,286	76
	V	W	83	529	887	938	51
			85	1,543	2,459	2,530	71
			86	102,510	39,073	44,064	4,991
AUSTRIA	V	E	82	2,044	3,272	3,524	252
			83	905	2,264	2,440	176
			84	1,463	3,201	3,578	377
			85	1,256	1,131	1,298	167
BELGIUM	V	E	82	11,286	8,313	9,416	1,103
			83	12,922	13,342	14,691	1,349
			84	22,689	11,978	14,434	2,456
			85	11,238	6,279	7,254	975
	V	W	83	2,808	1,835	2,062	227
			84	2,808	1,834	2,154	320
CANADA	O	E	83	280	406	700	294
	O	W	86	100,928	29,536	29,536	
	V	E	85	5,342	3,177	3,608	431
			86	6,420	1,908	2,142	234
CHILE	V	E	83	63,294	20,010	23,242	3,232
			84	105,744	27,951	33,073	5,122
CHINA M	V	E	81	2,857	2,107	2,323	216
			82	1,905	2,068	2,263	195
			83	264	363	426	63
			84	116,600	26,765	32,700	5,935
	V	H	82	675	591	646	55
			83	2,200	1,882	2,019	137
			84	2,808	2,861	3,073	212
			86	1,750	1,325	1,417	92
	V	W	82	713	1,123	1,195	72
			83	3,594	5,254	5,638	384
			84	6,921	8,130	8,789	659
			86	1,390	1,543	1,627	84
CHINA T	V	H	85	2,750	2,208	2,437	229
	V	W	83	867	814	883	69
COLOMB	V	E	84	39,286	8,730	10,687	1,957
CYPRUS	V	E	84	2,750	6,220	6,503	283
DENMARK	V	E	86	18,000	7,873	9,211	1,338
	V	W	86	798	1,451	2,002	551
FR GERM	A	E	81	68	307	313	6
	O	E	85	1,968	1,409	1,788	379
	V	E	83	360	269	309	40
			84	18,210	8,589	10,434	1,845
			85	204,959	104,732	123,810	19,078
			86	3,475	4,019	4,371	352
FRANCE	A	E	84	2,342	1,742	2,531	789
	O	E	81	1,778	2,043	2,343	300
			84	5,178	3,346	3,792	446
			86	2,249	3,646	3,786	140
	V	E	81	36,772	32,362	36,393	4,031
			82	49,846	40,348	46,168	5,820
			83	103,474	79,114	86,865	7,751
			84	145,697	82,741	93,538	10,797
			85	116,139	71,624	84,449	12,825
			86	192,725	190,326	216,572	26,246
	V	W	81	620	3,506	3,700	194
			82	1,840	4,724	5,069	345
			83	476	649	720	71
			84	21,562	15,121	17,146	2,025
			85	16,683	4,115	6,756	2,641
			86	4,589	9,785	10,885	1,100
GREECE	O	E	83	840	1,214	2,096	882
	V	E	82	295	287	331	44
			83	596	575	674	99
			84	735,373	234,444	289,783	55,339
			86	1,204,216	532,571	643,681	111,110
	V	W	82	300	300	332	32
			83	298	288	325	37
			84	600	550	628	78
HG KONG	O	W	82	938	1,041	1,109	68
	V	E	82	1,505	3,127	3,274	147

Crop
Product
TSUSA commodity number, description, and unit of quantity

Country	Mode	Reg	Yr	Quantity	F.A.S.	C.I.F.	Charges
			83	556	1,007	1,068	61
			84	2,762	3,346	3,797	451
	V	H	81	1,457	1,761	1,898	137
			82	500	459	494	35
			83	1,350	1,100	1,188	88
			84	1,675	1,823	2,023	200
	V	W	81	2,700	4,105	4,332	227
			82	2,931	3,740	3,992	252
			83	3,166	4,276	4,512	236
			84	1,810	2,731	2,889	158
HUNGARY	V	E	84	71,429	18,669	22,452	3,783
			86	52,911	4,601	8,172	3,571
	V	W	86	48,000	15,442	18,723	3,281
INDNSIA	V	E	86	80,552	28,049	31,177	3,128
ISRAEL	V	E	81	138,031	55,326	67,328	12,002
			82	201,006	75,261	91,208	15,947
			83	269,575	106,717	125,825	19,108
			84	211,042	102,944	124,542	21,598
			85	665,708	209,629	267,907	58,278
			86	840,916	259,769	319,108	59,339
ITALY	A	E	81	118	515	670	155
	O	E	85	460	1,131	1,396	265
	V	E	82	1,680	1,091	1,246	155
			83	51,337	12,571	14,824	2,253
			84	5,958	14,801	15,777	976
			85	3,218	11,933	12,874	941
			86	43,671	22,108	24,804	2,696
	V	W	83	114	372	386	14
			84	20,881	5,447	6,864	1,417
JAPAN	V	E	86	14,753	30,210	31,881	1,671
	V	W	82	51	278	298	20
			83	300	309	322	13
LEBANON	O	E	82	420	400	400	
	V	E	84	1,323	1,050	1,115	65
MACAO	V	H	83	300	529	575	46
MOROC	V	E	86	82,896	39,567	45,065	5,498
NETHLDS	O	E	85	21,600	6,468	6,468	
	V	E	83	6,007	4,782	5,240	458
			84	1,574	1,583	1,693	110
			85	45,420	21,706	26,027	4,321
			86	17,052	10,505	13,106	2,601
PORTUGL	A	E	84	2,208	6,670	9,114	2,444
REP SAF	O	E	84	6,703	1,195	1,195	
	V	E	81	20,160	8,153	9,912	1,759
			82	3,150	9,432	11,182	1,750
			83	35,532	9,536	11,286	1,750
			84	563,677	167,708	197,103	29,395
			85	222,032	75,231	88,944	13,713
ROMANIA	V	E	83	5,040	1,812	2,128	316
			84	86,548	31,604	35,880	4,276
			85	71,856	25,138	28,729	3,591
			86	21,083	5,200	6,327	1,127
SPAIN	N	E	84	6,514,234	1,514,422	1,879,499	365,077
			85	1,966,635	447,923	573,116	125,193
	O	E	84	2,745	6,502	8,247	1,745
			85	61,479	14,370	18,055	3,685
	V	E	81	171,621	47,750	63,065	15,315
			82	1,080,892	263,295	333,609	70,314
			83	6,963,635	1,564,944	1,915,710	350,766
			84	2,839,340	709,991	879,448	169,457
			85	5,843,670	1,236,715	1,580,925	344,210
			86	6,903,493	2,522,413	2,915,149	392,736
	V	W	83	333,702	88,981	111,601	22,620
			84	929,322	194,980	255,871	60,891
			85	819,419	172,364	232,929	60,565
			86	139,845	49,108	57,541	8,433
SWITZLD	V	E	81	3,645	1,597	1,978	381
			82	11,792	11,878	12,952	1,074
			83	15,922	15,268	16,486	1,218
			84	12,120	13,338	14,300	962
			85	12,898	13,570	15,041	1,471
			86	24,250	39,911	43,169	3,258
	V	W	84	476	492	527	35
			86	1,543	3,500	3,763	263
SYRIA	O	E	85	2,500	3,000	3,000	
	V	E	81	46,297	69,800	75,434	5,634
			82	30,313	34,405	37,481	3,076
			83	62,991	74,465	78,898	4,433
			84	28,034	37,905	40,625	2,720
			85	11,023	2,565	3,223	658
			86	20,074	14,866	15,607	741
	V	W	82	5,872	11,400	12,494	1,094
TURKEY	O	E	84	665	692	718	26
U KING	O	E	82	168	302	331	29

Country	Mode	Reg	Yr	Quantity	F.A.S.	C.I.F.	Charges
			83	705	1,277	1,405	128
	V	E	81	1,203	1,322	1,567	245
			82	13,311	14,722	16,810	2,088
			83	16,965	17,440	19,089	1,649
			84	1,462	1,205	1,389	184
			85	549	1,032	1,067	35
			86	4,751	4,839	5,278	439
	V	H	84	200	461	538	77
YUGOSLV	V	E	84	5,122	1,515	2,094	579
			85	53,625	9,777	15,000	5,223
			86	121,958	29,329	40,348	11,019

Arrowroot

Arrowroot, flour and starch**
1323540 ARROWRT A SAGO FLOUR A STRCH (LB)

Country	Mode	Reg	Yr	Quantity	F.A.S.	C.I.F.	Charges
TOTAL			81	3,289,353	1,035,154	1,238,436	203,282
			82	1,906,545	499,737	614,415	114,678
			83	2,168,932	620,650	743,605	122,955
			84	2,119,965	539,760	657,445	117,685
			85	2,012,363	475,073	611,076	136,003
			86	1,432,169	336,403	424,392	87,989
AUSTRAL	A	W	83	1,047	787	3,077	2,290
BRAZIL	O	E	84	10,000	5,727	5,727	
	V	E	81	241,246	137,374	151,430	14,056
			82	376,595	191,795	214,651	22,856
			83	422,400	54,529	76,647	22,118
			84	75,295	27,967	32,093	4,126
			85	22,000	11,000	12,355	1,355
			86	44,000	15,840	17,519	1,679
CANADA	A	W	85	1,100	1,360	1,492	132
	O	E	81	156,000	128,168	128,168	
			83	394	1,708	1,708	
			84	671	2,449	2,449	
			86	88	1,267	1,267	
CAYMAN	V	E	85	42,750	18,000	20,340	2,340
CHINA M	N	E	84	37,895	15,317	24,702	9,385
			85	18,907	6,071	10,159	4,088
	O	E	84	500	480	480	
	O	W	86	4,125	1,773	1,860	87
	V	E	81	68,332	22,282	28,045	5,763
			82	3,281	872	1,192	320
			83	21,246	14,955	17,119	2,164
			86	57,759	20,900	25,613	4,713
	V	W	81	3,494	1,859	2,032	173
			82	6,237	3,870	4,189	319
			83	14,084	12,039	12,971	932
			84	6,225	5,964	6,265	301
			85	23,105	9,138	12,176	3,038
CHINA T	A	E	85	4,800	1,200	2,516	1,316
	V	E	82	2,500	1,900	2,222	322
			83	2,500	1,550	1,770	220
	V	W	82	1,019	660	730	70
			83	1,444	1,100	1,195	95
			84	6,346	3,640	3,887	247
			85	1,253	1,100	1,192	92
COLOMB	V	E	84	15,939	6,641	7,553	912
DOM REP	A	E	83	2,241	750	1,050	300
F W IND	O	E	85	44,800	22,400	22,400	
	V	E	83	117,395	73,438	83,893	10,455
FINLAND	A	W	86	9,257	3,149	5,669	2,520
FRANCE	O	E	82	159,584	45,326	54,055	8,729
GUATMAL	A	W	81	750	255	450	195
			83	2,024	800	1,443	643
HG KONG	O	E	81	135	310	310	
	V	E	81	1,500	332	446	114
			82	111,343	11,886	17,856	5,970
			83	1,100	934	993	59
			84	1,250	320	396	76
			86	9,989	4,052	5,095	1,043
	V	H	81	2,400	744	796	52
	V	W	81	3,750	1,023	1,089	66
			83	1,577	1,335	1,464	129
			84	1,000	785	844	59
INDIA	V	E	82	50,706	14,425	18,027	3,602
			83	123,017	36,150	45,287	9,137
			84	34,444	7,449	10,515	3,066
			85	11,023	2,333	3,333	1,000
	V	W	81	33,069	8,945	11,550	2,605

Crop Product TSUSA commodity number, description, and unit of quantity Country	Mode	Reg	Yr	Quantity	F.A.S.	C.I.F.	Charges
			82	96,980	29,525	32,734	3,209
			83	11,000	3,842	4,513	671
			84	336	602	662	60
			85	36,222	6,306	8,856	2,550
INDNSIA	A	W	82	261	905	1,544	639
	V	E	81	80,000	13,801	16,902	3,101
			84	107,883	20,501	27,912	7,411
JAMAICA	V	E	85	45,000	19,800	22,050	2,250
			86	44,100	17,121	18,901	1,780
JAPAN	A	E	83	132	313	503	190
	O	E	81	1,720	4,410	4,536	126
			82	793	1,958	2,212	254
	V	E	81	5,078	12,933	13,767	834
			82	18,983	12,709	14,026	1,317
			83	19,258	19,580	21,052	1,472
			84	17,260	30,842	32,914	2,072
			85	47,542	30,003	32,374	2,371
			86	7,360	28,486	29,822	1,336
	V	H	83	88	329	366	37
	V	W	81	6,379	11,486	12,234	748
			82	56,121	21,618	24,619	3,001
			83	6,070	18,624	19,727	1,103
			84	20,503	43,324	46,630	3,306
			85	14,028	13,998	14,616	618
			86	4,835	11,630	11,905	275
KOR REP	V	E	86	1,200	2,554	2,728	174
MALAYSA	N	E	85	160,021	26,276	35,390	9,114
	O	W	85	39,600	4,585	7,546	2,961
	V	E	81	88,000	3,943	11,499	7,556
			82	230,521	28,774	44,643	15,869
			83	151,661	32,440	43,597	11,157
			84	530,184	113,905	134,805	20,900
			85	314,845	37,987	66,262	28,275
			86	240,054	37,722	51,324	13,602
	V	W	81	129,612	8,880	16,134	7,254
			82	427,098	61,837	85,756	23,919
			83	481,909	99,513	120,665	21,152
			84	621,038	121,804	145,654	23,850
			85	80,000	7,400	13,794	6,394
			86	346,439	54,331	77,141	22,810
PHIL R	V	E	84	1,800	425	486	61
	V	H	81	360	350	394	44
	V	W	81	995	952	1,120	168
			82	7,500	2,078	3,128	1,050
PORTUGL	V	E	81	1,628	627	770	143
			83	3,020	1,096	1,199	103
S VN GR	O	E	81	542,600	416,693	457,746	41,053
			85	45,000	9,450	11,800	2,350
	V	E	81	230	289	349	60
			83	300,800	151,125	165,245	14,120
			84	120,280	48,342	55,589	7,247
			85	315,000	121,030	137,340	16,310
			86	135,000	58,897	64,740	5,843
SENEGAL	V	E	85	38,991	7,966	11,246	3,280
SINGAPR	N	E	86	80,020	14,476	16,540	2,064
	O	E	83	44,000	14,843	14,843	
	V	E	81	1,205,200	171,298	257,820	86,522
			82	285,478	50,464	70,934	20,470
			83	202,900	41,072	54,475	13,403
			84	198,514	42,935	57,083	14,148
			85	370,413	61,743	92,114	30,371
			86	160,013	27,326	41,056	13,730
	V	W	83	112,456	21,148	26,319	5,171
			84	158,400	23,352	35,452	12,100
			85	159,022	24,384	30,968	6,584
			86	160,000	20,908	33,604	12,696
THAILND	V	E	81	716,875	88,200	120,849	32,649
			83	111,660	12,975	18,146	5,171
			84	154,037	16,584	24,909	8,325
			85	40,000	7,126	10,601	3,475
	V	H	82	2,502	550	654	104
	V	W	82	69,043	18,585	21,243	2,658
			83	10,509	2,625	2,928	303
			84	165	405	438	33
			85	91,941	7,850	11,256	3,406
			86	127,930	15,971	19,608	3,637
VENEZ	V	E	85	45,000	16,567	18,900	2,333
W SAMOA	A	W	83	3,000	1,050	1,410	360

Artichoke

Artichoke, in brine or pickled
1417600 ARTICHOKES, IN BRINE, ETC. (LB)

Crop Product TSUSA commodity number, description, and unit of quantity Country	Mode	Reg	Yr	Quantity	F.A.S.	C.I.F.	Charges
TOTAL			81	3,807,533	2,870,965	3,169,292	298,327
			82	4,567,074	3,374,990	3,759,623	384,633
			83	5,435,450	3,118,534	3,471,761	353,227
			84	9,966,556	5,869,044	6,654,896	785,852
			85	9,989,028	5,247,928	6,063,886	815,958
			86	9,980,480	5,564,957	6,324,407	759,450
BRAZIL	V	E	85	635	1,200	1,361	161
CANADA	O	E	81	1,260	911	911	
CHINA M	V	W	86	3,500	1,832	1,962	130
CHINA T	V	E	83	1,875	3,345	3,750	405
			84	637	500	615	115
			85	1,350	1,305	1,575	270
	V	W	82	3,492	2,846	3,114	268
			84	29,134	15,087	16,654	1,567
COLOMB	V	E	86	990	1,380	1,518	138
	V	W	86	19,950	16,363	18,513	2,150
FRANCE	V	E	82	210	1,155	1,215	60
			83	1,310	1,679	1,778	99
			85	9,228	15,927	19,103	3,176
			86	600	2,576	2,711	135
GREECE	O	E	82	420	313	358	45
ISRAEL	V	E	81	41,006	7,650	10,150	2,500
ITALY	A	E	84	813	2,568	3,210	642
	V	E	81	9,569	18,548	20,666	2,118
			82	38,143	45,996	51,288	5,292
			83	15,024	19,392	21,069	1,677
			84	197,906	116,612	130,239	13,627
			85	206,825	115,789	134,368	18,579
			86	12,038	10,594	11,227	633
	V	W	82	42,722	19,889	22,580	2,691
			83	71	275	416	141
			84	47,862	24,875	28,533	3,658
			85	28,379	18,409	21,516	3,107
			86	3,175	3,500	3,669	169
JAPAN	V	E	82	131	506	553	47
	V	W	81	2,271	2,410	2,603	193
			82	727	433	470	37
			84	22,376	18,052	20,879	2,827
			86	25,145	29,452	32,625	3,173
MEXICO	O	E	83	40,000	13,950	13,950	
	O	W	84	35,670	15,584	15,584	
MOROC	V	E	82	40,462	34,860	41,028	6,168
PHIL R	V	E	83	18,205	10,785	11,954	1,169
	V	W	83	520	296	328	32
			85	1,080	1,140	1,256	116
ROMANIA	V	E	81	10,648	11,900	13,550	1,650
			83	87,450	35,650	41,236	5,586
SPAIN	A	E	81	15,270	9,817	10,804	987
	N	E	82	2,413,500	2,092,561	2,320,478	227,917
	N	W	85	208,566	81,850	97,077	15,227
	O	E	81	46,139	19,396	24,421	5,025
			84	1,504	1,202	1,332	130
			85	39,021	14,800	17,237	2,437
			86	39,021	16,711	18,598	1,887
	V	E	81	2,545,158	2,191,786	2,408,881	217,095
			82	1,182,450	715,394	797,737	82,343
			83	3,677,678	2,159,301	2,391,224	231,923
			84	6,977,298	4,081,004	4,620,646	539,642
			85	6,797,627	3,667,211	4,211,197	543,986
			86	7,455,998	4,105,861	4,637,311	531,450
	V	W	81	1,136,212	608,547	677,306	68,759
			82	844,817	461,037	520,802	59,765
			83	1,677,462	906,659	1,024,210	117,551
			84	2,565,906	1,557,910	1,775,968	218,058
			85	2,696,317	1,330,297	1,559,196	228,899
			86	2,401,232	1,370,532	1,590,053	219,521
THAILND	V	W	83	3,305	2,852	3,082	230
			86	948	1,050	1,114	64
U KING	O	E	86	17,883	5,106	5,106	

Artichoke, prepared or preserved
1419200 ARTICHOKES PREP/PRES, EX FZ (LB)

			Yr	Quantity	F.A.S.	C.I.F.	Charges
TOTAL			81	13,694,941	6,613,774	7,444,883	831,109
			82	21,880,194	10,741,963	12,061,736	1,319,773
			83	23,249,884	12,103,222	13,422,894	1,319,672

Crop
Product
TSUSA commodity number, description, and unit of quantity

Country	Mode	Reg	Yr	Quantity	F.A.S.	C.I.F.	Charges
			84	30,054,382	15,085,286	17,123,768	2,038,482
			85	28,679,748	13,214,773	15,177,986	1,963,213
			86	31,809,801	14,041,097	16,028,543	1,987,446
BELGIUM	A	W	83	44	560	598	38
	V	E	82	4,630	1,676	1,984	308
			84	33,750	6,181	7,858	1,677
BRAZIL	V	E	86	34,400	24,892	27,515	2,623
CHILE	A	E	83	16,681	3,129	3,794	665
			84	16,823	5,202	16,175	10,973
	A	W	84	1,541	452	1,665	1,213
	N	E	84	349,259	114,397	182,844	68,447
	V	E	84	21,826	8,574	13,322	4,748
			85	54,894	18,600	29,232	10,632
	V	W	86	40,379	28,493	32,187	3,694
CHINA M	V	E	84	243,624	121,685	136,180	14,495
CHINA T	V	E	81	18,213	12,387	13,274	887
			83	4,500	3,600	3,965	365
			84	14,513	14,460	16,960	2,500
			86	68,936	68,901	73,211	4,310
	V	W	81	2,471	2,348	2,461	113
			82	12,771	10,190	10,645	455
			85	4,500	4,900	5,075	175
DENMARK	V	E	85	32,760	17,445	20,273	2,828
FRANCE	V	E	81	121,690	53,983	59,722	5,739
			82	46,723	34,156	37,303	3,147
			83	123,466	68,447	76,254	7,807
			84	88,766	42,316	47,717	5,401
			85	5,925	7,418	8,022	604
HG KONG	V	E	81	1,800	1,451	1,558	107
			83	41,667	20,337	20,350	13
			85	5,811	2,946	3,614	668
ISRAEL	V	W	85	35,250	19,688	23,415	3,727
ITALY	A	E	84	3,490	3,371	4,094	723
	N	E	81	2,809	5,096	5,660	564
	O	E	86	10,361	6,403	6,638	235
	V	E	81	13,508	19,636	22,630	2,994
			82	115,739	80,917	90,759	9,842
			83	111,419	88,905	99,412	10,507
			84	136,686	103,327	116,518	13,191
			85	129,203	77,268	87,287	10,019
			86	167,890	125,996	137,369	11,373
	V	W	82	3,321	5,383	5,978	595
			83	86,491	56,517	61,920	5,403
			84	6,374	5,194	5,749	555
			85	14,179	20,186	22,314	2,128
			86	3,585	11,801	15,459	3,658
MEXICO	O	W	81	2,156	490	490	
			82	2,100	800	800	
			84	1,665	3,315	3,315	
N ZEAL	A	E	81	593	352	629	277
			82	374	383	525	142
			83	374	382	559	177
	A	W	83	502	308	808	500
			84	792	274	449	175
			85	705	1,095	1,436	341
PORTUGL	V	E	84	32,670	17,771	19,827	2,056
ROMANIA	V	E	84	14,306	5,544	6,754	1,210
SPAIN	N	E	83	730,429	361,389	397,578	36,189
			85	5,976,143	2,777,111	3,148,615	371,504
			86	591,226	263,737	307,914	44,177
	N	W	82	248,209	124,277	137,866	13,589
			84	2,957,771	1,602,974	1,809,319	206,345
			85	204,735	141,936	164,570	22,634
			86	348,454	163,870	186,764	22,894
	O	E	84	107,552	43,027	48,251	5,224
			85	27,778	10,643	12,095	1,452
			86	19,312	7,810	8,846	1,036
	V	E	81	11,713,897	5,655,596	6,352,252	696,656
			82	18,359,905	9,025,066	10,118,389	1,093,323
			83	17,240,840	8,960,915	9,898,917	938,002
			84	22,849,123	11,420,770	12,906,547	1,485,777
			85	16,938,817	7,518,388	8,654,688	1,136,300
			86	25,939,901	11,276,888	12,832,625	1,555,737
	V	W	81	1,817,804	862,435	986,207	123,772
			82	3,086,422	1,459,115	1,657,487	198,372
			83	4,893,471	2,538,733	2,858,739	320,006
			84	3,173,851	1,566,452	1,780,224	213,772
			85	5,247,724	2,595,679	2,995,675	399,996
			86	4,585,357	2,062,306	2,400,015	337,709
TURKEY	V	E	85	1,324	1,470	1,675	205

Crop
Product
TSUSA commodity number, description, and unit of quantity
Country   Mode Reg Yr   Quantity   F.A.S.   C.I.F.   Charges

Asafetida

Asafetida, natural drug**
4350500 ALOES JALAP MATE ETC, CRUDE (LB)
(See Aloe, natural drug under Aloe)
4351000 ALOES,JALAP MANA,ETC ADVANCE (LB)
(See Aloe, natural drug under Aloe)

Asparagus

Asparagus, fresh
1350300 ASPARAGUS, 9/15-11/15, AIR (LB)

Country	Mode	Reg	Yr	Quantity	F.A.S.	C.I.F.	Charges
TOTAL			84	39,385	20,360	48,767	28,407
			85	2,036,631	1,121,980	2,165,117	1,043,137
			86	3,292,358	2,615,672	4,642,880	2,027,208
ARGENT	A	E	85	21,231	10,075	26,145	16,070
			86	36,806	23,714	46,602	22,888
	A	W	86	23,888	17,050	33,692	16,642
AUSTRAL	A	H	86	1,248	4,992	5,932	940
	A	W	85	85,430	119,614	161,776	42,162
			86	139,838	182,319	247,795	65,476
BRAZIL	A	E	85	12,043	11,988	18,755	6,767
	A	W	86	5,238	5,160	8,625	3,465
C RICA	A	E	86	3,263	2,640	3,640	1,000
CHILE	A	E	84	33,492	15,138	38,201	23,063
			85	1,203,732	626,263	1,411,292	785,029
			86	1,739,877	1,115,535	2,337,077	1,221,542
	A	W	85	13,483	16,828	27,471	10,643
			86	12,336	5,501	14,450	8,949
COLOMB	A	E	86	2,822	2,280	3,170	890
IVY CST	A	E	85	2,783	1,265	3,070	1,805
	A	W	86	2,607	1,183	3,058	1,875
MEXICO	A	E	85	292,596	96,133	147,521	51,388
			86	236,943	94,210	136,964	42,754
	A	W	85	286,823	89,728	151,188	61,460
			86	160,223	143,266	171,632	28,366
MONSRAT	A	W	85	17,284	5,600	9,203	3,603
N ZEAL	A	E	84	2,782	2,985	6,083	3,098
			85	2,527	2,237	4,515	2,278
			86	9,241	12,887	18,874	5,987
	A	H	84	1,347	824	1,799	975
			85	16,909	22,146	37,314	15,168
			86	138,444	150,828	255,996	105,168
	A	W	84	1,764	1,413	2,684	1,271
			85	74,445	112,363	156,730	44,367
			86	773,558	849,457	1,343,476	494,019
NETHLDS	A	E	85	5,940	5,940	7,240	1,300
PERU	A	E	85	1,405	1,800	2,897	1,097
	A	W	86	6,026	4,650	11,897	7,247

1350520 ASPARAGUS, FRESH OR CHILLED (LB)

Country	Mode	Reg	Yr	Quantity	F.A.S.	C.I.F.	Charges
TOTAL			81	1,953,977	1,193,341	1,248,056	54,715
			82	16,133,223	10,591,912	10,795,978	204,066
			83	20,226,285	13,462,662	14,524,798	1,062,136
			84	14,273,625	6,997,788	8,257,080	1,259,292
			85	15,993,230	9,392,485	10,192,820	800,335
			86	20,354,805	11,324,610	12,523,422	1,198,812
ARGENT	A	E	82	7,168	7,896	12,213	4,317
			83	15,888	5,197	14,954	9,757
			84	17,670	10,320	22,423	12,103
			86	3,439	1,872	3,781	1,909
	A	W	82	2,487	2,363	3,940	1,577
			83	4,238	1,500	4,432	2,932
			85	13,079	7,049	16,432	9,383
			86	17,696	7,225	10,343	3,118
AUSTRAL	A	E	82	2,778	1,339	3,591	2,252
			84	2,376	5,252	6,461	1,209
	A	H	86	4,630	5,745	7,764	2,019
	A	W	82	3,657	5,657	7,157	1,500
			83	4,306	5,421	6,743	1,322
			84	7,701	11,258	15,008	3,750
			85	59,037	69,823	100,160	30,337
			86	92,840	100,586	148,067	47,481
BELGIUM	A	E	82	6,063	2,205	3,150	945
			83	481	1,025	1,382	357
			84	1,019	4,410	4,981	571
	A	W	83	737	1,880	2,687	807

Crop
Product
TSUSA commodity number, description, and unit of quantity

Country	Mode	Reg	Yr	Quantity	F.A.S.	C.I.F.	Charges
			84	361	1,775	2,063	288
	O	E	84	176	355	480	125
BRAZIL	A	E	84	3,531	3,605	5,653	2,048
CANADA	A	E	81	747	2,428	3,163	735
	A	W	83	4,034	1,650	4,386	2,736
	O	E	82	800	900	900	
			86	4,400	3,078	3,078	
	O	W	83	13,870	10,727	10,727	
			85	83,023	53,155	53,155	
			86	12,870	8,438	8,438	
CHILE	A	E	81	4,373	4,604	6,901	2,297
			82	116,844	41,347	93,681	52,334
			83	1,348,653	600,166	1,292,397	692,231
			84	1,172,722	590,069	1,357,190	767,121
			85	635,755	418,869	853,763	434,894
			86	759,375	504,682	1,067,469	562,787
	A	W	82	16,217	5,070	12,487	7,417
			83	1,985	825	2,024	1,199
			84	10,475	6,018	12,368	6,350
			86	2,427	1,100	2,845	1,745
	N	E	84	161,847	86,967	170,010	83,043
	N	W	84	67,975	31,618	62,046	30,428
			85	10,559	5,491	9,956	4,465
			86	9,712	4,706	5,265	559
	O	E	84	13	440	440	
			86	21,096	1,830	1,830	
	O	W	83	31,812	15,816	20,620	4,804
	V	E	84	18,386	8,940	15,951	7,011
			85	21,826	10,800	11,655	855
			86	2,163	1,472	1,997	525
DOM REP	A	E	84	8,184	3,000	7,872	4,872
ECUADOR	A	E	84	1,910	1,330	2,728	1,398
			85	1,540	1,092	1,815	723
FR GERM	A	E	84	38	258	281	23
FRANCE	A	E	82	8,007	16,816	19,626	2,810
			83	4,801	9,546	12,051	2,505
			84	6,692	17,112	21,904	4,792
			86	693	2,279	2,931	652
	A	W	86	589	1,377	2,025	648
GUATMAL	A	E	84	2,400	657	1,957	1,300
	A	W	86	728	2,750	4,371	1,621
IVY CST	A	E	86	2,061	1,411	3,016	1,605
JAPAN	V	H	86	3,416	8,791	10,891	2,100
MEXICO	A	E	81	9,950	5,697	8,123	2,426
			82	284,103	106,111	160,653	54,542
			83	952,143	357,377	547,253	189,876
			84	278,138	84,659	132,651	47,992
			85	291,810	92,531	146,662	54,131
			86	365,189	119,773	183,448	63,675
	A	W	82	16,828	10,936	13,516	2,580
			83	613,874	245,302	345,142	99,840
			84	752,212	320,405	437,331	116,926
			85	376,696	117,438	179,256	61,818
			86	138,011	62,994	89,709	26,715
	N	E	83	2,597,197	870,960	873,227	2,267
			84	3,256,618	1,046,792	1,048,292	1,500
			85	3,594,159	1,230,063	1,232,415	2,352
			86	6,336,852	2,074,572	2,075,903	1,331
	N	W	82	36,827	16,512	20,616	4,104
			85	111,371	37,781	58,364	20,583
	O	E	81	1,594,336	965,847	965,847	
			82	3,281,465	1,596,342	1,596,348	6
			83	77,959	33,749	33,749	
			84	164,257	52,904	52,904	
			86	15,060	4,393	4,393	
	O	W	81	247,478	93,396	93,396	
			82	12,225,296	8,631,972	8,631,972	
			83	14,455,394	11,230,255	11,230,255	
			84	8,043,449	4,495,776	4,495,776	
			85	10,465,837	6,897,309	6,897,310	1
			86	11,807,207	7,593,513	7,593,517	4
MONSRAT	O	W	85	51,870	36,699	36,699	
MOZAMBQ	O	W	85	29,488	18,858	18,858	
N ZEAL	A	E	81	5,120	6,730	10,021	3,291
			82	7,800	6,823	10,044	3,221
			83	10,294	7,512	15,841	8,329
			84	11,707	7,716	17,121	9,405
			86	24,107	21,625	42,352	20,727
	A	H	81	522	416	543	127
			82	2,927	2,834	4,012	1,178
			83	820	2,449	2,887	438
			84	17,115	13,136	21,452	8,316
			85	825	1,106	1,598	492
			86	71,816	85,876	137,856	51,980

Crop
Product
TSUSA commodity number, description, and unit of quantity

Country	Mode	Reg	Yr	Quantity	F.A.S.	C.I.F.	Charges
	A	W	81	84,899	111,346	153,813	42,467
			82	94,276	111,049	166,587	55,538
			83	35,842	38,641	58,210	19,569
			84	256,707	173,618	314,839	141,221
			85	213,919	345,114	504,623	159,509
			86	83,468	104,950	163,683	58,733
	N	E	82	4,488	4,418	7,654	3,236
	N	W	86	508,289	492,495	798,772	306,277
NETHLDS	A	E	82	1,545	4,294	4,787	493
			83	264	827	925	98
			84	7,215	13,853	20,015	6,162
			85	7,053	11,264	14,414	3,150
			86	4,225	14,181	17,389	3,208
	A	W	83	156	643	720	77
			84	1,281	2,806	3,546	740
			85	1,378	3,811	4,799	988
			86	7,231	20,162	27,183	7,021
	O	E	85	1,191	2,419	2,419	
PERU	A	E	82	274	997	1,178	181
			83	48,880	18,968	40,521	21,553
			85	15,345	22,972	34,804	11,832
			86	28,797	32,738	45,888	13,150
	A	W	83	935	1,250	2,219	969
			86	6,438	5,862	11,565	5,703
REP SAF	A	E	82	13,373	16,031	21,866	5,835
			84	1,208	2,364	2,805	441
SENEGAL	A	E	83	42	328	328	
			84	242	375	532	157
SPAIN	A	E	83	1,680	648	1,118	470
			85	7,469	8,841	13,663	4,822
			86	13,142	26,184	35,445	9,261
SWITZLD	A	E	86	2,400	4,400	6,096	1,696
URUGUAY	A	E	81	6,552	2,877	6,249	3,372
			86	4,438	3,550	6,112	2,562

Asparagus, frozen
1350540 ASPARAGUS, FROZEN (LB)

Country	Mode	Reg	Yr	Quantity	F.A.S.	C.I.F.	Charges
TOTAL			81	392,357	242,178	242,720	542
			82	62,866	44,133	44,133	
			85	353,046	139,832	159,493	19,661
			86	1,584,498	910,756	943,635	32,879
CANADA	O	E	81	43,085	28,806	28,806	
CHILE	A	E	85	10,364	6,127	12,829	6,702
			86	13,867	6,303	15,908	9,605
	O	E	86	5,448	6,880	6,880	
CHINA T	V	E	81	2,808	1,418	1,810	392
	V	H	86	1,750	2,563	2,773	210
	V	W	85	17,436	12,675	14,175	1,500
			86	15,390	19,565	20,776	1,211
FRANCE	O	E	86	30,240	8,467	8,467	
GUATMAL	V	E	81	618	591	741	150
			86	69,500	16,243	21,344	5,101
MEXICO	A	E	85	12,356	4,050	6,417	2,367
			86	22,768	9,834	14,021	4,187
	A	W	85	9,877	2,836	4,893	2,057
	O	E	81	345,846	211,363	211,363	
			82	62,866	44,133	44,133	
			85	279,723	90,532	90,532	
			86	48,015	17,756	17,756	
	O	W	85	1,620	1,894	1,894	
			86	1,297,560	786,820	786,820	
N ZEAL	A	E	86	4,960	7,090	11,495	4,405
	A	H	85	6,061	4,480	8,652	4,172
	A	W	85	3,704	3,063	4,824	1,761
SALVADR	V	E	86	75,000	29,235	37,395	8,160
SPAIN	V	E	85	11,905	14,175	15,277	1,102

1384640 ASPARAGUS, FRZ, CUT, SLICED (LB)

Country	Mode	Reg	Yr	Quantity	F.A.S.	C.I.F.	Charges
TOTAL			82	333,769	199,604	211,830	12,226
			83	1,216,910	624,571	627,655	3,084
			84	529,412	233,871	262,490	28,619
			85	563,922	381,049	387,931	6,882
			86	999,025	430,219	440,677	10,458
BELGIUM	A	E	84	125	440	532	92
CANADA	O	E	86	88,326	55,293	55,293	
CHILE	A	E	82	968	340	725	385
	N	E	84	16,641	4,069	18,212	14,143
CHINA T	V	H	86	3,500	4,786	5,776	990
	V	W	82	55,951	49,734	55,990	6,256
			85	2,700	2,185	2,340	155

Country	Mode	Reg	Yr	Quantity	F.A.S.	C.I.F.	Charges
			86	111,168	116,724	123,375	6,651
COLOMB	V	E	85	5,000	10,400	10,400	
FRANCE	A	E	82	994	1,493	2,166	673
			83	139	371	432	61
GUATMAL	V	E	82	9,067	8,518	10,817	2,299
			83	10,420	7,066	8,179	1,113
MEXICO	A	W	83	9,699	3,170	5,080	1,910
			85	10,915	4,340	6,281	1,941
	O	E	82	262,015	134,214	134,214	
			83	1,184,924	599,092	599,092	
			84	456,131	181,969	181,969	
			85	417,223	223,163	223,165	2
			86	739,294	217,528	217,528	
	O	W	83	11,728	14,872	14,872	
			84	25,311	14,666	14,666	
			85	2,265	3,614	3,614	
			86	28,543	20,005	20,005	
N ZEAL	A	H	82	1,029	863	1,294	431
			85	1,812	3,423	5,054	1,631
	A	W	82	3,745	4,442	6,624	2,182
			84	27,592	24,974	38,477	13,503
NETHLDS	A	E	84	470	1,003	1,310	307
SPAIN	A	E	85	728	1,550	2,269	719
	O	E	85	123,279	132,374	134,808	2,434
			86	28,194	15,883	18,700	2,817
	V	E	84	3,142	6,750	7,324	574

Asparagus, prepared or preserved
1419300 ASPARAGUS, PREP OR PRES (LB)

Country	Mode	Reg	Yr	Quantity	F.A.S.	C.I.F.	Charges
TOTAL			81	3,076,671	2,338,719	2,459,333	120,614
			82	4,600,021	3,672,144	3,955,320	283,176
			83	2,944,330	2,561,000	2,731,818	170,818
			84	6,587,017	6,452,236	6,860,218	407,982
			85	5,251,118	4,749,288	4,945,924	196,636
			86	5,077,567	4,478,164	4,747,589	269,425
BELGIUM	V	E	83	13,488	10,630	11,595	965
			84	8,216	11,570	12,802	1,232
			85	40,807	51,664	59,968	8,304
			86	61,123	109,408	122,529	13,121
	V	W	86	33,660	54,071	59,185	5,114
BRAZIL	V	E	83	3,440	7,600	8,430	830
CANADA	A	E	82	224	467	525	58
	A	W	85	1,984	1,050	1,455	405
	O	E	84	1,050	643	643	
	O	W	85	143,400	72,542	72,542	
			86	72,000	40,715	40,715	
CHILE	V	E	84	4,286	2,160	3,671	1,511
			86	48,000	19,668	21,730	2,062
	V	W	86	19,688	16,530	17,129	599
CHINA M	O	E	86	28,629	9,500	9,500	
	V	E	84	20,858	22,602	23,734	1,132
	V	W	81	900	785	884	99
			82	450	341	374	33
			83	11,377	5,572	5,759	187
			84	86,932	80,633	84,826	4,193
			85	104,291	57,012	61,792	4,780
			86	60,108	31,368	33,650	2,282
CHINA T	N	E	81	17,215	13,704	15,056	1,352
			84	237,134	245,917	265,687	19,770
	N	W	84	144,069	139,128	145,613	6,485
	O	E	81	24,636	20,416	22,172	1,756
			82	20,669	16,481	17,982	1,501
			83	18,966	14,017	14,882	865
			84	6,750	6,840	7,480	640
			85	10,800	10,220	11,013	793
			86	23,469	15,015	16,945	1,930
	O	W	81	18,576	14,336	15,607	1,271
	V	E	81	564,027	471,971	510,586	38,615
			82	1,877,403	1,486,918	1,646,561	159,643
			83	1,060,553	945,452	1,027,048	81,596
			84	1,993,387	2,025,153	2,193,612	168,459
			85	1,145,761	1,134,676	1,228,277	93,601
			86	1,603,860	1,290,238	1,405,061	114,823
	V	H	81	75,637	71,847	75,759	3,912
			82	179,924	171,768	182,667	10,899
			83	106,639	112,891	119,822	6,931
			84	163,857	184,042	194,643	10,601
			85	54,155	61,780	64,963	3,183
			86	139,263	147,472	158,625	11,153
	V	W	81	1,252,103	1,034,921	1,102,207	67,286
			82	1,766,015	1,439,276	1,537,413	98,137

Country	Mode	Reg	Yr	Quantity	F.A.S.	C.I.F.	Charges
			83	1,335,696	1,163,092	1,221,120	58,028
			84	2,245,081	2,229,649	2,351,611	121,962
			85	932,966	840,722	888,798	48,076
			86	1,332,451	1,104,504	1,169,405	64,901
COLOMB	V	E	86	4,011	8,532	9,221	689
FR GERM	V	E	81	7,932	17,194	17,959	765
			82	2,447	6,586	7,264	678
			83	2,513	6,613	7,457	844
			84	2,381	3,037	3,691	654
FRANCE	A	E	86	974	2,394	2,930	536
	N	E	83	6,792	12,879	14,286	1,407
			84	25,998	30,929	33,940	3,011
	O	W	84	250	534	561	27
	V	E	81	1,680	3,758	4,194	436
			82	6,326	12,389	13,381	992
			83	1,359	2,285	2,437	152
			84	2,540	3,909	4,447	538
			85	4,646	6,790	7,307	517
			86	1,757	4,633	4,983	350
	V	W	81	633	1,077	1,157	80
			83	5,713	11,063	12,168	1,105
			84	2,387	5,290	5,617	327
			85	820	2,761	3,041	280
			86	1,797	6,651	7,498	847
GREECE	V	E	81	7,410	3,625	4,340	715
GUATMAL	V	E	81	1,069	824	1,047	223
HG KONG	V	E	82	1,161	588	658	70
			84	123,990	130,740	141,179	10,439
	V	H	85	1,455	1,061	1,141	80
	V	W	81	1,260	1,110	1,161	51
			83	7,177	6,422	6,826	404
			84	7,937	4,808	5,437	629
			85	87,799	70,103	73,784	3,681
			86	74,090	34,365	36,912	2,547
ITALY	V	E	86	3,790	8,729	9,011	282
JAPAN	O	E	82	16,762	13,186	14,418	1,232
	V	E	83	10,232	8,502	9,396	894
			84	18,383	18,216	19,763	1,547
	V	H	82	427	1,045	1,377	332
			83	69	268	281	13
			84	4,212	6,538	6,931	393
			85	1,665	2,109	2,255	146
			86	2,225	4,472	5,075	603
	V	W	82	26,250	24,200	25,448	1,248
			85	1,632	2,540	2,720	180
KOR REP	V	E	82	30,294	24,095	26,190	2,095
			83	4,064	3,500	3,762	262
			85	33,089	35,420	37,917	2,497
			86	31,759	26,961	28,646	1,685
MEXICO	A	W	85	5,092	2,630	3,073	443
			86	2,447	1,480	1,900	420
	O	E	81	174	357	357	
			82	601,413	415,120	415,120	
			83	143,603	86,082	86,082	
			84	2,174	2,560	2,560	
			85	245,650	97,348	97,348	
			86	63,368	6,336	6,336	
	O	W	81	1,046,866	634,817	634,817	
			84	914,261	788,935	788,935	
			85	2,247,231	2,083,559	2,083,559	
			86	1,051,420	1,162,951	1,162,951	
	V	E	83	32,679	17,306	20,084	2,778
N ZEAL	A	E	82	1,510	2,873	4,127	1,254
	A	W	85	4,867	8,480	11,330	2,850
	V	E	84	31,500	29,757	34,472	4,715
	V	W	86	22,860	11,284	14,884	3,600
NETHLDS	O	E	86	28,851	48,334	52,626	4,292
	V	E	86	3,441	6,174	6,774	600
PERU	V	E	81	30,219	21,709	23,304	1,595
			82	45,824	38,528	41,962	3,434
			83	55,814	49,315	53,496	4,181
			84	13,500	12,000	12,534	534
			85	18,000	18,400	19,981	1,581
			86	50,949	38,034	40,700	2,666
REP SAF	V	E	83	5,511	6,896	7,944	1,048
SPAIN	V	E	81	26,334	26,268	28,726	2,458
			82	15,666	12,463	13,518	1,055
			83	101,229	72,290	79,345	7,055
			84	487,057	425,564	470,634	45,070
			85	162,098	185,671	208,173	22,502
			86	256,689	213,893	241,639	27,746
	V	W	83	17,416	18,325	19,598	1,273
			84	8,452	10,369	11,758	1,389
			85	2,910	2,750	5,487	2,737

Crop Product TSUSA commodity number, description, and unit of quantity Country	Mode	Reg	Yr	Quantity	F.A.S.	C.I.F.	Charges
			86	42,273	40,324	45,782	5,458
THAILND	V	E	82	7,256	5,820	6,335	515
			84	30,375	30,713	33,437	2,724
	V	W	86	9,070	7,688	7,990	302
U KING	V	E	86	3,545	6,440	7,257	817

Avocado

Avocado, fresh or prepared or preserved
1463000 AVOCADOS,FRESH PREP OR PRES (LB)

Country	Mode	Reg	Yr	Quantity	F.A.S.	C.I.F.	Charges
TOTAL			81	1,928,708	188,042	382,978	194,936
			82	1,486,933	127,136	265,870	138,734
			83	3,393,231	445,216	772,796	327,580
			84	7,325,021	645,256	1,038,572	393,316
			85	3,742,205	828,345	1,351,357	523,012
			86	15,748,542	4,111,497	5,805,603	1,694,106
BAHAMAS	N	E	82	243,909	9,880	13,145	3,265
			85	34,854	4,755	7,021	2,266
	V	E	81	82,848	2,880	3,228	348
			83	314,588	13,332	16,297	2,965
			84	10,450	2,200	2,679	479
			85	165,110	6,270	7,607	1,337
			86	29,545	2,602	3,805	1,203
C RICA	V	E	83	509,272	169,326	238,529	69,203
			86	3,977,000	509,339	652,873	143,534
CANADA	O	E	86	77,708	15,387	15,387	
CHILE	A	E	84	2,200	950	2,244	1,294
			85	189,314	62,041	171,946	109,905
			86	761,160	307,276	676,700	369,424
	A	W	85	8,652	2,800	6,200	3,400
			86	5,109	1,500	1,588	88
	N	E	86	333,312	132,564	268,164	135,600
	V	E	81	348	1,856	3,350	1,494
			85	1,111,163	466,333	623,906	157,573
			86	4,641,132	1,846,867	2,425,310	578,443
	V	W	86	286,215	128,040	178,576	50,536
DENMARK	V	E	86	8,960	2,016	2,384	368
DOM REP	A	E	81	9,809	2,962	5,103	2,141
			82	11,200	1,120	3,650	2,530
			84	179,050	17,350	35,237	17,887
			85	42,330	16,029	18,680	2,651
			86	16,535	5,266	9,625	4,359
	N	E	81	1,835,703	180,344	371,297	190,953
			82	1,231,724	115,136	247,997	132,861
			83	2,508,993	252,803	502,955	250,152
			84	2,365,514	251,829	486,585	234,756
			85	2,026,158	209,023	439,236	230,213
			86	3,745,777	475,952	627,379	151,427
	V	E	83	47,310	5,982	10,443	4,461
			84	86,050	10,732	16,943	6,211
			85	125,965	51,752	61,769	10,017
			86	270,190	73,989	89,718	15,729
ECUADOR	A	E	83	3,598	1,600	2,179	579
	V	W	84	3,799,566	252,166	340,528	88,362
			86	1,595,899	610,699	854,094	243,395
FRANCE	V	E	84	5,920	553	1,034	481
GUATMAL	V	E	84	33,790	1,561	2,000	439
			85	5,964	4,426	5,351	925
HONDURA	V	E	84	805,281	101,544	144,951	43,407
IVY CST	A	E	85	6,250	3,000	7,725	4,725
MEXICO	O	E	84	37,200	6,371	6,371	
			85	26,445	1,916	1,916	
	O	W	83	6,890	1,399	1,399	
MONSRAT	V	E	82	100	1,000	1,078	78
TRINID	V	E	83	2,580	774	994	220

B

Babassu

Babassu, vegetable oil, edible
1760000 BABASSU OIL (LB)

Country	Mode	Reg	Yr	Quantity	F.A.S.	C.I.F.	Charges
TOTAL			81	138,181	81,397	92,336	10,939
			83	1,363,814	402,973	435,561	32,588
			84	1,277,555	705,357	738,907	33,550
			85	7,930,032	2,882,769	3,081,173	198,404
			86	87,314	51,399	59,584	8,185
BRAZIL	V	E	84	1,230,230	696,000	729,550	33,550
			85	7,903,669	2,877,249	3,075,653	198,404
	V	W	83	1,320,463	391,105	423,405	32,300
FRANCE	V	E	86	8,566	9,964	10,349	385
ITALY	V	E	81	107,317	59,502	68,814	9,312
			86	78,748	41,435	49,235	7,800
MEXICO	O	W	83	38,942	9,828	9,828	
			84	47,325	9,357	9,357	
			85	26,363	5,520	5,520	
SPAIN	V	E	81	30,864	21,895	23,522	1,627
			83	4,409	2,040	2,328	288

Balata

Gutta balata, rubber
4460510 GUTTA BALATA (LB)

Country	Mode	Reg	Yr	Quantity	F.A.S.	C.I.F.	Charges
TOTAL			81	220,968	105,599	114,206	8,607
			82	43,504	18,519	20,734	2,215
			84	702,856	351,216	374,272	23,056
			85	338,642	133,843	145,905	12,062
BRAZIL	A	E	85	25,586	19,190	19,899	709
CHINA T	V	E	82	6,821	3,132	3,319	187
GUYANA	A	E	81	65	315	395	80
			84	291	355	555	200
INDNSIA	V	E	84	70,547	26,760	33,776	7,016
	V	W	81	220,460	105,000	113,473	8,473
MALAYSA	O	E	84	279,858	141,702	141,702	
	V	E	81	443	284	338	54
			82	36,683	15,387	17,415	2,028
			84	161,668	83,855	90,855	7,000
			85	313,056	114,653	126,006	11,353
PANAMA	O	E	84	79,380	32,546	32,546	
SRI LKA	V	E	84	111,112	65,998	74,838	8,840

Balsa

Balsa, lumber**
2023200 BALSA/TEAK LUMBER ROUGH (MBF)

Country	Mode	Reg	Yr	Quantity	F.A.S.	C.I.F.	Charges
TOTAL			81	11,650	12,244,895	13,530,795	1,285,900
			82	8,819	10,348,993	11,669,028	1,320,035
			83	14,768	15,973,614	17,646,956	1,673,342
ARGENT	V	W	83	10	5,351	6,644	1,293
AUSTRAL	V	W	82	12	8,212	9,799	1,587
			83	6	5,219	6,236	1,017
BOLIVIA	V	E	82	24	13,691	17,933	4,242
BRAZIL	V	E	81	1,063	382,200	503,950	121,750
			82	1,074	339,659	561,548	221,889
			83	1,090	629,020	731,847	102,827
BURMA	N	W	82	134	328,817	353,495	24,678
			83	295	695,971	745,948	49,977
	O	E	81	11	33,195	33,195	
			83	16	50,953	50,953	
	V	E	81	1,645	2,927,642	3,213,075	285,433
			82	817	1,541,833	1,687,491	145,658
			83	983	988,974	1,094,785	105,811
	V	W	81	404	966,935	1,042,409	75,474
			82	65	195,603	211,304	15,701
			83	380	863,895	933,785	69,890

Crop / Product / TSUSA commodity number, description, and unit of quantity / Country	Mode	Reg	Yr	Quantity	F.A.S.	C.I.F.	Charges
C RICA	V	E	81	20	10,000	11,667	1,667
CANADA	O	E	81	93	15,181	15,181	
			82	50	14,368	14,368	
			83	17	2,585	2,585	
CHINA M	V	E	81	101	97,591	106,987	9,396
			82	14	33,352	39,751	6,399
			83	8	12,847	14,766	1,919
	V	W	81	148	288,399	323,234	34,835
			82	81	167,192	192,343	25,151
			83	214	412,283	461,450	49,167
CHINA T	N	E	83	*	360	418	58
	O	E	81	4	11,694	11,694	
	V	E	81	35	90,684	97,726	7,042
			82	168	271,903	291,384	19,481
			83	1,308	515,289	550,253	34,964
	V	W	81	53	151,992	157,528	5,536
			82	6	18,501	19,809	1,308
			83	84	216,714	229,865	13,151
COLOMB	V	E	82	64	47,280	51,757	4,477
ECUADOR	A	E	81	1	676	1,387	711
	N	E	81	2,850	894,467	1,005,147	110,680
			82	2,269	1,368,295	1,556,977	188,682
			83	1,795	1,021,878	1,213,741	191,863
	V	E	81	93	55,858	70,251	14,393
			82	66	33,729	43,310	9,581
			83	121	62,659	77,341	14,682
	V	W	81	446	248,609	306,307	57,698
			82	242	162,284	206,286	44,002
			83	141	65,669	88,147	22,478
FIJI	V	W	81	1	571	687	116
FR GERM	V	E	82	21	29,778	34,760	4,982
			83	398	42,362	47,725	5,363
	V	W	83	1	1,693	1,983	290
GUYANA	V	E	81	40	146,143	173,373	27,230
HG KONG	N	E	82	92	84,774	90,360	5,586
	V	E	81	753	1,578,762	1,689,848	111,086
			82	265	474,219	519,952	45,733
			83	3,228	1,526,514	1,704,798	178,284
	V	W	81	456	435,681	462,964	27,283
			82	118	126,428	136,038	9,610
			83	413	991,933	1,076,522	84,589
HONDURA	V	E	81	12	19,500	21,092	1,592
			82	11	14,556	15,393	837
			83	6	12,000	13,701	1,701
INDNSIA	N	W	83	238	486,744	522,586	35,842
	V	E	81	26	42,490	50,660	8,170
			82	599	603,923	710,534	106,611
			83	1,340	1,354,922	1,547,844	192,922
	V	W	81	864	901,969	1,043,141	141,172
			82	388	466,905	527,958	61,053
			83	294	463,444	500,025	36,581
JAPAN	V	W	81	22	53,641	58,221	4,580
MALAYSA	O	E	82	10	9,678	9,678	
	V	E	81	14	25,033	28,830	3,797
			82	18	9,618	13,509	3,891
			83	11	9,757	12,182	2,425
	V	W	81	10	36,522	38,660	2,138
			82	52	82,204	86,850	4,646
MEXICO	V	E	81	9	18,598	20,416	1,818
PERU	N	E	81	*	372	880	508
	V	E	82	4	3,520	3,922	402
	V	W	81	20	10,000	13,474	3,474
PHIL R	V	E	83	24	23,069	28,250	5,181
	V	W	81	23	35,744	41,805	6,061
			83	10	30,726	31,145	419
SINGAPR	N	W	81	46	137,407	142,564	5,157
	V	E	81	1,889	2,055,502	2,199,380	143,878
			82	1,380	2,675,182	2,887,691	212,509
			83	652	1,471,515	1,586,598	115,083
	V	W	81	164	432,516	463,389	30,873
			82	227	521,296	562,624	41,328
			83	1,397	3,608,663	3,900,942	292,279
SURINAM	V	E	81	21	10,809	14,417	3,608
			82	346	204,106	263,502	59,396
			83	191	120,542	153,915	33,373
THAILND	O	E	83	1	747	747	
	V	E	82	99	291,945	321,789	29,844
	V	W	81	1	4,411	4,597	186
			82	52	159,808	175,032	15,224
			83	44	124,558	131,509	6,951
U KING	V	E	81	51	40,437	45,517	5,080
			82	51	46,334	51,881	5,547
W SAMOA	V	W	83	26	95,478	103,884	8,406
YUGOSLV	V	E	83	26	59,280	73,836	14,556
ZAIRE	V	E	81	261	83,664	117,142	33,478

2023205 BALSA LUMBER, ROUGH (MBF)

Country	Mode	Reg	Yr	Quantity	F.A.S.	C.I.F.	Charges
TOTAL			84	3,486	1,876,385	2,254,565	378,180
			85	3,774	1,872,286	2,281,930	409,644
			86	4,686	2,344,833	2,848,317	503,484
BURMA	V	W	84	14	39,012	41,456	2,444
CANADA	O	E	84	16	6,477	6,477	
CHINA T	V	E	85	5	17,797	18,788	991
	V	W	86	14	17,846	18,946	1,100
ECUADOR	V	E	84	3,136	1,523,868	1,841,506	317,638
			85	3,675	1,758,014	2,152,007	393,993
			86	4,447	2,216,237	2,699,383	483,146
	V	W	84	89	58,693	70,467	11,774
			85	53	33,528	40,577	7,049
			86	108	62,886	79,294	16,408
GUATMAL	V	E	84	75	27,000	31,050	4,050
HG KONG	V	E	84	18	53,541	59,297	5,756
	V	W	84	8	15,912	16,912	1,000
			85	8	18,077	19,492	1,415
HONDURA	V	E	84	25	11,870	13,895	2,025
INDNSIA	V	E	84	10	5,735	7,909	2,174
			85	12	20,081	22,217	2,136
	V	W	84	8	17,396	18,583	1,187
JAPAN	V	E	86	93	21,824	22,435	611
PANAMA	V	W	84	9	7,541	8,893	1,352
			85	19	14,150	16,984	2,834
SALVADR	V	E	84	50	17,000	20,008	3,008
SINGAPR	V	E	84	10	29,500	31,937	2,437
	V	W	84	15	51,323	73,247	21,924
SPAIN	V	E	86	22	16,159	17,984	1,825
U KING	V	E	84	3	11,517	12,928	1,411
			85	2	10,639	11,865	1,226
			86	2	9,881	10,275	394

2023300 BALSA/TEAK LBR DSD EX SIDNG (MBF)

Country	Mode	Reg	Yr	Quantity	F.A.S.	C.I.F.	Charges
TOTAL			81	2,468	2,799,650	3,096,469	296,819
			82	2,199	2,426,876	2,696,153	269,277
			83	4,108	2,688,992	3,028,551	339,559
BOLIVIA	V	E	83	20	8,522	9,721	1,199
BRAZIL	V	E	82	10	10,750	12,672	1,922
	V	W	82	13	14,185	17,090	2,905
BURMA	N	W	81	15	46,066	48,038	1,972
	O	E	82	10	24,112	27,735	3,623
			83	2	7,458	7,458	
	O	W	82	2	612	612	
	V	E	82	134	310,825	347,682	36,857
			83	50	135,426	153,080	17,654
	V	W	81	89	235,170	257,759	22,589
			82	115	326,377	355,333	28,956
			83	32	89,314	95,169	5,855
C RICA	V	E	83	40	9,378	10,078	700
CANADA	O	E	81	191	33,661	33,661	
			82	63	33,944	33,944	
			83	102	31,385	31,385	
	O	W	81	18	43,031	43,031	
			82	5	4,582	4,582	
CHINA T	A	E	83	1	1,860	2,207	347
	V	E	81	14	44,778	47,237	2,459
			82	34	45,707	48,589	2,882
			83	1,211	317,967	347,965	29,998
	V	W	81	13	40,313	41,538	1,225
			82	58	14,613	15,775	1,162
			83	43	110,787	123,528	12,741
ECUADOR	N	E	81	452	215,711	241,131	25,420
	V	E	81	15	11,253	13,635	2,382
			82	520	216,769	259,532	42,763
			83	1,676	666,090	807,407	141,317
	V	W	81	90	53,835	70,213	16,378
			82	22	10,677	14,418	3,741
			83	10	7,560	9,230	1,670
FINLAND	A	E	81	2	1,246	4,361	3,115
FR GERM	V	E	83	66	49,212	58,229	9,017
GUATMAL	V	E	81	10	10,000	12,015	2,015
			82	10	10,000	11,711	1,711
			83	1	1,430	4,428	2,998
HG KONG	V	E	81	37	94,196	102,999	8,803
			82	53	107,913	122,073	14,160
			83	122	286,955	320,977	34,022
	V	W	81	552	1,051,374	1,142,877	91,503
			82	57	129,262	140,264	11,002
			83	14	32,192	34,863	2,671

Crop
Product
TSUSA commodity number, description, and unit of quantity

Country	Mode	Reg	Yr	Quantity	F.A.S.	C.I.F.	Charges
HONDURA	V	E	82	8	9,552	11,462	1,910
INDIA	V	W	81	3	1,913	2,179	266
INDNSIA	V	E	81	445	193,181	231,715	38,534
			82	230	134,618	165,798	31,180
			83	140	160,619	174,714	14,095
	V	W	81	142	56,123	65,952	9,829
			82	280	355,338	384,405	29,067
			83	298	230,620	259,318	28,698
ISRAEL	V	E	81	16	21,736	23,205	1,469
			82	303	71,623	77,055	5,432
ITALY	A	E	83	13	950	992	42
IVY CST	V	E	81	27	25,922	34,395	8,473
			82	5	5,696	6,888	1,192
			83	27	129,264	134,614	5,350
JAPAN	A	E	82	8	1,233	1,609	376
	V	W	83	1	6,087	6,300	213
MALAYSA	V	E	81	137	52,442	68,480	16,038
			82	40	25,685	34,313	8,628
	V	W	82	13	22,577	26,873	4,296
MEXICO	O	E	83	6	1,000	1,000	
	O	W	83	4	1,814	1,814	
	V	E	83	4	8,126	9,826	1,700
NICARAG	V	E	82	1	2,400	2,506	106
PHIL R	V	E	83	3	6,499	6,955	456
SINGAPR	V	E	81	129	388,225	415,680	27,455
			82	60	187,763	199,435	11,672
			83	25	81,935	87,941	6,006
	V	W	81	46	154,394	166,952	12,558
			82	64	190,478	201,889	11,411
			83	95	286,901	306,551	19,650
THAILND	N	W	83	*	2,483	2,525	42
	V	E	82	53	81,721	87,711	5,990
	V	W	81	25	25,080	29,416	4,336
			82	27	76,402	81,958	5,556
U KING	N	E	83	102	17,158	20,276	3,118
	V	E	82	1	1,462	2,239	777

2023305 BALSA LUMBER DRESSD EXCL SIDING (MBF)

Country	Mode	Reg	Yr	Quantity	F.A.S.	C.I.F.	Charges
TOTAL			84	1,303	513,819	597,744	83,925
			85	993	453,466	524,418	70,952
			86	382	87,351	118,000	30,649
ANTIGUA	V	W	86	20	17,785	20,762	2,977
BRAZIL	V	E	84	9	7,810	10,090	2,280
			85	45	7,497	7,534	37
CANADA	O	E	84	60	7,945	7,945	
			85	1	1,554	1,554	
ECUADOR	A	E	84	3	10,769	13,451	2,682
	V	E	84	652	258,945	307,537	48,592
			85	816	334,221	388,088	53,867
			86	362	69,566	97,238	27,672
	V	W	84	20	17,689	20,408	2,719
			85	102	90,008	104,406	14,398
FR GERM	A	E	84	10	1,896	2,388	492
	N	E	84	*	14,647	15,146	499
HONDURA	N	E	84	*	35,971	42,046	6,075
ISRAEL	V	E	84	322	72,432	75,660	3,228
			85	29	20,186	22,836	2,650
SALVADR	V	E	84	225	81,765	98,398	16,633
SRI LKA	V	E	84	2	3,950	4,675	725

Balsam Fir

Balsam fir, lumber
2021820 FIR LUMBER ROUGH (MBF)

Country	Mode	Reg	Yr	Quantity	F.A.S.	C.I.F.	Charges
TOTAL			81	51,339	11,667,911	14,356,469	2,677,490
			82	74,083	14,849,136	17,554,802	2,705,666
			83	138,252	31,754,124	37,497,963	5,743,839
			84	138,200	26,429,620	31,498,375	5,068,755
			85	136,466	29,770,874	34,696,705	4,925,831
			86	116,042	26,477,362	31,078,133	4,600,771
CANADA	N	E	83	16,958	3,644,153	4,525,538	881,385
			84	70,135	12,323,811	15,069,457	2,745,646
			85	73,634	14,983,762	18,948,437	3,964,675
			86	78,148	16,172,135	19,894,718	3,722,583
	N	W	81	11,724	3,913,502	3,930,825	7,255
			82	5,451	1,782,981	1,783,705	724
	O	E	81	1,103	231,557	231,557	
			82	10,824	1,938,392	1,938,392	
			83	25,623	5,039,819	5,039,819	
			84	19,787	3,578,363	3,578,363	
			85	11,233	2,070,123	2,070,123	
			86	4,385	896,096	896,096	
	O	W	81	96	23,227	23,227	
			82	36	7,360	7,360	
			83	10,744	3,706,004	3,706,004	
			84	10,229	3,009,139	3,009,139	
			85	13,289	4,840,636	4,842,080	1,444
			86	15,815	5,812,983	6,045,009	232,026
	V	E	81	37,183	7,344,088	9,985,161	2,640,073
			82	57,739	11,107,476	13,809,085	2,701,609
			83	84,919	19,363,120	24,225,335	4,862,215
			84	37,418	7,391,531	9,666,303	2,274,772
			85	34,745	7,091,123	7,913,297	822,174
			86	14,848	3,186,796	3,723,152	536,356
	V	W	81	1,233	155,537	185,699	30,162
			82	33	12,927	16,260	3,333
			83	8	1,028	1,267	239
			84	631	126,509	174,771	48,262
			85	2,906	645,705	747,549	101,844
			86	559	48,375	61,022	12,647
CHINA T	V	E	86	523	45,000	51,189	6,189
GERM DR	V	E	86	1,764	315,977	406,947	90,970
JAPAN	N	W	84	*	267	342	75
PHIL R	V	E	85	4	6,268	7,382	1,114
	V	W	85	32	6,406	7,979	1,573
U KING	V	E	85	623	126,851	159,858	33,007

2021840 FIR LBR DRSD WKD EXC SDG MLD (MBF)

Country	Mode	Reg	Yr	Quantity	F.A.S.	C.I.F.	Charges
TOTAL			81	483,328	92,531,754	108,505,683	15,865,062
			82	386,610	67,696,688	79,520,374	11,823,686
			83	570,386	122,113,058	142,634,142	20,521,084
			84	626,875	114,687,897	131,434,482	16,746,585
			85	655,327	136,109,761	155,885,763	19,776,002
			86	651,924	138,974,814	162,345,387	23,370,573
CANADA	N	E	82	20,261	4,346,323	5,055,015	708,692
			85	388,962	83,323,029	95,253,153	11,930,124
			86	96,990	18,701,963	18,712,699	10,736
	N	W	81	100,284	20,454,098	21,070,737	613,629
			82	53,098	10,300,130	10,301,459	1,329
			83	84,386	20,862,646	20,864,167	1,521
			84	90,620	19,677,046	19,678,052	1,006
	O	E	81	96,644	20,053,729	20,053,812	40
			82	120,759	22,580,908	22,712,702	131,794
			83	151,121	30,567,502	30,567,504	2
			84	234,706	44,346,033	44,346,033	
			85	16,998	3,205,256	3,205,256	
			86	68,533	13,639,940	13,639,942	2
	O	H	84	13	1,409	2,030	621
	O	W	81	890	142,995	142,995	
			82	1,885	201,048	201,048	
			83	898	146,251	146,251	
			84	1,059	145,832	145,832	
			85	87,118	20,316,954	20,316,960	6
			86	64,499	15,980,777	16,278,435	297,658
	V	E	81	276,301	50,389,932	65,491,407	14,995,661
			82	174,297	28,319,445	38,696,067	10,376,622
			83	327,640	68,903,145	89,180,731	20,277,586
			84	299,432	50,369,735	67,062,390	16,692,655
			85	156,556	28,216,353	35,869,042	7,652,689
			86	419,225	90,028,745	112,353,506	22,324,761
	V	W	81	9,181	1,484,418	1,734,491	250,073
			82	16,310	1,948,834	2,554,083	605,249
			83	6,341	1,633,514	1,875,489	241,975
			84	1,044	147,538	199,279	51,741
			85	2,793	540,669	645,852	105,183
			86	582	53,710	65,471	11,761
CHINA M	V	E	85	2,900	507,500	595,500	88,000
CZECHO	V	W	81	11	5,500	11,159	5,659
GABON	V	E	86	2,089	567,025	1,291,300	724,275
MEXICO	O	W	81	17	1,082	1,082	
REP SAF	V	E	86	6	2,654	4,034	1,380
SWITZLD	A	E	84	1	304	866	562

Crop / Product / TSUSA commodity number, description, and unit of quantity — Country	Mode	Reg	Yr	Quantity	F.A.S.	C.I.F.	Charges

Bamboo

Bamboo, basket
2224000 BASKETS AND BAGS BAMBOO (NO)

Country	Mode	Reg	Yr	Quantity	F.A.S.	C.I.F.	Charges
TOTAL			81	68,111,749	28,418,368	34,673,093	6,254,806
			82	62,176,382	23,790,610	30,080,295	6,287,675
			83	67,371,197	24,336,971	31,280,920	6,943,949
			84	70,243,826	27,544,507	36,275,291	8,730,784
			85	56,679,072	22,971,769	28,863,180	5,891,411
			86	55,909,638	20,613,271	25,587,367	4,974,096
AUSTRIA	V	W	81	457	1,218	1,372	154
			85	450	2,176	2,250	74
BELGIUM	A	E	83	100	2,802	3,542	740
BHUTAN	A	W	82	1,000	700	717	17
BNGLDSH	A	E	82	300	483	1,570	1,087
	N	E	81	11,506	9,544	17,478	7,934
	O	E	81	1,296	900	1,168	268
			84	2,932	2,490	3,799	1,309
	V	E	81	109,304	65,960	90,351	24,391
			82	59,856	41,271	68,672	27,401
			83	100,790	36,399	52,372	15,973
			84	154,435	64,602	87,665	23,063
			85	130,388	51,440	69,215	17,775
			86	76,338	22,371	34,307	11,936
	V	W	81	14,814	11,223	15,175	3,952
			82	13,819	11,193	14,824	3,631
			83	10,438	6,440	9,757	3,317
			84	667	673	758	85
			86	16,489	15,757	18,476	2,719
BOLIVIA	V	E	86	38,592	7,286	7,924	638
BRAZIL	A	W	81	140	1,344	1,548	204
	V	E	81	390	498	1,033	535
			82	1,450	4,535	7,588	3,053
			84	5,197	16,097	31,390	15,293
			85	4,956	2,681	6,506	3,825
BURMA	A	W	81	206	683	928	245
C RICA	A	E	84	45	287	481	194
	V	E	84	286	422	728	306
CAMROON	A	W	82	100	490	651	161
	V	W	85	3,172	5,141	5,834	693
CANADA	O	E	81	75	450	536	86
			84	6	288	288	
			85	100	1,019	1,019	
			86	1,000	3,804	3,804	
	O	W	81	29	300	300	
CHINA M	A	E	81	337	607	2,052	1,445
			83	5,397	1,980	3,091	1,111
			84	13,504	3,208	6,795	3,587
	A	H	81	1,000	2,028	3,041	1,013
			83	77	319	481	162
	A	W	84	151	476	745	269
	N	E	81	8,981,606	2,829,041	3,662,929	833,888
			82	9,573,291	3,335,161	4,566,714	1,231,553
			83	11,881,818	3,343,447	4,671,313	1,327,866
			84	8,261,150	2,054,317	3,016,025	961,708
			85	16,714	5,197	7,615	2,418
			86	5,258,285	925,117	1,311,986	386,869
	N	H	81	50,060	23,916	29,692	5,776
			83	23,765	16,378	20,737	4,359
	N	W	81	16,789,785	6,568,092	7,928,701	1,360,609
			82	17,450,558	6,140,841	7,606,454	1,465,613
			83	2,414,491	672,987	826,572	153,585
			84	5,950,794	1,629,783	1,999,739	369,956
			85	3,564,651	1,264,716	1,537,560	272,844
			86	136,373	48,217	57,960	9,743
	O	E	81	105,736	37,376	46,625	9,249
			82	46,770	33,764	38,510	4,746
			83	279,217	56,958	91,352	34,394
			84	238,806	98,575	113,869	15,294
			85	272,906	130,663	173,328	42,665
			86	603,626	150,807	211,013	60,206
	O	H	81	10,094	7,685	8,044	359
			82	99,471	55,786	65,535	9,749
			83	40,546	31,830	34,479	2,649
	O	W	81	400	1,710	1,799	89
			82	1,110	772	875	103
			83	12,477	34,988	37,143	2,155
	V	E	81	5,622,468	2,142,982	2,743,943	600,961
			82	5,392,092	1,924,916	2,633,504	708,588
			83	7,035,447	2,744,822	3,757,585	1,012,763
			84	9,867,758	4,065,446	5,792,463	1,727,017
			85	12,300,131	3,554,236	4,747,444	1,193,208
			86	8,033,218	2,144,070	2,836,029	691,959
	V	H	82	80,383	26,335	35,295	8,960
			84	15,642	10,673	13,249	2,576
			85	13,964	11,160	14,026	2,866
			86	7,112	3,696	5,578	1,882
	V	W	81	16,224,641	6,393,135	7,860,193	1,467,058
			82	10,446,752	4,175,984	5,163,449	987,465
			83	26,542,880	9,338,361	11,858,921	2,520,560
			84	26,275,583	9,729,228	12,595,524	2,866,296
			85	22,443,806	8,558,331	10,837,913	2,279,582
			86	26,793,927	8,224,079	10,047,736	1,823,657
CHINA T	A	E	81	12,048	3,339	8,677	5,338
			82	6,048	726	1,006	280
			83	400	924	1,054	130
			84	6,858	5,191	17,438	12,247
			86	39,564	18,474	61,200	42,726
	A	H	81	2,400	2,376	5,996	3,620
			83	72	765	1,562	797
	A	W	81	6,000	1,766	4,977	3,211
			84	150	361	483	122
	N	E	82	1,146,235	409,414	502,229	92,815
			83	1,075,038	508,300	594,948	86,648
			84	739,617	234,174	305,712	71,538
			86	233,805	170,865	206,373	35,508
	N	W	81	1,684,785	530,506	622,189	91,683
			82	1,761,121	578,681	683,361	104,680
			83	1,867,580	589,848	693,914	104,066
			84	1,680,986	551,252	695,690	144,438
			86	150,024	55,992	71,632	15,640
	O	E	82	74,916	16,204	20,556	4,352
			83	2,556	8,624	8,624	
			84	7,214	6,398	7,857	1,459
			85	15,043	3,793	5,147	1,354
			86	2,790	3,178	4,003	825
	O	W	81	1,633	2,880	3,366	486
			84	1,300	2,120	2,311	191
			85	7,020	2,225	2,979	754
	V	E	81	2,489,183	621,054	771,633	150,579
			82	1,998,602	387,311	510,896	123,585
			83	1,867,195	392,564	523,316	130,752
			84	1,159,642	492,953	669,043	176,090
			85	2,181,031	417,921	537,103	119,182
			86	821,150	417,283	526,794	109,511
	V	H	81	2,592	2,476	2,714	238
			82	22,368	1,814	2,145	331
			83	22,616	5,676	6,921	1,245
			85	21,600	3,114	3,571	457
	V	W	81	4,755,822	1,210,172	1,431,483	221,311
			82	4,856,401	1,154,207	1,403,412	249,205
			83	3,492,783	845,619	993,052	147,433
			84	3,288,446	1,388,045	1,609,744	221,699
			85	4,251,883	1,232,547	1,524,804	292,255
			86	2,965,482	963,005	1,123,483	160,478
COLOMB	A	E	81	276	1,386	1,788	402
			82	2,422	2,858	3,260	402
			83	22	780	840	60
			84	1,000	450	584	134
			85	29	1,016	1,086	70
			86	2,000	1,260	1,740	480
DOM REP	V	E	83	2,405	3,278	3,885	607
			86	99	3,471	4,064	593
ECUADOR	A	E	84	40	600	624	24
	A	W	83	31	384	480	96
FIJI	V	W	81	9,014	4,818	6,172	1,354
FINLAND	V	W	86	56,400	5,880	8,550	2,670
FR GERM	A	E	83	156	696	803	107
	A	W	82	53	620	655	35
	V	E	81	357	740	764	24
			82	12,116	6,531	9,466	2,935
			83	4,800	2,654	2,831	177
			84	4,100	2,515	2,644	129
			85	4,800	2,070	2,211	141
			86	4,800	2,496	2,759	263
FRANCE	V	E	82	29	460	479	19
			83	368	955	1,180	225
			84	2,616	2,901	2,975	74
	V	W	81	200	4,072	4,283	211
			82	120	3,056	3,631	575
			83	174	3,643	4,085	442
			84	325	6,376	7,284	908
			85	127	2,988	3,408	420
GAMBIA	V	E	84	1,168	2,287	3,216	929
GHANA	A	W	81	170	340	375	35

Crop
Product
TSUSA commodity number, description, and unit of quantity

Country	Mode	Reg	Yr	Quantity	F.A.S.	C.I.F.	Charges
HAITI	A	E	81	179	363	396	33
			83	4,172	4,570	7,475	2,905
	N	E	81	9,894	16,528	20,836	4,308
	V	E	81	50,707	40,730	52,299	11,569
			82	41,565	64,310	76,442	12,132
			83	33,915	42,266	52,425	10,159
			84	38,503	43,668	53,794	10,126
			85	21,453	68,698	76,820	8,122
			86	25,981	69,705	77,708	8,003
	V	W	83	6,868	9,538	12,726	3,188
			84	988	1,650	2,128	478
			85	800	1,336	1,618	282
HG KONG	A	E	84	15,300	8,457	15,132	6,675
			86	12,240	11,925	33,628	21,703
	A	H	84	11,016	4,781	15,195	10,414
	N	E	81	248,875	95,071	122,450	27,379
			82	1,535,062	265,709	365,583	99,874
			83	1,339,224	413,830	532,435	118,605
			84	859,458	174,520	252,235	77,715
			85	85,075	33,945	43,724	9,779
	N	W	81	589,734	297,175	358,741	61,566
			82	140,168	87,934	103,005	15,071
			84	1,951,547	631,605	796,317	164,712
			86	9,252	22,558	29,304	6,746
	O	E	81	4,968	5,914	7,366	1,452
			82	12,748	9,016	10,177	1,161
			83	10,600	11,157	12,142	985
			84	2,512	704	831	127
			85	10,840	5,484	6,704	1,220
	O	H	83	500	306	320	14
	V	E	81	425,396	154,243	188,713	34,470
			82	429,199	135,232	188,764	53,532
			83	1,002,328	343,326	469,822	126,496
			84	755,514	346,832	484,068	137,236
			85	1,205,418	489,256	638,105	148,849
			86	1,721,915	598,149	791,875	193,726
	V	H	82	724	427	604	177
			83	8,050	6,505	8,199	1,694
	V	W	81	754,962	264,201	312,610	48,409
			82	1,539,619	548,017	654,111	106,094
			83	1,818,963	589,652	740,151	150,499
			84	922,403	306,914	376,913	69,999
			85	2,730,518	954,842	1,182,854	228,012
			86	2,388,132	854,863	1,024,285	169,422
INDIA	V	E	81	19,109	21,168	40,666	19,498
			83	2,333	2,292	2,756	464
	V	W	81	2,240	7,049	14,871	7,822
			82	504	820	1,062	242
			83	1,636	6,272	7,677	1,405
			84	93	292	353	61
			85	4,098	8,409	9,792	1,383
INDNSIA	A	E	83	350	350	806	456
			85	88	1,550	1,914	364
	A	W	84	383	516	724	208
	N	W	81	55,158	64,779	74,110	9,331
			82	42,413	47,788	57,530	9,742
			83	21,778	20,183	23,234	3,051
	O	E	81	3,126	2,610	3,978	1,368
	V	E	81	12,621	19,857	24,942	5,085
			82	3,506	9,822	13,135	3,313
			84	2,484	2,994	4,806	1,812
			85	176	1,349	4,735	3,386
			86	6,290	11,344	20,711	9,367
	V	W	81	66,606	74,478	98,487	24,009
			82	37,059	69,653	98,652	28,999
			83	4,568	21,140	25,483	4,343
			84	104,590	101,612	116,655	15,043
			85	76,808	115,350	137,995	22,645
			86	46,489	62,966	73,243	10,277
IRAN	V	E	81	3,075	1,596	2,519	923
ISRAEL	V	E	81	1,145	3,297	3,669	372
ITALY	V	E	82	8,978	4,157	6,236	2,079
			83	302	1,593	2,000	407
			84	7,517	8,032	10,992	2,960
			85	95	1,073	1,138	65
	V	W	82	7,871	7,238	8,171	933
			83	3,158	1,954	2,349	395
			84	1,000	730	828	98
IVY CST	V	W	85	37	1,298	1,777	479
			86	64,560	15,239	21,074	5,835
JAMAICA	V	E	83	954	1,163	1,292	129
JAPAN	A	E	84	70	339	504	165
			86	675	1,664	2,929	1,265
	A	H	81	6	935	1,005	70

Crop
Product
TSUSA commodity number, description, and unit of quantity

Country	Mode	Reg	Yr	Quantity	F.A.S.	C.I.F.	Charges
	A	W	82	3	309	309	6
	N	E	81	42,767	21,989	28,568	6,579
			82	11,816	43,808	49,723	5,915
			84	7,665	19,357	27,938	8,581
	N	H	82	2,290	2,263	2,550	287
			86	768	7,959	9,256	1,297
	N	W	81	470	22,235	24,508	2,273
			82	12,425	21,014	23,298	2,284
			83	6,319	32,800	36,751	3,951
			84	45,254	38,506	44,280	5,774
	O	E	81	8	300	315	15
	V	E	81	13	520	541	21
			82	1,530	2,727	2,911	184
			83	8,614	22,166	25,317	3,151
			84	5	322	360	38
			85	9,280	14,093	18,883	4,790
			86	495	17,327	20,627	3,300
	V	H	81	1,172	2,267	2,481	214
			83	562	1,340	1,465	125
			84	284	1,246	1,395	149
			85	73	2,572	2,795	223
	V	W	81	21,296	88,281	97,048	8,848
			82	14,566	53,278	62,313	9,035
			83	141,109	62,411	70,837	8,426
			84	12,820	23,724	26,740	3,016
			85	2,919	36,495	40,847	4,352
			86	86,700	44,195	50,015	5,820
KENYA	A	E	81	250	325	511	186
			82	350	2,975	3,716	741
			84	3,250	18,070	22,770	4,700
			85	3,700	7,200	9,405	2,205
	A	W	81	5,500	2,889	4,181	1,292
			84	2,687	7,575	12,162	4,587
			85	1,514	7,087	11,587	4,500
	V	E	84	486	2,068	2,784	716
KOR REP	A	E	82	250	380	756	376
	V	E	81	3,354	2,077	2,420	343
			82	49,769	13,374	16,401	3,027
			83	2,976	1,114	1,467	353
			84	25,655	4,105	6,305	2,200
			85	4,268	9,431	12,805	3,374
			86	157,060	69,922	83,694	13,772
	V	H	82	20	2,125	2,226	101
	V	W	81	204,793	30,134	32,632	2,498
			82	64,051	28,250	31,920	3,670
			83	61,256	33,155	39,069	5,914
			84	29,158	20,665	24,114	3,449
			85	120,000	12,800	16,900	4,100
MACAO	V	E	82	10,080	3,604	4,102	498
			83	1,800	888	1,285	397
			84	576	684	1,024	340
	V	H	84	120	480	521	41
	V	W	81	4,457	1,054	1,337	283
			83	1,152	346	392	46
			84	78,474	22,540	31,766	9,226
			86	15,134	11,762	14,295	2,533
MALAYSA	V	E	84	13,980	6,062	7,862	1,800
	V	W	82	389	461	541	80
			82	385	343	352	9
			83	3,842	2,833	3,416	583
			85	12,338	5,224	6,032	808
MEXICO	A	E	82	472	881	961	80
	A	W	81	1,800	2,543	2,543	
			83	1,994	2,569	4,064	1,495
			84	14,331	10,834	10,834	
			86	1,544	3,503	5,467	1,964
	N	E	81	3,645,877	2,226,939	2,235,428	8,489
	O	E	81	92,454	72,260	73,366	1,106
			82	1,714,263	1,037,474	1,037,551	77
			83	2,236,417	892,867	893,667	800
			84	2,605,791	1,357,869	1,358,578	709
			85	2,532,330	2,479,377	2,481,756	2,379
			86	1,497,653	1,205,290	1,206,861	1,571
	O	W	81	463,658	385,347	386,363	1,016
			82	127,162	134,870	134,886	16
			83	76,174	47,696	47,696	
			84	135,307	99,747	99,924	177
			85	109,430	123,961	126,829	2,868
			86	55,261	61,363	61,461	98
	V	E	82	97,836	44,684	48,158	3,474
			83	3,624	3,203	4,979	1,776
			84	2,040	3,240	5,190	1,950
			85	1,220	2,133	5,309	3,176
			86	816	1,614	1,777	163

Crop
Product
TSUSA commodity number, description, and unit of quantity

Country	Mode	Reg	Yr	Quantity	F.A.S.	C.I.F.	Charges
MOROC	A	E	84	150	1,395	1,980	585
	V	E	84	700	1,190	1,515	325
			85	750	3,571	3,963	392
NEPAL	A	W	84	257	256	795	539
NIGERIA	A	E	84	85	679	797	118
PAKISTN	V	W	82	12,660	22,510	33,092	10,582
PANAMA	V	W	86	614	1,167	1,407	240
PERU	A	E	81	222	831	1,167	336
			83	200	1,056	1,339	283
			84	472	2,146	2,396	250
			85	1,010	1,009	1,875	866
PHIL R	A	E	82	416	5,142	10,151	5,009
			83	840	285	920	635
			84	205	940	2,352	1,412
			85	24,288	5,415	11,733	6,318
	A	W	82	4	300	1,013	713
			83	495	1,834	3,742	1,908
	N	E	81	483,335	259,961	344,863	84,902
			82	147,923	132,495	188,048	55,553
			83	171,245	152,960	211,467	58,507
			84	441,266	231,967	355,808	123,841
			85	20,658	38,340	60,494	22,154
			86	38,782	77,958	111,311	33,353
	N	H	81	28,000	42,747	58,371	15,624
	N	W	81	1,397,688	1,241,867	1,548,965	307,098
			82	619,968	507,349	659,550	152,201
			83	635,797	546,717	718,549	171,832
			84	1,637,198	1,250,122	1,698,606	448,484
			85	1,259,525	719,865	948,442	228,577
	O	E	81	5,858	3,378	4,095	717
			82	2,323	3,705	4,975	1,270
			83	1,603	2,378	2,965	587
			84	19,014	7,375	10,262	2,887
			85	900	1,208	2,769	1,561
			86	1,442	3,119	3,962	843
	O	W	84	93	2,318	2,446	128
	V	E	81	513,354	559,002	727,213	168,211
			82	758,016	625,627	842,092	216,465
			83	706,003	639,103	845,446	206,343
			84	928,590	743,660	1,049,191	305,531
			85	1,233,886	948,876	1,290,951	342,075
			86	638,233	996,607	1,231,842	235,235
	V	H	81	100	304	445	141
			82	27,979	60,741	83,471	22,730
			83	33,494	66,120	86,135	20,015
			84	18,893	24,050	37,099	13,049
			85	6,897	9,278	14,456	5,178
			86	10,813	15,600	21,219	5,619
	V	W	81	1,274,853	1,242,625	1,630,251	387,626
			82	1,191,999	1,134,159	1,464,991	330,832
			83	2,103,159	1,417,806	1,832,244	414,438
			84	1,646,800	1,352,410	1,937,365	584,955
			85	1,577,111	1,272,647	1,749,550	476,903
			86	3,432,907	3,033,853	3,845,251	811,398
PITCARN	V	W	86	2,554	1,021	1,566	545
POLAND	V	E	81	6,880	14,494	17,681	3,187
			82	1,248	3,869	4,955	1,086
			83	3,010	1,674	1,965	291
PORTUGL	A	E	82	75	653	1,056	403
	V	E	81	39,577	32,804	40,725	7,921
			85	10,469	16,161	22,282	6,121
ROMANIA	V	E	85	940	3,285	6,260	2,975
RWANDA	A	E	81	56	366	418	52
			82	24	290	567	277
			83	22	265	439	174
SALVADR	A	E	82	2,625	5,364	6,035	671
			83	2,000	4,145	4,854	709
			84	1,000	2,665	3,071	406
SINGAPR	A	W	84	236	1,755	2,799	1,044
	V	E	82	1,500	1,388	2,321	933
			84	1,080	1,567	2,429	862
			86	5,548	6,148	10,363	4,215
	V	W	81	3,987	9,421	13,292	3,871
			82	99	300	344	44
			83	3,200	2,816	3,469	653
			86	4,158	3,919	5,602	1,683
SPAIN	V	E	82	1,665	11,551	15,819	4,268
			83	2,577	26,671	30,592	3,921
			85	5,116	20,133	24,044	3,911
	V	W	85	3,964	2,011	2,344	333
SRI LKA	V	W	83	10,136	2,392	2,689	297
			84	542	2,801	3,108	307
			86	7,140	12,815	18,669	5,854
SWEDEN	V	E	82	30	302	332	30

Crop
Product
TSUSA commodity number, description, and unit of quantity
Country Mode Reg Yr Quantity F.A.S. C.I.F. Charges

Country	Mode	Reg	Yr	Quantity	F.A.S.	C.I.F.	Charges
SWITZLD	O	E	86	8,512	6,328	6,328	
	V	E	84	15	763	1,042	279
			85	75,843	43,908	62,995	19,087
			86	258,522	51,919	69,601	17,682
	V	W	85	96,794	41,129	52,336	11,207
			86	78,926	49,591	61,141	11,550
T PAC I	V	W	85	36,092	31,447	50,156	18,709
			86	14,400	3,690	3,874	184
THAILND	A	E	83	1,710	325	779	454
	A	W	84	50	1,234	3,050	1,816
	N	W	81	43,476	28,049	34,119	6,070
			84	14,263	24,611	29,856	5,245
	V	E	81	136,098	123,314	167,055	43,741
			82	138,652	58,613	78,606	19,993
			83	46,384	43,332	55,409	12,077
			84	39,009	63,826	92,229	28,403
			85	18,946	26,750	38,031	11,281
			86	8,796	16,137	22,886	6,749
	V	H	82	471	3,721	4,372	651
			83	600	927	1,028	101
			84	6	280	309	29
			85	150	2,273	2,594	321
	V	W	81	550,031	434,038	567,416	133,378
			82	314,336	251,434	320,391	68,957
			83	159,328	193,239	239,200	45,961
			84	138,651	158,550	202,700	44,150
			85	122,229	118,651	154,232	35,581
			86	53,383	68,651	88,402	19,751
TUNISIA	V	E	85	288	10,402	12,316	1,914
	V	W	85	10,404	6,777	9,267	2,490
U KING	A	E	81	5	531	709	178
	N	E	84	5,475	2,183	2,282	99
			85	1	1,106	1,122	16
	N	W	84	8,523	3,201	4,236	1,035
	V	E	81	200	301	316	15
			82	81	3,509	3,691	182
			83	56	369	381	12
			86	900	1,170	1,580	410
	V	W	81	45	1,532	2,183	651
			82	21	643	2,704	45
			83	50	314	346	32
YUGOSLV	O	E	83	111	337	425	88
	V	E	83	1,895	6,476	9,863	3,387
			84	9,574	19,635	22,423	2,788
			85	7,562	12,130	17,625	5,495
			86	11,969	5,122	8,742	3,620
	V	W	81	1,206	2,095	2,180	85
			82	200	350	660	310

Bamboo shoot, canned

1417800 BAMBOO SHOOTS, CANNED (LB)

Country	Mode	Reg	Yr	Quantity	F.A.S.	C.I.F.	Charges
TOTAL			81	35,348,304	16,592,968	18,463,131	1,870,163
			82	26,873,089	13,684,234	15,294,035	1,609,801
			83	30,522,148	14,490,272	16,162,135	1,671,863
			84	35,053,002	14,468,024	16,573,420	2,105,396
			85	41,403,274	17,290,500	19,611,832	2,321,332
			86	49,571,348	21,492,799	23,803,724	2,310,925
BRAZIL	V	E	86	28,500	97,900	98,617	717
BURKINA	V	W	81	3,900	3,150	3,300	150
CHINA M	O	E	81	21,675	16,810	16,810	
			84	27,600	9,840	9,840	
			86	22,084	18,847	19,973	1,126
	O	W	81	7,791	3,050	3,194	144
			86	5,842	3,160	3,331	171
	V	E	81	1,020,388	447,419	511,896	64,477
			82	486,489	248,757	280,508	31,751
			83	1,645,372	677,920	784,767	106,847
			84	375,603	166,129	193,835	27,706
			85	283,641	135,442	156,825	21,383
			86	1,242,765	506,090	587,719	81,629
	V	H	81	44,161	16,666	18,536	1,870
			82	4,458	1,512	1,790	278
			83	39,690	20,580	23,277	2,697
			84	39,923	13,481	15,433	1,952
			85	5,512	2,200	2,489	289
	V	W	81	1,453,132	587,977	658,803	70,826
			82	1,011,989	612,243	663,628	51,385
			83	981,806	428,285	477,727	49,442
			84	1,016,955	383,377	430,815	47,438
			85	528,996	239,289	263,036	23,747
			86	826,397	396,906	427,687	30,781

Crop
Product
TSUSA commodity number, description, and unit of quantity

Country	Mode	Reg	Yr	Quantity	F.A.S.	C.I.F.	Charges
CHINA T	N	E	81	5,386,362	2,510,303	2,867,937	357,634
			85	7,543,804	3,382,837	3,951,995	569,158
			86	120,526	37,054	42,820	5,766
	N	H	82	706,353	430,847	483,175	52,328
	N	W	81	193,912	101,639	110,102	8,463
			83	660,836	314,940	341,248	26,308
			84	2,685	1,230	1,276	46
			85	201,543	87,975	99,784	11,809
			86	277,811	114,372	126,219	11,847
	O	E	81	269,684	127,480	129,787	2,307
			82	25,500	16,575	16,575	
			84	36,538	17,936	18,101	165
			86	5,250	2,840	3,044	204
	V	E	81	7,263,783	3,550,809	4,028,621	477,812
			82	8,250,880	4,181,259	4,816,073	634,814
			83	9,680,845	4,556,922	5,263,641	706,719
			84	12,406,308	4,973,350	5,971,255	997,905
			85	7,253,512	3,016,285	3,569,890	553,605
			86	15,270,561	6,977,648	7,942,966	965,318
	V	H	81	1,014,754	536,019	590,591	54,572
			82	124,944	76,663	85,548	8,885
			83	960,602	528,551	586,110	57,559
			84	820,040	385,572	436,714	51,142
			85	931,422	516,553	570,025	53,472
			86	989,232	465,168	518,221	53,053
	V	W	81	17,088,709	8,019,647	8,777,530	757,883
			82	14,324,475	7,278,476	7,999,965	721,489
			83	14,339,735	7,065,905	7,680,878	614,973
			84	18,423,804	7,708,880	8,596,517	887,637
			85	21,683,174	8,842,584	9,793,428	950,844
			86	24,850,818	10,590,360	11,503,337	912,977
DENMARK	V	W	85	71,196	28,704	30,898	2,194
FRANCE	V	E	83	825	521	533	12
HG KONG	O	E	81	1,980	917	917	
			83	4,200	4,065	4,431	366
			85	14,104	4,523	5,438	915
	V	E	81	219,723	70,600	84,158	13,558
			82	106,181	39,285	45,857	6,572
			83	353,136	148,956	172,646	23,690
			84	79,450	27,588	35,615	8,027
			85	517,274	230,243	265,367	35,124
			86	956,210	402,478	446,408	43,930
	V	H	82	1,913	1,283	1,403	120
	V	W	81	154,087	70,146	75,991	5,845
			82	54,025	27,930	31,984	4,054
			83	455,111	173,764	195,801	22,037
			84	71,256	25,901	28,303	2,402
			85	91,190	40,480	43,424	2,944
			86	367,726	160,020	174,279	14,259
INDIA	V	E	82	60,550	25,840	28,669	2,829
INDNSIA	V	W	83	2,340	950	1,014	64
JAPAN	V	E	81	71,906	55,190	62,710	7,520
			82	95,882	71,351	82,477	11,126
			83	16,762	30,757	34,023	3,266
			84	64,119	48,965	55,609	6,644
			85	3,959	12,411	13,473	1,062
			86	11,614	14,440	16,523	2,083
	V	H	81	8,539	12,452	14,129	1,677
			82	12,447	22,473	25,970	3,497
			83	15,023	25,711	28,619	2,908
			84	31,135	25,792	29,147	3,355
			85	3,974	9,535	10,895	1,360
			86	7,501	24,305	26,525	2,220
	V	W	81	93,958	86,711	92,410	5,699
			82	76,111	58,866	63,291	4,425
			83	78,151	83,240	89,822	6,582
			84	65,700	89,778	96,087	6,309
			85	50,056	77,666	82,884	5,218
			86	75,749	100,722	105,415	4,693
KOR REP	V	E	81	12,974	7,993	8,808	815
			84	20,400	8,925	11,470	2,545
			86	22,944	10,611	12,070	1,459
	V	W	81	80,400	40,304	43,816	3,512
			83	11,376	3,760	4,065	305
			85	4,275	1,346	1,406	60
MACAO	V	E	84	1,275	625	752	127
MALAYSA	V	E	86	30,000	12,815	13,970	1,155
	V	W	83	2,925	775	828	53
MEXICO	O	W	86	5,225	4,320	4,320	
	V	E	83	4,500	3,420	3,874	454
PAKISTN	V	W	85	13,760	8,304	8,764	460
PHIL R	V	W	81	330	299	321	22
			83	2,500	800	863	63
			85	7,313	3,748	4,068	320

Crop
Product
TSUSA commodity number, description, and unit of quantity

Country	Mode	Reg	Yr	Quantity	F.A.S.	C.I.F.	Charges
SINGAPR	V	E	86	15,145	9,283	10,321	1,038
	V	W	81	9,312	3,877	4,230	353
			82	3,376	2,152	2,351	199
			84	5,313	3,643	3,825	182
			86	38,463	13,738	16,072	2,334
SPAIN	V	E	85	36,113	10,891	13,271	2,380
SWITZLD	V	E	85	60,000	24,870	28,012	3,142
THAILND	N	E	81	157,874	40,557	45,641	5,084
			85	33,981	11,534	13,335	1,801
			86	764,744	201,171	242,250	41,079
	N	W	84	653,034	212,824	233,541	20,717
	O	E	81	23,870	24,174	25,527	1,353
			82	9,612	3,020	3,322	302
			83	1,197	800	874	74
			86	7,341	1,468	1,657	189
	O	W	84	721	462	501	39
			85	26,563	12,930	14,227	1,297
	V	E	81	147,564	45,597	51,712	6,115
			82	665,915	286,751	324,653	37,902
			83	261,007	60,996	73,693	12,697
			84	273,255	75,886	91,150	15,264
			85	405,442	111,391	136,675	25,284
			86	66,109	21,779	24,601	2,822
	V	H	81	360	353	397	44
			82	5,403	3,551	4,107	556
			83	9,136	4,811	5,213	402
			84	8,267	4,762	5,452	690
			86	6,413	2,728	3,125	397
	V	W	81	595,170	211,560	233,913	22,353
			82	846,586	295,400	332,689	37,289
			83	995,073	353,843	388,188	34,345
			84	629,621	283,078	308,182	25,104
			85	1,632,470	478,759	532,223	53,464
			86	3,456,695	1,258,956	1,385,630	126,674
TUNISIA	V	W	86	99,683	43,620	46,624	3,004
U KING	V	W	81	2,006	1,269	1,344	75

Bamboo shoot, frozen**
1384000 BAMBOO SHOOTS, CHESTNUTS FZ (LB)

Country	Mode	Reg	Yr	Quantity	F.A.S.	C.I.F.	Charges
TOTAL			81	740,560	283,749	351,571	67,822
			82	1,238,051	553,071	705,757	152,686
			83	1,637,958	682,031	854,356	172,325
			84	2,495,499	980,384	1,257,854	277,470
			85	4,333,305	1,883,635	2,356,378	472,743
			86	3,629,028	1,709,269	1,970,055	260,786
CANADA	O	E	82	4,500	1,852	1,852	
			83	845	300	300	
CHINA M	N	E	84	4,465	1,778	3,485	1,707
	V	E	83	2,730	1,494	1,790	296
			86	57,167	27,204	33,811	6,607
	V	W	81	148,146	43,763	51,263	7,500
			84	9,750	3,244	4,493	1,249
CHINA T	N	E	85	206,160	123,089	146,781	23,692
	V	E	81	515,533	206,246	262,757	56,511
			82	999,851	441,987	572,832	130,845
			83	1,402,682	550,936	705,220	154,284
			84	2,031,980	765,110	1,004,065	238,955
			85	3,025,887	1,290,582	1,662,214	371,632
			86	1,972,316	809,596	979,086	169,490
	V	W	81	72,966	32,029	35,598	3,569
			82	230,480	106,863	128,408	21,545
			83	212,761	124,127	141,705	17,578
			84	444,957	207,065	242,081	35,016
			85	906,802	405,032	458,629	53,597
			86	1,562,790	853,258	934,838	81,580
DOM REP	V	E	81	1,904	476	573	97
HG KONG	O	E	84	580	650	660	10
	V	E	85	23,876	5,608	7,763	2,155
			86	13,227	3,240	4,973	1,733
	V	W	85	38,488	10,905	16,942	6,037
JAPAN	V	E	85	115,200	37,395	51,839	14,444
			86	4,154	6,464	7,596	1,132
	V	W	83	176	534	561	27
			85	1,185	1,724	1,809	85
			86	2,574	5,307	5,551	244
MEXICO	O	E	86	16,800	4,200	4,200	
PHIL R	V	W	84	849	800	879	79
THAILND	O	E	83	16,826	3,040	3,040	
	V	E	84	2,019	1,107	1,277	170
	V	W	81	2,011	1,235	1,380	145
			82	3,220	2,369	2,665	296

Crop Product TSUSA commodity number, description, and unit of quantity Country	Mode	Reg	Yr	Quantity	F.A.S.	C.I.F.	Charges
			83	1,938	1,600	1,740	140
			84	899	630	914	284
			85	15,707	9,300	10,401	1,101

Bamboo, stick**

2220590 BAMBOO/RAT STICKS ROUGH/CUT (NULL)

Country	Mode	Reg	Yr	Quantity	F.A.S.	C.I.F.	Charges
TOTAL			81	-	3,262,378	3,882,797	620,419
			82	-	3,320,153	3,840,462	520,309
			83	-	2,319,124	2,841,277	522,153
			84	-	2,159,598	2,699,629	540,031
			85	-	2,901,727	3,667,487	765,760
			86	-	2,766,865	3,281,238	514,373
BELIZE	N	E	86	-	10,875	11,480	605
BRAZIL	N	E	83	-	300	439	139
BURMA	N	E	81	-	5,040	13,263	8,223
			85	-	27,799	67,500	39,701
	N	W	81	-	14,175	25,677	11,502
			82	-	10,593	19,294	8,701
			83	-	10,337	20,224	9,887
CAMROON	N	E	86	-	14,008	18,509	4,501
CANADA	N	E	84	-	285	285	
			85	-	2,580	2,580	
			86	-	3,822	3,822	
	N	W	83	-	900	934	34
			86	-	1,606	1,606	
CHINA M	N	E	81	-	108,766	147,041	38,275
			82	-	49,902	72,300	22,398
			83	-	131,733	180,222	48,489
			84	-	200,724	288,398	87,674
			85	-	319,528	463,086	143,558
			86	-	197,233	275,513	78,280
	N	W	81	-	258,428	342,026	83,598
			82	-	275,885	370,238	94,353
			83	-	359,338	487,011	127,673
			84	-	192,900	259,931	67,031
			85	-	364,660	476,811	112,151
			86	-	387,636	481,451	93,815
CHINA T	N	E	81	-	282,097	371,445	89,348
			82	-	310,746	393,829	83,083
			83	-	370,057	432,039	61,982
			84	-	180,554	253,701	73,147
			85	-	207,494	273,087	65,593
			86	-	390,643	449,834	59,191
	N	H	81	-	2,510	3,039	529
			82	-	2,178	2,698	520
			83	-	2,082	2,592	510
			84	-	2,107	3,019	912
			85	-	4,797	6,348	1,551
			86	-	2,205	3,502	1,297
	N	W	81	-	455,097	536,534	81,437
			82	-	325,258	399,562	74,304
			83	-	174,998	225,787	50,789
			84	-	309,345	399,669	90,324
			85	-	337,614	448,722	111,108
			86	-	356,063	418,452	62,389
DOMINCA	N	E	86	-	6,087	7,637	1,550
ECUADOR	N	E	86	-	4,100	5,950	1,850
FRANCE	N	E	83	-	1,545	2,020	475
			84	-	256	262	6
	N	W	81	-	609	652	43
			83	-	1,247	1,295	48
			84	-	7,734	8,115	381
			85	-	10,714	11,197	483
			86	-	13,657	14,809	1,152
GERM DR	N	E	85	-	4,383	6,572	2,189
GUATMAL	N	E	86	-	3,125	4,625	1,500
HG KONG	N	E	81	-	372,333	432,640	60,307
			82	-	103,560	127,851	24,291
			83	-	260,987	340,479	79,492
			84	-	120,834	146,334	25,500
			85	-	119,092	143,525	24,433
			86	-	125,658	152,021	26,363
	N	W	81	-	154,148	186,615	32,467
			82	-	107,803	140,606	32,803
			83	-	35,156	41,653	6,497
			84	-	33,359	38,390	5,031
			85	-	42,778	50,798	8,020
			86	-	134,961	155,176	20,215
INDIA	N	E	84	-	2,796	4,077	1,281
			86	-	7,666	11,280	3,614
	N	H	85	-	1,795	3,236	1,441
	N	W	81	-	2,073	4,313	2,240
			82	-	1,249	2,000	751
			83	-	2,996	5,670	2,674
			84	-	2,083	2,160	77
			85	-	2,569	3,492	923
			86	-	13,544	15,617	2,073
INDNSIA	N	E	81	-	261,363	296,341	34,978
			82	-	240,513	264,490	23,977
			83	-	80,667	92,776	12,109
			84	-	227,488	257,535	30,047
			85	-	268,950	319,164	50,214
			86	-	202,022	227,383	25,361
	N	W	81	-	140,821	155,640	14,819
			82	-	30,330	33,122	2,792
			83	-	37,230	47,834	10,604
			85	-	11,903	13,424	1,521
			86	-	31,788	39,388	7,600
ITALY	N	E	85	-	1,063	1,109	46
			86	-	3,040	3,115	75
	N	W	85	-	3,000	5,532	2,532
JAPAN	N	E	81	-	36,595	41,711	5,116
			82	-	190,947	226,055	35,108
			83	-	97,514	113,923	16,409
			84	-	128,503	154,024	25,521
			85	-	218,527	266,310	47,783
			86	-	332,666	384,661	51,995
	N	H	81	-	9,109	11,340	2,231
			82	-	15,148	18,100	2,952
			83	-	12,140	12,770	630
			84	-	17,094	20,790	3,696
			85	-	10,921	11,746	825
			86	-	6,302	9,070	2,768
	N	W	81	-	524,146	588,719	64,573
			82	-	779,935	849,996	70,061
			83	-	391,235	454,655	63,420
			84	-	445,059	525,596	80,537
			85	-	267,067	347,111	80,044
			86	-	158,099	177,318	19,219
KENYA	N	E	81	-	1,144	1,250	106
			82	-	280	322	42
KOR REP	N	E	83	-	8,590	12,740	4,150
			86	-	12,180	12,328	148
	N	W	81	-	50,890	54,175	3,285
			83	-	2,353	2,463	110
			84	-	902	1,069	167
			86	-	18,457	19,756	1,299
MALAYSA	N	E	81	-	4,375	4,871	496
			82	-	19,508	21,045	1,537
			84	-	13,098	17,771	4,673
	N	W	83	-	6,081	7,559	1,478
MEXICO	N	E	83	-	2,655	2,655	
	N	W	82	-	1,400	1,400	
NETHLDS	N	E	81	-	5,588	5,878	290
			86	-	2,500	2,579	79
PHIL R	N	E	81	-	2,238	2,859	621
			82	-	1,039	1,229	190
			83	-	741	965	224
			84	-	257	358	101
			85	-	13,143	16,777	3,634
	N	H	81	-	346	3,131	2,785
			85	-	1,625	2,878	1,253
	N	W	81	-	15,413	19,444	4,031
			82	-	29,451	33,454	4,003
			83	-	1,711	2,095	384
			84	-	5,812	9,202	3,390
			85	-	41,862	47,711	5,849
			86	-	123,761	138,132	14,371
PITCARN	N	W	85	-	7,113	7,696	583
PORTUGL	N	E	81	-	17,607	33,862	16,255
SIER LN	N	E	86	-	1,148	2,050	902
SINGAPR	N	E	81	-	354,906	390,761	35,855
			82	-	246,875	256,701	9,826
			83	-	239,061	256,845	17,784
			84	-	220,972	250,469	29,497
			85	-	482,479	525,136	42,657
			86	-	180,142	201,422	21,280
	N	W	81	-	138,394	153,183	14,789
			82	-	550,367	568,947	18,580
			83	-	84,117	90,056	5,939
			84	-	42,450	46,491	4,041
			85	-	125,726	143,214	17,488
			86	-	13,916	17,513	3,597
SPAIN	N	E	81	-	711	889	178
			85	-	2,545	2,725	180

Crop Product TSUSA commodity number, description, and unit of quantity Country	Mode	Reg	Yr	Quantity	F.A.S.	C.I.F.	Charges
	N W	86	-	4,928	9,030	4,102	
THAILND	N E	81	-	35,770	47,243	11,473	
		82	-	25,325	35,240	9,915	
		84	-	2,800	9,663	6,863	
		86	-	3,027	6,209	3,182	
	N W	81	-	1,200	1,402	202	
U KING	N E	81	-	3,397	3,432	35	
		82	-	600	644	44	
		83	-	3,353	3,576	223	
		84	-	1,647	1,710	63	
	N W	81	-	647	700	53	
		82	-	1,261	1,339	78	
		84	-	539	610	71	
VENEZ	N E	81	-	2,442	2,721	279	

2221500 BAMBOO SPLIT (LB)

Country	Mode	Reg	Yr	Quantity	F.A.S.	C.I.F.	Charges
TOTAL		81	260,567	85,956	104,109	18,153	
		82	273,187	83,008	103,733	21,136	
		83	290,922	117,617	141,625	24,008	
		84	1,610,157	207,771	243,815	36,044	
		85	469,214	169,351	201,170	31,819	
		86	616,084	182,349	221,315	38,966	
C RICA	V E	85	89,541	4,051	9,726	5,675	
CAMROON	V E	86	42,187	8,960	10,163	1,203	
CHINA M	A W	85	10	1,028	1,078	50	
	O E	82	6,000	1,137	1,545	408	
	V E	81	123,413	20,192	28,409	8,217	
		82	64,810	10,826	15,654	4,828	
		83	45,535	8,592	11,824	3,232	
		84	1,199,927	46,157	57,678	11,521	
		85	71,743	19,886	23,081	3,195	
		86	113,129	33,825	39,214	5,389	
	V W	81	4,847	680	1,054	374	
		82	72,972	11,822	16,718	4,896	
		83	97,503	24,222	32,100	7,878	
		84	47,844	11,940	14,070	2,130	
		85	117,813	35,146	39,845	4,699	
		86	46,000	13,530	15,660	2,130	
CHINA T	A E	81	132	306	621	315	
	V E	81	42,944	19,118	22,829	3,711	
		82	48,645	14,576	18,391	3,815	
		83	79,830	39,117	46,349	7,232	
		84	257,148	90,751	104,434	13,683	
		85	155,449	87,912	102,135	14,223	
		86	48,488	21,530	25,917	4,387	
	V W	81	42,327	17,495	20,620	3,125	
		82	77,878	42,845	49,257	6,412	
		83	59,891	38,996	43,325	4,329	
		84	47,701	28,347	32,235	3,888	
		85	24,626	9,550	11,745	2,195	
		86	157,621	71,378	82,693	11,315	
FRANCE	A E	84	6	371	389	18	
HG KONG	V E	81	3,527	646	923	277	
		84	18,966	14,370	16,280	1,910	
		85	6,371	6,530	7,595	1,065	
	V W	86	38,089	12,705	17,421	4,716	
JAPAN	A W	82	411	665	665	411	
	V E	81	3,479	2,332	3,251	919	
		82	1,920	621	931	310	
		83	4,002	1,414	2,049	635	
		84	2,399	6,063	6,180	117	
		85	3,661	5,248	5,965	717	
	V W	83	2,096	1,461	1,736	275	
		84	8,109	5,912	6,995	1,083	
KOR REP	V E	84	120	750	786	36	
	V W	83	298	400	424	24	
MEXICO	O E	83	1,197	923	923		
	O W	81	30,864	5,443	5,443		
		84	20,000	950	950		
PHIL R	V E	81	551	345	455	110	
PORTUGL	V E	84	7,937	2,160	3,818	1,658	
		86	170,570	20,421	30,247	9,826	
SINGAPR	V E	81	3,000	10,312	10,730	418	
		83	570	2,492	2,895	403	
	V W	81	5,483	9,087	9,774	687	
THAILND	V W	82	551	516	572	56	

Bamboo, webbing**
2223000 WOV MTL BMBO RATN ETC F/BLDS (NULL)

Country	Mode	Reg	Yr	Quantity	F.A.S.	C.I.F.	Charges
TOTAL		81	-	345,323	387,850	42,527	
		82	-	187,537	231,907	44,370	
		83	-	173,423	212,923	39,500	
		84	-	147,377	183,635	36,258	
		85	-	267,556	319,036	51,480	
		86	-	316,905	380,314	63,409	
CAMROON	N E	86	-	7,002	7,080	78	
CHINA M	N E	81	-	1,621	2,077	456	
		82	-	28,658	44,255	15,597	
		84	-	5,440	6,852	1,412	
		85	-	13,438	17,858	4,420	
		86	-	20,951	27,452	6,501	
	N W	81	-	4,329	5,127	798	
		82	-	6,121	8,291	2,170	
		84	-	1,970	2,437	467	
		85	-	4,956	7,636	2,680	
CHINA T	N E	81	-	39,093	43,574	4,481	
		82	-	1,763	2,318	555	
		83	-	19,298	23,693	4,395	
		84	-	14,542	17,937	3,395	
		85	-	3,986	4,728	742	
		86	-	27,030	32,607	5,577	
	N H	81	-	10,117	11,182	1,065	
	N W	81	-	22,397	26,753	4,356	
		82	-	43,248	48,386	5,138	
		83	-	19,240	23,353	4,113	
		84	-	8,966	9,683	717	
		85	-	27,006	30,036	3,030	
		86	-	106,925	119,864	12,939	
FR GERM	N W	83	-	1,663	1,950	287	
HG KONG	N E	82	-	2,076	2,364	288	
	N H	84	-	696	1,337	641	
	N W	81	-	13,446	13,705	259	
		82	-	996	1,162	166	
		83	-	936	1,089	153	
		84	-	5,894	7,364	1,470	
		86	-	6,956	9,746	2,790	
INDNSIA	N E	83	-	278	304	26	
	N W	84	-	795	1,504	709	
IRELAND	N E	84	-	342	360	18	
ISRAEL	N E	81	-	53,035	58,260	5,225	
		82	-	15,164	17,238	2,074	
JAMAICA	N E	82	-	264	285	21	
JAPAN	N E	81	-	50,361	57,634	7,273	
		82	-	27,916	32,932	5,016	
		83	-	33,572	41,224	7,652	
		84	-	22,554	28,071	5,517	
		85	-	14,990	19,343	4,353	
	N H	82	-	3,704	4,039	335	
		83	-	2,102	2,319	217	
		84	-	17,767	19,800	2,033	
		85	-	8,139	9,070	931	
		86	-	9,207	10,111	904	
	N W	81	-	129,711	142,638	12,927	
		82	-	39,145	44,799	5,654	
		83	-	48,711	56,021	7,310	
		84	-	26,210	31,479	5,269	
		85	-	38,220	46,340	8,120	
		86	-	31,981	37,900	5,919	
KOR REP	N W	86	-	8,470	8,970	500	
MEXICO	N W	81	-	855	1,057	202	
PHIL R	N E	81	-	5,510	7,633	2,123	
		82	-	8,967	13,431	4,464	
		83	-	9,771	13,914	4,143	
		84	-	3,544	4,142	598	
		85	-	23,742	31,848	8,106	
		86	-	52,186	71,731	19,545	
	N H	81	-	2,406	3,368	962	
	N W	82	-	12,442	14,842	2,400	
		83	-	1,260	2,237	977	
		84	-	1,766	2,240	474	
		85	-	18,328	26,075	7,747	
		86	-	98,744	105,481	6,737	
SINGAPR	N E	85	-	11,847	14,799	2,952	
SPAIN	N E	82	-	8,255	10,170	1,915	
		84	-	1,760	2,104	344	
	N W	83	-	35,722	46,416	10,694	
		84	-	6,534	8,784	2,250	
		85	-	22,488	31,897	9,409	
		86	-	18,070	23,024	4,954	
THAILND	N E	84	-	4,121	4,392	271	
	N W	83	-	364	400	36	
YUGOSLV	N E	84	-	7,914	11,314	3,400	

Crop Product TSUSA commodity number, description, and unit of quantity Country	Mode	Reg	Yr	Quantity	F.A.S.	C.I.F.	Charges

Banana

Banana, dried
1464200 BANANAS, DRIED (LB)

Country	Mode	Reg	Yr	Quantity	F.A.S.	C.I.F.	Charges
TOTAL			81	1,316,703	1,208,381	1,294,174	86,724
			82	192,076	166,116	183,820	17,704
			83	1,150,685	850,321	920,859	70,538
			84	1,584,907	1,551,657	1,660,756	109,099
			85	1,707,308	1,518,004	1,690,914	172,910
			86	2,167,866	1,860,812	2,021,757	160,945
BRAZIL	A	E	84	1,488	2,504	4,815	2,311
			85	81,182	74,581	132,959	58,378
			86	81,978	142,197	182,568	40,371
	V	E	83	452	640	726	86
			84	5,996	7,901	9,327	1,426
			86	3,219	3,014	3,448	434
	V	W	82	4,975	7,988	9,901	1,913
			83	50,605	13,440	15,840	2,400
C RICA	A	W	81	6,660	3,063	3,063	931
			84	373	320	728	408
			86	1,520	1,500	2,313	813
	V	E	81	8,756	5,178	6,036	858
			83	44,814	39,108	43,962	4,854
			84	55,291	41,747	45,608	3,861
	V	W	82	2,500	1,850	2,050	200
			85	4,134	3,750	4,052	302
CHILE	V	E	85	107,302	18,720	27,848	9,128
CHINA M	V	W	81	300	364	417	53
CHINA T	V	E	86	69,450	22,919	25,471	2,552
	V	W	81	440	440	488	48
			83	438	540	565	25
			84	638	664	706	42
			85	46,760	21,510	25,810	4,300
COOK IS	A	H	81	1,000	2,360	2,699	339
ECUADOR	A	E	82	3,260	3,907	6,166	2,259
			85	10,000	11,000	12,733	1,733
	O	E	85	35,000	38,365	40,606	2,241
	V	E	81	965,020	933,920	988,739	54,819
			83	370,020	405,873	427,681	21,808
			84	783,235	1,020,333	1,066,036	45,703
			85	789,856	1,007,776	1,051,043	43,267
			86	933,288	1,258,884	1,308,824	49,940
	V	W	81	183,750	179,110	191,107	11,997
			82	115,000	116,147	123,156	7,009
			83	77,500	81,767	86,819	5,052
			84	70,000	77,000	80,857	3,857
			85	83,763	86,948	92,040	5,092
			86	44,500	47,145	51,322	4,177
HG KONG	V	H	86	750	1,041	1,123	82
HONDURA	V	E	82	20,625	3,422	3,767	345
ISRAEL	O	E	83	286	368	389	21
JAMAICA	A	E	85	1,429	1,058	1,608	550
	V	E	82	3,037	1,988	2,105	117
MEXICO	O	W	85	1,218	1,044	1,044	
			86	1,784	1,122	1,122	
	V	W	81	3,108	3,500	3,900	400
PHIL R	A	W	81	810	2,254	3,964	1,710
			82	1,200	1,200	3,604	2,404
	O	E	82	6,822	4,353	4,353	
			83	23,100	13,440	13,440	
	V	E	81	15,288	7,595	8,223	628
			83	208,082	103,944	120,241	16,297
			84	115,262	57,521	67,943	10,422
			85	368,249	145,600	181,159	35,559
			86	538,580	200,935	237,439	36,504
	V	H	86	11,217	3,752	5,520	1,768
	V	W	81	112,754	56,897	70,816	13,919
			82	26,054	13,847	16,135	2,288
			83	341,974	165,078	183,633	18,555
			84	523,264	319,757	356,995	37,238
			85	134,400	61,824	71,432	9,608
			86	477,080	174,149	198,279	24,130
PITCARN	V	W	85	35,000	38,500	40,878	2,378
SALVADR	V	W	84	14,811	14,354	17,645	3,291
SWITZLD	O	E	84	550	1,317	1,374	57
	V	E	83	1,542	898	959	61
THAILND	V	E	81	17,945	12,646	13,637	991
			82	250	377	425	48
			83	1,066	1,017	1,154	137
			84	908	1,207	1,351	144
	V	W	81	872	1,054	1,085	31

Country	Mode	Reg	Yr	Quantity	F.A.S.	C.I.F.	Charges
			82	8,353	11,037	12,158	1,121
			83	30,806	24,208	25,450	1,242
			84	11,901	5,219	5,493	274
			85	9,015	7,328	7,702	374
			86	4,500	4,154	4,328	174
U KING	O	E	84	1,190	1,813	1,878	65

Banana, flour**
1520000 BANANA AND PLANTAIN FLOUR (LB)

Country	Mode	Reg	Yr	Quantity	F.A.S.	C.I.F.	Charges
TOTAL			81	1,500	300	302	2
			82	2,024	1,466	1,980	514
			83	7,803	3,035	4,035	1,000
			84	33,411	16,944	20,747	3,803
			85	834,091	1,036,589	1,082,549	45,960
			86	191,293	102,308	109,817	7,509
ECUADOR	A	E	81	1,500	300	302	2
			82	2,000	347	740	393
			83	1,640	600	1,078	478
			85	30	1,500	2,005	505
	N	E	84	10,460	4,000	5,396	1,396
	O	E	86	7,750	3,554	3,554	
	V	E	84	2,500	1,500	1,708	208
			85	834,061	1,035,089	1,080,544	45,455
			86	14?,161	82,800	88,007	5,207
HONDURA	V	E	86	8,350	3,340	3,607	267
INDIA	V	W	84	1,168	1,325	1,414	89
ISRAEL	V	E	83	264	334	359	25
JAMAICA	A	E	84	1,830	659	1,482	823
	V	E	82	24	1,119	1,240	121
PANAMA	V	E	83	5,000	1,552	2,010	458
			84	10,000	4,000	4,657	657
			86	28,032	12,614	14,649	2,035
PHIL R	V	E	83	899	549	588	39
			84	243	404	453	49
	V	W	84	6,250	4,307	4,841	534
THAILND	V	W	84	960	749	796	47

Banana, fresh
1464000 BANANAS, FRESH (LB)

Country	Mode	Reg	Yr	Quantity	F.A.S.	C.I.F.	Charges
TOTAL			81	5,419,596,639	524,758,124	709,495,558	184,171,071
			82	5,695,745,594	560,783,657	760,432,762	199,649,105
			83	5,389,582,726	568,031,578	754,076,490	186,044,912
			84	5,681,671,462	626,874,414	826,312,300	199,437,886
			85	6,544,866,595	722,233,954	960,032,538	237,798,584
			86	6,488,003,925	707,013,118	933,531,322	226,518,204
AFGHAN	V	E	84	12,466,400	2,181,620	2,311,827	130,207
AUSTRAL	V	W	84	7,330,110	931,122	1,329,145	398,023
BAHAMAS	V	E	84	18,680,520	2,152,928	2,923,498	770,570
BELGIUM	V	W	86	1,122,930	129,012	184,260	55,248
BERMUDA	V	E	82	2,369,320	207,316	252,925	45,609
BOLIVIA	V	E	81	1,778,364	162,593	266,754	104,161
			82	3,415,566	312,280	512,335	200,055
			83	2,557,296	331,685	500,408	168,723
			84	9,630,534	1,018,571	1,545,948	527,377
	V	W	81	4,122,480	416,370	563,748	147,378
BRAZIL	V	E	81	662,480	38,921	55,483	16,562
			82	5,342,200	406,126	496,619	90,493
			83	13,835,382	1,448,339	1,636,035	187,696
			84	4,248,320	718,344	789,107	70,763
			85	8,761,440	1,533,252	1,558,203	24,951
			86	3,391,760	333,240	517,244	184,004
C RICA	N	E	83	318,480	21,015	37,607	16,592
	O	E	81	42,700	9,110	9,110	
			82	100,200	20,250	20,250	
			83	24,200	6,447	6,447	
			84	132,800	33,951	33,951	
			85	36,000	5,477	5,477	
			86	109,760	26,630	26,630	
	O	W	83	2,250	500	500	
	V	E	81	952,913,449	100,122,071	135,174,772	35,045,701
			82	889,069,858	96,763,645	128,841,622	32,077,977
			83	1,059,875,858	119,342,790	154,673,151	35,330,361
			84	1,144,164,463	131,031,477	170,320,687	39,289,210
			85	1,104,703,036	128,157,287	167,036,110	38,878,823
			86	1,163,295,369	139,982,638	180,599,780	40,617,142
	V	W	81	173,455,532	17,507,570	24,782,219	7,274,649
			82	257,021,719	23,101,146	32,821,689	9,720,543
			83	220,222,512	25,941,422	36,579,098	10,637,676

Crop
Product
TSUSA commodity number, description, and unit of quantity

Country	Mode	Reg	Yr	Quantity	F.A.S.	C.I.F.	Charges
			84	145,528,008	18,422,550	26,001,652	7,579,102
			85	73,545,006	8,021,116	11,443,376	3,422,260
			86	74,558,058	8,888,767	12,663,666	3,774,899
CANADA	A	E	85	8,900	2,300	2,731	431
	O	E	81	36,100	6,762	6,762	
			82	132,325	24,333	24,333	
			83	53,280	12,321	12,321	
			84	74,400	12,506	12,506	
			85	65,200	11,552	11,552	
	O	W	81	46,000	2,984	2,984	
			82	54,500	10,975	10,975	
			83	4,680	842	842	
	V	E	85	2,396,867	219,421	374,305	154,884
			86	414,397	44,009	75,074	31,065
	V	W	85	449,855	57,144	81,615	24,471
CHILE	V	E	82	425,840	31,938	53,230	21,292
	V	W	83	191,262	13,202	17,764	4,562
			85	3,388,194	534,978	891,630	356,652
CHINA T	V	E	83	29,365	7,104	8,716	1,612
COLOMB	N	E	83	86,007,824	9,844,182	14,754,677	4,910,495
			84	883,580,996	86,421,039	113,585,072	27,164,033
			85	418,597,466	44,201,612	59,803,077	15,601,465
	O	E	81	84,200	13,117	13,117	
			82	105,140	21,796	21,796	
			83	161,800	37,839	37,839	
			84	343,400	72,758	72,758	
			86	30,800	8,085	8,085	
	V	E	81	677,132,724	66,332,843	90,976,415	24,643,572
			82	856,431,289	87,074,438	119,984,728	32,910,290
			83	741,756,056	73,257,144	97,056,523	23,799,379
			84	149,860,573	15,171,736	22,570,992	7,399,256
			85	550,011,663	49,805,965	67,249,202	17,443,237
			86	1,128,020,843	107,123,190	149,991,630	42,868,440
	V	W	82	3,520,608	383,496	440,710	57,214
COOK IS	V	E	85	2,901,683	309,845	376,771	66,926
DOM REP	A	E	82	18,200	1,973	5,914	3,941
			84	44,343	5,811	13,049	7,238
			86	26,460	4,830	10,514	5,684
	N	E	81	353,268	44,252	94,798	50,446
			82	16,330,065	2,316,885	2,955,966	639,081
			83	2,586,603	228,115	324,418	96,303
			84	1,934,536	284,274	403,098	118,824
			85	746,660	74,351	119,392	45,041
			86	18,661	5,093	6,995	1,902
	V	E	81	32,930,395	4,308,181	5,827,727	1,519,546
			82	44,640	3,306	5,677	2,371
			83	1,599,596	195,543	295,162	99,619
			84	16,825	1,625	2,488	863
			85	1,008,660	167,351	232,016	64,665
			86	867,715	192,352	238,737	46,385
DOMINCA	V	E	86	194,733	44,686	49,577	4,891
ECUADOR	A	E	83	148,538	15,705	28,866	13,161
			84	30,200	3,604	6,361	2,757
			86	36,617	4,288	10,957	6,669
	N	E	82	123,921	7,850	16,801	8,951
			83	407,818,242	41,907,727	55,553,177	13,645,450
			84	420,611,563	58,257,588	72,239,144	13,981,556
			85	585,621,074	74,788,530	95,787,868	20,999,338
			86	767,462,684	96,005,589	122,716,761	26,711,172
	N	W	82	623,608,728	59,290,030	80,227,214	20,937,184
			85	722,849,024	68,281,869	94,933,566	26,651,697
	O	E	82	66,760	13,685	13,685	
			83	42,800	11,277	11,277	
			84	34,200	7,416	7,416	
			85	102,000	23,629	23,629	
			86	130,310	46,177	46,177	
	O	W	82	2,813,680	51,552	51,552	
	V	E	81	616,734,706	51,453,799	72,165,043	20,711,244
			82	690,265,201	59,454,092	84,404,158	24,950,066
			83	79,856,454	7,934,370	12,297,889	4,363,519
			84	139,127,075	13,559,654	20,787,263	7,227,609
			85	279,672,007	27,914,416	41,117,749	13,203,333
			86	117,757,911	11,693,056	17,516,719	5,823,663
	V	W	81	547,609,250	48,319,438	65,937,376	17,617,938
			82	3,228,831	449,814	583,913	134,099
			83	495,910,800	41,766,176	55,919,852	14,153,676
			84	541,664,337	48,550,743	65,279,677	16,728,934
			86	731,517,690	72,648,931	94,685,171	22,036,240
EGYPT	A	E	86	16,800	2,000	2,789	789
	V	E		3,173,973	251,025	386,874	135,849
EQ GUIN	V	E	84	4,669,440	507,802	768,123	260,321
F W IND	V	E	81	19,013	2,323	3,335	1,012
FINLAND	N	W	86	475,133	376,145	597,407	221,262
FRANCE	O	E	85	36,000	5,850	5,850	
	V	E	81	4,008,360	350,732	427,893	77,161
			85	29,400	4,252	5,975	1,723
			86	640	1,511	1,789	278
GREECE	V	E	85	3,087,760	173,687	243,162	69,475
			86	10,218,120	812,805	991,623	178,818
GUATMAL	N	E	81	852,444	94,815	120,960	26,145
			82	374,885	23,031	60,303	37,272
			83	286,524	27,786	58,486	30,700
	O	E	82	6,000	903	903	
	V	E	81	550,375,443	36,498,401	48,836,806	11,708,406
			82	556,231,214	35,614,986	46,560,339	10,945,353
			83	468,715,545	29,273,024	38,277,129	9,004,105
			84	402,948,999	24,003,082	31,080,868	7,077,786
			85	544,005,244	38,391,005	49,642,734	11,251,729
			86	622,410,106	42,179,630	56,997,802	14,818,172
	V	W	81	3,887,329	302,850	393,615	90,765
GUYANA	V	E	86	2,212,584	176,001	214,721	38,720
HAITI	A	E	83	68,010	8,620	16,912	8,292
			84	5,638	1,836	3,442	1,606
	N	E	82	99,961	10,749	21,581	10,832
HONDURA	A	E	81	3,748	288	723	435
	N	E	85	831,678,318	102,196,350	125,824,554	23,628,204
	O	E	81	64,600	14,241	14,241	
			82	68,040	12,901	12,901	
			83	53,800	14,022	14,022	
			84	41,440	10,299	10,299	
			85	28,200	7,226	7,226	
			86	6,400	2,186	2,186	
	V	E	81	1,282,462,591	141,399,711	183,980,818	42,573,843
			82	1,291,673,651	142,725,202	188,543,762	45,818,560
			83	1,100,674,640	127,198,892	164,185,560	36,986,668
			84	1,183,925,320	142,503,650	182,660,679	40,157,029
			85	421,732,318	50,086,210	67,263,708	17,177,498
			86	1,118,939,366	137,047,857	174,121,899	37,074,042
INDIA	V	W	81	1,764	2,052	2,704	652
			86	1,710	1,085	1,205	120
JAMAICA	A	E	84	5,600	400	936	536
			86	2,550	1,800	2,700	900
	N	E	83	94,177	14,019	21,655	7,636
	V	E	82	106,680	14,586	19,137	4,551
JAPAN	V	W	83	336,475	21,910	29,735	7,825
KIRIBAT	V	E	85	12,894,166	1,127,906	1,375,544	247,638
			86	8,237,508	701,294	895,777	194,483
MALAYSA	V	E	85	1,850,255	164,392	251,780	87,388
	V	W	85	1,558,656	236,160	283,770	47,610
MEXICO	A	E	81	3,503	685	2,077	1,392
			82	3,969	609	1,929	1,320
	N	W	85	8,026,113	1,035,637	1,064,779	29,142
	O	E	81	9,998,506	1,312,072	1,312,072	
			82	12,338,817	1,296,811	1,298,583	1,772
			83	52,741,778	4,741,487	4,741,487	
			84	56,539,312	6,159,259	6,159,262	3
			85	71,178,604	7,498,668	7,498,815	147
			86	130,235,235	12,576,646	12,576,646	
	O	W	81	8,178,168	971,450	971,450	
			82	12,771,805	1,749,281	1,750,081	800
			83	27,112,945	4,186,785	4,187,173	388
			84	10,617,826	1,168,825	1,168,825	
			85	79,600	8,177	8,177	
			86	7,623,320	923,889	923,889	
	V	E	81	2,021,628	85,549	110,943	25,394
			84	159,240	8,440	13,545	5,105
			85	12,181,336	1,402,433	1,904,741	502,308
			86	25,501,893	2,880,642	3,941,341	1,060,699
	V	W	83	1,436,247	190,920	275,186	84,266
			84	385,915	54,000	70,758	16,758
			85	967,520	115,261	181,575	66,314
			86	186,960	29,520	40,770	11,250
MONSRAT	O	W	85	18,360	1,836	1,836	
			86	9,000	1,224	1,224	
MOZAMBQ	O	E	85	163,490	8,854	8,854	
			86	37,200	6,975	6,975	
	V	E	82	114,000	5,985	15,138	9,153
N ANTIL	O	E	83	31,000	4,960	7,377	2,417
	V	E	81	20,000	3,625	4,554	929
N ZEAL	A	E	83	1,792	2,286	3,939	1,653
			84	1,954	3,500	5,144	1,635
NICARAG	N	W	84	149,917,728	23,508,564	33,080,483	9,571,919
	O	W	83	41,000	2,079	2,079	
	V	W	81	165,325,292	17,126,785	21,828,940	4,750,155
			82	83,564,960	9,557,922	12,023,980	2,466,058
			83	136,322,015	20,214,760	26,596,811	6,382,051
			85	102,970,890	16,335,427	22,992,675	6,657,248
PANAMA	A	E	83	11,830	677	2,684	2,007

Crop Product TSUSA commodity number, description, and unit of quantity Country	Mode	Reg	Yr	Quantity	F.A.S.	C.I.F.	Charges
	O	E	82	41,300	10,833	10,833	
			84	4,800	1,059	1,059	
			85	28,000	7,350	7,350	
	V	E	81	208,511,747	20,620,338	30,823,974	10,233,636
			82	170,691,315	17,904,465	27,136,884	9,232,419
			83	303,610,525	37,041,689	53,466,231	16,424,542
			84	194,953,285	24,886,387	35,318,944	10,432,557
			85	75,149,544	11,050,732	15,164,776	4,114,044
			86	76,986,944	10,244,046	14,302,138	4,058,092
	V	W	81	170,977,718	16,902,026	24,254,027	7,352,001
			82	209,567,837	21,518,361	30,748,140	9,229,779
			83	183,515,585	22,429,262	31,958,762	9,529,500
			84	195,218,527	24,694,050	34,907,150	10,213,100
			85	682,104,455	85,311,564	121,246,671	35,935,107
			86	478,953,758	59,811,082	85,623,788	25,812,706
PERU	V	E	82	552,840	39,725	64,988	25,263
	V	W	82	145,467	11,034	22,988	11,954
PHIL R	V	E	81	32,025	17,392	20,101	2,709
			82	2,550	744	860	116
			83	1,750	428	528	100
	V	W	81	23,040	12,215	13,564	1,349
			82	2,116	1,007	1,204	197
S LUCIA	V	E	85	40,707	5,046	8,646	3,600
			86	277,172	22,052	44,277	22,225
SALVADR	V	W	86	4,600,398	363,752	363,752	
SPAIN	A	E	86	19,500	8,466	9,111	645
	V	E	85	9,360,810	1,257,866	1,523,519	265,653
			86	4,774,668	488,633	730,690	242,057
SWITZLD	V	E	86	4,106,298	488,845	629,999	141,154
THAILND	V	E	81	2,906	3,449	3,936	487
	V	W	84	712	1,146	1,193	47
TRINID	V	E	83	3,480	564	764	200
U KING	V	E	86	2,815,040	165,477	214,596	49,119
VENEZ	A	E	83	1,489,612	323,863	462,407	138,544
			84	2,772,123	522,789	825,951	303,162
			85	623,772	119,750	230,732	110,982
			86	4,505,222	1,007,827	1,574,250	566,423
	N	E	85	2,928,071	832,350	1,219,947	387,597
	V	E	81	4,925,166	299,114	492,517	193,403
			82	2,899,596	337,596	392,136	54,540
W SAMOA	V	H	83	30,718	9,800	14,994	5,194

*Banana, paste and pulp***

1527200 BANANA, PLNTAIN PASTE, PULP (LB)

Country	Mode	Reg	Yr	Quantity	F.A.S.	C.I.F.	Charges
TOTAL			81	31,969,214	5,334,062	6,200,827	866,765
			82	20,851,183	3,479,252	4,207,775	728,523
			83	16,583,722	3,067,442	3,579,301	511,859
			84	21,044,552	4,407,835	5,053,893	646,058
			85	22,011,411	4,990,237	5,813,501	823,264
			86	25,819,290	6,493,224	7,196,973	703,749
BRAZIL	V	E	81	4,072	1,015	1,265	250
			85	10,172	1,935	2,501	566
			86	42,316	10,402	12,637	2,235
C RICA	N	E	85	4,081,002	888,065	1,218,402	330,337
	V	E	81	5,069,311	824,854	1,094,718	269,864
			82	5,307,419	924,591	1,310,470	385,879
			83	3,113,898	756,165	997,270	241,105
			84	5,126,716	1,046,282	1,410,975	364,693
			85	1,158,742	250,496	345,119	94,623
			86	5,203,986	1,200,287	1,609,408	409,121
	V	W	81	25,970	14,118	16,718	2,600
			84	77,694	15,676	21,458	5,782
			86	77,696	18,172	25,160	6,988
CANADA	O	E	85	13,746	2,240	2,240	
ECUADOR	A	E	83	2,500	500	743	243
	V	E	86	78,370	19,552	24,367	4,815
FR GERM	A	E	86	355	1,607	1,807	200
	V	E	81	132	322	365	43
GUATMAL	V	E	86	147,666	64,271	67,278	3,007
HAITI	V	E	81	692,848	84,827	96,432	11,605
HONDURA	N	E	81	3,310,603	464,314	558,066	93,752
			85	5,526,041	1,473,312	1,566,304	92,992
	V	E	81	12,370,167	1,898,879	2,166,754	267,875
			82	14,132,807	2,175,354	2,514,603	339,249
			83	7,199,982	1,247,452	1,430,754	183,302
			84	12,600,557	2,718,621	2,896,193	177,572
			85	3,814,615	866,284	955,799	89,515
			86	11,186,791	3,106,445	3,323,381	216,936
ITALY	V	E	83	212	391	418	27
MEXICO	O	E	81	3,510,219	945,273	945,273	
			82	913,760	269,669	269,669	

Crop Product TSUSA commodity number, description, and unit of quantity Country	Mode	Reg	Yr	Quantity	F.A.S.	C.I.F.	Charges

Country	Mode	Reg	Yr	Quantity	F.A.S.	C.I.F.	Charges
			83	1,745,719	427,392	427,392	
			84	931,847	246,542	246,542	
			85	1,548,999	358,767	358,767	
			86	935,240	242,769	242,769	
	O	W	81	880,472	205,950	205,950	
			82	325,939	80,980	80,980	
			83	381,090	85,551	85,551	
			86	34,028	7,826	7,826	
	V	W	81	400,000	100,000	126,125	26,125
			84	36,191	7,935	8,814	879
			85	156,337	35,957	41,559	5,602
			86	66,789	15,346	17,445	2,099
PANAMA	V	E	81	5,703,533	792,900	987,391	194,491
			82	153,537	21,570	24,965	3,395
			83	4,139,143	549,438	636,575	87,137
			84	2,270,329	372,181	469,196	97,015
			85	5,701,757	1,113,181	1,322,810	209,629
			86	8,026,519	1,801,958	1,858,693	56,735
PHIL R	V	W	81	520	452	488	36
			84	1,218	598	715	117
			86	17,600	3,514	4,742	1,228
REP SAF	A	E	81	992	543	605	62
	O	E	82	17,721	7,088	7,088	
THAILND	V	E	81	375	615	677	62
			86	1,934	1,075	1,460	385
	V	W	83	1,178	553	598	45

Banana, prepared or preserved

1464400 BANANAS, NSPF, PREP OR PRES (LB)

Country	Mode	Reg	Yr	Quantity	F.A.S.	C.I.F.	Charges
TOTAL			81	12,511,764	5,096,637	5,841,499	745,042
			82	9,063,879	4,475,798	5,111,965	636,167
			83	12,684,315	4,507,741	5,354,976	847,235
			84	22,259,718	8,089,460	9,534,746	1,445,286
			85	18,178,057	6,955,883	8,255,636	1,299,753
			86	22,286,611	6,870,561	8,215,286	1,344,725
BRAZIL	A	E	86	1,984	2,301	2,494	193
	V	E	84	35,000	58,250	62,616	4,366
			85	79,364	28,564	33,042	4,478
			86	35,507	7,954	9,671	1,717
	V	W	83	1,102	2,050	2,624	574
C RICA	N	E	84	1,402,274	292,254	438,579	146,325
	N	W	84	39,948	8,686	11,551	2,865
	V	E	81	16,500	8,580	9,916	1,336
			82	119,335	59,433	70,558	11,125
			83	4,254,217	939,528	1,285,494	345,966
			84	1,043,966	211,894	297,784	85,890
			85	3,203,151	702,104	1,023,176	321,072
			86	5,124,443	1,253,210	1,711,597	458,387
	V	W	83	193,776	44,328	58,465	14,137
			84	107,068	23,015	31,647	8,632
			85	264,650	60,329	87,687	27,358
			86	35,805	11,816	14,622	2,806
CANADA	O	E	81	750	443	443	
			85	16,772	11,404	13,260	1,856
	O	W	83	5,020	2,653	2,653	
			84	12,210	6,562	6,562	
			85	14,109	7,434	7,434	
			86	19,794	10,045	10,045	
CHILE	V	W	84	5,760	1,152	1,457	305
CHINA M	V	W	81	500	898	971	73
			84	20,440	9,558	11,038	1,480
CHINA T	V	E	81	22,905	12,598	14,294	1,696
			84	4,765	4,471	4,728	257
			85	6,415	6,213	6,979	766
	V	W	82	20,702	11,724	13,533	1,809
			83	45,360	20,445	22,680	2,235
			86	4,780	3,958	4,174	216
COLOMB	A	E	83	2	309	518	209
	V	E	86	1,209,418	125,956	190,147	64,191
DOM REP	A	E	82	200	280	649	369
			86	3,351	3,881	4,440	559
ECUADOR	V	E	81	46,200	46,740	49,456	2,716
			84	74,800	106,590	111,877	5,287
	V	W	81	2,204	2,499	2,595	96
			84	35,000	38,500	40,316	1,816
			86	39,153	9,768	11,317	1,549
F W IND	V	E	84	20,760	11,833	14,178	2,345
FR GERM	V	E	82	265	837	863	26
			83	450	1,440	1,508	68
			84	396	1,133	1,195	62
			86	265	1,036	1,073	37

Crop
Product
TSUSA commodity number, description, and unit of quantity

Country	Mode	Reg	Yr	Quantity	F.A.S.	C.I.F.	Charges
GREECE	O	E	83	110	881	887	6
GUATMAL	V	E	83	34,665	7,494	14,267	6,773
			84	14,357	4,968	8,870	3,902
			85	141,460	67,284	81,879	14,595
			86	93,130	33,660	42,043	8,383
	V	W	85	522,375	234,193	290,720	56,527
			86	325,400	146,430	173,579	27,149
HG KONG	V	E	85	22,500	9,675	11,775	2,100
	V	W	82	667	364	402	38
			83	1,125	1,475	1,607	132
			85	42,000	20,160	24,562	4,402
			86	85,142	51,165	56,939	5,774
HONDURA	N	E	81	221,312	54,096	62,995	8,899
			85	2,487,690	564,925	606,646	41,721
	V	E	81	4,212,201	548,533	653,813	105,460
			82	1,672,130	328,575	393,029	64,454
			83	2,148,356	425,478	498,617	73,139
			84	8,430,310	1,185,468	1,482,587	297,119
			85	1,145,771	282,364	324,061	41,697
			86	4,632,978	1,158,680	1,300,827	142,147
INDIA	V	E	86	29,333	76,816	78,637	1,821
	V	W	86	2,205	3,250	4,652	1,402
INDNSIA	V	E	84	42,000	23,100	26,077	2,977
JAMAICA	A	E	82	23	531	803	272
			83	9,900	17,812	19,369	1,557
			84	1,272	1,440	1,680	240
			85	1,224	1,026	1,942	916
			86	2,271	2,338	2,673	335
	V	E	82	8,100	14,128	14,893	765
			83	2,550	1,889	1,976	87
			85	7,650	3,750	4,120	370
JAPAN	V	E	84	1,215	949	1,020	71
	V	W	81	2,322	1,022	1,145	123
			82	20,790	11,515	12,890	1,375
			83	8,960	4,939	5,376	437
KIRIBAT	V	W	86	38,600	17,370	20,990	3,620
KOR REP	V	E	86	4,333	10,868	12,054	1,186
MALAYSA	V	E	81	2,500	3,313	3,660	347
			84	500	593	681	88
			86	19,050	6,668	7,368	700
	V	W	81	375	502	553	51
			86	3,600	2,871	3,101	230
MALI	V	E	84	46,200	20,790	37,950	17,160
MEXICO	O	E	82	66,176	28,510	28,510	
			85	113,785	12,779	12,779	
			86	195,642	45,278	45,278	
	V	W	82	75,170	17,289	20,043	2,754
			83	259,783	57,570	69,777	12,207
MOZAMBQ	V	E	82	107,500	124,000	137,669	13,669
PANAMA	V	E	81	38,800	6,392	7,882	1,490
			85	97,538	23,304	27,520	4,216
			86	1,691,191	456,366	516,994	60,628
PHIL R	A	E	81	1,493	881	3,925	3,044
			82	1,254	3,327	3,346	19
	N	E	81	2,777,579	1,552,887	1,788,089	235,202
			83	1,420	847	3,387	2,540
			84	341,855	192,663	225,605	32,942
			85	126,549	59,892	73,598	13,706
			86	1,171,607	403,760	491,045	87,285
	N	W	81	322,604	172,323	215,804	43,481
			83	81,648	38,801	43,159	4,358
	O	E	81	17,250	9,488	10,277	789
			82	1,283	1,100	2,447	1,347
			83	11,088	6,320	6,320	
			84	30,708	25,727	29,982	4,255
			86	46,760	15,291	18,786	3,495
	V	E	81	458,222	258,308	296,381	38,073
			82	2,339,971	1,289,443	1,492,425	202,982
			83	2,295,345	1,186,516	1,364,581	178,065
			84	4,148,154	2,201,259	2,573,734	372,475
			85	3,441,845	1,522,472	1,840,242	317,770
			86	1,714,580	677,165	807,215	130,050
	V	H	81	17,158	11,656	13,629	1,973
			82	19,005	11,583	13,497	1,914
			83	19,964	11,873	14,171	2,298
			84	48,845	28,170	32,465	4,295
			85	9,840	4,952	6,537	1,585
			86	4,389	2,520	2,895	375
	V	W	81	4,304,320	2,343,780	2,638,044	294,264
			82	4,535,704	2,489,043	2,813,482	324,439
			83	3,211,555	1,645,917	1,839,729	193,812
			84	6,293,127	3,582,188	4,027,020	444,832
			85	6,217,261	3,229,255	3,663,819	434,564
			86	5,126,121	2,023,047	2,326,327	303,280

Crop
Product
TSUSA commodity number, description, and unit of quantity

Country	Mode	Reg	Yr	Quantity	F.A.S.	C.I.F.	Charges
SINGAPR	V	E	86	1,750	2,048	2,415	367
	V	W	86	24,636	10,329	20,035	9,706
THAILND	V	E	81	11,359	13,855	15,306	1,451
			82	13,463	15,391	17,429	2,038
			83	27,260	28,834	32,070	3,236
			84	16,027	15,264	17,391	2,127
			85	12,863	9,705	10,978	1,273
			86	51,618	26,332	29,972	3,640
	V	H	81	250	358	403	45
			83	1,440	1,572	1,801	229
	V	W	81	34,721	47,099	51,507	4,408
			82	62,141	68,725	75,497	6,772
			83	48,219	47,889	51,130	3,241
			84	42,761	32,983	36,156	3,173
			85	203,245	94,099	102,880	8,781
			86	525,375	259,648	281,473	21,825
TURKEY	V	E	83	21,000	10,881	12,810	1,929
U KING	O	E	81	239	386	411	25
	V	W	86	22,400	8,736	10,408	1,672

Barbasco

*Barbasco, root***

4930200 CUBE DERRIS TUBE ROOT CRUDE (LB)

Country	Mode	Reg	Yr	Quantity	F.A.S.	C.I.F.	Charges
TOTAL			81	730,556	173,380	215,320	41,940
			82	167,119	63,167	74,471	11,304
			83	471,790	202,599	233,801	31,202
			84	505,918	255,330	286,424	31,094
			85	91,518	88,640	98,586	9,946
			86	113,149	67,731	78,140	10,409
CANADA	O	E	81	10,000	20,008	20,008	
FRANCE	V	E	86	1,543	24,185	24,494	309
INDIA	V	E	83	9,539	23,795	25,828	2,033
			84	482	1,205	1,340	135
			85	21,895	54,643	60,431	5,788
IRELAND	O	E	84	83,776	89,767	92,153	2,386
PAKISTN	V	E	85	28,838	11,797	13,587	1,790
PERU	V	E	81	720,556	153,372	195,312	41,940
			82	167,119	63,167	74,471	11,304
			83	462,251	178,804	207,973	29,169
			84	421,660	164,358	192,931	28,573
			85	40,785	22,200	24,568	2,368
			86	111,606	43,546	53,646	10,100

4930400 BARBASCO DERRIS TUBE ROOT AD (LB)

Country	Mode	Reg	Yr	Quantity	F.A.S.	C.I.F.	Charges
TOTAL			81	377,790	246,800	272,791	25,991
			82	519,216	366,282	415,416	49,134
			83	649,729	330,240	370,349	40,109
			84	599,095	349,467	390,824	41,357
			85	527,043	421,281	462,599	41,318
			86	506,104	409,265	446,772	37,507
ARGENT	V	W	85	47,831	21,696	23,996	2,300
BELGIUM	V	E	82	3,748	29,716	30,230	514
			85	9,921	61,225	64,418	3,193
FRANCE	N	E	83	34,438	72,775	74,619	1,844
			84	65,034	103,690	106,848	3,158
			85	17,614	91,100	95,839	4,739
	V	E	81	14,307	133,042	136,234	3,192
			82	18,433	152,487	160,994	8,507
			84	7,974	36,089	36,502	413
			86	29,433	183,500	186,022	2,522
PERU	V	E	81	343,055	106,345	127,647	21,302
			82	410,137	152,242	181,173	28,931
			83	472,577	181,987	210,346	28,359
			84	420,409	170,920	199,846	28,926
			85	451,677	247,260	278,346	31,086
			86	369,549	177,175	202,029	24,854
	V	W	81	20,428	7,413	8,910	1,497
			82	86,898	31,837	43,019	11,182
			83	95,314	34,954	43,084	8,130
			84	105,678	38,768	47,628	8,860
			86	107,122	48,590	58,721	10,131
U KING	V	E	83	47,400	40,524	42,300	1,776

Crop Product TSUSA commodity number, description, and unit of quantity Country	Mode	Reg	Yr	Quantity	F.A.S.	C.I.F.	Charges

Barberry

Barberry, dried
1466400 BARBERRIES, DRIED (LB)

Country	Mode	Reg	Yr	Quantity	F.A.S.	C.I.F.	Charges
TOTAL			81	595	1,255	1,330	75
			82	2,403	6,008	8,323	2,315
			83	1,205	1,644	3,270	1,626
			84	43,651	11,698	11,698	
			85	49,723	13,092	13,836	744
			86	42,000	25,200	25,200	
CANADA	O	E	86	42,000	25,200	25,200	
	O	W	84	43,651	11,698	11,698	
FRANCE	V	E	81	595	1,255	1,330	75
	V	W	82	1,190	2,279	4,555	2,276
IRAN	A	W	83	1,205	1,644	3,270	1,626
	V	W	82	1,213	3,729	3,768	39
			85	520	1,966	2,111	145
MEXICO	O	E	85	37,200	4,883	4,883	
U KING	V	W	85	12,003	6,243	6,842	599

Barley

Barley, grain
1301100 BARLEY, NSPF (BU)

Country	Mode	Reg	Yr	Quantity	F.A.S.	C.I.F.	Charges
TOTAL			81	173,069	751,477	782,583	31,106
			82	213,888	735,686	740,962	5,276
			83	1,135,035	3,107,395	3,349,666	242,271
			84	2,575,141	7,650,784	7,761,059	110,275
			85	2,145,182	5,294,805	5,671,698	376,893
			86	4,376,061	7,879,976	9,052,097	1,172,121
AUSTRAL	V	H	83	385,805	1,158,037	1,395,337	237,300
CANADA	N	W	81	26,155	210,206	211,568	1,362
	O	E	81	39,107	212,813	212,813	
			82	151,994	535,272	535,272	
			83	330,943	916,178	916,178	
			84	379,893	1,234,695	1,234,695	
			85	138,495	490,732	490,732	
			86	215,729	513,046	513,046	
	O	W	81	58,239	169,109	169,109	
			82	60,575	185,088	185,088	
			83	415,391	1,013,609	1,013,609	
			84	626,035	1,702,570	1,702,570	
			85	398,684	967,981	967,981	
			86	550,196	1,127,964	1,130,544	2,580
	V	H	81	48,849	147,484	174,448	26,964
			84	286,945	837,145	917,145	80,000
			86	2,162,209	3,641,370	4,233,880	592,510
CHINA M	V	E	84	10	600	676	76
			86	57	3,665	3,940	275
	V	W	81	14	290	334	44
			82	73	268	277	9
			83	11	547	603	56
			84	16	914	992	78
DENMARK	O	W	83	1,156	1,925	1,925	
FR GERM	O	E	81	53	598	598	
HG KONG	O	W	84	23	780	852	72
	V	W	83	37	1,212	1,315	103
ITALY	V	W	81	459	8,750	11,290	2,540
JAPAN	V	E	82	92	1,735	2,068	333
			83	1,358	4,665	6,326	1,661
			84	1,291	2,260	2,489	229
			85	9,717	8,128	8,966	838
			86	9,435	8,401	9,595	1,194
	V	W	81	27	595	629	34
			82	179	2,908	3,189	281
			83	72	5,466	5,831	365
			84	41	1,692	1,861	169
			85	1,878	3,546	4,315	769
KOR REP	V	E	83	15	1,612	1,779	167
			84	50	1,306	1,484	178
			85	4,744	4,236	4,671	435
			86	3,148	2,405	2,552	147
	V	W	81	166	1,632	1,794	162
MEXICO	A	W	84	9	400	500	100
N ZEAL	N	W	86	1,435,287	2,583,125	3,158,540	575,415
	V	H	84	1,280,722	3,865,865	3,893,750	27,885

Country	Mode	Reg	Yr	Quantity	F.A.S.	C.I.F.	Charges
			85	1,591,446	3,816,629	4,190,429	373,800
NETHLDS	V	W	82	827	6,734	9,920	3,186
			85	218	3,553	4,604	1,051
SWEDEN	V	W	83	112	787	1,915	1,128
THAILND	O	W	84	18	528	572	44
	V	W	82	11	431	460	29
U KING	V	E	82	137	3,250	4,688	1,438
			83	135	3,357	4,848	1,491
			84	88	2,029	3,473	1,444

Barley, grain, for malting
1300800 BARLEY FOR MALTING PURPOSES (BU)

Country	Mode	Reg	Yr	Quantity	F.A.S.	C.I.F.	Charges
TOTAL			81	5,662,913	24,077,005	24,269,995	192,990
			82	8,901,733	32,050,024	32,594,890	544,866
			83	5,347,636	16,954,386	16,977,419	23,033
			84	4,118,157	13,624,957	13,670,957	46,000
			85	2,675,362	9,152,013	9,152,015	2
			86	1,839,894	6,721,291	6,747,488	26,197
BELGIUM	V	W	86	1,534	7,015	10,630	3,615
CANADA	N	E	81	602,639	2,452,933	2,645,923	192,990
			82	8,352,860	30,639,407	31,182,785	543,378
			84	3,881,896	12,973,260	13,019,260	46,000
	O	E	81	5,060,274	21,624,072	21,624,072	
			82	548,567	1,408,775	1,408,775	
			83	5,089,255	16,086,874	16,086,874	
			84	232,932	645,557	645,557	
			85	2,557,786	8,730,900	8,730,902	2
			86	1,793,160	6,611,875	6,611,875	
	O	W	84	3,329	6,140	6,140	
			85	21,576	87,033	87,033	
			86	207	1,635	1,635	
	V	E	83	257,806	865,639	883,115	17,476
DENMARK	O	E	86	2,578	25,287	31,887	6,600
	V	E	82	300	1,170	2,203	1,033
			83	230	598	1,216	618
JAPAN	V	E	86	37,500	48,926	52,946	4,020
	V	W	83	285	669	687	18
MONGOLA	O	E	85	96,000	334,080	334,080	
NETHLDS	A	E	83	60	606	5,527	4,921
PORTUGL	V	E	82	6	672	1,127	455
U KING	O	E	86	4,662	21,633	33,119	11,486
	V	E	86	69	2,393	2,644	251
	V	W	86	184	2,527	2,752	225

Barley, malt
1322000 BARLEY AND OTHER MALTS, NSPF (CWT)

Country	Mode	Reg	Yr	Quantity	F.A.S.	C.I.F.	Charges
TOTAL			81	1,112,341	15,326,246	15,683,587	357,341
			82	896,590	13,088,908	13,387,546	298,638
			83	662,141	9,305,701	9,613,723	308,022
			84	692,553	9,427,967	9,583,539	155,572
			85	935,865	10,538,415	10,630,200	91,785
			86	861,616	10,184,012	10,263,779	79,767
AUSTRAL	V	W	86	71	1,494	1,665	171
BELGIUM	N	E	86	311	8,203	8,642	439
	V	E	86	402	5,151	7,151	2,000
	V	W	85	220	2,694	2,918	224
			86	368	3,932	7,471	3,539
C RICA	V	W	85	27	2,856	3,671	815
CANADA	A	E	83	448	6,884	9,212	2,328
			84	3,444	51,296	72,642	21,346
	N	E	85	527,502	5,671,298	5,689,298	18,000
			86	488,695	5,302,255	5,328,792	26,537
	O	E	81	1,086,107	14,884,115	15,160,645	276,530
			82	870,431	12,825,789	13,096,825	271,036
			83	626,210	8,848,646	9,135,130	286,484
			84	583,536	7,867,307	7,971,773	104,466
			85	252,808	3,132,809	3,132,809	
			86	249,955	3,278,973	3,278,973	
	O	W	81	8,933	158,727	158,727	
			82	4,522	66,313	66,313	
			83	24,628	312,575	312,575	
			84	91,811	1,324,319	1,324,319	
			85	80,437	1,041,953	1,041,953	
			86	91,131	1,230,420	1,230,420	
	V	E	81	12,456	154,958	206,933	51,975
			85	18,645	382,026	394,371	12,345
			86	8,556	135,109	137,406	2,297
CHINA M	V	W	86	39	1,781	1,916	135

Crop Product TSUSA commodity number, description, and unit of quantity Country	Mode	Reg	Yr	Quantity	F.A.S.	C.I.F.	Charges
DENMARK	V	E	84	132	601	1,587	986
	V	W	85	36,000	32,560	38,257	5,697
DOM REP	V	E	84	280	12,600	14,140	1,540
			85	134	3,379	3,720	341
FINLAND	V	E	83	40	647	1,118	471
FR GERM	V	E	83	43	768	1,691	923
			84	33	2,303	2,440	137
			85	476	11,426	14,631	3,205
			86	472	12,893	17,040	4,147
JAPAN	V	E	84	5,223	24,777	26,856	2,079
			85	9,875	75,616	86,119	10,503
			86	3,662	40,583	44,647	4,064
	V	H	84	4	624	732	108
	V	W	83	524	3,140	3,283	143
			84	1,202	9,952	10,338	386
			85	510	15,387	16,146	759
			86	1,130	7,523	7,857	334
KENYA	V	W	86	40	1,852	2,064	212
KOR REP	V	E	81	139	7,793	9,042	1,249
			82	495	12,255	13,775	1,520
			83	4,687	9,545	10,968	1,423
			84	2,002	10,690	11,994	1,304
			85	18	1,623	1,780	157
			86	3,641	6,438	7,055	617
	V	W	81	1,600	29,966	32,763	2,797
			82	14,409	44,948	48,545	3,597
			83	2,580	44,892	48,054	3,162
			84	1,767	22,730	24,313	1,583
			85	4,234	69,089	76,802	7,713
			86	6,562	30,328	32,745	2,417
MEXICO	O	W	82	234	2,611	2,611	
			83	161	730	730	
NETHLDS	V	E	85	67	1,432	1,588	156
	V	W	85	315	5,665	7,718	2,053
THAILND	V	E	83	63	1,281	1,529	248
U KING	A	E	82	7	286	597	311
	N	E	82	2,383	5,590	6,332	742
			85	530	3,213	3,438	225
			86	2,653	27,345	34,807	7,462
	O	E	81	82	2,153	2,503	350
			82	90	2,119	2,596	477
			83	147	4,591	5,152	561
			84	13	6,504	7,248	744
			85	353	4,594	4,594	
			86	776	13,224	17,669	4,445
	V	E	81	1,351	36,677	48,016	11,339
			82	2,416	75,699	87,171	11,472
			83	1,650	45,260	51,765	6,505
			84	1,974	59,278	69,799	10,521
			85	3,314	70,665	95,188	24,523
			86	2,752	63,383	82,260	18,877
	V	W	81	1,673	51,857	64,958	13,101
			82	1,603	53,298	62,781	9,483
			83	960	26,742	32,516	5,774
			84	1,132	34,986	45,358	10,372
			85	400	10,130	15,199	5,069
			86	400	13,125	15,199	2,074

Barley, milled for humans
1311200 BARLEY MILLED EDIBL EX PEARL (LB)

Country	Mode	Reg	Yr	Quantity	F.A.S.	C.I.F.	Charges
TOTAL			81	200,623	134,181	140,718	6,537
			82	181,570	82,062	91,617	9,555
			83	238,290	148,145	162,351	14,206
			84	308,343	174,999	196,201	21,202
			85	386,714	136,833	151,197	14,364
			86	203,646	123,387	137,139	13,752
AUSTRAL	V	W	81	2,259	886	1,016	130
CANADA	O	E	82	61,089	963	963	
			83	2,935	900	900	
			84	2,341	397	397	
			85	158,044	24,698	24,698	
			86	28,800	13,489	13,489	
CHINA M	V	E	83	5,898	5,134	5,662	528
			84	2,166	2,205	2,416	211
	V	W	81	5,746	10,821	11,343	522
			82	20,171	17,753	18,686	933
			83	25,366	27,053	28,280	1,227
			84	11,932	13,252	13,868	616
			85	8,550	4,826	5,562	736
			86	1,960	3,283	3,464	181
CHINA T	V	E	83	1,000	1,152	1,296	144
	V	H	82	2,000	761	989	228
ECUADOR	V	E	81	1,000	350	411	61
			83	1,000	300	376	76
			84	1,000	500	583	83
FINLAND	A	E	83	37,407	19,574	22,967	3,393
			84	44,737	19,004	22,548	3,544
			85	27,320	12,053	14,230	2,177
FR GERM	O	E	84	3,307	2,149	2,754	605
FRANCE	V	E	83	606	2,316	2,406	90
HG KONG	V	E	82	500	1,550	1,653	103
			83	5,000	4,696	5,208	512
			84	1,800	533	615	82
	V	H	83	500	396	456	60
	V	W	81	3,854	2,432	2,573	141
			82	2,760	5,417	5,707	290
			83	5,059	5,121	5,356	235
			84	6,750	8,322	8,831	509
ITALY	V	E	84	31,169	7,250	7,944	694
			85	4,200	5,040	5,746	706
JAPAN	V	E	81	8,264	4,513	4,948	435
			82	23,592	12,777	14,656	1,879
			83	56,468	30,301	34,081	3,780
			84	65,534	31,545	36,377	4,832
			85	92,127	39,781	45,786	6,005
			86	30,631	20,715	23,171	2,456
	V	H	81	10,846	6,441	7,449	1,008
			82	8,561	4,611	5,687	1,076
			83	13,164	7,367	8,500	1,133
			84	15,015	7,490	8,870	1,380
			85	9,000	4,242	5,257	1,015
			86	5,248	3,680	4,112	432
	V	W	81	54,684	29,604	31,689	2,085
			82	53,053	23,893	26,231	2,338
			83	77,281	40,019	42,645	2,626
			84	65,573	39,275	42,391	3,116
			85	80,679	41,371	44,378	3,007
			86	52,983	36,615	39,894	3,279
KOR REP	O	E	82	1,200	1,329	1,468	139
	V	E	81	6,600	1,686	1,799	113
			82	1,656	982	1,118	136
			83	1,008	602	658	56
			84	1,080	1,905	2,014	109
			85	1,680	1,403	1,646	243
			86	2,821	1,056	1,200	144
	V	H	85	1,200	1,060	1,237	177
			86	2,520	1,457	2,045	588
	V	W	81	5,681	2,763	2,962	199
			82	3,487	2,660	2,778	118
			83	3,159	1,531	1,634	103
			84	7,839	3,538	3,847	309
			85	3,914	2,359	2,657	298
			86	14,920	8,905	9,703	798
MEXICO	O	W	81	81,022	56,793	56,793	
PORTUGL	V	E	81	2,678	3,014	3,648	634
			82	3,501	9,366	11,681	2,315
			83	1,763	1,329	1,537	208
			84	2,749	3,715	4,177	462
THAILND	V	W	86	4,400	2,564	2,643	79
TURKEY	V	E	86	38,635	14,062	18,062	4,000
U KING	O	E	83	676	354	389	35
	V	E	81	17,989	14,878	16,087	1,209
			84	45,351	33,919	38,569	4,650
			86	20,728	17,561	19,356	1,795

Barley, milled not for humans
1315000 BARLEY, MIL N FOR HUMAN CONS (CWT)

Country	Mode	Reg	Yr	Quantity	F.A.S.	C.I.F.	Charges
TOTAL			81	75	4,374	4,559	185
			82	173	2,123	2,145	22
			83	31,006	163,633	163,633	
			84	12,612	92,852	92,852	
			85	4,358	41,797	49,008	7,211
			86	4,013	13,786	17,786	4,000
CANADA	O	E	82	171	1,010	1,010	
			83	21,270	108,981	108,981	
			84	6,378	42,865	42,865	
			85	927	6,842	6,842	
			86	2,381	8,726	8,726	
	O	W	83	9,736	54,652	54,652	
			84	6,234	49,987	49,987	
			85	2,192	15,837	15,837	
	V	W	86	1,632	5,060	9,060	4,000

Crop Product TSUSA commodity number, description, and unit of quantity Country	Mode	Reg	Yr	Quantity	F.A.S.	C.I.F.	Charges
CHINA M	V	W	81	9	3,009	3,107	98
			82	2	731	753	22
FR GERM	A	E	85	38	2,774	5,635	2,861
GREECE	N	E	82	*	382	382	
KOR REP	V	W	81	66	1,365	1,452	87
THAILND	V	W	85	1,201	16,344	20,694	4,350

Pearl barley, milled for humans
1311000 PEARL BARLEY, EDIBLE (LB)

Country	Mode	Reg	Yr	Quantity	F.A.S.	C.I.F.	Charges
TOTAL			81	947,842	159,720	163,318	3,598
			82	1,664,412	263,738	266,435	2,697
			83	2,473,109	431,073	451,669	20,596
			84	2,518,411	358,212	373,740	15,528
			85	2,034,040	245,060	246,660	1,600
			86	1,521,094	229,241	233,792	4,551
CANADA	O	E	81	899,816	123,918	123,918	
			82	1,629,248	236,050	236,050	
			83	1,959,202	272,968	272,968	
			84	2,144,095	240,207	240,207	
			85	2,004,536	225,052	225,052	
			86	1,459,267	185,852	185,852	
CHINA M	O	E	84	1,000	362	422	60
	V	E	81	21,130	10,856	12,420	1,564
			82	12,250	7,998	9,117	1,119
			83	35,612	30,465	35,228	4,763
			84	12,530	7,691	9,591	1,900
			85	2,475	1,972	2,471	499
			86	2,550	1,139	1,319	180
	V	W	81	19,524	15,474	16,556	1,082
			82	14,085	13,125	14,045	920
			83	31,078	33,033	35,353	2,320
			84	35,876	25,708	27,562	1,854
			85	9,909	9,764	10,189	425
			86	5,100	1,612	1,758	146
HG KONG	V	E	81	2,000	1,056	1,225	169
			82	5,900	3,882	4,304	422
			83	6,696	6,904	7,581	677
			84	9,100	5,072	5,979	907
	V	W	81	1,501	1,199	1,290	91
			82	1,450	1,071	1,126	55
			83	1,500	1,146	1,209	63
			84	8,207	4,348	4,954	606
			85	3,323	2,072	2,220	148
			86	4,013	1,431	1,545	114
JAPAN	O	E	84	952	2,424	2,653	229
			86	3,874	7,391	7,737	346
	V	E	84	661	1,444	1,593	149
			85	2,200	1,753	1,950	197
			86	529	1,117	1,173	56
	V	H	83	158	539	581	42
			84	132	425	476	51
	V	W	81	2,711	6,631	7,264	633
			82	979	1,177	1,324	147
			83	743	1,314	1,410	96
			84	3,201	7,216	7,734	518
			85	793	1,374	1,374	
			86	9,321	16,842	17,765	923
KOR REP	V	E	86	2,298	3,347	3,655	308
	V	W	84	3,120	1,546	1,689	143
MEXICO	O	E	84	39,683	4,167	4,167	
N ZEAL	A	W	86	10,809	4,191	5,085	894
PHIL R	V	W	82	500	435	469	34
SINGAPR	V	W	86	2,094	1,094	2,334	1,240
THAILND	O	W	84	12,800	4,224	4,778	554
	V	E	83	1,001	873	983	110
			84	500	592	691	99
	V	W	81	1,160	586	645	59
			83	437,119	83,831	96,356	12,525
			84	242,465	49,091	57,092	8,001
			85	10,804	3,073	3,404	331
			86	21,239	5,225	5,569	344
U KING	A	E	84	4,089	3,695	4,152	457

Basil

Basil, spice
1610300 BASIL, CRUDE OR NOT MFRD (LB)

Country	Mode	Reg	Yr	Quantity	F.A.S.	C.I.F.	Charges
TOTAL			81	1,642,253	685,905	800,314	114,409
			82	2,467,281	1,353,688	1,525,663	171,975
			83	2,544,660	1,536,505	1,714,769	178,264
			84	3,168,993	1,640,748	1,868,472	227,724
			85	4,028,882	2,187,449	2,537,174	349,725
			86	3,028,938	1,907,023	2,246,739	339,716
ALBANIA	V	E	82	57,108	31,688	37,415	5,727
			83	17,637	12,983	14,814	1,831
			85	13,657	11,312	12,353	1,041
AUSTRAL	A	E	84	265	1,718	2,668	950
CANADA	O	E	83	2,731	5,318	5,318	
CHINA M	V	E	83	22,046	20,095	23,320	3,225
CYPRUS	V	E	84	595	668	750	82
ECUADOR	V	E	81	11,000	4,080	4,644	564
EGYPT	N	E	82	1,561,904	765,720	853,118	87,398
			84	2,290,588	1,096,056	1,244,727	148,671
	O	W	84	882	1,499	1,712	213
	V	E	81	1,263,333	482,852	550,421	67,569
			82	44,092	21,327	24,027	2,700
			83	1,675,093	922,711	1,022,235	99,524
			84	44,092	17,025	22,000	4,975
			85	3,006,998	1,416,407	1,656,040	239,633
			86	2,234,564	1,193,854	1,428,813	234,959
	V	W	86	25,228	20,110	27,063	6,953
FR GERM	O	E	81	1,053	607	653	46
	V	E	82	20,326	7,550	9,497	1,947
FRANCE	A	E	84	49	272	286	14
	A	W	82	88	477	532	55
	N	E	84	353,804	230,439	257,789	27,350
	N	W	85	21,095	16,706	19,118	2,412
	O	E	83	200	911	943	32
			84	375	3,086	3,139	53
	V	E	81	313,055	164,960	208,580	43,620
			82	748,952	503,086	576,445	73,359
			83	527,803	358,496	406,342	47,846
			84	272,833	177,699	203,257	25,558
			85	980,983	717,750	813,043	95,293
			86	659,657	544,912	607,703	62,791
	V	W	82	2,205	1,848	1,963	115
GIBRAT	V	E	84	10,823	6,878	8,308	1,430
GREECE	V	E	86	25,708	10,554	12,868	2,314
INDIA	O	E	81	8,353	3,550	3,763	213
	V	E	83	82,673	39,884	50,937	11,053
INDNSIA	V	E	84	44,069	19,058	24,436	5,378
ISRAEL	V	E	83	87,575	83,333	96,814	13,481
			84	12,480	10,864	12,543	1,679
			86	22,046	13,766	16,548	2,782
ITALY	A	E	84	144	252	257	5
	V	E	82	92	506	557	51
			83	192	1,896	1,967	71
	V	W	82	56	303	303	
			83	47	289	335	46
MEXICO	O	E	81	3,307	2,315	2,315	
			82	22,046	7,407	7,407	
			83	123,393	80,169	80,169	
			84	8,703	4,839	4,839	
N ZEAL	A	E	85	306	4,387	9,067	4,680
			86	552	5,952	7,644	1,692
	A	W	83	40	263	294	31
			84	2,091	10,246	11,673	1,427
			85	5,643	19,884	26,390	6,506
			86	19,687	90,918	116,382	25,464
NETHLDS	A	E	81	341	2,048	2,386	338
			85	200	1,003	1,163	160
	O	E	81	200	802	833	31
			82	300	1,206	1,256	50
			83	300	1,208	1,258	50
			84	300	1,354	1,426	72
	V	E	83	703	2,130	2,324	194
			84	75	382	400	18
			86	39,600	21,848	24,088	2,240
PAKISTN	V	E	84	88,184	40,854	48,054	7,200
SPAIN	O	E	81	28,235	12,000	12,720	720
THAILND	N	E	82	274	2,615	2,821	206
	V	E	81	982	2,236	2,519	283
			82	125	295	356	61
			83	1,540	2,661	3,114	453
			84	390	1,251	1,407	156
			86	888	2,385	2,776	391
	V	W	81	2,394	6,395	6,879	484
			82	1,213	3,430	3,736	306
			83	2,687	4,158	4,585	427
			84	776	1,823	1,995	172
TURKEY	O	E	82	8,500	6,230	6,230	

Crop
Product
TSUSA commodity number, description, and unit of quantity

Country	Mode	Reg	Yr	Quantity	F.A.S.	C.I.F.	Charges
	V	E	81	10,000	4,060	4,601	541
			84	37,475	14,485	16,806	2,321
			86	1,000	1,210	1,283	73
U KING	A	E	86	8	1,514	1,571	57

1610500 BASIL, MANUFACTURED (LB)

Country	Mode	Reg	Yr	Quantity	F.A.S.	C.I.F.	Charges
TOTAL			81	7,075	16,568	17,846	1,278
			82	22,963	27,826	29,821	1,995
			83	77,058	71,781	77,050	5,269
			84	58,670	47,866	55,956	8,090
			85	15,760	22,569	26,408	3,839
			86	57,048	18,564	23,456	4,892
ARGENT	V	E	83	39,683	25,200	28,391	3,191
CANADA	O	E	81	733	2,444	2,444	
			82	11,010	11,730	11,730	
			83	23,405	25,436	25,436	
			84	3,706	7,694	7,694	
CHINA M	V	W	86	11,100	1,044	1,098	54
DENMARK	A	E	85	62	1,492	1,553	61
	N	E	86	21,262	8,099	8,513	414
	V	E	85	1,702	3,221	3,528	307
EGYPT	V	E	84	22,046	9,625	12,563	2,938
			85	10,000	8,259	10,501	2,242
			86	24,239	6,887	11,294	4,407
FIJI	A	E	84	2,700	1,140	1,951	811
FR GERM	O	E	82	1,010	546	614	68
FRANCE	V	E	81	297	3,969	4,142	173
			82	141	2,524	2,625	101
			83	215	3,475	3,589	114
			84	1,341	6,022	6,342	320
			85	420	1,386	1,486	100
			86	45	1,082	1,086	4
GREECE	V	E	84	840	471	535	64
	V	W	84	220	471	526	55
HG KONG	V	E	83	250	298	323	25
ITALY	A	E	83	411	1,833	2,133	300
	A	W	83	65	292	520	228
	V	E	83	201	590	652	62
			84	422	1,560	1,623	63
			85	2,226	7,131	8,146	1,015
MEXICO	O	W	84	5,400	548	548	
N ZEAL	A	W	84	359	617	774	157
PHIL R	V	E	84	156	320	338	18
REP SAF	V	E	83	3,858	3,224	3,798	574
			84	15,542	11,954	15,001	3,047
SPAIN	V	E	82	4,428	5,533	6,402	869
THAILND	N	W	84	4,428	4,663	5,015	352
	V	E	81	1,145	3,055	3,524	469
			82	3,580	2,860	3,420	560
			83	132	270	309	39
			84	220	282	317	35
	V	H	84	220	255	285	30
	V	W	81	2,620	4,102	4,440	338
			82	2,585	3,643	4,001	358
			83	8,482	8,984	9,634	650
			84	839	1,685	1,835	150
			85	1,350	1,080	1,194	114
			86	402	1,452	1,465	13
U KING	O	E	81	957	2,053	2,308	255
			82	24	272	292	20
	V	E	81	1,323	945	988	43
			82	185	718	737	19
			83	356	2,179	2,265	86
			84	231	559	609	50

Bay

Bay, rum or water

4611500 BAY RUM OR BAY WATER (LB)

Country	Mode	Reg	Yr	Quantity	F.A.S.	C.I.F.	Charges
TOTAL			81	43,435	158,764	164,745	5,981
			82	35,182	179,934	187,206	7,272
			83	27,143	132,781	138,029	5,248
			84	31,841	151,722	156,739	5,017
			85	23,207	96,583	99,234	2,651
			86	78,924	331,626	342,206	10,580
B VIRGN	V	E	82	30	312	316	4
BARBADO	V	E	83	736	1,058	1,137	79
			86	743	7,586	8,246	660

Country	Mode	Reg	Yr	Quantity	F.A.S.	C.I.F.	Charges
BERMUDA	V	E	81	7,879	85,671	87,373	1,702
			82	6,020	91,106	92,760	1,654
			83	11,198	75,004	77,144	2,140
			84	10,845	87,933	88,970	1,037
			85	10,831	76,070	77,373	1,303
			86	12,134	132,953	135,024	2,071
BRAZIL	A	E	84	844	12,520	13,210	690
CANADA	O	E	82	4,598	4,258	4,258	
			86	4,958	17,572	17,572	
CHINA M	V	E	85	81	1,628	1,668	40
FRANCE	A	E	82	629	1,333	1,612	279
	A	W	86	756	2,264	3,078	814
	N	E	81	7,560	33,894	34,701	807
			83	931	3,306	3,448	142
			84	3,363	16,503	17,088	585
			86	673	5,479	5,735	256
	O	W	84	14	460	481	21
	V	E	81	60	526	563	37
			83	10	483	488	5
			84	342	1,878	1,929	51
			85	90	1,125	1,138	13
			86	9,951	52,775	54,449	1,674
GUYANA	V	E	81	927	924	970	46
			82	4,792	21,282	22,345	1,063
			83	1,868	9,634	10,068	434
			84	1,041	6,492	6,642	150
HAITI	A	E	83	192	374	441	67
ITALY	V	E	82	989	3,347	3,615	268
			85	871	1,380	1,515	135
			86	1,012	2,635	2,834	199
JAMAICA	A	E	81	341	945	1,043	98
			82	443	7,303	7,993	690
	V	E	81	7,370	10,301	11,434	1,133
			82	9,550	13,973	15,006	1,033
			83	5,933	7,362	7,887	525
			84	9,040	11,345	12,053	708
			85	11,334	16,380	17,540	1,160
			86	12,344	11,800	12,433	633
JAPAN	V	H	82	42	392	416	24
MEXICO	O	W	83	425	2,140	2,140	
N ANTIL	V	E	81	16,632	18,786	20,047	1,261
			82	7,207	35,679	37,786	2,107
			83	5,737	31,766	33,514	1,748
			86	7,050	16,934	17,812	878
SPAIN	V	E	81	2,127	5,844	6,608	764
			84	225	448	531	83
			86	10,557	24,034	25,933	1,899
SWITZLD	O	E	84	1,215	2,518	2,616	98
	V	E	81	444	1,263	1,371	108
U KING	A	E	81	95	610	635	25
			82	882	949	1,099	150
			83	113	1,654	1,762	108
			84	1,059	2,769	3,211	442
	O	E	86	18,746	57,594	59,090	1,496
	V	E	84	3,853	8,856	10,008	1,152

Bean

Bean (not specified), dried

1401140 DRIED BEANS, NSPF (LB)

Country	Mode	Reg	Yr	Quantity	F.A.S.	C.I.F.	Charges
TOTAL			81	8,616,749	3,049,973	3,274,967	237,444
			82	7,018,172	2,414,517	2,479,036	64,519
			83	3,643,115	941,124	1,006,002	64,878
			84	2,880,527	897,875	951,346	53,471
			85	2,369,363	764,480	856,451	91,971
			86	2,571,879	802,492	883,681	81,189
ARGENT	V	E	82	20,943	6,455	7,720	1,265
			85	471,436	95,939	120,272	24,333
			86	357,132	110,154	129,759	19,605
AUSTRAL	O	E	85	7,960	1,997	2,352	355
	O	W	86	7,150	1,710	1,710	
	V	E	83	749	301	351	50
			84	4,409	1,129	1,360	231
			86	38,456	8,040	10,095	2,055
	V	W	81	17,417	5,147	6,050	903
			83	4,205	1,307	1,555	248
			84	17,637	4,024	4,850	826
			85	94,876	19,072	22,529	3,457
BELGIUM	O	E	83	32,340	7,486	7,486	

Crop
Product
TSUSA commodity number, description, and unit of quantity

Country	Mode	Reg	Yr	Quantity	F.A.S.	C.I.F.	Charges
	V	E	81	234,000	92,440	101,005	8,565
BRAZIL	V	E	81	930	999	1,114	115
			84	44,092	20,000	22,883	2,883
			85	79,366	27,000	31,440	4,440
CANADA	O	E	81	827,574	254,518	254,518	
			82	5,695,403	1,862,682	1,862,682	
			83	1,148,330	217,187	217,187	
			84	1,670,101	388,174	388,189	15
			85	489,868	128,342	128,342	
			86	901,112	208,561	208,561	
	O	W	81	187,000	52,739	52,739	
			82	191,700	38,203	38,203	
			83	1,052,319	139,775	139,775	
			84	223,000	45,080	45,080	
			85	89,000	9,774	9,774	
			86	29,500	3,831	3,831	
	V	E	81	19	300	324	24
CHILE	V	E	81	6,446,383	2,157,404	2,327,086	182,132
			82	179,985	53,170	62,896	9,726
			83	354,370	81,720	100,778	19,058
			85	179,741	59,129	67,031	7,902
			86	238,098	74,520	89,120	14,600
	V	W	81	79,350	22,003	27,720	5,717
			82	79,366	7,200	13,729	6,529
CHINA M	O	E	83	1,320	471	514	43
	V	E	81	35,771	17,089	18,765	1,676
			82	61,937	26,845	31,341	4,496
			83	6,880	2,265	2,606	341
			84	6,350	3,330	3,827	497
			85	10,850	4,405	5,151	746
			86	38,950	10,227	12,222	1,995
	V	H	81	1,962	3,062	3,402	340
			82	900	673	759	86
			84	1,700	769	844	75
			85	6,614	2,163	2,403	240
			86	15,000	3,755	4,176	421
	V	W	81	106,291	43,764	48,585	4,821
			82	137,701	57,783	64,778	6,995
			83	212,952	88,451	94,350	5,899
			84	72,113	29,524	32,106	2,582
			85	64,389	32,011	35,622	3,611
			86	68,569	27,946	30,084	2,138
CHINA T	N	W	82	10,765	8,129	9,601	1,472
	O	E	82	3,307	1,821	2,065	244
	V	E	81	9,004	5,060	5,873	813
			82	8,375	6,880	8,098	1,218
			83	8,750	4,666	5,268	602
			84	55,000	24,786	28,454	3,668
			85	43,798	16,666	19,629	2,963
			86	4,393	3,139	3,429	290
	V	H	81	71,032	37,775	40,444	2,669
			82	38,500	23,590	26,035	2,445
			83	55,491	23,923	26,999	3,076
			84	52,000	25,305	29,813	4,508
			85	70,800	29,151	33,011	3,860
			86	40,000	17,746	19,814	2,068
	V	W	81	116,416	84,860	90,370	5,510
			82	198,738	120,193	129,231	9,038
			83	201,350	85,934	92,434	6,500
			84	143,473	74,189	80,164	5,975
			85	120,952	56,082	61,353	5,271
			86	223,414	94,312	103,077	8,765
COLOMB	N	E	86	3,687	4,912	5,353	441
DOM REP	V	E	81	10,000	2,600	3,110	510
			82	4,950	1,287	1,493	206
ETHIOP	V	E	84	33,380	7,339	9,616	2,277
FR GERM	A	E	83	308	938	1,370	432
			84	15,400	5,210	6,446	1,236
			85	506	1,068	1,284	216
	O	E	81	2,068	3,277	3,578	301
	V	E	83	132	512	661	149
			86	60,083	28,782	32,300	3,518
FRANCE	A	E	83	2,205	3,000	3,100	100
	N	E	83	2,730	3,117	3,624	507
	V	E	81	5,831	4,310	4,659	349
			82	1,800	2,546	2,948	402
			84	1,116	730	802	72
			86	2,250	1,201	1,302	101
GUATMAL	A	W	83	2,794	2,094	3,404	1,310
	V	E	85	16,528	5,825	6,855	1,030
	V	W	84	6,000	3,048	3,612	564
HG KONG	O	W	82	4,950	2,559	2,727	168
	V	E	81	33,900	18,810	20,364	1,554
			82	12,930	6,012	6,846	834

Country	Mode	Reg	Yr	Quantity	F.A.S.	C.I.F.	Charges
			83	12,440	6,412	7,290	878
			84	2,646	650	768	118
			85	38,500	17,437	19,915	2,478
			86	34,760	12,821	15,091	2,270
	V	H	81	440	333	361	28
			84	3,300	1,223	1,282	59
	V	W	81	33,343	16,858	17,846	988
			82	113,855	59,717	64,375	4,658
			83	61,465	13,076	14,994	1,918
			84	13,126	6,157	6,572	415
			85	16,699	9,292	9,889	597
			86	13,615	6,373	7,019	646
INDIA	O	E	83	992	1,153	1,211	58
			84	1,176	1,804	1,984	180
			85	7,976	5,143	7,017	1,874
			86	7,700	3,595	3,595	
	O	W	84	1,320	457	485	28
	V	E	81	265	293	353	60
			83	940	898	1,023	125
			84	113,603	55,276	61,724	6,448
			85	10,803	3,750	4,418	668
			86	21,606	7,825	9,398	1,573
	V	W	83	3,028	2,351	2,715	364
			84	11,380	5,234	6,103	869
			85	104,243	40,466	46,051	5,585
			86	67,087	23,223	27,538	4,315
INDNSIA	V	W	83	960	350	374	24
			84	422	450	582	132
ISRAEL	A	W	83	385	613	1,162	549
	V	E	82	24,251	5,887	7,489	1,602
			85	12,472	5,305	5,336	31
			86	41,446	16,920	19,135	2,215
ITALY	V	E	81	11,022	10,000	11,445	1,445
			82	18,740	9,660	11,122	1,462
			83	39,683	5,193	7,199	2,006
JAPAN	V	E	81	32,388	10,134	11,919	1,785
			82	4,230	5,428	5,947	519
			83	7,365	12,951	14,226	1,275
			84	5,825	9,659	10,680	1,021
			85	5,931	6,504	7,151	647
			86	2,419	4,817	5,074	257
	V	H	82	1,640	2,541	2,982	441
			84	132	251	294	43
	V	W	81	1,339	2,385	2,551	166
			82	3,569	5,747	6,228	481
			83	93,182	82,393	88,937	6,544
			84	11,008	6,020	6,613	593
			86	20,169	10,316	10,926	610
KENYA	N	E	81	57,347	21,989	25,952	3,963
			84	11,617	4,879	5,480	601
	O	E	81	5,000	2,066	2,341	275
			82	2,090	1,972	1,972	
			83	16,318	6,218	6,404	186
			84	420	328	328	
			85	14,921	4,219	4,784	565
	V	E	81	9,150	2,822	3,062	240
			83	13,135	3,485	4,153	668
			84	14,109	5,680	6,888	1,208
			85	3,307	1,163	1,475	312
	V	W	82	5,225	2,058	2,299	241
			83	2,205	1,975	2,330	355
KOR REP	V	E	81	14,334	4,677	5,267	590
			83	120	490	538	48
			84	1,890	2,081	2,310	229
			85	47,548	25,991	29,987	3,996
			86	8,100	9,390	10,283	893
	V	W	82	11,800	7,480	8,137	657
			83	2,461	3,254	3,554	300
			86	45,325	25,343	28,856	3,513
LEBANON	V	E	85	15,000	1,470	1,897	427
	V	W	86	3,915	1,871	2,100	229
MADAGAS	V	E	84	119,049	66,487	71,188	4,701
MALAWI	O	E	81	1,100	799	879	80
			83	24,273	10,719	10,821	102
			84	19,581	9,020	9,300	280
	V	W	83	4,205	2,222	2,645	423
MEXICO	O	E	81	3,163	2,385	2,385	
			83	31,500	10,491	10,491	
			86	37,478	11,905	11,905	
	O	W	82	6,850	3,223	3,223	
			83	18,409	2,923	2,923	
			86	115,950	27,530	27,530	
	V	E	81	24,209	22,400	23,451	1,051
			82	13,750	15,125	17,067	1,942

Crop
Product
TSUSA commodity number, description, and unit of quantity

Country	Mode	Reg	Yr	Quantity	F.A.S.	C.I.F.	Charges
			83	33,069	16,842	18,926	2,084
MOROC	V	E	86	16,585	4,800	6,030	1,230
NEPAL	V	W	81	6,614	2,478	2,700	222
NETHLDS	V	W	86	7,426	4,072	4,308	236
PERU	O	E	85	8,818	3,636	4,102	466
	V	E	81	112,435	59,670	65,316	5,646
			84	35,420	11,781	13,620	1,839
			85	99,452	32,734	37,949	5,215
PHIL R	V	E	84	1,800	1,505	1,712	207
	V	H	82	1,400	952	1,039	87
			83	1,238	897	1,005	108
			85	1,760	1,126	1,285	159
	V	W	81	180	320	367	47
			83	900	775	840	65
			84	699	426	485	59
PORTUGL	V	E	81	79,641	68,849	72,185	3,336
			82	13,843	14,099	14,850	751
			83	113,831	66,618	71,595	4,977
			84	78,159	42,174	46,870	4,696
			85	185,184	86,073	93,510	7,437
			86	2,205	1,550	1,649	99
REP SAF	V	E	83	1,653	942	1,428	486
			85	4,928	13,562	14,969	1,407
SINGAPR	V	W	84	3,336	1,188	1,345	157
SPAIN	A	E	86	2,204	1,294	2,869	1,575
	V	W	82	7,165	6,500	7,073	573
			83	2,976	1,755	1,983	228
THAILND	O	E	84	2,200	1,245	1,245	
	V	E	81	12,006	3,954	4,583	629
			82	25,926	8,819	9,985	1,166
			83	15,194	5,055	5,779	724
			84	2,756	1,054	1,336	282
			86	44,350	11,940	13,243	1,303
	V	W	81	27,825	11,404	12,298	894
			82	111,588	39,281	44,096	4,815
			83	53,963	17,926	19,994	2,068
			84	64,540	25,166	28,247	3,081
			85	24,938	11,755	12,557	802
			86	18,687	6,759	7,426	667
TURKEY	O	E	86	5,500	3,383	3,734	351
	V	E	84	8,787	2,736	3,294	558
U KING	O	E	84	6,455	2,307	2,565	258
			85	20,199	6,230	7,111	881
			86	27,558	7,929	11,139	3,210

1401660 BEANS, DRY, NSPF, 9/1-4/30 (LB)

Country	Mode	Reg	Yr	Quantity	F.A.S.	C.I.F.	Charges
TOTAL			81	6,600,537	2,210,179	2,350,530	140,351
			82	8,976,795	2,870,747	3,025,120	154,373
			83	8,041,272	2,051,982	2,187,606	135,624
			84	6,689,901	1,667,785	1,791,486	123,701
			85	4,332,642	1,277,802	1,406,006	128,204
			86	5,861,289	1,764,392	1,913,160	148,768
AFGHAN	V	E	86	6,064	1,108	1,460	352
ARGENT	O	E	84	3,300	1,582	1,582	
	V	E	81	105,045	39,912	46,265	6,353
			82	118,894	38,803	46,094	7,291
			83	28,578	6,811	8,703	1,892
			84	340,695	83,338	102,108	18,770
			85	288,595	88,809	107,746	18,937
			86	393,998	122,274	141,950	19,676
AUSTRAL	O	E	83	2,200	650	720	70
	O	W	84	5,900	12,135	13,674	1,539
	V	E	81	40,168	11,511	14,291	2,780
			84	18,737	4,857	5,712	855
			85	77,115	12,766	17,804	5,038
			86	90,389	17,272	21,832	4,560
	V	W	81	12,809	4,431	5,229	798
			83	39,683	11,787	13,677	1,890
			85	43,208	12,084	14,186	2,102
AUSTRIA	V	E	84	43,210	19,890	22,820	2,930
BELGIUM	O	E	82	14,794	6,457	7,590	1,133
			83	16,310	6,671	7,145	474
			85	9,636	3,464	3,613	149
			86	8,800	1,816	1,816	
	V	E	81	2,249	352	622	270
			84	3,968	1,232	1,443	211
BRAZIL	V	E	82	2,205	510	639	129
			86	1,587	1,080	1,274	194
CANADA	O	E	81	3,906,007	911,791	911,791	
			82	6,029,565	1,678,691	1,678,691	
			83	3,082,060	540,065	562,289	22,224
			84	3,581,645	536,513	536,658	145
			85	1,429,016	242,217	242,217	

Crop
Product
TSUSA commodity number, description, and unit of quantity

Country	Mode	Reg	Yr	Quantity	F.A.S.	C.I.F.	Charges
			86	2,307,105	423,742	423,817	75
	O	W	81	54,550	13,922	13,922	
			82	95,400	12,819	12,819	
			83	2,728,775	454,145	454,149	4
			84	1,038,660	166,684	166,684	
			85	314,000	30,901	30,901	
			86	360,000	40,847	40,847	
CHILE	V	E	81	473,341	185,452	211,574	26,122
			82	704,639	101,856	136,409	34,553
			83	152,824	42,170	50,147	7,977
			84	345,843	98,317	116,743	18,426
			85	237,802	59,831	69,629	9,798
			86	448,515	107,864	128,525	20,661
	V	W	81	79,366	27,000	32,213	5,213
			82	36,000	2,856	2,856	
			83	43,651	5,556	11,916	6,360
CHINA M	O	E	81	7,614	2,549	2,978	429
	V	E	81	97,809	37,407	43,393	5,986
			82	96,648	41,730	48,160	6,430
			83	138,902	48,082	56,197	8,115
			84	91,581	41,357	51,055	9,698
			85	118,189	34,265	42,080	7,815
			86	261,349	53,560	63,052	9,492
	V	H	81	1,334	687	742	55
			83	893	508	574	66
			84	2,717	1,863	2,130	267
			85	18,728	5,435	5,803	368
			86	20,000	5,115	5,881	766
	V	W	81	151,132	69,076	73,835	4,759
			82	304,841	144,565	158,803	14,238
			83	230,358	108,858	118,366	9,508
			84	200,808	93,561	99,671	6,110
			85	103,655	62,872	68,307	5,435
			86	111,246	35,168	39,463	4,295
CHINA T	O	E	86	7,000	3,640	3,640	
	O	W	85	4,000	1,560	1,762	202
	V	E	81	42,094	19,354	21,107	1,753
			82	55,002	35,372	39,837	4,465
			83	119,785	59,386	65,750	6,364
			84	98,177	48,257	60,049	11,792
			85	75,411	19,424	23,606	4,182
			86	6,250	3,400	4,087	687
	V	H	81	47,500	27,333	30,237	2,904
			82	76,800	46,636	51,158	4,522
			83	67,109	26,226	30,621	4,395
			84	52,522	21,078	24,324	3,246
			85	101,632	39,062	44,994	5,932
			86	59,966	25,364	29,466	4,102
	V	W	81	331,665	193,914	208,480	14,566
			82	313,044	178,729	195,547	16,818
			83	560,407	251,942	274,488	22,546
			84	199,185	90,453	99,980	9,527
			85	700,563	270,342	295,695	25,353
			86	452,963	196,995	212,257	15,262
CYPRUS	A	E	85	40	1,814	3,658	1,844
	V	E	81	88,184	27,999	33,000	5,001
			82	13,552	4,685	5,005	320
			86	8,106	6,133	6,533	400
DOM REP	V	E	81	10,000	2,600	3,087	487
	V	W	83	1,047	1,002	1,104	102
FR GERM	A	E	82	462	1,494	2,056	562
			83	308	1,014	1,370	356
			86	2,200	8,676	9,943	1,267
	A	W	84	1,823	7,134	8,680	1,546
			86	1,092	1,298	2,301	1,003
	O	E	81	2,508	3,700	4,139	439
			82	462	654	781	127
	O	W	82	2,500	2,082	2,226	144
	V	E	83	132	559	605	46
			84	616	1,365	1,600	235
			86	1,653	1,560	1,592	32
	V	W	81	1,436	3,012	3,716	704
			82	380	1,505	2,183	678
			84	1,598	5,852	6,312	460
FRANCE	A	E	81	441	747	1,183	436
	N	E	84	10,670	6,661	7,084	423
			86	5,031	5,978	8,177	2,199
	O	E	86	1,400	2,281	2,984	703
	O	W	86	1,417	1,670	1,768	98
	V	E	81	4,307	4,681	5,139	458
			82	3,204	4,250	4,603	353
			83	5,874	4,485	4,787	302
			84	400	351	373	22
			85	547	1,128	1,247	119

Crop
Product
TSUSA commodity number, description, and unit of quantity

Country	Mode	Reg	Yr	Quantity	F.A.S.	C.I.F.	Charges
	V	W	81	1,400	1,705	1,804	99
			82	20,885	10,656	11,198	542
			83	14,398	8,073	9,346	1,273
			84	1,300	1,133	1,271	138
			85	18,659	7,804	8,541	737
			86	2,273	3,223	3,326	103
GREECE	O	E	83	1,200	280	280	
			84	766	373	373	
	V	E	84	4,409	3,360	3,735	375
			85	4,409	3,940	4,769	829
			86	11,023	9,575	10,722	1,147
GUATMAL	O	W	85	6,375	2,446	2,446	
HG KONG	V	E	81	38,000	21,115	22,972	1,857
			82	28,525	16,226	18,088	1,862
			83	13,080	6,101	6,855	754
			84	7,891	6,457	7,645	1,188
			85	14,133	7,573	8,226	653
			86	137,670	18,550	25,356	6,806
	V	H	83	13,200	4,605	5,270	665
			84	6,614	2,511	2,652	141
	V	W	81	165,100	82,656	87,079	4,423
			82	57,080	33,714	35,766	2,052
			83	53,283	20,659	22,025	1,366
			84	74,415	45,715	48,332	2,617
			85	19,220	12,198	13,227	1,029
			86	48,657	22,557	24,257	1,700
INDIA	O	E	81	15,094	14,113	15,167	1,054
			83	440	390	390	
			84	20,314	11,760	12,111	351
			85	7,575	4,670	4,670	
			86	3,190	2,151	2,151	
	O	W	83	850	501	546	45
	V	E	81	10,000	7,688	9,858	2,170
			82	3,000	549	640	91
			83	20,762	10,129	11,869	1,740
			84	73,628	33,689	38,680	4,991
			85	90,629	35,217	41,005	5,788
			86	114,489	43,783	49,667	5,884
	V	W	81	2,756	1,058	1,243	185
			82	750	865	982	117
			84	26,191	14,400	14,552	152
			85	124,794	57,369	66,261	8,892
			86	54,855	19,800	22,074	2,274
INDNSIA	V	W	84	165	269	285	16
			86	1,543	2,450	2,831	381
ISRAEL	V	E	82	90,736	25,180	30,484	5,304
			83	2,136	5,340	5,515	175
			85	4,496	11,220	11,230	10
			86	1,760	4,400	4,500	100
ITALY	O	E	83	396	279	279	
	V	E	81	23,037	14,282	16,340	2,058
			82	21,297	11,429	14,131	2,702
			83	12,401	5,940	7,157	1,217
			84	11,023	5,700	6,824	1,124
			85	18,839	8,312	10,018	1,706
			86	57,621	47,500	53,997	6,497
JAPAN	N	H	81	3,427	5,407	6,235	828
	N	W	83	4,974	9,248	11,179	1,931
	V	E	81	6,646	14,136	15,335	1,199
			82	6,822	11,582	12,797	1,215
			83	9,093	15,782	17,167	1,385
			84	14,175	24,373	26,325	1,952
			85	7,881	13,836	14,968	1,132
			86	2,092	4,775	5,029	254
	V	H	82	5,534	9,156	11,020	1,864
			83	11,187	15,874	17,542	1,668
			84	5,541	8,686	9,739	1,053
			85	4,645	5,370	5,879	509
			86	1,067	3,912	4,018	106
	V	W	81	4,606	9,016	9,542	526
			82	9,940	16,217	17,426	1,209
			83	3,622	6,054	6,424	370
			84	14,680	21,634	23,249	1,615
			85	6,705	10,415	10,903	488
			86	17,144	16,470	16,983	513
KENYA	O	E	81	550	292	292	
			82	7,062	3,216	3,508	292
			83	9,625	4,987	5,087	100
			84	45,633	15,163	16,570	1,407
			85	22,766	7,691	8,511	820
	O	W	82	1,433	766	842	76
	V	E	81	47,183	13,940	16,960	3,020
			82	1,653	365	433	68
			83	11,550	3,090	3,699	609
			84	6,063	2,945	3,330	385
			86	3,086	2,100	2,510	410
	V	W	82	4,023	2,064	2,309	245
KOR REP	V	E	82	2,042	2,058	2,304	246
			83	4,103	6,239	6,837	598
			84	3,720	4,152	4,597	445
			85	5,039	6,373	6,726	353
			86	4,569	4,527	5,033	506
	V	W	83	5,000	4,629	4,900	271
			84	9,126	4,052	4,554	502
			85	9,473	7,041	7,855	814
			86	17,680	18,001	19,184	1,183
LAOS	V	W	81	1,098	473	489	16
LEBANON	O	E	85	2,751	1,050	1,050	
	V	E	83	8,100	4,591	5,002	411
			84	5,512	1,440	1,644	204
			85	61,218	25,305	30,164	4,859
			86	1,162	1,279	1,417	138
MADAGAS	V	E	84	14,330	7,995	8,845	850
MALAWI	O	E	82	17,743	9,685	9,906	221
			83	6,614	3,649	3,821	172
			84	952	463	515	52
			85	18,189	6,744	6,744	
			86	28,641	10,670	10,670	
	V	W	83	22,046	6,979	7,749	770
			85	11,023	3,054	3,420	366
MEXICO	O	E	81	41,210	29,278	29,278	
			82	50,276	39,996	39,996	
			83	72,562	31,955	31,955	
			84	55,674	24,749	24,749	
			85	81,982	36,295	36,295	
			86	68,181	41,344	41,344	
	O	W	81	44,092	16,000	16,000	
			82	28,880	13,680	13,680	
			85	78,867	33,270	33,270	
			86	171,266	40,472	40,472	
	V	E	81	16,535	13,200	14,325	1,125
			83	87,115	36,446	40,378	3,932
MOROC	O	E	81	8,141	7,263	7,263	
	V	E	85	16,535	4,650	6,061	1,411
NETHLDS	O	E	81	1,653	460	501	41
			82	1,543	2,079	2,342	263
			86	2,004	1,235	1,235	
	V	E	81	5,000	3,128	3,628	500
			82	4,329	1,218	1,501	283
			83	2,002	4,256	4,606	350
			84	6,612	6,557	7,385	828
			85	105	4,624	4,840	216
			86	2,205	2,280	2,673	393
	V	W	81	4,995	2,105	2,899	794
			82	5,935	2,506	3,377	871
			83	5,632	2,139	2,943	804
			85	9,668	11,574	12,538	964
PERU	A	E	86	2,110	12,441	17,369	4,928
	V	E	81	109,866	37,964	43,035	5,071
			82	162,771	47,498	55,851	8,353
			83	2,597	1,200	1,344	144
			84	42,539	11,664	13,868	2,204
			85	1,984	4,097	5,144	1,047
			86	109,598	129,335	135,955	6,620
PHIL R	V	E	84	1,200	534	606	72
	V	H	81	1,320	950	1,067	117
			83	2,035	1,293	1,526	233
			84	721	598	683	85
	V	W	81	738	451	599	148
			82	2,201	1,522	1,688	166
			83	774	420	517	97
			84	2,608	2,048	2,267	219
			86	40	1,280	1,569	289
PORTUGL	O	E	81	2,220	1,776	1,776	
			86	24,452	11,143	11,143	
	V	E	81	339,777	228,932	251,205	22,273
			82	313,330	210,225	231,320	21,095
			83	205,513	134,206	146,039	11,833
			84	63,793	31,925	36,243	4,318
			85	50,697	25,103	27,542	2,439
			86	298,010	177,152	194,312	17,160
REP SAF	V	E	83	13,585	42,878	44,576	1,698
			84	21,840	82,626	87,360	4,734
SENEGAL	A	E	83	15,360	8,609	8,659	50
			84	152	1,368	1,820	452
SINGAPR	V	W	81	5,510	2,306	2,662	356
			82	13,233	8,140	9,049	909
			83	750	396	431	35

Crop
Product
TSUSA commodity number, description, and unit of quantity

Country	Mode	Reg	Yr	Quantity	F.A.S.	C.I.F.	Charges
			84	1,102	450	477	27
SWEDEN	V	E	83	798	377	503	126
SYRIA	O	E	81	3,000	523	523	
THAILND	N	E	83	11,451	4,147	4,728	581
	O	E	81	2,090	1,520	1,520	
			84	100	500	518	18
	V	E	81	50,150	18,818	20,823	2,005
			82	34,300	9,729	11,334	1,605
			83	9,150	2,863	3,154	291
			84	2,502	609	712	103
			85	75,369	19,080	23,129	4,049
			86	8,750	2,840	3,153	313
	V	W	81	118,300	38,741	43,902	5,161
			82	197,646	71,285	80,899	9,614
			83	117,225	47,981	52,454	4,473
			84	76,044	36,057	39,761	3,704
			85	5,200	1,210	1,357	147
			86	48,627	16,492	17,880	1,388
TURKEY	O	E	82	5,512	1,908	2,092	184
			85	5,530	1,894	2,092	198
			86	5,500	1,985	2,229	244
	V	E	81	17,397	7,200	8,481	1,281
			83	39,683	13,752	15,537	1,785
			84	4,976	1,672	1,923	251
			85	2,200	1,015	1,117	102
			86	33,051	12,464	14,171	1,707
	V	W	86	15,432	7,350	9,050	1,700
U KING	N	E	83	4,027	3,469	4,044	575
	O	E	81	5,811	2,053	2,282	229
			84	18,990	6,464	7,125	661
			85	12,538	5,616	6,139	523
			86	3,410	2,695	2,695	
	V	E	81	44,276	24,200	28,502	4,302
			82	2,205	600	855	255
			84	2,545	1,214	1,479	265
			85	6,602	4,652	5,347	695
			86	4,000	1,320	1,520	200
	V	W	82	7,717	2,939	3,845	906
			83	4,057	2,259	2,665	406
			85	4,409	1,120	1,274	154

Bean (not specified), fresh or frozen

1351600 BEANS, NSPF, FRESH OR FROZEN (LB)

Country	Mode	Reg	Yr	Quantity	F.A.S.	C.I.F.	Charges
TOTAL			81	19,868,609	6,721,673	6,989,135	264,516
			82	16,212,853	8,310,888	8,657,038	346,150
			83	23,589,816	8,240,258	8,740,543	500,285
			84	25,714,983	11,834,624	12,504,325	669,701
			85	25,400,673	9,391,972	9,889,873	497,901
			86	33,176,095	20,583,015	20,981,859	398,844
ARGENT	A	E	84	110	550	609	59
	V	E	83	39,682	2,700	4,342	1,642
AUSTRAL	O	E	85	5,500	2,006	2,006	
	V	E	82	2,544	4,137	4,602	465
	V	W	86	46,296	10,842	12,500	1,658
BAHAMAS	V	E	84	3,000	1,500	1,614	114
			85	11,322	7,290	7,724	434
BELGIUM	A	E	81	2,186	1,536	1,948	412
			82	6,164	13,756	17,923	4,167
			83	4,542	5,733	6,810	1,077
			84	29,342	42,321	57,944	15,623
			85	1,524	5,519	7,211	1,692
	N	E	84	8,027	3,350	3,506	156
			85	35,245	21,763	29,961	8,198
	O	E	85	130,953	32,547	39,964	7,417
			86	9,985	3,510	4,508	998
	V	E	86	4,800	1,560	2,000	440
CANADA	A	E	81	139	561	594	33
	O	E	81	199,745	40,960	40,960	
			82	388,463	128,061	128,061	
			83	1,112,366	330,402	330,469	67
			84	1,322,555	392,727	392,727	
			85	982,692	257,119	257,119	
			86	1,081,677	325,054	325,054	
	O	W	81	20,724	6,600	6,600	
			82	70,400	24,640	24,640	
			83	17,612	7,164	7,164	
			85	3,600	1,340	1,340	
	V	E	86	3,000	1,411	1,935	524
CHINA M	V	E	82	17,503	5,309	6,206	897
			83	44,740	12,304	16,540	4,236
	V	W	83	2,756	2,021	2,321	300
			85	39,021	9,237	10,850	1,613
			86	7,450	2,261	2,580	319
CHINA T	V	E	82	23,250	12,382	15,018	2,636
			83	33,000	18,198	21,155	2,957
			84	47,500	17,514	22,073	4,559
			85	52,320	28,417	32,133	3,716
			86	56,497	25,018	28,089	3,071
	V	H	82	17,508	12,574	15,007	2,433
			83	93,500	47,387	63,720	16,333
			84	90,008	48,163	57,005	8,842
			85	126,400	60,263	74,955	14,692
			86	83,560	47,365	56,284	8,919
	V	W	81	4,500	2,536	2,700	164
			82	22,032	10,024	12,118	2,094
			83	92,800	39,586	43,363	3,777
			84	42,096	21,474	23,457	1,983
			85	70,160	28,710	33,723	5,013
			86	393,900	217,483	237,488	20,005
COLOMB	A	E	86	11,924	14,904	17,655	2,751
DOM REP	A	E	81	2,400	840	1,080	240
			82	1,117,884	195,071	439,060	243,989
			83	605	284	330	46
			84	340,638	55,829	132,311	76,482
			85	231,532	40,926	74,073	33,147
			86	161,600	29,719	55,584	25,865
	N	E	81	981,704	161,596	369,461	205,820
			83	1,286,886	226,241	500,606	274,365
			84	1,263,627	217,872	504,652	286,780
			86	112,654	24,701	44,620	19,919
EGYPT	A	W	84	1,000	1,000	1,095	95
	V	E	85	4,409	1,950	2,047	97
	V	W	85	2,205	1,200	1,679	479
			86	7,716	2,100	2,863	763
FR GERM	A	E	81	110	305	346	41
			84	172	279	280	1
			85	10,000	1,700	3,103	1,403
	V	E	84	9,000	3,870	4,449	579
FRANCE	A	E	81	57,287	114,617	134,270	19,653
			82	78,195	134,647	170,931	36,284
			83	275,575	363,006	463,467	100,461
			84	253,097	386,252	495,689	109,437
			85	49,521	89,492	130,404	40,912
			86	29,995	72,773	105,529	32,756
	A	W	84	14,632	21,278	30,499	9,221
			85	20,027	22,740	36,690	13,950
			86	1,265	2,431	3,822	1,391
	N	E	85	383,812	464,248	620,022	155,774
			86	375,620	316,348	442,689	126,341
	O	E	81	18,651	28,085	28,085	
	O	W	86	6,254	4,240	4,240	
	V	E	86	11,027	5,182	6,146	964
GREECE	O	E	82	2,400	1,848	1,848	
GUATMAL	A	E	86	800	2,007	2,536	529
	A	W	81	3,297	1,591	2,473	882
			86	2,125	4,250	5,077	827
	N	E	82	67,877	16,562	21,374	4,812
			86	116,172	32,605	43,798	11,193
	V	E	81	9,601	2,595	3,387	792
			83	40,471	8,876	11,015	2,139
			84	14,133	3,972	4,664	692
			85	79,795	15,284	18,811	3,527
HAITI	A	E	85	2,679	2,416	2,808	392
			86	47,499	8,061	20,981	12,920
HG KONG	V	E	81	7,275	2,482	2,938	456
			84	43,641	13,660	19,720	6,060
			86	39,000	14,413	17,226	2,813
	V	W	82	220,462	54,113	60,400	6,287
INDIA	O	E	83	1,100	463	551	88
	V	W	84	653	653	766	113
ISRAEL	A	E	85	1,107	1,858	3,093	1,235
	V	E	86	17,136	6,146	8,688	2,542
ITALY	A	E	81	76	300	331	31
			83	1,818	2,810	3,317	507
			84	3,886	5,199	6,529	1,330
			85	1,478	3,613	4,482	869
			86	154	1,908	2,423	515
	V	W	83	36,111	10,974	16,173	5,199
			84	38,095	12,434	17,061	4,627
IVY CST	A	E	86	1,693	1,203	1,492	289
JAMAICA	A	E	84	30,000	4,925	11,506	6,581
			85	349,135	232,039	300,358	68,319
			86	81,543	30,011	45,095	15,084
	N	E	85	97,670	53,444	75,494	22,050
JAPAN	A	W	82	397	731	1,229	498

Crop Product TSUSA commodity number, description, and unit of quantity Country	Mode	Reg	Yr	Quantity	F.A.S.	C.I.F.	Charges
	V	E	81	7,664	7,463	10,521	3,058
			82	4,611	5,368	6,146	778
			83	4,292	5,470	5,927	457
			85	1,106	1,518	1,737	219
			86	1,540	2,130	2,607	477
	V	H	82	15,000	9,785	12,000	2,215
			83	1,644	1,738	1,791	53
			84	330	298	335	37
	V	W	81	9,277	8,947	9,625	678
			82	7,548	6,865	7,478	613
			83	3,150	3,495	3,870	375
			84	1,115	510	530	20
			86	6,825	6,617	6,847	230
KENYA	A	E	83	448	825	916	91
			85	1,412	1,915	2,808	893
	V	E	83	39,682	12,600	15,300	2,700
KOR REP	O	E	86	1,890	1,084	1,084	
	V	E	85	40,882	15,341	17,908	2,567
MALAYSA	O	W	86	2,006	1,360	1,360	
MEXICO	A	E	85	7,423	3,420	5,170	1,750
	A	W	81	1,248	1,270	1,633	363
			86	925	4,536	4,681	145
	N	W	85	50,012	44,346	51,494	7,148
	O	E	81	518,315	81,761	81,761	
			82	24,959	3,307	3,307	
			83	157,994	19,138	19,138	
			84	426,472	59,202	59,202	
			85	916,431	102,355	102,355	
			86	15,045	10,200	10,200	
	O	W	81	17,323,834	6,017,775	6,018,676	
			82	13,909,213	7,515,079	7,517,383	2,304
			83	19,966,980	6,943,491	6,943,491	
			84	21,116,389	10,146,634	10,146,634	
			85	21,190,128	7,569,440	7,569,440	
			86	29,809,513	19,049,299	19,049,300	1
MONSRAT	O	W	85	10,856	3,680	3,680	
MOROC	A	E	86	5,034	9,631	15,038	5,407
MOZAMBQ	O	W	85	61,744	20,930	20,930	
			86	12,686	8,600	8,600	
N ZEAL	A	W	85	1,144	1,384	1,860	476
NETHLDS	A	E	81	143	286	656	370
			82	13,644	30,669	35,114	4,445
			83	13,594	22,295	29,646	7,351
			84	330	627	1,187	560
			86	882	2,079	2,901	822
	N	E	84	80,281	59,905	81,402	21,497
	V	E	85	10,262	3,856	6,134	2,278
			86	19,587	7,556	9,293	1,737
	V	W	86	463	1,307	1,523	216
PHIL R	V	W	81	4,896	4,290	4,778	488
			82	1,600	1,200	1,347	147
			83	3,880	3,085	3,517	432
			84	3,067	3,093	3,501	408
			86	1,506	1,110	1,199	89
PORTUGL	A	E	83	1,050	252	486	234
	A	W	86	3,270	1,320	1,564	244
	O	E	81	550	744	744	
			82	9,820	6,902	6,902	
			84	260	476	476	
	V	E	81	95,479	50,001	59,446	9,445
			82	170,569	94,216	119,987	25,771
			83	86,093	44,079	55,600	11,521
			84	223,308	100,479	124,992	24,513
			85	216,318	67,528	90,572	23,044
			86	311,469	83,775	115,017	31,242
REP SAF	A	E	83	3,267	11,092	15,121	4,029
			85	19,315	15,726	21,090	5,364
S ARAB	A	E	85	5,079	1,689	3,064	1,375
SENEGAL	A	E	82	20,665	23,236	28,501	5,265
			83	111,921	50,821	106,196	55,375
			84	265,137	190,349	276,280	85,931
			85	157,812	138,620	202,325	63,705
			86	176,014	147,480	202,275	54,795
	A	W	85	1,693	1,336	2,474	1,138
SINGAPR	A	E	86	27,936	18,532	24,423	5,891
SPAIN	A	E	85	4,947	4,532	5,424	892
SWEDEN	A	E	86	23,050	6,719	8,886	2,167
THAILND	V	E	81	39,535	13,430	15,202	1,772
			86	1,020	2,474	2,744	270
	V	W	81	559,973	171,102	190,920	19,818
			83	79,683	26,660	30,930	4,270
			84	1,014	375	435	60
			85	6,139	6,500	7,165	665
			86	44,092	9,700	11,415	1,715

Crop Product TSUSA commodity number, description, and unit of quantity Country	Mode	Reg	Yr	Quantity	F.A.S.	C.I.F.	Charges
TURKEY	O	E	85	2,563	1,235	2,685	1,450
	V	W	84	1,786	390	457	67
U KING	A	E	82	145	406	456	50
			83	129	295	393	98
	O	E	83	32,445	16,773	16,878	105
	V	E	84	29,700	9,917	11,880	1,963
			85	3,300	1,500	1,508	8
YUGOSLV	V	W	84	10,582	7,547	8,858	1,311

Bean (not specified), in brine or pickled
1411000 BEANS NSPF IN BRINE OR SALT (LB)

Country	Mode	Reg	Yr	Quantity	F.A.S.	C.I.F.	Charges
TOTAL			81	139,356	47,663	52,382	4,719
			82	115,195	59,466	67,072	7,606
			83	247,206	99,298	114,767	15,469
			84	698,273	185,437	225,657	40,220
			85	627,458	151,249	177,554	26,305
			86	880,824	177,571	210,847	33,276
BELGIUM	V	E	82	7,703	2,965	3,573	608
			83	22,573	6,450	7,195	745
			84	53,283	9,395	11,984	2,589
			85	262,356	45,113	54,546	9,433
			86	192,660	51,394	62,070	10,676
	V	W	86	18,360	5,942	6,692	750
CANADA	O	E	81	47,935	8,830	8,830	
			82	178	1,275	1,275	
			83	21,340	3,776	3,776	
			84	72,723	16,344	16,344	
			85	38,081	10,593	10,593	
			86	13,104	4,490	4,490	
CHINA M	N	W	84	37,167	9,972	11,476	1,504
	V	E	81	1,200	1,133	1,404	271
			83	50,255	18,932	23,781	4,849
			84	27,686	8,196	11,394	3,198
			86	20,500	5,817	6,506	689
	V	W	81	1,020	576	605	29
			82	4,297	2,782	2,979	197
			83	37,633	14,026	15,662	1,636
			84	20,900	7,464	9,693	2,229
			85	35,311	9,090	11,009	1,919
			86	48,825	12,342	14,467	2,125
CHINA T	V	E	81	1,680	916	1,262	346
			83	892	310	386	76
	V	W	82	1,500	840	977	137
			83	2,312	1,941	2,029	88
			84	1,116	1,000	1,130	130
			85	2,646	1,055	1,120	65
			86	3,616	2,000	2,207	207
DOM REP	V	E	81	25,452	4,764	5,197	433
			84	8,250	330	537	207
ECUADOR	V	E	86	309,250	12,370	16,889	4,519
EGYPT	V	E	82	34,258	14,875	15,855	980
			85	10,044	3,667	4,112	445
FR GERM	V	E	82	1,088	608	665	57
			83	675	343	429	86
			84	1,115	770	878	108
			85	22,163	3,823	4,683	860
FRANCE	N	E	84	2,149	2,610	3,107	497
	V	E	81	14,867	4,797	5,784	987
			82	9,158	2,451	3,241	790
			83	1,607	1,980	2,112	132
			84	350,631	78,363	99,734	21,371
			86	7,542	2,592	2,959	367
	V	W	84	563	304	357	53
GREECE	V	E	86	107,926	11,475	17,112	5,637
GUATMAL	V	E	84	4,882	3,467	3,898	431
	V	W	86	2,027	2,955	3,147	192
HG KONG	V	E	81	23,635	12,530	13,814	1,284
			82	11,180	5,496	6,243	747
			83	25,220	10,869	12,999	2,130
			84	78,463	25,849	31,005	5,156
			86	10,481	5,927	6,475	548
	V	W	81	12,055	8,409	8,936	527
			82	14,680	8,541	9,356	815
			83	16,050	9,318	10,208	890
			84	15,740	8,508	9,477	969
			85	91,880	12,622	15,348	2,726
			86	25,476	12,377	13,244	867
INDIA	O	E	84	2,116	1,140	1,312	172
	V	E	81	5,820	2,565	3,130	565
			82	2,959	1,186	1,754	568
			83	15,513	7,327	8,508	1,181

Crop
Product
TSUSA commodity number, description, and unit of quantity

Country	Mode	Reg	Yr	Quantity	F.A.S.	C.I.F.	Charges
			84	3,175	1,252	1,512	260
			85	5,291	2,273	2,680	407
			86	32,789	12,693	14,521	1,828
	V	W	82	14,554	6,419	7,708	1,289
			83	9,524	4,725	5,820	1,095
			84	2,751	1,308	1,582	274
			86	9,590	4,649	5,242	593
INDNSIA	V	W	82	1,738	3,873	4,398	525
			83	1,295	2,075	2,298	223
ITALY	V	E	83	14,969	4,224	5,125	901
			86	8,844	4,060	4,733	673
	V	W	83	9,524	3,300	4,048	748
			84	4,233	1,584	1,740	156
			85	3,048	1,140	1,365	225
JAMAICA	V	E	85	30,000	17,000	18,585	1,585
JAPAN	V	E	84	3,036	3,712	4,182	470
	V	W	83	360	521	553	32
			86	582	1,252	1,337	85
LEBANON	O	E	84	979	406	450	44
	V	E	85	5,082	2,698	2,847	149
			86	12,504	4,209	4,615	406
N ZEAL	A	W	86	900	1,529	2,070	541
NETHLDS	O	E	86	33,182	9,134	9,386	252
	V	E	81	102	485	520	35
			82	463	1,266	1,371	105
			84	9	269	294	25
	V	W	81	230	288	311	23
			82	1,079	2,461	2,659	198
PHIL R	V	E	84	670	317	370	53
	V	W	82	782	810	874	64
			84	342	297	342	45
			86	1,560	1,450	1,612	162
PORTUGL	V	E	83	7,400	3,700	3,839	139
			84	2,517	1,496	1,526	30
			85	29,720	6,480	7,099	619
SINGAPR	O	W	81	360	270	270	
	V	E	83	1,509	1,195	1,385	190
			85	2,400	1,175	1,308	133
			86	9,860	3,563	4,562	999
	V	W	82	9,466	3,347	3,855	508
			83	2,710	1,814	2,002	188
			84	1,791	587	664	77
			86	2,381	1,225	1,327	102
SPAIN	V	E	84	1,984	497	669	172
			85	37,037	8,744	11,574	2,830
SWITZLD	V	E	82	112	271	289	18
THAILND	V	E	81	5,000	2,100	2,319	219
	V	W	83	2,995	1,172	1,312	140
TURKEY	V	E	86	4,605	2,394	2,692	298
U KING	O	E	83	2,850	1,300	1,300	
	V	E	85	52,399	25,776	30,685	4,909
			86	4,260	1,732	2,492	760

1411500 BEANS, PICKLD, EXCPT SOYBEAN (LB)

Country	Mode	Reg	Yr	Quantity	F.A.S.	C.I.F.	Charges
TOTAL			81	373,432	136,093	136,408	315
			82	4,398	3,287	3,609	322
			83	12,444	9,784	11,057	1,273
			84	5,874	9,230	9,755	525
BELGIUM	V	E	83	1,692	614	700	86
CANADA	O	E	81	371,000	133,946	133,946	
	O	W	84	690	4,830	4,830	
CHINA M	V	W	84	1,503	721	758	37
CHINA T	O	W	84	429	374	374	
	V	E	81	2,432	2,147	2,462	315
			82	2,813	2,257	2,487	230
	V	W	82	585	466	510	44
			83	2,509	1,052	1,130	78
FR GERM	V	E	83	1,238	465	498	33
			84	990	837	891	54
FRANCE	V	E	83	473	331	352	21
GUATMAL	A	E	84	960	449	615	166
HG KONG	V	W	82	1,000	564	612	48
			83	500	253	272	19
INDIA	V	E	83	5,583	6,142	7,125	983
ITALY	V	E	83	242	356	379	23
JAPAN	V	E	84	1,302	2,019	2,287	268
	V	W	83	198	270	300	30
NETHLDS	O	E	83	9	301	301	

Crop
Product
TSUSA commodity number, description, and unit of quantity

Bean (not specified), prepared or preserved

1412000 BEANS PREP ETC EXCEPT SOYA (LB)

Country	Mode	Reg	Yr	Quantity	F.A.S.	C.I.F.	Charges
TOTAL			81	1,586,732	805,713	890,662	84,949
			82	1,246,026	722,914	808,218	85,304
			83	2,259,704	1,121,510	1,234,282	112,772
			84	5,106,336	1,876,268	2,133,077	256,809
			85	16,404,324	4,325,798	4,728,829	403,031
			86	14,402,575	3,862,274	4,105,879	243,605
ARGENT	V	E	86	857	1,289	1,693	404
AUSTRAL	O	E	85	88,184	24,000	26,060	2,060
	V	E	81	70,350	30,084	35,205	5,121
			85	17,490	3,802	4,474	672
	V	W	83	1,209	1,024	1,130	106
BELGIUM	N	E	84	251,830	43,933	56,682	12,749
	O	E	86	5,320	1,994	1,994	
	V	E	81	14,064	6,167	7,140	973
			82	6,751	3,148	3,499	351
			83	20,308	7,940	8,768	828
			84	11,119	4,197	4,656	459
			85	309,426	68,964	85,536	16,572
			86	475,670	151,004	177,573	26,569
	V	W	81	5,291	501	575	74
			84	2,161	981	1,180	199
			85	17,136	4,696	6,376	1,680
			86	59,976	20,316	23,003	2,687
BRAZIL	V	E	81	1,175	1,173	1,302	129
			85	950	3,726	4,265	539
BURKINA	V	W	81	2,600	1,824	1,899	75
C RICA	V	W	83	528	262	451	189
CANADA	A	W	85	15,196	4,194	5,293	1,099
			86	17,995	4,806	5,816	1,010
	O	E	81	216,577	48,365	48,365	
			82	162,121	37,144	37,144	
			83	484,328	121,196	121,712	516
			84	1,049,110	235,043	235,156	113
			85	9,768,175	1,990,005	1,991,104	1,099
			86	10,194,539	2,077,000	2,077,000	
	O	W	81	314,734	94,011	94,011	
	V	E	86	6,000	2,510	2,510	
CHINA M	O	E	85	2,500	1,209	1,301	92
	O	W	84	315,000	78,354	96,600	18,246
	V	E	81	45,018	18,116	20,863	2,747
			82	39,610	19,243	22,913	3,670
			83	67,414	25,001	27,631	2,630
			84	104,775	34,048	43,379	9,331
			85	77,270	44,087	53,671	9,584
			86	99,383	44,967	51,382	6,415
	V	H	83	5,300	4,510	6,423	1,913
			84	2,200	1,868	2,599	731
			85	2,244	1,777	2,479	702
			86	2,310	2,934	3,789	855
	V	W	81	41,574	17,958	19,262	1,304
			82	42,365	28,029	30,894	2,865
			83	70,374	33,410	35,929	2,519
			84	342,427	101,446	114,959	13,513
			85	352,940	93,566	111,284	17,718
			86	121,327	40,842	45,218	4,376
CHINA T	N	W	84	97,381	46,405	51,150	4,745
	O	W	84	878	765	765	
	V	E	81	31,860	33,967	37,180	3,213
			82	36,803	25,276	28,893	3,617
			83	126,079	60,112	69,753	9,641
			84	92,481	60,300	69,594	9,294
			85	83,739	69,771	81,402	11,631
			86	155,958	67,613	79,717	12,104
	V	H	81	34,694	21,365	23,145	1,780
			82	3,780	2,310	2,554	244
			84	35,100	18,280	20,296	2,016
			85	4,232	2,680	3,601	921
	V	W	81	42,659	27,442	29,394	1,952
			82	133,399	88,867	95,956	7,089
			83	190,669	119,207	127,451	8,244
			84	159,820	99,785	105,518	5,733
			85	544,169	298,712	324,506	25,794
			86	252,171	140,836	149,916	9,080
COLOMB	N	E	86	33,384	18,818	21,321	2,503
	V	E	84	1,500	950	1,122	172
CYPRUS	V	E	85	8,004	4,080	5,100	1,020
DOM REP	A	E	82	3,880	660	938	278
			83	1,600	272	430	158
			84	10,435	1,796	3,214	1,418

Crop
Product
TSUSA commodity number, description, and unit of quantity

Country	Mode	Reg	Yr	Quantity	F.A.S.	C.I.F.	Charges
	V	E	83	12,000	1,500	2,335	835
			84	68,655	29,230	31,234	2,004
			85	32,400	12,488	13,203	715
			86	42,000	16,625	17,750	1,125
EGYPT	V	E	81	44,494	15,125	17,917	2,792
			82	19,000	9,000	10,020	1,020
			83	44,513	19,000	21,300	2,300
			86	6,300	1,925	2,279	354
	V	W	85	32,011	8,250	11,142	2,892
			86	37,196	10,450	12,895	2,445
FR GERM	N	W	81	2,200	3,175	4,694	1,519
	O	E	84	563	255	287	32
	V	E	81	1,642	1,485	1,735	250
			82	484	565	653	88
			86	29,470	9,018	9,978	960
	V	W	83	72,860	25,559	27,509	1,950
FRANCE	A	E	81	211	633	717	84
	N	E	82	30,244	16,001	20,373	4,372
			83	40,121	22,283	26,412	4,129
	N	W	84	22,274	10,258	14,765	4,507
	O	E	83	579	339	506	167
			84	1,125	421	459	38
	V	E	81	41,746	25,677	27,977	2,300
			82	2,656	2,030	2,202	172
			83	61,493	17,285	19,714	2,429
			84	463,248	122,704	155,240	32,536
			85	785,401	169,607	208,885	39,278
			86	624,862	141,834	170,489	28,655
	V	W	81	7,659	4,581	5,018	437
			82	10,236	3,457	3,744	287
			83	3,932	2,197	2,490	293
			84	67	830	879	49
			86	4,888	2,419	2,508	89
GREECE	N	E	82	44,959	19,379	23,938	4,559
			84	28,409	13,885	17,367	3,482
	V	E	81	62,170	24,780	30,047	5,267
			82	519	500	501	1
			83	23,204	18,500	20,775	2,275
			84	5,245	3,200	3,565	365
			85	96,393	58,164	65,430	7,266
			86	118,585	79,837	90,942	11,105
	V	W	82	6,612	5,000	5,602	602
			83	941	737	822	85
			84	794	700	765	65
GUATMAL	A	E	82	1,782	1,067	1,410	343
			84	930	360	573	213
	A	W	81	22,241	10,596	15,785	5,189
			82	23,173	12,478	17,980	5,502
			83	12,030	6,931	9,790	2,859
			85	4,275	6,762	8,477	1,715
	N	W	82	3,109	1,641	1,934	293
			83	15,259	9,088	11,384	2,296
			84	44,017	24,097	29,494	5,397
	O	E	85	2,771	1,439	1,439	
	O	W	84	14,650	5,828	5,828	
			85	27,765	14,143	14,143	
			86	98,669	32,117	32,117	
	V	E	85	13,906	10,190	10,933	743
			86	89,315	34,913	40,959	6,046
	V	W	85	40,685	21,704	26,775	5,071
			86	111,022	43,829	52,249	8,420
HG KONG	N	W	81	12,035	8,548	9,536	988
			84	27,836	16,934	17,977	1,043
	O	E	85	12,360	5,492	6,141	649
	O	W	84	3,000	1,847	1,981	134
	V	E	81	53,861	31,573	34,923	3,350
			82	39,351	26,248	29,105	2,857
			83	81,383	44,412	50,827	6,415
			84	78,489	50,796	59,283	8,487
			85	141,619	69,644	81,692	12,048
			86	24,437	16,759	18,465	1,706
	V	H	81	1,230	480	511	31
			82	1,200	512	579	67
	V	W	81	78,952	59,175	63,760	4,585
			82	56,794	37,744	40,660	2,916
			83	84,794	51,327	55,336	4,009
			84	108,215	64,734	68,992	4,258
			85	129,434	88,508	93,520	5,012
			86	176,474	109,178	116,809	7,631
HUNGARY	V	E	86	60,742	15,400	19,579	4,179
	V	W	86	30,371	6,860	8,529	1,669
INDIA	N	E	85	7,803	5,040	5,869	829
	O	E	81	1,762	1,580	1,769	189
			84	990	654	654	

Crop
Product
TSUSA commodity number, description, and unit of quantity

Country	Mode	Reg	Yr	Quantity	F.A.S.	C.I.F.	Charges
			86	17,209	14,996	17,478	2,482
	V	E	81	18,121	11,368	14,914	3,546
			82	23,943	14,353	18,051	3,698
			83	14,013	13,320	15,489	2,169
			84	38,171	15,229	17,741	2,512
			85	62,927	27,544	31,298	3,754
			86	72,250	30,251	33,371	3,120
	V	W	81	19,053	6,970	8,428	1,458
			82	5,243	4,463	5,373	910
			83	1,609	1,420	1,798	378
			86	21,605	7,766	8,999	1,233
INDNSIA	V	W	83	44	360	379	19
			85	2,150	3,288	4,010	722
ISRAEL	V	E	81	1,125	1,190	1,360	170
			85	4,947	2,328	2,813	485
ITALY	A	E	82	161	540	553	13
	N	E	85	2,387,202	544,004	690,968	146,964
	O	E	83	880	1,978	1,978	
	V	E	81	14,273	3,299	5,085	1,786
			83	83,564	25,532	29,380	3,848
			84	216,773	42,385	54,355	11,970
			85	10,687	2,505	3,592	1,087
			86	374,902	97,748	119,191	21,443
	V	W	85	21,160	7,920	8,845	925
JAMAICA	V	E	83	6,000	3,280	3,499	219
			84	856	485	518	33
			86	7,938	1,500	1,693	193
JAPAN	N	H	84	27,541	33,327	41,793	8,466
			86	9,316	15,942	19,798	3,856
	N	W	84	81,392	98,550	106,008	7,458
	V	E	81	13,509	18,445	20,243	1,798
			82	18,897	25,210	27,976	2,766
			83	28,640	34,751	38,299	3,548
			84	65,230	76,498	85,653	9,155
			85	51,588	62,590	69,981	7,391
			86	61,742	86,287	93,462	7,175
	V	H	81	12,026	16,298	19,805	3,507
			82	15,539	17,302	20,815	3,513
			83	24,032	26,604	32,666	6,062
			85	18,891	19,578	24,506	4,928
			86	1,166	1,190	1,611	421
	V	W	81	65,288	83,567	88,888	5,321
			82	81,344	98,689	105,037	6,348
			83	140,158	158,635	170,940	12,305
			84	33,254	34,615	36,999	2,384
			85	132,451	151,329	159,606	8,277
			86	116,829	163,649	172,304	8,655
KENYA	O	E	81	2,092	1,351	1,351	
			82	1,060	722	722	
			86	6,085	2,165	2,493	328
	V	W	83	33,731	10,800	13,543	2,743
KOR REP	V	E	81	798	1,400	1,498	98
			84	2,250	1,091	1,205	114
			85	26,580	29,231	33,297	4,066
			86	4,405	3,838	4,390	552
	V	H	82	2,950	1,344	1,624	280
			83	2,000	565	692	127
			84	12,599	7,105	8,384	1,279
	V	W	81	19,946	10,164	10,956	792
			82	40,549	26,435	28,807	2,372
			83	148,290	81,808	87,848	6,040
			84	259,425	135,092	146,589	11,497
			85	113,532	55,624	60,165	4,541
			86	183,250	94,270	102,292	8,022
LEBANON	O	E	81	4,021	1,130	1,538	408
	V	E	81	17,619	6,200	7,027	827
			82	21,362	8,925	9,844	919
			83	43,165	17,135	18,888	1,753
			84	6,223	3,040	3,227	187
			85	49,414	16,459	18,891	2,432
			86	14,443	4,716	5,456	740
	V	W	83	15,239	7,540	8,417	877
			84	979	525	551	26
			85	12,165	4,884	6,349	1,465
			86	8,548	3,781	4,226	445
LESOTHO	V	E	85	3,272	4,986	5,545	559
MACAO	V	H	83	500	470	511	41
MALAWI	O	E	82	16,534	7,951	7,951	
MEXICO	A	E	83	11,102	6,000	6,744	744
	O	E	81	13,570	13,950	13,950	
			83	7,500	3,158	3,158	
			84	9,080	4,586	4,586	
			86	3,480	1,312	1,312	
	O	W	81	33,877	18,023	18,023	

Crop Product TSUSA commodity number, description, and unit of quantity Country	Mode	Reg	Yr	Quantity	F.A.S.	C.I.F.	Charges
			82	86,652	26,526	26,526	
			83	63,282	13,836	13,836	
			84	113,534	35,255	35,255	
			85	71,453	21,246	21,246	
N ZEAL	V	E	81	867	794	922	128
NETHLDS	O	E	86	38,433	10,592	10,885	293
	V	E	81	8,637	6,898	7,594	696
			82	9,797	8,131	9,042	911
			83	4,656	2,980	3,388	408
			84	220,937	66,851	82,235	15,384
			85	339,829	102,661	123,859	21,198
			86	279,406	84,354	108,870	24,516
	V	W	81	1,723	2,967	3,806	839
			82	875	315	353	38
			83	6,890	2,563	2,796	233
			84	6,164	1,922	2,268	346
			85	4,409	2,214	2,470	256
			86	11,078	4,464	5,057	593
NIGER	V	E	81	1,688	888	1,033	145
PERU	V	E	85	28,101	8,730	10,530	1,800
			86	37,000	9,925	11,764	1,839
PHIL R	V	E	81	8,680	8,961	10,007	1,046
			82	10,915	11,721	13,297	1,576
			83	5,310	5,086	5,840	754
			84	13,777	8,667	10,395	1,728
			85	2,250	1,837	2,144	307
	V	H	81	2,880	3,023	3,482	459
			82	2,347	2,388	2,773	385
			83	500	340	378	38
			84	1,530	1,591	1,885	294
			85	1,950	1,205	1,412	207
			86	1,411	1,124	1,270	146
	V	W	81	30,353	31,239	34,962	3,723
			82	39,452	32,953	36,969	4,016
			83	33,559	31,443	36,113	4,670
			84	57,429	41,655	48,538	6,883
			85	22,599	23,387	26,213	2,826
			86	12,018	14,047	15,509	1,462
PORTUGL	A	W	85	2,750	2,200	2,445	245
	O	E	81	1,785	2,233	2,233	
			82	550	344	344	
	V	E	81	14,850	5,265	5,899	634
			82	10,493	4,447	5,827	1,380
			84	17,600	7,580	8,685	1,105
			86	79,335	21,986	27,411	5,425
ROMANIA	V	E	85	82,146	14,888	18,931	4,043
SALVADR	V	E	83	720	365	415	50
			84	1,155	636	729	93
	V	W	84	3,300	1,995	2,230	235
			85	3,300	1,884	2,230	346
SENEGAL	A	E	84	9,005	5,697	6,148	451
	A	W	84	5,079	4,574	8,127	3,553
SINGAPR	V	E	83	540	348	398	50
			84	1,323	595	790	195
	V	W	81	390	281	333	52
			82	7,272	3,590	3,861	271
			83	2,989	1,665	1,855	190
			84	12,752	6,472	7,435	963
			86	24,524	11,290	12,665	1,375
SPAIN	V	E	81	2,310	768	1,031	263
			82	35,481	9,613	11,404	1,791
			83	4,515	1,717	2,180	463
			84	2,100	580	883	303
	V	W	84	5,111	1,017	2,198	1,181
SWITZLD	V	W	85	5,000	2,050	2,220	170
			86	2,875	1,724	1,836	112
THAILND	V	E	81	7,900	3,002	3,457	455
			82	15,186	5,280	5,792	512
			83	63,387	22,854	25,722	2,868
			84	93,984	27,436	34,157	6,721
			85	19,375	4,700	5,674	974
			86	800	1,440	1,547	107
	V	H	83	1,045	290	310	20
	V	W	81	23,310	8,967	9,913	946
			82	28,471	15,083	16,407	1,324
			83	16,578	9,894	10,810	916
			84	250,078	65,513	72,362	6,849
			85	154,881	44,140	48,846	4,706
			86	26,102	12,092	13,151	1,059
TURKEY	V	E	83	2,640	1,440	1,781	341
			84	17,605	11,417	12,703	1,286
			86	11,997	8,135	9,136	1,001
U KING	A	E	82	1,177	1,056	1,208	152
	N	E	81	17,423	8,981	10,961	1,980

Crop Product TSUSA commodity number, description, and unit of quantity Country	Mode	Reg	Yr	Quantity	F.A.S.	C.I.F.	Charges
			82	23,692	12,149	14,735	2,586
			85	55,206	25,604	29,266	3,662
	N	W	82	4,687	3,191	4,801	1,610
	O	E	81	5,250	2,700	2,700	
			82	10,469	4,931	5,518	587
			84	28,185	12,387	14,878	2,491
			85	22,500	11,143	13,698	2,555
	V	E	81	66,833	33,874	42,704	8,830
			82	61,356	34,633	40,736	6,103
			83	66,490	38,031	41,356	3,325
			84	143,913	45,439	55,575	10,136
			85	36,348	15,990	17,017	1,027
			86	59,699	28,068	30,650	2,582
	V	W	81	5,736	3,136	3,829	693
			82	744	330	380	50
			83	5,218	3,210	3,997	787
			84	3,278	1,577	1,779	202
			85	36,783	22,949	26,661	3,712
			86	35,508	27,529	31,572	4,043

Kidney bean, canned
1418400 KIDNEY BEANS, CANNED (LB)

	Mode	Reg	Yr	Quantity	F.A.S.	C.I.F.	Charges
TOTAL			81	**5,040**	**1,104**	**1,104**	
			82	**1,932**	**1,180**	**1,216**	**36**
CANADA	O	E	81	5,040	1,104	1,104	
			82	1,575	384	384	
JAPAN	V	W	82	357	796	832	36

Kidney bean, dried
1401000 RED KIDNEY BEANS DRIED DEHYD (LB)

	Mode	Reg	Yr	Quantity	F.A.S.	C.I.F.	Charges
TOTAL			81	**518,947**	**193,640**	**200,570**	**6,930**
			82	**1,535,128**	**374,659**	**394,813**	**20,154**
			83	**665,842**	**114,374**	**130,723**	**16,349**
			84	**1,535,947**	**252,516**	**296,506**	**43,990**
			85	**208,224**	**60,141**	**70,824**	**10,683**
			86	**764,327**	**185,564**	**244,654**	**59,090**
ARGENT	V	E	85	60,000	20,625	25,164	4,539
			86	78,837	11,754	15,587	3,833
C RICA	V	E	82	93,660	5,901	8,828	2,927
			83	75,345	7,625	12,037	4,412
			84	61,200	3,600	3,679	79
CANADA	A	E	82	47,900	13,723	14,192	469
	O	E	81	390,100	158,493	158,493	
			82	933,198	266,659	271,188	4,529
			83	87,191	18,403	18,523	120
			84	325,101	103,609	103,609	
			85	89,000	30,806	30,806	
			86	150,000	41,870	41,870	
	O	W	83	63,111	19,089	19,089	
CHINA M	V	E	81	9,200	4,131	4,642	511
			82	46,009	21,764	24,645	2,881
			83	9,900	4,039	4,552	513
			84	74,988	22,086	29,107	7,021
			85	20,200	4,670	5,925	1,255
			86	11,400	3,353	3,964	611
	V	W	81	1,750	1,847	1,924	77
			82	6,559	2,614	2,945	331
			83	25,420	12,501	14,418	1,917
			84	26,732	6,222	8,062	1,840
			85	2,500	1,120	1,211	91
CHINA T	V	E	81	2,500	1,725	1,742	17
			83	18,000	5,705	6,476	771
	V	W	81	5,000	2,970	3,110	140
			82	21,500	13,390	14,342	952
			83	22,801	12,035	13,087	1,052
			84	20,300	8,278	8,903	625
			86	52,000	19,997	21,498	1,501
COLOMB	V	E	82	381,350	46,310	53,937	7,627
			83	300,850	27,077	30,176	3,099
			84	489,400	58,728	81,240	22,512
			86	163,873	30,000	38,126	8,126
DOM REP	V	E	81	103,020	17,877	21,210	3,333
			86	13,000	2,080	2,330	250
ECUADOR	A	E	83	25,000	2,500	4,662	2,162
			85	26,515	1,620	5,984	4,364
	V	E	81	3,500	2,450	5,005	2,555
			84	499,066	41,868	49,253	7,385
GUATMAL	A	W	83	3,480	657	1,424	767

Crop Product TSUSA commodity number, description, and unit of quantity Country	Mode	Reg	Yr	Quantity	F.A.S.	C.I.F.	Charges
HG KONG	V	E	81	720	418	454	36
			82	3,500	978	1,248	270
			84	500	271	882	611
			86	8,400	2,681	2,887	206
	V	W	81	500	415	442	27
			83	10,000	790	858	68
HONDURA	V	E	86	45,530	13,800	14,927	1,127
JAPAN	V	E	81	287	494	529	35
			82	1,320	3,059	3,204	145
			83	394	863	937	74
			86	331	1,051	1,116	65
	V	W	81	1,560	2,265	2,399	134
			82	132	261	284	23
			84	110	338	355	17
N ZEAL	V	H	86	234,638	57,768	100,386	42,618
PHIL R	V	W	81	810	555	620	65
			84	1,075	754	860	106
SINGAPR	V	W	83	20	608	659	51
THAILND	V	E	84	185	360	404	44
	V	W	85	10,009	1,300	1,734	434
VENEZ	A	E	83	24,330	2,482	3,825	1,343
			84	37,290	6,402	10,152	3,750
			86	6,318	1,210	1,963	753

1401640   RED KIDNY BEAN DRY 9/1-4/30 (LB)

Country	Mode	Reg	Yr	Quantity	F.A.S.	C.I.F.	Charges
TOTAL			81	680,940	242,902	251,547	8,645
			82	171,990	65,579	71,917	6,338
			83	738,700	257,342	265,140	7,798
			84	890,394	333,845	337,314	3,469
			85	366,564	113,218	117,332	4,114
			86	924,515	237,985	248,890	10,905
ARGENT	V	E	86	78,837	26,016	29,849	3,833
AUSTRAL	V	W	86	2,205	2,426	2,454	28
CANADA	O	E	81	534,000	183,869	184,244	375
			82	99,339	26,445	27,685	1,240
			83	580,877	191,237	191,237	
			84	824,334	305,838	305,838	
			85	287,870	77,170	77,170	
			86	632,500	137,258	137,258	
CHINA M	V	E	81	62,912	22,955	26,142	3,187
			82	34,446	15,596	17,985	2,389
			84	2,001	738	931	193
			85	5,000	1,897	2,325	428
			86	56,160	12,485	14,281	1,796
	V	H	84	924	280	319	39
	V	W	82	13,022	9,831	10,484	653
			83	19,824	11,321	12,463	1,142
			86	5,000	1,806	1,882	76
CHINA T	N	W	85	15,000	5,450	6,206	756
	V	E	81	8,378	2,000	2,333	333
			82	7,004	4,160	4,691	531
			83	15,000	4,950	5,487	537
			84	10,000	4,355	4,796	441
			85	5,000	2,450	2,811	361
			86	33,173	11,321	12,529	1,208
	V	W	81	27,000	14,493	15,473	980
			82	11,023	4,462	5,500	1,038
			83	15,000	6,600	7,368	768
			84	27,950	6,346	6,719	373
			85	34,871	16,522	17,744	1,222
			86	73,500	30,444	33,028	2,584
EGYPT	V	E	83	57,752	23,600	25,488	1,888
HG KONG	O	E	83	3,000	1,222	1,353	131
	V	E	83	42,121	14,304	16,813	2,509
			85	8,650	2,508	2,957	449
	V	W	81	1,250	656	687	31
JAPAN	V	E	81	29,400	10,573	12,912	2,339
			82	660	1,374	1,501	127
			83	683	1,160	1,288	128
			84	4,144	4,559	5,004	445
			85	1,365	1,460	1,592	132
			86	1,100	1,244	1,553	309
	V	H	82	184	290	342	52
			83	1,693	2,195	2,802	607
			85	1,217	1,530	1,696	166
	V	W	82	1,312	1,526	1,603	77
			84	660	1,564	1,665	101
			86	1,323	1,784	1,905	121
KOR REP	V	E	85	1,651	1,261	1,507	246
PERU	V	E	84	4,409	2,400	2,711	311
			85	5,940	2,970	3,324	354
			86	2,136	1,550	1,600	50
PHIL R	V	E	84	540	465	531	66

Country	Mode	Reg	Yr	Quantity	F.A.S.	C.I.F.	Charges
PORTUGL	V	E	81	10,000	5,153	6,167	1,014
			84	15,432	7,300	8,800	1,500
THAILND	V	W	81	8,000	3,203	3,589	386
			82	5,000	1,895	2,126	231
			83	2,750	753	841	88
VENEZ	V	E	86	38,581	11,651	12,551	900

Kidney bean, frozen
1382500   KIDNEY BEANS, FROZEN (LB)

Country	Mode	Reg	Yr	Quantity	F.A.S.	C.I.F.	Charges
TOTAL			83	45,084	2,288	2,288	
			84	16,250	2,763	3,598	835
			85	37,735	7,650	10,666	3,016
C RICA	V	E	85	37,735	7,650	10,666	3,016
DOM REP	V	E	84	16,250	2,763	3,598	835
MEXICO	O	E	83	45,084	2,288	2,288	

Lima bean, dried
1401120   LIMA BEANS DRY MAY 1-AUG 31 (LB)

Country	Mode	Reg	Yr	Quantity	F.A.S.	C.I.F.	Charges
TOTAL			81	17,716	13,713	13,713	
			82	53,202	30,521	36,525	6,004
			83	7,326	2,067	2,067	
			84	53,120	28,686	28,796	110
			85	305,191	91,249	93,049	1,800
			86	14,014	2,450	2,450	
CHINA M	V	E	84	750	508	618	110
MALAWI	O	E	82	9,900	6,005	12,009	6,004
MEXICO	O	W	81	17,716	13,713	13,713	
			82	43,302	24,516	24,516	
			83	7,326	2,067	2,067	
			84	52,370	28,178	28,178	
			85	266,691	82,404	82,404	
			86	14,014	2,450	2,450	
PERU	V	E	85	38,500	8,845	10,645	1,800

1401620   LIMA BEANS, DRIED, 9/1-4/30 (LB)

Country	Mode	Reg	Yr	Quantity	F.A.S.	C.I.F.	Charges
TOTAL			81	88,381	65,999	67,143	1,144
			82	141,342	84,242	85,021	779
			83	15,558	3,941	3,941	
			84	16,420	8,530	8,888	358
			85	40,444	13,652	13,652	
			86	108,741	41,194	42,217	1,023
CANADA	O	E	82	1,344	753	897	144
CHINA M	V	E	81	8,649	3,090	3,404	314
	V	W	81	11,111	2,665	3,175	510
			82	9,921	4,110	4,745	635
FRANCE	A	E	84	435	445	803	358
	O	E	81	441	574	638	64
			86	2,750	3,016	3,439	423
GREECE	V	E	86	10,768	10,568	10,768	200
HG KONG	V	W	81	1,000	508	544	36
KENYA	O	E	82	1,102	673	673	
MALAWI	O	E	82	13,228	7,200	7,200	
MEXICO	O	E	82	24,945	10,682	10,682	
			83	8,000	2,655	2,655	
	O	W	81	65,983	58,501	58,501	
			82	90,802	60,824	60,824	
			83	7,558	1,286	1,286	
			84	15,985	8,085	8,085	
			85	40,444	13,652	13,652	
			86	87,286	25,845	25,845	
PERU	V	E	86	7,937	1,765	2,165	400
PORTUGL	V	E	81	1,197	661	881	220

Lima bean, fresh or frozen
1351000   BEANS, LIMA, JUN1-OCT31 INCL (LB)

Country	Mode	Reg	Yr	Quantity	F.A.S.	C.I.F.	Charges
TOTAL			81	23,336	8,953	11,185	2,232
			82	148,529	52,534	58,075	5,541
			83	21,003	8,378	11,440	3,062
			84	125,451	40,056	48,088	8,032
			85	31,867	19,525	22,167	2,642
			86	50,615	17,444	23,490	6,046
BELGIUM	A	E	83	2,772	2,856	4,456	1,600
			84	297	357	427	70
			85	1,056	2,662	2,962	300
	A	W	83	2,900	3,125	4,060	935

Crop
Product
TSUSA commodity number, description, and unit of quantity

Country	Mode	Reg	Yr	Quantity	F.A.S.	C.I.F.	Charges
			86	2,798	4,218	5,319	1,101
CANADA	O	E	81	1,700	914	914	
			84	21,050	7,521	7,521	
			86	6,555	3,306	3,306	
DOM REP	A	E	84	5,250	893	2,090	1,197
FRANCE	A	E	84	423	618	882	264
	A	W	84	1,500	1,094	2,163	1,069
GREECE	V	E	85	9,374	9,518	10,581	1,063
ITALY	A	E	86	2,130	1,385	2,342	957
JAMAICA	A	E	84	1,980	1,000	1,526	526
JAPAN	V	E	84	440	280	350	70
MEXICO	O	E	81	3,360	416	416	
			82	97,611	27,275	27,275	
			83	12,559	1,199	1,199	
			84	8,424	1,465	1,465	
	O	W	81	7,253	2,023	2,023	
			82	12,702	6,144	6,144	
			84	53,335	13,805	13,805	
			85	10,414	4,095	4,095	
NETHLDS	A	E	82	425	984	1,084	100
			84	2,439	2,023	3,013	990
PORTUGL	V	E	81	11,023	5,600	7,832	2,232
			82	37,791	18,131	23,572	5,441
			83	2,772	1,198	1,725	527
			84	30,313	11,000	14,846	3,846
			85	11,023	3,250	4,529	1,279
			86	39,132	8,535	12,523	3,988

1351200 BEANS LIMA FR, FRZ ENTRY NOV (LB)

Country	Mode	Reg	Yr	Quantity	F.A.S.	C.I.F.	Charges
TOTAL			82	1,500	662	662	
			83	2,250	359	1,037	678
			84	1,375	1,528	1,562	34
			85	2,718	3,000	3,290	290
CANADA	O	E	82	1,500	662	662	
			84	1,243	1,093	1,093	
DOM REP	A	E	83	2,250	359	1,037	678
JAPAN	V	E	84	132	435	469	34
PORTUGL	V	E	85	2,718	3,000	3,290	290

1351400 BEANS,LIMA, DEC 1-MAY 31INCL (LB)

Country	Mode	Reg	Yr	Quantity	F.A.S.	C.I.F.	Charges
TOTAL			81	2,784	1,732	1,732	
			82	60,700	27,235	27,235	
			83	51,528	19,990	25,146	5,156
			84	88,306	32,935	34,413	1,478
			85	68,758	42,232	51,866	9,634
			86	24,886	14,731	15,612	881
CANADA	O	E	81	1,100	593	593	
			82	60,700	27,235	27,235	
			83	600	323	323	
			84	600	291	291	
			86	3,600	2,878	2,878	
FRANCE	A	E	86	265	1,144	1,144	
GREECE	V	E	85	2,600	1,820	2,029	209
			86	19,320	9,360	9,948	588
JAMAICA	A	E	84	3,000	600	1,400	800
	V	E	85	38,303	33,208	41,233	8,025
MEXICO	O	E	81	704	845	845	
			83	1,365	300	300	
			84	20,880	18,258	18,258	
	O	W	81	980	294	294	
			83	19,426	3,867	3,867	
			84	51,690	8,648	8,648	
			85	24,690	2,469	2,469	
NETHLDS	A	W	83	1,754	1,378	2,461	1,083
PHIL R	V	E	83	360	295	345	50
PORTUGL	V	E	83	28,023	13,827	17,850	4,023
			84	12,136	5,138	5,816	678
SENEGAL	A	E	85	3,165	4,735	6,135	1,400
TURKEY	V	E	86	1,701	1,349	1,642	293

Mung bean, dried
1400900 MUNG BEANS, DRIED, DEHYDRATD (LB)

Country	Mode	Reg	Yr	Quantity	F.A.S.	C.I.F.	Charges
TOTAL			81	7,505,777	2,445,087	2,789,754	344,667
			82	2,538,142	704,212	829,929	125,717
			83	2,331,426	648,150	746,212	98,062
			84	9,656,184	2,528,353	2,960,803	432,450
			85	15,827,423	2,487,537	2,943,964	456,427
			86	7,830,668	1,926,136	2,263,712	337,576
ANGOLA	V	E	86	46,298	9,975	13,804	3,829

Crop
Product
TSUSA commodity number, description, and unit of quantity

Country	Mode	Reg	Yr	Quantity	F.A.S.	C.I.F.	Charges
AUSTRAL	N	E	83	22,408	6,697	7,222	525
			85	259,388	66,030	76,811	10,781
			86	224,593	38,345	49,109	10,764
	N	W	84	449,490	136,798	155,116	18,318
	O	E	81	6,437	2,170	2,395	225
			82	8,818	3,245	3,680	435
			83	8,360	2,304	2,464	160
			84	39,572	8,328	10,976	2,648
	O	W	86	27,500	6,250	6,250	
	V	E	81	533,193	186,605	220,275	33,670
			82	96,983	28,756	31,461	2,705
			83	116,212	21,693	28,606	6,913
			84	1,692,303	441,290	522,298	81,008
			85	702,485	181,573	209,648	28,075
			86	1,848,193	383,930	484,891	100,961
	V	H	81	121,867	38,905	46,873	7,968
			84	38,580	15,590	17,325	1,735
			85	139,633	43,448	50,007	6,559
			86	138,864	33,320	40,283	6,963
	V	W	81	705,955	275,356	319,297	43,941
			82	17,600	4,472	5,303	831
			84	321,983	81,376	98,492	17,116
			85	1,813,452	440,561	522,943	82,382
			86	732,724	173,749	205,787	32,038
CANADA	O	E	82	20,000	9,728	9,728	
			86	56,100	20,412	20,412	
CHILE	V	E	86	36,000	10,260	12,003	1,743
CHINA M	O	E	84	5,500	2,035	2,035	
	V	E	81	18,049	8,282	8,995	713
			82	15,942	4,079	5,087	1,008
			83	60,268	21,321	25,934	4,613
			84	197,717	50,516	62,938	12,422
			85	102,400	25,014	31,573	6,559
			86	3,800	1,085	1,192	107
	V	H	81	2,150	1,338	1,455	117
			82	1,000	448	521	73
	V	W	81	196	275	290	15
			83	8,026	2,402	2,694	292
			84	109,095	46,802	51,539	4,737
			85	136,325	35,833	40,486	4,653
			86	718,364	142,334	163,222	20,888
CHINA T	V	E	81	2,500	2,100	2,121	21
			85	15,000	5,780	6,506	726
	V	W	81	5,661	2,621	2,781	160
			83	3,336	2,516	2,740	224
			84	202,913	9,894	12,808	2,914
			85	39,683	7,380	10,507	3,127
DOM REP	V	E	86	22,050	5,625	6,325	700
HG KONG	A	E	86	34,723	7,000	9,500	2,500
	V	E	82	8,300	2,386	3,157	771
			86	202,543	31,780	44,843	13,063
	V	H	81	540	353	381	28
	V	W	82	10,000	5,020	5,361	341
			84	37,500	17,009	18,240	1,231
			86	87,300	16,436	18,356	1,920
INDIA	O	E	83	11,023	384	720	336
			84	170,745	77,242	87,732	10,490
	O	W	81	1,210	518	518	
			86	2,000	1,014	1,014	
	V	E	81	265	293	353	60
			82	794	874	1,005	131
			83	800	640	800	160
			84	139,501	57,813	65,868	8,055
			85	99,365	36,649	43,080	6,431
			86	180,513	60,223	70,491	10,268
	V	W	81	496	674	748	74
			84	15,680	6,719	7,808	1,089
			85	36,043	15,605	17,281	1,676
			86	20,062	7,482	8,616	1,134
INDNSIA	V	W	83	269	360	430	70
KENYA	N	E	81	47,657	17,555	19,164	1,609
			82	65,722	21,587	24,653	3,066
			83	71,087	21,592	25,046	3,454
	O	E	81	96,538	35,019	39,863	4,844
			82	56,176	14,531	17,439	2,908
			83	80,676	25,498	27,904	2,406
			84	152,573	55,679	61,973	6,294
	V	E	82	83,774	25,080	30,159	5,079
			83	147,283	39,981	48,882	8,901
			84	16,635	6,031	7,023	992
			85	12,126	3,600	4,227	627
			86	11,023	2,740	3,250	510
	V	W	81	22,046	8,289	10,093	1,804
			82	16,645	8,549	10,824	2,275

Crop
Product
TSUSA commodity number, description, and unit of quantity

Country	Mode	Reg	Yr	Quantity	F.A.S.	C.I.F.	Charges
			83	30,515	9,861	11,996	2,135
			84	17,800	5,740	6,538	798
			85	34,562	10,316	11,525	1,209
KOR REP	V	E	84	1,800	2,250	2,538	288
	V	W	83	6,808	2,443	2,962	519
			86	37,400	12,207	12,893	686
MALAWI	O	E	81	39,683	14,554	16,504	1,950
			82	6,614	2,250	2,341	91
			83	49,278	20,195	20,195	
			84	11,239	4,244	4,661	417
			85	5,181	1,550	1,812	262
			86	22,000	8,638	8,638	
	V	E	84	2,750	965	1,107	142
	V	W	85	11,023	2,901	3,249	348
MEXICO	O	E	84	30,000	10,200	10,200	
N ZEAL	V	W	85	24,251	5,282	6,380	1,098
NEPAL	V	W	81	11,023	4,131	4,500	369
NETHLDS	V	E	81	10,000	4,492	4,872	380
PERU	N	E	86	511,153	141,082	164,496	23,414
	V	E	81	1,043,488	495,925	549,042	53,117
			82	704,189	196,627	231,263	34,636
			83	154,283	58,398	66,060	7,662
			84	77,161	29,050	33,045	3,995
			85	750,960	219,038	260,438	41,400
			86	165,974	46,541	55,149	8,608
PHIL R	V	E	81	1,980	1,813	2,131	318
			83	882	798	917	119
			84	2,160	1,614	1,900	286
	V	H	81	1,183	852	951	99
			82	1,000	672	769	97
			83	1,434	841	942	101
			84	1,296	641	729	88
	V	W	81	1,230	3,985	4,645	660
			82	662	1,376	1,574	198
			83	2,699	2,488	2,657	169
			84	6,201	3,596	4,048	452
			86	2,028	4,134	4,565	431
SINGAPR	O	E	82	2,183	644	732	88
	O	W	81	2,700	1,123	1,190	67
	V	E	81	4,410	1,791	2,065	274
	V	W	81	4,409	1,605	1,965	360
SRI LKA	V	W	81	4,409	2,281	2,673	392
SWITZLD	O	W	86	26,455	7,672	7,672	
	V	W	86	38,544	6,125	9,225	3,100
THAILND	N	E	84	207,849	52,007	64,757	12,750
	N	W	85	335,034	82,295	93,110	10,815
	O	E	81	56,100	27,080	27,080	
			84	660	363	363	
	V	E	81	288,794	79,417	93,277	13,860
			82	81,319	24,125	28,636	4,511
			83	339,203	105,684	120,936	15,252
			84	1,145,281	297,103	379,645	82,542
			85	8,834,552	814,999	955,237	140,238
			86	89,817	23,282	28,822	5,540
	V	H	82	768	390	423	33
			85	119,048	23,760	28,996	5,236
	V	W	81	4,443,422	1,215,065	1,391,079	176,014
			82	1,339,653	349,373	415,813	66,440
			83	1,191,704	294,372	337,686	43,314
			84	4,558,806	1,106,376	1,267,898	161,522
			85	2,356,912	465,923	570,148	104,225
			86	2,531,867	717,837	806,041	88,204
U KING	O	E	81	28,186	10,620	12,178	1,558
			83	11,012	3,171	3,409	238
			84	3,394	1,082	1,203	121
			86	12,780	6,658	6,863	205
	V	E	83	13,860	4,511	5,010	499

1401400 MUNG BEANS, 9/1-4/30, INCL (LB)

Country	Mode	Reg	Yr	Quantity	F.A.S.	C.I.F.	Charges
TOTAL			81	20,451,329	5,891,419	6,783,624	892,205
			82	3,035,802	899,947	1,053,405	153,458
			83	3,308,309	905,943	1,045,861	139,918
			84	9,734,877	2,755,937	3,202,957	447,020
			85	12,946,987	3,272,181	3,903,134	630,953
			86	8,889,748	2,068,586	2,414,074	345,488
AUSTRAL	N	E	81	316,631	105,761	131,153	25,392
			83	52,779	17,522	20,003	2,481
			84	414,583	123,257	138,856	15,599
			85	914,323	229,370	272,791	43,421
			86	50,310	15,169	17,371	2,202
	N	W	84	246,242	55,544	66,388	10,844
			85	519,440	119,640	141,917	22,277
			86	93,684	21,966	25,224	3,258

Crop
Product
TSUSA commodity number, description, and unit of quantity

Country	Mode	Reg	Yr	Quantity	F.A.S.	C.I.F.	Charges
	O	E	81	6,614	2,509	5,018	2,509
			82	2,205	796	796	
			84	52,140	18,029	18,172	143
	V	E	81	39,903	11,734	13,756	2,022
			82	72,003	19,777	24,809	5,032
			83	354,916	74,963	93,036	18,073
			84	1,171,259	296,912	349,821	52,909
			85	1,827,065	483,592	558,468	74,876
			86	797,464	170,426	221,069	50,643
	V	H	81	114,749	36,090	42,922	6,832
			82	39,705	10,404	12,600	2,196
			84	38,580	15,638	17,451	1,813
			85	92,592	21,943	26,543	4,600
			86	131,174	32,964	38,071	5,107
	V	W	81	104,789	33,174	39,234	6,060
			82	78,320	15,897	20,086	4,189
			83	25,080	7,419	8,837	1,418
			84	373,901	101,723	119,437	17,714
			85	1,652,108	434,195	516,151	81,956
			86	661,360	135,837	169,445	33,608
AUSTRIA	V	E	85	44,092	9,080	10,500	1,420
BRAZIL	V	E	82	8,267	2,570	3,222	652
CANADA	O	E	81	4,200	1,698	1,698	
			82	59,624	13,727	13,727	
			83	46,266	17,315	17,315	
			84	4,263	1,528	1,528	
			85	62,029	20,672	20,672	
	O	W	82	11,000	4,840	5,095	255
CHILE	V	E	85	40,000	14,438	17,200	2,762
CHINA M	O	E	82	6,600	2,086	2,328	242
			83	2,200	1,125	1,125	
	O	W	81	4,210	2,210	2,210	
	V	E	81	49,092	13,280	15,733	2,453
			82	28,047	8,137	10,174	2,037
			83	22,299	8,474	9,831	1,357
			84	42,483	11,930	14,690	2,760
			86	189,231	31,538	38,637	7,099
	V	H	82	800	345	379	34
			83	1,000	410	449	39
			84	745	292	347	55
	V	W	81	5,000	2,565	2,909	344
			82	800	274	297	23
			83	17,872	7,129	7,604	475
			84	39,032	23,022	24,730	1,708
			85	41,250	11,885	14,075	2,190
			86	634,299	114,510	138,986	24,476
CHINA T	O	E	84	3,960	1,933	1,933	
	V	E	85	1,112,389	250,348	319,252	68,904
			86	130,048	28,917	35,285	6,368
	V	W	81	2,500	2,677	2,865	188
			82	12,600	9,347	10,740	1,393
			83	33,000	10,540	12,210	1,670
			85	59,063	18,900	20,699	1,799
			86	70,650	16,169	18,167	1,998
DJIBUTI	O	E	84	4,365	1,470	1,623	153
DOM REP	V	E	86	20,000	4,700	5,229	529
FR GERM	A	E	86	1	1,279	1,351	72
	V	E	86	62,831	10,925	13,802	2,877
HG KONG	V	E	81	250	1,674	1,808	134
			83	2,001	658	879	221
			84	79,366	19,080	24,320	5,240
			85	25,000	6,000	7,298	1,298
	V	W	81	515,552	149,940	172,278	22,338
			84	30,000	12,384	13,008	624
			85	42,182	12,062	13,391	1,329
			86	195,381	42,785	45,951	3,166
INDIA	N	E	85	46,517	21,872	24,733	2,861
	O	E	81	4,929	2,439	2,695	256
			82	550	267	267	
			83	4,808	2,201	2,428	227
			84	10,334	7,448	7,715	267
			85	44,048	17,132	19,969	2,837
			86	12,982	5,598	5,901	303
	O	W	81	5,500	2,475	2,690	215
	V	E	81	48,492	16,454	20,691	4,237
			83	803	657	912	255
			84	307,063	144,337	162,681	18,344
			85	486,022	174,264	203,296	29,032
			86	392,921	139,154	160,685	21,531
	V	W	81	4,341	2,758	3,299	541
			82	2,586	2,459	2,879	420
			84	54,137	26,112	29,765	3,653
			85	38,918	20,823	24,287	3,464
			86	121,913	42,068	48,843	6,775

Crop
Product
TSUSA commodity number, description, and unit of quantity

Country	Mode	Reg	Yr	Quantity	F.A.S.	C.I.F.	Charges
JAPAN	V	E	81	2,205	1,030	1,396	366
	V	H	81	1,000	470	511	41
KENYA	N	E	83	42,155	15,721	17,338	1,617
	O	E	81	117,284	51,874	56,754	4,880
			82	167,853	64,759	71,000	6,241
			83	18,464	6,195	6,602	407
			84	227,169	74,316	86,756	12,440
			85	16,096	5,421	6,063	642
	O	W	82	17,042	6,186	6,803	617
			84	11,000	3,500	4,097	597
	V	E	81	66,138	25,170	29,674	4,504
			82	363,364	112,070	136,341	24,271
			83	345,554	95,441	114,886	19,445
			84	137,390	49,489	57,494	8,005
			85	42,389	9,642	13,348	3,706
			86	48,502	14,425	17,118	2,693
	V	W	82	109,878	40,459	50,761	10,302
			83	8,818	2,400	2,932	532
			84	2,205	600	707	107
			85	5,042	2,781	3,111	330
			86	7,716	2,175	2,454	279
KOR REP	V	E	82	15,549	8,011	9,112	1,101
			83	15,856	7,753	8,911	1,158
	V	W	82	17,890	8,217	8,559	342
			85	33,982	12,842	14,152	1,310
MALAWI	O	E	81	794	336	381	45
			82	107,113	38,466	38,606	140
			83	83,832	31,193	31,193	
			84	20,645	7,873	8,449	576
			85	32,019	15,035	15,286	251
			86	48,682	17,840	17,840	
	V	E	81	4,400	2,453	2,558	105
MALAYSA	O	E	82	4,409	1,500	1,500	
	V	E	84	39,088	14,550	17,100	2,550
MEXICO	O	W	84	44,092	7,920	7,920	
NEPAL	V	E	81	5,300	2,272	2,369	97
			86	79,366	27,180	32,149	4,969
PAKISTN	O	E	83	4,409	1,481	1,613	132
PERU	V	E	81	1,447,360	658,448	725,023	66,575
			82	703,782	213,276	249,024	35,748
			83	127,387	46,683	53,187	6,504
			84	540,946	197,618	223,164	25,546
			85	1,018,656	322,048	371,339	49,291
			86	934,382	262,089	307,775	45,686
	V	W	81	298,944	133,108	149,172	16,064
			82	40,000	9,600	12,594	2,994
PHIL R	V	E	81	450	442	472	30
			82	1,259	1,190	1,346	156
			83	720	620	724	104
			84	900	788	902	114
	V	H	82	1,440	835	1,009	174
			83	968	562	658	96
	V	W	81	19,516	13,329	14,631	1,302
			82	2,160	1,396	1,581	185
			83	1,052	737	831	94
SINGAPR	V	E	85	992,070	223,808	276,558	52,750
			86	476,192	97,616	109,828	12,212
	V	W	81	12,907	6,537	7,558	1,021
			82	5,512	2,172	2,230	58
			84	19,198	6,823	7,680	857
SPAIN	O	E	84	2	745	745	
SRI LKA	V	E	83	66,365	21,335	25,889	4,554
THAILND	N	E	81	220,742	78,179	87,797	9,618
			82	140,277	41,391	48,140	6,749
	O	E	81	39,600	19,755	19,755	
			82	2,205	729	792	63
			83	61,509	15,190	17,745	2,555
			85	39,682	15,079	15,079	
	O	W	84	3,200	11,840	13,446	1,606
	V	E	81	1,407,033	419,074	490,798	71,724
			82	574,298	128,755	161,064	32,309
			83	659,153	175,756	206,021	30,265
			84	2,106,406	536,462	660,337	123,875
			85	1,498,244	309,441	396,227	86,786
			86	2,520,516	494,517	565,802	71,285
	V	H	81	113,915	39,426	43,941	4,515
			82	1,000	428	467	39
			84	9,048	1,589	1,819	230
	V	W	81	15,411,609	4,030,566	4,665,572	635,006
			82	421,836	122,839	137,571	14,732
			83	1,275,588	326,470	371,457	44,987
			84	3,692,633	977,188	1,115,401	138,213
			85	2,208,981	484,846	575,467	90,621
			86	1,087,407	313,735	347,795	34,060

Crop
Product
TSUSA commodity number, description, and unit of quantity

Country	Mode	Reg	Yr	Quantity	F.A.S.	C.I.F.	Charges
TNZANIA	V	E	81	15,432	3,500	4,519	1,019
TURKEY	O	E	81	4,400	2,405	2,624	219
			83	13,161	3,651	4,134	483
	V	E	84	1,323	743	855	112
U KING	A	E	86	7,700	1,852	2,056	204
	N	E	84	7,179	3,254	3,620	366
	O	E	81	35,548	15,607	17,160	1,553
			82	15,828	6,742	7,506	764
			83	9,910	2,951	3,254	303
			85	4,510	1,702	1,702	
	V	E	83	10,384	3,391	3,857	466
			85	8,278	3,320	3,560	240
			86	17,670	5,739	6,530	791
VENEZ	A	E	86	18,000	4,550	5,350	800
	V	E	86	79,366	12,863	15,360	2,497

Beech

*Beech, hardwood flooring***
2025820 HARDWOOD FLOORING, MAPLE (MBF)

Country	Mode	Reg	Yr	Quantity	F.A.S.	C.I.F.	Charges
TOTAL			81	2,834	2,976,454	3,020,119	43,665
			82	2,594	2,410,364	2,481,782	71,418
			83	3,659	4,058,722	4,159,703	100,981
			84	6,823	7,709,764	8,177,532	467,768
			85	2,956	2,867,670	3,027,126	159,456
			86	3,699	3,721,625	3,794,001	72,376
ARGENT	V	E	83	28	14,037	16,281	2,244
BRAZIL	V	E	82	3	3,261	3,873	612
			86	2	1,269	1,490	221
C RICA	V	E	84	3	3,814	4,606	792
CANADA	A	E	81	1	637	920	283
	N	E	85	1,274	1,000,114	1,000,114	
	N	W	83	*	333	718	385
	O	E	81	2,640	2,634,090	2,634,090	
			82	2,264	1,860,731	1,860,731	
			83	3,130	3,313,508	3,313,508	
			84	4,031	4,338,772	4,338,775	3
			85	1,047	703,878	703,878	
			86	3,195	2,988,503	2,988,503	
	O	W	85	61	19,676	19,676	
			86	1	1,296	1,296	
DENMARK	A	E	82	5	8,730	15,755	7,025
			83	28	5,880	10,035	4,155
			84	1	400	802	402
	A	W	83	3	7,463	8,043	580
	V	E	81	182	308,573	351,031	42,458
			82	272	432,714	486,136	53,422
			83	226	529,681	591,770	62,089
			84	2,410	2,967,571	3,376,842	409,271
			85	466	913,392	1,043,575	130,183
			86	423	585,611	643,458	57,847
	V	W	82	27	56,078	61,980	5,902
			83	27	57,789	63,911	6,122
			84	141	65,715	76,623	10,908
			85	11	19,317	23,675	4,358
FINLAND	V	E	85	14	15,543	17,565	2,022
			86	18	12,681	14,029	1,348
	V	W	84	8	18,014	21,406	3,392
			86	18	19,375	22,356	2,981
FR GERM	V	E	83	4	6,189	6,875	686
			84	8	13,405	14,580	1,175
			85	1	3,169	3,365	196
			86	2	6,750	7,323	573
	V	W	84	1	5,698	6,948	1,250
GREECE	V	E	86	1	2,183	3,644	1,461
HG KONG	V	W	86	2	3,140	3,300	160
INDIA	A	E	82	1	480	1,150	670
ITALY	A	W	85	5	3,467	4,803	1,336
	V	E	86	7	8,705	9,199	494
JAPAN	V	E	85	1	5,031	5,126	95
	V	W	86	1	2,401	2,563	162
MALAYSA	V	W	86	6	3,609	4,259	650
NETHLDS	V	E	84	74	117,010	132,543	15,533
NORWAY	N	E	83	*	3,582	3,879	297
			86	*	1,229	1,374	145
	O	E	84	2	2,643	2,999	356
	V	E	84	87	108,375	123,945	15,570
			85	32	78,458	87,715	9,257
			86	3	7,865	8,631	766

Crop / Product / TSUSA commodity number, description, and unit of quantity / Country	Mode	Reg	Yr	Quantity	F.A.S.	C.I.F.	Charges
SWEDEN	V	E	81	10	32,409	33,184	775
			82	21	45,739	49,463	3,724
			83	211	118,845	143,156	24,311
			84	41	47,328	51,399	4,071
			85	41	99,594	111,214	11,620
			86	12	45,374	48,494	3,120
	V	W	82	1	2,631	2,694	63
			83	2	1,415	1,527	112
			84	4	6,137	6,844	707
			85	3	6,031	6,420	389
			86	4	14,848	16,248	1,400
SWITZLD	V	E	81	1	745	894	149
THAILND	V	E	86	4	16,786	17,834	1,048
U KING	V	E	84	12	14,882	19,220	4,338

Beech, lumber
2024235 LUMBER, BEECH, ROUGH (MBF)

Country	Mode	Reg	Yr	Quantity	F.A.S.	C.I.F.	Charges
TOTAL			81	470	181,671	181,671	
			82	224	80,392	80,392	
			83	251	114,602	116,391	1,789
			84	542	193,228	194,649	1,421
			85	488	127,491	127,858	367
			86	498	179,052	179,052	
AUSTRAL	V	W	83	1	521	645	124
CANADA	O	E	81	470	181,671	181,671	
			82	224	80,392	80,392	
			83	246	110,154	110,154	
			84	536	190,151	190,151	
			85	485	124,318	124,318	
			86	498	179,052	179,052	
CHILE	V	E	85	1	1,305	1,483	178
FR GERM	O	E	83	4	3,927	5,592	1,665
	V	E	84	2	1,290	1,557	267
FRANCE	V	E	85	2	1,868	2,057	189
SWITZLD	V	E	84	4	1,787	2,941	1,154

2024245 BEECH LUMBER, DRESSED (MBF)

Country	Mode	Reg	Yr	Quantity	F.A.S.	C.I.F.	Charges
TOTAL			81	427	193,301	193,947	646
			82	87	56,202	56,611	409
			83	111	71,149	72,665	1,516
			84	326	108,222	112,370	4,148
			85	290	144,213	144,984	771
			86	521	259,755	262,645	2,890
AUSTRAL	V	W	82	2	1,492	1,901	409
AUSTRIA	V	E	84	1	1,174	1,206	32
CANADA	O	E	81	412	189,301	189,301	
			82	85	54,710	54,710	
			83	110	69,119	69,119	
			84	276	97,853	97,853	
			85	276	138,483	138,483	
			86	379	239,676	239,676	
	O	W	84	1	638	638	
DENMARK	V	E	84	31	7,309	11,264	3,955
FR GERM	V	E	85	1	1,379	1,496	117
			86	25	14,050	15,236	1,186
FRANCE	O	E	81	14	2,890	3,299	409
ITALY	A	E	83	1	2,030	3,546	1,516
	A	W	86	100	3,600	4,082	482
MEXICO	O	E	84	15	409	409	
THAILND	V	W	81	1	1,110	1,347	237
U KING	A	E	86	17	2,429	3,651	1,222
	V	E	84	2	839	1,000	161
			85	13	4,351	5,005	654

Creosote oil
4012200 CREOSOTE OIL (GAL)

Country	Mode	Reg	Yr	Quantity	F.A.S.	C.I.F.	Charges
TOTAL			81	9,576,191	9,213,155	10,660,144	1,446,989
			82	8,963,080	9,492,987	10,548,244	1,055,257
			83	11,809,100	13,798,055	15,024,285	1,226,230
			84	7,296,117	6,927,006	7,608,895	681,889
			85	11,921,811	14,356,635	15,993,941	1,637,306
			86	10,404,499	7,304,567	8,768,964	1,464,397
BELGIUM	V	E	81	836,258	936,776	1,045,322	108,546
CANADA	O	E	81	937,520	585,868	585,868	
			82	2,276,731	1,857,570	1,857,570	
			83	1,545,397	1,333,552	1,333,552	
			84	478,248	396,555	396,555	

Country	Mode	Reg	Yr	Quantity	F.A.S.	C.I.F.	Charges
			86	48,372	61,209	61,209	
	O	W	81	3,850	1,895	1,895	
			82	4,000	1,875	1,875	
	V	E	81	1,119,283	1,044,757	1,224,583	179,826
DENMARK	V	E	86	3,743,791	2,098,018	2,784,888	686,870
FR GERM	A	W	86	59	3,703	4,061	358
	O	E	84	41	4,660	4,749	89
	V	E	81	2,808,639	3,195,193	3,561,650	366,457
			82	1,962,077	2,295,096	2,565,681	270,585
			83	1,913,468	2,298,831	2,545,754	246,923
			84	483,906	355,241	431,282	76,041
			85	2,574,512	3,939,967	4,250,110	310,143
			86	2,898,947	2,233,627	2,497,402	263,775
	V	W	81	1,473,496	1,026,994	1,444,027	417,033
			83	1,294,743	1,482,745	1,625,983	143,238
			85	1,304,190	1,467,214	1,583,662	116,448
			86	1,218,357	1,187,898	1,457,688	269,790
FRANCE	A	E	81	44	1,752	2,197	445
	V	E	81	988,892	798,895	969,114	170,219
			82	2,293,653	2,694,047	3,006,321	312,274
			83	838,030	990,308	1,097,896	107,588
			84	1,355,748	1,168,295	1,307,788	139,493
			85	4,000,168	4,166,169	4,600,611	434,442
			86	1,055,956	694,297	810,947	116,650
JAPAN	A	E	86	172	2,294	2,735	441
	A	W	84	1,673	11,975	14,741	2,766
MEXICO	O	E	83	77,884	38,577	38,577	
			84	816,573	248,006	248,006	
			85	237,439	14,964	14,964	
			86	152,812	80,365	80,365	
	V	E	82	783,720	838,593	1,063,174	224,581
NETHLDS	V	E	81	455,013	574,188	633,993	59,805
			82	510,940	552,166	638,675	86,509
			83	3,285,114	4,158,542	4,503,370	344,828
			84	4,159,928	4,742,274	5,205,774	463,500
			85	3,805,502	4,768,321	5,544,594	776,273
			86	1,211,411	886,881	1,006,854	119,973
SWEDEN	V	E	83	340	21,523	21,756	233
U KING	V	E	81	953,196	1,046,837	1,191,495	144,658
			82	1,131,959	1,253,640	1,414,948	161,308
			83	2,854,065	3,473,977	3,857,397	383,420
			86	74,622	56,275	62,815	6,540

Beet

Beet, dried pulp
1842000 BEET PULP, DRIED (STN)

Country	Mode	Reg	Yr	Quantity	F.A.S.	C.I.F.	Charges
TOTAL			81	59	10,317	10,317	
			82	1,242	144,248	144,248	
			83	725	133,534	145,608	12,074
			84	280	33,085	33,085	
			85	221	29,525	29,525	
			86	2,322	259,008	274,290	15,282
CANADA	O	E	81	59	10,317	10,317	
			82	676	83,943	83,943	
			83	189	23,263	23,263	
			84	245	30,585	30,585	
			85	221	29,525	29,525	
			86	790	84,658	84,658	
	O	W	82	566	60,305	60,305	
			84	35	2,500	2,500	
	V	H	86	1,532	174,350	189,632	15,282
ISRAEL	O	E	83	481	66,238	73,342	7,104
	V	E	83	55	44,033	49,003	4,970

Beet, fresh or frozen
1352000 BEETS, EXCEPT SUGAR FR OR FZ (LB)

Country	Mode	Reg	Yr	Quantity	F.A.S.	C.I.F.	Charges
TOTAL			81	432,864	31,869	31,869	
			82	668,102	34,726	34,901	175
			83	517,759	56,185	58,694	2,509
			84	2,396,058	104,707	104,944	237
			85	865,775	85,554	85,554	
			86	2,982,575	135,088	135,088	
CANADA	O	E	81	408,284	27,112	27,112	
			82	570,046	26,586	26,586	
			83	253,892	32,999	33,299	300
			84	2,303,960	92,195	92,195	

Crop
Product
TSUSA commodity number, description, and unit of quantity

Country	Mode	Reg	Yr	Quantity	F.A.S.	C.I.F.	Charges
			85	825,966	74,693	74,693	
			86	2,735,200	110,805	110,805	
CHINA M	O	E	86	880	1,320	1,320	
DOM REP	A	E	83	860	316	482	166
FRANCE	A	E	84	330	263	500	237
MALAYSA	O	W	86	19,440	4,320	4,320	
MEXICO	O	E	84	36,023	2,055	2,055	
	O	W	81	24,580	4,757	4,757	
			82	37,356	4,929	4,929	
			83	187,857	20,777	20,777	
			84	55,745	10,194	10,194	
			85	39,809	10,861	10,861	
			86	227,055	18,643	18,643	
NETHLDS	V	E	82	60,700	3,211	3,386	175
			83	75,150	2,093	4,136	2,043

Beet, seed
1260500 BEET SEED EXCEPT SUGAR BEET (LB)

Country	Mode	Reg	Yr	Quantity	F.A.S.	C.I.F.	Charges
TOTAL			81	52,999	64,856	71,008	6,152
			82	18,124	29,882	32,098	2,216
			83	12,075	24,692	25,870	1,178
			84	6,730	19,106	20,535	1,429
			85	12,873	46,481	48,617	2,136
			86	4,673	38,073	41,313	3,240
DENMARK	A	E	86	1,500	4,153	5,360	1,207
	V	W	83	210	658	871	213
			84	990	3,489	3,615	126
			85	525	3,764	4,134	370
FR GERM	A	E	85	1,058	8,609	9,386	777
	V	E	86	1,830	21,504	22,714	1,210
FRANCE	A	W	84	88	1,004	1,252	248
	O	E	81	10,000	11,930	13,131	1,201
	V	W	81	4,409	4,332	5,097	765
			82	6,614	12,644	13,363	719
			83	1,607	1,854	2,041	187
ISRAEL	V	E	81	11,023	12,378	13,170	792
	V	W	81	11,000	8,971	9,750	779
			83	6,614	4,536	4,745	209
ITALY	V	E	85	8,512	19,982	20,547	565
NETHLDS	A	E	81	18	390	477	87
			82	325	1,738	1,878	140
			86	220	1,109	1,327	218
	A	W	86	505	1,698	1,783	85
	N	W	84	3,022	8,171	8,666	495
	O	E	81	12,500	14,120	16,055	1,935
	V	E	81	2,049	7,135	7,370	235
			82	1,300	5,517	5,797	280
			83	500	1,391	1,544	153
			84	2,553	5,211	5,704	493
	V	W	81	2,000	5,600	5,958	358
			82	7,500	8,448	9,222	774
			83	3,000	12,453	12,729	276
			85	2,612	10,315	10,632	317
PHIL R	V	W	82	180	484	511	27
U KING	A	E	83	79	2,983	3,084	101
			84	37	390	420	30
			85	166	3,811	3,918	107
			86	618	9,609	10,129	520
	A	W	84	40	841	878	37
	V	E	83	65	817	856	39
	V	W	82	2,205	1,051	1,327	276

Begonia

Begonia, tuber
1253260 BEGONIA TUBERS SOIL ATTACHD (NO)

Country	Mode	Reg	Yr	Quantity	F.A.S.	C.I.F.	Charges
TOTAL			81	501,847	224,362	228,765	4,403
			82	665,631	408,572	410,703	2,131
			83	690,902	467,701	467,789	88
			84	586,248	524,427	524,653	226
			85	420,743	347,140	347,140	
			86	668,679	633,755	634,573	818
BELGIUM	A	W	82	75,000	13,050	13,800	750
	V	E	82	22,650	5,457	5,868	411
	V	W	81	383,550	92,936	97,339	4,403
CANADA	A	E	83	200	633	721	88
			84	1,296	795	991	196
	A	W	82	3,770	2,516	3,464	948
	O	E	81	118,297	131,426	131,426	
			82	539,211	387,149	387,149	
			83	690,702	467,068	467,068	
			84	553,672	516,613	516,613	
			85	420,743	347,140	347,140	
			86	542,699	603,768	603,768	
	O	W	84	5,780	5,744	5,744	
NETHLDS	A	W	84	25,500	1,275	1,305	30
	O	E	82	25,000	400	422	22
	V	E	86	125,980	29,987	30,805	818

1253460 BEGONIA TUBERS, NSPF (NO)

Country	Mode	Reg	Yr	Quantity	F.A.S.	C.I.F.	Charges
TOTAL			81	8,413,271	1,886,844	2,000,867	113,522
			82	8,870,891	1,928,336	2,040,579	112,243
			83	7,877,795	1,659,441	1,767,056	107,615
			84	22,538,313	2,744,366	2,862,859	118,493
			85	7,955,752	1,476,499	1,588,600	112,101
			86	10,081,508	2,081,260	2,241,948	160,688
BARBADO	A	E	84	12	497	581	84
BELGIUM	A	E	83	20,400	6,625	7,374	749
			84	4,100	735	889	154
	A	W	83	28,000	10,960	12,879	1,919
			84	61,650	24,341	28,410	4,069
			85	57,000	14,205	18,009	3,804
			86	35,141	24,160	34,824	10,664
	N	E	81	3,489,663	755,045	795,234	40,189
			82	3,995,055	795,342	834,981	39,639
			86	2,643,240	524,754	568,394	43,640
	N	W	82	131,600	31,797	33,160	1,363
			84	876,375	188,592	192,726	4,134
			85	336,375	77,125	81,841	4,716
	V	E	81	614,817	149,131	163,979	14,848
			82	611,882	133,850	147,165	13,315
			83	4,201,078	789,251	832,317	43,066
			84	4,817,776	1,662,207	1,712,290	50,083
			85	3,418,114	543,265	584,570	41,305
			86	2,863,401	506,334	542,578	36,244
	V	W	81	977,720	243,907	262,212	18,305
			82	1,096,925	215,467	234,544	19,077
			83	547,095	120,555	129,613	9,058
			84	334,200	65,481	70,081	4,600
			85	40,950	7,254	8,148	894
			86	1,351,425	267,108	284,049	16,941
CANADA	A	E	82	100	255	279	24
			83	576	360	417	57
			84	504	378	425	47
	O	E	81	3,200	3,178	3,178	
			82	86,550	89,732	89,732	
			84	41,460	6,068	6,068	
			86	7,400	4,754	4,754	
	O	W	81	4,667	11,076	11,076	
			82	17,080	2,621	2,621	
			83	1,905	2,039	2,039	
			84	26,065	10,676	10,676	
			85	650	2,045	2,045	
			86	317	1,651	1,651	
DENMARK	V	E	83	11,634	4,380	5,106	726
FR GERM	A	E	86	420	2,769	2,897	128
	O	E	81	360	1,180	1,209	29
			83	92	2,339	2,352	13
INDIA	A	E	84	54,050	2,595	6,230	3,635
JAPAN	A	W	82	50	290	348	58
MAURIT	A	W	83	6,000	2,100	2,500	400
			84	6,000	1,364	1,848	484
NETHLDS	A	E	81	6,000	2,880	3,089	209
			84	750	282	388	106
			85	42,200	8,108	9,414	1,306
	A	W	84	26,700	4,488	5,769	1,281
			85	45,000	9,296	13,343	4,047
			86	30,000	13,879	15,259	1,380
	N	E	82	1,645,796	438,120	458,751	20,631
			83	1,682,135	406,613	431,719	25,106
			84	12,589,398	437,166	461,476	24,310
			86	960,242	244,300	262,913	18,613
	N	W	85	345,334	70,565	77,924	7,359
	V	E	81	3,172,244	670,154	703,765	33,110
			82	812,638	83,310	89,745	6,435
			83	459,577	104,198	114,951	10,753
			84	1,017,073	211,545	228,617	17,072
			85	2,911,594	596,274	635,499	39,225
			86	1,838,092	409,917	434,999	25,082
	V	W	81	142,985	46,652	53,172	6,520

Crop Product TSUSA commodity number, description, and unit of quantity Country	Mode	Reg	Yr	Quantity	F.A.S.	C.I.F.	Charges
			82	471,480	130,373	141,768	11,395
			83	917,994	205,228	220,757	15,529
			84	229,220	22,763	27,051	4,288
			85	758,535	148,362	157,807	9,445
			86	351,830	81,634	89,630	7,996
REP SAF	V	E	84	2,407,260	90,869	94,570	3,701
U KING	A	E	81	1,615	3,641	3,953	312
			82	1,735	7,179	7,485	306
			83	1,309	4,793	5,032	239
	N	E	84	45,720	14,319	14,764	445

Belladonna

Belladonna, natural drug
4353500 BELLADONNA (LB)

Country	Mode	Reg	Yr	Quantity	F.A.S.	C.I.F.	Charges
TOTAL			81	7,542	9,994	10,783	789
			82	13,042	15,640	17,793	2,153
			83	2,194	2,725	2,949	224
			84	2,180	2,452	2,809	357
			86	5,004	3,273	5,094	1,821
BULGAR	V	E	82	6,482	7,888	8,865	977
BURMA	V	E	86	3,230	1,499	2,208	709
YUGOSLV	A	E	86	1,774	1,774	2,886	1,112
	V	E	81	7,542	9,994	10,783	789
			82	6,560	7,752	8,928	1,176
			83	2,194	2,725	2,949	224
			84	2,180	2,452	2,809	357

Bent Grass

Bent grass, seed
1260700 BENT GRASS SEED (LB)

Country	Mode	Reg	Yr	Quantity	F.A.S.	C.I.F.	Charges
TOTAL			81	888	4,654	5,418	764
			82	1,212	4,005	4,739	734
			83	1,202	7,903	8,248	345
			84	22,701	12,580	14,146	1,566
			85	88,787	94,766	101,782	7,016
			86	6,797	14,061	15,152	1,091
CANADA	O	E	83	100	2,840	2,840	
			85	300	1,800	1,800	
	O	W	86	5,000	7,018	7,018	
DOMINCA	V	E	85	33,068	32,467	34,060	1,593
FR GERM	V	W	85	44,092	41,988	45,415	3,427
JAPAN	V	W	84	22,000	9,900	11,012	1,112
NETHLDS	A	E	84	150	450	661	211
	A	W	84	110	452	550	98
			86	220	1,980	2,302	322
	N	W	86	772	2,528	3,088	560
	V	E	86	805	2,535	2,744	209
	V	W	82	794	2,431	2,541	110
			85	2,425	4,225	4,487	262
NORWAY	A	W	81	254	804	852	48
			82	198	503	1,012	509
	V	W	81	132	729	836	107
			82	220	1,071	1,186	115
			83	1,102	5,063	5,408	345
			84	441	1,778	1,923	145
SWEDEN	A	E	81	440	2,838	3,355	517
	V	W	85	8,902	14,286	16,020	1,734
U KING	A	E	81	62	283	375	92

Bergamot

Bergamot, essential oil
4520600 BERGAMOT OIL (LB)

Country	Mode	Reg	Yr	Quantity	F.A.S.	C.I.F.	Charges
TOTAL			81	41,165	1,072,515	1,096,823	24,073
			82	52,251	821,467	840,614	19,147
			83	69,063	917,759	941,549	23,790
			84	65,760	852,701	880,070	27,369
			85	69,275	656,723	683,428	26,705
			86	98,658	1,173,504	1,200,488	26,984

Country	Mode	Reg	Yr	Quantity	F.A.S.	C.I.F.	Charges
BRAZIL	A	E	81	66	750	901	151
	V	E	82	4,497	36,456	38,270	1,814
			85	4,497	28,380	30,015	1,635
CANADA	O	E	86	15,493	26,859	26,859	
FR GERM	A	E	81	1,233	7,281	7,821	540
			82	910	5,476	5,922	446
			83	187	1,613	1,690	77
			86	400	2,811	3,289	478
	N	E	84	5,020	26,547	27,626	1,079
			85	5,023	26,378	27,092	714
FRANCE	N	E	81	6,195	247,491	251,784	4,303
			82	6,038	190,246	193,915	3,669
			83	17,658	256,675	262,625	5,950
			84	11,501	226,376	234,521	8,145
			85	9,370	163,089	170,033	6,944
			86	15,168	252,909	259,082	6,173
HG KONG	V	E	81	9	485	508	23
INDNSIA	V	E	84	386	3,870	3,943	73
ITALY	N	E	81	25,608	642,365	657,435	15,031
			82	39,375	547,820	560,111	12,291
			83	36,906	507,447	520,343	12,896
			84	27,933	389,945	403,447	13,502
			85	30,709	285,504	298,203	12,699
			86	43,304	653,037	665,965	12,928
JAPAN	N	E	81	815	34,819	35,540	721
			83	463	18,303	19,232	929
	V	E	84	995	23,629	23,808	179
			85	1,102	10,004	10,249	245
NETHLDS	A	E	81	132	740	845	105
	N	E	83	1,620	24,443	24,931	488
			85	10,604	91,409	94,529	3,120
			86	4,145	54,016	55,427	1,411
	V	E	84	8,245	85,315	86,653	1,338
SPAIN	V	E	83	882	9,721	10,063	342
			86	395	9,137	9,337	200
SWITZLD	N	E	81	6,706	133,965	137,114	2,943
			82	452	12,445	12,738	293
			83	6,361	63,017	64,337	1,320
			84	6,930	60,765	63,021	2,256
			86	6,042	67,451	69,104	1,653
	V	E	85	4,884	29,150	29,997	847
U KING	N	E	82	891	25,695	26,244	549
			83	4,986	36,540	38,328	1,788
			84	4,750	36,254	37,051	797
			86	13,711	107,284	111,425	4,141
	V	E	81	401	4,619	4,875	256
			85	3,086	22,809	23,310	501
USSR	V	E	82	88	3,329	3,414	85

Birch

Birch, hardwood flooring**
2025820 HARDWOOD FLOORING, MAPLE (MBF)
 (See Beech, hardwood flooring under Beech)

Birch, logs
2003527 BIRCH LOG/TIMBER EXC PULPWD (MBF)

Country	Mode	Reg	Yr	Quantity	F.A.S.	C.I.F.	Charges
TOTAL			81	6,936	1,119,520	1,120,743	1,223
			82	7,961	1,513,279	1,513,294	15
			83	3,616	742,515	744,610	2,095
			84	3,970	871,097	871,104	7
			85	2,741	721,374	721,467	93
			86	2,632	893,439	893,439	
CANADA	N	W	82	4	1,341	1,356	15
	O	E	81	6,817	1,104,601	1,104,601	
			82	7,957	1,511,938	1,511,938	
			83	3,616	742,515	744,610	2,095
			84	3,937	865,477	865,484	7
			85	2,206	695,615	695,615	
			86	2,421	870,133	870,133	
	O	W	81	119	14,919	16,142	1,223
			84	28	5,080	5,080	
			85	534	24,579	24,579	
			86	211	23,306	23,306	
FR GERM	V	W	85	1	1,180	1,273	93
MEXICO	O	W	84	5	540	540	

Crop
Product
TSUSA commodity number, description, and unit of quantity

Birch, lumber

2024225 LUMBER, BIRCH, ROUGH (MBF)

Country	Mode	Reg	Yr	Quantity	F.A.S.	C.I.F.	Charges
TOTAL			81	8,818	4,474,917	4,474,918	
			82	8,977	4,301,736	4,304,350	2,614
			83	7,491	3,551,396	3,554,550	3,154
			84	7,194	3,556,836	3,570,997	14,161
			85	10,450	4,187,233	4,363,912	176,679
			86	8,852	4,289,200	4,297,598	8,398
CANADA	O	E	81	8,798	4,467,429	4,467,430	
			82	8,856	4,283,881	4,283,881	
			83	7,450	3,521,942	3,521,942	
			84	7,021	3,391,630	3,391,630	
			85	9,264	3,838,732	3,838,732	
			86	8,671	4,109,882	4,109,882	
	O	W	81	20	7,488	7,488	
			82	9	6,104	6,104	
			83	21	13,317	13,317	
			84	15	8,137	8,137	
			85	29	16,373	16,373	
			86	71	62,569	62,569	
	V	E	83	20	16,137	19,291	3,154
			84	58	53,771	63,059	9,288
	V	W	84	98	101,800	106,184	4,384
			85	141	122,451	139,969	17,518
			86	110	116,749	125,147	8,398
FR GERM	O	E	82	13	4,466	4,466	
	V	E	82	98	6,904	9,451	2,547
ITALY	A	E	84	2	1,498	1,987	489
MALAYSA	V	W	82	1	381	448	67
POLAND	V	E	85	7	1,857	3,299	1,442
USSR	V	E	85	1,009	207,820	365,539	157,719

2024230 LUMBER, BIRCH, DRESSED (MBF)

Country	Mode	Reg	Yr	Quantity	F.A.S.	C.I.F.	Charges
TOTAL			81	5,806	3,257,937	3,257,940	
			82	3,072	1,663,726	1,664,181	455
			83	5,078	2,538,238	2,538,238	
			84	5,222	2,668,948	2,678,182	9,234
			85	5,188	2,723,143	2,732,039	8,896
			86	5,127	2,797,603	2,804,714	7,111
BRAZIL	V	E	85	18	14,499	16,983	2,484
CANADA	N	W	86	83	19,917	22,754	2,837
	O	E	81	5,760	3,240,511	3,240,514	
			82	3,054	1,649,193	1,649,193	
			83	5,062	2,525,257	2,525,257	
			84	5,098	2,590,428	2,590,428	
			85	5,122	2,659,181	2,660,370	1,189
			86	4,708	2,728,979	2,728,979	
	O	W	81	9	5,651	5,651	
			82	8	6,565	6,565	
			83	16	12,981	12,981	
			84	54	25,096	25,096	
			86	24	10,601	10,601	
	V	W	84	70	53,424	62,658	9,234
			85	48	49,463	54,686	5,223
FINLAND	V	E	86	21	17,075	18,781	1,706
FR GERM	A	E	86	5	1,020	1,304	284
	N	W	86	260	10,278	11,777	1,499
	V	E	86	8	3,333	4,118	785
FRANCE	O	E	82	8	6,766	6,766	
JAPAN	V	W	82	2	1,202	1,657	455
MEXICO	O	W	81	1	500	500	
SP MQEL	O	E	86	18	6,400	6,400	
U KING	O	E	81	36	11,275	11,275	

Birch, plywood

2401420 PLYWD BIRCH FACED SPEC DIMS (MSF)

Country	Mode	Reg	Yr	Quantity	F.A.S.	C.I.F.	Charges
TOTAL			81	159,296	33,445,307	35,029,014	1,579,158
			82	144,257	29,291,152	30,713,375	1,422,223
			83	178,345	35,626,981	37,482,433	1,855,452
			84	193,319	42,100,611	44,080,205	1,979,594
			85	206,178	35,192,607	37,372,059	2,179,452
			86	193,419	36,477,925	38,920,063	2,442,138
CANADA	N	W	82	*	300	300	
	O	E	81	41,596	8,984,134	8,984,134	
			82	31,130	6,732,175	6,732,175	
			83	21,306	4,905,833	4,905,833	
			84	28,646	6,822,238	6,822,238	
			85	19,883	3,880,318	3,880,318	
			86	1,703	525,029	525,029	
	O	W	81	8	1,175	1,175	
			84	23	14,684	14,684	
			85	23	13,036	13,036	
			86	28	16,010	16,010	
	V	W	86	109	15,598	19,011	3,413
CHINA T	N	E	84	17,222	3,678,470	3,863,073	184,603
			85	328	75,924	80,267	4,343
			86	5,008	972,508	1,042,747	70,239
	N	W	85	3,320	589,283	635,133	45,850
	V	E	81	68,014	13,562,642	14,429,093	866,451
			82	72,229	14,042,716	14,889,769	847,053
			83	107,543	20,441,347	21,575,286	1,133,939
			84	100,315	20,637,462	21,770,660	1,133,198
			85	126,952	19,743,694	21,148,761	1,405,067
			86	128,929	22,864,207	24,412,446	1,548,239
	V	W	81	26,673	5,443,610	5,743,781	300,171
			82	22,907	4,527,756	4,791,789	264,033
			83	28,592	5,504,517	5,843,871	339,354
			84	29,405	6,476,491	6,826,069	349,578
			85	33,548	5,859,403	6,242,920	383,517
			86	31,991	6,222,737	6,607,459	384,722
FINLAND	V	E	81	47	34,075	37,632	3,557
			82	350	255,711	283,760	28,049
			83	277	164,083	181,871	17,788
			84	279	205,430	235,654	30,224
			85	659	331,343	380,182	48,839
			86	422	164,708	190,956	26,248
	V	W	81	41	16,744	18,722	1,978
			82	69	49,192	54,740	5,548
			83	222	132,034	151,542	19,508
			84	98	52,911	61,776	8,865
			85	97	44,541	54,119	9,578
FR GERM	O	E	83	2	9,919	10,336	417
ITALY	A	E	83	345	22,000	24,000	2,000
	V	E	86	271	55,639	58,876	3,237
JAPAN	N	E	85	979	199,492	213,648	14,156
	N	W	84	530	127,860	137,269	9,409
	V	E	81	10,479	2,703,498	2,955,469	250,979
			82	6,388	1,400,311	1,521,459	121,148
			83	6,328	1,445,020	1,556,761	111,741
			84	4,879	1,305,160	1,416,724	111,564
			85	5,032	1,132,918	1,214,784	81,866
			86	12,477	3,034,868	3,253,401	218,533
	V	W	81	11,919	2,593,281	2,746,883	150,045
			82	10,957	2,223,647	2,374,247	150,600
			83	13,204	2,880,930	3,100,417	219,487
			84	10,325	2,468,266	2,597,709	129,443
			85	13,027	2,936,975	3,079,686	142,711
			86	6,779	1,625,555	1,707,889	82,334
KOR REP	V	E	83	221	44,120	46,900	2,780
			84	804	147,001	155,358	8,357
			85	47	16,074	18,022	1,948
			86	303	58,485	62,095	3,610
	V	W	82	41	8,158	8,596	438
			83	163	32,379	34,933	2,554
			84	165	37,550	40,100	2,550
MEXICO	O	E	83	25	9,373	11,058	1,685
PHIL R	V	E	81	519	106,148	112,125	5,977
			82	139	28,385	30,165	1,780
			83	95	20,530	21,812	1,282
			85	375	61,770	66,537	4,767
	V	W	82	21	4,369	4,562	193
			84	124	24,270	25,564	1,294
SINGAPR	V	E	82	26	18,432	21,813	3,381
			83	22	14,896	17,813	2,917
			84	504	102,818	113,327	10,509
			85	1,838	295,262	330,932	35,670
			86	4,803	819,657	911,225	91,568
	V	W	85	70	12,574	13,714	1,140
			86	596	102,924	112,919	9,995

2401440 PLYWD BRCH FC NO FIN EXC DM (MSF)

Country	Mode	Reg	Yr	Quantity	F.A.S.	C.I.F.	Charges
TOTAL			81	71,609	23,808,748	26,234,520	2,423,050
			82	51,252	17,977,961	19,711,720	1,733,759
			83	64,772	21,418,585	23,626,105	2,207,520
			84	73,107	25,610,936	27,853,951	2,243,015
			85	85,877	27,335,570	29,729,803	2,394,233
			86	70,565	23,734,218	25,741,161	2,006,943
BRAZIL	V	E	85	105	21,061	26,905	5,844
CANADA	O	E	81	1,651	893,061	893,061	
			82	2,449	1,278,715	1,278,715	
			83	3,619	1,989,217	1,989,217	

Crop
Product
TSUSA commodity number, description, and unit of quantity

Country	Mode	Reg	Yr	Quantity	F.A.S.	C.I.F.	Charges
			84	9,720	5,264,830	5,264,830	
			85	11,265	5,604,618	5,604,798	180
			86	9,812	5,515,369	5,515,369	
	O	W	81	610	357,504	357,504	
			82	1,257	709,458	709,458	
			83	22	26,224	26,224	
			84	465	284,583	284,583	
			85	985	583,203	583,203	
			86	418	263,833	263,833	
CHILE	V	E	82	179	12,550	15,218	2,668
CHINA T	A	E	81	5	2,880	5,132	2,252
	O	E	85	107	18,206	19,712	1,506
	O	W	82	3	1,366	1,366	
	V	E	81	15,689	3,526,143	3,799,097	267,218
			82	11,675	2,559,266	2,744,909	185,643
			83	14,921	3,219,806	3,462,452	242,646
			84	17,359	4,208,083	4,525,335	317,252
			85	21,742	4,188,700	4,547,638	358,938
			86	20,506	3,874,242	4,195,040	320,798
	V	H	81	13	8,672	10,028	1,356
			83	6	1,728	2,133	405
			85	21	11,347	14,086	2,739
			86	71	38,328	46,339	8,011
	V	W	81	2,505	637,755	674,308	36,553
			82	3,184	725,908	766,881	40,973
			83	4,601	1,109,483	1,177,093	67,610
			84	2,363	596,049	636,330	40,281
			85	4,149	771,151	822,227	51,076
			86	5,693	1,204,501	1,287,985	83,484
ECUADOR	V	E	85	160	41,454	51,956	10,502
			86	205	14,692	15,450	758
FINLAND	A	E	81	8	5,791	11,552	5,761
	A	W	81	8	5,791	7,412	1,621
	N	W	83	63	52,868	60,328	7,460
			85	4,089	2,187,324	2,549,645	362,321
			86	145	101,393	120,459	19,066
	O	W	82	23	19,032	21,157	2,125
	V	E	81	5,344	3,366,558	3,702,689	336,932
			82	3,850	2,410,236	2,672,547	262,311
			83	2,941	1,996,501	2,218,835	222,334
			84	5,177	1,982,729	2,220,413	237,684
			85	3,076	1,895,639	2,134,874	239,235
			86	6,200	3,264,359	3,701,207	436,848
	V	W	81	2,669	1,712,340	1,888,782	176,817
			82	1,296	859,706	952,041	92,335
			83	1,677	1,194,248	1,343,715	149,467
			84	2,303	1,387,675	1,603,930	216,255
			85	579	298,954	356,499	57,545
			86	3,057	1,886,419	2,175,989	289,570
JAPAN	A	E	84	4	3,990	5,645	1,655
	N	W	84	113	31,729	34,148	2,419
			85	2,767	744,796	802,132	57,336
	V	E	81	9,192	4,240,178	4,669,300	429,122
			82	8,834	4,062,157	4,496,117	433,960
			83	10,953	4,924,632	5,428,371	503,739
			84	9,137	4,332,201	4,761,386	429,185
			85	13,172	4,754,245	5,237,343	483,098
			86	4,828	2,155,327	2,362,333	207,006
	V	W	81	18,516	5,761,854	6,153,215	393,199
			82	12,620	3,855,785	4,130,306	274,521
			83	14,161	4,360,334	4,643,101	282,767
			84	13,676	4,150,772	4,416,016	265,244
			85	15,824	4,517,433	4,817,691	300,258
			86	13,416	3,818,403	4,057,273	238,870
KOR REP	V	E	83	623	141,444	151,028	9,584
			84	517	169,547	181,650	12,103
			86	64	13,120	14,264	1,144
	V	W	82	5	1,003	1,057	54
			83	272	63,271	66,842	3,571
			84	2,161	555,102	597,550	42,448
			85	897	204,576	220,129	15,553
			86	547	127,856	137,192	9,336
MALAYSA	V	E	82	38	27,648	32,521	4,873
			83	10	6,384	7,634	1,250
	V	W	81	100	59,904	72,197	12,293
			82	73	51,872	61,449	9,577
PHIL R	V	E	81	22	18,746	21,278	2,532
			82	11	9,584	10,642	1,058
			83	33	7,393	7,820	427
			84	86	22,121	23,921	1,800
			85	79	22,664	25,122	2,458
			86	22	4,544	5,012	468
	V	W	82	1	504	513	9
			83	134	42,438	51,595	9,157
SINGAPR	V	W	82	16	11,520	14,158	2,638
U KING	V	W	82	6	7,377	7,577	200
USSR	N	E	81	13,924	2,889,056	3,581,113	692,057
	O	E	83	97	27,695	31,507	3,812
			85	30	10,690	10,690	
	V	E	81	245	47,651	59,061	11,410
			82	4,105	1,062,936	1,366,109	303,173
			83	8,107	1,724,180	2,231,764	507,584
			84	7,929	2,102,478	2,615,752	513,274
			85	4,310	1,109,753	1,438,912	329,159
			86	5,282	1,389,733	1,763,321	373,588
	V	W	81	1,108	274,864	328,791	53,927
			82	1,627	311,338	428,979	117,641
			83	2,532	530,739	726,446	195,707
			84	2,097	519,047	682,462	163,415
			85	2,520	349,756	466,241	116,485
			86	299	62,099	80,095	17,996

2401460 PLYWD BRCH FC CL FIN OV DIM (MSF)

Country	Mode	Reg	Yr	Quantity	F.A.S.	C.I.F.	Charges
TOTAL			**81**	**18,684**	**9,911,764**	**10,648,175**	**736,923**
			82	**23,136**	**9,437,566**	**10,051,149**	**613,583**
			83	**31,737**	**12,342,201**	**13,219,714**	**877,513**
			84	**43,520**	**14,960,859**	**16,298,196**	**1,337,337**
			85	**38,821**	**14,390,832**	**15,761,688**	**1,370,856**
			86	**63,034**	**18,036,223**	**19,710,219**	**1,673,996**
BRAZIL	V	E	85	272	204,858	259,962	55,104
			86	99	101,156	128,890	27,734
C RICA	V	E	82	59	19,836	23,592	3,756
			83	104	22,930	26,901	3,971
			86	77	34,092	38,949	4,857
CANADA	N	W	81	*	361	361	
	O	E	81	4,263	2,377,131	2,377,131	
			82	4,666	2,677,348	2,677,348	
			83	5,031	3,031,470	3,031,494	24
			84	3,421	2,116,957	2,116,957	
			85	7,276	3,064,377	3,064,377	
			86	4,346	2,122,412	2,124,487	2,075
	O	W	84	27	15,210	15,210	
			85	184	94,337	94,337	
			86	393	227,974	227,974	
CHINA T	N	E	85	403	76,550	82,023	5,473
			86	7,177	1,330,831	1,434,494	103,663
	N	W	85	37	14,362	15,511	1,149
	V	E	81	3,392	763,889	818,122	54,233
			82	8,440	1,637,389	1,741,902	104,513
			83	12,000	2,215,876	2,346,424	130,548
			84	14,729	3,034,398	3,228,531	194,133
			85	14,401	2,619,846	2,829,891	210,045
			86	30,232	5,274,942	5,637,319	362,377
	V	H	83	3	2,099	2,575	476
			85	3	1,482	1,796	314
			86	2	1,702	2,143	441
	V	W	81	378	81,414	85,389	3,975
			82	561	100,907	107,013	6,106
			83	1,716	362,504	392,572	30,068
			84	2,342	491,055	523,500	32,445
			85	472	117,682	126,397	8,715
			86	2,197	442,962	475,235	32,273
ECUADOR	V	E	84	4,386	1,046,563	1,265,149	218,586
			85	311	79,910	101,131	21,221
			86	347	104,647	123,922	19,275
FINLAND	N	E	85	4,168	2,364,189	2,651,955	287,766
	N	W	85	2,042	872,728	998,655	125,927
	V	E	81	7,388	4,976,522	5,491,178	515,168
			82	5,309	3,186,827	3,522,146	335,319
			83	6,982	4,014,145	4,463,022	448,877
			84	12,262	6,106,222	6,806,009	699,787
			85	7,355	4,178,843	4,737,673	558,830
			86	13,551	6,377,031	7,285,454	908,423
	V	W	81	685	679,886	745,895	66,009
			82	355	400,188	438,137	37,949
			83	1,250	1,124,563	1,254,066	129,503
			84	306	285,687	325,943	40,256
			85	175	98,753	138,361	39,608
			86	962	711,149	823,304	112,155
JAPAN	N	E	85	194	68,337	75,218	6,881
	V	E	81	2,040	820,062	898,768	78,706
			82	3,211	1,243,345	1,354,592	111,247
			83	1,928	742,850	817,940	75,090
			84	3,110	910,492	997,605	87,113
			85	918	344,696	381,448	36,752
			86	1,960	777,387	845,865	68,478
	V	W	81	490	188,217	201,529	13,312

Crop
Product
TSUSA commodity number, description, and unit of quantity

Country	Mode	Reg	Yr	Quantity	F.A.S.	C.I.F.	Charges
			82	484	153,957	166,354	12,397
			83	1,481	494,745	528,276	33,531
			84	2,601	858,887	915,926	57,039
			85	542	169,692	181,354	11,662
			86	1,652	509,559	540,861	31,302
KOR REP	V	E	82	1	529	647	118
			83	428	85,069	90,809	5,740
			84	230	65,280	69,983	4,703
			85	67	16,096	17,094	998
	V	W	83	798	239,710	258,081	18,371
			84	90	23,868	25,860	1,992
MALAYSA	V	E	83	16	6,240	7,554	1,314
PHIL R	V	E	84	16	6,240	7,523	1,283
POLAND	V	E	81	48	24,282	29,802	5,520
			82	50	17,240	19,418	2,178
			86	39	20,379	21,322	943
U KING	V	W	85	1	4,094	4,505	411

Birch, veneer
2400020 BIRCH VENR NT REINF OR BCKD (MSF)

Country	Mode	Reg	Yr	Quantity	F.A.S.	C.I.F.	Charges
TOTAL			81	567,280	34,084,414	34,123,900	37,809
			82	464,323	25,783,332	25,795,058	11,726
			83	595,802	35,689,308	35,736,950	47,642
			84	488,061	33,972,635	34,038,098	65,463
			85	458,585	27,031,388	27,062,591	31,203
			86	503,746	31,397,558	31,452,726	55,168
AUSTRIA	A	E	82	1	826	1,018	192
BRAZIL	V	E	84	188	61,468	78,071	16,603
			86	3,227	217,430	237,777	20,347
CANADA	A	E	83	14	2,060	2,139	79
	A	W	86	101	7,100	8,029	929
	N	E	85	26,719	1,736,640	1,736,640	
	O	E	81	529,170	30,719,250	30,720,955	28
			82	437,409	23,768,818	23,768,818	
			83	569,402	33,781,377	33,781,377	
			84	450,936	30,028,939	30,028,942	3
			85	412,563	23,759,166	23,759,169	3
			86	445,520	27,019,284	27,019,284	
	O	W	81	35,675	3,012,912	3,012,912	
			82	26,148	1,835,541	1,835,541	
			83	22,293	1,600,723	1,600,723	
			84	33,366	3,548,008	3,548,008	
			85	15,444	1,238,112	1,238,112	
			86	49,525	3,730,146	3,730,146	
CHINA T	V	E	81	821	145,202	154,797	9,595
			82	456	91,402	97,740	6,338
			84	122	26,322	26,842	520
			85	127	15,883	17,521	1,638
	V	W	81	551	109,258	123,356	14,098
			83	153	31,071	32,941	1,870
			84	10	4,371	4,555	184
			85	16	6,912	7,040	128
ECUADOR	V	E	84	45	17,473	20,607	3,134
FIJI	O	W	83	317	12,748	14,933	2,185
	V	W	83	2,241	86,780	102,886	16,106
			86	633	26,355	30,679	4,324
FINLAND	A	W	81	15	1,849	2,509	660
	O	E	83	13	1,929	1,929	
			84	11	1,553	1,553	
			85	19	3,815	3,815	
			86	36	5,370	5,370	
	V	E	83	24	19,153	24,639	5,486
			84	437	54,914	61,871	6,957
			85	278	43,573	49,259	5,686
			86	399	70,206	78,797	8,591
FR GERM	A	E	86	585	19,626	24,852	5,226
	O	E	83	9	1,237	1,237	
			86	75	70,868	70,868	
	V	E	82	13	6,891	7,247	356
			86	43	68,101	73,294	5,193
	V	W	85	4	3,978	4,212	234
FRANCE	O	E	85	13	8,139	8,242	103
INDNSIA	V	E	84	1,753	93,240	118,592	25,352
			85	507	39,101	47,623	8,522
			86	666	46,186	49,660	3,474
ITALY	A	E	84	10	414	535	121
	N	E	81	269	5,269	6,202	933
	O	E	85	364	28,502	28,502	
N CALDN	O	E	85	354	18,205	18,205	
NORWAY	O	E	84	14	2,111	2,111	
PANAMA	V	E	81	158	14,279	16,350	2,071

Crop
Product
TSUSA commodity number, description, and unit of quantity

Country	Mode	Reg	Yr	Quantity	F.A.S.	C.I.F.	Charges
PHIL R	V	E	81	504	25,696	32,865	7,169
			83	691	16,781	20,354	3,573
			85	957	29,282	36,019	6,737
			86	244	8,557	10,399	1,842
	V	W	83	208	5,824	7,025	1,201
			85	1,088	18,704	23,417	4,713
REP SAF	O	E	82	114	7,867	7,867	
SINGAPR	V	W	82	29	3,814	3,879	65
SWEDEN	V	E	85	1	4,700	4,971	271
U KING	A	E	81	117	50,699	53,954	3,255
			82	114	52,098	56,179	4,081
			83	206	102,032	115,538	13,506
			84	1	312	399	87
			85	1	1,607	1,843	236
	A	W	82	13	5,016	5,428	412
			83	38	11,767	12,849	1,082
			84	446	30,712	34,099	3,387
	N	E	82	26	11,059	11,341	282
			83	*	1,063	1,176	113
			84	131	78,832	86,654	7,822
			86	2,632	71,456	74,616	3,160
	V	E	83	193	14,763	17,204	2,441
			84	591	23,966	25,259	1,293
			85	117	73,989	76,853	2,864
			86	60	36,873	38,955	2,082
	V	W	85	13	1,080	1,148	68

2403400 WOOD-VNER PANEL BIRCH (MSF)

Country	Mode	Reg	Yr	Quantity	F.A.S.	C.I.F.	Charges
TOTAL			81	828	358,774	362,702	3,928
			82	1,229	375,776	381,444	5,668
			83	6,092	1,519,321	1,760,799	241,478
			84	1,068	283,948	301,969	18,021
			85	1,769	557,402	598,538	41,136
			86	7,772	1,290,135	1,383,970	93,835
CANADA	O	E	81	604	306,443	306,443	
			82	940	285,240	285,240	
			83	1,156	275,074	280,740	5,666
			84	625	177,733	177,733	
			85	245	134,515	134,515	
			86	270	116,099	116,099	
	O	W	81	1	675	675	
			82	1	528	528	
			84	2	1,434	1,434	
			86	12	8,695	8,695	
CHINA T	O	E	82	98	21,118	21,118	
	V	E	83	463	87,161	92,013	4,852
			84	72	16,259	17,018	759
			85	113	22,405	24,023	1,618
			86	1,454	291,041	311,601	20,560
	V	W	81	207	42,667	44,903	2,236
			84	32	9,120	9,761	641
			85	84	17,907	18,849	942
FINLAND	V	E	81	12	5,867	7,112	1,245
			82	135	48,538	52,901	4,363
			83	618	375,519	418,293	42,774
			84	23	10,959	12,304	1,345
	V	W	81	4	3,122	3,569	447
			84	10	6,541	7,463	922
			85	76	45,460	57,624	12,164
ITALY	N	E	86	423	130,464	143,694	13,230
	V	E	85	271	63,674	70,303	6,629
			86	5,434	694,170	754,215	60,045
JAPAN	V	E	85	2	2,371	2,450	79
	V	W	82	55	20,352	21,657	1,305
			84	61	13,952	14,922	970
			85	978	271,070	290,774	19,704
KOR REP	V	W	83	43	8,439	8,883	444
MEXICO	O	E	86	179	49,666	49,666	
SWEDEN	V	E	83	47	44,314	48,424	4,110
U KING	V	E	83	13	16,412	19,532	3,120
USSR	O	E	83	1,593	319,351	397,031	77,680
			84	220	47,400	60,519	13,119
	V	E	83	2,159	393,051	495,883	102,832
			84	23	550	815	265

2405400 WD-VNER PANLS, 1 SIDE BIRCH (MSF)

Country	Mode	Reg	Yr	Quantity	F.A.S.	C.I.F.	Charges
TOTAL			81	752	28,524	28,562	38
			82	67	10,445	10,573	128
			83	81	17,511	18,691	1,180
			84	75	19,380	20,882	1,502
			85	148	46,341	47,941	1,600
			86	641	130,122	140,914	10,792

Crop Product TSUSA commodity number, description, and unit of quantity Country	Mode	Reg	Yr	Quantity	F.A.S.	C.I.F.	Charges
CANADA	O	E	81	750	27,932	27,932	
			82	59	7,008	7,008	
			83	36	7,204	7,204	
			84	3	2,624	2,624	
			85	110	24,401	24,401	
	O	W	86	3	1,877	1,877	
CHINA T	V	E	86	617	113,720	121,924	8,204
	V	W	83	44	8,941	9,969	1,028
			84	43	9,424	10,280	856
FINLAND	V	E	83	1	1,366	1,518	152
			85	10	15,000	15,675	675
			86	21	14,525	17,113	2,588
FR GERM	V	E	81	2	592	630	38
ITALY	V	E	82	8	3,437	3,565	128
			85	4	1,660	2,076	416
JAPAN	V	W	84	29	7,332	7,978	646
			85	24	5,280	5,789	509

Bitter Orange

Pettigrain, essential oil
4525600 PETTIGRAIN OIL (LB)

Country	Mode	Reg	Yr	Quantity	F.A.S.	C.I.F.	Charges
TOTAL			81	492,327	3,665,750	3,821,917	156,167
			82	324,106	2,137,589	2,237,980	100,391
			83	343,156	1,738,823	1,827,350	88,527
			84	211,918	1,354,377	1,417,557	63,180
			85	174,342	1,296,793	1,352,383	55,590
			86	268,276	1,472,460	1,570,441	97,981
BRAZIL	N	E	81	80,809	386,136	401,008	14,872
			83	23,832	146,411	153,998	7,587
			84	15,169	119,139	126,654	7,515
			85	34,123	366,197	380,723	14,526
	V	E	82	96,355	761,467	794,137	32,670
			86	61,683	275,200	288,905	13,705
C RICA	A	E	81	110	1,250	1,390	140
FRANCE	N	E	81	1,942	54,331	55,737	1,406
			82	1,346	24,919	25,519	600
			83	7,354	83,095	85,489	2,394
			84	7,118	100,679	103,405	2,726
			85	3,529	36,640	37,926	1,286
			86	3,195	57,024	58,428	1,404
HG KONG	V	E	81	88	674	708	34
INDNSIA	A	E	81	88	2,034	2,045	11
ITALY	A	E	82	545	17,933	19,403	1,470
			84	1,052	47,209	49,546	2,337
			85	3,538	178,545	183,843	5,298
	N	E	83	677	23,971	25,780	1,809
			86	3,118	201,472	234,512	33,040
	V	E	81	110	3,499	3,676	177
NETHLDS	A	E	81	33	913	1,048	135
			82	101	12,607	12,822	215
			83	55	1,789	1,858	69
			84	66	1,827	2,002	175
	N	E	86	3,857	67,389	69,015	1,626
PARAGUA	A	E	83	794	5,389	5,539	150
	V	E	81	401,583	3,156,159	3,293,254	137,095
			82	223,521	1,312,503	1,377,478	64,975
			83	309,427	1,461,992	1,537,954	75,962
			84	185,393	1,036,318	1,084,600	48,282
			85	132,602	708,300	742,443	34,143
			86	184,523	767,372	811,311	43,939
PORTUGL	V	E	86	2,381	10,356	10,981	625
SPAIN	A	E	83	165	6,062	6,301	239
			85	55	2,250	2,370	120
	N	E	84	497	20,095	20,595	500
			86	1,826	58,019	59,868	1,849
SWITZLD	A	E	81	220	2,450	2,509	59
			82	306	3,742	3,843	101
			83	808	7,511	7,819	308
			85	495	4,861	5,078	217
			86	507	4,318	4,515	197
	N	E	84	2,359	17,314	18,807	1,493
U KING	A	E	81	201	1,975	2,129	154
			86	44	1,440	1,490	50
	N	E	82	1,932	4,418	4,778	360
			84	264	11,796	11,948	152
	V	E	83	44	2,603	2,612	9
URUGUAY	V	E	81	7,143	56,329	58,413	2,084
			86	7,142	29,870	31,416	1,546

Blueberry

Blueberry, fresh or in brine
1465000 BLUEBERRIES, FRESH O IN BRNE (LB)

Country	Mode	Reg	Yr	Quantity	F.A.S.	C.I.F.	Charges
TOTAL			81	4,568,058	2,066,664	2,083,123	16,459
			82	9,247,926	5,054,241	5,083,366	29,125
			83	8,396,457	4,492,102	4,615,990	123,888
			84	8,986,281	3,484,369	3,735,812	251,443
			85	11,871,035	4,819,399	5,241,777	422,378
			86	10,579,271	5,452,774	6,155,379	702,605
AUSTRAL	A	W	84	2,159	9,336	10,569	1,233
			85	403	2,000	2,522	522
			86	2,066	8,250	9,797	1,547
	V	W	86	22,910	16,834	19,758	2,924
BRAZIL	O	W	84	10,240	3,891	3,891	
CANADA	A	E	85	2,600	3,400	4,204	804
	A	W	81	101	922	970	48
			84	14,791	4,552	5,922	1,370
			86	1,338	5,710	6,933	1,223
	O	E	81	4,404,526	1,890,184	1,890,184	
			82	7,384,372	3,722,067	3,722,067	
			83	7,538,820	3,558,909	3,558,909	
			84	7,773,187	2,203,543	2,209,475	5,932
			85	10,391,311	3,353,971	3,353,971	
			86	8,315,010	2,793,412	2,793,414	2
	O	W	81	140,497	100,498	100,498	
			82	1,821,395	1,189,339	1,189,339	
			83	690,325	551,368	551,368	
			84	862,553	462,727	462,727	
			85	764,144	524,126	524,126	
			86	1,136,382	910,111	910,111	
CHILE	A	E	83	1,148	2,610	3,502	892
			84	8,702	10,411	19,213	8,802
			85	2,236	2,857	5,308	2,451
			86	4,169	4,729	10,585	5,856
CHINA M	V	W	81	210	284	305	21
ECUADOR	V	W	85	217,660	15,186	20,268	5,082
FR GERM	V	E	83	1,178	1,064	1,152	88
			84	847	1,551	1,695	144
FRANCE	V	E	84	11,648	6,374	7,209	835
ITALY	V	E	84	1,531	3,978	4,230	252
	V	W	84	2,091	7,272	7,830	558
JAPAN	A	H	84	99	328	485	157
	A	W	83	476	1,393	2,112	719
	V	E	85	29,950	29,860	33,128	3,268
MEXICO	A	E	85	5,500	1,500	2,434	934
	O	E	86	3,360	1,008	1,008	
	O	W	83	7,200	576	576	
			86	9,600	1,260	1,260	
N ZEAL	A	E	81	4,845	16,777	20,524	3,747
			82	9,351	27,524	34,216	6,692
			83	38,196	99,932	134,902	34,970
			84	37,962	102,589	133,548	30,959
			85	28,415	59,205	87,857	28,652
			86	4,945	8,820	13,588	4,768
	A	H	81	221	750	1,169	419
			82	1,857	5,354	6,373	1,019
			83	2,298	6,105	7,288	1,183
			84	12,924	26,665	37,003	10,338
			85	11,071	26,453	36,118	9,665
			86	30,703	52,985	81,440	28,455
	A	W	81	17,658	57,249	69,473	12,224
			82	30,951	109,957	131,371	21,414
			83	112,590	258,683	340,524	81,841
			84	247,315	640,109	830,838	190,729
			85	20,113	44,421	61,233	16,812
			86	2,841	7,120	11,636	4,516
	N	H	86	5,482	10,584	14,313	3,729
	N	W	83	3,204	8,282	10,912	2,630
			85	362,402	735,097	1,085,580	350,483
			86	1,040,033	1,629,501	2,279,086	649,585
	O	E	86	432	2,450	2,450	
NETHLDS	A	E	83	1,022	3,180	4,745	1,565
	A	W	84	232	1,043	1,177	134
U KING	V	E	85	35,230	21,323	25,028	3,705

Blueberry, frozen
1466800 BLUEBERRIES , FROZEN (LB)

Country	Mode	Reg	Yr	Quantity	F.A.S.	C.I.F.	Charges
TOTAL			81	5,662,050	3,639,153	3,639,153	

Crop Product TSUSA commodity number, description, and unit of quantity Country	Mode	Reg	Yr	Quantity	F.A.S.	C.I.F.	Charges
			82	4,402,395	3,513,513	3,513,513	
			83	9,096,963	6,979,279	6,979,279	
			84	10,693,097	6,129,781	6,133,533	3,752
			85	10,216,254	5,875,564	5,875,736	172
			86	10,112,997	5,647,037	5,667,304	20,267
AUSTRAL	V	W	86	19,700	14,124	14,598	474
CANADA	N	W	81	2,269,235	1,210,389	1,210,389	
	O	E	81	3,392,815	2,428,764	2,428,764	
			82	2,266,788	1,896,581	1,896,581	
			83	6,460,200	5,004,301	5,004,301	
			84	5,939,911	3,667,548	3,667,548	
			85	5,451,565	3,004,094	3,004,094	
			86	7,918,109	4,217,129	4,217,129	
	O	W	82	2,135,607	1,616,932	1,616,932	
			83	2,636,763	1,974,978	1,974,978	
			84	4,748,229	2,447,855	2,447,855	
			85	4,761,849	2,869,334	2,869,334	
			86	1,997,860	1,311,711	1,311,711	
FRANCE	V	E	86	2,557	3,019	3,444	425
N ZEAL	A	W	84	4,957	14,378	18,130	3,752
	V	E	86	62,654	33,726	41,405	7,679
	V	W	86	109,260	65,611	77,121	11,510
SWEDEN	V	W	85	2,840	2,136	2,308	172
			86	2,857	1,717	1,896	179

Blueberry, prepared or preserved
1467900 BLUEBERYS PREP OR PRES NSPF (LB)

Country	Mode	Reg	Yr	Quantity	F.A.S.	C.I.F.	Charges
TOTAL			81	541,456	161,785	180,219	18,434
			82	192,640	177,255	184,361	7,106
			83	212,283	190,713	202,792	12,079
			84	311,995	217,139	241,077	23,938
			85	357,240	275,849	309,395	33,546
			86	551,978	428,702	453,447	24,745
AUSTRIA	V	E	82	600	827	903	76
			83	3,723	5,748	6,220	472
			84	5,990	6,879	7,722	843
			85	3,484	4,378	5,024	646
BELGIUM	V	E	84	505	397	443	46
CANADA	O	E	83	1,500	3,419	3,569	150
			85	2,640	1,986	1,986	
	O	W	81	67,497	57,739	57,739	
			82	131,118	104,228	104,228	
			83	58,923	50,331	50,331	
			84	31,111	28,568	28,568	
			85	87,314	54,021	54,021	
			86	256,996	192,811	192,811	
	V	E	85	2,914	2,761	3,136	375
ECUADOR	V	E	81	400,600	27,541	37,556	10,015
FR GERM	V	E	81	2,665	8,291	8,862	571
			82	1,200	1,009	1,090	81
			83	1,472	2,576	2,879	303
			84	5,603	4,020	4,574	554
			85	2,197	1,455	1,716	261
			86	1,402	1,570	1,676	106
FRANCE	N	E	81	6,136	9,441	10,328	887
	O	E	81	5,994	9,461	9,911	450
			82	5,576	9,491	9,966	475
			84	6,038	4,292	5,019	727
			85	1,964	1,899	2,250	351
			86	6,938	14,811	15,972	1,161
	V	E	81	29,047	29,255	32,223	2,968
			82	42,429	46,384	51,539	5,155
			83	98,349	97,643	106,144	8,501
			84	196,722	113,432	128,898	15,466
			85	194,879	155,718	179,534	23,816
			86	275,255	206,537	228,814	22,277
	V	W	84	51,837	38,201	43,039	4,838
			85	10,019	8,594	9,592	998
			86	1,376	2,210	2,517	307
ITALY	V	E	82	131	304	337	33
N ZEAL	A	W	85	2,266	8,992	10,585	1,593
NETHLDS	V	E	83	675	991	1,033	42
			84	675	922	968	46
POLAND	O	E	84	1,300	1,820	2,181	361
	V	E	81	15,347	5,689	7,370	1,681
			83	17,325	9,800	11,115	1,315
			85	39,729	23,596	27,980	4,384
			86	4,850	2,220	2,754	534
SWEDEN	V	E	82	1,553	1,664	1,895	231
SWITZLD	V	E	81	14,170	14,368	16,230	1,862

Country	Mode	Reg	Yr	Quantity	F.A.S.	C.I.F.	Charges
			82	10,033	13,348	14,403	1,055
			83	8,603	11,187	11,859	672
			84	6,881	8,908	9,341	433
			85	2,923	3,734	4,140	406
			86	3,506	5,380	5,618	238
	V	W	84	476	553	591	38
U KING	O	E	84	4,857	9,147	9,733	586
			85	6,761	7,493	8,015	522
			86	1,655	3,163	3,285	122
	V	E	83	21,713	9,018	9,642	624
	V	W	85	150	1,222	1,416	194

Bluegrass

Bluegrass (not Kentucky), seed
1261100 BLUEGRASS SEED, NSPF (LB)

Country	Mode	Reg	Yr	Quantity	F.A.S.	C.I.F.	Charges
TOTAL			81	168,463	118,150	134,282	16,132
			82	169,907	101,714	121,310	19,596
			83	186,091	116,135	133,135	17,000
			84	342,520	242,777	273,909	31,132
			85	500,826	399,875	450,559	50,684
			86	377,611	481,369	514,414	33,045
AUSTRAL	A	W	84	66	288	397	109
CANADA	O	W	81	2,660	1,130	1,130	
			84	4,850	48,500	48,500	
			85	800	4,313	4,313	
			86	2,900	25,400	25,400	
DENMARK	O	E	82	44,052	22,898	26,343	3,445
			83	57,787	35,600	39,108	3,508
			84	43,649	28,224	31,493	3,269
	V	E	81	137,203	97,496	109,365	11,869
			82	40,664	25,261	30,503	5,242
			83	41,693	25,201	30,073	4,872
			84	127,413	73,660	87,356	13,696
			85	198,787	158,085	172,825	14,740
	V	W	81	28,600	19,524	23,787	4,263
			82	82,991	49,630	60,064	10,434
			83	85,619	54,672	63,154	8,482
			84	155,046	83,215	97,079	13,864
			85	206,437	165,551	189,069	23,518
			86	208,699	254,222	277,007	22,785
FR GERM	A	W	84	55	289	348	59
	V	E	86	158,729	178,597	186,504	7,907
	V	W	84	11,441	8,601	8,736	135
FRANCE	V	W	85	121	1,242	1,271	29
MEXICO	O	W	86	5,740	17,220	17,220	
NETHLDS	V	E	82	2,200	3,925	4,400	475
	V	W	83	992	662	800	138
			85	79,081	52,276	62,535	10,259
SWEDEN	A	W	86	1,543	5,930	8,283	2,353
U KING	V	E	85	15,600	18,408	20,546	2,138

Kentucky bluegrass, seed
1260900 BLUEGRASS SEED KENTUCKY (LB)

Country	Mode	Reg	Yr	Quantity	F.A.S.	C.I.F.	Charges
TOTAL			81	12,621	13,798	14,782	984
			82	47,080	14,544	15,319	775
			83	110,503	53,390	57,411	4,021
			84	665,830	437,016	477,545	40,529
			85	1,658,964	1,375,968	1,506,267	130,299
			86	891,211	938,114	993,861	55,747
CANADA	O	E	81	3,000	1,612	1,612	
			82	44,800	11,952	11,952	
			83	88,200	34,106	34,106	
			84	93,000	35,950	35,950	
			85	152,945	166,204	166,204	
			86	121,498	139,254	139,254	
DENMARK	V	E	85	592,518	415,783	463,459	47,676
			86	174,972	172,921	182,289	9,368
	V	W	83	11,013	8,095	9,959	1,864
			85	127,864	133,974	145,501	11,527
			86	22,045	24,771	26,895	2,124
FR GERM	O	E	86	39,690	51,216	51,216	
	V	E	85	66,092	48,949	54,472	5,523
			86	118,328	103,298	111,813	8,515
	V	W	85	66,138	74,880	81,350	6,470
			86	88,184	101,543	109,807	8,264
NETHLDS	A	E	82	1,380	2,097	2,872	775

Crop Product TSUSA commodity number, description, and unit of quantity Country	Mode	Reg	Yr	Quantity	F.A.S.	C.I.F.	Charges
			83	737	1,248	1,788	540
			85	993	2,731	3,677	946
	A	W	85	440	1,320	1,623	303
	N	W	85	434,820	347,138	388,503	41,365
			86	200,807	203,769	221,876	18,107
	O	E	85	44,000	50,600	53,110	2,510
	O	W	82	900	495	495	
	V	E	84	44,000	26,430	28,140	1,710
			85	85,154	65,629	71,765	6,136
			86	46,315	53,756	56,655	2,899
	V	W	81	9,511	11,674	12,552	878
			83	7,026	6,699	7,445	746
			84	528,830	374,636	413,455	38,819
			85	88,000	68,760	76,603	7,843
			86	79,372	87,586	94,056	6,470
NORWAY	V	W	81	110	512	618	106
SWEDEN	V	W	83	3,527	3,242	4,113	871

Boxwood

Boxwood, lumber**
2023820 BOXWD, JAP MAPLE LBR, ROUGH (MBF)

Country	Mode	Reg	Yr	Quantity	F.A.S.	C.I.F.	Charges
TOTAL			81	56	109,223	120,790	11,567
			82	1	799	1,574	775
			83	12	17,044	18,985	1,941
			84	*	2,480	3,011	531
			85	4	9,189	10,484	1,295
			86	1	1,527	1,850	323
AUSTRAL	V	W	85	4	9,189	10,484	1,295
CANADA	O	E	81	1	470	470	
			83	2	714	714	
FR GERM	N	E	81	*	2,478	2,600	122
			84	*	2,480	3,011	531
	V	E	81	1	1,301	1,528	227
			86	1	1,527	1,850	323
	V	W	83	1	1,911	2,018	107
FRANCE	V	E	82	1	799	1,574	775
JAPAN	V	W	81	54	104,974	116,192	11,218
			83	9	14,419	16,253	1,834

2023840 BOXWD, JAP MAP LBR, DRESSED (MBF)

Country	Mode	Reg	Yr	Quantity	F.A.S.	C.I.F.	Charges
TOTAL			81	87	17,652	19,745	2,093
			82	6	2,194	2,338	144
			84	82	36,878	42,346	5,468
			85	60	15,771	17,664	1,893
BRAZIL	V	E	85	25	10,521	12,414	1,893
CANADA	O	E	84	14	4,867	4,867	
			85	35	5,250	5,250	
	O	W	82	5	710	710	
FR GERM	V	E	84	1	3,209	3,393	184
FRANCE	V	E	84	67	28,802	34,086	5,284
JAPAN	V	W	81	87	17,652	19,745	2,093
U KING	V	E	82	1	1,484	1,628	144

Boysenberry

Boysenberry, frozen
1467000 BOYSENBERRIES, FROZEN (LB)

Country	Mode	Reg	Yr	Quantity	F.A.S.	C.I.F.	Charges
TOTAL			81	915,387	267,703	388,278	120,575
			82	2,544,407	582,295	891,036	308,741
			83	2,047,501	465,392	689,788	224,396
			84	1,142,221	406,901	548,881	141,980
			85	3,009,237	1,606,061	1,965,456	359,395
			86	4,597,502	2,691,832	3,272,578	580,746
CANADA	O	W	86	26,666	20,135	20,135	
CHILE	A	E	83	3,089	2,389	6,289	3,900
	V	E	85	6,636	3,318	4,182	864
			86	36,139	20,282	24,455	4,173
CHINA M	V	W	82	14,020	5,117	5,583	466
CHINA T	V	W	81	496	536	557	21
FRANCE	V	E	82	1,488	3,148	3,321	173
MEXICO	O	E	83	4,176	3,028	3,028	
N ZEAL	O	E	82	33,399	9,583	13,360	3,777
	V	E	81	879,370	256,875	373,177	116,302

Crop Product TSUSA commodity number, description, and unit of quantity Country	Mode	Reg	Yr	Quantity	F.A.S.	C.I.F.	Charges
			82	1,803,678	393,609	608,973	215,364
			83	662,422	151,459	226,669	75,210
			84	609,426	203,005	271,942	68,937
			85	935,528	500,169	606,967	106,798
			86	1,279,560	721,434	878,542	157,108
	V	W	81	35,521	10,292	14,544	4,252
			82	691,822	170,838	259,799	88,961
			83	1,377,814	308,516	453,802	145,286
			84	532,795	203,896	276,939	73,043
			85	2,067,073	1,102,574	1,354,307	251,733
			86	3,255,137	1,929,981	2,349,446	419,465

Brazil Nut

Brazil nut, nut, shelled, prepared or preserved
1454200 BRAZIL NUTS, SHELLED (LB)

Country	Mode	Reg	Yr	Quantity	F.A.S.	C.I.F.	Charges
TOTAL			81	7,782,171	6,980,898	7,786,491	805,593
			82	7,665,276	10,680,559	11,564,799	884,240
			83	7,858,956	10,289,893	11,150,169	860,276
			84	9,007,354	8,417,993	9,417,640	999,647
			85	9,715,336	7,525,806	8,625,986	1,100,180
			86	9,817,947	8,111,444	9,162,320	1,050,876
BNGLDSH	V	E	86	35,640	30,294	33,490	3,196
BOLIVIA	N	E	81	2,241,666	1,791,775	1,964,950	173,175
	O	E	81	660	707	707	
			83	3,406	3,968	3,968	
	V	E	81	33,660	25,931	29,177	3,246
			82	1,051,710	1,336,578	1,434,091	97,513
			83	344,454	476,520	504,167	27,647
			84	725,234	745,217	814,929	69,712
			85	377,130	291,709	322,051	30,342
			86	526,279	469,839	527,478	57,639
	V	W	81	183,876	149,042	164,826	15,784
			82	350,695	474,735	505,806	31,071
			83	116,890	171,752	181,702	9,950
			84	19,800	17,820	19,481	1,661
			85	51,612	42,319	47,353	5,034
			86	176,550	140,100	160,997	20,897
BRAZIL	A	W	83	463	2,121	2,621	500
	N	E	81	3,468,274	3,324,048	3,725,059	401,011
			82	3,256,728	4,482,624	4,880,777	398,153
			83	4,023,364	5,286,342	5,746,795	460,453
			84	4,210,272	3,799,689	4,281,932	482,243
	O	E	82	1,628	2,930	2,930	
			83	11,880	18,414	18,414	
			84	13,376	10,856	10,856	
			85	15,840	6,970	6,970	
	O	W	82	44,000	18,000	18,000	
	V	E	81	1,194,787	1,122,164	1,274,698	152,534
			82	1,257,124	1,822,554	2,018,929	196,375
			83	1,297,652	1,618,111	1,789,887	171,776
			84	1,678,580	1,643,396	1,878,202	234,806
			85	6,478,465	4,875,416	5,683,899	808,483
			86	6,704,693	5,540,834	6,294,230	753,396
	V	W	81	35,500	26,197	29,434	3,237
			82	119,790	178,596	189,851	11,255
			83	24,958	40,920	46,030	5,110
			84	196,416	153,719	180,204	26,485
			86	27,500	88,130	89,663	1,533
CANADA	O	E	81	19,800	18,018	18,018	
			83	200	307	307	
			84	19,767	19,752	19,752	
CHILE	V	E	82	44,946	50,969	55,147	4,178
			83	362,637	466,415	500,067	33,652
			84	127,446	145,994	157,003	11,009
	V	W	86	68,640	60,055	67,298	7,243
CHINA M	V	W	85	35,000	42,439	45,000	2,561
ECUADOR	A	E	85	37,000	38,500	44,561	6,061
	V	E	83	59,928	72,767	78,574	5,807
			84	8,250	10,560	11,161	601
			85	13,000	5,940	6,267	327
INDIA	V	E	82	14,991	4,528	5,120	592
			83	15,000	25,002	26,244	1,242
			85	36,800	76,800	80,500	3,700
	V	W	83	145,000	236,942	251,905	14,963
			85	5,750	13,303	13,732	429
			86	6,500	21,127	21,494	367
ITALY	V	E	83	44,092	40,745	43,403	2,658
KOR REP	V	E	86	13,376	11,029	12,905	1,876

Crop Product TSUSA commodity number, description, and unit of quantity Country	Mode	Reg	Yr	Quantity	F.A.S.	C.I.F.	Charges
MALAYSA	V	E	86	33,069	66,799	70,300	3,501
MOZAMBQ	V	E	85	35,000	55,050	58,039	2,989
NETHLDS	V	E	86	33,069	24,000	26,500	2,500
PERU	N	E	81	438,270	368,555	407,854	39,299
	V	E	81	10,296	8,400	9,364	964
			82	1,166,982	1,600,111	1,703,867	103,756
			83	1,135,174	1,444,787	1,541,213	96,426
			84	1,634,292	1,478,162	1,613,364	135,202
			85	2,113,570	1,575,108	1,755,979	180,871
			86	1,769,583	1,322,151	1,468,995	146,844
	V	W	81	155,382	146,061	162,404	16,343
			82	83,424	144,914	153,703	8,789
			83	231,019	296,980	321,242	24,262
			84	268,158	250,374	276,311	25,937
			85	363,299	268,342	310,487	42,145
			86	416,985	323,219	374,722	51,503
REP SAF	V	E	85	32,500	51,583	54,035	2,452
TNZANIA	V	E	82	204,500	351,237	372,914	21,677
TURKEY	V	E	85	88,184	107,800	116,906	9,106
U KING	N	E	84	61,763	99,774	105,617	5,843
	O	W	85	2,866	8,294	8,294	
	V	E	82	68,758	212,783	223,664	10,881
			83	23,039	64,700	67,841	3,141
			84	44,000	42,680	48,828	6,148
			85	29,320	66,233	71,913	5,680
			86	6,063	13,867	14,248	381
USSR	V	E	83	19,800	23,100	25,789	2,689

Brazil nut, nut, unshelled
1451400 BRAZIL NUTS NOT SHELLED (LB)

Country	Mode	Reg	Yr	Quantity	F.A.S.	C.I.F.	Charges
TOTAL			81	14,238,545	6,494,451	7,722,198	1,227,747
			82	14,238,145	7,418,389	8,773,752	1,355,363
			83	15,466,241	7,154,025	8,557,340	1,403,315
			84	14,366,253	5,929,060	7,240,267	1,311,207
			85	19,735,398	7,670,329	9,495,233	1,824,904
			86	9,750,022	2,754,411	3,491,093	736,682
BOLIVIA	V	E	82	25,542	30,657	33,201	2,544
	V	W	81	110,230	33,069	44,744	11,675
			82	110,230	37,478	47,228	9,750
			83	153,315	56,038	68,754	12,716
			85	72,402	68,782	76,259	7,477
BRAZIL	N	E	83	226,600	156,161	180,665	24,504
	N	W	82	464,100	195,134	255,881	60,747
	O	E	81	56,946	46,244	46,244	
			82	12,500	10,592	10,592	
			83	57,405	17,712	18,209	497
			84	1,814	2,298	2,298	
			86	58,419	52,461	52,461	
	O	W	82	4,950	2,025	2,025	
			84	3,080	4,312	4,312	
			85	9,843	6,128	6,128	
			86	1,600	1,184	1,184	
	V	E	81	13,643,343	6,262,227	7,440,631	1,178,404
			82	13,245,955	6,974,757	8,224,652	1,249,895
			83	14,718,382	6,797,108	8,140,710	1,343,602
			84	13,547,056	5,600,958	6,838,577	1,237,619
			85	17,819,628	6,665,375	8,274,696	1,609,321
			86	9,485,463	2,601,251	3,326,132	724,881
	V	W	81	88,185	33,440	44,307	10,867
			83	2,100	4,788	5,525	737
			84	483,744	170,294	213,586	43,292
			85	1,640,700	785,956	950,200	164,244
CANADA	O	E	86	86,840	8,600	8,600	
DOM REP	V	E	84	36,000	3,300	4,980	1,680
FRANCE	A	E	85	13,086	6,790	7,997	1,207
INDIA	V	W	85	13,200	8,525	10,089	1,564
JAMAICA	A	E	82	1,800	1,178	1,743	565
PERU	N	W	85	28,765	23,639	25,237	1,598
	O	E	84	14,269	7,652	7,652	
			85	6,402	5,105	5,105	
	O	W	83	32,340	5,508	6,302	794
	V	E	81	220,460	77,162	93,006	15,844
			82	211,030	98,512	114,806	16,294
			83	276,099	116,710	137,175	20,465
			84	122,605	49,333	60,575	11,242
			85	83,189	59,245	67,595	8,350
			86	33,000	26,565	28,468	1,903
	V	W	81	119,381	42,309	53,266	10,957
			82	162,038	68,056	83,624	15,568
			84	144,485	78,624	94,137	15,513
			85	46,860	38,148	68,686	30,538

Crop Product TSUSA commodity number, description, and unit of quantity Country	Mode	Reg	Yr	Quantity	F.A.S.	C.I.F.	Charges
			86	84,700	64,350	74,248	9,898
U KING	A	E	85	1,323	2,636	3,241	605
	V	E	84	13,200	12,289	14,150	1,861

Breadfruit

Breadfruit, fresh or frozen**
1379300 PUMPKIN, BREADFRUIT, FR, CH, FZ (LB)

Country	Mode	Reg	Yr	Quantity	F.A.S.	C.I.F.	Charges
TOTAL			83	3,545,070	548,483	809,645	261,162
			84	9,000,155	1,496,357	1,970,867	474,510
			85	8,670,519	1,026,273	1,469,759	443,486
			86	8,322,921	1,142,138	1,489,117	346,979
BAHAMAS	V	E	86	37,125	2,475	4,617	2,142
BELGIUM	A	E	83	5,086	3,252	4,546	1,294
BRAZIL	A	E	84	317	951	1,931	980
C RICA	N	E	83	20,402	2,533	3,304	771
	V	E	83	1,500	360	385	25
			84	97,060	9,080	13,095	4,015
			85	141,527	16,215	25,901	9,686
			86	594,344	89,339	120,121	30,782
CANADA	O	E	83	50,000	4,328	4,328	
			84	215,948	3,423	3,423	
DOM REP	A	E	86	17,856	12,628	15,900	3,272
	N	E	83	2,327,370	382,902	544,960	162,058
			84	3,964,956	506,238	746,552	240,314
			85	7,357,709	803,590	1,137,577	333,987
			86	2,486,145	237,381	321,681	84,300
	V	E	83	184,515	19,775	30,700	10,925
			84	443,994	54,298	74,576	20,278
			85	337,240	34,231	48,328	14,097
			86	4,329,522	519,875	657,396	137,521
DOMINCA	V	E	86	13,058	2,415	2,805	390
ECUADOR	A	E	86	2,800	1,935	2,100	165
FR GERM	V	E	86	50,000	5,000	6,691	1,691
FRANCE	A	E	84	8,415	4,611	7,852	3,241
GRENADA	A	E	85	8,021	3,449	9,316	5,867
			86	3,100	2,441	7,306	4,865
GUATMAL	V	E	84	30,750	26,690	29,435	2,745
HAITI	A	E	86	16,792	4,038	6,829	2,791
	V	E	84	29,400	15,000	16,822	1,822
HONDURA	V	E	83	205,121	6,752	23,509	16,757
			86	40,000	4,096	7,049	2,953
ITALY	A	E	86	7,669	3,585	5,182	1,597
JAMAICA	A	E	83	56,052	8,843	17,107	8,264
			85	140,567	31,448	54,289	22,841
			86	51,017	9,400	16,150	6,750
	N	E	83	621,699	113,281	172,069	58,788
			84	2,103,713	371,512	564,337	192,825
			85	542,254	102,675	157,662	54,987
			86	296,959	69,564	95,465	25,901
	O	E	85	5,000	1,453	1,453	
	V	E	83	9,500	1,045	1,721	676
			86	133,995	26,763	32,276	5,513
JAPAN	V	E	84	220	253	285	32
			86	1,012	1,424	1,609	185
	V	W	84	660	556	592	36
			86	1,430	1,440	1,489	49
KOR REP	V	E	85	450	2,234	2,450	216
MEXICO	O	E	83	6,975	322	322	
			84	516,487	24,923	24,923	
			85	125,771	27,058	27,058	
	O	W	83	47,250	3,780	3,780	
			84	1,548,524	469,294	469,294	
			85	8,180	2,360	2,360	
			86	88,784	57,433	57,433	
N ANTIL	A	E	85	3,800	1,560	3,365	1,805
			86	2,039	1,599	2,031	432
S LUCIA	A	E	84	32,105	9,108	16,635	7,527
			86	2,953	3,368	4,818	1,450
S VN GR	A	E	86	77,549	60,173	84,346	24,173
	V	E	86	5,400	2,302	2,524	222
SPAIN	A	E	86	9,072	3,015	5,178	2,163
TRINID	A	E	86	44,817	15,319	22,265	6,946
TURKEY	V	E	86	9,483	5,130	5,856	726
VENEZ	A	E	83	9,600	1,310	2,914	1,604
			84	7,606	420	1,115	695

				Crop Product TSUSA commodity number, description, and unit of quantity			
Country	Mode	Reg	Yr	Quantity	F.A.S.	C.I.F.	Charges

Broccoli

Broccoli, fresh**
1379730 BROCCOLI, FRESH OR CHILLED (LB)

Country	Mode	Reg	Yr	Quantity	F.A.S.	C.I.F.	Charges
TOTAL			81	159,301	39,379	41,663	2,284
			82	121,768	19,462	19,462	
			83	364,168	105,337	107,039	1,702
			84	3,611,738	594,055	599,302	5,247
			85	4,461,754	703,151	712,244	9,093
			86	8,344,016	897,136	921,418	24,282
BELGIUM	V	E	81	1,896	1,183	1,408	225
CANADA	O	E	81	5,550	2,477	2,477	
			82	121,768	19,462	19,462	
			83	153,152	37,101	37,101	
			84	117,495	19,916	19,916	
			85	224,572	29,178	29,178	
			86	276,224	41,175	41,175	
	O	W	83	2,880	1,031	1,031	
			85	184,480	55,552	55,552	
			86	18,600	2,256	2,256	
	V	E	86	1,984	1,118	1,451	333
DOM REP	A	E	83	1,015	261	487	226
			84	6,325	1,153	2,520	1,367
	V	E	83	4,464	884	1,118	234
GUATMAL	A	E	84	1,300	260	495	235
	N	E	84	28,726	5,046	8,691	3,645
	V	E	81	19,010	6,114	8,173	2,059
			85	32,945	8,197	12,945	4,748
			86	17,556	4,743	5,599	856
ISRAEL	V	E	86	42,660	24,198	30,797	6,599
MALAYSA	O	W	85	7,680	2,473	2,473	
MEXICO	O	E	81	106,745	19,216	19,216	
			83	60,997	10,588	10,588	
			84	824,655	83,855	83,855	
			85	2,440,423	223,577	223,577	
			86	4,783,108	360,105	361,048	943
	O	W	81	26,100	10,389	10,389	
			83	139,920	54,222	54,222	
			84	2,633,237	483,825	483,825	
			85	1,571,654	384,174	388,519	4,345
			86	3,024,883	392,530	395,137	2,607
MONSRAT	O	E	86	22,659	2,510	2,510	
PERU	A	E	83	1,740	1,250	2,492	1,242
SALVADR	V	E	86	112,500	53,238	61,614	8,376
	V	W	86	43,842	15,263	19,831	4,568

1380520 BROCCOLI ETC FR, CUT SLICED (LB)

Country	Mode	Reg	Yr	Quantity	F.A.S.	C.I.F.	Charges
TOTAL			81	1,759,187	259,877	259,877	
			82	788,090	97,330	97,635	305
			83	96,558	10,822	10,822	
			84	2,352,600	330,778	330,856	78
			85	423,563	106,611	115,297	8,686
			86	8,726,602	808,713	820,373	11,660
ARGENT	V	E	85	88,350	53,010	57,621	4,611
BELIZE	A	E	86	3,585	2,430	3,025	595
CANADA	O	E	81	4,000	1,500	1,500	
			82	21,320	3,327	3,327	
			83	3,250	564	564	
			84	23,100	5,151	5,151	
			85	47,830	7,858	7,858	
			86	131,676	24,477	24,477	
	V	E	86	4,584	2,568	3,386	818
CHINA T	V	W	84	3,968	1,700	1,778	78
DOM REP	V	E	85	2,940	1,764	1,972	208
GUATMAL	N	E	82	1,730	831	1,136	305
	V	E	85	20,500	2,400	5,016	2,616
			86	89,700	10,132	20,379	10,247
MEXICO	A	E	85	1,000	1,250	1,427	177
	O	E	81	1,755,187	258,377	258,377	
			82	765,040	93,172	93,172	
			83	79,483	7,493	7,493	
			84	2,325,532	323,927	323,927	
			85	219,158	28,417	28,419	2
			86	8,497,057	769,106	769,106	
	O	W	83	13,825	2,765	2,765	
			85	23,256	4,152	4,152	
THAILND	V	W	85	20,529	7,760	8,832	1,072

Broccoli, frozen
1380540 BROCCOLI FZ REDUCE IN SIZE (LB)

Country	Mode	Reg	Yr	Quantity	F.A.S.	C.I.F.	Charges
TOTAL			81	27,822,940	9,599,582	10,063,745	466,555
			82	31,870,425	9,669,595	10,089,512	419,917
			83	33,550,808	10,964,155	11,367,631	403,476
			84	65,404,438	21,288,381	21,961,006	672,625
			85	77,147,296	25,665,550	26,719,638	1,054,088
			86	117,149,539	34,494,527	36,009,682	1,515,155
C RICA	A	E	85	85,391	50,022	58,689	8,667
CANADA	O	E	81	28,307	6,336	6,336	
			82	600	265	265	
			83	36,060	12,976	12,976	
			85	43,700	20,719	20,719	
			86	249,120	82,261	82,261	
	O	W	82	68,400	30,780	30,780	
			83	12,000	4,570	4,570	
			84	1,250	450	450	
	V	E	86	1,177	1,052	1,162	110
DOM REP	V	E	84	61,563	27,087	30,718	3,631
FRANCE	O	E	85	52,560	12,600	12,600	
			86	94,480	32,148	32,148	
GREECE	V	E	85	14,832	3,856	4,833	977
GUATMAL	N	E	81	1,853,825	576,014	746,835	170,821
			85	10,723,929	3,216,286	3,979,060	762,774
			86	6,434,082	2,539,333	3,090,876	551,543
	O	E	85	27,994	6,993	7,263	270
			86	159,415	24,535	25,075	540
	V	E	81	3,307,315	1,111,426	1,397,715	287,259
			82	4,667,988	1,527,432	1,946,022	418,590
			83	5,461,603	1,727,158	2,092,861	365,703
			84	10,023,182	3,432,980	4,101,968	668,988
			85	1,904,093	878,518	1,059,102	180,584
			86	11,530,275	3,194,885	4,001,087	806,202
	V	W	82	6,831	2,249	2,967	718
			83	103,284	30,432	43,064	12,632
GUYANA	V	E	85	25,500	6,885	8,684	1,799
HONDURA	V	E	82	5,763	2,252	2,861	609
ISRAEL	V	E	83	157,620	66,178	89,115	22,937
			85	13,478	7,576	9,188	1,612
			86	57,750	31,503	40,570	9,067
KIRIBAT	N	E	85	689,334	269,143	318,786	49,643
	V	E	86	10,512	2,628	3,534	906
MEXICO	N	E	85	59,387,004	19,777,941	19,785,481	7,540
	O	E	81	22,541,993	7,880,246	7,878,824	
			82	27,120,843	8,106,617	8,106,617	
			83	27,708,089	9,096,845	9,096,845	
			84	55,311,143	17,827,065	17,827,071	6
			85	3,942,033	1,349,767	1,374,617	24,850
			86	96,830,323	28,006,018	28,019,276	13,258
	O	W	83	39,011	14,473	14,473	
			84	7,300	799	799	
			85	46,743	15,687	15,687	
			86	6,400	1,016	1,016	
MONGOLA	O	E	86	17,280	8,813	8,813	
MONSRAT	O	E	86	31,350	8,402	8,402	
MOZAMBQ	O	E	86	77,868	19,397	19,397	
NETHLDS	V	E	86	9,700	4,712	6,261	1,549
NICARAG	V	E	81	91,500	25,560	34,035	8,475
PANAMA	V	E	86	160,838	51,421	62,908	11,487
SALVADR	V	E	85	180,705	49,557	64,929	15,372
			86	1,436,619	479,618	597,758	118,140
SEYCHEL	V	E	86	42,350	6,785	9,138	2,353
SPAIN	V	E	83	33,141	11,523	13,727	2,204

Broomcorn

Broomcorn
1925500 BROOMCORN (STN)

Country	Mode	Reg	Yr	Quantity	F.A.S.	C.I.F.	Charges
TOTAL			81	9,195	13,412,911	13,424,874	11,963
			82	7,570	12,594,056	12,672,569	78,513
			83	9,392	14,252,904	14,481,339	228,435
			84	8,915	12,071,957	12,132,453	60,496
			85	9,562	9,946,695	9,979,379	32,684
			86	8,434	7,048,246	7,075,030	26,784
ARGENT	V	E	83	191	120,680	169,463	48,783
CANADA	O	E	81	14	20,604	20,604	
			84	24	5,856	5,856	

Crop Product TSUSA commodity number, description, and unit of quantity Country	Mode	Reg	Yr	Quantity	F.A.S.	C.I.F.	Charges
			85	16	2,473	2,473	
DJIBUTI	V	E	85	100	166,486	182,327	15,841
			86	32	54,801	62,399	7,598
DOM REP	V	E	86	48	65,355	76,749	11,394
ETHIOP	V	E	84	45	72,106	104,727	32,621
			86	45	54,245	61,837	7,592
FR GERM	V	E	83	43	55,961	66,255	10,294
FRANCE	V	E	85	26	52,156	59,727	7,571
HUNGARY	V	E	81	10	12,008	15,000	2,992
			82	248	288,523	336,442	47,919
			83	674	798,220	948,406	150,186
			84	57	90,725	105,219	14,494
			85	10	8,716	12,867	4,151
	V	W	83	10	13,407	16,472	3,065
ITALY	V	E	81	10	4,495	6,160	1,665
			83	20	29,287	34,033	4,746
			84	18	27,063	32,039	4,976
LESOTHO	V	E	82	128	67,903	91,501	23,598
			83	61	35,987	47,348	11,361
			84	13	6,941	9,477	2,536
			85	13	7,910	10,530	2,620
MEXICO	O	E	81	9,120	13,359,524	13,359,524	
			82	7,155	12,218,157	12,218,157	
			83	8,354	13,166,709	13,166,709	
			84	8,282	11,394,785	11,394,785	
			85	9,340	9,642,751	9,642,751	
			86	8,307	6,855,157	6,855,165	8
	O	W	83	39	32,653	32,653	
			84	448	454,008	454,008	
			85	25	30,195	30,195	
			86	2	1,285	1,285	
MOROC	O	E	85	10	18,014	18,014	
MOZAMBQ	O	E	85	9	7,332	7,332	
N ZEAL	N	W	86	*	17,403	17,595	192
PANAMA	V	E	81	4	6,905	7,705	800
			84	2	6,454	7,256	802
REP SAF	V	E	81	13	6,655	8,935	2,280
			82	39	19,473	26,469	6,996
			84	26	14,019	19,086	5,067
			85	13	10,662	13,163	2,501
TNZANIA	V	E	81	24	2,720	6,946	4,226

Brussels Sprouts

Brussels sprouts, fresh
1377120 BRUSSEL SPROUTS, FRSH, CHLD (LB)

Country	Mode	Reg	Yr	Quantity	F.A.S.	C.I.F.	Charges
TOTAL			81	8,314,090	1,632,184	1,632,566	382
			82	8,009,806	1,520,190	1,524,589	4,399
			83	6,922,131	1,673,977	1,677,559	3,582
			84	10,805,753	1,598,446	1,602,391	3,945
			85	12,060,864	2,067,699	2,067,789	90
			86	10,826,873	1,891,212	1,892,452	1,240
BELGIUM	A	E	83	642	415	576	161
CANADA	O	E	82	4,000	3,178	3,178	
			83	242,201	37,332	37,332	
	O	W	86	122,975	20,620	20,620	
CHILE	A	E	84	1,257	504	1,310	806
FRANCE	A	E	83	2,508	1,124	2,172	1,048
	O	W	86	21,900	2,453	2,453	
GUATMAL	A	E	84	4,330	1,590	2,779	1,189
	N	E	81	4,491	1,770	2,152	382
	V	E	83	15,960	4,965	6,485	1,520
			84	39,163	12,148	14,098	1,950
			86	21,600	3,600	3,816	216
MEXICO	O	E	81	988,975	137,271	137,271	
			82	692,074	71,447	72,102	655
			83	248,589	28,966	28,966	
			84	850,139	111,569	111,569	
			85	1,330,923	157,056	157,146	90
			86	417,971	50,405	50,405	
	O	W	81	7,320,624	1,493,143	1,493,143	
			82	7,308,892	1,443,616	1,446,063	2,447
			83	6,408,986	1,599,954	1,599,954	
			84	9,910,864	1,472,635	1,472,635	
			85	10,729,941	1,910,643	1,910,643	
			86	10,240,829	1,812,292	1,812,292	
NETHLDS	A	E	82	4,840	1,949	3,246	1,297
			83	3,245	1,221	2,074	853
SWITZLD	A	E	86	1,598	1,842	2,866	1,024

Brussels sprouts, frozen
1377140 BRUSSELS SPROUTS, FROZEN (LB)

Country	Mode	Reg	Yr	Quantity	F.A.S.	C.I.F.	Charges
TOTAL			81	3,982,366	1,613,815	1,696,144	82,329
			82	3,773,708	1,535,838	1,690,144	154,306
			83	5,729,805	2,097,118	2,282,946	185,828
			84	8,067,324	2,749,683	2,980,769	231,086
			85	7,913,409	2,507,798	2,800,888	293,090
			86	4,502,003	1,256,904	1,409,699	152,795
BELGIUM	O	E	84	88,845	21,353	24,486	3,133
			85	335,449	77,435	95,004	17,569
			86	25,184	10,755	12,087	1,332
	V	E	84	40,798	10,405	12,709	2,304
			85	443,939	102,833	137,321	34,488
			86	211,732	53,576	65,674	12,098
CANADA	O	E	81	20,300	9,653	9,653	
			82	10,643	5,253	5,253	
			83	20,438	9,475	9,475	
			84	377,298	123,981	123,981	
			85	11,400	4,913	4,913	
			86	15,000	6,667	6,667	
	O	W	82	392,400	124,201	198,649	74,448
			83	1,174,091	389,756	389,756	
			84	1,416,633	478,777	478,777	
			85	1,494,310	511,401	511,401	
			86	41,800	14,455	14,455	
DOM REP	V	E	84	1,280	576	654	78
FRANCE	O	E	84	44,092	11,244	13,744	2,500
	V	E	84	22,050	4,974	6,512	1,538
GUATMAL	N	E	81	367,836	115,863	148,671	32,808
			85	3,213,235	1,066,231	1,234,008	167,777
	O	E	81	2,394	766	945	179
			85	17,880	2,861	2,861	
	V	E	81	91,116	28,374	35,051	6,677
			82	804,697	270,887	349,976	79,089
			83	2,642,660	891,134	1,066,142	175,008
			84	3,443,635	1,161,238	1,351,178	189,940
			85	18,613	4,281	5,497	1,216
			86	2,019,388	500,033	618,002	117,969
	V	W	82	7,294	2,438	3,207	769
			86	42,000	12,040	15,540	3,500
MALAYSA	O	E	86	44,000	11,097	11,097	
MEXICO	O	E	81	3,253,805	1,353,463	1,353,463	
			82	2,558,674	1,133,059	1,133,059	
			83	1,719,230	764,328	764,328	
			84	2,155,054	816,584	816,584	
			85	1,207,250	461,977	461,977	
			86	1,811,848	555,387	555,388	1
	O	W	86	21,216	8,160	8,160	
	V	E	83	18,261	5,920	7,213	1,293
NETHLDS	O	E	85	89,758	30,192	33,320	3,128
	O	W	84	1,100	671	671	
	V	E	84	306,365	73,879	90,962	17,083
			85	710,056	160,283	206,942	46,659
			86	220,670	63,783	75,248	11,465
NORWAY	V	E	85	42,864	9,011	12,009	2,998
SINGAPR	V	W	83	1,525	3,089	3,337	248
			84	5,390	6,657	6,990	333
SPAIN	O	E	85	88,570	19,741	19,741	
	V	E	85	42,168	11,631	16,740	5,109
THAILND	V	W	85	13,888	13,365	16,570	3,205
			86	7,165	10,031	11,421	1,390
U KING	V	E	83	153,600	33,416	42,695	9,279
			84	164,784	39,344	53,521	14,177
			85	184,029	31,643	42,584	10,941
			86	42,000	10,920	15,960	5,040
	V	W	81	246,915	105,696	148,361	42,665

Buchu

Buchu, leaf, natural drug**
4350500 ALOES JALAP MATE ETC, CRUDE (LB)
(See Aloe, natural drug under Aloe)
4351000 ALOES,JALAP MANA,ETC ADVANCE (LB)
(See Aloe, natural drug under Aloe)

Crop / Product / TSUSA commodity number, description, and unit of quantity / Country	Mode	Reg	Yr	Quantity	F.A.S.	C.I.F.	Charges

Buckwheat

Buckwheat, hulled or unhulled
1301500 BUCKWHEAT, HULLD OR NT HULLD (CWT)

Country	Mode	Reg	Yr	Quantity	F.A.S.	C.I.F.	Charges
TOTAL			81	61,553	1,127,134	1,211,083	83,949
			82	107,521	1,385,778	1,514,402	128,624
			83	55,671	728,988	728,988	
			84	14,116	192,861	192,869	8
			85	6,734	88,156	88,156	
			86	44,498	559,911	594,441	34,530
BRAZIL	V	E	81	24,691	371,526	453,159	81,633
			82	77,160	856,158	984,115	127,957
			86	9,664	82,295	86,245	3,950
CANADA	O	E	81	36,228	741,225	741,225	
			82	29,508	514,795	514,795	
			83	54,721	699,943	699,943	
			84	14,116	192,861	192,869	8
			85	6,514	84,200	84,200	
			86	27,276	341,574	341,574	
	O	W	81	196	3,483	3,483	
			82	450	5,850	5,850	
			83	950	29,045	29,045	
			85	220	3,956	3,956	
			86	2,724	62,689	62,689	
CHINA M	V	W	86	3,953	49,331	72,842	23,511
FR GERM	O	E	82	100	1,842	1,842	
JAPAN	V	E	86	37	2,045	2,821	776
POLAND	V	E	86	396	12,600	14,800	2,200
USSR	V	E	81	438	10,900	13,216	2,316
			82	289	6,821	7,335	514
			86	448	9,377	13,470	4,093
	V	W	82	14	312	465	153

Buckwheat, milled for humans
1311500 BUCKWHEAT, MILLED, EDIBLE (LB)

Country	Mode	Reg	Yr	Quantity	F.A.S.	C.I.F.	Charges
TOTAL			81	229,298	62,889	64,251	1,362
			82	565,875	94,842	95,907	1,065
			83	143,964	30,541	33,095	2,554
			84	59,179	22,468	27,610	5,142
			85	121,041	25,294	28,269	2,975
			86	21,700	2,885	2,885	
BRAZIL	A	W	85	772	8,610	10,122	1,512
CANADA	O	E	81	197,154	52,148	52,148	
			82	544,218	88,014	88,014	
			83	115,053	15,614	15,616	2
			84	8,091	984	984	
			85	94,532	8,114	8,114	
			86	15,100	1,284	1,284	
	O	W	84	463	3,785	3,785	
INDIA	O	E	81	882	433	474	41
JAPAN	V	E	84	7,101	5,450	6,444	994
	V	H	81	2,910	1,364	1,602	238
			82	1,715	1,078	1,214	136
			83	5,828	3,590	4,205	615
			84	3,864	4,123	4,598	475
	V	W	81	825	926	999	73
			83	268	257	285	28
KOR REP	V	E	82	1,200	932	1,067	135
			83	9,312	8,006	8,802	796
			85	10,305	5,770	6,413	643
	V	W	81	201	766	819	53
			82	300	685	720	35
U KING	O	E	81	3,946	1,788	1,971	183
			83	2,480	1,036	1,139	103
			84	2,469	1,298	1,444	146
USSR	N	E	82	13,228	2,940	3,239	299
	O	E	81	23,380	5,464	6,238	774
			82	5,214	1,193	1,653	460
			86	6,600	1,601	1,601	
	V	E	83	11,023	2,038	3,048	1,010
			84	21,759	3,978	6,017	2,039
			85	15,432	2,800	3,620	820
	V	W	84	15,432	2,850	4,338	1,488

Buckwheat, milled not for humans
1315700 BUCKWHIT MLD NOT FOR HUM CONS (CWT)

C

Cabbage

Cabbage, fresh or frozen
1353000 CABBAGE, FRESH, CHLLD, FROZN (LB)

Country	Mode	Reg	Yr	Quantity	F.A.S.	C.I.F.	Charges
TOTAL			81	5,881,866	614,152	620,678	6,526
			82	26,574,115	2,370,524	2,783,861	413,337
			83	30,805,354	2,442,434	2,651,280	208,846
			84	143,191,581	13,054,638	14,476,944	1,422,306
			85	39,097,659	4,125,066	4,370,531	245,465
			86	28,044,663	2,956,006	3,009,160	53,154
ARGENT	V	E	84	66,138	21,000	28,209	7,209
BAHAMAS	N	E	84	20,150	4,316	4,641	325
	V	E	85	22,193	4,335	5,218	883
BELGIUM	A	E	82	2,049	3,167	4,317	1,150
			83	20,312	20,419	25,207	4,788
			85	20,713	32,486	43,522	11,036
			86	21,958	43,163	57,387	14,224
	A	W	82	260	337	480	143
	N	E	84	103,095	39,010	53,189	14,179
C RICA	V	E	82	144,600	41,368	51,766	10,398
			84	291,937	32,614	49,558	16,944
CANADA	A	H	84	5,750	1,065	1,885	820
	O	E	81	4,222,986	372,572	372,572	
			82	5,828,234	487,708	488,255	547
			83	13,094,477	1,288,501	1,288,501	
			84	20,261,994	3,752,235	3,753,465	1,230
			85	18,482,080	2,001,772	2,001,850	78
			86	24,140,984	2,579,529	2,579,529	
	O	W	82	2,100	672	672	
			84	35,995	3,883	3,883	
			85	166,500	10,681	10,681	
			86	707,736	85,229	85,229	
	V	E	86	40,000	4,000	6,228	2,228
CHILE	A	E	86	3,819	1,906	3,823	1,917
DOM REP	A	E	83	2,061	1,131	1,848	717
			84	10,330	1,033	2,093	1,060
	N	E	84	1,431,172	107,415	171,070	63,655
	V	E	84	212,771	32,000	49,223	17,223
			85	19,000	1,300	1,550	250
			86	66,098	14,962	18,256	3,294
ECUADOR	O	E	82	13,000	648	648	
FR GERM	O	E	84	171,950	45,634	45,634	
	V	E	84	381,473	72,320	90,514	18,194
			85	640,000	41,450	44,443	2,993
FRANCE	A	E	82	3,247	5,493	6,364	871
			83	2,403	1,795	2,738	943
			84	3,207	4,990	7,085	2,095
			85	724	1,027	1,316	289
GUATMAL	V	E	81	101,350	6,054	10,951	4,897
			82	50,500	5,555	7,636	2,081
			84	548,315	72,314	100,470	28,156
			85	40,250	9,525	14,860	5,335
			86	127,948	33,444	44,918	11,474
HONDURA	O	E	85	18,750	1,368	1,368	
	V	E	84	124,580	13,128	21,269	8,141
ITALY	A	E	82	86,511	27,986	38,902	10,916
			83	585,095	291,959	398,444	106,485
			84	463,852	506,585	734,643	228,058
			85	2,974	5,368	7,478	2,110
	N	E	85	237,307	366,434	511,675	145,241
JAMAICA	A	E	84	9,970	1,866	4,796	2,930
JAPAN	O	E	84	21,240	969	969	
	V	E	84	96,000	10,272	15,484	5,212
MEXICO	O	E	81	8,000	320	320	
			82	10,235,615	472,775	472,775	
			83	10,541,318	145,672	145,672	

Crop
Product
TSUSA commodity number, description, and unit of quantity

Country	Mode	Reg	Yr	Quantity	F.A.S.	C.I.F.	Charges
			84	92,604,332	4,453,882	4,453,882	
			85	8,714,818	289,035	289,271	236
			86	858,202	41,551	41,551	
	O	H	82	35,549	865	865	
	O	W	81	1,509,530	229,326	229,326	
			82	2,927,251	367,270	367,270	
			83	4,706,402	565,639	565,645	6
			84	8,437,428	1,011,942	1,011,942	
			85	6,999,275	1,017,909	1,017,909	
			86	1,190,093	79,246	79,246	
MONSRAT	O	W	85	26,537	3,846	3,846	
MOZAMBQ	O	W	85	23,860	4,010	4,010	
N ANTIL	V	E	84	90,000	10,086	15,134	5,048
NETHLDS	N	E	82	6,882,699	892,634	1,259,572	366,938
			83	1,642,252	113,961	197,103	83,142
			84	15,874,201	2,478,269	3,402,563	924,294
	O	E	84	868,050	199,763	206,704	6,941
			85	431,500	57,490	57,490	
	V	E	81	40,000	5,880	7,509	1,629
			82	362,500	64,046	84,339	20,293
			83	210,000	12,577	24,666	12,089
			84	1,026,051	174,887	243,199	68,312
			85	3,065,966	262,057	338,700	76,643
			86	886,800	71,579	91,010	19,431
NIGER	V	E	85	160,000	9,600	9,782	182
PANAMA	V	E	84	31,600	3,160	5,440	2,280
SENEGAL	A	E	85	25,212	5,373	5,562	189
SPAIN	A	E	86	1,025	1,397	1,983	586
SWITZLD	A	E	83	1,034	780	1,456	676

Cabbage, prepared or preserved
1413000 CABBAGE PREP,PRES,EXC SAUKRT (LB)

Country	Mode	Reg	Yr	Quantity	F.A.S.	C.I.F.	Charges
TOTAL			81	185,653	97,246	109,974	12,728
			82	411,945	162,337	182,036	19,699
			83	264,191	117,387	137,181	19,794
			84	503,389	190,347	217,705	27,358
			85	748,425	226,422	278,951	52,529
			86	831,003	318,431	375,755	57,324
AUSTRIA	V	W	83	925	667	689	22
BELGIUM	V	E	82	1,831	705	850	145
			83	2,000	1,879	2,060	181
			84	22,532	8,235	9,217	982
			85	63,878	21,714	26,253	4,539
			86	52,372	24,090	27,905	3,815
	V	W	84	1,872	849	1,022	173
CANADA	O	E	81	5,625	3,778	3,778	
			82	22,250	3,262	3,262	
			84	25,500	4,416	4,416	
			85	82,450	7,251	7,251	
			86	1,500	1,050	1,050	
	O	W	82	8,750	4,806	4,806	
CHINA M	V	E	81	585	330	363	33
			83	1,102	260	333	73
			84	8,454	5,203	6,328	1,125
			86	18,016	6,323	7,121	798
	V	H	84	1,575	1,154	1,267	113
			86	4,440	1,079	1,221	142
	V	W	81	21,761	10,282	11,146	864
			82	81,028	35,073	38,471	3,398
			83	23,854	9,945	10,836	891
			84	57,291	33,084	36,369	3,285
			85	18,787	9,921	10,838	917
			86	38,673	19,407	20,996	1,589
CHINA T	V	E	81	5,489	3,788	4,201	413
			82	5,470	5,883	6,528	645
			83	8,100	5,680	7,021	1,341
			84	7,540	4,432	5,063	631
			85	29,616	9,863	11,609	1,746
			86	20,550	19,523	21,351	1,828
	V	H	82	2,070	1,415	1,562	147
			85	3,157	1,365	1,517	152
	V	W	81	8,953	4,705	5,006	301
			82	27,155	18,960	20,425	1,465
			83	19,169	13,678	14,885	1,207
			84	4,380	2,682	2,933	251
			85	1,181	1,050	1,123	73
			86	26,495	17,595	19,487	1,892
CZECHO	O	E	81	2,025	623	784	161
DENMARK	V	E	85	2,822	1,181	1,548	367
	V	W	81	3,294	2,158	2,444	286
			85	627	1,762	1,955	193
			86	6,300	2,229	2,477	248
FR GERM	N	E	81	41,185	24,086	26,379	2,293
			82	14,995	7,221	8,434	1,213
	N	W	83	4,279	2,562	3,393	831
	O	E	81	14,234	7,719	9,469	1,750
			83	9,354	4,570	5,228	658
			84	5,114	2,278	2,577	299
			85	37,408	13,225	16,294	3,069
			86	11,444	5,936	6,615	679
	V	E	81	8,903	4,364	4,892	528
			82	62,931	30,804	34,570	3,766
			83	127,547	52,695	61,420	8,725
			84	274,386	89,139	103,789	14,650
			85	260,504	80,958	103,467	22,509
			86	260,081	107,728	126,656	18,928
	V	W	81	13,851	6,677	7,843	1,166
			82	58,650	13,442	14,636	1,194
			83	10,121	4,108	5,293	1,185
			84	34,285	11,414	13,599	2,185
			85	58,374	24,299	30,958	6,659
			86	33,507	13,265	15,473	2,208
FRANCE	O	E	86	848	3,918	3,918	
GUATMAL	V	E	85	64,425	28,992	33,919	4,927
			86	194,539	29,066	45,416	16,350
HG KONG	V	E	84	15,249	6,069	6,865	796
	V	H	86	850	1,074	1,180	106
	V	W	81	2,401	1,092	1,230	138
			82	7,006	4,189	4,570	381
			83	472	372	451	79
			84	1,587	950	1,171	221
			86	13,860	11,550	12,275	725
HUNGARY	V	E	82	66,000	11,160	14,400	3,240
JAPAN	V	E	81	402	619	675	56
			82	605	545	592	47
	V	W	82	2,640	1,695	1,778	83
			84	692	805	914	109
			86	16,012	12,178	13,654	1,476
KOR REP	V	E	83	900	581	620	39
	V	H	85	3,720	1,719	2,160	441
	V	W	81	14,940	10,899	11,580	681
			83	900	606	671	65
NETHLDS	O	E	86	19,044	5,812	5,892	80
	V	E	81	2,403	789	890	101
			82	2,867	1,039	1,149	110
			83	165	733	802	69
			85	22,038	5,141	7,025	1,884
			86	13,287	3,100	3,635	535
	V	W	81	1,532	539	584	45
			83	7,771	3,052	3,354	302
			84	5,632	1,675	1,904	229
			85	1,705	1,176	1,291	115
POLAND	O	E	82	9,600	2,720	4,014	1,294
			83	17,942	4,774	6,205	1,431
			84	3,770	928	1,296	368
	V	E	81	25,425	6,481	9,697	3,216
			82	6,434	1,353	1,665	312
			83	20,880	5,568	7,737	2,169
			84	11,148	3,117	3,879	762
			85	14,876	3,936	5,318	1,382
			86	7,585	1,920	2,545	625
ROMANIA	V	E	86	27,778	4,551	5,938	1,387
SWEDEN	V	E	81	2,528	2,512	2,642	130
			82	17,172	11,853	12,706	853
			83	3,274	2,823	3,116	293
			84	634	399	399	
			86	24,198	5,437	7,737	2,300
	V	W	82	1,298	896	1,052	156
			84	1,456	662	741	79
SWITZLD	V	E	84	4,032	2,688	2,970	282
THAILND	O	W	86	3,175	1,380	1,511	131
	V	E	81	838	340	441	101
			82	1,905	765	969	204
			83	608	328	359	31
	V	W	81	8,094	4,563	4,936	373
			82	9,981	3,950	4,961	1,011
			83	3,967	1,750	1,880	130
			84	13,041	7,903	8,501	598
			85	82,857	12,869	16,425	3,556
			86	36,449	20,220	21,702	1,482
TURKEY	V	E	84	3,219	2,265	2,485	220
U KING	V	W	81	1,185	902	994	92
			82	1,307	601	636	35
			83	861	756	828	72

Crop / Product / TSUSA commodity number, description, and unit of quantity							
Country	Mode	Reg	Yr	Quantity	F.A.S.	C.I.F.	Charges

Cabbage, seed
1261500 CABBAGE SEED (LB)

Country	Mode	Reg	Yr	Quantity	F.A.S.	C.I.F.	Charges
TOTAL			81	19,251	524,256	554,325	29,919
			82	16,877	690,188	711,664	21,476
			83	24,431	1,039,552	1,071,994	32,442
			84	35,359	966,777	998,144	31,367
			85	28,534	984,023	1,005,565	21,542
			86	28,479	888,348	910,336	21,988
AUSTRAL	A	H	86	438	10,945	11,376	431
	A	W	85	163	5,093	5,239	146
			86	1,423	38,610	39,751	1,141
CANADA	N	E	81	138	1,942	1,991	29
	O	E	82	10	900	900	
			84	8	358	358	
CHILE	V	W	85	955	2,627	2,685	58
CHINA M	A	H	83	120	448	845	397
	V	E	83	50	418	422	4
	V	H	85	1,800	3,410	3,676	266
	V	W	81	350	1,125	1,168	43
			82	990	2,849	3,096	247
			83	350	1,974	2,038	64
			84	350	1,367	1,413	46
			85	2,500	6,880	7,051	171
			86	550	2,088	2,146	58
CHINA T	A	W	81	31	45,957	46,506	549
			82	17	27,214	27,444	230
			83	42	64,407	64,980	573
			86	1,546	61,688	62,407	719
	N	E	81	7	8,624	8,664	40
	V	W	85	1,150	1,849	1,944	95
			86	945	1,031	1,198	167
DENMARK	A	E	81	55	1,877	2,082	205
			82	400	3,426	3,811	385
			83	16	676	697	21
			84	100	271	317	46
			85	100	1,301	1,389	88
	N	E	84	685	5,061	6,361	1,300
	O	W	82	6	410	420	10
	V	E	81	400	1,678	1,789	111
			82	100	872	965	93
			83	115	1,777	1,823	46
			84	2	750	766	16
			86	1,259	4,823	5,156	333
	V	W	84	11,013	5,737	6,883	1,146
FR GERM	A	E	86	1,491	256,478	260,330	3,852
	V	E	82	170	1,520	1,554	34
FRANCE	A	W	84	44	3,095	3,206	111
	V	E	82	1,990	2,700	2,778	78
	V	W	81	2,103	2,660	2,713	53
HG KONG	A	E	83	140	705	929	224
	A	W	83	40	569	803	234
	O	E	83	60	315	495	180
	V	W	81	160	653	676	23
			82	850	2,455	2,570	115
ISRAEL	V	W	84	1,764	2,200	2,286	86
ITALY	V	E	86	7,566	75,487	77,776	2,289
JAPAN	A	E	81	2,312	99,344	107,051	7,707
			82	782	76,437	79,475	3,038
			83	379	24,921	27,197	2,276
			84	906	52,209	56,347	4,138
			85	333	20,237	21,795	1,558
	A	H	85	198	12,442	12,712	270
	A	W	81	255	7,779	8,985	1,206
			82	313	7,036	8,006	970
			83	288	11,719	12,252	533
			84	118	2,964	3,600	636
			86	30	2,145	2,463	318
	N	E	81	1,761	59,215	62,718	3,463
			82	1,912	105,210	111,311	6,101
			83	1,085	59,522	63,873	4,351
			84	1,554	107,402	111,754	4,352
	N	H	81	60	2,599	2,719	120
			83	415	6,849	7,155	306
			84	814	14,221	15,079	858
	N	W	81	4,883	178,825	190,380	11,555
			82	5,415	261,208	268,079	6,871
			83	11,764	453,427	470,415	16,988
			84	10,313	454,599	466,781	12,182
			85	11,246	471,586	483,277	11,691
			86	5,831	222,824	231,241	8,417
	O	E	81	86	2,879	3,296	417
			82	170	5,724	6,308	584
			83	96	2,665	3,253	588
			84	15	1,104	1,207	103
			85	25	1,975	2,130	155
			86	30	1,768	1,768	
	O	W	82	50	1,500	1,888	388
	V	E	83	280	12,874	13,126	252
			84	20	820	846	26
			85	300	12,430	12,620	190
	V	H	82	290	11,459	11,765	306
			85	125	6,872	7,123	251
			86	550	12,404	12,645	241
	V	W	81	720	23,565	24,271	706
			82	1,946	58,655	59,001	346
			83	6,617	250,583	252,581	1,998
			84	3,482	138,007	139,375	1,368
			85	97	4,625	4,648	23
			86	225	10,575	10,723	148
KOR REP	A	E	81	85	2,129	2,459	330
			83	280	5,040	5,890	850
			84	301	5,799	6,666	867
			85	88	1,760	2,100	340
	A	W	81	400	7,200	8,274	1,074
			85	174	4,229	4,628	399
			86	110	2,300	2,533	233
	N	E	86	639	11,817	12,238	421
	V	E	85	350	8,328	8,495	167
	V	W	86	212	8,267	8,364	97
MALI	A	E	85	120	2,184	2,196	12
N ZEAL	A	W	82	13	690	724	34
NETHLDS	A	E	81	353	30,604	31,228	624
			82	1,011	114,820	116,361	1,541
			83	985	127,260	129,288	2,028
			84	3,004	101,407	103,155	1,748
			85	1,862	332,787	334,805	2,018
			86	3,941	74,422	75,304	882
	A	W	84	69	1,456	1,543	87
			86	1,607	88,491	90,711	2,220
	N	W	81	1,255	19,006	19,427	421
			83	938	3,843	4,049	206
			84	703	66,077	68,218	2,141
			85	2,667	70,239	72,724	2,485
	O	E	81	118	7,133	7,402	179
			82	26	1,763	1,763	
			83	51	6,930	7,040	110
			84	9	304	304	
			86	55	1,015	1,015	
	O	W	84	80	1,049	1,149	100
	V	E	81	234	1,573	1,653	80
			83	287	2,193	2,361	168
			85	450	2,369	2,519	150
	V	W	82	300	2,400	2,442	42
			83	33	437	482	45
REP SAF	V	W	85	3,777	6,263	7,000	737
SPAIN	V	W	81	3,307	4,219	4,584	365
U KING	A	E	81	151	8,554	9,024	470
			82	116	940	1,003	63
			84	5	520	530	10
	A	W	81	4	616	667	51
	N	E	85	54	4,537	4,809	272
	O	E	86	31	1,170	1,191	21
	O	W	81	23	4,500	4,598	98

Sauerkraut
1412500 SAUERKRAUT (LB)

Country	Mode	Reg	Yr	Quantity	F.A.S.	C.I.F.	Charges
TOTAL			81	613,547	157,628	195,230	37,602
			82	977,862	249,464	301,198	51,734
			83	983,568	236,511	283,313	46,802
			84	1,464,955	370,525	451,856	81,331
			85	1,672,424	352,375	461,648	109,273
			86	1,729,539	447,717	556,803	109,086
AUSTRIA	V	E	85	71,430	13,910	20,084	6,174
	V	W	83	1,327	1,104	1,184	80
			84	73,910	15,365	21,107	5,742
BELGIUM	V	E	83	94	1,162	1,282	120
			84	8,082	3,368	3,791	423
			85	36,993	7,513	9,506	1,993
			86	10,864	5,072	5,891	819
	V	W	84	2,876	1,304	1,569	265
CHINA T	V	W	81	1,224	1,404	1,465	61
			82	4,320	2,678	2,824	146

Crop
Product
TSUSA commodity number, description, and unit of quantity

Country	Mode	Reg	Yr	Quantity	F.A.S.	C.I.F.	Charges
CZECHO	O E	81		4,613	2,044	2,572	528
FR GERM	N E	81		291,817	93,365	106,148	12,783
		82		650,919	181,467	208,174	26,707
		83		522,743	136,058	155,255	19,197
		84		73,545	16,085	19,846	3,761
		85		55,517	19,156	25,815	6,659
		86		44,419	8,992	10,386	1,394
	N W	84		78,315	19,083	24,613	5,530
	O E	81		69,448	17,699	22,788	5,089
		83		5,934	3,192	3,857	665
		85		135,072	25,380	30,404	5,024
		86		7,098	1,600	1,600	
	O W	81		1,000	559	559	
		82		100	504	504	
	V E	81		5,823	1,818	1,976	158
		82		19,955	5,538	6,849	1,311
		83		75,993	25,517	28,714	3,197
		84		857,279	238,488	277,978	39,490
		85		627,950	159,245	197,001	37,756
		86		874,073	291,728	348,379	56,651
	V W	81		75,931	14,343	17,396	3,053
		82		36,455	12,060	14,978	2,918
		83		51,455	14,682	18,276	3,594
		84		83,125	22,121	26,286	4,165
		85		139,231	41,724	52,541	10,817
		86		90,911	32,747	35,791	3,044
FRANCE	V W	81		8,312	1,995	2,184	189
		82		225	321	342	21
		83		1,918	499	539	40
ISRAEL	V E	84		6,113	3,240	3,572	332
ITALY	V E	83		1,487	422	481	59
JAPAN	V E	83		788	975	1,062	87
MEXICO	O E	84		5,800	433	433	
		86		73,799	4,017	4,017	
	O W	84		4,980	512	512	
NETHLDS	N E	85		164,941	14,178	25,070	10,892
	O E	86		146,576	16,961	23,882	6,921
	V E	85		16,667	4,194	5,621	1,427
		86		71,636	18,341	23,881	5,540
NORWAY	V E	82		992	561	689	128
		84		48	580	648	68
	V W	81		1,835	682	1,125	443
		82		1,786	639	1,098	459
		83		1,786	614	900	286
		84		1,786	571	767	196
POLAND	N E	82		87,368	15,179	23,189	8,010
		84		119,571	20,750	30,516	9,766
	O E	82		114,026	19,350	27,418	8,068
		83		155,013	24,900	34,200	9,300
		85		105,820	15,500	23,408	7,908
		86		21,089	3,330	5,027	1,697
	V E	81		152,704	23,419	38,704	15,285
		82		61,716	11,167	15,133	3,966
		83		165,030	27,386	37,563	10,177
		84		145,255	24,070	35,263	11,193
		85		289,702	46,795	65,976	19,181
		86		389,074	64,929	97,949	33,020
ROMANIA	V E	85		29,101	4,780	6,222	1,442
SPAIN	V E	84		2,700	2,794	3,111	317
THAILND	V W	84		1,220	1,500	1,557	57
U KING	O E	84		350	261	287	26
YUGOSLV	O W	81		840	300	313	13

Camphor Tree

Camphor
4932000 NATURAL CAMPHOR CRUDE (LB)

Country	Mode	Reg	Yr	Quantity	F.A.S.	C.I.F.	Charges
TOTAL		81		55	548	552	4
		82		11,078	120,094	122,343	2,249
		83		81,477	52,827	56,843	4,016
		84		44,246	47,279	51,294	4,015
		85		1,102	1,070	1,094	24
		86		1,102	1,205	1,230	25
CANADA	O E	83		2,000	1,740	1,740	
CHINA M	V E	84		44	358	398	40
CHINA T	A E	84		110	1,323	1,447	124
	V E	82		11,023	119,367	121,606	2,239
FR GERM	V E	83		79,364	50,064	54,001	3,937
FRANCE	V E	84		44,092	45,598	49,449	3,851

Country	Mode	Reg	Yr	Quantity	F.A.S.	C.I.F.	Charges
ITALY	O W	83		20	404	426	22
NETHLDS	V E	85		1,102	1,070	1,094	24
		86		1,102	1,205	1,230	25
SWITZLD	A E	81		55	548	552	4
		82		55	727	737	10
		83		86	341	359	18
	O E	83		7	278	317	39

4932100 NATURAL CAMPHOR ADVANCED (LB)

Country	Mode	Reg	Yr	Quantity	F.A.S.	C.I.F.	Charges
TOTAL		81		81,376	639,126	652,646	13,520
		82		61,422	478,059	491,821	13,762
		83		5,454	12,606	14,211	1,605
		84		2,864	7,429	8,686	1,257
		85		40,701	36,706	40,302	3,596
		86		13,614	7,925	8,604	679
CANADA	O E	84		240	600	615	15
CHINA M	V E	81		354	299	361	62
		82		4,469	31,147	33,473	2,326
		83		5,000	8,300	9,000	700
		84		506	573	730	157
	V W	82		1,102	1,567	1,700	133
		84		790	1,618	1,658	40
CHINA T	A E	83		55	465	625	160
		84		55	678	754	76
	N E	81		46,517	368,737	375,661	6,924
		82		28,714	254,199	259,675	5,476
	V E	85		220	1,200	1,273	73
	V H	82		397	1,521	1,723	202
	V W	81		6,613	54,683	55,778	1,095
		86		12,200	3,120	3,301	181
FR GERM	V W	85		1,350	1,062	1,171	109
FRANCE	A E	82		66	689	742	53
HG KONG	V E	82		4,409	32,347	33,487	1,140
		84		1,000	1,473	1,610	137
		85		2,645	3,902	4,380	478
INDIA	O E	83		76	445	494	49
	V E	81		212	526	623	97
	V W	84		53	370	425	55
JAPAN	A E	83		88	759	1,136	377
		84		110	1,027	1,389	362
		85		110	1,132	1,510	378
		86		220	1,225	1,343	118
	A W	81		66	576	1,194	618
		84		110	1,090	1,505	415
	V E	81		27,559	213,572	218,150	4,578
		82		22,045	154,249	158,469	4,220
KOR REP	V E	85		2,205	3,251	3,650	399
MALAYSA	V W	83		15	300	340	40
N ZEAL	V E	85		33,069	24,989	27,116	2,127
NETHLDS	V E	85		1,102	1,170	1,202	32
		86		1,102	1,110	1,366	256
SWITZLD	A E	81		55	733	879	146
		82		110	1,127	1,283	156
		83		220	2,337	2,616	279
	O E	82		110	1,213	1,269	56
VENEZ	A E	86		92	2,470	2,594	124

Camphor, essential oil
4520800 CAMPHOR OIL (LB)

Country	Mode	Reg	Yr	Quantity	F.A.S.	C.I.F.	Charges
TOTAL		81		128,726	168,932	193,224	24,292
		82		126,168	138,256	150,339	12,083
		83		177,357	193,639	216,202	22,563
		84		128,207	170,546	184,302	13,756
		85		153,214	241,287	254,873	13,586
		86		54,529	68,030	74,894	6,864
CHINA M	N E	86		11,111	10,048	11,233	1,185
	O E	85		4,365	4,246	4,463	217
	V E	83		8,818	6,381	7,343	962
		84		48,501	62,488	68,021	5,533
CHINA T	N E	86		42,990	56,201	61,803	5,602
	V E	81		124,935	164,351	188,217	23,866
		82		121,759	131,805	143,384	11,579
		83		118,475	137,142	151,501	14,359
		84		79,674	107,698	115,911	8,213
		85		83,247	166,289	176,371	10,082
	V W	81		2,205	640	855	215
		82		4,409	6,451	6,955	504
		83		22,222	15,430	18,212	2,782
		85		63,492	60,530	63,426	2,896
FRANCE	A E	84		32	360	370	10

Crop / Product / TSUSA commodity number, description, and unit of quantity							
Country	Mode	Reg	Yr	Quantity	F.A.S.	C.I.F.	Charges
	V	E	81	1,586	3,941	4,152	211
			85	2,110	10,222	10,613	391
	V	W	86	428	1,781	1,858	77
JAPAN	V	E	83	27,842	34,686	39,146	4,460

Canary-grass

Canary, seed
1302000 CANARY SEED (LB)

Country	Mode	Reg	Yr	Quantity	F.A.S.	C.I.F.	Charges
TOTAL			81	16,973,894	2,835,191	2,848,791	13,800
			82	16,414,642	2,793,323	2,803,861	10,538
			83	17,284,873	1,928,762	1,942,172	13,410
			84	13,278,015	1,849,792	1,883,057	33,265
			85	20,226,795	2,745,714	2,802,678	56,964
			86	28,408,681	3,653,682	3,666,938	13,256
ARGENT	V	E	84	1,445	356	451	95
AUSTRAL	V	E	83	237,843	23,603	34,396	10,793
CANADA	N	E	86	3,600,230	442,991	444,091	1,100
	N	W	84	60,064	27,796	28,396	600
	O	E	81	14,015,609	2,280,272	2,280,272	
			82	11,095,155	1,911,305	1,911,305	
			83	10,516,657	1,121,032	1,121,032	
			84	7,980,677	1,077,070	1,077,070	
			85	12,211,692	1,538,961	1,541,261	2,300
			86	9,714,713	1,255,479	1,255,479	
	O	W	81	2,887,687	512,546	512,346	
			82	5,241,784	847,467	847,467	
			83	6,510,241	776,857	776,857	
			84	5,066,992	663,339	668,993	5,654
			85	7,616,133	1,037,158	1,037,158	
			86	14,995,013	1,927,140	1,927,142	2
CHINA M	V	W	82	77,703	34,551	45,089	10,538
			83	20,132	7,270	9,887	2,617
			84	142,144	66,197	89,050	22,853
			85	237,628	107,779	154,366	46,587
			86	97,918	26,905	38,993	12,088
CHINA T	V	W	85	11,014	4,145	4,392	247
DENMARK	V	E	86	807	1,167	1,233	66
ETHIOP	V	W	85	43,404	18,211	18,536	325
INDIA	O	E	81	37,280	22,804	24,850	2,046
	V	W	85	73,855	29,945	33,940	3,995
KOR REP	V	W	84	3,086	1,135	1,234	99
LEBANON	V	W	84	21,788	13,451	17,295	3,844
NEPAL	V	W	81	33,318	19,569	31,323	11,754
			85	33,069	9,515	13,025	3,510
NETHLDS	V	E	84	1,819	448	568	120

Candelilla

Candelilla, wax
4941000 VEGETABLE WAX CANDELILLA (LB)

Country	Mode	Reg	Yr	Quantity	F.A.S.	C.I.F.	Charges
TOTAL			81	834,731	855,168	855,168	
			82	1,985,579	1,594,057	1,596,716	2,659
			83	806,297	793,785	801,482	7,697
			84	913,295	803,628	807,140	3,512
			85	708,023	628,499	629,729	1,230
			86	988,140	856,201	856,201	
BRAZIL	V	E	83	15,432	6,736	8,350	1,614
CANADA	O	E	83	4,560	5,524	5,524	
FR GERM	V	E	83	22	278	431	153
			85	173	1,172	1,265	93
JAPAN	A	E	83	794	4,826	6,861	2,035
	A	W	83	1,528	5,274	9,169	3,895
			84	1,550	5,657	9,169	3,512
MEXICO	O	E	81	834,731	855,168	855,168	
			82	1,940,605	1,524,722	1,524,722	
			83	783,961	771,147	771,147	
			84	911,745	797,971	797,971	
			85	685,804	592,792	592,792	
			86	988,140	856,201	856,201	
	V	E	82	44,974	69,335	71,994	2,659
			85	22,046	34,535	35,672	1,137

Crop / Product / TSUSA commodity number, description, and unit of quantity							
Country	Mode	Reg	Yr	Quantity	F.A.S.	C.I.F.	Charges

Cantaloupe

Cantaloupe, fresh
1481000 CANTALOUP,FR,8-1 TO 9-15 (LB)

Country	Mode	Reg	Yr	Quantity	F.A.S.	C.I.F.	Charges
TOTAL			81	41,962	6,740	6,770	30
			82	170,645	20,613	28,384	7,771
			83	144,371	8,248	11,819	3,571
			84	756,001	51,851	91,342	39,491
			85	626,924	92,981	129,568	36,587
			86	62,751	19,358	63,192	43,834
C RICA	V	E	83	55,000	4,950	8,146	3,196
			84	64,120	6,325	9,798	3,473
			85	62,000	5,650	9,770	4,120
			86	491	4,800	7,816	3,016
CANADA	O	E	82	1,695	339	339	
			84	2,100	420	420	
			85	13	2,576	2,576	
			86	20,760	3,556	3,556	
	O	W	83	51,600	2,193	2,193	
COLOMB	V	E	82	168,950	20,274	28,045	7,771
			85	294,263	25,921	29,423	3,502
DOM REP	V	E	84	678,849	42,117	73,708	31,591
			85	75,088	13,648	23,079	9,431
			86	14,250	2,250	2,969	719
ECUADOR	A	E	83	2,640	275	650	375
FRANCE	A	E	81	34	270	300	30
			84	879	864	1,372	508
GUATMAL	A	W	84	9,053	852	3,492	2,640
	V	E	86	9,750	3,956	5,111	1,155
HONDURA	V	E	85	24,025	1,840	3,767	1,927
IVY CST	A	E	84	1,000	1,273	2,552	1,279
MEXICO	O	E	81	41,928	6,470	6,470	
			83	35,131	830	830	
	O	W	85	20,196	3,374	3,374	
PANAMA	A	E	85	104,075	26,252	35,515	9,263
VENEZ	A	E	85	47,264	13,720	22,064	8,344
			86	17,500	4,796	43,740	38,944

1481200 CANTALOUPES FRESH 12/1-3/31 (LB)

Country	Mode	Reg	Yr	Quantity	F.A.S.	C.I.F.	Charges
TOTAL			81	20,366,024	4,084,485	4,167,663	83,178
			82	47,668,959	7,246,007	7,399,256	153,249
			83	24,999,350	4,138,575	4,482,198	343,623
			84	72,791,240	9,066,835	9,933,766	866,931
			85	121,725,009	15,369,756	18,070,348	2,700,592
			86	114,221,094	14,252,088	17,548,625	3,296,537
BELIZE	A	E	84	43,886	23,800	28,095	4,295
BRAZIL	V	E	86	25,769	4,961	10,261	5,300
C RICA	N	E	81	488,810	138,142	181,058	42,916
			82	97,888	36,990	44,506	7,516
	V	E	83	127,764	31,663	42,937	11,274
			85	4,891	1,200	2,299	1,099
			86	1,243,257	203,465	301,255	97,790
	V	W	83	3,104	1,034	1,482	448
CAYMAN	V	E	82	19,866	2,000	2,435	435
CHILE	A	E	82	900	720	1,255	535
	V	E	83	61,440	7,680	14,415	6,735
			85	7,407	2,016	3,010	994
			86	204,606	35,251	56,133	20,882
	V	W	83	69,336	11,040	17,480	6,440
			84	127,000	26,702	37,741	11,039
			86	372,611	47,593	94,581	46,988
DOM REP	A	E	81	30,229	1,581	4,096	2,515
			83	12,037	1,067	2,390	1,323
	N	E	82	541,298	31,528	73,474	41,946
			83	1,281,639	138,345	226,134	87,789
			84	6,250,378	554,884	1,011,438	456,554
			85	9,357,409	747,124	1,356,189	609,065
			86	4,669,020	412,711	697,705	284,994
	O	E	84	2,520	1,531	1,531	
	V	E	82	546,692	87,558	115,875	28,317
			83	2,690,213	358,303	499,618	141,315
			84	5,659,000	387,437	685,875	298,438
			85	13,898,865	1,255,862	2,182,569	926,707
			86	12,614,642	874,837	1,880,024	1,005,187
	V	W	86	84,800	4,784	9,916	5,132
DOMINCA	A	E	86	94,810	5,292	13,141	7,849
	V	E	86	1,192,501	87,400	185,808	98,408
ECUADOR	A	E	82	45,002	11,378	11,892	514
	V	E	85	304,537	29,860	71,241	41,381
			86	591,025	94,209	159,554	65,345

Crop
Product
TSUSA commodity number, description, and unit of quantity

Country	Mode	Reg	Yr	Quantity	F.A.S.	C.I.F.	Charges
FRANCE	O	E	86	23,160	3,011	3,011	
	V	E	85	71,040	3,996	8,366	4,370
GERM DR	A	E	86	25,669	2,265	9,615	7,350
GUATMAL	A	E	84	26,000	1,463	4,583	3,120
	N	E	85	1,281,333	180,532	276,330	95,798
			86	453,166	66,593	113,028	46,435
	O	E	85	436,726	25,221	25,221	
			86	43,200	1,950	1,950	
	V	E	81	132,650	9,609	18,394	8,785
			82	53,694	2,826	6,381	3,555
			85	1,324,462	240,296	335,976	95,680
			86	3,680,243	444,166	706,326	262,160
HAITI	A	E	85	15,435	4,320	6,120	1,800
			86	12,000	2,280	4,503	2,223
HONDURA	N	E	82	625,180	87,754	143,130	55,376
			86	824,612	78,568	160,779	82,211
	O	E	86	40,000	13,488	13,488	
	V	E	81	1,567,157	231,854	260,816	28,962
			82	1,633,459	295,767	310,117	14,350
			83	4,055,389	964,113	1,027,092	62,979
			84	3,503,388	749,081	822,421	73,340
			85	8,670,992	1,485,527	1,962,844	477,317
			86	12,465,898	1,742,929	2,481,509	738,580
JAMAICA	A	E	83	39,553	11,776	18,470	6,694
			85	38,165	11,295	15,286	3,991
			86	44,360	11,631	20,687	9,056
	N	E	85	1,702,884	516,270	602,920	86,650
			86	1,131,987	153,237	219,319	66,082
	V	E	82	33,264	5,000	5,705	705
			86	46,504	2,736	5,452	2,716
MALAYSA	O	W	86	47,520	6,480	6,480	
MEXICO	A	E	84	10,792	639	2,019	1,380
	O	E	81	16,270,478	3,400,037	3,400,037	
			82	40,376,262	6,232,648	6,232,648	
			83	14,447,267	2,304,926	2,323,552	18,626
			84	50,291,613	6,326,527	6,326,671	144
			85	75,113,505	9,162,598	9,170,617	8,019
			86	57,843,313	6,858,731	6,858,737	6
	O	W	81	1,876,700	303,262	303,262	
			82	3,695,454	451,838	451,838	
			83	2,211,608	308,628	308,628	
			84	6,738,614	931,637	931,637	
			85	6,400,369	942,459	942,460	1
			86	11,390,850	1,714,526	1,715,570	1,044
MONSRAT	O	E	85	47,650	4,384	4,384	
			86	17,280	1,363	1,363	
MOZAMBQ	O	E	85	23,400	2,340	2,340	
PANAMA	A	E	85	747,184	188,010	286,515	98,505
	N	E	85	1,069,258	253,305	360,077	106,772
			86	2,000,572	788,455	981,330	192,875
	N	W	84	16,605	5,561	7,129	1,568
	V	E	84	3,770	1,027	1,118	91
			85	480,584	161,009	191,664	30,655
			86	322,248	136,702	163,834	27,132
	V	W	85	88,213	24,510	31,154	6,644
			86	794,545	239,295	283,280	43,985
SALVADR	O	E	85	29,820	3,408	3,408	
	V	E	84	48,374	5,966	11,723	5,757
			85	425,321	47,048	99,978	52,930
			86	1,920,917	213,179	389,986	176,807
VENEZ	A	E	84	69,300	50,580	61,785	11,205
			85	185,559	77,166	129,380	52,214

1481700 CANTALOUPES, FRESH, NSPF (LB)

Country	Mode	Reg	Yr	Quantity	F.A.S.	C.I.F.	Charges
TOTAL			81	117,633,262	18,761,997	18,782,564	21,567
			82	134,641,877	19,174,433	19,223,050	48,617
			83	140,953,023	22,390,155	22,637,097	246,942
			84	173,120,857	21,948,985	22,640,498	691,513
			85	123,681,620	14,945,331	15,640,984	695,653
			86	202,947,036	22,697,276	23,652,508	955,232
ANTIGUA	N	E	86	72,544	10,435	12,945	2,510
C RICA	O	E	82	31,914	9,870	12,448	2,578
	V	E	81	29,680	2,226	4,881	2,655
CANADA	O	E	82	218,897	23,867	23,867	
			83	35,992	4,642	4,642	
			85	124,000	24,169	24,169	
	O	W	85	44,528	3,006	3,006	
CHILE	V	E	84	2,249	1,020	1,386	366
			85	9,045	1,268	2,712	1,444
			86	38,317	10,309	14,583	4,274
COLOMB	A	E	83	2,205	500	1,130	630
DENMARK	V	E	85	62,700	4,950	7,530	2,580
DOM REP	A	E	82	1,880	282	421	139

Crop
Product
TSUSA commodity number, description, and unit of quantity

Country	Mode	Reg	Yr	Quantity	F.A.S.	C.I.F.	Charges
	N	E	82	712,500	42,190	71,772	29,582
			83	2,535,535	160,893	322,330	161,437
			84	5,577,074	721,664	1,108,059	386,395
			85	1,246,624	80,834	167,923	87,089
	O	E	83	37,800	2,362	4,243	1,881
	V	E	82	71,630	4,241	6,979	2,738
			83	1,404,676	195,588	261,107	65,519
			84	4,032,983	369,707	626,125	256,418
			85	7,150,645	647,279	1,167,656	520,377
			86	7,599,319	606,999	1,145,780	538,781
DOMINCA	V	E	86	656,637	45,435	100,402	54,967
FRANCE	A	E	83	147	254	316	62
			84	115	500	661	161
GUATMAL	O	W	85	65,640	9,005	9,005	
	V	E	81	75,845	5,736	10,726	4,990
			84	530,670	54,881	83,775	28,894
			85	739,159	47,937	105,915	57,978
			86	3,566,232	329,456	562,650	233,194
	V	W	86	89,558	37,005	44,205	7,200
HAITI	V	E	84	35,000	6,000	8,400	2,400
HONDURA	A	E	85	8,592	2,348	3,505	1,157
	V	E	83	7,074	1,655	3,663	2,008
			85	54,594	9,602	15,085	5,483
			86	2,100,217	340,060	401,399	61,339
ISRAEL	A	E	86	3,030	1,305	4,231	2,926
JAMAICA	A	E	85	6,000	8,940	9,792	852
			86	7,500	1,875	6,340	4,465
	V	E	84	80,909	25,024	29,286	4,262
MEXICO	O	E	81	77,501,614	13,485,575	13,487,575	
			82	94,223,009	12,690,220	12,703,800	13,580
			83	62,330,739	10,720,920	10,732,974	12,054
			84	80,238,620	9,215,130	9,215,166	36
			85	82,465,891	10,273,765	10,273,801	36
			86	116,976,588	13,716,056	13,716,068	12
	O	W	81	40,016,298	5,267,477	5,277,375	12,898
			82	39,382,047	6,403,763	6,403,763	
			83	74,575,184	11,288,309	11,289,135	826
			84	82,532,056	11,535,343	11,535,487	144
			85	31,497,326	3,790,057	3,790,060	3
			86	71,435,970	7,444,172	7,444,957	785
NICARAG	A	E	81	9,825	983	2,007	1,024
PANAMA	A	E	85	16,572	6,510	8,640	2,130
	N	E	86	57,258	30,233	37,721	7,488
	V	E	84	68,345	14,542	25,233	10,691
			85	88,130	25,490	33,020	7,530
	V	W	84	22,836	5,174	6,920	1,746
			85	16,000	3,960	5,143	1,183
			86	39,180	7,836	10,730	2,894
SALVADR	V	E	85	86,174	6,211	14,022	7,811
VENEZ	A	E	83	23,671	15,032	17,557	2,525
			86	9,505	4,950	7,970	3,020
	N	E	86	295,181	111,150	142,527	31,377

Caper

Caper, spice
1610600 CAPERS IN CONTAINR OV 7.5LB (LB)

Country	Mode	Reg	Yr	Quantity	F.A.S.	C.I.F.	Charges
TOTAL			82	1,118,579	1,790,504	1,901,193	110,689
			83	1,047,599	2,023,660	2,123,217	99,557
			84	1,173,869	2,033,706	2,156,811	123,105
			85	1,261,175	1,837,982	1,983,475	145,493
			86	1,117,977	1,557,588	1,708,025	150,437
AUSTRAL	V	W	85	37,200	28,874	33,666	4,792
CHINA T	V	W	86	22,928	40,000	42,300	2,300
CYPRUS	V	E	82	899	1,455	1,620	165
			83	217	301	342	41
FRANCE	V	E	83	3,612	4,761	5,100	339
			86	52,026	60,186	65,116	4,930
	V	W	85	2,222	7,104	7,601	497
			86	17,637	35,000	37,575	2,575
GREECE	V	W	84	22,487	30,288	32,270	1,982
			85	683	2,120	2,370	250
			86	1,737	5,256	6,269	1,013
ITALY	V	E	83	220	321	346	25
			84	919	1,856	2,003	147
			85	644	1,695	1,860	165
			86	3,709	9,860	10,526	666
	V	W	85	926	1,139	1,257	118
			86	5,295	4,712	5,047	335

Crop Product TSUSA commodity number, description, and unit of quantity Country	Mode	Reg	Yr	Quantity	F.A.S.	C.I.F.	Charges
MACAO	V	E	85	31,746	65,062	67,162	2,100
MOROC	O	E	82	340,631	302,846	328,432	25,586
			83	39,154	62,783	66,508	3,725
			85	11,025	19,400	26,874	7,474
	V	E	82	633,773	1,273,239	1,338,056	64,817
			83	666,184	1,393,093	1,444,161	51,068
			84	811,371	1,302,564	1,374,868	72,304
			85	696,381	850,876	909,439	58,563
			86	400,800	383,717	420,888	37,171
	V	W	82	16,314	43,586	46,367	2,781
			84	50,706	129,147	137,809	8,662
			85	78,042	155,738	164,122	8,384
			86	81,317	139,292	149,838	10,546
SPAIN	N	E	86	41,420	78,541	90,159	11,618
	V	E	82	118,230	145,248	160,000	14,752
			83	203,459	270,796	292,299	21,503
			84	173,079	310,313	335,369	25,056
			85	181,952	344,645	378,852	34,207
			86	160,657	369,149	408,920	39,771
	V	W	82	8,732	24,130	26,718	2,588
			83	131,446	285,380	307,937	22,557
			84	115,307	259,538	274,492	14,954
			85	156,219	252,649	277,297	24,648
			86	209,948	339,163	362,010	22,847
TOKELAU	V	W	86	16,755	15,987	19,366	3,379
TURKEY	V	E	83	3,307	6,225	6,524	299
			85	64,135	108,680	112,975	4,295
			86	103,748	76,725	90,011	13,286

1610700 CAPERS (LB)

	Mode	Reg	Yr	Quantity	F.A.S.	C.I.F.	Charges
TOTAL			81	1,669,961	3,703,438	3,957,118	285,763
			82	367,401	777,448	831,149	53,701
CYPRUS	V	E	81	1,350	448	582	134
			82	421	690	824	134
FR GERM	O	E	82	55	308	346	38
	V	E	81	1,590	3,791	4,003	212
			82	213	633	655	22
FRANCE	N	E	81	14,220	29,073	30,987	1,914
			82	3,270	1,575	2,240	665
	O	E	81	1,019	3,878	4,311	433
	V	E	81	133	818	869	51
			82	158	879	959	80
	V	W	81	19,070	33,104	35,135	2,031
			82	5,291	20,448	21,228	780
ITALY	O	E	81	452	951	1,045	94
	V	E	81	4,460	7,706	8,495	789
			82	12,257	17,481	19,181	1,700
MOROC	N	E	81	271,632	690,662	688,095	29,516
	O	E	81	429,784	1,034,302	1,123,002	88,700
			82	47,173	88,780	94,218	5,438
	V	E	81	200,728	270,112	296,947	26,835
			82	93,526	248,366	256,361	7,995
NETHLDS	V	E	81	315	699	808	109
SENEGAL	O	E	81	4,409	5,985	6,358	373
SPAIN	V	E	81	519,413	1,125,622	1,219,283	93,661
			82	163,272	285,293	313,600	28,307
	V	W	81	201,386	496,287	537,198	40,911
			82	41,765	112,995	121,537	8,542

1610800 CAPERS, NSPF (LB)

	Mode	Reg	Yr	Quantity	F.A.S.	C.I.F.	Charges
TOTAL			82	275,504	811,416	876,432	65,016
			83	463,480	1,281,285	1,396,899	115,614
			84	779,068	1,777,515	1,932,787	155,272
			85	1,091,061	2,051,027	2,275,890	224,863
			86	1,037,931	2,162,502	2,358,559	196,057
BELGIUM	A	E	85	1,422	1,684	2,864	1,180
	O	E	86	600	2,313	2,496	183
BRAZIL	V	E	86	2,361	7,995	9,218	1,223
CYPRUS	V	E	82	1,350	669	875	206
			83	1,117	1,711	1,878	167
			84	2,051	3,690	4,074	384
			85	2,660	3,326	3,737	411
			86	118	1,591	1,888	297
	V	W	86	1,000	1,622	2,102	480
DOM REP	V	E	82	536	1,341	1,645	304
EGYPT	V	E	84	11,023	3,960	4,530	570
FR GERM	A	E	86	196	3,399	3,617	218
	V	E	82	5,518	4,581	4,867	286
			83	2,604	2,154	2,300	146
			84	4,891	3,608	3,974	366
			86	6,303	4,527	5,162	635
FRANCE	O	E	84	1,313	5,826	6,361	535

Country	Mode	Reg	Yr	Quantity	F.A.S.	C.I.F.	Charges
	V	E	82	1,988	3,633	4,016	383
			83	4,210	14,212	14,888	676
			84	3,299	5,239	6,124	885
			85	6,463	11,071	12,091	1,020
			86	8,024	23,491	24,508	1,017
	V	W	82	198	362	412	50
			83	116	672	699	27
			84	291	5,930	6,627	697
			85	639	2,210	2,408	198
			86	35,274	78,500	82,838	4,338
GREECE	V	E	84	8,057	4,517	5,134	617
			85	17,600	43,599	46,683	3,084
	V	W	84	4,564	5,500	6,137	637
			85	1,292	3,843	4,283	440
			86	2,447	7,770	9,142	1,372
ISRAEL	V	E	85	1,586	1,762	1,950	188
ITALY	O	E	83	1,350	4,615	5,308	693
	V	E	82	1,103	2,745	3,059	314
			83	913	2,214	2,418	204
			84	5,172	5,532	6,289	757
			85	6,331	7,306	8,727	1,421
			86	3,775	10,236	10,908	672
	V	W	82	2,653	3,348	3,907	559
			84	130	301	359	58
			85	1,984	2,613	3,108	495
			86	948	1,233	1,303	70
MOROC	V	E	82	18,225	59,249	61,074	1,825
			85	35,273	30,095	34,571	4,476
	V	W	82	2,520	6,129	6,520	391
SPAIN	N	E	85	16,762	29,607	32,329	2,722
	O	E	85	476	2,800	3,166	366
			86	4,586	4,205	4,756	551
	V	E	82	180,616	504,192	548,146	43,954
			83	343,797	924,116	1,009,253	85,137
			84	588,939	1,221,374	1,325,817	104,443
			85	728,616	1,300,157	1,448,539	148,382
			86	688,261	1,427,175	1,557,751	130,576
	V	W	82	60,797	225,167	241,911	16,744
			83	109,373	331,591	360,155	28,564
			84	130,433	455,902	497,329	41,427
			85	232,509	502,449	555,422	52,973
			86	265,982	529,114	580,606	51,492
U KING	O	E	86	16,540	48,636	51,156	2,520
	V	E	84	18,905	56,136	60,032	3,896
			85	37,448	108,505	116,012	7,507
	V	W	86	1,516	10,695	11,108	413

Caraway

Caraway, essential oil
4521000 CARAWAY OIL (LB)

	Mode	Reg	Yr	Quantity	F.A.S.	C.I.F.	Charges
TOTAL			81	25,078	559,124	573,788	14,664
			82	18,620	385,892	397,602	11,710
			83	22,791	401,302	411,101	9,799
			84	12,619	220,367	226,784	6,417
			85	13,244	196,646	201,472	4,826
			86	14,737	233,949	239,069	5,120
AUSTRAL	V	E	83	121	1,868	1,912	44
			85	220	2,923	2,961	38
			86	591	19,256	19,605	349
BELGIUM	V	E	83	860	17,279	17,613	334
FR GERM	N	E	83	665	12,896	13,253	357
	O	E	81	380	12,850	12,850	
	V	E	84	1,091	18,801	19,246	445
			85	2,624	44,493	45,413	920
			86	3,307	50,376	51,111	735
FRANCE	N	E	81	2,581	52,569	54,831	2,262
			82	2,589	64,369	66,153	1,784
			83	1,652	38,756	40,034	1,278
			84	1,355	37,421	38,209	788
			85	3,003	50,150	51,609	1,459
	V	E	86	3,202	49,154	49,816	662
HUNGARY	O	E	84	220	2,500	2,500	
			85	2,249	22,500	22,500	
NETHLDS	V	E	81	11,727	254,689	260,373	5,684
			82	10,797	206,558	211,519	4,961
			83	12,314	216,278	222,450	6,172
			84	9,512	154,265	159,130	4,865
			85	2,811	43,854	45,392	1,538

Crop Product TSUSA commodity number, description, and unit of quantity Country	Mode	Reg	Yr	Quantity	F.A.S.	C.I.F.	Charges
			86	5,203	78,662	81,416	2,754
POLAND	N	E	81	10,390	239,016	245,734	6,718
			82	5,234	114,965	119,930	4,965
	V	E	83	7,164	113,898	115,493	1,595
			84	441	7,380	7,699	319
			85	2,337	32,726	33,597	871
			86	2,434	36,501	37,121	620
U KING	A	E	83	15	327	346	19

Caraway, spice
1610900 CARAWAY (LB)

				Quantity	F.A.S.	C.I.F.	Charges
TOTAL			81	6,682,514	3,162,058	3,520,227	358,169
			82	7,915,559	4,035,779	4,471,191	435,412
			83	7,361,749	3,522,086	3,861,756	339,670
			84	8,758,195	5,302,589	5,744,001	441,412
			85	7,930,637	5,473,810	5,917,005	443,195
			86	8,135,584	4,202,026	4,685,522	483,496
AUSTRAL	V	E	86	69,000	12,238	17,991	5,753
BELGIUM	O	E	85	30,800	19,127	21,252	2,125
	V	E	83	59,910	30,669	31,994	1,325
			85	74,381	56,470	59,911	3,441
	V	W	82	11,000	5,459	6,320	861
			85	30,800	18,324	20,329	2,005
			86	30,800	18,742	19,727	985
BRAZIL	V	E	85	44,400	28,460	30,813	2,353
CANADA	O	E	81	352	384	384	
			82	15,420	7,402	7,402	
			83	69,439	37,029	37,029	
			84	69,512	56,974	56,974	
			85	114,083	80,955	80,955	
	O	W	81	199,400	92,937	92,937	
			82	219,889	78,245	78,245	
			83	43,700	20,870	20,870	
			84	68,095	39,981	39,981	
			85	57,200	31,379	31,379	
DENMARK	V	E	81	61,184	29,416	32,498	3,082
			82	31,001	18,180	19,621	1,441
EGYPT	N	E	85	71,695	39,567	44,859	5,292
	V	E	81	687,926	247,113	279,818	32,705
			82	1,207,564	451,705	518,952	67,247
			83	626,175	246,151	279,291	33,140
			84	1,987,165	948,563	1,056,553	107,990
			85	967,494	508,302	559,623	51,321
			86	1,461,537	643,110	711,734	68,624
FR GERM	O	E	81	460	841	948	107
			82	478	300	337	37
			83	556	502	508	6
			84	46,001	21,911	24,311	2,400
	V	E	81	108,770	52,028	57,606	5,578
			84	31,206	21,573	23,198	1,625
			85	44,000	22,000	23,910	1,910
FRANCE	V	E	83	94	323	340	17
G BISAU	V	W	85	30,000	22,099	28,752	6,653
GUATMAL	N	W	86	6,614	22,500	23,384	884
HUNGARY	V	E	83	30,800	15,380	16,555	1,175
INDIA	V	E	81	1,452	1,556	1,842	286
			82	1,155	1,345	1,527	182
			83	2,587	2,130	2,381	251
			84	1,706	2,554	2,826	272
			85	5,640	5,541	5,917	376
			86	3,905	3,639	3,960	321
	V	W	83	22,427	7,350	7,594	244
INDNSIA	V	E	84	99,207	59,224	71,970	12,746
ITALY	V	E	83	827	892	934	42
JAMAICA	A	E	84	400	600	795	195
NETHLDS	N	E	81	2,715,373	1,292,325	1,428,317	135,992
			82	3,912,580	2,085,880	2,285,061	199,181
			83	3,980,078	1,921,011	2,092,526	171,515
			84	1,175,745	699,571	760,322	60,751
			85	1,254,582	965,000	1,041,573	76,573
			86	3,100,259	1,665,430	1,846,966	181,536
	O	E	82	1,120	1,013	1,072	59
			86	59,000	30,266	35,071	4,805
	O	W	83	28,300	13,608	14,926	1,318
	V	E	81	1,821,740	930,018	1,032,242	102,224
			82	1,536,354	867,104	955,652	88,548
			83	1,132,469	580,185	626,240	46,055
			84	4,666,221	3,020,088	3,234,365	214,277
			85	4,288,612	3,063,303	3,295,579	232,276
			86	1,448,422	771,650	849,913	78,263
	V	W	81	428,191	202,598	246,003	43,405

Crop Product TSUSA commodity number, description, and unit of quantity Country	Mode	Reg	Yr	Quantity	F.A.S.	C.I.F.	Charges
			82	492,535	269,815	317,085	47,270
			83	796,481	389,078	438,120	49,042
			84	400,650	266,657	293,730	27,073
			85	659,893	459,719	500,735	41,016
			86	660,287	359,248	398,101	38,853
NIGER	V	E	85	62,900	40,334	43,884	3,550
			86	30,800	16,855	18,572	1,717
PAKISTN	V	E	86	790	2,927	3,104	177
POLAND	N	E	82	378,092	195,695	220,791	25,096
	V	E	81	505,061	234,192	259,166	24,974
			82	55,116	24,938	28,750	3,812
			83	486,237	219,305	248,080	28,775
			84	52,911	41,664	46,126	4,462
			85	189,828	111,859	125,825	13,966
			86	1,192,966	619,142	716,955	97,813
SPAIN	V	E	82	19,842	15,758	15,758	
			83	17,600	11,172	13,376	2,204
SWEDEN	V	E	81	31,108	18,018	19,895	1,877
	V	W	83	20,000	9,207	10,149	942
TURKEY	V	E	81	95,625	46,730	53,265	6,535
			82	33,069	11,249	12,871	1,622
			83	44,069	17,224	20,843	3,619
			84	96,022	69,746	76,190	6,444
			85	4,329	1,371	1,709	338
			86	26,759	13,379	14,915	1,536
	V	W	84	1,653	1,090	1,242	152
			86	2,205	1,200	1,361	161
U KING	O	E	82	187	808	828	20
			84	101	318	343	25
	V	E	81	25,872	13,902	15,306	1,404
			82	157	883	919	36
			84	61,600	52,075	55,075	3,000
			86	42,240	21,700	23,768	2,068

Cardamom

Cardamom, spice
1611100 CARDAMON (LB)

				Quantity	F.A.S.	C.I.F.	Charges
TOTAL			81	184,530	491,338	520,168	28,830
			82	262,416	785,186	830,640	45,454
			83	192,103	598,174	622,408	24,234
			84	176,481	1,116,090	1,155,200	39,110
			85	447,298	1,580,302	1,649,046	68,744
			86	292,906	788,358	827,504	39,146
C RICA	A	W	85	917	4,487	5,786	1,299
	O	E	85	792	7,795	7,795	
	V	E	83	1,000	5,000	5,352	352
			84	3,306	27,548	28,236	688
			85	27,001	81,267	84,789	3,522
			86	17,640	46,511	49,169	2,658
CANADA	O	E	81	432	1,696	1,696	
			82	1,325	5,170	5,196	26
			83	105	3,333	3,333	
			84	1,939	7,068	7,068	
			85	12	2,027	2,027	
			86	880	4,995	4,995	
	O	W	81	186	1,362	1,439	77
			82	330	2,475	2,605	130
	V	E	85	308	3,080	3,311	231
CHINA M	N	E	83	33,069	24,603	26,103	1,500
	V	E	84	22,487	16,900	18,191	1,291
			85	44,092	18,543	21,500	2,957
			86	2,205	5,976	6,313	337
	V	W	85	1,250	2,592	2,810	218
ECUADOR	A	E	85	528	3,300	4,127	827
	V	W	85	4,409	15,141	15,680	539
FR GERM	A	E	82	55	463	597	134
FRANCE	A	W	84	441	869	1,177	308
	V	E	83	38	899	946	47
			84	32	837	845	8
			85	38	1,617	1,778	161
	V	W	83	132	493	523	30
			85	56	2,460	2,819	359
GUATMAL	A	E	84	3,324	22,817	23,836	1,019
			85	5,113	16,463	18,530	2,067
	A	W	83	1,606	12,175	12,798	623
	N	E	81	98,401	213,104	226,260	13,156
			82	13,327	45,940	48,063	2,123
			83	97,745	309,325	323,489	14,164

Crop Product TSUSA commodity number, description, and unit of quantity Country	Mode	Reg	Yr	Quantity	F.A.S.	C.I.F.	Charges
			84	76,233	554,983	566,654	11,671
			85	6,989	55,849	57,571	1,722
			86	102,440	283,887	295,937	12,050
	N	W	81	11,344	41,000	43,762	2,762
			82	25,925	74,857	79,381	4,524
			84	29,381	146,960	157,153	10,193
			85	45,953	265,567	278,830	13,263
			86	35,390	126,454	138,051	11,597
	O	E	81	440	879	1,132	253
			82	110	766	766	
			84	880	7,504	7,533	29
			85	4,004	23,753	24,492	739
			86	6,504	30,842	30,967	125
	O	W	85	25,080	25,080	25,080	
	V	E	81	8,488	24,215	25,263	1,048
			82	174,779	396,752	422,512	25,760
			83	31,573	126,357	129,146	2,789
			84	18,949	148,015	153,962	5,947
			85	176,722	669,141	688,856	19,715
			86	32,403	88,014	91,353	3,339
	V	W	81	14,999	46,789	48,143	1,354
			82	13,589	32,886	34,320	1,434
			84	4,410	31,000	31,464	464
			85	10,615	60,652	64,307	3,655
			86	8,818	22,000	23,200	1,200
GUINEA	V	E	85	771	4,418	4,749	331
HONDURA	O	E	86	10,050	37,891	37,891	
	V	E	85	3,349	3,762	4,783	1,021
			86	2,200	7,750	8,050	300
INDIA	N	E	82	14,745	109,561	115,540	5,979
			84	6,041	92,030	94,278	2,248
			85	54,650	111,204	120,276	9,072
			86	2,100	4,828	5,313	485
	N	W	81	2,556	4,623	5,335	712
			84	1,189	8,619	9,502	883
	O	E	81	366	3,288	3,288	
			82	605	3,561	3,762	201
			83	1,102	1,393	1,393	
			84	458	2,897	3,042	145
			85	991	2,680	2,824	144
			86	1,430	4,340	4,340	
	V	E	81	8,173	64,935	67,721	2,786
			82	2,000	32,500	33,379	879
			83	8,415	53,777	55,660	1,883
			84	506	2,266	2,320	54
			85	5,743	65,349	66,604	1,255
			86	19,408	67,228	71,218	3,990
	V	W	81	4,461	6,741	7,965	1,224
			82	3,171	8,580	9,884	1,304
			83	4,449	7,002	8,195	1,193
			84	700	2,837	3,474	637
			85	4,824	37,665	40,250	2,585
			86	3,360	9,281	10,081	800
JAMAICA	V	E	81	551	4,683	4,974	291
JAPAN	V	W	83	1,102	1,278	1,461	183
KIRIBAT	V	E	85	1,102	4,279	4,596	317
			86	2,205	4,000	4,156	156
MEXICO	A	W	83	243	1,150	1,233	83
			86	3,080	10,710	11,754	1,044
	O	W	86	39,600	21,780	21,780	
	V	E	83	3,307	10,684	10,929	245
MOROC	V	E	83	2,205	14,882	15,032	150
NEPAL	V	E	81	17,637	22,400	25,228	2,828
NETHLDS	O	E	82	1,276	4,650	4,804	154
NEW GUI	V	W	85	21,517	79,900	82,181	2,281
OMAN	V	E	84	2,205	18,186	18,632	446
PAKISTN	O	E	84	88	1,605	1,742	137
S HELNA	V	E	84	1,102	12,685	13,596	911
SALVADR	V	W	81	7,000	22,462	23,075	613
SINGAPR	V	H	81	19	283	322	39
SPAIN	A	E	85	268	9,946	10,250	304
SRI LKA	O	E	86	2,205	6,032	6,432	400
	V	E	81	8,977	24,753	26,161	1,408
			82	6,615	23,531	24,743	1,212
			83	4,410	24,912	25,779	867
	V	W	82	2,205	9,615	10,048	433
THAILND	V	E	82	109	535	640	105
	V	W	82	250	844	949	105
			85	110	1,010	1,095	85
			86	481	3,315	3,532	217
TNZANIA	A	E	85	94	1,275	1,350	75
			86	66	1,128	1,389	261
TURKEY	V	E	84	2,700	8,385	10,326	1,941
	V	W	86	441	1,396	1,583	187

Crop Product TSUSA commodity number, description, and unit of quantity Country	Mode	Reg	Yr	Quantity	F.A.S.	C.I.F.	Charges
U KING	A	E	84	110	2,079	2,169	90
	V	E	81	500	8,125	8,404	279
			82	2,000	32,500	33,451	951
			83	1,602	911	1,036	125

Carnation

Carnation, fresh
1921700 MINIATURE CARNATIONS, FRESH (NO)

Country	Mode	Reg	Yr	Quantity	F.A.S.	C.I.F.	Charges
TOTAL			81	32,835,605	2,733,627	4,266,794	1,509,362
			82	45,775,823	4,937,887	7,213,676	2,275,789
			83	72,682,172	7,285,537	9,834,505	2,548,968
			84	80,863,531	11,479,976	14,877,456	3,397,480
			85	66,508,645	11,736,202	15,453,832	3,717,630
			86	80,160,625	10,345,093	13,892,602	3,547,509
ALGERIA	A	E	82	18,170	2,541	3,017	476
ARGENT	A	E	84	3,300	264	1,316	1,052
AUSTRIA	A	E	82	1,550	403	469	66
C RICA	A	E	81	5,333	2,800	3,242	442
			83	321,172	23,807	29,127	5,320
			84	235,460	28,610	38,513	9,903
			85	515,441	62,312	69,863	7,551
			86	1,329,438	208,365	247,572	39,207
	A	W	83	1,100	748	1,073	325
			84	3,500	363	425	62
			85	12,500	1,316	1,595	279
			86	150,830	131,732	159,932	28,200
CANADA	A	E	83	6,860	6,138	6,973	835
			85	1,500	1,200	1,504	304
			86	110,620	17,995	21,143	3,148
	O	E	81	14,360	27,102	27,102	
			82	17,840	31,001	31,001	
			83	32,766	53,313	53,313	
			84	14,260	16,963	16,963	
			85	43,562	19,416	19,416	
			86	128,048	23,662	23,662	
	O	W	84	225	652	652	
CHILE	A	E	83	6,350	2,439	3,055	616
			84	8,750	8,493	10,354	1,861
			86	13,800	1,242	1,721	479
COLOMB	A	E	81	2,417,641	334,681	427,288	69,192
			82	17,415,814	1,879,606	2,205,563	325,957
			83	33,708	4,384	5,041	657
			84	266,440	30,644	35,610	4,966
			85	22,822,275	5,923,998	7,029,676	1,105,678
			86	3,084,085	946,955	1,209,471	262,516
	A	W	81	1,337	702	976	274
	N	E	81	5,194,552	755,298	1,008,457	252,499
			83	29,943,000	3,224,335	3,746,191	521,856
			84	26,457,649	5,712,786	6,620,829	908,043
			86	36,401,762	3,907,343	4,912,905	1,005,562
	O	E	86	233	1,057	1,057	
DENMARK	A	W	84	2,675	1,664	1,874	210
DOM REP	A	E	82	10,154	900	1,149	249
ECUADOR	A	E	81	2,229	1,170	1,530	360
			82	1,476	959	1,235	276
			83	1,149,094	157,006	201,832	44,826
			84	205,541	10,989	17,560	6,571
			85	3,229,568	355,454	463,837	108,383
			86	873,040	138,945	169,026	30,081
	A	H	85	1,240	1,708	2,006	298
	A	W	86	120	1,643	3,366	1,723
	N	E	84	1,703,695	389,720	473,792	84,072
EGYPT	A	E	85	15,000	1,500	1,710	210
FR GERM	A	E	83	9,100	3,345	4,019	674
			84	6,251	1,710	1,995	285
	N	E	85	130,800	5,290	10,822	5,532
FRANCE	A	E	82	14,060	2,499	2,781	282
			83	156,711	29,990	35,274	5,284
			84	89,552	24,674	30,705	6,031
			85	14,500	5,018	6,364	1,346
			86	923	1,796	2,266	470
	A	W	83	2,400	253	483	230
			84	800	1,280	1,614	334
GERM DR	A	E	85	4,700	3,057	4,417	1,360
GREECE	A	E	83	46,500	4,507	6,429	1,922
			84	11,884	1,426	1,726	300
			86	24,000	3,266	4,659	1,393
GUATMAL	A	E	81	10,200	816	1,067	251

Crop
Product
TSUSA commodity number, description, and unit of quantity

Country	Mode	Reg	Yr	Quantity	F.A.S.	C.I.F.	Charges
			85	27,015	3,382	4,245	863
HONDURA	A	E	83	24,250	2,449	2,776	327
ICELAND	A	E	85	16,500	1,800	3,634	1,834
ISRAEL	A	E	81	18,441,773	538,572	1,462,357	924,055
			82	18,636,925	1,178,754	2,633,382	1,454,628
			83	19,798,624	882,270	2,030,950	1,148,680
			84	17,426,723	1,203,951	2,294,579	1,090,628
	.		85	2,400,745	354,518	525,215	170,697
			86	20,756,538	2,532,115	3,737,571	1,205,456
	A	W	82	22,500	4,160	7,839	3,679
			84	11,965	6,730	8,859	2,129
			85	373,487	178,977	263,363	84,386
			86	567,180	101,517	187,106	85,589
	N	E	85	16,809,608	1,666,941	2,853,739	1,186,798
ITALY	A	E	81	295,680	41,018	54,356	13,338
			82	35,200	5,848	7,892	2,044
			83	620,480	121,874	142,833	20,959
			84	461,740	80,547	103,312	22,765
			85	279,625	54,367	71,130	16,763
			86	124,073	26,591	36,167	9,576
	A	W	83	111	302	316	14
			84	48,600	10,236	12,849	2,613
JAMAICA	A	E	84	18,600	800	1,428	628
JAPAN	A	E	85	27,000	1,336	2,735	1,399
			86	22,000	2,621	4,866	2,245
KENYA	A	E	81	26,000	3,332	4,446	1,114
			82	1,002,800	34,475	67,277	32,802
			83	1,977,271	127,499	238,400	110,901
			84	3,830,372	167,522	308,774	141,252
			85	3,290,981	168,234	346,490	178,256
			86	2,553,454	150,401	247,673	97,272
	A	W	84	2,400	2,284	2,936	652
MACAO	A	E	85	25,000	2,500	2,976	476
MALI	A	E	85	9,300	1,093	2,044	951
MEXICO	A	E	82	44,950	5,179	6,284	1,105
			84	68,477	15,772	19,542	3,770
			86	110,000	41,674	42,652	978
	A	W	81	45,991	4,100	6,145	2,045
			84	1,500	268	318	50
	O	W	81	50,571	7,420	7,420	
			82	71,960	5,429	5,429	
			84	245,031	9,151	9,151	
N ANTIL	A	E	85	307,660	28,459	43,942	15,483
			86	120,000	2,340	2,533	193
N CALDN	A	E	86	59,702	1,226	1,837	611
NETHLDS	A	E	81	5,388,032	767,539	946,306	178,767
			82	2,900,903	226,846	273,917	47,071
			83	6,413,165	1,155,850	1,450,635	294,785
			84	1,724,078	209,981	275,429	65,448
			85	697,012	119,976	156,165	36,189
			86	3,253,686	696,501	955,408	258,907
	A	W	81	3,128	552	1,000	448
			82	30,787	13,589	17,369	3,780
			83	33,220	9,538	11,962	2,424
			84	780,112	121,200	159,017	37,817
			85	332,328	71,259	91,301	20,042
			86	754,807	95,284	132,003	36,719
	N	E	81	32,000	3,040	3,296	256
			82	4,446,679	669,740	851,642	181,902
			83	104,660	21,791	24,466	2,675
			84	10,060,556	1,580,272	2,069,827	489,555
			85	3,953,773	723,441	1,004,645	281,204
	N	W	86	49,900	9,552	13,337	3,785
	O	E	85	1,000	2,400	2,565	165
			86	21,828	7,768	10,468	2,700
	V	E	84	38,370	6,945	8,864	1,919
PANAMA	A	E	86	43,000	2,150	3,155	1,005
PERU	A	E	81	267,877	194,922	246,148	51,226
			82	22,270	17,438	22,628	5,190
			83	51,400	5,481	6,903	1,422
			84	39,560	4,827	5,903	1,076
			85	10,513,961	1,901,809	2,351,254	449,445
			86	8,750,517	1,180,527	1,602,481	421,954
	A	W	81	29,850	25,269	36,237	10,968
			82	16,450	13,880	18,912	5,032
	N	E	82	934,925	822,246	1,027,174	204,928
			83	11,686,061	1,414,551	1,784,533	369,982
			84	16,852,123	1,796,570	2,291,867	495,297
PORTUGL	A	E	84	15,000	3,300	4,637	1,337
			86	7,650	1,490	1,735	245
REP SAF	A	E	82	50,990	4,720	6,246	1,526
			83	7,060	1,794	2,049	255
			84	13,700	2,941	3,513	572
			85	19,600	2,310	3,020	710

Country	Mode	Reg	Yr	Quantity	F.A.S.	C.I.F.	Charges
SINGAPR	A	E	83	10,270	2,066	2,504	438
			84	3,050	590	671	81
			85	26,410	3,980	5,195	1,215
			86	14,770	3,268	3,959	691
SPAIN	A	E	82	26,290	1,596	2,696	1,100
			83	237,195	27,867	40,985	13,118
			84	143,371	14,007	26,617	12,610
			85	487,400	23,272	43,119	19,847
			86	809,000	95,896	141,972	46,076
	A	W	83	1,164	263	327	64
			86	17,621	4,668	4,911	243
THAILND	A	E	83	3,760	747	905	158
			84	8,725	4,110	5,421	1,311
			85	15,665	4,433	7,039	2,606
			86	2,500	4,373	4,483	110
U KING	A	E	81	609,051	25,294	29,421	4,127
			82	53,130	16,078	19,774	3,696
			83	4,720	930	1,151	221
			84	54,296	7,008	9,168	2,160
			85	103,489	41,446	58,806	17,360
			86	5,500	1,130	1,505	375
	A	W	84	5,200	726	846	120

1922130 STANDARD CARNATIONS, FRESH (NO)

Country	Mode	Reg	Yr	Quantity	F.A.S.	C.I.F.	Charges
TOTAL			83	522,909,322	38,512,749	44,373,807	5,861,058
			84	637,242,150	50,777,346	59,561,666	8,784,320
			85	620,325,528	42,889,494	53,028,389	10,138,895
			86	623,259,256	38,609,531	49,869,716	11,260,185
BELGIUM	A	E	86	10,650	2,190	3,252	1,062
BOLIVIA	A	E	86	43,000	3,230	4,685	1,455
BULGAR	O	E	86	13,620	4,343	4,343	
C RICA	A	E	83	677,350	37,950	46,753	8,803
			84	629,725	51,463	60,195	8,732
			85	392,735	44,279	50,816	6,537
			86	1,081,128	111,272	126,784	15,512
	A	W	84	12,000	1,461	1,674	213
			85	14,000	2,374	2,633	259
			86	27,000	2,892	3,343	451
CANADA	A	E	83	158,000	9,889	11,586	1,697
			85	3,387,975	214,302	264,229	49,927
			86	398,520	26,651	33,974	7,323
	A	W	86	22,820	2,537	5,044	2,507
	O	E	83	28,445	13,041	13,041	
			84	67,342	21,950	21,950	
			85	61,050	14,687	14,687	
			86	56,784	23,181	23,181	
	O	W	86	37,750	2,844	2,844	
CHILE	A	E	83	460,350	21,701	35,954	14,253
			84	103,540	8,807	13,735	4,928
			85	2,189,250	90,947	193,184	102,237
			86	1,885,449	65,179	143,146	77,967
	A	W	84	104,361	24,400	27,651	3,251
			85	105,625	7,030	10,294	3,264
			86	215,509	20,965	33,652	12,687
	N	E	84	1,563,395	99,319	167,748	68,429
CHINA M	A	E	86	51,600	2,106	3,009	903
COCOS I	A	E	86	164,900	9,378	12,362	2,984
COLOMB	A	E	83	1,131,454	100,673	118,101	17,428
			84	2,129,819	190,976	233,180	42,204
			85	6,123,176	404,042	494,224	90,182
			86	2,090,898	155,306	198,261	42,955
	A	H	86	57,900	2,728	3,725	997
	A	W	85	40,350	3,000	4,428	1,428
	N	E	83	501,018,044	36,749,265	42,464,596	5,715,331
			84	608,894,655	48,261,300	56,595,388	8,334,088
			85	591,176,969	40,759,807	50,403,680	9,643,873
			86	597,123,578	36,448,489	47,151,369	10,702,880
	O	E	86	15,850	3,733	3,733	
DOM REP	A	E	85	56,425	5,155	7,188	2,033
			86	106,800	8,725	10,723	1,998
	N	E	84	887,400	40,142	51,127	10,985
ECUADOR	A	E	83	26,022	5,074	6,213	1,139
			84	300,228	42,181	54,372	12,191
			85	3,323,516	197,972	271,873	73,901
			86	4,251,360	251,888	323,253	71,365
	A	W	86	140,603	8,755	16,957	8,202
EGYPT	A	E	86	22,700	1,022	1,418	396
F W IND	A	E	84	3,500	525	597	72
FR GERM	A	E	85	15,000	2,549	2,975	426
			86	800	1,723	1,723	
FRANCE	A	E	83	127,350	22,620	28,461	5,841
			84	16,590	4,045	4,880	835
			85	162	1,557	2,040	483

Crop Product TSUSA commodity number, description, and unit of quantity Country	Mode	Reg	Yr	Quantity	F.A.S.	C.I.F.	Charges
			86	34,500	7,004	8,610	1,606
	A	W	85	550	4,202	4,374	172
GREECE	A	E	83	24,800	2,372	3,472	1,100
			86	71,000	11,666	13,618	1,952
GUATMAL	A	E	83	7,680	888	1,310	422
			84	20,890	1,940	2,876	936
			85	32,550	2,989	3,716	727
HONDURA	A	E	84	536,400	33,612	42,309	8,697
			85	170,000	1,726	1,878	152
ISRAEL	A	E	83	106,821	7,983	15,805	7,822
			84	1,418,749	170,318	301,805	131,487
			85	143,760	21,226	29,036	7,810
			86	553,700	68,357	108,260	39,903
	A	W	84	5,360	1,200	1,689	489
			85	91,542	19,957	41,006	21,049
			86	344,470	47,395	82,231	34,836
ITALY	A	E	83	204,900	33,836	39,838	6,002
			84	484,417	84,451	108,277	23,826
			85	494,130	88,798	118,347	29,549
			86	297,280	64,431	83,886	19,455
	A	W	84	4,000	612	914	302
KENYA	A	E	83	6,000	828	1,002	174
			85	107,350	4,297	10,220	5,923
			86	143,786	15,125	32,691	17,566
KIRIBAT	A	E	85	26,400	1,680	2,076	396
KOR REP	A	E	86	1,600	2,142	2,983	841
MACAO	A	E	85	185,000	12,948	15,816	2,868
MEXICO	A	E	85	3,575,713	329,587	364,880	35,293
			84	4,177,214	381,780	424,175	42,395
			85	560,942	57,695	67,363	9,668
			86	3,809,540	362,028	411,403	49,375
	A	W	83	420,970	33,813	42,140	8,327
			84	1,388,225	112,356	141,232	28,876
			85	1,097,225	69,848	84,694	14,846
			86	957,456	116,176	148,746	32,570
	N	E	83	605,485	47,132	50,131	2,999
			84	209,912	18,044	20,455	2,411
			85	1,458,225	136,451	149,041	12,590
			86	711,800	53,690	54,245	555
	O	E	83	26,800	2,020	2,274	254
			86	45,000	2,989	2,989	
	O	W	83	12,818,289	952,297	953,581	1,284
			84	12,721,617	978,922	978,922	
			85	7,358,591	512,514	512,514	
			86	6,786,920	457,570	471,855	14,285
MONSRAT	A	E	85	39,000	2,720	3,030	310
	A	W	85	18,600	1,558	1,796	238
	O	W	85	38,250	2,295	2,295	
N ANTIL	A	E	85	28,400	4,150	4,724	574
			86	10,800	1,368	1,496	128
N ZEAL	A	W	84	4,910	761	837	76
NETHLDS	A	E	83	352,344	62,984	76,064	13,080
			84	791,840	165,757	206,245	40,488
			85	18,534	10,857	14,411	3,554
			86	563,008	114,424	167,193	52,769
	A	W	83	16,545	2,015	2,818	803
			84	86,631	18,744	24,320	5,576
			85	30,903	9,246	13,028	3,782
			86	93,148	11,073	14,608	3,535
	N	E	85	402,443	96,253	116,949	20,696
	O	E	86	64,718	12,987	14,667	1,680
	V	E	84	7,740	3,667	4,296	629
PANAMA	A	E	86	277,100	13,825	19,444	5,619
PERU	A	E	83	475,910	37,471	47,469	9,998
			84	589,090	49,553	57,091	7,538
			85	200,700	37,098	45,913	8,815
			86	139,020	15,864	20,953	5,089
POLAND	A	E	83	545,150	33,881	41,743	7,862
REP SAF	A	E	85	3,350	1,316	1,747	431
SINGAPR	A	W	85	11,500	1,831	2,131	300
SPAIN	A	E	83	79,100	3,730	4,363	633
			84	82,200	8,325	12,767	4,442
			85	915,500	39,833	59,891	20,058
			86	398,001	59,128	83,253	24,125
	O	E	86	700	1,224	1,224	
U KING	A	E	85	9,200	1,621	1,889	268
			86	35,940	5,821	7,677	1,856
	A	W	83	800	579	795	216
	O	E	86	97,200	4,791	5,156	365
VENEZ	A	E	83	15,000	1,120	1,417	297
			84	400	735	959	224

Carnauba Palm

Carnauba, wax
4941200 VEGETABLE WAX CARNAUBA (LB)

Country	Mode	Reg	Yr	Quantity	F.A.S.	C.I.F.	Charges
TOTAL			81	6,023,038	5,096,739	5,855,527	758,788
			82	5,887,875	4,793,329	5,532,822	739,493
			83	8,271,247	4,898,443	5,715,926	817,483
			84	7,296,087	3,876,325	4,596,459	720,134
			85	6,634,665	4,247,590	4,771,725	524,135
			86	7,362,401	5,890,047	6,359,593	469,546
AUSTRIA	V	E	81	110	492	500	8
BELIZE	V	E	85	264,092	160,954	182,039	21,085
			86	6,614	4,491	4,901	410
BRAZIL	A	E	85	6,614	10,733	15,346	4,613
	N	E	81	5,576,723	4,676,223	5,378,727	702,504
			85	5,219,436	3,211,064	3,632,098	421,034
	O	E	82	10,000	9,272	9,272	
	V	E	81	280,572	252,415	289,772	37,357
			82	5,530,106	4,405,783	5,112,744	706,961
			83	8,144,283	4,786,404	5,588,097	801,693
			84	7,101,556	3,623,299	4,309,154	685,855
			85	602,028	445,860	496,293	50,433
			86	6,874,193	5,391,640	5,842,621	450,981
	V	W	81	151,045	154,798	173,512	18,714
			82	187,071	188,856	211,096	22,240
			83	102,320	89,245	103,522	14,277
			84	45,569	28,469	35,262	6,793
			85	84,824	56,011	69,171	13,160
			86	45,183	49,865	57,850	7,985
CANADA	O	E	81	14,563	11,239	11,239	
			83	150	390	390	
DENMARK	V	E	85	34,171	25,007	28,754	3,747
DOM REP	V	E	85	29,900	44,564	46,281	1,717
			86	29,900	40,884	42,662	1,778
FR GERM	V	E	83	1,164	1,327	1,479	152
			84	11,024	5,056	6,241	1,185
	V	W	86	1,200	4,254	4,716	462
HG KONG	V	W	82	120	464	480	16
IRELAND	O	E	82	119,820	161,549	166,549	5,000
ITALY	V	E	84	40	304	364	60
	V	W	85	1,753	2,113	2,439	326
JAPAN	A	E	84	4,650	27,710	38,281	10,571
	A	W	84	2,262	8,549	13,854	5,305
	V	E	84	88,184	62,995	70,400	7,405
			86	55,115	54,890	61,050	6,160
	V	W	83	13,310	16,834	17,090	256
			84	12,890	75,119	76,268	1,149
			85	9,601	45,640	46,166	526
			86	30,216	42,193	42,572	379
MEXICO	O	E	82	31,822	15,658	18,350	2,692
			85	266,356	201,641	201,641	
			86	305,165	289,691	289,691	
N ZEAL	V	E	85	66,138	56,067	60,185	4,118
SINGAPR	A	E	82	99	500	789	289
SPAIN	V	E	82	8,800	10,542	12,707	2,165
			83	10,000	3,974	5,025	1,051
U KING	V	E	84	12	260	354	94
			85	79,652	32,500	37,593	5,093
			86	14,043	10,827	12,152	1,325
	V	W	81	25	1,572	1,777	205
			82	37	705	835	130
			83	20	269	323	54
VENEZ	V	E	86	772	1,312	1,378	66

Carob

Carob, gum
1883820 LOCUST BEAN GUM, NATURAL (LB)

Country	Mode	Reg	Yr	Quantity	F.A.S.	C.I.F.	Charges
TOTAL			81	5,500,184	8,644,740	9,048,269	404,572
			82	4,119,812	8,258,830	8,565,640	306,810
			83	5,204,544	9,359,644	9,720,640	360,996
			84	5,560,707	9,808,568	10,198,997	390,429
			85	3,645,677	9,516,920	9,814,666	297,746
			86	4,911,710	23,411,133	23,917,921	506,788
AUSTRAL	V	E	83	11,795	1,715	2,836	1,121
BRAZIL	V	E	82	39,727	65,550	70,196	4,646

Crop
Product
TSUSA commodity number, description, and unit of quantity

Country	Mode	Reg	Yr	Quantity	F.A.S.	C.I.F.	Charges
CANADA	O	E	83	70,000	136,596	136,596	
DENMARK	A	E	86	33,070	49,526	54,418	4,892
	V	E	81	37,500	55,875	61,463	5,588
			82	3,307	18,035	18,559	524
			83	4,409	27,187	28,546	1,359
			84	110	754	778	24
			85	4,409	26,989	27,695	706
			86	21,715	31,666	33,551	1,885
	V	W	84	4,409	28,064	28,609	545
FRANCE	A	E	83	55	310	359	49
			85	221	1,495	1,870	375
	V	E	86	22,046	103,750	105,340	1,590
GREECE	V	E	86	10,031	50,822	51,676	854
GUATMAL	V	E	82	32,858	59,144	61,840	2,696
INDIA	V	E	82	40,000	88,700	91,565	2,865
	V	W	82	56,689	17,586	20,338	2,752
IRAN	V	E	83	44,092	77,234	79,807	2,573
			84	220,643	425,370	438,430	13,060
ITALY	A	E	86	7,000	36,547	42,940	6,393
	V	E	81	1,377,297	2,125,490	2,238,042	112,552
			82	946,553	1,933,511	2,008,028	74,517
			83	1,534,124	2,732,371	2,836,748	104,377
			84	1,539,480	2,896,556	3,008,896	112,340
			85	837,339	1,700,124	1,769,710	69,586
			86	1,781,489	8,347,078	8,543,398	196,320
	V	W	81	84,333	143,259	151,492	8,233
			82	81,600	169,271	176,581	7,310
			83	77,500	128,760	134,650	5,890
			84	315,110	596,511	618,688	22,177
			85	119,112	224,041	233,027	8,986
			86	80,026	484,579	491,003	6,424
JAPAN	V	E	85	84,000	331,756	338,289	6,533
NETHLDS	V	E	81	5,512	29,980	30,653	673
			82	40,000	65,500	68,340	2,840
			83	4,409	7,870	8,402	532
PAKISTN	V	E	81	114,002	81,186	89,732	8,546
PORTUGL	V	E	81	1,043,150	1,625,892	1,688,736	62,844
			82	820,032	1,581,649	1,631,879	50,230
			83	689,216	1,244,678	1,292,229	47,551
			84	716,910	1,316,223	1,374,595	58,372
			85	200,080	743,962	760,079	16,117
			86	736,648	3,306,375	3,342,643	36,268
	V	W	81	79,400	126,167	130,470	4,303
			82	39,910	77,486	80,194	2,708
			83	60,000	104,630	110,400	5,770
			84	40,000	79,130	82,400	3,270
SPAIN	A	E	85	15,983	74,667	86,328	11,661
	N	E	85	1,108,074	3,082,973	3,175,609	92,636
			86	923,420	4,672,819	4,849,807	176,988
	O	E	82	95,450	219,006	219,006	
			83	52,050	103,872	103,872	
			84	10,192	19,978	19,978	
	V	E	81	2,565,990	4,186,050	4,373,234	188,227
			82	1,745,687	3,624,823	3,768,324	143,501
			83	2,545,571	4,596,653	4,781,221	184,568
			84	2,595,749	4,222,282	4,394,220	171,938
			85	1,056,338	3,001,630	3,082,204	80,574
			86	1,212,173	6,222,671	6,294,697	72,026
	V	W	81	191,000	266,446	279,847	13,401
			82	175,999	333,814	345,830	12,016
			83	110,772	196,938	203,982	7,044
			84	118,104	223,700	232,403	8,703
			85	100,014	186,798	194,408	7,610
SWEDEN	V	E	85	40,741	72,643	75,605	2,962
SWITZLD	V	E	81	2,000	4,395	4,600	205
			82	2,000	4,755	4,960	205
			83	551	830	992	162
			86	40,000	80,000	80,670	670
U KING	V	E	85	79,366	69,842	69,842	
			86	44,092	25,300	27,778	2,478

Carrot

Carrot, canned

1418200 CARROTS, CANNED (LB)

				Quantity	F.A.S.	C.I.F.	Charges
TOTAL			81	8,565,204	2,290,702	2,679,187	388,485
			82	7,717,792	1,839,834	2,149,962	310,128
			83	8,947,142	1,797,357	2,117,307	319,950
			84	9,938,711	2,011,836	2,445,382	433,546
			85	12,267,174	2,478,570	3,102,269	623,699

Crop
Product
TSUSA commodity number, description, and unit of quantity

Country	Mode	Reg	Yr	Quantity	F.A.S.	C.I.F.	Charges
			86	14,134,577	3,435,706	4,147,045	711,339
AUSTRIA	N	E	83	254,286	96,843	107,313	10,470
			85	229,601	100,357	117,612	17,255
	V	E	81	138,317	41,484	49,014	7,530
			82	134,931	49,456	53,871	4,415
			84	278,918	93,983	103,250	9,267
			85	9,750	2,594	3,051	457
			86	124,695	34,893	41,472	6,579
	V	W	83	21,450	6,352	7,309	957
			84	16,710	3,779	4,523	744
BELGIUM	N	E	81	1,956,904	526,235	610,363	84,128
			82	2,337,073	526,012	609,213	83,201
			83	2,676,465	502,112	587,852	85,740
			85	784,337	161,164	196,706	35,542
	O	E	81	146,763	35,762	43,793	8,031
			82	54,811	12,296	15,093	2,797
			84	37,699	6,385	8,507	2,122
			85	71,832	11,310	15,370	4,060
	V	E	81	3,028,789	839,095	991,422	152,327
			82	2,921,651	715,362	842,692	127,330
			83	3,295,664	654,794	765,482	110,688
			84	6,498,647	1,259,298	1,535,888	276,590
			85	8,030,990	1,489,757	1,873,197	383,440
			86	10,092,135	2,439,982	2,918,757	478,775
	V	W	81	1,307,892	348,929	410,958	62,029
			82	881,660	212,005	254,849	42,844
			83	1,070,167	220,528	271,034	50,506
			84	984,193	183,506	233,896	50,390
			85	1,145,244	286,790	362,945	76,155
			86	953,965	251,271	298,156	46,885
BULGAR	V	E	85	94,909	19,715	22,630	2,915
			86	262,490	54,630	67,170	12,540
CANADA	O	E	81	373,698	61,835	61,835	
			82	102,747	20,135	20,135	
			83	45,902	9,788	9,788	
			84	145,640	27,487	27,487	
			85	139,307	26,715	26,715	
			86	74,760	15,187	15,187	
CHINA T	V	E	83	15,640	7,480	8,069	589
			84	25,265	10,050	11,781	1,731
	V	W	83	5,100	2,278	2,384	106
			85	33,660	12,377	13,477	1,100
DENMARK	V	E	83	33,730	6,480	7,691	1,211
FR GERM	V	E	82	77,317	16,897	18,952	2,055
			83	74,024	15,187	17,404	2,217
			84	25,587	5,116	5,774	658
			85	40,304	11,665	14,008	2,343
			86	68,641	20,274	22,402	2,128
FRANCE	N	E	83	3,934	1,957	2,574	617
			85	19,316	3,272	4,344	1,072
	V	E	81	11,738	4,729	5,558	829
			82	8,330	3,579	4,454	875
			83	5,429	1,463	1,742	279
			84	910,378	184,407	236,624	52,217
			85	759,109	128,290	167,605	39,315
			86	774,518	141,940	175,821	33,881
	V	W	81	2,714	728	859	131
			82	12,854	3,711	3,908	197
			83	10,384	1,775	3,210	1,435
			84	30,260	10,151	11,470	1,319
			85	12,222	3,368	4,076	708
HG KONG	V	W	84	513	353	415	62
HUNGARY	O	E	84	5,000	7,026	7,026	
			86	5,016	9,340	9,340	
ISRAEL	V	E	81	73,089	23,537	28,485	4,948
			82	97,156	22,110	27,491	5,381
			83	24,839	6,310	7,133	823
			85	118,737	51,285	66,331	15,046
			86	369,002	128,236	178,068	49,832
ITALY	V	E	85	29,762	4,108	5,346	1,238
MALI	V	E	85	33,750	6,500	8,931	2,431
MALTA	V	E	84	40,183	6,356	7,777	1,421
N ANTIL	V	E	81	134,943	37,869	43,204	5,335
NETHLDS	O	E	86	24,424	7,571	7,731	160
	V	E	81	1,322,857	351,098	410,586	59,488
			82	1,055,512	248,826	288,410	39,584
			83	1,329,678	248,565	299,064	50,499
			84	692,961	133,289	156,845	23,556
			85	577,988	115,697	147,136	31,439
			86	725,277	143,286	194,787	51,501
	V	W	81	67,500	19,401	23,110	3,709
			83	33,731	6,780	8,526	1,746
			84	101,250	21,620	28,461	6,841

Crop
Product
TSUSA commodity number, description, and unit of quantity

Country	Mode	Reg	Yr	Quantity	F.A.S.	C.I.F.	Charges
NIGER	V	E	85	70,876	13,067	17,369	4,302
			86	141,752	27,941	35,442	7,501
PORTUGL	V	E	84	39,683	6,633	8,224	1,591
			86	39,683	7,411	9,520	2,109
SPAIN	V	E	82	33,750	9,445	10,894	1,449
			84	67,527	30,830	34,966	4,136
	V	W	83	37,699	6,062	7,727	1,665
SWAZLND	V	E	84	18,452	6,090	6,724	634
SWEDEN	V	E	86	29,597	6,951	8,358	1,407
SWITZLD	V	E	83	9,020	2,603	3,005	402
			84	19,845	15,477	15,744	267
			85	33,480	23,497	26,895	3,398
			86	290,280	97,081	110,763	13,682
THAILND	V	W	86	46,892	23,345	25,257	1,912
U KING	V	E	85	18,500	4,575	5,534	959
			86	111,450	26,367	28,814	2,447
VENEZ	V	E	85	13,500	2,467	2,991	524

Carrot, dried
1405400 CARROTS, DRIED DEHYDRTD ETC (LB)

Country	Mode	Reg	Yr	Quantity	F.A.S.	C.I.F.	Charges
TOTAL			81	91,742	166,487	175,982	9,495
			82	158,457	227,026	247,362	20,336
			83	270,964	428,722	457,462	28,740
			84	481,763	744,914	802,153	57,239
			85	881,760	1,249,243	1,362,410	113,167
			86	1,313,013	1,471,439	1,597,565	126,126
ARGENT	V	E	82	2,205	2,420	2,601	181
			83	4,409	5,105	5,699	594
CANADA	O	E	81	18,758	56,412	56,412	
			82	29,290	68,502	69,062	560
			83	41,112	96,826	96,826	
			84	32,031	56,783	56,783	
			86	5,040	9,305	9,305	
	O	W	82	5,040	7,488	7,488	
CHINA M	V	E	81	2,150	1,490	1,614	124
	V	W	81	6,614	4,244	5,291	1,047
			85	9,900	12,346	14,389	2,043
			86	29,068	9,018	10,171	1,153
CHINA T	V	E	85	22,205	23,993	27,254	3,261
			86	6,250	6,670	7,201	531
	V	W	84	26,684	25,551	27,183	1,632
			85	33,675	35,051	36,515	1,464
			86	33,015	43,775	45,678	1,903
FR GERM	A	E	84	320	317	337	20
	A	W	86	2,110	2,271	3,395	1,124
	O	E	81	1,012	3,520	3,796	276
			83	2,396	3,527	3,715	188
			85	5,148	5,262	5,778	516
			86	3,999	6,694	7,215	521
	V	E	83	538	1,089	1,268	179
			84	5,235	6,457	7,032	575
			85	5,400	4,684	4,980	296
			86	124,332	139,161	146,518	7,357
	V	W	81	1,557	2,884	3,389	505
			86	20,475	17,649	20,475	2,826
HG KONG	V	E	85	5,515	5,037	6,671	1,634
ISRAEL	A	E	82	196	760	830	70
	N	E	85	49,552	59,028	79,191	20,163
	O	E	81	4,620	5,666	5,666	
			82	196	738	760	22
			83	128,089	192,982	208,915	15,933
			86	11,968	14,578	15,293	715
	V	E	81	32,005	38,597	43,072	4,475
			82	60,334	82,629	92,534	9,905
			83	80,660	115,639	124,511	8,872
			84	353,517	565,763	611,145	45,382
			85	681,559	995,004	1,074,422	79,418
			86	1,006,011	1,160,872	1,263,025	102,153
	V	W	81	25,026	53,674	56,742	3,068
			82	54,776	57,876	67,474	9,598
			84	10,162	12,704	14,025	1,321
			86	56,715	51,648	58,392	6,744
ITALY	A	E	83	8,000	8,946	11,920	2,974
	V	E	84	34,062	44,842	48,068	3,226
			85	6,320	7,707	8,785	1,078
MEXICO	O	E	82	6,420	6,613	6,613	
			83	4,320	3,456	3,456	
			85	33,120	82,800	82,800	
	O	W	83	1,440	1,152	1,152	
			84	12,115	9,692	9,692	
			85	6,186	6,373	6,373	

Crop
Product
TSUSA commodity number, description, and unit of quantity

Country	Mode	Reg	Yr	Quantity	F.A.S.	C.I.F.	Charges
POLAND	V	E	84	2,205	800	921	121
			85	17,636	7,740	9,607	1,867
			86	11,023	4,650	5,333	683
REP SAF	V	E	85	5,544	4,218	5,645	1,427
SPAIN	V	E	86	3,007	5,148	5,564	416
SWITZLD	A	E	84	4,409	20,740	25,599	4,859
TURKEY	V	E	84	1,023	1,265	1,368	103

Carrot, fresh or frozen
1354100 CARROTS UNDER 4IN, FRSH, FZ (LB)

Country	Mode	Reg	Yr	Quantity	F.A.S.	C.I.F.	Charges
TOTAL			81	395,436	96,050	96,147	97
			82	926,759	150,520	168,747	18,227
			83	1,819,718	645,795	765,863	120,068
			84	2,385,009	635,125	775,432	140,307
			85	4,289,517	1,120,313	1,382,344	262,031
			86	5,049,016	1,389,455	1,756,085	366,630
BELGIUM	N	E	85	1,302,570	302,938	380,788	77,850
	O	E	83	44,092	10,144	12,008	1,864
			84	88,092	20,444	25,388	4,944
			85	88,184	19,576	19,576	
			86	1,155,103	343,159	448,568	105,409
	V	E	84	56,484	17,491	23,039	5,548
			85	407,712	111,393	149,996	38,603
			86	957,182	251,930	337,121	85,191
	V	W	85	5,992	1,003	1,187	184
			86	160,552	59,234	72,768	13,534
C RICA	V	E	82	75,552	2,913	7,017	4,104
CANADA	O	E	81	395,328	95,658	95,658	
			82	720,635	110,210	110,210	
			83	465,696	150,697	150,697	
			84	646,150	134,364	137,348	2,984
			85	636,422	149,209	149,209	
			86	1,204,974	239,390	239,390	
CHILE	V	E	84	45,000	13,034	16,499	3,465
CHINA T	V	W	86	41,400	21,231	21,581	350
FRANCE	A	E	81	108	392	489	97
	V	E	85	44,000	8,605	11,855	3,250
			86	46,538	18,358	23,058	4,700
	V	W	82	4,491	1,285	1,357	72
ISRAEL	O	E	85	15,015	8,671	8,671	
			86	42,659	11,314	16,426	5,112
	V	E	82	85,580	29,013	38,571	9,558
			83	820,413	348,879	421,379	72,500
			84	681,936	202,333	255,208	52,875
			85	820,230	244,429	335,247	90,818
			86	1,072,911	343,643	466,251	122,608
	V	W	84	44,893	11,611	19,210	7,599
			85	173,832	61,155	82,968	21,813
MEXICO	O	E	86	17,500	4,186	4,186	
	O	W	85	36,557	4,032	4,032	
NETHLDS	N	E	85	340,103	94,369	121,216	26,847
	O	E	84	249,731	72,398	87,232	14,834
			85	343,300	100,126	100,126	
			86	265,187	76,077	98,165	22,088
	O	W	84	1,650	1,018	1,018	
	V	E	82	40,501	7,099	11,592	4,493
			83	489,517	136,075	181,779	45,704
			84	553,409	158,634	205,150	46,516
			86	85,010	20,933	28,571	7,638
U KING	V	E	84	17,664	3,798	5,340	1,542
			85	75,600	14,807	17,473	2,666

1354200 CARROTS NOT UN 4IN FRSH, FZ (LB)

Country	Mode	Reg	Yr	Quantity	F.A.S.	C.I.F.	Charges
TOTAL			81	87,485,264	8,764,445	8,765,495	1,050
			82	104,199,524	8,317,499	8,317,499	
			83	124,848,386	13,425,470	13,426,598	1,128
			84	159,105,103	14,868,816	14,875,373	6,557
			85	143,499,278	12,597,053	12,612,309	15,256
			86	108,905,013	12,734,747	12,829,992	95,245
BELGIUM	A	E	84	770	592	622	30
	V	E	85	170,400	48,047	61,974	13,927
			86	511,973	100,857	146,418	45,561
CANADA	N	E	84	14,275,720	1,857,001	1,857,001	
			85	57,171,163	4,503,600	4,503,600	
	O	E	81	84,982,272	8,568,110	8,569,160	1,050
			82	102,950,544	8,249,737	8,249,737	
			83	119,042,108	13,167,514	13,168,354	840
			84	134,033,973	12,458,473	12,462,415	3,942
			85	76,646,175	7,519,617	7,519,709	92
			86	101,810,939	12,089,779	12,089,789	10

Crop
Product
TSUSA commodity number, description, and unit of quantity

Country	Mode	Reg	Yr	Quantity	F.A.S.	C.I.F.	Charges
	O	W	83	10,000	1,136	1,136	
			84	18,000	1,156	1,156	
	V	E	85	20,700	3,096	3,518	422
DOM REP	V	E	83	1,400	400	490	90
ECUADOR	O	E	82	7,880	1,562	1,562	
FRANCE	O	E	84	38,400	5,336	5,336	
	V	E	85	2,881	1,214	1,343	129
			86	38,644	14,405	18,087	3,682
HONDURA	O	E	85	1,500	1,341	1,341	
ISRAEL	V	E	86	140,744	46,511	61,976	15,465
	V	W	86	252,490	84,636	114,441	29,805
MALAYSA	O	W	85	11,080	1,662	1,662	
MEXICO	O	E	81	2,261,583	176,037	176,037	
			82	1,241,100	66,200	66,200	
			83	4,804,915	173,849	173,849	
			84	9,366,979	390,205	392,550	2,345
			85	7,380,436	259,987	259,987	
			86	4,552,211	179,964	179,964	
	O	W	81	241,409	20,298	20,298	
			83	940,630	72,949	72,949	
			84	1,343,508	152,172	152,172	
			85	2,049,506	244,949	244,949	
			86	1,548,394	210,656	210,656	
N ZEAL	V	H	84	26,455	2,983	3,066	83
NETHLDS	A	E	83	1,760	1,045	1,243	198
			84	1,298	898	1,055	157
			85	1,389	1,050	1,736	686
	O	E	85	44,048	12,490	12,490	
	V	E	86	8,818	2,938	3,660	722
REP SAF	O	E	83	47,567	8,577	8,577	
			86	40,800	5,001	5,001	

Carrot, seed
1261700 CARROT SEED (LB)

Country	Mode	Reg	Yr	Quantity	F.A.S.	C.I.F.	Charges
TOTAL			81	9,864	42,367	48,877	6,500
			82	12,536	63,763	68,404	4,641
			83	22,245	121,763	132,637	10,874
			84	10,112	94,997	100,602	5,605
			85	83,031	288,432	302,973	14,541
			86	67,598	388,202	417,594	29,392
AUSTRAL	A	H	86	18,300	131,558	141,722	10,164
	A	W	85	20,680	36,727	40,236	3,509
			86	395	3,622	3,647	25
CANADA	O	E	81	954	2,730	2,730	
			86	265	4,738	4,738	
CHILE	V	W	81	763	2,335	2,426	91
			85	23,372	90,144	92,403	2,259
			86	4,627	6,978	7,080	102
DENMARK	A	E	82	360	3,746	4,163	417
			83	250	2,629	2,923	294
			84	375	4,225	4,623	398
	A	W	81	230	357	816	459
			84	290	290	684	394
			85	979	1,017	1,907	890
	O	E	81	30	321	331	
	V	E	82	200	2,012	2,143	131
			86	4,659	12,740	14,380	1,640
	V	W	83	439	428	444	16
			84	828	1,274	1,439	165
FR GERM	A	E	85	32	1,550	1,573	23
FRANCE	A	E	81	40	473	505	32
			82	110	3,904	4,195	291
			84	650	3,902	3,994	92
			85	4,710	15,257	16,196	939
			86	1,045	20,087	21,732	1,645
	A	W	81	441	2,384	2,783	399
			84	244	1,912	2,238	326
			85	187	1,283	1,465	182
			86	1,677	11,929	14,467	2,538
	N	E	84	1,337	33,466	34,112	646
	O	E	82	127	1,792	1,824	32
			83	126	2,096	2,186	90
			84	65	715	715	
			86	230	2,726	2,726	
	V	E	84	18	285	304	19
			85	408	9,788	9,913	125
			86	3,527	31,902	33,314	1,412
	V	W	81	4,152	9,292	10,066	774
			82	200	1,366	1,459	93
			83	250	1,695	1,707	12
			85	11,023	17,657	19,565	1,908

Crop
Product
TSUSA commodity number, description, and unit of quantity

Country	Mode	Reg	Yr	Quantity	F.A.S.	C.I.F.	Charges
			86	1,764	4,058	4,894	836
ITALY	A	E	83	794	6,796	7,905	1,109
	V	W	86	3,307	6,993	7,752	759
JAPAN	A	E	83	150	1,800	2,494	694
	A	W	81	200	1,240	2,042	802
			82	11	499	575	76
			86	31	1,232	1,287	55
	N	W	83	116	785	1,254	469
			84	29	1,075	1,106	31
MEXICO	O	E	82	250	500	500	
N ZEAL	V	W	84	550	4,800	4,886	86
NETHLDS	A	E	81	831	2,029	4,074	2,045
			82	1,347	13,903	15,448	1,545
			83	1,674	23,786	25,856	2,070
			84	319	3,811	4,137	326
			85	1,856	13,719	14,691	972
			86	4,612	18,753	22,660	3,907
	A	W	81	250	440	660	220
			82	220	383	668	285
			83	1,890	4,912	7,055	2,143
			84	1,190	10,303	11,324	1,021
			86	4,678	18,015	19,652	1,637
	N	W	81	1,633	17,890	19,006	1,116
			82	1,124	3,410	3,553	143
			83	1,791	5,194	6,118	924
			85	1,051	20,878	21,328	450
			86	15,838	90,000	92,658	2,658
	O	E	82	350	1,366	1,526	160
			85	6,189	9,914	10,598	684
	V	E	83	1,200	2,409	2,584	175
			86	886	2,640	3,540	900
	V	W	82	2,205	5,847	6,083	236
			83	1,069	2,153	2,410	257
			84	1,102	2,682	2,882	200
			85	1,453	7,226	7,536	310
REP SAF	A	E	82	311	1,822	1,999	177
	N	W	82	5,486	21,312	22,239	927
	V	E	83	11,539	34,312	34,783	471
			84	228	4,792	4,892	100
			85	8,336	39,102	39,868	766
	V	W	86	1,208	1,223	1,309	86
SWEDEN	A	E	81	26	561	653	92
			86	350	3,980	4,299	319
	A	W	83	201	2,413	2,598	185
	V	E	85	304	2,992	3,278	286
U KING	A	E	81	308	1,851	2,263	412
			82	235	1,901	2,029	128
			83	506	25,795	27,585	1,790
			84	2,816	19,884	21,589	1,705
			85	480	9,999	10,452	453
			86	90	10,532	11,157	625
	A	W	81	6	464	522	58
	N	E	84	71	1,581	1,677	96
			85	185	5,577	5,834	257
	O	E	86	109	4,496	4,580	84
	V	E	83	250	4,560	4,735	175
	V	W	85	1,786	5,602	6,130	528

Cashew

Cashew apple, fresh or prepared or preserved**
1468700 CASHEW APPLES,ETC FR OR PRES (LB)

Country	Mode	Reg	Yr	Quantity	F.A.S.	C.I.F.	Charges
TOTAL			81	712,241	389,713	455,056	65,343
			82	469,530	259,500	305,699	46,199
			83	815,373	279,427	327,898	48,471
			84	1,068,689	496,427	576,753	80,326
			85	904,116	420,997	495,316	74,319
			86	1,031,845	554,434	620,306	65,872
BRAZIL	V	E	84	990	750	825	75
C RICA	N	E	83	8,759	6,449	7,749	1,300
	V	E	81	169,491	121,505	161,290	39,785
			82	68,352	35,769	45,820	10,051
			83	3,568	3,040	3,457	417
			84	4,566	1,370	1,703	333
			85	36,435	14,240	17,617	3,377
			86	2,100	1,071	1,155	84
	V	W	82	4,424	3,024	4,708	1,684
CANADA	O	E	84	171	557	557	
COLOMB	V	E	81	3,315	3,465	3,879	414

Crop Product TSUSA commodity number, description, and unit of quantity Country	Mode	Reg	Yr	Quantity	F.A.S.	C.I.F.	Charges
			82	6,400	3,756	4,176	420
			83	5,304	7,528	8,221	693
			86	19,248	16,443	17,228	785
DOM REP	A	E	81	3,244	2,450	3,049	599
			82	8,394	828	1,659	831
	N	E	81	455,310	225,188	240,982	15,794
			82	35,195	30,353	34,284	3,931
	V	E	81	21,570	4,634	5,206	572
			82	136,282	82,297	90,413	8,116
			83	369,248	134,945	152,990	18,045
			84	207,424	97,028	107,921	10,893
			85	412,884	247,977	279,525	31,548
			86	812,245	470,516	529,006	58,490
ECUADOR	A	E	81	43,021	20,623	26,485	5,862
			82	6,780	1,320	2,336	1,016
			83	20,333	4,553	7,167	2,614
	V	E	84	31,588	10,207	12,390	2,183
FR GERM	A	E	82	14	320	335	15
GERM DR	V	E	85	4,725	3,165	3,578	413
GUATMAL	A	E	81	15,690	11,233	13,501	2,268
			82	8,002	4,418	5,266	848
	N	E	82	152,367	74,000	87,620	13,620
	V	E	83	405,984	120,956	145,969	25,013
			84	823,950	386,515	453,357	66,842
			85	381,698	114,418	144,419	30,001
			86	112,047	56,735	62,959	6,224
INDNSIA	V	W	83	657	843	955	112
JAMAICA	V	E	81	600	615	664	49
KIRIBAT	V	E	86	3,115	1,780	2,069	289
MEXICO	A	E	82	10,336	8,433	11,674	3,241
			85	34,272	30,516	35,689	5,173
	O	E	86	83,090	7,889	7,889	
	V	E	83	1,520	1,113	1,390	277
N ANTIL	V	E	82	32,984	14,982	17,408	2,426
VENEZ	N	E	85	34,102	10,681	14,488	3,807

Cashew apple, jelly or jam**
1530200 CASHEW APPLE, MANGO JELLY (LB)

Country	Mode	Reg	Yr	Quantity	F.A.S.	C.I.F.	Charges
TOTAL			81	9,779	8,686	9,412	726
			82	99,002	62,618	71,535	8,917
			83	176,329	103,330	113,131	9,801
			84	114,415	52,708	61,506	8,798
			85	87,379	51,398	60,634	9,236
			86	199,419	213,750	231,253	17,503
BRAZIL	A	E	84	424	725	1,376	651
C RICA	V	E	82	1,106	291	361	70
CANADA	O	E	83	5,447	2,517	2,517	
			86	22,932	16,329	16,329	
CHINA M	A	E	84	10,311	7,498	9,005	1,507
	V	E	85	125	1,057	1,240	183
	V	W	84	40,124	11,200	12,565	1,365
CHINA T	V	W	81	1,050	760	828	68
			83	1,042	1,138	1,243	105
COLOMB	A	E	85	994	1,273	1,607	334
DOM REP	V	E	81	4,710	1,157	1,250	93
			83	105,096	32,399	35,210	2,811
			84	29,449	7,648	9,010	1,362
			85	7,875	1,680	2,013	333
FR GERM	V	E	82	1,080	653	1,074	421
			84	597	409	459	50
			85	24,645	14,240	16,197	1,957
	V	W	85	1,976	1,019	1,485	466
FRANCE	N	W	85	2,431	3,609	4,645	1,036
	O	E	81	1,368	2,304	2,454	150
			82	533	996	1,071	75
			86	450	1,138	1,160	22
	V	E	81	2,605	4,214	4,599	385
			82	1,805	2,339	2,531	192
			83	1,681	3,451	3,713	262
			84	1,457	2,509	2,777	268
			85	968	1,619	1,838	219
			86	688	1,147	1,278	131
	V	W	86	975	2,095	2,248	153
HUNGARY	V	E	86	51,852	7,622	13,038	5,416
INDIA	O	E	84	736	357	397	40
	V	E	86	3,170	1,487	1,636	149
	V	W	86	7,376	7,250	8,851	1,601
ISRAEL	V	E	85	32,392	15,866	18,000	2,134
ITALY	V	E	82	60	316	360	44
	V	W	86	2,438	5,063	5,357	294
JAMAICA	V	E	83	151	524	540	16

Crop Product TSUSA commodity number, description, and unit of quantity Country	Mode	Reg	Yr	Quantity	F.A.S.	C.I.F.	Charges
			86	1,305	1,360	1,512	152
JAPAN	V	W	83	674	1,040	1,092	52
			84	714	1,229	1,331	102
LEBANON	V	E	85	3,968	2,400	2,652	252
MEXICO	O	W	83	1,397	287	287	
			84	798	968	968	
NETHLDS	V	E	86	1,620	2,949	3,404	455
	V	W	84	2,172	499	631	132
PERU	V	E	86	2,931	3,876	4,180	304
PHIL R	V	E	83	270	278	374	96
			84	1,874	1,111	1,267	156
	V	W	83	900	713	798	85
			84	12,760	9,552	10,309	757
			86	2,700	2,828	2,993	165
POLAND	O	E	82	9,600	4,480	5,361	881
PORTUGL	O	E	86	2,645	1,200	1,241	41
	V	E	83	3,533	1,958	2,318	360
			84	814	792	876	84
			85	6,400	2,578	2,778	200
			86	14,550	4,927	5,391	464
SWEDEN	V	E	85	3,171	3,547	5,363	1,816
	V	W	83	12,654	11,673	11,870	197
SWITZLD	V	E	83	4,943	5,964	6,376	412
U KING	A	E	81	46	251	281	30
			83	1,033	2,562	2,699	137
			84	1	1,302	2,102	800
	N	E	85	2,434	2,510	2,816	306
	N	W	86	7,526	9,250	10,456	1,206
	O	E	82	225	365	379	14
			86	3,409	1,945	2,173	228
	V	E	83	433	971	1,340	369
			84	127	322	394	72
			86	4,621	10,959	12,037	1,078
	V	W	82	84,593	53,178	60,398	7,220
			83	28,190	32,971	37,194	4,223
			84	1,171	1,384	1,846	462
			86	68,231	132,325	137,969	5,644
YUGOSLV	V	E	83	8,885	4,884	5,560	676
			84	10,886	5,203	6,193	990

Cashew apple, paste and pulp**
1524300 FRUIT PASTE, CASHEW APPL ETC (LB)

Country	Mode	Reg	Yr	Quantity	F.A.S.	C.I.F.	Charges
TOTAL			81	507,759	250,480	287,158	36,678
			82	677,310	261,589	301,043	39,454
			83	568,427	288,879	326,390	37,511
			84	373,169	152,728	178,797	26,069
			85	406,909	131,237	158,792	27,555
			86	1,576,943	629,477	725,456	95,979
C RICA	V	E	81	17,430	15,057	24,020	8,963
			82	24,998	12,366	14,493	2,127
COLOMB	A	E	84	1,746	2,453	2,867	414
			85	581	1,062	1,289	227
	N	E	86	146,007	106,402	110,304	3,902
DOM REP	N	E	84	82,409	9,725	15,314	5,589
			85	192,986	33,218	45,346	12,128
	V	E	81	481,139	230,915	257,546	26,631
			82	593,242	225,642	257,750	32,108
			83	426,540	189,580	220,485	30,905
			84	280,480	135,461	154,948	19,487
			85	148,701	54,928	64,468	9,540
			86	855,567	305,262	356,041	50,779
ECUADOR	A	E	81	8,000	3,740	4,824	1,084
			86	10,151	3,854	5,500	1,646
	N	E	82	9,738	3,003	4,277	1,274
GUATMAL	V	E	82	34,016	18,937	21,390	2,453
			83	141,887	99,299	105,905	6,606
			84	8,534	5,089	5,668	579
			86	188,722	92,646	109,777	17,131
HONDURA	V	E	82	15,316	1,641	3,133	1,492
KIRIBAT	V	E	86	76,264	37,334	43,462	6,128
MEXICO	O	E	81	1,190	768	768	
			86	7,920	1,236	1,236	
VENEZ	V	E	85	64,641	42,029	47,689	5,660
			86	292,312	82,743	99,136	16,393

Cashew, nut shell, gum resin
1883855 CASHEW NUT SHELL LIQUID (LB)

Country	Mode	Reg	Yr	Quantity	F.A.S.	C.I.F.	Charges
TOTAL			81	20,612,201	3,749,256	4,762,491	1,013,235
			82	14,369,242	1,392,125	2,043,960	651,835

Crop
Product
TSUSA commodity number, description, and unit of quantity

Country	Mode	Reg	Yr	Quantity	F.A.S.	C.I.F.	Charges
			83	21,045,154	1,719,626	2,671,893	952,267
			84	22,277,599	2,819,115	3,657,641	838,526
			85	20,971,877	3,214,826	3,968,660	753,834
			86	16,128,155	2,642,968	3,192,355	549,387
BELIZE	V	E	85	881,840	152,357	185,476	33,119
BRAZIL	V	E	81	9,560,546	1,888,273	2,285,868	397,595
			82	6,959,803	746,660	1,041,087	294,427
			83	13,455,723	1,250,940	1,771,574	520,634
			84	20,095,409	2,605,775	3,346,002	740,227
			85	20,090,037	3,062,469	3,783,184	720,715
			86	15,244,125	2,522,663	3,042,206	519,543
CANADA	O	E	84	665	280	280	
INDIA	V	E	81	833,339	137,259	210,400	73,141
KENYA	V	E	81	2,972,178	472,472	631,247	158,775
			83	896,774	67,989	118,174	50,185
MOZAMBQ	V	E	81	4,604,658	754,530	988,207	233,677
			82	6,968,519	606,315	938,677	332,362
			83	5,366,472	291,125	607,010	315,885
			84	1,345,982	102,360	182,268	79,908
PORTUGL	V	E	83	3,545	1,899	2,295	396
			86	18,519	10,349	11,899	1,550
SPAIN	V	E	83	881,840	72,000	104,717	32,717
			84	835,543	110,700	129,091	18,391
			86	865,511	109,956	138,250	28,294
TNZANIA	V	E	81	2,641,480	496,722	646,769	150,047
			82	440,920	39,150	64,196	25,046
			83	440,800	35,673	68,123	32,450

Cashew, nut, shelled, prepared or preserved
1454400 CASHEW NUTS SHELLED ETC (LB)

Country	Mode	Reg	Yr	Quantity	F.A.S.	C.I.F.	Charges
TOTAL			81	60,848,297	140,127,048	147,796,557	7,669,409
			82	78,419,827	126,346,810	135,786,412	9,439,602
			83	95,155,913	151,142,883	160,814,290	9,671,407
			84	82,832,347	175,507,779	184,442,322	8,934,543
			85	105,781,540	206,052,202	217,186,822	11,134,620
			86	95,778,678	241,110,949	250,356,522	9,245,573
AFGHAN	V	E	84	27,500	76,230	80,447	4,217
			86	1,103	3,608	3,671	63
ARGENT	V	E	82	7,500	12,000	13,081	1,081
			83	82,500	106,113	116,548	10,435
			84	8,000	15,536	16,735	1,199
AUSTRIA	V	E	81	162,500	452,203	457,584	5,381
			85	65,000	112,672	117,942	5,270
			86	32,500	93,600	97,950	4,350
B IND O	V	E	81	50,000	124,213	136,788	12,575
BELGIUM	N	E	86	107,000	161,783	169,430	7,647
	O	E	82	65,000	79,350	82,550	3,200
			83	111,950	139,607	143,894	4,287
	V	E	84	48,000	91,993	125,728	33,735
			85	186,000	233,488	248,650	15,162
			86	18,157	41,789	44,684	2,895
	V	W	86	150,000	214,650	218,823	4,173
BENIN	V	E	81	47,300	95,340	98,083	2,743
BNGLDSH	V	E	84	37,500	91,722	94,926	3,204
BOLIVIA	V	E	81	405,240	348,150	381,275	33,125
			82	6,750	10,868	11,968	1,100
			84	20,000	16,493	18,236	1,743
			86	73,128	64,654	71,587	6,933
BRAZIL	A	E	86	16,436	31,152	43,890	12,738
	N	E	81	20,907,350	46,310,779	48,995,272	2,684,493
			82	25,829,483	44,004,132	47,280,704	3,276,572
			83	28,487,421	45,782,028	49,290,459	3,508,431
			84	18,205,760	38,138,210	40,518,633	2,380,423
			85	33,805,207	62,644,802	67,177,748	4,532,946
			86	27,034,165	59,865,867	63,075,684	3,209,817
	O	E	81	49,750	153,988	157,595	3,607
			82	73,400	120,080	120,080	
			83	52,050	106,353	106,353	
			84	24,847	62,693	62,693	
			85	212,250	463,252	463,252	
			86	459,047	1,332,109	1,335,084	2,975
	O	W	85	4,550	11,603	11,603	
	V	E	81	3,079,500	7,957,611	8,371,188	413,577
			82	3,985,185	7,742,670	8,293,312	550,642
			83	5,092,119	8,203,365	8,892,675	689,310
			84	5,804,500	12,184,577	12,992,796	808,219
			85	9,627,134	18,239,207	19,537,068	1,297,861
			86	10,997,125	27,781,424	29,274,665	1,493,241
	V	W	81	257,500	738,773	770,772	31,999
			82	11,250	31,850	32,750	900
			85	142,790	279,098	303,181	24,083
			86	199,700	450,999	466,576	15,577
CANADA	O	E	81	123,600	339,611	339,611	
			82	35,925	82,168	82,734	566
			83	32,268	46,182	47,643	1,461
			84	93,193	195,340	195,340	
			85	112,550	238,277	238,277	
			86	60,410	148,658	148,658	
	O	W	81	250	1,134	1,134	
			82	500	2,212	2,212	
			83	930	4,049	4,049	
			84	560	2,305	2,305	
			85	2,500	4,560	4,560	
CHILE	V	E	83	57,354	81,336	86,745	5,409
CHINA M	A	E	84	50	400	445	45
	N	E	84	1,569,520	3,044,633	3,197,373	152,740
			85	1,485,500	2,911,970	3,069,808	157,838
	O	E	83	155,850	295,546	295,546	
			84	54,480	147,872	147,872	
			85	15,000	38,880	38,880	
	V	E	81	13,645	28,900	29,998	1,098
			82	1,850	5,514	6,161	647
			83	1,321,900	2,009,400	2,145,412	136,012
			85	17,500	35,429	37,233	1,804
			86	439,804	1,153,213	1,183,496	30,283
	V	H	81	470	1,486	1,600	114
			82	1,600	5,418	5,923	505
			83	1,650	3,243	3,488	245
			84	1,149	3,293	3,644	351
			85	1,735	4,950	5,353	403
			86	3,300	10,864	11,421	557
	V	W	81	97,773	273,780	283,047	9,267
			82	83,798	189,606	198,684	9,078
			83	462,370	678,500	751,113	72,613
			84	1,030,299	2,086,501	2,169,663	83,162
			85	913,985	1,752,227	1,852,774	100,547
			86	225,650	588,907	602,495	13,588
CHINA T	V	E	82	10,000	31,574	32,500	926
			83	35,000	35,643	40,397	4,754
			84	30,000	58,090	60,900	2,810
			86	9,750	25,553	26,612	1,059
	V	W	81	775	898	938	40
			82	150	508	545	37
			83	83,500	93,455	96,520	3,065
COLOMB	V	E	82	30,000	76,000	80,327	4,327
CR N AN	O	E	85	31,250	44,531	47,375	2,844
	V	E	84	12,500	15,071	27,750	12,679
DOM REP	V	E	81	1,325	1,532	1,575	43
			86	35,000	103,250	107,503	4,253
ECUADOR	V	E	82	20,000	17,000	19,812	2,812
EGYPT	V	E	83	20,000	21,274	24,120	2,846
FR GERM	V	E	81	905	4,209	4,542	333
			82	671	3,289	3,475	186
			83	81,193	100,681	107,363	6,682
			84	32,965	45,892	48,986	3,094
			85	225,001	424,400	442,509	18,109
	V	W	81	60	289	318	29
FRANCE	V	E	81	414	748	794	46
			82	73,000	167,500	177,742	10,242
			86	132,000	324,676	339,078	14,402
	V	W	81	60	291	317	26
GUATMAL	V	E	85	20,600	41,309	44,895	3,586
			86	200,466	451,699	468,995	17,296
	V	W	86	14,600	20,105	22,059	1,954
HG KONG	O	E	85	5,000	11,849	12,303	454
	V	E	81	5,000	10,229	10,546	317
			82	2,500	7,327	7,447	120
			83	224,500	385,673	405,685	20,012
			84	320,450	688,917	718,223	29,306
			85	278,800	531,439	557,016	25,577
			86	85,000	216,178	223,980	7,802
	V	H	81	150	283	307	24
			83	250	561	631	70
			85	500	1,199	1,296	97
	V	W	81	20,500	58,952	61,766	2,814
			82	35,500	106,673	109,328	2,655
			83	115,950	201,031	213,391	12,360
			84	68,400	122,169	125,988	3,819
			85	139,428	249,748	258,904	9,156
			86	177,278	377,728	387,557	9,829
HONDURA	A	E	86	1,500	1,725	1,973	248
	V	E	85	43,659	37,000	39,856	2,856
			86	660	1,200	1,350	150
ICELAND	V	E	86	21,250	62,534	86,854	24,320

Crop
Product
TSUSA commodity number, description, and unit of quantity

Country	Mode	Reg	Yr	Quantity	F.A.S.	C.I.F.	Charges
	V	W	85	3,750	8,079	8,875	796
INDIA	A	E	84	1,214	682	784	102
	N	E	81	6,925,046	20,244,757	21,021,005	776,248
			82	6,257,324	13,289,922	13,896,570	606,648
			83	31,102,508	50,806,552	53,397,305	2,590,753
			84	30,394,710	66,255,932	68,937,954	2,682,022
			85	25,764,097	52,629,353	54,751,885	2,122,532
			86	33,190,563	89,735,595	92,167,430	2,431,835
	N	W	81	380,306	1,125,097	1,170,851	45,754
			84	51,250	83,843	89,559	5,716
	O	E	81	130,100	369,119	369,119	
			82	67,029	160,613	160,613	
			83	404,004	695,289	695,532	243
			84	1,006,008	2,312,257	2,430,897	118,640
			85	155,400	354,910	356,232	1,322
			86	80,000	258,206	258,206	
	V	E	81	785,000	2,354,113	2,438,271	84,158
			82	1,785,750	4,296,925	4,469,239	172,314
			83	8,954,575	14,662,188	15,469,918	807,730
			84	7,089,658	15,829,007	16,474,093	645,086
			85	18,007,453	38,849,813	40,130,617	1,280,804
			86	12,828,651	34,533,647	35,513,119	979,472
	V	H	81	32,500	117,096	119,275	2,179
			84	100	286	323	37
	V	W	81	619,012	1,813,990	1,882,940	68,950
			82	2,467,980	5,635,645	5,868,418	232,773
			83	4,267,492	6,883,139	7,322,826	439,687
			84	4,425,174	9,124,517	9,601,677	477,160
			85	3,741,005	7,568,408	7,934,034	365,626
			86	2,356,921	6,744,057	6,978,104	234,047
INDNSIA	V	E	81	31,000	86,774	90,147	3,373
			82	40,000	95,925	99,620	3,695
			83	468,070	873,340	921,478	48,138
			84	695,890	1,492,058	1,553,159	61,101
			85	418,620	747,991	783,433	35,442
			86	1,040,298	2,656,846	2,715,094	58,248
	V	W	81	85,559	192,664	203,504	10,840
			83	2,000	3,871	3,960	89
			84	62,000	117,900	172,180	54,280
			85	44,750	66,570	68,690	2,120
			86	185,020	484,493	493,701	9,208
IRAN	V	E	81	5,000	17,053	17,600	547
			86	38,500	35,882	39,358	3,476
ISRAEL	V	E	85	1,800	6,400	6,843	443
			86	554	2,403	2,752	349
ITALY	V	E	84	32,500	76,053	79,682	3,629
			85	97,500	210,491	217,550	7,059
			86	1,711	3,924	4,333	409
IVY CST	V	E	81	17,000	40,000	42,577	2,577
JAPAN	V	E	86	10,000	22,000	23,355	1,355
	V	H	83	500	1,443	1,533	90
	V	W	82	18,000	49,802	52,063	2,261
KENYA	O	E	81	102,650	307,300	307,300	
			82	32,600	77,818	78,543	725
			84	575	1,330	1,330	
			85	27,950	47,423	47,423	
	V	E	81	467,750	1,100,707	1,158,951	58,244
			82	1,047,550	1,661,355	1,745,653	84,298
			83	812,450	1,274,329	1,337,356	63,027
			84	1,144,600	2,575,197	2,678,076	102,879
			85	1,364,783	2,328,074	2,444,374	116,300
			86	1,337,125	3,179,401	3,303,711	124,310
	V	W	85	44,000	74,991	78,838	3,847
			86	6,250	11,875	12,238	363
KOR REP	V	E	82	5,000	8,300	8,564	264
	V	W	86	32,000	92,580	105,780	13,200
MACAO	V	E	84	33,750	69,789	72,420	2,631
MADAGAS	V	E	84	12,500	25,000	26,097	1,097
MALAYSA	V	W	82	63,646	70,112	75,913	5,801
MAURIT	V	E	86	44,100	86,260	89,962	3,702
MEXICO	V	E	86	35,000	99,250	103,186	3,936
MOROC	V	E	86	16,250	46,200	47,125	925
MOZAMBQ	N	E	81	18,066,146	37,277,075	39,652,672	2,375,597
			82	24,044,404	28,962,133	31,838,372	2,876,239
			83	8,225,400	10,821,018	11,599,130	778,112
			84	4,244,473	8,018,860	8,646,087	627,227
	N	W	86	21,350	23,995	25,551	1,556
	O	E	81	50,000	112,858	112,858	
			82	78,025	170,072	170,072	
			83	7,350	9,776	9,776	
			85	86,050	158,691	158,691	
	O	W	85	5,000	13,794	13,794	
	V	E	81	2,400,450	6,342,978	6,682,207	339,229
			82	3,242,500	6,283,141	6,712,014	428,873
			83	360,650	593,907	637,184	43,277
			84	435,650	848,456	912,815	64,359
			85	4,899,660	8,171,050	8,820,678	649,628
			86	2,420,666	5,785,026	6,123,270	338,244
	V	W	85	13,500	30,446	31,320	874
N ZEAL	V	E	85	35,000	85,793	91,455	5,662
			86	66,500	145,702	153,273	7,571
NAURU	V	E	85	15,000	37,500	38,719	1,219
NEPAL	V	E	83	5,500	7,535	8,015	480
NETHLDS	N	E	83	153,450	234,837	245,251	10,414
	O	E	86	34,350	97,281	99,271	1,990
	V	E	81	5,000	16,475	17,225	750
			82	161,350	203,823	210,132	6,309
			84	460,816	1,093,546	1,137,151	43,605
			85	517,411	1,024,381	1,069,714	45,333
			86	321,260	731,213	765,249	34,036
	V	W	83	32,500	64,865	65,000	135
			84	35,000	95,717	98,000	2,283
			85	65,000	139,241	142,416	3,175
			86	271,521	838,888	856,526	17,638
NICARAG	V	E	85	419	1,305	1,381	76
NORFOLK	V	E	82	140,000	313,538	325,192	11,654
NORWAY	V	E	82	35,000	96,501	100,128	3,627
PAKISTN	V	E	85	45,000	83,354	87,625	4,271
PERU	V	E	82	25,700	53,620	56,035	2,415
			83	19,800	25,193	26,979	1,786
			84	221,650	273,307	290,511	17,204
			85	248,782	159,763	179,252	19,489
			86	49,720	39,713	43,638	3,925
	V	W	85	34,650	27,968	32,340	4,372
			86	17,204	32,010	36,868	4,858
PHIL R	V	E	81	15,926	8,983	10,602	1,619
			83	2,250	1,585	1,740	155
			84	1,032	403	550	147
			86	91,688	39,780	45,596	5,816
	V	W	81	60	300	405	5
			83	1,008	684	745	61
PORTUGL	V	E	83	15,000	35,008	36,448	1,440
REP SAF	N	E	81	493,375	1,308,759	1,358,038	49,279
	O	E	81	20,000	51,600	51,600	
			82	32,400	65,772	65,772	
	V	E	83	287,500	558,787	583,413	24,626
			84	348,600	709,838	743,546	33,708
			85	69,350	165,917	169,997	4,080
			86	260,000	534,047	566,397	32,350
S HELNA	V	E	84	456,930	1,049,568	1,091,018	41,450
			85	40,000	69,300	72,295	2,995
	V	W	84	31,250	74,207	77,500	3,293
SALVADR	V	E	85	41,750	50,428	53,550	3,122
SIER LN	V	E	82	70,000	113,750	120,125	6,375
SINGAPR	A	W	81	56	442	679	237
	V	E	81	14,250	42,656	44,634	1,978
			82	75,000	97,352	107,333	9,981
			83	274,551	474,676	496,648	21,972
			85	125,000	325,250	330,987	5,737
	V	W	82	20,000	41,150	43,282	2,132
			83	100,000	185,763	193,382	7,619
SPAIN	V	E	82	12,500	31,238	32,939	1,701
			83	102,746	153,275	164,547	11,272
			84	253,000	662,925	695,564	32,639
			85	35,000	55,000	59,854	4,854
SRI LKA	N	E	81	218,900	383,710	412,550	28,840
			86	53,818	135,508	141,283	5,775
	V	E	83	18,227	27,087	29,821	2,734
			84	24,042	44,591	47,986	3,395
			85	208,218	375,532	397,892	22,360
	V	W	81	40,550	89,791	94,397	4,606
			82	14,632	21,705	23,661	1,956
			83	59,365	94,912	103,264	8,352
			84	5,000	9,533	10,250	717
			86	30,000	84,612	87,479	2,867
SURINAM	V	E	84	15,000	44,000	46,260	2,260
SWEDEN	V	E	84	32,500	79,635	81,656	2,021
SWITZLD	V	E	82	227,500	399,333	407,215	7,882
			84	314,582	753,146	765,699	12,553
			85	62,500	137,964	141,711	3,747
	V	W	81	4,750	3,905	4,180	275
THAILND	V	E	86	22,074	62,378	65,250	2,872
	V	W	86	2,205	6,000	6,261	261
TNZANIA	N	E	81	4,013,206	8,178,168	8,730,161	551,993
			82	5,971,650	7,345,880	8,142,303	796,423
			83	2,798,000	4,000,995	4,303,920	302,925
			84	2,626,640	4,665,933	4,950,975	285,042
	O	E	81	254,230	460,604	460,604	

Crop
Product
TSUSA commodity number, description, and unit of quantity

Country	Mode	Reg	Yr	Quantity	F.A.S.	C.I.F.	Charges
			82	80,375	153,281	153,281	
			85	17,892	41,331	41,331	
	V	E	81	413,908	1,091,525	1,151,247	59,722
			82	2,043,100	3,813,905	4,110,764	296,859
			83	107,500	150,851	164,719	13,868
			84	286,273	533,357	567,014	33,657
			85	1,185,949	1,744,173	1,880,117	135,944
	V	W	83	32,800	48,535	50,285	1,750
TRINID	V	E	83	29,012	42,068	43,546	1,478
TUNISIA	V	E	82	7,500	4,050	5,057	1,007
			85	363,250	727,950	752,972	25,022
			86	130,000	357,725	366,452	8,727
TURKEY	O	E	83	22,000	21,758	23,722	1,964
			84	33,000	33,699	36,645	2,946
			85	44,092	23,950	23,950	
	V	E	82	20,000	37,400	41,916	4,516
U KING	N	E	84	476,057	1,059,503	1,098,388	38,885
	O	E	81	32,500	85,150	85,908	758
	V	E	82	34,250	65,760	69,636	3,876
			83	70,950	95,577	104,815	9,238
			84	130,000	313,884	321,068	7,184
			85	486,020	931,538	977,890	46,352
			86	287,850	675,027	699,854	24,827
	V	W	84	32,500	57,133	59,475	2,342
			85	130,000	266,190	277,614	11,424
USSR	V	E	82	25,000	31,250	34,652	3,402
VENEZ	A	E	86	500	1,500	2,775	1,275
ZMBABWE	V	E	84	28,750	34,750	37,250	2,500

Cashew, nut, unshelled
1451600 CASHEW NUTS NOT SHELLED (LB)

Country	Mode	Reg	Yr	Quantity	F.A.S.	C.I.F.	Charges
TOTAL			81	85,229	220,662	227,065	6,403
			82	351,977	556,336	588,097	31,761
			83	643,171	1,027,413	1,088,063	60,650
			84	752,477	1,274,709	1,343,195	68,486
			85	2,526,483	4,657,451	4,956,046	298,595
			86	3,375,354	8,648,704	9,070,896	422,192
BRAZIL	N	E	81	22,410	53,000	55,751	2,751
			86	1,907,427	4,764,671	5,014,212	249,541
	O	E	82	40,000	46,750	46,750	
			84	1,500	3,393	3,393	
			85	11,600	38,173	38,173	
	V	E	82	80,058	152,625	161,711	9,086
			83	155,000	283,020	304,671	21,651
			84	262,500	478,432	509,720	31,288
			85	1,115,264	1,843,828	2,007,939	164,111
			86	137,600	387,066	405,947	18,881
	V	W	85	30,000	78,530	80,100	1,570
CANADA	A	E	83	99	450	577	127
	O	E	82	375	1,074	1,366	292
			83	2,735	8,571	10,222	1,651
			84	2,600	6,279	6,279	
CHINA M	O	E	83	23,400	43,107	43,107	
	V	E	84	4,800	8,256	8,857	601
			85	62,336	106,449	113,500	7,051
	V	W	81	51,500	151,771	155,224	3,453
			82	24,500	69,348	69,953	605
			83	79,150	111,203	116,960	5,757
			84	3,482	4,833	4,953	120
			85	63,866	127,116	131,514	4,398
			86	12,500	36,760	37,810	1,050
CHINA T	V	W	81	674	654	701	47
			82	35,000	27,791	30,848	3,057
			84	59,524	141,392	143,292	1,900
			85	6,000	13,041	13,800	759
FR GERM	V	E	86	457	1,546	2,013	467
GUATMAL	V	E	84	2,376	264	600	336
HG KONG	V	E	85	27,500	54,391	56,336	1,945
			86	2,500	9,016	9,770	754
	V	W	81	750	2,175	2,294	119
			83	7,150	9,740	10,725	985
			84	542	1,085	1,142	57
			85	11,463	21,287	22,500	1,213
			86	30,000	94,540	95,220	680
HONDURA	A	E	83	527	712	820	108
			85	2,367	4,202	4,576	374
			86	5,330	6,129	7,315	1,186
	V	E	84	7,950	11,930	13,442	1,512
			85	5,042	7,616	8,524	908
			86	3,034	3,489	4,286	797
INDIA	N	E	84	195,020	125,396	140,357	14,961

Crop
Product
TSUSA commodity number, description, and unit of quantity

Country	Mode	Reg	Yr	Quantity	F.A.S.	C.I.F.	Charges
		O	E	82	22,568	63,275	63,275	
			83	85,200	139,435	139,435	
			84	30,750	80,873	80,873	
			85	6,750	17,213	17,213	
	V	E	82	20,000	27,203	30,056	2,853
			83	3,750	7,237	7,518	281
			85	705,000	1,519,481	1,580,629	61,148
			86	712,256	1,839,719	1,922,798	83,079
	V	H	85	750	1,725	1,809	84
	V	W	83	135,001	234,530	246,973	12,443
			84	106,750	244,212	257,141	12,929
			85	65,000	125,629	132,159	6,530
INDNSIA	V	E	85	54,950	125,178	129,404	4,226
			86	32,500	85,476	94,676	9,200
	V	W	86	31,000	90,730	93,454	2,724
KENYA	O	E	82	425	1,278	1,724	446
MALAYSA	V	W	82	12,042	20,724	20,880	156
MOZAMBQ	N	E	82	81,515	92,812	102,902	10,090
	O	E	81	9,800	12,696	12,696	
	V	E	82	35,000	51,557	56,560	5,003
			83	136,159	164,558	182,205	17,647
			85	48,000	72,891	80,759	7,868
			86	458,250	1,198,313	1,251,320	53,007
N ANTIL	V	E	82	485	1,500	1,629	129
NETHLDS	V	E	84	11,023	21,846	22,846	1,000
			85	331	1,348	1,372	24
	V	W	85	264	1,085	1,096	11
PHIL R	V	W	82	9	399	443	44
REP SAF	O	E	83	15,000	24,850	24,850	
SINGAPR	A	E	81	95	366	399	33
	V	W	84	303	856	1,000	144
SWITZLD	V	W	86	10,000	24,893	25,705	812
THAILND	V	W	84	1,607	900	977	77
TNZANIA	V	E	85	310,000	498,268	534,643	36,375
U KING	V	E	84	61,750	144,762	148,323	3,561
			86	32,500	106,356	106,370	14

Cassava

Cassava, flour and starch
1323520 TAPIOCA CASSAVA FLR A STARCH (LB)

Country	Mode	Reg	Yr	Quantity	F.A.S.	C.I.F.	Charges
TOTAL			81	79,904,462	11,415,627	15,221,989	3,806,362
			82	65,503,354	8,591,448	12,152,995	3,561,547
			83	63,111,324	8,170,497	11,391,023	3,220,526
			84	80,002,449	10,600,535	14,933,962	4,333,427
			85	96,612,660	9,607,177	13,039,132	3,431,955
			86	88,360,056	9,703,613	13,203,909	3,500,296
BELGIUM	O	E	81	40,000	13,773	16,069	2,296
	V	E	81	36,000	11,236	13,196	1,960
BRAZIL	V	E	81	6,643,192	1,113,713	1,466,136	352,423
			82	4,884,649	842,780	1,149,056	306,276
			83	2,975,854	446,463	618,796	172,333
			84	1,396,328	259,790	334,982	75,192
			85	886,591	166,923	209,128	42,205
			86	1,499,190	262,116	331,428	69,312
	V	W	81	4,409	800	1,027	227
			83	74,200	11,967	16,737	4,770
			84	35,999	7,240	9,818	2,578
			85	81,907	16,039	20,222	4,183
BURMA	V	E	82	46,343	7,860	10,335	2,475
C RICA	V	E	81	39,200	7,840	10,112	2,272
			84	40,500	8,100	12,326	4,226
	V	W	82	3,354	1,039	1,290	251
CANADA	O	E	86	10,000	2,000	2,000	
	V	W	82	8,250	1,650	1,822	172
CHINA M	N	W	84	79,072	10,877	12,948	2,071
	O	W	86	80	2,135	2,187	52
	V	E	81	108,492	18,999	25,050	6,051
			82	407,344	79,225	80,771	1,546
			83	585,945	77,606	116,833	39,227
			84	20,501	5,719	7,353	1,634
			85	1,091,271	163,350	276,971	113,621
	V	H	81	660	1,120	1,289	169
			83	2,750	318	356	38
	V	W	81	50,010	7,973	9,567	1,594
			82	4,000	1,098	1,201	103
			83	2,570	792	866	74
			84	24,500	3,668	4,856	1,188
			85	41,821	18,420	20,374	1,954

Crop
Product
TSUSA commodity number, description, and unit of quantity

Country	Mode	Reg	Yr	Quantity	F.A.S.	C.I.F.	Charges
			86	67,199	30,597	33,635	3,038
CHINA T	V	E	81	2,917,056	382,372	519,664	137,292
			82	941,442	94,887	146,031	51,144
			83	1,060,019	188,591	244,643	56,052
			84	679,017	96,391	128,774	32,383
			85	575,107	60,431	94,762	34,331
			86	1,268,001	154,593	212,741	58,148
	V	W	81	6,125	1,632	1,835	203
			82	371,185	33,715	53,625	19,910
			83	641,147	89,994	113,899	23,905
			84	706,349	102,575	125,981	23,406
			85	599,211	71,725	94,190	22,465
			86	181,568	26,736	34,218	7,482
COLOMB	A	E	84	13,223	9,100	11,471	2,371
			85	41,600	18,332	24,982	6,650
			86	8,700	8,113	12,563	4,450
	V	E	81	22,000	10,050	10,854	804
			83	22,266	15,000	16,741	1,741
DENMARK	V	E	86	350,000	35,000	51,101	16,101
DOM REP	N	E	82	47,576	28,291	34,114	5,823
			83	22,117	9,544	12,660	3,116
	V	E	84	39,251	15,847	20,407	4,560
			85	22,530	7,976	9,901	1,925
FIJI	V	H	83	24,285	9,924	12,817	2,893
FRANCE	N	E	83	305,353	112,630	131,880	19,250
			86	80,000	34,600	41,900	7,300
	N	W	85	105,691	43,154	54,584	11,430
	O	E	81	320,684	106,304	119,457	13,153
			82	280,000	103,940	119,819	15,879
			83	240,150	84,886	98,697	13,811
			84	441,000	154,966	184,779	29,813
			85	320,000	114,640	142,549	27,909
	V	E	81	235,683	77,369	91,667	14,298
			82	280,184	80,150	93,687	13,537
			83	200,000	76,273	87,047	10,774
			84	720,000	133,711	156,380	22,669
			85	360,000	134,138	157,603	23,465
			86	768,184	243,368	311,253	67,885
	V	W	81	80,000	27,151	31,770	4,619
			82	80,000	30,406	34,366	3,960
			83	40,000	15,800	18,240	2,440
			84	40,000	13,787	16,800	3,013
			86	40,000	15,750	18,000	2,250
G BISAU	V	E	81	220	869	1,240	371
GHANA	V	E	83	2,000	500	788	288
			86	69,366	40,135	45,730	5,595
GIBRAT	O	E	81	39,683	14,286	16,086	1,800
GREECE	V	E	81	4,381	2,838	3,239	401
GUATMAL	A	W	81	16,100	6,761	9,660	2,899
			84	17,050	2,015	4,651	2,636
	V	E	81	2,559	590	752	162
HG KONG	V	E	81	262,115	29,781	42,970	13,189
			82	304,655	44,754	61,640	16,886
			83	368,768	44,427	72,217	27,790
			84	9,935	4,155	4,911	756
			85	44,480	2,929	5,565	2,636
			86	543,070	96,444	136,985	40,541
	V	H	83	3,000	354	391	37
	V	W	82	44,092	6,400	6,531	131
			83	91,912	16,870	18,789	1,919
			84	1,050	764	819	55
			85	48,584	5,933	7,899	1,966
			86	250,139	42,346	50,249	7,903
INDIA	N	E	84	18,084	5,208	6,149	941
	O	E	81	2,480	775	879	104
			83	1,984	650	726	76
	V	E	81	237,860	30,081	41,962	11,881
			82	14,888	3,986	4,901	915
			83	24,217	8,188	9,442	1,254
			84	26,248	9,025	10,406	1,381
			85	20,009	6,375	8,040	1,665
			86	21,878	10,108	11,038	930
	V	W	81	7,934	2,559	3,362	803
			82	17,901	5,616	6,620	1,004
			83	7,777	2,260	3,274	1,014
			84	12,224	4,274	5,408	1,134
INDNSIA	V	E	81	73,999	9,050	12,828	3,778
			82	78,999	10,982	13,937	2,955
	V	W	81	80,023	18,880	21,280	2,400
			82	4,084	4,090	4,719	629
			83	852	1,325	1,498	173
			86	992	1,395	1,694	299
ISRAEL	V	E	85	86,790	15,017	20,269	5,252
ITALY	V	E	81	36,000	12,142	14,101	1,959

Crop
Product
TSUSA commodity number, description, and unit of quantity

Country	Mode	Reg	Yr	Quantity	F.A.S.	C.I.F.	Charges
			85	39,293	6,862	8,718	1,856
IVY CST	V	E	83	2,646	1,130	1,332	202
			84	3,000	1,500	1,782	282
JAMAICA	V	E	83	11,000	4,086	4,399	313
			84	11,000	3,313	3,850	537
JAPAN	V	E	81	114,227	13,223	18,902	5,679
			82	37,000	4,241	6,078	1,837
			84	73,999	8,589	12,785	4,196
			86	10,080	2,138	2,360	222
	V	H	83	37,188	6,655	7,981	1,326
	V	W	81	74,600	8,079	11,571	3,492
			82	148,000	15,157	21,457	6,300
			84	2,202	408	418	10
			85	1,800	1,159	1,309	150
KOR REP	V	E	84	396,003	54,714	79,329	24,615
	V	W	86	57,811	11,688	13,949	2,261
LIBERIA	V	E	81	42,047	16,155	21,304	5,149
			82	61,710	21,690	27,054	5,364
			83	1,865	285	491	206
MALAYSA	V	E	81	43,741	15,485	18,003	2,518
			82	120,621	31,677	37,145	5,468
			83	65,621	18,899	23,333	4,434
			84	59,835	22,091	25,920	3,829
			85	87,322	21,616	27,382	5,766
			86	30,357	7,249	8,684	1,435
	V	W	81	86,535	22,171	24,877	2,706
			82	93,673	23,401	26,075	2,674
			83	57,663	10,918	12,344	1,426
			85	35,963	8,547	9,275	728
NETHLDS	V	H	81	4,400	896	970	74
			82	7,700	1,545	1,694	149
			83	13,750	2,612	2,928	316
			84	11,110	3,140	3,587	447
			85	4,400	1,012	1,248	236
			86	24,200	4,596	5,701	1,105
	V	W	85	6,614	1,315	1,628	313
NIGERIA	A	W	84	400	480	971	491
PHIL R	V	E	81	11,286	3,818	4,498	680
			82	7,925	3,583	4,052	469
			83	9,196	3,980	4,553	573
			84	26,074	12,833	15,599	2,766
			85	90,000	55,800	63,709	7,909
			86	4,479	2,164	2,474	310
	V	H	81	1,680	1,400	1,709	309
			82	2,550	2,669	3,120	451
			83	2,836	1,773	2,069	296
			84	3,251	2,185	2,610	425
			85	2,188	1,144	1,519	375
			86	3,925	2,198	2,562	364
	V	W	81	15,558	5,251	6,033	782
			82	47,641	12,910	16,275	3,365
			83	93,197	27,119	34,370	7,251
			84	105,744	32,527	38,491	5,964
			85	133,965	41,126	48,443	7,317
			86	126,705	35,132	40,993	5,861
PORTUGL	V	E	81	3,897	2,126	2,623	497
			82	9,632	3,979	4,580	601
			86	3,000	1,624	1,807	183
REP SAF	V	E	83	5,000	3,750	4,303	553
			85	4,050	2,002	2,394	392
S HELNA	V	E	86	132,000	15,312	22,281	6,969
SIER LN	N	E	81	8,680	7,225	8,846	1,621
	V	E	81	1,990	400	1,045	645
			82	12,900	6,353	9,922	3,569
			83	4,200	2,089	2,453	364
			84	106,712	47,946	58,512	10,566
			85	28,392	17,360	20,407	3,047
			86	7,800	1,833	2,682	849
SINGAPR	N	E	85	2,477,245	384,361	532,908	148,547
	V	E	81	714,952	82,306	117,800	35,494
			82	1,193,115	114,401	176,217	61,816
			83	603,747	64,672	95,940	31,268
			84	2,282,907	316,628	452,792	136,164
			85	80,999	12,258	16,890	4,632
			86	2,684,219	474,119	605,940	131,821
	V	W	81	118,221	15,759	20,879	5,120
			82	81,113	8,745	13,046	4,301
			83	37,000	4,179	6,135	1,956
			84	249,767	38,105	52,120	14,015
			85	9,688	1,910	2,107	197
			86	72,083	19,848	23,597	3,749
THAILND	N	E	82	23,132,796	2,369,189	3,664,022	1,294,833
			83	30,694,690	3,227,267	4,770,779	1,543,512
			84	18,627,827	2,091,286	3,115,094	1,023,808

Crop
Product
TSUSA commodity number, description, and unit of quantity

Country	Mode	Reg	Yr	Quantity	F.A.S.	C.I.F.	Charges
			85	48,596,941	5,049,230	7,054,221	2,004,991
	N	W	85	2,887,146	270,136	324,341	54,205
	O	E	81	75,290	11,381	11,381	
			85	42,290	7,012	7,879	867
	O	W	84	1,850	351	381	30
			86	28,081	9,565	10,432	867
	V	E	81	60,602,013	8,416,430	11,302,292	2,885,862
			82	27,964,978	3,897,221	5,395,279	1,498,058
			83	21,188,280	2,944,200	4,022,095	1,077,895
			84	42,645,659	5,566,729	7,949,685	2,382,956
			85	14,717,155	1,863,383	2,580,154	716,771
			86	68,349,562	7,387,069	10,246,691	2,859,622
	V	H	81	199,346	36,993	44,793	7,800
			82	163,877	30,162	35,441	5,279
			83	158,291	30,138	37,890	7,752
			84	184,974	33,280	38,940	5,660
			85	195,515	30,367	36,596	6,229
			86	9,413,756	368,558	488,619	120,061
	V	W	81	6,519,134	847,585	1,118,411	270,826
			82	4,277,175	635,481	841,612	206,131
			83	3,427,988	602,383	760,291	157,908
			84	10,856,735	1,509,943	2,012,106	502,163
			85	22,846,102	985,195	1,150,965	165,770
			86	2,252,529	353,884	427,059	73,175
U KING	V	E	84	33,069	7,275	9,771	2,496
VENEZ	A	E	86	1,102	1,200	1,356	156
YUGOSLV	V	E	82	322,002	28,175	45,461	17,286

Cassia

Cassia, essential oil
4521200 CASSIA OIL (LB)

Country	Mode	Reg	Yr	Quantity	F.A.S.	C.I.F.	Charges
TOTAL			81	140,631	4,648,708	4,682,791	34,083
			82	212,448	7,506,211	7,554,227	48,016
			83	203,268	6,788,710	6,829,804	41,094
			84	215,227	6,893,836	6,937,429	43,593
			85	554,191	11,780,288	11,873,148	92,860
			86	421,373	8,732,685	8,867,129	134,444
ARGENT	V	E	85	3,583	105,699	105,944	245
BAHAMAS	V	E	83	6,300	228,060	228,656	596
			85	947	35,045	35,179	134
CANADA	O	E	82	800	13,570	13,784	214
			83	33	1,147	1,147	
CHINA M	A	E	82	1,940	84,480	84,866	386
			83	2,646	111,000	111,967	967
	N	E	85	385,825	7,614,134	7,680,111	65,977
			86	299,962	5,068,898	5,169,092	100,194
	V	E	81	77,159	2,860,429	2,884,727	24,298
			82	55,153	1,854,571	1,863,847	9,276
			83	120,692	3,869,484	3,890,272	20,788
			84	98,162	3,166,636	3,187,463	20,827
			85	19,604	345,641	347,725	2,084
			86	33,476	877,120	879,787	2,667
	V	W	81	9,701	411,441	414,649	3,208
			82	39,243	1,552,674	1,565,884	13,210
			83	5,292	198,216	199,880	1,664
			84	8,378	275,427	277,107	1,680
			85	882	33,148	33,384	236
			86	8,496	334,633	337,283	2,650
CHINA T	A	E	81	2,840	139,411	140,790	1,379
			83	2,640	110,769	111,405	636
	V	E	81	26,715	841,523	842,067	544
FR GERM	V	E	85	9,220	271,990	272,387	397
FRANCE	A	E	82	144	5,166	5,361	195
			83	1	1,081	1,112	31
			84	59	3,713	3,782	69
			86	6	1,023	1,082	59
GUATMAL	V	E	84	9,700	17,512	18,241	729
HG KONG	A	E	86	9,502	87,500	102,682	15,182
	V	E	82	1,323	58,645	59,400	755
			84	1,323	48,160	48,844	684
			85	3,858	92,789	94,078	1,289
INDNSIA	V	E	85	32,755	405,411	410,049	4,638
ISRAEL	V	E	81	11,905	36,785	38,447	1,662
			82	13,227	40,903	42,677	1,774
			83	7,496	22,018	22,981	963
			84	11,024	19,872	20,931	1,059
			85	11,025	26,923	28,727	1,804
JAPAN	V	E	81	8,060	332,583	334,391	1,808

Crop
Product
TSUSA commodity number, description, and unit of quantity

Country	Mode	Reg	Yr	Quantity	F.A.S.	C.I.F.	Charges
			82	95,188	3,855,877	3,876,412	20,535
			83	58,168	2,246,935	2,262,384	15,449
			84	86,570	3,361,769	3,380,161	18,392
			85	86,492	2,849,508	2,865,564	16,056
			86	69,828	2,356,842	2,370,447	13,605
MOROC	V	E	81	2,205	14,286	14,666	380
SPAIN	V	E	81	2,046	12,250	13,054	804
			82	5,430	40,325	41,996	1,671
SWITZLD	A	E	84	11	747	900	153
U KING	N	E	86	103	6,669	6,756	87

Cassia, spice
1611300 CASSIA, CAS BUD A VERA UNGRD (LB)

Country	Mode	Reg	Yr	Quantity	F.A.S.	C.I.F.	Charges
TOTAL			81	18,018,307	9,466,704	11,552,947	2,086,243
			82	18,264,393	9,024,500	11,246,832	2,222,332
			83	19,541,343	8,302,333	10,727,879	2,425,546
			84	23,840,959	10,671,241	13,459,057	2,787,816
			85	24,092,258	11,238,246	14,204,900	2,966,654
			86	25,665,228	14,814,856	17,357,821	2,542,965
AFGHAN	V	E	86	2,756	2,947	3,107	160
BRAZIL	V	E	86	69,138	45,251	54,814	9,563
CANADA	O	E	83	150	415	415	
	O	W	82	827	1,365	1,421	56
			83	1,582	2,548	2,652	104
			84	595	770	770	
			85	1,872	2,930	2,930	
			86	1,058	2,232	2,232	
CHINA M	N	E	83	247,687	377,951	408,782	30,831
			84	337,326	398,115	441,787	43,672
			86	1,431,301	1,120,262	1,243,139	122,877
	N	W	81	230,200	232,997	249,419	16,422
	O	E	81	20,110	23,729	23,758	29
			84	1,102	1,986	2,218	232
	V	E	81	327,662	342,486	379,723	37,237
			82	400,226	520,773	570,577	49,804
			85	398,136	477,123	525,148	48,025
			86	84,740	54,064	61,542	7,478
	V	W	81	39,683	37,856	40,648	2,792
			82	289,086	379,901	405,503	25,602
			83	105,270	144,296	154,165	9,869
			84	304,644	338,992	364,949	25,957
			85	277,328	218,595	239,302	20,707
			86	903,244	527,386	594,515	67,129
CHINA T	V	E	81	221,853	48,448	70,865	22,417
			82	44,092	26,244	31,098	4,854
			83	111,130	17,037	28,317	11,280
			84	103,616	34,292	45,927	11,635
			85	22,046	9,203	12,159	2,956
			86	97,015	25,396	31,596	6,200
	V	W	81	22,088	3,773	5,620	1,847
			82	11,023	1,875	2,770	895
			83	22,046	3,597	4,956	1,359
			84	33,069	6,017	8,240	2,223
			85	88,184	30,398	38,652	8,254
			86	22,046	4,259	5,740	1,481
COMOROS	V	E	84	22,046	86,073	88,484	2,411
DENMARK	V	E	84	22,046	7,519	10,500	2,981
EGYPT	V	E	82	4,408	6,304	6,557	253
			84	16,534	7,170	7,920	750
			85	39,686	24,756	29,408	4,652
			86	33,067	19,651	21,724	2,073
FR GERM	V	E	83	6,182	15,758	16,691	933
FRANCE	V	E	85	12,447	8,523	10,142	1,619
GRENADA	V	E	85	33,600	20,160	21,460	1,300
HG KONG	V	E	82	6,781	9,716	10,259	543
			83	22,400	20,541	22,991	2,450
			85	22,046	38,268	38,826	558
			86	36,376	33,382	36,453	3,071
	V	W	84	15,432	23,123	24,673	1,550
			85	55,115	43,650	46,010	2,360
			86	263,238	236,846	263,613	26,767
INDIA	O	E	82	600	819	819	
			83	1,102	2,643	3,123	480
			85	44,092	27,778	27,778	
	V	E	81	21,737	9,391	11,132	1,741
			82	11,056	2,820	3,691	871
			83	11,056	2,227	2,287	60
			84	58,901	26,069	30,920	4,851
			85	387,472	171,468	220,982	49,514
			86	551,828	311,710	365,325	53,615
	V	W	83	11,056	2,081	2,873	792

Crop Product TSUSA commodity number, description, and unit of quantity Country	Mode	Reg	Yr	Quantity	F.A.S.	C.I.F.	Charges
			85	101,412	52,986	62,344	9,358
			86	156,016	75,177	89,511	14,334
INDNSIA	N	E	81	13,343,184	6,759,858	8,419,930	1,660,072
			82	13,952,497	6,321,740	8,148,773	1,827,033
			83	13,959,903	5,511,509	7,310,199	1,798,690
			84	18,696,934	7,660,852	9,952,306	2,291,454
			85	17,715,442	7,753,248	10,069,803	2,316,555
			86	17,227,561	9,697,514	11,451,401	1,753,887
	N	W	85	879,385	393,918	490,758	96,840
	V	E	81	1,377,875	645,749	809,615	163,866
			82	986,559	445,256	572,391	127,135
			83	2,122,168	823,062	1,102,139	279,077
			84	1,053,798	430,491	560,874	130,383
			85	291,006	138,328	173,139	34,811
			86	1,635,813	935,795	1,122,488	186,693
	V	W	81	2,136,857	1,196,565	1,349,847	153,282
			82	2,039,255	1,058,233	1,200,735	142,502
			83	2,787,245	1,281,167	1,560,792	279,625
			84	3,042,042	1,571,506	1,823,469	251,963
			85	3,456,075	1,682,430	2,022,957	340,527
			86	3,079,798	1,706,020	1,993,119	287,099
JAPAN	N	E	84	23,157	8,241	10,624	2,383
	V	W	81	43,741	28,099	30,678	2,579
			82	88,184	41,809	47,534	5,725
			84	33,069	34,500	39,036	4,536
MACAO	V	E	82	22,046	9,635	12,563	2,928
			84	11,023	7,246	8,902	1,656
MALAYSA	V	E	81	55,115	33,103	39,970	6,867
	V	W	82	44,092	25,162	27,917	2,755
MEXICO	O	E	86	6,580	3,657	3,657	
NETHLDS	N	E	83	50,892	24,690	26,514	1,824
	V	E	84	33,069	12,919	17,519	4,600
			85	30,482	19,277	21,977	2,700
PANAMA	O	E	86	33,069	16,339	19,416	3,077
PERU	V	E	85	22,046	5,470	7,221	1,751
SINGAPR	V	E	81	110,297	67,987	80,846	12,859
			82	88,184	31,925	43,231	11,306
			83	76,977	69,030	76,746	7,716
			84	4,409	2,966	3,603	637
			85	5,512	4,029	4,774	745
			86	21,990	21,369	21,996	627
	V	W	81	66,138	32,676	36,478	3,802
			82	251,915	134,275	151,715	17,440
			84	22,046	8,547	11,019	2,472
			85	136,086	66,368	79,210	12,842
SRI LKA	V	E	84	2,400	1,147	2,279	1,132
			86	22,046	5,071	7,071	2,000
	V	W	82	22,046	4,574	7,023	2,449
			85	3,650	4,089	5,106	1,017
			86	52,686	14,219	18,424	4,205
THAILND	V	E	81	563	837	960	123
			83	1,921	1,400	1,552	152
			84	1,549	1,100	1,276	176
	V	W	81	1,204	3,150	3,458	308
			82	1,516	2,074	2,255	181
			83	2,576	2,381	2,685	304
			84	2,152	1,600	1,762	162
			86	3,000	1,560	1,752	192

1611500 CASSIA AND BUDS VERA GROUND (LB)

TOTAL			81	593,957	245,578	320,177	74,599
			82	943,979	416,634	540,129	123,495
			83	632,639	386,379	464,161	77,782
			84	689,285	383,661	445,018	61,357
			85	598,700	275,630	347,362	71,732
			86	665,037	423,735	489,720	65,985
ARGENT	V	E	84	38,578	13,173	15,859	2,686
			86	159,429	122,710	143,922	21,212
AUSTRIA	V	E	84	94,338	96,621	107,104	10,483
CANADA	O	E	82	7,090	8,041	8,041	
CHINA M	V	E	83	9,750	11,911	12,966	1,055
			84	250	1,122	1,219	97
			85	2,264	2,518	2,830	312
	V	H	81	500	418	447	29
	V	W	81	1,000	1,379	1,459	80
			83	250	449	477	28
			86	4,549	1,800	1,944	144
CHINA T	V	W	84	1,193	2,310	2,359	49
			85	98,546	46,891	54,723	7,832
DOM REP	A	E	81	300	450	600	150
EGYPT	O	E	84	220	448	448	
	V	E	83	10,520	11,582	12,180	598
			84	24,428	20,635	22,393	1,758

Crop Product TSUSA commodity number, description, and unit of quantity Country	Mode	Reg	Yr	Quantity	F.A.S.	C.I.F.	Charges
			86	46,290	17,718	22,370	4,652
	V	W	86	11,020	6,512	8,609	2,097
FR GERM	V	E	83	5,205	5,850	6,272	422
			84	182,738	89,357	96,128	6,771
	V	W	82	530	1,361	1,491	130
			83	23,296	14,893	19,917	5,024
FRANCE	O	E	81	49,065	34,725	38,830	4,105
	V	E	81	2,954	10,098	10,303	205
			82	193	374	459	85
			83	999	1,923	2,038	115
			85	25,189	14,213	17,278	3,065
GHANA	V	E	86	17,317	3,465	5,287	1,822
HG KONG	V	E	82	720	1,884	2,087	203
			83	4,500	5,409	5,985	576
			84	500	1,174	1,377	203
HUNGARY	V	W	84	873	433	497	64
INDIA	O	E	81	75	276	281	5
	V	E	81	6,000	5,394	5,938	544
			82	55,181	22,945	30,146	7,201
	V	W	82	1,460	3,909	4,401	492
			85	88,184	39,323	49,229	9,906
			86	33,069	15,386	17,904	2,518
INDNSIA	V	E	81	531,309	184,211	250,937	66,726
			82	870,817	360,745	471,202	110,457
			83	268,545	157,017	197,187	40,170
			84	93,696	40,713	51,949	11,236
			85	275,574	112,421	150,668	38,247
			86	209,437	147,662	165,867	18,205
	V	W	81	344	491	529	38
			83	66,138	31,221	42,346	11,125
			84	220,462	87,606	109,960	22,354
			85	60,320	28,997	35,797	6,800
			86	154,322	80,671	93,707	13,036
ISRAEL	V	E	86	2,205	1,416	1,500	84
ITALY	V	E	81	2,500	7,514	10,142	2,628
JAPAN	V	E	86	1,364	3,832	4,087	255
	V	W	82	4,409	4,431	4,720	289
			84	200	371	406	35
KOR REP	V	E	86	950	2,515	2,655	140
	V	W	81	94	434	460	26
			82	94	470	500	30
MALAYSA	V	E	84	22,046	5,579	8,494	2,915
MEXICO	O	E	84	213	799	799	
	O	W	83	46,073	24,673	24,673	
REP SAF	V	E	83	135,219	80,146	88,917	8,771
			86	25,085	20,048	21,868	1,820
SINGAPR	A	E	84	7,940	21,583	24,080	2,497
	V	W	85	47,812	29,035	34,445	5,410
SPAIN	V	E	82	2,462	8,822	12,984	4,162
			83	3,780	15,904	18,522	2,618
SWITZLD	A	E	82	368	779	1,147	368
THAILND	V	E	84	818	721	846	125
	V	W	83	614	1,467	1,497	30
			84	480	364	412	48
			85	811	2,232	2,392	160
TRINID	A	E	81	40	290	371	81
U KING	O	E	82	311	2,382	2,422	40
	V	E	81	120	389	409	20
			84	312	652	688	36
YUGOSLV	V	E	83	57,750	23,934	31,184	7,250

Castor Bean

Castor bean

1750600 CASTOR BEANS (LB)

TOTAL			82	5,072	2,231	2,638	407
			83	790	1,285	1,297	12
			84	2,320	4,640	4,640	
			85	220	1,272	1,516	244
			86	75,830	19,258	20,264	1,006
CHINA M	V	E	83	150	325	337	12
FR GERM	A	E	85	220	1,272	1,516	244
HAITI	V	E	82	5,072	2,231	2,638	407
KOR REP	V	W	86	75,330	15,488	15,984	496
MEXICO	O	W	86	640	960	960	
			84	2,320	4,640	4,640	
NETHLDS	A	E	86	500	3,770	4,280	510

Crop Product TSUSA commodity number, description, and unit of quantity Country	Mode	Reg	Yr	Quantity	F.A.S.	C.I.F.	Charges

Castor bean, soap
4662000 SOAP CONT CASTOR OIL (LB)

Country	Mode	Reg	Yr	Quantity	F.A.S.	C.I.F.	Charges
TOTAL			82	43,422	16,081	16,102	21
			83	110,037	36,004	37,745	1,741
			84	10,575	10,150	10,217	67
			85	153,491	89,445	99,171	9,726
			86	34,281	33,340	36,202	2,862
CANADA	O	E	82	40,764	13,656	13,656	
			83	45,514	12,697	12,697	
			84	7,398	7,499	7,499	
			85	948	8,613	8,613	
			86	18,090	19,143	19,143	
	O	W	83	5,040	4,842	4,842	
CHINA T	V	W	85	1,845	4,111	4,576	465
FR GERM	V	E	83	39,683	13,333	15,074	1,741
FRANCE	V	E	85	148,036	72,836	81,461	8,625
			86	14,000	8,065	9,371	1,306
GREECE	V	E	85	1,500	1,100	1,243	143
ITALY	O	E	84	3,039	2,363	2,363	
	V	W	85	1,162	2,785	3,278	493
JAPAN	O	E	82	12	356	377	21
	V	E	86	2,191	6,132	7,688	1,556
MEXICO	O	W	82	2,646	2,069	2,069	
			83	19,800	5,132	5,132	
NETHLDS	A	W	84	138	288	355	67

Castor bean, vegetable oil, edible
1760100 CASTOR OIL, NOT OVER 20 CTS (LB)

Country	Mode	Reg	Yr	Quantity	F.A.S.	C.I.F.	Charges
TOTAL			84	4,000	378	428	50
			85	1,102,300	42,330	45,536	3,206
			86	3,040,625	556,852	638,179	81,327
BRAZIL	V	E	85	1,102,300	42,330	45,536	3,206
			86	2,865,980	524,165	603,465	79,300
INDIA	V	E	86	165,825	31,507	33,398	1,891
ITALY	V	E	86	8,820	1,180	1,316	136
JAPAN	A	E	84	4,000	378	428	50

1761400 CASTOR OIL OV 20CT LOVIBOND (LB)

Country	Mode	Reg	Yr	Quantity	F.A.S.	C.I.F.	Charges
TOTAL			81	87,900,300	32,629,295	34,958,529	2,329,234
			82	63,255,270	23,116,359	24,877,530	1,761,171
			83	66,371,574	27,259,687	29,025,607	1,765,920
			84	76,879,263	42,696,681	45,362,400	2,665,719
			85	79,593,594	27,592,874	29,843,711	2,250,837
			86	77,787,760	19,676,070	21,941,851	2,265,781
BRAZIL	N	E	85	58,348,601	19,845,798	21,305,652	1,459,854
	V	E	81	86,544,485	32,087,028	34,406,673	2,319,645
			82	52,741,305	19,402,856	20,787,290	1,384,434
			83	47,720,324	19,779,590	21,072,700	1,293,110
			84	52,129,292	28,038,826	29,968,944	1,930,118
			85	41,800	20,251	20,549	298
			86	70,794,521	17,570,092	19,654,464	2,084,372
	V	W	81	31,746	13,744	16,053	2,309
			86	3,968	1,479	1,695	216
CHINA M	V	E	84	95,617	9,429	18,858	9,429
CHINA T	V	E	86	33,863	11,240	13,517	2,277
DOM REP	V	E	82	6,154	2,010	2,178	168
ECUADOR	V	E	81	1,324,069	528,523	535,803	7,280
			84	1,657,571	869,544	904,836	35,292
			85	830,515	242,984	261,604	18,620
			86	3,187,649	1,041,620	1,114,870	73,250
FR GERM	V	W	86	4,689	4,277	4,316	39
INDIA	V	E	82	7,644,426	2,677,429	2,983,768	306,339
			83	8,715,312	3,393,293	3,634,824	241,531
			84	16,761,757	10,018,350	10,539,738	521,388
			85	19,367,430	7,160,166	7,897,177	737,011
ITALY	V	E	84	13,307	8,400	8,741	341
LAOS	V	E	84	649,433	766,623	787,552	20,929
NIGER	V	E	83	551,271	202,545	217,798	15,253
PHIL R	V	W	85	35,200	12,636	14,784	2,148
THAILND	V	E	82	2,863,385	1,034,064	1,104,294	70,230
			83	9,384,667	3,884,259	4,100,285	216,026
			84	5,572,286	2,985,509	3,133,731	148,222
			85	970,048	311,039	343,945	32,906
			86	3,763,070	1,047,362	1,152,989	105,627

1761500 CASTOR OIL OV 20 CT LB NSPF (LB)

Country	Mode	Reg	Yr	Quantity	F.A.S.	C.I.F.	Charges
TOTAL			81	1,141,021	510,181	518,661	8,480
			82	1,442,422	580,575	621,564	40,989

Country	Mode	Reg	Yr	Quantity	F.A.S.	C.I.F.	Charges
			83	7,878,157	4,018,989	4,221,467	202,478
			84	1,326,367	839,132	878,753	39,621
			85	1,290,812	669,904	691,892	21,988
			86	2,197,456	619,329	668,435	49,106
BRAZIL	V	E	82	1,426,466	572,694	612,968	40,274
			83	3,730,143	1,788,989	1,891,658	102,669
			84	992,070	678,000	704,676	26,676
			85	1,128,300	602,521	618,637	16,116
			86	1,120,000	310,000	338,553	28,553
CANADA	O	E	81	1,000	929	929	
			82	565	381	381	
			84	1,036	1,261	1,261	
CHINA T	V	W	84	3,436	3,155	3,283	128
			86	13,974	6,080	6,396	316
DOM REP	V	E	82	15,391	7,500	8,215	715
ECUADOR	V	E	81	1,102,904	475,260	481,438	6,178
			84	34,392	18,480	20,280	1,800
	V	W	85	34,392	18,720	21,322	2,602
FR GERM	V	E	81	37,117	33,992	36,294	2,302
			83	27,842	20,048	21,303	1,255
			84	9,189	1,260	1,762	502
FRANCE	V	W	86	4,662	2,238	2,658	420
INDIA	V	E	83	4,120,172	2,209,952	2,308,506	98,554
			84	248,324	107,970	116,533	8,563
			85	35,274	16,775	19,568	2,793
			86	82,544	22,466	23,815	1,349
ITALY	V	E	84	4,057	7,212	7,648	436
			85	2,646	3,024	3,501	477
MEXICO	O	E	85	90,200	28,864	28,864	
			86	276,123	92,147	92,147	
THAILND	V	E	86	666,290	176,153	192,517	16,364
	V	W	84	33,863	21,794	23,310	1,516
			86	33,863	10,245	12,349	2,104

Cauliflower

Cauliflower, fresh**
1380520 BROCCOLI ETC FR, CUT SLICED (LB)
(See Broccoli, fresh under Broccoli)

Cauliflower, fresh or frozen
1355000 CAULIFLOWR, JUN5-OCT15 INCL (LB)

Country	Mode	Reg	Yr	Quantity	F.A.S.	C.I.F.	Charges
TOTAL			81	6,624,807	1,207,975	1,208,067	92
			82	8,224,579	1,432,794	1,433,027	233
			83	9,477,359	1,657,637	1,676,598	18,961
			84	8,950,498	1,609,218	1,624,494	15,276
			85	11,593,664	2,022,425	2,070,913	48,488
			86	8,150,147	1,434,950	1,497,135	62,185
BELGIUM	N	E	85	13,039	6,730	8,445	1,715
	V	E	85	28,752	5,751	8,379	2,628
			86	100,800	28,780	40,993	12,213
CANADA	O	E	81	6,522,115	1,190,098	1,190,098	
			82	8,149,009	1,416,920	1,416,923	3
			83	9,239,510	1,610,673	1,610,673	
			84	8,409,265	1,457,302	1,457,302	
			85	10,776,974	1,773,961	1,773,961	
			86	7,215,093	1,191,347	1,191,347	
	O	W	83	35,200	1,100	1,100	
			84	5,516	1,379	1,379	
CHILE	V	W	86	34,127	6,531	12,289	5,758
ECUADOR	O	E	82	9,000	729	729	
FRANCE	O	E	86	176,368	63,200	72,352	9,152
	V	E	85	30,960	11,146	13,051	1,905
GREECE	V	E	86	40,800	16,728	18,754	2,026
GUATMAL	V	E	81	1,010	313	405	92
			83	91,643	32,090	50,417	18,327
			84	104,000	37,872	48,369	10,497
			85	493,065	185,117	223,738	38,621
			86	412,520	103,810	134,406	30,596
ITALY	A	E	83	12,310	3,588	4,128	540
JAMAICA	A	E	86	15,531	3,654	4,380	726
JAPAN	V	E	82	1,640	1,017	1,247	230
KOR REP	V	W	85	7,937	6,221	6,500	279
MEXICO	O	E	82	64,930	14,128	14,128	
			83	42,470	2,572	2,572	
			84	243,091	55,895	55,895	
			85	165,521	23,233	23,233	

Crop / Product / TSUSA commodity number, description, and unit of quantity							
Country	Mode	Reg	Yr	Quantity	F.A.S.	C.I.F.	Charges
			86	14,900	2,235	2,235	
	O	W	81	101,682	17,564	17,564	
			83	39,726	4,479	4,479	
			84	85,570	12,790	12,790	
			86	134,018	15,030	15,030	
NETHLDS	A	E	86	579	2,595	3,767	1,172
	O	E	85	77,416	10,266	13,606	3,340
	V	E	83	16,500	3,135	3,229	94
			84	90,222	38,280	42,369	4,089
PHIL R	V	W	84	12,834	5,700	6,390	690
U KING	V	E	86	5,411	1,040	1,582	542

1355100 CAULIFLOWR, OCT16-JUN4 INCL (LB)

Country	Mode	Reg	Yr	Quantity	F.A.S.	C.I.F.	Charges
TOTAL			81	4,565,111	705,094	702,827	733
			82	2,559,278	409,832	409,832	
			83	3,069,126	569,125	596,550	27,425
			84	4,549,507	781,762	792,607	10,845
			85	4,702,691	882,154	967,033	84,879
			86	4,974,919	699,493	796,939	97,446
BELGIUM	V	E	84	35,273	12,343	16,578	4,235
			85	191,346	58,761	78,478	19,717
			86	132,000	39,302	53,664	14,362
CANADA	O	E	81	227,038	30,412	30,412	
			82	816,510	104,837	104,837	
			83	1,000,605	133,975	133,975	
			84	1,954,524	214,380	214,380	
			85	1,133,554	194,702	197,123	2,421
			86	437,130	65,095	65,095	
	O	W	83	200	400	400	
DOM REP	A	E	81	1,480	324	642	318
FRANCE	V	E	84	22,062	5,530	7,069	1,539
			86	25,534	9,023	11,287	2,264
GUATMAL	N	E	83	89,752	48,948	69,166	20,218
	V	E	84	25,507	4,084	5,868	1,784
			85	486,064	152,482	191,320	38,838
			86	271,117	63,421	86,169	22,748
HONDURA	V	E	83	6,000	3,600	5,610	2,010
ISRAEL	V	E	85	40,744	19,150	23,331	4,181
			86	184,142	74,544	97,441	22,897
	V	W	84	33,069	9,450	12,669	3,219
KIRIBAT	V	E	85	2,266	1,224	1,409	185
MEXICO	O	E	81	1,396,988	118,871	118,871	
			82	757,056	64,303	64,303	
			83	336,941	33,303	33,303	
			84	130,472	21,434	21,434	
			85	815,667	89,890	90,610	720
			86	582,026	76,171	76,801	630
	O	W	81	2,939,605	555,487	552,902	415
			82	985,712	240,692	240,692	
			83	1,615,938	335,903	335,903	
			84	2,348,102	514,061	514,061	
			85	1,722,286	299,452	299,452	
			86	2,994,463	292,977	292,977	
MOZAMBQ	O	W	85	20,504	2,296	2,296	
NETHLDS	A	E	84	498	480	548	68
SALVADR	V	E	83	19,690	12,996	18,193	5,197
SPAIN	O	E	85	251,106	54,166	70,083	15,917
			86	158,732	35,761	47,653	11,892
	V	E	85	39,154	10,031	12,931	2,900
			86	189,775	43,199	65,852	22,653

Cauliflower, frozen

1380560 CAULIFLOWER FZ, CUT, SLICED (LB)

Country	Mode	Reg	Yr	Quantity	F.A.S.	C.I.F.	Charges
TOTAL			81	13,573,703	4,891,342	5,188,578	298,911
			82	20,570,025	7,089,003	7,673,361	584,358
			83	21,085,376	6,973,338	7,201,873	228,535
			84	30,834,702	10,287,562	10,499,527	211,965
			85	36,823,083	11,517,697	11,801,748	284,051
			86	37,843,231	10,753,311	11,006,201	252,890
BELGIUM	O	E	86	91,109	20,324	30,859	10,535
	V	E	85	124,292	25,523	37,048	11,525
CANADA	O	E	81	60,966	20,506	20,506	
			82	35,343	9,919	9,919	
			83	122,813	43,796	43,796	
			84	132,339	43,156	43,156	
			85	74,292	24,697	24,697	
			86	179,619	43,436	51,038	7,602
	O	W	82	125,550	47,435	47,435	
			83	153,363	74,287	74,287	
			86	40,200	14,461	14,461	

Country	Mode	Reg	Yr	Quantity	F.A.S.	C.I.F.	Charges
CZECHO	O	E	86	13,590	3,533	3,533	
DOM REP	V	E	84	9,861	5,226	5,927	701
GUATMAL	N	E	81	605,784	190,326	245,815	55,500
			82	4,226,495	1,494,479	1,802,961	308,482
			83	3,029,660	1,097,148	1,305,466	208,318
			85	2,550,356	668,069	830,655	162,586
	V	E	81	2,483,878	831,580	1,074,978	243,411
			82	2,792,470	908,683	1,177,849	269,166
			83	208,538	68,946	89,163	20,217
			84	3,109,872	1,100,931	1,309,772	208,841
			85	284,867	116,715	135,402	18,687
			86	2,158,689	554,556	693,984	139,428
	V	W	82	64,121	18,751	25,461	6,710
HG KONG	O	E	86	32,400	8,100	8,100	
ISRAEL	V	E	85	26,286	9,386	12,091	2,705
			86	22,752	8,367	11,680	3,313
MEXICO	O	E	81	10,412,308	3,842,687	3,841,036	
			82	13,326,046	4,609,736	4,609,736	
			83	17,571,002	5,689,161	5,689,161	
			84	27,559,230	9,132,282	9,132,282	
			85	32,868,614	10,477,284	10,477,291	7
			86	34,318,152	9,873,395	9,875,747	2,352
	O	W	81	10,767	6,243	6,243	
			86	29,323	7,331	7,331	
MONSRAT	O	E	86	28,080	9,828	9,828	
MOZAMBQ	O	E	86	31,350	10,502	10,502	
REP SAF	V	E	86	37,953	9,048	14,571	5,523
SPAIN	O	E	85	245,924	52,862	72,424	19,562
			86	832,291	188,182	264,580	76,398
	V	E	85	204,751	37,558	60,752	23,194
	V	W	85	35,274	7,334	12,333	4,999
U KING	V	E	84	23,400	5,967	8,390	2,423
			85	380,347	88,441	129,227	40,786
			86	55,803	12,076	19,815	7,739

Cauliflower, seed

1261900 CAULIFLOWER SEED (LB)

Country	Mode	Reg	Yr	Quantity	F.A.S.	C.I.F.	Charges
TOTAL			81	32,162	301,063	312,623	7,226
			82	34,558	422,009	434,090	6,201
			83	27,648	600,149	614,724	14,575
			84	41,318	1,171,838	1,191,015	19,177
			85	19,798	565,429	574,740	9,311
			86	24,472	670,008	678,012	8,004
AUSTRAL	A	H	86	105	1,832	1,975	143
	A	W	81	121	3,851	4,250	399
			84	849	13,708	15,029	1,321
			85	339	9,542	10,181	639
			86	5,809	7,881	8,517	636
	N	W	84	204	4,494	4,698	204
	V	W	83	209	3,290	3,413	123
CANADA	O	E	81	9	1,038	1,048	
			82	54	2,841	2,841	
			84	400	7,824	7,824	
			86	1,728	7,258	7,258	
CHINA T	A	E	82	22	392	457	65
	V	H	82	134	1,216	1,242	26
DENMARK	A	E	81	25	800	863	63
			83	55	3,688	3,879	191
			84	130	6,237	6,769	532
			85	55	3,688	3,951	263
			86	55	4,050	4,264	214
	N	W	84	1,100	38,500	38,965	465
	V	E	83	20	1,239	1,297	58
			86	329	1,012	1,075	63
	V	W	81	1,275	25,500	26,027	527
			83	850	26,373	26,806	433
			84	968	23,627	24,124	497
FR GERM	V	E	82	20	961	982	21
FRANCE	A	E	86	22	4,302	4,478	176
JAPAN	A	E	81	7	982	1,019	37
			82	263	22,104	22,931	827
			83	94	8,904	9,086	182
			84	390	18,038	18,796	758
			85	478	71,313	73,012	1,699
			86	88	8,400	8,903	503
	A	W	81	55	5,250	5,519	269
			83	94	7,657	8,154	497
			84	1,240	8,900	9,290	390
			85	10	1,500	1,573	73
	N	E	81	340	30,932	32,482	1,550
			83	1,389	153,374	157,648	4,274

Crop
Product
TSUSA commodity number, description, and unit of quantity

Country	Mode	Reg	Yr	Quantity	F.A.S.	C.I.F.	Charges
			84	599	82,171	83,199	1,028
	N W		83	238	34,379	36,554	2,175
			84	2,924	226,609	228,742	2,133
			85	1,281	78,582	80,252	1,670
			86	88	10,344	10,639	295
	O E		81	236	27,483	28,732	1,239
			82	49	6,801	7,094	293
			83	40	5,480	5,742	262
			84	7	1,250	1,349	99
			86	10	2,000	2,000	
	O W		82	51	5,601	5,939	338
	V E		84	4	713	738	25
	V W		82	281	14,401	20,459	178
			84	200	27,466	27,695	229
			86	10	1,699	1,711	12
MEXICO	A E		83	17	748	748	
	O E		81	3,240	13,873	13,873	
	O W		81	23,911	46,040	46,040	
			82	29,033	97,272	97,272	
			83	13,838	58,201	58,201	
			84	15,799	36,041	36,041	
			85	12,836	39,212	39,212	
			86	8,119	24,224	24,224	
N ANTIL	A W		82	1,150	85,963	86,624	661
N ZEAL	A W		81	683	10,540	11,085	545
	V W		84	6	1,800	1,832	32
NETHLDS	A E		81	862	61,807	62,976	1,169
			82	562	52,134	53,208	1,074
			83	605	9,198	9,416	218
			84	2,255	22,904	23,352	448
			85	25	2,713	2,787	74
	A W		81	1,166	62,422	67,889	1,173
			82	2,872	128,969	131,629	2,660
			83	834	75,952	77,582	1,630
			85	1,035	104,700	106,089	1,389
			86	1,200	123,906	125,328	1,422
	N W		83	9,264	208,993	213,413	4,420
			84	13,009	634,498	645,172	10,674
			85	2,764	203,820	206,857	3,037
			86	6,079	467,489	471,898	4,409
	O E		81	8	1,125	1,145	
			82	10	1,838	1,847	9
			83	16	560	560	
	O W		82	5	1,100	1,121	21
	V E		86	830	5,611	5,742	131
	V W		81	150	8,199	8,369	170
			83	32	413	456	43
			85	950	47,875	48,225	350
U KING	A E		82	52	416	444	28
	A W		81	3	462	487	25
			83	22	621	647	26
			84	1,234	17,058	17,400	342
			85	9	1,406	1,453	47
	N E		81	71	759	819	60
			83	31	1,079	1,122	43
	O E		85	16	1,078	1,148	70

Cedar

Cedar, leaf, essential oil
4521400 CEDAR LEAF OIL (LB)

Country	Mode	Reg	Yr	Quantity	F.A.S.	C.I.F.	Charges
TOTAL			81	3,787	58,702	58,726	24
			82	18,973	232,152	232,647	495
			83	9,897	147,938	148,041	103
			84	21,445	366,478	366,759	281
			85	23,717	363,940	364,181	241
			86	25,197	329,715	331,200	1,485
AUSTRIA	A E		81	20	298	299	1
BRAZIL	V E		86	375	5,542	5,717	175
CANADA	O E		81	3,620	54,475	54,475	
			82	16,989	220,387	220,387	
			83	9,765	142,418	142,503	85
			84	20,906	353,081	353,081	
			85	22,117	358,930	358,930	
			86	22,398	301,280	301,615	335
FR GERM	A E		81	147	3,929	3,952	23
			82	214	5,302	5,332	30
			83	110	4,767	4,782	15
			86	105	9,206	9,322	116

Crop
Product
TSUSA commodity number, description, and unit of quantity

Country	Mode	Reg	Yr	Quantity	F.A.S.	C.I.F.	Charges
	N E		84	539	13,397	13,678	281
FRANCE	V E		82	1,764	5,889	6,350	461
			85	1,600	5,010	5,251	241
JAPAN	A E		82	6	574	578	4
MEXICO	N E		86	2,319	13,687	14,546	859
PORTUGL	A E		83	22	753	756	3

Cedar, lumber**
2022720 WESTERN RED CEDAR, RGH LBR (MBF)

Country	Mode	Reg	Yr	Quantity	F.A.S.	C.I.F.	Charges
TOTAL			81	168,187	55,699,908	57,470,697	1,757,475
			82	155,483	49,381,762	51,817,015	2,435,253
			83	221,097	89,022,677	93,298,550	4,275,873
			84	203,934	77,186,313	80,059,768	2,873,455
			85	217,795	72,981,874	76,751,607	3,769,733
			86	213,815	74,913,459	80,138,584	5,225,125
BELIZE	O E		83	10	9,375	9,375	
	V E		83	2	2,000	2,297	297
CANADA	N E		85	1,790	561,871	731,302	169,431
	N W		82	91,490	29,235,611	29,236,306	695
			83	111,624	44,558,034	44,591,425	33,391
			84	127,975	49,799,611	49,914,347	114,736
			85	129,817	47,249,151	47,345,775	96,624
			86	141,779	51,856,968	54,153,907	2,296,939
	O E		81	33,026	12,155,565	12,173,122	17,557
			82	20,785	6,798,048	6,798,048	
			83	43,354	17,368,654	17,368,654	
			84	17,853	7,651,051	7,651,051	
			85	12,259	4,376,969	4,377,069	100
			86	5,219	1,681,927	1,681,927	
	O W		81	111,682	35,722,717	35,742,156	10,655
			82	2,649	674,813	674,813	
			83	6,615	1,766,619	1,766,619	
			84	11,186	2,943,335	2,943,335	
			85	8,677	2,158,432	2,158,432	
			86	10,588	4,407,440	4,407,447	7
	V E		81	21,569	7,005,053	8,663,843	1,654,260
			82	37,957	12,064,600	14,436,340	2,371,740
			83	59,247	25,207,635	29,439,524	4,231,889
			84	43,982	15,677,092	18,334,466	2,657,374
			85	56,027	14,659,554	17,536,089	2,876,535
			86	45,282	14,002,618	16,489,494	2,486,876
	V W		81	1,910	816,573	891,576	75,003
			82	2,602	608,690	671,508	62,818
			83	245	110,360	120,656	10,296
			84	2,918	1,108,773	1,210,118	101,345
			85	9,044	3,917,549	4,544,592	627,043
			86	4,504	1,606,734	1,818,808	212,074
CHINA M	O E		85	131	43,097	43,097	
	V E		86	6,298	1,312,010	1,541,239	229,229
COLOMB	O W		85	23	12,645	12,645	
GABON	O W		85	27	2,606	2,606	
			86	16	3,594	3,594	
USSR	O W		86	129	42,168	42,168	
YEMEN A	O W		84	20	6,451	6,451	

2022740 WESTERN RED CEDAR ETC, NSPF (MBF)

Country	Mode	Reg	Yr	Quantity	F.A.S.	C.I.F.	Charges
TOTAL			81	391,007	117,447,373	119,079,035	1,603,649
			82	367,714	103,307,243	105,999,153	2,691,910
			83	419,810	147,784,971	150,515,035	2,730,064
			84	473,900	156,482,600	158,183,301	1,700,701
			85	561,958	158,935,836	162,928,249	3,992,413
			86	540,181	165,858,633	172,180,567	6,321,934
BRAZIL	V E		81	12	8,307	10,544	2,237
			86	24	12,931	16,192	3,261
CANADA	N E		83	30,591	9,257,281	10,988,107	1,730,826
			86	1,551	798,926	798,926	
	N H		81	21	10,142	12,205	2,063
			82	46	21,821	24,007	2,186
			83	11	7,847	8,118	271
			86	37	16,521	17,041	520
	N W		81	216,578	60,660,034	60,851,572	219,899
			82	218,806	58,524,067	58,700,667	176,600
			83	236,806	79,987,988	80,023,392	35,404
			84	294,267	95,077,646	95,124,860	47,214
			85	335,757	96,221,803	96,519,632	297,829
			86	342,229	104,003,187	106,864,195	2,861,008
	O E		81	145,951	49,516,176	49,516,178	
			82	106,187	31,154,959	31,172,754	17,795
			83	137,250	53,235,248	53,244,424	9,176
			84	126,881	45,987,474	45,989,093	1,619

Crop Product TSUSA commodity number, description, and unit of quantity Country	Mode	Reg	Yr	Quantity	F.A.S.	C.I.F.	Charges
			85	135,312	43,815,433	43,938,940	123,507
			86	108,423	39,727,233	39,765,887	38,654
	O	H	84	12	8,943	8,943	
	O	W	81	6,838	1,455,359	1,455,359	
			82	9,537	2,302,813	2,302,813	
			83	6,870	2,017,755	2,017,755	
			84	8,046	2,326,659	2,326,659	
			85	10,621	2,808,403	2,808,403	
			86	11,704	3,449,543	3,449,543	
	V	E	81	21,607	5,797,355	7,233,177	1,379,450
			82	33,138	11,303,583	13,798,912	2,495,329
			83	5,395	1,970,075	2,683,643	713,568
			84	42,479	12,486,761	14,036,900	1,550,139
			85	79,590	15,812,496	19,380,108	3,567,612
			86	72,268	16,460,978	19,734,340	3,273,362
	V	W	83	2,887	1,308,777	1,549,596	240,819
			84	2,189	588,313	690,042	101,729
			85	96	59,628	62,573	2,945
			86	3,780	1,333,420	1,479,069	145,649
CHINA M	O	E	85	523	194,887	194,887	
COCOS I	O	W	85	22	6,665	6,665	
ISRAEL	O	W	84	26	6,804	6,804	
LAOS	O	W	86	25	18,780	18,780	
N CALDN	O	W	86	24	9,985	9,985	
USSR	O	W	86	153	43,650	43,650	

2022760 CDR,EX W/RED,LUMBER,ROUGH (MBF)

Country	Mode	Reg	Yr	Quantity	F.A.S.	C.I.F.	Charges
TOTAL			81	5,294	2,276,603	2,339,308	62,705
			82	5,252	1,872,158	1,970,636	98,478
			83	10,944	3,969,077	4,098,364	129,287
			84	10,708	3,737,419	3,897,890	160,471
			85	8,303	2,834,109	2,887,461	53,352
			86	13,706	5,023,295	5,141,581	118,286
BELIZE	A	E	82	2	849	1,889	1,040
			83	2	1,422	3,081	1,659
	V	E	82	2	2,201	2,225	24
BERMUDA	A	E	84	10	5,034	5,313	279
BRAZIL	V	E	82	93	46,949	59,966	13,017
			83	44	27,255	38,467	11,212
			84	840	209,929	255,367	45,438
			85	28	16,610	18,780	2,170
			86	195	72,746	87,231	14,485
C RICA	V	E	81	20	9,000	13,585	4,585
			82	21	4,000	5,605	1,605
			83	23	16,000	17,957	1,957
CANADA	N	E	84	157	57,590	68,651	11,061
			86	865	159,525	197,061	37,536
	N	W	81	4,156	1,898,039	1,933,528	35,489
			84	4,595	1,849,297	1,949,410	100,113
	O	E	81	800	270,686	270,686	
			82	1,535	402,965	402,965	
			83	2,600	775,804	775,804	
			84	3,727	1,225,919	1,225,919	
			85	2,681	817,837	817,839	2
			86	4,895	1,620,160	1,620,426	266
	O	W	81	101	30,270	30,270	
			82	1,132	447,285	447,285	
			83	2,358	794,639	794,639	
			84	1,334	364,006	364,006	
			85	4,587	1,749,985	1,749,985	
			86	5,888	2,889,267	2,889,267	
	V	E	81	3	4,306	5,745	1,439
			82	1,626	517,455	583,708	66,253
			83	416	184,279	216,031	31,752
			84	20	7,108	9,515	2,407
			85	794	212,491	255,039	42,548
			86	588	177,997	231,134	53,137
	V	W	82	840	448,481	464,890	16,409
			83	4,780	2,154,469	2,224,876	70,407
			84	25	18,536	19,709	1,173
			85	213	37,186	45,818	8,632
			86	1,275	103,600	116,462	12,862
CHILE	V	E	83	720	14,580	26,880	12,300
COLOMB	V	E	81	181	39,697	55,540	15,843
ITALY	N	E	81	•	531	746	215
NETHLDS	O	E	83	1	629	629	
PARAGUA	V	W	81	12	5,600	6,742	1,142
PERU	V	W	81	20	18,000	21,992	3,992
U KING	O	E	81	1	474	474	
	V	W	82	1	1,973	2,103	130

2022780 CDR EX W/RED D/W LBR, NSPF (MBF)

Country	Mode	Reg	Yr	Quantity	F.A.S.	C.I.F.	Charges
TOTAL			81	9,873	2,728,896	2,782,112	53,023

Country	Mode	Reg	Yr	Quantity	F.A.S.	C.I.F.	Charges
			82	10,560	3,064,604	3,240,841	176,237
			83	12,242	4,063,813	4,091,179	27,366
			84	15,590	4,870,343	4,919,855	49,512
			85	19,880	5,464,096	5,525,629	61,533
			86	32,908	8,570,495	9,217,860	647,365
BELGIUM	V	W	82	3	1,835	2,040	205
BELIZE	V	E	84	64	9,600	10,955	1,355
BRAZIL	V	E	81	87	49,130	63,253	14,123
			82	40	7,931	14,439	6,508
			84	179	19,056	29,383	10,327
			85	1,865	39,979	47,650	7,671
			86	42	19,969	24,292	4,323
C RICA	V	E	82	34	5,500	5,846	346
CANADA	N	E	84	264	106,665	124,728	18,063
	O	E	81	2,465	719,052	720,296	1,244
			82	3,545	1,016,012	1,023,808	7,796
			83	6,512	2,098,208	2,101,025	2,817
			84	6,426	1,997,144	1,997,235	91
			85	7,953	2,308,273	2,309,773	1,500
			86	8,118	2,240,021	2,241,736	1,715
	O	H	83	5	4,853	5,733	880
	O	W	81	4,836	1,762,344	1,762,344	
			82	4,660	1,429,371	1,429,371	
			83	5,190	1,843,477	1,843,477	
			84	8,413	2,630,122	2,630,122	
			85	9,060	2,888,762	2,888,762	
			86	13,687	2,954,554	2,955,523	969
	V	E	81	74	18,576	21,619	2,850
			82	2,211	568,686	720,510	151,824
			83	179	47,110	58,666	11,556
			84	187	85,304	103,068	17,764
			85	590	171,211	211,489	40,278
			86	9,889	2,922,024	3,557,734	635,710
	V	W	81	1,185	116,141	144,754	28,613
			82	67	35,269	44,827	9,558
			83	176	65,165	73,060	7,895
			84	57	22,452	24,364	1,912
			85	60	13,648	17,613	3,965
			86	50	3,774	5,946	2,172
CHILE	V	E	83	180	5,000	9,218	4,218
GUATMAL	V	E	81	417	47,063	49,846	2,783
			85	24	32,401	34,639	2,238
HONDURA	V	E	81	5	4,711	5,640	929
	V	W	81	3	2,115	2,505	390
INDIA	V	W	86	13	5,540	5,740	200
JAPAN	A	W	86	5	2,679	4,030	1,351
	V	W	86	21	18,898	19,823	925
MEXICO	O	W	86	1,083	403,036	403,036	
PARAGUA	V	E	85	328	9,822	15,703	5,881
PERU	V	E	81	800	9,180	10,567	1,387
U KING	A	E	81	1	584	1,288	704

2023500 SPN CDR EBONY ETC LUMBR RGH (MBF)

Country	Mode	Reg	Yr	Quantity	F.A.S.	C.I.F.	Charges
TOTAL			81	467	489,335	549,818	60,483
			82	457	229,547	276,825	47,278
			83	573	316,731	366,673	49,942
			84	1,263	367,089	445,284	78,195
			85	905	235,371	263,580	28,209
			86	561	340,788	398,709	57,921
AUSTRAL	V	W	83	21	21,758	27,445	5,687
BELIZE	O	E	82	1	537	872	335
	V	E	82	17	6,073	6,884	811
			83	18	11,866	14,323	2,457
			86	6	7,946	8,628	682
BOLIVIA	V	E	81	177	96,597	126,252	29,655
			82	31	25,024	31,002	5,978
	V	W	83	2	1,071	1,321	250
BRAZIL	V	E	81	106	74,763	88,073	13,310
			82	185	82,767	113,776	31,009
			83	203	153,457	176,378	22,921
			84	1,052	210,757	276,253	65,496
			85	288	51,750	56,722	4,972
			86	406	180,480	221,549	41,069
BURMA	V	E	86	11	18,982	21,439	2,457
CAMROON	O	E	84	1	392	392	
CANADA	O	E	81	12	1,554	1,554	
			82	48	13,366	13,366	
			83	6	1,603	1,603	
			84	79	37,450	37,450	
			85	92	35,143	35,143	
			86	22	5,263	5,263	
	O	W	82	8	1,200	1,200	

Crop
Product
TSUSA commodity number, description, and unit of quantity

Country	Mode	Reg	Yr	Quantity	F.A.S.	C.I.F.	Charges
			83	15	3,861	3,861	
FR GERM	A	E	82	1	463	482	19
	N	E	83	*	2,996	3,032	36
			85	*	2,096	2,236	140
			86	*	3,270	3,786	516
	O	W	81	1	564	594	30
	V	E	81	14	27,046	28,051	1,005
			83	2	9,042	9,956	914
			84	2	2,650	2,806	156
			86	1	2,059	2,175	116
	V	W	81	1	1,337	1,397	60
			82	1	993	1,147	154
			83	1	253	297	44
			85	352	6,630	7,599	969
			86	1	3,094	3,225	131
GABON	V	E	83	12	3,581	8,202	4,621
GUATMAL	V	E	82	10	9,004	9,964	960
			83	73	61,650	69,248	7,598
			84	120	106,485	118,015	11,530
			85	40	24,466	28,938	4,472
			86	80	52,375	58,297	5,922
HONDURA	V	E	84	1	715	810	95
INDIA	N	W	86	*	3,752	3,944	192
	O	E	86	1	2,220	2,220	
	V	E	81	76	61,586	64,796	3,210
			82	82	4,802	5,394	592
			84	2	2,862	3,115	253
			85	2	3,828	4,053	225
	V	W	81	55	119,065	122,366	3,301
			82	35	14,574	15,486	912
			85	12	6,722	7,035	313
INDNSIA	O	E	82	1	3,001	3,001	
	V	E	81	3	15,190	16,300	1,110
	V	W	83	1	8,228	9,149	921
			85	2	16,915	17,591	676
JAPAN	V	E	83	9	13,512	14,440	928
			86	17	10,697	12,221	1,524
	V	W	82	3	14,948	16,294	1,346
			86	2	6,554	7,627	1,073
MEXICO	V	E	82	3	29,521	30,416	895
	V	W	86	6	1,379	2,979	1,600
NIGERIA	V	E	81	9	15,733	22,557	6,824
PERU	V	E	82	31	23,274	27,541	4,267
			83	15	17,373	20,151	2,778
			85	67	49,606	61,382	11,776
SINGAPR	V	E	86	2	12,661	13,101	440
	V	W	81	13	75,900	77,878	1,978
			85	50	38,215	42,881	4,666
			86	6	30,056	32,255	2,199
SRI LKA	N	W	84	*	5,097	5,467	370
	V	E	83	194	5,720	6,206	486
U KING	A	W	84	6	681	976	295
	V	W	83	1	760	1,061	301

2023700 SPN CDR ETC LUMBER DRSD ETC (MBF)

Country	Mode	Reg	Yr	Quantity	F.A.S.	C.I.F.	Charges
TOTAL			81	1,070	782,433	882,094	99,661
			82	53	77,983	85,670	7,687
			83	196	118,511	141,132	22,621
			84	134	53,018	61,181	8,163
			85	262	142,852	171,471	28,619
			86	37	27,260	30,923	3,663
BOLIVIA	V	E	81	43	37,898	44,778	6,880
BRAZIL	V	E	81	462	353,687	437,581	83,894
			82	15	9,768	13,390	3,622
			83	102	62,041	79,726	17,685
			85	135	45,914	55,688	9,774
			86	35	14,385	16,888	2,503
C RICA	V	E	84	3	11,741	14,366	2,625
CANADA	O	E	83	71	20,857	20,857	
			85	38	7,502	7,502	
	O	W	85	17	4,109	4,109	
CHINA M	V	W	83	7	13,884	16,136	2,252
DOM REP	V	E	84	1	2,367	2,539	172
FR GERM	A	E	85	8	7,264	8,145	881
	O	E	81	480	277,889	282,451	4,562
			82	1	8,382	8,645	263
	V	E	85	15	6,506	8,436	1,930
			86	2	12,875	14,035	1,160
	V	W	83	1	1,510	1,625	115
			84	1	629	703	74
FRANCE	A	E	84	3	10,395	11,595	1,200
GUATMAL	N	E	84	*	420	420	
	V	E	81	19	19,334	20,484	1,150

Crop
Product
TSUSA commodity number, description, and unit of quantity

Country	Mode	Reg	Yr	Quantity	F.A.S.	C.I.F.	Charges
HG KONG	V	E	85	16	49,965	55,952	5,987
	V	W	81	4	8,275	8,950	675
HONDURA	V	E	82	1	1,850	2,538	688
			84	2	1,638	2,606	968
INDIA	N	E	82	*	5,500	5,642	142
			84	*	1,150	1,150	
	V	E	81	23	76,210	78,036	1,826
			82	33	42,528	44,850	2,322
			84	1	1,964	2,215	251
	V	W	83	1	1,507	1,764	257
INDNSIA	V	E	82	1	8,193	8,593	400
			84	113	8,868	10,385	1,517
JAPAN	V	E	81	38	8,798	9,472	674
			85	3	5,975	6,558	583
MEXICO	O	E	84	1	660	660	
NICARAG	O	W	81	1	342	342	
			82	1	486	486	
PANAMA	V	E	82	1	1,276	1,526	250
PARAGUA	V	E	85	20	5,899	9,445	3,546
PERU	V	E	83	13	12,155	13,672	1,517
			84	7	10,136	11,010	874
SRI LKA	V	E	83	1	6,557	7,352	795
			84	2	3,050	3,532	482
U KING	A	E	85	10	9,718	15,636	5,918

Cedar, plywood
2401000 PLYWD, PLY SPANISH CDR FACE (MSF)

Country	Mode	Reg	Yr	Quantity	F.A.S.	C.I.F.	Charges
TOTAL			81	578	216,452	255,978	39,526
			82	2,113	807,616	963,494	155,878
			83	4,061	1,209,727	1,406,180	196,453
			84	8,183	2,186,573	2,583,342	396,769
			85	11,950	3,073,983	3,587,595	513,612
			86	15,836	3,989,067	4,579,502	590,435
AUSTRIA	A	E	82	1	355	715	360
BRAZIL	V	E	81	535	208,217	247,311	39,094
			82	1,934	753,692	897,101	143,409
			83	4,039	1,206,927	1,403,112	196,185
			84	7,956	2,123,107	2,512,945	389,838
			85	11,141	2,979,800	3,468,545	488,745
			86	15,833	3,986,490	4,576,777	590,287
C RICA	V	E	81	23	5,600	6,025	425
			82	176	53,284	65,349	12,065
CANADA	O	E	81	19	2,100	2,100	
	O	W	86	3	1,356	1,356	
CHINA T	V	E	83	22	2,800	3,068	268
			84	77	33,180	36,663	3,483
			85	9	3,783	4,150	367
	V	W	85	800	90,400	114,900	24,500
FINLAND	V	E	81	1	535	542	7
FRANCE	V	W	84	150	30,286	33,734	3,448
JAPAN	N	E	86	*	1,221	1,369	148
SPAIN	V	E	82	2	285	329	44

Cedar, shingles
2008520 RED CEDAR SHINGLES A SHAKES (SQ)

Country	Mode	Reg	Yr	Quantity	F.A.S.	C.I.F.	Charges
TOTAL			81	2,888,636	125,015,349	125,563,197	546,639
			82	2,624,204	99,108,281	99,222,189	113,908
			83	3,213,878	144,932,420	145,035,545	103,125
			84	3,662,860	162,516,895	162,610,205	93,310
			85	3,994,353	156,848,243	156,878,727	30,484
			86	4,087,649	148,326,263	148,338,463	12,200
CANADA	A	E	86	10	2,060	3,203	1,143
	N	E	82	11,180	142,895	142,895	
			85	9,342	188,240	188,240	
	N	W	81	2,087,153	90,377,667	90,892,973	515,096
			82	2,035,034	79,306,657	79,419,138	112,481
			83	2,855,525	130,963,052	131,038,998	75,946
			84	3,265,593	149,642,946	149,730,238	87,292
			85	3,463,986	140,183,646	140,202,824	19,178
	O	E	81	790,290	34,143,355	34,145,986	1,632
			82	571,523	19,407,569	19,407,569	
			83	350,224	13,523,147	13,523,147	
			84	392,999	12,658,329	12,659,262	933
			85	515,040	16,211,398	16,211,402	4
			86	839,006	20,915,183	20,918,253	3,070
	O	H	84	48	1,452	1,452	
	O	W	81	5,364	220,355	220,355	
			82	5,223	195,778	195,778	

Crop Product TSUSA commodity number, description, and unit of quantity Country	Mode	Reg	Yr	Quantity	F.A.S.	C.I.F.	Charges
			83	1,339	75,867	75,867	
			84	2,986	148,243	148,243	
			85	1,870	90,728	90,728	
			86	3,245,904	127,302,889	127,304,933	2,044
	V	E	81	45	1,906	2,561	655
			82	669	28,713	29,675	962
			83	896	44,625	48,340	3,715
			84	733	37,546	40,742	3,196
			85	346	23,152	28,502	5,350
			86	429	16,779	19,687	2,908
	V	H	81	600	32,604	39,534	6,930
	V	W	81	4,840	218,812	241,138	22,326
			82	339	15,683	16,148	465
			83	5,874	323,903	347,249	23,346
			84	501	28,379	30,268	1,889
			85	1,977	88,797	94,749	5,952
			86	1,103	43,294	46,329	3,035
CHINA M	O	E	85	376	19,914	19,914	
CZECHO	O	W	85	179	8,234	8,234	
JAPAN	V	W	83	20	1,826	1,944	118
LAOS	O	W	86	249	7,899	7,899	
MEXICO	O	E	85	60	1,781	1,781	
	O	W	81	344	20,650	20,650	
			82	236	10,986	10,986	
			86	948	38,159	38,159	
USSR	O	W	85	1,177	32,353	32,353	

Cedar, veneer
2403000 WD-VENR PANEL SPANISH CEDAR (MSF)

Country	Mode	Reg	Yr	Quantity	F.A.S.	C.I.F.	Charges
TOTAL			81	1	276	358	82
			82	232	2,273	2,599	326
			83	186	8,066	8,133	67
			84	174	57,086	65,780	8,694
			85	465	118,882	142,386	23,504
			86	309	67,046	78,031	10,985
BRAZIL	V	E	84	100	42,562	49,518	6,956
			85	175	26,523	32,837	6,314
			86	144	33,204	41,990	8,786
C RICA	A	E	82	128	400	726	326
CANADA	O	E	82	104	1,873	1,873	
			83	135	7,417	7,417	
CHINA T	V	W	86	165	33,842	36,041	2,199
JAPAN	V	W	83	51	649	716	67
NAURU	V	E	85	290	92,359	109,549	17,190
PHIL R	V	E	84	74	14,524	16,262	1,738
YUGOSLV	V	E	81	1	276	358	82

2405000 WD-VNER PANLS,1 SDE SPAN CDR (MSF)

Country	Mode	Reg	Yr	Quantity	F.A.S.	C.I.F.	Charges
TOTAL			81	88	4,957	5,086	129
			82	13	2,179	2,219	40
			84	18	3,989	4,157	168
			85	300	32,893	34,295	1,402
			86	29	16,449	16,948	499
BRAZIL	V	E	85	7	2,673	3,366	693
CANADA	O	E	82	12	1,676	1,676	
			85	97	20,758	20,758	
			86	6	11,847	11,847	
CHINA M	V	W	85	18	1,136	1,227	91
CHINA T	V	W	85	2	3,490	3,824	334
			86	17	3,064	3,438	374
FR GERM	N	E	81	55	950	990	40
FRANCE	A	E	84	16	513	526	13
			85	176	4,836	5,120	284
HG KONG	V	W	82	1	503	543	40
MACAO	V	W	86	6	1,538	1,663	125
PERU	V	E	84	2	3,476	3,631	155
SWITZLD	A	E	81	33	4,007	4,096	89

Cedar, woodsiding
2024720 WOOD SIDNG, RED CEDR, RESAWN (MSF)

Country	Mode	Reg	Yr	Quantity	F.A.S.	C.I.F.	Charges
TOTAL			81	97,488	38,097,623	38,100,252	733
			82	91,873	34,358,436	34,358,638	202
			83	160,292	72,389,073	72,389,077	4
			84	184,375	81,755,824	81,755,830	6
			85	228,091	92,050,682	92,088,563	37,881
			86	239,683	95,345,771	97,602,586	2,256,815
CANADA	N	E	86	125	64,313	64,313	

Country	Mode	Reg	Yr	Quantity	F.A.S.	C.I.F.	Charges
	N	W	84	107,803	47,169,201	47,169,207	6
			86	139,200	53,341,456	55,579,936	2,238,480
	O	E	81	36,733	16,414,342	16,416,238	
			82	34,429	13,942,451	13,942,653	202
			83	58,235	26,329,945	26,329,945	
			84	75,148	33,930,443	33,930,443	
			85	97,711	40,657,045	40,676,480	19,435
			86	98,357	41,214,143	41,232,478	18,335
	O	W	81	60,743	21,680,176	21,680,176	
			82	57,444	20,415,985	20,415,985	
			83	102,057	46,059,128	46,059,132	4
			84	1,424	656,180	656,180	
			85	129,146	50,916,469	50,933,872	17,403
			86	1,872	681,511	681,511	
CHINA M	O	E	85	842	350,468	350,468	
GABON	O	E	86	80	35,463	35,463	
	O	W	86	49	8,885	8,885	
INDIA	O	W	85	65	35,499	35,499	
JAPAN	V	E	85	15	10,735	11,778	1,043
LAOS	O	W	85	217	50,105	50,105	
N CALDN	O	E	85	44	12,314	12,314	
PHIL R	V	E	81	12	3,105	3,838	733
USSR	O	W	85	51	18,047	18,047	

2024800 WD SIDING NSPF W. RED CEDAR (MSF)

Country	Mode	Reg	Yr	Quantity	F.A.S.	C.I.F.	Charges
TOTAL			81	64,479	21,663,132	21,671,601	
			82	46,675	15,808,863	15,808,920	57
			83	70,758	29,185,035	29,185,035	
			84	77,793	31,411,375	31,411,380	5
			85	74,275	23,566,926	23,568,807	1,881
			86	65,144	22,325,678	22,726,218	400,540
CANADA	N	E	82	*	1,400	1,400	
	N	W	86	51,233	17,296,661	17,692,157	395,496
	O	E	81	24,198	8,155,743	8,155,742	
			82	16,517	5,637,245	5,637,245	
			83	21,389	8,747,787	8,747,787	
			84	13,786	5,996,855	5,996,855	
			85	19,283	5,239,843	5,239,843	
			86	13,405	4,847,345	4,851,094	3,749
	O	W	81	40,281	13,507,389	13,515,859	
			82	30,157	10,169,553	10,169,553	
			83	49,369	20,437,248	20,437,248	
			84	64,007	25,414,520	25,414,525	5
			85	54,779	18,267,812	18,269,693	1,881
			86	494	170,018	170,018	
CHINA M	O	E	85	186	54,173	54,173	
MALAYSA	V	W	86	12	11,654	12,949	1,295
PHIL R	V	W	82	1	665	722	57
USSR	O	W	85	27	5,098	5,098	

Cedarwood, essential oil
4528005 CEDARWOOD (LB)

Country	Mode	Reg	Yr	Quantity	F.A.S.	C.I.F.	Charges
TOTAL			81	435,816	401,123	462,014	60,891
			82	703,722	939,418	1,041,368	101,950
			83	316,127	848,073	906,357	58,284
			84	516,007	1,311,100	1,390,010	78,910
			85	373,957	415,127	458,673	43,546
			86	926,865	847,056	918,164	71,108
AUSTRAL	A	E	86	628	18,829	19,593	764
CHINA M	O	E	81	115,874	103,628	119,473	15,845
			82	87,302	144,689	157,753	13,064
			83	12,302	26,526	28,401	1,875
	V	E	81	164,683	141,657	165,664	24,007
			82	148,413	183,996	205,624	21,628
			83	229,998	646,526	691,957	45,431
			84	423,718	1,063,045	1,126,630	63,585
			85	367,844	400,580	443,555	42,975
			86	839,488	708,702	771,880	63,178
	V	W	81	146,032	125,934	145,761	19,827
			82	444,446	572,142	636,780	64,638
			83	62,301	139,475	149,413	9,938
CHINA T	V	W	82	11,905	16,393	18,210	1,817
FR GERM	A	E	84	22	1,286	1,387	101
	V	E	83	165	999	1,040	41
FRANCE	O	E	83	1,519	8,212	8,353	141
	V	E	81	1,763	5,906	6,177	271
			82	8,820	15,470	15,969	499
			83	6,000	15,794	16,200	406
			84	864	2,402	2,628	226
			85	2,145	8,089	8,238	149

Crop
Product
TSUSA commodity number, description, and unit of quantity

Country	Mode	Reg	Yr	Quantity	F.A.S.	C.I.F.	Charges
HG KONG	V	E	84	77,381	211,690	224,080	12,390
			86	44,445	33,854	37,155	3,301
INDIA	V	E	85	3,968	6,458	6,880	422
JAPAN	V	E	83	425	1,088	1,201	113
			86	1,462	5,961	6,270	309
	V	W	86	125	1,612	1,730	118
KENYA	V	E	81	6,583	20,138	20,932	794
			84	14,022	32,677	35,285	2,608
MOROC	V	E	82	441	1,541	1,706	165
NETHLDS	V	E	82	838	1,480	1,501	21
			86	425	1,994	2,035	41
SPAIN	A	E	86	963	1,627	2,396	769
U KING	N	E	83	3,417	9,453	9,792	339
	O	E	86	39,329	74,477	77,105	2,628
	V	E	81	881	3,860	4,007	147
			82	1,557	3,707	3,825	118

Celery

Celery, fresh or frozen
1356000 CELERY, APR 15-JULY 31 INCL (LB)

Country	Mode	Reg	Yr	Quantity	F.A.S.	C.I.F.	Charges
TOTAL			81	543,575	104,222	104,222	
			82	593,445	108,017	108,367	350
			83	288,238	49,196	52,419	3,223
			84	540,981	101,871	104,794	2,923
			85	1,136,413	148,782	176,590	27,808
			86	1,494,578	209,337	222,730	13,393
BELGIUM	A	E	84	1,086	955	1,735	780
			86	35	1,348	1,837	489
CANADA	O	E	81	530,387	100,022	100,022	
			82	549,585	92,114	92,114	
			83	242,440	36,040	36,040	
			84	525,305	94,118	94,185	67
			85	357,630	62,500	62,500	
			86	442,745	76,437	76,437	
	O	W	84	9,000	1,500	1,500	
FRANCE	A	E	83	935	2,217	2,562	345
			84	670	2,234	2,655	421
			85	1,745	3,138	4,412	1,274
	A	W	84	952	996	1,569	573
GUATMAL	V	E	85	403,297	38,261	64,795	26,534
			86	188,643	22,557	35,122	12,565
ISRAEL	V	E	83	44,445	10,080	12,760	2,680
ITALY	A	E	86	864	2,394	2,733	339
MEXICO	O	E	85	10,508	1,065	1,065	
	O	W	81	13,188	4,200	4,200	
			82	33,360	11,000	11,000	
			85	363,233	43,818	43,818	
			86	862,291	106,601	106,601	
NETHLDS	A	E	84	3,968	2,068	3,150	1,082
SENEGAL	A	E	83	418	859	1,057	198
SPAIN	V	E	82	10,500	4,903	5,253	350

1356100 CELERY FRESH OR FROZEN NSPF (LB)

Country	Mode	Reg	Yr	Quantity	F.A.S.	C.I.F.	Charges
TOTAL			81	6,882,614	895,130	904,075	8,945
			82	9,612,100	1,063,463	1,064,480	1,017
			83	10,141,695	1,471,527	1,473,235	1,708
			84	6,707,188	746,953	754,970	8,017
			85	11,619,445	1,327,634	1,404,065	76,431
			86	13,268,974	1,684,941	1,838,334	153,393
BELGIUM	A	E	82	238	492	844	352
			84	783	1,008	1,353	345
C RICA	V	E	82	4,904	420	445	25
CANADA	O	E	81	6,771,115	866,723	866,723	
			82	9,566,092	1,053,143	1,053,143	
			83	10,095,122	1,460,385	1,460,385	
			84	6,046,674	669,863	669,863	
			85	7,786,745	871,649	871,649	
			86	6,549,288	930,350	930,350	
	O	W	83	17,375	2,693	2,693	
			84	281,650	37,560	37,560	
			86	43,081	4,097	4,097	
CHINA M	V	E	81	44,092	9,972	12,462	2,490
CHINA T	A	E	86	3,000	4,800	10,201	5,401
	V	E	85	39,571	8,817	9,045	228
DOM REP	N	E	81	21,284	5,974	12,319	6,345
	V	E	82	750	375	486	111
			84	4,680	1,685	1,898	213

Crop
Product
TSUSA commodity number, description, and unit of quantity

Country	Mode	Reg	Yr	Quantity	F.A.S.	C.I.F.	Charges
			86	4,770	1,908	2,128	220
FR GERM	O	E	85	1,158	2,734	2,953	219
	V	E	83	3,290	1,323	1,426	103
FRANCE	A	E	81	205	270	340	70
			83	21,752	3,510	4,407	897
			86	1,283	2,619	3,847	1,228
	N	E	84	3,108	1,721	1,843	122
	V	E	82	1,019	422	461	39
			84	238	319	336	17
	V	W	82	39,097	8,611	9,101	490
GUATMAL	V	E	84	134,768	11,169	16,228	5,059
			85	1,262,064	117,515	183,304	65,789
			86	2,569,695	225,951	363,294	137,343
GUYANA	O	E	86	37,664	2,495	2,993	498
ICELAND	V	E	85	119,026	27,423	32,518	5,095
ISRAEL	V	E	85	117,064	22,950	28,050	5,100
			86	161,400	65,634	70,923	5,289
ITALY	A	E	83	1,650	2,682	3,390	708
			84	598	1,397	1,946	549
KIRIBAT	V	E	86	38,038	4,292	6,319	2,027
MEXICO	O	E	84	172,789	8,625	8,625	
			85	58,333	4,452	4,452	
	O	W	84	45,640	11,833	11,833	
			83	2,506	934	934	
			84	42,059	8,298	8,298	
			85	2,235,484	272,094	272,094	
			86	3,846,001	440,136	440,136	
NETHLDS	V	E	84	19,841	5,308	7,020	1,712
U KING	V	E	81	278	358	398	40
			86	14,754	2,659	4,046	1,387

Celery, seed
1262100 CELERY SEEDS (LB)

Country	Mode	Reg	Yr	Quantity	F.A.S.	C.I.F.	Charges
TOTAL			81	4,499,374	1,375,857	1,713,278	337,421
			82	4,318,831	1,325,975	1,655,962	329,987
			83	5,095,146	1,778,041	2,139,093	361,052
			84	4,795,939	2,964,518	3,349,668	385,150
			85	5,617,728	2,911,317	3,345,406	434,089
			86	5,679,047	2,149,847	2,575,947	426,100
CANADA	O	E	83	1,275	2,167	2,167	
CHINA M	V	E	81	767,977	187,433	219,907	32,474
			82	408,874	95,738	120,897	25,159
			83	137,302	40,613	48,360	7,747
			84	204,773	120,147	133,101	12,954
			85	336,142	225,773	254,922	29,149
			86	89,800	37,558	44,306	6,748
	V	W	81	33,069	8,554	9,245	691
			82	154,322	34,544	43,366	8,822
			83	22,046	5,564	6,734	1,170
			84	33,950	20,196	24,031	3,835
			85	192,947	137,615	148,682	11,067
CHINA T	V	E	85	11,022	8,726	9,464	738
COLOMB	V	E	81	44,092	10,174	12,450	2,276
EGYPT	O	E	84	24,200	10,174	11,383	1,009
FRANCE	A	E	84	50	339	455	116
	N	E	82	9,515	8,097	9,641	1,544
			83	7,026	4,904	5,483	579
	V	E	81	22,346	13,372	17,288	3,916
			82	11,023	4,883	6,001	1,118
			84	57,259	43,365	50,462	7,097
			85	19,140	19,172	22,173	3,001
			86	40,720	40,161	43,800	3,639
	V	W	81	110	660	701	41
			82	100	401	412	11
			86	441	1,728	1,880	152
GREECE	V	E	83	26,276	8,328	10,228	1,900
HG KONG	V	E	81	101,853	27,678	29,598	1,920
			83	45,018	13,086	14,298	1,212
			85	56,471	28,252	30,132	1,880
			86	62,544	24,105	27,995	3,890
	V	W	81	88	305	334	29
INDIA	N	E	82	3,013,586	953,541	1,191,656	238,115
			83	3,909,266	1,386,363	1,666,397	280,034
			86	1,084,261	420,829	502,156	81,327
	N	W	82	510,192	156,629	194,416	37,787
	V	E	81	3,206,489	1,015,577	1,283,651	268,074
			82	154,844	49,875	62,326	12,451
			83	522,766	173,685	210,679	36,994
			84	4,180,923	2,578,960	2,914,302	335,342
			85	4,802,637	2,373,607	2,744,837	371,230
			86	4,257,518	1,562,576	1,879,416	316,840

Crop
Product
TSUSA commodity number, description, and unit of quantity

Country	Mode	Reg	Yr	Quantity	F.A.S.	C.I.F.	Charges
	V	W	81	280,487	95,420	119,632	24,212
			82	55,434	16,224	20,736	4,512
			83	421,679	130,244	161,404	31,160
			84	165,475	101,646	116,279	14,633
			85	156,108	87,254	101,175	13,921
			86	142,688	56,886	70,104	13,218
INDNSIA	N	E	85	38,723	20,774	23,783	3,009
	V	E	81	39,802	11,035	14,543	3,508
ITALY	A	E	82	100	391	627	236
	V	E	82	302	1,867	1,923	56
	V	W	81	485	1,853	1,972	119
			82	350	1,423	1,457	34
			83	1,022	3,844	3,914	70
			84	234	2,336	2,360	24
			86	1,075	6,004	6,290	286
JAPAN	A	E	82	5	1,264	1,360	96
			84	1	302	318	16
	N	W	84	7	2,318	2,366	48
	O	E	83	4	1,007	1,066	59
	O	W	84	5	1,516	1,564	48
	V	E	83	5	1,529	1,552	23
KUWAIT	V	E	84	21,860	20,406	22,331	1,925
MEXICO	O	W	81	2,466	2,989	2,989	
			83	1,351	4,728	4,728	
			84	18,143	15,207	15,207	
			85	4,508	9,027	9,027	
NETHLDS	A	E	81	60	302	427	125
			82	175	790	819	29
	A	W	83	10	1,527	1,598	71
			85	30	1,117	1,211	94
	V	E	81	50	505	541	36
			83	100	452	485	33
PAKISTN	V	W	84	7,716	8,911	9,877	966
S HELNA	V	E	84	64,824	32,250	37,846	5,596
TURKEY	V	E	84	16,519	6,245	7,786	1,541
U KING	A	W	82	9	308	325	17

Chayote

Chayote, fresh or frozen
1377500 CHAYOTE, FRSH, CHLD OR FRZN (LB)

Country	Mode	Reg	Yr	Quantity	F.A.S.	C.I.F.	Charges
TOTAL			81	6,810,862	1,216,755	1,636,212	419,457
			82	8,715,627	1,570,250	2,162,012	591,762
			83	10,245,293	1,559,087	2,268,474	709,387
			84	11,126,946	1,691,480	2,304,421	612,941
			85	11,309,118	2,108,881	2,769,689	660,808
			86	12,435,002	2,414,799	3,042,106	627,307
BERMUDA	V	E	82	2,183	263	460	197
C AF RP	V	W	85	36,201	13,082	17,146	4,064
C RICA	N	E	85	6,271,149	1,118,652	1,591,152	472,500
	O	E	86	32,000	3,920	6,571	2,651
	V	E	81	5,925,822	1,003,138	1,364,741	361,603
			82	7,004,421	1,168,381	1,615,242	446,861
			83	8,367,656	1,244,586	1,787,496	542,910
			84	8,949,564	1,181,351	1,721,963	540,612
			85	2,841,231	380,386	522,272	141,886
			86	8,776,587	1,320,663	1,924,188	603,525
	V	W	81	530,894	153,837	203,211	49,374
			82	1,497,716	348,918	488,149	139,231
			83	1,529,625	253,742	416,271	162,529
			84	595,171	89,541	155,894	66,353
			85	292,202	81,386	115,896	34,510
			86	87,375	27,683	37,405	9,722
CANADA	O	E	86	693	1,915	1,915	
	V	E	86	3,600	1,024	1,320	296
CHILE	V	E	86	27,368	4,875	6,896	2,021
COLOMB	A	E	81	91,800	15,300	23,300	8,000
DOM REP	A	E	83	4,809	495	835	340
	N	E	84	5,500	700	1,066	366
	V	E	82	4,000	400	514	114
			83	4,200	672	895	223
			84	35,390	4,224	6,776	2,552
			85	14,079	1,250	2,053	803
			86	80,000	16,000	21,131	5,131
GUATMAL	V	E	85	24,280	1,821	1,875	54
	V	W	83	33,000	3,750	7,135	3,385
			85	34,000	1,063	1,116	53
HONDURA	V	E	85	40,392	3,250	6,326	3,076
JAMAICA	N	E	85	29,527	8,020	11,882	3,862

Country	Mode	Reg	Yr	Quantity	F.A.S.	C.I.F.	Charges
KIRIBAT	V	E	86	16,000	3,200	5,184	1,984
MEXICO	A	W	84	7,937	1,300	3,120	1,820
	O	E	81	27,025	4,389	4,389	
			82	8,770	1,016	1,016	
			83	6,736	2,008	2,008	
			84	171,160	12,388	12,388	
	O	W	81	227,521	39,291	39,291	
			82	143,510	32,552	32,822	270
			83	299,267	53,834	53,834	
			84	1,346,224	399,576	399,576	
			85	1,726,057	499,971	499,971	
			86	3,391,762	1,026,085	1,026,085	
NICARAG	V	W	82	55,027	18,720	23,809	5,089
PANAMA	A	E	86	19,617	9,434	11,411	1,977
	V	E	81	7,800	800	1,280	480
			84	16,000	2,400	3,638	1,238

Cherry

Cherry, candied
1540500 CHERRIES, CANDIED,GLACE,ETC (LB)

Country	Mode	Reg	Yr	Quantity	F.A.S.	C.I.F.	Charges
TOTAL			81	1,382	2,517	2,901	384
			82	174,503	116,947	133,415	16,468
			83	359,092	221,909	251,978	30,069
			84	496,935	412,321	470,320	57,999
			85	922,230	576,678	654,422	77,744
			86	1,796,359	1,278,662	1,409,873	131,211
AUSTRAL	N	H	83	484	878	1,265	387
CANADA	O	E	83	1,292	1,392	1,426	34
			84	1,619	1,651	1,668	17
			86	4,000	3,590	3,590	
	O	W	86	12,000	13,401	13,401	
FR GERM	V	E	81	245	1,049	1,146	97
			83	456	878	916	38
			84	226	659	708	49
FRANCE	A	E	83	180	860	890	30
			84	96	788	1,121	333
	O	E	86	22,046	21,000	22,475	1,475
	V	E	82	172,995	115,456	131,806	16,350
			83	283,203	157,244	179,379	22,135
			84	463,781	379,890	432,555	52,665
			85	733,975	458,852	520,485	61,633
			86	1,727,981	1,216,654	1,343,566	126,912
GREECE	V	E	81	476	660	780	120
ITALY	A	E	83	264	381	817	436
	V	E	82	1,508	1,491	1,609	118
			84	29,921	27,973	32,177	4,204
			85	54,464	45,783	53,627	7,844
PORTUGL	V	E	81	441	541	687	146
SPAIN	A	W	84	485	450	1,125	675
	V	E	81	220	267	288	21
			83	73,213	60,276	67,285	7,009
			85	133,791	72,043	80,310	8,267
			86	28,012	20,121	22,817	2,696
SWITZLD	V	E	84	807	910	966	56
U KING	V	E	86	2,320	3,896	4,024	128

Cherry, canned
1469100 CHERRIES,FR,IN AIRTITE CONT (LB)

Country	Mode	Reg	Yr	Quantity	F.A.S.	C.I.F.	Charges
TOTAL			81	15,165	20,534	22,701	2,167
			82	13,380	6,529	6,529	
			83	3,134	3,446	4,638	1,192
			84	7,066	5,913	9,661	3,748
			85	52,553	48,016	66,212	18,196
			86	80,170	14,214	19,389	5,175
BELGIUM	A	E	83	782	602	1,047	445
	V	E	85	4,428	3,272	3,714	442
	V	W	85	2,238	1,650	2,023	373
CANADA	O	E	82	13,380	6,529	6,529	
			86	528	1,545	1,545	
CHILE	A	E	84	4,950	3,600	7,100	3,500
			85	14,183	9,493	18,917	9,424
	V	E	85	26,515	26,515	34,204	7,689
FRANCE	V	E	84	2,116	2,313	2,561	248
	V	W	85	2,675	2,735	2,896	161
GREECE	A	W	85	1,200	1,440	1,507	67
	V	E	81	10,800	14,792	16,517	1,725

Crop
Product
TSUSA commodity number, description, and unit of quantity

Country	Mode	Reg	Yr	Quantity	F.A.S.	C.I.F.	Charges
			86	1,320	1,265	1,471	206
N ZEAL	A	E	83	986	1,371	2,027	656
SWITZLD	V	E	86	1,778	2,275	2,408	133
	V	W	86	1,750	2,472	2,588	116
U KING	V	E	83	1,366	1,473	1,564	91
			85	1,314	2,911	2,951	40
YUGOSLV	V	E	81	4,365	5,742	6,184	442
			86	74,794	6,657	11,377	4,720

Cherry, dried
1469300 CHERRIES, DRIED (LB)

Country	Mode	Reg	Yr	Quantity	F.A.S.	C.I.F.	Charges
TOTAL			81	15,987	16,622	17,440	818
			82	57,400	39,477	42,714	3,237
			83	64,706	39,778	43,801	4,023
			84	39,817	31,929	33,990	2,061
			85	23,642	28,599	28,599	
			86	54,207	35,152	41,354	6,202
AFGHAN	V	W	84	1,707	600	697	97
			86	9,969	3,482	4,214	732
CANADA	O	E	81	7,140	8,818	8,818	
			82	10,000	13,500	13,500	
			83	7,700	11,620	12,206	586
			84	7,098	16,696	16,696	
			85	23,642	28,599	28,599	
			86	5,000	5,043	5,263	220
CHINA T	V	H	86	1,000	1,210	1,350	140
FR GERM	V	W	83	6,614	6,720	7,200	480
LEBANON	O	E	81	220	274	274	
SWITZLD	A	E	86	2,006	2,006	3,806	1,800
	V	E	84	935	3,143	3,272	129
TURKEY	V	E	81	4,141	2,443	2,624	181
			82	47,400	25,977	29,214	3,237
			83	50,392	21,438	24,395	2,957
			84	16,849	6,600	7,611	1,011
			86	17,802	9,834	11,881	2,047
	V	W	84	13,228	4,890	5,714	824
			86	18,430	13,577	14,840	1,263
YUGOSLV	V	E	81	4,486	5,087	5,724	637

Cherry, fresh
1469000 CHERRIES, FRESH NOT CANNED (LB)

Country	Mode	Reg	Yr	Quantity	F.A.S.	C.I.F.	Charges
TOTAL			81	137,716	174,343	237,962	63,619
			82	298,220	386,892	534,101	147,209
			83	987,936	738,934	1,264,163	525,229
			84	1,571,539	1,068,270	1,723,090	654,820
			85	4,059,421	2,258,348	2,755,817	497,469
			86	1,777,593	1,106,357	1,646,700	540,343
ARGENT	A	E	84	10,251	7,830	16,086	8,256
BELGIUM	V	E	83	1,865	1,437	1,687	250
			84	8,646	5,449	6,601	1,152
C RICA	V	W	86	8,400	3,850	7,400	3,550
CANADA	O	E	81	4,140	2,902	2,902	
			82	31,510	17,418	17,418	
			83	13,354	5,216	5,216	
			84	276,608	133,816	133,816	
			85	154,907	99,585	99,585	
			86	17,060	10,689	10,689	
	O	W	83	2,000	1,353	1,353	
			84	17,600	9,680	9,680	
			85	2,454,243	1,180,351	1,180,351	
			86	304,937	51,767	51,767	
CHILE	A	E	81	80,245	82,107	124,953	42,846
			82	220,419	293,041	407,018	113,977
			83	670,373	519,594	939,244	419,650
			84	85,630	68,566	124,043	55,477
			85	525,266	345,717	690,569	344,852
			86	548,746	439,526	839,681	400,155
	A	W	82	6,807	7,698	15,733	8,035
			84	11,783	14,094	22,081	7,987
			85	13,102	9,468	17,287	7,819
			86	24,359	21,400	39,251	17,851
	N	E	84	925,140	694,946	1,240,730	545,784
	N	W	83	85,072	58,911	114,528	55,617
	O	W	84	11,244	15,940	15,940	
	V	E	83	147,166	52,662	74,227	21,565
			84	115,638	64,280	78,775	14,495
			85	873,473	570,506	691,316	120,810
			86	842,210	542,951	645,823	102,872

Crop
Product
TSUSA commodity number, description, and unit of quantity

Country	Mode	Reg	Yr	Quantity	F.A.S.	C.I.F.	Charges
CHINA M	A	E	85	5,768	3,220	7,636	4,416
ECUADOR	A	E	84	9,838	7,280	12,988	5,708
FR GERM	V	E	86	529	3,149	3,262	113
FRANCE	V	E	84	5,762	3,264	3,580	316
GREECE	V	E	86	1,200	1,050	1,230	180
GUATMAL	A	E	84	6,462	9,683	11,791	2,108
JAMAICA	V	E	84	19,600	2,000	2,050	50
N ZEAL	A	E	82	5,037	6,611	10,545	3,934
			83	4,178	6,058	8,616	2,558
			84	18,810	6,348	8,304	1,956
	A	H	81	4,204	6,600	7,738	1,138
			82	1,430	2,083	2,631	548
			83	1,007	1,484	1,932	448
			84	132	335	435	100
			85	926	1,723	2,275	552
	A	W	81	48,677	81,714	101,286	19,572
			82	32,961	59,701	80,380	20,679
			83	62,921	92,219	117,360	25,141
			84	9,815	18,039	27,098	9,059
			85	21,004	40,389	57,246	16,857
			86	5,337	15,265	18,735	3,470
PERU	A	E	84	38,580	6,720	9,092	2,372
			86	9,914	6,000	11,400	5,400
PHIL R	V	W	86	4,177	3,437	3,794	357
SWITZLD	A	E	86	10,724	7,273	13,668	6,395
	N	E	85	10,732	7,389	9,552	2,163
	V	E	81	450	1,020	1,083	63
U KING	V	E	82	56	340	376	36

Cherry, frozen
1469700 CHERRIES, FROZEN (LB)

Country	Mode	Reg	Yr	Quantity	F.A.S.	C.I.F.	Charges
TOTAL			81	27,760	11,058	11,058	
			83	565,238	92,345	92,345	
			85	137,971	45,418	51,648	6,230
			86	306,316	109,534	126,391	16,857
CANADA	O	E	83	49,560	32,880	32,880	
	O	W	81	27,760	11,058	11,058	
			83	515,678	59,465	59,465	
			85	80,000	29,207	29,207	
			86	167,145	70,416	70,416	
DOM REP	V	E	85	8,610	6,027	6,890	863
FRANCE	V	E	86	1,102	1,149	1,332	183
HUNGARY	V	E	86	21,600	10,549	12,060	1,511
YUGOSLV	V	E	85	49,361	10,184	15,551	5,367
			86	116,469	27,420	42,583	15,163

Cherry, in brine
1469500 CHERRIES,IN BRINE WITH PITS (LB)

Country	Mode	Reg	Yr	Quantity	F.A.S.	C.I.F.	Charges
TOTAL			81	3,896	3,594	3,905	311
			83	4,377	4,298	5,157	859
			84	1,823	2,946	3,096	150
			85	198,854	102,928	129,758	26,830
			86	260,717	159,092	183,335	24,243
FR GERM	V	E	86	1,640	2,208	2,318	110
FRANCE	A	E	84	147	347	410	63
	V	E	81	2,708	2,047	2,285	238
	V	W	86	43,970	31,266	36,331	5,065
ITALY	V	E	84	88	697	730	33
			86	26,989	15,992	19,002	3,010
	V	W	85	198,854	102,928	129,758	26,830
			86	180,528	108,108	124,166	16,058
MEXICO	O	W	86	7,590	1,518	1,518	
N ZEAL	A	W	83	997	1,336	2,079	743
SWITZLD	V	E	81	1,188	1,547	1,620	73
			83	3,380	2,962	3,078	116
			84	1,588	1,902	1,956	54

1469600 CHERRIES,IN BRINE, NO PITS (LB)

Country	Mode	Reg	Yr	Quantity	F.A.S.	C.I.F.	Charges
TOTAL			81	621,959	398,912	477,449	78,537
			82	988,530	675,309	782,543	107,234
			83	1,313,724	825,443	961,025	135,582
			84	2,157,993	1,387,981	1,603,246	215,265
			85	3,389,371	2,105,437	2,446,644	341,207
			86	6,862,671	4,674,809	5,375,597	700,788
CANADA	O	E	86	19,404	23,056	23,056	
FR GERM	O	E	85	3,537	1,427	1,835	408
	V	E	84	3,450	1,505	1,668	163

Crop / Product / TSUSA commodity number, description, and unit of quantity Country	Mode	Reg	Yr	Quantity	F.A.S.	C.I.F.	Charges
	V	W	84	247	307	340	33
			86	87,744	107,985	119,738	11,753
FRANCE	O	E	86	1,584	5,257	5,553	296
	V	E	85	27,500	12,650	15,400	2,750
			86	1,358	2,601	2,756	155
	V	W	86	2,571	6,591	6,956	365
HUNGARY	V	E	82	4,500	1,814	2,325	511
			84	10,930	4,051	5,647	1,596
			85	22,180	3,998	7,191	3,193
			86	30,904	10,113	13,087	2,974
ITALY	N	E	85	2,463,084	1,585,694	1,827,682	241,988
	V	E	81	618,174	395,269	473,526	78,257
			82	810,149	575,314	664,223	88,909
			83	1,133,601	725,482	845,473	119,991
			84	2,091,282	1,352,841	1,562,605	209,764
			85	490,343	274,331	327,417	53,086
			86	4,160,238	2,932,097	3,364,355	432,258
	V	W	85	142,864	97,358	113,039	15,681
			86	1,656,325	1,119,643	1,296,369	176,726
SPAIN	N	E	86	49,384	26,880	32,453	5,573
	V	E	82	173,018	96,195	113,924	17,729
			83	170,738	91,575	106,765	15,190
			84	47,620	24,366	27,916	3,550
			85	223,103	121,731	145,271	23,540
			86	819,699	415,701	483,115	67,414
	V	W	86	23,810	13,130	15,714	2,584
SWITZLD	V	E	81	3,785	3,643	3,923	280
			82	863	1,986	2,071	85
			83	9,385	8,386	8,787	401
			84	4,464	4,911	5,070	159
			86	3,418	4,335	4,652	317
	V	W	86	6,232	7,420	7,793	373
THAILND	V	W	85	12,600	7,000	7,561	561
YUGOSLV	O	E	85	4,160	1,248		

Cherry, prepared or preserved
1469900 CHERRIES PREP OR PRES, NSPF (LB)

Country	Mode	Reg	Yr	Quantity	F.A.S.	C.I.F.	Charges
TOTAL			**81**	**348,963**	**292,536**	**331,610**	**39,073**
			82	**427,060**	**416,246**	**464,053**	**47,807**
			83	**521,631**	**513,026**	**566,270**	**53,244**
			84	**777,349**	**741,300**	**817,401**	**76,101**
			85	**1,531,779**	**941,877**	**1,076,697**	**134,820**
			86	**2,411,884**	**1,868,452**	**2,122,671**	**254,219**
AUSTRIA	V	E	82	1,894	3,023	3,242	219
			84	1,890	2,316	2,615	299
BELGIUM	V	E	82	10,449	7,204	8,166	962
			83	19,032	22,751	25,567	2,816
			84	25,948	16,436	18,919	2,483
			85	16,923	11,123	12,635	1,512
			86	3,281	1,736	1,920	184
	V	W	83	3,989	2,827	3,177	350
			84	3,677	2,587	3,038	451
BULGAR	V	E	81	48,055	16,269	20,100	3,831
			82	11,508	4,608	5,755	1,147
CANADA	O	E	82	700	980	980	
			83	2,566	3,592	3,592	
			84	212	572	572	
			85	23,117	21,999	21,999	
			86	6,328	5,712	5,712	
	O	W	81	23,110	14,463	14,463	
			82	34,500	23,370	23,885	515
			83	10,800	7,169	7,169	
			84	3,663	4,789	4,789	
			85	104,960	53,154	53,154	
			86	500	1,436	1,436	
	V	E	85	1,943	1,565	1,777	212
			86	3,012	1,917	2,152	235
CHINA T	V	H	84	2,249	1,786	1,800	14
			86	2,406	4,994	5,498	504
	V	W	83	1,778	1,956	2,195	239
COLOMB	A	E	84	2,718	5,771	6,251	480
CYPRUS	V	E	84	360	900	941	41
DENMARK	V	E	81	1,442	705	927	222
			86	32,400	18,131	21,107	2,976
DOM REP	V	E	83	1,500	400	498	98
FR GERM	V	E	81	2,520	2,478	2,641	163
			82	20,699	16,605	18,443	1,838
			83	28,746	25,502	27,783	2,281
			84	54,111	26,469	31,135	4,666
			85	119,053	76,114	88,657	12,543
			86	27,697	28,579	31,132	2,553
FRANCE	V	W	86	19,840	27,371	31,471	4,100
	A	E	84	890	469	477	8
	A	W	86	608	1,023	1,706	683
	N	E	82	46,476	49,836	55,112	5,276
			84	111,000	86,184	96,202	10,018
			85	3,141	3,710	4,500	790
			86	316,928	563,619	578,188	14,569
	O	E	81	7,112	10,397	11,246	849
			84	11,972	8,696	10,080	1,384
			85	43,200	26,294	26,294	
			86	7,750	10,981	11,570	589
	O	W	86	782	1,152	1,217	65
	V	E	81	29,723	39,530	43,639	4,109
			82	7,772	8,395	9,253	858
			83	77,909	93,473	101,874	8,401
			84	19,815	18,594	21,124	2,530
			85	242,211	181,854	200,831	18,977
			86	303,722	275,177	308,966	33,789
	V	W	81	368	1,802	1,903	101
			82	1,891	6,520	6,932	412
			83	978	1,324	1,403	79
			84	37,730	34,280	38,462	4,182
			85	2,666	9,844	10,531	687
			86	15,998	19,132	20,893	1,761
GREECE	V	E	81	46,644	57,316	64,757	7,441
			82	44,265	47,380	55,037	7,657
			83	2o,127	29,940	34,883	4,943
			84	27,054	26,001	30,116	4,115
			85	38,182	40,640	47,674	7,034
			86	40,647	39,266	43,220	3,954
	V	W	81	8,400	11,850	13,525	1,675
			82	34,033	45,550	51,607	6,057
			83	21,337	27,000	30,278	3,278
			84	30,154	35,325	40,202	4,877
			85	26,198	29,700	33,173	3,473
			86	38,393	40,250	45,684	5,434
HG KONG	V	H	81	500	703	748	45
HUNGARY	V	E	81	19,840	5,511	6,972	1,461
			82	39,600	17,317	22,260	4,943
			83	25,206	9,279	11,520	2,241
			84	107,620	45,431	52,081	6,650
			85	230,348	83,834	105,542	21,708
			86	404,731	121,327	187,040	65,713
	V	W	83	2,778	984	1,580	596
			84	10,567	3,142	4,633	1,491
			85	75,032	31,591	40,495	8,904
			86	111,528	33,835	44,087	10,252
ITALY	A	E	81	188	895	1,164	269
	O	E	85	633	1,686	2,081	395
	V	E	81	5,539	9,767	10,665	898
			82	25,888	51,314	54,486	3,172
			83	40,702	78,969	84,557	5,588
			84	63,120	153,854	165,725	11,871
			85	39,122	103,477	112,998	9,521
			86	348,721	223,573	263,332	39,759
	V	W	81	1,349	1,431	1,619	188
			82	4,863	9,116	10,307	1,191
			83	20,177	34,546	37,692	3,146
			84	20,164	33,287	35,704	2,417
			86	5,800	9,938	10,434	496
JAPAN	V	E	86	1,419	1,191	1,355	164
NETHLDS	O	E	85	21,600	6,597	6,597	
	V	E	83	8,255	7,634	8,215	581
			86	10,039	5,526	7,423	1,897
POLAND	N	E	81	11,500	3,965	5,250	1,285
			82	33,275	14,621	18,811	4,190
	O	E	82	9,905	3,640	4,623	983
	V	E	81	58,954	19,991	26,099	6,108
			83	41,775	15,430	18,714	3,284
			84	14,051	4,550	5,418	868
			85	56,862	20,985	26,155	5,170
			86	27,427	9,605	12,012	2,407
PORTUGL	V	E	81	496	718	829	111
			86	65,008	40,269	45,976	5,707
ROMANIA	V	E	83	14,856	6,127	6,982	855
			84	74,991	105,270	109,713	4,443
			85	45,572	16,858	19,604	2,746
			86	52,910	16,006	18,941	2,935
SPAIN	V	E	83	1,235	681	741	60
			84	1,759	2,610	3,082	472
			85	209,365	102,649	121,410	18,761
			86	349,306	223,531	260,385	36,854
SWITZLD	V	E	81	55,750	54,983	61,998	7,015
			82	54,592	61,388	66,518	5,130

Crop Product TSUSA commodity number, description, and unit of quantity Country	Mode	Reg	Yr	Quantity	F.A.S.	C.I.F.	Charges
			83	59,848	65,003	69,652	4,649
			84	35,913	39,649	41,937	2,288
			85	40,015	40,146	44,016	3,870
			86	49,238	61,965	67,817	5,852
	V	W	84	952	1,107	1,186	79
TURKEY	A	E	86	1,200	1,050	1,172	122
	V	E	83	10,587	6,797	7,999	1,202
			86	3,574	2,212	2,526	314
U KING	N	E	81	8,901	15,224	16,302	1,078
	O	E	81	984	2,327	2,627	300
			82	718	1,213	1,288	75
			83	3,174	5,184	5,839	655
			84	21,798	37,430	39,146	1,716
			85	11,159	23,398	24,488	1,090
			86	17,085	38,797	40,714	1,917
	V	E	81	8,817	16,856	17,735	878
			82	26,182	33,745	35,823	2,078
			83	34,169	43,748	47,400	3,652
			84	24,404	20,602	23,017	2,415
			85	7,358	7,138	8,167	1,029
			86	5,850	5,588	6,225	637
	V	W	81	377	679	785	106
			82	711	1,857	2,008	151
			83	585	1,037	1,125	88
			84	8,371	3,631	4,242	611
			85	957	3,648	4,187	539
USSR	N	E	83	42,474	16,578	19,585	3,007
	V	E	81	5,537	2,366	3,020	654
			82	17,139	8,564	9,517	953
			84	10,125	5,625	5,951	326
			85	33,085	12,208	16,208	4,000
			86	29,762	7,425	8,875	1,450
	V	W	84	2,829	1,022	1,556	534
YUGOSLV	O	E	84	8,465	3,794	4,560	766
			85	6,300	2,300	2,300	
			86	50,560	8,846	8,846	
	V	E	81	2,857	2,310	2,596	286
			83	19,048	5,095	6,250	1,155
			84	38,777	9,121	12,727	3,606
			85	132,777	29,365	41,224	11,859
			86	57,434	17,292	23,639	6,347

Chestnut

Chestnut, nut, candied
1541000 CHESTNUTS,CANDIED, PREP, ETC (LB)

Country	Mode	Reg	Yr	Quantity	F.A.S.	C.I.F.	Charges
TOTAL			81	90,405	87,836	96,797	8,961
			82	31,181	45,953	50,861	4,908
			83	33,396	65,971	72,593	6,622
			84	86,094	86,360	98,819	12,459
			85	54,469	48,021	57,024	9,003
			86	70,511	119,427	134,316	14,889
CANADA	O	E	84	1,800	2,088	2,088	
			86	900	1,350	1,350	
CHINA M	V	W	81	64,500	27,053	31,269	4,216
CHINA T	V	W	82	9,775	4,285	4,549	264
FR GERM	V	E	84	23,850	6,270	8,224	1,954
FRANCE	A	E	81	63	612	672	60
			83	35	356	396	40
			86	291	2,926	3,291	365
	A	W	84	15	350	461	111
	N	E	81	18,769	48,691	52,347	3,656
			82	16,470	30,144	33,460	3,316
			83	24,422	44,658	47,934	3,276
			84	34,141	45,800	51,694	5,894
			86	27,432	33,534	37,086	3,552
	V	E	81	3,578	3,074	3,477	403
			82	954	2,821	2,966	145
			83	551	1,756	1,979	223
			84	16,087	7,032	7,527	495
			85	25,454	26,059	31,597	5,538
			86	2,904	6,205	6,789	584
	V	W	81	501	4,565	4,791	226
			82	297	282	329	47
			83	311	278	322	44
			84	371	2,648	2,853	205
HG KONG	A	E	81	2,500	3,118	3,451	333
ITALY	A	E	86	780	3,348	3,894	546
	N	E	82	2,314	5,425	6,046	621

Crop Product TSUSA commodity number, description, and unit of quantity Country	Mode	Reg	Yr	Quantity	F.A.S.	C.I.F.	Charges
			83	3,747	11,612	13,141	1,529
			84	5,320	14,409	16,207	1,798
	O	E	84	1,200	1,368	1,368	
	V	E	85	601	2,268	2,789	521
			86	22,567	48,590	50,950	2,360
	V	W	82	661	1,836	2,068	232
JAPAN	A	H	84	158	2,000	3,037	1,037
			85	197	2,960	3,895	935
			86	451	3,216	4,986	1,770
	N	H	83	314	1,765	2,645	880
	V	E	83	106	254	283	29
			84	106	274	312	38
			86	396	1,986	2,204	218
	V	W	82	110	348	522	174
			83	195	478	507	29
			84	390	980	1,053	73
KOR REP	V	E	85	4,207	6,960	7,438	478
			86	1,376	2,300	2,483	183
	V	W	84	392	646	686	40
			85	22,046	8,748	10,000	1,252
PORTUGL	A	E	86	9,367	5,464	5,792	328
SPAIN	A	E	86	608	3,954	5,448	1,494
SWITZLD	V	E	81	494	723	790	67
			82	600	812	921	109
			83	1,894	2,209	2,586	377
			84	2,277	2,732	3,511	779
			86	1,455	2,378	2,526	148
	V	W	83	1,429	1,959	2,114	155
			84	379	409	484	75
TURKEY	A	W	86	1,984	4,176	7,517	3,341
U KING	V	E	85	1,964	1,026	1,305	279

Chestnut, nut, dried
1450100 CHESTNUTS, CRUDE, DRIED, BKD (LB)

Country	Mode	Reg	Yr	Quantity	F.A.S.	C.I.F.	Charges
TOTAL			81	10,824,854	6,134,004	8,337,408	2,203,404
			82	9,661,759	6,408,644	8,202,802	1,794,158
			83	9,478,030	5,888,179	7,514,120	1,625,941
			84	8,361,025	6,337,506	8,280,127	1,942,621
			85	11,662,508	8,464,595	10,416,479	1,951,884
			86	9,976,764	7,111,319	8,689,927	1,578,608
BELGIUM	V	E	83	428	452	571	119
BOLIVIA	A	E	84	1,653	815	1,483	668
CANADA	A	E	82	3,025	3,530	3,774	244
	A	W	81	3,190	4,785	5,132	347
	O	E	83	500	400	400	
			86	41,950	53,731	53,731	
	O	W	81	45,000	40,530	40,530	
			86	5,500	3,575	3,575	
CHILE	A	E	83	2,253	716	1,559	843
	A	W	84	2,211	900	2,194	1,294
	V	E	86	195,768	88,800	107,715	18,915
CHINA M	O	W	81	64,000	94,545	94,545	
			82	35,000	32,000	32,000	
	V	E	81	23,400	26,509	28,912	2,403
			82	10,324	13,236	14,216	980
			83	70,595	65,014	69,936	4,922
			84	14,780	15,031	16,464	1,433
			85	67,264	60,419	66,056	5,637
			86	58,029	39,687	44,381	4,694
	V	H	81	29,955	44,708	51,535	6,827
			82	34,413	40,161	48,197	8,036
			83	21,858	32,372	36,577	4,205
			84	59,365	88,623	101,544	12,921
	V	W	81	45,450	28,780	32,832	4,052
			82	61,264	62,162	69,110	6,948
			83	49,858	50,053	55,283	5,230
			84	66,880	61,843	65,768	3,925
			85	58,554	46,515	50,716	4,201
			86	57,023	49,235	53,006	3,771
CHINA T	V	H	81	4,927	7,306	8,493	1,187
	V	W	84	500	542	585	43
DOM REP	N	E	84	128,500	42,800	55,725	12,925
	V	E	81	69,491	47,313	50,456	3,143
			82	229,000	43,600	55,700	12,100
			83	276,800	52,800	67,878	15,078
			84	3,300	300	440	140
			86	22,000	3,300	4,502	1,202
FR GERM	V	E	85	41,887	42,800	50,200	7,400
FRANCE	A	E	82	2,926	1,949	3,268	1,319
			85	21,384	22,244	33,464	11,220
	A	W	83	2,646	1,354	2,670	1,316

Crop
Product
TSUSA commodity number, description, and unit of quantity

Country	Mode	Reg	Yr	Quantity	F.A.S.	C.I.F.	Charges
	N W		82	2,987	3,369	4,284	915
	O E		81	794	630	700	70
			83	1,058	673	713	40
	V E		82	1,798	2,182	2,293	111
			83	4,206	7,833	8,334	501
			84	5,500	7,967	8,707	740
			85	5,954	5,763	6,106	343
			86	24,626	30,686	32,686	2,000
	V W		83	1,750	1,977	2,100	123
			84	3,873	3,762	4,385	623
			86	2,116	1,131	1,227	96
GREECE	O E		83	50	750	750	
HG KONG	O E		83	750	884	979	95
	V E		82	3,100	2,210	2,441	231
			83	12,857	16,699	18,277	1,578
			84	14,367	21,579	22,966	1,387
			85	42,271	25,351	28,713	3,362
			86	14,154	21,484	22,949	1,465
	V H		82	368	468	511	43
			84	650	689	780	91
	V W		81	1,250	2,121	2,318	197
			82	11,300	17,135	18,287	1,152
			83	7,020	6,754	7,267	513
			84	11,250	15,913	17,036	1,123
			85	16,564	18,115	20,135	2,020
			86	199,785	91,636	99,017	7,381
INDIA	V W		86	10,500	5,040	5,358	318
ITALY	A E		81	102,444	71,805	116,958	45,153
			82	2,205	254	2,096	1,842
			84	331	390	735	345
	A W		84	19,842	17,075	27,854	10,779
	N E		81	7,167,822	4,312,078	6,129,122	1,817,044
			82	8,752,765	5,832,066	7,524,380	1,692,314
			83	5,252,227	3,799,851	4,913,465	1,113,614
			84	5,544,226	4,325,437	5,983,744	1,658,307
			85	4,286,447	3,337,492	4,485,606	1,148,114
			86	2,950,219	2,304,769	3,249,379	944,610
	N W		84	27,721	26,777	32,542	5,765
	O E		81	147,550	124,570	124,570	
			82	48,250	51,516	51,516	
			83	48,098	49,710	49,710	
			84	533,720	555,030	555,030	
			85	1,250	1,400	1,400	
			86	200,696	247,037	247,037	
	O W		85	6,325	7,274	7,274	
	V E		81	2,989,428	1,201,800	1,504,329	302,529
			82	196,059	89,040	115,139	26,099
			83	3,668,492	1,762,456	2,230,130	467,674
			84	1,705,689	992,415	1,195,769	203,354
			85	6,565,276	4,498,189	5,190,420	692,231
			86	5,693,787	3,889,612	4,424,572	534,960
	V W		81	17,056	20,004	21,440	1,436
			82	17,502	19,251	20,944	1,693
			83	2,242	2,360	2,787	427
			85	13,480	14,121	14,958	837
			86	31,453	33,912	35,682	1,770
JAPAN	V E		84	825	1,394	1,433	39
			86	660	3,178	3,247	69
	V H		81	39,846	29,569	38,999	9,430
			83	98	271	327	56
			85	26,455	40,422	45,827	5,405
	V W		81	27,009	28,995	34,560	5,565
			82	34,444	30,988	36,734	5,746
			83	141	332	344	12
			84	629	1,256	1,323	67
			86	49,353	30,079	37,712	7,633
KENYA	A W		86	3,000	2,040	5,329	3,289
KOR REP	N W		85	196,054	120,430	139,654	19,224
	V E		83	900	1,716	1,873	157
			84	134,684	100,778	112,912	12,134
			85	92,100	56,714	66,941	10,227
			86	21,000	12,870	16,612	3,742
	V H		83	249	318	372	54
			84	220	408	472	64
			85	14,267	9,250	11,300	2,050
	V W		82	209,517	159,887	191,113	31,226
			83	21,444	8,053	12,219	4,166
			84	44,962	21,898	29,999	8,101
			86	151,138	88,985	96,952	7,967
NETHLDS	V E		85	117,346	88,171	99,097	10,926
			86	4,423	1,440	1,475	35
PHIL R	V E		84	5,400	7,560	8,370	810
PORTUGL	A E		82	5,512	3,640	6,799	3,159
			83	5,511	1,811	3,065	1,254
			85	41,046	22,081	44,031	21,950
			86	45,470	25,639	35,134	9,495
SPAIN	A E		86	5,500	3,750	9,914	6,164
	N E		85	46,484	44,884	51,420	6,536
	V E		81	44,092	46,429	50,250	3,821
			83	25,999	22,570	26,534	3,964
			84	28,660	24,827	30,099	5,272
			86	182,320	74,540	93,552	19,012
SWITZLD	O W		86	5,500	4,125	4,125	
	V E		84	952	1,083	1,219	136
			85	2,100	2,960	3,161	201
			86	794	1,038	1,058	20
THAILND	V E		81	2,150	1,527	1,727	200
U KING	V E		84	335	414	549	135

Chestnut, nut, prepared or preserved
1450200 CHESTNUTS, PREP, PRES, NSPF (LB)

Country	Mode	Reg	Yr	Quantity	F.A.S.	C.I.F.	Charges
TOTAL			81	377,222	384,973	419,408	34,435
			82	422,065	428,054	474,562	46,508
			83	491,844	486,740	544,279	57,539
			84	484,670	499,906	561,848	61,942
			85	420,196	454,061	512,045	57,984
			86	393,717	479,160	520,493	41,333
CANADA	V E		85	2,525	1,616	1,835	219
CHILE	V W		86	18,500	17,925	20,835	2,910
CHINA M	V E		82	441	630	717	87
			86	52,966	33,919	37,589	3,670
	V W		81	8,134	2,340	2,516	176
			82	33,150	9,350	10,760	1,410
			83	30,730	13,913	15,970	2,057
			84	48,297	61,313	69,241	7,928
			85	4,640	7,044	7,330	286
			86	900	1,528	1,612	84
CHINA T	V E		82	4,350	3,615	4,185	570
			83	1,744	2,950	3,206	256
			84	16,126	10,699	12,389	1,690
	V W		82	55,683	27,036	29,833	2,797
			83	52,800	26,400	28,600	2,200
			84	36,743	18,401	20,511	2,110
			85	28,034	13,530	14,604	1,074
FR GERM	O E		83	2,287	1,491	1,622	131
	V E		83	229	603	641	38
FRANCE	A E		84	502	836	1,037	201
	N E		81	158,443	165,401	176,895	11,494
			82	137,154	138,898	151,382	12,484
			83	206,987	217,957	238,613	20,656
			84	178,159	161,125	184,193	23,068
			85	152,626	162,328	178,874	16,546
	N W		84	29,034	25,311	29,690	4,379
			85	39,700	46,523	53,131	6,608
	O E		81	1,484	850	945	95
			82	2,162	1,273	1,383	110
			83	3,621	2,217	2,574	357
			84	488	279	308	29
	V E		81	22,687	20,293	22,690	2,397
			82	31,935	27,532	29,244	1,712
			83	28,898	26,567	29,274	2,707
			84	32,003	44,355	48,734	4,379
			85	37,864	46,291	52,088	5,797
			86	139,144	214,392	228,770	14,378
	V W		81	35,829	47,199	51,324	4,125
			82	47,548	59,202	64,185	4,983
			83	30,105	36,581	40,586	4,005
			86	32,705	42,264	45,474	3,210
HG KONG	V E		82	1,200	1,590	1,713	123
			83	1,200	1,172	1,279	107
			84	41,000	24,491	26,924	2,433
			85	47,069	28,031	32,179	4,148
			86	31,109	17,683	19,746	2,063
	V W		82	585	2,069	2,179	110
			83	317	485	524	39
			84	22,500	40,309	43,469	3,160
			85	15,000	18,810	21,299	2,489
			86	36,630	31,213	34,635	3,422
INDIA	V W		82	55	490	556	66
ITALY	A E		83	25,500	15,000	24,681	9,681
			85	9,900	24,000	33,932	9,932
	A W		84	1,100	1,300	2,145	845
	N E		83	3,598	6,837	7,518	681
	O E		81	9,100	10,436	10,436	
			82	2,250	359	359	

Crop Product TSUSA commodity number, description, and unit of quantity Country	Mode	Reg	Yr	Quantity	F.A.S.	C.I.F.	Charges
			83	9,625	12,000	12,000	
	V	E	81	2,577	7,649	8,700	1,051
			82	9,847	26,029	27,392	1,363
			84	2,215	1,839	1,981	142
			85	2,590	3,678	4,945	1,267
			86	575	4,960	5,473	513
	V	W	82	2,281	4,076	4,804	728
			83	1,829	6,786	7,444	658
			84	359	1,397	1,514	117
JAPAN	V	E	81	1,939	6,256	6,973	717
			82	3,606	9,379	10,254	875
			83	1,397	3,603	3,758	155
			84	5,884	18,293	20,267	1,974
			85	1,688	5,631	6,155	524
			86	1,010	4,250	4,365	115
	V	H	81	1,961	5,371	6,235	864
			82	2,254	6,005	6,915	910
			83	915	2,602	3,019	417
			84	2,293	6,179	6,906	727
			85	390	1,106	1,157	51
			86	580	2,645	2,896	251
	V	W	81	3,352	8,659	9,102	443
			82	4,027	10,632	11,384	752
			83	5,522	16,573	18,565	1,992
			84	7,026	13,503	14,349	846
			85	5,799	12,393	14,180	1,787
			86	14,330	24,737	28,096	3,359
KOR REP	N	W	82	30,608	47,378	56,205	8,827
	V	E	82	979	1,791	1,930	139
			83	10,562	13,741	14,626	885
			84	4,894	6,525	7,205	680
			85	11,382	12,415	14,068	1,653
			86	8,850	10,431	11,577	1,146
	V	H	85	5,505	4,143	5,081	938
			86	10,655	9,325	10,157	832
	V	W	81	11,825	18,510	19,439	929
			82	7,831	14,429	15,325	896
			83	25,302	35,436	37,940	2,504
			84	28,531	39,952	42,284	2,332
			85	33,910	45,729	48,216	2,487
			86	22,769	28,741	30,858	2,117
NETHLDS	V	E	85	5,952	6,630	7,386	756
			86	5,952	8,590	9,129	539
PHIL R	V	E	85	900	1,205	1,500	295
	V	W	81	50,000	29,475	32,141	2,666
PORTUGL	A	E	82	10,616	1,876	4,905	3,029
SPAIN	A	E	86	897	3,187	4,185	998
	V	E	81	39,683	29,417	36,054	6,637
			82	13,228	9,453	11,809	2,356
			83	31,993	20,642	26,847	6,205
			84	16,007	10,604	14,227	3,623
			86	2,100	2,000	2,319	319
SWITZLD	O	E	84	952	1,230	1,310	80
	V	E	81	27,562	32,002	34,720	2,718
			82	19,323	23,691	25,782	2,091
			83	14,779	20,572	22,225	1,653
			84	10,557	11,965	13,164	1,199
			85	9,762	11,083	12,055	972
			86	14,045	21,370	22,777	1,407
	V	W	82	952	1,271	1,361	90
			83	1,904	2,612	2,767	155
THAILND	V	E	81	882	350	399	49
	V	W	81	1,764	765	839	74
			85	4,960	1,875	2,030	155

Chestnut, nut, tannin**
4702300 CHESTNUT NOT CRUDE OR PROC (LB)

Country	Mode	Reg	Yr	Quantity	F.A.S.	C.I.F.	Charges
TOTAL			81	2,548,518	863,198	1,004,441	141,243
			82	2,693,986	941,167	1,091,502	150,335
			83	1,863,053	691,214	790,756	99,542
			84	2,326,559	872,121	998,494	126,373
			85	1,903,036	710,901	799,582	88,681
			86	3,242,783	1,126,171	1,299,956	173,785
CANADA	O	E	82	41,800	13,324	13,324	
			83	34,480	10,560	10,560	
			86	43,541	16,545	16,545	
FRANCE	O	E	81	44,092	15,436	18,136	2,700
			82	32,544	11,387	13,007	1,620
	V	E	81	881,840	315,784	350,903	35,119
			82	1,928,500	682,124	789,932	107,808
			83	997,108	367,671	422,902	55,231

Crop Product TSUSA commodity number, description, and unit of quantity Country	Mode	Reg	Yr	Quantity	F.A.S.	C.I.F.	Charges
			84	1,742,432	649,790	741,687	91,897
			85	1,515,026	556,026	621,378	65,352
			86	1,943,058	689,199	782,818	93,619
ITALY	V	E	81	1,622,586	531,978	635,402	103,424
			82	691,142	234,332	275,239	40,907
			83	787,373	295,161	337,115	41,954
			84	584,127	222,331	256,807	34,476
			85	388,010	154,875	178,204	23,329
			86	1,256,184	420,427	500,593	80,166
SPAIN	V	E	83	44,092	17,822	20,179	2,357

Chickpea

Chickpea, dried
1402000 CHICKPEAS OR GARBANZOS SPLIT (LB)

Country	Mode	Reg	Yr	Quantity	F.A.S.	C.I.F.	Charges
TOTAL			81	788,702	266,617	307,429	40,812
			82	1,234,125	375,561	446,640	71,079
			83	727,889	229,641	263,027	33,386
			84	1,481,098	452,274	525,579	73,305
			85	2,073,812	671,982	771,269	99,287
			86	1,803,464	510,053	606,729	96,676
AUSTRAL	O	E	83	6,174	2,698	2,947	249
			85	16,500	5,610	5,610	
	V	E	81	38,801	9,926	12,226	2,300
			82	145,382	46,011	55,823	9,812
			83	61,683	19,146	22,710	3,564
			84	352,838	95,258	110,325	15,067
			85	343,341	88,487	100,887	12,400
			86	570,708	113,865	133,973	20,108
	V	W	82	56,183	18,860	22,682	3,822
			83	88,954	31,720	36,051	4,331
			84	14,734	4,575	5,639	1,064
			85	61,398	14,328	16,893	2,565
			86	107,893	24,899	29,833	4,934
AUSTRIA	V	E	84	43,210	13,260	15,213	1,953
BRAZIL	V	E	82	3,858	1,575	1,974	399
BURMA	V	E	81	22,000	9,460	10,762	1,302
CANADA	O	E	82	5,708	2,994	3,117	123
			83	31,957	12,516	12,516	
			84	13,778	5,396	5,396	
			85	12,671	5,681	5,681	
			86	7,159	2,865	2,865	
CHILE	V	E	82	17,637	4,665	5,845	1,180
			85	39,683	11,398	13,222	1,824
			86	19,841	4,639	5,519	880
CHINA M	V	E	81	1,320	771	807	36
			83	3,125	940	1,350	410
	V	W	84	1,250	962	1,031	69
CHINA T	V	E	83	12,500	1,482	2,250	768
			84	1,250	1,150	1,287	137
CYPRUS	V	E	82	1,000	425	455	30
HG KONG	V	E	83	1,500	573	722	149
			85	2,500	1,050	1,379	329
	V	W	81	1,200	587	639	52
			84	2,500	1,764	1,863	99
INDIA	N	E	85	37,518	14,105	16,261	2,156
	O	E	83	20,675	5,726	6,322	596
			84	114,578	40,136	47,271	7,135
			85	44,677	15,077	17,908	2,831
			86	53,045	16,460	19,524	3,064
	O	W	86	11,990	5,006	5,006	
	V	E	81	4,017	2,888	3,518	630
			82	1,968	1,519	1,807	288
			83	21,000	6,494	7,714	1,220
			84	260,174	82,007	96,937	14,930
			85	477,949	157,633	184,569	26,936
			86	532,650	177,703	206,597	28,894
	V	W	81	4,214	2,768	3,280	512
			82	5,621	3,155	3,704	549
			84	24,735	10,621	12,199	1,578
			85	166,919	71,310	82,370	11,060
			86	130,068	48,691	55,889	7,198
IRAN	V	W	85	13,228	2,859	3,664	805
ISRAEL	V	W	85	13,294	4,221	5,267	1,046
JAPAN	V	W	82	74	290	303	13
			83	110	426	547	121
KENYA	N	E	81	39,600	19,800	22,540	2,740
			82	38,876	15,525	16,978	1,453
	O	E	81	127,412	63,717	70,230	6,513

Crop / Product / TSUSA commodity number, description, and unit of quantity Country	Mode	Reg	Yr	Quantity	F.A.S.	C.I.F.	Charges
			83	15,350	4,585	4,940	355
			84	42,077	17,709	20,854	3,145
	V	E	81	72,751	30,847	37,262	6,415
			82	195,106	68,390	83,337	14,947
			83	206,354	65,211	78,547	13,336
			84	131,158	42,517	50,398	7,881
			86	33,069	9,425	11,161	1,736
	V	W	83	79,366	29,760	35,760	6,000
			84	5,229	3,692	4,449	757
LEBANON	O	E	81	5,291	1,978	2,119	141
MALAWI	O	E	81	25,855	19,394	20,333	939
			82	34,865	15,107	15,360	253
			83	44,093	18,222	18,222	
			84	24,778	10,268	10,726	458
			85	27,480	11,626	12,041	415
			86	60,579	22,659	22,659	
	V	E	82	19,841	7,158	9,453	2,295
			83	13,228	4,438	5,100	662
			86	3,968	1,690	2,073	383
	V	W	83	4,762	2,211	2,705	494
MEXICO	O	E	84	99,207	12,600	14,950	2,350
	O	W	81	198,414	34,002	34,002	
			82	44,092	9,400	9,400	
			83	88,184	13,800	13,800	
			85	69,445	10,890	10,890	
MOROC	O	E	81	4,180	1,963	2,253	290
			82	3,307	911	1,043	132
N ZEAL	V	W	85	6,614	1,540	1,860	320
NEPAL	O	E	82	3,300	1,836	1,836	
			83	4,730	2,244	2,244	
	V	E	81	179,234	39,431	54,997	15,566
			82	189,376	62,291	73,210	10,919
			84	4,409	1,000	1,313	313
SINGAPR	V	E	81	2,205	894	1,031	137
			82	39,683	13,050	15,322	2,272
	V	W	81	2,755	1,099	1,330	231
SRI LKA	V	E	81	11,023	2,818	3,764	946
			82	39,683	13,966	17,248	3,282
	V	W	82	11,023	4,193	5,146	953
THAILND	V	E	82	3,520	1,297	1,407	110
			84	11,023	1,555	2,214	659
TNZANIA	O	E	81	3,240	1,261	1,346	85
	V	E	86	38,968	8,100	10,487	2,387
TURKEY	O	E	82	1,125	560	560	
	V	E	82	362,425	78,053	95,460	17,407
			83	19,823	5,461	6,344	883
			84	316,625	100,470	114,854	14,384
			85	735,645	254,683	291,007	36,324
			86	227,062	70,125	97,013	26,888
	V	W	84	7,074	3,080	3,845	765
			85	4,950	1,484	1,760	276
U KING	A	E	86	4,400	1,805	2,009	204
	O	E	81	36,951	19,381	21,049	1,668
			82	7,716	3,589	4,065	476
			83	2,205	850	942	92
			84	10,471	4,254	4,815	561
			86	2,064	2,121	2,121	
	V	E	81	8,239	3,632	3,941	309
			83	2,116	1,138	1,294	156
	V	W	82	2,756	741	1,105	364

1402100 CHICKPEAS OR GARBANZOS, NSPF (LB)

Country	Mode	Reg	Yr	Quantity	F.A.S.	C.I.F.	Charges
TOTAL			81	27,820,685	8,825,956	9,273,123	447,167
			82	19,136,060	6,754,328	6,963,158	208,830
			83	29,799,941	6,585,434	6,673,833	88,399
			84	25,139,788	6,156,724	6,304,467	147,743
			85	19,010,097	5,547,068	5,675,758	128,690
			86	23,688,981	6,788,609	6,932,040	143,431
AUSTRAL	N	E	81	33,012	13,646	14,358	712
	O	E	81	7,714	3,142	3,486	344
			82	2,750	1,100	1,155	55
			83	23,050	7,969	8,096	127
			85	3,190	1,120	1,120	
	O	W	86	4,730	1,371	1,371	
	V	E	81	26,400	13,200	13,656	456
			83	57,371	12,772	16,024	3,252
	.		84	2,205	515	620	105
			85	211,013	46,185	54,142	7,957
			86	44,093	8,393	9,888	1,495
	V	W	81	17,636	6,809	7,467	658
			83	5,500	1,870	2,228	358
			84	22,042	6,132	7,514	1,382
			85	8,818	1,546	1,901	355

Country	Mode	Reg	Yr	Quantity	F.A.S.	C.I.F.	Charges
BELGIUM	O	E	83	14,300	4,808	4,808	
			84	2,200	492	492	
			85	5,500	1,401	1,401	
	V	E	81	43,692	17,130	19,291	2,161
			82	118,689	44,312	50,036	5,724
			83	62,000	17,630	19,506	1,876
	V	W	85	2,094	1,226	1,386	160
BRAZIL	V	E	82	1,654	480	602	122
BURMA	V	E	81	11,000	4,147	4,730	583
CANADA	O	E	81	605	1,295	1,295	
			82	22,406	7,258	7,258	
			83	105,820	45,072	50,712	5,640
			84	35,358	11,131	11,131	
			85	53,082	27,068	27,068	
			86	49,592	18,082	18,082	
	O	W	82	44,092	15,600	15,600	
			83	132,276	26,700	26,700	
CHILE	V	E	81	218,230	69,525	82,358	12,833
			82	434,558	120,183	144,707	24,524
			85	309,525	88,074	102,050	13,976
			86	498,240	157,436	175,452	18,016
	V	W	85	39,683	12,230	15,015	2,785
DJIBUTI	O	E	84	4,365	1,634	1,804	170
DOM REP	V	E	82	36,000	18,750	20,781	2,031
GREECE	O	E	81	1,188	574	574	
	V	E	84	2,194	1,244	1,336	92
GUATMAL	V	E	81	551,150	167,475	199,562	32,087
INDIA	O	E	83	2,149	919	1,000	81
			84	12,391	4,168	4,759	591
			85	8,360	3,800	3,800	
			86	5,000	1,204	1,204	
	O	W	81	13,250	6,625	7,101	476
			84	3,850	1,267	1,346	79
	V	E	81	1,726	1,582	1,895	313
			82	882	1,049	1,272	223
			83	1,000	420	455	35
			84	59,231	20,194	23,395	3,201
			85	51,798	14,131	17,280	3,149
			86	49,643	17,738	20,309	2,571
	V	W	81	1,939	1,476	1,712	236
			82	4,357	2,143	2,592	449
			83	1,107	957	1,153	196
			86	19,070	7,575	9,252	1,677
IRAN	V	W	85	14,330	4,860	6,228	1,368
ISRAEL	V	E	82	55,115	15,844	19,310	3,466
			85	2,850	1,250	1,373	123
			86	2,882	1,200	1,298	98
ITALY	A	E	82	225	350	474	124
	N	E	86	26,504	17,036	18,585	1,549
	O	E	86	8,818	5,284	5,844	560
	V	E	82	13,228	4,640	5,290	650
KENYA	O	E	81	53,380	16,083	18,489	2,406
			82	10,869	3,824	4,174	350
			83	4,365	1,413	1,530	117
			84	11,346	4,351	4,786	435
			85	36,400	10,374	13,670	3,296
	V	E	81	90,389	46,050	52,112	6,062
			82	30,864	7,360	9,011	1,651
			83	159,237	43,630	52,829	9,199
			84	93,649	25,075	30,263	5,188
			86	52,910	9,975	12,520	2,545
	V	W	81	15,432	7,700	9,564	1,864
			82	39,233	15,649	19,179	3,530
			83	6,409	2,370	2,881	511
			84	8,409	2,762	3,125	363
LEBANON	V	E	82	52,910	18,278	20,814	2,536
			83	13,261	2,880	4,003	1,123
			85	6,614	2,250	2,460	210
			86	1,281	1,410	1,562	152
	V	W	85	9,028	3,800	4,477	677
MALAWI	O	E	81	41,610	17,199	18,241	1,042
			82	8,818	3,100	3,364	264
			83	30,450	11,106	11,639	533
			84	37,736	11,673	13,061	1,388
			85	39,458	13,358	14,708	1,350
			86	33,048	11,473	11,886	413
	V	E	82	9,921	2,742	3,621	879
			83	2,205	944	1,085	141
MEXICO	A	W	82	44,092	17,000	18,782	1,782
			84	49,500	14,175	17,672	3,497
	N	E	83	396,831	121,050	132,757	11,707
			85	346,500	98,919	123,398	24,479
	N	W	86	20,263,741	5,790,474	5,792,034	1,560
	O	E	81	1,383,390	502,988	541,745	38,757

Crop Product TSUSA commodity number, description, and unit of quantity Country	Mode	Reg	Yr	Quantity	F.A.S.	C.I.F.	Charges
			82	1,119,506	434,602	466,800	32,198
			83	182,477	35,225	37,601	2,376
			84	51,700	11,910	15,407	3,497
			85	40,000	14,200	14,200	
	O	W	81	19,491,911	6,676,149	6,676,149	
			82	14,837,614	5,421,774	5,421,774	
			83	27,487,875	5,938,736	5,938,736	
			84	21,821,706	5,240,976	5,240,976	
			85	16,404,105	4,784,350	4,784,352	2
			86	285,927	77,972	77,972	
	V	E	84	88,000	24,000	26,466	2,466
MOROC	O	E	81	14,300	3,241	3,720	479
	V	E	81	39,683	10,396	13,115	2,719
			82	48,501	18,590	20,711	2,121
N ZEAL	V	W	85	8,818	1,788	2,160	372
NEPAL	V	E	84	79,370	18,000	21,050	3,050
NETHLDS	O	E	85	11,023	5,550	6,486	936
			86	11,023	7,000	7,700	700
	V	E	81	99,207	31,101	33,998	2,897
PAKISTN	O	E	84	4,409	1,290	1,417	127
PERU	V	E	82	22,068	6,507	7,688	1,181
			83	43,652	12,613	13,955	1,342
			85	39,683	11,500	13,520	2,020
PHIL R	V	E	84	540	585	668	83
	V	W	81	720	775	839	64
			83	1,800	2,300	2,463	163
			84	270	265	305	40
PORTUGL	O	E	81	102	333	333	
	V	E	81	3,858	2,408	2,529	121
SINGAPR	V	W	81	2,989	1,450	1,667	217
SPAIN	V	W	83	8,377	8,360	9,001	641
SYRIA	V	E	83	1,433	981	1,031	50
TNZANIA	V	E	81	15,432	4,200	5,423	1,223
			82	26,506	6,900	8,868	1,968
TURKEY	N	E	81	20,935	6,759	7,829	1,070
			82	19,800	5,704	6,579	875
			84	61,344	17,653	19,675	2,022
			85	21,487	5,275	5,797	522
	N	W	84	4,505	2,349	2,668	319
	O	E	81	43,539	8,930	10,072	1,142
			82	108,464	33,381	37,389	4,008
			83	29,950	7,514	7,933	419
			84	13,222	4,484	4,484	
			86	20,075	6,891	8,075	1,184
	O	W	82	8,267	2,243	2,467	224
	V	E	81	5,505,492	1,163,140	1,495,345	332,205
			82	2,010,262	523,694	641,442	117,748
			83	1,014,252	270,520	318,504	47,984
			84	2,606,060	706,658	823,115	116,457
			85	1,321,183	385,867	450,095	64,228
			86	2,259,534	623,283	729,441	106,158
	V	W	81	64,428	17,654	21,405	3,751
			83	5,410	1,441	1,636	195
			84	11,023	6,560	7,651	1,091
			85	6,614	3,000	3,284	284
			86	41,887	20,750	24,967	4,217
U KING	O	E	81	6,346	2,774	3,063	289
			82	4,409	1,271	1,418	147
			83	6,506	4,804	5,078	274
			84	53,163	17,181	19,281	2,100
	V	E	83	878	430	489	59
			86	10,983	4,062	4,598	536
	V	W	85	5,083	2,121	2,373	252
YUGOSLV	V	E	85	3,858	1,825	2,014	189

Chickpea, fresh or frozen
1357000 CHICKPEAS OR GARBANZOS FR FZ (LB)

Country	Mode	Reg	Yr	Quantity	F.A.S.	C.I.F.	Charges
TOTAL			81	34,073	12,482	14,620	2,138
			82	113,758	27,031	32,299	5,268
			83	360,502	136,779	143,427	6,648
			84	525,614	112,446	140,644	28,198
			85	827,563	211,341	249,279	37,938
			86	1,364,243	370,986	411,182	40,196
ARGENT	V	E	83	246,818	115,702	118,125	2,423
AUSTRAL	V	E	86	46,297	4,572	7,321	2,749
BELGIUM	O	E	85	5,500	2,143	2,143	
CANADA	O	E	82	11,000	5,009	5,009	
			84	2,210	1,228	1,228	
			85	40,300	13,600	13,600	
			86	10,500	2,407	2,407	
COMOROS	V	E	85	79,366	21,240	24,964	3,724

Crop Product TSUSA commodity number, description, and unit of quantity Country	Mode	Reg	Yr	Quantity	F.A.S.	C.I.F.	Charges
DOM REP	V	E	84	18,823	3,982	5,441	1,459
INDIA	O	E	84	110	414	414	
	V	E	84	10,719	3,456	4,369	913
	V	W	85	12,170	5,178	6,305	1,127
ITALY	V	E	82	317	1,048	1,087	39
MEXICO	O	E	81	840	316	316	
			83	32,310	2,585	2,585	
			85	44,092	16,280	19,291	3,011
	O	W	82	8,310	1,500	1,500	
			85	70,431	17,636	17,636	
			86	454,101	137,676	137,676	
NETHLDS	A	E	83	328	1,640	2,078	438
PHIL R	V	E	85	1,800	2,164	2,446	282
	V	W	81	450	541	589	48
			82	558	700	772	72
			83	1,680	1,912	2,099	187
			84	450	432	505	73
SPAIN	O	E	84	55	371	371	
SWITZLD	V	E	86	220,460	52,000	60,760	8,760
TURKEY	O	E	81	4,510	1,647	1,647	
			82	5,500	2,310	2,310	
	V	E	81	27,273	9,449	11,539	2,090
			82	88,073	16,464	21,621	5,157
			83	79,366	14,940	18,540	3,600
			84	483,531	98,944	123,510	24,566
			85	573,904	133,100	162,894	29,794
			86	632,885	174,331	203,018	28,687
	V	W	84	7,716	2,750	3,563	813
U KING	O	E	81	1,000	529	529	
	V	W	84	2,000	869	1,243	374

Chickpea, prepared or preserved
1413500 CHICKPEAS OR GARBANZOS PRES (LB)

Country	Mode	Reg	Yr	Quantity	F.A.S.	C.I.F.	Charges
TOTAL			81	849,301	362,780	427,963	65,183
			82	896,700	396,267	452,758	56,491
			83	1,373,359	489,887	567,530	77,643
			84	2,176,883	553,707	653,627	99,920
			85	1,410,193	468,957	554,804	85,847
			86	772,941	310,485	348,856	38,371
AUSTRAL	O	E	85	8,047	2,611	2,611	
			86	41,800	9,452	9,452	
AUSTRIA	V	E	84	1,125	855	968	113
BELGIUM	N	E	86	4,111	8,827	9,292	465
CANADA	O	E	81	36,141	11,081	11,081	
			82	24,051	7,746	7,746	
			83	57,255	16,731	16,731	
			84	153,716	55,097	55,981	884
			85	32,790	9,176	9,268	92
			86	72,043	27,585	29,087	1,502
CHILE	V	E	81	44,092	12,612	15,123	2,511
CHINA T	V	E	86	2,960	3,600	4,354	754
DOM REP	V	E	83	195,657	104,525	116,006	11,481
			84	23,085	6,362	8,018	1,656
			86	85,200	30,525	33,226	2,701
EGYPT	V	E	83	25,000	10,899	12,879	1,980
GREECE	O	E	82	2,905	2,165	2,239	74
			84	354	585	599	14
INDIA	N	E	84	6,609	1,969	2,558	589
	O	E	81	881	790	884	94
			82	353	359	359	
			83	11,653	4,240	4,560	320
			84	1,425	471	471	
			85	1,653	1,119	1,256	137
			86	2,500	2,298	2,298	
	V	E	81	25,983	16,915	20,920	4,005
			82	11,633	6,710	7,842	1,132
			83	17,953	8,842	10,167	1,325
			84	7,076	4,583	5,192	609
			86	23,391	12,888	14,078	1,190
	V	W	81	14,103	7,467	9,342	1,875
			82	11,702	6,053	7,101	1,048
			83	6,281	2,653	3,073	420
			84	1,653	845	1,042	197
			86	38,645	18,685	21,640	2,955
ISRAEL	V	E	82	6,563	2,835	3,141	306
			83	57	267	302	35
			86	3,060	1,210	1,393	183
	V	W	83	110	283	314	31
ITALY	V	E	81	8,457	1,505	2,559	1,054
			83	2,138	552	670	118
			85	776,200	188,435	232,789	44,354

Crop Product TSUSA commodity number, description, and unit of quantity Country	Mode	Reg	Yr	Quantity	F.A.S.	C.I.F.	Charges
			86	51,375	12,687	16,882	4,195
JAMAICA	V	E	84	875	270	297	27
JORDAN	V	E	84	1,950	973	1,007	34
KENYA	O	E	82	5,512	2,456	2,726	270
	V	E	81	6,614	2,850	3,311	461
			83	10,670	3,204	3,524	320
			85	6,614	1,570	1,832	262
KOR REP	V	E	84	600	734	800	66
LEBANON	V	E	81	56,077	39,550	43,867	4,317
			82	67,841	43,000	47,633	4,633
			83	87,259	53,507	58,506	4,999
			84	15,600	8,800	9,631	831
			85	199,082	94,284	108,027	13,743
			86	69,215	30,225	33,872	3,647
	V	W	82	10,053	6,871	7,995	1,124
			83	28,149	18,050	19,923	1,873
			85	79,407	34,113	42,078	7,965
			86	10,849	5,720	6,585	865
LESOTHO	V	E	85	7,238	6,649	6,664	15
MALAWI	V	E	86	15,410	5,671	5,769	98
MEXICO	O	W	81	19,643	2,475	2,475	
			84	756	1,880	1,982	102
MOROC	O	E	81	855	261	261	
PERU	V	E	82	22,068	4,404	5,317	913
PHIL R	V	E	81	3,420	4,213	4,606	393
			82	5,670	6,948	7,695	747
			83	3,150	3,670	4,136	466
			84	5,766	4,601	5,375	774
			85	3,330	3,632	4,243	611
			86	880	1,315	1,574	259
	V	H	81	990	1,229	1,420	191
			82	288	296	341	45
			83	180	265	309	44
	V	W	81	17,403	20,855	22,209	1,354
			82	19,243	19,458	21,404	1,946
			83	15,324	16,293	18,904	2,611
			84	17,652	14,938	16,934	1,996
			85	4,993	7,869	8,885	1,016
			86	5,598	5,775	6,290	515
PORTUGL	V	E	82	5,745	2,858	3,363	505
			86	16,650	4,698	5,840	1,142
REP SAF	O	E	82	8,000	4,160	4,160	
SPAIN	V	E	82	7,560	2,010	2,283	273
			85	36,960	8,279	11,109	2,830
			86	32,319	16,368	18,565	2,197
	V	W	84	1,575	518	611	93
SYRIA	V	E	81	4,282	2,768	3,064	296
TURKEY	N	E	82	53,267	16,264	18,311	2,047
	O	E	81	3,950	2,586	2,586	
			82	2,090	1,100	1,100	
			83	3,190	1,835	1,835	
			84	3,168	1,878	1,878	
			85	3,300	1,063	1,157	94
	V	E	81	576,736	218,073	265,995	47,922
			82	629,951	259,614	300,916	41,302
			83	909,333	244,071	295,691	51,620
			84	1,932,465	446,714	538,489	91,775
			85	217,620	91,037	102,460	11,423
			86	267,129	101,324	115,236	13,912
	V	W	81	19,974	12,050	12,463	413
			85	32,959	19,120	22,425	3,305
			86	29,806	11,632	13,423	1,791
U KING	O	E	82	2,205	960	1,086	126
			84	1,433	1,634	1,794	160
	V	W	81	9,700	5,500	5,797	297

Chicory

Chicory, root, crude
1603000 CHICORY ROOTS, CRUDE (LB)

Country	Mode	Reg	Yr	Quantity	F.A.S.	C.I.F.	Charges
TOTAL			81	5,512,609	817,675	1,146,629	328,954
			82	1,865,385	405,934	487,442	81,508
			83	2,345,405	535,347	613,268	77,921
			84	1,461,839	291,739	316,128	24,389
			85	3,314,383	675,558	776,165	100,607
			86	2,367,897	473,322	599,561	126,239
BELGIUM	A	E	83	165	360	554	194
			85	595	1,425	1,873	448
	N	E	84	44,752	10,047	12,197	2,150

Crop Product TSUSA commodity number, description, and unit of quantity Country	Mode	Reg	Yr	Quantity	F.A.S.	C.I.F.	Charges
	V	E	82	132,801	57,265	61,899	4,634
			86	13,227	5,144	6,144	1,000
BRAZIL	V	E	86	141,300	14,376	17,866	3,490
CANADA	O	E	81	38,086	7,643	7,643	
			83	4,765	2,506	2,506	
	O	W	83	45	408	408	
CHINA M	V	W	82	500	844	896	52
FINLAND	O	W	86	190	1,845	2,262	417
FR GERM	O	E	83	44,092	11,710	11,853	143
	V	E	82	590,390	120,508	157,426	36,918
			83	26,455	23,515	24,868	1,353
FRANCE	V	E	83	65,093	128,545	133,681	5,136
ITALY	A	E	83	192	304	459	155
			84	1,649	2,155	3,478	1,323
MEXICO	A	W	85	3,307	1,500	2,107	607
	O	W	86	8,800	2,000	2,000	
N ZEAL	A	H	85	1,487	1,413	1,946	533
	O	E	81	616	700	859	159
NETHLDS	A	E	84	270	475	581	106
	V	E	85	2,205	1,144	1,344	200
POLAND	V	E	81	4,329,537	694,323	930,080	235,757
			82	1,141,694	227,317	267,221	39,904
			83	2,204,598	367,999	438,939	70,940
			84	1,415,168	279,062	299,872	20,810
			85	3,306,789	670,076	768,895	98,819
			86	2,204,380	449,957	571,289	121,332
PORTUGL	V	E	81	1,144,370	115,009	208,047	93,038

Chicory, root, ground
1603500 CHICORY, GROUND OR OTWS PREP (LB)

Country	Mode	Reg	Yr	Quantity	F.A.S.	C.I.F.	Charges
TOTAL			81	4,771,307	1,840,068	2,172,053	331,985
			82	3,731,065	1,184,451	1,415,994	231,543
			83	4,562,035	1,433,614	1,667,535	233,921
			84	4,591,972	1,466,725	1,743,546	276,821
			85	3,804,433	1,311,208	1,648,808	337,600
			86	6,164,272	2,607,112	3,140,687	533,575
AUSTRAL	A	W	86	17,935	16,473	22,417	5,944
AUSTRIA	V	E	81	238,098	99,515	118,552	19,037
	V	W	81	396,829	165,155	194,732	29,577
BELGIUM	N	E	82	41,965	18,285	21,082	2,797
			83	66,781	25,674	29,563	3,889
			84	91,004	58,628	67,799	9,171
			85	99,776	45,855	55,259	9,404
	V	E	81	49,841	17,992	22,699	4,707
			82	66,525	20,674	26,605	5,931
			85	260,745	82,150	99,325	17,175
			86	606,445	227,455	298,316	70,861
	V	W	85	7,500	3,427	3,560	133
			86	7,500	3,973	5,473	1,500
BRAZIL	A	E	85	3,802	4,372	5,280	908
C RICA	V	E	83	45,000	22,500	24,000	1,500
CANADA	O	E	84	3,000	1,320	1,820	500
CYPRUS	V	W	86	38,500	16,492	19,454	2,962
CZECHO	V	E	86	38,581	15,689	16,132	443
	V	W	86	501,146	222,635	262,311	39,676
FR GERM	A	E	81	4,455	4,925	7,632	2,707
			83	551	1,417	1,615	198
			84	2,669	2,303	4,533	2,230
	V	E	81	370,373	137,242	166,256	29,014
			82	265,000	89,606	105,460	15,854
			84	8,606	22,673	23,244	571
			85	10,022	32,535	32,900	365
			86	122,000	135,386	174,581	39,195
	V	W	81	383,601	146,401	176,358	29,957
			85	38,500	15,982	19,649	3,667
			86	982,077	445,216	523,709	78,493
FRANCE	N	E	81	588,570	345,818	397,614	51,796
			83	329,147	104,904	126,484	21,580
			84	319,795	94,283	121,407	27,124
	O	E	81	792	815	815	
			83	88,050	28,294	30,974	2,680
			84	1,875	825	1,038	213
	V	E	81	2,727,498	917,686	1,081,080	163,394
			82	3,350,075	1,052,993	1,259,432	206,439
			83	3,870,687	1,159,516	1,349,680	190,164
			84	2,394,642	715,025	859,928	144,903
			85	2,303,013	697,948	889,812	191,864
			86	2,309,043	878,864	1,088,950	210,086
	V	W	81	11,250	4,519	6,315	1,796
			82	7,500	2,893	3,415	522
			83	34,388	12,382	16,041	3,659

Crop
Product
TSUSA commodity number, description, and unit of quantity

Country	Mode	Reg	Yr	Quantity	F.A.S.	C.I.F.	Charges
			84	42,331	13,816	17,372	3,556
			85	29,568	9,368	13,339	3,971
			86	16,039	9,686	11,468	1,782
NETHLDS	A	E	83	6,816	6,328	7,699	1,371
			84	3,248	2,794	3,856	1,062
	A	W	86	1,278	1,218	1,840	622
	V	E	83	41,250	10,942	13,230	2,288
			84	133,092	49,409	59,332	9,923
			85	261,875	95,034	118,580	23,546
			86	41,250	13,692	17,732	4,040
	V	W	84	1,102	1,440	1,585	145
			85	1,968	1,452	1,637	185
POLAND	O	E	86	3,031	1,274	1,274	
	V	E	84	788,120	155,508	159,058	3,550
			85	77,000	30,102	37,927	7,825
			86	590,579	122,332	131,278	8,946
	V	W	84	578,722	181,174	230,632	49,458
			85	539,889	188,740	245,915	57,175
PORTUGL	V	E	85	38,500	15,982	19,641	3,659
	V	W	86	771,134	385,963	437,133	51,170
REP SAF	V	E	86	11,914	16,157	20,030	3,873
SWITZLD	V	E	83	79,365	61,657	68,249	6,592
			84	185,185	154,229	174,186	19,957
			85	132,275	88,261	105,984	17,723
			86	105,820	94,607	108,589	13,982
	V	W	84	38,581	13,298	17,756	4,458

Chrysanthemum

Chrysanthemum, fresh
1922110 POMPOM CHRYSANTHEMUMS, FRESH (NO)

Country	Mode	Reg	Yr	Quantity	F.A.S.	C.I.F.	Charges
TOTAL			83	270,921,237	33,094,870	39,996,762	6,901,892
			84	308,798,829	39,134,280	48,247,950	9,113,670
			85	263,474,911	37,951,591	47,884,975	9,933,384
			86	288,078,310	34,407,955	46,423,927	12,015,972
AUSTRAL	A	E	84	846	427	447	20
C RICA	A	E	83	73,141	17,088	21,372	4,284
			84	1,487,361	718,510	892,165	173,655
			85	2,299,526	1,196,913	1,465,545	268,632
			86	6,005,179	1,189,018	1,470,493	281,475
	A	W	84	47,061	26,873	36,292	9,419
			85	1,224	2,040	2,297	257
			86	96,360	66,780	81,905	15,125
	N	E	83	2,278,392	455,730	596,932	141,202
			86	5,908,611	748,336	919,845	171,509
CANADA	A	E	83	45,530	38,245	44,370	6,125
			85	385,466	31,248	41,394	10,146
			86	103,160	7,588	12,519	4,931
	N	E	85	38,843	80,790	80,790	
	O	E	83	396,677	595,988	595,988	
			84	481,144	748,318	748,318	
			85	32,630	50,692	50,692	
			86	59,665	123,866	123,866	
	O	W	84	1,709	863	863	
CHILE	A	E	83	270	270	405	135
			85	30,000	4,374	8,836	4,462
			86	60,000	2,640	5,488	2,848
CHINA M	A	E	86	67,200	3,672	5,202	1,530
COCOS I	A	E	86	236,400	18,028	24,312	6,284
COLOMB	A	E	83	379,450	50,991	62,445	11,454
			84	7,490,117	1,144,282	1,502,208	357,926
			85	7,188,566	1,206,448	1,593,841	387,393
			86	5,677,947	942,160	1,278,796	336,636
	A	H	85	1,200	1,020	1,313	293
			86	51,750	3,105	4,544	1,439
	A	W	83	26,700	2,346	2,868	522
*			84	2,856	756	1,006	250
			85	7,440	6,697	7,697	1,000
	N	E	83	260,666,002	31,019,479	37,455,007	6,435,528
			84	288,789,476	35,364,841	43,594,910	8,230,069
			85	246,439,298	34,024,447	43,009,364	8,984,917
			86	263,238,686	30,536,833	41,442,255	10,905,422
	O	E	85	1,755	1,579	2,008	429
DOM REP	A	E	83	518,165	49,600	76,288	26,688
			84	111,015	38,646	51,991	13,345
			85	555,640	92,981	128,218	35,237
			86	521,371	70,974	98,453	27,479
	N	E	84	1,305,383	82,106	129,367	47,261
ECUADOR	A	E	83	244,166	92,007	127,747	35,740
			84	393,156	117,814	162,469	44,655
			85	373,640	48,222	66,651	18,429
			86	218,969	35,543	50,943	15,400
F W IND	A	E	84	777	768	844	76
FR GERM	A	E	85	13,920	2,112	2,975	863
FRANCE	A	E	84	800	720	935	215
			86	49,280	6,336	8,103	1,767
GREECE	A	E	86	16,400	1,066	1,492	426
GUATMAL	A	E	83	59,610	9,127	12,847	3,720
			84	84,860	14,696	20,541	5,845
			86	65,000	2,650	3,611	961
	N	E	83	376,731	73,597	101,462	27,865
HONDURA	A	E	84	98,800	8,645	10,670	2,025
			85	6,150	1,657	1,839	182
ISRAEL	A	E	84	12,300	2,583	13,324	10,741
ITALY	A	E	86	9,940	2,176	3,386	1,210
IVY CST	A	E	86	15,600	1,092	1,477	385
JAMAICA	A	E	83	1,903	295	370	75
			86	300	2,277	2,485	208
JAPAN	A	E	86	58,240	4,032	5,280	1,248
KIRIBAT	A	E	85	7,200	5,760	7,029	1,269
LIBERIA	A	E	83	132,480	17,664	20,963	3,299
MEXICO	A	E	83	295,266	51,160	59,000	7,840
			84	1,207,983	163,730	196,656	32,926
			85	1,274,889	426,416	483,380	56,964
			86	3,256,900	236,180	286,805	50,625
	A	W	83	37,630	1,136	1,330	194
			84	11,200	3,531	4,399	868
			85	31,900	3,816	5,360	1,544
			86	127,676	18,382	24,837	6,455
	N	E	83	9,596	1,347	1,465	118
	O	E	85	3,600	2,860	2,860	
			86	1,200	1,320	1,320	
	O	W	83	502,986	48,135	48,805	670
			84	1,948,209	203,892	204,788	896
			85	1,597,886	176,870	176,872	2
			86	854,872	93,104	93,104	
MONSRAT	A	E	85	20,210	4,991	5,783	792
N ANTIL	A	E	86	245,580	51,255	88,110	36,855
NETHLDS	A	E	83	32,451	11,190	15,363	4,173
			84	35,071	15,136	21,419	6,283
			85	22,370	5,813	7,597	1,784
			86	11,380	2,126	4,028	1,902
	A	W	83	2,256	937	1,236	299
			85	22,030	5,557	7,280	1,723
	N	E	83	64,826	28,819	32,530	3,711
			86	378,376	118,562	202,124	83,562
	O	E	83	282	475	475	
			84	240	619	619	
NORWAY	A	E	85	10,500	3,415	3,730	315
PANAMA	A	E	83	1,200	1,035	1,148	113
			84	26,720	17,953	22,311	4,358
			85	12,200	9,760	12,180	2,420
			86	93,200	8,340	10,195	1,855
PERU	A	E	83	166,560	27,019	33,887	6,868
			84	387,776	49,998	62,560	12,562
			85	3,091,828	552,169	706,350	154,181
			86	622,968	107,250	164,973	57,723
	N	E	83	4,442,772	478,060	653,014	174,954
			84	4,873,969	408,573	568,848	160,275
POLAND	A	E	83	164,280	21,904	27,625	5,721
PORTUGL	A	E	86	6,100	1,464	1,798	334
SPAIN	A	E	83	1,355	292	407	115
SUDAN	A	E	86	20,000	1,800	2,178	378
THAILND	A	E	85	5,000	2,944	3,094	150
U KING	A	E	83	50	500	864	364
VENEZ	A	E	83	510	434	549	115

1922120 CHRYSTHEMUMS, NSPF, FRESH (NO)

Country	Mode	Reg	Yr	Quantity	F.A.S.	C.I.F.	Charges
TOTAL			83	38,982,749	7,878,534	9,225,662	1,347,128
			84	38,698,750	9,342,111	11,350,999	2,008,888
			85	39,684,789	7,761,151	9,770,152	2,009,001
			86	57,293,728	8,317,349	10,687,422	2,370,073
AUSTRAL	A	E	84	1,838	294	615	321
	A	W	84	608	1,824	2,347	523
BRAZIL	A	E	84	59,200	3,583	8,633	5,050
C RICA	A	E	83	81,644	39,796	46,950	7,154
			84	596,774	436,113	520,211	84,098
			85	51,944	28,591	38,347	9,756
			86	294,642	37,262	50,049	12,787
	A	W	86	2,000	1,680	2,137	457
CANADA	A	E	84	23,500	683	801	118
			85	115,440	16,512	19,092	2,580

Crop Product TSUSA commodity number, description, and unit of quantity Country	Mode	Reg	Yr	Quantity	F.A.S.	C.I.F.	Charges
			86	62,872	4,523	7,076	2,553
	O	E	83	98,840	123,246	123,246	
			84	169,208	217,768	217,768	
			85	255,473	125,123	125,123	
			86	420,918	64,588	64,588	
	O	W	83	1,000	285	285	
			84	300	676	676	
CHILE	A	E	84	1,000	300	351	51
CHINA M	A	E	86	33,072	2,797	4,071	1,274
	V	E	85	1,375	2,820	3,315	495
COLOMB	A	E	83	5,708	2,295	2,591	296
			84	1,089,608	158,167	208,437	50,270
			85	80,118	19,148	24,180	5,032
			86	6,582,884	1,312,001	1,697,464	385,463
	A	W	85	1,200	1,140	1,300	160
	N	E	83	34,455,033	6,800,471	7,902,331	1,101,860
			84	31,732,569	7,341,322	8,851,142	1,509,820
			85	35,829,456	6,818,164	8,517,857	1,699,693
			86	47,835,461	6,348,299	8,077,519	1,729,220
DOM REP	A	E	83	239,537	16,086	23,986	7,900
			84	824,960	41,896	65,569	23,673
			85	20,720	1,184	2,429	1,245
ECUADOR	A	E	83	4,272	3,792	4,621	829
			84	264,218	32,227	42,486	10,259
			85	60,103	18,487	23,707	5,220
			86	98,366	8,991	14,497	5,506
F W IND	A	E	86	96	1,317	1,954	637
FR GERM	A	E	83	14,150	2,480	3,215	735
			84	1,000	320	379	59
FRANCE	A	E	83	3,390	3,517	4,337	820
			84	7,032	994	1,291	297
GUATMAL	A	E	83	57,170	13,701	17,677	3,976
			84	38,050	4,516	5,584	1,068
HONDURA	A	E	84	53,760	10,752	13,656	2,904
ISRAEL	A	E	83	19,320	2,555	4,316	1,761
			84	100,574	12,667	27,423	14,756
			85	484,230	18,397	38,170	19,773
ITALY	A	E	83	8,460	1,892	2,112	220
			84	40,400	6,920	8,276	1,356
KENYA	A	E	83	4,005	506	579	73
LIBERIA	A	E	83	24,840	704	1,222	518
MALTA	A	E	85	6,480	2,282	2,641	359
MEXICO	A	E	83	17,760	1,642	1,642	
			84	73,472	8,408	10,643	2,235
			85	66,210	8,240	11,782	3,542
			86	252,320	23,758	28,402	4,644
	A	W	83	4,800	890	1,066	176
	N	E	83	6,263	721	756	35
	O	E	83	2,280	383	383	
	O	W	83	109,020	1,230	1,230	
			86	18,000	1,080	1,080	
N CALDN	A	W	86	3,927	1,778	2,676	898
N ZEAL	A	W	85	4,420	1,543	2,605	1,062
NETHLDS	A	E	83	3,381,648	777,003	973,981	196,978
			84	3,274,028	955,255	1,224,598	269,343
			85	343,829	90,565	130,017	39,452
			86	395,129	126,611	194,460	67,849
	A	W	83	14,486	7,152	9,264	2,112
			84	41,699	7,847	10,091	2,244
			85	179,551	17,396	25,610	8,214
			86	4,281	2,393	3,427	1,034
	N	E	83	49,532	21,733	24,632	2,899
			84	49,400	28,136	35,311	7,175
			85	1,909,233	540,455	736,847	196,392
			86	660,201	254,228	354,149	99,921
	O	E	83	2,721	4,484	4,484	
			84	9,360	4,048	4,048	
			85	59,123	10,919	13,419	2,500
			86	8,165	7,058	8,358	1,300
	V	E	84	14,103	6,834	8,808	1,974
NORWAY	A	E	85	4,765	1,017	1,394	377
PANAMA	A	E	84	4,680	1,267	1,550	283
PERU	A	E	83	262,888	29,043	39,743	10,700
			84	22,800	4,560	5,165	605
			85	19,600	2,100	2,866	766
			86	218,730	14,688	19,730	5,042
POLAND	A	E	83	44,640	7,589	9,394	1,805
REP SAF	A	E	83	7,000	1,540	2,112	572
			84	512	1,007	1,146	139
			85	150,565	25,323	33,795	8,472
			86	122,727	33,007	44,076	11,069
SINGAPR	A	E	83	730	256	500	244
SPAIN	A	E	83	53,630	10,703	15,056	4,353
			84	170,154	30,843	46,106	15,263

Crop Product TSUSA commodity number, description, and unit of quantity Country	Mode	Reg	Yr	Quantity	F.A.S.	C.I.F.	Charges
			85	35,869	10,445	14,064	3,619
			86	186,476	39,016	62,729	23,713
	A	W	86	1,218	1,023	1,106	83
THAILND	A	E	83	2,120	569	919	350
			84	4,654	1,126	2,164	1,038
			86	84,879	28,908	44,513	15,605
	A	W	83	360	439	961	522
			84	3,400	527	1,235	708
U KING	A	E	83	5,502	1,831	2,071	240
			84	10,159	3,345	4,410	1,065
			85	5,085	1,300	1,592	292
			86	4,664	1,321	1,844	523
	A	W	86	2,700	1,022	1,517	495
	O	E	84	3,420	726	726	
VENEZ	A	E	84	12,310	17,160	19,353	2,193

Cinchona

Cinchona, alkaloid

4370860 CINCHONA BARK ALKALOID NSPF (AOZ)

Country	Mode	Reg	Yr	Quantity	F.A.S.	C.I.F.	Charges
TOTAL			81	352,836	717,750	727,882	10,132
			82	329,019	630,671	662,500	31,829
			83	537,563	465,482	489,460	23,978
			84	513,459	960,053	997,487	37,434
			85	800,237	1,387,492	1,462,231	74,739
			86	1,153,453	2,493,337	2,604,043	110,706
BAHAMAS	V	E	81	133,488	156,379	157,280	901
CANADA	A	E	81	66	995	1,030	35
FR GERM	A	E	81	55,000	94,052	95,700	1,648
			82	1,128	2,983	3,133	150
			83	309,792	44,057	44,524	467
			84	62,047	164,138	164,966	828
	O	E	81	247	309	338	29
			82	176	660	785	125
	V	E	85	22	1,295	1,994	699
			86	73,842	206,207	207,774	1,567
FRANCE	A	E	82	19,008	34,166	35,015	849
			83	1,485	6,684	6,894	210
			84	35,200	91,925	93,473	1,548
			85	36,031	91,507	93,331	1,824
GUATMAL	V	E	84	52,912	3,071	3,675	604
			85	4,034	3,570	4,483	913
INDIA	A	E	86	1,373	1,950	3,610	1,660
INDNSIA	A	E	82	293,040	562,565	592,463	29,898
			83	225,195	412,728	435,838	23,110
			84	230,382	481,650	509,660	28,010
			85	746,041	1,250,208	1,321,511	71,303
			86	1,078,115	2,284,116	2,391,566	107,450
ISRAEL	A	E	81	6,417	2,475	2,500	25
ITALY	A	E	81	114,098	379,757	385,771	6,014
			84	40,565	129,950	132,200	2,250
NETHLDS	A	E	81	39,110	70,024	70,994	970
			82	15,667	30,297	31,104	807
			83	1,091	2,013	2,204	191
			84	91,857	87,726	91,870	4,144
			86	123	1,064	1,093	29
	O	E	85	14,109	40,912	40,912	
U KING	A	E	81	4,410	13,759	14,269	510
			84	496	1,593	1,643	50

Cinchona, natural drug

4353000 BARK CINCHONA ETC QUININE (LB)

Country	Mode	Reg	Yr	Quantity	F.A.S.	C.I.F.	Charges
TOTAL			81	2,637	2,627	2,788	161
			82	8,299	8,484	9,993	1,509
			83	40,208	21,496	24,969	3,473
			85	98,307	58,746	60,639	1,893
			86	109,957	41,913	49,251	7,338
BRAZIL	A	E	83	619	750	1,859	1,109
	V	E	86	5,071	2,803	3,400	597
CHILE	V	E	86	88,184	26,408	31,601	5,193
CHINA T	V	E	85	80,000	46,392	46,392	
	V	W	85	15,000	9,450	10,572	1,122
ECUADOR	V	E	81	2,205	1,800	1,957	157
			82	1,641	1,778	2,039	261
			83	1,089	636	702	66
			86	2,152	2,381	2,740	359
FR GERM	V	W	81	432	827	831	4

Crop
Product
TSUSA commodity number, description, and unit of quantity

Country	Mode	Reg	Yr	Quantity	F.A.S.	C.I.F.	Charges
GUATMAL	V	E	82	3,351	3,328	4,052	724
			85	3,307	2,904	3,675	771
			86	3,307	3,878	4,350	472
KOR REP	V	W	83	38,500	20,110	22,408	2,298
NETHLDS	V	E	82	3,307	3,378	3,902	524
PERU	V	E	86	11,243	6,443	7,160	717

Quinidine, alkaloid
4370840 QUINIDINE AND ITS SALTS (AOZ)

Country	Mode	Reg	Yr	Quantity	F.A.S.	C.I.F.	Charges
TOTAL			81	5,472,727	14,844,028	15,080,721	235,812
			82	5,160,464	13,793,610	13,974,399	180,789
			83	5,737,260	16,847,623	17,017,317	169,694
			84	7,430,736	21,555,581	21,908,137	352,556
			85	6,026,490	16,874,362	17,149,421	275,059
			86	6,608,618	20,558,161	20,838,592	280,431
BELGIUM	A	E	81	1,000	3,300	3,336	36
			82	84,568	235,022	236,956	1,934
			83	181,280	514,823	518,413	3,590
			85	19,408	51,060	51,684	624
			86	28,219	95,759	97,400	1,641
FR GERM	A	E	81	35,280	111,116	112,021	905
			82	17,728	38,454	40,013	1,559
			85	1,600	10,665	10,765	100
	N	E	81	2,567,078	6,850,814	6,929,569	77,874
			82	2,538,122	6,871,771	6,956,197	84,426
			83	2,386,808	6,440,662	6,512,293	71,631
			84	4,150,460	11,855,839	12,085,939	230,100
			85	2,856,666	7,151,490	7,299,112	147,622
			86	3,634,724	10,766,450	10,889,949	123,499
	O	E	81	49,559	138,237	138,258	21
			82	33,274	91,983	91,994	11
			83	65,256	239,778	239,778	
			84	109,413	357,418	357,437	19
			85	101,248	276,304	276,304	
			86	75,838	305,020	305,020	
FRANCE	A	E	81	843,335	2,080,999	2,165,956	84,957
			82	687,882	1,487,787	1,519,554	31,767
			83	503,662	1,675,697	1,695,614	19,917
			84	357,390	998,753	1,017,604	18,851
			85	175,470	1,303,393	1,313,053	9,660
			86	228,163	812,000	826,101	14,101
GERM DR	V	E	83	1,984	98,316	98,727	411
INDNSIA	A	E	81	348,724	732,400	744,101	11,701
			84	56,438	179,009	181,164	2,155
			85	35,274	60,380	62,000	1,620
IRELAND	A	E	82	705	1,200	1,342	142
			84	432	750	1,102	352
			85	7,280	19,955	20,255	300
ITALY	A	E	81	470,469	1,368,560	1,387,972	19,412
			82	657,493	1,846,520	1,875,615	29,095
			83	845,098	2,663,411	2,686,227	22,816
			84	639,505	1,932,986	1,961,923	28,937
			85	755,397	2,124,413	2,156,287	31,874
			86	554,315	1,987,277	2,021,042	33,765
NETHLDS	A	E	81	835,223	2,684,561	2,708,459	23,898
			82	1,112,472	3,140,275	3,170,972	30,697
			83	1,638,538	4,869,585	4,913,866	44,281
			84	1,979,830	5,796,444	5,862,017	65,573
			86	2,087,359	6,591,655	6,699,080	107,425
	A	W	83	114,634	345,351	352,399	7,048
			84	102,068	335,213	339,886	4,673
	N	E	85	1,939,202	5,491,011	5,568,897	77,886
	O	E	85	25,789	71,596	71,596	
SPAIN	A	E	85	73,882	216,610	219,868	3,258
SWITZLD	A	E	82	21,164	65,430	66,348	918
U KING	A	E	81	300,895	806,155	822,429	16,274
			82	7,056	15,168	15,408	240
			84	35,200	99,169	101,065	1,896
			85	35,274	97,485	99,600	2,115
USSR	A	E	81	21,164	67,886	68,620	734

Quinine, alkaloid
4370820 QUININE AND ITS SALTS (AOZ)

Country	Mode	Reg	Yr	Quantity	F.A.S.	C.I.F.	Charges
TOTAL			81	2,068,627	4,457,334	4,542,366	84,480
			82	2,305,563	4,532,172	4,643,544	111,372
			83	2,092,382	5,465,691	5,550,513	84,822
			84	2,612,832	4,814,986	4,908,620	93,634
			85	3,216,377	6,056,876	6,226,684	169,808
			86	2,050,719	4,487,425	4,581,289	93,864

Crop
Product
TSUSA commodity number, description, and unit of quantity

Country	Mode	Reg	Yr	Quantity	F.A.S.	C.I.F.	Charges
BELGIUM	A	E	81	15,937	43,351	44,561	1,210
			82	193,515	406,734	410,878	4,144
			83	50,000	100,836	101,976	1,140
			84	233,568	429,112	441,334	12,222
			85	24,692	43,279	44,800	1,521
			86	51,990	101,008	106,061	5,053
	A	W	83	50,000	100,480	102,344	1,864
	N	E	81	170,054	387,086	392,048	4,962
			82	69,672	109,147	111,810	2,663
			83	224,054	532,055	537,350	5,295
	O	E	81	3,779	6,403	6,787	384
			82	10,000	32,618	33,000	382
	V	W	81	34,000	74,654	75,938	1,284
CANADA	O	E	82	2,000	4,640	4,640	
			83	2,500	6,625	6,625	
			84	1,810	6,148	6,457	309
CHINA M	A	E	84	10,582	16,645	17,100	455
	V	E	84	43,589	73,424	74,201	777
FR GERM	A	E	81	105,808	229,875	238,512	8,637
			84	320	466	565	99
			85	1,411	2,342	2,551	209
			86	3,540	8,588	8,934	346
	N	E	81	572,959	1,382,215	1,407,274	24,507
			82	434,770	851,556	864,231	12,675
			83	550,169	1,672,135	1,694,805	22,670
			84	471,109	930,883	943,792	12,909
			85	1,012,912	2,212,827	2,269,864	57,037
			86	490,677	1,202,749	1,219,236	16,487
	O	E	81	77,192	148,640	148,668	28
			82	32,929	74,865	74,865	
			83	51,570	117,885	117,913	28
			84	8,900	19,060	19,060	
			85	9,700	21,556	21,556	
			86	2,000	5,200	5,200	
FRANCE	A	E	81	50,756	107,549	111,129	3,580
			82	392,011	787,172	830,748	43,576
			83	125,802	267,157	270,365	3,208
			84	211,831	457,576	467,440	9,864
			85	58,165	116,263	126,531	10,268
			86	14,314	32,974	33,578	604
	A	W	83	15,000	30,781	31,631	850
INDIA	V	E	86	35,280	59,000	59,573	573
	V	W	85	35,280	53,000	53,977	977
INDNSIA	A	E	81	445,604	906,803	927,827	21,024
			82	713,298	1,295,622	1,330,462	34,840
			83	27,573	52,199	53,261	1,062
			85	2,992	4,748	4,875	127
			86	1,764	3,955	4,050	95
	N	E	83	316,003	918,991	944,183	25,192
			84	739,970	1,282,399	1,307,805	25,406
			85	548,773	833,930	862,285	28,355
			86	288,813	581,000	587,335	6,335
	V	W	84	133,456	205,378	208,963	3,585
ITALY	A	E	83	65,091	284,529	289,118	4,589
NETHLDS	A	E	81	386,066	783,797	793,241	9,444
			82	446,475	952,649	965,319	12,670
			83	502,400	1,146,566	1,160,572	14,006
			84	550,373	1,023,546	1,042,150	18,604
			85	825,693	1,636,738	1,669,730	32,992
			86	1,031,038	2,175,697	2,231,832	56,135
	A	W	83	5,291	11,874	12,121	247
			84	50,655	61,126	63,352	2,226
	V	E	85	5,296	8,925	9,128	203
SINGAPR	A	E	84	5,291	9,300	10,114	814
SWITZLD	A	E	83	61,729	124,463	127,344	2,881
U KING	A	E	81	206,472	386,961	396,381	9,420
			82	10,893	17,169	17,591	422
			83	45,200	99,115	100,905	1,790
			84	161,960	316,568	323,387	6,819
			85	680,881	1,106,623	1,144,287	37,664
			86	131,303	317,254	325,490	8,236

Cinnamon

Cinnamon, essential oil
4521600 CINNAMON OIL (LB)

Country	Mode	Reg	Yr	Quantity	F.A.S.	C.I.F.	Charges
TOTAL			81	40,163	115,856	124,069	8,213
			82	78,925	238,094	249,859	11,765
			83	84,892	314,665	329,066	14,401

Crop Product TSUSA commodity number, description, and unit of quantity Country	Mode	Reg	Yr	Quantity	F.A.S.	C.I.F.	Charges
			84	72,620	241,135	252,372	11,237
			85	140,894	385,792	403,416	17,624
			86	89,119	247,479	256,119	8,640
CHINA T	V E		85	2,205	5,049	5,290	241
FR GERM	A E		81	18	1,881	1,922	41
			84	750	1,883	2,076	193
	A W		83	45	1,047	1,063	16
	V E		83	1,264	3,413	3,431	18
			84	1,760	4,400	4,662	262
FRANCE	A E		81	248	3,140	3,212	72
			82	96	6,753	6,895	142
			83	66	2,351	2,409	58
			84	8	718	734	16
			85	20	2,009	2,018	9
			86	11	1,464	1,486	22
JAPAN	A E		81	39	467	657	190
			83	66	1,304	1,686	382
	V W		83	220	4,246	4,349	103
MADAGAS	A E		82	110	1,370	1,375	5
MEXICO	O E		85	71	2,019	2,019	
NETHLDS	A E		82	2	363	365	2
NORWAY	A E		85	14	1,300	1,358	58
SEYCHEL	V E		81	494	4,142	4,262	120
			82	509	4,461	4,583	122
SINGAPR	V E		86	2,241	5,264	5,483	219
SPAIN	V E		82	1,680	32,578	33,425	847
SRI LKA	N E		81	39,287	97,654	105,075	7,421
			82	76,478	185,451	194,958	9,507
			83	83,172	295,727	309,331	13,604
			84	65,630	212,030	221,982	9,952
			85	126,915	312,081	326,889	14,808
			86	82,425	225,483	233,314	7,831
	V W		84	4,409	12,517	13,086	569
			85	11,420	29,363	30,794	1,431
			86	4,409	9,873	10,219	346
SWITZLD	A E		81	44	5,518	5,662	144
			82	50	7,118	8,258	1,140
			83	39	6,193	6,379	186
			85	18	2,732	3,534	802
			86	33	5,395	5,617	222
	N E		84	63	9,587	9,832	245
U KING	A E		81	33	3,054	3,279	225
			83	20	384	418	34
	N E		85	231	31,239	31,514	275

Cinnamon, spice

1611700 CINNAMON AND CHIPS UNGROUND (LB)

Country	Mode	Reg	Yr	Quantity	F.A.S.	C.I.F.	Charges
TOTAL			81	1,861,637	1,417,978	1,752,296	334,318
			82	1,800,297	1,454,362	1,780,934	326,572
			83	2,099,954	1,710,975	2,088,846	377,871
			84	6,050,107	3,822,370	4,772,727	950,357
			85	3,270,874	2,691,336	3,211,014	519,678
			86	2,101,770	1,753,476	2,077,526	324,050
BRAZIL	V W		85	6,614	10,950	11,909	959
CANADA	O E		81	150	430	430	
			82	1,000	1,518	1,518	
			83	8,741	6,957	6,957	
			84	96,000	6,704	6,704	
	O W		82	330	577	607	30
CHINA M	N E		82	22,604	6,897	9,562	2,665
			84	93	689	719	30
			86	9,077	10,068	11,658	1,590
	O E		82	1,102	2,864	3,192	328
			83	1,100	2,243	2,405	162
			84	331	641	705	64
			85	3,205	4,214	4,681	467
	V E		81	44,170	11,637	16,823	5,186
			85	5,500	6,389	6,474	85
	V W		81	185	1,551	1,654	103
			82	11,558	4,131	5,544	1,413
			83	150	303	320	17
			84	700	1,428	1,477	49
			86	80,069	49,075	54,945	5,870
CHINA T	O E		83	110	274	274	
	V W		82	11,023	1,663	2,544	881
			84	20,000	12,096	15,180	3,084
			85	32,660	25,266	30,272	5,006
			86	80,164	261,436	289,392	27,956
FR GERM	V E		81	661	1,688	1,765	77
			82	1,653	3,630	3,778	148
			83	661	1,428	1,467	39
FRANCE	V E		81	163	327	348	21
			83	25	323	340	17
			84	119	377	399	22
HAITI	A E		82	116	338	391	53
HG KONG	V E		81	125	273	280	7
	V W		82	5	384	390	6
			86	116	1,396	1,427	31
INDIA	V E		82	33,620	13,538	17,998	4,460
			83	20,040	16,999	20,884	3,885
			84	114	374	480	106
			85	33,023	20,159	24,601	4,442
	V W		81	132	382	471	89
			83	55	325	355	30
			84	31,636	29,890	33,248	3,358
INDNSIA	O E		82	600	977	977	
			84	9,300	5,565	5,565	
	V E		81	110,230	35,181	49,412	14,231
			82	291,448	135,307	173,720	38,413
			83	67,902	30,592	39,665	9,073
			84	194,005	81,575	106,672	25,097
			85	443,947	183,844	242,106	58,262
			86	56,765	32,045	38,788	6,743
	V W		81	33,069	14,066	19,015	4,949
			83	66,138	35,517	41,939	6,422
			84	32,000	29,966	33,120	3,154
			85	68,343	41,149	47,470	6,321
			86	88,184	60,536	68,870	8,334
ITALY	V E		84	3,307	4,086	4,586	500
JAPAN	V W		83	9,698	9,076	10,561	1,485
KENYA	O E		85	1,100	1,237	1,419	182
MADAGAS	V E		81	22,046	11,500	15,411	3,911
			84	11,139	41,909	43,024	1,115
			86	4,652	1,937	3,166	1,229
MEXICO	O E		81	109	464	464	
			83	110	469	469	
	O W		84	198	251	251	
NETHLDS	V W		81	9,170	13,464	13,604	140
PHIL R	V W		85	888	2,897	3,071	174
			86	1,183	1,561	1,655	94
REP SAF	V E		81	99,175	34,605	53,640	19,035
SEYCHEL	O E		83	2,160	1,164	1,164	
	V E		81	229,647	87,393	129,848	42,455
SINGAPR	O E		82	661	806	899	93
	V W		82	220	503	516	13
			83	12,000	11,260	12,281	1,021
			84	220	400	424	24
SPAIN	V E		83	22,000	16,500	18,047	1,547
SRI LKA	N E		86	1,188,982	843,577	1,018,671	175,094
	V E		81	739,252	526,052	645,950	119,898
			82	863,638	633,274	782,742	149,468
			83	904,116	607,751	756,993	149,242
			84	1,085,177	539,293	705,083	165,790
			85	372,319	256,745	316,711	59,966
			86	23,525	2,502	4,802	2,300
	V W		81	572,934	677,255	801,119	123,864
			82	557,141	634,825	762,613	127,788
			83	962,655	925,962	1,127,680	201,718
			84	4,531,357	3,014,759	3,757,657	742,898
			85	2,302,341	2,137,236	2,520,951	383,715
			86	553,542	473,808	566,282	92,474
THAILND	V E		82	45	308	421	113
			84	250	404	458	54
	V W		82	601	1,476	1,630	154
			83	1,503	2,361	2,598	237
			84	2,262	3,573	3,842	269
			85	934	1,250	1,349	99
			86	15,511	15,535	17,870	2,335
TURKEY	V E		84	20,000	14,631	17,000	2,369
U KING	N E		83	19,688	38,671	41,437	2,766
			84	11,899	33,759	36,133	2,374
	O E		83	1,102	2,800	3,010	210
	V E		82	2,932	11,346	11,892	546
	V W		81	419	1,710	2,062	352

1611900 CINNAMON A CINN CHIPS GROUND (LB)

Country	Mode	Reg	Yr	Quantity	F.A.S.	C.I.F.	Charges
TOTAL			81	97,476	115,616	123,410	7,794
			82	119,526	125,194	127,869	2,675
			83	232,058	181,210	184,764	3,554
			84	102,279	106,209	117,755	11,546
			85	31,641	35,884	40,581	4,697
			86	64,386	57,596	63,639	6,043
BELGIUM	O E		81	331	412	445	33

Crop Product TSUSA commodity number, description, and unit of quantity Country	Mode	Reg	Yr	Quantity	F.A.S.	C.I.F.	Charges
CANADA	O	E	81	52,726	54,860	54,860	
			82	77,500	63,782	63,782	
			83	200,544	159,779	159,779	
			84	26,783	23,473	23,605	132
			85	1,465	2,160	2,160	
			86	149	4,120	4,120	
	O	W	81	4,307	5,853	5,853	
CHINA M	O	E	82	205	804	882	78
			83	110	412	442	30
	V	E	83	529	1,423	1,458	35
			84	524	1,318	1,410	92
	V	W	81	125	312	372	60
			82	22,150	30,759	30,948	189
			83	1,000	341	377	36
			84	625	1,069	1,180	111
CHINA T	V	E	83	22,046	3,781	5,726	1,945
	V	W	81	32	316	355	39
COLOMB	A	E	83	335	317	535	218
			84	45	529	569	40
FR GERM	O	E	83	46	290	304	14
	V	E	81	606	1,797	1,885	88
			84	331	757	784	27
FRANCE	V	E	83	192	2,081	2,126	45
GUATMAL	V	W	83	47	384	455	71
HG KONG	V	E	83	1,650	835	895	60
INDIA	O	E	81	550	1,046	1,138	92
			83	220	449	489	40
	V	W	83	496	390	474	84
			84	1,102	747	901	154
INDNSIA	O	E	81	12,280	8,984	8,984	
			86	1,345	1,013	1,013	
	V	E	83	716	2,780	2,862	82
ITALY	V	E	83	419	3,044	3,259	215
KENYA	O	E	81	132	555	613	58
KOR REP	V	W	81	93	592	684	92
			82	216	1,670	1,734	64
			83	93	617	690	73
			84	1,246	2,705	2,915	210
MEXICO	O	E	83	1	408	408	
			86	30,864	1,400	1,400	
NETHLDS	O	E	81	6,886	9,528	10,103	575
			82	11,121	18,262	18,865	603
			84	17,050	24,020	26,172	2,152
	V	E	81	550	869	993	124
			82	298	413	446	33
			83	331	448	502	54
			84	2,308	2,612	2,813	201
			86	3,868	8,648	8,857	209
	V	W	82	1,100	1,753	2,024	271
			85	1,705	2,514	2,729	215
			86	771	1,271	1,407	136
SEYCHEL	V	E	84	206	328	379	51
SINGAPR	A	E	84	3,220	7,475	8,335	860
	V	W	82	1,102	808	913	105
SPAIN	V	E	84	127	409	448	39
SRI LKA	V	E	84	39,921	34,496	40,844	6,348
			86	10,000	9,693	12,079	2,386
	V	W	81	16,470	23,296	29,462	6,166
			82	4,409	2,587	3,693	1,106
			83	2,600	1,364	1,704	340
			84	7,300	3,128	3,932	804
			85	28,191	23,936	28,418	4,482
			86	16,033	17,131	20,372	3,241
THAILND	V	E	84	263	480	535	55
	V	W	82	1,173	1,964	2,089	125
			83	325	598	666	68
			84	912	1,614	1,813	199
			86	904	1,185	1,256	71
U KING	N	E	81	444	1,651	1,699	48
	O	E	81	1,764	4,930	5,314	384
			82	89	1,650	1,735	85
			83	107	524	635	111
			84	47	420	432	12
			85	280	7,274	7,274	
			86	452	13,135	13,135	
	V	E	81	180	615	650	35
			82	163	742	758	16
			83	251	945	978	33
			84	269	629	688	59

Citron

Citron, candied
1541500 CITRONS, CANDIED, GLACE, ETC (LB)

Country	Mode	Reg	Yr	Quantity	F.A.S.	C.I.F.	Charges
TOTAL			81	500	579	609	30
			82	1,000	1,074	1,129	55
			83	51,187	30,414	36,357	5,943
			84	16,831	5,614	7,321	1,707
			85	776	1,355	1,399	44
ARGENT	V	W	83	47,880	29,563	35,258	5,695
BRAZIL	V	E	83	3,307	851	1,099	248
			84	15,432	4,995	6,573	1,578
FRANCE	V	E	85	776	1,355	1,399	44
HG KONG	V	W	81	500	579	609	30
			82	1,000	1,074	1,129	55
JAPAN	O	W	84	1,399	619	748	129

Citron, fresh or dried or in brine
1470000 CITRON, FRSH, DRD, IN BRINE (LB)

Country	Mode	Reg	Yr	Quantity	F.A.S.	C.I.F.	Charges
TOTAL			81	20,795	144,488	166,800	22,312
			82	77,934	681,482	754,855	73,373
			83	45,585	407,578	446,864	39,286
			84	36,617	477,358	510,027	32,669
			85	86,156	529,875	571,366	41,491
			86	40,317	316,491	352,082	35,591
CHINA M	V	W	85	37,511	13,384	14,745	1,361
COLOMB	A	E	86	2,006	3,950	5,326	1,376
ICELAND	A	E	85	1,048	12,098	14,264	2,166
INDIA	A	E	86	2,000	4,000	4,450	450
IRAN	A	E	86	276	1,750	1,969	219
ISRAEL	A	E	81	20,760	143,848	166,070	22,222
			86	34,825	300,770	334,230	33,460
	N	E	82	75,715	677,362	747,788	70,426
			83	44,022	405,525	443,647	38,122
			84	33,651	470,976	502,009	31,033
			85	46,701	486,393	523,356	36,963
ITALY	A	E	82	2,219	4,120	7,067	2,947
			83	1,563	2,053	3,217	1,164
			84	60	2,000	2,163	163
			85	896	18,000	19,001	1,001
			86	1,210	6,021	6,107	86
JAPAN	V	E	84	66	600	634	34
MOROC	A	E	81	35	640	730	90
			84	2,500	3,000	4,182	1,182
N ZEAL	A	W	84	340	782	1,039	257

Citron, peel
1521000 CITRON PEEL CRUDE, DRIED ETC (LB)

Country	Mode	Reg	Yr	Quantity	F.A.S.	C.I.F.	Charges
TOTAL			83	38,130	4,739	5,151	412
			84	57	402	564	162
			85	14,889	6,846	8,641	1,795
CANADA	O	E	85	20	3,978	3,978	
CHINA T	V	E	83	37,530	4,400	4,787	387
FRANCE	A	E	84	57	402	564	162
HG KONG	V	W	83	600	339	364	25
ITALY	V	E	85	13,767	1,689	3,363	1,674
JAPAN	V	W	85	1,102	1,179	1,300	121

1522600 CITRN PEEL PRES O PREP NSPF (LB)

Country	Mode	Reg	Yr	Quantity	F.A.S.	C.I.F.	Charges
TOTAL			81	1,917	2,055	2,147	92
			82	30	402	417	15
			83	2,914	6,275	6,481	206
			84	43,976	25,415	27,983	2,568
			85	210	3,082	3,164	82
CHINA M	N	W	84	1,718	11,135	11,523	388
	V	W	81	1,917	2,055	2,147	92
			83	2,641	5,129	5,252	123
			85	210	3,082	3,164	82
CHINA T	V	W	82	30	402	417	15
JAPAN	V	W	83	273	1,146	1,229	83
			84	42,258	14,280	16,460	2,180

Crop Product TSUSA commodity number, description, and unit of quantity Country	Mode	Reg	Yr	Quantity	F.A.S.	C.I.F.	Charges

1542000 CITRON PEEL CANDIED ETC (LB)

Citron, prepared or preserved
1470200 CITRONS, PREP OR PRES, NSPF (LB)

Country	Mode	Reg	Yr	Quantity	F.A.S.	C.I.F.	Charges
TOTAL			82	66	350	360	10
			83	667	1,309	1,421	112
			84	14,004	4,026	5,573	1,547
			86	39,553	16,926	20,385	3,459
DOM REP	A	E	84	13,490	1,775	3,125	1,350
FR GERM	O	E	86	1,153	1,126	2,305	1,179
FRANCE	V	E	84	161	1,005	1,131	126
GREECE	V	E	83	601	750	852	102
ISRAEL	V	E	86	38,400	15,800	18,080	2,280
JAPAN	V	E	82	66	350	360	10
			83	66	559	569	10
			84	353	1,246	1,317	71

Citronella Grass

Citronella, essential oil
4521800 CITRONELLA OIL (LB)

Country	Mode	Reg	Yr	Quantity	F.A.S.	C.I.F.	Charges
TOTAL			81	1,647,967	4,754,462	4,997,513	242,704
			82	1,189,839	2,974,523	3,226,931	252,408
			83	1,461,906	2,763,368	2,970,095	206,727
			84	1,860,269	3,280,836	3,538,625	257,789
			85	1,369,755	2,401,645	2,590,121	188,476
			86	1,557,201	3,831,113	4,000,362	169,249
ARGENT	V	E	81	146,029	414,937	446,324	31,072
			82	212,918	469,652	514,680	45,028
			83	121,474	216,035	240,244	24,209
			85	44,092	77,335	85,857	8,522
			86	129,293	188,397	207,933	19,536
BRAZIL	V	E	81	13,492	33,150	37,107	3,957
			82	39,754	101,090	109,696	8,606
			83	3,175	5,525	6,535	1,010
			84	77,161	116,938	136,048	19,110
			85	92,417	144,149	166,722	22,573
			86	27,728	43,815	46,215	2,400
CHINA M	N	E	85	826,184	1,401,014	1,510,312	109,298
			86	1,004,351	2,813,382	2,922,191	108,809
	V	E	81	593,384	1,763,105	1,847,787	84,682
			82	204,364	558,970	605,453	46,483
			83	646,901	1,125,551	1,219,749	94,198
			84	1,278,527	2,072,141	2,243,009	170,868
			86	71,429	121,576	131,513	9,937
	V	W	81	45,447	128,393	133,679	5,286
			82	400,001	989,422	1,085,187	95,765
			83	156,824	282,736	306,048	23,312
			85	39,683	67,467	70,029	2,562
			86	50,705	92,149	99,671	7,522
CHINA T	N	E	86	75,353	190,137	196,877	6,740
	V	E	81	213,236	753,627	778,517	24,890
			82	34,251	139,666	144,177	4,511
			83	197,731	519,696	544,266	24,570
			84	211,242	551,333	577,856	26,523
			85	44,092	111,028	115,663	4,635
	V	W	81	29,352	86,928	90,402	3,474
			82	15,873	49,831	51,998	2,167
			84	25,353	59,350	62,751	3,401
			85	32,408	90,132	94,116	3,984
FR GERM	V	E	84	2,206	761	864	103
FRANCE	A	E	82	60	1,858	1,917	59
			84	487	1,117	1,342	225
	V	E	81	4,806	13,985	14,866	849
GUATMAL	V	E	81	6,400	24,841	25,505	664
			86	2,000	6,600	6,883	283
INDNSIA	N	E	85	229,587	382,131	408,753	26,622
	V	E	81	349,247	850,081	899,249	49,168
			82	191,930	487,808	523,543	35,735
			83	235,781	414,491	439,542	25,051
			84	119,544	205,677	222,150	16,473
			86	72,916	145,045	149,879	4,834
	V	W	81	118,936	319,935	336,490	16,555
			84	4,762	6,517	7,905	1,388
JAPAN	V	E	84	22,222	39,975	42,692	2,717
			86	11,112	22,856	23,688	832
MACAO	V	E	81	11,574	29,954	32,856	2,902

Crop Product TSUSA commodity number, description, and unit of quantity Country	Mode	Reg	Yr	Quantity	F.A.S.	C.I.F.	Charges
NETHLDS	V	E	81	11,577	23,304	23,767	463
			86	24,306	48,446	50,164	1,718
SINGAPR	V	E	82	16,755	33,259	34,494	1,235
			83	22,486	35,198	37,814	2,616
			85	2,240	5,040	5,427	387
SPAIN	V	E	81	16,754	62,869	66,449	3,580
SRI LKA	N	E	85	54,753	113,560	122,897	9,337
			86	83,246	150,793	157,065	6,272
	V	E	81	87,568	248,473	263,556	15,083
			82	73,426	140,393	152,944	12,551
			83	59,544	109,720	118,762	9,042
			84	99,677	188,859	204,125	15,266
	V	W	85	2,094	4,689	5,080	391
			86	4,762	7,917	8,283	366
SWITZLD	A	E	81	55	300	306	6
	V	E	83	17,990	54,416	57,135	2,719
U KING	A	E	81	110	580	653	73
			82	507	2,574	2,842	268
	V	E	84	19,088	38,168	39,883	1,715
			85	2,205	5,100	5,265	165

Citronellol
4608010 CITRONELLOL (LB)

Country	Mode	Reg	Yr	Quantity	F.A.S.	C.I.F.	Charges
TOTAL			81	69,574	305,638	320,304	14,666
			82	35,822	158,725	166,327	7,602
			83	101,606	399,741	411,501	11,760
			84	138,874	541,374	556,430	15,056
			85	144,600	499,042	511,684	12,642
			86	187,647	580,270	602,963	22,693
BELGIUM	V	E	84	2,205	6,246	6,446	200
BRAZIL	V	E	83	175	732	818	86
CHINA T	V	E	86	764	3,601	4,140	539
FR GERM	N	E	81	727	8,575	8,833	258
			82	10,852	37,156	37,961	805
			83	48,247	143,934	146,680	2,746
			84	94,996	265,138	271,347	6,209
			85	75,238	187,685	192,323	4,638
	V	E	86	62,458	139,109	148,065	8,956
FRANCE	A	E	84	242	6,583	6,813	230
			85	1,102	8,635	9,273	638
	N	E	83	8,402	40,381	42,077	1,696
	V	E	81	33,069	88,416	96,144	7,728
			82	1,600	7,552	7,911	359
			86	5,200	23,148	23,558	410
INDNSIA	V	E	83	1,764	5,847	6,391	544
			86	6,614	16,795	19,304	2,509
	V	W	81	11,243	41,504	42,395	891
ISRAEL	A	E	82	26	378	481	103
ITALY	A	E	82	1,984	9,891	10,530	639
JAPAN	A	E	86	2	1,010	1,025	15
	N	E	83	11,342	42,780	43,976	1,196
			84	12,466	62,783	64,451	1,668
	V	E	81	55	397	402	5
			85	48,000	206,486	211,738	5,252
			86	34,269	150,996	154,452	3,456
NETHLDS	V	E	83	441	273	280	7
			84	772	2,402	2,457	55
			85	772	2,301	2,366	65
SWITZLD	A	E	81	44	503	516	13
			82	33	372	407	35
U KING	N	E	81	17,095	110,465	113,940	3,475
			82	21,327	103,376	109,037	5,661
			83	28,149	152,320	157,350	5,030
			84	28,193	198,222	204,916	6,694
			86	23,985	113,196	116,804	3,608
	V	E	81	7,341	55,778	58,074	2,296
			83	3,086	13,474	13,929	455
			85	19,488	93,935	95,984	2,049
			86	54,355	132,415	135,615	3,200

Clove

Clove, essential oil
4522000 CLOVE OIL (LB)

Country	Mode	Reg	Yr	Quantity	F.A.S.	C.I.F.	Charges
TOTAL			81	931,049	1,913,277	2,060,405	147,128
			82	1,375,467	2,627,143	2,828,422	201,279
			83	864,583	1,534,148	1,672,586	138,438
			84	1,793,686	3,440,192	3,693,694	253,502

Crop
Product
TSUSA commodity number, description, and unit of quantity

Country	Mode	Reg	Yr	Quantity	F.A.S.	C.I.F.	Charges
			85	1,298,313	2,210,921	2,368,896	157,975
			86	1,629,379	2,811,282	2,981,081	169,799
BRAZIL	N	E	83	573	3,842	4,611	769
			84	1,322	8,225	9,239	1,014
			85	4,189	28,725	32,315	3,590
	V	E	81	3,968	20,550	21,591	1,041
			82	397	2,332	2,415	83
			83	2,205	8,180	10,838	2,658
			86	35,979	146,900	155,945	9,045
	V	W	85	5,549	19,920	21,501	1,581
CANADA	O	E	81	4,850	9,585	9,585	
			82	2,425	6,063	6,063	
ETHIOP	A	E	84	22	305	308	3
FR GERM	A	E	81	114	613	670	57
			82	165	710	781	71
			84	110	393	455	62
	V	E	83	1,323	16,347	16,884	537
			86	1,323	14,256	14,647	391
FRANCE	N	E	81	6,960	78,534	81,612	3,078
			82	3,720	49,339	50,459	1,120
			83	18,196	119,670	123,395	3,725
			84	79,673	214,469	231,196	16,727
			85	27,698	125,398	136,932	11,534
			86	29,421	174,318	182,956	8,638
INDIA	V	E	84	1,653	3,075	3,757	682
INDNSIA	N	E	85	638,014	879,201	945,053	65,852
			86	1,003,694	1,372,754	1,461,042	88,288
	V	E	81	547,930	842,442	919,914	77,472
			82	1,034,707	1,642,551	1,777,368	134,817
			83	661,204	837,377	926,574	89,197
			84	646,831	1,129,687	1,193,922	64,235
	V	W	81	229,278	260,516	287,447	26,931
			82	196,368	331,175	351,000	19,825
			84	161,377	340,768	363,861	23,093
			85	76,058	126,747	136,237	9,490
			86	41,888	79,508	82,705	3,197
IRELAND	V	E	85	606	7,210	7,348	138
JAPAN	V	E	81	1,587	14,345	14,594	249
MADAGAS	N	E	81	115,570	490,786	523,026	32,240
			82	136,234	588,919	634,084	45,165
			83	172,595	526,267	566,007	39,740
			84	811,070	1,557,804	1,695,994	138,190
			85	475,523	838,595	896,141	57,546
			86	380,146	751,829	799,611	47,782
	O	E	84	111	1,653	1,653	
	V	E	84	71,453	123,178	130,319	7,141
MALAYSA	V	E	81	13,474	182,024	186,442	4,418
			84	11,155	22,210	22,763	553
NETHLDS	A	E	81	220	838	893	55
			84	18	777	831	54
	N	E	82	385	1,422	1,467	45
			83	771	3,192	3,506	314
	V	E	86	39,683	69,114	72,720	3,606
PHIL R	V	E	81	6,614	8,870	10,342	1,472
REP SAF	V	E	85	52,910	139,480	145,134	5,654
SINGAPR	V	E	85	4,409	8,909	9,369	460
			86	6,614	13,265	14,036	771
SPAIN	V	E	85	4,750	7,844	8,702	858
			86	4,409	8,687	9,000	313
SRI LKA	V	E	83	6,720	11,129	12,364	1,235
			84	6,720	22,548	23,683	1,135
SWITZLD	A	E	81	484	4,174	4,289	115
			82	231	2,710	2,793	83
			83	539	6,774	6,951	177
			84	869	11,353	11,856	503
			85	2,436	14,971	15,450	479
			86	352	8,404	8,707	303
U KING	N	E	82	835	1,922	1,992	70
			83	457	1,370	1,456	86
			84	1,302	3,747	3,857	110
	V	E	85	1,543	8,104	8,287	183
			86	85,870	172,247	179,712	7,465
VENEZ	V	E	85	4,628	5,817	6,427	610

Clove, spice
1612100 CLOVES AND CLOVE STMS, UNGD (LB)

Country	Mode	Reg	Yr	Quantity	F.A.S.	C.I.F.	Charges
TOTAL			81	2,081,628	8,099,627	8,391,500	291,873
			82	2,437,884	10,997,851	11,365,238	367,387
			83	1,463,072	5,622,081	5,826,754	204,673
			84	2,323,454	6,667,444	6,982,996	315,552
			85	2,474,971	4,444,245	4,735,100	290,855

Crop
Product
TSUSA commodity number, description, and unit of quantity

Country	Mode	Reg	Yr	Quantity	F.A.S.	C.I.F.	Charges
			86	2,303,323	4,305,680	4,547,004	241,324
AFGHAN	V	E	86	4,134	7,427	7,647	220
BELGIUM	V	E	84	5,492	17,970	18,563	593
			85	22,219	34,970	36,217	1,247
BRAZIL	N	E	85	783,372	1,194,454	1,303,757	109,303
	O	E	81	6,469	24,547	24,547	
	V	E	81	701,630	2,686,413	2,784,917	98,504
			82	269,893	1,012,068	1,052,088	40,020
			83	514,707	1,961,823	2,036,556	74,733
			84	822,156	2,027,436	2,142,091	114,655
			85	165,345	265,858	287,844	21,986
			86	769,222	1,312,856	1,414,431	101,575
	V	W	81	33,069	121,309	125,664	4,355
			82	12,201	30,281	32,106	1,825
			83	33,080	93,358	98,030	4,672
			84	45,194	123,643	129,925	6,282
			85	86,738	153,532	165,688	12,156
			86	23,338	30,970	34,641	3,671
CANADA	O	E	81	972	1,852	1,852	
			83	6,729	4,990	4,990	
			84	2,441	6,295	6,295	
			85	1,099	2,633	2,633	
			86	767	9,641	9,641	
	O	W	81	68	378	378	
CHINA M	V	E	81	44,277	10,983	13,544	2,561
			82	200	940	1,066	126
			83	50	374	378	4
	V	W	81	50	313	327	14
			82	175	1,155	1,328	173
			83	50	363	405	42
			85	1,500	4,222	4,511	289
			86	475	1,482	1,516	34
CHINA T	V	W	84	50	304	326	22
			86	8,960	47,488	48,175	687
COMOROS	N	E	81	50,708	219,423	224,500	5,077
			84	41,844	112,870	129,171	16,301
	V	E	81	22,046	83,400	86,802	3,402
			83	88,166	364,928	385,729	20,801
			85	92,450	174,538	190,089	15,551
FR GERM	V	E	82	22,046	107,474	108,546	1,072
			85	32,104	55,013	60,289	5,276
FRANCE	V	E	81	68,688	292,770	299,609	6,839
			82	55,430	246,367	254,383	8,016
			83	38,609	167,846	173,010	5,164
			84	102,121	283,749	293,580	9,831
			85	167,544	360,456	376,815	16,359
			86	224,556	488,889	510,488	21,599
HG KONG	V	E	81	751	555	559	4
			83	125	956	967	11
	V	W	81	50	331	351	20
INDIA	O	E	82	110	668	668	
			83	110	574	625	51
			84	372	844	855	11
	V	E	81	22,018	11,572	13,545	1,973
			84	11,023	33,450	36,004	2,554
			85	22,046	16,376	17,725	1,349
			86	33,069	10,338	12,783	2,445
	V	W	81	602	783	992	209
INDNSIA	V	E	81	7,636	13,351	14,370	1,019
			82	3,307	5,108	5,762	654
			83	20,077	42,103	45,009	2,906
			84	47,819	39,538	44,113	4,575
			86	64,150	151,420	157,698	6,278
	V	W	81	35,269	157,388	161,009	3,621
			82	4,480	35,392	35,680	288
			84	8,818	57,459	58,259	800
			85	66,000	33,999	35,489	1,490
IRAN	V	E	86	52,745	25,792	27,992	2,200
ITALY	V	E	83	176	2,191	2,266	75
JAMAICA	A	E	82	144	432	477	45
KENYA	V	E	84	174	934	948	14
KOR REP	O	E	86	480	2,518	2,678	160
	V	E	83	6,614	14,404	15,075	671
MADAGAS	N	E	82	1,203,570	5,447,146	5,601,712	154,566
			83	462,923	1,951,081	2,009,389	58,308
			84	887,166	2,918,951	3,023,466	104,515
			86	757,507	1,482,897	1,542,837	59,940
	O	E	81	11,010	11,962	11,962	
			85	1,020	1,791	1,791	
	V	E	81	564,334	2,398,919	2,488,588	89,669
			82	44,092	190,696	198,416	7,720
			83	44,092	188,988	191,358	2,370
			84	98,477	357,141	367,335	10,194

Crop Product TSUSA commodity number, description, and unit of quantity Country	Mode	Reg	Yr	Quantity	F.A.S.	C.I.F.	Charges
			85	836,007	1,588,029	1,658,453	70,424
			86	27,227	42,820	44,696	1,876
	V	H	82	22,046	93,400	96,300	2,900
	V	W	81	17,637	79,094	80,612	1,518
			82	44,117	200,507	206,698	6,191
			84	16,588	48,939	50,748	1,809
			85	21,075	42,393	44,970	2,577
			86	30,796	54,583	59,420	4,837
MALAYSA	A	E	84	6,720	33,628	45,511	11,883
	N	E	86	8,889	31,943	34,491	2,548
	V	E	81	112,171	512,902	525,695	12,793
			82	40,515	315,412	335,160	19,748
			83	4,480	32,250	33,993	1,743
			84	8,960	43,285	46,239	2,954
			85	22,312	116,168	125,099	8,931
			86	17,850	91,924	97,027	5,103
	V	W	81	27,492	206,373	213,839	7,466
			82	69,373	491,235	504,572	13,337
			83	42,418	344,791	350,933	6,142
			84	104,006	254,676	262,102	7,426
			85	31,187	162,134	172,189	10,055
			86	28,836	152,172	157,171	4,999
MEXICO	A	E	84	1	518	523	5
	O	E	83	69	951	951	
NETHLDS	V	E	83	5,511	22,538	23,151	613
			84	38,630	133,143	141,318	8,175
			85	34,755	62,085	65,801	3,716
			86	10,385	17,759	18,642	883
	V	W	85	11,102	29,975	30,218	243
NIGERIA	V	E	86	22,046	36,376	38,276	1,900
NIUE	V	E	85	23,000	35,286	35,667	381
NORWAY	V	E	85	20,862	28,844	30,250	1,406
PERU	O	E	85	5,890	9,975	9,975	
REP SAF	V	E	86	60,947	113,959	116,692	2,733
SEYCHEL	V	E	86	2,224	1,360	1,653	293
SINGAPR	V	E	81	79,361	352,376	360,718	8,342
			82	6,614	10,699	11,759	1,060
			83	22,046	89,791	91,948	2,157
			84	15,198	22,348	26,238	3,890
			85	10,075	13,842	17,019	3,177
			86	8,928	9,393	12,198	2,805
	V	W	81	17,747	78,456	81,285	2,829
			82	13,625	59,159	62,197	3,038
			84	218	1,089	1,156	67
SPAIN	V	E	83	3,300	2,508	2,726	218
			84	11,052	25,591	26,099	508
			86	24,251	55,564	57,275	1,711
SRI LKA	N	E	86	75,052	62,815	71,136	8,321
	V	E	81	99,874	156,247	172,038	15,791
			82	16,623	72,478	76,132	3,654
			83	48,112	121,316	131,703	10,387
			84	35,388	73,159	79,142	5,983
			85	16,608	56,096	60,945	4,849
	V	W	81	51,884	277,413	290,206	12,793
			82	30,227	72,283	78,294	6,011
			83	81,992	46,499	52,294	5,795
			84	2,204	12,452	13,271	819
			86	24,249	12,831	15,186	2,355
THAILND	O	E	81	2,200	2,200	2,200	
	V	W	82	313	425	468	43
			86	549	3,827	4,078	251
TNZANIA	V	E	81	103,615	398,317	411,391	13,074
			82	462,966	2,071,293	2,152,368	81,075
			84	162	330	370	40
			86	21,691	46,636	48,536	1,900
	V	W	82	50,781	228,512	233,174	4,662
			85	661	1,576	1,666	90
TUNISIA	V	E	82	26,455	123,382	128,307	4,925
TURKEY	V	E	82	16,535	79,927	81,019	1,092
U KING	V	E	82	22,046	101,412	106,558	5,146
			83	39,636	167,458	175,268	7,810
			84	180	433	493	60
URUGUAY	V	E	84	11,000	37,269	38,855	1,586

1612300 CLOVES A CLOVE STEMS, GROUND (LB)

Country	Mode	Reg	Yr	Quantity	F.A.S.	C.I.F.	Charges
TOTAL			81	766	1,579	1,579	
			82	1,883	7,638	7,795	157
			83	15,993	50,203	50,408	205
			84	37,963	35,946	38,451	2,505
			86	3,226	6,741	8,047	1,306
BRAZIL	A	E	86	2,220	3,424	4,635	1,211
	O	E	83	600	2,710	2,710	
			86	256	1,050	1,050	

Crop Product TSUSA commodity number, description, and unit of quantity Country	Mode	Reg	Yr	Quantity	F.A.S.	C.I.F.	Charges
CANADA	O	E	81	592	862	862	
			82	1,000	5,481	5,481	
			83	13,771	44,278	44,278	
			84	4,186	7,794	7,794	
	O	W	81	174	717	717	
FRANCE	V	E	83	66	532	560	28
	V	W	83	132	291	309	18
HG KONG	V	W	82	850	1,781	1,936	155
			83	1,000	1,372	1,505	133
			86	750	2,267	2,362	95
INDIA	O	E	83	35	268	276	8
			84	250	260	270	10
	V	E	84	33,069	26,620	29,031	2,411
NETHLDS	V	E	82	33	376	378	2
PAKISTN	O	E	84	290	611	645	34
SPAIN	V	E	84	48	382	417	35
U KING	V	E	83	389	752	770	18
			84	120	279	294	15

Clover

Alsike clover, seed
1262300 CLOVER SEED ALSIKE (LB)

Country	Mode	Reg	Yr	Quantity	F.A.S.	C.I.F.	Charges
TOTAL			81	2,846,685	616,659	616,659	
			82	2,955,056	693,802	693,802	
			83	9,852,736	3,931,891	3,931,891	
			84	2,551,961	764,101	764,101	
			85	3,087,279	918,963	918,963	
			86	5,087,865	2,007,852	2,007,852	
CANADA	O	E	81	2,293,247	514,945	514,945	
			82	2,647,118	623,884	623,884	
			83	8,901,911	3,558,248	3,558,248	
			84	2,226,791	674,796	674,796	
			85	2,692,730	807,635	807,635	
			86	4,370,667	1,737,971	1,737,971	
	O	W	81	553,438	101,714	101,714	
			82	307,938	69,918	69,918	
			83	950,825	373,643	373,643	
			84	325,170	89,305	89,305	
			85	394,549	111,328	111,328	
			86	717,198	269,881	269,881	

Clover (not specified), seed
1263300 CLOVER SEED, NSPF (LB)

Country	Mode	Reg	Yr	Quantity	F.A.S.	C.I.F.	Charges
TOTAL			81	229,881	246,455	267,605	21,150
			82	235,221	196,705	225,419	28,714
			83	690,580	652,843	691,877	39,034
			84	692,392	539,322	566,021	26,699
			85	789,379	406,550	445,159	38,609
			86	677,929	338,456	359,774	21,318
AUSTRAL	N	W	81	13,850	63,688	66,251	2,563
			82	3,527	14,703	17,613	2,910
			83	20,950	47,439	50,177	2,738
	V	E	81	52,911	47,566	52,320	4,754
			82	100,420	64,347	74,330	9,983
			83	128,732	119,643	128,072	8,429
			84	116,844	37,689	42,850	5,161
			85	204,697	64,362	73,864	9,502
			86	132,573	43,785	48,751	4,966
	V	H	83	1,320	3,147	3,355	208
			84	220	484	518	34
			85	1,100	3,000	3,120	120
			86	3,000	10,108	10,350	242
	V	W	81	102,625	101,594	114,936	13,342
			82	120,111	109,272	123,757	14,485
			83	395,004	368,018	392,277	24,259
			84	286,433	341,890	361,166	19,276
			85	379,975	257,259	278,931	21,672
			86	344,769	160,841	174,991	14,150
AUSTRIA	A	W	82	441	1,786	2,628	842
	V	E	83	39,000	34,003	36,000	1,997
	V	W	83	4,409	11,820	12,400	580
			84	13,988	31,706	32,619	913
BRAZIL	V	E	85	44,092	24,216	27,181	2,965
CANADA	O	E	81	57,960	32,621	32,621	
			82	8,040	2,131	2,131	
			83	58,560	44,233	44,233	

Crop Product TSUSA commodity number, description, and unit of quantity Country	Mode	Reg	Yr	Quantity	F.A.S.	C.I.F.	Charges
			84	75,000	44,578	44,578	
			85	104,500	39,858	39,858	
			86	85,200	45,187	45,187	
	O	W	83	35,000	9,235	9,235	
			84	180,000	70,000	70,000	
			85	3,031	3,000	3,000	
			86	73,745	49,279	49,279	
FR GERM	A	E	82	26	1,374	1,423	49
	V	E	82	2,646	1,720	2,116	396
	V	W	83	7,385	14,242	14,976	734
INDIA	V	W	85	51,984	14,855	19,205	4,350
ITALY	V	W	86	3,307	3,151	3,512	361
JAPAN	A	E	84	35	2,826	3,236	410
			86	35	2,415	2,459	44
	V	W	86	35,274	22,514	23,967	1,453
N ZEAL	V	E	81	2,535	986	1,477	491
	V	H	83	220	1,063	1,152	89
NETHLDS	A	E	82	10	1,372	1,421	49
			84	4	3,077	3,124	47
			86	26	1,176	1,278	102
NORFOLK	V	W	84	19,868	7,072	7,930	858

Crimson clover, seed
1262500 CLOVER SEED, CRIMSON (LB)

Country	Mode	Reg	Yr	Quantity	F.A.S.	C.I.F.	Charges
TOTAL			82	10,530	4,643	4,858	215
			83	8	1,444	1,513	69
			84	88,184	47,104	52,260	5,156
			85	42,000	10,665	10,665	
CANADA	O	E	85	42,000	10,665	10,665	
	O	W	82	10,500	2,205	2,205	
CHINA M	V	E	84	88,184	47,104	52,260	5,156
JAPAN	O	E	82	30	2,438	2,653	215
U KING	V	E	83	8	1,444	1,513	69

Red clover, seed
1262700 CLOVER SEED, RED (LB)

Country	Mode	Reg	Yr	Quantity	F.A.S.	C.I.F.	Charges
TOTAL			81	10,477,070	3,002,372	3,006,664	4,292
			82	13,727,308	4,687,812	4,690,646	2,834
			83	22,524,523	12,355,637	12,363,974	8,337
			84	10,093,420	4,914,382	4,919,349	4,967
			85	5,303,063	2,181,492	2,183,256	1,764
			86	11,020,792	6,184,913	6,185,813	900
AUSTRAL	V	W	84	2,205	1,452	1,600	148
			85	1,102	2,890	3,000	110
CANADA	O	E	81	9,264,255	2,662,419	2,662,419	
			82	12,954,255	4,460,166	4,460,166	
			83	21,123,263	11,625,576	11,625,576	
			84	8,564,398	4,149,474	4,149,474	
			85	4,791,379	1,950,627	1,950,627	
			86	10,770,511	6,034,629	6,034,631	2
	O	W	81	1,167,369	301,399	301,399	
			82	764,140	210,123	210,123	
			83	1,275,470	582,736	582,736	
			84	1,520,203	748,173	748,173	
			85	504,677	206,081	206,081	
			86	236,462	125,000	125,000	
FR GERM	A	E	82	2,315	5,209	7,004	1,795
	O	W	86	5,512	5,126	5,126	
	V	W	83	1,213	2,186	2,304	118
			84	220	485	739	254
FRANCE	A	E	84	381	705	1,072	367
	O	E	84	191	836	836	
INDIA	V	E	81	33,069	11,037	13,558	2,521
JAPAN	A	W	84	912	3,375	6,005	2,630
	N	W	84	800	1,187	2,087	900
			85	5,905	21,894	23,548	1,654
	V	W	81	8,695	16,957	17,838	881
			82	6,190	11,222	12,114	892
			83	4,477	20,016	20,738	722
			84	2,908	5,146	5,573	427
			86	7,095	15,888	16,595	707
N ZEAL	V	W	81	2,204	8,220	8,600	380
NETHLDS	V	W	83	1,104	3,192	3,312	120
NORWAY	V	W	82	110	300	333	33
SWEDEN	O	E	83	118,996	121,931	129,308	7,377
SWITZLD	V	W	81	1,478	2,340	2,850	510
			82	298	792	906	114
			84	1,202	3,549	3,790	241

Crop Product TSUSA commodity number, description, and unit of quantity Country	Mode	Reg	Yr	Quantity	F.A.S.	C.I.F.	Charges
			86	1,212	4,270	4,461	191

Sweet clover, seed
1262900 CLOVER SEED, SWEET (LB)

Country	Mode	Reg	Yr	Quantity	F.A.S.	C.I.F.	Charges
TOTAL			81	6,750,305	1,648,058	1,648,058	
			82	8,501,372	1,937,463	1,937,463	
			83	21,853,566	7,310,205	7,310,275	70
			84	7,543,634	2,091,545	2,093,034	1,489
			85	6,978,932	1,658,250	1,658,252	2
			86	13,240,651	4,766,769	4,768,173	1,404
CANADA	O	E	81	6,332,865	1,554,948	1,554,948	
			82	8,201,972	1,869,924	1,869,924	
			83	21,433,886	7,186,130	7,186,130	
			84	6,983,270	1,921,844	1,921,844	
			85	6,702,802	1,595,788	1,595,788	
			86	12,743,342	4,586,091	4,587,495	1,404
	O	W	81	417,440	93,110	93,110	
			82	299,400	67,539	67,539	
			83	419,306	123,415	123,415	
			84	514,864	139,340	139,340	
			85	276,130	62,462	62,464	2
			86	497,309	180,678	180,678	
ITALY	V	E	83	374	660	730	70
NETHLDS	V	E	84	45,500	30,361	31,850	1,489

White clover, seed
1263100 CLOVER SEED, WHITE A LADINO (LB)

Country	Mode	Reg	Yr	Quantity	F.A.S.	C.I.F.	Charges
TOTAL			81	1,022,152	905,609	984,656	79,047
			82	334,239	346,741	379,420	32,679
			83	1,036,988	949,023	1,014,172	65,149
			84	944,899	580,980	629,292	48,312
			85	1,143,994	729,163	793,973	64,810
			86	642,761	498,772	537,801	39,029
ARGENT	O	E	86	11,500	9,307	9,307	
	V	E	85	202,823	103,786	118,400	14,614
			86	39,683	38,187	41,400	3,213
	V	W	85	22,046	13,918	15,655	1,737
AUSTRAL	V	H	81	400	2,787	2,898	111
	V	W	81	220	803	867	64
			85	4,409	2,898	3,100	202
CANADA	O	E	81	10,197	3,433	3,433	
			83	2,685	2,968	2,968	
			84	48,266	32,297	32,297	
			85	46,926	41,292	41,292	
			86	46,500	37,780	37,780	
	O	W	81	187,643	61,214	61,214	
			82	75,790	17,998	17,998	
			83	96,883	26,337	26,337	
			84	259,130	60,037	60,037	
			85	97,600	48,724	48,724	
			86	68,874	35,605	35,605	
DENMARK	A	E	82	441	1,863	2,313	450
	A	W	82	1,023	793	1,048	255
			84	106	360	618	258
	V	W	82	1,091	4,540	4,832	292
			83	540	2,226	2,338	112
			84	886	3,070	3,251	181
FR GERM	A	E	83	220	669	907	238
FRANCE	V	W	82	2,161	7,113	7,563	450
IRELAND	A	E	82	165	975	1,342	367
ISRAEL	A	E	82	507	3,450	4,586	1,136
	V	W	81	772	5,250	5,551	301
			84	5,400	3,528	3,813	285
N ZEAL	A	W	86	770	4,235	5,642	1,407
	N	W	81	313,382	310,836	322,886	12,050
			82	84,991	116,083	124,515	8,432
			83	458,191	456,910	479,114	22,204
			84	294,447	230,010	250,676	20,666
			85	286,026	201,483	214,395	12,912
	O	E	81	59,880	65,077	68,827	3,750
			83	12,511	8,178	8,178	
			84	22,446	19,540	19,540	
			85	20,550	15,411	15,411	
	O	W	81	77,434	76,961	82,551	5,590
			85	20,172	11,796	13,386	1,590
	V	E	81	55,525	57,330	68,482	11,152
			83	54,869	55,898	63,055	7,157
			85	89,172	53,061	60,081	7,020

Crop Product TSUSA commodity number, description, and unit of quantity Country	Mode	Reg	Yr	Quantity	F.A.S.	C.I.F.	Charges
	V	W	81	315,902	317,949	362,872	44,923
			82	167,450	192,614	213,080	20,466
			83	408,669	385,620	420,559	34,939
			84	313,043	227,513	253,749	26,236
			85	351,680	226,128	251,795	25,667
			86	440,238	327,994	358,344	30,350
NETHLDS	V	W	86	32,320	34,784	38,084	3,300
U KING	A	E	81	528	2,798	3,462	664
			82	100	320	479	159
			84	300	1,096	1,351	255
			85	300	1,191	1,602	411
	A	W	81	269	1,171	1,613	442
			82	520	992	1,664	672
			84	84	272	531	259
			85	150	1,307	1,538	231
	V	W	83	2,420	10,217	10,716	499
			84	791	3,257	3,429	172
			85	2,140	8,168	8,594	426
			86	2,876	10,880	11,639	759

Coca

Coca, leaf, natural drug
4354000 COCA LEAVES (LB)

Country	Mode	Reg	Yr	Quantity	F.A.S.	C.I.F.	Charges
TOTAL			81	705,710	702,088	786,866	84,778
			82	701,870	627,376	708,623	81,247
			83	440,000	560,000	618,695	58,695
			84	337,348	401,905	442,270	40,365
			86	150,000	150,000	169,896	19,896
BOLIVIA	V	E	82	250,000	200,000	224,762	24,762
CHINA M	O	E	84	37,348	13,905	15,036	1,131
INDIA	V	E	81	50,000	64,000	70,241	6,241
PERU	V	E	81	655,710	638,088	716,625	78,537
			82	451,870	427,376	483,861	56,485
			83	440,000	560,000	618,695	58,695
			84	300,000	388,000	427,234	39,234
			86	150,000	150,000	169,896	19,896

Cocculus Indicus

Cocculus indicus, natural drug**
4350500 ALOES JALAP MATE ETC, CRUDE (LB)
(See Aloe, natural drug under Aloe)
4351000 ALOES,JALAP MANA,ETC ADVANCE (LB)
(See Aloe, natural drug under Aloe)

Cocoa

Chocolate, sweetened
1562500 CHOC,SWEET,BARS NOT UND 1OLB (LB)

Country	Mode	Reg	Yr	Quantity	F.A.S.	C.I.F.	Charges
TOTAL			81	3,005,404	3,598,048	3,839,865	241,817
			82	4,216,797	4,886,203	5,201,144	314,941
			83	11,776,620	9,933,890	10,729,362	795,472
			84	17,970,909	16,115,815	17,397,655	1,281,840
			85	29,371,739	26,850,803	28,574,998	1,724,195
			86	60,926,422	52,924,477	54,432,486	1,508,009
ARGENT	V	E	85	800	1,840	2,033	193
AUSTRAL	V	W	83	33,069	35,090	39,325	4,235
			84	112,420	127,669	137,101	9,432
			85	224,279	219,941	239,786	19,845
AUSTRIA	V	E	84	38,880	47,239	49,362	2,123
BELGIUM	A	E	82	5,000	7,850	10,595	2,745
			84	5,159	6,767	9,352	2,585
			85	4,449	6,526	9,249	2,723
			86	2,615	5,165	8,556	3,391
	A	H	84	551	1,323	1,948	625
	N	E	81	327,425	453,700	486,792	33,092
			82	663,322	753,873	809,435	55,562
			83	772,590	814,813	853,676	38,863
			84	1,249,353	1,425,849	1,523,719	97,870
			85	1,960,026	2,230,929	2,406,139	175,210
	N	W	83	9,422	15,440	16,139	699

Country	Mode	Reg	Yr	Quantity	F.A.S.	C.I.F.	Charges
			84	91,860	103,364	114,982	11,618
			85	2,021,696	2,391,116	2,638,864	247,748
	O	E	81	1,047	1,422	1,647	225
			82	1,444	1,323	1,481	158
			83	1,213	1,346	1,546	200
			84	67,460	94,220	98,323	4,103
			85	2,205	2,821	3,096	275
	O	W	81	880	1,839	1,839	
			82	1,211	1,856	1,856	
			85	60,927	27,384	30,863	3,479
			86	4,186	10,326	10,326	
	V	E	81	160,492	216,139	230,986	14,847
			82	631,710	699,361	757,660	58,299
			83	1,794,649	1,832,838	1,952,126	119,288
			84	4,338,305	4,507,638	4,945,220	437,582
			85	5,335,890	5,736,174	6,351,318	615,144
			86	7,690,681	9,580,594	10,273,048	692,454
	V	W	81	264,552	362,467	386,907	24,440
			82	484,012	595,531	641,136	45,605
			83	713,882	784,307	860,509	76,202
			84	432,615	480,488	530,656	50,168
			86	1,893,817	2,424,784	2,631,734	206,950
BNGLDSH	O	W	86	386	1,035	1,035	
BRAZIL	V	E	81	291,008	221,754	247,313	25,559
			82	79,019	50,386	57,090	6,704
			83	2,902,282	1,667,424	1,892,508	225,084
			84	3,847,577	2,699,705	2,967,022	267,317
			85	6,282,456	4,359,254	4,791,521	432,267
			86	7,087,549	4,460,420	4,955,919	495,499
	V	W	84	79,366	61,740	73,030	11,290
			86	37,478	22,977	25,753	2,776
C RICA	A	E	82	530	1,063	1,416	353
			83	530	1,063	1,411	348
	V	E	83	100,700	75,778	82,011	6,233
			84	300,000	245,952	262,620	16,668
			85	161,764	122,517	130,539	8,022
			86	206,764	139,911	149,094	9,183
CANADA	O	E	83	1,526	1,588	1,728	140
			84	384,732	404,508	404,508	
			85	9,637,147	8,171,332	8,171,332	
			86	42,677,598	34,346,661	34,346,661	
	O	H	84	276	519	713	194
	O	W	81	450	361	361	
			82	1,102	2,062	2,062	
			83	331	735	735	
			84	2,753	3,606	3,606	
			85	13,051	14,912	14,912	
			86	4,076	4,397	4,397	
COLOMB	N	E	86	6,250	9,283	9,850	567
	V	E	83	13,400	23,059	23,577	518
			84	15,698	15,154	16,103	949
			86	3,307	4,200	4,440	240
DOM REP	V	E	81	45,000	30,105	31,524	1,419
ECUADOR	V	E	81	421,411	367,150	392,634	25,484
			82	104,696	66,063	71,605	5,542
			83	1,712,351	1,156,863	1,267,565	110,702
			84	562,171	359,210	393,484	34,274
			85	460,761	466,040	493,128	27,088
			86	110,230	129,484	136,762	7,278
	V	W	84	640	1,648	1,760	112
FR GERM	N	E	83	86,742	108,287	113,549	5,262
	V	E	82	10,301	9,671	9,977	306
			84	7,154	7,837	8,355	518
			85	56,120	64,075	69,205	5,130
			86	23,700	33,497	36,028	2,531
	V	W	82	3,086	7,032	7,093	61
			85	39,958	55,075	59,075	4,000
FRANCE	A	E	81	264	804	1,308	504
			84	319	994	1,210	216
			86	2,977	10,026	12,289	2,263
	N	E	85	63,382	92,404	100,084	7,680
	O	E	84	2,205	2,593	2,764	171
			85	4,630	5,797	6,668	871
	O	W	86	2,864	5,324	5,449	125
	V	E	81	163,613	246,299	256,735	10,436
			82	38,867	44,404	46,658	2,254
			83	52,090	95,547	98,260	2,713
			84	64,870	94,585	100,704	6,119
			85	17,560	27,965	29,787	1,822
			86	493,026	713,806	741,078	27,272
	V	W	81	2,249	2,621	2,839	218
			86	111,645	134,777	147,667	12,890
ISRAEL	V	E	83	37,082	50,310	53,471	3,161
			84	119,691	145,326	158,035	12,709

Crop
Product
TSUSA commodity number, description, and unit of quantity

Country	Mode	Reg	Yr	Quantity	F.A.S.	C.I.F.	Charges
ITALY	O	E	86	42,009	34,490	34,490	
IVY CST	V	E	81	198,415	209,845	224,460	14,615
			83	1,425,281	863,310	965,277	101,967
			84	5,428,786	4,229,791	4,488,430	258,639
			85	1,744,765	1,233,389	1,313,389	80,000
JAMAICA	A	E	84	3,929	6,308	7,906	1,598
JAPAN	A	W	84	192	959	1,099	140
	V	E	84	64	1,053	1,200	147
MEXICO	O	E	84	58,153	51,431	51,431	
			85	11,295	11,295	11,295	
	V	E	83	40,000	30,400	32,443	2,043
NETHLDS	V	E	81	2,205	4,581	4,764	183
			82	217,393	286,998	303,329	16,331
			83	78,640	94,183	96,170	1,987
			84	151,123	185,853	198,228	12,375
			85	201,224	99,835	118,478	18,643
			86	40,013	58,500	62,020	3,520
	V	W	84	40,597	41,161	45,086	3,925
			86	40,565	57,869	62,946	5,077
PANAMA	V	E	84	44,092	100,751	104,223	3,472
PORTUGL	V	E	84	3,907	2,275	2,481	206
SINGAPR	V	E	83	115,742	192,698	198,594	5,896
SPAIN	V	E	85	42,500	12,203	15,848	3,645
SWEDEN	A	E	84	77	452	462	10
SWITZLD	A	E	85	297	1,304	1,659	355
	A	W	84	873	2,572	3,130	558
	N	E	84	65,433	84,095	89,528	5,433
			85	120,428	206,036	216,945	10,909
			86	283,919	437,873	454,270	16,397
	N	W	85	51,652	73,888	79,031	5,143
			86	5,161	17,646	22,158	4,512
	O	E	81	4,557	8,080	8,563	483
			82	14,120	22,451	23,844	1,393
			83	3,748	5,145	5,511	366
			84	33,338	50,044	52,177	2,133
			85	48,154	68,181	73,072	4,891
			86	6,614	12,548	12,971	423
	O	W	85	1,848	2,526	2,692	166
	V	E	81	1,108,679	1,448,648	1,537,843	89,195
			82	1,960,306	2,334,257	2,453,235	118,978
			83	1,877,147	2,072,386	2,161,140	88,754
			84	402,477	498,176	523,668	25,492
			85	797,986	1,137,920	1,186,211	48,291
			86	146,611	264,171	278,549	14,378
	V	W	81	1,581	3,711	3,933	222
			83	4,203	11,280	12,091	811
			84	882	1,725	1,848	123
			85	4,489	8,124	8,779	655
			86	2,381	4,713	4,996	283
U KING	V	E	81	11,576	18,522	19,417	895
			84	12,931	21,235	22,181	946
VENEZ	A	E	82	678	2,022	2,672	650

1563020 CHOC SWEET, CANDY-CONFECTON (LB)

Country	Mode	Reg	Yr	Quantity	F.A.S.	C.I.F.	Charges
TOTAL			81	6,259,900	11,419,918	11,977,854	579,783
			82	12,261,954	17,825,022	18,602,916	778,291
			83	11,771,234	18,714,538	19,844,574	1,130,036
			84	15,659,093	24,562,374	26,209,154	1,646,780
			85	16,073,001	25,256,504	27,030,659	1,774,155
			86	9,361,498	18,860,141	20,046,861	1,186,720
ARGENT	A	W	86	2,248	3,024	4,523	1,499
AUSTRAL	A	E	81	165	427	593	166
	A	H	86	214	1,381	1,440	59
	A	W	84	755	1,767	3,470	1,703
			86	27,299	29,872	40,836	10,964
	V	E	82	6,582	14,423	15,176	753
			86	858	1,487	1,607	120
	V	H	82	379	650	719	69
	V	W	85	50,957	60,180	74,720	14,540
AUSTRIA	A	E	81	1,647	4,054	4,844	790
	A	W	82	8,629	21,252	30,421	9,169
			85	2,811	7,797	10,186	2,389
	N	E	81	6,632	20,865	22,169	1,304
			83	4,063	9,904	10,590	686
			84	66,605	154,967	164,462	9,495
			85	263,986	332,204	354,748	22,544
			86	7,315	28,654	32,634	3,980
	N	W	83	1,557	3,959	5,034	1,075
			84	6,787	15,290	19,134	3,844
	O	E	85	23,119	31,320	34,277	2,957
			86	4,400	2,261	2,261	
	V	E	82	18,563	31,448	34,533	3,085
			84	5,740	15,795	21,376	5,581

Crop
Product
TSUSA commodity number, description, and unit of quantity

Country	Mode	Reg	Yr	Quantity	F.A.S.	C.I.F.	Charges
			85	20,757	59,153	71,339	12,186
			86	50,805	125,337	132,747	7,410
	V	W	84	3,032	3,229	4,410	1,181
			85	4,478	10,135	10,851	716
BELGIUM	A	E	81	1,777	12,096	13,848	1,752
			82	3,854	15,504	20,277	4,773
			83	11,832	41,785	47,402	5,617
			84	6,704	17,926	22,038	4,112
			85	10,650	25,559	32,438	6,879
			86	17,408	84,320	102,564	18,244
	A	W	81	1,848	9,118	10,822	1,704
			82	88	788	1,294	506
			83	392	2,057	2,561	504
			84	617	3,142	3,697	555
			86	651	2,708	3,485	777
	N	E	81	19,372	130,796	138,528	7,732
			82	102,400	165,751	182,039	16,288
			83	337,028	401,985	438,174	36,189
			84	464,276	803,079	888,885	85,806
			85	623,899	859,343	961,153	101,810
			86	228,779	415,999	461,174	45,175
	N	W	82	51,814	93,927	103,116	9,189
			83	9,269	30,443	33,083	2,640
			84	30,041	61,087	71,177	10,090
			85	50,379	81,184	94,357	13,173
			86	58,824	151,494	177,154	25,660
	O	E	86	7,002	22,488	24,108	1,620
	O	W	83	75	427	427	
	V	E	81	41,452	88,579	94,589	6,010
			82	13,756	13,047	14,495	1,448
			83	1,630	5,659	5,903	244
			84	107,814	177,860	185,916	8,056
			85	62,178	120,163	127,933	7,770
			86	73,973	212,157	233,074	20,917
	V	W	83	6,376	7,322	8,665	1,343
			85	11,954	26,764	29,727	2,963
			86	30,752	57,554	62,096	4,542
BRAZIL	A	E	81	209	337	814	477
			82	254	800	1,441	641
	V	E	82	32,170	35,710	37,556	1,846
			83	60,427	72,671	83,583	10,912
			84	222,510	174,709	191,903	17,194
			85	222,832	138,086	154,854	16,768
			86	3,385	1,480	1,687	207
C RICA	V	E	81	38,600	26,011	29,761	3,750
			82	109,793	83,451	95,576	12,125
			86	88,184	191,786	195,945	4,159
CANADA	A	E	81	1,370	1,939	2,431	492
			82	202	300	361	61
			83	2,972	25,365	27,685	2,320
			84	1,711	2,915	3,764	849
			85	3,750	2,382	2,382	
			86	400	3,871	4,171	300
	A	W	85	108	1,767	1,949	182
	N	E	81	14,304	49,641	51,830	2,189
			82	57,692	158,860	159,766	906
			83	563,510	615,541	616,818	1,277
			84	738,228	898,443	899,774	1,331
			85	211,389	357,801	358,799	998
			86	141,930	227,733	227,781	48
	O	E	81	1,793,647	3,131,218	3,131,218	
			82	6,193,721	7,091,393	7,091,645	252
			83	2,767,668	3,336,568	3,337,794	1,226
			84	3,850,831	4,775,811	4,777,039	1,228
			85	4,680,499	5,883,382	5,886,175	2,793
			86	2,868,888	3,995,213	3,995,213	
	O	W	81	8,652	14,599	14,599	
			82	2,947	12,036	12,036	
			83	105	431	431	
			84	664	2,519	2,519	
			85	1,600	5,106	5,106	
			86	13,475	11,122	11,122	
	V	E	86	3,028	20,571	21,275	704
CHINA M	V	E	83	911	2,284	2,409	125
			84	647	1,413	1,492	79
	V	W	82	200	499	524	25
			83	540	546	586	40
			84	7,739	2,754	3,020	266
CHINA T	A	E	86	276	1,854	2,690	836
COLOMB	A	E	83	842	880	920	40
			86	1,429	1,584	1,969	385
	N	E	83	15,334	22,436	24,721	2,285
			84	7,750	9,501	10,529	1,028
			85	46,639	61,185	70,752	9,567

Crop
Product
TSUSA commodity number, description, and unit of quantity

Country	Mode	Reg	Yr	Quantity	F.A.S.	C.I.F.	Charges
			86	26,866	27,530	31,861	4,331
	V	E	81	15,298	19,206	22,815	3,609
			82	3,805	5,940	6,427	487
			84	10,233	11,790	12,448	658
			85	3,675	6,750	7,083	333
			86	6,614	6,000	6,449	449
CYPRUS	A	E	81	255	594	1,335	741
	A	W	86	1,173	4,767	7,171	2,404
	V	E	82	2,434	4,609	4,940	331
CZECHO	N	E	85	18,184	49,793	57,776	7,983
	O	E	85	540	1,417	1,417	
	V	E	81	29,968	67,145	77,546	10,401
			82	23,951	54,614	60,298	5,684
			83	42,706	99,972	107,517	7,545
			84	33,934	80,494	88,793	8,299
			86	31,598	82,590	96,735	14,145
	V	W	81	1,963	4,149	4,286	137
DENMARK	A	E	81	44	313	458	145
	N	E	82	6,823	16,544	18,139	1,595
			83	5,253	29,923	32,944	3,021
			84	4,862	10,710	13,419	2,709
	O	E	81	583	3,177	3,680	503
	V	E	81	3,746	13,990	14,923	933
			84	2,252	4,364	4,501	137
			85	18,213	30,687	31,946	1,259
			86	99,781	127,764	136,096	8,332
	V	W	81	122	328	376	48
			82	6,908	29,003	31,442	2,439
			83	2,985	6,560	7,409	849
			85	2,028	4,490	7,508	3,018
DOM REP	A	E	81	5,375	1,625	2,153	528
			83	568	610	686	76
			84	7,176	7,958	9,167	1,209
			85	11,150	9,803	11,249	1,446
			86	18,832	16,555	19,492	2,937
	N	E	82	8,748	3,418	5,242	1,824
	V	E	81	65,675	95,664	99,091	3,427
			82	45,000	23,198	24,834	1,636
			83	400	400	599	199
			84	45,000	37,544	39,650	2,106
			85	49,500	30,875	35,409	4,534
ECUADOR	A	E	81	607	1,336	2,131	795
	V	E	82	1,584	3,468	3,658	190
FINLAND	A	E	81	581	1,267	2,443	1,176
			82	2,154	9,354	10,582	1,228
			83	212	1,429	1,469	40
			84	486	1,929	2,029	100
	A	W	82	385	796	796	397
	V	E	83	22,242	20,869	24,299	3,430
			84	18,462	19,789	21,157	1,368
	V	W	83	18,519	16,668	20,230	3,562
			84	73,571	69,168	78,960	9,792
FR GERM	A	E	81	346	1,236	1,570	334
			82	9	396	403	7
			83	804	867	1,518	651
			84	8,319	22,044	25,150	3,106
			85	3,681	14,878	18,980	4,102
	A	W	82	23	502	575	73
	N	E	81	636,339	1,181,586	1,269,261	87,675
			82	1,072,717	2,325,755	2,449,875	124,120
			83	1,050,127	1,798,187	1,927,400	129,213
			84	3,094,161	3,849,071	4,165,174	316,103
			85	1,831,557	3,380,183	3,757,059	376,876
			86	935,460	2,102,704	2,252,875	150,171
	N	W	83	43,137	84,439	96,771	12,332
			84	51,871	88,791	102,811	14,020
			85	98,656	208,007	244,467	36,460
			86	138,847	380,763	417,665	36,902
	O	E	81	39,009	79,124	84,923	5,799
			82	7,000	10,091	10,806	715
			83	7,604	27,427	29,161	1,734
			84	21,580	52,452	54,575	2,123
			85	66,916	95,878	95,878	
			86	31,115	86,186	94,031	7,845
	O	W	81	60	423	423	
			82	117	876	876	
	V	E	81	855,150	998,019	1,066,024	68,005
			82	1,230,645	1,192,996	1,300,184	107,188
			83	1,602,061	1,443,747	1,569,013	125,266
			84	273,972	443,541	493,642	50,101
			85	1,397,813	1,798,766	1,978,652	179,886
			86	510,104	883,819	973,930	90,111
	V	W	81	82,567	217,536	245,498	27,962
			82	104,100	229,015	258,386	29,371

Crop
Product
TSUSA commodity number, description, and unit of quantity

Country	Mode	Reg	Yr	Quantity	F.A.S.	C.I.F.	Charges
			83	70,728	126,042	145,836	19,794
			84	64,842	125,916	151,643	25,727
			85	89,590	140,216	160,038	19,822
			86	33,077	65,824	72,552	6,728
FRANCE	A	E	82	897	2,319	2,979	660
			83	1,033	4,706	5,956	1,250
			84	3,362	13,170	16,081	2,911
			86	800	4,293	5,164	871
	A	W	83	319	1,480	2,058	578
			84	1,870	9,400	10,652	1,252
			86	3,143	18,130	20,924	2,794
	N	E	81	26,556	57,363	67,486	10,123
			82	74,488	165,869	178,128	12,259
			83	52,016	83,863	94,906	11,043
			84	321,631	872,698	955,895	83,197
			85	481,492	888,595	980,200	91,605
			86	275,347	554,554	602,564	48,010
	N	W	81	1,555	2,241	2,695	454
			82	43,176	98,078	114,599	16,521
			83	23,536	63,301	71,387	8,086
			84	16,682	43,693	49,251	5,558
			85	25,435	45,249	59,529	14,280
			86	19,817	84,272	96,493	12,221
	O	E	82	3,148	3,602	4,074	472
			83	9,811	14,056	14,881	825
			84	15,207	21,813	24,186	2,373
			85	25,509	46,186	52,842	6,656
			86	39,233	39,233	48,553	9,320
	V	E	82	776	2,000	2,196	196
			83	14,073	22,549	23,399	850
			84	73,434	107,156	116,494	9,338
			85	257,424	337,891	360,120	22,229
			86	197,851	473,046	507,442	34,396
	V	W	86	1,482	11,870	12,586	716
GABON	O	E	86	26,076	42,255	42,255	
GERM DR	V	E	83	340	405	585	180
			84	4,762	7,087	7,785	698
			86	2,397	11,712	12,526	814
GREECE	A	E	81	1,676	2,911	3,989	1,078
			83	7,822	14,608	21,352	6,744
			84	777	1,506	2,430	924
			85	3,792	6,492	10,772	4,280
	A	W	82	4,598	9,293	13,326	4,033
	N	E	84	7,896	16,617	23,302	6,685
	O	E	83	106	286	286	
			84	269	492	492	
	V	E	81	1,120	1,355	1,574	219
			82	2,415	1,670	2,002	332
			83	871	450	534	84
			85	38,582	58,494	65,092	6,598
			86	5,620	11,534	12,761	1,227
GUATMAL	A	W	82	450	337	425	88
	V	E	85	7,592	7,003	7,510	507
HG KONG	V	E	81	825	5,108	5,254	146
			83	3,457	16,209	16,539	330
			84	11,034	51,821	53,388	1,567
			85	1,199	7,686	7,877	191
	V	W	83	936	3,113	3,240	127
			84	235	780	817	37
HUNGARY	N	E	84	8,680	20,835	22,152	1,317
	O	E	82	1,944	2,492	2,913	421
	V	E	82	3,386	5,701	7,636	1,935
			83	2,909	7,258	8,448	1,190
			85	77,282	87,793	103,245	15,452
			86	111,673	148,374	172,734	24,360
	V	W	81	2,543	4,124	5,541	1,417
			86	8,858	10,894	12,837	1,943
ICELAND	O	E	85	80,000	43,227	46,673	3,446
IRAN	O	E	85	124,000	83,965	90,728	6,763
			86	40,000	21,171	22,700	1,529
IRELAND	O	E	84	163	309	368	59
	V	E	81	2,560	4,355	5,303	948
			83	750	288	588	300
ISRAEL	A	E	84	8,254	28,018	38,890	10,872
			85	9,012	15,840	16,493	653
	N	E	83	205,071	306,881	329,566	22,685
	O	E	83	833	566	566	
			84	499	1,429	1,429	
	V	E	81	237,619	513,507	541,671	28,164
			82	279,428	515,647	547,434	31,787
			83	113,565	224,234	239,616	15,382
			84	358,354	718,923	777,014	58,091
			85	406,993	767,138	820,723	53,585
			86	163,662	329,261	362,619	33,358

Crop
Product
TSUSA commodity number, description, and unit of quantity

Country	Mode	Reg	Yr	Quantity	F.A.S.	C.I.F.	Charges
	V	W	83	5,031	9,508	9,958	450
			84	3,860	8,503	8,991	488
			86	8,642	16,877	18,655	1,778
ITALY	A	E	82	411	1,847	2,687	840
			83	209	534	1,284	750
			84	4,718	11,130	15,358	4,228
			85	5,368	12,836	17,729	4,893
			86	1,829	8,154	11,407	3,253
	A	W	83	3,110	6,225	8,315	2,090
			86	2,230	5,117	7,420	2,303
	N	E	82	133,966	456,460	492,684	36,224
			83	289,244	998,135	1,068,102	69,967
			84	220,932	977,033	1,060,079	83,046
			85	167,144	671,974	736,790	64,816
			86	59,249	196,838	225,992	29,154
	N	W	85	31,432	86,114	104,878	18,764
			86	26,039	95,982	108,948	12,966
	O	E	81	119	788	849	61
			82	10,956	20,460	21,483	1,023
			83	12,704	23,311	24,466	1,155
			84	3,207	6,327	6,637	310
			86	1,562	9,570	9,570	
	O	W	84	1,124	4,305	5,494	1,189
	V	E	81	209,986	630,465	697,277	66,812
			82	627	933	1,045	112
			84	12,508	15,844	18,778	2,934
			85	35,398	113,853	122,975	9,122
			86	37,779	190,416	217,026	26,610
	V	W	81	1,151	5,696	6,460	764
			84	6,054	13,765	14,841	1,076
			85	898	5,396	6,212	816
JAMAICA	A	E	81	960	4,326	4,826	500
			82	2,040	6,489	7,289	800
			83	225	340	860	520
			84	2,543	3,199	4,706	1,507
			85	3,962	5,431	6,310	879
	N	E	86	25,778	34,877	39,205	4,328
	V	E	82	525	978	1,183	205
JAPAN	A	E	81	145	315	822	507
			82	2,000	12,381	15,851	3,470
			84	15	286	300	14
	A	W	82	115	608	797	189
			86	539	4,537	6,060	1,523
	N	E	81	40,158	75,014	81,804	6,790
			84	5,520	21,433	26,349	4,916
			85	6,499	28,236	32,717	4,481
	N	H	83	1,389	10,780	12,833	2,053
	N	W	82	2,686	11,036	15,277	4,241
			83	42,889	223,595	240,085	16,490
			84	30,869	165,954	175,558	9,604
			85	15,643	87,062	97,420	10,358
			86	15,256	44,652	50,297	5,645
	O	E	82	124	966	966	
	V	E	82	26,075	130,717	145,649	14,932
			83	11,310	78,903	89,221	10,318
			84	147	822	905	83
			86	3,206	7,112	9,104	1,992
	V	W	81	376	745	833	88
			82	100	393	409	16
			83	124	595	622	27
			84	183	1,191	1,388	197
			86	8,191	35,068	37,227	2,159
KIRIBAT	O	E	85	310	1,240	1,291	51
KOR REP	V	W	86	1,975	2,764	3,198	434
LEBANON	A	E	83	2,740	26,353	31,604	5,251
	A	W	83	210	2,882	2,917	35
			86	3,432	5,148	8,221	3,073
	V	E	85	1,377	1,630	1,747	117
MEXICO	A	W	84	220	800	850	50
	O	E	81	238,771	311,106	311,106	
			82	251,221	217,810	217,810	
			83	209,075	138,206	138,206	
			84	323,837	236,343	236,343	
			85	183,943	217,604	217,604	
			86	125,520	101,829	101,829	
	O	W	82	3,481	2,325	2,325	
			85	62,924	54,494	54,494	
N ZEAL	A	W	83	12	422	479	57
	V	E	85	280	1,343	1,384	41
			86	2,205	3,885	5,000	1,115
NETHLDS	A	E	82	152	281	544	263
			83	256	883	992	109
			84	6,631	13,873	18,444	4,571
	A	W	84	602	2,034	2,384	350
			86	11,384	4,898	9,582	4,684
	N	E	81	3,752	6,673	7,211	538
			83	745,609	1,595,039	1,710,895	115,856
			84	591,929	1,164,501	1,262,580	98,079
			85	917,341	1,748,112	1,880,845	132,733
			86	477,489	1,356,955	1,438,119	81,164
	N	W	82	18,629	41,475	47,870	6,395
			83	327,567	764,292	842,856	78,564
			84	46,095	52,089	57,720	5,631
			85	35,147	70,855	84,196	13,341
	O	E	81	10	263	263	
			82	7,729	20,952	22,804	1,852
			83	35,302	63,742	65,496	1,754
			84	12,835	22,510	24,000	1,490
			85	28,137	66,844	67,985	1,141
			86	7,644	17,607	19,336	1,729
	O	W	83	72	305	305	
	V	E	81	584,863	994,697	1,047,757	53,060
			82	458,383	946,390	989,904	43,514
			83	165,777	282,533	306,892	24,359
			84	33,786	48,411	54,515	6,104
			85	64,326	153,364	164,208	10,844
			86	183,741	423,052	446,807	23,755
	V	W	81	4,766	11,737	13,569	1,832
			82	1,071	2,179	2,734	555
			86	27,785	89,141	95,165	6,024
NORWAY	A	E	85	543	1,861	3,310	1,449
	A	W	83	220	765	897	132
			84	231	712	1,327	615
			86	555	2,078	2,750	672
	N	E	81	4,454	8,672	9,741	1,069
			83	15,825	32,740	37,002	4,262
			85	15,986	36,522	39,151	2,629
			86	7,559	18,511	20,847	2,336
	O	W	81	508	1,313	1,415	102
			82	135	307	345	38
	V	E	82	31,757	50,532	55,913	5,381
			83	838	1,757	2,080	323
			84	23,174	40,821	46,599	5,778
			85	2,703	4,935	5,685	750
	V	W	81	108	256	284	28
			82	2,463	4,912	5,485	573
PANAMA	A	E	86	1,017	1,086	2,003	917
PERU	V	E	85	554	1,088	1,288	200
			86	1,739	3,602	3,759	157
PHIL R	V	W	84	635	387	441	54
POLAND	N	E	82	16,932	34,197	36,533	2,336
	O	E	83	12,698	26,918	28,455	1,537
	V	E	81	23,589	25,078	26,895	1,817
			86	3,175	5,223	5,663	440
PORTUGL	A	E	84	1,309	7,112	9,324	2,212
			85	2,138	3,382	5,136	1,754
	N	E	85	6,314	21,297	24,004	2,707
	O	E	83	1,500	2,695	2,695	
	V	E	81	14,333	29,831	33,328	3,497
			82	4,295	5,891	6,442	551
			83	2,444	4,599	4,779	180
			84	2,331	7,215	7,369	154
			86	9,582	26,628	29,435	2,807
	V	W	85	73	2,533	2,602	69
REP SAF	A	E	82	224	505	1,180	675
SINGAPR	V	W	82	8,831	29,315	32,615	3,300
			83	37,818	107,721	120,418	12,697
			85	27,865	78,311	85,521	7,210
			86	14,349	34,096	36,453	2,357
SPAIN	O	E	85	4,500	5,832	5,832	
	V	E	81	2,866	9,581	10,265	684
			82	4,927	7,670	8,927	1,257
			84	75,303	60,016	67,266	7,250
			85	17,629	32,867	35,854	2,987
			86	28,153	89,405	94,511	5,106
SRI LKA	V	E	85	866	1,836	1,902	66
SWEDEN	A	E	83	145	721	762	41
			84	1	304	723	419
			86	12,143	31,874	40,476	8,602
	A	W	86	304	1,037	1,427	390
	N	E	84	244,916	512,340	567,187	54,847
			85	249,175	569,205	617,732	48,527
	V	E	82	18,871	4,682	5,458	776
			83	87,654	104,691	118,504	13,813
			84	220	466	496	30
			86	457,883	1,085,407	1,152,583	67,176
	V	W	81	2,103	2,523	2,732	209
			83	17,367	29,433	31,631	2,198

Crop Product TSUSA commodity number, description, and unit of quantity Country	Mode	Reg	Yr	Quantity	F.A.S.	C.I.F.	Charges
SWITZLD	A E		81	2,249	6,583	9,992	3,409
			82	1,774	6,636	8,667	2,031
			83	4,511	36,930	37,711	781
			84	9,258	42,174	49,886	7,712
			85	3,167	15,331	17,929	2,598
			86	14,372	86,953	107,060	20,107
	A W		86	550	2,896	3,959	1,063
	N E		81	1,108,395	2,263,578	2,376,413	134,682
			82	1,051,094	2,199,971	2,326,070	126,099
			83	1,439,601	3,069,755	3,221,517	151,762
			84	1,184,744	2,320,101	2,517,455	197,354
			85	963,021	1,922,993	2,074,997	152,004
			86	952,670	2,313,760	2,424,968	111,208
	N W		82	28,509	58,826	63,758	4,932
			83	210,726	383,401	422,477	39,076
			84	79,207	160,909	178,430	17,521
			85	66,489	118,502	129,903	11,401
			86	114,021	532,951	565,085	32,134
	O E		81	147	271	504	233
			84	65,862	125,092	128,948	3,856
			85	7,237	13,008	13,087	79
			86	318	2,015	2,264	249
	O W		86	13,264	32,493	36,276	3,783
	V E		81	4,585	9,303	10,162	859
			82	47,977	90,807	102,648	11,841
			83	163,865	254,857	269,214	14,357
			84	363,283	1,012,525	1,048,622	36,097
			85	355,947	594,890	650,322	55,432
			86	206,379	554,085	588,095	34,010
	V W		81	1,926	3,810	4,504	694
			82	1,764	3,110	3,348	238
			84	7,525	25,917	28,924	3,007
			85	76,278	205,756	221,437	15,681
			86	40,650	49,840	58,121	8,281
TURKEY	O E		85	80,000	43,360	45,832	2,472
U KING	A E		81	687	3,631	5,171	1,540
			82	6,033	6,318	9,814	3,496
			83	6,762	12,171	14,950	2,779
			84	2,403	5,271	6,766	1,495
			85	9,799	16,072	22,314	6,242
			86	5,327	15,369	19,941	4,572
	A W		81	1,279	1,261	1,599	338
			83	1,150	4,397	5,118	721
			84	3,198	3,790	5,854	2,064
			85	2,500	7,797	10,606	2,809
			86	1,615	8,020	9,309	1,289
	N E		81	28,062	133,916	143,720	9,804
			82	230,439	262,253	286,478	24,225
			83	308,162	559,024	604,846	45,822
			84	2,189,997	3,549,743	3,845,635	295,892
			85	88,519	187,975	210,278	22,303
			86	9,799	12,353	16,781	4,428
	N W		81	1,849	7,662	8,546	884
			83	742	3,887	4,544	657
			84	4,508	9,163	12,240	3,077
			85	66,247	105,639	113,255	7,616
			86	9,785	9,327	11,713	2,386
	O E		82	17,177	51,213	57,618	6,405
			83	113,948	142,773	157,954	15,181
			84	3,429	4,594	4,727	133
			85	1,024,056	1,677,896	1,747,046	69,150
	O W		84	170	814	814	
	V E		81	20,834	65,950	70,776	4,826
			82	137,095	322,693	342,934	20,241
			83	357,035	634,779	677,801	43,022
			84	11,854	18,482	21,979	3,497
			85	5,640	12,591	14,589	1,998
			86	32,582	67,233	73,083	5,850
	V W		82	184,356	338,113	379,279	41,166
			86	12,202	46,360	51,174	4,814
URUGUAY	A E		85	2,643	3,625	5,522	1,897
	V E		83	34,857	52,661	57,381	4,720
USSR	O E		81	5,782	18,300	18,300	
	V W		81	340	513	627	114
VENEZ	A E		84	797	1,602	1,825	223
			85	4,255	2,959	3,092	133
			86	1,620	2,417	3,119	702
	N E		86	1,359	3,400	3,668	268
YUGOSLV	A E		84	392	770	1,796	1,026
	O E		84	420	583	583	
	O W		81	85	260	260	
	V E		81	8,845	18,439	21,348	2,909
			82	12,857	14,969	15,943	974
			83	11,178	19,624	21,905	2,281
			84	10,030	17,603	19,368	1,765
			85	6,928	11,240	12,636	1,396
			86	16,255	28,192	31,599	3,407

1563045 CHOC SWT, NO BFT/MILK SOLID (LB)

Country	Mode	Reg	Yr	Quantity	F.A.S.	C.I.F.	Charges
TOTAL			81	7,906,516	8,142,339	8,317,532	175,553
			82	10,744,477	9,585,302	9,875,697	290,395
			83	23,125,062	24,075,916	25,270,868	1,194,952
			84	47,867,770	41,935,900	43,273,102	1,337,202
			85	41,130,914	34,001,621	35,971,685	1,970,064
			86	33,360,469	28,286,584	29,887,887	1,601,303
AUSTRAL	A W		81	200	532	1,198	666
AUSTRIA	A E		83	100	255	332	77
			84	329	1,217	1,537	320
BELGIUM	A E		81	758	6,808	7,101	293
			82	1,286	2,047	2,895	848
			84	2,116	890	1,850	960
			85	1,398	3,312	4,129	817
	N E		84	2,901	7,576	8,482	906
			86	12,567	20,448	22,731	2,283
	N W		82	25,556	40,068	44,356	4,288
			84	43,446	60,467	68,390	7,923
	O W		84	150	975	975	
			85	1,653	1,977	2,228	251
	V E		82	11,023	16,403	16,836	433
			83	3,850	8,259	9,046	787
			84	49,347	66,930	74,654	7,724
			85	60,789	53,648	62,313	8,665
			86	51,731	60,979	69,066	8,087
	V W		81	13,552	21,920	23,453	1,533
			83	47,779	52,938	59,318	6,380
			85	43,535	56,450	62,421	5,971
			86	52,575	76,784	83,843	7,059
BRAZIL	A E		83	2,381	289	2,658	2,369
	N E		85	90,962	63,560	63,560	
	V E		81	47,399	20,890	24,706	3,816
			83	3,411,021	8,389,112	8,975,556	586,444
			84	11,302,873	8,492,689	9,288,883	796,194
			85	18,457,389	13,562,344	14,917,832	1,355,488
			86	10,493,629	7,394,273	8,044,333	650,060
C RICA	V E		81	135,000	90,900	99,807	8,907
			82	74,162	13,600	17,268	3,668
			83	74,014	88,182	94,115	5,933
			84	27,599	23,092	25,760	2,668
			85	600,895	467,372	495,503	28,131
			86	200,144	129,075	137,679	8,604
CAMROON	V E		86	158,731	35,981	44,520	8,539
CANADA	A E		81	3,400	3,059	4,079	1,020
			82	951	922	1,074	152
			84	2,540	2,574	3,547	973
	A W		84	126	279	344	65
	N E		84	5,725,183	5,792,502	5,792,502	
			85	1,478,537	1,399,570	1,399,570	
	N W		84	4,720	12,654	12,654	
	O E		81	5,063,986	5,728,480	5,728,985	865
			82	6,578,574	6,264,287	6,264,287	
			83	10,752,631	9,112,186	9,112,441	255
			84	23,506,707	20,725,479	20,725,575	96
			85	12,353,082	11,221,194	11,221,194	
			86	10,736,102	10,273,797	10,273,797	
	O W		82	1,199	3,466	3,466	
			83	5,766	16,517	16,517	
			84	317	266	266	
			85	126,445	148,221	148,221	
			86	147,333	149,165	149,165	
	V E		86	38,650	33,001	33,001	
CHINA M	V E		85	1,190	1,288	1,425	137
COLOMB	A E		84	3,142	2,850	3,370	520
			86	5,000	7,000	8,030	1,030
	V E		81	66,961	62,263	68,192	5,929
			82	4,409	5,680	5,995	315
			83	6,159	7,084	7,414	330
			84	3,307	3,375	3,515	140
			85	5,732	3,900	7,098	3,198
DENMARK	A E		81	220	328	501	173
	V E		81	11,068	55,084	59,099	4,015
			82	12,666	70,851	76,712	5,861
			83	50,567	196,039	212,039	16,000
			84	39,134	207,682	232,550	24,868
			85	49,227	301,305	337,041	35,736
			86	70,677	387,004	437,397	50,393
	V W		81	6,622	39,542	43,327	3,785
			82	3,523	20,397	23,074	2,677

Crop
Product
TSUSA commodity number, description, and unit of quantity

Country	Mode	Reg	Yr	Quantity	F.A.S.	C.I.F.	Charges
			83	1,976	12,405	13,492	1,087
			84	8,888	50,010	60,307	10,297
			85	21,708	57,533	69,111	11,578
			86	27,293	144,805	167,954	23,149
DOM REP	V	E	81	1,620,000	995,439	1,109,815	114,376
			82	1,629,608	1,039,605	1,152,819	113,214
			83	2,115,000	1,234,663	1,358,736	124,073
			84	3,240,600	2,567,609	2,732,232	164,623
			85	1,710,000	1,209,657	1,321,476	111,819
			86	2,610,600	2,179,062	2,342,553	163,491
ECUADOR	V	E	81	58,069	52,102	55,814	3,712
			82	1,068,027	643,136	710,353	67,217
			83	5,043,793	3,295,530	3,614,034	318,504
			84	2,396,014	2,041,207	2,186,553	145,346
			85	912,025	808,720	865,014	56,294
			86	1,028,450	741,757	798,374	56,617
FR GERM	A	E	82	146	788	989	201
			83	140	511	640	129
			84	1,370	4,416	4,978	562
			85	6,086	27,779	32,332	4,553
			86	1,190	2,158	3,491	1,333
	A	W	81	20	330	377	47
			86	2,021	12,896	15,950	3,054
	N	E	82	54,061	89,043	94,792	5,749
			83	82,138	111,642	118,901	7,259
			84	48,327	71,028	77,463	6,435
			85	69,897	117,128	126,484	9,356
			86	93,456	200,635	211,190	10,555
	N	W	83	3,790	14,114	15,584	1,470
			84	8,371	20,637	22,366	1,729
			85	6,359	22,068	26,374	4,306
			86	1,641	7,713	9,802	2,089
	O	E	81	35	258	340	82
			83	236	303	360	57
			84	441	609	698	89
			85	963	3,785	4,268	483
	O	W	82	1,887	5,217	5,217	
	V	E	81	24,938	31,140	33,774	2,634
			83	9,204	42,251	43,572	1,321
			84	11,550	50,645	55,557	4,912
			85	12,788	49,402	52,659	3,257
			86	35,220	140,885	147,183	6,298
	V	W	82	6,206	14,544	16,138	1,594
			83	3,609	20,527	22,747	2,220
			84	25,733	68,049	82,610	14,561
			85	29,442	60,639	73,571	12,932
			86	5,794	10,045	10,829	784
FRANCE	A	E	81	284	1,887	2,539	652
			82	392	1,917	2,072	155
	N	E	82	7,457	17,413	18,506	1,093
			83	65,193	119,058	127,909	8,851
			84	120,224	173,581	187,018	13,437
			85	53,382	101,710	107,384	5,674
			86	73,622	173,708	182,672	8,964
	N	W	82	46,561	65,252	70,319	5,067
			84	47,445	65,030	72,427	7,397
			85	39,220	65,756	80,827	15,071
	O	E	82	94	356	356	
			85	2,879	4,027	4,577	550
			86	3,502	4,727	5,298	571
	O	W	85	5,732	5,727	6,922	1,195
	V	E	81	23,034	38,620	40,205	1,585
			82	3,317	3,920	4,384	464
			83	15,223	15,082	16,460	1,378
			84	16,485	25,153	26,156	1,003
			85	18,222	31,478	33,776	2,298
			86	65,971	111,007	137,576	26,569
	V	W	81	40,896	68,191	74,822	6,631
			83	60,026	85,281	94,040	8,759
			84	423	1,133	1,221	88
			85	5,468	6,707	7,894	1,187
			86	5,504	11,773	13,079	1,306
GREECE	V	W	84	1,323	1,807	2,040	233
INDIA	V	E	82	1,905	4,702	4,908	206
	V	W	83	420	610	660	50
INDNSIA	V	W	82	444,460	474,800	515,400	40,600
ISRAEL	V	E	82	2,297	1,750	1,988	238
			86	7,200	3,600	3,947	347
ITALY	A	E	84	223	1,098	1,521	423
			85	2,023	12,076	12,496	420
			86	111	1,324	1,492	168
	O	E	85	88,404	72,178	72,178	
	V	E	85	2,182	2,685	2,838	153
			86	1,800	5,424	5,629	205

Crop
Product
TSUSA commodity number, description, and unit of quantity

Country	Mode	Reg	Yr	Quantity	F.A.S.	C.I.F.	Charges
IVY CST	V	E	83	79,445	42,128	48,072	5,944
			85	3,941,402	2,743,884	2,921,884	178,000
			86	6,786,960	4,603,008	5,066,011	463,003
JAMAICA	N	E	82	6,915	15,498	17,970	2,472
	V	E	83	525	1,136	1,397	261
JAPAN	A	W	81	371	2,069	3,161	1,092
			82	456	2,852	4,245	1,393
			84	47	387	528	141
KIRIBAT	V	E	85	219,909	149,600	159,600	10,000
MEXICO	O	E	81	421,426	502,681	502,681	
			82	306,609	289,112	289,112	
			83	299,866	206,266	206,266	
			84	253,201	200,730	200,730	
			85	36,375	32,001	32,001	
			86	61,725	43,707	43,707	
	O	W	81	83,802	87,186	87,186	
			82	166,002	112,559	112,559	
			83	52,744	20,182	20,182	
			86	89,100	32,400	32,400	
NAMIBIA	V	E	85	7,937	7,574	8,096	522
NETHLDS	A	E	81	88	333	395	62
			82	1,565	6,668	6,979	311
			83	3,115	10,809	13,447	2,638
			84	2,115	6,557	7,950	1,393
			85	5,839	18,300	23,509	5,209
			86	8,414	29,983	44,274	14,291
	A	W	81	250	971	1,548	577
			82	2,839	10,997	13,847	2,850
			84	913	3,419	4,888	1,469
			85	5,893	20,864	32,055	11,191
			86	778	3,044	5,418	2,374
	N	E	83	236,643	143,564	164,435	20,871
			84	229,040	107,968	131,121	23,153
	N	W	84	9,841	17,126	18,605	1,479
			85	706	2,658	3,167	509
			86	8,223	23,114	32,087	8,973
	O	W	83	30	255	255	
	V	E	81	31,680	34,038	35,402	1,364
			82	152,152	69,916	77,247	7,331
			83	42,619	25,006	28,073	3,067
	V	W	86	8,936	21,875	25,946	4,071
NORWAY	V	E	83	383	1,231	1,297	66
PHIL R	V	E	84	1,352	393	571	178
PORTUGL	V	E	81	4,431	2,211	2,728	517
			83	2,610	6,936	7,126	190
			84	8,052	8,052	9,952	1,900
			85	1,344	9,152	9,704	552
			86	11,835	13,537	14,779	1,242
SPAIN	V	E	83	377,993	249,309	284,471	35,162
			84	248,480	167,238	189,657	22,419
			85	89,987	58,179	67,638	9,459
			86	22,553	14,397	16,965	2,568
SWEDEN	V	E	81	3,605	7,325	7,711	386
			84	6,667	8,737	10,873	2,136
			86	2,205	4,703	4,864	161
SWITZLD	A	E	81	198	1,245	1,599	354
			82	2,691	3,916	5,232	1,316
			83	446	1,566	1,804	238
			84	1,582	1,567	2,656	1,089
			85	5,948	22,278	26,736	4,458
			86	1,622	8,418	9,775	1,357
	A	W	81	735	2,613	2,969	356
	N	E	81	27,346	54,768	58,481	3,713
			82	20,725	48,140	50,613	2,473
			83	98,777	179,357	186,754	7,397
			84	243,291	415,543	433,037	17,494
			85	13,778	31,752	35,185	3,433
	N	W	82	5,516	15,473	17,656	2,183
			83	4,959	14,661	16,199	1,538
			85	6,443	13,241	15,424	2,183
			86	10,985	22,123	25,137	3,014
	O	E	81	55	290	390	100
			84	320	851	906	55
			85	13,241	24,893	27,224	2,331
			86	27,544	60,474	63,157	2,683
	O	W	85	7,035	14,091	15,189	1,098
	V	E	81	54,078	112,603	118,435	5,832
			82	76,295	181,624	193,788	12,164
			83	138,251	302,512	320,246	17,734
			84	186,878	387,181	427,479	40,298
			85	491,503	858,662	914,735	56,073
			86	386,650	1,078,785	1,134,017	55,232
	V	W	81	179	509	539	30
			82	2,205	2,697	2,941	244

Crop
Product
TSUSA commodity number, description, and unit of quantity

Country	Mode	Reg	Yr	Quantity	F.A.S.	C.I.F.	Charges
			83	529	861	898	37
			84	14,762	34,375	38,844	4,469
			85	8,939	22,290	23,976	1,686
			86	2,425	7,990	8,769	779
TRINID	A	E	82	740	604	819	215
U KING	A	E	85	1,200	1,217	2,066	849
	A	W	81	188	420	636	216
	N	E	83	1,024	2,511	2,797	286
			84	660	1,609	2,517	908
	N	W	84	*	738	743	5
	O	E	81	158,731	109,030	109,030	
			84	1,130	1,147	1,206	59
	V	E	81	2,528	5,043	5,210	167
			82	20,000	25,082	28,485	3,403
			83	29,198	42,850	48,508	5,658
			84	18,085	28,773	32,838	4,065
			85	15,361	26,613	29,455	2,842
	V	W	83	1,272	3,169	3,367	198
			85	460	1,176	1,325	149

1563050 CHOC SWEET OV 5.5% BF QUOTA (LB)

TOTAL			81	11,690,770	7,955,920	8,423,197	467,277
			82	18,827,296	10,312,428	11,389,251	1,076,823
			83	16,239,705	8,188,493	8,857,817	669,324
			84	13,393,283	6,281,221	6,844,955	563,734
			85	19,328,959	10,714,765	12,100,313	1,385,548
			86	15,982,832	8,678,992	9,714,869	1,035,877
AUSTRAL	O	E	85	35,274	17,021	19,521	2,500
	V	E	85	2,709,022	1,591,094	1,818,933	227,839
	V	W	84	493,665	212,625	243,502	30,877
			86	246,915	91,020	102,441	11,421
BELGIUM	V	E	82	1,324	1,523	1,664	141
CANADA	O	E	81	1,500	2,072	2,072	
			82	500	442	442	
			84	550	729	983	254
ECUADOR	V	E	85	44,511	34,163	36,995	2,832
FRANCE	V	E	83	39,683	71,600	73,632	2,032
			85	1,323	1,777	1,893	116
IRELAND	A	W	82	4,640	1,192	1,592	400
	N	E	82	648,898	344,801	380,181	35,380
			84	9,082,500	4,242,707	4,603,436	360,729
	O	E	82	86,000	324,776	330,076	5,300
			83	3,150,000	1,544,075	1,644,321	100,246
			84	40,000	22,061	23,297	1,236
			85	9,700,000	5,552,175	6,221,294	669,119
			86	8,703,800	4,956,858	5,498,809	541,951
	V	E	81	5,339,959	3,383,697	3,716,360	332,663
			82	11,289,789	5,605,973	6,282,408	676,435
			83	6,465,665	3,121,267	3,414,121	292,854
			84	990,000	492,960	550,110	57,150
			85	520,001	278,867	317,000	38,133
			86	600,000	334,851	373,448	38,597
NETHLDS	A	E	83	1,011	3,041	4,019	978
	A	W	83	6,039	4,997	5,615	618
SWITZLD	A	E	81	3	344	346	2
	V	E	81	132	336	358	22
U KING	A	E	82	2,046	1,835	2,100	265
			86	4,844	3,852	6,825	2,973
	N	E	82	4,968,695	2,924,966	3,194,580	269,614
			83	436,678	226,120	246,976	20,856
			86	386,829	232,732	262,747	30,015
	O	E	81	5,238,060	3,752,042	3,831,264	79,222
			82	1,825,404	1,106,920	1,196,208	89,288
			83	5,267,607	2,764,895	2,980,399	215,504
			84	2,786,568	1,310,139	1,423,627	113,488
			85	6,263,736	3,206,893	3,646,943	440,050
			86	5,762,664	2,898,443	3,287,123	388,680
	V	E	81	1,111,116	817,429	872,797	55,368
			83	873,022	452,498	488,734	36,236
			85	55,092	32,775	37,734	4,959
			86	277,780	161,236	183,476	22,240

1563065 CHOC SWT NOV 5.5% BF QUOTA (LB)

TOTAL			81	1,025,553	650,050	705,649	55,599
			82	740,279	471,269	511,097	39,828
			83	1,252,621	1,092,493	1,156,422	63,929
			84	69,521	78,953	85,516	6,563
			85	2,001,409	1,172,291	1,290,777	118,486
			86	957,161	558,989	615,357	56,368
BELGIUM	A	E	81	821	4,984	5,450	466
	O	W	82	188	928	928	
	V	E	82	1,189	1,486	1,605	119

Country	Mode	Reg	Yr	Quantity	F.A.S.	C.I.F.	Charges
CANADA	A	E	82	218	2,767	2,901	134
	O	E	81	572	1,227	1,227	
	O	W	81	7,025	3,634	3,634	
FR GERM	O	W	81	240	1,692	1,692	
IRELAND	A	E	83	84	350	564	214
			84	84	745	824	79
	O	E	81	559,998	363,250	392,824	29,574
			82	440,000	257,718	275,550	17,832
			83	680,000	368,423	391,748	23,325
			84	40,000	22,061	23,297	1,236
			85	2,000,000	1,168,030	1,286,041	118,011
			86	720,000	415,770	457,160	41,390
	V	E	81	362,406	206,244	224,312	18,068
			82	165,000	95,613	106,288	10,675
			83	228,482	162,214	174,833	12,619
			86	160,000	83,266	92,641	9,375
	V	W	81	80,000	57,385	62,400	5,015
			82	120,082	82,525	89,614	7,089
ITALY	A	E	84	486	1,743	2,054	311
NETHLDS	A	E	84	2,833	6,086	7,699	1,613
SWITZLD	A	E	84	84	638	785	147
	N	E	83	90,558	159,342	168,675	9,333
	V	E	81	445	996	1,062	66
			84	16,407	31,993	34,081	2,088
	V	W	84	7,391	12,696	13,572	876
U KING	A	E	82	1,075	1,383	2,281	898
			83	14,200	14,071	15,212	1,141
			84	712	1,869	1,927	58
	N	E	83	159,297	345,689	359,350	13,661
	O	E	82	200	337	337	
			84	1,524	1,122	1,277	155
	O	W	82	418	2,000	2,000	
	V	E	81	14,286	12,330	14,740	2,410
			82	11,669	24,820	27,901	3,081
			83	80,000	42,404	46,040	3,636
			85	1,409	4,261	4,736	475
			86	77,161	59,953	65,556	5,603

Chocolate, unsweetened
1562000 CHOCOLATE, UNSWEETENED (LB)

TOTAL			81	72,992,837	84,251,859	89,196,049	4,971,190
			82	69,266,826	67,787,987	72,372,158	4,584,171
			83	100,256,331	91,665,768	98,170,891	6,505,123
			84	100,413,369	127,278,520	133,982,918	6,704,398
			85	116,936,797	137,167,827	144,500,769	7,332,942
			86	111,783,632	125,425,650	132,043,452	6,617,802
ARGENT	O	E	83	44,096	54,679	54,679	
	V	E	84	220,460	128,000	141,107	13,107
BELGIUM	A	E	83	1,708	2,496	2,592	96
			85	9,936	13,275	18,555	5,280
	N	E	85	36,925	42,046	44,461	2,415
	V	E	83	551	900	953	53
			84	73,065	87,560	92,483	4,923
			85	950	1,945	2,133	188
			86	13,219	28,313	29,304	991
	V	W	83	39,959	48,602	52,347	3,745
			86	1,323	2,357	2,540	183
BRAZIL	N	E	81	495,968	580,650	620,148	39,498
			82	515,014	436,853	482,224	45,371
	O	E	83	176,108	218,374	218,374	
	V	E	81	27,771,880	32,537,274	34,614,540	2,104,266
			82	24,117,973	24,323,781	26,114,275	1,790,494
			83	48,790,074	46,921,398	50,150,413	3,229,015
			84	51,517,037	64,753,757	68,324,386	3,570,629
			85	49,928,552	59,181,715	62,501,791	3,320,076
			86	48,052,279	54,858,253	57,925,044	3,066,791
	V	W	81	1,341,891	1,751,503	1,863,364	111,861
			82	379,501	355,546	396,908	41,362
			83	1,829,819	2,248,167	2,408,344	160,177
			84	347,225	464,934	494,677	29,743
			85	113,713	137,182	145,443	8,261
			86	308,700	390,287	424,262	33,975
C RICA	V	E	81	220,151	305,999	321,224	15,225
CANADA	A	E	83	309	540	706	166
	O	E	81	1,908,970	3,463,590	3,463,590	
			82	2,199,828	3,823,685	3,823,685	
			83	1,749,720	2,422,203	2,422,203	
			84	1,982,771	2,883,141	2,883,141	
			85	2,414,629	3,684,203	3,684,203	
			86	1,752,227	2,453,478	2,453,479	1
CHILE	V	E	85	238,097	278,335	290,325	11,990

Crop
Product
TSUSA commodity number, description, and unit of quantity

Country	Mode	Reg	Yr	Quantity	F.A.S.	C.I.F.	Charges
COLOMB	N	E	84	158,038	227,187	240,019	12,832
			85	370,567	522,076	550,109	28,033
			86	29,324	50,850	53,735	2,885
	V	E	81	5,512	11,710	12,461	751
			82	26,613	51,760	56,705	4,945
			83	123,678	161,535	171,348	9,813
			84	2,307,333	2,924,856	3,096,579	171,723
			85	1,571,885	1,883,550	1,994,033	110,483
			86	238,075	306,188	323,277	17,089
	V	W	81	10,009	13,362	13,969	607
			84	37,478	51,850	54,336	2,486
			85	899,477	1,029,843	1,127,561	97,718
			86	450,096	498,180	521,659	23,479
DOM REP	V	E	81	60,210	47,612	51,550	3,938
			82	100,020	87,295	93,430	6,135
			84	244,831	222,428	241,159	18,731
			85	225,000	365,814	382,139	16,325
			86	339,762	700,576	727,604	27,028
ECUADOR	A	E	82	240	420	708	288
	N	E	81	1,869,941	2,192,923	2,304,030	111,107
			83	24,399,979	19,445,003	20,976,785	1,531,782
			84	2,037,068	2,718,847	2,873,245	154,398
			85	17,977,934	20,148,395	21,276,956	1,128,561
	V	E	81	26,825,031	29,869,824	31,457,298	1,587,474
			82	31,436,733	28,307,749	30,259,891	1,952,142
			83	3,585,961	2,789,342	3,019,109	229,767
			84	18,937,269	23,356,097	24,573,457	1,217,360
			85	20,785,690	23,200,324	24,391,703	1,191,379
			86	31,954,514	34,351,974	36,093,637	1,741,663
	V	W	81	2,160,882	2,122,289	2,241,055	118,766
			82	2,996,112	2,359,329	2,547,250	187,921
			83	2,570,074	2,403,217	2,586,062	182,845
			84	3,948,970	5,029,622	5,282,821	253,199
			85	3,802,348	4,395,453	4,643,511	248,058
			86	4,337,617	4,499,546	4,720,511	220,965
FR GERM	O	E	85	1,213	1,565	1,635	70
	V	E	81	15,800	32,151	33,604	1,453
			82	1,904	1,544	1,686	142
			83	12,128	53,324	54,574	1,250
			84	88,014	102,060	107,703	5,643
			85	105,419	166,322	175,348	9,026
	V	W	81	80,002	46,304	51,477	5,173
			84	84,092	107,423	113,115	5,692
			85	44,000	26,606	29,920	3,314
			86	1,102	1,228	1,244	16
FRANCE	A	E	82	179	328	580	252
			83	1,189	1,413	1,850	437
			84	642	2,781	3,515	734
	A	W	84	220	366	1,649	1,283
	N	E	82	5,395	5,700	6,667	967
			84	10,192	16,407	17,443	1,036
			86	48,832	69,700	73,227	3,527
	V	E	81	37,776	46,974	50,060	3,086
			82	2,813	5,074	5,367	293
			83	3,735	4,137	4,537	400
			84	3,817	6,528	6,805	277
			85	10,747	18,127	19,055	928
			86	4,079	7,577	7,916	339
	V	W	83	10,155	12,309	13,696	1,387
			84	4,200	6,496	7,337	841
GHANA	V	E	81	110,230	98,642	107,673	9,031
GUATMAL	V	E	84	562	260	349	89
HG KONG	V	W	83	115,742	20,888	28,088	7,200
INDNSIA	V	W	82	440,860	474,800	515,400	40,600
IRELAND	O	E	82	40,000	23,100	25,410	2,310
ISRAEL	V	E	82	4,000	7,072	7,380	308
ITALY	A	E	82	101	279	474	195
	V	E	83	1,323	2,794	2,985	191
IVY CST	N	E	84	8,074,081	10,332,581	10,797,999	465,418
	O	E	86	19,998	16,998	16,998	
	V	E	81	5,217,025	5,649,521	6,123,111	473,590
			82	2,063,295	2,407,753	2,531,792	124,039
			83	5,789,353	5,288,635	5,696,831	408,196
			84	449,804	584,812	619,866	35,054
			85	10,945,855	12,948,017	13,552,288	604,271
			86	17,013,641	19,112,627	20,076,472	963,845
JAPAN	N	E	86	11,985	25,240	30,037	4,797
	V	W	86	11,242	23,107	24,396	1,289
MEXICO	O	W	82	2,511	1,449	1,449	
	V	E	83	1,986,675	1,507,905	1,587,222	79,317
N ZEAL	V	E	86	6,000	11,468	11,976	508
NAMIBIA	V	E	85	132,040	232,379	243,733	11,354
			86	106,000	199,275	207,413	8,138
NAURU	V	E	85	257,277	300,432	316,747	16,315

Crop
Product
TSUSA commodity number, description, and unit of quantity

Country	Mode	Reg	Yr	Quantity	F.A.S.	C.I.F.	Charges
NETHLDS	A	E	84	397	615	868	253
	A	W	81	475	1,894	2,593	699
	N	E	81	66,667	112,166	117,432	5,266
			83	48,013	78,544	85,374	6,830
			84	276,767	554,935	572,853	17,918
	O	E	81	9,026	10,583	14,640	4,057
			84	160,052	261,261	270,682	9,421
			85	322,353	506,989	527,570	20,581
			86	242,065	314,647	328,104	13,457
	V	E	81	34,000	62,137	64,464	2,327
			82	209,507	259,795	271,041	11,246
			83	705,112	1,178,806	1,213,319	34,513
			84	336,220	553,704	576,184	22,480
			85	164,371	279,776	291,271	11,495
			86	64,000	116,526	122,041	5,515
	V	W	81	40,013	65,136	68,022	2,886
			83	170,366	167,320	178,980	11,660
			84	90,026	157,253	164,347	7,094
			85	53,077	78,419	82,681	4,262
			86	4,000	7,532	8,075	543
NIGERIA	V	E	84	406,237	462,472	501,135	38,663
PANAMA	V	E	84	584,772	855,120	899,308	44,188
			85	637,194	806,155	839,289	33,134
			86	1,821,441	1,849,500	1,945,077	95,577
PERU	N	E	81	25,161	66,492	69,746	3,254
	V	E	81	4,402,149	4,786,769	5,125,946	339,177
			82	4,073,871	4,035,425	4,372,604	337,179
			83	5,919,783	5,224,003	5,681,855	457,852
			84	3,991,415	5,095,297	5,409,817	314,520
			85	3,736,690	4,301,325	4,570,948	269,623
			86	2,419,550	2,689,890	2,868,408	178,518
	V	W	82	238,100	213,621	230,225	16,604
			83	833,424	880,682	934,426	53,744
			84	2,828,202	3,762,688	3,962,882	200,194
			85	2,023,775	2,476,017	2,641,715	165,698
			86	1,190,521	1,281,908	1,379,978	98,070
PHIL R	V	E	83	77,161	13,925	18,725	4,800
	V	W	81	344	1,052	1,093	41
			83	1,033,847	230,202	302,202	72,000
PORTUGL	V	E	84	121	286	316	30
	V	W	85	118	3,741	3,839	98
SINGAPR	V	E	81	11,338	10,000	10,560	560
	V	W	82	79,366	86,050	92,772	6,722
SPAIN	V	E	86	630,516	690,915	729,471	38,556
SWEDEN	A	E	82	1,021	1,513	2,495	982
SWITZLD	A	E	82	265	759	917	158
			84	815	1,227	5,227	4,000
			85	1,807	3,578	4,668	1,090
	O	E	83	131	271	271	
			85	2,204	5,194	5,389	195
			86	1,322	5,404	5,586	182
	V	E	81	1,054	4,402	4,482	80
			84	5,511	15,516	16,559	1,043
			85	7,049	15,116	15,938	822
			86	35,172	93,022	97,210	4,188
	V	W	85	1,682	4,653	5,007	354
			86	441	1,634	1,688	54
U KING	A	E	84	1,034	1,608	2,267	659
			85	895	1,173	1,290	117
	N	E	85	113,328	108,087	119,515	11,428
	O	E	81	38,592	65,992	65,992	
			82	217,318	345,846	352,104	6,258
			83	81,836	108,564	111,844	3,280
			84	39,715	46,872	46,872	
			86	40,320	62,940	62,940	
	V	E	81	232,640	294,638	321,464	26,826
			82	114,286	171,461	178,719	7,258
			84	617,289	852,768	887,680	34,912
			86	38,123	65,210	68,150	2,940
VENEZ	V	E	83	110,230	119,250	128,729	9,479
			84	547,402	648,114	691,846	43,732
			86	596,146	639,300	701,993	62,693
	V	W	83	44,092	56,340	61,468	5,128
W SAMOA	A	W	81	100	270	461	191
YUGOSLV	V	E	84	225	791	884	93

Cocoa, bean
1561000 COCOA BEANS (LB)

		Yr	Quantity	F.A.S.	C.I.F.	Charges
TOTAL		81	548,712,039	466,155,714	501,345,788	35,190,084
		82	435,038,300	323,382,572	352,526,895	29,144,323
		83	478,661,303	349,336,600	382,783,035	33,446,435
		84	427,569,047	411,190,276	441,086,595	29,896,319

Crop Product TSUSA commodity number, description, and unit of quantity Country	Mode	Reg	Yr	Quantity	F.A.S.	C.I.F.	Charges
			85	595,971,190	564,213,182	603,762,570	39,549,388
			86	451,391,538	417,621,514	449,404,940	31,783,426
AFGHAN	V	E	82	132,276	114,000	122,631	8,631
ARGENT	V	E	83	308,644	196,474	208,806	12,332
	V	W	82	55,115	48,125	50,741	2,616
BARBADO	V	E	85	233,200	244,860	266,319	21,459
BELGIUM	A	E	83	2,700	3,480	6,380	2,900
	V	E	81	264,552	252,000	272,395	20,395
BELIZE	V	E	81	9,091	9,091	9,738	647
			82	29,375	27,455	29,337	1,882
			83	116,660	100,122	105,285	5,163
			84	107,828	122,106	127,096	4,990
			85	152,945	173,789	180,531	6,742
			86	186,050	203,242	211,848	8,606
BENIN	V	E	81	579,612	407,444	423,077	15,633
BRAZIL	N	E	81	808,888	673,602	720,494	46,892
			83	31,514,927	23,315,523	25,433,066	2,117,543
			85	28,100,161	26,823,262	28,785,230	1,961,968
			86	35,301,766	30,757,811	32,958,672	2,200,861
	O	E	81	238,098	337,490	337,490	
			85	575,924	675,528	675,528	
			86	3,307	3,711	3,711	
	V	E	81	78,165,621	67,492,119	72,828,212	5,336,093
			82	88,793,621	63,080,555	69,290,699	6,210,144
			83	32,295,124	23,238,559	25,378,214	2,139,655
			84	53,841,713	53,632,773	57,188,773	3,556,000
			85	38,107,361	35,973,424	38,680,645	2,707,221
			86	37,794,420	34,926,991	37,289,737	2,362,746
	V	W	81	132,276	117,637	126,320	8,683
			82	2,050,002	1,452,196	1,599,937	147,741
			83	1,663,645	1,238,478	1,364,615	126,137
			84	2,623,442	2,838,806	3,008,103	169,297
			85	2,049,036	1,917,284	2,054,330	137,046
			86	5,138,479	4,476,321	4,812,721	336,400
C RICA	A	E	83	145	270	399	129
	N	E	82	599,597	467,562	506,963	39,401
	V	E	81	1,586,423	1,308,233	1,421,520	113,287
			82	1,555,990	1,291,139	1,399,320	108,181
			83	76,059	47,638	52,306	4,668
			84	240,000	170,568	182,408	11,840
			85	1,895,559	1,726,199	1,839,981	113,782
			86	1,062,416	842,202	887,889	45,687
CAMROON	V	E	81	14,620,468	13,337,407	14,119,187	781,780
			82	1,103,410	1,022,265	1,102,560	80,295
			83	1,322,870	1,341,600	1,410,619	69,019
			85	954,678	1,018,991	1,058,900	39,909
			86	1,103,402	1,364,470	1,457,854	93,384
CANADA	O	E	81	29,394	42,584	42,584	
			85	91,221	99,406	99,406	
			86	3,307	3,612	3,612	
CHINA T	V	E	81	89,599	77,485	86,464	8,979
	V	W	81	231,483	182,110	202,650	20,540
COLOMB	V	E	82	33,334	29,862	32,170	2,308
			84	3,539,612	3,573,440	3,789,422	215,982
			85	1,953,879	1,789,636	1,909,050	119,414
			86	66,510	55,800	59,780	3,980
	V	W	85	223,378	205,000	217,645	12,645
DOM REP	N	E	82	48,145,155	30,929,348	33,918,154	2,988,806
			85	38,082,020	33,112,639	35,853,912	2,741,273
			86	39,148,856	30,091,170	32,870,185	2,779,015
	V	E	81	58,636,965	44,543,703	47,883,692	3,339,989
			82	31,692,279	20,444,518	22,333,269	1,888,751
			83	70,279,947	50,478,766	55,355,245	4,876,479
			84	74,116,952	73,959,372	79,276,042	5,316,670
			85	31,146,960	26,368,654	28,566,715	2,198,061
			86	36,165,780	27,303,517	29,645,618	2,342,101
	V	W	86	540,127	387,170	424,920	37,750
DOMINCA	V	E	86	1,003,093	704,674	773,584	68,910
ECUADOR	N	E	83	13,383,674	8,285,280	9,078,162	792,882
			85	37,249,974	34,347,057	36,424,735	2,077,678
			86	1,477,100	1,196,102	1,316,717	120,615
	V	E	81	19,734,713	16,591,804	17,711,899	1,120,095
			82	56,885,048	40,334,672	43,540,561	3,205,889
			83	1,635,261	999,642	1,092,224	92,582
			84	53,404,865	52,664,860	55,901,462	3,236,602
			85	68,171,677	61,922,287	65,449,349	3,527,062
			86	23,745,626	19,948,252	21,153,581	1,205,329
	V	W	81	3,506,761	2,916,104	3,111,930	195,826
			82	3,992,972	2,704,915	2,960,139	255,224
			83	2,409,779	1,539,032	1,723,088	184,056
			84	3,034,451	3,102,147	3,346,180	244,033
			85	5,600,093	4,994,561	5,347,512	352,951
			86	7,170,277	6,027,856	6,496,560	468,704
EGYPT	V	E	85	456,352	372,600	398,549	25,949
F W IND	V	E	83	167,200	158,840	175,111	16,271
			84	605,413	627,323	681,829	54,506
			85	41,800	43,890	44,653	763
			86	75,310	94,372	101,374	7,002
FIJI	A	W	84	1,098	1,155	1,414	259
	V	W	85	3,418	3,459	3,745	286
FR GERM	V	E	81	112,589	113,321	115,922	2,601
			82	55,253	59,273	60,064	791
			83	4,041	5,072	5,238	166
			84	220,460	585,529	604,139	18,610
			85	77,758	67,575	73,902	6,327
FRANCE	V	E	81	1,476,592	1,100,702	1,206,710	106,008
			82	551,701	397,945	438,063	40,118
			83	1,359,427	1,073,150	1,174,586	101,436
			84	2,873,530	2,815,237	3,059,086	243,849
			85	4,449,976	4,046,548	4,348,661	302,113
	V	W	82	44,836	116,088	149,394	33,306
			83	23,567	55,330	73,064	17,734
			84	69,266	150,296	202,676	52,380
			85	5,939	16,562	21,141	4,579
GHANA	N	E	85	12,353,541	12,681,670	13,597,817	916,147
	V	E	81	32,845,596	32,382,009	34,159,747	1,777,738
			82	29,209,023	25,213,402	27,134,281	1,920,879
			83	31,585,586	24,622,625	26,733,281	2,110,656
			84	13,109,352	14,818,793	15,739,599	920,806
			85	19,403,134	21,197,502	22,752,301	1,554,799
			86	66,675,596	70,967,696	76,213,089	5,245,393
	V	W	83	551,150	409,351	452,636	43,285
			84	769,575	811,142	890,505	79,363
GIBRAT	V	E	86	2,536,061	2,887,269	3,084,829	197,560
GRENADA	V	E	81	88,000	105,600	113,269	7,669
			82	88,000	105,600	112,548	6,948
			84	146,988	154,337	167,571	13,234
			85	66,000	69,300	75,242	5,942
			86	242,660	254,100	265,152	11,052
GUATMAL	V	E	81	404,956	429,414	453,007	23,593
			83	1,834,546	1,003,735	1,092,056	88,321
			84	2,145,000	2,229,117	2,359,156	130,039
			85	935,364	902,228	961,008	58,780
			86	2,800,567	2,563,972	2,689,049	125,077
GUINEA	V	E	86	44,352	42,134	44,289	2,155
	V	W	81	220,800	223,600	244,947	21,347
			84	220,800	225,993	244,440	18,447
HAITI	N	E	81	3,107,701	2,311,638	2,510,960	199,322
			82	1,000,791	721,329	783,819	62,490
	V	E	81	402,592	293,440	318,541	25,101
			82	1,251,996	803,778	882,662	78,884
			83	1,841,315	1,304,975	1,438,837	133,862
			84	702,407	695,702	747,996	52,294
			85	513,673	482,352	505,969	23,617
			86	493,637	444,611	470,972	26,361
HEARD I	V	E	86	35,200	25,946	28,554	2,608
HG KONG	V	E	82	110,230	76,271	81,750	5,479
			85	77,264	107,091	111,526	4,435
HONDURA	V	E	81	1,118,816	1,236,586	1,326,437	89,851
			82	169,428	147,984	157,697	9,713
			83	344,170	258,566	283,086	24,520
			84	1,441,569	1,521,339	1,621,002	99,663
			85	1,254,244	1,141,581	1,226,887	85,306
			86	2,211,556	1,805,592	1,936,230	130,638
INDIA	V	E	86	165,345	153,765	162,041	8,276
INDNSIA	V	E	81	492,805	465,746	504,377	38,631
			82	848,253	631,629	728,363	96,734
			83	1,029,322	740,453	842,805	102,352
			84	2,355,989	2,424,776	2,624,489	199,713
			85	1,767,520	1,693,410	1,864,869	171,459
			86	3,606,972	3,205,362	3,421,043	215,681
	V	W	81	189,982	148,560	165,507	16,947
			83	55,000	43,277	46,297	3,020
			84	362,381	367,201	384,267	17,066
			86	83,731	74,305	81,327	7,022
ITALY	N	E	85	378,169	464,670	514,440	49,770
	V	E	85	760,000	748,267	838,711	90,444
			86	479,325	480,668	538,110	57,442
	V	W	86	131,069	60,825	65,518	4,693
IVY CST	N	E	81	103,654,060	85,695,944	93,038,048	7,342,104
			82	6,412,056	4,928,784	5,143,393	214,609
			85	139,406,016	131,447,857	140,520,779	9,072,922
	O	E	84	362,662	443,682	443,682	
			85	453,362	471,933	471,933	
	O	W	85	40,040	45,177	47,177	2,000
	V	E	81	132,536,964	113,372,290	121,954,016	8,581,726
			82	112,618,481	91,630,617	99,794,153	8,163,536

Crop
Product
TSUSA commodity number, description, and unit of quantity

Country	Mode	Reg	Yr	Quantity	F.A.S.	C.I.F.	Charges
			83	196,785,502	142,002,374	157,085,886	15,083,512
			84	163,021,013	144,520,958	156,596,728	12,075,770
			85	107,120,933	105,038,042	112,668,239	7,630,197
			86	150,585,355	147,138,904	158,740,492	11,601,588
	V	W	82	1,106,644	764,167	835,129	70,962
			84	551,701	599,332	641,000	41,668
			85	14,187	15,259	16,448	1,189
JAMAICA	V	E	85	88,900	151,870	159,793	7,923
KENYA	V	E	83	83,600	79,420	86,966	7,546
KIRIBAT	V	E	86	220,680	204,158	215,614	11,456
LIBERIA	V	E	81	2,352,000	2,006,941	2,191,591	184,650
			82	1,008,000	896,916	978,286	81,370
MADAGAS	V	E	82	44,092	27,500	31,390	3,890
MALAYSA	N	E	84	1,742,783	1,778,805	1,840,940	62,135
	V	E	81	9,178,296	7,313,984	8,131,867	817,893
			82	5,526,520	4,091,146	4,565,411	474,265
			83	10,242,921	7,552,102	8,190,617	638,515
			84	9,084,861	9,224,925	9,850,513	625,588
			85	4,186,073	3,801,005	4,092,795	291,790
			86	4,070,693	3,542,891	3,752,388	209,497
	V	W	81	4,406,119	3,709,655	4,058,380	348,725
			82	4,430,863	3,510,642	3,859,185	348,543
			83	5,993,677	4,053,437	4,371,132	317,695
			84	4,400,029	4,388,763	4,635,031	246,268
			85	797,432	799,010	850,461	51,451
			86	440,834	380,553	401,107	20,554
MEXICO	O	E	83	141,226	65,113	65,113	
			86	539,665	417,725	417,725	
	V	E	83	15,335,725	11,252,599	11,801,181	548,582
			84	2,314,748	2,490,895	2,582,186	91,291
			85	1,653,626	1,696,440	1,772,547	76,107
			86	557,801	533,500	553,764	20,264
N ZEAL	V	E	81	39,683	33,868	36,540	2,672
NAMIBIA	V	E	85	10,527	18,916	19,735	819
			86	19,565	35,565	37,071	1,506
NETHLDS	A	E	82	11	655	714	59
			86	2,039	2,273	3,976	1,703
	N	E	81	2,189,542	2,454,817	2,515,221	60,404
	V	E	82	1,103,676	698,451	761,235	62,784
			83	38,581	35,911	38,534	2,623
			84	43,260	47,001	50,504	3,503
			85	1,886,370	1,896,982	2,044,851	147,869
			86	837,814	965,149	1,013,579	48,430
NEW GUI	V	E	81	899,036	978,808	1,003,231	24,423
			82	3,728	4,664	4,792	128
			84	665,018	691,838	741,258	49,420
	V	W	81	17,803,347	16,132,653	17,507,179	1,374,526
			82	10,560,569	7,800,967	8,584,733	783,766
			83	12,692,224	11,642,481	12,569,818	927,337
			84	6,934,615	7,673,965	8,179,324	505,359
			85	11,740,407	11,606,089	12,384,928	778,839
			86	14,019,627	12,350,552	13,306,194	955,642
NICARAG	V	E	81	78,651	83,712	88,976	5,264
NIGER	V	E	82	881,840	678,114	747,161	69,047
NIGERIA	V	E	81	38,449,996	29,829,495	31,884,401	2,054,906
			82	15,647,625	11,794,897	12,860,823	1,065,926
			83	30,477,342	22,517,679	24,468,805	1,951,126
			84	8,299,358	8,881,571	9,470,529	588,958
			85	22,921,822	22,927,981	24,619,707	1,691,726
			86	4,629,661	5,018,269	5,330,932	312,663
NORFOLK	V	E	83	44,092	31,149	34,974	3,825
NORWAY	A	W	82	406	604	634	30
	V	E	85	77,161	67,516	73,510	5,994
PANAMA	V	E	81	122,454	190,030	198,982	8,952
			85	158,876	153,039	160,820	7,781
			86	90,000	78,000	85,425	7,425
PARAGUA	V	E	81	132,276	123,000	132,505	9,505
			84	76,407	78,371	83,179	4,808
PERU	N	E	81	760,707	680,980	725,228	44,248
	V	E	81	418,931	366,611	391,728	25,117
			82	1,168,451	857,415	931,928	74,513
			83	633,712	479,245	512,611	33,366
			84	55,335	36,976	40,601	3,625
	V	W	83	330,690	342,815	374,771	31,956
			84	330,693	401,568	424,851	23,283
PHIL R	V	E	85	154,322	99,400	121,677	22,277
			86	147,708	154,212	164,400	10,188
	V	W	84	54,233	55,017	58,908	3,891
			85	52,910	45,600	49,120	3,520
REP SAF	V	E	84	2,206,805	1,205,166	1,380,174	175,008
			86	1,103,402	951,984	1,044,362	92,378
S LUCIA	O	E	85	35,145	42,174	44,291	2,117
	V	E	81	36,000	42,174	43,512	1,338
			83	36,630	43,956	46,003	2,047

Crop
Product
TSUSA commodity number, description, and unit of quantity

Country	Mode	Reg	Yr	Quantity	F.A.S.	C.I.F.	Charges
			84	70,925	85,110	88,741	3,631
			85	73,650	87,912	91,768	3,856
			86	60,060	72,072	75,754	3,682
S VN GR	V	E	83	83,600	79,420	86,965	7,545
SALVADR	V	E	84	40,789	31,955	34,933	2,978
	V	W	86	324,000	259,500	285,482	25,982
SAO T P	V	E	81	1,984,140	1,643,398	1,825,263	181,865
SIER LN	V	E	81	4,934,275	4,748,961	4,841,683	92,722
			86	38,580	28,549	30,799	2,250
SINGAPR	V	E	81	823,867	679,975	755,448	75,473
			82	551,035	376,996	417,450	40,454
			83	1,113,293	731,343	811,331	79,988
			84	4,113,392	3,722,131	3,958,940	236,809
			85	630,868	809,887	845,534	35,647
	V	W	81	110,230	90,457	98,000	7,543
			82	572,441	560,889	630,758	69,869
			83	336,890	257,097	279,317	22,220
			84	499,618	513,091	541,061	27,970
			85	83,775	80,540	86,256	5,716
SPAIN	V	E	85	627,179	573,159	608,317	35,158
			86	66,138	66,000	70,036	4,036
SWITZLD	A	E	81	330	872	1,037	165
	N	E	81	7,730	17,611	18,340	729
TOGO	V	E	81	1,979,857	1,712,141	1,792,647	80,506
TRINID	N	E	81	3,316,548	3,579,464	3,930,969	351,505
			82	1,750,000	1,490,841	1,706,694	215,853
	V	E	81	80,000	94,400	99,123	4,723
			82	151,050	187,403	207,054	19,651
			83	1,872,059	1,504,993	1,734,808	229,815
			84	1,566,143	1,599,423	1,805,548	206,125
			85	517,261	582,555	652,480	69,925
			86	880,000	848,583	961,697	113,114
U KING	V	E	81	242,437	228,507	235,802	7,295
			83	1,178,085	863,940	911,131	47,191
			85	1,837,442	2,057,664	2,161,276	103,612
			86	793,987	981,409	1,064,829	83,420
VANUATA	V	E	81	61,039	61,039	66,087	5,048
VENEZ	V	E	81	2,288,142	2,524,260	2,654,245	129,985
			82	2,535,831	2,415,987	2,562,750	146,763
			83	5,437,923	3,849,557	4,161,083	311,526
			84	4,551,065	4,616,499	4,849,708	233,209
			85	3,527,360	3,586,000	3,724,550	138,550
			86	2,278,538	2,074,000	2,207,209	133,209
W SAMOA	A	H	81	1,815	1,706	2,917	1,211
			82	4,680	6,298	7,592	1,294
	A	W	81	800	1,352	1,703	351
			82	540	972	1,353	381
	V	E	82	22,046	15,521	17,154	1,633
			83	42,769	40,973	42,601	1,628
			84	195,817	198,842	202,451	3,609
	V	W	81	728,394	657,180	704,043	46,863
			82	540,030	422,215	462,001	39,786
			83	1,956,003	1,450,758	1,583,982	133,224
			84	455,086	412,380	438,150	25,770
			85	743,328	679,893	724,369	44,476
			86	193,866	164,148	173,539	9,391

Cocoa, bean shell
1565000 COCOA BEAN SHELLS (LB)

Country	Mode	Reg	Yr	Quantity	F.A.S.	C.I.F.	Charges
TOTAL			81	448,200	14,004	24,152	10,148
			82	75,510	2,805	6,661	3,856
			84	32,705	2,287	2,596	309
			86	44,092	2,456	4,900	2,444
C RICA	V	E	86	44,092	2,456	4,900	2,444
DOM REP	V	E	81	360,000	12,240	22,031	9,791
			82	75,510	2,805	6,661	3,856
ECUADOR	V	E	81	88,200	1,764	2,121	357
IVY CST	O	E	84	32,408	1,575	1,575	
N ZEAL	A	E	84	297	712	1,021	309

Cocoa, bean waste
1565500 COCOA BEAN WASTES EX SHELLS (LB)

Country	Mode	Reg	Yr	Quantity	F.A.S.	C.I.F.	Charges
TOTAL			81	1,852,773	620,554	715,183	94,629
			82	856,189	1,257,010	1,309,962	52,952
			83	4,098,134	3,661,786	3,933,838	272,052
			84	2,596,823	1,796,473	1,937,843	141,370
			85	1,799,666	684,646	761,555	76,909
			86	3,028,205	3,033,740	3,232,641	198,901

Crop Product TSUSA commodity number, description, and unit of quantity Country	Mode	Reg	Yr	Quantity	F.A.S.	C.I.F.	Charges
BRAZIL	O	E	81	40,542	14,023	14,023	
	V	E	81	1,234,577	444,767	508,295	63,528
			82	27,558	6,775	8,968	2,193
			83	3,739,429	3,504,975	3,757,632	252,657
			84	2,005,747	1,436,959	1,547,933	110,974
			85	694,449	248,805	273,442	24,637
			86	2,323,391	2,000,271	2,154,906	154,635
C RICA	V	E	84	80,000	46,376	48,476	2,100
			85	160,001	97,542	105,030	7,488
			86	5,112	5,822	6,396	574
CANADA	O	E	82	12,000	4,790	4,790	
CYPRUS	V	E	86	57,250	13,168	15,914	2,746
DOM REP	V	E	83	45,000	11,250	12,632	1,382
			84	90,000	53,127	56,635	3,508
			85	180,000	57,893	65,164	7,271
			86	90,600	22,388	25,417	3,029
ECUADOR	A	E	86	1,102	2,204	3,213	1,009
	V	E	81	286,598	42,365	57,512	15,147
			83	110,230	6,500	12,486	5,986
			84	110,230	12,500	18,193	5,693
			85	606,243	118,397	149,291	30,894
	V	W	81	30,266	40,050	41,803	1,753
			86	37,478	43,350	45,505	2,155
FR GERM	V	E	85	40,014	60,258	61,462	1,204
FRANCE	A	E	84	459	894	923	29
	V	E	83	200	494	548	54
GHANA	V	E	81	220,460	34,333	43,593	9,260
ISRAEL	V	E	83	1,575	3,960	4,396	436
IVY CST	O	E	85	31,875	7,969	7,969	
	V	E	86	471,784	933,267	964,429	31,162
JAMAICA	V	E	83	967	1,871	1,924	53
MALAYSA	V	E	81	20,000	35,900	39,539	3,639
			84	262,347	154,202	170,794	16,592
NETHLDS	N	W	83	10,118	13,952	15,001	1,049
	V	E	81	20,000	8,762	10,000	1,238
			82	20,000	11,600	13,556	1,956
			83	99,968	80,561	86,110	5,549
			84	46,000	90,034	92,320	2,286
			85	42,000	78,734	80,640	1,906
			86	40,000	11,256	14,600	3,344
NIGERIA	V	E	84	1,543	2,107	2,262	155
PANAMA	V	E	83	88,184	35,374	40,085	4,711
			85	44,092	13,000	16,265	3,265
PHIL R	V	E	81	330	354	418	64
	V	W	82	509	311	351	40
			83	1,139	679	749	70
			84	497	274	307	33
PORTUGL	V	E	85	992	2,048	2,292	244
SWITZLD	V	E	83	1,324	2,170	2,275	105
U KING	A	E	86	1,488	2,014	2,261	247
	O	E	82	796,122	1,233,534	1,282,297	48,763

Cocoa butter

1563500 COCOA BUTTER (LB)

Country	Mode	Reg	Yr	Quantity	F.A.S.	C.I.F.	Charges
TOTAL			81	95,230,707	220,165,441	228,115,074	7,951,436
			82	82,287,721	164,849,489	171,325,512	6,476,023
			83	105,778,768	189,757,479	197,008,658	7,251,179
			84	114,002,923	244,551,984	252,344,372	7,792,388
			85	154,644,270	333,342,916	343,893,229	10,550,313
			86	154,903,107	322,910,530	333,189,589	10,279,059
BELGIUM	A	E	83	386	981	997	16
	V	E	84	10	314	364	50
			85	992	2,902	3,017	115
			86	39,683	81,000	82,550	1,550
BOLIVIA	V	E	81	154,315	396,178	411,146	14,968
			82	131,819	192,071	204,574	12,503
			83	192,903	355,049	370,176	15,127
			84	157,598	333,200	350,212	17,012
			85	502,098	1,062,775	1,112,350	49,575
			86	508,117	1,030,000	1,079,881	49,881
BRAZIL	N	E	85	49,665,843	104,615,264	108,429,718	3,814,454
	O	E	81	66,138	149,360	149,360	
			83	224	448	448	
			85	3,302	7,810	7,810	
	V	E	81	34,841,756	80,645,363	83,595,156	2,949,793
			82	20,753,364	36,864,751	38,592,037	1,727,286
			83	28,312,305	48,756,936	50,844,091	2,087,155
			84	34,827,856	72,196,043	74,770,866	2,574,823
			85	6,714,421	14,567,536	15,081,080	513,544
			86	66,496,576	138,755,361	143,533,221	4,777,860
	V	W	81	50,838	114,817	120,198	5,381

Country	Mode	Reg	Yr	Quantity	F.A.S.	C.I.F.	Charges
			82	169,754	312,634	331,678	19,044
			83	467,377	823,377	868,219	44,842
			84	1,653,450	3,388,757	3,542,160	153,403
			85	231,483	497,242	518,993	21,751
			86	154,322	312,341	342,063	29,722
C RICA	V	E	81	1,538,153	3,564,609	3,715,262	150,653
			82	1,631,618	3,326,326	3,424,134	97,808
			83	758,916	1,438,998	1,486,886	47,888
			84	1,802,238	4,125,272	4,241,910	116,638
			85	1,880,825	4,200,290	4,318,416	118,126
			86	2,168,065	4,830,172	4,936,612	106,440
CAMROON	V	E	82	110,230	249,545	259,088	9,543
			83	39,683	50,566	54,000	3,434
			86	238,097	491,602	506,112	14,510
CANADA	O	E	81	4,354	17,141	17,371	230
			82	41,628	113,307	113,307	
			83	161,352	393,744	393,744	
			84	859,735	2,084,504	2,084,504	
			85	1,182,836	2,804,021	2,804,021	
			86	39,867	93,978	93,978	
	O	W	82	43,450	116,880	116,880	
CHILE	V	E	84	150,000	245,000	260,155	15,155
			85	44,092	104,000	108,662	4,662
			86	87,026	181,000	189,834	8,834
CHINA M	V	E	81	372,578	908,629	932,168	23,539
			82	4,497,270	10,035,350	10,349,534	314,184
			83	4,085,128	7,327,679	7,606,321	278,642
			84	3,447,995	6,914,486	7,139,551	225,065
			85	6,544,354	14,777,517	15,261,580	484,063
			86	4,294,606	9,906,605	10,207,112	300,507
	V	W	81	402,179	770,667	810,081	39,414
			82	1,655,653	3,914,391	4,031,993	117,602
			83	337,305	586,107	609,832	23,725
			84	787,041	1,720,396	1,779,038	58,642
			85	240,720	452,200	462,952	10,752
			86	151,200	318,500	338,188	19,688
CHINA T	V	E	86	702,796	1,581,126	1,640,450	59,324
	V	W	82	37,478	88,074	90,514	2,440
			86	74,956	148,814	153,624	4,810
COLOMB	V	E	81	1,620,634	3,725,566	3,841,160	115,594
			82	2,392,041	4,565,350	4,732,502	167,152
			83	2,623,474	4,477,944	4,681,348	203,404
			84	3,540,595	7,803,606	8,104,298	300,692
			85	1,773,499	4,031,872	4,141,563	109,691
			86	2,291,468	4,859,467	5,031,307	171,840
	V	W	83	354,860	318,000	349,566	31,566
			84	110,230	235,000	244,356	9,356
			85	775,691	1,738,162	1,798,479	60,317
			86	1,043,648	1,708,142	1,796,881	88,739
DOM REP	A	E	81	297	528	645	117
	N	E	81	111,066	241,267	257,517	16,250
			85	1,092,103	2,413,772	2,514,644	100,872
	V	E	81	1,456,435	3,241,453	3,363,006	121,553
			82	1,880,644	3,901,206	4,078,785	177,579
			83	2,077,969	3,694,917	3,860,350	165,433
			84	1,561,439	3,564,371	3,688,796	124,425
			85	1,617,792	3,615,620	3,775,603	159,983
			86	2,374,192	4,940,549	5,138,367	197,818
ECUADOR	N	E	83	2,618,631	4,467,948	4,650,887	182,939
	V	E	81	5,971,433	12,369,282	12,815,600	446,318
			82	2,304,543	3,982,234	4,149,035	166,801
			83	623,904	910,068	954,020	43,952
			84	2,746,799	5,732,923	5,932,339	199,416
			85	3,847,284	7,335,032	7,610,102	275,070
			86	746,258	1,438,612	1,486,502	47,890
	V	W	81	40,013	97,441	100,823	3,382
			82	87,200	144,600	150,067	5,467
			83	58,808	106,700	111,562	4,862
			84	734,133	1,642,062	1,695,714	53,652
			85	754,125	1,358,176	1,407,256	49,080
			86	521,770	909,473	939,868	30,395
FR GERM	N	E	84	970,951	2,394,087	2,471,715	77,628
	O	W	86	46	1,590	1,590	
	V	E	81	401,898	1,051,517	1,076,296	24,779
			82	293,098	800,052	817,192	17,140
			83	509,702	1,024,789	1,052,663	27,874
			84	44,092	100,714	103,128	2,414
			85	124,449	285,769	294,281	8,512
			86	222	1,131	1,211	80
FRANCE	V	E	81	1,018,943	2,670,410	2,738,016	67,606
			82	2,003,748	4,407,440	4,500,803	93,363
			83	2,174,492	3,464,325	3,545,979	81,654
			84	96,099	203,417	208,850	5,433
			85	15,963	33,670	35,768	2,098

Crop
Product
TSUSA commodity number, description, and unit of quantity

Country	Mode	Reg	Yr	Quantity	F.A.S.	C.I.F.	Charges
	V	W	84	20	260	281	21
GHANA	V	E	81	859,794	1,947,723	2,032,766	85,043
			83	551,150	1,096,236	1,121,000	24,764
			84	636,027	1,468,639	1,515,865	47,226
GREECE	V	E	86	88,184	209,714	213,963	4,249
HG KONG	V	E	84	113,312	276,908	286,048	9,140
			86	40,020	80,440	82,040	1,600
	V	W	85	40,020	90,045	94,280	4,235
			86	160,080	308,754	321,517	12,763
INDIA	V	E	82	28,662	64,731	68,347	3,616
			84	279,984	598,670	616,741	18,071
INDNSIA	V	E	81	39,682	106,346	110,390	4,044
			82	119,049	305,350	314,280	8,930
			83	79,366	197,280	201,882	4,602
			84	521,727	1,124,800	1,214,310	89,510
			86	81,570	158,204	164,735	6,531
	V	W	81	831,135	1,972,441	2,076,131	103,690
			84	37,478	95,717	100,991	5,274
ISRAEL	V	E	82	4,200	5,100	5,536	436
			86	1,270	1,037	1,184	147
IVY CST	N	E	83	11,004,917	20,516,806	21,354,167	837,361
	O	E	81	20,505	69,494	69,494	
			83	22,128	43,259	43,259	
			86	119,686	283,447	283,447	
	V	E	81	14,720,156	32,850,994	34,079,638	1,228,644
			82	14,105,765	28,574,640	29,501,767	927,127
			84	22,598,895	49,763,428	51,178,342	1,414,914
			85	35,975,474	77,681,599	80,067,954	2,386,355
			86	36,260,440	73,645,949	76,056,937	2,410,988
JAMAICA	V	E	81	56,000	123,364	129,218	5,854
			83	215,331	377,355	401,147	23,792
			84	322,581	718,178	754,289	36,111
			85	330,249	730,073	770,710	40,637
			86	379,649	857,815	892,997	35,182
	V	W	84	44,800	88,249	93,650	5,401
JAPAN	V	E	85	3,750	4,991	7,241	2,250
			86	379,412	889,545	908,143	18,598
	V	W	82	220,460	465,422	483,506	18,084
			83	6,614	10,874	11,617	743
			84	112,435	283,792	292,612	8,820
KIRIBAT	V	E	85	79,366	154,724	158,724	4,000
MADAGAS	V	E	86	36,682	89,620	93,327	3,707
MALAYSA	V	E	81	3,253,973	8,101,132	8,426,275	325,143
			82	4,858,977	9,962,511	10,508,927	546,416
			83	5,831,004	10,890,936	11,283,465	392,529
			84	8,860,348	19,319,056	19,879,969	560,913
			85	11,119,766	24,773,862	25,473,698	699,836
			86	11,900,897	25,672,700	26,340,097	667,397
	V	W	81	764,943	1,704,981	1,781,254	76,273
			82	478,841	1,060,375	1,102,835	42,460
			83	39,683	69,289	69,750	461
			84	506,982	1,106,827	1,144,289	37,462
			85	715,450	1,606,474	1,648,113	41,639
			86	45,432	92,261	93,961	1,700
MAURIT	V	E	85	39,683	78,837	81,014	2,177
			86	119,048	240,121	243,361	3,240
MEXICO	A	W	84	22,575	53,750	57,027	3,277
	N	E	83	1,504,310	2,486,213	2,587,242	101,029
	O	E	81	48,941	139,516	139,516	
			82	424,235	664,888	664,888	
			83	595,547	859,331	859,331	
			84	1,720,855	2,953,237	2,953,237	
			85	3,824,934	7,380,186	7,380,975	789
			86	2,617,028	5,054,644	5,054,644	
	V	E	81	3,174,400	7,473,883	7,674,120	200,237
			82	1,335,746	2,077,340	2,151,149	73,809
			83	895,302	1,370,000	1,403,795	33,795
			84	5,095,368	12,390,488	12,671,740	281,252
			85	7,533,414	17,226,873	17,619,228	392,355
			86	6,633,800	14,130,656	14,521,548	390,892
NAMIBIA	V	E	85	96,410	235,841	242,309	6,468
			86	211,862	492,657	506,772	14,115
NETHLDS	A	E	83	1,102	2,988	3,484	496
			84	121	508	678	170
	N	E	84	317,824	751,133	770,563	19,430
			85	960,323	2,375,902	2,443,722	67,820
	N	W	84	3,472	5,352	6,523	1,171
	O	E	83	3,326	12,205	12,205	
			84	771	8,640	8,640	
			85	18,088	44,150	45,150	1,000
			86	2,480	12,932	12,932	
	V	E	81	1,818,349	4,294,175	4,387,052	92,877
			82	984,061	1,977,199	2,029,655	52,456
			83	1,534,387	3,095,696	3,178,421	82,725

Country	Mode	Reg	Yr	Quantity	F.A.S.	C.I.F.	Charges
			84	1,160,445	2,430,090	2,523,173	93,083
			85	474,184	1,038,173	1,076,965	38,792
			86	1,053,083	2,432,945	2,491,362	58,417
	V	W	81	6,063	15,050	15,881	831
			82	6,282	13,850	14,322	472
			83	3,031	6,123	6,329	206
			85	5,000	9,643	10,439	796
			86	70,296	136,687	141,217	4,530
NIGERIA	O	E	83	660	660	660	
	V	E	81	4,661,627	10,829,659	11,223,419	393,760
			82	575,456	1,016,719	1,066,735	50,016
			83	992,070	1,526,181	1,611,116	84,935
			84	3,003,986	6,651,560	6,907,502	255,942
			85	220,460	470,634	470,634	
NORWAY	V	E	86	255,500	458,382	474,736	16,354
	V	W	83	551	359	511	152
PANAMA	V	E	81	176,368	399,518	411,409	11,891
			82	903,886	1,759,529	1,826,895	67,366
			83	870,541	1,517,537	1,578,853	61,316
			84	1,014,106	2,265,824	2,343,626	77,802
			85	1,300,711	2,938,948	3,048,816	109,868
			86	1,367,674	2,892,105	2,988,664	96,559
	V	W	82	88,184	152,163	158,984	6,821
			83	220,460	368,735	384,456	15,721
			84	352,736	779,677	805,457	25,780
PERU	V	E	81	2,765,788	6,186,861	6,450,243	263,382
			82	2,489,744	5,460,840	5,705,374	244,534
			83	2,309,323	4,068,404	4,313,301	244,897
			84	1,819,866	3,719,046	3,854,924	135,878
			85	2,552,451	5,653,227	5,824,455	171,228
			86	1,029,185	2,119,957	2,183,806	63,849
	V	W	81	91,533	208,595	215,921	7,326
			82	92,911	213,333	221,304	7,971
			83	341,714	604,975	633,712	28,737
			84	115,743	239,625	249,039	9,414
			85	173,062	375,800	391,946	16,146
			86	14,330	31,200	33,278	2,078
PHIL R	N	W	83	360	320	320	
	O	E	81	37,305	61,462	62,812	1,350
	V	E	81	5,592,485	12,800,374	13,225,458	425,084
			82	10,317,240	21,488,926	22,295,814	806,888
			83	10,073,111	18,761,588	19,503,801	742,213
			84	2,189,468	4,248,935	4,405,275	156,340
			85	3,184,970	6,658,757	6,873,772	215,015
			86	3,032,967	6,045,604	6,233,802	188,162
	V	W	81	2,226,842	5,003,782	5,169,681	165,899
			82	1,542,895	3,043,781	3,164,966	121,185
			83	851,634	1,465,514	1,518,499	52,985
			84	754,931	1,384,348	1,444,394	60,046
			85	376,723	767,577	798,274	30,697
			86	112,434	254,200	261,918	7,718
PORTUGL	V	E	81	79,366	184,531	194,648	10,117
			82	39,683	88,881	92,700	3,819
			83	158,732	252,593	268,560	15,967
			84	39,683	95,842	98,100	2,258
REP SAF	V	E	81	33,600	66,002	69,562	3,560
SENEGAL	V	E	81	119,048	280,886	290,876	9,990
SINGAPR	V	E	81	2,972,520	7,656,470	7,969,291	312,821
			82	2,328,777	5,367,238	5,619,329	252,091
			83	17,780,905	33,203,429	34,235,540	1,032,111
			84	5,861,050	12,781,375	13,066,018	284,643
			85	6,759,012	15,536,843	15,971,981	435,138
			86	3,613,338	7,936,391	8,098,682	162,291
	V	W	81	558,282	1,534,362	1,629,484	95,122
			82	211,642	527,542	548,267	20,725
			83	1,967,624	3,452,560	3,527,680	75,120
			84	554,559	937,681	962,080	24,399
			85	79,366	203,630	208,014	4,384
			86	1,669,841	3,546,119	3,622,320	76,201
SPAIN	V	E	81	200,949	370,023	392,858	22,835
			82	282,190	599,600	623,986	24,386
			83	39,683	67,837	71,820	3,983
			84	227,074	520,696	544,540	23,844
			85	35,716	84,629	90,974	6,345
			86	150,795	337,349	360,558	23,209
	V	W	83	44,092	74,730	77,823	3,093
SWEDEN	V	W	81	441	1,514	1,594	80
SWITZLD	O	E	83	110	339	356	17
			84	330	927	986	59
	V	E	81	1,762	5,967	6,272	305
			82	1,811	6,064	6,431	367
			83	1,936	6,062	6,434	372
			84	3,413	9,690	10,621	931
			85	1,857	4,161	4,354	193

Crop Product TSUSA commodity number, description, and unit of quantity Country	Mode	Reg	Yr	Quantity	F.A.S.	C.I.F.	Charges
			86	12,688	28,539	30,005	1,466
	V	W	82	88	264	290	26
			83	330	981	1,023	42
			84	551	1,664	1,891	227
			85	441	1,106	1,170	64
			86	441	1,737	1,794	57
U KING	A	E	81	1,734	3,152	4,149	997
	A	W	82	639	1,044	1,656	612
	O	E	81	924,511	3,128,344	3,140,790	14,249
			82	2,081,989	5,550,387	5,749,959	199,572
			83	873,282	2,028,938	2,070,130	41,192
			84	115,798	365,206	365,206	
	V	E	81	396,221	920,950	963,867	42,917
			82	47,344	88,682	91,136	2,454
			83	971,791	2,043,010	2,090,977	47,967
			84	701,063	1,490,610	1,530,966	40,356
			86	88,184	207,512	212,000	4,488
VENEZ	V	E	81	745,354	1,759,662	1,827,200	67,538
			82	683,426	1,298,879	1,364,351	65,472
			83	595,242	1,079,560	1,134,903	55,343
			84	1,402,285	2,937,404	3,066,823	129,419
			85	1,731,515	3,312,601	3,402,022	89,421
			86	1,421,896	2,671,808	2,764,491	92,683

Cocoa, confectionery
1564700 CONFECTIONERS COATINGS,ETC (LB)

Country	Mode	Reg	Yr	Quantity	F.A.S.	C.I.F.	Charges
TOTAL			81	826,920	872,607	930,325	57,718
			82	1,915,078	1,341,637	1,416,794	75,157
			83	4,111,629	2,423,432	2,519,014	95,582
			84	11,452,200	6,108,536	6,216,282	107,746
			85	6,947,403	4,393,931	4,647,274	253,343
			86	11,227,452	6,354,013	6,595,397	241,384
BELGIUM	A	W	83	337	1,798	2,093	295
	O	W	82	253	299	299	
	V	E	84	2,756	3,473	3,612	139
			85	5,512	7,605	8,091	486
			86	10,052	7,019	7,627	608
BRAZIL	V	E	82	36,376	24,367	27,050	2,683
			83	12,240	4,920	6,354	1,434
			85	77,161	84,397	90,267	5,870
CANADA	N	E	85	3,160,998	1,507,666	1,507,666	
	N	W	84	267,122	137,923	137,923	
	O	E	81	406,002	317,422	317,422	
			82	1,348,228	626,248	626,248	
			83	3,330,930	1,512,496	1,512,496	
			84	10,306,092	5,007,143	5,007,143	
			85	795,785	412,833	413,064	231
			86	8,031,664	3,588,359	3,588,359	
	O	W	83	7,143	4,286	4,286	
			85	498,916	302,157	302,157	
			86	558,588	301,729	301,729	
CHINA M	V	E	86	18,414	23,601	24,955	1,354
DENMARK	V	E	82	8,053	9,748	10,406	658
			83	2,116	2,483	2,592	109
			84	3,520	3,122	3,241	119
			86	1,534	1,904	2,157	253
	V	W	82	3,968	4,296	4,860	564
			83	2,646	2,893	3,199	306
			84	5,346	7,412	8,214	802
			86	4,195	6,943	8,102	1,159
DOM REP	V	E	81	3,103	1,816	2,035	219
			82	2,000	1,440	1,560	120
FR GERM	A	E	81	196	517	542	25
			82	375	2,035	2,303	268
			83	138	266	522	256
	N	W	84	2,441	5,237	6,456	1,219
	O	E	84	79	349	349	
			86	27,000	10,736	12,045	1,309
	V	E	81	2,483	2,537	3,055	518
			83	749	764	806	42
			84	840	844	942	98
			85	64,687	50,336	54,494	4,158
			86	1,416	4,393	4,795	402
	V	W	82	2,935	5,989	6,741	752
			83	1,970	1,862	2,119	257
			84	220	560	605	45
			85	47,179	44,297	50,794	6,497
FRANCE	A	E	82	152	356	406	50
			84	110	327	408	81
	A	W	85	900	4,248	7,292	3,044
	N	E	84	7,072	9,395	10,432	1,037

Country	Mode	Reg	Yr	Quantity	F.A.S.	C.I.F.	Charges
	O	E	86	2,690	4,080	4,125	45
	O	W	86	5,036	5,631	5,765	134
	V	E	83	1,384	1,693	1,851	158
			84	4,718	4,156	4,495	339
			85	42,057	34,593	36,942	2,349
			86	148,009	140,407	147,568	7,161
	V	W	82	2,200	4,446	4,746	300
			86	6,015	5,364	5,941	577
GERM DR	V	W	83	2,228	2,682	3,044	362
ITALY	A	W	85	2,011	4,642	6,152	1,510
	O	E	84	177	353	353	
	V	E	84	1,320	1,692	2,228	536
IVY CST	V	E	85	119,048	50,241	59,968	9,727
MEXICO	A	E	86	10	4,200	4,265	65
N ZEAL	V	E	86	10,750	4,363	5,146	783
NETHLDS	A	W	85	855	2,300	3,645	1,345
	N	E	85	17,250	10,738	12,282	1,544
			86	448,569	221,553	248,669	27,116
	O	E	84	26,644	26,103	27,710	1,607
			85	3,679	2,677	2,856	179
	V	E	82	1,244	1,149	1,295	146
			83	99,389	40,221	49,266	9,045
			84	58,171	23,602	27,781	4,179
			85	556,799	260,271	298,409	38,138
			86	448,918	208,796	237,921	29,125
	V	W	86	51,492	21,518	25,176	3,658
NIGER	V	E	85	56,468	25,949	29,688	3,739
			86	1,667	1,559	1,719	160
PORTUGL	V	E	84	5,000	4,750	6,310	1,560
SPAIN	V	E	85	34,033	30,311	36,726	6,415
			86	45,358	48,264	53,249	4,985
SWEDEN	N	E	85	35,076	44,054	48,156	4,102
	N	W	81	199,737	255,018	292,518	37,500
			84	334,492	374,331	418,892	44,561
	O	E	85	21,117	50,295	53,201	2,906
	O	W	84	31,890	37,802	42,789	4,987
			85	31,254	39,476	46,344	6,868
	V	E	81	52,670	66,335	71,418	5,083
			82	69,102	90,037	97,060	7,023
			83	129,530	161,043	177,136	16,093
			84	123,092	161,420	174,664	13,244
			85	73,181	95,357	102,173	6,816
			86	123,409	159,069	169,670	10,601
	V	H	85	15,444	19,615	24,257	4,642
			86	49,896	64,808	77,377	12,569
	V	W	81	15,510	19,926	23,662	3,736
			82	282,263	348,890	397,268	48,378
			83	291,922	342,708	385,570	42,862
			84	43,126	56,711	64,118	7,407
			85	522,400	634,189	723,533	89,344
			86	453,923	551,208	622,668	71,460
SWITZLD	A	E	83	459	890	1,515	625
			84	573	1,088	1,719	631
			85	3,175	3,136	5,286	2,150
			86	3,307	5,457	8,071	2,614
	N	E	86	31,108	58,905	65,620	6,715
	O	E	81	21,463	37,571	39,352	1,781
			84	3,086	3,733	4,040	307
			85	39,360	46,123	48,710	2,587
			86	29,368	52,255	54,955	2,700
	O	W	85	9,033	8,770	9,437	667
	V	E	81	111,978	154,576	161,802	7,226
			82	148,867	215,225	228,593	13,368
			83	218,020	329,994	351,999	22,005
			84	175,402	180,679	200,367	19,688
			85	355,859	423,545	443,356	19,811
			86	360,859	595,893	628,971	33,078
	V	W	81	13,778	16,889	18,519	1,630
			82	5,865	6,524	7,178	654
			83	10,428	12,433	14,166	1,733
			84	48,911	56,331	61,491	5,160
			85	27,660	33,044	35,482	2,438
			86	14,363	26,292	27,480	1,188
U KING	N	E	85	247,021	115,919	132,887	16,968
			86	73,833	37,706	42,318	4,612
	O	E	85	53,485	29,845	35,809	5,964
			86	91,812	51,900	59,301	7,401
	V	E	82	3,197	588	781	193
			85	30,000	15,302	18,150	2,848
			86	86,013	54,901	60,191	5,290
VENEZ	V	E	86	88,184	85,200	89,462	4,262

1571040 CONFECTIONERY CON CHOC NSPF (LB)

Country	Mode	Reg	Yr	Quantity	F.A.S.	C.I.F.	Charges
TOTAL			81	25,842,654	40,112,207	42,590,288	2,552,817

Crop
Product
TSUSA commodity number, description, and unit of quantity

Country	Mode	Reg	Yr	Quantity	F.A.S.	C.I.F.	Charges
			82	35,456,597	50,870,401	54,417,719	3,547,468
			83	47,324,004	69,832,700	75,053,444	5,220,744
			84	78,558,280	105,737,418	115,499,188	9,761,770
			85	70,632,895	102,493,173	112,237,022	9,743,849
ARGENT	V	E	81	19,506	11,786	13,308	1,522
			82	42,940	24,851	27,477	2,626
			83	76,030	42,003	48,025	6,022
			84	228,302	136,494	150,109	13,615
			85	313,575	155,013	178,688	23,675
	V	W	81	1,683	1,031	1,177	146
			83	22,860	12,506	15,430	2,924
			84	370	2,889	4,319	1,430
AUSTRAL	A	E	84	529	1,032	2,082	1,050
	A	W	81	718	1,446	2,750	1,304
			83	218	315	1,044	729
			84	692	1,716	2,865	1,149
	N	E	81	340,055	511,687	608,543	96,856
			84	29,416	29,347	32,745	3,398
	N	H	81	21,190	48,512	62,777	14,265
			82	1,979	5,678	7,078	1,400
	N	W	83	1,480,563	1,633,370	2,048,713	415,343
			84	103,900	163,513	191,942	28,429
			85	252,250	270,755	310,005	39,250
	V	E	81	260,458	260,816	307,414	46,598
			82	1,022,408	1,398,168	1,672,356	274,188
			83	111,087	113,009	134,586	21,577
			85	21,300	16,574	18,657	2,083
	V	H	83	16,928	53,631	59,570	5,939
			84	5,297	18,369	21,043	2,674
			85	8,366	26,048	30,527	4,479
	V	W	81	31,868	39,722	49,303	9,581
			85	10,950	19,551	23,117	3,566
AUSTRIA	A	E	82	182	479	709	230
			83	15,711	38,508	47,015	8,507
			84	12,990	33,136	41,057	7,921
			85	3,111	4,330	6,208	1,878
	A	W	81	85	352	678	326
			82	858	2,425	3,419	994
	N	E	81	30,412	95,585	102,625	7,040
			82	48,542	115,508	123,808	8,300
			83	65,499	187,794	201,352	13,558
			84	167,288	238,801	278,027	39,226
			85	1,374,229	1,531,076	1,670,727	139,651
	N	W	81	2,545	3,121	4,067	946
			83	10,606	42,186	47,974	5,788
			84	14,501	42,940	54,886	11,946
			85	4,782	15,555	20,118	4,563
	O	E	81	2,163	1,607	1,729	122
			82	3,275	2,600	2,837	237
			83	6,491	9,940	9,940	
			84	1,404	11,144	12,121	977
			85	7,562	13,878	13,878	
	V	E	81	898	1,435	1,637	202
			85	385,106	400,702	455,309	54,607
	V	W	81	2,301	4,988	5,777	789
			82	2,143	6,844	7,653	809
			83	4,196	5,338	6,077	739
			84	21,626	22,965	27,491	4,526
			85	58,636	56,700	67,083	10,383
BAHAMAS	V	E	84	38,174	31,352	35,537	4,185
BELGIUM	A	E	81	39,297	212,109	235,765	23,656
			82	8,743	37,894	44,817	6,923
			83	10,851	43,360	50,997	7,637
			84	78,959	315,449	375,668	60,219
			85	150,364	531,700	604,932	73,232
	A	H	84	247	1,125	1,548	423
	A	W	81	820	3,108	3,900	792
			82	2,217	8,449	10,458	2,009
			83	7,829	27,136	33,330	6,194
			84	13,450	56,214	74,353	18,139
			85	8,452	29,371	39,379	10,008
	N	E	81	428,639	986,916	1,046,098	59,292
			82	322,808	833,609	924,052	90,443
			83	804,728	2,154,923	2,363,616	208,693
			84	1,181,676	2,819,131	3,207,504	388,373
			85	1,440,079	3,347,040	3,843,940	496,900
	N	W	81	9,033	39,746	44,182	4,436
			82	68,291	77,414	89,013	11,599
			83	99,719	109,893	132,112	22,219
			84	87,807	168,568	219,345	50,777
			85	81,704	145,468	200,789	55,321
	O	E	81	2,684	4,312	4,312	
			82	1,369	2,055	2,325	270

Crop
Product
TSUSA commodity number, description, and unit of quantity

Country	Mode	Reg	Yr	Quantity	F.A.S.	C.I.F.	Charges
			84	19,518	12,861	14,200	1,339
			85	93,007	59,915	68,971	9,056
	O	W	82	1,027	3,252	4,113	861
	V	E	81	2,028	8,069	8,340	271
			82	23,540	19,386	22,182	2,796
			83	18,508	22,819	25,284	2,465
			84	60,568	75,647	80,721	5,074
			85	196,849	320,743	351,363	30,620
BRAZIL	A	E	84	3,244	3,097	5,677	2,580
			85	4,216	15,675	18,399	2,724
	A	W	81	1,000	1,000	1,167	167
	N	E	81	118,231	51,801	63,142	11,341
			82	106,273	139,742	156,535	16,793
			84	59,332	29,540	37,764	8,224
	V	E	81	105,168	62,484	71,274	8,790
			82	85,948	41,450	48,444	6,994
			83	1,065,992	879,746	943,857	64,111
			84	267,127	188,645	208,558	19,913
			85	829,527	597,972	674,610	76,638
	V	W	82	1,010	9,088	10,533	1,445
			85	26,852	11,206	12,639	1,433
BULGAR	O	E	84	1,000	1,503	1,503	
	V	E	85	6,000	2,997	3,495	498
C RICA	N	E	81	351,257	281,148	320,864	39,716
	V	E	81	73,658	75,689	84,200	8,511
			82	812,708	597,294	686,372	89,078
			83	770,546	689,670	774,637	84,967
			84	398,776	337,887	371,289	33,402
			85	385,051	335,906	367,249	31,343
	V	W	83	1,740	592	1,020	428
CANADA	A	E	81	553	3,234	3,321	87
			82	120	496	535	39
			83	314	508	683	175
			84	137	972	1,168	196
			85	467	2,567	2,836	269
	A	W	81	1,012	2,991	3,257	266
			83	503	1,107	1,410	303
			84	280	1,477	2,055	578
			85	3,713	9,537	10,487	950
	N	E	81	868,029	1,221,745	1,220,880	6,655
			82	5,229,267	6,849,928	6,854,736	4,808
			83	7,222,808	9,315,929	9,321,487	5,558
			84	3,877,063	5,793,898	5,796,859	2,961
			85	5,314,751	8,123,773	8,125,409	1,636
	N	W	82	1,455	2,569	2,718	149
	O	E	81	4,834,553	6,934,258	6,921,969	
			82	1,935,268	1,973,563	1,974,465	902
			83	601,339	992,400	992,400	
			84	3,628,770	4,762,374	4,762,813	439
			85	2,436,022	4,017,188	4,032,354	15,166
	O	W	81	71,567	148,654	149,358	704
			82	54,102	170,733	170,733	
			83	64,967	203,245	203,245	
			84	128,198	277,510	277,849	339
			85	207,439	341,387	341,387	
	V	E	83	781	640	744	104
	V	W	85	1,800	5,040	5,358	318
CHILE	A	E	83	441	488	943	455
	V	E	82	1,000	454	671	217
			84	47,704	61,428	68,184	6,756
			85	15,929	7,730	8,729	999
	V	W	82	179	1,008	1,271	263
			83	2,840	2,589	3,286	697
			84	716	878	1,138	260
			85	8,173	6,908	8,854	1,946
CHINA M	A	E	83	1,600	600	636	36
			85	280	2,014	2,387	373
	O	E	84	1,095	708	826	118
	V	E	81	1,760	1,984	2,244	260
			83	9,034	8,960	9,944	984
			84	206	507	539	32
			85	6,580	5,866	6,511	645
	V	H	82	2,083	3,188	3,413	225
	V	W	81	540	1,317	1,379	62
			82	11,400	4,871	5,252	381
			83	10,494	9,036	9,736	700
			84	13,998	12,702	13,756	1,054
			85	8,380	4,596	5,089	493
CHINA T	V	E	84	2,482	4,060	4,552	492
			85	1,250	1,560	1,783	223
	V	H	83	750	990	1,160	170
			84	3,201	4,815	5,556	741
			85	1,045	1,500	1,707	207
	V	W	81	31,931	41,519	45,045	3,526

Crop
Product
TSUSA commodity number, description, and unit of quantity

Country	Mode	Reg	Yr	Quantity	F.A.S.	C.I.F.	Charges
			82	7,005	8,418	9,199	781
			83	6,814	3,178	3,444	266
			84	4,159	5,561	5,993	432
			85	12,086	15,143	17,639	2,496
COLOMB	A	E	84	1,180	1,640	2,369	729
			85	3,992	11,103	12,930	1,827
	N	E	81	99,155	52,557	60,348	7,791
	O	W	84	1,500	4,500	4,838	338
	V	E	81	81,377	68,885	80,164	11,279
			82	207,687	146,983	169,706	22,723
			83	4,013	5,245	5,837	592
			84	8,377	4,800	5,334	534
			85	10,000	4,788	5,451	663
	V	W	85	3,000	8,400	9,077	677
CYPRUS	V	E	81	57,530	146,291	153,583	7,292
			82	25,820	39,848	43,999	4,151
CZECHO	V	E	81	47,611	16,495	22,223	5,728
DENMARK	A	E	82	1,450	2,926	5,480	2,554
			83	1,936	3,603	6,501	2,898
			84	2,413	6,044	8,375	2,331
			85	646	1,834	3,150	1,316
	A	W	82	582	934	1,578	644
			84	790	1,659	2,338	679
	N	E	82	213,187	340,907	363,711	22,804
			83	287,384	339,126	361,878	22,752
			84	247,421	367,944	395,836	27,892
			85	232,843	329,433	362,112	32,679
	N	W	85	2,082	5,820	7,067	1,247
	O	E	81	99	315	340	25
			84	1,940	1,848	1,848	
	V	E	81	232,870	321,120	343,776	22,656
			83	39,551	47,013	51,561	4,548
			84	25,462	60,297	64,477	4,180
			85	39,600	18,845	20,520	1,675
	V	W	81	691	1,861	2,133	272
			82	630	1,316	1,614	298
			83	775	1,445	1,620	175
			85	3,581	6,770	8,892	2,122
DOM REP	A	E	81	6,550	2,007	2,756	749
			83	969	257	374	117
			84	8,782	811	1,160	349
			85	29,743	31,025	34,485	3,460
	N	E	83	17,501	7,598	9,987	2,389
			84	32,245	8,852	14,479	5,627
	V	E	81	48,579	84,093	86,112	2,019
			82	15,607	5,965	6,618	653
			83	48,582	84,720	89,441	4,721
			84	3,655	1,540	1,716	176
			85	9,114	3,301	4,155	854
ECUADOR	A	E	83	2,003	1,010	1,292	282
	V	E	85	70,696	63,960	68,354	4,394
	V	W	85	36,900	33,982	35,682	1,700
F W IND	A	E	85	7,236	19,993	27,567	7,574
FINLAND	A	W	82	280	693	1,020	327
			83	309	2,000	2,450	450
			84	411	1,353	1,656	303
	N	E	82	148,536	165,420	188,337	22,917
			83	448,516	402,683	456,612	53,929
			84	1,007,373	815,732	947,401	131,669
			85	645,064	734,682	876,307	141,625
	N	W	84	460,134	423,527	523,043	99,516
			85	1,098,078	1,170,003	1,536,913	366,910
	O	E	83	286	316	316	
	V	E	81	520,471	536,249	604,499	68,250
			82	521,626	680,191	754,222	74,031
			83	784,719	771,111	903,705	132,594
			84	1,171,864	1,284,114	1,554,485	270,371
			85	738,988	868,959	1,053,475	184,516
	V	W	81	719,994	926,509	1,043,903	117,394
			82	421,618	593,312	677,729	84,417
			83	256,348	299,975	376,167	76,192
FR GERM	A	E	81	1,704	2,957	3,277	320
			82	1,262	5,338	6,103	765
			83	1,988	6,145	7,543	1,398
			84	1,836	5,802	7,774	1,972
			85	3,291	15,354	19,316	3,962
	A	W	82	249	750	1,240	490
			83	6,855	11,548	21,545	9,997
			84	2,114	4,826	8,805	3,979
	N	E	81	2,158,953	3,105,082	3,366,045	260,963
			82	2,820,915	3,945,910	4,266,041	320,131
			83	3,605,448	4,524,352	4,897,162	372,810
			84	4,647,302	6,103,488	6,718,936	615,448
			85	7,293,657	8,665,781	9,560,939	895,158

Crop
Product
TSUSA commodity number, description, and unit of quantity

Country	Mode	Reg	Yr	Quantity	F.A.S.	C.I.F.	Charges
	N	W	82	142,956	236,673	266,580	29,907
			83	180,423	292,825	326,950	34,125
			84	501,572	556,064	647,764	91,700
			85	286,125	404,217	466,327	62,110
	O	E	81	5,367	5,740	5,740	
			82	25,463	47,077	48,372	1,295
			83	21,849	41,069	42,616	1,547
			84	21,976	12,805	12,944	139
			85	261,120	279,836	281,470	1,634
	V	E	81	202,506	453,284	490,907	37,623
			82	79,507	196,185	216,643	20,458
			83	162,591	289,715	307,056	17,341
			84	531,565	582,117	634,856	52,739
			85	390,706	662,548	717,641	55,093
	V	W	81	350,683	499,804	560,542	60,738
			82	91,625	118,232	137,368	19,136
			83	205,604	206,788	259,333	52,545
			84	46,169	56,579	77,655	21,076
			85	588,750	382,118	474,303	92,185
FRANCE	A	E	81	5,019	32,637	36,578	3,941
			82	32,512	103,098	119,926	16,828
			83	71,490	121,937	164,925	42,988
			84	19,792	60,000	77,286	17,286
			85	61,404	185,297	235,318	50,021
	A	H	84	653	2,996	3,970	974
	A	W	81	1,781	12,862	14,535	1,673
			82	168	1,463	1,706	243
			83	1,880	24,378	26,284	1,906
			84	1,171	6,285	7,792	1,507
			85	5,922	24,791	32,887	8,096
	N	E	81	113,529	377,875	408,889	31,014
			82	261,415	570,397	612,751	42,354
			83	370,518	805,609	895,644	90,035
			84	1,140,450	1,875,530	2,054,224	178,694
			85	1,727,444	3,843,495	4,175,107	331,612
	N	W	82	11,887	43,860	52,522	8,662
			83	44,252	169,066	195,951	26,885
			84	53,751	159,371	186,222	26,851
			85	40,751	104,766	128,665	23,899
	O	E	82	225	503	503	
			83	174	2,330	2,395	65
			84	7,778	16,392	16,392	
			85	6,170	13,200	14,014	814
	V	E	81	1,158	3,174	3,342	168
			82	273	1,794	1,974	180
			83	103,779	163,374	172,591	9,217
			84	24,476	49,662	52,950	3,288
			85	68,058	182,718	196,575	13,857
	V	W	81	1,102	3,666	4,152	486
			82	1,195	4,204	4,508	304
			84	2,000	6,860	7,260	400
			85	4,681	16,470	18,814	2,344
GERM DR	V	E	82	240	580	630	50
			84	121,022	67,399	77,050	9,651
GREECE	A	E	83	7,592	10,112	15,637	5,525
			84	2,966	5,146	7,817	2,671
			85	5,700	8,120	9,561	1,441
	N	E	83	169,081	141,997	171,367	29,370
			84	141,965	122,536	165,896	43,360
	N	W	83	11,795	13,656	25,820	12,164
	O	E	82	221	474	474	
			83	379	518	916	398
	V	E	81	60,035	48,780	54,436	5,656
			82	106,627	102,657	118,516	15,859
			83	2,865	1,848	2,231	383
			84	7,220	5,033	5,701	668
			85	189,708	152,736	170,585	17,849
	V	W	81	6,614	5,150	5,737	587
GUATMAL	A	E	82	231	924	1,042	118
	A	W	83	5,961	4,800	6,558	1,758
	N	W	84	2,359	2,053	2,270	217
HG KONG	N	E	84	6,696	10,240	11,060	820
	N	W	82	3,872	6,268	8,274	2,006
	V	E	81	51,000	57,872	61,993	4,121
			82	7,880	12,922	13,459	537
			83	23,251	50,656	55,043	4,387
			84	4,570	6,699	7,309	610
			85	21,823	8,726	10,268	1,542
	V	H	82	132	343	386	43
			84	250	269	312	43
	V	W	81	7,434	7,806	8,340	534
			82	26,338	20,175	21,661	1,486
			83	66,318	74,451	79,600	5,149
			84	41,698	104,770	116,269	11,499

Crop
Product
TSUSA commodity number, description, and unit of quantity

Country	Mode	Reg	Yr	Quantity	F.A.S.	C.I.F.	Charges
			85	20,296	24,300	26,301	2,001
HUNGARY	N	E	84	60,638	97,081	108,040	10,959
	V	E	81	7,461	13,210	14,042	832
			82	8,016	7,966	9,413	1,447
			83	20,054	41,758	45,220	3,462
			84	20,328	15,739	19,798	4,059
			85	67,772	127,709	148,378	20,669
	V	W	81	1,039	1,680	2,259	579
			85	3,527	3,520	3,655	135
ICELAND	O	E	85	478	1,200	1,200	
	V	E	85	40,396	49,029	53,195	4,166
INDIA	V	E	81	1,210	843	1,058	215
			82	606	511	626	115
	V	W	83	1,384	1,075	1,355	280
INDNSIA	V	E	84	3,000	1,834	2,045	211
IRELAND	A	E	81	430	1,069	1,471	402
			83	212	370	658	288
	N	E	81	26,038	44,391	51,301	6,910
	O	E	84	31,946	37,584	41,084	3,500
	V	E	81	11,664	8,943	10,783	1,840
			82	2,225	1,801	2,025	224
			83	68,380	109,897	120,528	10,631
			84	62,198	69,552	81,147	11,595
			85	27,290	28,155	34,816	6,661
	V	W	81	4,094	3,454	3,977	523
			83	8,541	5,127	6,265	1,138
			84	2,673	1,798	2,180	382
			85	3,655	2,487	3,087	600
ISRAEL	N	E	82	53,833	74,304	81,358	7,054
			84	558,234	540,660	607,925	67,265
			85	145,300	124,424	139,349	14,925
	O	E	81	14,114	36,057	38,249	2,192
			83	429	291	291	
			84	23,788	15,719	17,611	1,892
	V	E	81	520,395	690,024	744,744	54,720
			82	743,613	1,020,941	1,135,498	114,557
			83	950,631	907,331	1,003,622	96,291
			84	918,946	1,142,158	1,264,289	122,131
			85	1,365,070	1,708,707	1,864,541	155,834
	V	W	81	492	582	625	43
			82	794	2,400	2,731	331
			83	14,368	19,858	21,358	1,500
			84	184,869	226,681	255,914	29,233
			85	41,905	50,965	57,414	6,449
ITALY	A	E	81	1,903	7,307	11,663	4,356
			82	5,757	22,139	24,335	2,196
			83	580	796	875	79
			84	15,548	33,085	41,940	8,855
			85	740	2,229	4,067	1,838
	N	E	81	1,093,788	2,874,324	3,050,558	175,604
			82	1,828,679	4,398,887	4,711,550	312,663
			83	2,481,415	7,056,370	7,565,151	508,781
			84	4,024,408	12,553,793	13,760,378	1,206,585
			85	4,899,364	13,508,617	14,780,697	1,272,080
	N	W	81	2,285	3,109	4,233	1,124
			83	22,256	50,217	55,130	4,913
			84	406,078	343,381	394,239	50,858
			85	383,071	494,407	557,158	62,751
	O	E	81	33,998	57,850	61,088	3,238
			82	27,866	47,682	50,682	3,000
			83	22,372	56,098	59,209	3,111
			84	52,177	78,753	83,329	4,576
			85	50,428	127,025	130,306	3,281
	V	E	81	199,467	394,898	433,757	38,859
			82	116,246	229,041	259,398	30,357
			83	161,015	371,708	408,822	37,114
			84	215,767	538,849	637,739	98,890
			85	277,299	659,753	768,617	108,864
	V	W	81	15,993	34,785	37,918	3,133
			82	15,586	27,882	29,976	2,094
			83	16,973	30,552	34,652	4,100
IVY CST	A	E	82	220	276	468	192
JAMAICA	A	E	83	705	1,205	1,409	204
JAPAN	A	E	81	1,491	7,418	11,343	3,925
			82	32	317	337	20
			83	419	345	1,748	1,403
	A	H	83	1,124	2,154	3,157	1,003
	A	W	81	597	6,034	8,866	2,832
			83	1,529	5,930	10,566	4,636
	N	E	81	7,121	32,407	36,312	3,905
			82	54,848	187,930	206,970	19,040
			83	9,086	32,148	35,445	3,297
			84	22,431	54,146	61,533	7,387
	N	H	81	501	3,848	5,201	1,353
			82	512	3,125	4,070	945
			84	5,280	16,537	20,194	3,657
			85	7,934	18,403	21,889	3,486
	N	W	81	8,039	38,571	40,911	2,340
			82	9,339	35,282	38,330	3,048
			83	79,975	298,272	333,929	35,657
			84	101,384	374,746	403,678	28,932
			85	72,304	270,669	287,253	16,584
	O	E	84	40	304	304	
	O	W	85	2,381	10,704	12,000	1,296
	V	E	82	620	1,191	1,322	131
			83	2,948	7,689	8,463	774
			84	2,051	6,162	6,882	720
			85	6,431	17,981	19,755	1,774
	V	H	83	3,226	11,743	13,947	2,204
	V	W	81	4,816	29,888	31,038	1,150
			82	2,425	11,675	12,188	513
			83	32,536	28,090	31,275	3,185
			84	3,637	9,798	10,618	820
			85	14,260	55,139	58,000	2,861
KOR REP	V	E	83	5,000	2,018	2,187	169
			84	37,143	13,179	15,195	2,016
			85	431	1,517	1,649	132
	V	H	84	1,185	1,124	1,396	272
	V	W	81	825	1,792	1,904	112
			82	3,073	2,071	2,254	183
			83	3,051	1,978	2,161	183
			84	2,000	1,500	1,580	80
			85	4,497	8,639	9,501	862
LEBANON	A	E	83	3,338	14,106	18,613	4,507
	V	E	83	18,330	17,365	18,104	739
			84	16,875	13,959	15,325	1,366
			85	29,757	23,994	27,358	3,364
	V	W	83	5,952	7,375	8,268	893
MEXICO	A	E	84	2,400	2,490	2,764	274
	O	E	81	793,920	584,520	584,520	
			82	2,269,341	1,254,057	1,282,967	28,910
			83	1,638,807	812,730	836,543	23,813
			84	2,392,977	1,498,936	1,506,225	7,289
			85	2,928,302	1,781,681	1,788,822	7,141
	O	W	81	67,136	80,392	80,392	
			82	57,948	50,501	50,501	
			83	32,348	12,597	12,597	
			84	48,828	33,022	33,022	
			85	141,363	178,679	178,679	
N ZEAL	A	H	85	6,163	14,772	19,191	4,419
	A	W	84	58	1,745	2,317	572
			85	1,200	2,345	3,150	805
	N	W	85	4,375	5,077	6,168	1,091
	V	E	81	600	337	460	123
			85	2,010	7,810	8,812	1,002
	V	W	83	32,381	26,844	30,041	3,197
NETHLDS	A	E	82	205	1,113	1,576	463
			83	2,565	2,728	3,638	910
			84	110	697	836	139
			85	336	1,100	1,521	421
	A	H	85	994	2,074	4,229	2,155
	A	W	83	134	1,081	1,146	65
			84	1,289	617	1,799	1,182
			85	298	1,620	2,201	581
	N	E	81	370,431	745,984	793,906	47,922
			82	432,959	776,923	824,811	47,888
			83	847,177	1,241,743	1,329,771	88,028
			84	17,373,971	16,581,670	18,485,070	1,903,400
			85	1,736,965	1,918,025	2,155,865	237,840
	N	W	81	52,376	82,182	97,102	14,920
			82	54,110	74,240	83,292	9,052
			83	163,187	301,851	352,283	50,432
			84	55,889	55,069	59,935	4,866
			85	177,992	259,378	313,786	54,408
	O	E	81	177,979	109,357	115,440	6,083
			82	30,387	75,618	75,618	
			83	37,027	25,159	26,868	1,709
			84	160,076	106,729	115,398	8,669
			85	43,308	49,111	52,911	3,800
	V	E	81	364,705	374,923	414,821	39,898
			82	371,872	362,212	405,545	43,333
			83	2,280,643	2,173,167	2,393,205	220,038
			84	1,149,340	1,095,294	1,215,709	120,415
			85	451,885	513,916	572,742	58,826
	V	W	81	65	281	286	5
			82	150	3,400	3,420	20
			83	41,460	48,835	54,344	5,509
			84	7,440	20,847	25,018	4,171

Crop
Product
TSUSA commodity number, description, and unit of quantity

Country	Mode	Reg	Yr	Quantity	F.A.S.	C.I.F.	Charges
			85	49,556	76,047	91,577	15,530
NORWAY	A	E	81	445	1,055	1,487	432
			82	524	1,547	1,859	312
			83	264	453	733	280
			85	3,853	10,037	13,753	3,716
	A	W	84	120	568	976	408
	N	E	81	19,384	42,005	45,633	3,628
			84	3,736	10,043	13,343	3,300
	N	W	81	6,258	15,150	16,963	1,813
			82	2,570	6,736	7,379	643
			83	5,501	10,579	13,096	2,517
			85	30,411	59,915	72,316	12,401
	V	E	81	1,335	3,208	3,474	266
			82	31,332	55,312	61,419	6,107
			83	24,088	50,547	56,360	5,813
			84	1,738	4,010	4,644	634
			85	9,045	10,600	11,699	1,099
	V	W	81	1,867	4,230	4,736	506
			82	3,719	6,728	7,925	1,197
			83	2,424	4,559	5,106	547
			84	6,094	13,366	16,107	2,741
OMAN	A	E	84	555	3,028	3,608	580
PERU	A	W	85	409	1,668	2,292	624
	V	E	84	618	903	1,074	171
PHIL R	A	W	82	128	376	376	150
	V	E	84	2,250	1,181	1,354	173
	V	W	81	158	458	500	42
			82	1,049	1,081	1,194	113
			83	3,795	3,921	4,491	570
			84	5,607	5,468	6,306	838
			85	4,423	2,904	3,218	314
POLAND	N	E	82	24,589	17,907	20,193	2,286
			84	3,995	2,803	4,064	1,261
			85	8,387	14,158	19,888	5,730
	O	E	82	40,450	33,444	37,404	3,960
			83	17,359	43,200	45,684	2,484
	V	E	81	246,343	191,336	217,419	26,083
			82	15,065	36,690	39,992	3,302
			83	76,371	61,583	69,486	7,903
			84	93,231	94,566	103,778	9,212
			85	194,755	107,171	121,412	14,241
PORTUGL	A	E	82	6,194	19,654	22,850	3,196
			83	3,268	7,594	9,585	1,991
			84	4,522	11,450	15,894	4,444
			85	5,942	18,959	23,425	4,466
	A	W	83	1,577	4,333	5,400	1,067
	N	E	83	6,118	14,081	14,755	674
	O	E	82	120	400	400	
			84	1,809	3,855	3,855	
	V	E	81	6,574	15,642	17,223	1,581
			82	38,899	52,591	57,263	4,672
			83	18,438	44,604	47,647	3,043
			84	27,070	62,477	66,347	3,870
			85	19,922	17,967	20,587	2,620
	V	W	82	3,009	5,943	6,273	330
REP SAF	N	E	84	156,650	80,757	92,795	12,038
	V	E	81	144,170	76,852	88,348	11,496
			82	103,800	52,993	62,532	9,539
			83	145,032	71,303	83,961	12,658
			84	12,287	5,882	6,752	870
			85	45,328	22,467	26,002	3,535
	V	W	83	1,440	715	857	142
SALVADR	A	E	83	350	280	506	226
SINGAPR	A	W	84	243	496	1,274	778
	V	W	84	17,511	27,807	35,392	7,585
			85	24,786	73,686	80,906	7,220
SPAIN	A	E	83	462	589	858	269
	A	W	81	130	474	624	150
	N	E	81	22,003	54,694	64,807	10,113
			82	164,189	259,206	278,176	18,970
			84	231,826	314,245	369,720	55,475
			85	321,051	499,327	549,089	49,762
	O	E	85	7,633	8,090	8,960	870
	V	E	81	591,945	816,960	882,159	65,199
			82	89,581	151,424	158,370	6,946
			83	346,929	526,807	564,384	37,577
			84	261,232	399,592	436,132	36,540
			85	205,002	281,107	309,066	27,959
	V	W	84	714	1,609	1,753	144
			85	41,142	34,474	37,774	3,300
SWAZLND	V	E	85	10,726	40,480	43,095	2,615
SWEDEN	A	E	82	12,994	31,144	44,024	12,880
			83	326	424	772	348
			84	1,323	4,992	6,418	1,426

Crop
Product
TSUSA commodity number, description, and unit of quantity

Country	Mode	Reg	Yr	Quantity	F.A.S.	C.I.F.	Charges
			85	3,433	8,718	11,290	2,572
	N	E	81	1,374,200	2,197,597	2,383,849	186,252
			82	1,131,658	1,320,878	1,444,052	123,174
			83	580,021	889,767	973,774	84,007
			84	551,510	840,200	947,918	107,718
	N	W	82	15,530	16,121	19,489	3,368
			83	4,926	6,883	7,623	740
			85	10,541	15,667	21,266	5,599
	O	E	83	975	1,590	1,590	
	V	E	81	37,392	52,585	59,163	6,578
			82	13,407	16,974	20,088	3,114
			83	27,645	35,326	38,505	3,179
			84	71,639	101,693	108,359	6,666
			85	487,675	717,764	815,241	97,477
	V	W	81	35,544	36,263	39,537	3,274
			83	5,707	1,933	4,753	2,820
			84	102,918	148,834	184,595	35,761
			85	93,496	121,047	150,136	29,089
SWITZLD	A	E	81	3,943	19,276	22,179	2,903
			82	37,715	133,976	153,220	19,244
			83	31,365	130,478	152,221	21,743
			84	19,732	74,060	92,686	18,626
			85	21,078	104,562	125,116	20,554
	A	H	84	2,209	8,725	14,852	6,127
			85	823	3,015	5,135	2,120
	A	W	81	1,088	3,729	5,345	1,616
			83	477	3,909	4,866	957
			84	227	368	909	541
			85	5,042	15,518	19,273	3,755
	N	E	81	2,604,649	5,614,924	5,836,752	277,276
			82	2,246,692	4,893,478	5,126,107	232,629
			83	2,729,505	6,417,567	6,731,181	313,614
			84	4,172,501	8,204,603	8,802,113	597,510
			85	3,767,412	8,737,729	9,555,585	817,856
	N	W	81	32,169	162,937	187,064	24,127
			82	85,894	351,924	397,090	45,166
			83	233,145	661,604	719,233	57,629
			84	512,122	1,176,491	1,311,720	135,229
			85	331,908	846,494	942,915	96,421
	O	E	82	1,798	3,992	4,307	315
			83	28,259	50,815	53,961	3,146
			84	216,134	341,443	355,624	14,181
			85	56,058	92,982	102,689	9,707
	O	W	82	380	935	935	
			85	2,684	2,635	2,808	173
	V	E	81	22,393	92,621	104,333	11,712
			82	54,491	169,873	186,311	16,438
			83	282,762	673,582	712,352	38,770
			84	457,464	838,707	894,522	55,815
			85	768,028	1,355,587	1,485,452	129,865
	V	W	82	6,512	26,724	30,027	3,303
			83	23,717	95,402	101,480	6,078
			84	81,311	231,742	251,980	20,238
			85	130,359	313,435	352,871	39,436
THAILND	V	E	82	250	318	351	33
	V	W	82	1,500	1,628	1,760	132
			83	2,999	2,356	2,590	234
			85	900	1,570	1,798	228
TRINID	A	E	81	3,500	2,571	3,901	1,330
			82	114	375	603	228
			84	2,877	3,803	4,837	1,034
	V	E	85	85,000	61,489	66,089	4,600
TUNISIA	A	W	81	423	347	624	277
			82	846	957	1,591	634
TURKEY	V	E	84	1,323	874	1,010	136
			85	39,907	24,722	27,952	3,230
	V	W	85	7,024	4,699	5,280	581
U KING	A	E	81	9,566	13,754	16,338	2,584
			82	16,010	34,332	43,419	9,087
			83	9,025	23,789	29,060	5,271
			84	40,884	90,929	118,753	27,824
			85	15,746	43,284	55,664	12,380
	A	H	83	442	1,046	1,719	673
	A	W	81	98	912	1,494	582
			83	2,079	7,009	7,546	537
	N	E	81	2,111,268	3,075,577	3,315,076	239,499
			82	7,851,862	11,512,930	12,359,069	846,139
			83	3,739,785	5,183,986	5,488,866	304,880
			84	18,702,193	23,571,271	25,549,715	1,978,444
			85	12,609,529	15,027,419	16,687,902	1,660,483
	N	W	81	843,615	1,234,325	1,357,801	123,475
			82	957,985	1,247,292	1,410,437	163,145
			83	2,610,216	3,586,608	4,024,225	437,617
			84	492,975	724,574	805,193	80,619

Crop
Product
TSUSA commodity number, description, and unit of quantity

Country	Mode	Reg	Yr	Quantity	F.A.S.	C.I.F.	Charges
			85	1,166,264	1,403,788	1,608,838	205,050
	O	E	81	40,682	82,847	87,947	5,100
			82	55,396	99,673	104,113	4,440
			83	1,557,115	2,160,104	2,271,538	111,434
			84	140,232	118,429	126,065	7,636
			85	4,801,119	5,738,476	6,010,885	272,409
	V	E	81	1,398,852	2,108,340	2,222,922	114,582
			82	1,055,323	1,445,824	1,524,033	78,209
			83	6,124,778	9,635,026	10,326,797	691,771
			84	2,132,453	2,518,263	2,759,817	241,554
			85	4,061,429	5,078,784	5,638,290	559,506
	V	W	82	239,462	344,528	389,648	45,120
			83	9,336	16,363	19,244	2,881
			84	1,188,346	1,552,558	1,751,959	199,401
			85	455,024	584,792	695,764	110,972
USSR	N	E	81	7,209	10,165	10,725	560
	O	E	81	3,656	4,394	4,838	444
			83	2,183	1,485	1,485	
			84	15,055	22,490	23,795	1,305
			85	3,146	1,779	1,779	
	V	E	82	31,992	40,396	41,794	1,398
			83	21,837	26,395	27,132	737
			85	13,252	17,301	19,060	1,759
VENEZ	A	E	82	701	2,104	2,918	814
			83	679	380	590	210
			84	8,772	10,260	12,202	1,942
			85	1,971	3,241	3,827	586
YUGOSLV	N	E	84	30,248	34,580	43,678	9,098
	O	E	83	6,614	17,073	17,073	
	O	W	81	162	526	526	
	V	E	81	49,206	68,750	79,441	10,691
			82	51,249	58,772	65,600	6,828
			83	58,260	70,526	83,090	12,564
			84	7,922	10,347	11,333	986
			85	185,143	116,403	142,255	25,852
	V	W	83	95,080	27,840	35,820	7,980

1571050 CONFECTIONERY CON CHOC NSPF (LB)

Country	Mode	Reg	Yr	Quantity	F.A.S.	C.I.F.	Charges
TOTAL			86	15,581,842	27,189,200	29,419,234	2,230,034
ARGENT	V	E	86	268,293	165,715	185,401	19,686
AUSTRAL	N	E	86	41,149	69,963	87,462	17,499
	N	W	86	34,722	94,695	106,288	11,593
	V	W	86	180,031	229,310	262,859	33,549
AUSTRIA	A	E	86	2,008	9,339	12,702	3,363
	A	W	86	2,027	8,357	11,507	3,150
	N	E	86	3,789	17,505	18,728	1,223
	V	E	86	72,267	137,427	142,117	4,690
BELGIUM	A	E	86	59,892	260,344	325,123	64,779
	A	H	86	1,145	7,230	9,471	2,241
	A	W	86	14,903	49,545	70,131	20,586
	N	E	86	296,787	801,994	927,057	125,063
	N	W	86	88,744	223,331	255,449	32,118
	O	E	86	250	2,800	2,840	40
	V	E	86	80,251	128,823	135,120	6,297
BRAZIL	V	E	86	169,023	77,898	89,429	11,531
BULGAR	A	E	86	367	2,170	2,270	100
	V	W	86	1,859	3,836	4,147	311
C RICA	V	E	86	89,404	75,802	82,341	6,539
CANADA	A	E	86	611	3,583	3,767	184
	A	W	86	9,480	8,146	9,980	1,834
	N	E	86	821,891	906,585	906,705	120
	O	E	86	805,065	1,071,898	1,071,898	
	O	W	86	580	1,072	1,072	
CHILE	V	E	86	145,004	138,131	149,877	11,746
CHINA M	V	W	86	975	1,667	1,750	83
CHINA T	V	E	86	45,282	46,782	50,533	3,751
COLOMB	V	E	86	3,800	1,710	1,950	240
DENMARK	V	E	86	58,489	61,416	65,397	3,981
DOM REP	V	E	86	9,833	3,650	3,908	258
ECUADOR	A	E	86	918	1,796	2,005	209
	V	E	86	28,095	24,648	26,062	1,414
FINLAND	A	E	86	1,166	3,431	5,381	1,950
	N	E	86	94,638	96,188	108,754	12,566
	N	W	86	166,179	202,390	267,776	65,386
	V	E	86	28,880	71,250	86,014	14,764
	V	W	86	89,280	137,140	179,860	42,720
FR GERM	A	E	86	2,865	13,826	17,306	3,480
	N	E	86	2,298,130	2,841,075	3,072,717	231,642
	N	W	86	44,055	104,656	123,289	18,633
	O	E	86	126,533	164,054	175,252	11,198
	V	E	86	284,290	323,178	352,913	29,735
	V	W	86	301,911	394,692	435,004	40,312
FRANCE	A	E	86	18,382	85,673	105,623	19,950
	A	W	86	212	1,234	1,710	476
	N	E	86	244,429	674,059	712,238	38,179
	N	W	86	9,207	15,256	19,392	4,136
	V	E	86	133,632	295,924	324,481	28,557
GREECE	V	E	86	60,271	47,444	55,528	8,084
HG KONG	V	E	86	29,942	43,515	45,068	1,553
	V	W	86	13,796	26,750	28,858	2,108
HUNGARY	V	E	86	83,701	82,475	95,822	13,347
IRELAND	V	E	86	31,624	33,130	39,289	6,159
ISRAEL	O	E	86	5,077	2,854	3,141	287
	V	E	86	613,734	1,004,610	1,072,204	67,594
ITALY	A	E	86	110	1,140	1,367	227
	A	W	86	196	1,894	2,040	146
	N	E	86	770,050	1,854,448	2,060,362	205,914
	O	E	86	2,430	17,477	18,422	945
	V	E	86	1,574,715	4,103,593	4,422,282	318,689
	V	W	86	35,641	139,709	150,319	10,610
JAMAICA	A	E	86	2,143	1,940	4,683	2,743
JAPAN	A	W	86	492	2,392	2,669	277
	V	E	86	5,787	18,109	19,358	1,249
	V	H	86	3,141	4,572	5,165	593
	V	W	86	31,197	73,857	77,276	3,419
KOR REP	V	E	86	533	1,468	1,640	172
LEBANON	V	E	86	2,472	2,266	2,362	96
	V	W	86	4,762	5,162	5,474	312
MEXICO	O	E	86	2,700	3,854	3,854	
	O	W	86	147,446	118,177	118,177	
N ZEAL	V	W	86	4,497	3,279	3,905	626
NETHLDS	A	E	86	2,225	9,808	13,684	3,876
	N	E	86	11,965	36,347	40,158	3,811
	N	W	86	3,895	8,687	12,930	4,243
	O	E	86	19,306	39,436	40,788	1,352
	V	E	86	89,511	113,681	123,784	10,103
NORWAY	A	E	86	722	1,794	2,714	920
	A	W	86	3,419	11,035	15,550	4,515
	V	E	86	20,749	47,744	53,629	5,885
PERU	V	E	86	9,053	17,123	18,347	1,224
PHIL R	V	W	86	11,758	5,882	6,483	601
POLAND	A	E	86	988	1,071	1,971	900
	V	E	86	154,913	112,710	126,371	13,661
PORTUGL	A	E	86	1,565	5,919	8,630	2,711
	A	W	86	1,567	6,300	8,268	1,968
REP SAF	V	E	86	41,300	58,271	68,637	10,366
S HELNA	V	E	86	33,000	16,466	18,966	2,500
SINGAPR	V	W	86	4,800	14,000	15,350	1,350
SPAIN	A	E	86	6,263	14,380	20,286	5,906
	A	W	86	3,731	1,379	5,379	4,000
	V	E	86	70,809	80,931	90,861	9,930
	V	W	86	8,824	26,721	28,048	1,327
SWEDEN	A	E	86	6,064	20,171	26,524	6,353
	V	E	86	49,798	68,680	78,609	9,929
SWITZLD	A	E	86	18,599	101,103	120,665	19,562
	A	W	86	15,071	122,282	139,449	17,167
	N	E	86	1,809,203	4,944,899	5,068,054	123,155
	N	W	86	3,707	8,867	9,739	872
	O	E	86	23,155	47,989	48,550	561
	V	E	86	197,102	505,332	532,027	26,695
U KING	A	E	86	8,617	16,836	23,954	7,118
	N	E	86	1,719,824	2,459,341	2,720,860	261,519
	N	W	86	146,737	125,118	153,609	28,491
	O	E	86	130,007	86,796	89,514	2,718
	V	E	86	280,759	325,029	351,966	26,937
	V	W	86	793	4,412	4,499	87
USSR	O	E	86	1,660	1,162	1,162	
	V	E	86	15,594	14,306	15,560	1,254
VENEZ	A	E	86	2,788	4,050	5,404	1,354
	N	E	86	15,708	19,872	22,472	2,600
YUGOSLV	V	E	86	29,113	27,961	33,462	5,501

Cocoa, powder

1564000 COCOA UNSWEET AND COCOA CAKE (LB)

Country	Mode	Reg	Yr	Quantity	F.A.S.	C.I.F.	Charges
TOTAL			81	171,692,128	71,183,746	80,665,930	9,545,417
			82	133,517,666	50,178,653	57,514,815	7,336,162
			83	174,097,313	68,578,696	77,962,323	9,383,627
			84	198,365,967	138,983,504	150,188,160	11,204,656
			85	180,282,212	105,594,377	116,368,004	10,773,627
			86	197,211,237	97,501,051	108,744,985	11,243,934
ARGENT	V	E	83	231,483	91,886	105,540	13,654
BAHRAIN	V	E	86	881,840	213,678	282,032	68,354
BELGIUM	A	E	83	220	330	463	133
	N	E	85	76,000	21,570	35,040	13,470

Crop Product TSUSA commodity number, description, and unit of quantity — Country	Mode	Reg	Yr	Quantity	F.A.S.	C.I.F.	Charges
	O	E	81	40,000	18,741	21,400	2,659
			84	45,086	52,306	54,405	2,099
	V	E	82	2,337	2,879	3,103	224
			83	4,739	5,428	5,651	223
			84	988,178	809,754	859,520	49,766
			85	217,852	223,650	242,793	19,143
			86	225,875	147,055	165,010	17,955
	V	W	86	40,000	36,864	40,200	3,336
BERMUDA	V	E	84	1,400	1,232	1,566	334
BRAZIL	N	E	83	465,600	46,946	58,021	11,075
			84	41,347,394	24,451,138	27,013,231	2,562,093
			86	309,792	83,293	99,401	16,108
	O	E	83	45,603	11,555	11,555	
			85	8,289	1,243	1,243	
	V	E	81	35,740,723	9,814,284	12,009,226	2,195,122
			82	31,707,417	6,459,465	8,492,589	2,033,124
			83	38,685,952	10,413,027	12,810,690	2,397,663
			84	14,393,254	8,221,687	9,082,539	860,852
			85	50,482,356	22,170,588	25,190,258	3,019,670
			86	45,243,647	14,592,834	17,171,616	2,578,782
	V	W	81	467,376	116,807	152,022	35,215
			82	566,363	94,643	136,590	41,947
			83	562,174	157,912	197,922	40,010
			84	573,197	358,765	402,176	43,411
			85	231,571	96,785	114,434	17,649
C RICA	V	E	81	808,558	234,169	284,423	50,254
			82	1,478,529	328,891	381,928	53,037
			83	486,350	118,173	139,513	21,340
			84	720,004	475,685	510,422	34,737
			85	1,120,002	391,191	455,189	63,998
			86	1,204,988	574,885	653,796	78,911
CAMROON	V	E	81	6,706,027	2,459,458	2,758,751	298,884
			82	555,560	190,154	209,762	19,608
			83	1,309,529	366,790	415,700	48,910
			84	1,936,352	1,557,655	1,634,220	76,565
			85	634,924	239,844	272,244	32,400
			86	2,427,099	1,012,277	1,131,917	119,640
CANADA	O	E	81	76,793	14,658	14,658	
			82	343,298	105,054	105,054	
			83	241,342	100,114	100,114	
			84	122,231	79,718	79,718	
			85	373,659	174,690	181,690	7,000
			86	175,377	30,429	30,429	
	O	W	82	21,835	31,661	31,661	
			83	165	317	317	
			84	250	266	266	
			85	34,650	28,387	31,636	3,249
CHILE	V	E	86	77,500	21,041	25,075	4,034
CHINA M	V	E	84	97,604	37,097	44,898	7,801
			86	72,851	43,625	51,228	7,603
	V	W	84	24,250	10,574	13,045	2,471
CHINA T	V	E	83	270,064	40,295	52,589	12,294
			84	40,000	47,661	50,000	2,339
COLOMB	V	E	81	637,131	122,944	164,268	41,324
			82	524,695	92,650	129,604	36,954
			83	260,145	54,980	73,361	18,381
			84	2,628,050	3,220,284	3,433,452	213,168
			86	451,105	115,358	142,895	27,537
DENMARK	V	E	82	120,000	60,756	68,231	7,475
			83	43,942	42,039	44,000	1,961
			84	40,000	32,100	34,000	1,900
			85	43,942	44,864	47,475	2,611
	V	W	83	40,000	23,293	25,787	2,494
DOM REP	N	E	85	425,938	134,468	151,132	16,664
	V	E	81	1,491,330	703,343	790,134	86,791
			82	1,035,000	228,917	289,565	60,648
			83	855,000	192,074	247,371	55,297
			84	568,605	385,925	418,107	32,182
			85	1,386,691	580,428	672,946	92,518
			86	1,573,040	648,630	745,784	97,154
ECUADOR	O	E	83	12,456	2,922	3,214	292
	V	E	81	10,791,896	3,705,859	4,314,837	608,978
			82	4,456,910	781,319	1,025,910	244,591
			83	4,866,643	860,033	1,124,521	264,488
			84	5,071,181	1,396,203	1,686,825	290,622
			85	5,462,741	1,147,959	1,436,022	288,063
			86	6,102,091	1,869,984	2,180,780	310,796
	V	W	83	216,710	292,498	301,658	9,160
FR GERM	N	E	81	6,988,129	5,326,385	5,709,359	382,974
			82	7,229,187	4,034,049	4,406,725	372,676
			84	7,915,454	6,879,204	7,348,346	469,142
			85	8,122,640	6,116,167	6,593,507	477,340
			86	155,998	91,276	99,840	8,564
	N	W	83	1,038,714	612,385	672,416	60,031
			85	517,095	366,292	408,603	42,311
	O	E	82	28,000	49,134	49,134	
			84	34,367	35,652	35,652	
			85	42,000	28,980	28,980	
			86	2,720	2,500	2,500	
	V	E	81	1,171,009	726,372	811,942	62,066
			82	1,644,000	836,055	922,774	86,719
			83	7,607,112	4,692,530	5,050,403	357,873
			84	1,862,643	1,576,443	1,687,393	110,950
			85	1,351,537	985,885	1,074,238	88,353
			86	7,435,429	5,345,968	5,727,601	381,633
	V	W	81	1,159,507	698,581	771,923	73,342
			82	706,693	450,448	500,848	50,400
			83	140,592	79,818	89,130	9,312
			84	161,412	138,914	151,195	12,281
			85	333,152	283,754	308,265	24,511
			86	791,228	561,361	613,349	51,988
FRANCE	A	E	81	617	770	3,016	2,246
			82	110	482	523	41
	N	E	84	28,615	52,323	56,941	4,618
	V	E	81	11,169,513	4,541,366	5,102,370	561,065
			82	2,743,403	1,310,745	1,436,370	125,625
			83	1,753,672	721,429	802,368	80,939
			84	1,445,188	1,153,476	1,230,174	76,698
			85	2,287,090	1,382,507	1,523,044	140,537
			86	771,035	505,901	546,387	40,486
	V	W	85	40,000	36,835	39,999	3,164
GHANA	V	E	81	5,526,491	1,260,969	1,672,798	411,829
			82	220,460	40,589	57,841	17,252
			83	1,102,300	218,735	302,390	83,655
			84	661,380	443,390	472,701	29,311
			86	1,565,266	390,668	513,574	122,906
GUATMAL	A	W	82	300	284	340	56
	V	E	83	149,913	104,939	114,465	9,526
HG KONG	V	E	84	270,064	49,373	62,089	12,716
			86	2,400	10,429	12,273	1,844
INDIA	V	E	83	648	1,685	1,884	199
INDNSIA	V	E	81	220,460	74,424	83,399	8,975
			82	66,138	12,026	15,788	3,762
			84	307,542	185,275	241,045	55,770
			85	250,222	152,975	168,457	15,482
ISRAEL	V	E	81	1,587	3,960	4,069	109
			82	28,100	23,585	24,612	1,027
			84	3,150	5,641	6,740	1,099
			85	40,000	38,125	40,000	1,875
			86	2,919	2,242	2,521	279
ITALY	N	E	85	13,056	27,880	31,986	4,106
	N	W	85	5,684	10,588	11,955	1,367
			86	45,837	44,129	49,334	5,205
	V	E	83	3,006	4,913	5,592	679
			84	8,817	22,179	24,092	1,913
			86	8,732	23,231	25,467	2,236
	V	W	84	12,949	34,621	35,495	874
IVY CST	N	E	83	19,979,847	3,757,571	5,029,686	1,272,115
			84	201,611	104,466	112,948	8,482
	O	E	81	31,967	9,870	9,870	
			83	4,409	1,168	1,168	
			86	158,732	46,504	46,504	
	V	E	81	31,526,217	7,931,311	9,474,630	1,539,125
			82	24,142,668	4,816,550	6,034,002	1,217,452
			83	6,753,932	1,311,390	1,637,736	326,346
			84	25,101,493	13,175,558	14,610,561	1,435,003
			85	34,432,229	15,227,129	17,260,609	2,033,480
			86	50,230,412	14,975,632	17,816,349	2,840,717
JAMAICA	A	E	84	1,415	296	795	499
	V	E	83	1,725	4,829	5,051	222
			84	64,800	40,816	45,663	4,847
JAPAN	V	E	83	54,000	25,078	28,669	3,591
			86	40,000	37,817	40,000	2,183
	V	W	84	661	938	1,289	351
KIRIBAT	V	E	86	1,851,864	567,318	668,031	100,713
MALAYSA	A	E	81	298	572	1,164	592
	O	E	83	12,500	3,376	3,714	338
	V	E	81	2,468,307	682,020	872,401	190,381
			82	2,584,935	584,202	784,659	200,457
			83	3,865,295	940,564	1,150,089	209,525
			84	7,434,542	4,207,686	4,619,521	411,835
			85	4,582,152	1,608,468	1,885,303	276,835
			86	2,239,317	717,297	811,939	94,642
	V	W	82	158,732	38,133	50,425	12,292
			83	213,846	59,365	71,263	11,898
			85	44,092	8,486	10,636	2,150
MALI	V	E	84	40,000	37,287	40,000	2,713
MEXICO	O	E	86	352,736	96,000	96,000	

Crop
Product
TSUSA commodity number, description, and unit of quantity

Country	Mode	Reg	Yr	Quantity	F.A.S.	C.I.F.	Charges
	V	E	83	2,204,600	533,050	619,125	86,075
			84	224,869	110,960	126,050	15,090
			86	440,920	130,000	155,800	25,800
N ANTIL	V	E	82	40,000	25,960	27,839	1,879
			83	11,250	12,915	13,500	585
N CALDN	V	E	86	40,500	38,644	40,500	1,856
N ZEAL	V	E	86	31,200	28,964	30,247	1,283
	V	W	86	40,000	25,101	27,700	2,599
NAMIBIA	V	E	85	3,891,713	3,499,463	3,719,033	219,570
			86	2,947,800	2,710,312	2,878,502	168,190
NETHLDS	A	E	83	800	584	1,134	550
			84	630	903	1,502	599
			85	331	1,100	1,294	194
	N	E	81	27,767,591	19,157,956	20,363,670	1,296,813
			82	28,519,020	16,733,977	17,999,140	1,265,163
			83	30,749,016	21,451,880	22,736,976	1,285,096
			84	35,353,530	33,499,566	35,158,298	1,658,732
			85	28,537,339	23,158,606	24,579,235	1,420,629
			86	25,088,875	20,586,602	21,852,172	1,265,570
	N	W	82	3,188,951	2,229,123	2,414,343	185,220
			84	3,126,075	3,554,310	3,749,779	195,469
			85	1,128,000	1,020,151	1,122,831	102,680
	O	E	81	432,600	262,823	291,299	28,476
			82	240,000	126,532	139,405	12,873
			83	970,000	690,454	750,669	60,215
			84	3,841,000	2,981,951	3,125,437	143,486
			85	7,128,313	5,829,301	6,314,186	484,885
			86	3,640,863	2,738,344	3,021,110	282,766
	V	E	81	6,670,467	4,872,502	5,223,759	351,257
			82	8,958,770	5,939,331	6,398,771	459,440
			83	13,547,334	9,497,288	10,148,450	651,162
			84	16,289,673	13,795,688	14,690,449	894,761
			85	9,438,903	7,820,663	8,442,687	622,024
			86	14,676,193	11,864,785	12,684,876	820,091
	V	W	81	6,170,526	4,884,026	5,290,253	406,227
			82	2,846,052	2,113,845	2,284,636	170,791
			83	7,766,743	5,965,301	6,412,346	447,045
			84	3,922,500	3,948,214	4,217,072	268,858
			85	8,242,485	7,326,109	7,985,904	659,795
			86	10,716,569	9,043,501	9,767,067	723,566
NIGER	V	E	85	81,000	73,499	78,322	4,823
NIGERIA	N	E	84	74,747	40,502	50,528	10,026
	V	E	81	8,684,625	1,919,563	2,422,988	503,425
			82	4,454,503	796,355	1,127,532	331,177
			83	6,171,403	578,416	993,552	415,136
			84	2,051,071	815,890	958,642	142,752
			85	1,091,277	417,541	490,423	72,882
			86	220,460	69,762	81,570	11,808
NORWAY	V	E	85	220,460	84,077	89,347	5,270
			86	50,510	52,081	56,493	4,412
PANAMA	V	E	81	132,276	25,332	34,518	9,186
			82	507,098	86,151	114,165	28,014
			83	877,173	170,250	225,681	55,431
			84	1,015,877	487,611	556,581	68,970
			85	353,000	83,320	103,667	20,347
			86	1,396,035	327,793	397,683	69,890
PERU	V	E	81	264,560	55,287	74,379	19,092
			82	556,420	54,573	86,000	31,427
			83	1,185,370	248,968	313,988	65,020
			84	757,587	335,975	376,764	40,789
			85	887,382	217,800	235,365	17,565
			86	569,237	175,343	199,182	23,839
	V	W	82	1,087	1,250	1,299	49
			83	119,048	108,501	117,383	8,882
PHIL R	O	E	84	83,057	20,141	23,469	3,328
	V	E	82	189,596	242,790	255,522	12,732
			83	2,462,530	329,993	465,575	135,582
	V	W	82	33,069	10,701	12,914	2,213
			83	179,093	37,921	52,956	15,035
POLAND	V	E	84	36,000	49,454	51,120	1,666
PORTUGL	O	E	83	694	1,000	1,000	
			84	400	400	400	
REP SAF	V	E	83	39,683	22,189	25,020	2,831
SENEGAL	V	E	81	716,495	117,513	164,864	47,351
SINGAPR	O	E	85	3,306	2,182	2,182	
			86	40,000	20,175	23,600	3,425
	V	E	81	2,124,038	603,700	826,125	222,425
			82	2,282,614	532,229	704,072	171,843
			83	15,109,219	2,615,781	3,361,885	746,104
			84	11,287,084	5,032,771	5,664,745	631,974
			85	2,783,582	1,072,847	1,259,803	186,956
			86	3,281,305	1,034,701	1,210,358	175,657
	V	W	81	119,997	40,389	52,118	11,729
			83	176,368	28,371	42,800	14,429
			84	172,276	37,313	53,500	16,187
			85	402,673	194,559	230,930	36,371
			86	3,322,102	1,650,291	1,914,053	263,762
SPAIN	O	E	86	39,683	24,984	27,484	2,500
	V	E	81	330,690	69,351	90,000	20,649
			82	46,297	21,657	25,840	4,183
			83	118,720	60,543	72,602	12,059
			84	413,270	296,254	325,787	29,533
			86	182,707	113,938	134,599	20,661
SWEDEN	V	E	81	220	533	561	28
			83	40,000	20,468	22,960	2,492
			84	40,000	31,995	33,999	2,004
	V	W	83	20,000	8,373	8,600	227
			84	81,000	107,154	110,970	3,816
SWITZLD	A	E	85	1,323	1,592	2,429	837
	N	E	85	11,928	12,799	14,027	1,228
	O	E	82	1,102	3,396	3,609	213
			83	3,990	7,267	7,864	597
			84	882	1,899	2,023	124
			85	661	1,435	1,586	151
			86	1,984	4,029	4,228	199
	V	E	81	3,637	9,262	9,712	450
			82	11,648	28,392	30,030	1,638
			83	28,606	43,858	47,792	3,934
			84	8,677	16,872	18,475	1,603
			85	21,799	35,942	37,307	1,365
			86	88,610	125,991	134,475	8,484
	V	W	82	441	926	1,018	92
			83	4,188	8,383	8,970	587
			84	45,952	48,442	51,708	3,266
			85	3,528	5,264	5,571	307
			86	2,205	4,290	4,444	154
TRINID	V	E	85	625	1,548	2,122	574
U KING	A	E	86	2,000	3,280	5,012	1,732
	N	E	82	329,732	139,401	159,466	20,065
			84	108,202	72,775	78,464	5,689
			86	565,083	378,337	416,571	38,234
	O	E	83	117,110	155,927	159,329	3,402
	V	E	81	1,250,245	717,794	793,908	76,114
			82	862,654	465,651	514,785	49,134
			83	847,948	545,159	588,678	43,519
			84	5,117,969	4,256,900	4,493,279	236,379
			85	3,371,520	3,114,796	3,332,434	217,638
			86	5,305,564	3,454,839	3,793,423	338,584
	V	W	82	40,000	22,359	24,594	2,235
			84	120,000	98,948	107,339	8,391
			85	121,500	90,045	99,635	9,590
			86	81,002	86,738	92,004	5,266
USSR	V	E	83	661	469	582	113
VENEZ	V	E	82	43,942	31,383	31,797	414
			83	66,138	75,000	78,895	3,895
W SAMOA	A	H	81	29	312	376	64
	A	W	81	196	540	740	200
YEMAN S	V	E	84	40,500	59,028	60,750	1,722

Cocoa, sweetened
1564500 COCOA, SWEETENED (LB)

Country	Mode	Reg	Yr	Quantity	F.A.S.	C.I.F.	Charges
TOTAL			81	1,681,081	1,314,885	1,414,513	99,628
			82	4,292,891	2,917,525	3,159,876	242,351
			83	7,421,414	3,371,160	3,553,589	182,429
			84	22,022,976	9,379,881	9,459,776	79,895
			85	10,595,416	5,156,991	5,266,338	109,347
			86	3,284,495	1,285,807	1,326,822	41,015
ARGENT	A	E	82	443	302	592	290
AUSTRAL	A	W	85	2,293	4,874	6,303	1,429
AUSTRIA	V	W	84	1,350	1,047	1,510	463
B VIRGN	V	E	86	183	1,414	1,435	21
BELGIUM	V	E	82	1,102	1,212	1,259	47
BRAZIL	O	E	83	1,917	405	556	151
	V	E	84	551,150	605,771	643,542	37,771
			85	424,386	443,714	473,843	30,129
			86	385,805	386,883	413,381	26,498
C RICA	V	E	83	191,050	52,596	61,568	8,972
			84	240,000	84,800	97,929	13,129
			85	40,000	12,400	14,249	1,849
CANADA	N	E	84	3,970,625	1,413,101	1,413,101	
	O	E	82	553,297	128,377	128,377	
			83	4,413,917	1,348,588	1,348,588	
			84	16,864,585	6,911,229	6,913,129	1,900
			85	8,993,347	3,531,856	3,537,121	5,265
			86	2,694,925	776,713	779,589	2,876

Crop Product TSUSA commodity number, description, and unit of quantity Country	Mode	Reg	Yr	Quantity	F.A.S.	C.I.F.	Charges
	O	W	84	750	397	397	
COLOMB	A	E	86	1,247	1,550	1,791	241
	V	E	84	13,228	17,372	18,044	672
DOM REP	A	E	84	1,200	925	1,008	83
	N	E	82	136,025	56,443	61,053	4,610
	V	E	81	45,000	28,215	29,634	1,419
			83	540,000	137,702	156,217	18,515
			84	65,412	66,618	73,161	6,543
			85	107,406	74,202	79,263	5,061
			86	15,210	4,487	5,154	667
ECUADOR	V	E	81	1,634,210	1,284,024	1,381,431	97,407
			82	3,400,576	2,630,973	2,852,879	221,906
			83	2,086,714	1,639,995	1,780,288	140,293
			84	66,138	87,975	92,276	4,301
			85	674,608	770,906	817,392	46,486
FR GERM	V	E	84	46,547	27,146	29,530	2,384
	V	W	82	40,296	19,154	21,654	2,500
			83	44,000	21,248	23,998	2,750
			84	48,546	31,475	33,694	2,219
			85	25,000	18,900	21,000	2,100
			86	25,000	18,000	20,150	2,150
FRANCE	A	E	85	882	1,510	2,155	645
	O	E	86	111,795	12,521	12,521	
	V	E	82	629	1,473	1,579	106
			84	1,429	742	797	55
GREECE	A	E	83	220	252	382	130
	O	E	84	643	593	723	130
ISRAEL	V	E	84	960	1,700	1,914	214
ITALY	A	E	83	282	586	910	324
	V	W	82	1,370	2,087	2,134	47
JAMAICA	A	E	82	2,249	370	533	163
	V	E	82	16,800	33,120	34,479	1,359
			83	50,853	52,758	57,020	4,262
			85	6,300	4,050	4,676	626
MEXICO	O	E	83	13,600	5,308	5,308	
			85	96,898	75,855	75,855	
	O	W	81	811	1,095	1,095	
			85	44,372	33,888	33,888	
NETHLDS	A	E	81	606	497	957	460
			82	3,197	2,471	4,931	2,460
			83	3,307	2,775	3,780	1,005
	V	E	83	16,431	25,158	26,469	1,311
			84	46,547	26,952	29,890	2,938
			85	71,734	84,126	87,927	3,801
	V	W	83	9,350	8,334	9,326	992
			85	100,750	91,154	99,715	8,561
NIGERIA	A	E	84	274	320	588	268
NORWAY	V	E	82	992	2,201	2,394	193
	V	W	86	1,204	1,834	2,064	230
PERU	V	E	82	129,250	28,563	36,190	7,627
PHIL R	V	E	84	40,013	20,207	22,536	2,329
	V	W	82	26	486	540	54
			84	773	376	431	55
			86	2,750	1,578	1,808	230
PORTUGL	V	E	81	322	752	1,010	258
SWITZLD	V	E	82	6,438	9,976	10,659	683
			83	16,704	24,002	24,912	910
	V	W	83	33,069	51,453	54,267	2,814
			84	15,256	24,158	26,525	2,367
U KING	A	E	85	7,440	9,556	12,951	3,395
	A	W	82	201	317	623	306
	O	E	84	47,268	55,798	57,645	1,847
	V	E	84	282	1,179	1,406	227
			86	46,376	80,827	88,929	8,102
	V	W	81	132	302	386	84

Theobromine, alkaloid
4371800 THEOBROMINE (LB)

Country	Mode	Reg	Yr	Quantity	F.A.S.	C.I.F.	Charges
TOTAL			81	110	1,796	1,821	25
			82	55	1,070	1,183	113
			83	15,915	12,493	13,464	971
			84	245	2,706	2,852	146
			85	62	1,120	1,160	40
			86	55	2,427	2,607	180
FR GERM	A	E	84	110	1,115	1,125	10
	O	E	83	15,750	9,453	10,133	680
GUYANA	V	E	84	80	316	329	13
SPAIN	A	E	82	55	1,070	1,183	113
			83	165	3,040	3,331	291
			84	55	1,275	1,398	123
			85	62	1,120	1,160	40

Crop Product TSUSA commodity number, description, and unit of quantity Country	Mode	Reg	Yr	Quantity	F.A.S.	C.I.F.	Charges
			86	55	2,427	2,607	180
USSR	A	E	81	110	1,796	1,821	25

Coconut Palm

Coconut, copra
1750900 COPRA (LB)

Country	Mode	Reg	Yr	Quantity	F.A.S.	C.I.F.	Charges
TOTAL			82	115,000	47,800	53,932	6,132
			85	100	4,729	4,838	109
NETHLDS	V	W	85	100	4,729	4,838	109
PHIL R	V	E	82	115,000	47,800	53,932	6,132

Coconut, in shell
1450400 COCONUTS IN SHELL (NO)

Country	Mode	Reg	Yr	Quantity	F.A.S.	C.I.F.	Charges
TOTAL			81	22,037,339	3,888,623	4,880,141	991,758
			82	23,898,597	3,893,680	4,902,276	1,008,596
			83	29,101,207	4,242,197	5,468,936	1,226,739
			84	22,404,234	3,336,938	4,318,307	981,369
			85	22,239,596	3,363,980	4,307,017	943,037
			86	20,887,309	3,093,324	3,958,733	865,409
BAHAMAS	V	E	84	49,000	5,600	6,569	969
C RICA	N	E	81	1,262,822	190,074	252,076	62,002
	V	E	81	197,577	33,810	41,519	7,709
			82	1,955,343	240,835	312,022	71,187
			83	4,022,379	529,869	684,053	154,184
			84	378,664	61,262	85,047	23,785
			85	299,929	49,333	63,105	13,772
			86	71,360	16,170	23,300	7,130
	V	W	81	4,096	833	1,029	196
			83	57,028	22,720	30,761	8,041
			84	15,486	12,395	16,985	4,590
			85	300	1,200	2,091	891
CANADA	O	E	83	204	447	460	13
	O	W	83	2,000	900	900	
CHILE	V	E	83	93,500	17,600	22,440	4,840
CHINA M	V	W	86	2,600	1,144	1,257	113
CHINA T	V	W	84	2,136	1,658	1,910	252
COLOMB	V	E	84	884	300	400	100
CR N AN	V	E	81	25,000	4,000	6,193	2,193
DOM REP	A	E	84	1,350	490	777	287
	N	E	81	10,186,929	1,854,310	2,391,837	537,527
			82	10,525,237	1,822,298	2,317,659	495,361
			83	11,024,826	1,854,216	2,449,346	595,130
			84	4,958,736	588,999	800,132	211,133
			85	13,952,877	2,032,016	2,659,503	627,487
			86	5,291,292	578,488	729,223	150,735
	O	E	81	8,350	1,825	1,825	
			84	30	428	428	
	V	E	81	3,452,425	631,843	770,934	139,091
			82	4,180,956	690,610	866,368	175,758
			83	4,017,369	514,609	680,788	166,179
			84	10,816,528	1,790,320	2,393,234	602,914
			85	3,357,776	523,292	688,902	165,610
			86	11,377,680	1,795,918	2,368,612	572,694
	V	W	86	220,000	16,060	20,020	3,960
DOMINCA	V	E	81	55,000	4,400	6,217	1,817
ECUADOR	A	E	86	15,512	2,400	5,138	2,738
	V	W	82	2,000	600	1,123	523
F W IND	V	E	81	18,500	2,960	5,390	2,430
			82	173,950	20,812	29,333	8,521
FIJI	V	W	85	49,340	11,601	16,101	4,500
FR GERM	V	E	84	22,000	2,750	3,515	765
FRANCE	V	E	84	82,000	6,900	9,807	2,907
			85	122,000	19,030	21,191	2,161
GUATMAL	V	E	86	14,978	2,515	3,060	545
	V	W	83	360	279	412	133
HAITI	V	E	84	42,700	3,030	5,606	2,576
HG KONG	A	E	81	6	397	431	34
	V	E	85	21,000	9,763	11,559	1,796
HONDURA	V	E	81	3,197,415	462,214	571,674	109,700
			82	3,078,296	432,521	535,941	103,420
			83	4,577,679	662,397	813,581	151,184
			84	2,351,231	363,456	454,131	90,675
			85	1,697,906	286,730	350,940	64,210
			86	1,772,437	294,479	351,282	56,803
INDIA	V	E	85	350,000	71,290	73,500	2,210
ITALY	A	E	82	17,300	9,200	15,823	6,623

Crop
Product
TSUSA commodity number, description, and unit of quantity

Country	Mode	Reg	Yr	Quantity	F.A.S.	C.I.F.	Charges
	V	E	81	38,500	28,000	33,775	5,775
JAMAICA	V	E	81	67,740	49,944	61,592	11,648
			82	110,325	83,750	98,485	14,735
			83	76,300	62,993	72,779	9,786
			84	253,300	60,865	69,385	8,520
			85	177,129	89,194	103,698	14,504
			86	78,576	63,105	73,022	9,917
JAPAN	V	E	85	7,000	1,068	1,391	323
KIRIBAT	V	H	83	4,520	1,247	1,581	334
MEXICO	O	E	81	1,852,767	283,084	283,084	
			82	1,431,442	112,906	113,272	366
			83	2,151,406	100,160	100,160	
			84	1,818,074	107,672	107,672	
			85	1,016,027	67,963	67,963	
			86	655,085	39,744	39,744	
	O	W	81	489,163	134,058	134,058	
			82	737,578	183,018	183,018	
			83	1,308,684	267,527	267,527	
			84	1,140,008	222,726	222,726	
			85	473,990	84,094	84,094	
			86	770,134	164,642	164,642	
	V	E	85	40,368	6,264	7,412	1,148
MOZAMBQ	O	W	86	4,060	1,054	1,054	
N ZEAL	O	W	81	2,100	761	761	
OMAN	V	E	81	22,232	3,390	4,661	1,271
PANAMA	V	E	81	7,380	3,763	5,562	1,799
PHIL R	V	E	82	22,000	4,125	5,810	1,685
			83	500,000	38,000	44,306	6,306
			84	50,000	27,500	29,394	1,894
			85	24,750	3,795	4,165	370
	V	W	81	13,500	25,650	28,310	2,660
			82	190,000	70,500	83,275	12,775
			83	5,440	7,493	8,462	969
			84	26,523	16,251	18,632	2,381
			85	5,898	5,665	6,613	948
			86	3,000	1,817	2,065	248
PORTUGL	V	E	84	50	660	720	60
SALVADR	V	E	83	9,030	2,542	4,816	2,274
	V	W	83	12,282	2,009	6,609	4,600
THAILND	V	W	83	2,240	896	1,133	237
			84	13,124	15,610	17,544	1,934
			85	11,816	5,086	5,659	573
			86	2,500	1,250	1,250	
W SAMOA	O	H	84	15,440	1,694	2,977	1,283
	O	W	84	1,500	525	648	123
	V	W	81	1,135,837	173,307	279,213	105,906
			82	1,474,170	222,505	340,147	117,642
			83	1,235,960	156,293	278,822	122,529
			84	365,470	45,847	70,068	24,221
			85	631,490	96,596	139,130	42,534
			86	608,095	114,538	175,064	60,526

Coconut, meat, prepared or preserved
1450700 COCONUT MT FZN NOV10% SUG AD (LB)

Country	Mode	Reg	Yr	Quantity	F.A.S.	C.I.F.	Charges
TOTAL			81	1,379,825	599,509	685,083	85,574
			82	1,999,040	863,179	1,014,228	151,049
			83	1,970,467	872,434	1,044,836	172,402
			84	2,763,978	1,159,789	1,380,471	220,682
			85	4,725,559	2,176,734	2,540,028	363,294
			86	2,189,787	874,379	1,032,123	157,744
BELGIUM	V	W	86	796	1,897	1,915	18
BRAZIL	V	E	81	2,113	3,308	3,737	429
C RICA	V	E	81	65,200	32,826	36,022	3,196
			83	43,655	12,420	15,904	3,484
			84	72,940	18,774	25,427	6,653
			85	284,111	139,479	168,841	29,362
			86	229,813	113,851	131,966	18,115
	V	W	84	9,836	2,000	2,256	256
CANADA	A	E	81	4,482	747	1,205	458
	O	E	82	5,000	1,805	1,805	
	O	W	83	25	331	331	
CHINA M	V	E	81	750	1,483	1,571	88
			82	225	424	447	23
			86	1,188	2,424	2,561	137
	V	H	84	84	352	397	45
	V	W	82	750	884	940	56
			84	425	511	547	36
			86	2,375	2,752	2,897	145
CHINA T	V	W	84	5,732	6,900	8,184	1,284
DOM REP	N	E	81	66,631	18,768	21,599	2,831
			82	23,993	8,323	11,272	2,949

Crop
Product
TSUSA commodity number, description, and unit of quantity

Country	Mode	Reg	Yr	Quantity	F.A.S.	C.I.F.	Charges
			84	314,478	69,894	85,928	16,034
	V	E	81	434,171	108,922	124,015	15,093
			82	749,140	357,091	395,665	38,574
			83	677,601	266,848	297,158	30,310
			84	1,094,902	350,212	406,761	56,549
			85	1,896,226	597,320	692,444	95,124
			86	345,378	109,261	131,148	21,887
	V	W	82	42,439	4,400	6,883	2,483
FIJI	N	H	82	259,143	103,126	145,228	42,102
			83	347,147	131,823	198,899	67,076
			84	280,278	98,501	156,887	58,386
			85	199,676	66,268	106,060	39,792
			86	55,190	27,346	36,987	9,641
	V	H	81	295,923	128,864	158,350	29,486
FRANCE	V	W	86	641	1,603	1,999	396
GUATMAL	V	E	82	27,350	3,777	6,456	2,679
			83	5,867	900	1,202	302
HAITI	A	E	81	4,942	1,148	1,274	126
HG KONG	V	E	83	3,063	5,105	5,336	231
			85	80,000	45,760	52,389	6,629
			86	1,443	1,875	2,297	422
	V	W	85	288	1,572	1,691	119
			86	16,255	9,340	10,198	858
JAMAICA	A	E	84	2,001	1,587	1,837	250
JAPAN	V	E	81	2,500	1,625	1,851	226
			82	400	524	571	47
MALAYSA	V	E	85	25,000	9,718	11,918	2,200
	V	W	81	2,204	1,670	1,843	173
MEXICO	O	W	81	827	540	540	
PHIL R	A	W	82	450	295	1,122	827
	N	W	81	12,500	4,109	4,209	100
			86	114,668	56,220	62,188	5,968
	O	E	81	5,000	3,028	3,028	
			83	10,915	2,673	2,673	
			84	886	721	721	
			86	27,980	14,528	14,528	
	V	E	81	70,410	37,921	44,724	6,803
			82	9,800	6,515	7,633	1,118
			83	99,960	43,487	50,438	6,951
			84	390,116	246,542	275,694	29,152
			85	585,534	316,862	366,449	49,587
			86	710,752	255,352	301,799	46,447
	V	H	82	24,800	20,150	23,440	3,290
			83	33,212	27,176	31,387	4,211
			84	26,504	21,463	25,755	4,292
			85	51,779	42,437	51,597	9,160
			86	38,700	26,012	32,143	6,131
	V	W	81	396,128	242,800	268,448	25,648
			82	664,428	275,575	319,698	44,123
			83	726,338	367,393	425,255	57,862
			84	467,094	286,763	326,697	39,934
			85	1,446,053	868,996	989,498	120,502
			86	237,223	86,587	107,155	20,568
SALVADR	V	E	82	159,222	58,020	67,727	9,707
			83	7,065	4,474	5,189	715
			84	44,000	20,680	23,012	2,332
			85	44,000	21,120	23,607	2,487
			86	37,800	5,670	8,490	2,820
SINGAPR	V	E	82	4,435	3,815	4,030	215
SPAIN	V	W	84	45,000	27,788	32,351	4,563
SRI LKA	V	E	86	113,125	29,317	38,169	8,852
THAILND	V	E	82	12,614	7,169	8,635	1,466
			83	2,004	1,550	1,732	182
			84	7,891	5,161	5,650	489
			85	31,522	22,529	26,691	4,162
			86	2,500	1,300	1,639	339
	V	W	81	11,133	6,279	6,746	467
			82	5,401	3,286	3,744	458
			83	12,740	7,700	8,723	1,023
			84	1,811	1,940	2,367	427
			85	79,620	41,908	46,078	4,170
			86	219,077	100,399	110,342	9,943
U KING	O	E	83	875	554	609	55
			85	1,750	2,765	2,765	
	V	E	81	4,911	5,471	5,921	450
			86	34,883	28,645	33,702	5,057
W SAMOA	V	W	82	9,450	8,000	8,932	932

1450800 COCONUT MEAT, SHREDDED, ETC (LB)

Country	Mode	Reg	Yr	Quantity	F.A.S.	C.I.F.	Charges
TOTAL			81	85,760,144	49,219,455	54,916,955	5,673,842
			82	86,663,697	33,672,977	39,128,664	5,455,687
			83	93,829,203	37,114,209	43,176,718	6,062,509
			84	80,471,006	48,569,505	54,799,357	6,229,852
			85	96,074,888	56,143,806	63,253,056	7,109,250

Crop
Product
TSUSA commodity number, description, and unit of quantity

Country	Mode	Reg	Yr	Quantity	F.A.S.	C.I.F.	Charges
			86	80,384,729	28,329,959	33,554,666	5,224,707
AUSTRAL	N	H	82	2,381	1,772	2,094	322
BRAZIL	V	E	82	300	780	950	170
			85	1,056	1,920	2,551	631
			86	2,900	1,800	1,890	90
BURKINA	V	E	84	1,080	756	838	82
C RICA	V	E	81	1,550	516	547	31
			82	149,040	45,783	56,541	10,758
			83	194,720	63,393	79,181	15,788
			84	186,160	62,056	77,020	14,964
CANADA	O	E	81	21,500	14,813	14,813	
			82	24,600	12,090	12,090	
			85	3,750	1,742	1,742	
			86	40,000	15,600	15,600	
	O	W	81	28,004	30,574	30,574	
			82	22,675	25,650	25,650	
			83	28,549	31,916	31,916	
			84	16,075	18,035	18,035	
CHINA M	N	E	81	1,875	2,644	4,027	1,383
	O	E	84	170	298	298	
	V	W	81	1,500	905	988	83
			85	750	1,436	1,541	105
CHINA T	N	E	86	95,545	32,675	39,030	6,355
	O	E	85	252,400	133,252	155,518	22,266
			86	290,863	131,062	147,232	16,170
	V	E	82	134,960	41,677	49,543	7,866
			84	360,003	232,200	265,846	33,646
			85	1,230,000	647,904	738,538	90,634
			86	501,020	225,636	258,309	32,673
	V	W	81	44,000	25,080	27,483	2,403
			84	51,213	33,640	38,076	4,436
			85	733,551	448,025	502,621	54,596
			86	333,663	127,803	149,016	21,213
DOM REP	N	E	84	31,192	15,572	18,680	3,108
			85	1,177,549	420,976	484,498	63,522
			86	776,816	141,894	183,184	41,290
	V	E	81	305,973	131,028	148,766	17,738
			82	346,892	111,756	128,053	16,297
			83	278,216	63,684	75,810	12,126
			84	118,448	51,337	56,675	5,338
			85	589,081	171,473	204,044	32,571
			86	426,745	201,335	221,682	20,347
	V	W	81	12,000	5,400	6,662	1,262
DOMINCA	V	E	85	4,500	1,500	3,015	1,515
ECUADOR	V	E	85	43,281	22,880	25,627	2,747
FIJI	A	H	82	12,510	4,861	8,989	4,128
			85	58,313	25,523	38,595	13,072
	N	H	86	133,827	60,130	84,686	24,556
	V	H	81	94,184	40,293	49,046	8,753
FR GERM	V	E	81	220	413	434	21
			83	551	688	727	39
			85	36,000	4,320	6,156	1,836
GUATMAL	V	E	83	133,127	37,840	44,362	6,522
			85	43,120	12,016	14,763	2,747
HG KONG	O	E	86	95,000	42,800	47,654	4,854
	V	E	81	50,000	29,500	32,380	2,880
			83	146,250	72,332	83,016	10,684
			84	50,219	32,760	37,597	4,837
			85	191,325	125,774	142,854	17,080
			86	503,926	213,047	244,631	31,584
	V	W	85	55,000	24,911	28,719	3,808
			86	388,603	164,443	190,430	25,987
HONDURA	V	E	82	11,910	1,918	4,808	2,890
INDIA	V	W	86	25,008	8,913	11,450	2,537
INDNSIA	A	E	85	2,000	1,244	5,163	3,919
	V	W	84	50,000	31,500	34,404	2,904
			86	143,463	48,711	64,789	16,078
IVY CST	V	E	86	57,320	17,185	20,635	3,450
JAPAN	V	E	81	1,108,000	678,519	763,859	85,340
			82	50,000	15,000	17,994	2,994
			83	300,000	93,000	108,600	15,600
			84	285,000	183,350	208,396	25,046
			85	565,000	338,150	383,492	45,342
			86	100,000	44,000	48,800	4,800
	V	W	81	94,000	53,080	58,390	5,310
			82	22,498	7,831	9,141	1,310
			83	38,000	61,026	63,840	2,814
			84	25,000	15,850	18,050	2,200
			85	177,552	94,825	106,060	11,235
			86	23,213	11,000	12,560	1,560
KOR REP	V	E	82	100,000	46,320	53,020	6,700
LIBERIA	V	W	86	50,706	13,642	16,973	3,331
MACAO	V	W	83	24,250	7,599	9,007	1,408
MALAYSA	V	E	82	20,201	7,929	9,800	1,871
			85	49,150	22,718	28,028	5,310
	V	W	85	47,826	27,261	31,219	3,958
MEXICO	O	W	82	1,378	847	847	
			83	1,157	386	386	
			84	1,433	682	682	
			86	102,314	33,051	33,051	
	V	W	81	19,949	15,338	16,193	855
PHIL R	N	E	81	25,374,647	13,848,935	15,441,166	1,592,231
			82	28,971,134	11,213,424	12,984,668	1,771,244
			84	27,190,970	16,131,160	18,111,414	1,980,254
			85	630,864	397,160	442,082	44,922
			86	23,713,952	8,326,505	9,709,145	1,382,640
	N	W	82	629,745	222,747	261,921	39,174
			85	3,090,736	1,716,927	1,938,023	221,096
	O	E	81	184,400	109,858	124,041	14,183
			82	178,609	77,230	86,216	8,986
			83	56,700	24,140	24,140	
			84	40,322	7,989	7,989	
			85	25,000	15,750	18,293	2,543
			86	111,000	40,273	40,273	
	O	W	85	1,080	1,215	1,339	124
	V	E	81	34,435,119	20,667,480	23,115,440	2,422,310
			82	21,388,979	8,497,715	9,871,406	1,373,691
			83	55,960,048	21,573,698	25,136,254	3,562,556
			84	16,065,477	9,569,667	10,844,141	1,274,474
			85	54,633,954	32,082,537	35,880,754	3,798,217
			86	26,046,067	9,453,642	11,205,695	1,752,053
	V	H	81	47,750	29,075	32,248	3,173
			82	52,125	22,756	26,550	3,794
			83	22,250	7,670	9,119	1,449
			84	5,125	4,344	4,833	489
	V	W	81	23,920,495	13,527,247	15,039,548	1,514,293
			82	33,879,506	13,054,331	15,212,055	2,157,724
			83	35,546,413	14,765,323	17,129,128	2,363,805
			84	35,222,560	21,785,672	24,611,859	2,826,187
			85	29,172,297	17,655,017	20,061,912	2,406,895
			86	20,719,242	7,315,408	8,730,083	1,414,675
PORTUGL	V	E	82	2,646	3,000	3,442	442
SALVADR	V	E	82	357,824	152,251	174,952	22,701
			83	713,193	187,198	233,009	45,811
			84	638,588	282,620	316,150	33,530
			85	873,601	403,494	443,973	40,479
			86	851,455	250,353	278,965	28,612
SINGAPR	V	E	83	539	533	611	78
			86	10,104	6,085	8,108	2,023
	V	W	84	25,000	13,250	14,950	1,700
			85	20,833	12,473	14,167	1,694
			86	2,500	1,450	1,495	45
SRI LKA	N	E	86	2,164,056	601,298	779,841	178,543
	O	E	82	770	460	460	
	V	E	81	13,228	7,200	8,573	1,373
			82	22,046	8,497	10,633	2,136
			84	81,055	79,993	94,593	14,600
			85	1,971,049	1,084,579	1,259,661	175,082
			86	502,810	148,673	190,129	41,456
	V	W	82	52,668	26,902	32,134	5,232
			85	141,518	88,056	101,926	13,870
			86	1,036,717	287,732	362,473	74,741
T PAC I	V	W	86	192,810	50,113	65,832	15,719
THAILND	V	E	82	3,300	1,950	2,099	149
			83	1,000	560	634	74
			84	25,300	16,356	18,374	2,018
			85	50,000	25,180	34,125	8,945
			86	193,865	60,456	69,017	8,561
	V	H	83	6,614	5,683	6,420	737
	V	W	82	225,000	67,500	82,608	15,108
			83	150,876	48,886	57,464	8,578
			84	616	418	457	39
			85	102,502	63,751	75,125	11,374
			86	44,223	21,000	23,529	2,529
U KING	O	E	81	1,750	1,557	1,777	220
			83	1,750	1,154	1,230	76
			85	5,250	5,967	5,967	
	V	E	83	225,000	67,500	81,864	14,364
			85	95,000	63,850	70,965	7,115
			86	674,999	229,604	294,439	64,835
W SAMOA	V	W	86	29,997	2,640	4,040	1,400

1450900 COCONUT MEAT NSPF PREP PRES (LB)

Country	Mode	Reg	Yr	Quantity	F.A.S.	C.I.F.	Charges
TOTAL			81	3,942,308	1,927,921	2,141,357	213,436
			82	3,838,142	1,977,523	2,219,538	242,015
			83	3,531,514	1,630,074	1,823,023	192,949
			84	3,358,368	1,798,547	2,005,490	206,943

Crop / Product / TSUSA commodity number, description, and unit of quantity — Country	Mode	Reg	Yr	Quantity	F.A.S.	C.I.F.	Charges
			85	4,750,868	2,726,922	2,984,799	257,877
			86	6,869,122	3,565,089	3,949,004	383,915
BRAZIL	A	E	84	220	303	461	158
	V	E	83	26,062	9,807	12,430	2,623
			84	60,216	20,532	25,646	5,114
	V	W	82	2,884	5,132	7,339	2,207
			83	2,001	5,037	5,999	962
C RICA	V	E	81	401,062	208,323	232,109	23,786
			82	624,466	220,124	265,998	45,874
			83	338,107	117,081	143,518	26,437
			84	216,486	63,587	81,329	17,742
			85	205,940	85,892	105,907	20,015
			86	320,406	171,651	201,656	30,005
	V	W	85	6,033	12,214	14,025	1,811
CANADA	A	E	82	80	261	344	83
	O	E	83	39,300	10,379	10,379	
			84	40,000	30,000	30,000	
			85	40,000	7,600	7,600	
	O	W	82	1,000	1,300	1,368	68
			84	19,850	22,041	22,041	
			85	45,125	48,729	48,729	
			86	41,000	43,637	43,637	
CHINA M	V	E	81	2,865	4,526	4,765	239
			83	8,450	6,002	6,972	970
			84	3,125	5,294	5,834	540
			86	1,250	1,734	1,879	145
	V	W	82	2,125	4,083	4,360	277
			84	4,681	6,965	7,610	645
			85	6,811	7,539	8,108	569
			86	1,000	1,074	1,147	73
CHINA T	V	E	81	1,350	1,684	1,917	233
			82	3,420	4,651	5,084	433
			83	293	258	307	49
			86	33,492	11,700	13,684	1,984
	V	W	82	550	874	945	71
			83	490	1,733	1,917	184
			84	3,099	2,430	2,857	427
			85	106,653	64,507	72,295	7,788
DOM REP	N	E	82	74,478	8,800	11,533	2,733
			84	304,736	136,753	150,790	14,037
	O	E	83	83,915	42,840	46,116	3,276
	V	E	81	2,558,426	970,502	1,075,600	105,098
			82	1,670,209	707,284	768,862	61,578
			83	1,836,007	661,740	721,042	59,302
			84	1,357,715	479,759	524,592	44,833
			85	2,814,427	1,470,752	1,578,891	108,139
			86	4,111,619	1,997,961	2,180,237	182,276
FIJI	A	H	81	68	288	421	133
	V	W	81	555	489	578	89
			84	720	440	531	91
FR GERM	V	W	86	3,200	2,130	2,747	617
FRANCE	A	E	85	1,502	2,059	3,052	993
	V	E	83	169	255	274	19
			86	4,401	6,589	7,349	760
GUATMAL	V	E	81	88,848	46,794	52,192	5,398
			82	8,970	3,140	3,772	632
			84	1,440	1,020	1,125	105
HG KONG	V	E	81	4,235	7,682	8,044	362
			82	2,000	3,826	4,051	225
			83	1,500	2,764	3,193	429
			84	1,000	1,767	1,931	164
			85	3,250	4,933	5,321	388
			86	3,023	4,064	4,420	356
	V	W	82	875	1,841	1,940	99
			83	2,750	2,200	2,752	552
			84	375	577	639	62
			85	2,500	3,734	4,023	289
			86	6,425	6,534	6,996	462
INDIA	O	E	84	437	500	544	44
			86	3,750	1,874	1,926	52
INDNSIA	V	W	84	339	555	587	32
ITALY	V	E	83	631	1,532	1,639	107
JAMAICA	A	E	81	30	460	550	90
			85	2,622	2,500	4,143	1,643
JAPAN	V	E	81	2,499	2,214	2,618	404
	V	W	85	401	3,547	3,948	401
			86	8,256	5,150	5,969	819
KOR REP	V	W	82	1,957	3,309	3,468	159
			85	3,400	1,817	2,217	400
MALAYSA	V	W	81	30,000	26,070	27,286	1,216
			85	2,218	2,164	2,379	215
			86	6,398	2,037	2,500	463
MEXICO	O	E	86	15,879	9,239	9,239	
	O	W	82	4,248	1,023	1,023	
PHIL R	N	E	83	73,620	23,438	25,166	1,728
			84	40,335	26,864	28,904	2,040
	N	W	83	119,135	45,024	52,860	7,836
	O	E	84	40,000	7,600	7,600	
			85	121,080	24,158	24,460	302
	V	E	81	107,585	102,062	113,496	11,434
			82	95,909	94,830	107,547	12,717
			83	43,983	44,594	50,116	5,522
			84	73,623	72,974	83,882	10,908
			85	42,609	32,578	38,168	5,590
			86	399,112	202,456	235,424	32,968
	V	H	81	14,984	16,302	19,162	2,860
			82	24,483	27,204	31,695	4,491
			83	24,447	25,725	30,437	4,712
			84	39,862	40,803	49,743	8,940
			85	42,721	40,775	48,045	7,270
			86	40,914	43,945	50,145	6,200
	V	W	81	394,143	344,997	381,881	36,884
			82	744,062	486,191	551,114	64,923
			83	641,298	420,030	475,444	55,414
			84	613,843	441,620	507,919	66,299
			85	804,775	598,859	667,653	68,794
			86	481,950	394,147	441,882	47,735
SALVADR	N	E	81	296,556	159,770	181,173	21,403
	V	E	82	220,168	133,677	150,596	16,919
			83	53,326	40,151	47,888	7,737
SINGAPR	V	E	82	8,413	6,648	7,197	549
			83	2,392	1,890	2,116	226
			84	7,071	4,240	4,977	737
			86	2,545	2,348	2,746	398
	V	W	81	1,740	1,461	1,613	152
			82	4,732	2,281	2,480	199
			83	12,837	6,969	7,661	692
			84	8,842	4,494	4,980	486
			86	14,655	7,693	8,363	670
SRI LKA	O	E	82	1,870	1,246	1,246	
			86	3,052	1,096	2,211	1,115
	V	E	85	25,000	9,447	11,056	1,609
	V	W	84	38,580	29,028	33,198	4,170
			85	57,450	31,791	36,999	5,208
			86	70,249	16,392	21,252	4,860
THAILND	O	E	82	961	980	1,078	98
	O	W	85	31,746	9,750	10,905	1,155
	V	E	81	8,955	9,470	10,562	1,092
			82	19,611	16,457	17,873	1,416
			83	2,340	2,570	2,849	279
			84	7,257	3,739	4,234	495
			85	38,272	17,600	19,850	2,250
			86	126,142	46,213	53,091	6,878
	V	H	81	1,920	1,387	1,520	133
			82	9,231	6,015	6,861	846
			83	29,965	25,163	27,476	2,313
			86	6,981	3,600	4,038	438
	V	W	81	14,294	9,503	10,337	834
			82	87,505	57,750	62,416	4,666
			83	50,587	28,916	31,540	2,624
			84	167,997	97,025	105,810	8,785
			85	125,397	55,380	62,420	7,040
			86	993,229	482,438	536,899	54,461
TURKEY	V	W	85	1,356	1,774	2,217	443
U KING	N	E	81	10,618	12,399	13,839	1,440
			82	220,890	177,333	197,978	20,645
			83	134,944	101,611	110,401	8,790
			84	304,531	295,572	315,252	19,680
			85	179,433	153,345	166,280	12,935
			86	103,694	58,188	64,280	6,092
	O	E	81	875	774	846	72
			83	350	380	380	
			84	788	805	897	92
			85	8,575	7,883	7,883	
	V	E	83	2,615	1,985	2,151	166
			85	17,500	18,500	20,097	1,597
			86	66,500	41,199	45,287	4,088
	V	W	81	700	764	848	84
			82	3,045	1,263	1,370	107
			85	5,116	2,805	3,368	563
W SAMOA	V	H	84	1,200	1,260	1,577	317
	V	W	85	8,956	4,290	4,760	470

Crop Product TSUSA commodity number, description, and unit of quantity						
Country	Mode	Reg	Yr	Quantity	F.A.S.	C.I.F.	Charges

Coconut, oil, fatty acid**

4902408 OTH FATTY ACIDS FR PALM OIL (LB)

Country	Mode	Reg	Yr	Quantity	F.A.S.	C.I.F.	Charges
TOTAL			86	26,166,775	7,901,827	9,272,091	1,370,264
BELGIUM	V	E	86	111,852	66,221	75,034	8,813
CANADA	O	E	86	639,810	219,743	219,743	
CHINA M	V	E	86	959,007	1,237,304	1,342,977	105,673
DENMARK	A	E	86	1,102	1,643	2,792	1,149
	V	E	86	169,200	154,486	164,824	10,338
FR GERM	O	E	86	112,391	76,225	85,410	9,185
	V	E	86	6,504,687	2,523,040	2,954,763	431,723
MALAYSA	V	E	86	5,479,776	1,054,475	1,173,404	118,929
	V	W	86	2,087,929	631,362	659,433	28,071
MOROC	V	E	86	99,207	16,150	21,150	5,000
NETHLDS	O	E	86	32,627	25,062	28,059	2,997
	V	E	86	875,891	343,261	405,992	62,731
PHIL R	V	E	86	8,870,101	1,427,526	1,997,743	570,217
	V	W	86	43,122	11,996	15,061	3,065
SINGAPR	V	W	86	47,355	21,488	23,628	2,140
TURKEY	V	E	86	32,573	17,785	20,093	2,308
U KING	N	E	86	2,090	6,528	7,699	1,171
	V	E	86	98,055	67,532	74,286	6,754

4902410 FATTY ACIDS FR PALM OIL ETC (LB)

Country	Mode	Reg	Yr	Quantity	F.A.S.	C.I.F.	Charges
TOTAL			81	4,296,920	2,009,385	2,319,532	310,147
			82	4,489,623	1,966,267	2,195,306	229,039
			83	7,473,907	3,283,004	3,678,910	395,906
			84	14,378,823	7,205,743	7,900,240	694,497
			85	9,129,433	3,932,779	4,468,183	535,404
CANADA	O	E	82	17,860	10,946	10,946	
			83	570	364	364	
DENMARK	V	E	81	764,761	296,404	359,076	62,672
			82	260,429	92,983	111,659	18,676
			83	1,188,192	575,082	657,451	82,369
			84	795,005	615,933	679,741	63,808
			85	328,619	174,212	195,934	21,722
	V	W	83	75,133	53,224	60,649	7,425
FR GERM	A	E	83	1,433	1,382	1,969	587
	N	E	82	73,546	67,303	71,184	3,881
	O	E	83	18,188	12,601	13,201	600
			84	801,302	292,798	354,663	61,865
			85	60,318	60,063	64,844	4,781
	V	E	81	3,037,494	1,439,460	1,649,588	210,128
			82	3,260,325	1,372,026	1,521,240	149,214
			83	4,181,401	1,772,162	1,950,370	178,208
			84	4,694,538	2,752,230	3,031,330	279,100
			85	3,531,134	1,948,373	2,208,144	259,771
	V	W	85	37,456	5,315	5,849	534
FRANCE	N	E	85	3,968	3,801	6,294	2,493
GERM DR	V	E	85	43,122	43,814	47,433	3,619
INDNSIA	V	E	85	1,097,230	162,001	188,628	26,627
	V	W	83	33,069	10,988	11,161	173
JAPAN	A	W	85	3,355	4,974	7,366	2,392
	V	E	81	126,984	96,558	104,112	7,554
			82	279,188	179,969	199,800	19,831
			83	397	489	594	105
	V	W	81	55,953	43,862	48,574	4,712
			82	44,092	16,049	19,400	3,351
MALAYSA	V	E	82	330,745	116,855	133,723	16,868
			83	1,359,617	637,862	724,400	86,538
			84	3,854,485	1,553,725	1,753,221	199,496
			85	2,916,698	868,425	1,036,826	168,401
	V	W	83	51,588	16,901	19,928	3,027
			85	111,343	40,190	47,649	7,459
MOROC	V	E	85	49,604	16,361	19,687	3,326
NETHLDS	O	E	83	41,277	31,986	35,086	3,100
			85	1,077	7,545	8,393	848
	V	E	81	289,482	121,547	143,717	22,170
			82	147,624	78,842	89,058	10,216
			83	302,779	107,424	122,295	14,871
			84	275,127	121,161	139,808	18,647
			85	82,099	75,075	78,775	3,700
PHIL R	V	E	84	1,642,065	864,053	897,892	33,839
	V	W	84	2,278,735	998,136	1,032,509	34,373
			85	689,106	409,854	420,186	10,332
SINGAPR	V	E	85	130,512	101,743	114,725	12,982
SWEDEN	V	E	82	15,540	7,203	9,516	2,313
			83	145,284	37,104	51,070	13,966
			84	37,566	7,707	11,076	3,369
			85	38,338	6,667	10,145	3,478
U KING	A	E	85	4,409	2,443	5,372	2,929

Country	Mode	Reg	Yr	Quantity	F.A.S.	C.I.F.	Charges
	N	E	81	15,897	8,962	11,168	2,206
	V	E	81	6,349	2,592	3,297	705
			82	60,274	24,091	28,780	4,689
			83	74,979	25,435	30,372	4,937
			85	1,045	1,923	1,933	10

4902420 OTH FATTY ACIDS FR PALM OIL (LB)

Country	Mode	Reg	Yr	Quantity	F.A.S.	C.I.F.	Charges
TOTAL			81	4,320,282	2,467,784	2,708,646	241,472
			82	3,010,302	1,342,612	1,456,573	113,961
			83	3,565,031	1,910,600	2,038,988	128,388
			84	5,800,255	3,908,115	4,217,301	309,186
			85	13,572,844	6,538,266	6,953,751	415,485
BELGIUM	V	E	83	5,512	1,903	2,524	621
			85	80,000	39,737	44,872	5,135
CANADA	A	W	84	551	1,780	2,036	256
	O	E	81	591,360	288,911	288,301	
			82	415,745	189,033	189,033	
			83	1,110,282	554,218	554,218	
			84	409,020	190,397	190,397	
			85	1,168,140	451,386	451,386	
CHINA M	V	E	85	210,345	349,297	370,335	21,038
	V	W	84	202,824	311,024	332,442	21,418
CHINA T	V	W	85	44,092	14,924	16,069	1,145
DENMARK	A	E	85	2,204	2,635	2,635	
	V	E	81	36,774	13,733	17,299	3,566
			82	163,564	61,638	72,137	10,499
			83	92,113	52,119	58,028	5,909
			84	121,354	59,410	66,747	7,337
			85	36,652	14,500	17,144	2,644
	V	W	83	229,327	162,451	184,738	22,287
			84	351,736	249,533	282,975	33,442
FR GERM	A	E	83	2,315	1,214	1,951	737
	A	W	81	5	1,206	1,406	200
			84	5,015	9,316	18,423	9,107
			85	1,543	1,284	3,336	2,052
	O	E	84	40,124	27,795	30,485	2,690
	V	E	81	2,311,002	1,645,642	1,822,474	176,832
			82	1,284,807	855,327	920,643	65,316
			83	1,494,057	785,579	849,231	63,652
			84	2,403,569	1,760,299	1,873,569	113,270
			85	4,876,904	3,150,577	3,327,549	176,972
	V	W	84	31,746	28,371	30,705	2,334
HG KONG	V	E	82	404	5,346	5,742	396
INDIA	A	E	83	356	1,285	2,077	792
			84	4	860	900	40
	N	E	82	2,006	4,000	4,304	304
	V	E	83	391	600	664	64
JAPAN	A	E	84	441	820	1,116	296
	A	W	83	388	2,634	4,056	1,422
			84	2	470	513	43
	O	E	83	7	388	393	5
	V	E	81	98,105	102,096	111,750	9,654
			82	39,916	61,301	65,641	4,340
			83	3,571	6,661	7,102	441
			84	159,559	214,962	231,046	16,084
			85	3,175	3,371	3,787	416
MALAYSA	O	E	81	913,182	236,138	267,182	31,044
	V	E	81	33,069	12,031	13,800	1,769
			82	936,069	77,101	98,802	21,701
			83	218,250	69,222	80,119	10,897
			84	1,240,723	565,938	611,660	45,722
			85	946,365	286,387	317,959	31,572
	V	W	84	132,938	64,706	75,380	10,674
			85	384,810	275,222	311,396	36,174
MALI	V	E	85	2,447	2,152	2,347	195
MEXICO	O	W	81	17,129	15,520	15,520	
NETHLDS	O	E	85	74,977	35,298	39,146	3,848
	V	E	81	248,547	131,217	145,785	14,568
			82	125,816	80,776	89,264	8,488
			83	369,705	214,015	231,947	17,932
			84	202,344	139,954	154,111	14,157
			85	614,990	265,011	309,191	44,180
	V	W	84	109,478	81,640	92,785	11,145
NORWAY	V	E	82	43,651	11,461	14,534	3,073
PHIL R	V	E	84	321,495	137,507	149,173	11,666
			85	5,106,328	1,606,094	1,691,834	85,740
	V	W	84	3,858	1,072	1,543	471
SPAIN	A	E	84	486	800	912	112
	V	E	83	1,323	454	537	83
SWITZLD	A	E	83	4	331	370	39
			84	22	299	304	5
THAILND	V	E	83	9,921	10,333	10,980	647
U KING	A	E	81	55	1,096	1,159	63

Crop Product TSUSA commodity number, description, and unit of quantity Country	Mode	Reg	Yr	Quantity	F.A.S.	C.I.F.	Charges
			84	386	265	313	48
	A	W	84	7,135	11,299	15,124	3,825
			85	2,809	4,294	6,138	1,844
	N	E	82	330	629	777	148
			83	27,504	47,193	50,053	2,860
			84	53,439	45,598	50,338	4,740
	V	E	81	71,054	20,194	23,970	3,776
			85	17,063	36,097	38,627	2,530

Coconut, oil, fatty ester**
4909200 ESTERS FROM COCONUT ETC (LB)

Country	Mode	Reg	Yr	Quantity	F.A.S.	C.I.F.	Charges
TOTAL			81	154,731	116,844	131,699	14,755
			82	349,596	248,442	277,788	29,346
			83	638,687	371,239	404,730	33,491
			84	767,322	535,931	578,716	42,785
			85	2,037,730	1,161,805	1,260,662	98,857
			86	2,249,101	1,363,336	1,476,842	113,506
AUSTRAL	V	E	83	33,124	17,447	21,531	4,084
BELGIUM	V	E	83	11,398	8,169	9,369	1,200
CANADA	O	E	83	113,182	86,394	86,394	
			84	86,482	65,166	65,166	
			85	249,144	183,201	183,201	
			86	160,200	99,870	99,870	
CHINA T	V	E	85	16,535	13,051	14,262	1,211
DENMARK	V	E	85	40,168	41,627	45,271	3,644
FR GERM	N	E	83	376,184	184,377	206,248	21,871
			85	1,429,986	700,056	765,097	65,041
	O	E	86	91,995	28,780	35,418	6,638
	V	E	81	63,383	61,506	67,083	5,477
			82	108,246	56,666	64,648	7,982
			83	21,820	8,795	11,700	2,905
			84	611,616	390,290	428,494	38,204
			85	39,683	34,463	38,088	3,625
			86	1,740,624	1,039,813	1,128,563	88,750
FRANCE	A	E	82	9,921	13,725	19,025	5,300
	V	E	81	5,864	9,544	9,842	298
			82	33,510	51,072	53,200	2,128
			83	29,762	4,405	5,870	1,465
			84	40,873	58,436	60,839	2,403
			85	14,682	17,542	19,277	1,735
			86	17,857	27,892	29,970	2,078
ITALY	A	E	83	108	25,900	25,950	50
NETHLDS	V	E	85	1,764	1,254	1,629	375
			86	16,755	18,985	20,145	1,160
NORWAY	V	E	81	23,645	12,444	14,153	1,709
			82	85,483	49,591	56,752	7,161
			83	53,109	35,752	37,668	1,916
			85	40,013	43,415	46,249	2,834
U KING	O	E	84	242	311	311	
	V	E	81	61,839	33,350	40,621	7,271
			82	112,436	77,388	84,163	6,775
			84	28,109	21,728	23,906	2,178
			85	205,755	127,196	147,588	20,392
			86	221,670	147,996	162,876	14,880

Coconut, oil, fatty salt**
4904800 SALTS FROM COCONUT ETC (LB)

Country	Mode	Reg	Yr	Quantity	F.A.S.	C.I.F.	Charges
TOTAL			82	7,549	11,347	11,347	
			83	2,914	4,897	4,897	
			84	661	616	744	128
			85	14,330	6,100	8,450	2,350
			86	66,523	34,249	40,813	6,564
CANADA	O	E	82	7,549	11,347	11,347	
			83	2,914	4,897	4,897	
CHINA T	V	E	86	38,162	17,706	23,245	5,539
	V	W	85	14,330	6,100	8,450	2,350
FR GERM	V	E	84	661	616	744	128
			86	518	1,780	1,931	151
FRANCE	V	E	86	27,843	14,763	15,637	874

Coconut, surface-active agent**
4652500 SALTS FROM OILS, FATS NSPF (LB)

Country	Mode	Reg	Yr	Quantity	F.A.S.	C.I.F.	Charges
TOTAL			81	289	1,924	3,205	1,281
			82	27,798	26,661	30,464	3,803
			83	165,473	53,082	54,632	1,550
			84	70,647	167,998	175,504	7,506
			85	68,949	88,401	96,450	8,049

Crop Product TSUSA commodity number, description, and unit of quantity Country	Mode	Reg	Yr	Quantity	F.A.S.	C.I.F.	Charges
			86	357,646	297,472	331,430	33,958
BELGIUM	V	E	86	26,367	9,438	11,066	1,628
C RICA	V	W	85	2,976	1,800	2,658	858
CANADA	O	E	81	51	954	1,058	104
			84	11,010	15,807	15,807	
			85	16,015	24,801	24,801	
			86	25,773	35,032	35,032	
	O	W	83	152,100	16,237	16,237	
CAYMAN	V	E	83	5,954	31,251	32,184	933
			84	23,812	126,473	128,736	2,263
			86	143,997	105,345	107,279	1,934
CHINA T	A	W	81	238	970	2,147	1,177
FR GERM	A	E	86	9,757	19,128	28,029	8,901
	V	E	85	1,940	1,015	1,126	111
			86	40,886	43,284	49,800	6,516
FRANCE	V	E	82	1,799	684	813	129
			83	441	1,039	1,099	60
HG KONG	V	E	82	2,250	2,009	2,300	291
			83	5,736	3,289	3,718	429
			85	6,523	6,938	8,365	1,427
JAPAN	V	E	82	22,818	21,646	24,840	3,194
			84	25,243	21,262	24,961	3,699
			85	21,495	15,451	19,500	4,049
			86	46,396	37,490	45,380	7,890
	V	W	85	20,000	38,396	40,000	1,604
KOR REP	V	W	83	581	687	786	99
MEXICO	A	W	82	682	1,809	1,933	124
SWEDEN	V	E	84	10,582	4,456	6,000	1,544
SWITZLD	V	E	83	661	579	608	29
U KING	V	E	82	249	513	578	65
			86	64,470	47,755	54,844	7,089

4653500 FATTY ACIDS SULPH COCONUT (LB)

Country	Mode	Reg	Yr	Quantity	F.A.S.	C.I.F.	Charges
TOTAL			81	24,190	8,772	8,772	
			82	53,302	32,115	36,317	4,202
			83	69,932	65,168	69,631	4,463
			84	86,479	50,645	55,159	4,514
			85	20,480	10,416	10,999	583
			86	250,031	68,808	70,775	1,967
BELGIUM	V	E	82	10,251	4,501	6,594	2,093
			83	10,979	4,255	5,659	1,404
CANADA	O	E	81	24,190	8,772	8,772	
			82	28,060	11,415	11,415	
			83	23,293	14,838	14,838	
			84	35,624	29,557	29,557	
			85	5,920	3,321	3,321	
			86	225,900	50,364	50,364	
FR GERM	A	E	84	2,687	2,599	4,497	1,898
	N	E	82	8,818	14,255	16,364	2,109
	O	E	84	33,069	8,992	10,642	1,650
	V	E	83	35,660	46,075	49,134	3,059
			84	14,947	6,658	7,429	771
FRANCE	A	E	84	152	2,839	3,034	195
	V	E	85	14,560	7,095	7,678	583
MEXICO	O	E	82	6,173	1,944	1,944	
U KING	V	E	86	24,131	18,444	20,411	1,967

4654500 FATTY ACHL SULPH COCONUT ETC (LB)

Country	Mode	Reg	Yr	Quantity	F.A.S.	C.I.F.	Charges
TOTAL			81	1,374,319	1,201,584	1,340,369	138,785
			82	1,551,917	1,292,459	1,437,932	145,473
			83	2,001,546	1,515,865	1,690,468	174,603
			84	2,393,188	1,966,090	2,146,825	180,735
			85	2,594,755	2,417,098	2,608,121	191,023
			86	4,297,176	2,868,235	3,043,080	174,845
BELGIUM	V	W	85	44,092	24,641	27,860	3,219
CANADA	O	E	84	268,835	60,865	60,865	
			85	422,638	109,342	112,249	2,907
			86	783,051	173,107	173,107	
CAYMAN	V	E	84	39,680	29,992	30,600	608
			85	85,412	518,988	526,727	7,739
			86	370,355	649,406	657,490	8,084
CHINA T	V	E	86	36,831	32,190	34,090	1,900
FR GERM	A	E	83	4,024	6,160	8,157	1,997
			85	2,756	4,556	6,619	2,063
			86	1,984	1,485	3,507	2,022
	A	W	81	2,292	6,829	9,561	2,732
	N	E	82	433,300	353,844	383,410	29,566
			83	293,350	246,534	262,569	16,035
			84	282,479	280,156	297,412	17,256
			85	596,415	455,496	498,268	42,772
			86	2,133,712	1,231,375	1,317,958	86,583

Crop
Product
TSUSA commodity number, description, and unit of quantity

Country	Mode	Reg	Yr	Quantity	F.A.S.	C.I.F.	Charges
	O	E	85	1,323	1,011	1,308	297
	V	E	81	409,330	334,230	360,730	26,500
			82	46,825	24,321	28,017	3,696
			83	116,117	69,351	77,719	8,368
			84	104,647	91,316	101,536	10,220
			86	256,330	206,029	224,080	18,051
	V	W	82	9,038	5,788	7,467	1,679
			83	2,259	7,570	8,252	682
			84	134,922	92,497	102,410	9,913
			85	44,445	25,947	28,961	3,014
FRANCE	N	E	83	19,885	5,129	5,950	821
			85	27,160	9,253	12,375	3,122
	V	E	82	27,160	6,808	9,031	2,223
			84	18,430	7,069	8,289	1,220
			86	107,780	59,666	67,519	7,853
ITALY	O	E	84	30,518	29,224	32,281	3,057
	V	E	83	121,428	97,791	109,389	11,598
			84	73,891	62,892	68,782	5,890
JAPAN	V	E	81	68,784	69,665	81,120	11,455
			82	79,047	75,854	86,052	10,198
			83	64,485	50,028	61,425	11,397
			84	72,642	62,731	73,940	11,209
			85	28,660	27,311	30,550	3,239
NETHLDS	V	E	83	31,078	30,111	32,874	2,763
	V	W	84	88,184	54,022	59,410	5,388
SPAIN	V	E	85	3,527	1,902	3,200	1,298
U KING	A	E	82	33	9,967	10,092	125
			83	94	5,351	5,714	363
			84	55	14,352	14,477	125
			85	55	12,666	12,676	10
			86	77	16,753	16,853	100
	N	E	81	1,235	1,385	1,579	194
			82	416,308	356,036	402,575	46,539
			83	415,075	369,434	409,984	40,550
			84	831,375	798,518	870,999	72,481
			85	683,800	666,804	729,055	62,251
			86	31,747	21,452	23,434	1,982
	O	E	81	280,193	274,751	306,064	31,313
			82	434,432	367,988	407,464	39,476
			83	614,226	365,357	410,511	45,154
			84	38,581	30,286	34,755	4,469
			86	263,777	266,648	289,307	22,659
	V	E	81	612,485	514,724	581,315	66,591
			82	105,774	91,853	103,824	11,971
			83	319,525	263,049	297,924	34,875
			84	408,949	352,170	391,069	38,899
			85	654,472	559,181	618,273	59,092
			86	311,532	210,124	235,735	25,611

4656500 COCONUT PALM KERNEL A PM OIL (LB)

Country	Mode	Reg	Yr	Quantity	F.A.S.	C.I.F.	Charges
TOTAL			81	958	1,181	1,294	113
			82	1,320	1,000	1,071	71
			83	177,334	30,540	32,263	1,723
			84	1,088,997	233,327	245,160	11,833
			85	5,838,395	1,932,072	2,095,634	163,562
			86	1,067,131	260,864	302,811	41,947
C RICA	V	E	82	1,320	1,000	1,071	71
			86	13,914	9,983	11,779	1,796
CANADA	O	E	83	155,420	14,911	14,911	
			84	18,961	11,778	11,778	
			85	456	1,019	1,019	
CHINA T	V	W	86	249,208	50,401	57,091	6,690
DOM REP	V	E	83	11,625	8,750	9,250	500
FR GERM	A	W	84	838	889	2,139	1,250
	O	E	84	4,950	10,593	11,227	634
	V	E	83	7,408	4,797	5,263	466
			84	45,283	23,390	26,605	3,215
			86	7,716	5,642	6,442	800
GUATMAL	V	E	85	145,887	56,030	65,336	9,306
			86	36,316	7,540	8,840	1,300
GUYANA	V	E	85	39,465	13,389	16,044	2,655
HG KONG	V	W	85	121,605	22,322	26,207	3,885
INDNSIA	V	E	85	2,212,911	683,383	737,721	54,338
JAPAN	A	W	86	2,382	1,181	8,572	7,391
	N	W	84	4,151	24,375	27,187	2,812
LIBERIA	V	E	84	714	880	993	113
MALAYSA	A	E	85	1,164	2,711	5,160	2,449
			86	1,190	2,268	4,368	2,100
	A	W	85	2,094	1,464	5,758	4,294
	V	E	85	3,386,418	1,170,373	1,260,751	90,378
	V	W	86	616,516	117,193	133,903	16,710
NETHLDS	V	E	85	50,000	3,703	3,845	142
NORWAY	V	W	86	18,284	44,334	45,609	1,275

Country	Mode	Reg	Yr	Quantity	F.A.S.	C.I.F.	Charges
PHIL R	V	W	84	1,008,000	151,293	153,853	2,560
REP SAF	A	E	84	398	253	667	414
	V	E	84	5,000	9,265	10,000	735
S LUCIA	V	E	84	405	265	305	40
S VN GR	V	E	81	170	482	532	50
			83	220	986	1,116	130
SIER LN	V	E	83	2,661	1,096	1,723	627
U KING	O	E	81	788	699	762	63
	V	W	84	297	346	406	60

Coconut, vegetable oil
1761720 COCONUT OIL, CRUDE (LB)

Country	Mode	Reg	Yr	Quantity	F.A.S.	C.I.F.	Charges
TOTAL			81	992,312,994	237,721,238	260,389,173	22,667,935
			82	833,795,640	171,365,199	189,470,112	18,104,913
			83	907,963,263	203,951,822	222,672,727	18,720,905
			84	776,029,944	322,538,578	339,950,552	17,411,974
			85	909,160,493	255,235,703	275,911,981	20,676,278
			86	1,110,881,569	163,904,670	188,182,418	24,277,748
BRAZIL	V	E	84	3,240,762	1,592,688	1,686,557	93,869
CANADA	O	E	81	1,600	656	656	
			84	48,510	31,532	31,532	
			86	44,290	18,336	18,336	
DOM REP	V	E	84	13,939,496	6,585,716	6,824,863	239,147
			85	3,242,062	1,196,254	1,252,815	56,561
DOMINCA	V	E	85	1,322,760	526,165	542,231	16,066
F W IND	V	E	82	2,242,230	460,458	513,922	53,464
FIJI	V	E	81	10,098,174	2,556,892	2,709,855	152,963
			82	13,879,297	2,971,245	3,390,847	419,602
			83	19,876,163	5,770,769	6,233,227	462,458
			84	15,498,060	7,567,711	8,065,415	497,704
			85	12,771,975	4,891,673	5,250,471	358,798
	V	W	86	534,160	60,627	71,221	10,594
FINLAND	V	E	85	562,173	187,428	203,359	15,931
FR POLY	V	E	81	3,192,040	831,465	909,732	78,267
FRANCE	O	E	83	516	626	676	50
G BISAU	V	E	85	1,680,752	560,367	607,998	47,631
GUINEA	V	E	85	1,680,750	634,992	688,966	53,974
HG KONG	V	E	84	2,748	2,478	2,757	279
INDIA	V	E	85	1,656,249	543,523	571,695	28,172
	V	W	85	3,308,867	906,506	984,543	78,037
INDNSIA	N	E	85	15,482,890	4,968,551	5,381,451	412,900
	V	E	81	1,119,498	269,898	293,868	23,970
			85	35,957,033	11,797,273	12,238,737	441,464
	V	W	85	38,671,179	10,940,948	12,111,674	1,170,726
			86	2,178,099	507,058	555,658	48,600
IVY CST	V	E	83	3,299,964	1,032,696	1,113,082	80,386
JAMAICA	V	E	83	207	403	415	12
MALAYSA	O	E	84	96,746	34,356	34,356	
	V	E	81	8,960,097	2,411,239	2,668,368	257,129
			82	10,139,458	2,134,765	2,409,109	274,344
			83	25,427,312	6,874,196	7,533,916	659,720
			84	38,871,197	19,119,554	20,464,773	1,345,219
			85	50,531,587	17,868,186	18,713,528	845,342
			86	29,548,875	4,293,718	4,785,653	491,935
	V	W	82	1,118,034	252,287	279,530	27,243
			83	3,969,713	1,455,568	1,552,329	96,761
			84	17,258,950	9,411,983	9,887,218	475,235
			85	18,694,585	7,319,468	7,854,318	534,850
			86	2,284,798	206,092	291,448	85,356
MEXICO	O	E	83	44,000	18,920	18,920	
	O	W	83	465,509	150,947	150,947	
			86	2,083,966	902,551	902,551	
NETHLDS	V	E	81	2,200,818	491,830	545,288	53,458
NEW GUI	V	E	81	9,104,376	2,459,151	2,621,652	162,501
			82	3,393,806	733,911	795,505	61,594
			83	6,840,840	1,271,719	1,419,022	147,303
			85	7,818,372	2,052,704	2,250,797	198,093
			86	5,341,066	510,181	661,989	151,808
	V	W	84	2,475,483	1,391,390	1,451,904	60,514
			86	2,186,031	511,703	571,995	60,292
PANAMA	V	E	85	3,359,838	752,229	842,964	90,735
PHIL R	N	E	81	117,941,162	28,494,530	31,624,244	3,129,714
			84	106,014,515	47,264,034	49,230,395	1,966,361
	O	E	81	55,373,472	14,712,589	16,188,530	1,475,941
			82	663,620	140,871	157,600	16,729
			83	151,897	24,428	27,921	3,493
			85	8,960,000	2,926,400	2,926,400	
	O	W	81	3,489,877	756,346	865,400	109,054
	V	E	81	260,910,195	62,749,138	68,515,415	5,766,277
			82	325,587,280	66,968,631	74,119,545	7,150,914
			83	332,602,270	68,467,811	75,595,247	7,127,436

Crop
Product
TSUSA commodity number, description, and unit of quantity

Country	Mode	Reg	Yr	Quantity	F.A.S.	C.I.F.	Charges
			84	116,075,085	48,981,530	52,069,591	3,088,061
			85	233,722,328	60,283,146	64,679,608	4,396,462
			86	455,803,564	65,427,062	74,439,171	9,012,109
	V	W	81	485,206,247	113,471,800	124,142,581	10,670,781
			82	445,889,625	91,771,228	101,159,039	9,387,811
			83	471,053,699	107,694,276	116,885,148	9,190,872
			84	423,833,940	160,209,041	168,966,965	8,757,924
			85	386,419,110	99,837,058	109,836,637	9,999,579
			86	564,747,051	85,307,065	98,592,983	13,285,918
REP SAF	V	E	86	3,310,006	312,849	339,441	26,592
S LUCIA	V	E	84	906,091	588,959	601,596	12,637
			85	826,725	322,500	333,891	11,391
SINGAPR	V	E	82	2,252,570	576,471	603,971	27,500
			83	1,120,000	458,185	461,576	3,391
			84	2,193,673	1,017,257	1,077,954	60,697
			85	13,800,923	6,010,387	6,208,882	198,495
	V	W	84	5,530,887	3,284,738	3,399,373	114,635
			85	3,373,723	1,082,408	1,183,413	101,005
SOMALIA	V	E	82	3,706,416	765,563	856,056	90,493
SRI LKA	V	E	81	17,454,009	4,301,403	4,713,686	412,283
			82	10,201,266	2,189,206	2,432,866	243,660
			83	13,230,007	3,826,855	4,158,104	331,249
			84	7,324,778	4,573,810	4,726,725	152,915
			85	33,117,526	9,593,727	10,373,688	779,961
			86	40,290,886	6,322,135	7,325,203	1,003,068
	V	W	83	2,222,147	543,661	599,274	55,613
			84	1,160,760	413,419	443,378	29,959
			85	1,088,944	374,161	400,821	26,660
SWITZLD	A	E	86	20,000	31,193	31,815	622
	O	E	85	131	1,056	1,075	19
T PAC I	V	E	81	6,258,779	1,542,517	1,689,871	147,354
	V	W	81	10,995,122	2,669,180	2,896,039	226,859
			82	7,745,922	1,227,601	1,363,013	135,412
			83	8,312,952	1,693,709	1,863,732	170,023
			84	10,050,636	4,881,715	5,115,388	233,673
			85	8,286,672	2,500,629	2,697,628	196,999
			86	6,778,774	908,354	1,069,500	161,146
THAILND	V	E	85	4,223,125	1,234,043	1,310,936	76,893
	V	W	85	3,712,241	1,269,557	1,394,017	124,460
U KING	O	E	84	864	723	796	73
	V	E	82	8,550	8,380	9,577	1,197
W SAMOA	V	E	82	2,888,603	397,715	505,650	107,935
			83	13,565,156	3,085,238	3,333,306	248,068
			84	5,190,142	2,525,429	2,693,102	167,673
			85	11,621,147	3,903,614	4,231,730	328,116
	V	W	81	7,528	2,604	3,988	1,384
			82	4,078,963	766,867	873,882	107,015
			83	5,780,911	1,581,815	1,725,885	144,070
			84	4,232,655	2,157,964	2,273,363	115,399
			85	1,080,795	239,047	265,713	26,666

1761740 COCONUT OIL, REFINED (LB)

Country	Mode	Reg	Yr	Quantity	F.A.S.	C.I.F.	Charges
TOTAL			81	44,569,780	11,395,099	12,389,506	994,407
			82	55,966,353	12,732,178	13,958,183	1,226,005
			83	82,752,489	19,125,817	21,150,208	2,024,391
			84	57,136,583	19,758,557	20,878,788	1,120,231
			85	83,342,794	23,785,920	25,632,528	1,846,608
			86	67,196,294	9,745,232	11,275,055	1,529,823
C RICA	A	W	81	620	273	497	224
	V	E	82	1,480	1,200	1,350	150
			83	1,135	588	907	319
	V	W	83	1,830	984	1,141	157
			84	6,260	4,217	5,420	1,203
			85	15,520	5,400	7,753	2,353
CANADA	O	E	82	2,061	3,571	3,571	
			86	297,268	46,796	46,796	
DENMARK	V	E	86	79,721	83,282	90,777	7,495
DOM REP	V	E	84	3,031,693	1,962,371	2,019,777	57,406
F W IND	V	E	82	2,240,050	505,600	559,013	53,413
FIJI	V	E	82	7,700,497	1,862,091	2,039,189	177,098
FR GERM	A	E	84	76	2,536	2,587	51
	V	W	85	33,120	16,890	18,140	1,250
FR POLY	A	W	83	65	295	590	295
	V	E	81	7,712	3,315	3,680	365
FRANCE	O	E	82	302	413	490	77
	V	E	85	54,982	39,048	43,938	4,890
			86	56,085	37,634	41,576	3,942
	V	W	83	12,517	11,120	11,870	750
GREECE	A	E	83	22	308	381	73
GRENADA	V	E	82	1,150	749	829	80
GUATMAL	V	E	84	81,261	42,434	47,184	4,750
HG KONG	V	E	82	800	342	460	118
INDIA	O	E	84	480	543	591	48

Country	Mode	Reg	Yr	Quantity	F.A.S.	C.I.F.	Charges
	V	E	81	666	3,417	3,780	363
			82	95	307	333	26
	V	W	82	612	1,413	1,643	230
			85	2,212,532	508,883	561,761	52,878
INDNSIA	V	E	84	1,102,300	207,439	219,082	11,643
			85	3,318,717	881,114	953,054	71,940
	V	W	85	3,323,291	1,170,146	1,231,796	61,650
JAMAICA	V	E	81	9,600	9,600	10,900	1,300
			82	41,768	40,568	43,805	3,237
			83	23,316	23,516	25,355	1,839
			84	4,800	4,500	4,704	204
			85	12,684	12,042	12,710	668
JAPAN	V	E	86	19,200	19,200	20,496	1,296
MALAYSA	V	E	82	2,246,176	500,086	527,850	27,764
			84	2,139,210	881,074	923,614	42,540
			85	2,238,996	800,627	860,402	59,775
MEXICO	O	E	83	352,580	138,208	138,208	
			84	458,111	109,435	109,435	
NEW GUI	V	E	83	2,246,518	405,386	460,436	55,050
			85	4,516,654	831,516	994,077	162,561
PERU	V	E	85	1,120,000	212,670	240,800	28,130
PHIL R	N	E	81	5,588,635	1,389,570	1,533,520	143,950
	O	E	81	5,580,322	1,475,586	1,620,821	145,235
	V	E	81	19,979,308	5,069,010	5,475,379	406,369
			82	26,780,008	5,775,570	6,442,035	666,465
			83	35,727,087	8,757,838	9,757,536	999,698
			84	14,609,991	7,686,928	7,946,077	259,149
			85	21,837,011	7,753,136	8,184,496	431,360
			86	42,843,773	5,670,880	6,587,960	917,080
	V	W	81	5,637,716	1,428,763	1,545,000	116,237
			82	16,925,952	4,029,717	4,324,630	294,913
			83	38,015,112	8,604,246	9,411,775	807,529
			84	35,692,298	8,846,122	9,587,984	741,862
			85	35,794,377	8,244,111	9,043,631	799,520
S LUCIA	V	E	85	992,070	608,855	622,523	13,668
S VN GR	V	E	84	360	357	395	38
SINGAPR	V	E	85	2,225,687	685,663	728,435	42,772
SRI LKA	V	E	81	7,728,080	1,985,483	2,163,639	178,156
			82	22,046	6,925	8,927	2,002
			83	6,364,150	1,177,329	1,335,353	158,024
			85	5,645,327	2,013,483	2,126,450	112,967
			86	21,577,094	3,522,320	4,065,135	542,815
SWEDEN	V	E	86	39,332	36,551	41,483	4,932
SWITZLD	A	E	86	10,000	9,593	9,783	190
THAILND	V	W	86	32,593	11,700	12,764	1,064
U KING	N	E	84	6,231	7,449	8,434	985
	O	E	81	37,121	30,082	32,290	2,208
			82	2,754	2,863	3,206	343
			83	4,923	3,407	3,848	441
			85	927	1,138	1,281	143
	O	W	86	900	1,034	1,151	117
	V	E	83	2,286	1,769	1,917	148
			84	1,862	1,233	1,351	118
	V	W	82	602	763	852	89
			83	948	823	891	68
			84	1,650	1,919	2,153	234
			85	899	1,198	1,281	83
			86	869	1,117	1,218	101
W SAMOA	V	E	86	2,239,459	305,125	355,916	50,791

Coir, fiber, raw and waste
3040600 COIR RAW AND WASTES (LTN)

Country	Mode	Reg	Yr	Quantity	F.A.S.	C.I.F.	Charges
TOTAL			81	9,070	2,316,993	3,353,991	1,037,825
			82	10,850	2,015,120	3,371,604	1,356,484
			83	7,858	1,604,210	2,577,119	972,909
			84	7,984	1,529,910	2,561,320	1,031,410
			85	9,476	1,923,370	3,053,524	1,130,154
			86	13,406	2,529,731	4,098,873	1,569,142
CANADA	O	E	81	18	3,408	2,581	
			84	40	4,846	6,476	1,630
CHINA M	A	E	85	13	8,574	9,596	1,022
INDIA	V	E	81	636	203,029	248,548	45,519
			82	364	53,103	102,362	49,259
			84	436	113,956	168,585	54,629
			86	200	54,142	78,863	24,721
	V	W	85	12	6,264	7,197	933
LIBERIA	V	E	86	119	32,241	47,146	14,905
MEXICO	O	E	81	262	53,954	53,954	
			83	19	4,405	4,405	
NORWAY	V	E	82	10	4,457	6,601	2,144
SRI LKA	N	E	84	2,948	535,407	924,729	389,322

Crop Product TSUSA commodity number, description, and unit of quantity Country	Mode	Reg	Yr	Quantity	F.A.S.	C.I.F.	Charges
		O E	85	4,623	929,413	1,452,850	523,437
			81	1,152	252,026	404,226	152,200
			83	3,979	768,044	1,230,444	462,400
			84	579	145,329	215,419	70,090
			86	2,904	481,875	769,150	287,275
		V E	81	6,365	1,597,817	2,423,733	825,916
			82	10,476	1,957,560	3,262,641	1,305,081
			83	3,860	831,761	1,342,270	510,509
			84	3,981	730,372	1,246,111	515,739
			85	4,828	979,119	1,583,881	604,762
			86	10,142	1,945,226	3,180,047	1,234,821
		V W	81	626	202,426	214,571	12,145
			86	41	16,247	23,667	7,420
SWITZLD	V	E	81	11	4,333	6,378	2,045

Lauric acid
4902404 LAURIC ACID (LB)

Country	Mode	Reg	Yr	Quantity	F.A.S.	C.I.F.	Charges
TOTAL			86	876,329	145,600	197,898	52,298
DENMARK	A	E	86	1,873	2,793	4,728	1,935
	V	E	86	81,003	13,784	19,054	5,270
FR GERM	V	E	86	310,763	59,477	77,059	17,582
MALAYSA	V	E	86	44,092	3,850	6,819	2,969
MEXICO	O	E	86	38,955	12,368	12,368	
NETHLDS	O	E	86	36,382	5,413	6,963	1,550
	V	E	86	363,261	47,915	70,907	22,992

Coffee

Coffee, crude
1601020 COFFEE, CRUDE (LB)

Country	Mode	Reg	Yr	Quantity	F.A.S.	C.I.F.	Charges
TOTAL			81	2,189,855,243	2,621,712,359	2,769,649,404	147,947,531
			82	2,303,668,299	2,718,234,482	2,875,572,258	157,337,776
			83	2,175,745,270	2,592,246,156	2,733,246,757	141,000,601
			84	2,345,723,979	3,061,015,199	3,211,754,586	150,739,387
			85	2,473,311,973	3,127,676,686	3,281,094,936	153,418,250
			86	2,577,116,002	4,287,537,580	4,426,498,930	138,961,350
AFGHAN	A	E	81	46,296	55,965	61,057	5,092
	V	E	81	264,000	316,800	339,680	22,880
ANGOLA	V	E	81	2,728,891	2,905,988	3,168,218	262,230
			82	8,368,540	7,634,586	8,324,944	690,358
			83	3,544,467	4,009,573	4,287,376	277,803
			84	660,322	873,276	901,649	28,373
			86	661,380	780,000	866,215	86,215
		V W	81	61,987	72,276	77,499	5,223
			86	188,493	240,551	256,755	16,204
ANTIGUA	V	E	81	19,015	26,250	28,327	2,077
ARGENT	V	E	81	2,894,583	2,687,255	2,890,286	203,031
			82	916,738	1,155,090	1,192,065	36,975
			84	152,196	202,421	208,021	5,600
			85	296,342	379,124	400,710	21,586
			86	1,465,023	1,695,419	1,814,127	118,708
AUSTRAL	V	W	82	1,050	1,691	2,090	399
			86	363,759	454,699	480,725	26,026
AUSTRIA	V	E	85	304,236	376,500	382,200	5,700
BELGIUM	A	E	83	264	526	625	99
	V	E	81	868,190	1,213,481	1,244,006	30,525
			82	141,041	160,402	167,428	7,026
			83	197,753	242,247	260,018	17,771
			84	46,164	74,557	77,523	2,966
			85	321,839	513,880	531,639	17,759
			86	1,942,561	3,878,580	3,987,784	109,204
		V W	85	77,236	130,980	135,793	4,813
			86	202,459	422,732	435,197	12,465
BELIZE	A	E	83	342	987	1,299	312
	V	E	81	2,308,672	1,986,360	2,140,784	154,424
			82	1,597,233	1,217,019	1,309,418	92,399
			86	240,434	276,786	282,759	5,973
BENIN	V	E	82	1,544,382	1,304,998	1,387,411	82,413
BNGLDSH	V	E	86	77,161	91,000	97,385	6,385
BOLIVIA	N	E	86	165,433	211,125	223,830	12,705
	V	E	81	2,734,231	2,818,941	2,974,602	155,661
			82	3,472,805	3,953,140	4,166,884	213,744
			83	2,042,744	2,208,016	2,334,271	126,255
			84	749,700	852,054	896,158	44,104
			85	3,047,739	3,641,089	3,830,344	189,255
			86	1,565,739	2,701,443	2,806,891	105,448
		V W	82	610,674	731,456	783,319	51,863

Crop Product TSUSA commodity number, description, and unit of quantity Country	Mode	Reg	Yr	Quantity	F.A.S.	C.I.F.	Charges
BOTSWAN	V	E	81	21,785	10,675	12,453	1,778
BRAZIL	A	E	82	396	594	619	25
			86	10,833	64,912	73,812	8,900
	N	E	81	142,247,045	248,598,182	260,966,355	12,368,173
			82	111,961,311	146,131,404	156,736,124	10,604,720
			83	199,437,497	250,363,867	267,204,993	16,841,126
			84	139,662,349	188,132,333	200,233,097	12,100,764
			85	469,329,485	572,306,440	611,785,871	39,479,431
			86	118,754,358	206,615,619	216,548,027	9,932,408
	N	W	82	38,270,552	50,047,578	54,025,383	3,977,805
			83	99,869	116,716	128,228	11,512
			86	12,130,723	20,458,208	21,347,640	889,432
	O	E	81	302,470	· 369,461	369,461	
			82	7,507	14,141	14,141	
			83	93,680	137,895	137,895	
			84	6,394	12,024	12,024	
			85	534,562	808,300	827,327	19,027
			86	79,936	128,790	128,790	
	V	E	81	246,330,339	350,854,362	372,389,288	21,534,926
			82	294,870,031	360,920,951	388,096,028	27,175,077
			83	215,964,685	261,690,436	280,090,247	18,399,811
			84	324,773,583	419,663,502	446,663,882	27,000,380
			85	46,542,473	56,013,404	59,953,371	3,939,967
			86	159,887,803	274,476,323	287,838,936	13,362,613
	V	W	81	40,124,518	70,024,680	73,848,722	3,824,042
			82	931,913	1,177,600	1,278,838	101,238
			83	36,454,811	47,409,563	51,181,377	3,771,814
			84	46,895,830	62,940,903	67,277,032	4,336,129
			85	32,276,744	40,454,997	43,204,150	2,749,153
			86	107,339	171,252	179,372	8,120
BURMA	V	W	83	948,948	1,149,934	1,222,802	72,868
BURUNDI	V	E	81	27,202,890	27,794,919	30,173,297	2,378,378
			82	34,533,978	41,279,304	44,316,050	3,036,746
			83	2,332,296	2,747,689	2,931,171	183,482
			84	493,201	663,653	710,414	46,761
			85	525,052	618,220	653,387	35,167
			86	1,586,312	1,881,089	1,995,883	114,794
	V	W	84	661,380	909,001	959,001	50,000
			85	391,986	403,745	431,858	28,113
			86	5,401,893	7,866,456	8,263,376	396,920
C AF RP	V	E	82	1,000,008	991,333	1,040,922	49,589
			84	739,347	930,690	930,691	1
C RICA	N	E	81	10,667,194	13,134,598	13,797,610	663,012
			82	6,596,896	8,265,013	8,713,550	448,537
			84	8,937,009	12,067,135	12,605,032	537,897
			86	1,407,085	2,614,500	2,645,734	31,234
	N	W	84	1,626,069	2,116,422	2,236,835	120,413
			85	1,915,513	2,584,886	2,701,020	116,134
			86	228,145	534,811	543,321	8,510
	O	E	85	76,059	34,500	50,145	15,645
			86	16,126	37,023	37,023	
	V	E	81	8,243,776	9,868,322	10,337,778	469,456
			82	18,452,834	22,495,246	23,429,963	934,717
			83	21,859,825	26,694,330	28,137,466	1,443,136
			84	20,639,436	28,046,378	29,232,180	1,185,802
			85	38,613,801	50,592,204	52,452,563	1,860,359
			86	45,477,028	78,688,151	80,535,420	1,847,269
	V	W	81	11,039,178	12,052,062	12,850,587	798,525
			82	7,755,029	10,189,967	10,813,148	623,181
			83	8,061,140	9,977,888	10,590,037	612,149
			84	2,968,163	4,165,644	4,370,069	204,425
			85	6,994,876	9,580,451	9,971,637	391,186
			86	7,452,058	13,666,188	13,943,312	277,124
CAMROON	O	E	82	1,650	2,129	2,129	
	V	E	81	30,381,165	32,824,601	35,436,962	2,612,361
			82	30,830,085	30,936,675	33,208,478	2,271,803
			83	20,535,770	20,207,761	21,503,473	1,295,712
			84	10,713,983	14,058,786	14,662,694	603,908
			85	10,401,368	12,435,025	13,103,025	668,000
			86	11,574,055	15,376,777	16,130,374	753,597
	V	W	83	222,223	243,201	260,001	16,800
			85	1,763,834	1,740,810	1,858,165	117,355
			86	227,162	320,298	331,198	10,900
CANADA	N	E	84	9,771	13,716	13,852	136
	O	E	81	321,483	390,695	394,794	4,099
			82	164,575	216,731	216,731	
			83	47,710	70,192	70,488	296
			84	44,103	57,313	57,313	
			85	4,000	7,641	7,641	
			86	1,745	4,716	4,716	
	O	W	81	40,850	36,704	36,704	
			85	40,926	26,942	26,942	
			86	1,500	4,800	4,800	
CHILE	V	E	81	912,704	638,893	653,293	14,400

Crop
Product
TSUSA commodity number, description, and unit of quantity

Country	Mode	Reg	Yr	Quantity	F.A.S.	C.I.F.	Charges
			85	681,220	759,506	801,655	42,149
			86	154,323	184,286	193,971	9,685
	V	W	83	532,194	711,636	760,943	49,307
CHINA M	O	E	82	9,568	11,441	11,935	494
	O	W	85	177,700	139,383	148,720	9,337
			86	220,460	97,160	110,000	12,840
	V	E	82	3,516,459	2,692,768	2,977,632	284,864
			85	266,889	285,571	302,500	16,929
	V	W	81	76,915	32,273	37,174	4,901
			82	1,870,792	1,297,508	1,412,789	115,281
			83	1,983,036	1,444,031	1,582,271	138,240
			86	492,525	354,563	390,373	35,810
CHINA T	V	E	86	346,827	374,302	398,508	24,206
	V	W	81	2,000	1,500	1,565	65
CO BRAZ	V	E	86	554,400	550,004	593,962	43,958
COCOS I	V	E	86	215,019	196,878	211,747	14,869
COLOMB	A	E	81	15,432	18,655	22,055	3,400
			82	89,651	127,431	158,283	30,852
			83	76,808	96,625	105,521	8,896
	A	W	82	77,161	103,085	111,557	8,472
	N	E	81	91,255,330	128,022,920	134,129,601	6,106,681
			82	101,790,202	142,025,200	149,559,711	7,534,511
			83	120,466,665	155,516,290	165,855,954	10,339,664
			84	88,404,690	120,964,526	127,456,031	6,491,505
			85	148,412,264	202,959,957	213,370,418	10,410,461
			86	144,860,926	275,975,029	285,868,816	9,893,787
	N	W	81	191,217	289,000	294,858	5,858
			83	92,475	127,624	133,053	5,429
			85	1,315,646	1,854,146	1,948,301	94,155
	O	E	81	270	526	526	
			83	96,841	153,503	156,541	3,038
			84	44,015	67,424	67,424	
			85	25,992	33,634	33,634	
			86	176,587	374,421	375,403	982
	O	W	81	38,033	54,800	57,481	2,681
	V	E	81	86,386,116	115,986,349	121,934,465	5,948,116
			82	66,845,790	94,202,548	98,991,170	4,788,622
			83	54,377,343	70,928,564	74,736,598	3,808,034
			84	126,110,768	172,343,768	181,441,982	9,098,214
			85	117,578,137	157,464,721	166,117,766	8,653,045
			86	119,463,373	222,567,494	230,669,788	8,102,294
	V	W	81	50,585,099	68,781,864	72,103,990	3,322,126
			82	57,336,646	80,865,556	84,721,058	3,855,502
			83	56,985,274	73,083,709	77,186,719	4,103,010
			84	72,528,994	98,746,283	103,980,640	5,234,357
			85	70,537,001	96,179,036	101,347,168	5,168,132
			86	83,247,146	157,835,783	163,547,369	5,711,586
COMOROS	V	E	82	33,098	44,434	46,518	2,084
CR N AN	V	E	86	39,518	81,802	82,452	650
DOM REP	N	E	81	25,319,868	27,874,648	29,468,059	1,593,411
			82	53,486,640	61,638,596	63,511,021	1,872,425
			83	12,015,717	13,931,884	14,606,323	674,439
			84	13,741,884	18,016,191	18,667,437	651,246
			85	38,081,239	49,077,768	50,527,613	1,449,845
	O	E	84	82,500	106,345	106,345	
	V	E	81	21,870,027	23,784,698	25,027,614	1,242,916
			82	12,617,629	15,841,702	16,615,567	773,865
			83	44,869,357	53,439,442	54,902,191	1,462,749
			84	45,308,220	59,390,089	61,035,817	1,645,728
			85	19,992,645	25,590,046	26,776,941	1,186,895
			86	64,526,477	109,971,856	112,856,631	2,884,775
	V	W	81	330,524	383,405	413,199	29,794
ECUADOR	N	E	81	41,317,651	41,499,191	44,148,954	2,649,763
			83	13,006,751	13,763,825	14,582,355	818,530
			84	45,620,998	54,489,619	56,380,972	1,891,353
			86	80,839,711	112,604,583	117,274,451	4,669,868
	O	E	86	588,169	478,008	505,436	27,428
	V	E	81	37,626,746	38,863,920	40,963,013	2,099,093
			82	87,369,430	92,287,673	96,808,552	4,520,879
			83	89,755,635	100,226,391	103,989,953	3,763,562
			84	73,486,045	89,118,711	92,711,546	3,592,835
			85	120,450,626	142,149,299	147,862,467	5,713,168
			86	83,991,739	121,713,790	126,092,874	4,379,084
	V	W	81	13,824,137	13,490,242	14,421,479	931,237
			82	14,927,035	16,668,159	17,792,257	1,124,098
			83	10,544,892	11,722,046	12,451,652	729,606
			84	8,027,454	10,144,012	10,665,278	521,266
			85	8,409,124	10,200,233	10,659,601	459,368
			86	15,910,616	22,405,128	23,367,286	962,158
EGYPT	V	E	84	211,141	252,729	262,001	9,272
			86	152,117	500,000	517,536	17,536
EQ GUIN	V	E	81	304,235	191,668	211,752	20,084
ETHIOP	N	E	82	35,235,598	43,648,733	46,942,676	3,293,943
			84	23,185,608	30,338,483	32,434,753	2,096,270

Crop
Product
TSUSA commodity number, description, and unit of quantity

Country	Mode	Reg	Yr	Quantity	F.A.S.	C.I.F.	Charges
			85	7,237,168	9,582,986	10,188,935	605,949
	O	E	86	3,020	6,962	6,962	
	V	E	81	62,691,456	68,911,889	74,274,440	5,362,551
			82	34,708,771	43,392,323	46,517,624	3,125,301
			83	66,344,078	76,864,437	82,905,111	6,040,674
			84	31,290,830	41,041,569	43,936,097	2,894,528
			85	17,876,688	22,862,969	24,463,361	1,600,392
			86	31,882,470	62,259,928	64,569,934	2,310,006
	V	W	81	9,658,360	10,511,920	11,389,236	877,316
			82	6,533,325	8,457,771	9,020,128	562,357
			83	2,262,090	2,756,871	2,942,132	185,261
			84	1,515,213	2,100,010	2,221,307	121,297
			85	642,371	876,752	937,707	60,955
			86	226,264	470,668	486,434	15,766
FINLAND	V	E	86	677,160	1,023,743	1,081,048	57,305
FR GERM	N	E	81	7,197,093	10,472,942	10,912,250	439,308
			83	9,872,383	14,331,645	14,749,736	418,091
			85	23,707,275	37,162,491	38,631,701	1,469,210
			86	32,578,019	66,167,623	67,699,382	1,531,759
	N	W	83	146,794	232,784	241,067	8,283
			86	2,150,072	4,431,828	4,585,874	154,046
	O	E	81	801	2,067	2,738	671
			86	8,838	17,749	18,412	663
	O	W	85	77,307	117,604	120,434	2,830
	V	E	81	5,622,384	7,974,158	8,198,643	224,485
			82	9,641,912	13,831,400	14,359,515	528,115
			83	5,288,740	8,197,364	8,468,272	270,908
			84	31,966,255	50,771,060	52,529,201	1,758,141
			85	11,110,707	17,983,928	18,613,131	629,203
			86	17,161,832	33,568,891	34,491,947	923,056
	V	W	81	169,106	281,548	295,759	14,211
			82	1,343,183	2,261,983	2,362,609	100,626
			83	2,127,203	3,575,663	3,721,834	146,171
			84	5,252,670	9,229,255	9,599,474	370,219
			85	4,160,560	6,745,631	7,067,353	321,722
			86	1,728,731	3,909,335	4,021,290	111,955
FR POLY	V	E	85	76,587	93,750	99,071	5,321
FRANCE	N	E	83	3,856,012	5,612,006	5,797,779	185,773
			84	6,275,549	9,454,570	9,818,922	364,352
			85	597,650	767,530	801,035	33,505
			86	3,900,267	5,515,054	5,690,970	175,916
	V	E	81	6,570,208	8,582,482	8,896,979	314,497
			82	7,613,362	10,995,779	11,422,755	426,976
			83	3,152,554	4,356,958	4,524,569	167,611
			84	760,615	1,123,843	1,155,780	31,937
			85	9,340,274	13,170,265	13,683,511	513,246
			86	5,287,053	10,268,139	10,559,375	291,236
	V	W	82	442,181	649,785	676,285	26,500
			83	790,170	1,284,662	1,340,898	56,236
			84	302,109	450,709	469,334	18,625
			85	311,113	524,627	547,086	22,459
			86	904,772	614,569	669,047	54,478
GERM DR	V	E	85	44,180	74,749	76,029	1,280
GHANA	V	E	81	224,472	220,130	237,941	17,811
GIBRAT	V	E	86	31,296	64,360	66,137	1,777
GREECE	V	E	84	11,000	9,350	11,061	1,711
			85	228,176	302,963	316,884	13,921
			86	465,729	1,077,246	1,096,759	19,513
GUATMAL	N	E	81	56,679,856	69,066,376	72,255,980	3,189,604
			82	19,002,659	25,150,749	26,376,583	1,225,834
			83	58,206,624	72,619,320	75,939,701	3,320,381
			84	56,599,150	76,066,703	79,491,889	3,425,186
			85	67,370,564	90,922,580	94,407,758	3,485,178
			86	176,869,672	307,125,550	314,747,381	7,621,831
	N	W	82	1,860,094	2,273,023	2,404,182	131,159
			84	351,075	528,327	552,504	24,177
			85	6,499,203	8,721,015	9,086,919	365,904
			86	647,113	1,378,873	1,400,620	21,747
	O	E	81	38,031	45,000	48,430	3,430
			82	1,800	2,323	2,323	
			85	6,968	9,994	9,994	
			86	196,456	405,932	406,595	663
	V	E	81	25,712,209	32,067,830	33,383,776	1,315,946
			82	90,453,824	113,327,835	118,007,775	4,679,940
			83	53,680,261	65,469,995	68,753,541	3,283,546
			84	79,200,896	104,508,335	109,028,225	4,519,890
			85	63,975,812	85,058,453	88,262,788	3,204,335
			86	31,645,366	55,868,888	57,418,877	1,549,989
	V	W	81	2,867,758	3,483,231	3,691,141	207,910
			82	262,229	360,442	380,456	20,014
			83	5,463,951	6,227,261	6,614,591	387,330
			84	11,750,833	15,735,899	16,604,373	868,474
			85	1,547,263	2,149,103	2,244,556	95,453
			86	9,990,036	18,255,461	18,642,919	387,458

Crop
Product
TSUSA commodity number, description, and unit of quantity

Country	Mode	Reg	Yr	Quantity	F.A.S.	C.I.F.	Charges
GUINEA	O	E	86	7,526	15,022	15,572	550
	V	E	81	1,361,424	1,512,437	1,568,454	56,017
			83	5,849,280	6,416,328	6,681,700	265,372
			84	899,508	1,009,690	1,043,430	33,740
			86	489,421	921,445	950,000	28,555
	V	W	81	279,984	332,602	350,657	18,055
			82	1,106,708	1,135,804	1,219,112	83,308
			83	92,593	116,818	124,012	7,194
			84	701,340	702,817	751,460	48,643
			85	267,859	349,920	368,488	18,568
			86	119,048	218,662	230,423	11,761
GUYANA	V	E	81	1,001,405	1,108,367	1,173,561	65,194
			82	86,508	116,964	119,920	2,956
HAITI	N	E	81	2,388,654	2,251,409	2,387,995	136,586
			83	4,785,410	5,214,722	5,360,843	146,121
	V	E	81	2,194,493	2,367,027	2,476,377	109,350
			82	15,636,081	17,700,094	18,478,004	777,910
			83	12,024,451	12,982,948	13,673,190	690,242
			84	13,618,690	17,023,501	17,697,799	674,298
			85	9,005,183	10,905,965	11,361,711	455,746
			86	3,589,505	5,523,118	5,684,406	161,288
	V	W	82	198,414	236,739	253,712	16,973
			83	177,634	186,816	202,356	15,540
			84	312,833	409,026	436,027	27,001
			85	89,948	106,080	113,194	7,114
HEARD I	V	E	85	152,117	202,500	212,788	10,288
HG KONG	V	E	85	132,000	159,322	170,136	10,814
			86	253,705	310,117	317,668	7,551
	V	W	82	2,202,107	1,674,035	1,805,728	131,693
HONDURA	A	E	81	66,171	76,995	81,203	4,208
	N	E	81	35,802,118	41,667,599	43,483,580	1,815,981
			82	13,918,102	17,267,006	17,794,014	527,008
			83	4,690,390	5,411,081	5,720,298	309,217
			84	8,692,134	10,714,238	11,184,003	469,765
			85	13,419,640	16,979,738	17,633,124	653,386
			86	33,672,920	62,730,113	64,259,544	1,529,431
	N	W	84	182,352	318,353	321,589	3,236
			85	190,147	246,743	262,974	16,231
	O	E	84	1,520	3,183	3,183	
			85	342,264	460,890	477,493	16,603
			86	1,576	3,828	3,828	
	V	E	81	8,107,285	9,542,432	10,138,164	595,732
			82	15,042,153	19,522,946	20,442,372	919,426
			83	29,429,559	35,096,636	36,891,788	1,795,152
			84	28,289,809	35,903,890	37,498,168	1,594,278
			85	20,721,599	26,844,473	28,044,593	1,200,120
			86	19,268,316	33,404,823	34,054,738	649,915
	V	W	81	864,773	998,545	1,063,793	65,248
			82	262,403	353,342	366,577	13,235
			83	123,207	147,848	157,632	9,784
			84	570,439	732,563	775,967	43,404
			85	76,059	139,688	143,828	4,140
INDIA	N	E	81	18,774,614	16,941,042	18,166,877	1,225,835
			86	28,632,109	37,116,502	38,631,991	1,515,489
	O	E	82	33,000	41,842	41,842	
			84	8,580	9,771	9,771	
			86	36,168	43,845	43,845	
	V	E	81	30,276,400	29,655,649	31,698,366	2,042,717
			82	28,295,799	29,228,612	31,015,115	1,786,503
			83	18,047,114	20,196,956	21,271,581	1,074,625
			84	13,243,322	16,085,870	16,922,449	836,579
			85	21,235,060	24,140,265	25,516,918	1,376,653
			86	12,536,921	17,853,639	18,679,910	826,271
	V	W	81	13,192,693	12,437,783	13,344,051	906,268
			82	8,535,256	9,916,758	10,492,782	576,024
			83	2,866,736	3,434,132	3,635,296	201,164
			84	7,036,849	9,251,633	9,706,244	454,611
			85	11,806,731	14,320,593	15,047,394	726,801
			86	8,700,898	11,963,069	12,476,813	513,744
INDNSIA	N	E	81	79,359,073	67,454,571	74,320,923	6,866,252
			84	20,559,003	23,702,882	25,440,633	1,737,751
			85	80,818,049	86,246,264	92,837,387	6,591,123
			86	55,482,609	67,796,238	71,196,040	3,399,802
	O	E	84	40,713	52,945	52,945	
			85	568,089	486,024	515,950	29,926
			86	6,600	16,866	16,866	
	O	W	81	11,094	14,415	15,049	634
			82	1,100,679	741,049	806,871	65,822
	V	E	81	68,790,188	58,064,858	64,312,959	6,248,101
			82	101,417,085	88,752,850	97,347,553	8,594,703
			83	86,076,027	85,512,107	92,180,018	6,667,911
			84	57,968,302	66,489,262	71,308,022	4,818,760
			85	17,960,433	19,247,491	20,580,999	1,333,508
			86	74,685,593	87,979,356	92,797,123	4,817,767

Crop
Product
TSUSA commodity number, description, and unit of quantity

Country	Mode	Reg	Yr	Quantity	F.A.S.	C.I.F.	Charges
	V	W	81	52,317,258	48,634,493	52,547,347	3,912,854
			82	45,356,490	42,734,272	46,302,219	3,567,947
			83	56,653,297	61,850,150	66,243,214	4,393,064
			84	57,706,625	68,913,502	73,393,646	4,480,144
			85	38,379,076	41,712,919	44,540,033	2,827,114
			86	47,887,566	61,252,302	64,163,731	2,911,429
IRELAND	V	E	86	88,019	115,364	122,823	7,459
ISRAEL	V	E	81	1,010,420	1,196,413	1,278,707	82,294
ITALY	A	W	85	1,860	6,186	6,394	208
			86	496	2,407	5,544	3,137
	N	E	83	8,620	16,340	17,882	1,542
	O	E	82	80	259	259	
			83	4,100	2,180	2,180	
			84	612	3,325	3,325	
	V	E	81	357,885	389,015	422,352	33,337
			82	809,279	1,193,747	1,264,402	70,655
			83	1,257,093	1,610,247	1,714,394	104,147
			84	16,466	28,719	31,902	3,183
			85	547,063	844,906	901,283	56,377
			86	790,964	975,468	1,013,880	38,412
	V	W	81	23,173	34,476	36,563	2,087
			82	234,173	311,029	332,022	20,993
			83	188,393	236,752	252,577	15,825
			84	50,690	73,055	77,707	4,652
IVY CST	N	E	83	28,657,203	30,060,820	31,992,492	1,931,672
			84	11,251,061	11,918,112	12,531,011	612,899
			85	49,256,929	55,919,176	59,631,000	3,711,824
			86	13,663,083	19,866,465	20,794,902	928,437
	O	E	85	34,375	45,719	45,719	
			86	198,400	218,281	218,281	
	V	E	81	78,260,990	78,855,219	84,580,096	5,725,687
			82	123,786,661	122,174,068	131,084,110	8,910,042
			83	51,427,765	54,909,583	58,056,575	3,146,992
			84	112,067,913	132,246,185	139,545,772	7,299,587
			85	48,601,971	56,584,457	59,686,596	3,102,139
			86	70,225,787	94,401,028	98,954,836	4,553,808
	V	W	81	1,367,782	1,447,936	1,554,493	106,557
			82	8,162,988	8,990,625	9,571,188	580,563
			83	9,008,993	10,405,803	11,061,134	655,331
			84	27,943,064	34,624,953	36,632,682	2,007,729
			85	27,891,694	29,109,452	30,587,065	1,477,613
			86	7,679,617	10,772,627	11,104,418	331,791
JAMAICA	A	E	82	60	392	544	152
			84	17,920	70,616	75,782	5,166
			85	839	7,117	7,299	182
			86	4,490	31,456	34,341	2,885
	A	W	84	400	4,728	4,728	
	N	E	81	45,957	148,996	158,961	9,965
			83	20,270	103,160	110,611	7,451
			86	48,960	199,828	212,736	12,908
	N	W	83	120,713	347,127	360,061	12,934
			84	25,825	89,320	94,713	5,393
			85	24,120	96,450	99,037	2,587
	O	E	82	100	385	435	50
	V	E	81	20,000	67,275	69,196	1,921
			82	33,901	82,725	86,718	3,993
			83	962	10,469	10,712	243
			84	49,415	238,724	245,123	6,399
			85	8,808	65,777	67,555	1,778
			86	7,527	34,472	36,335	1,863
	V	W	82	30,400	75,800	79,021	3,221
			83	37,919	77,425	79,520	2,095
JAPAN	N	E	86	187,027	283,795	284,131	336
	O	E	82	6,160	12,320	12,320	
	V	W	83	1,103	564	610	46
			84	26	363	388	25
			85	14,750	50,765	52,531	1,766
			86	23,000	95,830	97,838	2,008
KENYA	N	W	86	6,341,526	10,269,538	10,717,719	448,181
	O	E	83	40,337	57,473	57,473	
			84	948	2,335	2,335	
			86	36,080	97,968	97,968	
	V	E	81	22,546,235	23,181,186	24,901,965	1,720,779
			82	24,788,126	28,471,785	30,423,387	1,951,602
			83	30,551,916	34,036,522	36,384,102	2,347,580
			84	20,204,254	25,303,303	26,863,695	1,560,392
			85	27,334,288	33,155,012	35,376,710	2,221,698
			86	39,966,790	64,692,364	67,238,100	2,545,736
	V	W	81	1,669,122	2,015,481	2,164,576	149,095
			82	1,527,375	2,389,841	2,523,339	133,498
			83	4,216,683	4,777,187	5,143,915	366,728
			84	2,477,120	3,229,517	3,459,202	229,685
			85	7,082,327	7,473,853	8,059,564	585,711
			86	10,647,099	13,392,197	14,122,634	729,885

Crop
Product
TSUSA commodity number, description, and unit of quantity

Country	Mode	Reg	Yr	Quantity	F.A.S.	C.I.F.	Charges
KIRIBAT	O	E	86	16,000	23,040	23,040	
	V	E	85	934,887	1,029,870	1,079,249	49,379
			86	3,207,545	5,824,328	6,026,080	201,752
	V	W	86	38,029	73,125	74,430	1,305
KOR REP	V	E	85	71,032	86,304	91,729	5,425
			86	253,600	292,659	304,490	11,831
	V	W	83	440,924	476,602	510,477	33,875
KUWAIT	V	E	83	1,100	1,996	2,346	350
LAOS	V	W	82	661,380	675,323	725,313	49,990
			83	2,006,184	2,269,107	2,411,862	142,755
LIBERIA	O	E	82	147	273	273	
	V	E	81	4,156,320	4,292,452	4,611,635	319,183
			82	4,373,167	4,128,251	4,453,483	325,232
			83	5,144,051	5,454,366	5,851,001	396,635
			84	2,568,130	3,103,350	3,295,717	192,367
			85	1,121,177	1,398,849	1,476,959	78,110
			86	1,599,251	2,275,634	2,386,042	110,408
MACAO	V	E	81	110,230	103,390	113,226	9,836
			82	374,782	299,385	333,144	33,759
			86	382,279	736,289	747,677	11,388
MADAGAS	N	E	85	4,235,393	5,012,987	5,392,661	379,674
	V	E	81	32,508,526	33,806,268	36,235,663	2,429,395
			82	14,416,431	14,172,631	15,198,471	1,025,840
			83	9,596,992	10,288,051	10,937,395	649,344
			84	6,383,784	7,694,654	8,096,034	401,380
			85	3,226,309	3,897,511	4,109,783	212,272
			86	7,826,697	9,144,878	9,544,523	399,645
	V	W	82	4,072,625	4,255,714	4,567,018	311,304
			83	7,069,456	8,172,546	8,728,326	555,780
			84	4,670,913	5,642,558	5,975,978	333,420
			85	1,172,492	1,339,685	1,406,990	67,305
MALAWI	V	E	82	33,069	38,029	41,349	3,320
			86	66,138	88,790	93,363	4,573
	V	W	84	33,069	43,372	46,842	3,470
			86	33,075	57,846	60,334	2,488
MALAYSA	A	E	81	1,137	1,394	1,564	170
	O	E	83	440,920	393,260	419,230	25,970
	O	W	81	797,020	825,090	875,221	50,131
			82	1,046,702	833,512	866,212	32,700
			83	569,505	487,912	511,157	23,245
			85	1,059,813	827,398	874,671	47,273
	V	E	81	1,217,600	1,181,535	1,255,533	73,998
			82	1,070,417	671,752	722,007	50,255
			84	52,917	61,913	62,710	797
			85	428,199	483,925	532,427	48,502
			86	628,463	997,645	1,016,894	19,249
	V	W	81	3,898,997	3,784,117	4,010,266	226,149
			82	2,640,193	2,507,917	2,693,443	185,526
			83	1,245,848	1,329,630	1,453,532	123,902
			84	33,069	39,750	41,452	1,702
			86	195,367	335,990	344,027	8,037
MALDIVE	V	E	85	66,138	74,575	75,200	625
	V	W	82	110,186	145,943	152,055	6,112
			84	264,554	367,200	378,000	10,800
MEXICO	N	E	85	27,569,008	36,997,038	38,136,632	1,139,594
			86	241,689,119	468,642,160	468,646,287	4,127
	N	W	84	10,785	16,875	17,163	288
			85	41,998	56,834	60,878	4,044
	O	E	81	179,713,780	228,783,004	228,788,182	5,178
			82	165,090,616	226,270,101	226,270,101	
			83	177,926,398	228,271,852	228,274,352	2,500
			84	165,507,269	235,445,795	235,445,798	3
			85	201,273,793	282,668,607	282,669,943	1,336
			86	898,246	1,370,925	1,371,260	335
	O	H	84	304,235	432,013	432,013	
	O	W	81	2,874,623	3,637,574	3,637,574	
			82	548,445	662,040	662,040	
			83	13,651	19,173	19,173	
			84	29,184	39,137	39,137	
			85	55,736	80,534	80,534	
			86	1,903,647	2,084,866	2,084,866	
	V	E	81	1,586,645	2,062,365	2,138,811	76,446
			82	16,309,085	22,570,237	23,195,047	624,810
			83	11,827,919	14,431,965	14,829,374	397,409
			84	28,373,672	39,287,032	40,406,343	1,119,311
			85	2,433,045	3,415,657	3,547,933	132,276
			86	28,645,733	54,131,036	55,338,661	1,207,625
	V	W	81	88,274	120,469	127,883	7,414
			82	202,092	276,598	285,901	9,303
			83	7,967,705	10,419,805	10,712,297	292,492
			84	11,259,916	15,409,903	15,959,462	549,559
			85	8,296,251	11,229,219	11,547,515	318,296
			86	7,976,337	14,165,454	14,498,992	333,538
MONSRAT	V	E	85	264,393	291,332	309,414	18,082
	V	W	85	304,238	443,882	452,372	8,490
MOZAMBQ	V	E	86	37,037	40,556	42,878	2,322
N ANTIL	V	E	81	2,067,999	1,704,306	1,839,246	134,940
			82	175,318	175,318	180,314	4,996
			86	4,223,004	8,087,419	8,208,771	121,352
N ZEAL	V	E	81	43,812	73,331	75,095	1,764
			82	147,312	197,398	210,135	12,737
			85	145,505	178,971	190,587	11,616
NAMIBIA	V	E	86	330,203	511,600	517,335	5,735
NAURU	V	E	85	66,138	80,850	87,250	6,400
NETHLDS	A	E	81	1,323	1,708	2,456	748
			83	2,116	2,291	4,221	1,930
			86	440	1,384	1,509	125
	N	E	83	2,301,298	3,409,291	3,704,086	294,795
			86	6,073,707	9,404,416	9,731,063	326,647
	V	E	81	2,804,264	3,853,042	4,014,844	161,802
			82	2,596,461	3,583,978	3,706,868	122,890
			83	87,633	113,924	122,834	8,910
			84	4,318,849	6,752,036	7,266,017	513,981
			85	4,841,488	7,365,484	8,029,844	664,360
			86	6,169,970	12,362,007	12,816,098	454,091
	V	W	81	117,660	210,681	220,148	9,467
			82	124,383	201,770	210,722	8,952
			83	21,737	37,758	39,344	1,586
			84	2,884,457	3,529,940	3,669,406	139,466
			85	625,190	1,099,953	1,156,217	56,264
			86	848,106	1,924,717	1,993,623	68,906
NEW GUI	V	E	82	5,163	10,233	10,585	352
			83	5,036	8,742	9,014	272
			85	45,680	74,403	77,336	2,933
			86	1,989	4,420	4,535	115
	V	W	81	4,695,270	4,985,260	5,333,797	348,537
			82	4,690,839	6,068,512	6,452,611	384,099
			83	5,118,760	5,985,932	6,374,604	388,672
			84	8,615,958	11,026,752	11,702,332	675,580
			85	6,283,053	7,924,487	8,368,330	443,843
			86	12,250,501	21,132,053	21,846,331	714,278
NICARAG	V	E	81	12,073,905	16,630,902	17,338,083	707,181
			82	1,787,999	2,700,747	2,822,146	121,399
			83	383,622	545,032	566,199	21,167
			84	3,527,781	4,526,648	4,663,465	136,817
			85	1,134,477	1,465,955	1,517,238	51,283
	V	W	81	4,693,450	6,204,964	6,505,984	301,020
			82	697,928	919,956	976,650	56,694
			83	380,715	473,459	501,417	27,958
			84	697,495	952,163	1,003,740	51,577
			85	25,307	37,425	40,476	3,051
NIGERIA	V	E	84	608,885	756,481	805,827	49,346
NORWAY	V	E	86	491,736	693,841	722,780	28,939
PANAMA	N	W	81	4,099,128	5,028,182	5,347,749	319,567
	O	E	86	3,300	5,478	5,478	
	V	E	81	1,506,644	1,988,033	2,081,046	93,013
			82	3,989,811	4,994,766	5,180,223	185,457
			83	3,157,738	3,994,501	4,163,946	169,445
			84	3,666,810	4,802,166	4,992,587	190,421
			85	5,201,031	6,897,941	7,208,479	310,538
			86	12,789,302	23,296,274	23,834,525	538,251
	V	W	81	714,635	838,453	892,205	53,752
			82	2,795,492	3,710,070	3,954,289	244,219
			83	4,558,998	5,854,134	6,256,856	402,722
			84	4,505,162	5,987,715	6,347,291	359,576
			85	4,319,773	5,768,427	6,092,166	323,739
			86	6,061,124	11,062,368	11,371,065	308,697
PARAGUA	V	E	81	16,236,136	16,095,108	17,383,194	1,288,086
			82	10,730,729	11,822,162	12,631,232	809,070
			83	17,407,112	19,036,993	20,250,365	1,213,372
			84	16,264,282	19,656,644	20,725,119	1,068,475
			85	7,841,868	12,455,690	12,950,220	494,530
			86	9,969,114	17,028,627	17,575,268	546,641
PERU	N	E	81	29,132,374	30,979,776	32,675,762	1,695,986
			82	30,312,287	35,944,637	37,835,506	1,890,869
			84	24,866,285	31,276,543	32,983,926	1,707,383
			85	20,281,377	26,141,742	27,523,521	1,381,779
			86	21,212,706	35,582,525	36,881,939	1,299,414
	N	W	81	1,175,395	1,294,194	1,378,821	84,627
			82	448,057	566,104	595,325	29,221
			84	89,922	135,662	140,901	5,239
	O	E	85	3,042	4,259	4,259	
	V	E	81	18,352,465	20,195,231	21,286,404	1,091,173
			82	18,932,738	23,077,997	24,178,960	1,100,963
			83	41,355,868	47,208,622	49,877,351	2,668,729
			84	23,499,481	29,485,091	30,873,354	1,388,263
			85	27,517,040	34,530,787	36,505,259	1,974,472
			86	50,025,013	82,427,492	85,459,913	3,032,421

Country	Mode	Reg	Yr	Quantity	F.A.S.	C.I.F.	Charges
Crop							
Product							
TSUSA commodity number, description, and unit of quantity							
	V	W	81	27,176,379	29,833,045	31,954,048	2,121,003
			82	18,201,067	23,422,125	24,942,320	1,520,195
			83	16,736,420	19,812,089	21,035,597	1,223,508
			84	25,220,966	32,628,431	34,368,720	1,740,289
			85	24,077,530	30,029,473	31,686,484	1,657,011
			86	18,069,804	30,861,485	32,127,717	1,266,232
PHIL R	N	E	85	5,624,972	5,908,405	6,272,823	364,418
	N	W	86	28,938,893	38,662,810	40,021,398	1,358,588
	O	E	85	71,447	68,825	73,438	4,613
	V	E	81	6,778,869	6,181,276	6,687,314	506,038
			82	7,483,346	6,673,719	7,251,030	577,311
			83	5,634,802	5,544,358	5,914,285	369,927
			84	1,079,264	1,262,503	1,352,935	90,432
			85	5,513,204	6,230,871	6,600,673	369,802
			86	16,308,704	22,121,421	23,085,310	963,889
	V	W	81	28,994,794	26,475,405	28,500,860	2,025,455
			82	33,283,482	31,251,890	33,358,904	2,107,014
			83	30,931,177	32,402,222	34,208,128	1,805,906
			84	38,063,250	44,577,655	46,944,845	2,367,190
			85	42,658,400	44,005,563	46,150,029	2,144,466
			86	12,892,208	16,449,549	17,052,033	602,484
PITCARN	V	E	85	46,297	63,037	64,868	1,831
POLAND	V	E	86	152,117	244,500	255,145	10,645
PORTUGL	N	E	83	3,500	4,955	5,791	836
	V	E	85	52,800	75,915	81,589	5,674
REP SAF	N	E	85	152,117	200,735	211,677	10,942
			86	378,254	644,171	668,768	24,597
	O	E	86	7,014	14,509	15,025	516
	O	W	83	19,286	19,119	20,858	1,739
			85	87,964	44,243	52,631	8,388
	V	E	81	66,138	66,600	72,579	5,979
			82	1,185,205	1,188,095	1,235,055	46,960
			83	2,218,077	2,488,434	2,559,358	70,924
			85	233,114	271,199	292,487	21,288
			86	72,752	156,585	163,094	6,509
	V	W	82	99,208	112,500	121,000	8,500
RWANDA	V	E	81	35,253,776	38,091,075	40,597,268	2,506,193
			82	23,500,069	30,809,753	32,551,748	1,741,995
			83	21,690,301	26,227,746	27,501,443	1,273,697
			84	8,533,022	11,774,953	12,373,064	598,111
			85	1,405,263	1,643,201	1,743,056	99,855
			86	4,021,344	6,336,686	6,529,486	192,800
	V	W	81	132,276	121,214	132,891	11,677
			82	330,702	412,334	436,434	24,100
			84	472,886	645,498	670,696	25,198
			86	436,231	654,356	692,721	38,365
S ARAB	O	E	82	12,194	12,190	12,921	731
	V	W	81	25,097	44,436	46,065	1,629
SALVADR	A	W	81	1,075	1,313	2,018	705
	N	E	81	29,469,037	35,862,020	37,756,668	1,894,648
			82	58,720,094	74,609,923	78,386,218	3,776,295
			84	42,603,399	54,834,164	56,976,781	2,142,617
			85	63,464,557	93,590,303	96,827,385	3,237,082
			86	53,336,658	96,928,228	99,363,595	2,435,367
	N	W	85	2,557,022	3,609,033	3,735,660	126,627
	O	E	82	3,359,102	4,932,750	5,301,914	369,164
			83	7,268,196	9,603,994	10,436,456	832,462
			85	5,625	7,481	7,481	
	O	W	82	51,680	70,339	70,339	
			86	152,117	352,918	359,393	6,475
	V	E	81	47,108,504	57,190,022	60,323,277	3,133,255
			82	41,781,083	56,186,756	59,058,176	2,871,420
			83	125,137,912	153,984,344	160,358,691	6,374,347
			84	63,869,391	90,026,058	93,702,611	3,676,553
			85	74,124,524	93,453,530	96,976,878	3,523,348
			86	56,686,813	96,836,997	99,650,115	2,813,118
	V	W	81	26,422,161	30,434,381	32,227,047	1,792,666
			82	17,676,544	22,461,314	23,860,046	1,398,732
			83	28,170,015	36,700,996	38,724,105	2,023,109
			84	32,647,312	45,667,251	47,992,766	2,325,515
			85	40,532,563	53,312,435	55,397,244	2,084,809
			86	36,410,876	68,891,728	70,570,343	1,678,615
SAO T P	V	E	86	228,176	438,188	445,404	7,216
SEYCHEL	V	E	85	662,015	813,954	841,430	27,476
			86	112,435	160,392	163,710	3,318
SIER LN	V	E	81	4,522,652	4,902,656	5,144,055	241,399
			82	16,240,237	15,308,306	16,339,579	1,031,273
			83	13,887,156	14,545,120	15,578,975	1,033,855
			84	18,486,026	22,244,551	23,592,288	1,347,737
SINGAPR	O	E	85	327,179	346,858	363,975	17,117
			86	1,106,394	1,451,928	1,511,003	59,075
	V	E	81	220,460	171,570	185,668	14,098
			82	1,851,804	1,634,484	1,789,875	155,391
			84	121,115	149,050	157,047	7,997
			85	2,904,159	3,264,012	3,401,529	137,517
			86	10,248,155	14,141,196	14,526,160	384,964
	V	W	81	2,604,522	2,395,872	2,548,294	152,422
			82	12,616,868	12,725,588	13,582,067	856,479
			83	3,702,880	4,104,647	4,358,310	253,663
			84	2,053,703	2,514,351	2,639,495	125,144
			85	7,837,364	8,568,393	9,078,843	510,450
			86	3,755,873	4,133,153	4,352,834	219,681
SPAIN	O	E	83	11,000	6,930	7,801	871
	V	E	81	442,749	635,361	672,808	37,447
			82	577,523	879,908	930,093	50,185
			83	628,443	934,249	978,585	44,336
			84	44,136	74,675	78,750	4,075
			85	709,376	820,228	872,406	52,178
			86	638,159	1,073,641	1,114,477	40,836
	V	W	84	140,876	218,134	227,728	9,594
SRI LKA	V	E	81	88,096	69,071	77,858	8,787
			82	2,682,074	2,265,846	2,498,390	232,544
			83	3,785,122	3,645,414	4,018,002	372,588
			84	296,739	317,422	345,704	28,282
			85	595,242	541,925	601,232	59,307
			86	3,024,712	3,103,123	3,319,448	216,325
	V	W	82	315,390	260,934	288,820	27,886
			83	529,636	517,070	560,663	43,593
			84	456,661	517,608	556,193	38,585
			86	396,829	505,657	535,257	29,600
SURINAM	O	E	81	39,683	46,876	46,876	
	V	E	81	132,000	248,160	260,600	12,440
SWAZLND	V	E	86	43,560	140,134	144,184	4,050
SWEDEN	N	E	83	18,970	35,385	37,705	2,320
	V	E	82	16,596	39,615	50,487	10,872
			83	308,644	194,752	216,352	21,600
			84	1,537	7,200	7,578	378
SWITZLD	A	E	83	18,144	29,678	35,975	6,297
	O	E	82	158,731	190,477	201,500	11,023
	V	E	81	593,149	921,499	967,505	46,006
			82	375,715	718,622	744,824	26,202
			83	600,750	1,087,347	1,128,507	41,160
			84	1,286,168	2,517,820	2,618,350	100,530
			85	3,050,549	4,972,827	5,182,243	209,416
			86	2,147,644	4,864,928	4,980,202	115,274
	V	W	81	104,620	170,438	178,108	7,670
			82	106,454	192,869	201,149	8,280
			83	261,360	493,612	516,101	22,489
			84	202,301	430,164	448,863	18,699
			85	492,970	1,041,676	1,089,961	48,285
			86	224,615	630,594	649,875	19,281
THAILND	O	E	86	1,102,254	1,818,719	1,862,291	43,572
	V	E	81	771,610	824,927	871,542	46,615
			82	306,441	584,953	613,010	28,057
			83	791,853	827,158	876,110	48,952
			84	158,732	188,928	200,115	11,187
			85	4,938,920	6,041,923	6,313,173	271,250
			86	12,757,069	18,257,090	18,914,148	657,058
	V	W	81	4,187,698	3,956,990	4,250,124	293,134
			82	11,345,715	11,774,586	12,579,422	804,836
			83	13,931,201	15,997,105	17,048,273	1,051,168
			84	10,970,723	13,596,010	14,313,378	717,368
			85	9,860,338	10,816,564	11,265,787	449,223
			86	22,277,536	31,288,342	32,255,865	967,523
TNZANIA	O	E	83	1,890	2,684	2,684	
			85	8,986	12,830	12,830	
			86	11,900	27,598	27,598	
	V	E	81	3,752,459	3,719,746	4,028,252	308,506
			82	6,157,673	7,161,414	7,634,829	473,415
			83	1,691,582	2,013,215	2,152,965	139,750
			84	961,841	1,278,148	1,345,520	67,372
			85	1,465,965	1,843,359	1,962,231	118,872
			86	3,740,449	5,859,649	6,140,248	280,599
	V	W	81	74,489	88,584	96,063	7,479
			82	42,605	52,775	55,990	3,215
			83	66,138	76,389	81,714	5,325
			84	247,678	367,536	388,695	21,159
			85	798,997	900,098	948,533	48,435
			86	118,799	221,980	231,532	9,552
TOGO	V	E	82	11,909,861	9,765,443	10,470,765	705,322
			83	13,865,327	15,586,862	16,356,066	769,204
			84	14,287,434	18,018,267	19,114,099	1,095,832
	V	W	83	3,750,287	4,188,390	4,498,771	310,381
			84	12,126,133	15,955,355	16,598,877	643,522
TRINID	V	E	81	211,642	232,805	238,904	6,099
			82	2,460,334	2,622,369	2,778,908	156,539
			83	741,195	692,823	741,549	48,726
			84	533,750	420,000	463,076	43,076

Crop
Product
TSUSA commodity number, description, and unit of quantity

Country	Mode	Reg	Yr	Quantity	F.A.S.	C.I.F.	Charges
			85	427,826	469,177	527,097	57,920
			86	305,000	432,718	455,464	22,746
TUNISIA	V	E	86	403,995	366,129	389,017	22,888
	V	W	86	57,099	55,944	58,811	2,867
U KING	A	W	84	160	1,236	1,439	203
	N	E	81	296,147	288,635	306,746	18,111
			82	173,737	189,689	205,526	15,837
	O	E	83	17,342	24,972	24,972	
	V	E	82	41,358	66,300	68,251	1,951
			83	1,188	9,163	9,447	284
			84	132,276	177,949	190,473	12,524
			85	304,235	454,500	468,672	14,172
			86	1,571,189	3,482,708	3,558,418	75,710
	V	W	85	433,208	423,721	456,121	32,400
			86	41,667	85,004	88,594	3,590
UGANDA	N	E	85	14,111,575	17,214,055	18,185,736	971,681
			86	23,210,929	32,065,210	33,607,073	1,541,863
	O	E	85	40,920	55,282	55,282	
	V	E	81	113,851,392	100,580,643	108,065,129	7,494,262
			82	155,980,160	148,390,630	159,090,269	10,699,639
			83	88,428,460	94,536,028	100,682,789	6,146,761
			84	64,896,488	79,443,212	83,487,608	4,044,396
			85	78,803,583	90,133,523	95,327,086	5,193,563
			86	70,094,157	94,126,278	98,734,641	4,608,363
	V	W	81	313,592	297,845	324,650	26,805
			82	6,579,213	7,005,395	7,451,041	445,646
			83	7,998,319	9,060,633	9,622,693	562,060
			84	10,491,009	13,030,110	13,892,184	862,074
			85	4,761,662	5,026,500	5,277,877	251,377
			86	4,214,338	6,147,708	6,413,516	265,808
URUGUAY	V	E	84	388,317	388,317	412,480	24,163
USSR	V	E	85	70,768	67,335	71,312	3,977
			86	228,176	314,546	323,854	9,308
VANUATA	V	W	81	35,834	43,001	45,014	2,013
VENEZ	N	E	84	448,741	608,353	636,419	28,066
	O	E	86	1,000	2,474	2,474	
	V	E	81	3,594,398	4,671,192	4,917,174	245,982
			82	2,163,166	2,939,756	3,045,059	105,303
			83	3,187,325	4,086,913	4,263,611	176,698
			84	11,169,128	14,743,323	15,203,638	460,315
			85	13,850,224	18,933,821	19,833,885	900,064
			86	29,634,723	44,900,103	46,093,177	1,193,074
	V	W	83	220,504	302,582	305,018	2,436
			85	267,858	722,089	733,266	11,177
YEMAN S	O	W	85	52,910	209,358	216,224	6,866
	V	E	82	55,115	115,000	124,468	9,468
	V	W	81	88,555	261,812	283,330	21,518
			82	7,230	14,104	15,156	1,052
YEMEN A	O	E	85	55,115	110,000	120,250	10,250
	V	W	81	180,630	437,927	458,767	20,840
			82	100,790	199,096	214,891	15,795
			85	49,173	99,900	107,251	7,351
YUGOSLV	V	E	86	837,553	1,465,013	1,524,938	59,925
ZAIRE	N	E	81	14,811,732	15,355,224	16,331,279	976,055
	O	E	83	1,980	7,485	7,485	
			86	9,200	18,177	18,177	
	V	E	81	15,282,768	17,290,017	18,321,420	1,031,403
			82	12,766,959	12,006,558	12,984,215	977,657
			83	2,866,009	2,689,034	2,873,551	184,517
			84	1,640,636	1,977,965	2,065,436	87,471
			85	3,568,469	4,087,078	4,356,468	269,390
			86	9,666,157	13,875,261	14,512,238	636,977
	V	W	83	66,000	77,712	79,487	1,775
			86	224,880	311,459	330,009	18,550
ZAMBIA	V	E	82	33,069	33,300	36,190	2,890
ZMBABWE	V	E	81	802,119	786,969	857,703	70,734
			82	1,049,485	1,184,622	1,275,388	90,766
			83	1,185,316	1,328,538	1,415,531	86,993
			84	529,104	750,900	799,945	49,045
			85	833,339	1,047,295	1,121,571	74,276
			86	1,665,931	2,420,100	2,518,501	98,401
	V	W	81	330,702	360,000	389,982	29,982
			82	1,818,807	2,176,217	2,324,378	148,161
			83	2,182,556	2,582,939	2,773,876	190,937
			84	2,380,968	3,256,710	3,426,615	169,905
			85	453,046	525,690	565,430	39,740
			86	560,920	1,212,819	1,245,272	32,453

Coffee, extract

1602100 COFFEE ESSENCE, EXTRACT ETC (LB)

Country	Mode	Reg	Yr	Quantity	F.A.S.	C.I.F.	Charges
TOTAL			81	2,458,620	5,012,137	5,311,407	299,270
			82	2,435,991	5,232,491	5,625,865	393,374
			83	2,802,618	5,722,360	6,013,080	290,720
			84	3,485,681	6,855,268	7,252,295	397,027
			85	3,426,274	7,306,906	7,853,931	547,025
			86	3,445,602	10,184,465	10,663,279	478,814
AUSTRIA	O	E	82	984	1,593	1,593	
BELGIUM	O	E	85	9,232	22,611	22,677	66
	V	E	81	332,671	674,628	713,279	38,651
			82	199,735	442,580	465,342	22,762
			83	69,478	138,694	145,518	6,824
			84	13,413	70,216	78,313	8,097
BRAZIL	A	E	81	285	6,606	7,342	736
			82	2,589	58,951	62,963	4,012
			83	6,511	20,450	22,328	1,878
			84	629	5,165	6,583	1,418
			85	3,973	3,001	4,561	1,560
	N	E	85	22,655	90,417	95,466	5,049
	V	E	82	27,005	103,950	104,127	177
			84	766,350	1,096,271	1,158,321	62,050
			85	13,228	50,160	53,964	3,804
			86	8,910	54,802	56,641	1,839
	V	W	82	1,563	3,153	4,316	1,163
			84	13,228	52,800	56,409	3,609
C RICA	A	E	82	100	700	800	100
	A	W	86	1,148	4,918	7,235	2,317
	V	E	82	432	1,080	1,980	900
CANADA	A	E	82	110	325	400	75
	O	E	81	1,809	4,365	4,365	
			82	5,426	12,327	12,885	558
			83	8,730	43,243	43,243	
			84	1,260	8,059	8,087	28
			85	7,826	45,270	49,311	4,041
			86	1,316	3,531	3,531	
CHINA T	V	W	85	2,646	1,200	1,314	114
			86	5,873	2,300	2,741	441
COLOMB	O	E	86	10,236	23,265	23,265	
	V	E	86	123,458	712,000	737,666	25,666
DENMARK	A	E	85	243	2,000	2,200	200
FR GERM	A	E	81	4,623	2,030	3,549	1,519
			83	140	291	419	128
	A	W	84	100	2,895	3,223	328
			85	4,724	24,890	27,822	2,932
	N	E	85	77,092	241,692	262,464	20,772
	O	E	85	2,634	4,820	4,909	89
	V	E	82	9,722	48,319	49,584	1,265
			84	6,963	14,934	15,626	692
			85	11,177	18,704	26,204	7,500
FRANCE	A	E	81	5	3,351	3,458	107
			85	441	4,000	4,400	400
			86	1,750	17,728	19,932	2,204
	N	E	83	408	1,366	1,513	147
	N	W	84	2,129	6,184	7,016	832
			86	760	3,607	4,398	791
	V	E	83	245	927	992	65
			84	907	1,406	1,575	169
			86	2,568	4,805	5,294	489
	V	W	82	2,209	9,442	9,778	336
			85	3,364	6,993	7,719	726
GERM DR	A	W	83	90	1,425	1,523	98
GREECE	O	E	84	156	516	516	
HG KONG	A	E	82	952	21,375	129,167	107,792
	A	W	83	124	399	587	188
INDIA	V	E	83	2,200	1,179	1,297	118
ITALY	A	E	81	608	696	1,000	304
			82	101	1,256	1,563	307
	N	E	83	6,276	17,920	20,295	2,375
	O	E	86	12,274	18,879	20,663	1,784
	V	E	81	757	2,130	2,375	245
			82	1,497	3,649	3,932	283
			83	598	2,054	2,561	507
			84	2,019	5,056	5,728	672
			85	2,994	8,400	9,656	1,256
			86	6,698	32,122	33,915	1,793
JAMAICA	A	E	83	640	926	1,726	800
	V	W	84	5,840	30,220	31,290	1,070
JAPAN	A	E	83	102	402	871	469
	V	E	82	495	329	364	35
			84	3,180	1,734	1,959	225
	V	W	82	883	689	732	43
			83	4,604	3,800	4,107	307
			84	801	1,527	1,662	135
			85	21,536	11,727	12,497	770
			86	16,400	72,170	73,851	1,681
KENYA	A	E	83	15,471	18,599	41,156	22,557

Crop Product TSUSA commodity number, description, and unit of quantity Country	Mode	Reg	Yr	Quantity	F.A.S.	C.I.F.	Charges
			84	998	2,354	2,635	281
MEXICO	O	W	86	51,496	164,020	164,020	
	V	E	86	375	4,680	5,105	425
NETHLDS	A	E	81	1,548	2,795	3,467	672
			83	8,076	17,363	19,742	2,379
			84	3,565	8,713	10,071	1,358
			85	8,730	22,747	23,272	525
			86	1,600	5,258	7,036	1,778
	O	E	85	3,378	12,237	12,237	
			86	4,375	13,919	13,919	
	V	E	81	1,830,504	3,706,960	3,917,141	210,181
			82	2,130,205	4,374,754	4,620,482	245,728
			83	2,403,657	4,905,395	5,132,018	226,623
			84	2,361,618	4,939,695	5,222,243	282,548
			85	2,912,982	6,120,144	6,508,893	388,749
			86	3,008,457	8,448,186	8,841,180	392,994
	V	W	81	241,458	503,108	542,255	39,147
			83	257,608	518,764	542,249	23,485
			84	171,438	388,739	409,098	20,359
			85	294,270	592,851	698,096	105,245
			86	164,785	534,561	568,592	34,031
POLAND	V	E	84	1,587	1,701	1,889	188
PORTUGL	V	E	84	725	2,328	3,098	770
			86	8,435	7,280	7,780	500
SALVADR	A	E	85	5,873	10,377	12,075	1,698
			86	4,267	7,565	9,199	1,634
	V	E	82	10,000	52,000	54,109	2,109
			84	68,844	121,355	127,696	6,341
	V	W	86	3,672	16,249	18,733	2,484
SWEDEN	V	E	82	34,193	73,110	77,634	4,524
SWITZLD	A	E	83	203	282	454	172
	N	E	81	6,090	30,845	33,980	3,135
	O	E	82	5,054	10,079	10,079	
	V	E	81	2,520	8,250	8,386	136
			82	1,984	10,707	11,513	806
			83	16,647	25,168	26,370	1,202
	V	W	81	198	647	685	38
THAILND	V	E	84	737	525	622	97
	V	W	81	1,351	1,298	1,388	90
			84	23,244	17,023	18,711	1,688
			85	17,276	12,665	14,194	1,529
			86	3,364	2,016	2,157	141
U KING	A	E	82	400	1,200	1,451	251
			84	226	529	619	90
			86	331	1,625	1,949	324
	N	E	82	352	923	1,071	148
	O	E	83	810	3,713	4,111	398
	V	E	81	34,193	64,428	68,737	4,309
			84	35,724	75,323	79,305	3,982
			86	2,254	26,355	31,133	4,778
YUGOSLV	V	E	86	800	2,624	3,344	720

Coffee, instant

1602000 SOLBL OR INST COFFEE NO ADD (LB)

Country	Mode	Reg	Yr	Quantity	F.A.S.	C.I.F.	Charges
TOTAL			81	56,992,748	214,791,086	227,321,125	12,524,024
			82	50,047,008	145,075,272	156,427,008	11,351,736
			83	51,833,407	140,979,920	151,576,181	10,596,261
			84	54,669,251	152,804,095	164,037,566	11,233,471
			85	50,571,588	138,691,445	148,484,711	9,793,266
			86	47,291,647	182,859,702	189,538,936	6,679,234
ARGENT	V	E	86	57,684	152,737	164,692	11,955
AUSTRAL	A	W	81	240	629	1,269	640
AUSTRIA	V	E	81	8,929	47,500	49,008	1,508
BELGIUM	A	E	81	66	434	516	82
			82	1,455	7,500	9,414	1,914
			83	1,250	8,841	10,053	1,212
	N	E	81	17,894	93,199	96,623	3,424
	O	E	82	1,601	9,286	9,286	
	V	E	81	14,724	110,764	116,685	5,921
			82	206,550	896,709	925,989	29,280
			83	121,373	497,123	512,683	15,560
			84	421,068	1,764,737	1,812,697	47,960
			85	171,873	685,678	707,070	21,392
			86	90,742	486,298	496,434	10,136
BRAZIL	A	E	81	53,791	221,864	283,090	61,226
			83	220	880	1,256	376
			85	6,614	23,771	30,309	6,538
			86	383	1,713	2,317	604
	N	E	81	20,599,072	80,208,255	85,055,849	4,847,594
			82	11,984,702	35,714,347	38,641,831	2,927,484
			84	12,022,120	34,826,057	37,413,702	2,587,645
			85	465,003	1,642,266	1,772,953	130,687
			86	1,857,109	5,717,847	6,052,859	335,012
	N	W	84	6,311,900	17,764,084	19,478,596	1,714,512
	O	E	81	9,206	15,249	15,249	
			82	84,180	260,958	260,958	
			83	85,186	256,983	256,983	
			84	5,066	18,448	18,448	
			85	319,285	1,381,321	1,390,335	9,014
			86	32,832	128,334	128,334	
	V	E	81	18,247,807	71,374,178	75,743,801	4,369,623
			82	18,622,048	52,738,831	57,350,219	4,611,388
			83	31,889,500	88,549,378	95,275,535	6,726,157
			84	23,693,092	67,320,962	72,468,226	5,147,264
			85	33,180,453	86,122,967	93,286,046	7,163,079
			86	24,529,043	78,273,851	82,757,090	4,483,239
	V	W	81	6,134,068	25,891,718	27,537,738	1,646,020
			82	7,649,124	22,269,832	24,413,070	2,143,238
			83	7,486,281	20,340,604	22,389,221	2,048,617
			85	3,558,021	9,666,237	10,494,802	828,565
			86	1,131,586	3,699,209	3,941,405	242,196
C RICA	V	E	82	54,167	123,480	127,550	4,070
CANADA	A	E	81	1,171	2,593	2,653	60
			82	1,625	1,837	2,316	479
			83	1,117	1,558	1,898	340
			84	570	1,077	1,334	257
			86	2,560	6,549	6,549	
	A	W	81	350	956	1,056	100
	N	E	84	66	585	595	10
	N	W	86	•	2,345	3,605	1,260
	O	E	81	11,718	90,452	90,452	
			82	46,397	238,881	238,881	
			83	3,630	16,426	16,426	
			84	8,109	20,082	20,082	
			85	2,071,372	11,287,069	11,287,069	
			86	8,034,652	52,972,041	52,972,041	
	O	W	84	3,968	15,441	16,062	621
			86	13,860	132,686	132,686	
CAYMAN	V	E	81	1,335	2,646	2,746	100
CHINA M	V	W	85	2,187	3,748	3,949	201
CHINA T	V	W	86	18,506	74,205	74,979	774
COLOMB	A	E	82	175	349	369	20
			85	22,000	84,700	90,303	5,603
	N	E	81	647,832	2,694,641	2,858,747	164,106
			82	585,381	2,034,323	2,157,800	123,477
			83	1,434,968	4,110,137	4,411,907	301,770
			84	2,144,926	6,059,491	6,478,847	419,356
			85	2,416,943	6,134,981	6,601,694	466,713
			86	168,595	666,784	691,027	24,243
	O	E	82	260	705	705	
	V	E	81	22,000	87,250	92,266	5,016
			82	11,000	44,000	46,674	2,674
			83	308,660	972,279	1,044,063	71,784
			84	222,161	559,996	607,092	47,096
			85	69,820	307,286	323,148	15,862
			86	1,756,595	6,510,023	6,810,731	300,708
	V	W	81	176,115	627,680	677,192	49,512
			82	142,058	457,020	491,258	34,238
			83	1,220,494	3,125,581	3,382,164	256,583
			84	769,983	1,986,468	2,138,067	151,599
			85	532,353	1,435,861	1,541,103	105,242
			86	429,650	1,820,100	1,903,765	83,665
DOM REP	V	E	84	184,087	536,218	554,729	18,511
			85	25,353	91,250	94,665	3,415
DOMINCA	V	E	86	10,560	50,123	54,773	4,650
ECUADOR	A	E	82	13,227	54,363	55,378	1,015
	N	E	82	2,326,248	5,592,522	6,033,119	440,597
			85	2,444,625	5,668,439	5,991,167	322,728
	O	E	81	13,228	54,111	54,111	
			83	113,200	308,498	308,498	
			85	4,630	15,392	15,392	
			86	27,251	102,199	102,199	
	V	E	81	2,863,836	6,824,417	7,288,416	463,999
			82	2,077,272	4,043,168	4,262,424	219,256
			83	3,613,047	8,364,138	8,962,535	598,397
			84	4,509,129	10,054,625	10,589,344	534,719
			85	778,259	1,878,276	1,960,418	82,142
			86	3,576,214	11,453,851	11,961,826	507,975
	V	W	81	1,129,922	2,131,610	2,349,048	217,438
			82	773,766	1,527,022	1,691,515	164,493
			83	534,145	1,211,225	1,314,841	103,616
			84	760,620	1,877,734	2,001,895	124,161
			85	338,738	794,355	861,279	66,924
			86	732,164	2,432,250	2,517,831	85,581
ETHIOP	V	E	84	13,228	32,400	34,400	2,000

Crop
Product
TSUSA commodity number, description, and unit of quantity

Country	Mode	Reg	Yr	Quantity	F.A.S.	C.I.F.	Charges
FR GERM	A	E	84	96	317	579	262
			86	220	1,140	1,406	266
	N	E	81	579,735	1,815,575	1,888,257	72,682
			84	623,178	1,842,294	1,890,914	48,620
			86	920,356	3,599,544	3,723,665	124,121
	O	E	83	19,529	41,454	44,983	3,529
			84	11,878	39,589	41,259	1,670
			85	44,559	122,053	124,053	2,000
	V	E	81	812,074	4,699,599	4,764,277	64,678
			82	1,289,032	5,311,478	5,437,697	126,219
			83	1,233,136	4,319,674	4,417,196	97,522
			84	329,194	1,340,715	1,386,357	45,642
			85	1,785,550	5,015,867	5,194,039	178,172
			86	1,884,025	6,906,948	7,083,885	176,937
	V	W	81	243	1,289	1,634	345
			82	132	851	913	62
			84	42,079	122,011	130,317	8,306
			86	19,498	84,638	87,725	3,087
FRANCE	A	E	83	434	3,752	4,158	406
			84	8,141	46,572	52,338	5,766
			85	5,998	47,948	53,222	5,274
	N	E	81	812,580	4,754,603	4,831,212	76,609
			83	21,415	162,317	179,688	17,371
			84	132,572	195,719	201,468	5,749
			85	155,584	965,280	1,008,915	43,635
	O	E	82	11	541	596	55
			83	449	897	960	63
	V	E	82	905,180	5,075,989	5,167,463	91,474
			86	30,718	344,347	374,403	30,056
GUATMAL	A	E	82	924	1,600	1,754	154
	A	W	81	30,173	79,183	89,291	10,108
	V	E	81	416,580	1,290,691	1,353,949	63,258
			83	57,068	122,800	130,474	7,674
			84	24,323	58,954	64,017	5,063
			85	59,415	104,662	111,654	6,992
			86	58,969	184,038	192,593	8,555
	V	W	84	77,491	140,161	145,849	5,688
HONDURA	V	E	82	51,652	123,480	127,622	4,142
			85	76,059	98,250	103,523	5,273
ISRAEL	A	E	82	1,584	8,955	11,101	2,146
ITALY	A	E	81	240	4,400	4,784	384
			82	95	1,240	1,539	299
			83	309	3,799	4,508	709
			84	84	1,500	1,802	302
			85	225	2,441	2,709	268
			86	562	5,247	5,824	577
	N	E	84	3,102	9,957	11,339	1,382
			85	19,420	52,698	55,587	2,889
	V	E	81	1,058	2,802	3,083	281
			82	37	1,037	1,051	14
			83	5,319	35,593	38,061	2,468
			84	2,319	6,570	7,446	876
	V	W	86	7,048	8,720	9,460	740
IVY CST	V	E	82	2,386	12,161	13,297	1,136
JAMAICA	A	E	82	1,080	10,562	11,547	985
	V	E	83	323	2,928	3,406	478
			84	712	8,002	8,871	869
			86	2,175	26,084	26,728	644
JAPAN	A	E	82	48	320	560	240
			84	110	567	965	398
	V	W	82	31	324	346	22
			83	11,106	7,515	12,911	5,396
			84	80	1,292	1,372	80
			85	94	1,108	1,152	44
			86	45	1,144	1,148	4
MEXICO	O	E	81	792,921	2,071,772	2,071,772	
			82	2,249	13,500	13,500	
			83	523,646	1,343,593	1,343,593	
			84	84,016	229,121	229,121	
			85	40,000	137,200	137,200	
			86	295,189	1,520,929	1,520,929	
	O	W	81	113,396	421,899	421,899	
			82	15,370	47,392	47,392	
			83	6,469	22,140	22,140	
			84	4,575	22,560	22,560	
			85	750	3,000	3,000	
			86	143,146	382,989	382,989	
NETHLDS	A	E	81	450	897	1,797	900
			83	1,800	13,162	14,048	886
	A	W	86	247	2,034	3,130	1,096
	N	E	82	7,302	13,802	17,178	3,376
			84	233,085	566,402	599,942	33,540
			85	58,202	171,200	203,673	32,473
	N	H	86	51,430	316,744	338,326	21,582

Crop
Product
TSUSA commodity number, description, and unit of quantity

Country	Mode	Reg	Yr	Quantity	F.A.S.	C.I.F.	Charges
	O	E	83	86	764	789	25
			85	1,588	10,360	11,360	1,000
			86	1,588	10,136	10,136	
	V	E	81	869,568	1,939,908	2,044,420	98,497
			82	674,076	1,419,791	1,493,536	73,745
			83	1,092,820	2,312,687	2,406,626	93,939
			84	909,748	2,049,200	2,139,464	90,264
			85	730,694	1,665,414	1,767,257	101,843
			86	380,163	1,475,229	1,536,698	61,469
	V	H	85	10,201	107,906	113,452	5,546
	V	W	81	250,967	484,944	522,715	37,771
			82	396,757	914,455	966,711	52,056
			83	333,774	740,641	782,014	41,373
			84	299,415	842,075	887,329	45,254
			85	314,357	619,953	671,446	51,493
			86	388,775	1,021,875	1,080,480	58,605
NICARAG	A	E	83	400	1,120	1,615	495
	V	E	81	395,841	983,325	1,008,933	25,608
			82	254,266	593,632	622,035	28,403
			83	25,200	64,260	66,150	1,890
	V	W	81	1,083,600	2,813,580	2,930,335	116,755
			82	911,200	2,142,008	2,246,706	104,698
			83	277,600	676,388	709,302	32,914
PARAGUA	V	E	85	238,096	445,241	483,186	37,945
			86	185,547	602,101	631,546	29,445
PERU	V	E	82	120,834	379,833	409,973	30,140
			83	168,057	295,701	315,667	19,966
			84	13,426	48,412	51,377	2,965
PORTUGL	V	E	81	715	2,528	3,413	885
			82	226	952	978	26
			83	4,252	3,260	3,655	395
			84	18	632	643	11
			85	5,039	6,065	6,621	556
			86	1,349	5,199	5,840	641
RWANDA	V	E	83	99,192	119,031	124,725	5,694
SALVADR	N	E	81	252,185	866,836	912,600	45,764
			82	91,238	310,124	329,910	19,786
			83	205,934	365,958	376,461	10,503
			85	221,274	591,130	620,481	29,351
	O	E	81	36,700	102,995	103,754	759
	V	E	81	10,600	53,530	54,360	830
			82	281,360	913,355	962,527	49,172
			83	406,455	1,109,300	1,168,733	59,433
			84	234,811	821,769	875,621	53,852
			85	72,043	259,500	274,352	14,852
			86	162,505	668,100	693,912	25,812
	V	W	81	452,544	1,668,219	1,726,139	57,920
			82	248,584	933,199	972,865	39,666
			83	450,280	1,331,895	1,393,352	61,457
			84	461,161	1,327,669	1,387,892	60,223
			85	305,284	915,656	953,163	37,507
			86	207,113	719,863	741,747	21,884
SPAIN	A	E	81	9	266	333	67
			85	313	9,365	9,773	408
	O	E	84	1,045	5,759	5,759	
	V	E	82	149,760	723,366	738,126	14,760
			84	156	1,633	1,815	182
			85	6,085	13,260	14,156	896
	V	W	86	26,455	111,840	116,064	4,224
SWEDEN	A	E	81	132	292	420	128
	O	E	84	1,059	7,038	7,550	512
SWITZLD	A	E	82	463	1,452	1,702	250
	N	E	81	98,633	188,676	198,496	9,820
			84	44,161	100,457	104,092	3,635
	V	E	82	42,277	87,595	91,459	3,864
			83	73,255	105,021	110,707	5,686
			84	26,455	19,503	22,238	2,735
			86	46,356	116,454	123,832	7,378
THAILND	V	E	83	600	530	580	50
	V	W	81	900	817	900	83
TNZANIA	V	E	84	22,046	58,500	65,193	6,693
U KING	A	E	81	2,542	6,029	7,912	1,883
			82	70	596	650	54
			83	1,112	4,081	4,871	790
			84	712	4,381	5,374	993
			85	225	2,886	3,282	396
	A	W	84	179	465	713	248
	N	E	81	25,058	56,285	57,925	1,640
			83	316	6,008	6,745	737
			84	143	3,309	5,177	1,868
	N	W	84	7,329	35,565	39,299	3,734
	O	E	84	36	976	976	
	V	E	84	223	6,044	6,422	378
			85	13,004	99,405	105,753	6,348

Crop Product TSUSA commodity number, description, and unit of quantity Country	Mode	Reg	Yr	Quantity	F.A.S.	C.I.F.	Charges
			86	8,182	61,214	71,327	10,113
ZAIRE	V	E	82	17,548	16,349	17,518	1,169

Coffee, mixed with substitutes
1604000 COFFEE SUBSTITUTES, NSPF (LB)

Country	Mode	Reg	Yr	Quantity	F.A.S.	C.I.F.	Charges
TOTAL			81	471,487	1,161,386	1,273,952	112,566
			82	397,577	911,805	985,415	75,933
			83	476,976	1,093,755	1,200,303	106,548
			84	481,258	1,081,671	1,178,468	96,797
			85	437,662	818,429	916,227	97,798
			86	450,282	1,165,714	1,248,287	82,573
BELGIUM	N	E	86	1,205	5,357	5,629	272
	V	E	81	10,809	15,460	17,426	1,966
			82	26,539	39,383	44,053	4,670
			83	10,229	31,050	34,612	3,562
			84	7,546	19,588	20,309	721
			86	132	1,220	1,354	134
	V	W	81	5,756	14,650	15,332	682
			85	1,557	2,311	2,551	240
BRAZIL	A	E	84	5,512	26,250	26,252	2
			85	13,316	50,310	56,650	6,340
BULGAR	V	E	81	13,007	20,050	21,351	1,301
			83	4,416	6,809	7,213	404
			85	3,307	4,946	5,729	783
BURMA	V	E	85	7,760	8,642	10,967	2,325
CANADA	O	E	82	5,330	6,924	6,924	
			83	48	302	302	
			84	9,008	20,481	20,481	
	O	W	82	2,600	3,736	3,736	
CHINA T	V	E	86	2,400	1,200	1,301	101
FR GERM	A	E	85	1,984	2,798	3,954	1,156
	N	E	83	209,996	551,591	596,469	44,878
			85	74,439	133,107	153,388	20,281
			86	114,673	390,414	414,171	23,757
	N	W	82	5,172	17,387	18,738	1,351
	O	E	82	12,197	30,896	32,792	1,896
			83	498	2,081	2,081	
			84	10,076	19,178	20,948	1,770
			85	23,747	38,408	41,543	3,135
			86	21,515	80,293	81,293	1,000
	O	W	83	723	4,384	4,384	
			84	2,734	4,894	4,894	
			85	2,600	4,384	4,384	
			86	5,196	9,040	9,040	
	V	E	81	240,753	625,293	678,330	53,037
			82	245,412	581,028	626,325	45,297
			83	89,017	183,499	204,222	20,723
			84	259,841	616,158	667,227	51,069
			85	155,156	393,207	431,043	37,836
			86	143,674	393,053	427,142	34,089
	V	W	81	75,107	181,064	197,313	16,249
			82	39,922	70,734	73,137	2,403
			83	47,699	92,903	103,806	10,903
			84	33,474	93,123	105,013	11,890
			85	28,324	45,835	48,951	3,116
			86	6,235	15,133	16,119	986
GERM DR	V	W	85	999	2,726	3,244	518
GREECE	O	E	84	180	473	473	
HG KONG	V	W	85	28,274	35,625	45,896	10,271
HUNGARY	V	E	81	10,670	46,297	48,746	2,449
	V	W	82	1,537	2,316	2,316	2,323
INDIA	V	E	85	2,385	1,229	1,472	243
IRELAND	V	E	84	1,014	814	1,054	240
ITALY	V	E	83	2,429	6,750	7,461	711
JAMAICA	A	E	81	2,000	7,358	8,609	1,251
JAPAN	V	E	83	992	2,759	3,090	331
			84	10,763	5,908	7,524	1,616
	V	H	83	218	910	1,052	142
	V	W	81	70	416	459	43
			84	14,431	14,365	15,735	1,370
			85	3,129	4,669	5,115	446
PERU	V	W	86	2,249	2,796	2,862	66
POLAND	O	E	82	6,672	6,197	8,978	2,781
	V	E	81	32,592	29,891	44,032	14,141
			83	45,061	34,533	43,523	8,990
			84	21,638	19,729	22,240	2,511
			85	36,740	30,312	34,840	4,528
			86	64,592	48,576	57,250	8,674
	V	W	82	2,447	3,617	3,784	167
			84	9,425	11,875	15,098	3,223
PORTUGL	V	E	81	12,152	18,984	27,681	8,697

Country	Mode	Reg	Yr	Quantity	F.A.S.	C.I.F.	Charges
			82	1,713	3,083	3,379	296
			83	8,018	18,694	22,719	4,025
			84	1,740	2,633	3,112	479
			85	8,527	12,925	15,470	2,545
			86	17,986	30,322	34,621	4,299
	V	W	84	548	1,145	1,717	572
			85	2,625	1,285	1,835	550
ROMANIA	V	E	81	3,808	4,843	5,589	746
			86	6,612	10,676	11,563	887
SWITZLD	N	E	83	26,837	112,038	118,790	6,752
	V	E	81	53,906	178,679	188,631	9,952
			82	41,650	139,339	153,286	13,947
			84	37,783	141,652	152,527	10,875
			85	9,161	28,340	30,045	1,705
			86	32,816	141,839	147,901	6,062
	V	W	81	5,291	11,711	13,012	1,301
THAILND	V	W	81	3,742	3,371	3,737	366
			82	3,628	3,310	3,642	332
			83	3,304	2,292	2,506	214
			84	2,771	1,489	1,619	130
			85	33,632	17,370	19,150	1,780
			86	24,262	10,069	10,962	893
U KING	V	E	83	313	1,063	1,163	100
			84	656	460	529	69
YUGOSLV	V	E	81	548	705	782	77
			82	2,218	3,350	3,749	399
			83	27,491	43,160	48,073	4,913
			84	51,787	80,730	90,894	10,164
			86	6,735	25,726	27,079	1,353
	V	W	81	963	1,551	1,759	208
			82	540	505	576	71
			84	331	726	822	96

Coffee, roasted or ground
1601040 COFFEE ROASTED OR GROUND (LB)

Country	Mode	Reg	Yr	Quantity	F.A.S.	C.I.F.	Charges
TOTAL			81	26,797,277	39,675,948	40,564,336	888,388
			82	24,025,887	34,572,342	35,278,631	706,509
			83	21,943,992	32,103,997	32,753,320	649,323
			84	31,611,958	50,469,055	51,779,753	1,310,698
			85	28,675,333	48,573,425	49,408,948	835,523
			86	29,763,663	63,854,230	65,133,238	1,279,008
ARGENT	A	E	82	200	600	600	220
AUSTRAL	V	W	84	2,500	3,201	3,461	260
AUSTRIA	A	E	84	1,141	2,494	3,220	726
			86	304	1,297	1,997	700
	A	W	82	1,220	4,121	5,712	1,591
			83	661	2,682	3,534	852
	N	W	86	224,585	632,846	650,652	17,806
	V	E	84	70,264	154,484	160,740	6,256
			85	39,034	84,965	86,940	1,975
	V	W	85	458,329	890,100	946,502	56,402
BELGIUM	A	E	84	1,177	5,654	8,161	2,507
			86	161	1,085	1,480	395
	N	E	81	31,154	121,375	133,121	11,746
			82	96,812	281,696	299,438	17,742
			83	76,949	193,985	209,739	15,754
			84	140,678	461,253	504,155	42,902
			85	114,473	290,600	314,608	24,008
			86	63,385	218,796	234,865	16,069
	N	W	83	51,137	150,018	163,967	13,949
	V	E	82	7,800	23,669	25,222	1,553
			83	8,500	22,810	24,180	1,370
			85	40,847	105,706	115,708	10,002
			86	23,980	86,223	90,985	4,762
	V	W	81	864	3,291	4,302	1,011
			82	32,569	95,317	100,320	5,003
			84	99,694	308,020	316,235	8,215
			85	16,831	57,587	67,207	9,620
BELIZE	V	E	83	437	683	1,667	984
BOLIVIA	V	E	82	46,297	51,389	54,269	2,880
BRAZIL	A	E	81	1,322	3,932	5,473	1,541
			83	1,070	2,339	2,867	528
			84	2,240	5,928	9,026	3,098
			86	1,865	3,970	5,829	1,859
	N	E	81	16,102	45,750	48,135	2,385
			83	4,519	8,847	11,378	2,531
			84	566,051	785,400	844,135	58,735
			85	158,371	235,253	258,263	23,010
	N	W	85	4,806	11,188	13,064	1,876
	O	E	81	12,000	28,234	28,234	

Crop
Product
TSUSA commodity number, description, and unit of quantity

Country	Mode	Reg	Yr	Quantity	F.A.S.	C.I.F.	Charges
			82	23,018	48,965	49,215	250
			83	108,943	181,839	181,893	54
			84	70,529	162,979	162,979	
			85	476	1,017	1,017	
			86	178,091	356,216	356,935	719
	V	E	81	1,223,553	2,494,635	2,609,833	115,198
			82	645,827	866,561	926,115	59,554
			83	3,475,073	3,977,939	4,297,915	319,976
			84	4,767,612	6,171,201	6,616,796	445,595
			85	117,423	160,437	171,630	11,193
			86	317,382	1,093,459	1,117,246	23,787
	V	W	83	2,425	7,214	7,747	533
			84	4,409	14,600	15,817	1,217
			85	3,702	10,950	11,365	415
			86	3,044	11,160	11,632	472
C RICA	A	E	86	609	1,211	1,445	234
	O	E	84	75	289	289	
			85	687,250	494,820	532,618	37,798
			86	2,167	3,302	3,302	
	O	W	85	11,409	16,657	16,657	
	V	E	82	5,003,024	5,777,820	6,034,694	256,874
			84	2,028,399	1,923,245	2,049,488	126,243
	V	W	82	1,278	1,534	1,667	133
			85	6,389	13,020	13,912	892
CAMROON	V	E	85	2,205	6,750	6,951	201
	V	W	84	1,625	5,009	5,408	399
CANADA	A	E	81	1,696	5,331	7,087	1,756
			82	120	510	565	55
			83	120	487	556	69
			84	2,873	6,731	8,724	1,993
	A	W	81	106	397	397	
			84	200	670	814	144
			86	9,750	22,651	34,936	12,285
	N	E	81	688	1,282	1,536	254
			82	4,314	12,031	12,334	303
			83	436	1,779	1,927	148
			84	398	1,048	1,048	
	O	E	81	172,024	433,137	433,933	796
			82	88,841	236,289	236,289	
			83	203,820	403,920	403,920	
			84	184,104	397,961	404,113	6,152
			85	252,302	476,594	477,732	1,138
			86	623,972	1,185,569	1,185,665	96
	O	W	81	1,035,227	2,831,296	2,831,296	
			82	1,182,864	3,152,517	3,152,517	
			83	302,185	827,104	827,104	
			84	219,148	565,609	565,609	
			85	642,481	1,454,225	1,454,225	
			86	852,487	2,570,408	2,570,537	129
	V	E	85	1,600	14,516	14,855	339
CHINA M	O	E	85	1,587	3,800	3,800	
CHINA T	V	W	84	27,514	15,100	17,583	2,483
			85	16,800	6,720	7,520	800
			86	5,999	2,900	3,517	617
COLOMB	A	E	83	5,179	7,728	10,892	3,164
			84	267	1,100	1,437	337
			85	39,278	51,045	61,482	10,437
	A	W	81	34	288	451	163
	N	E	82	1,412,201	901,451	959,954	58,503
			83	308,744	182,908	204,637	21,729
	N	W	85	1,984	5,124	6,087	963
	O	E	81	4,880	12,478	12,538	60
			82	1,274	3,267	3,267	
			83	6,375	15,244	15,269	25
			84	3,380	9,356	9,356	
			85	18,281	27,890	27,890	
			86	133,292	323,577	323,682	105
	O	W	83	11,400	13,434	13,434	
			85	2,875	8,197	8,197	
	V	E	81	187,840	353,807	359,041	5,234
			82	466,974	633,000	667,451	34,451
			86	4,109,409	6,660,649	6,830,298	169,649
	V	W	82	76,896	103,250	108,421	5,171
			83	199,936	269,858	282,621	12,763
			86	37,192	85,235	88,075	2,840
CYPRUS	V	E	81	500	276	358	82
			82	2,294	6,477	7,010	533
			83	4,996	11,960	13,568	1,608
			84	2,281	4,664	5,032	368
			85	1,000	2,575	2,669	94
			86	17,226	42,294	44,536	2,242
DOM REP	N	E	82	125,726	125,550	129,965	4,415
	O	E	81	170	398	398	
			83	1,725	3,625	3,650	25

Crop
Product
TSUSA commodity number, description, and unit of quantity

Country	Mode	Reg	Yr	Quantity	F.A.S.	C.I.F.	Charges
			86	1,000	2,900	2,900	
	V	E	81	11,515,276	13,529,491	13,795,919	266,428
			82	4,099,603	5,036,997	5,120,563	83,566
			83	87,610	109,918	120,867	10,949
			84	57,780	47,910	55,255	7,345
			85	551,700	716,525	732,770	16,245
			86	1,545,275	3,046,270	3,073,582	27,312
ECUADOR	A	W	83	1,398	3,311	3,682	371
	O	E	81	4,800	13,000	13,780	780
			84	1,064	1,485	1,485	
	V	E	82	188,740	182,885	193,028	10,143
			83	52,466	57,147	64,094	6,947
			84	4,440	1,987	2,437	450
			85	585,882	669,553	697,846	28,293
			86	1,834,319	3,133,480	3,255,428	121,948
ETHIOP	O	E	81	90	252	252	
			84	110	431	431	
			86	11,515	25,390	25,390	
FINLAND	A	E	82	356	847	897	50
FR GERM	A	E	82	188	612	986	374
			83	3,376	33,859	38,171	4,312
			84	182	630	910	280
			85	882	2,492	3,266	774
			86	772	9,127	9,864	737
	N	E	81	1,009	3,407	3,577	170
			82	5,964	20,503	23,429	2,926
			83	4,684	15,589	18,014	2,425
			84	34,542	97,495	112,746	15,251
			85	73,302	186,949	200,557	13,608
			86	94,767	288,308	303,325	15,017
	O	E	81	6,916	15,683	16,469	786
			82	233	746	746	
			83	9,989	19,031	20,311	1,280
			84	39,384	87,146	87,146	
			85	5,790	17,808	18,743	935
	O	W	83	6,489	33,785	33,785	
			84	37,753	83,366	83,483	117
	V	E	81	153,092	958,279	994,420	36,141
			82	3,326	10,121	11,206	1,085
			83	54,678	181,843	198,479	16,636
			84	20,066	82,487	88,420	5,933
			85	214,953	410,424	426,765	16,341
			86	695,031	1,575,331	1,624,462	49,131
	V	W	81	42,927	67,769	70,969	3,200
			82	4,173	12,768	13,998	1,230
			83	36,398	68,280	72,931	4,651
			84	2,590	9,623	10,357	734
			85	744	2,547	2,614	67
			86	46,335	105,012	108,488	3,476
FRANCE	A	E	82	441	1,397	1,517	120
			86	476	1,364	1,865	501
	N	E	83	7,085	17,403	18,362	959
			84	3,078	8,749	9,442	693
			86	8,291	32,468	37,596	5,128
	N	W	84	4,311	13,496	17,143	3,647
	O	E	81	768	3,387	4,040	653
			82	33,604	142,136	142,136	
	O	W	85	46,297	75,357	76,343	986
	V	E	81	198,500	1,695,070	1,821,280	126,210
			82	45,118	108,382	113,827	5,445
			83	2,913	9,384	9,484	100
			84	46,504	92,758	96,060	3,302
			85	39,942	325,651	336,565	10,914
			86	46,138	80,464	82,988	2,524
	V	W	81	6,305	23,246	25,109	1,863
			82	860	2,857	2,996	139
			83	2,320	15,928	16,735	807
			85	22,216	49,342	58,726	9,384
GREECE	N	E	82	92,341	230,112	242,556	12,444
			83	147,879	341,782	363,908	22,126
	O	E	82	612	1,636	1,636	
	V	E	81	187,259	447,337	469,553	22,216
			84	265,147	637,800	679,132	41,332
			85	199,969	551,510	586,305	34,795
			86	177,404	522,275	549,405	27,130
GUATMAL	A	E	83	1,291	1,378	2,569	1,191
			84	1,961	4,038	5,329	1,291
			85	9,127	10,508	13,906	3,398
	A	W	81	641	978	1,133	155
	N	E	82	130,413	155,611	163,618	8,007
			83	145,337	197,933	210,280	12,347
	N	W	85	56,734	86,567	90,993	4,426
	O	E	81	170	398	398	
			82	114,059	168,047	168,047	

Crop
Product
TSUSA commodity number, description, and unit of quantity

Country	Mode	Reg	Yr	Quantity	F.A.S.	C.I.F.	Charges
			86	66,865	126,834	126,834	
	O	W	82	43,600	62,894	62,894	
	V	E	81	130,208	130,107	134,722	4,615
			83	38,029	46,125	49,121	2,996
			84	39,284	60,000	62,808	2,808
			86	15,467	26,744	29,449	2,705
	V	W	81	22,818	35,462	36,965	1,503
			84	38,029	52,214	54,828	2,614
HAITI	A	E	81	496	1,500	1,876	376
			84	200	475	707	232
			85	832	2,070	2,427	357
	V	E	81	9,530	31,264	32,659	1,395
	V	W	85	529	1,436	1,600	164
HG KONG	V	E	84	1,250	4,055	4,722	667
	V	W	85	6,168	13,385	13,556	171
HONDURA	V	E	84	79,471	126,877	132,994	6,117
			86	34,500	128,438	134,859	6,421
	V	W	84	10,433	66,583	73,103	6,520
			85	529	1,453	1,619	166
INDIA	O	E	86	2,806	6,485	6,485	
	V	E	84	240,964	305,140	321,921	16,781
			85	38,360	41,812	44,049	2,237
			86	279,105	256,204	272,286	16,082
	V	W	81	20,503	26,088	27,622	1,534
			86	36,375	46,094	48,017	1,923
INDNSIA	O	E	83	1,935	3,300	3,300	
			84	2,200	6,226	6,226	
			86	738	1,610	1,610	
	V	E	81	58,713	55,151	61,238	6,087
			82	8,459	21,405	23,022	1,617
			83	551,150	562,007	592,371	30,364
			84	1,083,066	1,281,746	1,375,669	93,923
			85	218,337	232,840	238,761	5,921
			86	220,460	234,834	247,174	12,340
	V	W	82	3,827	10,798	12,292	1,494
			83	3,801	10,900	11,907	1,007
			84	1,327	4,091	4,417	326
			85	33,598	42,563	45,305	2,742
			86	2,642	7,710	8,295	585
IRELAND	A	E	81	94	313	450	137
ISRAEL	A	E	84	39	360	809	449
	V	E	82	2,100	5,760	5,969	209
ITALY	A	E	81	3,529	4,682	7,281	2,599
			82	539	2,335	3,002	667
			83	3,411	16,656	20,423	3,767
			84	448	2,987	3,880	893
			85	441	4,500	5,352	852
			86	1,839	5,594	8,384	2,790
	A	W	85	928	3,725	5,005	1,280
	N	E	81	62,183	159,596	173,258	13,662
			83	81,995	228,709	248,552	19,843
			84	218,514	563,100	611,106	48,006
			85	338,242	912,538	979,291	66,753
			86	611,992	1,062,358	1,184,412	122,054
	N	W	81	11,902	70,913	78,593	7,680
			82	10,432	29,970	32,944	2,974
			83	25,091	110,975	116,175	5,200
			84	42,293	198,872	220,044	21,172
			85	36,196	95,653	104,218	8,565
			86	15,012	72,924	75,524	2,600
	O	E	81	3,033	8,116	8,398	282
			82	3,179	9,415	9,415	
			83	2,393	7,527	7,527	
			84	8,662	26,159	26,909	750
			85	4,515	14,095	14,309	214
			86	6,299	26,244	29,136	2,892
	V	E	81	12,678	36,179	39,714	3,535
			82	120,013	267,127	289,901	22,774
			83	38,215	144,371	158,124	13,753
			84	43,834	124,467	139,689	15,222
			85	121,092	305,340	333,299	27,959
			86	8,908	34,622	36,809	2,187
	V	W	82	14,182	76,852	81,924	5,072
			83	14,758	35,688	40,035	4,347
			84	6,811	14,512	16,178	1,666
			85	87,204	288,282	310,557	22,275
			86	179,764	773,450	831,977	58,527
JAMAICA	A	E	81	34,581	136,452	151,903	15,451
			82	72,908	329,505	362,518	33,013
			83	38,984	193,545	210,124	16,579
			84	62,057	341,593	363,809	22,216
			85	33,444	219,999	235,736	15,737
			86	48,528	325,335	340,805	15,470
	A	W	84	5,140	28,958	31,769	2,811

Crop
Product
TSUSA commodity number, description, and unit of quantity

Country	Mode	Reg	Yr	Quantity	F.A.S.	C.I.F.	Charges
			85	2,450	14,451	15,836	1,385
	N	E	85	41,336	188,409	202,154	13,745
			86	52,270	266,787	278,148	11,361
	V	E	81	5,000	16,819	17,383	564
			82	53	1,475	1,600	125
			83	37	433	483	50
			85	15,000	38,000	41,272	3,272
			86	903	6,230	7,000	770
	V	W	83	7,040	112,640	113,857	1,217
			85	17,200	71,990	74,356	2,366
			86	1,600	12,772	13,088	316
JAPAN	A	E	85	5,295	18,165	20,117	1,952
			86	911	2,011	6,221	4,210
	A	W	82	529	374	1,988	1,614
	N	H	83	1,829	7,190	8,165	975
	V	H	82	1,102	4,483	4,964	481
			84	3,440	14,325	15,663	1,338
			85	1,400	5,199	5,847	648
	V	W	82	11,023	41,414	46,561	5,147
			84	1,785	12,409	12,742	333
			86	284	1,642	1,820	178
KENYA	A	W	82	119	413	673	260
	O	E	81	170	401	401	
			83	456	553	553	
			84	572	1,395	1,395	
			86	2,063	4,627	4,627	
	O	W	85	1,995	3,412	3,412	
	V	E	85	9,922	16,899	17,678	779
			86	3,307	8,301	9,051	750
	V	W	82	774	2,523	2,742	219
			85	397	1,075	1,198	123
			86	1,236,792	1,100,727	1,195,181	94,454
KOR REP	V	E	81	1,201	800	921	121
			82	1,200	1,959	2,160	201
			86	1,928	2,082	2,372	290
LEBANON	V	E	84	1,279	3,312	3,497	185
			85	1,264	3,000	3,239	239
			86	2,802	2,255	2,482	227
	V	W	86	6,613	2,665	3,110	445
MADAGAS	O	E	83	536	650	650	
MALAYSA	V	W	84	926	2,151	2,550	399
MEXICO	A	E	84	50	1,820	1,877	57
	N	W	85	37,979	60,556	60,690	134
	O	E	81	6,458,419	9,277,931	9,277,931	
			82	8,402,049	12,979,579	12,979,579	
			83	13,905,620	20,130,437	20,130,437	
			84	17,759,615	28,994,916	28,994,919	3
			85	17,633,929	28,748,323	28,748,323	
			86	11,265,604	25,909,374	25,909,374	
	O	W	81	1,027,738	1,849,895	1,849,895	
			82	993,530	1,648,979	1,648,979	
			83	1,397,986	2,100,010	2,100,010	
			84	1,561,808	2,571,124	2,571,124	
			85	2,555,140	4,363,168	4,363,170	2
			86	1,937,563	4,669,594	4,669,594	
	V	E	84	177,800	302,261	314,098	11,837
			85	100,001	153,001	159,001	6,000
N ANTIL	V	E	81	3,617,954	3,974,597	4,154,706	180,109
			82	44,000	44,000	46,215	2,215
N ZEAL	A	W	81	1,004	1,642	1,946	304
	V	E	82	33,069	38,693	41,465	2,772
NETHLDS	A	E	81	3,623	8,491	10,161	1,670
			82	110	360	438	78
			83	366	2,384	3,094	710
			84	187	1,017	1,465	448
	N	E	81	79,043	138,743	148,717	9,974
			82	6,374	14,263	16,081	1,818
			83	8,177	74,405	83,100	8,695
			84	13,723	29,067	34,679	5,612
			85	9,517	16,189	18,832	2,643
			86	34,664	119,610	128,856	9,246
	N	W	81	2,227	6,587	7,650	1,063
	O	E	83	6,285	15,468	16,012	544
	V	E	81	265	562	665	103
			82	58,135	243,581	260,517	16,936
			83	86,227	206,811	219,600	12,789
			84	47,104	116,538	124,525	7,987
			85	61,544	162,559	172,642	10,083
			86	266,834	738,491	763,957	25,466
	V	W	82	529	1,187	1,322	135
			83	3,631	9,438	10,249	811
			84	22,693	58,557	59,955	1,398
			85	19,025	52,433	53,713	1,280
			86	33,084	131,656	133,893	2,237

Crop
Product
TSUSA commodity number, description, and unit of quantity

Country	Mode	Reg	Yr	Quantity	F.A.S.	C.I.F.	Charges
NEW GUI	O	W	81	40,200	45,635	45,635	
	V	W	85	450	1,020	1,265	245
NICARAG	V	E	85	9,920	53,401	56,468	3,067
	V	W	81	125,000	178,750	192,138	13,388
			83	820	2,735	3,052	317
			86	6,111	18,620	19,766	1,146
NORWAY	A	E	83	68	300	391	91
	V	E	84	17,774	36,579	42,026	5,447
PANAMA	A	E	86	1,100	2,310	2,739	429
	O	E	86	1,241	2,329	2,329	
	V	E	85	1,190,000	1,356,900	1,397,700	40,800
PERU	O	E	81	1,440	3,960	4,197	237
	O	W	84	38,030	50,531	50,531	
	V	E	83	115,170	141,750	148,241	6,491
PHIL R	O	E	83	804	975	975	
	V	W	81	184,800	176,484	192,213	15,729
			82	158,672	157,661	169,664	12,003
			83	44,047	47,619	49,952	2,333
			84	145,505	164,537	170,885	6,348
PORTUGL	V	E	81	110	1,921	2,122	201
			82	4,458	8,724	9,419	695
			86	2,580	4,314	4,883	569
SALVADR	A	E	81	600	714	1,186	472
			82	114	653	722	69
	O	E	83	770	934	934	
	O	W	83	14,675	16,361	16,361	
	V	E	81	37,375	54,562	56,140	1,578
			82	58,323	90,876	97,475	6,599
			84	10,000	27,000	28,780	1,780
			86	20,238	85,000	87,865	2,865
	V	W	81	26,400	122,433	125,429	2,996
			83	66,139	105,000	109,096	4,096
SINGAPR	A	E	86	1,320	2,600	4,885	2,285
	V	E	83	13,331	75,207	80,640	5,433
SPAIN	A	E	81	309	431	489	58
			83	308	481	648	167
			84	624	1,588	1,879	291
SRI LKA	V	W	85	33,069	35,384	38,803	3,419
SWEDEN	A	E	81	215	413	715	302
			83	1,725	6,108	7,764	1,656
			84	55,684	142,114	192,678	50,564
			85	860	1,817	2,713	896
			86	7,933	30,664	41,431	10,767
	A	W	83	119	256	368	112
	N	E	82	21,108	47,168	55,896	8,728
			83	71,095	187,708	201,681	13,973
	V	E	83	1,575	4,373	5,086	713
			84	812,301	2,028,088	2,191,709	163,621
			85	1,123,566	2,668,625	2,884,668	216,043
			86	2,160,893	5,077,390	5,389,406	312,016
	V	W	83	714	1,701	1,881	180
			84	794	2,106	2,274	168
			85	3,175	10,865	12,854	1,989
SWITZLD	A	E	84	4,440	27,569	34,275	6,706
			85	8,602	40,397	50,224	9,827
			86	14,529	110,546	128,062	17,516
	N	E	82	3,108	6,383	7,420	1,037
			83	2,734	9,251	9,613	362
			86	21,831	82,327	98,560	16,233
	O	E	81	650	2,904	3,307	403
			82	650	2,765	3,236	471
			83	121	341	341	
	V	E	81	650	2,517	2,713	196
			83	623	2,091	2,482	391
			84	2,017	4,720	5,060	340
			85	90,021	200,885	207,218	6,333
			86	46,930	112,867	115,615	2,748
	V	W	83	849	1,871	2,495	624
THAILND	O	E	82	116	1,139	1,194	55
	V	E	81	480	280	336	56
			83	280	798	893	95
			84	450	765	854	89
	V	W	81	1,503	1,140	1,252	112
			82	6,431	10,549	11,028	479
TNZANIA	O	E	83	670	813	813	
			86	1,822	1,624	1,624	
TURKEY	V	E	86	331	2,040	2,161	121
U KING	A	E	84	9,902	26,958	29,031	2,073
			85	5,978	64,765	71,165	6,400
			86	3,232	18,174	21,506	3,332
	A	W	83	408	1,289	1,989	700
			84	240	782	1,145	363
			85	485	1,635	1,733	98
			86	1,554	5,122	5,924	802
	N	E	81	1,080	8,142	8,730	588
			83	6,043	34,513	39,732	5,219
	N	W	82	299	1,034	1,492	458
	O	E	81	440	1,167	1,167	
	V	E	84	363	1,051	1,183	132
			85	2,489	12,229	14,696	2,467
			86	21,740	43,066	46,515	3,449
	V	W	85	529	1,373	1,530	157
VENEZ	O	E	81	3,200	8,000	8,480	480
			86	4,475	4,496	4,796	300
	V	E	83	44,092	46,016	47,500	1,484
			84	320,126	450,103	461,351	11,248
			85	308,460	455,000	463,810	8,810
YUGOSLV	V	E	85	12,169	22,128	24,734	2,606
ZAIRE	V	E	85	1,903	6,044	6,438	394
	V	W	82	265	650	704	54
			83	317	2,310	2,386	76
			84	3,233	11,860	12,613	753
			85	529	1,129	1,258	129
			86	1,058	11,200	11,434	234

Copaiba

Copaiba, balsam
1881800 BALSAMS, COPAIBA (LB)

Country	Mode	Reg	Yr	Quantity	F.A.S.	C.I.F.	Charges
TOTAL			81	37,828	101,361	110,185	8,824
			82	92,904	200,995	222,101	21,106
			83	106,066	175,105	197,348	22,243
			84	128,395	133,815	158,766	24,951
			85	44,616	41,491	49,875	8,384
			86	14,690	21,930	25,244	3,314
BOLIVIA	V	E	82	15,873	23,490	27,300	3,810
BRAZIL	O	E	83	1,190	1,791	1,791	
	V	E	81	37,828	101,361	110,185	8,824
			82	77,031	177,505	194,801	17,296
			83	104,082	170,457	192,700	22,243
			84	128,395	133,815	158,766	24,951
			85	44,616	41,491	49,875	8,384
			86	12,690	11,930	14,827	2,897
CANADA	O	E	83	794	2,857	2,857	
SALVADR	V	E	86	2,000	10,000	10,417	417

Coriander

Coriander, spice
1612500 CORIANDER (LB)

Country	Mode	Reg	Yr	Quantity	F.A.S.	C.I.F.	Charges
TOTAL			81	10,280,949	1,887,608	2,156,737	269,129
			82	9,901,843	1,867,366	2,104,997	237,631
			83	9,223,129	1,721,544	2,005,517	283,973
			84	13,977,693	2,391,079	2,762,220	371,141
			85	5,437,991	993,387	1,256,543	263,156
			86	7,320,580	1,372,028	1,722,325	350,297
ALGERIA	V	E	82	39,683	9,900	12,513	2,613
ARGENT	V	E	81	256,000	61,675	80,549	18,874
			82	154,450	36,547	45,213	8,666
			84	54,208	13,383	17,434	4,051
AUSTRAL	V	E	86	19,842	4,500	5,750	1,250
AUSTRIA	V	E	84	1,100	693	785	92
BNGLDSH	O	E	84	4,950	1,297	1,297	
CANADA	O	E	81	20,642	5,150	5,150	
			82	6,606	3,076	3,076	
			83	14,539	12,112	12,112	
			84	9,143	5,588	5,588	
			86	217	1,293	1,293	
	O	W	81	42,650	9,903	9,903	
			82	13,116	1,901	1,901	
CHINA M	N	E	81	553,512	92,452	123,147	30,695
	V	E	81	88,184	17,687	19,130	1,443
			83	45,195	9,710	12,649	2,939
			84	82,430	18,442	24,042	5,600
			85	165,808	22,350	34,104	11,754
			86	443,280	57,369	81,429	24,060
	V	W	81	123,353	20,033	26,345	6,312
			84	39,683	8,979	11,173	2,194
			85	16,314	2,397	3,330	933

Crop Product TSUSA commodity number, description, and unit of quantity Country	Mode	Reg	Yr	Quantity	F.A.S.	C.I.F.	Charges
			86	18,000	2,676	3,000	324
CHINA T	V	E	84	39,683	13,464	16,031	2,567
COLOMB	A	E	84	25	331	358	27
DOM REP	A	E	81	2,874	1,267	1,733	466
			83	1,128	395	672	277
			85	30,822	10,788	15,128	4,340
			86	26,737	13,656	16,403	2,747
	N	E	81	83,304	38,209	54,072	15,863
			82	8,270	2,919	3,456	537
			84	51,944	15,317	21,222	5,905
EGYPT	N	E	86	88,211	22,180	30,215	8,035
	V	E	82	32,319	7,938	9,648	1,710
			83	130,676	31,890	44,405	12,515
			84	898,683	229,249	309,438	80,189
			85	94,798	16,017	23,423	7,406
ETHIOP	V	E	83	22,046	3,200	5,528	2,328
FR GERM	V	E	84	62,710	23,897	29,565	5,668
			85	10,362	2,930	3,632	702
	V	W	83	8,672	2,515	3,343	828
FRANCE	V	E	81	150	439	665	226
			82	400	634	704	70
			83	800	1,127	1,187	60
			84	237,497	65,565	79,647	14,082
			85	316,743	52,610	73,619	21,009
			86	504,836	90,140	124,435	34,295
	V	W	83	77	354	376	22
GREECE	O	E	83	1,102	393	445	52
HG KONG	V	E	84	17,640	3,618	5,518	1,900
INDIA	A	E	84	742	417	480	63
	N	E	81	13,946	10,050	12,005	1,955
			82	46,521	24,762	30,447	5,685
			84	73,682	36,879	42,689	5,810
			86	66,707	47,457	53,639	6,182
	O	E	82	2,430	1,477	1,477	
			83	6,953	4,197	4,282	85
			84	1,000	738	738	
			85	22,482	10,750	12,217	1,467
	V	E	81	7,690	4,911	5,911	1,000
			82	17,429	8,166	9,896	1,730
			83	103,382	45,100	53,634	8,534
			84	70,938	26,714	31,530	4,816
			85	73,790	37,841	43,241	5,400
			86	6,878	6,323	6,956	633
	V	W	81	20,106	13,049	15,027	1,978
			82	54,585	25,002	29,520	4,518
			83	43,958	22,595	26,416	3,821
			84	34,974	14,868	18,178	3,310
			85	3,307	1,080	1,231	151
			86	26,639	17,071	18,676	1,605
ITALY	O	E	84	7,896	14,040	14,240	200
	V	E	86	38,963	7,350	9,949	2,599
JAPAN	V	E	83	360	2,375	2,488	113
KENYA	V	E	84	15,743	4,705	5,772	1,067
MACAO	V	E	82	41,006	12,050	12,135	85
			85	39,683	7,780	11,035	3,255
			86	39,683	7,370	9,950	2,580
MALAWI	O	E	81	704	571	627	56
			84	881	500	500	
MEXICO	O	E	81	1,701,692	427,050	427,050	
			82	1,779,519	288,116	288,116	
			83	1,813,817	222,493	222,493	
			84	2,741,080	335,860	335,860	
			85	749,108	133,392	133,392	
			86	982,295	179,758	179,758	
	O	W	81	3,865,381	473,525	473,525	
			82	4,206,084	619,286	620,494	1,208
			83	2,669,376	337,583	337,583	
			84	5,788,925	646,124	646,124	
			85	166,548	29,149	29,149	
			86	633,518	101,597	101,597	
MOROC	N	E	83	2,434,746	619,241	775,885	156,644
	O	E	84	8,800	3,168	3,168	
	V	E	81	1,358,079	289,107	375,985	86,878
			82	2,027,612	469,686	600,770	131,084
			83	119,049	30,094	37,919	7,825
			84	2,910,099	702,571	891,721	189,150
			85	2,526,592	429,206	576,574	147,368
			86	2,819,772	557,377	728,479	171,102
	V	W	83	39,683	11,913	13,568	1,655
			84	48,987	9,600	14,396	4,796
			85	39,683	7,050	9,900	2,850
			86	59,524	12,222	15,400	3,178
MOZAMBQ	O	E	85	5,159	1,217	1,217	
			86	6,504	1,180	1,180	

Crop Product TSUSA commodity number, description, and unit of quantity Country	Mode	Reg	Yr	Quantity	F.A.S.	C.I.F.	Charges
NETHLDS	V	E	81	7,214	3,123	3,412	289
			85	20,930	6,471	8,400	1,929
			86	39,683	5,107	7,896	2,789
	V	W	84	250	553	624	71
PAKISTN	O	E	82	551	674	747	73
	V	E	85	1,968	1,466	1,676	210
			86	7,874	3,039	3,416	377
	V	W	84	2,205	998	1,250	252
			85	1,425	1,064	1,239	175
ROMANIA	V	E	81	2,107,401	411,531	513,276	101,745
			82	1,423,318	329,616	404,078	74,462
			83	1,680,276	345,020	426,764	81,744
			84	743,691	183,801	221,202	37,401
			85	1,150,174	217,634	271,473	53,839
			86	1,434,018	225,915	310,362	84,447
SINGAPR	V	W	82	2,208	893	1,009	116
SPAIN	V	E	81	19,841	3,508	4,519	1,011
			86	10,000	2,442	2,997	555
SWEDEN	O	E	81	265	620	620	
THAILND	V	E	83	1,446	1,095	1,249	154
			84	216	1,296	1,540	244
	V	W	82	250	270	297	27
TURKEY	V	E	84	13,228	2,751	3,587	836
			86	47,399	6,006	9,545	3,539
	V	W	83	3,307	862	982	120
U KING	N	E	82	27,671	16,718	20,908	4,190
	O	E	81	7,889	3,388	3,696	308
			82	15,615	6,913	7,671	758
			83	6,817	3,727	4,087	360
			84	8,046	3,538	4,012	474
			85	2,295	2,195	2,563	368
	V	E	81	72	360	390	30
			82	2,200	822	921	99
			84	3,307	1,273	1,529	256
YUGOSLV	V	E	83	79,031	14,415	18,432	4,017

Cork Oak

Cork, manufactured
2202500 VUL SHEETS, ETC OF CORK-RUB (LB)

Country	Mode	Reg	Yr	Quantity	F.A.S.	C.I.F.	Charges
TOTAL			81	5,095,288	2,601,356	2,832,622	231,266
			82	5,648,238	2,824,219	3,095,914	271,695
			83	3,792,010	1,752,304	1,907,258	154,954
			84	4,353,635	1,954,260	2,247,775	293,515
			85	6,631,013	2,827,187	3,187,817	360,630
			86	6,474,614	3,169,232	3,481,827	312,595
BELIZE	V	W	85	5,122	5,088	6,178	1,090
			86	4,030	4,176	4,803	627
BRAZIL	V	W	83	8,514	7,726	9,131	1,405
			84	3,360	3,079	3,618	539
CANADA	A	E	81	128	311	409	98
	A	W	83	1	325	350	25
	N	E	83	115,204	263,927	263,927	
	O	E	81	158,013	364,194	364,194	
			82	87,159	223,683	223,685	2
			83	1,865	6,480	6,480	
			84	116,828	271,472	271,472	
			85	113,281	254,521	254,521	
			86	125,183	287,424	287,424	
	O	W	84	31,730	10,573	10,573	
CHINA T	A	E	86	88	1,515	1,797	282
DENMARK	A	E	84	240	295	485	190
FR GERM	A	E	83	95	445	535	90
	V	E	81	273	1,403	1,514	111
JAPAN	A	E	84	2,160	8,000	8,800	800
			85	1,320	10,721	13,962	3,241
	A	W	84	184	1,912	2,501	589
	N	E	84	4,756	45,614	59,775	14,161
NETHLDS	V	W	82	9,339	7,685	8,568	883
			83	7,589	7,181	7,941	760
PORTUGL	A	E	81	295	490	880	390
			84	47	260	392	132
	O	E	86	4,150	2,325	2,325	
	V	E	81	4,393,633	2,009,149	2,219,870	210,721
			82	5,529,987	2,569,061	2,836,746	267,685
			83	3,656,314	1,459,541	1,611,991	152,450
			84	4,187,137	1,597,075	1,872,409	275,334
			85	6,495,461	2,531,145	2,883,844	352,699
			86	6,287,792	2,837,572	3,144,238	306,666

Crop Product TSUSA commodity number, description, and unit of quantity Country	Mode	Reg	Yr	Quantity	F.A.S.	C.I.F.	Charges
SPAIN	V	E	85	12,211	6,634	9,167	2,533
			86	50,788	15,263	19,473	4,210
SWEDEN	V	E	85	2,342	8,793	9,209	416
U KING	A	E	84	794	4,050	4,442	392
			85	365	1,480	1,973	493
	N	E	81	594	5,123	5,223	100
			82	542	2,653	2,982	329
			83	2,153	6,297	6,521	224
	O	E	86	917	6,934	6,934	
	O	W	83	275	382	382	
			84	908	1,257	1,257	
			85	200	1,521	1,521	
	V	E	81	4,585	4,037	4,606	569
			82	21,211	21,137	23,933	2,796
			84	5,491	10,673	12,051	1,378
			85	711	7,284	7,442	158
			86	1,666	14,023	14,833	810
YUGOSLV	V	E	81	537,767	216,649	235,926	19,277

2203000 CORK INSULATION BLOCKS ETC (BFT)

TOTAL			81	7,134,138	2,122,637	2,642,769	520,132
			82	5,850,259	1,482,108	1,850,667	368,559
			83	4,474,848	1,295,635	1,632,149	336,514
			84	5,232,999	1,104,941	1,430,464	325,523
			85	3,602,489	1,059,912	1,386,978	327,066
			86	2,823,061	1,056,513	1,327,175	270,662
BRAZIL	V	E	84	5,742	1,132	1,308	176
CANADA	O	E	81	26	374	575	201
			85	1,657	7,638	7,638	
FR GERM	A	E	82	48	291	336	45
	N	E	85	*	1,701	1,960	259
	V	E	86	2,539	5,147	5,532	385
FRANCE	V	E	84	4,514	6,788	9,056	2,268
ITALY	V	E	82	2,563	15,864	19,400	3,536
JAPAN	N	E	84	1	2,804	5,291	2,487
	V	W	84	2	704	729	25
NETHLDS	V	E	81	45,742	13,351	17,477	4,126
PORTUGL	N	E	82	66,960	13,522	18,892	5,370
	V	E	81	942,887	261,929	350,509	88,580
			82	1,124,435	249,323	331,733	82,410
			83	572,988	210,338	265,448	55,110
			84	531,693	147,871	205,486	57,615
			85	298,422	129,658	177,001	47,343
			86	493,833	241,534	301,107	59,573
	V	W	81	658,310	61,127	84,981	23,854
			82	350,337	40,676	53,414	12,738
			83	406,311	43,018	60,717	17,699
			84	770,697	26,191	37,213	11,022
			85	165,888	11,959	20,799	8,840
SPAIN	N	E	85	473,421	77,736	103,491	25,755
			86	865,129	381,417	464,409	82,992
	N	W	84	591,557	127,208	169,323	42,115
	O	E	81	1,064	5,921	5,921	
	V	E	81	4,599,201	1,559,781	1,897,922	338,141
			82	4,074,488	1,084,836	1,328,865	244,029
			83	2,652,615	948,167	1,183,392	235,225
			84	3,328,056	784,423	990,922	206,499
			85	2,327,987	666,003	855,762	189,759
			86	1,012,294	237,725	307,815	70,090
	V	W	81	842,412	200,254	262,018	61,764
			82	231,428	77,596	98,027	20,431
			83	842,070	93,499	121,469	27,970
			84	730	7,086	10,391	3,305
			85	335,114	165,217	220,327	55,110
			86	449,266	190,690	248,312	57,622
SWITZLD	V	E	84	7	734	745	11
U KING	V	E	83	864	613	1,123	510
YUGOSLV	V	E	81	44,496	19,900	23,366	3,466

2203100 CORK INSULATION, FITTNGS,ETC (LB)

TOTAL			81	1,698	2,000	4,844	2,844
			83	168	1,184	1,358	174
			84	44	1,600	1,702	102
			86	12,051	13,896	15,721	1,825
JAPAN	A	E	83	90	630	720	90
PORTUGL	A	E	81	1,698	2,000	4,844	2,844
	V	E	83	78	554	638	84
			84	44	1,600	1,702	102
			86	12,051	13,896	15,721	1,825

2203500 TAPER CORK STPRS, HLW O PERF (LB)

TOTAL			81	3,828	35,092	38,707	3,615

Crop Product TSUSA commodity number, description, and unit of quantity Country	Mode	Reg	Yr	Quantity	F.A.S.	C.I.F.	Charges
			82	5,887	31,797	36,424	4,627
			83	5,967	32,371	34,539	2,168
			84	27,788	185,041	194,701	9,660
			85	12,872	40,896	46,347	5,451
			86	4,549	13,453	14,692	1,239
CANADA	O	E	86	841	1,968	1,968	
CHILE	V	E	82	1,275	1,450	1,573	123
FRANCE	A	W	82	704	3,950	4,685	735
HG KONG	O	E	84	138	938	1,013	75
PORTUGL	A	E	81	1,284	18,722	20,852	2,130
			84	331	1,100	1,530	430
			85	5,756	7,810	11,212	3,402
	A	W	82	45	258	467	209
	N	E	82	3,172	21,581	24,545	2,964
			84	528	4,541	4,991	450
	V	E	81	1,979	11,646	12,818	1,172
			83	5,396	28,647	30,400	1,753
			84	7,265	49,418	52,446	3,028
			85	7,116	33,086	35,135	2,049
			86	2,572	10,257	10,787	530
	V	W	81	565	4,724	5,037	313
			82	691	4,558	5,154	596
			83	440	3,171	3,380	209
			84	19,251	125,886	131,488	5,602
			86	1,136	1,228	1,937	709
SPAIN	V	E	83	85	300	489	189
SWITZLD	A	E	84	275	3,158	3,233	75
U KING	V	E	83	46	253	270	17

2203600 CORK STOP N/HLW PER NOV 3/4 (LB)

TOTAL			81	90,555	543,805	586,657	42,852
			82	201,896	855,948	910,440	54,492
			83	118,881	700,069	738,207	38,138
			84	129,093	489,494	534,972	45,478
			85	75,812	354,897	383,353	28,456
			86	142,555	724,728	768,472	43,744
BELGIUM	V	E	84	1,676	7,200	9,420	2,220
CANADA	O	E	82	400	1,000	1,000	
CHINA T	A	W	84	7	1,285	1,378	93
	V	W	85	91	8,940	9,940	1,000
FR GERM	A	E	85	992	7,584	7,961	377
			86	120	1,200	1,356	156
	A	W	81	20	266	301	35
			86	474	4,042	5,636	1,594
	O	E	84	924	834	995	161
	V	E	85	1,996	14,721	15,234	513
FRANCE	A	E	81	928	5,666	6,514	848
			82	1,625	11,685	12,554	869
	A	W	85	1,002	3,696	4,712	1,016
			86	186	12,494	12,977	483
	N	E	82	120	1,367	1,591	224
	N	W	85	2,368	16,158	17,912	1,754
	V	E	83	16	504	649	145
			84	150	4,963	5,041	78
			85	816	2,575	2,918	343
	V	W	86	8,078	24,543	25,678	1,135
HG KONG	O	E	83	75	925	1,011	86
ITALY	A	E	83	333	3,710	4,616	906
	O	E	86	425	4,000	4,457	457
	V	E	81	51	776	800	24
			83	7	257	303	46
			84	208	766	1,042	276
	V	W	83	20	638	713	75
JAPAN	V	E	86	2,000	7,839	8,000	161
NETHLDS	V	E	84	240	1,127	1,215	88
PHIL R	V	W	85	54	1,284	1,334	50
PORTUGL	A	E	81	78	1,105	1,526	421
			82	15	569	718	149
			83	380	342	1,000	658
			84	466	2,524	3,298	774
			86	55	1,177	1,448	271
	A	W	84	27	981	1,217	236
	N	E	81	65,710	385,080	414,469	29,389
			82	110,084	463,275	496,483	33,208
			83	62,513	364,920	384,138	19,218
			84	83,770	307,686	331,185	23,499
			85	48,266	240,475	254,683	14,208
	N	W	84	2,051	8,663	10,322	1,659
	O	E	82	317	446	446	
			84	452	2,108	2,486	378
			85	394	2,045	2,972	927
			86	862	4,230	5,259	1,029

Crop
Product
TSUSA commodity number, description, and unit of quantity

Country	Mode	Reg	Yr	Quantity	F.A.S.	C.I.F.	Charges
	V	E	81	21,476	143,137	154,008	10,871
			82	72,068	229,874	242,531	12,657
			83	49,689	304,184	319,598	15,414
			84	31,834	115,289	128,474	13,185
			85	19,137	53,558	61,368	7,810
			86	114,612	602,326	635,301	32,975
	V	W	81	712	2,763	3,076	313
			82	14,297	140,895	147,178	6,283
			83	748	3,339	3,665	326
			84	649	1,803	2,009	206
			86	6,733	25,991	28,491	2,500
SPAIN	A	E	81	83	340	468	128
			82	181	1,167	1,503	336
			84	298	1,219	1,665	446
	O	E	84	300	300	342	42
	V	E	81	1,330	3,278	3,732	454
			82	143	390	440	50
			83	5,100	21,250	22,514	1,264
			85	513	2,800	3,173	373
			86	4,022	6,115	7,303	1,188
	V	W	81	140	413	546	133
			82	2,646	5,280	5,996	716
			84	4,519	26,950	28,482	1,532
			86	4,885	29,766	31,561	1,795
U KING	N	E	84	1,549	6,777	7,618	841
	O	E	86	103	1,005	1,005	
	V	E	85	183	1,061	1,146	85

2203700 CORK DISK N/HLW PER NOV 3/4 (LB)

Country	Mode	Reg	Yr	Quantity	F.A.S.	C.I.F.	Charges
TOTAL			81	1,510	14,374	15,533	1,159
			82	6,466	27,657	31,304	3,647
			83	9,561	45,598	49,584	3,986
			84	29,086	83,972	90,577	6,605
			85	54,384	216,661	237,167	20,506
			86	10,974	33,741	36,479	2,738
CHINA T	V	E	82	318	586	702	116
FR GERM	N	E	83	767	4,973	5,460	487
FRANCE	A	W	82	30	313	448	135
	V	E	84	96	469	535	66
ITALY	A	E	85	2,058	12,488	14,687	2,199
	V	E	84	19	385	408	23
			86	894	6,238	6,588	350
PORTUGL	A	E	81	77	262	453	191
			84	853	7,882	8,262	380
	N	E	85	14,383	64,900	72,544	7,644
			86	8,406	17,015	19,112	2,097
	O	E	83	13	334	364	30
			86	11	1,400	1,400	
	V	E	82	2,371	16,538	17,349	811
			83	6,675	26,720	28,827	2,107
			84	24,863	64,411	69,601	5,190
			85	35,999	134,174	143,201	9,027
			86	1,243	5,029	5,171	142
	V	W	81	1,433	14,112	15,080	968
			82	3,549	9,419	11,715	2,296
			83	2,106	13,571	14,933	1,362
			84	2,307	7,962	8,597	635
			85	1,944	5,099	6,735	1,636
SPAIN	A	E	82	198	801	1,090	289
	V	E	86	420	4,059	4,208	149
	V	W	84	948	2,863	3,174	311

2203900 CORK STOP N/HLW PERF OV3/4 (LB)

Country	Mode	Reg	Yr	Quantity	F.A.S.	C.I.F.	Charges
TOTAL			81	128,055	486,305	531,044	44,739
			82	269,627	687,815	759,341	71,526
			83	226,767	628,509	687,890	59,381
			84	271,391	1,038,997	1,132,581	93,584
			85	181,174	774,717	830,882	56,165
			86	178,826	692,546	748,577	56,031
BELGIUM	A	E	86	3,252	2,485	5,117	2,632
BRAZIL	V	E	84	46	263	306	43
CANADA	O	E	81	386	3,956	3,956	
FR GERM	A	E	84	256	1,798	2,271	473
			85	397	4,025	4,515	490
	A	W	85	176	1,238	1,970	732
	N	W	86	706	6,100	6,428	328
	V	E	82	1,929	11,032	12,051	1,019
			86	462	5,743	6,232	489
	V	W	82	772	6,022	6,804	782
			83	8,035	40,613	44,597	3,984
			84	4,912	46,700	48,300	1,600
FRANCE	A	E	82	258	1,610	2,063	453

Crop
Product
TSUSA commodity number, description, and unit of quantity

Country	Mode	Reg	Yr	Quantity	F.A.S.	C.I.F.	Charges
			83	269	1,050	1,142	92
			85	1,407	9,804	11,000	1,196
			86	1,918	11,446	13,166	1,720
	A	W	85	357	3,241	3,834	593
	V	E	86	35	2,004	2,008	4
	V	W	82	1,825	16,619	17,487	868
			83	1,521	7,041	7,714	673
			84	4,966	25,276	27,266	1,990
ITALY	O	E	86	901	11,750	12,051	301
	V	E	81	4	356	372	16
JAPAN	V	W	86	792	3,457	3,831	374
NETHLDS	V	E	81	3,979	18,216	19,628	1,412
			86	12,037	25,662	28,186	2,524
POLAND	V	E	82	236	546	630	84
			84	406	3,029	3,352	323
			86	995	2,803	3,246	443
PORTUGL	A	E	82	1,269	7,750	10,006	2,256
			84	128	2,419	2,669	250
			85	417	2,667	3,152	485
	A	W	83	1,500	14,200	14,968	768
			84	745	7,000	8,500	1,500
	N	E	81	49,899	158,130	172,870	14,740
			82	58,826	200,040	220,384	20,344
			83	103,159	261,271	285,983	24,712
			84	96,425	261,053	285,572	24,519
	N	W	84	28,397	176,713	183,592	6,879
			86	7,285	43,072	46,371	3,299
	O	E	82	800	5,601	5,775	174
			84	618	3,502	3,630	128
			85	1,874	5,484	6,240	756
	V	E	81	70,526	292,684	319,938	27,254
			82	179,197	267,612	304,269	36,657
			83	94,808	150,373	167,194	16,821
			84	35,408	106,751	122,440	15,689
			85	103,384	351,899	381,838	29,939
			86	117,120	296,597	329,988	33,391
	V	W	81	1,078	7,805	8,277	472
			82	17,555	135,540	142,291	6,751
			83	16,207	146,009	157,175	11,166
			84	5,823	52,797	56,193	3,396
			85	32,839	223,437	235,411	11,974
			86	33,323	281,427	291,953	10,526
SPAIN	A	E	81	49	450	599	149
			82	1,102	4,700	5,728	1,028
			83	190	570	655	85
	A	W	84	418	2,000	2,418	418
	V	E	81	2,134	4,708	5,404	696
			82	559	3,925	4,198	273
			83	1,078	7,382	8,462	1,080
			84	82,922	320,267	345,977	25,710
			85	32,980	126,072	136,044	9,972
	V	W	82	5,299	26,818	27,655	837
			85	7,343	46,850	46,878	28
U KING	V	W	84	9,921	29,429	40,095	10,666

2204100 CORK DISK N/HLW PERF OV 3/4 (LB)

Country	Mode	Reg	Yr	Quantity	F.A.S.	C.I.F.	Charges
TOTAL			81	7,047	21,276	23,742	2,466
			82	15,601	52,678	58,422	5,744
			83	5,870	23,734	28,015	4,281
			84	36,221	136,188	150,388	14,200
			85	21,794	61,701	71,064	9,363
			86	55,294	101,770	111,618	9,848
CHINA M	V	W	84	2,734	11,709	12,402	693
CHINA T	V	E	84	233	397	449	52
FR GERM	A	E	85	1,731	1,659	1,659	
			86	89	1,122	1,163	41
FRANCE	A	E	83	10	944	1,131	187
	V	E	86	810	7,796	7,921	125
	V	W	81	2,329	3,996	4,583	587
ITALY	V	E	84	52	459	546	87
JAPAN	V	W	83	154	1,659	1,691	32
KOR REP	V	E	82	328	777	895	118
	V	W	82	142	339	383	44
NETHLDS	A	E	84	3	644	651	7
PORTUGL	A	E	81	60	302	497	195
			82	393	693	1,385	692
			83	985	5,761	7,458	1,697
			84	49	2,775	2,965	190
	N	E	84	6,226	22,006	25,364	3,358
			85	8,429	24,933	28,930	3,997
			86	2,612	11,008	11,881	873
	O	E	82	5,510	5,898	5,898	
			84	527	1,815	2,374	559

Crop
Product
TSUSA commodity number, description, and unit of quantity

Country	Mode	Reg	Yr	Quantity	F.A.S.	C.I.F.	Charges
	V	E	81	2,117	10,649	11,563	914
			82	6,762	37,608	41,560	3,952
			83	150	574	672	98
			84	7,723	30,791	33,767	2,976
			85	9,501	28,647	32,157	3,510
			86	51,783	81,844	90,653	8,809
	V	W	81	2,541	6,329	7,099	770
			82	1,126	4,851	5,424	573
			83	1,103	5,318	5,985	667
			84	177	611	660	49
			85	2,013	5,276	6,968	1,692
SPAIN	A	E	83	174	318	607	289
	V	E	82	1,340	2,512	2,877	365
			83	3,294	9,160	10,471	1,311
			84	16,292	61,981	68,180	6,199
U KING	A	E	85	120	1,186	1,350	164
	V	E	84	2,205	3,000	3,030	30

2204700 CORK STOPPERS NSPF N TAPERD (LB)

Country	Mode	Reg	Yr	Quantity	F.A.S.	C.I.F.	Charges
TOTAL			81	2,189,295	16,237,161	16,803,068	565,907
			82	1,741,109	11,877,243	12,371,726	494,483
			83	2,058,585	13,119,511	13,589,934	470,423
			84	2,163,289	13,619,394	14,268,795	649,401
			85	2,131,589	13,941,702	14,651,073	709,371
			86	2,399,995	14,897,110	15,555,073	657,963
BELGIUM	V	E	85	1,444	8,282	9,590	1,308
	V	W	84	6,012	37,960	40,350	2,390
			86	10,441	88,236	90,600	2,364
BRAZIL	V	W	85	5,882	41,735	44,460	2,725
CANADA	A	W	86	55	2,652	2,732	80
	O	E	81	21,797	138,789	138,789	
			82	17,672	123,564	123,564	
			83	6,121	41,135	41,135	
			84	1,775	11,757	11,757	
			85	1,370	8,194	8,194	
			86	2,160	13,579	13,579	
CHINA T	V	W	85	176	1,558	1,731	173
FR GERM	A	E	84	335	2,223	3,084	861
			85	324	2,159	3,038	879
	A	W	81	241	735	848	113
	N	W	81	79,668	550,805	574,709	23,904
			82	19,958	143,026	150,104	7,078
			84	2,225	21,236	21,763	527
			85	11,173	80,374	84,128	3,754
	V	E	81	8,019	73,704	77,698	3,994
			82	3,825	36,381	38,717	2,336
			84	20,208	120,886	133,728	12,842
			85	8,289	50,142	54,980	4,838
	V	W	84	15,900	82,422	89,446	7,024
			85	1,631	10,797	12,691	1,894
			86	21,595	143,400	151,973	8,573
FRANCE	A	E	82	550	5,197	5,809	612
			83	1,717	13,220	15,941	2,721
			84	95	1,702	1,834	132
	A	W	84	277	1,098	1,815	717
	N	E	81	8,756	52,360	55,902	3,542
	N	W	83	2,567	14,341	16,208	1,867
			84	21,328	146,992	158,300	11,308
			85	5,297	35,137	39,355	4,218
			86	40,595	203,018	216,589	13,571
	V	E	85	95	2,392	2,544	152
			86	1,194	10,983	11,701	718
	V	W	81	5,670	32,405	34,028	1,623
			82	27,964	133,809	141,995	8,186
			83	7,513	55,704	58,807	3,103
			84	4,686	30,079	32,022	1,943
			85	2,410	16,160	17,892	1,732
			86	2,380	16,567	17,394	827
HG KONG	V	W	86	1,706	12,607	13,225	618
ITALY	A	E	82	93	340	785	445
	O	E	83	510	2,345	2,345	
			84	2,550	10,066	10,066	
	V	E	81	9,083	68,150	70,616	2,466
	V	W	83	44	535	633	98
MAURITN	O	E	84	80	598	598	
NETHLDS	V	E	85	3,011	9,836	11,748	1,912
			86	1,803	16,922	17,531	609
	V	W	81	381	542	705	163
			83	18,820	84,771	88,447	3,676
			84	28,247	113,617	118,875	5,258
			85	24,158	172,148	179,358	7,210
			86	38,068	192,660	207,318	14,658
PORTUGL	A	E	81	463	3,185	3,772	587

Crop
Product
TSUSA commodity number, description, and unit of quantity

Country	Mode	Reg	Yr	Quantity	F.A.S.	C.I.F.	Charges
			82	755	5,185	7,281	2,096
			83	390	3,433	4,090	657
			84	132	1,252	1,487	235
			85	315	3,206	3,847	641
			86	119	2,520	2,663	143
	A	W	81	2,221	20,904	23,914	3,010
			83	151	1,026	1,382	356
			84	661	8,268	9,716	1,448
			86	569	8,980	11,038	2,058
	N	E	81	48,515	413,056	443,845	30,789
			82	47,764	336,214	358,471	22,257
			83	77,466	471,274	493,322	22,048
			84	62,316	407,733	427,833	20,100
			86	456	3,841	4,336	495
	N	W	81	1,177,421	8,879,343	9,168,602	289,259
			82	1,150,752	8,220,103	8,554,954	334,851
			83	1,259,740	8,460,168	8,760,914	300,746
			84	1,293,593	7,961,184	8,357,566	396,382
			85	1,170,879	7,716,762	8,125,967	409,205
			86	1,245,046	7,957,357	8,277,776	320,419
	O	E	82	2,172	15,633	15,726	93
			83	17,207	111,170	111,170	
			84	21,706	154,988	155,529	541
			85	20,725	152,201	152,201	
			86	14,663	110,044	110,413	369
	V	E	81	685,053	5,271,047	5,443,652	172,605
			82	296,699	2,077,343	2,148,342	70,999
			83	436,821	2,833,367	2,920,359	86,992
			84	551,928	3,912,209	4,066,917	154,708
			85	692,414	4,666,135	4,864,093	197,958
			86	387,850	2,607,932	2,718,841	110,909
	V	W	81	26,092	190,816	197,237	6,421
			82	2,733	14,860	15,797	937
			83	9,758	65,292	67,758	2,466
			85	99,349	649,142	689,292	40,150
			86	483,482	2,936,431	3,069,370	132,939
S LUCIA	V	E	81	2,440	22,391	23,549	1,158
SPAIN	A	E	85	2,036	6,930	8,823	1,893
	N	W	82	1,345	9,231	10,380	1,149
			83	27,707	152,000	161,754	9,754
			86	77,039	338,380	367,319	28,939
	V	E	81	89,180	376,169	394,508	18,339
			82	128,636	548,593	579,012	30,419
			83	191,667	808,280	844,057	35,777
			84	62,964	276,252	284,659	8,407
			86	9,507	23,016	26,500	3,484
	V	W	81	24,295	142,760	150,694	7,934
			82	40,191	207,764	220,789	13,025
			83	386	1,450	1,612	162
			84	66,141	316,202	340,689	24,487
			85	79,182	303,104	330,496	27,392
			86	61,267	207,985	224,175	16,190
U KING	A	E	85	1,429	5,308	6,645	1,337
	O	E	84	130	670	761	91

2204800 CORK DISKS NES, NOT TAPERED (LB)

Country	Mode	Reg	Yr	Quantity	F.A.S.	C.I.F.	Charges
TOTAL			81	1,547,815	6,178,887	6,515,761	336,874
			82	1,348,876	5,455,489	5,758,040	302,551
			83	1,039,403	4,161,524	4,400,963	239,439
			84	1,056,979	3,960,921	4,247,615	286,694
			85	1,240,956	5,206,188	5,624,679	418,491
			86	893,117	4,554,009	4,838,718	284,709
ARAB EM	V	W	86	14,907	88,349	91,891	3,542
BRAZIL	V	E	84	16,335	39,976	43,756	3,780
			85	3,835	10,946	11,498	552
CANADA	O	E	82	2,846	18,374	18,374	
			83	600	4,067	4,067	
			86	3,420	17,784	17,784	
CHINA T	A	E	86	103	1,280	2,036	756
	N	E	84	1,040	1,896	2,696	800
	V	E	83	446	401	470	69
			85	9,120	5,472	6,797	1,325
	V	W	82	99	586	674	88
			83	844	2,149	2,331	182
			84	3,050	7,756	8,538	782
			85	412	1,836	1,906	70
			86	256	2,100	2,234	134
FR GERM	A	E	81	320	255	507	252
			83	733	10,223	10,907	684
			85	20	1,421	1,492	71
	A	W	82	96	481	640	159
	N	W	85	57,773	468,786	475,100	6,314
	O	E	82	668	2,267	2,489	222

Crop
Product
TSUSA commodity number, description, and unit of quantity

Country	Mode	Reg	Yr	Quantity	F.A.S.	C.I.F.	Charges
	V	E	81	464	4,635	4,810	175
			84	231	2,755	3,198	443
			85	2,260	8,770	9,312	542
	V	W	81	3,792	35,661	37,128	1,467
			82	14,434	104,288	108,846	4,558
			86	6,450	61,760	63,770	2,010
FRANCE	A	E	82	95	383	649	266
			83	7,759	34,249	39,405	5,156
			84	792	3,326	4,259	933
			85	20,420	85,102	101,819	16,717
			86	1,000	1,119	1,618	499
	A	W	82	60	1,135	1,315	180
			83	7,607	38,541	44,667	6,126
			85	1,723	2,534	3,080	546
			86	626	6,778	8,512	1,734
	N	E	84	168	3,244	3,496	252
	N	W	83	107,235	563,280	600,069	36,789
			84	194,927	951,215	1,035,409	84,194
			85	175,058	809,907	893,939	84,032
	O	W	86	1,459	13,109	13,725	616
	V	E	81	28,682	168,928	182,048	13,120
			82	28,070	144,657	153,156	8,499
			83	27,820	136,147	144,674	8,527
			85	226	1,022	1,070	48
			86	223	1,059	1,073	14
	V	W	81	63,833	350,527	372,906	22,379
			82	124,104	645,109	690,837	45,728
			85	589	8,000	8,113	113
			86	124,886	714,381	757,708	43,327
HG KONG	V	E	84	6,075	6,919	8,054	1,135
			85	1,535	5,746	6,800	1,054
IRELAND	A	E	85	1,416	5,141	6,043	902
ITALY	A	E	82	1,054	6,826	8,362	1,536
	A	W	84	217	408	674	266
	V	E	81	600	2,788	2,981	193
			82	4,810	2,373	3,694	1,321
			83	1,020	3,183	3,947	764
	V	W	81	9,698	26,226	28,160	1,934
JAPAN	A	W	82	2	324	333	9
	V	E	83	220	2,303	2,336	33
			84	255	615	623	8
			85	67	3,468	3,584	116
			86	294	8,223	8,315	92
	V	W	81	17,652	60,301	65,389	5,088
MEXICO	O	W	81	100	350	350	
NETHLDS	O	E	81	150	1,186	1,259	73
	V	E	81	2,963	14,665	15,801	1,136
			86	36,327	73,247	79,472	6,225
	V	W	86	18,461	38,464	45,083	6,619
POLAND	V	E	84	640	1,700	1,882	182
			85	905	1,705	2,048	343
PORTUGL	A	E	82	916	2,316	3,606	1,290
			83	3,432	10,803	14,236	3,433
			84	2,298	11,458	14,542	3,084
			85	3,280	3,880	7,650	3,770
			86	457	9,021	9,824	803
	A	W	82	722	7,150	8,117	967
			83	1,080	10,850	12,036	1,186
			84	332	3,919	4,804	885
			85	12,111	18,424	28,242	9,818
	N	E	81	316,565	948,212	1,034,123	85,911
			82	170,667	576,155	618,581	42,426
			83	116,103	333,468	358,975	25,507
			84	51,592	168,342	180,749	12,407
			85	11,222	47,402	51,735	4,333
			86	44,413	185,492	198,758	13,266
	N	W	81	650,643	2,715,551	2,813,543	97,992
			82	2,828	11,673	13,641	1,968
			83	487,858	1,829,833	1,899,504	69,671
			84	415,973	1,399,207	1,476,651	77,444
			85	336,352	1,274,090	1,361,980	87,890
			86	206,843	1,253,539	1,318,517	64,978
	O	E	83	3,800	5,205	5,205	
			84	42	500	500	
			86	550	9,295	9,415	120
	V	E	81	132,278	512,069	534,696	22,627
			82	125,452	394,525	411,400	16,875
			83	22,348	163,879	171,089	7,210
			84	51,538	187,748	197,782	10,034
			85	78,847	290,327	314,982	24,655
			86	63,012	253,508	270,946	17,438
	V	W	81	7,595	35,856	38,296	2,440
			82	602,092	2,482,659	2,582,948	100,289
			83	11,411	87,806	89,914	2,108
			84	5,243	29,562	30,573	1,011
			86	66,276	438,151	454,153	16,002
SPAIN	A	E	83	1,012	3,468	4,404	936
			85	1,726	9,707	11,823	2,116
	N	E	81	86,808	360,567	382,326	21,759
	N	W	81	160,078	643,382	684,814	41,432
			82	106,501	436,055	469,743	33,688
			83	160,739	638,339	686,210	47,871
			84	198,354	824,177	888,258	64,081
			85	323,651	1,398,322	1,508,342	110,020
	V	E	81	38,779	167,471	178,745	11,274
			82	140,752	521,388	557,255	35,867
			83	30,664	100,975	109,767	8,792
			84	38,143	80,853	88,703	7,850
			85	152,061	556,528	603,205	46,677
			86	136,687	600,346	643,309	42,963
	V	W	81	26,758	129,423	137,020	7,597
			82	22,608	96,765	103,380	6,615
			83	46,672	182,355	196,750	14,395
			84	40,021	162,705	176,228	13,523
			85	46,347	187,652	204,119	16,467
			86	134,475	670,514	725,552	55,038
SWEDEN	O	W	81	15	285	287	2
SWITZLD	V	E	84	1,570	1,708	1,922	214
TOKELAU	V	E	86	4,810	3,538	3,976	438
U KING	A	E	81	42	549	572	23
			84	441	300	636	336
	V	W	84	27,702	70,632	73,682	3,050
			86	10,692	26,452	29,152	2,700
W SAHAR	V	E	86	16,490	76,500	81,895	5,395

2204900 CORK DSKS ETC NSPF CAN APTA (LB)

Country	Mode	Reg	Yr	Quantity	F.A.S.	C.I.F.	Charges
TOTAL			**81**	**3,822**	**9,933**	**9,933**	
			82	**2,622**	**6,453**	**6,630**	**177**
			83	**6,814**	**33,906**	**33,949**	**43**
			84	**657**	**3,200**	**3,200**	
CANADA	A	E	82	33	331	483	152
	N	E	82	2,239	3,911	3,936	25
			83	526	1,875	1,918	43
	O	E	81	3,822	9,933	9,933	
			82	350	2,211	2,211	
			83	6,288	32,031	32,031	
			84	657	3,200	3,200	

2205000 CORK MANUFACTURES NSPF (NULL)

Country	Mode	Reg	Yr	Quantity	F.A.S.	C.I.F.	Charges
TOTAL			**81**	-	**2,071,161**	**2,280,868**	**209,707**
			82	-	**1,833,693**	**2,040,360**	**206,667**
			83	-	**1,614,059**	**1,819,757**	**205,698**
			84	-	**2,299,716**	**2,581,734**	**282,018**
			85	-	**2,399,686**	**2,641,089**	**241,403**
			86	-	**2,136,867**	**2,328,786**	**191,919**
ALGERIA	N	E	85	-	1,200	1,450	250
AUSTRAL	N	W	84	-	724	854	130
BRAZIL	N	E	81	-	12,705	14,014	1,309
			82	-	3,526	3,870	344
			83	-	6,264	6,871	607
			84	-	527	594	67
	N	W	84	-	327	600	273
C RICA	N	E	83	-	3,048	3,307	259
CANADA	N	E	81	-	101,099	101,154	55
			82	-	250,141	250,141	
			83	-	117,897	117,899	2
			84	-	160,811	160,839	28
			85	-	347,718	347,718	
			86	-	237,901	237,981	80
	N	W	84	-	8,640	9,661	1,021
CHINA M	N	E	81	-	194,179	215,250	21,071
			82	-	159,170	185,450	26,280
			83	-	124,525	144,744	20,219
			84	-	269,289	299,380	30,091
			85	-	189,344	208,024	18,680
			86	-	194,510	217,272	22,762
	N	H	81	-	153,027	166,803	13,776
			82	-	124,499	136,713	12,214
			83	-	53,055	59,561	6,506
			84	-	48,008	55,478	7,470
			85	-	38,766	44,521	5,755
			86	-	30,358	34,588	4,230
	N	W	81	-	363,548	394,004	30,456
			82	-	223,121	250,492	27,371
			83	-	314,709	348,804	34,095
			84	-	276,040	306,896	30,856

Crop
Product
TSUSA commodity number, description, and unit of quantity

Country	Mode	Reg	Yr	Quantity	F.A.S.	C.I.F.	Charges
			85	-	614,405	672,191	57,786
			86	-	531,818	579,465	47,647
CHINA T	N	E	81	-	8,657	9,710	1,053
			82	-	4,356	5,361	1,005
			83	-	20,967	22,851	1,884
			84	-	11,669	14,275	2,606
			86	-	430,812	450,983	20,171
	N	H	83	-	1,967	2,234	267
			84	-	5,356	6,142	786
			85	-	2,831	3,207	376
			86	-	3,931	4,301	370
	N	W	81	-	18,020	19,477	1,457
			82	-	13,774	14,879	1,105
			83	-	32,428	35,078	2,650
			84	-	96,248	104,970	8,722
			85	-	66,113	71,518	5,405
			86	-	57,446	65,285	7,839
DENMARK	N	E	81	-	743	858	115
			82	-	2,700	3,502	802
			83	-	731	781	50
			84	-	4,868	5,318	450
			86	-	1,305	1,457	152
FINLAND	N	E	82	-	1,584	1,626	42
			83	-	1,586	1,638	52
			84	-	856	870	14
FR GERM	N	E	81	-	53,011	55,700	2,689
			82	-	41,554	44,993	3,439
			83	-	5,830	6,188	358
			84	-	6,209	7,141	932
			85	-	54,389	56,910	2,521
			86	-	21,895	23,155	1,260
	N	W	81	-	19,178	20,525	1,347
			82	-	103,110	105,745	2,635
			83	-	1,300	1,524	224
			85	-	4,472	5,035	563
FRANCE	N	E	82	-	1,215	1,458	243
			83	-	2,994	3,084	90
			85	-	21,105	23,703	2,598
	N	W	81	-	285	373	88
			82	-	1,051	1,077	26
			83	-	1,051	1,073	22
			84	-	1,764	1,854	90
GREECE	N	E	81	-	1,617	1,678	61
			82	-	1,540	1,818	278
			83	-	860	1,069	209
			84	-	950	1,164	214
			85	-	2,511	2,922	411
HG KONG	N	E	81	-	35,084	38,899	3,815
			82	-	16,087	17,842	1,755
			83	-	58,602	66,620	8,018
			84	-	83,170	94,392	11,222
			85	-	82,075	89,492	7,417
			86	-	5,420	5,861	441
	N	H	82	-	3,113	3,448	335
			84	-	890	1,108	218
	N	W	81	-	41,866	47,263	5,397
			82	-	96,814	100,711	3,897
			83	-	26,502	28,870	2,368
			84	-	43,570	47,820	4,250
			85	-	45,903	49,433	3,530
			86	-	48,168	53,819	5,651
IRELAND	N	E	86	-	5,393	6,219	826
ISRAEL	N	E	82	-	4,255	4,523	268
			83	-	1,288	1,836	548
			84	-	19,493	21,630	2,137
			86	-	3,076	3,242	166
ITALY	N	E	81	-	34,100	37,229	3,129
			82	-	54,122	58,860	4,738
			83	-	19,767	22,637	2,870
			84	-	19,394	21,531	2,137
			85	-	7,340	8,085	745
			86	-	37,560	40,904	3,344
	N	W	82	-	7,086	7,333	247
			83	-	2,379	2,388	9
			84	-	931	1,065	134
IVY CST	N	H	86	-	2,041	2,510	469
JAPAN	N	E	81	-	270	442	172
			82	-	2,693	3,456	763
			83	-	9,869	11,525	1,656
			84	-	24,637	28,172	3,535
			85	-	44,414	47,487	3,073
			86	-	4,436	4,812	376
	N	H	81	-	373	396	23
	N	W	81	-	641	725	84
			82	-	1,835	2,032	197
			83	-	18,891	20,078	1,187
			84	-	45,955	51,154	5,199
			85	-	5,796	6,628	832
KOR REP	N	E	81	-	132,256	136,658	4,402
			82	-	5,304	5,644	340
			83	-	4,806	5,244	438
			84	-	9,813	10,429	616
	N	W	81	-	995	1,087	92
			82	-	2,220	4,301	2,081
			85	-	1,087	1,212	125
			86	-	7,501	8,890	1,389
MACAO	N	W	82	-	4,217	4,645	428
			84	-	351	382	31
			85	-	1,401	1,516	115
MEXICO	N	E	83	-	269	269	
			85	-	3,850	3,850	
	N	W	82	-	286	286	
			84	-	340	340	
N ZEAL	N	E	84	-	13,505	14,580	1,075
	N	H	84	-	255	281	26
	N	W	81	-	3,175	3,500	325
NETHLDS	N	E	81	-	653	678	25
			83	-	1,344	1,360	16
			85	-	3,135	3,463	328
			86	-	9,500	9,738	238
	N	W	86	-	7,543	8,715	1,172
NORWAY	N	E	81	-	823	867	44
	N	W	82	-	496	548	52
PHIL R	N	E	84	-	2,098	2,708	610
	N	W	81	-	1,641	1,861	220
			83	-	1,440	1,628	188
POLAND	N	E	85	-	8,999	10,079	1,080
PORTUGL	N	E	81	-	617,779	694,969	77,190
			82	-	495,828	575,048	79,220
			83	-	567,220	647,903	80,683
			84	-	952,959	1,085,899	132,940
			85	-	595,418	678,931	83,513
			86	-	244,250	280,329	36,079
	N	W	81	-	21,564	25,272	3,708
			82	-	15,520	18,438	2,918
			83	-	8,813	10,062	1,249
			84	-	13,373	16,817	3,444
			85	-	27,590	35,094	7,504
			86	-	35,558	39,423	3,865
SINGAPR	N	W	81	-	1,500	2,031	531
SPAIN	N	E	81	-	223,707	255,615	31,908
			82	-	173,900	205,502	31,602
			83	-	117,801	142,505	24,704
			84	-	108,702	131,558	22,856
			85	-	149,197	178,470	29,273
			86	-	129,291	148,283	18,992
	N	W	81	-	4,769	6,202	1,433
			83	-	17,152	21,411	4,259
			84	-	4,181	4,675	494
			85	-	17,517	22,222	4,705
			86	-	2,812	3,040	228
SWEDEN	N	E	81	-	343	360	17
			83	-	1,200	1,675	475
			84	-	9,721	10,947	1,226
	N	W	81	-	651	1,067	416
			86	-	19,091	28,367	9,276
SWITZLD	N	E	84	-	7,009	7,512	503
			85	-	1,605	1,699	94
			86	-	10,923	11,880	957
	N	H	85	-	9,132	10,626	1,494
	N	W	81	-	4,771	5,048	277
			82	-	1,574	1,818	244
			83	-	12,106	12,490	384
			84	-	805	990	185
			85	-	23,703	25,270	1,567
THAILND	N	W	84	-	360	551	191
U KING	N	E	81	-	12,347	13,846	1,499
			82	-	16,315	17,799	1,484
			83	-	16,506	17,923	1,417
			84	-	44,970	49,763	4,793
			85	-	28,670	30,333	1,663
			86	-	52,728	56,667	3,939
	N	W	83	-	828	918	90
			84	-	297	327	30
			86	-	1,600	1,600	
VENEZ	N	E	81	-	6,435	8,374	1,939
			82	-	687	1,001	314
			83	-	34,832	42,117	7,285

Crop Product TSUSA commodity number, description, and unit of quantity Country	Mode	Reg	Yr	Quantity	F.A.S.	C.I.F.	Charges
	N	W	83		3,232	3,592	360

Cork, not manufactured
2200500 NAT CORK UNMFD A CORK WASTE (LB)

Country	Mode	Reg	Yr	Quantity	F.A.S.	C.I.F.	Charges
TOTAL			81	14,869,978	1,921,684	3,442,890	1,521,306
			82	5,049,244	623,330	1,209,861	586,531
			83	7,216,484	672,362	1,270,542	598,180
			84	9,014,755	1,127,022	1,941,119	814,097
			85	1,507,378	297,792	461,668	163,876
			86	7,272,885	1,022,943	1,588,533	565,590
CANADA	O	E	82	20	253	253	
			84	39,600	1,980	1,980	
CHINA T	V	E	84	53,280	13,005	17,902	4,897
DENMARK	O	E	84	585	1,518	1,570	52
FR GERM	N	E	84	*	2,172	2,728	556
	V	E	84	52,359	9,025	18,461	9,436
G BISAU	V	E	81	45,144	8,986	17,606	8,620
MOROC	V	E	83	892,713	74,416	167,516	93,100
			84	1,160,000	198,000	282,000	84,000
NETHLDS	V	E	82	85,561	19,403	35,813	16,410
			86	56,216	9,983	20,726	10,743
	V	W	85	6,973	5,728	9,333	3,605
PAKISTN	V	E	85	72,311	22,500	31,710	9,210
PORTUGL	A	E	83	127	300	400	100
	V	E	81	12,054,688	1,678,832	2,854,599	1,175,867
			82	2,766,438	416,927	682,153	265,226
			83	6,001,320	573,194	1,056,433	483,239
			84	5,195,789	622,414	1,070,655	448,241
			85	1,197,790	229,907	371,303	141,396
			86	5,872,424	853,320	1,286,586	433,266
	V	W	81	6,971	5,107	6,847	1,740
			82	4,343	2,983	4,011	1,028
			83	3,230	2,630	3,247	617
			84	20,496	14,059	21,706	7,647
			86	143,057	27,491	42,142	14,651
SPAIN	V	E	81	110,230	9,750	22,191	12,441
			82	882	1,184	1,301	117
			83	319,094	21,822	42,946	21,124
			84	2,492,646	264,849	524,117	259,268
			85	230,304	39,657	49,322	9,665
			86	1,201,188	132,149	239,079	106,930
TUNISIA	V	E	81	2,452,044	198,650	502,400	303,750
			82	2,192,000	182,580	486,330	303,750
YUGOSLV	V	E	81	200,901	20,359	39,247	18,888

2201000 CORK GRANLTD ETC NOV 6LB CFT (LB)

Country	Mode	Reg	Yr	Quantity	F.A.S.	C.I.F.	Charges
TOTAL			81	3,077,586	710,200	1,039,581	329,381
			82	4,699,857	1,035,096	1,505,098	470,002
			83	8,162,529	1,317,293	1,945,404	628,111
			84	11,727,395	2,529,342	3,745,215	1,215,873
			85	5,727,236	1,492,633	2,209,937	717,304
			86	4,232,333	1,131,995	1,599,864	467,869
FINLAND	V	E	84	21,627	3,139	5,990	2,851
NETHLDS	V	E	86	17,408	9,888	12,500	2,612
NORFOLK	V	E	84	55,684	16,974	25,554	8,580
PARAGUA	V	E	82	16,547	5,959	7,690	1,731
PORTUGL	V	E	81	3,000,754	694,611	1,011,041	316,430
			82	4,632,483	1,017,589	1,475,715	458,126
			83	8,044,633	1,293,917	1,909,068	615,151
			84	11,523,348	2,492,195	3,679,954	1,187,759
			85	5,727,236	1,492,633	2,209,937	717,304
			86	4,214,925	1,122,107	1,587,364	465,257
	V	W	82	1,102	261	300	39
SPAIN	V	E	81	76,832	15,589	28,540	12,951
			82	49,725	11,287	21,393	10,106
			83	117,896	23,376	36,336	12,960
			84	126,736	17,034	33,717	16,683

2201500 CORK GRANLTD, ETC OV 6LB CFT (LB)

Country	Mode	Reg	Yr	Quantity	F.A.S.	C.I.F.	Charges
TOTAL			81	723,506	186,613	242,179	55,566
			82	337,077	75,053	107,868	32,815
			83	707,821	121,798	184,478	62,680
			84	1,117,785	213,556	362,450	148,894
			85	1,759,479	333,168	522,810	189,642
			86	1,466,708	214,095	303,976	89,881
CANADA	O	E	81	20	320	320	
			82	25	698	698	
			83	20	330	330	
	O	W	83	34	424	424	

Country	Mode	Reg	Yr	Quantity	F.A.S.	C.I.F.	Charges
CHINA T	V	E	86	877	1,849	1,998	149
HAITI	V	E	85	18,555	7,422	10,890	3,468
PORTUGL	A	W	82	235	1,350	2,027	677
	O	E	81	32,408	3,750	5,139	1,389
			84	1,248	1,342	1,342	
			86	28,505	13,786	13,786	
	V	E	81	622,677	163,724	200,832	37,108
			82	326,562	70,679	100,562	29,883
			83	671,342	114,159	170,981	56,822
			84	1,114,537	209,892	358,636	148,744
			85	1,740,924	325,746	511,920	186,174
			86	1,437,326	198,460	288,192	89,732
	V	W	81	2,991	559	731	172
SPAIN	V	E	81	65,410	18,260	35,157	16,897
			82	10,255	2,326	4,581	2,255
			83	36,425	6,885	12,743	5,858
			84	2,000	2,322	2,472	150

2202000 CORK NA COMP N/ADV EX/CUT ETC (LB)

Country	Mode	Reg	Yr	Quantity	F.A.S.	C.I.F.	Charges
TOTAL			81	3,431,762	2,449,856	2,864,137	414,281
			82	3,447,320	2,295,547	2,680,080	384,533
			83	4,038,779	2,430,530	2,873,073	442,543
			84	3,918,284	2,524,382	3,012,044	487,662
			85	4,718,714	3,371,409	4,024,254	652,845
			86	5,881,970	3,753,026	4,417,000	663,974
BRAZIL	V	E	84	98,623	75,521	83,678	8,157
			86	234	1,006	1,133	127
	V	W	83	4,152	3,215	3,832	617
			85	2,526	2,479	2,960	481
CANADA	O	E	81	10,585	13,580	13,580	
			82	14,970	20,488	20,516	28
			83	9,082	5,862	5,862	
			84	33,077	16,380	16,380	
			85	80,684	71,856	71,856	
			86	10,546	12,651	12,651	
CHINA T	V	E	86	32,174	69,444	74,322	4,878
	V	W	86	273	4,455	4,753	298
CZECHO	V	W	86	7,143	11,385	14,438	3,053
FR GERM	A	E	84	375	322	586	264
	V	E	81	790	4,600	4,760	160
			82	237	4,325	4,488	163
			83	322	15,465	15,750	285
			85	341	1,243	1,311	68
			86	1,764	4,795	4,988	193
	V	W	81	21	378	390	12
FRANCE	A	W	86	798	3,509	3,613	104
	V	E	81	180	370	392	22
			83	331	499	524	25
	V	W	81	27,950	16,550	22,063	5,513
			84	328	4,764	4,952	188
GIBRAT	V	E	81	16,786	18,867	20,795	1,928
ICELAND	V	E	85	6,041	1,217	3,864	2,647
ISRAEL	A	W	86	200	1,748	2,080	332
ITALY	A	E	84	110	296	441	145
	O	E	81	510	2,327	2,477	150
	V	E	85	450	1,512	1,806	294
JAPAN	A	E	83	19	805	883	78
			84	37	1,611	1,765	154
	V	E	81	28	255	261	6
KOR REP	A	W	82	456	1,350	1,850	500
NETHLDS	V	E	81	25,983	18,470	21,300	2,830
			85	1,200	1,443	2,185	742
			86	102,673	77,045	86,370	9,325
	V	W	86	157,101	128,394	140,756	12,362
NORFOLK	V	E	84	21,111	16,856	32,228	15,372
POLAND	V	E	82	926	1,129	1,303	174
			85	19,118	11,348	12,710	1,362
PORTUGL	A	E	82	21	300	358	58
			85	90	2,715	2,859	144
			86	143	3,372	3,741	369
	A	W	84	3,516	6,026	11,560	5,534
	N	E	81	2,172,102	1,376,737	1,597,088	220,351
			83	2,339,605	1,150,740	1,384,553	233,813
			84	908,453	630,624	743,022	112,398
			85	846,448	539,011	640,380	101,369
			86	811,067	560,410	646,116	85,706
	N	W	83	249,478	168,508	203,388	34,880
	O	E	81	75	507	507	
			83	3,615	2,085	2,085	
			84	8,157	5,880	6,862	982
			85	1	1,977	2,110	133
			86	245	13,382	13,543	161
	V	E	81	729,646	642,931	748,366	105,435

Crop
Product
TSUSA commodity number, description, and unit of quantity

Country	Mode	Reg	Yr	Quantity	F.A.S.	C.I.F.	Charges
			82	2,936,986	1,909,597	2,220,116	310,519
			83	1,053,306	804,185	909,662	105,477
			84	2,133,139	1,290,648	1,505,536	214,888
			85	3,091,498	2,252,324	2,678,811	426,487
			86	4,287,146	2,460,693	2,932,378	471,685
	V	W	81	109,488	74,596	94,095	19,499
			82	159,170	96,016	113,736	17,720
			83	9,016	4,699	6,715	2,016
			84	224,734	133,839	164,763	30,924
			85	328,593	183,760	240,945	57,185
			86	96,909	63,180	75,939	12,759
SPAIN	A	E	83	909	15,430	17,505	2,075
			84	445	16,200	17,996	1,796
			85	2,672	13,361	14,853	1,492
	A	W	82	146	5,000	5,576	576
			84	1,146	19,940	23,004	3,064
			86	471	17,940	21,013	3,073
	N	E	85	140,708	123,383	142,803	19,420
	N	W	83	148,903	114,714	144,392	29,678
			84	167,608	113,686	152,471	38,785
			85	1,435	25,821	28,001	2,180
	O	W	81	5,089	3,000	3,808	808
	V	E	81	244,060	195,288	236,216	40,928
			82	257,229	189,217	228,380	39,163
			83	210,294	137,541	166,081	28,540
			84	309,973	177,863	228,509	50,646
			85	65,540	37,742	50,505	12,763
			86	239,678	206,873	237,258	30,385
	V	W	81	88,467	80,990	97,623	16,633
			82	77,179	68,125	83,757	15,632
			83	7,915	5,462	6,862	1,400
			84	5,352	10,662	14,535	3,873
			85	130,470	98,089	123,844	25,755
			86	133,405	112,744	141,908	29,164
SWITZLD	A	E	81	2	410	416	6
			83	906	274	930	656
	V	E	85	899	2,128	2,451	323
U KING	V	E	84	238	666	749	83
VENEZ	A	E	83	926	1,046	4,049	3,003
	V	E	84	1,862	2,598	3,007	409

Corn Mint

Corn mint, essential oil**
4522200 CORNMINT OIL & PEP OIL NSPF (LB)

Country	Mode	Reg	Yr	Quantity	F.A.S.	C.I.F.	Charges
TOTAL			81	548,678	1,930,390	2,031,270	100,880
			82	442,857	1,951,635	2,044,534	92,899
			83	649,329	2,883,558	2,997,953	114,395
			84	633,137	2,994,522	3,101,226	106,704
			85	291,773	1,468,764	1,530,848	62,084
			86	210,520	726,759	757,419	30,660
AUSTRAL	V	E	86	3,629	32,455	33,781	1,326
BELGIUM	V	E	84	3,157	539	990	451
BRAZIL	V	E	81	183,055	885,183	929,801	44,618
			82	231,516	1,220,957	1,280,861	59,904
			83	165,079	1,088,171	1,129,887	41,716
			84	283,943	1,493,141	1,545,884	52,743
			85	181,538	881,270	929,674	48,404
			86	54,012	218,682	231,326	12,644
	V	W	81	26,280	127,623	132,840	5,217
			82	15,078	82,240	85,837	3,597
			83	16,270	157,660	160,490	2,830
			85	3,968	14,250	14,902	652
CANADA	A	W	78	11	1,300	1,378	78
CHINA M	N	E	86	76,387	212,835	222,417	9,582
	V	E	81	89,507	253,693	267,738	14,045
			82	38,778	122,444	128,603	6,159
			83	310,263	907,847	955,405	47,558
			84	203,979	756,896	787,538	30,642
			85	54,398	277,026	282,024	4,998
	V	W	81	209,878	586,093	617,430	31,337
			82	92,412	258,148	272,867	14,719
			84	10,417	35,775	37,282	1,507
CHINA T	V	E	82	11,905	48,203	50,030	1,827
			83	86,506	433,621	446,798	13,177
			84	38,028	224,274	230,511	6,237
			85	9,921	59,539	61,083	1,544
			86	7,200	50,049	51,357	1,308
	V	W	83	1,984	7,963	8,285	322

Crop
Product
TSUSA commodity number, description, and unit of quantity

Country	Mode	Reg	Yr	Quantity	F.A.S.	C.I.F.	Charges
			84	397	3,114	3,239	125
FRANCE	N	E	82	7,562	4,751	5,436	685
			85	1,989	10,465	10,800	335
	V	E	81	5,952	4,553	4,901	348
			83	12,787	31,282	32,497	1,215
			84	5,361	6,454	6,663	209
			86	882	7,311	7,435	124
INDIA	V	E	85	15,873	54,628	56,901	2,273
INDNSIA	V	E	81	22,046	16,964	19,637	2,673
JAPAN	V	E	83	11,111	57,346	59,227	1,881
MADAGAS	V	E	84	22,311	40,061	43,228	3,167
N ZEAL	V	E	86	661	7,800	8,003	203
NETHLDS	V	E	81	55	425	447	22
			84	7,038	49,180	50,598	1,418
			85	2,205	15,560	16,242	682
			86	6,559	21,254	21,629	375
PARAGUA	V	E	85	365	1,530	1,600	70
			86	2,381	7,512	7,978	466
	V	W	81	7,143	36,306	37,991	1,685
SINGAPR	V	E	81	4,762	19,550	20,485	935
			82	21,841	99,460	101,925	2,465
			83	17,858	81,739	83,342	1,603
			84	31,747	206,167	210,033	3,866
	V	W	82	15,872	67,000	68,840	1,840
			83	15,874	70,182	71,110	928
			84	9,921	72,569	74,332	1,763
SPAIN	V	E	82	3,925	25,383	26,523	1,140
			83	11,597	47,747	50,912	3,165
			84	5,528	41,292	44,221	2,929
			85	1,323	9,336	9,741	405
			86	4,410	33,041	34,053	1,012
U KING	N	E	84	11,310	65,060	66,707	1,647
			86	54,388	134,520	138,062	3,542
	V	E	82	3,968	23,049	23,612	563
			85	12,477	109,272	111,353	2,081
	V	W	85	7,716	35,888	36,528	640

Cotton

Cotton, fiber, linters
3003000 COTTON LINTERS WH BLCH OR PURF (LB)

Country	Mode	Reg	Yr	Quantity	F.A.S.	C.I.F.	Charges
TOTAL			81	17,448,718	2,707,709	2,847,642	139,933
			82	10,973,942	1,722,894	1,840,061	117,167
			83	31,464,159	5,521,976	6,318,577	796,601
			84	63,060,550	12,824,697	14,846,153	2,021,456
			85	46,632,509	8,358,627	9,412,958	1,054,331
			86	79,397,344	5,432,949	6,612,893	1,179,944
ARGENT	V	E	84	3,079,055	655,819	803,626	147,807
AUSTRAL	V	E	83	2,222,587	206,871	292,271	85,400
			84	4,495,840	458,779	591,202	132,423
			85	4,162,064	445,592	597,160	151,568
BRAZIL	O	E	84	350,389	111,016	126,824	15,808
	V	E	81	242,610	32,750	46,866	14,116
			82	438,149	92,428	109,024	16,596
			83	14,635,784	1,546,082	2,164,976	618,894
			84	21,953,165	2,906,089	3,763,054	856,965
			85	18,665,516	1,619,067	1,979,271	360,204
			86	15,997,096	872,623	1,157,699	285,076
	V	W	84	348,707	60,079	79,007	18,928
CANADA	O	E	81	1,680	1,470	1,470	
			82	75	325	325	
			83	530	1,440	1,440	
			84	45,173	19,127	19,127	
			85	750	2,700	2,700	
			86	150	900	900	
	O	W	86	44,069	4,531	4,531	
CHINA M	O	E	84	351,102	123,055	123,055	
	V	E	81	2,447,041	398,611	507,326	108,715
			82	1,703,814	284,941	372,521	87,580
			83	1,406,892	319,793	361,642	41,849
			84	5,585,978	1,215,017	1,433,639	218,622
			85	47,907	8,398	13,579	5,181
			86	1,204,643	108,698	137,944	29,246
	V	W	82	389,851	97,365	110,356	12,991
			83	221,943	54,103	61,043	6,940
			86	528,222	79,714	105,528	25,814
CHINA T	O	E	84	43,823	15,361	15,361	
			85	50	907	907	
FR GERM	V	E	84	36,779	22,041	23,710	1,669

Crop Product TSUSA commodity number, description, and unit of quantity Country	Mode	Reg	Yr	Quantity	F.A.S.	C.I.F.	Charges
FRANCE	A	W	85	462	2,363	2,795	432
GUATMAL	V	E	84	330,669	59,520	79,550	20,030
			85	1,589,510	281,991	368,000	86,009
			86	333,215	38,986	51,272	12,286
	V	W	84	624,471	98,010	126,999	28,989
			85	299,850	53,973	72,319	18,346
INDIA	V	E	86	2,209,860	132,315	209,833	77,518
JAPAN	O	E	86	50	360	360	
	V	W	84	77	291	301	10
MEXICO	O	E	81	4,641,122	1,188,597	1,188,597	
			82	3,362,904	880,512	880,512	
			83	8,108,948	2,676,539	2,676,539	
			84	6,850,318	3,344,374	3,344,374	
			85	5,915,391	2,658,641	2,658,641	
			86	24,697,668	1,692,645	1,692,645	
	O	W	81	9,783,346	1,051,282	1,051,282	
			82	5,079,149	367,323	367,323	
			83	3,922,312	443,103	443,103	
			84	6,670,916	1,411,902	1,411,902	
			85	6,566,838	897,616	897,616	
			86	11,543,206	784,362	784,817	455
MOROC	O	E	86	500	720	720	
PAKISTN	V	E	85	20,031	13,449	15,949	2,500
	V	W	85	3,000	1,517	1,950	433
REP SAF	V	E	81	332,919	34,999	52,101	17,102
SALVADR	V	E	84	695,391	114,405	169,389	54,984
SUDAN	V	E	84	1,655,957	225,342	324,855	99,513
TURKEY	V	E	84	8,219,132	1,621,101	1,957,244	336,143
			85	4,263,717	874,649	1,154,395	279,746
			86	19,479,668	1,363,831	1,977,048	613,217
	V	W	84	386,041	54,283	81,554	27,271
U KING	A	E	84	891	565	1,011	446
	V	E	83	51,915	13,124	16,668	3,544
			84	219,759	72,520	81,883	9,363
			85	648,474	327,452	393,393	65,941
			86	83,835	51,823	62,751	10,928
	V	W	83	342,589	133,857	153,356	19,499
			84	74,218	17,556	22,598	5,042
USSR	O	E	83	550,659	127,064	147,539	20,475
VENEZ	V	E	84	1,042,699	218,445	265,888	47,443
			85	4,448,949	1,170,312	1,254,283	83,971
			86	3,275,162	301,441	426,845	125,404

Cotton, fiber, raw
3001020 RAW COT ROUGH STPL UN 3V4 IN (LB)

	Mode	Reg	Yr	Quantity	F.A.S.	C.I.F.	Charges
TOTAL			81	74,518	49,592	54,959	5,367
			82	16,464	9,055	10,869	1,814
			83	184,060	123,757	144,836	21,079
			84	125,983	76,603	91,600	14,997
			85	117,809	50,179	64,441	14,262
			86	169,453	98,396	116,600	18,204
BARBADO	V	E	86	2,099	1,000	2,319	1,319
CANADA	O	E	81	1,000	1,787	1,787	
CHINA M	V	E	85	40,749	5,372	9,359	3,987
	V	W	84	36,348	12,690	14,694	2,004
INDIA	V	E	82	8,640	4,732	5,443	711
			83	10,198	5,951	7,001	1,050
			84	50,243	36,175	44,368	8,193
PAKISTN	O	E	83	67,540	41,258	46,366	5,108
	V	E	82	7,824	4,323	5,426	1,103
			83	66,438	46,037	54,452	8,415
			84	39,392	27,738	32,538	4,800
			85	77,060	44,807	55,082	10,275
			86	167,354	97,396	114,281	16,885
SINGAPR	V	E	81	73,518	47,805	53,172	5,367
SUDAN	O	E	83	39,884	30,511	37,017	6,506

3001040 RAW COT NSPF STPL UN 1-1/8 (LB)

	Mode	Reg	Yr	Quantity	F.A.S.	C.I.F.	Charges
TOTAL			81	7,903,877	5,187,659	5,245,898	462,719
			82	13,302,443	7,318,480	7,318,480	
			83	1,111,561	662,323	725,990	63,667
			84	1,205,527	779,775	802,300	22,525
			85	17,818,355	9,294,248	9,372,958	78,710
			86	177,165	144,858	158,096	13,238
ARGENT	V	E	83	1,045	543	1,262	719
BRAZIL	A	E	86	140	276	395	119
CHINA M	V	E	86	31,588	13,063	17,133	4,070
	V	W	84	496	3,820	3,962	142
FRANCE	A	E	81	653	383	771	388
MEXICO	N	E	81	3,011,655	1,545,686	1,546,060	

	Mode	Reg	Yr	Quantity	F.A.S.	C.I.F.	Charges
	O	E	81	350,595	285,985	285,985	
			82	13,302,443	7,318,480	7,318,480	
			83	533,419	277,458	277,458	
			84	1,005,397	640,983	641,548	565
			85	11,397,403	6,162,227	6,222,795	60,568
			86	29,442	18,401	18,401	
	O	W	81	3,152,629	2,520,884	2,520,884	
			85	6,239,131	3,003,786	3,003,786	
	V	W	81	404,745	219,574	219,574	404,854
PAKISTN	A	E	84	500	400	1,664	1,264
	A	W	84	605	484	860	376
	N	E	83	187,091	116,069	133,791	17,722
	V	E	84	151,989	105,661	121,639	15,978
			85	181,821	128,235	146,377	18,142
			86	115,995	113,118	122,167	9,049
	V	W	81	19,683	13,146	15,574	2,428
SUDAN	O	E	83	174,690	133,638	162,132	28,494
	V	E	83	214,917	133,939	150,443	16,504
			84	46,540	28,427	32,627	4,200
SWITZLD	A	E	83	399	676	904	228
USSR	V	E	81	963,917	602,001	657,050	55,049

3001520 HAR COT ST 1-5/32 TO 1-3/8 INCH (LB)

	Mode	Reg	Yr	Quantity	F.A.S.	C.I.F.	Charges
TOTAL			81	10,654	9,993	10,786	793
			86	1,477,829	749,301	749,301	
MEXICO	O	E	86	1,477,829	749,301	749,301	
PERU	V	E	81	10,654	9,993	10,786	793

3001540 OTH COT ST 1-1/8 TO 1-3/8 INCH (LB)

	Mode	Reg	Yr	Quantity	F.A.S.	C.I.F.	Charges
TOTAL			82	36,586	32,837	35,490	2,653
			83	79,534	48,000	48,000	
			84	2,802,625	2,037,296	2,038,825	1,529
			85	3,649,466	1,933,489	2,008,562	75,073
			86	1,504,116	809,662	809,662	
EGYPT	V	E	82	3,937	3,583	3,752	169
MEXICO	O	E	83	79,534	48,000	48,000	
			84	2,802,625	2,037,296	2,038,825	1,529
			85	3,649,466	1,933,489	2,008,562	75,073
			86	1,504,116	809,662	809,662	
SUDAN	V	E	82	32,649	29,254	31,738	2,484

3001560 OT R COT ST 1-3/8 TO 1-11/16 IN (LB)

	Mode	Reg	Yr	Quantity	F.A.S.	C.I.F.	Charges
TOTAL			81	206,548	280,830	290,419	9,589
			82	2,004,105	1,798,396	1,912,900	114,504
			83	1,799,064	1,590,326	1,715,027	124,701
			84	563,618	689,432	726,501	37,069
			86	50,898	30,397	30,796	399
CANADA	O	E	82	2,760	5,794	5,794	
EGYPT	V	E	81	206,548	280,830	290,419	9,589
			82	977,986	855,662	899,647	43,985
			83	496,371	515,955	546,371	30,416
			84	356,524	502,870	525,330	22,460
GERM DR	V	E	82	177,713	198,321	206,938	8,617
ITALY	A	E	86	375	1,851	2,250	399
MEXICO	O	E	86	50,523	28,546	28,546	
	O	W	84	807	293	293	
PERU	V	E	82	388,279	370,869	396,410	25,541
SUDAN	O	E	84	844	687	687	
	V	E	82	457,367	367,750	404,111	36,361
			83	1,302,693	1,074,371	1,168,656	94,285
			84	205,443	185,582	200,191	14,609

3002000 RAW COT STP 1-11/16 IN OR MORE (LB)

	Mode	Reg	Yr	Quantity	F.A.S.	C.I.F.	Charges
TOTAL			82	3,921,971	3,973,595	4,144,225	170,630
			83	746,755	862,266	889,681	27,415
			84	1,059,917	1,502,341	1,566,502	64,161
			85	672,714	990,682	1,020,704	30,022
EGYPT	O	E	84	141,083	199,814	204,993	5,179
	V	E	82	2,507,992	2,644,222	2,723,850	79,628
			83	746,755	862,266	889,681	27,415
			84	918,834	1,302,527	1,361,509	58,982
			85	656,464	989,366	1,019,388	30,022
MEXICO	O	E	85	16,250	1,316	1,316	
PERU	V	E	82	1,413,979	1,329,373	1,420,375	91,002

Cotton, fiber, waste
3004010 OT S WSTE CD STPS UN 1-3/16 (LB)

	Mode	Reg	Yr	Quantity	F.A.S.	C.I.F.	Charges
TOTAL			81	79,396	6,580	6,580	

Crop
Product
TSUSA commodity number, description, and unit of quantity

Country	Mode	Reg	Yr	Quantity	F.A.S.	C.I.F.	Charges
			82	76,229	7,968	8,115	147
			84	1,082	908	908	
			86	266	1,338	1,338	
CANADA	O	E	81	79,396	6,580	6,580	
			82	75,695	7,521	7,521	
			84	1,082	908	908	
ITALY	A	E	86	266	1,338	1,338	
U KING	V	E	82	534	447	594	147

3004015 COT S WASTE CD ETC 1-3/16AOV (LB)

Country	Mode	Reg	Yr	Quantity	F.A.S.	C.I.F.	Charges
TOTAL			81	108,991	11,904	14,504	2,600
			83	90,602	11,800	15,000	3,200
			84	64,285	10,831	10,942	111
CANADA	O	E	81	30,991	4,559	4,559	
			83	15,466	2,321	2,321	
			84	25,999	4,242	4,242	
HG KONG	V	W	81	78,000	7,345	9,945	2,600
			83	75,136	9,479	12,679	3,200
			84	38,286	6,589	6,700	111

3004025 COT COMB WASTE STP U 1-3/16 (LB)

Country	Mode	Reg	Yr	Quantity	F.A.S.	C.I.F.	Charges
TOTAL			81	310,919	162,933	159,242	6,309
CANADA	O	E	81	193,319	103,778	93,778	
JAPAN	V	E	81	117,600	59,155	65,464	6,309

3004030 COT S WASTE C OTH 1-3/16AOV (LB)

Country	Mode	Reg	Yr	Quantity	F.A.S.	C.I.F.	Charges
TOTAL			81	131,628	65,897	70,118	4,221
CANADA	O	E	81	53,228	25,430	25,430	
JAPAN	V	E	81	78,400	40,467	44,688	4,221

3004035 COT S WASTE INCL LAP SL ROV (LB)

Country	Mode	Reg	Yr	Quantity	F.A.S.	C.I.F.	Charges
TOTAL			82	1,411	851	2,035	1,184
			84	39,496	6,261	7,915	1,654
			85	9,122	2,281	2,281	
CANADA	O	E	84	1,101	1,142	1,142	
			85	9,122	2,281	2,281	
CZECHO	V	E	82	1,411	851	2,035	1,184
HG KONG	V	W	84	38,395	5,119	6,773	1,654

3004060 COT WASTES, SOFT, NSPF (LB)

Country	Mode	Reg	Yr	Quantity	F.A.S.	C.I.F.	Charges
TOTAL			81	1,536,684	281,570	349,473	67,903
			82	916,657	96,405	128,329	31,924
			83	2,049,156	225,824	303,898	78,074
			84	3,809,840	537,673	838,036	300,363
			85	1,576,313	218,205	277,454	59,249
			86	1,113,363	100,704	138,705	38,001
AUSTRAL	V	E	85	82,692	26,213	27,796	1,583
BELGIUM	A	E	84	2	312	334	22
			85	40	255	255	
BRAZIL	V	E	81	322,978	31,893	45,395	13,502
			82	220,758	21,676	31,515	9,839
			83	707,138	82,036	113,192	31,156
			84	1,027,159	137,783	189,685	51,902
			85	596,957	46,316	69,468	23,152
			86	232,872	12,666	23,108	10,442
CANADA	O	E	82	67,229	8,219	8,219	
			83	199,158	11,909	11,909	
			84	129,673	15,022	15,022	
			85	112,135	24,666	24,666	
			86	134,832	16,582	16,582	
CHINA T	V	W	85	1,681	2,258	2,525	267
			86	154	806	896	90
FRANCE	A	E	85	251	287	644	357
			86	154	636	834	198
	V	E	81	1,763	968	1,024	56
			86	46,186	10,756	13,687	2,931
GUATMAL	V	E	81	570,266	176,866	209,562	32,696
			86	2,527	450	504	54
HG KONG	N	W	82	194,770	21,488	27,387	5,899
	V	E	81	278,165	29,302	39,889	10,587
			82	278,000	29,853	39,848	9,995
			83	333,800	37,433	49,830	12,397
			84	112,823	18,373	23,313	4,940
			85	200,448	35,984	46,190	10,206
			86	150,912	13,805	20,665	6,860
	V	H	82	77,900	7,438	10,769	3,331
			83	77,900	7,791	11,100	3,309
			84	116,900	13,639	20,830	7,191
			85	114,117	17,945	23,445	5,500
	V	W	81	271,000	23,797	34,224	10,427
			82	78,000	7,731	10,591	2,860
			83	661,750	74,031	101,862	27,831
			84	533,638	74,140	97,471	23,331
			85	464,315	63,084	81,055	17,971
			86	544,860	43,914	61,117	17,203
ISRAEL	V	E	85	3,118	756	848	92
JAPAN	A	E	84	20	380	896	516
	V	E	84	39,000	8,382	8,886	504
KOR REP	V	W	83	263	634	731	97
			85	559	441	562	121
			86	866	1,089	1,312	223
NETHLDS	V	E	84	23,038	5,225	7,573	2,348
SPAIN	V	E	81	5,512	4,410	5,045	635
SYRIA	V	E	84	1,747,035	247,119	452,586	205,467
TURKEY	V	E	84	4,028	2,457	2,918	461
U KING	V	E	83	69,147	11,990	15,274	3,284
			84	76,524	14,841	18,522	3,681
USSR	O	E	81	87,000	14,334	14,334	

3004070 COT HARD WASTE YARN & THRD WSTE (LB)

Country	Mode	Reg	Yr	Quantity	F.A.S.	C.I.F.	Charges
TOTAL			81	741,148	113,966	114,276	310
			82	482,363	103,770	105,240	1,470
			83	393,734	101,507	107,269	5,762
			84	321,248	72,666	72,666	
			85	159,126	47,067	51,331	4,264
			86	58,358	19,505	28,283	8,778
CANADA	O	E	81	737,945	112,835	112,835	
			82	478,428	96,292	96,292	
			83	351,860	89,358	89,935	577
			84	321,248	72,666	72,666	
			85	83,412	26,648	26,648	
CHINA T	V	W	82	3,935	7,478	8,948	1,470
			83	16,762	8,134	10,802	2,668
HG KONG	V	E	85	36,137	7,024	8,852	1,828
INDIA	V	W	81	3,203	1,131	1,441	310
			83	3,086	1,234	1,636	402
JAPAN	V	E	86	56,639	17,996	26,334	8,338
KOR REP	V	W	86	1,499	1,089	1,329	240
PAKISTN	V	E	85	39,577	13,395	15,831	2,436
PERU	V	W	86	220	420	620	200
TURKEY	V	W	83	22,026	2,781	4,896	2,115

3004500 COT WASTE ADV ETC UN 1-1/8 (LB)

Country	Mode	Reg	Yr	Quantity	F.A.S.	C.I.F.	Charges
TOTAL			81	261,277	73,891	85,326	11,435
			82	500,573	218,847	232,747	13,900
			83	656,697	183,153	188,665	5,512
			84	521,608	185,494	207,595	22,101
			85	282,058	227,317	252,696	25,379
			86	1,921,579	356,036	406,161	50,125
AUSTRAL	V	E	86	1,169,646	233,929	272,153	38,224
	V	W	86	676,197	75,383	79,905	4,522
BRAZIL	V	E	84	450	342	817	475
CANADA	O	E	81	529	1,058	1,211	153
			82	250,814	28,690	28,690	
			83	563,083	62,776	62,776	
			84	215,011	29,243	29,243	
			85	4,266	1,644	1,644	
CHINA M	N	E	81	179,684	39,895	46,706	6,811
FR GERM	A	E	83	23	279	371	92
FRANCE	A	E	85	547	1,569	2,195	626
HG KONG	V	E	84	174,852	66,554	78,760	12,206
	V	W	81	35,376	16,327	18,468	2,141
ITALY	V	E	81	88	432	448	16
			82	19,091	100,913	103,896	2,983
			83	16,429	84,754	87,574	2,820
			86	20	534	600	66
JAPAN	V	E	81	45,600	16,179	18,493	2,314
			82	192,000	71,825	80,886	9,061
			84	77,162	34,780	38,754	3,974
			86	38,581	16,391	18,190	1,799
	V	W	82	38,400	15,880	17,280	1,400
			83	77,162	35,344	37,944	2,600
SWITZLD	A	E	85	83	305	405	100
			86	3	375	380	5
U KING	A	E	82	268	1,539	1,995	456
	O	E	85	82,525	73,635	78,654	5,019
	V	E	84	54,133	54,575	60,021	5,446
			85	194,637	150,164	169,798	19,634
			86	37,132	29,424	34,933	5,509

Crop Product TSUSA commodity number, description, and unit of quantity Country	Mode	Reg	Yr	Quantity	F.A.S.	C.I.F.	Charges

3005000 COT WASTE ADV ETC 1-1/8 AOV (LB)

Country	Mode	Reg	Yr	Quantity	F.A.S.	C.I.F.	Charges
TOTAL			82	670	606	848	242
			83	727	1,203	1,986	783
			84	185	1,196	1,292	96
			85	2,561	7,138	9,372	2,234
			86	1,750	8,770	11,139	2,369
CANADA	O	E	84	185	1,196	1,292	96
			85	1,454	5,025	6,489	1,464
FR GERM	A	E	86	659	2,510	4,551	2,041
JAPAN	A	E	85	168	1,470	2,071	601
	V	W	85	650	295	354	59
PAKISTN	V	W	83	22	339	475	136
SWITZLD	A	E	83	705	864	1,511	647
	V	E	82	670	606	848	242
U KING	A	E	85	289	348	458	110
	V	E	86	1,091	6,260	6,588	328

Cottonseed
1751500 COTTONSEED (LB)

Country	Mode	Reg	Yr	Quantity	F.A.S.	C.I.F.	Charges
TOTAL			81	349,980	26,250	30,275	4,025
			82	189,731	19,338	19,338	
			83	100,780	14,630	14,630	
			84	86,349	9,825	9,825	
			85	4,425,670	230,245	398,741	168,496
			86	3,618,073	189,343	324,473	135,130
AUSTRAL	V	H	85	4,380,518	225,328	393,824	168,496
			86	3,458,069	177,462	312,592	135,130
CANADA	O	E	82	189,731	19,338	19,338	
			83	100,780	14,630	14,630	
			84	86,349	9,825	9,825	
			85	45,152	4,917	4,917	
			86	160,004	11,881	11,881	
HAITI	V	E	81	349,980	26,250	30,275	4,025

Cottonseed, oil cake and oil-cake meal**
1845200 SOYA,COTTONSD OIL CAKE/MEAL (LB)

Country	Mode	Reg	Yr	Quantity	F.A.S.	C.I.F.	Charges
TOTAL			81	16,547,218	1,239,646	1,649,871	410,225
			82	66,480,241	5,119,688	5,645,623	525,935
			83	67,106,611	4,985,083	5,393,616	408,533
			84	10,210,375	819,835	1,072,316	252,481
			85	16,971,831	943,820	1,269,703	325,883
			86	32,828,357	2,079,646	2,791,772	712,126
ARGENT	V	E	82	5,490,115	476,544	537,053	60,509
AUSTRAL	V	H	82	394,688	28,839	45,981	17,142
			83	2,692,151	178,447	284,484	106,037
			84	5,454,954	362,251	566,100	203,849
			85	6,778,816	329,415	536,235	206,820
			86	19,265,110	1,080,837	1,715,357	634,520
	V	W	84	400,580	37,254	52,254	15,000
BRAZIL	A	E	84	4,409	1,200	5,209	4,009
	V	E	85	4,391,103	244,908	288,298	43,390
CANADA	O	E	81	1,304,291	121,429	121,429	
			82	21,449,353	1,888,084	1,888,084	
			83	30,844,126	3,062,148	3,062,148	
			84	3,298,523	331,686	331,686	
			85	360,936	32,256	32,256	
			86	4,280,641	363,283	363,283	
	O	W	81	48,832	3,237	3,237	
			84	37,562	3,755	3,755	
			85	55,900	5,590	5,590	
			86	32,980	3,298	3,298	
HAITI	V	E	82	38,637,383	2,572,138	2,984,284	412,146
			83	33,301,703	1,679,837	1,970,653	290,816
			84	977,621	63,384	89,287	25,903
			85	5,137,931	256,361	309,963	53,602
			86	663,151	34,216	37,600	3,384
INDNSIA	V	W	83	892	1,175	1,371	196
ISRAEL	V	E	85	163,471	33,671	44,044	10,373
			86	32,959	6,008	7,758	1,750
JAMAICA	V	E	86	8,524,780	575,300	643,055	67,755
JAPAN	A	E	83	880	2,193	3,182	989
	V	E	82	328,492	91,948	112,800	20,852
			83	74,691	20,296	25,011	4,715
			84	2,315	829	867	38
			85	4,713	3,600	4,669	1,069
	V	W	82	4,317	3,254	3,654	400

Country	Mode	Reg	Yr	Quantity	F.A.S.	C.I.F.	Charges
			83	5,857	4,664	5,226	562
			84	9,411	5,402	5,908	506
			85	511	1,359	1,438	79
KOR REP	V	W	82	800	424	454	30
MEXICO	O	E	83	121,936	14,505	14,505	
SALVADR	V	E	81	14,770,975	1,076,900	1,478,900	402,000
T PAC I	V	H	81	423,120	38,080	46,305	8,225
U KING	A	E	86	2,170	3,400	4,532	1,132
	O	E	84	25,000	14,074	17,250	3,176
			85	78,450	36,660	47,210	10,550
			86	26,566	13,304	16,889	3,585
	V	E	82	175,093	58,457	73,313	14,856
			83	64,375	21,818	27,036	5,218

Cottonseed, vegetable oil
1761800 COTTONSEED OIL (LB)

Country	Mode	Reg	Yr	Quantity	F.A.S.	C.I.F.	Charges
TOTAL			81	93,302	14,512	14,593	81
			83	20,000,990	4,554,370	4,765,766	211,396
			85	97,567	9,458	9,458	
			86	403,448	35,465	35,560	95
BRAZIL	O	E	83	20,000,990	4,554,370	4,765,766	211,396
CANADA	O	E	81	92,690	13,931	13,931	
			85	97,567	9,458	9,458	
			86	40:,861	32,753	32,753	
JAPAN	V	E	81	612	581	662	81
	V	W	86	1,587	2,712	2,807	95

Cowberry

Lingonberry, fresh or in brine**
1465200 LINGON OR PARTRIDGE BERRIES (LB)

Country	Mode	Reg	Yr	Quantity	F.A.S.	C.I.F.	Charges
TOTAL			81	19,528	19,988	21,690	1,702
			82	595	1,069	1,386	317
			83	7,904	12,354	13,468	1,114
			84	43,086	35,222	39,918	4,696
			85	66,849	100,712	113,034	12,322
			86	3,547	8,890	10,293	1,403
DENMARK	V	W	85	1,530	2,534	2,811	277
FR GERM	A	E	82	595	1,069	1,386	317
FRANCE	V	E	86	330	1,143	1,301	158
HUNGARY	V	E	84	5,291	1,752	2,340	588
N ZEAL	A	H	86	554	1,627	2,380	753
	A	W	84	134	646	894	248
			85	3,597	13,357	17,943	4,586
			86	32	1,128	1,154	26
SWEDEN	A	E	84	11,253	1,772	2,642	870
	V	E	81	19,528	19,988	21,690	1,702
			83	2,078	2,598	2,794	196
			85	22,648	31,309	34,218	2,909
	V	W	83	5,207	8,928	9,729	801
			84	15,728	24,076	26,076	2,000
			85	39,074	53,512	58,062	4,550
			86	2,631	4,992	5,458	466
THAILND	V	E	83	619	828	945	117
			84	10,680	6,976	7,966	990

Lingonberry, frozen**
1466900 BLACK CURRANTS, ETC, FROZEN (LB)

Country	Mode	Reg	Yr	Quantity	F.A.S.	C.I.F.	Charges
TOTAL			81	37,561	53,709	53,954	245
			82	24,724	32,367	33,292	925
			83	22,350	37,011	38,491	1,480
			84	75,176	34,084	40,833	6,749
			85	98,463	82,267	87,038	4,771
			86	89,010	57,102	64,356	7,254
CANADA	O	E	81	37,340	53,320	53,320	
			82	12,950	20,749	20,749	
			83	14,475	27,307	27,307	
			84	2,500	4,000	4,000	
			85	57,500	62,400	62,400	
			86	11,960	10,338	10,338	
	O	W	84	6,000	6,377	6,377	
			86	2,000	1,400	1,400	
FRANCE	A	E	84	551	698	1,311	613
	V	E	86	8,810	11,881	13,094	1,213

Crop
Product
TSUSA commodity number, description, and unit of quantity

Country	Mode	Reg	Yr	Quantity	F.A.S.	C.I.F.	Charges
	V	W	86	1,109	1,323	1,341	18
IRELAND	V	E	82	11,436	11,191	11,949	758
N ZEAL	A	W	81	221	389	634	245
			82	338	427	594	167
			83	432	588	1,236	648
	V	E	84	35,450	13,444	16,671	3,227
	V	W	84	30,422	9,204	12,059	2,855
			85	24,886	10,040	12,548	2,508
			86	32,055	14,177	17,954	3,777
POLAND	V	E	85	9,904	3,640	4,747	1,107
SWEDEN	N	W	85	6,173	6,187	7,343	1,156
	V	E	83	3,978	5,785	6,394	609
	V	W	86	33,076	17,983	20,229	2,246
U KING	V	E	83	3,465	3,331	3,554	223
	V	W	84	253	361	415	54

Lingonberry, prepared or preserved**
1468200 BLACK CURRNT ETC PREP, PRES (LB)

Country	Mode	Reg	Yr	Quantity	F.A.S.	C.I.F.	Charges
TOTAL			81	387,348	433,755	478,697	44,942
			82	511,844	627,883	680,049	52,166
			83	634,470	696,322	761,382	65,060
			84	730,582	803,789	884,377	80,588
			85	714,017	714,249	788,306	74,057
			86	582,887	708,533	776,710	68,177
AUSTRIA	V	E	82	488	1,551	1,610	59
			83	390	1,002	1,075	73
			84	755	1,513	1,697	184
BELGIUM	V	E	83	48,846	12,648	13,650	1,002
			84	5,904	2,828	3,317	489
			85	2,715	1,514	1,735	221
	V	W	83	2,106	1,376	1,546	170
			84	2,106	1,376	1,616	240
CANADA	O	W	81	8,456	6,642	6,642	
			82	6,979	5,709	5,709	
			83	5,280	4,164	4,654	490
			84	2,900	3,210	3,210	
			85	1,600	1,224	1,224	
	V	E	83	3,415	4,716	5,075	359
CHILE	V	E	85	49,008	6,270	10,506	4,236
CHINA M	V	E	83	1,575	708	898	190
CHINA T	V	W	81	3,000	1,850	1,962	112
			82	450	300	323	23
DENMARK	V	E	86	14,515	24,733	26,144	1,411
	V	W	86	426	1,155	1,195	40
ECUADOR	A	E	83	10,020	3,914	5,232	1,318
FR GERM	O	E	85	3,600	1,321	1,736	415
			86	1,725	1,054	1,199	145
	V	E	81	15,012	25,216	26,545	1,329
			82	7,858	10,335	10,941	606
			83	47,118	38,599	42,318	3,719
			84	52,216	64,698	69,082	4,384
			85	31,102	29,767	31,850	2,083
			86	27,462	36,654	40,069	3,415
	V	W	83	1,512	1,452	1,711	259
FRANCE	A	E	84	2,877	3,838	5,001	1,163
	N	E	82	972	1,975	2,223	248
			83	13,374	18,756	20,547	1,791
	O	E	81	535	847	893	46
			83	334	268	295	27
			84	589	393	465	72
			86	4,704	4,003	4,245	242
	V	E	81	2,875	4,215	4,524	309
			82	2,789	4,638	4,947	309
			83	487	664	701	37
			84	5,688	7,483	8,355	872
			86	27,371	32,535	36,927	4,392
	V	W	81	2,638	4,244	4,697	453
			82	3,371	5,160	5,366	206
			83	5,653	6,452	7,282	830
			84	11,920	12,739	13,784	1,045
HUNGARY	V	E	82	1,080	3,885	4,860	975
			84	21,585	6,432	9,259	2,827
			85	12,493	5,829	6,520	691
			86	6,643	1,539	2,136	597
	V	W	85	7,200	2,467	3,129	662
			86	14,400	3,681	5,279	1,598
INDIA	A	E	86	16,590	11,000	12,489	1,489
	V	E	83	529	373	1,136	763
	V	W	83	952	845	960	115
IRELAND	V	E	81	304	345	374	29
			82	257	358	363	5

Crop
Product
TSUSA commodity number, description, and unit of quantity

Country	Mode	Reg	Yr	Quantity	F.A.S.	C.I.F.	Charges
JAMAICA	A	E	82	1,025	513	813	300
MEXICO	O	E	84	4,519	990	990	
N ZEAL	A	W	81	179	277	382	105
			83	709	1,731	2,621	890
			84	252	540	738	198
			85	506	1,410	1,580	170
	V	E	85	25,860	9,814	13,447	3,633
NETHLDS	V	E	82	1,830	1,498	1,569	71
			85	3,600	2,698	3,122	424
NORWAY	V	E	83	1,076	5,042	5,524	482
POLAND	O	E	82	3,715	1,365	1,733	368
	V	E	81	81,654	27,006	35,825	8,819
			82	40,296	15,640	19,031	3,391
			83	61,854	23,640	28,292	4,652
			84	19,031	6,870	8,416	1,546
			85	56,537	19,373	24,449	5,076
			86	26,900	8,700	10,497	1,797
ROMANIA	V	E	84	8,948	5,179	5,732	553
			85	8,069	4,127	4,639	512
SWEDEN	A	E	86	1,628	6,255	9,132	2,877
	N	E	85	45,678	64,974	72,000	7,026
			86	122,984	177,034	190,086	13,052
	O	E	81	26,475	32,771	35,805	3,034
			82	18,200	43,791	46,584	2,793
			83	17,928	29,940	32,649	2,709
			84	42,434	71,626	76,621	4,995
	O	W	86	15,181	18,406	18,406	
	V	E	81	132,097	181,903	199,269	17,366
			82	285,818	369,373	397,844	28,471
			83	235,341	347,591	372,458	24,867
			84	189,552	253,916	276,693	22,777
			85	310,912	396,650	426,301	29,651
			86	177,702	205,368	224,289	18,921
	V	W	81	57,373	71,375	78,247	6,872
			82	47,282	60,494	66,470	5,976
			83	28,142	41,769	46,505	4,736
			84	41,285	52,023	58,845	6,822
			85	25,951	31,131	35,591	4,460
			86	28,679	41,067	45,106	4,039
SWITZLD	O	E	84	41,739	73,353	80,795	7,442
	V	E	83	6,209	10,910	11,820	910
			84	19,985	29,976	32,615	2,639
	V	W	84	476	553	591	38
THAILND	V	E	81	600	495	555	60
			82	600	522	651	129
			83	2,200	1,890	2,208	318
	V	W	83	13,452	11,804	12,472	668
			85	2,400	1,345	1,468	123
U KING	N	E	81	48,504	63,672	68,707	5,035
			82	24,012	30,638	33,295	2,657
	O	E	81	5,811	8,666	9,591	925
			82	1,458	2,051	2,276	225
			83	12,477	15,248	16,812	1,564
			84	54,428	45,494	47,621	2,127
			85	27,284	54,468	57,242	2,774
			86	24,053	47,431	49,835	2,404
	V	E	81	735	990	1,157	167
			82	62,741	66,817	72,055	5,238
			83	112,782	109,605	121,619	12,014
			84	149,399	137,817	151,298	13,481
			85	65,537	64,357	72,354	7,997
			86	71,924	87,918	99,676	11,758
	V	W	81	1,100	3,241	3,522	281
			82	623	1,270	1,386	116
			83	709	1,215	1,322	107
			84	6,418	2,644	3,093	449
			85	881	2,802	3,205	403
USSR	V	E	84	45,576	18,298	24,543	6,245
			85	33,084	12,708	16,208	3,500

Cowpea

Cowpea, dried
1402500 COWPEAS, BLACK-EYE, DRIED ETC (LB)

Country	Mode	Reg	Yr	Quantity	F.A.S.	C.I.F.	Charges
TOTAL			81	1,903	1,079	1,460	381
			83	4,090	1,645	1,650	5
			84	7,453	4,014	4,410	396
			85	4,594	4,113	4,744	631
			86	172,040	11,049	11,369	320

Crop Product TSUSA commodity number, description, and unit of quantity Country	Mode	Reg	Yr	Quantity	F.A.S.	C.I.F.	Charges
AUSTRAL	O	E	84	2,183	709	809	100
CANADA	O	E	81	800	310	620	310
			83	3,000	1,290	1,290	
JAPAN	V	E	84	726	1,298	1,390	92
KENYA	O	E	84	1,587	827	889	62
MALAWI	O	E	84	2,205	750	822	72
MEXICO	O	W	86	165,440	8,772	8,772	
PERU	O	E	83	1,090	355	360	5
	V	E	86	6,600	2,277	2,597	320
THAILND	V	E	85	4,594	4,113	4,744	631
U KING	O	E	81	1,103	769	840	71
			84	752	430	500	70

1402600 COWPEAS, EXCEPT BLACKEYE DRD (LB)

Country	Mode	Reg	Yr	Quantity	F.A.S.	C.I.F.	Charges
TOTAL			81	263,108	77,865	79,147	1,282
			82	23,177	7,684	9,286	1,602
			83	256,540	23,460	24,178	718
			84	124,208	20,033	21,044	1,011
			85	356,832	42,130	44,888	2,758
			86	45,300	5,437	7,350	1,913
AUSTRAL	V	E	83	8,818	2,204	2,605	401
			84	948	291	403	112
			86	45,300	5,437	7,350	1,913
	V	W	85	46,826	8,064	10,699	2,635
CANADA	O	E	84	600	432	432	
CHINA M	V	E	83	1,750	1,680	1,974	294
	V	W	81	4,900	1,198	1,274	76
GUATMAL	N	E	82	12,561	2,621	3,810	1,189
INDIA	O	E	81	4,459	5,218	5,523	305
JAPAN	O	E	81	2,778	4,151	4,414	263
			82	1,125	1,887	2,108	221
	V	E	81	6,478	9,439	10,077	638
			82	1,091	2,336	2,528	192
			84	1,720	3,003	3,217	214
			85	660	1,006	1,129	123
KENYA	O	E	83	1,323	309	332	23
			84	2,535	857	954	97
MEXICO	O	E	81	244,493	57,859	57,859	
			82	8,400	840	840	
			83	244,649	19,267	19,267	
			84	106,200	12,000	12,000	
			85	309,346	33,060	33,060	
PERU	V	E	84	10,000	2,850	3,370	520
TURKEY	O	E	84	2,205	600	668	68

Cowpea, fresh or frozen
1358000 COWPEAS, BLACKEYE FRSH, FRZN (LB)

Country	Mode	Reg	Yr	Quantity	F.A.S.	C.I.F.	Charges
TOTAL			81	541,237	266,104	319,013	52,909
			82	385,969	193,944	225,524	31,580
			83	81,110	13,856	20,695	6,839
			84	208,480	44,198	55,130	10,932
			85	261,107	110,801	119,410	8,609
			86	126,660	40,783	48,186	7,403
DOM REP	A	E	83	2,310	630	869	239
	V	E	82	43,970	17,533	20,061	2,528
GUATMAL	V	E	86	42,825	12,933	16,451	3,518
INDIA	V	E	85	28,779	11,812	15,396	3,584
MEXICO	O	E	81	2,360	307	307	
			83	6,800	816	816	
			84	80,000	20,328	20,328	
			85	79,500	8,845	8,845	
			86	46,335	5,560	5,560	
NICARAG	V	E	81	515,984	255,514	306,691	51,177
			82	36,000	13,320	16,543	3,223
	V	W	81	22,893	10,283	12,015	1,732
			82	305,999	163,091	188,920	25,829
			83	72,000	12,410	19,010	6,600
PANAMA	A	E	84	2,480	350	650	300
SALVADR	V	E	84	126,000	23,520	34,152	10,632
			85	42,000	11,812	14,700	2,888
	V	W	86	37,500	22,290	26,175	3,885
THAILND	V	E	85	110,828	78,332	80,469	2,137

1358100 COWPEAS, FRES, FROZEN, NSPF (LB)

Country	Mode	Reg	Yr	Quantity	F.A.S.	C.I.F.	Charges
TOTAL			81	2,119,335	270,238	279,624	9,386
			82	3,701,924	414,515	414,762	247
			83	6,689,829	731,791	732,273	482
			84	6,485,883	671,442	671,442	
			85	3,213,557	394,349	402,498	8,149
			86	1,665,251	202,320	208,387	6,067
CANADA	O	E	83	25,310	3,927	3,927	
			84	9,900	1,348	1,348	
DOM REP	V	E	83	2,400	1,200	1,520	320
			85	74,400	30,063	31,099	1,036
GUATMAL	A	E	85	15,628	3,135	6,023	2,888
			86	21,438	5,778	10,028	4,250
	A	W	81	36,645	36,421	45,807	9,386
			82	1,000	453	700	247
			83	480	480	642	162
GUYANA	A	E	86	3,833	1,080	2,058	978
INDIA	V	W	85	24,339	10,452	12,726	2,274
MEXICO	O	E	81	2,082,690	233,817	233,817	
			82	3,650,524	408,518	408,518	
			83	6,661,639	726,184	726,184	
			84	6,472,503	669,746	669,746	
			85	3,065,440	341,774	341,774	
			86	1,637,034	191,954	191,954	
	O	W	82	50,400	5,544	5,544	
			84	3,480	348	348	
NETHLDS	V	E	85	33,750	8,925	10,876	1,951
U KING	V	W	86	2,946	3,508	4,347	839

Cowpea, in brine or pickled
1414000 COWPEAS,BLCKEYE,SALTD,PICKLD (LB)

Country	Mode	Reg	Yr	Quantity	F.A.S.	C.I.F.	Charges
TOTAL			81	15,730	7,503	10,083	2,580
			82	33,914	18,914	21,643	2,729
			83	4,086	2,009	2,158	149
			84	630	390	610	220
			85	26,243	13,314	15,628	2,314
			86	55,116	29,998	32,984	2,986
CHINA T	A	W	83	1,000	644	708	64
COLOMB	V	E	86	7,680	5,478	5,892	414
FR GERM	V	E	86	1,368	1,721	1,847	126
INDIA	O	E	81	1,974	1,294	2,588	1,294
			82	22,222	9,962	11,836	1,874
			85	25,185	11,285	13,328	2,043
			86	5,210	7,394	7,394	
	V	E	81	13,756	6,209	7,495	1,286
			85	1,058	2,029	2,300	271
			86	12,694	5,602	6,600	998
	V	W	82	2,116	948	1,124	176
			86	28,164	9,803	11,251	1,448
JAPAN	V	W	83	3,086	1,365	1,450	85
PORTUGL	V	E	82	2,100	879	1,007	128
SALVADR	A	E	84	630	390	610	220
SPAIN	V	E	82	7,327	5,633	6,163	530
U KING	O	E	82	149	1,492	1,513	21

Cranberry

Cranberry, frozen
1467100 CRANBERRIES, FROZEN (LB)

Country	Mode	Reg	Yr	Quantity	F.A.S.	C.I.F.	Charges
TOTAL			82	2,130	2,394	2,394	
			85	9,409	6,739	6,848	109
			86	76,850	55,178	56,501	1,323
CANADA	O	E	82	2,130	2,394	2,394	
	O	W	85	7,980	5,378	5,378	
			86	63,800	43,511	43,511	
	V	E	86	11,948	9,975	11,115	1,140
FRANCE	V	E	86	1,102	1,692	1,875	183
SWEDEN	V	W	85	1,429	1,361	1,470	109

Cranberry, prepared or preserved
1468300 CRANBERRIES PREP, PRES NSPF (LB)

Country	Mode	Reg	Yr	Quantity	F.A.S.	C.I.F.	Charges
TOTAL			82	2,061	1,840	1,901	61
			83	5,759	3,916	4,294	378
			84	6,390	6,671	7,551	880
			85	11,318	12,937	14,667	1,730
			86	1,290	2,102	2,207	105
BELGIUM	V	E	84	932	1,094	1,204	110
			85	5,063	5,665	6,729	1,064
CANADA	O	W	82	1,800	1,350	1,350	
CHINA T	V	W	83	4,500	2,200	2,460	260

Crop Product TSUSA commodity number, description, and unit of quantity Country	Mode	Reg	Yr	Quantity	F.A.S.	C.I.F.	Charges
			84	157	370	405	35
FR GERM	O	E	82	261	490	551	61
	V	E	83	990	1,414	1,516	102
			84	4,034	4,627	5,274	647
			85	2,197	1,682	1,984	302
ITALY	V	E	84	1,267	580	668	88
JAPAN	V	E	85	1,341	1,191	1,351	160
U KING	O	E	85	2,717	4,399	4,603	204
			86	1,290	2,102	2,207	105
	V	E	83	269	302	318	16

Crocus

Crocus, corms
1252000 CROCUS CORMS (NO)

Country	Mode	Reg	Yr	Quantity	F.A.S.	C.I.F.	Charges
TOTAL			81	46,294,132	2,320,802	2,453,582	133,686
			82	51,572,252	2,308,030	2,467,530	159,500
			83	59,974,825	2,271,253	2,435,652	164,399
			84	66,067,390	2,346,531	2,547,325	200,794
			85	74,441,586	2,204,084	2,412,722	208,638
			86	71,270,268	2,673,901	2,918,635	244,734
ALBANIA	V	E	85	84,000	3,429	3,842	413
BELGIUM	V	E	83	62,949	4,918	5,065	147
			86	329,700	44,331	47,090	2,759
FR GERM	V	E	81	6,425	485	510	25
			85	447,145	12,969	15,462	2,493
FRANCE	V	E	81	35,500	1,495	1,556	61
			84	27,063	818	899	81
ISRAEL	V	E	81	561,319	31,516	33,063	1,547
			82	751,715	23,277	24,779	1,502
			83	580,066	35,160	38,781	3,621
			84	718,500	21,507	23,751	2,244
			85	677,487	30,102	31,718	1,616
			86	58,392	2,443	2,620	177
	V	W	84	46,244	1,979	2,082	103
ITALY	V	E	86	19,000	1,104	1,309	205
JAPAN	N	W	82	18	700	774	74
			84	24	789	912	123
	O	W	83	28	940	1,064	124
	V	W	81	149,000	5,622	5,962	569
			86	536,000	47,605	54,177	6,572
MALI	N	E	86	10	2,245	2,535	290
	V	E	85	57,150	1,586	1,766	180
NETHLDS	A	E	81	52,500	3,478	4,421	943
			82	27,026	2,206	2,682	476
			83	52,282	1,934	2,377	443
			84	54,985	1,333	1,880	547
			85	44,600	1,934	2,999	1,065
			86	87,600	5,780	6,942	1,162
	A	W	84	28,000	1,084	1,854	770
	N	E	81	35,546,961	1,770,131	1,862,719	93,265
			82	36,885,777	1,669,175	1,771,437	102,262
			83	41,119,675	1,586,382	1,693,890	107,508
			84	46,939,909	1,713,534	1,844,951	131,417
			85	57,869,788	1,663,426	1,811,114	147,688
			86	53,598,707	2,007,668	2,181,044	173,376
	N	W	82	911,977	35,332	45,730	10,398
			83	1,438,467	62,021	69,192	7,171
			84	1,562,524	67,552	80,329	12,777
			85	1,520,506	68,936	78,032	9,096
			86	380,807	17,730	20,540	2,810
	O	E	81	4,600	274	274	
			82	4,605	259	263	4
			85	55	1,163	1,163	
			86	35,700	2,120	2,120	
	V	E	81	7,444,648	369,304	391,844	22,540
			82	11,578,350	505,482	542,331	36,849
			83	15,947,275	551,143	594,352	43,209
			84	16,446,742	529,843	581,076	51,233
			85	13,473,905	410,794	454,985	44,191
			86	14,633,267	458,568	503,941	45,373
	V	W	81	2,424,589	135,559	150,133	14,574
			82	1,059,449	58,167	64,419	6,252
			83	348,924	12,589	13,789	1,200
			84	243,399	8,092	9,591	1,499
			85	266,950	9,745	11,641	1,896
			86	1,237,085	73,515	80,334	6,819
REP SAF	V	E	83	167,159	9,450	9,874	424
U KING	A	W	82	82,000	2,730	3,782	1,052

Country	Mode	Reg	Yr	Quantity	F.A.S.	C.I.F.	Charges
	V	E	81	46,000	1,545	1,651	106
			82	240,000	9,222	9,761	539
			83	258,000	6,716	7,268	552
			86	354,000	10,792	15,983	5,191
	V	W	81	22,590	1,393	1,449	56
YEMAN S	V	E	82	31,335	1,480	1,572	92

Croton

Croton, vegetable oil
1762000 CROTON OIL (LB)

Country	Mode	Reg	Yr	Quantity	F.A.S.	C.I.F.	Charges
TOTAL			81	37,468	24,539	26,943	2,404
			82	12,285	17,717	19,285	1,568
			83	121,670	63,466	72,117	8,651
			84	97,252	111,439	117,149	5,710
			85	46,026	26,857	30,711	3,854
			86	119,405	110,635	152,113	41,478
BELGIUM	A	E	81	22	646	661	15
			83	22	1,075	1,095	20
FR GERM	A	E	82	173	3,306	3,746	440
			83	53	1,227	1,484	257
			84	110	1,833	2,079	246
			85	110	1,994	2,136	142
	A	W	83	99	1,776	2,053	277
	O	W	82	22	391	448	57
	V	W	85	220	4,105	4,371	266
FRANCE	A	E	81	69	457	480	23
	V	E	86	2,486	5,407	5,566	159
GREECE	V	E	83	5,644	4,000	4,800	800
INDNSIA	V	W	86	116,919	105,228	146,547	41,319
ITALY	O	W	82	218	364	387	23
	V	E	85	41,887	18,050	21,295	3,245
NETHLDS	A	E	83	22	1,100	1,131	31
	V	E	84	42,784	33,080	35,044	1,964
			85	3,809	2,708	2,909	201
SPAIN	O	E	84	54,358	76,526	80,026	3,500
	V	E	81	37,377	23,436	25,802	2,366
			82	11,872	13,656	14,704	1,048
			83	115,830	54,288	61,554	7,266

Cucumber

Cucumber, fresh or frozen
1359000 CUCUMBERS FRSH CHILLED O FRZ (LB)

Country	Mode	Reg	Yr	Quantity	F.A.S.	C.I.F.	Charges
TOTAL			81	374,641,733	56,522,638	56,973,039	449,401
			82	234,641,478	45,515,284	45,807,549	292,265
			83	239,669,042	30,860,549	31,094,952	234,403
			84	253,955,758	30,804,736	31,338,550	533,814
			85	269,728,235	58,106,437	59,108,483	1,002,046
			86	288,057,615	41,831,405	42,605,331	773,926
ANTIGUA	V	E	85	25,200	3,780	5,460	1,680
			86	220,879	30,751	48,236	17,485
AUSTRIA	A	E	86	1,786	1,310	1,875	565
BAHAMAS	A	E	85	44,400	3,161	5,325	2,164
	N	E	81	9,249,340	520,250	644,241	123,991
			82	14,311,289	624,585	790,011	165,426
			84	11,879,119	501,108	639,216	138,108
	V	E	81	9,338,162	582,323	699,518	117,195
			82	960,479	58,350	70,857	12,507
			83	12,462,170	527,280	635,065	107,785
			84	646,800	26,400	31,680	5,280
			85	11,075,659	454,283	571,718	117,435
			86	4,887,385	199,542	229,514	29,972
BELGIUM	A	E	85	14,120	8,408	13,816	5,408
			86	9,922	10,112	15,805	5,693
BELIZE	A	E	86	58,512	14,808	21,645	6,837
	O	E	86	8,063	3,135	3,135	
	V	E	86	11,872	1,792	2,741	949
C RICA	V	E	82	36,000	2,400	5,490	3,090
			84	40,000	1,921	4,862	2,941
			86	77,072	5,130	12,720	7,590
CANADA	O	E	81	1,868,745	610,757	610,757	
			82	283,050	134,550	134,550	
			83	71,698	32,850	32,850	
			84	100,366	54,087	54,087	

Crop
Product
TSUSA commodity number, description, and unit of quantity

Country	Mode	Reg	Yr	Quantity	F.A.S.	C.I.F.	Charges
			85	138,007	51,439	51,439	
			86	107,820	83,805	83,805	
	O	W	81	201,782	46,725	46,725	
			82	16,786	6,912	6,912	
			83	597,839	120,252	120,252	
			84	133,755	12,240	12,240	
			85	2,250	2,175	2,175	
			86	4,250	4,200	4,200	
CHILE	A	E	86	15,695	7,134	12,952	5,818
CHINA M	V	E	81	150	1,103	1,155	52
COLOMB	A	E	84	84,927	34,725	59,137	24,412
			85	84,562	50,589	87,426	36,837
			86	227,274	147,065	209,396	62,331
	O	W	81	28,483	2,760	2,760	
DOM REP	A	E	81	9,668	1,316	2,087	771
			82	176,560	10,573	28,331	17,758
			83	166,538	8,513	17,612	9,099
			86	22,910	4,104	7,929	3,825
	N	E	82	89,043	6,345	15,226	8,881
			84	517,165	29,764	60,662	30,898
			85	1,429,423	98,809	178,724	79,915
	V	E	84	297,218	21,229	42,285	21,056
			85	470,213	42,107	74,465	32,358
FRANCE	A	E	82	19,648	1,261	3,261	2,000
	O	W	83	2,592	876	876	
			85	78,077	25,515	25,516	1
			86	58,479	11,160	11,160	
	V	E	85	24,096	2,510	3,938	1,428
GUATMAL	A	W	81	720	266	432	166
	O	E	85	88,800	12,800	13,340	540
	V	E	82	78,750	1,500	6,404	4,904
			83	36,210	1,775	4,172	2,397
			84	1,182,640	59,535	138,163	78,628
			85	400,286	20,332	56,766	36,434
			86	905,868	41,978	112,491	70,513
HAITI	A	E	84	119,216	12,916	20,240	7,324
	V	E	81	3,978	4,819	7,088	2,269
			86	130,805	22,649	33,432	10,783
HONDURA	N	E	86	2,093,447	159,599	335,506	175,907
	V	E	81	1,026,206	112,736	175,886	63,150
			82	972,000	18,750	72,745	53,995
			83	1,120,781	49,865	142,353	92,488
			84	1,858,201	77,629	189,839	112,210
			85	4,091,500	236,135	582,055	345,920
			86	264,176	18,313	41,409	23,096
ISRAEL	V	E	85	1,693	1,776	3,552	1,776
ITALY	O	E	85	99,132	2,810	2,810	
JAMAICA	A	E	84	18,389	7,808	10,948	3,140
	N	E	84	250,804	117,310	150,283	32,973
			85	3,778,673	883,552	1,063,923	180,371
			86	4,898,375	692,022	970,904	278,882
	V	E	82	79,518	8,706	16,015	7,309
JAPAN	V	W	86	1,188	1,438	1,664	226
MALAYSA	O	W	86	57,800	11,680	11,680	
MEXICO	A	E	85	5,280	2,400	4,921	2,521
	O	E	81	62,208,304	6,817,594	6,817,594	
			82	46,792,935	3,013,393	3,013,393	
			83	58,061,014	2,534,080	2,534,080	
			84	68,514,361	4,892,121	4,892,121	
			85	65,723,757	3,162,246	3,162,246	
			86	41,150,814	1,045,734	1,045,736	2
	O	W	81	289,858,399	47,487,668	47,493,568	4,900
			82	170,789,773	41,607,418	41,618,965	11,547
			83	167,028,282	27,536,134	27,536,143	9
			84	167,928,288	24,775,790	24,775,790	
			85	181,490,061	52,712,769	52,718,149	5,380
			86	232,573,094	39,154,273	39,154,276	3
MOZAMBQ	O	W	85	13,066	3,525	3,525	
			86	43,674	11,720	11,720	
N ZEAL	A	W	86	1,614	2,603	4,048	1,445
NETHLDS	A	E	81	2,761	1,668	2,320	652
			83	12,337	11,044	18,247	7,203
			84	31,234	17,967	24,874	6,907
			85	190,947	143,722	205,479	61,757
			86	86,250	64,702	102,491	37,789
	A	W	83	2,866	2,052	3,224	1,172
			84	5,656	3,931	9,023	5,092
			85	16,679	17,890	24,741	6,851
			86	8,972	14,073	17,019	2,946
	N	E	84	23,445	19,498	24,255	4,757
	O	E	84	550	518	518	
PANAMA	A	E	84	6,800	342	1,015	673
	N	E	85	155,020	22,807	35,115	12,308
PHIL R	V	W	82	4,000	1,840	2,600	760

Crop
Product
TSUSA commodity number, description, and unit of quantity

Country	Mode	Reg	Yr	Quantity	F.A.S.	C.I.F.	Charges
S VN GR	V	E	86	67,226	14,212	19,827	5,615
SPAIN	A	E	83	10,912	8,883	11,798	2,915
			84	2,204	1,460	2,095	635
			85	5,774	6,349	8,503	2,154
			86	58,846	51,096	76,615	25,519
	A	W	84	485	278	519	241
			85	5,181	3,620	6,743	3,123
	N	E	84	314,135	136,159	194,698	58,539
			85	209,988	115,151	172,314	57,163
	N	W	85	13,398	6,494	9,601	3,107
	V	E	81	845,035	332,653	468,908	136,255
			82	31,647	18,701	22,789	4,088
			83	56,053	26,007	34,440	8,433
			85	50,794	6,997	11,218	4,221
SURINAM	V	E	83	39,750	938	3,840	2,902
U KING	A	W	85	2,199	2,286	3,480	1,194
YUGOSLV	V	E	86	3,545	1,265	1,400	135

1359500 CUCUMBERS, FR, FZ, 3/1-4/30 (LB)

Country	Mode	Reg	Yr	Quantity	F.A.S.	C.I.F.	Charges
TOTAL			82	44,619,823	12,938,943	12,987,051	48,108
			83	102,808,643	17,811,635	18,022,851	211,216
			84	97,522,093	8,872,082	8,968,634	96,552
			85	86,263,064	18,571,128	18,701,184	130,056
			86	100,942,700	16,496,953	16,654,315	157,362
ANTIGUA	A	E	86	23,778	3,616	7,257	3,641
BAHAMAS	A	E	82	13,095	2,025	2,575	550
	N	E	82	739,649	49,950	62,808	12,858
			84	1,912,659	83,448	107,345	23,897
			85	2,117,547	89,010	110,612	21,602
	V	E	83	2,409,375	275,288	296,816	21,528
			86	109,820	7,640	9,630	1,990
BELIZE	A	E	85	141,536	14,100	34,899	20,799
			86	98,474	16,911	29,229	12,318
C RICA	V	E	83	2,835	2,835	4,574	1,739
			85	234,763	19,987	29,426	9,439
			86	121,887	10,500	17,010	6,510
CANADA	A	H	86	4,852	3,449	4,306	857
	O	E	82	209,828	96,201	96,201	
			83	305,090	171,966	171,966	
			84	156,828	84,474	84,474	
			85	362,214	229,796	229,796	
			86	765,770	337,492	337,492	
	O	W	82	12,000	3,179	3,179	
			83	2,070	1,553	1,553	
			84	92,642	13,694	13,694	
			85	54,632	28,086	28,086	
			86	210,162	96,339	96,339	
COLOMB	A	E	84	12,250	3,062	6,600	3,538
			86	10,307	5,332	8,532	3,200
DOM REP	A	E	84	33,755	1,741	3,117	1,376
			85	4,875	1,040	3,429	2,389
			86	24,056	2,096	5,696	3,600
	N	E	83	973,858	58,114	163,935	105,821
			84	494,282	40,958	63,322	22,364
	V	E	83	29,460	4,100	5,319	1,219
			84	25,640	3,766	5,704	1,938
			85	421,169	51,520	69,722	18,202
GUATMAL	N	E	84	164,900	14,005	22,663	8,658
	O	E	84	142,580	6,259	8,755	2,496
	V	E	84	138,000	7,200	12,838	5,638
			85	119,250	10,874	15,689	4,815
			86	68,275	3,340	5,677	2,337
HAITI	V	E	86	12,290	2,130	3,440	1,310
HG KONG	V	E	84	1,200	900	1,069	169
			86	2,400	1,617	1,929	312
HONDURA	V	E	82	230,500	9,277	22,654	13,377
			83	402,804	49,422	77,725	28,303
			84	1,321,241	65,625	88,048	22,423
			85	501,659	26,736	40,795	14,059
			86	160,000	7,061	9,125	2,064
ITALY	A	E	82	184	483	581	98
JAMAICA	A	E	83	285,988	44,863	97,469	52,606
			84	54,705	25,841	34,884	9,043
	N	E	86	1,708,957	178,598	282,784	104,186
	V	E	82	232,116	25,413	46,638	21,225
			83	928,910	208,110	240,131	32,021
MEXICO	O	E	82	2,955,632	141,079	141,079	
			83	28,206,763	953,224	953,224	
			84	34,149,675	2,773,671	2,773,671	
			85	23,039,071	1,103,223	1,103,225	2
			86	19,323,274	520,958	520,958	
	O	W	82	40,226,819	12,611,336	12,611,336	
			83	70,190,400	16,250,270	16,250,270	

Crop
Product
TSUSA commodity number, description, and unit of quantity

Country	Mode	Reg	Yr	Quantity	F.A.S.	C.I.F.	Charges
			84	58,983,223	5,758,220	5,760,940	2,720
			85	58,203,897	16,737,273	16,737,276	3
			86	78,109,598	15,269,379	15,270,709	1,330
MONSRAT	O	W	85	33,696	9,720	9,720	
MOZAMBQ	O	W	85	39,576	12,660	12,660	
N ZEAL	A	W	86	589	1,251	2,020	769
NETHLDS	A	E	84	2,778	2,870	3,676	806
			85	23,409	20,253	25,906	5,653
			86	20,941	15,416	19,412	3,996
	A	W	84	635	353	497	144
			85	2,205	3,160	3,470	310
S VN GR	V	E	86	4,770	1,440	2,036	596
SPAIN	A	E	85	28,655	1,563	2,013	450
YEMAN S	O	E	85	3,600	2,400	2,400	

1359700 CUCUMBER 5/1-6/30 9/1-11/30 (LB)

Country	Mode	Reg	Yr	Quantity	F.A.S.	C.I.F.	Charges
TOTAL			82	24,040,031	4,419,569	4,431,002	11,433
			83	41,920,350	5,016,245	5,041,991	25,746
			84	34,560,327	5,920,840	6,057,650	136,810
			85	21,926,611	5,489,478	5,642,484	153,006
			86	27,598,843	4,847,123	4,898,225	51,102
BAHAMAS	V	E	85	26,500	2,650	2,970	320
BELGIUM	A	E	84	2,475	1,740	2,440	700
			85	13,737	4,202	7,712	3,510
			86	22,140	10,513	16,124	5,611
	A	W	85	3,240	2,215	4,200	1,985
C RICA	V	E	82	36,000	2,400	4,407	2,007
			83	33,600	2,400	5,407	3,007
CANADA	A	H	84	6,600	2,891	3,746	855
	O	E	82	736,789	288,168	288,168	
			83	712,991	289,208	291,328	2,120
			84	1,143,397	433,512	433,512	
			85	1,136,060	474,019	474,351	332
			86	1,776,540	814,610	814,610	
	O	W	82	56,600	15,229	15,229	
			83	86,700	31,272	31,272	
			84	245,415	85,662	85,662	
			85	240,635	87,016	87,016	
			86	407,877	154,821	154,821	
CHINA T	V	E	86	67,500	53,325	60,125	6,800
COLOMB	A	E	83	1,514	502	922	420
			84	39,179	8,960	20,086	11,126
			85	31,022	12,912	25,100	12,188
DOM REP	A	E	82	9,776	489	1,589	1,100
	O	E	84	2,150	258	259	1
	V	E	83	250	480	858	378
FRANCE	A	E	83	758	309	597	288
	V	E	83	2,786	4,190	4,413	223
GUATMAL	V	E	83	37,500	1,500	4,015	2,515
			86	24,240	2,525	2,572	47
JAMAICA	A	E	84	23,093	1,488	3,029	1,541
			86	31,415	4,968	6,818	1,850
JAPAN	V	E	83	1,000	2,255	2,424	169
			85	1,100	1,144	1,401	257
	V	W	86	8,064	12,581	13,172	591
MEXICO	A	E	85	4,092	1,432	3,415	1,983
	O	E	82	6,503,200	342,475	342,475	
			83	15,987,094	595,520	595,520	
			84	13,037,109	997,469	997,469	
			85	2,932,919	184,000	184,000	
			86	5,922,704	119,525	119,525	
	O	W	82	16,651,105	3,743,208	3,743,208	
			83	24,911,679	4,013,232	4,013,236	4
			84	19,604,166	4,151,525	4,151,525	
			85	17,114,701	4,477,166	4,477,166	
			86	19,178,786	3,562,899	3,563,583	684
NETHLDS	A	E	83	18,627	7,085	11,187	4,102
			84	171,767	90,353	137,516	47,163
			85	240,302	159,601	241,813	82,212
			86	56,079	54,787	69,256	14,469
	A	W	84	16,193	5,640	11,297	5,657
			86	9,186	4,673	8,610	3,937
NIGER	A	E	86	992	1,100	1,265	165
SPAIN	A	E	85	6,783	7,620	11,398	3,778
	N	E	84	254,332	136,335	203,477	67,142
			85	31,262	3,995	6,445	2,450
	O	E	83	15,565	8,913	8,913	
			84	8,388	4,194	4,194	
	V	E	82	46,561	27,600	35,926	8,326
			83	110,286	59,379	71,899	12,520
			85	144,258	71,506	115,497	43,991
			86	93,320	50,796	67,744	16,948
SWITZLD	A	E	84	6,063	813	3,438	2,625

Crop
Product
TSUSA commodity number, description, and unit of quantity

1359900 CUCUMBERS, JUL 1-AUG31 INCL (LB)

Country	Mode	Reg	Yr	Quantity	F.A.S.	C.I.F.	Charges
TOTAL			82	1,244,948	298,474	298,474	
			83	6,187,626	778,138	782,191	4,053
			84	2,242,887	580,567	584,850	4,283
			85	2,550,423	616,680	633,538	16,858
			86	8,407,960	1,435,503	1,441,267	5,764
CANADA	O	E	82	992,791	270,841	270,841	
			83	815,221	273,739	273,739	
			84	1,059,422	344,386	344,386	
			85	795,944	313,083	313,083	
			86	1,400,955	517,611	517,611	
	O	W	82	64,000	17,154	17,154	
			83	66,500	24,413	24,413	
			84	352,665	123,115	123,115	
			85	176,460	69,799	69,799	
			86	314,385	117,555	117,555	
COLOMB	A	E	84	6,838	1,554	3,499	1,945
DOM REP	V	E	84	8,800	719	915	196
			85	28,550	2,884	4,080	1,196
JAPAN	V	E	83	20,000	3,965	5,600	1,635
	V	W	86	1,966	2,807	2,875	68
MEXICO	O	E	82	188,157	10,479	10,479	
			83	3,197,699	357,673	357,673	
			84	730,469	95,157	95,157	
			85	222,519	40,888	40,888	
	O	W	83	2,079,956	115,575	115,575	
			84	76,699	10,887	10,887	
			85	1,288,448	164,268	164,268	
			86	6,679,852	787,689	787,689	
NETHLDS	A	E	83	8,250	2,773	5,191	2,418
			84	7,994	4,749	6,891	2,142
			85	36,297	24,660	38,976	14,316
			86	10,802	9,841	15,537	5,696
	A	W	85	2,205	1,098	2,444	1,346

Cucumber, in brine or pickled

1417720 CUCUMBERS IN SALT BRINE ETC (LB)

Country	Mode	Reg	Yr	Quantity	F.A.S.	C.I.F.	Charges
TOTAL			81	6,733,787	1,409,999	1,603,337	193,338
			82	9,511,122	1,631,009	1,831,891	200,882
			83	9,031,668	1,912,352	2,099,709	187,357
			84	9,681,725	2,602,710	2,942,399	339,689
			85	13,194,331	3,266,242	3,785,013	518,771
			86	14,741,767	3,949,789	4,506,590	556,801
AUSTRAL	V	W	83	1,755	1,813	2,001	188
AUSTRIA	V	E	81	1,646	580	642	62
	V	W	86	10,000	4,694	8,894	4,200
BELGIUM	O	E	81	18,497	7,606	8,622	1,016
	V	E	86	10,519	4,440	4,820	380
BRAZIL	V	E	84	85,626	42,253	48,399	6,146
			85	60,715	18,174	21,197	3,023
C RICA	V	E	81	5,385	1,785	2,085	300
	V	W	86	5,639	1,949	1,949	
CANADA	O	E	81	283,920	78,071	78,071	
			82	520,297	128,551	128,551	
			83	2,216,547	354,249	354,249	
			84	759,865	218,319	218,319	
			85	192,448	46,103	46,103	
			86	27,525	8,658	8,658	
	O	W	85	175,440	8,918	8,918	
	V	E	83	712	395	451	56
CHILE	V	E	86	23,766	11,544	13,044	1,500
CHINA M	V	E	84	660	1,226	1,288	62
	V	W	82	1,074	1,156	1,255	99
			83	2,175	1,426	1,507	81
			84	6,750	2,543	3,080	537
			85	15,000	5,125	5,560	435
			86	5,947	3,150	3,280	130
CHINA T	O	E	84	3,241	1,430	1,571	141
	V	E	81	1,234	858	962	104
			82	6,681	4,700	5,295	595
			83	11,311	6,757	7,883	1,126
			84	40,782	22,296	26,979	4,683
			85	70,089	48,166	55,175	7,009
			86	60,553	40,582	44,308	3,726
	V	H	81	3,900	2,540	2,688	148
	V	W	81	180,474	107,122	114,884	7,762
			82	270,316	145,703	160,995	15,292
			83	246,192	138,291	153,867	15,576
			84	354,586	213,359	236,238	22,879

Crop
Product
TSUSA commodity number, description, and unit of quantity

Country	Mode	Reg	Yr	Quantity	F.A.S.	C.I.F.	Charges
			85	219,082	143,052	155,968	12,916
			86	615,189	304,406	323,395	18,989
COLOMB	V	E	85	39,158	19,689	21,670	1,981
CYPRUS	V	E	82	375	400	469	69
			83	375	400	453	53
			84	878	1,070	1,228	158
	V	W	86	615	1,163	1,507	344
CZECHO	O	E	81	1,725	1,080	1,359	279
DENMARK	V	E	81	1,347	1,211	1,488	277
			82	841	780	920	140
			83	569	660	887	227
			86	2,282	1,387	1,590	203
	V	W	81	10,032	10,765	12,402	1,637
			85	507	3,865	4,288	423
			86	1,189	3,224	3,583	359
FR GERM	N	E	81	228,857	136,659	152,974	16,315
			82	95,442	45,547	54,932	9,385
			86	19,445	21,781	24,049	2,268
	O	E	81	57,809	24,529	30,372	5,843
			83	12,730	1,020	1,211	191
			84	95,359	24,004	28,913	4,909
			85	81,256	37,642	47,818	10,176
			86	41,019	9,295	12,195	2,900
	V	E	82	465,750	181,002	204,309	23,307
			83	427,381	207,212	233,733	26,521
			84	456,936	230,761	263,247	32,486
			85	705,116	339,450	405,550	66,100
			86	904,490	512,331	589,642	77,311
	V	W	81	24,374	8,937	10,734	1,797
			82	26,832	9,710	12,140	2,430
			83	27,060	10,399	12,715	2,316
			84	105,809	44,961	53,601	8,640
			85	100,929	56,305	68,438	12,133
			86	80,563	45,235	52,104	6,869
FRANCE	N	E	81	215,397	256,356	278,074	21,718
			84	127,059	153,477	171,129	17,652
			85	15,963	17,054	19,636	2,582
			86	117,643	156,480	178,409	21,929
	O	E	81	5,839	9,302	11,050	1,748
			82	5,253	2,113	3,096	983
			83	10,108	9,653	10,620	967
			84	2,315	2,330	2,623	293
	V	E	81	22,414	18,767	21,114	2,347
			82	224,830	242,507	270,502	27,995
			83	299,408	348,333	380,813	32,480
			84	65,506	67,135	81,466	14,331
			85	221,825	225,931	264,506	38,575
			86	60,785	107,685	121,352	13,667
	V	W	81	27,387	25,264	28,884	3,620
			82	21,459	22,101	26,046	3,945
			83	28,393	33,171	39,507	6,336
			84	28,173	40,878	47,448	6,570
			85	57,438	58,031	72,730	14,699
			86	73,073	96,605	107,730	11,125
GREECE	V	E	81	73,963	17,112	20,148	3,036
			82	261,950	60,881	70,454	9,573
			83	111,982	23,354	32,847	9,493
			84	167,813	57,618	74,469	16,851
			85	335,807	57,843	85,358	27,515
			86	88,846	19,378	29,256	9,878
	V	W	81	6,511	1,220	1,760	540
			83	26,455	4,800	7,011	2,211
			86	30,424	3,795	6,463	2,668
GUATMAL	V	E	81	162,231	16,680	27,745	11,065
			83	95,722	46,907	54,370	7,463
			84	140,880	50,932	60,810	9,878
			85	187,798	38,804	53,613	14,809
			86	352,347	52,400	65,400	13,000
HAITI	V	E	81	52,300	16,042	18,196	2,154
HG KONG	V	E	81	2,040	1,998	2,264	266
			82	5,460	5,381	6,036	655
			83	9,000	6,066	7,008	942
			84	9,660	7,383	8,246	863
			85	6,720	4,809	5,718	909
			86	44,067	22,376	24,729	2,353
	V	W	81	13,155	9,715	10,210	495
			82	4,500	3,438	3,663	225
			83	15,895	11,309	12,154	845
			84	7,945	7,315	7,755	440
			85	5,880	5,600	5,910	310
			86	16,740	11,486	12,093	607
HUNGARY	V	E	82	165,000	27,924	35,800	7,876
			83	25,943	6,114	7,590	1,476
			84	58,409	13,211	20,494	7,283

Crop
Product
TSUSA commodity number, description, and unit of quantity

Country	Mode	Reg	Yr	Quantity	F.A.S.	C.I.F.	Charges
			85	25,200	4,521	7,739	3,218
			86	4,050	1,051	1,407	356
	V	W	84	19,048	4,700	6,975	2,275
			85	63,388	16,080	21,349	5,269
INDIA	O	E	82	675	400	400	
			83	41	786	786	
	V	E	83	11,475	7,973	9,677	1,704
			84	2,745	2,804	3,380	576
			85	38,139	8,978	11,977	2,999
			86	42,015	17,712	23,310	5,598
	V	W	81	795	498	659	161
			82	8,246	9,554	11,212	1,658
			83	794	552	678	126
			84	6,303	3,438	4,058	620
IRAN	V	E	86	75,000	20,384	23,184	2,800
	V	W	86	25,445	13,940	15,820	1,880
ISRAEL	N	E	81	8,006	3,064	3,848	784
			83	2,141	1,195	1,318	123
	V	E	81	47,834	17,429	20,809	3,380
			82	67,012	26,438	31,389	4,951
			83	71,947	36,235	41,930	5,695
			84	237,041	121,543	135,144	13,601
			85	578,420	212,240	244,436	32,196
			86	479,789	204,449	236,861	32,412
	V	W	84	124,750	69,595	77,401	7,806
			85	283,811	124,033	144,229	20,196
			86	192,509	106,237	128,739	22,502
ITALY	O	E	81	265	347	381	34
			85	1,836	3,654	4,024	370
			86	734	1,890	2,055	165
	V	E	82	110,226	43,284	51,200	7,916
			83	11,134	3,785	4,394	609
			85	14,724	7,320	8,474	1,154
			86	2,924	2,477	2,867	390
	V	W	84	3,750	4,036	4,364	328
			86	3,675	5,291	5,660	369
JAMAICA	N	E	85	188,338	33,311	43,437	10,126
	V	E	84	34,200	22,230	24,268	2,038
JAPAN	N	E	81	4,262	9,970	11,762	1,792
			84	32,352	42,776	47,777	5,001
	N	W	84	10,045	9,220	10,667	1,447
	O	H	83	374	319	446	127
	V	E	81	126	787	844	57
			82	5,362	7,480	8,231	751
			83	20,681	25,043	27,571	2,528
			84	9,759	12,921	14,165	1,244
			85	17,465	17,901	19,633	1,732
			86	56,771	66,547	72,228	5,681
	V	H	81	2,952	2,677	3,657	980
			84	304	260	293	33
	V	W	81	4,789	7,428	8,084	656
			82	18,113	18,819	20,668	1,849
			83	24,440	26,363	28,913	2,550
			84	6,526	9,362	10,142	780
			85	25,416	18,056	19,228	1,172
			86	29,042	45,266	48,107	2,841
KOR REP	V	E	83	3,210	2,307	2,502	195
			84	1,190	595	650	55
			86	14,130	1,010	1,123	113
	V	W	82	30,761	8,927	9,728	801
			83	5,316	3,700	4,034	334
			84	2,558	1,556	1,800	244
			85	2,403	1,719	1,920	201
			86	27,069	34,445	37,121	2,676
LEBANON	N	E	84	21,764	7,341	8,112	771
	V	E	83	1,638	1,159	1,456	297
			85	37,261	17,669	19,792	2,123
			86	26,370	13,443	15,601	2,158
	V	W	85	12,677	4,250	5,599	1,349
			86	6,746	2,700	3,058	358
LESOTHO	V	E	85	141	1,994	2,150	156
MEXICO	O	E	81	1,433,219	142,587	142,587	
			82	2,586,279	248,089	248,228	139
			83	1,236,033	196,354	196,354	
			84	1,870,303	286,848	286,848	
			85	2,735,332	508,255	508,257	2
			86	5,863,441	687,998	687,998	
	O	W	81	2,881,025	168,183	168,183	
			82	3,795,673	120,412	120,412	
			83	3,265,384	86,857	86,857	
			84	2,830,094	128,402	128,402	
			85	3,408,235	140,424	140,424	
			86	998,145	41,840	41,840	
MOROC	V	E	83	61,596	40,559	46,269	5,710

Crop Product TSUSA commodity number, description, and unit of quantity Country	Mode	Reg	Yr	Quantity	F.A.S.	C.I.F.	Charges
N ZEAL	V	E	85	7,980	8,654	9,477	823
NETHLDS	V	E	81	30,947	14,644	16,922	2,278
			82	1,376	874	1,014	140
			83	1,429	587	698	111
			84	9,487	4,797	5,903	1,106
			85	17,808	7,844	9,659	1,815
			86	42,362	19,398	24,461	5,063
	V	W	81	450	269	300	31
			84	2,155	1,338	1,478	140
			86	262,800	2,768	3,089	321
PHIL R	V	E	81	8,100	5,400	5,967	567
			84	1,410	409	595	186
POLAND	N	E	82	413,074	104,825	146,708	41,883
			83	39,547	12,240	15,685	3,445
			84	69,484	16,016	21,702	5,686
	O	E	82	30,583	10,400	13,983	3,583
	V	E	81	630,327	132,982	205,494	72,512
			82	91,442	22,109	31,543	9,434
			83	469,530	109,930	149,499	39,569
			84	825,341	193,509	259,476	65,967
			85	1,157,748	280,499	380,062	99,563
			86	1,038,125	243,572	326,640	83,068
	V	W	83	22,500	5,200	8,070	2,870
PORTUGL	V	E	83	2,965	1,095	1,219	124
			84	19,718	9,595	10,852	1,257
ROMANIA	V	E	84	41,135	10,149	12,708	2,559
			85	144,855	30,264	38,796	8,532
			86	31,588	6,686	8,135	1,449
SPAIN	V	E	81	229,469	125,117	147,773	22,656
			82	194,631	78,122	94,999	16,877
			83	118,990	58,587	63,674	5,087
			84	850,899	342,754	402,470	59,716
			85	1,769,913	579,106	676,389	97,283
			86	1,363,865	483,901	572,440	88,539
	V	W	83	1,746	309	433	124
			85	59,216	19,829	24,455	4,626
			86	1,303,750	340,669	421,913	81,244
SWEDEN	V	E	81	1,530	557	640	83
			82	1,110	923	996	73
			83	1,080	648	703	55
			84	900	599	639	40
	V	W	84	2,063	1,928	2,158	230
SWITZLD	O	E	82	1,190	1,101	1,493	392
			84	1,240	492	537	45
	V	E	81	754	1,014	1,074	60
			82	2,224	2,444	2,704	260
			83	8,121	7,023	7,465	442
			84	14,386	12,209	12,802	593
			85	32,668	21,644	22,990	1,346
			86	3,694	4,262	4,393	131
	V	W	82	728	882	1,082	200
			83	765	673	714	41
SYRIA	O	E	84	4,013	4,351	4,491	140
	V	E	84	160	520	638	118
			85	2,600	3,072	3,249	177
THAILND	V	E	83	360	276	303	27
	V	W	81	720	473	501	28
			82	2,734	1,495	1,687	192
			83	2,387	1,044	1,130	86
			84	1,125	805	879	74
			86	10,794	6,900	7,298	398
TURKEY	V	E	86	6,614	1,133	1,249	116
	V	W	86	17,024	8,102	13,355	5,253
U KING	A	E	82	892	800	915	115
	N	W	82	2,250	2,028	3,056	1,028
	O	E	81	165	338	338	
			83	34,815	36,387	38,786	2,399
			84	34,023	35,623	38,779	3,156
	V	E	81	2,693	4,106	4,558	452
			82	16,939	23,104	25,571	2,467
			83	17,436	21,164	23,283	2,119
			84	22,787	24,076	27,134	3,058
			85	56,795	53,017	59,724	6,707
			86	68,481	86,564	92,516	5,952
	V	W	81	7,566	5,630	6,546	916
			83	4,155	4,112	5,299	1,187
			86	9,977	7,006	8,000	994
USSR	O	E	82	4,409	938	1,104	166
	V	E	81	2,593	620	694	74
			82	7,857	2,226	2,756	530
YUGOSLV	O	E	86	19,206	5,460	5,460	
	V	E	81	34,763	11,680	14,988	3,308
			82	41,276	13,441	16,349	2,908
			83	19,925	7,561	8,686	1,125

Crop Product TSUSA commodity number, description, and unit of quantity Country	Mode	Reg	Yr	Quantity	F.A.S.	C.I.F.	Charges
			84	50,415	13,412	17,409	3,997
			85	20,791	7,347	9,388	2,041
			86	122,966	22,644	32,212	9,568

Cummin

Cummin, spice
1612700 CUMMIN (LB)

TOTAL			81	10,420,198	6,122,959	6,980,492	857,533
			82	8,888,675	5,993,674	6,651,823	658,149
			83	7,038,630	4,837,470	5,306,811	469,341
			84	9,700,057	5,329,092	6,023,640	694,548
			85	8,688,236	3,296,166	3,884,098	587,932
			86	8,030,151	4,033,374	4,548,204	514,830
ARAB EM	V	E	81	418,523	249,806	281,525	31,719
			82	4,523	1,155	1,573	418
			85	76,110	37,096	39,527	2,431
			86	53,352	25,655	27,969	2,314
	V	W	84	600	428	496	68
			85	3,086	1,874	2,326	452
AUSTRIA	V	E	84	550	649	735	86
C RICA	V	E	84	291	1,590	1,718	128
CANADA	O	E	81	8,340	9,023	9,046	23
			82	75,050	79,981	79,981	
			83	51,807	56,203	56,203	
			84	1,769	4,263	4,263	
	V	E	81	8,500	9,146	10,199	1,053
CHINA M	N	E	83	1,714,103	1,258,060	1,364,690	106,630
	V	E	81	11,023	6,789	7,437	648
			82	681,508	495,727	540,647	44,920
			83	303,641	224,731	244,702	19,971
			84	877,780	654,714	706,582	51,868
			85	1,184,889	516,732	596,522	79,790
			86	2,253,453	1,034,688	1,179,867	145,179
	V	W	82	982,554	717,584	785,220	67,636
			83	719,671	549,228	593,945	44,717
			84	192,240	144,255	151,294	7,039
			85	436,513	197,318	214,146	16,828
			86	166,226	70,020	80,304	10,284
CHINA T	V	E	85	55,116	15,823	19,480	3,657
EGYPT	V	E	81	22,040	13,801	15,429	1,628
			82	314,096	297,959	312,340	14,381
			83	152,558	77,729	85,856	8,127
			84	176,368	88,201	97,488	9,287
			85	22,046	11,025	12,186	1,161
ETHIOP	V	E	82	22,046	9,412	11,598	2,186
			83	11,023	5,506	6,533	1,027
FR GERM	V	W	84	53,630	28,924	34,341	5,417
FRANCE	V	E	83	260	970	1,021	51
			85	83,200	41,584	46,980	5,396
	V	W	83	265	354	376	22
GREECE	V	E	81	11,000	15,342	17,853	2,511
			82	26,455	20,880	22,843	1,963
			84	27,558	11,225	12,887	1,662
HG KONG	V	E	83	246,651	189,465	209,720	20,255
			84	44,100	30,960	34,773	3,813
			85	88,184	37,127	42,727	5,600
	V	W	82	132,276	96,530	103,694	7,164
			83	158,081	119,588	126,471	6,883
			84	11,023	8,100	9,000	900
INDIA	A	E	84	587	330	380	50
	N	E	81	6,524,100	3,805,734	4,359,428	553,694
			82	1,347,997	788,208	900,408	112,200
			83	947,747	652,323	721,833	69,510
			84	3,346,328	1,961,510	2,230,347	268,837
			85	973,111	498,030	581,955	83,925
	N	W	86	46,682	28,121	31,601	3,480
	O	E	81	2,376	2,406	2,445	39
			82	220	312	312	
			83	3,669	3,924	4,328	404
			84	4,124	3,807	3,807	
			86	33,009	30,695	34,773	4,078
	V	E	81	542,345	313,758	358,937	45,179
			82	151,961	97,708	108,755	11,047
			83	103,938	75,344	83,217	7,873
			84	427,522	240,968	276,051	35,083
			85	157,886	80,376	99,392	19,016
			86	1,227,632	754,796	846,594	91,798
	V	W	81	1,701,506	1,005,527	1,138,599	133,072

Crop / Product / TSUSA commodity number, description, and unit of quantity Country	Mode	Reg	Yr	Quantity	F.A.S.	C.I.F.	Charges
			82	328,847	198,158	225,996	27,838
			83	179,893	141,066	156,504	15,438
			84	733,865	475,675	540,352	64,677
			85	329,510	187,966	220,864	32,898
			86	167,090	106,460	119,779	13,319
INDNSIA	V	W	82	25,000	18,833	19,623	790
IRAN	N	E	82	260,301	202,036	221,201	19,165
	V	E	81	421,839	257,758	283,920	26,162
			82	2,304	2,171	2,457	286
			84	99,427	59,532	65,260	5,728
			85	296,525	130,482	149,547	19,065
			86	1,886,755	1,255,418	1,354,750	99,332
	V	W	83	364	378	446	68
			84	4,444	3,905	4,383	478
			85	6,415	4,237	5,171	934
ISRAEL	V	E	86	4,409	3,778	4,001	223
ITALY	V	E	86	22,046	10,652	12,956	2,304
JAPAN	V	E	83	855	2,160	2,282	122
			85	44,092	19,226	22,026	2,800
	V	W	85	945	2,016	2,119	103
KENYA	O	E	83	1,102	1,276	1,395	119
LEBANON	V	E	82	22,040	14,931	16,530	1,599
MALAWI	O	E	84	705	628	689	61
MEXICO	N	E	83	14,925	9,900	10,521	621
	O	E	81	4,410	3,428	3,428	
			82	107,870	76,607	76,607	
	O	W	84	2,640	400	400	
MOROC	V	E	83	6,614	4,102	4,776	674
NETHLDS	V	W	81	220	291	317	26
PAKISTN	N	E	81	271,616	160,619	184,192	23,573
			82	3,049,650	1,951,692	2,197,492	245,800
	O	E	81	1,122	553	608	55
			82	308	1,076	1,193	117
			83	440	1,251	1,364	113
			84	269	566	598	32
	V	E	81	1,388	1,286	1,589	303
			82	562,772	359,168	402,318	43,150
			84	441	950	1,176	226
			86	2,143	3,280	3,560	280
	V	W	81	44,320	26,464	30,202	3,738
			82	208,116	127,002	145,297	18,295
			83	64,021	50,491	56,481	5,990
			84	2,425	2,134	2,710	576
PORTUGL	V	E	82	163	318	585	267
S HELNA	V	E	84	65,534	35,505	41,055	5,550
			85	46,297	22,865	26,820	3,955
SINGAPR	V	E	86	2,205	1,665	1,807	142
	V	W	82	2,248	2,096	2,368	272
SPAIN	V	E	83	220	383	444	61
			84	63,157	38,322	42,874	4,552
SRI LKA	V	W	84	27,558	19,730	23,129	3,399
SWEDEN	V	W	83	205	341	486	145
SWITZLD	O	E	81	1	327	366	39
THAILND	V	W	81	250	390	416	26
			83	213	332	354	22
			84	250	548	595	47
TUNISIA	V	E	86	9,829	9,829	11,329	1,500
TURKEY	O	E	83	330	264	264	
			84	880	835	835	
			86	20,848	13,969	13,969	
	V	E	81	397,414	219,808	250,262	30,454
			82	566,580	416,297	453,058	36,761
			83	2,282,815	1,356,967	1,511,281	154,314
			84	3,411,672	1,444,224	1,658,776	214,552
			85	4,093,388	1,256,848	1,505,309	248,461
			86	1,723,865	565,654	675,042	109,388
	V	W	81	21,825	11,811	14,065	2,254
			83	58,697	40,800	45,551	4,751
			84	118,595	62,780	72,826	10,046
			85	785,390	231,926	292,995	61,069
			86	410,607	118,694	149,903	31,209
U KING	O	E	81	4,929	7,781	8,455	674
			82	13,239	15,864	17,516	1,652
			83	14,522	14,334	15,767	1,433
			84	1,520	1,546	1,688	142
	V	E	84	2,205	1,888	2,132	244
			85	1,760	1,515	1,713	198
	V	W	82	551	1,969	2,211	242
			85	3,773	2,100	2,293	193
YEMEN A	A	E	81	1,111	1,111	1,774	663

Currant

Black currant, frozen**
1466900 BLACK CURRANTS, ETC, FROZEN (LB)
  (See Lingonberry, frozen under Cowberry)

Black currant, prepared or preserved**
1468200 BLACK CURRNT ETC PREP, PRES (LB)
  (See Lingonberry, prepared or preserved under Cowberry)

D

Dasheen

Dasheen, fresh or frozen
1360000 DASHEENS, FRSH, CHLD OR FROZ (LB)

Country	Mode	Reg	Yr	Quantity	F.A.S.	C.I.F.	Charges
TOTAL			81	38,070,301	7,059,386	9,723,301	2,663,615
			82	38,412,933	6,384,885	8,719,788	2,334,903
			83	37,498,699	6,513,157	8,809,047	2,295,890
			84	42,701,357	7,138,655	9,756,198	2,617,543
			85	55,862,428	9,057,144	12,139,522	3,082,378
			86	47,430,616	8,334,944	11,040,893	2,705,949
ARGENT	V	E	85	77,161	19,250	26,000	6,750
BELGIUM	V	E	83	8,400	10,731	12,044	1,313
BRAZIL	A	W	82	15,890	4,941	13,851	8,910
			83	33,376	6,715	24,892	18,177
			84	37,788	5,082	27,874	22,792
			85	14,943	3,370	10,519	7,149
	N	E	85	89,962	21,938	33,953	12,015
			86	230,590	40,569	61,643	21,074
	V	E	83	30,500	8,890	12,452	3,562
			85	25,556	5,796	8,947	3,151
	V	W	86	12,698	2,880	4,917	2,037
C AF RP	V	W	85	11,483	2,349	3,223	874
C RICA	N	E	83	1,025,958	216,245	285,159	68,914
	O	E	81	6,000	1,800	1,848	48
	V	E	81	195,646	30,222	40,731	10,509
			82	336,926	56,414	76,841	20,427
			83	136,266	26,928	32,568	5,640
			84	1,687,740	266,105	376,578	110,473
			85	1,277,718	194,103	274,051	79,948
			86	1,939,130	308,094	429,741	121,647
	V	W	81	82,450	10,565	21,713	11,148
			82	6,305	2,035	2,597	562
			83	11,066	5,005	6,948	1,943
			84	3,803	675	1,082	407
			85	67,111	20,950	29,653	8,703
			86	56,533	17,865	24,495	6,630
CANADA	O	E	81	3,120	688	688	
			84	1,870	561	561	
			85	18,000	2,513	2,513	
	O	W	85	1,236	2,872	2,872	
CHINA M	A	E	84	3,600	540	1,418	878
	V	W	81	36,540	4,860	6,841	1,981
			82	138,699	18,709	25,568	6,859
			83	137,329	15,876	21,864	5,988
			84	120,788	17,726	24,176	6,450
			85	90,706	16,415	23,371	6,956
			86	119,847	20,618	28,110	7,492
CHINA T	V	E	85	39,682	5,580	12,135	6,555
	V	W	84	9,710	7,904	8,517	613
			85	1,560	1,404	1,659	255
			86	99,326	35,390	38,708	3,318
COLOMB	A	E	84	3,510	674	2,814	2,140
DOM REP	A	E	81	67,775	8,037	14,067	6,030
			82	21,180	2,520	3,698	1,178
			83	10,912	1,658	2,841	1,183
			84	2,960	1,332	1,681	349
	N	E	81	33,653,210	5,848,543	7,863,540	2,014,997

Crop
Product
TSUSA commodity number, description, and unit of quantity

Country	Mode	Reg	Yr	Quantity	F.A.S.	C.I.F.	Charges
			82	34,283,799	5,275,618	7,047,443	1,771,825
			83	32,842,473	5,215,023	6,825,332	1,610,309
			84	36,006,498	5,524,129	7,215,913	1,691,784
			85	43,382,881	6,176,835	8,171,062	1,994,227
			86	34,547,795	5,255,308	6,882,984	1,627,676
	N	W	84	33,350	7,827	10,850	3,023
	V	E	81	1,419,603	246,016	324,970	78,954
			82	1,312,890	254,379	322,903	68,524
			83	177,350	24,899	33,641	8,742
			84	790,402	93,268	137,761	44,493
			85	6,626,804	1,304,106	1,707,983	403,877
			86	7,219,841	1,489,545	1,944,809	455,264
	V	W	84	5,526	2,818	3,633	815
DOMINCA	V	E	81	1,995	750	903	153
			83	690	680	994	314
			86	38,601	11,594	13,254	1,660
FIJI	A	H	84	3,150	764	1,445	681
	A	W	83	96,541	32,058	58,042	25,984
			84	387,097	115,088	222,911	107,823
			85	15,650	5,634	9,763	4,129
			86	91,000	21,501	43,893	22,392
	V	H	83	1,500	1,225	1,582	357
FINLAND	A	H	86	9,306	3,165	5,695	2,530
	N	W	86	53,251	18,901	30,961	12,060
FR GERM	V	E	86	13,400	1,608	2,468	860
FR POLY	A	H	84	1,980	720	1,951	1,231
FRANCE	A	E	81	14,195	1,758	2,883	1,125
			83	5,000	500	970	470
	V	E	81	5,000	600	820	220
			84	3,000	356	656	300
GUATMAL	A	E	82	12,831	5,774	8,337	2,563
	V	E	84	18,550	1,484	3,312	1,828
HAITI	A	E	81	32,490	3,942	7,075	3,133
			82	5,400	648	1,144	496
			83	25,515	5,400	8,096	2,696
			85	25,000	6,750	9,750	3,000
	N	E	82	60,868	7,653	11,849	4,196
HG KONG	V	W	82	17,920	2,667	3,684	1,017
			83	17,500	2,871	3,963	1,092
			84	21,910	2,262	3,281	1,019
			86	31,818	8,482	10,251	1,769
HONDURA	V	E	81	79,620	8,332	12,748	4,416
			84	44,032	4,768	7,762	2,994
			85	46,800	5,940	8,464	2,524
			86	36,000	4,000	6,510	2,510
ITALY	A	E	83	3,571	640	1,240	600
			85	3,439	2,866	3,743	877
			86	8,089	4,400	5,734	1,334
JAMAICA	A	E	81	2,895	354	597	243
			83	3,677	968	1,565	597
			84	32,284	7,292	13,952	6,660
			85	137,033	30,613	56,772	26,159
			86	14,425	6,869	8,942	2,073
	N	E	81	324,523	110,148	155,313	45,165
			82	468,500	97,972	147,799	49,827
			83	926,547	189,999	330,294	140,295
			84	1,513,599	292,058	510,652	218,594
			85	1,205,201	368,506	562,450	193,944
			86	1,203,228	457,056	606,309	149,253
	V	E	85	29,000	3,863	5,095	1,232
			86	1,451	1,520	2,620	1,100
JAPAN	N	E	86	39,385	29,187	34,529	5,342
	N	H	84	8,352	7,969	10,105	2,136
	V	E	81	27,500	35,979	47,574	11,595
			82	37,937	52,235	64,056	11,821
			83	53,472	33,064	42,159	9,095
			84	41,138	53,952	65,534	11,582
			85	27,500	24,668	28,330	3,662
			86	2,420	2,398	2,562	164
	V	H	81	1,320	2,394	2,799	405
			83	6,934	6,148	8,205	2,057
			85	7,700	7,075	8,030	955
			86	3,080	3,897	4,720	823
	V	W	81	71,531	78,608	85,589	6,981
			82	82,962	90,124	96,725	6,601
			83	99,417	95,686	103,268	7,582
			84	134,160	155,341	166,244	10,903
			85	231,381	179,502	198,409	18,907
			86	271,198	194,786	212,560	17,774
KOR REP	A	W	81	12,500	4,086	7,375	3,289
MEXICO	O	E	81	40,500	24,300	24,300	
			83	71,232	24,085	24,085	
			84	60,342	1,916	1,916	
			85	156,700	49,673	49,673	

Crop
Product
TSUSA commodity number, description, and unit of quantity

Country	Mode	Reg	Yr	Quantity	F.A.S.	C.I.F.	Charges
	O	W	82	32,400	7,560	7,560	
			83	85,153	17,071	17,071	
			84	243,080	72,856	72,856	
			85	52,134	10,835	10,835	
			86	40,686	13,008	13,008	
N ANTIL	V	E	81	3,550	305	411	106
N ZEAL	A	W	83	600	996	1,321	325
NETHLDS	V	E	85	15,000	1,750	2,438	688
NICARAG	V	E	81	41,325	8,265	12,007	3,742
PARAGUA	V	W	86	36,700	4,100	5,100	1,000
PHIL R	A	E	85	8,432	2,486	8,380	5,894
PORTUGL	A	E	81	15,872	4,680	12,482	7,802
			82	116,347	36,363	86,121	49,758
			83	169,340	59,109	124,205	65,096
			84	125,111	39,884	94,156	54,272
			85	23,907	7,131	18,796	11,665
			86	38,691	11,251	28,759	17,508
	N	E	81	270,411	72,620	137,567	64,947
			82	187,562	61,119	100,167	39,048
			83	141,218	53,588	75,177	21,589
			84	272,760	95,375	183,098	87,723
			85	370,148	114,060	194,714	80,654
			86	274,513	87,925	199,999	112,074
	V	E	81	37,479	11,820	17,928	6,108
			82	10,406	3,210	5,272	2,062
			83	17,800	6,944	9,003	2,059
			86	23,076	7,297	10,944	3,647
S LUCIA	A	E	84	938	825	1,188	363
S VN GR	A	E	86	1,640	1,099	1,477	378
	V	E	86	28,875	7,012	7,998	986
SPAIN	A	E	81	3,527	1,260	3,258	1,998
TONGA	V	W	82	7,630	1,526	2,682	1,156
			85	39,683	4,858	7,500	2,642
TRINID	A	E	82	663	332	847	515
			83	450	500	1,190	690
			84	3,610	3,721	4,987	1,266
			86	10,186	8,300	12,592	4,292
	N	E	81	27,885	7,025	11,375	4,350
	V	E	83	2,100	462	572	110
VENEZ	A	E	83	257,594	66,239	88,545	22,306
			84	31,856	9,641	13,383	3,742
			85	20,000	4,000	6,429	2,429
	N	E	84	121,265	23,786	34,204	10,418
	V	E	85	87,088	7,960	14,845	6,885
			86	45,635	11,700	14,717	3,017
W SAHAR	A	H	81	10,000	3,488	5,400	1,912
	A	W	81	10,000	3,000	5,631	2,631
W SAMOA	A	E	86	6,000	3,600	5,266	1,666
	A	H	81	292,214	99,025	188,040	89,015
			82	34,660	9,270	18,585	9,315
			83	27,000	10,322	14,249	3,927
			84	67,657	24,611	40,007	15,396
			85	80,352	15,426	34,289	18,863
	A	W	81	397,696	140,884	250,398	109,214
			82	2,500	750	1,714	964
			83	17,550	5,460	9,935	4,475
	N	H	81	866,504	280,250	447,533	167,283
			82	1,072,391	349,593	587,418	237,825
			83	823,881	289,877	510,642	220,765
			84	599,537	204,646	373,547	168,901
			85	472,290	147,209	238,801	91,592
	N	W	81	15,425	4,782	8,897	4,115
			82	146,267	43,473	82,927	39,454
			83	230,787	77,295	114,933	37,638
			84	215,660	83,870	106,030	22,160
	O	W	84	9,000	2,565	3,608	1,043
	V	W	84	33,744	4,264	6,555	2,291
			85	1,163,539	294,284	388,364	94,080
			86	801,850	224,593	300,329	75,736

Date Palm

Date, fresh or dried
1473800 CHIANI DATES FR DRD NOV10LB (LB)

Country	Mode	Reg	Yr	Quantity	F.A.S.	C.I.F.	Charges
TOTAL			81	450	1,183	1,234	51
			83	60,402	40,423	51,280	10,857
			84	55,172	53,186	62,956	9,770
			86	11,022	6,400	31,382	24,982
CHINA M	V	W	83	2,000	2,766	2,957	191

Crop
Product
TSUSA commodity number, description, and unit of quantity

Country	Mode	Reg	Yr	Quantity	F.A.S.	C.I.F.	Charges
CHINA T	V E	83	1,500	1,389	1,549	160
	V W	81	100	319	330	11
HG KONG	V W	81	350	864	904	40
ISRAEL	A E	86	11,022	6,400	31,382	24,982
	V E	83	56,902	36,268	46,774	10,506
		84	55,172	53,186	62,956	9,770

1474100 DATES NSPF FR PITS, NOV10LB (LB)

Country	Mode	Reg	Yr	Quantity	F.A.S.	C.I.F.	Charges
TOTAL		81	262,037	333,101	358,402	25,301
		82	224,047	267,180	287,978	20,798
		83	226,396	203,280	222,418	19,138
		84	260,635	281,954	300,217	18,263
		85	308,282	394,853	417,372	22,519
		86	166,166	160,175	167,301	7,126
ARAB EM	V W	84	1,564	1,187	1,309	122
CHINA M	A W	84	15,000	14,551	14,971	420
	N W	84	151,159	179,249	189,529	10,280
	O E	81	500	665	777	112
		84	2,705	1,007	1,181	174
	V E	81	117,767	126,792	138,970	12,178
		82	89,275	103,555	113,094	9,539
		83	123,846	79,366	91,926	12,560
		84	16,061	18,567	21,250	2,683
		85	1,250	1,589	1,819	230
		86	2,100	1,045	1,144	99
	V H	81	1,830	3,336	3,567	231
		82	1,059	1,374	1,538	164
	V W	81	97,298	147,494	156,385	8,891
		82	104,814	130,342	139,047	8,705
		83	67,637	80,831	85,095	4,264
		84	26,188	17,679	18,874	1,195
		85	289,275	386,005	407,129	21,124
		86	142,306	140,147	146,388	6,241
CHINA T	V E	83	1,500	1,434	1,616	182
	V W	81	1,653	1,625	1,958	333
		84	1,000	1,286	1,363	77
HG KONG	O E	81	900	972	1,050	78
	V E	81	11,769	13,714	14,592	878
		82	11,999	11,571	12,686	1,115
		83	2,580	2,126	2,387	261
		84	1,602	1,829	2,029	200
		85	3,307	3,277	4,135	858
	V H	81	100	256	276	20
		82	950	1,269	1,380	111
	V W	81	22,957	29,158	30,619	1,461
		82	14,300	17,365	18,433	1,068
		83	30,833	39,523	41,394	1,871
		84	41,300	35,037	36,821	1,784
		85	14,450	3,982	4,289	307
		86	2,950	2,862	3,011	149
ISRAEL	V E	81	6,563	8,400	9,432	1,032
JAPAN	V H	81	200	269	292	23
KOR REP	V W	84	2,350	6,405	6,724	319
MACAO	V E	82	1,650	1,704	1,800	96
		86	15,900	11,521	11,908	387
PAKISTN	V W	84	665	490	539	49
REP SAF	V E	81	500	420	484	64
SPAIN	V E	81	1,041	4,667	5,627	960
TUNISIA	A W	86	2,910	4,600	4,850	250

1474200 DATES,FR,DRD,PITS,OV 1O LBS (LB)

Country	Mode	Reg	Yr	Quantity	F.A.S.	C.I.F.	Charges
TOTAL		81	3,713,241	1,471,225	1,757,177	285,952
		82	2,858,741	1,675,997	1,941,217	265,220
		83	7,827,167	4,537,282	5,092,152	554,870
		84	8,690,890	5,089,106	5,747,351	658,245
		85	13,157,196	7,910,324	8,989,478	1,079,154
		86	1,943,916	1,123,446	1,194,400	70,954
ALGERIA	O E	85	22,090	13,778	15,847	2,069
BELGIUM	A E	84	221	355	475	120
CANADA	A W	85	1,587	2,235	2,368	133
CHINA M	A W	84	10,200	12,326	12,682	356
	N W	84	52,524	57,345	61,397	4,052
	V E	81	63,725	58,939	64,236	5,297
		82	55,487	49,670	54,986	5,316
		83	66,233	53,570	60,293	6,723
		84	4,615	4,389	5,065	676
		85	1,000	1,072	1,225	153
	V H	81	1,424	1,967	2,078	111
		82	1,323	1,735	1,785	50
		83	200	315	343	28
	V W	81	53,189	56,240	58,074	1,834
		82	78,884	73,510	79,522	6,012
		83	7,063	4,532	4,868	336
		84	2,100	2,918	3,179	261
		85	59,850	76,589	87,416	10,827
		86	71,873	62,641	66,207	3,566
CHINA T	V E	81	1,500	2,754	2,855	101
		83	1,969	1,770	2,171	401
	V W	81	986	1,250	1,274	24
FRANCE	A E	84	265	617	786	169
GREECE	V E	81	2,646	1,600	1,892	292
		84	33,000	13,042	16,542	3,500
HG KONG	V E	81	4,225	5,304	5,626	322
		82	4,446	5,163	5,671	508
		83	9,750	3,918	4,610	692
		85	2,500	2,510	2,747	237
		86	26,350	28,572	31,128	2,556
	V H	81	150	306	322	16
	V W	81	3,387	5,151	5,546	395
		82	3,990	3,854	4,209	355
		83	5,250	4,431	4,629	198
		84	400	564	610	46
		85	5,425	2,170	2,577	407
INDIA	O E	82	2,205	678	764	86
		84	798	679	739	60
	V E	81	1,124	314	432	118
INDNSIA	V W	86	33,550	35,368	36,481	1,113
IRAN	O E	82	438,733	279,162	297,295	18,133
		83	4,260,766	2,358,514	2,662,203	303,689
		84	4,037,059	2,315,720	2,616,107	300,387
		85	5,114,837	3,091,034	3,478,700	387,666
		86	1,659,671	891,031	931,341	40,310
	V E	82	272,432	131,857	147,175	15,318
		83	896,211	657,637	694,382	36,745
		85	186,307	104,091	115,744	11,653
		86	69,184	35,500	43,048	7,548
	V W	84	1,549,137	769,284	857,560	88,276
		85	4,864,122	2,851,152	3,201,558	350,406
IRAQ	O E	81	3,565,815	1,327,889	1,604,107	276,218
	V E	81	2,686	342	455	113
		82	1,998,930	1,128,885	1,348,166	219,281
		83	751,186	450,103	502,954	52,851
		84	1,091,277	860,785	928,126	67,341
IRELAND	O E	85	68,290	38,788	43,924	5,136
ISRAEL	A E	83	9,923	5,405	27,384	21,979
		86	7,712	21,000	36,108	15,108
	N E	84	70,582	65,175	113,305	48,130
		85	123,542	175,661	267,287	91,626
	O E	85	3,960	4,320	5,593	1,273
	V E	86	2,331	6,808	7,039	231
JAPAN	V E	81	2,750	2,030	2,421	391
KOR REP	V W	81	6,489	4,905	5,298	393
MACAO	V W	86	13,950	14,509	15,031	522
MEXICO	O E	85	18,721	2,425	2,425	
	O W	84	31,085	13,073	13,073	
		85	46,000	21,950	21,950	
		86	59,295	28,017	28,017	
PAKISTN	N E	84	164,079	69,289	79,518	10,229
	O E	82	2,311	1,483	1,644	161
		83	1,068,202	593,721	674,527	80,806
		84	1,611,431	891,187	1,022,191	131,004
		85	1,651,934	1,046,878	1,204,737	157,859
	V E	81	2,205	1,007	1,282	275
		83	749,314	402,644	453,006	50,362
		85	41,887	26,600	27,081	481
	V W	83	1,100	722	782	60
		85	119,049	51,969	62,100	10,131
SWITZLD	V E	85	5,512	5,783	5,944	161
TUNISIA	O E	85	188,915	162,097	177,489	15,392
	V E	84	31,897	11,357	14,917	3,560
	V W	85	631,668	229,222	262,766	33,544
U KING	O E	84	220	1,001	1,079	78
	V E	81	440	279	289	10
	V W	81	500	948	990	42

1474400 DATES,FR,DRD,NO PITS NOV10LB (LB)

Country	Mode	Reg	Yr	Quantity	F.A.S.	C.I.F.	Charges
TOTAL		81	22,566	26,048	27,680	1,632
		82	42,485	46,425	49,949	3,524
		83	79,176	66,466	73,431	6,965
		84	43,200	40,808	43,756	2,948
		85	42,767	66,089	177,391	111,302
		86	24,847	17,108	18,341	1,233
CANADA	O E	85	2,425	3,025	3,025	
CHINA M	O E	83	55,119	41,667	45,194	3,527
	V E	81	2,150	3,734	4,035	301

Crop
Product
TSUSA commodity number, description, and unit of quantity

Country	Mode	Reg	Yr	Quantity	F.A.S.	C.I.F.	Charges
			82	9,943	13,138	14,404	1,266
			84	1,543	1,939	2,146	207
			86	2,500	2,545	2,638	93
	V	H	81	450	938	995	57
			82	350	592	663	71
	V	W	81	17,416	17,267	18,280	1,013
			82	23,146	22,396	23,927	1,531
			83	14,239	15,374	17,761	2,387
			84	22,613	26,748	28,120	1,372
			85	2,750	2,295	2,396	101
			86	12,266	8,336	8,839	503
CHINA T	V	E	82	325	270	313	43
			84	1,000	1,020	1,152	132
EGYPT	V	W	86	6,614	2,550	2,974	424
HG KONG	O	W	81	400	495	543	48
	V	E	81	1,750	3,060	3,239	179
			82	2,000	2,169	2,350	181
			84	812	1,250	1,400	150
	V	W	81	400	554	588	34
			82	2,581	2,977	3,177	200
			83	3,000	3,206	3,403	197
			84	1,313	1,110	1,465	355
ISRAEL	A	E	85	15,546	31,324	133,415	102,091
	V	E	82	4,140	4,883	5,115	232
			83	3,968	4,680	5,258	578
			84	11,111	5,040	5,632	592
			85	22,046	29,445	38,555	9,110
			86	2,579	2,652	2,865	213
KOR REP	O	W	84	3,600	2,880	2,880	
MEXICO	A	E	84	375	339	419	80
PAKISTN	O	E	84	833	482	542	60
	V	E	83	2,600	1,180	1,434	254
THAILND	V	W	83	250	359	381	22
TUNISIA	O	E	86	888	1,025	1,025	

1474600 DATES,FR,DRD,NO PITS OV1OLBS (LB)

Country	Mode	Reg	Yr	Quantity	F.A.S.	C.I.F.	Charges
TOTAL			81	2,386,905	774,326	878,682	104,356
			82	9,785,182	5,905,954	6,306,630	400,676
			83	12,717,600	8,286,184	8,854,354	568,170
			84	13,575,126	9,648,033	10,411,037	763,004
			85	14,621,009	8,360,523	9,083,149	722,626
			86	4,742,373	2,753,062	2,980,079	227,017
AUSTRAL	V	E	82	32,462	14,498	16,198	1,700
			86	79,344	15,847	20,047	4,200
CANADA	O	E	82	41,887	24,713	24,713	
			83	149,587	103,647	108,328	4,681
			86	11,022	6,240	6,240	
	O	W	82	120,000	94,000	94,000	
			84	19,841	15,974	15,974	
			85	39,694	31,758	34,933	3,175
			86	39,683	31,746	31,746	
CHILE	V	E	86	16,565	6,927	9,359	2,432
CHINA M	A	E	82	59,750	36,590	42,382	5,792
	N	E	82	1,268,064	681,773	754,989	73,216
			83	242,718	100,495	114,452	13,957
	N	W	82	200,000	165,000	165,000	
			83	1,733,995	1,046,393	1,143,552	97,159
	O	E	82	884,764	553,289	594,703	41,414
			83	853,944	573,735	587,956	14,221
	O	W	82	1,369,508	968,075	968,075	
			83	80,000	66,000	66,000	
	V	E	81	8,228	8,505	9,254	749
			82	697	745	868	123
			84	141,095	73,936	83,954	10,018
			85	184,036	100,385	113,650	13,265
			86	37,478	15,600	17,085	1,485
	V	H	81	1,020	1,128	1,210	82
			82	8,591	7,956	8,589	633
	V	W	81	1,480	2,433	2,501	68
			82	650,681	300,728	327,109	26,381
			83	53	269	280	11
			84	370,373	138,894	150,894	12,000
			85	6,832	9,621	10,127	506
CHINA T	O	E	82	97,554	37,820	38,268	448
			83	276	373	384	11
			86	1,984	2,100	2,100	
	V	E	85	35,274	17,736	20,099	2,363
FR GERM	O	E	86	255,002	144,463	145,856	1,393
	V	E	85	29,156	18,963	21,359	2,396
			86	529	1,632	1,815	183
HG KONG	O	E	82	163,488	60,975	67,119	6,144
	V	E	81	33,569	13,797	15,670	1,873
			82	135,741	59,408	67,796	8,388

Crop
Product
TSUSA commodity number, description, and unit of quantity

Country	Mode	Reg	Yr	Quantity	F.A.S.	C.I.F.	Charges
			83	294,860	125,984	141,978	15,994
			84	70,547	29,860	34,411	4,551
	V	W	81	322	283	289	6
			82	1,102,190	410,030	449,955	39,925
			83	4,222	5,663	5,886	223
INDIA	O	E	82	110	381	381	
IRAN	N	W	84	233,997	150,400	164,051	13,651
	O	E	82	155,204	106,959	112,099	5,140
			83	2,594,921	1,309,090	1,407,572	98,482
			84	3,460,258	2,225,914	2,429,891	203,977
			85	4,889,981	1,641,585	1,760,238	118,653
			86	49,823	28,205	28,205	
	O	W	83	26,558	25,508	25,508	
	V	E	81	94,798	54,525	62,661	8,136
			82	968,828	634,097	684,205	50,108
			83	2,768,483	2,210,805	2,309,064	98,259
			84	5,848,485	4,594,335	4,882,486	288,151
			85	4,193,449	3,017,518	3,253,081	235,563
			86	2,202,351	1,415,622	1,480,642	65,020
	V	W	83	1,164,580	792,524	852,388	59,864
			84	74,498	47,646	52,146	4,500
			85	1,823,646	1,140,660	1,266,233	125,573
IRAQ	A	W	85	1,000	1,082	1,150	68
	O	E	81	2,176,232	650,929	739,096	88,167
			82	80,000	60,000	60,000	
			83	308,810	173,140	190,857	17,717
			84	703,378	632,242	670,642	38,400
			85	786,602	698,296	738,667	40,371
	V	E	81	66,138	38,734	43,718	4,984
			82	2,403,667	1,665,582	1,803,710	138,128
			83	1,978,850	1,427,987	1,543,842	115,855
			84	860,786	739,558	798,627	59,069
			85	476,194	426,017	447,048	21,031
ISRAEL	A	E	81	229	432	437	5
			84	1,102	528	3,050	2,522
	N	E	85	10,630	16,394	21,573	5,179
			86	65,598	96,612	106,052	9,440
	O	E	83	154	264	279	15
	V	E	85	18,518	26,542	28,924	2,382
JAPAN	V	W	85	94,050	48,165	51,615	3,450
JORDAN	V	E	86	7,275	5,031	5,283	252
KOR REP	V	W	81	3,238	2,789	2,938	149
MEXICO	O	W	86	41,760	16,704	16,704	
N ZEAL	A	W	82	108	332	461	129
PAKISTN	N	E	84	1,096,992	575,179	649,346	74,167
	O	E	81	551	368	408	40
			82	3,638	2,194	2,386	192
			83	3,304	1,633	1,831	198
			84	635,903	389,451	437,987	48,536
			85	265,875	165,928	186,269	20,341
	O	W	83	20,000	18,400	18,400	
			84	19,841	15,873	15,873	
			85	89,658	65,495	65,495	
			86	3,086	2,160	2,160	
	V	E	81	1,100	403	500	97
			82	37,699	20,445	23,221	2,776
			83	450,176	271,491	301,420	29,929
			84	4,409	2,260	2,799	539
			85	1,311,392	713,948	807,295	93,347
			86	943,046	417,523	482,167	64,644
	V	W	84	33,621	15,983	18,906	2,923
			85	188,493	132,525	147,555	15,030
TUNISIA	O	E	85	38,301	24,170	26,003	1,833
			86	987,827	546,650	624,618	77,968
	V	W	85	135,803	62,304	80,404	18,100
TURKEY	O	E	85	2,425	1,431	1,431	
U KING	O	E	83	4,410	5,229	5,670	441
	V	E	83	37,699	27,554	28,707	1,153
	V	W	82	551	364	403	39

Date, prepared or preserved

1474800 DATES, PREP OR PRES, NSPF (LB)

Country	Mode	Reg	Yr	Quantity	F.A.S.	C.I.F.	Charges
TOTAL			81	28,692	19,243	21,082	1,839
			82	18,525	14,724	15,996	1,272
			83	13,348	11,207	12,011	804
			84	8,085	3,032	3,389	357
			85	27,682	26,081	31,543	5,462
			86	53,751	30,261	33,353	3,092
CANADA	O	E	86	40,320	20,160	22,410	2,250
CHINA M	V	E	81	14,429	6,740	7,696	956
			82	892	1,173	1,301	128

Crop Product TSUSA commodity number, description, and unit of quantity Country	Mode	Reg	Yr	Quantity	F.A.S.	C.I.F.	Charges
			83	3,135	2,595	2,926	331
			85	800	2,915	3,119	204
	V	H	81	613	709	795	86
			82	613	776	875	99
			83	364	326	370	44
	V	W	81	10,143	8,407	8,953	546
			82	15,421	11,430	12,340	910
			83	9,236	6,357	6,767	410
			84	1,050	909	997	88
			85	3,000	3,605	3,793	188
			86	3,000	1,806	2,000	194
CHINA T	V	W	81	1,096	1,404	1,481	77
GUATMAL	A	E	85	30	1,267	1,555	288
HG KONG	V	E	81	1,500	1,020	1,132	112
			82	911	1,062	1,174	112
			85	1,031	1,097	1,386	289
	V	H	81	250	348	372	24
	V	W	81	661	615	653	38
			82	688	283	306	23
			83	344	331	350	19
			86	5,250	2,360	2,493	133
ISRAEL	V	E	85	22,821	17,197	21,690	4,493
PAKISTN	V	W	84	3,307	1,125	1,238	113
PORTUGL	O	E	83	269	1,598	1,598	
SPAIN	V	E	86	1,984	4,655	5,098	443
THAILND	V	W	84	3,728	998	1,154	156
			86	3,197	1,280	1,352	72

Derris

Derris, root**
4930200 CUBE DERRIS TUBE ROOT CRUDE (LB)
  (See Barbasco, root under Barbasco)
4930400 BARBASCO DERRIS TUBE ROOT AD (LB)
  (See Barbasco, root under Barbasco)

Digitalis

Digitalis (Lanata), natural drug**
4350500 ALOES JALAP MATE ETC, CRUDE (LB)
  (See Aloe, natural drug under Aloe)
4351000 ALOES,JALAP MANA,ETC ADVANCE (LB)
  (See Aloe, natural drug under Aloe)

Digitalis (Purpurea), natural drug
4354500 DIGITALIS (PURPUREA) (LB)

Country	Mode	Reg	Yr	Quantity	F.A.S.	C.I.F.	Charges
TOTAL			81	9	14,216	14,344	128
			84	1	1,000	1,015	15
FR GERM	O	E	84	1	1,000	1,015	15
U KING	A	E	81	9	14,216	14,344	128

Dill

Dill, spice
1613100 DILL (LB)

Country	Mode	Reg	Yr	Quantity	F.A.S.	C.I.F.	Charges
TOTAL			81	1,185,374	500,079	594,170	94,091
			82	1,329,309	517,375	618,948	101,573
			83	1,317,512	533,111	621,985	88,874
			84	1,633,198	621,709	752,331	130,622
			85	988,593	359,969	446,451	86,482
			86	1,657,563	823,707	958,149	134,442
BRAZIL	V	E	86	26,460	15,600	18,800	3,200
CANADA	O	E	81	8	304	304	
			83	11,839	11,545	11,545	
			84	3,102	8,432	8,432	
			85	1,465	1,968	1,968	
	O	W	81	304	687	687	
			84	273	300	318	18
CHINA M							
CHINA T	V	E	86	24,063	10,974	12,235	1,261
	V	W	86	44,080	16,266	19,096	2,830
DENMARK	A	E	81	200	644	775	131

Crop Product TSUSA commodity number, description, and unit of quantity Country	Mode	Reg	Yr	Quantity	F.A.S.	C.I.F.	Charges
			82	810	2,255	2,738	483
			83	200	544	803	259
	N	E	84	1,200	3,591	3,917	326
	V	E	85	2,384	3,320	3,744	424
			86	3,440	7,947	8,252	305
EGYPT	V	E	81	119,089	159,063	166,264	7,201
			82	179,589	175,820	183,953	8,133
			83	153,568	178,329	186,948	8,619
			84	162,135	166,047	176,324	10,277
			85	87,698	66,136	78,394	12,258
			86	131,468	136,645	157,678	21,033
FR GERM	V	E	82	6,513	13,442	14,804	1,362
			83	9,834	25,429	26,553	1,124
			84	176	347	405	58
			85	9,751	8,744	9,568	824
			86	5,178	8,727	9,416	689
FRANCE	V	E	81	200	369	396	27
			83	34	411	432	21
			86	11,620	8,265	9,953	1,688
HUNGARY	V	E	82	4,431	11,410	12,408	998
			86	20,305	20,685	24,242	3,557
INDIA	V	E	81	895,952	281,796	356,258	74,462
			82	951,873	254,649	328,813	74,164
			83	898,582	226,707	290,275	63,568
			84	1,187,357	349,040	444,900	95,860
			85	798,527	240,687	306,202	65,515
			86	986,177	412,141	484,013	71,872
	V	W	81	165,747	55,417	67,596	12,179
			82	109,370	30,118	38,272	8,154
			83	154,487	39,729	51,739	12,010
			84	263,455	80,234	103,033	22,799
			85	67,957	20,533	26,878	6,345
			86	139,338	122,304	132,370	10,066
INDNSIA	V	E	82	44,092	20,392	26,069	5,677
			86	44,092	22,686	28,305	5,619
	V	W	82	32,628	8,941	11,531	2,590
MALI	V	E	85	2,504	8,064	8,726	662
MEXICO	O	E	84	7,219	2,382	2,382	
NETHLDS	O	E	84	3,000	4,950	5,666	716
	V	E	83	621	1,099	1,150	51
			84	749	791	964	173
			85	1,552	2,475	2,618	143
	V	W	81	426	599	618	19
			83	277	447	478	31
PAKISTN	V	E	86	221,342	41,467	53,789	12,322
SINGAPR	V	E	83	55,115	38,270	38,470	200
SPAIN	O	E	81	3,448	1,200	1,272	72
THAILND	V	E	83	2,162	1,350	1,504	154
TURKEY	V	E	83	8,680	3,729	5,021	1,292
			84	4,408	4,212	4,499	287
			85	16,755	8,042	8,353	311
U KING	A	E	82	3	348	360	12
	V	E	84	124	1,383	1,491	108
YEMEN A	V	E	83	22,113	5,522	7,067	1,545

Divi-divi

Divi-divi, tannin**
4702300 CHESTNUT NOT CRUDE OR PROC (LB)
  (See Chestnut, nut, tannin under Chestnut)

Douglas Fir

Douglas fir, christmas tree
1921020 EVRGRN XMAS TREES, DOUG FIR (NO)

Country	Mode	Reg	Yr	Quantity	F.A.S.	C.I.F.	Charges
TOTAL			81	342,677	785,413	789,641	4,228
			82	327,432	558,838	561,667	2,829
			83	236,969	535,896	539,144	3,248
			84	238,443	573,628	573,628	
			85	291,617	625,709	625,709	
			86	232,234	486,810	486,810	
CANADA	A	H	81	1,799	6,376	10,604	4,228
			82	1,008	884	3,713	2,829
			83	612	3,204	6,452	3,248
	O	E	81	160,782	341,250	341,250	
			82	170,359	180,359	180,359	
			83	54,875	74,591	74,591	

Crop Product TSUSA commodity number, description, and unit of quantity Country	Mode	Reg	Yr	Quantity	F.A.S.	C.I.F.	Charges
			84	69,113	208,389	208,389	
			85	42,399	163,058	163,058	
			86	33,026	114,260	114,260	
	O	W	81	180,096	437,787	437,787	
			82	156,065	377,595	377,595	
			83	181,482	458,101	458,101	
			84	169,330	365,239	365,239	
			85	246,878	456,107	456,107	
			86	199,208	372,550	372,550	
CHINA M	O	E	85	2,340	6,544	6,544	

Douglas fir, lumber
2021520 LUMBER,DOUGLAS-FIR, ROUGH (MBF)

Country	Mode	Reg	Yr	Quantity	F.A.S.	C.I.F.	Charges
TOTAL			81	22,030	4,766,780	5,738,270	971,480
			82	20,974	4,028,865	5,007,348	978,483
			83	79,481	20,629,794	24,990,392	4,360,598
			84	108,086	22,768,735	28,631,949	5,863,214
			85	127,313	28,784,138	36,398,384	7,614,246
			86	60,055	13,941,029	16,969,816	3,028,787
CANADA	N	E	85	71,472	16,256,968	21,696,781	5,439,813
	N	W	81	6,924	1,405,236	1,462,866	57,620
			83	2,268	520,296	588,703	68,407
			84	23,528	5,986,801	6,928,134	941,333
			85	9,688	2,608,460	2,609,254	794
			86	9,595	3,298,753	3,320,185	21,432
	O	E	81	955	171,039	171,039	
			82	1,039	263,320	263,320	
			83	13,347	3,772,040	3,772,040	
			84	10,907	2,562,080	2,562,080	
			85	6,154	1,291,772	1,291,774	2
			86	2,211	518,873	518,873	
	O	W	81	1,073	117,695	117,695	
			82	5,177	877,334	877,334	
			83	8,516	2,197,467	2,197,467	
			84	277	13,196	13,196	
			85	744	58,581	58,581	
			86	158	21,485	21,485	
	V	E	81	13,071	3,071,387	3,984,839	913,452
			82	12,696	2,626,843	3,544,088	917,245
			83	55,350	14,139,991	18,432,182	4,292,191
			84	73,348	14,201,359	19,122,069	4,920,710
			85	20,471	3,913,954	4,825,266	911,312
			86	39,743	8,630,370	11,391,458	2,761,088
	V	W	81	7	1,423	1,831	408
			82	2,062	261,368	322,606	61,238
			85	18,784	4,654,403	5,916,728	1,262,325
			86	8,307	1,435,020	1,675,268	240,248
CHILE	V	E	84	8	4,097	4,932	835
JAPAN	V	W	84	18	1,202	1,538	336
N ZEAL	V	E	86	41	36,528	42,547	6,019

2021540 DOUG FIR LBR DRSD EXC SDG ETC (MBF)

Country	Mode	Reg	Yr	Quantity	F.A.S.	C.I.F.	Charges
TOTAL			81	461,318	89,957,219	100,073,597	10,092,625
			82	483,291	77,640,312	84,815,952	7,175,640
			83	520,856	103,020,031	110,065,139	7,045,108
			84	494,868	92,526,312	98,984,241	6,457,929
			85	637,783	124,602,174	132,379,666	7,777,492
			86	626,121	128,667,543	143,272,944	14,605,401
CANADA	N	E	81	617	124,361	145,652	21,291
			84	182,168	35,308,656	35,308,656	
			86	94,933	18,142,336	18,142,338	2
	N	H	82	844	203,679	245,005	41,326
			83	1,062	304,440	386,163	81,723
	N	W	81	147,299	28,964,935	30,738,019	1,773,084
			82	109,401	17,335,231	18,215,874	880,643
			83	83,360	14,888,106	14,929,240	41,134
			84	152,165	28,057,440	29,485,571	1,428,131
			85	98,926	16,710,188	16,710,861	673
			86	76,271	16,892,933	19,443,400	2,550,467
	O	E	81	155,228	31,104,853	31,123,518	18,665
			82	261,030	41,617,779	41,645,863	28,084
			83	301,003	58,966,241	58,966,241	
			84	53,999	8,354,773	8,354,773	
			85	312,706	58,505,070	58,521,821	16,751
			86	185,604	34,607,092	34,640,999	33,907
	O	H	81	8	11,898	13,676	1,778
	O	W	81	9,545	1,651,580	1,651,580	
			82	10,448	1,483,532	1,483,532	
			83	23,519	4,849,085	4,849,085	
			84	30,917	5,342,332	5,342,332	

Country	Mode	Reg	Yr	Quantity	F.A.S.	C.I.F.	Charges
			85	40,675	6,794,171	6,794,171	
			86	86,079	15,371,888	15,654,956	283,068
	V	E	81	147,244	27,905,665	36,170,302	8,240,884
			82	98,947	16,609,992	22,764,664	6,154,672
			83	73,715	15,480,539	21,091,353	5,610,814
			84	74,380	14,997,258	19,984,329	4,987,071
			85	78,877	17,043,055	21,713,665	4,670,610
			86	183,138	43,633,625	55,371,582	11,737,957
	V	H	85	650	149,883	194,312	44,429
	V	W	81	1,361	189,904	226,827	36,923
			82	2,621	390,099	461,014	70,915
			83	38,197	8,531,620	9,843,057	1,311,437
			84	430	97,027	113,313	16,286
			85	105,196	25,190,098	28,227,799	3,037,701
CHILE	V	E	84	24	17,288	20,605	3,317
			85	11	7,950	9,400	1,450
CHINA M	O	E	85	8	7,403	7,403	
COLOMB	O	E	84	84	10,288	10,288	
	V	E	85	62	6,726	12,601	5,875
GABON	V	W	85	321	116,091	116,094	3
HONDURA	V	E	84	15	5,529	7,249	1,720
JAPAN	V	W	84	398	281,900	286,900	5,000
MALI	O	E	85	152	35,867	35,867	
MEXICO	O	W	81	16	4,023	4,023	
			84	21	10,135	10,135	
			86	19	5,879	5,879	
MOROC	O	E	85	146	29,120	29,120	
NETHLDS	A	E	84	81	18,130	18,130	
SPAIN	V	E	84	186	25,556	41,960	16,404
U KING	O	E	86	77	13,790	13,790	
USSR	O	W	85	53	6,552	6,552	

E

Ebony

Ebony, lumber**
2023500 SPN CDR EBONY ETC LUMBR RGH (MBF)
  (See Cedar, lumber under Cedar)
2023700 SPN CDR ETC LUMBER DRSD ETC (MBF)
  (See Cedar, lumber under Cedar)

Eggplant

Eggplant, fresh or frozen
1362000 EGGPLANT, APR 1-NOV 30 INCL (LB)

Country	Mode	Reg	Yr	Quantity	F.A.S.	C.I.F.	Charges
TOTAL			81	7,727,666	2,324,285	2,381,322	57,037
			82	6,969,590	1,555,123	1,597,941	42,818
			83	11,698,237	2,775,197	2,879,368	104,171
			84	8,043,004	1,821,149	1,997,735	176,586
			85	5,450,033	1,459,923	1,491,890	31,967
			86	8,000,757	2,211,138	2,255,162	44,024
CANADA	O	E	81	4,375	700	700	
			82	25,155	3,635	3,635	
			83	122,060	19,336	19,336	
			84	77,435	13,446	13,446	
			85	24,500	4,900	4,900	
	O	W	85	23,202	6,629	6,629	
CHINA T	V	W	85	14,270	9,521	9,941	420
DENMARK	A	E	83	1,925	308	715	407
DOM REP	A	E	81	37,316	5,807	9,776	3,969
			82	210,204	31,246	73,620	42,374
			83	42,895	6,058	11,897	5,839
			84	186,400	28,052	63,387	35,335
			86	76,002	13,012	25,463	12,451
	A	W	84	8,121	922	3,385	2,463
	N	E	81	352,402	40,120	92,814	52,694

Crop Product TSUSA commodity number, description, and unit of quantity Country	Mode	Reg	Yr	Quantity	F.A.S.	C.I.F.	Charges
			82	4,356	610	925	315
			83	480,518	75,730	173,400	97,670
			84	657,110	103,550	233,307	129,757
			85	134,180	14,717	22,972	8,255
	V	E	84	8,780	1,512	1,776	264
			85	203,697	32,806	46,913	14,107
			86	180,282	18,765	27,042	8,277
DOMINCA	V	E	86	72,298	18,606	27,006	8,400
GREECE	V	E	81	3,000	3,213	3,587	374
			83	551	475	475	
			85	5,863	3,811	4,452	641
HG KONG	V	W	83	3,086	789	828	39
ISRAEL	V	E	82	1,530	1,371	1,500	129
			84	220	850	960	110
ITALY	A	E	84	600	877	1,148	271
	O	E	83	220	372	372	
	V	E	84	23,438	16,263	17,998	1,735
			85	16,204	12,625	15,938	3,313
JAMAICA	A	E	84	5,670	2,520	3,780	1,260
			85	23,085	10,664	15,794	5,130
	N	E	86	185,493	32,876	43,477	10,601
JAPAN	V	W	84	659	1,430	1,715	285
LEBANON	V	E	85	392	1,004	1,017	13
			86	1,720	1,188	1,290	102
MEXICO	A	W	86	1,101	1,201	1,450	249
	O	E	83	59,623	7,300	7,300	
			84	25,845	2,310	2,310	
	O	W	81	7,330,573	2,274,445	2,274,445	
			82	6,728,345	1,518,261	1,518,261	
			83	10,986,157	2,663,729	2,663,729	
			84	7,019,402	1,637,430	1,637,430	
			85	5,002,545	1,361,992	1,361,993	1
			86	7,481,098	2,123,834	2,127,692	3,858
SPAIN	V	E	84	27,866	10,782	15,668	4,886
THAILND	V	E	84	1,458	1,205	1,425	220
	V	W	83	1,202	1,100	1,316	216
			85	2,095	1,254	1,341	87
			86	2,763	1,656	1,742	86

1362200 EGGPLANT, FRSH, CHLD OR FROZ (LB)

Country	Mode	Reg	Yr	Quantity	F.A.S.	C.I.F.	Charges
TOTAL			81	27,016,595	6,383,897	6,401,166	17,275
			82	27,361,245	6,045,478	6,076,229	30,751
			83	27,588,798	6,548,145	6,618,326	70,181
			84	31,571,566	6,687,061	6,795,780	108,719
			85	26,586,605	7,495,605	7,522,740	27,135
			86	27,662,147	7,295,790	7,384,210	88,420
CANADA	O	W	81	2,997	708	708	
			83	114,562	27,328	27,328	
CHILE	A	E	84	992	945	1,434	489
COLOMB	O	W	81	6,401	1,260	1,260	
DOM REP	A	E	81	98,041	16,710	33,979	17,275
			82	77,295	10,318	17,626	7,308
			83	209,253	29,360	58,210	28,850
			84	33,617	5,460	12,773	7,313
			85	96,661	18,387	33,181	14,794
			86	180,770	29,936	68,670	38,734
	N	E	82	137,864	19,703	42,272	22,569
			83	192,870	28,106	66,593	38,487
			84	668,835	112,171	211,842	99,671
			85	105,114	13,803	24,046	10,243
	V	E	82	16,212	2,683	3,557	874
			83	1,188	528	1,855	1,327
			84	25,950	4,189	5,422	1,233
			86	20,888	2,340	3,336	996
FRANCE	O	W	83	14,773	3,738	3,738	
GREECE	O	E	85	17,825	3,565	3,565	
	V	W	85	4,762	3,000	4,023	1,023
GUATMAL	A	E	83	2,300	322	822	500
HAITI	V	E	86	24,556	3,634	6,222	2,588
ITALY	V	E	86	3,771	3,432	3,810	378
JAMAICA	N	E	86	786,944	111,451	157,167	45,716
JAPAN	V	W	85	1,200	1,985	2,104	119
LEBANON	V	E	85	3,016	1,305	1,523	218
MALAYSA	O	W	86	34,978	9,996	9,996	
MEXICO	O	E	81	6,370	1,235	1,235	
			82	24,892	4,900	4,900	
			83	163,781	11,141	11,141	
			84	577,816	62,301	62,301	
			85	29,258	6,082	6,082	
			86	45,276	12,936	12,936	
	O	W	81	26,902,786	6,363,984	6,363,984	
			82	27,104,982	6,007,874	6,007,874	
			83	26,887,267	6,444,762	6,444,762	
			84	30,264,356	6,501,995	6,502,008	13
			85	26,324,702	7,444,334	7,444,336	2
			86	26,545,560	7,116,521	7,116,529	8
MOZAMBQ	O	W	86	19,404	5,544	5,544	
NETHLDS	A	E	85	1,664	1,814	2,296	482
THAILND	V	E	83	2,804	2,860	3,877	1,017
	V	W	85	2,403	1,330	1,584	254

Endive

Endive, fresh or frozen

1361000 ENDIVES INCL WITLOOF CHICORY (LB)

Country	Mode	Reg	Yr	Quantity	F.A.S.	C.I.F.	Charges
TOTAL			81	2,113,412	2,112,846	2,475,183	362,337
			82	3,310,750	2,904,851	3,521,552	616,701
			83	4,227,454	3,650,272	4,483,158	832,886
			84	5,635,209	5,323,422	6,649,853	1,326,431
			85	6,242,311	5,517,659	7,474,264	1,956,605
			86	6,936,053	6,379,996	8,997,406	2,617,410
AUSTRIA	A	E	82	1,841	3,545	5,593	2,048
			84	2,183	2,970	3,735	765
	A	W	83	1,250	1,493	2,529	1,036
BARBADO	A	W	84	2,840	3,906	5,111	1,205
BELGIUM	A	E	81	17,088	25,941	35,351	9,410
			82	93,323	116,967	156,536	39,569
			83	231,552	303,853	393,727	89,874
			84	330,906	420,664	560,204	139,540
			85	252,447	281,578	391,916	110,338
			86	249,534	296,290	416,404	120,114
	A	W	81	183,518	265,530	366,470	100,940
			82	333,494	353,863	497,493	143,630
			83	610,646	653,102	879,110	226,008
			84	152,831	170,834	241,452	70,618
			85	118,701	139,887	212,313	72,426
			86	343,545	230,365	425,013	194,648
	N	E	81	1,240,321	1,576,602	1,792,416	215,814
			82	1,694,647	1,728,238	2,053,945	325,707
			83	2,054,289	2,109,237	2,468,745	359,508
			84	2,453,273	2,635,964	3,183,361	547,397
			85	3,090,149	3,055,957	3,859,148	803,191
			86	3,674,617	3,567,208	4,417,684	850,476
	N	W	84	616,200	701,674	914,764	213,090
			85	627,409	516,747	835,385	318,638
			86	482,762	408,264	678,099	269,835
	O	E	85	4,380	3,942	3,942	
	V	E	83	882	1,291	1,411	120
			84	1,818	1,375	1,502	127
			85	19,471	18,728	23,361	4,633
BELIZE	A	E	83	2,400	3,540	4,567	1,027
BRAZIL	A	E	85	11,149	14,386	19,720	5,334
			86	16,310	10,415	18,500	8,085
	A	W	85	2,975	5,286	7,579	2,293
			86	2,745	1,038	3,252	2,214
	V	E	82	396,828	236,709	264,647	27,938
			85	48,678	11,040	17,193	6,153
BRUNEI	A	E	85	8,312	9,883	15,650	5,767
BULGAR	A	E	85	1,058	1,686	2,130	444
	A	W	85	2,101	1,551	2,420	869
C RICA	V	E	83	13,750	2,475	3,325	850
CANADA	A	E	81	1,600	2,480	2,967	487
			83	320	336	459	123
	A	W	83	2,480	1,250	3,003	1,753
	O	E	81	347,153	76,498	76,498	
			82	321,648	68,898	68,898	
			83	375,759	115,008	115,008	
			84	406,436	111,078	111,086	8
			85	136,092	34,449	34,449	
			86	92,700	21,240	21,240	
	O	W	81	900	1,290	1,290	
			82	250	313	313	
			84	3,300	4,478	4,478	
			85	2,420	3,104	3,104	
			86	2,750	3,619	3,619	
CHILE	A	E	81	9,365	8,000	11,485	3,485
			82	28,908	23,360	36,883	13,523
			83	41,580	19,500	36,950	17,450
			84	60,073	30,668	61,176	30,508
			85	39,225	17,793	40,516	22,723
			86	21,883	13,178	26,820	13,642
	A	W	82	5,976	5,724	8,853	3,129

Crop
Product
TSUSA commodity number, description, and unit of quantity

Country	Mode	Reg	Yr	Quantity	F.A.S.	C.I.F.	Charges
			83	1,437	725	1,742	1,017
			84	1,984	1,000	2,400	1,400
CHINA T	A	W	85	2,820	2,975	4,630	1,655
DENMARK	A	W	82	2,756	1,813	2,758	945
DOM REP	A	E	82	10,100	1,804	2,783	979
			83	9,180	4,531	6,648	2,117
			85	1,485	1,680	2,036	356
	N	E	84	66,800	10,066	12,591	2,525
	V	E	81	11,750	2,655	3,301	646
			83	58,800	7,056	8,942	1,886
			84	392,280	315,928	343,638	27,710
			85	521,584	56,595	84,610	28,015
DOMINCA	V	E	86	5,038	1,439	1,759	320
FIJI	A	W	83	15,999	4,800	8,725	3,925
			84	18,300	4,758	9,715	4,957
FINLAND	A	E	84	1,991	684	896	212
FR GERM	A	E	83	1,210	2,000	2,552	552
			84	3,277	3,780	13,492	9,712
			86	5,258	5,682	8,356	2,674
	A	W	85	5,523	6,701	9,921	3,220
			86	3,670	4,844	8,965	4,121
	N	E	85	23,348	17,780	23,469	5,689
	V	E	86	2,698	5,400	6,377	977
FRANCE	A	E	81	758	1,987	2,475	488
			82	1,927	2,856	3,713	857
			83	10,810	10,282	15,839	5,557
			84	3,809	4,109	6,143	2,034
			85	5,067	4,563	7,000	2,437
			86	22,672	20,441	35,588	15,147
	A	W	82	1,873	1,759	3,179	1,420
			83	7,744	8,505	12,006	3,501
			84	10,637	2,546	3,978	1,432
	N	E	82	46,446	45,739	53,252	7,513
			84	46,063	53,471	65,736	12,265
			85	46,417	45,972	53,786	7,814
			86	21,365	13,102	17,833	4,731
IRELAND	A	E	85	1,667	1,101	1,717	616
ITALY	A	E	83	13,598	14,824	19,111	4,287
			84	97,415	131,340	193,760	62,420
			85	360,926	493,714	748,433	254,719
			86	449,679	587,069	986,386	399,317
	A	W	82	10,479	6,151	8,658	2,507
			83	8,164	12,972	18,518	5,546
			84	72,820	95,741	147,869	52,128
			85	142,981	223,000	334,739	111,739
			86	166,709	212,128	383,532	171,404
	N	E	84	1,882	1,909	3,760	1,851
			86	490,081	406,436	733,346	326,910
JAMAICA	A	E	83	32,024	13,673	19,750	6,077
			84	6,705	939	1,610	671
			86	20,586	10,525	14,741	4,216
MAURIT	A	W	86	13,526	17,817	28,070	10,253
MEXICO	A	E	82	10,613	10,821	13,526	2,705
	A	W	85	35,358	31,987	37,876	5,889
	O	E	81	16,404	5,277	5,277	
			83	14,970	4,946	4,946	
	O	W	81	204,022	43,222	43,222	
			82	232,868	139,997	139,997	
			83	445,487	75,291	75,291	
			84	476,816	180,049	180,911	862
			85	342,024	101,228	101,228	
			86	486,052	102,321	102,321	
N ZEAL	A	E	83	4,743	10,427	13,691	3,264
			84	1,224	2,554	3,450	896
	A	H	83	149	352	442	90
			84	211	1,643	1,737	94
	A	W	81	22,378	39,691	50,035	10,344
			82	28,486	68,296	82,554	14,258
			83	506	1,303	1,693	390
			84	25,177	39,890	54,449	14,559
			85	2,190	2,176	3,498	1,322
			86	14,382	16,496	24,811	8,315
	N	W	83	26,151	35,037	49,602	14,565
			85	17,527	24,413	39,511	15,098
NETHLDS	A	E	81	32,178	40,865	53,677	12,812
			82	52,501	52,813	71,579	18,766
			83	135,422	146,779	193,726	46,947
			84	84,518	87,791	117,506	29,715
			85	30,510	39,840	57,312	17,472
			86	231,001	287,581	412,782	125,201
	A	W	81	12,277	17,688	21,284	3,596
			82	19,732	24,765	29,823	5,058
			83	28,407	33,847	52,750	18,903
			84	72,486	100,592	130,910	30,318

Crop
Product
TSUSA commodity number, description, and unit of quantity

Country	Mode	Reg	Yr	Quantity	F.A.S.	C.I.F.	Charges
			85	80,202	82,077	127,829	45,752
			86	10,048	8,908	13,008	4,100
	N	E	84	170,798	185,065	243,023	57,958
			85	236,674	254,918	351,785	96,867
	N	W	84	2,228	2,316	3,519	1,203
			86	82,087	97,219	160,916	63,697
	O	E	83	26	2,239	2,279	40
			84	550	989	1,010	21
NIGER	A	W	86	2,394	2,323	4,200	1,877
NORWAY	A	E	86	2,381	3,600	5,269	1,669
OMAN	N	E	83	47,719	40,628	47,261	6,633
PANAMA	A	W	86	1,745	1,424	3,552	2,128
SENEGAL	A	E	84	1,041	2,570	3,513	943
			85	2,332	2,185	2,823	638
SPAIN	A	E	84	4,619	2,645	5,111	2,466
			85	2,700	1,800	2,477	677
			86	2,750	2,528	5,043	2,515
SWEDEN	A	W	86	4,891	7,752	11,338	3,586
SWITZLD	A	E	86	2,659	4,020	5,607	1,587
	A	W	84	2,877	3,081	4,231	1,150
U KING	A	E	82	132	264	297	33
			85	748	1,091	1,415	324
			86	2,098	3,570	4,322	752
	A	W	82	5,872	7,031	9,244	2,213
			84	441	355	726	371
			85	4,411	3,034	5,653	2,619
			86	5,437	5,754	8,653	2,899
VENEZ	V	E	84	38,400	4,000	7,300	3,300
W SAMOA	A	H	82	2,500	875	1,867	992
			83	20,000	6,470	12,636	6,166
	A	W	81	13,700	5,120	9,435	4,315
			82	7,550	2,250	5,161	2,911
			83	10,000	2,500	6,174	3,674
	V	W	85	11,250	2,812	3,690	878

Eucalyptus

Eucalyptus, essential oil
4522400 EUCALYPTUS OIL (LB)

Country	Mode	Reg	Yr	Quantity	F.A.S.	C.I.F.	Charges
TOTAL			81	671,092	1,170,511	1,273,389	102,878
			82	534,661	1,098,881	1,191,414	92,533
			83	669,284	1,428,091	1,534,796	106,705
			84	846,875	1,908,983	2,034,570	125,587
			85	498,597	1,022,944	1,087,152	64,208
			86	645,528	1,206,860	1,286,313	79,453
AUSTRAL	V	E	81	19,290	6,670	7,007	337
			82	10,681	25,834	27,817	1,983
			83	23,348	24,191	26,526	2,335
			84	7,059	18,627	19,476	849
			85	26,675	76,319	80,269	3,950
			86	794	1,369	1,447	78
	V	W	81	1,254	3,227	3,450	223
			85	1,318	3,211	3,362	151
			86	794	2,366	2,520	154
AUSTRIA	V	E	85	10,031	27,412	29,789	2,377
BELGIUM	V	E	86	4,233	8,776	9,312	536
BRAZIL	V	E	81	15,819	27,649	30,698	3,049
			82	9,574	19,416	21,594	2,178
			83	57,100	81,431	92,606	11,175
			84	95,294	103,665	119,784	16,119
			86	14,816	20,698	23,544	2,846
CANADA	A	E	81	399	2,576	2,766	190
CHINA M	N	E	85	130,512	199,092	216,204	17,112
			86	457,452	819,061	871,843	52,782
	O	E	81	4,762	39,890	40,719	829
	V	E	81	183,334	327,671	357,532	29,861
			82	136,350	252,303	272,451	20,148
			83	302,169	631,945	678,396	46,451
			84	369,843	819,420	873,223	53,803
			86	13,492	26,557	28,668	2,111
	V	W	81	180,158	306,314	330,999	24,685
			82	174,208	336,288	362,197	25,909
			83	107,517	209,812	224,425	14,613
			84	125,221	307,350	324,396	17,046
			86	7,936	15,294	16,110	816
CHINA T	O	E	81	33,333	47,893	52,961	5,068
FR GERM	O	W	84	12	298	325	27
	V	E	81	661	2,865	2,970	105
			86	6,283	6,661	7,043	382

Crop Product TSUSA commodity number, description, and unit of quantity Country	Mode	Reg	Yr	Quantity	F.A.S.	C.I.F.	Charges
FRANCE	V	E	81	101,279	144,800	155,829	11,029
			82	20,020	24,477	26,867	2,390
			83	22,790	49,329	52,527	3,198
			84	4,299	9,697	10,296	599
			85	2,205	4,672	4,775	103
			86	21,991	33,915	36,296	2,381
HG KONG	V	E	84	4,762	11,609	12,277	668
			85	7,500	14,332	15,300	968
			86	8,730	15,734	17,028	1,294
	V	W	82	3,968	8,824	9,180	356
JAMAICA	V	E	82	63	1,609	1,705	96
			83	56	1,350	1,435	85
			85	1,802	2,663	2,812	149
			86	700	4,930	5,191	261
JAPAN	A	E	81	24	1,468	1,681	213
			82	4	321	370	49
	V	E	85	4,409	9,224	9,881	657
KOR REP	V	W	85	1,186	3,371	3,573	202
MEXICO	O	E	84	7,606	17,511	18,616	1,105
NETHLDS	V	E	84	437	668	684	16
			85	11,005	23,967	24,683	716
			86	5,390	10,399	10,732	333
PARAGUA	V	E	82	21,825	37,950	42,547	4,597
PORTUGL	V	E	81	87,691	160,418	182,067	21,649
			82	92,094	193,476	217,245	23,769
			83	81,877	200,170	217,108	16,938
			84	144,788	340,669	366,220	25,551
			85	154,850	325,722	350,282	24,560
			86	60,138	117,791	127,194	9,403
	V	W	81	14,392	27,076	29,184	2,108
			84	5,079	10,977	11,621	644
			85	8,532	20,803	21,665	862
REP SAF	V	E	81	11,192	9,037	9,857	820
			82	22,381	19,902	21,289	1,387
			84	11,023	12,653	13,581	928
			85	20,852	30,331	32,033	1,702
			86	11,191	16,976	18,591	1,615
SPAIN	O	E	81	4,409	10,278	10,278	
	V	E	82	9,921	20,583	22,491	1,908
			83	41,226	90,495	97,128	6,633
			84	35,274	91,292	93,913	2,621
			85	105,821	223,813	231,961	8,148
			86	15,714	34,930	36,531	1,601
U KING	N	E	81	13,095	52,679	55,391	2,712
			82	33,572	157,898	165,661	7,763
			83	33,201	139,368	144,645	5,277
			84	36,178	164,547	170,158	5,611
	V	E	85	11,899	58,012	60,563	2,551
			86	15,874	71,403	74,263	2,860

European Fan Palm

Crin Vegetal, fiber, raw and waste
3040800 CRIN VEGETAL RAW AND WASTES (LB)

F

Fennel

Fennel, spice
1613300 FENNEL (LB)

Country	Mode	Reg	Yr	Quantity	F.A.S.	C.I.F.	Charges
TOTAL			81	3,121,757	1,271,639	1,509,193	237,554
			82	3,042,082	1,287,209	1,486,410	199,201
			83	3,840,456	2,130,387	2,387,092	256,705
			84	4,378,826	1,783,915	2,133,605	349,690
			85	3,545,299	1,021,540	1,292,339	270,799
			86	4,915,265	1,562,837	1,895,286	332,449
AUSTRIA	V	E	84	990	1,148	1,300	152
BELGIUM	A	E	84	3,326	2,850	4,112	1,262

Crop Product TSUSA commodity number, description, and unit of quantity Country	Mode	Reg	Yr	Quantity	F.A.S.	C.I.F.	Charges
	A	W	85	2,755	2,253	4,492	2,239
			86	2,149	2,868	3,915	1,047
BULGAR	V	E	85	26,000	8,163	9,648	1,485
CANADA	O	E	81	10,320	7,228	7,228	
			82	43,850	36,368	36,368	
			83	63,263	61,205	61,205	
			84	6,345	5,920	5,920	
CHINA M	N	E	81	144,377	44,297	56,340	12,043
	N	W	84	31,364	14,266	15,879	1,613
	V	E	82	214,265	71,899	88,469	16,570
			83	491,507	201,741	235,919	34,178
			84	271,880	115,337	130,337	15,000
			85	232,725	44,929	56,712	11,783
			86	541,086	82,531	114,015	31,484
	V	W	81	253,523	66,911	79,971	13,060
			82	85,979	25,600	27,751	2,151
			83	174,041	62,289	75,327	13,038
			84	62,963	25,327	30,518	5,191
			85	94,797	17,870	20,280	2,410
			86	30,358	4,149	6,000	1,851
CHINA T	V	E	83	11,146	4,600	7,400	2,800
			86	19,000	6,945	8,745	1,800
ECUADOR	V	E	86	26,455	6,959	7,839	880
EGYPT	N	E	84	650,852	313,513	351,966	38,453
	O	E	84	375	323	323	
	V	E	81	560,955	196,938	233,431	36,493
			82	1,624,340	667,635	762,189	94,554
			83	1,848,097	911,563	1,017,684	106,121
			84	33,069	16,700	18,750	2,050
			85	408,988	105,877	129,755	23,878
			86	2,251,042	613,032	740,627	127,595
	V	W	86	13,167	3,378	4,804	1,426
FIJI	A	E	86	2,250	1,048	2,207	1,159
FR GERM	V	E	81	116	759	839	80
			82	311	1,115	1,195	80
			83	650	2,197	2,359	162
			84	252	827	886	59
			86	1,838	2,721	2,833	112
	V	W	81	1,790	2,617	2,885	268
			83	1,030	3,530	3,995	465
			84	188	649	733	84
FRANCE	A	E	81	269	571	686	115
	N	E	82	1,737	2,003	2,528	525
			83	8,928	7,420	11,063	3,643
			84	3,333	3,280	4,618	1,338
	N	W	83	1,429	2,815	3,394	579
	O	E	81	326	753	778	25
	V	E	81	154	320	335	15
			83	68	323	340	17
GERM DR	V	E	82	22,046	10,000	11,488	1,488
			83	30,247	16,450	18,065	1,615
			84	24,251	14,080	15,200	1,120
HG KONG	V	E	83	22,000	8,150	9,849	1,699
			84	19,842	5,130	5,281	151
			85	33,069	7,056	9,360	2,304
	V	W	82	22,046	7,070	7,750	680
			83	66,039	26,627	31,057	4,430
			84	33,069	11,191	13,531	2,340
			86	13,228	3,815	5,400	1,585
INDIA	A	E	84	587	330	380	50
	N	E	81	1,795,842	807,630	957,919	150,289
			82	3,523	2,246	2,430	184
	O	E	82	380	383	425	42
			83	9,135	9,588	10,163	575
			84	7,286	5,553	6,250	697
			86	4,409	2,200	2,529	329
	V	E	81	180,583	81,627	96,827	15,200
			82	971,613	429,358	507,456	78,098
			83	909,253	696,322	762,977	66,655
			84	2,860,392	1,089,963	1,325,447	235,484
			85	1,968,601	608,523	768,697	160,174
			86	1,220,514	606,297	703,617	97,320
	V	W	81	70,258	33,286	39,562	6,276
			82	23,972	12,992	15,299	2,307
			83	23,076	20,216	22,948	2,732
			84	77,249	36,753	44,728	7,975
			85	63,473	21,763	27,457	5,694
			86	56,178	20,828	24,601	3,773
INDNSIA	V	E	83	11,023	3,186	4,653	1,467
			84	33,168	10,516	13,206	2,690
			85	123,848	63,928	76,716	12,788
			86	44,092	23,806	29,529	5,723
ITALY	A	E	84	43,128	29,424	43,567	14,143
			85	9,058	6,725	12,941	6,216

Crop
Product
TSUSA commodity number, description, and unit of quantity

Country	Mode	Reg	Yr	Quantity	F.A.S.	C.I.F.	Charges
			86	11,983	8,082	16,318	8,236
	N	E	82	617	1,046	1,255	209
			83	3,492	4,223	5,672	1,449
	V	E	82	500	3,050	3,192	142
	V	W	82	356	834	975	141
MACAO	V	W	84	79	270	288	18
MEXICO	O	E	84	4,863	2,918	2,918	
MOROC	V	E	83	39,682	7,943	9,543	1,600
			84	44,092	7,650	9,450	1,800
			85	66,092	12,152	16,617	4,465
N ZEAL	A	W	86	1,270	1,081	2,184	1,103
NETHLDS	A	E	83	4,505	6,450	8,297	1,847
			84	13,074	13,160	17,874	4,714
			85	1,102	1,400	1,890	490
			86	8,851	12,149	14,892	2,743
	A	W	84	1,880	1,256	2,262	1,006
			85	2,753	2,597	4,336	1,739
			86	5,723	5,000	7,163	2,163
	N	W	81	1,141	3,348	3,983	635
	O	E	83	200	802	827	25
			84	100	4,506	4,516	10
PAKISTN	V	E	82	23,810	13,264	15,110	1,846
			83	22,046	12,825	14,394	1,569
S HELNA	V	E	84	145,988	46,814	58,877	12,063
SINGAPR	V	E	85	39,542	11,318	15,862	4,544
SPAIN	O	E	81	61,176	13,000	13,780	780
SWEDEN	V	E	86	3,042	2,343	2,423	80
SWITZLD	V	E	81	1,800	1,567	1,680	113
			82	2,737	2,346	2,530	184
			83	1,216	1,031	1,099	68
			84	3,955	3,365	3,518	153
			85	7,438	5,846	6,326	480
			86	5,005	4,069	4,303	234
	V	W	85	22,000	11,000	12,500	1,500
THAILND	V	E	83	125	2,240	2,460	220
	V	W	84	441	850	870	20
TUNISIA	V	E	83	33,069	16,700	18,750	2,050
TURKEY	V	E	81	39,127	10,787	12,949	2,162
			83	64,814	39,628	47,329	7,701
			85	443,058	90,140	118,750	28,610
			86	653,212	147,462	189,078	41,616
U KING	O	E	84	820	369	423	54
	V	E	86	413	2,074	2,264	190

Fern

Fiddlehead fern, fresh or frozen
1377800 FIDDLEHEAD FERNS FR, CH, FZ (LB)

Country	Mode	Reg	Yr	Quantity	F.A.S.	C.I.F.	Charges
TOTAL			81	46,746	27,874	28,444	570
			82	60,773	71,851	75,221	3,370
			83	54,519	60,487	61,270	783
			84	70,726	58,589	59,158	569
			85	70,786	105,408	107,830	2,422
			86	108,505	104,731	104,731	
CANADA	A	E	82	5,030	7,228	8,370	1,142
			83	135	390	440	50
			85	7,008	12,336	14,213	1,877
	A	W	81	1,741	2,014	2,584	570
			82	2,928	5,448	7,676	2,228
			83	3,000	3,779	4,088	309
			84	200	322	422	100
			85	1,500	2,835	3,047	212
	N	W	83	3,316	5,779	6,203	424
			84	10,313	14,544	15,013	469
			85	9,172	20,706	21,039	333
	O	E	81	15,030	14,844	14,844	
			82	44,642	48,195	48,195	
			83	48,068	50,539	50,539	
			84	33,813	39,938	39,938	
			85	53,106	69,531	69,531	
			86	94,854	87,314	87,314	
	O	W	81	29,975	11,016	11,016	
			82	8,173	10,980	10,980	
			86	13,651	17,417	17,417	
MEXICO	O	W	84	26,400	3,785	3,785	

Crop
Product
TSUSA commodity number, description, and unit of quantity

Fescue

Creeping red fescue, seed
1263500 CREEPING RED FESCUE SEED (LB)

Country	Mode	Reg	Yr	Quantity	F.A.S.	C.I.F.	Charges
TOTAL			81	8,903,257	6,196,595	6,201,087	4,492
			82	9,561,438	4,591,027	4,600,720	9,693
			83	7,059,110	2,993,148	2,993,675	527
			84	8,477,629	2,984,743	2,988,656	3,913
			85	14,111,440	5,046,443	5,095,529	49,086
			86	17,979,637	8,554,031	8,556,532	2,501
CANADA	N	E	85	2,593,025	861,739	861,739	
	O	E	81	4,882,297	3,422,065	3,422,065	
			82	6,440,824	2,898,465	2,898,465	
			83	5,760,239	2,395,923	2,395,923	
			84	5,962,955	2,088,736	2,088,736	
			85	7,558,420	2,682,470	2,682,818	348
			86	12,346,680	5,766,276	5,767,108	832
	O	W	81	4,010,818	2,749,494	2,751,009	1,515
			82	3,023,208	1,461,226	1,461,476	250
			83	1,297,500	594,981	594,981	
			84	2,469,340	879,268	879,268	
			85	3,442,318	1,305,522	1,305,522	
			86	5,588,768	2,764,873	2,764,873	
CZECHO	O	E	86	40,000	15,434	15,434	
DENMARK	V	W	81	170	421	461	40
			83	436	541	655	114
			85	64,920	22,028	28,365	6,337
DOM REP	V	E	82	92,241	220,250	228,822	8,572
FR GERM	A	E	83	218	470	653	183
	V	E	84	39,322	9,044	10,417	1,373
	V	W	84	882	1,403	1,628	225
NETHLDS	A	E	81	1,250	2,613	4,058	1,445
			82	436	990	1,212	222
	A	W	84	606	1,025	1,564	539
			86	1,543	3,859	5,128	1,269
	N	W	84	2,017	2,388	3,293	905
			85	186,575	71,189	90,689	19,500
	O	E	81	2,834	5,720	6,158	438
	V	E	85	37,075	13,830	16,875	3,045
	V	W	81	1,204	2,475	2,618	143
			82	3,616	6,796	7,232	436
			83	276	279	389	110
			84	1,515	1,242	1,435	193
			85	227,784	88,607	107,252	18,645
NORWAY	V	W	81	176	493	598	105
			83	441	954	1,074	120
SWEDEN	A	W	85	1,323	1,058	2,269	1,211
	V	W	86	2,646	3,589	3,989	400
U KING	A	W	82	110	300	313	13
	V	E	81	4,508	13,314	14,120	806
			82	1,003	3,000	3,200	200
	V	W	84	992	1,637	2,315	678

Fescue (not Red or Meadow), seed
1263900 FESCUE SEED, NSPF (LB)

Country	Mode	Reg	Yr	Quantity	F.A.S.	C.I.F.	Charges
TOTAL			81	52,794	48,900	54,532	5,632
			82	66,629	63,386	71,309	7,923
			83	83,250	97,518	105,568	8,050
			84	469,036	148,810	173,251	24,441
			85	165,195	110,026	125,567	15,541
			86	493,721	322,803	346,499	23,696
AUSTRAL	A	E	83	220	2,000	2,230	230
	V	E	82	26,000	22,869	25,870	3,001
			85	32,000	28,019	29,730	1,711
	V	W	85	26,350	14,493	15,848	1,355
			86	172,686	45,269	53,681	8,412
BELGIUM	V	W	83	386	351	464	113
			84	39,682	7,584	10,416	2,832
BELIZE	A	E	84	4,500	500	1,232	732
BRAZIL	A	E	82	1,120	1,371	2,218	847
			84	265	360	625	265
	A	W	85	75	2,409	2,936	527
C RICA	A	E	81	145	1,950	2,159	209
			82	323	5,150	5,656	506
			83	183	2,750	3,022	272
			84	42	510	570	60
			86	40	1,817	2,017	200
CANADA	O	E	81	15,000	4,551	4,551	

Crop
Product
TSUSA commodity number, description, and unit of quantity

Country	Mode	Reg	Yr	Quantity	F.A.S.	C.I.F.	Charges
			83	41,000	28,350	28,350	
			86	7,020	2,948	2,948	
	O	W	81	650	1,041	1,041	
			82	7,000	3,220	3,220	
			83	14,500	39,875	39,875	
			84	18,672	20,016	20,016	
			85	6,239	4,968	4,968	
			86	41,025	37,438	37,438	
DENMARK	A	E	84	200	1,062	1,248	186
	A	W	85	1,085	1,230	2,383	1,153
	O	W	85	5,005	4,004	4,004	
			86	24,340	22,518	22,518	
	V	E	86	37,423	28,807	31,250	2,443
	V	W	81	2,200	814	1,047	233
			82	2,160	2,170	2,310	140
			83	1,060	1,166	1,386	220
			84	1,080	1,225	1,360	135
			86	42,438	32,624	35,224	2,600
FR GERM	A	E	84	1,400	9,000	9,301	301
	N	W	84	42,990	20,807	23,328	2,521
			85	19,511	8,493	9,587	1,094
	O	W	86	39,664	27,795	27,795	
	V	E	83	10,823	8,103	9,260	1,157
			84	314,577	70,720	83,391	12,671
			86	39,682	17,700	19,841	2,141
	V	W	81	22,046	23,589	25,985	2,396
			85	1,213	1,997	2,355	358
			86	39,682	36,334	38,927	2,593
FRANCE	A	E	83	1,885	4,210	5,804	1,594
	V	W	82	560	1,843	1,960	117
			84	904	1,761	1,950	189
GERM DR	O	W	86	33,000	33,880	33,880	
	V	E	82	21,845	17,052	18,958	1,906
			85	1,531	1,456	1,543	87
	V	W	83	6,063	2,631	3,304	673
HAITI	A	E	82	231	1,200	1,327	127
ITALY	A	E	81	353	406	714	308
JAPAN	A	E	85	350	20,988	22,132	1,144
MEXICO	O	E	81	1,815	978	978	
			82	3,072	1,537	1,537	
NETHLDS	A	E	81	600	1,854	2,521	667
			83	288	374	525	151
	A	W	82	220	300	526	226
			83	661	655	1,319	664
	N	W	83	2,699	2,892	5,167	2,275
			84	40,300	8,119	11,847	3,728
			86	4,008	5,641	8,001	2,360
	O	E	84	990	1,022	1,022	
	V	E	81	5,025	5,679	6,693	1,014
			86	8,304	23,794	25,766	1,972
	V	W	81	4,934	7,752	8,519	767
			82	3,568	5,432	6,278	846
			83	2,821	2,753	3,027	274
			84	2,988	5,270	5,818	548
			85	71,836	21,969	30,081	8,112
			86	4,409	6,238	7,213	975
NORWAY	V	W	82	420	942	1,057	115
			84	331	586	727	141
POLAND	V	E	84	115	268	400	132
U KING	A	E	81	26	286	324	38
			83	661	1,408	1,835	427
	A	W	82	110	300	392	92

Meadow fescue, seed
1263700 MEADOW FESCUE SEED (LB)

Country	Mode	Reg	Yr	Quantity	F.A.S.	C.I.F.	Charges
TOTAL			81	21,392	20,171	21,520	1,349
			82	992	922	922	
			83	13,930	11,629	15,994	4,365
			84	55,643	30,997	34,659	3,662
			85	17,841	14,285	14,285	
			86	2,000	1,200	1,200	
CANADA	A	W	84	181	332	511	179
	O	E	81	15,010	10,606	10,606	
			83	10,000	7,032	7,032	
			84	25,000	16,365	16,365	
			85	17,841	14,285	14,285	
	O	W	81	650	3,478	3,478	
			82	992	922	922	
			84	2,200	1,914	1,914	
			86	2,000	1,200	1,200	
DENMARK	V	W	84	28,262	12,386	15,869	3,483

Crop
Product
TSUSA commodity number, description, and unit of quantity

Country	Mode	Reg	Yr	Quantity	F.A.S.	C.I.F.	Charges
JAPAN	A	W	83	1,399	1,364	4,364	3,000
NETHLDS	V	E	83	660	1,020	1,188	168
POLAND	A	E	83	110	485	549	64
	V	E	83	218	502	600	98
SWEDEN	A	E	83	1,543	1,226	2,261	1,035
	V	E	81	5,732	6,087	7,436	1,349

Fig

Ficin**
4374880 CRUDE FICIN AND PAPAIN (LB)

Country	Mode	Reg	Yr	Quantity	F.A.S.	C.I.F.	Charges
TOTAL			81	75,362	396,081	429,896	33,815
			82	24,536	172,380	182,627	10,247
			83	71,597	747,073	821,391	74,318
			84	37,676	337,480	358,207	20,727
			85	42,179	158,346	173,571	15,225
			86	30,889	215,319	223,881	8,562
BELGIUM	A	E	81	3,131	35,486	36,510	1,024
			84	108	830	896	66
	A	W	84	991	6,382	6,855	473
	V	E	83	2,205	18,507	18,701	194
DENMARK	A	W	81	168	2,259	2,769	510
HONDURA	A	E	85	1,662	3,350	4,275	925
INDIA	A	E	84	2,240	28,448	31,233	2,785
			85	11,663	34,284	39,417	5,133
			86	970	11,777	14,220	2,443
	A	W	84	110	1,500	2,130	630
	V	E	82	2,205	14,109	15,099	990
			84	2,255	28,186	30,843	2,657
	V	W	82	500	5,000	5,240	240
IRELAND	A	E	86	2,362	50,198	52,959	2,761
JAPAN	V	E	85	110	1,300	1,698	398
KENYA	A	E	82	3,853	27,688	29,006	1,318
	V	E	81	1,146	6,755	7,500	745
			83	55	615	626	11
LESOTHO	A	E	84	1,102	7,800	8,138	338
MEXICO	O	E	84	110	3,600	3,600	
REP SAF	A	E	81	2,200	11,750	12,337	587
	V	E	81	25,595	108,021	115,211	7,190
	V	W	85	8,818	37,392	39,112	1,720
SRI LKA	A	E	83	220	2,016	2,509	493
	A	H	83	1,102	11,398	12,822	1,424
	A	W	83	3,968	33,950	39,488	5,538
	V	E	82	5,842	42,019	45,179	3,160
			86	2,205	9,259	10,000	741
U KING	A	E	85	772	1,887	2,687	800
	V	E	81	4,321	14,444	15,381	937
UGANDA	A	E	83	2,136	18,169	18,944	775
			84	2,210	17,276	18,043	767
	N	W	83	21,078	179,994	192,898	12,904
	V	E	81	17,416	80,085	84,458	4,373
			82	2,072	12,910	13,216	306
ZAIRE	A	E	81	2,205	19,225	19,995	770
			83	38,786	463,390	515,059	51,669
			84	3,565	44,909	47,909	3,000
	N	E	81	17,097	111,042	128,029	16,987
			82	7,352	51,690	55,289	3,599
			84	11,023	79,943	82,500	2,557
	V	E	81	2,083	7,014	7,706	692
			82	2,712	18,964	19,598	634
			84	7,168	54,699	57,275	2,576
			85	10,115	41,372	43,081	1,709
			86	14,329	84,641	86,676	2,035
	V	W	83	2,047	19,034	20,344	1,310
			84	6,794	63,907	68,785	4,878
			85	9,039	38,761	43,301	4,540
			86	11,023	59,444	60,026	582

Fig, dried
1475100 FIGS, DRIED, OVER 1 LB EACH (LB)

Country	Mode	Reg	Yr	Quantity	F.A.S.	C.I.F.	Charges
TOTAL			81	1,289,705	999,429	1,122,733	123,304
			82	1,601,412	934,421	1,064,231	129,810
			83	1,272,061	667,743	779,495	111,752
			84	1,059,117	570,872	655,116	84,244
			85	752,513	391,093	448,604	57,511
			86	297,750	170,686	191,886	21,200
AUSTRAL	V	E	84	2,705	6,844	7,111	267

Crop
Product
TSUSA commodity number, description, and unit of quantity

Country	Mode	Reg	Yr	Quantity	F.A.S.	C.I.F.	Charges
	V	H	82	221	441	461	20
	V	W	83	441	860	895	35
			85	661	1,003	1,036	33
CANADA	O	E	81	2,100	1,416	1,416	
			82	15,480	13,307	15,948	2,641
			85	19,051	11,268	11,268	
CHINA M	V	H	84	300	519	570	51
GREECE	O	E	82	1,313	736	736	
			84	28,605	10,034	10,034	
			85	41,180	22,129	22,129	
	V	E	81	62,420	41,074	45,236	4,162
			82	614,623	340,046	391,279	51,233
			83	368,047	164,028	206,238	42,210
			84	459,792	220,156	269,819	49,663
			85	314,775	128,090	166,530	38,440
			86	79,200	32,000	42,000	10,000
	V	W	81	782,000	549,741	617,891	68,150
			82	759,000	413,912	475,139	61,227
			83	396,000	196,470	225,720	29,250
ITALY	V	E	81	16,458	20,387	21,634	1,247
			86	2,860	4,342	4,660	318
PAKISTN	V	E	83	1,323	690	780	90
PORTUGL	O	E	85	3,096	1,806	1,806	
	V	E	81	13,064	12,365	13,971	1,606
			82	35,824	10,351	12,391	2,040
			83	27,754	8,620	10,019	1,399
ROMANIA	V	E	81	40,000	20,710	27,290	6,580
SPAIN	V	E	83	14,319	16,033	18,760	2,727
			84	17,048	17,791	20,932	3,141
SYRIA	O	E	85	670	1,180	1,180	
TURKEY	N	E	83	419,673	258,287	292,408	34,121
	O	E	81	2,475	2,890	2,890	
			82	310	373	373	
			83	44,504	22,755	24,675	1,920
			84	207	783	783	
	V	E	81	371,188	350,846	392,405	41,559
			82	174,641	155,255	167,904	12,649
			84	550,460	314,745	345,867	31,122
			85	373,080	225,617	244,655	19,038
			86	215,690	134,344	145,226	10,882

1475300 FIGS, DRIED, NOT OVER 1 LB (LB)

Country	Mode	Reg	Yr	Quantity	F.A.S.	C.I.F.	Charges
TOTAL			81	3,670,398	2,839,557	3,245,477	405,920
			82	3,880,844	2,459,750	2,831,724	371,974
			83	4,377,728	2,388,976	2,835,982	447,006
			84	5,003,124	2,657,025	3,157,766	500,741
			85	7,521,766	3,971,374	4,727,495	756,121
			86	5,649,812	2,971,200	3,514,754	543,554
ARGENT	V	E	86	1,433	2,243	2,320	77
AUSTRAL	V	E	82	5,512	9,375	9,867	492
			83	176	344	363	19
			84	420	891	925	34
			85	880	2,144	2,232	88
	V	W	81	1,323	2,726	2,810	84
			85	661	1,067	1,110	43
			86	1,102	2,203	2,261	58
BELGIUM	V	W	86	6,614	2,967	3,374	407
BRAZIL	A	E	85	3,174	4,949	6,727	1,778
			86	2,222	3,083	4,268	1,185
	V	E	83	298	331	362	31
			85	36,750	20,752	25,137	4,385
CANADA	O	E	81	2,100	2,113	2,113	
			82	41,750	26,341	27,441	1,100
			83	15,100	7,950	7,950	
			84	20,865	12,475	12,475	
			85	99,020	54,346	54,346	
			86	50,567	33,088	33,574	486
	V	E	85	18,840	8,664	9,535	871
CHILE	V	E	81	13,270	11,376	18,069	6,693
CHINA M	V	H	84	200	393	432	39
	V	W	82	750	441	474	33
COLOMB	V	E	84	3,000	1,850	2,101	251
			86	27,241	20,460	22,570	2,110
FRANCE	V	E	84	900	420	463	43
G BISAU	V	E	82	5,512	900	1,108	208
GREECE	A	E	82	882	967	1,615	648
	N	E	81	3,562,702	2,736,818	3,130,313	393,495
			82	3,300,470	2,101,384	2,433,735	332,351
			83	3,589,126	1,967,004	2,362,129	395,125
			85	5,220,371	2,583,487	3,181,082	597,595
	O	E	81	10,314	8,925	8,925	
			82	25,410	21,271	21,271	
			83	27,461	13,751	13,751	

Crop
Product
TSUSA commodity number, description, and unit of quantity

Country	Mode	Reg	Yr	Quantity	F.A.S.	C.I.F.	Charges
			84	144,811	87,382	87,870	488
			85	280,874	177,141	177,141	
			86	69,615	42,383	42,383	
	V	E	83	73,500	49,154	56,280	7,126
			84	3,976,388	2,075,396	2,509,526	434,130
			85	78,750	41,025	50,010	8,985
			86	4,335,291	2,138,809	2,597,878	459,069
	V	W	82	16,800	9,626	11,226	1,600
			83	38,430	24,863	28,014	3,151
			84	408,735	235,690	271,773	36,083
			85	898,999	490,063	566,114	76,051
			86	411,345	226,521	264,031	37,510
HG KONG	V	H	83	200	290	340	50
IRAN	V	W	85	4,345	4,927	6,295	1,368
ITALY	N	E	83	16,093	23,298	25,615	2,317
			85	18,834	24,635	26,742	2,107
	O	E	86	17,850	12,325	12,325	
	V	E	84	134,514	99,997	111,609	11,612
			84	12,910	16,719	18,116	1,397
			86	12,120	19,416	20,839	1,423
N ZEAL	A	W	86	9,702	12,500	15,500	3,000
PAKISTN	V	E	84	937	340	530	190
	V	W	82	340	269	316	47
			83	882	340	529	189
PORTUGL	O	E	82	1,701	1,050	1,050	
	V	E	81	14,400	9,000	11,703	2,703
			82	12,700	6,185	7,777	1,592
			83	8,809	7,413	8,630	1,217
			84	15,636	7,319	9,949	2,630
			85	6,026	6,263	6,988	725
			86	8,923	7,834	8,768	934
SPAIN	V	E	82	6,384	4,658	5,615	957
			83	34,228	27,586	33,161	5,575
			84	27,219	19,048	22,787	3,739
			85	81,157	48,696	60,011	11,315
			86	103,263	79,770	85,873	6,103
TOKELAU	V	E	85	12,000	39,000	41,019	2,019
			86	20,988	13,304	14,971	1,667
TURKEY	N	E	83	66,382	40,984	45,221	4,237
	O	E	81	22,898	25,069	25,069	
			82	2,438	2,613	2,613	
			84	2,442	2,606	2,606	
	V	E	81	43,391	43,530	46,475	2,945
			82	325,681	174,673	196,007	21,334
			83	507,043	225,668	253,637	27,969
			84	388,661	196,496	218,213	21,717
			85	758,985	462,915	511,706	48,791
			86	563,820	349,604	378,502	28,898
	V	W	86	7,716	4,690	5,317	627
U KING	O	E	85	2,100	1,300	1,300	

Fig, fresh or in brine
1475000 FIGS, FRESH OR IN BRINE (LB)

Country	Mode	Reg	Yr	Quantity	F.A.S.	C.I.F.	Charges
TOTAL			81	24,194	16,346	16,380	34
			82	132,380	52,963	60,719	7,756
			83	5,815	3,594	3,594	
			84	31,342	15,432	18,254	2,822
			85	33,360	16,988	17,147	159
			86	30,100	3,188	3,188	
BELGIUM	A	E	84	147	545	770	225
CANADA	O	E	81	4,800	4,020	4,020	
			85	20,000	6,200	6,200	
COLOMB	V	E	84	13,061	8,600	8,600	
			85	2,800	3,000	3,159	159
DOM REP	A	E	84	9,625	963	3,053	2,090
FR GERM	O	E	82	29,762	7,711	10,058	2,347
GREECE	O	E	81	12,960	11,057	11,057	
			83	5,815	3,594	3,594	
			84	1,872	1,100	1,100	
			85	10,560	7,788	7,788	
	V	E	82	39,599	25,984	28,718	2,734
			84	6,637	4,224	4,731	507
HG KONG	V	W	81	750	420	454	34
MEXICO	O	E	81	2,800	503	503	
			82	23,019	738	738	
	O	W	81	2,884	346	346	
			86	30,100	3,188	3,188	
PORTUGL	O	E	82	40,000	18,530	21,205	2,675

Crop / Product / TSUSA commodity number, description, and unit of quantity							
Country	Mode	Reg	Yr	Quantity	F.A.S.	C.I.F.	Charges

Fig, paste and pulp
1525000 FIG PASTE AND PULP (LB)

Country	Mode	Reg	Yr	Quantity	F.A.S.	C.I.F.	Charges
TOTAL			81	9,686,815	5,393,438	6,034,548	641,110
			82	8,969,038	4,334,147	4,891,278	557,131
			83	7,990,207	3,227,868	3,713,964	486,096
			84	11,897,994	3,981,493	4,803,341	821,848
			85	8,289,913	2,095,823	2,734,172	638,349
			86	6,560,893	1,709,258	2,230,395	521,137
BRAZIL	V	E	85	21,120	6,040	7,580	1,540
CHINA M	V	E	84	40,000	12,084	15,276	3,192
DENMARK	V	E	81	1,596	800	894	94
			84	40,000	12,248	15,352	3,104
DOM REP	V	E	84	8,000	800	1,514	714
GREECE	V	E	81	1,040,000	611,001	686,711	75,710
			82	640,000	319,304	368,421	49,117
			83	317,368	130,122	154,406	24,284
			84	2,000,000	741,300	900,000	158,700
			85	640,000	183,847	227,143	43,296
	V	W	81	40,000	25,440	28,600	3,160
			82	120,000	62,014	71,685	9,671
			83	40,000	17,269	20,140	2,871
ISRAEL	V	E	84	85,000	32,462	38,956	6,494
MEXICO	O	E	86	26,189	2,884	2,884	
NETHLDS	V	E	85	40,000	11,395	13,467	2,072
PORTUGL	N	E	84	672,500	222,733	259,331	36,598
	O	E	81	430,000	233,987	264,194	30,207
			82	194,950	78,648	90,344	11,696
			83	320,000	125,194	144,622	19,428
	V	E	81	1,560,000	870,501	984,813	114,312
			82	990,000	467,296	535,811	68,515
			83	635,000	253,981	298,224	44,243
			85	1,082,584	295,506	365,648	70,142
			86	240,000	68,653	81,260	12,607
SPAIN	N	E	81	4,179,600	2,426,356	2,695,144	268,788
			85	4,058,288	1,105,307	1,441,109	335,802
	O	E	81	1,069,952	615,236	685,765	70,529
			82	401,750	201,528	227,161	25,633
			83	486,000	196,422	227,276	30,854
			84	940,250	304,421	368,889	64,468
			85	1,952,859	313,328	472,542	159,214
			86	1,772,350	308,680	489,557	180,877
	V	E	81	388,728	188,254	211,828	23,574
			82	5,138,386	2,622,296	2,932,361	310,065
			83	3,937,144	1,772,978	2,021,540	248,562
			84	5,878,892	2,055,790	2,487,381	431,582
			86	3,736,200	1,066,315	1,356,755	290,440
SURINAM	V	E	85	40,000	11,770	14,820	3,050
THAILND	V	E	81	200,000	130,823	134,000	3,177
TURK IS	V	E	84	74,736	9,273	13,002	3,729
TURKEY	N	E	81	651,949	234,936	279,588	44,652
			84	1,973,438	500,027	600,797	100,770
	O	E	81	124,990	56,104	63,011	6,907
			82	712,620	341,072	384,602	43,530
			83	397,556	184,112	203,764	19,652
			84	185,178	90,346	102,843	12,497
	V	E	82	769,999	240,204	279,011	38,807
			83	1,852,120	542,859	638,645	95,786
			85	455,062	168,630	191,863	23,233
			86	786,154	262,726	299,939	37,213
U KING	V	E	82	1,333	1,785	1,882	97
			83	5,019	4,931	5,347	416

Fig, prepared or preserved
1475400 FIGS, PREP OR PRES, NSPF (LB)

Country	Mode	Reg	Yr	Quantity	F.A.S.	C.I.F.	Charges
TOTAL			81	86,548	70,171	78,844	8,673
			82	101,512	71,917	81,556	9,639
			83	149,862	109,663	127,277	17,614
			84	451,045	312,077	359,953	47,876
			85	288,538	147,555	179,158	31,603
			86	76,520	76,781	82,839	6,058
BELGIUM	V	E	84	1,591	1,546	1,822	276
BRAZIL	V	E	83	2,279	2,495	2,843	348
			86	2,714	1,200	1,362	162
	V	W	83	281	276	358	82
COLOMB	A	E	83	14,660	14,149	17,083	2,934
	O	E	85	6,270	4,569	5,165	596
	V	E	81	54,276	33,745	39,276	5,531
			82	52,020	33,756	38,711	4,955
			83	65,248	40,339	47,067	6,728

Country	Mode	Reg	Yr	Quantity	F.A.S.	C.I.F.	Charges
			84	212,398	158,091	179,439	21,348
			85	18,505	16,998	18,706	1,708
			86	19,859	15,115	15,831	716
CYPRUS	V	E	83	243	600	634	34
DENMARK	V	W	83	1,125	1,928	2,163	235
ECUADOR	V	E	83	2,013	2,090	2,216	126
			84	3,600	2,160	2,391	231
			85	6,000	3,800	4,227	427
FRANCE	O	E	81	2,689	3,672	3,972	300
			82	5,583	1,074	1,224	150
			86	540	1,068	1,088	20
	V	E	81	2,764	3,796	4,111	315
			82	2,099	2,788	3,116	328
			83	2,256	2,964	3,272	308
			84	3,382	4,387	4,834	447
GREECE	O	E	81	1,722	1,785	1,785	
			83	1,050	817	817	
			84	17,762	16,150	16,353	203
	V	E	81	6,531	5,984	7,013	1,029
			82	5,991	3,900	4,569	669
			83	47,542	25,730	31,158	5,428
			84	161,396	84,974	103,841	18,867
			85	239,036	99,516	126,660	27,144
	V	W	82	2,138	1,800	2,046	246
			83	889	863	966	103
			84	2,093	1,925	2,199	274
			85	1,190	1,100	1,263	163
HG KONG	V	W	86	3,500	4,720	4,836	116
ISRAEL	V	E	81	6,000	2,300	2,643	343
			86	3,244	4,067	4,320	253
ITALY	O	E	84	3,250	1,689	1,689	
	V	E	81	12,566	18,889	20,044	1,155
			82	33,681	28,599	31,890	3,291
			83	8,911	13,376	14,247	871
			84	6,480	11,243	12,176	933
			85	9,188	14,574	15,781	1,207
			86	9,360	19,937	21,398	1,461
KOR REP	V	W	84	765	1,811	2,023	212
MEXICO	O	W	85	1,575	1,275	1,275	
PORTUGL	A	E	84	2,304	5,184	7,735	2,551
	O	E	85	2,904	1,232	1,232	
	V	E	83	618	1,033	1,142	109
			84	1,781	1,454	1,874	420
			86	5,401	3,185	3,653	468
SPAIN	V	E	86	10,714	6,888	7,665	777
THAILND	V	W	86	11,001	12,546	13,615	1,069
TURKEY	V	E	84	32,804	19,752	21,651	1,899
			86	9,287	6,835	7,721	886
U KING	V	E	83	2,747	3,003	3,311	308
			84	1,439	1,711	1,926	215
			85	270	1,191	1,247	56
			86	900	1,220	1,350	130
VENEZ	O	E	85	3,600	3,300	3,602	302

Filbert

Filbert, nut, shelled, prepared or preserved
1454600 FILBERT NUTS, SHELLED, ETC (LB)

Country	Mode	Reg	Yr	Quantity	F.A.S.	C.I.F.	Charges
TOTAL			81	3,139,901	5,207,399	5,450,387	242,988
			82	5,712,335	6,322,627	6,760,127	437,500
			83	5,387,356	5,848,241	6,281,797	433,556
			84	8,570,840	8,811,793	9,508,024	696,231
			85	7,746,061	9,643,352	10,286,941	643,589
			86	3,209,821	5,301,206	5,572,250	271,044
BELGIUM	A	W	84	150	256	334	78
	N	E	82	3,483	4,141	4,414	273
	O	E	81	1,102	2,039	2,114	75
			84	2,590	2,625	2,823	198
	V	E	81	121,361	191,305	200,272	8,967
			82	99,205	122,373	133,746	11,373
			83	68,520	72,937	80,507	7,570
			84	144,993	137,877	154,232	16,355
			85	118,031	148,222	162,291	14,069
			86	113,263	186,911	199,405	12,494
	V	W	86	13,977	32,947	35,089	2,142
BRAZIL	V	E	84	21,604	26,200	28,041	1,841
BULGAR	V	E	86	793	4,772	4,920	148
CANADA	O	E	81	2,690	4,084	4,084	
			83	475	992	992	

Crop
Product
TSUSA commodity number, description, and unit of quantity

Country	Mode	Reg	Yr	Quantity	F.A.S.	C.I.F.	Charges
			84	988	2,029	2,029	
CHINA T	V	E	83	6,000	4,300	4,594	294
COLOMB	V	E	85	1,120	3,552	4,186	634
DENMARK	V	E	86	1,323	1,642	1,860	218
	V	W	86	1,323	1,615	1,860	245
FR GERM	A	E	85	1,100	1,560	2,210	650
	N	E	81	23,565	42,161	44,415	2,254
			82	1,130	3,240	3,475	235
	O	E	83	84,000	100,200	104,200	4,000
			84	82,364	84,172	91,121	6,949
	V	E	83	13,882	13,926	15,065	1,139
			84	751	1,891	2,017	126
			86	30,610	50,492	52,882	2,390
	V	W	81	525	477	569	92
			82	1,102	1,765	1,780	15
			85	776	1,230	1,330	100
FRANCE	N	E	83	13,563	24,887	26,523	1,636
	V	E	81	2,115	3,606	3,814	208
			82	441	794	835	41
			84	856	1,550	1,730	180
			85	3,705	4,818	5,333	515
			86	15,282	29,316	30,731	1,415
	V	W	82	1,386	3,294	3,347	53
			83	1,649	3,541	3,824	283
			84	172	440	470	30
INDNSIA	V	E	85	21,606	24,000	25,495	1,495
IRAN	V	E	85	54,013	65,425	67,963	2,538
			86	74,956	116,363	122,823	6,460
ISRAEL	V	E	86	554	2,403	2,752	349
ITALY	A	E	82	101	291	365	74
	N	E	82	269,853	324,019	345,147	21,128
			83	241,847	243,485	259,269	15,784
	O	E	81	87,692	160,600	170,203	9,603
			82	958,685	1,191,202	1,251,964	60,762
			83	693,290	822,724	861,356	38,632
			84	432,108	493,992	518,406	24,414
			85	22,000	24,000	25,710	1,710
	V	E	81	106,556	194,187	209,084	14,897
			82	44,092	44,000	46,674	2,674
			83	268	954	1,021	67
			84	576,005	587,554	625,141	37,587
			85	5,765	9,565	11,542	1,977
			86	44,707	71,626	77,513	5,887
	V	W	81	1,728	2,468	2,572	104
			82	43,585	53,315	59,756	6,441
			83	6,614	10,578	11,623	1,045
			84	231,484	270,489	286,921	16,432
MEXICO	O	E	81	360,420	376,272	376,272	
	O	W	81	1,056	317	317	
NETHLDS	V	E	81	370	367	419	52
			82	3,593	2,945	3,205	260
			83	300	1,753	1,856	103
			85	1,378	2,095	2,215	120
	V	W	81	370	410	458	48
			85	1,753	1,304	1,382	78
SPAIN	O	E	82	33,165	34,378	37,123	2,745
	V	E	82	662	1,809	1,990	181
			83	2,981	4,466	5,162	696
			84	1,031	1,852	2,050	198
			85	1,031	2,026	2,026	
			86	913	3,024	3,351	327
SWITZLD	O	E	85	3,391	4,915	5,054	139
	O	W	85	1,787	2,195	2,339	144
	V	E	81	1,650	4,397	4,610	213
			82	4,122	9,698	10,401	703
			83	23,821	32,688	34,933	2,245
			84	4,048	8,622	9,519	897
			85	1,270	3,089	3,273	184
			86	2,141	7,396	8,225	829
	V	W	82	1,482	2,286	2,496	210
			83	159	370	415	45
			84	159	335	397	62
			85	397	1,005	1,111	106
THAILND	V	E	83	600	626	688	62
TOKELAU	O	E	86	44,092	77,000	80,422	3,422
TURKEY	N	E	82	1,678,664	1,735,636	1,871,995	136,359
			83	2,100,396	2,134,167	2,324,459	190,292
			84	3,523,562	3,558,181	3,858,157	299,976
			86	4,738	9,842	10,155	313
	O	E	81	1,168,954	2,050,264	2,141,363	91,099
			82	2,259,216	2,455,733	2,629,018	173,285
			83	1,875,527	2,093,002	2,248,803	155,801
			84	1,791,489	1,846,022	1,996,718	150,696
			85	2,015,281	2,389,448	2,539,791	150,343

Crop
Product
TSUSA commodity number, description, and unit of quantity

Country	Mode	Reg	Yr	Quantity	F.A.S.	C.I.F.	Charges
			86	719,339	1,070,920	1,126,781	55,861
	O	W	86	58,000	37,700	39,555	1,855
	V	E	81	1,259,747	2,174,445	2,289,821	115,376
			82	297,345	317,858	337,691	19,833
			83	253,464	282,645	296,507	13,862
			84	1,647,594	1,672,156	1,804,253	132,097
			85	5,373,348	6,823,653	7,281,553	457,900
			86	2,083,810	3,597,237	3,773,926	176,689
	V	W	82	11,023	13,850	14,705	855
			84	108,892	115,550	123,665	8,115
			85	118,309	131,250	142,137	10,887

Filbert, nut, unshelled
1451800 FILBERTS NOT SHELLED (LB)

Country	Mode	Reg	Yr	Quantity	F.A.S.	C.I.F.	Charges
TOTAL			81	11,016	7,038	7,068	30
			82	1,526,664	913,033	985,680	72,647
			83	250,468	118,692	134,668	15,976
			84	623,652	236,665	262,078	25,413
			85	143,378	149,398	160,197	10,799
			86	23,744	35,937	38,147	2,210
CANADA	O	E	81	10,016	6,538	6,538	
			84	166,250	22,268	22,268	
FRANCE	V	W	84	27,500	13,400	15,400	2,000
INDIA	O	E	82	350	800	818	18
ITALY	O	E	82	44,092	20,300	23,046	2,746
	V	E	82	1,056,221	661,687	702,698	41,011
			83	162,276	78,678	89,357	10,679
			84	361,559	155,967	175,035	19,068
			85	44,092	26,400	30,503	4,103
	V	W	82	426,001	230,246	259,118	28,872
			83	88,192	40,014	45,311	5,297
SPAIN	V	E	84	46,297	20,030	22,050	2,020
SWITZLD	V	E	86	1,102	1,776	1,891	115
TURKEY	O	E	81	1,000	500	530	30
			85	25,432	27,778	27,778	
	V	E	84	22,046	25,000	27,325	2,325
			85	73,854	95,220	101,916	6,696
			86	22,045	32,100	33,725	1,625
U KING	A	E	86	597	2,061	2,531	470

Flax

Flax, fiber, hackled
3041600 FLAX HACKLED (LB)

Country	Mode	Reg	Yr	Quantity	F.A.S.	C.I.F.	Charges
TOTAL			81	93,694	84,930	90,056	5,126
			82	163,533	120,234	128,531	8,297
			83	102,307	82,321	89,082	6,761
			84	242,198	250,467	270,246	19,779
			85	91,629	90,414	98,062	7,648
			86	88,401	77,228	84,419	7,191
BELGIUM	A	E	83	2,117	3,697	4,811	1,114
			84	5,678	6,567	9,696	3,129
			86	518	1,224	1,718	494
	N	E	83	92,628	63,832	68,645	4,813
			84	158,179	160,821	169,640	8,819
			85	3,392	7,734	8,959	1,225
	O	E	86	40,410	32,006	34,606	2,600
	V	E	81	92,152	81,609	86,475	4,866
			82	162,503	117,047	125,105	8,058
			83	6,432	11,942	12,495	553
			84	77,793	81,420	89,089	7,669
			85	84,674	76,168	82,074	5,906
			86	1,860	3,983	4,387	404
FRANCE	V	W	81	970	1,602	1,716	114
			83	619	1,311	1,516	205
			86	326	457	588	131
IRELAND	A	E	82	550	1,649	1,863	214
			85	124	604	674	70
	V	E	86	559	1,664	1,846	182
ITALY	V	E	86	38,195	32,677	35,291	2,614
NETHLDS	V	E	85	3,439	5,908	6,355	447
U KING	V	E	81	572	1,719	1,865	146
			82	480	1,538	1,563	25
			83	511	1,539	1,615	76
			84	548	1,659	1,821	162
			86	6,533	5,217	5,983	766

Crop Product TSUSA commodity number, description, and unit of quantity Country	Mode	Reg	Yr	Quantity	F.A.S.	C.I.F.	Charges

Flax, fiber, processed
3041400 FLAX PROCESSED NO CRD NO HCK (LB)

Country	Mode	Reg	Yr	Quantity	F.A.S.	C.I.F.	Charges
TOTAL			85	7,937	11,858	12,816	958
BELGIUM	V	E	85	7,937	11,858	12,816	958

3041800 FLAX FIBERS, PROCESS, NSPF (LB)

Country	Mode	Reg	Yr	Quantity	F.A.S.	C.I.F.	Charges
TOTAL			81	800,369	687,731	738,709	50,978
			82	689,841	514,003	558,389	44,386
			83	1,326,822	1,111,100	1,188,758	77,658
			84	1,688,208	1,714,898	1,816,635	101,737
			85	562,116	626,601	718,476	91,875
			86	739,265	773,871	847,557	73,686
BELGIUM	A	E	86	303	363	619	256
	N	E	81	139,026	248,948	258,952	10,004
	O	E	81	19,095	18,325	19,980	1,655
	V	E	81	622,050	390,292	426,495	36,203
			82	641,568	405,928	439,880	33,952
			83	1,216,906	861,915	918,485	56,570
			84	1,416,556	1,340,908	1,414,854	73,946
			85	401,007	338,179	393,146	54,967
			86	535,491	385,089	427,912	42,823
	V	W	85	381	776	904	128
BULGAR	V	E	85	31,049	30,905	33,035	2,130
			86	41,925	45,844	49,189	3,345
CANADA	A	E	84	2,337	1,500	1,650	150
	O	E	86	29	369	465	96
CHINA M	V	E	85	9,039	15,662	17,807	2,145
DENMARK	A	E	85	643	2,260	2,591	331
EGYPT	V	E	81	1,100	800	864	64
			84	11,000	7,500	8,250	750
			85	22,046	15,000	17,200	2,200
FR GERM	V	E	85	306	681	884	203
FRANCE	A	E	81	119	300	315	15
			83	3,057	8,637	10,068	1,431
			84	1,483	7,246	7,979	733
			85	2,125	7,895	9,497	1,602
			86	1,052	1,445	2,265	820
	O	E	85	1,392	1,940	2,939	999
			86	19,075	31,037	33,937	2,900
	V	E	81	1,499	4,047	4,660	613
			83	185	450	474	24
			84	11,375	25,132	27,047	1,915
			85	35,122	57,203	61,242	4,039
			86	35,991	34,048	40,133	6,085
	V	W	81	90	398	433	35
			86	498	1,226	1,426	200
IRELAND	A	E	83	4,569	10,301	11,940	1,639
			85	7,158	12,196	16,777	4,581
	N	E	83	33,424	76,128	78,865	2,737
			84	22,784	72,107	74,282	2,175
	V	E	85	16,901	54,334	60,844	6,510
			86	33,307	88,562	96,677	8,115
ITALY	A	E	82	123	663	808	145
			83	3,541	14,175	15,912	1,737
			84	1,732	4,262	6,004	1,742
			86	317	675	1,013	338
	A	W	84	113	435	461	26
			85	110	400	532	132
SPAIN	V	E	86	17,793	47,892	50,327	2,435
SWEDEN	A	E	85	82	1,389	1,581	192
U KING	A	E	82	1,000	2,179	2,690	511
			83	9,002	16,012	19,982	3,970
			84	8,188	19,288	22,715	3,427
			85	111	441	534	93
	N	E	82	47,150	105,233	115,011	9,778
			83	54,721	122,172	129,552	7,380
			84	193,755	172,440	184,847	12,407
			86	20,791	94,609	98,893	4,284
	V	E	81	17,390	24,621	27,010	2,389
			83	1,417	1,310	3,480	2,170
			84	18,885	64,080	68,546	4,466
			85	34,644	87,340	98,963	11,623
			86	32,693	42,712	44,701	1,989

Flax, fiber, raw
3041000 FLAX, RAW (LB)

Country	Mode	Reg	Yr	Quantity	F.A.S.	C.I.F.	Charges
TOTAL			81	25,526	24,748	27,087	2,339
			82	2,013	5,056	5,570	514
			83	441	357	357	

Country	Mode	Reg	Yr	Quantity	F.A.S.	C.I.F.	Charges
			85	291	582	678	96
			86	2,028	2,123	2,373	250
BELGIUM	O	E	81	24,997	23,990	26,157	2,167
			86	1,730	1,421	1,421	
	V	E	86	298	702	952	250
	V	W	85	291	582	678	96
CANADA	O	E	83	441	357	357	
FRANCE	V	E	81	413	492	517	25
PORTUGL	V	E	82	2,013	5,056	5,570	514
U KING	A	E	81	116	266	413	147

Flax, fiber, waste
3041200 FLAX WASTE A ADV WASTE (LB)

Country	Mode	Reg	Yr	Quantity	F.A.S.	C.I.F.	Charges
TOTAL			81	2,819,602	1,871,461	1,993,819	122,358
			82	7,606,157	1,655,402	2,008,592	353,190
			83	3,654,895	1,668,481	1,836,581	168,100
			84	4,592,044	3,061,633	3,292,991	231,358
			85	2,896,787	1,995,476	2,158,302	162,826
			86	2,875,911	2,098,745	2,260,200	161,455
BELGIUM	A	E	81	600	750	942	192
			82	18,967	19,868	25,433	5,565
			83	5	688	938	250
			84	1,210	1,079	1,578	499
			85	7,239	9,479	14,256	4,777
			86	7,084	12,671	17,380	4,709
	N	E	81	91,328	72,369	77,215	4,846
			82	49,381	30,177	34,264	4,087
			83	19,541	14,506	16,437	1,931
			84	241,732	214,979	228,022	13,043
			85	43,286	26,523	29,896	3,373
	O	E	86	423	298	322	24
	V	E	81	2,629,882	1,764,324	1,876,446	112,122
			82	1,389,348	757,627	819,846	62,219
			83	2,348,518	1,345,528	1,442,524	96,996
			84	4,054,549	2,606,055	2,800,355	194,300
			85	2,687,817	1,849,471	1,992,820	143,349
			86	2,780,475	2,034,536	2,185,400	150,864
	V	W	84	91,010	55,613	60,731	5,118
BULGAR	V	E	85	103,418	55,752	61,593	5,841
			86	44,493	20,863	24,369	3,506
CHINA M	V	E	85	10,935	17,184	19,537	2,353
EGYPT	V	E	81	40,726	4,387	7,374	2,987
			82	6,143,307	835,387	1,115,138	279,751
			83	986,338	138,621	193,724	55,103
FRANCE	A	E	81	185	254	352	98
	V	E	81	13,272	757	768	11
			83	122,070	43,968	46,143	2,175
			86	43,436	30,377	32,729	2,352
NETHLDS	V	E	83	43,669	34,244	35,874	1,630
			84	40,225	47,944	50,317	2,373
PORTUGL	V	E	82	5,154	12,343	13,911	1,568
SPAIN	V	E	83	83,102	56,443	62,057	5,614
			84	163,318	135,963	151,988	16,025
U KING	V	E	81	43,609	28,620	30,722	2,102
			83	51,652	34,483	38,884	4,401
			85	44,092	37,067	40,200	3,133

Flax, straw
1926000 FLAX STRAW (LB)

Country	Mode	Reg	Yr	Quantity	F.A.S.	C.I.F.	Charges
TOTAL			81	20,585,678	489,392	489,392	
			82	71,000	5,806	5,806	
			83	261,204	41,632	45,253	3,621
			84	329,394	39,750	39,784	34
			85	36,000	3,978	3,978	
			86	938,322	182,900	183,466	566
BELGIUM	V	E	83	3,758	2,442	2,954	512
BRAZIL	V	E	83	38,896	12,192	15,301	3,109
CANADA	O	E	81	20,581,269	488,863	488,863	
			82	71,000	5,806	5,806	
			83	218,550	26,998	26,998	
			84	280,395	30,423	30,423	
			85	36,000	3,978	3,978	
			86	936,644	179,590	179,590	
CHINA T	V	W	86	387	1,094	1,253	159
HG KONG	V	W	86	727	1,011	1,147	136
JAPAN	V	E	86	564	1,205	1,476	271
MEXICO	O	E	84	48,644	8,756	8,756	

Crop
Product
TSUSA commodity number, description, and unit of quantity

Country	Mode	Reg	Yr	Quantity	F.A.S.	C.I.F.	Charges
	O	W	81	4,409	529	529	
PHIL R	V	W	84	355	571	605	34

Flaxseed
1751800 FLAXSEED, LINSEED (LB)

Country	Mode	Reg	Yr	Quantity	F.A.S.	C.I.F.	Charges
TOTAL			81	260,280,388	37,405,072	37,406,143	728
			82	112,255,390	13,402,884	13,402,884	
			83	192,881,938	23,718,095	23,718,095	
			84	167,942,740	22,192,168	22,192,178	10
			85	276,816,730	32,857,936	32,903,303	45,367
			86	133,166,746	11,850,175	11,851,012	837
CANADA	N	E	85	27,519,700	3,151,835	3,195,235	43,400
	O	E	81	259,904,288	37,354,228	37,355,299	728
			82	112,059,760	13,375,131	13,375,131	
			83	192,710,576	23,695,407	23,695,407	
			84	167,026,217	22,067,992	22,068,002	10
			85	248,535,425	29,605,178	29,607,145	1,967
			86	132,923,691	11,818,534	11,819,371	837
	O	W	81	376,100	50,844	50,844	
			82	195,630	27,753	27,753	
			83	171,362	22,688	22,688	
			84	916,523	124,176	124,176	
			85	761,605	100,923	100,923	
			86	243,055	31,641	31,641	

Flaxseed, chaff
1844500 FLAXSEED SCREENNG,CHAFF,ETC (STN)

Country	Mode	Reg	Yr	Quantity	F.A.S.	C.I.F.	Charges
TOTAL			81	22,261	2,361,268	2,361,398	
			82	10,406	1,003,055	1,004,916	1,861
			83	12,227	1,197,771	1,200,370	2,599
			84	11,798	1,361,190	1,363,890	2,700
			85	14,249	1,198,107	1,198,179	72
			86	6,521	483,242	487,322	4,080
CANADA	N	E	84	1,833	139,435	142,135	2,700
			85	3,894	231,140	231,140	
			86	534	31,943	33,516	1,573
	O	E	81	21,198	2,264,299	2,264,429	
			82	9,271	916,394	916,398	4
			83	11,089	1,123,147	1,123,147	
			84	9,561	1,181,178	1,181,178	
			85	10,167	951,586	951,586	
			86	5,851	435,179	435,179	
	O	W	81	1,063	96,969	96,969	
			82	1,135	86,661	88,518	1,857
			83	807	60,205	60,205	
			84	404	40,577	40,577	
			85	128	13,343	13,343	
	V	E	86	87	4,316	5,416	1,100
FRANCE	V	E	83	325	12,293	14,518	2,225
JAPAN	V	E	86	17	3,353	3,607	254
	V	W	85	60	2,038	2,110	72
NETHLDS	V	E	86	32	8,451	9,604	1,153
SPAIN	A	E	83	6	2,126	2,500	374

Linseed, oil
1782500 OIL MIXTUR, CHIEFLY LINSEED (LB)

Country	Mode	Reg	Yr	Quantity	F.A.S.	C.I.F.	Charges
TOTAL			81	1,902	11,723	11,982	259
			82	993	8,947	9,122	175
			83	9,428	9,416	9,567	151
			84	76,269	37,966	39,879	1,913
			85	163,679	17,994	18,136	142
			86	180,073	39,092	41,820	2,728
BRAZIL	V	E	86	40,001	8,800	10,626	1,826
MEXICO	O	E	83	1,333	878	878	
			85	162,072	11,995	11,995	
	O	W	86	132,040	6,602	6,602	
NETHLDS	V	E	81	5	465	470	5
U KING	N	E	81	1,347	9,657	9,896	239
	O	E	81	550	1,601	1,616	15
	V	E	82	993	8,947	9,122	175
			83	8,095	8,538	8,689	151
			84	76,269	37,966	39,879	1,913
			85	1,607	5,999	6,141	142
			86	8,032	23,690	24,592	902

Linseed, oil cake and oil-cake meal
1845000 LINSEED OIL CAKE AND MEAL (LB)

Country	Mode	Reg	Yr	Quantity	F.A.S.	C.I.F.	Charges
TOTAL			81	2,859,333	349,970	349,970	
			82	3,436,455	342,551	342,551	
			83	4,656,391	409,083	409,083	
			84	1,170,432	119,037	119,037	
			85	5,050,219	321,178	324,178	3,000
			86	5,378,854	385,525	385,525	
BRAZIL	O	E	81	48,000	5,710	5,710	
CANADA	O	E	81	1,922,590	245,405	245,405	
			82	1,746,642	184,696	184,696	
			83	2,724,969	249,465	249,465	
			84	672,446	66,086	66,086	
			85	2,993,958	166,562	166,562	
			86	1,467,571	106,181	106,181	
	O	W	81	888,743	98,855	98,855	
			82	1,689,813	157,855	157,855	
			83	1,931,422	159,618	159,618	
			84	497,986	52,951	52,951	
			85	1,810,261	122,458	122,458	
			86	3,911,283	279,344	279,344	
ITALY	V	E	85	246,000	32,158	35,158	3,000

Linseed, oil, fatty acid
4902000 FATTY ACID FROM LINSEED OIL (LB)

Country	Mode	Reg	Yr	Quantity	F.A.S.	C.I.F.	Charges
TOTAL			81	68	253	270	17
			82	113,388	47,136	52,129	4,993
			83	54,718	27,342	29,667	2,325
			84	53,971	121,398	127,801	6,403
			85	62	1,420	1,432	12
			86	159,207	57,778	67,113	9,335
BAHAMAS	O	E	85	62	1,420	1,432	12
CANADA	O	E	82	12,000	7,276	7,276	
DENMARK	V	E	81	68	253	270	17
			82	100	329	365	36
			84	906	2,278	2,427	149
FR GERM	A	E	82	56	533	690	157
	V	E	82	98,057	35,384	39,801	4,417
			83	54,718	27,342	29,667	2,325
			86	157,674	52,547	61,327	8,780
JAPAN	V	E	84	11,574	25,798	27,367	1,569
	V	W	84	41,491	93,322	98,007	4,685
NETHLDS	A	W	86	100	2,364	2,539	175
U KING	V	E	82	3,175	3,614	3,997	383
			86	1,433	2,867	3,247	380

Linseed, oil, fatty salt
4904400 OTHER FATTY SALTS F LIN OIL (LB)

Country	Mode	Reg	Yr	Quantity	F.A.S.	C.I.F.	Charges
TOTAL			82	15,550	20,265	21,198	933
			84	2,227	1,992	3,546	1,554
			85	441	1,324	1,542	218
			86	221	1,043	1,129	86
CANADA	O	E	82	12,250	15,097	15,097	
FR GERM	V	E	82	2,500	3,737	4,621	884
			85	441	1,324	1,542	218
HG KONG	V	W	82	800	1,431	1,480	49
ITALY	A	W	84	2,205	1,144	2,668	1,524
SWITZLD	V	E	86	221	1,043	1,129	86
U KING	A	E	84	22	848	878	30

Linseed, vegetable oil
1762600 LINSEED OR FLAXSEED OIL (LB)

Country	Mode	Reg	Yr	Quantity	F.A.S.	C.I.F.	Charges
TOTAL			81	30,692	18,404	18,635	231
			82	8,737	9,076	12,827	3,751
			83	6,746	4,239	4,531	292
			84	95,629	83,244	85,306	2,062
			85	23,525	52,939	54,693	1,754
			86	784,729	236,273	245,691	9,418
BELGIUM	V	E	84	10,450	3,323	4,037	714
CANADA	O	E	81	28,500	12,526	12,526	
			84	58,561	48,618	48,618	
			86	464,975	76,555	76,555	
	O	W	86	159,000	42,083	42,083	

Crop Product TSUSA commodity number, description, and unit of quantity Country	Mode	Reg	Yr	Quantity	F.A.S.	C.I.F.	Charges
COLOMB	A	E	86	46,000	14,918	15,669	751
DENMARK	V	E	81	745	1,778	1,912	134
			82	1,088	2,346	2,509	163
			83	1,517	2,361	2,500	139
FR GERM	A	W	86	1,840	4,137	6,242	2,105
	O	E	81	275	338	348	10
			82	879	513	574	61
	V	E	84	514	887	1,026	139
			85	5,864	3,406	3,645	239
			86	76,653	41,239	43,563	2,324
	V	W	83	4,951	933	1,063	130
FRANCE	V	E	81	62	262	282	20
			82	420	575	617	42
			84	936	1,810	1,947	137
			86	336	1,454	1,509	55
MEXICO	A	E	85	40	5,000	5,059	59
NETHLDS	O	E	83	278	945	968	23
			86	1,416	3,180	3,294	114
	V	E	84	654	3,643	3,699	56
			85	913	1,701	1,820	119
NORWAY	V	W	86	15,707	14,922	16,768	1,846
SPAIN	V	E	86	9,132	7,800	8,769	969
U KING	A	E	82	6,350	5,642	9,127	3,485
	V	E	81	1,110	3,500	3,567	67
			84	24,514	24,963	25,979	1,016
			85	16,708	42,832	44,169	1,337
			86	9,670	29,985	31,239	1,254

G

Galia Melon

Galia melon, fresh**
1481900 OGEN/GALIA MELONS 12/1-5/31 (LB)

Country	Mode	Reg	Yr	Quantity	F.A.S.	C.I.F.	Charges
TOTAL			81	114,512	24,402	42,333	17,931
			82	246,945	60,087	129,005	68,918
			83	150,390	30,358	77,791	47,433
			84	660,026	197,327	488,122	290,795
			85	472,360	153,309	284,969	131,660
			86	248,516	81,324	337,943	256,619
ANTIGUA	A	E	86	7,822	7,422	8,784	1,362
CHILE	V	E	84	351,420	85,480	123,069	37,589
			85	76,190	15,120	23,760	8,640
GUATMAL	V	E	82	34,877	4,746	7,359	2,613
HONDURA	A	E	85	41,218	7,938	13,459	5,521
ISRAEL	A	E	81	14,348	10,014	21,695	11,681
			82	93,508	40,337	106,642	66,305
			83	150,390	30,358	77,791	47,433
			84	181,457	49,798	292,484	242,686
			85	314,322	51,654	149,618	97,964
			86	240,694	73,902	329,159	255,257
JAMAICA	A	E	84	39,770	48,557	58,691	10,134
			85	18,236	8,812	11,483	2,671
	V	E	85	22,394	69,785	86,649	16,864
MEXICO	O	E	82	118,560	15,004	15,004	
			84	1,750	467	467	
	O	W	84	85,160	12,774	12,774	
NICARAG	V	E	81	100,164	14,388	20,638	6,250
SPAIN	A	E	84	469	251	637	386

1482200 OGEN/GALIA MELONS 6/1-11/30 (LB)

Country	Mode	Reg	Yr	Quantity	F.A.S.	C.I.F.	Charges
TOTAL			81	67,282	4,771	5,468	697
			82	168,655	12,758	14,508	1,750
			83	345,775	50,171	79,621	29,450
			84	198,803	45,656	116,452	70,796
			85	328,204	68,078	177,726	109,648
			86	407,241	119,215	178,646	59,431
ANTIGUA	N	E	86	96,062	42,148	56,763	14,615
	V	E	86	33,720	15,736	17,598	1,862
C RICA	A	E	86	5,252	1,604	2,731	1,127

Crop Product TSUSA commodity number, description, and unit of quantity Country	Mode	Reg	Yr	Quantity	F.A.S.	C.I.F.	Charges
CANADA	A	E	82	1,000	977	1,319	342
	O	E	85	2,545	2,097	2,097	
	O	W	85	27,460	7,873	7,873	
FRANCE	A	E	84	605	352	618	266
ISRAEL	A	E	81	14,340	2,204	2,901	697
			82	36,022	8,875	10,283	1,408
			83	257,845	45,263	74,713	29,450
			84	198,198	45,304	115,834	70,530
			85	259,618	56,883	166,531	109,648
			86	272,207	59,727	101,554	41,827
MEXICO	O	E	81	52,942	2,567	2,567	
			82	131,633	2,906	2,906	
			83	87,930	4,908	4,908	
			85	38,581	1,225	1,225	

Gambier

Gambier, tannin
4704000 GAMBIER (LB)

Country	Mode	Reg	Yr	Quantity	F.A.S.	C.I.F.	Charges
TOTAL			81	19,842	8,393	9,555	1,162
			82	4,340	2,026	2,337	311
			83	11,023	7,790	9,118	1,328
FRANCE	V	E	81	19,842	8,393	9,555	1,162
			82	4,340	2,026	2,337	311
			83	11,023	7,790	9,118	1,328

Garlic

Garlic, dried
1403000 GARLIC, DRIED, DEHYDRATED (LB)

Country	Mode	Reg	Yr	Quantity	F.A.S.	C.I.F.	Charges
TOTAL			81	262,168	155,719	181,951	26,232
			82	3,520,640	2,098,528	2,540,170	441,642
			83	843,666	571,442	648,293	76,851
			84	396,751	296,995	322,065	25,070
			85	621,253	331,585	391,279	59,694
			86	2,952,648	1,233,544	1,502,754	269,210
AUSTRIA	O	E	84	1,534	1,740	1,835	95
	V	E	84	1,050	1,320	1,569	249
CANADA	O	E	81	41,627	18,527	18,527	
			82	3,000	2,649	2,649	
			83	16,400	13,024	13,024	
			86	5,000	4,202	6,500	2,298
CHINA M	O	W	85	55	1,477	1,477	
	V	E	81	27,786	18,023	20,512	2,489
			82	15,384	11,208	12,983	1,775
			83	61,133	28,061	31,332	3,271
			84	11,102	10,333	11,638	1,305
			85	74,555	44,318	51,800	7,482
			86	164,340	92,611	108,026	15,415
	V	H	83	500	454	503	49
			84	1,800	2,071	2,330	259
	V	W	81	177,865	107,242	129,628	22,386
			82	3,428,238	1,986,318	2,418,781	432,463
			83	695,514	448,878	519,675	70,797
			84	303,480	226,015	238,960	12,945
			85	79,132	36,941	41,166	4,225
			86	2,540,270	1,026,584	1,265,823	239,239
CHINA T	O	W	82	1,102	700	700	
	V	E	81	9,884	5,120	5,862	742
			82	500	620	719	99
			84	14,375	4,334	5,994	1,660
			85	386,607	176,477	217,403	40,926
	V	W	82	17,946	6,921	8,539	1,618
			83	4,409	3,500	3,681	181
			85	38,810	30,757	33,796	3,039
			86	15,000	9,416	9,638	222
FR GERM	V	E	81	60	3,159	3,281	122
			82	24,558	71,771	73,937	2,166
			83	34,836	60,281	61,791	1,510
			84	320	2,467	2,682	215
FRANCE	V	E	81	3,715	445	638	193
			85	3,087	3,996	4,302	306
GUATMAL	V	E	84	20,000	23,196	26,286	3,090
			86	20,100	9,045	11,640	2,595
HG KONG	V	E	82	1,900	1,140	1,291	151

Crop
Product
TSUSA commodity number, description, and unit of quantity

Country	Mode	Reg	Yr	Quantity	F.A.S.	C.I.F.	Charges
			83	7,300	5,239	5,900	661
			84	2,360	2,714	3,067	353
			85	4,400	4,382	5,016	634
	V	H	84	500	679	755	76
	V	W	81	250	277	300	23
			82	1,000	1,050	1,114	64
			83	1,602	1,282	1,370	88
			84	8,874	6,435	6,866	431
			85	14,968	8,326	8,980	654
			86	145,590	57,719	62,565	4,846
INDIA	V	E	82	2,689	2,053	2,321	268
			83	1,843	1,365	1,592	227
			84	1,429	1,128	1,287	159
			86	22,046	8,130	10,430	2,300
	V	W	82	2,313	1,824	2,133	309
			84	970	1,020	1,151	131
IRAN	V	E	85	2,034	3,900	4,108	208
ITALY	V	E	81	441	2,333	2,513	180
			84	302	497	538	41
			86	19,550	7,776	8,475	699
JAPAN	A	E	85	14,400	18,480	19,997	1,517
			86	13,885	13,264	14,148	884
	V	W	84	825	1,473	1,555	82
			86	6,614	3,153	3,865	712
KOR REP	V	E	84	540	610	701	91
	V	W	84	746	444	528	84
MEXICO	O	W	82	869	701	701	
			83	19,663	8,714	8,714	
SINGAPR	V	W	82	19,842	9,830	12,422	2,592
SPAIN	V	E	83	441	344	404	60
			84	26,455	10,247	14,031	3,784
			85	2,205	1,500	2,077	577
SWITZLD	V	E	85	1,000	1,031	1,157	126
THAILND	V	E	81	540	593	690	97
			82	1,200	1,175	1,299	124
U KING	O	E	84	89	272	292	20
			86	253	1,644	1,644	
	V	E	82	99	568	581	13
			83	25	300	307	7

Garlic, essential oil**
4528023 ONION AND GARLIC (LB)

Country	Mode	Reg	Yr	Quantity	F.A.S.	C.I.F.	Charges
TOTAL			81	22,529	1,237,356	1,247,086	9,730
			82	10,592	740,741	750,041	9,300
			83	13,623	840,721	850,565	9,844
			84	16,913	797,905	806,946	9,041
			85	13,371	744,719	755,970	11,251
			86	28,758	1,473,370	1,500,037	26,667
AUSTRIA	A	E	84	22	4,251	4,310	59
BELGIUM	A	E	81	385	13,256	13,882	626
			82	110	4,296	4,421	125
			83	110	17,500	17,632	132
			86	670	17,803	18,810	1,007
CHINA M	O	E	86	110	4,943	5,025	82
	V	W	81	1,763	87,644	88,336	692
EGYPT	A	E	81	965	114,997	118,060	3,063
			82	1,300	126,107	129,709	3,602
			83	1,750	123,686	127,234	3,548
			84	1,249	81,128	83,434	2,306
			85	2,522	144,418	149,776	5,358
			86	6,066	372,437	389,042	16,605
FRANCE	A	E	81	36	3,737	3,785	48
ITALY	A	E	81	1,763	250,000	251,550	1,550
			82	916	95,345	96,173	828
			83	661	70,000	70,353	353
			84	704	39,785	40,460	675
			85	1,494	93,554	94,615	1,061
			86	221	45,000	45,261	261
MEXICO	A	E	81	2,446	105,650	107,678	2,028
			82	3,976	198,789	202,465	3,676
			83	4,118	179,250	182,824	3,574
			84	1,981	63,250	65,064	1,814
			85	2,083	53,725	55,210	1,485
			86	6,770	234,628	239,828	5,200
	O	E	81	13,122	532,785	532,785	
			82	2,742	70,460	70,460	
			83	5,982	313,275	313,275	
			84	10,492	277,009	277,009	
			85	5,340	141,246	141,246	
			86	11,971	462,207	462,207	
NETHLDS	A	E	81	2,049	129,287	131,010	1,723

Crop
Product
TSUSA commodity number, description, and unit of quantity

Country	Mode	Reg	Yr	Quantity	F.A.S.	C.I.F.	Charges
			82	1,548	245,744	246,813	1,069
			83	892	135,545	137,646	2,101
			84	1,329	198,291	199,743	1,452
			85	1,104	185,987	187,751	1,764
			86	2,510	260,396	262,864	2,468
SWITZLD	A	E	83	110	1,465	1,601	136
			84	1,136	134,191	136,926	2,735
			85	828	125,789	127,372	1,583
			86	440	75,956	77,000	1,044

Garlic, flour
1406000 GARLIC FLOUR (LB)

Country	Mode	Reg	Yr	Quantity	F.A.S.	C.I.F.	Charges
TOTAL			81	165,076	119,969	130,600	17,505
			82	332,028	251,253	276,829	25,576
			83	63,719	48,830	51,756	2,926
			84	42,871	49,882	54,365	4,483
			85	257,821	180,391	199,669	19,278
			86	129,497	95,830	112,987	17,157
BELGIUM	A	E	85	18,000	9,000	9,904	904
CANADA	O	E	81	3,349	3,287	3,287	
			82	2,000	2,001	2,001	
			83	1,338	2,371	2,371	
			85	1,221	3,338	3,338	
	O	W	81	337	584	584	
CHILE	V	E	83	550	394	440	46
CHINA M	N	E	86	50,263	18,943	22,814	3,871
	V	E	81	4,257	3,364	3,658	294
			82	28,616	17,733	20,316	2,583
			84	1,000	561	676	115
			85	103,513	76,778	84,401	7,623
			86	5,412	1,791	2,220	429
	V	W	81	63,104	40,089	44,760	4,671
			82	55,116	37,679	43,121	5,442
			83	11,023	6,384	6,914	530
			84	14,624	11,205	12,061	856
			85	26,458	14,364	16,763	2,399
			86	6,889	3,403	3,973	570
CHINA T	V	E	85	20,000	5,443	7,459	2,016
	V	W	83	2,705	2,401	2,561	160
			84	2,352	2,070	2,192	122
			85	20,538	12,976	13,828	852
			86	38,524	22,799	23,899	1,100
EGYPT	O	E	84	200	379	417	38
	V	E	82	11,023	7,350	8,139	789
FR GERM	A	E	83	1,059	1,165	1,631	466
	N	E	82	10,548	15,705	17,138	1,433
	V	E	82	311	3,267	3,549	282
			83	17,491	19,616	20,412	796
			84	5,282	4,447	4,824	377
			86	4,312	8,764	9,385	621
FRANCE	A	E	82	127	269	359	90
			86	12,322	25,669	33,458	7,789
	A	W	84	109	367	436	69
	O	E	82	93,991	88,591	93,915	5,324
	V	E	81	39,687	37,655	40,422	2,767
			82	55,067	61,270	65,623	4,353
			83	131	532	560	28
			84	15,994	27,316	29,552	2,236
			85	50,423	40,893	43,915	3,022
	V	W	83	394	291	309	18
			85	263	1,151	1,561	410
HG KONG	V	E	84	1,240	737	1,014	277
	V	W	82	1,000	1,004	1,060	56
			83	2,579	4,138	4,378	240
			84	500	545	573	28
INDIA	N	E	84	1,243	1,215	1,486	271
	V	E	82	4,894	3,673	4,161	488
			83	366	317	366	49
			85	2,231	1,243	1,426	183
ITALY	V	E	81	176	766	955	189
			82	353	2,340	2,442	102
			83	5,397	6,143	6,643	500
JAPAN	A	E	85	12,200	9,219	10,000	781
	A	W	85	273	4,636	5,585	949
	V	W	81	4,074	26,405	27,456	1,051
			82	92	703	726	23
			83	970	652	745	93
MEXICO	O	E	86	455	1,137	1,137	
	O	W	83	19,716	4,426	4,426	
	V	E	81	44,092	3,128	4,787	1,659
			82	66,138	4,692	8,490	3,798

Crop Product TSUSA commodity number, description, and unit of quantity Country	Mode	Reg	Yr	Quantity	F.A.S.	C.I.F.	Charges
PERU	A	E	82	2,200	1,935	2,538	603
SWITZLD	A	E	86	3,924	8,668	11,194	2,526
THAILND	V	E	81	6,000	4,691	4,691	6,874
	V	W	85	2,701	1,350	1,489	139
			86	7,396	4,656	4,907	251
U KING	O	E	82	552	3,041	3,251	210
			84	327	1,040	1,134	94

Garlic, fresh or frozen
1363000 GARLIC, FRESH, CHILLED, FROZ (LB)

Country	Mode	Reg	Yr	Quantity	F.A.S.	C.I.F.	Charges
TOTAL			81	18,844,841	8,606,026	8,936,104	329,936
			82	24,080,334	14,906,922	15,633,740	726,818
			83	27,831,300	10,427,244	11,354,942	927,698
			84	37,931,010	9,726,770	10,818,247	1,091,477
			85	33,674,422	10,771,039	11,814,157	1,043,118
			86	37,250,638	20,481,407	21,969,688	1,488,281
ARGENT	O	E	83	9,000	5,500	5,500	
			86	5,040	2,520	2,520	
	V	E	81	977,880	679,634	770,970	91,336
			82	1,061,471	1,173,162	1,263,756	90,594
			83	4,602,217	2,125,728	2,563,624	437,896
			84	4,375,911	1,230,730	1,632,643	401,913
			85	2,770,538	932,072	1,184,886	252,814
			86	6,373,243	3,635,961	4,168,612	532,651
	V	W	83	220,460	85,000	107,566	22,566
			84	341,575	104,000	138,986	34,986
			85	440,724	162,439	175,842	13,403
			86	916,266	631,089	712,953	81,864
AUSTRIA	V	E	85	13,707	4,998	7,010	2,012
BRAZIL	V	E	86	77,889	54,800	60,417	5,617
C RICA	V	E	82	18,293	6,525	9,605	3,080
			86	14,912	1,800	2,713	913
	V	W	81	2,840	2,059	3,254	1,195
CANADA	O	E	82	40,476	9,628	9,628	
			83	1,085	1,396	1,396	
			85	40,000	4,000	4,000	
			86	35,467	7,162	7,162	
	O	W	86	37,600	4,000	4,000	
CHILE	O	E	81	3,300	2,897	2,897	
			86	16,660	8,330	8,330	
	V	E	81	429,973	244,611	279,377	34,766
			82	400,926	374,100	430,175	56,075
			83	231,490	132,859	166,474	33,615
			84	154,388	42,024	57,115	15,091
			85	166,889	68,225	82,942	14,717
			86	1,442,525	726,656	852,111	125,455
	V	W	86	450,274	292,348	346,441	54,093
CHINA M	V	E	86	79,365	41,925	51,525	9,600
	V	H	86	59,250	21,430	29,831	8,401
	V	W	81	32,738	12,859	13,780	921
			83	23,600	8,204	9,534	1,330
			86	593,449	164,455	210,277	45,822
CHINA T	A	E	82	44	560	760	200
	N	W	86	74,000	35,230	39,593	4,363
	O	E	85	28,658	6,853	6,853	
	V	E	81	507,058	245,550	290,855	45,305
			82	666,492	375,815	430,862	55,047
			83	7,122	6,941	7,774	833
			84	2,906	2,850	3,253	403
			85	278,230	114,119	150,382	36,263
			86	77,161	34,274	40,078	5,804
	V	H	82	19,841	15,873	17,173	1,300
			84	19,841	6,480	8,586	2,106
			86	20,800	11,062	14,255	3,193
	V	W	81	713,000	281,089	329,914	48,825
			82	1,792,528	848,941	1,002,316	153,375
			83	19,500	8,247	10,062	1,815
			84	68,949	19,032	26,108	7,076
			85	255,526	110,370	131,142	20,772
			86	1,102,745	476,917	547,918	71,001
DOM REP	A	E	83	5,280	660	1,168	508
	V	E	83	35,000	4,200	5,358	1,158
			84	216,290	31,742	39,214	7,472
			85	80,300	9,636	13,045	3,409
			86	204,702	30,314	43,100	12,786
FRANCE	A	E	84	2,750	2,030	2,030	
	A	W	82	727	3,051	3,653	602
			85	12,249	13,507	15,058	1,551
	O	E	83	1,323	1,727	1,907	180
	V	E	81	2,538	2,057	2,130	73
			82	22,046	19,141	20,944	1,803
			83	49,010	19,335	20,605	1,270
			84	98,613	44,949	60,134	15,185
			85	186,135	130,844	155,915	25,071
			86	28,660	30,166	36,100	5,934
GUATMAL	A	E	82	3,990	798	1,584	786
	A	W	82	5,000	4,229	5,500	1,271
	N	E	81	114,514	63,481	73,771	10,290
			82	853,611	196,284	244,547	48,263
			83	10,050	1,379	2,529	1,150
			84	24,160	6,250	8,783	2,533
	O	E	85	24,038	3,709	3,709	
	V	E	81	277,513	130,617	148,761	18,144
			82	394,224	235,741	265,972	30,231
			85	266,834	82,094	103,839	21,745
			86	227,323	103,616	122,554	18,938
	V	W	85	157,536	67,968	80,926	12,958
HAITI	A	E	82	7,550	1,510	2,410	900
HG KONG	V	E	82	39,000	19,299	24,180	4,881
			86	22,050	4,000	7,680	3,680
	V	W	85	41,800	14,660	16,720	2,060
			86	307,115	68,112	85,202	17,090
INDIA	V	W	81	523	364	448	84
ISRAEL	A	E	82	5,732	7,560	20,860	13,300
			84	3,307	750	7,633	6,883
ITALY	N	E	83	67,810	41,692	51,495	9,803
			84	79,305	46,176	62,091	15,915
	O	E	81	4,380	6,360	6,360	
			86	12,000	9,000	9,000	
	V	E	82	47,980	51,904	58,084	6,180
			85	8,800	8,640	9,139	499
			86	32	1,406	1,494	88
JAMAICA	A	E	85	2,652	1,352	2,311	959
JAPAN	A	E	85	55	4,070	4,383	313
	A	W	82	220	600	1,153	553
	V	E	84	330	328	365	37
			86	550	1,384	1,458	74
	V	W	84	1,320	1,778	1,877	99
KOR REP	V	W	81	2,400	3,257	3,600	343
MALAYSA	O	E	86	40,500	39,838	39,838	
MEXICO	A	E	85	77,792	16,380	29,701	13,321
	N	E	83	72,600	35,656	41,361	5,705
			86	62,328	18,220	18,768	548
	O	E	81	11,115,780	5,323,989	5,324,131	
			82	12,085,295	7,434,051	7,435,693	1,642
			83	13,289,586	3,724,736	3,725,736	1,000
			84	21,264,003	3,858,636	3,858,636	
			85	18,897,669	5,285,578	5,292,777	7,199
			86	18,108,289	9,452,518	9,452,518	
	O	W	81	3,995,507	1,031,667	1,031,667	
			82	4,516,775	2,707,744	2,707,744	
			83	6,059,893	2,886,017	2,886,017	
			84	7,454,036	3,083,563	3,083,563	
			85	4,044,996	1,704,533	1,704,533	
			86	3,607,955	2,090,807	2,090,807	
	V	E	84	3,270	460	460	
N ZEAL	V	H	84	1,499	1,394	1,550	156
			85	4,235	2,193	3,842	1,649
NETHLDS	O	E	85	44,092	12,000	18,050	6,050
	V	E	84	18,000	39,062	48,975	9,913
			85	1,513,500	97,038	108,942	11,904
PERU	A	E	86	192,593	109,804	162,913	53,109
	N	E	82	147,202	124,051	153,820	29,769
	V	E	81	384,809	267,839	304,700	36,861
			82	88,000	79,200	85,300	6,100
			83	174,010	85,853	103,415	17,562
			86	33,562	19,756	25,756	6,000
PHIL R	A	E	86	5,571	3,500	5,125	1,625
ROMANIA	V	W	84	1,560	507	547	40
SINGAPR	V	W	84	493	368	386	18
SPAIN	N	E	85	442,519	189,412	257,119	67,707
	O	E	85	188,705	68,480	74,003	5,523
			86	104,582	37,952	43,502	5,550
	V	E	81	280,088	307,696	349,489	41,793
			82	1,860,880	1,215,845	1,436,549	220,704
			83	2,951,963	1,251,048	1,642,035	390,987
			84	3,796,619	1,201,085	1,772,356	571,271
			85	3,686,243	1,655,869	2,177,088	521,219
			86	2,812,542	2,272,046	2,677,386	405,340
SWITZLD	A	E	83	173	268	557	289
	V	E	86	49,207	30,368	34,310	3,942
	V	W	86	54,431	8,641	13,441	4,800
THAILND	V	E	82	1,671	995	1,117	122
			84	1,200	1,000	1,122	122
	V	W	82	360	315	355	40

Crop Product TSUSA commodity number, description, and unit of quantity Country	Mode	Reg	Yr	Quantity	F.A.S.	C.I.F.	Charges
			84	616	1,300	1,540	240
U KING	V	E	83	128	798	829	31
			84	69	276	294	18

Gentian

Gentian, natural drug
4355500 GENTIAN (LB)

Country	Mode	Reg	Yr	Quantity	F.A.S.	C.I.F.	Charges
TOTAL			81	11,525	24,818	27,118	2,300
			82	20,949	40,671	44,942	4,271
			83	9,530	21,714	23,204	1,490
			84	18,584	31,126	33,982	2,856
			85	8,278	10,326	11,656	1,330
			86	25,013	31,314	35,429	4,115
CHINA M	V	E	83	3,307	11,498	12,247	749
FR GERM	V	E	81	223	454	510	56
			82	437	809	922	113
	V	W	81	648	1,541	1,560	19
			82	1,538	3,182	3,429	247
			84	2,137	9,180	10,465	1,285
			85	1,825	3,147	3,447	300
			86	7,578	7,270	7,437	167
FRANCE	V	E	81	3,329	9,071	9,792	721
			82	7,606	13,360	14,724	1,364
			83	4,400	6,971	7,515	544
			84	11,994	15,966	17,094	1,128
			85	6,453	7,179	8,209	1,030
			86	8,777	10,365	12,661	2,296
SPAIN	V	E	81	6,020	10,916	12,385	1,469
			82	6,851	13,688	14,780	1,092
			83	1,823	3,245	3,442	197
			84	4,453	5,980	6,423	443
			86	8,658	13,679	15,331	1,652
	V	W	81	1,305	2,836	2,871	35
			82	2,271	4,368	5,315	947
YUGOSLV	V	E	82	2,246	5,264	5,772	508

Geranium

Geranium, essential oil
4522600 GERANIUM OIL (LB)

Country	Mode	Reg	Yr	Quantity	F.A.S.	C.I.F.	Charges
TOTAL			81	111,086	2,700,772	2,769,494	68,583
			82	100,564	2,167,262	2,221,401	54,139
			83	119,780	2,444,633	2,512,963	68,330
			84	134,270	3,018,737	3,088,550	69,813
			85	107,866	2,589,301	2,651,414	62,113
			86	122,157	2,551,694	2,601,957	50,263
ALGERIA	A	E	84	110	2,239	2,284	45
	N	E	83	541	10,275	10,441	166
	V	E	81	3,087	76,967	77,833	866
			82	3,362	78,606	79,719	1,113
BELGIUM	A	E	83	10	605	684	79
CHINA M	N	E	85	13,515	318,520	324,104	5,584
			86	27,326	623,009	629,841	6,832
	V	E	81	2,204	29,915	30,529	614
			83	15,962	186,625	192,211	5,586
			84	17,705	335,151	341,085	5,934
	V	W	81	1,146	15,509	15,855	346
			84	4,409	103,700	105,400	1,700
			85	5,556	137,252	138,685	1,433
COMOROS	A	E	84	441	13,025	13,480	455
EGYPT	N	E	81	36,841	606,333	628,549	22,196
			82	27,139	489,158	501,739	12,581
			83	21,288	466,466	485,355	18,889
			84	34,683	884,797	910,027	25,230
			85	18,164	454,441	477,608	23,167
			86	29,663	431,088	443,972	12,884
F IND O	A	E	83	2,205	57,000	58,853	1,853
	N	E	81	13,999	434,393	444,679	10,286
			82	3,527	99,848	102,277	2,429
			85	4,189	108,493	110,747	2,254
			86	1,874	75,104	76,587	1,483
	V	E	84	1,543	36,460	37,094	634
FR GERM	A	E	81	177	1,974	2,093	119
			82	176	2,044	2,221	177

Country	Mode	Reg	Yr	Quantity	F.A.S.	C.I.F.	Charges
			83	286	3,279	3,434	155
			84	2,055	17,836	18,882	1,046
			85	136	2,038	2,694	656
FRANCE	A	W	84	13	291	354	63
	N	E	81	43,862	1,175,081	1,200,926	25,845
			82	53,143	1,289,133	1,321,259	32,126
			83	51,758	1,181,250	1,207,783	26,533
			84	54,013	1,152,626	1,179,207	26,581
			85	63,223	1,460,913	1,489,161	28,248
			86	52,757	1,107,808	1,134,334	26,526
	V	E	82	2,205	37,270	38,265	995
ISRAEL	N	E	83	8,855	130,707	133,313	2,606
	V	E	82	1,851	34,858	35,364	506
			84	4,116	98,175	99,091	916
			85	661	14,818	15,035	217
			86	719	16,695	16,922	227
MOROC	A	E	81	5,511	131,594	136,477	4,883
			82	1,058	24,293	25,200	907
			83	11,001	246,348	256,600	10,252
			84	7,119	191,078	195,861	4,783
NETHLDS	A	E	82	55	526	647	121
			83	132	1,347	1,545	198
			86	3,800	57,000	57,496	496
	N	E	84	1,025	20,759	21,105	346
PARAGUA	V	E	82	4,762	31,620	32,875	1,255
REP SAF	A	E	81	551	98,750	99,527	777
SPAIN	A	E	84	110	2,994	3,100	106
SWITZLD	N	E	81	231	5,917	6,591	615
			82	2,585	54,347	55,415	1,068
			83	7,228	150,809	152,565	1,756
			84	6,345	149,766	151,357	1,591
			86	5,523	229,052	230,547	1,495
	V	E	85	2,378	91,770	92,302	532
U KING	N	E	82	701	25,559	26,420	861
			83	514	9,922	10,179	257
			84	583	9,840	10,223	383
			86	495	11,938	12,258	320
	V	E	81	672	23,619	23,978	299
			85	44	1,056	1,078	22
USSR	V	E	81	2,805	100,720	102,457	1,737

Rhodinol
4606500 RHODINOL NOT ARTIFICIAL MIXT (LB)

Country	Mode	Reg	Yr	Quantity	F.A.S.	C.I.F.	Charges
TOTAL			81	1,813	22,149	23,091	942
			82	2,621	43,888	45,215	1,327
			83	2,397	64,758	66,743	1,985
			84	5,473	143,947	148,554	4,607
			85	6,370	181,727	186,598	4,871
			86	3,779	155,133	158,085	2,952
FRANCE	A	E	86	902	38,348	39,137	789
	N	E	81	1,813	22,149	23,091	942
			82	2,610	42,602	43,908	1,306
			83	2,397	64,758	66,743	1,985
			84	5,473	143,947	148,554	4,607
			85	6,370	181,727	186,598	4,871
			86	2,877	116,785	118,948	2,163
U KING	V	E	82	11	1,286	1,307	21

Ginger

Ginger, root, candied
1544000 GINGER ROOT, CANDIED ETC (LB)

Country	Mode	Reg	Yr	Quantity	F.A.S.	C.I.F.	Charges
TOTAL			81	400,823	460,707	497,216	36,509
			82	315,288	352,196	384,915	32,719
			83	2,462,381	909,000	1,151,093	242,093
			84	638,328	488,231	541,614	53,383
			85	644,273	484,132	533,370	49,238
			86	432,618	413,107	451,097	37,990
AUSTRAL	N	E	84	32,772	40,439	44,431	3,992
			86	17,166	26,875	28,872	1,997
	N	H	84	941	1,430	1,912	482
	N	W	82	23,481	37,711	41,103	3,392
			86	45,090	59,462	67,751	8,289
	O	E	82	250	533	796	263
			83	300	666	855	189
			84	1,700	2,464	2,531	67
	V	E	81	51,293	67,235	74,084	6,849

Crop
Product
TSUSA commodity number, description, and unit of quantity

Country	Mode	Reg	Yr	Quantity	F.A.S.	C.I.F.	Charges
			82	33,213	45,454	50,257	4,803
			83	50,900	65,292	71,980	6,688
			84	5,070	7,215	7,854	639
			85	33,072	47,000	50,683	3,683
			86	5,649	7,432	8,154	722
	V	W	81	26,114	41,601	43,507	1,906
			82	5,793	6,681	7,580	899
			83	26,521	33,322	36,098	2,776
			84	33,871	53,383	55,940	2,557
			85	32,270	42,613	46,179	3,566
			86	5,931	7,160	7,679	519
AUSTRIA	V	E	82	1,400	1,709	1,913	204
			84	4,107	5,423	5,933	510
	V	W	84	3,646	2,818	3,275	457
BRAZIL	V	E	85	220,460	72,592	85,564	12,972
C RICA	V	E	84	12,250	4,900	5,732	832
	V	W	83	1,102	950	1,224	274
			84	1,825	707	959	252
CANADA	O	E	82	507	1,052	1,052	
			83	152	340	500	160
	V	W	81	4,800	7,000	7,400	400
CHINA M	V	E	81	6,263	5,868	6,784	916
			82	375	320	384	64
			83	14,734	7,205	8,882	1,677
			84	200	272	311	39
	V	H	84	250	316	344	28
	V	W	81	500	306	322	16
			83	2,458	2,798	2,998	200
			84	450	781	821	40
			86	3,518	3,788	4,026	238
CHINA T	O	E	81	540	820	820	
			82	1,800	2,700	2,874	174
			84	302	515	566	51
	V	E	81	161,949	168,745	184,645	15,900
			82	90,859	84,472	93,921	9,449
			83	154,872	149,517	164,022	14,505
			84	125,720	118,011	130,585	12,574
			85	140,796	110,244	124,119	13,875
			86	125,339	96,720	106,379	9,659
	V	H	81	200	432	464	32
			82	250	420	480	60
	V	W	81	107,751	120,981	127,647	6,666
			82	139,296	150,542	161,795	11,253
			83	162,096	176,549	187,217	10,668
			84	135,862	142,273	151,673	9,400
			85	154,150	151,671	162,791	11,120
			86	121,584	118,923	127,586	8,663
FIJI	A	W	83	2,530	945	1,773	828
			84	2,411	2,846	3,694	848
	V	W	81	9,461	10,773	11,599	826
			83	52,920	19,345	24,734	5,389
			84	17,280	6,649	9,291	2,642
FR GERM	V	E	83	253	968	1,179	211
GUATMAL	A	E	83	36,214	11,312	15,239	3,927
	V	E	84	121,080	37,704	48,189	10,485
HG KONG	A	E	86	1,769	1,436	2,252	816
	V	E	81	19,894	24,311	26,196	1,885
			82	13,718	15,517	17,243	1,726
			83	27,585	25,600	29,249	3,649
			84	133,184	50,322	55,914	5,592
			85	4,725	8,253	9,584	1,331
			86	6,825	13,392	14,871	1,479
	V	H	81	1,500	2,003	2,123	120
			82	1,096	1,225	1,317	92
			83	1,880	2,366	2,746	380
			84	400	501	563	62
	V	W	81	2,669	4,071	4,305	234
			82	2,770	3,480	3,719	239
			83	9,615	12,712	13,560	848
			84	1,793	2,152	2,289	137
			85	18,800	13,640	14,450	810
			86	44,081	24,739	25,691	952
JAPAN	A	E	83	220	347	419	72
	V	E	81	3,706	2,400	2,628	228
			84	118	271	285	14
	V	W	81	2,394	1,927	2,248	321
			83	2,415	4,028	4,338	310
			84	1,011	2,194	3,587	1,393
			86	600	1,050	1,090	40
KOR REP	V	E	83	9,300	10,993	12,351	1,358
	V	W	81	500	397	420	23
			84	628	1,594	1,725	131
MAURIT	V	E	83	1,900,761	380,083	567,471	187,388
MEXICO	O	E	83	250	554	567	13

Country	Mode	Reg	Yr	Quantity	F.A.S.	C.I.F.	Charges
N ZEAL	V	W	81	440	477	571	94
NETHLDS	V	E	85	40,000	38,119	40,000	1,881
			86	14,600	14,348	15,065	717
	V	W	86	36,250	31,703	34,185	2,482
PANAMA	A	E	83	5,100	2,700	3,248	548
			86	688	3,097	4,308	1,211
THAILND	V	E	81	696	682	724	42
			82	480	380	481	101
			86	1,323	1,101	1,188	87
	V	W	86	2,205	1,881	2,000	119
U KING	O	E	84	593	569	646	77
	V	E	81	153	678	729	51
			84	864	2,482	2,564	82
	V	W	83	203	408	443	35

Ginger, root, spice

1613500 GINGER ROOT, UNGROUND (LB)

Country	Mode	Reg	Yr	Quantity	F.A.S.	C.I.F.	Charges
TOTAL			81	9,533,827	3,861,500	5,133,878	1,272,378
			82	10,476,235	4,164,341	5,719,659	1,555,318
			83	7,849,489	3,664,145	4,686,666	1,022,521
			84	9,196,452	5,792,758	7,012,509	1,219,751
			85	12,347,766	7,184,488	9,166,187	1,981,699
			86	11,228,862	4,824,006	6,204,622	1,380,616
AUSTRAL	A	W	81	9,045	10,325	14,417	4,092
			82	9,300	13,893	20,723	6,830
			86	7,500	3,075	4,996	1,921
	V	E	81	70,594	81,020	87,783	6,763
			82	33,280	37,191	40,599	3,408
			83	50,889	59,375	65,016	5,641
			84	406	634	734	100
			85	67,152	75,897	85,059	9,162
			86	15,409	16,868	18,559	1,691
BELGIUM	O	E	86	12	1,116	1,127	11
BELIZE	A	E	85	5,291	1,440	4,352	2,912
BRAZIL	A	E	81	9,251	3,721	8,199	4,478
			82	9,170	2,912	7,604	4,692
	A	W	82	21,618	7,640	17,639	9,999
			83	34,539	12,832	20,175	7,343
	N	E	81	220,724	75,222	127,939	52,717
			82	243,230	104,836	186,632	81,796
			83	564,749	158,860	282,879	124,019
			84	764,041	307,516	541,123	233,607
			85	2,503,751	682,563	1,152,017	469,454
			86	2,108,699	555,250	891,401	336,151
	N	W	81	54,773	23,105	39,714	16,609
			86	149,289	49,432	72,989	23,557
	O	W	82	500	600	600	
	V	E	83	84,288	20,737	31,350	10,613
			84	22,046	14,702	18,700	3,998
			85	20,238	4,590	5,916	1,326
			86	322,275	102,861	146,022	43,161
	V	W	85	116,128	63,977	87,237	23,260
C RICA	A	E	86	5,517	4,643	6,193	1,550
	N	E	82	269,327	93,887	115,448	21,561
			83	471,426	169,048	203,016	33,968
	N	W	82	31,785	19,187	26,129	6,942
	O	E	82	9,950	6,000	6,210	210
	V	E	81	67,044	24,075	26,270	2,195
			82	93,942	28,552	31,828	3,276
			83	48,042	10,072	11,762	1,690
			84	342,162	86,101	108,943	22,842
			85	173,922	22,970	32,617	9,647
			86	79,492	16,594	21,334	4,740
	V	W	81	2,650	901	1,424	523
			83	45,935	14,515	19,951	5,436
			84	80,156	29,114	34,986	5,872
			85	7,960	2,894	3,690	796
CANADA	O	E	81	15,250	18,255	18,255	
			82	4,000	1,600	1,600	
			84	35	725	725	
	O	W	81	539	865	865	
			82	15,900	12,040	12,040	
			83	8,100	7,125	7,125	
			86	18,600	12,090	12,090	
CHILE	A	E	81	14,494	1,512	3,308	1,796
			83	21,120	5,376	16,076	10,700
CHINA M	N	E	84	760,233	662,769	730,183	67,414
			85	855,372	626,156	699,533	73,377
			86	909,235	378,836	448,227	69,391
	V	E	81	2,315,753	747,410	916,115	168,705
			82	2,069,047	547,723	758,277	210,554

188 Table 1. U.S. Import Statistics for Crop-Specific Commodities by Crop Name

Crop
Product
TSUSA commodity number, description, and unit of quantity

Country	Mode	Reg	Yr	Quantity	F.A.S.	C.I.F.	Charges
			83	1,343,951	655,271	784,868	129,597
			84	99,207	71,166	78,683	7,517
			85	126,103	70,251	95,596	25,345
			86	73,413	28,083	31,979	3,896
	V	W	81	334,336	103,042	122,440	19,398
			82	588,904	172,341	216,640	44,299
			83	279,442	95,913	118,304	22,391
			84	922,603	882,439	964,953	82,514
			85	441,377	371,862	402,097	30,235
			86	198,143	88,492	104,974	16,482
CHINA T	N	W	82	323,710	127,266	150,698	23,432
			86	37,800	22,227	23,802	1,575
	O	E	85	17,460	8,041	8,041	
	O	W	81	3,065	2,827	2,827	
			85	7,500	3,375	3,375	
	V	E	81	44,818	11,037	16,512	5,475
			82	81,532	49,562	60,861	11,299
			83	97,946	42,539	48,093	5,554
			84	50,060	39,262	45,723	6,461
			85	166,659	69,374	84,541	15,167
	V	H	85	28,050	9,734	13,430	3,696
	V	W	81	138,656	51,593	62,610	11,017
			82	283,458	140,792	165,072	24,280
			83	26,310	10,225	12,992	2,767
			84	56,470	10,819	16,093	5,274
			85	184,116	54,476	74,685	20,209
			86	92,141	49,777	54,236	4,459
DOM REP	A	E	81	18,755	2,691	5,281	2,590
			82	2,400	1,080	1,790	710
			84	18,223	5,112	7,440	2,328
			86	10,800	2,160	3,611	1,451
	N	E	81	481,023	85,769	142,668	56,899
			82	287,026	45,138	64,474	19,336
			83	178,538	39,374	54,983	15,609
			84	225,708	58,132	84,724	26,592
			85	77,800	33,205	41,954	8,749
			86	93,197	37,999	49,927	11,928
	V	E	81	24,505	5,578	7,720	2,142
			82	26,505	6,381	8,084	1,703
			83	54,800	12,413	15,946	3,533
			84	20,222	4,684	6,136	1,452
			85	13,444	5,884	7,382	1,498
			86	35,000	9,710	11,477	1,767
ECUADOR	V	E	81	64,360	19,308	21,820	2,512
			82	60,420	21,360	24,844	3,484
			84	18,535	5,022	7,149	2,127
			86	4,672	2,628	2,855	227
EGYPT	V	E	83	10,563	10,563	12,063	1,500
EQ GUIN	A	H	84	1,890	687	1,570	883
FIJI	A	E	81	109,120	75,389	108,922	33,533
			82	5,400	2,646	5,491	2,845
			84	7,800	2,495	6,200	3,705
			85	85,320	32,399	59,265	26,866
			86	79,539	36,016	57,444	21,428
	A	H	82	9,780	6,156	10,100	3,944
			83	5,400	3,726	4,653	927
			84	8,280	2,649	4,746	2,097
			85	50,651	22,272	35,324	13,052
			86	53,957	23,241	39,042	15,801
	A	W	81	25,878	12,598	23,435	10,837
			82	48,000	23,218	40,985	17,767
			83	56,701	21,964	43,645	21,681
			84	11,445	3,656	6,467	2,811
			85	27,835	14,195	24,114	9,919
			86	31,320	13,449	25,618	12,169
	N	E	82	463,165	185,578	337,176	151,598
			83	276,133	116,677	199,033	82,356
			84	515,748	219,310	384,842	165,532
	N	H	81	529,991	267,170	413,484	146,314
			82	480,992	230,179	352,203	122,024
			83	249,089	90,931	133,697	42,766
			84	134,280	42,187	65,492	23,305
			85	234,420	107,693	150,421	42,728
			86	335,860	138,543	198,363	59,820
	N	W	81	2,069,427	1,094,936	1,538,758	443,822
			82	2,662,030	1,263,094	1,809,280	546,186
			83	1,829,223	704,480	1,033,456	328,976
			84	2,848,117	763,006	1,128,499	365,493
			85	2,972,550	1,321,919	1,841,643	519,724
			86	3,001,828	1,274,507	1,789,800	515,293
	O	E	81	19,550	13,218	13,218	
			82	11,175	9,150	9,150	
			83	4,500	2,850	2,850	
			84	6,000	3,701	3,701	

Country	Mode	Reg	Yr	Quantity	F.A.S.	C.I.F.	Charges
	O	W	83	155,325	100,373	100,373	
			84	89,400	55,890	55,890	
	V	W	82	25,500	11,522	16,029	4,507
			86	18,000	7,380	9,828	2,448
FINLAND	A	H	86	2,790	1,144	1,846	702
	N	W	85	88,530	41,445	57,225	15,780
			86	114,532	51,696	56,211	4,515
	V	W	86	19,215	7,380	10,053	2,673
FR GERM	V	E	81	3,000	450	1,021	571
FR POLY	A	H	84	440	320	867	547
FRANCE	A	E	81	101	730	775	45
			86	12,736	27,279	29,692	2,413
	A	W	83	3	728	759	31
	O	E	86	41	1,107	1,171	64
	V	E	83	123,285	78,134	84,209	6,075
			85	43,254	28,263	30,464	2,201
GREECE	V	E	84	22,000	16,005	18,843	2,838
GUATMAL	A	E	81	8,100	2,106	2,873	767
			82	10,562	3,797	5,581	1,784
			83	1,140	331	724	393
			84	3,845	1,865	3,520	1,655
	A	W	81	907	363	618	255
	V	W	85	34,120	12,906	16,979	4,073
			86	31,080	7,770	11,270	3,500
HAITI	V	E	81	36,000	56,055	59,934	3,879
HG KONG	O	E	86	7,104	14,656	14,751	95
	V	E	81	22,024	7,679	9,287	1,608
			83	135,561	58,463	73,421	14,958
			84	241,002	180,915	201,295	20,380
			85	245,180	136,900	154,919	18,019
			86	20,437	7,042	8,549	1,507
	V	W	81	32,287	16,545	18,969	2,424
			82	43,982	10,478	14,963	4,485
			83	2,205	1,973	2,094	121
			84	71,523	81,304	89,555	8,251
			85	54,255	30,505	34,495	3,990
HONDURA	V	E	83	2,520	360	668	308
			84	1,520	320	367	47
INDIA	A	E	86	221	3,166	3,763	597
	N	E	81	875,124	249,321	322,413	73,092
			85	2,651,671	2,376,097	2,901,889	525,792
	O	E	81	33,069	9,588	11,953	2,365
			83	3,080	1,516	1,516	
	V	E	81	34,021	11,789	14,448	2,659
			82	379,504	214,557	244,184	29,627
			83	203,312	191,488	204,567	13,079
			84	1,003,688	1,179,346	1,245,220	65,874
			85	160,936	109,153	120,316	11,163
			86	2,278,183	1,075,781	1,201,213	125,432
	V	W	81	122,620	33,653	44,640	10,987
			82	110,936	71,393	81,277	9,884
			84	33,069	33,068	36,756	3,688
			85	59,524	38,212	45,031	6,819
			86	265,000	115,299	133,226	17,927
INDNSIA	N	E	85	37,982	26,197	38,418	12,221
	V	E	81	44,092	27,508	33,019	5,511
			82	10,913	8,730	9,467	737
			83	10,838	8,955	10,457	1,502
			84	22,046	17,804	19,498	1,694
			86	26,455	12,169	13,763	1,594
	V	W	81	22,046	6,193	7,992	1,799
			85	22,046	12,531	14,077	1,546
IVY CST	V	E	84	43,004	28,754	33,015	4,261
			85	226,820	168,224	189,083	20,859
			86	127,467	62,816	71,865	9,049
JAMAICA	A	E	82	810	628	780	152
			83	2,850	1,038	1,232	194
			86	6,940	5,950	9,715	3,765
	N	E	83	237,871	253,429	272,650	19,221
	V	E	81	99,210	146,610	155,729	9,119
			82	94,104	97,573	104,078	6,505
			84	108,322	241,123	253,294	12,171
			85	103,608	273,257	284,770	11,513
			86	100,534	229,074	238,683	9,609
	V	W	82	49,520	58,494	63,692	5,198
			83	34,040	33,894	38,410	4,516
			84	11,058	11,433	12,759	1,326
			85	22,046	63,332	66,218	2,886
			86	22,046	51,323	53,856	2,533
JAPAN	A	W	85	5,580	2,623	4,083	1,460
	V	E	83	1,323	751	897	146
			84	28,124	15,907	19,340	3,433
			85	20,882	16,098	16,291	193
	V	W	83	19,740	6,909	10,143	3,234

Crop Product TSUSA commodity number, description, and unit of quantity Country	Mode	Reg	Yr	Quantity	F.A.S.	C.I.F.	Charges
			85	16,440	6,707	9,307	2,600
KOR REP	V	W	81	375	981	1,011	30
			84	200	255	271	16
			86	18,600	7,626	10,276	2,650
MALAYSA	V	W	82	1,227	573	636	63
MEXICO	O	E	85	6,393	1,508	1,508	
	O	W	81	45,884	3,412	3,412	
			82	24,295	1,395	1,395	
			83	18,267	1,137	1,854	717
MOROC	V	E	83	11,200	9,216	9,902	686
N ZEAL	A	H	82	5,610	2,749	4,692	1,943
	A	W	85	10,290	4,789	7,840	3,051
			86	7,738	3,510	5,742	2,232
	V	W	81	6,914	3,296	6,554	3,258
NEPAL	V	E	81	49,167	16,838	19,463	2,625
NETHLDS	A	W	84	7,500	2,088	4,005	1,917
NICARAG	N	E	81	589,637	149,948	230,308	80,360
	N	W	81	73,092	32,830	42,661	9,831
	V	E	82	379,852	128,484	161,800	33,316
			83	85,552	21,563	27,977	6,414
			84	67,600	16,900	22,333	5,433
	V	W	83	116,840	37,727	49,948	12,221
NIGERIA	N	E	83	379,660	168,590	208,761	40,171
	O	E	83	15,675	15,119	17,064	1,945
			84	365,940	448,658	482,040	33,382
			86	4,124	3,615	3,615	
	V	E	81	165,369	51,303	53,119	1,816
			82	649,784	164,891	231,933	67,042
			85	142,628	138,334	150,135	11,801
			86	232,383	141,004	159,148	18,144
NORWAY	A	E	85	27,110	7,845	9,246	1,401
PANAMA	A	E	82	9,478	3,384	5,051	1,667
			83	2,700	999	2,161	1,162
			85	9,960	6,474	7,545	1,071
			86	2,200	1,100	1,511	411
	N	E	85	28,500	4,600	7,455	2,855
	V	E	86	213,910	106,786	123,044	16,258
PERU	V	E	84	21,495	15,393	16,784	1,391
PHIL R	A	E	82	3,978	1,999	2,203	204
	V	E	81	25,540	10,887	14,238	3,351
	V	W	81	53,340	11,880	17,850	5,970
			82	12,250	2,625	4,266	1,641
			85	67,790	15,408	23,094	7,686
			86	12,285	1,871	4,607	2,736
REP SAF	V	E	85	40,840	30,630	31,056	426
S HELNA	V	E	84	22,046	29,103	30,403	1,300
S LUCIA	A	E	84	3,733	900	1,255	355
	V	E	85	23,897	14,500	18,260	3,760
S VN GR	V	E	86	12,400	2,480	3,111	631
SIER LN	N	E	81	535,626	269,546	323,164	53,618
			84	97,260	193,841	203,610	9,769
	V	E	82	437,334	183,845	232,282	48,437
			83	502,580	385,118	412,610	27,492
SPAIN	A	E	84	15,024	3,408	11,308	7,900
SRI LKA	A	E	82	110	1,800	2,133	333
SWITZLD	V	W	85	10,681	6,793	7,710	917
T PAC I	A	W	81	7,500	3,525	6,713	3,188
	N	W	82	42,060	20,983	30,575	9,592
	V	W	83	18,030	6,671	9,062	2,391
THAILND	A	H	85	3,175	4,718	5,133	415
	N	E	81	2,141	2,920	3,250	330
	O	W	85	529	1,272	1,351	79
	V	E	82	202	483	544	61
			83	251	269	286	17
			86	1,250	1,750	1,937	187
	V	W	81	2,625	2,577	2,836	259
			82	37,825	12,445	18,304	5,859
			83	6,274	6,665	7,278	613
			84	2,946	2,270	2,469	199
			86	7,233	5,635	6,110	475
TONGA	A	W	83	7,440	4,363	7,625	3,262
U KING	O	E	82	223	522	576	54
	V	E	81	415	1,400	1,644	244
			82	630	989	1,041	52
	V	W	83	223	455	485	30
VENEZ	A	E	83	10,020	3,045	7,600	4,555

1613700 GINGER ROOT, GRND, N CANDIED (LB)

TOTAL			81	119,258	66,040	74,118	8,078
			82	117,881	87,068	91,484	4,416
			83	178,779	132,366	141,712	9,346
			84	80,179	91,902	97,210	5,308
			85	56,547	55,396	58,235	2,839
			86	65,086	32,566	40,085	7,519

Crop Product TSUSA commodity number, description, and unit of quantity — Country Mode Reg Yr Quantity F.A.S. C.I.F. Charges

Country	Mode	Reg	Yr	Quantity	F.A.S.	C.I.F.	Charges
AUSTRAL	V	W	84	206	283	310	27
BRAZIL	O	E	85	8,350	8,249	8,249	
	V	E	83	35,494	11,512	17,179	5,667
			85	6,608	6,756	7,350	594
			86	27,888	6,325	11,124	4,799
C RICA	V	E	84	146	635	686	51
CANADA	N	W	82	3,300	2,288	2,508	220
	O	E	81	28,205	15,787	15,787	
			82	64,000	45,014	45,014	
			83	100,016	71,878	71,878	
			84	17,213	19,977	19,977	
			85	10,955	10,009	10,009	
			86	1,000	1,345	1,345	
	O	W	82	5,000	2,700	2,700	
CHINA M	O	E	84	276	278	306	28
	V	E	81	27,850	12,840	15,186	2,346
			82	5,200	4,786	5,438	652
			83	11,261	11,786	12,457	671
			84	3,125	3,653	4,099	446
			85	1,250	1,050	1,267	217
	V	W	81	27,752	14,051	15,457	1,406
			82	8,940	5,531	5,873	342
			83	2,725	2,897	3,184	287
			84	5,438	7,244	7,782	538
			85	11,023	11,602	12,500	898
			86	14,050	6,480	6,824	344
CHINA T	V	E	83	384	1,816	1,882	66
			84	563	2,432	2,637	205
			86	37	1,225	1,275	50
	V	W	82	476	693	779	86
			84	5,230	7,000	7,294	294
DOM REP	A	E	82	2,400	480	780	300
FIJI	A	H	86	7,500	3,075	4,241	1,166
	A	W	81	3,000	1,440	2,552	1,112
HG KONG	V	E	81	1,938	2,611	2,808	197
			83	1,360	1,590	1,792	202
			84	1,095	1,288	1,451	163
			86	1,058	1,076	1,207	131
	V	W	81	2,655	2,392	2,626	234
			82	1,620	1,743	1,916	173
			83	1,332	1,340	1,484	144
			84	250	316	331	15
			86	1,500	1,195	1,245	50
INDIA	O	E	81	880	616	616	
			82	750	459	459	
	V	E	82	1,543	1,421	1,612	191
			84	33,895	37,406	39,675	2,269
	V	W	81	22,046	5,376	7,148	1,772
			82	2,340	1,481	1,717	236
			83	953	1,317	1,514	197
			85	1,949	1,934	2,080	146
INDNSIA	V	W	83	353	400	429	29
JAMAICA	N	E	81	886	1,270	1,381	111
	V	E	82	2,076	1,705	1,887	182
JAPAN	V	E	82	9,921	2,902	3,418	516
			83	2,645	1,380	1,564	184
			84	4,514	2,822	3,245	423
	V	W	81	67	396	414	18
			82	114	590	632	42
			83	19,485	17,807	19,231	1,424
			84	209	1,014	1,065	51
			85	9,357	6,899	7,067	168
KOR REP	V	W	81	94	528	559	31
			82	314	890	939	49
			83	1,159	5,002	5,236	234
			85	198	1,296	1,400	104
			86	2,317	2,798	2,995	197
MEXICO	O	W	84	3,024	1,665	1,665	
NETHLDS	V	W	84	83	448	480	32
NIGERIA	V	E	84	214	330	382	52
PAKISTN	V	W	85	1,194	1,687	1,965	278
PHIL R	V	W	81	263	321	353	32
S ARAB	V	E	85	4,023	4,627	4,973	346
SINGAPR	V	W	81	375	1,240	1,364	124
SWITZLD	A	E	84	333	743	1,076	333
THAILND	V	E	82	3,935	5,150	5,662	512
	V	W	81	2,784	5,444	5,979	535
			82	5,952	9,235	10,150	915
			83	1,216	2,366	2,527	161
			84	3,738	2,998	3,265	267
			85	1,640	1,287	1,375	88
			86	9,736	9,047	9,829	782
U KING	O	E	81	384	1,299	1,429	130

Crop
Product
TSUSA commodity number, description, and unit of quantity

Country	Mode	Reg	Yr	Quantity	F.A.S.	C.I.F.	Charges
			83	132	294	322	28
			84	495	1,024	1,127	103
	V	E	81	79	429	459	30
			83	212	582	596	14
			84	132	346	357	11
	V	W	83	52	399	437	38

Sweet ginger, processed
1418700 SWEET GINGER (LB)

Country	Mode	Reg	Yr	Quantity	F.A.S.	C.I.F.	Charges
TOTAL			81	120,665	110,263	119,385	9,122
			82	238,741	184,650	201,806	17,156
			83	574,070	394,993	437,895	42,902
			84	647,195	415,653	468,542	52,889
			85	893,608	404,567	466,402	61,835
			86	954,882	575,451	640,043	64,592
AUSTRAL	A	W	84	177	295	471	176
	N	W	82	9,221	10,436	12,735	2,299
	O	E	83	3,968	4,968	4,968	
			84	1,563	2,905	2,905	
	V	E	82	6,032	5,720	6,548	828
			83	9,401	8,659	9,385	726
			84	10,481	7,185	8,662	1,477
			85	17,193	16,924	18,979	2,055
			86	19,969	23,810	26,036	2,226
	V	W	81	10,911	12,275	13,279	1,004
			83	40,831	41,658	46,509	4,851
			84	17,709	18,605	20,418	1,813
			85	17,760	18,557	20,011	1,454
			86	13,136	14,047	15,943	1,896
CANADA	O	W	83	2,232	2,261	2,261	
CHINA M	O	W	83	810	576	603	27
			84	737	625	673	48
	V	E	81	4,183	2,592	2,872	280
			82	2,470	1,773	2,038	265
			83	3,211	4,092	4,774	682
			84	3,335	3,296	3,773	477
			85	5,220	3,354	3,928	574
	V	H	81	4,365	1,474	1,782	308
			82	6,614	4,903	5,400	497
	V	W	81	6,890	7,251	7,818	567
			82	32,884	9,625	10,270	645
			83	5,169	4,624	4,958	334
			84	3,655	3,575	4,031	456
			85	2,500	3,155	3,399	244
			86	5,000	6,343	6,555	212
CHINA T	N	W	81	3,746	4,955	5,454	499
	V	E	81	9,937	5,040	5,674	634
			82	250	480	493	13
			83	70,650	41,141	46,325	5,184
			84	50,867	32,760	38,434	5,674
			85	108,238	69,080	79,101	10,021
			86	162,302	69,453	82,062	12,609
	V	H	81	300	528	560	32
	V	W	81	375	615	659	44
			82	41,732	17,986	20,562	2,576
			83	113,035	43,159	48,886	5,727
			84	287,466	156,244	172,338	16,094
			85	375,983	105,413	125,843	20,430
			86	140,852	66,719	74,373	7,654
DOM REP	V	E	84	18,000	4,324	6,324	2,000
FIJI	A	E	83	2,700	2,031	3,196	1,165
HG KONG	N	W	82	13,125	23,808	25,784	1,976
	O	W	82	500	505	538	33
	V	E	81	31,942	34,867	37,493	2,626
			82	10,780	12,458	13,206	748
			83	20,013	13,338	15,759	2,421
			84	52,850	48,515	57,148	8,633
			85	32,627	32,777	36,984	4,207
			86	57,984	50,712	56,146	5,434
	V	H	81	3,222	2,950	3,095	145
	V	W	81	14,910	16,921	17,983	1,062
			82	29,346	29,427	31,480	2,053
			83	68,862	71,852	81,232	9,380
			84	30,103	24,706	27,792	3,086
			85	29,692	22,621	23,922	1,301
			86	34,724	29,080	30,891	1,811
INDIA	V	E	81	794	1,039	1,255	216
			82	3,178	3,216	4,221	1,005
JAPAN	N	E	85	58,647	39,186	44,201	5,015
	V	E	81	9,084	8,374	9,102	728
			82	8,451	11,443	12,536	1,093
			83	48,544	38,958	43,899	4,941
			84	60,926	51,492	58,059	6,567
			85	22,604	16,118	19,367	3,249
			86	131,147	117,148	128,983	11,835
	V	W	81	13,302	8,575	9,368	793
			82	66,822	45,181	47,669	2,488
			83	169,498	106,689	113,085	6,396
			84	46,223	32,096	34,256	2,160
			85	47,101	26,742	30,113	3,371
			86	175,476	124,221	133,598	9,377
KOR REP	V	E	86	3,067	3,131	3,297	166
	V	W	84	250	660	700	40
			86	218	1,734	1,910	176
SPAIN	V	E	83	11,246	7,931	8,754	823
THAILND	V	E	82	3,307	3,300	3,548	248
			83	2,337	1,275	1,385	110
			84	841	700	856	156
			86	7,615	4,160	4,413	253
	V	W	81	6,400	1,978	2,098	120
			82	3,603	3,357	3,676	319
			83	1,563	1,781	1,916	135
			84	56,755	20,962	24,470	3,508
			85	176,043	50,640	60,554	9,914
			86	200,852	59,820	70,639	10,819
U KING	V	E	81	304	829	893	64
			82	203	510	543	33
			84	5,257	6,708	7,232	524
			86	2,540	5,073	5,197	124
	V	W	82	223	522	559	37

Ginseng

Ginseng, crude
1932540 GINSENG, CRUDE (LB)

Country	Mode	Reg	Yr	Quantity	F.A.S.	C.I.F.	Charges
TOTAL			81	3,745	64,038	67,215	3,177
			82	8,210	346,019	361,778	15,759
			83	18,859	497,640	521,637	23,997
			84	3,064	106,536	111,025	4,489
			85	11,276	522,955	538,799	15,844
			86	22,779	867,683	898,465	30,782
CANADA	A	E	84	896	41,377	41,557	180
			86	7,376	313,254	316,862	3,608
	A	W	85	500	15,029	15,142	113
	N	E	83	329	28,800	28,915	115
			85	4,780	333,357	336,303	2,946
	O	E	81	10	800	800	
			82	30	700	700	
			83	387	15,543	15,543	
			84	15	830	830	
			85	245	11,623	11,623	
			86	964	35,773	35,773	
CHINA M	A	E	82	40	9,392	10,527	1,135
			85	27	1,388	1,486	98
	A	W	86	556	23,000	24,112	1,112
	V	E	81	3,028	11,857	12,218	361
			83	88	1,341	1,378	37
	V	W	82	1,044	41,623	42,667	1,044
			83	485	25,176	25,759	583
			84	800	17,835	18,345	510
CHINA T	V	E	85	1,229	35,652	38,390	2,738
	V	W	85	110	3,000	3,026	26
GUATMAL	A	W	84	3	325	864	539
HG KONG	A	E	81	575	36,760	38,571	1,811
			83	3,210	77,262	80,864	3,602
			85	3,906	90,646	98,329	7,683
	N	E	82	1,386	84,231	87,706	3,475
			86	8,376	322,488	339,321	16,833
	V	W	83	5	1,254	1,304	50
			85	13	2,756	2,910	154
INDIA	N	E	86	244	16,475	17,386	911
	V	E	85	77	6,650	7,554	904
JAPAN	A	E	81	132	14,621	15,626	1,005
			82	3,278	121,709	129,151	7,442
			83	14,120	337,670	356,769	19,099
			84	735	33,804	35,184	1,380
			85	133	11,378	11,805	427
			86	533	15,683	16,600	917
	N	W	86	809	18,441	18,983	542
	V	W	83	23	970	993	23

Crop Product TSUSA commodity number, description, and unit of quantity Country	Mode	Reg	Yr	Quantity	F.A.S.	C.I.F.	Charges
			86	66	7,594	8,170	576
KOR REP	A	E	84	112	2,761	3,200	439
			86	2,028	54,685	57,200	2,515
	N	E	82	572	33,484	35,347	1,863
			86	537	20,476	23,336	2,860
	N	W	86	719	26,270	26,753	483
	O	E	83	50	1,711	1,711	
			86	195	7,182	7,182	
	V	E	83	142	5,504	5,623	119
	V	W	84	503	9,604	11,045	1,441
			85	231	8,939	9,694	755
			86	376	6,362	6,787	425
MEXICO	O	W	85	25	2,537	2,537	
NETHLDS	V	E	83	20	2,409	2,778	369
PHIL R	V	W	82	1,860	54,880	55,680	800

Ginseng, root
4391050 GINSENG ROOTS (LB)

Country	Mode	Reg	Yr	Quantity	F.A.S.	C.I.F.	Charges
TOTAL			81	125,648	2,893,678	2,950,745	57,067
			82	93,647	2,585,453	2,639,581	54,128
			83	62,581	1,802,152	1,841,673	39,521
			84	83,391	1,958,916	2,002,890	43,974
			85	103,861	2,439,646	2,489,333	49,687
			86	95,688	1,559,547	1,609,620	50,073
CANADA	A	E	84	3,829	267,313	268,392	1,079
			85	100	3,169	3,201	32
			86	6,170	231,313	234,253	2,940
	A	W	81	610	30,695	31,033	338
			83	700	40,437	40,960	523
			84	1,050	56,298	56,950	652
			85	343	15,357	15,678	321
			86	160	9,417	9,481	64
	N	E	81	1,201	97,354	99,098	1,744
			83	642	45,090	45,376	286
			85	6,176	313,328	320,735	7,407
			86	1,750	54,162	55,556	1,394
	O	E	81	2,295	14,398	14,398	
			82	5	1,000	1,025	25
			83	2,159	22,275	22,275	
			85	2,263	34,174	34,174	
			86	781	22,860	22,860	
CHILE	V	E	84	2,218	1,062	1,222	160
CHINA M	A	W	86	535	17,525	19,314	1,789
	N	E	81	5,891	202,808	207,405	4,597
			82	14,938	57,345	62,549	5,204
			83	1,760	43,567	45,903	2,336
			84	2,467	121,921	125,751	3,830
			85	8,663	128,821	131,460	2,639
			86	10,538	90,234	93,606	3,372
	N	W	82	422	22,247	23,633	1,386
			83	1,363	51,111	53,549	2,438
			85	3,287	115,362	120,959	5,597
			86	6,933	213,453	222,458	9,005
	O	E	84	90	388	455	67
	V	E	84	54	454	521	67
	V	H	83	113	3,256	3,324	68
			85	80	3,520	3,640	120
	V	W	81	26,666	62,543	63,358	815
			82	737	19,068	19,602	534
			83	3,312	23,833	24,397	564
			84	1,212	50,122	50,453	331
			85	293	34,430	34,680	250
			86	4,409	3,229	3,800	571
CHINA T	A	E	81	462	13,006	14,709	1,703
			82	143	6,490	6,822	332
	V	E	86	4,358	16,959	17,441	482
	V	W	83	4,400	2,874	3,426	552
FR GERM	V	E	83	129	3,908	4,133	225
GREECE	V	E	81	220	499	583	84
HG KONG	A	E	81	360	20,120	21,368	1,248
			83	7,570	422,792	435,295	12,503
			85	15,207	740,508	746,675	6,167
	A	H	85	417	10,798	11,348	550
	A	W	83	667	12,340	13,717	1,377
			84	2,154	111,561	114,435	2,874
	N	E	81	10,179	249,453	258,060	8,607
			82	8,909	453,427	465,172	11,745
			84	6,817	343,847	354,869	11,022
			86	10,282	228,038	235,894	7,856
	N	W	83	403	6,080	6,481	401
			85	4,026	118,729	125,982	7,253

Country	Mode	Reg	Yr	Quantity	F.A.S.	C.I.F.	Charges
			86	1,458	63,660	67,125	3,465
	V	W	81	7,642	15,971	17,158	1,187
			82	4,148	13,385	14,590	1,205
			85	220	8,634	8,861	227
			86	874	42,557	42,698	141
INDIA	N	E	84	30,127	10,656	15,918	5,262
	V	E	81	6,614	5,318	6,650	1,332
			82	6,614	5,295	6,650	1,355
			83	22,029	4,512	7,132	2,620
			86	11,023	10,750	12,090	1,340
	V	W	82	4,189	986	1,284	298
JAPAN	A	W	85	463	26,005	26,229	224
	N	E	81	8,038	511,804	524,948	13,144
			82	4,657	250,702	255,958	5,256
			83	2,827	83,431	88,916	5,485
			84	4,635	84,161	88,367	4,206
			85	9,726	319,840	326,062	6,222
			86	8,205	148,327	155,234	6,907
	N	W	82	631	37,263	39,379	2,116
			83	295	10,340	11,124	784
			84	300	11,539	12,064	525
	V	H	81	4	476	498	22
			83	71	1,519	1,551	32
	V	W	81	12	1,199	1,215	16
			82	521	30,009	30,306	297
			83	455	19,082	19,333	251
			85	805	35,017	35,629	612
			86	1,241	43,174	44,009	835
KOR REP	A	E	81	727	47,002	47,309	307
			84	10	416	499	83
			85	794	28,159	29,732	1,573
	A	W	82	58	540	732	192
	N	E	81	1,761	51,440	57,379	5,939
			83	1,054	50,282	51,460	1,178
			84	4,124	98,200	102,789	4,589
			86	9,532	150,813	155,859	5,046
	N	W	81	51,643	1,479,592	1,495,183	15,591
			82	37,954	1,534,907	1,555,802	20,895
			83	4,190	150,863	155,660	4,797
			84	4,734	158,427	161,833	3,406
			85	39,202	468,595	476,341	7,746
			86	6,539	202,812	206,994	4,182
	O	E	83	567	108,137	108,137	
	V	E	82	66	2,563	2,637	74
	V	W	81	1,323	90,000	90,393	393
			83	5,772	695,497	698,318	2,821
			84	8,850	637,808	642,983	5,175
			85	1,036	31,343	33,075	1,732
MOROC	V	E	82	7,848	101,486	103,773	2,287
SINGAPR	A	W	86	170	5,589	6,160	571
	N	E	82	1,507	36,939	37,667	728
	V	W	82	300	11,801	12,000	199
YUGOSLV	V	E	83	2,103	926	1,206	280
			84	10,720	4,743	5,389	646
			85	10,760	3,857	4,872	1,015
			86	10,730	4,675	4,788	113

4393050 GINSENG IN ADVANCED FORM (LB)

Country	Mode	Reg	Yr	Quantity	F.A.S.	C.I.F.	Charges
TOTAL			81	165,257	2,855,668	2,997,728	142,060
			82	259,527	3,410,552	3,522,125	111,573
			83	268,124	2,556,146	2,651,516	95,370
			84	218,925	2,989,945	3,093,615	103,670
			85	252,133	4,029,413	4,116,036	86,623
			86	423,564	4,280,210	4,394,946	114,736
AUSTRAL	V	W	81	5	469	476	7
BRAZIL	A	E	81	1,102	118,443	119,308	865
CANADA	A	E	82	15	1,088	1,121	33
	A	W	81	133	531	569	38
			84	50	1,975	2,000	25
			86	150	3,678	3,869	191
	O	E	82	771	3,020	3,045	25
	O	W	85	800	4,420	4,920	500
CHINA M	A	E	81	114	297	384	87
			83	325	10,801	11,774	973
			84	221	10,786	11,170	384
	A	H	81	440	5,619	6,383	764
	N	E	81	496	15,057	15,348	291
			82	4,494	7,696	8,758	1,062
			83	373	11,393	12,253	860
	N	W	81	55,424	845,595	901,417	55,822
			82	132,998	1,213,098	1,261,079	47,981
			83	146,799	861,179	905,162	43,983
			84	88,881	670,842	688,900	18,058

Crop Product TSUSA commodity number, description, and unit of quantity Country	Mode	Reg	Yr	Quantity	F.A.S.	C.I.F.	Charges
			85	64,701	740,282	763,997	23,715
			86	167,920	920,300	955,366	35,066
	O	E	84	265	416	488	72
	V	E	85	992	9,011	9,619	608
			86	11,204	46,081	48,830	2,749
	V	W	81	20	577	583	6
			82	3,085	30,236	31,021	785
			83	1,586	8,724	9,048	324
			85	9,925	76,670	79,017	2,347
			86	11,827	229,450	234,421	4,971
CHINA T	A	W	84	1,047	32,340	34,672	2,332
			86	200	9,428	9,729	301
	N	W	81	11,155	11,832	12,980	1,148
	V	W	82	31	600	621	21
			84	110	880	959	79
			86	1,102	8,220	8,336	116
FR GERM	A	E	83	82	272	367	95
	V	E	81	1,065	3,749	4,007	258
			82	2,158	4,783	5,094	311
			84	21,826	40,363	44,513	4,150
FRANCE	A	E	83	11	2,124	2,163	39
HG KONG	A	E	81	377	30,070	30,719	649
			82	150	4,930	5,183	253
			85	625	16,800	16,820	20
			86	1,300	62,923	65,000	2,077
	A	W	86	900	43,850	45,405	1,555
	N	W	83	2,798	71,699	73,334	1,635
			84	213	4,051	4,172	121
			85	11,326	118,836	122,866	4,030
			86	787	32,190	33,251	1,061
	O	E	86	500	1,270	1,411	141
	V	E	84	68	1,240	1,347	107
	V	W	82	2,068	44,635	44,878	243
			83	4,938	25,126	25,730	604
			85	9,330	37,494	38,122	628
			86	7,397	27,403	28,404	1,001
INDIA	A	E	81	4,413	12,486	19,214	6,728
	O	E	82	4	1,567	1,692	125
JAPAN	A	W	81	827	2,647	4,550	1,903
			84	228	13,822	14,378	556
	N	W	81	13,731	106,819	118,379	11,560
			82	9,737	181,423	189,801	8,378
			83	416	21,515	22,655	1,140
			84	1,435	79,154	83,057	3,903
			86	1,193	58,530	61,247	2,717
	V	E	81	260	2,548	2,637	89
			82	323	37,751	39,410	1,659
			84	120	639	652	13
	V	W	83	3,456	75,359	76,664	1,305
			84	2,969	24,646	25,525	879
			85	7,851	202,654	209,753	7,099
			86	14,298	145,693	149,642	3,949
KENYA	A	E	86	1,122	7,020	7,244	224
	V	E	85	2,896	90,140	91,983	1,843
KOR REP	A	E	83	1,984	30,147	35,641	5,494
	A	H	81	1,020	2,857	3,985	1,128
	A	W	83	13	400	454	54
			84	685	16,831	17,747	916
			85	154	1,130	1,130	
			86	156	26,523	26,807	284
	N	E	81	8,957	92,626	100,982	8,356
			82	33,366	616,187	630,770	14,583
			83	16,360	459,410	468,125	8,715
			84	8,719	284,163	296,567	12,404
			85	13,584	405,963	415,022	9,059
			86	36,741	333,624	347,449	13,825
	N	W	81	62,071	1,501,644	1,551,045	49,401
			82	19,173	608,829	630,654	21,825
			83	52,406	596,399	611,075	14,676
			84	17,537	199,062	205,404	6,342
			85	206	28,317	28,495	178
			86	133,070	2,033,339	2,064,415	31,076
	O	E	81	880	19,953	19,953	
			82	1,794	77,408	77,408	
			83	888	18,897	18,897	
			84	220	5,710	5,710	
			85	88	2,284	2,284	
	O	W	83	30	1,200	1,200	
	V	E	82	26	1,600	1,678	78
			84	13,774	77,260	84,088	6,828
			85	7,650	44,276	47,401	3,125
			86	3,478	32,097	33,325	1,228
	V	H	81	18	1,974	2,280	306
			82	462	10,350	11,020	670

Crop Product TSUSA commodity number, description, and unit of quantity Country	Mode	Reg	Yr	Quantity	F.A.S.	C.I.F.	Charges
			85	301	6,054	6,407	353
	V	W	81	2,696	79,567	82,196	2,629
			82	48,871	562,859	576,286	13,427
			83	34,659	361,171	376,588	15,417
			84	60,557	1,525,765	1,572,266	46,501
			85	121,704	2,245,082	2,278,200	33,118
			86	27,268	253,001	264,883	11,882
MALAYSA	V	H	81	53	308	333	25
ROMANIA	V	E	86	2,554	3,744	3,894	150
SINGAPR	V	W	83	1,000	330	386	56
SWITZLD	A	E	82	1	2,492	2,606	114
YUGOSLV	V	E	86	397	1,846	2,018	172

Gladiolus

Gladiolus, corms

1253240 GLADIOLUS CORMS, WITH SOIL (NO)

	Mode	Reg	Yr	Quantity	F.A.S.	C.I.F.	Charges
TOTAL			83	**1,210,000**	**14,750**	**18,542**	**3,792**
			86	**1,269**	**2,370**	**2,370**	
CANADA	O	E	86	1,269	2,370	2,370	
NETHLDS	A	E	83	1,210,000	14,750	18,542	3,792

1253440 GLADIOLUS CORMS, NSPF (NO)

	Mode	Reg	Yr	Quantity	F.A.S.	C.I.F.	Charges
TOTAL			81	**67,623,422**	**1,207,313**	**1,374,120**	**171,625**
			82	**73,058,190**	**1,097,634**	**1,254,327**	**156,693**
			83	**76,057,062**	**1,196,222**	**1,374,350**	**178,128**
			84	**80,952,122**	**1,263,989**	**1,450,464**	**186,475**
			85	**73,221,530**	**1,212,010**	**1,408,750**	**196,740**
			86	**118,568,656**	**1,593,774**	**1,862,847**	**269,073**
BELGIUM	V	E	83	188,530	12,797	13,803	1,006
			84	698,791	37,354	41,246	3,892
			85	377,000	12,190	14,986	2,796
			86	200,400	2,034	2,177	143
	V	W	83	128,400	30,025	31,794	1,769
CANADA	O	E	81	169	376	376	
			82	370,500	10,290	10,290	
			83	80,000	1,695	1,695	
			86	100,000	2,675	2,675	
	O	W	81	22,823	7,129	7,129	
			82	847,800	23,780	23,780	
			83	85,000	4,760	4,760	
			84	75,000	1,599	1,599	
			85	184,500	6,973	6,973	
			86	108,800	5,537	5,537	
FR GERM	V	E	85	42	1,007	1,175	168
HONDURA	A	E	84	11,400	377	480	103
ISRAEL	V	E	83	22,000	1,119	1,214	95
JAPAN	V	W	85	12,000	1,876	2,058	182
MALI	V	E	86	449,325	14,207	20,614	6,407
NETHLDS	A	E	82	19,000	2,526	3,511	985
			83	926,000	6,787	9,805	3,018
			84	2,060,000	6,484	9,322	2,838
	A	W	86	22,500	1,037	1,659	622
	N	E	81	58,515,137	881,123	975,304	99,681
			82	62,239,843	757,444	859,791	102,347
			83	64,472,704	859,420	979,330	119,910
			84	66,327,423	957,360	1,088,551	131,191
			85	41,557,030	791,723	906,000	114,277
			86	69,046,716	818,154	944,313	126,159
	N	W	84	281,590	18,842	23,923	5,081
			85	1,118,480	27,468	34,639	7,171
	O	W	85	382,900	12,161	14,291	2,130
	V	E	81	7,802,143	271,321	335,719	63,716
			82	6,902,370	203,276	235,793	32,517
			83	8,829,340	227,270	271,975	44,705
			84	9,832,174	178,118	212,094	33,976
			85	28,531,478	325,922	389,119	63,197
			86	46,974,707	691,483	816,282	124,799
	V	W	81	1,283,150	47,364	55,592	8,228
			82	2,032,850	72,695	85,708	13,013
			83	1,006,188	35,105	41,286	6,181
			84	1,121,660	36,558	43,610	7,052
			85	1,058,100	32,690	39,509	6,819
			86	1,666,208	58,647	69,590	10,943
REP SAF	V	E	83	285,900	15,631	16,941	1,310
			84	167,075	15,752	16,530	778
U KING	V	E	82	645,827	27,623	35,454	7,831
			83	33,000	1,613	1,747	134

Crop Product TSUSA commodity number, description, and unit of quantity Country	Mode	Reg	Yr	Quantity	F.A.S.	C.I.F.	Charges
			84	377,009	11,545	13,109	1,564

Gooseberry

Gooseberry, frozen**
1466900 BLACK CURRANTS, ETC, FROZEN (LB)
  (See Lingonberry, frozen under Cowberry)

Gooseberry, prepared or preserved**
1468200 BLACK CURRNT ETC PREP, PRES (LB)
  (See Lingonberry, prepared or preserved under Cowberry)

Grape

Champagne
1671020 CHAMPAGNE WINE NOV $6 GAL (GAL)

Country	Mode	Reg	Yr	Quantity	F.A.S.	C.I.F.	Charges
TOTAL			81	1,720,055	6,305,522	7,426,497	1,120,975
			82	1,196,052	5,225,703	6,374,114	1,148,411
			83	1,540,760	6,215,987	7,465,436	1,249,449
			84	3,554,007	15,716,019	19,169,751	3,453,732
			85	4,015,480	19,000,538	23,487,638	4,487,100
			86	1,563,670	7,586,340	9,159,903	1,573,563
ARGENT	O	E	84	1,428	5,508	6,443	935
	V	E	84	713	2,754	3,526	772
	V	W	84	1,903	8,640	11,409	2,769
AUSTRAL	V	E	82	2,852	16,274	20,630	4,356
	V	W	82	165	290	325	35
			83	4,993	29,063	33,967	4,904
			86	463	2,124	2,337	213
AUSTRIA	O	E	81	399	2,303	2,600	297
			85	238	1,261	1,716	455
	V	E	81	799	4,485	5,063	578
			82	399	2,016	2,542	526
			83	2,523	14,686	16,421	1,735
			84	6,535	12,290	12,314	24
	V	W	82	274	1,002	1,145	143
BELGIUM	A	E	83	97	382	425	43
	O	E	82	755	3,445	4,622	1,177
			83	209	1,045	1,208	163
			85	1,509	6,204	8,223	2,019
	V	E	84	11,909	41,294	48,328	7,034
			85	297	1,331	1,670	339
			86	365	1,556	1,790	234
	V	W	86	2,478	11,052	12,252	1,200
BENIN	V	E	86	404	2,253	2,836	583
BERMUDA	O	E	83	951	4,668	5,729	1,061
BRAZIL	V	E	81	330,690	655,050	682,925	27,875
			85	1,545	6,792	8,972	2,180
			86	12,951	50,160	52,791	2,631
BULGAR	V	W	83	428	2,440	2,678	238
CANADA	O	E	81	10,169	49,350	49,350	
			82	9,656	44,206	47,187	2,981
			83	10,031	47,611	47,611	
			84	8,042	37,726	37,726	
			85	14,322	69,722	71,589	1,867
			86	8,793	37,013	37,013	
	O	W	85	262	1,456	1,456	
	V	E	81	2,017	10,416	12,812	2,396
CHILE	V	E	83	119	705	804	99
			84	118	692	777	85
			86	556	3,105	3,535	430
FR GERM	A	E	84	118	700	1,569	869
	N	E	81	857	4,808	5,368	560
			82	978	5,492	6,113	621
			84	8,033	44,092	52,656	8,564
			85	8,308	39,121	47,257	8,136
	O	E	81	9,803	51,414	61,115	9,701
			82	23,774	112,696	134,241	21,545
			83	14,182	64,051	74,802	10,751
			84	13,178	61,128	74,020	12,892
			85	7,100	33,075	40,816	7,741
			86	3,584	15,480	17,867	2,387
	O	W	84	178	884	1,423	539
	V	E	81	53,605	205,993	242,861	36,868
			82	46,356	211,172	266,219	55,047
			83	115,226	250,640	286,415	35,775
			84	60,750	198,505	231,941	33,436
			85	44,377	214,675	264,323	49,648
			86	19,603	88,739	107,854	19,115
	V	W	81	8,499	41,118	48,784	7,666
			82	10,930	54,821	66,403	11,582
			83	9,915	43,422	50,013	6,591
			84	16,553	75,287	88,602	13,315
			85	30,334	138,506	170,219	31,713
			86	12,241	54,128	61,902	7,774
FRANCE	A	E	85	594	2,214	6,448	4,234
	N	E	83	2,820	14,255	17,102	2,847
			84	100,333	404,187	530,965	126,778
			85	17,597	81,917	108,554	26,637
	N	W	83	52,005	234,158	280,884	46,726
			84	26,591	116,123	139,661	23,538
			85	59,206	245,626	299,513	53,887
	O	E	81	33,700	134,660	154,479	19,819
			82	67,732	312,774	386,397	73,623
			83	100,590	452,929	554,609	101,680
			84	168,885	595,979	715,035	119,056
			85	116,910	514,964	641,590	126,626
			86	65,157	292,372	360,564	68,192
	O	H	85	1,427	6,931	8,738	1,807
			86	741	3,866	4,839	973
	O	W	81	265	980	1,319	339
			82	1,741	8,313	9,841	1,528
			83	2,825	13,351	16,422	3,071
			84	19,936	92,628	108,270	15,642
			85	3,696	16,459	21,016	4,557
			86	8,651	35,352	43,835	8,483
	V	E	81	64,375	315,890	358,619	42,729
			82	102,174	477,528	581,294	103,766
			83	221,397	960,257	1,163,920	203,663
			84	196,649	852,805	1,044,903	192,098
			85	285,146	1,245,357	1,588,981	343,624
			86	254,412	1,083,461	1,248,856	165,395
	V	W	81	12,377	58,170	68,002	9,832
			82	27,603	136,388	163,267	26,879
			83	10,961	48,187	57,521	9,334
			84	38,002	153,807	190,619	36,812
			85	98,135	456,613	549,709	93,096
			86	51,468	255,127	296,100	40,973
GERM DR	V	W	83	200	1,171	1,331	160
			85	793	2,028	2,129	101
GREECE	O	E	81	399	2,310	2,539	229
HG KONG	V	W	83	2,500	1,018	1,069	51
HUNGARY	O	E	81	400	2,324	2,678	354
			82	299	1,580	1,950	370
			84	437	2,344	2,790	446
			86	5,831	26,050	26,050	
	V	E	81	2,853	17,100	19,245	2,145
			82	600	3,275	4,126	851
			83	2,853	15,450	16,950	1,500
	V	W	82	1,845	10,995	12,888	1,893
			83	200	992	1,360	368
			84	713	3,470	4,220	750
IRELAND	V	E	84	20,000	38,880	42,380	3,500
ISRAEL	O	E	84	7,288	23,916	31,234	7,318
			85	4,156	20,159	24,328	4,169
	V	E	84	7,483	25,443	33,171	7,728
			85	5,372	27,111	33,964	6,853
			86	618	3,120	3,661	541
	V	W	83	357	2,085	2,286	201
			84	3,196	10,914	13,697	2,783
			85	2,019	10,200	12,957	2,757
ITALY	N	E	81	251,330	1,050,311	1,259,348	209,037
			82	21,980	84,853	104,938	20,085
			83	216,164	960,599	1,133,613	173,014
			84	608,636	2,864,372	3,484,179	619,807
			85	399,028	1,836,793	2,272,021	435,228
			86	10,104	54,929	65,591	10,662
	N	W	84	60,808	297,464	355,392	57,928
			85	29,960	144,930	178,021	33,091
	O	E	81	140,373	581,679	682,228	100,549
			82	153,576	669,293	791,071	121,778
			83	157,032	652,412	784,854	132,442
			84	580,886	2,709,497	3,289,798	580,301
			85	484,773	2,240,170	2,726,851	486,681
			86	267,974	1,314,993	1,609,343	294,350
	O	W	81	3,085	11,439	14,018	2,579
			82	5,470	21,455	26,820	5,365
			83	594	2,430	2,873	443
			84	3,193	15,352	18,528	3,176
			85	7,686	36,980	45,188	8,208

Crop
Product
TSUSA commodity number, description, and unit of quantity

Country	Mode	Reg	Yr	Quantity	F.A.S.	C.I.F.	Charges
			86	237	1,299	1,698	399
	V	E	81	240,647	1,077,625	1,290,502	212,877
			82	462,245	1,805,445	2,201,810	396,365
			83	323,966	1,241,861	1,500,045	258,184
			84	1,134,856	5,127,390	6,276,610	1,149,220
			85	1,589,312	7,629,511	9,383,621	1,754,110
			86	589,155	2,957,920	3,606,321	648,401
	V	W	81	61,917	238,821	302,771	63,950
			82	40,611	143,644	179,373	35,729
			83	28,328	102,437	131,603	29,166
			84	112,827	500,237	613,038	112,801
			85	259,315	1,133,811	1,418,947	285,136
			86	51,350	262,400	317,664	55,264
JAPAN	V	E	82	281	1,662	1,858	196
			83	603	1,372	1,487	115
	V	H	81	937	1,898	2,201	303
			83	132	336	378	42
	V	W	83	165	312	329	17
			84	255	846	885	39
MALTA	V	E	81	2,259	11,305	14,145	2,840
MEXICO	O	E	86	2,179	6,218	6,361	143
	O	W	81	182,540	222,827	222,827	
NETHLDS	O	E	81	178	675	716	41
			84	1,919	2,078	2,264	186
			86	1,189	5,647	7,276	1,629
	V	E	81	4,992	7,546	8,268	722
			82	832	11,025	12,197	1,172
			83	1,373	3,525	4,056	531
			84	2,615	12,232	14,558	2,326
			85	1,690	2,071	3,527	1,456
NORWAY	V	E	84	16,191	27,298	30,834	3,536
PORTUGL	O	E	81	59	340	365	25
			84	3,208	18,023	21,080	3,057
			85	3,943	22,535	27,160	4,625
			86	237	1,400	1,780	380
	O	W	81	150	840	977	137
	V	E	83	5,456	16,162	20,750	4,588
			84	9,001	48,087	59,171	11,084
			85	9,231	45,968	55,089	9,121
			86	16,736	93,303	105,369	12,066
	V	W	85	47,549	247,300	322,220	74,920
ROMANIA	O	E	85	508	2,354	2,542	188
	V	E	82	416	1,418	1,658	240
			84	3,065	11,670	14,058	2,388
			85	1,664	9,355	11,283	1,928
SPAIN	A	W	83	138	811	1,044	233
	N	E	82	3,687	19,890	24,724	4,834
			83	2,914	14,302	17,549	3,247
			84	47,347	219,437	271,907	52,470
	N	W	81	14,078	80,060	104,201	24,141
	O	E	81	34,824	173,506	213,218	39,712
			82	34,505	184,348	230,510	46,162
			83	49,884	246,931	296,536	49,605
			84	64,670	310,798	371,779	60,981
			85	54,588	280,151	333,012	52,861
			86	56,183	301,978	373,199	71,221
	O	W	81	10,118	50,907	59,849	8,942
			82	2,102	11,674	14,012	2,338
			83	4,339	22,210	33,273	11,063
			84	9,042	31,413	42,807	11,394
			85	33,570	188,869	240,112	51,243
			86	5,592	28,680	34,437	5,757
	V	E	81	189,342	977,575	1,211,443	233,868
			82	116,560	613,164	766,057	152,893
			83	122,902	478,574	582,136	103,562
			84	110,700	414,824	509,545	94,721
			85	260,538	1,337,123	1,683,451	346,328
			86	67,228	345,538	437,126	91,588
	V	W	81	51,677	260,773	320,567	59,794
			82	55,654	255,565	309,896	54,331
			83	37,168	173,876	215,962	42,086
			84	52,375	234,855	291,921	57,066
			85	112,582	623,906	774,026	150,120
			86	43,317	226,982	283,895	56,913
SWEDEN	V	E	85	948	4,960	5,778	818
SWITZLD	O	E	83	3,210	9,585	12,599	3,014
	V	W	85	2,656	10,628	12,999	2,371
U KING	O	E	81	342	1,024	1,094	70
			83	3,516	17,239	18,858	1,619
			84	12,429	54,776	67,394	12,618
			85	12,351	59,959	75,913	15,954
			86	561	3,245	3,811	566
	O	W	84	713	4,200	5,070	870
			85	245	1,442	1,709	267

Crop
Product
TSUSA commodity number, description, and unit of quantity

Country	Mode	Reg	Yr	Quantity	F.A.S.	C.I.F.	Charges
			86	1,902	10,920	13,320	2,400
	V	E	83	27,494	68,447	73,964	5,517
	V	W	84	300	1,174	1,254	80
YUGOSLV	V	E	86	1,410	5,930	8,630	2,700

1671040 CHAMPAGNE AND WNE OV $6 GAL (GAL)

Country	Mode	Reg	Yr	Quantity	F.A.S.	C.I.F.	Charges
TOTAL			81	5,937,096	120,312,449	127,968,086	7,666,234
			82	7,156,559	125,043,169	133,897,488	8,854,319
			83	9,566,817	166,497,296	177,479,244	10,981,948
			84	11,354,441	209,315,207	224,738,124	15,422,917
			85	11,740,693	237,527,770	255,868,362	18,340,592
			86	12,738,041	270,847,295	289,730,972	18,766,416
ARGENT	O	E	83	119	1,100	1,166	66
			84	831	7,700	8,304	604
			85	355	3,300	3,741	441
			86	846	7,831	8,732	901
	V	E	82	238	2,000	2,317	317
			83	476	4,000	4,497	497
			86	3,564	40,500	40,500	
	V	W	85	119	1,200	1,338	138
			86	119	2,000	2,200	200
AUSTRAL	A	W	85	1,113	14,147	16,422	2,275
	N	H	86	1,332	17,841	20,883	3,042
	N	W	83	1,488	22,251	24,306	2,055
			84	2,177	14,355	16,879	2,524
	O	E	82	154	2,098	2,468	370
			83	24	350	378	28
			84	40	416	453	37
			86	237	2,960	3,093	133
	O	H	83	357	4,968	5,514	546
			84	1,275	17,720	19,361	1,641
	O	W	81	1,783	26,445	28,172	1,727
			82	299	7,573	8,063	490
	V	E	81	476	6,554	7,390	836
			82	142	1,824	1,998	174
			83	703	10,517	11,626	1,109
			84	671	36,476	41,115	4,639
			85	2,261	31,853	35,969	4,116
			86	3,586	79,385	85,173	5,788
	V	H	81	379	6,052	6,604	552
			82	321	5,227	5,566	339
			85	500	6,537	7,451	914
			86	142	1,877	2,117	240
	V	W	81	8,548	73,442	79,564	6,122
			82	4,756	46,622	51,477	4,855
			83	1,632	39,807	42,338	2,531
			84	179	2,519	2,803	284
			85	1,149	16,471	18,195	1,724
			86	1,221	18,807	20,214	1,407
AUSTRIA	A	E	81	12	263	403	140
			84	225	2,560	4,173	1,613
			85	59	1,143	1,886	743
	N	E	81	810	10,991	13,729	2,738
			82	1,496	19,153	23,799	4,646
			84	305	5,818	6,476	658
	O	E	81	143	2,361	2,501	140
			82	2,045	24,541	31,156	6,615
			83	1,917	25,040	27,704	2,664
			84	360	3,618	3,952	334
			85	574	9,022	10,036	1,014
	O	W	85	179	3,148	3,523	375
			86	604	13,070	13,826	756
	V	E	81	2,651	42,142	46,693	4,551
			82	214	4,734	5,147	413
			83	4,526	63,700	70,742	7,042
			84	9,369	112,962	125,871	12,909
			85	3,655	43,521	49,145	5,624
			86	1,832	43,500	46,988	3,488
	V	W	81	138	3,240	3,394	154
			82	587	10,070	11,302	1,232
			83	2,848	34,276	36,159	1,883
			84	288	5,055	5,538	483
			85	2,953	25,392	29,806	4,414
			86	712	7,859	8,642	783
BELGIUM	A	E	82	28	442	567	125
	N	E	81	2,447	22,928	24,595	1,667
			85	251	11,514	12,593	1,079
	O	E	82	2,890	21,498	25,346	3,848
			83	7,012	152,910	159,398	6,488
			84	831	12,015	12,850	835
			85	30,622	1,633,844	1,678,042	44,198
			86	48,091	2,825,277	2,922,248	96,971
	V	E	81	10,058	77,289	90,385	13,096

Crop
Product
TSUSA commodity number, description, and unit of quantity

Country	Mode	Reg	Yr	Quantity	F.A.S.	C.I.F.	Charges
			82	247	2,075	2,347	272
			84	12,173	345,762	359,625	13,863
			85	18,639	613,760	641,582	27,822
			86	10,531	387,133	407,724	20,591
	V	W	85	2,787	76,430	80,753	4,323
			86	2,402	30,485	33,172	2,687
BENIN	V	E	86	1,664	10,500	13,219	2,719
BRAZIL	O	E	82	1,318	46,925	48,868	1,943
	V	E	81	56,922	754,226	871,411	117,185
			85	476	41,519	42,275	756
BULGAR	V	W	83	64	708	777	69
CANADA	O	E	83	871	8,706	8,853	147
			84	38	1,102	1,102	
			85	8,810	62,531	65,733	3,202
			86	8,998	127,302	142,051	14,749
	O	W	84	71	900	1,467	567
	V	E	81	2,445	18,142	21,138	2,996
CHILE	O	E	81	948	8,202	9,391	1,189
			82	1,105	11,236	12,619	1,383
			83	83	725	811	86
	V	E	81	1,462	12,825	14,383	1,558
			82	1,844	38,508	42,344	3,836
			83	1,057	9,318	10,857	1,539
			84	3,187	23,477	26,910	3,433
			85	831	7,263	8,759	1,496
			86	1,604	13,604	15,794	2,190
	V	W	81	488	4,620	5,557	937
			86	356	3,600	4,197	597
CHINA T	O	E	84	475	7,700	8,547	847
CZECHO	O	E	85	2,044	18,060	18,060	
			86	180	5,485	5,485	
DENMARK	A	E	83	177	27,114	28,968	1,854
	O	E	86	6,151	73,262	78,772	5,510
	V	E	84	24	980	983	3
	V	W	84	2,424	21,711	24,621	2,910
F W IND	V	E	85	276	11,584	11,666	82
FINLAND	O	E	83	45	1,062	1,125	63
FR GERM	N	E	81	34,346	437,803	481,407	40,279
			82	13,139	184,440	202,388	17,948
			83	61,834	868,906	940,020	71,114
			84	32,330	356,691	401,490	44,799
			85	39,275	433,959	496,073	62,114
			86	56,531	667,889	750,648	82,759
	N	W	83	13,904	146,729	160,413	13,684
			84	18,548	168,222	191,714	23,492
			85	21,110	169,874	208,815	38,941
			86	7,262	128,322	137,074	8,752
	O	E	81	35,355	463,719	500,811	37,092
			82	57,594	989,858	1,053,085	63,227
			83	52,113	947,210	1,003,948	56,738
			84	51,205	752,402	817,690	65,288
			85	42,857	1,106,464	1,180,601	74,137
			86	30,816	406,196	452,483	46,287
	O	W	81	4,367	59,035	65,376	6,341
			82	2,229	17,985	20,169	2,184
			83	1,543	17,237	18,984	1,747
			84	3,576	63,852	68,188	4,336
			85	9,719	86,825	96,594	9,769
			86	9,566	79,988	97,179	17,191
	V	E	81	64,424	760,935	841,417	80,482
			82	86,232	1,033,703	1,143,945	110,242
			83	51,710	576,653	635,629	58,976
			84	73,938	906,351	1,007,180	100,829
			85	84,937	1,568,882	1,714,789	145,907
			86	84,258	1,431,657	1,563,878	132,221
	V	W	81	18,598	201,728	225,346	23,618
			82	21,488	265,908	295,279	29,371
			83	15,620	162,020	179,080	17,060
			84	22,141	206,538	232,619	26,081
			85	37,156	265,453	307,043	41,590
			86	12,887	142,026	154,376	12,350
FRANCE	A	E	81	1,442	251,547	263,951	12,404
			82	5,508	654,627	683,996	29,369
			83	2,877	285,857	307,727	21,870
			84	3,378	406,372	517,499	111,127
			85	459	23,739	32,078	8,339
			86	1,065	92,157	96,522	4,365
	A	W	83	13	2,900	3,116	216
			84	10	2,774	2,817	43
			85	485	50,097	53,697	3,600
	N	E	81	571,293	21,156,845	22,029,123	872,278
			82	525,581	18,113,483	18,940,655	827,172
			83	818,557	28,940,833	30,072,118	1,131,285
			84	1,134,042	38,073,744	39,888,067	1,814,323
			85	1,230,276	43,588,754	46,580,376	2,991,622
			86	1,153,290	47,546,401	49,628,166	2,081,765
	N	W	81	209,863	7,825,690	8,147,901	322,211
			82	167,495	6,133,963	6,371,732	237,769
			83	366,137	14,895,489	15,525,651	630,162
			84	630,910	26,774,294	28,018,397	1,244,103
			85	913,896	39,400,559	41,092,023	1,691,464
			86	704,051	31,698,689	32,541,460	842,771
	O	E	81	652,033	30,358,204	31,354,337	996,133
			82	591,480	25,034,270	25,865,609	831,339
			83	676,570	30,208,185	31,159,658	951,473
			84	825,656	38,671,618	40,175,496	1,503,878
			85	875,676	40,506,560	42,090,788	1,584,228
			86	936,179	46,967,660	48,870,648	1,902,988
	O	H	81	1,504	54,405	56,292	1,887
			82	6,101	226,667	235,195	8,528
			83	4,238	164,372	169,587	5,215
			85	3,042	112,427	117,543	5,116
			86	6,202	256,765	265,728	8,963
	O	W	81	83,448	4,834,166	4,993,928	159,762
			82	88,593	4,780,808	4,907,211	126,403
			83	78,636	4,126,046	4,229,146	103,100
			84	73,460	2,552,596	2,646,553	93,957
			85	89,328	3,551,187	3,756,155	204,968
			86	103,401	5,297,962	5,421,916	123,954
	V	E	81	280,329	10,298,244	10,730,581	430,961
			82	251,965	9,416,101	9,843,518	427,417
			83	263,854	9,427,431	9,793,298	365,867
			84	426,316	13,651,845	14,383,237	731,392
			85	577,089	17,114,836	18,223,850	1,109,014
			86	885,790	34,789,361	36,579,431	1,790,070
	V	H	86	1,188	8,833	10,607	1,774
	V	W	81	38,782	1,198,050	1,255,218	57,168
			82	39,402	1,340,529	1,396,996	56,467
			83	13,144	436,403	457,791	21,388
			84	13,402	343,777	368,236	24,459
			85	24,725	697,613	746,612	48,999
			86	81,031	2,975,484	3,091,700	116,216
GERM DR	O	E	85	1,485	35,062	37,340	2,278
	V	W	82	194	6,152	6,646	494
			83	694	5,115	5,930	815
GIBRAT	V	E	81	635	39,517	40,056	539
			83	313	3,564	3,892	328
GREECE	O	E	81	114	3,474	3,818	344
	V	E	83	71	960	1,207	247
			84	1,450	12,315	15,203	2,888
			85	118	1,124	1,461	337
			86	118	1,270	1,591	321
GUATMAL	V	W	83	178	2,004	2,231	227
HG KONG	O	E	85	2,401	31,092	34,550	3,458
	V	E	83	710	19,080	19,811	731
HUNGARY	O	E	81	357	2,925	3,238	313
			83	143	3,970	4,113	143
			86	1,758	14,626	16,672	2,046
	V	E	81	7,368	48,174	56,180	8,006
			82	3,109	22,175	26,212	4,037
			83	676	4,690	5,224	534
			84	1,531	10,039	11,802	1,763
	V	W	81	766	5,743	7,231	1,488
			82	1,950	12,590	14,459	1,869
			83	386	2,850	3,187	337
			84	778	6,699	7,346	647
			86	235	2,471	2,914	443
IRAN	V	E	85	247	1,596	1,931	335
			86	154	1,365	1,683	318
IRELAND	O	E	85	2,429	93,392	99,401	6,009
	V	W	85	629	11,495	12,277	782
ISRAEL	N	E	81	951	8,821	10,530	1,709
	O	E	81	4,392	40,610	45,454	4,844
			82	4,350	40,763	46,321	5,558
			83	4,219	41,861	46,455	4,594
			84	2,809	29,291	32,001	2,710
			85	941	9,805	10,432	627
	V	E	81	904	8,379	10,295	1,916
			82	1,544	14,331	17,051	2,720
			83	2,628	27,389	33,716	6,327
			84	2,316	23,909	28,100	4,191
			85	2,325	21,302	26,132	4,830
			86	2,589	23,945	28,067	4,122
	V	W	81	3,316	25,695	31,238	5,543
			82	1,017	9,536	11,377	1,841
			83	366	3,803	4,798	995
			84	130	1,359	1,697	338

Crop
Product
TSUSA commodity number, description, and unit of quantity

Country	Mode	Reg	Yr	Quantity	F.A.S.	C.I.F.	Charges
ITALY	N	E	81	546,702	5,875,449	6,470,787	595,338
			82	644,212	7,235,434	7,937,042	701,608
			83	835,188	9,475,237	10,323,669	848,432
			84	1,518,231	18,858,326	20,625,888	1,767,562
			85	1,020,498	13,292,088	14,648,691	1,356,603
			86	843,848	9,886,893	10,981,931	1,095,038
	N	W	81	35,609	378,279	430,435	52,156
			82	71,898	843,217	936,993	93,776
			83	157,700	2,005,024	2,202,454	197,430
			84	409,067	4,777,430	5,294,975	517,545
			85	325,246	4,258,561	4,677,031	418,470
			86	206,817	2,355,067	2,606,775	251,708
	O	E	81	610,931	7,168,561	7,842,067	673,506
			82	750,779	8,608,000	9,349,633	741,633
			83	1,096,774	12,696,137	13,761,315	1,065,178
			84	936,133	11,368,363	12,373,118	1,004,755
			85	901,924	11,449,376	12,503,149	1,053,773
			86	1,127,232	13,737,747	15,063,355	1,325,608
	O	H	81	36	263	293	30
			82	238	1,579	1,738	159
	O	W	81	37,377	475,049	525,231	50,182
			82	58,433	776,533	846,782	70,249
			83	41,381	619,780	674,602	54,822
			84	53,352	833,357	899,383	66,026
			85	45,947	708,152	759,427	51,275
			86	56,007	889,164	964,754	75,590
	V	E	81	1,654,292	18,229,606	19,987,075	1,762,263
			82	2,005,251	23,023,032	25,207,047	2,184,015
			83	2,417,996	27,962,149	30,409,990	2,447,841
			84	1,951,364	22,367,192	24,706,790	2,339,598
			85	2,107,165	25,777,366	28,478,921	2,701,555
			86	2,346,481	28,997,917	32,168,144	3,170,227
	V	H	84	1,486	24,179	27,060	2,881
			85	238	2,062	2,680	618
			86	3,138	33,641	41,030	7,389
	V	W	81	289,231	3,352,214	3,756,258	404,044
			82	246,321	2,868,710	3,191,840	323,130
			83	196,981	2,483,029	2,734,026	250,997
			84	92,095	1,052,869	1,169,546	116,677
			85	161,878	1,930,469	2,157,269	226,800
			86	276,698	3,941,375	4,317,004	375,629
JAPAN	V	E	82	59	579	692	113
			85	4,615	210,406	219,723	9,317
KOR REP	O	E	86	59	1,640	1,733	93
	V	E	85	39	2,811	2,856	45
MALI	O	E	85	178	1,702	1,702	
MALTA	V	E	83	535	8,779	9,684	905
MAURIT	V	E	85	261	10,874	11,238	364
			86	95	4,341	4,421	80
MEXICO	O	E	82	4,857	41,468	42,867	1,399
			85	1,823	16,722	17,725	1,003
			86	118	3,950	4,146	196
	O	W	82	118	1,050	1,150	100
			83	892	6,928	7,939	1,011
MOROC	V	E	85	278	3,276	3,725	449
N ANTIL	A	E	82	450	9,425	9,645	220
	V	E	85	178	13,409	13,503	94
			86	297	15,393	15,567	174
N ZEAL	O	W	85	119	2,248	2,539	291
			86	927	17,541	19,614	2,073
	V	E	84	180	1,691	1,885	194
	V	W	82	2,803	32,540	37,116	4,576
			83	2,358	26,202	29,535	3,333
			84	1,044	10,732	12,254	1,522
			85	1,262	12,998	15,055	2,057
			86	133	1,355	1,568	213
NAMIBIA	V	E	85	214	2,160	2,210	50
NETHLDS	A	W	84	493	31,612	34,656	3,044
			85	437	41,108	44,099	2,991
	O	E	81	21	639	671	32
			82	1,724	24,728	27,555	2,827
			83	24	3,500	3,534	34
			84	5,491	64,225	69,624	5,399
			85	11,273	134,475	147,656	13,181
			86	6,275	290,155	299,599	9,444
	O	W	86	2,139	92,482	95,569	3,087
	V	E	81	2,416	34,922	37,132	2,210
			82	473	4,676	5,563	887
			83	14,537	164,803	181,819	17,016
			84	3,659	48,322	52,763	4,441
			85	15,172	385,207	420,118	34,911
			86	12,597	320,504	339,249	18,745
	V	W	82	1,427	20,275	22,105	1,830
			85	1,741	76,805	80,080	3,275

Crop
Product
TSUSA commodity number, description, and unit of quantity

Country	Mode	Reg	Yr	Quantity	F.A.S.	C.I.F.	Charges
			86	1,733	75,242	194,060	1,557
NIGERIA	O	E	83	5	345	355	10
NORWAY	O	E	85	142	2,220	2,417	197
	O	W	81	58	1,455	1,499	44
PANAMA	O	E	83	60	2,475	2,577	102
			85	535	5,083	5,084	1
POLAND	O	E	83	357	6,146	6,318	172
PORTUGL	A	E	81	5	932	959	27
			82	9	544	554	10
			83	84	14,826	15,535	709
			84	69	7,049	7,479	430
			85	14	3,488	3,659	171
	A	W	82	56	8,183	8,860	677
	N	E	83	629	5,346	6,068	722
			84	656	5,671	6,810	1,139
			85	495	7,791	8,793	1,002
			86	10,088	76,009	83,741	7,732
	O	E	81	808	7,470	8,756	1,286
			82	519	5,252	5,836	584
			83	672	5,686	6,381	695
			84	1,330	30,533	31,719	1,186
			85	3,208	30,625	34,397	3,772
			86	9,501	91,347	103,923	12,576
	O	W	81	12	1,111	1,226	115
			85	356	2,250	2,308	58
			86	2,615	20,900	24,214	3,314
	V	E	81	1,299	12,857	14,685	1,828
			82	2,796	24,896	29,298	4,402
			83	1,213	10,151	11,925	1,774
			84	6,240	47,132	55,859	8,727
			85	35,916	360,623	404,979	44,356
			86	78,468	672,260	781,655	109,395
	V	W	81	59	550	644	94
			83	238	14,500	15,188	688
			84	574	4,156	5,174	1,018
			85	6,551	81,220	87,476	6,256
			86	16,910	127,461	148,253	20,792
REP SAF	O	E	84	119	1,303	1,406	103
			85	1,018	14,852	16,649	1,797
			86	308	3,702	4,054	352
	O	W	83	95	1,635	1,732	97
			84	286	4,903	5,308	405
	V	E	81	1,371	11,335	13,234	1,899
			82	2,401	21,455	25,597	4,142
			83	3,563	34,374	39,964	5,590
			84	2,031	23,357	25,917	2,560
			85	118	1,608	1,845	237
	V	W	83	820	6,165	7,629	1,464
			84	1,071	13,025	14,798	1,773
ROMANIA	O	E	82	4,470	28,426	36,344	7,918
			83	1,966	12,504	15,643	3,139
			84	235	1,990	2,149	159
	V	E	82	19,277	131,054	158,412	27,358
			84	5,479	42,245	50,549	8,304
			85	7,083	49,079	63,258	14,179
			86	535	3,628	4,804	1,176
	V	W	84	237	2,000	2,428	428
			85	747	4,722	6,506	1,784
			86	615	4,162	5,206	1,044
SEYCHEL	O	E	85	59	4,050	4,155	105
SINGAPR	O	E	82	24	312	337	25
SPAIN	N	E	81	168,197	1,385,605	1,619,530	233,925
			82	70,928	571,792	671,619	99,827
			83	597,864	4,705,620	5,333,008	627,388
			84	958,901	7,930,056	9,146,298	1,216,242
			85	65,297	559,025	659,673	100,648
			86	198,164	1,764,682	2,065,555	300,873
	N	W	81	13,351	112,254	129,551	17,297
			83	205,118	1,629,147	1,852,250	223,103
			84	490,866	4,056,577	4,594,570	537,993
			85	460,013	4,209,053	4,760,837	551,784
			86	321,403	2,787,297	3,137,608	350,311
	O	E	81	92,345	799,510	923,907	124,397
			82	241,097	2,116,224	2,442,100	325,876
			83	401,785	3,326,679	3,766,859	440,180
			84	463,850	4,001,125	4,563,522	562,397
			85	493,683	4,436,134	5,076,382	640,248
			86	558,749	5,277,508	6,055,578	778,070
	O	H	83	1,130	10,266	11,142	876
			85	3,787	33,496	42,062	8,566
			86	10,859	240,487	262,165	21,678
	O	W	81	12,697	116,219	133,432	17,213
			82	18,979	164,818	187,237	22,419
			83	33,953	260,540	305,010	44,470

Crop Product TSUSA commodity number, description, and unit of quantity Country	Mode	Reg	Yr	Quantity	F.A.S.	C.I.F.	Charges
			84	66,586	745,716	821,655	75,939
			85	36,355	370,535	421,120	50,585
			86	66,275	576,446	663,288	86,842
	V	E	81	270,752	2,115,007	2,483,691	379,188
			82	827,551	6,767,523	7,824,871	1,057,348
			83	805,940	6,538,267	7,457,952	919,685
			84	875,718	7,389,032	8,508,221	1,119,189
			85	1,779,226	15,332,664	17,897,810	2,565,146
			86	1,899,078	17,381,456	20,073,300	2,691,844
	V	H	86	7,310	61,484	80,871	19,387
	V	W	81	76,560	599,699	695,833	96,134
			82	270,366	2,159,923	2,463,834	303,911
			83	258,970	2,104,740	2,396,267	291,527
			84	122,217	987,646	1,149,719	162,073
			85	173,397	1,442,883	1,694,149	251,266
			86	422,511	3,704,539	4,267,926	563,387
SWEDEN	O	E	85	832	14,000	14,600	600
	O	W	83	1,190	19,250	20,886	1,636
	V	E	84	144	4,753	4,895	142
			86	9,556	79,397	92,809	13,412
SWITZLD	A	E	82	8	503	520	17
	O	E	83	2,021	22,950	24,383	1,433
	V	E	81	2,378	16,746	19,615	2,869
			82	3,566	29,500	29,900	400
			83	15	484	583	99
			86	3,116	32,671	38,837	6,166
	V	W	86	7,972	92,166	100,520	8,354
TRINID	V	E	86	356	5,875	6,596	721
TUNISIA	V	E	84	1,699	60,443	61,685	1,242
U KING	A	E	81	441	75,103	79,351	4,248
			82	1,282	186,041	198,066	12,025
			83	232	29,111	30,195	1,084
			84	799	77,887	82,132	4,245
			85	319	48,826	54,350	5,524
			86	159	25,886	27,844	1,958
	A	W	81	421	60,304	62,087	1,783
			82	535	74,949	78,222	3,273
			84	1	295	501	206
			85	38	6,120	6,582	462
	N	W	82	6,024	566,129	595,543	29,414
			83	100	1,748	1,890	142
			84	320	49,033	51,455	2,422
			85	4,331	199,768	207,439	7,671
	O	E	81	5,266	100,099	107,397	7,298
			82	7,198	115,813	124,529	8,716
			83	21,210	344,664	367,526	22,862
			84	17,814	599,877	623,063	23,186
			85	27,711	429,714	492,394	62,680
			86	47,041	777,147	846,104	68,957
	O	H	81	74	751	781	30
			82	12	556	572	16
	O	W	81	7	332	355	23
			83	5,965	176,350	183,714	7,364
			84	4,167	72,621	77,836	5,215
			85	247	1,813	2,074	261
			86	832	38,500	39,278	778
	V	E	81	5,641	164,924	173,769	8,845
			82	2,158	20,821	24,141	3,320
			83	1,272	20,847	22,902	2,055
			84	3,630	50,161	53,832	3,671
			85	471	29,517	30,431	914
			86	41	7,465	7,535	70
	V	W	81	43	7,376	7,728	352
			86	987	28,637	30,083	1,446
USSR	A	E	86	134	3,451	3,451	
	O	E	81	1,328	11,340	13,178	1,838
			82	1,081	9,514	10,594	1,080
			86	6,846	46,080	56,720	10,640
	V	E	84	203	3,994	4,263	269
YUGOSLV	A	E	86	238	4,500	9,625	5,125
	O	E	81	2,952	41,377	46,072	4,695
			82	524	5,280	5,506	226
			83	24	303	323	20
			84	399	2,520	2,746	226
	V	E	83	1,427	12,500	14,523	2,023
			84	2,956	20,435	23,162	2,727
	V	W	81	119	1,680	1,819	139
			84	380	3,840	4,669	829

Grape, dried
1477500 DRIED GRAPES EXCEPT RAISINS (LB)

Country	Mode	Reg	Yr	Quantity	F.A.S.	C.I.F.	Charges
TOTAL			82	7,963	1,753	2,571	818

Country	Mode	Reg	Yr	Quantity	F.A.S.	C.I.F.	Charges
C RICA	V	E	82	7,200	800	1,398	598
HG KONG	V	E	82	675	690	781	91
JAPAN	V	H	82	88	263	392	129

Grape, fresh
1476000 GRAPES, FRESH, HOTHOUSE (LB)

Country	Mode	Reg	Yr	Quantity	F.A.S.	C.I.F.	Charges
TOTAL			81	297,975	245,784	248,915	3,131
			82	22,630	12,284	21,632	9,348
			83	190,149	97,672	126,638	28,966
			84	254,189	107,447	134,868	27,421
			85	319,831	153,737	241,715	87,978
			86	1,860,689	838,546	1,062,135	223,589
BELGIUM	A	E	81	288	415	529	114
			83	141	929	978	49
			84	938	1,518	1,700	182
			86	1,521	2,625	3,438	813
	A	W	82	225	585	764	179
			83	331	285	335	50
BRAZIL	A	E	85	2,400	2,000	3,388	1,388
CHILE	A	E	82	11,828	6,102	9,620	3,518
			84	17,780	11,850	23,066	11,216
			85	87,029	62,832	124,212	61,380
	A	W	82	7,524	4,500	10,032	5,532
	O	E	86	24,160	2,080	2,080	
	V	E	81	13,427	3,748	6,765	3,017
			83	135,221	59,840	80,933	21,093
			84	119,693	31,153	46,332	15,179
			86	65,513	21,294	30,079	8,785
	V	W	83	54,403	36,345	44,098	7,753
			85	189,369	61,248	85,916	24,668
			86	1,381,248	623,625	813,039	189,414
CHINA M	V	E	82	1,672	542	596	54
DOM REP	A	E	86	4,000	1,269	1,593	324
FRANCE	A	E	83	53	273	294	21
			84	201	273	474	201
	V	E	82	1,381	555	620	65
ITALY	A	E	84	1,711	1,122	1,420	298
			86	51,475	21,549	45,802	24,253
MEXICO	O	W	81	284,260	241,621	241,621	
			84	113,088	60,256	60,256	
			85	39,644	25,228	25,228	
			86	332,772	166,104	166,104	
N ZEAL	A	W	85	1,389	2,429	2,971	542
NETHLDS	A	E	84	778	1,275	1,620	345

1476100 FR GRAPE NSPF FEB 15-MAR 31 (LB)

Country	Mode	Reg	Yr	Quantity	F.A.S.	C.I.F.	Charges
TOTAL			81	49,494,314	19,164,125	29,994,878	10,830,751
			82	70,936,071	25,711,579	37,980,077	12,268,498
			83	131,745,768	42,809,850	64,397,904	21,588,054
			84	149,552,807	46,547,844	66,123,850	19,576,006
			85	178,923,177	64,887,586	87,912,279	23,024,693
			86	177,987,934	60,166,298	81,959,668	21,793,370
ARGENT	V	E	86	359,486	146,757	234,848	88,091
BRAZIL	O	E	83	30,019	25,224	25,224	
			84	6,600	6,000	6,000	
	V	E	83	143,000	91,000	106,730	15,730
			84	14,357	20,510	26,415	5,905
			86	69,594	27,115	42,415	15,300
CANADA	O	E	86	24,586	14,320	14,320	
	O	W	83	21,396	15,576	15,576	
CHILE	A	E	81	69,400	28,285	31,396	3,111
			85	2,242	1,268	2,683	1,415
	N	E	84	38,233	7,816	16,530	8,714
			86	108,981,257	36,598,154	49,934,736	13,336,582
	N	W	81	75,260	30,620	42,399	11,779
			82	8,342,872	3,239,921	4,952,520	1,712,599
			83	342,858	150,633	195,557	44,924
			84	31,485,634	10,456,630	14,441,446	3,984,816
			85	672,336	245,516	337,870	92,354
			86	21,317,525	7,274,203	9,766,871	2,492,668
	O	E	81	21,910	18,059	18,059	
			83	61,286	32,587	35,337	2,750
			84	62,999	9,024	15,737	6,713
	V	E	81	44,624,749	16,996,968	26,591,140	9,594,170
			82	62,521,020	22,442,993	32,987,050	10,544,057
			83	109,257,378	35,933,865	54,286,180	18,352,315
			84	117,755,874	35,987,976	51,530,526	15,542,550
			85	131,532,963	47,866,309	65,232,380	17,366,071
			86	26,080,483	9,224,500	12,185,292	2,960,792

Crop
Product
TSUSA commodity number, description, and unit of quantity

Country	Mode	Reg	Yr	Quantity	F.A.S.	C.I.F.	Charges
	V	W	81	4,702,995	2,090,193	3,311,884	1,221,691
			82	72,179	28,665	40,507	11,842
			83	21,889,831	6,560,965	9,733,300	3,172,335
			84	188,890	59,328	86,324	26,996
			85	46,219,474	16,554,233	22,080,392	5,526,159
			86	20,572,676	6,626,166	9,487,297	2,861,131
COOK IS	V	E	86	41,362	11,441	16,493	5,052
GREENLD	V	W	86	228,094	66,491	94,006	27,515
N ZEAL	A	H	84	220	560	872	312
	A	W	85	3,180	6,682	8,827	2,145
			86	2,873	7,977	14,216	6,239
REP SAF	O	E	85	161,150	94,249	94,249	
			86	309,998	169,174	169,174	
	V	E	85	293,653	106,104	137,261	31,157
SIER LN	V	W	85	38,179	13,225	18,617	5,392

1476300 FR GRAPE NSPF APR 1-JUNE 30 (LB)

Country	Mode	Reg	Yr	Quantity	F.A.S.	C.I.F.	Charges
TOTAL			81	61,630,639	26,918,228	37,046,644	10,131,416
			82	117,189,295	49,009,486	63,718,619	14,709,133
			83	113,680,458	41,288,629	56,041,969	14,753,340
			84	125,439,020	49,332,834	63,547,128	14,214,294
			85	176,502,950	72,588,547	90,628,124	18,039,577
			86	159,466,129	57,593,171	71,194,417	13,601,246
ARGENT	O	E	86	114,540	50,688	65,285	14,597
BERMUDA	V	W	84	59,365	14,721	22,003	7,282
BRAZIL	O	E	82	6,250	5,510	5,510	
	V	E	86	37,832	9,458	19,658	10,200
CANADA	O	E	81	42,356	36,237	36,237	
			82	26,448	21,480	21,480	
			83	33,000	26,886	26,886	
	O	W	82	34,560	20,028	20,028	
CHILE	A	E	82	21,840	14,560	22,160	7,600
	N	E	82	97,740	53,964	80,843	26,879
			83	72,590,749	21,224,087	32,928,807	11,704,720
	N	W	81	193,203	119,469	138,142	18,673
			82	344,237	164,107	192,020	27,913
			83	299,136	122,528	154,025	31,497
			84	12,733,958	4,468,895	6,133,061	1,664,166
			85	30,602,521	10,727,238	14,823,378	4,096,140
	O	E	81	24,144	12,072	12,072	
			83	377,095	344,148	344,148	
			84	1,872	1,742	1,742	
	V	E	81	44,280,974	16,315,879	25,074,803	8,758,924
			82	73,367,040	26,576,793	38,620,004	12,043,211
			83	708,843	173,320	278,185	104,865
			84	90,888,883	30,959,357	43,370,688	12,411,331
			85	106,410,857	36,181,664	50,123,086	13,941,422
			86	85,314,445	26,396,557	36,858,444	10,461,887
	V	W	81	6,047,268	2,085,192	3,386,285	1,301,093
			82	15,214,952	6,306,497	8,908,848	2,602,351
			83	16,115,809	4,688,538	7,246,445	2,557,907
			84	282,438	83,568	135,562	51,994
			86	22,628,317	7,459,028	10,327,803	2,868,775
CHINA T	V	E	83	1,885,289	634,104	950,139	316,035
COOK IS	V	E	86	218,754	73,815	98,883	25,068
ECUADOR	V	E	86	11,704	3,696	5,115	1,419
FRANCE	O	W	85	60,720	42,504	42,504	
			86	141,064	65,020	65,020	
GREECE	V	E	81	600	643	717	74
ITALY	V	W	81	24,762	7,776	13,508	5,732
IVY CST	V	E	86	45,366	1,260	1,800	540
MEXICO	O	E	82	7,753	2,053	2,053	
			83	456,126	81,168	81,168	
			84	38,825	27,100	27,100	
			86	22,280	7,721	7,721	
	O	W	81	10,501,944	7,981,021	8,024,941	46,920
			82	27,179,335	15,316,001	15,316,001	
			83	20,709,493	13,692,278	13,692,278	
			84	20,355,443	13,135,509	13,135,509	
			85	38,745,722	25,337,158	25,337,305	147
			86	50,620,689	23,417,409	23,417,409	
N ZEAL	A	H	85	1,698	2,984	4,297	1,313
	A	W	84	4,264	13,932	16,540	2,608
REP SAF	O	E	81	515,388	359,939	359,939	
			82	204,754	161,083	161,083	
			83	228,536	173,941	173,941	
			84	286,930	175,091	175,091	
			85	83,673	70,850	70,850	
	V	E	82	684,386	367,410	368,589	1,179
			83	276,382	127,631	165,947	38,316
			84	787,042	452,919	529,832	76,913
			85	593,919	222,818	223,373	555
			86	289,332	102,228	317,760	215,532

Crop
Product
TSUSA commodity number, description, and unit of quantity

Country	Mode	Reg	Yr	Quantity	F.A.S.	C.I.F.	Charges
SWITZLD	O	E	85	3,840	3,331	3,331	
	V	E	86	21,806	6,291	9,519	3,228

1476400 FRSH GRAPE EX HOTHOUSE NSPF (LB)

Country	Mode	Reg	Yr	Quantity	F.A.S.	C.I.F.	Charges
TOTAL			81	15,564,293	6,715,209	8,510,062	1,794,853
			82	21,567,057	9,836,618	11,730,385	1,893,767
			83	35,564,607	20,005,602	23,378,960	3,373,358
			84	47,392,257	15,846,163	21,031,914	5,185,751
			85	75,995,993	31,700,531	42,773,526	11,072,995
			86	115,712,898	44,142,607	56,774,927	12,632,320
ARGENT	A	E	85	2,145	1,268	2,668	1,400
	V	E	83	302,549	334,720	381,720	47,000
CANADA	O	E	81	2,532,686	297,785	297,785	
			82	5,123,689	587,156	588,143	987
			83	2,783,500	337,112	337,112	
			84	4,938,867	543,075	543,075	
			85	5,228,000	432,700	432,700	
			86	15,949,104	1,683,599	1,683,599	
	O	W	83	52,290	34,860	34,860	
			84	188,170	42,637	42,637	
			85	3,181	1,299	1,674	375
CHILE	A	E	81	431,631	217,263	381,371	164,108
			82	1,568,986	1,580,779	2,375,136	794,357
			83	495,861	311,993	506,392	194,399
			84	49,429	18,080	48,974	30,894
			85	17,748	10,139	20,772	10,633
			86	105,537	60,925	138,823	77,898
	N	E	83	509,653	481,966	799,433	317,467
			84	94,837	49,220	103,733	54,513
	N	W	81	391,995	134,348	232,300	97,952
			82	478,972	233,749	369,097	135,348
			83	1,853,989	855,405	1,157,390	301,985
			85	13,264,115	5,325,332	8,799,572	3,474,240
			86	1,339,823	554,674	720,474	165,800
	V	E	81	6,720,097	2,720,490	4,242,900	1,522,410
			82	5,385,009	2,548,072	3,419,016	870,944
			83	13,704,113	7,572,590	9,874,268	2,301,678
			84	29,054,738	9,551,865	13,368,173	3,816,308
			85	44,623,176	18,306,529	25,441,597	7,135,068
			86	78,609,912	33,687,133	43,661,500	9,974,367
	V	W	81	28,158	8,843	15,956	7,113
			84	7,587,597	2,626,210	3,570,121	943,911
			86	17,129,399	7,083,665	9,322,111	2,238,446
DOM REP	A	E	82	14,465	10,400	15,400	5,000
GREECE	A	E	84	10,984	3,109	6,896	3,787
			85	8,556	2,824	7,984	5,160
ITALY	A	E	81	6,636	7,000	10,270	3,270
			83	478,985	350,193	541,844	191,651
			84	825,278	415,108	734,964	319,856
			85	726,005	419,712	764,151	344,439
			86	209,210	137,021	248,106	111,085
	N	E	82	290,271	111,109	180,715	69,606
	O	E	83	34,363	31,169	31,169	
			84	77,128	63,780	63,780	
			85	1,323	1,079	1,079	
			86	70,286	62,383	62,383	
	V	E	83	63,630	23,370	25,370	2,000
JAPAN	V	W	86	456,771	150,093	201,317	51,224
KOR REP	V	E	83	19,488	5,746	8,765	3,019
MEXICO	O	E	81	28,512	19,008	19,008	
			83	207,806	56,521	56,521	
			84	419,986	40,848	40,848	
			85	239,640	15,420	15,420	
			86	119,962	5,782	5,782	
	O	W	81	5,424,578	3,310,472	3,310,472	
			82	8,521,726	4,717,533	4,717,533	
			83	14,962,520	9,550,935	9,550,935	
			84	3,792,981	2,361,580	2,361,580	
			85	10,366,673	6,647,422	6,647,422	
			86	1,576,614	655,412	655,412	
NETHLDS	A	E	84	220	338	478	140
PERU	A	E	82	16,056	9,420	15,820	6,400
PORTUGL	A	E	83	1,466	485	1,222	737
REP SAF	A	E	85	93,688	115,118	144,477	29,359
	O	E	85	1,323	1,080	1,080	
			86	36,280	15,420	15,420	
SPAIN	O	E	84	35,264	9,600	9,600	
			85	295,854	124,886	124,886	
	V	E	82	167,883	38,400	49,525	11,125
			83	94,394	58,537	71,959	13,422
			84	316,778	120,713	137,055	16,342
			85	1,124,566	295,723	368,044	72,321
			86	110,000	46,500	60,000	13,500

Crop / Product / TSUSA commodity number, description, and unit of quantity / Country	Mode	Reg	Yr	Quantity	F.A.S.	C.I.F.	Charges

Grape, juice, concentrated
1654040 GRAPE JUC CNCNTRT FZ,NT MIX (GAL)

Country	Mode	Reg	Yr	Quantity	F.A.S.	C.I.F.	Charges
TOTAL			81	370,178	355,287	421,061	65,774
			82	431,382	311,785	388,972	77,187
			83	233,531	193,252	240,036	46,784
			84	116,602	135,211	154,535	19,324
			85	55,693	58,009	63,811	5,802
			86	107,508	94,242	110,437	16,195
ARGENT	V	E	84	83,413	34,603	41,332	6,729
			86	15,180	8,391	10,231	1,840
BELGIUM	V	E	86	872	2,186	2,448	262
BRAZIL	O	E	81	363,756	341,605	403,370	61,765
			82	200,682	160,545	201,679	41,134
			83	227,247	181,797	228,378	46,581
	V	E	84	13,104	16,879	19,003	2,124
			86	41,756	25,149	30,300	5,151
	V	W	82	58,038	44,925	59,414	14,489
CANADA	O	E	82	330	1,309	1,309	
			83	4,284	7,175	7,175	
			85	33,782	30,780	30,780	
			86	5,395	15,550	15,550	
CHINA M	V	W	86	4,366	14,200	15,786	1,586
DENMARK	V	E	81	5,972	12,308	16,317	4,009
FR GERM	V	E	85	713	3,883	4,886	1,003
KOR REP	V	W	83	2,000	4,280	4,483	203
MEXICO	O	E	81	450	1,374	1,374	
			85	3,514	2,761	2,761	
REP SAF	V	E	86	39,939	28,766	36,122	7,356
SPAIN	V	E	82	172,332	105,006	126,570	21,564
			85	17,684	20,585	25,384	4,799
SWITZLD	V	E	84	20,085	83,729	94,200	10,471

1654060 GRAPE JUC CNCNTRT NT MIX/FZ (GAL)

Country	Mode	Reg	Yr	Quantity	F.A.S.	C.I.F.	Charges
TOTAL			81	758,442	751,015	866,898	115,883
			82	1,106,210	1,081,344	1,274,554	193,210
			83	2,297,170	1,376,507	1,757,846	381,339
			84	6,752,256	3,290,055	4,267,050	976,995
			85	7,477,077	4,092,704	5,210,079	1,117,375
			86	7,550,394	5,398,281	6,346,255	947,974
ANTIGUA	V	E	85	33,120	16,264	21,835	5,571
			86	64,160	30,604	40,003	9,399
	V	W	85	3,754	6,894	7,583	689
ARGENT	O	E	81	215,408	182,024	209,250	27,226
			86	19,958	19,399	19,399	
	V	E	81	88,641	129,019	139,571	10,552
			82	47,501	38,914	44,502	5,588
			83	1,147,793	520,644	680,750	160,106
			84	4,329,951	1,522,084	2,130,262	608,178
			85	4,213,606	2,046,239	2,664,885	618,646
			86	2,532,292	1,436,698	1,779,728	343,030
	V	W	83	161,485	55,979	81,083	25,104
			84	392,870	121,383	164,142	42,759
			85	395,121	184,047	255,949	71,902
			86	71,480	63,630	80,527	16,897
AUSTRAL	O	W	81	545	1,526	1,526	
			82	1,004	2,600	2,600	
			83	441	1,638	1,638	
			84	154	537	537	
	V	E	82	6,300	16,446	18,494	2,048
			83	10,800	21,194	26,174	4,980
			84	15,061	38,899	42,892	3,993
AUSTRIA	O	E	81	120	299	299	
	O	W	82	197	447	447	
	V	E	85	155,824	70,777	94,966	24,189
BELGIUM	V	E	85	507	1,728	2,222	494
			86	748	2,123	2,886	763
BRAZIL	O	E	81	289,329	215,442	268,699	53,257
			82	483,080	375,681	470,832	95,151
			83	675,386	433,563	570,826	137,263
			84	1,129,303	800,177	1,010,691	210,514
			85	1,117,751	607,817	809,151	201,334
			86	1,274,377	760,386	1,002,979	242,593
	V	E	81	72,188	64,375	75,467	11,092
			83	72,998	81,963	95,418	13,455
			84	527,181	441,230	509,126	67,896
			85	440,325	372,671	430,157	57,486
			86	1,563,771	1,335,979	1,503,088	167,109
	V	W	83	83,019	47,435	64,015	16,580
			84	65,044	24,297	27,922	3,625
			85	99,694	88,215	105,424	17,209

Country	Mode	Reg	Yr	Quantity	F.A.S.	C.I.F.	Charges
			86	466,047	458,987	519,778	60,791
C RICA	V	E	86	32,080	15,681	20,016	4,335
CANADA	O	E	81	24,138	35,275	35,368	93
			82	113	1,271	1,271	
			83	16,878	52,582	52,582	
			84	8,597	29,572	29,572	
			85	148,377	162,551	162,551	
			86	667,794	695,406	696,306	900
CHILE	O	E	86	5,280	2,970	2,970	
	V	E	83	3,960	10,692	12,123	1,431
			84	13,860	27,856	32,856	5,000
			85	15,776	8,696	10,096	1,400
			86	479,130	300,972	355,126	54,154
	V	W	86	29,400	13,993	20,338	6,345
COLOMB	A	E	83	18	408	489	81
DENMARK	V	W	85	45	2,583	2,842	259
FR GERM	A	E	86	50	1,251	2,301	1,050
	O	E	81	483	2,255	2,638	383
	V	E	83	280	1,392	1,698	306
			84	303	369	441	72
	V	W	82	4,008	58,797	61,839	3,042
FRANCE	O	E	81	6,669	21,008	21,008	
			82	6,083	20,333	20,333	
			83	966	3,293	3,293	
			86	15,120	31,541	31,941	400
	V	E	83	3,340	17,595	20,726	3,131
			84	118	480	531	51
			85	1,584	8,151	9,350	1,199
			86	703	3,268	3,792	524
ISRAEL	V	E	85	403	5,160	5,386	226
			86	2,272	7,282	9,079	1,797
ITALY	A	E	84	458	1,232	2,464	1,232
	O	E	81	9,316	28,883	28,883	
			82	7,890	26,230	26,230	
			83	1,100	3,829	3,829	
			86	2,420	6,915	8,591	1,676
	O	W	84	442	1,705	1,705	
	V	E	81	5,110	9,855	11,749	1,894
			82	11,006	15,929	18,015	2,086
			83	13,235	18,694	21,675	2,981
			84	5,105	7,548	8,736	1,188
			85	3,915	4,703	5,891	1,188
JAPAN	V	E	85	1,346	6,847	8,164	1,317
			86	769	6,048	6,433	385
	V	W	83	34	510	546	36
KOR REP	V	E	83	338	2,130	2,155	25
LEBANON	V	E	82	8	1,867	2,058	191
MEXICO	N	E	84	23,028	109,259	113,234	3,975
			85	6,817	20,494	22,992	2,498
	O	E	82	113	330	330	
	O	W	86	22,925	22,053	22,053	
	V	E	86	2,642	7,013	7,595	582
PORTUGL	V	E	86	586	1,675	2,048	373
REP SAF	O	E	83	713	4,469	4,856	387
	V	E	81	37,278	37,043	45,387	8,344
			82	15,390	12,970	15,503	2,533
			83	92,868	85,037	98,480	13,443
			84	46,270	42,707	47,683	4,976
			85	160,627	80,764	98,024	17,260
			86	262,878	145,374	174,404	29,030
	V	W	86	13,392	7,710	9,663	1,953
SPAIN	O	E	81	1,298	3,532	3,532	
			82	1,107	3,383	3,383	
			83	1,817	5,878	5,878	
			84	297	988	988	
	V	E	81	7,919	20,479	23,521	3,042
			82	522,410	506,146	588,717	82,571
			83	9,970	8,789	10,641	1,852
			84	194,185	118,691	141,990	23,299
			85	677,682	395,695	490,048	94,353
			86	18,910	18,073	21,852	3,779
U KING	V	E	83	69	923	1,126	203
			84	29	1,041	1,278	237
			85	384	1,132	1,287	155
			86	872	1,120	1,204	84
USSR	O	W	85	419	1,276	1,276	

Grape, juice, not concentrated
1654020 GRAPE JUC NT CNCNTRT NT MIX (GAL)

Country	Mode	Reg	Yr	Quantity	F.A.S.	C.I.F.	Charges
TOTAL			81	244,762	900,715	963,622	62,907
			82	261,991	940,494	956,676	16,182
			83	181,652	609,038	678,302	69,264

Crop
Product
TSUSA commodity number, description, and unit of quantity

Country	Mode	Reg	Yr	Quantity	F.A.S.	C.I.F.	Charges
			84	195,022	553,334	652,909	99,575
			85	281,045	733,609	851,254	117,645
			86	390,418	1,033,703	1,219,573	185,870
ARGENT	V	E	86	26,628	18,582	23,448	4,866
AUSTRAL	N	W	85	9,964	45,138	55,097	9,959
	V	E	86	4,797	22,807	26,849	4,042
	V	H	85	314	2,498	2,727	229
	V	W	81	45,256	228,691	268,418	39,727
			82	3,064	17,753	21,106	3,353
			83	18,728	76,594	90,800	14,206
			84	3,412	13,425	16,277	2,852
			85	1,665	8,272	10,994	2,722
AUSTRIA	A	E	85	1,204	2,195	6,681	4,486
	V	E	86	20,377	42,145	61,323	19,178
BELGIUM	O	E	84	1,420	3,656	4,336	680
			85	1,695	3,617	5,100	1,483
	V	E	83	2,266	6,744	7,767	1,023
			84	19,313	44,990	57,804	12,814
			85	21,037	47,850	61,187	13,337
			86	8,055	22,527	26,958	4,431
	V	W	86	1,220	3,071	3,635	564
CANADA	O	E	81	22,220	53,960	53,960	
			82	62,347	198,787	198,787	
			83	72,171	231,885	231,885	
			84	77,517	190,446	190,446	
			85	123,945	283,578	283,578	
			86	100,349	231,069	231,069	
	O	W	81	147,184	498,550	498,550	
			82	178,712	660,687	660,687	
			83	9,677	48,121	48,121	
CHINA T	V	W	85	661	1,274	1,461	187
DENMARK	V	E	82	1,445	3,526	4,199	673
			83	18,274	23,144	28,892	5,748
	V	W	83	3,050	8,970	10,476	1,506
FR GERM	N	E	83	11,739	48,441	56,944	8,503
			85	6,371	23,734	29,760	6,026
	O	E	83	211	903	1,083	180
			84	386	2,993	3,374	381
	V	E	81	14,154	60,104	69,157	9,053
			82	13,492	51,803	62,413	10,610
			83	222	2,131	2,366	235
			84	7,616	32,924	38,675	5,751
			85	3,095	8,361	11,685	3,324
			86	9,558	28,533	38,087	9,554
	V	H	86	737	3,232	4,087	855
	V	W	81	242	1,128	1,138	10
			82	135	460	537	77
			83	396	1,658	1,945	287
			84	72	1,230	1,454	224
			85	986	6,578	7,831	1,253
			86	2,712	14,545	15,924	1,379
FRANCE	N	E	85	24,051	85,729	104,706	18,977
	O	E	82	228	740	740	
			86	1,755	10,241	10,841	600
	V	E	82	1,810	3,853	4,525	672
			83	8,388	35,982	43,812	7,830
			84	19,091	70,407	89,515	19,108
			85	12,153	36,982	45,379	8,397
			86	58,843	254,427	309,934	55,507
	V	W	83	247	808	891	83
			84	9,915	33,183	42,854	9,671
			85	21,244	75,879	95,923	20,044
			86	5,862	24,724	29,554	4,830
HG KONG	V	E	86	1,257	1,503	1,625	122
	V	W	84	620	1,458	1,678	220
ICELAND	V	E	86	2,063	7,150	9,420	2,270
ISRAEL	N	E	86	65,961	64,238	75,286	11,048
	O	E	83	2,372	9,381	11,826	2,445
	V	E	81	6,668	24,615	30,821	6,206
			83	2,615	11,385	13,463	2,078
			84	8,503	32,605	41,604	8,999
			85	2,784	9,693	12,917	3,224
			86	6,214	20,878	25,708	4,830
	V	W	84	1,722	7,395	8,926	1,531
			86	1,031	3,593	4,856	1,263
ITALY	O	E	82	170	556	556	
			86	4,341	12,930	13,130	200
	V	E	85	15,321	53,939	68,725	14,786
			86	34,779	132,240	168,844	36,604
	V	W	83	10,902	29,870	40,398	10,528
			84	32,572	88,312	120,998	32,686
			85	19,971	8,001	11,073	3,072
			86	4,148	12,156	16,829	4,673

Crop
Product
TSUSA commodity number, description, and unit of quantity

Country	Mode	Reg	Yr	Quantity	F.A.S.	C.I.F.	Charges
JAPAN	A	H	82	60	268	637	369
	V	E	84	1,688	11,610	12,815	1,205
			85	3,152	2,164	2,566	402
			86	4,605	15,309	17,925	2,616
	V	W	86	375	2,760	2,893	133
KOR REP	V	W	81	2	444	480	36
MEXICO	O	E	83	676	1,500	1,500	
			85	405	1,098	1,098	
	O	W	84	3,584	3,185	3,185	
PORTUGL	V	E	86	1,640	4,502	5,305	803
REP SAF	V	E	81	2,592	4,487	5,029	542
			83	14,514	53,307	62,568	9,261
			85	5,771	12,084	12,844	760
			86	7,761	6,347	6,533	186
	V	W	81	2,670	11,827	14,975	3,148
SPAIN	V	E	83	3,975	11,050	13,105	2,055
			84	5,241	7,214	8,214	1,000
			85	4,645	11,988	16,265	4,277
			86	7,372	19,745	25,082	5,337
SWITZLD	V	E	81	1,368	9,278	11,812	2,534
			82	528	2,061	2,489	428
			83	903	4,549	7,295	2,746
			84	1,218	5,085	6,744	1,659
			85	611	2,957	3,657	700
			86	1,817	10,474	13,546	3,072
	V	W	83	22	330	430	100
			86	1,894	10,529	12,979	2,450
U KING	V	E	83	234	1,308	1,668	360
			84	95	591	676	85
			86	2,892	21,962	24,906	2,944
	V	W	83	70	977	1,067	90
VENEZ	V	E	86	1,375	11,484	12,997	1,513
YUGOSLV	V	E	81	2,406	7,631	9,282	1,651
			84	594	1,409	1,864	455
	V	W	84	443	1,216	1,470	254

Grape, prepared or preserved
1477700 GRAPES, PREP OR PRES (LB)

Country	Mode	Reg	Yr	Quantity	F.A.S.	C.I.F.	Charges
TOTAL			81	389,485	75,844	77,456	1,612
			82	6,536,670	1,614,440	1,864,620	250,180
			83	70,762	18,723	19,282	559
			84	40,346	26,000	32,265	6,265
			85	47,577	21,516	24,286	2,770
			86	86,925	69,777	73,254	3,477
ARGENT	V	W	82	6,530,623	1,605,000	1,854,000	249,000
			84	27,664	11,777	17,266	5,489
CANADA	O	E	83	220	256	256	
			85	480	1,344	1,344	
			86	39,775	24,263	24,263	
	O	W	81	376,215	66,760	66,760	
CHILE	V	E	86	8,362	6,655	7,735	1,080
CHINA M	V	E	83	500	498	547	49
			84	660	825	1,057	232
CHINA T	V	E	82	2,249	1,790	1,993	203
	V	W	86	11,803	5,552	5,741	189
FRANCE	V	E	81	96	483	517	34
			86	8,000	16,800	16,911	111
	V	W	82	50	337	358	21
			83	317	432	480	48
GREECE	V	E	81	3,799	3,432	4,108	676
			82	1,500	1,250	1,459	209
			83	2,695	2,610	2,963	353
			84	1,200	1,050	1,355	305
			86	4,500	3,800	4,195	395
	V	W	82	467	300	350	50
HG KONG	V	E	84	220	257	312	55
ISRAEL	V	E	81	7,125	3,500	4,258	758
ITALY	O	E	82	500	344	344	
	V	E	82	39	266	433	167
			86	5,265	6,951	7,933	982
JAPAN	V	H	84	162	345	405	60
	V	W	82	1,125	4,711	4,800	89
			84	1,125	4,920	5,014	94
KOR REP	V	E	86	4,500	3,303	3,704	401
	V	W	81	2,250	1,669	1,813	144
			84	675	567	597	30
			85	8,997	6,280	6,940	660
MEXICO	O	E	83	64,626	13,437	13,437	
SOMALIA	V	E	85	38,100	13,892	16,002	2,110
THAILND	O	W	83	1,202	745	805	60
	V	W	83	1,202	745	794	49

Crop Product TSUSA commodity number, description, and unit of quantity Country	Mode	Reg	Yr	Quantity	F.A.S.	C.I.F.	Charges
TONGA	A	W	82	117	442	883	441
TURKEY	O	E	84	8,640	6,259	6,259	
	V	E	86	4,720	2,453	2,772	319

Grape, wine
1673005 WINE GRAPE RED NOV 1 GL, NOV $4 (GAL)

Country	Mode	Reg	Yr	Quantity	F.A.S.	C.I.F.	Charges
TOTAL			83	19,320,399	54,550,449	68,788,862	14,238,413
			84	21,269,981	57,421,572	74,173,401	16,751,829
			85	18,387,312	48,512,404	64,097,989	15,585,585
			86	10,029,948	30,362,858	38,633,843	8,270,985
ALGERIA	N	E	84	25,294	73,829	85,476	11,647
	O	E	83	28,710	76,178	95,214	19,036
			84	55,896	165,667	202,862	37,195
			85	11,483	33,810	39,059	5,249
			86	27,561	81,144	85,201	4,057
	O	W	84	13,780	40,572	46,871	6,299
	V	E	83	84,308	244,822	283,610	38,788
			84	2,297	6,762	7,762	1,000
			85	4,326	12,740	14,624	1,884
	V	W	84	712	2,581	3,172	591
ANTIGUA	V	E	85	1,426	4,625	5,762	1,137
			86	1,427	5,344	6,641	1,297
ARGENT	O	E	84	1,712	5,764	7,053	1,289
			85	1,254	3,563	4,516	953
			86	2,290	6,830	9,078	2,248
	V	E	83	23,311	70,185	87,624	17,439
			84	38,494	106,056	136,711	30,655
			85	26,784	90,661	109,330	18,669
			86	16,058	50,091	64,116	14,025
	V	W	83	1,854	6,543	8,093	1,550
			85	5,467	14,830	19,006	4,176
			86	1,782	4,956	6,440	1,484
AUSTRAL	O	E	85	7,713	9,000	9,588	588
			86	380	1,512	1,512	
	V	E	83	1,569	2,365	3,067	702
	V	W	85	891	2,956	3,614	658
AUSTRIA	O	E	85	3,506	2,996	3,451	455
	V	E	83	3,227	3,263	3,772	509
			84	4,557	17,032	22,090	5,058
			85	1,901	6,730	9,246	2,516
B IND O	V	E	84	4,636	13,350	15,350	2,000
BELGIUM	O	E	86	827	1,376	1,431	55
	V	E	83	9,416	29,812	35,177	5,365
			84	7,184	21,270	28,234	6,964
BERMUDA	O	E	83	119	300	433	133
	V	E	84	5,084	15,230	20,372	5,142
			86	1,117	3,760	5,540	1,780
BOLIVIA	O	E	85	475	1,100	1,644	544
			86	979	3,914	4,227	313
BRAZIL	V	E	85	712	2,840	3,536	696
			86	1,838	6,272	7,184	912
BULGAR	N	W	84	3,791	10,177	15,233	5,056
	O	E	83	20,392	72,100	91,723	19,623
			84	30,461	98,382	120,333	21,951
			85	22,286	79,929	89,374	9,445
			86	19,434	75,577	84,708	9,131
	V	E	83	144,547	508,376	655,723	147,347
			84	170,581	609,526	756,243	146,717
			85	83,634	312,448	393,290	80,842
			86	131,798	486,036	599,940	113,904
	V	W	83	12,605	29,076	49,719	20,643
			84	5,609	16,939	23,373	6,434
			85	3,889	3,215	4,911	1,696
			86	3,636	10,814	15,277	4,563
BURMA	O	E	86	4,921	19,684	26,837	7,153
	V	E	86	1,403	5,565	6,465	900
CANADA	O	E	83	357	1,175	1,500	325
			84	1,767	5,819	7,451	1,632
			85	2,663	1,058	1,058	
			86	1,284	4,779	4,779	
	V	E	86	3,197	10,388	13,159	2,771
CHILE	O	E	86	1,307	4,000	5,282	1,282
	O	W	83	1,753	4,593	6,499	1,906
	V	E	83	6,202	22,521	27,048	4,527
			84	20,942	75,866	93,793	17,927
			85	36,272	115,566	136,943	21,377
			86	34,690	109,372	126,919	17,547
	V	W	83	1,664	6,380	7,863	1,483
			84	2,994	11,466	13,542	2,076
			86	749	2,993	3,947	954
COLOMB	O	E	84	252	848	1,130	282
CYPRUS	V	E	83	240	905	1,130	225
			84	476	1,600	2,097	497
			85	936	1,450	1,843	393
DENMARK	V	E	83	1,962	5,201	7,354	2,153
			85	2,892	8,263	10,843	2,580
	V	W	83	416	1,654	1,970	316
			86	9,000	15,132	16,132	1,000
FR GERM	N	E	83	6,136	16,989	22,332	5,343
			84	6,646	23,063	28,505	5,442
			85	1,625	5,417	7,141	1,724
	N	W	84	380	946	1,099	153
			85	5,230	14,036	17,291	3,255
			86	2,568	7,999	9,342	1,343
	O	E	83	2,177	5,361	6,955	1,594
			84	20,192	42,533	51,532	8,999
			85	12,527	41,978	46,189	4,211
			86	12,838	44,912	58,912	14,000
	O	W	85	713	2,700	3,195	495
	V	E	83	71,777	212,737	266,455	53,718
			84	62,319	143,991	181,960	37,969
			85	28,913	95,838	125,746	29,908
			86	11,833	36,588	48,203	11,615
	V	W	83	6,024	20,193	25,498	5,305
			84	12,529	37,675	49,174	11,499
			85	4,991	12,684	15,701	3,017
FRANCE	A	E	84	4,512	11,976	13,307	1,331
			85	348	1,282	1,422	140
			86	1,483	1,272	1,399	127
	N	E	83	574,801	1,729,312	2,136,047	406,735
			84	949,925	2,673,606	3,381,917	708,311
			85	1,107,135	3,016,102	3,960,336	944,234
			86	505,559	939,279	1,129,404	190,125
	N	W	83	38,997	117,668	139,650	21,982
			84	79,554	247,397	299,477	52,080
			85	10,801	25,710	33,305	7,595
			86	14,416	22,864	28,556	5,692
	O	E	83	166,584	513,011	650,851	137,840
			84	179,616	472,439	615,079	142,640
			85	181,300	509,223	662,673	153,450
			86	54,783	177,549	229,522	51,973
	O	W	83	119	474	534	60
			84	2,437	4,168	4,886	718
			85	4,575	15,332	18,208	2,876
	V	E	83	369,567	1,194,722	1,481,082	286,360
			84	1,002,349	3,003,239	3,822,789	819,550
			85	669,578	2,074,423	2,790,800	716,377
			86	358,481	979,690	1,226,136	246,446
	V	W	83	104,052	346,700	420,340	73,640
			84	157,819	486,850	604,552	117,702
			85	238,577	697,568	906,118	208,550
			86	68,060	207,345	241,608	34,263
GIBRAT	V	E	84	1,295	4,177	4,864	687
GREECE	N	E	84	4,171	13,305	18,426	5,121
			86	10,264	34,949	40,894	5,945
	O	E	83	6,494	19,558	24,284	4,726
			84	4,965	16,665	20,864	4,199
			85	9,088	25,801	34,653	8,852
			86	1,465	4,780	6,370	1,590
	V	E	83	40,584	136,146	175,332	39,186
			84	47,931	160,831	212,991	52,160
			85	53,053	157,042	214,224	57,182
			86	27,893	89,602	117,181	27,579
	V	W	83	2,526	8,795	10,832	2,037
			85	713	2,025	2,636	611
			86	1,843	6,530	8,357	1,827
HUNGARY	N	E	83	3,864	15,123	17,689	2,566
	O	E	83	6,463	20,617	25,327	4,710
			84	2,683	9,235	11,597	2,362
			85	6,989	22,074	30,638	8,564
			86	9,726	36,845	37,619	774
	V	E	83	48,538	178,751	222,982	44,231
			84	63,087	194,783	241,497	46,714
			85	15,851	39,853	56,124	16,271
			86	23,701	73,965	101,437	27,472
	V	W	83	4,161	14,662	17,379	2,717
			84	12,599	40,925	51,608	10,683
			85	5,467	13,300	18,491	5,191
			86	1,188	4,250	5,159	909
ICELAND	V	E	85	7,075	15,802	21,010	5,208
	V	W	86	832	3,015	3,733	718
IRAN	O	E	85	475	1,176	1,776	600
	V	E	85	6,470	18,525	23,913	5,388
			86	3,578	13,142	16,200	3,058
IRELAND	O	E	84	273	863	1,102	239

Crop
Product
TSUSA commodity number, description, and unit of quantity

Country	Mode	Reg	Yr	Quantity	F.A.S.	C.I.F.	Charges
	V	W	85	884	2,823	3,764	941
ISRAEL	O	E	83	1,289	4,950	6,140	1,190
			84	3,092	9,750	12,071	2,321
			85	1,346	4,550	5,621	1,071
			86	475	1,680	2,021	341
	V	E	84	10,254	30,707	38,448	7,741
			85	6,923	21,447	27,515	6,068
			86	28,567	102,018	127,625	25,607
	V	W	83	1,938	5,909	8,179	2,270
			85	3,268	10,666	13,992	3,326
			86	1,723	6,160	8,269	2,109
ITALY	N	E	83	7,005,282	19,375,623	24,217,110	4,841,487
			84	5,741,434	15,409,086	19,539,144	4,130,058
			85	5,433,696	13,782,637	18,159,507	4,376,870
			86	101,277	317,029	412,612	95,583
	N	W	83	763,134	2,156,254	2,806,573	650,319
			84	878,017	2,363,347	3,117,714	754,367
			85	353,269	911,720	1,229,131	317,411
			86	160,646	530,767	666,714	135,947
	O	E	83	780,028	2,141,728	2,690,525	548,797
			84	759,912	1,957,478	2,447,946	490,468
			85	886,304	2,433,759	3,093,536	659,777
			86	268,764	815,256	1,050,206	234,950
	O	W	83	37,796	116,960	145,360	28,400
			84	12,809	32,102	43,543	11,441
			85	8,930	25,456	29,861	4,405
			86	80,404	242,567	318,146	75,579
	V	E	83	6,830,919	18,844,464	23,773,206	4,928,742
			84	8,941,324	23,432,678	30,596,064	7,163,386
			85	6,981,142	17,891,968	23,680,160	5,788,192
			86	6,664,112	20,682,889	26,290,385	5,607,496
	V	H	84	1,469	4,510	7,045	2,535
			85	16,948	47,320	81,132	33,812
			86	4,607	15,711	25,222	9,511
	V	W	83	939,682	2,717,199	3,560,142	842,943
			84	420,353	1,144,814	1,506,923	362,109
			85	876,076	2,350,305	3,156,966	806,661
			86	427,756	1,357,437	1,737,655	380,218
JAPAN	O	E	83	285	781	1,086	305
	V	E	85	475	1,008	1,497	489
			86	3,364	9,840	12,773	2,933
	V	W	86	1,783	5,406	7,471	2,065
KOR REP	V	E	83	750	969	1,095	126
KUWAIT	O	E	85	713	1,810	2,998	1,188
LIBERIA	O	E	85	7,926	2,800	4,022	1,222
MACAO	V	E	84	1,831	5,429	6,817	1,388
MALAYSA	V	W	85	1,029	2,859	3,778	919
MALI	V	E	83	356	915	1,216	301
			85	1,069	2,550	3,499	949
MALTA	V	E	84	3,946	13,146	15,707	2,561
MEXICO	O	E	83	357	263	282	19
			84	10,373	33,388	36,627	3,239
			85	1,268	4,800	4,800	
			86	1,141	3,269	4,751	1,482
	O	W	84	1,520	4,338	5,098	760
	V	W	84	5,699	14,655	17,922	3,267
			85	653	1,913	2,252	339
MOROC	A	E	84	1,185	3,493	8,895	5,402
	V	E	85	4,566	12,547	17,401	4,854
			86	2,694	9,366	11,791	2,425
	V	W	83	2,140	6,750	9,215	2,465
			84	2,733	10,211	13,477	3,266
			86	356	1,423	1,852	429
NETHLDS	O	E	86	1,260	3,780	4,007	227
	V	E	83	13,618	37,578	46,254	8,676
			84	10,231	31,280	41,156	9,876
			85	10,930	32,687	37,639	4,952
			86	7,317	21,274	26,970	5,696
	V	W	84	1,783	5,831	7,502	1,671
			85	2,766	9,787	12,552	2,765
PERU	O	E	86	1,874	4,754	10,007	5,253
	V	E	85	713	2,012	2,604	592
POLAND	O	E	83	119	461	596	135
PORTUGL	N	E	84	12,680	24,217	35,223	11,006
	O	E	83	3,636	13,041	15,812	2,771
			84	1,112	2,198	2,797	599
			85	475	1,660	2,103	443
			86	832	3,000	3,717	717
	V	E	83	243,741	816,527	1,021,926	205,399
			84	269,190	774,014	985,235	211,221
			85	247,447	742,146	991,764	249,618
			86	189,155	547,570	712,134	164,564
	V	W	83	232,707	800,849	990,715	189,866
			84	186,322	564,484	884,847	320,363
			85	37,698	113,963	151,535	37,572
			86	528	1,160	1,593	433
ROMANIA	N	E	84	3,875	8,132	11,579	3,447
			85	12,836	43,275	57,003	13,728
			86	4,279	14,400	17,848	3,448
	O	E	83	1,462	4,460	7,967	3,507
			84	4,484	12,301	16,252	3,951
			85	2,579	8,253	8,915	662
			86	9,616	18,913	22,418	3,505
	V	E	83	141,478	428,604	579,984	151,380
			84	158,482	431,069	602,305	171,236
			85	123,391	415,207	581,236	166,029
			86	131,249	440,584	609,206	168,622
	V	W	83	12,953	39,498	54,323	14,825
			84	6,561	20,011	31,773	11,762
			85	7,072	24,000	33,464	9,464
			86	5,348	18,000	24,274	6,274
SINGAPR	O	E	86	1,531	5,622	7,111	1,489
SPAIN	N	E	84	18,626	55,007	70,507	15,500
			85	3,978	10,974	13,315	2,341
	O	E	83	5,755	16,086	21,055	4,969
			84	28,948	86,247	113,800	27,553
			85	9,919	28,805	38,001	9,196
			86	7,184	20,583	27,589	7,006
	O	W	83	5,989	19,908	26,103	6,195
			84	155	390	428	38
			86	3,835	14,112	16,481	2,369
	V	E	83	201,011	539,661	688,666	149,005
			84	324,084	837,103	1,111,884	274,781
			85	255,684	696,953	922,284	225,331
			86	158,972	466,132	602,895	136,763
	V	W	83	12,805	32,764	45,306	12,542
			84	15,576	45,774	59,253	13,479
			85	14,666	42,696	56,979	14,283
			86	4,944	17,140	21,477	4,337
SWITZLD	O	E	84	475	1,887	2,117	230
	V	E	85	356	1,323	1,714	391
THAILND	V	E	83	1,783	4,575	6,514	1,939
U KING	A	E	83	2,400	2,808	2,834	26
			85	5,469	11,820	12,884	1,064
	A	W	85	2,852	4,179	4,383	204
	N	E	85	11,503	40,267	46,623	6,356
	O	E	83	9,700	27,249	33,235	5,986
			84	9,500	27,296	33,078	5,782
			85	4,178	13,041	16,629	3,588
			86	16,928	25,254	33,716	8,462
	O	W	86	691	1,640	1,738	98
	V	E	83	1,958	6,027	7,612	1,585
			84	7,528	17,369	22,546	5,177
			85	2,496	9,656	11,386	1,730
			86	7,136	24,479	30,757	6,278
	V	W	83	71	257	274	17
			84	1,188	4,622	6,399	1,777
URUGUAY	V	E	85	951	2,400	3,145	745
USSR	O	E	86	1,615	6,460	8,164	1,704
YUGOSLV	N	E	85	129,383	338,418	479,695	141,277
			86	4,635	12,460	17,727	5,267
	N	W	85	3,438	9,469	12,780	3,311
	O	E	83	6,216	16,484	22,255	5,771
			84	8,558	25,280	32,371	7,091
			85	18,363	49,484	68,171	18,687
			86	13,293	39,171	56,499	17,328
	V	E	83	249,383	693,649	931,996	238,347
			84	379,074	1,054,110	1,414,514	360,404
			85	293,213	810,094	1,127,973	317,879
			86	309,991	893,094	1,204,689	311,595
	V	W	83	14,142	40,930	54,218	13,288
			84	13,797	36,415	48,020	11,605
			85	11,905	30,695	41,332	10,637
			86	20,439	58,874	77,606	18,732

1673015 WINE, GRAPE WH NOV 1 GL, NOV $4 (GAL)

Country	Mode	Reg	Yr	Quantity	F.A.S.	C.I.F.	Charges
TOTAL			83	27,593,006	81,024,434	100,948,422	19,923,988
			84	36,532,812	105,316,200	133,905,069	28,588,869
			85	33,300,213	93,842,200	122,065,202	28,223,002
			86	15,086,164	46,976,639	59,437,198	12,460,559
ALBANIA	O	E	84	2,080	7,875	8,878	1,003
ALGERIA	O	E	83	22,452	53,310	59,952	6,642
			84	19,757	58,057	73,371	15,314
			85	38,734	114,044	128,742	14,698
			86	27,559	81,144	93,739	12,595
	V	E	84	54,880	159,383	182,473	23,090
ANTIGUA	V	E	85	475	1,600	1,980	380

Crop
Product
TSUSA commodity number, description, and unit of quantity

Country	Mode	Reg	Yr	Quantity	F.A.S.	C.I.F.	Charges
			86	1,189	4,061	5,046	985
ARGENT	N	E	84	28,461	68,872	92,461	23,589
	O	E	84	1,565	5,295	6,480	1,185
			85	4,278	14,460	18,255	3,795
			86	475	1,180	1,180	
	V	E	83	37,113	104,707	134,672	29,965
			84	19,106	50,350	64,015	13,665
			85	22,496	79,685	97,343	17,658
			86	15,551	32,418	43,085	10,667
	V	W	83	2,318	7,428	8,429	1,001
			85	2,257	6,375	8,242	1,867
			86	475	1,300	1,536	236
AUSTRAL	A	E	85	1,058	3,869	4,750	881
	V	E	85	3,043	6,487	6,871	384
			86	1,783	1,611	4,510	2,899
	V	W	85	13,219	10,899	13,784	2,885
AUSTRIA	A	E	83	143	459	966	507
	N	E	84	5,837	20,885	28,073	7,188
	O	E	83	6,182	12,131	15,339	3,208
			84	3,288	10,483	13,277	2,794
			85	540	1,471	1,633	162
	V	E	83	23,424	75,452	95,742	20,290
			84	21,126	62,234	81,191	18,957
			85	15,788	48,963	64,759	15,796
BELGIUM	N	E	83	5,403	18,097	23,690	5,593
	O	E	83	3,209	12,560	14,360	1,800
			84	476	1,782	2,316	534
			85	356	1,125	1,547	422
			86	3,963	6,595	6,860	265
	O	W	86	475	1,238	1,748	510
	V	E	83	14,039	38,295	47,025	8,730
			84	38,022	96,077	116,633	20,556
			85	34,717	124,587	158,078	33,491
			86	2,008	6,551	8,686	2,135
	V	W	85	3,458	10,405	12,520	2,115
BERMUDA	O	E	83	1,037	2,616	3,772	1,156
	V	E	84	2,596	10,116	13,062	2,946
			86	1,070	3,600	5,304	1,704
BOLIVIA	O	E	85	951	2,200	3,288	1,088
			86	399	1,596	1,724	128
BRAZIL	V	E	86	1,902	4,800	6,419	1,619
BULGAR	N	W	84	2,817	7,672	11,316	3,644
	O	E	83	19,555	70,002	82,109	12,107
			84	17,478	60,500	71,960	11,460
			85	18,418	66,477	74,651	8,174
			86	14,528	54,846	60,768	5,922
	V	E	83	114,997	409,726	527,051	117,325
			84	140,710	505,130	630,354	125,224
			85	65,471	242,302	301,543	59,241
			86	119,771	450,056	556,632	106,576
	V	W	83	10,400	23,302	40,931	17,629
			84	3,520	10,022	13,788	3,766
			85	2,548	8,468	13,121	4,653
			86	950	2,827	4,020	1,193
BURMA	O	E	86	5,958	23,826	29,989	6,163
	V	E	85	2,330	9,310	10,629	1,319
			86	5,516	21,984	25,470	3,486
CANADA	A	E	86	2,155	6,681	10,601	3,920
	O	E	83	4,128	13,589	17,110	3,521
			84	7,095	14,087	17,865	3,778
			85	2,942	2,086	2,086	
			86	11,042	21,409	26,788	5,379
CHILE	O	W	83	2,260	5,035	7,248	2,213
	V	E	83	9,759	37,090	42,459	5,369
			84	13,398	39,697	49,843	10,146
			85	78,598	228,444	288,581	60,137
			86	86,195	263,846	330,900	67,054
	V	W	83	3,031	11,325	13,958	2,633
			84	3,299	12,074	14,037	1,963
			85	2,317	8,698	11,566	2,868
			86	1,177	4,703	6,140	1,437
CHINA M	V	E	85	3,566	11,303	14,755	3,452
CHINA T	V	E	85	3,328	9,058	12,676	3,618
COLOMB	O	E	84	364	1,224	1,631	407
CYPRUS	V	E	84	476	1,600	2,097	497
	V	W	85	1,188	4,500	5,450	950
DENMARK	O	W	86	1,983	6,163	7,613	1,450
	V	E	83	3,150	8,320	11,581	3,261
			85	6,419	8,355	17,402	9,047
DOMINCA	V	E	85	6,418	24,330	28,574	4,244
FR GERM	A	E	83	2,995	8,714	11,045	2,331
	N	E	83	554,104	1,740,070	2,118,332	378,262
			84	1,101,730	3,508,371	4,401,771	893,400
			85	359,930	1,049,193	1,350,105	300,912
			86	41,302	35,005	40,199	5,194
	N	W	84	254,008	685,093	808,389	123,296
			85	17,547	50,582	63,599	13,017
			86	13,990	17,499	21,093	3,594
	O	E	83	237,710	728,826	900,512	171,686
			84	355,745	1,114,868	1,428,088	313,220
			85	189,789	535,631	694,316	158,685
			86	27,810	73,227	93,854	20,627
	O	W	84	547	2,077	2,768	691
			85	6,537	16,041	23,610	7,569
			86	33,630	59,525	62,936	3,411
	V	E	83	983,169	2,969,728	3,661,418	691,690
			84	2,055,545	6,295,760	8,049,489	1,753,729
			85	1,477,889	4,831,919	6,342,730	1,510,811
			86	180,979	349,636	459,568	109,932
	V	H	85	3,982	15,153	22,839	7,686
	V	W	83	309,877	937,338	1,120,270	182,932
			84	479,458	1,583,391	1,979,647	396,256
			85	435,029	1,390,264	1,748,692	358,428
			86	3,918	10,027	13,165	3,138
FRANCE	A	E	83	683	2,415	2,799	384
			84	476	1,899	4,476	2,577
			86	988	1,434	1,636	202
	A	W	84	80	270	1,387	1,117
	N	E	83	1,145,310	3,643,248	4,490,981	847,733
			84	2,335,740	7,128,359	9,055,834	1,927,475
			85	2,390,679	6,731,400	8,809,469	2,078,069
			86	61,702	113,582	134,364	20,782
	N	W	83	164,142	484,980	568,872	83,892
			84	232,103	752,934	908,138	155,204
			85	204,410	645,644	844,530	198,886
	O	E	83	341,709	1,033,881	1,296,484	262,603
			84	423,792	1,223,337	1,560,320	336,983
			85	526,925	1,537,158	2,042,058	504,900
			86	261,441	822,984	1,068,725	245,741
	O	W	83	1,427	5,658	7,487	1,829
			84	8,912	27,140	31,535	4,395
			85	11,019	36,681	47,462	10,781
	V	E	83	1,160,885	3,604,788	4,491,084	886,296
			84	2,069,260	6,490,299	8,288,421	1,798,122
			85	1,984,960	6,071,960	8,077,513	2,005,553
			86	1,253,935	4,027,859	5,193,642	1,165,783
	V	W	83	253,157	812,035	980,378	168,343
			84	350,788	1,092,527	1,359,665	267,138
			85	413,964	1,302,030	1,663,509	361,479
			86	92,132	266,375	328,728	62,353
GERM DR	V	E	83	2,225	5,480	9,620	4,140
			84	3,428	12,788	16,647	3,859
			86	880	2,335	3,442	1,107
GIBRAT	O	E	83	7,133	15,480	19,920	4,440
			84	428	1,082	1,393	311
	V	E	84	4,757	15,257	18,062	2,805
GREECE	N	E	83	4,509	14,280	18,079	3,799
			84	11,095	3,150	4,162	1,012
			86	22,376	59,590	81,290	21,700
	O	E	83	4,083	14,755	19,540	4,785
			84	22,359	81,580	104,858	23,278
			85	47,296	170,109	221,243	51,134
			86	57,391	204,074	258,058	53,984
	O	W	85	960	3,573	3,894	321
	V	E	83	52,707	110,434	146,815	36,381
			84	112,840	381,691	520,545	138,854
			85	121,493	395,851	533,907	138,056
			86	94,578	289,027	393,483	104,456
	V	W	84	9,204	30,371	39,917	9,546
			85	29,512	104,574	138,317	33,743
			86	18,900	68,992	87,360	18,368
GUATMAL	V	W	85	1,331	5,308	6,800	1,492
HUNGARY	N	E	83	3,329	12,975	15,023	2,048
			84	11,201	37,978	46,871	8,893
	O	E	83	3,047	11,797	14,404	2,607
			84	2,349	8,238	10,078	1,840
			85	1,216	4,064	5,563	1,499
			86	523	2,090	2,619	529
	V	E	83	24,550	86,931	107,107	20,176
			84	9,333	28,580	32,870	4,290
			85	34,118	75,577	110,168	34,591
			86	47,812	160,476	217,965	57,489
	V	W	83	4,874	17,512	20,784	3,272
			84	3,846	12,036	15,429	3,393
			85	16,640	27,508	37,522	10,014
			86	475	1,700	2,063	363
ICELAND	V	E	85	3,091	6,589	8,853	2,264
IRAN	V	E	85	1,426	3,425	4,805	1,380

Crop
Product
TSUSA commodity number, description, and unit of quantity

Country	Mode	Reg	Yr	Quantity	F.A.S.	C.I.F.	Charges
IRELAND	O	E	85	1,383	4,729	6,487	1,758
	V	W	85	1,792	5,749	7,665	1,916
ISRAEL	O	E	85	3,661	2,187	2,554	367
	V	E	84	5,087	12,136	15,310	3,174
			85	4,619	12,493	17,106	4,613
			86	6,608	23,397	30,690	7,293
	V	W	83	856	2,610	3,612	1,002
			86	356	1,170	1,424	254
ITALY	N	E	83	8,582,952	24,849,064	30,611,351	5,762,287
			84	11,976,571	33,418,923	42,105,229	8,686,306
			85	10,838,109	29,447,060	37,781,724	8,334,664
			86	558,002	1,807,240	2,262,659	455,419
	N	W	83	658,273	1,977,131	2,514,406	537,275
			84	1,075,027	2,975,845	3,834,185	858,340
			85	217,143	609,697	803,876	194,179
			86	111,222	362,220	456,820	94,600
	O	E	83	1,597,072	4,345,786	5,559,354	1,213,568
			84	1,985,629	5,147,840	6,601,547	1,453,707
			85	1,699,612	4,548,439	5,834,314	1,285,875
			86	971,536	2,976,922	3,682,201	705,279
	O	W	83	23,566	72,295	92,343	20,048
			84	23,005	75,053	94,490	19,437
			85	17,565	35,146	46,119	10,973
			86	106,190	330,447	443,831	113,384
	V	E	83	8,775,796	25,205,039	31,363,051	6,158,012
			84	8,723,795	24,695,007	31,532,536	6,837,529
			85	8,811,351	24,427,625	31,857,182	7,429,557
			86	9,113,266	28,671,657	36,049,467	7,377,810
	V	H	84	1,636	5,689	8,893	3,204
			85	32,174	98,773	158,421	59,648
			86	12,107	41,649	66,298	24,649
	V	W	83	1,117,954	3,416,197	4,515,643	1,099,446
			84	615,771	1,721,805	2,235,040	513,235
			85	1,477,654	4,003,610	5,270,249	1,266,639
			86	666,253	2,173,930	2,749,002	575,072
JAPAN	A	E	84	3,328	11,636	14,146	2,510
	O	E	83	1,118	3,338	4,640	1,302
	O	W	85	653	2,241	2,621	380
	V	E	84	1,448	3,920	5,461	1,541
			85	475	1,008	1,497	489
			86	439	1,471	1,931	460
KOR REP	V	E	86	475	1,736	2,317	581
LIBERIA	O	E	85	1,822	6,287	9,032	2,745
MACAO	V	E	84	832	2,468	3,099	631
MALI	V	E	83	1,545	3,966	5,270	1,304
			85	2,258	5,375	7,379	2,004
MEXICO	N	W	84	10,526	28,343	35,549	7,206
	O	E	84	14,488	47,588	50,392	2,804
			85	4,634	16,664	19,249	2,585
			86	987	3,757	4,091	334
	O	W	83	4,176	2,700	2,700	
			84	2,658	7,310	8,775	1,465
	V	E	86	2,964	7,578	8,651	1,073
	V	W	84	1,699	4,590	5,611	1,021
			85	1,347	3,613	4,254	641
MOROC	A	E	84	475	1,400	2,103	703
	O	W	83	1,189	4,500	7,481	2,981
	V	E	86	10,164	33,851	39,449	5,598
NETHLDS	O	E	83	1,102	3,051	3,923	872
			84	1,803	5,989	7,301	1,312
			85	11,888	12,935	14,290	1,355
			86	13,511	14,203	16,481	2,278
	O	W	86	531	1,260	1,336	76
	V	E	83	25,279	75,434	90,174	14,740
			84	78,226	218,356	267,997	49,641
			85	61,363	159,083	206,718	47,635
			86	17,230	43,198	52,541	9,343
	V	W	84	4,398	15,807	20,065	4,258
			85	7,405	25,824	32,595	6,771
NIGERIA	O	E	83	1,583	4,602	5,054	452
PERU	V	E	85	1,132	3,534	4,573	1,039
PORTUGL	N	E	85	174,614	596,836	751,459	154,623
	O	E	83	1,591	6,077	7,260	1,183
			84	21,739	21,729	27,061	5,332
			85	2,139	7,080	8,640	1,560
			86	10,737	38,399	49,157	10,758
	O	W	85	2,495	5,587	9,755	4,168
	V	E	83	414,257	1,383,367	1,711,348	327,981
			84	501,553	1,642,059	2,099,930	457,871
			85	207,555	652,449	861,859	209,410
			86	194,970	616,077	776,741	160,664
	V	W	83	227,205	785,650	986,399	200,749
			84	191,273	621,722	863,493	241,771
			85	106,593	356,920	483,218	126,298
			86	28,775	95,935	119,776	23,841
REP SAF	V	E	84	1,390	5,025	6,509	1,484
	V	W	83	345	877	1,006	129
			84	169	662	842	180
ROMANIA	N	E	85	14,167	44,954	56,679	11,725
			86	5,539	18,640	22,518	3,878
	O	E	83	1,165	3,463	6,201	2,738
			84	1,211	3,670	5,440	1,770
			85	860	2,737	2,956	219
			86	1,915	6,448	6,964	516
	V	E	83	85,636	272,545	368,509	95,964
			84	91,378	280,561	388,490	107,929
			85	103,104	345,761	485,111	139,350
			86	106,763	360,070	502,262	142,192
	V	W	83	11,369	34,190	47,106	12,916
			84	4,611	14,066	22,337	8,271
			85	5,966	20,080	27,841	7,761
			86	10,339	34,800	50,646	15,846
SPAIN	N	E	84	13,930	33,102	40,985	7,883
			85	77,594	177,758	246,298	68,540
	O	E	83	1,766	3,967	4,821	854
			84	3,285	8,236	10,962	2,726
			85	6,437	17,244	21,410	4,166
			86	1,378	4,595	6,102	1,507
	O	W	83	21,929	68,926	85,322	16,396
			84	1,248	4,175	5,429	1,254
			85	1,128	3,226	4,341	1,115
	V	E	83	103,839	268,151	352,487	84,336
			84	241,721	637,370	844,162	206,792
			85	119,014	322,989	431,809	108,820
			86	100,495	284,874	375,974	91,100
	V	W	83	11,130	32,197	41,701	9,504
			84	11,435	26,795	34,528	7,733
			85	23,728	44,870	59,201	14,331
			86	2,657	9,155	11,295	2,140
SWITZLD	A	E	83	119	300	430	130
			84	1,367	1,385	1,785	400
	V	E	83	5,658	20,722	25,640	4,918
			84	9,519	30,173	38,218	8,045
			85	2,615	9,507	12,316	2,809
THAILND	V	E	83	1,426	3,623	5,158	1,535
TUNISIA	O	E	85	515	1,169	1,585	416
TURKEY	V	E	84	554	2,100	2,988	888
U KING	N	E	85	3,388	13,068	15,055	1,987
	O	E	83	7,038	14,782	18,072	3,290
			84	15,805	52,448	63,338	10,890
			85	5,611	18,139	23,361	5,222
			86	16,490	57,126	72,458	15,332
	V	E	83	5,396	14,173	18,332	4,159
			84	14,775	42,813	56,419	13,606
			85	19,975	67,034	85,813	18,779
			86	11,728	38,202	49,231	11,029
	V	W	85	2,733	9,468	13,169	3,701
YUGOSLV	N	E	84	1,772	6,052	9,252	3,200
			85	200,564	529,841	746,295	216,454
			86	4,753	12,601	17,720	5,119
	N	W	85	6,809	17,299	23,671	6,372
			86	4,323	11,544	15,521	3,977
	O	E	83	7,357	19,482	25,896	6,414
			84	18,507	52,900	64,029	11,129
			85	10,722	28,061	38,800	10,739
			86	8,951	29,635	35,951	6,316
	V	E	83	338,748	933,002	1,257,928	324,926
			84	593,012	1,652,078	2,212,851	560,773
			85	366,409	994,180	1,381,455	387,275
			86	445,489	1,242,525	1,683,617	441,092
	V	W	83	10,346	28,458	38,456	9,998
			84	20,781	54,883	72,411	17,528
			85	22,782	64,136	80,870	16,734
			86	18,135	52,455	69,128	16,673

1673020 WINE NOV 14%, NOV$4,NOV 1GL (GAL)

Country	Mode	Reg	Yr	Quantity	F.A.S.	C.I.F.	Charges
TOTAL			81	49,549,537	151,496,895	189,569,977	38,134,125
			82	53,291,168	153,175,727	193,797,395	40,621,668
ALGERIA	O	E	81	6,494	15,224	20,531	5,307
			82	30,757	79,722	103,317	23,595
	O	W	81	2,418	5,744	7,858	2,114
	V	E	81	39,530	102,837	128,364	25,527
			82	91,292	248,046	314,492	66,446
ARGENT	O	E	81	2,274	7,914	9,243	1,329
			82	65	252	300	48
	V	E	81	54,302	178,725	224,496	45,771
			82	45,311	137,584	172,833	35,249

Crop
Product
TSUSA commodity number, description, and unit of quantity

Country	Mode	Reg	Yr	Quantity	F.A.S.	C.I.F.	Charges
	V	W	81	4,815	15,413	19,476	4,063
			82	1,843	6,163	7,242	1,079
AUSTRAL	A	W	82	227	252	327	75
	O	E	81	602	1,629	1,946	317
	O	W	82	321	1,102	1,164	62
	V	E	82	2,095	6,691	10,354	3,663
	V	W	81	357	858	1,273	415
AUSTRIA	O	E	82	5,549	6,145	6,382	237
	V	E	81	6,061	20,995	26,412	5,417
			82	5,548	13,625	15,260	1,635
BAHAMAS	O	E	81	240	795	861	66
BELGIUM	O	E	81	321	958	1,059	101
	V	E	82	8,044	15,285	18,432	3,147
BRAZIL	V	E	82	4,260	9,677	15,703	6,026
BULGAR	O	E	81	46,246	105,385	136,587	31,202
			82	51,923	145,391	186,077	40,686
	V	E	81	132,892	424,890	551,216	126,326
			82	220,511	787,659	998,877	211,218
	V	W	81	4,160	14,962	20,439	5,477
			82	10,400	25,356	45,314	19,958
CANADA	O	E	81	17,125	55,180	65,889	10,709
			82	794	3,067	3,067	
	V	E	81	12,147	30,753	40,013	9,260
			82	3,271	9,816	11,966	2,150
CHILE	O	E	81	7,463	24,572	29,817	5,245
			82	3,740	13,327	16,912	3,585
	V	E	81	1,331	5,296	5,886	590
CHINA M	V	W	82	1,664	6,650	7,634	984
CYPRUS	O	E	81	507	1,747	2,233	486
	V	E	82	1,069	4,068	5,076	1,008
FR GERM	N	E	81	89,324	300,465	351,853	63,584
			82	128,932	336,367	418,271	81,904
	N	W	82	922	2,902	3,988	1,086
	O	E	81	41,104	131,994	163,039	31,045
			82	52,987	137,964	170,565	32,601
	O	W	81	333	1,218	1,593	375
			82	10,230	29,511	34,457	4,946
	V	E	81	184,226	553,417	682,963	129,546
			82	236,844	483,883	623,157	139,274
	V	W	81	45,735	147,274	178,299	31,025
			82	40,242	67,348	83,729	16,381
FRANCE	A	E	81	152	503	1,583	1,080
			82	71	255	781	526
	N	E	81	865,752	2,837,375	3,557,875	720,500
			82	1,133,239	3,601,081	4,515,990	914,909
	O	E	81	240,883	725,401	907,459	182,058
			82	426,249	1,296,519	1,634,011	337,492
	O	W	82	3,817	5,149	5,731	582
	V	E	81	683,172	2,008,737	2,486,843	478,866
			82	1,156,732	3,518,031	4,395,684	877,653
	V	W	81	176,258	595,151	733,154	138,003
			82	215,280	709,760	888,348	178,588
GERM DR	V	W	82	857	2,302	3,165	863
GIBRAT	O	E	81	1,217	3,172	3,848	676
	V	E	82	3,844	9,533	11,904	2,371
GREECE	O	E	81	15,571	55,434	72,071	16,637
			82	44,280	125,684	169,748	44,064
	V	E	81	142,161	473,091	631,159	158,068
			82	138,002	491,850	662,126	170,276
	V	W	81	5,865	21,800	28,783	6,983
			82	5,797	21,625	28,195	6,570
HUNGARY	N	E	82	11,388	44,625	55,833	11,208
	O	E	81	7,944	25,265	30,120	4,855
			82	144	450	572	122
	V	E	81	76,626	275,655	343,915	68,260
			82	94,681	367,161	460,334	93,173
	V	W	81	13,885	47,778	58,619	10,841
			82	38,260	145,077	177,707	32,630
IRELAND	O	E	82	566	1,404	1,516	112
ISRAEL	O	E	81	2,494	7,274	9,454	2,180
			82	5,022	16,077	19,143	3,066
ITALY	N	E	81	20,695,624	62,893,562	77,940,870	15,076,612
			82	18,308,335	51,914,956	65,090,728	13,175,772
	N	W	81	1,343,846	4,200,779	5,598,527	1,397,608
			82	1,593,400	4,636,780	6,065,897	1,429,117
	O	E	81	2,589,804	7,699,017	9,628,133	1,926,824
			82	3,278,767	9,089,590	11,576,628	2,487,038
	O	W	81	80,049	269,129	333,122	63,993
			82	149,752	460,505	565,647	105,142
	V	E	81	18,257,290	55,823,411	69,547,750	13,738,564
			82	21,394,937	61,005,121	77,176,024	16,170,903
	V	W	81	2,302,097	7,279,231	9,610,817	2,338,528
			82	2,127,173	6,330,229	8,417,429	2,087,200
JAPAN	V	E	81	28,755	95,655	105,771	10,116

Country	Mode	Reg	Yr	Quantity	F.A.S.	C.I.F.	Charges
			82	4,362	12,045	13,701	1,656
MALAYSA	V	E	82	1,427	3,800	4,634	834
MALTA	O	E	81	3,130	9,818	10,986	1,168
MEXICO	O	E	81	119	449	449	
			82	666	874	1,342	468
	O	W	81	713	2,694	2,695	1
MOROC	V	W	82	4,754	18,450	21,875	3,425
N ZEAL	V	E	82	7,323	14,035	15,183	1,148
	V	W	82	846	1,512	1,760	248
NETHLDS	O	E	82	2,437	5,490	6,805	1,315
	V	E	81	24,794	90,436	108,597	18,161
			82	36,907	106,729	129,967	23,238
	V	W	81	5,229	14,669	20,222	5,553
			82	5,659	21,276	26,324	5,048
POLAND	V	E	82	2,734	6,352	8,350	1,998
PORTUGL	O	E	81	11,513	28,742	35,470	6,728
			82	5,017	10,432	12,981	2,549
	O	W	81	599	460	508	48
			82	2,140	6,690	7,766	1,076
	V	E	81	278,426	885,518	1,099,592	214,074
			82	595,171	1,889,040	2,220,491	331,451
	V	W	81	37,364	137,083	169,859	32,776
			82	204,251	691,873	798,802	106,929
ROMANIA	N	E	82	102,873	311,865	410,027	98,162
	O	E	81	29,780	84,295	113,318	29,023
			82	26,630	82,028	114,184	32,156
	V	E	81	162,103	491,663	698,819	207,156
			82	110,329	335,793	482,684	146,891
	V	W	81	19,162	57,288	83,416	26,128
			82	19,614	59,815	98,306	38,491
SINGAPR	V	E	81	2,378	7,500	10,067	2,567
SPAIN	N	E	82	4,474	13,136	17,263	4,127
	O	E	81	16,139	53,496	70,991	17,495
			82	10,397	31,120	38,159	7,039
	V	E	81	411,130	1,191,517	1,566,202	374,733
			82	446,978	1,298,099	1,693,082	394,983
	V	W	81	22,325	63,807	87,822	24,015
			82	60,277	195,821	246,182	50,361
SWITZLD	V	E	81	3,329	9,006	11,456	2,450
			82	10,659	32,520	39,616	7,096
U KING	O	E	81	9,507	29,337	37,966	8,629
			82	17,642	56,104	71,363	15,259
	V	E	82	5,723	13,990	15,620	1,630
	V	W	82	945	3,440	4,420	980
YUGOSLV	N	E	82	62,103	192,197	253,255	61,058
	O	E	81	12,224	43,943	54,636	10,693
			82	24,678	79,324	108,220	28,896
	V	E	81	258,752	777,559	1,045,539	267,980
			82	422,358	1,298,632	1,719,267	420,635
	V	W	81	5,646	17,960	24,528	6,568
			82	8,083	25,618	33,349	7,731

1673025 WINE GRAPE NSPF NOV 1GL, NOV $4 (GAL)

Country	Mode	Reg	Yr	Quantity	F.A.S.	C.I.F.	Charges
TOTAL			83	12,012,544	34,810,410	43,861,618	9,051,208
			84	7,109,145	20,231,295	25,773,659	5,542,364
			85	6,043,049	16,743,178	21,785,323	5,042,145
			86	3,901,947	12,154,735	15,360,508	3,205,773
ALGERIA	O	E	83	12,609	32,776	39,036	6,260
			84	16,078	47,235	54,235	7,000
			85	45,936	135,240	145,529	10,289
			86	4,594	13,524	14,335	811
	V	E	83	9,187	24,188	29,001	4,813
			84	11,484	33,810	35,444	1,634
	V	W	84	118	362	467	105
ARGENT	O	E	83	228	888	1,645	757
	V	E	83	3,077	9,995	12,468	2,473
			84	11,761	40,070	50,018	9,948
			85	9,793	33,773	42,728	8,955
			86	3,923	13,150	15,054	1,904
	V	W	83	713	2,400	2,805	405
			85	2,139	6,200	7,886	1,686
			86	713	1,999	2,712	713
AUSTRAL	O	H	84	2,640	6,390	7,417	1,027
			85	3,379	8,179	9,687	1,508
AUSTRIA	O	E	83	492	338	447	109
	V	E	83	468	1,799	1,953	154
			84	118	383	534	151
BELGIUM	O	E	83	257	767	793	26
			84	972	2,959	4,046	1,087
	V	E	83	3,233	12,613	15,997	3,384
	V	W	85	285	1,066	1,315	249
BULGAR	O	E	83	1,426	3,954	4,272	318
	V	E	83	6,241	23,625	30,668	7,043

Crop
Product
TSUSA commodity number, description, and unit of quantity

Country	Mode	Reg	Yr	Quantity	F.A.S.	C.I.F.	Charges
CHILE	A	E	84	80	319	319	
	V	E	83	718	2,696	3,262	566
			84	5,368	18,222	22,071	3,849
			85	20,387	59,567	72,015	12,448
			86	1,901	7,173	8,764	1,591
	V	W	83	942	3,240	3,880	640
			86	582	2,058	2,632	574
FR GERM	N	E	83	57,724	215,869	264,132	48,263
			84	5,014	15,230	20,525	5,295
	O	E	83	11,058	35,440	45,257	9,817
			84	40,157	143,325	175,057	31,732
			85	3,233	8,471	11,264	2,793
			86	868	3,401	3,401	
	O	W	83	6,138	6,807	10,584	3,777
	V	E	83	89,004	269,390	345,776	76,386
			84	28,486	95,399	121,650	26,251
			85	18,673	59,252	75,242	15,990
			86	7,411	25,820	30,359	4,539
	V	W	83	13,913	45,847	56,325	10,478
			84	5,478	17,530	21,274	3,744
			85	2,804	10,154	13,164	3,010
FRANCE	A	E	86	3,700	3,729	3,747	18
	N	E	83	147,974	488,190	608,465	120,275
			84	120,275	407,905	518,087	110,182
			85	81,837	247,671	324,807	77,136
			86	2,567	4,591	5,499	908
	N	W	84	21,352	75,432	92,603	17,171
	O	E	83	102,417	293,258	373,787	80,529
			84	49,895	166,372	212,964	46,592
			85	64,597	188,302	208,546	20,244
			86	30,118	58,015	75,882	17,867
	O	W	83	262	724	925	201
			84	833	2,440	2,826	386
			86	7,711	18,235	19,329	1,094
	V	E	83	203,838	648,278	806,799	158,521
			84	277,076	878,946	1,103,085	224,139
			85	160,757	519,804	697,023	177,219
			86	54,065	128,918	167,405	38,487
	V	W	83	90,372	261,596	310,296	48,700
			84	12,878	37,794	47,885	10,091
			85	46,433	158,100	198,407	40,307
			86	4,283	16,362	20,075	3,713
GREECE	O	E	83	9,612	34,392	46,044	11,652
			84	28,752	90,132	112,368	22,236
			85	8,497	28,187	36,249	8,062
			86	17,749	56,875	73,091	16,216
	V	E	83	39,127	129,897	172,389	42,492
			84	58,294	178,458	240,361	61,903
			85	98,006	284,840	405,881	121,041
			86	91,030	263,044	368,380	105,336
	V	W	83	7,374	16,730	21,101	4,371
			84	3,073	10,355	12,932	2,577
			85	5,090	18,950	23,995	5,045
			86	2,956	10,740	13,787	3,047
HUNGARY	O	E	83	1,092	3,750	4,941	1,191
			86	25,151	91,339	92,243	904
	V	E	83	26,628	103,602	133,582	29,980
			84	356	914	1,258	344
IRAN	V	E	85	475	1,142	1,602	460
IRELAND	V	W	85	361	1,068	1,424	356
ISRAEL	O	E	84	1,585	5,000	6,083	1,083
	V	E	84	990	2,873	3,639	766
			85	1,837	4,369	6,259	1,890
			86	7,845	28,070	36,128	8,058
	V	W	83	238	940	960	20
ITALY	A	E	83	247	790	1,605	815
	N	E	83	3,115,184	8,880,585	11,065,563	2,184,978
			84	2,094,438	5,807,110	7,214,738	1,407,628
			85	1,763,282	4,873,100	6,264,786	1,391,686
			86	552,264	1,648,281	2,061,886	413,605
	N	W	83	138,492	387,211	519,339	132,128
			84	205,931	575,547	762,714	187,167
			86	33,103	105,917	137,127	31,210
	O	E	83	681,568	1,879,610	2,371,770	492,160
			84	231,505	641,392	845,156	203,764
			85	310,423	906,108	1,138,772	232,664
			86	160,546	506,573	644,465	137,892
	O	W	83	22,211	68,004	87,160	19,156
			84	2,502	6,969	9,097	2,128
			85	12,980	38,874	51,484	12,610
			86	19,968	61,055	80,014	18,959
	V	E	83	5,367,016	15,105,703	19,004,745	3,899,042
			84	2,897,067	7,945,129	10,226,714	2,281,585
			85	2,455,067	6,389,141	8,338,281	1,949,140
			86	2,405,928	7,608,719	9,559,965	1,951,246
	V	H	85	6,750	19,518	33,097	13,579
			86	4,023	13,464	22,100	8,636
	V	W	83	676,080	1,918,712	2,492,688	573,976
			84	80,673	226,494	292,028	65,534
			85	336,514	912,909	1,232,382	319,473
			86	150,139	479,162	620,577	141,415
JAPAN	O	E	83	143	413	574	161
	V	W	84	1,493	4,633	5,278	645
LIBERIA	O	E	85	1,822	1,461	2,099	638
MACAO	V	E	84	499	1,481	1,860	379
MAURITN	V	E	84	1,284	4,803	5,909	1,106
MEXICO	O	E	83	357	263	282	19
MOROC	V	W	84	178	664	860	196
NETHLDS	O	E	83	9,987	29,012	36,242	7,230
	V	E	83	5,741	13,934	18,272	4,338
			84	6,543	22,883	34,381	11,498
			85	4,077	7,097	7,808	711
			86	1,925	3,239	4,254	1,015
NORFOLK	V	E	83	958	3,596	4,238	642
PANAMA	A	E	83	530	326	371	45
PORTUGL	O	E	83	4,304	5,429	8,340	2,911
			84	7,639	23,402	30,039	6,637
			85	2,496	7,363	9,417	2,054
			86	4,698	8,075	11,340	3,265
	V	E	83	909,744	3,124,367	3,961,009	836,642
			84	645,829	1,995,443	2,582,251	586,808
			85	331,048	1,064,839	1,410,801	345,962
			86	239,357	821,426	1,072,756	251,330
	V	W	83	52,828	196,157	244,550	48,393
			84	131,658	420,659	527,427	106,768
			85	187,546	595,393	806,289	210,896
			86	43,768	98,278	128,195	29,917
ROMANIA	O	E	83	3,567	10,875	13,251	2,376
	V	E	83	8,083	24,310	35,065	10,755
			84	2,139	6,525	6,851	326
SPAIN	O	E	83	3,197	9,769	12,214	2,445
			84	1,559	4,865	6,504	1,639
	O	W	83	120	480	494	14
	V	E	83	64,683	163,709	223,120	59,411
			84	45,607	120,512	159,507	38,995
			85	37,321	105,750	140,557	34,807
			86	10,631	31,440	38,722	7,282
	V	W	83	5,587	17,410	22,866	5,456
			84	491	1,796	2,226	430
			85	543	1,180	1,663	483
			86	1,521	5,791	7,252	1,461
SWITZLD	V	E	83	297	770	921	151
			86	4,950	10,242	10,668	426
TURKEY	V	E	84	178	637	907	270
U KING	O	E	83	20,510	66,374	83,356	16,982
			84	12,268	41,172	55,779	14,607
			85	1,402	3,664	4,625	961
			86	499	1,732	2,387	655
	O	W	85	475	1,332	1,742	410
	V	E	83	118	389	559	170
			84	713	2,707	3,364	657
			86	748	2,108	3,053	945
YUGOSLV	O	E	83	8,899	26,734	40,025	13,291
			84	571	1,415	1,958	543
	V	E	83	63,709	194,331	255,942	61,611
			84	33,035	93,365	125,970	32,605
			85	15,357	37,304	53,381	16,077
			86	712	2,190	2,924	734
	V	W	83	2,022	7,158	9,467	2,309
			84	2,232	3,837	4,993	1,156
			85	1,427	3,810	5,116	1,306

1673030 WINE, GRAPE RED NOV 1 GL OV $4 (GAL)

Country	Mode	Reg	Yr	Quantity	F.A.S.	C.I.F.	Charges
TOTAL			83	13,494,417	135,044,339	149,513,677	14,469,338
			84	16,189,774	173,079,134	192,333,147	19,254,013
			85	15,939,392	197,448,191	220,050,243	22,602,052
			86	15,224,270	210,394,568	230,965,904	20,571,336
ALGERIA	O	E	83	1,522	10,792	12,641	1,849
	V	E	86	713	5,400	6,615	1,215
	V	W	84	832	5,117	6,030	913
			86	266	1,106	1,177	71
ANTIGUA	V	E	85	534	3,750	4,177	427
ARGENT	N	E	83	20,811	117,635	138,334	20,699
			84	15,089	94,586	110,228	15,642
			85	32,667	197,608	228,372	30,764
	O	E	83	3,210	18,070	20,205	2,135
			84	12,744	76,287	86,745	10,458

Crop
Product
TSUSA commodity number, description, and unit of quantity

Country	Mode	Reg	Yr	Quantity	F.A.S.	C.I.F.	Charges
			85	16,415	91,632	104,797	13,165
			86	4,249	26,250	29,343	3,093
	V	E	83	25,656	138,385	163,618	25,233
			84	34,723	247,322	281,496	34,174
			85	26,438	157,721	182,178	24,457
			86	57,825	344,162	399,261	55,099
	V	W	83	4,046	27,053	31,609	4,556
			84	3,292	20,861	23,564	2,703
			85	11,539	68,579	82,784	14,205
			86	9,835	82,011	92,869	10,858
AUSTRAL	A	W	84	2,377	34,734	37,665	2,931
	N	H	86	1,159	18,942	21,514	2,572
	N	W	84	23,504	243,150	265,525	22,375
			85	18,364	168,306	188,799	20,493
			86	28,647	312,681	334,683	22,002
	O	E	83	3,453	27,446	32,660	5,214
			84	1,438	9,953	12,032	2,079
			85	1,722	14,908	16,775	1,867
			86	393	5,998	6,307	309
	O	H	83	107	1,627	1,849	222
			84	414	4,743	5,105	362
	O	W	84	2,998	35,377	38,775	3,398
			85	694	9,536	10,336	800
			86	239	1,858	1,970	112
	V	E	83	16,801	171,782	194,189	22,407
			84	18,556	233,182	260,532	27,350
			85	23,201	251,948	281,978	30,030
			86	53,846	711,042	776,194	65,152
	V	H	83	159	2,879	3,181	302
			84	75	1,017	1,169	152
			85	140	1,319	1,526	207
	V	W	83	32,078	328,729	360,051	31,322
			84	8,511	78,867	88,549	9,682
			85	26,058	232,118	260,586	28,468
			86	25,357	267,033	289,995	22,962
AUSTRIA	A	E	84	476	2,311	2,765	454
	N	E	84	1,080	9,029	10,458	1,429
			86	1,386	22,357	41,016	18,659
	O	E	83	255	2,840	3,076	236
			84	530	2,630	3,153	523
			85	2,752	15,754	19,769	4,015
			86	121	1,712	2,198	486
	O	W	85	666	7,326	8,326	1,000
			86	332	3,671	3,671	
	V	E	83	11,603	91,534	103,478	11,944
			84	15,465	108,285	128,667	20,382
			85	2,674	19,181	21,807	2,626
			86	4,229	34,108	39,543	5,435
	V	H	84	143	1,290	1,537	247
	V	W	83	1,588	9,338	10,295	957
			84	978	7,829	9,029	1,200
			85	2,049	11,568	13,013	1,445
			86	238	2,207	2,321	114
BAHAMAS	V	E	83	2,853	15,459	18,028	2,569
			84	2,484	12,833	15,346	2,513
BELGIUM	A	E	83	3	1,155	1,266	111
			84	476	3,399	7,502	4,103
			85	521	17,249	18,240	991
	N	E	83	3,436	30,737	32,995	2,258
			84	2,396	56,714	59,146	2,432
			85	3,751	63,350	69,804	6,454
			86	1,552	21,002	22,824	1,822
	O	E	83	1,331	12,146	13,486	1,340
			85	2,432	10,803	13,949	3,146
			86	605	5,974	6,632	658
	V	E	83	3,060	20,819	23,784	2,965
			84	3,875	22,221	26,639	4,418
			85	9,126	48,355	59,443	11,088
			86	6,318	45,236	49,916	4,680
	V	W	85	4,368	43,929	47,548	3,619
			86	12,688	298,459	311,112	12,653
BERMUDA	V	E	84	227	1,123	1,396	273
BRAZIL	V	E	85	2,615	20,661	24,791	4,130
			86	5,584	47,300	54,476	7,176
	V	W	85	969	10,022	11,877	1,855
BULGAR	O	E	83	8,321	45,150	51,002	5,852
			84	9,010	46,914	54,951	8,037
			85	5,570	34,113	38,419	4,306
			86	3,053	21,027	22,519	1,492
	V	E	83	11,308	114,698	126,853	12,155
			84	19,495	96,425	115,974	19,549
			85	48,398	286,005	337,553	51,548
			86	25,976	143,146	170,892	27,746
	V	W	83	4,816	21,681	27,460	5,779
			84	2,330	9,849	11,907	2,058
			85	9,189	41,318	52,609	11,291
			86	11,258	48,572	61,002	12,430
BURKINA	V	E	85	2,280	15,092	17,669	2,577
BURMA	O	E	86	665	3,234	4,077	843
	V	E	86	3,232	18,686	21,230	2,544
CANADA	A	E	86	442	3,348	3,962	614
	A	W	85	266	1,859	2,045	186
	O	E	83	9,772	61,165	64,544	3,379
			84	9,209	47,712	49,371	1,659
			85	10,830	63,205	66,066	2,861
			86	760	8,677	8,775	98
	O	W	83	1,751	8,390	8,390	
	V	E	84	95	454	789	335
			85	832	4,733	6,000	1,267
			86	1,179	16,511	22,055	5,544
	V	W	84	1,811	31,199	33,189	1,990
CHILE	A	W	85	238	1,200	5,450	4,250
	N	E	83	36,728	607,058	703,069	96,011
	N	W	83	3,686	32,773	38,329	5,556
	O	E	83	3,196	16,081	18,822	2,741
			84	6,153	39,658	44,493	4,835
			85	4,410	21,926	25,977	4,051
			86	1,330	6,051	7,361	1,310
	O	W	83	238	1,708	2,048	340
			84	1,020	8,260	9,905	1,645
	V	E	83	88,250	806,584	886,984	80,400
			84	122,398	1,048,130	1,166,474	118,344
			85	133,546	1,052,732	1,196,621	143,889
			86	170,451	1,312,415	1,499,463	187,048
	V	W	83	10,027	93,751	107,063	13,312
			84	20,865	174,040	199,451	25,411
			85	16,635	113,028	135,032	22,004
			86	17,455	110,492	131,423	20,931
CHINA M	V	E	83	5,294	33,854	37,186	3,332
			84	1,367	12,866	14,293	1,427
			85	1,188	6,129	8,727	2,598
			86	297	2,063	2,804	741
	V	W	84	711	4,420	5,523	1,103
			85	309	2,210	2,723	513
			86	237	1,720	2,532	812
CHINA T	A	E	86	713	6,333	6,966	633
	V	E	84	1,188	5,816	6,776	960
	V	W	84	149	1,337	1,562	225
			85	370	2,745	3,261	516
COLOMB	O	E	84	506	2,403	2,970	567
COOK IS	O	E	86	594	3,332	4,012	680
CYPRUS	O	E	85	1,011	6,965	8,474	1,509
			86	1,544	7,563	9,412	1,849
	V	E	83	2,139	11,275	13,407	2,132
			84	3,328	18,550	21,498	2,948
			85	1,664	8,400	10,431	2,031
	V	W	84	834	5,933	7,138	1,205
			85	3,329	21,150	23,783	2,633
			86	476	2,910	3,591	681
CZECHO	O	E	86	225	4,943	4,943	
DENMARK	V	E	84	15	488	513	25
	V	W	83	177	3,524	3,713	189
ECUADOR	V	E	83	1,069	10,644	11,608	964
ETHIOP	V	E	86	2,758	12,740	13,240	500
FINLAND	O	E	83	143	3,456	3,660	204
			85	133	1,299	1,403	104
	O	W	85	499	9,069	9,069	
FR GERM	A	E	83	118	1,050	2,372	1,322
			84	7	377	504	127
			85	118	1,118	2,826	1,708
			86	282	3,662	7,328	3,666
	N	E	83	16,437	116,478	130,662	14,184
			84	34,090	219,172	259,696	40,524
			85	32,449	309,482	348,612	39,130
			86	20,321	170,861	199,903	29,042
	N	W	83	19,694	207,808	226,848	19,040
			84	24,438	234,409	257,643	23,234
			85	5,306	46,515	55,088	8,573
	O	E	83	11,405	104,247	115,939	11,692
			84	17,107	117,076	137,164	20,088
			85	35,275	251,741	300,273	48,532
			86	6,766	95,820	109,406	13,586
	O	W	83	54	1,246	1,284	38
			84	471	8,841	10,384	1,543
			85	356	2,520	2,982	462
	V	E	83	126,723	1,030,349	1,166,192	135,843
			84	134,032	1,252,994	1,415,188	162,194
			85	82,065	650,394	762,049	111,655

Crop
Product
TSUSA commodity number, description, and unit of quantity

Country	Mode	Reg	Yr	Quantity	F.A.S.	C.I.F.	Charges
			86	67,964	592,674	678,809	86,135
	V	W	83	7,310	46,317	52,406	6,089
			84	1,191	13,516	15,472	1,956
			85	7,431	83,684	92,760	9,076
			86	6,859	188,200	196,170	7,970
FRANCE	A	E	83	11,751	947,341	1,013,652	66,311
			84	22,627	1,092,970	1,242,923	149,953
			85	15,844	558,686	713,626	154,940
			86	19,160	473,121	594,165	121,044
	A	W	83	1,409	73,639	87,133	13,494
			84	730	32,561	38,944	6,383
			85	499	16,748	24,240	7,492
			86	237	2,591	4,592	2,001
	N	E	83	4,252,140	51,732,836	56,394,910	4,662,074
			84	5,435,999	71,977,152	78,848,230	6,871,078
			85	5,501,870	86,298,736	95,328,226	9,029,490
			86	5,028,825	87,615,620	95,615,077	7,999,457
	N	H	85	1,544	17,052	22,990	5,938
			86	213	3,090	5,504	2,414
	N	W	83	847,260	13,444,925	14,438,086	993,161
			84	1,096,237	17,935,822	19,553,718	1,617,896
			85	1,426,980	27,854,947	30,134,636	2,279,689
			86	1,229,854	28,505,135	30,008,504	1,503,369
	O	E	83	470,738	5,803,339	6,398,399	595,060
			84	407,294	5,074,583	5,608,419	533,836
			85	342,424	5,410,526	5,867,504	456,978
			86	294,596	3,807,208	4,217,588	410,380
	O	W	83	20,259	210,161	227,274	17,113
			84	23,155	302,777	330,706	27,929
			85	9,003	188,037	204,084	16,047
			86	28,387	538,576	565,951	27,375
	V	E	83	826,441	9,031,596	9,910,043	878,447
			84	1,443,546	16,763,501	18,574,054	1,810,553
			85	1,177,552	16,633,665	18,590,818	1,957,153
			86	1,504,293	24,164,628	26,482,697	2,318,069
	V	H	86	529	4,919	5,712	793
	V	W	83	51,287	549,222	601,258	52,036
			84	79,985	869,031	975,115	106,084
			85	69,529	1,094,551	1,200,000	105,449
			86	102,265	1,312,623	1,412,400	99,777
GAMBIA	A	E	84	119	729	1,402	673
GHANA	O	E	85	1,611	18,298	20,142	1,844
GIBRAT	O	E	83	190	1,052	1,200	148
	V	E	83	7,028	66,775	72,595	5,820
			84	296	2,808	3,483	675
	V	W	84	2,175	26,907	27,855	948
GREECE	N	E	83	46,407	233,811	295,121	61,310
			84	415	1,925	2,491	566
			85	3,269	21,126	26,423	5,297
	O	E	83	7,373	36,935	45,901	8,966
			84	9,179	42,738	54,311	11,573
			85	18,634	83,783	110,409	26,626
			86	11,048	54,995	69,535	14,540
	O	W	85	244	1,037	1,231	194
	V	E	83	35,335	186,519	241,445	54,926
			84	70,446	372,135	477,883	105,748
			85	48,086	284,830	357,774	72,944
			86	37,958	209,670	269,353	59,683
	V	W	83	5,592	39,481	46,221	6,740
			84	1,645	7,415	9,349	1,934
			85	7,628	43,446	54,084	10,638
			86	8,046	50,174	60,899	10,725
GUATMAL	V	W	85	237	3,896	4,991	1,095
HAITI	A	E	83	24	360	425	65
HG KONG	A	E	84	14	12,224	12,362	138
	V	E	83	2,652	26,112	28,943	2,831
HUNGARY	A	E	84	2	520	533	13
	N	E	84	1,829	10,714	12,351	1,637
			85	998	5,313	6,317	1,004
			86	17,882	129,831	152,048	22,217
	N	W	86	3,570	21,528	24,614	3,086
	O	E	83	15,074	99,565	114,172	14,607
			84	15,071	85,039	99,538	14,499
			85	6,331	37,695	44,411	6,716
			86	7,201	42,293	43,687	1,394
	V	E	83	42,795	263,103	310,707	47,604
			84	90,637	565,179	658,635	93,456
			85	58,840	373,536	441,105	67,569
			86	24,577	160,573	190,529	29,956
	V	W	83	15,955	101,561	115,277	13,716
			84	18,844	118,146	135,375	17,229
			85	13,432	79,815	93,673	13,858
			86	5,176	35,267	39,434	4,167
IRAN	V	E	86	1,882	16,251	18,972	2,721

Crop
Product
TSUSA commodity number, description, and unit of quantity
Country Mode Reg Yr Quantity F.A.S. C.I.F. Charges

Country	Mode	Reg	Yr	Quantity	F.A.S.	C.I.F.	Charges
IRELAND	V	W	86	178	1,451	1,515	64
	O	W	86	663	2,993	3,723	730
ISRAEL	V	W	85	2,924	40,788	44,153	3,365
	N	E	83	27,340	150,102	183,670	33,568
	O	E	83	50,233	254,311	300,438	46,127
			84	48,433	303,449	368,656	65,207
			85	44,396	229,883	273,570	43,687
			86	5,989	67,570	73,333	5,763
	V	E	83	35,772	180,314	227,638	47,324
			84	60,381	338,246	405,675	67,429
			85	65,597	357,854	426,681	68,827
			86	48,988	319,213	375,218	56,005
	V	W	83	24,904	128,308	157,383	29,075
			84	11,610	63,040	77,968	14,928
			85	14,253	78,155	97,687	19,532
ITALY			86	6,298	37,598	46,103	8,505
	A	E	83	790	11,412	16,877	5,465
			84	187	3,498	5,297	1,799
			85	2,424	27,300	42,466	15,166
	A	W	83	21	540	1,080	540
	N	E	83	2,076,231	15,690,500	17,559,256	1,868,756
			84	2,352,306	20,462,606	22,919,210	2,456,604
			85	2,209,663	19,373,315	22,021,790	2,648,475
			86	2,026,464	19,784,903	22,152,006	2,367,103
	N	W	83	573,151	5,046,036	5,671,823	625,787
			84	396,044	2,777,646	3,186,734	409,088
			85	444,846	3,333,170	3,830,761	497,591
			86	120,539	958,298	1,089,669	131,371
	O	E	83	435,885	2,801,258	3,158,409	357,151
			84	345,126	2,462,395	2,784,775	322,380
			85	310,978	2,297,299	2,587,985	290,686
			86	354,328	3,378,205	3,771,537	393,332
	O	W	83	18,322	1,121,528	1,690,504	568,976
			84	17,397	129,344	153,846	24,502
			85	16,892	185,705	200,516	14,811
			86	20,141	247,994	270,968	22,974
	V	E	83	2,165,489	14,607,207	16,447,825	1,840,618
			84	2,250,137	14,510,171	16,803,342	2,293,171
			85	2,003,823	14,464,064	16,706,166	2,242,102
			86	2,033,905	15,600,920	17,824,804	2,223,884
	V	H	83	1,388	8,266	8,591	325
			85	1,566	7,565	10,317	2,752
			86	1,367	18,425	26,816	8,391
	V	W	83	64,690	637,819	717,196	79,377
			84	324,944	3,077,390	3,425,197	347,807
			85	367,351	3,257,880	3,665,861	407,981
			86	619,255	6,178,788	6,861,809	683,021
JAPAN	A	W	85	237	2,000	9,013	7,013
	O	W	85	748	5,446	6,370	924
	V	E	83	534	3,804	4,391	587
			84	2,068	18,075	21,061	2,986
			85	831	10,183	11,009	826
			86	927	5,956	6,935	979
	V	W	83	1,087	7,784	9,839	2,055
			84	1,367	10,195	11,225	1,030
			85	93	1,984	2,836	852
			86	962	11,462	11,989	527
KIRIBAT	O	E	85	237	1,225	1,522	297
KOR REP	V	E	86	7,306	110,636	119,899	9,263
LEBANON	V	E	84	2,389	50,325	52,746	2,421
			85	3,703	26,559	30,338	3,779
	V	W	86	713	6,642	7,800	1,158
LESOTHO	V	E	84	1,664	12,000	13,339	1,339
MALAYSA	V	W	85	356	1,443	1,834	391
MALI	V	E	86	1,644	24,814	27,549	2,735
MAURIT	O	E	85	199	1,748	1,778	30
	V	E	85	178	37,472	37,472	
MEXICO	N	E	83	546	3,105	3,115	10
	O	E	83	1,378	8,167	9,156	989
			84	7,159	34,727	36,690	1,963
			85	6,127	47,343	48,957	1,614
			86	569	9,533	10,052	519
	O	W	83	2,548	17,324	17,324	
			84	2,019	12,508	12,531	23
			85	1,380	7,910	7,910	
			86	1,213	7,312	7,408	96
	V	E	86	1,069	5,800	6,840	1,040
	V	W	84	1,168	5,900	6,839	939
MOROC	V	E	85	763	7,062	8,248	1,186
			86	951	5,600	6,738	1,138
	V	W	84	1,189	12,000	14,991	2,991
			86	1,379	7,658	12,886	5,228
N ZEAL	O	W	86	119	1,306	1,475	169
	V	E	83	497	4,031	4,746	715

Crop
Product
TSUSA commodity number, description, and unit of quantity

Country	Mode	Reg	Yr	Quantity	F.A.S.	C.I.F.	Charges
			84	123	1,155	1,306	151
			86	133	1,086	1,225	139
	V	W	83	1,075	10,190	11,426	1,236
			84	1,125	12,846	14,504	1,658
			85	4,391	44,929	50,291	5,362
			86	1,630	12,920	15,024	2,104
NAURU	A	W	84	2,347	21,454	46,281	24,827
NETHLDS	A	E	83	974	5,342	6,683	1,341
			85	1,120	11,565	19,138	7,573
	N	E	85	1,874	26,174	32,138	5,964
	N	W	85	5,714	126,996	136,123	9,127
	O	E	84	1,588	14,844	16,965	2,121
			85	498	4,007	4,629	622
			86	2,231	16,924	18,370	1,446
	V	E	83	17,235	140,732	153,933	13,201
			84	18,233	114,186	128,925	14,739
			85	34,191	395,990	447,526	51,536
			86	27,588	463,698	515,045	51,347
	V	W	84	1,817	22,944	24,667	1,723
			85	1,752	18,660	20,998	2,338
			86	7,897	72,716	80,604	7,888
NORWAY	V	W	86	118	2,384	3,080	696
PANAMA	V	E	86	4,095	36,091	40,980	4,889
POLAND	V	E	85	1,421	13,933	15,509	1,576
PORTUGL	A	E	83	767	119,313	122,620	3,307
			84	445	144,964	148,974	4,010
			85	528	100,145	104,179	4,034
			86	1,249	79,437	83,569	4,132
	A	W	84	41	4,089	4,936	847
	N	E	83	14,129	118,797	133,374	14,577
			84	181,154	1,226,982	1,425,527	198,545
			85	101,927	792,855	922,543	129,688
			86	84,740	735,648	848,735	113,087
	N	W	83	35,620	307,103	358,521	51,418
			84	21,260	225,283	258,088	32,805
			85	52,304	478,913	550,430	71,517
			86	6,077	70,293	78,276	7,983
	O	E	83	31,045	182,583	207,580	24,997
			84	20,527	115,335	131,762	16,427
			85	15,721	111,738	126,218	14,480
			86	11,521	89,719	109,730	20,011
	V	E	83	168,118	1,131,153	1,292,108	160,955
			84	127,550	847,058	971,973	124,915
			85	258,949	1,739,049	2,004,725	265,676
			86	177,531	1,567,388	1,787,067	219,679
	V	H	86	119	1,008	1,097	89
	V	W	83	7,048	46,906	59,114	12,208
			84	38,639	256,582	303,943	47,361
			85	9,877	59,509	71,358	11,849
			86	12,743	146,436	162,200	15,764
REP SAF	A	E	86	150	2,546	5,105	2,559
	O	E	83	1,089	10,487	11,724	1,237
			84	1,301	14,145	15,303	1,158
			85	1,477	19,140	21,769	2,629
			86	5,028	49,632	53,991	4,359
	O	W	83	1,575	16,170	18,168	1,998
			84	1,095	10,982	12,362	1,380
	V	E	83	8,712	106,119	115,208	9,089
			84	8,858	82,770	93,732	10,962
			85	4,976	51,716	58,851	7,135
			86	3,692	25,261	29,801	4,540
	V	W	83	4,914	49,351	56,486	7,135
			84	297	2,829	3,234	405
			85	2,115	17,198	20,397	3,199
			86	971	4,672	5,654	982
ROMANIA	N	E	85	12,576	78,511	97,607	19,096
	O	E	84	894	4,512	5,852	1,340
			85	2,169	11,962	13,283	1,321
			86	3,166	27,066	31,084	4,018
	O	W	85	1,902	10,640	13,728	3,088
	V	E	83	28,287	142,766	170,788	28,022
			84	7,668	45,200	62,625	17,425
			85	19,842	115,181	142,552	27,371
			86	29,865	159,123	200,577	41,454
	V	W	86	1,902	10,640	13,708	3,068
SINGAPR	O	E	86	313	1,254	1,354	100
SPAIN	A	E	86	68	4,261	4,454	193
	A	W	84	3	475	510	35
	N	E	83	138,674	1,268,909	1,397,092	128,183
			84	193,805	1,686,848	1,891,535	204,687
			85	159,618	1,494,159	1,695,962	201,803
			86	197,034	2,063,847	2,287,624	223,777
	N	W	83	32,217	291,061	324,437	33,376
			86	39,694	376,421	427,105	50,684

Crop
Product
TSUSA commodity number, description, and unit of quantity

Country	Mode	Reg	Yr	Quantity	F.A.S.	C.I.F.	Charges
	O	E	83	16,793	111,202	128,719	17,517
			84	15,334	112,873	128,220	15,347
			85	28,640	219,153	242,476	23,323
			86	20,057	141,369	163,729	22,360
	O	W	83	2,766	22,754	28,437	5,683
			84	2,527	17,176	18,641	1,465
			85	2,294	22,380	24,888	2,508
			86	3,775	30,031	34,568	4,537
	V	E	83	249,047	2,042,843	2,325,775	282,932
			84	297,443	2,406,932	2,760,820	353,888
			85	236,917	2,017,519	2,329,038	311,519
			86	295,902	3,257,640	3,630,908	373,268
	V	W	83	27,275	313,701	348,805	35,104
			84	67,056	519,495	608,943	89,448
			85	95,923	773,192	899,503	126,311
			86	76,761	653,013	739,479	86,466
SWAZLND	V	E	85	666	10,080	10,357	277
SWEDEN	V	E	84	583	12,236	12,936	700
			85	1,427	8,400	10,115	1,715
			86	93	18,370	20,210	1,840
	V	W	85	1,664	10,347	12,434	2,087
			86	570	4,299	4,964	665
SWITZLD	A	E	83	34	904	1,403	499
			84	16	535	808	273
	N	E	83	4,094	34,870	38,493	3,623
			86	581	16,027	16,960	933
	O	E	83	499	11,304	12,286	982
			85	945	16,238	17,895	1,657
			86	714	12,147	13,425	1,278
	V	E	83	302	7,691	9,126	1,435
			84	5,763	90,687	96,337	5,650
			85	4,571	37,098	39,814	2,716
			86	9,003	77,729	91,872	14,143
	V	H	85	59	1,500	1,718	218
	V	W	83	131	2,834	3,013	179
			84	1,153	19,499	20,009	510
			86	357	6,750	7,333	583
THAILND	V	E	83	1,010	12,404	13,658	1,254
			85	1,968	11,282	13,022	1,740
TRINID	A	E	86	16	1,404	1,683	279
	O	E	86	133	1,557	1,707	150
	V	E	86	776	4,007	4,965	958
TUNISIA	O	E	83	285	2,174	2,568	394
			84	903	5,609	6,944	1,335
			85	594	3,630	4,281	651
	V	E	83	1,242	8,796	10,318	1,522
			84	1,069	6,156	7,353	1,197
			85	237	1,224	1,476	252
			86	237	1,401	1,509	108
TURKEY	V	E	84	1,500	7,322	9,188	1,866
U KING	A	E	83	742	86,287	95,614	9,327
			84	852	169,916	177,978	8,062
			85	685	139,980	147,438	7,458
			86	353	49,601	51,644	2,043
	A	W	83	57	9,269	9,844	575
			85	994	27,997	29,837	1,840
			86	293	114,886	119,389	4,503
	N	E	83	306	58,820	60,588	1,768
			84	895	158,572	164,804	6,232
			85	14,125	459,010	481,728	22,718
			86	957	127,919	135,533	7,614
	N	W	83	3,035	73,102	77,195	4,093
			84	6,613	98,371	104,605	6,234
			85	8,841	193,161	202,102	8,941
			86	1,694	400,193	404,347	4,154
	O	E	83	18,086	144,352	160,046	15,694
			84	5,641	56,557	63,559	7,002
			85	3,806	97,935	108,548	10,613
			86	17,036	143,670	165,187	21,517
	O	W	83	286	6,803	7,058	255
			84	401	3,227	3,602	375
			86	600	11,672	12,103	431
	V	E	83	493	5,857	6,691	834
			84	4,976	43,864	50,674	6,810
			85	15,813	166,593	189,225	22,632
			86	3,255	126,520	131,596	5,076
	V	W	83	16	4,189	4,324	135
			85	1,715	20,340	22,941	2,601
URUGUAY	V	E	85	357	1,470	1,926	456
USSR	O	E	86	698	5,828	7,022	1,194
YUGOSLV	N	E	83	3,137	26,017	30,155	4,138
			84	2,375	12,446	14,978	2,532
			85	3,185	14,865	18,385	3,520
	O	E	83	552	2,796	3,216	420

210　　Table 1.　U.S. Import Statistics for Crop-Specific Commodities by Crop Name

Crop
Product
TSUSA commodity number, description, and unit of quantity

Country	Mode	Reg	Yr	Quantity	F.A.S.	C.I.F.	Charges
			84	1,427	7,163	8,128	965
			85	237	1,200	1,636	436
	O W	83		1,015	8,496	9,566	1,070
	V E	83		27,536	152,199	178,319	26,120
			84	29,420	148,328	178,131	29,803
			85	20,442	133,831	157,220	23,389
			86	28,341	176,855	207,999	31,144
	V W	83		4,065	22,235	26,247	4,012
			84	3,711	22,193	26,147	3,954
			85	833	3,465	3,585	120
			86	1,428	6,550	8,468	1,918

1673040 WINE OV 14%, OV $4, NOV 1GL (GAL)

Country	Mode	Reg	Yr	Quantity	F.A.S.	C.I.F.	Charges
TOTAL			81	48,658,141	408,234,154	455,483,926	47,286,289
			82	51,440,876	432,391,850	483,550,836	51,158,986
ALGERIA	O E	81		594	4,216	4,938	722
	V E	81		2,368	15,088	17,253	2,165
ARGENT	A E	82		67	608	2,863	2,255
	N E	81		67,745	377,485	439,837	62,352
	O E	81		1,170	5,355	6,447	1,092
		82		981	6,179	6,579	400
	V E	81		46,528	305,554	354,891	49,337
		82		105,255	637,400	734,497	97,097
	V W	81		15,726	91,856	106,093	14,237
		82		23,421	154,830	180,089	25,259
AUSTRAL	A W	81		130	1,728	3,649	1,921
		82		200	1,726	3,951	2,225
	N E	81		855	10,486	12,879	2,393
	N H	81		1,135	11,295	12,644	1,349
	N W	81		63,789	634,804	699,464	64,660
		82		65,495	706,037	771,491	65,454
	O E	81		11,718	190,469	212,354	21,885
		82		5,842	50,379	58,831	8,452
	O W	81		6,262	41,050	46,583	5,533
		82		5,028	52,409	55,751	3,342
	V E	81		45,689	458,647	508,994	50,347
		82		33,830	365,056	415,053	49,997
	V H	81		873	7,546	8,759	1,213
		82		251	2,811	3,322	511
	V W	81		19,307	188,176	207,932	19,756
		82		11,651	133,944	144,182	10,238
AUSTRIA	N E	81		3,455	31,682	37,216	5,534
		82		31,680	304,043	338,253	34,210
	O E	81		34,396	262,009	298,731	36,732
		82		15,734	124,456	142,201	17,745
	O W	82		36	345	448	103
	V E	81		168,456	1,314,276	1,497,670	183,394
		82		119,821	876,827	1,008,639	131,812
	V W	81		25,483	272,122	306,680	34,558
		82		16,254	198,912	216,766	17,854
BELGIUM	N E	81		12,960	122,566	135,270	12,704
		82		45,166	388,601	422,676	34,075
	O E	81		2,530	55,919	58,628	2,709
		82		119	869	961	92
	V E	81		27,349	180,245	200,004	19,759
		82		12,670	109,555	120,978	11,423
	V W	81		5,589	55,210	60,747	5,537
		82		498	5,077	5,835	758
BERMUDA	V E	82		2,378	14,600	16,326	1,726
BRAZIL	V E	81		1,248	5,775	7,831	2,056
BULGAR	V E	81		280	7,000	8,313	1,313
		82		9,294	49,193	57,082	7,889
	V W	82		2,080	8,356	9,890	1,534
CANADA	A E	82		47	405	430	25
	A W	81		31	2,100	2,254	154
		82		100	1,576	2,036	460
	N E	81		22,558	153,753	160,177	13,583
		82		1,554	14,084	14,149	65
	O E	81		19,560	114,613	120,785	6,172
		82		12,562	96,847	102,618	5,771
	O W	81		734	4,255	4,255	
		82		530	9,264	9,264	
	V E	81		9,411	48,823	64,163	15,340
CHILE	A E	81		178	960	1,332	372
	N E	82		70,315	533,471	623,251	89,780
	N W	81		10,033	83,696	97,847	14,151
	O E	81		3,992	25,191	29,965	4,774
		82		3,682	23,921	28,395	4,474
	O W	81		1,963	12,902	15,472	2,570
		82		5,921	39,005	46,775	7,770
	V E	81		242,124	1,834,105	2,132,652	298,547
		82		181,890	1,309,157	1,514,265	205,108
	V W	81		5,142	49,491	56,792	7,301
		82		21,547	155,156	182,078	26,922
CHINA M	V E	82		4,683	47,113	54,186	7,073
	V W	81		476	3,558	3,968	410
		82		9,797	112,639	123,469	10,830
CHINA T	O E	81		21	400	502	102
	V E	82		3,424	20,912	23,499	2,587
COLOMB	A E	81		12	407	591	184
	O E	81		119	697	809	112
CYPRUS	O E	81		5,403	27,364	33,670	6,306
		82		2,794	14,533	17,775	3,242
	V E	81		9,017	51,358	62,756	11,398
		82		10,301	49,413	60,384	10,971
	V W	81		60	300	392	92
		82		4,920	27,465	35,793	8,328
CZECHO	V E	82		2,020	16,905	19,405	2,500
DENMARK	V E	81		1,885	14,025	15,804	1,779
ECUADOR	V E	82		4,537	31,945	36,201	4,256
EGYPT	A E	81		29	1,000	1,670	670
		82		59	300	305	5
F W IND	O E	82		7	277	286	9
FR GERM	A E	81		5	870	1,080	210
		82		201	6,017	8,680	2,663
	N E	81		5,569,808	42,276,011	47,592,535	5,328,372
		82		4,749,939	37,764,560	42,399,196	4,634,636
	N W	81		1,528,148	12,244,968	13,708,219	1,463,251
		82		928,149	7,095,299	8,013,174	917,875
	O E	81		1,617,003	11,815,273	13,316,354	1,501,081
		82		1,214,753	8,909,719	10,090,364	1,180,645
	O W	81		85,347	608,524	685,807	77,283
		82		88,215	720,326	796,970	76,644
	V E	81		3,092,373	23,552,257	26,446,109	2,896,902
		82		4,674,985	34,594,161	39,366,925	4,772,764
	V H	82		3,328	20,530	24,999	4,469
	V W	81		780,544	5,722,344	6,465,668	743,324
		82		1,067,849	8,360,822	9,366,218	1,005,396
FRANCE	A E	81		5,119	807,942	846,306	38,364
		82		12,334	1,156,560	1,223,184	66,624
	A W	82		176	20,446	22,516	2,070
	N E	81		7,222,293	89,747,880	97,595,186	7,815,575
		82		9,047,511	101,042,499	111,148,267	10,105,768
	N W	81		1,982,739	29,734,203	32,072,543	2,338,341
		82		1,987,252	29,513,748	31,679,910	2,166,162
	O E	81		1,025,667	13,873,303	14,970,379	1,097,076
		82		1,288,851	15,629,064	17,069,851	1,440,787
	O H	82		476	15,000	15,571	571
	O W	81		32,198	571,815	605,655	33,840
		82		46,368	722,566	772,341	49,775
	V E	81		2,677,335	30,026,247	32,888,304	2,888,774
		82		2,523,254	28,991,611	31,765,803	2,774,192
	V H	82		292	2,454	2,933	479
	V W	81		137,150	1,895,691	2,048,665	152,974
		82		200,203	2,287,521	2,500,147	212,626
G BISAU	V E	81		7,690	52,705	59,914	7,209
	V W	81		33,880	151,288	180,899	29,611
GERM DR	V E	81		10,874	118,807	129,025	10,218
		82		23,072	176,251	198,899	22,648
	V W	82		14,297	149,583	163,159	13,576
GIBRAT	A E	82		1,188	10,438	16,359	5,921
	O E	81		1,198	6,048	7,054	1,006
	V E	81		3,259	25,599	28,114	2,515
		82		4,255	34,182	37,686	3,504
GREECE	N E	82		208,486	1,039,533	1,305,728	266,195
	O E	81		78,092	374,385	445,035	71,556
		82		54,721	271,097	338,905	67,808
	V E	81		312,257	1,553,626	1,943,033	398,675
		82		152,189	777,865	991,440	213,575
	V W	81		15,424	69,793	93,963	24,170
		82		23,656	110,106	140,949	30,843
GUATMAL	O E	82		2,045	59,654	61,164	1,510
HG KONG	V W	81		357	7,473	7,644	171
		82		2,142	23,553	26,570	3,017
HUNGARY	A E	82		18	445	803	358
	N E	81		67,050	410,249	473,217	62,968
		82		30,977	175,157	204,566	29,409
	O E	81		37,427	260,623	298,037	37,414
		82		15,855	119,291	136,172	16,881
	V E	81		73,243	474,249	558,321	84,072
		82		70,135	419,159	497,130	77,971
	V W	81		29,416	201,671	234,801	33,130
		82		24,967	170,012	194,989	24,977
IRELAND	V E	82		15	457	520	63
ISRAEL	N E	81		117,983	663,082	803,168	140,086
	O E	81		95,697	523,866	604,411	80,545
		82		107,307	630,104	731,404	101,300

Crop Product TSUSA commodity number, description, and unit of quantity Country	Mode	Reg	Yr	Quantity	F.A.S.	C.I.F.	Charges
	V	E	81	57,989	316,481	386,959	70,478
			82	120,797	672,154	827,299	155,145
	V	W	81	36,733	199,732	248,075	48,343
			82	24,820	158,147	191,710	33,563
ITALY	A	E	81	158	18,231	19,509	1,278
			82	104	1,427	1,851	424
	A	W	81	127	592	3,540	2,948
	N	E	81	5,418,910	34,917,534	39,574,121	4,653,577
			82	5,601,220	36,218,430	41,030,631	4,812,201
	N	W	81	97,715	648,543	753,548	105,005
			82	293,017	2,190,614	2,481,417	290,803
	O	E	81	1,564,135	9,505,071	10,805,074	1,300,003
			82	1,712,566	11,378,997	12,932,368	1,553,371
	O	W	81	76,225	454,525	516,340	61,815
			82	57,002	381,826	437,180	55,354
	V	E	81	6,456,297	39,281,310	44,742,311	5,461,401
			82	7,386,403	47,260,090	53,666,280	6,406,190
	V	W	81	977,241	6,815,384	7,929,783	1,114,399
			82	1,120,611	7,958,272	9,143,245	1,184,973
JAMAICA	O	E	81	264	1,172	1,519	347
JAPAN	V	E	81	475	3,200	4,030	830
	O	E	82	72	971	1,073	102
	V	E	81	6,420	42,917	48,048	5,131
			82	1,818	13,513	15,946	2,433
	V	W	81	5,865	34,319	43,588	9,269
			82	7,015	42,169	55,068	12,899
LEBANON	A	E	81	28	316	920	604
	O	E	81	1,106	15,110	16,796	1,686
	V	E	81	9,219	137,950	147,667	9,717
			82	2,259	37,457	38,313	856
MALAYSA	O	E	82	59	355	414	59
	V	E	81	1,189	6,000	7,317	1,317
MEXICO	O	E	81	3,851	27,060	28,064	1,004
			82	12,486	79,290	85,836	6,546
	O	W	81	1,545	10,360	10,360	
			82	6,642	38,438	38,438	
	V	E	81	6,420	43,048	44,798	1,750
			82	3,200	22,585	24,929	2,344
MOROC	A	E	82	28	500	780	280
	V	E	82	5,943	25,594	31,451	5,857
	V	W	82	1,189	10,300	14,085	3,785
N ZEAL	N	W	81	11,579	103,535	119,081	15,546
			82	10,700	92,306	105,252	12,946
	V	E	81	2,375	22,977	26,624	3,647
			82	2,767	19,469	23,522	4,053
	V	H	81	418	2,757	3,467	710
			82	534	3,669	4,569	900
	V	W	81	4,154	161,281	167,114	5,833
			82	5,690	55,363	60,687	5,324
NETHLDS	O	E	81	4,799	57,097	63,027	5,930
			82	8,236	64,558	72,396	7,838
	O	W	82	332	6,259	6,532	273
	V	E	81	76,695	590,469	681,709	91,240
			82	144,633	1,144,485	1,280,275	135,790
	V	W	81	45,754	426,813	475,635	48,822
			82	7,807	60,298	68,974	8,676
NORFOLK	V	E	81	756	13,291	14,374	1,083
			82	737	3,483	4,105	622
NORWAY	O	W	81	26	629	666	37
PORTUGL	A	E	81	277	7,403	9,843	2,440
			82	530	76,905	80,683	3,778
	N	E	81	1,384,180	8,437,174	9,562,661	1,125,487
			82	1,083,147	6,873,010	7,683,299	810,289
	N	W	81	515,775	2,844,468	3,341,414	496,946
			82	530,220	3,235,431	3,826,572	591,141
	O	E	81	503,510	2,966,234	3,353,331	387,097
			82	491,320	3,211,419	3,601,991	390,572
	O	W	81	74,905	456,750	531,427	74,677
			82	20,658	128,404	144,873	16,469
	V	E	81	2,115,066	12,448,456	14,462,369	2,016,573
			82	1,961,161	11,809,074	13,647,304	1,838,230
	V	W	81	383,648	2,418,260	2,808,680	390,420
			82	85,113	547,874	657,910	110,036
REP SAF	A	E	81	71	390	3,982	3,592
			82	2	437	535	98
	N	E	81	1,783	17,224	19,599	2,375
	O	E	81	1,855	18,474	20,728	2,254
			82	2,391	22,000	24,453	2,453
	V	E	81	31,254	260,074	298,653	38,579
			82	96,012	912,851	1,018,661	105,810
	V	W	81	454	21,877	26,060	4,183
			82	14,550	144,669	165,887	21,218
ROMANIA	O	E	82	9,007	45,456	58,998	13,542
	V	E	81	77,743	373,148	467,991	104,082

Crop Product TSUSA commodity number, description, and unit of quantity Country	Mode	Reg	Yr	Quantity	F.A.S.	C.I.F.	Charges
			82	81,714	422,411	545,912	123,501
	V	W	82	2,615	13,200	17,755	4,555
SENEGAL	V	W	81	773	4,869	5,717	848
SINGAPR	V	E	81	2,158	11,065	12,980	1,915
SPAIN	A	E	82	26	789	834	45
	N	E	81	442,616	3,402,839	3,865,871	463,032
			82	292,876	2,356,416	2,651,005	294,589
	O	E	81	67,532	538,904	606,567	67,663
			82	41,914	310,262	351,016	40,754
	O	W	81	457	3,565	4,085	520
			82	1,013	15,349	17,090	1,741
	V	E	81	436,290	3,141,728	3,636,634	494,906
			82	532,894	4,089,077	4,692,543	603,466
	V	W	81	66,197	580,485	664,417	83,932
			82	108,089	871,314	987,175	115,861
SWEDEN	O	W	82	1,249	10,100	10,888	788
SWITZLD	A	E	81	846	12,989	16,338	3,349
			82	249	4,877	6,494	1,617
	N	E	81	4,842	82,919	89,353	6,434
			82	7,048	93,146	104,356	11,210
	O	E	81	238	5,153	5,459	306
			82	1,423	33,102	36,256	3,154
	V	E	81	6,436	70,290	76,635	6,345
			82	2,866	20,683	22,863	2,180
	V	W	81	1,427	27,783	29,315	1,532
			82	4,377	84,032	88,422	4,390
TUNISIA	V	E	81	266	1,497	1,787	290
TURKEY	V	E	82	1,308	15,580	16,987	1,407
U KING	A	E	81	1,247	192,927	201,876	8,949
			82	1,291	189,017	200,600	11,583
	A	W	81	148	35,320	36,791	1,471
			82	1,179	201,537	211,262	9,725
	N	E	81	3,690	95,896	102,697	6,801
			82	4,893	212,599	225,836	13,237
	O	E	81	10,196	175,008	187,824	12,816
			82	21,197	284,617	303,298	18,681
	O	W	81	1,046	58,488	60,422	1,934
			82	1,546	12,102	13,388	1,286
	V	E	81	39,334	320,656	346,883	26,227
			82	34,388	232,492	260,456	27,964
	V	W	81	272	90,386	93,045	2,659
			82	34	874	977	103
USSR	V	E	81	3,091	22,367	24,424	2,057
YUGOSLV	A	E	82	72	386	1,679	1,293
	N	E	81	15,666	85,131	104,117	18,986
	O	E	81	8,084	51,104	57,837	6,733
			82	6,035	44,587	59,371	14,784
	O	W	81	166	1,039	1,251	212
	V	E	81	44,874	223,563	268,283	44,720
			82	35,497	179,459	210,572	31,113
	V	W	81	4,198	23,744	27,791	4,047
			82	3,486	25,356	28,905	3,549

1673045 WINE, GRAPE WHITE NOV 1GL OV $4 (GAL)

Country	Mode	Reg	Yr	Quantity	F.A.S.	C.I.F.	Charges
TOTAL			83	30,204,922	244,899,254	272,649,707	27,750,453
			84	31,933,748	266,193,022	299,525,447	33,332,425
			85	32,941,229	291,983,957	331,741,227	39,757,270
			86	34,468,691	336,120,075	375,868,514	39,748,439
ALGERIA	O	E	85	6,186	27,048	31,247	4,199
	V	E	86	238	1,800	2,205	405
ARGENT	O	E	83	2,854	14,860	16,400	1,540
			84	7,013	44,253	49,271	5,018
			85	4,333	24,258	27,444	3,186
			86	2,160	17,337	19,080	1,743
	V	E	83	29,352	154,968	181,904	26,936
			84	21,848	133,967	161,652	27,685
			85	43,102	254,154	299,525	45,371
			86	29,310	187,256	220,433	33,177
	V	W	83	2,448	15,447	17,644	2,197
			84	1,271	7,655	8,552	897
			85	6,920	43,387	51,520	8,133
			86	6,666	56,854	63,875	7,021
AUSTRAL	A	E	85	892	4,055	4,797	742
	A	W	83	49	1,008	1,729	721
			84	1,031	24,695	25,713	1,018
			85	118	1,176	2,390	1,214
	N	W	84	5,830	65,089	72,071	6,982
			85	1,072	10,906	14,994	4,088
	O	E	84	1,260	11,715	12,994	1,279
			84	1,908	26,701	29,359	2,658
			85	1,579	19,893	21,730	1,837
			86	1,789	39,285	40,242	957
	O	H	83	178	1,909	2,168	259

Crop
Product
TSUSA commodity number, description, and unit of quantity

Country	Mode	Reg	Yr	Quantity	F.A.S.	C.I.F.	Charges
			84	500	5,413	5,905	492
	O	W	84	6,456	45,085	50,323	5,238
			85	1,711	13,434	14,561	1,127
			86	239	1,858	1,970	112
	V	E	83	23,121	201,637	233,247	31,610
			84	17,227	210,865	237,514	26,649
			85	32,989	433,890	476,766	42,876
			86	77,494	898,333	983,019	84,686
	V	H	83	2,404	27,220	30,293	3,073
			84	531	7,942	8,994	1,052
			85	166	1,309	1,514	205
			86	1,824	14,404	16,524	2,120
	V	W	83	50,365	503,060	551,371	48,311
			84	51,042	527,016	569,317	42,301
			85	69,318	676,344	743,455	67,111
			86	145,867	1,397,657	1,502,376	104,719
AUSTRIA	A	E	83	58	1,763	2,261	498
			84	1,436	12,094	13,465	1,371
	N	E	83	24,260	448,641	477,126	28,485
			84	24,053	205,614	237,086	31,472
	O	E	83	6,756	55,613	66,268	10,655
			84	4,482	31,270	37,043	5,773
			85	17,878	141,035	159,143	18,108
			86	3,492	22,363	26,399	4,036
	O	W	84	106	1,897	1,934	37
			85	1,577	18,328	20,084	1,756
			86	2,413	35,111	37,242	2,131
	V	E	83	59,771	461,525	525,807	64,282
			84	75,549	626,147	710,954	84,807
			85	43,836	540,037	601,137	61,100
			86	15,182	126,716	149,203	22,487
	V	H	84	119	1,075	1,281	206
	V	W	83	7,252	61,717	67,749	6,032
			84	6,641	73,269	84,252	10,983
			85	8,084	91,336	100,776	9,440
			86	1,069	9,807	10,810	1,003
BAHAMAS	V	E	83	8,012	43,984	51,621	7,637
			84	476	2,419	2,893	474
BELGIUM	A	E	84	122	1,459	1,777	318
	N	E	83	19,114	141,445	156,347	14,902
			85	46,373	347,088	396,643	49,555
			86	3,518	42,844	48,665	5,821
	O	E	83	11,149	68,818	78,536	9,718
			84	910	5,727	6,092	365
			85	21,637	143,754	171,624	27,870
			86	9,082	82,104	92,133	10,029
	V	E	83	17,402	122,452	134,410	11,958
			84	40,179	298,653	340,791	42,138
			85	134,340	1,151,958	1,325,965	174,007
			86	50,695	715,642	787,412	71,770
	V	W	83	950	12,598	13,956	1,358
			84	1,140	4,964	5,574	610
			85	11,805	69,798	86,543	16,745
			86	21,244	197,211	223,066	25,855
BERMUDA	V	E	85	9,510	83,247	89,968	6,721
BRAZIL	O	E	85	1,806	10,564	12,296	1,732
			86	523	3,058	3,058	
	V	E	85	4,910	42,782	49,274	6,492
			86	18,182	167,208	183,043	15,835
	V	W	85	396	3,001	3,586	585
BULGAR	O	E	83	1,884	9,011	11,168	2,157
			84	5,793	30,045	34,673	4,628
			85	5,746	32,301	35,948	3,647
			86	1,569	14,216	15,636	1,420
	O	H	86	237	1,005	1,222	217
	V	E	83	11,054	61,534	73,324	11,790
			84	23,813	128,663	155,905	27,242
			85	40,172	250,629	290,985	40,356
			86	39,905	261,390	300,429	39,039
	V	W	83	3,044	13,567	17,484	3,917
			85	6,036	27,376	33,508	6,132
			86	8,376	38,291	47,651	9,360
BURMA	O	E	86	1,117	5,275	6,690	1,415
	V	E	85	6,880	32,558	36,833	4,275
			86	5,122	29,561	32,831	3,270
CANADA	N	E	84	11,214	63,629	63,634	5
			85	5,069	30,875	32,920	2,045
			86	3,899	30,042	34,546	4,504
	O	E	83	13,798	83,155	94,296	11,141
			84	4,884	32,045	32,502	457
			85	4,774	37,236	39,798	2,562
			86	7,718	58,624	62,704	4,080
	O	W	83	3,574	20,354	20,354	
			84	2,958	26,887	28,610	1,723
			85	2,929	26,488	26,488	
	V	E	84	95	438	761	323
			85	462	3,560	4,112	552
CHILE	N	E	83	71,020	490,438	549,269	58,831
	N	W	83	3,674	29,483	33,934	4,451
	O	E	83	1,492	7,773	9,004	1,231
			84	3,578	22,054	25,137	3,083
			85	3,907	17,745	20,767	3,022
			86	4,099	17,736	21,750	4,014
	O	W	83	952	5,768	6,649	881
			84	2,045	13,692	16,465	2,773
	V	E	83	73,133	682,007	748,136	66,129
			84	100,460	806,382	897,424	91,042
			85	108,171	787,098	896,431	109,333
			86	133,422	983,043	1,126,102	143,059
	V	W	83	10,718	92,429	105,044	12,615
			84	11,621	79,646	93,838	14,192
			85	16,289	117,619	137,673	20,054
			86	17,571	101,102	121,377	20,275
CHINA M	A	E	83	24	512	1,675	1,163
	O	E	84	7,725	71,059	80,726	9,667
			85	5,348	46,615	53,729	7,114
	O	H	84	497	5,211	6,353	1,142
	V	E	83	9,764	83,013	97,667	14,654
			84	1,010	6,805	7,560	755
			85	6,989	37,480	50,174	12,694
			86	20,103	189,496	215,467	25,971
	V	W	83	595	5,186	5,413	227
			84	4,754	49,700	55,376	5,676
			85	11,886	136,925	155,831	18,906
			86	15,203	136,864	162,986	26,122
CHINA T	O	E	85	1,188	7,500	9,000	1,500
	V	E	84	1,664	8,813	10,269	1,456
	V	W	84	2,370	14,801	17,851	3,050
			85	1,169	5,708	6,781	1,073
COOK IS	O	E	86	1,169	10,570	11,041	471
CYPRUS	O	E	85	1,549	8,546	10,459	1,913
			86	3,208	15,547	19,428	3,881
	V	E	83	4,279	18,000	21,858	3,858
			84	2,495	10,500	12,172	1,672
			85	1,901	11,250	13,563	2,313
	V	W	83	237	1,300	1,808	508
			84	2,077	11,446	13,813	2,367
			85	3,231	16,748	19,676	2,928
			86	1,545	8,750	10,797	2,047
CZECHO	O	E	86	344	3,352	3,352	
DENMARK	O	W	86	4,593	48,242	51,848	3,606
	V	E	83	6,142	81,799	87,338	5,539
			84	3,143	13,617	16,467	2,850
	V	W	83	2,615	15,246	17,295	2,049
			85	10,460	46,700	55,440	8,740
DOMINCA	O	E	85	2,544	18,927	21,859	2,932
	V	E	85	25,890	199,670	228,566	28,896
			86	4,980	47,630	53,706	6,076
ECUADOR	V	E	84	1,545	15,577	16,988	1,411
ETHIOP	V	E	86	2,948	12,466	12,966	500
F W IND	V	E	85	60	4,941	4,971	30
FINLAND	O	W	85	119	2,474	2,474	
FR GERM	A	E	83	529	8,689	9,893	1,204
			84	180	3,046	4,322	1,276
			85	216	4,859	7,054	2,195
			86	363	6,674	14,685	8,011
	A	W	84	1	257	276	19
	N	E	83	4,287,966	33,088,936	36,959,615	3,870,679
			84	4,701,186	35,671,994	40,559,935	4,887,941
			85	4,785,687	35,334,309	40,885,923	5,551,614
			86	2,284,743	21,526,114	24,113,858	2,587,744
	N	W	83	1,304,451	9,836,963	10,852,817	1,015,854
			84	1,355,814	10,344,962	11,513,595	1,168,633
			85	1,359,075	11,189,609	12,648,922	1,459,313
			86	381,889	3,458,604	3,760,713	302,109
	O	E	83	845,723	6,213,972	6,925,801	711,829
			84	632,771	4,741,258	5,365,116	623,858
			85	473,001	3,606,439	4,150,847	544,408
			86	531,724	4,708,296	5,298,729	590,433
	O	H	83	2,425	37,260	39,269	2,009
	O	W	83	126,478	915,632	1,002,320	86,688
			84	56,247	485,307	530,008	44,701
			85	47,295	319,645	357,759	38,114
			86	25,922	258,672	285,414	26,742
	V	E	83	4,331,048	32,417,945	36,468,793	4,050,848
			84	3,910,848	28,740,714	32,955,713	4,214,999
			85	4,232,476	30,422,842	35,800,898	5,378,056
			86	4,638,017	40,746,677	46,466,566	5,719,889

Crop
Product
TSUSA commodity number, description, and unit of quantity

Country	Mode	Reg	Yr	Quantity	F.A.S.	C.I.F.	Charges
	V	H	83	1,767	23,433	25,604	2,171
			85	821	16,540	18,146	1,606
	V	W	83	470,488	3,227,101	3,647,765	420,664
			84	423,448	3,266,616	3,674,265	407,649
			85	541,694	3,883,602	4,549,551	665,949
			86	1,026,567	9,742,418	10,611,201	868,783
FRANCE	A	E	83	2,138	185,794	200,951	15,157
			84	1,727	134,274	142,295	8,021
			85	2,240	109,995	118,356	8,361
			86	1,055	49,737	57,281	7,544
	A	W	83	267	8,367	12,787	4,420
			84	22	2,126	2,289	163
	N	E	83	5,067,885	53,556,590	58,572,889	5,016,299
			84	5,841,465	63,995,540	70,707,225	6,711,685
			85	5,616,074	71,140,369	78,787,033	7,646,664
			86	6,713,991	89,310,184	98,019,722	8,709,538
	N	W	83	1,379,792	14,822,091	16,141,604	1,319,513
			84	1,608,708	17,879,567	19,563,770	1,684,203
			85	1,904,430	22,177,774	24,645,806	2,468,032
			86	1,968,568	28,468,817	30,235,728	1,766,911
	O	E	83	700,295	7,803,851	8,543,162	739,311
			84	575,796	6,531,912	7,165,566	633,654
			85	570,789	6,969,796	7,711,724	741,928
			86	592,396	6,791,495	7,527,606	736,111
	O	W	83	24,399	285,616	307,034	21,418
			84	31,797	267,619	299,746	32,127
			85	32,678	640,396	679,604	39,208
			86	19,904	295,602	315,495	19,893
	V	E	83	1,752,777	16,722,355	18,528,393	1,806,038
			84	2,015,732	20,756,298	23,112,144	2,355,846
			85	2,141,400	23,609,496	26,683,954	3,074,458
			86	3,369,720	36,499,431	41,154,571	4,655,140
	V	H	85	868	13,522	15,500	1,978
			86	1,490	31,023	36,252	5,229
	V	W	83	114,426	1,201,262	1,357,571	156,309
			84	143,717	1,546,699	1,731,970	185,271
			85	131,789	1,686,765	1,896,423	209,658
			86	230,092	2,627,174	2,851,837	224,663
GERM DR	O	E	83	2,053	15,556	16,762	1,206
			85	41,959	249,322	293,987	44,665
			86	309	6,139	6,416	277
	V	E	83	13,384	102,863	114,493	11,630
			84	7,599	54,740	62,140	7,400
			85	211	5,198	5,305	107
			86	1,664	8,838	11,216	2,378
	V	W	84	2,142	9,366	11,117	1,751
			85	11,487	68,867	76,018	7,151
GHANA	O	E	85	166	3,036	3,281	245
			86	424	4,000	4,414	414
GIBRAT	O	E	84	11,258	52,940	62,654	9,714
	V	E	83	1,888	21,346	22,798	1,452
			84	891	6,490	7,796	1,306
	V	W	84	1,069	10,323	10,783	460
GREECE	N	E	83	101,947	504,117	637,459	133,342
			84	2,972	14,100	18,173	4,073
			85	7,935	45,357	56,557	11,200
			86	1,653	8,224	9,500	1,276
	O	E	83	18,776	86,577	110,281	23,704
			84	20,335	105,778	128,204	22,426
			85	15,219	68,588	87,584	18,996
			86	29,825	157,916	193,173	35,257
	V	E	83	72,092	354,084	449,182	95,098
			84	110,780	580,771	723,109	142,338
			85	70,887	372,903	472,351	99,448
			86	70,005	399,480	497,412	97,932
	V	W	83	14,081	78,749	95,037	16,288
			84	2,613	10,947	14,333	3,386
			85	7,570	43,933	52,923	8,990
			86	21,630	179,172	201,123	21,951
HG KONG	V	E	83	860	13,847	15,167	1,320
	V	W	83	3,329	18,256	20,401	2,145
			85	3,088	17,461	20,660	3,199
			86	1,331	9,010	10,704	1,694
HUNGARY	A	E	84	52	303	731	428
	N	E	84	1,782	12,427	14,737	2,310
			85	9,677	64,814	75,890	11,076
			86	9,794	83,986	95,641	11,655
	O	E	83	10,355	108,640	125,807	17,167
			84	10,653	82,606	95,607	13,001
			85	2,819	17,651	21,185	3,534
			86	1,288	8,744	9,897	1,153
	V	E	83	33,787	240,477	281,137	40,660
			84	52,872	342,931	399,152	56,221
			85	19,517	186,178	211,440	25,262
			86	16,060	111,854	130,165	18,311
	V	W	83	7,916	53,879	62,572	8,693
			84	16,062	117,139	131,631	14,492
			85	15,820	101,377	122,632	21,255
			86	12,673	81,842	95,193	13,351
ICELAND	V	E	85	1,902	13,968	16,068	2,100
	V	W	86	1,486	7,955	9,849	1,894
IRAN	V	E	85	531	2,920	3,533	613
			86	2,496	15,120	18,638	3,518
	V	W	86	238	2,554	2,667	113
IRELAND	O	E	85	2,540	28,318	30,567	2,249
	O	W	86	2,128	9,576	11,912	2,336
	V	W	85	3,985	64,954	69,438	4,484
ISRAEL	N	E	83	26,020	177,224	214,973	37,749
			84	36,285	228,493	269,757	41,264
			86	49,959	359,868	419,242	59,374
	O	E	83	36,350	267,433	301,753	34,320
			84	40,472	263,223	299,683	36,460
			85	32,676	213,007	241,989	28,982
			86	12,146	67,818	79,162	11,344
	V	E	83	27,648	178,514	221,354	42,840
			84	19,228	129,790	158,945	29,155
			85	77,631	564,425	655,393	90,968
			86	44,725	313,566	369,327	55,761
	V	W	83	14,395	79,440	96,518	17,078
			84	11,859	83,917	102,954	19,037
			85	14,471	90,150	112,017	21,867
			86	10,732	76,878	91,084	14,206
ITALY	A	E	83	33	335	460	125
			84	299	1,887	2,228	341
			85	238	1,280	3,009	1,729
	A	W	85	2,020	10,466	11,231	765
	N	E	83	3,313,418	21,853,037	24,574,538	2,721,501
			84	2,792,933	18,686,844	21,375,562	2,688,718
			85	3,668,088	25,038,645	29,024,467	3,985,822
			86	3,799,518	27,509,751	31,474,058	3,964,307
	N	W	83	330,460	2,260,687	2,568,788	308,101
			84	295,780	1,924,286	2,212,190	287,904
			85	114,540	692,766	808,492	115,726
			86	135,307	807,980	945,923	137,943
	O	E	83	761,664	4,116,368	4,728,008	611,640
			84	896,337	8,230,213	9,038,459	808,246
			85	824,805	6,442,112	7,243,658	801,546
			86	1,048,740	7,355,233	8,392,138	1,036,905
	O	W	83	27,963	207,908	224,249	16,341
			84	16,481	127,777	143,672	15,895
			85	13,892	131,969	148,479	16,510
			86	20,569	164,638	194,724	30,086
	V	E	83	2,851,841	17,720,689	20,046,130	2,325,441
			84	3,877,545	23,974,835	27,605,905	3,631,070
			85	3,065,734	23,354,506	26,429,593	3,075,087
			86	4,283,533	29,314,587	33,890,159	4,575,572
	V	H	83	428	2,464	2,547	83
			84	178	1,119	1,750	631
			85	209	6,234	10,481	4,247
			86	1,932	9,125	13,310	4,185
	V	W	83	317,351	2,492,176	2,814,797	322,621
			84	316,393	2,380,140	2,693,268	313,128
			85	649,321	4,490,828	5,192,445	701,617
			86	674,813	5,224,372	5,911,842	687,470
IVY CST	O	E	85	713	3,000	3,699	699
JAMAICA	V	E	85	3,566	24,371	28,878	4,507
JAPAN	A	E	84	17	302	503	201
	O	W	85	1,379	11,534	11,729	195
	V	E	83	1,545	9,876	11,614	1,738
			85	4,229	23,390	27,723	4,333
			86	2,096	13,615	15,942	2,327
	V	W	83	136	1,638	1,807	169
			85	2,377	10,750	13,047	2,297
KIRIBAT	O	E	85	237	1,225	1,522	297
KOR REP	V	E	84	1,426	10,400	12,154	1,754
			86	8,421	114,263	124,801	10,538
LEBANON	V	E	85	1,313	8,994	10,273	1,279
	V	W	86	987	6,040	7,093	1,053
LESOTHO	V	E	84	951	7,000	7,766	766
MALI	V	E	86	1,069	22,539	25,024	2,485
MALTA	V	E	84	832	5,023	6,002	979
MAURIT	O	E	85	684	5,668	5,789	121
	O	W	84	71	299	359	60
	V	E	86	1,534	27,918	29,096	1,178
MAURITN	V	E	84	464	1,873	2,275	402
MEXICO	N	E	83	784	4,455	4,465	10
	O	E	83	2,350	13,392	14,761	1,369
			84	11,676	57,162	62,731	5,569

Crop
Product
TSUSA commodity number, description, and unit of quantity

Country	Mode	Reg	Yr	Quantity	F.A.S.	C.I.F.	Charges
			85	4,489	30,120	30,868	748
			86	118	2,043	2,276	233
	O	W	83	3,592	21,920	21,920	
			84	2,434	13,615	13,615	
			85	1,452	7,825	7,825	
			86	843	6,065	6,065	
	V	E	86	1,307	6,650	7,842	1,192
	V	W	84	1,999	10,550	12,293	1,743
MONGOLA	O	E	86	1,578	8,347	10,147	1,800
MOROC	V	E	85	1,043	18,325	22,053	3,728
			86	2,496	12,377	14,885	2,508
N ANTIL	V	E	86	184	4,149	4,251	102
N ZEAL	O	E	85	411	3,000	3,397	397
			86	1,095	6,375	6,885	510
	O	W	84	628	6,585	7,522	937
			85	7,504	77,007	87,173	10,166
			86	7,287	71,200	80,521	9,321
	V	E	83	2,987	26,569	31,073	4,504
			84	1,541	15,860	19,230	3,370
			85	2,519	22,248	29,525	7,277
			86	2,217	19,848	22,979	3,131
	V	H	86	237	3,759	4,509	750
	V	W	83	12,601	305,286	319,514	14,228
			84	14,161	139,147	157,779	18,632
			85	18,896	169,977	194,691	24,714
			86	10,139	94,687	108,789	14,102
NETHLDS	N	E	83	5,230	29,618	36,649	7,031
			86	144	2,571	2,897	326
	N	W	85	5,605	41,104	46,574	5,470
	O	E	83	83	728	786	58
			84	3,187	40,509	45,279	4,770
			85	6,953	74,322	82,683	8,361
			86	15,913	113,423	132,777	19,354
	O	W	85	1,188	12,699	14,360	1,661
	V	E	83	87,184	596,597	673,147	76,550
			84	49,227	383,683	431,780	48,097
			85	136,210	1,146,199	1,310,037	163,838
			86	74,730	743,669	844,228	100,559
	V	W	83	2,642	19,027	23,071	4,044
			84	7,809	59,048	64,765	5,717
			85	6,251	52,539	62,048	9,509
			86	15,226	125,365	153,405	28,040
PANAMA	V	E	86	7,059	89,249	97,840	8,591
PERU	V	E	85	794	4,585	5,924	1,339
			86	8,440	49,211	58,016	8,805
POLAND	V	E	85	1,137	11,101	11,361	260
	V	W	85	688	6,916	7,680	764
PORTUGL	A	E	83	73	6,903	7,349	446
			84	182	26,790	28,498	1,708
	N	E	83	15,295	104,178	116,737	12,559
			84	372,409	2,141,466	2,506,182	364,716
			85	231,872	1,558,123	1,805,066	246,943
	N	W	83	54,290	336,846	387,670	50,824
			84	142,246	795,177	966,028	170,851
			85	4,826	30,818	36,536	5,718
	O	E	83	93,197	638,897	715,013	76,116
			84	78,913	482,185	555,904	73,719
			85	98,449	828,058	927,130	99,072
			86	71,115	550,138	630,130	79,992
	O	W	83	9,284	55,886	63,050	7,164
			85	4,515	47,044	52,223	5,179
			86	475	2,740	3,282	542
	V	E	83	455,976	3,026,283	3,454,225	427,942
			84	348,873	2,258,761	2,684,210	425,449
			85	395,609	2,873,626	3,367,801	494,175
			86	856,057	6,271,511	7,264,578	993,067
	V	H	86	1,617	14,488	15,766	1,278
	V	W	83	51,810	383,816	425,936	42,120
			84	23,780	150,048	177,742	27,694
			85	223,222	1,482,222	1,768,285	286,063
			86	91,785	532,524	628,556	96,032
REP SAF	A	E	83	38	311	1,057	746
			84	33	560	1,007	447
	O	E	83	1,654	14,181	15,936	1,755
			84	902	8,108	8,902	794
			85	1,379	12,073	13,437	1,364
			86	1,917	17,227	17,327	100
	O	W	83	2,460	20,902	23,354	2,452
			84	2,219	17,844	19,917	2,073
			85	416	3,634	4,056	422
	V	E	83	66,268	569,375	634,260	64,885
			84	14,986	120,924	142,939	22,015
			85	12,082	106,860	122,372	15,512
			86	1,062	7,276	8,557	1,281
	V	W	83	5,451	46,372	53,259	6,887
			84	727	6,041	7,200	1,159
			85	4,377	34,804	40,688	5,884
			86	777	3,835	4,641	806
ROMANIA	N	E	85	4,778	26,658	33,535	6,877
			86	1,046	6,029	6,653	624
	O	E	84	119	600	778	178
			85	6,488	38,979	46,230	7,251
			86	5,007	64,363	71,442	7,079
	O	W	85	951	5,320	6,864	1,544
	V	E	83	7,752	39,149	47,451	8,302
			84	28,143	169,292	195,549	26,257
			85	13,151	71,058	89,859	18,801
			86	30,003	212,350	257,996	45,646
	V	W	85	3,218	18,614	22,354	3,740
			86	5,224	40,466	49,264	8,798
SPAIN	N	E	83	2,910	26,306	29,640	3,334
			84	2,122	15,750	17,892	2,142
			85	92,350	620,775	718,767	97,992
			86	8,498	61,600	71,367	9,767
	N	W	83	1,235	10,555	12,007	1,452
			84	28,007	172,323	199,092	26,769
			86	21,752	133,323	153,758	20,435
	O	E	83	11,505	74,825	88,412	13,587
			84	19,409	125,225	141,881	16,656
			85	16,976	117,276	133,980	16,704
			86	15,700	102,650	116,341	13,691
	O	W	83	1,711	17,122	20,051	2,929
			84	3,185	16,380	18,819	2,439
			85	1,189	9,075	10,357	1,282
			86	1,069	6,755	7,676	921
	V	E	83	260,986	1,819,498	2,072,158	252,660
			84	338,611	2,289,728	2,636,371	346,643
			85	174,342	1,181,981	1,389,589	207,608
			86	301,051	2,039,909	2,375,264	335,355
	V	W	83	34,580	239,505	274,032	34,527
			84	29,826	214,224	249,390	35,166
			85	71,514	453,426	525,972	72,546
			86	51,738	291,794	345,303	53,509
SWAZLND	V	E	85	2,011	26,460	27,187	727
SWEDEN	O	E	86	739	7,004	8,240	1,236
	V	E	84	1,815	38,125	39,423	1,298
			86	2,835	12,222	14,636	2,414
	V	W	85	1,105	4,557	5,476	919
			86	1,307	17,853	19,069	1,216
SWITZLD	A	E	85	71	1,023	1,746	723
			86	166	3,161	3,323	162
	N	E	83	15,185	113,572	126,868	13,296
	N	W	84	380	5,898	6,411	513
	O	E	83	3,101	74,140	80,882	6,742
			84	22,222	145,410	164,904	19,494
			85	4,940	135,162	146,512	11,350
			86	20,354	187,968	206,512	18,544
	V	E	83	2,306	24,004	26,704	2,700
			84	10,826	165,721	179,507	13,786
			85	11,958	119,057	134,787	15,730
			86	11,514	124,974	145,450	20,476
	V	H	85	62	1,560	1,786	226
	V	W	83	555	10,939	11,633	694
			84	1,588	24,381	24,381	
			85	4,338	18,926	21,636	2,710
			86	14,507	147,227	162,051	14,824
THAILND	V	E	85	3,257	18,712	21,599	2,887
TRINID	V	E	85	5,044	23,343	28,995	5,652
TURKEY	V	E	84	2,139	10,400	13,095	2,695
			86	3,066	38,331	43,531	5,200
U KING	A	E	83	215	13,856	15,090	1,234
			84	98	13,578	14,387	809
			85	273	26,408	28,089	1,681
			86	179	31,541	32,106	565
	A	W	83	72	82,677	83,337	660
			85	12	1,598	1,719	121
			86	96	29,303	30,391	1,088
	N	E	83	19,511	130,395	147,009	16,614
			84	3,972	59,734	67,460	7,726
			85	7,618	86,328	97,586	11,258
			86	4,070	53,098	59,327	6,229
	N	W	83	3,041	51,582	55,034	3,452
			84	188	19,342	19,962	620
			85	3,453	168,548	176,517	7,969
			86	3,660	209,077	214,292	5,215
	O	E	83	25,168	212,472	236,705	24,233
			84	15,019	88,734	103,655	14,921
			85	22,834	204,161	229,707	25,546

Crop
Product
TSUSA commodity number, description, and unit of quantity

Country	Mode	Reg	Yr	Quantity	F.A.S.	C.I.F.	Charges
			86	15,352	129,465	145,646	16,181
	O W	83		3,626	44,114	48,020	3,906
		84		2,837	24,752	27,880	3,128
	V E	83		17,194	146,740	163,206	16,466
		84		12,371	123,794	140,196	16,402
		85		19,016	137,741	163,873	26,132
		86		14,612	137,458	155,975	18,517
	V W	83		14	565	583	18
		84		332	9,423	10,186	763
		85		10,862	71,900	83,138	11,238
		86		2,911	19,705	22,553	2,848
USSR	V E	85		95	1,497	1,703	206
YUGOSLV	N E	83		925	5,498	6,737	1,239
		84		1,820	10,608	13,576	2,968
		86		3,003	18,605	21,962	3,357
	O E	83		1,759	8,630	10,171	1,541
		84		3,639	21,179	23,714	2,535
		85		2,471	12,015	15,336	3,321
	O W	83		742	4,765	7,321	2,556
	V E	83		26,445	133,911	162,584	28,673
		84		11,238	74,153	89,832	15,679
		85		11,186	77,539	87,526	9,987
		86		24,946	166,355	192,605	26,250
	V W	83		3,807	19,900	22,393	2,493
		84		4,209	19,455	23,412	3,957
		85		1,547	6,500	8,203	1,703
		86		1,783	11,850	11,850	

1673060 WINE, GRAPE NSPF NOV 1 GL OV $4 (GAL)

Country	Mode	Reg	Yr	Quantity	F.A.S.	C.I.F.	Charges
TOTAL			83	8,215,473	62,969,019	70,955,505	7,986,486
			84	4,977,583	35,857,940	40,906,225	5,048,285
			85	4,602,808	32,214,576	37,423,173	5,208,597
			86	4,098,447	28,837,400	33,388,993	4,551,593
ANTIGUA	V E	86		3,808	19,070	22,460	3,390
ARGENT	O E	83		1,594	7,060	8,374	1,314
		84		140	590	710	120
		85		776	7,947	9,269	1,322
		86		1,489	7,731	8,872	1,141
	V E	83		20,759	152,198	171,621	19,423
		84		8,265	50,430	60,275	9,845
		85		13,443	70,829	81,764	10,935
		86		40,418	232,758	266,851	34,093
	V W	83		238	1,080	1,319	239
		85		335	2,015	2,357	342
		86		652	4,552	5,243	691
AUSTRAL	A H	84		59	966	4,272	3,306
	A W	84		285	4,540	8,249	3,709
	O E	83		1,938	27,410	29,641	2,231
		84		238	1,317	1,633	316
		85		1,752	16,788	16,788	
	O H	84		1,848	9,669	10,416	747
	V E	83		1,320	9,518	11,607	2,089
		84		1,090	9,591	11,345	1,754
		85		1,926	18,462	21,764	3,302
		86		399	2,184	2,409	225
	V H	83		67	1,201	1,298	97
	V W	83		5,548	66,878	72,136	5,258
		84		556	5,862	6,462	600
		85		2,439	12,899	15,574	2,675
		86		1,484	12,262	13,276	1,014
AUSTRIA	A E	84		71	370	438	68
	N E	83		799	11,869	13,632	1,763
	O E	83		447	5,389	6,370	981
		84		805	12,314	13,271	957
	O H	83		333	2,773	3,390	617
	V E	83		17,845	130,375	145,285	14,910
		84		6,788	46,353	51,805	5,452
		85		1,738	15,015	16,439	1,424
	V W	83		3,426	27,314	32,233	4,919
		84		17	261	266	5
BAHAMAS	V E	83		4,612	25,397	30,033	4,636
BELGIUM	A E	83		22	308	637	329
		85		36	16,262	17,734	1,472
	A W	83		59	8,575	9,465	890
	O E	86		9,046	79,602	88,075	8,473
	V E	83		3,110	39,573	46,773	7,200
		84		53	270	290	20
		85		2,175	12,605	15,584	2,979
		86		8,776	55,637	63,636	7,999
	V W	83		1,026	8,569	9,605	1,036
BRAZIL	A E	84		71	900	1,080	180
	V E	86		237	1,144	1,455	311
BULGAR	V E	83		4,280	19,710	22,734	3,024

Crop
Product
TSUSA commodity number, description, and unit of quantity

Country	Mode	Reg	Yr	Quantity	F.A.S.	C.I.F.	Charges
			85	237	1,827	2,070	243
			86	1,665	9,981	11,961	1,980
	V W	85		476	3,170	4,295	1,125
C RICA	V E	86		214	1,030	1,391	361
CANADA	A E	83		19	268	321	53
		85		851	7,835	7,835	
	O E	83		310	26,630	28,117	1,487
		84		7,769	72,696	75,414	2,718
		85		5,761	31,136	36,134	4,998
		86		1,354	6,477	7,775	1,298
	V E	85		1,189	6,003	6,163	160
CHILE	N E	83		629	3,610	4,092	482
	O E	83		2,009	13,398	15,914	2,516
		84		1,986	12,722	14,724	2,002
		85		237	1,100	1,301	201
	V E	83		9,707	415,156	484,702	69,546
		84		12,558	70,101	81,098	10,997
		85		3,488	30,107	33,791	3,684
		86		3,969	28,879	32,852	3,973
	V W	83		2,864	24,899	27,412	2,513
		84		178	1,140	1,383	243
		85		2,260	20,764	24,464	3,700
		86		266	2,408	2,693	285
CHINA M	A E	83		100	1,260	1,357	97
	V W	83		714	5,577	5,961	384
		86		3,850	21,060	24,960	3,900
CYPRUS	O E	83		178	1,022	1,261	239
		85		128	1,215	1,349	134
	V W	85		1,664	9,800	11,000	1,200
DENMARK	V E	86		2,337	17,340	19,538	2,198
FINLAND	O E	83		12	283	300	17
FR GERM	A E	83		141	1,766	2,935	1,169
		84		105	1,141	1,690	549
		86		45	2,368	2,980	612
	N E	83		337,572	2,610,548	2,952,621	342,073
		84		184,545	1,543,896	1,726,918	183,022
		85		56,305	513,361	586,453	73,092
	N W	83		150,439	1,219,461	1,351,126	131,665
	O E	83		154,477	1,155,142	1,296,383	141,241
		84		30,359	219,448	247,724	28,276
		85		23,369	167,488	193,204	25,716
		86		12,014	106,603	121,053	14,450
	O W	83		3,072	165,519	168,211	2,692
		84		554	7,655	8,285	630
	V E	83		434,322	3,236,781	3,682,424	445,643
		84		82,557	619,426	717,736	98,310
		85		93,750	635,585	752,711	117,126
		86		37,208	303,879	348,055	44,176
	V W	83		46,041	338,694	383,217	44,523
		84		524	12,728	13,875	1,147
		85		3,417	25,804	29,400	3,596
		86		247	3,040	3,304	264
FRANCE	A E	83		1,057	134,091	140,441	6,350
		84		713	6,900	12,582	5,682
		85		1,942	26,123	46,212	20,089
		86		476	7,949	10,902	2,953
	A W	83		154	1,730	2,595	865
	N E	83		891,483	9,127,540	10,162,831	1,035,291
		84		432,769	4,954,447	5,561,589	607,142
		85		220,804	2,845,090	3,254,702	409,612
		86		243,724	2,823,085	3,164,826	341,741
	N W	83		292,934	3,383,484	3,704,926	321,442
		84		48,372	366,896	408,913	42,017
		85		39,825	287,746	349,240	61,494
		86		34,578	326,326	371,590	45,264
	O E	83		202,630	2,692,136	2,901,801	209,665
		84		109,375	1,272,272	1,388,168	115,896
		85		47,624	727,417	786,723	59,306
		86		35,641	276,782	314,901	38,119
	O W	83		18,066	142,807	157,964	15,157
		84		2,800	18,411	20,443	2,032
		85		820	9,206	9,664	458
		86		215	19,399	21,650	2,251
	V E	83		438,293	3,899,308	4,386,149	486,841
		84		219,632	1,939,212	2,184,691	245,479
		85		189,706	1,709,842	1,950,565	240,723
		86		339,772	2,743,688	3,187,189	443,501
	V W	83		8,613	85,702	94,494	8,792
		84		14,750	125,328	142,695	17,367
		85		6,680	43,726	50,997	7,271
		86		47,501	345,502	385,222	39,720
GERM DR	O E	85		285	1,616	1,995	379
	V E	83		8,382	96,603	106,304	9,701
	V W	83		1,521	22,964	26,407	3,443

Crop
Product
TSUSA commodity number, description, and unit of quantity

Country	Mode	Reg	Yr	Quantity	F.A.S.	C.I.F.	Charges
GIBRAT	V	E	83	811	6,485	7,080	595
GREECE	N	E	83	64,950	291,518	373,260	81,742
			84	9,648	45,414	57,505	12,091
			85	1,962	10,378	13,066	2,688
	O	E	83	17,616	83,494	102,207	18,713
			84	6,819	34,397	42,850	8,453
			85	2,537	12,883	16,377	3,494
			86	1,948	9,934	12,723	2,789
	V	E	83	22,768	116,209	150,768	34,559
			84	16,669	84,116	103,906	19,790
			85	26,812	130,903	163,813	32,910
			86	10,998	60,981	77,870	16,889
	V	W	83	3,028	23,175	27,053	3,878
			85	297	1,338	1,659	321
			86	535	2,950	3,499	549
HUNGARY	O	E	83	2,254	21,465	23,641	2,176
			84	119	1,430	1,531	101
	V	E	83	34,528	212,154	254,085	41,931
			84	154	1,067	1,505	438
			85	7,643	58,123	66,882	8,759
	V	W	83	3,998	21,704	25,194	3,490
			85	1,569	11,953	14,110	2,157
ICELAND	V	W	86	237	1,090	1,349	259
IRAN	V	E	85	265	1,355	1,640	285
IRELAND	O	W	86	398	1,796	2,234	438
	V	W	85	1,228	21,414	22,803	1,389
ISRAEL	N	E	83	6,551	36,962	44,399	7,437
	O	E	83	7,996	72,372	80,373	8,001
			84	16,959	96,829	108,654	11,825
			85	8,985	46,306	53,259	6,953
			86	1,543	7,920	8,668	748
	V	E	83	8,490	41,285	53,394	12,109
			84	15,920	85,023	106,238	21,215
			85	14,876	76,115	93,688	17,573
			86	10,077	60,810	72,338	11,528
	V	W	83	1,592	9,396	11,734	2,338
			84	1,368	8,129	10,214	2,085
			85	499	2,539	3,224	685
			86	1,485	8,020	9,848	1,828
ITALY	A	E	83	72	649	1,270	621
	N	E	83	652,589	4,317,341	4,859,265	541,924
			84	557,828	4,065,930	4,598,055	532,125
			85	837,221	4,404,022	5,248,062	844,040
			86	627,837	3,597,471	4,259,919	662,448
	N	W	83	125,070	877,605	1,014,716	137,111
			84	12,797	64,180	75,902	11,722
			85	57,224	301,930	371,385	69,455
			86	7,669	51,687	59,669	7,982
	O	E	83	491,067	3,147,873	3,568,617	420,744
			84	430,136	2,334,867	2,686,787	351,920
			85	328,833	1,891,557	2,173,506	281,949
			86	273,436	1,647,115	1,903,050	255,935
	O	W	83	10,172	308,887	441,059	132,172
			84	821	3,725	4,477	752
			86	2,560	16,442	19,599	3,157
	V	E	83	2,071,413	12,383,969	14,083,479	1,699,510
			84	1,301,993	6,999,755	8,204,205	1,204,450
			85	977,718	5,873,948	6,862,661	988,713
			86	827,077	5,354,405	6,227,511	873,106
	V	H	86	332	10,069	10,705	636
	V	W	83	25,444	326,774	347,694	20,920
			84	32,853	215,023	251,564	36,541
			85	17,666	106,184	121,379	15,195
			86	71,252	459,243	514,448	55,205
JAMAICA	V	E	85	288	5,385	6,315	930
JAPAN	A	E	84	3	301	574	273
	V	E	84	2,853	21,276	27,219	5,943
			85	5,026	42,940	52,700	9,760
			86	4,077	34,471	41,403	6,932
	V	W	83	1,070	6,718	7,407	689
			84	154	2,462	2,804	342
			85	4,111	34,600	37,580	2,980
			86	1,722	19,607	20,908	1,301
KOR REP	V	E	84	1,426	8,000	9,350	1,350
			86	237	1,002	1,293	291
LEBANON	V	E	85	2,036	15,327	17,507	2,180
	V	W	86	737	4,517	5,305	788
MALI	O	E	85	237	1,707	2,032	325
MAURIT	O	E	85	1,483	12,274	12,724	450
MEXICO	N	E	83	284	1,620	1,627	7
	O	E	83	4,350	23,282	30,507	7,225
			84	59	336	437	101
			86	237	1,138	1,369	231
	O	W	83	2,324	14,033	14,033	
			84	686	4,223	4,223	
MOROC	V	E	86	475	2,800	3,370	570
N ZEAL	A	E	83	19	313	673	360
	V	E	83	237	1,272	1,470	198
			84	118	1,232	1,907	675
	V	W	83	3,041	26,477	29,931	3,454
NETHLDS	O	E	83	5,350	37,888	42,306	4,418
			84	615	3,682	4,376	694
			85	3,134	22,944	24,372	1,428
			86	6,704	39,558	44,645	5,087
	V	E	83	15,396	120,637	136,747	16,110
			84	3,800	24,948	33,599	8,651
			85	14,335	99,163	114,562	15,399
			86	5,167	52,101	58,519	6,418
	V	W	83	1,607	15,497	18,068	2,571
			85	1,379	12,621	14,294	1,673
POLAND	V	E	83	1,284	9,824	11,891	2,067
			85	1,286	14,873	16,833	1,960
			86	1,427	8,750	10,850	2,100
	V	W	85	606	5,790	6,438	648
PORTUGL	A	E	83	402	25,446	26,445	999
			85	146	58,291	60,001	1,710
	N	E	83	371,585	2,581,993	2,899,033	317,040
			84	436,554	2,660,210	3,070,996	410,786
			85	373,681	2,864,080	3,299,976	435,896
			86	325,703	2,299,227	2,626,195	326,968
	N	W	85	11,148	68,841	83,081	14,240
	O	E	83	199,029	1,347,817	1,510,556	162,739
			84	97,121	580,797	663,468	82,671
			85	119,999	954,275	1,065,838	111,563
			86	117,072	872,838	998,816	125,978
	O	W	83	10,139	60,563	68,657	8,094
			85	19,039	138,689	159,950	21,261
			86	5,598	34,197	40,609	6,412
	V	E	83	652,536	4,479,041	5,101,821	622,780
			84	577,463	4,814,798	5,459,613	644,815
			85	621,624	4,664,762	5,401,368	736,606
			86	745,566	5,260,082	6,149,404	889,322
	V	H	86	1,141	10,401	11,319	918
	V	W	83	160,797	1,219,826	1,338,157	118,331
			84	195,646	1,138,346	1,320,535	182,189
			85	334,076	2,174,166	2,590,936	416,770
			86	157,417	954,317	1,125,869	171,552
REP SAF	A	E	84	90	1,368	2,330	962
	O	E	83	423	2,900	3,146	246
	V	E	83	20,630	175,208	197,824	22,616
			84	981	6,367	7,902	1,535
	V	W	83	547	18,264	19,818	1,554
ROMANIA	O	E	83	946	4,776	5,223	447
	V	E	83	475	2,400	3,162	762
			85	1,949	10,909	13,612	2,703
SPAIN	A	W	83	91	374	477	103
	N	E	83	22,935	166,303	191,048	24,745
			84	11,378	74,928	88,381	13,453
	O	E	83	13,946	91,470	105,063	13,593
			84	4,358	34,308	37,604	3,296
			85	2,135	12,705	14,750	2,045
			86	2,386	17,379	19,207	1,828
	O	W	83	476	2,695	3,238	543
	V	E	83	67,803	505,053	580,822	75,769
			84	51,712	396,797	450,009	53,212
			85	57,125	374,397	439,167	64,770
			86	42,380	293,098	344,620	51,522
	V	W	83	7,145	57,252	74,595	17,343
			84	2,254	15,984	18,091	2,107
			85	2,233	13,684	15,970	2,286
			86	3,488	62,199	65,845	3,646
SWEDEN	V	E	85	1,545	8,125	10,337	2,212
			86	380	2,275	2,661	386
SWITZLD	A	E	83	72	1,672	2,271	599
			84	409	99,716	103,687	3,971
	N	E	84	62	1,620	1,986	366
	O	E	83	23	581	607	26
			84	25	512	691	179
			86	3,209	16,605	19,802	3,197
	V	E	83	512	11,538	11,955	417
	V	W	85	1,664	7,347	8,607	1,260
THAILND	V	E	85	984	5,640	6,510	870
U KING	A	E	83	723	90,080	94,625	4,545
			84	30	6,108	7,008	900
			85	174	52,188	55,082	2,894
			86	75	7,913	9,167	1,254
	A	W	83	14	1,793	1,996	203
			86	7	1,805	2,008	203

Crop
Product
TSUSA commodity number, description, and unit of quantity

Country	Mode	Reg	Yr	Quantity	F.A.S.	C.I.F.	Charges
	N	E	84	8,409	471,345	489,758	18,413
			85	1,629	18,641	22,060	3,419
			86	287	69,680	72,225	2,545
	N	W	84	1,673	23,142	25,808	2,666
	O	E	83	9,636	71,530	80,232	8,702
			84	3,734	20,771	23,460	2,689
			85	1,429	31,369	33,265	1,896
			86	951	5,188	6,856	1,668
	O	W	83	974	10,111	10,867	756
			84	57	1,007	1,060	53
			86	23	1,477	1,568	91
	V	E	83	3,886	61,706	66,308	4,602
			84	1,454	7,397	8,584	1,187
			85	8,925	264,783	279,360	14,577
YUGOSLV	O	E	83	2,848	21,198	28,845	7,647
	O	W	83	86	540	608	68
	V	E	83	6,716	40,310	47,402	7,092
			84	543	8,222	8,932	710
			85	154	2,454	3,228	774
			86	3,212	14,106	16,611	2,505

1673200 GRP WNE,NOV 14% ALHL OV 1 GL (GAL)

Country	Mode	Reg	Yr	Quantity	F.A.S.	C.I.F.	Charges
TOTAL			81	104,975	342,949	422,623	79,674
			82	117,154	409,017	495,663	86,646
			83	264,929	734,446	890,246	155,800
			84	340,455	907,638	1,127,564	219,926
			85	432,259	1,151,397	1,443,023	291,626
			86	354,400	868,781	1,110,433	241,652
ANTIGUA	V	E	86	2,113	4,000	4,873	873
ARGENT	N	E	85	20,116	38,080	46,638	8,558
	V	E	82	12,445	14,962	20,662	5,700
			83	22,401	25,187	33,197	8,010
			84	17,564	24,800	33,247	8,447
			85	11,043	16,720	21,674	4,954
			86	54,894	57,146	78,535	21,389
AUSTRAL	A	W	81	95	1,416	2,852	1,436
	O	H	83	10,935	35,127	40,045	4,918
			84	13,760	67,345	72,865	5,520
			85	5,491	11,587	13,891	2,304
	V	E	86	135	1,773	1,924	151
BRAZIL	V	E	81	27,694	62,899	96,536	33,637
			82	19,173	43,546	67,545	23,999
			83	19,172	39,410	60,573	21,163
			84	10,650	21,774	32,811	11,037
			85	8,522	15,322	21,510	6,188
			86	8,520	15,322	22,415	7,093
CANADA	O	E	82	85	300	300	
CHILE	V	W	83	1,309	995	2,081	1,086
FR GERM	N	E	83	7,385	24,385	28,443	4,058
			84	1,627	6,180	7,036	856
	O	E	83	196	891	985	94
	V	E	83	7,281	27,383	30,305	2,922
			84	5,292	21,108	24,311	3,203
			85	1,849	10,133	11,659	1,526
			86	3,102	16,889	21,056	4,167
	V	W	83	17,656	65,830	77,714	11,884
			84	9,333	31,828	38,893	7,065
			85	3,672	9,646	12,921	3,275
			86	396	2,569	2,811	242
FRANCE	A	E	81	114	1,227	1,568	341
			82	859	18,911	21,977	3,066
			83	877	9,982	12,226	2,244
			84	396	4,550	7,127	2,577
			85	364	5,028	8,199	3,171
			86	2	3,949	4,025	76
	A	W	81	75	831	1,537	706
			82	106	1,272	2,050	778
			83	213	2,610	4,641	2,031
			84	174	1,760	3,485	1,725
	N	E	82	3,052	58,826	64,095	5,269
			83	6,555	79,080	86,173	7,093
			84	21,656	162,386	175,794	13,408
			85	10,613	140,608	162,233	21,625
			86	3,467	69,856	78,793	8,937
	N	W	82	262	5,063	8,712	3,649
			83	13,699	43,735	51,651	7,916
			84	10,184	36,394	48,150	11,756
	O	E	82	2,529	16,772	20,061	3,289
			83	96	617	778	161
			84	20	833	886	53
			85	3,534	13,050	13,198	148
			86	2	3,558	4,768	1,210
	O	W	82	2	853	866	13

Country	Mode	Reg	Yr	Quantity	F.A.S.	C.I.F.	Charges
	V	E	81	3,940	17,038	18,988	1,950
			82	1,269	13,854	14,867	1,013
			83	1,572	10,616	12,580	1,964
			84	519	6,874	7,514	640
			85	448	8,819	9,606	787
			86	366	6,447	6,921	474
	V	W	81	414	43,913	45,280	1,367
			82	354	19,965	20,362	397
			83	3	320	349	29
			84	1,575	32,032	32,821	789
			85	8,570	77,573	82,056	4,483
			86	597	27,749	28,368	619
GREECE	V	E	81	1,374	3,055	3,788	733
ITALY	N	E	84	8,193	19,494	23,985	4,491
	N	W	84	3,017	10,133	11,831	1,698
	O	E	83	159	1,080	1,176	96
			85	475	1,732	1,973	241
	O	W	83	222	502	626	124
	V	E	82	264	1,943	2,128	185
			83	11,953	38,595	47,840	9,245
			84	278	1,393	1,569	176
			85	18,756	64,181	85,257	21,076
			86	1,814	6,720	8,180	1,460
	V	W	81	384	3,353	4,028	675
			83	224	2,213	2,455	242
			84	66	493	559	66
			85	608	4,850	5,741	891
JAPAN	V	E	86	5,239	14,755	21,265	6,510
MEXICO	O	E	85	6,794	17,690	17,690	
	O	W	85	27,260	103,660	103,662	2
NAURU	A	W	84	356	4,671	5,478	807
NETHLDS	A	E	85	4,060	8,500	9,557	1,057
PERU	V	E	85	401	7,150	9,911	2,761
PORTUGL	N	E	84	38,442	62,707	93,562	30,855
			85	114,478	243,213	325,718	82,505
	N	W	83	609	2,586	2,967	381
	O	E	81	1,057	4,108	4,444	336
			82	2,219	6,510	7,607	1,097
			84	5,996	13,937	15,498	1,561
			85	3,116	5,493	8,803	3,310
			86	3,011	5,842	8,093	2,251
	V	E	81	60,039	181,480	216,279	34,799
			82	72,723	199,986	235,976	35,990
			83	138,958	315,145	382,148	67,003
			84	183,444	359,656	467,377	107,721
			85	168,103	313,154	424,646	111,492
			86	268,661	618,584	803,944	185,360
	V	W	84	1,890	4,478	5,884	1,406
			85	4,359	9,850	13,192	3,342
			86	1,449	3,287	4,127	840
SPAIN	O	E	86	594	7,125	7,125	
	V	E	81	423	1,425	1,829	404
			82	1,812	6,254	8,455	2,201
			83	3,454	8,157	11,293	3,136
			84	6,023	12,812	16,881	4,069
			85	9,627	25,358	33,288	7,930
	V	W	81	845	2,850	3,498	648
U KING	V	E	86	38	3,210	3,210	
URUGUAY	V	E	81	8,521	19,354	21,996	2,642

1673400 MARSALA WNE OV 14% AL NOV1GL (GAL)

Country	Mode	Reg	Yr	Quantity	F.A.S.	C.I.F.	Charges
TOTAL			81	151,282	1,070,891	1,206,197	135,306
			82	139,949	971,895	1,105,117	133,222
			83	157,441	1,039,227	1,165,070	125,843
			84	197,125	1,283,309	1,460,101	176,792
			85	167,663	1,133,730	1,316,317	182,587
			86	184,008	1,295,633	1,511,345	215,712
FRANCE	A	E	81	12	360	585	225
			82	89	6,563	6,956	393
	O	E	81	24	443	471	28
			82	2,139	18,335	20,581	2,246
	V	E	81	6,075	61,274	67,883	6,609
			82	261	3,461	3,864	403
	V	W	82	59	1,309	1,339	30
ITALY	N	E	82	315	2,261	2,717	456
			84	682	3,633	4,316	683
			86	11,341	67,551	78,803	11,252
	N	W	85	3,932	25,663	31,760	6,097
	O	E	81	73,557	532,128	594,393	62,265
			82	70,979	518,810	582,054	63,244
			83	67,964	489,659	538,144	48,485
			84	42,841	312,274	350,649	38,375
			85	61,591	463,870	522,014	58,144

Crop
Product
TSUSA commodity number, description, and unit of quantity

Country	Mode	Reg	Yr	Quantity	F.A.S.	C.I.F.	Charges
			86	52,324	375,521	432,020	56,499
	O	W	81	13,363	101,250	114,232	12,982
			82	2,554	19,332	22,045	2,713
			86	3,481	25,968	29,509	3,541
	V	E	81	41,924	249,144	285,956	36,812
			82	55,506	351,597	405,973	54,376
			83	78,454	469,880	535,701	65,821
			84	132,972	847,955	965,113	117,158
			85	88,701	560,430	662,716	102,286
			86	99,963	707,825	830,582	122,757
	V	H	85	332	2,622	2,912	290
	V	W	81	14,354	92,834	107,191	14,357
			82	8,047	50,227	59,588	9,361
			83	10,819	62,385	73,672	11,287
			84	20,630	119,447	140,023	20,576
			85	13,107	81,145	96,915	15,770
			86	16,899	118,768	140,431	21,663
JAPAN	V	W	81	1,664	21,000	22,510	1,510
PORTUGL	A	E	83	204	17,303	17,553	250
	V	W	81	309	12,458	12,976	518

1673520 SHERRY WINE NOT OVER 1 GAL (GAL)

Country	Mode	Reg	Yr	Quantity	F.A.S.	C.I.F.	Charges
TOTAL			81	2,381,737	35,334,524	37,775,923	2,441,399
			82	2,076,469	26,488,361	28,512,266	2,023,905
			83	2,063,599	26,725,818	28,630,918	1,905,100
			84	2,140,119	26,609,762	28,782,473	2,172,711
			85	1,878,333	22,720,200	24,842,890	2,122,690
			86	1,760,607	23,717,556	25,687,599	1,970,043
ARGENT	O	E	83	3,169	6,497	7,667	1,170
AUSTRAL	N	E	82	59	358	389	31
	V	W	81	499	3,529	3,840	311
			82	20,993	38,798	41,005	2,207
			84	13	314	314	
CANADA	O	E	81	7,920	66,799	66,799	
			82	3,965	34,315	35,174	859
CYPRUS	N	E	81	35	353	464	111
	O	E	82	59	538	651	113
	V	E	82	59	538	643	105
FRANCE	A	E	82	41	5,730	5,972	242
	O	E	81	1,512	14,914	16,784	1,870
	V	E	82	1,012	9,401	9,766	365
GREECE	O	E	81	2,615	13,050	15,784	2,734
	V	E	82	83	495	627	132
ISRAEL	V	E	81	48	331	402	71
ITALY	O	E	81	119	3,675	3,795	120
MEXICO	O	E	81	1,189	5,750	5,750	
			82	357	2,250	2,250	
	O	W	82	1,189	7,500	7,500	
N ZEAL	V	E	83	76	698	837	139
	V	W	81	200	1,985	2,301	316
			82	1,028	8,904	10,251	1,347
PORTUGL	A	E	82	47	13,685	13,908	223
	O	W	81	26	743	785	42
	V	E	83	4,704	87,351	91,856	4,505
REP SAF	V	E	82	435	3,404	3,918	514
			83	399	3,125	3,442	317
			84	47	372	398	26
	V	W	82	380	2,976	3,440	464
			83	285	2,232	2,666	434
			84	131	2,955	3,121	166
SPAIN	A	E	82	2	322	340	18
			83	68	8,465	9,145	680
			84	61	4,111	5,025	914
			85	1,467	36,777	40,415	3,638
			86	1,114	15,839	16,994	1,155
	A	W	84	2	616	662	46
	N	E	81	676,458	7,506,904	8,189,567	682,663
			82	760,588	8,226,680	8,939,180	712,500
			83	774,664	8,653,785	9,328,775	674,990
			84	846,374	8,968,147	9,839,792	871,645
			85	634,938	6,877,042	7,561,236	684,194
			86	794,937	9,221,773	10,041,364	819,591
	N	W	82	71,779	913,173	990,459	77,286
			83	170,635	2,122,097	2,295,412	173,315
			84	117,260	1,285,946	1,417,795	131,849
			85	107,658	1,425,017	1,548,206	123,189
	O	E	81	789,312	13,773,946	14,484,928	710,982
			82	531,800	8,229,717	8,712,891	483,174
			83	471,406	7,080,420	7,481,082	400,662
			84	492,754	6,968,507	7,438,266	469,759
			85	428,921	5,700,354	6,182,831	482,477
			86	327,160	5,207,196	5,553,321	346,125
	O	W	81	115,948	1,940,970	2,094,238	153,268
			82	81,008	1,105,659	1,213,415	107,756
			83	71,740	976,676	1,062,472	85,796
			84	54,865	750,684	797,288	46,604
			85	73,599	914,916	990,871	75,955
			86	53,962	762,919	829,429	66,510
	V	E	81	497,933	6,818,764	7,407,092	588,328
			82	504,273	6,388,485	6,932,387	543,902
			83	552,521	7,665,410	8,204,415	539,005
			84	615,923	8,499,773	9,134,553	634,780
			85	534,138	6,861,524	7,501,600	640,076
			86	453,429	7,266,027	7,857,229	591,202
	V	W	81	75,851	1,153,933	1,246,556	92,623
			82	40,277	583,485	631,367	47,882
			83	13,228	110,295	133,469	23,174
			84	12,659	128,039	144,956	16,917
			85	97,612	904,570	1,017,731	113,161
			86	130,005	1,243,802	1,389,262	145,460
U KING	N	E	81	12,724	273,454	284,444	10,990
	O	E	81	77,803	1,634,212	1,720,656	86,444
			82	9,141	176,766	183,655	6,889
			83	288	3,719	3,907	188
			84	30	298	303	5
	O	W	81	9,672	258,611	271,389	12,778
			82	2,778	64,319	68,021	3,702
	V	E	81	93,223	1,579,237	1,656,853	77,616
			82	30,300	492,637	515,775	23,138
			83	416	5,048	5,773	725
	V	W	81	18,650	283,364	303,496	20,132
			82	14,816	178,226	189,282	11,056

1673540 SHERRY WINE OVER 1 GAL (GAL)

Country	Mode	Reg	Yr	Quantity	F.A.S.	C.I.F.	Charges
TOTAL			81	21,773	147,759	171,983	24,224
			82	38,682	391,463	427,991	36,528
			83	54,990	676,494	737,542	61,048
			84	11,094	108,889	130,723	21,834
			85	20,025	281,514	309,695	28,181
			86	24,433	206,177	225,935	19,758
CANADA	O	E	81	216	1,614	1,614	
SPAIN	A	E	85	114	14,378	15,704	1,326
			86	736	22,290	22,851	561
	A	W	85	330	4,003	4,189	186
	N	E	82	3,669	37,457	42,163	4,706
	O	E	81	632	6,610	7,343	733
			83	852	15,898	16,543	645
			84	2,788	22,537	32,921	10,384
			85	3,991	28,023	31,586	3,563
			86	383	3,024	3,384	360
	O	W	83	95	2,615	2,819	204
			84	94	2,156	2,308	152
	V	E	81	20,509	131,274	154,270	22,996
			82	32,169	322,409	351,859	29,450
			83	52,527	639,824	698,650	58,826
			84	8,200	83,850	95,135	11,285
			85	10,631	152,502	167,325	14,823
			86	21,539	156,877	172,175	15,298
	V	W	83	1,516	18,157	19,530	1,373
			84	12	346	359	13
			85	4,959	82,608	90,891	8,283
			86	1,775	23,986	27,525	3,539
U KING	O	E	81	416	8,261	8,756	495
	V	E	82	2,844	31,597	33,969	2,372

1673700 GRAPE WINE OV14% ALCHL NSPF (GAL)

Country	Mode	Reg	Yr	Quantity	F.A.S.	C.I.F.	Charges
TOTAL			81	266,737	3,892,120	4,214,552	319,094
			82	350,066	5,210,444	5,656,708	446,264
			83	354,257	6,066,748	6,548,508	481,760
			84	488,273	8,299,895	9,019,744	719,849
			85	500,314	9,843,862	10,587,638	743,776
			86	475,852	11,457,413	12,147,167	689,754
ARGENT	V	E	85	2,734	41,700	45,700	4,000
			86	1,427	4,050	5,432	1,382
AUSTRAL	O	E	81	291	3,952	4,495	543
			82	121	1,865	2,049	184
			83	265	3,381	3,934	553
	O	W	82	71	1,440	1,519	79
	V	E	81	427	5,898	6,799	901
			82	756	32,068	34,251	2,183
			83	2,336	35,535	38,264	2,729
			84	1,089	27,846	31,506	3,660
			85	1,260	15,232	18,998	3,766
			86	1,643	36,712	39,691	2,979
	V	H	84	141	1,726	1,957	231

Crop
Product
TSUSA commodity number, description, and unit of quantity

Country	Mode	Reg	Yr	Quantity	F.A.S.	C.I.F.	Charges
	V	W	81	4,841	97,164	101,395	4,231
			82	9,767	179,417	190,729	11,312
			83	1,747	30,046	32,546	2,500
			84	3,094	46,330	49,411	3,081
			85	728	16,855	18,588	1,733
			86	3,520	60,682	63,690	3,008
BELGIUM	V	E	84	142	7,643	7,895	252
			85	223	3,400	4,025	625
			86	269	6,620	7,054	434
	V	W	85	266	1,415	1,415	
			86	5,159	224,785	229,560	4,775
BULGAR	V	E	81	2,080	5,815	7,000	1,185
CANADA	O	E	82	1,396	10,387	10,989	602
			83	369	18,675	19,652	977
			84	947	12,210	14,836	2,626
			85	1,203	1,203	1,203	
			86	133	1,205	1,205	
CHILE	O	E	82	95	1,000	1,113	113
	V	E	85	434	6,049	6,620	571
CHINA M	V	E	84	1,426	8,202	11,142	2,940
			86	416	2,888	3,978	1,090
	V	W	84	1,902	12,745	15,600	2,855
			85	1,783	11,172	14,025	2,853
CHINA T	V	E	84	475	4,092	5,187	1,095
	V	W	85	237	1,700	1,787	87
CYPRUS	V	E	84	356	2,025	2,543	518
	V	W	84	659	4,718	5,443	725
			85	1,190	8,575	8,853	278
CZECHO	O	E	83	847	5,084	5,458	374
			84	480	2,885	3,307	422
DENMARK	N	E	86	4,280	48,538	54,078	5,540
	O	E	81	285	1,724	2,076	352
			82	3,328	5,945	6,897	952
			83	1,829	12,104	14,144	2,040
			84	840	11,355	14,645	3,290
			85	9,057	68,456	76,840	8,384
	V	E	81	90	666	757	91
			82	1,427	9,684	10,935	1,251
			83	4,278	28,994	33,518	4,524
			84	1,902	11,953	14,425	2,472
			85	6,205	51,710	58,722	7,012
			86	507	7,577	8,925	1,348
	V	W	82	532	3,615	4,261	646
			83	133	936	1,087	151
			85	1,763	12,586	15,572	2,986
FINLAND	O	E	81	834	6,095	7,088	993
			82	961	6,066	6,966	900
			84	446	4,264	4,987	723
	O	W	86	2,974	33,191	39,813	6,622
FR GERM	A	E	83	490	7,181	7,446	265
	A	W	82	22	1,577	1,786	209
	O	E	81	810	6,365	7,066	701
			83	526	8,743	9,702	959
			84	288	6,711	7,573	862
			85	1,222	15,953	18,410	2,457
	O	W	83	152	3,881	4,037	156
			84	53	2,462	2,561	99
			85	24	1,044	1,086	42
	V	E	81	235	1,816	2,149	333
			82	28	476	481	5
			84	653	14,981	16,411	1,430
			85	463	14,053	15,607	1,554
			86	119	4,750	4,972	222
	V	W	83	14	1,647	1,670	23
			84	239	6,494	7,156	662
			85	133	1,960	2,203	243
			86	411	6,548	7,442	894
FRANCE	A	E	81	237	16,826	17,802	976
			82	163	17,123	18,061	938
			83	2,232	81,026	89,121	8,095
			84	257	39,104	41,234	2,130
			85	20	5,295	5,513	218
			86	38	7,681	8,160	479
	A	W	83	271	43,257	45,028	1,771
			84	235	4,324	4,774	450
	N	E	81	9,548	125,565	135,989	10,424
			82	14,472	221,089	237,688	16,599
			83	10,534	135,180	148,253	13,073
			84	35,226	449,741	516,788	67,047
			85	19,258	246,189	273,636	27,447
			86	2,414	54,992	61,018	6,026
	N	W	82	6,293	137,992	148,077	10,085
			83	4,251	67,881	73,826	5,945
			84	8,992	186,963	201,315	14,352
			85	16,207	516,304	542,727	26,423
			86	5,019	85,936	90,471	4,535
	O	E	81	4,879	46,401	53,180	6,779
			82	44,780	405,716	459,346	53,630
			83	57,030	425,806	492,664	66,858
			84	33,909	293,693	334,602	40,909
			85	49,211	437,001	497,335	60,334
			86	30,318	317,368	358,638	41,270
	O	W	81	537	12,140	13,227	1,087
			82	127	3,193	3,480	287
			83	1,319	13,937	15,352	1,415
			84	405	4,491	4,880	389
			85	195	4,582	5,190	608
			86	1,069	12,900	13,752	852
	V	E	81	5,344	56,465	66,681	6,878
			82	7,603	93,640	103,916	10,276
			83	7,964	83,707	93,545	9,838
			84	5,105	51,548	61,703	10,155
			85	10,094	118,867	135,549	16,682
			86	21,589	342,543	374,162	31,619
	V	W	81	4,018	34,325	38,336	4,011
			82	2,130	24,967	27,273	2,306
			83	36	418	448	30
			85	3,304	67,741	72,292	4,551
			86	15,973	536,590	553,777	17,187
G BISAU	V	E	81	62	20,077	20,398	321
GIBRAT	V	E	83	36	492	520	28
GREECE	O	E	81	4,243	23,030	28,441	5,411
			82	5,198	31,277	40,346	9,069
			83	4,939	28,315	34,596	6,281
			84	4,429	21,853	27,141	5,288
			85	7,267	36,748	46,697	9,949
			86	13,097	65,285	82,576	17,291
	V	E	81	16,151	108,910	130,573	21,663
			82	17,800	116,233	144,955	28,722
			83	13,638	96,494	120,499	24,005
			84	12,605	81,314	100,514	19,200
			85	7,285	51,248	62,639	11,391
			86	2,254	22,603	25,597	2,994
	V	W	82	714	4,210	5,257	1,047
			83	797	7,505	8,661	1,156
			84	213	990	1,250	260
IRELAND	O	W	86	990	6,373	7,389	1,016
ISRAEL	N	E	83	993	6,710	7,709	999
	O	E	81	190	1,599	1,938	339
			82	119	1,000	1,231	231
			83	60	500	560	60
			84	580	4,899	5,387	488
			86	1,545	128,284	131,099	2,815
	V	E	81	274	2,300	2,768	468
			82	451	3,440	4,253	813
			84	142	1,200	1,444	244
			86	2,359	5,104	7,806	2,702
	V	W	83	59	1,043	1,144	101
ITALY	A	E	81	9	765	986	221
			85	119	1,628	2,696	1,068
	N	E	83	10,463	406,780	420,986	14,206
	O	E	81	2,560	50,517	52,924	2,407
			82	3,404	64,316	68,152	3,836
			83	8,499	115,969	125,566	9,597
			84	10,224	179,515	194,754	15,239
			85	7,034	212,611	221,056	8,445
			86	4,051	214,903	223,332	8,429
	O	W	82	171	1,728	1,940	212
			83	171	1,728	1,939	211
			84	46	489	567	78
	V	E	81	13,657	127,182	143,540	16,358
			82	22,365	363,323	394,857	31,534
			83	3,664	38,850	43,443	4,593
			84	29,309	366,797	411,028	44,231
			85	10,000	171,148	191,474	20,326
			86	22,205	369,068	403,109	34,041
	V	W	81	308	6,781	7,430	649
			82	3,517	28,984	33,129	4,145
			83	1,271	16,883	18,328	1,445
			84	6,071	61,926	68,122	6,196
			85	8,914	101,179	113,350	12,171
			86	3,863	97,660	103,999	6,339
JAPAN	V	E	84	120	1,344	1,700	356
			85	285	5,083	5,814	731
			86	564	4,125	5,215	1,090
	V	W	82	328	3,402	3,936	534
			83	1,370	8,888	10,750	1,862
			84	25	376	388	12

Table 1. U.S. Import Statistics for Crop-Specific Commodities by Crop Name

Crop
Product
TSUSA commodity number, description, and unit of quantity

Country	Mode	Reg	Yr	Quantity	F.A.S.	C.I.F.	Charges
MEXICO	O E		82	119	675	711	36
			83	713	4,050	4,050	
			84	238	1,353	1,353	
	O W		82	1,486	9,375	9,375	
			83	133	560	560	
			84	133	560	560	
N ANTIL	V E		85	2,251	8,104	8,927	823
N ZEAL	O W		85	119	1,306	1,475	169
			86	99	1,097	1,254	157
	V W		83	133	1,288	1,473	185
			84	2,225	29,575	33,031	3,456
			85	123	1,057	1,196	139
			86	133	1,124	1,288	164
NETHLDS	A E		82	14	1,176	1,226	50
	O E		82	48	458	516	58
			85	164	2,936	3,580	644
			86	511	4,623	5,460	837
	V E		81	501	22,505	22,908	403
			85	554	6,584	7,586	1,002
			86	11,586	285,616	300,117	14,501
	V W		83	1,720	30,216	32,169	1,953
			84	206	5,171	5,645	474
			86	4,002	77,972	84,068	6,096
POLAND	A W		85	342	6,038	6,257	219
	O E		81	1,870	15,300	18,153	2,853
			82	1,150	12,194	13,950	1,756
			83	1,188	14,700	16,603	1,903
			84	80	1,550	1,850	300
	V E		84	3,500	31,475	36,325	4,850
			86	1,283	13,500	15,480	1,980
PORTUGL	A E		81	49	4,460	4,735	275
			82	1,703	140,939	147,947	7,008
			83	2,684	208,283	219,178	10,895
			84	3,413	199,223	221,538	22,315
			85	1,670	113,943	119,660	5,717
			86	179	26,715	28,962	2,247
	A W		83	15	839	1,257	418
			84	542	35,221	38,524	3,303
			85	174	22,672	24,761	2,089
	N E		81	51,204	980,605	1,032,184	51,579
			82	71,029	1,347,187	1,426,378	79,191
			83	66,373	1,570,259	1,669,518	99,259
			84	129,550	2,838,062	3,007,237	169,175
			85	138,362	3,331,382	3,519,821	188,439
			86	143,264	3,715,917	3,907,127	191,210
	N W		82	22,659	641,975	685,697	43,722
			83	26,622	837,007	892,146	55,139
			84	47,578	1,065,669	1,139,633	73,964
			85	72,181	1,816,443	1,919,040	102,597
			86	40,458	1,621,579	1,704,252	82,673
	O E		81	22,532	407,201	438,978	31,777
			82	7,780	141,780	151,129	9,349
			83	6,811	136,888	145,956	9,068
			84	9,087	175,839	188,578	12,739
			85	13,697	381,270	403,344	22,074
			86	14,505	399,232	416,747	17,515
	O W		81	624	17,206	18,114	908
			82	2,085	33,417	36,729	3,312
			83	367	6,833	7,263	430
			84	504	10,391	10,871	480
			85	37	4,987	5,436	449
	V E		81	27,965	579,867	623,541	43,674
			82	23,801	449,048	480,238	31,190
			83	31,773	652,556	699,028	46,472
			84	56,296	1,006,750	1,083,808	77,058
			85	18,861	458,423	493,150	34,727
			86	37,281	1,237,760	1,300,266	62,506
	V W		81	22,024	505,810	535,636	29,826
			82	1,712	32,539	35,252	2,713
			83	4,279	70,512	73,279	2,767
			84	2,919	70,572	76,375	5,803
			85	735	19,862	21,483	1,621
			86	20,832	595,746	630,849	35,103
REP SAF	O W		83	90	3,131	3,492	361
	V E		82	322	10,397	10,980	583
			83	902	20,121	21,875	1,754
			84	3,293	62,440	70,024	7,584
			85	90	2,792	2,996	204
	V W		82	95	3,124	3,545	421
			83	142	4,858	5,509	651
SPAIN	A E		82	21	533	731	198
	N E		81	10,681	73,610	85,769	12,159
			83	15,097	157,008	169,773	12,765
			84	12,839	116,868	131,032	14,164

Crop
Product
TSUSA commodity number, description, and unit of quantity

Country	Mode	Reg	Yr	Quantity	F.A.S.	C.I.F.	Charges
			85	18,410	177,289	202,956	25,667
	N W		83	1,998	25,814	28,836	3,022
	O E		81	5,296	84,334	88,680	4,346
			82	5,651	88,711	93,919	5,208
			83	3,211	42,543	45,179	2,636
			84	4,869	74,834	79,602	4,768
			85	2,942	39,299	43,264	3,965
			86	8,853	132,094	143,815	11,721
	O W		81	26	743	782	39
			82	31	626	665	39
			83	155	1,893	2,026	133
			84	149	1,660	2,701	1,041
	V E		81	21,573	146,971	165,478	18,507
			82	32,484	275,232	314,067	38,835
			83	21,430	228,490	247,909	19,419
			84	22,105	198,880	223,376	24,496
			85	13,687	123,428	143,523	20,095
			86	17,468	192,585	213,873	21,288
	V W		81	1,731	15,407	17,485	2,078
			82	11,513	64,737	72,765	8,028
			83	3,422	33,742	37,251	3,509
			84	3,804	21,448	26,217	4,769
			85	12,963	100,749	117,892	17,143
			86	2,509	34,956	39,088	4,132
SWEDEN	O E		81	1,379	11,020	12,433	1,413
			84	1,799	28,659	35,100	6,441
			85	563	7,209	7,865	656
	V E		81	126	1,100	1,853	753
			84	458	4,182	4,857	675
	V W		81	1,189	8,000	8,786	786
			82	1,331	16,115	18,623	2,508
			85	1,545	6,630	9,130	2,500
			86	266	1,994	2,600	606
SWITZLD	V E		83	56	1,597	1,643	46
			84	118	1,949	2,019	70
TURKEY	V E		84	59	325	462	137
U KING	A E		81	32	4,046	4,572	526
			82	96	6,043	6,377	334
			83	807	43,325	45,754	2,429
			84	607	24,619	26,955	2,336
			85	875	137,936	146,411	8,475
			86	111	9,441	11,286	1,845
	A W		81	31	2,892	3,080	188
			82	21	2,115	2,202	87
			85	498	74,445	78,616	4,171
			86	351	61,898	65,197	3,299
	N E		82	503	16,300	17,566	1,266
			83	9,164	99,496	107,457	7,961
			84	4,838	82,317	88,772	6,455
			85	7,884	391,979	418,522	26,543
			86	8,089	99,730	110,764	11,034
	N W		83	632	30,903	31,946	1,043
			84	2,095	135,704	141,427	5,723
			86	268	67,971	68,701	730
	O E		81	2,639	36,283	38,342	2,059
			82	363	7,801	8,170	369
			83	564	11,676	12,106	430
			84	544	9,651	9,937	286
			85	891	7,519	8,497	978
			86	6,985	130,944	137,551	6,607
	O W		82	181	2,398	2,564	166
			84	69	823	869	46
	V E		81	9,897	99,119	109,670	10,551
			82	8,816	77,663	84,834	7,171
			83	123	2,856	2,987	131
			84	3,410	62,742	66,615	3,873
			85	419	8,328	9,231	903
			86	309	4,737	5,076	339
	V W		81	36	5,465	5,726	261
			83	10	1,265	1,290	25
			84	36	962	1,046	84
			85	2,258	110,173	116,226	6,053
USSR	O E		81	5,507	44,547	50,896	6,349
			82	5,199	41,193	48,957	7,764
			83	9,029	73,851	82,077	8,226
			84	5,917	49,281	55,039	5,758
			85	10,384	107,520	120,895	13,375
			86	10,552	89,913	100,830	10,917
	O H		81	254	2,180	2,655	475
	O W		81	1,730	14,438	16,923	2,485
			82	190	1,800	2,195	395
			84	1,017	6,871	7,930	1,059
			85	1,277	8,111	9,746	1,635
			86	254	6,131	6,131	

Crop Product TSUSA commodity number, description, and unit of quantity Country	Mode	Reg	Yr	Quantity	F.A.S.	C.I.F.	Charges
	V	E	81	67	661	685	24
			85	4,488	34,539	41,442	6,903
W SAMOA	V	W	86	26	3,068	3,117	49
YUGOSLV	O	E	81	2,773	22,752	26,989	4,237
			86	326	2,475	2,723	248
	O	W	83	294	2,122	2,389	267
	V	E	81	3,091	23,220	26,461	3,241
			82	890	5,920	6,605	685
			83	1,261	7,790	8,881	1,091
			84	317	1,700	2,000	300
			85	871	4,250	5,020	770
			86	1,148	7,606	8,673	1,067
	V	W	82	634	3,800	4,922	1,122
			83	476	2,700	3,252	552
			84	634	3,360	4,260	900

Raisin

1476600 CURRANTS, RAISINS, NO SEEDS (LB)

Country	Mode	Reg	Yr	Quantity	F.A.S.	C.I.F.	Charges
TOTAL			81	123,200	77,569	87,500	9,931
			82	136,500	79,935	91,336	11,401
			83	123,431	54,918	64,109	9,191
			84	34,383	14,776	17,694	2,918
			85	22,271	7,392	10,459	3,067
			86	87,659	39,545	46,925	7,380
AUSTRAL	O	E	86	7,441	4,286	4,286	
CHILE	V	E	83	564	2,240	4,169	1,929
	V	W	85	22,271	7,392	10,459	3,067
GREECE	O	E	82	81,200	47,595	54,124	6,529
			83	39,200	22,271	25,480	3,209
	V	E	81	123,200	77,569	87,500	9,931
			82	54,200	31,565	36,197	4,632
			83	47,600	25,459	29,512	4,053
			84	30,211	11,117	13,384	2,267
			86	43,501	19,575	23,150	3,575
INDIA	V	E	82	1,100	775	1,015	240
MEXICO	O	E	83	36,067	4,948	4,948	
N ZEAL	A	W	84	597	2,186	2,680	494
			86	1,617	4,143	5,888	1,745
REP SAF	V	E	84	3,575	1,473	1,630	157
TURKEY	V	E	86	35,100	11,541	13,601	2,060

1476800 SULTANA RAISINS, NO SEEDS (LB)

Country	Mode	Reg	Yr	Quantity	F.A.S.	C.I.F.	Charges
TOTAL			81	178,500	122,573	122,980	407
			82	1,486,250	947,771	1,037,029	89,258
			83	332,948	182,238	204,885	22,647
			84	672,469	274,633	295,561	20,928
			85	57,624	27,407	31,782	4,375
			86	696,706	248,323	277,591	29,268
ARGENT	V	E	84	12,787	6,306	7,521	1,215
			85	13,228	7,202	7,920	718
AUSTRAL	O	E	82	312,360	279,749	287,069	7,320
			83	9,859	6,871	14,925	8,054
			84	10,945	9,697	9,815	118
			86	23,810	13,585	13,585	
AUSTRIA	O	E	85	2,976	1,347	1,347	
CANADA	O	E	81	93,000	68,100	68,100	
			82	113,190	84,279	84,279	
			83	43,177	42,752	42,752	
			84	7,011	3,492	3,492	
CHILE	V	E	84	1,102	405	465	60
CYPRUS	V	E	82	825	561	609	48
			83	873	963	1,090	127
			84	10,800	6,152	6,773	621
GREECE	O	E	82	64,500	36,195	41,280	5,085
			86	100	1,078	1,078	
	V	E	81	85,500	54,473	54,880	407
			82	829,480	464,916	534,513	69,597
			83	42,000	20,965	25,832	4,867
			84	67,308	24,073	29,598	5,525
IRAN	V	W	85	18,300	9,360	11,614	2,254
REP SAF	V	E	84	28,050	14,376	15,788	1,412
			85	23,120	9,498	10,901	1,403
TURKEY	O	E	82	462	323	323	
			83	115,742	53,813	56,788	2,975
			84	293,984	115,245	115,245	
	O	W	84	1,543	665	665	
	V	E	82	165,433	81,748	88,956	7,208
			83	121,297	56,874	63,498	6,624
			84	238,939	94,222	106,199	11,977
			86	672,796	233,660	262,928	29,268

1477000 RAISINS FR SEEDLESS GRAPES (LB)

Country	Mode	Reg	Yr	Quantity	F.A.S.	C.I.F.	Charges
TOTAL			81	7,768	9,883	10,572	689
			82	5,436,401	2,224,199	2,245,668	21,469
			83	7,606,991	2,682,261	2,709,346	27,085
			84	1,957,144	958,122	1,014,912	56,790
			85	4,929,557	1,213,876	1,251,562	37,686
			86	12,147,461	2,359,254	2,366,208	6,954
AFGHAN	V	E	82	74,956	41,172	43,690	2,518
			84	110,230	28,980	32,370	3,390
AUSTRAL	O	E	82	56,535	40,338	40,338	
			84	3,307	1,650	1,650	
			85	14,510	7,349	7,349	
CANADA	O	E	82	3,900	1,742	2,112	370
			84	3,300	1,420	1,420	
			85	3,556	3,897	3,897	
			86	2,100	2,068	2,068	
	O	W	82	44,092	17,111	17,111	
			83	42,711	17,148	17,148	
			85	84,134	23,216	23,216	
			86	19,740	7,624	7,624	
CHILE	V	E	83	35,274	21,808	24,784	2,976
CHINA M	O	E	82	276	321	368	47
	V	W	81	4,200	5,246	5,475	229
			82	440	685	753	68
			84	1	577	613	36
CHINA T	V	E	83	250	291	320	29
	V	H	86	1,000	1,139	1,200	61
	V	W	82	309	570	716	146
CYPRUS	V	E	84	93,900	50,940	56,037	5,097
EGYPT	O	E	84	440	387	447	60
FR GERM	V	E	81	1,944	3,023	3,206	183
			82	8,757	13,902	22,761	8,859
			83	4,724	6,143	6,568	425
			84	1,390	1,721	1,841	120
	V	W	81	162	256	282	26
FRANCE	V	W	81	162	258	281	23
GREECE	O	E	84	4,134	1,875	1,875	
			85	13,228	5,375	5,375	
	V	E	81	600	500	589	89
ITALY	V	W	82	254	540	610	70
			83	680	1,494	1,625	131
JAPAN	A	W	84	91	271	626	355
MEXICO	O	E	82	127,112	52,002	52,002	
			83	320,592	166,081	173,365	7,284
			85	730,596	138,465	138,465	
			86	420,564	150,691	150,691	
	O	W	82	5,117,633	2,053,997	2,063,073	9,076
			83	6,926,540	2,286,543	2,286,993	450
			84	865,650	423,425	423,425	
			85	3,396,699	775,722	775,722	
			86	11,584,314	2,145,281	2,145,303	22
PAKISTN	V	E	84	882	600	675	75
			86	1,543	1,050	1,400	350
	V	W	82	320	319	364	45
REP SAF	N	E	84	445,096	226,323	249,260	22,937
	O	E	83	37,632	20,463	21,415	952
			84	44,373	24,301	25,406	1,105
	V	E	83	230,398	157,294	171,214	13,920
			84	325,337	166,501	187,629	21,128
			85	571,864	218,336	250,245	31,909
			86	76,200	35,101	39,922	4,821
	V	W	83	5,280	3,219	3,921	702
			84	38,100	17,005	19,430	2,425
SOMALIA	V	E	85	112,500	39,521	45,000	5,479
SPAIN	V	E	81	700	600	739	139
			82	1,817	1,500	1,770	270
			83	2,910	1,777	1,993	216
			84	220	318	380	62
			85	2,470	1,995	2,293	298
TURKEY	O	E	84	20,693	11,828	11,828	
	V	E	86	42,000	16,300	18,000	1,700

1477200 RAISINS MADE FRM SEED GRAPES (LB)

Country	Mode	Reg	Yr	Quantity	F.A.S.	C.I.F.	Charges
TOTAL			81	486	353	409	56
			82	54,532	23,477	25,235	1,758
			83	28,240	12,102	14,677	2,575
			84	131,306	76,827	82,613	5,786
			85	372,780	132,944	172,639	39,695
			86	132,468	29,687	42,052	12,365
AFGHAN	V	W	84	11,023	5,000	5,811	811
			86	9,319	6,167	7,463	1,296

Crop
Product
TSUSA commodity number, description, and unit of quantity

Country	Mode	Reg	Yr	Quantity	F.A.S.	C.I.F.	Charges
ARGENT	V	E	83	24,251	6,600	8,581	1,981
	V	W	84	8,819	3,460	4,305	845
AUSTRAL	O	E	83	992	1,076	1,108	32
			84	29,700	13,050	13,050	
AUSTRIA	O	E	83	469	345	366	21
			84	490	351	372	21
CANADA	O	E	83	265	279	293	14
			84	41,824	39,594	39,594	
CHILE	V	E	82	9,881	3,984	5,274	1,290
			84	31,270	9,209	12,859	3,650
			85	372,780	132,944	172,639	39,695
			86	123,149	23,520	34,589	11,069
FRANCE	V	W	82	651	1,693	2,161	468
INDIA	V	W	83	212	413	459	46
MEXICO	O	E	82	44,000	17,800	17,800	
PAKISTN	V	E	81	486	353	409	56
REP SAF	O	E	83	826	869	921	52
			84	2,675	2,629	2,674	45
SPAIN	V	E	83	1,225	2,520	2,949	429
			84	545	969	1,140	171
TURKEY	V	E	84	4,960	2,565	2,808	243

Vermouth

1674000 VERMOUTH IN CONT NOV 1 GAL (GAL)

Country	Mode	Reg	Yr	Quantity	F.A.S.	C.I.F.	Charges
TOTAL			81	2,858,286	17,224,780	19,574,471	2,359,018
			82	2,644,586	16,536,625	18,715,470	2,178,845
			83	2,768,765	17,211,044	19,427,084	2,216,040
			84	2,921,515	18,244,377	20,843,756	2,599,379
			85	3,078,253	18,554,333	21,425,130	2,870,797
			86	2,669,158	17,142,828	19,789,372	2,646,544
BELGIUM	V	E	83	773	2,548	2,954	406
CANADA	O	E	81	603	3,937	4,560	623
			82	79	350	350	
			83	571	2,160	2,160	
			85	266	1,344	1,344	
			86	8,347	63,430	70,279	6,849
	V	E	81	5,468	25,254	29,646	4,392
CHINA M	V	W	81	119	1,036	1,106	70
			82	131	2,439	2,514	75
			83	345	2,649	2,828	179
			84	166	1,358	1,467	109
			85	475	4,940	5,969	1,029
			86	237	2,444	2,748	304
CHINA T	O	E	84	1,637	12,215	13,558	1,343
CYPRUS	O	E	81	63	290	354	64
DENMARK	V	E	81	2,853	19,879	21,972	2,093
FR GERM	O	E	83	2,257	30,818	32,851	2,033
			85	3,896	19,698	23,921	4,223
	V	E	81	1,704	11,338	13,076	1,738
			82	2,901	18,066	20,830	2,764
			86	2,853	14,376	18,153	3,777
	V	W	81	214	1,328	1,633	305
			85	939	3,950	4,826	876
FRANCE	N	E	82	4,399	14,419	18,441	4,022
			84	120,973	776,862	896,087	119,225
			85	8,133	23,187	29,254	6,067
			86	20,505	119,679	139,405	19,726
	O	E	81	36,202	234,582	265,969	31,387
			82	30,413	186,737	211,606	24,869
			83	15,106	92,871	104,899	12,028
			84	24,137	215,493	237,558	22,065
			85	63,271	449,365	492,381	43,016
			86	33,621	202,033	228,257	26,224
	O	W	81	4,354	26,958	32,093	5,135
			82	3,571	23,600	27,111	3,511
			83	3,330	22,763	26,268	3,505
			84	4,698	32,202	36,704	4,502
			85	357	2,934	3,200	266
			86	24	1,254	1,329	75
	V	E	81	399,249	2,362,947	2,756,593	393,646
			82	267,776	1,615,022	1,879,830	264,808
			83	342,014	2,110,115	2,430,472	320,357
			84	199,111	1,360,811	1,562,838	202,027
			85	334,705	1,690,216	1,988,741	298,525
			86	260,152	1,779,151	2,087,285	308,134
	V	H	86	808	5,795	7,085	1,290
	V	W	81	28,197	186,076	218,566	32,490
			82	18,187	125,493	145,560	20,067
			83	16,532	126,785	144,871	18,086
			84	34,825	209,464	242,029	32,565
			85	21,852	148,515	172,999	24,484

Crop
Product
TSUSA commodity number, description, and unit of quantity

Country	Mode	Reg	Yr	Quantity	F.A.S.	C.I.F.	Charges
			86	21,685	156,116	179,289	23,173
GIBRAT	O	E	81	307	2,516	2,906	390
			82	3,329	12,180	14,343	2,163
			84	324	3,063	3,336	273
	V	E	81	1,664	12,005	13,699	1,694
GREECE	V	W	81	119	700	892	192
HG KONG	V	W	81	119	1,125	1,200	75
			82	119	3,228	3,288	60
ISRAEL	O	E	81	440	2,594	2,970	376
			82	436	2,189	2,604	415
			83	321	1,717	2,039	322
			84	118	650	765	115
	V	E	81	3,312	9,179	12,107	2,928
			82	408	2,072	2,507	435
			83	71	390	459	69
			84	466	2,831	3,081	250
ITALY	N	E	81	566,637	3,101,760	3,540,481	438,721
			82	107,615	674,473	769,515	95,042
			83	592,519	3,501,747	3,961,799	460,052
			84	876,108	5,130,338	5,859,761	729,423
			85	223,522	924,387	1,095,443	171,056
			86	169,492	1,029,404	1,219,493	190,089
	N	W	82	26,898	189,443	213,998	24,555
			84	83,220	540,075	604,295	64,220
	O	E	81	393,921	2,609,928	2,905,148	295,220
			82	477,406	3,102,379	3,469,266	366,887
			83	524,939	3,252,432	3,653,141	400,709
			84	435,676	2,706,588	3,063,868	357,280
			85	578,711	3,704,093	4,200,073	495,980
			86	460,954	3,044,430	3,355,290	310,860
	O	W	81	21,257	165,116	185,274	20,158
			82	23,372	194,043	211,388	17,345
			83	41,537	334,645	365,975	31,330
			84	42,620	332,964	369,719	36,755
			85	24,704	192,160	210,553	18,393
			86	26,540	195,408	218,555	23,147
	V	E	81	1,271,187	7,599,191	8,599,549	1,009,685
			82	1,600,800	9,818,544	11,098,505	1,279,961
			83	1,131,065	7,095,068	7,980,680	885,612
			84	1,058,722	6,637,007	7,629,189	992,182
			85	1,651,810	10,220,938	11,874,968	1,654,030
			86	1,490,184	9,520,822	11,087,446	1,566,624
	V	H	84	990	7,815	9,510	1,695
	V	W	81	107,328	765,782	871,209	105,427
			82	59,048	429,297	486,072	56,775
			83	78,125	525,932	592,753	66,821
			84	23,463	186,812	207,869	21,057
			85	146,209	1,026,262	1,157,554	131,292
			86	129,253	913,920	1,069,901	155,981
JAPAN	V	E	83	350	1,113	1,180	67
			84	2,695	12,053	14,986	2,933
MALTA	V	E	83	1,347	10,560	11,648	1,088
MEXICO	O	E	81	1,070	7,655	8,880	1,225
	O	W	86	24,569	7,988	7,988	
NETHLDS	V	E	81	2,164	17,596	19,281	1,685
			83	1,042	5,123	5,675	552
			84	2,909	28,698	31,447	2,749
PORTUGL	O	E	85	275	3,005	3,338	333
	V	E	84	634	5,000	6,022	1,022
			86	2,798	20,547	23,067	2,520
SINGAPR	O	E	82	1,648	16,999	18,340	1,341
SPAIN	O	E	81	1,724	12,565	14,601	2,036
			83	456	3,205	3,605	400
			84	1,361	4,175	5,152	977
			85	3,624	15,484	18,168	2,684
			86	713	4,995	5,845	850
	V	E	81	2,618	9,234	11,726	2,492
			82	7,506	39,330	45,097	5,767
			83	5,310	13,576	17,427	3,851
			84	3,162	19,617	23,801	4,184
			85	2,708	32,477	35,577	3,100
SWEDEN	O	W	81	119	800	937	137
			82	357	2,400	2,811	411
			83	2,292	16,844	18,521	1,677
TRINID	V	E	86	2,282	19,581	21,986	2,405
U KING	O	E	81	4,494	28,136	32,242	4,106
			82	5,366	41,686	47,197	5,511
			83	7,850	53,103	59,305	6,202
			84	3,276	16,406	18,699	2,293
			85	11,021	79,338	92,139	12,801
			86	12,429	32,599	34,833	2,234
	O	W	81	182	1,328	1,498	170
			83	213	1,760	2,093	333
			84	224	1,880	2,015	135

Crop Product TSUSA commodity number, description, and unit of quantity Country	Mode	Reg	Yr	Quantity	F.A.S.	C.I.F.	Charges
	V	E	81	598	3,945	4,303	358
			82	2,821	22,236	24,297	2,061
			83	400	3,120	3,481	361
			85	1,775	12,040	14,682	2,642
YUGOSLV	V	E	86	1,712	8,856	11,138	2,282

1674200 VERMOUTH IN CONT OV 1 GAL (GAL)

TOTAL			81	8,211	45,111	51,811	6,700
			82	1,664	9,600	11,372	1,772
			83	594	4,726	5,021	295
			84	72	2,934	3,245	311
			85	951	2,955	3,795	840
			86	4,718	36,702	42,368	5,666
FR GERM	O	W	81	2	258	303	45
FRANCE	O	E	81	3,407	12,677	15,377	2,700
ITALY	O	W	84	72	2,934	3,245	311
	V	E	81	4,802	32,176	36,131	3,955
			83	594	4,726	5,021	295
			85	951	2,955	3,795	840
			86	3,230	24,240	27,345	3,105
	V	W	82	1,664	9,600	11,372	1,772
			86	1,488	12,462	15,023	2,561

Grapefruit

Grapefruit, essential oil
4522800 GRAPEFRUIT OIL (LB)

TOTAL			81	92,503	88,076	99,856	11,780
			82	65,689	61,018	65,557	4,539
			83	110,014	208,718	218,302	9,584
			84	37,358	84,204	88,742	4,538
			85	189,415	229,570	250,768	21,198
			86	212,849	321,152	343,543	22,391
ARGENT	V	E	85	794	4,758	4,903	145
			86	6,997	17,794	19,235	1,441
AUSTRAL	V	E	86	23,145	34,791	38,128	3,337
BELGIUM	A	E	82	265	622	819	197
	N	E	83	561	1,304	1,632	328
			84	308	703	968	265
	V	E	81	110	266	401	135
BELIZE	O	E	81	14,087	13,308	14,764	1,456
	V	E	81	2,006	2,047	2,128	81
			84	13,978	10,658	11,323	665
			85	35,327	28,841	29,886	1,045
			86	45,234	34,131	37,546	3,415
BRAZIL	V	E	85	52,723	50,807	59,848	9,041
			86	56,328	73,528	77,427	3,899
CANADA	O	E	84	1,929	481	481	
CHINA M	O	E	85	1,146	25,721	26,101	380
FR GERM	A	E	82	74	3,178	3,367	189
			83	110	5,767	6,047	280
FRANCE	V	E	84	110	2,205	2,291	86
			86	110	1,576	1,600	24
	V	W	83	265	1,140	1,280	140
			84	970	4,180	4,765	585
ISRAEL	N	E	81	71,820	65,268	74,856	9,588
			84	16,163	11,389	13,076	1,687
			85	95,219	108,472	118,044	9,572
			86	47,286	65,583	70,564	4,981
	V	E	82	34,589	28,614	31,740	3,126
			83	96,867	52,199	60,684	8,485
			86	26,590	35,316	38,512	3,196
	V	W	82	30,761	28,604	29,631	1,027
JAMAICA	V	E	85	3,600	2,489	3,053	564
JAPAN	O	E	84	35	1,040	1,047	7
	V	W	84	661	8,730	9,090	360
MEXICO	O	E	83	12,000	144,000	144,000	
			84	2,055	35,868	35,868	
NETHLDS	A	E	81	49	552	583	31
			83	33	866	894	28
			84	275	845	885	40
REP SAF	V	E	81	4,365	4,142	4,518	376
			86	4,894	7,268	7,941	673
SPAIN	A	E	83	101	1,826	2,003	177
			84	99	1,381	1,637	256
			86	186	2,683	3,069	386
SWITZLD	A	E	81	66	2,493	2,606	113
			83	77	1,616	1,762	146

Crop Product TSUSA commodity number, description, and unit of quantity Country	Mode	Reg	Yr	Quantity	F.A.S.	C.I.F.	Charges
			84	775	6,724	7,311	587
			85	606	8,482	8,933	451
			86	298	3,796	4,186	390
	N	E	86	794	12,727	13,045	318
U KING	A	W	86	976	29,422	29,728	306
	O	E	86	11	2,537	2,562	25

Grapefruit, fresh
1470300 GRAPEFRUIT, FRESH, 8/1-9/30 (LB)

TOTAL			81	1,450,277	208,257	208,257	
			82	517,782	64,971	67,237	2,266
			83	148,458	14,377	18,030	3,653
			84	197,038	50,164	69,930	19,766
			85	39,675	13,656	17,116	3,460
			86	110,964	12,776	19,594	6,818
DOM REP	A	E	84	5,040	2,016	3,124	1,108
	V	E	83	10,920	1,917	2,487	570
			84	17,410	1,695	2,248	553
			86	14,109	1,600	2,336	736
HAITI	A	E	82	18,730	4,402	6,668	2,266
			83	24,000	5,000	8,083	3,083
			84	73,950	19,200	32,379	13,179
			86	8,400	1,596	3,108	1,512
INDIA	V	E	84	79,366	25,200	30,126	4,926
ISRAEL	V	E	85	39,675	13,656	17,116	3,460
JAMAICA	V	E	86	88,455	9,580	14,150	4,570
MEXICO	O	E	81	1,450,277	208,257	208,257	
			82	499,052	60,569	60,569	
			83	113,538	7,460	7,460	
			84	21,272	2,053	2,053	

1470700 GRAPEFRUIT, FRESH, OCT ONLY (LB)

TOTAL			81	1,920,206	258,699	259,104	405
			82	4,439,323	233,428	239,462	6,034
			83	1,496,781	128,282	128,614	332
			84	3,129,251	203,309	217,834	14,525
			85	232,081	32,683	39,660	6,977
			86	84,000	7,200	9,690	2,490
BAHAMAS	V	E	84	1,133,650	43,050	55,167	12,117
			85	161,950	6,150	7,090	940
CANADA	O	E	85	1,375	1,422	1,422	
DOM REP	A	E	81	4,050	675	1,080	405
	N	E	85	15,288	4,598	5,368	770
	V	E	83	9,920	882	1,214	332
			85	17,680	6,460	7,457	997
DOMINCA	V	E	84	44,213	6,685	9,093	2,408
ECUADOR	V	E	82	38,130	7,812	13,846	6,034
JAMAICA	V	E	86	84,000	7,200	9,690	2,490
MALAYSA	V	E	85	2,189	1,577	1,752	175
MEXICO	O	E	81	1,916,156	258,024	258,024	
			82	4,401,193	225,616	225,616	
			83	1,486,861	127,400	127,400	
			84	1,951,388	153,574	153,574	
PHIL R	V	W	85	1,350	1,134	1,353	219
REP SAF	V	E	85	32,249	11,342	15,218	3,876

1471500 GRAPEFRUIT, FRESH 11/1-7/31 (LB)

TOTAL			81	209,241	27,246	28,534	1,288
			82	372,697	36,010	38,304	2,294
			83	179,242	11,961	16,965	5,004
			84	2,777,192	209,338	218,376	9,038
			85	1,480,095	74,901	89,932	15,031
			86	4,150,578	218,224	235,770	17,546
BAHAMAS	V	E	83	122,450	4,650	5,616	966
			84	560,900	21,300	26,915	5,615
			85	1,238,720	47,040	58,320	11,280
			86	2,201,133	82,260	92,215	9,955
CANADA	O	E	86	35,620	3,580	3,580	
DOM REP	A	E	84	4,000	300	765	465
	V	E	81	12,610	2,032	2,572	540
			83	8,890	910	1,238	328
			84	3,920	392	505	113
			85	38,600	2,316	4,151	1,835
			86	23,000	2,340	3,320	980
DOMINCA	V	E	86	52,056	10,855	13,505	2,650
ISRAEL	V	E	81	14,928	2,279	3,027	748
			82	41,754	5,587	7,881	2,294
			83	41,152	5,418	9,128	3,710
			84	23,065	3,199	6,044	2,845

Crop Product TSUSA commodity number, description, and unit of quantity Country	Mode	Reg	Yr	Quantity	F.A.S.	C.I.F.	Charges
			85	26,970	12,566	14,482	1,916
			86	57,228	20,770	24,281	3,511
JAMAICA	V	E	86	13,650	2,625	3,075	450
MEXICO	O	E	81	181,703	22,935	22,935	
			82	330,943	30,423	30,423	
			83	6,750	983	983	
			84	2,185,307	184,147	184,147	
			85	175,805	12,979	12,979	
			86	1,767,891	95,794	95,794	

Grapefruit, prepared or preserved
1470500 GRAPEFRUIT, PREP, 8/1-9/30 (LB)

Country	Mode	Reg	Yr	Quantity	F.A.S.	C.I.F.	Charges
TOTAL			81	1,028,177	321,099	369,874	48,775
			82	543,183	162,435	169,548	7,113
			83	1,059,913	290,784	330,754	39,970
			84	2,301,390	699,116	820,214	121,098
			85	3,442,957	867,250	1,012,977	145,727
			86	3,447,777	1,322,418	1,521,681	199,263
ARGENT	V	E	86	52,249	9,480	14,280	4,800
BRAZIL	V	E	85	34,888	13,350	15,349	1,999
CANADA	A	H	84	13,975	14,759	16,435	1,676
			85	5,145	5,510	6,240	730
			86	18,031	19,313	21,845	2,532
	A	W	85	2,565	2,631	3,110	479
	O	E	83	4,880	4,850	4,850	
			84	6,978	8,014	8,014	
			85	20,338	23,454	23,454	
			86	34,907	36,015	36,015	
	O	W	84	2,950	2,444	2,444	
			85	11,646	9,983	9,983	
			86	26,672	25,490	25,490	
ECUADOR	V	E	81	76,260	17,670	22,890	5,220
			84	436,806	91,015	111,585	20,570
			85	180,500	69,350	85,350	16,000
GREECE	V	E	86	4,469	5,328	5,763	435
HONDURA	V	E	84	23,732	1,047	2,546	1,499
			85	488,900	23,900	59,087	35,187
IRELAND	V	E	85	34,888	14,050	17,182	3,132
ISRAEL	V	E	81	328,439	116,569	146,635	30,066
			82	52,560	19,651	23,691	4,040
			83	236,032	91,345	115,532	24,187
			84	356,520	130,343	150,235	19,892
			85	1,774,066	429,873	498,994	69,121
			86	2,354,140	914,354	1,066,924	152,570
	V	W	81	34,581	15,072	17,738	2,666
			82	29,325	10,732	13,161	2,429
			83	34,500	13,160	15,500	2,340
			84	80,136	32,342	42,130	9,788
			85	85,596	31,964	39,034	7,070
			86	196,627	79,938	92,602	12,664
ITALY	V	E	81	22,425	8,189	9,419	1,230
KOR REP	V	E	85	6,746	4,539	4,920	381
MEXICO	O	E	81	496,472	142,461	142,461	
			82	461,298	132,052	132,696	644
			83	675,622	146,779	147,426	647
			84	747,129	204,199	204,201	2
			85	700,961	204,614	204,614	
			86	493,137	116,253	116,253	
REP SAF	V	E	81	70,000	21,138	30,731	9,593
			83	108,879	34,650	47,446	12,796
			84	633,164	214,953	282,624	67,671
			85	96,718	34,032	45,660	11,628
			86	267,545	116,247	142,509	26,262

1470900 GRAPEFRUIT, PREP, ENTRY OCT (LB)

Country	Mode	Reg	Yr	Quantity	F.A.S.	C.I.F.	Charges
TOTAL			81	1,494,965	456,084	499,341	43,257
			82	1,070,580	230,708	252,744	22,036
			83	860,238	165,869	166,939	1,070
			84	1,562,419	452,604	490,304	37,700
			85	2,079,521	533,873	599,382	65,509
			86	4,450,970	1,455,035	1,577,735	122,700
ARGENT	V	E	85	88,184	16,000	26,242	10,242
			86	32,574	8,152	12,652	4,500
AUSTRAL	V	E	82	1,102	1,825	1,924	99
CANADA	A	H	84	9,585	10,074	11,251	1,177
			85	7,485	8,018	8,975	957
			86	5,125	5,652	6,461	809
	O	E	82	400	390	390	
			83	258	260	260	
			84	16,895	19,787	19,787	

Country	Mode	Reg	Yr	Quantity	F.A.S.	C.I.F.	Charges
			85	5,561	6,374	6,374	
			86	26,284	26,522	26,522	
	O	W	84	3,485	3,562	3,562	
			85	26,472	19,380	19,380	
			86	8,262	7,173	7,173	
DOM REP	A	E	84	2,900	400	553	153
	V	E	84	2,800	343	433	90
ECUADOR	V	E	82	192,510	44,075	57,831	13,756
			84	78,197	19,530	23,618	4,088
HG KONG	O	E	86	26,880	12,096	12,096	
HONDURA	V	E	84	121,158	5,592	13,398	7,806
			85	390,500	19,400	43,776	24,376
			86	122,000	6,000	14,241	8,241
ISRAEL	N	E	86	125,003	47,302	54,685	7,383
	V	E	81	206,220	77,549	95,569	18,020
			82	72,900	30,970	34,780	3,810
			83	19,047	8,077	9,147	1,070
			84	182,540	73,860	87,171	13,311
			85	425,905	167,299	194,627	27,328
			86	859,189	331,567	406,638	75,071
	V	W	81	140,904	52,766	68,424	15,658
			82	36,111	14,190	18,561	4,371
			84	20,020	8,080	10,348	2,268
			85	34,888	14,400	17,006	2,606
			86	36,032	15,630	18,375	2,745
JAPAN	V	E	84	87,163	44,088	52,865	8,777
MEXICO	O	E	81	1,080,641	305,801	305,801	
			82	767,557	139,258	139,258	
			83	840,933	157,532	157,532	
			84	1,037,316	266,993	266,993	
			85	1,100,526	283,002	283,002	
			86	3,112,874	960,796	972,892	12,096
PHIL R	V	W	84	360	295	325	30
REP SAF	V	E	81	67,200	19,968	29,547	9,579
			86	96,747	34,145	46,000	11,855

1471700 GRAPEFRUIT, PREP, 11/1-7/31 (LB)

Country	Mode	Reg	Yr	Quantity	F.A.S.	C.I.F.	Charges
TOTAL			81	9,118,443	2,776,027	3,129,434	353,407
			82	9,231,554	2,411,984	2,667,081	255,097
			83	8,690,950	2,097,947	2,338,252	240,305
			84	10,692,334	3,287,368	3,639,103	351,735
			85	14,540,685	5,143,871	5,805,104	661,233
			86	24,912,849	6,917,696	7,870,122	952,426
ARGENT	V	E	86	398,906	72,416	85,154	12,738
BAHAMAS	V	E	86	3,995,030	151,710	178,336	26,626
BELGIUM	V	E	86	37,920	15,228	16,748	1,520
CANADA	A	H	84	8,375	8,837	9,849	1,012
			85	59,852	65,101	72,296	7,195
			86	52,883	53,408	59,649	6,241
	O	E	83	18,566	14,360	14,360	
			84	140,742	153,959	153,959	
			85	90,148	103,640	103,640	
			86	129,093	130,055	130,055	
	O	W	82	240	259	259	
			85	111,957	88,441	88,441	
			86	191,079	141,596	141,596	
CYPRUS	V	E	83	121	300	317	17
			84	32,625	13,725	16,023	2,298
DOM REP	A	E	84	24,696	1,764	4,768	3,004
	N	E	86	43,360	11,649	15,372	3,723
	V	E	86	985,010	421,383	456,538	35,155
ECUADOR	V	E	81	470,420	101,070	128,844	27,774
			82	294,730	72,111	97,873	25,762
			85	132,574	26,087	35,687	9,600
FR GERM	V	E	84	20,019	8,080	10,209	2,129
HG KONG	V	E	83	10,800	612	736	124
HONDURA	V	E	84	82,104	3,732	9,156	5,424
			85	622,306	37,605	82,761	45,156
			86	450,498	54,435	85,640	31,205
ICELAND	V	E	85	538,847	202,825	232,901	30,076
			86	192,903	64,025	72,750	8,725
ISRAEL	N	E	85	3,727,731	1,525,176	1,829,179	304,003
			86	676,219	259,392	297,930	38,538
	O	E	84	29,325	10,928	12,830	1,902
			86	39,600	17,070	19,758	2,688
	V	E	81	3,235,075	1,146,271	1,436,164	289,893
			82	2,329,417	937,409	1,144,481	207,072
			83	1,794,345	715,049	902,876	187,827
			84	3,076,484	1,288,743	1,559,711	270,968
			85	3,415,031	1,352,875	1,575,460	222,585
			86	11,427,397	4,078,773	4,774,073	695,300
	V	W	81	227,836	89,043	112,002	22,959
			82	150,465	60,359	72,339	11,980

Crop Product TSUSA commodity number, description, and unit of quantity Country	Mode	Reg	Yr	Quantity	F.A.S.	C.I.F.	Charges
			83	314,035	121,419	153,082	31,663
			84	608,403	244,669	301,958	57,289
			85	375,918	146,112	183,054	36,942
			86	586,962	243,972	304,179	60,207
MEXICO	O	E	81	5,077,352	1,405,337	1,405,337	
			82	6,290,667	1,296,745	1,296,745	
			83	6,303,307	1,164,224	1,164,224	
			84	6,391,970	1,500,330	1,500,330	
			85	5,376,092	1,568,473	1,568,475	2
			86	5,228,076	1,056,268	1,057,820	1,552
	O	W	81	4,160	1,381	1,381	
			82	35,280	6,544	6,544	
			84	182,888	20,715	20,715	
			85	24,464	3,375	3,375	
			86	184,970	16,466	16,466	
REP SAF	V	E	81	103,600	32,925	45,706	12,781
			82	130,755	38,557	48,840	10,283
			83	216,236	71,162	89,736	18,574
			84	94,118	31,440	39,104	7,664
			85	31,265	11,580	15,217	3,637
			86	225,743	103,342	126,418	23,076
	V	W	83	33,540	10,821	12,921	2,100
SPAIN	V	E	85	34,500	12,581	14,618	2,037
U KING	V	E	84	585	446	491	45
	V	W	86	67,200	26,508	31,640	5,132

Great Laurel

Brierroot
2004500 BRIERROOT, ROUGH OR BLOCK (GR)

Country	Mode	Reg	Yr	Quantity	F.A.S.	C.I.F.	Charges
TOTAL			81	24,326	1,486,013	1,594,000	107,987
			82	12,634	1,061,767	1,138,578	76,811
			83	8,744	703,923	761,335	57,412
			84	12,397	780,239	843,581	63,342
			85	11,738	805,234	883,680	78,446
			86	7,131	440,011	482,812	42,801
FRANCE	A	E	84	10	1,055	1,372	317
			86	1	2,235	2,521	286
	O	E	83	60	6,037	6,037	
			86	86	4,691	4,691	
	O	W	84	12	644	644	
GREECE	A	E	85	123	1,481	1,505	24
	V	E	81	9,372	916,408	974,158	57,750
			82	5,352	502,024	535,618	33,594
			83	3,497	334,528	359,619	25,091
			84	5,361	434,201	470,684	36,483
			85	3,104	322,944	350,086	27,142
			86	1,489	156,253	170,140	13,887
	V	W	81	111	2,670	3,067	397
			82	35	12,150	12,711	561
			83	12	8,260	8,647	387
ISRAEL	V	E	83	162	9,273	9,878	605
ITALY	N	E	82	475	56,135	58,797	2,662
			84	3,379	135,155	142,060	6,905
			85	1,612	82,574	88,717	6,143
	V	E	81	7,456	161,954	173,382	11,428
			82	939	162,820	168,728	5,908
			83	1,896	178,286	190,355	12,069
			84	1,313	119,647	125,413	5,766
			85	3,918	248,100	270,759	22,659
			86	4,020	192,796	207,985	15,189
MOROC	V	E	83	232	24,000	26,352	2,352
SPAIN	V	E	81	7,387	404,981	443,393	38,412
			82	5,827	325,338	359,140	33,802
			83	2,885	143,539	160,447	16,908
			84	2,322	89,537	103,408	13,871
			85	2,706	147,735	169,401	21,666
			86	1,530	83,011	96,145	13,134
	V	W	82	6	3,300	3,584	284
			85	275	2,400	3,212	812
			86	5	1,025	1,330	305

Guar

Guar, gum
1883810 GUAR GUM, NATURAL (LB)

Country	Mode	Reg	Yr	Quantity	F.A.S.	C.I.F.	Charges
TOTAL			81	165,862,585	86,227,951	97,033,431	10,808,480
			82	135,293,707	62,223,515	70,995,038	8,771,523
			83	51,650,581	15,399,922	18,719,295	3,319,373
			84	67,331,809	16,554,266	21,004,561	4,450,295
			85	96,914,297	24,749,892	30,650,144	5,900,252
			86	65,891,209	27,043,364	30,188,635	3,145,271
AUSTRIA	V	E	81	22,500	14,033	15,271	1,238
BELGIUM	V	E	83	2,262	476	576	100
BOLIVIA	O	E	82	152,003	103,422	114,934	11,512
CANADA	O	E	81	700	832	915	83
			85	43,310	18,900	19,517	617
	O	W	83	2,000	2,595	2,595	
CHINA T	V	E	85	87,000	33,060	37,996	4,936
	V	W	84	178,516	54,097	65,082	10,985
FR GERM	A	E	85	331	1,148	1,391	243
	O	E	81	900	995	1,084	89
	V	E	81	44,000	17,175	19,600	2,425
			85	21,495	66,080	70,150	4,070
FRANCE	A	E	82	1,184	3,909	4,927	1,018
	V	E	81	65,999	80,855	85,060	4,205
			83	9,064	6,969	7,621	652
			84	6,600	4,469	5,148	679
			86	14,409	20,000	22,314	2,314
GHANA	V	W	85	39,683	20,720	24,424	3,704
HG KONG	V	E	85	37,556	8,520	11,203	2,683
HUNGARY	V	E	81	110,230	57,750	65,196	7,446
INDIA	N	E	83	184,505	63,040	76,156	13,116
			84	4,082,452	1,180,607	1,462,360	281,753
			86	11,231,859	3,541,401	4,124,499	583,098
	O	E	81	32,500	22,408	24,921	2,513
			82	672,504	375,375	425,538	50,163
			83	38,534	10,003	12,361	2,358
			84	52,300	20,857	20,857	
	O	W	85	44,912	11,572	14,560	2,988
	V	E	81	138,270,085	71,308,634	80,376,240	9,070,606
			82	105,866,102	48,063,715	54,960,373	6,896,658
			83	39,716,505	10,681,276	13,202,205	2,520,929
			84	40,228,660	8,435,642	11,021,301	2,585,659
			85	71,752,817	16,828,888	21,015,826	4,186,938
			86	33,414,026	13,423,113	14,910,707	1,487,594
	V	W	81	856,764	437,409	506,193	68,784
			82	754,378	344,769	404,288	59,519
			83	1,265,501	408,775	495,286	86,511
			84	2,002,563	574,277	741,055	166,778
			85	2,050,343	596,207	767,003	170,796
			86	674,290	306,329	345,823	39,494
INDNSIA	V	E	85	75,000	22,448	26,972	4,524
IRAN	V	E	85	46,670	58,452	59,202	750
ITALY	A	E	81	450	473	885	412
			82	3,991	3,320	5,683	2,363
	O	E	81	772	2,411	2,411	
	V	E	81	568,200	496,227	538,169	41,942
			82	234,330	347,741	365,159	17,418
			83	82,682	85,835	90,478	4,643
			84	1,047,659	284,955	306,497	21,542
			85	132,661	70,318	78,158	7,840
			86	288,494	613,490	632,317	18,827
JAPAN	A	E	83	50	350	632	282
	V	E	84	425,926	79,440	106,569	27,129
			86	119,048	64,152	70,433	6,281
	V	W	81	1,548	3,240	3,440	200
			82	1,689	4,645	5,075	430
			85	59,547	18,407	23,465	5,058
KENYA	V	E	86	41,800	13,775	13,871	96
LAOS	V	E	84	39,683	9,900	12,776	2,876
MALAWI	V	E	81	4,279,680	477,548	627,713	150,165
MEXICO	O	W	81	193,674	33,578	33,578	
			82	15,212	4,564	4,564	
			84	132,276	7,557	7,557	
NETHLDS	O	E	83	1,101	1,503	1,503	
	V	E	82	2,000	4,035	4,240	205
			86	4,410	4,669	5,300	631
PAKISTN	N	E	83	4,915,152	1,846,345	2,167,095	320,750
			84	320,504	98,194	125,424	27,230
			85	1,289,009	399,119	491,853	92,734
			86	1,831,915	732,648	826,686	94,038
	N	W	83	672,528	232,143	274,554	42,411

Crop
Product
TSUSA commodity number, description, and unit of quantity

Country	Mode	Reg	Yr	Quantity	F.A.S.	C.I.F.	Charges
			84	912,154	253,592	307,583	53,991
	O	E	82	246,553	129,483	148,138	18,655
			83	48,000	39,358	39,358	
			86	44,092	11,778	14,471	2,693
	O	W	84	119,049	58,050	58,050	
			85	98,766	13,380	17,758	4,378
	V	E	81	20,205,085	12,318,539	13,679,385	1,360,846
			82	16,400,254	7,452,014	8,499,199	1,047,185
			83	1,767,048	612,109	726,699	114,590
			84	13,208,105	3,566,262	4,443,445	877,183
			85	16,193,089	4,480,440	5,538,068	1,057,628
			86	13,213,483	5,231,429	5,845,603	614,174
	V	W	81	892,501	596,699	667,087	70,388
			82	1,339,773	517,447	617,068	99,621
			83	1,717,348	644,593	773,305	128,712
			84	2,533,379	766,815	960,975	194,160
			85	1,825,255	567,916	690,552	122,636
			86	789,860	298,565	350,859	52,294
PHIL R	V	E	85	40,000	13,200	14,124	924
	V	W	86	114,500	47,551	54,916	7,365
PITCARN	V	E	85	18,348	27,840	32,136	4,296
PORTUGL	V	E	83	39,700	67,490	67,700	210
	V	W	86	125,661	27,398	36,190	8,792
S HELNA	V	E	84	39,651	7,657	9,895	2,238
SINGAPR	V	E	81	29,120	13,341	15,410	2,069
SPAIN	O	E	82	6,000	3,000	3,000	
	V	E	81	250,510	317,949	340,236	22,287
			82	327,002	323,914	343,078	19,164
			83	218,201	143,202	158,613	15,411
			84	291,000	247,657	266,200	18,543
			85	571,866	512,052	547,867	35,815
			86	166,503	135,264	145,944	10,680
SWEDEN	V	E	83	77,422	26,057	30,936	4,879
			84	37,500	12,053	14,763	2,710
SWITZLD	A	E	82	1,819	3,324	4,694	1,370
			83	110	303	353	50
			84	1,952	3,885	5,016	1,131
	N	E	86	37,900	26,730	33,609	6,879
	O	E	84	22,050	9,900	10,601	701
	V	E	81	992	1,468	1,582	114
			82	8,992,810	4,354,173	4,881,491	527,318
			83	35,000	23,946	26,363	2,417
			84	3,307	4,057	4,567	510
			85	4,740	7,857	8,218	361
	V	W	82	1,102	3,205	3,362	157
			83	1,102	2,861	3,001	140
THAILND	V	E	86	44,800	6,213	6,213	
U KING	N	W	86	930,480	632,384	678,382	45,998
	O	E	81	36,375	26,387	29,055	2,668
			84	151,384	83,945	119,491	35,546
			85	95,900	45,221	55,721	10,500
			86	1,525,400	1,110,068	1,192,304	82,236
	V	E	82	159,920	102,062	116,212	14,150
			83	408,010	234,632	256,097	21,465
			84	973,971	521,598	640,415	118,817
			85	1,477,083	502,720	607,365	104,645
			86	1,190,095	737,340	816,627	79,287
	V	W	82	115,081	79,398	84,015	4,617
			83	448,756	266,061	305,808	39,747
			84	521,168	268,800	288,934	20,134
			85	908,916	425,427	496,615	71,188
			86	88,184	59,067	61,567	2,500

Guar, seed
1922200 GUAR SEEDS (LB)

Country	Mode	Reg	Yr	Quantity	F.A.S.	C.I.F.	Charges
TOTAL			81	6,881,727	772,449	1,129,717	357,268
			82	5,628	2,429	2,785	356
			83	391,419	92,899	106,147	13,248
			84	277,512	15,178	15,488	310
			85	1,773,077	83,079	85,212	2,133
			86	665,062	24,544	26,887	2,343
BRAZIL	A	E	83	45,752	46,484	56,767	10,283
	A	W	83	4,409	17,000	19,432	2,432
COLOMB	A	E	81	73,900	12,798	14,607	1,809
			82	5,047	1,536	1,673	137
			83	26,000	2,470	3,003	533
			84	9,000	804	921	117
			85	22,500	3,825	5,130	1,305
			86	7,320	3,660	6,003	2,343
MALAWI	V	E	81	6,807,827	759,651	1,115,110	355,459
MEXICO	O	W	83	315,258	26,945	26,945	

Crop
Product
TSUSA commodity number, description, and unit of quantity

Country	Mode	Reg	Yr	Quantity	F.A.S.	C.I.F.	Charges
			84	264,552	14,028	14,028	
			85	1,736,387	76,348	76,348	
			86	657,742	20,884	20,884	
MOROC	V	W	82	581	893	1,112	219
NETHLDS	A	E	84	3,960	346	539	193
			85	14,190	2,906	3,734	828

Guava

Guava, fresh or dried or pickled
1478000 GUAVAS,FR,DRD,PCKLD,IN BRINE (LB)

Country	Mode	Reg	Yr	Quantity	F.A.S.	C.I.F.	Charges
TOTAL			81	6,179	1,389	2,991	1,602
			82	139,615	60,186	69,540	9,354
			83	36,523	19,880	27,574	7,694
			84	54,719	18,988	29,804	10,816
			85	11,855	6,076	7,230	1,154
			86	11,922	11,515	16,097	4,582
BELGIUM	A	W	83	1,129	1,217	1,763	546
BRAZIL	V	E	82	60,000	21,875	27,061	5,186
			83	2,921	890	1,130	240
			85	971	1,008	1,083	75
CHINA T	V	W	82	16,800	8,638	9,829	1,191
DOM REP	V	E	83	22,737	4,000	4,714	714
			84	5,724	1,908	2,265	357
			85	10,179	4,000	4,560	560
JAMAICA	A	E	84	32,400	4,608	6,754	2,146
N ZEAL	A	E	81	432	366	618	252
			84	229	253	364	111
	A	W	81	1,338	719	2,069	1,350
			83	8,525	13,140	19,156	6,016
			84	10,738	10,371	18,216	7,845
			85	705	1,068	1,587	519
			86	4,919	9,072	13,360	4,288
NETHLDS	O	E	81	4,409	304	304	
PHIL R	V	E	84	800	280	376	96
	V	W	82	960	580	670	90
			83	1,211	633	811	178
			84	1,342	558	647	89
THAILND	V	E	82	1,584	711	834	123
			84	840	350	394	44
	V	W	82	60,271	28,382	31,146	2,764
			84	2,646	660	788	128
			86	7,003	2,443	2,737	294

Guava, jelly or jam
1530800 GUAVA JELLY, JAM, ETC (LB)

Country	Mode	Reg	Yr	Quantity	F.A.S.	C.I.F.	Charges
TOTAL			81	640,209	145,362	167,072	21,710
			82	1,094,666	274,420	318,463	44,043
			83	792,754	177,538	208,906	31,368
			84	894,042	211,870	251,648	39,778
			85	1,379,877	257,369	312,583	55,214
			86	766,544	176,575	198,903	22,328
BRAZIL	V	E	81	103,800	29,614	35,483	5,869
			82	235,595	61,216	79,847	18,631
			83	202,254	49,088	62,829	13,741
			84	280,334	76,937	92,192	15,255
			85	303,987	75,462	95,560	20,098
			86	24,639	6,009	7,408	1,399
	V	W	81	2,400	526	659	133
			82	4,800	1,440	1,745	305
			84	4,800	1,440	1,955	515
C RICA	V	E	82	14,775	4,681	5,632	951
			83	16,000	7,272	7,712	440
			84	4,802	3,069	3,297	228
			85	103,692	19,860	24,846	4,986
			86	95,025	19,988	23,915	3,927
COLOMB	A	E	86	886	1,520	1,596	76
	N	E	84	32,433	13,324	16,876	3,552
	V	E	84	15,475	10,140	11,074	934
			85	34,070	12,333	17,190	4,857
DOM REP	N	E	82	403,292	71,154	81,029	9,875
			86	253,268	54,497	61,099	6,602
	V	E	81	490,384	94,461	107,272	12,811
			82	411,289	120,851	130,358	9,507
			83	513,537	81,166	94,948	13,782
			84	536,986	91,489	109,335	17,846
			85	888,038	133,347	157,571	24,224

Crop Product TSUSA commodity number, description, and unit of quantity Country	Mode	Reg	Yr	Quantity	F.A.S.	C.I.F.	Charges
			86	373,454	82,945	92,469	9,524
FRANCE	O	E	81	1,329	1,803	1,953	150
			82	782	1,075	1,225	150
	V	E	81	524	780	822	42
			82	639	803	895	92
			83	1,013	1,109	1,219	110
			84	1,996	2,992	3,337	345
INDIA	V	W	81	2,333	2,364	2,667	303
JAMAICA	N	E	82	4,426	1,981	5,145	3,164
	V	E	81	35,093	14,171	16,538	2,367
			82	10,085	8,564	9,846	1,282
			83	22,885	17,245	18,995	1,750
			84	7,455	4,905	5,430	525
			85	9,750	6,440	7,129	689
			86	1,885	1,360	1,568	208
	V	W	84	1,800	1,010	1,346	336
MEXICO	O	E	84	50	509	509	
			85	11,776	2,560	2,560	
			86	3,732	3,433	3,433	
	O	W	81	3,960	1,391	1,391	
			82	8,400	1,795	1,795	
			83	1,206	354	354	
			84	3,929	1,949	1,949	
			85	26,224	5,567	5,567	
PHIL R	V	E	82	185	272	290	18
			83	257	341	377	36
	V	W	81	386	252	287	35
			82	398	588	656	68
			83	360	283	329	46
			84	150	254	274	20
SWITZLD	V	E	84	3,814	3,530	3,727	197
TRINID	V	E	83	1,222	2,050	2,122	72
			85	2,340	1,800	2,160	360
U KING	O	E	86	1,412	2,316	2,591	275
	V	E	84	18	322	347	25
VENEZ	V	E	83	34,020	18,630	20,021	1,391
			86	12,243	4,507	4,824	317

Guava, paste and pulp

1525400 GUAVA PASTE AND PULP (LB)

Country	Mode	Reg	Yr	Quantity	F.A.S.	C.I.F.	Charges
TOTAL			**81**	**5,728,538**	**1,363,002**	**1,598,114**	**235,112**
			82	**8,320,041**	**2,088,246**	**2,490,387**	**402,141**
			83	**7,331,563**	**1,785,406**	**2,148,267**	**362,861**
			84	**7,976,405**	**1,844,273**	**2,232,725**	**388,452**
			85	**8,450,885**	**1,944,343**	**2,341,879**	**397,536**
			86	**13,878,143**	**2,788,540**	**3,345,370**	**556,830**
ARGENT	V	E	83	24,000	3,600	3,780	180
AUSTRAL	V	E	86	28,550	6,456	10,778	4,322
	V	W	86	686,675	103,615	156,835	53,220
BRAZIL	N	E	85	1,604,742	416,134	524,895	108,761
	O	E	86	22,200	2,022	2,685	663
	V	E	81	1,912,958	496,383	619,823	123,440
			82	3,444,493	1,023,389	1,275,910	252,521
			83	4,042,641	1,018,384	1,287,171	268,787
			84	3,654,898	956,700	1,203,250	246,550
			85	1,896,600	527,544	649,446	121,902
			86	6,676,690	1,131,591	1,354,449	222,858
	V	W	81	65,980	16,032	20,326	4,294
			82	121,304	35,811	45,413	9,602
			83	93,410	23,116	29,904	6,788
			84	54,900	13,341	17,803	4,462
			85	112,465	27,831	36,064	8,233
			86	809,897	198,809	246,441	47,632
C RICA	V	E	81	24,511	7,288	10,551	3,263
			82	283,047	85,160	109,579	24,419
			83	101,033	41,879	45,028	3,149
			84	140,826	65,883	72,190	6,307
			86	23,333	6,925	8,245	1,320
CHINA T	V	W	83	2,850	1,250	1,350	100
COLOMB	A	E	83	2,230	1,188	1,625	437
			84	38,545	18,291	24,967	6,676
			86	4,300	2,000	3,380	1,380
	N	E	83	23,200	18,816	21,605	2,789
			84	32,837	11,960	15,503	3,543
			85	157,287	87,375	116,479	29,104
			86	360,162	183,508	204,970	21,462
	O	E	85	1,874	1,092	1,234	142
	V	E	81	393,908	175,811	207,167	31,356
			82	62,910	49,207	53,339	4,132
			83	87,010	52,356	58,733	6,377
			84	159,735	106,875	119,039	12,164
			85	7,910	3,760	4,634	874
DOM REP	A	E	82	972	394	545	151
	N	E	82	3,686,731	666,425	756,400	89,975
			86	1,941,170	349,753	413,677	63,924
	V	E	81	2,464,498	444,913	502,460	57,547
			82	46,676	9,823	11,147	1,324
			83	2,126,842	442,532	496,083	53,551
			84	2,737,390	469,821	556,322	86,501
			85	4,290,004	796,429	917,424	120,995
			86	1,842,324	457,866	501,505	43,639
ECUADOR	A	E	82	30,093	13,909	18,000	4,091
	V	E	82	11,747	6,840	7,695	855
FIJI	V	W	81	79,964	43,818	50,377	6,559
			82	139,609	62,037	75,038	13,001
			83	10,648	4,831	5,808	977
			86	162,015	38,394	51,870	13,476
FINLAND	V	W	86	64,815	14,800	20,748	5,948
FRANCE	A	E	84	214	334	900	566
	V	E	84	23,275	14,817	17,060	2,243
			86	2,817	5,215	5,930	715
	V	W	82	132	297	302	5
GUATMAL	V	E	85	29,931	3,174	3,573	399
HAITI	V	E	81	17,100	5,250	5,801	551
INDIA	V	W	84	35,053	6,996	10,601	3,605
			86	46,500	16,821	19,687	2,866
ISRAEL	V	W	83	20,160	5,180	6,654	1,474
ITALY	V	E	86	101,271	31,931	36,431	4,500
JAPAN	V	E	86	22,046	9,600	12,998	3,398
MEXICO	O	E	81	211,700	41,879	41,879	
			82	139,380	26,751	26,751	
			83	394,107	59,090	59,090	
			84	666,897	73,424	73,424	
			85	153,481	36,319	36,319	
			86	26,236	4,725	4,725	
	O	W	81	494,510	112,506	112,506	
			82	330,002	98,524	98,524	
			83	195,855	43,548	43,548	
			84	205,266	30,051	30,051	
			85	84,439	19,520	19,520	
			86	146,052	22,607	22,607	
PHIL R	V	E	83	85,978	25,948	33,260	7,312
			84	72,200	28,664	37,376	8,712
			86	44,092	11,187	16,305	5,118
	V	W	84	134	377	445	68
			85	381	1,785	1,983	198
			86	7,872	1,988	2,682	694
REP SAF	V	E	83	108,467	19,694	28,973	9,279
			85	29,632	4,380	6,223	1,843
			86	429,934	77,144	106,420	29,276
	V	W	81	63,409	19,122	27,224	8,102
			86	369,775	96,861	123,124	26,263
SPAIN	O	E	84	273	1,752	1,789	37
SWITZLD	V	E	83	1,499	408	492	84
U KING	V	E	83	233	1,586	1,678	92
VENEZ	A	E	83	11,400	22,000	23,485	1,485
	V	E	82	22,945	9,679	11,744	2,065
			84	153,962	44,987	52,005	7,018
			85	82,139	19,000	24,085	5,085
			86	59,417	14,722	18,878	4,156

Guava, prepared or preserved

1478500 GUAVAS,PREP AND PRES, NSPF (LB)

Country	Mode	Reg	Yr	Quantity	F.A.S.	C.I.F.	Charges
TOTAL			**81**	**1,114,012**	**423,435**	**488,894**	**65,459**
			82	**1,483,069**	**683,330**	**766,308**	**82,978**
			83	**1,370,660**	**537,237**	**631,754**	**94,517**
			84	**1,335,625**	**510,785**	**582,765**	**71,980**
			85	**1,136,479**	**383,173**	**447,464**	**64,291**
			86	**1,613,617**	**541,409**	**625,412**	**84,003**
BRAZIL	N	E	82	238,454	129,023	149,191	20,168
	V	E	81	817,267	306,412	361,890	55,478
			82	512,654	211,910	249,375	37,465
			83	980,890	414,690	492,600	77,910
			84	600,969	248,325	286,362	38,037
			85	555,491	192,253	234,769	42,516
			86	1,085,236	374,922	437,875	62,953
	V	W	81	32,400	11,226	14,029	2,803
			82	30,000	11,998	14,644	2,646
			83	64,206	22,861	28,157	5,296
			84	54,000	22,300	27,291	4,991
C RICA	V	E	82	49,089	17,560	20,133	2,573
			83	54,171	9,692	12,756	3,064

Crop
Product
TSUSA commodity number, description, and unit of quantity

Country	Mode	Reg	Yr	Quantity	F.A.S.	C.I.F.	Charges
			84	3,800	3,168	3,468	300
	V	W	84	1,500	330	526	196
CHINA M	V	W	82	6,400	2,830	3,185	355
CHINA T	V	W	82	2,849	1,575	1,684	109
			83	675	315	334	19
			86	5,004	2,750	3,294	544
COLOMB	A	E	83	865	1,082	1,512	430
	N	E	84	38,088	16,810	20,400	3,590
			85	17,718	17,283	20,839	3,556
			86	21,941	21,106	25,223	4,117
	V	E	81	1,045	500	600	100
			84	9,436	5,100	5,739	639
DOM REP	A	E	81	2,847	2,120	2,600	480
	N	E	82	5,397	3,700	4,625	925
	V	E	81	62,474	23,175	25,501	2,326
			82	149,556	69,054	75,379	6,325
			83	160,478	57,054	63,734	6,680
			84	108,597	34,419	38,616	4,197
			85	321,971	100,480	111,375	10,895
			86	250,871	73,089	79,375	6,286
FRANCE	V	W	84	2,700	4,261	4,483	222
GUATMAL	V	E	84	945	607	683	76
HG KONG	V	E	86	1,329	2,270	2,707	437
INDIA	V	E	81	2,115	823	1,129	306
			82	2,622	954	1,281	327
	V	W	84	1,266	777	997	220
JAMAICA	V	E	84	15,200	4,869	5,372	503
MALAYSA	V	W	85	2,324	1,350	1,450	100
MEXICO	O	E	81	36,518	11,686	11,686	
			82	10,554	8,215	8,215	
			83	23,100	4,200	4,200	
			84	65,294	25,355	25,355	
			85	11,118	4,860	4,860	
	O	W	81	112,033	49,386	49,386	
			82	320,311	164,565	164,565	
			83	73,764	17,379	17,379	
			84	266,985	92,357	92,357	
			85	180,473	51,108	51,108	
			86	107,497	28,791	28,791	
PERU	V	E	86	14,400	6,520	7,353	833
PHIL R	V	E	81	7,201	380	408	28
			82	45,310	13,802	17,881	4,079
			83	939	3,062	3,184	122
			84	12,460	4,427	4,646	219
	V	W	81	1,425	763	889	126
			82	4,100	2,371	2,670	299
			83	11,572	6,902	7,898	996
			84	6,550	3,450	4,019	569
			85	490	1,450	1,537	87
REP SAF	V	E	81	37,629	16,338	20,047	3,709
			82	44,672	15,109	19,228	4,119
			85	28,660	6,075	11,959	5,884
			86	92,391	14,418	21,942	7,524
SPAIN	V	E	81	1,058	626	729	103
SWITZLD	V	E	84	143,299	41,823	59,800	17,977
THAILND	V	E	82	14,641	7,481	8,519	1,038
			84	1,477	500	606	106
			85	16,434	6,445	7,317	872
	V	W	82	46,460	23,183	25,733	2,550
			84	3,059	1,907	2,045	138
			86	12,218	5,500	5,980	480
U KING	V	E	85	1,800	1,869	2,250	381
VENEZ	V	E	86	22,730	12,043	12,872	829

Gum Arabic Tree

Gum arabic, gum

1883600 GUM ARABIC (LB)

Country	Mode	Reg	Yr	Quantity	F.A.S.	C.I.F.	Charges
TOTAL			81	19,058,914	13,151,845	14,409,122	1,257,277
			82	14,678,958	10,287,231	11,084,865	797,634
			83	19,063,675	12,895,648	13,955,112	1,059,464
			84	25,515,371	17,794,636	19,040,514	1,245,878
			85	15,884,792	11,538,570	12,325,553	786,983
			86	14,067,950	17,255,562	18,085,393	829,831
AFGHAN	V	E	86	44,753	98,160	104,540	6,380
ARGENT	A	E	85	13,448	72,827	89,169	16,342
AUSTRAL	V	E	81	38,492	5,516	8,730	3,214
CANADA	O	E	81	1,417	1,486	1,486	
			83	51,984	63,389	63,389	

Crop
Product
TSUSA commodity number, description, and unit of quantity

Country	Mode	Reg	Yr	Quantity	F.A.S.	C.I.F.	Charges
			84	15,200	17,853	17,853	
			85	22,540	45,385	45,385	
			86	36,265	79,420	79,420	
CHINA M	V	W	84	290	600	623	23
CHINA T	V	W	83	1,943	4,400	4,702	302
			84	1,551	3,060	3,258	198
EGYPT	V	E	82	56,250	188,750	191,913	3,163
ETHIOP	V	E	82	6,614	10,500	11,905	1,405
			86	7,420	10,303	11,003	700
FR GERM	N	E	84	112,581	54,900	59,114	4,214
			86	69,627	159,804	171,220	11,416
	O	E	81	1,202	844	1,001	157
			84	1,050	288	315	27
	V	E	81	40,282	23,400	24,450	1,050
			83	86	360	418	58
			84	61,729	60,518	63,718	3,200
			85	406,369	252,880	267,896	15,016
			86	16,093	31,494	33,968	2,474
FRANCE	A	E	82	110	935	1,136	201
			85	20,064	44,550	56,033	11,483
	A	W	83	5,500	4,420	4,768	348
	N	E	82	718,203	530,776	572,892	42,116
			83	881,879	665,961	708,382	42,421
			85	2,039,797	2,070,169	2,232,747	162,578
	N	W	85	50,600	55,066	67,928	12,862
	O	E	82	586,408	451,319	485,038	33,719
			83	861,275	549,302	585,757	36,455
			84	114,180	96,699	106,755	10,056
	V	E	81	1,172,848	607,739	666,723	58,984
			82	5,550	4,456	4,689	233
			83	395,630	339,201	360,385	21,184
			84	2,113,855	1,861,686	2,040,315	178,629
			85	1,899,709	1,868,348	2,006,317	137,969
			86	4,596,297	6,501,384	6,902,473	401,089
	V	W	85	39,600	25,821	29,304	3,483
			86	78,600	103,707	110,544	6,837
GERM DR	V	E	86	22,266	78,872	88,337	9,465
GREECE	V	E	85	11,023	36,000	36,635	635
HEARD I	V	E	86	44,090	147,300	164,976	17,676
INDIA	V	E	82	199,948	143,880	182,881	39,001
			83	312,046	251,384	273,094	21,710
			84	793,656	517,968	561,204	43,236
			85	198,773	129,872	136,852	6,980
			86	77,329	59,713	65,207	5,494
	V	W	81	400	611	678	67
			83	441	581	688	107
IRAN	V	E	81	44,092	32,000	36,409	4,409
ITALY	A	E	86	1,381	6,745	8,525	1,780
IVY CST	V	E	85	185,186	66,115	79,266	13,151
			86	326,626	133,436	154,454	21,018
JAPAN	V	E	83	469	383	391	8
	V	W	83	1,214	1,738	2,015	277
			86	331	1,688	1,874	186
MADAGAS	O	E	84	14,992	17,383	17,383	
MALI	V	E	86	398,155	174,621	199,825	25,204
MEXICO	A	E	84	529	1,758	2,280	522
			86	57	4,000	4,076	76
	O	E	86	19,974	77,282	77,282	
MOROC	O	E	84	5,000	5,541	5,541	
NETHLDS	O	E	86	695	1,408	1,478	70
	V	E	81	56	816	824	8
			83	254	1,429	1,886	457
			85	202,013	205,459	211,819	6,360
NICARAG	V	E	85	11,680	10,137	10,704	567
NIGERIA	V	E	84	374,724	151,626	161,657	10,031
			85	925,047	913,536	962,835	49,299
NORWAY	V	E	85	150,050	53,245	61,511	8,266
PAKISTN	V	E	82	1,449,246	924,180	1,012,703	88,523
S ARAB	V	E	86	80,106	182,325	203,254	20,929
SENEGAL	V	E	86	44,000	248,566	250,876	2,310
SPAIN	V	E	81	44,092	29,088	32,476	3,388
			86	84,000	466,135	470,685	4,550
SUDAN	N	E	82	11,594,154	7,975,545	8,559,101	583,556
			83	14,757,274	9,781,249	10,644,322	863,073
			84	16,973,886	11,438,262	12,278,348	840,086
	O	E	84	162,023	182,122	182,122	
			85	162,276	678,232	690,182	11,950
	V	E	81	17,659,122	12,408,283	13,584,645	1,176,362
			84	619,493	433,482	454,583	21,101
			85	8,064,193	3,876,128	4,126,142	250,014
			86	7,718,347	7,866,766	8,126,609	259,843
SWEDEN	V	E	83	110,000	71,940	79,583	7,643
			84	44,092	29,560	31,960	2,400
SWITZLD	V	E	85	6,971	11,368	11,849	481

Crop Product TSUSA commodity number, description, and unit of quantity Country	Mode	Reg	Yr	Quantity	F.A.S.	C.I.F.	Charges
TUNISIA	V	E	84	44,092	32,789	34,832	2,043
U KING	A	E	85	1,984	7,282	8,375	1,093
	N	E	81	56,631	38,767	48,313	9,546
			82	746	5,854	5,979	125
			83	1,637,787	1,128,184	1,189,943	61,759
			85	1,436,542	1,078,848	1,155,444	76,596
			86	334,959	720,855	748,669	27,814
	O	E	84	309	268	304	36
	V	E	81	280	3,295	3,387	92
			82	61,729	51,036	56,628	5,592
			83	45,893	31,727	35,389	3,662
			84	4,062,139	2,888,273	3,018,349	130,076
			85	11,023	7,329	8,037	708
			86	66,579	101,578	106,098	4,520
YEMAN S	V	E	85	14,881	18,003	18,753	750
YEMEN A	V	E	85	11,023	11,970	12,370	400

Gutta-Percha

Gutta-percha, rubber
4460520 GUTTA-PERCHA & GUTTAS, NSPF (LB)

Country	Mode	Reg	Yr	Quantity	F.A.S.	C.I.F.	Charges
TOTAL			81	1,858,442	1,718,952	1,834,931	115,979
			82	599,305	705,094	740,060	34,966
			83	4,062,141	2,175,423	2,404,115	228,692
			84	4,679,335	2,323,481	2,677,648	354,167
			85	7,651,621	3,060,535	3,404,559	344,024
			86	14,120,416	5,213,143	5,781,184	568,041
BRAZIL	A	E	83	102	8,429	8,653	224
			85	6,961	78,583	81,695	3,112
			86	4,358	10,292	10,764	472
	O	E	85	79,366	41,024	41,024	
	O	W	86	59,248	20,392	20,392	
	V	E	86	11,356	6,691	7,251	560
CAMBOD	O	E	84	100	346	390	44
	V	W	84	44	391	422	31
HG KONG	A	W	81	85	8,625	8,846	221
INDNSIA	A	E	83	11,210	42,424	43,927	1,503
	A	W	82	41	4,052	4,214	162
			83	329	5,174	5,433	259
	N	W	84	1,284,259	538,553	587,337	48,784
	O	E	83	83	342	342	
	O	W	82	47,223	18,417	18,417	
			83	46,000	13,585	13,585	
	V	E	81	18,819	61,034	66,897	5,863
			83	623,906	265,889	294,009	28,120
			84	220,460	115,467	126,617	11,150
			85	499,563	145,940	166,099	20,159
			86	687,196	343,087	382,561	39,474
KOR REP	A	E	83	4,989	79,688	82,006	2,318
			84	1,259	18,159	19,218	1,059
			85	1,471	5,952	6,976	1,024
	A	W	81	508	55,552	56,762	1,210
			83	408	28,279	29,520	1,241
			84	109	11,346	11,755	409
			86	2,340	13,585	13,982	397
	N	E	85	18,282	22,771	23,397	626
	V	E	86	24,566	12,425	14,575	2,150
MALAYSA	A	E	84	700	6,286	6,448	162
	A	W	83	1,690	16,892	16,971	79
	O	E	81	441	624	624	
			85	79,366	40,278	40,278	
	V	E	81	1,560,812	1,441,121	1,526,274	85,153
			82	255,744	167,864	178,429	10,565
			83	292,275	150,740	165,578	14,838
			84	1,942,480	927,112	1,120,300	193,188
			85	5,145,328	1,881,305	2,105,344	224,039
			86	12,016,470	4,299,419	4,765,028	465,609
NIGERIA	V	E	85	188,857	66,699	72,139	5,440
			86	235,950	75,082	82,016	6,934
SINGAPR	V	E	85	1,011,170	492,071	531,900	39,829
			86	478,398	168,937	188,570	19,633
SRI LKA	A	E	84	2,400	18,531	18,931	400
	V	E	81	277,777	151,996	175,528	23,532
			82	296,297	514,761	539,000	24,239
			83	3,081,149	1,563,981	1,744,091	180,110
			84	1,227,524	687,290	786,230	98,940
			85	621,257	285,912	335,707	49,795
			86	600,534	263,233	296,045	32,812

H

Hemlock

Hemlock, lumber
2022120 HEMLOCK LUMBER ROUGH (MBF)

Country	Mode	Reg	Yr	Quantity	F.A.S.	C.I.F.	Charges
TOTAL			81	90,686	27,509,375	31,304,968	3,786,402
			82	75,590	19,989,772	23,351,980	3,362,208
			83	170,957	50,229,946	58,597,597	8,367,651
			84	199,733	48,964,474	59,093,964	10,129,490
			85	220,456	51,642,945	61,746,763	10,103,818
			86	105,081	30,035,807	34,089,757	4,053,950
CANADA	N	E	85	67,717	15,304,898	20,406,647	5,101,749
	N	W	81	46,957	16,434,319	16,775,378	341,059
			82	26,596	9,132,500	9,215,460	82,960
			83	49,697	19,658,845	19,776,969	118,124
			84	59,318	19,500,944	20,099,499	598,555
			85	49,369	16,044,277	16,223,751	179,474
			86	38,093	14,074,341	14,476,595	402,254
	O	E	81	1,623	421,734	421,734	
			82	1,903	474,034	474,034	
			83	3,493	783,388	783,388	
			84	12,033	1,930,270	1,930,270	
			85	4,231	839,463	839,463	
			86	3,159	739,749	740,880	1,131
	O	W	83	90	23,592	23,592	
			84	36	6,166	6,166	
			85	54	11,875	11,875	
			86	16	5,598	5,598	
	V	E	81	42,062	10,641,579	14,093,299	3,442,529
			82	38,965	9,390,965	12,505,803	3,114,838
			83	106,169	27,616,184	35,644,949	8,028,765
			84	128,346	27,527,094	37,058,029	9,530,935
			85	80,480	16,526,349	20,642,505	4,116,156
			86	52,070	12,939,951	16,112,414	3,172,463
	V	W	81	37	7,521	9,679	2,158
			82	8,126	992,273	1,156,683	164,410
			83	11,497	2,147,056	2,367,665	220,609
			85	18,505	2,899,459	3,601,815	702,356
			86	8,462	1,018,543	1,244,366	225,823
CHINA M	V	E	86	3,253	1,246,046	1,498,325	252,279
JAPAN	V	W	81	5	3,562	4,218	656
LAOS	O	W	86	28	11,579	11,579	
PHIL R	V	W	85	100	16,624	20,707	4,083
U KING	A	W	83	11	881	1,034	153
	O	E	81	2	660	660	

2022140 HEM LBR DRSD WKD EXC SDG MLD (MBF)

Country	Mode	Reg	Yr	Quantity	F.A.S.	C.I.F.	Charges
TOTAL			81	376,348	83,741,791	92,797,989	9,064,478
			82	218,277	45,839,963	53,267,497	7,427,534
			83	245,733	58,256,012	65,864,499	7,608,487
			84	315,189	70,570,269	79,747,279	9,177,010
			85	423,440	94,481,546	106,954,091	12,472,545
			86	383,326	93,059,339	105,624,810	12,565,471
CANADA	N	E	81	5,757	1,043,309	1,310,970	267,661
			83	27,344	7,974,078	9,510,653	1,536,575
	N	W	81	124,092	31,787,365	32,866,988	1,087,945
			82	64,279	18,922,913	19,888,422	965,509
			83	49,629	19,395,249	19,403,852	8,603
			84	69,767	25,556,309	26,196,726	640,417
			85	114,730	30,536,131	32,060,569	1,524,438
			86	129,192	33,867,263	36,254,849	2,387,586
	O	E	81	107,214	25,256,268	25,256,268	
			82	47,828	8,750,498	8,764,016	13,518
			83	52,911	10,547,135	10,547,135	
			84	76,071	12,765,638	12,765,638	
			85	64,741	11,542,687	11,542,687	
			86	47,672	10,102,140	10,102,140	
	O	W	81	858	153,113	155,907	2,794
			82	792	128,912	128,912	
			83	2,290	410,159	410,159	
			84	4,290	661,274	661,274	
			85	4,808	785,389	785,389	
			86	2,751	491,939	491,939	
	V	E	81	137,449	25,352,542	33,016,638	7,664,054
			82	103,114	17,680,540	24,069,781	6,389,241
			83	57,423	12,269,956	16,425,747	4,155,791
			84	103,598	22,194,000	28,365,524	6,171,524

Crop
Product
TSUSA commodity number, description, and unit of quantity

Country	Mode	Reg	Yr	Quantity	F.A.S.	C.I.F.	Charges
			85	206,737	45,404,770	55,184,491	9,779,721
			86	203,711	48,597,997	58,775,882	10,177,885
	V	W	81	973	148,426	190,450	42,024
			82	2,245	354,220	413,486	59,266
			83	55,932	7,621,742	9,524,133	1,902,391
			84	58,795	8,717,730	10,901,544	2,183,814
			85	29,523	5,691,539	6,744,927	1,053,388
CHINA M	O	E	85	8	7,403	7,403	
	V	W	85	2,115	414,934	473,046	58,112
CHINA T	O	W	81	3	266	266	
	V	W	83	204	37,693	42,820	5,127
COLOMB	V	E	85	267	26,106	50,266	24,160
SEYCHEL	V	E	84	23	4,049	6,094	2,045
SPAIN	V	E	84	378	50,979	84,209	33,230
			85	511	72,587	105,313	32,726
U KING	O	E	81	2	502	502	
			82	19	2,880	2,880	
	V	E	84	2,267	620,290	766,270	145,980

Hemlock, tannin**
4702300 CHESTNUT NOT CRUDE OR PROC (LB)
   (See Chestnut, nut, tannin under Chestnut)

Hemp

Hemp, fiber, hackled
3042400 HEMP HACKLED (LB)

Hemp, fiber, processed
3042200 HEMP PROCESSED NO CRD NO HCK (LB)

3042600 HEMP FIBERS, PROCESS, NSPF (LB)

Country	Mode	Reg	Yr	Quantity	F.A.S.	C.I.F.	Charges
TOTAL			81	798	1,093	1,233	140
			82	99	537	542	5
			83	3,187	9,600	10,066	466
			84	4,600	13,844	14,372	528
			85	45,141	36,627	41,903	5,276
			86	3,514	13,317	13,609	292
AUSTRAL	A	E	85	409	2,370	2,828	458
CANADA	O	E	86	882	2,075	2,075	
ECUADOR	A	E	84	27	405	528	123
FRANCE	V	E	81	798	1,093	1,233	140
			82	99	537	542	5
			83	2,710	8,075	8,261	186
			84	3,860	10,724	11,008	284
			85	2,948	6,182	6,574	392
			86	2,632	11,242	11,534	292
IRELAND	A	E	85	1,106	3,973	4,632	659
ITALY	A	E	84	713	2,715	2,836	121
JAPAN	V	W	83	250	670	717	47
			85	20	832	908	76
PHIL R	V	W	85	40,658	23,270	26,961	3,691
U KING	A	E	83	227	855	1,088	233

Hemp, fiber, raw and waste
3042000 HEMP RAW AND WASTES (LB)

Country	Mode	Reg	Yr	Quantity	F.A.S.	C.I.F.	Charges
TOTAL			81	58,812	19,636	23,490	3,854
			82	840,636	239,700	307,834	68,134
			83	2,296,449	668,774	848,593	179,819
			84	95,825	29,318	38,703	9,385
			86	3,180,821	1,071,159	1,263,652	192,493
CANADA	O	E	82	3,543	1,878	1,878	
FR GERM	V	E	86	45,852	10,217	14,247	4,030
INDIA	V	E	84	4,885	1,678	2,168	490
PHIL R	V	E	82	837,093	237,822	305,956	68,134
			83	2,120,265	606,362	771,293	164,931
			84	46,848	13,532	18,275	4,743
			86	2,945,779	1,053,425	1,234,650	181,225
	V	W	83	176,184	62,412	77,300	14,888
			84	44,092	14,108	18,260	4,152
SINGAPR	V	W	86	189,190	7,517	14,755	7,238
THAILND	V	E	81	18,812	7,232	8,533	1,301
	V	W	81	40,000	12,404	14,957	2,553

Hempseed
1752100 HEMPSEED (LB)

Country	Mode	Reg	Yr	Quantity	F.A.S.	C.I.F.	Charges
TOTAL			81	526,243	160,180	189,569	29,389
			82	291,486	79,677	94,063	14,386
			83	146,680	43,217	52,587	9,370
			84	598,931	148,161	182,059	33,898
			85	817,643	180,514	222,029	41,515
			86	691,745	134,773	168,264	33,491
CHINA M	O	E	81	25,413	6,882	8,358	1,476
			82	93,815	25,668	30,849	5,181
			83	22,046	12,346	14,196	1,850
	V	E	81	139,970	49,876	57,153	7,277
			83	69,555	13,818	17,269	3,451
			84	333,109	74,667	94,844	20,177
			85	32,738	6,533	8,679	2,146
			86	229,832	44,644	56,786	12,142
	V	W	82	197,671	54,009	63,214	9,205
			83	34,079	6,322	8,233	1,911
			84	232,753	61,946	73,740	11,794
			85	616,161	137,093	166,185	29,092
			86	461,913	90,129	111,478	21,349
FR GERM	V	E	81	84,106	44,536	48,196	3,660
			83	21,000	10,731	12,889	2,158
GUINEA	V	E	85	66,451	12,660	16,661	4,001
JAPAN	V	E	85	33,951	8,922	11,396	2,474
LEBANON	V	E	81	131,660	26,306	37,484	11,178
TURKEY	V	E	81	145,094	32,580	38,378	5,798
			84	33,069	11,548	13,475	1,927
			85	68,342	15,306	19,108	3,802

Hempseed, fatty acid**
4902200 FATTY ACIDS DRVD HMP KPK ETC (LB)

Country	Mode	Reg	Yr	Quantity	F.A.S.	C.I.F.	Charges
TOTAL			81	2,191,328	1,903,874	2,066,012	162,138
			82	1,493,773	1,196,136	1,314,910	118,774
			83	3,007,714	2,381,464	2,548,592	167,128
			84	2,452,914	2,061,789	2,198,929	137,140
			85	2,646,312	2,041,340	2,237,536	196,196
			86	4,287,047	1,893,948	2,056,641	162,693
BELGIUM	V	E	85	43,563	53,084	57,698	4,614
	V	W	82	36,153	40,115	45,100	4,985
CANADA	O	E	81	84,340	102,054	102,054	
			83	190,340	15,502	15,626	124
			84	266,260	207,928	207,928	
			85	253,200	108,122	108,122	
			86	521,744	99,838	99,838	
	O	W	81	415,885	86,929	86,929	
			82	415,990	76,594	76,594	
			83	517,100	95,417	95,417	
			84	565,224	122,310	122,310	
			85	426,750	81,185	81,185	
			86	2,010,090	198,109	198,109	
CHINA M	V	E	81	420	554	621	67
FR GERM	N	E	81	951,661	1,003,142	1,081,726	78,584
			84	893,569	981,036	1,055,002	73,966
			85	297,109	313,262	351,224	37,962
			86	248,591	249,274	274,660	25,386
	O	E	81	40,388	41,726	45,799	4,073
			82	79,454	83,786	93,344	9,558
			83	495,197	482,252	517,182	34,930
			84	441	371	396	25
	V	E	81	518,959	504,258	557,098	52,840
			82	676,349	704,674	775,762	71,088
			83	1,318,762	1,288,769	1,383,224	94,455
			84	521,064	533,053	576,244	43,191
			85	1,286,414	1,119,573	1,234,110	114,537
			86	801,035	655,313	715,614	60,301
	V	W	82	40,785	41,895	48,174	6,279
FRANCE	A	E	84	1,918	2,020	3,231	1,211
NETHLDS	O	E	83	65,168	64,874	68,857	3,983
	V	E	81	30,953	31,461	33,555	2,094
			84	40,917	44,112	48,362	4,250
			85	46,771	42,973	48,258	5,285
U KING	A	E	81	496	802	1,062	260
	O	E	81	331	581	581	
			84	38,140	43,510	46,081	2,571
			85	40,036	41,325	45,400	4,075
			86	86,508	82,853	89,467	6,614
	V	E	81	147,895	132,367	156,587	24,220
			82	168,476	168,389	188,281	19,892

Crop Product TSUSA commodity number, description, and unit of quantity Country	Mode	Reg	Yr	Quantity	F.A.S.	C.I.F.	Charges
			83	345,132	353,999	380,585	26,586
			84	125,381	127,449	139,375	11,926
			85	252,469	281,816	311,539	29,723
			86	619,079	608,561	678,953	70,392
	V	W	82	76,566	80,683	87,655	6,972
			83	76,015	80,651	87,701	7,050

Hempseed, fatty salt**
4904600 FATTY SALTS OF SESAME ETC (LB)

Country	Mode	Reg	Yr	Quantity	F.A.S.	C.I.F.	Charges
TOTAL			81	11,334	18,995	25,098	6,103
			82	2,756	4,312	5,404	1,092
			83	3,565	7,581	8,489	908
			84	7,177	6,870	9,970	3,100
			85	5,914	7,927	9,023	1,096
			86	44,092	42,294	44,450	2,156
FR GERM	N	E	83	3,029	5,208	5,995	787
	V	E	81	11,334	18,995	25,098	6,103
			82	2,756	4,312	5,404	1,092
			84	397	312	360	48
FRANCE	A	E	84	2,205	1,988	3,388	1,400
	V	E	84	4,444	3,840	5,459	1,619
			85	4,409	4,800	4,999	199
			86	44,092	42,294	44,450	2,156
JAPAN	V	W	83	536	2,373	2,494	121
			84	131	730	763	33
			85	270	1,096	1,162	66
NETHLDS	A	E	85	1,235	2,031	2,862	831

Hempseed, vegetable oil
1762200 HEMPSEED OIL (LB)

Country	Mode	Reg	Yr	Quantity	F.A.S.	C.I.F.	Charges
TOTAL			82	5,713	3,008	3,318	310
NETHLDS	V	E	82	5,713	3,008	3,318	310

Henbane

Henbane, natural drug
4356000 HENBANE (LB)

Henequen

Henequen, fiber, processed**
3044800 SISAL A HENEQUEN FIB PROCESS (LB)

Country	Mode	Reg	Yr	Quantity	F.A.S.	C.I.F.	Charges
TOTAL			81	66,066	29,591	34,179	4,588
			82	241,102	94,533	107,944	13,411
			83	170,881	45,422	54,882	9,460
			84	598,219	177,481	228,677	51,196
			85	1,204,917	255,817	335,905	80,088
			86	440,779	100,346	126,097	25,751
ARGENT	V	E	86	68,195	14,170	17,612	3,442
BRAZIL	A	E	83	957	522	1,701	1,179
	O	E	83	31,526	7,110	7,110	
	V	E	81	53,281	13,833	16,858	3,025
			82	128,688	36,400	43,706	7,306
			83	137,760	36,789	44,978	8,189
			84	481,377	117,316	153,339	36,023
			85	1,031,219	176,364	240,620	64,256
			86	38,644	8,572	10,500	1,928
	V	W	86	55,534	14,343	18,308	3,965
CANADA	O	E	81	2,317	2,887	2,887	
CHINA T	V	E	81	10,270	11,857	13,134	1,277
			82	1,317	3,394	3,642	248
			83	73	490	541	51
			84	7,858	6,555	9,113	2,558
			86	1,193	6,243	6,614	371
	V	W	83	565	511	552	41
			84	15,874	12,960	14,473	1,513
FR GERM	A	E	84	362	3,199	3,641	442
	V	E	84	150	1,184	1,379	195
HAITI	V	E	84	27,708	7,464	9,166	1,702
			85	150,235	75,440	88,156	12,716
HG KONG	V	W	86	456	2,266	2,346	80

Country	Mode	Reg	Yr	Quantity	F.A.S.	C.I.F.	Charges
ITALY	A	E	86	148	442	442	
	V	E	81	198	1,014	1,300	286
			85	114	901	1,234	333
KENYA	A	E	84	849	1,379	2,238	859
KOR REP	V	E	86	115	590	678	88
MEXICO	O	E	82	26,972	17,053	17,053	
	O	W	82	24,500	12,275	12,275	
	V	E	85	23,349	3,112	5,895	2,783
PORTUGL	V	E	82	45,925	20,426	24,800	4,374
			86	5,350	2,826	3,363	537
REP SAF	V	E	82	13,700	4,985	6,468	1,483
S ARAB	A	E	86	900	500	1,400	900
THAILND	V	E	84	64,041	27,424	35,328	7,904
VENEZ	V	E	86	270,244	50,394	64,834	14,440

Henequen, fiber, raw and waste**
3044600 SISAL A HENEQ RAW A WASTES (LTN)

Country	Mode	Reg	Yr	Quantity	F.A.S.	C.I.F.	Charges
TOTAL			81	3,468	1,708,416	2,227,784	519,368
			82	1,022	537,480	714,049	176,569
			83	2,493	1,100,830	1,430,944	330,114
			84	1,530	624,346	793,988	169,642
			85	2,059	554,459	768,017	213,558
			86	940	394,570	476,162	81,592
BELGIUM	O	E	86	13	10,625	10,625	
	V	E	85	35	12,512	17,391	4,879
BRAZIL	O	E	82	1	308	308	
			83	15	8,460	8,460	
			84	99	33,454	33,454	
			85	32	15,801	15,801	
			86	34	18,288	18,288	
	V	E	81	1,717	619,463	803,434	183,971
			82	199	56,765	82,718	25,953
			83	1,580	617,794	817,358	199,564
			84	844	236,766	326,635	89,869
			85	1,610	319,186	470,827	151,641
			86	798	330,495	409,725	79,230
	V	W	81	30	8,910	13,382	4,472
CANADA	O	E	81	4	1,100	1,100	
			83	4	450	450	
ECUADOR	V	E	85	2	1,150	2,350	1,200
GERM DR	N	W	85	*	747	752	5
HAITI	V	E	81	155	118,791	132,652	13,861
			82	43	31,008	35,771	4,763
			83	96	54,920	66,379	11,459
KENYA	V	E	81	1,259	776,102	1,056,671	280,569
			82	649	382,175	519,871	137,696
			83	688	368,902	485,807	116,905
			84	199	134,044	166,322	32,278
			85	144	84,014	106,161	22,147
MEXICO	O	E	81	84	35,287	35,287	
			82	90	43,889	43,889	
			83	92	40,007	40,007	
			84	96	42,566	42,566	
			85	53	24,562	24,562	
			86	77	31,468	31,468	
PHIL R	V	E	82	40	23,335	31,492	8,157
PORTUGL	V	E	85	36	6,356	11,537	5,181
			86	18	3,694	6,056	2,362
REP SAF	V	E	83	18	10,297	12,483	2,186
			84	17	11,927	14,229	2,302
TNZANIA	V	E	81	219	148,763	185,258	36,495
			84	275	165,589	210,782	45,193
			85	147	90,131	118,636	28,505

Hop

Beer
1670515 BEER, ETC NOV1GL,GLASS CNTR (GAL)

Country	Mode	Reg	Yr	Quantity	F.A.S.	C.I.F.	Charges
TOTAL			81	143,553,389	366,859,773	425,928,159	59,121,489
			82	159,641,819	431,884,625	498,285,040	66,400,415
			83	172,915,508	472,678,448	544,220,802	71,542,354
			84	197,028,501	527,193,561	609,512,410	82,318,849
			85	216,830,072	577,719,479	672,100,006	94,380,527
			86	241,060,535	713,486,776	811,421,605	97,934,829
ALBANIA	V	E	85	3,150	7,439	9,070	1,631
ALGERIA	V	E	83	51,032	142,105	167,074	24,969
ARGENT	V	E	85	7,456	18,200	24,533	6,333

Table 1. U.S. Import Statistics for Crop-Specific Commodities by Crop Name

Crop
Product
TSUSA commodity number, description, and unit of quantity

Country	Mode	Reg	Yr	Quantity	F.A.S.	C.I.F.	Charges
			86	5,218	10,579	14,832	4,253
	V	W	85	8,746	16,852	24,561	7,709
AUSTRAL	A	W	81	271	452	2,598	2,146
			84	195	662	1,966	1,304
	N	E	84	346,947	876,688	1,281,766	405,078
			86	21,263	56,507	74,887	18,380
	N	W	84	177,053	412,286	572,126	159,840
	O	E	81	720	2,731	3,354	623
			85	1,793	7,610	9,320	1,710
	O	W	82	5,482	12,220	14,651	2,431
	V	E	81	219,415	506,565	767,746	261,181
			82	240,239	539,674	829,101	289,427
			83	485,958	1,075,455	1,586,662	511,207
			84	153,189	409,521	568,466	158,945
			85	548,103	1,342,926	1,965,899	622,973
			86	938,579	2,407,479	3,169,267	761,788
	V	H	83	1,578	3,556	5,045	1,489
			84	12,694	30,732	40,978	10,246
			85	2,309	5,344	7,362	2,018
			86	11,364	32,268	41,123	8,855
	V	W	81	203,790	524,372	678,207	153,835
			82	231,745	657,085	858,755	201,670
			83	473,250	1,157,159	1,574,343	417,184
			84	150,677	484,994	616,583	131,589
			85	480,234	1,254,418	1,696,920	442,502
			86	631,281	1,607,904	2,100,603	492,699
AUSTRIA	N	E	81	63,859	164,144	206,653	42,509
			82	31,242	82,467	106,721	24,224
			84	47,059	115,004	149,051	34,047
			85	29,669	65,292	85,402	20,110
	N	W	84	52,002	111,975	147,403	35,428
	O	E	81	2,120	5,398	7,648	2,250
			83	42,134	125,970	153,425	27,455
			86	14,571	41,981	51,895	9,914
	V	E	81	24,823	67,350	89,331	21,981
			82	27,158	71,381	87,515	16,134
			83	26,135	65,021	82,343	17,322
			84	117,397	354,526	442,397	87,871
			85	176,984	467,884	612,541	144,657
			86	115,217	414,651	505,926	91,275
	V	W	81	16,917	44,995	57,698	12,703
			82	14,948	35,066	48,456	13,390
			83	4,129	9,685	12,532	2,847
			84	30,983	79,361	101,539	22,178
			85	54,871	109,470	155,569	46,099
			86	37,114	82,271	111,291	29,020
BARBADO	V	E	81	113	485	587	102
BELGIUM	A	E	81	40	308	674	366
			83	56	270	315	45
			84	69	266	779	513
	N	E	83	29,818	92,056	113,261	21,205
			84	69,792	204,547	248,211	43,664
			85	125,493	280,262	346,072	65,810
			86	818	6,500	7,689	1,189
	O	E	83	10,920	29,350	38,557	9,207
			84	5,751	18,147	21,426	3,279
			85	2,163	6,808	9,223	2,415
			86	2,247	11,612	13,986	2,374
	V	E	81	113,884	356,840	432,190	75,350
			82	40,710	120,194	147,160	26,966
			83	58,784	204,955	240,087	35,132
			84	81,077	279,702	332,454	52,752
			85	256,798	877,278	1,094,932	217,654
			86	219,711	1,001,495	1,219,914	218,419
	V	W	81	14,879	54,578	65,167	10,589
			82	23,550	87,024	103,954	16,930
			83	21,408	75,379	91,309	15,930
			84	65,979	177,703	230,138	52,435
			85	211,643	722,426	915,224	192,798
			86	124,737	464,094	576,047	111,953
BELIZE	V	E	82	7,983	21,998	30,508	8,510
			84	1,130	4,141	5,237	1,096
BRAZIL	O	E	84	576	1,024	1,473	449
	V	E	81	13,978	27,971	39,975	12,004
			82	8,673	17,037	25,056	8,019
			83	37,386	68,416	99,776	31,360
			84	26,682	41,709	55,045	13,336
			85	143,888	368,403	473,730	105,327
			86	75,654	182,138	225,373	43,235
	V	W	81	6,979	7,106	10,891	3,785
			82	1,584	3,231	4,801	1,570
			83	14,423	22,055	32,950	10,895
			84	30,768	52,986	78,704	25,718
			85	16,020	23,720	35,426	11,706
			86	5,040	7,816	9,531	1,715
BULGAR	V	E	85	5,319	23,886	29,970	6,084
	V	W	85	1,102	5,488	6,522	1,034
C RICA	V	E	85	6,066	14,828	19,828	5,000
	V	W	85	5,512	13,476	18,184	4,708
CAMROON	V	E	85	2,511	9,009	11,599	2,590
CANADA	A	E	84	8	972	1,201	229
	N	E	81	8,124,517	14,394,839	14,406,950	17,111
			83	15,034,719	35,238,376	35,238,381	5
			84	8,999,363	22,944,728	22,946,070	1,342
			85	30,821,780	73,483,060	73,503,453	20,393
			86	25,564	87,440	96,045	8,605
	N	W	82	328,649	1,105,539	1,110,430	4,891
			83	2,459,783	6,435,906	7,876,737	1,440,831
			85	1,886,231	4,858,755	6,004,374	1,145,619
	O	E	81	37,953,284	79,593,276	79,696,150	102,995
			82	48,381,569	108,410,443	108,426,558	16,115
			83	33,343,789	76,222,451	76,246,247	23,796
			84	42,358,892	96,573,721	96,618,026	44,305
			85	19,877,395	47,617,177	47,617,184	7
			86	50,698,956	124,211,998	124,217,971	5,973
	O	H	81	648	1,650	1,650	
	O	W	81	47,685	156,821	156,821	
			82	23,938	67,871	67,871	
			83	190,945	602,121	602,121	
			84	62,303	206,102	206,102	
			85	70,180	151,216	153,576	2,360
			86	2,483,361	6,501,270	6,501,277	7
	V	E	81	278,446	644,465	792,433	147,968
			82	128,905	337,369	417,005	79,636
			83	68,238	175,893	224,662	48,769
			84	98,079	229,416	289,432	60,016
			85	405,851	1,039,496	1,357,816	318,320
			86	35,472	81,537	90,692	9,155
	V	W	81	1,219,000	3,009,060	3,800,051	790,991
			82	1,450,088	3,738,989	5,225,032	1,486,043
			83	336,873	866,582	1,115,742	249,160
			84	3,283,680	8,469,934	10,547,438	2,077,504
			85	711,275	1,834,548	2,381,733	547,185
			86	1,420,411	3,662,997	4,589,299	926,302
CHILE	V	E	86	18,337	36,192	47,176	10,984
	V	W	86	7,617	17,628	26,822	9,194
CHINA M	O	E	86	9,005	31,200	36,000	4,800
	V	E	81	442,048	728,208	1,007,232	279,024
			82	566,893	1,096,968	1,352,411	255,443
			83	735,635	1,542,101	1,966,937	424,836
			84	814,214	1,536,675	2,338,763	802,088
			85	1,010,292	1,804,325	2,926,479	1,122,154
			86	1,537,462	3,133,805	4,951,517	1,817,712
	V	H	83	8,213	19,432	22,468	3,036
			84	4,206	6,623	11,269	4,646
			85	4,185	6,920	11,858	4,938
			86	2,093	4,073	6,231	2,158
	V	W	81	296,603	566,504	798,229	231,725
			82	301,395	528,121	789,510	261,389
			83	485,735	851,529	1,353,590	502,061
			84	766,018	1,332,465	2,048,578	716,113
			85	975,089	1,681,792	2,770,725	1,088,933
			86	1,175,906	2,574,101	3,834,240	1,260,139
CHINA T	N	E	85	21,602	59,520	80,738	21,218
	O	E	85	11,250	31,000	39,859	8,859
	O	W	85	12,794	35,254	43,783	8,529
			86	4,862	1,638	1,638	
	V	E	81	56,361	116,447	149,569	33,122
			82	5,811	15,727	21,019	5,292
			83	68,633	152,680	215,200	62,520
			84	20,314	53,219	84,015	30,796
			85	55,821	158,552	214,346	55,794
			86	39,888	109,579	146,986	37,407
	V	H	86	2,211	3,488	5,037	1,549
	V	W	81	20,506	48,172	65,985	17,813
			82	10,257	16,878	25,633	8,755
			83	21,776	63,157	83,098	19,941
			84	12,759	29,590	39,996	10,406
			85	122,703	260,895	354,072	93,177
			86	62,851	188,800	240,142	51,342
COLOMB	O	E	84	1,192	4,108	4,108	
	V	E	81	9,000	30,240	38,927	8,687
			82	4,082	13,715	17,566	3,851
			83	2,250	7,560	9,785	2,225
			85	24,723	75,044	90,893	15,849
			86	13,558	18,630	24,230	5,600
	V	W	84	4,925	15,750	20,370	4,620
			85	29,413	89,100	115,891	26,791

Crop
Product
TSUSA commodity number, description, and unit of quantity

Country	Mode	Reg	Yr	Quantity	F.A.S.	C.I.F.	Charges
CR N AN	V	E	84	307	1,292	1,422	130
CYPRUS	V	E	81	2,549	10,200	12,747	2,547
			82	1,805	8,075	10,783	2,708
CZECHO	O	E	81	1,000	3,520	4,159	639
	V	E	81	274,752	660,739	864,692	203,953
			82	313,200	770,570	1,021,891	251,321
			83	335,299	1,029,314	1,320,662	291,348
			84	355,142	987,540	1,296,602	309,062
			85	347,366	965,393	1,254,809	289,416
			86	295,488	913,455	1,162,511	249,056
	V	W	81	10,368	27,734	38,841	11,107
			82	15,552	38,844	53,498	14,654
			83	38,880	117,642	161,183	43,541
			84	103,481	330,869	428,669	97,800
			85	132,158	402,215	531,293	129,078
			86	90,699	313,109	395,656	82,547
DENMARK	N	E	82	215,854	626,754	767,909	141,155
			84	4,800	14,902	18,889	3,987
	N	W	85	35,732	111,161	152,877	41,716
	O	E	81	63,740	137,741	162,656	24,915
			82	35,489	105,619	125,784	20,165
			83	17,573	47,217	62,076	14,859
			84	15,556	45,067	52,641	7,574
			85	16,369	45,954	59,852	13,898
			86	22,713	110,950	136,550	25,600
	O	W	81	3,244	9,165	13,227	4,062
			82	313	886	1,085	199
			83	832	2,081	2,748	667
			85	494	1,357	1,717	360
	V	E	81	283,316	941,568	1,159,658	218,090
			82	174,571	566,478	731,530	165,052
			83	514,127	1,610,669	2,027,060	416,391
			84	691,784	2,086,803	2,713,830	627,027
			85	603,376	1,649,056	2,173,073	524,017
			86	958,866	2,863,813	3,658,027	794,214
	V	W	81	243,321	775,161	1,011,221	236,060
			82	269,189	801,934	1,072,974	271,040
			83	313,267	939,153	1,205,953	266,800
			84	340,960	1,006,384	1,276,920	270,536
			85	203,584	557,748	747,055	189,307
			86	62,494	158,217	218,971	60,754
DOM REP	A	E	84	225	505	1,016	511
	N	E	84	188,886	550,810	598,099	47,289
	V	E	81	23,626	61,376	75,081	13,705
			82	3,015	8,275	10,699	2,424
			83	26,082	76,260	85,971	9,711
			84	327,517	932,917	1,066,818	133,901
			85	49,359	131,023	151,429	20,406
			86	8,640	24,770	28,550	3,780
	V	W	86	2,268	7,682	9,626	1,944
ECUADOR	V	E	82	5,062	14,625	18,722	4,097
EGYPT	A	E	86	1,584	3,616	5,066	1,450
F GUIAN	V	E	81	6,801	22,200	26,508	4,308
F W IND	V	W	83	5,184	10,627	14,065	3,438
FINLAND	V	E	81	17,228	56,216	76,161	19,945
			82	5,753	15,390	22,894	7,504
			86	13,635	59,226	69,226	10,000
	V	W	81	9,324	27,483	36,120	8,637
			82	2,373	5,255	7,530	2,275
			83	2,485	6,946	9,052	2,106
			84	2,489	7,504	11,085	3,581
			85	2,520	6,468	9,854	3,386
FR GERM	N	E	81	5,349,944	15,391,089	19,473,587	4,082,498
			82	7,300,989	21,840,845	26,843,807	5,002,962
			83	14,072,744	43,733,930	52,951,192	9,217,262
			84	2,740,412	9,073,545	10,916,376	1,842,831
			85	19,839,556	62,961,834	76,350,311	13,388,477
			86	6,694,799	24,858,618	29,524,938	4,666,320
	N	W	81	98,016	292,431	371,953	79,522
			84	1,964,133	6,694,621	8,266,230	1,571,609
			85	5,504,313	19,403,902	24,689,787	5,285,885
			86	369,130	1,191,053	1,442,215	251,162
	O	E	81	473,257	1,741,665	2,056,877	315,212
			82	139,706	449,584	539,715	90,131
			83	217,830	779,593	918,741	139,148
			84	170,545	460,141	574,557	114,416
			85	44,321	119,083	151,322	32,239
			86	62,813	175,331	219,874	44,543
	O	H	84	3,164	6,025	9,508	3,483
	O	W	81	107	692	802	110
			82	314	1,095	1,396	301
			83	2,316	6,162	7,162	1,000
			84	3,264	11,911	16,735	4,824
			85	5,138	14,195	16,153	1,958
	V	E	81	7,342,077	23,244,114	28,433,538	5,187,476
			82	10,370,536	34,032,737	41,236,971	7,204,234
			83	7,342,994	23,746,184	28,782,365	5,036,181
			84	23,586,631	74,164,778	89,914,843	15,750,065
			85	10,929,414	35,200,485	42,824,977	7,624,492
			86	23,516,522	75,704,921	92,201,392	16,496,471
	V	H	82	5,400	17,728	24,253	6,525
			85	14,071	37,698	57,223	19,525
			86	38,489	130,092	159,250	29,158
	V	W	81	2,442,304	8,039,908	10,437,731	2,402,914
			82	3,012,497	10,000,925	12,900,890	2,899,965
			83	4,705,004	16,946,380	20,817,599	3,871,219
			84	3,396,533	12,356,128	15,203,905	2,847,777
			85	202,575	719,629	937,859	218,230
			86	5,003,698	18,250,125	22,957,764	4,707,639
FR POLY	A	H	81	187	350	2,627	2,277
	O	H	82	23,137	109,840	134,564	24,724
			83	7,902	40,826	48,432	7,606
	V	H	85	2,494	12,163	15,400	3,237
	V	W	82	18,019	104,826	116,977	12,151
			83	18,414	65,152	77,566	12,414
			84	12,492	67,838	79,895	12,057
			85	7,163	39,094	45,635	6,541
			86	5,440	28,444	31,850	3,406
FRANCE	N	E	81	99,864	354,319	407,083	52,764
			82	838,368	2,844,521	3,279,590	435,069
			83	419,926	1,387,029	1,657,126	270,097
			84	33,412	127,115	154,476	27,361
			85	60,268	216,545	263,076	46,531
			86	23,439	77,358	97,716	20,358
	N	W	81	92,389	312,633	401,512	88,879
			84	108,795	346,996	436,088	89,092
	O	E	81	10,487	38,973	48,944	9,971
			82	23,584	89,394	108,790	19,396
			83	155,598	543,163	648,906	105,743
			84	34,150	122,152	146,091	23,939
			85	24,039	67,861	78,761	10,900
			86	15,523	50,103	58,023	7,920
	O	W	81	1,350	4,478	5,774	1,296
	V	E	81	1,245,748	4,084,710	4,802,373	715,170
			82	623,040	2,143,626	2,522,311	378,685
			83	384,472	1,311,845	1,563,560	251,715
			84	1,456,781	4,874,077	5,875,259	1,001,182
			85	973,275	2,825,172	3,533,511	708,339
			86	1,024,095	3,001,633	3,698,181	696,548
	V	H	86	3,150	8,529	11,988	3,459
	V	W	81	56,445	211,040	259,473	48,433
			82	241,358	846,008	1,036,933	190,925
			83	260,520	850,484	1,085,346	234,862
			84	203,771	642,090	820,815	178,725
			85	280,226	810,354	1,065,508	255,154
			86	209,579	650,135	827,816	177,681
GAMBIA	V	W	82	5,580	20,010	29,760	9,750
GERM DR	O	E	83	11,550	9,163	17,063	7,900
			84	1,958	4,507	5,411	904
	O	W	84	3,105	2,001	4,163	2,162
	V	E	81	2,378	9,705	11,150	1,445
			82	7,353	23,653	27,678	4,025
			83	38,756	32,719	48,223	15,504
			84	5,487	20,983	26,199	5,216
			85	29,700	80,964	100,368	19,404
			86	13,733	9,901	22,059	12,158
	V	W	82	2,430	7,992	10,490	2,498
			83	48,346	76,740	111,073	34,333
			84	3,067	2,176	4,106	1,930
			86	12,845	25,116	38,244	13,128
GREECE	N	E	85	14,174	38,762	57,054	18,292
	N	W	85	21,157	64,984	89,311	24,327
			86	19,507	56,789	79,614	22,825
	O	E	83	825	2,400	3,378	978
			85	8,250	19,200	23,536	4,336
	V	E	81	23,375	60,172	83,349	23,177
			82	26,892	76,805	105,251	28,446
			83	49,142	165,062	222,278	57,216
			84	39,513	124,350	169,193	44,843
			85	99,863	276,825	374,379	97,554
			86	57,777	169,909	234,551	64,642
	V	W	81	2,475	6,720	10,043	3,323
			83	13,405	42,426	59,443	17,017
			84	5,606	19,305	25,525	6,220
			86	11,937	35,185	46,568	11,383
GUATMAL	V	E	82	9,720	21,640	26,248	4,608
			83	8,640	28,775	34,318	5,543
			84	13,800	52,733	65,406	12,673

Crop
Product
TSUSA commodity number, description, and unit of quantity

Country	Mode	Reg	Yr	Quantity	F.A.S.	C.I.F.	Charges
			85	8,775	26,156	31,096	4,940
			86	17,550	36,192	45,695	9,503
	V	W	84	2,880	7,078	9,461	2,383
			85	8,775	21,060	27,259	6,199
			86	8,775	15,717	21,916	6,199
GUINEA	O	W	83	405	2,237	2,371	134
	V	H	83	4,959	18,356	25,544	7,188
	V	W	85	111,672	477,784	550,172	72,388
HAITI	O	H	83	1,771	9,248	10,949	1,701
	V	E	86	7,065	18,830	22,493	3,663
HG KONG	O	E	86	2,700	7,800	11,675	3,875
	V	E	81	17,265	27,713	43,964	16,251
			82	2,813	12,125	13,936	1,811
			83	2,126	2,980	4,804	1,824
			84	1,729	2,774	4,610	1,836
			85	12,554	34,911	42,851	7,940
			86	5,400	15,600	20,940	5,340
	V	W	81	43,096	99,920	131,787	31,867
			82	4,032	8,385	10,858	2,473
			83	15,279	27,943	33,550	5,607
			84	3,911	7,545	10,065	2,520
			85	50,990	107,933	143,290	35,357
			86	20,880	55,535	65,525	9,990
HONDURA	A	W	82	45	360	1,760	1,400
	V	E	83	5,274	18,752	22,182	3,430
			84	28,318	102,512	128,372	25,860
			85	40,356	146,726	170,980	24,254
			86	33,228	85,768	121,098	35,330
ICELAND	V	E	84	2,970	8,818	10,808	1,990
INDIA	N	E	85	4,570	11,688	18,038	6,350
	N	W	85	22,922	58,806	91,044	32,238
	O	W	84	1,236	3,178	4,834	1,656
	V	E	81	13,756	29,250	52,472	23,222
			82	12,668	30,734	50,185	19,451
			83	43,014	119,086	176,814	57,728
			84	43,362	170,036	224,560	54,524
			85	52,441	122,785	169,551	46,766
			86	33,909	84,965	124,706	39,741
	V	W	81	5,876	14,885	25,863	10,978
			82	11,752	31,748	54,150	22,402
			83	20,331	60,132	90,763	30,631
			84	36,455	96,474	145,651	49,177
			85	39,092	100,836	159,074	58,238
			86	69,947	259,237	336,567	77,330
INDNSIA	V	E	83	5,400	16,176	19,022	2,846
			85	2,970	10,565	13,337	2,772
			86	2,970	8,818	10,374	1,556
	V	W	84	4,845	21,638	23,104	1,466
IRAN	V	E	85	16,605	52,030	62,509	10,479
			86	9,507	28,703	35,309	6,606
	V	W	85	1,800	5,956	7,745	1,789
			86	16,470	49,652	64,835	15,183
IRELAND	A	E	84	45	454	488	34
	N	E	85	90,990	296,284	370,283	73,999
			86	25,380	84,832	105,984	21,152
	N	W	85	82,754	237,560	303,596	66,036
			86	215,640	653,554	821,052	167,498
	O	E	81	428	1,188	1,222	34
			83	12,403	35,021	37,122	2,101
	V	E	81	1,802,860	6,210,784	7,484,479	1,273,668
			82	1,935,146	6,528,713	7,752,394	1,223,681
			83	1,777,703	5,674,258	6,710,100	1,035,842
			84	2,735,808	8,157,389	9,817,433	1,660,044
			85	2,574,277	7,842,387	9,344,124	1,501,737
			86	3,817,140	11,238,971	13,477,165	2,238,194
	V	W	81	58,734	185,803	241,597	55,794
			82	59,526	185,512	239,322	53,810
			83	81,305	256,381	320,037	63,656
			84	209,278	623,821	783,735	159,914
			85	52,020	154,527	206,626	52,099
			86	75,195	230,091	295,125	65,034
ISRAEL	V	E	82	3,038	7,965	10,476	2,511
			83	5,175	17,848	21,293	3,445
			84	16,425	45,620	58,788	13,168
			85	9,494	19,144	27,633	8,489
	V	W	85	5,231	16,511	22,830	6,319
ITALY	N	E	86	8,010	27,590	37,492	9,902
	N	W	83	6,085	14,579	19,990	5,411
			84	10,906	26,546	36,709	10,163
			85	15,434	43,642	57,541	13,899
			86	21,402	60,275	78,093	17,818
	O	E	83	1,350	3,905	4,835	930
			84	1,005	3,126	3,870	744
			85	7,275	32,003	37,559	5,556
			86	1,651	1,963	3,421	1,458
	V	E	81	140,759	362,965	488,212	125,247
			82	281,689	874,409	1,078,635	204,226
			83	128,222	411,374	515,117	103,743
			84	174,254	393,502	549,870	156,368
			85	149,613	339,826	496,480	156,654
			86	224,713	548,479	769,793	221,314
	V	W	81	32,525	76,305	120,061	43,756
			82	61,648	151,789	220,370	68,581
			83	54,015	155,189	202,426	47,237
			84	54,446	124,793	174,082	49,289
			85	80,414	209,509	285,419	75,910
			86	78,055	215,427	292,143	76,716
IVY CST	V	E	85	7,030	26,880	35,832	8,952
			86	11,405	57,036	74,279	17,243
	V	W	86	10,480	32,271	34,724	2,453
JAMAICA	O	E	85	2,881	8,320	11,142	2,822
	V	E	81	83,822	264,903	340,957	76,054
			82	72,114	235,141	298,360	63,219
			83	145,793	444,334	562,518	118,184
			84	322,353	914,919	1,174,510	259,591
			85	204,969	632,269	795,125	162,856
			86	335,069	942,057	1,169,912	227,855
	V	W	84	14,403	41,600	55,041	13,441
			85	37,447	115,520	156,184	40,664
			86	8,442	24,420	34,190	9,770
JAPAN	N	E	84	856,326	2,720,795	3,627,692	906,897
	N	H	84	168,159	355,666	503,254	147,588
			86	160,779	360,076	553,721	193,645
	N	W	84	1,580,698	5,427,800	6,455,538	1,027,738
			85	57,797	207,225	261,109	53,884
			86	1,191,354	4,091,219	4,743,786	652,567
	O	E	85	74,371	236,241	315,643	79,402
			86	67,827	199,904	269,234	69,330
	O	H	86	1,446	3,184	5,136	1,952
	O	W	83	33	315	338	23
	V	E	81	560,162	1,602,855	2,111,232	508,377
			82	573,078	1,635,645	2,153,820	518,175
			83	798,941	2,273,506	3,021,166	747,660
			84	348,894	1,022,663	1,394,885	372,222
			85	1,010,291	2,949,143	3,971,931	1,022,788
			86	1,305,627	3,942,148	5,125,695	1,183,547
	V	H	81	139,678	318,604	419,211	100,607
			82	139,278	330,833	433,851	103,018
			83	153,633	373,022	501,641	128,619
			85	171,320	388,210	572,494	184,284
			86	23,906	54,789	81,211	26,422
	V	W	81	780,748	2,371,239	2,917,782	546,543
			82	989,538	3,232,026	3,908,605	676,579
			83	1,416,022	4,805,887	5,660,576	854,689
			84	230,064	761,575	975,745	214,170
			85	2,032,615	6,917,580	8,359,026	1,441,446
			86	1,268,965	4,384,845	5,058,137	673,292
KENYA	V	E	86	7,533	17,409	24,397	6,988
	V	W	86	2,510	5,803	8,582	2,779
KIRIBAT	V	E	86	2,925	5,239	7,190	1,951
KOR REP	A	E	84	4,185	7,421	10,253	2,832
	O	E	85	32,069	80,932	103,616	22,684
			86	24,008	60,755	72,274	11,519
	V	E	81	2,808	8,174	10,578	2,404
			82	2,808	8,088	10,853	2,765
			84	62,697	183,332	247,928	64,596
			85	41,590	119,730	154,102	34,372
			86	100,392	305,869	365,470	59,601
	V	H	84	8,072	10,645	14,951	4,306
	V	W	83	23,313	73,946	89,427	15,481
			84	33,388	124,774	144,810	20,036
			85	61,774	190,729	236,069	45,340
			86	93,484	283,033	330,959	47,926
LEBANON	V	W	86	8,584	15,006	19,495	4,489
LIBERIA	V	W	82	2,880	5,584	8,341	2,757
MACAO	V	E	86	2,268	5,194	7,358	2,164
	V	W	82	2,880	5,584	8,166	2,582
MALI	V	E	85	94,233	237,937	289,443	51,506
			86	223,335	773,065	882,680	109,615
	V	W	86	9,450	31,581	40,280	8,699
MALTA	V	E	85	24,948	104,355	118,189	13,834
			86	2,322	10,320	12,290	1,970
MAURIT	V	E	85	2,970	9,915	11,718	1,803
			86	6,600	36,693	44,019	7,326
MEXICO	N	E	82	46,011	115,201	121,232	6,031
			83	18,428	40,538	56,158	15,620
	N	W	84	18,333	43,858	51,889	8,031
			85	262,900	588,641	713,404	124,763

Crop Product TSUSA commodity number, description, and unit of quantity Country	Mode	Reg	Yr	Quantity	F.A.S.	C.I.F.	Charges
	O	E	81	2,557,101	5,938,717	5,979,543	36,318
			82	2,984,711	7,411,778	7,418,735	6,957
			83	2,980,876	7,286,627	7,321,454	34,827
			84	4,114,515	9,975,939	10,064,092	88,153
			85	8,003,064	21,003,103	21,023,825	20,722
			86	15,017,712	39,279,436	39,280,763	1,327
	O	W	81	4,747,573	11,704,512	11,704,831	220
			82	4,694,274	12,236,738	12,236,738	
			83	5,486,165	13,075,564	13,075,567	3
			84	7,084,376	16,359,446	16,366,435	6,989
			85	9,949,398	24,882,047	24,882,152	105
			86	20,883,937	52,889,167	52,889,175	8
	V	E	84	404,676	1,020,566	1,238,794	218,228
			85	503,748	1,243,014	1,574,777	331,763
			86	207,060	581,111	726,821	145,710
	V	W	81	23,133	44,905	50,592	5,687
			83	2,672	9,261	11,155	1,894
			84	41,578	100,270	138,120	37,850
			85	1,130,546	3,194,243	4,170,410	976,167
			86	3,221,213	8,320,692	11,122,103	2,801,411
MONSRAT	V	E	86	5,544	14,488	18,288	3,800
	V	W	86	20,718	52,646	74,104	21,458
MOROC	A	E	84	681	1,470	3,272	1,802
	O	W	85	3,087	7,820	7,820	
			86	3,087	8,163	8,163	
	V	E	85	6,996	27,628	36,160	8,532
MOZAMBQ	V	W	85	2,698	7,592	9,986	2,394
N ANTIL	V	E	81	2,970	7,712	9,394	1,682
			84	9,135	23,918	28,179	4,261
			85	6,273	34,962	50,359	15,397
	V	W	86	5,954	21,775	25,878	4,103
N CALDN	V	E	85	12,600	30,264	36,027	5,763
N ZEAL	N	E	84	4,786	7,701	13,553	5,852
			85	9,190	38,281	56,940	18,659
	N	W	84	214,541	603,913	784,821	180,908
	O	E	81	2,259	4,210	6,934	2,724
			82	2,269	11,995	12,969	974
			84	2,465	6,742	9,073	2,331
	V	E	81	34,618	92,747	135,380	42,633
			82	36,218	95,175	133,782	38,607
			83	72,813	205,963	289,407	83,444
			84	96,759	275,265	378,113	102,848
			85	84,895	222,967	294,856	71,889
			86	93,633	331,164	446,710	115,546
	V	H	81	116,346	273,184	378,529	105,345
			82	189,359	492,903	658,459	165,556
			83	237,970	627,300	821,669	194,369
			84	283,307	732,102	953,731	221,629
			85	331,943	899,207	1,157,566	258,359
			86	348,685	955,070	1,214,504	259,434
	V	W	81	117,976	344,442	460,336	115,894
			82	164,279	500,344	655,556	155,212
			83	321,280	923,495	1,212,889	289,394
			84	155,123	428,473	582,881	154,408
			85	432,421	1,272,348	1,626,882	354,534
			86	348,842	1,102,931	1,379,368	276,437
NETHLDS	N	E	81	3,782,043	10,388,940	12,370,185	1,982,300
			82	27,758,857	78,145,211	94,036,973	15,891,762
			83	28,985,071	81,556,728	97,111,993	15,555,265
			84	5,407,410	13,756,924	16,721,263	2,964,339
			85	34,610,150	87,840,207	106,271,496	18,431,289
			86	30,320,456	104,972,677	120,758,183	15,785,506
	N	W	84	5,321,116	14,547,245	17,720,837	3,173,592
			85	70,120	185,546	239,696	54,150
			86	4,332,076	14,304,675	17,779,900	3,475,225
	O	E	81	1,234,780	3,459,405	4,087,531	628,126
			82	628,219	1,760,266	2,059,973	299,707
			83	1,314,898	3,592,018	4,174,023	582,005
			84	91,416	249,370	298,922	49,552
			85	75,056	198,117	238,658	40,541
			86	56,638	181,926	209,553	27,627
	O	H	85	311,613	726,922	959,488	232,566
			86	165,694	480,073	617,167	137,094
	O	W	81	320	1,966	2,524	558
			82	1,056	3,522	4,737	1,215
			83	331	22,037	22,309	272
			84	2,272	7,950	9,366	1,416
			85	4,329	13,771	16,335	2,564
			86	18,160	53,351	66,937	13,586
	V	E	81	46,338,135	127,585,417	153,632,217	26,054,714
			82	26,882,357	77,295,807	91,280,878	13,985,071
			83	27,829,789	79,172,056	94,001,122	14,829,066
			84	59,825,374	157,968,857	188,769,583	30,800,726
			85	37,894,781	96,728,131	116,621,960	19,893,829
			86	46,076,209	146,320,976	171,513,054	25,192,078
	V	H	83	1,732	4,652	6,049	1,397
			85	13,796	36,466	60,782	24,316
			86	64,431	213,452	275,512	62,060
	V	W	81	8,983,006	24,756,096	32,326,887	7,609,808
			82	11,829,814	33,671,582	42,903,539	9,231,957
			83	12,457,761	35,468,165	43,906,455	8,438,290
			84	6,136,657	16,438,818	20,046,850	3,608,032
			85	9,881,340	24,924,614	31,331,412	6,406,798
			86	5,029,581	16,083,598	19,834,754	3,751,156
NEW GUI	N	H	83	10,145	42,041	52,988	10,947
	N	W	84	64,105	311,923	359,176	47,253
	O	H	83	4,620	19,862	24,267	4,405
			84	3,526	18,618	21,001	2,383
	O	W	83	16,311	89,429	93,237	3,808
			84	20,491	102,111	123,257	21,146
	V	H	84	36,982	176,372	205,524	29,152
			85	41,160	204,947	233,199	28,252
			86	20,610	99,422	112,022	12,600
	V	W	83	5,394	28,745	33,511	4,766
			84	148,533	676,018	805,988	129,970
			85	462,573	2,021,652	2,310,607	288,955
			86	124,603	354,415	426,648	72,233
NICARAG	O	E	86	3,150	10,919	12,569	1,650
	V	E	83	2,700	8,700	10,228	1,528
NIGER	O	E	85	12,600	35,628	57,080	21,452
	V	E	85	3,150	8,391	10,044	1,653
			86	131,355	411,763	483,419	71,656
	V	W	86	12,600	39,777	44,682	4,905
NIGERIA	V	H	86	5,983	28,258	31,858	3,600
NIUE	V	W	86	2,457	7,278	7,470	192
NORFOLK	V	E	82	2,700	7,368	9,132	1,764
NORWAY	A	E	81	171	578	2,245	1,667
	N	E	82	152,888	478,540	586,806	108,266
			85	4,176	17,188	18,634	1,446
	O	E	81	120,721	359,888	432,987	73,099
			82	130,036	324,423	394,527	70,104
			83	83,786	242,579	291,958	49,379
			84	42,217	108,911	138,203	29,292
			85	32,526	85,184	117,559	32,375
			86	40,708	98,780	135,458	36,678
	O	W	81	3,967	15,112	17,081	1,969
			82	2,746	8,296	10,262	1,966
			83	4,455	14,622	17,644	3,022
			84	309	750	1,050	300
			85	517	4,951	5,448	497
			86	309	1,050	1,113	63
	V	E	81	249,608	776,033	957,573	181,540
			82	138,464	434,354	549,316	114,962
			83	210,199	628,202	784,390	156,188
			84	219,260	705,802	890,543	184,741
			85	188,630	536,000	688,578	152,578
			86	123,490	388,704	497,988	109,284
	V	W	81	88,681	298,319	366,188	67,869
			82	66,984	252,805	312,743	59,938
			83	88,727	270,543	340,151	69,608
			84	107,174	252,965	307,758	54,793
			85	70,024	231,693	292,348	60,655
			86	76,588	257,889	324,295	66,406
PAKISTN	V	W	83	4,755	15,750	18,525	2,775
PANAMA	N	W	84	8,330	35,233	40,289	5,056
	V	E	85	6,048	17,195	20,795	3,600
			86	63,509	191,193	225,833	34,640
	V	W	84	10,445	52,224	58,443	6,219
			85	88,084	275,267	320,463	45,196
			86	59,002	169,439	200,225	30,786
PERU	N	W	84	7,500	20,400	33,398	12,998
			85	77,843	276,795	351,171	74,376
			86	15,759	42,336	60,401	18,065
	O	E	81	394	700	1,276	576
			84	2,377	5,600	8,017	2,417
	O	W	85	1,968	5,400	7,540	2,140
	V	E	81	22,273	47,926	78,898	31,012
			82	20,139	41,880	69,080	27,200
			83	16,201	33,880	55,651	21,771
			84	86,298	213,157	297,969	84,812
			85	75,599	206,991	268,537	61,546
			86	39,020	101,410	134,299	32,889
	V	W	83	1,875	5,000	8,767	3,767
			84	1,875	5,000	8,569	3,569
			85	1,701	4,470	6,258	1,788
PHIL R	N	H	84	37,800	58,200	86,362	28,162
	O	E	82	1,728	3,158	5,754	2,596
	O	W	84	4,406	8,154	10,548	2,394

Crop
Product
TSUSA commodity number, description, and unit of quantity

Country	Mode	Reg	Yr	Quantity	F.A.S.	C.I.F.	Charges
			85	1,728	2,726	4,196	1,470
	V	E	81	115,776	192,796	307,383	114,587
			82	118,656	226,827	334,338	107,511
			83	163,267	330,303	474,349	144,046
			84	138,820	245,046	389,323	144,277
			85	233,886	339,063	558,314	219,251
			86	76,351	115,164	174,826	59,662
	V	H	81	75,912	120,000	175,292	55,292
			82	51,848	96,146	131,496	35,350
			83	80,622	167,135	221,094	53,959
			85	52,902	75,184	123,211	48,027
			86	29,347	46,287	67,982	21,695
	V	W	81	968,813	1,669,615	2,357,599	687,984
			82	963,409	1,862,428	2,520,148	657,720
			83	929,914	1,889,544	2,527,599	638,055
			84	995,600	1,708,979	2,373,129	664,150
			85	1,263,384	1,599,457	2,333,656	734,199
			86	934,632	1,452,222	1,979,375	527,153
POLAND	N	E	81	11,308	19,315	31,175	11,860
	O	E	82	13,433	25,640	42,440	16,800
			83	1,962	3,468	5,468	2,000
	V	E	81	203,282	266,539	450,446	183,907
			82	96,733	139,912	237,933	98,021
			83	118,186	173,995	279,794	105,799
			84	99,299	147,934	249,185	101,251
			85	57,888	87,261	157,159	69,898
			86	60,662	93,610	160,225	66,615
	V	W	81	26,719	33,435	73,343	39,908
			82	900	1,300	2,330	1,030
			83	900	1,300	3,624	2,324
			84	5,458	8,189	13,894	5,705
			85	10,682	16,338	27,137	10,799
			86	4,110	6,286	12,128	5,842
PORTUGL	V	E	81	59,944	131,644	191,857	60,213
			82	46,859	103,656	147,105	43,449
			83	74,182	147,882	225,675	77,793
			84	71,038	133,278	199,718	66,440
			85	142,344	294,686	423,168	128,482
			86	134,430	308,007	433,090	125,083
	V	W	82	1,729	3,628	5,771	2,143
			83	11,636	23,065	35,343	12,278
			84	4,527	8,221	11,948	3,727
			85	5,050	9,246	15,276	6,030
			86	3,168	8,096	10,530	2,434
REP SAF	V	E	83	2,790	11,880	14,880	3,000
			84	3,120	14,560	19,751	5,191
			85	4,290	16,640	19,124	2,484
SALVADR	O	E	85	2,016	9,184	11,184	2,000
			86	2,016	9,184	9,919	735
	O	W	83	2,916	5,897	5,897	
	V	E	84	2,016	7,138	9,184	2,046
			85	2,016	7,148	9,184	2,036
			86	26,208	72,576	88,146	15,570
	V	W	83	18,144	77,480	92,343	14,863
			84	22,896	95,014	113,515	18,501
			85	16,992	69,025	81,630	12,605
			86	25,056	92,316	113,681	21,365
SINGAPR	N	W	85	4,869	19,143	21,899	2,756
	O	E	84	2,548	11,078	13,273	2,195
	V	E	83	5,625	18,557	21,805	3,248
			84	9,619	30,355	37,375	7,020
			85	9,900	27,244	36,744	9,500
			86	46,382	154,111	197,085	42,974
	V	H	83	2,636	11,077	13,377	2,300
			86	8,304	41,148	47,348	6,200
	V	W	81	5,440	14,655	20,065	5,410
			82	2,722	7,543	10,477	2,934
			83	10,783	26,044	29,815	3,771
			84	33,841	110,696	127,561	16,865
			85	15,128	53,279	64,548	11,269
			86	169,296	543,299	646,638	103,339
SPAIN	O	E	84	3,564	11,405	14,644	3,239
			85	756	2,520	3,300	780
			86	1,944	6,480	8,485	2,005
	O	W	86	1,620	5,760	6,743	983
	V	E	81	57,919	138,781	204,497	65,716
			82	65,236	157,066	222,754	65,688
			83	57,020	162,529	216,762	54,233
			84	298,277	730,266	909,275	179,009
			85	41,153	109,051	145,070	36,019
			86	33,975	86,022	114,391	28,369
	V	W	83	5,622	18,743	23,376	4,633
			84	12,449	43,526	54,083	10,557
SWAZLND	V	E	85	2,512	8,583	10,568	1,985
SWEDEN	N	E	81	79,389	196,247	248,781	52,534
	O	E	81	756	2,801	3,560	759
			84	155	367	461	94
	V	E	81	30,225	90,895	109,284	18,389
			82	105,067	277,912	361,673	83,761
			83	113,948	329,657	417,863	88,206
			84	526,830	2,241,085	2,696,232	455,147
			85	537,753	2,208,395	2,639,596	431,201
			86	143,146	602,823	727,076	124,253
	V	W	81	2,867	14,202	16,790	2,588
			82	8,306	22,383	31,200	8,817
			83	5,984	15,350	20,356	5,006
			84	107,615	431,436	518,164	86,728
			85	133,357	568,598	690,650	122,052
			86	108,560	460,817	562,988	102,171
SWITZLD	A	E	81	39	732	2,952	2,220
	N	E	84	84,333	288,116	338,731	50,615
			86	6,968	24,744	30,275	5,531
	N	W	82	10,048	36,997	46,233	9,236
	O	E	81	5,606	12,220	18,783	6,563
			82	873	4,006	4,806	800
			83	20,119	70,981	87,760	16,779
			84	2,521	20,521	24,357	3,836
			85	13,487	45,092	59,452	14,360
			86	13,809	47,485	58,079	10,594
	V	E	81	80,570	287,267	350,561	63,294
			82	153,715	554,041	657,880	103,839
			83	201,874	711,247	833,821	122,574
			84	155,847	583,530	714,850	131,320
			85	199,480	709,866	850,886	141,020
			86	229,591	732,574	924,494	191,920
	V	W	81	75,388	275,060	338,659	63,599
			82	53,187	197,442	250,383	52,941
			83	96,710	367,357	444,645	77,288
			84	106,957	386,935	459,985	73,050
			85	94,615	310,547	400,118	89,571
			86	111,865	331,796	409,373	77,577
THAILND	O	H	82	619	4,006	4,463	457
			83	1,444	5,320	6,387	1,067
			86	2,475	7,625	10,090	2,465
	V	E	81	20,717	88,357	114,089	25,732
			82	35,295	145,079	176,467	31,388
			83	54,037	221,088	257,981	36,893
			84	72,563	319,879	379,328	59,449
			85	93,694	335,263	409,973	74,710
			86	130,572	524,430	595,825	71,395
	V	H	83	2,250	8,150	9,672	1,522
			84	5,400	20,125	23,150	3,025
			85	5,400	18,783	21,984	3,201
			86	2,708	9,371	11,136	1,765
	V	W	81	43,472	136,784	184,182	47,398
			82	90,294	328,579	428,583	100,004
			83	112,045	460,542	593,986	133,444
			84	105,042	385,873	485,664	99,791
			85	223,265	659,679	802,246	142,567
			86	227,508	656,494	780,715	124,221
TOKELAU	V	W	84	4,734	13,996	18,439	4,443
TRINID	A	E	86	450	1,473	2,398	925
	V	E	86	1,190	7,381	8,621	1,240
TURKEY	O	E	85	2,875	4,821	7,329	2,508
			86	8,748	14,463	15,254	791
	V	E	81	11,412	25,320	36,936	11,616
			86	37,915	65,160	107,594	42,434
U KING	N	E	81	422,515	1,529,515	1,823,581	294,066
			82	531,236	2,026,412	2,411,711	385,299
			83	900,372	3,231,286	3,808,094	576,808
			84	1,176,957	4,291,117	5,093,281	802,164
			85	1,475,498	5,145,262	6,237,777	1,092,515
			86	69,233	323,182	413,941	90,759
	N	W	82	73,682	312,967	384,410	71,443
			84	436,914	1,473,253	1,805,156	331,903
			85	584,840	2,034,969	2,541,997	507,028
			86	326,191	1,367,883	1,651,627	283,744
	O	E	81	25,504	102,035	124,675	22,640
			82	11,848	48,391	57,939	9,548
			83	37,569	134,156	148,200	14,044
			84	38,709	118,469	148,019	29,550
			85	13,756	40,849	50,425	9,576
			86	21,316	68,475	73,070	4,595
	O	W	83	698	4,435	4,715	280
			84	660	1,446	1,856	410
			85	5,913	10,489	12,475	1,986
	V	E	81	1,026,527	3,441,183	4,194,346	750,303
			82	992,458	3,379,013	4,079,284	700,271

Crop Product TSUSA commodity number, description, and unit of quantity Country	Mode	Reg	Yr	Quantity	F.A.S.	C.I.F.	Charges
			83	1,085,497	3,625,389	4,381,408	756,019
			84	1,370,140	4,403,194	5,363,988	960,794
			85	1,329,511	4,245,243	5,149,164	903,921
			86	2,541,749	9,050,764	10,825,537	1,774,773
	V	W	81	745,583	2,723,685	3,459,363	742,478
			82	767,597	2,697,705	3,410,208	712,503
			83	820,729	3,141,016	3,828,192	687,176
			84	507,142	1,962,903	2,392,644	429,741
			85	628,586	2,238,746	2,847,634	608,888
			86	649,968	2,318,714	2,901,384	582,670
URUGUAY	V	E	85	12,438	20,160	34,180	14,020
			86	2,276	4,500	6,593	2,093
	V	W	86	2,126	7,830	9,849	2,019
USSR	V	E	82	2,739	7,313	10,271	2,958
			83	17,325	51,034	60,339	9,305
	V	W	85	2,250	7,100	8,987	1,887
VENEZ	N	E	85	25,539	35,742	68,614	32,872
	V	E	86	41,223	66,832	103,522	36,690
W SAMOA	V	W	83	4,208	22,936	26,169	3,233
			84	2,295	11,174	13,164	1,990
YUGOSLV	N	E	82	4,797	11,520	17,297	5,777
			83	8,398	12,148	19,126	6,978
	O	E	83	9,141	21,231	29,367	8,136
			84	7,701	13,971	21,351	7,380
			85	4,653	12,540	16,379	3,839
			86	2,705	6,144	8,787	2,643
	O	W	83	4,226	11,539	19,175	7,636
	V	E	81	32,062	75,097	107,196	32,099
			82	19,459	46,365	65,849	19,484
			83	31,068	73,757	95,943	22,186
			84	20,844	45,877	64,934	19,057
			85	13,175	28,051	39,717	11,666
			86	27,599	59,701	86,196	26,495
	V	W	81	7,494	17,117	27,613	10,496
			82	5,032	11,430	15,682	4,252
			83	14,442	35,536	47,062	11,526
			84	5,071	10,508	14,000	3,492
			85	10,010	23,210	31,992	8,782
			86	2,705	5,760	8,192	2,432
ZAIRE	V	E	85	6,240	32,240	38,354	6,114
			86	8,136	70,117	78,867	8,750

1670530 BEER, ETC NT OV 1 GAL, NSPF (GAL)

Country	Mode	Reg	Yr	Quantity	F.A.S.	C.I.F.	Charges
TOTAL			81	6,445,462	16,165,407	18,089,185	1,921,902
			82	6,528,336	16,615,942	18,856,464	2,240,522
			83	8,769,321	20,612,962	23,794,869	3,181,907
			84	10,529,094	25,453,243	29,169,948	3,716,705
			85	13,018,856	30,537,219	34,915,796	4,378,577
			86	14,944,181	39,846,222	44,345,577	4,499,355
ALGERIA	V	E	83	496	1,470	1,638	168
AUSTRAL	N	E	85	7,242	28,243	34,246	6,003
	N	W	86	105,705	292,531	352,410	59,879
	O	E	81	13,715	43,630	51,843	8,213
			82	3,516	6,908	10,787	3,879
			84	5,557	16,022	19,497	3,475
			85	1,264	7,000	8,902	1,902
	V	E	81	657,208	1,342,215	1,916,884	574,669
			82	898,603	1,695,478	2,511,374	815,896
			83	1,197,099	2,213,391	3,124,399	911,008
			84	1,378,141	3,428,799	4,499,611	1,070,812
			85	1,554,464	3,047,653	4,266,046	1,218,393
			86	1,842,610	4,664,772	5,720,611	1,055,839
	V	H	81	41,304	89,030	118,998	29,968
			82	46,047	116,283	148,489	32,206
			83	50,575	111,261	149,434	38,173
			84	48,293	118,425	153,942	35,517
			85	38,221	72,501	101,411	28,910
			86	44,285	111,795	140,463	28,668
	V	W	81	719,154	1,606,933	2,093,363	486,430
			82	587,147	1,215,866	1,636,263	420,397
			83	888,252	1,797,994	2,449,472	651,478
			84	825,630	1,867,223	2,454,073	586,850
			85	1,114,216	2,309,067	3,105,268	796,201
			86	1,052,584	2,689,500	3,351,214	661,714
AUSTRIA	A	E	84	137	1,843	4,907	3,064
	O	E	81	836	2,213	2,733	520
			82	1,109	3,675	3,885	210
			84	11,809	26,383	28,956	2,573
	V	E	81	1,255	2,739	3,666	927
			82	2,824	7,693	11,503	3,810
			84	8,532	21,670	27,474	5,804
			85	5,218	13,540	13,708	168
	V	W	82	8,296	20,492	26,162	5,670

Country	Mode	Reg	Yr	Quantity	F.A.S.	C.I.F.	Charges
			83	21,287	44,896	54,965	10,069
			85	4,078	8,035	12,536	4,501
BARBADO	V	E	81	562	1,852	2,251	399
BELGIUM	A	E	83	56	279	324	45
	N	E	83	5,754	24,566	31,090	6,524
			85	9,468	36,005	43,429	7,424
	O	E	83	13,163	24,711	30,100	5,389
			84	2,184	7,735	9,985	2,250
			85	1,394	3,069	3,338	269
	V	E	81	5,986	16,807	19,734	2,927
			82	605	1,398	1,867	469
			83	10,998	36,207	41,250	5,043
			84	20,282	96,467	112,500	16,033
			85	32,170	111,786	145,847	34,061
			86	20,610	113,323	131,847	18,524
	V	W	83	4,820	8,986	11,059	2,073
			84	10,242	19,607	24,474	4,867
			85	7,915	23,183	29,574	6,391
			86	3,108	8,755	10,836	2,081
BRAZIL	V	E	81	522	1,160	1,587	427
			83	2,250	4,600	6,535	1,935
			84	4,752	6,547	8,898	2,351
			85	13,464	18,950	25,111	6,161
			86	16,072	22,583	28,529	5,946
	V	W	82	22,500	38,069	52,010	13,941
			83	20,340	35,226	47,004	11,778
			84	3,937	6,455	9,963	3,508
C RICA	V	E	86	990	3,235	3,582	347
CANADA	A	E	81	316	742	1,284	542
			82	209	705	1,196	491
			84	392	1,342	1,648	306
	A	W	81	90	1,020	1,043	23
	N	W	83	3,690	9,900	12,387	2,487
			86	1,038	5,400	5,400	
	O	E	81	5,367	5,500	5,500	
			82	454,675	1,215,246	1,215,400	154
			83	613,520	1,438,013	1,439,091	1,078
			84	590,494	1,333,309	1,334,312	1,003
			85	352,139	887,870	887,870	
			86	544,467	1,355,218	1,355,218	
	O	W	82	140	579	579	
			85	21,982	56,396	56,396	
			86	8,459	17,127	17,127	
	V	E	81	34,015	82,174	84,727	2,553
			82	10,187	21,811	27,936	6,125
			83	450	1,210	1,341	131
			84	29,070	55,142	61,042	5,900
			85	18,648	44,730	49,285	4,555
			86	7,560	20,094	23,278	3,184
	V	W	82	69,975	186,275	221,482	35,207
			83	2,250	5,975	7,895	1,920
			84	36,358	93,105	111,051	17,946
			85	28,791	79,760	94,124	14,364
			86	35,798	70,615	89,863	19,248
CHINA M	V	E	86	6,279	20,367	45,010	24,643
	V	W	81	20,932	26,621	47,245	20,624
			82	3,375	3,875	6,057	2,182
			85	4,050	13,600	15,600	2,000
COLOMB	N	E	84	5,353	15,828	19,572	3,744
	V	E	83	11,250	34,000	39,816	5,816
			84	7,560	21,168	25,414	4,246
			85	2,565	6,840	8,410	1,570
CZECHO	V	E	81	10,368	22,535	28,334	5,799
			84	2,592	5,198	7,856	2,658
DENMARK	O	E	81	2,010	4,982	7,126	2,144
			82	2,177	7,701	7,701	
	V	E	84	5,688	19,389	25,150	5,761
			85	3,792	6,082	10,080	3,998
	V	W	84	4,755	11,024	13,181	2,157
DOM REP	N	E	84	340,489	1,024,977	1,103,195	78,218
	V	E	84	33,306	99,234	110,503	11,269
			85	10,920	29,848	32,607	2,759
ECUADOR	V	E	81	4,016	5,649	8,160	2,511
F W IND	V	E	84	77	990	1,096	106
FR GERM	A	E	82	40	396	613	217
			83	79	277	315	38
			84	113	323	415	92
			86	900	3,183	7,139	3,956
	N	E	81	45,184	170,301	196,081	25,780
			82	35,997	123,007	146,306	23,299
			83	28,039	88,086	106,168	18,082
			84	58,316	149,836	196,339	46,503
			85	17,588	58,729	77,773	19,044
	N	W	81	24,803	81,383	101,467	20,084

Crop
Product
TSUSA commodity number, description, and unit of quantity

Country	Mode	Reg	Yr	Quantity	F.A.S.	C.I.F.	Charges
			84	54,848	141,448	171,996	30,548
			85	32,436	116,745	146,704	29,959
	O	E	81	7,811	25,818	29,275	3,457
			82	1,998	5,035	5,846	811
			83	31,685	112,577	132,643	20,066
			85	6,408	16,060	25,642	9,582
			86	52,113	54,239	64,056	9,817
	O	W	82	103	328	383	55
			84	1,727	6,800	7,539	739
	V	E	81	155,512	464,343	561,984	97,641
			82	139,047	371,316	451,218	79,902
			83	493,613	1,128,730	1,399,130	270,400
			84	634,358	1,634,721	1,972,343	337,622
			85	575,135	1,617,375	1,999,600	382,225
			86	923,099	3,047,455	3,556,925	509,470
	V	W	81	11,195	35,298	44,483	9,185
			82	122,602	270,871	340,012	69,141
			83	122,247	300,766	358,951	58,185
			84	58,016	150,315	180,268	29,953
			85	29,889	105,205	129,118	23,913
			86	101,571	304,251	377,538	73,287
FRANCE	O	E	83	2,825	10,824	12,825	2,001
			84	1,931	5,911	6,884	973
			86	1,488	5,685	6,771	1,086
	V	E	81	6,026	20,360	24,456	4,096
			82	3,150	10,154	12,072	1,918
			83	5,670	22,020	27,450	5,430
			84	26,319	79,185	93,995	14,810
			85	11,114	42,083	51,248	9,165
			86	4,482	32,694	36,438	3,744
	V	W	81	33,314	109,114	139,372	30,258
			82	3,013	7,603	9,341	1,738
			83	8,440	34,136	40,440	6,304
			84	6,300	20,430	25,092	4,662
			85	1,797	8,033	9,691	1,658
			86	13,188	32,232	40,933	8,701
GERM DR	V	E	83	3,087	2,176	2,279	103
	V	W	83	3,072	2,176	4,420	2,244
GREECE	O	E	85	14,359	30,047	35,001	4,954
			86	9,488	22,080	26,529	4,449
	V	E	84	675	1,800	2,534	734
GUINEA	V	W	85	3,935	14,593	17,380	2,787
HG KONG	V	W	86	3,745	10,252	12,367	2,115
INDIA	V	E	84	2,250	5,800	6,090	290
	V	W	86	5,636	21,362	26,682	5,320
IRELAND	V	E	81	18,477	23,717	33,526	9,809
			82	748	2,341	2,716	375
			84	29,430	87,840	103,372	15,532
			85	136,179	203,885	269,076	65,191
			86	4,995	15,277	19,162	3,885
	V	W	82	2,508	2,993	4,786	1,793
			84	5,130	6,460	9,342	2,882
ISRAEL	O	E	86	4,752	12,358	14,721	2,363
	V	E	81	2,784	7,959	10,284	2,325
ITALY	O	E	82	3,518	9,583	11,777	2,194
	V	E	83	2,430	7,031	9,401	2,370
			84	2,835	8,190	10,395	2,205
			85	7,110	21,423	33,272	11,849
			86	7,560	25,038	32,630	7,592
	V	W	82	3,118	5,156	8,171	3,015
JAMAICA	V	E	83	2,880	9,540	12,160	2,620
			84	25,920	78,880	91,346	12,466
			85	100,307	388,434	469,334	80,900
			86	237,567	973,904	1,168,850	194,946
JAPAN	N	E	83	33,380	104,938	164,503	59,565
	N	H	82	30,409	74,971	96,370	21,399
			84	33,780	78,072	106,024	27,952
	N	W	81	36,909	112,595	136,806	24,211
			84	130,395	497,974	574,199	76,225
	O	E	86	618	2,175	3,033	858
	O	W	83	824	1,600	2,117	517
	V	E	81	22,434	58,293	75,843	17,550
			82	30,572	78,858	102,449	23,591
			83	34,030	91,250	121,785	30,535
			84	83,112	277,341	369,370	92,029
			85	65,497	243,171	298,957	55,786
			86	216,701	767,669	918,706	151,037
	V	H	81	29,546	61,467	79,450	17,983
			83	30,188	81,350	101,793	20,443
			85	41,158	100,147	133,026	32,879
			86	41,396	102,144	148,463	46,319
	V	W	81	15,814	51,440	61,994	10,554
			82	41,741	144,214	166,495	22,281
			83	292,122	1,137,765	1,265,290	127,525
			84	213,867	783,961	892,557	108,596
			85	624,408	2,241,724	2,568,489	326,765
			86	697,841	2,468,919	2,761,418	292,499
KOR REP	V	E	85	2,520	7,166	10,016	2,850
	V	W	84	2,476	8,415	9,611	1,196
			86	5,018	10,080	11,882	1,802
LEBANON	V	E	82	225	375	377	2
MALAYSA	O	E	85	11,057	24,382	24,382	
MALI	V	E	85	990	2,377	3,314	937
			86	16,583	58,365	64,457	6,092
MEXICO	N	E	82	1,125	2,500	2,860	360
	N	W	84	5,850	12,400	12,719	319
			86	18,270	44,890	54,500	9,610
	O	E	81	1,667,356	4,027,156	4,062,131	34,948
			82	872,580	2,134,957	2,141,731	6,774
			83	890,042	1,840,475	1,840,825	350
			84	1,249,198	2,656,047	2,659,897	3,850
			85	1,747,388	3,849,770	3,849,869	99
			86	1,466,398	3,349,703	3,350,455	752
	O	W	81	1,835,426	4,838,816	4,838,816	
			82	1,827,846	5,100,690	5,114,500	13,810
			83	2,044,558	4,318,905	4,318,905	
			84	2,309,264	4,691,295	4,691,295	
			85	3,839,491	8,378,533	8,378,536	3
			86	4,817,254	10,518,764	10,518,764	
	V	W	81	21,060	45,863	51,299	5,436
			84	1,800	3,391	4,611	1,220
			85	1,800	3,600	4,661	1,061
N ANTIL	V	E	84	572	1,724	2,056	332
			85	25	1,072	1,227	155
N ZEAL	V	H	82	2,645	6,160	7,884	1,724
	V	W	84	2,442	4,798	6,934	2,136
			86	2,419	5,049	7,688	2,639
NETHLDS	N	E	81	44,273	118,818	135,040	16,222
			82	414,532	1,186,063	1,357,691	171,628
			83	89,901	258,522	302,979	44,457
			84	107,990	276,487	336,632	60,145
			85	510,222	1,242,611	1,462,851	220,240
			86	610,063	2,037,362	2,275,269	237,907
	N	W	84	120,241	338,551	396,773	58,222
	O	E	81	11,016	33,484	38,330	4,846
			82	20,128	49,290	56,740	7,450
			83	62,296	168,082	197,866	29,784
			84	5,495	15,007	16,954	1,947
			85	1,804	4,178	6,476	2,298
			86	2,929	8,923	10,323	1,400
	O	H	85	13,332	12,830	16,919	4,089
			86	3,218	9,558	12,222	2,664
	V	E	81	729,524	2,042,814	2,364,340	319,677
			82	566,065	1,653,449	1,904,755	251,306
			83	1,344,692	3,965,609	4,548,441	582,832
			84	1,672,317	4,238,414	4,969,686	731,272
			85	1,355,507	3,604,413	4,215,936	611,523
			86	1,582,293	5,317,166	6,084,230	767,064
	V	H	83	990	2,738	3,291	553
			86	2,227	7,559	9,177	1,618
	V	W	81	136,433	391,809	477,895	86,086
			82	200,775	581,761	703,883	122,122
			83	248,254	690,661	831,009	140,348
			84	133,210	346,751	416,388	69,637
			85	203,235	505,075	625,067	119,992
			86	229,038	754,476	906,535	152,059
NEW GUI	O	H	83	951	3,972	4,492	520
	O	W	83	166	857	879	22
			84	3,685	18,213	18,840	627
	V	H	82	18,804	66,295	86,590	20,295
			84	230	1,141	1,341	200
			85	521	2,614	3,025	411
	V	W	84	6,415	25,844	32,063	6,219
NIGER	V	E	86	1,485	4,198	4,618	420
NORWAY	O	E	81	5,994	17,607	20,791	3,184
			82	1,898	5,732	6,716	984
			83	2,465	5,819	8,319	2,500
			84	1,040	2,450	3,290	840
	V	E	85	5,850	9,100	13,270	4,170
PANAMA	A	W	84	187	650	1,817	1,167
	V	E	86	3,024	10,621	12,306	1,685
PERU	V	E	85	4,498	17,508	20,404	2,896
PHIL R	V	E	86	17,766	48,354	63,532	15,178
	V	W	82	3,456	6,317	9,724	3,407
			84	3,026	5,549	7,476	1,927
			85	1,944	2,480	3,642	1,162
			86	3,167	7,272	8,457	1,185
POLAND	V	E	81	4,726	6,280	10,962	4,682

Crop Product TSUSA commodity number, description, and unit of quantity Country	Mode	Reg	Yr	Quantity	F.A.S.	C.I.F.	Charges
			82	9,449	13,651	22,756	9,105
			83	5,370	9,500	16,010	6,510
			84	7,088	10,238	17,106	6,868
			85	2,496	3,413	5,622	2,209
			86	4,726	7,350	16,269	8,919
	V	W	81	900	1,148	2,221	1,073
			84	2,648	3,716	6,026	2,310
PORTUGL	V	E	84	2,940	6,906	9,993	3,087
SINGAPR	V	W	85	2,475	6,731	9,037	2,306
SPAIN	V	E	85	3,279	6,210	7,779	1,569
SWAZLND	V	E	86	33,488	71,867	86,985	15,118
SWEDEN	V	E	81	248	784	972	188
			84	5,940	17,636	21,461	3,825
			86	7,354	20,320	25,209	4,889
	V	W	85	13,300	21,611	30,793	9,182
SWITZLD	N	W	84	27,457	109,809	130,410	20,601
	V	E	81	2,512	10,569	10,919	350
			83	22,419	70,451	84,415	13,964
			84	6,545	27,612	31,770	4,158
			85	11,263	45,327	51,909	6,582
			86	11,506	36,997	44,704	7,707
	V	W	83	16,364	67,335	82,892	15,557
			85	4,773	20,149	24,688	4,539
			86	12,328	43,662	54,975	11,313
TRINID	A	E	84	94	975	1,072	97
U KING	A	E	81	37	266	572	306
			82	37	279	602	323
	N	E	83	17,319	40,131	49,497	9,366
			85	11,363	37,057	43,966	6,909
	O	E	81	186	540	620	80
			82	2,402	5,000	6,415	1,415
			84	547	4,106	4,695	589
			85	2,978	11,537	13,373	1,836
			86	8,300	7,876	8,307	431
	V	E	81	40,431	108,790	131,234	22,444
			82	41,757	123,970	149,258	25,288
			83	31,626	104,745	124,448	19,703
			84	96,331	290,354	343,568	53,214
			85	343,782	646,613	806,033	159,420
			86	51,005	121,773	153,193	31,420
	V	W	81	17,875	42,773	53,544	10,771
			82	12,233	28,337	37,719	9,382
			83	48,572	129,581	162,084	32,503
			84	9,114	21,595	27,064	5,469
			85	14,642	43,005	56,112	13,107
			86	7,603	20,616	26,342	5,726
USSR	V	E	83	2,475	7,652	9,047	1,395
VENEZ	V	E	85	5,418	7,585	8,070	485
			86	10,014	27,189	37,429	10,240
YUGOSLV	V	E	82	2,430	2,236	5,017	2,781
			85	2,772	6,300	8,560	2,260
ZAIRE	O	W	85	810	2,160	2,160	

1670540 ALE,PORTER,STOUT,BEER,OV GAL (GAL)

Country	Mode	Reg	Yr	Quantity	F.A.S.	C.I.F.	Charges
TOTAL			81	11,849,388	15,852,555	19,278,164	3,425,595
			82	12,217,480	17,089,995	20,582,633	3,492,638
			83	14,036,427	21,943,469	25,870,251	3,926,782
			84	15,744,058	24,362,187	28,904,635	4,542,448
			85	15,551,397	24,300,735	29,136,437	4,835,702
			86	17,973,628	30,753,711	36,282,861	5,529,150
ALGERIA	V	E	83	1,373	2,041	2,581	540
AUSTRAL	V	E	81	3,496	7,653	11,211	3,558
			82	77,219	142,869	202,317	59,448
			83	69,018	121,657	174,601	52,944
			84	4,082	15,904	18,651	2,747
			85	14,201	25,920	35,512	9,592
	V	W	83	2,534	4,281	5,454	1,173
AUSTRIA	N	E	83	8,834	16,552	19,311	2,759
	O	E	81	951	2,520	3,556	1,036
	V	E	81	20,620	27,245	37,408	10,163
			82	13,572	23,104	29,937	6,833
			83	6,787	23,760	27,260	3,500
			84	20,621	39,567	53,796	14,229
			85	15,820	17,285	31,747	14,462
			86	15,848	23,697	41,697	18,000
BAHAMAS	V	E	82	3,802	5,449	7,027	1,578
BELGIUM	N	E	85	13,267	17,359	23,111	5,752
	O	E	84	3,801	5,097	6,747	1,650
	V	E	81	330	442	539	97
			83	4,752	7,141	10,069	2,928
			84	4,962	6,732	8,669	1,937
			85	20,905	37,397	62,451	25,054
			86	18,753	44,503	55,614	11,111

Crop Product TSUSA commodity number, description, and unit of quantity Country	Mode	Reg	Yr	Quantity	F.A.S.	C.I.F.	Charges
	V	W	81	3,043	8,235	9,960	1,725
			83	2,006	2,883	4,105	1,222
			86	4,858	8,729	12,086	3,357
BULGAR	V	W	85	1,800	4,350	5,991	1,641
C RICA	V	E	86	950	1,603	2,006	403
CANADA	N	E	81	421,310	436,605	436,651	47
			85	3,558,987	3,798,651	3,798,651	
	O	E	81	3,770,113	3,796,634	3,796,534	
			82	4,172,763	4,113,514	4,113,514	
			83	4,324,253	4,378,564	4,383,873	5,309
			84	4,704,632	4,868,662	4,874,519	5,857
			85	1,008,760	1,408,775	1,408,781	6
			86	5,256,407	6,260,731	6,261,412	681
	O	W	82	93,744	260,670	260,670	
			83	877,139	2,971,534	2,971,534	
			84	893,405	3,262,321	3,262,321	
			85	967,056	3,375,493	3,375,494	1
			86	714,892	2,305,079	2,305,079	
	V	E	85	4,038	5,508	7,111	1,603
	V	W	83	214	605	788	183
			85	20,192	26,244	33,975	7,731
			86	96,609	131,774	177,867	46,093
CHILE	V	W	83	2,565	3,304	4,703	1,399
CHINA M	V	W	85	1,188	1,620	1,840	220
			86	22,200	50,173	72,719	22,546
CZECHO	V	W	85	3,715	4,848	5,319	471
DENMARK	V	E	82	29,160	87,913	106,239	18,326
			83	3,645	4,590	6,213	1,623
			85	7,656	8,321	11,245	2,924
			86	4,115	3,296	8,492	5,196
	V	W	81	4,992	8,322	11,634	3,312
			82	1,268	2,899	3,806	907
DOM REP	V	E	85	5,020	6,315	8,168	1,853
F GUIAN	V	E	81	2,074	2,896	3,608	712
FR GERM	N	E	81	1,498,700	2,229,181	2,937,644	708,463
			82	34,175	74,814	89,136	14,322
			83	1,369,989	2,571,712	3,240,085	668,373
			84	50,037	90,263	106,831	16,568
			85	220,605	436,693	562,405	125,712
			86	145,802	297,188	367,126	69,938
	N	W	82	83,901	229,754	274,674	44,920
			83	87,766	224,384	266,877	42,493
			85	89,440	173,078	225,255	52,177
	O	E	81	2,160	5,705	7,252	1,547
			82	317	975	1,138	163
			83	56,527	169,337	192,105	22,768
			84	20,882	43,826	48,551	4,725
			85	15,753	27,926	38,963	11,037
			86	7,341	15,422	20,234	4,812
	O	W	83	4,338	16,416	18,516	2,100
			84	2,249	8,528	9,746	1,218
	V	E	81	676,194	1,155,128	1,496,900	341,772
			82	2,156,553	3,554,786	4,538,397	983,611
			83	705,077	1,225,727	1,582,034	356,307
			84	2,327,432	4,254,327	5,388,654	1,134,327
			85	2,333,990	4,103,596	5,397,935	1,294,339
			86	2,617,430	5,541,738	6,914,693	1,372,955
	V	W	81	101,077	185,509	239,060	53,551
			82	57,656	163,900	198,232	34,332
			83	153,265	435,455	538,018	102,563
			84	177,441	434,527	533,262	98,735
			85	117,610	294,049	374,068	80,019
			86	228,424	626,276	772,525	146,249
FRANCE	A	E	82	48	360	643	283
	O	E	84	476	648	792	144
	O	W	83	2,846	10,824	10,824	
	V	E	81	15,277	30,744	39,070	8,326
			82	5,707	21,828	25,034	3,206
			83	2,824	10,824	12,364	1,540
			84	66,450	122,190	182,968	60,778
			85	21,205	24,041	35,129	11,088
			86	102,993	142,897	190,630	47,733
	V	W	81	33,313	139,742	152,950	13,208
			82	3,723	7,750	10,275	2,525
			85	12,152	23,875	33,731	9,856
			86	475	1,372	2,042	670
GERM DR	V	E	81	3,333	3,977	5,451	1,474
GHANA	V	W	85	2,565	3,267	5,478	2,211
GREECE	V	E	83	2,092	7,075	9,943	2,868
INDNSIA	V	W	85	2,565	3,230	5,311	2,081
IRAN	V	W	85	4,455	5,610	9,049	3,439
IRELAND	O	W	81	3,564	4,253	6,802	2,549
	V	E	81	314,992	397,132	559,278	162,146
			82	421,926	550,622	746,467	195,845

Crop
Product
TSUSA commodity number, description, and unit of quantity

Country	Mode	Reg	Yr	Quantity	F.A.S.	C.I.F.	Charges
			83	531,666	684,389	908,834	224,445
			84	747,262	962,570	1,305,009	342,439
			85	764,710	1,075,060	1,443,562	368,502
			86	1,264,785	1,675,984	2,255,569	579,585
	V	W	81	19,272	22,768	37,673	14,905
			82	46,290	55,674	84,839	29,165
			83	57,183	72,661	105,329	32,668
			84	100,860	134,377	190,228	55,851
			85	120,645	153,251	242,273	89,022
			86	313,025	397,986	591,366	193,380
ISRAEL	V	E	85	4,455	5,739	7,876	2,137
ITALY	O	E	82	95	1,120	1,201	81
	V	E	85	1,267	1,847	2,304	457
	V	W	85	1,800	4,350	5,637	1,287
			86	475	3,200	3,753	553
JAMAICA	V	E	83	2,880	10,150	12,800	2,650
JAPAN	N	H	82	1,083	3,876	8,421	4,545
	V	E	83	8,185	21,725	28,586	6,861
			85	3,412	12,090	14,915	2,825
	V	H	83	159	388	564	176
	V	W	82	4,769	15,588	18,215	2,627
			83	4,783	18,790	24,974	6,184
			84	47,805	164,955	199,221	34,266
			85	14,847	52,876	60,501	7,625
			86	18,065	79,395	88,568	9,173
KOR REP	V	W	86	1,255	2,520	2,888	368
MALI	V	E	85	3,801	4,706	6,461	1,755
			86	26,928	48,923	59,920	10,997
MEXICO	A	E	81	47	1,800	2,053	253
	O	W	86	75,638	76,379	76,379	
N ZEAL	V	E	82	2,476	9,641	12,045	2,404
	V	H	86	11,436	12,990	18,861	5,871
NETHLDS	N	E	81	301,191	449,963	505,032	55,069
			82	90,223	130,544	193,308	62,764
			83	388,875	587,296	768,001	180,705
			84	474,968	665,124	856,897	191,773
			85	1,308,574	1,687,383	2,161,069	473,686
			86	938,744	1,730,808	2,065,496	334,688
	N	W	84	242,174	334,981	453,810	118,829
	O	E	81	52,990	74,845	89,334	14,489
			82	38,863	57,487	66,727	9,240
			83	173,336	257,052	326,820	69,768
			84	2,762	3,666	4,485	819
			86	1,267	2,386	3,109	723
	O	H	85	2,534	3,282	5,405	2,123
			86	3,168	4,810	7,468	2,658
	V	E	81	3,283,225	4,745,752	6,025,650	1,279,898
			82	3,233,781	4,849,185	5,970,101	1,120,916
			83	3,153,395	4,694,831	5,829,061	1,134,230
			84	3,543,629	4,849,387	6,193,592	1,344,205
			85	2,240,523	3,065,749	3,977,140	911,391
			86	2,332,294	4,168,087	5,089,011	920,924
	V	H	83	844	1,169	1,702	533
			86	2,323	3,919	5,870	1,951
	V	W	81	333,925	474,331	667,124	192,793
			82	531,167	785,243	1,090,066	304,823
			83	575,133	849,963	1,158,157	308,194
			84	286,099	453,494	588,148	134,654
			85	507,770	708,825	966,518	257,693
			86	574,595	1,050,315	1,333,575	283,260
NIGER	O	E	85	3,801	5,540	7,190	1,650
NORWAY	O	E	84	2,295	8,407	12,363	3,956
	V	E	84	2,475	8,771	11,241	2,470
			85	2,378	10,370	13,301	2,931
	V	W	84	2,982	11,760	14,044	2,284
			85	2,615	10,692	13,157	2,465
PERU	V	E	85	845	2,304	2,690	386
PHIL R	V	W	86	2,402	6,400	7,294	894
POLAND	V	W	81	3,496	4,248	5,382	1,134
SWEDEN	V	E	81	1,940	3,065	3,719	654
	V	W	85	2,054	5,672	7,353	1,681
SWITZLD	N	E	84	756	3,456	3,514	58
			86	1,521	8,791	10,968	2,177
	O	E	84	187	3,456	4,279	823
			86	1,775	7,126	8,732	1,606
	V	E	83	508	2,304	3,423	1,119
			84	34,149	155,568	174,346	18,778
			85	20,972	75,011	88,088	13,077
			86	4,818	22,511	26,338	3,827
	V	W	83	1,480	13,304	15,315	2,011
			84	7,520	36,864	41,080	4,216
			85	8,622	35,307	41,298	5,991
			86	6,275	23,815	28,350	4,535
THAILND	V	W	86	2,700	9,794	10,991	1,197
U KING	N	E	82	109,655	164,365	211,622	47,257
			85	138,354	237,830	293,866	56,036
	N	W	84	304,444	557,108	705,348	148,240
			85	367,237	698,554	928,659	230,105
	O	E	81	3,603	7,100	8,945	1,845
			82	2,402	5,000	6,275	1,275
			83	27,054	55,904	67,689	11,785
			84	3,511	6,650	8,585	1,935
	V	E	81	602,387	948,553	1,248,011	299,358
			82	613,893	1,035,250	1,327,903	292,653
			83	872,213	1,471,499	1,838,335	366,836
			84	1,286,784	2,088,723	2,663,645	574,922
			85	1,321,503	2,169,886	2,743,566	573,680
			86	2,446,186	4,549,977	5,573,892	1,023,915
	V	W	81	371,773	678,207	929,733	251,511
			82	384,741	730,400	975,558	245,158
			83	550,889	993,378	1,299,403	306,025
			84	374,300	753,942	971,763	217,821
			85	245,733	440,960	606,888	165,928
			86	704,874	1,409,817	1,804,174	394,357
VENEZ	V	E	86	1,982	3,300	6,067	2,767
YUGOSLV	V	W	82	2,508	5,415	8,846	3,431
			84	2,626	6,336	7,530	1,194

Hop, extract
1923000 HOP EXTRACT (LB)

Country	Mode	Reg	Yr	Quantity	F.A.S.	C.I.F.	Charges
TOTAL			81	1,256	10,432	12,254	1,822
			82	1,558	8,977	10,449	1,472
			83	673	6,550	6,980	430
			84	2,893	19,068	21,433	2,365
			85	125,709	26,237	27,252	1,015
			86	59,905	53,130	57,612	4,482
AUSTRAL	A	W	81	291	312	1,284	972
CANADA	O	E	83	45	1,715	1,715	
COLOMB	V	E	86	59,525	49,245	53,017	3,772
FR GERM	A	E	81	90	1,362	1,654	292
	A		84	225	1,561	1,738	177
	A	W	82	1,323	5,274	6,592	1,318
			84	2,378	14,574	16,378	1,804
			85	275	1,913	2,137	224
			86	160	1,679	2,100	421
	V	E	82	129	653	663	10
			83	30	452	467	15
	V	W	81	92	2,142	2,177	35
			82	52	1,395	1,411	16
			83	53	601	615	14
			84	133	1,664	1,704	40
MEXICO	O	E	81	126	1,408	1,408	
	O	W	85	125,000	19,750	19,750	
U KING	A	E	81	657	5,208	5,731	523
			82	54	1,655	1,783	128
			84	55	513	608	95
			85	434	4,574	5,365	791
			86	220	2,206	2,495	289
	O	W	83	545	3,782	4,183	401
	V	E	84	102	756	1,005	249

Hop, pellet
1922510 HOP PELLETS (LB)

Country	Mode	Reg	Yr	Quantity	F.A.S.	C.I.F.	Charges
TOTAL			82	610,257	1,613,236	1,654,468	41,232
			83	760,528	1,925,611	1,979,401	53,790
			84	905,912	1,952,494	2,044,259	91,765
			85	438,457	971,664	1,015,232	43,568
			86	1,064,132	2,250,688	2,350,867	100,179
CANADA	A	E	84	800	1,080	1,320	240
	O	W	86	8,466	22,119	22,119	
CZECHO	A	E	84	5,002	11,266	16,400	5,134
	V	E	83	22,705	87,927	89,684	1,757
			84	9,400	16,675	17,839	1,164
			86	224,078	445,045	458,518	13,473
FR GERM	A	E	83	1,102	1,639	2,441	802
			84	8,840	8,353	16,386	8,033
			86	4,090	10,277	13,247	2,970
	A	W	84	750	3,737	4,361	624
			85	548	1,098	1,543	445
	N	E	85	331,893	808,063	843,098	35,035
	O	E	84	1,771	7,335	7,907	572
			85	4,378	10,855	11,979	1,124

Crop Product TSUSA commodity number, description, and unit of quantity Country	Mode	Reg	Yr	Quantity	F.A.S.	C.I.F.	Charges
			86	14,727	123,165	124,864	1,699
	O	W	86	5,234	12,442	12,442	
	V	E	82	358,887	1,016,188	1,040,533	24,345
			83	613,359	1,535,413	1,578,770	43,357
			84	834,585	1,866,258	1,938,102	71,844
			85	95,900	140,486	146,572	6,086
			86	546,115	1,144,757	1,202,210	57,453
	V	W	84	4,956	18,283	19,142	859
JAPAN	V	E	84	37,400	13,785	16,404	2,619
KOR REP	V	W	86	71,121	12,500	15,839	3,339
U KING	O	W	85	738	1,815	2,040	225
	V	W	82	245	1,226	1,342	116
			83	344	743	962	219
			84	2,408	5,722	6,398	676
USSR	V	E	85	5,000	9,347	10,000	653
YUGOSLV	V	E	82	251,125	595,822	612,593	16,771
			83	123,018	299,889	307,544	7,655
			86	190,301	480,383	501,628	21,245

Hops
1922520 HOPS, NSPF (LB)

Country	Mode	Reg	Yr	Quantity	F.A.S.	C.I.F.	Charges
TOTAL			82	14,500,441	30,985,344	31,768,217	782,873
			83	12,731,751	30,386,667	31,277,399	890,732
			84	13,279,223	31,548,751	32,408,988	860,237
			85	17,801,903	46,274,233	47,592,637	1,318,404
			86	14,008,251	36,397,151	37,853,792	1,456,641
AUSTRAL	V	W	82	241,811	498,264	559,888	61,624
			83	77,408	143,688	164,308	20,620
			84	81,087	28,177	48,404	20,227
BELGIUM	V	E	82	22,046	45,335	48,729	3,394
			83	62,280	113,173	116,859	3,686
			85	25,000	41,041	43,130	2,089
	V	W	86	25,000	50,019	53,619	3,600
C RICA	A	E	83	10,051	2,994	5,178	2,184
			84	2,822	1,920	2,588	668
CANADA	O	E	82	3,277	5,080	5,080	
			83	31,741	53,921	53,921	
			84	19,310	30,104	30,104	
			85	4,869	9,034	9,034	
			86	6,007	9,310	9,310	
	O	W	82	90,142	124,028	124,028	
			83	179,068	285,149	285,149	
			84	120,045	106,513	106,513	
			85	61,917	52,765	52,765	
			86	109,496	88,812	88,812	
CHILE	V	W	83	2,729	1,714	1,848	134
CHINA M	A	W	83	639	436	752	316
CHINA T	V	W	84	900	1,095	1,148	53
COLOMB	A	E	85	1,160	1,160	1,430	270
CRIST I	V	E	86	160,189	523,348	536,635	13,287
CZECHO	N	E	85	1,041,175	1,989,037	2,103,865	114,828
	V	E	82	2,423,388	5,639,848	5,775,203	135,355
			83	1,445,295	2,930,681	3,031,184	100,503
			84	2,963,275	6,107,820	6,336,423	228,603
			85	720,974	1,390,864	1,434,680	43,816
			86	3,776,162	8,703,169	9,017,294	314,125
	V	W	86	1,984	3,393	3,743	350
FR GERM	A	E	84	616	3,077	3,581	504
			85	6,486	9,905	13,198	3,293
	N	E	85	6,140,016	16,956,799	17,404,823	448,024
			86	1,404,066	3,732,591	3,857,751	125,160
	O	E	84	2,500	5,794	5,794	
			86	5,334	24,491	24,491	
	V	E	82	9,884,424	21,068,438	21,553,679	485,241
			83	9,199,561	23,173,912	23,837,585	663,673
			84	9,052,141	23,042,107	23,587,238	545,131
			85	8,648,633	22,679,479	23,312,566	633,087
			86	7,549,268	21,111,873	22,046,407	934,534
	V	W	82	2,459	858	967	109
			83	4,442	2,101	2,321	220
			84	48,258	102,101	105,254	3,153
			85	200,034	648,109	661,893	13,784
			86	162,973	372,674	386,958	14,284
FRANCE	V	E	82	320,138	649,058	666,382	17,324
			83	400,157	848,369	869,137	20,768
			84	240,317	532,888	546,389	13,501
			85	360,123	876,894	897,518	20,624
			86	320,194	567,530	586,765	19,235
GUATMAL	A	E	82	9,081	6,220	8,775	2,555
			83	5,449	1,295	2,595	1,300
			84	45,791	8,163	17,861	9,698

Crop Product TSUSA commodity number, description, and unit of quantity Country	Mode	Reg	Yr	Quantity	F.A.S.	C.I.F.	Charges
	O	E	84	30,570	8,279	8,549	270
			85	7,955	12,330	15,012	2,682
HG KONG	V	W	84	3,307	323	713	390
ISRAEL	V	E	85	39,998	95,417	97,595	2,178
JAPAN	V	E	84	110	426	438	12
KOR REP	V	W	86	1,323	3,000	3,687	687
MEXICO	O	E	83	67,200	18,980	18,980	
			84	25,920	7,217	7,217	
			85	1,450	5,964	5,964	
			86	880	2,398	2,398	
	O	W	83	2,171	625	625	
NETHLDS	A	E	86	254	1,098	1,368	270
POLAND	O	E	86	40,000	126,481	129,200	2,719
	V	E	82	1,417,547	2,784,154	2,854,677	70,523
			83	1,239,627	2,802,816	2,878,354	75,538
			84	640,059	1,554,845	1,592,574	37,729
			85	519,624	1,480,909	1,513,214	32,305
			86	400,062	1,018,555	1,042,260	23,705
REP SAF	A	E	82	397	362	624	262
SPAIN	A	E	83	53	300	331	31
SUDAN	V	W	82	2,125	1,190	1,202	12
U KING	A	W	83	907	1,889	2,730	841
	O	E	82	933	4,637	4,697	60
			83	331	538	561	23
	V	E	82	176	767	776	9
			83	542	1,027	1,066	39
			84	820	1,927	1,957	30
			85	2,489	4,115	4,549	434
			86	3,341	6,332	7,556	1,224
	V	W	84	1,375	5,975	6,243	268
			86	1,704	3,700	5,119	1,419
YUGOSLV	A	E	82	800	7,186	8,865	1,679
	A	W	83	2,100	3,059	3,915	856
	V	E	82	81,697	149,919	154,645	4,726
			85	20,000	20,411	21,401	990
			86	40,014	48,377	50,419	2,042

Lupulin
1923500 LUPULIN (LB)

Country	Mode	Reg	Yr	Quantity	F.A.S.	C.I.F.	Charges
TOTAL			81	255	1,615	2,486	871
			82	1,782	8,633	10,452	1,819
			83	1,000	592	643	51
			85	1,190	1,542	1,613	71
			86	614	1,999	2,860	861
AUSTRAL	A	E	81	55	582	1,402	820
CANADA	O	E	82	13	1,579	1,579	
FR GERM	V	E	86	614	1,999	2,860	861
HG KONG	V	E	83	1,000	592	643	51
	V	W	81	200	1,033	1,084	51
INDIA	V	W	82	1,769	7,054	8,873	1,819
JAPAN	V	W	85	1,190	1,542	1,613	71

Horseradish

Horseradish, fresh or frozen
1364000 HORSERADISH, FRESH OR FROZEN (LB)

Country	Mode	Reg	Yr	Quantity	F.A.S.	C.I.F.	Charges
TOTAL			81	1,080,499	267,461	272,771	5,310
			82	1,343,795	395,583	396,661	1,078
			83	1,679,539	405,610	409,106	3,496
			84	1,852,884	669,277	718,929	49,652
			85	7,766,004	1,469,317	1,834,411	365,094
			86	11,583,012	1,935,241	1,963,314	28,073
AUSTRIA	V	E	84	164,905	78,419	95,133	16,714
			85	594,770	107,453	183,088	75,635
			86	114,573	32,591	44,683	12,092
CANADA	N	E	85	1,641,941	481,713	481,713	
	O	E	81	1,024,300	236,946	236,946	
			82	1,339,700	381,655	381,655	
			83	1,640,300	391,434	391,434	
			84	1,349,595	382,581	382,581	
			85	415,245	121,294	121,294	
			86	2,285,113	673,074	673,074	
CHINA T	A	W	83	231	972	1,645	673
			84	287	562	1,560	998
	V	E	86	1,857	2,343	2,583	240
DOM REP	V	E	81	20,000	3,795	5,295	1,500
FR GERM	N	E	85	6,522	5,705	7,384	1,679

Crop
Product
TSUSA commodity number, description, and unit of quantity

Country	Mode	Reg	Yr	Quantity	F.A.S.	C.I.F.	Charges
			86	*	3,989	4,008	19
	V	E	82	785	865	933	68
			83	320	293	311	18
			84	276,808	141,124	164,706	23,582
			85	122,912	49,426	62,473	13,047
			86	82,317	39,066	48,990	9,924
FRANCE	A	E	81	220	278	335	57
	V	E	85	84,456	38,639	48,984	10,345
HONDURA	V	E	85	4,774,030	594,550	848,700	254,150
			86	9,061,328	1,127,784	1,128,017	233
ITALY	A	E	84	1,012	902	1,287	385
			86	2,914	3,150	4,962	1,812
JAPAN	A	H	81	11	280	334	54
	N	E	84	2,585	10,179	11,455	1,276
	O	E	84	562	1,528	1,528	
	V	E	81	60	391	420	29
			82	840	4,139	4,503	364
			83	23,992	6,864	7,872	1,008
			84	7,860	18,277	20,667	2,390
			85	7,542	20,541	23,483	2,942
			86	7,494	32,163	34,040	1,877
	V	W	81	568	2,980	3,046	66
			82	1,311	6,704	7,204	500
			83	283	1,520	1,692	172
			84	2,224	7,767	8,325	558
			85	33,785	22,862	24,620	1,758
			86	15,102	16,745	17,706	961
KOR REP	V	E	82	85	291	309	18
MEXICO	O	W	81	8,700	1,183	1,183	
			84	3,456	786	786	
			85	19,785	6,805	6,805	
			86	6,600	2,336	2,336	
NETHLDS	A	W	84	3,190	1,577	2,791	1,214
	V	E	81	25,066	18,296	21,642	3,346
	V	W	84	40,000	25,095	27,600	2,505
PHIL R	V	W	84	400	480	510	30
POLAND	V	E	86	5,714	2,000	2,915	915
SWEDEN	V	E	85	32,628	9,431	14,800	5,369
U KING	N	E	82	1,074	1,929	2,057	128
	O	E	85	31,500	8,505	8,505	
	V	E	81	1,574	3,312	3,570	258
			83	14,413	4,527	6,152	1,625
			85	888	2,393	2,562	169

Hyacinth

Hyacinth, bulbs
1250500 HYACINTH BULBS (NO)

Country	Mode	Reg	Yr	Quantity	F.A.S.	C.I.F.	Charges
TOTAL			81	21,465,304	4,130,522	4,490,957	357,526
			82	22,563,199	4,342,528	4,754,798	412,270
			83	24,588,698	4,394,524	4,821,074	426,140
			84	27,015,886	4,443,879	4,973,310	529,431
			85	31,213,258	4,895,541	5,482,704	587,163
			86	29,903,771	5,249,588	5,852,917	603,329
AUSTRAL	A	E	86	105,000	40,541	48,079	7,538
BELGIUM	V	E	83	27,876	4,622	4,932	310
CANADA	O	E	81	4,500	845	845	
			82	4,604	5,242	5,242	
			84	1,596	2,398	2,398	
			85	1,812	8,418	8,418	
			86	400	1,136	1,136	
FRANCE	V	E	81	24,680	4,469	4,880	411
			82	12,355	2,692	4,306	1,614
			83	2,730	693	782	89
			84	8,004	1,586	1,792	206
			85	11,044	2,475	2,737	262
ISRAEL	V	E	81	57,283	10,149	11,248	1,099
			82	91,357	19,237	21,020	1,783
			83	91,826	24,917	28,022	3,105
			84	193,516	32,856	36,374	3,518
			85	267,313	39,283	42,585	3,302
	V	W	84	14,714	2,869	3,139	270
JAPAN	N	W	83	22,007	5,380	5,869	489
	V	E	82	25,000	4,073	4,486	413
			83	59,350	12,754	14,120	1,366
			84	17,600	3,585	3,800	215
	V	W	81	46,505	8,020	8,713	846
			82	67,507	14,605	15,993	1,388
			83	50,000	11,072	11,823	751

Crop
Product
TSUSA commodity number, description, and unit of quantity

Country	Mode	Reg	Yr	Quantity	F.A.S.	C.I.F.	Charges
			84	57,005	11,619	12,704	1,085
			85	57,000	11,623	12,720	1,097
			86	53,500	10,663	11,923	1,260
MALI	V	E	86	42,509	8,498	9,817	1,319
N ANTIL	A	E	86	23,595	5,578	9,876	4,298
NETHLDS	A	E	82	2,000	304	514	210
			83	42,960	7,931	10,413	2,482
			84	6,000	969	1,291	322
			85	8,655	1,776	2,418	642
	A	W	83	4,500	979	1,553	574
			84	12,600	1,987	3,399	1,412
			86	300	1,150	1,419	269
	N	E	81	17,007,977	3,239,657	3,524,379	281,660
			82	17,320,520	3,303,347	3,601,661	298,314
			83	18,594,254	3,348,887	3,659,644	310,757
			84	19,731,312	3,328,659	3,709,078	380,419
			85	23,322,479	3,669,505	4,099,419	429,914
			86	23,261,581	4,014,370	4,472,673	458,303
	N	W	82	835,383	163,406	189,342	25,936
			83	760,647	134,361	156,250	21,889
			84	819,887	109,383	130,148	20,765
			85	452,605	47,546	56,524	8,978
			86	132,531	27,491	31,670	4,179
	O	E	81	39,699	11,351	11,351	
			82	38,415	9,549	9,589	40
			83	48,592	11,243	11,373	130
			84	52,346	8,198	8,319	121
			85	268,717	42,608	42,608	
			86	241,585	47,232	47,232	
	V	E	81	3,441,769	689,687	745,117	55,430
			82	3,835,444	753,183	827,909	74,726
			83	4,737,102	807,327	889,028	81,291
			84	5,751,033	892,150	1,004,861	112,711
			85	6,003,943	950,366	1,072,544	122,178
			86	5,413,723	979,476	1,090,262	110,786
	V	W	81	815,806	163,180	180,985	17,805
			82	141,284	22,633	25,401	2,768
			83	95,404	14,670	16,781	2,111
			84	181,989	27,056	31,592	4,536
			85	819,690	121,941	142,731	20,790
			86	628,675	111,505	126,733	15,228
U KING	A	E	84	9,500	1,035	1,502	467
			86	372	1,948	2,097	149
	A	W	82	4,900	938	1,299	361
	V	E	81	16,000	2,031	2,221	190
			82	24,300	3,735	4,103	368
			83	51,450	9,688	10,484	796
			84	158,784	19,529	22,913	3,384
	V	W	81	11,085	1,133	1,218	85
YEMAN S	V	E	82	160,130	39,584	43,933	4,349

I

Indigo

Indigo, dye**
4102440 ALIZARIN A INDIGO NATURAL (LB)

Country	Mode	Reg	Yr	Quantity	F.A.S.	C.I.F.	Charges
TOTAL			81	4,790	33,570	35,751	2,181
			82	9,720	41,345	43,834	2,489
			83	43,798	224,491	233,591	9,100
			84	40,037	190,652	196,887	6,235
			85	155,302	425,724	456,434	30,710
			86	223,022	588,074	637,702	49,628
CANADA	A	E	85	9	1,017	1,082	65
	O	E	86	650	1,443	1,443	
CHINA M	O	E	83	11,024	74,206	74,426	220
CHINA T	A	E	82	926	1,763	1,768	5
FR GERM	A	E	81	64	1,318	1,693	375
			82	331	3,953	4,113	160
			83	716	4,659	5,000	341
			84	880	8,564	8,787	223

Crop
Product
TSUSA commodity number, description, and unit of quantity

Country	Mode	Reg	Yr	Quantity	F.A.S.	C.I.F.	Charges
			85	110	1,414	1,639	225
	A	W	85	24	5,093	5,193	100
	N	E	83	4,418	34,334	35,392	1,058
			84	8,879	59,005	61,624	2,619
			85	15,660	148,730	151,181	2,451
			86	18,251	187,247	192,670	5,423
	O	E	83	3,575	25,155	25,368	213
			84	726	747	798	51
			85	880	6,475	6,535	60
	V	E	82	1,484	11,930	12,128	198
			83	4,959	43,032	43,640	608
			84	3,794	35,058	35,444	386
			86	3,340	32,822	34,235	1,413
FRANCE	A	E	82	110	1,103	1,144	41
			83	110	1,026	1,118	92
			86	937	1,801	2,823	1,022
	V	E	82	131	378	453	75
			83	139	449	542	93
HG KONG	A	E	82	88	620	953	333
INDIA	O	E	86	1,102	5,148	5,480	332
ITALY	V	E	85	4,409	14,339	14,992	653
			86	4,409	14,484	14,992	508
	V	W	84	721	990	1,122	132
JAPAN	A	E	85	772	12,390	13,302	912
	A	H	85	1,102	8,000	10,058	2,058
	A	W	83	2,425	15,020	18,633	3,613
	N	E	85	123,034	194,598	215,837	21,239
	O	E	81	2	803	829	26
	V	E	83	15,220	21,399	24,064	2,665
			84	5,661	17,413	18,654	1,241
			86	175,985	169,031	202,125	33,094
	V	W	81	2,205	7,652	8,000	348
			82	6,650	21,598	23,275	1,677
			84	8,000	9,527	9,527	
			85	8,200	27,149	29,872	2,723
			86	18,051	166,937	173,783	6,846
KOR REP	V	E	84	551	1,656	1,687	31
NETHLDS	V	E	84	4,410	17,046	17,478	432
PAKISTN	V	W	86	187	1,403	1,618	215
POLAND	O	E	84	6,393	40,173	41,257	1,084
SWITZLD	O	E	81	314	2,261	2,271	10
U KING	A	E	84	22	473	509	36
			86	110	7,758	8,533	775
	N	E	83	1,212	5,211	5,408	197
	V	E	81	2,205	21,536	22,958	1,422
			85	1,102	6,519	6,743	224

Ipecac

Ipecac, natural drug**
4350500 ALOES JALAP MATE ETC, CRUDE (LB)
(See Aloe, natural drug under Aloe)
4351000 ALOES,JALAP MANA,ETC ADVANCE (LB)
(See Aloe, natural drug under Aloe)

Iris

Iris, bulbs
1253220 IRIS BULBS, SOIL ATTACHED (NO)

Country	Mode	Reg	Yr	Quantity	F.A.S.	C.I.F.	Charges
TOTAL			81	12,900	3,380	3,477	97
			83	72,805	3,098	3,414	316
			84	5,999	320	347	27
			86	21,500	2,650	2,999	349
BELGIUM	V	E	83	70,530	1,503	1,667	164
CANADA	O	E	81	900	327	327	
JAPAN	V	W	81	12,000	3,053	3,150	97
			83	2,275	1,595	1,747	152
NETHLDS	A	E	84	5,999	320	347	27
	A	W	86	21,500	2,650	2,999	349

1253420 IRIS BULBS, NSPF (NO)

Country	Mode	Reg	Yr	Quantity	F.A.S.	C.I.F.	Charges
TOTAL			81	54,754,642	1,695,678	1,875,832	180,290
			82	59,109,334	1,633,399	1,814,772	181,373
			83	67,811,437	1,790,483	2,005,086	214,603
			84	95,533,964	2,355,498	2,699,554	344,056
			85	93,670,291	2,424,041	2,826,284	402,243
			86	99,143,029	2,896,951	3,272,859	375,908
BELGIUM	V	E	84	194,191	12,823	13,992	1,169
			85	602,650	74,928	79,398	4,470
FRANCE	V	E	82	36,800	1,480	1,574	94
			83	170,199	8,864	9,245	381
			84	438,336	21,746	23,135	1,389
	V	W	85	1,300,000	34,130	40,216	6,086
HG KONG	V	W	83	57,892	1,944	2,064	120
ISRAEL	N	E	81	918,710	44,649	51,342	6,693
			82	794,650	38,895	45,738	6,843
			83	1,462,200	61,889	75,734	13,845
	V	E	81	341,606	6,024	6,933	909
			82	585,897	27,976	30,159	2,183
			83	3,728,648	158,085	168,383	10,298
			84	2,049,319	98,145	105,293	7,148
			85	1,814,146	68,457	79,322	10,865
			86	442,850	20,687	24,278	3,591
	V	W	81	994,575	44,917	51,880	6,963
			82	1,192,180	51,144	57,545	6,401
			83	1,040,172	44,473	50,704	6,231
			84	666,370	29,044	29,607	563
			85	587,500	26,175	31,995	5,820
			86	437,300	18,978	23,002	4,024
JAPAN	A	W	84	18,000	9,810	13,534	3,724
	N	W	82	1,002	2,495	2,663	168
			85	188,300	102,889	111,437	8,548
	V	E	81	1,500	543	584	41
			82	6,400	3,230	3,496	266
			83	15,805	7,538	8,246	708
			84	37,310	10,528	11,687	1,159
			85	46,700	25,313	27,360	2,047
			86	5,500	3,099	3,305	206
	V	W	82	15,225	8,450	9,158	708
			83	7,000	4,344	4,701	357
			84	63,800	31,783	33,617	1,834
			85	28,000	6,836	7,499	663
			86	37,000	11,784	12,871	1,087
KOR REP	V	E	84	9,700	564	609	45
MALI	V	E	85	189,950	5,677	6,167	490
			86	31,250	1,609	1,733	124
NEPAL	V	E	85	13,500	8,370	10,992	2,622
NETHLDS	A	E	81	178,250	4,036	5,723	1,687
			82	77,900	1,777	2,251	474
			83	745,231	23,768	31,519	7,751
			84	58,391	4,875	6,451	1,576
			86	50,000	1,819	2,057	238
	A	W	86	6,749	4,927	5,463	536
	N	E	81	17,974,553	641,763	688,604	46,941
			82	19,741,630	626,024	679,278	53,254
			83	23,759,860	594,048	647,299	53,251
			84	31,466,446	899,378	997,630	98,252
			85	28,149,911	778,419	856,424	78,005
			86	34,884,043	1,013,482	1,109,633	96,151
	N	W	81	3,472,303	81,699	95,071	13,372
			82	18,896,977	464,666	528,423	63,757
			83	19,484,935	456,596	534,214	77,618
			84	44,962,020	873,354	1,050,639	177,285
			85	38,008,811	749,166	948,974	199,808
			86	27,300,546	848,523	993,967	145,444
	O	E	84	673,000	20,153	24,353	4,200
			85	2,062,750	73,503	73,503	
			86	685,000	15,612	15,612	
	V	E	81	12,002,791	315,287	346,469	31,218
			82	15,894,309	356,375	398,219	41,844
			83	16,446,070	390,183	428,603	38,420
			84	11,985,956	274,647	307,842	33,195
			85	17,790,536	391,597	446,903	55,306
			86	11,737,453	387,033	426,636	39,603
	V	W	81	18,454,718	542,745	613,929	71,184
			82	720,350	15,897	18,260	2,363
			83	709,845	32,576	37,461	4,885
			84	2,031,216	34,095	44,170	10,075
			85	2,887,537	78,581	106,094	27,513
			86	23,481,273	567,505	652,182	84,677
REP SAF	V	E	81	135,469	4,832	5,232	400
			82	786,438	26,186	27,597	1,411
			83	21,830	1,488	1,627	139
			84	24,420	1,583	1,630	47
	V	W	81	228,548	7,622	8,384	762
			82	110,948	3,958	4,489	531
TURKEY	V	E	83	26,000	452	562	110
U KING	A	E	83	6,750	522	704	182
	V	E	81	35,000	1,236	1,301	65

Crop Product TSUSA commodity number, description, and unit of quantity Country	Mode	Reg	Yr	Quantity	F.A.S.	C.I.F.	Charges
			82	248,628	4,846	5,922	1,076
			83	129,000	3,713	4,020	307
			84	855,489	32,970	35,365	2,395
			86	44,065	1,893	2,120	227
	V	W	81	16,619	325	380	55

J

Jalap

Jalap, natural drug**

4350500 ALOES JALAP MATE ETC, CRUDE (LB)
(See Aloe, natural drug under Aloe)
4351000 ALOES,JALAP MANA,ETC ADVANCE (LB)
(See Aloe, natural drug under Aloe)

Jelutong

Jelutong, rubber
4460530 JELUTONG OR PONTIANAK (LB)

Country	Mode	Reg	Yr	Quantity	F.A.S.	C.I.F.	Charges
TOTAL			81	3,405,466	6,428,289	6,751,792	323,503
			82	3,189,145	5,037,866	5,352,813	314,947
			83	3,312,699	5,066,523	5,459,678	393,155
			84	2,818,013	5,568,760	5,868,838	300,078
			85	2,833,124	5,028,010	5,312,020	284,010
			86	2,702,114	4,598,749	4,871,669	272,920
MALAYSA	V	E	84	70,603	11,223	15,245	4,022
SINGAPR	A	E	86	2,000	3,500	3,594	94
	V	E	81	3,052,737	5,706,637	5,989,933	283,296
			82	2,746,566	4,377,286	4,648,287	271,001
			83	1,947,887	2,834,325	3,095,339	261,014
			84	2,481,142	4,888,772	5,152,555	263,783
			85	2,215,625	3,765,579	3,985,923	220,344
			86	2,523,076	4,212,903	4,467,060	254,157
	V	W	81	352,729	721,652	761,859	40,207
			82	442,579	660,580	704,526	43,946
			83	1,319,832	2,214,780	2,343,021	128,241
			84	266,268	668,765	701,038	32,273
			85	617,499	1,262,431	1,326,097	63,666
			86	177,038	382,346	401,015	18,669
SRI LKA	V	E	83	44,980	17,418	21,318	3,900

Jicama

Jicama, fresh
1377900 JICAMAS, FRESH OR CHILLED (LB)

Country	Mode	Reg	Yr	Quantity	F.A.S.	C.I.F.	Charges
TOTAL			81	12,627,493	2,356,882	2,356,882	
			82	13,681,904	2,142,272	2,145,737	3,465
			83	11,277,208	1,700,548	1,702,398	1,850
			84	17,157,221	2,162,954	2,164,831	1,877
			85	12,917,299	1,947,289	1,948,646	1,357
			86	18,657,134	3,213,893	3,214,960	1,067
CANADA	O	W	81	5,120	870	870	
			82	4,400	792	792	
FRANCE	O	W	81	18,280	3,656	3,656	
			84	8,640	1,133	1,133	
MEXICO	N	W	85	4,489,588	805,518	805,520	2
	O	E	81	447,312	38,262	38,262	
			82	147,224	12,999	12,999	
			83	168,541	23,137	23,137	
			84	405,805	35,307	35,307	
			85	50,350	8,217	8,217	
			86	6,872	3,726	3,726	
	O	W	81	12,156,781	2,314,094	2,314,094	

Crop Product TSUSA commodity number, description, and unit of quantity Country	Mode	Reg	Yr	Quantity	F.A.S.	C.I.F.	Charges
			82	13,530,280	2,128,481	2,131,946	3,465
			83	11,103,867	1,675,731	1,675,731	
			84	16,742,776	2,126,514	2,128,391	1,877
			85	8,377,361	1,133,554	1,134,909	1,355
			86	18,492,054	3,181,997	3,183,064	1,067
MOZAMBQ	O	W	86	158,208	28,170	28,170	
W SAMOA	A	W	83	4,800	1,680	3,530	1,850

Jimsonweed

Stramonium, natural drug
4357500 STRAMONIUM (LB)

Country	Mode	Reg	Yr	Quantity	F.A.S.	C.I.F.	Charges
TOTAL			82	22,547	5,235	6,162	927
			84	300	443	650	207
			85	33	1,350	1,390	40
ALBANIA	V	W	82	11,949	2,464	3,215	751
JAPAN	A	H	84	300	443	650	207
MEXICO	A	E	85	33	1,350	1,390	40
YUGOSLV	V	W	82	10,598	2,771	2,947	176

Jute

Jute, fiber, processed
3043600 JUTE FIB PROCESSED NOT SLIV (LB)

Country	Mode	Reg	Yr	Quantity	F.A.S.	C.I.F.	Charges
TOTAL			81	320	894	908	14
			82	5,445	2,314	2,630	316
			83	27,046	12,694	16,629	3,935
			84	1,272,005	332,955	434,280	101,325
			85	652,002	202,839	247,984	45,145
			86	663,852	170,853	207,826	36,973
BNGLDSH	O	E	81	300	544	558	14
			86	374,421	25,164	50,064	24,900
	V	E	83	5,442	2,130	2,814	684
			84	1,094,840	229,380	323,525	94,145
			85	466,526	92,721	119,639	26,918
			86	95,467	20,450	25,304	4,854
	V	W	86	29,211	9,776	12,385	2,609
BRAZIL	V	E	85	1,102	625	710	85
CANADA	N	E	82	875	761	761	
	O	E	83	11,124	334	334	
			84	11,120	4,000	4,000	
			86	6,000	7,568	7,568	
CHINA T	V	E	83	5,821	4,591	5,781	1,190
			84	5,226	4,623	5,923	1,300
			85	4,968	7,384	8,658	1,274
			86	408	2,291	2,316	25
	V	W	85	5,068	16,746	17,564	818
			86	8,888	15,847	18,180	2,333
COLOMB	A	E	83	2,621	1,150	2,221	1,071
FR GERM	V	E	83	228	345	358	13
FRANCE	A	W	86	83	1,172	1,298	126
INDIA	A	E	83	906	741	1,122	381
			84	360	450	687	237
			85	542	1,114	1,212	98
	O	E	81	20	350	350	
			82	150	425	425	
			84	175	350	350	
			86	320	1,250	1,250	
	V	E	85	67,922	36,964	44,190	7,226
	V	W	85	25,269	4,411	6,784	2,373
ITALY	A	W	85	190	1,049	1,407	358
			86	94	521	742	221
JAPAN	A	W	83	72	655	778	123
NETHLDS	A	E	82	4,270	728	1,044	316
	V	E	85	823	1,478	2,381	903
PHIL R	N	E	83	232	2,332	2,764	432
	V	W	83	600	416	457	41
			84	1,216	689	831	142
			85	4,000	261	308	47
			86	600	405	491	86
THAILND	O	E	84	130,484	80,795	80,795	
			85	45,700	26,904	26,904	
			86	128,810	77,415	77,415	
	V	W	85	19,292	8,982	10,627	1,645
			86	19,550	8,994	10,813	1,819

Crop Product TSUSA commodity number, description, and unit of quantity Country	Mode	Reg	Yr	Quantity	F.A.S.	C.I.F.	Charges
U KING	O	E	82	150	400	400	
			84	19,994	9,965	12,735	2,770
	V	E	84	8,590	2,703	5,434	2,731
			85	10,600	4,200	7,600	3,400

Jute, fiber, raw and waste
3043220 JUTE BUTTS A WASTES (LTN)

Country	Mode	Reg	Yr	Quantity	F.A.S.	C.I.F.	Charges
TOTAL			81	9,102	976,329	1,446,977	470,648
			82	3,880	618,959	826,194	207,235
			83	5,060	702,801	1,128,145	425,344
			84	3,658	499,181	703,657	204,476
			85	7,784	1,410,481	2,252,627	842,146
			86	7,476	1,011,861	1,602,746	590,885
BELGIUM	V	E	85	124	52,271	62,634	10,363
BNGLDSH	N	E	83	150	39,132	56,286	17,154
	O	E	86	41	5,853	11,686	5,833
	V	E	81	2,018	168,628	253,687	85,059
			82	1,759	327,115	441,439	114,324
			83	1,327	169,517	267,029	97,512
			84	966	124,248	187,083	62,835
			85	1,457	274,715	443,965	169,250
			86	2,189	242,428	353,902	111,474
	V	W	82	522	145,689	206,076	60,387
			83	200	26,918	30,256	3,338
			85	305	71,586	116,725	45,139
			86	1,440	182,059	318,655	136,596
CANADA	O	E	81	17	1,643	1,643	
			82	7	433	433	
			84	6	379	379	
CHINA T	N	W	86	*	483	581	98
	V	E	83	110	23,699	34,502	10,803
			85	51	10,174	15,193	5,019
	V	W	81	51	9,727	13,092	3,365
FR GERM	V	E	86	366	82,207	117,853	35,646
HG KONG	V	E	81	169	2,833	4,107	1,274
	V	W	81	58	7,683	10,586	2,903
INDIA	N	E	81	624	66,156	81,317	15,161
	O	E	82	2	486	486	
	V	E	81	1,056	127,064	156,375	29,311
			82	1,476	124,787	145,299	20,512
			83	1,972	231,230	411,249	180,019
			84	2,050	264,455	346,434	81,979
			85	3,698	601,602	1,046,720	445,118
			86	2,483	343,230	540,506	197,276
	V	W	85	15	2,991	5,000	2,009
INDNSIA	V	E	85	64	10,416	19,951	9,535
			86	769	111,703	197,941	86,238
ITALY	V	E	86	126	30,800	41,690	10,890
JAPAN	V	E	85	240	44,592	68,097	23,505
NETHLDS	V	E	85	41	5,792	9,904	4,112
			86	20	3,960	5,902	1,942
NO KOR	V	E	81	68	9,724	10,457	733
NORWAY	V	E	81	1	1,302	1,332	30
PAKISTN	O	E	81	2	355	355	
	V	E	85	886	108,522	158,390	49,868
			86	36	3,570	7,570	4,000
PHIL R	V	E	81	300	35,342	38,947	3,605
	V	W	85	26	1,950	2,252	302
			86	6	5,568	6,460	892
SINGAPR	V	E	85	143	23,361	31,313	7,952
THAILND	V	E	81	226	29,988	53,529	23,541
			82	25	4,466	7,449	2,983
			83	1,301	212,305	328,823	116,518
			84	371	52,449	86,085	33,636
	V	W	81	4,512	515,884	821,550	305,666
			82	89	15,983	25,012	9,029
			84	265	57,650	83,676	26,026
			85	734	202,509	272,483	69,974

3043240 RAW JUTE FIBERS, NSPF (LTN)

Country	Mode	Reg	Yr	Quantity	F.A.S.	C.I.F.	Charges
TOTAL			81	8,158	2,230,220	3,008,630	778,410
			82	13,755	1,893,572	2,610,885	717,313
			83	10,117	1,618,159	2,495,220	877,061
			84	5,705	1,082,270	1,585,206	502,936
			85	6,466	1,875,431	2,527,721	652,290
			86	5,790	1,209,877	1,751,799	541,922
AUSTRIA	V	E	84	123	16,953	25,954	9,001
BELGIUM	V	E	85	458	166,040	220,540	54,500
BNGLDSH	N	E	81	562	224,883	240,691	15,808
			82	656	232,540	270,161	37,621
			83	701	231,218	286,656	55,438
			84	187	101,113	122,050	20,937
	O	E	84	101	39,371	49,818	10,447
			85	152	103,278	125,099	21,821
			86	123	15,780	33,471	17,691
	V	E	81	3,239	1,122,665	1,590,511	467,846
			82	10,376	1,206,503	1,680,397	473,894
			83	4,141	577,817	955,032	377,215
			84	1,874	278,395	399,525	121,130
			85	2,042	569,051	863,160	294,109
			86	3,892	793,606	1,131,877	338,271
	V	W	82	507	102,888	128,429	25,541
			83	1,966	303,365	416,950	113,585
			84	326	46,392	84,942	38,550
CANADA	O	E	84	1	289	289	
	O	W	83	1	948	948	
CHINA M	V	E	85	1,000	840,410	1,062,777	222,367
			86	679	264,663	403,193	138,530
CHINA T	V	E	81	586	221,156	320,787	99,631
			82	116	35,480	55,802	20,322
			83	173	33,070	54,498	21,428
			84	506	168,389	266,237	97,848
			85	148	42,877	67,116	24,239
			86	147	57,206	58,679	1,473
	V	W	81	276	37,634	49,882	12,248
FINLAND	V	E	82	12	936	1,002	66
FR GERM	A	E	86	270	4,172	4,461	289
	V	E	85	16	1,780	3,946	2,166
HG KONG	V	W	81	516	71,018	108,160	37,142
			83	329	41,194	66,214	25,020
INDIA	N	E	85	2,330	67,620	68,620	1,000
	V	E	81	40	19,719	27,723	8,004
			82	107	56,255	74,454	18,199
			83	1,331	167,985	302,633	134,648
			84	1,299	167,278	264,572	97,294
			85	156	44,852	58,856	14,004
			86	38	17,271	24,293	7,022
	V	W	81	28	2,475	2,899	424
			82	80	4,050	6,342	2,292
			83	757	116,833	193,302	76,469
			84	256	31,947	42,986	11,039
ITALY	V	E	85	47	6,669	9,364	2,695
JAPAN	V	W	84	78	13,984	21,232	7,248
LAOS	V	E	81	216	261,278	306,580	45,302
MALAYSA	V	W	81	312	6,680	10,805	4,125
NETHLDS	V	E	84	23	7,861	10,859	2,998
			85	19	2,708	4,745	2,037
PAKISTN	O	E	84	6	1,563	1,563	
	V	E	83	160	50,589	78,973	28,384
PHIL R	N	W	83	*	340	401	61
	V	E	83	61	8,468	9,429	961
	V	W	82	2	334	357	23
SINGAPR	V	E	81	806	92,603	122,826	30,223
	V	W	83	158	32,002	47,152	15,150
			84	442	87,605	122,243	34,638
			86	641	57,179	95,825	38,646
THAILND	V	E	81	977	88,485	98,950	10,465
			82	1,861	248,965	384,793	135,828
			83	112	32,523	52,333	19,810
			84	198	28,088	42,142	14,054
			85	98	30,146	43,498	13,352
	V	W	81	600	81,016	128,191	47,175
			82	38	5,621	9,148	3,527
			83	227	21,807	30,699	8,892
			84	285	93,042	130,794	37,752
U KING	N	E	81	*	608	625	17

Jute, sliver
3043400 JUTE SLIVER (LB)

Country	Mode	Reg	Yr	Quantity	F.A.S.	C.I.F.	Charges
TOTAL			86	700	742	742	
CANADA	O	E	86	700	742	742	

Crop Product TSUSA commodity number, description, and unit of quantity Country	Mode	Reg	Yr	Quantity	F.A.S.	C.I.F.	Charges

K

Kale

Kale, seed
1265100 KALE GARDEN SEEDS (LB)

Country	Mode	Reg	Yr	Quantity	F.A.S.	C.I.F.	Charges
TOTAL			81	1,181	2,448	2,602	154
			82	1,566	10,636	12,331	1,695
			83	820	11,108	11,962	854
			84	11,551	39,382	40,929	1,547
			85	13,250	41,141	42,405	1,264
			86	14,527	32,350	34,680	2,330
AUSTRAL	V	E	86	13,227	1,920	2,257	337
CHINA M	V	E	83	60	449	454	5
	V	W	81	100	313	325	12
			84	500	1,358	1,448	90
			85	1,000	2,770	2,823	53
CHINA T	V	W	84	500	1,000	1,018	18
DENMARK	V	E	83	55	256	268	12
FR GERM	V	W	81	661	887	929	42
			82	661	660	774	114
			84	220	875	1,129	254
FRANCE	A	E	86	51	2,444	2,591	147
HG KONG	A	E	83	50	267	352	85
	V	W	81	120	462	505	43
			83	150	350	355	5
JAPAN	A	E	83	3	387	452	65
			84	11	1,222	1,328	106
	A	W	82	25	319	422	103
	N	W	84	5,030	10,327	10,665	338
			85	12,110	25,631	26,149	518
			86	125	11,012	11,611	599
	O	E	82	77	980	1,408	428
			83	48	7,057	7,269	212
	O	W	84	20	300	412	112
N ZEAL	V	E	81	287	407	448	41
NETHLDS	A	E	83	15	1,313	1,383	70
			84	5,175	20,475	20,911	436
			85	140	12,740	13,433	693
			86	1,124	16,974	18,221	1,247
	O	E	84	20	1,820	1,883	63
U KING	A	E	82	207	6,072	6,527	455
	A	W	83	439	1,029	1,429	400
			84	75	2,005	2,135	130
	N	W	82	596	2,605	3,200	595
	V	E	81	13	379	395	16

Kapok Tree

Kapok, fatty acid**
4902200 FATTY ACIDS DRVD HMP KPK ETC (LB)
(See Hempseed, fatty acid under Hemp)

Kapok, fatty salt**
4904600 FATTY SALTS OF SESAME ETC (LB)
(See Hempseed, fatty salt under Hemp)

Kapok, fiber, processed
3044000 KAPOK FIBER PROCESSED (LB)

Country	Mode	Reg	Yr	Quantity	F.A.S.	C.I.F.	Charges
TOTAL			81	33,595	17,454	20,747	3,293
			82	44,655	18,322	22,524	4,202
			83	22,503	9,942	10,930	988
			84	41,623	19,563	23,924	4,361
			85	96,477	40,088	48,603	8,515
			86	20,314	16,504	24,547	8,043
FRANCE	A	E	81	716	3,316	3,815	499
JAPAN	V	E	82	220	276	410	134
PHIL R	V	W	84	41,623	19,563	23,924	4,361
			85	51,090	21,206	24,330	3,124
SINGAPR	V	E	86	10,240	8,176	10,551	2,375
THAILND	V	E	82	22,002	8,840	10,871	2,031

Crop Product TSUSA commodity number, description, and unit of quantity Country	Mode	Reg	Yr	Quantity	F.A.S.	C.I.F.	Charges
			85	22,045	8,588	11,213	2,625
			86	10,074	8,328	13,996	5,668
	V	W	81	32,879	14,138	16,932	2,794
			82	22,433	9,206	11,243	2,037
			83	21,879	9,434	10,365	931
			85	23,342	10,294	13,060	2,766
U KING	V	E	83	624	508	565	57

Kapok, fiber, raw and waste
3043800 KAPOK, RAW AND WASTES (LTN)

Country	Mode	Reg	Yr	Quantity	F.A.S.	C.I.F.	Charges
TOTAL			81	2,347	2,054,947	2,494,070	439,123
			82	1,310	1,224,326	1,531,813	307,487
			83	1,645	1,432,078	1,797,538	365,460
			84	2,086	1,848,354	2,330,688	482,334
			85	1,175	1,024,092	1,291,390	267,298
			86	1,462	1,035,474	1,359,241	323,767
CHINA T	V	E	81	33	31,929	37,837	5,908
			82	20	17,891	22,445	4,554
			84	31	25,933	33,840	7,907
			85	130	108,986	140,673	31,687
			86	43	30,273	39,093	8,820
GERM DR	V	W	81	10	11,610	13,762	2,152
HG KONG	V	W	83	20	17,382	22,204	4,822
JAPAN	V	E	85	29	38,444	43,920	5,476
	V	W	83	40	34,814	45,670	10,856
			84	20	17,656	22,679	5,023
KOR REP	V	E	86	11	7,822	10,171	2,349
MALAYSA	V	E	86	19	15,890	20,478	4,588
SINGAPR	O	E	86	54	38,163	49,744	11,581
	V	E	83	22	16,596	21,048	4,452
			85	53	44,719	57,635	12,916
			86	110	77,583	102,091	24,508
	V	W	81	20	17,154	21,464	4,310
			86	35	24,277	32,020	7,743
SRI LKA	V	E	82	40	27,600	40,795	13,195
	V	W	81	10	7,000	8,655	1,655
			82	23	16,875	23,736	6,861
			84	57	43,932	55,975	12,043
			85	12	8,453	11,180	2,727
THAILND	N	E	86	154	97,119	127,140	30,021
	O	E	81	17	26,764	26,764	
	V	E	81	1,473	1,505,452	1,824,016	318,564
			82	1,085	1,042,777	1,296,359	253,582
			83	1,332	1,163,365	1,459,096	295,731
			84	1,665	1,472,408	1,868,585	396,177
			85	863	756,408	951,250	194,842
			86	929	670,757	882,912	212,155
	V	W	81	784	455,038	561,572	106,534
			82	142	119,183	148,478	29,295
			83	231	199,921	249,520	49,599
			84	313	288,425	349,609	61,184
			85	88	67,082	86,732	19,650
			86	107	73,590	95,592	22,002

Kapok, seed
1752400 KAPOK SEED (LB)

Country	Mode	Reg	Yr	Quantity	F.A.S.	C.I.F.	Charges
TOTAL			82	92	500	787	287
THAILND	A	E	82	92	500	787	287

Kapok, vegetable oil
1762400 KAPOK OIL (LB)

Country	Mode	Reg	Yr	Quantity	F.A.S.	C.I.F.	Charges
TOTAL			82	33,684	33,345	35,622	2,277
			83	965	924	1,033	109
			86	9,934	5,473	6,283	810
GREECE	V	E	83	965	924	1,033	109
SPAIN	V	E	82	33,684	33,345	35,622	2,277
			86	9,934	5,473	6,283	810

Crop Product TSUSA commodity number, description, and unit of quantity Country	Mode	Reg	Yr	Quantity	F.A.S.	C.I.F.	Charges

Karaya Gum

Karaya, gum
1883850 KARAYA GUM, NATURAL (LB)

Country	Mode	Reg	Yr	Quantity	F.A.S.	C.I.F.	Charges
TOTAL			81	6,437,646	4,819,295	5,330,155	510,860
			82	8,874,945	7,352,778	7,982,095	629,317
			83	4,698,940	4,884,493	5,179,931	295,438
			84	5,471,332	6,145,039	6,553,408	408,369
			85	3,354,899	3,742,460	4,003,987	261,527
			86	2,806,042	2,066,649	2,243,360	176,711
BELGIUM	V	E	85	109,586	86,914	90,804	3,890
CHILE	V	E	85	22,009	26,783	26,970	187
CHINA T	V	E	81	32,738	26,050	28,924	2,874
FR GERM	V	E	84	44,093	46,000	48,267	2,267
FRANCE	A	E	84	330	528	802	274
	N	E	81	67,239	34,200	37,920	3,720
	O	E	83	440	806	844	38
	V	E	82	44,092	27,022	29,652	2,630
			83	36,000	49,878	51,939	2,061
			84	365,780	447,230	466,245	19,015
			85	163,533	223,127	237,012	13,885
			86	44,000	30,000	30,400	400
INDIA	N	E	81	6,203,382	4,660,048	5,150,656	490,608
			82	6,073,938	5,355,076	5,800,648	445,572
			83	3,913,261	4,241,198	4,520,605	279,407
			84	4,876,341	5,545,975	5,924,967	378,992
			86	2,722,359	2,000,281	2,174,353	174,072
	V	E	83	66,552	86,898	91,704	4,806
			84	1,400	2,776	2,940	164
			85	2,883,787	3,189,135	3,420,597	231,462
	V	W	81	43,986	38,707	46,557	7,850
IRELAND	A	E	85	2,100	4,492	6,105	1,613
ITALY	V	E	82	44,101	94,019	97,942	3,923
JAPAN	V	E	81	21,958	17,004	18,669	1,665
			82	11,027	10,480	11,326	846
PAKISTN	V	E	83	39,000	16,965	19,677	2,712
			84	37,577	13,214	14,139	925
PERU	V	E	81	43,916	13,342	14,940	1,598
PHIL R	V	E	84	88,528	23,030	24,872	1,842
PORTUGL	N	E	85	79,700	175,389	180,789	5,400
	V	E	81	21,958	20,289	21,975	1,686
	V	W	83	39,700	62,526	65,817	3,291
REP SAF	V	E	86	1,102	1,460	1,625	165
S HELNA	V	E	84	35,274	35,274	38,621	3,347
SINGAPR	V	E	82	39,998	4,808	7,964	3,156
SUDAN	V	E	81	2,469	9,655	10,514	859
			82	2,661,789	1,861,373	2,034,563	173,190
			83	555,559	362,578	362,578	
			84	22,009	31,012	32,555	1,543
			85	88,184	21,880	24,162	2,282
SWEDEN	V	E	83	44,018	59,224	62,307	3,083
U KING	A	E	85	6,000	14,740	17,548	2,808
	V	E	83	4,410	4,420	4,460	40
			86	38,581	34,908	36,982	2,074

Kiwi

Kiwifruit, fresh
1494800 CHINESE GOOSEBERY (KIWI FRT) FR (LB)

Country	Mode	Reg	Yr	Quantity	F.A.S.	C.I.F.	Charges
TOTAL			81	4,534,622	4,217,991	5,472,567	1,258,152
			82	4,139,283	4,586,088	5,793,072	1,206,984
			83	11,868,504	8,076,435	10,437,425	2,360,990
			84	12,764,794	10,395,915	12,608,250	2,212,335
			85	17,675,601	11,061,654	13,771,327	2,709,673
			86	18,421,899	16,349,832	19,794,352	3,444,520
AUSTRAL	A	E	82	2,507	3,874	4,689	815
			83	21,498	21,397	35,469	14,072
	A	W	81	2,663	2,710	4,073	1,363
	V	E	83	86,189	51,156	76,156	25,000
			85	117,246	68,557	90,335	21,778
	V	W	83	18,350	15,804	19,074	3,270
			84	50,066	85,886	96,947	11,061
			85	104,955	95,353	102,687	7,334
			86	43,836	52,435	61,932	9,497
AUSTRIA	V	E	84	16,111	18,717	24,101	5,384
BELGIUM	A	W	86	5,412	5,863	12,623	6,760

Country	Mode	Reg	Yr	Quantity	F.A.S.	C.I.F.	Charges
C RICA	A	E	82	2,916	2,106	3,028	922
CANADA	O	E	83	36,053	27,840	27,840	
			86	24,210	16,140	16,140	
	O	W	81	1,008	1,440	1,440	
			82	770	1,403	1,403	
			83	567	828	828	
CHILE	V	E	85	37,705	34,372	40,523	6,151
			86	92,738	49,208	68,205	18,997
CHINA T	V	W	86	28,200	13,442	14,102	660
DOM REP	V	E	84	18,366	5,142	6,484	1,342
FIJI	A	W	82	8,677	4,998	9,672	4,674
FR GERM	O	E	86	2,471	1,944	2,070	126
HG KONG	V	H	85	15,985	9,609	12,542	2,933
INDNSIA	V	W	83	697	893	1,009	116
ITALY	A	W	82	14,491	19,048	23,320	4,272
JAPAN	A	W	82	10,498	12,768	14,634	1,866
			83	1,994	995	2,106	1,111
KOR REP	V	E	85	1,481	2,873	3,120	247
N ZEAL	A	E	81	18,821	10,681	15,041	4,360
			82	314,133	342,169	419,296	77,127
			83	8,496	8,996	13,874	4,878
			84	303	457	619	162
	A	H	81	100,959	130,894	161,788	30,894
			82	142,837	163,948	201,155	37,207
			83	37,191	28,433	39,502	11,069
			84	148	300	752	452
			86	2,092	2,202	3,720	1,518
	A	W	81	180,077	144,650	194,882	50,232
			82	332,077	389,461	489,149	99,688
			83	275,593	252,634	418,586	165,952
			84	1,686	2,895	4,564	1,669
			85	855	1,500	2,506	1,006
			86	1,309	1,991	2,976	985
	N	E	81	1,483,526	1,319,143	1,765,952	446,809
			82	1,355,624	1,382,051	1,888,194	506,143
			83	3,397,742	2,615,840	3,569,838	953,998
			85	3,043,638	2,078,690	2,574,997	496,307
			86	9,146,779	8,863,474	10,443,374	1,579,900
	N	H	84	96,386	77,846	102,771	24,925
			85	219,883	145,932	188,293	42,361
			86	291,342	174,617	231,502	56,885
	N	W	81	2,691,558	2,554,290	3,259,446	708,732
			82	1,884,118	2,225,454	2,680,567	455,113
			83	7,582,312	4,606,147	5,708,702	1,102,555
			84	4,886,273	3,970,043	4,612,765	642,722
			85	13,728,414	8,367,648	10,453,190	2,085,542
			86	8,473,309	6,917,575	8,661,148	1,743,573
	O	E	83	16,111	18,753	18,753	
			84	79,379	54,348	54,348	
			85	147,486	150,947	150,947	
			86	203,055	163,716	163,716	
	V	E	81	56,010	54,183	69,945	15,762
			82	58,058	23,593	38,763	15,170
			83	383,773	425,879	504,793	78,914
			84	3,262,258	2,491,356	3,226,713	735,357
			85	176,341	50,443	78,150	27,707
			86	107,146	87,225	112,844	25,619
	V	W		4,353,818	3,688,925	4,478,186	789,261
NAMIBIA	V	W	85	16,340	10,493	13,572	3,079
NETHLDS	A	E	82	3,044	4,007	4,698	691
	A	W	82	9,533	11,208	14,504	3,296
	V	E	85	65,272	45,237	60,465	15,228
THAILND	V	W	83	1,938	840	895	55

Kohlrabi

Kohlrabi, seed
1265300 KOHLRABI SEEDS (LB)

Country	Mode	Reg	Yr	Quantity	F.A.S.	C.I.F.	Charges
TOTAL			81	920	10,302	11,383	1,081
			82	597	25,146	26,924	1,778
			83	605	16,466	17,348	882
			84	75	1,443	1,585	142
			85	35	2,023	2,151	128
			86	58	4,203	4,498	295
DENMARK	A	E	84	35	843	906	63
	O	E	84	40	600	679	79
	V	E	81	200	808	862	54
	V	W	81	15	340	392	52
FRANCE	V	W	81	441	772	798	26

Crop Product TSUSA commodity number, description, and unit of quantity Country	Mode	Reg	Yr	Quantity	F.A.S.	C.I.F.	Charges
JAPAN	A	E	81	130	5,840	6,515	675
			82	254	11,442	12,818	1,376
			85	35	2,023	2,151	128
	A	W	81	30	1,311	1,491	180
			83	50	2,011	2,202	191
	N	E	82	184	8,918	9,223	305
	O	E	83	25	665	754	89
	V	E	83	135	6,435	6,925	490
	V	W	82	103	4,328	4,394	66
			83	145	6,953	7,036	83
NETHLDS	A	E	86	10	1,015	1,051	36
	V	E	81	100	378	405	27
			83	250	402	431	29
SWITZLD	A	E	86	33	1,298	1,401	103
	O	E	81	4	853	920	67
U KING	A	E	82	56	458	489	31
			86	15	1,890	2,046	156

Kumquat

Kumquat, candied**
1544300 KUMQUATS, ETC, CANDIED, ETC (LB)

Country	Mode	Reg	Yr	Quantity	F.A.S.	C.I.F.	Charges
TOTAL			81	26,123	16,697	18,204	1,507
			82	62,520	64,200	71,115	6,915
			83	68,325	72,039	76,942	4,903
			84	156,683	249,484	271,485	22,001
			85	244,367	289,666	321,671	32,005
			86	158,838	301,225	325,003	23,778
AUSTRAL	V	E	82	1,102	2,385	4,770	2,385
CHINA M	A	E	81	1,048	1,013	1,530	517
	V	E	83	4,800	4,416	4,919	503
			84	635	426	504	78
			85	19,315	20,833	22,634	1,801
			86	1,674	1,273	1,410	137
	V	W	82	6,651	4,779	5,227	448
			83	750	2,016	2,080	64
			84	1,238	1,823	1,936	113
			86	2,188	1,277	1,486	209
CHINA T	O	E	84	159	278	306	28
	V	E	81	15,908	2,809	2,994	185
			82	2,920	5,086	5,906	820
			83	2,918	2,768	2,981	213
			84	41,819	70,373	77,178	6,805
			85	70,714	89,644	101,040	11,396
			86	27,077	55,629	61,070	5,441
	V	W	81	6,612	9,762	10,088	326
			82	48,366	42,224	44,036	1,812
			84	23,349	33,885	35,409	1,524
			85	51,806	69,019	71,655	2,636
			86	56,435	123,661	128,617	4,956
FR GERM	V	E	81	197	806	837	31
			82	443	1,846	1,901	55
			83	136	628	725	97
			84	487	1,745	1,819	74
FRANCE	V	E	84	668	1,376	1,491	115
			85	882	1,643	3,443	1,800
HAITI	A	E	83	11,215	3,457	4,718	1,261
HG KONG	V	E	83	1,452	2,581	2,928	347
			84	7,161	22,997	24,756	1,759
			85	17,312	23,986	26,482	2,496
			86	812	2,570	2,757	187
	V	W	81	628	678	715	37
			82	200	280	316	36
			83	4,122	6,211	6,559	348
			84	719	1,100	1,155	55
			85	563	1,080	1,157	77
			86	1,031	2,304	2,371	67
INDIA	V	W	81	530	346	420	74
JAPAN	V	E	84	21,810	11,600	12,156	556
			85	7,000	13,090	13,759	669
			86	9,000	21,831	23,909	2,078
MEXICO	O	W	83	27,904	12,800	12,800	
PHIL R	N	E	82	2,838	7,600	8,959	1,359
	V	W	83	15,028	37,162	39,232	2,070
			84	47,615	80,381	90,295	9,914
			85	75,035	66,279	77,068	10,789
			86	54,562	77,157	86,686	9,529
SWITZLD	V	E	86	6,059	15,523	16,697	1,174
THAILND	V	E	84	11,023	23,500	24,480	980

Crop Product TSUSA commodity number, description, and unit of quantity Country	Mode	Reg	Yr	Quantity	F.A.S.	C.I.F.	Charges
			85	661	1,161	1,209	48
	V	W	81	1,200	1,283	1,620	337
			85	1,079	2,931	3,224	293

Kumquat, canned
1473000 KUMQUATS, CANNED (LB)

Country	Mode	Reg	Yr	Quantity	F.A.S.	C.I.F.	Charges
TOTAL			81	41,297	17,613	18,754	1,141
			82	146,323	60,016	71,624	11,608
			83	25,803	19,203	20,651	1,448
			84	133,642	23,484	28,263	4,779
			85	882,215	282,393	354,099	71,706
			86	873,153	220,504	288,793	68,289
CHILE	V	E	86	2,364	4,346	6,342	1,996
	V	W	84	250	430	480	50
CHINA M	O	E	86	2,400	1,189	1,387	198
	V	H	82	320	459	502	43
	V	W	83	2,608	3,496	3,793	297
			84	1,576	1,685	1,786	101
CHINA T	V	E	81	8,234	11,044	11,983	939
			82	92,440	36,600	42,891	6,291
			83	14,741	9,344	10,041	697
			84	12,273	7,578	8,467	889
			85	324,939	154,148	179,609	25,461
			86	12,400	7,597	8,072	475
	V	H	81	500	360	384	24
			82	2,490	4,720	5,132	412
	V	W	81	2,403	1,670	1,755	85
			82	45,298	17,137	21,450	4,313
			83	7,680	5,059	5,434	375
			84	1,830	1,651	1,789	138
			86	2,400	1,562	1,666	104
DOM REP	A	E	82	5,400	450	963	513
	V	E	86	69,552	5,796	10,725	4,929
GUATMAL	O	E	84	113,600	9,088	12,188	3,100
HG KONG	V	E	83	300	494	525	31
	V	H	81	850	850	915	65
			84	188	338	366	28
	V	W	81	650	677	705	28
			82	375	650	686	36
			84	250	274	278	4
INDIA	V	E	83	474	810	858	48
JAMAICA	A	E	84	2,938	2,080	2,480	400
	N	E	85	521,576	119,320	162,315	42,995
	V	E	85	35,700	8,925	12,175	3,250
			86	784,037	200,014	260,601	60,587
MEXICO	O	E	81	28,660	3,012	3,012	
PERU	V	E	84	737	360	429	69

L

Lancewood

Lancewood, lumber**
2023500 SPN CDR EBONY ETC LUMBR RGH (MBF)
  (See Cedar, lumber under Cedar)
2023700 SPN CDR ETC LUMBER DRSD ETC (MBF)
  (See Cedar, lumber under Cedar)

Larch

Larch, lumber
2022420 LARCH LUMBER, ROUGH (MBF)

Country	Mode	Reg	Yr	Quantity	F.A.S.	C.I.F.	Charges
TOTAL			81	389	93,045	141,035	47,990
			82	1,911	159,432	199,043	39,611
			83	1,930	215,492	298,360	82,868
			84	1,092	124,511	155,730	31,219
			85	2,908	191,242	222,006	30,764

Crop Product TSUSA commodity number, description, and unit of quantity Country	Mode	Reg	Yr	Quantity	F.A.S.	C.I.F.	Charges
			86	5,700	1,113,967	1,168,232	54,265
BRAZIL	V	E	83	102	66,786	87,051	20,265
			86	2,744	319,417	373,682	54,265
CANADA	N	E	86	*	1,175	1,175	
	O	E	81	157	36,511	36,511	
			82	469	101,787	101,787	
			83	151	40,521	40,521	
			84	286	35,301	35,301	
			85	543	94,986	94,986	
			86	6	2,925	2,925	
	O	W	81	10	3,876	3,876	
			82	16	1,844	1,844	
			83	73	11,998	11,998	
			84	151	39,896	39,896	
			85	138	15,210	15,210	
			86	62	11,860	11,860	
	V	E	86	2,888	778,590	778,590	
N ZEAL	V	H	81	222	52,658	100,648	47,990
			82	1,426	55,801	95,412	39,611
			83	1,604	96,187	158,790	62,603
			84	655	49,314	80,533	31,219
			85	2,227	81,046	111,810	30,764

2022440 LARCH LUMBER, DRESSED (MBF)

Country	Mode	Reg	Yr	Quantity	F.A.S.	C.I.F.	Charges
TOTAL			81	5,962	1,307,609	1,310,153	2,544
			82	8,094	1,413,536	1,415,412	1,876
			83	14,794	3,028,701	3,033,920	5,219
			84	6,919	1,362,884	1,367,853	4,969
			85	9,936	1,653,229	1,712,070	58,841
			86	11,985	2,068,184	2,087,800	19,616
BRAZIL	V	E	81	11	9,000	9,798	798
CANADA	N	E	84	*	3,300	3,300	
	O	E	81	4,090	947,379	947,379	
			82	6,162	1,076,102	1,076,102	
			83	11,545	2,323,296	2,323,296	
			84	4,268	788,025	788,025	
			85	7,657	1,344,901	1,344,901	
			86	11,550	1,950,256	1,950,256	
	O	W	81	1,818	347,402	347,402	
			82	1,923	333,289	333,289	
			83	3,167	687,754	687,754	
			84	2,589	516,500	516,500	
			85	400	56,578	56,578	
			86	187	34,643	45,710	11,067
	V	E	85	87	14,576	22,286	7,710
	V	W	83	43	9,322	11,039	1,717
			85	1,792	237,174	288,305	51,131
			86	226	63,415	70,364	6,949
CHILE	V	E	84	53	50,655	53,600	2,945
INDNSIA	V	E	83	30	4,187	5,611	1,424
MALAYSA	V	W	86	22	19,870	21,470	1,600
N ZEAL	V	H	81	43	3,828	5,574	1,746
			82	9	4,145	6,021	1,876
			83	9	4,142	6,220	2,078
			84	9	4,404	6,428	2,024

Laurel

Laurel, leaf, spice
1613900 LAUREL LEAVES, CRUDE (LB)

Country	Mode	Reg	Yr	Quantity	F.A.S.	C.I.F.	Charges
TOTAL			81	868,521	654,452	739,918	85,466
			82	1,029,710	592,495	699,419	106,972
			83	963,649	497,803	596,366	98,563
			84	1,218,504	506,327	634,069	127,742
			85	891,157	495,213	607,146	111,933
			86	1,222,959	893,737	1,037,833	144,096
ALBANIA	V	E	81	43,887	18,630	24,919	6,289
			86	29,233	33,260	38,017	4,757
CANADA	O	W	81	542	293	293	
CHINA M	V	W	82	450	296	317	21
CHINA T	V	E	85	10,803	16,965	18,712	1,747
	V	W	86	8,405	4,699	6,046	1,347
COLOMB	A	E	83	335	317	535	218
EGYPT	V	E	82	11,464	5,330	5,606	276
FR GERM	V	W	82	483	347	367	20
FRANCE	N	E	84	571	652	743	91
	V	E	81	670	292	401	109
			82	551	2,161	2,250	89
			86	67,621	80,612	88,112	7,500
GREECE	V	E	81	26,300	17,755	20,068	2,313
			83	40,314	19,349	21,376	2,027
			85	4,345	2,011	2,454	443
HG KONG	V	E	84	165	306	322	16
INDIA	V	E	82	17,912	6,949	8,461	1,512
			83	992	2,110	2,340	230
	V	W	83	194	294	349	55
			84	90	324	397	73
ISRAEL	V	E	86	110	4,344	4,600	256
ITALY	O	E	86	2,309	2,446	2,867	421
	V	E	82	92	506	557	51
			83	82	1,426	1,467	41
	V	W	82	48	260	260	48
JAMAICA	A	E	83	8	294	299	5
MEXICO	O	E	86	5,000	3,250	3,250	
MOROC	V	E	86	11,000	16,720	19,250	2,530
NETHLDS	V	E	82	88	394	424	30
	V	W	81	198	269	291	22
PORTUGL	V	E	86	58,926	37,429	44,554	7,125
SINGAPR	V	W	81	20	272	300	28
SPAIN	V	E	86	14,681	20,706	22,704	1,998
THAILND	V	E	81	264	378	409	31
	V	W	82	376	1,376	1,511	135
			83	125	320	339	19
TURKEY	N	E	84	1,124,528	485,932	606,474	120,542
	V	E	81	795,549	615,996	692,485	76,489
			82	987,223	556,166	659,717	103,551
			83	921,599	473,693	569,661	95,968
			84	93,150	19,113	26,133	7,020
			85	876,009	476,237	585,980	109,743
			86	1,004,881	678,031	793,685	115,654
	V	W	82	11,023	18,710	19,949	1,239
			86	11,975	7,228	8,316	1,088
YUGOSLV	V	E	86	8,818	5,012	6,432	1,420
	V	W	81	1,091	567	752	185

1614100 LAUREL LEAVES, EXCEPT CRUDE (LB)

Country	Mode	Reg	Yr	Quantity	F.A.S.	C.I.F.	Charges
TOTAL			81	3,367	3,044	3,805	761
			82	6,714	7,376	7,672	296
			83	1,182	3,659	3,818	159
			84	33,793	25,187	28,439	3,252
			85	6,000	2,697	3,438	741
			86	648	1,010	1,084	74
CANADA	O	E	82	5,000	4,992	4,992	
CHINA M	V	E	84	330	613	677	64
FRANCE	V	E	83	45	323	340	17
			84	119	377	399	22
HG KONG	V	E	84	330	613	652	39
INDIA	V	W	81	2,540	1,444	2,000	556
			82	1,190	1,076	1,277	201
INDNSIA	V	W	83	287	326	376	50
JAPAN	V	E	86	648	1,010	1,084	74
NETHLDS	V	W	82	329	397	423	26
SINGAPR	V	W	81	20	270	300	30
SPAIN	V	E	84	33,000	23,051	26,148	3,097
THAILND	V	W	82	188	541	590	49
TURKEY	V	W	85	6,000	2,697	3,438	741
U KING	O	E	81	807	1,330	1,505	175
			82	7	370	390	20
			84	14	533	563	30
USSR	V	E	83	850	3,010	3,102	92

Lavender

Lavender, essential oil
4523200 LAVENDER A SPIKE LAVENDR OIL (LB)

Country	Mode	Reg	Yr	Quantity	F.A.S.	C.I.F.	Charges
TOTAL			81	200,222	1,974,386	2,039,927	65,312
			82	184,984	1,290,864	1,339,399	48,535
			83	233,178	1,683,802	1,738,332	54,530
			84	200,511	1,242,995	1,300,165	57,170
			85	135,790	908,845	942,255	33,410
			86	152,848	1,353,072	1,393,200	40,128
AUSTRAL	V	E	82	110	1,654	1,755	101
			83	441	3,718	3,860	142
			85	441	3,262	3,384	122
BULGAR	V	E	81	4,696	41,108	41,599	491

Crop
Product
TSUSA commodity number, description, and unit of quantity

Country	Mode	Reg	Yr	Quantity	F.A.S.	C.I.F.	Charges
			82	2,315	17,760	18,142	382
			84	4,409	31,500	31,934	434
			85	4,630	24,570	25,535	965
			86	4,630	32,291	33,279	988
FR GERM	N E		85	550	4,114	4,218	104
	V E		82	714	1,125	1,375	250
			84	1,294	8,442	8,943	501
			86	330	3,002	3,196	194
FRANCE	A E		82	110	1,212	1,363	151
			84	109	727	870	143
	A W		86	200	1,799	2,024	225
	N E		81	114,381	1,153,099	1,190,699	37,600
			82	92,854	740,312	766,916	26,604
			83	104,383	814,577	844,042	29,465
			84	121,398	797,394	832,805	35,411
			85	76,204	589,145	610,857	21,712
			86	80,939	915,621	936,519	20,898
	O E		84	959	3,840	3,969	129
	V E		82	441	5,105	5,234	129
IRELAND	A E		84	441	3,540	3,681	141
ITALY	A E		82	573	5,844	6,049	205
	V E		81	882	10,427	10,607	180
NETHLDS	A E		81	4,850	25,274	26,875	1,601
			82	55	277	301	24
	N E		83	10,106	51,619	52,860	1,241
			84	11,700	64,138	66,000	1,892
			85	1,875	12,132	12,497	365
			86	7,496	58,061	60,085	2,024
	V E		81	1,600	8,579	9,169	557
SPAIN	A W		83	51	541	644	103
	N E		81	62,777	632,026	654,058	22,003
			82	84,936	489,752	509,213	19,461
			83	113,543	773,556	795,100	21,544
			84	56,623	298,361	315,473	17,112
			85	48,815	258,853	268,640	9,787
			86	50,269	282,262	295,305	13,043
SWITZLD	A E		86	66	1,188	1,244	56
	N E		81	3,506	49,137	50,107	803
			83	2,386	23,802	24,923	1,121
			84	1,281	12,931	13,209	278
	V E		82	772	9,150	9,412	262
			85	386	3,364	3,441	77
U KING	A E		83	22	408	445	37
			86	99	1,517	1,604	87
	N E		81	5,743	41,646	42,958	1,312
			82	1,718	14,330	15,226	896
			83	923	4,320	4,520	200
			84	1,975	18,841	19,892	1,051
			86	1,323	6,831	7,320	489
	O E		84	322	3,281	3,359	78
	V E		85	2,889	13,405	13,683	278
	V W		81	1	383	469	86
URUGUAY	V E		86	7,496	50,500	52,624	2,124
USSR	V E		81	860	7,850	7,986	136
YUGOSLV	V E		81	926	4,857	5,400	543
			82	386	4,343	4,413	70
			83	1,323	11,261	11,938	677

Lemon

Lemon, essential oil
4523400 LEMON OIL (LB)

Country	Mode	Reg	Yr	Quantity	F.A.S.	C.I.F.	Charges
TOTAL			81	706,320	7,201,368	7,418,821	217,453
			82	983,469	6,527,192	6,801,637	274,445
			83	1,645,116	7,940,964	8,326,651	385,687
			84	1,363,347	7,418,361	7,709,470	291,109
			85	2,200,425	12,471,073	13,042,769	571,696
			86	2,021,217	14,185,572	14,653,493	467,921
ARGENT	A E		85	5,200	26,000	29,156	3,156
	N E		82	247,941	1,356,779	1,428,722	71,943
			83	367,273	1,357,549	1,441,173	83,624
	O E		81	104,100	1,248,153	1,291,473	43,320
			82	138,522	1,025,945	1,068,271	42,326
			83	53,334	231,136	241,144	10,008
			85	9,524	56,040	58,350	2,310
			86	34,128	206,942	218,846	11,904
	V E		81	204,727	1,835,209	1,900,086	64,877
			82	202,150	1,481,114	1,527,426	46,312
			83	742,384	4,197,161	4,398,722	201,561

Crop
Product
TSUSA commodity number, description, and unit of quantity

Country	Mode	Reg	Yr	Quantity	F.A.S.	C.I.F.	Charges
			84	727,106	3,689,290	3,859,105	169,815
			85	1,294,643	7,542,451	7,855,545	313,094
			86	1,170,370	7,205,065	7,468,469	263,404
	V W		82	5,953	46,980	48,651	1,671
			83	7,920	43,150	45,068	1,918
			85	111,949	704,832	736,327	31,495
			86	121,827	704,581	734,118	29,537
AUSTRAL	O E		81	25,410	323,350	328,866	5,516
			83	21,000	113,787	117,416	3,629
	V E		81	37,515	381,274	389,691	8,417
			82	30,879	116,909	124,565	7,656
			83	7,716	15,897	17,498	1,601
			84	19,274	68,531	72,383	3,852
			85	27,709	104,972	112,512	7,540
			86	12,390	41,070	43,035	1,965
	V W		84	7,700	31,361	32,146	785
			86	34,901	238,753	240,444	1,691
BRAZIL	O E		82	11,580	134,610	137,921	3,311
	V E		81	48,873	367,112	379,739	12,627
			82	126,231	678,191	726,082	47,891
			83	89,424	355,628	376,309	20,681
			84	96,537	374,777	393,886	19,109
			85	52,849	188,978	198,872	9,894
			86	83,075	494,845	514,275	19,430
CANADA	O E		81	77,655	316,045	316,045	
			82	20,103	53,038	53,038	
			83	66,215	166,504	169,800	3,296
			84	89,661	288,306	288,306	
			85	82,058	292,212	295,905	3,693
			86	38,873	177,369	177,369	
CHILE	V E		84	8,287	17,965	19,927	1,962
			85	3,858	10,997	11,789	792
			86	6,173	19,936	21,411	1,475
CYPRUS	V E		84	4,409	28,127	28,680	553
DOM REP	V E		81	172	1,883	1,937	54
ECUADOR	V E		85	1,124	1,588	1,690	102
FR GERM	A E		81	1,212	51,049	52,020	971
			83	413	22,776	23,439	663
	N E		82	535	40,482	41,281	799
			84	2,073	133,703	136,146	2,443
			85	19,446	105,295	109,606	4,311
			86	53,319	165,252	172,132	6,880
FRANCE	A E		82	3,293	40,330	41,355	1,025
			86	951	31,997	32,302	305
	N E		81	33,530	397,486	412,559	15,073
			83	4,592	40,067	41,941	1,874
			84	9,711	87,919	90,304	2,385
			85	8,755	72,927	74,949	2,022
			86	7,764	80,126	81,546	1,420
	O E		84	44	2,730	2,730	
GREECE	V E		81	14,435	232,986	236,277	3,291
			83	646	4,698	4,812	114
			84	2,487	16,376	16,828	452
			85	14,881	93,755	95,694	1,939
INDNSIA	V E		82	16,204	37,575	42,074	4,499
			83	17,747	36,930	40,176	3,246
			84	11,133	27,074	28,473	1,399
			85	8,853	25,263	27,861	2,598
	V W		86	13,896	39,583	43,323	3,740
IRELAND	A E		84	30	12,031	12,306	275
	N E		83	86,807	78,834	86,823	7,989
			85	31,746	31,747	34,647	2,900
			86	38,306	72,925	77,964	5,039
	O E		84	23,810	21,527	23,810	2,283
ISRAEL	V E		83	21,502	90,021	92,411	2,390
			84	25,179	152,231	155,413	3,182
			85	28,080	125,306	128,988	3,682
			86	48,212	261,614	269,021	7,407
ITALY	A E		82	21,815	180,492	188,872	8,380
	N E		81	134,815	1,770,595	1,824,958	54,363
			82	133,366	1,097,636	1,129,388	31,752
			83	96,508	702,183	725,284	23,101
			84	165,000	1,390,454	1,433,853	43,399
			85	183,843	1,206,013	1,313,895	107,882
			86	140,279	1,480,971	1,513,044	32,073
	V E		82	14,027	117,679	121,304	3,625
			83	3,175	22,248	22,412	164
			84	18,800	138,358	143,217	4,859
			85	61,518	416,302	427,109	10,807
			86	26,867	226,758	233,489	6,731
	V W		85	26,983	184,883	190,361	5,478
IVY CST	V E		81	15,498	160,792	167,280	6,488
			84	26,389	119,950	123,805	3,855
JAPAN	A E		83	505	3,439	5,700	2,261

Crop Product TSUSA commodity number, description, and unit of quantity Country	Mode	Reg	Yr	Quantity	F.A.S.	C.I.F.	Charges
			85	309	2,632	3,820	1,188
			86	849	6,278	9,882	3,604
	N	E	84	52	2,546	2,867	321
	V	E	83	14	1,132	1,157	25
			85	21,584	53,568	54,077	509
			86	50,778	160,495	168,878	8,383
MEXICO	O	E	85	12,000	37,200	37,200	
	V	E	81	2,000	25,000	25,125	125
			86	2,150	10,006	10,213	207
N ZEAL	V	E	84	1,543	6,853	7,251	398
NETHLDS	A	E	81	132	3,139	3,519	380
			83	74	5,647	5,938	291
			84	43	8,975	9,057	82
			85	2,486	342,999	348,387	5,388
			86	7,503	1,694,487	1,714,291	19,804
	N	E	82	904	13,921	14,076	155
			83	1,764	21,176	21,690	514
			84	10,865	70,000	71,630	1,630
PERU	A	E	86	2,695	16,891	19,439	2,548
	V	E	83	6,746	14,571	15,970	1,399
PHIL R	V	W	84	11,524	31,667	33,045	1,378
			85	23,368	54,552	57,343	2,791
			86	17,727	54,681	57,069	2,388
REP SAF	V	E	81	2,000	20,747	21,693	946
			82	1,757	9,234	9,465	231
			83	6,437	23,040	25,043	2,003
			84	27,734	106,414	109,265	2,851
			85	18,559	72,991	76,458	3,467
			86	19,034	68,413	71,114	2,701
SPAIN	N	E	83	8,399	48,715	50,236	1,521
			84	24,353	102,833	108,686	5,853
	O	E	84	4,000	1,762	1,939	177
			85	7,285	40,277	42,297	2,020
	V	E	83	3,940	16,739	18,148	1,409
			85	43,960	211,453	230,533	19,080
			86	579	2,556	2,730	174
SWITZLD	A	E	81	4,135	63,933	64,901	968
			82	8,123	95,605	98,410	2,805
			84	19	1,425	1,487	62
			85	9,756	192,560	205,313	12,753
			86	3,782	67,489	70,563	3,074
	N	E	83	15,071	227,727	234,771	7,044
			84	16,747	320,349	329,903	9,554
			86	10,316	186,308	199,344	13,036
THAILND	V	W	82	68	360	402	42
U KING	A	E	81	110	2,149	2,176	27
			82	18	312	334	22
			83	55	606	853	247
			84	13	946	971	25
	N	E	83	10,054	87,930	90,015	2,085
			86	1,257	17,250	18,614	1,364
	O	E	81	1	466	476	10
	V	E	85	62,062	134,110	139,160	5,050
			86	12,765	51,435	52,961	1,526
URUGUAY	V	E	84	28,824	163,881	172,051	8,170
			85	19,864	124,750	129,805	5,055
			86	56,593	388,717	404,075	15,358
VENEZ	V	E	83	5,401	11,673	12,702	1,029
			85	6,173	14,420	15,120	700
			86	3,858	12,779	13,532	753

Lemon, fresh
1471900 LEMONS, FRESH (LB)

Country	Mode	Reg	Yr	Quantity	F.A.S.	C.I.F.	Charges
TOTAL			81	124,210	18,101	25,548	7,447
			82	12,425,316	3,952,800	4,608,842	656,042
			83	3,341,893	626,817	902,223	275,406
			84	12,829,445	2,970,342	4,231,051	1,260,709
			85	24,832,545	4,783,083	6,962,530	2,179,447
			86	20,118,048	2,352,671	3,430,088	1,077,417
BAHAMAS	V	E	84	204,131	11,910	16,324	4,414
			85	5,022,626	154,860	196,012	41,152
			86	8,399,060	261,570	309,687	48,117
CANADA	O	E	82	116,400	44,550	44,550	
			85	37,340	32,999	32,999	
CHILE	O	E	85	3,800	1,248	1,248	
	V	E	83	2,554,911	415,497	650,411	234,914
			84	1,394,243	267,219	412,021	144,802
			85	13,859,068	2,911,675	4,551,695	1,640,020
			86	6,787,624	1,139,515	1,772,264	632,749
	V	W	83	111,182	17,624	31,770	14,146
			84	568,894	120,752	190,386	69,634

Crop Product TSUSA commodity number, description, and unit of quantity Country	Mode	Reg	Yr	Quantity	F.A.S.	C.I.F.	Charges
DOM REP	A	E	84	18,517	4,237	6,181	1,944
	N	E	81	94,610	13,501	18,331	4,830
			82	23,573	2,833	4,422	1,589
			83	30,351	4,067	6,354	2,287
			84	157,365	27,096	38,022	10,926
	V	E	84	882	300	400	100
			86	1,750	1,900	1,980	80
ECUADOR	A	E	84	3,100	800	1,312	512
GUATMAL	V	E	81	10,000	1,800	2,511	711
			85	131,137	16,588	31,307	14,719
			86	108,000	6,578	17,713	11,135
HONDURA	A	E	86	4,950	1,250	1,400	150
ISRAEL	V	E	81	19,600	2,800	4,706	1,906
			86	42,924	13,120	14,494	1,374
ITALY	A	E	86	5,820	1,683	2,007	324
	N	E	85	61,484	14,404	28,628	14,224
	O	E	83	465,608	158,400	162,600	4,200
	V	E	82	65,256	14,550	25,647	11,097
			83	77,225	15,438	23,114	7,676
MEXICO	O	E	82	41,930	1,915	1,915	
			84	96,554	10,030	10,030	
			85	313,711	36,473	36,473	
			86	60,686	3,153	3,153	
	O	W	86	322,018	56,495	56,495	
SPAIN	N	E	82	11,595,605	3,670,821	4,303,428	632,607
	O	E	82	485,251	190,631	190,631	
			84	210,020	48,710	48,710	
			86	191,375	57,827	66,879	9,052
	V	E	82	97,301	27,500	38,249	10,749
			83	102,616	15,791	27,974	12,183
			84	10,090,219	2,469,414	3,494,191	1,024,777
			85	5,403,379	1,614,836	2,084,168	469,332
			86	4,193,841	809,580	1,184,016	374,436
TURKEY	V	E	84	85,520	9,874	13,474	3,600

Lemon, juice, concentrated
1653650 LEMON JUICE UNMIXED CONCENTRATD (GAL)

Country	Mode	Reg	Yr	Quantity	F.A.S.	C.I.F.	Charges
TOTAL			84	1,041,644	701,297	824,881	123,584
			85	1,079,606	1,122,592	1,239,997	117,405
			86	10,882,508	11,008,614	12,650,426	1,641,812
ANTIGUA	V	E	86	232,824	302,671	340,363	37,692
ARGENT	O	E	86	857,547	973,219	1,088,678	115,459
	O	W	86	1,912,525	2,010,008	2,335,647	325,639
	V	E	84	371,000	77,390	128,145	50,755
			85	112,893	100,918	120,183	19,265
			86	4,093,335	4,265,623	4,887,911	622,288
	V	W	85	181,376	191,840	225,247	33,407
			86	1,269,815	1,340,074	1,592,023	251,949
AUSTRAL	V	E	86	47,736	41,440	49,346	7,906
	V	W	86	466,685	338,700	429,694	90,994
BRAZIL	O	E	84	260,827	242,200	265,181	22,981
			85	398,365	561,821	604,854	43,033
			86	276,559	248,705	277,475	28,770
	V	E	84	97,060	241,689	285,688	43,999
			85	287,112	176,443	191,727	15,284
			86	805,723	641,499	712,359	70,860
FR GERM	V	W	84	9,016	26,673	27,757	1,084
			85	3,848	16,372	18,632	2,260
FRANCE	A	E	84	66	1,354	1,719	365
			85	125	1,500	2,481	981
			86	185	3,938	5,578	1,640
	V	E	85	12,390	26,632	29,434	2,802
			86	3,900	18,240	21,134	2,894
GREECE	O	E	84	158	750	750	
ISRAEL	V	E	86	2,278	9,186	11,232	2,046
	V	W	85	2,165	1,087	1,460	373
ITALY	V	E	84	5,921	21,878	25,417	3,539
MEXICO	O	E	84	293,330	83,809	83,809	
			85	81,332	45,979	45,979	
			86	423,680	275,092	275,092	
NETHLDS	O	W	86	320,320	364,096	418,430	54,334
	V	E	86	169,049	173,176	202,362	29,186
	V	W	84	21	483	507	24
PHIL R	V	W	84	3,705	5,071	5,908	837
			86	347	2,947	3,102	155

Lemon, peel
1521800 LEMN PEEL, CRUDE, DRIED BRNE (LB)

Country	Mode	Reg	Yr	Quantity	F.A.S.	C.I.F.	Charges
TOTAL			81	190,463	173,364	199,034	25,670

Crop
Product
TSUSA commodity number, description, and unit of quantity

Country	Mode	Reg	Yr	Quantity	F.A.S.	C.I.F.	Charges
			82	150,270	121,750	141,145	19,395
			83	146,627	65,329	88,606	23,277
			84	125,994	54,152	74,124	19,972
			85	73,439	62,188	73,813	11,625
			86	196,361	233,585	265,531	31,946
CANADA	O	E	83	3,210	4,575	4,575	
CHINA M	V	E	81	250	378	406	28
			82	500	1,163	1,302	139
	V	W	81	950	435	482	47
			84	250	500	543	43
FR GERM	A	W	82	500	660	1,155	495
	O	E	82	1,102	1,985	2,093	108
	V	E	81	36,409	41,349	44,795	3,446
			82	12,126	17,750	18,258	508
			84	3,728	2,765	3,119	354
			85	3,677	3,387	3,759	372
			86	1,112	1,590	1,725	135
GUATMAL	V	W	85	11,023	11,227	12,880	1,653
HG KONG	V	E	83	450	780	855	75
INDIA	V	E	81	450	382	473	91
			83	740	454	529	75
ITALY	V	E	81	58,800	20,959	25,448	4,489
			82	39,585	18,407	21,389	2,982
			85	19,000	16,500	17,750	1,250
KIRIBAT	V	E	86	2,275	5,373	5,698	325
OMAN	V	E	81	4,409	5,393	7,758	2,365
PAKISTN	V	E	81	3,469	2,479	2,727	248
SPAIN	A	W	83	3,000	3,730	6,396	2,666
	V	E	81	51,116	58,186	66,388	8,202
			82	92,891	79,291	94,170	14,879
			83	138,977	55,506	75,944	20,438
			84	118,794	47,756	66,774	19,018
			85	39,739	31,074	39,424	8,350
			86	181,951	213,963	244,149	30,186
	V	W	81	34,610	43,803	50,557	6,754
			82	3,000	1,886	2,135	249
			84	1,250	1,392	1,537	145
			86	11,023	12,659	13,959	1,300
SWITZLD	V	E	82	441	320	322	2
			84	1,763	1,385	1,758	373
THAILND	V	W	82	125	288	321	33
			83	250	284	307	23
			84	209	354	393	39

1523400 LEMON PEEL PRES O PREP NSPF (LB)

Country	Mode	Reg	Yr	Quantity	F.A.S.	C.I.F.	Charges
TOTAL			81	20,062	26,555	28,937	2,382
			82	3,061	4,865	5,245	380
			83	1,828	3,101	3,374	273
			84	24,573	37,692	48,422	10,730
			85	8,818	4,920	5,442	522
			86	1,926	6,176	6,643	467
CANADA	O	E	84	3,683	7,847	7,847	
CHINA M	V	H	86	700	2,010	2,164	154
	V	W	82	375	526	583	57
FR GERM	N	E	81	3,312	4,849	5,175	326
	V	E	82	656	2,220	2,352	132
			83	844	1,425	1,539	114
			84	359	967	1,021	54
			86	785	2,956	3,104	148
	V	W	81	1,080	2,570	2,711	141
			83	434	548	637	89
			84	637	569	657	88
GREECE	V	E	84	6,036	4,577	5,098	521
HG KONG	V	E	81	500	850	906	56
			82	1,550	1,859	1,998	139
			83	300	716	753	37
	V	W	81	331	786	839	53
			83	250	412	445	33
SPAIN	A	W	84	12,500	22,249	31,791	9,542
	V	E	85	8,818	4,920	5,442	522
			86	441	1,210	1,375	165
	V	W	81	14,839	17,500	19,306	1,806
THAILND	V	E	82	480	260	312	52
U KING	A	E	84	1,035	1,147	1,663	516
	V	E	84	323	336	345	9

1542500 LEMON PEEL, CANDIED ETC (LB)

Country	Mode	Reg	Yr	Quantity	F.A.S.	C.I.F.	Charges
TOTAL			81	122,743	70,493	78,182	7,689
			82	178,531	100,073	110,395	10,322
			83	169,906	97,878	106,693	8,815
			84	117,339	60,127	66,455	6,328
			85	220,388	117,452	129,420	11,968
			86	220,330	102,248	114,008	11,760
AUSTRAL	V	E	81	114,850	57,057	63,654	6,597
			82	178,110	98,806	109,050	10,244
			83	163,692	89,519	97,673	8,154
			84	109,128	56,128	61,296	5,168
			85	216,568	111,962	122,554	10,592
			86	217,495	97,453	108,584	11,131
	V	W	86	1,142	1,843	1,923	80
CANADA	O	E	83	45	2,673	2,673	
FR GERM	O	E	81	2,603	6,482	6,972	490
	V	E	81	5,290	6,954	7,556	602
			82	311	838	897	59
			83	511	1,521	1,698	177
			85	1,064	2,426	3,034	608
FRANCE	V	E	84	1,290	1,029	1,153	124
HG KONG	V	E	83	500	385	450	65
INDIA	V	E	82	110	429	448	19
	V	W	85	1,764	1,600	2,091	491
SPAIN	V	E	84	5,488	1,984	2,930	946
SWITZLD	V	E	83	2,205	1,422	1,567	145
	V	W	84	1,433	986	1,076	90
U KING	V	W	83	2,953	2,358	2,632	274
			85	992	1,464	1,741	277
			86	1,693	2,952	3,501	549

Lemon, prepared or preserved

1472100 LEMONS, PREP OR PRESERVED (LB)

Country	Mode	Reg	Yr	Quantity	F.A.S.	C.I.F.	Charges
TOTAL			81	187,857	214,682	233,216	18,084
			82	232,356	271,263	295,817	24,554
			83	305,051	353,433	388,088	34,655
			84	362,384	391,783	434,387	42,604
			85	189,701	220,918	241,682	20,764
			86	267,372	247,819	268,473	20,654
ARAB EM	V	E	83	6,614	11,530	13,217	1,687
			85	8,981	12,222	13,682	1,460
	V	W	81	11,023	2,725	4,995	2,270
			84	2,327	3,874	4,273	399
CANADA	O	E	84	550	3,248	3,248	
	O	W	81	6,050	2,789	2,789	
			82	6,050	2,767	2,767	
CHINA M	O	E	84	375	568	662	94
	V	E	81	1,777	2,990	3,204	214
			82	10,550	8,779	9,870	1,091
			83	2,625	3,850	4,303	453
			84	2,431	3,106	3,430	324
			85	10,825	10,310	11,368	1,058
			86	11,933	15,687	17,722	2,035
	V	H	81	1,105	2,647	2,858	211
			82	8,873	10,093	10,814	721
			83	14,939	20,499	22,606	2,107
			84	5,259	9,916	10,783	867
			85	15,300	17,257	18,623	1,366
			86	9,500	7,945	8,710	765
	V	W	81	4,615	7,921	8,442	521
			82	9,058	12,031	12,851	820
			83	7,975	9,957	10,684	727
			84	12,401	21,972	23,366	1,394
			85	7,415	15,384	16,985	1,601
			86	23,811	42,549	44,309	1,760
CHINA T	O	H	86	3,500	4,977	5,250	273
	V	E	81	2,125	3,120	3,354	234
			82	2,075	3,502	3,797	295
			83	875	1,645	1,843	198
			84	800	1,164	1,302	138
	V	H	81	2,050	2,323	2,498	175
			82	2,550	4,288	4,533	245
			83	450	756	876	120
			84	749	1,175	1,247	72
			85	1,500	1,125	1,295	170
			86	4,000	3,873	4,080	207
	V	W	81	2,160	2,667	2,819	152
			82	500	880	990	110
			83	600	341	356	15
			84	427	340	357	17
DENMARK	A	E	81	62	350	551	201
			82	220	1,198	1,467	269
FR GERM	A	E	81	529	1,829	2,085	256
	O	E	86	2,569	5,422	5,422	
	V	E	81	529	1,926	1,943	17
			82	1,058	3,657	5,129	1,472

Crop Product TSUSA commodity number, description, and unit of quantity Country	Mode	Reg	Yr	Quantity	F.A.S.	C.I.F.	Charges
FRANCE	A	E	86	5,629	17,112	18,122	1,010
	A	E	84	1,383	1,991	2,769	778
	V	E	81	458	833	873	40
			82	164	282	307	25
			83	1,323	985	1,343	358
			84	7,055	5,104	6,245	1,141
			85	4,960	8,530	9,632	1,102
			86	1,190	1,346	1,559	213
GREECE	V	E	81	596	600	684	84
			82	295	288	332	44
HG KONG	V	E	81	7,866	11,524	12,395	871
			82	8,196	12,796	14,084	1,288
			83	10,025	11,188	12,268	1,080
			84	14,795	19,551	22,156	2,605
			85	3,098	4,390	4,938	548
			86	9,916	15,093	16,673	1,580
	V	H	81	82,480	106,864	112,302	5,438
			82	104,637	138,151	146,259	8,108
			83	127,248	150,389	159,368	8,979
			84	136,724	140,247	148,913	8,666
			85	69,340	54,230	57,131	2,901
			86	51,489	38,038	40,371	2,333
	V	W	81	19,466	25,398	26,997	1,599
			82	14,802	19,780	21,174	1,394
			83	14,129	20,928	22,384	1,456
			84	26,514	37,394	39,796	2,402
			85	10,808	25,738	26,831	1,093
			86	10,750	21,679	22,227	548
INDIA	N	E	84	11,517	7,624	8,602	978
			85	3,557	3,218	3,655	437
	O	E	81	675	1,100	1,204	104
	V	E	81	14,719	11,966	14,807	2,841
			82	18,790	12,901	15,871	2,970
			83	21,722	24,431	27,814	3,383
			84	11,296	8,191	9,438	1,247
			85	4,410	2,602	2,952	350
			86	1,571	1,864	2,109	245
	V	W	81	5,281	3,240	4,091	851
			82	8,385	7,907	9,449	1,542
			83	20,420	24,539	28,610	4,071
			84	7,718	13,686	15,517	1,831
			85	2,553	2,897	3,614	717
			86	9,466	7,265	8,461	1,196
IRAN	V	E	82	6,614	11,726	13,434	1,708
	V	W	84	8,167	12,400	14,950	2,550
			85	1,146	2,704	3,024	320
			86	6,889	3,165	3,389	224
ISRAEL	O	E	83	550	826	873	47
	V	E	82	135	285	409	124
			85	10,335	7,926	8,629	703
			86	42,704	16,499	21,805	5,306
	V	W	81	6,172	7,305	7,849	544
ITALY	A	E	84	2,049	814	3,365	2,551
	V	E	83	302	639	766	127
			84	2,128	3,788	4,481	693
	V	W	84	1,428	4,976	5,357	381
JAPAN	V	W	83	32,014	16,498	18,696	2,198
KOR REP	V	E	83	188	450	461	11
			86	550	1,525	1,672	147
MACAO	V	H	83	250	448	487	39
MEXICO	O	E	83	4,023	7,099	8,012	913
			86	48,150	9,154	9,154	
MOROC	A	E	84	2,037	952	2,113	1,161
OMAN	V	E	83	6,600	12,075	13,413	1,338
	V	W	82	11,464	16,383	19,204	2,821
			84	2,205	5,000	5,426	426
			85	20,984	33,839	38,067	4,228
PHIL R	V	E	85	4,168	6,011	7,789	1,778
			86	2,643	7,800	8,177	377
	V	W	86	4,346	10,932	11,808	876
SPAIN	V	E	84	33,000	12,038	17,909	5,871
SWITZLD	V	E	85	1,389	1,190	1,269	79
	V	W	85	154	2,248	2,390	142
THAILND	V	E	81	1,925	2,250	2,513	263
			82	7,815	5,536	6,323	787
			83	2,338	3,329	3,823	494
			84	2,468	2,405	2,753	348
			86	2,651	2,752	2,977	225
	V	H	81	3,175	2,195	2,381	186
			82	5,291	3,665	4,008	343
			84	12,630	15,105	15,943	838
			86	5,820	5,843	6,389	546
	V	W	81	13,019	10,120	11,582	1,012
			82	16,298	10,751	11,949	1,198

Crop Product TSUSA commodity number, description, and unit of quantity Country	Mode	Reg	Yr	Quantity	F.A.S.	C.I.F.	Charges
			83	11,120	7,838	8,476	638
			84	15,418	10,738	11,658	920
			85	5,400	3,600	3,868	268
			86	4,920	2,716	2,965	249
U KING	N	E	83	7,257	6,810	8,205	1,395
	O	E	84	1,234	1,308	1,373	65
			86	3,375	4,583	5,122	539
	V	E	84	37,135	42,844	46,660	3,816
			85	1,090	1,178	1,319	141
	V	W	84	164	264	295	31
			85	2,288	4,319	4,621	302

Lemongrass

Citral, aldehyde
4602500 CITRAL NOV 10% ALC NOT MIXT (LB)

Country	Mode	Reg	Yr	Quantity	F.A.S.	C.I.F.	Charges
TOTAL			81	199,794	858,960	882,602	23,389
			82	114,717	480,183	494,391	14,208
			83	176,815	742,128	772,648	30,520
			84	187,786	795,085	826,760	31,675
			85	143,783	550,722	571,297	20,575
			86	130,795	516,391	535,023	18,632
CANADA	O	E	86	900	1,414	1,414	
FR GERM	N	E	83	28,426	94,426	96,373	1,947
			84	41,913	162,482	165,299	2,817
			85	28,424	107,536	109,304	1,768
	V	E	82	17,206	69,672	70,943	1,271
			86	11,968	42,709	44,633	1,924
FRANCE	N	E	82	23,236	89,419	92,194	2,775
			85	7,355	32,550	33,472	922
	V	E	81	5,088	31,703	32,909	1,206
			86	6,614	28,868	29,489	621
GUATMAL	O	E	81	53	350	350	
ITALY	V	E	85	8,488	28,688	30,205	1,517
JAPAN	V	E	81	385	3,030	3,102	72
			82	277	1,965	2,099	134
			83	633	4,412	4,538	126
MEXICO	O	W	86	9,846	6,975	6,975	
NETHLDS	A	E	81	66	819	878	59
			85	187	2,138	2,356	218
	N	E	84	253	1,938	2,010	72
	V	E	82	55	647	658	11
SWITZLD	N	E	83	119,328	470,785	493,388	22,603
			84	114,544	406,297	426,154	19,857
			86	81,791	359,839	373,154	13,315
	V	E	81	175,926	685,713	704,346	18,380
			82	64,816	248,232	256,047	7,815
			85	86,807	290,738	302,388	11,650
			86	19,676	76,586	79,358	2,772
U KING	A	E	82	9,127	70,248	72,450	2,202
	N	E	81	18,276	137,345	141,017	3,672
			83	17,240	130,446	134,438	3,992
			84	31,076	224,368	233,297	8,929
			85	12,522	89,072	93,572	4,500
USSR	V	E	83	11,188	42,059	43,911	1,852

Lemon grass, essential oil
4523600 LEMON GRASS OIL (LB)

Country	Mode	Reg	Yr	Quantity	F.A.S.	C.I.F.	Charges
TOTAL			81	246,911	718,109	745,632	27,523
			82	216,760	739,747	764,045	24,298
			83	234,627	795,588	829,051	33,463
			84	185,300	726,202	756,683	30,481
			85	135,518	396,092	414,355	18,263
			86	170,649	434,772	464,809	30,037
BRAZIL	V	E	83	397	1,425	1,479	54
CANADA	A	E	82	11,000	12,641	12,677	36
	O	E	85	1,499	1,499	1,499	
CHINA M	V	W	84	20,238	102,770	105,772	3,002
DOM REP	V	E	86	2,000	2,000	2,439	439
F GUIAN	V	E	83	20,000	72,310	74,899	2,589
FR GERM	A	E	83	1	653	653	18
FRANCE	V	E	82	4,409	17,790	18,466	676
GUATMAL	A	E	81	800	3,000	3,640	640
	N	E	86	147,350	361,136	386,375	25,239
	V	E	81	196,287	539,945	554,734	14,789
			82	186,383	641,189	660,992	19,803
			83	156,885	524,551	542,285	17,734

Crop
Product
TSUSA commodity number, description, and unit of quantity

Country	Mode	Reg	Yr	Quantity	F.A.S.	C.I.F.	Charges
			84	116,174	392,515	407,598	15,083
			85	133,225	389,596	407,316	17,720
HAITI	A	E	82	2,250	23,575	24,259	684
INDIA	V	E	81	27,778	96,709	103,492	6,783
			82	7,540	25,802	27,629	1,827
			83	46,428	158,727	169,457	10,730
			84	34,525	161,713	170,020	8,307
			86	7,937	36,700	38,774	2,074
	V	W	81	22,046	78,455	83,766	5,311
			82	3,968	13,475	14,440	965
			83	7,173	25,505	27,237	1,732
			84	14,286	68,895	72,976	4,081
MEXICO	A	E	85	794	4,997	5,540	543
SALVADR	V	E	86	10,000	22,425	23,889	1,464
SRI LKA	N	E	86	3,362	12,511	13,332	821
	V	E	83	441	1,527	1,590	63
	V	W	83	2,205	7,250	7,680	430
THAILND	V	E	82	23	460	525	65
	V	W	82	32	555	640	85
U KING	O	E	83	1,097	3,658	3,771	113
	V	E	82	1,155	4,260	4,417	157
			84	77	309	317	8

Lentil

Lentil, dried

1403500 LENTILS, DRIED, DEHYDRATED (LB)

Country	Mode	Reg	Yr	Quantity	F.A.S.	C.I.F.	Charges
TOTAL			81	1,159,805	388,273	447,357	59,084
			82	2,250,435	583,719	633,883	50,164
			83	2,233,957	480,011	540,189	60,178
			84	2,751,398	690,867	747,274	56,407
			85	2,065,880	672,733	716,860	44,127
			86	3,802,972	1,370,471	1,465,371	94,900
AFGHAN	V	E	86	11,852	4,432	5,120	688
AUSTRAL	O	E	83	2,200	516	559	43
			84	1,430	498	498	
	V	E	81	22,923	8,349	8,464	115
			84	35,200	8,873	10,315	1,442
			85	8,800	1,502	1,840	338
	V	W	82	5,502	1,418	1,783	365
			84	660	269	296	27
			86	11,023	2,850	3,379	529
BELGIUM	O	E	82	5,500	1,792	1,792	
			83	23,650	7,816	7,816	
			85	5,500	2,154	2,154	
			86	2,750	1,165	1,165	
	V	E	86	44,092	16,110	17,900	1,790
BELIZE	V	E	86	35,274	28,593	30,415	1,822
CANADA	O	E	81	218,643	58,410	58,426	16
			82	984,802	207,463	209,601	2,138
			83	766,012	159,882	159,942	60
			84	793,081	209,269	209,269	
			85	640,650	171,677	171,677	
			86	1,862,349	593,691	593,691	
	O	W	82	380,817	85,317	85,577	260
			83	191,000	44,720	44,720	
			84	755,410	160,761	160,761	
			85	669,500	250,308	250,308	
			86	563,000	197,466	197,466	
CHILE	V	E	82	21,936	7,100	8,123	1,023
CHINA M	V	W	83	500	500	523	23
			84	2,000	3,475	3,727	252
			85	1,000	1,839	1,950	111
DOM REP	V	W	83	1,047	1,156	1,274	118
FR GERM	A	E	84	1,452	632	1,525	893
	O	E	81	9,988	16,226	17,927	1,701
			85	4,850	4,155	4,437	282
	V	E	83	2,904	2,230	2,846	616
FRANCE	O	E	86	1,400	1,312	1,716	404
	V	W	81	400	287	298	11
			82	8,259	3,657	3,896	239
			83	2,000	2,921	3,121	200
			84	1,500	1,617	1,844	227
INDIA	O	E	81	6,702	2,239	2,451	212
			83	550	282	305	23
			84	3,660	2,156	2,183	27
			85	2,750	1,091	1,091	
			86	12,100	3,589	3,589	
	O	W	81	550	268	268	

Crop
Product
TSUSA commodity number, description, and unit of quantity

Country	Mode	Reg	Yr	Quantity	F.A.S.	C.I.F.	Charges
	V	E	83	5,434	3,470	3,657	187
			84	213,024	98,272	108,555	10,283
			85	40,300	21,707	25,046	3,339
			86	93,738	32,154	40,296	8,142
	V	W	81	881	732	923	191
			82	397	436	515	79
			86	3,968	1,764	2,003	239
ITALY	V	E	81	54	676	760	84
			82	9,921	3,450	3,933	483
JAPAN	A	W	83	27	663	670	7
KENYA	O	E	82	22,562	8,218	9,083	865
			83	13,512	4,321	4,802	481
			84	42,844	11,428	12,795	1,367
			85	15,400	5,334	6,178	844
	V	E	81	26,455	14,258	16,400	2,142
			82	6,614	2,100	2,543	443
			83	38,958	11,224	13,707	2,483
			84	33,000	8,050	10,154	2,104
			86	30,864	10,500	12,300	1,800
	V	W	84	6,800	2,920	3,212	292
LEBANON	V	E	81	39,600	15,616	17,101	1,485
			82	8,818	2,800	3,614	814
			84	6,614	1,431	1,634	203
			86	216,382	90,904	119,497	28,593
	V	W	86	200,336	99,854	113,629	13,775
MALAWI	O	E	81	26,416	12,106	13,238	1,132
			82	11,000	3,328	3,693	365
			83	11,000	3,190	3,190	
			84	4,409	2,136	2,319	183
			85	2,200	1,466	1,684	218
MALAYSA	O	E	83	495	304	322	18
MEXICO	O	E	82	719	285	285	
			83	5,250	1,307	1,307	
			84	1,598	1,034	1,034	
			86	14,600	2,847	2,847	
MOZAMBQ	V	E	81	10,825	4,281	5,075	794
NEPAL	V	W	83	17,637	5,004	6,216	1,212
NETHLDS	O	E	84	1,455	724	1,249	525
	V	E	82	1,940	1,336	1,539	203
SWITZLD	O	E	86	8,690	4,311	4,311	
THAILND	V	W	84	4,409	1,569	1,761	192
			85	17,637	5,441	7,214	1,773
TURKEY	N	E	81	22,956	9,355	10,407	1,052
			82	35,200	14,315	16,696	2,381
			83	27,557	7,702	8,751	1,049
			84	48,422	10,787	11,539	752
	O	E	81	97,075	40,371	46,033	5,662
			82	92,898	35,747	40,204	4,457
			83	122,304	28,257	31,072	2,815
			84	84,176	22,068	25,355	3,287
			85	107,542	43,779	51,443	7,664
			86	71,893	21,765	25,495	3,730
	O	W	81	550	288	305	17
			82	6,614	2,264	2,490	226
	V	E	81	643,398	190,987	234,200	43,213
			82	527,820	142,936	171,636	28,700
			83	816,371	148,745	189,615	40,870
			84	546,044	111,247	136,484	25,237
			85	348,338	102,970	120,330	17,360
			86	488,402	198,991	222,636	23,645
	V	W	81	3,123	1,482	1,645	163
			82	19,700	14,122	16,135	2,013
			83	47,150	7,395	10,702	3,307
			84	127,867	19,275	27,406	8,131
			85	136,126	32,282	42,047	9,765
			86	44,092	20,200	23,600	3,400
U KING	A	E	82	1,127	1,011	1,157	146
	N	E	81	14,895	6,274	6,769	495
			82	22,022	8,156	9,074	918
			84	15,576	4,585	5,068	483
	O	E	81	13,537	5,410	5,954	544
			82	36,364	14,809	16,353	1,544
			83	95,894	24,745	29,739	4,994
			84	15,817	5,478	5,776	298
			85	65,287	27,028	29,461	2,433
			86	46,484	25,648	29,453	3,805
	V	E	81	834	658	713	55
			83	25,470	8,202	9,154	952
			84	4,950	2,313	2,515	202
			86	39,683	12,325	14,863	2,538
	V	W	82	39,903	21,659	24,161	2,502
			83	17,035	5,459	6,179	720

Crop Product / TSUSA commodity number, description, and unit of quantity

Lentil, fresh or frozen
1365000 LENTILS, FRESH, CHLLD, FROZN (LB)

Country	Mode	Reg	Yr	Quantity	F.A.S.	C.I.F.	Charges
TOTAL			81	215,345	55,135	60,744	5,609
			82	461,872	108,151	121,615	13,464
			83	151,412	31,733	39,783	8,050
			84	533,906	106,222	108,998	2,776
			85	536,999	177,421	185,329	7,908
			86	1,331,696	450,290	466,860	16,570
BELGIUM	O	E	82	4,950	1,646	1,646	
			84	1,100	440	440	
	V	E	86	220,460	71,809	83,120	11,311
CANADA	A	W	85	3,500	1,225	1,551	326
			86	4,950	2,550	2,930	380
	O	E	81	142,550	31,842	31,842	
			82	183,650	36,811	36,811	
			83	87,500	14,560	14,560	
			84	361,550	75,452	75,452	
			85	388,650	133,952	133,952	
			86	1,034,250	344,917	344,981	64
	O	W	82	135,000	23,333	23,333	
			84	39,600	4,400	4,400	
			85	20,000	5,800	5,800	
CHINA T	A	E	85	3	1,733	1,914	181
DOM REP	A	E	82	3,507	350	721	371
			84	3,650	365	528	163
FRANCE	A	W	83	9,900	2,509	7,980	5,471
INDIA	V	E	84	10,719	2,944	3,722	778
KENYA	V	E	82	39,683	12,137	14,907	2,770
			83	39,682	11,400	13,750	2,350
MEXICO	A	E	84	3,240	380	840	460
	O	E	81	795	541	541	
	O	W	84	14,296	1,715	1,715	
TURKEY	O	E	83	14,330	3,264	3,493	229
			84	20,358	6,572	6,572	
	V	E	81	72,000	22,752	28,361	5,609
			82	87,082	31,314	40,034	8,720
			84	39,600	5,238	6,578	1,340
			85	109,446	28,411	34,312	5,901
			86	69,831	29,914	34,716	4,802
U KING	O	E	84	39,793	8,716	8,751	35
	V	W	86	2,205	1,100	1,113	13
W SAMOA	A	H	82	8,000	2,560	4,163	1,603
	V	W	85	15,400	6,300	7,800	1,500

Lettuce

Lettuce, fresh or frozen
1366000 LETTUCE, JUN 1-OCT 31 INCL (LB)

Country	Mode	Reg	Yr	Quantity	F.A.S.	C.I.F.	Charges
TOTAL			81	5,587,076	961,228	972,600	11,372
			82	7,511,485	1,012,577	1,036,512	23,935
			83	8,889,180	1,182,868	1,189,356	6,488
			84	17,139,050	2,366,966	2,417,629	50,663
			85	16,430,740	1,874,159	1,953,787	79,628
			86	6,180,794	872,332	891,438	19,106
BELGIUM	A	E	81	15,598	17,696	25,325	7,629
			82	23,982	37,900	56,409	18,509
			83	4,577	3,546	4,789	1,243
			84	13,358	19,414	26,291	6,877
			85	1,360	5,560	6,660	1,100
			86	6,078	4,890	7,918	3,028
	A	W	84	450	258	435	177
BRAZIL	A	E	81	759	755	957	202
C RICA	V	E	86	8,232	1,568	1,857	289
CANADA	O	E	81	5,329,661	891,103	891,107	4
			82	7,244,288	902,779	902,798	19
			83	8,591,718	1,088,504	1,089,053	549
			84	15,704,474	2,023,586	2,023,586	
			85	15,646,369	1,665,595	1,665,595	
			86	4,975,135	600,895	600,897	2
	O	W	81	133,720	27,563	27,563	
			82	23,470	8,665	8,665	
			83	207,024	66,557	66,557	
			84	1,026,480	164,775	164,775	
			85	528,304	126,478	126,478	
			86	1,081,380	196,400	196,400	
CHINA T	V	W	85	38,500	15,463	18,813	3,350
			86	1,799	1,150	1,212	62

Country	Mode	Reg	Yr	Quantity	F.A.S.	C.I.F.	Charges
DOM REP	A	E	83	2,550	255	621	366
			84	4,356	600	1,088	488
			86	9,350	1,122	2,522	1,400
	V	E	81	60,000	11,750	13,776	2,026
			82	27,500	3,300	5,664	2,364
			83	2,000	384	484	100
			84	35,900	4,308	5,402	1,094
			85	99,815	17,781	23,481	5,700
FRANCE	A	E	81	1,610	1,503	1,829	326
			82	1,766	1,987	3,107	1,120
			83	1,862	3,496	4,356	860
			84	4,041	9,793	13,435	3,642
			85	440	1,260	1,594	334
			86	1,586	2,531	4,352	1,821
	O	E	85	24,000	2,736	2,736	
GUATMAL	A	W	83	5,850	1,755	3,508	1,753
	V	E	81	2,400	300	419	119
ISRAEL	A	E	85	21,660	5,502	58,871	53,369
ITALY	A	E	81	598	1,873	2,723	850
			82	1,650	2,736	3,556	820
			84	48,699	58,820	89,394	30,574
			85	1,408	1,135	1,861	726
			86	3,938	5,865	10,012	4,147
	A	W	84	3,230	5,224	8,097	2,873
			85	576	1,040	1,640	600
			86	3,760	2,867	7,547	4,680
MAURIT	A	E	86	475	1,102	1,808	706
MEXICO	A	E	82	1,445	1,927	2,408	481
	O	E	81	39,661	7,285	7,285	
			82	40,502	28,351	28,351	
			83	41,521	3,252	3,252	
			84	185,787	58,482	58,482	
			85	39,000	7,800	7,800	
			86	66,875	32,319	32,319	
	O	W	82	137,794	20,192	20,192	
			83	28,764	3,480	3,480	
			84	93,628	7,109	7,109	
			86	14,148	6,490	6,490	
N ZEAL	A	W	85	3,672	5,178	7,715	2,537
NETHLDS	A	E	83	3,314	11,639	13,256	1,617
			84	13,027	12,057	14,717	2,660
			85	9,687	11,608	17,077	5,469
			86	8,038	15,133	18,104	2,971
	A	W	82	450	1,140	1,279	139
			85	6,349	4,773	10,466	5,693
SPAIN	A	E	84	4,420	2,021	4,241	2,220
THAILND	V	W	81	3,069	1,400	1,616	216
			82	6,138	2,800	2,931	131
			84	1,200	519	577	58
W SAMOA	A	H	82	2,500	800	1,152	352
	V	W	85	9,600	2,250	3,000	750

1366100 LETTUCE, FRESH, CHLLD, FROZN (LB)

Country	Mode	Reg	Yr	Quantity	F.A.S.	C.I.F.	Charges
TOTAL			81	5,816,235	1,032,743	1,044,169	11,426
			82	7,085,520	2,885,311	2,913,993	28,682
			83	12,547,013	2,559,138	2,594,438	35,300
			84	15,418,839	3,441,322	3,552,215	110,893
			85	21,355,544	4,402,565	4,499,710	97,145
			86	14,260,041	2,812,330	2,833,833	21,503
BELGIUM	A	E	81	15,547	22,544	29,244	6,700
			82	27,265	46,242	60,807	14,565
			83	33,405	48,312	59,858	11,546
			84	38,288	67,523	90,295	22,772
			85	67,064	87,015	112,442	25,427
			86	8,387	11,221	17,209	5,988
	A	W	81	880	824	1,500	676
			82	630	868	1,260	392
			83	1,245	1,788	2,611	823
			84	73	264	345	81
			85	4,800	4,288	6,183	1,895
C RICA	V	E	85	12,751	1,500	2,280	780
CANADA	A	E	83	5,952	5,400	8,701	3,301
	A	H	84	6,889	7,515	10,812	3,297
	O	E	81	656,290	191,994	191,994	
			82	525,155	164,724	164,724	
			83	750,828	251,760	251,760	
			84	804,673	270,202	270,202	
			85	516,720	145,436	145,540	104
			86	104,260	32,090	32,090	
	O	W	82	30,895	19,505	19,505	
			83	127,926	94,482	94,482	
			84	168,653	144,657	144,657	
			85	141,847	89,747	89,747	

Crop
Product
TSUSA commodity number, description, and unit of quantity

Country	Mode	Reg	Yr	Quantity	F.A.S.	C.I.F.	Charges
			86	180,146	109,804	109,804	
CHINA T	V	E	84	669	357	396	39
	V	W	82	3,616	2,700	2,955	255
			83	3,599	3,003	3,260	257
			84	2,701	1,371	1,625	254
COLOMB	A	E	83	2,742	1,020	1,493	473
DOM REP	A	E	82	3,650	438	832	394
FRANCE	A	E	81	4,855	15,960	18,817	2,857
			82	9,541	16,695	21,094	4,399
			83	12,890	31,936	39,151	7,215
			84	17,445	34,256	47,706	13,450
			85	132	1,331	1,581	250
			86	232	3,440	3,600	160
	A	W	83	1,653	2,660	3,628	968
	N	E	85	22,258	6,647	8,789	2,142
GUATMAL	V	E	82	15,600	3,600	5,936	2,336
			85	333,447	44,208	58,499	14,291
ITALY	A	E	81	598	1,322	2,181	859
			83	5,377	2,960	5,525	2,565
			84	83,797	113,981	170,100	56,119
			85	65,584	106,976	153,735	46,759
			86	5,179	7,795	12,342	4,547
	A	W	83	3,120	2,488	6,070	3,582
			84	950	763	763	
			85	1,653	2,100	6,796	4,696
			86	6,777	5,286	11,595	6,309
MALAYSA	O	W	85	3,451	1,015	1,015	
MEXICO	A	E	85	302	1,032	1,313	281
	A	W	86	1,683	1,011	1,432	421
	O	E	81	23,207	2,048	2,048	
			82	31,434	2,300	2,300	
			84	18,924	1,447	1,447	
			86	61,965	9,102	9,102	
	O	W	81	5,114,547	797,457	797,721	264
			82	6,404,944	2,600,467	2,600,467	
			83	11,586,185	2,103,433	2,103,433	
			84	14,228,670	2,738,553	2,738,553	
			85	20,184,479	3,909,990	3,909,990	
			86	13,835,250	2,601,353	2,601,361	8
N ZEAL	A	E	83	99	638	748	110
NETHLDS	A	E	81	311	594	664	70
			82	15,485	19,424	24,948	5,524
			83	9,424	6,878	9,856	2,978
			84	13,198	7,975	11,291	3,316
			85	1,056	1,280	1,800	520
			86	1,092	2,085	2,966	881
	A	W	83	250	437	1,641	1,204
			86	2,207	4,790	5,490	700
	N	E	84	25,722	45,035	54,871	9,836
PORTUGL	A	E	84	373	395	636	241
SENEGAL	A	E	83	154	755	908	153
			84	945	3,025	3,929	904
THAILND	V	E	82	5,029	2,748	3,176	428
			83	664	374	413	39
			84	4,203	2,505	2,884	379
	V	W	82	12,276	5,600	5,989	389
			83	1,500	814	900	86
			84	2,666	1,498	1,703	205
			86	52,378	20,283	22,372	2,089
TURKEY	A	W	86	485	4,070	4,470	400

Licorice

Licorice, extract

1924500 LICORICE EXTRACT (LB)

Country	Mode	Reg	Yr	Quantity	F.A.S.	C.I.F.	Charges
TOTAL			81	6,323,124	8,629,146	9,186,353	557,207
			82	8,559,879	12,045,359	12,736,003	690,644
			83	8,576,599	11,277,309	11,908,419	631,110
			84	9,507,338	11,779,542	12,777,041	997,499
			85	11,597,459	16,845,208	18,077,349	1,232,141
			86	8,243,795	12,172,505	13,043,122	870,617
AFGHAN	V	E	84	1,872,857	556,357	627,673	71,316
CANADA	O	E	83	24,553	22,137	22,156	19
CHINA M	V	E	81	233,514	310,630	352,015	41,385
			82	3,095,748	3,895,211	4,109,129	213,918
			83	2,490,218	3,030,731	3,178,977	148,246
			84	1,243,000	1,634,338	1,711,110	76,772
			85	3,736,164	5,052,598	5,295,885	243,287
			86	535,584	721,651	754,196	32,545

Crop
Product
TSUSA commodity number, description, and unit of quantity

Country	Mode	Reg	Yr	Quantity	F.A.S.	C.I.F.	Charges
	V	W	81	34,100	40,764	43,597	2,833
			82	784,796	1,025,150	1,104,023	78,873
			83	57,157	73,827	80,060	6,233
			84	250	489	527	38
CHINA T	V	E	83	212,800	250,350	262,200	11,850
			86	11,023	17,500	18,416	916
	V	W	83	186,648	229,090	235,810	6,720
COLOMB	A	E	84	700	3,062	3,351	289
FR GERM	V	E	81	44,092	67,585	69,733	2,148
			82	210,003	264,171	290,240	26,069
			84	163,676	424,502	469,606	45,104
			85	3,104,314	4,433,816	4,944,603	510,787
			86	1,996,803	2,929,170	3,240,255	311,085
FRANCE	A	E	84	441	767	2,090	1,323
	V	E	85	2,966	5,150	5,820	670
			86	4,402	8,184	8,838	654
HG KONG	V	E	82	630,071	757,180	795,979	38,799
			83	112,000	137,595	142,500	4,905
			84	500	666	781	115
			85	992,070	1,333,525	1,375,000	41,475
			86	970,024	1,315,340	1,349,646	34,306
INDIA	V	E	84	33,069	49,834	55,500	5,666
INDNSIA	O	E	84	40,124	70,217	73,033	2,816
IRAN	N	E	81	1,058,198	1,118,600	1,193,235	74,635
			82	546,200	620,379	708,611	88,232
	O	E	83	81,604	177,036	180,910	3,874
	V	E	81	1,756,684	2,260,150	2,463,526	203,376
			82	120,248	202,992	214,452	11,460
			83	3,186,064	3,670,421	3,998,154	327,733
			84	3,469,483	4,692,406	5,240,599	548,193
			85	1,620,261	2,268,637	2,529,411	260,774
			86	2,359,248	3,547,922	3,856,755	308,833
IRAQ	O	E	84	661,380	810,000	869,800	59,800
	V	E	81	246,653	313,240	335,640	22,400
			82	519,823	660,282	709,549	49,267
			83	526,150	718,750	733,750	15,000
			84	661,380	810,000	886,050	76,050
			85	220,460	270,000	299,350	29,350
			86	661,336	809,946	878,066	68,120
IRELAND	V	E	86	2,205	3,415	3,703	288
ISRAEL	O	E	82	177,596	386,598	398,224	11,626
			86	17,196	35,291	44,329	9,038
	V	E	81	1,485,885	2,908,622	2,984,001	75,379
			82	1,319,340	2,839,817	2,918,249	78,432
			83	805,455	1,814,334	1,869,491	55,157
			84	752,768	1,649,946	1,703,576	53,630
			85	1,034,552	2,478,867	2,561,805	82,938
			86	594,276	1,425,784	1,480,508	54,724
ITALY	A	W	84	110	740	894	154
	V	E	83	220	442	456	14
			84	74,956	68,500	72,081	3,581
			85	701,062	626,448	667,899	41,451
			86	881,880	971,903	997,118	25,215
JAPAN	A	W	82	154	2,513	2,990	477
			83	110	4,078	4,581	503
			84	77	3,381	3,695	314
	V	E	81	105,885	162,156	178,173	16,017
			82	134,191	196,523	218,519	21,996
			83	142,630	208,189	229,686	21,497
			84	118,611	215,371	236,216	20,845
			85	44,007	103,502	112,124	8,622
			86	46,436	89,794	97,990	8,196
	V	W	85	881	5,217	5,314	97
			86	10,828	34,468	36,953	2,485
N ZEAL	V	E	81	1,798	1,978	2,699	721
NETHLDS	V	E	81	220,460	239,290	278,790	39,500
	V	W	84	141	388	420	32
REP SAF	O	E	84	3,000	1,871	1,871	
SINGAPR	V	W	83	18	270	295	25
SWITZLD	A	W	84	493	3,250	3,990	740
SYRIA	V	E	84	1,102	742	767	25
TURKEY	N	E	81	92,148	207,905	220,973	13,068
			82	169,215	425,550	438,603	13,053
			84	131,473	456,263	469,444	13,181
	V	E	81	1,003,583	928,009	990,938	62,929
			82	852,494	768,993	827,435	58,442
			83	750,972	940,059	969,393	29,334
			84	302,648	326,304	345,567	19,263
			85	140,722	267,448	280,138	12,690
			86	152,554	262,137	276,349	14,212
	V	W	84	9,921	67,050	67,738	688
U KING	O	E	84	5,302	3,315	3,695	380

Crop Product TSUSA commodity number, description, and unit of quantity Country	Mode	Reg	Yr	Quantity	F.A.S.	C.I.F.	Charges

Licorice, root
1924000 LICORICE ROOT (LB)

Country	Mode	Reg	Yr	Quantity	F.A.S.	C.I.F.	Charges
TOTAL			81	26,421,337	7,666,659	8,236,037	569,378
			82	44,395,828	13,988,975	15,120,905	1,131,930
			83	26,877,693	8,902,831	9,581,714	678,883
			84	28,404,701	9,036,161	9,696,914	660,753
			85	13,362,535	4,058,171	4,280,108	221,937
			86	29,990,507	9,585,655	10,114,132	528,477
AFGHAN	V	E	81	10,119,482	2,904,941	3,092,506	187,565
			82	12,298,587	3,392,554	3,758,183	365,629
			83	6,494,430	1,881,875	2,035,379	153,504
			84	9,278,722	2,873,073	3,127,528	254,455
BELGIUM	O	E	81	6,788	10,385	11,524	1,139
BRAZIL	V	E	84	1,296	1,160	1,248	88
CANADA	A	W	85	12,100	11,269	11,558	289
CHILE	V	W	83	6,462	6,070	6,543	473
CHINA M	V	E	81	11,036,165	3,141,497	3,341,968	200,471
			82	21,086,852	6,353,466	6,809,146	455,680
			83	11,025,719	3,824,133	4,104,677	280,544
			84	11,225,995	3,682,689	3,865,302	182,613
			86	7,275,180	2,310,000	2,364,120	54,120
	V	H	82	1,323	2,049	2,156	107
			83	300	372	410	38
			84	1,200	1,711	1,966	255
			85	1,500	2,253	2,445	192
	V	W	81	127,055	60,853	70,190	9,337
			82	95,940	42,527	49,867	7,340
			83	17,974	18,211	20,175	1,964
			84	1,008	2,332	2,597	265
			85	43,138	24,566	26,504	1,938
			86	44,821	29,448	37,984	8,536
CHINA T	V	E	82	2,205	2,831	3,060	229
			83	4,000	5,566	6,120	554
FINLAND	V	E	82	130,263	131,527	143,890	12,363
FR GERM	N	E	82	4,920	5,092	5,853	761
	N	W	84	14,616	14,780	20,071	5,291
	O	E	83	7,144	7,549	8,959	1,410
			84	2,122	1,390	1,558	168
			85	11,215	9,896	10,209	313
			86	6,614	8,176	8,331	155
	V	E	81	36,209	29,260	34,381	5,121
			82	18,430	16,646	19,459	2,813
			83	53,624	55,430	61,265	5,835
			84	22,490	24,052	26,467	2,415
			85	43,260	36,445	42,830	6,385
			86	103,562	76,758	84,143	7,385
	V	W	81	15,209	11,935	12,265	330
			82	37,991	35,578	39,214	3,636
			83	40,276	37,316	40,973	3,657
			85	41,592	37,238	41,454	4,216
			86	57,451	54,248	59,096	4,848
HG KONG	V	E	81	200	854	865	11
			82	500	434	488	54
			84	927	1,581	1,672	91
	V	H	81	1,080	1,613	1,705	92
			82	661	817	926	109
			86	2,250	3,332	3,667	335
	V	W	82	829	776	820	44
			83	250	1,116	1,221	105
INDNSIA	V	E	85	1,118	1,363	1,496	133
IRAN	O	E	82	8,300	5,055	5,541	486
	V	E	86	1,543	1,981	2,382	401
ITALY	V	E	81	40,312	18,048	21,910	3,862
			82	6,276	11,815	12,640	825
			83	5,437	8,253	9,068	815
			85	1,213	1,642	1,816	174
			86	2,200	4,351	4,865	514
	V	W	81	1,120	1,923	1,932	9
			83	616	1,135	1,219	84
			84	240	409	411	2
JAPAN	V	E	81	2,456,692	742,602	770,452	27,850
KIRIBAT	V	E	86	1,144	1,064	1,224	160
PAKISTN	V	E	81	727,518	234,300	247,500	13,200
			82	6,131,139	2,446,926	2,598,529	151,603
			83	2,297,193	661,850	716,034	54,184
			84	1,763,680	502,400	570,608	68,208
			85	9,666,377	2,807,707	2,910,218	102,511
			86	19,372,927	6,085,897	6,459,276	373,379
	V	W	84	2,204	783	1,005	222
ROMANIA	V	E	82	3,452	6,137	6,745	608
SPAIN	V	E	81	653	523	575	52
	V	W	86	6,911	8,081	8,500	419
SYRIA	V	E	81	777,611	176,500	227,055	50,555
			83	4,582	2,523	2,761	238
TURKEY	O	E	86	5,380	8,009	8,607	598
	V	E	81	1,075,243	331,425	401,209	69,784
			82	4,568,160	1,534,745	1,664,388	129,643
			83	6,761,793	2,302,570	2,473,528	170,958
			84	6,090,201	1,929,801	2,076,481	146,680
			85	3,541,022	1,125,792	1,231,578	105,786
			86	3,110,524	994,310	1,071,937	77,627
USSR	O	E	83	157,893	88,862	93,382	4,520

Lignum Vitae

Lignum vitae, lumber**
2023500 SPN CDR EBONY ETC LUMBR RGH (MBF)
(See Cedar, lumber under Cedar)
2023700 SPN CDR ETC LUMBER DRSD ETC (MBF)
(See Cedar, lumber under Cedar)

Lily

Lily, bulbs
1251000 LILY BULBS (NO)

Country	Mode	Reg	Yr	Quantity	F.A.S.	C.I.F.	Charges
TOTAL			81	6,002,583	1,151,618	1,285,168	133,410
			82	5,728,090	1,104,634	1,240,107	135,473
			83	7,673,787	1,228,202	1,368,460	140,258
			84	15,514,431	2,220,646	2,504,697	284,051
			85	25,960,038	3,511,964	3,951,173	439,209
			86	35,760,841	5,628,417	6,272,619	644,202
BELGIUM	V	E	82	177,936	32,185	34,119	1,934
			84	55,555	2,501	2,655	154
CANADA	A	E	81	2,087	1,591	1,827	236
			82	551	1,093	1,158	65
	O	E	85	19,402	15,622	15,622	
	O	W	82	15,088	13,321	13,321	
			86	1,077	1,264	1,264	
FR GERM	V	E	85	11,000	5,010	8,000	2,990
FRANCE	A	E	81	13	590	976	386
	V	E	81	21,020	10,400	10,868	468
			82	8,890	4,757	5,074	317
			83	17,442	13,582	14,180	598
			84	9,775	7,122	7,533	411
INDIA	A	E	81	94,552	2,772	3,322	550
			82	94,200	3,694	10,651	6,957
	O	E	85	21,000	1,475	2,391	916
ISRAEL	N	E	84	20,000	7,145	10,585	3,440
	V	E	83	1,443	274	301	27
			84	37,981	10,821	11,982	1,161
			85	58,360	22,942	25,437	2,495
			86	9,000	2,000	2,151	151
JAPAN	N	E	81	43,675	10,852	15,018	4,166
			82	34,430	13,469	18,315	4,846
			83	45,330	14,826	18,188	3,362
			84	41,370	13,871	19,115	5,244
	N	W	82	121,780	32,627	34,694	2,067
			84	1	585	639	54
	V	E	81	169,705	55,772	64,649	8,877
			82	161,320	52,786	60,999	8,213
			83	9,500	1,513	1,645	132
			84	8	460	578	118
			85	68,330	31,327	36,616	5,289
			86	62,586	40,840	45,796	4,956
	V	W	81	125,695	38,512	42,098	3,586
			82	19,415	10,007	10,868	861
			83	148,970	36,998	39,678	2,680
			84	109,790	50,590	55,294	4,704
			85	171,750	57,405	64,096	6,691
			86	161,580	69,148	75,870	6,722
MALI	V	W	85	279,075	47,587	54,020	6,433
N ANTIL	A	E	84	10,150	1,827	2,762	935
			85	96,559	18,397	20,918	2,521
			86	13,217	3,518	3,786	268
	V	E	84	299,400	19,526	19,837	311
N ZEAL	A	E	84	20,000	17,321	18,503	1,182
			86	30,000	10,196	10,313	117

Crop
Product
TSUSA commodity number, description, and unit of quantity

Country	Mode	Reg	Yr	Quantity	F.A.S.	C.I.F.	Charges
	A	W	81	45,320	38,917	45,930	7,013
			82	27,400	23,360	28,075	4,715
			83	11,250	9,900	12,305	2,405
			85	8,002	15,691	17,281	1,590
			86	32,754	38,199	42,404	4,205
NETHLDS	A	E	82	99,499	25,794	34,934	9,140
			83	136,685	41,741	48,229	6,488
			84	59,915	21,635	26,149	4,514
			85	77,310	28,564	35,748	7,184
			86	64,175	17,542	19,970	2,428
	A	W	82	54,300	7,902	11,181	3,279
			84	2,425	2,709	4,272	1,563
			86	3,000	1,626	1,918	292
	N	E	81	1,495,432	295,027	319,224	24,197
			82	2,257,768	415,088	461,327	46,239
			83	1,939,038	363,676	402,277	38,601
			84	5,528,376	893,649	986,553	92,904
			85	9,491,614	1,606,684	1,773,290	166,606
			86	11,487,613	2,433,742	2,654,809	221,067
	N	W	81	1,133,025	187,519	226,625	39,106
			82	1,959,921	323,761	357,411	33,650
			83	1,852,324	265,751	306,086	40,335
			84	5,835,288	733,235	857,219	123,984
			85	3,519,020	514,921	560,128	45,207
			86	12,479,607	1,654,718	1,880,875	226,157
	O	E	84	2,900	798	898	100
			86	14,000	10,303	10,303	
	V	E	81	1,239,219	277,792	296,367	18,435
			82	365,982	87,110	94,640	7,530
			83	1,940,294	282,166	300,513	18,347
			84	2,723,454	370,145	400,782	30,637
			85	928,739	202,087	221,493	19,406
			86	569,182	152,545	165,362	12,817
	V	W	81	1,632,840	231,874	258,264	26,390
			82	327,080	55,962	61,547	5,585
			83	1,541,296	192,938	219,336	26,398
			84	279,878	12,038	16,357	4,319
			85	11,209,877	944,252	1,116,133	171,881
			86	10,757,000	1,183,210	1,344,967	161,757
NICARAG	A	E	86	76,050	9,566	12,831	3,265
REP SAF	V	E	82	2,530	1,718	1,793	75
			83	2,715	1,636	1,778	142
			84	5,595	3,167	3,296	129
U KING	A	E	83	27,500	3,201	3,944	743
	A	W	84	1,179	2,089	3,339	1,250
	N	W	84	426,150	38,293	44,412	6,119
	V	E	84	45,241	11,119	11,937	818

1252500 LILY OF THE VALLEY PIPS (NO)

Country	Mode	Reg	Yr	Quantity	F.A.S.	C.I.F.	Charges
TOTAL			81	1,832,719	143,667	154,083	10,416
			82	1,881,664	147,731	156,590	8,859
			83	1,754,632	148,895	158,782	9,887
			84	3,125,328	241,229	258,745	17,516
			85	58,687,861	790,705	897,411	106,706
			86	20,337,440	740,441	844,837	104,396
BELGIUM	V	E	82	5,000	2,405	2,487	82
			85	35,000	1,542	1,710	168
			86	84,000	3,474	3,719	245
CANADA	O	E	85	1,300	2,949	2,949	
FR GERM	A	E	82	52,165	8,863	9,448	585
HG KONG	V	W	86	10,000	4,992	5,154	162
ITALY	A	E	84	515	592	730	138
	O	E	81	115	263	275	12
JAPAN	A	E	82	2,500	813	935	122
			85	1,600	1,856	3,030	1,174
	V	W	81	10,000	2,818	3,220	402
NETHLDS	A	E	82	43,000	2,268	2,628	360
			83	36,000	1,952	2,364	412
			84	14,000	4,319	5,014	695
			86	20,000	1,216	1,503	287
	N	E	81	1,444,664	95,307	101,788	6,481
			82	1,438,011	89,232	94,224	4,992
			83	1,047,757	91,663	96,511	4,848
			84	2,582,338	183,050	194,867	11,817
			85	58,314,961	743,548	844,292	100,744
			86	12,982,037	340,485	396,757	56,272
	N	W	86	296,182	12,936	16,745	3,809
	V	E	81	40,000	1,871	2,056	185
			82	51,000	2,109	2,312	203
			83	322,105	14,454	15,806	1,352
			84	190,370	14,333	15,418	1,085
			85	62,500	3,942	4,361	419
			86	6,048,341	231,625	264,294	32,669

Country	Mode	Reg	Yr	Quantity	F.A.S.	C.I.F.	Charges
	V	W	81	284,940	39,397	41,886	2,489
			82	289,988	42,041	44,556	2,515
			83	348,770	40,826	44,101	3,275
			84	328,065	38,478	42,250	3,772
			85	272,500	36,868	41,069	4,201
			86	603,480	55,273	61,602	6,329
SWEDEN	A	E	86	278,150	89,008	93,521	4,513
U KING	A	E	81	53,000	4,011	4,858	847
	V	E	84	10,040	457	466	9
			86	15,250	1,432	1,542	110

Lime

Lime, citrate
4261200 LIME CITRATE (LB)

Country	Mode	Reg	Yr	Quantity	F.A.S.	C.I.F.	Charges
TOTAL			81	48,501	70,525	74,310	3,785
			82	64,132	90,024	95,730	5,706
			83	56,352	79,669	86,146	6,477
			84	225,457	241,872	255,867	13,995
			85	242,507	72,410	78,000	5,590
			86	112,226	196,643	209,495	12,852
FR GERM	A	E	86	17,637	35,911	40,079	4,168
	O	E	85	242,507	72,410	78,000	5,590
			86	22,046	36,296	39,000	2,704
	V	E	81	48,501	70,525	74,310	3,785
			82	64,132	90,024	95,730	5,706
			83	56,218	77,326	83,701	6,375
			84	225,457	241,872	255,867	13,995
			86	55,116	92,148	97,518	5,370
JAPAN	V	E	86	2,204	5,661	5,788	127
	V	W	86	13,518	24,742	25,154	412
THAILND	V	W	86	1,705	1,885	1,956	71
U KING	A	E	83	134	2,343	2,445	102

Lime, essential oil
4523800 LIME OIL (LB)

Country	Mode	Reg	Yr	Quantity	F.A.S.	C.I.F.	Charges
TOTAL			81	1,171,563	13,860,656	14,026,970	166,314
			82	714,369	9,062,232	9,183,196	120,964
			83	1,354,277	15,894,892	16,036,401	141,509
			84	1,188,383	14,329,394	14,516,244	186,850
			85	1,373,394	13,486,247	13,723,183	236,936
			86	1,392,596	8,550,042	8,664,385	114,343
ARGENT	V	E	81	110	542	603	61
			82	36,324	822,105	824,221	2,116
			83	27,276	757,944	759,393	1,449
			84	16,849	532,445	533,512	1,067
			85	21,607	258,531	261,224	2,693
			86	28,321	151,816	156,136	4,320
BAHAMAS	A	E	81	35	6,475	6,520	45
	V	E	83	32,000	359,336	360,615	1,279
			85	30,000	373,800	375,764	1,964
BRAZIL	N	E	84	58,753	370,773	387,690	16,917
			85	187,538	1,407,751	1,467,781	60,030
	V	E	81	220,689	55,191	70,677	15,486
			82	26,659	147,759	154,694	6,935
			83	52,325	227,661	240,632	12,971
			84	8,000	79,529	80,800	1,271
			85	23,496	207,544	216,071	8,527
			86	20,604	235,094	244,000	8,906
CANADA	O	E	81	48	516	516	
			82	2,989	41,873	41,873	
			83	64	6,448	6,448	
			84	1,082	9,415	9,415	
			85	827	7,691	7,691	
			86	22	2,083	2,083	
CHINA M	V	E	83	17,775	196,020	196,436	416
DOM REP	V	E	81	12,292	132,625	136,892	4,267
			82	10,313	109,720	112,831	3,111
			83	10,859	103,378	105,653	2,275
			84	7,185	78,206	80,552	2,346
			85	4,427	38,072	39,602	1,530
			86	5,771	40,052	41,474	1,422
DOMINCA	V	E	85	5,843	58,070	60,548	2,478
			86	10,665	63,700	67,780	4,080
F W IND	V	E	84	4,000	43,316	44,036	720
FR GERM	A	E	82	11	3,290	3,355	65
			83	55	9,976	10,104	128

Crop / Product / TSUSA commodity number, description, and unit of quantity Country	Mode	Reg	Yr	Quantity	F.A.S.	C.I.F.	Charges
			85	22	3,283	3,530	247
	N	E	81	334	27,615	28,664	1,049
			84	153	13,985	14,412	427
	V	E	86	5,952	61,366	62,157	791
FRANCE	A	E	82	88	918	934	16
			86	126	3,873	4,010	137
	A	W	82	16	313	332	19
	N	E	84	4,420	4,698	5,418	720
	V	E	85	3,087	22,613	23,108	495
GHANA	V	E	82	6,000	66,084	67,613	1,529
GREECE	V	E	86	408	1,869	2,108	239
GUATMAL	N	E	84	10,080	124,732	126,639	1,907
			86	11,942	62,760	67,132	4,372
	V	E	81	23,277	280,596	285,290	4,694
			82	9,249	75,922	77,118	1,196
			83	13,648	153,277	157,240	3,963
			84	9,400	115,888	118,430	2,542
			85	8,365	65,591	67,140	1,549
HAITI	A	E	83	8,000	86,136	88,877	2,741
			84	9,611	114,271	117,983	3,712
	N	E	81	146,369	1,503,935	1,544,206	40,271
			82	104,692	1,056,887	1,091,167	34,280
			83	194,004	1,526,645	1,572,303	45,658
			84	131,328	1,540,181	1,587,014	46,833
			85	93,886	758,588	790,541	31,953
			86	66,297	409,829	424,268	14,439
	O	E	85	1,140	11,462	11,976	514
	V	E	81	2,800	29,568	30,567	999
			84	25,600	200,911	205,888	4,977
			85	12,409	75,160	78,280	3,120
			86	17,727	145,598	150,346	4,748
HG KONG	A	E	85	500	6,425	6,425	
INDIA	A	E	83	2,205	105,000	108,749	3,749
	V	E	86	6,000	48,305	50,100	1,795
INDNSIA	V	E	83	18,000	504,000	510,070	6,070
IRELAND	N	E	84	4,416	4,245	4,867	622
ITALY	V	E	81	1,984	21,387	22,104	717
IVY CST	A	E	81	3,800	189,050	189,897	847
			82	12,000	126,576	131,639	5,063
	V	E	81	10,973	103,821	106,418	2,597
			82	12,516	106,900	110,243	3,343
			83	12,832	128,317	130,950	2,633
			84	31,540	351,787	361,985	10,198
			85	24,544	237,226	243,924	6,698
			86	47,575	269,531	279,858	10,327
JAMAICA	N	E	81	33,222	304,671	311,884	7,213
			82	53,310	487,895	497,778	9,883
			83	79,124	718,913	733,372	14,459
	V	E	83	4,000	35,547	36,000	453
			84	80,477	788,936	803,964	15,028
			85	27,792	253,340	259,880	6,540
			86	1,190	9,942	10,196	254
JAPAN	A	E	81	11	3,250	3,324	74
			83	24	411	625	214
			85	2,400	81,840	86,759	4,919
MEXICO	A	E	83	882	82,896	83,725	829
			84	51	347	394	47
	N	E	81	199,165	3,314,555	3,346,990	32,435
			82	240,023	3,717,709	3,729,250	11,541
			83	668,381	8,613,958	8,621,846	7,888
			84	490,951	6,723,827	6,746,693	22,866
			85	569,902	6,306,955	6,344,975	38,020
	O	E	81	304,180	4,048,428	4,060,259	11,831
			82	7,554	103,955	103,955	
			86	766,859	4,446,508	4,446,948	440
	V	E	81	38,541	1,799,562	1,802,890	3,328
			82	10,443	160,300	161,212	912
			83	42,400	611,929	614,247	2,318
			84	29,616	340,716	344,531	3,815
			85	27,625	535,252	538,405	3,153
			86	210,321	1,415,578	1,437,710	22,132
NETHLDS	A	E	81	224	9,108	9,777	669
			82	11	429	443	14
			83	14	672	709	37
			84	17	753	802	49
			86	66	6,096	6,351	255
PARAGUA	V	E	84	2,381	14,244	14,834	590
PERU	N	E	82	130,368	1,418,516	1,447,855	29,339
			85	298,391	2,408,608	2,454,480	45,872
	V	E	81	108,879	1,305,879	1,329,848	23,969
			83	147,836	1,334,740	1,356,983	22,243
			84	208,871	2,513,900	2,550,531	36,631
			85	4,000	39,000	39,621	621
			86	139,608	823,486	842,606	19,120
SPAIN	V	E	81	7,936	102,975	103,325	350
			84	4,299	11,641	12,099	458
SWITZLD	A	E	84	33	2,027	2,128	101
			86	11	1,408	1,408	
	N	E	86	1,104	13,692	13,959	267
TRINID	O	E	81	5,390	64,593	65,649	1,056
	V	E	82	4,000	42,299	42,984	685
U KING	A	E	81	15,200	179,368	183,325	3,957
			82	5,000	215,793	217,008	1,215
	N	E	81	36,104	376,946	387,345	10,399
			82	42,803	356,989	366,691	9,702
			83	18,573	153,534	162,310	8,776
			84	49,270	348,621	361,627	13,006
			85	11,593	99,635	106,171	6,536
			86	8,009	59,262	60,240	978
	V	E	83	4,000	178,154	179,114	960
			85	14,000	229,810	239,287	9,477
			86	44,018	278,194	293,515	15,321

Lime, fresh or in brine
1472200 LIMES FRESH OR IN BRINE (LB)

Country	Mode	Reg	Yr	Quantity	F.A.S.	C.I.F.	Charges
TOTAL			81	46,858,957	3,961,548	4,079,767	118,219
			82	23,560,611	1,917,912	2,091,415	173,503
			83	36,539,087	2,708,616	2,847,164	138,548
			84	49,387,802	3,753,881	4,015,166	261,285
			85	69,946,742	5,043,761	5,242,958	199,197
			86	56,626,775	4,047,909	4,276,400	228,491
AFGHAN	V	E	84	14,278	4,088	4,250	162
ANTIGUA	A	E	82	463	269	326	57
BAHAMAS	A	E	84	8,847	3,168	5,132	1,964
			85	9,040	6,480	8,635	2,155
	N	E	82	1,384,263	53,854	70,354	16,500
			83	4,868,836	149,940	184,275	34,335
	V	E	84	7,248,746	227,074	308,012	80,938
			85	8,927,425	295,339	375,920	80,581
			86	5,492,226	186,110	229,110	43,000
BELIZE	A	E	81	4,800	3,360	3,740	380
			82	2	455	734	279
			84	14,070	8,040	10,202	2,162
C RICA	A	E	85	3,500	1,327	2,091	764
	N	E	84	51,794	10,384	16,116	5,732
			86	184,657	59,338	100,495	41,157
	O	E	81	1,710	472	539	67
	V	E	81	1,693	568	691	123
			82	6,470	1,580	1,995	415
			83	4,762	945	1,525	580
	V	W	86	30,062	3,750	7,753	4,003
CANADA	O	E	83	67,738	2,677	2,677	
COLOMB	A	E	84	47	300	372	72
DOM REP	A	E	83	17,308	800	2,655	1,855
			84	2,600	1,170	1,477	307
			85	6,605	1,332	2,412	1,080
			86	12,720	1,908	3,693	1,785
	N	E	84	169,577	26,431	45,271	18,840
			85	120,416	19,328	32,600	13,272
	V	E	83	24,585	3,410	4,386	976
			84	2,110	520	770	250
			85	20,700	3,930	6,235	2,305
DOMINCA	V	E	86	7,755	3,567	3,967	400
ECUADOR	A	E	81	27,540	3,500	7,401	3,901
			82	11,528	1,960	3,770	1,810
			84	7,800	1,200	2,247	1,047
	N	E	86	462,302	127,493	133,950	6,457
	V	E	81	405,217	108,357	123,922	15,565
			82	301,535	89,098	98,163	9,065
			83	131,187	32,367	37,122	4,755
			84	102,664	33,631	35,146	1,515
			85	274,877	80,030	81,791	1,761
			86	120,890	39,244	39,824	580
F W IND	A	E	85	1,536	1,536	1,943	407
GUATMAL	A	E	83	4,000	400	917	517
			84	23,360	936	2,857	1,921
	O	E	83	38,750	3,500	4,700	1,200
			85	90,950	6,800	6,800	
	V	E	84	63,945	15,171	19,847	4,676
			85	177,263	10,373	25,592	15,219
			86	222,620	14,520	35,522	21,002
HAITI	A	E	81	742,331	395,359	474,349	78,990
			82	118,020	68,655	92,837	24,182
			84	278,652	62,686	93,848	31,162
			86	52,644	14,342	23,999	9,657

Crop
Product
TSUSA commodity number, description, and unit of quantity

Country	Mode	Reg	Yr	Quantity	F.A.S.	C.I.F.	Charges
	N	E	82	710,154	205,661	284,088	78,427
			83	453,016	128,748	174,399	45,651
			85	217,487	50,752	80,131	29,379
HONDURA	A	E	81	3,870	1,591	2,077	486
			82	168,992	22,285	42,050	19,765
			83	118,365	17,033	31,987	14,954
	A	W	81	10,355	1,300	2,538	1,238
	N	E	81	134,444	16,082	32,101	16,019
			82	231,459	63,243	86,159	22,916
			83	447,800	149,042	182,701	33,659
			84	911,891	206,773	294,702	87,929
			85	587,371	80,616	128,349	47,733
			86	1,149,645	142,817	242,414	99,597
	V	E	84	114,460	15,118	24,585	9,467
			85	31,760	3,176	5,750	2,574
INDIA	V	E	84	2,296	1,673	1,944	271
	V	W	83	179	379	417	38
ITALY	A	E	84	2,789	5,079	6,529	1,450
MEXICO	A	W	84	13,007	3,540	5,176	1,636
	O	E	81	45,355,146	3,391,322	3,392,652	1,330
			82	20,557,395	1,397,632	1,397,632	
			83	30,169,059	2,125,276	2,125,276	
			84	40,208,428	3,067,999	3,068,382	383
			85	59,311,447	4,457,178	4,457,582	404
			86	48,823,913	3,442,663	3,442,671	8
	O	H	81	25,287	1,114	1,114	
	O	W	81	145,459	36,735	36,735	
			82	69,775	12,356	12,356	
			83	193,021	93,780	93,780	
			84	32,123	3,709	3,709	
			85	99,028	12,970	12,970	
			86	59,110	9,060	9,060	
MOZAMBQ	O	E	85	56,104	4,203	4,203	
SALVADR	V	E	84	104,121	45,685	53,342	7,657
THAILND	V	E	84	600	360	431	71
	V	W	83	481	319	347	28
U KING	A	E	84	4,000	1,200	1,717	517
	O	E	82	555	864	951	87
			84	4,133	6,145	7,007	862
			85	7,927	6,891	7,725	834
			86	731	1,097	1,242	145
	V	E	81	1,105	1,788	1,908	120
			84	1,144	1,339	1,529	190
	V	W	84	320	462	566	104
VENEZ	A	E	85	3,306	1,500	2,229	729
			86	7,500	2,000	2,700	700

Lime, juice, concentrated
1652540 LIME-JUICE UNMXD CONCNTRTD (GAL)

Country	Mode	Reg	Yr	Quantity	F.A.S.	C.I.F.	Charges
TOTAL			81	883,082	797,186	838,504	41,318
			82	1,038,808	1,349,450	1,390,035	40,585
			83	317,018	258,831	259,532	701
			84	789,472	503,908	562,630	58,722
			85	503,247	478,437	514,599	36,162
			86	1,504,371	1,212,150	1,243,865	31,715
BRAZIL	O	E	81	371,000	260,500	299,380	38,880
			83	970	323	406	83
			84	602,236	323,319	375,728	52,409
			85	75,600	52,849	59,876	7,027
			86	53,646	27,328	30,414	3,086
	V	E	85	47,719	31,769	36,528	4,759
			86	7,663	15,456	20,456	5,000
CANADA	O	E	86	57,184	149,490	149,490	
DOMINCA	V	E	86	33,183	47,692	52,190	4,498
FR GERM	A	W	85	528	2,508	2,848	340
	V	E	82	5,010	18,312	19,250	938
GHANA	V	E	81	999	2,589	2,796	207
ITALY	V	E	83	900	5,777	6,395	618
			84	1,904	6,416	7,705	1,289
JAMAICA	V	E	81	1,656	12,180	13,482	1,302
			82	6,835	11,920	12,988	1,068
JAPAN	V	W	82	1,369	9,303	11,213	1,910
KOR REP	V	E	86	1,476	5,777	6,415	638
MEXICO	O	E	81	230,870	245,994	246,923	929
			82	584,149	584,374	584,374	
			83	147,259	115,423	115,423	
			84	33,981	46,695	46,695	
			85	167,304	132,135	132,135	
			86	1,216,555	807,259	807,259	
	O	W	81	278,557	275,923	275,923	
			82	160,893	137,556	137,556	
			83	167,889	137,308	137,308	
			84	101,551	79,677	79,677	
			85	30,834	28,461	28,461	
			86	75,140	73,482	73,482	
	V	E	85	6,816	10,100	10,941	841
	V	W	84	46,800	43,770	48,445	4,675
			85	116,220	127,296	139,792	12,496
			86	49,920	53,820	61,317	7,497
PERU	V	E	86	9,424	30,640	41,404	10,764
	V	W	84	3,000	4,031	4,380	349
			85	21,463	23,369	25,844	2,475
PHIL R	V	W	86	180	1,206	1,438	232
THAILND	V	W	82	462	645	753	108
U KING	V	E	82	280,090	587,340	623,901	36,561
			85	36,763	69,950	78,174	8,224

Lime, juice, not concentrated
1652520 LIME JCE UNMXD N CONCENTRATD (GAL)

Country	Mode	Reg	Yr	Quantity	F.A.S.	C.I.F.	Charges
TOTAL			81	33,630	171,802	199,059	27,257
			82	14,835	97,048	107,740	10,692
			83	4,822	26,839	30,680	3,841
			84	16,732	65,522	85,648	20,126
			85	45,267	99,852	118,104	18,252
			86	37,775	108,935	127,094	18,159
AUSTRAL	V	W	86	475	1,691	2,613	922
CANADA	O	E	85	4,940	3,946	3,946	
			86	849	7,226	7,226	
	O	W	86	1,496	9,266	9,266	
CYPRUS	V	E	82	365	2,538	2,613	75
DOM REP	V	E	84	4,800	3,600	4,106	506
			85	23,554	23,624	26,124	2,500
			86	22,900	25,772	29,572	3,800
EGYPT	O	E	84	188	1,050	1,050	
HAITI	A	E	85	55	2,700	2,925	225
HG KONG	V	E	81	674	1,915	2,124	209
	V	W	85	428	1,272	1,392	120
ITALY	O	E	83	76	412	412	
			84	229	1,035	1,057	22
	V	E	81	25,553	148,230	173,400	25,170
			82	13,125	85,181	94,399	9,218
			83	4,539	25,528	29,221	3,693
			84	5,256	25,587	29,874	4,287
			85	10,156	41,283	51,623	10,340
			86	7,738	39,728	49,256	9,528
	V	W	81	938	5,494	7,372	1,878
			83	207	899	1,047	148
			86	750	4,887	5,829	942
KOR REP	V	E	85	2,480	9,625	10,950	1,325
MEXICO	O	E	81	6,465	16,163	16,163	
			86	342	2,142	2,142	
SPAIN	V	E	82	1,312	8,909	10,276	1,367
SWITZLD	V	E	84	1,961	14,910	16,883	1,973
			85	3,654	17,402	21,144	3,742
			86	3,225	18,223	21,190	2,967
THAILND	V	E	82	33	420	452	32
TRINID	V	E	84	4,298	19,340	32,678	13,338

Lime, prepared or preserved
1472600 LIMES, PREP OR PRES, NSPF (LB)

Country	Mode	Reg	Yr	Quantity	F.A.S.	C.I.F.	Charges
TOTAL			81	31,391	27,075	32,002	4,927
			82	41,046	23,622	27,847	4,225
			83	17,941	19,186	21,349	2,163
			84	29,611	25,452	29,170	3,718
			85	200,133	59,138	63,348	4,210
			86	13,691	12,108	13,671	1,563
BELGIUM	V	W	85	1,125	1,355	1,532	177
FRANCE	A	E	84	1,718	2,234	2,955	721
INDIA	N	E	81	9,854	7,472	9,522	2,050
	O	E	81	562	516	577	61
			83	300	429	474	45
			85	3,962	1,304	1,528	224
	V	E	81	1,923	919	1,224	305
			82	7,667	6,860	8,743	1,883
			83	5,503	7,743	8,527	784
			84	4,944	3,073	3,485	412
			85	8,765	4,636	5,492	856
			86	6,063	3,823	4,420	597
	V	W	81	8,281	4,608	5,865	1,257

Crop Product TSUSA commodity number, description, and unit of quantity Country	Mode	Reg	Yr	Quantity	F.A.S.	C.I.F.	Charges
			82	6,843	2,879	3,682	803
			83	688	345	403	58
			84	5,723	3,668	4,309	641
			85	2,143	1,236	1,412	176
			86	1,984	1,206	1,339	133
JAPAN	V	E	83	708	1,184	1,347	163
MEXICO	O	E	85	160,296	26,595	26,595	
PAKISTN	V	E	81	619	535	664	129
			83	6,188	5,739	6,439	700
			85	7,023	6,705	7,546	841
			86	1,288	1,113	1,276	163
	V	W	82	1,858	1,868	2,269	401
			84	1,758	2,666	3,269	603
SINGAPR	V	W	81	1,049	1,680	1,848	168
THAILND	V	E	81	162	312	373	61
			82	2,414	1,646	1,838	192
			83	1,440	964	1,064	100
	V	W	81	4,209	3,824	4,135	311
			82	20,464	7,971	8,714	743
			83	2,101	1,415	1,614	199
			84	9,504	6,425	7,138	713
U KING	N	E	81	1,867	3,217	3,395	178
			84	2,355	2,940	3,295	355
	O	E	81	2,865	3,992	4,399	407
			82	1,050	1,367	1,476	109
			83	1,013	1,367	1,481	114
			85	13,473	15,145	16,538	1,393
			86	4,356	5,966	6,636	670
	V	E	82	375	542	586	44
			84	3,392	4,153	4,376	223
	V	W	82	375	489	539	50
			84	217	293	343	50
			85	3,346	2,162	2,705	543

Litchi

Litchi, nut, canned**
1456500 LITCHI OR LONGAN, CANNED (LB)

Country	Mode	Reg	Yr	Quantity	F.A.S.	C.I.F.	Charges
TOTAL			81	4,573,910	2,322,200	2,557,405	235,205
			82	4,152,914	2,370,979	2,606,659	235,680
			83	4,623,613	2,541,956	2,767,515	225,559
			84	6,937,823	3,295,397	3,666,392	370,995
			85	5,532,986	2,715,618	3,032,086	316,468
			86	8,080,329	4,432,558	4,826,502	393,944
CHINA M	O	E	81	2,994	1,657	1,873	216
			84	9,000	4,873	5,615	742
	O	W	83	125	459	480	21
	V	E	81	76,337	49,446	54,356	4,910
			82	65,838	51,482	56,793	5,311
			83	5,197	8,194	8,726	532
			84	52,208	29,266	34,026	4,760
			85	23,450	9,692	11,625	1,933
			86	6,300	2,730	3,133	403
	V	H	82	200	254	278	24
	V	W	81	60,626	34,776	38,049	3,273
			82	82,848	40,643	44,236	3,593
			83	29,294	20,490	22,317	1,827
			84	78,032	44,281	48,164	3,883
			85	2,456	4,395	4,495	100
			86	48,848	25,073	25,994	921
CHINA T	O	E	81	12,300	6,586	6,973	387
			85	6,750	2,100	2,470	370
	V	E	81	1,332,672	655,369	755,452	100,083
			82	1,279,483	655,457	744,375	88,918
			83	1,147,229	601,164	680,636	79,472
			84	1,371,552	601,716	708,389	106,673
			85	1,400,333	603,020	703,386	100,366
			86	1,581,496	748,965	855,498	106,533
	V	H	81	157,911	70,772	78,727	7,955
			82	183,495	89,427	99,246	9,819
			83	138,976	68,187	74,383	6,196
			84	266,373	107,423	122,119	14,696
			85	246,852	115,298	129,327	14,029
			86	274,292	144,463	159,462	14,999
	V	W	81	2,671,572	1,258,867	1,360,082	101,215
			82	2,025,812	1,099,510	1,192,506	92,996
			83	2,704,593	1,347,229	1,448,683	101,454
			84	4,341,214	1,788,056	1,970,414	182,358
			85	2,724,807	1,174,217	1,294,983	120,766

Crop Product TSUSA commodity number, description, and unit of quantity Country	Mode	Reg	Yr	Quantity	F.A.S.	C.I.F.	Charges
			86	3,619,397	1,648,908	1,775,656	126,748
GUATMAL	V	E	81	1,285	514	630	116
HG KONG	N	E	84	11,641	8,507	9,550	1,043
	O	W	85	6,000	3,600	4,046	446
	V	E	81	825	480	529	49
			82	9,000	4,438	4,840	402
			83	49,008	30,957	34,886	3,929
			84	1,320	2,340	2,772	432
			86	39,680	18,480	20,480	2,000
	V	W	81	14,608	10,872	11,759	887
			82	11,850	7,997	8,462	465
			83	15,310	8,077	8,716	639
			84	18,688	11,835	13,212	1,377
			85	2,040	2,756	2,933	177
			86	49,500	22,935	24,094	1,159
INDNSIA	V	E	86	3,003	1,800	2,032	232
JAPAN	V	E	83	6,300	6,150	7,013	863
			85	6,000	2,488	2,961	473
KENYA	V	W	86	506	1,094	1,219	125
KOR REP	V	W	82	3,000	1,449	1,576	127
MEXICO	A	E	83	2,200	1,750	2,090	340
PHIL R	V	E	84	6,900	6,173	6,627	454
			85	4,500	3,565	3,961	396
			86	3,600	2,925	3,269	344
SINGAPR	V	E	86	10,575	4,935	5,450	515
	V	W	86	63,600	53,350	56,485	3,135
SWITZLD	V	E	82	115	252	268	16
THAILND	O	E	84	3,109	4,039	4,645	606
			85	2,989	2,600	3,283	683
	V	E	81	26,715	29,563	32,467	2,904
			82	39,260	35,392	38,794	3,402
			83	73,459	66,155	71,360	5,205
			84	187,714	185,688	202,562	16,874
			85	184,438	149,147	168,962	19,815
			86	334,790	237,234	262,604	25,370
	V	H	81	4,200	4,210	4,646	436
			82	2,395	2,079	2,446	367
			83	7,181	6,064	6,581	517
			84	8,976	8,116	9,200	1,084
			85	1,495	1,244	1,464	220
			86	5,100	2,916	3,289	373
	V	W	81	211,865	199,088	211,862	12,774
			82	449,618	382,599	412,839	30,240
			83	444,741	377,080	401,644	24,564
			84	581,096	493,084	529,097	36,013
			85	920,876	641,496	698,190	56,694
			86	2,039,642	1,516,750	1,627,837	111,087

Loganberry

Loganberry, fresh or in brine**
1465400 RASPBERRIES AND LOGANBERRIES, 7/1-8/31 (LB)

Country	Mode	Reg	Yr	Quantity	F.A.S.	C.I.F.	Charges
TOTAL			81	6,141,929	3,781,388	3,790,973	225
			82	10,372,212	8,899,228	8,899,728	500
			83	6,581,147	3,586,268	3,589,854	3,586
			84	14,446,492	8,488,523	8,493,559	5,036
			85	13,678,341	9,101,852	9,106,841	4,989
			86	15,762,930	14,388,084	14,398,478	10,394
BELIZE	O	W	85	37,600	23,782	23,782	
BRAZIL	O	W	83	51,200	25,600	25,600	
			84	22,400	12,320	12,320	
CANADA	O	E	83	43,540	13,994	13,994	
			85	1,776	3,271	3,271	
	O	W	81	6,141,465	3,779,909	3,789,269	
			82	10,371,024	8,896,978	8,896,978	
			83	6,446,044	3,532,955	3,532,955	
			84	14,409,243	8,457,708	8,457,708	
			85	13,634,711	9,069,078	9,069,090	12
			86	15,723,803	14,364,084	14,369,866	5,782
CHILE	A	E	82	726	2,250	2,750	500
			83	2,296	3,855	5,351	1,496
			85	3,791	3,774	8,613	4,839
	A	W	83	1,497	3,780	5,819	2,039
			84	1,036	940	1,585	645
DENMARK	V	E	86	4,312	7,718	8,419	701
FR GERM	V	E	83	570	684	735	51
ITALY	V	E	85	463	1,947	2,085	138
JAPAN	V	E	84	500	1,220	1,304	84
MEXICO	O	E	83	36,000	5,400	5,400	

Crop Product TSUSA commodity number, description, and unit of quantity Country	Mode	Reg	Yr	Quantity	F.A.S.	C.I.F.	Charges
N ZEAL	A	W	81	464	1,479	1,704	225
			84	13,313	16,335	20,642	4,307
	V	E	86	34,815	16,282	20,193	3,911

1465600 RASPBERRIES AND LOGANBERRIES, 9/1-6/30 (LB)

Country	Mode	Reg	Yr	Quantity	F.A.S.	C.I.F.	Charges
TOTAL			81	90,446	112,272	130,940	18,668
			82	74,985	193,475	238,681	45,206
			83	750,236	1,084,144	1,375,718	291,574
			84	508,909	1,270,480	1,655,783	385,303
			85	785,410	1,860,640	2,601,195	740,555
			86	1,237,577	2,679,050	3,742,736	1,063,686
ARGENT	A	E	84	4,666	5,950	10,645	4,695
			85	6,599	7,840	13,545	5,705
			86	1,534	2,784	3,889	1,105
AUSTRAL	A	W	84	1,450	604	1,807	1,203
			86	8,112	26,993	33,388	6,395
AUSTRIA	V	E	86	26,061	132,632	137,128	4,496
BRAZIL	A	E	85	3,452	5,628	9,553	3,925
			86	7,204	11,180	19,262	8,082
C RICA	A	E	86	13,464	7,020	10,240	3,220
CANADA	A	H	85	2,250	2,025	2,508	483
	A	W	86	2,077	6,072	7,399	1,327
	O	E	81	2,880	1,299	1,299	
	O	W	81	63,688	66,607	66,607	
			82	25,539	43,239	43,239	
			83	362,434	268,423	268,423	
			84	80,684	131,886	131,886	
			85	112,089	192,040	192,042	2
			86	185,014	298,150	298,150	
CHILE	A	E	81	395	1,080	1,610	530
			82	16,324	53,635	66,938	13,303
			83	293,888	439,994	656,607	216,613
			84	145,412	185,343	341,826	156,483
			85	332,763	431,186	803,516	372,330
			86	626,760	917,144	1,576,963	659,819
	A	W	81	7,214	17,802	30,269	12,467
			82	9,435	28,632	40,391	11,759
			83	1,496	3,285	4,130	845
			85	2,877	4,303	8,361	4,058
			86	1,510	1,370	1,497	127
	N	E	84	36,882	40,481	71,024	30,543
	N	W	84	4,488	6,387	8,458	2,071
CHINA M	V	E	81	565	1,153	1,262	109
			84	250	1,684	1,991	307
	V	W	82	330	1,398	1,496	98
CHINA T	A	E	85	1,323	4,200	7,255	3,055
	V	E	82	1,125	837	954	117
			83	900	670	750	80
			84	2,060	1,060	1,199	139
	V	W	81	2,205	2,419	3,100	681
			84	656	6,000	6,075	75
COLOMB	A	E	86	575	1,044	1,804	760
FR GERM	A	E	84	33	333	407	74
FRANCE	A	E	86	94	2,100	2,686	586
	V	E	84	293	508	541	33
GREECE	V	E	81	7,800	4,982	5,764	782
GUATMAL	A	E	84	1,810	2,052	3,422	1,370
HG KONG	V	E	84	35	280	304	24
IVY CST	A	E	85	1,320	2,400	3,947	1,547
JAPAN	V	H	83	750	3,083	3,420	337
	V	W	81	35	288	292	4
			83	56	367	395	28
KIRIBAT	A	E	86	2,657	2,410	6,010	3,600
LAOS	A	E	86	4,000	3,220	4,720	1,500
N ZEAL	A	E	81	643	1,524	1,812	288
			82	1,354	5,130	7,490	2,360
			83	12,979	45,024	55,400	10,376
			84	18,219	61,945	78,865	16,920
			85	1,964	7,596	9,881	2,285
			86	238	1,157	1,379	222
	A	H	82	287	1,135	1,390	255
			83	1,198	5,384	6,078	694
			84	2,280	10,122	12,348	2,226
			85	4,074	13,831	19,552	5,721
			86	13,218	49,867	67,943	18,076
	A	W	81	5,021	15,118	18,925	3,807
			82	17,004	55,606	72,375	16,769
			83	70,176	301,941	363,022	61,081
			84	186,078	797,289	964,929	167,640
			85	308,639	1,177,305	1,512,356	335,051
			86	321,477	1,190,254	1,536,627	346,373
	N	W	83	1,092	6,207	7,160	953
	O	W	83	1,381	5,586	5,586	

Country	Mode	Reg	Yr	Quantity	F.A.S.	C.I.F.	Charges
NETHLDS	A	W	84	307	948	1,070	122
			85	1,084	4,195	5,964	1,769
			86	619	3,900	4,997	1,097
PORTUGL	V	E	86	4,401	11,267	12,786	1,519
SWITZLD	A	E	85	6,976	8,091	12,715	4,624
			86	2,308	3,365	5,817	2,452
THAILND	V	E	82	3,587	3,863	4,408	545
			83	3,886	4,180	4,747	567
			84	18,000	16,100	17,324	1,224
	V	W	84	5,306	1,508	1,662	154
VENEZ	A	E	86	1,574	2,352	3,922	1,570
W SAMOA	V	W	86	14,680	4,769	6,129	1,360

Loganberry, frozen**
1466900 BLACK CURRANTS, ETC, FROZEN (LB)
  (See Lingonberry, frozen under Cowberry)

Loganberry, prepared or preserved**
1468200 BLACK CURRNT ETC PREP, PRES (LB)
  (See Lingonberry, prepared or preserved under Cowberry)

Logwood

Logwood, dye
4701600 LOGWOOD NOT CRUDE OR PROC (LB)

Country	Mode	Reg	Yr	Quantity	F.A.S.	C.I.F.	Charges
TOTAL			81	32,408	92,550	99,145	6,595
			82	32,389	81,003	86,080	5,077
			83	37,292	93,705	99,378	5,673
			84	37,650	72,576	76,288	3,712
			85	28,416	150,912	156,692	5,780
			86	28,889	117,988	121,119	3,131
CANADA	O	W	83	350	406	406	
FR GERM	O	E	83	14	1,225	1,290	65
			84	60	9,465	9,669	204
			85	80	10,298	10,493	195
			86	75	17,838	18,094	256
	V	E	82	6,614	12,697	13,384	687
			83	8,818	17,609	18,340	731
			84	8,819	18,147	19,010	863
			86	6,393	13,189	13,725	536
FRANCE	A	E	85	214	17,031	17,500	469
			86	44	3,630	3,738	108
	N	E	82	4,459	8,495	8,801	306
	V	E	81	21,385	68,400	72,284	3,884
			82	2,756	4,751	4,938	187
			83	2,205	3,678	3,923	245
			84	4,000	5,139	5,707	568
			85	661	50,687	50,867	180
			86	331	28,331	28,500	169
JAPAN	V	W	82	1,500	1,500	1,838	338
			85	2,205	2,896	3,280	384
MEXICO	V	E	81	11,023	24,150	26,861	2,711
			82	17,060	53,560	57,119	3,559
			83	23,686	66,400	70,865	4,465
			84	24,771	39,825	41,902	2,077
			85	25,256	70,000	74,552	4,552
			86	22,046	55,000	57,062	2,062
SPAIN	V	E	83	70	1,853	1,923	70
U KING	O	E	83	2,149	2,534	2,631	97

Longan

Longan, canned**
1456500 LITCHI OR LONGAN, CANNED (LB)
  (See Litchi, nut, canned under Litchi)

Lupine

Lupine, dried
1403800 LUPINES, DRIED, DEHYDRATED (LB)

Country	Mode	Reg	Yr	Quantity	F.A.S.	C.I.F.	Charges
TOTAL			81	482,077	308,025	351,189	43,164

Crop Product TSUSA commodity number, description, and unit of quantity Country	Mode	Reg	Yr	Quantity	F.A.S.	C.I.F.	Charges
			82	340,816	182,303	212,438	30,135
			83	395,381	183,557	218,179	34,622
			84	376,996	180,833	218,137	37,304
			85	362,994	190,086	223,973	33,887
			86	464,101	207,752	243,858	36,106
ARGENT	V	E	81	11,111	6,829	7,538	709
			85	21,384	6,094	7,153	1,059
			86	39,640	13,053	14,971	1,918
AUSTRAL	V	E	86	90,389	10,460	14,300	3,840
BELGIUM	O	E	83	11,000	6,146	6,146	
CANADA	O	E	81	255	311	311	
CHILE	V	E	85	30,864	7,148	8,049	901
			86	61,728	9,765	12,483	2,718
CHINA T	V	W	83	3,430	2,826	2,945	119
ITALY	N	E	85	180,988	115,658	135,427	19,769
	V	E	81	290,506	244,689	275,344	30,655
			82	230,712	140,960	163,106	22,146
			83	300,794	149,100	177,427	28,327
			84	297,278	162,804	193,822	31,018
			85	41,336	23,550	28,687	5,137
			86	136,355	118,080	137,213	19,133
	V	W	81	22,046	17,550	20,492	2,942
			82	22,046	15,500	18,245	2,745
			83	22,046	11,614	15,066	3,452
			84	11,023	5,750	7,431	1,681
			85	22,046	13,200	15,902	2,702
			86	22,023	19,300	22,705	3,405
MOROC	V	E	81	88,184	15,671	19,349	3,678
			83	32,770	8,676	10,602	1,926
			84	62,691	10,185	14,142	3,957
			86	44,092	11,600	13,646	2,046
PORTUGL	V	E	81	67,814	21,072	25,770	4,698
			82	88,058	25,843	31,087	5,244
			83	25,341	5,195	5,993	798
			84	5,511	1,150	1,756	606
			85	66,376	24,436	28,755	4,319
			86	51,874	22,394	24,525	2,131
SPAIN	O	E	81	2,161	1,903	2,385	482
U KING	A	E	84	493	944	986	42
VENEZ	V	E	86	18,000	3,100	4,015	915

Lupine, fresh or frozen
1367000 LUPINES, FRESH, CHLLD, FROZN (LB)

Country	Mode	Reg	Yr	Quantity	F.A.S.	C.I.F.	Charges
TOTAL			81	88,222	35,950	40,773	4,823
			83	22,046	11,000	13,202	2,202
			84	11,012	6,675	8,067	1,392
			85	18,962	4,959	5,770	811
			86	20,421	9,228	10,495	1,267
CHILE	V	E	85	18,962	4,959	5,770	811
DOM REP	A	E	81	4,950	779	1,051	272
	V	E	81	31,250	3,750	5,123	1,373
ITALY	V	E	81	19,841	18,383	20,674	2,291
			83	22,046	11,000	13,202	2,202
			84	11,012	6,675	8,067	1,392
MEXICO	O	E	81	7,930	668	668	
PORTUGL	V	E	81	24,251	12,370	13,257	887
			86	20,421	9,228	10,495	1,267

M

Macadamia

Macadamia, nut, shelled or blanched
1455810 MACADAMIA NUTS SHELL/BLANCH (LB)

Country	Mode	Reg	Yr	Quantity	F.A.S.	C.I.F.	Charges
TOTAL			82	539,655	1,982,177	2,045,128	62,951
			83	548,778	1,922,740	1,989,874	67,134
			84	1,009,225	2,565,030	2,681,044	116,014
			85	1,514,602	4,846,668	4,989,622	142,954
			86	1,646,820	6,179,085	6,357,484	178,399

Crop Product TSUSA commodity number, description, and unit of quantity Country	Mode	Reg	Yr	Quantity	F.A.S.	C.I.F.	Charges
AUSTRAL	A	E	84	7,055	28,420	35,840	7,420
	A	W	84	96	402	452	50
	N	H	86	118,033	470,882	480,196	9,314
	V	E	84	46,296	159,724	164,124	4,400
			85	172,841	665,105	676,772	11,667
			86	101,677	440,028	445,939	5,911
	V	H	85	213,259	810,684	823,505	12,821
			86	1,653	6,393	6,525	132
	V	W	82	21,771	74,629	76,849	2,220
			84	122,306	387,965	398,899	10,934
			85	269,292	885,647	907,390	21,743
			86	451,115	1,997,478	2,030,775	33,297
BRAZIL	A	E	86	5,423	18,020	22,797	4,777
C RICA	N	E	85	8,010	30,293	32,033	1,740
	V	E	84	3,086	1,214	1,828	614
			85	10,020	42,586	43,910	1,324
			86	18,000	64,500	67,116	2,616
	V	W	86	60,000	243,000	251,250	8,250
CHINA M	V	E	82	1,000	806	902	96
			84	518	2,633	2,712	79
	V	W	85	1,075	6,572	6,812	240
FR GERM	V	E	82	6,118	45,686	48,256	2,570
GUATMAL	A	E	86	5,130	20,500	22,728	2,228
	A	W	86	1,000	2,000	2,366	366
	O	E	86	375	1,694	1,844	150
	V	E	82	150,200	567,224	581,066	13,842
			86	22,696	79,770	83,157	3,387
	V	H	85	56,300	56,300	63,300	7,000
			86	32,500	97,500	101,000	3,500
	V	W	83	171,500	628,048	654,228	26,180
			84	271,200	271,200	313,905	42,705
			85	166,825	299,750	319,081	19,331
			86	353,070	1,005,290	1,044,147	38,857
HG KONG	V	E	85	345	1,756	1,833	77
KENYA	V	E	84	32,857	44,553	45,832	1,279
			85	35,060	93,777	99,634	5,857
	V	H	82	115,437	412,132	427,147	15,015
			83	208,983	700,582	725,468	24,886
			84	26,801	93,147	96,482	3,335
			85	10,844	33,247	34,699	1,452
	V	W	82	102,177	370,922	384,024	13,102
			83	29,709	103,231	106,956	3,725
			84	26,184	81,608	85,098	3,490
MALAWI	V	E	83	2,205	8,269	8,954	685
			84	14,220	36,581	38,394	1,813
			85	13,228	39,960	41,171	1,211
	V	W	86	72,755	273,233	280,733	7,500
REP SAF	N	E	84	35,200	104,650	109,795	5,145
			85	15,213	52,976	58,413	5,437
	O	E	86	17,188	25,850	25,850	
	V	E	82	110,851	388,100	398,900	10,800
			83	136,381	482,610	494,268	11,658
			84	356,201	1,125,280	1,155,595	30,315
			85	486,067	1,680,369	1,720,253	39,884
			86	222,888	841,201	859,191	17,990
	V	W	82	32,101	122,678	127,984	5,306
			84	66,130	221,081	225,276	4,195
			85	46,826	128,038	137,686	9,648
			86	132,145	473,758	486,631	12,873
U KING	V	E	85	10,472	26,180	29,942	3,762
ZMBABWE	A	E	86	31,172	117,988	145,239	27,251

Macadamia, nut, shelled, prepared or preserved
1457010 MACADAMIA NUTS PICKLED,PREP (LB)

Country	Mode	Reg	Yr	Quantity	F.A.S.	C.I.F.	Charges
TOTAL			82	6,300	5,282	5,946	664
			83	9,146	33,682	36,063	2,381
			84	11,971	13,175	15,192	2,017
			85	65,850	143,360	152,841	9,481
			86	67,813	157,268	164,783	7,515
AUSTRAL	O	E	85	7,165	22,068	22,068	
	V	W	83	1,323	5,834	6,008	174
			85	41,336	68,876	70,947	2,071
C RICA	V	E	86	32,500	136,375	140,439	4,064
CHINA M	V	E	82	6,300	5,282	5,946	664
	V	W	84	4,201	2,077	2,229	152
CHINA T	V	W	86	9,000	3,624	4,050	426
GUATMAL	A	E	83	7,823	27,848	30,055	2,207
			86	5,325	5,019	7,184	2,165
	N	E	84	7,770	11,098	12,963	1,865
INDNSIA	V	W	85	1,102	1,250	1,309	59

Crop Product TSUSA commodity number, description, and unit of quantity Country	Mode	Reg	Yr	Quantity	F.A.S.	C.I.F.	Charges
MEXICO	A	E	85	1,725	2,438	3,983	1,545
THAILND	V	W	86	20,988	12,250	13,110	860
U KING	O	E	85	1,980	1,510	1,510	
ZAMBIA	A	E	85	8,794	31,357	35,864	4,507
ZMBABWE	A	E	85	3,748	15,861	17,160	1,299

Macadamia, nut, unshelled
1453010 MACADAMIA NUTS, NOT SHELLED (LB)

Country	Mode	Reg	Yr	Quantity	F.A.S.	C.I.F.	Charges
TOTAL			82	6,612	4,240	4,818	578
			84	2,032	1,367	1,643	276
			85	24,220	64,204	70,220	6,016
			86	43,721	185,755	192,638	6,883
AUSTRAL	O	E	85	4,010	17,938	17,938	
	V	E	86	35,935	161,370	165,864	4,494
	V	W	82	6,612	4,240	4,818	578
C RICA	V	E	85	5,010	21,293	21,911	618
CHINA M	V	E	86	169	1,297	1,433	136
	V	W	84	2,032	1,367	1,643	276
GUATMAL	A	E	85	5,461	7,713	11,601	3,888
			86	4,525	11,313	13,566	2,253
HG KONG	V	E	85	5,339	1,873	2,050	177
REP SAF	A	E	85	4,400	15,387	16,720	1,333
	O	E	86	3,092	11,775	11,775	

Madder

Alizarin, dye**
4102440 ALIZARIN A INDIGO NATURAL (LB)
  (See Indigo, dye under Indigo)

Mahogany

Mahogany, logs
2003537 LOGS MAHOGANY, EXC PULPWOOD (MBF)

Country	Mode	Reg	Yr	Quantity	F.A.S.	C.I.F.	Charges
TOTAL			81	611	332,243	498,526	166,283
			82	803	382,492	571,180	188,688
			83	321	125,781	181,351	55,570
			84	520	292,810	423,327	130,517
			85	331	182,137	248,305	66,168
			86	1,260	215,350	281,091	65,741
BELIZE	A	E	81	2	1,727	2,207	480
	V	E	83	12	5,338	7,124	1,786
			84	45	40,500	62,250	21,750
BOLIVIA	V	E	83	4	4,482	6,481	1,999
BRAZIL	O	E	85	3	3,986	3,986	
	V	E	83	19	9,405	13,609	4,204
			84	51	39,076	39,271	195
			85	24	6,720	7,877	1,157
	V	W	85	73	58,668	73,336	14,668
CAMROON	V	E	83	23	11,879	17,996	6,117
			84	17	7,861	12,391	4,530
			85	18	11,128	16,039	4,911
			86	14	9,716	13,916	4,200
CANADA	O	E	83	34	5,869	5,869	
			85	13	2,299	2,299	
CHILE	V	E	85	18	11,143	15,274	4,131
FR GERM	V	E	83	3	2,223	2,567	344
			84	55	37,406	52,096	14,690
	V	W	85	43	18,702	18,957	255
GABON	V	E	84	19	12,966	16,532	3,566
GUATMAL	V	E	82	8	6,241	8,090	1,849
IVY CST	N	E	84	312	144,977	224,990	80,013
	V	E	81	582	316,881	475,068	158,187
			82	770	363,271	543,473	180,202
			83	226	86,585	127,705	41,120
			84	21	10,024	15,797	5,773
			85	139	69,491	110,537	41,046
			86	157	97,289	126,586	29,297
KIRIBAT	V	E	86	52	12,994	18,112	5,118
LIBERIA	V	E	81	18	9,531	14,885	5,354
			82	25	12,980	19,617	6,637
REP SAF	V	E	86	12	10,922	15,545	4,623
U KING	V	E	86	11	5,921	6,127	206
ZAIRE	V	E	81	9	4,104	6,366	2,262

Crop Product TSUSA commodity number, description, and unit of quantity Country	Mode	Reg	Yr	Quantity	F.A.S.	C.I.F.	Charges
			86	1,014	78,508	100,805	22,297

Mahogany, lumber
2023420 LBR MAHOGNY RGH EXC SDG FLG (MBF)

Country	Mode	Reg	Yr	Quantity	F.A.S.	C.I.F.	Charges
TOTAL			81	35,622	25,906,512	31,655,622	5,749,110
			82	16,683	11,131,980	14,023,512	2,891,532
			83	33,950	21,469,870	27,573,465	6,103,595
			84	43,777	28,273,504	35,696,911	7,423,407
			85	50,256	26,520,263	32,781,118	6,260,855
			86	38,586	20,970,758	25,272,608	4,301,850
ALGERIA	V	W	84	24	8,990	12,808	3,818
ARGENT	V	E	85	18	12,533	16,523	3,990
	V	W	86	3	2,196	2,546	350
AUSTRAL	V	E	86	6	7,482	9,903	2,421
	V	W	83	20	21,502	27,437	5,935
			84	10	9,881	11,987	2,106
			86	18	11,549	13,987	2,438
BELGIUM	V	E	85	37	22,463	27,940	5,477
BELIZE	O	E	82	26	18,629	20,435	1,806
			83	8	6,750	6,750	
			84	3	2,319	2,319	
			86	2	1,518	2,129	611
	V	E	81	4	2,907	3,221	314
			82	91	31,690	35,923	4,233
			83	158	92,633	106,470	13,837
			84	56	53,162	62,182	9,020
			85	88	72,256	78,817	6,561
			86	55	24,858	27,787	2,929
BOLIVIA	A	E	81	4	3,046	3,542	496
	N	E	81	36	30,301	40,897	10,596
	V	E	81	6,544	4,453,359	5,507,673	1,054,314
			82	415	214,463	259,880	45,417
			83	587	477,345	557,553	80,208
			84	937	352,878	484,541	131,663
			85	22	25,838	30,038	4,200
			86	148	84,000	106,526	22,526
BRAZIL	N	E	83	*	311	311	
			85	3,727	1,737,828	2,206,945	469,117
	O	E	81	5	7,808	7,808	
			82	115	22,214	22,214	
			83	52	48,254	48,254	
			84	20	14,882	14,882	
			85	39	21,137	21,137	
			86	30	42,180	42,180	
	V	E	81	27,231	19,927,162	24,294,945	4,367,783
			82	14,630	9,973,474	12,659,596	2,686,122
			83	31,717	19,788,291	25,637,369	5,849,078
			84	40,203	26,051,198	32,907,379	6,856,181
			85	40,291	20,935,036	25,945,234	5,010,198
			86	34,719	18,353,859	22,213,821	3,859,962
	V	W	81	373	307,349	377,853	70,504
			82	194	188,644	233,884	45,240
			83	179	143,259	183,078	39,819
			84	497	307,174	403,966	96,792
			85	776	534,840	680,143	145,303
			86	83	80,691	99,445	18,754
BURMA	O	E	83	2	3,375	3,375	
C RICA	V	E	81	61	23,212	35,466	12,254
			82	61	22,309	30,087	7,778
CAMROON	V	E	84	20	20,232	23,922	3,690
			85	11	5,488	7,123	1,635
CANADA	N	E	83	*	746	746	
	O	E	81	39	16,305	16,305	
			82	118	63,277	63,277	
			83	20	7,162	7,162	
			84	22	14,744	14,744	
			85	56	26,947	26,947	
			86	47	54,223	54,223	
	O	W	82	13	7,854	7,854	
			83	3	3,753	3,753	
			84	13	9,914	9,914	
	V	W	84	22	4,480	5,929	1,449
CHILE	V	E	81	154	115,250	145,040	29,790
			82	12	10,849	12,619	1,770
			84	108	84,460	99,108	14,648
			85	500	193,004	251,130	58,126
			86	194	107,731	122,134	14,403
	V	W	84	2	448	583	135
			85	146	48,692	64,112	15,420
CHINA T	V	E	82	12	9,800	11,722	1,922
			84	12	24,307	50,114	25,807

Crop Product TSUSA commodity number, description, and unit of quantity Country	Mode	Reg	Yr	Quantity	F.A.S.	C.I.F.	Charges
	V	W	85	40	29,845	37,313	7,468
FIJI	V	W	83	2	1,552	1,804	252
			84	9	6,968	8,058	1,090
FINLAND	V	W	85	2	2,261	2,555	294
FR GERM	O	E	82	1	1,023	1,380	357
	V	E	82	1	674	724	50
			84	125	83,583	93,459	9,876
	V	W	85	8	10,217	12,172	1,955
			86	39	71,884	85,470	13,586
FRANCE	V	E	83	10	7,876	8,009	133
			86	7	7,991	11,491	3,500
	V	W	82	10	8,769	11,665	2,896
			84	306	114,638	165,602	50,964
			85	128	46,282	68,190	21,908
GAMBIA	V	E	86	16	32,542	42,955	10,413
GHANA	V	E	84	34	24,949	32,352	7,403
			85	98	64,599	95,620	31,021
			86	473	205,806	268,485	62,679
GUATMAL	V	E	81	465	399,895	449,714	49,819
			82	236	220,337	245,264	24,927
			83	562	466,363	508,609	42,246
			84	452	443,874	493,627	49,753
			85	756	554,593	604,697	50,104
			86	1,411	989,336	1,088,300	98,964
GUYANA	N	E	84	*	300	330	30
HG KONG	V	E	83	38	21,383	26,936	5,553
HONDURA	O	E	81	33	39,092	39,092	
			86	2	3,939	3,939	
	O	W	82	1	1,428	1,428	
	V	E	81	1	1,413	1,470	57
			82	23	24,814	27,727	2,913
			83	30	15,641	18,278	2,637
			84	6	5,157	5,931	774
			85	10	10,379	12,541	2,162
			86	23	19,180	22,991	3,811
INDNSIA	V	E	86	31	29,339	35,579	6,240
	V	W	86	14	7,867	9,356	1,489
ISRAEL	O	E	85	125	46,705	52,870	6,165
	V	E	86	43	129,988	142,318	12,330
ITALY	V	E	84	8	8,050	10,730	2,680
IVY CST	O	E	86	33	37,903	37,903	
	V	E	81	37	31,349	43,271	11,922
			82	369	64,014	88,884	24,870
			83	119	74,379	98,383	24,004
			84	403	271,372	357,237	85,865
			85	391	255,562	331,818	76,256
			86	250	205,753	259,899	54,146
JAMAICA	V	E	86	1	1,480	1,555	75
KIRIBAT	V	E	85	63	38,404	45,534	7,130
LIBERIA	V	E	81	32	26,342	32,506	6,164
			82	40	28,476	39,701	11,225
LIBYA	V	E	81	8	9,382	11,698	2,316
MALAYSA	O	W	82	156	83,882	83,882	
	V	E	84	23	14,950	20,359	5,409
	V	H	84	3	1,080	1,873	793
	V	W	83	82	12,823	14,357	1,534
			86	294	121,797	161,207	39,410
MALI	V	E	85	23	22,093	26,687	4,594
			86	24	24,438	29,343	4,905
MEXICO	O	W	83	37	22,381	22,381	
			85	8	11,363	11,363	
N ZEAL	V	W	84	20	17,765	21,900	4,135
NETHLDS	V	E	85	269	290,602	329,178	38,576
	V	W	84	43	16,974	21,981	5,007
NICARAG	V	E	83	62	27,255	29,595	2,340
NIGERIA	V	E	85	15	15,000	15,500	500
PAKISTN	V	E	84	11	5,618	8,142	2,524
PANAMA	V	E	85	16	14,400	15,738	1,338
PERU	V	E	81	91	93,923	109,582	15,659
			82	48	38,799	45,636	6,837
			83	225	196,031	225,614	29,583
			84	195	170,278	192,337	22,059
			85	477	452,705	513,737	61,032
			86	79	65,819	80,710	14,891
	V	W	81	32	33,682	39,388	5,706
			82	18	17,208	21,735	4,527
			83	1	1,448	1,623	175
			85	166	77,274	94,027	16,753
PHIL R	V	W	84	31	33,321	36,625	3,304
PORTUGL	V	E	85	1,504	742,581	934,936	192,355
REP SAF	V	E	81	19	15,826	20,714	4,888
			83	23	12,258	16,987	4,729
			84	20	11,108	15,393	4,285
			86	13	10,000	13,068	3,068

Crop Product TSUSA commodity number, description, and unit of quantity Country	Mode	Reg	Yr	Quantity	F.A.S.	C.I.F.	Charges
SINGAPR	V	E	85	228	72,410	77,973	5,563
SWITZLD	V	E	86	80	17,868	25,596	7,728
THAILND	V	W	83	8	9,149	10,104	955
U KING	N	E	82	*	399	399	
	V	E	84	56	35,068	46,275	11,207
			85	91	84,788	90,593	5,805
			86	183	137,171	151,876	14,705
VENEZ	V	E	85	67	25,342	32,069	6,727
W SAMOA	V	W	83	5	7,950	8,527	577
YUGOSLV	V	E	84	52	15,759	19,959	4,200
ZAIRE	V	E	81	453	368,909	475,437	106,528
			82	93	78,954	97,596	18,642
			84	31	33,623	40,363	6,740
			85	60	16,796	19,918	3,122
ZAMBIA	V	E	86	265	80,370	105,886	25,516

2023440 LBR,MAHOGNY DRSD EXC SDG,FLG (MBF)

Country	Mode	Reg	Yr	Quantity	F.A.S.	C.I.F.	Charges
TOTAL			81	7,117	5,472,260	6,660,371	1,188,111
			82	10,165	7,278,301	9,175,045	1,896,744
			83	6,970	4,369,324	5,678,335	1,309,011
			84	4,149	2,408,853	2,938,275	529,422
			85	11,443	7,144,847	8,251,030	1,106,183
			86	16,624	8,178,618	9,077,321	898,703
ARAB EM	V	E	84	48	30,394	40,468	10,074
AUSTRAL	V	E	85	27	13,385	15,888	2,503
	V	W	81	5	5,122	6,312	1,190
			86	17	11,669	12,569	900
BARBADO	O	E	86	2	3,497	3,497	
BELIZE	O	E	86	10	6,811	6,811	
	V	E	82	47	36,816	42,408	5,592
			83	147	65,299	75,349	10,050
			84	7	6,596	7,665	1,069
			85	97	65,022	82,383	17,361
			86	3	1,409	1,786	377
BOLIVIA	A	E	81	2	4,004	4,274	270
	V	E	81	464	329,070	404,806	75,736
			82	31	36,162	43,033	6,871
			83	62	54,790	64,217	9,427
			84	181	160,981	175,704	14,723
			85	164	115,009	137,164	22,155
BRAZIL	N	E	84	*	659	659	
			85	1,481	665,883	829,630	163,747
	O	E	81	64	109,930	109,930	
			82	134	229,166	229,166	
			83	33	55,779	55,779	
			84	86	134,721	134,721	
			85	41	65,203	65,203	
			86	414	172,306	172,306	
	V	E	81	5,938	4,576,020	5,606,115	1,030,095
			82	9,350	6,528,108	8,341,684	1,813,576
			83	5,876	3,620,294	4,865,523	1,245,229
			84	3,351	1,716,316	2,164,611	448,295
			85	7,945	5,190,378	5,928,358	737,980
			86	13,753	6,945,287	7,684,782	739,495
	V	W	81	105	105,716	128,435	22,719
			82	59	49,198	50,507	1,309
			84	33	25,549	29,629	4,080
			85	88	43,219	49,018	5,799
			86	106	79,350	100,850	21,500
C RICA	V	E	83	13	11,324	12,992	1,668
CANADA	O	E	81	131	76,205	76,205	
			82	36	58,250	58,250	
			83	143	83,969	83,969	
			84	51	26,350	26,350	
			85	72	74,183	74,183	
			86	208	99,437	99,437	
	O	W	81	35	24,150	24,150	
			82	3	2,745	2,745	
			83	54	41,376	41,376	
			84	46	51,838	51,838	
			85	111	112,136	112,136	
			86	95	113,566	113,566	
	V	W	86	9	6,296	7,506	1,210
CAYMAN	V	E	85	1	1,359	1,552	193
CHILE	V	E	82	35	28,183	32,045	3,862
			83	92	85,494	98,125	12,631
			85	57	39,651	50,820	11,169
			86	118	9,470	11,705	2,235
	V	W	86	34	23,541	28,754	5,213
CHINA T	A	E	86	5	1,090	2,140	1,050
	V	E	83	25	8,944	12,639	3,695
	V	W	83	26	9,025	12,325	3,300
			85	2	5,210	5,608	398

Crop
Product
TSUSA commodity number, description, and unit of quantity

Country	Mode	Reg	Yr	Quantity	F.A.S.	C.I.F.	Charges
			86	27	18,474	20,759	2,285
COLOMB	V	E	81	54	14,185	24,500	10,315
			82	139	36,496	56,056	19,560
F W IND	V	E	83	3	4,027	4,268	241
FR GERM	V	E	83	10	2,566	2,943	377
			85	18	14,918	15,362	444
	V	W	84	1	2,706	2,854	148
			85	5	1,749	2,318	569
FRANCE	V	E	85	22	10,711	13,356	2,645
	V	W	83	9	8,126	11,001	2,875
			85	43	28,200	30,012	1,812
GHANA	O	E	85	1	3,788	3,788	
	V	E	85	13	27,564	30,281	2,717
			86	770	146,084	173,136	27,052
	V	W	86	20	15,812	24,462	8,650
GUATMAL	V	E	82	28	25,446	29,294	3,848
			84	15	5,196	7,649	2,453
			85	489	356,949	404,444	47,495
			86	338	160,017	186,844	26,827
HG KONG	V	E	85	47	17,993	25,107	7,114
HONDURA	O	W	86	7	10,411	10,411	
	V	E	81	6	6,289	7,469	1,180
			82	40	32,182	38,941	6,759
			83	87	77,094	85,142	8,048
			85	2	3,000	3,806	806
			86	44	28,799	32,958	4,159
	V	W	81	1	913	1,050	137
INDIA	V	E	84	2	1,065	1,433	368
			86	24	11,810	15,530	3,720
INDNSIA	A	W	85	8	6,600	7,841	1,241
	V	W	85	74	15,978	20,071	4,093
			86	22	17,110	20,327	3,217
ISRAEL	V	E	86	310	116,612	126,887	10,275
ITALY	A	W	85	8	9,608	11,432	1,824
IVY CST	O	E	83	14	14,548	14,548	
			84	14	20,663	20,663	
	V	E	84	75	49,271	66,040	16,769
			85	41	16,235	21,658	5,423
			86	50	40,828	52,105	11,277
JAMAICA	V	E	82	18	24,379	28,000	3,621
KENYA	O	E	83	28	29,762	29,762	
LIBERIA	V	W	85	11	5,646	7,078	1,432
MALAYSA	O	W	81	14	12,455	12,455	
			82	18	14,156	14,156	
			83	3	2,086	2,086	
			84	3	2,907	2,907	
			86	4	4,270	4,270	
	V	W	85	154	66,196	86,841	20,645
			86	87	44,823	54,689	9,866
MEXICO	O	E	84	1	1,430	1,430	
	O	W	85	12	15,910	15,910	
N ZEAL	V	E	83	14	9,342	11,877	2,535
NETHLDS	V	E	83	27	18,426	23,396	4,970
PANAMA	V	E	84	61	32,538	44,816	12,278
PERU	V	E	81	298	208,201	254,670	46,469
			82	211	158,500	190,246	31,746
			83	193	108,866	109,639	773
			84	83	85,121	95,019	9,898
			85	368	140,552	184,670	44,118
			86	5	5,958	6,561	603
	V	W	85	25	8,136	8,763	627
PHIL R	O	E	82	15	16,956	16,956	
	V	W	84	83	46,977	55,494	8,517
POLAND	V	E	86	84	64,437	76,289	11,852
REP SAF	O	E	82	1	1,558	1,558	
			83	1	2,166	2,166	
			84	4	5,555	5,555	
SINGAPR	V	E	83	80	14,631	16,951	2,320
U KING	V	E	86	1	1,389	1,498	109
	V	W	83	1	2,163	3,035	872
VENEZ	V	E	84	4	2,020	2,770	750
			85	16	4,476	6,349	1,873
ZAIRE	O	E	83	29	39,227	39,227	
	V	E	86	57	18,055	24,886	6,831

Mahogany, plywood

2402340 PLYWOOD, FACE PLY MAHOGANY (MSF)

Country	Mode	Reg	Yr	Quantity	F.A.S.	C.I.F.	Charges
TOTAL			81	9,589	3,936,599	4,580,793	644,194
			82	6,037	2,169,973	2,527,828	357,855
			83	8,875	2,781,966	3,252,478	470,512
			84	10,691	3,174,407	3,700,698	526,291
			85	11,541	3,404,740	3,914,036	509,296

Crop
Product
TSUSA commodity number, description, and unit of quantity

Country	Mode	Reg	Yr	Quantity	F.A.S.	C.I.F.	Charges
			86	16,626	3,541,562	4,095,543	553,981
BRAZIL	V	E	81	8,773	3,634,986	4,236,261	601,275
			82	5,503	1,968,533	2,300,459	331,926
			83	8,022	2,448,006	2,880,566	432,560
			84	9,343	2,686,361	3,175,831	489,470
			85	10,173	2,922,656	3,407,294	484,638
			86	7,519	2,357,278	2,705,182	347,904
	V	W	84	166	13,615	16,462	2,847
			85	42	14,584	15,247	663
C RICA	V	E	81	310	111,476	132,242	20,766
			82	22	7,000	8,967	1,967
			83	227	58,020	68,611	10,591
			84	213	57,605	67,965	10,360
			85	46	14,336	15,486	1,150
			86	184	43,472	49,634	6,162
CANADA	O	E	81	4	4,263	4,263	
			82	17	24,823	24,823	
			83	108	55,706	55,706	
			84	282	117,770	117,770	
			85	229	188,977	188,977	
			86	267	135,797	135,797	
	O	W	81	3	4,457	4,457	
			82	3	2,218	2,218	
			83	2	324	324	
			84	9	3,258	3,258	
			85	32	15,804	15,804	
			86	46	34,474	34,474	
	V	E	83	13	10,735	11,622	887
CHILE	V	E	86	57	28,865	40,701	11,836
CHINA T	V	E	84	256	70,379	72,861	2,482
COLOMB	V	E	85	35	13,410	14,473	1,063
DENMARK	V	E	84	20	23,439	25,979	2,540
ECUADOR	V	E	85	96	8,285	9,828	1,543
			86	1,219	66,282	69,615	3,333
FR GERM	A	E	83	1	1,386	1,960	574
	O	E	85	333	56,634	58,190	1,556
	V	E	81	6	9,400	10,095	695
	V	W	86	44	29,325	33,969	4,644
FRANCE	A	E	83	1	685	1,585	900
	N	E	83	3	4,030	7,037	3,007
	V	E	83	116	33,565	40,821	7,256
			84	126	38,937	42,013	3,076
HONDURA	V	E	81	246	62,290	72,183	9,893
			82	1	535	609	74
			86	37	13,835	15,483	1,648
INDIA	V	W	85	3	2,325	3,025	700
INDNSIA	V	E	83	8	6,000	7,060	1,060
			85	68	9,419	10,948	1,529
			86	6,155	544,763	673,159	128,396
	V	W	86	138	18,388	22,820	4,432
ISRAEL	V	W	84	24	7,727	8,214	487
ITALY	A	E	86	4	8,174	8,971	797
	V	E	82	125	10,070	12,304	2,234
			83	115	15,998	17,758	1,760
			85	10	10,542	11,450	908
			86	27	14,047	14,406	359
KOR REP	V	E	82	61	12,192	13,566	1,374
MACAO	V	E	86	354	24,998	30,100	5,102
MEXICO	O	E	85	3	1,056	1,056	
NETHLDS	V	E	81	114	34,799	37,828	3,029
			82	94	56,103	64,116	8,013
			83	45	62,643	67,367	4,724
			84	61	43,078	46,984	3,906
			85	44	50,748	55,914	5,166
			86	46	50,642	53,611	2,969
	V	W	81	13	15,179	17,086	1,907
			82	6	4,779	5,740	961
			83	25	30,720	33,314	2,594
			84	58	68,852	75,011	6,159
			85	15	7,760	7,915	155
			86	29	31,184	32,495	1,311
PHIL R	V	E	82	152	42,204	50,878	8,674
			83	52	15,371	18,146	2,775
			84	89	22,352	26,246	3,894
			85	14	3,384	3,925	541
	V	H	86	444	117,076	149,558	32,482
	V	W	83	70	6,336	7,048	712
			84	26	2,304	2,575	271
			85	321	29,852	35,893	6,041
REP SAF	V	E	81	63	26,374	27,669	1,295
SINGAPR	V	H	81	41	18,507	23,293	4,786
			86	50	16,992	19,192	2,200
SPAIN	V	E	85	30	3,172	4,762	1,590

Crop Product TSUSA commodity number, description, and unit of quantity Country	Mode	Reg	Yr	Quantity	F.A.S.	C.I.F.	Charges
U KING	V	E	81	1	537	742	205
			82	28	15,863	17,939	2,076
			83	49	14,502	14,810	308
			85	40	42,474	44,116	1,642
	V	W	81	15	14,331	14,674	343
			82	25	25,653	26,209	556
			83	18	17,939	18,743	804
			84	18	18,730	19,529	799
			85	7	9,322	9,733	411
			86	6	5,970	6,376	406

Maize

Corn, canned
1418300 CORN IN AIRTIGHT CONTAINERS (LB)

Country	Mode	Reg	Yr	Quantity	F.A.S.	C.I.F.	Charges
TOTAL			81	4,462,451	1,843,502	2,066,970	223,468
			82	5,204,071	2,060,218	2,356,215	295,997
			83	8,587,165	3,615,604	4,040,937	425,333
			84	10,116,757	4,082,536	4,685,816	603,280
			85	11,306,837	4,377,821	4,996,126	618,305
			86	14,582,894	5,235,608	5,896,013	660,405
AUSTRIA	V	E	83	840	1,275	1,368	93
C RICA	V	E	81	768	649	722	73
			84	1,800	2,400	3,112	712
CANADA	N	E	82	88,792	36,583	41,553	4,970
	O	E	81	79,567	34,722	39,166	4,444
			82	30,800	9,798	9,798	
			83	636,778	200,077	208,399	8,322
			84	680,839	220,345	236,095	15,750
			85	650,000	121,133	121,133	
			86	382,144	99,270	99,270	
	V	E	81	38,700	16,481	18,689	2,208
CHINA M	V	E	84	4,216	3,000	3,284	284
			85	9,000	4,158	4,342	184
			86	4,500	1,940	2,134	194
	V	W	83	5,737	900	971	71
CHINA T	N	E	83	129,070	43,180	50,797	7,617
			85	2,162,894	900,358	1,056,168	155,810
	N	W	84	1,206,489	479,028	526,160	47,132
			86	589,964	261,403	286,864	25,461
	O	E	85	15,300	8,336	9,691	1,355
	O	W	85	4,560	3,056	3,331	275
			86	17,081	10,720	10,840	120
	V	E	81	2,484,659	1,008,920	1,142,734	133,814
			82	3,069,903	1,112,982	1,305,098	192,116
			83	3,368,919	1,460,195	1,669,287	209,092
			84	3,776,476	1,515,583	1,807,919	292,336
			85	1,013,266	389,077	468,701	79,624
			86	2,377,522	896,909	1,029,794	132,885
	V	H	81	130,483	53,034	60,773	7,739
			82	96,426	42,266	48,300	6,034
			83	160,798	67,925	75,985	8,060
			84	155,157	68,712	80,654	11,942
			85	132,183	56,513	64,777	8,264
			86	123,869	56,654	64,126	7,472
	V	W	81	1,513,017	636,722	699,019	62,297
			82	1,419,909	588,898	650,561	61,663
			83	2,865,523	1,160,843	1,279,795	118,952
			84	2,097,556	846,675	947,818	101,143
			85	3,203,752	1,219,975	1,350,513	130,538
			86	2,524,227	894,109	978,297	84,188
DENMARK	V	W	85	2,640	1,056	1,137	81
DOM REP	V	E	85	2,835	1,134	1,295	161
FR GERM	V	E	81	99	324	352	28
			83	859	1,286	1,378	92
			84	1,493	4,473	5,058	585
			85	2,092	5,202	5,628	426
			86	3,520	7,304	7,874	570
	V	W	84	1,347	3,668	3,857	189
			85	661	1,725	2,780	1,055
FRANCE	A	E	84	897	261	877	616
	V	E	81	11,020	4,290	4,403	113
			83	32	954	1,283	329
			84	4,629	6,035	6,743	708
			85	4,748	6,822	7,198	376
			86	21,728	8,146	9,294	1,148
	V	W	84	8,086	6,011	6,620	609
GAMBIA	V	W	81	4,320	2,772	3,022	250
GUATMAL	A	W	83	706	731	932	201

Country	Mode	Reg	Yr	Quantity	F.A.S.	C.I.F.	Charges
	V	E	82	47,412	35,084	37,283	2,199
			83	5,602	4,794	5,176	382
			85	2,400	1,800	2,189	389
HG KONG	V	E	84	2,250	980	1,038	58
	V	W	83	18,000	8,342	9,643	1,301
			84	3,825	990	1,074	84
			86	89,100	33,103	39,160	6,057
INDIA	V	W	82	309	325	455	130
JAPAN	V	E	81	42,694	17,669	19,869	2,200
			84	23,897	10,290	12,151	1,861
			85	20,839	9,325	11,039	1,714
			86	19,049	11,079	12,274	1,195
	V	W	83	145	534	582	48
			84	2,946	3,814	4,302	488
			85	37,875	17,296	20,257	2,961
KOR REP	V	E	81	41,513	11,310	14,070	2,760
			83	11,250	3,948	4,436	488
			84	34,425	5,905	8,095	2,190
	V	H	82	1,200	609	718	109
	V	W	81	4,200	1,750	1,912	162
			82	3,375	1,590	1,730	140
			83	4,800	1,957	2,149	192
			84	35,532	14,214	15,587	1,373
			85	36,060	13,784	15,206	1,422
MACAO	V	E	86	9,563	3,875	4,357	482
MALAYSA	V	E	84	32,513	15,052	17,000	1,948
			86	38,250	7,900	9,347	1,447
MEXICO	O	W	84	22,496	4,912	4,912	
			85	13,228	4,800	4,800	
PHIL R	V	H	84	646	939	1,068	129
	V	W	83	270	262	287	25
SALVADR	V	E	83	7,452	5,394	5,817	423
			84	600	790	855	65
	V	W	84	1,200	1,628	1,819	191
			85	1,800	2,306	2,729	423
SINGAPR	V	E	86	120,549	32,930	38,304	5,374
	V	W	85	38,262	11,920	13,505	1,585
			86	31,746	11,405	12,750	1,345
SPAIN	V	E	85	130,844	47,808	79,378	31,570
SWITZLD	V	E	85	2,690	4,176	4,309	133
THAILND	O	E	86	12,750	11,500	11,500	
	V	E	81	34,425	15,725	19,163	3,438
			82	217,478	109,592	125,387	15,795
			83	920,586	424,987	473,232	48,245
			84	1,539,697	633,828	734,706	100,878
			85	2,882,773	1,116,435	1,278,305	161,870
			86	5,396,033	1,818,492	2,083,840	265,348
	V	H	83	1,495	871	945	74
			84	4,734	2,307	2,640	333
			86	3,646	1,585	1,787	202
	V	W	81	76,986	39,134	43,076	3,942
			82	228,467	122,491	135,332	12,841
			83	448,303	227,149	248,475	21,326
			84	473,011	230,696	252,372	21,676
			85	936,135	429,626	467,715	38,089
			86	2,817,653	1,067,284	1,194,201	126,917

Corn, fresh or frozen
1357500 CORN ON COB FRSH CHLD O FROZ (LB)

Country	Mode	Reg	Yr	Quantity	F.A.S.	C.I.F.	Charges
TOTAL			81	365,841	57,930	60,252	2,322
			82	327,738	39,107	41,512	2,405
			83	2,269,155	299,021	299,143	122
			84	8,632,662	1,219,524	1,221,080	1,556
			85	6,808,799	1,038,979	1,043,645	4,666
			86	7,679,529	1,182,486	1,273,148	90,662
C RICA	V	E	81	11,400	1,950	2,642	692
			82	37,776	1,118	1,512	394
CANADA	O	E	81	327,909	42,241	42,241	
			82	32,000	2,074	2,074	
			83	85,774	7,099	7,099	
			84	779,113	115,766	115,766	
			85	18,000	2,793	2,793	
			86	859,200	60,388	60,388	
	O	W	84	35,500	3,856	3,856	
			86	80,000	7,218	7,218	
	V	E	86	3,310	2,568	3,057	489
CHILE	A	E	84	817	275	1,193	918
			85	6,859	3,060	7,726	4,666
	V	E	86	623,867	110,121	193,190	83,069
CHINA T	A	W	86	1,800	1,872	4,750	2,878
	V	H	84	4,992	4,903	5,541	638

Crop
Product
TSUSA commodity number, description, and unit of quantity

Country	Mode	Reg	Yr	Quantity	F.A.S.	C.I.F.	Charges
	V	W	86	68,080	57,322	61,548	4,226
GUATMAL	A	W	83	300	305	427	122
MEXICO	O	E	81	3,362	574	574	
	O	W	81	2,378	406	406	
			82	245,797	25,107	25,107	
			83	2,183,081	291,617	291,617	
			84	7,812,240	1,094,724	1,094,724	
			85	6,783,940	1,033,126	1,033,126	
			86	6,043,272	942,997	942,997	
NICARAG	V	W	81	20,792	12,759	14,389	1,630
			82	12,165	10,808	12,819	2,011

Corn, milled for humans
1312000 CORN, MILLED, EDIBLE (CWT)

Country	Mode	Reg	Yr	Quantity	F.A.S.	C.I.F.	Charges
TOTAL			81	43,634	546,335	554,658	8,323
			82	34,980	543,482	556,751	13,269
			83	36,939	553,632	573,042	19,410
			84	104,905	708,383	724,941	16,558
			85	383,255	3,365,264	3,655,087	289,823
			86	75,436	1,237,542	1,335,491	97,949
ARGENT	V	E	85	264,042	1,434,226	1,651,101	216,875
			86	28,478	238,028	301,245	63,217
BRAZIL	V	E	81	168	3,739	4,400	661
			82	92	5,980	6,697	717
			84	5	360	384	24
			85	22,025	123,000	175,000	52,000
CANADA	O	E	81	16,036	448,615	448,615	
			82	16,898	429,866	429,866	
			83	18,018	432,849	432,849	
			84	22,289	598,516	598,516	
			85	44,798	997,921	997,921	
			86	36,276	823,292	823,292	
	O	W	81	239	10,500	10,500	
CHINA M	V	W	83	2,100	1,756	1,847	91
CHINA T	V	W	82	231	735	779	44
COLOMB	A	E	86	22	2,300	3,560	1,260
	N	E	85	770	24,127	28,167	4,040
	O	E	85	1,102	31,500	35,608	4,108
	V	E	81	2,293	2,495	2,636	141
			82	374	14,450	16,449	1,999
			83	356	15,300	18,267	2,967
			84	56,444	47,206	54,908	7,702
			85	389	12,916	15,060	2,144
			86	389	12,916	16,000	3,144
DOM REP	A	E	83	5	285	297	12
ECUADOR	A	E	85	18	2,300	2,739	439
	V	E	81	71	1,450	1,702	252
			82	26	1,000	1,210	210
			83	115	4,375	5,359	984
			84	308	9,180	11,856	2,676
			85	190	4,500	6,046	1,546
			86	180	10,800	12,760	1,960
FR GERM	V	E	86	48	1,055	1,971	916
FRANCE	A	E	83	44	2,200	3,918	1,718
	V	E	82	457	10,286	12,066	1,780
			85	3	3,113	3,262	149
GREECE	O	E	83	25	1,067	1,067	
GUATMAL	A	W	84	10	990	1,863	873
HG KONG	V	W	84	2,425	2,370	2,546	176
HONDURA	V	E	82	5	468	519	51
ITALY	N	E	83	21	713	2,275	1,562
	V	E	81	5,458	4,665	5,448	783
			83	23	2,304	2,619	315
			84	9	815	1,585	770
			86	62	1,960	2,235	275
	V	W	81	11	309	399	90
			82	13	379	468	89
			83	69	2,301	2,827	526
			84	42	1,586	1,792	206
			85	116	1,676	2,282	606
JAPAN	A	W	86	315	16,432	27,280	10,848
	V	H	84	14	1,416	1,583	167
	V	W	82	2	327	357	30
			83	1	2,250	2,718	468
KOR REP	V	E	81	1,200	1,295	1,367	72
			82	4,074	23,974	24,554	580
			83	2,499	9,352	10,259	907
			84	86	3,807	4,418	611
			85	114	4,410	6,185	1,775
			86	31	1,160	1,318	158
	V	W	81	25	2,546	2,808	262

Crop
Product
TSUSA commodity number, description, and unit of quantity

Country	Mode	Reg	Yr	Quantity	F.A.S.	C.I.F.	Charges
			83	26	1,827	2,031	204
			85	50	2,691	3,035	344
			86	100	4,116	4,812	696
MEXICO	O	E	85	41,036	649,022	649,022	
	O	W	81	9,978	23,684	23,684	
			82	7,008	13,241	13,241	
			83	435	6,889	6,889	
			84	13,635	31,054	31,054	
			85	1,384	22,496	22,496	
			86	108	1,680	1,680	
NETHLDS	A	E	85	44	1,003	3,407	2,404
	V	E	83	42	1,313	1,488	175
PERU	V	E	84	1,653	1,200	1,292	92
			85	70	6,000	6,360	360
			86	4,122	10,220	11,205	985
PORTUGL	V	E	81	7,355	27,345	31,707	4,362
			82	5,347	15,108	17,840	2,732
			83	53	1,214	1,511	297
			84	5,789	5,723	6,329	606
			85	950	1,200	1,538	338
			86	35	2,217	2,412	195
SALVADR	A	W	84	2,000	2,000	2,827	827
	V	W	86	400	17,831	19,747	1,916
THAILND	V	W	81	800	19,692	21,392	1,700
U KING	V	E	83	23	317	363	46
	V	W	82	13	307	422	115
VENEZ	A	E	82	100	7,599	9,459	1,860
			83	242	5,984	8,707	2,723
			84	196	2,160	3,988	1,828
	N	E	82	340	19,762	22,824	3,062
			83	12,836	60,916	67,331	6,415
	O	E	83	6	420	420	
	V	E	85	6,154	43,163	45,858	2,695
			86	4,870	93,535	105,914	12,379

Corn, milled not for humans
1316000 CORN NFIT HUMAN CONSUMPTION (CWT)

Country	Mode	Reg	Yr	Quantity	F.A.S.	C.I.F.	Charges
TOTAL			81	68,071	715,371	821,671	106,300
			82	154,326	1,707,360	1,756,982	49,622
			83	279,304	3,228,982	3,368,513	139,531
			84	347,912	3,579,301	3,659,734	80,433
			85	393,364	3,517,651	3,711,403	193,752
			86	142,161	931,103	999,201	68,098
ARGENT	V	E	83	1,458	11,902	15,539	3,637
AUSTRAL	V	E	83	66	1,184	1,923	739
BRAZIL	V	E	81	38,285	337,395	443,695	106,300
			82	19,400	162,800	206,454	43,654
			83	41,857	293,189	427,924	134,735
			84	77,427	428,201	498,831	70,630
			85	171,033	875,540	1,069,197	193,657
			86	26,981	150,531	216,413	65,882
CANADA	O	E	81	29,786	377,976	377,976	
			82	134,926	1,544,560	1,550,528	5,968
			83	235,835	2,921,360	2,921,360	
			84	270,470	3,150,761	3,160,409	9,648
			85	222,331	2,642,111	2,642,206	95
			86	113,793	771,925	771,925	
COLOMB	V	E	86	45	2,750	3,125	375
ECUADOR	A	E	86	37	1,260	2,570	1,310
FRANCE	V	E	84	15	339	494	155
KOR REP	V	E	86	1,305	4,637	5,168	531
U KING	V	E	83	88	1,347	1,767	420

Corn, seed
1303000 CORN OR MAIZE CERTFIED SEED (BU)

Country	Mode	Reg	Yr	Quantity	F.A.S.	C.I.F.	Charges
TOTAL			81	384,851	12,611,825	13,351,134	739,357
			82	345,785	11,579,086	12,473,537	894,451
			83	219,055	5,939,349	5,945,151	5,802
			84	692,925	22,288,711	23,180,249	891,538
			85	495,009	14,044,540	14,322,810	278,270
			86	333,884	9,160,482	9,184,258	23,776
ARGENT	V	E	81	41,630	1,624,197	1,764,055	139,858
			86	2,793	79,160	83,118	3,958
BRAZIL	V	E	81	19,948	189,950	256,617	66,667
			82	116	2,074	2,350	276
			83	237	4,950	7,420	2,470
			84	72	1,661	1,884	223
CANADA	N	E	85	362,556	9,413,028	9,413,028	

Crop Product TSUSA commodity number, description, and unit of quantity Country	Mode	Reg	Yr	Quantity	F.A.S.	C.I.F.	Charges
	O	E	81	162,640	5,241,067	5,241,019	
			82	164,583	4,983,659	4,983,659	
			83	217,747	5,908,597	5,908,597	
			84	307,392	9,125,617	9,125,617	
			85	28,475	939,792	939,792	
			86	318,221	8,704,239	8,704,239	
CHILE	A	E	84	182	5,552	11,148	5,596
			86	111	3,059	3,375	316
	V	E	84	212,973	6,900,350	7,258,486	358,136
			85	58,295	2,079,193	2,202,091	122,898
			86	450	18,500	20,036	1,536
ECUADOR	A	E	81	145	1,219	1,965	746
	V	E	84	232	6,500	7,715	1,215
			85	415	13,200	13,304	104
			86	170	5,750	6,741	991
FR GERM	V	E	82	39,959	1,454,485	1,555,246	100,761
FRANCE	A	E	82	8	2,047	2,384	337
	O	E	84	465	23,810	23,810	
	V	E	81	11,815	228,281	236,185	7,904
			82	12	586	782	196
			86	21	1,263	1,433	170
HUNGARY	O	E	85	1,810	79,874	83,845	3,971
			86	2,835	75,600	75,600	
	V	E	81	34,705	1,263,264	1,367,581	104,317
			82	66,828	2,401,417	2,958,674	557,257
			84	23,931	871,044	985,140	114,096
			86	7,848	170,022	184,902	14,880
INDIA	V	E	83	962	17,198	19,850	2,652
			84	777	16,204	19,047	2,843
ITALY	A	E	81	95	10,644	14,251	3,607
			82	25	4,464	5,128	664
	V	E	81	888	102,823	108,841	6,018
			82	385	43,411	48,844	5,433
			83	109	8,604	9,284	680
			84	15	2,333	2,495	162
			85	59	3,885	4,311	426
			86	289	19,406	21,331	1,925
KOR REP	V	W	85	15	1,742	1,953	211
MEXICO	O	E	81	39	421	421	
			84	43	1,320	1,320	
			86	126	3,259	3,259	
PERU	V	E	84	984	25,000	28,011	3,011
ROMANIA	A	E	82	7	260	690	430
	O	E	85	118	7,898	7,898	
			86	1,020	80,224	80,224	
	V	E	81	89,130	3,244,403	3,512,883	268,480
			82	72,547	2,639,756	2,856,328	216,572
			84	132,669	4,829,177	5,219,067	389,890
			85	6,023	219,245	243,579	24,334
SPAIN	V	E	82	1,315	46,927	59,452	12,525
			85	3,937	150,442	175,000	24,558
YUGOSLV	V	E	81	23,816	705,556	847,316	141,760
			84	13,190	480,143	496,509	16,366
			85	33,306	1,136,241	1,238,009	101,768

1303200 YELLOW DENT CORN EX CERTIFD (BU)

Country	Mode	Reg	Yr	Quantity	F.A.S.	C.I.F.	Charges
TOTAL			**81**	**225,770**	**1,047,272**	**1,389,301**	**342,028**
			82	**405,350**	**1,002,383**	**1,212,789**	**210,406**
			83	**361,943**	**1,227,366**	**1,461,377**	**234,011**
			84	**613,995**	**2,040,412**	**2,190,785**	**150,373**
			85	**1,016,561**	**2,910,932**	**3,089,408**	**178,476**
			86	**8,076,152**	**19,309,724**	**19,638,236**	**328,512**
ARGENT	V	E	81	48,187	246,024	309,672	63,648
			82	136,816	401,265	551,851	150,586
			83	144,398	535,350	708,751	173,401
			84	78,735	373,804	483,822	110,018
			85	236,136	953,541	1,025,784	72,243
			86	468,816	1,232,812	1,561,153	328,341
BRAZIL	V	E	81	147,549	716,100	994,300	278,200
			82	34,643	123,200	182,290	59,090
			83	32,046	115,060	175,670	60,610
CANADA	O	E	81	29,980	84,398	84,399	
			82	233,867	476,449	476,449	
			83	185,499	576,956	576,956	
			84	398,539	1,121,041	1,121,041	
			85	622,332	1,426,198	1,426,198	
			86	7,605,386	18,068,449	18,068,505	56
	O	W	84	23,110	88,886	88,886	
	V	H	84	113,398	453,868	493,868	40,000
			85	158,093	531,193	637,426	106,233
CHILE	A	E	84	38	2,288	2,540	252
ECUADOR	V	E	81	54	750	930	180
FR GERM	O	E	86	1,949	6,436	6,436	

Crop Product TSUSA commodity number, description, and unit of quantity Country	Mode	Reg	Yr	Quantity	F.A.S.	C.I.F.	Charges
FRANCE	A	E	84	175	525	628	103
ITALY	A	E	86	1	2,027	2,142	115
MEXICO	O	E	82	24	1,469	2,199	730

1303700 CORN EX CERTIFIED SEED NSPF (BU)

Country	Mode	Reg	Yr	Quantity	F.A.S.	C.I.F.	Charges
TOTAL			**81**	**598,282**	**2,406,045**	**3,236,696**	**831,003**
			82	**183,319**	**919,853**	**1,133,757**	**213,904**
			83	**234,206**	**959,819**	**1,070,431**	**110,612**
			84	**1,448,318**	**5,711,263**	**6,380,760**	**669,497**
			85	**937,445**	**2,842,392**	**3,175,704**	**333,312**
			86	**1,614,843**	**5,008,670**	**5,859,342**	**850,672**
ARGENT	V	E	81	483,702	1,683,032	2,295,701	612,669
			82	94,032	277,073	372,615	95,542
			83	184,118	751,667	789,250	37,583
			84	1,405,061	5,614,950	6,279,131	664,181
			85	908,762	2,660,412	2,990,959	330,547
			86	1,482,567	4,490,421	5,334,913	844,492
AUSTRAL	A	E	83	73	334	1,774	1,440
	V	E	82	118	2,777	3,221	444
BRAZIL	V	E	81	106,296	552,100	753,637	201,537
			82	64,171	224,000	329,910	105,910
			83	33,306	104,920	158,170	53,250
CANADA	A	E	84	10	803	1,311	508
	O	E	81	5,942	135,146	135,146	
			82	17,369	344,417	344,417	
			83	5,975	29,402	29,402	
			84	28,497	59,445	59,445	
			85	17,390	152,251	152,251	
			86	73,008	402,674	402,674	
	O	W	84	2,780	10,652	10,652	
			86	2,379	4,828	4,828	
CHILE	A	E	83	34	1,720	2,902	1,182
	V	W	86	72	4,190	4,461	271
CHINA T	V	E	84	40	1,000	1,213	213
COLOMB	A	E	83	28	500	1,490	990
ECUADOR	A	E	82	912	13,590	22,396	8,806
	N	E	81	1,219	15,986	28,049	12,415
			83	1,212	17,489	26,842	9,353
	V	E	81	161	4,900	6,153	1,253
			82	89	1,750	2,156	406
			85	324	8,835	9,582	747
			86	253	8,700	9,119	419
FR GERM	A	E	83	187	1,557	2,642	1,085
			84	9	1,900	2,317	417
FRANCE	A	E	82	58	11,938	13,435	1,497
			83	62	10,477	12,197	1,720
			84	9	281	548	267
HUNGARY	A	E	83	960	2,590	3,790	1,200
			84	1,623	3,800	6,019	2,219
ISRAEL	V	W	82	220	287	294	7
ITALY	A	E	82	8	386	426	40
	V	E	81	63	2,285	2,625	340
			82	5,513	8,450	9,060	610
			85	2,183	1,247	1,501	254
JAPAN	V	E	84	4	423	471	48
	V	W	84	395	3,958	4,212	254
			85	12	1,232	1,306	74
KOR REP	V	E	85	3,999	1,631	1,800	169
			86	3,148	2,355	2,499	144
	V	W	81	675	10,125	11,126	1,001
MEXICO	O	E	82	543	33,396	33,396	
			83	1,970	12,100	12,100	
			84	179	2,126	2,126	
			86	5,024	37,713	37,713	
	O	W	81	5	347	347	
			83	48	652	652	
			84	159	2,100	2,100	
			85	4,331	11,084	11,084	
			86	25,238	26,658	26,658	
NICARAG	A	E	81	21	924	2,447	1,523
PERU	V	E	83	985	21,989	24,000	2,011
			85	89	1,200	1,560	360
			86	22,445	18,831	21,618	2,787
	V	W	86	591	10,500	12,500	2,000
PHIL R	V	W	82	188	539	764	225
PORTUGL	V	E	81	198	1,200	1,465	265
			82	98	1,250	1,667	417
			83	5,248	4,422	5,220	798
			84	9,552	9,825	11,215	1,390
			85	355	4,500	5,661	1,161
			86	118	1,800	2,359	559

Crop Product TSUSA commodity number, description, and unit of quantity							
Country	Mode	Reg	Yr	Quantity	F.A.S.	C.I.F.	Charges

Corn, vegetable oil
1761600 CORN OIL (LB)

Country	Mode	Reg	Yr	Quantity	F.A.S.	C.I.F.	Charges
TOTAL			81	44,066	30,000	32,632	2,632
			82	11,033	9,708	13,216	3,508
			83	88,785	33,346	35,880	2,534
			84	331,047	114,084	124,141	10,057
			85	189,212	111,184	118,828	7,644
			86	99,130	58,203	63,914	5,711
BRAZIL	V	E	81	843	711	792	81
CANADA	O	E	81	7,159	1,820	1,820	
			82	40	476	533	57
			83	50,201	3,421	3,421	
			84	12,521	5,826	5,826	
	V	E	81	13,460	2,939	3,174	235
CHINA M	V	W	83	13,500	6,562	6,887	325
			84	221,422	48,825	51,359	2,534
			85	30,137	18,801	19,808	1,007
			86	31,392	12,421	13,156	735
FR GERM	A	E	81	2,218	444	1,273	829
	V	E	86	7,716	6,472	8,072	1,600
FRANCE	N	E	82	4,087	4,460	6,303	1,843
			84	3,620	1,979	3,403	1,424
	V	E	81	14,148	20,500	21,612	1,112
			83	428	286	315	29
			86	2,315	2,082	2,110	28
GREECE	V	E	86	2,820	2,270	2,570	300
HG KONG	V	E	84	30,685	18,912	22,360	3,448
			86	36,631	21,776	23,399	1,623
	V	W	83	3,600	1,878	2,019	141
			84	49,788	29,718	31,363	1,645
			85	139,917	81,035	86,323	5,288
JAPAN	O	H	81	1,280	1,736	1,947	211
	V	E	81	549	471	535	64
			82	36	251	298	47
			84	613	518	609	91
			85	919	1,429	1,585	156
	V	H	82	436	261	344	83
			83	1,200	328	603	275
			84	363	300	338	38
	V	W	85	4,800	2,750	2,926	176
KOR REP	V	E	85	4,500	2,056	2,237	181
	V	W	86	2,610	1,505	1,656	151
NETHLDS	V	E	81	4,409	1,379	1,479	100
PORTUGL	V	E	84	2,435	3,806	4,459	653
			85	8,939	5,113	5,949	836
			86	15,646	11,677	12,951	1,274
REP SAF	V	W	83	3,600	1,878	2,019	141
			84	9,600	4,200	4,424	224
SWITZLD	A	E	82	1,279	1,924	3,005	1,081
U KING	A	E	83	178	289	512	223
USSR	O	E	82	2,668	1,273	1,562	289
	V	E	82	2,487	1,063	1,171	108
VENEZ	V	E	83	16,078	18,704	20,104	1,400

Mamey Colorado

Mamey colorado, fresh or prepared or preserved**
1468700 CASHEW APPLES,ETC FR OR PRES (LB)
(See Cashew apple, fresh or prepared or preserved under Cashew)

Mamey colorado, jelly or jam**
1530200 CASHEW APPLE, MANGO JELLY (LB)
(See Cashew apple, jelly or jam under Cashew)

Mamey colorado, paste and pulp**
1524300 FRUIT PASTE, CASHEW APPL ETC (LB)
(See Cashew apple, paste and pulp under Cashew)

Mangel Beet

Mangelwurzel, seed
1265500 MANGELWURZEL SEED (LB)

Country	Mode	Reg	Yr	Quantity	F.A.S.	C.I.F.	Charges
TOTAL			82	562	4,869	5,419	550

Crop Product TSUSA commodity number, description, and unit of quantity							
Country	Mode	Reg	Yr	Quantity	F.A.S.	C.I.F.	Charges

Country	Mode	Reg	Yr	Quantity	F.A.S.	C.I.F.	Charges
			83	25,326	25,325	27,490	2,165
			84	1,349	1,434	1,656	222
			86	2,205	1,039	1,680	641
FR GERM	A	E	82	562	4,869	5,419	550
			83	25,326	25,325	27,490	2,165
			84	110	1,007	1,100	93
PHIL R	V	W	84	1,239	427	556	129
U KING	V	W	86	2,205	1,039	1,680	641

Mango

Mango, candied**
1544300 KUMQUATS, ETC, CANDIED, ETC (LB)
(See Kumquat, candied under Kumquat)

Mango, fresh
1479800 MANGOES, FRESH NOV 1-APR 30 (LB)

Country	Mode	Reg	Yr	Quantity	F.A.S.	C.I.F.	Charges
TOTAL			81	8,025,332	1,738,911	2,157,596	418,685
			82	5,914,509	984,713	1,258,714	274,001
BRAZIL	A	E	81	2,081	858	1,840	982
			82	30,613	9,730	22,692	12,962
	N	E	81	64,770	29,153	63,141	33,988
CHILE	A	E	81	499	516	826	310
CHINA T	V	W	81	750	1,040	1,064	24
DOM REP	A	E	81	75,870	7,604	22,125	14,521
			82	86,197	8,504	23,886	15,382
	V	E	81	7,050	915	1,669	754
HAITI	A	E	81	284,247	86,573	141,337	54,764
	N	E	81	4,524,699	1,098,158	1,410,983	312,825
			82	1,946,778	465,340	709,840	244,500
HG KONG	V	E	82	540	565	630	65
INDIA	V	E	81	2,249	2,407	2,762	355
	V	W	82	50	600	735	135
JAMAICA	V	E	82	15,525	1,118	1,800	682
MALAYSA	V	W	82	4,204	2,489	2,764	275
MEXICO	O	E	81	2,920,805	497,006	497,006	
			82	3,830,602	496,367	496,367	
	O	W	81	141,061	11,253	11,253	
PHIL R	V	W	81	860	2,973	3,084	111
THAILND	V	W	81	391	455	506	51

1480000 MANGOES, FRESH MAY 1-OCT 31 (LB)

Country	Mode	Reg	Yr	Quantity	F.A.S.	C.I.F.	Charges
TOTAL			81	34,385,637	13,289,007	13,603,870	313,573
			82	278,092	55,807	85,382	29,575
C RICA	O	E	81	12,495	2,677	3,174	497
CHINA T	V	E	81	625	1,125	1,179	54
DOM REP	A	E	81	15,200	1,520	4,789	3,269
	N	E	81	73,862	9,600	17,840	8,237
HAITI	A	E	81	440,495	98,268	182,614	83,059
			82	238,483	52,542	82,117	29,575
	N	E	81	4,237,982	860,097	1,051,740	191,643
JAMAICA	A	E	81	2,122	1,865	2,389	524
MEXICO	A	E	81	16,000	8,000	15,535	7,535
	N	W	81	33,352	17,461	17,986	525
	O	E	81	10,168,332	1,761,482	1,761,482	
			82	39,609	3,265	3,265	
	O	W	81	19,383,192	10,525,922	10,543,994	18,072
PHIL R	V	W	81	1,980	990	1,148	158

1480300 MANGOES FRESH SEPT 1-MAY 31 (LB)

Country	Mode	Reg	Yr	Quantity	F.A.S.	C.I.F.	Charges
TOTAL			82	17,094,669	4,545,510	5,157,424	611,914
			83	35,505,799	8,055,875	9,612,075	1,556,200
			84	34,327,487	8,899,275	11,426,739	2,527,464
			85	31,455,835	7,909,511	10,094,081	2,184,570
			86	32,410,349	9,456,661	11,208,496	1,751,835
AUSTRAL	V	E	84	485	1,000	1,038	38
BAHAMAS	V	E	85	15,750	5,250	5,900	650
BELIZE	A	E	86	203,331	74,763	119,496	44,733
	N	E	83	875,268	200,803	323,495	122,692
			84	939,810	281,793	508,763	226,970
BRAZIL	A	E	82	11,967	6,199	12,615	6,416
			83	69,401	28,192	63,444	35,252
			84	80,027	41,257	73,190	31,933
			85	463,230	121,571	368,229	246,658
			86	68,604	25,951	58,365	32,414

Crop Product TSUSA commodity number, description, and unit of quantity Country	Mode	Reg	Yr	Quantity	F.A.S.	C.I.F.	Charges
	A	W	85	4,409	2,380	4,998	2,618
			86	27,225	30,875	48,892	18,017
	N	E	84	302,344	87,111	238,749	151,638
			86	313,934	194,824	291,281	96,457
CANADA	O	E	83	57,159	4,326	4,326	
			84	52,928	8,066	8,066	
			85	34,086	3,588	3,588	
	O	W	82	26,860	8,058	8,058	
			83	2,560	1,280	1,280	
			85	25	2,814	2,814	
CHINA T	V	E	82	500	785	817	32
			83	5,344	3,051	3,491	440
	V	W	86	9,457	11,609	12,909	1,300
COLOMB	A	E	83	7	2,100	3,000	900
			84	3,850	2,323	3,469	1,146
DOM REP	A	E	82	18,385	1,839	5,973	4,134
			83	6,800	340	1,781	1,441
			84	33,930	5,061	10,132	5,071
	N	E	82	21,450	3,230	6,901	3,671
			83	181,472	26,363	48,222	21,859
			84	202,772	22,939	60,609	37,670
	V	E	84	86,140	9,125	11,555	2,430
GUATMAL	A	E	84	3,170	270	1,357	1,087
			85	20,876	3,092	8,641	5,549
	N	E	85	17,738	2,782	7,276	4,494
	O	W	85	30,810	13,055	13,055	
	V	E	85	8,000	1,200	2,221	1,021
HAITI	A	E	82	155,619	59,366	87,475	28,109
			83	517,015	213,042	306,652	93,610
			84	1,082,524	384,238	587,851	203,613
			85	121,602	41,654	68,540	26,886
			86	48,000	9,120	17,175	8,055
	N	E	82	5,064,645	1,094,070	1,653,892	559,822
			83	10,568,616	2,518,065	3,779,507	1,261,442
			84	14,069,424	2,962,187	4,748,739	1,786,552
			85	15,421,183	3,349,689	5,239,603	1,889,914
			86	11,964,207	2,652,660	4,187,390	1,534,730
	V	E	82	36,000	8,250	11,474	3,224
			84	108,000	15,750	23,391	7,641
			86	176,300	55,440	67,229	11,789
HONDURA	A	E	83	24,000	6,000	9,015	3,015
INDIA	O	E	85	7,923	2,608	3,057	449
			86	1,761	2,710	3,003	293
	V	E	82	660	351	526	175
			83	8,278	2,577	3,229	652
			84	4,268	3,519	4,190	671
			85	6,429	5,168	6,075	907
			86	2,201	2,407	2,738	331
	V	W	82	400	460	523	63
			84	1,350	1,000	1,250	250
INDNSIA	V	W	83	194	262	298	36
JAMAICA	A	E	82	19,581	4,424	9,466	5,042
			83	1,325	1,112	1,297	185
			84	10,764	4,400	7,036	2,636
MALAYSA	V	W	82	3,063	1,433	1,590	157
MEXICO	A	W	85	4,000	1,610	4,403	2,793
	O	E	82	7,057,576	1,372,639	1,372,639	
			83	14,497,701	1,871,670	1,871,670	
			84	8,637,501	1,337,041	1,337,041	
			85	9,062,241	1,545,456	1,545,456	
			86	9,170,940	1,404,247	1,404,247	
	O	W	82	4,625,578	1,967,126	1,967,126	
			83	8,499,476	3,051,166	3,051,166	
			84	8,336,431	3,508,668	3,508,668	
			85	6,218,158	2,792,333	2,792,334	1
			86	10,403,352	4,969,631	4,969,631	
MONSRAT	V	E	82	4,000	2,200	2,371	171
PERU	A	E	84	48,766	33,522	52,194	18,672
	O	E	84	3,750	3,188	6,736	3,548
PHIL R	V	E	83	67,461	16,340	16,950	610
			84	2,600	1,310	1,454	144
			85	500	1,600	1,904	304
	V	W	82	48,385	15,080	15,978	898
			83	1,758	2,448	2,706	258
			84	360	291	323	32
			86	19,537	21,100	24,670	3,570
THAILND	V	E	83	7,004	3,294	3,778	484
			84	8,551	3,600	4,069	469
			85	5,675	5,601	6,529	928
			86	1,500	1,324	1,470	146
VENEZ	A	E	83	114,960	103,444	116,768	13,324
			84	307,742	181,616	226,869	45,253
			85	13,200	8,060	9,458	1,398

1480600 MANGOES FRESH JUNE 1-AUG 31 (LB)

Country	Mode	Reg	Yr	Quantity	F.A.S.	C.I.F.	Charges
TOTAL			82	41,516,147	14,552,956	14,983,712	430,756
			83	51,794,313	14,957,133	15,409,429	452,296
			84	47,434,462	13,271,204	13,463,917	192,713
			85	49,816,506	14,693,985	14,927,037	233,052
			86	66,073,940	19,566,263	20,048,902	482,639
BELIZE	A	E	84	28,500	8,550	16,030	7,480
			86	231,045	88,200	139,030	50,830
	N	E	83	587,670	137,625	204,238	66,613
	O	E	86	100,034	35,496	35,496	
BRAZIL	A	E	84	17,441	7,044	12,620	5,576
			85	4,506	1,024	3,512	2,488
	A	W	85	8,786	2,048	2,348	300
CHINA T	V	W	82	2,645	900	982	82
DOM REP	A	E	83	36,920	8,491	13,405	4,914
			84	7,980	616	1,810	1,194
	N	E	82	29,120	5,447	10,179	4,732
			83	30,540	3,264	4,294	1,030
			84	142,335	12,546	29,707	17,161
	V	E	83	99,600	30,696	38,004	7,308
			84	2	3,000	5,242	2,242
			86	42,800	11,700	13,078	1,378
DOMINCA	V	E	86	40,571	14,119	14,839	720
FRANCE	O	W	85	35,306	14,960	14,960	
GUATMAL	A	E	84	8,429	2,400	3,900	1,500
	O	W	85	73,745	29,985	29,985	
	V	E	85	388,588	80,999	103,552	22,553
			86	235,611	18,360	54,638	36,278
	V	W	85	35,000	24,500	28,609	4,109
HAITI	A	E	82	424,767	145,417	211,831	66,414
			83	410,163	155,471	230,965	75,494
			84	338,915	115,906	168,102	52,196
			85	33,000	9,000	16,920	7,920
	N	E	82	2,822,468	627,422	975,549	348,127
			83	2,160,247	505,808	784,215	278,407
			84	766,926	239,545	325,348	85,803
			85	1,736,037	454,435	649,578	195,143
			86	4,052,070	783,357	1,168,275	384,918
	V	E	86	31,460	7,800	10,675	2,875
HG KONG	V	E	85	990	1,340	1,740	400
INDIA	O	E	83	5,844	3,494	3,494	
	V	E	82	1,786	1,854	2,485	631
			84	4,200	2,705	2,750	45
JAMAICA	A	E	82	43,860	16,659	23,445	6,786
			83	25,850	6,395	10,586	4,191
			84	3,737	1,739	2,470	731
MEXICO	A	E	84	23,248	7,593	10,692	3,099
	O	E	82	14,863,605	2,007,460	2,009,632	2,172
			83	20,514,515	2,392,359	2,396,393	4,034
			84	18,920,327	2,079,494	2,079,994	500
			85	19,345,310	1,824,862	1,824,868	6
			86	24,747,898	1,844,816	1,844,818	2
	O	W	82	23,321,982	11,746,368	11,746,368	
			83	27,838,096	11,686,616	11,686,616	
			84	27,084,249	10,729,089	10,729,089	
			85	28,154,797	12,249,810	12,249,810	
			86	36,552,156	16,749,311	16,754,949	5,638
N ZEAL	O	E	86	40,295	13,104	13,104	
PHIL R	V	E	83	525	263	352	89
	V	W	82	2,714	471	2,179	1,708
			84	403	382	445	63
S LUCIA	A	E	82	2,719	1,176	2,022	846
THAILND	V	E	83	960	316	361	45
	V	W	82	3,200	958	1,062	104
			85	441	1,022	1,155	133
TRINID	A	E	84	5,400	2,509	2,998	489
VENEZ	A	E	83	83,383	26,335	36,506	10,171
			84	79,651	56,910	70,698	13,788

Mango, jelly or jam**
1530200 CASHEW APPLE, MANGO JELLY (LB)
(See Cashew apple, jelly or jam under Cashew)

Mango, paste and pulp
1525800 MANGO PASTE AND PULP (LB)

Country	Mode	Reg	Yr	Quantity	F.A.S.	C.I.F.	Charges
TOTAL			81	1,982,916	907,615	1,034,511	126,896
			82	1,867,535	941,225	1,068,585	127,360
			83	2,268,231	935,961	1,051,937	115,976
			84	2,319,138	961,515	1,092,073	130,558

Crop
Product
TSUSA commodity number, description, and unit of quantity

Country	Mode	Reg	Yr	Quantity	F.A.S.	C.I.F.	Charges
			85	4,043,463	1,298,482	1,467,929	169,447
			86	3,468,298	1,487,774	1,704,458	216,684
AUSTRAL	V	H	81	765	443	487	44
AUSTRIA	V	W	81	694	359	522	163
BELGIUM	V	W	86	796	1,274	1,278	4
BRAZIL	V	E	82	30,184	17,114	19,415	2,301
	V	W	81	37,699	9,556	11,295	1,739
C RICA	V	E	81	164,510	58,363	70,747	12,384
			82	78,079	23,295	30,728	7,433
			83	1,050	368	556	188
			84	38,912	8,970	11,829	2,859
			85	10,626	2,695	3,828	1,133
			86	24,297	7,690	9,590	1,900
CANADA	O	E	82	900	426	426	
CHINA T	V	E	82	1,250	1,800	1,913	113
	V	W	81	133,102	55,779	63,153	7,374
			82	3,879	1,600	1,894	294
			83	2,868	1,407	1,547	140
			84	1,724	1,404	1,617	213
			85	89,729	34,526	42,802	8,276
COLOMB	A	E	84	1,413	1,201	1,510	309
	V	E	81	19,687	8,000	10,100	2,100
DOM REP	N	E	82	72,384	13,184	16,487	3,303
	V	E	81	102,276	31,127	34,030	2,903
			82	140,945	42,283	48,069	5,786
			83	156,445	30,231	34,977	4,746
			84	314,287	49,675	61,798	12,123
			85	607,872	113,347	133,047	19,700
			86	778,634	234,466	257,519	23,053
ECUADOR	V	E	83	14,944	1,665	1,775	110
FRANCE	N	E	86	7,716	12,457	14,509	2,052
	V	E	84	2,070	2,849	3,161	312
			86	7,211	12,683	14,196	1,513
	V	W	82	132	321	326	5
			84	132	267	289	22
			85	623	1,335	1,443	108
			86	1,771	2,908	3,081	173
GUATMAL	V	E	81	2,064	1,651	1,659	8
			84	55,620	15,781	21,055	5,274
			85	11,976	8,320	9,366	1,046
			86	52,760	19,345	23,021	3,676
HAITI	V	E	82	75,338	27,911	33,124	5,213
			83	182,116	65,778	73,913	8,135
			84	168,673	55,384	61,621	6,237
			85	371,387	121,930	135,405	13,475
			86	112,218	37,255	41,192	3,937
	V	W	85	39,900	14,303	16,340	2,037
HG KONG	V	E	81	609	1,995	2,041	46
			86	43,395	21,076	26,037	4,961
HONDURA	V	E	85	32,802	16,401	19,393	2,992
INDIA	A	E	84	1,031	579	666	87
	N	E	82	140,603	122,318	134,008	11,690
			84	161,905	115,116	128,284	13,168
			85	153,297	101,780	113,750	11,970
			86	70,599	61,111	66,411	5,300
	O	E	81	34,665	25,670	26,857	1,187
			82	8,992	8,213	8,873	660
			83	5,638	4,643	5,053	410
			84	28,122	16,897	17,004	107
			85	3,367	3,281	3,281	
	V	E	81	272,712	206,322	241,168	34,846
			82	298,243	217,027	248,399	31,372
			83	595,701	409,081	459,658	50,577
			84	704,880	430,964	480,360	49,396
			85	450,147	320,687	357,947	37,260
			86	884,475	592,868	650,597	57,729
	V	W	81	47,919	29,548	35,556	6,008
			82	255,582	163,947	190,908	26,961
			83	25,561	22,798	25,874	3,076
			84	124,152	67,046	76,761	9,715
			85	101,392	61,487	69,353	7,866
			86	89,142	51,986	59,976	7,990
JAPAN	V	W	83	90	1,008	1,048	40
KIRIBAT	V	E	86	10,000	4,877	5,631	754
MEXICO	O	E	81	175,296	69,407	69,407	
			82	79,099	17,274	17,274	
			83	703,235	123,121	123,121	
			84	342,365	58,565	58,565	
			85	1,356,304	148,407	148,407	
			86	24,990	7,168	7,168	
	O	W	81	11,024	1,963	1,963	
			82	232,909	74,703	74,703	
			83	5,915	605	605	

Crop
Product
TSUSA commodity number, description, and unit of quantity

Country	Mode	Reg	Yr	Quantity	F.A.S.	C.I.F.	Charges
			85	59,044	4,964	4,964	
	V	E	86	7,442	10,449	11,345	896
	V	W	81	69,700	26,066	30,260	4,194
NETHLDS	V	E	86	99,535	25,433	31,007	5,574
PERU	V	E	86	85,979	15,297	26,910	11,613
	V	W	86	364,059	74,099	109,266	35,167
PHIL R	A	E	84	2,530	1,322	6,449	5,127
			85	2,205	1,150	4,468	3,318
	N	W	86	543,767	184,454	209,279	24,825
	V	E	81	80,025	36,649	43,213	6,564
			82	84,410	40,411	47,425	7,014
			83	122,960	61,864	72,555	10,691
			84	140,822	66,622	77,571	10,949
			85	129,835	58,975	72,286	13,311
			86	184,592	86,981	108,720	21,739
	V	W	81	787,423	324,539	369,408	44,869
			82	357,522	166,045	190,794	24,749
			83	441,337	209,987	246,501	36,514
			84	230,500	68,873	83,533	14,660
			85	622,957	284,894	331,849	46,955
			86	30,998	11,359	14,057	2,698
SWITZLD	V	E	83	9,524	2,592	3,128	536
THAILND	V	W	81	39,896	16,825	18,935	2,110
			82	7,084	3,353	3,819	466
TRINID	V	E	86	1,512	1,800	2,930	1,130
TURKEY	O	E	83	847	813	1,626	813
U KING	O	E	81	2,850	3,353	3,710	357
	V	E	86	42,410	10,738	10,738	

Mango, prepared or preserved
1480800 MANGOES, PREPARED PRESERVED (LB)

Country	Mode	Reg	Yr	Quantity	F.A.S.	C.I.F.	Charges
TOTAL			81	1,568,757	1,178,409	1,343,575	165,166
			82	2,720,298	1,849,374	2,069,137	219,763
			83	2,359,771	1,532,327	1,708,649	176,322
			84	2,896,271	1,800,183	2,011,338	211,155
			85	2,723,837	1,655,020	1,849,195	194,175
			86	4,017,730	2,160,658	2,440,503	279,845
AUSTRIA	V	E	84	13,332	13,255	15,008	1,753
BELGIUM	V	W	85	6,373	6,319	7,144	825
BRAZIL	A	E	84	110	301	563	262
BURMA	V	E	82	720	255	309	54
C RICA	V	E	81	4,305	1,722	2,320	598
			82	74,003	31,918	36,571	4,653
			83	95,579	30,645	40,498	9,853
			84	5,576	1,332	1,783	451
			85	11,970	4,091	4,941	850
			86	9,300	3,534	4,208	674
	V	W	83	38,911	9,378	12,728	3,350
CANADA	O	E	81	960	974	974	
			82	8,165	7,699	7,699	
			83	10,370	4,680	4,680	
			84	6,082	3,848	3,848	
			85	4,512	1,987	1,987	
	O	W	82	5,080	2,265	2,384	119
CHILE	A	W	85	9,210	4,500	7,803	3,303
CHINA M	O	W	83	3,072	480	480	
	V	E	81	3,563	3,808	4,207	399
			83	2,563	8,857	9,302	445
			84	281	720	793	73
			85	1,102	1,575	1,682	107
			86	472	1,708	1,871	163
	V	H	82	2,345	3,229	3,514	285
			83	3,200	5,611	6,040	429
			84	3,500	5,033	5,362	329
			85	9,060	7,144	7,676	532
	V	W	81	1,000	1,025	1,104	79
			82	1,606	5,106	5,423	317
			83	2,630	3,938	4,272	334
			84	1,612	3,163	3,307	144
			85	875	3,900	3,920	20
			86	7,398	10,399	10,984	585
CHINA T	O	E	83	4,500	1,480	1,707	227
	V	E	81	30,538	18,294	20,046	1,752
			82	77,689	45,908	51,854	5,946
			83	63,203	29,497	33,952	4,455
			84	58,778	37,782	42,758	4,976
			85	51,522	34,195	37,411	3,216
			86	90,776	74,959	84,278	9,319
	V	H	81	48,953	74,405	80,087	5,682
			82	38,934	61,108	65,582	4,474
			83	32,406	54,167	57,940	3,773

Crop
Product
TSUSA commodity number, description, and unit of quantity

Country	Mode	Reg	Yr	Quantity	F.A.S.	C.I.F.	Charges
			84	33,995	51,720	55,329	3,609
			85	26,626	46,748	50,033	3,285
			86	20,821	30,424	32,637	2,213
	V	W	81	115,292	54,097	59,713	5,616
			82	21,389	21,724	23,280	1,556
			83	29,476	11,395	12,710	1,315
			84	28,024	29,464	31,631	2,167
			85	18,010	27,072	28,610	1,538
			86	82,486	84,755	91,343	6,588
COLOMB	V	E	81	255	268	300	32
DOM REP	A	W	85	2,800	1,457	2,221	764
	V	E	81	155,818	60,472	65,956	5,484
			82	214,197	82,240	89,922	7,682
			83	201,455	73,282	79,962	6,680
			84	207,462	74,857	84,411	9,554
			85	219,527	79,236	88,247	9,011
			86	167,578	64,678	87,528	22,850
FRANCE	V	W	84	2,700	4,261	4,483	222
GUATMAL	A	W	84	1,803	516	1,020	504
	V	E	82	1,360	332	408	76
			83	3,661	565	678	113
			84	77,649	32,237	40,513	8,276
			86	20,440	9,250	10,834	1,584
	V	W	86	13,000	1,167	1,843	676
GUYANA	V	E	81	216	458	497	39
HAITI	A	E	84	48,581	8,080	13,949	5,869
	N	E	83	107,170	33,859	41,864	8,005
			86	208,300	44,820	71,045	26,225
	V	E	82	49,310	13,933	18,191	4,258
			83	187,107	71,198	80,090	8,892
			84	38,975	13,502	14,796	1,294
			86	92,624	29,424	33,265	3,841
	V	W	83	121,777	63,020	69,222	6,202
			86	42,000	14,805	16,955	2,150
HG KONG	V	E	81	300	292	310	18
			83	1,973	2,289	2,524	235
			84	1,615	2,461	2,615	154
	V	H	81	74,131	63,044	66,322	3,278
			82	79,156	76,735	80,825	4,090
			83	82,593	79,225	83,934	4,709
			84	84,240	75,769	79,766	3,997
			85	92,770	93,401	98,268	4,867
			86	47,770	52,027	54,672	2,645
	V	W	81	4,950	3,392	3,583	191
			82	7,250	5,195	5,495	300
			83	9,204	11,225	11,774	549
			84	6,391	14,410	14,953	543
			85	4,850	9,467	9,949	482
			86	6,779	10,923	11,450	527
INDIA	N	E	81	274,890	147,759	196,620	48,861
			83	36,567	11,266	13,936	2,670
			84	83,303	58,991	67,142	8,151
			85	78,459	61,152	67,086	5,934
			86	12,161	12,083	13,640	1,557
	N	W	84	7,665	8,234	9,047	813
	O	E	81	28,147	32,115	34,525	2,410
			82	19,520	18,293	21,644	3,351
			83	7,636	7,754	7,986	232
			84	113,267	49,684	55,260	5,576
			85	8,338	6,885	8,099	1,214
			86	8,758	13,345	14,099	754
	O	W	86	4,546	8,854	9,376	522
	V	E	81	73,272	54,777	65,241	10,464
			82	526,536	305,249	370,401	65,152
			83	432,500	257,358	299,698	42,340
			84	767,982	398,232	460,916	62,684
			85	625,621	299,160	350,390	51,230
			86	843,608	360,777	411,019	50,242
	V	W	81	201,973	106,958	135,180	28,222
			82	179,575	130,431	155,843	25,412
			83	140,010	94,068	113,828	19,760
			84	93,052	59,375	71,741	12,366
			85	118,326	89,403	103,953	14,550
			86	117,049	69,084	80,725	11,641
INDNSIA	V	W	83	75	294	315	21
ISRAEL	V	E	82	540	1,142	1,639	497
JAMAICA	A	E	82	528	330	424	94
	N	E	84	28,360	9,469	10,979	1,510
	V	E	81	38,700	17,415	19,577	2,162
			82	5,400	2,190	2,665	475
			83	6,068	4,151	4,725	574
			84	25,999	10,168	11,028	860
			85	70,357	24,832	27,522	2,690
			86	155,526	39,411	50,609	11,198

Crop
Product
TSUSA commodity number, description, and unit of quantity

Country	Mode	Reg	Yr	Quantity	F.A.S.	C.I.F.	Charges
JAPAN	V	H	86	2,500	2,189	2,356	167
	V	W	83	1,653	1,366	1,561	195
KENYA	O	E	82	1,420	1,055	1,172	117
			84	4,497	1,245	1,396	151
KOR REP	V	E	81	337	324	373	49
			83	469	1,125	1,152	27
LEBANON	O	E	84	2,224	1,570	1,570	
MACAO	V	H	83	1,250	1,691	1,837	146
MALAWI	O	E	84	1,701	2,248	2,465	217
MALAYSA	V	E	81	25,342	27,030	30,185	3,155
			82	2,395	2,728	3,063	335
	V	W	81	34,104	31,104	33,840	2,736
			85	2,300	2,338	2,541	203
			86	5,723	5,149	5,490	341
MEXICO	O	E	81	9,557	5,729	5,729	
			82	230,678	72,947	72,947	
			83	213,058	46,885	46,885	
			84	363,873	117,965	117,965	
			85	466,492	71,078	71,078	
			86	505,804	115,687	115,687	
	O	W	81	19,375	13,472	13,472	
			82	115,142	46,952	46,952	
			83	62,165	21,643	21,643	
			84	91,075	44,398	44,398	
			85	35,941	14,019	14,019	
			86	137,682	55,499	55,499	
PAKISTN	O	E	82	310	451	470	19
			84	4,905	3,349	3,666	317
	O	W	86	2,116	2,902	3,074	172
	V	E	81	1,030	891	1,105	214
			83	15,687	15,766	17,782	2,016
			84	2,100	2,120	2,671	551
			85	11,642	10,440	11,807	1,367
			86	44,938	40,025	46,049	6,024
	V	W	81	2,172	2,100	2,912	812
			82	6,779	5,769	7,200	1,431
			84	6,899	10,050	11,963	1,913
			85	3,862	3,883	4,656	773
PERU	V	E	84	737	360	443	83
			86	14,400	5,600	6,428	828
PHIL R	O	W	83	550	712	712	
			86	505	2,254	2,254	
	V	E	81	47,279	105,559	112,954	7,395
			82	137,757	177,587	196,049	18,462
			83	60,038	140,299	150,576	10,277
			84	108,597	112,671	126,633	13,962
			85	126,569	141,971	160,590	18,619
			86	273,431	167,026	192,712	25,686
	V	H	81	116	528	584	56
			82	2,274	6,871	7,599	728
			83	1,348	4,849	5,847	998
			85	1,468	2,966	3,520	554
	V	W	81	154,350	184,468	200,173	15,705
			82	446,346	400,952	439,451	38,499
			83	104,564	206,227	222,295	16,068
			84	158,786	259,873	282,136	22,263
			85	159,114	182,540	203,965	21,425
			86	318,201	347,972	392,534	44,562
S HELNA	V	E	84	10,009	3,800	5,205	1,405
S LUCIA	V	E	81	85,050	32,195	40,273	8,078
			82	18,000	8,640	10,373	1,733
			83	53,550	24,633	28,698	4,065
			84	26,100	8,352	11,052	2,700
			85	70,200	22,464	28,710	6,246
S VN GR	V	E	82	19,800	9,306	9,906	600
SALVADR	V	E	85	44,086	22,880	25,627	2,747
SINGAPR	V	E	86	41,296	22,330	25,333	3,003
	V	H	83	500	458	483	25
	V	W	83	44	254	279	25
			84	456	340	357	17
SRI LKA	O	E	81	315	252	252	
THAILND	N	W	85	121,734	72,245	80,258	8,013
	O	E	86	5,889	2,730	2,972	242
	O	W	82	23,789	12,403	12,403	
			83	11,023	2,812	3,040	228
	V	E	81	20,891	11,790	13,329	1,539
			82	57,386	32,877	37,189	4,312
			83	18,535	15,223	16,963	1,740
			84	102,324	51,794	59,935	8,141
			85	48,121	76,121	79,995	3,874
			86	131,670	63,649	72,075	8,426
	V	H	84	679	1,180	1,331	151
	V	W	81	55,880	42,579	46,842	4,263
			82	282,323	168,070	185,825	17,755

Crop Product TSUSA commodity number, description, and unit of quantity							
Country	Mode	Reg	Yr	Quantity	F.A.S.	C.I.F.	Charges
			83	100,695	75,007	81,285	6,278
			84	130,074	83,170	91,049	7,879
			85	86,382	45,735	49,907	4,172
			86	492,079	267,698	289,392	21,694
TRINID	N	E	86	8,537	14,858	16,726	1,868
TUNISIA	V	W	86	3,197	1,665	1,807	142
TURKEY	O	E	83	1,124	813	1,626	813
	V	E	83	547	804	840	36
U KING	N	E	81	14,658	22,018	23,895	1,877
			84	136,138	122,718	137,479	14,761
			85	90,238	98,523	108,857	10,334
			86	41,137	54,238	58,948	4,710
	O	E	81	40,288	55,781	59,636	3,855
			82	57,326	79,969	86,113	6,144
			83	79,210	95,320	102,782	7,462
			84	375	557	557	
			85	55,759	52,594	58,048	5,454
			86	31,480	43,558	48,591	5,033
	V	E	82	1,313	1,889	2,047	158
			83	10,055	6,758	7,518	760
			84	3,753	4,282	4,539	257
			85	4,795	2,432	2,681	249
			86	4,815	7,808	8,785	977
	V	W	81	750	1,314	1,459	145
			82	3,957	5,626	6,305	679
			84	635	1,277	1,527	250
			85	34,826	30,267	35,994	5,727
			86	938	1,394	1,410	16

Manna Ash

Manna, natural drug**

4350500 ALOES JALAP MATE ETC, CRUDE (LB)
  (See Aloe, natural drug under Aloe)
4351000 ALOES,JALAP MANA,ETC ADVANCE (LB)
  (See Aloe, natural drug under Aloe)

Maple

Maple, hardwood flooring**

2025820 HARDWOOD FLOORING, MAPLE (MBF)
  (See Beech, hardwood flooring under Beech)

Maple, logs

2003529 MAPLE LOG/TIMBER EXC PULPWD (MBF)

Country	Mode	Reg	Yr	Quantity	F.A.S.	C.I.F.	Charges
TOTAL			81	1,734	256,665	258,435	1,770
			82	2,211	355,298	361,991	6,693
			83	1,445	256,027	262,499	6,472
			84	430	102,747	103,467	720
			85	165	110,380	110,380	
			86	394	121,333	122,976	1,643
CANADA	O	E	81	1,277	187,847	187,847	
			82	1,613	223,503	223,503	
			83	747	150,700	150,700	
			84	348	98,151	98,151	
			85	165	110,380	110,380	
			86	265	110,500	110,500	
	V	W	81	452	67,993	69,763	1,770
			82	598	131,795	138,488	6,693
			83	698	105,327	111,799	6,472
			84	82	4,596	5,316	720
			86	100	7,147	8,381	1,234
FR GERM	N	E	86	*	1,979	2,064	85
	V	E	86	29	1,707	2,031	324
U KING	O	E	81	5	825	825	

Maple, lumber**

2023820 BOXWD, JAP MAPLE LBR, ROUGH (MBF)
  (See Boxwood, lumber under Boxwood)
2023840 BOXWD, JAP MAP LBR, DRESSED (MBF)
  (See Boxwood, lumber under Boxwood)
2024210 MAPLE LUMBER, NSPF, ROUGH (MBF)

Country	Mode	Reg	Yr	Quantity	F.A.S.	C.I.F.	Charges
TOTAL			81	21,038	7,923,581	7,925,504	1,923

Country	Mode	Reg	Yr	Quantity	F.A.S.	C.I.F.	Charges
			82	16,658	5,927,429	5,928,408	979
			83	14,038	5,294,425	5,295,998	1,573
			84	15,236	5,826,210	5,834,635	8,425
			85	13,063	5,087,184	5,091,970	4,786
			86	27,213	6,632,507	6,646,052	13,545
AUSTRAL	V	W	85	27	29,752	30,303	551
AUSTRIA	V	E	85	85	2,756	3,085	329
BRAZIL	V	E	84	19	9,180	13,558	4,378
BURMA	O	E	83	1	353	353	
CANADA	N	E	85	9,938	3,804,297	3,804,297	
	O	E	81	20,505	7,892,990	7,892,990	
			82	16,640	5,918,997	5,918,997	
			83	14,023	5,279,416	5,279,881	465
			84	15,146	5,797,794	5,797,794	
			85	2,760	1,166,030	1,166,030	
			86	25,519	6,483,947	6,483,947	
	O	W	81	11	6,924	6,924	
			82	1	647	647	
			83	2	1,415	1,415	
			85	9	3,908	3,908	
			86	14	2,013	2,013	
	V	E	83	5	2,355	2,580	225
			84	21	1,571	1,571	
	V	W	84	12	4,661	6,957	2,296
			85	19	20,148	21,397	1,249
			86	85	75,476	84,584	9,108
CHINA M	O	E	81	9	4,023	4,023	
FR GERM	A	E	82	6	3,445	3,791	346
			83	4	4,760	4,869	109
			84	2	1,455	1,679	224
			86	3	9,903	11,189	1,286
	A	W	86	55	5,133	5,571	438
	N	E	81	*	1,044	1,474	430
			82	11	4,340	4,973	633
			84	2	973	1,013	40
			85	*	1,170	1,297	127
			86	*	1,400	1,574	174
	N	W	85	*	1,964	2,041	77
	O	W	84	15	310	379	69
	V	E	81	503	7,220	7,424	204
			83	3	6,126	6,900	774
			84	17	8,320	9,573	1,253
			85	224	53,420	55,834	2,414
			86	1,537	54,635	57,174	2,539
	V	W	81	10	11,380	12,669	1,289
			84	2	1,946	2,111	165
			85	1	3,739	3,778	39

2024215 MAPLE LUMBER, NSPF, DRESSED (MBF)

Country	Mode	Reg	Yr	Quantity	F.A.S.	C.I.F.	Charges
TOTAL			81	6,314	3,407,275	3,408,355	1,080
			82	3,756	2,094,264	2,096,163	1,899
			83	4,550	2,260,492	2,261,419	927
			84	4,503	2,083,318	2,086,295	2,977
			85	5,254	2,040,371	2,042,171	1,800
			86	6,205	2,779,561	2,783,290	3,729
AUSTRIA	V	E	83	1	1,301	1,405	104
CAMROON	O	E	84	1	572	572	
CANADA	N	W	84	*	602	602	
	O	E	81	6,303	3,395,819	3,395,819	
			82	3,716	2,054,386	2,054,386	
			83	4,440	2,206,349	2,206,349	
			84	4,477	2,061,855	2,061,946	91
			85	5,243	2,024,174	2,024,174	
			86	6,138	2,748,524	2,748,524	
	O	W	83	88	29,741	29,741	
			84	10	5,888	5,888	
	V	W	84	13	10,101	12,356	2,255
			85	9	9,955	11,147	1,192
			86	12	11,894	12,013	119
CHILE	V	E	86	48	10,239	13,403	3,164
CHINA T	V	W	82	1	2,370	2,590	220
FR GERM	A	E	81	1	452	791	339
			82	1	1,595	1,994	399
			83	8	1,622	1,744	122
			84	1	2,380	2,804	424
			86	1	2,376	2,545	169
	N	E	81	*	3,695	4,229	534
	O	E	81	10	7,309	7,516	207
			82	22	23,976	24,486	510
			83	12	19,505	20,141	636
			84	1	1,920	2,127	207
	V	E	82	3	5,136	5,709	573

Crop Product TSUSA commodity number, description, and unit of quantity Country	Mode	Reg	Yr	Quantity	F.A.S.	C.I.F.	Charges
			83	1	1,974	2,039	65
			85	2	6,242	6,850	608
			86	6	6,528	6,805	277
	V	W	82	1	2,092	2,289	197
ITALY	O	E	82	12	4,709	4,709	

Maple, sugar
1555000 MAPLE SUGAR (LB)

Country	Mode	Reg	Yr	Quantity	F.A.S.	C.I.F.	Charges
TOTAL			81	1,059,593	1,204,589	1,208,647	4,057
			82	747,313	847,721	849,046	1,325
			83	766,999	895,694	900,550	4,856
			84	752,409	783,873	784,098	225
			85	488,816	756,410	756,410	
			86	726,670	1,073,752	1,078,760	5,008
CANADA	A	E	81	210	552	552	
			84	318	384	550	166
			85	17,182	11,435	11,435	
	A	W	81	313	600	1,138	538
			82	56	297	435	138
	N	W	83	18,233	21,981	22,974	993
	O	E	81	1,022,070	1,196,383	1,197,584	1,200
			82	746,737	846,150	847,337	1,187
			83	686,746	799,289	799,289	
			84	752,055	783,227	783,227	
			85	468,914	736,842	736,842	
			86	656,123	1,047,558	1,047,560	2
	V	E	81	37,000	7,054	9,373	2,319
			86	70,547	26,194	31,200	5,006
	V	W	83	62,020	74,424	78,287	3,863
F W IND	O	E	85	2,720	8,133	8,133	
FRANCE	A	W	84	36	262	321	59
REP SAF	O	E	82	520	1,274	1,274	

Maple, syrup
1555500 MAPLE SIRUP (LB)

Country	Mode	Reg	Yr	Quantity	F.A.S.	C.I.F.	Charges
TOTAL			81	11,539,500	12,308,010	12,309,162	1,115
			82	12,729,101	13,705,586	13,707,006	1,420
			83	14,201,525	14,755,809	14,777,319	21,510
			84	13,765,447	15,701,125	15,702,616	1,491
			85	14,590,833	19,242,526	19,245,126	2,600
			86	18,447,633	31,287,538	31,289,538	2,000
BRAZIL	V	E	83	148,811	20,091	30,082	9,991
CANADA	A	E	81	1,255	3,305	4,208	903
			82	319	1,200	1,392	192
			83	57	650	690	40
			84	110	1,000	1,096	96
	A	H	83	83	326	636	310
	A	W	82	189	485	485	
			84	598	1,306	1,608	302
			85	2,326	5,238	7,838	2,600
	N	E	81	70,957	117,134	117,239	105
			83	41,866	42,989	43,054	65
			84	295,128	410,282	410,486	204
	N	W	83	57,590	108,315	114,475	6,160
			84	1,590	3,819	4,708	889
	O	E	81	11,446,413	12,138,600	12,138,744	107
			82	12,684,795	13,657,294	13,658,522	1,228
			83	13,833,134	14,404,861	14,404,861	
			84	13,460,554	15,263,562	15,263,562	
			85	14,545,252	19,172,142	19,172,142	
			86	18,396,261	31,227,150	31,229,150	2,000
	O	W	81	19,435	46,314	46,314	
			82	5,520	14,127	14,127	
			83	6,767	7,832	7,834	2
			84	6,417	19,446	19,446	
			85	3,255	10,418	10,418	
			86	51,372	60,388	60,388	
	V	W	83	49,945	90,405	94,297	3,892
COLOMB	A	E	83	63,272	80,340	81,390	1,050
F W IND	O	E	85	40,000	54,728	54,728	
JAPAN	O	E	81	1,440	2,657	2,657	
KOR REP	O	E	82	660	1,250	1,250	
REP SAF	O	E	82	37,618	31,230	31,230	
U KING	A	E	84	1,050	1,710	1,710	

Maple, veneer
2400040 MAPLE VENR NT REINF OR BCKD (MSF)

Country	Mode	Reg	Yr	Quantity	F.A.S.	C.I.F.	Charges
TOTAL			81	37,787	2,729,865	2,734,126	4,261
			82	42,472	3,022,214	3,026,830	4,616
			83	42,041	3,408,623	3,417,636	9,013
			84	49,179	3,416,681	3,430,834	14,153
			85	42,897	3,593,789	3,613,797	20,008
			86	53,509	4,062,791	4,107,176	44,385
BRAZIL	V	E	86	1,031	83,377	109,106	25,729
CANADA	A	E	83	6	5,720	5,880	160
			85	2	4,044	4,186	142
			86	30	11,490	11,725	235
	A	W	85	2	3,342	3,534	192
	O	E	81	37,008	2,678,393	2,678,393	
			82	41,573	2,934,617	2,934,617	
			83	41,576	3,290,315	3,290,315	
			84	39,631	3,288,390	3,288,390	
			85	36,626	3,212,948	3,212,948	
			86	48,198	3,835,472	3,835,472	
	O	W	81	190	7,675	7,675	
			82	58	8,033	8,033	
			83	38	3,304	3,304	
			84	185	15,127	15,127	
			85	203	19,417	19,417	
			86	745	34,199	34,199	
FR GERM	A	E	85	45	23,911	26,593	2,682
	A	W	86	1,228	35,242	38,153	2,911
	O	E	84	21	12,857	13,193	336
			85	62	5,531	5,531	
			86	26	5,284	5,284	
	V	E	81	80	20,837	22,857	2,020
			84	77	37,293	38,171	878
			85	16	9,335	10,009	674
			86	10	2,836	2,907	71
FRANCE	A	E	83	125	38,676	43,042	4,366
			84	83	20,054	26,221	6,167
	A	W	86	15	16,529	18,286	1,757
	O	W	86	2	2,501	2,501	
	V	E	81	10	4,730	4,915	185
			83	40	24,710	25,185	475
	V	W	85	16	6,182	6,432	250
GREECE	V	E	82	10	5,940	6,122	182
ITALY	A	E	83	146	1,799	2,343	544
			85	65	11,336	14,824	3,488
			86	71	15,281	21,588	6,307
	N	E	81	310	9,454	11,061	1,607
			84	8,809	31,415	38,025	6,610
	O	E	85	1	1,456	1,456	
	V	E	85	2,788	220,860	224,514	3,654
			86	107	5,562	5,872	310
NETHLDS	A	E	83	29	17,225	18,797	1,572
SWITZLD	A	E	83	31	18,011	19,226	1,215
			85	2,937	54,598	62,691	8,093
			86	2,046	15,018	22,083	7,065
	N	E	85	134	20,829	21,662	833
	V	E	82	53	18,098	19,380	1,282
			84	372	11,264	11,392	128
U KING	A	E	81	189	8,776	9,225	449
			82	778	55,526	58,678	3,152
			83	50	8,863	9,544	681
			84	1	281	315	34

Marjoram

Marjoram, spice
1615100 MARJORAM, CRUDE OR NOT MFRD (LB)

Country	Mode	Reg	Yr	Quantity	F.A.S.	C.I.F.	Charges
TOTAL			81	756,241	371,713	416,290	44,577
			82	1,133,683	621,955	680,781	58,916
			83	711,437	649,162	707,172	58,010
			84	1,101,633	1,067,013	1,160,593	93,580
			85	870,058	405,479	481,788	76,309
			86	1,181,369	450,440	566,758	116,318
CANADA	O	E	82	173,788	28,610	28,610	
			83	1,860	2,920	2,920	
			84	151	2,260	2,260	
			86	222,210	25,411	25,411	
	O	W	82	46,460	6,969	6,969	

Crop Product TSUSA commodity number, description, and unit of quantity Country	Mode	Reg	Yr	Quantity	F.A.S.	C.I.F.	Charges
CHILE	V	E	83	47,399	30,600	35,361	4,761
			85	19,676	10,237	12,059	1,822
DOM REP	A	E	83	8,520	2,983	5,635	2,652
			84	3,410	955	1,810	855
	V	E	81	5,960	1,649	2,549	900
			84	5,129	7,353	8,337	984
			85	5,400	4,500	4,686	186
EGYPT	O	E	83	210	342	342	
	V	E	81	659,620	310,174	347,067	36,893
			82	774,164	476,506	521,818	45,312
			83	534,380	486,954	525,683	38,729
			84	1,003,958	948,020	1,029,025	81,005
			85	779,036	347,016	413,640	66,624
			86	899,043	391,769	503,273	111,504
	V	W	85	6,870	3,509	4,655	1,146
			86	17,416	8,302	8,302	
FR GERM	O	E	81	1,067	849	913	64
			82	994	744	836	92
	V	E	81	353	431	593	162
			82	19,800	20,650	21,978	1,328
			83	781	1,676	1,846	170
FRANCE	A	E	82	20	377	401	24
	A	W	82	75	364	364	90
	N	E	84	66,790	93,637	102,468	8,831
	V	E	81	60,793	44,300	50,108	5,808
			82	98,497	74,569	84,609	10,040
			83	84,985	95,789	105,579	9,790
			85	31,751	22,686	26,963	4,277
			86	18,357	13,884	16,084	2,200
GERM DR	V	E	82	19,665	11,517	13,525	2,008
			84	11,023	7,442	8,292	850
GREECE	V	E	85	285	1,440	1,469	29
INDIA	O	E	81	10,055	4,600	4,870	270
JAPAN	V	W	82	120	547	554	7
NETHLDS	A	E	83	65	772	827	55
			86	99	1,352	1,505	153
	O	E	81	2,000	2,210	2,240	30
			82	100	1,102	1,117	15
			83	100	1,640	1,655	15
			84	149	2,276	2,316	40
	V	E	83	10,000	10,006	10,100	94
	V	W	85	5,000	6,834	7,062	228
PERU	V	E	83	17,637	12,800	14,383	1,583
			84	11,023	5,070	6,085	1,015
PHIL R	V	E	86	24,244	9,722	12,183	2,461
SPAIN	O	E	81	16,393	7,500	7,950	450
	V	E	85	22,040	9,257	11,254	1,997
THAILND	O	E	83	5,500	2,680	2,841	161

1615300 MARJORAM, OTHER THAN CRUDE (LB)

Country	Mode	Reg	Yr	Quantity	F.A.S.	C.I.F.	Charges
TOTAL			81	24,053	11,708	14,958	3,250
			82	775	876	876	
			83	3,830	5,726	6,465	739
			84	7,007	10,927	11,591	664
C RICA	V	E	84	146	1,017	1,099	82
CANADA	O	E	81	480	388	388	
			82	775	876	876	
			83	2,600	3,564	3,564	
			84	800	1,071	1,071	
DOM REP	V	E	81	1,030	630	669	39
EGYPT	V	E	84	5,510	6,888	7,199	311
FRANCE	V	E	83	25	323	323	
INDIA	A	W	83	1,102	1,250	1,975	725
	V	E	81	22,046	9,852	13,063	3,211
JAPAN	V	E	84	396	726	787	61
MEXICO	O	E	81	497	838	838	
NETHLDS	A	E	84	36	945	1,120	175
U KING	V	E	83	103	589	603	14
			84	119	280	315	35

Marsh Mallow

Marsh mallow, natural drug**

4350500 ALOES JALAP MATE ETC, CRUDE (LB)
(See Aloe, natural drug under Aloe)
4351000 ALOES,JALAP MANA,ETC ADVANCE (LB)
(See Aloe, natural drug under Aloe)

Mate

Mate, crude
1606000 MATE, CRUDE (LB)

Country	Mode	Reg	Yr	Quantity	F.A.S.	C.I.F.	Charges
TOTAL			81	52,723	52,536	57,484	4,948
			82	161,358	97,394	112,951	15,557
			83	34,574	18,268	21,639	3,371
			84	195,941	171,416	199,049	27,633
			85	49,384	44,865	51,834	6,969
			86	156,883	136,617	154,325	17,708
ARGENT	O	E	86	4,409	4,699	4,699	
	V	E	83	8,362	5,162	6,180	1,018
			84	6,779	4,912	5,522	610
			85	28,492	18,218	20,686	2,468
	V	W	81	22,046	24,000	27,138	3,138
			82	26,173	18,673	20,403	1,730
BNGLDSH	V	E	84	26,670	33,779	38,865	5,086
BRAZIL	N	E	84	6,740	3,213	6,195	2,982
	O	E	81	12,654	13,900	13,900	
			86	4,410	4,180	4,180	
	V	E	82	33,069	14,500	17,367	2,867
			83	25,348	11,496	13,727	2,231
			84	2,205	978	1,141	163
			86	22,046	13,600	15,499	1,899
	V	W	81	13,228	9,683	10,918	1,235
			83	431	369	374	5
CHINA M	V	E	84	43,651	41,511	45,738	4,227
CHINA T	V	E	84	441	554	600	46
FR GERM	V	E	81	4,795	4,953	5,528	575
HG KONG	V	E	84	21,341	10,483	12,677	2,194
	V	H	85	642	1,230	1,360	130
INDIA	V	E	85	14,650	18,311	22,117	3,806
	V	W	86	79,683	84,066	95,733	11,667
INDNSIA	V	E	82	25,353	15,347	17,811	2,464
			86	25,463	17,325	19,155	1,830
	V	W	85	2,921	3,666	3,949	283
			86	20,872	12,747	15,059	2,312
JAPAN	V	E	82	270	858	944	86
			83	433	1,241	1,358	117
	V	W	85	2,679	3,440	3,722	282
MOROC	V	E	82	276	316	330	14
MOZAMBQ	V	E	82	75,781	46,984	55,264	8,280
SRI LKA	V	W	84	85,974	72,217	84,102	11,885
U KING	V	E	82	436	716	832	116
			84	2,140	3,769	4,209	440

Mate, prepared
1606500 MATE, PREPARED (LB)

Country	Mode	Reg	Yr	Quantity	F.A.S.	C.I.F.	Charges
TOTAL			81	434,245	445,306	484,536	39,230
			82	742,511	394,149	448,337	54,188
			83	268,178	161,807	188,503	26,696
			84	497,300	331,181	377,222	46,041
			85	334,407	232,594	266,212	33,618
			86	516,173	345,366	392,030	46,664
ARGENT	A	E	86	22,091	11,500	11,652	152
	N	E	84	188,245	131,856	150,432	18,576
	O	E	82	110	2,250	2,250	
			83	11,247	10,000	10,000	
			84	3,174	2,640	2,640	
			85	7,936	7,196	7,196	
			86	37,659	24,295	24,295	
	V	E	81	161,149	197,028	211,334	14,306
			82	246,892	201,865	226,631	24,766
			83	80,254	40,928	46,993	6,065
			84	36,684	22,751	26,123	3,372
			85	184,074	118,853	135,998	17,145
			86	256,216	162,015	190,642	28,627
	V	W	81	100,940	113,779	125,227	11,448
			82	178,927	116,321	136,657	20,336
			83	121,967	72,765	88,836	16,071
			84	137,228	84,158	96,813	12,655
			85	54,397	37,342	42,894	5,552
			86	68,658	39,040	45,533	6,493
AUSTRIA	V	E	81	39,683	15,088	18,087	2,999
			86	22,377	14,260	17,116	2,856
BRAZIL	A	E	86	1,229	3,141	4,191	1,050
	N	E	84	93,437	58,530	66,532	8,002
	O	E	81	12,502	20,097	20,097	

Crop
Product
TSUSA commodity number, description, and unit of quantity

Country	Mode	Reg	Yr	Quantity	F.A.S.	C.I.F.	Charges
			82	110	2,250	2,250	
			83	11,247	10,000	10,000	
			84	17,724	15,984	15,984	
			85	13,227	11,590	11,590	
			86	43,988	39,417	39,417	
	V	E	81	48,987	39,189	43,162	3,973
			82	305,134	59,880	68,116	8,236
			83	30,594	17,440	20,873	3,433
			85	26,455	12,235	14,599	2,364
			86	28,365	26,576	29,609	3,033
	V	W	81	38,096	31,686	36,103	4,417
			83	6,614	2,520	3,187	667
			84	15,419	7,926	9,413	1,487
			85	4,409	2,960	3,476	516
			86	5,600	5,400	7,203	1,803
CANADA	O	E	81	3,735	6,557	6,557	
			82	4,189	4,275	4,275	
			84	44	980	980	
			86	2,469	2,800	2,800	
CHINA M	V	W	83	1,563	2,964	3,124	160
CHINA T	V	H	82	3,000	1,944	2,195	251
	V	W	83	3,200	2,556	2,711	155
			84	882	1,755	1,851	96
FR GERM	A	E	85	1,052	3,666	6,287	2,621
	V	E	81	14,483	13,767	14,986	1,219
			82	4,104	4,803	5,385	582
FRANCE	V	E	82	45	561	578	17
			84	264	1,034	1,178	144
HG KONG	V	W	83	963	2,141	2,286	145
JAPAN	V	W	81	194	1,891	1,958	67
			84	385	967	1,028	61
			86	216	1,505	1,621	116
KOR REP	V	W	86	7,771	11,655	12,200	545
MEXICO	O	W	81	9,559	2,209	2,209	
			83	529	493	493	
PARAGUA	V	E	81	4,409	2,937	3,475	538
	V	W	84	3,814	2,600	4,248	1,648
			86	19,534	3,762	5,751	1,989
SRI LKA	V	W	85	42,857	38,752	44,172	5,420
U KING	A	E	81	508	1,078	1,341	263

Millet

Millet, seed
1265700 MILLET SEED (LB)

Country	Mode	Reg	Yr	Quantity	F.A.S.	C.I.F.	Charges
TOTAL			81	345,459	211,280	236,701	25,421
			82	305,421	222,273	251,264	28,991
			83	519,646	213,948	251,699	37,751
			84	462,288	297,874	368,089	70,215
			85	419,538	378,148	457,751	79,603
			86	244,662	235,572	262,505	26,933
AUSTRAL	V	E	81	13,492	3,050	4,366	1,316
			83	116,958	16,113	22,328	6,215
	V	W	84	131,725	19,776	27,891	8,115
CANADA	O	E	81	198,716	95,922	95,922	
			82	108,241	89,405	89,405	
			83	290,099	92,826	92,826	
			84	129,397	82,178	82,178	
			85	86,870	52,046	52,046	
			86	72,680	48,818	48,818	
CHINA M	V	E	84	30,076	22,824	29,198	6,374
			85	53,002	34,706	41,539	6,833
	V	W	86	30,718	14,718	15,598	880
CHINA T	V	E	81	115,810	99,207	122,398	23,191
			82	158,208	107,202	131,156	23,954
			83	79,574	73,635	92,908	19,273
			84	73,872	65,327	78,581	13,254
			85	148,544	168,399	211,898	43,499
			86	82,851	111,606	126,940	15,334
	V	W	81	12,073	7,404	7,975	571
			82	30,823	19,858	23,140	3,282
			83	10,735	9,748	11,378	1,630
			84	9,901	10,314	12,533	2,219
FR GERM	V	E	82	220	469	579	110
			83	165	307	317	10
FRANCE	N	E	85	55,333	34,923	39,014	4,091
	O	E	82	4,409	4,325	5,425	1,100
JAPAN	A	W	83	342	706	1,417	711
	N	E	84	52,708	54,533	68,314	13,781

Crop
Product
TSUSA commodity number, description, and unit of quantity

Country	Mode	Reg	Yr	Quantity	F.A.S.	C.I.F.	Charges
	V	W	82	2,420	314	659	345
			85	11,023	6,580	8,750	2,170
KOR REP	N	E	84	31,862	41,290	67,600	26,310
	V	E	81	959	386	440	54
			83	21,773	20,613	30,525	9,912
			85	63,326	80,168	103,017	22,849
			86	58,413	60,430	71,149	10,719
	V	W	82	1,100	700	900	200
			84	2,747	1,632	1,794	162
			85	1,440	1,326	1,487	161
U KING	V	E	81	4,409	5,311	5,600	289

Mint

Mint, leaf, spice
1615500 MINT LEAVES, CRUDE NOT MFRD (LB)

Country	Mode	Reg	Yr	Quantity	F.A.S.	C.I.F.	Charges
TOTAL			81	473,354	301,370	347,880	46,510
			82	499,202	290,080	328,489	38,409
			83	362,443	275,471	308,807	33,336
			84	318,069	203,494	232,891	29,397
			85	406,135	227,129	261,782	34,653
			86	314,409	148,551	182,801	34,250
BULGAR	O	E	86	1,087	1,902	1,902	
	V	E	81	71,901	48,364	59,484	11,120
			82	105,146	40,211	47,810	7,599
			84	42,432	20,346	28,095	7,749
			85	18,783	14,279	17,125	2,846
	V	W	82	22,024	8,886	13,986	5,100
CANADA	A	E	86	345	1,140	1,302	162
	O	E	81	723	1,808	1,926	118
			82	132	277	302	25
CHINA M	V	E	82	2,050	1,192	1,369	177
	V	W	82	500	735	777	42
			86	50,904	19,419	22,668	3,249
DOM REP	V	E	83	22,000	7,700	8,492	792
EGYPT	N	E	81	361,429	214,230	244,289	30,059
			82	330,870	214,977	235,626	20,649
	N	W	84	13,400	8,048	8,395	347
	V	E	82	7,729	4,595	5,259	664
			83	232,613	168,190	186,197	18,007
			84	198,043	123,651	140,233	16,582
			85	361,033	197,221	227,089	29,868
			86	235,144	112,152	135,822	23,670
	V	W	85	11,020	5,099	5,154	55
			86	22,520	11,338	18,003	6,665
FR GERM	O	E	82	3,095	1,508	1,818	310
	V	E	81	36,486	32,806	37,443	4,637
			82	760	412	488	76
			83	7,342	12,252	13,654	1,402
			84	166	414	463	49
			85	1,102	2,922	3,530	608
	V	W	85	10,031	4,095	4,611	516
FRANCE	A	E	81	22	743	786	43
			82	9	406	427	21
	V	E	84	9,479	8,886	9,455	569
	V	W	85	4,166	3,513	4,273	760
GREECE	O	E	84	572	871	871	
	V	E	82	23,876	13,378	16,542	3,164
			83	73,083	51,628	62,862	11,234
			84	42,699	30,668	34,013	3,345
INDIA	N	E	81	1,476	1,528	1,666	138
	O	E	81	110	291	339	48
			84	110	307	353	46
	V	E	83	309	266	299	33
			84	276	760	874	114
JAMAICA	A	E	81	613	839	1,136	297
			82	662	1,676	1,881	205
			83	120	285	435	150
MEXICO	O	W	83	7,950	19,240	19,240	
			84	2,500	327	327	
NETHLDS	A	E	81	6	261	281	20
	V	E	82	144	267	296	29
ROMANIA	V	E	84	551	1,319	1,436	117
SPAIN	O	E	81	588	500	530	30
			84	471	400	424	24
	V	E	83	7,345	7,926	8,891	965
	V	W	82	2,205	1,560	1,908	348
SYRIA	V	E	83	198	360	381	21
			84	207	412	546	134

Crop Product TSUSA commodity number, description, and unit of quantity Country	Mode	Reg	Yr	Quantity	F.A.S.	C.I.F.	Charges
TURKEY	V E		83	11,020	6,723	7,302	579
			84	7,163	7,085	7,406	321
			86	4,409	2,600	3,104	504
YUGOSLV	O E		83	463	901	1,054	153

1615700 MINT LEAVES, MANUFACTURED (LB)

Country	Mode	Reg	Yr	Quantity	F.A.S.	C.I.F.	Charges
TOTAL			81	75,540	175,589	191,328	15,739
			82	181,063	268,217	287,890	19,673
			83	295,468	379,065	413,773	34,708
			84	216,621	317,600	348,023	30,423
			85	171,783	290,264	311,551	21,287
			86	203,308	399,743	428,810	29,067
CANADA	O E		84	180	318	318	
CHINA M	V W		84	159	263	271	8
DOM REP	V E		84	4,200	1,200	1,425	225
EGYPT	O E		83	50	495	495	
			84	748	1,660	1,697	37
	V E		81	11,020	3,925	4,762	837
			82	11,020	4,010	4,984	974
			83	12,612	12,476	13,787	1,311
			84	12,401	14,701	15,970	1,269
			85	16,583	10,190	14,864	4,674
			86	76,809	42,200	51,712	9,512
FR GERM	N E		84	1,420	5,824	6,184	360
			85	127,942	223,773	233,938	10,165
	O E		81	1,968	3,602	4,064	462
			82	2,079	5,360	6,454	1,094
	V E		81	57,315	144,773	156,391	11,618
			82	55,390	127,921	136,624	8,703
			83	150,449	215,419	234,432	19,013
			84	98,374	169,678	186,255	16,577
			85	16,358	23,852	26,007	2,155
			86	115,239	305,385	319,904	14,519
	V W		81	3,162	9,389	10,881	1,492
			82	110,332	121,332	129,441	8,109
			83	106,001	119,297	127,787	8,490
			84	86,044	93,520	102,221	8,701
			85	4,456	17,826	19,745	1,919
			86	1,672	10,403	11,229	826
FRANCE	V W		83	203	1,008	1,070	62
GREECE	V E		83	22,046	13,661	18,090	4,429
HAITI	V E		83	349	990	1,102	112
INDIA	V E		86	2,094	5,279	5,534	255
	V W		82	185	309	340	31
			83	109	279	350	71
IRAN	V W		85	3,441	3,331	4,425	1,094
ITALY	V E		81	529	3,148	3,491	343
			82	625	1,695	1,811	116
			83	812	1,997	2,068	71
			85	506	2,159	2,403	244
			86	290	1,196	1,266	70
JAMAICA	A E		83	421	1,000	1,248	248
			84	434	264	573	309
LEBANON	V E		83	110	260	305	45
MACAO	V W		84	169	796	848	52
PAKISTN	V E		86	474	1,675	1,884	209
POLAND	V E		84	1,923	9,634	10,142	508
SPAIN	V E		83	514	2,236	2,393	157
TURKEY	V E		84	1,349	522	663	141
	V W		84	6,455	6,600	7,252	652
U KING	N E		81	1,470	10,027	10,974	947
	O E		81	34	376	391	15
			84	39	299	319	20
	V E		81	42	349	374	25
			82	1,432	7,590	8,236	646
			83	1,792	9,947	10,646	699
			84	2,726	12,321	13,885	1,564
			85	2,497	9,133	10,169	1,036
			86	6,730	33,605	37,281	3,676

Monkshood

Aconite, natural drug**

4350500 ALOES JALAP MATE ETC, CRUDE (LB)
(See Aloe, natural drug under Aloe)
4351000 ALOES,JALAP MANA,ETC ADVANCE (LB)
(See Aloe, natural drug under Aloe)

Mulberry

Mulberry, jelly or jam
1530500 MULBERRY JAM,MARMALADE,ETC (LB)

Country	Mode	Reg	Yr	Quantity	F.A.S.	C.I.F.	Charges
TOTAL			83	186,176	148,998	157,412	8,414
			84	125,919	85,265	95,307	10,042
			85	606,744	151,339	164,611	13,272
			86	180,440	79,696	98,493	18,797
AUSTRAL	V E		85	3,619	6,569	7,358	789
AUSTRIA	V E		83	360	427	458	31
BELGIUM	O E		85	258	1,658	2,172	514
	V E		83	3,707	2,511	2,850	339
			84	3,053	1,530	1,795	265
			85	504,000	53,310	54,520	1,210
CANADA	O E		83	720	391	391	
			84	45,100	9,071	9,071	
	O W		83	85,850	70,500	70,990	490
			84	4,000	3,130	3,130	
			85	16,162	13,340	13,340	
CHINA T	V W		83	889	883	1,002	119
DENMARK	V W		85	2,100	1,059	1,284	225
FR GERM	V E		83	1,296	1,052	1,158	106
			84	960	783	861	78
	V W		83	3,000	3,173	3,564	391
			85	4,104	2,407	3,250	843
FRANCE	V E		83	26,905	21,471	24,195	2,724
			84	13,747	12,200	13,878	1,678
			85	5,679	5,906	6,618	712
			86	20,114	18,815	21,469	2,654
	V W		83	17,609	3,038	3,414	376
			86	992	1,101	1,560	459
HUNGARY	V E		86	134,310	24,959	36,657	11,698
IRAN	V W		85	2,756	1,440	1,845	405
ITALY	V E		84	6,429	8,841	10,951	2,110
JAPAN	V H		84	13,402	10,625	12,503	1,878
	V W		83	18,449	14,006	15,135	1,129
KOR REP	V E		84	9,518	6,841	7,950	1,109
MEXICO	O W		83	4,429	4,352	4,352	
NETHLDS	O E		86	9,000	4,162	5,061	899
	V E		85	5,127	7,659	8,465	806
			86	1,557	3,420	3,735	315
PORTUGL	V E		84	6,613	7,500	7,698	198
SWITZLD	V E		83	8,135	7,537	8,087	550
			84	385	2,569	2,638	69
			85	1,190	1,238	1,404	166
	V W		83	180	494	535	41
U KING	N E		83	8,985	12,245	13,480	1,235
	O E		85	7,572	6,613	7,170	557
	V E		83	2,232	2,793	3,192	399
			84	16,957	16,851	18,696	1,845
			85	41,518	38,548	44,263	5,715
			86	12,417	24,691	27,198	2,507
	V W		83	3,430	4,125	4,609	484
			84	5,755	5,324	6,136	812
			85	12,659	11,592	12,922	1,330
			86	2,050	2,548	2,813	265

Mushroom

Mushroom, dried
1441200 MUSHROOMS, DRIED (LB)

Country	Mode	Reg	Yr	Quantity	F.A.S.	C.I.F.	Charges
TOTAL			81	1,508,817	12,128,776	12,809,141	680,365
			82	431,348	2,323,683	2,458,876	135,193
BELGIUM	V E		81	1,124	4,413	4,568	155
CANADA	A W		81	360	5,974	6,305	331
	O E		81	2,216	31,583	31,583	
			82	220	3,352	3,454	102
CHILE	O E		81	10,659	15,559	16,818	1,259
	V E		81	19,166	29,705	31,737	2,032
			82	60,308	95,404	101,894	6,490
	V W		81	143,303	225,229	246,354	21,125
			82	110,241	212,226	229,179	16,953
CHINA M	V E		81	17,402	145,907	155,484	9,577
			82	1,555	4,565	4,739	174
	V H		81	200	1,175	1,258	83
	V W		81	1,877	8,151	8,647	496

Crop / Product / TSUSA commodity number, description, and unit of quantity — Country	Mode	Reg	Yr	Quantity	F.A.S.	C.I.F.	Charges
			82	6,610	19,023	19,964	941
CHINA T	N	E	81	42,863	356,531	383,318	26,787
	O	E	81	21,282	94,125	99,605	5,480
	O	W	82	1,320	12,555	12,555	
	V	E	81	6,574	79,376	84,732	5,356
			82	9,740	82,118	87,536	5,418
	V	H	82	1,000	7,581	8,300	719
	V	W	81	155,430	1,459,364	1,541,699	82,335
			82	17,829	153,975	161,908	7,933
FR GERM	N	W	82	3,617	20,185	22,435	2,250
	O	E	81	5,870	27,093	28,648	1,555
			82	22	412	418	6
	V	E	81	13,238	106,323	112,367	6,044
			82	2,659	19,257	20,277	1,020
	V	W	81	5,103	36,053	39,729	3,676
FRANCE	A	E	81	52	2,935	3,068	133
	N	E	81	7,554	134,239	139,736	5,497
			82	1,110	20,478	21,678	1,200
	N	W	81	1,948	68,391	71,227	2,836
			82	595	17,883	18,727	844
	O	E	81	82	1,745	1,745	
	V	E	81	631	2,010	2,251	241
			82	212	6,112	7,420	1,308
	V	W	81	144	7,470	8,265	795
			82	24	1,251	1,389	138
HAITI	N	E	81	1,332	2,542	2,947	405
HG KONG	N	W	81	198	1,572	1,878	306
	V	E	81	1,042	7,290	7,879	589
			82	50	578	626	48
	V	H	81	193	1,940	2,061	121
			82	100	773	827	54
	V	W	81	319	2,211	2,391	180
INDIA	A	E	81	4,534	183,677	198,341	14,664
			82	410	18,135	19,023	888
	O	E	81	22	1,000	1,150	150
ITALY	A	W	81	359	8,001	14,891	6,890
			82	251	5,780	6,723	943
	N	E	81	5,276	82,454	90,064	7,610
	O	E	81	16	298	330	32
	V	E	82	6,504	35,159	36,134	975
JAPAN	N	E	81	351,199	2,997,893	3,183,535	185,642
	N	W	81	123,149	1,012,356	1,063,444	51,088
			82	39,451	278,375	290,592	12,217
	O	E	81	500	5,000	5,000	
	V	E	81	6,938	60,685	65,002	4,317
			82	47,535	368,026	387,604	19,578
	V	H	81	55,246	514,776	575,318	60,542
			82	8,486	76,106	84,010	7,904
	V	W	81	338,280	3,055,482	3,161,740	106,258
			82	91,148	670,319	703,765	33,446
KOR REP	N	W	81	111,648	823,104	856,033	32,929
	O	E	81	500	4,533	4,533	
	V	E	81	28,442	212,408	224,044	11,636
			82	148	1,810	1,980	170
	V	H	81	1,400	9,286	10,461	1,175
	V	W	81	4,635	28,575	30,817	2,242
			82	14,185	99,315	103,725	4,410
NETHLDS	A	E	81	220	9,248	9,559	311
PAKISTN	A	W	81	1,454	52,198	55,069	2,871
			82	772	27,143	30,000	2,857
SWEDEN	V	E	81	8	265	279	14
SWITZLD	A	E	81	1,511	54,535	56,302	1,767
			82	547	18,053	18,618	565
	A	W	81	312	13,826	14,704	878
	V	E	81	141	4,823	5,110	287
			82	290	13,676	14,206	530
SYRIA	V	E	81	300	1,758	2,103	345
U KING	A	E	81	1,110	4,994	5,987	993
YUGOSLV	A	E	81	11,455	128,695	139,025	10,330
			82	4,409	34,058	39,170	5,112

1441400 MUSHROOMS, AIR OR SUN DRIED (LB)

Country	Mode	Reg	Yr	Quantity	F.A.S.	C.I.F.	Charges
TOTAL			82	466,501	3,070,003	3,226,865	156,862
			83	953,922	7,996,926	8,335,973	339,047
			84	1,327,341	9,475,348	9,950,083	474,735
			85	1,289,264	8,003,118	8,448,114	444,996
			86	1,304,482	8,620,730	9,048,107	427,377
AUSTRAL	V	H	83	200	1,956	2,038	82
	V	W	83	495	3,411	3,448	37
AUSTRIA	A	E	83	600	10,964	11,343	379
			84	600	8,455	8,955	500
BELGIUM	A	E	83	66	3,298	3,449	151
			84	220	1,691	1,775	84

Country	Mode	Reg	Yr	Quantity	F.A.S.	C.I.F.	Charges
CANADA	A	E	85	157	2,458	2,543	85
			86	101	4,461	4,696	235
	O	E	83	1,100	14,232	14,232	
			84	1,548	19,761	19,782	21
			85	1,400	18,513	18,513	
			86	10,314	69,574	71,198	1,624
	O	W	84	40	854	854	
			86	16,907	176,021	176,021	
CHILE	V	E	82	9,709	16,399	17,463	1,064
			83	92,089	147,979	159,423	11,444
			84	123,743	135,316	149,215	13,899
			85	18,442	17,308	19,370	2,062
			86	82,265	62,888	71,874	8,986
	V	W	82	125,562	239,646	259,165	19,519
			83	211,870	424,275	459,262	34,987
			84	295,926	573,653	616,022	42,369
			85	239,725	362,592	403,172	40,580
			86	129,895	224,109	247,135	23,026
CHINA M	N	W	85	3,926	16,251	16,952	701
	O	E	85	3,000	2,045	2,328	283
	V	E	82	1,413	7,007	7,225	218
			83	6,205	34,959	36,876	1,917
			84	1,850	15,518	17,116	1,598
			85	330	3,474	3,500	26
			86	4,122	28,882	30,085	1,203
	V	H	82	265	1,885	2,034	149
			83	192	3,456	3,707	251
	V	W	82	148	692	741	49
			83	15,504	98,973	103,457	4,484
			84	4,113	39,301	41,452	2,151
			85	6,216	15,376	16,447	1,071
			86	29,295	47,243	51,354	4,111
CHINA T	A	E	86	3,307	13,500	21,636	8,136
	A	W	86	750	2,212	3,147	935
	N	E	85	27,676	96,486	110,494	14,008
	N	W	85	70,978	282,132	299,237	17,105
			86	68,405	292,846	304,843	11,997
	O	E	83	2,368	7,415	8,146	731
	O	W	83	165	1,248	1,248	
	V	E	82	4,952	37,337	39,027	1,690
			83	15,856	147,952	152,539	4,587
			84	8,212	40,444	44,406	3,962
			85	562	1,200	1,502	302
			86	39,228	154,870	164,695	9,825
	V	H	86	701	8,412	9,180	768
	V	W	82	15,075	68,881	72,317	3,436
			83	24,026	80,377	85,883	5,506
			84	35,146	139,855	154,769	14,914
			85	15,986	65,065	68,556	3,491
			86	20,385	73,186	76,187	3,001
DENMARK	A	E	84	22	470	496	26
FR GERM	A	E	84	50	558	751	193
			85	363	2,803	3,055	252
			86	1,980	4,653	6,159	1,506
	A	W	84	237	2,267	2,494	227
			85	165	1,552	1,701	149
			86	98	1,035	1,220	185
	N	E	83	4,673	22,758	23,980	1,222
			84	12,215	41,520	44,338	2,818
			86	6,523	36,080	39,525	3,445
	O	E	85	6,024	35,084	37,549	2,465
	V	E	82	12,720	90,745	97,479	6,734
			83	13,432	68,597	73,279	4,682
			84	11,863	56,215	59,716	3,501
			85	4,800	16,004	17,605	1,601
			86	26,273	143,448	150,899	7,451
	V	W	82	954	7,365	8,066	701
			83	616	6,796	7,362	566
			86	422	3,142	3,279	137
FRANCE	A	E	83	272	9,719	10,726	1,007
			84	1,449	40,083	44,634	4,551
			85	960	34,724	37,352	2,628
			86	2,236	26,203	29,117	2,914
	A	W	84	62	2,240	2,389	149
			86	869	5,815	8,099	2,284
	N	E	82	5,142	67,965	70,660	2,695
			83	5,559	104,297	109,621	5,324
			84	3,831	101,113	103,721	2,608
			85	10,042	233,120	241,490	8,370
			86	4,795	94,127	98,139	4,012
	N	W	83	202	5,054	5,386	332
			84	1,714	35,512	37,906	2,394
			85	10,315	125,155	133,965	8,810
			86	3,007	29,378	31,378	2,000

Crop
Product
TSUSA commodity number, description, and unit of quantity

Country	Mode	Reg	Yr	Quantity	F.A.S.	C.I.F.	Charges
	O	E	82	1,273	29,774	30,740	966
			83	24	1,006	1,140	134
			84	336	10,540	11,268	728
			86	133	6,138	8,789	2,651
	O	W	86	510	12,096	12,804	708
	V	E	82	270	11,641	11,742	101
			83	2,844	37,861	39,243	1,382
			84	2,919	19,768	20,151	383
			85	23,208	40,782	44,077	3,295
			86	4,943	13,818	14,858	1,040
	V	W	82	601	18,364	18,744	380
			83	1,352	44,765	46,005	1,240
			86	1,080	39,617	40,807	1,190
GREECE	A	E	85	400	3,400	3,693	293
HAITI	A	E	82	132	832	877	45
			83	116	1,286	1,364	78
			84	399	2,394	2,783	389
	V	E	83	516	2,826	3,092	266
HG KONG	A	E	82	33	686	732	46
	A	W	84	88	1,400	1,619	219
	V	E	83	4,713	13,576	14,024	448
			84	250	2,010	2,252	242
			86	1,035	9,636	10,880	1,244
	V	H	83	25	255	288	33
	V	W	82	880	11,215	11,714	499
			84	1,196	5,812	6,137	325
			85	1,670	7,479	7,720	241
			86	2,885	13,211	14,471	1,260
INDIA	A	E	82	2,960	90,941	95,918	4,977
			83	2,237	58,917	62,958	4,041
			84	4,624	162,416	168,105	5,689
			85	4,876	199,023	204,589	5,566
			86	3,557	225,780	230,148	4,368
	A	W	83	240	9,150	10,496	1,346
ITALY	A	E	82	328	4,551	5,089	538
			83	250	2,950	3,629	679
			84	1,602	13,364	15,358	1,994
			85	1,577	16,508	19,148	2,640
			86	3,568	51,114	56,058	4,944
	A	W	83	313	4,507	4,846	339
			84	110	1,730	1,892	162
			85	7,193	79,967	91,149	11,182
			86	183	3,385	3,743	358
	N	E	82	849	19,770	20,937	1,167
			83	3,522	68,081	72,257	4,176
			84	3,979	65,750	71,519	5,769
			85	9,932	149,271	160,073	10,802
			86	14,044	160,125	171,724	11,599
	N	W	84	3,480	39,678	47,069	7,391
			86	6,913	102,469	113,274	10,805
	V	E	83	248	3,228	3,621	393
			84	851	3,459	3,745	286
			85	220	1,412	1,834	422
			86	8,373	109,579	112,502	2,923
	V	W	83	2,224	29,607	30,077	470
JAPAN	A	W	86	2,800	7,000	7,106	106
	N	E	84	158,413	2,047,299	2,133,999	86,700
	N	W	82	71,685	569,512	585,729	16,217
			83	170,820	2,118,807	2,183,266	64,459
			84	60,503	621,792	647,847	26,055
			85	87,558	618,227	645,210	26,983
			86	70,552	563,210	581,281	18,071
	O	H	84	77	1,394	1,687	293
	O	W	83	331	5,324	5,640	316
			85	5,940	40,093	41,580	1,487
	V	E	82	128,246	1,121,007	1,175,236	54,229
			83	137,794	1,876,962	1,949,223	72,261
			84	4,359	57,805	62,060	4,255
			85	229,822	2,019,075	2,129,236	110,161
			86	199,113	1,917,880	2,012,759	94,879
	V	H	82	15,196	140,785	155,320	14,535
			83	17,618	230,390	248,773	18,383
			84	24,873	275,278	302,453	27,175
			85	19,434	205,135	233,958	28,823
			86	19,632	180,543	203,422	22,879
	V	W	82	25,729	206,117	215,050	8,933
			83	877	14,048	15,046	998
			84	241,903	2,030,289	2,098,316	68,027
			85	202,292	1,496,741	1,549,895	53,154
			86	109,843	900,738	922,944	22,206
KOR REP	N	E	82	2,134	2,738	3,020	282
			84	26,194	223,566	244,364	20,798
			86	37,148	268,611	278,682	10,071
	N	W	83	102,239	1,008,228	1,037,173	28,945

Country	Mode	Reg	Yr	Quantity	F.A.S.	C.I.F.	Charges
	V	E	82	2,427	19,705	21,121	1,416
			83	24,984	272,373	286,915	14,542
			84	1,000	11,294	11,709	415
			85	21,199	121,234	128,298	7,064
			86	6,046	44,046	47,321	3,275
	V	H	84	1,188	11,861	13,647	1,786
			85	1,000	9,397	9,755	358
			86	4,039	33,070	36,957	3,887
	V	W	82	29,373	186,509	196,596	10,087
			83	74,292	785,072	815,654	30,582
			84	250,506	2,288,057	2,365,106	77,049
			85	236,601	1,404,800	1,464,701	59,901
			86	343,952	2,108,884	2,203,498	94,614
MALAYSA	A	W	85	132	3,960	4,232	272
MAURIT	A	E	86	22	1,986	2,004	18
MEXICO	A	W	84	176	5,450	5,872	422
			85	838	27,455	28,967	1,512
			86	902	37,027	37,678	651
	V	W	83	1,170	11,119	11,565	446
PAKISTN	A	E	82	639	24,327	25,741	1,414
			83	986	32,590	35,784	3,194
			84	1,122	41,913	44,829	2,916
			85	766	33,727	34,546	819
			86	850	65,750	68,255	2,505
	A	W	82	471	14,000	15,088	1,088
			83	1,607	59,534	64,446	4,912
			84	2,134	94,700	111,182	16,482
			85	1,838	84,016	89,578	5,562
			86	219	13,700	14,571	871
PERU	V	E	84	5,505	5,404	6,004	600
POLAND	A	E	84	1,102	12,000	13,742	1,742
			86	265	1,161	1,440	279
ROMANIA	A	E	84	220	2,667	3,500	833
	V	W	84	2,656	3,815	4,138	323
SINGAPR	V	W	84	461	900	945	45
SPAIN	V	E	85	241	3,564	3,804	240
SWEDEN	V	E	85	551	2,945	3,509	564
SWITZLD	A	E	82	60	3,039	3,120	81
			83	2,306	78,014	81,186	3,172
			84	1,152	30,642	31,942	1,300
			85	1,686	63,937	66,374	2,437
			86	2,890	142,181	148,025	5,844
	A	W	84	240	11,820	12,193	373
			85	271	5,277	5,508	231
	N	E	82	255	7,902	8,358	456
	O	E	84	120	5,575	5,689	114
	V	E	82	354	10,218	10,957	739
			83	36	618	663	45
			84	342	9,152	9,739	587
			86	1,559	11,578	12,176	598
	V	W	83	35	1,866	2,094	228
THAILND	V	E	84	896	605	691	86
	V	W	82	66	480	532	52
			83	1,415	3,434	3,692	258
			84	1,405	2,035	2,238	203
			85	5,482	7,611	8,201	590
TURKEY	A	E	83	216	6,864	7,991	1,127
			84	881	33,846	35,266	1,420
			85	220	7,619	8,069	450
			86	48	2,700	2,904	204
U KING	V	E	85	390	5,493	5,579	86
YUGOSLV	A	E	82	6,600	37,968	40,327	2,359
			83	3,082	15,952	18,417	2,465
			84	17,238	63,042	78,236	15,194
			85	2,860	13,628	19,500	5,872
			86	5,500	71,612	77,160	5,548

1441600 MUSHROOMS, DRIED, NSPF (LB)

Country	Mode	Reg	Yr	Quantity	F.A.S.	C.I.F.	Charges
TOTAL			82	351,601	3,131,544	3,306,238	174,694
			83	631,296	7,641,779	7,997,641	355,862
			84	800,301	8,163,879	8,663,279	499,400
			85	905,056	8,401,310	8,996,849	595,539
			86	947,873	9,107,681	9,549,550	441,869
AUSTRIA	V	E	82	512	11,776	11,814	38
BELGIUM	A	E	85	279	1,493	1,588	95
	V	E	86	900	12,729	13,431	702
CANADA	A	E	85	60	1,424	1,498	74
	O	E	82	209	3,139	3,304	165
			83	620	9,278	9,449	171
			84	50	1,106	1,106	
			85	975	9,555	9,555	
	O	W	84	126	3,354	3,457	103
CHILE	V	E	82	3,360	5,597	5,944	347

Crop
Product
TSUSA commodity number, description, and unit of quantity

Country	Mode	Reg	Yr	Quantity	F.A.S.	C.I.F.	Charges
			83	10,794	18,454	19,780	1,326
	V	W	82	16,433	31,343	33,816	2,473
CHINA M	O	E	84	469	588	606	18
	V	E	82	128	1,160	1,207	47
			83	2,380	13,508	14,628	1,120
			84	1,583	21,679	22,556	877
			85	2,660	28,329	28,331	2
			86	11,720	125,076	131,523	6,447
	V	H	83	231	3,500	3,711	211
			84	3,266	31,085	32,588	1,503
			86	1,233	10,333	10,692	359
	V	W	82	6,324	11,306	12,077	771
			83	1,689	12,142	12,501	359
			84	7,935	94,271	96,018	1,747
			85	2,780	10,914	11,136	222
			86	1,875	17,970	19,023	1,053
CHINA T	N	E	85	150,180	1,438,793	1,605,387	166,594
	N	W	84	78,419	848,179	889,889	41,710
			86	8,680	98,411	101,801	3,390
	V	E	82	13,300	95,877	100,913	5,036
			83	73,829	751,577	802,495	50,918
			84	118,316	1,146,300	1,243,610	97,310
			85	17,060	181,602	198,006	16,404
			86	116,915	1,253,372	1,324,011	70,639
	V	W	82	49,846	549,364	579,273	29,909
			83	73,956	791,613	823,679	32,066
			84	11,437	105,441	111,295	5,854
			85	146,686	1,269,137	1,324,417	55,280
			86	200,444	1,644,906	1,701,719	56,813
DENMARK	V	E	83	38	1,014	1,092	78
FR GERM	A	E	82	204	2,533	2,969	436
			83	522	4,807	5,402	595
			84	802	6,199	6,472	273
			86	672	7,585	9,398	1,813
	A	W	84	110	1,058	1,084	26
	N	E	84	3,283	17,104	18,004	900
			85	16,879	75,163	84,861	9,698
			86	11,756	70,554	80,275	9,721
	V	E	82	201	6,198	6,687	489
			83	7,014	49,429	52,023	2,594
			84	4,490	27,270	29,824	2,554
			85	921	4,617	4,848	231
			86	17,381	78,525	84,714	6,189
	V	W	82	1,488	16,380	17,276	896
			83	5,425	38,876	42,006	3,130
			85	5,512	23,438	26,252	2,814
FRANCE	A	E	82	1,530	32,231	34,527	2,296
			83	3,002	68,333	72,690	4,357
			84	2,788	52,859	56,537	3,678
			85	1,679	57,046	59,297	2,251
			86	198	4,357	4,796	439
	A	W	82	390	15,328	16,054	726
			83	49	1,077	1,160	83
	N	E	82	7,876	14,264	15,317	1,053
			83	7,501	71,606	74,836	3,230
			84	40,136	229,459	248,201	18,742
			85	19,188	142,116	149,275	7,159
			86	12,219	157,681	169,837	12,156
	N	W	83	3,097	65,779	71,037	5,258
			84	4,118	79,497	84,167	4,670
			85	9,022	62,236	68,340	6,104
			86	490	16,543	18,127	1,584
	O	E	82	61	1,831	2,020	189
			83	6	279	279	
			84	90	4,866	4,882	16
			85	11,001	57,697	60,808	3,111
	V	E	82	1,643	8,837	9,135	298
			83	1,177	16,986	17,515	529
			84	761	7,101	7,291	190
			85	5,220	38,509	40,473	1,964
			86	5,340	111,513	113,787	2,274
	V	W	82	36	1,949	2,163	214
			83	180	8,500	9,500	1,000
			84	7,454	113,123	123,656	10,533
			85	1,242	29,426	31,468	2,042
			86	2,367	33,079	35,043	1,964
GUATMAL	A	E	85	240	11,602	11,821	219
HAITI	A	E	82	455	455	683	228
			83	400	500	613	113
			86	250	1,950	2,155	205
	V	E	84	1,014	5,577	6,552	975
			86	242	1,334	1,694	360
HG KONG	N	E	83	687	6,467	6,884	417
	V	E	83	7	297	386	89
			84	519	8,081	8,886	805
			85	209	3,744	4,042	298
	V	H	84	25	410	427	17
			86	125	1,712	1,835	123
	V	W	82	33	378	391	13
			83	463	4,339	4,710	371
			84	6,790	74,209	77,353	3,144
			85	1,069	13,872	14,467	595
			86	2,348	15,180	15,870	690
INDIA	A	E	82	850	30,705	32,767	2,062
			83	420	16,590	17,579	989
			84	1,414	45,693	48,292	2,599
			85	757	25,962	29,359	3,397
IRELAND	V	W	85	196	1,758	1,869	111
ITALY	A	E	82	961	13,115	15,331	2,216
			83	1,458	19,443	23,007	3,564
			84	1,589	20,813	23,820	3,007
			85	4,102	38,072	43,344	5,272
			86	614	6,144	7,210	1,066
	A	W	82	830	27,875	30,384	2,509
			85	2,258	22,038	26,449	4,411
			86	225	3,790	4,417	627
	N	E	82	14,943	91,694	102,565	10,871
			83	10,298	97,040	105,154	8,114
			84	36,168	334,117	359,834	25,717
			85	15,094	195,172	216,479	21,307
			86	7,732	89,698	98,321	8,623
	N	W	83	438	3,870	4,684	814
			84	1,646	15,441	18,583	3,142
			85	3,020	34,898	37,552	2,654
			86	3,501	14,865	15,929	1,064
	V	E	82	110	2,053	2,336	283
			83	68	1,343	1,481	138
			84	406	5,236	5,454	218
			85	1,751	9,506	10,964	1,458
			86	3,412	39,421	43,032	3,611
	V	W	86	300	4,402	5,409	1,007
JAPAN	A	E	84	22	674	748	74
	N	E	83	166,389	2,153,155	2,230,653	77,498
			84	166,916	1,647,190	1,729,986	82,796
	N	H	82	26,652	286,148	319,747	33,599
			83	25,732	384,690	419,318	34,628
			84	32,830	431,242	483,952	52,710
	N	W	82	60,374	525,610	550,119	24,509
			83	196,423	2,528,457	2,615,553	87,096
			84	188,545	2,032,812	2,111,720	78,908
			85	131,006	1,263,377	1,339,089	75,712
			86	118,838	1,412,505	1,476,129	63,624
	O	E	84	206	4,771	5,255	484
	O	H	84	123	1,574	1,997	423
	O	W	85	300	1,800	1,947	147
			86	450	6,469	6,728	259
	V	E	82	41,683	388,993	406,157	17,164
			83	12,116	144,878	155,642	10,764
			84	12,357	138,809	150,460	11,651
			85	182,183	1,579,484	1,659,315	79,831
			86	176,674	1,597,493	1,669,909	72,416
	V	H	85	25,266	325,716	369,155	43,439
			86	18,964	266,669	299,938	33,269
	V	W	82	95,404	835,824	865,630	29,806
			83	12,283	188,337	200,654	12,317
			84	39,749	398,769	423,541	24,772
			85	125,555	1,177,002	1,236,887	59,885
			86	161,563	1,503,971	1,553,478	49,507
KOR REP	O	E	84	165	2,310	2,310	
	V	E	82	365	4,587	4,997	410
			83	4,000	42,318	47,969	5,651
			84	1,214	19,068	19,494	426
			86	7,570	64,604	70,569	5,965
	V	H	84	23	259	300	41
			85	896	8,477	8,912	435
			86	2,591	20,584	22,808	2,224
	V	W	82	2,782	20,606	21,881	1,275
			83	3,278	34,057	35,369	1,312
			84	8,181	86,940	91,725	4,785
			85	7,796	62,893	67,742	4,849
			86	26,402	157,313	166,566	9,253
MOROC	O	E	84	464	561	561	
	V	E	86	284	1,836	1,905	69
NETHLDS	A	E	85	4,405	78,831	88,386	9,555
NORWAY	A	E	85	127	1,616	1,854	238
PAKISTN	A	E	83	78	2,870	3,066	196
	A	W	82	440	16,400	18,000	1,600
REP SAF	A	E	84	3,191	13,113	17,932	4,819

Crop Product TSUSA commodity number, description, and unit of quantity Country	Mode	Reg	Yr	Quantity	F.A.S.	C.I.F.	Charges
			85	659	2,400	3,140	740
			86	689	2,504	3,304	800
SINGAPR	V	E	86	5,540	62,048	64,948	2,900
SOMALIA	A	E	85	441	1,600	2,000	400
SPAIN	V	E	84	5,100	12,236	16,125	3,889
SWITZLD	A	E	82	2,068	77,388	80,091	2,703
			83	1,548	52,657	55,119	2,462
			84	2,400	62,846	64,869	2,023
			85	5,526	83,625	89,051	5,426
	A	W	85	724	20,801	21,863	1,062
	N	E	83	240	9,443	9,817	374
	V	E	83	35	622	655	33
			86	99	1,761	1,838	77
THAILND	V	W	82	110	600	663	63
			83	655	780	831	51
			86	650	1,830	2,017	187
TURKEY	A	E	85	132	5,569	5,622	53
	V	E	86	16,620	186,964	195,364	8,400
U KING	A	E	83	1	1,000	1,010	10
	V	E	84	2,266	1,995	2,111	116
YUGOSLV	A	E	83	2,769	21,868	23,704	1,836
			84	1,345	8,594	9,749	1,155

Mushroom, fresh
1441000 MUSHROOMS, FRESH (LB)

Country	Mode	Reg	Yr	Quantity	F.A.S.	C.I.F.	Charges
TOTAL			81	474,579	366,827	373,471	6,564
			82	760,660	697,910	713,180	15,270
			83	1,400,557	724,687	766,412	41,725
			84	633,325	731,438	899,665	168,227
			85	252,163	485,597	694,403	208,806
			86	1,373,006	900,547	1,170,766	270,219
BELGIUM	A	E	81	1,229	2,384	3,046	662
			82	1,186	3,143	4,067	924
			84	878	1,826	2,439	613
			85	520	2,174	2,416	242
	A	W	82	82	309	448	139
			84	15	375	525	150
			85	3,413	10,287	12,458	2,171
			86	456	2,220	3,306	1,086
BRAZIL	A	E	81	224	621	787	166
CANADA	A	E	81	3,666	14,583	16,634	2,051
			82	4,163	12,999	15,033	2,034
			83	13,365	34,086	40,246	6,160
			84	5,332	23,781	26,440	2,659
			85	498	2,229	3,004	775
	A	H	81	255	1,531	1,663	132
			82	110	1,447	1,513	66
			84	5,222	5,067	5,643	576
			86	1,100	1,085	1,186	101
	A	W	81	236	1,586	1,695	109
			82	507	7,570	7,811	241
			83	100	371	501	130
			84	6,807	16,924	19,754	2,830
			85	4,451	8,868	10,785	1,917
			86	608	4,083	4,563	480
	N	W	81	458,780	313,435	313,481	46
			82	739,922	597,091	597,110	19
			83	796,522	517,554	517,604	50
	O	E	81	5,768	5,319	5,399	
			82	608	1,953	1,953	
			83	100	494	494	
			85	62,465	45,871	45,871	
			86	797,136	225,117	225,117	
	O	W	83	3,229	2,496	2,496	
			84	431,857	276,203	276,203	
			85	8,150	12,096	12,096	
			86	384,577	245,782	245,782	
CHILE	A	E	83	5,494	4,305	7,455	3,150
CHINA T	A	E	86	9,389	7,334	18,231	10,897
	A	W	84	159	648	1,294	646
			85	4,679	4,254	4,824	570
			86	9,419	12,663	15,662	2,999
	O	E	86	600	1,600	1,715	115
ECUADOR	V	E	83	552,920	43,542	53,185	9,643
FR GERM	A	E	86	1,763	3,506	6,250	2,744
FRANCE	A	E	81	2,133	12,711	15,282	2,571
			82	12,318	62,618	73,199	10,581
			83	16,974	84,064	96,143	12,079
			84	33,520	127,843	151,165	23,322
			85	15,407	61,344	74,685	13,341
			86	10,868	42,286	52,599	10,313

Country	Mode	Reg	Yr	Quantity	F.A.S.	C.I.F.	Charges
	A	W	83	2,133	2,215	3,671	1,456
			84	86	666	816	150
			85	285	5,236	5,874	638
			86	4,665	23,949	29,026	5,077
	O	E	81	981	8,405	8,405	
HAITI	A	E	81	390	397	568	171
HG KONG	V	E	81	487	289	346	57
ISRAEL	A	E	86	8,487	20,650	50,871	30,221
ITALY	A	E	81	41	385	402	17
			82	240	4,059	4,473	414
			83	4,351	7,407	12,281	4,874
			84	86,035	135,290	194,294	59,004
			85	92,236	194,999	275,123	80,124
			86	100,043	250,714	366,332	115,618
	A	W	81	132	2,412	2,614	202
			84	6,944	10,591	16,440	5,849
			85	1,885	6,600	8,717	2,117
			86	270	1,068	1,731	663
	O	W	84	6,000	3,777	3,777	
	V	E	85	253	1,062	1,121	59
JAPAN	A	E	81	102	414	466	52
			86	270	1,388	1,528	140
	A	H	81	7	443	495	52
			83	47	1,861	2,057	196
			84	88	496	788	292
	A	W	84	20,488	71,334	115,353	44,019
			85	53,641	113,362	213,795	100,433
			86	16,359	29,395	63,980	34,585
	N	H	85	295	2,696	3,671	975
	N	W	86	23,282	19,361	70,280	50,919
	V	E	83	1,500	18,825	19,520	695
KOR REP	A	H	81	59	1,563	1,793	230
MEXICO	A	E	84	42	333	376	43
MOROC	A	W	86	407	1,827	2,275	448
N ZEAL	A	W	83	396	372	425	53
NETHLDS	A	E	81	89	349	395	46
			82	1,478	6,372	7,181	809
			83	252	1,611	1,723	112
			84	2,181	9,510	10,622	1,112
			85	201	1,019	1,112	93
			86	1,334	2,157	3,066	909
	A	W	84	463	903	1,320	417
			85	1,214	4,505	5,707	1,202
REP SAF	A	E	84	485	2,146	3,221	1,075
			85	363	1,320	1,720	400
SENEGAL	A	E	83	244	934	1,149	215
			84	580	1,366	1,523	157
			86	165	1,403	1,556	153
SINGAPR	A	E	86	551	1,250	3,251	2,001
	A	W	84	1,063	1,837	4,822	2,985
			85	1,415	6,287	9,872	3,585
SPAIN	A	E	83	2,930	4,550	7,462	2,912
			84	24,010	37,408	58,601	21,193
SWITZLD	A	W	84	977	2,758	3,768	1,010
			86	1,257	1,709	2,459	750
THAILND	V	W	85	792	1,388	1,552	164
U KING	A	E	82	46	349	392	43
			84	93	356	481	125

Mushroom, frozen
1442005 MUSHROOMS, FROZEN (LB)

Country	Mode	Reg	Yr	Quantity	F.A.S.	C.I.F.	Charges
TOTAL			81	775,423	911,723	949,100	37,377
			82	382,136	386,629	402,905	16,276
			83	39,872	70,367	77,922	7,555
			84	950,864	1,030,534	1,067,326	36,792
			85	1,567,851	1,658,085	1,756,287	98,202
			86	2,581,128	2,971,856	3,130,265	158,409
BRAZIL	V	E	81	52,800	51,744	58,623	6,879
CANADA	A	H	83	1,129	3,386	3,813	427
			85	3,264	5,612	5,990	378
			86	4,200	6,010	6,474	464
	O	E	81	420,628	589,445	589,445	
			82	210,530	246,835	246,835	
			83	23,436	27,363	27,363	
			84	694,541	790,511	790,511	
			85	640,709	712,415	712,415	
			86	701,352	785,534	785,534	
	O	W	81	3,968	6,010	6,010	
			85	8,442	11,134	11,134	
			86	158,619	222,184	222,186	2
CHINA M	V	W	86	166,388	59,360	78,045	18,685

Crop Product TSUSA commodity number, description, and unit of quantity Country	Mode	Reg	Yr	Quantity	F.A.S.	C.I.F.	Charges
CHINA T	V	E	81	185,760	160,991	181,991	21,000
			82	15,750	9,450	10,227	777
			84	54,113	31,040	36,633	5,593
			85	85,200	71,555	79,586	8,031
	V	H	83	1,200	1,200	1,351	151
			84	6,192	7,149	8,088	939
	V	W	81	112,152	103,110	112,593	9,483
			82	153,698	118,198	131,935	13,737
			83	8,268	8,074	8,991	917
			84	172,280	108,057	121,491	13,434
			85	756,150	654,945	713,142	58,197
			86	1,427,780	1,598,551	1,686,225	87,674
FRANCE	A	E	83	502	3,149	3,454	305
			84	44	710	745	35
			85	44	1,339	1,380	41
	A	W	84	474	2,446	3,046	600
	V	E	85	19,258	12,745	15,591	2,846
			86	24,614	15,970	20,039	4,069
ITALY	A	E	82	2,068	11,766	13,160	1,394
			83	1,980	9,972	11,164	1,192
			84	431	3,213	3,713	500
			86	10,074	67,550	80,171	12,621
	A	W	82	90	380	748	368
			83	1,188	6,447	9,990	3,543
			84	5,574	26,628	34,876	8,248
			85	6,220	31,855	43,809	11,954
			86	7,020	48,000	67,857	19,857
	N	E	84	2,363	12,855	14,328	1,473
			85	7,418	45,753	52,866	7,113
	V	E	86	4,212	33,824	36,107	2,283
JAPAN	A	H	85	1,520	5,320	5,692	372
	V	E	84	6,000	8,250	9,160	910
	V	W	81	115	423	438	15
			84	49	267	281	14
			85	3,388	17,062	17,745	683
			86	45,000	33,300	35,100	1,800
KOR REP	V	E	84	540	622	756	134
	V	W	84	560	718	785	67
MEXICO	O	E	86	5,608	6,775	6,775	
NETHLDS	A	E	84	308	1,250	1,567	317
REP SAF	O	E	86	2,178	2,645	2,645	
SPAIN	A	E	84	6,573	34,018	38,221	4,203
			85	14,192	78,295	86,882	8,587
			86	2,221	7,892	10,363	2,471
	O	E	85	22,046	10,055	10,055	
	V	E	86	20,367	82,991	91,383	8,392
SWITZLD	A	E	83	2,169	10,776	11,796	1,020
	V	E	84	822	2,800	3,125	325
THAILND	V	W	86	1,495	1,270	1,361	91

9225605 MUSHROOMS FZ, ARBITRARY NO. (LB)

Country	Mode	Reg	Yr	Quantity	F.A.S.	C.I.F.	Charges
TOTAL			82	513,370	478,032	503,588	25,556
			83	935,538	879,313	916,608	37,295
CANADA	O	E	82	261,227	277,804	279,130	1,326
			83	452,881	490,311	490,311	
	O	W	82	646	1,116	1,116	
			83	1,386	1,439	1,439	
CHINA T	V	E	83	810	1,440	1,607	167
	V	W	82	251,008	197,000	219,771	22,771
			83	294,002	216,496	240,378	23,882
ITALY	A	W	82	489	2,112	3,571	1,459
			83	699	4,507	6,607	2,100
KOR REP	V	W	83	185,760	165,120	176,266	11,146

Mushroom, prepared or preserved

1442027 MUSHROOM WHOLE PREP/PRES NOV9OZ (LB)

Country	Mode	Reg	Yr	Quantity	F.A.S.	C.I.F.	Charges
TOTAL			81	4,505,106	5,906,169	6,382,659	476,490
			82	2,440,269	3,278,364	3,543,655	265,291
			83	740,068	858,855	930,503	71,648
			84	6,375,077	8,262,160	8,964,332	702,172
			85	6,385,408	8,327,400	8,984,670	657,270
			86	6,731,779	8,016,546	8,681,930	665,384
BELGIUM	V	E	85	48,323	64,541	71,039	6,498
			86	43,124	75,992	85,163	9,171
	V	W	86	13,338	27,101	29,903	2,802
CANADA	O	E	84	1,905	2,129	2,129	
			86	574	2,040	2,040	
	O	W	85	4,333	17,893	17,893	
			86	1,395	3,515	3,515	
CHINA M	N	W	86	45,324	40,205	42,787	2,582
	O	W	82	104,084	88,557	106,541	17,984
	V	E	81	10,500	11,711	13,119	1,408
			82	16,590	16,403	18,731	2,328
			84	23,400	30,400	33,980	3,580
			85	28,560	33,018	36,883	3,865
			86	361,349	289,017	317,048	28,031
	V	H	81	102,696	124,459	132,914	8,455
			82	15,675	17,290	18,746	1,456
			83	14,850	17,640	18,840	1,200
			84	132,143	162,147	173,388	11,241
			85	109,763	134,680	146,072	11,392
			86	128,198	142,414	161,062	18,648
	V	W	81	105,010	99,005	121,754	22,749
			82	56,109	69,912	76,933	7,021
			83	2,730	1,247	1,356	109
			84	483,920	507,041	554,434	47,393
			85	298,346	346,321	371,717	25,396
			86	322,640	366,448	399,127	32,679
CHINA T	N	E	82	161,429	169,074	190,668	21,594
	N	W	84	1,798,348	2,258,859	2,410,113	151,254
	O	E	83	29,490	34,628	39,610	4,982
			84	6,804	9,297	9,746	449
	V	E	81	1,947,723	2,403,417	2,626,356	222,939
			82	1,072,238	1,440,470	1,548,722	108,252
			83	233,710	217,974	241,674	23,700
			84	2,386,142	3,207,031	3,547,826	340,795
			85	2,051,970	2,765,133	3,046,458	281,325
			86	2,203,117	2,869,182	3,148,009	278,827
	V	H	81	138,566	179,539	191,193	11,654
			82	89,039	103,131	111,020	7,889
			83	24,078	25,646	27,700	2,054
			84	183,393	227,059	242,118	15,059
			85	154,811	191,795	207,450	15,655
			86	61,462	70,178	76,038	5,860
	V	W	81	1,590,535	2,154,588	2,292,302	137,714
			82	572,974	744,158	795,599	51,441
			83	417,862	513,590	550,248	36,658
			84	1,040,441	1,381,298	1,475,772	94,474
			85	3,020,006	3,959,000	4,228,299	269,290
			86	2,683,131	3,139,174	3,352,004	212,830
FR GERM	A	E	82	1,005	2,660	3,469	809
	V	E	81	8,523	48,139	50,433	2,294
			82	6,394	36,781	38,434	1,653
			83	810	5,920	6,250	330
			84	4,226	19,124	20,362	1,238
			85	31,795	106,796	110,398	3,602
			86	3,840	8,396	9,051	655
	V	H	86	1,815	9,483	10,269	786
	V	W	82	2,213	7,579	8,019	440
			84	1,080	6,698	7,239	541
			86	3,600	30,124	30,428	304
FRANCE	A	E	82	645	2,450	2,788	338
			83	317	782	862	80
			84	210	475	515	40
	A	W	82	97	265	297	32
	N	E	82	2,400	15,963	18,836	2,873
	O	E	81	480	3,172	3,312	140
			82	480	3,172	3,312	140
	V	E	81	5,868	25,473	26,718	1,245
			82	6,255	38,443	40,365	1,922
			83	1,916	11,606	11,980	374
			84	51,669	92,397	96,087	3,690
			85	18,111	63,884	67,623	3,739
			86	28,968	82,803	89,049	6,246
	V	W	81	3,364	24,314	25,970	1,656
			82	15,178	84,080	88,030	3,950
			83	3,480	11,295	12,035	740
			84	3,016	8,296	8,691	395
			85	2,868	16,983	18,182	1,199
GERM DR	V	E	86	3,000	26,218	26,864	646
HG KONG	O	E	81	18,000	19,800	21,746	1,946
			85	258,600	171,878	172,271	393
	V	E	82	600	760	842	82
			84	7,200	7,926	8,715	789
			85	21,600	27,980	30,742	2,762
			86	199,767	117,032	128,769	11,737
	V	H	86	11,400	13,205	14,036	831
	V	W	81	34,875	31,995	34,177	2,182
			83	4,200	2,500	2,741	241
			84	41,108	40,528	43,435	2,907
			85	122,565	130,964	137,039	6,075
			86	143,143	143,640	158,473	14,833
INDNSIA	V	W	85	14,400	13,230	14,687	1,457
			86	50,220	64,589	69,637	5,048

Crop
Product
TSUSA commodity number, description, and unit of quantity

Country	Mode	Reg	Yr	Quantity	F.A.S.	C.I.F.	Charges
ITALY	A E	84	153	318	408	90
	A W	84	14	277	329	52
	N E	81	2,950	7,952	9,229	1,277
	O E	81	180	330	362	32
	V E	82	1,575	2,921	3,328	407
	V W	84	1,620	8,188	8,501	313
JAPAN	V E	81	11,974	22,749	24,726	1,977
		82	9,022	15,809	17,453	1,644
		83	2,148	4,994	5,389	395
		84	18,800	34,387	37,282	2,895
		85	3,643	12,716	13,581	865
		86	5,150	16,849	19,071	2,222
	V H	81	880	2,516	2,844	328
		82	15,824	17,256	18,681	1,425
		83	676	931	1,143	212
		84	484	952	1,091	139
		86	3,191	5,178	5,850	672
	V W	81	5,263	12,999	13,640	641
		82	8,201	12,958	13,919	961
		83	3,104	8,393	8,847	454
		84	4,634	13,780	14,392	612
		85	9,394	23,085	24,458	1,373
		86	1,993	7,422	7,712	290
KOR REP	V E	81	172,013	226,545	247,184	20,639
		82	92,063	121,169	132,141	10,972
		83	697	1,709	1,828	119
		84	50,473	65,048	73,092	8,044
		85	16,960	28,418	31,153	2,735
		86	28,008	29,635	32,847	3,212
	V H	85	16,800	20,160	23,698	3,538
		86	59,400	63,195	68,595	5,400
	V W	81	337,282	465,371	500,484	35,113
		82	186,090	257,620	276,259	18,639
		84	92,995	134,264	145,516	11,252
		85	80,004	114,935	122,342	7,407
		86	243,750	315,681	332,360	16,679
MACAO	V E	86	5,400	6,750	7,268	518
	V W	82	1,188	747	788	41
		85	1,920	1,720	1,803	83
MEXICO	O E	85	895	1,325	1,325	
	O W	85	6,941	13,471	13,471	
	V W	86	1,114	2,649	2,668	19
NETHLDS	A E	81	276	305	660	355
	V E	81	2,210	6,671	6,944	273
		82	1,200	3,334	3,792	458
		84	1,650	3,696	4,007	311
		86	7,906	9,454	10,677	1,223
RWANDA	V W	85	3,126	4,187	4,475	288
SPAIN	V E	84	25,587	19,497	21,641	2,144
		85	58,804	55,102	62,759	7,657
SWITZLD	O E	85	870	8,185	8,852	667
	V E	81	5,938	35,119	36,592	1,473
		82	603	4,762	5,213	451
		84	1,536	4,756	5,290	534
		86	348	4,886	5,288	402
	V W	86	2,196	8,134	8,819	685
THAILND	V E	84	12,126	16,292	18,233	1,941
	V W	82	1,098	640	729	89
		86	62,832	24,650	26,034	1,384
U KING	V E	86	1,086	1,307	1,469	162

1442031 MUSHROOM SLICED NT FZ NT OV 9OZ (LB)

Country	Mode	Reg	Yr	Quantity	F.A.S.	C.I.F.	Charges
TOTAL		81	6,629,801	8,766,530	9,433,459	666,929
		82	5,843,590	8,414,547	9,072,226	657,679
		83	734,723	1,035,426	1,100,722	65,296
		84	15,479,566	20,839,798	22,562,801	1,723,003
		85	15,480,465	21,949,754	23,704,096	1,754,342
		86	16,657,604	21,023,486	22,849,499	1,826,013
BELGIUM	V E	85	63,632	68,036	74,168	6,132
		86	42,944	73,296	82,228	8,932
	V W	85	1,482	1,728	2,342	614
		86	9,894	19,047	20,947	1,900
CHINA M	O E	81	21,675	22,175	22,175	
	O W	83	84,000	84,577	89,277	4,700
	V E	81	33,691	21,008	23,345	2,337
		82	3,300	3,272	3,545	273
		84	282,708	306,476	335,608	29,132
		85	350,688	397,394	439,793	42,399
		86	2,334,910	1,805,899	2,051,687	245,788
	V W	81	52,695	47,128	49,896	2,768
		82	180,140	243,741	269,032	25,291
		84	409,401	449,409	489,670	40,261
		85	846,296	952,365	1,010,731	58,366
		86	663,221	714,289	787,598	73,309
CHINA T	N E	85	541,818	742,203	820,819	78,616
	N W	84	6,186,507	8,136,615	8,643,420	506,805
	O E	83	43,140	56,394	61,693	5,299
		84	10,584	14,994	15,720	726
		86	16,500	13,880	13,880	
	V E	81	3,772,286	4,783,241	5,180,791	397,550
		82	3,829,052	5,608,128	6,060,665	452,537
		83	74,891	105,053	114,168	9,115
		84	5,614,153	8,074,448	8,920,569	846,121
		85	4,565,729	6,919,158	7,606,722	687,564
		86	5,522,709	7,812,458	8,496,428	683,970
	V H	81	8,925	12,620	13,471	851
		82	19,425	21,680	23,207	1,527
		83	413	550	610	60
		84	2,190	4,150	4,475	325
		85	2,625	3,580	3,863	283
		86	2,025	2,550	2,692	142
	V W	81	2,196,414	3,202,573	3,413,885	211,312
		82	1,431,626	2,013,524	2,148,169	134,645
		83	517,104	772,365	815,027	42,662
		84	1,762,505	2,533,054	2,712,316	179,262
		85	7,760,223	11,324,730	12,082,154	757,424
		86	6,070,484	8,364,072	8,992,690	628,618
FR GERM	V E	81	9,600	7,598	7,862	264
		82	840	5,041	5,326	285
		84	111	568	639	71
FRANCE	A W	84	21	770	804	34
	V E	81	1,358	3,794	3,919	125
		82	420	1,861	2,005	144
		83	2,100	3,442	4,007	565
		84	180	366	391	25
		85	13,618	28,901	31,389	2,488
		86	30,378	73,249	79,535	6,286
HG KONG	V E	82	1,320	1,309	1,449	140
		83	9,206	8,123	9,977	1,854
		84	227,945	180,355	201,414	21,059
		85	99,634	78,867	87,992	9,125
		86	340,196	209,548	227,801	18,253
	V W	83	3,600	3,870	4,091	221
		84	284,625	305,014	323,758	18,744
		85	171,776	160,152	170,113	9,961
		86	271,483	213,804	233,016	19,212
INDIA	V E	86	50,220	66,785	74,249	7,464
INDNSIA	V E	86	149,823	203,367	222,395	19,028
	V W	85	434,202	582,257	624,802	42,545
		86	573,525	756,032	819,248	63,216
ISRAEL	V E	86	30,690	40,741	45,352	4,611
ITALY	A E	81	40	357	411	54
		83	269	1,052	1,872	820
	O E	86	1,586	8,465	8,825	360
	V E	84	178	728	908	180
		85	6,170	6,580	7,041	461
		86	498	1,426	1,546	120
	V W	84	210	2,654	2,736	82
JAPAN	A H	86	26	1,032	1,466	434
	N E	82	412	3,018	3,238	220
	O E	84	756	1,071	1,129	58
	V E	81	5,760	8,244	9,022	778
		84	7,405	10,165	11,176	1,011
		85	4,152	6,090	6,676	586
		86	765	2,106	2,234	128
	V H	84	2,365	6,200	7,241	1,041
	V W	81	17,314	24,256	24,457	201
		82	6,615	8,996	9,709	713
		84	11,430	16,560	17,889	1,329
		85	16,717	27,676	29,507	1,831
		86	28,864	45,536	47,711	2,175
KOR REP	O E	85	21,675	16,166	18,356	2,190
	V E	81	131,700	174,826	192,564	17,738
		82	151,275	197,137	216,735	19,598
		84	122,240	159,239	178,858	19,619
		85	2,168	2,380	2,692	312
		86	77,352	67,614	74,952	7,338
	V H	81	1,200	1,780	1,907	127
	V W	81	376,850	456,427	489,231	32,804
		82	219,165	306,840	329,146	22,306
		84	443,217	511,929	555,851	43,922
		85	363,456	474,349	513,468	39,119
		86	417,921	490,262	519,510	29,248
MACAO	V E	86	5,400	7,470	8,043	573
	V W	86	20,400	18,840	19,756	916
MEXICO	O E	85	9,863	15,651	15,651	
		86	2,400	3,932	3,932	

Crop / Product / TSUSA commodity number, description, and unit of quantity Country	Mode	Reg	Yr	Quantity	F.A.S.	C.I.F.	Charges
	V	W	86	1,219	1,676	2,053	377
NETHLDS	V	E	81	293	503	523	20
			84	16,350	23,508	26,027	2,519
			85	108,561	74,288	82,295	8,007
			86	11,228	12,547	15,104	2,557
SPAIN	V	E	84	80,625	81,575	90,004	8,429
			85	25,529	14,734	17,049	2,315
SWITZLD	O	E	86	218	3,703	4,094	391
	V	E	85	39,551	19,564	21,869	2,305
THAILND	V	E	84	13,860	19,950	22,198	2,248
			86	1,125	8,700	10,283	1,583
	V	W	85	10,500	14,065	14,848	783

1442037 MUSHRM PREP NT FZ NSPF, NOV 9OZ (LB)

Country	Mode	Reg	Yr	Quantity	F.A.S.	C.I.F.	Charges
TOTAL			81	12,821,112	13,897,531	15,151,606	1,254,075
			82	7,393,694	7,242,426	8,001,998	759,572
			83	2,032,441	2,019,463	2,255,007	235,544
			84	28,389,996	30,829,175	33,878,267	3,049,092
			85	28,450,744	28,714,225	31,634,894	2,920,669
			86	31,129,757	26,415,583	28,993,027	2,577,444
BELGIUM	V	E	85	19,200	18,144	20,190	2,046
			86	22,205	21,651	25,795	4,144
CANADA	O	E	84	4,026	11,805	11,805	
			85	150	1,200	1,200	
			86	675	2,400	2,400	
	O	W	85	2,628	6,033	6,033	
			86	54,882	48,833	48,833	
CHILE	V	E	85	16,208	9,517	10,746	1,229
CHINA M	N	W	82	1,293,656	1,043,192	1,158,212	115,020
	O	E	81	276,654	242,500	283,103	40,603
			82	535,146	460,444	553,031	92,587
			83	387,834	349,538	413,258	63,720
			84	814,639	769,015	898,123	129,108
			85	892,500	682,130	779,780	97,650
			86	416,925	284,191	329,146	44,955
	O	H	81	1,733	1,512	1,665	153
			82	3,218	2,808	3,085	277
	O	W	81	898,472	915,349	1,029,385	114,036
			82	516,120	472,705	509,813	37,108
			84	90,000	93,434	99,505	6,071
			85	268,171	328,056	358,500	30,444
			86	1,066,440	931,097	991,014	59,917
	V	E	81	1,100,094	1,111,946	1,252,284	140,338
			82	738,026	847,413	933,854	86,441
			83	169,166	155,416	177,127	21,711
			84	4,063,958	3,870,935	4,391,886	520,951
			85	6,177,572	5,922,612	6,717,487	794,875
			86	4,826,262	3,649,174	4,117,021	467,847
	V	H	81	135,777	144,435	155,239	10,804
			82	9,900	10,500	11,242	742
			83	15,360	16,256	18,756	2,500
			84	110,849	117,164	126,691	9,527
			85	37,875	41,310	45,022	3,712
			86	91,996	86,083	95,813	9,730
	V	W	81	3,618,666	3,709,783	4,040,994	331,211
			82	815,274	650,471	716,690	66,219
			83	410,928	388,778	425,677	36,899
			84	3,778,429	3,694,642	4,055,765	361,123
			85	4,818,642	4,521,669	4,990,965	469,296
			86	5,139,031	4,008,211	4,460,638	452,427
CHINA T	A	W	84	214	430	698	268
	N	E	85	150,287	169,692	189,973	20,281
	N	W	84	2,911,528	3,478,378	3,722,915	244,537
			85	731,400	733,506	789,168	55,662
	O	E	83	357,256	382,455	423,262	40,807
			84	237,666	247,357	267,577	20,220
			85	5,220	4,421	4,962	541
			86	98,813	86,258	98,626	12,368
	O	W	85	95,562	99,033	109,063	10,030
	V	E	81	2,588,776	3,087,467	3,352,181	264,714
			82	1,251,697	1,390,819	1,544,601	153,782
			83	306,215	314,698	352,864	38,166
			84	5,456,975	6,323,743	7,037,786	714,043
			85	2,821,491	3,303,558	3,671,864	368,306
			86	3,649,978	3,580,383	3,935,319	354,936
	V	H	81	74,939	88,413	94,286	5,873
			82	30,650	33,065	35,690	2,625
			83	25,311	24,323	26,397	2,074
			84	139,046	157,911	170,173	12,262
			85	160,588	166,328	181,058	14,730
			86	66,038	67,829	74,298	6,469
	V	W	81	1,914,243	2,123,700	2,269,799	146,099
			82	1,260,155	1,288,244	1,388,169	99,925
			83	216,278	217,444	232,518	15,074
			84	5,375,646	6,177,011	6,625,720	448,709
			85	5,711,579	6,181,658	6,603,341	421,683
			86	8,206,787	7,523,628	8,107,156	583,528
DENMARK	V	E	84	42,687	38,920	43,559	4,639
FR GERM	A	E	82	201	544	709	165
			84	715	3,095	3,647	552
	O	E	81	480	3,184	3,419	235
			85	1,023	2,721	2,967	246
			86	1,056	2,640	2,787	147
	V	E	81	240	1,570	1,645	75
			82	1,500	8,559	8,973	414
			83	1,830	8,329	8,867	538
			84	3,518	21,328	21,824	496
			85	21,000	39,615	42,836	3,221
			86	10,053	19,210	20,167	957
	V	W	82	12,000	76,239	81,701	5,462
			84	780	4,690	5,047	357
			85	2,400	18,814	19,797	983
			86	900	7,533	8,243	710
FRANCE	A	E	84	81	553	628	75
	N	E	82	2,001	9,945	10,837	892
	V	E	81	21,625	40,427	43,367	2,940
			82	447	2,597	2,871	274
			83	2,619	11,794	11,948	154
			84	45,011	82,066	87,740	5,674
			85	67,458	154,791	163,712	8,921
			86	62,516	154,095	162,831	8,736
	V	W	81	815	6,860	7,539	679
			82	289	5,111	5,611	500
			83	525	7,401	7,829	428
			84	5,176	19,160	19,697	537
			85	4,303	43,300	45,962	2,662
			86	913	9,416	10,508	1,092
GERM DR	O	E	81	360	2,984	3,123	139
HG KONG	O	E	82	16,667	8,266	9,021	755
	V	E	81	431,115	422,748	462,176	39,428
			82	147,880	118,489	134,647	16,158
			83	67,320	56,760	61,819	5,059
			84	499,500	470,870	520,879	50,009
			85	712,292	555,416	621,309	65,893
			86	1,253,760	733,850	826,625	92,775
	V	W	81	423,159	446,222	480,779	34,557
			82	105,414	94,967	102,618	7,651
			84	202,810	217,989	227,603	9,614
			85	341,487	311,492	342,573	31,081
			86	405,103	264,551	286,327	21,776
INDIA	V	E	86	67,200	61,051	67,874	6,823
INDNSIA	V	E	86	84,894	85,993	94,010	8,017
	V	W	85	434,772	467,154	479,177	12,023
			86	623,490	571,004	625,845	54,841
ISRAEL	V	E	86	14,400	13,059	14,537	1,478
ITALY	O	E	81	208	2,809	3,084	275
			84	79	401	409	8
	V	E	82	2,270	4,754	5,159	405
			83	1,510	5,129	5,426	297
			84	2,849	15,432	16,985	1,553
			85	1,001	5,931	6,382	451
			86	3,292	10,442	11,157	715
	V	W	82	139	788	883	95
JAPAN	A	E	84	4,900	9,108	9,674	566
	N	E	83	210	473	514	41
			84	26,585	42,739	47,327	4,588
	N	H	84	11,513	28,234	32,663	4,429
	N	W	83	1,515	9,862	11,204	1,342
			84	65,529	102,502	109,997	7,495
			85	104,378	154,396	165,862	11,466
			86	1,534	16,225	19,521	3,296
	O	E	85	407	2,112	2,293	181
	V	E	81	13,192	19,542	21,414	1,872
			82	1,358	2,838	3,118	280
			83	213	779	865	86
			84	44,070	41,231	45,808	4,577
			85	16,412	24,028	26,643	2,615
			86	6,260	15,681	16,678	997
	V	H	81	9,146	19,117	21,830	2,713
			82	3,521	8,520	9,946	1,426
			83	3,442	6,725	8,262	1,537
			85	3,292	8,797	10,643	1,846
			86	9,568	20,063	22,940	2,877
	V	W	81	40,780	55,774	59,260	3,486
			82	23,503	35,721	38,055	2,334
			83	198	431	472	41
			84	5,955	17,669	18,676	1,007

Crop
Product
TSUSA commodity number, description, and unit of quantity

Country	Mode	Reg	Yr	Quantity	F.A.S.	C.I.F.	Charges
			85	3,737	17,578	18,445	867
			86	80,060	108,843	115,600	6,757
KOR REP	O H	82	5,198	4,536	4,983	447
	V E	81	393,067	446,115	486,585	40,470
			82	240,240	249,740	274,809	25,069
			84	1,304,710	1,412,769	1,596,564	183,795
			85	1,075,611	1,016,381	1,146,528	130,147
			86	1,623,845	1,311,433	1,471,560	160,127
	V H	81	8,250	9,460	10,346	886
			84	67,200	77,840	85,872	8,032
			85	82,425	75,300	87,232	11,932
			86	116,475	99,905	109,125	9,220
	V W	81	760,567	865,293	927,806	62,513
			82	364,815	386,381	427,020	40,639
			83	22,680	23,814	25,922	2,108
			84	2,091,595	2,329,284	2,523,330	194,046
			85	2,701,344	2,678,195	2,906,612	228,417
			86	2,641,968	2,191,212	2,342,752	151,540
KUWAIT	V W	85	16,800	16,240	17,490	1,250
MACAO	V E	81	68,176	48,633	52,728	4,095
			82	8,400	6,650	7,382	732
			83	36,888	17,150	19,370	2,220
			84	79,997	64,710	71,916	7,206
			86	32,925	21,343	24,022	2,679
	V H	81	13,388	11,813	12,628	815
	V W	84	80,750	59,200	63,095	3,895
N ANTIL	V E	85	21,600	16,235	18,300	2,065
NETHLDS	O E	85	12,768	15,091	17,341	2,250
			86	104,736	77,260	87,700	10,440
	V E	84	104,509	120,313	129,334	9,021
			85	198,352	165,782	182,585	16,803
			86	60,501	39,643	43,741	4,098
PHIL R	V E	85	36,000	37,500	42,767	5,267
POLAND	V E	81	3,600	12,439	14,400	1,961
			82	2,400	10,848	11,341	493
			84	8,021	21,377	23,784	2,407
			85	21,350	78,568	86,380	7,812
			86	10,721	42,608	46,350	3,742
PORTUGL	A E	82	315	490	664	174
	V E	86	960	1,045	1,147	102
SPAIN	N E	85	183,038	155,545	176,402	20,857
	V E	84	572,595	546,298	607,971	61,673
			85	398,362	328,771	379,168	50,397
			86	165,790	142,876	160,708	17,832
	V W	84	90,000	96,900	109,373	12,473
			86	20,183	29,132	31,877	2,745
SWITZLD	N E	82	416	3,031	3,429	398
			85	12,156	42,436	43,847	1,411
	V E	81	6,790	38,256	39,981	1,725
			82	878	3,751	3,834	83
			83	3,655	20,983	21,648	665
			85	7,477	40,214	41,621	1,407
			86	640	7,612	8,022	410
	V W	85	201	1,985	2,197	212
THAILND	V E	84	7,500	8,695	9,695	1,000
			85	43,425	32,910	39,061	6,151
			86	14,400	11,760	13,098	1,338
	V W	81	16,800	19,180	20,560	1,380
			83	1,488	925	1,002	77
			84	38,385	33,977	36,526	2,549
			85	16,800	18,060	19,410	1,350
			86	70,613	55,133	59,837	4,704
U KING	V E	86	969	1,227	1,379	152

1442043 MUSHRM WHOLE PREP NT FRZ OV 9OZ (LB)

Country	Mode	Reg	Yr	Quantity	F.A.S.	C.I.F.	Charges
TOTAL			81	3,808,741	3,815,742	4,075,097	259,355
			82	1,306,462	1,562,945	1,667,501	104,556
			83	289,444	302,200	325,081	22,881
			84	5,074,543	5,159,110	5,572,288	413,178
			85	5,873,326	5,944,747	6,427,017	482,270
			86	5,203,345	4,770,026	5,175,892	405,866
BELGIUM	V E	85	7,482	10,912	13,099	2,187
CANADA	O E	81	2,728	3,431	3,431	
			84	2,555	3,024	3,024	
	O W	85	1,930	3,320	3,320	
CHILE	V E	85	22,752	13,554	15,305	1,751
CHINA M	O E	81	20,910	16,620	18,803	2,183
	V E	81	343,753	172,083	191,347	19,264
			83	2,550	2,100	2,325	225
			84	274,128	183,250	210,846	27,596
			85	538,497	389,729	436,232	46,503
			86	251,743	179,113	201,049	21,936
	V H	81	7,200	7,250	7,714	464

Crop
Product
TSUSA commodity number, description, and unit of quantity

Country	Mode	Reg	Yr	Quantity	F.A.S.	C.I.F.	Charges
			84	1,200	1,225	1,366	141
			85	4,195	3,531	3,870	339
			86	27,773	22,950	24,699	1,749
	V W	81	421,616	225,809	244,713	18,904
			82	79,230	65,490	70,238	4,748
			83	22,500	16,737	18,599	1,862
			84	376,504	318,130	344,129	25,999
			85	365,792	271,743	294,031	22,288
			86	99,731	69,833	75,161	5,328
CHINA T	N E	81	26,851	27,661	29,694	2,033
			84	186,681	212,761	235,431	22,670
			85	150,048	166,094	186,247	20,153
	N W	84	1,117,678	1,131,923	1,193,996	62,073
			85	934,222	1,023,956	1,102,465	78,509
	O E	81	33,696	40,258	43,043	2,785
			82	17,844	16,439	17,787	1,348
			83	2,231	740	740	
			84	4,318	4,110	4,110	
			85	20,400	23,290	25,292	2,002
			86	9,127	11,250	12,150	900
	O W	82	1,344	1,596	1,794	198
			86	3,600	3,900	4,165	265
	V E	81	1,027,698	1,161,677	1,243,557	81,880
			82	348,631	397,419	429,371	31,952
			83	114,038	77,969	85,718	7,749
			84	939,981	955,131	1,057,073	101,942
			85	1,305,543	1,347,481	1,478,220	130,739
			86	1,675,775	1,671,934	1,834,668	162,734
	V H	81	42,854	52,103	55,127	3,024
			82	15,744	18,762	20,135	1,373
			83	9,600	10,400	11,173	773
			84	24,450	24,049	25,755	1,706
			85	82,938	74,851	82,110	7,259
			86	131,044	123,867	135,185	11,318
	V W	81	966,459	1,146,475	1,207,034	60,559
			82	527,009	549,233	583,739	34,506
			83	109,651	98,151	104,522	6,371
			84	935,501	1,019,207	1,091,292	72,085
			85	1,410,702	1,534,214	1,624,876	90,662
			86	1,606,769	1,554,426	1,644,827	90,401
DOM REP	V E	82	62,623	35,100	37,443	2,343
FR GERM	V E	81	7,557	46,824	48,909	2,085
			82	30,919	98,726	101,778	3,052
			83	2,160	14,413	15,050	637
			84	9,090	43,552	46,937	3,385
			85	4,800	32,737	33,622	885
			86	18,454	44,884	49,239	4,355
	V W	81	3,480	22,896	23,924	1,028
			82	3,000	19,759	20,443	684
			84	1,260	6,660	7,271	611
			85	5,700	27,178	28,177	999
			86	1,068	5,999	6,679	680
FRANCE	N E	85	974	4,937	5,245	308
	N W	81	7,053	36,836	39,237	2,401
			84	21,878	52,990	57,406	4,416
	O E	81	16,200	26,565	28,074	1,509
			86	360	2,523	3,612	1,089
	V E	81	49,612	88,426	96,392	7,966
			82	26,199	56,056	62,383	6,327
			83	5,496	11,646	12,276	630
			84	82,136	112,638	122,413	9,775
			85	40,940	69,009	74,172	5,163
			86	29,682	58,203	63,306	5,103
	V W	81	8,969	25,554	28,109	2,555
			83	5,544	24,024	26,048	2,024
			85	22,593	77,536	79,449	1,913
			86	27,564	76,606	79,065	2,459
HG KONG	O E	82	12,720	12,190	13,350	1,160
	V E	81	155,520	147,616	161,297	13,681
			82	29,638	25,955	28,142	2,187
			83	2,856	2,352	2,508	156
			84	80,754	84,976	94,359	9,383
			85	244,265	204,005	224,347	20,342
			86	498,667	288,531	314,635	26,104
	V H	85	1,275	1,200	1,301	101
			86	4,080	3,365	3,688	323
	V W	81	478,787	315,788	339,240	23,452
			82	52,559	46,562	49,405	2,843
			84	639,797	560,722	594,621	33,899
			85	528,384	462,905	494,884	31,979
			86	634,804	406,981	458,754	51,773
INDIA	A E	85	25,500	10,200	10,390	190
			86	48,687	67,676	68,887	1,211
ITALY	A E	84	234	991	1,253	262

Crop Product TSUSA commodity number, description, and unit of quantity Country	Mode	Reg	Yr	Quantity	F.A.S.	C.I.F.	Charges
	N	E	84	4,926	9,287	11,143	1,856
			85	368	3,459	3,845	386
			86	2,120	7,477	8,168	691
	N	W	86	3,804	25,719	28,270	2,551
	O	E	81	399	612	612	
			84	23,288	23,460	25,576	2,116
	V	E	81	512	1,644	1,807	163
			84	808	5,449	5,947	498
			85	1,512	7,633	8,385	752
	V	W	81	66	382	486	104
			82	614	5,336	5,656	320
			84	1,311	7,992	8,396	404
JAPAN	V	E	81	3,569	5,778	6,172	394
			82	1,122	2,698	2,809	111
			83	1,680	3,967	4,302	335
			84	1,470	3,344	3,612	268
			86	26,759	30,930	32,826	1,896
	V	H	82	1,470	2,697	2,920	223
	V	W	81	2,400	1,850	1,923	73
			82	158	324	339	15
			83	720	4,149	4,779	630
			84	29,773	24,417	25,504	1,087
			85	595	1,208	1,283	75
			86	735	2,533	2,616	83
KOR REP	V	E	81	50,121	44,197	48,318	4,121
			84	135,760	115,437	128,176	12,739
			85	2,194	2,236	2,530	294
	V	H	84	1,032	2,035	2,250	215
	V	W	81	17,710	21,524	22,575	1,051
			84	21,675	19,125	20,908	1,783
			86	3,000	3,912	4,660	748
MACAO	V	E	81	43,920	47,949	51,003	3,054
			82	21,900	23,034	24,601	1,567
	V	H	81	1,200	1,300	1,387	87
	V	W	81	52,680	50,455	53,463	3,008
			82	18,600	14,736	15,863	1,127
			84	30,986	29,614	31,327	1,713
			85	17,214	17,249	18,273	1,024
			86	19,701	11,250	11,784	534
MEXICO	O	W	85	1,322	2,349	2,349	
NETHLDS	O	E	85	37,422	20,925	23,375	2,450
	V	E	85	900	1,692	2,032	340
			86	29,716	23,811	29,860	6,049
PAKISTN	A	E	86	4,642	18,570	18,960	390
POLAND	V	E	81	14,013	67,456	70,268	2,812
			82	13,500	63,720	65,864	2,144
SPAIN	V	E	84	58,343	53,013	60,057	7,044
			85	67,969	71,889	81,766	9,877
			86	1,852	1,015	1,203	188
	V	W	85	3,150	2,092	2,633	541
SWITZLD	A	E	86	441	6,848	7,668	820
	N	E	83	394	2,700	2,833	133
			85	2,194	14,021	14,665	644
	O	E	81	1,058	7,139	7,574	435
			82	1,936	10,259	10,582	323
			83	4,392	10,614	11,002	388
			84	12,175	18,910	20,745	1,835
			86	774	4,868	5,226	358
	V	E	81	5,080	23,738	24,286	548
			82	13,528	52,060	53,882	1,822
			83	5,632	22,238	23,206	968
			84	23,094	84,775	87,286	2,511
			85	10,416	33,452	34,069	617
			86	1,198	4,351	4,738	387
	V	W	82	106	745	812	67
			84	5,505	17,264	18,463	1,199
			85	1,347	9,707	10,306	599
THAILND	V	E	82	14,400	17,045	18,465	1,420
			85	3,307	2,058	2,298	240
			86	20,400	22,100	24,215	2,115
	V	W	81	4,039	3,400	3,687	287
			82	3,000	1,450	1,591	141
			84	855	821	896	75
			85	4,484	2,395	2,554	159
			86	19,275	14,601	15,929	1,328
U KING	V	E	84	25,397	28,828	30,720	1,892

1442047 MUSHRM SLICED PREP NT FZ OV 9OZ (LB)

TOTAL			81	4,154,223	4,092,208	4,378,843	286,635
			82	1,709,226	1,529,430	1,670,935	141,505
			83	480,064	414,201	448,552	34,351
			84	6,869,472	6,736,938	7,335,046	598,108
			85	9,718,031	8,965,092	9,767,972	802,880
			86	8,611,710	6,502,955	7,077,655	574,700

Crop Product TSUSA commodity number, description, and unit of quantity Country	Mode	Reg	Yr	Quantity	F.A.S.	C.I.F.	Charges
BELGIUM	O	E	84	96,840	86,661	92,817	6,156
	V	E	84	44,829	46,734	49,786	3,052
			85	1,482	2,105	2,574	469
CANADA	O	E	83	1,100	4,957	4,957	
			86	320	4,210	4,210	
	O	W	85	15,300	10,500	12,026	1,526
			86	26,000	22,567	22,567	
CHINA M	O	E	81	21,675	21,675	21,675	
			85	353,813	262,661	302,928	40,267
	O	W	81	20,999	20,822	22,744	1,922
	V	E	81	594,326	558,147	606,145	47,998
			82	320,905	279,433	308,444	29,011
			83	12,189	12,790	14,453	1,663
			84	430,525	358,967	406,858	47,891
			85	882,821	679,246	747,144	67,898
			86	1,532,408	1,025,333	1,152,483	127,150
	V	H	81	15,035	15,375	16,493	1,118
			84	3,600	3,925	4,488	563
			85	6,350	5,583	6,202	619
			86	145,322	111,937	122,659	10,722
	V	W	81	368,456	287,935	308,298	20,363
			82	88,111	76,771	83,061	6,290
			83	242,505	179,231	190,807	11,576
			84	1,081,841	949,915	1,032,285	82,370
			85	888,187	752,490	815,229	62,739
			86	990,421	715,036	760,016	44,980
CHINA T	N	E	85	872,029	1,015,801	1,112,301	96,500
	N	W	84	609,059	635,248	671,092	35,844
			85	797,306	922,270	971,480	49,210
			86	288,569	288,688	302,438	13,750
	O	E	81	20,739	25,783	27,672	1,889
			83	4,320	4,586	4,911	325
			85	8,160	9,553	10,276	723
			86	9,000	12,450	13,446	996
	O	W	83	6,768	7,251	7,784	533
			86	1,200	1,360	1,452	92
	V	E	81	429,466	493,843	529,608	35,765
			82	129,945	151,451	166,883	15,432
			83	43,988	47,408	51,157	3,749
			84	1,333,917	1,480,505	1,619,194	138,689
			85	374,110	358,034	396,549	38,515
			86	1,076,280	972,736	1,070,446	97,710
	V	H	81	30,552	39,466	41,766	2,300
			82	13,200	16,225	17,314	1,089
			84	24,300	28,530	30,613	2,083
			85	30,580	36,643	40,228	3,585
			86	107,625	86,961	95,227	8,266
	V	W	81	504,285	603,029	634,061	31,032
			82	185,402	199,864	211,689	11,825
			83	11,434	20,408	21,227	819
			84	404,079	467,569	503,518	35,949
			85	854,118	878,197	942,376	64,179
			86	446,516	409,443	436,673	27,230
FR GERM	V	E	84	180	1,060	1,095	35
			86	2,200	12,179	12,648	469
	V	W	86	189	1,406	1,467	61
FRANCE	A	E	83	7,060	15,122	18,109	2,987
			84	5,160	7,490	9,212	1,722
	V	E	81	1,680	5,191	5,449	258
			82	3,720	6,393	7,230	837
			83	5,100	8,616	9,969	1,353
			84	115,664	117,627	126,817	9,190
			86	1,279	2,016	2,230	214
	V	W	83	893	14,374	15,799	1,425
HG KONG	N	W	85	24,767	25,102	26,666	1,564
	O	E	81	9,371	5,512	5,914	402
			82	36,975	24,288	26,168	1,880
			85	10,073	6,715	6,715	
	V	E	81	1,022,882	992,132	1,066,165	74,033
			82	547,111	453,732	499,734	46,002
			83	56,301	34,408	38,113	3,705
			84	741,955	722,561	797,673	75,112
			85	1,999,520	1,800,145	1,987,270	187,125
			86	1,876,194	1,368,237	1,488,614	120,377
	V	H	81	2,550	2,500	2,707	207
			84	2,805	2,970	3,414	444
			85	9,104	9,639	10,434	795
			86	2,160	1,686	1,799	113
	V	W	81	849,714	763,029	815,330	52,301
			82	216,549	170,250	183,125	12,875
			83	17,850	15,400	16,279	879
			84	751,126	718,248	762,117	43,869
			85	1,545,021	1,301,769	1,379,152	77,383

288   Table 1. U.S. Import Statistics for Crop-Specific Commodities by Crop Name

Crop
Product
TSUSA commodity number, description, and unit of quantity

Country	Mode	Reg	Yr	Quantity	F.A.S.	C.I.F.	Charges
			86	1,490,483	1,030,398	1,102,659	72,261
ITALY	A	E	84	308	2,169	2,618	449
			86	110	1,611	1,899	288
	A	H	86	138	1,253	1,845	592
	V	E	81	154	1,186	1,366	180
			84	1,417	10,538	11,390	852
			85	238	1,102	1,333	231
	V	W	82	1,000	6,903	7,317	414
			84	215	2,328	2,401	73
JAPAN	N	H	84	6,310	15,004	19,790	4,786
	O	W	84	176	2,190	2,338	148
	V	E	81	6,263	7,831	8,480	649
			84	45,984	44,889	49,666	4,777
			85	50,968	46,618	51,011	4,393
			86	26,760	26,286	27,702	1,416
	V	H	81	2,463	5,492	6,183	691
			82	2,508	5,101	5,872	771
			85	4,975	10,893	13,113	2,220
			86	1,870	6,022	7,264	1,242
	V	W	85	440	4,599	4,813	214
			86	1,815	3,905	4,060	155
KOR REP	V	E	81	22,440	18,500	20,471	1,971
			82	65,025	54,400	59,895	5,495
			83	21,675	16,660	18,443	1,783
			84	181,782	148,362	166,167	17,805
			85	133,875	102,260	118,610	16,350
			86	32,025	24,152	26,912	2,760
	V	W	81	81,045	77,519	82,648	5,129
			82	20,400	16,936	18,379	1,443
			85	79,739	55,493	62,809	7,316
MACAO	V	E	81	118,448	117,782	124,563	6,781
			82	15,975	17,256	18,822	1,566
			83	11,475	10,665	11,504	839
			84	92,978	92,981	102,090	9,109
			86	327,738	200,458	222,079	21,621
	V	W	81	31,680	29,459	31,105	1,646
			82	53,175	40,679	44,894	4,215
			84	83,438	78,719	82,662	3,943
			85	83,438	79,154	84,051	4,897
			86	11,815	5,700	5,955	255
MEXICO	O	E	84	11,700	13,200	13,200	
	O	W	84	10,500	13,200	13,200	
NETHLDS	O	E	84	63,281	45,439	49,389	3,950
			86	55,543	51,378	51,832	454
	V	E	84	71,144	71,538	76,025	4,487
			85	46,399	37,934	44,038	6,104
			86	8,377	9,364	12,906	3,542
SPAIN	V	E	82	7,425	7,535	9,711	2,176
			83	37,406	22,325	25,040	2,715
			84	617,616	528,256	587,725	59,469
			85	640,434	545,627	610,493	64,866
			86	95,355	57,595	71,024	13,429
	V	W	84	35,123	33,609	38,175	4,566
			85	4,453	3,408	6,476	3,068
SWITZLD	V	E	84	990	4,304	4,724	420
			85	331	1,551	1,675	124
			86	2,106	14,787	15,788	1,001
	V	W	84	265	1,624	1,863	239
			86	21,292	11,581	13,351	1,770
THAILND	V	E	82	1,800	2,213	2,397	184
			84	365	578	644	66
	V	W	86	8,160	9,020	9,375	355
U KING	V	E	86	22,440	13,200	14,629	1,429

1442053 MUSHRM PREP NT FRZ NSPF, OV 9OZ (LB)

Country	Mode	Reg	Yr	Quantity	F.A.S.	C.I.F.	Charges
TOTAL			81	52,032,197	43,026,775	46,805,244	3,778,469
			82	28,858,381	21,532,972	23,930,319	2,397,347
			83	6,816,611	5,587,386	6,098,000	510,614
			84	100,793,243	88,811,399	97,532,957	8,721,558
			85	80,601,614	60,629,476	67,631,545	7,002,069
			86	84,349,699	50,415,978	56,216,724	5,800,746
BELGIUM	A	E	81	386	1,705	1,882	177
			82	661	3,027	3,313	286
	N	E	84	114,750	108,372	116,793	8,421
	O	E	83	17,943	15,288	16,913	1,625
			84	57,187	43,649	46,875	3,226
	V	E	84	870,092	769,794	817,567	47,773
			85	44,160	33,170	37,106	3,936
			86	23,775	11,070	12,931	1,861
BRAZIL	V	E	84	43,350	34,574	39,392	4,818
CAMROON	V	E	86	122,400	62,664	75,640	12,976
CANADA	A	E	81	7	390	426	36
			85	66	1,350	1,424	74
	A	H	81	220	770	925	155
	O	E	81	14,875	53,262	53,262	
			82	2,490	16,108	16,108	
			84	3,584	4,959	4,959	
			86	200	2,479	2,479	
	O	W	83	22,412	36,700	36,700	
			86	7,407	21,504	21,504	
	V	E	86	48,960	28,800	32,300	3,500
CHINA M	N	E	85	6,451,987	5,126,304	5,818,834	692,530
	N	W	81	709,236	584,741	628,640	43,899
			82	4,274,049	3,049,999	3,359,936	309,937
			84	327,172	301,788	320,326	18,538
			85	7,091,558	5,484,884	6,046,430	561,546
	O	E	81	1,246,790	1,131,736	1,260,825	129,089
			82	1,390,185	1,001,341	1,183,905	182,564
			83	136,553	110,178	121,810	11,632
			84	566,865	482,198	537,804	55,606
			85	839,460	666,818	754,369	87,551
			86	989,679	590,337	640,550	50,213
	O	W	81	1,705,089	1,397,655	1,550,266	152,611
			82	1,783,244	1,424,980	1,552,259	127,279
			83	1,699,684	1,532,212	1,658,676	126,464
			84	651,029	590,215	642,847	52,632
			85	601,056	461,927	492,068	30,141
			86	4,614,660	2,881,165	3,145,711	264,546
	V	E	81	6,437,062	4,958,877	5,471,070	512,193
			82	4,664,908	3,244,628	3,692,330	447,702
			83	1,110,590	828,493	910,908	82,415
			84	17,576,177	13,418,704	15,073,712	1,655,008
			85	8,881,306	6,352,709	7,215,112	862,403
			86	15,568,509	8,892,612	10,280,490	1,387,878
	V	H	81	40,646	35,493	38,047	2,554
			82	34,808	25,868	28,377	2,509
			84	15,300	15,300	16,490	1,190
			86	38,760	24,791	27,931	3,140
	V	W	81	9,041,586	7,199,569	7,915,970	716,401
			82	1,647,857	1,202,791	1,324,001	121,210
			83	1,070,510	863,651	926,269	62,618
			84	13,308,705	11,322,277	12,242,205	919,928
			85	5,235,624	3,735,729	4,172,279	436,550
			86	7,198,323	4,206,497	4,705,704	499,207
CHINA T	A	W	85	3,375	1,780	2,213	433
	N	E	81	219,428	201,507	219,197	17,690
			85	1,810,032	1,792,849	1,998,181	205,332
	N	W	82	418,513	350,064	390,051	39,987
			83	495	645	695	50
			84	4,079,319	3,740,450	3,982,169	241,719
			85	1,499,310	1,403,569	1,510,565	106,996
			86	26,760	19,120	22,210	3,090
	O	E	81	144,789	133,895	144,650	10,755
			82	8,775	7,540	8,409	869
			83	204,394	181,845	199,027	17,182
			84	50,025	47,735	51,361	3,626
			85	255,000	167,900	195,800	27,900
			86	503,128	337,687	391,834	54,147
	O	W	82	38,149	29,159	31,734	2,575
			83	3,111	2,684	2,776	92
	V	E	81	1,013,160	868,927	955,142	86,215
			82	2,484,588	1,973,643	2,202,774	229,131
			83	205,822	117,036	134,696	17,660
			84	8,447,884	8,159,178	9,075,331	916,153
			85	1,677,233	1,561,554	1,737,996	176,442
			86	5,665,294	3,912,275	4,408,930	496,655
	V	H	81	116,295	115,767	123,203	7,436
			82	55,686	44,881	48,238	3,357
			84	399,588	394,277	420,829	26,552
			85	333,787	290,072	313,187	23,115
			86	307,091	189,135	209,211	20,076
	V	W	81	1,730,105	1,548,077	1,656,405	108,328
			82	1,481,798	1,242,115	1,358,250	116,135
			83	121,774	88,719	95,111	6,392
			84	5,589,277	5,432,638	5,905,843	473,205
			85	1,565,304	1,377,613	1,472,213	94,600
			86	4,602,387	3,047,079	3,259,913	212,834
COLOMB	V	E	86	792	1,200	1,320	120
CZECHO	V	E	86	250,104	115,244	120,507	5,263
DENMARK	V	E	84	69,615	62,140	69,008	6,868
			86	3,000	23,310	23,903	593
DOM REP	V	E	81	47,520	43,200	47,644	4,444
FR GERM	A	E	84	495	2,060	2,326	266
			85	6,173	3,222	6,730	3,508
	A	W	81	594	9,960	10,594	634
			82	66	1,089	1,167	78
	O	E	81	569	2,944	3,301	357

Crop
Product
TSUSA commodity number, description, and unit of quantity

Country	Mode	Reg	Yr	Quantity	F.A.S.	C.I.F.	Charges
			83	19,181	15,983	17,835	1,852
			85	1,056	2,376	2,640	264
	O	W	84	2,100	12,215	12,810	595
	V	E	81	1,770	7,003	7,765	762
			82	9,338	31,679	33,345	1,666
			83	3,465	19,374	20,301	927
			84	133,337	237,531	247,666	10,135
			85	66,439	203,627	216,284	12,657
			86	23,749	117,044	121,923	4,879
	V	W	86	44,880	24,640	26,440	1,800
FRANCE	A	E	82	44	508	606	98
			83	53	348	400	52
			84	159	2,962	3,309	347
			85	360	17,861	18,437	576
			86	7,599	24,096	32,502	8,406
	A	W	84	88	257	320	63
	N	E	82	5,918	28,722	30,156	1,434
			83	220,342	175,340	193,377	18,037
			84	1,106,207	1,038,876	1,136,518	97,642
			85	229,949	280,219	303,461	23,242
			86	22,321	31,435	34,582	3,147
	N	W	82	1,205	4,299	5,153	854
			84	19,911	79,085	83,091	4,006
			86	2,775	21,260	22,765	1,505
	O	E	84	582	1,112	1,251	139
			85	229	3,592	4,051	459
			86	450	3,088	3,574	486
	V	E	81	44,893	70,038	75,169	5,131
			82	1,639	7,087	7,458	371
			83	40,604	21,045	22,150	1,105
			84	260,789	240,373	260,319	19,946
			85	21,526	31,251	33,643	2,392
			86	22,039	43,734	44,853	1,119
	V	W	81	1,958	11,022	11,858	836
			84	40,560	21,022	21,238	216
			85	19,256	72,982	77,684	4,702
			86	330	4,478	4,991	513
HG KONG	A	W	84	21,675	22,950	25,050	2,100
	N	E	84	497,183	458,515	509,792	51,277
			85	220,645	150,662	166,343	15,681
			86	7,353,705	4,204,014	4,656,501	452,487
	N	W	84	1,727,194	1,593,197	1,679,485	86,288
			85	459,052	331,244	353,438	22,194
	O	E	81	175,075	128,803	141,673	12,870
			82	36,982	21,249	23,933	2,684
			83	43,350	38,250	41,318	3,068
			84	328,746	282,020	314,962	32,942
	O	W	81	22,185	17,140	18,705	1,565
			82	12,750	9,945	10,804	859
			83	3,188	2,375	2,528	153
			85	205,243	144,598	156,529	11,931
			86	15	1,550	1,634	84
	V	E	81	13,036,709	10,486,918	11,395,492	908,574
			82	5,014,863	3,626,887	4,065,272	438,385
			83	418,808	333,288	377,859	44,571
			84	11,064,762	9,996,150	11,061,168	1,065,018
			85	16,545,584	11,328,069	12,661,048	1,332,979
			86	19,089,830	10,928,103	12,097,328	1,169,225
	V	H	81	2,576	2,133	2,303	170
			85	49,260	34,648	37,448	2,800
			86	2,550	1,400	1,553	153
	V	W	81	6,816,068	5,459,214	5,848,818	389,604
			82	2,372,562	1,728,009	1,856,764	128,755
			83	849,648	672,891	738,981	66,090
			84	5,187,178	4,803,796	5,163,540	359,744
			85	7,456,115	5,213,653	5,634,719	421,066
			86	7,542,344	4,171,129	4,519,633	348,504
INDIA	A	E	84	228	1,348	1,546	198
			85	4,750	16,170	16,523	353
			86	12,240	16,840	17,220	380
	V	E	84	18,000	17,785	19,154	1,369
	V	W	82	22,185	16,530	17,970	1,440
INDNSIA	O	E	86	216,750	132,940	149,940	17,000
	V	E	86	71,250	43,452	48,488	5,036
ISRAEL	V	E	84	21,675	20,910	23,133	2,223
			86	115,704	88,828	97,799	8,971
ITALY	A	E	81	150	1,700	2,049	349
			83	506	2,788	4,400	1,612
			84	4,190	8,025	8,291	266
	N	E	81	2,383	10,969	11,766	797
			85	35,894	41,390	46,381	4,991
			86	2,129	8,540	9,422	882
	O	E	84	318	574	574	
	V	E	82	4,610	13,750	14,596	846

Crop
Product
TSUSA commodity number, description, and unit of quantity

Country	Mode	Reg	Yr	Quantity	F.A.S.	C.I.F.	Charges
			83	8,936	40,346	43,460	3,114
			84	66,494	123,226	133,404	10,178
			85	6,409	10,683	11,830	1,147
			86	65,978	95,338	101,273	5,935
	V	W	85	3,725	5,255	6,011	756
			86	5,341	16,467	18,196	1,729
JAPAN	A	E	84	267	4,224	5,073	849
	N	E	84	158,551	167,477	187,195	19,718
	N	H	84	6,955	17,076	21,079	4,003
	N	W	84	33,361	54,029	58,806	4,777
			85	38,951	67,063	76,446	9,383
	V	E	81	241,716	207,681	226,853	19,172
			82	253	345	374	29
			83	1,262	3,203	3,359	156
			84	244,825	210,596	236,814	26,218
			85	357,222	291,573	332,327	40,754
			86	104,757	81,297	94,392	13,095
	V	H	81	6,334	13,288	15,773	2,485
			82	4,281	9,260	10,553	1,293
			85	7,579	14,627	17,664	3,037
			86	4,620	13,908	16,006	2,098
	V	W	81	422	977	1,029	52
			82	22,623	20,660	22,306	1,646
			84	40,042	42,605	45,813	3,208
			85	934	2,290	2,406	116
			86	22,622	16,668	18,840	2,172
KOR REP	N	E	84	150,450	141,185	158,474	17,289
			85	890,715	674,750	770,221	95,471
	O	E	81	196,248	173,407	187,557	14,150
			82	107,202	93,418	101,055	7,637
			85	21,114	12,903	14,795	1,892
			86	10,251	6,227	7,144	917
	O	W	81	21,675	21,250	22,392	1,142
			82	43,350	42,500	44,962	2,462
	V	E	81	2,585,025	2,354,822	2,560,044	205,222
			82	774,813	609,330	675,376	66,046
			83	63,000	50,475	56,879	6,404
			84	3,611,243	3,333,924	3,716,216	382,292
			85	2,911,228	2,210,184	2,512,787	302,603
			86	1,884,123	1,181,418	1,340,330	158,912
	V	H	81	86,700	76,033	82,273	6,240
	V	W	81	4,152,267	3,725,503	3,992,862	267,359
			82	684,478	536,525	579,817	43,292
			83	65,025	48,875	52,824	3,949
			84	3,371,851	3,088,342	3,341,795	253,453
			85	1,660,699	1,302,278	1,425,769	123,491
			86	483,975	308,490	343,463	34,973
MACAO	O	E	81	150,581	121,620	132,429	10,809
			83	21,675	16,405	17,786	1,381
	O	W	81	21,675	18,700	19,828	1,128
	V	E	81	1,199,916	1,030,257	1,112,286	82,029
			82	902,557	668,497	743,821	75,324
			83	31,725	24,710	27,170	2,460
			84	1,177,062	1,005,524	1,123,114	117,590
			85	723,010	509,531	571,848	62,317
			86	1,470,110	856,945	952,708	95,763
	V	H	81	6,900	6,188	6,624	436
	V	W	81	583,815	511,205	543,282	32,077
			82	467,527	351,678	381,712	30,034
			84	337,902	301,239	323,975	22,736
			85	356,813	257,438	276,828	19,390
			86	139,975	92,632	97,860	5,228
MALAYSA	V	E	82	22,440	16,896	18,808	1,912
	V	W	86	36,495	14,994	15,944	950
MEXICO	O	W	86	45,237	41,411	41,411	
MOROC	V	E	86	46,256	27,382	31,035	3,653
N ANTIL	V	E	84	22,950	21,488	23,377	1,889
NETHLDS	N	E	84	1,585,224	1,419,102	1,545,272	126,170
			85	983,031	712,162	796,608	84,446
	O	E	83	45,900	39,901	43,274	3,373
			84	96,036	59,900	63,441	3,541
			85	45,600	35,092	37,232	2,140
			86	131,850	58,003	62,096	4,093
	V	E	83	96,268	85,434	90,927	5,493
			84	3,115,225	2,799,292	3,029,436	230,144
			85	1,390,936	1,024,744	1,209,319	184,575
			86	502,438	246,425	284,905	38,480
	V	W	84	22,440	20,680	21,674	994
NORWAY	V	E	86	24,225	14,249	15,840	1,591
POLAND	V	E	81	13,500	65,861	68,604	2,743
			86	2,535	3,744	4,502	758
REP SAF	V	E	85	23,409	15,885	17,442	1,557
			86	117,630	87,747	96,249	8,502
ROMANIA	V	E	85	33,730	16,903	18,325	1,422

Crop
Product
TSUSA commodity number, description, and unit of quantity

Country	Mode	Reg	Yr	Quantity	F.A.S.	C.I.F.	Charges
RWANDA	V	W	85	13,440	10,055	10,746	691
SINGAPR	V	E	86	168,000	105,000	116,725	11,725
	V	W	84	22,440	22,000	24,435	2,435
SPAIN	N	E	84	7,107,670	6,050,084	6,722,138	672,054
			85	5,983,565	4,401,009	4,965,606	564,597
			86	2,169,720	1,306,379	1,471,816	165,437
	N	W	85	518	3,502	3,784	282
	O	E	81	25,500	21,850	24,078	2,228
			84	32,368	20,688	22,238	1,550
			85	10,140	7,523	8,314	791
	V	E	81	147,141	120,885	134,325	13,440
			83	282,433	182,000	201,651	19,651
			84	6,620,991	5,718,729	6,333,682	614,953
			85	3,168,658	2,365,169	2,661,190	296,021
			86	1,839,479	1,134,760	1,286,666	151,906
	V	W	84	118,818	104,348	118,404	14,056
			86	45,392	22,872	26,422	3,550
SWITZLD	N	E	81	6,225	36,103	36,995	892
			85	128,311	124,137	137,107	12,970
	O	E	81	4,608	5,177	6,009	832
			85	1,740	17,558	19,156	1,598
			86	14,980	29,859	32,015	2,156
	V	E	81	2,862	6,453	6,912	459
			82	4,763	31,620	33,035	1,415
			83	7,354	36,494	37,488	994
			84	18,218	120,412	122,378	1,966
			85	135,772	103,664	115,970	12,306
			86	280,149	272,758	301,783	29,025
	V	W	81	5,791	24,820	26,635	1,815
			82	1,770	5,170	5,537	367
			84	2,898	8,763	9,247	484
			85	49,269	58,723	64,530	5,807
			86	3,524	18,471	19,330	859
THAILND	O	E	82	2,989	2,350	2,585	235
			86	1,764	1,045	1,179	134
	O	W	85	1,495	1,005	1,111	106
	V	E	82	49,809	37,811	42,342	4,531
			84	153,457	127,043	140,042	12,999
			86	203,637	117,071	132,575	15,504
	V	W	81	1,172	1,280	1,407	127
			82	1,653	1,014	1,127	113
			83	600	410	452	42
			84	47,769	39,732	43,628	3,896
			85	32,896	22,908	24,868	1,960
			86	22,747	10,878	11,803	925
TUNISIA	V	E	85	7,800	8,970	9,614	644
U KING	V	E	85	2,116	8,100	8,555	455
	V	W	84	22,440	20,680	22,753	2,073

9225627 MUSHROM WH PREP NOV9OZ/ARB# (LB)

Country	Mode	Reg	Yr	Quantity	F.A.S.	C.I.F.	Charges
TOTAL			82	2,509,682	3,236,155	3,513,958	277,803
			83	4,398,806	5,768,765	6,199,999	431,234
BELGIUM	V	E	83	129	350	366	16
CHINA M	O	W	82	149,388	140,716	153,788	13,072
	V	E	*82	4,800	6,518	7,206	688
			83	78,430	74,780	83,597	8,817
	V	H	82	136,820	158,119	173,171	15,052
			83	127,725	147,849	157,821	9,972
	V	W	82	120,845	127,153	139,725	12,572
			83	155,986	177,834	192,010	14,176
CHINA T	N	E	83	327,739	387,676	424,717	37,041
	N	W	83	182,992	231,791	244,141	12,350
	O	E	82	13,200	15,362	16,667	1,305
			83	21,336	28,699	31,048	2,349
	V	E	82	384,324	511,490	560,909	49,419
			83	1,014,078	1,398,337	1,520,679	122,342
	V	H	82	47,376	57,482	62,083	4,601
			83	77,583	92,045	99,251	7,206
	V	W	82	1,277,117	1,743,437	1,886,061	142,624
			83	1,935,833	2,582,552	2,745,623	163,071
FR GERM	V	E	82	165	563	606	43
FRANCE	A	E	83	135	1,901	2,126	225
	O	E	82	360	3,323	3,415	92
			83	2,701	1,575	1,889	314
	V	E	82	60	397	413	16
			83	1,860	8,419	8,827	408
	V	W	82	51	814	834	20
			83	1,577	9,485	10,286	801
HG KONG	V	E	82	78,600	77,933	85,919	7,986
			83	50,115	34,412	39,486	5,074
	V	H	83	14,850	16,368	17,568	1,200
	V	W	82	72,594	70,408	76,717	6,309
			83	37,925	39,739	43,206	3,467

Crop
Product
TSUSA commodity number, description, and unit of quantity

Country	Mode	Reg	Yr	Quantity	F.A.S.	C.I.F.	Charges
ITALY	N	E	83	382	920	1,083	163
	V	W	83	105	601	621	20
JAPAN	V	E	82	2,407	5,037	5,395	358
			83	1,519	2,696	2,922	226
	V	H	82	126	271	302	31
			83	210	663	712	49
	V	W	82	1,511	3,647	3,762	115
			83	6,124	17,149	18,397	1,248
KOR REP	V	E	82	9,671	15,402	16,551	1,149
			83	107,904	150,070	163,267	13,197
	V	W	82	194,823	277,290	297,537	20,247
			83	241,144	347,561	374,339	26,778
MACAO	V	E	83	4,620	4,042	4,453	411
MEXICO	O	E	83	4,604	3,044	3,044	
SWITZLD	V	E	82	468	1,340	1,479	139
			83	1,200	8,207	8,520	313
THAILND	V	E	82	14,976	19,453	21,418	1,965

9225631 MUSHROOM SLICED NOV 9OZ/ARB# (LB)

Country	Mode	Reg	Yr	Quantity	F.A.S.	C.I.F.	Charges
TOTAL			82	4,870,652	6,838,739	7,421,370	582,631
			83	10,470,194	14,355,204	15,374,395	1,019,191
BELGIUM	V	E	83	150	1,051	1,099	48
CHINA M	V	E	82	116,736	126,208	142,330	16,122
			83	175,872	183,001	206,243	23,242
	V	H	83	1,387	1,343	1,493	150
	V	W	82	259,718	278,046	306,105	28,059
			83	767,961	772,957	832,714	59,757
CHINA T	N	W	83	106,279	135,067	141,300	6,233
	O	E	83	23,208	32,392	34,911	2,519
	V	E	82	1,527,174	2,239,795	2,469,706	229,911
			83	3,528,647	5,116,124	5,535,009	418,885
	V	H	82	1,200	1,250	1,336	86
			83	12,975	16,522	17,493	971
	V	W	82	2,626,279	3,721,722	3,992,440	270,718
			83	4,682,514	6,576,646	6,956,437	379,791
HG KONG	V	E	83	17,100	20,837	22,898	2,061
	V	W	82	13,050	13,183	14,210	1,027
			83	113,943	105,413	111,457	6,044
JAPAN	V	E	82	1,800	2,499	2,768	269
			83	2,325	3,958	4,272	314
	V	H	83	319	689	763	74
	V	W	83	661	1,264	1,336	72
KOR REP	V	E	82	55,155	69,410	76,500	7,090
			83	285,024	424,164	462,825	38,661
	V	W	82	254,804	366,590	393,891	27,301
			83	731,399	947,426	1,025,826	78,400
MACAO	V	E	83	16,830	11,550	13,047	1,497
PHIL R	V	E	83	3,600	4,800	5,272	472
THAILND	V	E	82	14,736	20,036	22,084	2,048

9225637 MUSHRM NSPF PRP NOV9OZ/ARB# (LB)

Country	Mode	Reg	Yr	Quantity	F.A.S.	C.I.F.	Charges
TOTAL			82	8,461,083	8,221,393	9,065,973	844,580
			83	17,142,085	17,182,410	18,754,422	1,572,012
BNGLDSH	V	E	83	5,100	5,525	6,126	601
CHINA M	N	W	83	420,489	424,902	457,539	32,637
	O	W	82	1,015,830	902,935	979,874	76,939
			83	399,666	375,571	412,871	37,300
	V	E	82	1,128,719	1,033,930	1,171,898	137,968
			83	2,821,475	2,491,586	2,816,040	324,454
	V	H	82	216,061	196,123	218,134	22,011
			83	128,445	128,522	137,921	9,399
	V	W	82	2,016,912	1,921,972	2,132,629	210,657
			83	2,780,466	2,566,111	2,814,025	247,914
CHINA T	N	W	83	2,032,470	2,178,959	2,330,333	151,374
	O	E	82	16,800	18,200	20,224	2,024
			83	301,680	321,147	348,371	27,224
	V	E	82	1,149,736	1,186,071	1,322,011	135,940
			83	2,516,955	2,698,883	2,957,630	258,747
	V	H	82	9,600	10,195	11,197	1,002
			83	29,858	31,919	34,060	2,141
	V	W	82	2,153,001	2,237,616	2,421,322	183,706
			83	3,505,168	3,701,712	3,953,651	251,939
FR GERM	A	E	83	198	934	1,091	157
	V	E	83	750	4,290	4,491	201
FRANCE	V	E	82	180	694	716	22
			83	3,981	19,656	20,537	881
HG KONG	V	E	82	333,636	266,523	299,548	33,025
			83	144,507	125,801	139,969	14,168
	V	W	82	120,000	112,059	122,712	10,653
			83	103,995	87,041	94,462	7,421
ITALY	V	E	82	1,320	3,850	4,197	347
			83	935	3,312	3,858	546

Crop
Product
TSUSA commodity number, description, and unit of quantity

Country	Mode	Reg	Yr	Quantity	F.A.S.	C.I.F.	Charges
JAPAN	N	H	83	7,355	18,777	22,014	3,237
	V	E	82	2,417	3,506	3,891	385
			83	29,468	42,315	46,862	4,547
	V	H	82	4,714	8,705	10,180	1,475
	V	W	82	18,702	23,124	24,659	1,535
			83	46,965	60,208	68,647	8,439
KOR REP	V	E	82	33,967	40,795	44,613	3,818
			83	401,013	405,309	450,580	45,271
	V	W	82	200,442	214,701	232,909	18,208
			83	1,265,187	1,325,854	1,450,351	124,497
MACAO	V	E	83	57,750	48,724	53,678	4,954
	V	W	83	2,400	2,400	2,634	234
PHIL R	V	E	83	8,592	9,168	10,069	901
SPAIN	V	E	83	125,498	94,671	106,854	12,183
SWEDEN	V	E	82	576	1,646	1,820	174
SWITZLD	N	E	83	1,719	9,113	9,758	645
THAILND	V	E	82	37,872	38,338	42,977	4,639
	V	W	82	598	410	462	52

9225643 MUSHROOM WH PREP OV 9OZ ARB# (LB)

Country	Mode	Reg	Yr	Quantity	F.A.S.	C.I.F.	Charges
TOTAL			82	2,229,331	2,421,526	2,623,495	201,969
			83	2,275,222	2,338,198	2,523,480	185,282
BELGIUM	A	W	83	20	530	567	37
	V	E	83	13,200	20,246	21,558	1,312
CANADA	O	E	83	2,550	2,551	2,551	
CHINA M	N	W	83	55,522	41,233	43,829	2,596
	O	W	82	36,000	32,992	35,958	2,966
	V	E	82	89,396	76,952	84,958	8,006
			83	3,074	2,387	3,006	619
	V	H	82	10,446	6,571	7,127	556
	V	W	82	76,517	57,619	61,916	4,297
			83	78,778	52,445	57,730	5,285
CHINA T	N	E	83	21,675	22,892	24,903	2,011
	O	E	82	4,032	4,790	5,116	326
			83	12,000	13,750	14,938	1,188
	V	E	82	842,205	935,535	1,022,039	86,504
			83	710,925	729,230	800,354	71,124
	V	H	82	33,072	39,176	42,161	2,985
			83	27,120	30,807	33,941	3,134
	V	W	82	777,153	880,370	945,729	65,359
			83	999,481	1,062,840	1,128,742	65,902
FR GERM	V	E	82	1,163	4,138	4,436	298
FRANCE	O	E	82	225	1,071	1,208	137
	V	E	82	31,260	68,251	73,190	4,939
			83	44,753	74,092	80,056	5,964
	V	W	82	4,566	10,999	13,189	2,190
HG KONG	V	E	82	27,882	27,674	30,473	2,799
			83	104,770	91,035	100,375	9,340
	V	H	82	14,861	6,020	6,490	470
	V	W	82	161,504	136,698	147,852	11,154
			83	123,867	102,311	111,003	8,692
ITALY	V	E	83	733	714	787	73
JAPAN	O	W	82	2,400	2,850	3,203	353
	V	E	82	24,252	25,873	28,337	2,464
			83	5,670	8,681	9,433	752
KOR REP	O	E	82	20,400	24,226	26,228	2,002
	V	W	82	21,000	19,487	20,845	1,358
			83	8,400	11,599	12,200	601
MACAO	V	E	82	6,984	8,389	9,345	956
			83	32,475	27,463	30,269	2,806
	V	H	82	960	560	595	35
	V	W	82	41,445	33,870	36,524	2,654
			83	24,135	22,126	23,270	1,144
SWITZLD	V	E	82	3,978	20,738	21,805	1,067
			83	1,508	10,267	10,779	512
	V	W	82	2,196	7,676	7,960	284

9225647 MUSHROOM SL PREP OV 9OZ ARB# (LB)

Country	Mode	Reg	Yr	Quantity	F.A.S.	C.I.F.	Charges
TOTAL			82	2,854,602	2,550,531	2,793,481	242,950
			83	6,348,329	5,477,282	5,954,670	477,388
CANADA	O	E	83	25,500	23,288	23,288	
	O	W	83	12,000	16,061	16,061	
CHINA M	N	W	83	10,296	3,178	3,406	228
	V	E	82	452,413	359,221	404,431	45,210
			83	1,292,276	1,040,665	1,165,024	124,359
	V	H	83	17,574	14,033	15,438	1,405
	V	W	82	349,786	304,103	329,515	25,412
			83	957,460	717,331	753,918	36,587
CHINA T	N	E	83	51,285	57,393	62,773	5,380
	O	E	83	4,800	5,500	5,830	330
	O	W	82	1,344	1,652	1,787	135
	V	E	82	277,872	312,416	340,931	28,515

Crop
Product
TSUSA commodity number, description, and unit of quantity

Country	Mode	Reg	Yr	Quantity	F.A.S.	C.I.F.	Charges
			83	937,309	918,421	1,001,337	82,916
	V	H	82	36,939	35,660	38,775	3,115
			83	16,200	19,038	20,418	1,380
	V	W	82	423,264	432,915	465,848	32,933
			83	549,393	587,509	624,183	36,674
HG KONG	V	E	82	818,608	708,179	780,596	72,417
			83	970,737	798,360	878,506	80,146
	V	H	83	10,328	10,275	11,756	1,481
	V	W	82	240,928	209,573	225,419	15,846
			83	702,966	604,460	644,000	39,540
INDNSIA	V	W	83	2,270	2,002	2,071	69
ITALY	V	W	83	180	1,182	1,216	34
JAPAN	V	E	83	25,155	22,185	24,773	2,588
	V	H	82	2,730	4,763	5,459	696
	V	W	83	22,650	16,303	17,438	1,135
KOR REP	O	E	83	10,200	7,880	8,836	956
	V	E	83	215,475	170,874	193,093	22,219
	V	H	83	22,530	22,496	24,397	1,901
	V	W	83	38,475	34,398	38,924	4,526
MACAO	V	E	82	88,125	60,206	67,796	7,590
			83	177,809	150,898	164,640	13,208
	V	W	82	162,413	121,509	132,564	11,055
			83	62,271	47,063	49,811	2,748
NETHLDS	O	E	83	22,695	18,957	19,685	728
	V	E	83	50,848	43,567	46,306	2,739
SPAIN	V	E	83	139,647	123,965	137,542	13,577
SWITZLD	V	E	82	180	334	360	26

9225653 MUSHRM NSPF PREP OV9OZ,ARB# (LB)

Country	Mode	Reg	Yr	Quantity	F.A.S.	C.I.F.	Charges
TOTAL			82	29,095,962	21,806,152	24,130,037	2,323,885
			83	56,597,956	43,731,440	48,028,482	4,297,042
BELGIUM	O	E	83	35,888	32,476	35,411	2,935
BNGLDSH	V	E	83	14,790	13,108	14,439	1,331
CANADA	A	E	83	144	1,072	1,098	26
	O	E	82	74,150	74,372	74,372	
			83	28,769	30,836	30,838	2
CHINA M	N	E	82	2,880,881	2,058,586	2,296,834	238,248
			83	324,768	250,174	281,941	31,767
	N	W	82	1,032,701	751,571	809,511	57,940
			83	6,183,666	4,737,256	5,108,392	371,136
	O	E	82	1,010,986	711,293	824,289	112,996
			83	820,671	586,659	665,233	78,574
	O	W	82	1,346,157	1,038,102	1,109,387	71,285
			83	1,852,028	1,485,067	1,597,161	112,094
	V	E	82	3,209,885	2,220,337	2,500,585	280,248
			83	9,530,416	6,776,334	7,598,646	822,312
	V	H	82	113,195	75,432	82,436	7,004
			83	15,300	11,902	13,301	1,399
	V	W	82	2,263,358	1,644,460	1,824,592	180,132
			83	2,265,680	1,469,471	1,615,046	145,575
CHINA T	N	E	83	3,542,764	2,994,405	3,357,050	362,645
	N	W	83	1,078,788	980,373	1,041,985	61,612
	O	E	82	474,991	381,651	424,218	42,567
			83	270,468	231,949	256,069	24,120
	O	W	82	54,830	43,684	47,336	3,652
			83	21,675	17,000	18,379	1,379
	V	E	82	3,874,782	3,087,026	3,432,505	345,479
			83	3,297,832	2,820,658	3,086,832	266,174
	V	H	82	87,572	71,319	77,766	6,447
			83	224,231	189,310	203,403	14,093
	V	W	82	3,788,453	3,108,740	3,394,547	285,807
			83	3,731,037	3,251,133	3,497,144	246,011
FR GERM	V	E	82	5,040	19,905	20,443	538
			83	45,990	39,527	41,757	2,230
FRANCE	A	E	82	44	1,740	1,777	37
	N	E	83	175,339	136,055	150,751	14,696
	O	E	82	203	928	1,012	84
			83	34,804	27,003	30,200	3,197
	V	E	83	1,842	4,088	4,273	185
HG KONG	N	E	83	305,040	226,247	254,625	28,378
	N	W	83	1,094,018	864,947	919,211	54,264
	O	E	82	67,080	51,920	57,444	5,524
			83	23,715	18,600	20,384	1,784
	O	W	82	9,435	7,360	7,995	635
	V	E	82	3,143,608	2,217,071	2,484,966	267,895
			83	9,153,913	6,925,467	7,643,019	717,552
	V	H	82	21,675	16,575	18,227	1,652
			83	26,530	19,998	21,892	1,894
	V	W	82	2,539,010	1,851,378	2,008,300	156,922
			83	2,591,922	2,008,369	2,147,791	139,422
ITALY	V	E	82	1,435	1,994	2,314	320
			83	19,254	36,937	39,406	2,469
JAPAN	N	W	83	387	1,515	1,632	117

Crop
Product
TSUSA commodity number, description, and unit of quantity

Country	Mode	Reg	Yr	Quantity	F.A.S.	C.I.F.	Charges
	O	E	83	21,675	16,830	19,029	2,199
	V	E	82	180	1,755	1,925	170
			83	154,148	139,372	155,233	15,861
	V	H	82	3,572	6,345	7,176	831
			83	7,733	14,666	17,057	2,391
	V	W	82	68,466	55,671	61,041	5,370
			83	43,560	34,474	37,888	3,414
KOR REP	O	E	82	21,675	18,785	20,368	1,583
			83	31,875	26,290	29,265	2,975
	O	W	82	21,675	19,550	20,821	1,271
			83	59,033	46,352	50,188	3,836
	V	E	82	866,295	657,000	732,831	75,831
			83	3,124,787	2,379,591	2,647,256	267,665
	V	W	82	521,139	416,745	456,567	39,822
			83	1,270,960	1,026,741	1,114,786	88,045
MACAO	O	E	82	43,635	32,925	36,459	3,534
	V	E	82	1,003,212	746,745	837,102	90,357
			83	1,893,866	1,450,966	1,605,667	154,701
	V	W	82	495,496	364,668	399,863	35,195
			83	932,904	716,026	778,128	62,102
MOROC	O	E	83	220	457	457	
N ANTIL	V	E	83	22,950	20,268	21,394	1,126
NETHLDS	O	E	83	209,003	144,392	152,460	8,068
	V	E	83	312,853	230,752	254,479	23,727
PHIL R	V	E	83	20,400	17,425	19,051	1,626
SINGAPR	V	W	82	19,511	15,229	16,504	1,275
SPAIN	O	E	82	22,440	18,182	20,048	1,866
	V	E	82	28,560	19,600	22,499	2,899
			83	1,697,445	1,163,275	1,304,774	141,499
	V	W	83	2,550	1,815	1,981	166
SWITZLD	N	E	83	4,704	18,118	18,707	589
	V	E	82	2,175	15,075	15,340	265
			83	3,547	9,124	9,660	536
	V	W	83	15,894	43,130	45,638	2,508
THAILND	N	W	83	450	369	407	38
	V	E	83	21,375	16,678	18,378	1,700
	V	W	82	900	615	685	70
			83	11,529	6,250	6,750	500
U KING	A	E	83	386	1,961	2,492	531

Mushroom spawn seed
1265900 MUSHROOM SPAWN SEED (LB)

Country	Mode	Reg	Yr	Quantity	F.A.S.	C.I.F.	Charges
TOTAL			81	63,000	81,511	118,018	36,507
			82	209,952	176,921	210,580	33,659
			83	3,536	63,834	80,053	16,219
			84	51,389	95,336	131,854	36,518
			85	157,600	133,507	186,209	52,702
			86	477,749	384,231	460,549	76,318
CANADA	A	E	82	3,600	1,858	2,668	810
	O	W	81	700	630	630	
DOM REP	V	E	85	29,792	12,162	19,490	7,328
FRANCE	A	E	81	40	1,665	2,640	975
			82	260	10,004	12,830	2,826
			84	24,679	68,552	88,999	20,447
			85	5,830	10,041	14,537	4,496
			86	22,150	56,507	77,762	21,255
	A	W	81	4,686	40,993	60,335	19,342
			82	980	39,212	51,588	12,376
			83	120	4,756	5,839	1,083
			84	17,819	14,466	20,528	6,062
			85	25,990	48,654	73,749	25,095
			86	584	1,226	1,295	69
	N	E	83	3,416	59,078	74,214	15,136
	V	E	81	50,400	28,714	41,032	12,318
			82	203,084	121,641	138,615	16,974
			85	58,642	38,262	52,090	13,828
			86	96,340	71,297	87,369	16,072
JAPAN	A	W	81	125	395	842	447
KOR REP	A	E	84	8,891	12,318	22,327	10,009
NETHLDS	A	E	81	4,079	2,934	5,145	2,211
	V	E	83	35,274	22,171	22,841	670
			86	323,269	226,112	262,534	36,422
SWITZLD	A	E	85	2,072	2,217	3,502	1,285
U KING	A	E	81	2,970	6,180	7,394	1,214
	V	E	82	2,028	4,206	4,879	673
			86	35,406	29,089	31,589	2,500

Crop
Product
TSUSA commodity number, description, and unit of quantity

Straw mushroom, prepared or preserved
1442009 STRAW MUSHROOMS PREP PRES NT FZ (LB)

Country	Mode	Reg	Yr	Quantity	F.A.S.	C.I.F.	Charges
TOTAL			81	3,908,279	3,633,847	3,957,438	323,591
			82	2,256,150	2,314,056	2,529,298	215,242
			83	2,166,735	2,040,445	2,230,662	190,217
			84	5,120,472	4,056,932	4,559,489	502,557
			85	7,256,074	6,829,113	7,487,282	658,169
			86	6,424,670	5,500,386	5,971,793	471,407
CANADA	O	E	82	201	395	490	95
CHINA M	N	E	82	16,860	13,424	13,445	21
	V	E	81	77,638	49,927	55,868	5,941
			83	1,800	1,350	1,707	357
			84	449,738	192,654	223,870	31,216
			85	2,400	1,800	2,091	291
			86	25,290	28,433	31,266	2,833
	V	W	81	14,619	8,586	9,248	662
			82	8,857	6,955	7,679	724
			83	412	1,057	1,115	58
			84	6,852	4,297	4,853	556
			85	2,249	1,298	1,384	86
			86	42,844	36,297	38,555	2,258
CHINA T	N	E	81	1,467,522	1,573,361	1,730,877	157,516
			85	2,840,416	2,942,370	3,251,449	309,079
	O	E	81	3,600	4,500	4,862	362
			82	100,116	102,608	112,126	9,518
			83	4,463	1,200	1,200	
	O	H	86	9,900	4,638	5,369	731
	V	E	81	690,695	553,953	607,699	53,746
			82	960,236	1,042,342	1,151,954	109,612
			83	1,328,813	1,279,169	1,408,310	129,141
			84	2,251,480	1,996,292	2,275,228	278,936
			85	920,368	858,087	956,965	98,878
			86	2,737,486	2,604,182	2,861,935	257,753
	V	H	81	85,937	86,404	93,216	6,812
			82	93,252	100,648	109,964	9,316
			83	107,693	120,612	131,988	11,376
			84	165,572	170,574	188,642	18,068
			85	222,881	217,520	238,033	20,513
			86	189,196	149,352	164,018	14,666
	V	W	81	1,529,364	1,316,891	1,412,048	95,157
			82	1,040,103	1,008,079	1,090,483	82,404
			83	718,052	631,287	679,954	48,667
			84	2,212,429	1,654,897	1,824,663	169,766
			85	3,113,998	2,674,437	2,889,711	215,274
			86	3,168,898	2,483,455	2,657,428	173,973
FRANCE	V	E	82	985	3,340	3,517	177
			85	18,000	24,335	26,169	1,834
GAMBIA	V	W	81	4,800	4,086	4,376	290
HG KONG	V	E	84	17,400	19,575	22,093	2,518
			86	9,000	5,640	5,640	
	V	W	81	2,400	2,800	2,876	76
			82	1,200	1,400	1,480	80
			84	4,800	3,440	3,732	292
			86	19,320	19,729	20,713	984
JAPAN	V	E	82	16,800	19,053	21,027	1,974
			83	3,102	3,330	3,750	420
			84	1,600	1,650	1,852	202
			86	56,880	48,108	52,766	4,658
	V	H	84	9,413	12,110	12,936	826
	V	W	86	132	255	280	25
KOR REP	V	E	81	31,704	33,339	36,368	3,029
			86	33,731	26,460	28,362	1,902
	V	W	83	2,400	2,440	2,638	198
MALAYSA	V	E	86	20,280	9,900	11,040	1,140
SPAIN	V	E	85	25,575	19,525	21,987	2,462
SWITZLD	V	E	85	18,912	25,269	28,376	3,107
THAILND	V	E	83	15,291	14,662	15,833	1,171
			84	1,056	1,188	1,340	152
			85	56,400	47,504	52,823	5,319
			86	69,950	44,584	51,950	7,366
	V	W	82	2,249	1,150	1,300	150
			85	34,875	16,968	18,294	1,326
			86	30,495	27,550	29,897	2,347
TUNISIA	V	W	86	11,400	12,058	12,854	796

9225609 STRAW MUSHROOMS NT FZ, ARB# (LB)

Country	Mode	Reg	Yr	Quantity	F.A.S.	C.I.F.	Charges
TOTAL			82	722,024	612,294	671,269	58,975
			83	1,535,001	1,203,851	1,328,910	125,059
CHINA M	V	E	83	31,674	27,388	31,079	3,691
CHINA T	O	E	82	2,400	2,900	3,159	259

Crop Product TSUSA commodity number, description, and unit of quantity Country	Mode	Reg	Yr	Quantity	F.A.S.	C.I.F.	Charges
	V	E	82	215,631	204,130	226,425	22,295
			83	690,329	579,937	645,717	65,780
	V	H	82	4,800	5,250	5,543	293
			83	26,850	31,645	34,751	3,106
	V	W	82	494,693	395,239	430,947	35,708
			83	768,580	550,371	601,094	50,723
HG KONG	V	W	83	7,200	8,346	9,652	1,306
JAPAN	V	W	83	267	414	464	50
KOR REP	V	W	82	4,500	4,775	5,195	420
THAILND	V	W	83	10,101	5,750	6,153	403

Musk Plant

Musk
4606000 MUSK IN GR OR PODS NOT MIXT (OZ)

Country	Mode	Reg	Yr	Quantity	F.A.S.	C.I.F.	Charges
TOTAL			83	882	453	750	297
			84	39,032	73,148	78,911	5,763
			85	951	497,190	498,893	1,703
			86	502	141,498	142,738	1,240
FRANCE	A	E	85	951	497,190	498,893	1,703
			86	282	134,105	134,393	288
JAPAN	A	E	83	882	453	750	297
			84	26	10,544	14,880	4,336
			86	220	7,393	8,345	952
U KING	V	E	84	39,006	62,604	64,031	1,427

Mustard

Mustard, seed, spice
1616100 MUSTARD SEEDS WHOLE (LB)

Country	Mode	Reg	Yr	Quantity	F.A.S.	C.I.F.	Charges
TOTAL			81	77,361,636	11,232,819	11,237,916	5,077
			82	69,786,076	11,549,028	11,552,035	3,007
			83	70,393,629	10,599,880	10,604,784	4,904
			84	82,102,690	13,071,697	13,158,687	86,990
			85	87,830,658	14,257,199	14,277,200	20,001
			86	91,032,792	13,367,163	13,395,208	28,045
CANADA	N	E	85	9,003,734	1,409,069	1,429,069	20,000
			86	12,909,520	1,739,821	1,759,599	19,778
	O	E	81	60,538,611	8,841,706	8,842,111	405
			82	55,343,930	9,227,017	9,227,017	
			83	57,805,250	8,564,788	8,564,791	3
			84	65,274,172	10,199,879	10,199,879	
			85	60,934,464	9,913,628	9,913,629	1
			86	61,721,723	9,180,309	9,188,478	8,169
	O	W	81	16,784,667	2,362,539	2,362,559	
			82	14,407,377	2,296,829	2,296,829	
			83	12,469,844	2,002,114	2,002,114	
			84	15,310,428	2,394,787	2,394,787	
			85	17,454,400	2,882,491	2,882,491	
			86	16,376,183	2,442,439	2,442,439	
	V	E	83	600	588	647	59
			84	637,037	261,401	286,873	25,472
CHINA M	O	E	84	120,482	31,189	37,718	6,529
			85	438,060	52,011	52,011	
	V	E	84	75,563	8,309	12,056	3,747
CHINA T	V	W	82	66	327	360	33
FRANCE	V	E	83	36,673	8,284	10,419	2,135
	V	W	81	3,894	4,064	5,041	977
HG KONG	V	E	83	500	268	296	28
INDIA	O	E	82	904	977	1,130	153
			86	22,500	3,394	3,394	
	V	E	81	176	346	400	54
			82	1,653	415	655	240
INDNSIA	V	E	82	27,778	19,455	21,112	1,657
ITALY	V	E	81	33,069	22,915	26,426	3,511
			83	33,069	16,500	16,514	14
			84	33,069	13,965	15,983	2,018
JAPAN	V	W	81	259	600	695	95
N ZEAL	V	W	84	48,171	12,018	14,480	2,462
NETHLDS	O	E	84	107,145	20,520	27,234	6,714
SWEDEN	V	E	84	162,038	70,916	75,992	5,076
THAILND	V	W	86	2,866	1,200	1,298	98
U KING	O	E	84	85,980	15,014	25,620	10,606
	V	E	81	960	649	684	35
			82	4,368	4,008	4,932	924

Country	Mode	Reg	Yr	Quantity	F.A.S.	C.I.F.	Charges
			83	47,693	7,338	10,003	2,665
			84	248,605	43,699	68,065	24,366

Mustard, spice
1615800 MUSTARD, GROUND (LB)

Country	Mode	Reg	Yr	Quantity	F.A.S.	C.I.F.	Charges
TOTAL			81	2,477,542	1,811,903	1,975,321	163,418
			82	2,709,238	1,753,466	1,869,293	115,827
			83	3,473,517	1,985,574	2,140,227	154,653
			84	6,012,352	2,886,170	3,068,775	182,605
			85	7,048,791	3,085,012	3,293,310	208,298
			86	8,044,111	3,591,809	3,808,487	216,678
BELGIUM	V	E	85	16,830	2,813	3,254	441
			86	21,039	8,996	9,767	771
	V	W	83	13,515	10,556	12,396	1,840
CANADA	O	E	81	1,149,915	513,249	513,249	
			82	1,277,242	620,644	620,644	
			83	1,869,038	740,496	740,496	
			84	4,179,649	1,616,809	1,616,809	
			85	5,092,383	1,821,656	1,821,656	
			86	5,882,211	1,996,228	1,996,228	
	O	W	81	689	859	859	
			82	44,100	14,024	14,024	
			83	45,000	13,351	13,351	
			84	143,550	50,108	50,108	
			85	131,868	36,931	36,931	
			86	87,120	26,921	26,921	
CHINA M	V	E	82	4,900	2,673	2,859	186
	V	W	83	500	292	315	23
			84	4,000	2,624	2,761	137
			86	2,500	1,755	1,993	238
CHINA T	V	W	81	47	276	293	17
			82	79	517	573	56
			83	54	259	273	14
			84	1,629	1,627	1,718	91
DENMARK	V	E	81	608	983	1,172	189
			82	290	260	377	117
FR GERM	O	E	81	2,920	3,173	3,421	248
	V	E	83	8,047	5,285	6,412	1,127
			84	688	942	1,005	63
			86	26,071	11,282	12,956	1,674
	V	W	83	17,684	9,764	11,350	1,586
			85	10,116	5,445	6,969	1,524
FRANCE	N	E	81	391	2,779	3,074	295
			82	5,423	3,704	4,495	791
			86	211,135	122,401	137,312	14,911
	N	W	81	7,211	7,011	7,352	341
	O	E	84	1,604	5,333	6,003	670
			86	9,067	5,293	5,529	236
	V	E	81	30,883	27,375	30,319	2,944
			82	108,492	35,284	40,265	4,981
			83	106,052	45,527	50,868	5,341
			84	363,840	156,095	183,984	27,889
			85	188,424	46,572	59,948	13,376
			86	399,480	149,880	173,818	23,938
	V	W	81	86,803	26,361	30,651	4,290
			82	45,151	18,332	22,367	4,035
			83	81,368	55,844	66,351	10,507
			84	20,317	10,615	13,925	3,310
			85	134,690	55,936	67,348	11,412
			86	240,660	79,785	96,862	17,077
HG KONG	V	E	82	600	346	408	62
			83	500	269	299	30
JAPAN	V	E	81	937	2,249	2,467	218
			82	4,941	16,213	17,481	1,268
			83	4,700	11,433	12,384	951
			84	8,219	30,564	32,753	2,189
			85	13,926	19,702	21,369	1,667
			86	4,574	22,516	26,772	4,256
	V	H	81	135	345	382	37
			82	135	349	389	40
			83	135	404	453	49
			84	821	2,229	2,571	342
			86	293	1,187	1,350	163
	V	W	81	15,697	31,967	33,632	1,665
			82	15,193	29,408	30,984	1,576
			83	23,322	50,310	52,701	2,391
			84	16,880	33,276	35,171	1,895
			85	25,201	46,245	49,363	3,118
			86	34,418	82,342	86,338	3,996
KOR REP	V	E	81	308	790	845	55
			82	197	300	352	52

Crop
Product
TSUSA commodity number, description, and unit of quantity

Country	Mode	Reg	Yr	Quantity	F.A.S.	C.I.F.	Charges
			83	1,389	1,502	1,618	116
			84	1,671	2,058	2,364	306
			86	1,520	1,749	1,953	204
	V	W	81	4,328	10,634	11,093	459
			82	2,386	4,108	4,477	369
			83	2,817	4,504	4,690	186
			84	6,372	9,187	11,796	2,609
			85	1,549	2,659	2,816	157
			86	773	1,096	1,210	114
NETHLDS	O	E	84	198	251	271	20
	V	E	82	244	300	323	23
			83	243	324	350	26
NORWAY	V	W	83	2,205	668	917	249
ROMANIA	V	W	84	154	320	350	30
SPAIN	O	E	86	2,215	1,107	1,107	
SWEDEN	V	E	82	476	1,021	1,376	355
THAILND	V	W	84	901	488	524	36
U KING	N	E	83	1,296,948	1,034,786	1,165,003	130,217
			85	1,430,389	1,039,237	1,215,002	175,765
			86	844,490	852,220	968,437	116,217
	V	E	81	1,160,594	1,162,982	1,311,343	148,361
			82	1,198,490	1,003,978	1,105,460	101,482
			84	1,261,859	963,644	1,106,662	143,018
			86	276,545	227,051	259,934	32,883
	V	W	81	16,076	20,870	25,169	4,299
			82	899	2,005	2,439	434
			85	3,415	7,816	8,654	838

1616000 MUSTARD, PREPARED (LB)

Country	Mode	Reg	Yr	Quantity	F.A.S.	C.I.F.	Charges
TOTAL			**81**	**2,465,057**	**2,173,260**	**2,456,672**	**283,412**
			82	**2,888,145**	**2,423,043**	**2,754,692**	**331,649**
			83	**3,545,074**	**2,831,149**	**3,181,573**	**350,424**
			84	**4,102,302**	**2,943,869**	**3,368,858**	**424,989**
			85	**4,855,184**	**3,139,676**	**3,610,111**	**470,435**
			86	**5,072,638**	**4,268,498**	**4,723,022**	**454,524**
ARGENT	V	W	83	529	541	570	29
AUSTRAL	V	E	86	1,616	2,044	2,218	174
	V	W	83	7,620	8,224	9,077	853
			86	1,301	1,022	1,134	112
AUSTRIA	A	E	83	313	720	906	186
	N	W	84	23,709	23,880	32,746	8,866
	O	E	84	4,362	3,964	4,465	501
	V	E	81	1,100	1,817	2,009	192
			82	1,103	1,020	1,282	262
			83	1,322	2,579	2,887	308
			84	2,653	2,978	3,601	623
	V	W	83	9,452	4,559	7,312	2,753
BELGIUM	N	E	85	127,594	103,268	118,561	15,293
	O	E	81	573	537	609	72
			85	10,787	4,879	7,064	2,185
	V	E	82	13,610	6,056	6,788	732
			83	54,078	40,925	44,575	3,650
			84	124,095	75,220	85,763	10,543
			85	23,827	16,544	19,445	2,901
			86	126,482	94,108	105,397	11,289
	V	W	85	5,548	5,075	5,540	465
			86	15,205	21,858	24,660	2,802
CANADA	O	E	81	52,352	88,236	88,236	
			82	114,084	171,096	171,096	
			83	178,771	335,958	335,958	
			84	273,121	345,654	345,654	
			85	716,637	601,560	601,560	
			86	547,675	884,585	884,585	
	O	W	85	925	1,428	1,428	
	V	E	83	1,411	1,587	1,729	142
CHINA M	O	W	84	500	283	303	20
	V	E	81	1,300	351	396	45
			82	1,350	725	831	106
			83	3,690	6,086	6,532	446
			84	3,500	1,368	1,625	257
			85	2,700	1,319	1,547	228
	V	W	81	1,500	942	1,013	71
			82	1,500	938	988	50
CHINA T	O	W	84	585	630	630	
	V	E	81	3,440	2,110	2,281	171
			82	5,063	3,345	3,739	394
			83	2,805	1,955	2,410	455
			84	14,983	7,149	8,381	1,232
			85	13,187	6,193	7,527	1,334
			86	3,513	3,635	4,210	575
	V	W	81	2,220	1,855	2,026	171
			82	610	725	772	47
			83	12,305	13,220	14,215	995
			84	8,886	5,719	6,362	643
			85	21,588	7,836	8,850	1,014
			86	20,532	11,031	11,763	732
DENMARK	A	W	84	308	1,003	1,369	366
	V	E	86	2,160	3,605	3,868	263
	V	W	81	446	442	603	161
F GUIAN	V	E	82	17,307	17,309	20,716	3,407
FR GERM	N	E	81	96,779	87,151	96,960	9,809
			82	19,758	19,392	23,369	3,977
			84	55,504	37,805	44,016	6,211
			85	149,662	104,791	124,731	19,940
			86	11,650	11,539	13,088	1,549
	N	W	84	2,228	1,523	2,239	716
	O	E	81	30,335	33,694	38,934	5,240
			83	14,279	11,587	12,987	1,400
			84	250	337	337	
			85	1,597	1,774	1,886	112
	O	W	82	2,145	2,416	2,952	536
	V	E	81	22,796	11,735	13,339	1,604
			82	158,131	139,057	153,623	14,566
			83	140,571	128,254	140,223	11,969
			84	250,060	174,719	195,677	20,958
			85	42,823	33,786	38,127	4,341
			86	226,081	231,701	260,525	28,824
	V	W	81	30,108	30,771	36,593	5,822
			82	62,493	45,502	52,151	6,649
			83	59,485	43,133	53,113	9,980
			84	54,973	46,874	56,535	9,661
			85	55,419	38,454	47,521	9,067
			86	56,104	51,302	58,379	7,077
FRANCE	A	E	81	94	480	557	77
			83	6,046	4,237	9,920	5,683
			84	1,032	1,010	1,384	374
	A	W	84	248	435	506	71
	N	E	81	1,301,909	1,048,926	1,178,677	129,751
			82	1,431,116	1,121,629	1,284,254	162,625
			83	1,921,485	1,272,968	1,446,443	173,475
			84	2,161,672	1,269,567	1,491,552	221,985
			85	1,998,960	1,219,986	1,438,212	218,226
			86	1,933,917	1,456,188	1,672,257	216,069
	N	W	82	56,156	42,106	49,678	7,572
			83	261,511	162,061	186,769	24,708
			84	398,491	243,822	284,060	40,238
			85	403,337	188,312	226,443	38,131
	O	E	81	42,101	54,601	60,912	6,311
			82	23,000	23,502	25,619	2,117
			83	11,079	8,707	9,765	1,058
			85	3,334	5,768	6,497	729
			86	53,204	42,248	46,937	4,689
	O	W	81	1	378	388	10
			85	1,463	1,592	1,951	359
	V	E	81	319,564	274,283	311,910	37,627
			82	440,812	360,836	421,655	60,819
			83	371,194	351,597	399,997	48,400
			84	280,522	265,526	301,229	35,703
			85	652,884	381,776	449,878	68,102
			86	1,097,061	716,348	812,537	96,189
	V	W	81	308,812	237,298	269,274	31,976
			82	166,042	128,821	144,895	16,074
			83	105,061	105,511	115,551	10,040
			84	12,833	12,028	13,427	1,399
			85	272,285	161,415	197,564	36,149
			86	615,174	394,103	444,357	50,254
HG KONG	V	E	81	1,875	2,491	2,747	256
			82	6,530	5,578	6,325	747
			83	11,488	8,561	10,016	1,455
			84	5,123	6,463	7,226	763
			85	3,520	7,812	8,827	1,015
			86	7,698	11,336	12,474	1,138
	V	W	81	1,000	759	773	14
			84	2,210	811	858	47
			86	1,668	1,152	1,217	65
INDIA	V	E	81	1,102	617	759	142
			82	1,102	650	710	60
			83	1,102	590	680	90
	V	W	83	551	317	364	47
			84	438	394	433	39
INDNSIA	V	E	84	51,698	35,289	40,351	5,062
	V	W	84	28,164	20,421	21,686	1,265
ISRAEL	V	E	82	2,622	2,195	2,500	305
ITALY	O	E	85	21,060	11,433	12,591	1,158
	V	E	81	2,310	6,913	7,548	635
			82	1,420	1,839	1,955	116
			83	612	895	1,021	126

Crop Product TSUSA commodity number, description, and unit of quantity Country	Mode	Reg	Yr	Quantity	F.A.S.	C.I.F.	Charges
			84	1,918	1,139	1,192	53
			85	32,847	19,893	22,658	2,765
			86	932	2,331	2,630	299
	V	W	86	5,093	8,990	9,512	522
JAPAN	O	E	84	110	306	306	
	V	E	81	3,071	8,444	9,136	692
			82	3,830	10,772	11,613	841
			83	4,272	12,540	13,555	1,015
			84	4,481	16,001	17,532	1,531
			85	1,045	3,106	3,401	295
			86	2,695	12,121	12,654	533
	V	H	82	74	265	297	32
			83	108	612	681	69
			84	336	1,190	1,424	234
	V	W	81	2,500	9,795	10,303	508
			82	2,133	8,497	8,956	459
			83	8,254	24,277	25,851	1,574
			84	3,802	15,462	16,327	865
			85	3,965	8,106	8,573	467
			86	2,476	9,567	10,020	453
KOR REP	V	E	81	568	1,065	1,165	100
			82	154	300	327	27
			85	2,280	4,479	4,775	296
			86	32,856	12,930	15,401	2,471
	V	H	82	280	537	618	81
	V	W	81	310	725	778	53
			82	825	1,376	1,433	57
			83	660	826	958	132
			84	200	506	514	8
MACAO	V	W	84	3,476	5,425	5,775	350
MEXICO	O	W	82	396	560	560	
NETHLDS	N	E	84	39,395	23,166	30,266	7,100
	O	E	82	602	593	683	90
	V	E	81	18,079	11,553	12,389	836
			82	22,793	17,356	19,866	2,510
			83	64,176	43,299	49,385	6,086
			84	36,389	22,369	26,374	4,005
			85	94,874	70,297	82,674	12,377
			86	17,774	16,887	18,548	1,661
	V	W	81	264	352	393	41
			82	368	317	353	36
			83	2,611	2,220	2,451	231
			84	3,163	1,983	2,539	556
			86	14,287	8,941	10,413	1,472
NORWAY	V	E	83	36	684	749	65
	V	W	81	882	326	450	124
			82	2,535	1,090	1,354	264
			83	1,110	713	783	70
			85	1,719	1,308	1,729	421
PORTUGL	V	E	83	1,485	1,041	1,321	280
SINGAPR	V	E	86	37	2,775	3,245	470
SPAIN	V	E	82	985	1,463	1,650	187
			84	1,598	5,325	6,050	725
SWEDEN	N	E	84	994	1,548	2,375	827
			86	5,303	3,373	4,117	744
	N	W	84	575	846	893	47
	O	E	84	1,429	1,494	2,050	556
	V	E	81	3,620	4,337	5,440	1,103
			82	5,552	6,469	8,068	1,599
			83	6,432	7,477	9,098	1,621
			84	2,389	2,819	3,573	754
			85	4,286	4,409	6,067	1,658
			86	1,429	2,033	2,450	417
	V	W	81	952	1,047	1,292	245
			82	945	1,022	1,221	199
			83	794	828	1,004	176
SWITZLD	O	E	83	1,350	2,165	2,345	180
			86	1,905	2,490	3,318	828
	V	W	86	4,445	1,160	1,221	61
THAILND	O	W	86	13,404	5,536	6,062	526
	V	E	81	1,534	997	1,200	203
			86	21,833	9,815	10,984	1,169
	V	W	84	8,200	4,589	5,181	592
			86	113,148	48,839	53,627	4,788
U KING	A	E	82	53	322	355	33
			83	175	616	830	214
			84	162	354	512	158
	N	E	81	13,620	22,333	24,652	2,319
			82	221,599	129,148	157,540	28,392
			83	221,690	196,940	235,378	38,438
			85	160,189	88,793	114,258	25,465
	N	W	84	7,716	9,203	10,948	1,745
	O	E	81	10,906	13,445	14,130	685
			82	3,072	4,311	4,689	378

Crop Product TSUSA commodity number, description, and unit of quantity Country	Mode	Reg	Yr	Quantity	F.A.S.	C.I.F.	Charges
			83	45,194	6,647	6,747	100
			84	11,935	15,191	15,968	777
			85	7,996	12,107	12,821	714
			86	80,927	128,178	136,996	8,818
	V	E	81	185,673	208,021	253,867	45,846
			82	90,641	132,504	146,300	13,796
			83	5,801	11,097	12,105	1,008
			84	209,390	224,434	259,819	35,385
			85	1,405	1,958	2,653	695
			86	30,923	51,042	58,104	7,062
	V	W	81	1,361	4,433	4,933	500
			82	5,354	11,440	12,911	1,507
			83	1,786	4,137	4,845	708
			84	2,496	5,647	6,825	1,178
			85	15,441	20,219	24,752	4,533
			86	2,130	3,685	4,114	429
USSR	V	E	83	2,380	258	467	209

Myrobalan

*Myrobalan, tannin***
4705500 MYROBALAN AND SUMAC (LB)

	Mode	Reg	Yr	Quantity	F.A.S.	C.I.F.	Charges
TOTAL			81	539,421	437,898	474,063	36,165
			82	215,934	124,264	136,575	12,311
			83	204,985	202,242	214,702	12,460
			84	1,526,608	582,386	681,975	99,589
			85	266,828	84,027	99,347	15,320
			86	1,250,533	451,557	555,052	103,495
CANADA	O	W	82	5	855	855	
CYPRUS	V	E	84	585,531	186,843	214,672	27,829
			85	136,757	38,905	46,945	8,040
FRANCE	V	E	81	341,713	231,838	250,250	18,412
			82	90,179	53,672	58,972	5,300
			83	142,949	50,493	56,282	5,789
			84	132,276	44,687	51,000	6,313
			85	130,071	45,122	52,402	7,280
			86	103,694	53,507	58,961	5,454
ITALY	V	E	81	54,409	160,671	168,728	8,057
			82	15,520	32,799	34,496	1,697
			83	62,036	151,749	158,420	6,671
			84	590,612	266,007	316,776	50,769
			86	485,453	178,000	219,550	41,550
SPAIN	V	E	84	44,092	14,000	17,906	3,906
TURKEY	V	E	84	165,279	64,849	74,671	9,822
			86	661,386	220,050	276,541	56,491
	V	W	84	8,818	6,000	6,950	950
YUGOSLV	V	E	81	143,299	45,389	55,085	9,696
			82	110,230	36,938	42,252	5,314

N

Narcissus

Narcissus, bulbs
1251500 NARCISSUS BULBS (NO)

	Mode	Reg	Yr	Quantity	F.A.S.	C.I.F.	Charges
TOTAL			81	52,174,688	6,004,092	6,838,359	834,600
			82	51,818,250	6,196,830	7,048,287	849,595
			83	59,597,887	6,716,345	7,655,932	939,587
			84	72,863,813	7,801,664	9,104,780	1,303,116
			85	84,929,216	8,753,956	10,340,436	1,586,480
			86	89,219,909	10,046,938	11,592,988	1,546,050
ALBANIA	V	E	85	24,500	3,306	4,033	727
BELGIUM	V	E	83	75,045	9,868	11,468	1,600
			84	41,363	1,569	1,778	209
			86	35,800	10,037	10,475	438
CANADA	O	E	82	1,821	915	915	
			85	1,630	4,637	4,637	

Crop
Product
TSUSA commodity number, description, and unit of quantity

Country	Mode	Reg	Yr	Quantity	F.A.S.	C.I.F.	Charges
			86	1,048	2,096	2,096	
CHINA M	N	H	81	720	2,748	3,397	649
			83	1,250	3,039	3,737	698
			85	2,400	4,534	5,563	1,029
			86	1,900	2,054	2,738	684
	V	E	85	9,000	3,419	3,719	300
	V	H	82	652	3,371	5,473	240
			84	17,703	8,627	9,603	976
	V	W	84	1,750	1,786	1,900	114
			85	80,000	13,358	14,168	810
FR GERM	V	E	85	499,600	31,350	43,450	12,100
FRANCE	V	E	81	225,035	36,885	40,208	3,323
			82	53,360	9,512	11,713	2,201
			83	75,538	15,807	17,142	1,335
			84	310,571	43,255	49,243	5,988
HG KONG	A	W	85	6,000	7,000	9,072	2,072
			86	1,200	1,200	1,200	
	V	W	81	2,500	4,000	4,074	74
			85	10,000	7,372	7,750	378
IRAQ	V	E	84	1,545	292	312	20
ISRAEL	N	E	81	3,859,657	367,954	443,643	75,689
			82	3,476,850	346,138	404,423	58,285
	V	E	81	1,323,910	226,454	255,724	29,271
			82	2,728,765	425,632	475,315	49,683
			83	7,038,961	823,043	944,382	121,339
			84	6,407,869	878,443	1,000,245	121,802
			85	8,053,965	998,881	1,141,789	142,908
			86	9,125,595	1,251,552	1,408,941	157,389
	V	W	81	733,546	73,304	86,439	13,135
			82	385,546	46,922	52,902	5,980
			83	124,589	13,747	15,491	1,744
			84	456,614	57,417	60,262	2,845
			85	148,488	14,214	17,779	3,565
			86	41,262	6,740	7,809	1,069
ITALY	V	W	86	7,000	1,456	1,623	167
JAPAN	N	W	82	12,549	3,405	3,809	404
	V	E	81	13,000	1,829	2,015	186
			82	12,500	4,356	4,687	331
			83	33,500	17,693	19,250	1,557
	V	H	81	600	1,300	1,412	112
	V	W	81	161,300	27,829	29,768	2,264
			82	120,500	21,780	23,346	1,566
			83	143,250	24,878	27,196	2,318
			84	146,500	27,788	30,269	2,481
			85	119,450	25,646	27,782	2,136
			86	208,326	79,386	83,017	3,631
KOR REP	V	E	84	18,400	3,165	3,465	300
MALI	V	E	85	114,000	7,703	9,988	2,285
			86	99,705	11,859	13,749	1,890
NETHLDS	A	E	82	24,707	3,750	5,251	1,501
			83	121,538	14,181	17,586	3,405
			84	10,867	2,065	2,481	416
			85	7,630	1,109	1,653	544
			86	22,700	3,581	4,290	709
	A	W	84	3,600	1,840	2,254	414
	N	E	81	27,253,406	3,382,137	3,831,174	449,044
			82	27,508,177	3,566,175	4,050,949	484,774
			83	32,977,153	4,000,366	4,527,983	527,617
			84	43,460,393	4,868,276	5,691,818	823,542
			85	46,198,173	5,222,914	6,084,046	861,132
			86	48,017,499	6,205,172	7,091,304	886,132
	N	W	82	1,201,698	136,062	164,072	28,010
			83	1,341,729	150,868	170,750	19,882
			84	1,802,747	183,105	218,400	35,295
			85	1,529,856	145,873	179,854	33,981
			86	264,271	42,617	48,787	6,170
	O	E	81	16,669	2,484	2,484	
			82	20,672	3,031	3,080	49
			83	15,276	1,633	1,778	145
			84	50,200	3,560	3,773	213
			85	54,813	12,632	12,632	
			86	59,500	10,576	10,576	
	V	E	81	9,046,703	1,035,393	1,188,936	153,543
			82	7,928,739	1,038,972	1,183,893	144,921
			83	12,348,025	1,293,573	1,479,774	186,201
			84	16,207,716	1,471,857	1,713,379	241,522
			85	11,847,682	1,395,178	1,618,324	223,146
			86	9,844,866	1,104,250	1,239,712	135,462
	V	W	81	1,814,131	210,981	252,852	41,871
			82	465,532	48,496	57,002	8,506
			83	820,033	94,976	115,231	20,255
			84	391,740	40,187	48,450	8,263
			85	763,105	78,769	93,279	14,510
			86	1,579,072	183,158	211,293	28,135

Crop
Product
TSUSA commodity number, description, and unit of quantity

Country	Mode	Reg	Yr	Quantity	F.A.S.	C.I.F.	Charges
REP SAF	V	E	83	4,000	773	828	55
			84	17,771	736	1,210	474
U KING	A	E	84	12,475	868	1,260	392
	V	E	81	5,909,016	484,961	525,431	40,470
			82	6,897,682	463,974	516,889	52,915
			83	4,456,500	241,046	289,473	48,427
			84	3,138,989	190,244	247,815	57,571
			85	14,795,094	738,478	1,008,026	269,548
			86	18,657,379	1,047,945	1,357,745	309,800
	V	W	81	1,814,495	145,833	170,802	24,969
			82	955,000	69,469	79,162	9,693
			83	21,500	10,854	13,863	3,009
			84	365,000	16,584	16,863	279
			85	663,830	37,583	52,892	15,309
			86	1,252,786	83,259	97,633	14,374
YEMAN S	V	E	82	23,500	4,870	5,406	536

Nutmeg

Mace, spice
1614300 MACE, BOMBAY OR WILD, UNGRND (LB)

Country	Mode	Reg	Yr	Quantity	F.A.S.	C.I.F.	Charges
TOTAL			81	46,299	43,054	51,688	8,634
			82	160	491	518	27
			83	47,399	51,233	60,751	9,518
			84	37,731	104,021	106,870	2,849
			85	42,204	118,993	124,743	5,750
			86	49,482	172,357	179,904	7,547
BELGIUM	V	E	85	6,132	20,506	21,506	1,000
FR GERM	V	E	85	4,535	9,226	9,476	250
INDIA	V	E	82	160	491	518	27
INDNSIA	V	E	81	40,787	38,828	44,548	5,720
			83	47,399	51,233	60,751	9,518
			84	37,731	104,021	106,870	2,849
			85	27,559	77,240	80,790	3,550
			86	38,459	140,489	146,637	6,148
	V	W	81	5,512	4,226	7,140	2,914
			86	11,023	31,868	33,267	1,399
NETHLDS	V	E	85	3,978	12,021	12,971	950

1614500 MACE, BOMBAY OR WILD, GROUND (LB)

Country	Mode	Reg	Yr	Quantity	F.A.S.	C.I.F.	Charges
TOTAL			83	7,050	2,468	5,112	2,644
FIJI	A	E	83	7,050	2,468	5,112	2,644

1614700 MACE, UNGROUND, NSPF (LB)

Country	Mode	Reg	Yr	Quantity	F.A.S.	C.I.F.	Charges
TOTAL			81	530,785	488,766	556,690	67,924
			82	474,711	594,614	645,900	51,286
			83	563,045	949,930	1,016,598	66,668
			84	478,841	1,227,574	1,299,857	72,283
			85	636,916	1,815,994	1,927,708	111,714
			86	380,647	1,418,685	1,463,036	44,351
BELGIUM	V	E	83	7,127	14,943	15,755	812
			85	4,506	16,447	16,959	512
BRAZIL	V	E	81	163	391	402	11
C RICA	V	E	86	1,488	4,755	5,065	310
CHINA T	V	E	85	20,944	53,997	62,221	8,224
FRANCE	V	E	83	15,778	18,662	20,557	1,895
			85	34,024	80,058	83,219	3,161
GRENADA	V	E	81	2,539	1,911	2,339	428
			82	1,120	625	782	157
			83	4,480	4,032	4,288	256
INDIA	V	E	81	11,052	11,973	12,995	1,022
			85	40,888	127,394	137,118	9,724
	V	W	85	6,614	22,643	23,216	573
INDNSIA	N	E	86	338,180	1,289,544	1,329,225	39,681
	V	E	81	406,270	371,448	422,737	51,289
			82	392,041	496,484	538,058	41,574
			83	457,897	793,688	851,619	57,931
			84	442,068	1,141,132	1,210,145	69,013
			85	480,586	1,428,350	1,510,183	81,833
			86	23,115	99,861	101,536	1,675
	V	W	81	22,047	20,940	24,348	3,408
			82	6,614	7,032	7,329	297
			83	24,295	35,371	37,794	2,423
			86	6,614	23,400	26,085	2,685
MEXICO	O	E	86	11,250	1,125	1,125	
NETHLDS	V	E	83	18,167	31,299	32,453	1,154
	V	W	85	4,519	15,626	16,608	982

Crop Product TSUSA commodity number, description, and unit of quantity Country	Mode	Reg	Yr	Quantity	F.A.S.	C.I.F.	Charges
NEW GUI	V	E	81	13,228	9,001	9,642	641
SINGAPR	V	E	81	57,849	56,591	63,034	6,443
			82	57,300	66,053	72,358	6,305
			83	35,301	51,935	54,132	2,197
			84	33,025	75,629	78,224	2,595
			85	29,807	63,257	67,663	4,406
	V	W	81	17,637	16,511	21,193	4,682
			82	17,636	24,420	27,373	2,953
SRI LKA	V	E	84	3,748	10,813	11,488	675
	V	W	85	15,028	8,222	10,521	2,299

1614900 MACE, NSPF, GROUND (LB)

Country	Mode	Reg	Yr	Quantity	F.A.S.	C.I.F.	Charges
TOTAL			81	11,376	9,977	13,434	3,457
			82	18,437	23,526	26,173	2,647
			83	2,805	4,075	4,319	244
			85	11,023	30,137	34,564	4,427
			86	2,205	6,023	6,314	291
CANADA	O	E	81	352	545	545	
			82	250	447	447	
			83	600	1,404	1,404	
INDIA	V	W	82	550	397	440	43
INDNSIA	V	E	81	11,024	9,432	12,889	3,457
			82	17,637	22,682	25,286	2,604
			85	11,023	30,137	34,564	4,427
	V	W	86	2,205	6,023	6,314	291
SINGAPR	V	W	83	2,205	2,671	2,915	244

Nutmeg, essential oil
4528020 NUTMEG OIL (LB)

Country	Mode	Reg	Yr	Quantity	F.A.S.	C.I.F.	Charges
TOTAL			81	163,392	1,027,533	1,066,407	38,874
			82	211,076	1,380,427	1,423,794	43,367
			83	206,171	1,364,993	1,403,575	38,582
			84	233,480	1,859,243	1,926,236	66,993
			85	239,292	1,994,616	2,048,009	53,393
			86	311,219	3,179,811	3,247,219	67,408
BAHAMAS	V	E	85	4,000	35,800	35,959	159
BRAZIL	V	E	85	4,409	32,296	33,037	741
CANADA	O	E	86	110	1,090	1,166	76
CHINA M	V	E	85	4,000	35,800	35,862	62
			86	2,000	25,000	25,117	117
CHINA T	V	E	84	13,228	53,777	58,103	4,326
FR GERM	V	E	82	13,228	92,903	95,059	2,156
FRANCE	N	E	84	992	8,169	8,408	239
	V	E	82	1,543	11,617	11,774	157
			85	220	1,672	1,700	28
			86	1,642	16,420	16,662	242
HAITI	V	E	82	2,200	19,800	20,365	565
INDIA	A	E	82	1,800	11,413	11,861	448
	O	E	86	200	1,838	1,838	
	V	E	83	1,102	6,796	7,035	239
			86	1,962	15,209	15,578	369
INDNSIA	N	E	85	224,663	1,874,231	1,926,178	51,947
			86	282,678	2,895,982	2,959,096	63,114
	O	E	81	399	3,193	3,404	211
			83	2,000	14,000	14,430	430
	V	E	81	160,189	1,003,043	1,041,127	38,084
			82	183,443	1,193,294	1,230,445	37,151
			83	201,052	1,340,933	1,378,544	37,611
			84	180,193	1,425,394	1,475,785	50,391
			85	2,000	14,817	15,273	456
			86	7,124	68,622	69,603	981
	V	W	82	8,730	49,880	52,490	2,610
			84	30,297	313,893	323,193	9,300
JAPAN	V	E	83	1,984	2,846	3,050	204
			84	1,587	10,495	10,721	226
MALAYSA	V	E	84	2,379	18,096	18,751	655
MEXICO	O	E	84	4,804	29,419	31,275	1,856
	V	E	81	600	6,150	6,162	12
NETHLDS	A	E	82	132	1,520	1,800	280
			83	33	418	516	98
			86	331	2,600	2,631	31
SINGAPR	V	E	81	2,204	15,147	15,714	567
			86	6,710	62,551	63,542	991
U KING	N	E	86	4,462	58,149	58,986	837
	V	E	86	4,000	32,350	33,000	650

Nutmeg, spice
1616300 NUTMEGS, UNGROUND (LB)

Crop Product TSUSA commodity number, description, and unit of quantity Country	Mode	Reg	Yr	Quantity	F.A.S.	C.I.F.	Charges
TOTAL			81	4,784,646	3,526,622	3,890,158	363,536
			82	5,337,743	3,576,882	3,932,966	356,084
			83	4,544,658	2,954,544	3,244,028	289,484
			84	4,350,450	2,967,154	3,307,620	340,466
			85	4,665,917	3,275,858	3,623,892	348,034
			86	4,017,612	6,877,866	7,140,803	262,937
ALBANIA	V	E	84	44,139	26,993	31,716	4,723
BARBADO	V	E	83	11,354	8,063	8,663	600
BELGIUM	V	E	84	48,966	34,605	35,821	1,216
			85	22,046	16,850	17,650	800
C RICA	V	E	86	3,241	6,209	6,613	404
CANADA	O	E	84	220	264	264	
CHINA M	N	E	83	11,076	7,755	8,260	505
	V	E	81	106	375	385	10
			84	36	256	261	5
CHINA T	V	E	85	6,614	3,957	4,797	840
F W IND	V	E	82	11,023	8,143	9,416	1,273
			86	1,553	4,160	4,336	176
FR GERM	V	E	84	28,660	17,804	19,669	1,865
			85	29,150	25,742	27,588	1,846
FRANCE	A	W	84	99	287	461	174
	V	E	81	246,433	209,704	223,853	14,149
			82	83,130	65,131	69,417	4,286
			83	79,394	47,751	52,495	4,744
			84	99,386	64,768	72,980	8,212
			85	161,156	111,114	122,044	10,930
			86	97,036	169,346	175,138	5,792
	V	W	81	30,437	24,654	26,951	2,297
			83	31,429	22,314	22,814	500
GREECE	V	E	84	11,023	6,834	8,134	1,300
GRENADA	N	E	86	318,480	493,739	507,175	13,436
	V	E	81	244,240	182,093	196,878	14,785
			82	378,289	240,268	278,174	37,906
			83	317,355	193,158	215,413	22,255
			84	166,267	140,790	152,184	11,394
			85	236,415	151,741	157,063	5,322
HAITI	V	E	85	42,000	33,600	34,600	1,000
HG KONG	V	E	85	30,864	19,839	23,766	3,927
INDIA	N	E	83	175,012	116,370	124,807	8,437
			84	121,446	92,860	101,689	8,829
	V	E	81	137,691	101,007	108,893	7,886
			82	49,471	40,917	42,637	1,720
			83	441	733	823	90
			84	31,075	21,751	24,332	2,581
			85	231,442	155,386	176,500	21,114
			86	394,634	913,036	938,745	25,709
	V	W	82	220	293	354	61
			83	1,263	888	1,056	168
			84	860	1,087	1,224	137
INDNSIA	N	E	81	3,003,364	2,114,830	2,378,435	263,605
			83	3,097,330	2,016,819	2,224,663	207,844
			85	2,669,047	1,834,366	2,054,526	220,160
			86	2,663,987	4,415,534	4,595,318	179,784
	V	E	81	220,847	163,837	177,082	13,245
			82	3,708,551	2,467,797	2,713,185	245,388
			83	224,780	144,859	158,557	13,698
			84	3,405,620	2,319,515	2,592,242	272,727
			85	520,638	390,030	424,723	34,693
			86	307,356	481,005	503,025	22,020
	V	W	81	246,323	174,671	186,683	12,012
			82	169,119	112,954	121,579	8,625
			83	73,524	39,712	42,896	3,184
			85	79,808	81,480	88,676	7,196
ITALY	V	E	82	57	433	477	44
			83	20,622	14,124	15,286	1,162
	V	W	82	34	260	260	
			83	84	469	544	75
JAMAICA	A	E	82	41	349	390	41
			83	2,750	4,550	4,570	20
	V	E	86	4,410	10,000	10,400	400
JAPAN	V	E	82	62,831	34,634	38,099	3,465
			83	29,762	14,222	15,939	1,717
MADAGAS	V	E	85	4,630	3,403	3,651	248
			86	26,235	22,132	22,956	824
MEXICO	O	W	85	3,210	2,236	2,236	
N ANTIL	V	E	84	28,660	18,721	20,471	1,750
NEPAL	V	E	82	22,388	17,921	19,185	1,264
NETHLDS	N	E	83	358,971	264,943	282,636	17,693
	O	E	86	2,401	5,544	5,544	

Crop
Product
TSUSA commodity number, description, and unit of quantity

Country	Mode	Reg	Yr	Quantity	F.A.S.	C.I.F.	Charges
	V E	81	532,180	439,154	467,515	28,361
		82	669,983	478,935	513,796	34,861
		84	255,923	174,239	189,855	15,616
		85	453,538	329,622	356,967	27,345
		86	159,994	301,949	312,062	10,113
	V W	85	22,597	20,003	21,259	1,256
		86	28,660	31,689	33,877	2,188
NEW GUI	V E	82	6,614	4,641	4,986	345
		83	12,566	3,598	4,067	469
NIGER	V E	85	43,802	30,423	33,375	2,952
PAKISTN	V E	84	55,115	15,155	22,155	7,000
		85	28,660	8,297	12,138	3,841
S LUCIA	V E	84	1,147	4,250	4,614	364
S VN GR	V E	86	2,990	6,279	7,379	1,100
SALVADR	V E	85	42,300	25,546	28,335	2,789
SINGAPR	V E	81	66,344	75,018	79,768	4,750
		82	52,977	31,061	38,367	7,306
		84	51,808	26,975	29,548	2,573
		85	38,000	32,223	33,998	1,775
		86	6,635	17,244	18,235	991
	V W	81	56,681	41,279	43,715	2,436
		82	122,615	70,453	79,863	9,410
		83	54,945	29,016	32,939	3,923
SPAIN	V E	83	42,000	25,200	27,600	2,400
U KING	O E	82	167	1,054	1,079	25
	V E	82	233	1,638	1,702	64

1616500 NUTMEGS, GROUND (LB)

Country	Mode	Reg	Yr	Quantity	F.A.S.	C.I.F.	Charges
TOTAL		81	70,939	80,956	82,625	1,669
		82	56,050	50,211	53,649	3,438
		83	57,773	59,492	62,001	2,509
		84	104,802	62,200	68,652	6,452
		85	35,078	36,835	38,303	1,468
		86	18,017	20,083	22,467	2,384
ARGENT	V E	83	39,477	35,529	37,322	1,793
		84	38,704	13,614	15,736	2,122
CANADA	O E	81	14,538	14,643	14,643	
		82	10,224	11,829	11,829	
		83	10,047	14,667	14,667	
		84	9,457	10,638	10,638	
		86	968	1,919	1,919	
	O W	81	328	731	731	
COLOMB	A E	83	335	317	535	218
DENMARK	V E	82	441	704	751	47
F W IND	O E	81	5,040	14,383	14,383	
FRANCE	A W	84	166	299	413	114
	V E	82	44,092	33,886	37,037	3,151
		83	45	494	520	26
		85	4,564	9,102	9,960	858
		86	12,331	6,973	8,722	1,749
GRENADA	O E	81	2,180	4,805	4,805	
	V E	84	42,223	21,630	24,177	2,547
		85	19,836	15,428	16,038	610
INDNSIA	O E	81	19,519	18,072	18,072	
		83	6,800	2,097	2,097	
		85	10,678	12,305	12,305	
	V E	84	11,343	9,528	10,776	1,248
ISRAEL	V E	86	4,409	8,599	9,001	402
ITALY	V E	81	265	1,866	2,010	144
		82	243	2,340	2,442	102
		83	466	4,680	5,010	330
		86	309	2,592	2,825	233
JAMAICA	A E	83	100	300	300	
JAPAN	V E	82	1,050	1,452	1,590	138
		83	242	413	445	32
	V W	84	2,090	3,709	3,920	211
NETHLDS	V E	81	28,660	24,687	26,182	1,495
SPAIN	V E	84	178	539	590	51
THAILND	V W	84	63	280	297	17
U KING	O E	81	139	809	839	30
		83	74	371	466	95
		84	458	1,684	1,811	127
	V E	81	270	960	960	
		83	187	624	639	15
		84	120	279	294	15

Crop
Product
TSUSA commodity number, description, and unit of quantity

O

Oak

Oak, hardwood flooring
2025600 HARDWOOD FLOORING, OAK STRP (MBF)

Country	Mode	Reg	Yr	Quantity	F.A.S.	C.I.F.	Charges
TOTAL		81	536	380,545	392,503	11,958
		82	451	497,743	514,249	16,506
		83	5,108	1,500,791	1,567,638	66,847
		84	2,167	1,794,277	1,933,226	138,949
		85	5,459	3,896,737	4,193,440	296,703
		86	5,893	3,820,837	4,075,578	254,741
AUSTRAL	V E	83	112	16,660	20,747	4,087
		85	3	7,518	9,349	1,831
		86	40	24,255	29,043	4,788
BELGIUM	V E	86	9	30,771	32,645	1,874
	V W	85	7	20,703	23,006	2,303
BOLIVIA	V W	82	28	28,570	32,038	3,468
CANADA	A W	81	1	722	1,667	945
	O E	81	351	239,190	239,190	
		82	276	223,771	223,771	
		83	580	612,712	612,712	
		84	403	560,985	560,985	
		85	1,741	809,894	809,894	
		86	587	558,277	558,277	
	O W	83	1	505	505	
		84	2	6,962	6,962	
		85	3	14,710	14,710	
	V H	86	1	1,729	1,729	
CHINA T	V W	86	29	34,022	35,638	1,616
DENMARK	V E	82	2	4,316	4,492	176
		83	15	28,333	31,795	3,462
		84	29	51,219	57,531	6,312
		85	4	11,149	12,935	1,786
		86	1	6,342	7,234	892
FINLAND	V W	86	7	40,498	45,264	4,766
FR GERM	A E	86	15	2,251	3,350	1,099
	N W	86	24	53,433	58,204	4,771
	O E	81	1	725	725	
		82	1	767	767	
		83	1	1,429	1,429	
		86	9	10,369	10,369	
	V E	83	10	15,973	17,743	1,770
		84	101	66,998	74,011	7,013
		85	1,193	827,218	912,733	85,515
		86	863	682,697	712,642	29,945
	V W	84	52	55,435	66,954	11,519
		85	7	24,696	27,359	2,663
		86	10	19,531	21,990	2,459
FRANCE	N E	82	•	396	507	111
		85	•	1,296	3,697	2,401
	O E	84	3	6,824	8,243	1,419
	V E	83	9	15,262	16,352	1,090
		84	62	10,519	13,265	2,746
		85	62	128,813	144,901	16,088
		86	14	15,420	16,314	894
	V W	84	38	64,242	69,550	5,308
GREECE	V W	84	101	2,316	2,658	342
ITALY	A E	85	4	11,042	13,138	2,096
	N E	84	256	24,019	24,575	556
	V E	86	1	1,324	1,375	51
JAMAICA	V E	86	12	31,706	33,673	1,967
KOR REP	V E	83	1	1,004	1,178	174
		85	30	17,612	18,913	1,301
		86	261	288,254	303,895	15,641
	V W	84	1	930	1,071	141
MEXICO	A E	81	5	4,569	6,244	1,675
	N E	83	•	624	624	
	O E	86	274	6,807	6,807	
	O W	82	57	62,927	62,927	
		83	40	30,184	30,184	
		84	460	43,053	43,053	
		85	59	53,999	53,999	
		86	5	23,876	23,876	
NAMIBIA	V E	85	8	27,050	28,550	1,500
NETHLDS	V E	86	6	16,607	18,059	1,452
NORWAY	N E	83	•	9,667	10,469	802
	V E	83	3	5,065	5,994	929
		84	221	123,526	138,937	15,411

Crop Product TSUSA commodity number, description, and unit of quantity Country	Mode	Reg	Yr	Quantity	F.A.S.	C.I.F.	Charges
			85	154	283,887	310,367	26,480
			86	190	294,974	321,865	26,891
	V	W	85	35	96,939	101,494	4,555
			86	138	147,735	155,934	8,199
PERU	V	E	81	44	3,480	4,490	1,010
			85	1	1,591	1,764	173
			86	3	2,359	2,540	181
PHIL R	V	E	85	25	3,000	3,246	246
SINGAPR	V	E	86	27	50,236	58,043	7,807
	V	W	81	18	24,253	28,253	4,000
SPAIN	V	E	85	1	3,480	3,876	396
SRI LKA	A	E	86	1	5,250	6,090	840
	V	E	86	28	42,989	48,817	5,828
	V	W	85	16	31,415	36,851	5,436
			86	72	187,580	210,465	22,885
SWEDEN	N	E	82	52	91,147	98,925	7,778
	N	W	84	14	18,751	21,252	2,501
	V	E	81	32	57,206	60,108	2,902
			82	17	49,514	53,648	4,134
			83	2,063	624,539	669,001	44,462
			84	385	689,231	769,966	80,735
			85	615	1,013,684	1,102,315	88,631
			86	302	774,127	843,601	69,474
	V	W	82	18	36,335	37,174	839
			83	2,273	138,834	148,905	10,071
			84	38	68,999	73,866	4,867
			85	1,491	507,041	560,343	53,302
			86	2,758	404,502	433,540	29,038
THAILND	A	E	86	2	1,750	5,326	3,576
	V	W	81	84	50,400	51,826	1,426
			86	204	61,166	68,973	7,807
U KING	V	E	84	1	268	347	79

Oak, lumber**

2023820 BOXWD, JAP MAPLE LBR, ROUGH (MBF)
(See Boxwood, lumber under Boxwood)
2023840 BOXWD, JAP MAP LBR, DRESSED (MBF)
(See Boxwood, lumber under Boxwood)
2024250 OAK LUMBER, ROUGH (MBF)

Country	Mode	Reg	Yr	Quantity	F.A.S.	C.I.F.	Charges
TOTAL			81	1,304	682,121	701,066	18,945
			82	1,403	791,607	821,354	29,747
			83	1,726	1,002,399	1,053,801	51,402
			84	3,008	1,776,245	1,835,665	59,420
			85	2,481	1,771,517	1,814,059	42,542
			86	2,763	2,121,346	2,156,843	35,497
AUSTRAL	V	E	82	55	42,305	58,403	16,098
			85	14	13,802	18,951	5,149
			86	87	13,923	18,486	4,563
	V	H	84	1	822	926	104
	V	W	82	14	1,632	4,514	2,882
			83	120	119,341	137,988	18,647
			84	276	192,490	227,471	34,981
			85	116	133,411	154,406	20,995
			86	128	136,700	152,723	16,023
BRAZIL	V	E	83	202	233,704	253,568	19,864
CANADA	N	E	85	747	475,678	475,678	
	O	E	81	1,225	552,350	552,350	
			82	1,093	573,378	573,378	
			83	1,218	531,156	531,156	
			84	1,941	1,221,485	1,221,485	
			85	1,285	907,635	907,635	
			86	2,412	1,817,992	1,817,994	2
	O	W	81	33	28,615	28,615	
			82	84	88,063	88,063	
			83	18	24,575	24,575	
			84	43	59,738	59,738	
			85	49	56,955	56,955	
			86	14	21,100	21,100	
	V	E	86	29	34,188	36,398	2,210
	V	W	83	52	57,656	64,069	6,413
			84	700	231,263	245,997	14,734
			85	233	157,599	171,651	14,052
			86	81	81,537	89,832	8,295
CHILE	V	E	84	7	2,114	3,846	1,732
	V	W	83	100	7,322	9,472	2,150
DENMARK	V	E	86	10	7,504	10,605	3,101
FR GERM	V	E	81	2	1,435	2,407	972
FRANCE	O	W	82	27	11,909	13,254	1,345
	V	E	81	11	18,845	20,843	1,998
	V	W	84	21	40,474	44,416	3,942
HONDURA	V	E	83	1	502	811	309

Country	Mode	Reg	Yr	Quantity	F.A.S.	C.I.F.	Charges
JAPAN	V	W	81	5	10,689	11,645	956
MALAYSA	V	W	85	15	7,263	9,609	2,346
MEXICO	O	E	82	1	960	960	
	O	W	85	22	19,174	19,174	
PHIL R	V	E	84	13	10,332	12,150	1,818
U KING	N	W	81	*	697	886	189
	O	E	82	116	31,146	34,831	3,685
			84	3	7,191	7,191	
			86	1	5,534	5,534	
	V	E	81	28	69,490	84,320	14,830
			82	13	42,214	47,951	5,737
			83	15	28,143	32,162	4,019
			84	3	10,336	12,445	2,109
	V	W	86	1	2,868	4,171	1,303

2024255 OAK LUMBER, DRESSED, WORKED (MBF)

Country	Mode	Reg	Yr	Quantity	F.A.S.	C.I.F.	Charges
TOTAL			81	1,116	842,869	843,949	1,078
			82	843	599,559	624,840	25,281
			83	1,865	1,569,022	1,642,276	73,254
			84	4,618	2,021,426	2,078,617	57,191
			85	4,635	2,002,920	2,058,359	55,439
			86	2,566	1,808,093	1,839,001	30,908
AUSTRAL	V	E	83	129	60,739	80,873	20,134
			84	4	1,691	2,078	387
			85	19	4,618	5,093	475
	V	W	83	37	31,671	40,756	9,085
			84	2	4,394	5,001	607
			85	39	44,933	53,008	8,075
			86	96	109,452	123,189	13,737
CANADA	N	E	84	*	455	656	201
			85	1,690	451,661	451,661	
	N	W	84	*	401	401	
	O	E	81	991	778,246	778,248	
			82	715	450,041	450,041	
			83	894	572,370	572,376	6
			84	1,584	1,000,040	1,000,068	28
			85	1,334	938,432	938,432	
			86	2,243	1,403,546	1,403,546	
	O	W	81	118	58,539	58,539	
			82	68	70,600	70,600	
			83	108	217,000	217,000	
			84	96	73,470	73,470	
			85	130	184,561	184,561	
			86	66	158,656	158,656	
	V	E	83	9	9,196	9,691	495
			84	8	6,681	7,091	410
			85	2	6,362	8,647	2,285
			86	4	13,771	14,157	386
	V	W	84	48	44,465	49,561	5,096
			85	57	52,046	57,758	5,712
			86	35	26,172	29,841	3,669
CHILE	V	E	83	9	6,073	7,893	1,820
			84	15	9,254	10,804	1,550
CHINA T	V	E	83	27	47,522	50,659	3,137
FR GERM	A	E	86	11	8,396	10,014	1,618
	N	W	86	13	20,949	22,772	1,823
	V	E	86	2	3,768	4,635	867
FRANCE	A	E	84	1	2,206	3,300	1,094
	O	E	84	14	16,499	19,929	3,430
	V	E	85	18	20,205	24,055	3,850
	V	W	82	5	12,411	13,693	1,282
			83	633	605,369	641,321	35,952
			84	2,591	801,068	839,460	38,392
			85	1,339	275,519	297,279	21,760
HONDURA	V	E	81	7	6,084	7,162	1,078
ITALY	A	E	84	2	1,498	1,972	474
	V	E	84	58	3,625	4,231	606
KOR REP	V	W	86	4	5,400	6,480	1,080
MEXICO	O	E	84	183	25,509	25,509	
	O	W	82	5	3,034	3,034	
			83	3	1,018	1,018	
NETHLDS	A	W	83	13	12,638	13,954	1,316
			84	3	14,966	17,816	2,850
PANAMA	V	E	82	2	2,539	3,036	497
PHIL R	V	W	86	40	15,940	18,579	2,639
REP SAF	V	E	84	9	10,220	12,057	1,837
SPAIN	V	E	82	40	52,007	71,232	19,225
SWEDEN	A	E	82	3	5,927	7,817	1,890
	V	E	86	52	42,043	47,132	5,089
U KING	A	E	85	6	20,704	33,814	13,110
	N	E	84	*	400	400	
	N	W	84	*	4,584	4,813	229
	V	E	83	3	5,426	6,735	1,309

Crop Product TSUSA commodity number, description, and unit of quantity Country	Mode	Reg	Yr	Quantity	F.A.S.	C.I.F.	Charges
			85	1	3,879	4,051	172
	V	W	82	5	3,000	5,387	2,387

Valonia, dye or tannin
4706000 VALONIA CRUDE OR PROCESD (LB)

TOTAL			83	22,046	5,900	9,851	3,951
TURKEY	V	E	83	22,046	5,900	9,851	3,951

4706500 VALONIA NOT CRUDE OR PROC (LB)

TOTAL			81	485,642	137,761	180,084	42,323
			82	44,296	12,716	16,090	3,374
			83	242,506	68,672	84,273	15,601
			84	44,092	12,800	15,439	2,639
			85	27,557	8,000	10,042	2,042
			86	19	2,466	2,578	112
DOM REP	V	E	81	630	315	348	33
FRANCE	A	E	86	19	2,466	2,578	112
PHIL R	V	W	82	250	300	336	36
TURKEY	V	E	81	485,012	137,446	179,736	42,290
			82	44,046	12,416	15,754	3,338
			83	242,506	68,672	84,273	15,601
			84	44,092	12,800	15,439	2,639
			85	27,557	8,000	10,042	2,042

Oat

Oat, hulled or unhulled
1304500 OATS, HULLED OR UNHULLED (BU)

TOTAL			81	884,520	2,094,070	2,094,070	
			82	1,874,416	3,840,752	3,872,640	31,888
			83	19,088,472	27,567,741	29,650,374	2,082,633
			84	28,279,369	48,934,900	52,801,591	3,866,691
			85	30,682,220	50,706,533	56,272,113	5,565,580
			86	30,116,561	36,815,274	42,213,194	5,397,920
ARGENT	V	E	82	3,062	10,553	14,600	4,047
			83	7,652	17,447	30,523	13,076
			85	72,284	111,741	152,136	40,395
AUSTRAL	V	E	84	909,449	1,934,444	2,073,111	138,667
	V	W	82	1,171	2,819	6,596	3,777
			85	7,441	14,023	24,841	10,818
			86	689	1,183	3,700	2,517
CANADA	N	E	82	1,187,159	2,163,957	2,184,115	20,158
			83	9,240,807	13,572,040	13,902,757	330,717
			84	4,291,542	6,494,675	6,566,585	71,910
			85	1,542,613	2,455,352	2,466,352	11,000
			86	5,034,739	4,414,726	4,552,326	137,600
	N	W	84	16,377	59,334	70,803	11,469
	O	E	81	840,475	1,992,122	1,992,122	
			82	627,322	1,544,521	1,544,521	
			83	1,443,785	2,752,805	2,756,933	4,128
			84	1,816,007	3,846,715	3,846,728	13
			85	499,534	1,134,114	1,134,114	
			86	1,206,103	1,709,620	1,709,626	6
	O	W	81	43,701	99,677	99,677	
			82	52,086	103,100	103,100	
			83	35,829	75,236	76,236	1,000
			84	79,073	141,421	141,421	
			85	117,439	221,577	221,577	
			86	284,293	497,553	497,553	
	V	E	83	840,504	1,250,502	1,374,511	124,009
			86	869,835	878,678	1,046,469	167,791
	V	W	82	3,272	11,300	13,800	2,500
FINLAND	V	E	84	16,213,839	27,346,764	30,061,678	2,714,914
			85	3,892,273	6,275,356	7,221,581	946,225
			86	8,600,594	8,543,774	10,492,744	1,948,970
FR GERM	O	E	81	344	2,271	2,271	
JAMAICA	A	E	84	3	400	420	20
JAPAN	V	W	82	344	4,502	5,908	1,406
MEXICO	O	E	84	965	2,545	2,545	
NETHLDS	V	E	85	723,384	1,312,500	1,448,759	136,259
			86	215	1,404	1,681	277
PAKISTN	V	W	84	2,000	859	1,006	147
SWEDEN	N	E	85	22,998,208	37,918,350	42,218,897	4,300,547
	V	E	83	7,519,895	9,899,711	11,509,414	1,609,703
			84	4,950,114	9,107,743	10,037,294	929,551
			85	829,044	1,263,520	1,383,856	120,336

Crop Product TSUSA commodity number, description, and unit of quantity Country	Mode	Reg	Yr	Quantity	F.A.S.	C.I.F.	Charges
			86	14,120,093	20,768,336	23,909,095	3,140,759

Oat, milled for humans
1312500 OATS, MILLD, EDBLE NOV $8CWT (CWT)

TOTAL			81	451	3,929	3,929	
			82	9,062	9,299	10,220	921
			83	47,487	18,608	18,725	117
			84	80	355	355	
			85	40,501	42,577	45,803	3,226
			86	4,270	17,776	18,061	285
BELGIUM	V	E	85	9,119	6,486	6,886	400
CANADA	O	E	82	400	3,110	3,110	
			83	1,000	6,849	6,849	
			85	894	6,946	6,946	
			86	3,229	13,807	13,807	
	O	W	81	451	3,929	3,929	
			83	45,715	8,756	8,756	
COLOMB	V	E	82	3,262	2,173	2,349	176
			85	21,429	15,694	18,222	2,528
	V	W	85	8,862	10,301	10,420	119
FR GERM	A	E	86	1,041	3,969	4,254	285
FRANCE	V	E	83	772	3,003	3,120	117
INDIA	O	E	84	80	355	355	
IRELAND	V	E	82	5,400	4,016	4,761	745
ITALY	A	E	85	197	3,150	3,329	179

1312700 OATS, MILLD, EDBLE OV $8 CWT (CWT)

TOTAL			81	18,849	1,182,109	1,332,887	150,778
			82	22,712	1,381,311	1,553,980	172,669
			83	19,592	1,311,341	1,462,568	151,227
			84	17,445	1,202,873	1,343,036	140,163
			85	23,480	1,283,709	1,423,710	140,001
			86	35,314	1,682,737	1,826,666	143,929
AUSTRAL	O	E	84	18	904	904	
BELGIUM	V	E	85	61	3,499	4,046	547
CANADA	O	E	82	709	14,160	14,160	
			83	405	15,722	15,722	
			84	195	7,738	7,738	
			85	5,586	69,929	69,929	
			86	10,236	149,406	149,406	
	V	E	86	770	57,630	62,488	4,858
CHINA M	V	E	81	5	312	365	53
CHINA T	A	E	83	1	291	567	276
COLOMB	V	E	81	15,843	1,015,731	1,133,985	118,254
			82	19,913	1,248,199	1,393,840	145,641
			83	16,781	1,161,376	1,288,174	126,798
			84	14,561	1,041,155	1,150,028	108,873
			85	15,070	1,066,457	1,179,027	112,570
			86	19,508	1,200,930	1,303,603	102,673
	V	W	82	14	1,063	1,225	162
FR GERM	O	E	86	128	5,547	6,934	1,387
	V	E	86	212	11,397	12,520	1,123
IRELAND	O	E	84	38	2,717	3,611	894
			85	30	1,966	2,206	240
	V	E	81	1,765	90,206	111,350	21,144
			82	1,817	100,796	122,947	22,151
			83	1,307	74,349	86,369	12,020
			84	1,040	61,780	70,421	8,641
			85	2,008	124,368	142,722	18,354
			86	1,967	112,396	127,677	15,281
	V	W	81	190	13,935	17,678	3,743
			82	164	11,442	15,699	4,257
			84	300	20,404	27,513	7,109
			86	86	5,148	6,343	1,195
ITALY	N	E	84	*	472	499	27
JAMAICA	V	E	84	42	3,712	4,799	1,087
			86	24	2,080	2,171	91
MEXICO	O	W	81	77	769	769	
	V	E	81	854	53,099	58,534	5,435
NETHLDS	V	E	85	317	3,722	7,940	4,218
			86	230	11,252	13,252	2,000
THAILND	V	E	86	400	5,695	7,200	1,505
U KING	A	E	82	20	451	529	78
	O	E	85	158	5,563	6,457	894
	V	E	81	106	7,657	9,041	1,384
			82	75	5,200	5,580	380
			83	997	50,786	60,242	9,456
			84	1,251	63,991	77,523	13,532
			85	250	8,205	11,383	3,178
			86	1,340	96,007	107,461	11,454

Crop Product TSUSA commodity number, description, and unit of quantity Country	Mode	Reg	Yr	Quantity	F.A.S.	C.I.F.	Charges
	V	W	83	101	8,817	11,494	2,677
VENEZ	A	E	81	9	400	1,165	765
	V	E	86	413	25,249	27,611	2,362

Oat, milled not for humans
1316500 OATS MILLED N FIT HUM CONS (CWT)

			Yr	Quantity	F.A.S.	C.I.F.	Charges
TOTAL			81	20,925	135,861	135,861	
			82	14,545	120,570	120,807	237
			83	54,990	455,550	456,729	1,179
			84	34,724	358,742	358,742	
			85	53,204	394,168	403,310	9,142
			86	228,602	826,581	946,716	120,135
ARGENT	V	E	85	1,078	7,493	13,711	6,218
	V	W	85	5,498	8,347	8,687	340
CANADA	N	E	85	9,603	77,845	77,845	
	O	E	81	20,495	134,141	134,141	
			82	14,332	118,936	118,936	
			83	54,990	455,550	456,729	1,179
			84	23,184	248,470	248,470	
			85	11,188	92,932	94,211	1,279
			86	7,804	78,601	78,601	
	O	W	81	430	1,720	1,720	
			82	40	397	397	
			84	11,540	110,272	110,272	
			85	25,705	206,348	206,348	
			86	26,121	223,686	223,686	
ITALY	A	E	86	1,304	4,432	6,376	1,944
JAMAICA	V	E	86	735	4,320	4,548	228
N ZEAL	V	H	85	132	1,203	2,508	1,305
NETHLDS	V	E	82	20	905	1,092	187
SWEDEN	V	E	86	192,638	515,542	633,505	117,963
U KING	A	E	82	153	332	382	50

Ogen Melon

Ogen melon, fresh**
1481900 OGEN/GALIA MELONS 12/1-5/31 (LB)
  (See Galia melon, fresh under Galia Melon)
1482200 OGEN/GALIA MELONS 6/1-11/30 (LB)
  (See Galia melon, fresh under Galia Melon)

Oil Palm

Palm kernel, vegetable oil, edible
1763320 PALM KERNL OIL EDIBLE CRUDE (LB)

	Mode	Reg	Yr	Quantity	F.A.S.	C.I.F.	Charges
TOTAL			81	137,814,080	35,699,203	39,280,904	3,581,701
			82	195,182,656	39,698,602	44,081,262	4,382,660
			83	221,213,175	53,079,907	58,261,461	5,181,554
			84	176,301,066	77,625,054	82,413,075	4,788,021
			85	228,324,957	68,802,417	74,571,100	5,768,683
			86	300,896,296	41,467,979	48,757,149	7,289,170
BELGIUM	V	E	81	2,211,237	574,918	663,378	88,460
BRAZIL	V	E	85	44,092	14,220	14,466	246
CANADA	O	E	84	122,920	34,525	34,525	
GUATMAL	V	E	84	169,530	99,166	108,401	9,235
			85	65,098	41,460	45,894	4,434
INDNSIA	V	E	85	40,314,461	12,132,867	13,200,658	1,067,791
			86	30,343,154	3,687,288	4,434,529	747,241
	V	W	86	15,081,189	2,209,922	2,574,805	364,883
IVY CST	V	E	81	2,758,231	696,453	716,753	20,300
			82	4,468,636	880,439	1,008,281	127,842
			83	2,932	1,068	1,308	240
LIBERIA	V	E	82	1,604	1,540	1,997	457
			84	1,834	450	676	226
			86	4,501	3,424	4,739	1,315
MACAO	V	E	86	11,012,716	1,113,695	1,380,044	266,349
MALAYSA	N	E	85	40,418,838	11,535,261	12,514,267	979,006
	O	E	81	240,301	59,595	66,083	6,488
			82	480,000	105,024	111,773	6,749
			83	154,282	20,754	25,046	4,292
	V	E	81	93,905,233	23,567,220	26,018,860	2,451,640
			82	140,962,147	30,220,458	33,730,552	3,510,094
			83	128,608,585	28,648,047	31,769,165	3,121,118
			84	144,815,495	62,400,976	66,393,113	3,992,137

Crop Product TSUSA commodity number, description, and unit of quantity Country	Mode	Reg	Yr	Quantity	F.A.S.	C.I.F.	Charges
			85	98,074,150	27,859,705	30,355,278	2,495,573
			86	189,399,202	27,409,559	32,089,898	4,680,339
	V	W	81	21,104,227	5,293,491	5,793,465	499,974
			82	40,552,256	4,609,168	5,128,511	519,343
			83	83,711,355	19,269,687	21,127,072	1,857,385
			84	27,646,993	13,145,597	13,807,843	662,246
			85	38,449,589	11,204,492	12,095,385	890,893
			86	48,262,086	5,586,947	6,656,324	1,069,377
NETHLDS	N	E	85	2,093,724	1,409,012	1,529,742	120,730
	O	E	84	40,010	32,398	35,369	2,971
			85	40,032	30,444	34,288	3,844
	V	E	81	3,303,260	1,982,089	2,086,701	104,612
			82	5,547,593	3,068,253	3,198,706	130,453
			83	7,625,886	4,942,706	5,110,509	167,803
			84	1,332,161	1,029,176	1,099,008	69,832
			85	3,866,477	3,348,185	3,463,528	115,343
			86	1,210,708	642,324	699,072	56,748
NIGER	V	E	86	44,092	10,031	11,829	1,798
NIGERIA	V	E	81	14,291,591	3,525,437	3,935,664	410,227
			82	923,727	335,200	360,759	25,559
PHIL R	V	E	82	2,246,693	478,520	540,683	62,163
			83	1,110,135	197,645	228,361	30,716
			84	2,172,123	882,766	934,140	51,374
			85	547,717	171,704	178,008	6,304
			86	4,419,268	690,459	760,620	70,161
REP SAF	V	E	85	4,000	4,000	4,576	576
SINGAPR	V	E	85	4,406,779	1,051,067	1,135,010	83,943
SRI LKA	V	E	86	1,118,900	114,330	145,289	30,959

1763340 PALM KRNL OIL,EDBLE,REFINED (LB)

	Mode	Reg	Yr	Quantity	F.A.S.	C.I.F.	Charges
TOTAL			81	14,892,237	8,608,349	9,160,353	552,004
			82	14,561,673	8,606,977	9,272,781	665,804
			83	13,679,386	7,915,867	8,509,728	593,861
			84	25,723,977	15,422,800	16,450,338	1,027,538
			85	51,820,106	21,304,002	22,973,643	1,669,641
			86	73,030,091	21,280,424	23,492,905	2,212,481
CANADA	O	E	82	9,600	3,990	3,990	
			83	1,103	899	1,681	782
			84	203,500	173,132	173,132	
			85	91,060	29,633	29,633	
	O	W	85	48,490	10,767	10,767	
			86	50,000	12,000	12,000	
CHILE	V	E	85	84,224	46,225	50,787	4,562
DENMARK	N	E	83	1,250,781	848,317	887,550	39,233
			84	259,261	214,222	229,702	15,480
	V	E	81	1,185,182	944,130	989,725	45,595
			82	2,725,040	1,680,739	1,771,246	90,507
			83	6,614	6,040	6,416	376
			84	556,049	495,519	528,243	32,724
			85	887,918	687,976	751,536	63,560
			86	1,147,121	652,001	724,587	72,586
DOMINCA	V	E	81	1,000	300	397	97
FR GERM	O	E	81	875	886	982	96
	V	E	81	222,212	178,623	187,079	8,456
			82	75,387	58,537	61,388	2,851
			84	2,074	2,162	2,494	332
	V	W	82	2,150	8,052	8,284	232
INDNSIA	V	E	84	1,653,459	345,674	388,564	42,890
			85	6,731,599	2,310,052	2,470,744	160,692
			86	4,409,301	480,899	602,899	122,000
	V	W	85	1,102,300	359,864	401,044	41,180
IVY CST	V	E	83	2,822	1,431	1,742	311
LIBERIA	V	E	81	959	980	1,085	105
			83	5,400	8,774	11,879	3,105
			84	1,612	300	509	209
MALAYSA	N	E	82	1,106,011	207,930	243,863	35,933
	V	E	81	3,362,032	828,276	919,436	91,160
			83	1,669,628	504,315	533,443	29,128
			84	5,489,495	1,878,744	2,011,320	132,576
			85	22,114,897	5,492,360	5,910,369	418,009
			86	46,030,726	11,497,030	12,539,640	1,042,610
	V	W	81	1,352,815	409,600	436,848	27,248
			82	37,478	20,664	24,829	4,165
			84	4,466,151	1,474,008	1,567,914	93,906
			85	1,126,901	262,056	288,890	26,834
			86	4,682,771	557,696	679,239	121,543
N ANTIL	V	E	85	85,566	73,418	77,268	3,850
N ZEAL	V	E	85	82,880	61,030	65,383	4,353
			86	251,201	132,116	143,621	11,505
NETHLDS	A	E	84	1,323	1,506	2,174	668
	N	E	84	3,438,918	2,739,679	2,936,069	196,390
			85	2,017,744	1,316,267	1,466,733	150,466
	V	E	81	8,563,175	6,055,993	6,421,187	365,194

Crop
Product
TSUSA commodity number, description, and unit of quantity

Country	Mode	Reg	Yr	Quantity	F.A.S.	C.I.F.	Charges
			82	10,393,123	6,491,402	7,002,498	511,096
			83	10,392,214	6,298,398	6,771,441	473,043
			84	8,699,417	7,406,953	7,872,912	465,959
			85	11,034,170	7,841,095	8,456,830	615,735
			86	11,615,686	6,155,780	6,887,691	731,911
	V	W	81	120,358	83,250	92,374	9,124
			82	112,435	67,735	80,191	12,456
			83	313,346	217,856	261,370	43,514
			84	224,478	89,521	103,792	14,271
NIUE	V	E	86	42,784	22,079	23,959	1,880
PARAGUA	V	E	82	441	264	338	74
REP SAF	V	E	81	525	400	506	106
			82	2,640	2,800	3,516	716
SIER LN	V	E	82	12,920	10,880	14,483	3,603
			85	4,500	1,085	1,891	806
SINGAPR	A	E	84	463	498	1,848	1,350
	A	W	84	106	960	1,312	352
	V	E	84	729,745	602,084	632,847	30,763
			85	6,405,783	2,810,012	2,989,274	179,262
			86	4,800,501	1,770,823	1,879,269	108,446
U KING	V	E	81	83,104	105,911	110,734	4,823
			82	84,448	53,984	58,155	4,171
	V	W	83	37,478	29,837	34,206	4,369

Palm kernel, vegetable oil, inedible
1763200 PALM-KERNEL OIL, INEDIBLE (LB)

Country	Mode	Reg	Yr	Quantity	F.A.S.	C.I.F.	Charges
TOTAL			81	5	369	381	12
			82	1,097,906	236,215	266,593	30,378
			84	96,903	47,799	52,319	4,520
			85	2,724,470	1,052,909	1,101,039	48,130
FRANCE	V	W	81	5	369	381	12
GUATMAL	V	E	84	44,907	25,412	27,646	2,234
			85	165,862	64,884	74,839	9,955
INDNSIA	V	E	85	1,101,125	373,102	385,890	12,788
MALAYSA	V	E	82	1,097,906	236,215	266,593	30,378
			85	1,369,299	577,886	599,873	21,987
NETHLDS	V	E	84	51,698	21,662	23,860	2,198
			85	88,184	37,037	40,437	3,400
U KING	O	E	84	298	725	813	88

Palm, nut and kernel
1752800 PALM-NUT KRNLS A PALM NUTS (LB)

Country	Mode	Reg	Yr	Quantity	F.A.S.	C.I.F.	Charges
TOTAL			81	18,970	17,335	20,518	3,183
			82	58,081	39,042	42,739	3,697
			83	85,292	54,633	61,056	6,423
			84	82,699	64,034	75,543	11,509
			85	113,837	83,689	91,280	7,591
			86	149,211	82,999	92,422	9,423
AUSTRAL	A	E	84	1,565	12,660	18,405	5,745
BRAZIL	V	W	81	7,500	6,750	7,150	400
C RICA	V	W	85	72,686	59,526	64,426	4,900
CHINA T	A	W	83	36	413	566	153
	V	E	84	7,075	4,000	4,366	366
IVY CST	V	E	83	31,746	15,908	18,649	2,741
LIBERIA	V	E	81	10,680	8,980	11,600	2,620
MALAYSA	V	E	86	4,486	1,401	1,454	53
PERU	V	E	86	41,336	28,500	31,400	2,900
PHIL R	V	E	83	1,080	1,271	1,534	263
			84	3,780	3,528	4,191	663
			85	2,698	3,032	3,426	394
	V	W	81	178	427	519	92
			82	2,815	2,332	2,634	302
			83	4,728	4,179	4,619	440
			84	10,242	8,312	9,373	1,061
			85	3,036	2,571	2,914	343
			86	13,937	7,668	9,221	1,553
THAILND	A	E	81	12	798	811	13
	V	E	82	1,196	764	905	141
			83	26,700	17,837	19,463	1,626
			84	24,000	14,000	15,875	1,875
	V	W	81	600	380	438	58
			82	54,070	35,946	39,200	3,254
			83	21,002	15,025	16,225	1,200
			84	36,037	21,534	23,333	1,799
			85	35,417	18,560	20,514	1,954
			86	89,452	45,430	50,347	4,917

Crop
Product
TSUSA commodity number, description, and unit of quantity
Country   Mode   Reg   Yr   Quantity   F.A.S.   C.I.F.   Charges

Palm, oil, fatty acid**
4902408 OTH FATTY ACIDS FR PALM OIL (LB)
(See Coconut, oil, fatty acid under Coconut Palm)
4902410 FATTY ACIDS FR PALM OIL ETC (LB)
(See Coconut, oil, fatty acid under Coconut Palm)
4902420 OTH FATTY ACIDS FR PALM OIL (LB)
(See Coconut, oil, fatty acid under Coconut Palm)

Palm, oil, fatty ester**
4909200 ESTERS FROM COCONUT ETC (LB)
(See Coconut, oil, fatty ester under Coconut Palm)

Palm, oil, fatty salt**
4904800 SALTS FROM COCONUT ETC (LB)
(See Coconut, oil, fatty salt under Coconut Palm)

Palm, surface-active agent**
4652500 SALTS FROM OILS, FATS NSPF (LB)
(See Coconut, surface-active agent under Coconut Palm)
4653500 FATTY ACIDS SULPH COCONUT (LB)
(See Coconut, surface-active agent under Coconut Palm)
4654500 FATTY ACHL SULPH COCONUT ETC (LB)
(See Coconut, surface-active agent under Coconut Palm)
4656500 COCONUT PALM KERNEL A PM OIL (LB)
(See Coconut, surface-active agent under Coconut Palm)

Palm, vegetable oil
1763420 PALM OIL, CRUDE (LB)

Country	Mode	Reg	Yr	Quantity	F.A.S.	C.I.F.	Charges
TOTAL			81	5,961,768	1,305,171	1,466,764	161,593
			82	8,333,982	1,877,636	2,087,895	210,259
			83	17,778,965	3,695,145	4,003,783	308,638
			84	11,184,200	3,319,388	3,533,979	214,591
			85	50,433,519	15,416,936	16,698,280	1,281,344
			86	18,301,858	2,578,799	2,948,134	369,335
BRAZIL	V	E	84	96,318	43,698	50,784	7,086
CANADA	O	E	81	149,920	53,123	53,123	
			84	88,620	31,301	31,301	
			85	88,140	27,323	27,323	
FRANCE	A	E	81	48	335	350	15
			82	1,113	640	857	217
			83	882	448	990	542
	N	E	84	3,527	1,849	2,937	1,088
	V	E	85	9,039	5,024	5,476	452
			86	8,818	6,166	6,410	244
INDNSIA	O	E	82	458,140	188,314	191,939	3,625
	V	E	84	33,069	11,890	12,977	1,087
			85	1,102,436	232,831	266,336	33,505
IVY CST	V	E	83	64,815	30,446	34,288	3,842
			84	29,397	9,375	12,080	2,705
LIBERIA	V	E	82	29,000	10,969	14,500	3,531
			84	2,175	400	651	251
			85	39,000	2,000	3,910	1,910
MALAYSA	N	E	81	2,222,712	491,607	560,304	68,697
			82	1,123,494	254,611	289,256	34,645
	O	E	81	194,840	60,744	60,744	
	V	E	81	2,254,043	406,237	473,428	67,191
			82	4,422,442	916,573	1,025,009	108,436
			83	1,143,230	142,767	192,198	49,431
			84	1,174,846	234,427	267,881	33,454
			85	46,944,336	14,672,784	15,873,556	1,200,772
			86	4,951,700	714,136	856,193	142,057
	V	W	81	1,122,443	279,375	303,060	23,685
			82	2,248,247	490,548	543,932	53,384
			83	16,567,833	3,521,050	3,775,624	254,574
			84	9,621,421	2,929,982	3,090,612	160,630
			85	2,247,945	475,774	519,837	44,063
			86	11,101,340	1,594,547	1,794,331	199,784
NETHLDS	V	E	84	81,570	36,299	40,499	4,200
PHIL R	V	E	86	2,240,000	263,950	291,200	27,250
SIER LN	V	E	81	17,762	13,750	15,755	2,005
			82	51,546	15,981	22,402	6,421
			83	2,205	434	683	249
			84	8,147	1,504	2,404	900
			85	2,623	1,200	1,842	642
THAILND	V	E	84	2,061	932	1,592	660
U KING	V	E	84	39,154	16,640	18,823	2,183

Crop Product TSUSA commodity number, description, and unit of quantity Country	Mode	Reg	Yr	Quantity	F.A.S.	C.I.F.	Charges
VENEZ	V	E	84	3,895	1,091	1,438	347

1763440 PALM OIL, REFINED (LB)

Country	Mode	Reg	Yr	Quantity	F.A.S.	C.I.F.	Charges
TOTAL			81	262,761,482	58,454,622	65,158,543	6,703,921
			82	241,673,642	46,715,030	52,252,742	5,537,712
			83	310,955,868	57,061,354	63,868,454	6,807,100
			84	314,445,892	88,805,638	95,957,440	7,151,802
			85	446,501,129	105,231,701	115,925,293	10,693,592
			86	587,186,504	85,127,712	97,872,551	12,744,839
ARGENT	V	E	84	1,089,894	343,898	370,426	26,528
BELGIUM	O	E	85	39,184	16,082	18,673	2,591
	V	E	85	1,102,300	364,014	390,969	26,955
BRAZIL	V	E	83	220	500	624	124
			84	3,380	2,400	2,672	272
			86	5,104	2,230	2,542	312
	V	W	84	2,425	3,200	5,307	2,107
CANADA	N	E	82	4,275	5,139	5,335	196
	O	E	81	92,140	27,982	27,982	
			83	601,721	443,619	444,493	874
			84	880,253	688,809	688,809	
			85	1,619,242	616,446	616,446	
			86	21,168	18,267	18,267	
FRANCE	O	E	83	5,400	2,925	3,125	200
	V	E	85	1,114,914	218,978	244,820	25,842
GHANA	V	E	86	200,138	55,321	64,239	8,918
INDIA	V	E	84	281	423	445	22
			86	2,300,399	501,512	526,329	24,817
	V	W	83	612	563	609	46
INDNSIA	V	E	81	4,436,580	847,565	1,002,347	154,782
			82	23,156,000	3,768,712	4,295,797	527,085
			83	31,224,786	5,712,098	6,428,306	716,208
			84	33,694,994	6,280,246	6,818,946	538,700
			85	46,071,732	10,042,653	11,215,041	1,172,388
			86	16,439,961	2,369,678	2,712,978	343,300
	V	W	82	2,312,516	387,355	436,548	49,193
			84	7,826,147	2,215,871	2,386,481	170,610
			85	15,467,283	2,955,629	3,516,179	560,550
			86	19,742,415	2,157,250	2,845,829	688,579
IVY CST	V	E	83	52,403	17,759	21,947	4,188
			84	21,197	4,142	7,342	3,200
			85	35,388	17,897	21,424	3,527
JAPAN	V	W	84	70,796	41,645	49,945	8,300
			85	107,228	78,505	91,183	12,678
			86	72,842	40,717	45,030	4,313
LIBERIA	V	E	81	4,911	5,400	6,002	602
			82	2,124	1,250	1,550	300
			83	10,382	4,533	6,158	1,625
			84	5,468	1,568	2,567	999
			86	558	2,796	3,496	700
MACAO	V	E	85	558,072	100,781	116,223	15,442
MALAYSA	A	E	81	1,444	415	462	47
			85	2,283	3,175	13,110	9,935
	N	E	81	24,378,817	5,386,874	6,058,026	671,152
			82	38,931,227	7,382,388	8,393,663	1,011,275
	O	E	81	90,200	29,676	29,676	
			82	400,000	83,460	89,084	5,624
			83	1,271,392	151,244	181,844	30,600
			84	1,129,690	354,083	358,268	4,185
			85	3,520,087	1,008,458	1,008,458	
	V	E	81	116,027,471	25,624,530	28,761,907	3,137,377
			82	74,237,066	14,485,728	16,146,169	1,660,441
			83	151,954,944	28,797,669	32,157,365	3,359,696
			84	150,502,836	45,248,777	48,676,591	3,427,814
			85	212,349,437	49,792,970	54,039,719	4,246,749
			86	404,341,522	58,198,295	65,706,564	7,508,269
	V	W	81	117,651,307	26,498,941	29,238,346	2,739,405
			82	99,301,531	20,013,036	22,196,468	2,183,432
			83	118,292,679	20,774,408	23,349,335	2,574,927
			84	114,719,267	32,048,908	34,909,244	2,860,336
			85	111,922,828	27,601,824	31,334,656	3,732,832
			86	113,882,365	16,271,478	19,999,400	3,727,922
MAURIT	O	E	85	45,680	14,161	14,161	
MEXICO	V	E	85	2,170,017	543,374	590,983	47,609
MOROC	V	E	85	2,209,172	422,992	435,681	12,689
			86	3,916,057	648,024	688,714	40,690
NETHLDS	V	E	81	74,748	30,774	30,897	123
			84	1,139,741	840,384	853,104	12,720
			86	2,199,188	476,789	529,313	52,524
	V	W	85	127,907	32,152	35,259	3,107
NIGERIA	V	E	86	62,655	41,650	43,747	2,097
PHIL R	V	E	82	2,204,793	385,228	469,965	84,737
			85	2,179,191	550,767	577,951	27,184
			86	5,600,000	480,706	600,600	119,894
	V	W	85	7,655,983	1,698,213	1,986,449	288,236
SIER LN	V	E	81	2,904	1,800	2,160	360
			82	10,212	10,000	11,222	1,222
			83	6,403	3,860	4,593	733
			84	49,040	16,835	19,323	2,488
			85	44,249	17,000	18,987	1,987
SINGAPR	V	E	83	7,534,926	1,152,176	1,270,055	117,879
			84	3,272,864	681,774	773,694	91,920
			85	37,009,577	8,834,801	9,308,171	473,370
			86	18,365,916	3,849,295	4,069,104	219,809
	V	W	84	35,274	31,568	32,874	1,306
			85	1,111,149	285,020	312,936	27,916
SPAIN	V	E	82	1,103,906	187,773	201,418	13,645
TOGO	V	E	84	1,984	778	1,032	254
U KING	O	E	82	9,028	4,354	4,841	487
			84	361	329	370	41
			86	33,786	11,896	14,483	2,587
	V	E	85	38,226	15,809	17,814	2,005
			86	2,430	1,808	1,916	108
	V	W	81	960	665	738	73
			82	964	607	682	75
			82	964	607	682	75

Okra

Okra, fresh or frozen**

1368000 OKRA, FRSH, CHLLD, OR FROZEN (LB)

Country	Mode	Reg	Yr	Quantity	F.A.S.	C.I.F.	Charges
TOTAL			81	23,480,530	3,077,081	3,341,001	263,850
			82	38,824,755	4,639,434	4,963,875	324,441
			83	42,102,182	4,179,720	4,365,910	186,190
			84	44,987,471	4,634,271	4,920,791	286,520
			85	30,485,949	4,072,048	4,318,484	246,436
			86	26,040,859	4,073,842	4,292,782	218,940
BELIZE	A	E	82	10,957	6,521	8,414	1,893
			83	2,865	568	891	323
			86	7,052	4,792	5,796	1,004
BRAZIL	A	E	82	1,925	925	1,875	950
			84	3,307	750	2,532	1,782
C RICA	A	E	84	39,544	5,548	13,118	7,570
	A	W	84	4,936	848	2,118	1,270
CANADA	O	E	82	21,740	2,042	2,042	
			83	27,140	3,201	3,201	
			84	413	600	600	
			85	39,540	4,595	4,595	
DOM REP	A	E	83	1,813	653	873	220
			84	5,123	574	1,328	754
	N	E	83	38,613	12,147	14,817	2,670
	V	E	82	456,367	178,128	204,430	26,302
			85	444,646	128,591	165,259	36,668
			86	1,165,812	862,295	924,976	62,681
ECUADOR	V	W	85	58,801	12,329	16,072	3,743
EGYPT	A	W	84	1,205	759	892	133
	V	E	85	7,716	5,250	5,463	213
			86	20,944	19,000	22,372	3,372
	V	W	85	33,307	2,100	2,937	837
			86	23,148	16,450	21,851	5,401
GREECE	O	E	82	1,050	913	1,026	113
			84	2,134	949	949	
			86	1,827	1,169	1,169	
	V	E	84	5,291	2,250	2,506	256
			85	12,516	3,254	4,078	824
GUATMAL	A	E	81	1,410	846	930	84
			82	12,051	5,423	7,896	2,473
			83	24,148	4,873	9,813	4,940
			84	6,836	766	1,772	1,006
	A	W	81	15,720	6,393	10,383	3,990
			82	4,113	2,082	3,085	1,003
			83	46,660	13,972	29,272	15,300
			84	13,338	6,002	9,896	3,894
			85	1,530	1,530	1,791	261
	N	E	81	1,366,276	424,936	589,664	164,658
			82	1,583,642	539,690	688,671	148,981
			83	810,743	241,435	326,924	85,489
			84	1,423,716	477,302	562,196	84,894
			86	30,760	8,183	14,796	6,613
	V	E	81	38,446	11,287	15,064	3,777
			82	172,346	54,351	70,946	16,595
			85	1,485,844	403,401	490,415	87,014
			86	1,202,299	294,562	367,148	72,586

Crop
Product
TSUSA commodity number, description, and unit of quantity

Country	Mode	Reg	Yr	Quantity	F.A.S.	C.I.F.	Charges
HAITI	A	E	82	3,628	2,204	3,793	1,589
			83	8,400	840	2,725	1,885
			84	112,784	11,912	32,606	20,694
HONDURA	A	E	82	1,550	570	790	220
	N	E	82	25,672	11,278	13,988	2,710
JAMAICA	A	E	82	6,730	2,526	3,933	1,407
			84	62,894	46,042	62,182	16,140
			86	61,563	31,960	49,876	17,916
	V	E	84	25	260	282	22
MEXICO	A	E	81	8,593	1,172	2,500	1,328
			84	309,609	37,829	82,158	44,329
			85	253,192	58,817	95,196	36,379
			86	17,702	7,355	10,392	3,037
	A	W	81	56,889	18,818	24,755	5,937
			82	101,347	28,415	44,463	16,048
			83	60,736	7,305	16,141	8,836
			84	40,465	17,655	25,354	7,699
			85	83,627	20,576	27,640	7,064
			86	34,289	12,806	17,313	4,507
	N	E	83	291,772	57,346	104,247	46,901
	O	E	81	20,846,707	2,191,058	2,191,312	254
			82	35,228,453	3,452,818	3,453,818	1,000
			83	40,557,258	3,782,266	3,785,418	3,152
			84	42,117,718	3,677,836	3,677,836	
			85	27,411,180	3,182,541	3,188,840	6,299
			86	23,122,636	2,681,510	2,681,510	
	O	W	81	45,600	18,246	18,246	
			83	62,899	7,166	7,166	
			84	9,308	1,780	1,780	
			86	10,110	1,578	1,578	
MOROC	O	E	83	600	600	600	
MOZAMBQ	O	E	86	11,790	1,415	1,415	
NICARAG	V	W	81	483,069	242,657	281,744	39,087
			82	360,364	112,836	145,950	33,114
			83	102,535	27,538	37,505	9,967
PANAMA	A	E	84	215,108	128,012	165,644	37,632
SALVADR	V	E	81	580,500	151,905	190,470	38,565
			82	832,820	238,712	308,755	70,043
			83	31,800	9,550	12,657	3,107
			84	380,376	125,589	149,059	23,470
			85	378,000	99,979	128,379	28,400
			86	100,813	25,399	32,175	6,776
	V	W	81	37,320	9,763	15,933	6,170
			83	34,200	10,260	13,660	3,400
			84	100,005	64,603	78,203	13,600
			85	276,050	149,085	187,819	38,734
			86	226,744	102,019	136,084	34,065
SPAIN	V	E	84	133,336	26,405	47,780	21,375
TURKEY	V	E	86	2,570	2,040	2,484	444
U KING	A	E	86	800	1,309	1,847	538

1380520 BROCCOLI ETC FR, CUT SLICED (LB)
  (See Broccoli, fresh under Broccoli)

Okra, frozen

1380580 OKRA, FRZN, REDUCED IN SIZE (LB)

Country	Mode	Reg	Yr	Quantity	F.A.S.	C.I.F.	Charges
TOTAL			81	14,557,742	4,721,197	5,396,014	674,921
			82	24,175,388	7,761,277	8,938,196	1,176,919
			83	22,308,673	6,944,187	8,254,202	1,310,015
			84	18,237,042	4,457,385	5,370,826	913,441
			85	19,423,399	5,275,178	6,543,244	1,268,066
			86	14,759,585	4,092,681	5,010,044	917,363
BELIZE	A	E	83	2,480	336	707	371
			86	6,105	4,035	5,058	1,023
CANADA	O	E	83	40,000	7,200	7,200	
DOM REP	N	E	82	9,441,524	3,356,534	3,735,708	379,174
	V	E	81	5,767,333	1,972,040	2,201,320	229,280
			82	1,030,692	368,888	415,142	46,254
			83	10,390,640	3,569,662	4,133,217	563,555
			84	8,416,873	1,605,974	2,044,914	438,940
			85	9,027,358	2,572,026	3,143,027	571,001
			86	5,294,197	1,683,343	1,965,236	281,893
	V	W	85	464,082	115,292	152,180	36,888
ECUADOR	V	E	83	276,815	91,647	117,514	25,867
GUATMAL	N	E	81	2,684,925	708,156	924,020	215,968
			82	4,966,933	1,449,443	1,761,739	312,296
			83	5,877,866	1,643,810	1,971,349	327,539
	O	E	81	1,955	1,253	1,433	180
			86	40,297	4,661	4,661	
	V	E	81	619,814	159,144	212,959	53,815
			82	1,469,958	409,153	540,500	131,347
			83	1,159,216	306,510	416,690	110,180

Crop
Product
TSUSA commodity number, description, and unit of quantity

Country	Mode	Reg	Yr	Quantity	F.A.S.	C.I.F.	Charges
			84	3,368,383	933,726	1,126,371	192,645
			85	3,701,319	817,362	1,012,230	194,868
			86	3,909,155	916,691	1,161,028	244,337
HONDURA	V	E	82	11,093	3,317	4,215	898
JAMAICA	V	E	82	60,240	18,250	21,230	2,980
MEXICO	O	E	81	3,021,669	1,099,747	1,099,747	
			82	3,067,832	1,021,727	1,021,727	
			83	911,915	309,151	309,151	
			84	1,888,165	670,989	670,989	
			85	165,925	51,978	51,978	
			86	82,590	20,465	20,465	
	V	E	83	43,728	11,738	14,211	2,473
NICARAG	V	E	81	315,945	184,985	217,131	32,146
			82	330,000	83,028	107,685	24,657
	V	W	81	160,613	73,577	86,307	12,730
			82	115,396	38,784	49,437	10,653
			83	129,481	42,774	56,116	13,342
PANAMA	A	E	84	2,655	1,700	2,100	400
SALVADR	N	E	81	1,985,488	522,295	653,097	130,802
			86	3,150,000	836,614	1,054,635	218,021
	V	E	82	3,681,720	1,012,153	1,280,813	268,660
			83	3,442,332	951,099	1,214,387	263,288
			84	4,560,966	1,244,996	1,526,452	281,456
			85	6,039,710	1,705,848	2,167,676	461,828
			86	2,235,241	616,779	785,367	168,588
	V	W	83	34,200	10,260	13,660	3,400
			85	25,005	12,672	16,153	3,481
SEYCHEL	V	E	86	42,000	10,093	13,594	3,501

Olive

Olive, dried

1485200 OLIVES, DRIED, NOT RIPE (LB)

Country	Mode	Reg	Yr	Quantity	F.A.S.	C.I.F.	Charges
TOTAL			81	7,436	5,066	5,622	556
			82	16,814	9,594	11,016	1,422
			83	5,328	4,968	5,289	321
			84	77,379	49,917	59,786	9,869
			85	79,433	39,553	46,899	7,346
			86	99,653	64,563	76,723	12,160
CHILE	V	E	86	26,444	16,793	18,727	1,934
CHINA M	V	E	82	1,400	633	741	108
	V	W	82	10,805	5,713	6,539	826
			83	1,150	1,635	1,729	94
GREECE	V	E	81	6,686	4,308	4,831	523
			84	64,151	33,157	40,499	7,342
			85	51,547	25,128	30,609	5,481
			86	22,928	9,880	13,556	3,676
	V	W	82	4,409	2,740	3,214	474
HG KONG	V	E	83	900	811	878	67
	V	W	81	500	408	427	19
			82	200	508	522	14
			83	1,250	946	1,012	66
ITALY	V	E	85	1,431	1,265	1,470	205
	V	W	83	2,028	1,576	1,670	94
MOROC	V	E	84	11,023	15,250	17,509	2,259
			85	26,455	13,160	14,820	1,660
			86	35,274	18,510	20,960	2,450
PERU	V	E	86	5,556	8,820	9,320	500
SPAIN	O	E	86	9,451	10,560	14,160	3,600
THAILND	V	W	81	250	350	364	14
TURKEY	V	W	84	2,205	1,510	1,778	268

1485400 OLIVES, DRIED, RIPE (LB)

Country	Mode	Reg	Yr	Quantity	F.A.S.	C.I.F.	Charges
TOTAL			81	1,486,282	940,614	1,030,686	90,072
			82	1,269,680	777,124	857,755	80,631
			83	1,478,729	807,069	883,607	76,538
			84	1,052,012	606,825	668,792	61,967
			85	1,140,018	563,727	633,664	69,937
			86	1,661,408	838,126	930,717	92,591
CANADA	O	E	81	72,500	42,747	44,611	1,864
			82	7,441	7,655	7,655	
			84	11,000	10,157	10,157	
CHINA M	V	E	81	2,000	712	875	163
			82	2,650	1,232	1,562	330
			83	2,000	1,291	1,447	156
			84	661	318	422	104
			85	5,950	2,709	3,256	547
	V	W	81	930	332	345	13

Crop Product TSUSA commodity number, description, and unit of quantity Country	Mode	Reg	Yr	Quantity	F.A.S.	C.I.F.	Charges
			84	1,790	1,444	1,624	180
			86	625	1,591	1,674	83
FR GERM	V	E	82	1,543	980	1,126	146
FRANCE	V	E	83	203	260	288	28
			84	1,054	2,347	2,426	79
			86	38,818	17,635	19,723	2,088
	V	W	85	662	1,022	1,105	83
			86	2,551	5,026	5,502	476
GREECE	V	E	81	2,205	1,380	1,570	190
			82	42,367	20,038	23,656	3,618
			83	47,590	25,754	28,744	2,990
			84	16,378	8,754	10,709	1,955
			85	6,615	3,560	4,472	912
			86	4,410	2,400	2,993	593
	V	W	81	400	310	372	62
			83	4,409	2,200	2,581	381
			84	8,818	4,140	5,137	997
			85	8,819	4,800	5,844	1,044
			86	9,259	5,128	6,082	954
HG KONG	V	E	82	1,538	1,558	1,662	104
			86	2,925	3,252	3,597	345
	V	W	81	4,000	2,806	2,915	109
			83	2,250	1,018	1,090	72
			86	5,818	6,115	6,469	354
ISRAEL	V	E	86	23,397	9,641	10,649	1,008
ITALY	O	E	84	3,970	2,508	2,508	
	V	E	81	209	440	496	56
			82	450	650	741	91
			83	643	946	1,006	60
JAPAN	V	E	83	37,500	21,375	23,411	2,036
MACAO	V	E	85	55,272	26,652	32,052	5,400
			86	33,750	19,800	21,900	2,100
MOROC	O	E	81	34,320	35,747	35,747	
			82	440	264	264	
			83	41,950	37,660	37,660	
			84	12,100	10,984	10,984	
			85	29,344	30,000	30,000	
			86	19,965	17,957	17,957	
	V	E	81	1,369,718	856,140	943,755	87,615
			82	1,209,503	741,935	817,794	75,859
			83	1,341,940	716,195	786,958	70,763
			84	995,434	565,363	623,913	58,550
			85	915,895	441,736	497,078	55,342
			86	1,452,067	715,367	795,794	80,427
	V	W	85	37,533	17,025	19,175	2,150
NETHLDS	V	E	86	37,500	21,603	23,889	2,286
ROMANIA	V	E	82	3,748	2,812	3,295	483
SPAIN	V	E	85	79,928	36,223	40,682	4,459
THAILND	V	E	83	244	370	422	52
			84	807	810	912	102
TURKEY	V	E	86	30,323	12,611	14,488	1,877

Olive, fresh
1484000 OLIVES FRESH (LB)

Country	Mode	Reg	Yr	Quantity	F.A.S.	C.I.F.	Charges
TOTAL			**81**	**61,891**	**33,504**	**38,934**	**5,430**
			82	**78,245**	**58,347**	**68,015**	**9,668**
			83	**1,672,431**	**197,431**	**232,868**	**35,437**
			84	**1,735,460**	**178,306**	**203,796**	**25,490**
			85	**6,611,558**	**1,152,435**	**1,595,019**	**442,584**
			86	**762,448**	**230,295**	**262,944**	**32,649**
CHINA M	V	E	85	3,620	2,838	3,290	452
	V	W	81	251	485	506	21
			82	661	1,815	1,885	70
COLOMB	V	E	83	38,150	47,800	75,285	27,485
DOM REP	N	E	86	78,624	6,048	11,118	5,070
FRANCE	V	E	82	215	382	419	37
			84	2,925	3,840	4,212	372
			86	14,345	17,156	18,236	1,080
	V	W	84	415	324	422	98
GREECE	O	E	84	10,679	5,496	5,496	
	V	E	81	55,360	31,230	36,480	5,250
			82	59,619	43,302	50,813	7,511
			83	68,784	45,120	52,942	7,822
			84	20,178	11,311	13,853	2,542
			85	56,060	32,229	38,712	6,483
			86	183,872	109,663	127,659	17,996
GUATMAL	V	E	84	1,081,088	45,748	59,328	13,580
			86	21,060	9,477	12,654	3,177
HG KONG	V	W	81	500	486	520	34
HONDURA	V	E	84	33,363	9,108	12,904	3,796
ISRAEL	V	E	82	14,550	11,788	13,627	1,839

Country	Mode	Reg	Yr	Quantity	F.A.S.	C.I.F.	Charges
			84	6,547	15,129	16,598	1,469
			86	68,355	39,457	42,944	3,487
MEXICO	O	E	85	75,320	6,079	6,079	
			86	78,120	3,720	3,720	
	O	W	81	3,280	328	328	
			82	2,700	540	540	
			83	1,564,197	102,959	102,959	
			84	553,108	68,685	68,685	
			85	1,173,892	59,285	59,285	
			86	294,033	31,001	31,001	
PANAMA	V	W	85	5,164,453	981,323	1,401,697	420,374
PORTUGL	V	E	86	9,396	4,535	5,139	604
SPAIN	V	E	84	20,800	14,500	17,643	3,143
			85	90,203	37,501	45,575	8,074
			86	8,643	8,153	8,729	576
	V	W	84	6,357	4,165	4,655	490
			85	38,510	30,224	35,391	5,167
THAILND	V	E	81	2,500	975	1,100	125
			82	500	520	731	211
TURKEY	V	E	83	1,300	1,552	1,682	130
VENEZ	A	E	85	9,500	2,956	4,990	2,034
			86	6,000	1,085	1,744	659

Olive, in brine
1484200 OLIVES IN BRINE NT RIPE ETC (LB)

Country	Mode	Reg	Yr	Quantity	F.A.S.	C.I.F.	Charges
TOTAL			81	3,734,732	2,586,441	2,970,458	384,017
			82	4,014,698	2,791,846	3,223,752	431,906
			83	4,077,484	2,613,960	3,069,959	455,999
			84	5,794,778	2,863,717	3,498,916	635,199
			85	10,746,853	3,573,915	4,518,278	944,363
			86	5,729,122	3,156,623	3,784,999	628,376
CANADA	O	E	86	8,923	7,137	7,137	
CHILE	N	E	83	92,682	73,751	83,364	9,613
	V	E	82	95,899	85,350	96,811	11,461
			84	15,000	10,000	11,900	1,900
			85	29,718	24,264	27,396	3,132
			86	77,778	64,008	71,108	7,100
CYPRUS	V	E	82	16,380	11,306	13,335	2,029
			84	2,866	1,950	2,294	344
			85	1,433	1,098	1,322	224
FRANCE	V	E	81	29,982	13,617	16,653	3,036
			84	13,648	14,170	15,842	1,672
	V	W	86	1,543	1,790	1,940	150
GREECE	N	E	82	2,149,532	1,510,499	1,746,771	236,272
			86	3,677,196	1,954,118	2,354,421	400,303
	O	E	82	7,050	6,345	6,345	
	V	E	81	3,008,966	2,183,582	2,486,856	303,274
			82	1,188,015	814,265	933,707	119,442
			83	3,640,120	2,324,980	2,735,882	410,902
			84	4,299,739	2,185,052	2,673,109	488,057
			85	4,198,235	2,045,636	2,514,293	468,657
			86	1,416,856	799,422	961,455	162,033
	V	W	81	182,405	136,508	166,572	30,064
			82	181,004	133,262	159,131	25,869
			83	133,313	94,363	110,296	15,933
			84	177,301	114,645	138,006	23,361
			85	240,101	135,895	166,240	30,345
			86	303,073	192,053	231,877	39,824
HG KONG	V	E	83	960	739	835	96
INDIA	V	W	82	1,984	1,843	2,089	246
ISRAEL	V	E	84	2,799	1,460	1,495	35
ITALY	V	E	81	30,450	21,705	24,789	3,084
			82	39,469	25,059	30,229	5,170
			83	83,954	58,760	68,895	10,135
			84	45,169	20,300	23,339	3,039
			85	11,750	14,125	16,090	1,965
	V	W	83	1,978	276	296	20
			86	9,787	9,113	9,548	435
MEXICO	O	W	84	4,288	5,588	5,588	
			85	1,610,096	213,187	213,187	
MOROC	O	E	81	21,362	7,722	8,459	737
			82	28,560	8,948	9,945	997
	V	E	81	308,434	147,923	173,482	25,559
			82	98,872	49,405	59,941	10,536
			83	39,028	14,960	17,848	2,888
			84	199,041	99,128	112,220	13,092
			85	106,923	40,280	48,979	8,699
			86	143,282	67,411	77,683	10,272
PERU	V	E	82	49,383	39,200	44,234	5,034
			85	52,588	36,582	39,865	3,283
			86	24,000	18,564	21,116	2,552

Crop
Product
TSUSA commodity number, description, and unit of quantity

Country	Mode	Reg	Yr	Quantity	F.A.S.	C.I.F.	Charges
PORTUGL	O	E	81	3,800	1,515	1,515	
	V	E	81	132,338	67,667	85,021	17,354
			82	158,550	106,364	121,214	14,850
			83	38,763	21,384	24,894	3,510
			84	75,352	33,798	41,094	7,296
			85	24,640	13,138	16,420	3,282
			86	7,540	1,600	1,762	162
	V	W	81	2,910	510	665	155
REP SAF	V	E	86	27,778	18,900	21,000	2,100
SPAIN	O	E	86	8,438	7,418	7,418	
	V	E	81	14,085	5,692	6,446	754
			83	46,686	24,747	27,649	2,902
			84	896,850	353,546	443,828	90,282
			85	45,299	24,281	29,825	5,544
	V	W	84	62,725	24,080	30,201	6,121
			85	4,408,070	1,016,621	1,433,316	416,695
U KING	V	E	85	18,000	8,808	11,345	2,537
			86	22,928	15,089	18,534	3,445

1484420 OLIVES N BRINE NT OV 0.3GAL (LB)

Country	Mode	Reg	Yr	Quantity	F.A.S.	C.I.F.	Charges
TOTAL			**81**	**2,464,769**	**2,086,405**	**2,376,162**	**290,384**
			82	**2,751,318**	**2,036,770**	**2,348,609**	**311,839**
			83	**3,605,807**	**2,090,901**	**2,492,540**	**401,639**
			84	**3,099,683**	**2,364,509**	**2,760,029**	**395,520**
			85	**3,965,912**	**2,197,874**	**2,704,557**	**506,683**
			86	**3,439,884**	**2,084,215**	**2,415,256**	**331,041**
BRAZIL	V	E	82	3,203	1,842	2,091	249
CANADA	O	E	81	2,187	1,456	1,531	75
CHINA M	V	W	82	2,182	812	868	56
CYPRUS	V	E	82	716	419	550	131
FRANCE	O	E	83	360	522	559	37
			84	661	529	566	37
			85	4,784	3,604	4,317	713
	V	E	81	4,583	8,303	9,199	896
			82	1,258	2,788	2,940	152
			83	1,354	1,151	1,247	96
			84	7,440	7,393	8,048	655
			86	1,090	2,735	3,022	287
	V	W	84	1,050	3,000	3,234	234
			85	1,350	2,529	3,315	786
GREECE	O	E	82	8,156	8,575	9,023	448
			84	616	606	606	
	V	E	81	128,876	80,359	92,770	12,411
			82	2,050	1,770	1,922	152
			83	56,021	28,140	34,913	6,773
			84	21,478	11,152	14,325	3,173
			85	11,464	4,853	5,689	836
			86	80,516	47,729	59,785	12,056
	V	W	83	5,732	2,782	3,458	676
			85	21,696	7,886	10,039	2,153
ISRAEL	O	E	83	1,313	1,640	1,856	216
	V	E	81	64,513	55,784	62,334	6,550
			82	31,486	28,552	31,182	2,630
			83	41,941	32,125	36,169	4,044
			84	31,583	23,755	26,385	2,630
			85	64,415	48,170	55,850	7,680
			86	49,906	29,057	34,081	5,024
	V	W	84	432	288	318	30
			86	13,924	12,470	15,577	3,107
ITALY	V	E	81	231	374	427	53
			82	22,037	14,924	16,407	1,483
			83	20,643	8,124	9,413	1,289
			84	25,159	17,642	21,324	3,682
			85	61,668	63,132	72,863	9,731
			86	88,178	106,522	117,634	11,112
	V	W	83	767	962	1,019	57
			84	497	458	527	69
KOR REP	V	W	84	882	670	796	126
LEBANON	V	E	84	265	290	331	41
MOROC	V	E	82	7,937	2,704	3,656	952
PORTUGL	V	E	81	31,317	28,217	32,634	4,417
			82	103,818	68,110	78,615	10,505
			83	43,665	26,948	33,298	6,350
			84	132,436	66,876	79,226	12,350
			85	21,742	8,774	11,023	2,249
			86	9,721	6,839	7,658	819
	V	W	85	4,800	2,800	4,034	1,234
SPAIN	N	E	85	634,538	341,894	424,577	82,683
			86	1,252,967	904,559	1,031,299	126,740
	O	E	83	2,250	4,415	4,415	
			84	3,227	3,326	3,856	530
			86	9,453	8,308	8,308	
	V	E	81	2,183,166	1,868,389	2,126,083	258,321
			82	2,355,494	1,768,727	2,039,922	271,195
			83	3,041,767	1,798,086	2,146,064	347,978
			84	2,531,638	1,987,288	2,318,858	331,570
			85	2,603,339	1,421,810	1,753,476	331,666
			86	1,578,756	724,155	855,131	130,976
	V	W	81	49,896	43,523	51,184	7,661
			82	212,981	137,547	161,433	23,886
			83	389,994	186,006	220,129	34,123
			84	338,820	237,991	278,112	40,121
			85	536,116	292,422	359,374	66,952
			86	355,373	241,841	282,761	40,920
THAILND	O	W	84	1,049	875	929	54
TURKEY	V	E	84	2,450	2,370	2,588	218

1484440 OLIVES IN BRINE OVER 0.3GAL (LB)

Country	Mode	Reg	Yr	Quantity	F.A.S.	C.I.F.	Charges
TOTAL			**81**	**6,230,679**	**3,083,478**	**3,571,802**	**490,228**
			82	**14,789,585**	**6,565,087**	**7,838,911**	**1,273,824**
			83	**7,338,563**	**2,818,069**	**3,469,001**	**650,932**
			84	**5,863,811**	**2,627,584**	**3,127,380**	**499,796**
			85	**14,594,482**	**4,034,944**	**4,838,897**	**803,953**
			86	**8,093,033**	**3,637,575**	**4,297,452**	**659,877**
ARGENT	V	E	85	35,000	7,956	10,751	2,795
CANADA	O	E	81	4,092	1,629	1,629	
			84	3,528	1,733	1,733	
			85	27,526	22,619	22,619	
			86	18,264	11,988	11,988	
CHINA M	V	E	84	8,957	5,185	5,937	752
			86	20,800	14,112	16,557	2,445
	V	W	84	1,272	512	563	51
CYPRUS	V	E	82	9,902	5,711	7,027	1,316
			83	1,746	1,626	1,813	187
FR GERM	V	E	84	24,647	16,934	19,451	2,517
FRANCE	V	E	81	308	334	371	37
			82	2,234	1,623	1,812	189
			83	1,051	1,128	1,240	112
			85	13,097	14,678	16,057	1,379
			86	11,223	14,944	16,684	1,740
	V	W	81	3,902	5,299	5,884	585
			85	2,156	3,826	5,986	2,160
GABON	O	E	85	2,201	1,657	1,657	
GREECE	N	E	83	134,276	124,337	127,494	3,157
	O	E	81	137,531	128,561	128,561	
			82	145,810	143,869	143,869	
			83	25,027	20,756	20,756	
			84	140,780	114,990	114,990	
			85	103,279	86,321	86,321	
			86	199,082	150,621	150,621	
	O	W	82	6,000	5,370	6,216	846
	V	E	81	943,154	541,419	633,993	92,574
			82	883,223	463,443	550,410	86,967
			83	905,175	432,124	534,071	101,947
			84	1,290,727	545,860	679,222	133,362
			85	824,599	350,759	446,255	95,496
			86	1,085,118	477,986	590,992	113,006
	V	W	81	40,620	18,329	23,275	4,946
			82	57,960	28,814	37,263	8,449
			83	44,757	17,583	20,878	3,295
			84	41,091	16,389	19,911	3,522
			85	132,694	56,255	69,784	13,529
			86	101,764	41,908	54,888	12,980
ISRAEL	N	E	82	350,353	124,848	153,086	28,238
	V	E	81	708,105	244,353	303,527	59,174
			82	275,493	88,827	108,152	19,325
			84	404,400	123,188	145,688	22,500
			85	108,121	43,043	50,551	7,508
			86	81,477	22,470	29,223	6,753
	V	W	82	55,821	24,006	28,343	4,337
			84	75,798	35,342	40,539	5,197
			85	22,068	7,101	8,680	1,579
			86	24,810	3,268	3,922	654
ITALY	O	E	84	23	406	448	42
	V	E	81	118,104	83,682	97,742	14,060
			82	34,794	21,517	24,565	3,048
			83	103,140	49,754	63,743	13,989
			84	39,386	22,891	25,635	2,744
			85	57,167	48,948	57,210	8,262
			86	148,966	120,210	140,666	20,456
	V	W	83	3,131	2,615	2,771	156
			85	4,826	4,026	4,313	287
MAURIT	V	E	86	10,395	7,863	9,299	1,436
MEXICO	O	E	81	18,430	7,003	7,003	
	O	W	81	225,744	68,854	68,854	
			82	233,743	30,595	30,595	

Crop
Product
TSUSA commodity number, description, and unit of quantity

Country	Mode	Reg	Yr	Quantity	F.A.S.	C.I.F.	Charges
			85	5,662,828	760,303	760,305	2
			86	1,029,678	155,376	155,376	
MOROC	O	E	82	413	283	283	
	V	E	81	55,291	11,526	17,226	5,700
			82	161,240	61,042	76,038	14,996
			86	31,283	2,001	4,701	2,700
NETHLDS	V	E	86	24,367	18,322	20,571	2,249
PAKISTN	V	E	85	22,905	11,456	12,666	1,210
PERU	V	E	82	9,921	7,800	8,701	901
PORTUGL	V	E	81	178,205	99,417	119,347	19,930
			82	314,249	175,700	204,620	28,920
			83	306,852	143,849	177,906	34,057
			84	310,964	142,124	168,068	25,944
			85	513,985	219,272	264,967	45,695
			86	680,591	292,901	355,567	62,666
	V	W	82	4,400	3,100	3,502	402
			83	7,500	6,250	7,716	1,466
			84	6,375	4,950	5,481	531
SPAIN	N	E	82	1,698,760	697,265	815,232	117,967
			83	1,508,900	558,699	679,107	120,408
			84	919,328	373,641	437,610	63,969
			86	988,559	642,978	750,909	107,931
	O	E	81	23,766	12,358	14,385	2,027
			82	13,920	5,829	6,797	968
			83	36,767	19,904	23,071	3,167
			85	2,376	1,089	1,452	363
			86	1,188	1,620	1,832	212
	V	E	81	3,614,251	1,767,076	2,041,650	276,478
			82	2,339,874	1,265,286	1,467,429	202,143
			83	3,219,546	1,176,312	1,466,796	290,484
			84	2,518,322	1,181,363	1,414,083	232,720
			85	6,145,455	2,140,294	2,658,957	518,663
			86	2,812,804	1,310,408	1,570,791	260,383
	V	W	81	159,176	93,638	108,355	14,717
			82	8,166,828	3,393,225	4,145,520	752,295
			83	1,032,354	253,908	332,415	78,507
			84	102,860	59,010	67,472	8,462
			85	899,199	247,961	350,875	102,914
			86	805,689	344,524	407,471	62,947
SURINAM	O	E	83	8,341	9,224	9,224	
U KING	V	E	85	15,000	7,380	9,491	2,111
	V	W	86	16,975	4,075	5,394	1,319

1484600 OLIVES IN BRINE RIPE ETC (LB)

Country	Mode	Reg	Yr	Quantity	F.A.S.	C.I.F.	Charges
TOTAL			**81**	**449,188**	**284,268**	**327,837**	**43,569**
			82	**553,097**	**397,156**	**447,997**	**50,841**
			83	**826,978**	**576,254**	**667,567**	**91,313**
			84	**3,963,457**	**1,256,988**	**1,640,727**	**383,739**
			85	**824,934**	**485,020**	**591,035**	**106,015**
			86	**1,288,440**	**646,285**	**782,218**	**135,933**
CANADA	O	E	83	900	534	534	
			85	850	1,614	1,614	
CHILE	V	E	84	13,117	11,900	13,459	1,559
ECUADOR	V	E	82	3,307	3,764	4,050	286
FRANCE	O	E	84	385	563	619	56
	V	E	81	1,800	2,729	2,929	200
			82	5,952	6,201	6,675	474
			83	18,785	18,783	20,244	1,461
			84	1,218	839	1,136	297
			85	37,119	15,610	19,043	3,433
			86	1,864	3,441	3,785	344
	V	W	82	2,822	3,966	4,219	253
			83	5,509	7,079	7,900	821
			84	2,950	3,161	3,427	266
			86	1,658	3,562	3,947	385
G BISAU	V	E	81	1,500	1,300	1,468	168
GREECE	N	E	82	19,716	14,306	16,841	2,535
	N	W	81	18,000	15,081	18,231	3,150
			84	47,315	28,731	35,102	6,371
			85	28,830	20,159	23,675	3,516
	O	E	81	36,250	22,594	22,594	
			82	18,598	14,020	14,020	
			83	543	946	946	
			86	9,749	8,346	8,346	
	O	W	82	42,000	36,960	38,360	1,400
			84	11,970	7,805	9,325	1,520
	V	E	81	311,162	200,807	235,805	34,998
			82	279,556	207,800	239,006	31,206
			83	636,851	433,979	506,125	72,146
			84	495,553	293,568	349,120	55,552
			85	329,257	194,792	240,772	45,980
			86	620,565	295,319	360,957	65,638
	V	W	81	11,440	8,237	10,004	1,767

Crop
Product
TSUSA commodity number, description, and unit of quantity

Country	Mode	Reg	Yr	Quantity	F.A.S.	C.I.F.	Charges
			82	76,144	42,352	49,860	7,508
			83	106,399	72,269	84,508	12,239
			84	33,414	23,794	29,900	6,106
			85	340,117	188,555	230,463	41,908
			86	428,765	206,324	257,145	50,821
ITALY	O	E	83	850	627	627	
			84	440	265	265	
	V	E	81	8,078	2,935	3,697	762
			82	400	756	861	105
			85	27,337	28,200	32,862	4,662
			86	2,100	2,280	2,664	384
	V	W	83	529	351	375	24
			84	970	560	600	40
MEXICO	O	W	81	18,430	7,004	7,004	
MOROC	V	E	83	25,132	27,600	29,712	2,112
			85	16,755	7,303	8,072	769
			86	102,536	48,936	57,560	8,624
PORTUGL	V	E	81	37,278	20,641	23,165	2,524
			83	31,480	14,086	16,596	2,510
			84	57,375	31,144	36,859	5,715
			86	32,268	13,234	15,491	2,257
	V	W	82	9,621	3,480	4,205	725
SPAIN	O	E	81	5,250	2,940	2,940	
	V	E	82	89,888	60,926	66,881	5,955
			84	2,504,300	652,857	884,420	231,563
			85	42,569	27,662	33,254	5,592
			86	88,935	64,843	72,323	7,480
	V	W	82	5,093	2,625	3,019	394
			84	794,450	201,801	276,495	74,694
THAILND	V	E	85	2,100	1,125	1,280	155

1484800 OLIVES IN BRINE RIPE, NSPF (LB)

Country	Mode	Reg	Yr	Quantity	F.A.S.	C.I.F.	Charges
TOTAL			**81**	**315,518**	**213,971**	**238,007**	**24,036**
			82	**3,901,803**	**3,480,305**	**3,893,663**	**413,358**
			83	**3,016,795**	**1,985,971**	**2,297,830**	**311,859**
			84	**3,997,198**	**2,479,863**	**2,914,237**	**434,374**
			85	**7,288,810**	**3,871,574**	**4,726,678**	**855,104**
			86	**7,371,787**	**4,409,182**	**5,228,529**	**819,347**
ALGERIA	V	E	85	20,779	12,933	15,983	3,050
CANADA	O	E	81	19,980	15,253	15,253	
			82	2,200	2,520	2,520	
			84	4,149	3,079	3,079	
CHINA M	V	W	86	43,350	22,057	26,269	4,212
FRANCE	O	E	81	399	540	615	75
			82	728	1,880	2,105	225
	V	E	81	3,779	9,846	10,198	352
			82	4,270	6,723	7,171	448
			83	6,184	8,408	8,883	475
			84	24,394	33,692	37,315	3,623
			85	75,092	84,226	91,001	6,775
			86	49,279	70,076	76,406	6,330
	V	W	81	9,850	6,605	7,153	548
			82	3,091	5,008	5,609	601
			83	11,101	13,354	14,691	1,337
			84	10,854	14,870	16,830	1,960
			85	37,256	29,543	33,605	4,062
			86	22,087	36,725	39,501	2,776
GREECE	A	E	83	3,307	2,880	4,562	1,682
	O	E	81	2,250	2,237	2,237	
			82	11,315	12,572	12,572	
			83	11,072	11,407	11,407	
			84	907	1,255	1,255	
			86	141,939	46,683	54,034	7,351
	O	W	84	7,980	4,019	5,032	1,013
	V	E	81	107,958	73,685	82,325	8,640
			82	136,361	102,918	121,020	18,102
			83	186,462	112,389	132,704	20,315
			84	159,057	86,627	104,995	18,368
			85	155,787	70,772	90,930	20,158
			86	228,477	128,507	156,198	27,691
	V	W	81	13,783	8,823	10,952	2,129
			82	25,434	19,994	23,199	3,205
			83	36,840	24,508	28,377	3,869
			84	2,850	1,710	1,965	255
			85	73,187	30,671	38,348	7,677
			86	92,279	56,930	75,248	18,318
HG KONG	V	W	81	4,800	4,592	4,785	193
			82	1,666	3,310	3,454	144
			84	960	797	885	88
IRELAND	V	E	86	22,619	5,130	7,465	2,335
ISRAEL	A	E	86	8,400	3,472	3,998	526
	V	E	84	35,190	17,748	19,883	2,135
			85	50,400	14,571	18,016	3,445

Crop Product TSUSA commodity number, description, and unit of quantity Country	Mode	Reg	Yr	Quantity	F.A.S.	C.I.F.	Charges
			86	33,305	24,524	27,566	3,042
ITALY	O	E	81	256	448	448	
			83	441	722	722	
			86	1,812	1,180	1,303	123
	V	E	81	3,607	3,449	3,800	351
			82	4,840	2,941	3,066	125
			83	41	507	538	31
			84	20,417	15,378	18,464	3,086
			85	9,963	7,696	9,002	1,306
			86	19,160	11,077	13,751	2,674
	V	W	82	689	958	1,113	155
			84	5,943	4,423	4,788	365
			85	8,510	10,778	11,692	914
			86	2,712	2,996	3,173	177
JAPAN	V	E	84	167	475	526	51
MEXICO	O	W	85	6,063	2,873	2,873	
			86	2,860	1,544	1,544	
MOROC	V	E	81	5,842	2,003	2,312	309
			85	17,850	16,150	19,799	3,649
			86	38,269	29,515	35,393	5,878
N ZEAL	V	W	86	19,241	9,605	12,404	2,799
NETHLDS	V	E	85	4,950	2,117	2,518	401
	V	W	86	11,088	6,048	7,029	981
PORTUGL	A	E	83	1,058	796	796	
	N	E	82	3,771	2,542	2,796	254
	O	E	81	3,256	2,299	2,299	
			82	2,640	1,980	1,980	
			83	4,440	3,670	3,670	
			86	3,840	2,565	2,565	
	V	E	81	7,187	4,685	5,444	759
			82	25,697	12,335	14,889	2,554
			83	16,322	4,198	5,047	849
			84	5,178	4,571	4,941	370
			85	3,480	2,753	3,226	473
			86	11,949	5,410	6,111	701
	V	W	82	2,646	1,020	1,232	212
			84	1,594	1,575	1,744	169
			85	2,400	1,700	2,225	525
			86	7,600	3,625	4,322	697
REP SAF	V	E	83	16,050	18,620	20,877	2,257
ROMANIA	V	E	83	4,000	3,405	3,989	584
SPAIN	N	E	83	516,356	342,458	393,812	51,354
			86	2,191,648	1,141,598	1,334,308	192,710
	O	E	82	7,129	3,921	3,921	
			84	43,210	14,672	14,672	
	V	E	81	132,018	78,844	89,463	10,619
			82	2,799,982	2,574,738	2,842,640	267,902
			83	1,852,672	1,298,547	1,493,485	194,938
			84	3,501,576	2,144,014	2,521,998	377,984
			85	6,348,625	3,319,982	4,062,555	742,573
			86	3,881,723	2,421,737	2,892,444	470,707
	V	W	81	553	662	723	61
			82	868,984	724,665	844,066	119,401
			83	350,449	140,102	174,270	34,168
			84	154,284	121,690	144,853	23,163
			85	446,837	245,453	302,437	56,984
			86	506,413	349,258	415,642	66,384
THAILND	V	W	82	360	280	310	30
TOKELAU	V	E	86	192	1,486	1,670	184
TUNISIA	V	E	86	4,938	3,684	4,086	402
TURKEY	V	E	84	18,488	9,268	11,012	1,744
			85	20,631	13,236	15,320	2,084
			86	26,607	23,750	26,099	2,349
	V	W	85	7,000	6,120	7,148	1,028

1485020 OLIVES, PITTED NT OV 0.3GAL (LB)

Country	Mode	Reg	Yr	Quantity	F.A.S.	C.I.F.	Charges
TOTAL			81	1,205,104	1,185,790	1,357,412	171,622
			82	1,808,994	1,940,892	2,225,189	284,297
			83	2,361,715	1,937,165	2,284,811	347,646
			84	2,949,153	2,378,377	2,791,762	413,385
			85	4,204,182	2,973,893	3,638,075	664,182
			86	4,475,695	3,275,193	3,857,603	582,410
BRAZIL	V	E	82	907	1,560	1,771	211
CHINA M	V	W	82	2,181	734	792	58
			84	3,345	1,449	1,528	79
DOM REP	V	E	82	473	1,029	1,262	233
FR GERM	V	E	85	4,455	4,590	5,236	646
			86	784	1,313	1,477	164
FRANCE	V	E	81	974	1,259	1,413	154
			82	2,758	3,152	3,283	131
			83	3,643	5,080	5,249	169
			84	7,377	12,331	13,981	1,650
			85	18,136	25,453	27,635	2,182

Crop Product TSUSA commodity number, description, and unit of quantity Country	Mode	Reg	Yr	Quantity	F.A.S.	C.I.F.	Charges
			86	1,984	6,077	6,307	230
	V	W	82	660	1,018	1,038	20
			83	644	933	1,056	123
			84	4,379	5,471	6,720	1,249
			85	1,873	2,704	3,734	1,030
			86	13,816	12,873	14,163	1,290
GREECE	O	E	81	16,874	16,223	16,223	
			84	2,640	1,044	1,044	
	V	E	83	19,594	21,375	23,490	2,115
			85	10,681	4,560	5,898	1,338
			86	3,456	3,456	4,022	566
	V	W	85	14,890	9,233	10,953	1,720
HG KONG	V	W	84	1,605	1,280	1,406	126
			86	1,920	1,486	1,612	126
ISRAEL	N	E	81	7,425	7,060	8,556	1,496
	V	E	81	46,383	56,288	64,007	7,719
			82	675	1,139	1,291	152
			83	23,340	13,249	14,747	1,498
			84	103,541	43,288	50,487	7,199
			85	33,437	12,354	14,590	2,236
			86	28,117	19,696	21,685	1,989
	V	W	86	20,000	15,624	18,099	2,475
ITALY	V	E	82	1,013	880	1,003	123
			86	62,481	48,837	61,152	12,315
MACAO	V	E	85	43,651	13,844	16,586	2,742
MOROC	V	E	81	4,850	1,595	1,860	265
			82	70,171	36,968	45,474	8,506
			83	19,510	8,192	10,896	2,704
			84	15,983	7,250	8,850	1,600
			85	66,264	52,360	67,001	14,641
			86	132,041	57,989	73,612	15,623
NETHLDS	V	W	86	20,790	15,120	17,666	2,546
SPAIN	N	E	85	306,520	252,596	305,525	52,929
			86	1,038,787	953,432	1,102,199	148,767
	O	E	83	2,963	4,724	4,724	
	V	E	81	1,128,328	1,102,660	1,264,562	161,902
			82	1,691,123	1,831,363	2,099,380	268,017
			83	2,120,918	1,709,222	2,026,962	317,740
			84	2,572,089	2,084,386	2,455,017	370,631
			85	2,904,138	2,095,981	2,553,352	457,371
			86	2,744,400	1,848,612	2,192,847	344,235
	V	W	81	270	705	791	86
			82	39,033	63,049	69,895	6,846
			83	171,103	174,390	197,687	23,297
			84	238,194	221,878	252,729	30,851
			85	800,137	500,218	627,565	127,347
			86	407,119	290,678	342,762	52,084

1485040 OLIVES, PITTED, OVER 0.3GAL (LB)

Country	Mode	Reg	Yr	Quantity	F.A.S.	C.I.F.	Charges
TOTAL			81	3,233,212	2,093,945	2,392,000	296,857
			82	6,667,958	6,077,581	6,777,868	700,287
			83	6,695,881	4,295,838	5,076,771	780,933
			84	7,236,563	4,601,265	5,387,737	786,472
			85	10,961,967	5,799,385	7,154,629	1,355,244
			86	15,603,579	9,401,353	11,040,566	1,639,213
ARGENT	V	E	82	33,896	17,111	21,556	4,445
BELGIUM	V	W	86	23,100	15,120	17,070	1,950
CANADA	O	E	82	2,717	1,882	1,882	
CHINA M	V	E	84	2,570	3,290	3,744	454
	V	W	84	17,315	10,656	11,891	1,235
			85	22,806	13,274	14,509	1,235
FR GERM	V	E	85	20,790	14,767	17,549	2,782
FRANCE	A	E	84	176	332	414	82
	O	E	81	992	709	759	50
	V	E	83	11,398	13,045	13,834	789
			86	11,420	11,120	11,710	590
	V	W	82	291	383	472	89
			83	3,836	4,698	5,235	537
			84	1,012	1,808	2,015	207
			85	705	1,186	1,302	116
			86	11,710	6,566	6,648	82
GREECE	O	E	81	1,540	1,457	1,457	
			84	1,375	700	700	
	V	E	84	42,785	24,500	29,179	4,679
	V	W	83	18,662	11,950	14,627	2,677
			84	4,630	1,375	1,709	334
			86	2,865	1,495	1,766	271
HG KONG	V	W	84	600	520	540	20
INDIA	O	E	83	418	774	774	
IRELAND	V	E	85	18,164	7,754	10,080	2,326
ISRAEL	N	E	82	311,499	184,957	210,577	25,620
	V	E	81	281,674	159,390	185,729	26,339
			82	257,844	162,755	187,346	24,591

Crop
Product
TSUSA commodity number, description, and unit of quantity

Country	Mode	Reg	Yr	Quantity	F.A.S.	C.I.F.	Charges
			83	163,809	86,919	99,086	12,167
			84	416,787	174,118	205,393	31,275
			85	51,732	24,627	29,697	5,070
			86	120,026	74,580	83,409	8,829
	V	W	81	16,384	10,791	12,657	1,866
			82	14,245	9,834	11,147	1,313
			83	29,676	15,309	17,983	2,674
			84	28,637	10,499	13,641	3,142
			86	5,432	1,916	2,272	356
ITALY	V	E	81	986	959	1,097	138
			83	49,212	41,925	48,180	6,255
			84	6,506	5,287	5,946	659
			85	25,499	10,226	12,147	1,921
			86	21,751	17,517	20,390	2,873
	V	W	86	20,785	14,112	16,745	2,633
JAPAN	V	E	82	1,552	960	1,081	121
			83	1,575	1,188	1,343	155
			84	1,575	1,458	1,670	212
	V	W	86	77,491	27,288	30,423	3,135
MAURIT	V	E	86	9,639	7,863	9,299	1,436
MEXICO	O	W	81	137,388	52,206	52,206	
			82	139,948	83,623	83,623	
			85	2,645	1,587	1,587	
			86	16,200	6,000	6,000	
MOROC	A	E	84	2,056	796	1,425	629
	V	E	81	54,563	20,011	24,891	4,880
			82	147,707	58,505	70,260	11,755
			83	91,872	27,081	32,758	5,677
			86	35,956	25,380	30,751	5,371
NETHLDS	V	E	85	3,240	2,466	2,933	467
			86	9,183	4,420	5,279	859
	V	W	86	54,432	39,984	46,648	6,664
PERU	V	E	83	992	1,000	1,112	112
PORTUGL	O	E	86	4,092	2,325	2,325	
	V	E	81	56,173	18,772	26,273	7,501
			85	22,046	9,665	12,647	2,982
S ARAB	V	E	85	4,296	3,817	4,461	644
SPAIN	N	E	83	99,627	70,562	84,225	13,663
			84	172,345	154,517	179,387	24,870
			85	993,528	609,101	738,178	129,077
			86	2,175,191	1,471,846	1,700,677	228,831
	N	W	85	1,352,677	736,411	893,775	157,364
	O	E	81	3,758	2,472	3,045	573
			83	6,318	2,596	3,088	492
			84	64,479	37,476	42,953	5,477
			85	8,485	4,246	5,661	1,415
	V	E	81	2,648,558	1,798,520	2,051,675	251,957
			82	5,616,559	5,457,223	6,077,924	620,701
			83	6,080,863	3,929,157	4,650,748	721,591
			84	5,677,617	3,611,581	4,233,036	621,455
			85	8,016,245	4,135,968	5,124,737	988,769
			86	9,147,102	6,430,103	7,565,721	1,135,618
	V	W	81	31,196	28,658	32,211	3,553
			82	141,700	100,348	112,000	11,652
			83	136,301	88,635	102,695	14,060
			84	795,613	562,092	653,779	91,687
			85	419,109	224,290	285,366	61,076
			86	3,857,204	1,243,718	1,483,433	239,715
THAILND	V	W	84	485	260	315	55
TURKEY	V	E	83	1,322	999	1,083	84

1485065 OLIVES STUFFED NT OV 0.3GAL (LB)

Country	Mode	Reg	Yr	Quantity	F.A.S.	C.I.F.	Charges
TOTAL			81	3,392,897	6,120,676	6,766,789	651,786
			82	3,385,527	5,944,630	6,610,429	665,799
			83	4,077,605	5,350,079	6,121,030	770,951
			84	3,822,584	5,373,454	6,146,426	772,972
			85	3,872,784	5,045,910	5,915,435	869,525
			86	4,241,810	6,781,880	7,691,988	910,108
CHINA M	V	E	84	1,263	1,728	1,949	221
	V	W	84	1,613	2,710	3,079	369
DENMARK	V	E	83	10,637	16,531	18,219	1,688
FRANCE	V	E	81	356	753	844	91
GREECE	V	E	82	9,600	11,100	12,840	1,740
	V	W	85	779	1,214	1,417	203
ISRAEL	V	E	85	1,458	2,257	2,830	573
			86	1,071	1,750	1,876	126
ITALY	V	E	84	2,211	3,876	4,604	728
			85	30,415	36,026	45,069	9,043
			86	8,061	14,193	16,070	1,877
JAPAN	V	E	84	4,484	6,557	7,669	1,112
			85	2,411	4,012	5,034	1,022
NETHLDS	V	E	86	22,577	9,760	10,879	1,119
PORTUGL	V	E	85	1,381	1,831	2,322	491

Country	Mode	Reg	Yr	Quantity	F.A.S.	C.I.F.	Charges
SPAIN	N	E	85	457,698	511,000	602,596	91,596
			86	1,072,791	2,127,101	2,396,785	269,684
	N	W	85	549,771	857,107	991,067	133,960
	O	E	81	159	539	582	43
			83	3,938	8,333	8,333	
	V	E	81	3,151,762	5,650,997	6,245,441	600,117
			82	3,032,303	5,322,037	5,916,032	593,995
			83	3,211,815	4,173,989	4,803,374	629,385
			84	3,172,316	4,420,409	5,065,185	644,776
			85	2,787,778	3,598,743	4,226,150	627,407
			86	2,765,420	3,864,882	4,413,201	548,319
	V	W	81	240,620	468,387	519,922	51,535
			82	343,624	611,493	681,557	70,064
			83	851,215	1,151,226	1,291,104	139,878
			84	640,697	938,174	1,063,940	125,766
			85	41,093	33,720	38,950	5,230
			86	371,890	764,194	853,177	88,983

1485070 OLIVES STUFD NSPF NOV0.3GAL (LB)

Country	Mode	Reg	Yr	Quantity	F.A.S.	C.I.F.	Charges
TOTAL			81	28,673,393	30,077,212	33,985,392	3,905,805
			82	32,784,490	35,682,116	40,279,822	4,597,706
			83	39,786,456	31,498,717	37,075,241	5,576,524
			84	39,699,519	35,432,142	41,205,323	5,773,181
			85	50,585,021	35,725,649	43,558,087	7,832,438
			86	46,149,213	38,466,351	44,519,285	6,052,934
BRAZIL	V	E	82	76,896	73,713	83,668	9,955
			86	16,469	12,562	14,485	1,923
CANADA	O	E	86	10,125	15,142	15,142	
CHINA M	V	E	84	35,940	28,374	33,840	5,466
	V	W	84	21,369	16,436	18,650	2,214
			85	9,126	9,372	10,606	1,234
DOM REP	V	E	82	945	1,579	1,936	357
FR GERM	V	E	85	33,660	32,647	37,242	4,595
FRANCE	V	E	83	724	1,125	1,226	101
			85	31,909	28,983	35,632	6,649
			86	37,873	13,170	15,186	2,016
	V	W	84	657	630	722	92
GREECE	V	E	82	5,910	4,000	4,734	734
			83	8,730	4,066	5,349	1,283
			84	46,052	16,375	17,360	985
			85	12,154	10,391	12,922	2,531
			86	24,786	31,470	35,977	4,507
	V	W	85	50,615	50,384	59,944	9,560
			86	23,333	33,610	37,092	3,482
HG KONG	V	W	83	720	446	470	24
			84	720	389	416	27
IRELAND	V	E	85	35,648	13,482	16,296	2,814
			86	41,343	10,988	13,314	2,326
ISRAEL	N	E	81	24,511	23,035	27,049	4,014
			83	33,052	52,032	57,992	5,960
	V	E	81	177,343	249,421	280,598	31,177
			82	308,384	343,410	392,193	48,783
			83	479,813	275,347	316,382	41,035
			84	557,560	401,245	462,093	60,848
			85	348,790	268,205	314,641	46,436
			86	886,750	553,397	636,730	83,333
	V	W	84	42,893	17,400	21,308	3,908
ITALY	V	E	82	556	803	887	84
			83	7,920	5,837	7,324	1,487
			84	74,723	69,720	79,698	9,978
			85	74,270	56,296	70,103	13,807
			86	17,445	13,712	15,535	1,823
	V	W	83	6,804	14,047	19,717	5,670
JAPAN	V	E	84	10,945	10,150	11,871	1,721
			85	10,864	5,703	7,156	1,453
MACAO	V	E	85	58,034	26,573	32,085	5,512
			86	42,758	12,429	15,201	2,772
MEXICO	O	W	86	392,362	157,536	157,536	
MOROC	V	E	85	235,021	140,137	169,583	29,446
			86	141,094	81,322	96,956	15,634
NETHLDS	V	E	85	10,890	7,889	9,383	1,494
			86	251,172	119,938	138,764	18,826
PHIL R	V	E	85	16,977	12,661	15,086	2,425
PORTUGL	V	E	81	377	1,046	1,490	444
			82	1,846	4,560	5,261	701
			84	62,034	47,054	57,498	10,444
			85	14,504	14,117	17,429	3,312
REP SAF	V	E	85	43,982	23,625	26,526	2,901
SPAIN	N	E	82	173,497	83,410	97,162	13,752
			84	17,943,152	15,925,758	18,502,911	2,577,153
			85	8,420,109	5,927,621	7,166,552	1,238,931
			86	18,376,502	15,094,446	17,315,355	2,220,909
	O	E	81	765	1,056	1,146	90

Crop
Product
TSUSA commodity number, description, and unit of quantity

Country	Mode	Reg	Yr	Quantity	F.A.S.	C.I.F.	Charges
			84	47,066	44,715	51,884	7,169
			86	334,616	303,414	352,401	48,987
	V	E	81	27,452,808	28,585,530	32,281,903	3,693,998
			82	30,426,740	32,880,484	37,106,402	4,225,918
			83	34,871,531	26,468,513	31,351,605	4,883,092
			84	16,746,174	14,540,450	16,984,861	2,444,411
			85	34,460,309	22,998,982	28,320,544	5,321,562
			86	20,132,971	16,267,656	19,012,202	2,744,546
	V	W	81	1,017,589	1,217,124	1,393,206	176,082
			82	1,772,000	2,267,571	2,562,119	294,548
			83	4,358,229	4,659,916	5,294,983	635,067
			84	4,110,234	4,313,446	4,962,211	648,765
			85	6,718,159	6,098,581	7,236,357	1,137,776
			86	5,419,614	5,745,559	6,647,409	901,850
THAILND	V	W	82	17,716	22,586	25,460	2,874
			83	18,933	17,388	20,193	2,805

1485080 OLIVES, STUFFED OVER 0.3GAL (LB)

Country	Mode	Reg	Yr	Quantity	F.A.S.	C.I.F.	Charges
TOTAL			81	39,508,386	27,486,924	30,716,427	3,235,550
			82	36,140,919	27,645,505	30,965,179	3,319,674
			83	39,608,485	21,294,448	24,822,482	3,528,034
			84	42,304,058	23,889,186	27,679,998	3,790,812
			85	40,189,169	20,686,161	25,212,372	4,526,211
			86	44,341,185	29,746,432	34,722,787	4,976,355
ARGENT	V	E	82	76,058	42,522	51,199	8,677
CANADA	O	E	83	27,161	11,760	12,485	725
			84	28,518	12,222	14,422	2,200
			86	46,848	12,198	12,758	560
	V	E	85	60,553	20,595	25,265	4,670
CHINA M	V	E	84	34,918	35,070	38,890	3,820
			86	65,835	43,092	46,755	3,663
	V	W	84	1,913	2,196	2,495	299
			85	22,692	36,047	39,863	3,816
FRANCE	V	E	85	43,740	28,640	36,100	7,460
GERM DR	V	E	82	13,920	14,871	16,966	2,095
GREECE	V	E	81	4,032	3,031	3,419	388
			82	52,118	25,818	30,535	4,717
			83	3,968	1,642	2,167	525
			84	73,633	33,767	40,893	7,126
			85	1,980	1,052	1,309	257
			86	122,221	20,900	32,900	12,000
	V	W	81	57,038	40,732	45,588	4,856
			82	19,950	13,788	16,526	2,738
ICELAND	V	E	85	28,056	7,137	8,982	1,845
ISRAEL	N	E	84	466,578	239,316	264,937	25,621
			85	57,036	25,961	30,342	4,381
	N	W	84	346,807	167,661	194,252	26,591
	V	E	81	1,444,259	906,481	1,022,184	115,703
			82	1,990,149	1,317,816	1,480,617	162,801
			83	2,107,048	1,027,048	1,170,484	143,436
			84	1,844,251	952,412	1,081,386	128,974
			85	301,555	177,833	204,504	26,671
			86	298,265	165,997	194,543	28,546
	V	W	81	116,030	78,700	88,605	9,905
			82	420,645	326,790	356,252	29,462
			83	270,615	163,199	187,686	24,487
			84	28,704	15,735	17,891	2,156
			85	32,253	22,445	23,887	1,442
			86	112,033	57,119	67,004	9,885
ITALY	O	W	86	10,800	9,450	10,877	1,427
	V	E	81	60,025	34,866	39,993	5,127
			82	329,633	197,540	220,317	22,777
			83	214,498	99,699	116,888	17,189
			84	96,793	63,213	71,329	8,116
			85	86,178	56,291	67,422	11,131
			86	100,596	68,538	78,917	10,379
	V	W	81	12,571	11,640	11,842	202
			82	28,858	17,595	20,234	2,639
			83	38,483	50,819	59,559	8,740
			84	30,714	17,588	19,800	2,212
JAPAN	N	E	84	990	968	1,072	104
	V	E	82	55,673	46,690	52,409	5,719
			83	43,519	11,800	14,196	2,396
			84	14,084	17,279	19,797	2,518
KOR REP	V	E	86	21,945	14,364	15,585	1,221
	V	W	84	8,033	4,958	5,891	933
LESOTHO	V	E	86	144,193	152,430	172,142	19,712
MACAO	V	E	86	124,161	28,321	34,856	6,535
MEXICO	O	W	86	51,836	18,004	18,004	
MOROC	N	E	85	294,886	77,574	93,246	15,672
	V	E	81	15,983	8,338	10,280	1,942
			82	489,002	229,180	261,589	32,409
			83	641,329	190,357	224,703	34,346

Crop
Product
TSUSA commodity number, description, and unit of quantity

Country	Mode	Reg	Yr	Quantity	F.A.S.	C.I.F.	Charges
			84	564,686	169,547	199,675	30,128
			86	31,040	6,720	8,620	1,900
NETHLDS	V	E	85	108,173	44,393	54,932	10,539
			86	164,582	89,302	103,758	14,456
PHIL R	V	E	84	28,864	17,340	19,736	2,396
PORTUGL	V	E	81	133,974	50,411	60,726	10,315
			82	161,603	136,487	148,683	12,196
			83	116,004	102,595	114,873	12,278
			84	124,932	88,296	98,960	10,664
			85	54,320	44,576	49,150	4,574
			86	111,232	54,448	63,141	8,693
S ARAB	V	E	85	64,270	28,549	34,978	6,429
SPAIN	N	E	82	4,457,798	2,639,667	2,973,351	333,684
			83	9,242,089	3,972,749	4,699,293	726,544
			84	15,997,042	7,134,390	8,389,336	1,254,946
			85	3,409,404	2,128,699	2,590,660	461,961
			86	14,899,331	9,680,304	11,328,621	1,648,317
	N	W	81	66,893	77,556	90,106	12,550
			82	54,966	55,838	65,109	9,271
			83	75,220	51,797	59,968	8,171
			84	2,454,322	1,897,017	2,141,263	244,246
			85	64,950	57,860	68,579	10,719
	O	E	81	287,144	198,611	231,707	33,096
			82	222,871	164,656	185,372	20,716
			83	509,830	228,740	263,198	34,458
			84	87,550	38,265	41,020	2,755
			85	48,427	23,520	23,520	
			86	39,600	22,950	29,350	6,400
	V	E	81	32,110,478	22,052,268	24,619,176	2,569,955
			82	23,544,668	19,177,671	21,455,634	2,277,963
			83	23,641,204	13,612,469	15,873,219	2,260,750
			84	19,866,353	12,826,718	14,842,428	2,015,710
			85	32,483,882	15,975,389	19,639,850	3,664,461
			86	25,606,607	16,927,290	19,892,845	2,965,555
	V	H	86	18,900	8,100	10,776	2,676
	V	W	81	5,199,959	4,024,290	4,492,801	471,511
			82	4,223,007	3,238,576	3,630,386	391,810
			83	2,677,517	1,769,774	2,023,763	253,989
			84	204,373	155,228	174,525	19,297
			85	3,026,814	1,929,600	2,219,783	290,183
			86	2,371,160	2,366,905	2,601,335	234,430

Olive, prepared or preserved

1485600 OLIVES PREP OR PRES, NSPF (LB)

Country	Mode	Reg	Yr	Quantity	F.A.S.	C.I.F.	Charges
TOTAL			81	2,517,234	1,751,585	2,010,371	258,729
			82	4,231,694	2,663,387	3,110,670	447,283
			83	2,451,447	1,555,980	1,844,340	288,360
			84	3,078,671	1,902,605	2,281,502	378,897
			85	3,236,838	1,650,914	2,030,162	379,248
			86	3,950,386	2,257,120	2,694,824	437,704
BRAZIL	V	E	82	23,400	9,360	11,655	2,295
CANADA	O	E	81	7,476	3,828	3,953	125
			84	750	690	690	
			86	75,150	115,537	115,537	
CHILE	N	E	84	44,512	41,481	50,716	9,235
	V	E	82	49,603	44,475	50,499	6,024
			86	25,926	16,464	18,646	2,182
CHINA M	N	W	84	889	1,255	1,278	23
	V	E	81	3,960	2,842	3,071	229
			82	18,746	8,285	10,258	1,973
			84	2,100	1,201	1,662	461
			85	3,000	1,615	2,028	413
			86	5,050	2,729	3,021	292
	V	W	81	6,670	2,053	2,253	200
			82	11,733	6,720	7,319	599
			83	19,315	10,052	10,876	824
			84	6,676	4,882	5,335	453
			85	34,646	19,525	23,283	3,758
			86	4,885	4,100	4,456	356
CHINA T	V	E	81	1,653	390	439	49
			82	250	420	485	65
			83	935	1,943	2,079	136
	V	H	81	7,700	10,183	10,939	756
	V	W	82	3,233	5,822	6,518	696
			83	3,449	2,058	2,208	150
			84	3,650	7,414	8,053	639
			85	1,938	2,450	2,702	252
FR GERM	A	E	81	62	280	286	6
FRANCE	A	E	84	60	294	408	114
	N	W	82	1,703	2,629	3,177	548
	O	E	81	146	542	721	179

Crop Product TSUSA commodity number, description, and unit of quantity Country	Mode	Reg	Yr	Quantity	F.A.S.	C.I.F.	Charges
			84	1,037	1,372	1,520	148
			85	2,006	2,547	2,830	283
			86	2,873	6,208	7,432	1,224
	V	E	81	31,928	51,583	56,288	4,705
			82	41,680	53,776	58,791	5,015
			83	32,767	54,643	59,797	5,154
			84	41,904	58,544	68,809	10,265
			85	15,908	20,811	22,907	2,096
			86	18,027	35,436	38,511	3,075
	V	W	83	236	726	746	20
			84	5,614	7,967	8,713	746
			85	482	1,610	1,888	278
			86	5,604	9,296	10,266	970
GREECE	N	E	82	2,110,070	1,479,072	1,712,165	233,093
	N	W	86	7,374	3,593	4,312	719
	O	E	82	31,305	11,047	14,269	3,222
			84	2,208	1,949	1,949	
			85	5,513	2,450	2,450	
	V	E	81	2,181,547	1,457,997	1,674,932	216,935
			82	265,724	179,372	208,991	29,619
			83	1,941,167	1,144,394	1,372,071	227,677
			84	2,223,394	1,205,611	1,471,811	266,200
			85	1,817,723	823,874	1,020,916	197,042
			86	2,111,661	935,674	1,157,919	222,245
	V	W	81	37,019	25,696	31,251	5,555
			82	106,493	80,606	94,826	14,220
			83	152,383	117,655	138,155	20,500
			84	122,609	77,988	92,073	14,085
			85	135,147	76,967	93,042	16,075
			86	118,220	65,506	80,102	14,596
GUATMAL	V	E	85	21,781	8,176	10,647	2,471
HG KONG	V	E	81	1,250	2,018	2,137	119
			82	1,750	1,290	1,469	179
			83	1,000	752	822	70
			84	2,170	1,309	1,504	195
			85	6,759	5,811	7,032	1,221
	V	H	81	420	292	317	25
	V	W	81	11,180	9,769	10,161	392
			82	23,910	19,103	20,731	1,628
			83	17,418	11,268	12,327	1,059
			84	5,112	4,661	4,955	294
			85	3,482	3,291	3,526	235
			86	2,880	2,186	2,408	222
ISRAEL	O	E	86	20,031	10,738	10,738	
	V	E	81	69,341	48,900	55,316	6,416
			82	99,820	78,696	87,779	9,083
			83	75,093	50,800	56,450	5,650
			84	91,877	62,843	69,480	6,637
			85	40,238	24,554	27,540	2,986
			86	172,050	110,287	125,770	15,483
	V	W	85	2,968	1,003	1,214	211
			86	29,902	19,121	22,682	3,561
ITALY	N	E	81	66,406	58,561	70,870	12,309
			82	143,408	113,661	130,204	16,543
			83	110,832	90,969	105,808	14,839
	O	E	81	1,059	1,270	1,394	124
			84	731	860	860	
	V	E	83	1,543	4,210	4,682	472
			84	211,549	178,039	204,095	26,056
			85	133,317	137,774	157,931	20,157
			86	225,155	273,289	302,941	29,652
	V	W	82	3,139	4,019	4,461	442
			83	688	1,319	1,398	79
			84	2,328	3,051	3,721	670
			85	2,480	1,633	1,942	309
			86	68,246	56,927	66,275	9,348
KOR REP	V	W	81	500	291	308	17
			85	914	1,116	1,252	136
MACAO	O	E	86	3,547	4,250	4,250	
MALAYSA	V	E	83	243	464	501	37
MOROC	O	E	82	16,500	16,575	16,575	
			83	1,008	576	576	
			84	7,870	4,972	4,972	
	V	E	81	17,976	9,783	12,731	2,948
			84	5,625	8,094	8,819	725
			85	20,000	8,748	9,669	921
PERU	V	E	81	19,048	17,280	19,161	1,881
			85	24,074	18,564	21,209	2,645
PORTUGL	V	E	81	14,500	18,215	19,763	1,548
			82	4,243	8,488	9,142	654
			83	3,150	8,488	9,134	646
			84	1,620	8,070	9,194	1,124
			85	3,681	8,834	10,578	1,744
			86	3,798	9,204	11,004	1,800

Crop Product TSUSA commodity number, description, and unit of quantity Country	Mode	Reg	Yr	Quantity	F.A.S.	C.I.F.	Charges
ROMANIA	V	E	82	66	465	545	80
SPAIN	V	E	81	36,291	29,552	33,717	4,108
			82	102,617	100,947	113,517	12,570
			83	85,648	51,325	61,901	10,576
			84	97,812	61,927	74,211	12,284
			85	649,707	290,454	372,148	81,694
			86	933,403	490,827	607,277	116,450
	V	W	82	1,165,193	434,561	542,857	108,296
			83	945	698	892	194
			84	180,501	148,688	174,637	25,949
			85	296,305	180,660	223,523	42,863
			86	108,195	81,745	96,921	15,176
THAILND	V	E	81	1,102	260	363	103
			84	1,052	750	788	38
	V	W	82	7,108	3,998	4,437	439
			84	9,718	6,859	8,037	1,178
			85	3,505	2,000	2,267	267
			86	8,409	4,003	4,356	353
TURKEY	N	W	84	4,931	1,565	2,874	1,309
	V	E	83	3,627	3,640	3,917	277
			84	372	269	338	69
			85	2,949	2,254	2,456	202
	V	W	85	2,315	1,590	1,835	245
U KING	V	E	85	6,000	2,603	3,347	744

Olive, vegetable oil, edible
1762900 OLIVE OIL PKG UNDER 40 LBS (LB)

Country	Mode	Reg	Yr	Quantity	F.A.S.	C.I.F.	Charges
TOTAL			81	33,402,667	28,257,696	30,669,490	2,405,094
			82	36,214,076	28,801,694	31,422,233	2,620,539
			83	45,456,126	32,349,294	35,479,007	3,129,713
			84	62,077,803	40,134,020	44,989,659	4,855,639
			85	68,455,179	40,585,032	45,903,805	5,318,773
			86	78,588,274	57,582,259	63,230,825	5,648,566
ARGENT	V	W	84	36,773	21,360	23,946	2,586
BELGIUM	V	E	82	463	616	637	21
			83	264	330	342	12
			84	31,031	21,815	23,094	1,279
			85	40,713	29,270	32,092	2,822
BRAZIL	O	E	81	768	1,018	1,018	
	V	E	81	750	405	456	51
			86	11,023	15,923	16,910	987
CANADA	O	E	81	14,208	12,839	13,014	175
			82	3,945	4,649	4,649	
			83	7,083	9,990	9,990	
			84	23,330	27,535	27,610	75
			85	11,183	14,548	14,548	
			86	82,368	62,455	62,455	
CYPRUS	V	E	85	595	802	869	67
DOM REP	V	E	85	41,877	16,582	19,547	2,965
FR GERM	O	E	83	2,739	2,220	2,451	231
			84	1,290	1,998	2,298	300
	V	E	83	661	717	764	47
			86	14,890	20,650	22,913	2,263
	V	W	86	35,194	24,290	27,040	2,750
FRANCE	A	E	84	8,047	4,643	9,371	4,728
	N	E	81	155,641	154,100	174,429	20,329
			82	287,309	255,448	285,648	30,200
			83	703,319	518,260	559,228	40,968
			84	889,044	621,286	689,647	68,361
			85	315,494	348,018	391,923	43,905
			86	443,605	585,118	644,482	59,364
	N	W	82	3,400	3,484	4,039	555
			84	58,020	72,787	79,829	7,042
			85	56,536	77,945	86,236	8,291
	O	E	81	6,060	9,400	10,477	1,077
			82	5,961	8,851	9,531	680
			83	1,599	1,869	2,017	148
			84	975	1,612	1,741	129
			85	8,972	10,709	11,252	543
			86	6,713	9,858	12,546	2,688
	V	E	81	92,025	71,889	82,411	10,522
			82	262,665	195,291	217,537	22,246
			83	293,349	242,894	263,155	20,261
			84	257,851	174,014	195,644	21,630
			85	159,181	143,156	162,389	19,233
			86	151,619	186,325	208,612	22,287
	V	W	81	35,742	40,331	45,678	5,347
			82	22,912	32,049	34,379	2,330
			83	54,959	72,253	79,362	7,109
			84	7,994	14,803	16,509	1,706
			85	5,779	10,718	11,884	1,166

Crop Product Country	Mode	Reg	Yr	Quantity	F.A.S.	C.I.F.	Charges
			86	23,231	37,181	38,367	1,186
G BISAU	V	E	81	9,120	7,100	8,015	915
GIBRAT	A	E	82	5,695	11,405	13,671	2,266
GREECE	A	E	84	50	340	460	120
	N	E	82	716,302	594,381	655,256	60,875
			83	882,898	602,117	687,478	85,361
	N	W	84	11,570	8,918	9,829	911
	O	E	81	18,308	22,279	22,279	
			82	51,741	61,271	61,271	
			83	75,745	86,152	86,152	
			84	53,836	56,585	56,585	
			85	71,739	69,687	69,687	
			86	41,594	43,111	43,111	
	O	W	82	14,706	14,526	15,706	1,180
			83	1,427	1,119	1,119	
			85	2,853	3,986	3,986	
	V	E	81	1,204,446	1,120,931	1,218,822	97,891
			82	317,997	289,088	316,461	27,373
			83	128,593	109,117	123,705	14,588
			84	1,079,861	734,785	849,002	114,217
			85	1,272,004	877,724	971,235	93,511
			86	1,698,626	1,277,841	1,411,989	134,148
	V	W	82	6,552	5,342	5,842	500
			83	50,853	52,694	57,644	4,950
			84	55,546	49,800	55,309	5,509
			85	138,095	101,307	114,893	13,586
			86	160,355	118,369	133,772	15,403
INDIA	O	E	83	300	1,200	1,200	
IRAN	V	W	86	118,105	114,454	124,540	10,086
ISRAEL	O	W	85	5,389	9,989	9,989	
	V	E	81	47,132	90,996	95,306	4,310
			85	101,408	62,850	69,769	6,919
	V	W	81	31,411	57,975	59,842	1,867
ITALY	A	E	83	1,469	3,266	5,118	1,852
			84	6,687	13,962	16,898	2,936
			86	1,409	3,085	4,022	937
	A	W	84	600	2,076	2,772	696
	N	E	82	15,817,845	12,789,450	13,838,091	1,048,641
			83	18,650,776	13,663,541	14,943,845	1,280,304
			84	28,412,901	18,736,888	20,950,786	2,213,898
			85	32,174,936	18,726,099	21,046,481	2,320,382
			86	31,392,917	23,348,011	25,346,953	1,998,942
	N	W	82	132,185	109,063	119,710	10,647
			83	6,844,459	4,924,007	5,426,044	502,037
			84	1,703,919	1,160,228	1,382,089	221,861
			85	12,155,685	7,373,964	8,559,012	1,185,048
			86	17,151,802	12,737,234	14,170,748	1,433,514
	O	E	81	27,245	45,059	46,969	1,910
			83	27,203	33,694	35,267	1,573
			84	111,151	99,219	99,299	80
			85	39,590	47,375	47,925	550
			86	62,971	58,540	60,827	2,287
	O	W	82	1,213	2,585	2,748	163
			86	2,090	3,834	4,422	588
	V	E	81	16,106,434	13,825,854	14,859,682	1,036,828
			82	3,167,438	2,706,063	3,000,776	294,713
			83	3,504,096	2,832,279	3,086,921	254,642
			84	3,034,059	2,160,184	2,443,982	283,798
			85	5,829,044	3,861,586	4,360,970	499,384
			86	11,773,682	8,380,563	9,213,138	832,575
	V	W	81	6,910,983	5,729,342	6,393,711	654,369
			82	6,535,937	4,907,267	5,459,734	552,467
			83	1,639,453	1,200,366	1,333,240	132,874
			84	10,007,860	6,374,015	7,223,290	849,275
			85	3,404	4,787	5,410	623
			86	1,344,516	964,277	1,071,883	107,606
JAMAICA	V	E	84	250	272	287	15
JAPAN	V	W	86	38,834	42,124	45,407	3,283
LEBANON	O	E	81	774	316	394	78
	V	E	84	159	288	329	41
MAURIT	V	E	86	8,467	20,354	21,683	1,329
N ANTIL	O	E	84	27,534	18,707	19,418	711
			85	24,300	16,038	16,661	623
			86	5,400	3,264	3,264	
NETHLDS	O	E	84	2,191	6,204	6,609	405
			85	29,620	18,804	19,206	402
			86	16,791	9,487	9,603	116
	V	E	84	543	374	406	32
			85	2,796	1,869	2,027	158
	V	W	86	84,930	63,866	69,486	5,620
PORTUGL	O	E	81	2,750	3,006	3,006	
			82	7,150	7,790	7,790	
			83	22,000	24,000	24,000	
			84	1,350	888	897	9
			86	9,000	5,250	5,250	
	V	E	81	934,238	904,123	978,851	74,728
			82	968,307	999,369	1,060,978	61,609
			83	1,004,239	925,077	994,963	69,886
			84	962,624	806,064	875,124	69,060
			85	843,523	607,296	663,585	56,289
			86	1,049,870	769,554	841,119	71,565
	V	W	82	26,780	26,200	29,601	3,401
			83	9,104	7,000	7,950	950
			84	8,452	7,500	8,686	1,186
			85	18,914	14,175	17,501	3,326
			86	8,362	5,950	6,847	897
SPAIN	N	E	83	5,441,546	2,940,816	3,262,228	321,412
			85	4,290,365	2,113,711	2,343,855	230,144
	N	W	81	222,015	161,961	179,755	17,794
			82	202,573	138,261	155,504	17,243
			83	242,607	170,354	189,937	19,583
			84	243,435	154,419	172,752	18,333
			85	141,079	101,943	113,563	11,620
			86	207,787	137,986	151,069	13,083
	O	E	81	695,425	645,398	677,534	32,136
			82	185,857	151,308	157,932	6,624
			83	213,973	171,281	178,235	6,954
			84	135,557	100,656	104,855	4,199
			85	84,209	59,730	64,092	4,362
			86	139,141	93,523	99,446	5,923
	O	W	82	960	964	984	20
	V	E	81	6,633,900	5,147,594	5,570,557	423,263
			82	7,198,543	5,259,603	5,713,737	454,134
			83	4,889,527	3,261,650	3,574,857	313,207
			84	14,159,980	8,220,549	9,126,418	905,869
			85	9,495,300	5,153,958	5,875,137	721,179
			86	11,086,374	7,348,660	8,135,427	786,767
	V	W	81	252,892	204,490	225,633	21,143
			82	268,905	225,435	247,743	22,308
			83	496,812	375,613	412,093	36,480
			84	503,482	323,810	363,713	39,903
			85	981,889	634,784	713,577	78,793
			86	1,253,560	943,284	1,045,462	102,178
SURINAM	O	E	83	3,016	1,129	1,129	
SWEDEN	V	E	85	39,059	29,475	32,297	2,822
TUNISIA	A	E	86	20,793	12,513	34,839	22,326
	O	E	83	10,392	8,422	8,846	424
	V	E	85	53,014	28,253	37,897	9,644
TURKEY	V	E	83	251,651	104,809	118,573	13,764
			84	237,189	131,589	146,157	14,568
			85	1,402	1,187	1,299	112
	V	W	85	2,196	1,080	1,451	371
			86	4,735	3,205	3,888	683
U KING	A	E	81	400	1,290	1,651	361
			82	735	1,935	2,278	343
			83	14	1,058	1,154	96
	V	E	84	127	1,026	1,130	104
VENEZ	V	E	86	137,520	132,120	139,305	7,185
YUGOSLV	O	W	84	1,940	2,019	2,019	
			85	13,631	12,429	12,429	

1763000 OLIVE OIL NOT UNDER 40 LBS (LB)

Country	Mode	Reg	Yr	Quantity	F.A.S.	C.I.F.	Charges
TOTAL			81	27,662,840	18,389,572	20,209,547	1,819,975
			82	28,150,452	18,387,767	20,184,258	1,796,491
			83	27,454,976	15,114,705	16,781,472	1,666,767
			84	28,601,825	15,606,744	17,345,126	1,738,382
			85	28,323,209	14,975,163	16,837,148	1,861,985
			86	36,388,870	22,300,078	24,047,815	1,747,737
ARGENT	V	E	86	68,078	41,422	45,035	3,613
	V	W	85	146,738	81,967	92,902	10,935
			86	147,091	94,494	105,599	11,105
BRAZIL	V	E	81	480	720	803	83
			83	8,580	562	685	123
			84	1,386	1,021	1,176	155
CANADA	A	W	86	12,300	10,230	10,894	664
	O	E	82	882	792	792	
			86	43,200	9,452	9,452	
CHINA T	V	E	86	2,094,370	1,489,600	1,584,496	94,896
DENMARK	V	E	84	30,864	18,172	20,244	2,072
FRANCE	N	E	83	356,756	192,730	202,069	9,339
			84	129,464	55,544	63,756	8,212
	O	E	84	2,159	2,168	2,423	255
			85	3,910	6,696	7,492	796
	V	E	81	77,636	53,760	59,360	5,600
			82	2,828,270	1,372,063	1,530,497	158,434
			83	2,941,080	1,384,354	1,529,726	145,372
			84	84,515	68,457	77,401	8,944

Crop
Product
TSUSA commodity number, description, and unit of quantity

Country	Mode	Reg	Yr	Quantity	F.A.S.	C.I.F.	Charges
			85	134,485	103,267	112,215	8,948
			86	67,806	73,183	79,902	6,719
	V	W	81	2,205	1,764	2,040	276
			82	39,989	33,524	38,044	4,520
			83	38,646	17,491	20,333	2,842
			84	473	1,458	1,646	188
			85	2,205	1,904	2,175	271
			86	3,074	3,698	4,149	451
GREECE	N	E	86	32,098	20,334	23,513	3,179
	V	E	81	54,203	49,449	54,555	5,106
			82	36,022	30,126	36,584	6,458
			83	58,936	45,821	53,237	7,416
			84	45,238	28,602	32,715	4,113
			85	80,976	57,014	66,283	9,269
			86	53,831	40,768	46,385	5,617
	V	W	82	5,049	5,006	5,392	386
			83	882	1,040	1,209	169
			84	9,557	8,463	9,828	1,365
			85	12,540	10,125	12,786	2,661
			86	7,296	6,380	7,812	1,432
INDIA	V	W	86	30,095	43,445	47,140	3,695
ISRAEL	V	E	86	20,607	15,188	18,642	3,454
ITALY	A	E	84	700	283	483	200
			85	1,940	1,470	3,099	1,629
	A	W	85	1,511	1,470	3,470	2,000
	N	E	81	7,884,001	3,985,264	4,411,209	425,945
			82	5,983,151	2,972,133	3,328,030	355,897
			83	4,814,992	2,015,203	2,305,660	290,457
			84	6,681,670	2,795,758	3,215,894	420,136
			85	4,250,446	1,907,717	2,188,910	281,193
	N	W	85	1,556,006	734,053	864,668	130,615
	O	E	82	77,110	35,326	38,495	3,169
			83	114	2,164	2,290	126
			84	1,775,339	722,709	772,745	50,036
			85	2,688,779	1,117,246	1,199,052	81,806
			86	2,806,786	1,609,333	1,690,425	81,092
	O	W	83	1,091	2,740	2,839	99
			85	24,391	13,776	16,949	3,173
	V	E	81	4,704,038	2,724,168	3,136,857	412,689
			82	4,182,133	2,170,792	2,538,138	367,346
			83	4,531,617	2,029,998	2,392,224	362,226
			84	3,631,226	1,727,242	2,010,109	282,867
			85	3,203,952	1,513,459	1,749,312	235,853
			86	10,422,673	5,751,883	6,258,621	506,738
	V	H	85	34,391	13,464	16,633	3,169
	V	W	81	714,998	422,753	493,701	70,948
			82	731,224	396,679	457,688	61,009
			83	1,495,787	682,686	797,988	115,302
			84	1,240,538	536,964	639,294	102,330
			85	6,081	10,362	12,023	1,661
			86	2,371,987	1,361,776	1,577,413	215,637
JAPAN	V	E	85	33,069	19,200	22,402	3,202
	V	H	84	381	402	425	23
			86	2,859	3,091	3,437	346
	V	W	85	1,403	2,000	2,073	73
LEBANON	O	E	85	2,569	1,700	1,818	118
MALTA	V	W	84	41,102	17,530	20,855	3,325
MEXICO	O	W	85	6,390	7,348	7,348	
			86	75,898	55,621	55,621	
MOROC	V	E	86	37,500	20,361	22,956	2,595
NETHLDS	V	W	84	42,075	17,186	20,926	3,740
PORTUGL	O	E	81	5,300	4,920	4,920	
			82	8,000	9,000	9,000	
			84	2,500	3,000	3,000	
			85	2,500	1,750	1,750	
	V	E	82	33,670	36,175	39,004	2,829
			83	49,783	49,370	52,613	3,243
			84	121,773	111,390	119,549	8,159
			85	145,419	130,706	144,703	13,997
			86	249,468	162,098	177,146	15,048
SPAIN	A	E	82	440	532	657	125
	N	E	81	46,304	35,905	38,798	2,893
			85	370,040	215,284	246,788	31,504
			86	271,164	191,149	212,078	20,929
	N	W	83	130,512	80,479	89,789	9,310
			84	149,656	96,597	108,626	12,029
	O	E	83	882	681	722	41
			84	12,000	9,000	9,325	325
			86	1,554,194	929,216	960,616	31,400
	V	E	81	11,268,270	8,962,323	9,664,062	701,739
			82	10,919,044	8,635,323	9,336,200	700,877
			83	9,883,672	6,349,375	6,964,540	615,165
			84	9,142,223	5,988,048	6,630,520	642,472
			85	9,200,818	5,433,480	6,184,469	750,989
			86	7,674,866	5,379,712	5,806,356	426,644
	V	W	81	267,637	220,097	240,800	20,703
			82	239,277	186,429	206,067	19,638
			83	158,731	100,367	114,147	13,780
			84	251,332	153,621	174,468	20,847
			85	748,078	407,185	477,467	70,282
			86	876,083	590,786	662,849	72,063
SWEDEN	V	W	85	35,274	16,440	19,968	3,528
			86	35,274	17,840	20,972	3,132
SWITZLD	V	E	85	87,964	37,212	43,501	6,289
	V	W	85	42,990	17,535	21,405	3,870
THAILND	V	W	82	1,452	2,138	2,251	113
TUNISIA	V	E	81	2,637,768	1,928,449	2,102,442	173,993
			82	3,027,260	2,480,734	2,593,938	113,204
			83	2,644,080	1,977,900	2,053,600	75,700
			84	3,196,670	2,204,000	2,318,489	114,489
			85	3,086,440	1,904,000	2,033,040	129,040
			86	2,915,209	1,929,201	2,066,720	137,519
TURKEY	V	E	82	37,479	20,995	23,481	2,486
			83	338,835	181,744	197,801	16,057
			84	1,967,097	1,013,379	1,063,626	50,247
			85	2,411,724	1,206,111	1,280,997	74,886
			86	4,495,706	2,436,281	2,534,886	98,605
U KING	A	E	85	180	1,222	1,450	228
	O	E	84	8,375	7,198	7,208	10
	V	E	84	32,672	16,506	17,806	1,300
			86	6,129	3,861	4,111	250
	V	W	84	840	2,046	2,589	543
			86	13,228	9,675	10,589	914

Olive, vegetable oil, inedible

1762800 OLIVE OIL, INEDIBLE (LB)

Country	Mode	Reg	Yr	Quantity	F.A.S.	C.I.F.	Charges
TOTAL			81	45,194	38,152	41,193	3,041
			82	87,580	51,778	56,208	4,430
			83	90,389	66,930	71,444	4,514
			84	31,879	22,861	24,441	1,580
			85	132,983	89,620	105,962	16,342
			86	129,395	100,220	112,105	11,885
FR GERM	A	E	86	18	1,344	1,391	47
FRANCE	A	W	85	2,158	3,232	4,852	1,620
	O	E	83	22,046	15,520	16,522	1,002
			84	4,409	3,104	3,305	201
	V	E	81	1,102	1,089	1,238	149
ISRAEL	A	E	86	7,168	5,376	5,921	545
	V	E	85	20,964	15,640	16,250	610
ITALY	A	E	85	5,212	4,221	10,831	6,610
	O	E	82	19,716	9,032	9,842	810
			85	20,944	12,033	13,663	1,630
	V	E	84	574	483	531	48
			85	200	3,345	3,761	416
			86	32,058	24,731	28,310	3,579
	V	W	85	49,259	28,274	32,208	3,934
			86	33,713	30,724	34,949	4,225
PORTUGL	V	E	86	18,188	10,670	11,749	1,079
SPAIN	O	E	81	44,092	37,063	39,955	2,892
			82	28,660	23,516	24,761	1,245
			83	68,343	51,410	54,922	3,512
			84	26,896	19,274	20,605	1,331
	V	E	85	39,204	19,230	21,605	2,375
			85	34,246	22,875	24,397	1,522
			86	38,250	27,375	29,785	2,410

Onion

Onion, dried

1404000 ONIONS, DRIED, DEHYDRATED (LB)

Country	Mode	Reg	Yr	Quantity	F.A.S.	C.I.F.	Charges
TOTAL			81	219,609	101,743	114,689	15,679
			82	26,160	34,353	42,018	7,665
			83	32,020	26,041	30,735	4,694
			84	243,703	169,073	203,472	34,399
			85	121,249	97,361	111,486	14,125
			86	58,348	19,134	20,307	1,173
BELGIUM	V	E	81	169,563	69,575	75,735	6,160
CANADA	O	E	81	450	295	295	
			83	1,050	3,349	3,349	
			85	680	3,100	3,100	
			86	44,000	5,830	5,830	

Crop
Product
TSUSA commodity number, description, and unit of quantity

Country	Mode	Reg	Yr	Quantity	F.A.S.	C.I.F.	Charges
	O	W	81	325	944	944	
			83	113	909	909	
CHILE	V	E	85	496	1,686	1,860	174
	V	W	84	148,820	130,319	153,907	23,588
			85	77,000	66,916	79,201	12,285
CHINA M	V	E	82	810	393	454	61
			84	1,170	1,799	1,996	197
	V	W	81	1,690	861	1,034	173
			82	9,125	2,961	3,715	754
			83	4,077	2,056	2,380	324
			84	5,805	5,116	5,565	449
CHINA T	V	E	81	2,500	2,896	3,209	313
			82	3,123	3,407	3,971	564
			83	300	729	906	177
			84	2,500	2,800	3,189	389
	V	W	84	123	260	289	29
			86	1,250	1,600	1,943	343
DENMARK	A	W	84	496	1,064	1,617	553
FR GERM	A	E	86	173	1,767	2,163	396
	O	E	85	63,250	10,964	15,180	4,216
			85	38,225	13,489	14,359	870
	V	E	84	1,846	3,489	3,830	341
	V	W	82	5,494	14,645	19,805	5,160
FRANCE	A	E	82	700	616	1,031	415
			83	6,072	3,764	5,837	2,073
			84	5,992	1,826	3,949	2,123
	A	W	84	149	312	417	105
	V	E	81	17,637	3,948	6,556	2,608
	V	W	85	292	1,919	2,199	280
HG KONG	V	W	82	650	455	523	68
			86	1,562	2,437	2,742	305
INDIA	O	E	84	1,435	3,263	3,589	326
INDNSIA	V	W	84	240	256	331	75
IRAN	V	W	82	2,205	1,457	1,511	54
			83	3,131	3,689	4,324	635
			84	10,034	3,835	5,290	1,455
IRELAND	V	W	85	1,715	2,261	2,404	143
ISRAEL	V	E	81	2,659	1,790	1,790	2,733
	V	W	81	22,057	11,326	14,007	2,681
ITALY	V	E	81	441	2,333	2,513	180
			84	302	497	538	41
JAPAN	V	H	81	24	941	1,033	92
			82	18	708	788	80
			83	158	614	659	45
	V	W	83	127	657	708	51
MEXICO	A	E	86	11,363	7,500	7,629	129
MOROC	A	E	84	573	1,016	1,340	324
NETHLDS	V	E	81	1,783	5,391	6,040	649
			82	3,085	5,729	6,038	309
			83	925	3,263	3,303	40
			85	1,496	3,280	3,491	211
	V	W	81	480	1,443	1,533	90
			82	585	1,546	1,686	140
			83	1,082	2,530	2,710	180
			84	765	1,280	1,397	117
			85	772	1,330	1,410	80
PERU	A	E	84	110	650	701	51
	V	E	85	573	3,380	3,462	82
REP SAF	A	E	83	14,960	4,224	5,386	1,162
U KING	O	E	82	206	1,218	1,243	25
			84	93	327	347	20
	V	E	82	159	1,218	1,253	35
			83	25	257	264	7

Onion, essential oil**
4528023 ONION AND GARLIC (LB)
(See Garlic, essential oil under Garlic)

Onion, flour
1406500 ONION FLOUR (LB)

Country	Mode	Reg	Yr	Quantity	F.A.S.	C.I.F.	Charges
TOTAL			81	9,691	6,644	7,203	559
			82	857	3,532	3,860	328
			83	10,351	14,535	15,347	812
			84	6,169	8,095	8,839	744
			85	21,542	32,507	34,597	2,090
			86	7,039	8,185	9,072	887
CANADA	O	E	81	2,250	1,249	1,249	
			83	803	1,371	1,371	
CHINA M	V	E	81	250	993	1,032	39
			86	6,510	4,945	5,541	596

Country	Mode	Reg	Yr	Quantity	F.A.S.	C.I.F.	Charges
	V	W	81	4,409	2,517	2,764	247
			82	250	650	695	45
			83	1,160	1,043	1,088	45
CHINA T	V	E	85	1,006	2,992	3,110	118
FRANCE	A	E	82	254	542	723	181
HG KONG	V	W	83	2,579	4,138	4,378	240
ISRAEL	V	E	85	19,841	25,278	27,000	1,722
	V	W	84	5,737	6,699	7,359	660
ITALY	V	E	81	2,782	1,885	2,158	273
			82	353	2,340	2,442	102
			83	5,309	5,558	5,918	360
			84	57	629	674	45
			86	529	3,240	3,531	291
JAPAN	V	W	85	695	4,237	4,487	250
KOR REP	V	W	83	500	2,425	2,592	167
NETHLDS	V	W	84	375	767	806	39

Onion, fresh or frozen
1369000 ONION SETS, FRESH OR FROZEN (LB)

Country	Mode	Reg	Yr	Quantity	F.A.S.	C.I.F.	Charges
TOTAL			81	2,206,274	795,408	896,828	101,360
			82	1,829,196	623,516	766,600	143,084
			83	2,417,639	693,713	864,543	170,830
			84	3,253,721	841,134	997,630	156,496
			85	3,427,539	748,384	878,151	129,767
			86	2,231,405	598,078	739,374	141,296
AUSTRIA	A	W	82	13,200	5,438	5,674	236
BELGIUM	A	E	83	1,760	1,232	1,689	457
			86	2,029	1,500	1,915	415
	V	E	81	14,286	10,221	12,004	1,783
			82	33,567	16,401	19,043	2,642
			83	2,909	2,555	2,739	184
			84	4,830	5,202	5,782	580
			85	15,450	7,984	9,538	1,554
			86	6,149	4,370	5,214	844
CANADA	O	E	81	926,591	295,083	295,991	908
			82	309,354	92,664	92,664	
			83	402,295	76,256	76,256	
			84	574,904	134,576	134,576	
			85	916,763	89,883	89,883	
			86	489,916	57,294	57,294	
CHINA T	V	W	86	42,500	24,829	26,332	1,503
DOM REP	A	E	83	4,400	484	937	453
			85	2,075	1,038	1,332	294
	V	E	81	11,850	2,487	3,103	616
			85	33,900	4,745	6,960	2,215
FRANCE	A	E	81	600	450	836	386
			82	700	448	502	54
			84	4,850	3,069	7,145	4,076
GUATMAL	V	E	86	10,200	3,570	5,996	2,426
ISRAEL	V	E	84	1,170	1,145	1,315	170
			86	6,060	1,830	2,909	1,079
JAPAN	V	W	85	11,000	10,364	12,225	1,861
MEXICO	O	E	81	89,370	3,411	3,411	
			84	320,600	31,498	31,498	
			85	90,680	9,637	9,637	
	O	W	81	65,888	8,557	8,557	
			82	36,936	6,156	6,156	
			83	37,954	8,028	8,028	
			84	468,330	37,899	37,899	
			85	151,989	45,473	45,473	
			86	179,307	49,804	49,804	
NETHLDS	A	E	86	1,887	1,666	2,191	525
	N	E	83	1,661,599	513,413	654,865	141,452
	V	E	81	1,088,345	465,288	561,479	96,131
			82	1,422,257	492,818	630,583	137,765
			83	281,535	77,848	102,123	24,275
			84	1,797,900	592,675	735,980	143,305
			85	1,654,996	528,886	648,379	119,493
			86	1,447,263	447,756	575,166	127,410
	V	W	81	9,344	9,911	11,447	1,536
			82	13,182	9,591	11,978	2,387
			83	25,187	13,897	17,906	4,009
			84	17,624	12,681	15,787	3,106
			85	2,923	1,599	2,201	602
			86	44,000	4,371	9,770	5,399
REP SAF	V	E	84	7,031	6,011	6,757	746
			85	7,062	4,920	5,812	892
SPAIN	A	E	85	2,205	1,200	1,996	796
	V	E	85	538,496	42,655	44,715	2,060
U KING	A	E	86	2,094	1,088	2,783	1,695
	V	E	84	56,482	16,378	20,891	4,513

Crop Product TSUSA commodity number, description, and unit of quantity Country	Mode	Reg	Yr	Quantity	F.A.S.	C.I.F.	Charges

1369300 ONIONS NSPF FRSH, CHLD, FRZ (LB)

Country	Mode	Reg	Yr	Quantity	F.A.S.	C.I.F.	Charges
TOTAL			81	133,109,401	22,556,187	23,142,186	581,232
			82	163,914,321	24,324,556	25,379,261	1,054,705
			83	202,426,319	24,570,568	25,034,469	463,901
			84	262,404,934	38,119,417	40,105,303	1,985,886
			85	259,669,705	39,748,146	40,996,989	1,248,843
			86	244,380,376	40,384,509	41,410,745	1,026,236
AUSTRAL	V	H	85	30,864	3,179	5,390	2,211
BELGIUM	A	E	81	9,790	6,894	9,416	2,522
			82	26,147	20,500	27,822	7,322
			83	92,718	52,296	69,106	16,810
			84	70,790	45,843	66,228	20,385
			85	27,071	18,635	27,522	8,887
			86	22,661	26,214	37,079	10,865
	A	W	81	6,613	4,984	8,330	3,346
			82	2,885	2,390	3,060	670
			83	19,514	14,950	20,462	5,512
			84	3,337	2,325	2,948	623
			85	44,584	13,917	33,613	19,696
			86	11,756	6,022	11,529	5,507
	N	E	81	152,260	70,694	92,362	21,668
			82	147,071	79,057	97,639	18,582
			83	252,548	143,206	192,910	49,704
			84	369,212	176,561	254,359	77,798
			85	376,951	153,990	209,375	55,385
			86	445,527	317,064	407,145	90,081
	N	W	81	117,297	47,097	79,427	32,330
			82	109,527	53,159	85,887	32,728
			83	122,965	52,211	77,059	24,848
			84	111,672	44,106	66,957	22,851
	O	E	85	38,575	9,107	12,003	2,896
			86	68,200	21,141	23,339	2,198
	V	E	81	24,000	13,200	13,287	87
BELIZE	A	E	83	551	380	408	28
BRAZIL	A	E	85	1,760	1,067	2,102	1,035
C RICA	V	E	84	40,500	8,100	12,325	4,225
CANADA	A	E	86	2,700	5,407	5,574	167
	A	H	82	1,988	2,187	2,342	155
	N	E	84	246,250	41,988	49,718	7,730
			85	27,259,638	1,964,562	1,964,562	
			86	270,350	33,039	38,943	5,904
	O	E	81	14,624,725	2,453,659	2,453,659	
			82	8,911,818	1,170,716	1,170,716	
			83	25,521,584	2,681,273	2,681,273	
			84	37,967,566	5,185,284	5,185,284	
			85	7,526,363	674,904	676,606	1,702
			86	35,560,481	2,782,973	2,782,975	2
	O	W	81	47,742	14,181	14,181	
			82	41,266	15,100	15,100	
			83	5,124	2,072	2,072	
			84	19,950	2,123	2,123	
			85	251,304	83,679	83,679	
			86	364,204	75,398	75,398	
	V	E	85	460,950	53,421	62,127	8,706
			86	711,400	86,823	105,392	18,569
CHILE	N	W	81	225,500	18,038	42,526	24,488
			84	1,435,780	155,445	248,109	92,664
	O	E	81	80,000	25,079	25,079	
	O	W	82	5,472	936	936	
	V	E	81	3,696,184	373,703	614,706	241,003
			82	6,719,870	807,719	1,259,642	451,923
			84	15,890,235	1,855,682	2,820,841	965,159
			85	2,776,456	307,300	473,736	166,436
			86	669,105	66,531	96,507	29,976
	V	W	81	240,954	16,632	34,825	18,193
			82	432,516	36,480	67,520	31,040
			86	210,554	20,491	43,081	22,590
CHINA M	N	W	84	9,945	3,054	4,243	1,189
	V	E	81	762	476	545	69
	V	W	81	23,460	8,354	10,557	2,203
			82	32,834	13,380	17,573	4,193
			83	31,295	7,892	11,015	3,123
			84	10,380	2,222	3,028	806
			86	6,057	2,208	2,499	291
CHINA T	O	W	81	1,320	1,567	1,567	
	V	E	86	1,500	1,409	1,575	166
	V	H	86	19,717	3,253	4,047	794
	V	W	82	317	416	477	61
			86	42,500	26,613	29,750	3,137
COLOMB	O	W	81	5,324	1,276	1,276	
CRIST I	O	E	86	35,700	3,490	3,490	
DOM REP	A	E	82	6,000	600	1,140	540

Country	Mode	Reg	Yr	Quantity	F.A.S.	C.I.F.	Charges
	V	E	84	150,850	35,014	43,704	8,690
			85	409,900	44,405	61,861	17,456
			86	44,900	2,665	4,449	1,784
ECUADOR	V	E	84	90,865	9,408	15,519	6,111
FINLAND	A	E	84	992	2,000	2,618	618
FR GERM	A	E	84	209	330	444	114
	V	E	81	44,000	18,480	22,149	3,669
FRANCE	A	E	81	33,234	15,465	31,453	15,988
			82	50,395	33,475	53,484	20,009
			83	69,760	36,701	67,722	31,021
			84	58,522	21,905	42,337	20,432
			85	30,634	19,632	32,799	13,167
			86	35,646	36,440	68,360	31,920
	A	W	84	22,600	7,209	12,533	5,324
			86	9,480	11,656	16,846	5,190
	N	E	81	340,470	208,447	272,890	64,443
			82	420,884	208,109	268,619	60,510
			83	468,983	286,104	375,483	89,379
			84	982,973	455,901	598,425	142,524
			85	1,256,028	575,592	749,090	173,498
			86	1,040,790	685,121	878,957	193,836
	N	W	81	306,363	106,184	159,299	53,115
			82	883,907	371,008	475,155	104,147
			83	737,814	369,358	474,472	105,114
			84	983,567	383,094	541,107	158,013
			85	1,809,034	513,310	794,553	281,243
			86	1,009,341	483,549	625,720	142,171
	O	E	84	10,000	1,524	3,090	1,566
			85	99,320	3,992	3,992	
	O	W	85	78,960	14,616	14,616	
	V	E	82	83,319	26,759	37,119	10,360
			83	187,671	76,329	99,534	23,205
			84	210,511	73,456	96,347	22,891
			85	207,013	50,436	69,765	19,329
			86	587,115	330,333	402,362	72,029
	V	W	81	22,046	9,541	11,476	1,935
			86	472,101	265,649	326,732	61,083
GIBRAT	V	W	85	36,200	4,517	10,980	6,463
GUATMAL	A	E	81	760	456	525	69
	N	E	81	169,099	14,621	27,091	12,470
	V	E	81	2,702	912	1,190	278
			82	197,498	14,833	27,506	12,673
			83	101,950	5,123	10,233	5,110
			84	45,867	2,293	4,355	2,062
			86	951,459	104,266	210,167	105,901
HAITI	A	W	81	3,050	1,708	2,857	1,149
HG KONG	V	W	81	1,875	752	828	76
			82	3,520	1,466	1,988	522
			83	38,580	9,832	11,149	1,317
			84	3,445	746	886	140
IRAN	V	E	82	7,919	10,651	12,130	1,479
ISRAEL	V	E	81	1,879	612	681	69
			85	27,456	14,826	17,274	2,448
			86	204,586	60,188	77,795	17,607
	V	W	86	48,677	16,523	21,661	5,138
ITALY	A	E	86	3,115	2,490	4,215	1,725
	A	W	84	1,181	730	845	115
	N	E	83	412,300	104,588	143,889	39,301
			85	448,091	117,025	197,510	80,485
	N	W	83	26,033	17,099	20,865	3,766
	V	E	81	244,555	119,026	153,002	33,976
			82	562,100	183,574	250,374	66,800
			84	532,600	193,356	252,554	59,198
			86	300,668	71,915	113,573	41,658
	V	W	86	34,000	5,568	11,561	5,993
JAMAICA	A	E	83	988	280	372	92
JAPAN	A	H	81	528	943	2,542	1,599
			82	572	712	1,921	1,209
	A	W	81	313	920	1,498	578
	N	W	85	123,855	10,915	15,544	4,629
	V	H	83	990	1,275	1,706	431
			84	1,188	1,532	1,920	388
			85	409	1,328	1,887	559
	V	W	83	440	467	478	11
MALTA	O	W	85	258,533	64,056	64,056	
MEXICO	O	E	81	69,424,294	5,713,272	5,713,302	
			82	95,209,828	5,857,495	5,878,298	20,803
			83	112,703,643	3,308,734	3,308,734	
			84	129,322,837	5,788,521	5,788,521	
			85	113,757,198	7,024,288	7,024,288	4
			86	84,969,886	3,935,664	3,935,664	
	O	W	81	42,832,631	13,148,810	13,156,648	5,250
			82	47,831,281	14,948,385	14,955,945	7,560
			83	60,761,135	17,227,493	17,230,855	3,362

Crop
Product
TSUSA commodity number, description, and unit of quantity

Country	Mode	Reg	Yr	Quantity	F.A.S.	C.I.F.	Charges
			84	69,438,579	22,796,133	22,801,658	5,525
			85	97,330,530	27,475,369	27,495,441	20,072
			86	114,737,187	30,542,511	30,544,770	2,259
MOROC	A	E	86	2,645	4,200	5,400	1,200
	O	E	81	10,388	3,700	4,118	418
	V	E	84	34,480	18,852	20,712	1,860
MOZAMBQ	O	W	85	63,328	16,305	16,305	
			86	20,958	8,888	8,888	
N ZEAL	N	W	81	17,250	4,963	4,963	
			83	40,264	2,683	4,703	2,020
			86	28,800	33,823	41,901	8,078
	O	W	82	23,500	5,524	5,524	
			85	4,400	1,200	1,200	
	V	E	84	104,021	14,090	25,397	11,307
	V	H	81	123,457	17,576	27,296	9,720
			82	572,176	82,170	134,163	51,993
			83	282,276	13,629	33,909	20,280
			84	1,494,759	289,031	425,376	136,345
			85	2,626,162	197,710	368,678	170,968
			86	1,046,103	65,148	145,438	80,290
	V	W	81	30,800	6,899	9,231	2,332
			82	101,347	21,241	35,501	14,260
			84	966,682	209,580	274,815	65,235
			86	26,455	6,366	8,612	2,246
NETHLDS	A	E	81	6,451	4,430	5,770	1,340
			82	3,570	2,747	3,985	1,238
			83	17,731	17,574	22,539	4,965
			84	19,982	10,744	15,864	5,120
			85	1,232	3,197	3,871	674
			86	6,073	6,976	10,222	3,246
	A	W	82	23,604	12,458	19,581	7,123
			83	23,100	14,295	21,275	6,980
			86	54,145	23,195	48,447	25,252
	N	E	82	808,000	230,777	280,234	49,457
			85	94,392	41,697	52,314	10,617
			86	6,878	4,952	6,115	1,163
	N	W	81	60,793	15,120	24,243	9,123
			82	34,824	25,665	32,472	6,807
			84	92,419	34,721	53,231	18,510
			85	168,918	76,979	111,973	34,994
	O	E	86	37,400	9,350	13,086	3,736
	V	E	81	54,344	14,551	21,694	4,994
			82	43,999	12,411	18,480	6,069
			83	323,593	110,625	125,570	14,945
			84	111,810	45,491	54,512	9,021
			86	89,755	42,597	49,939	7,342
	V	W	81	122,188	72,965	85,697	12,732
			85	44,092	14,617	21,766	7,149
			86	124,765	124,849	137,966	13,117
NICARAG	V	W	84	269,900	26,990	28,786	1,796
NIGERIA	V	E	84	2,028	270	313	43
PHIL R	V	W	86	49,223	16,442	20,686	4,244
SENEGAL	A	E	83	290	325	486	161
SPAIN	O	E	86	16,821	3,434	5,114	1,680
	V	E	82	614,367	72,456	136,928	64,472
			83	181,879	13,265	25,615	12,350
			84	1,117,550	151,315	231,817	80,502
			85	1,904,071	157,218	281,907	124,689
THAILND	V	E	85	2,750	1,104	1,104	
	V	W	83	600	509	575	66
U KING	A	E	86	2,297	1,273	1,867	594
	V	E	84	1,998	1,155	1,183	28
			85	39,683	12,887	16,651	3,764
			86	10,695	5,970	7,470	1,500
	V	W	84	6,607	2,700	2,994	294
VENEZ	A	E	85	19,000	1,600	5,288	3,688
	V	E	84	150,295	18,593	47,277	28,684

Onion, in brine or pickled
1414500 ONIONS IN BRINE OR PICKLED (LB)

Country	Mode	Reg	Yr	Quantity	F.A.S.	C.I.F.	Charges
TOTAL			81	2,958,447	1,348,850	1,607,361	258,511
			82	2,968,460	1,420,344	1,672,948	252,604
			83	3,108,669	1,340,087	1,547,935	207,848
			84	3,698,953	1,388,738	1,634,892	246,154
			85	4,017,444	1,312,858	1,616,766	303,908
			86	3,262,158	1,231,788	1,455,073	223,285
BELGIUM	V	E	81	3,375	1,306	1,606	300
			83	12,222	4,640	5,062	422
			84	106,430	50,201	55,727	5,526
			85	56,860	18,972	23,158	4,186
			86	148,503	60,097	66,310	6,213

Crop
Product
TSUSA commodity number, description, and unit of quantity

Country	Mode	Reg	Yr	Quantity	F.A.S.	C.I.F.	Charges
	V	W	82	26,400	15,441	17,116	1,675
			85	13,500	4,718	5,958	1,240
			86	25,201	13,583	14,883	1,300
BRAZIL	V	E	83	360	680	747	67
BULGAR	V	E	85	450	2,904	3,194	290
CANADA	O	E	82	17,200	10,062	10,062	
			85	11,600	5,112	5,112	
			86	336,150	135,673	135,673	
CHINA M	V	E	81	33,416	11,909	13,630	1,721
			82	52,052	18,884	22,381	3,497
			83	2,548	886	1,090	204
			84	3,381	1,443	1,831	388
	V	H	81	816	382	408	26
			82	8,175	3,969	4,358	389
			83	13,365	5,039	6,304	1,265
			84	20,361	7,513	9,377	1,864
			85	91,493	35,742	40,256	4,514
			86	38,903	16,373	19,416	3,043
	V	W	81	15,786	6,966	7,688	722
			82	82,700	31,206	35,317	4,111
			83	25,220	8,213	8,906	693
			84	98,564	32,429	37,126	4,697
			85	77,401	28,342	30,835	2,493
			86	81,883	30,981	34,070	3,089
CHINA T	V	E	84	875	1,733	1,789	56
	V	H	82	4,950	3,100	3,429	329
			83	2,475	1,550	1,746	196
			84	7,437	3,240	3,812	572
			86	4,960	2,000	2,430	430
	V	W	81	4,960	1,873	2,107	234
			82	476	790	861	71
DOM REP	V	E	84	175,000	22,817	32,492	9,675
FR GERM	O	E	81	585	647	718	71
			82	110	485	545	60
	V	E	81	3,444	3,005	3,302	297
			82	4,028	3,390	3,753	363
			83	5,668	4,098	4,488	390
			84	11,672	7,917	8,784	867
			85	18,255	11,865	14,249	2,384
			86	11,046	8,835	9,807	972
FRANCE	V	E	81	64	283	293	10
			83	29	290	307	17
			84	635	954	1,136	182
			85	3,072	2,196	2,581	385
			86	23,774	24,175	26,468	2,293
	V	W	82	3,307	2,479	2,689	210
			84	1,515	1,010	1,105	95
GREECE	V	E	86	125	2,087	3,208	1,121
GUATMAL	V	E	83	2,817	1,660	1,895	235
HG KONG	V	E	81	17,969	13,425	14,558	1,133
			82	4,740	3,662	4,157	495
			83	3,390	3,069	3,487	418
			84	1,620	1,106	1,260	154
			85	2,160	1,530	1,712	182
			86	3,213	3,283	3,577	294
	V	H	86	12,188	5,160	6,049	889
	V	W	81	7,695	6,251	6,643	392
			82	10,725	7,033	7,780	747
			83	2,681	2,401	2,635	234
			84	4,603	1,589	1,686	97
			85	4,551	1,665	1,746	81
			86	6,507	2,635	2,924	289
INDIA	V	E	81	595	573	718	145
			86	441	374	419	45
			86	44,048	14,983	17,390	2,407
	V	W	84	6,429	3,309	3,900	591
IRELAND	V	E	83	2,143	2,063	2,558	495
ISRAEL	A	W	83	1,030	1,200	1,566	366
	N	E	83	6,094	3,913	4,323	410
	O	E	81	938	522	671	149
	V	E	81	899,119	354,916	437,919	83,003
			82	1,198,296	470,791	574,996	104,205
			83	1,099,488	387,608	455,333	67,725
			84	1,126,591	431,656	505,391	73,735
			85	1,264,038	310,394	378,729	68,335
			86	679,988	223,568	277,233	53,665
	V	W	81	403,215	139,719	180,581	40,862
			82	251,741	82,622	107,644	25,022
			83	579,624	187,770	232,965	45,195
			84	649,683	231,228	271,629	40,401
			85	978,933	325,837	406,345	80,508
			86	496,105	152,907	181,198	28,291
ITALY	O	E	81	971	779	855	76
			82	23,810	13,683	15,370	1,687

Country	Mode	Reg	Yr	Quantity	F.A.S.	C.I.F.	Charges
			84	481	361	361	
	V	E	81	5,724	3,898	4,752	854
			82	1,169	788	878	90
			83	4,924	3,035	3,403	368
			84	5,088	4,137	4,573	436
			85	4,370	1,354	1,651	·297
			86	12,163	19,035	20,565	1,530
	V	W	84	196	280	303	23
JAPAN	V	E	81	2,981	6,244	6,793	549
			82	1,270	2,534	2,734	200
			83	609	1,336	1,450	114
			84	2,052	4,981	5,477	496
			86	2,097	6,398	6,772	374
	V	H	81	11,712	22,930	25,935	3,005
			82	21,098	42,367	49,481	7,114
			83	19,143	37,790	43,367	5,577
			84	13,107	27,180	30,914	3,734
			85	4,067	7,356	8,520	1,164
			86	5,312	11,263	12,585	1,322
	V	W	81	8,528	17,130	18,243	1,113
			82	6,240	12,008	12,887	879
			83	15,143	30,361	32,096	1,735
			84	12,351	23,981	25,911	1,930
			85	16,419	19,481	20,436	955
			86	4,115	9,260	9,841	581
KOR REP	V	E	83	109	329	354	25
	V	W	81	15,926	10,991	12,101	1,110
			82	7,226	7,866	8,452	586
N ZEAL	V	E	85	15,960	15,976	17,496	1,520
	V	W	85	3,200	2,267	2,519	252
NETHLDS	N	E	82	73,041	30,263	36,403	6,140
			83	175,224	84,380	92,339	7,959
	O	E	81	328,942	129,391	147,119	17,728
			82	473,874	254,619	292,371	37,752
			83	443,672	220,472	243,307	22,835
			84	581,264	161,935	199,363	37,428
			85	763,056	203,981	275,482	71,501
			86	380,281	106,137	125,953	19,816
	V	E	81	830,929	374,626	430,957	56,331
			82	521,146	261,065	298,020	36,955
			83	599,577	267,212	304,204	36,992
			84	725,477	261,870	305,131	43,261
			85	456,939	149,466	187,053	37,587
			86	715,847	220,164	285,477	65,313
	V	W	81	256,730	121,611	151,485	29,874
			82	107,259	61,559	69,170	7,611
			83	8,881	4,528	5,509	981
			84	31,058	12,835	15,601	2,766
			85	6,478	2,868	3,926	1,058
			86	82,053	25,236	30,726	5,490
PAKISTN	O	E	85	7,788	27,258	27,258	
PERU	V	E	85	39,683	9,900	11,700	1,800
PHIL R	V	W	83	270	338	373	35
POLAND	O	E	84	2,600	700	978	278
	V	E	81	13,895	3,816	5,520	1,704
			83	10,800	2,880	3,914	1,034
			84	4,800	1,400	1,833	433
			85	9,158	1,652	2,153	501
REP SAF	V	W	83	2,250	2,580	3,046	466
SPAIN	V	E	81	720	2,448	2,791	343
			82	3,892	2,134	2,750	616
			85	16,351	12,884	15,982	3,098
			86	58,430	38,875	46,130	7,255
	V	W	84	8,879	1,621	2,173	552
			86	1,943	2,488	3,482	994
SWEDEN	V	E	82	504	330	356	26
SWITZLD	O	E	85	32,166	16,909	16,909	
THAILND	V	E	83	360	262	303	41
			84	721	556	623	67
	V	W	83	1,195	1,311	1,407	96
			84	720	636	693	57
U KING	A	E	82	1,116	1,002	1,146	144
			84	939	625	862	237
	N	E	85	3,278	3,904	4,694	790
	O	E	81	1,625	2,244	2,636	392
			82	4,007	4,073	5,162	1,089
			83	1,853	2,252	2,737	485
			84	5,415	6,619	7,622	1,003
			85	5,700	8,189	10,436	2,247
	V	E	81	62,826	81,674	93,316	11,642
			82	38,140	47,230	53,360	6,130
			83	38,675	39,004	44,749	5,745
			84	53,355	48,323	56,134	7,811
			85	62,181	46,212	55,527	9,315
			86	65,691	73,343	84,772	11,429
	V	W	81	24,961	29,291	34,016	4,725
			82	19,768	24,909	29,320	4,411
			83	26,830	26,937	31,965	5,028
			84	35,213	32,179	38,876	6,697
			85	36,337	29,601	35,908	6,307
			86	21,632	23,249	28,134	4,885
VENEZ	V	E	85	12,000	4,323	5,241	918

Onion, prepared or preserved
1415000 ONIONS PRES NT SALTD PICKLED (LB)

Country	Mode	Reg	Yr	Quantity	F.A.S.	C.I.F.	Charges
TOTAL			81	5,348,793	3,286,298	3,352,279	66,071
			82	5,786,961	3,401,251	3,475,279	74,028
			83	6,372,653	3,730,201	3,786,654	56,453
			84	8,431,159	5,412,553	5,531,874	119,321
			85	10,014,435	6,553,052	6,673,319	120,267
			86	8,921,636	6,185,123	6,306,806	121,683
BELGIUM	N	E	81	186,747	68,779	76,766	7,987
			82	173,707	62,711	69,047	6,336
			83	249,486	99,528	109,238	9,710
	O	E	83	10,145	2,721	3,069	348
			85	4,002	1,219	1,701	482
	V	E	81	180,801	70,363	80,466	10,103
			82	287,140	102,803	116,626	13,823
			83	249,901	94,172	106,644	12,472
			84	453,147	163,077	190,656	27,579
			85	412,158	151,581	177,393	25,812
			86	233,495	107,712	121,274	13,562
	V	W	81	115,911	40,433	47,140	6,707
			82	156,389	50,089	58,609	8,520
			83	192,815	58,590	69,165	10,575
			84	181,169	72,524	86,116	13,592
			85	130,238	56,294	68,377	12,083
			86	85,097	45,747	53,114	7,367
CANADA	O	E	81	4,191,593	2,905,597	2,905,497	
			82	4,690,343	2,981,019	2,981,019	
			83	5,375,822	3,284,281	3,284,281	
			84	7,228,322	4,874,222	4,874,222	
			85	8,471,800	5,991,485	5,991,485	
			86	7,612,617	5,529,104	5,529,665	561
	O	W	83	19,866	10,885	10,885	
			85	24,409	17,184	17,184	
			86	13,024	9,186	9,186	
CHINA M	O	E	85	6,297	1,490	1,706	216
	V	E	81	16,678	5,362	6,547	1,185
			82	4,556	1,819	1,979	160
			83	29,272	10,218	12,217	1,999
			84	4,063	2,380	2,901	521
			85	6,942	3,135	4,000	865
			86	14,186	4,592	5,095	503
	V	H	84	1,219	474	535	61
	V	W	81	4,410	1,812	1,939	127
			82	8,000	3,813	3,989	176
			84	4,079	1,574	1,684	110
			85	33,182	11,954	13,586	1,632
			86	16,312	3,800	4,061	261
CHINA T	V	E	82	3,743	5,100	5,803	703
			83	8,270	11,451	12,649	1,198
			84	2,280	3,131	3,364	233
			85	16,114	5,973	6,631	658
			86	5,000	6,420	7,010	590
	V	W	81	4,656	6,028	6,370	342
			82	6,842	9,566	10,431	865
			83	7,255	11,632	12,409	777
			84	38,358	21,082	23,215	2,133
			85	20,235	18,323	20,763	2,440
			86	17,194	26,333	27,747	1,414
DENMARK	V	E	81	1,102	1,817	1,984	167
			85	610	1,192	1,346	154
			86	14,030	17,664	20,846	3,182
	V	W	81	551	528	598	70
DOM REP	V	E	81	42,327	14,967	16,318	1,351
			83	72,000	37,500	41,392	3,892
			86	32,400	12,150	12,899	749
FR GERM	A	E	83	1,400	3,027	3,919	892
	O	E	82	398	1,271	1,271	
			83	331	1,275	1,275	
			84	446	941	965	24
	V	E	84	765	655	785	130
			85	13,419	7,581	8,786	1,205
			86	28,785	17,031	18,353	1,322

Crop Product TSUSA commodity number, description, and unit of quantity Country	Mode	Reg	Yr	Quantity	F.A.S.	C.I.F.	Charges
FRANCE	N	E	84	33,481	13,492	16,081	2,589
			85	4,246	2,508	3,576	1,068
	O	E	83	635	665	742	77
	V	E	82	10,006	4,407	4,912	505
			83	33	432	581	149
			84	3,603	2,426	2,670	244
			86	12,348	8,660	9,721	1,061
	V	W	84	1,403	690	732	42
HG KONG	V	E	81	6,495	5,652	6,214	562
			82	3,510	2,688	2,918	230
			83	3,105	1,744	2,022	278
			84	3,240	5,296	5,652	356
			85	2,700	2,070	2,399	329
			86	2,565	1,843	2,070	227
	V	W	81	5,130	4,140	4,368	228
			82	3,240	2,761	2,971	210
			83	5,700	3,833	4,072	239
			84	4,515	2,694	2,872	178
			85	810	1,133	1,219	86
INDNSIA	V	W	83	453	537	619	82
ISRAEL	O	E	84	24,600	11,524	15,767	4,243
	V	E	81	1,256	1,535	1,677	142
			82	10,721	4,941	5,596	655
			83	81,678	40,846	47,624	6,778
			84	408,034	168,905	230,752	61,847
			85	445,745	182,279	242,959	60,680
			86	492,056	207,321	276,851	69,530
	V	W	81	453,537	92,456	121,825	29,369
			82	409,683	135,986	175,314	39,328
			83	36,488	13,623	18,015	4,392
			85	311,240	21,054	25,604	4,550
			86	58,098	21,340	26,731	5,391
ITALY	A	W	86	372	1,236	1,961	725
	O	E	81	485	863	890	27
	V	E	82	2,474	3,407	3,978	571
			84	9,582	14,663	15,775	1,112
			85	21,995	32,907	35,941	3,034
			86	4,004	8,911	10,169	1,258
JAPAN	V	E	81	447	884	961	77
			82	1,348	3,293	3,642	349
			83	2,082	4,375	4,800	425
			84	2,921	7,526	8,324	798
			85	625	2,338	2,588	250
	V	H	81	212	634	764	130
			83	138	396	440	44
			86	742	1,014	1,110	96
	V	W	81	8,780	15,041	15,868	817
			82	11,506	22,248	23,513	1,265
			83	16,354	30,173	31,652	1,479
			84	19,713	39,837	41,937	2,100
			85	3,960	4,442	4,708	266
			86	30,326	17,548	18,511	963
KOR REP	V	E	83	1,200	1,150	1,252	102
MEXICO	O	E	86	72,327	53,339	53,339	
NETHLDS	A	E	86	1,515	1,059	2,680	1,621
	A	W	84	1,008	816	1,506	690
	O	E	81	31,746	14,543	16,392	1,849
			86	4,922	2,717	2,744	27
	V	E	81	93,041	33,382	38,085	4,703
			85	52,858	18,368	21,697	3,329
			86	59,034	23,492	27,192	3,700
	V	W	81	794	476	532	56
			84	3,492	2,655	2,860	205
			85	11,016	5,916	6,385	469
			86	72,379	22,149	25,799	3,650
REP SAF	O	E	86	7,480	5,644	5,644	
SPAIN	V	E	83	1,500	589	629	40
			84	1,481	1,580	2,029	449
			85	3,364	1,552	2,016	464
			86	22,982	18,579	21,553	2,974
THAILND	V	E	81	2,094	1,006	1,078	72
			83	660	1,650	1,784	134
			84	238	389	474	85
			86	966	2,325	2,565	240
	V	W	83	6,064	4,908	5,279	371
			85	375	1,450	1,645	195
			86	5,322	6,879	7,413	534
U KING	V	E	85	4,941	1,789	1,789	
			86	2,058	1,328	1,503	175
	V	W	82	5,355	3,329	3,661	332
YEMAN S	O	E	85	11,154	7,835	7,835	

Onion, seed
1266100 ONION SEED (LB)

Country	Mode	Reg	Yr	Quantity	F.A.S.	C.I.F.	Charges
TOTAL			81	485,991	1,910,490	1,964,249	53,749
			82	525,384	3,075,910	3,138,029	62,119
			83	281,363	1,852,373	1,898,452	46,079
			84	372,502	2,180,206	2,240,118	59,912
			85	343,441	1,515,856	1,571,496	55,640
			86	290,807	1,710,697	1,767,720	57,023
ARGENT	A	W	83	101	505	842	337
AUSTRAL	A	W	81	71	923	1,173	250
			83	99	394	644	250
			84	758	4,420	6,912	2,492
			85	150	1,508	1,652	144
			86	165	2,607	2,740	133
	N	W	81	492	3,622	3,935	313
			83	628	4,156	4,516	360
	O	W	82	33	336	358	22
	V	W	85	7,277	24,758	25,033	275
			86	771	6,012	6,283	271
AUSTRIA	A	W	83	39	2,532	2,704	172
BRAZIL	A	W	82	66	528	714	186
	N	W	82	538	4,880	4,908	28
CANADA	O	E	81	11,194	34,070	34,070	
			82	3,090	7,508	7,508	
			86	55	2,340	2,340	
	O	W	83	1,250	350	350	
CHILE	V	W	81	477	8,074	8,133	59
			84	1,753	19,234	19,474	240
			86	11,841	61,685	62,093	408
DENMARK	A	E	82	440	6,072	6,584	512
			84	50	704	820	116
	V	E	81	1,100	8,346	8,758	412
			83	1,102	3,635	3,801	166
			84	882	3,000	3,140	140
			85	7,716	26,320	27,060	740
			86	3,249	11,079	11,861	782
	V	W	81	18,730	62,170	65,569	3,399
			82	6,393	20,183	21,379	1,196
			83	13,338	43,321	45,926	2,605
			84	2,769	10,702	11,059	357
			85	2,141	7,303	7,748	445
FR GERM	O	E	82	1	714	744	30
	V	W	81	268	3,919	4,030	111
			84	2,205	4,020	4,446	426
FRANCE	A	E	84	110	1,375	1,385	10
	A	W	86	670	9,654	10,545	891
	N	E	81	1,310	8,681	10,924	2,243
	N	W	82	10,481	35,292	36,452	1,160
	O	E	83	100	455	455	
	V	E	82	1,102	5,778	5,945	167
			84	523	4,046	4,456	410
	V	W	81	39,833	129,334	136,704	7,370
			82	7,914	29,907	31,108	1,201
			83	24,433	85,126	89,022	3,896
			84	20,730	74,037	78,811	4,774
ICELAND	V	W	85	661	7,215	7,380	165
INDIA	V	W	83	849	471	582	111
			86	1,431	1,149	1,358	209
ISRAEL	A	E	82	882	4,242	6,755	2,513
			84	104	431	466	35
			86	1,433	11,752	13,241	1,489
	A	W	85	1,280	7,312	10,774	3,462
			86	1,499	12,257	14,087	1,830
	N	E	83	1,273	8,599	9,559	960
	N	W	84	21,163	104,645	109,064	4,419
			86	20,562	90,514	97,574	7,060
	O	E	81	1,200	11,415	13,815	2,400
			84	600	4,350	5,405	1,055
	V	E	81	4,893	26,357	27,632	1,275
			82	300	2,175	2,291	116
			85	1,500	8,550	9,050	500
			86	1,900	10,706	11,032	326
	V	W	81	123,195	674,943	691,497	16,554
			82	53,345	323,746	331,912	8,166
			83	49,352	346,631	354,729	8,098
			84	19,988	123,546	126,528	2,982
			85	122,897	458,856	477,111	18,255
			86	37,650	242,570	248,860	6,290
ITALY	A	E	83	75	327	535	208
	A	W	86	243	3,134	3,684	550
	O	E	81	18,452	55,910	55,910	

Crop
Product
TSUSA commodity number, description, and unit of quantity

Country	Mode	Reg	Yr	Quantity	F.A.S.	C.I.F.	Charges
			82	26,820	103,316	103,316	
			83	16,060	64,143	64,143	
			84	8,250	32,931	32,931	
			86	8,140	40,630	40,630	
	V	E	81	3,308	13,537	13,842	305
			82	1,764	10,869	11,193	324
			85	6,836	30,442	31,722	1,280
			86	3,968	14,623	15,242	619
	V	W	81	5,968	20,745	21,429	684
			82	5,300	24,487	25,435	948
			83	3,408	31,965	32,407	442
			84	2,642	20,443	20,864	421
			85	1,213	7,040	7,671	631
JAMAICA	A	W	84	3,948	6,870	9,976	3,106
JAPAN	A	E	81	98	1,908	2,348	440
			82	150	10,040	10,833	793
			83	500	4,593	4,927	334
			84	61	2,231	2,438	207
			85	1,072	20,080	22,899	2,819
			86	500	9,425	11,904	2,479
	A	W	81	91	3,461	3,885	424
			82	50	1,063	1,156	93
			84	55	538	661	123
			85	125	2,500	2,909	409
	N	W	81	2,429	35,006	35,977	971
			82	850	11,358	13,698	2,340
			83	77	882	1,046	164
			84	4,115	54,348	58,262	3,914
			85	4,257	96,225	99,456	3,231
			86	13,010	265,027	271,675	6,648
	O	E	82	100	1,800	1,980	180
			83	75	1,376	1,865	489
			85	451	13,477	13,477	
			86	891	33,901	33,901	
	V	E	81	400	6,000	6,120	120
			82	230	3,853	3,910	57
			83	200	3,461	3,587	126
			84	493	8,183	8,674	491
	V	H	81	44	594	627	33
			82	70	1,072	1,137	65
			83	33	714	739	25
			84	33	707	741	34
	V	W	83	1,299	22,679	23,036	357
			84	258	352	390	38
KOR REP	V	W	84	850	3,720	3,909	189
			85	1,102	11,250	11,419	169
			86	330	1,875	1,991	116
MALI	A	E	85	1,000	25,000	25,848	848
MEXICO	A	W	82	971	17,664	18,590	926
	O	W	81	151,784	290,873	290,873	
			82	136,573	646,933	646,933	
			83	51,006	77,240	77,240	
			84	30,727	56,515	56,515	
			85	18,254	30,354	30,354	
			86	13,775	3,118	3,118	
N ZEAL	A	H	81	220	2,304	2,646	342
			85	3,224	4,856	5,193	337
	A	W	81	1,375	16,988	18,092	1,104
			82	1,019	28,572	30,430	1,858
			83	593	8,336	8,823	487
			84	616	8,008	8,564	556
			86	353	4,435	4,758	323
	N	W	84	209	2,043	2,235	192
	V	W	86	220	3,000	3,090	90
NETHLDS	A	E	81	200	3,605	3,760	155
			82	22	1,750	1,763	13
			83	21	588	627	39
			84	110	728	808	80
			86	400	10,000	10,529	529
	A	W	83	164	3,367	3,549	182
			84	55	385	593	208
			86	290	7,250	7,852	602
	N	E	81	800	9,590	10,120	520
			85	2,995	17,638	18,720	1,082
	N	W	84	766	3,560	4,022	462
			85	22,566	161,706	164,273	2,567
			86	45,889	317,538	324,235	6,697
	O	E	81	5,400	24,650	25,475	825
			82	11,898	44,678	48,795	4,117
			83	3,470	14,844	15,290	446
			84	2,200	7,847	8,111	264
			86	500	4,875	4,875	
	V	E	81	39,130	103,136	108,365	5,229
			83	2,418	16,345	17,177	832
			84	22,228	234,869	238,477	3,608
			85	400	1,445	1,476	31
			86	4,607	27,271	28,293	1,022
	V	W	81	34,528	225,052	229,181	4,129
			82	14,017	126,629	128,347	1,718
			83	2,099	41,277	41,601	324
			84	20,284	88,288	91,142	2,854
			85	441	1,232	1,469	237
			86	2,205	9,074	9,536	462
PHIL R	A	W	86	100	1,410	1,836	426
REP SAF	V	E	81	10,152	60,910	62,944	2,034
			82	57,051	375,694	384,295	8,601
			83	28,992	470,341	479,257	8,916
			84	165,622	1,149,626	1,169,588	19,962
			85	43,644	271,033	275,714	4,681
	V	W	81	8,830	62,316	64,245	1,929
			82	183,891	1,223,396	1,248,139	24,743
			83	75,057	572,451	587,165	14,714
			84	35,968	133,481	138,367	4,886
			85	92,239	279,756	293,088	13,332
			86	114,098	486,431	503,070	16,639
U KING	A	E	82	23	1,375	1,421	46
			83	258	8,906	9,716	810
			84	1,360	9,262	10,092	830
			86	17	1,832	1,901	69
	A	W	81	4	754	819	65
	O	E	84	17	761	792	31
			86	45	3,523	3,586	63
	V	E	81	15	1,297	1,351	54
			83	2,994	12,363	12,592	229

Opium Poppy

Opium, alkaloid
4371400 OPIUM ALKALOIDS (AOZ)

Country	Mode	Reg	Yr	Quantity	F.A.S.	C.I.F.	Charges
TOTAL			81	72,808	123,891	129,111	5,220
			82	489	8,302	8,388	86
			83	79	19,884	20,035	151
			84	65	4,044	4,186	142
			85	31,738	308,867	317,763	8,896
			86	1,523	75,193	75,659	466
AUSTRAL	A	E	85	27,122	71,521	71,881	360
	A	W	85	123	17,826	17,910	84
CANADA	O	E	86	368	3,400	3,400	
FRANCE	A	E	84	64	3,484	3,595	111
			85	869	94,031	94,686	655
			86	768	17,081	17,244	163
HUNGARY	V	E	81	35,200	44,200	45,826	1,626
NETHLDS	A	E	85	35	4,286	4,370	84
			86	212	27,150	27,233	83
	N	E	83	1	252	319	67
SENEGAL	A	E	86	48	5,949	6,000	51
SWITZLD	A	E	81	35	3,511	3,579	68
			85	26	2,263	2,330	67
			86	112	18,619	18,703	84
U KING	A	E	81	95	26,711	26,865	154
			82	489	8,302	8,388	86
			83	78	19,632	19,716	84
			85	3,563	118,940	126,586	7,646
			86	15	2,994	3,079	85
	A	W	84	1	560	591	31
	V	E	81	37,478	49,469	52,841	3,372

Opium, natural drug
4357000 OPIUM (CLB)

Country	Mode	Reg	Yr	Quantity	F.A.S.	C.I.F.	Charges
TOTAL			81	25,284	4,799,349	4,916,419	117,070
			82	175,142	10,515,804	10,692,902	177,098
			83	148,877	14,659,603	14,910,420	250,817
			84	76,600	11,548,777	12,164,043	615,266
			85	144,291	13,098,492	13,561,783	463,291
			86	74,872	8,980,941	9,230,816	249,875
FRANCE	A	E	81	1,978	234,703	237,914	3,211
HUNGARY	A	E	81	22	5,000	5,116	116
INDIA	A	E	82	119,077	1,702,792	1,715,943	13,151
			85	8,333	870,540	980,118	109,578
			86	3,684	598,276	610,947	12,671
	N	E	83	24,907	3,715,766	3,915,590	199,824

Crop Product TSUSA commodity number, description, and unit of quantity Country	Mode	Reg	Yr	Quantity	F.A.S.	C.I.F.	Charges
			84	47,375	7,355,119	7,866,016	510,897
	V	E	81	23,284	4,559,646	4,673,389	113,743
			82	56,065	8,813,012	8,976,959	163,947
			83	123,970	10,943,837	10,994,830	50,993
			84	29,225	4,193,658	4,298,027	104,369
			85	135,958	12,227,952	12,581,665	353,713
			86	71,188	8,382,665	8,619,869	237,204

Poppy, seed
1753600 POPPY SEED (CWT)

Country	Mode	Reg	Yr	Quantity	F.A.S.	C.I.F.	Charges
TOTAL			81	62,657	2,336,235	2,728,643	392,408
			82	73,053	4,231,192	4,685,044	453,852
			83	68,360	4,312,109	4,735,094	422,985
			84	95,809	3,196,886	3,648,729	451,843
			85	78,473	1,936,930	2,455,916	518,986
			86	104,774	2,087,376	2,614,608	527,232
AUSTRAL	N	E	85	992	25,245	27,574	2,329
			86	3,686	73,822	99,413	25,591
	O	E	86	1,066	20,916	27,609	6,693
	V	E	81	13,063	451,935	551,892	99,957
			82	17,201	875,011	1,012,794	137,783
			83	19,049	1,175,627	1,340,291	164,664
			84	27,956	1,117,631	1,338,711	221,080
			85	29,360	633,949	856,837	222,888
			86	34,502	694,544	929,209	234,665
	V	W	81	4,682	164,618	195,378	30,760
			82	4,908	242,104	280,166	38,062
			83	4,431	272,794	304,115	31,321
			84	2,423	107,868	128,646	20,778
			85	13,136	310,728	417,804	107,076
			86	15,358	341,495	441,348	99,853
AUSTRIA	V	E	83	353	26,984	29,599	2,615
			84	2,043	85,685	102,840	17,155
BELGIUM	V	W	82	310	20,224	22,076	1,852
			83	310	22,688	24,455	1,767
			84	310	13,823	15,764	1,941
			85	441	16,583	20,768	4,185
			86	630	18,511	22,111	3,600
CANADA	O	E	82	9	798	798	
			83	369	2,349	2,349	
			84	280	24,627	24,627	
FR GERM	A	W	84	4	359	503	144
	V	E	83	310	21,390	22,390	1,000
HONDURA	V	E	83	880	38,377	41,169	2,792
INDIA	N	E	83	11	1,260	1,310	50
	O	E	83	18	1,084	1,157	73
			84	20	1,665	1,891	226
			85	11	1,326	1,562	236
	V	E	81	52	3,059	3,730	671
			82	274	5,896	7,266	1,370
			83	135	4,147	4,530	383
			84	825	8,196	9,119	923
			85	50	9,827	10,855	1,028
	V	W	81	97	6,408	7,546	1,138
			82	45	2,722	3,238	516
			83	26	2,065	2,415	350
			84	9	989	1,176	187
			85	11	1,116	1,200	84
JAPAN	V	W	83	6	564	645	81
KOR REP	V	E	84	22	750	815	65
MEXICO	V	E	81	353	12,143	14,639	2,496
N ZEAL	V	W	85	360	9,720	12,726	3,006
NETHLDS	N	E	83	20,144	1,274,153	1,360,768	86,615
			85	1,293	34,780	41,865	7,085
	O	E	81	2,996	106,322	119,563	13,241
			82	1,232	68,535	73,620	5,085
			83	769	45,849	49,049	3,200
			84	1,254	64,068	70,475	6,407
			86	505	12,262	14,831	2,569
	O	W	83	25	1,488	1,638	150
	V	E	81	13,855	575,901	648,747	72,846
			82	32,635	2,030,336	2,199,205	168,869
			83	4,389	323,137	345,438	22,301
			84	20,100	1,013,013	1,107,278	94,265
			85	17,157	498,698	585,343	86,645
			86	12,274	423,204	486,713	63,509
	V	W	81	1,823	81,585	93,263	11,678
			82	2,023	150,881	167,564	16,683
			83	3,514	251,807	277,468	25,661
			84	13,107	137,458	151,600	14,142
			85	4,204	124,663	148,551	23,888

Country	Mode	Reg	Yr	Quantity	F.A.S.	C.I.F.	Charges
			86	21,989	134,040	153,368	19,328
PAKISTN	O	E	83	17	991	1,074	83
	V	E	85	44	1,654	2,005	351
			86	125	4,880	5,645	765
POLAND	V	E	81	331	13,880	15,256	1,376
			82	330	17,163	18,645	1,482
ROMANIA	V	E	81	4,916	206,235	225,617	19,382
			82	1,060	78,916	84,866	5,950
			84	440	15,400	18,261	2,861
			85	1,290	27,720	34,673	6,953
			86	3,086	65,412	79,724	14,312
SALVADR	V	E	85	740	24,364	27,764	3,400
SINGAPR	V	E	81	433	14,605	17,688	3,083
SPAIN	V	E	83	2,110	111,673	127,024	15,351
SWEDEN	V	W	83	110	6,785	7,479	694
TOKELAU	V	E	85	20	4,774	5,039	265
TURKEY	V	E	81	18,753	655,981	782,275	126,294
			82	13,026	738,606	814,806	76,200
			83	11,053	703,422	763,960	60,538
			84	27,016	605,354	677,023	71,669
			85	9,364	211,783	261,350	49,567
			86	8,949	230,498	276,941	46,443
	V	W	83	331	23,475	26,771	3,296
USSR	V	E	86	2,604	67,792	77,696	9,904
YUGOSLV	V	E	81	1,303	43,563	53,049	9,486

Poppy, seed, vegetable oil
1764200 POPPY SEED OIL (LB)

Country	Mode	Reg	Yr	Quantity	F.A.S.	C.I.F.	Charges
TOTAL			81	6,983	9,125	48,867	1,971
			82	81	775	792	17
			83	14,576	16,429	22,244	5,815
			84	190	945	984	39
			85	13,058	17,489	18,925	1,436
			86	113,658	97,906	108,090	10,184
AUSTRAL	V	W	86	36,000	6,878	9,360	2,482
FR GERM	V	E	81	6,702	7,695	47,408	1,942
			83	13,916	14,653	20,439	5,786
			85	13,058	17,489	18,925	1,436
			86	77,658	91,028	98,730	7,702
U KING	N	E	81	281	1,430	1,459	29
	V	E	82	81	775	792	17
			83	660	1,776	1,805	29
			84	190	945	984	39

Poppy, straw extract, natural drug
4357200 POPPY STRAW EXTRACT (LB)

Country	Mode	Reg	Yr	Quantity	F.A.S.	C.I.F.	Charges
TOTAL			81	39,487	4,823,002	4,882,279	59,277
			82	28,365	3,402,452	3,442,178	39,726
			83	61,915	5,852,821	5,965,861	113,040
			84	39,783	4,409,398	4,488,134	78,736
			85	23,955	2,440,057	2,474,365	34,308
			86	19,679	1,759,340	1,793,857	34,517
AUSTRAL	A	E	81	3,301	405,191	413,465	8,274
			82	7,315	847,816	866,593	18,777
			83	4,579	513,008	523,717	10,709
			84	13,228	1,402,727	1,427,147	24,420
			85	12,621	1,273,491	1,288,597	15,106
			86	11,420	1,235,283	1,257,373	22,090
	A	W	81	26	3,458	3,681	223
			82	8,147	911,607	914,380	2,773
			86	2,194	204,057	207,984	3,927
	N	E	83	12,423	1,248,910	1,270,305	21,395
AUSTRIA	A	E	82	1,281	165,765	171,500	5,735
DENMARK	A	E	81	99	1,890	2,135	245
FRANCE	A	E	81	11,960	1,372,950	1,392,704	19,754
			82	705	89,856	90,388	532
			83	7,466	594,953	600,904	5,951
			84	1,991	151,806	153,362	1,556
HUNGARY	V	E	81	2	407	450	43
NETHLDS	A	E	81	22,510	2,850,646	2,879,383	28,737
			82	10,800	1,370,277	1,381,800	11,523
TURKEY	A	E	82	117	17,131	17,517	386
			83	37,447	3,495,950	3,570,935	74,985
			84	24,564	2,854,865	2,907,625	52,760
			85	11,334	1,166,566	1,185,768	19,202
			86	6,065	320,000	328,500	8,500
U KING	A	E	81	1,589	188,460	190,461	2,001

Crop Product TSUSA commodity number, description, and unit of quantity Country	Mode	Reg	Yr	Quantity	F.A.S.	C.I.F.	Charges

Orange

Neroli, essential oil
4524200 ORANGE FLOWER OR NEROLI OIL (LB)

Country	Mode	Reg	Yr	Quantity	F.A.S.	C.I.F.	Charges
TOTAL			81	849	189,541	191,787	2,246
			82	1,247	254,014	258,184	4,170
			83	14,046	303,409	313,403	9,994
			84	1,403	278,380	285,115	6,735
			85	750	357,065	360,827	3,762
			86	10,720	665,725	675,419	9,694
BRAZIL	A	E	83	397	3,060	3,469	409
FR GERM	A	E	85	110	1,175	1,206	31
			86	400	4,583	4,998	415
FRANCE	A	E	81	832	181,346	183,474	2,128
			83	2	1,118	1,139	21
			84	1,378	268,865	275,521	6,656
	N	E	82	1,247	254,014	258,184	4,170
			83	1,521	220,970	224,748	3,778
			85	640	355,890	359,621	3,731
			86	1,478	552,477	560,368	7,891
INDNSIA	V	E	86	8,818	73,786	75,070	1,284
JAPAN	V	W	83	12,125	77,822	83,599	5,777
MOROC	A	E	81	3	1,168	1,170	2
NETHLDS	A	E	86	22	31,460	31,473	13
SPAIN	A	E	81	6	1,950	2,002	52
SWITZLD	A	E	81	2	1,113	1,145	32
			83	1	439	448	9
			86	2	3,419	3,510	91
TUNISIA	A	E	81	4	2,295	2,298	3
			84	25	9,515	9,594	79
USSR	V	E	81	2	1,669	1,698	29

Orange, essential oil
4524400 ORANGE OIL (LB)

Country	Mode	Reg	Yr	Quantity	F.A.S.	C.I.F.	Charges
TOTAL			81	4,657,642	2,029,743	2,350,768	321,025
			82	4,138,836	1,520,767	1,817,797	297,030
			83	9,638,104	1,786,960	2,332,858	545,898
			84	6,979,381	2,828,242	3,258,757	430,515
			85	9,845,097	6,329,473	7,135,885	806,412
			86	7,291,210	4,224,393	4,787,139	562,746
ARGENT	V	E	81	56,217	18,437	22,972	4,535
			84	150,575	57,741	67,840	10,099
			85	4,000	3,400	3,409	9
AUSTRAL	V	E	86	29,260	8,658	11,618	2,960
BAHAMAS	V	E	82	13,035	4,302	5,214	912
			83	8,800	7,463	7,488	25
			85	14,000	26,500	26,689	189
BELIZE	O	E	81	21,456	10,161	12,089	1,928
			82	7,960	4,393	4,870	477
	V	E	81	55,655	28,851	31,587	2,736
			82	20,048	10,614	11,387	773
			83	69,142	27,270	31,140	3,870
			84	135,384	54,717	60,434	5,717
			85	200,057	106,610	112,163	5,553
			86	162,105	65,108	75,935	10,827
BRAZIL	N	E	83	5,431,124	650,130	949,258	299,128
			84	11,784	32,575	35,564	2,989
			85	7,571,638	3,682,656	4,275,149	592,493
	O	E	83	138,602	12,260	19,038	6,778
			84	76,279	10,386	14,152	3,766
	V	E	81	4,340,681	1,266,012	1,545,066	279,054
			82	3,926,116	767,124	1,032,426	265,302
			83	3,814,886	473,185	680,064	206,879
			84	6,287,099	1,754,311	2,122,665	368,354
			85	1,545,280	1,030,640	1,150,223	119,583
			86	6,604,423	2,886,494	3,351,655	465,161
	V	W	85	22,486	11,730	13,925	2,195
CANADA	O	E	84	15	978	978	
			85	27	1,718	1,718	
			86	89	5,560	5,560	
CHINA M	V	E	86	6,000	12,400	12,607	207
DOM REP	N	E	82	20,754	170,063	175,068	5,005
	V	E	81	32,859	232,541	239,597	7,056
			82	14,931	112,110	115,528	3,418
			83	18,663	133,452	137,469	4,017
			84	16,294	117,417	121,594	4,177
			85	23,789	170,633	176,247	5,614
			86	24,271	172,149	178,097	5,948
DOMINCA	V	E	85	1,862	13,452	13,980	528
			86	3,200	23,118	24,056	938
FR GERM	A	E	82	71	3,092	3,278	186
			83	298	5,865	6,089	224
			84	33	1,337	1,391	54
			86	55	1,070	1,099	29
	N	E	81	33,113	11,136	13,332	2,196
	V	E	81	62	3,072	3,279	207
			82	48	2,134	2,318	184
			83	118	5,377	5,569	192
			84	126	4,734	5,199	465
			85	278	6,437	6,801	364
			86	58	2,445	3,025	580
FRANCE	N	E	81	14,668	108,224	111,740	3,516
			82	12,303	64,503	66,928	2,425
			83	15,004	57,112	59,541	2,429
			84	12,737	33,113	34,325	1,212
			85	27,101	72,497	74,362	1,865
			86	35,920	116,629	120,053	3,424
	V	E	84	1,292	5,213	6,041	828
			85	220	1,133	1,170	37
			86	8,868	16,930	18,949	2,019
	V	W	83	2,142	9,234	10,023	789
			84	3,036	13,082	14,258	1,176
			85	3,511	15,134	16,552	1,418
			86	3,513	16,417	18,956	2,539
GREECE	V	E	86	1,984	4,202	4,500	298
GUINEA	N	E	83	1,851	3,965	4,465	500
	V	E	81	1,190	3,286	3,452	166
			82	441	800	819	19
HAITI	A	E	83	800	6,119	6,430	311
	N	E	85	8,522	64,711	66,971	2,260
	V	E	81	5,165	57,424	58,963	1,539
			82	6,409	38,869	40,098	1,229
			83	3,200	24,609	25,648	1,039
			84	3,438	26,391	27,566	1,175
			86	7,063	62,849	64,501	1,652
INDNSIA	V	E	83	1,200	2,940	2,975	35
ISRAEL	N	E	81	71,210	91,228	99,644	8,416
			82	80,798	54,783	62,543	7,760
			83	115,439	110,105	121,482	11,377
			84	73,211	105,896	113,940	8,044
			85	202,322	177,927	196,527	18,600
			86	301,108	229,358	270,985	41,627
	V	E	82	14,319	14,421	15,794	1,373
			84	6,000	5,100	5,117	17
			85	21,009	15,915	18,296	2,381
			86	27,853	36,944	37,936	992
ITALY	A	E	81	110	2,681	2,813	132
			83	651	10,911	12,147	1,236
			84	176	4,445	4,869	424
			85	771	14,230	15,536	1,306
			86	1,720	32,184	35,235	3,051
	N	E	82	6,250	25,272	26,487	1,215
	V	E	84	132	2,700	3,283	583
			85	234	3,938	4,359	421
IVY CST	V	E	86	794	7,172	7,384	212
JAMAICA	V	E	85	32,000	18,913	22,637	3,724
JAPAN	A	E	85	198	1,440	2,077	637
	V	W	81	110	530	565	35
MEXICO	A	E	84	11,464	57,200	63,496	6,296
	O	E	84	139,880	42,726	42,726	
MOROC	V	E	83	2,094	692	1,187	495
			86	2,094	8,732	9,315	583
NETHLDS	A	E	81	351	29,463	30,124	661
			82	275	18,951	19,445	494
			83	96	9,962	10,256	294
			84	1,470	10,699	11,704	1,005
			85	534	13,511	14,918	1,407
			86	2,039	70,199	74,376	4,177
	N	E	81	110	9,102	9,380	278
			83	435	8,409	8,940	531
	V	E	81	110	9,256	9,553	297
			82	220	18,489	18,793	304
			83	297	29,964	30,180	216
			84	88	7,798	7,952	154
REP SAF	N	E	81	16,521	12,613	14,978	2,365
	V	E	86	2,447	1,832	2,266	434
SINGAPR	V	E	84	1,102	19,735	19,985	250
SPAIN	A	E	81	110	563	609	46
	V	E	83	397	613	734	121
SWITZLD	A	E	81	6,618	108,649	112,446	3,797
			82	14,646	172,919	178,483	5,564
			84	26,380	387,428	397,134	9,706

Crop
Product
TSUSA commodity number, description, and unit of quantity

Country	Mode	Reg	Yr	Quantity	F.A.S.	C.I.F.	Charges
			85	18,551	508,308	537,180	28,872
			86	3,605	176,523	180,735	4,212
	N	E	83	11,461	136,819	140,756	3,937
			86	7,828	123,564	129,112	5,548
	V	E	81	899	18,223	19,778	1,555
			83	1,204	22,400	23,554	1,154
			84	683	11,250	11,733	483
			86	662	17,529	17,780	251
U KING	A	E	81	61	6,776	7,260	484
			82	212	37,928	38,318	390
			83	200	38,104	38,425	321
			84	794	19,882	20,208	326
			85	322	13,221	13,619	398
			86	600	25,244	26,469	1,225
	N	E	84	18,709	39,834	42,803	2,969
	V	E	81	146	933	948	15
			84	1,200	1,554	1,800	246
			85	145,985	352,459	368,867	16,408
			86	53,651	101,083	104,935	3,852
	V	W	85	400	2,360	2,510	150
USSR	V	E	81	220	582	593	11

Orange, fresh
1473140 ORANGES, NSPF, FRESH (LB)

Country	Mode	Reg	Yr	Quantity	F.A.S.	C.I.F.	Charges
TOTAL			81	15,566,351	2,064,945	2,267,028	202,083
			82	31,313,364	3,325,927	3,810,893	484,966
			83	13,182,042	1,965,171	2,212,665	247,494
			84	44,579,090	8,165,290	9,843,737	1,678,447
			85	54,061,380	11,726,971	14,560,940	2,833,969
			86	54,552,397	9,284,887	10,493,977	1,209,090
ARGENT	V	E	86	1,190	1,733	1,792	59
BAHAMAS	V	E	85	76,867	2,370	4,046	1,676
			86	199,143	6,930	7,882	952
BELIZE	A	E	84	2,888	397	784	387
BRAZIL	A	E	86	1,973	2,685	3,929	1,244
C RICA	V	E	82	35,360	3,978	7,739	3,761
CANADA	O	E	82	17,820	6,826	6,826	
			84	39,683	21,600	21,600	
			85	237,240	115,806	115,806	
			86	42,462	21,600	21,600	
CHILE	A	E	82	3,748	1,000	1,110	110
			83	52,527	20,096	51,119	31,023
CHINA M	V	W	83	990	690	760	70
			84	750	1,200	1,268	68
CHINA T	V	E	83	25,763	13,925	24,858	10,933
			86	25,782	11,465	12,972	1,507
	V	W	84	250	500	534	34
COLOMB	V	E	84	1,984	1,100	1,100	
DENMARK	V	E	86	7,200	1,296	1,533	237
DOM REP	N	E	81	73,446	14,090	19,858	5,768
			82	33,937	3,050	5,110	2,060
			84	4,783,832	568,330	766,983	198,653
			85	3,391,686	471,269	611,503	140,234
			86	3,668,905	530,096	689,934	159,838
	V	E	81	242,252	35,194	45,897	10,703
			82	20,900	4,547	5,818	1,271
			83	1,054,743	91,675	128,330	36,655
			84	1,995,862	225,887	316,456	90,569
			85	4,687,618	498,010	708,494	210,484
			86	586,342	139,688	169,624	29,936
DOMINCA	V	E	86	19,829	6,580	7,930	1,350
FRANCE	A	E	83	4,552	923	2,788	1,865
	N	E	84	170,475	34,410	53,215	18,805
	O	E	82	79,200	33,935	33,935	
	V	E	83	1,323	750	937	187
			86	2,870	8,716	10,577	1,861
GREECE	V	E	81	4,200	3,325	3,923	598
			82	1,200	900	1,100	200
			83	27,007	4,350	5,295	945
			84	7,594	5,168	5,832	664
			85	4,800	2,660	3,099	439
			86	6,600	4,075	5,087	1,012
GUATMAL	V	E	86	8,944	1,073	1,528	455
HG KONG	V	W	82	750	1,691	1,861	170
HONDURA	V	E	82	450,283	28,300	59,150	30,850
ISRAEL	N	E	85	7,483,270	1,116,928	1,453,838	336,910
	O	E	82	1,557,061	246,473	387,504	141,031
			83	1,148,510	227,192	227,192	
			84	826,064	195,583	229,394	33,811
			85	629,700	81,900	109,500	27,600
	V	E	81	1,322,049	240,506	342,294	101,788

Crop
Product
TSUSA commodity number, description, and unit of quantity

Country	Mode	Reg	Yr	Quantity	F.A.S.	C.I.F.	Charges
			82	2,515,440	407,860	643,410	235,550
			83	160,723	21,538	37,607	16,069
			84	11,845,988	2,843,914	3,708,108	864,194
			85	109,440	15,135	26,898	11,763
			86	13,682,159	4,260,442	4,654,925	394,483
	V	W	83	19,163	7,711	10,326	2,615
ITALY	A	E	83	32,811	11,041	26,219	15,178
	N	E	84	168,252	24,597	57,534	32,937
	O	E	85	74,954	20,868	27,087	6,219
	V	E	85	70,805	14,757	30,481	15,724
JAMAICA	A	E	84	31,744	5,456	8,516	3,060
	V	E	84	1,027,260	92,583	165,312	72,729
			85	7,556,746	566,962	886,279	319,317
			86	4,945,714	409,040	608,731	199,691
JAPAN	V	W	84	1,299,509	616,506	721,138	104,632
			85	208,656	101,314	119,977	18,663
MACAO	V	E	85	4,524,227	984,960	1,096,092	111,132
			86	2,363,111	480,300	528,330	48,030
MEXICO	O	E	81	12,663,483	1,198,983	1,198,983	
			82	25,154,549	1,931,758	1,931,758	
			83	8,265,056	537,090	537,090	
			84	14,910,751	1,263,085	1,263,085	
			85	376,984	32,555	32,555	
			86	22,303,050	1,313,084	1,313,084	
	O	W	84	941,976	167,566	167,566	
			86	1,043,104	198,394	198,394	
	V	E	84	28,000	4,000	6,000	2,000
MOROC	O	E	81	345,610	175,573	175,573	
			82	341,292	165,290	165,290	
			83	558,360	271,331	271,331	
			84	2,046,162	597,700	608,200	10,500
	V	E	82	70,547	19,200	27,389	8,189
			83	867,731	401,787	443,607	41,820
			84	1,845,172	585,270	668,880	83,610
			85	6,017,882	1,899,292	2,019,516	120,224
N ZEAL	A	E	82	570	713	1,408	695
	A	W	81	1,379	1,187	2,288	1,101
			82	10,113	9,469	14,826	5,357
NETHLDS	A	E	84	3,220	1,169	2,610	1,441
PORTUGL	O	E	86	42,462	21,600	21,600	
REP SAF	O	E	82	39,600	19,860	19,860	
			84	414,711	97,713	116,382	18,669
SPAIN	N	E	81	834,732	363,105	445,230	82,125
	O	E	81	79,200	32,982	32,982	
			82	441,176	208,460	208,460	
			83	66,000	30,971	30,971	
			84	660,376	306,675	306,675	
			85	1,748,738	804,658	810,958	6,300
			86	525,219	207,723	232,811	25,088
	V	E	82	539,818	232,617	288,339	55,722
			83	892,863	323,415	413,439	90,024
			84	1,526,455	504,627	646,303	141,676
			85	16,641,307	4,975,754	6,481,187	1,505,433
			86	5,076,338	1,658,367	2,001,714	343,347
SWITZLD	V	E	84	132	254	262	8
TRINID	V	E	83	3,920	686	796	110
VENEZ	V	E	85	220,460	21,773	23,624	1,851

Orange, juice, concentrated
1652900 ORANGE JUICE CONCENTRATED (GAL)

Country	Mode	Reg	Yr	Quantity	F.A.S.	C.I.F.	Charges
TOTAL			81	214,230,552	178,168,440	199,108,345	20,939,905
			82	396,072,399	320,168,873	354,118,080	33,949,207
			83	364,768,963	293,500,568	319,962,832	26,462,264
			84	558,118,130	595,527,033	635,147,177	39,620,144
			85	581,427,069	695,387,546	735,239,982	39,852,436
			86	547,040,924	385,996,430	419,390,497	33,394,067
AFGHAN	O	E	82	257,943	229,569	247,625	18,056
ARGENT	N	E	81	285	771	1,931	1,160
	O	E	81	1,487,657	1,249,496	1,401,192	151,696
			82	920,592	516,748	568,564	51,816
			84	1,116,933	930,879	1,089,903	159,024
	V	W	81	26,373	18,060	21,901	3,841
AUSTRAL	V	W	86	215,644	247,544	282,682	35,138
BAHRAIN	V	E	85	4,050	1,109	1,440	331
BELGIUM	O	E	86	80,484	108,666	113,829	5,163
	V	E	85	839	5,417	7,147	1,730
			86	861	3,949	4,450	501
BELIZE	O	E	81	2,620,582	2,296,525	2,452,511	155,986
			82	2,043,258	1,826,810	1,959,105	132,295
	V	E	84	2,123,083	3,296,374	3,423,236	126,862
			85	3,784,998	6,130,533	6,349,285	218,752

Crop Product TSUSA commodity number, description, and unit of quantity Country	Mode	Reg	Yr	Quantity	F.A.S.	C.I.F.	Charges
			86	6,724,549	6,371,488	6,787,267	415,779
BRAZIL	A	E	83	2,403	4,766	9,005	4,239
			84	284	411	3,034	2,623
	N	E	81	32,743,606	26,171,785	29,743,771	3,571,986
			82	40,326,715	33,342,919	36,403,579	3,060,660
			83	56,781,024	45,459,537	49,740,191	4,280,654
			84	132,263,114	141,534,117	150,915,624	9,381,507
			85	54,891,279	62,731,991	67,333,542	4,601,551
	N	W	84	1,720,427	2,001,514	2,227,929	226,415
			85	32,056	33,128	36,278	3,150
			86	284,570	211,519	249,169	37,650
	O	E	81	141,284,582	122,781,583	136,398,065	13,616,482
			82	302,615,538	243,313,293	269,923,933	26,610,640
			83	244,345,202	198,432,812	216,000,658	17,567,846
			84	358,672,735	381,032,907	406,026,716	24,993,809
			85	476,859,945	572,787,336	604,787,478	32,000,142
			86	312,224,787	231,583,559	252,643,437	21,059,878
	O	W	81	10,815,420	6,980,629	8,302,319	1,321,690
			82	9,110,260	7,219,371	8,392,190	1,172,819
			83	12,966,584	9,303,138	10,793,081	1,489,943
			84	8,831,461	7,910,006	8,565,668	655,662
			85	2,481,459	2,926,899	3,150,681	223,782
			86	1,395,076	1,171,812	1,325,871	154,059
	V	E	81	2,043,184	1,554,547	1,749,502	194,955
			82	3,474,838	2,810,454	3,224,803	414,349
			83	1,054,429	875,289	947,455	72,166
			84	2,458,757	3,227,510	3,475,685	248,175
			85	10,218,796	12,382,766	13,105,947	723,181
			86	168,206,306	108,066,340	118,185,864	10,119,524
	V	W	81	16,217,032	11,276,646	13,154,864	1,878,218
			82	18,460,465	13,800,449	16,091,197	2,290,748
			83	22,014,082	16,634,282	19,496,452	2,862,170
			84	29,651,614	30,779,344	34,211,727	3,432,383
			85	17,961,773	19,001,269	20,683,434	1,682,165
			86	18,728,980	11,283,506	12,424,630	1,141,124
CANADA	A	H	82	320	781	1,169	388
	O	E	81	14,711	24,864	24,864	
			82	322,897	310,616	310,628	12
			83	353,222	368,519	382,763	14,244
			84	116,478	161,336	161,336	
			85	1,997,544	3,975,908	3,975,908	
			86	3,523,120	4,936,622	4,936,622	
	O	W	81	7,707	54,030	54,245	215
			82	220,947	245,509	245,509	
			83	1,284	6,516	6,516	
			84	2,800	7,199	7,199	
			85	4,215	29,968	29,968	
			86	14,400	17,142	17,142	
	V	E	86	20,092	21,196	25,720	4,524
CHINA T	V	W	86	52	1,680	1,844	164
COLOMB	O	E	85	28,849	25,051	25,051	
DENMARK	V	E	82	788	1,403	2,048	645
DOM REP	V	E	82	20,219	10,327	12,504	2,177
			83	9,447	10,712	11,924	1,212
			85	90,491	115,018	134,072	19,054
			86	17,223	3,946	4,831	885
F W IND	V	E	84	26,936	41,059	45,050	3,991
FR GERM	A	E	84	420	608	1,400	792
			86	1,765	2,896	5,292	2,396
	N	E	85	1,420	3,491	5,577	2,086
	O	E	83	210,000	1,865,900	1,880,600	14,700
	V	E	81	3,404	15,441	16,059	618
			82	236,857	851,905	928,269	76,364
	V	W	82	56,112	199,554	220,365	20,811
			83	10,010	12,311	13,362	1,051
			85	237	1,112	1,272	160
FRANCE	O	E	86	60,740	30,699	30,699	
	O	W	82	210,000	188,399	203,099	14,700
	V	E	82	17,784	39,151	42,740	3,589
			83	61,369	147,114	159,730	12,616
			84	232,229	541,433	590,620	49,187
			85	311,683	669,712	727,860	58,148
			86	405,957	1,311,541	1,399,778	88,237
	V	W	82	19,286	45,684	50,278	4,594
			83	82,967	202,822	219,576	16,754
			86	58,504	67,742	75,972	8,230
GERM DR	V	E	82	188,585	96,160	102,502	6,342
GREECE	V	E	82	928	1,500	1,949	449
GUATMAL	V	E	85	564,700	385,888	456,489	70,601
			86	625,520	303,186	366,652	63,466
	V	W	85	33,642	49,903	59,862	9,959
HG KONG	V	E	83	253	560	616	56
			86	3,403	3,233	3,805	572
HONDURA	O	E	85	361,035	447,855	453,105	5,250

Crop Product TSUSA commodity number, description, and unit of quantity Country	Mode	Reg	Yr	Quantity	F.A.S.	C.I.F.	Charges
			86	8,415	35,510	35,510	
	V	E	84	252,532	372,154	381,780	9,626
			85	1,157,885	1,224,722	1,317,615	92,893
			86	447,647	448,636	505,632	56,996
ISRAEL	A	E	81	127	405	534	129
	N	E	82	719	1,010	2,590	1,580
	O	E	86	135,399	117,979	145,211	27,232
	V	E	81	5,980	4,804	6,040	1,236
			82	2,440	1,962	2,442	480
			86	1,712	3,815	5,075	1,260
	V	W	85	3,885	2,538	3,408	870
ITALY	V	E	83	20,640	17,401	21,069	3,668
			85	1,088	2,590	2,775	185
JAMAICA	V	E	84	1,615,008	2,331,113	2,465,618	134,505
			85	956,566	1,246,610	1,322,041	75,431
			86	1,033,339	847,763	934,894	87,131
JAPAN	A	E	83	4	414	539	125
			84	115	2,828	4,445	1,617
	V	E	83	563	2,937	3,293	356
			84	375	1,958	2,148	190
			85	2,303	8,397	9,647	1,250
			86	1,616	10,005	10,741	736
	V	W	81	8	467	502	35
			82	195	1,094	1,253	159
			83	1,068	5,464	5,875	411
			84	103	948	1,002	54
			85	7,060	14,862	16,564	1,702
			86	3,505	17,353	18,453	1,100
KOR REP	V	E	86	2,322	10,012	11,057	1,045
	V	W	84	1,984	8,040	9,078	1,038
			85	16,648	61,767	68,927	7,160
			86	11,627	42,201	46,724	4,523
MEXICO	A	E	82	1,001	1,700	2,786	1,086
	N	E	82	29,460	22,656	22,721	65
			84	1,960,196	2,167,805	2,169,327	1,522
			85	8,745	23,029	25,357	2,328
	O	E	81	6,398,559	5,330,078	5,362,074	31,996
			82	16,698,006	14,394,628	14,422,616	27,988
			83	26,009,430	19,594,194	19,605,595	11,401
			84	15,361,256	17,467,871	17,505,298	37,427
			85	9,014,024	10,363,549	10,382,513	18,964
			86	31,503,635	17,671,263	17,676,440	5,177
	O	W	81	561,328	407,733	417,330	9,597
			82	627,946	524,856	544,866	20,010
			83	105,563	89,073	90,934	1,861
			84	308,448	366,710	379,287	12,577
			85	145,600	165,304	165,313	9
			86	828,358	579,772	583,488	3,716
	V	E	82	96,250	84,582	86,777	2,195
			86	3,434	7,013	7,595	582
MONSRAT	A	E	86	437	1,373	1,373	
NETHLDS	V	E	82	84	264	298	34
	V	W	82	66	258	284	26
OMAN	A	E	81	7	576	641	65
PANAMA	V	E	84	424,562	639,817	714,513	74,696
			86	364,000	385,749	437,753	52,004
PORTUGL	V	E	86	1,733	4,000	5,781	1,781
REP SAF	V	E	86	68,909	32,870	41,126	8,256
SINGAPR	V	W	86	8,200	16,072	18,252	2,180
SPAIN	O	E	84	22,357	26,407	27,749	1,342
			85	369,131	476,787	497,190	20,403
	O	W	84	260	319	319	
	V	E	84	372,610	441,714	462,971	21,257
			85	312	1,250	1,513	263
SURINAM	O	E	82	111,768	84,900	98,559	13,659
SWITZLD	V	E	83	1,040	4,709	5,568	859
			84	33	995	1,074	79
U KING	A	E	83	32	320	530	210
	A	W	82	132	361	832	471
	O	E	85	26,825	30,956	32,707	1,751
	V	E	84	13,336	18,451	22,469	4,018
	V	W	83	99	478	760	282
VENEZ	O	E	83	447,048	276,780	340,876	64,096
			86	24,603	16,778	19,836	3,058
	V	E	83	291,200	184,520	225,864	41,344
			84	567,684	215,206	254,972	39,766
			85	87,468	59,386	68,065	8,679
YUGOSLV	V	E	85	518	1,445	1,951	506

Orange, juice, not concentrated
1652700 ORANGE JUICE UNMXD NOT CONCENTD (GAL)

TOTAL			84	17,111,810	30,846,997	31,016,463	169,466

Crop Product TSUSA commodity number, description, and unit of quantity Country	Mode	Reg	Yr	Quantity	F.A.S.	C.I.F.	Charges
			85	284,393	659,567	693,311	33,744
			86	274,235	568,662	667,810	99,148
AUSTRIA	A	E	85	1,261	2,299	6,997	4,698
	V	E	86	36,213	75,113	115,352	40,239
BELGIUM	A	E	84	112	537	1,060	523
	O	E	84	584	1,576	1,865	289
			85	1,739	3,082	4,349	1,267
	V	E	84	8,513	20,957	27,490	6,533
			85	1,474	2,954	4,013	1,059
			86	4,263	11,434	14,308	2,874
BRAZIL	A	E	84	776	1,728	8,686	6,958
	O	E	84	1,507,757	1,950,589	2,041,187	90,598
			86	8,112	32,527	36,158	3,631
	V	E	84	7,078	10,607	12,879	2,272
			85	5,638	5,993	8,008	2,015
	V	W	84	372,610	430,963	475,816	44,853
CANADA	A	H	84	459	1,173	1,761	588
	O	E	84	3,035,173	4,795,364	4,795,364	
			85	236,910	507,844	507,844	
CHINA M	V	W	84	374	840	907	67
CHINA T	V	W	86	1,389	3,720	3,974	254
DENMARK	V	E	85	535	1,187	1,680	493
FR GERM	V	E	85	578	1,383	1,801	418
	V	W	86	186	1,296	1,419	123
GAZA ST	O	E	84	753	1,238	1,238	
HG KONG	V	E	84	223	598	798	200
	V	W	84	3,227	8,165	9,503	1,338
ISRAEL	V	E	86	40,876	99,900	127,438	27,538
ITALY	A	E	84	590	1,555	3,555	2,000
	V	W	86	1,116	2,027	3,238	1,211
JAMAICA	V	E	84	1,426	4,000	4,332	332
JAPAN	V	E	84	2,499	9,162	10,380	1,218
			85	2,250	8,244	9,774	1,530
			86	961	4,860	5,170	310
	V	H	84	6,294	24,531	30,360	5,829
			85	3,356	12,535	15,610	3,075
	V	W	84	7,640	36,958	39,569	2,611
			85	5,935	22,549	24,858	2,309
			86	4,354	24,284	25,593	1,309
KOR REP	V	E	85	10,583	39,435	47,298	7,863
			86	10,757	44,098	49,287	5,189
	V	W	84	8,734	35,107	37,057	1,950
			85	10,271	39,671	44,487	4,816
			86	20,942	84,640	94,736	10,096
MEXICO	A	E	85	423	1,359	2,076	717
	O	E	84	12,142,157	23,499,832	23,499,957	125
			86	132,156	151,282	151,282	
	O	W	84	2,521	6,115	6,115	
PORTUGL	O	E	84	945	1,907	1,907	
	V	E	84	27	408	548	140
			86	5,563	14,537	17,979	3,442
	V	W	84	191	284	496	212
S ARAB	V	W	84	167	841	1,671	830
SINGAPR	A	E	85	2	2,095	3,555	1,460
SPAIN	V	E	85	2,880	7,870	9,830	1,960
			86	2,430	7,259	8,469	1,210
TRINID	V	E	86	4,687	10,000	11,602	1,602
U KING	V	E	86	230	1,685	1,805	120
YUGOSLV	V	E	85	558	1,067	1,131	64
ZAIRE	O	E	84	980	1,962	1,962	

Orange, marmalade
1531600 ORANGE MARMALADE (LB)

Country	Mode	Reg	Yr	Quantity	F.A.S.	C.I.F.	Charges
TOTAL			81	2,040,983	1,489,175	1,628,492	139,317
			82	1,857,331	1,377,019	1,509,225	132,206
			83	2,277,838	1,697,027	1,853,579	156,552
			84	2,449,228	1,803,357	2,018,304	214,947
			85	2,440,488	1,823,368	2,045,761	222,393
			86	2,155,954	1,825,342	2,008,872	183,530
AUSTRAL	V	E	85	5,990	10,374	11,687	1,313
			86	1,313	1,056	1,172	116
	V	W	86	1,313	1,056	1,172	116
AUSTRIA	V	E	82	504	627	690	63
			86	1,650	2,732	4,974	2,242
	V	W	86	3,876	5,133	5,581	448
BELGIUM	N	E	84	7,241	5,295	6,063	768
	O	E	84	37,458	23,309	26,560	3,251
			85	7,943	3,634	4,777	1,143
	V	E	84	41,108	21,455	25,475	4,020
			85	10,955	6,033	6,972	939
			86	6,193	3,591	3,989	398
BRAZIL	V	W	85	2,520	1,146	1,404	258
	V	E	81	1,652	2,170	2,444	274
			82	1,514	1,640	1,922	282
			84	9,387	11,298	13,465	2,167
C RICA	V	E	83	3,000	2,244	2,380	136
			84	1,452	2,244	2,411	167
CANADA	O	E	81	137,892	40,017	40,017	
			82	139,128	52,288	52,288	
			83	100,128	60,868	60,868	
			84	143,915	77,860	79,219	1,359
			85	153,619	75,883	75,883	
			86	119,921	57,109	57,109	
	O	W	81	171,920	109,311	109,311	
			82	174,961	107,212	107,212	
			83	167,564	95,132	95,622	490
			84	131,014	76,711	76,711	
			85	155,018	96,335	96,335	
			86	120,920	79,645	79,645	
	V	E	85	733	1,289	1,473	184
			86	5,124	2,496	2,802	306
CHILE	V	E	85	13,080	9,728	10,713	985
CHINA T	V	E	81	9,600	3,992	4,303	311
CYPRUS	V	E	81	549	729	946	217
			83	485	1,200	1,268	68
DENMARK	V	E	83	10,120	14,790	15,690	900
			84	1,058	1,029	1,142	113
			85	16,052	4,931	5,786	855
			86	72,407	33,152	38,524	5,372
	V	W	86	198,011	85,130	97,475	12,345
DOM REP	N	E	86	20,713	6,786	7,504	718
	V	E	81	222,400	42,052	48,271	6,219
			82	232,662	44,536	50,870	6,334
			83	222,124	44,976	51,614	6,638
			84	114,895	19,610	24,009	4,399
			85	148,813	20,962	25,651	4,689
			86	79,731	20,001	22,414	2,413
ECUADOR	A	E	84	2,100	524	863	339
	V	E	85	10,500	3,500	4,230	730
			86	12,345	3,000	3,468	468
FR GERM	O	E	83	2,477	1,632	1,774	142
			84	120,789	60,188	69,656	9,468
			85	24,645	12,280	14,165	1,885
			86	37,511	19,832	22,531	2,699
	V	E	82	4,139	3,359	3,745	386
			83	49,036	28,193	31,166	2,973
			84	131,153	66,870	76,400	9,530
			85	200,393	100,851	118,366	17,515
			86	99,209	61,875	67,890	6,015
	V	W	82	1,000	679	763	84
			83	480	375	421	46
			84	1,200	882	1,035	153
			85	3,329	2,572	2,942	370
FRANCE	N	E	83	136,804	121,654	135,395	13,741
			84	188,561	144,650	165,319	20,669
			86	10,295	12,055	14,115	2,060
	O	E	81	825	699	769	70
			83	3,938	2,900	3,316	416
			84	1,416	804	876	72
			85	2,328	1,461	1,731	270
			86	4,388	4,974	4,989	15
	V	E	81	74,923	61,192	68,799	7,607
			82	109,953	91,921	105,577	13,656
			83	39,473	25,869	29,024	3,155
			84	38,853	25,984	29,890	3,906
			85	177,998	138,725	161,720	22,995
			86	146,983	145,880	161,743	15,863
	V	W	81	3,820	3,344	3,649	305
			82	8,352	7,324	8,307	983
			83	33,511	28,735	33,007	4,272
			84	73,250	55,377	62,698	7,321
			85	11,537	16,662	17,942	1,280
			86	7,280	15,484	17,039	1,555
GREECE	V	E	81	360	360	416	56
			83	834	500	587	87
			85	8,800	8,000	8,976	976
			86	23,627	28,659	32,332	3,673
IRELAND	N	E	81	21,298	15,941	17,878	1,937
			83	5,720	4,553	5,174	621
	O	E	84	866	1,068	1,382	314
	V	E	82	11,307	8,970	9,912	942
			84	1,728	1,059	1,330	271
			85	13,339	7,274	8,605	1,331
			86	11,979	7,047	7,819	772

Crop Product TSUSA commodity number, description, and unit of quantity Country	Mode	Reg	Yr	Quantity	F.A.S.	C.I.F.	Charges
ISRAEL	N	E	85	52,165	26,464	30,319	3,855
	V	E	81	62,327	28,942	34,263	5,321
			82	72,467	39,400	45,233	5,833
			83	141,286	83,248	94,038	10,790
			84	77,483	48,634	54,548	5,914
			85	68,123	30,784	36,119	5,335
			86	60,879	32,436	37,997	5,561
ITALY	V	E	82	253	864	943	79
	V	W	83	187	424	492	68
			86	1,853	2,875	3,042	167
JAMAICA	V	E	81	150	1,042	1,180	138
			82	180	266	322	56
			83	1,902	1,337	1,573	236
			84	5,704	2,467	2,824	357
JAPAN	V	E	84	1,100	669	794	125
			86	2,195	1,217	1,385	168
	V	W	83	1,950	1,462	1,656	194
LEBANON	V	E	81	2,646	1,600	1,830	230
MEXICO	O	E	84	50	586	586	
NETHLDS	V	E	82	540	1,138	1,168	30
			83	2,361	2,247	2,362	115
			84	10,475	4,701	5,544	843
			85	37,115	35,197	39,126	3,929
			86	6,124	7,115	7,888	773
NORWAY	V	E	86	9,062	13,790	14,196	406
PAKISTN	V	E	85	7,579	8,423	9,515	1,092
PERU	V	E	86	1,659	4,171	4,498	327
PORTUGL	V	E	81	1,500	948	1,051	103
			82	2,646	1,750	1,861	111
			83	5,250	2,020	2,325	305
			84	350	636	662	26
			86	4,409	2,672	3,260	588
REP SAF	V	W	84	595	729	934	205
SPAIN	V	E	84	16,967	9,257	13,814	4,557
			85	16,404	8,945	10,722	1,777
	V	W	81	11,574	6,850	8,118	1,268
			82	7,128	4,988	5,680	692
SWITZLD	O	E	85	1,058	1,222	1,222	
			86	3,107	4,091	4,583	492
	V	E	81	54,940	44,283	48,533	4,250
			82	53,510	55,123	59,494	4,371
			83	58,929	60,653	65,202	4,549
			84	66,507	84,355	89,062	4,707
			85	66,683	70,418	76,374	5,956
			86	139,789	199,470	214,450	14,980
	V	W	81	3,933	3,713	4,227	514
			82	1,698	1,898	2,210	312
			83	6,642	8,475	9,089	614
			84	12,269	12,311	13,318	1,007
			85	23,921	31,487	34,116	2,629
			86	26,154	33,365	35,193	1,828
U KING	A	E	82	65	397	438	41
			84	1,429	2,213	3,313	1,100
	N	E	81	697,406	688,777	749,700	60,923
			82	885,612	812,808	896,147	83,339
			83	509,077	462,186	508,010	45,824
			84	398,703	390,881	445,808	54,927
			85	329,203	251,277	287,543	36,266
			86	199,594	192,804	212,457	19,653
	N	W	81	71,701	48,668	55,639	6,971
			82	10,721	13,098	14,711	1,613
			84	79,504	69,212	76,909	7,697
			86	27,096	28,060	33,825	5,765
	O	E	81	132,056	87,864	97,535	9,671
			82	3,395	3,826	4,166	340
			83	221,648	172,684	190,460	17,776
			84	373,907	279,431	310,595	31,164
			85	48,933	81,848	87,713	5,865
			86	84,831	115,580	122,400	6,820
	O	W	85	5,103	2,937	3,461	524
	V	E	81	274,738	228,961	252,694	23,733
			82	99,996	88,821	96,937	8,116
			83	469,970	410,815	446,062	35,247
			84	278,104	230,309	255,993	25,684
			85	673,654	618,802	696,499	77,697
			86	483,322	476,614	532,133	55,519
	V	H	85	843	1,440	1,618	178
	V	W	81	82,773	67,720	76,919	9,199
			82	35,600	34,086	38,629	4,543
			83	82,942	57,855	65,004	7,149
			84	78,277	70,483	78,777	8,294
			85	142,112	132,484	152,056	19,572
			86	121,091	114,389	127,278	12,889
YUGOSLV	V	E	84	360	266	319	53

Crop Product TSUSA commodity number, description, and unit of quantity Country	Mode	Reg	Yr	Quantity	F.A.S.	C.I.F.	Charges

Orange, paste and pulp
1526200 ORANGE PASTE AND PULP (LB)

Country	Mode	Reg	Yr	Quantity	F.A.S.	C.I.F.	Charges
TOTAL			81	74,560	27,149	30,424	3,275
			82	125,886	51,069	59,310	8,241
			83	85,024	11,678	16,012	4,334
			84	194,529	74,158	88,052	13,894
			85	1,049,618	241,452	294,781	53,329
			86	271,000	82,401	103,387	20,986
BRAZIL	O	E	84	55,376	22,460	28,295	5,835
			85	870,100	207,005	250,591	43,586
			86	56,799	16,597	18,890	2,293
	O	W	85	3,520	1,408	1,408	
	V	E	83	74,956	6,800	10,634	3,834
			84	74,868	42,826	48,160	5,334
			85	18,916	3,317	4,290	973
CANADA	O	E	82	517	1,071	1,173	102
			84	550	578	578	
DOM REP	N	E	82	63,070	24,943	27,322	2,379
	V	E	81	64,029	23,702	25,911	2,209
			82	20,632	6,564	8,508	1,944
			83	10,068	4,878	5,378	500
			84	63,555	7,886	10,547	2,661
			85	150,094	25,358	33,426	8,068
			86	37,662	6,693	7,481	788
FRANCE	V	E	85	222	1,046	1,168	122
			86	827	1,253	1,435	182
HG KONG	V	W	81	610	1,799	1,946	147
ITALY	V	E	84	180	408	472	64
			86	5,509	1,223	1,697	474
JAPAN	V	W	85	5,655	2,312	2,724	412
SPAIN	V	E	81	9,921	1,648	2,567	919
			82	41,667	18,491	22,307	3,816
			86	168,953	54,969	72,123	17,154
SWITZLD	V	E	85	1,111	1,006	1,174	168
			86	1,250	1,666	1,761	95

Orange, peel
1521400 ORANGE PEEL CRUDE, DRIED ETC (LB)

Country	Mode	Reg	Yr	Quantity	F.A.S.	C.I.F.	Charges
TOTAL			81	1,036,499	372,866	466,515	93,649
			82	1,408,784	476,173	584,572	108,399
			83	1,678,177	428,464	559,984	131,520
			84	874,697	282,190	347,177	64,987
			85	632,430	211,971	252,033	40,062
			86	1,037,645	368,483	437,485	69,002
CANADA	O	E	83	266	2,236	2,236	
			84	525	1,579	1,579	
CHINA M	V	E	81	6,075	11,164	12,142	978
			82	5,778	17,573	18,367	794
			83	13,348	21,237	23,137	1,900
			84	8,605	7,244	7,828	584
			86	750	1,596	1,712	116
	V	H	81	1,102	750	888	138
	V	W	81	3,263	13,447	14,189	742
			82	3,461	6,934	7,358	424
			83	3,263	3,285	3,513	228
			84	8,479	13,544	14,578	1,034
			85	7,451	10,873	11,541	668
			86	1,856	1,188	1,340	152
CHINA T	V	E	86	768	1,190	1,248	58
DOM REP	A	E	81	1,500	420	557	137
	V	E	81	4,163	1,400	1,590	190
			85	5,967	2,400	2,712	312
FR GERM	A	W	82	500	365	639	274
	N	E	85	56,622	45,803	50,372	4,569
	O	E	81	2,223	2,607	2,804	197
	V	E	81	55,624	45,416	49,088	3,672
			82	42,674	25,115	28,913	3,798
			83	26,403	22,574	25,113	2,539
			84	42,620	36,101	39,411	3,310
			86	29,727	32,626	33,601	975
FRANCE	V	E	83	264	272	283	11
			84	942	345	362	17
HAITI	V	E	81	647,958	142,699	188,589	45,890
			82	714,230	135,933	186,039	50,106
			83	626,137	134,322	178,940	44,618
			84	630,855	140,137	181,653	41,516
			85	512,341	127,394	153,701	26,307
			86	764,680	184,533	219,881	35,348
	V	W	83	3,747	903	940	37

Crop
Product
TSUSA commodity number, description, and unit of quantity

Country	Mode	Reg	Yr	Quantity	F.A.S.	C.I.F.	Charges
HG KONG	V	E	81	1,750	1,618	1,766	148
			82	2,975	3,121	3,389	268
			83	2,039	3,023	3,407	384
			84	15,323	9,646	11,170	1,524
	V	H	81	100	480	510	30
	V	W	81	625	681	732	51
			82	3,751	3,432	3,599	167
			83	1,257	1,818	1,956	138
			84	4,729	5,233	5,609	376
			86	100	1,535	1,539	4
IRAN	V	E	82	531	1,321	1,358	37
			86	4,304	2,054	2,344	290
ISRAEL	V	E	83	550,788	72,452	116,924	44,472
ITALY	V	E	81	30,000	10,657	13,134	2,477
			82	26,400	9,834	11,891	2,057
JAMAICA	V	E	82	1,100	488	567	79
JAPAN	V	W	81	2,200	754	957	203
			82	263,950	99,020	112,069	13,049
			83	153,029	55,055	62,172	7,117
			84	42,258	14,280	16,580	2,300
MEXICO	O	E	83	20,084	4,072	4,072	
			84	3,528	1,762	1,879	117
	O	W	83	52,800	744	744	
PAKISTN	V	E	83	5,908	1,407	2,159	752
ROMANIA	V	E	85	5,484	3,563	4,012	449
SPAIN	A	E	83	1,885	2,420	3,419	999
	N	E	86	143,001	102,097	121,369	19,272
	V	E	81	279,916	140,773	179,569	38,796
			82	273,970	133,267	164,770	31,503
			83	216,078	101,548	129,776	28,228
			84	115,070	50,934	65,090	14,156
			85	44,565	21,938	29,695	7,757
			86	92,459	41,664	54,451	12,787
	V	W	82	69,023	39,450	45,291	5,841
SWITZLD	V	E	82	441	320	322	2
			83	662	455	493	38
			84	1,763	1,385	1,438	53
THAILND	V	W	83	219	641	700	59

1523000 ORNGE PEEL PRES O PREP NSPF (LB)

Country	Mode	Reg	Yr	Quantity	F.A.S.	C.I.F.	Charges
TOTAL			81	159,859	108,954	119,292	10,338
			82	268,486	130,246	144,722	14,476
			83	354,890	141,498	166,529	25,031
			84	480,403	204,747	235,346	30,599
			85	599,954	248,628	281,670	33,042
			86	504,562	212,873	234,761	21,888
AUSTRAL	V	E	82	198	379	396	17
BRAZIL	V	E	81	19,200	6,963	8,352	1,389
			82	68,376	22,343	28,013	5,670
			83	116,856	37,746	47,410	9,664
			84	124,890	42,943	52,337	9,394
			85	45,899	12,601	15,930	3,329
			86	44,769	11,868	14,345	2,477
	V	W	82	1,184	625	771	146
			83	3,600	1,125	1,425	300
			85	6,150	2,206	2,966	760
CANADA	O	E	82	711	1,409	1,409	
			83	8,896	4,605	4,605	
CHINA M	O	E	83	316	1,190	1,316	126
	O	W	84	844	1,763	1,880	117
	V	E	81	1,718	6,008	6,181	173
			82	3,514	5,743	6,165	422
			83	9,460	13,033	14,155	1,122
			84	431	1,139	1,215	76
			85	3,900	1,872	2,433	561
	V	W	81	5,538	19,462	20,722	1,260
			82	3,053	10,210	10,816	606
			83	3,616	9,429	10,133	704
			84	7,945	19,469	20,685	1,216
			85	2,953	7,471	7,842	371
			86	5,101	15,146	15,842	696
CHINA T	V	E	82	1,313	1,730	1,867	137
	V	W	83	1,425	350	373	23
DOM REP	A	E	81	3,000	550	778	228
	V	E	81	93,451	32,430	36,859	4,429
			82	127,826	51,125	55,069	3,944
			83	53,454	20,064	22,397	2,333
			84	60,240	18,816	20,605	1,789
			85	148,058	45,497	49,452	3,955
			86	62,020	21,578	22,943	1,365
ECUADOR	V	E	84	6,248	2,000	2,783	783
FR GERM	V	E	81	6,063	5,108	5,362	254
			82	3,306	2,528	2,792	264

Crop
Product
TSUSA commodity number, description, and unit of quantity

Country	Mode	Reg	Yr	Quantity	F.A.S.	C.I.F.	Charges
			83	672	727	814	87
			84	132	264	279	15
	V	W	81	11,196	21,471	21,525	54
			82	24,731	17,290	18,258	968
			83	2,161	1,762	2,047	285
			84	1,512	1,378	1,578	200
FRANCE	A	E	83	136	560	590	30
	V	E	84	41	321	348	27
GREECE	V	E	81	3,383	3,015	3,634	619
			82	1,500	1,250	1,459	209
			83	3,636	2,747	3,174	427
			84	6,240	5,310	6,021	711
			85	2,400	1,400	1,797	397
			86	1,800	1,275	1,440	165
	V	W	81	480	480	551	71
			82	2,400	2,400	2,654	254
			83	5,925	5,750	6,445	695
			84	2,977	2,750	3,118	368
			85	4,764	4,400	4,911	511
			86	2,381	2,000	2,295	295
HAITI	V	E	81	6,614	1,200	1,900	700
			83	11,000	2,353	2,954	601
			86	13,528	3,005	3,655	650
	V	W	83	127,608	32,304	40,190	7,886
HG KONG	V	E	82	250	374	384	10
			83	1,810	2,735	2,926	191
			84	1,109	1,533	1,662	129
			85	3,000	10,745	11,997	1,252
	V	W	81	1,237	3,158	3,348	190
			82	919	1,686	1,849	163
			83	1,618	3,099	3,282	183
			84	1,625	2,734	2,953	219
			85	5,203	14,382	15,238	856
JAPAN	V	E	86	2,475	1,295	1,388	93
	V	W	82	27,000	9,720	11,126	1,406
			84	204,000	75,248	85,168	9,920
			85	377,627	148,054	169,104	21,050
			86	296,441	129,946	145,596	15,650
PORTUGL	V	E	81	772	609	703	94
			86	54,001	3,185	3,233	48
SPAIN	V	E	82	2,205	1,434	1,694	260
			84	43,651	21,287	25,344	4,057
			86	22,046	23,575	24,024	449
	V	W	81	7,207	8,500	9,377	877
			84	18,518	7,792	9,370	1,578
THAILND	V	W	83	109	332	356	24
U KING	O	W	83	2,592	1,587	1,937	350

1543000 ORANGE PEEL, CANDIED ETC (LB)

Country	Mode	Reg	Yr	Quantity	F.A.S.	C.I.F.	Charges
TOTAL			81	252,617	106,272	122,914	16,642
			82	388,508	172,175	194,653	22,478
			83	232,286	140,113	151,861	11,748
			84	217,289	108,122	120,979	12,857
			85	168,085	94,863	104,955	10,092
			86	250,657	132,769	154,576	21,807
AUSTRAL	V	E	81	76,488	36,839	41,829	4,990
			82	167,462	92,634	102,297	9,663
			83	145,504	81,721	88,943	7,222
			84	125,052	65,634	71,551	5,917
			85	162,004	83,178	91,190	8,012
			86	219,016	98,144	115,798	17,654
	V	W	83	1,213	1,039	1,081	42
			84	349	949	992	43
BRAZIL	V	E	81	4,993	10,759	12,050	1,291
			83	2,205	679	877	198
			84	23,148	5,770	8,251	2,481
CANADA	A	E	82	1,235	2,418	2,841	423
	O	E	81	17	1,100	1,100	
			82	913	3,120	3,120	
			83	60,021	15,282	15,282	
			84	40,000	8,365	8,365	
CHINA M	V	E	81	1,100	1,831	1,978	147
			82	125	480	496	16
			83	1,380	5,978	6,646	668
			84	925	870	1,008	138
	V	W	81	782	2,012	2,150	138
			82	400	309	322	13
			83	125	553	572	19
			84	175	1,255	1,305	50
FR GERM	V	E	81	495	1,304	1,367	63
			82	839	2,751	2,857	106
			83	1,261	3,613	4,172	559
			84	4,171	3,390	3,573	183

Crop
Product
TSUSA commodity number, description, and unit of quantity

Country	Mode	Reg	Yr	Quantity	F.A.S.	C.I.F.	Charges
			85	1,100	1,188	1,238	50
	V	W	85	1,064	2,426	3,029	603
FRANCE	A	E	81	238	686	913	227
	V	E	82	247	1,267	1,357	90
			83	2,438	2,168	2,457	289
			85	761	2,336	2,471	135
GREECE	V	E	86	2,400	2,757	3,070	313
HAITI	V	E	82	19,836	5,058	6,838	1,780
HG KONG	V	E	81	125	1,512	1,636	124
			83	1,937	7,945	8,511	566
			84	2,500	1,734	2,148	414
			86	1,600	3,870	4,228	358
	V	W	83	250	287	310	23
INDIA	V	E	82	220	584	610	26
ISRAEL	V	W	84	551	500	670	170
ITALY	N	E	83	4,982	5,854	6,244	390
JAPAN	V	W	81	4,515	1,677	2,355	678
N ZEAL	A	W	85	577	1,291	2,045	754
PORTUGL	A	E	83	1,389	1,440	2,441	1,001
	V	E	81	1,499	1,136	1,415	279
REP SAF	V	E	81	158,800	43,651	52,170	8,519
			82	191,000	55,211	64,940	9,729
SPAIN	V	E	82	2,206	2,379	2,512	133
			83	4,685	6,250	6,507	257
			84	14,616	10,555	13,000	2,445
			86	24,801	22,381	25,285	2,904
SWITZLD	V	E	81	3,565	3,765	3,951	186
			82	3,886	5,642	6,119	477
			83	3,862	5,348	5,701	353
			84	2,600	4,542	5,090	548
			86	1,147	2,665	2,694	29
	V	W	82	139	322	344	22
			83	1,034	1,956	2,117	161
			84	3,202	4,558	5,026	468
			85	1,587	2,980	3,241	261
U KING	V	W	85	992	1,464	1,741	277
			86	1,693	2,952	3,501	549

Orange, prepared or preserved
1473160 ORANGES, NSPF (LB)

Country	Mode	Reg	Yr	Quantity	F.A.S.	C.I.F.	Charges
TOTAL			81	8,563,456	3,275,462	3,607,576	332,114
			82	6,240,410	2,232,313	2,411,102	178,789
			83	8,339,156	2,769,573	3,099,119	329,546
			84	9,833,265	3,822,714	4,143,774	321,060
			85	8,791,926	3,528,606	3,886,884	358,278
			86	9,768,635	3,474,908	3,843,467	368,559
ARGENT	V	E	86	132,938	24,120	27,116	2,996
AUSTRAL	V	E	83	176	315	333	18
			84	2,772	7,281	7,566	285
			85	4,960	9,756	10,160	404
	V	H	82	331	614	644	30
	V	W	82	4,325	8,147	8,493	346
			83	7,666	13,607	14,205	598
			84	3,968	7,221	7,443	222
			85	873	1,382	1,426	44
			86	4,167	7,690	7,793	103
BELGIUM	V	E	84	1,270	781	846	65
BOTSWAN	V	E	86	13,200	2,809	3,696	887
BRAZIL	V	E	81	156,807	59,746	71,500	11,754
			82	103,823	41,960	51,586	9,626
			83	191,918	37,031	50,303	13,272
			85	12,000	4,250	5,333	1,083
	V	W	81	3,360	1,170	1,465	295
			82	3,600	1,275	1,622	347
			83	3,600	578	750	172
CANADA	A	H	84	33,260	37,300	41,706	4,406
			85	81,144	94,631	105,438	10,807
			86	92,764	109,848	123,608	13,760
	A	W	85	2,745	3,091	3,640	549
	O	E	83	31,483	24,181	24,181	
			84	166,122	184,400	184,400	
			85	105,862	128,686	128,686	
			86	195,804	216,545	216,545	
	O	W	82	240	269	269	
			84	11,612	13,524	13,524	
			85	218,783	167,579	167,579	
			86	265,019	205,979	205,979	
	V	E	85	1,457	1,195	1,357	162
CHINA M	O	W	81	656	750	782	32
	V	E	81	17,951	8,684	11,417	2,733
			82	4,135	1,959	2,464	505
			83	3,900	4,485	5,131	646
			84	57,938	20,505	24,880	4,375
			85	938	2,015	2,026	11
			86	5,000	5,459	5,851	392
	V	H	83	550	620	665	45
			84	1,250	1,378	1,501	123
	V	W	82	10,928	15,703	16,982	1,279
			83	16,478	24,217	26,095	1,878
			84	38,826	25,847	28,380	2,533
			85	1,313	2,541	2,654	113
			86	1,544	2,414	2,543	129
CHINA T	V	E	83	7,063	4,761	5,239	478
			85	2,000	3,455	3,743	288
			86	45,250	21,695	24,178	2,483
	V	H	84	1,496	1,509	1,686	177
			86	5,000	2,779	3,100	321
	V	W	81	2,111	2,310	2,411	101
			82	6,844	9,158	9,486	328
			83	9,891	9,675	10,395	720
			84	7,595	7,525	8,223	698
			85	3,371	1,047	1,120	73
			86	26,455	10,880	11,525	645
COLOMB	V	E	81	20,850	12,440	14,186	1,746
			82	23,625	4,582	5,018	436
			83	13,462	12,955	14,333	1,378
			84	8,678	6,243	7,101	858
			86	2,994	1,200	1,320	120
DENMARK	V	E	86	10,800	4,708	5,516	808
DOM REP	N	E	81	19,925	10,988	14,178	3,190
			82	21,969	14,210	16,773	2,563
			86	30,400	9,770	12,536	2,766
	V	E	82	16,566	6,364	6,892	528
			83	41,589	10,276	12,179	1,903
			84	132,794	36,533	45,557	9,024
			85	263,790	258,221	291,949	33,728
			86	284,029	113,998	131,847	17,849
ECUADOR	A	E	83	2,244	340	673	333
	V	E	84	8,700	7,250	8,025	775
			85	7,500	6,500	7,138	638
FR GERM	O	E	86	1,215	1,076	2,212	1,136
	V	E	83	360	365	405	40
			84	43,560	19,809	23,806	3,997
			86	960	3,239	3,684	445
FRANCE	A	E	84	1,476	1,928	2,535	607
	N	E	83	17,068	6,445	12,371	5,926
			84	11,464	8,037	10,014	1,977
	N	W	83	490	1,412	1,628	216
	O	E	81	3,233	5,961	6,386	425
			82	1,849	2,374	2,524	150
	V	E	81	3,811	5,436	5,826	390
			82	6,728	11,009	11,784	775
			83	1,889	2,265	2,495	230
			84	12,064	10,672	12,098	1,426
			85	4,093	4,261	4,772	511
			86	14,475	20,229	22,781	2,552
	V	W	82	50	336	357	21
			83	840	695	778	83
			84	2,340	1,805	2,015	210
GREECE	V	E	81	12,162	12,320	14,458	2,138
			82	2,972	2,950	3,352	402
			83	13,492	13,345	14,962	1,617
			84	596	562	637	75
			85	21,600	20,520	23,261	2,741
	V	W	82	595	600	683	83
			84	1,488	1,375	1,565	190
			86	1,488	1,250	1,399	149
GUATMAL	V	E	85	969,428	45,480	106,517	61,037
			86	230,842	12,369	24,140	11,771
HG KONG	V	E	82	31,802	16,663	18,571	1,908
			83	1,338	1,466	1,662	196
			84	386	1,903	1,988	85
	V	H	82	1,250	1,446	1,531	85
			83	510	563	672	109
			84	995	1,163	1,285	122
	V	W	82	1,938	2,718	2,899	181
			83	7,283	12,509	13,339	830
			84	4,644	6,826	7,196	370
HONDURA	V	E	84	96,101	42,546	48,584	6,038
			85	220,424	14,619	31,953	17,334
			86	18,739	3,372	4,907	1,535
IRAN	V	E	86	3,450	1,200	1,398	198
ISRAEL	N	E	84	11,175	4,478	5,067	589
			85	1,401,876	564,173	719,315	155,142
	V	E	81	2,479,658	884,465	1,149,527	265,062

Crop
Product
TSUSA commodity number, description, and unit of quantity

Country	Mode	Reg	Yr	Quantity	F.A.S.	C.I.F.	Charges
			82	1,320,821	521,475	657,406	135,931
			83	2,113,332	839,774	1,077,168	237,394
			84	1,780,038	715,582	892,553	176,971
			85	269,134	103,479	123,240	19,761
			86	1,518,009	623,529	771,290	147,761
	V	W	81	288,786	118,074	149,435	31,361
			82	90,305	35,475	46,651	11,176
			83	256,904	101,211	133,938	32,727
			84	441,650	178,613	230,068	51,455
			85	231,628	93,017	120,589	27,572
			86	449,504	188,382	247,136	58,754
ITALY	N	E	83	19,373	8,115	14,585	6,470
	V	E	81	15,525	5,865	6,756	891
			82	281	270	316	46
			84	885	2,822	3,009	187
			85	4,298	12,755	14,022	1,267
			86	271	1,495	1,548	53
	V	W	84	900	2,147	2,322	175
JAMAICA	V	E	82	975	439	488	49
JAPAN	V	E	81	396	482	538	56
	V	W	84	11,171	5,748	6,261	513
			85	8,250	4,243	4,692	449
KOR REP	V	E	86	498	2,675	2,929	254
	V	W	86	14,438	5,985	6,397	412
MEXICO	O	E	81	5,385,552	2,075,545	2,075,545	
			82	4,421,629	1,459,054	1,459,054	
			83	5,347,754	1,551,170	1,552,060	890
			84	6,464,058	2,250,495	2,250,495	
			85	4,641,812	1,849,227	1,849,227	
			86	5,379,471	1,478,355	1,479,156	801
	O	W	81	9,600	3,820	3,820	
			84	4,800	1,875	1,875	
			86	10,752	3,701	3,701	
MOROC	O	E	82	3,836	1,131	1,131	
PORTUGL	V	E	84	1,003	660	803	143
REP SAF	V	E	81	33,600	11,125	15,878	4,753
			82	50,260	16,343	23,451	7,108
			83	100,453	33,721	46,316	12,595
			84	123,480	49,261	66,283	17,022
			85	95,705	39,774	51,671	11,897
			86	441,833	176,953	227,649	50,696
SALVADR	V	E	86	32,000	4,500	10,000	5,500
SPAIN	A	E	84	3,968	1,206	3,104	1,898
	O	E	82	39,600	18,000	18,000	
	V	E	81	100,489	48,839	55,036	6,197
			82	63,367	32,957	37,119	4,162
			83	111,277	43,711	50,471	6,760
			84	302,516	135,455	165,878	30,423
			85	197,807	79,367	89,169	9,802
			86	492,371	177,471	213,944	36,473
	V	W	83	5,184	3,175	3,685	510
SWITZLD	A	E	82	330	1,204	1,352	148
	V	E	82	139	317	325	8
			85	4,846	5,758	6,278	520
			86	2,859	3,810	4,205	395
U KING	N	E	81	8,984	7,442	8,432	990
			84	13,794	5,794	7,440	1,646
	O	E	85	5,880	2,654	2,837	183
			86	7,792	3,939	4,897	958
	V	E	82	5,297	3,311	3,879	568
			83	8,997	5,052	6,409	1,357
			84	2,182	2,638	2,752	114
			85	8,409	4,930	7,092	2,162
			86	32,304	21,484	26,941	5,457
	V	W	83	2,592	1,538	1,693	155
			84	20,250	12,017	13,303	1,286

Orchard Grass

Orchard grass, seed
1266300 ORCHARD GRASS SEED (LB)

Country	Mode	Reg	Yr	Quantity	F.A.S.	C.I.F.	Charges
TOTAL			81	183,296	92,137	110,354	18,217
			82	121,779	60,439	69,659	9,220
			83	231,208	111,575	123,741	12,166
			84	155,068	61,924	72,317	10,393
			85	115,972	37,846	45,905	8,059
			86	217,640	74,366	89,885	15,519
AUSTRAL	V	W	85	112,170	35,503	43,032	7,529
			86	35,274	12,119	14,109	1,990

Country	Mode	Reg	Yr	Quantity	F.A.S.	C.I.F.	Charges
CANADA	A	E	83	350	338	584	246
	O	E	85	3,000	1,110	1,110	
			86	1,870	1,612	1,612	
	O	W	82	365	572	572	
			83	440	880	880	
			84	992	1,888	2,012	124
			86	2,640	4,208	4,208	
DENMARK	O	E	83	79,263	37,565	40,535	2,970
	V	E	81	98,694	50,764	58,514	7,750
			82	72,644	35,719	39,483	3,764
			83	146,842	68,887	77,266	8,379
			84	153,272	58,854	69,018	10,164
			86	177,856	56,427	69,956	13,529
	V	W	81	37,445	16,019	19,972	3,953
			82	45,011	20,735	25,525	4,790
FR GERM	V	E	81	43,348	20,653	23,348	2,695
JAPAN	A	W	81	448	877	2,310	1,433
	N	W	81	836	1,463	3,389	1,926
	V	W	81	1,733	1,037	1,386	349
			82	3,759	3,413	4,079	666
			83	2,069	1,661	1,998	337
			84	804	1,182	1,287	105
NETHLDS	V	W	81	792	1,324	1,435	111
			83	2,244	2,244	2,478	234
U KING	A	W	85	802	1,233	1,763	530

Orchid

Dendrobium orchid, fresh
1922150 ORCHIDS, DENDROBIUM, FRESH (NO)

Country	Mode	Reg	Yr	Quantity	F.A.S.	C.I.F.	Charges
TOTAL			86	509,465	94,306	153,150	58,844
CHINA T	A	E	86	11,742	3,070	4,888	1,818
MEXICO	A	W	86	11,707	2,400	2,895	495
NETHLDS	A	E	86	26,924	10,251	14,260	4,009
THAILND	A	E	86	449,092	75,285	124,840	49,555
	A	W	86	10,000	3,300	6,267	2,967

Orchid (not specified), fresh
1922160 ORCHIDS, NSPF, FRESH (NO)

Country	Mode	Reg	Yr	Quantity	F.A.S.	C.I.F.	Charges
TOTAL			86	6,144,341	1,926,777	2,647,787	721,010
AUSTRAL	A	E	86	233,528	192,137	227,166	35,029
	A	W	86	185,615	94,764	109,831	15,067
BRAZIL	A	E	86	38,700	9,898	13,382	3,484
CANADA	O	W	86	1,128	1,196	1,196	
CHILE	A	W	86	72,000	1,725	2,700	975
CHINA T	A	W	86	9,000	5,070	5,133	63
COLOMB	A	E	86	25,420	4,635	5,727	1,092
DOM REP	A	E	86	9,319	1,724	3,018	1,294
FRANCE	A	E	86	16,360	3,787	5,285	1,498
ISRAEL	A	E	86	19,800	3,299	4,319	1,020
JAPAN	A	W	86	26,930	10,141	14,861	4,720
N ZEAL	A	E	86	27,102	19,044	25,158	6,114
	A	W	86	25,177	12,448	16,057	3,609
	N	W	86	364,371	197,598	256,696	59,098
NETHLDS	A	E	86	1,741,548	429,335	556,826	127,491
	A	W	86	58,508	25,559	37,474	11,915
REP SAF	A	E	86	6,250	3,754	4,380	626
SEYCHEL	A	W	86	5,730	2,170	3,196	1,026
SINGAPR	A	E	86	146,250	42,366	66,722	24,356
	A	W	86	172,671	65,564	94,932	29,368
SPAIN	A	W	86	99,085	38,919	57,840	18,921
THAILND	A	E	86	1,991,982	450,846	715,824	264,978
	A	W	86	867,867	310,798	420,064	109,266

Orchid, plant
1257000 ORCHID PLANTS (NO)

Country	Mode	Reg	Yr	Quantity	F.A.S.	C.I.F.	Charges
TOTAL			81	167,368	345,881	422,081	76,200
			82	197,508	381,042	473,355	92,313
			83	214,083	455,698	555,386	99,688
			84	255,645	605,917	742,405	136,488
			85	220,875	533,438	613,785	80,347
			86	377,513	832,207	944,129	111,922
ARGENT	A	E	82	2,410	7,780	8,695	915
AUSTRAL	A	E	82	2,228	3,486	5,367	1,881

Crop
Product
TSUSA commodity number, description, and unit of quantity

Country	Mode	Reg	Yr	Quantity	F.A.S.	C.I.F.	Charges
			83	787	5,957	8,605	2,648
			84	3,585	6,887	11,863	4,976
			85	450	1,680	1,801	121
			86	200	12,000	12,689	689
	A	H	82	210	530	577	47
			84	30	1,614	1,651	37
			85	24	1,396	1,438	42
	A	W	81	3,284	7,642	8,847	1,205
			82	4,039	9,108	10,598	1,490
			83	147	1,548	1,807	259
			84	100	300	525	225
			86	768	2,250	2,510	260
AUSTRIA	A	E	84	650	384	527	143
BELIZE	A	E	82	14,616	3,090	4,592	1,502
			83	7,409	1,350	1,917	567
	O	E	83	2,752	450	450	
BOLIVIA	A	E	81	737	2,115	2,267	152
BRAZIL	A	E	81	6,929	22,222	26,157	3,935
			82	4,754	16,749	20,849	4,100
			83	19,163	67,014	74,262	7,248
			84	14,135	53,128	61,257	8,129
			85	11,476	38,072	43,517	5,445
			86	11,374	31,840	36,368	4,528
	A	W	81	3,481	13,882	17,039	3,157
			82	1,616	8,932	10,884	1,952
			83	3,044	12,369	16,136	3,767
			84	4,463	14,158	17,468	3,310
			85	3,773	12,691	15,899	3,208
			86	5,308	8,572	11,350	2,778
C RICA	A	E	81	605	3,824	3,850	26
			82	2,374	4,656	4,976	320
			84	210	1,395	1,490	95
			85	420	1,260	1,342	82
	A	W	84	103	831	953	122
CANADA	A	E	84	2,990	2,032	2,188	156
	A	W	81	100	450	525	75
	O	E	86	340	3,887	3,887	
	O	W	81	240	650	650	
			84	24	336	336	
			85	402	3,993	3,993	
CHINA M	A	W	84	525	12,250	12,477	227
CHINA T	A	E	81	192	384	1,088	704
			82	80	400	475	75
			83	18	312	362	50
			84	872	5,608	7,125	1,517
			85	170	15,880	15,936	56
			86	27,500	13,750	13,875	125
	A	H	84	480	480	1,707	1,227
	A	W	82	1,484	1,244	1,842	598
			83	1,315	3,000	4,370	1,370
			84	3,870	4,040	5,378	1,338
			85	500	1,386	1,690	304
			86	63,644	70,353	76,426	6,073
	V	W	83	120	480	603	123
COLOMB	A	E	81	870	6,395	6,595	200
			82	640	2,020	2,388	368
			83	490	1,651	1,770	119
			84	1,000	1,700	2,772	1,072
			85	179	1,525	1,560	35
			86	608	6,683	6,877	194
	A	W	81	1,326	2,887	3,411	524
			82	520	1,560	1,725	165
			83	257	998	1,191	193
			86	1	1,320	1,390	70
FR GERM	A	E	81	3,869	15,669	16,652	983
			82	1,450	2,896	3,026	130
			83	2,860	7,616	8,325	709
			84	2,149	1,979	2,980	1,001
			85	15,490	13,388	14,456	1,068
			86	1,757	8,812	9,524	712
	A	W	81	109	886	1,225	339
			83	400	1,000	1,175	175
			84	380	755	1,005	250
			85	3,500	6,507	6,744	237
			86	960	1,175	2,409	1,234
FRANCE	A	E	81	3,424	16,620	17,397	777
			82	3,092	9,130	9,923	793
			83	5,627	12,103	13,277	1,174
			84	4,383	72,223	82,818	10,595
			85	27,724	39,844	42,196	2,352
			86	39,993	97,615	102,615	5,000
	A	W	81	866	6,042	7,045	1,003
			82	1,320	9,946	10,568	622
			83	8,921	16,687	17,410	723
			84	1,499	2,445	2,740	295
			86	3,558	3,367	3,489	122
GUATMAL	A	E	81	3,762	5,034	5,684	650
			82	1,150	1,480	2,276	796
			84	6,813	15,177	17,510	2,333
	A	W	81	3,674	6,558	8,160	1,602
			82	3,300	3,665	4,491	826
			84	3,255	4,055	4,831	776
HAITI	A	E	85	3,600	1,440	2,193	753
HG KONG	A	W	84	100	2,000	2,065	65
			85	340	6,800	6,909	109
HONDURA	A	E	81	11,799	4,559	5,679	1,120
			82	5,945	3,282	4,062	780
			83	4,277	2,191	3,232	1,041
			84	10,186	3,507	4,417	910
			85	2,100	1,050	1,168	118
			86	5,360	1,480	1,622	142
	A	W	81	755	426	590	164
			82	1,285	745	1,022	277
INDIA	A	E	81	8,045	5,251	10,312	5,061
			82	3,511	4,060	5,908	1,848
			83	11,010	8,786	15,072	6,286
			84	27,079	12,255	21,858	9,603
			85	9,880	9,150	12,259	3,109
			86	3,795	4,085	6,499	2,414
	A	W	81	6,804	7,219	11,383	4,164
			82	7,914	5,398	10,407	5,009
			83	750	438	538	100
			85	1,500	1,050	1,423	373
			86	2,475	1,421	2,542	1,121
	V	E	81	1,068	833	1,657	824
INDNSIA	A	E	85	542	2,005	2,055	50
	A	W	81	703	981	1,304	323
			82	470	1,255	1,697	442
			84	290	2,613	2,970	357
			85	12	3,500	3,535	35
			86	100	2,000	2,106	106
ITALY	A	E	86	20,290	25,062	27,365	2,303
JAMAICA	A	W	81	595	450	629	179
JAPAN	A	E	81	470	1,670	2,560	890
			82	850	3,305	3,916	611
			83	1,020	682	1,103	421
			84	95	338	497	159
			85	2,125	3,120	3,975	855
			86	1,615	6,610	7,385	775
	A	H	81	12,349	11,053	13,687	2,634
			82	8,903	7,013	8,374	1,361
			83	858	3,098	4,132	1,034
			84	20,039	22,021	24,368	2,347
			85	5,488	9,808	10,636	828
			86	30,268	43,069	47,678	4,609
	A	W	81	4,040	20,078	22,519	2,541
			82	2,349	9,824	12,306	2,482
			83	6,478	10,757	13,454	2,697
			84	2,526	5,982	6,650	668
			85	5,946	29,115	32,548	3,433
			86	4,321	13,681	15,415	1,734
	V	E	81	1,500	2,207	2,400	193
KOR REP	A	W	81	1,515	1,594	2,342	748
MADAGAS	A	E	81	3,500	1,500	1,560	60
			83	200	400	659	259
			84	180	260	340	80
MALAYSA	A	E	81	305	420	740	320
			82	200	877	1,052	175
			83	160	829	988	159
			84	170	680	946	266
			85	172	8,318	9,001	683
			86	1,588	3,195	3,551	356
	A	W	81	400	400	1,053	653
			83	897	2,225	2,481	256
			84	1,450	1,729	2,615	886
			85	235	1,395	1,708	313
MEXICO	A	E	81	14,350	3,487	3,607	120
			82	1,590	1,635	1,728	93
			83	300	500	533	33
			84	1,565	18,014	18,318	304
	A	W	81	838	1,933	2,131	198
			82	2,265	3,289	3,790	501
			83	1,990	2,870	3,278	408
			84	3,652	10,593	11,400	807
			85	1,030	2,727	2,962	235
	N	E	84	544	955	1,215	260
	O	E	84	14	350	350	
	O	W	83	2,500	290	290	

Crop
Product
TSUSA commodity number, description, and unit of quantity

Country	Mode	Reg	Yr	Quantity	F.A.S.	C.I.F.	Charges
N ANTIL	A E		85	250	1,448	1,886	438
N ZEAL	A E		82	6,000	3,000	3,786	786
			83	588	1,033	1,451	418
			84	11	1,080	1,394	314
	A H		85	3,500	3,440	3,677	237
	A W		82	1,488	3,838	4,435	597
			84	132	3,496	4,720	1,224
			85	3,630	4,812	5,380	568
			86	2,550	10,529	11,426	897
NEPAL	A E		82	2,900	1,624	2,584	960
NETHLDS	A E		81	2,208	10,725	12,013	1,288
			82	9,424	41,739	49,045	7,306
			83	18,843	76,287	89,118	12,831
			84	42,121	159,799	184,028	24,229
			85	46,127	162,132	186,247	24,115
			86	40,592	223,076	254,642	31,566
	A W		81	19,552	69,677	81,059	11,382
			82	56,966	127,592	154,590	26,998
			83	27,110	72,710	87,810	15,100
			84	27,252	48,611	54,216	5,605
			85	19,726	49,086	54,354	5,268
			86	36,528	106,783	121,792	15,009
	N W		86	2,270	7,356	9,134	1,778
NEW GUI	A H		81	252	894	940	46
			82	100	535	691	156
			83	170	999	1,275	276
	A W		82	800	4,394	5,206	812
			83	1,700	2,253	2,724	471
PANAMA	A E		83	617	1,580	1,692	112
			84	600	1,090	1,377	287
	A W		83	300	900	980	80
PERU	A E		81	400	1,380	1,659	279
			82	400	800	1,017	217
			83	3,000	2,490	3,094	604
			84	1,500	2,250	2,907	657
	A W		81	585	1,070	1,284	214
			82	1,970	3,570	4,783	1,213
			83	3,046	6,391	7,725	1,334
			84	500	500	682	182
			86	2,590	2,969	4,363	1,394
PHIL R	A E		81	1,626	6,208	7,565	1,357
			83	2,128	3,927	4,766	839
			84	6,496	10,606	14,518	3,912
			85	3,219	7,319	10,035	2,716
	A W		81	8,734	8,574	13,224	4,650
			82	4,040	4,897	6,842	1,945
			83	6,163	10,942	13,697	2,755
			84	9,419	8,142	12,138	3,996
			85	30	1,500	1,950	450
REP SAF	A W		84	100	750	780	30
S ARAB	A E		84	40	480	534	54
			85	73	1,020	1,283	263
SINGAPR	A E		81	44	362	442	80
			83	1,000	2,000	3,059	1,059
			84	1,305	1,338	1,961	623
			86	1,810	2,997	4,480	1,483
	A H		84	438	11,167	11,861	694
	A W		81	1,251	1,755	2,436	681
			82	453	375	591	216
			84	7,673	4,661	6,618	1,957
SURINAM	A E		84	300	1,500	4,514	3,014
			85	6,500	11,281	13,081	1,800
			86	2,000	2,500	2,700	200
THAILND	A E		81	23,972	46,343	63,680	17,337
			82	17,822	26,930	39,722	12,792
			83	43,487	55,642	82,726	27,084
			84	22,544	31,449	46,359	14,910
			85	25,834	41,797	59,736	17,939
			86	34,517	40,288	54,639	14,351
	A H		84	767	1,324	2,019	695
			86	1,387	8,661	10,828	2,167
	A W		81	3,711	6,094	8,111	2,017
			82	8,460	6,502	10,904	4,402
			83	6,924	6,211	9,628	3,417
			84	10,508	9,732	14,439	4,707
			85	10,569	12,422	14,547	2,125
			86	9,289	8,811	11,491	2,680
	V W		82	289	1,480	2,210	730
U KING	A E		81	465	3,200	3,611	411
			82	240	1,293	1,314	21
			83	1,725	8,709	9,552	843
			84	3,511	18,357	32,152	13,795
			86	7,018	38,306	40,048	1,742
	A W		81	1,857	13,402	14,071	669

Crop
Product
TSUSA commodity number, description, and unit of quantity

Country	Mode	Reg	Yr	Quantity	F.A.S.	C.I.F.	Charges
			82	5,591	25,118	28,121	3,003
			83	12,845	36,668	37,214	546
			84	1,012	6,044	7,080	1,036
			85	4,339	20,081	20,665	584
			86	11,139	17,704	21,014	3,310
	O E		83	10	262	281	19
			84	10	467	498	31
VENEZ	A E		83	677	1,093	1,174	81
	A W		81	207	876	1,141	265

Oregano

Origanum, essential oil
4524600 ORIGANUM OIL (LB)

Country	Mode	Reg	Yr	Quantity	F.A.S.	C.I.F.	Charges
TOTAL			81	5,732	86,743	89,094	2,351
			82	4,257	58,794	60,611	1,817
			83	5,292	67,245	69,333	2,088
			84	10,262	145,605	149,560	3,955
			85	5,558	65,707	68,044	2,337
			86	7,717	111,944	114,955	3,011
BRAZIL	A E		85	641	3,492	4,202	710
FRANCE	A E		84	55	1,071	1,086	15
SPAIN	N E		81	5,732	86,743	89,094	2,351
			82	4,257	58,794	60,611	1,817
			85	4,520	59,170	60,724	1,554
			86	7,717	111,944	114,955	3,011
	V E		83	5,292	67,245	69,333	2,088
			84	10,207	144,534	148,474	3,940
TURKEY	V E		85	397	3,045	3,118	73

Origanum, spice
1616700 ORIGANUM, CRUDE OR NOT MFRD (LB)

Country	Mode	Reg	Yr	Quantity	F.A.S.	C.I.F.	Charges
TOTAL			81	6,763,535	5,119,440	5,641,764	522,324
			82	8,360,476	6,917,608	7,510,631	593,023
			83	7,921,392	6,198,339	6,818,989	620,650
			84	9,563,782	4,876,969	5,547,367	670,398
			85	7,905,598	4,174,254	4,735,276	561,022
			86	11,699,631	7,902,894	8,599,707	696,813
ALBANIA	V E		82	19,420	21,883	24,275	2,392
BULGAR	V E		81	20,000	16,246	18,584	2,338
CANADA	O E		82	3,040	4,419	4,419	
			83	35,406	14,790	14,790	
			84	52,371	11,524	11,631	107
			85	1,099	1,025	1,025	
CHILE	V E		85	3,224	1,463	1,646	183
			86	54,957	44,604	50,383	5,779
CHINA T	V W		86	10,450	8,598	11,062	2,464
COLOMB	A E		83	335	317	535	218
DOM REP	A E		81	500	400	484	84
	N E		81	45,037	9,234	12,543	3,309
			82	30,013	8,658	11,784	3,126
			83	15,361	4,310	7,103	2,793
			84	3,975	2,320	2,764	444
			86	19,310	10,526	12,255	1,729
	V E		81	1,020	618	841	223
			82	513	425	452	27
			84	30,400	8,693	12,151	3,458
			85	2,113	1,902	1,976	74
			86	24,186	29,232	32,799	3,567
EGYPT	V E		81	205,893	97,722	108,636	10,914
			82	98,673	52,849	58,196	5,347
			83	64,138	56,360	60,631	4,271
			84	4,408	5,514	5,795	281
			85	54,115	28,633	31,094	2,461
FR GERM	O E		81	979	1,128	1,213	85
			82	8	431	474	43
	V E		81	11,020	8,318	9,680	1,362
			82	20,778	17,898	19,947	2,049
			83	26,455	23,290	25,397	2,107
FRANCE	O E		84	1,481	1,000	1,060	60
	V E		82	227,219	221,819	246,239	24,420
			83	50,047	37,682	42,520	4,838
			84	8,818	6,478	6,883	405
			85	76,596	40,632	48,369	7,737
			86	162,111	147,959	164,374	16,415
GREECE	N E		81	1,976,767	1,873,809	2,136,520	262,711
	V E		81	71,492	67,179	76,927	9,748

Crop Product TSUSA commodity number, description, and unit of quantity Country	Mode	Reg	Yr	Quantity	F.A.S.	C.I.F.	Charges
			82	1,698,362	1,940,555	2,156,350	215,795
			83	1,780,720	1,903,878	2,126,051	222,173
			84	1,750,775	1,328,168	1,558,199	230,031
			85	1,608,034	1,173,220	1,374,317	201,097
			86	1,712,419	1,788,426	2,019,079	230,653
	V	W	82	33,890	37,305	43,908	6,603
			83	19,842	22,702	27,699	4,997
			84	2,949	2,520	3,034	514
			85	53,066	43,248	55,524	12,276
			86	44,086	33,942	42,061	8,119
INDIA	N	E	81	17,272	11,795	13,289	1,494
	V	E	83	32,576	14,046	17,537	3,491
INDNSIA	V	E	81	11,000	11,330	12,798	1,468
			85	44,092	35,274	36,115	841
			86	33,069	31,605	33,305	1,700
IRAN	V	E	86	22,080	23,891	26,624	2,733
ISRAEL	V	E	81	102,732	96,120	107,176	11,056
			82	180,843	168,028	195,842	27,814
			83	201,499	215,622	246,086	30,464
			84	142,697	118,680	136,697	18,017
			85	143,289	99,490	117,181	17,691
			86	205,010	157,519	181,332	23,813
ITALY	A	E	82	15	705	801	96
	V	E	82	143,078	139,070	153,126	14,056
			83	3,938	5,596	5,779	183
			84	25,662	17,747	19,263	1,516
			86	12,132	12,334	12,955	621
	V	W	82	56	303	303	
			83	46	289	335	46
LEBANON	O	E	84	1,111	756	860	104
	V	E	82	14,320	12,830	14,491	1,661
			84	2,205	2,050	2,164	114
			85	2,222	1,798	1,887	89
MEXICO	N	E	81	821,364	601,725	642,458	40,733
			82	442,688	432,414	468,757	36,343
			83	433,362	412,240	442,862	30,622
	O	E	81	1,332,063	768,121	768,121	
			82	2,736,125	1,563,363	1,563,363	
			83	2,133,041	938,461	938,462	1
			84	3,273,144	960,333	960,333	
			85	2,651,187	718,759	718,759	
			86	5,503,119	2,009,599	2,009,601	2
	O	W	81	491,180	367,058	367,058	
			82	450,544	345,834	345,834	
			83	359,388	166,938	167,363	425
			84	282,993	160,208	160,208	
			85	326,012	98,111	98,111	
			86	220,523	91,629	91,629	
	V	E	81	114,392	80,990	88,419	7,429
			82	320,627	274,507	297,328	22,821
			83	112,931	97,740	105,499	7,759
			84	217,892	123,315	139,314	15,999
			85	18,611	5,722	7,572	1,850
MOROC	V	E	81	60,626	15,181	22,047	6,866
			82	103,156	42,502	59,156	16,654
			86	118,819	71,526	86,569	15,043
NETHLDS	V	E	81	22,038	20,056	22,564	2,508
PANAMA	V	E	86	19,836	15,428	18,619	3,191
PERU	V	E	84	26,373	14,324	16,702	2,378
			86	24,253	19,800	22,344	2,544
PORTUGL	V	E	84	159	277	374	97
SPAIN	O	E	81	66,100	54,065	58,623	4,558
	V	E	81	22,000	19,800	22,601	2,801
			86	38,500	26,565	29,665	3,100
SWITZLD	V	E	86	20,143	24,671	25,771	1,100
SYRIA	O	E	82	750	948	948	
THAILND	V	E	85	22,046	5,130	5,378	248
TUNISIA	V	E	85	22,000	14,740	16,623	1,883
			86	22,500	21,650	24,371	2,721
TURKEY	N	E	86	2,468,777	2,433,675	2,701,995	268,320
	O	E	82	5,530	7,595	7,595	
	V	E	81	1,370,060	998,545	1,151,182	152,637
			82	1,830,828	1,623,267	1,837,043	213,776
			83	2,652,307	2,284,078	2,590,340	306,262
			84	3,693,900	2,097,846	2,489,615	391,769
			85	2,791,512	1,864,996	2,172,128	307,132
			86	941,311	883,846	983,966	100,120
	V	W	84	10,000	3,906	6,000	2,094
U KING	V	E	85	86,380	40,111	47,571	7,460
			86	22,040	15,869	18,948	3,079
YUGOSLV	V	E	84	32,469	11,310	14,320	3,010

1616900 ORIGANUM, EXCEPT CRUDE (LB)

Country	Mode	Reg	Yr	Quantity	F.A.S.	C.I.F.	Charges
TOTAL			**81**	**124,090**	**68,870**	**71,110**	**2,240**

Crop Product TSUSA commodity number, description, and unit of quantity Country	Mode	Reg	Yr	Quantity	F.A.S.	C.I.F.	Charges
			82	**661,879**	**247,366**	**249,344**	**1,978**
			83	**72,146**	**63,919**	**65,354**	**1,435**
			84	**27,141**	**19,882**	**24,083**	**4,201**
			85	**206,549**	**148,303**	**180,227**	**31,924**
			86	**140,832**	**102,989**	**114,063**	**11,074**
ARGENT	V	W	83	138	384	405	21
CANADA	O	E	82	356,370	95,071	95,071	
			83	40,839	46,729	46,729	
CHILE	V	E	85	15,322	10,008	11,241	1,233
COLOMB	A	E	83	335	317	535	218
DENMARK	N	E	86	19,532	8,950	9,401	451
	V	E	85	2,043	3,378	3,744	366
			86	110	3,140	3,465	325
DOM REP	A	E	81	1,875	830	1,189	359
			82	1,800	932	1,315	383
			83	2,400	750	798	48
			84	2,498	721	1,045	324
	N	E	81	9,035	2,428	3,074	646
	V	E	82	2,500	750	940	190
			83	2,400	385	577	192
			86	400	1,500	1,573	73
FR GERM	O	E	82	953	1,174	1,319	145
			83	2,064	2,167	2,189	22
FRANCE	V	E	81	237	4,867	5,031	164
			82	120	2,159	2,244	85
			83	168	2,422	2,505	83
			84	227	2,116	2,178	62
	V	W	85	6,000	4,453	6,695	2,242
GREECE	V	E	81	2,240	2,016	2,255	239
			82	1,780	2,264	2,563	299
			83	2,080	3,443	3,652	209
			84	531	298	339	41
	V	W	84	2,220	1,658	2,035	377
			86	529	1,680	1,881	201
IRAN	V	W	85	6,452	3,300	4,095	795
ISRAEL	V	E	84	21,094	13,058	16,289	3,231
			85	166,732	118,270	143,115	24,845
			86	1,904	2,000	2,202	202
ITALY	O	W	83	11	458	503	45
	V	E	84	551	1,762	1,908	146
JAPAN	V	E	82	4,776	5,898	6,695	797
			83	4,581	2,754	3,096	342
LEBANON	V	E	86	1,323	1,020	1,105	85
	V	W	86	1,417	1,600	1,714	114
MALAYSA	V	W	82	1,554	727	806	79
MEXICO	O	E	81	104,572	52,286	52,286	
			82	132,450	112,730	112,730	
			86	22,978	9,881	9,881	
	O	W	81	5,509	3,684	3,684	
			82	23,536	6,565	6,565	
THAILND	V	E	81	525	728	800	72
TURKEY	O	E	82	136,040	19,096	19,096	
	V	E	83	4,630	882	1,137	255
			86	92,639	73,218	82,841	9,623
	V	W	85	10,000	8,894	11,337	2,443
U KING	O	E	81	62	1,574	2,314	740
			83	12,500	3,228	3,228	
			84	20	269	289	20
	V	E	81	35	457	477	20

Orris

Orris, essential oil
4524800 ORRIS OIL (LB)

Country	Mode	Reg	Yr	Quantity	F.A.S.	C.I.F.	Charges
TOTAL			81	992	394,516	400,457	5,941
			82	2,454	315,803	322,372	6,569
			83	1,138	276,280	280,862	4,582
			84	980	226,966	232,569	5,603
			85	2,559	636,185	645,665	9,480
			86	2,250	757,110	768,393	11,283
FR GERM	A	E	81	1	596	619	23
			83	4	496	527	31
			86	1	1,014	1,043	29
	V	E	85	838	1,148	1,197	49
			86	837	1,488	1,554	66
FRANCE	A	E	83	1	419	427	8
			86	312	176,416	180,277	3,861
	N	E	81	984	392,607	398,500	5,893

Crop Product TSUSA commodity number, description, and unit of quantity Country	Mode	Reg	Yr	Quantity	F.A.S.	C.I.F.	Charges
			82	2,452	313,896	320,421	6,525
			83	1,122	272,719	277,193	4,474
			84	975	221,715	227,237	5,522
			85	1,709	628,871	638,079	9,208
			86	1,059	566,645	573,520	6,875
ISRAEL	V	E	83	11	2,646	2,715	69
SWITZLD	A	E	81	7	1,313	1,338	25
			82	1	1,550	1,588	38
			84	5	5,251	5,332	81
			85	12	6,166	6,389	223
			86	41	11,547	11,999	452
U KING	V	E	82	1	357	363	6

Ouricury Palm

Ouricury, wax
4941600 VEGETABLE WAX OURICURY (LB)

Country	Mode	Reg	Yr	Quantity	F.A.S.	C.I.F.	Charges
TOTAL			81	13,452	27,602	29,504	1,902
			82	52,921	76,260	80,977	4,717
			83	15,100	32,446	34,861	2,415
			84	54,400	39,653	45,773	6,120
			85	9,005	16,870	18,175	1,305
			86	6,000	11,160	11,888	728
BRAZIL	V	E	81	13,452	27,602	29,504	1,902
			82	52,921	76,260	80,977	4,717
			83	15,000	32,100	34,479	2,379
			84	54,400	39,653	45,773	6,120
			85	9,005	16,870	18,175	1,305
			86	6,000	11,160	11,888	728
U KING	V	E	83	100	346	382	36

P

Papaya

Papain**
4374880 CRUDE FICIN AND PAPAIN (LB)
  (See Ficin under Fig)

Papaya, fresh
1486000 PAPAYAS, FRESH (LB)

Country	Mode	Reg	Yr	Quantity	F.A.S.	C.I.F.	Charges
TOTAL			81	1,365,963	255,824	335,675	79,851
			82	2,280,058	471,941	578,401	106,460
			83	4,096,186	603,097	689,989	86,892
			84	4,260,017	793,494	961,143	167,649
			85	2,070,189	491,139	610,652	119,513
			86	2,625,217	491,400	538,045	46,645
BAHAMAS	A	E	83	70,828	11,932	20,366	8,434
			84	32,004	5,331	8,168	2,837
	N	E	82	29,250	13,196	16,667	3,471
			84	1,545,228	360,006	455,259	95,253
			85	1,541,869	366,110	451,393	85,283
			86	769,405	150,412	191,766	41,354
	V	E	86	28,000	6,450	7,690	1,240
BELGIUM	A	E	81	8,533	2,100	6,030	3,930
	V	E	85	21,000	7,000	7,510	510
BERMUDA	V	E	85	52,500	17,500	19,270	1,770
BRAZIL	A	E	82	170,899	57,980	145,077	87,097
			83	129,225	29,590	88,379	58,789
	A	W	84	1,985	1,610	2,912	1,302
	N	E	81	219,504	59,499	131,170	71,671
			84	82,219	14,250	47,535	33,285
C RICA	V	E	81	5,010	1,754	2,581	827
			82	1,791	418	608	190
			83	50,221	10,883	14,862	3,979
			84	10,436	4,175	5,684	1,509

Country	Mode	Reg	Yr	Quantity	F.A.S.	C.I.F.	Charges
CHINA T	V	E	84	688	800	890	90
	V	W	82	1,852	1,900	1,984	84
COLOMB	A	E	82	28,858	11,366	19,534	8,168
			83	30,624	10,510	17,286	6,776
	V	E	83	8,686	3,948	6,841	2,893
DOM REP	A	E	81	34,158	4,349	7,718	3,369
			84	52,808	10,157	21,512	11,355
	N	E	82	59,744	8,402	14,861	6,459
			83	44,247	5,416	9,068	3,652
			85	62,385	11,353	16,424	5,071
	V	E	82	10,550	1,122	1,465	343
			83	6,750	675	1,070	395
			84	2,850	828	1,113	285
			85	22,280	7,306	8,350	1,044
			86	9,600	3,000	3,270	270
GUATMAL	V	E	85	14,451	3,468	4,184	716
			86	1,898	1,898	2,112	214
HAITI	A	E	83	5,000	1,500	2,848	1,348
	V	E	84	18,900	7,200	7,790	590
HG KONG	V	E	85	2,000	1,084	1,436	352
JAMAICA	A	E	82	2,703	877	1,525	648
			84	76,487	27,020	38,638	11,618
			85	48,334	23,386	47,563	24,177
			86	36,575	17,806	21,373	3,567
MEXICO	O	E	81	345,758	39,555	39,555	
			82	272,762	35,912	35,912	
			83	463,597	18,931	18,931	
			84	530,859	30,160	30,160	
			85	5,093	1,058	1,058	
			86	203,531	12,253	12,253	
	O	W	81	752,100	147,879	147,879	
			82	1,701,649	340,768	340,768	
			83	3,285,262	508,349	508,349	
			84	1,802,846	311,339	311,339	
			85	283,477	47,274	47,274	
			86	1,576,208	299,581	299,581	
N ZEAL	A	W	83	489	813	1,255	442
			84	1,000	2,092	2,764	672
PHIL R	V	E	84	3,449	2,796	3,095	299
	V	W	81	900	688	742	54
			84	126	954	1,054	100
SALVADR	V	E	84	97,232	13,860	22,210	8,350
SPAIN	V	E	85	16,800	5,600	6,190	590
THAILND	V	W	83	1,257	550	734	184
U KING	V	E	84	900	916	1,020	104

Papaya, jelly or jam
1532000 PAPAYA JELLY, JAM, ETC (LB)

Country	Mode	Reg	Yr	Quantity	F.A.S.	C.I.F.	Charges
TOTAL			81	320	279	863	584
			83	2,055	790	959	169
			84	282,468	47,794	60,793	12,999
			85	346,034	64,187	75,609	11,422
			86	187,848	66,570	74,618	8,048
ARGENT	A	E	86	5,069	3,000	4,185	1,185
BAHAMAS	A	E	86	8,000	1,200	1,850	650
C RICA	V	E	85	15,178	4,601	5,509	908
CHILE	A	E	81	320	279	863	584
DOM REP	V	E	84	196,302	30,360	37,580	7,220
			85	329,776	57,212	67,724	10,512
			86	161,781	59,164	64,683	5,519
FRANCE	V	E	84	829	962	1,063	101
			85	1,080	2,374	2,376	2
HONDURA	V	E	84	77,998	8,397	13,621	5,224
JAMAICA	V	E	84	1,800	1,450	1,476	26
PHIL R	V	E	83	2,055	790	959	169
ROMANIA	V	E	86	12,998	3,206	3,900	694
U KING	O	E	84	5,036	6,287	6,681	394
	O	W	84	503	338	372	34

Papaya, paste and pulp
1526500 PAPAYA PASTE AND PULP (LB)

Country	Mode	Reg	Yr	Quantity	F.A.S.	C.I.F.	Charges
TOTAL			81	462,713	115,013	135,101	20,088
			82	231,364	59,446	72,665	13,219
			83	741,254	181,946	228,597	46,651
			84	722,994	172,637	205,042	32,405
			85	571,433	174,392	205,479	31,087
			86	1,138,482	246,304	287,259	40,955
C RICA	V	E	81	276,738	52,999	66,064	13,065

Crop
Product
TSUSA commodity number, description, and unit of quantity

Country	Mode	Reg	Yr	Quantity	F.A.S.	C.I.F.	Charges
			83	195,706	47,633	59,891	12,258
			84	197,350	41,542	51,610	10,068
			85	238,138	97,025	116,114	19,089
			86	495,712	118,459	147,674	29,215
	V	W	83	258,000	61,080	79,851	18,771
CANADA	O	E	84	86,000	19,114	19,114	
			85	178,000	43,020	43,020	
			86	411,320	61,698	61,698	
CHINA T	V	W	82	1,984	772	906	134
DOM REP	A	E	82	3,000	450	740	290
	V	E	81	120,180	43,384	47,861	4,477
			82	112,743	34,227	39,395	5,168
			83	89,533	26,687	31,258	4,571
			84	258,522	64,512	76,308	11,796
			85	106,880	20,893	29,953	9,060
			86	132,907	40,008	46,019	6,011
ECUADOR	V	E	83	12,516	1,341	1,428	87
FRANCE	V	E	82	178	269	283	14
GUATMAL	V	E	83	85,895	16,312	24,709	8,397
			85	7,410	1,778	2,392	614
			86	87,594	21,992	27,086	5,094
	V	W	84	36,350	4,385	4,494	109
INDIA	V	E	82	71,759	18,636	26,249	7,613
			84	100,459	29,019	37,801	8,782
			85	41,005	11,676	14,000	2,324
	V	W	83	46,202	17,055	17,481	426
			84	44,313	14,065	15,715	1,650
KIRIBAT	V	E	86	7,029	1,687	1,982	295
MEXICO	O	E	81	17,729	10,941	10,941	
			82	39,600	4,554	4,554	
			83	4,407	1,234	1,234	
	O	W	82	2,100	538	538	
	V	E	81	48,066	7,689	10,235	2,546
PANAMA	V	E	83	40,000	7,952	9,544	1,592
			86	3,920	2,460	2,800	340
SWITZLD	V	E	83	8,995	2,652	3,201	549

Papaya, prepared or preserved
1486500 PAPAYAS, PREP OR PRES (LB)

Country	Mode	Reg	Yr	Quantity	F.A.S.	C.I.F.	Charges
TOTAL			81	2,283,397	994,133	1,133,364	139,231
			82	3,209,397	1,289,904	1,482,394	192,490
			83	3,854,614	1,880,456	2,105,030	224,574
			84	3,896,764	1,805,787	2,029,062	223,275
			85	4,020,319	1,673,746	1,912,302	238,556
			86	4,518,515	2,023,737	2,232,686	208,949
BAHAMAS	A	E	84	3,000	1,200	1,900	700
BRAZIL	A	E	84	110	595	904	309
	V	E	81	697,554	261,229	307,971	46,742
			82	821,512	290,469	352,905	62,436
			83	866,088	288,493	355,278	66,785
			84	565,236	185,486	226,691	41,205
			85	702,152	224,848	279,282	54,434
			86	484,824	149,276	176,259	26,983
	V	W	81	15,600	5,323	6,646	1,323
			82	16,800	5,905	7,512	1,607
			83	8,400	2,108	2,689	581
			84	10,800	3,500	4,471	971
			85	9,600	2,900	3,786	886
C RICA	V	E	81	90,111	35,193	43,559	8,366
			82	465,551	185,412	224,730	39,318
			83	259,948	91,133	114,766	23,633
			84	240,781	69,404	88,188	18,784
			85	63,495	24,188	29,839	5,651
			86	22,327	6,773	7,397	624
	V	W	83	3,045	608	953	345
CHILE	V	E	83	4,200	3,570	4,068	498
	V	W	85	17,460	19,971	22,232	2,261
			86	18,929	12,720	14,561	1,841
CHINA M	V	E	81	320	754	805	51
			85	14,330	9,170	9,791	621
	V	W	83	840	1,796	1,909	113
CHINA T	A	E	82	1,000	1,050	2,225	1,175
	N	E	84	322,001	229,090	246,016	16,926
			86	565,387	364,312	386,618	22,306
	N	W	85	83,775	51,435	54,555	3,120
	O	E	81	5,808	6,292	6,292	
			82	661	798	1,492	694
			83	6,526	6,656	6,656	
			85	12,320	8,792	8,792	
	O	W	82	630	835	872	37
	V	E	81	5,175	1,639	1,902	263
			82	65,666	56,776	62,327	5,551
			83	793,860	645,760	691,301	45,541
			84	511,849	378,309	409,193	30,884
			85	731,803	470,135	504,985	34,850
			86	117,284	68,475	73,416	4,941
	V	H	86	21,605	9,800	10,753	953
	V	W	81	139,878	119,018	125,621	6,603
			82	113,903	103,850	109,425	5,575
			83	339,062	297,380	317,891	20,511
			84	313,470	219,612	231,664	12,052
			85	180,227	118,801	129,301	10,500
			86	166,929	107,492	112,043	4,551
COLOMB	A	E	83	19,383	15,033	17,222	2,189
	V	E	82	979	725	790	65
DOM REP	A	E	82	2,754	450	740	290
			85	2,600	1,222	1,884	662
	A	W	85	2,541	2,541	3,268	727
	N	E	81	281,409	104,819	120,399	15,580
			82	1,260,645	457,631	504,627	46,996
			84	14,115	3,484	4,884	1,400
	V	E	81	632,677	233,706	261,693	27,987
			82	53,659	25,818	28,306	2,488
			83	1,296,182	423,959	474,799	50,840
			84	1,318,505	437,378	496,701	59,323
			85	1,579,669	470,670	530,899	60,229
			86	1,921,598	659,973	728,370	68,397
DOMINCA	V	E	85	9,030	3,341	3,741	400
GERM DR	V	E	85	17,535	6,488	7,334	846
GREECE	O	E	83	309	389	713	324
	V	E	85	14,370	6,319	8,006	1,687
			86	14,330	7,171	8,978	1,807
GUATMAL	N	E	81	135,995	64,327	75,492	11,165
	V	E	81	76,259	29,711	37,348	7,637
			82	300,974	85,257	104,387	19,130
			83	111,721	23,907	30,021	6,114
			84	100,168	28,852	36,486	7,634
			85	235,739	58,692	72,660	13,968
HAITI	V	E	82	6,830	2,913	3,694	781
			85	11,000	23,500	24,000	590
HG KONG	V	E	83	847	547	592	45
			84	3,098	1,987	2,296	309
	V	W	81	826	529	555	26
			83	9,822	8,778	9,237	459
			84	1,825	1,870	1,993	123
			86	10,608	6,148	6,913	765
HONDURA	O	E	83	10,141	1,825	2,092	267
	V	E	82	5,040	540	1,031	491
INDIA	V	W	83	1,630	1,680	2,007	327
ISRAEL	V	W	83	11,040	3,404	4,372	968
JAMAICA	A	E	82	5,710	3,080	4,140	1,060
			84	13,070	4,002	8,232	4,230
			85	1,935	1,261	3,136	1,875
	N	E	83	2,985	3,003	3,437	434
	V	E	86	1,298	2,184	2,279	95
JAPAN	V	E	84	17,159	13,372	14,376	1,004
	V	H	85	505	1,474	1,733	259
KOR REP	V	E	81	5,625	2,152	2,487	335
			84	35,274	24,440	26,371	1,931
MEXICO	O	E	81	3,751	365	365	
			84	38,115	2,945	2,945	
	O	W	83	5,830	873	873	
			85	31,500	1,943	1,943	
N ANTIL	V	E	82	7,000	1,566	1,820	254
PERU	V	E	84	1,135	555	672	117
PHIL R	V	E	81	1,710	1,749	1,945	196
			82	4,824	5,174	5,950	776
			83	2,650	2,281	2,587	306
			84	18,951	13,062	14,440	1,378
			85	26,516	15,000	16,619	1,619
	V	H	83	220	275	440	165
	V	W	81	174,257	116,349	127,996	11,647
			82	8,625	7,525	8,341	816
			83	7,782	6,922	7,705	783
			84	251,938	104,360	120,482	16,122
			85	178,615	72,531	83,033	10,502
			86	505,962	189,301	225,739	36,438
SINGAPR	V	W	83	15,487	12,964	13,462	498
			84	13,227	12,059	12,566	507
THAILND	A	W	85	50,584	43,882	74,194	30,312
	O	E	82	12,302	11,468	11,468	
	V	E	82	12,865	12,061	13,013	952
			83	14,109	12,160	12,887	727
			84	44,972	32,407	37,273	4,866
			85	28,218	20,043	21,858	1,815

Crop Product TSUSA commodity number, description, and unit of quantity Country	Mode	Reg	Yr	Quantity	F.A.S.	C.I.F.	Charges
			86	625,712	423,652	461,764	38,112
	V	W	81	10,052	8,208	8,827	619
			82	41,467	30,601	32,599	1,998
			83	31,457	11,439	12,551	1,112
			84	26,915	24,593	25,893	1,300
			85	14,800	14,599	15,341	742
TURK IS	A	E	81	6,390	2,770	3,461	691
VENEZ	V	E	83	31,050	13,513	14,522	1,009
			84	31,050	13,225	14,425	1,200
			86	41,722	16,460	17,596	1,136

Parsley

Parsley, seed
1266500 PARSLEY SEED (LB)

Country	Mode	Reg	Yr	Quantity	F.A.S.	C.I.F.	Charges
TOTAL			81	27,981	55,317	62,828	7,511
			82	40,500	69,974	79,745	9,771
			83	45,238	77,560	83,692	6,132
			84	38,781	66,877	72,840	5,963
			85	58,421	228,705	249,516	20,811
			86	61,756	106,652	120,315	13,663
ARGENT	A	E	85	2,785	74,088	81,972	7,884
CANADA	A	E	83	150	500	585	85
CHILE	V	W	81	77	270	277	7
CHINA M	V	E	81	300	496	517	21
			82	200	365	382	17
	V	W	81	30	279	290	11
DENMARK	A	E	81	225	1,114	1,508	394
	V	W	84	6,614	13,110	14,003	893
FR GERM	V	E	82	125	501	512	11
			86	1,010	5,456	5,738	282
FRANCE	A	E	81	1,600	3,757	4,803	1,046
			83	1,700	3,692	4,768	1,076
			85	2,314	3,841	5,620	1,779
			86	3,810	7,772	10,267	2,495
	N	E	81	4,300	9,236	10,743	1,507
			82	6,700	15,770	17,202	1,432
	N	W	85	24,121	102,375	108,088	5,713
			86	30,025	49,992	54,525	4,533
	O	E	83	76	330	330	
	V	E	81	1,150	2,755	3,055	300
			82	8,082	15,983	17,300	1,317
			83	6,000	11,908	13,173	1,265
			84	7,920	14,515	16,518	2,003
			85	8,916	14,715	17,612	2,897
			86	7,947	15,383	17,809	2,426
	V	W	81	17,301	29,667	32,804	3,137
			82	18,216	21,549	27,669	6,120
			83	21,595	33,540	36,624	3,084
			84	17,719	27,337	29,952	2,615
			85	6,614	10,609	11,676	1,067
			86	12,505	16,693	19,721	3,028
ISRAEL	V	W	81	500	790	858	68
			82	1,000	1,322	1,472	150
ITALY	V	E	82	2,679	7,227	7,442	215
	V	W	82	3,144	6,040	6,280	240
			83	9,149	17,233	17,679	446
			84	2,535	4,610	4,681	71
			85	3,483	7,761	7,924	163
MEXICO	O	W	83	5,062	7,593	7,593	
			84	485	605	605	
			85	2,733	4,784	4,784	
			86	1,630	2,852	2,852	
NETHLDS	A	E	81	100	350	385	35
	A	W	81	698	1,758	2,361	603
			82	150	437	671	234
	O	E	83	1,500	2,250	2,400	150
	V	E	81	1,200	3,889	4,176	287
			82	200	402	424	22
			84	992	1,419	1,481	62
			85	1,190	2,489	2,542	53
			86	400	1,206	1,326	120
	V	W	84	2,500	4,065	4,359	294
			85	3,510	4,661	5,414	753
			86	4,415	5,873	6,602	729
U KING	A	E	82	4	378	391	13
			86	14	1,425	1,475	50
	V	E	81	500	956	1,051	95
			83	6	514	540	26
			84	16	1,216	1,241	25
	V	W	85	2,755	3,382	3,884	502

Parsley, spice
1617300 PARSLEY, CRUDE N MANUFACTURD (LB)

Country	Mode	Reg	Yr	Quantity	F.A.S.	C.I.F.	Charges
TOTAL			81	303,989	145,601	200,759	55,158
			82	626,488	284,625	364,189	79,564
			83	691,338	264,679	358,758	94,079
			84	1,613,396	622,811	699,369	76,558
			85	1,018,535	499,303	542,973	43,670
			86	1,750,177	799,104	861,635	62,531
BRAZIL	A	E	83	10,000	3,825	6,029	2,204
C RICA	A	E	85	3,528	2,100	2,879	779
CANADA	O	E	81	16,529	10,456	10,456	
			82	104,660	36,906	36,906	
			83	44,322	24,841	24,841	
			84	77,516	28,312	28,312	
			85	74,133	35,403	35,403	
			86	71,600	7,914	7,914	
	O	W	83	450	300	300	
CHILE	V	E	86	2,205	1,299	1,449	150
DOM REP	A	E	81	226,884	97,628	148,520	50,892
			82	255,380	100,459	157,743	57,284
			83	356,326	133,343	213,378	80,035
			84	26,896	11,176	17,414	6,238
	N	E	84	168,033	70,958	112,565	41,607
	V	E	84	9,630	1,795	2,278	483
EGYPT	V	E	81	14,330	16,394	17,393	999
			82	22,713	29,607	30,961	1,354
FIJI	A	E	82	53,850	25,030	36,817	11,787
			83	5,400	2,268	3,456	1,188
FR GERM	V	E	81	1,333	1,644	1,921	277
			82	2,205	3,581	3,852	271
			84	1,984	3,177	3,234	57
			85	350	1,211	1,306	95
FRANCE	N	E	82	37,514	47,128	52,561	5,433
	V	E	83	54,834	61,186	71,786	10,600
			84	30,270	38,470	45,937	7,467
			85	96,328	61,733	71,398	9,665
ICELAND	V	E	85	35,000	16,457	18,951	2,494
INDIA	V	E	86	15,245	7,846	10,006	2,160
INDNSIA	V	E	84	33,069	13,371	18,171	4,800
			85	35,000	19,943	22,018	2,075
			86	27,558	31,519	33,069	1,550
ISRAEL	V	E	81	7,722	12,259	15,249	2,990
			84	78,602	108,930	123,044	14,114
			85	108,095	177,183	204,857	27,674
			86	234,113	355,526	409,283	53,757
	V	W	86	12,785	20,000	24,124	4,124
ITALY	V	E	83	156	1,879	1,931	52
MEXICO	O	E	81	3,108	1,676	1,676	
			82	14,330	2,060	2,060	
			83	75,920	7,477	7,477	
			84	344,607	74,503	74,503	
			85	15,432	3,500	3,500	
	O	W	81	34,083	5,544	5,544	
			82	126,238	26,379	26,379	
			83	143,930	29,560	29,560	
			84	834,857	253,235	253,237	2
			85	644,055	176,811	176,811	
			86	1,380,920	364,038	364,038	
NEPAL	V	E	82	4,193	3,873	5,261	1,388
NETHLDS	V	E	82	4,400	8,745	10,648	1,903
			84	7,771	18,607	20,298	1,691
			86	4,709	8,030	8,085	55
	V	W	85	6,614	4,962	5,850	888
TRINID	A	E	86	1,042	2,932	3,667	735
TURKEY	V	E	82	1,005	857	1,001	144
U KING	V	E	84	161	277	376	99

1617500 PARSLEY, MANUFACTURED (LB)

Country	Mode	Reg	Yr	Quantity	F.A.S.	C.I.F.	Charges
TOTAL			81	98,237	132,637	146,237	13,600
			82	161,801	197,134	229,631	32,497
			83	214,207	286,642	321,407	34,765
			84	151,707	207,255	232,761	25,506
			85	396,518	554,725	633,675	78,950
			86	327,683	302,740	348,290	45,550
BELGIUM	A	E	83	2,205	3,820	4,299	479
BRAZIL	V	E	85	83,100	81,623	89,938	8,315
	V	W	85	11,880	15,184	19,400	4,216

Crop Product TSUSA commodity number, description, and unit of quantity Country	Mode	Reg	Yr	Quantity	F.A.S.	C.I.F.	Charges
CANADA	O	E	81	7,530	13,096	13,096	
			82	11,407	21,022	21,022	
			83	20,452	40,508	40,508	
			84	4,515	10,622	10,622	
			86	105,600	38,212	38,212	
CHILE	V	E	86	1,985	2,051	2,171	120
COLOMB	A	E	84	28	330	357	27
DENMARK	V	E	85	1,702	2,504	2,808	304
			86	115	2,178	2,262	84
DOM REP	V	E	81	1,410	376	686	310
EGYPT	V	E	81	401	455	489	34
FR GERM	N	E	85	24,687	44,690	52,851	8,161
	N	W	83	25,176	11,896	14,845	2,949
	O	E	82	4,482	3,838	4,199	361
			83	13,585	20,123	21,745	1,622
			85	5,214	4,696	5,217	521
			86	23,869	34,635	39,418	4,783
	V	E	81	19,895	28,913	32,527	3,614
			83	36,777	62,077	68,115	6,038
			84	24,631	29,318	34,728	5,410
			85	14,425	21,970	24,861	2,891
			86	81	1,445	1,480	35
	V	W	81	10,032	3,712	3,757	45
			82	18,745	7,607	11,575	3,968
			84	3,677	6,148	7,062	914
FRANCE	A	E	86	6,935	19,597	24,708	5,111
	N	E	81	11,344	18,707	21,606	2,899
			82	7,151	14,059	15,935	1,876
	O	E	82	18,739	8,147	10,795	2,648
	V	E	83	29,732	31,637	37,298	5,661
			85	2,205	5,032	5,387	355
HUNGARY	O	E	84	4,409	5,873	6,085	212
	V	E	81	46,570	64,754	71,118	6,364
			82	4,418	5,761	6,470	709
			83	6,614	9,193	10,613	1,420
			84	13,500	12,007	13,597	1,590
			85	1,543	2,069	2,296	227
	V	W	84	4,187	4,984	6,155	1,171
INDIA	V	E	84	226	302	305	3
ISRAEL	N	E	82	60,783	95,618	111,094	15,476
	V	E	82	36,076	41,082	48,541	7,459
			83	79,510	107,124	123,710	16,586
			84	86,944	122,396	134,744	12,348
			85	244,778	366,094	416,810	50,716
			86	139,690	174,908	206,408	31,500
	V	W	86	1,995	1,358	1,496	138
ITALY	A	E	86	505	1,152	1,152	
KOR REP	V	W	81	1,010	2,268	2,597	329
			83	156	264	274	10
LEBANON	O	E	81	45	356	361	5
	V	E	86	3,541	2,354	2,691	337
MEXICO	O	W	86	4,397	6,616	6,616	
NETHLDS	V	W	84	9,466	13,892	17,615	3,723
			85	6,984	10,863	14,107	3,244
SPAIN	V	E	86	38,500	17,033	20,405	3,372
TRINID	A	E	86	470	1,201	1,271	70
U KING	V	E	84	124	1,383	1,491	108

Parsnip

Parsnip, fresh or frozen
1378000 PARSNIPS, FRSH, CHLD OR FRZ (LB)

Country	Mode	Reg	Yr	Quantity	F.A.S.	C.I.F.	Charges
TOTAL			81	513,373	128,387	132,110	3,723
			82	185,949	49,475	50,175	700
			83	68,042	19,167	19,759	592
			84	413,316	99,464	106,364	6,900
			85	187,155	45,632	54,434	8,802
			86	562,118	129,948	149,762	19,814
BRAZIL	V	E	85	35,200	17,600	21,902	4,302
			86	102,000	23,000	28,443	5,443
CANADA	O	E	81	482,998	115,242	115,248	6
			82	101,799	34,904	34,904	
			83	48,097	16,985	16,985	
			84	204,750	51,006	51,006	
			85	23,500	6,568	6,568	
			86	139,180	35,517	35,517	
	O	W	86	6,250	2,225	2,225	
COLOMB	V	E	84	102,900	21,000	22,082	1,082
			86	141,300	34,948	38,605	3,657

Country	Mode	Reg	Yr	Quantity	F.A.S.	C.I.F.	Charges
DOM REP	V	E	83	10,950	1,547	2,139	592
			84	43,300	11,552	14,585	3,033
			86	20,000	1,600	1,979	379
ECUADOR	O	E	82	720	255	255	
JAMAICA	A	E	81	13,410	7,527	11,244	3,717
			82	5,850	2,381	3,081	700
			84	20,489	6,213	8,998	2,785
			85	11,224	1,757	1,757	
			86	5,580	1,638	2,388	750
	N	E	86	43,412	19,110	24,850	5,740
	V	E	85	84,000	10,070	14,570	4,500
			86	75,611	6,800	10,645	3,845
MEXICO	O	E	81	16,965	5,618	5,618	
			83	8,995	635	635	
	O	W	82	77,580	11,935	11,935	
			84	41,877	9,693	9,693	
			85	33,231	9,637	9,637	
			86	28,785	5,110	5,110	

Parsnip, seed
1266700 PARSNIP SEED (LB)

Country	Mode	Reg	Yr	Quantity	F.A.S.	C.I.F.	Charges
TOTAL			81	77	2,176	2,503	327
			82	338	2,615	2,759	144
			83	110	2,670	2,807	137
			84	1,926	4,907	5,150	243
			85	121	2,620	2,807	187
			86	229	5,216	5,758	542
NETHLDS	V	E	82	250	403	425	22
			84	606	1,821	1,922	101
U KING	A	E	86	108	2,452	2,713	261
	A	W	81	77	2,176	2,503	327
			85	121	2,620	2,807	187
			86	121	2,764	3,045	281
	V	W	82	88	2,212	2,334	122
			83	110	2,670	2,807	137
			84	1,320	3,086	3,228	142

Partridgeberry

*Partridgeberry, fresh or in brine***
1465200 LINGON OR PARTRIDGE BERRIES (LB)
   (See Lingonberry, fresh or in brine under Cowberry)

*Partridgeberry, frozen***
1466900 BLACK CURRANTS, ETC, FROZEN (LB)
   (See Lingonberry, frozen under Cowberry)

*Partridgeberry, prepared or preserved***
1468200 BLACK CURRNT ETC PREP, PRES (LB)
   (See Lingonberry, prepared or preserved under Cowberry)

Patchouli

Patchouli, essential oil
4525200 PATCHOULI OIL (LB)

Country	Mode	Reg	Yr	Quantity	F.A.S.	C.I.F.	Charges
TOTAL			81	455,002	5,287,725	5,409,315	121,517
			82	665,362	9,591,276	9,777,353	186,077
			83	749,716	10,673,942	10,845,216	171,274
			84	725,846	9,047,027	9,303,679	256,652
			85	544,857	4,459,722	4,557,196	97,474
			86	655,244	5,688,023	5,787,981	99,958
BRAZIL	A	E	83	44	847	970	123
	V	E	82	882	12,784	13,239	455
CHINA M	N	E	81	21,274	238,973	243,630	4,657
	V	E	82	69,887	786,863	801,739	14,876
			83	203,271	2,734,947	2,776,081	41,134
			84	171,081	1,930,686	1,959,365	28,679
			85	66,138	732,843	744,128	11,285
	V	W	82	58,423	652,934	663,918	10,984
			83	19,841	231,427	234,932	3,505
			84	11,023	119,720	121,494	1,774
CHINA T	V	E	83	1,764	20,894	21,284	390

Crop
Product
TSUSA commodity number, description, and unit of quantity

Country	Mode	Reg	Yr	Quantity	F.A.S.	C.I.F.	Charges
FR GERM	A	E	82	110	2,839	3,002	163
			83	110	3,223	3,261	38
			84	110	2,576	2,678	102
	N	E	81	1,863	24,648	24,990	342
	V	E	81	22,046	136,510	138,499	1,989
FRANCE	A	E	82	18	374	399	25
			86	4,761	120,805	123,702	2,897
	N	E	81	3,644	100,938	103,218	2,260
			82	4,786	84,058	86,220	2,162
			83	15,297	184,411	190,098	5,687
			84	32,540	501,572	513,023	11,451
			85	16,932	221,648	226,418	4,770
HG KONG	V	E	82	882	12,367	12,709	342
			83	2,205	24,768	25,179	411
			84	4,409	53,249	54,041	792
	V	W	84	2,205	24,736	25,144	408
INDIA	A	E	83	15	3,349	3,472	123
	V	E	81	1,587	15,469	16,379	910
			86	33,069	298,287	304,464	6,177
	V	W	86	441	5,055	5,211	156
INDNSIA	N	E	82	452,862	6,793,462	6,919,859	126,397
			83	475,394	6,948,107	7,058,784	110,677
			85	457,621	3,446,393	3,525,875	79,482
			86	560,076	4,869,490	4,950,242	80,752
	V	E	81	381,831	4,506,186	4,610,833	104,612
			83	26,455	408,647	415,358	6,711
			84	479,293	6,010,811	6,124,769	113,958
			86	7,858	68,827	70,209	1,382
	V	W	81	22,046	254,254	260,782	6,528
			82	69,688	1,110,911	1,136,057	25,146
			83	2,205	35,391	36,103	712
			84	16,316	200,478	205,726	5,248
			86	40,564	295,853	302,982	7,129
IRELAND	A	E	83	441	9,000	9,500	500
	N	E	82	3,968	67,178	68,653	1,475
ISRAEL	V	E	84	50	850	884	34
ITALY	A	E	82	220	4,161	4,317	156
JAPAN	A	E	84	44	16,807	17,200	393
MALAYSA	V	E	82	1,323	16,291	17,207	916
NETHLDS	N	E	83	13	520	548	28
	V	E	82	220	3,408	3,579	171
SINGAPR	A	E	82	1,323	26,787	29,100	2,313
SPAIN	V	E	84	441	2,380	2,498	118
SWITZLD	A	E	83	2,339	56,713	57,668	955
			86	990	11,153	11,953	800
	N	E	81	611	9,417	9,631	196
			82	682	15,263	15,727	464
			84	6,942	163,684	256,941	93,257
			85	2,865	44,602	46,218	1,616
U KING	A	E	82	88	1,596	1,628	32
	N	E	83	283	7,252	7,492	240
			84	1,047	14,749	15,067	318
			85	1,301	14,236	14,557	321
			86	7,485	18,553	19,218	665
	O	E	83	39	4,446	4,486	40
			84	345	4,729	4,849	120
USSR	V	E	81	100	1,330	1,353	23

Pea

Pea, dried

1404500 PEAS,SPLIT,DRIED, DEHYDRATED (LB)

Country	Mode	Reg	Yr	Quantity	F.A.S.	C.I.F.	Charges
TOTAL			81	1,487,071	787,320	877,662	90,342
			82	1,685,991	539,367	598,807	59,440
			83	1,974,913	552,795	629,008	76,213
			84	2,439,528	597,365	647,103	49,738
			85	2,295,747	690,625	785,486	94,861
			86	4,127,589	982,276	1,096,829	114,553
AUSTRAL	O	E	82	9,900	3,479	3,479	
			83	31,350	11,939	11,939	
			84	20,350	4,626	4,626	
			85	16,500	5,610	5,610	
	V	E	84	123,459	32,780	38,780	6,000
			85	105,822	22,255	26,834	4,579
			86	365,964	65,569	82,709	17,140
	V	W	81	17,820	6,765	7,695	930
			83	26,455	7,385	9,031	1,646
			85	15,250	5,535	6,720	1,185
BELGIUM	V	E	83	9,563	2,879	3,342	463

Crop
Product
TSUSA commodity number, description, and unit of quantity

Country	Mode	Reg	Yr	Quantity	F.A.S.	C.I.F.	Charges
			85	199,683	43,040	55,776	12,736
BRAZIL	V	E	82	14,881	7,425	9,308	1,883
BURMA	V	E	82	551	303	368	65
CANADA	O	E	81	98,271	34,879	34,879	
			82	641,308	95,632	96,407	775
			83	510,390	93,411	93,591	180
			84	1,180,814	199,470	199,470	
			85	673,865	111,035	111,035	
			86	1,625,792	240,846	240,857	11
	O	W	83	144,711	9,733	9,733	
			84	265,820	15,641	15,641	
			85	5,000	1,750	1,750	
			86	45,000	6,188	6,188	
CR N AN	V	E	85	5,000	1,671	1,919	248
FR GERM	V	E	86	104,719	28,500	36,006	7,506
INDIA	N	E	82	41,877	15,441	18,303	2,862
	O	E	82	770	468	468	
			83	6,169	3,139	3,139	
			84	133,364	60,450	68,572	8,122
			85	14,580	6,598	6,598	
			86	22,301	10,003	11,049	1,046
	V	E	81	6,382	2,685	2,879	194
			82	882	350	420	70
			83	10,629	4,971	5,512	541
			84	81,791	30,870	36,062	5,192
			85	468,081	178,490	206,593	28,103
			86	297,660	104,668	122,525	17,857
	V	W	81	5,291	3,118	3,595	477
			85	69,665	31,759	36,429	4,670
			86	148,924	53,585	61,489	7,904
IRELAND	V	E	85	4,500	2,266	2,866	600
ISRAEL	V	W	85	26,289	9,540	11,904	2,364
JAPAN	V	W	85	288	2,173	2,259	86
KENYA	N	E	81	114,263	79,928	88,623	8,695
			82	116,831	46,228	53,872	7,644
			84	61,330	23,480	27,182	3,702
			86	116,940	38,700	45,700	7,000
	O	E	81	121,518	81,943	86,457	4,514
			82	86,783	41,324	42,834	1,510
			83	29,805	10,665	11,122	457
			84	41,233	15,271	18,263	2,992
	O	W	86	2,750	1,100	1,100	
	V	E	81	209,834	119,746	133,835	14,089
			82	452,647	176,285	211,720	35,435
			83	810,213	250,384	300,985	50,601
			84	221,738	62,286	76,585	14,299
			85	170,773	59,705	70,967	11,262
			86	624,766	182,136	210,017	27,881
	V	W	81	6,614	3,504	3,890	386
			82	17,368	9,002	10,654	1,652
			83	2,000	574	574	
			84	11,023	4,750	5,603	853
			85	14,881	12,066	13,591	1,525
			86	106,460	29,549	35,558	6,009
MALAWI	N	E	81	121,440	92,513	100,528	8,015
	O	E	81	104,431	56,491	60,997	4,506
			82	130,324	65,257	66,240	983
			83	38,481	17,674	17,674	
			84	131,825	73,107	73,389	282
			85	72,877	40,102	41,256	1,154
			86	83,318	42,149	42,149	
	O	W	86	5,082	2,313	2,313	
	V	E	81	79,366	42,540	51,686	9,146
			82	14,881	7,544	9,328	1,784
			83	227,399	84,788	100,411	15,623
			84	8,598	4,142	4,771	629
			86	39,683	17,211	19,585	2,374
	V	W	83	40,476	18,901	20,955	2,054
			85	9,149	3,644	3,956	312
MALAYSA	O	E	82	22,046	12,500	12,500	
MEXICO	O	E	85	664	1,420	1,460	40
	O	W	86	57,584	20,154	20,154	
NEPAL	O	E	82	55,220	31,315	31,315	
			83	2,200	977	977	
			85	120,702	49,731	56,629	6,898
	V	E	81	349,152	128,562	141,714	13,152
			85	85,979	30,030	35,491	5,461
	V	W	81	4,409	1,652	1,800	148
NETHLDS	N	E	86	39,281	13,173	14,855	1,682
	V	W	85	882	2,123	2,369	246
PERU	V	E	84	82,928	26,476	30,560	4,084
			85	111,314	29,214	35,514	6,300
			86	399,895	111,092	126,855	15,763
PHIL R	A	W	84	127	509	1,181	672

Crop Product TSUSA commodity number, description, and unit of quantity Country	Mode	Reg	Yr	Quantity	F.A.S.	C.I.F.	Charges
REP SAF	O	E	82	16,530	6,760	7,436	676
	V	E	81	39,683	25,850	33,506	7,656
			83	39,000	15,775	18,875	3,100
SINGAPR	O	E	82	8,818	4,685	5,271	586
	V	W	81	1,110	579	650	71
THAILND	V	E	83	6,389	2,307	2,656	349
			85	2,579	1,035	1,278	243
TNZANIA	O	E	81	6,900	4,063	4,349	286
	V	E	81	39,683	10,800	13,593	2,793
			82	38,400	8,900	11,445	2,545
			85	39,683	9,000	11,548	2,548
TURKEY	O	E	81	2,200	809	890	81
			82	8,818	3,123	3,529	406
			85	5,622	3,057	3,510	453
	V	E	82	2,756	821	1,125	304
			84	598	336	386	50
	V	W	86	4,409	2,608	2,825	217
U KING	O	E	81	40,052	24,211	26,065	1,854
			82	4,400	2,525	2,785	260
			83	39,683	17,293	18,492	1,199
			84	70,033	40,856	43,346	2,490
			85	9,971	4,573	5,345	772
			86	23,545	7,190	8,655	1,465
	V	E	81	118,652	66,682	80,031	13,349
			84	4,497	2,315	2,686	371
			86	13,516	5,542	6,240	698
	V	W	85	46,148	23,203	26,279	3,076

1404600 PEAS, NSPF, DRIED, DEHYDRATE (LB)

Country	Mode	Reg	Yr	Quantity	F.A.S.	C.I.F.	Charges
TOTAL			81	6,627,956	1,810,627	2,006,382	195,755
			82	9,594,083	2,004,056	2,187,231	183,175
			83	11,598,857	1,890,436	2,076,365	185,929
			84	9,014,423	1,793,719	1,906,904	113,185
			85	13,819,286	2,494,356	2,709,718	215,362
			86	21,409,089	3,141,691	3,297,813	156,122
AUSTRAL	O	E	81	36,540	20,535	20,818	283
			82	3,300	1,565	1,565	
			83	1,102	298	307	9
			84	13,750	3,521	3,521	
			85	8,800	2,425	2,425	
	V	E	81	46,297	11,951	16,184	4,233
			82	40,476	4,287	6,701	2,414
			83	1,102	401	460	59
			84	97,191	20,529	24,856	4,327
			85	21,384	4,234	5,119	885
			86	55,005	8,827	11,555	2,728
	V	W	85	22,046	4,909	5,999	1,090
BELGIUM	N	E	82	80,000	22,314	25,592	3,278
	O	E	81	129,301	39,492	46,684	7,192
			83	161,950	43,420	50,366	6,946
			84	48,000	15,331	16,976	1,645
			85	2,750	1,070	1,070	
	V	E	81	55,084	16,422	17,076	654
			82	37,500	11,311	12,118	807
			83	32,046	9,732	10,228	496
			85	137,813	43,141	55,661	12,520
			86	87,892	19,809	27,311	7,502
BRAZIL	V	E	82	1,102	280	351	71
BURMA	O	E	82	100	599	648	49
CANADA	A	E	86	22,050	5,101	5,966	865
	N	E	85	3,992,823	452,531	452,531	
	O	E	81	2,832,588	366,703	366,778	75
			82	5,651,900	598,777	598,777	
			83	7,039,476	740,431	740,691	260
			84	5,103,895	605,062	605,062	
			85	5,366,500	656,572	656,572	
			86	16,080,035	1,840,707	1,840,709	2
	O	W	81	327,464	38,479	38,479	
			82	698,290	89,862	89,862	
			83	1,535,508	150,731	150,731	
			84	1,954,466	186,880	186,880	
			85	1,625,399	176,168	176,168	
			86	3,031,222	322,978	322,978	
CHILE	V	E	85	39,286	7,740	9,471	1,731
CHINA M	V	E	84	221	547	699	152
			85	5,380	5,006	6,097	1,091
			86	38,460	5,391	7,851	2,460
	V	W	86	1,688	1,320	1,383	63
CHINA T	O	E	83	90	775	839	64
	V	E	85	945	1,066	1,205	139
	V	W	82	1,050	1,390	1,746	356
			83	2,664	6,457	6,705	248
			84	6,343	6,597	7,221	624

Country	Mode	Reg	Yr	Quantity	F.A.S.	C.I.F.	Charges
COLOMB	A	E	84	400	278	528	250
DOM REP	A	E	84	4,720	802	1,793	991
	V	E	82	46,000	18,085	20,595	2,510
			83	11,197	1,750	2,291	541
			84	21,400	9,510	10,496	986
			85	39,216	15,258	21,160	5,902
			86	83,400	36,100	38,489	2,389
FR GERM	A	E	84	1,110	2,582	3,053	471
			85	1,000	2,379	2,849	470
	A	W	84	2,331	5,869	7,705	1,836
	O	E	81	11,220	13,964	14,972	1,008
	V	E	86	10,020	3,972	5,408	1,436
	V	W	84	1,110	2,805	3,025	220
FRANCE	A	E	83	3,543	4,500	7,124	2,624
GUATMAL	V	E	81	9,500	2,813	3,420	607
HG KONG	V	W	84	1,002	578	679	101
INDIA	O	E	81	23,144	13,684	14,994	1,310
			82	1,100	405	405	
			83	11,023	4,264	4,632	368
			85	23,640	5,396	6,379	983
			86	2,200	1,084	1,084	
	O	W	81	9,570	10,510	11,000	490
			82	2,480	3,129	3,441	312
	V	E	81	110,341	35,035	40,590	5,555
			84	1,984	962	1,131	169
			85	3,688	2,680	3,038	358
			86	13,693	5,696	6,631	935
	V	W	85	51,101	23,879	26,719	2,840
IRELAND	O	E	81	67,205	73,505	80,151	6,646
			84	67,200	114,017	120,272	6,255
			85	134,400	208,800	226,770	17,970
			86	907	2,533	2,788	255
	V	E	82	67,200	101,946	108,640	6,694
			83	45,973	69,871	74,661	4,790
			84	25,400	40,136	43,838	3,702
			85	67,256	106,199	115,312	9,113
			86	143,331	221,240	240,405	19,165
	V	W	81	26,810	35,304	39,289	3,985
			82	3,300	7,425	10,395	2,970
			83	5,700	18,607	19,140	533
			85	3,304	10,326	11,370	1,044
			86	20,499	7,660	8,160	500
ISRAEL	V	E	85	7,128	13,115	14,255	1,140
ITALY	V	E	83	7,260	1,304	1,680	376
JAPAN	V	E	83	180	1,046	1,124	78
	V	W	81	1,323	848	919	71
			83	159	276	315	39
			86	7,480	7,076	7,588	512
KENYA	N	E	81	294,400	76,170	91,875	15,705
	O	E	81	200,000	59,448	73,077	13,629
			82	9,315	5,701	6,307	606
			83	9,720	6,406	6,681	275
			85	15,873	12,870	14,075	1,205
	O	W	84	12,000	9,270	9,847	577
	V	E	81	371,000	101,723	117,006	15,283
			82	1,261,116	305,691	375,192	69,501
			83	977,246	242,908	292,621	49,713
			84	805,007	243,338	286,006	42,668
			85	389,214	113,279	141,812	28,533
			86	354,000	90,274	113,666	23,392
	V	W	82	27,558	9,160	11,730	2,570
			83	17,637	6,400	7,820	1,420
KOR REP	V	E	84	772	1,115	1,227	112
MALAWI	N	E	81	20,298	9,335	10,625	1,290
	O	E	82	36,376	19,024	20,677	1,653
			83	23,495	13,209	13,537	328
	O	W	82	6,614	3,783	4,160	377
	V	E	83	2,579	866	1,055	189
			84	970	347	418	71
			86	44,092	11,015	12,900	1,885
	V	W	85	2,200	1,424	1,438	14
MOZAMBQ	O	E	82	40,000	11,105	12,796	1,691
			83	80,300	24,427	27,052	2,625
			84	80,601	24,368	27,968	3,600
	V	E	82	80,000	24,533	26,269	1,736
			83	40,000	11,960	13,143	1,183
N ZEAL	A	H	85	4,409	1,500	4,027	2,527
	A	W	83	4,455	14,402	18,791	4,389
	V	E	81	592,220	99,807	146,598	46,791
			82	355,662	67,099	98,227	31,128
			83	1,019,495	127,719	201,009	73,290
			84	222,224	22,713	30,406	7,693
			85	166,732	18,799	30,439	11,640
			86	139,993	17,466	27,111	9,645

Crop
Product
TSUSA commodity number, description, and unit of quantity

Country	Mode	Reg	Yr	Quantity	F.A.S.	C.I.F.	Charges
	V	W	81	39,154	5,847	8,829	2,982
			82	193,700	32,182	44,795	12,613
			83	246,191	51,314	63,842	12,528
			86	29,185	48,838	56,618	7,780
NEPAL	V	E	81	11,000	5,808	6,540	732
			85	119,049	42,390	50,417	8,027
NETHLDS	O	E	81	41,142	11,899	13,741	1,842
			83	1,323	666	718	52
			84	7,511	4,523	5,047	524
	V	E	82	11,210	4,558	5,097	539
			84	4,700	1,868	1,975	107
			85	5,000	2,350	2,712	362
			86	2,909	1,972	2,145	173
	V	W	81	3,960	1,261	1,371	110
			82	1,870	718	773	55
			83	1,430	319	344	25
			84	2,042	685	754	69
PERU	V	E	81	611,988	177,308	197,858	20,550
			82	254,541	78,610	89,645	11,035
			83	21,826	5,305	5,587	282
			84	278,732	82,140	96,972	14,832
			85	1,429,821	382,521	474,426	91,905
			86	718,548	190,054	229,954	39,900
PHIL R	V	E	84	360	314	411	97
	V	W	84	1,323	780	855	75
REP SAF	O	E	82	40,000	10,964	12,796	1,832
	V	E	82	32,427	49,144	50,263	1,119
			83	75,298	111,111	116,737	5,626
			84	74,048	140,278	147,670	7,392
			85	32,146	56,207	59,634	3,427
			86	245,520	40,888	43,963	3,075
SINGAPR	V	W	81	17,628	7,498	8,660	1,162
SWITZLD	O	E	86	4,160	2,170	2,170	
THAILND	V	E	81	126	457	523	66
			84	132	475	579	104
TNZANIA	N	E	81	333,219	93,839	108,053	14,214
	O	E	81	2,200	991	1,093	102
	V	E	81	80,000	20,139	24,250	4,111
			82	105,821	24,000	31,348	7,348
TURKEY	O	E	82	3,300	1,248	1,248	
	V	E	83	75,990	17,010	20,076	3,066
			84	2,539	1,061	1,298	237
			85	1,044	1,034	1,128	94
U KING	N	E	81	10,467	4,463	4,973	510
			82	434,301	421,384	436,294	14,910
			85	11,900	7,034	8,938	1,904
			86	75,042	90,569	103,127	12,558
	O	E	81	178,308	276,079	286,700	10,621
			82	11,670	8,917	9,447	530
			83	105,431	187,201	196,947	9,746
			84	147,164	232,156	243,941	11,785
			85	63,789	77,134	82,624	5,490
			86	13,580	6,542	7,307	765
	O	W	84	9,251	7,400	7,749	349
	V	E	81	24,251	37,278	39,408	2,130
			82	7,412	7,628	8,224	596
			83	14,714	7,334	8,890	1,556
			84	10,115	3,800	4,608	808
			85	24,250	34,920	37,878	2,958
			86	138,112	140,510	156,315	15,805
	V	W	81	110,208	142,032	153,848	11,816
			82	47,392	57,232	61,107	3,875
			83	22,754	8,016	10,221	2,205
			84	4,409	1,082	1,438	356
			86	46,066	11,899	14,231	2,332

Pea, fresh
1369500 PEAS NSPF FR, CHLD 7/1-9/30 (LB)

Country	Mode	Reg	Yr	Quantity	F.A.S.	C.I.F.	Charges
TOTAL			81	71,580	51,461	65,003	13,542
			82	184,762	58,437	79,093	20,656
			83	319,985	129,844	181,389	51,545
			84	883,047	339,018	485,807	146,789
			85	2,253,447	751,390	1,058,606	307,216
			86	1,308,875	434,585	633,623	199,038
CANADA	O	E	81	1,500	544	544	
			82	84,720	18,783	18,783	
			83	666	258	258	
			84	152,167	16,980	16,980	
			85	661,018	88,152	88,152	
			86	175,740	27,830	27,830	
CHINA T	A	H	84	397	1,080	2,594	1,514

Crop
Product
TSUSA commodity number, description, and unit of quantity

Country	Mode	Reg	Yr	Quantity	F.A.S.	C.I.F.	Charges
	V	W	86	21,600	17,705	19,048	1,343
DOM REP	A	E	82	79,244	32,526	49,607	17,081
			83	127,363	73,409	100,516	27,107
			84	468,005	184,591	285,222	100,631
			85	816,734	257,192	435,951	178,759
			86	295,423	133,124	197,754	64,630
	N	E	81	16,104	7,093	10,747	3,654
	V	E	84	3,600	1,380	1,680	300
			86	40,416	13,500	14,625	1,125
FRANCE	V	E	85	2,881	1,498	1,657	159
GUATMAL	A	E	81	25,147	19,503	23,072	3,569
			82	12,728	5,154	7,504	2,350
			83	2,200	550	1,076	526
			84	8,950	3,580	5,492	1,912
			86	112,461	34,179	63,706	29,527
	A	W	81	23,510	22,295	28,314	6,019
			83	12,237	13,552	17,753	4,201
			84	16,512	7,000	12,604	5,604
			86	5,120	1,536	3,376	1,840
	N	E	83	167,044	40,182	59,223	19,041
			84	199,293	112,319	149,147	36,828
			85	656,242	368,795	478,109	109,314
			86	601,813	185,761	280,521	94,760
	N	W	85	39,240	13,787	24,101	10,314
	V	E	85	16,592	4,880	7,455	2,575
HONDURA	A	E	86	36,408	16,204	22,017	5,813
	V	E	83	8,000	1,200	1,870	670
MEXICO	A	W	81	2,669	946	1,246	300
			85	17,000	4,250	10,345	6,095
	O	W	81	2,650	1,080	1,080	
			82	5,070	1,014	1,014	
			83	2,475	693	693	
			84	34,123	12,088	12,088	
			85	43,740	12,836	12,836	
			86	19,894	4,746	4,746	
W SAMOA	A	W	82	3,000	960	2,185	1,225

1370410 PEAS NSPF, FR/CH 10/1-6/30 (LB)

Country	Mode	Reg	Yr	Quantity	F.A.S.	C.I.F.	Charges
TOTAL			81	8,704,951	4,083,413	4,478,334	395,920
			82	10,723,255	6,120,920	6,796,218	675,298
			83	13,993,304	7,469,673	8,621,728	1,152,055
			84	17,994,931	8,368,224	9,987,406	1,619,182
			85	14,308,737	6,662,891	7,818,259	1,155,368
			86	6,934,237	3,484,371	3,544,889	60,518
BELGIUM	A	W	83	462	517	611	94
	O	E	82	12,150	3,293	3,293	
	V	E	84	37,699	7,117	8,244	1,127
BRAZIL	A	E	81	720	288	446	158
			82	2,500	600	1,804	1,204
CANADA	O	E	81	120,000	32,585	32,585	
			82	223,797	35,448	35,448	
			83	177,352	27,173	27,173	
			84	293,422	65,398	65,398	
			85	536,820	25,353	25,353	
			86	194,255	34,382	34,382	
CHINA M	O	E	84	400	500	500	
CHINA T	V	E	85	67,095	52,996	62,345	9,349
			86	33,750	25,288	29,438	4,150
	V	W	85	62,891	42,458	47,832	5,374
			86	622,334	432,810	463,203	30,393
COLOMB	A	E	81	11,900	4,760	6,066	1,306
			83	21,918	3,397	4,483	1,086
			84	9,900	3,469	5,218	1,749
			85	2,640	2,112	3,276	1,164
	N	E	86	7,849	9,630	10,146	516
DOM REP	A	E	81	740,596	288,182	435,511	147,329
			82	1,115,690	379,738	617,449	237,711
			83	187,974	46,142	84,770	38,628
			84	616,318	189,402	313,168	123,766
			85	2,438,376	919,613	1,398,192	478,579
			86	33,293	20,720	27,767	7,047
	N	E	83	1,595,692	650,370	990,802	340,432
			84	2,132,426	743,551	1,208,458	464,907
	O	E	84	1,186	484	484	
	V	E	86	94,000	33,250	35,866	2,616
FRANCE	A	E	84	4,740	806	1,801	995
			85	6,360	2,090	5,290	3,200
	O	W	86	2,904	2,904	2,904	
	V	W	82	6,837	1,151	1,221	70
GUATMAL	A	E	81	53,354	30,351	38,622	8,271
			82	178,544	99,178	130,926	31,748
			83	30,161	14,382	25,453	11,071
			84	298,518	110,257	200,625	90,368

Crop Product TSUSA commodity number, description, and unit of quantity Country	Mode	Reg	Yr	Quantity	F.A.S.	C.I.F.	Charges
			85	36,341	20,179	29,245	9,066
	A	W	81	116,619	62,827	93,444	30,617
			82	195,716	91,439	146,969	55,530
			83	257,244	123,884	207,183	83,299
			84	173,714	90,217	143,490	53,273
			85	12,000	4,800	9,279	4,479
			86	55,664	20,068	35,864	15,796
	N	E	81	1,577,434	796,285	994,151	197,866
			82	2,072,358	1,042,920	1,386,091	343,171
			83	3,113,386	1,397,169	2,064,377	667,208
			84	3,917,674	1,770,477	2,632,809	862,332
			85	2,562,028	1,106,577	1,638,429	531,852
	N	W	85	314,411	257,184	329,678	72,494
	O	E	85	16,560	5,776	6,046	270
	V	E	81	24,990	11,289	13,816	2,527
HAITI	A	E	81	2,100	1,050	1,466	416
			82	21,160	8,732	12,277	3,545
			84	8,300	3,320	4,848	1,528
HONDURA	A	E	84	36,910	61,215	72,547	11,332
			85	600	3,600	4,380	780
INDIA	O	E	82	525	318	318	
JAMAICA	A	E	81	100	275	312	37
			85	5,027	3,199	4,210	1,011
KIRIBAT	A	E	85	84,558	28,640	46,722	18,082
MALAYSA	O	W	85	4,422	1,474	1,474	
			86	16,095	6,105	6,105	
MEXICO	A	E	84	6,135	4,169	6,073	1,904
	A	W	81	13,906	5,400	6,705	1,305
			82	2,721	1,240	1,440	200
			83	4,800	2,400	3,987	1,587
			84	3,657	1,760	2,728	968
			85	43,292	47,258	55,119	7,861
	O	E	82	621	270	270	
	O	W	81	6,043,232	2,850,121	2,855,210	6,088
			82	6,890,386	4,456,093	4,458,173	2,080
			83	8,561,175	5,181,725	5,181,725	
			84	10,441,557	5,311,380	5,311,380	
			85	7,992,042	4,104,624	4,104,625	1
			86	5,874,093	2,899,214	2,899,214	
MONSRAT	V	E	82	250	500	539	39
MOZAMBQ	O	W	85	30,838	14,069	14,069	
N ZEAL	V	E	85	86,440	18,569	29,821	11,252
NETHLDS	A	E	84	132	320	406	86
	O	E	83	10,101	9,061	9,061	
	V	W	83	19,841	6,346	8,032	1,686
PANAMA	A	E	83	8,020	4,698	10,512	5,814
			84	4,048	920	2,858	1,938
PERU	A	E	84	6,370	2,732	5,260	2,528
PORTUGL	A	E	83	3,600	1,620	2,412	792
SWEDEN	A	E	83	1,578	789	1,147	358
TURKEY	V	W	85	5,996	2,320	2,874	554
VENEZ	A	E	84	1,825	730	1,111	381

Pea, frozen

1369700 PEAS, FROZEN, NSPF 7/1-9/30 (LB)

Country	Mode	Reg	Yr	Quantity	F.A.S.	C.I.F.	Charges
TOTAL			81	2,899,301	1,231,272	1,308,095	76,823
			82	7,829,253	2,913,581	3,197,410	283,829
			83	5,496,655	2,067,062	2,225,409	158,347
			84	9,444,485	3,437,856	3,739,631	301,775
			85	4,115,379	1,563,786	1,661,120	97,334
			86	3,597,838	1,808,808	1,971,783	162,975
CANADA	O	E	81	2,300,407	716,434	716,434	
			82	3,622,201	1,263,884	1,263,884	
			83	3,192,403	1,131,269	1,131,269	
			84	5,563,669	1,790,529	1,790,529	
			85	3,034,447	866,017	866,017	
			86	1,794,944	429,556	429,556	
	O	W	82	579,000	215,448	215,448	
			83	686,125	283,612	283,612	
			84	123,789	48,227	48,227	
CHINA T	V	E	81	475,043	406,886	473,091	66,205
			82	438,759	378,217	443,026	64,809
			83	415,736	297,803	352,435	54,632
			84	868,998	722,920	850,156	127,236
			85	332,859	247,152	293,049	45,897
			86	602,447	533,278	607,890	74,612
	V	H	81	15,600	13,223	14,586	1,363
			83	2,205	2,522	2,800	278
			85	15,600	10,666	12,529	1,863
			86	15,600	12,409	14,109	1,700
	V	W	81	84,725	76,455	83,076	6,621

Country	Mode	Reg	Yr	Quantity	F.A.S.	C.I.F.	Charges
			82	108,450	91,645	103,096	11,451
			83	143,922	121,157	133,704	12,547
			84	385,894	223,103	252,378	29,275
			85	345,520	266,949	292,721	25,772
			86	1,073,858	810,492	886,939	76,447
DOM REP	V	E	81	19,520	14,640	15,811	1,171
			84	34,310	10,575	12,415	1,840
			85	8,400	3,650	4,200	550
FRANCE	V	E	82	2,205,010	725,927	853,378	127,451
GUATMAL	A	W	81	1,520	380	774	394
	V	E	84	9,850	8,422	9,591	1,169
			85	21,826	19,465	20,588	1,123
INDIA	O	E	84	990	792	792	
JAPAN	V	E	85	95,850	74,762	88,182	13,420
MEXICO	O	W	82	2,700	540	540	
			86	4,940	1,596	1,596	
N ZEAL	V	E	84	358,800	109,149	117,512	8,363
	V	W	84	118,800	23,175	35,108	11,933
NETHLDS	O	E	84	313,083	84,538	101,767	17,229
	V	E	84	97,410	25,684	35,070	9,386
NICARAG	V	E	82	108,000	25,812	35,182	9,370
PORTUGL	V	E	81	2,486	3,254	4,323	1,069
SALVADR	V	E	85	43,182	16,864	21,056	4,192
			86	15,460	4,567	5,733	1,166
SWEDEN	N	E	85	128,385	36,152	36,152	
	O	E	83	882,720	192,260	270,644	78,384
			84	1,238,024	301,839	382,268	80,429
			85	45,210	8,438	12,955	4,517
			86	90,589	16,910	25,960	9,050
	O	W	84	44,136	13,814	13,814	
	V	E	82	220,680	54,054	70,915	16,861
			83	173,544	38,439	50,945	12,506
			84	132,408	39,639	43,776	4,137
	V	W	82	544,453	158,054	211,941	53,887
U KING	O	E	84	154,324	35,450	46,228	10,778
			85	44,100	13,671	13,671	

1370440 PEAS, FROZEN NSPF 10/1-6/30 (LB)

Country	Mode	Reg	Yr	Quantity	F.A.S.	C.I.F.	Charges
TOTAL			81	6,098,527	3,155,170	3,498,347	343,757
			82	8,516,551	4,926,307	5,593,048	666,741
			83	9,953,574	4,588,589	5,146,345	557,756
			84	12,816,430	7,243,469	8,027,491	784,022
			85	12,258,211	5,165,052	5,795,625	630,573
			86	13,949,088	7,278,925	7,949,056	670,131
BELGIUM	V	E	85	48,210	69,213	74,569	5,356
C RICA	V	E	85	150,766	25,200	34,642	9,442
CANADA	O	E	81	3,379,464	939,238	938,958	
			82	2,147,529	749,772	749,772	
			83	4,616,357	1,606,202	1,606,202	
			84	4,725,019	1,555,111	1,558,201	3,090
			85	5,762,652	1,650,260	1,650,263	3
			86	4,911,325	1,170,684	1,170,686	2
	O	W	83	2,100	812	812	
			84	264,694	83,780	83,780	
CHINA M	V	W	86	22,500	18,908	20,251	1,343
CHINA T	N	E	86	1,175,889	876,761	984,047	107,286
	O	E	81	20,250	19,045	22,027	2,982
	V	E	81	1,466,442	1,236,389	1,431,101	194,712
			82	1,938,737	1,673,736	1,930,150	256,414
			83	1,719,691	1,237,112	1,449,374	212,262
			84	2,642,393	2,186,926	2,524,861	337,935
			85	2,067,515	1,548,001	1,823,118	275,117
			86	1,970,017	1,435,719	1,648,976	213,257
	V	H	81	31,200	24,603	28,255	3,652
			82	62,400	51,193	57,530	6,337
			83	15,600	10,936	12,324	1,388
			84	62,400	51,222	57,924	6,702
			85	31,200	21,613	25,183	3,570
			86	51,000	41,300	45,117	3,817
	V	W	81	693,191	585,061	650,964	65,903
			82	1,522,923	1,217,073	1,370,096	153,023
			83	1,309,626	952,873	1,077,591	124,718
			84	3,343,237	2,584,396	2,869,883	285,487
			85	1,676,160	1,182,968	1,326,790	143,822
			86	4,321,174	3,224,565	3,467,981	243,416
DENMARK	V	E	83	439,633	127,919	159,533	31,614
DOM REP	A	E	83	2,625	1,313	1,937	624
	N	E	81	6,108	4,098	4,768	670
	O	E	84	1,378	308	308	
			85	14,000	2,380	2,380	
	V	E	81	4,830	1,242	1,467	225
			83	37,950	28,556	31,624	3,068
			84	2,919	2,131	2,450	319

Crop Product TSUSA commodity number, description, and unit of quantity Country	Mode	Reg	Yr	Quantity	F.A.S.	C.I.F.	Charges
FR GERM	V	E	83	30,825	30,209	34,554	4,345
FRANCE	V	E	85	1,333,914	278,446	388,223	109,777
			86	54,321	22,067	27,425	5,358
GUATMAL	A	E	81	2,250	2,812	2,845	33
			82	8,952	6,352	7,980	1,628
	A	W	83	4,875	2,431	4,042	1,611
			86	4,400	1,320	2,904	1,584
	N	E	81	156,159	135,128	171,882	37,054
			82	283,224	298,599	361,535	62,936
			83	437,793	298,918	382,547	83,629
			84	565,783	452,002	512,816	60,814
	V	E	81	135,649	98,260	120,943	22,683
			82	45,135	35,226	42,540	7,314
			83	159,265	51,771	64,919	13,148
			84	69,822	49,994	57,157	7,163
			85	344,150	190,719	224,400	33,681
			86	658,717	198,308	254,172	55,864
HAITI	A	E	83	3,250	910	1,628	718
JAPAN	V	H	82	1,012	723	810	87
	V	W	81	15,600	11,419	13,067	1,648
			86	18,000	14,936	14,936	
KIRIBAT	V	E	85	6,303	2,206	2,598	392
MEXICO	A	E	81	5,100	2,000	2,654	654
	O	E	82	41,720	4,722	4,722	
			86	98,645	55,302	55,302	
	O	W	81	6,833	3,673	3,673	
			85	21,520	8,107	8,107	
			86	16,392	15,026	15,026	
N ZEAL	V	E	85	211,071	34,095	52,260	18,165
NETHLDS	V	E	83	661,412	107,047	147,271	40,224
			86	11,839	5,795	7,347	1,552
NICARAG	V	E	81	45,514	24,953	28,533	3,580
	V	W	81	129,080	66,702	76,512	9,810
PHIL R	V	W	82	2,600	2,077	2,459	382
PORTUGL	V	E	81	857	547	698	151
			84	2,208	861	1,074	213
SALVADR	V	E	83	63,975	19,724	24,528	4,804
			86	33,750	17,480	20,448	2,968
	V	W	86	138,454	50,914	63,260	12,346
SWEDEN	O	E	83	4,000	1,621	1,621	
			84	384,341	102,983	123,817	20,834
			85	468,464	113,245	140,045	26,800
			86	435,170	116,257	133,765	17,508
	V	E	83	220,680	48,050	61,864	13,814
			84	397,532	89,467	124,397	34,930
	V	W	83	132,717	36,213	49,496	13,283
THAILND	V	E	85	7,187	11,600	12,075	475
U KING	O	E	83	2,880	1,204	1,204	
			84	260,144	62,776	81,268	18,492
			85	44,098	12,788	12,788	
	V	E	82	1,972,898	738,985	879,653	140,668
			83	88,320	24,768	33,274	8,506
			84	94,560	21,512	29,555	8,043
			85	71,001	14,211	18,184	3,973
	V	W	82	489,421	147,849	185,801	37,952
USSR	V	W	86	27,495	13,583	17,413	3,830

Pea, pod, frozen**
1384100 MIX PEA POD/WATER CHSTNT FZ (LB)

Country	Mode	Reg	Yr	Quantity	F.A.S.	C.I.F.	Charges
TOTAL			82	159,819	138,850	155,118	16,268
			83	111,000	77,620	88,355	10,735
			84	283,405	250,919	276,926	26,007
			85	748,471	581,961	675,395	93,434
			86	218,731	179,119	192,646	13,527
CHINA M	V	W	83	22,200	8,203	10,677	2,474
			86	13,500	11,344	12,149	805
CHINA T	V	E	83	8,325	7,326	8,513	1,187
			84	27,675	24,354	28,060	3,706
			85	569,625	446,930	526,472	79,542
			86	33,988	29,910	33,511	3,601
	V	W	82	159,819	138,850	155,118	16,268
			83	80,475	62,091	69,165	7,074
			84	255,730	226,565	248,866	22,301
			85	145,346	119,956	131,121	11,165
			86	171,243	137,865	146,986	9,121
GUATMAL	V	E	85	33,500	15,075	17,802	2,727

Pea, prepared or preserved
1415500 PEAS PREP, PRES, EXC DRIED (LB)

Country	Mode	Reg	Yr	Quantity	F.A.S.	C.I.F.	Charges
TOTAL			81	11,252,925	4,285,758	4,801,940	516,182
			82	10,489,472	4,270,642	4,709,173	438,531
			83	16,046,843	6,858,135	7,527,268	669,133
			84	30,843,635	10,386,077	11,461,353	1,075,276
			85	25,434,299	7,808,546	8,604,513	795,967
			86	20,130,314	7,389,511	7,976,501	586,990
BAHAMAS	V	E	84	540	440	476	36
BELGIUM	O	E	85	33,750	9,000	10,500	1,500
	V	E	81	47,025	13,181	15,181	2,000
			82	2,000	671	749	78
			83	167,994	41,354	47,010	5,656
			84	1,264,252	291,689	361,715	70,026
			85	2,468,430	570,574	708,699	138,125
			86	627,639	224,369	261,834	37,465
	V	W	81	2,250	1,066	1,296	230
			84	478,280	78,941	97,988	19,047
			85	140,721	25,494	30,001	4,507
			86	88,128	38,775	43,624	4,849
C RICA	V	E	83	1,334	739	860	121
			84	48,621	19,787	22,284	2,497
			85	7,770	4,137	5,404	1,267
CANADA	N	E	86	591,500	114,099	114,099	
	O	E	81	959,706	206,794	206,794	
			82	1,052,462	221,568	221,568	
			83	2,077,053	486,087	486,612	525
			84	5,996,827	1,566,942	1,566,942	
			85	4,178,689	905,764	905,764	
			86	2,289,855	424,525	424,525	
CHINA M	O	E	85	3,600	2,787	3,357	570
	V	E	82	960	341	414	73
	V	W	84	104,722	21,689	24,681	2,992
			86	4,200	2,460	4,160	1,700
CHINA T	N	E	86	*	3,909	4,179	270
	O	E	82	7,870	10,710	11,947	1,237
	V	E	82	760	460	703	243
			83	6,345	3,642	4,186	544
			84	21,598	12,638	15,739	3,101
			85	11,573	6,993	9,550	2,557
			86	3,600	2,467	2,901	434
	V	H	83	2,540	3,269	3,745	476
			84	1,058	1,398	1,519	121
			86	2,160	1,959	2,137	178
	V	W	82	12,015	10,466	11,860	1,394
			83	1,874	2,977	3,322	345
			84	7,200	3,526	4,220	694
			85	17,294	17,239	18,610	1,371
			86	42,274	27,344	31,233	3,889
DENMARK	V	E	85	33,750	8,730	10,522	1,792
	V	W	83	583	264	302	38
DOM REP	N	E	82	900,884	384,591	417,318	32,727
			85	9,750,304	3,473,063	3,727,945	254,882
			86	10,181,910	4,288,853	4,595,915	307,062
	V	E	81	9,681,898	3,736,267	4,207,542	471,275
			82	7,873,754	3,318,184	3,684,573	366,389
			83	12,949,044	5,914,773	6,527,790	613,017
			84	17,474,135	6,883,658	7,540,433	656,775
			85	3,626,466	1,361,735	1,460,870	99,135
			86	4,349,127	1,592,689	1,709,512	116,823
	V	W	81	33,750	15,000	18,164	3,164
			83	36,000	19,500	23,229	3,729
			84	36,000	15,750	19,631	3,881
FR GERM	V	E	82	38,640	16,303	18,508	2,205
			85	16,205	4,870	5,859	989
			86	25,323	7,862	8,785	923
	V	W	81	44	264	363	99
			82	44	337	507	170
FRANCE	N	E	85	27,527	5,434	7,215	1,781
	O	E	84	2,100	773	844	71
	V	E	81	10,993	5,757	6,489	732
			82	79,190	37,649	42,881	5,232
			83	162,817	56,658	62,702	6,044
			84	1,863,982	451,426	568,815	117,389
			85	2,082,069	440,372	555,259	114,887
			86	961,357	225,880	276,463	50,583
	V	W	82	3,075	2,869	3,342	473
			83	3,595	1,257	1,345	88
			84	59,332	24,505	29,950	5,445
			85	12,222	4,031	4,878	847
GREECE	V	E	83	9,370	9,905	11,477	1,572

Crop Product TSUSA commodity number, description, and unit of quantity Country	Mode	Reg	Yr	Quantity	F.A.S.	C.I.F.	Charges
			84	529	310	423	113
GUATMAL	A	E	85	7,000	7,000	8,959	1,959
HAITI	V	E	82	196,800	73,800	82,551	8,751
			83	206,544	96,170	109,945	13,775
			85	144,000	51,000	54,045	3,045
HG KONG	V	E	83	213	1,240	1,405	165
	V	W	84	300	513	541	28
INDIA	N	E	85	30,423	15,226	17,828	2,602
			86	10,379	4,461	4,970	509
	O	E	83	4,409	2,194	2,194	
			85	950	1,129	1,129	
	O	W	81	10,450	7,271	7,904	633
	V	E	81	12,243	7,246	9,304	2,058
			82	3,675	1,636	2,124	488
			83	9,377	3,893	4,613	720
			84	95,817	35,840	42,179	6,339
			85	244,161	100,128	113,374	13,246
			86	72,413	28,910	32,807	3,897
	V	W	81	1,347	637	828	191
			82	8,691	4,530	5,800	1,270
			83	2,498	2,409	3,050	641
			84	3,630	2,049	2,465	416
			86	28,275	13,914	16,339	2,425
INDNSIA	V	W	83	275	437	468	31
IRELAND	V	E	84	4,500	2,301	3,622	1,321
ITALY	V	E	84	1,105,966	208,811	267,497	58,686
			85	82,393	15,690	21,669	5,979
JAMAICA	V	E	83	48,540	27,023	28,639	1,616
			84	3,030	1,431	1,734	303
JAPAN	N	W	85	117,731	84,497	97,687	13,190
	V	E	82	173	263	295	32
			83	1,095	1,456	1,728	272
			84	413	600	788	188
			85	4,500	3,723	4,140	417
			86	11,370	15,861	16,966	1,105
	V	H	81	1,753	3,194	3,736	542
			82	1,524	1,737	1,924	187
			83	6,547	7,887	9,060	1,173
			84	13,276	14,878	17,122	2,244
			85	825	1,030	1,072	42
			86	8,237	12,283	13,592	1,309
	V	W	81	86,261	79,934	87,648	7,714
			82	152,596	119,673	132,257	12,584
			83	135,275	93,988	103,212	9,224
			84	122,334	100,491	110,683	10,192
			85	107,048	81,932	88,792	6,860
			86	145,951	131,150	143,378	12,228
KENYA	N	E	84	265,105	130,730	147,708	16,978
	O	E	84	39,683	30,393	32,563	2,170
	V	E	81	200,619	132,597	149,902	17,305
			82	6,614	3,000	3,628	628
			83	121,115	38,551	45,837	7,286
			84	158,732	61,200	71,847	10,647
			85	141,462	70,092	81,418	11,326
			86	58,642	18,305	21,888	3,583
	V	W	81	1,203	622	905	283
LEBANON	V	E	85	3,245	1,725	1,930	205
MALAWI	N	E	81	69,090	27,676	30,890	3,214
	O	E	82	75,838	37,996	38,096	100
			83	66,189	30,759	30,759	
			84	42,876	26,309	26,309	
			85	36,895	21,719	21,719	
			86	71,118	33,355	33,355	
	V	E	84	2,645	1,765	1,975	210
	V	W	85	2,646	2,098	2,347	249
MALAYSA	O	E	86	7,667	4,423	4,922	499
	V	E	81	221	1,573	1,810	237
MEXICO	O	W	83	480	400	400	
N ZEAL	V	E	85	44,092	3,440	3,512	72
			86	46,296	6,421	9,450	3,029
NEPAL	O	E	82	11,550	6,519	6,519	
			83	1,100	605	605	
	V	E	81	36,579	13,233	14,907	1,674
			85	72,752	30,690	35,021	4,331
			86	41,887	11,020	13,698	2,678
NETHLDS	O	E	83	54	678	731	53
			85	141,060	40,196	44,045	3,849
			86	42,538	19,802	20,142	340
	V	E	81	3,280	953	1,089	136
			82	7,011	2,367	2,715	348
			83	5,716	1,745	1,970	225
			84	907,362	206,540	249,574	43,034
			85	1,308,916	304,113	382,028	77,915
			86	339,831	98,071	123,808	25,737
	V	W	81	3,500	1,222	1,323	101
			82	2,175	698	783	85
			83	12,233	4,146	4,559	413
			84	8,850	2,548	2,947	399
			85	3,131	1,762	1,987	225
			86	12,140	4,337	4,912	575
PANAMA	V	E	84	44,906	16,500	17,853	1,353
PERU	V	E	81	80,000	24,800	28,910	4,110
			84	158,911	44,813	52,915	8,102
			85	117,700	32,898	38,427	5,529
			86	36,000	10,200	12,060	1,860
PHIL R	V	E	82	360	350	412	62
	V	W	81	395	496	568	72
			83	1,581	1,428	1,574	146
			84	760	588	667	79
			85	190	1,339	1,443	104
PORTUGL	V	E	82	607	293	443	150
ROMANIA	V	E	85	202,243	33,591	42,841	9,250
SPAIN	V	E	82	37,800	7,740	10,188	2,448
			84	439,285	97,892	124,655	26,763
			85	118,995	29,517	35,732	6,215
	V	W	84	1,575	502	592	90
SWITZLD	V	E	82	112	283	302	19
			84	787	599	621	22
THAILND	V	E	85	24,624	16,438	18,573	2,135
			86	24,630	18,012	20,572	2,560
	V	W	86	1,728	1,008	1,074	66
TRINID	V	E	84	51,030	19,656	21,393	1,737
U KING	A	E	82	685	615	704	89
			84	1,751	620	856	236
	N	W	82	7,015	2,804	3,435	631
	O	E	81	9,259	5,422	5,778	356
			82	2,205	1,324	1,498	174
			85	4,308	2,387	2,751	364
	V	E	82	1,340	537	742	205
			84	3,500	2,146	2,756	610
			85	52,366	12,276	14,234	1,958
			86	4,139	2,787	3,201	414
	V	W	81	1,059	553	609	56
			82	1,047	328	387	59
			83	5,053	2,701	3,939	1,238
			84	7,435	2,890	3,831	941
			85	10,273	2,687	3,377	690

Peach

Peach, dried
1487400 PEACHES, DRIED (LB)

Country	Mode	Reg	Yr	Quantity	F.A.S.	C.I.F.	Charges
TOTAL			81	220	1,397	1,665	268
			82	20,983	9,569	9,814	245
			83	20,775	32,538	35,657	3,119
			84	117,437	62,916	67,988	5,072
			85	96,136	90,971	95,031	4,060
			86	9,608	11,893	13,972	2,079
AUSTRAL	N	W	85	8,595	17,446	17,521	75
	V	E	84	641	1,772	1,841	69
			85	661	1,680	1,749	69
	V	W	82	20,078	4,460	4,647	187
			83	3,747	7,301	7,578	277
			84	2,204	4,347	4,517	170
			85	76,608	54,098	56,659	2,561
			86	3,748	7,589	7,730	141
CANADA	O	E	81	88	1,067	1,067	
			82	355	4,760	4,760	
			83	20	266	266	
			84	100	1,195	1,195	
			85	100	1,406	1,406	
CHILE	A	E	84	1,455	792	922	130
	A	W	81	132	330	598	268
CHINA M	V	E	82	550	349	407	58
	V	W	86	3,300	2,534	2,678	144
CYPRUS	V	E	84	2,750	3,143	3,286	143
HG KONG	V	W	84	150	288	305	17
ITALY	A	E	83	159	475	754	279
	N	E	85	6,041	11,699	12,662	963
	V	E	83	7,178	14,978	15,840	862
			84	54,670	10,590	11,263	673
N ZEAL	A	W	86	2,560	1,770	3,564	1,794
PANAMA	A	E	83	1,006	2,079	2,754	675

Crop
Product
TSUSA commodity number, description, and unit of quantity

Country	Mode	Reg	Yr	Quantity	F.A.S.	C.I.F.	Charges
REP SAF	V	E	83	8,589	6,614	7,514	900
			84	54,891	39,944	43,749	3,805
			85	4,131	4,642	5,034	392
SPAIN	V	E	84	366	509	565	56
THAILND	V	W	84	210	336	345	9
U KING	O	E	83	76	825	951	126

Peach, fresh or in brine

1487000 PEACHES IMPORTED JUN1-NOV30 (LB)

Country	Mode	Reg	Yr	Quantity	F.A.S.	C.I.F.	Charges
TOTAL			82	263,612	118,933	144,257	25,324
			83	772,031	159,759	196,698	36,939
			84	1,126,312	293,414	418,116	124,702
			85	2,169,326	628,889	794,871	165,982
			86	1,453,800	481,754	788,129	306,375
ARGENT	A	E	84	49,898	27,826	62,673	34,847
	V	E	85	135,596	32,550	40,453	7,903
			86	33,331	6,723	8,627	1,904
BELGIUM	A	E	83	325	289	503	214
	V	E	85	2,136	1,229	1,253	24
CANADA	O	E	82	65,415	24,243	24,243	
			83	467,679	78,822	78,822	
			84	46,395	9,121	9,121	
			85	1,188,848	348,338	348,338	
			86	462,965	150,711	150,711	
	O	W	83	32,254	9,446	9,446	
			84	197,151	38,978	38,978	
			85	140,533	41,319	41,319	
			86	31,596	3,949	3,949	
CHILE	A	E	82	1,007	610	1,203	593
			83	56,396	26,785	57,362	30,577
			84	63,281	29,627	69,254	39,627
			85	152,472	70,680	180,420	109,740
			86	374,262	177,742	450,176	272,434
	N	W	86	32,825	10,326	12,195	1,869
	V	E	82	2,116	600	899	299
			83	2,603	547	580	33
			85	15,765	5,128	6,944	1,816
	V	W	85	229,717	61,987	93,104	31,117
			86	97,239	26,912	38,196	11,284
CHINA T	V	W	86	5,000	2,605	3,050	445
DOM REP	V	E	86	42,600	2,403	4,234	1,831
FRANCE	N	E	84	9,700	6,437	7,674	1,237
	V	E	83	1,323	733	916	183
GREECE	V	E	85	39,365	12,480	14,530	2,050
			86	92,526	31,319	38,147	6,828
HG KONG	V	W	84	49,790	4,979	5,299	320
JAPAN	V	H	82	66,000	44,820	62,848	18,028
MEXICO	O	E	82	119,074	40,859	40,859	
			84	31,680	6,732	6,732	
			85	36,280	2,676	2,676	
	O	W	83	102,720	14,665	14,665	
			84	36,876	5,268	5,268	
			86	25,900	1,247	1,247	
N ZEAL	A	W	82	10,000	7,801	14,205	6,404
			83	595	405	714	309
			85	1,458	1,507	2,419	912
	V	E	84	183,713	43,574	65,646	22,072
REP SAF	V	E	84	100,839	36,493	41,898	5,405
			86	130,710	28,758	33,613	4,855
SALVADR	V	E	86	41,945	15,228	17,749	2,521
SPAIN	V	E	83	108,136	28,067	33,690	5,623
			84	343,966	81,495	102,403	20,908
			85	227,156	50,995	63,415	12,420
			86	41,250	9,393	11,725	2,332
SUDAN	V	E	86	41,651	14,438	14,510	72
THAILND	V	W	84	13,023	2,884	3,170	286

1487200 PEACHES FRESH IN BRINE NSPF (LB)

Country	Mode	Reg	Yr	Quantity	F.A.S.	C.I.F.	Charges
TOTAL			81	7,013,282	2,326,002	3,607,731	1,281,729
			82	12,476,102	5,034,288	7,391,609	2,357,321
			83	27,783,836	9,382,744	13,656,095	4,273,351
			84	35,942,776	10,452,052	15,079,328	4,627,276
			85	61,722,447	18,994,268	26,875,599	7,881,331
			86	70,151,759	19,996,386	27,861,634	7,865,248
ARGENT	A	E	83	4,233	3,768	4,182	414
			84	15,035	6,820	17,491	10,671
			85	9,244	7,188	7,411	223
AUSTRAL	A	W	82	864	975	1,497	522
			83	4,445	10,109	12,609	2,500
	V	W	85	661	1,047	1,080	33
BELGIUM	A	W	83	721	694	1,363	669
	V	E	84	1,454	894	959	65
BOLIVIA	A	E	84	2,436	912	5,112	4,200
BRAZIL	V	E	81	26,671	4,536	9,441	4,905
C RICA	V	E	86	18,100	10,000	12,400	2,400
CANADA	O	E	81	850	875	875	
			86	441	1,336	1,336	
	O	W	85	10,159	2,765	4,021	1,256
CHILE	A	E	81	295,717	174,448	289,619	115,171
			82	509,252	254,963	442,448	187,485
			83	474,901	237,764	415,323	177,559
			84	327,327	153,609	347,937	194,328
			85	472,173	192,477	442,538	250,061
			86	84,472	31,231	72,262	41,031
	A	W	85	2,006	3,290	4,446	1,156
	N	E	82	739,392	461,968	822,986	361,018
			83	586,719	329,970	658,158	328,188
			84	25,882,311	7,246,796	10,578,236	3,331,440
	N	W	82	904,683	350,147	501,150	151,003
			83	11,110	5,486	6,781	1,295
			84	8,402,908	2,397,394	3,281,290	883,896
			85	12,701,244	3,778,130	5,362,516	1,584,386
			86	11,462,161	2,703,413	3,668,485	965,072
	O	W	84	31,757	21,930	22,416	486
	V	E	81	6,228,330	1,867,706	2,892,225	1,024,519
			82	9,992,660	3,660,893	5,152,645	1,491,752
			83	21,970,325	6,756,946	9,857,812	3,100,866
			84	232,995	68,851	106,845	37,994
			85	47,289,951	14,471,520	20,385,784	5,914,264
			86	54,016,756	15,691,008	22,006,007	6,314,999
	V	W	81	192,773	55,462	86,223	30,761
			83	3,150,884	1,125,277	1,582,608	457,331
			86	2,853,866	763,001	1,126,329	363,328
CHINA T	V	H	86	9,921	2,163	3,000	837
COCOS I	V	E	86	17,778	4,838	6,745	1,907
DOM REP	A	E	82	9,878	4,480	7,780	3,300
			84	1,501	546	886	340
FRANCE	V	E	84	1,323	669	835	166
GREECE	V	E	85	135,407	31,593	38,091	6,498
			86	124,987	31,489	38,762	7,273
INDIA	V	E	85	36,541	9,360	15,269	5,909
ITALY	V	E	83	193	284	302	18
JAPAN	A	H	84	5,733	4,352	7,247	2,895
MEXICO	O	W	83	967,163	532,440	532,440	
			84	452,126	208,050	208,050	
			85	444,615	204,060	204,060	
			86	1,087,129	488,637	488,637	
N ZEAL	A	E	81	891	1,380	2,222	842
			82	19,838	18,184	31,210	13,026
			83	15,674	22,643	38,793	16,150
			84	595	391	660	269
			85	1,861	1,116	2,420	1,304
	A	H	81	77,821	52,828	85,111	32,283
			82	13,641	14,270	23,120	8,850
			83	20,034	14,688	23,979	9,291
			84	94,570	80,622	125,231	44,609
			85	67,620	76,149	105,968	29,819
			86	25,104	21,056	37,592	16,536
	A	W	81	190,229	168,767	242,015	73,248
			82	24,145	28,104	43,189	15,085
			83	221,852	262,302	423,495	161,193
			84	34,577	35,121	63,266	28,145
			85	56,201	79,712	128,227	48,515
			86	153,415	138,157	237,150	98,993
	N	H	82	93,993	62,091	98,646	36,555
			86	95,220	60,104	101,660	41,556
	N	W	82	152,740	172,711	258,849	86,138
			84	102,883	127,086	194,747	67,661
	O	W	83	192	297	297	
NETHLDS	A	W	86	964	1,620	2,076	456
PERU	A	E	82	2,811	1,350	2,350	1,000
	V	E	82	12,205	4,152	5,739	1,587
REP SAF	V	E	84	63,325	22,716	26,790	4,074
			85	272,160	87,476	98,011	10,535
	V	W	86	136,003	24,945	33,444	8,499
SPAIN	V	E	83	355,390	80,076	97,953	17,877
			84	286,948	72,127	86,977	14,850
			85	168,694	41,529	51,233	9,704
SUDAN	V	E	86	27,743	15,288	16,049	761
SWITZLD	A	E	85	53,910	6,856	24,524	17,668
	V	E	86	37,699	8,100	9,700	1,600
THAILND	V	W	84	900	529	575	46
U KING	A	W	84	2,072	2,637	3,778	1,141

Crop
Product
TSUSA commodity number, description, and unit of quantity

Peach, kernel**
1750300 APRICOT AND PEACH KERNELS (LB)
(See Apricot, kernel under Apricot)

Peach, prepared or preserved
1487700 WHITE FLESHED PEACHES, PREP (LB)

Country	Mode	Reg	Yr	Quantity	F.A.S.	C.I.F.	Charges
TOTAL			81	16,276	10,813	12,098	1,285
			82	6,142	9,173	10,140	967
			83	93,393	33,168	37,131	3,963
			84	58,988	31,389	34,673	3,284
			85	65,879	35,369	40,616	5,247
			86	213,536	63,130	77,767	14,637
ARGENT	V	E	84	224	376	447	71
CHILE	A	E	86	2,823	1,755	4,039	2,284
CHINA M	V	W	81	6,750	2,243	2,626	383
			83	57,327	20,767	22,873	2,106
			84	31,126	10,000	11,170	1,170
CHINA T	V	W	86	3,347	2,508	2,586	78
COLOMB	A	E	83	3,881	800	836	36
FR GERM	V	E	86	1,730	4,587	4,741	154
FRANCE	V	E	82	1,025	3,783	3,928	145
			83	1,885	2,358	2,474	116
			84	1,587	4,519	5,215	696
			85	22,784	19,998	23,298	3,300
			86	11,461	16,699	17,931	1,232
GREECE	V	E	86	149,031	24,125	33,346	9,221
INDIA	V	E	83	8,200	1,818	2,578	760
ITALY	V	E	83	864	530	640	110
			84	795	3,944	4,225	281
			85	833	4,007	4,291	284
JAPAN	V	E	81	450	446	499	53
			84	185	346	383	37
	V	H	81	1,313	2,184	2,551	367
			82	656	1,131	1,228	97
	V	W	81	1,013	990	1,049	59
			82	2,249	2,029	2,177	148
			83	1,394	1,195	1,267	72
			84	2,843	2,572	2,718	146
KOR REP	V	E	81	6,750	4,950	5,373	423
			84	9,000	5,832	6,497	665
			86	11,250	6,200	7,816	1,616
	V	W	85	4,497	2,500	2,719	219
			86	8,550	3,800	3,852	52
MEXICO	O	W	86	25,344	3,456	3,456	
N ZEAL	A	E	82	2,212	2,230	2,807	577
SPAIN	V	E	83	19,842	5,700	6,463	763
			84	13,228	3,800	4,018	218
SWITZLD	V	E	85	37,765	8,864	10,308	1,444

1487800 PEACHES, PREP OR PRES, NSPF (LB)

Country	Mode	Reg	Yr	Quantity	F.A.S.	C.I.F.	Charges
TOTAL			81	485,672	116,270	127,433	11,163
			82	741,271	127,190	133,358	6,168
			83	7,930,019	2,209,629	2,608,131	398,502
			84	72,347,893	20,268,789	24,271,032	4,002,243
			85	69,289,476	18,096,768	21,768,750	3,671,982
			86	40,236,187	9,808,291	11,914,059	2,105,768
ANTIGUA	V	E	85	78,075	17,160	20,755	3,595
ARGENT	O	E	84	174,176	31,372	38,841	7,469
			85	188,456	27,027	39,497	12,470
			86	11,529	2,802	3,376	574
	V	E	83	15,760	5,078	7,364	2,286
			84	8,464,230	2,206,274	2,704,880	498,606
			85	2,741,445	720,481	885,462	164,981
			86	29,841	7,520	9,506	1,986
	V	W	85	13,492	3,480	4,409	929
AUSTRAL	V	E	85	664,797	164,882	203,819	38,937
	V	W	85	1,127,857	290,875	348,341	57,466
BELGIUM	V	E	83	1,563	1,399	1,643	244
			84	19,567	15,208	18,120	2,912
			85	55,233	24,264	28,780	4,516
	V	W	83	952	853	959	106
			84	1,054	944	1,109	165
			85	2,192	1,891	2,274	383
BRAZIL	V	E	83	1,449	1,637	1,829	192
			84	243,811	85,466	114,002	28,536
			85	214,650	47,188	58,908	11,720
	V	W	86	42,930	10,236	13,316	3,080
C RICA	V	E	81	4,913	3,365	3,833	468
	V	W	82	2,213	450	608	158

Crop
Product
TSUSA commodity number, description, and unit of quantity

Country	Mode	Reg	Yr	Quantity	F.A.S.	C.I.F.	Charges
			83	18,853	6,650	8,643	1,993
CANADA	O	E	83	125	492	492	
	O	W	82	2,800	1,406	1,406	
			85	1,069	1,420	1,420	
	V	E	85	2,914	1,515	1,721	206
CHILE	O	E	84	52,331	14,958	17,144	2,186
			85	22,396	10,313	10,733	420
			86	27,612	6,457	6,734	277
	V	E	84	5,631,755	1,656,479	1,907,878	251,399
			85	10,898,509	3,079,315	3,525,909	446,594
			86	6,803,201	1,663,459	1,959,157	295,698
	V	W	84	245,570	70,745	84,517	13,772
			85	68,081	18,824	23,886	5,062
			86	39,270	8,549	11,273	2,724
CHINA M	V	E	81	4,409	2,248	2,435	187
			82	5,025	2,896	3,024	128
			83	3,750	2,017	2,078	61
			85	22,275	4,689	6,262	1,573
	V	H	82	1,641	957	1,054	97
			83	665	407	437	30
			84	10,767	7,842	8,426	584
			85	32,148	26,308	28,494	2,186
			86	12,150	12,367	13,404	1,037
	V	W	81	500	386	418	32
			82	7,097	3,906	4,316	410
			83	750	377	406	29
			84	88,148	29,048	34,076	5,028
			85	138,108	47,562	52,534	4,972
			86	37,304	39,633	41,361	1,728
CHINA T	O	H	86	1,000	1,137	1,200	63
	V	H	81	91	255	284	29
			85	26,420	23,270	25,097	1,827
			86	2,550	2,458	2,663	205
	V	W	81	10,500	4,165	4,563	398
			83	52,000	24,652	27,080	2,428
			84	9,790	4,233	4,446	213
			85	1,482	1,365	1,443	78
			86	2,460	2,277	2,362	85
COLOMB	A	E	82	725	1,500	1,745	245
			83	814	1,660	1,967	307
			84	458	1,548	1,711	163
CR N AN	V	E	85	39,000	10,162	11,871	1,709
DENMARK	V	E	86	14,400	6,331	7,419	1,088
DOM REP	V	E	85	106,498	23,723	33,296	9,573
FR GERM	O	E	86	5,990	4,931	8,151	3,220
	V	E	84	17,834	8,220	9,886	1,666
			85	75,518	38,077	46,800	8,723
			86	62,201	23,405	27,158	3,753
FRANCE	A	E	84	175	265	340	75
	O	E	81	2,311	2,929	3,229	300
			82	1,067	1,350	1,500	150
			84	1,578	817	910	93
			85	926	1,114	1,199	85
			86	1,800	2,479	2,616	137
	V	E	81	4,663	2,432	2,832	400
			82	14,630	9,543	10,912	1,369
			83	34,274	20,401	22,763	2,362
			84	8,957	7,714	8,703	989
			85	33,694	23,156	27,910	4,754
			86	87,423	79,069	87,610	8,541
	V	W	83	952	1,297	1,440	143
			84	900	828	956	128
GIBRAT	V	E	86	1,045,890	265,237	332,967	67,730
GREECE	N	E	86	204,810	63,465	75,900	12,435
	O	E	84	108,360	27,303	37,236	9,933
			86	46,669	13,871	18,058	4,187
	V	E	83	86,368	14,492	20,492	6,000
			84	8,436,102	1,748,582	2,271,959	523,377
			85	12,328,611	2,984,538	3,631,882	647,344
			86	19,610,059	4,857,349	5,979,593	1,122,244
	V	W	85	39,240	10,371	13,171	2,800
			86	91,233	18,608	25,584	6,976
GUATMAL	V	E	85	6,300	3,900	4,187	287
HG KONG	V	E	82	653	967	1,036	69
			84	375	315	391	76
	V	H	81	2,200	1,118	1,207	89
			83	2,000	1,800	2,009	209
			84	4,250	6,016	6,699	683
			85	3,600	6,945	7,212	267
			86	14,620	18,465	19,811	1,346
	V	W	82	5,687	2,623	3,222	599
ISRAEL	V	E	81	9,900	5,775	6,688	913
			83	1,800	1,000	1,124	124
ITALY	O	E	86	79,500	7,101	7,101	

Crop
Product
TSUSA commodity number, description, and unit of quantity

Country	Mode	Reg	Yr	Quantity	F.A.S.	C.I.F.	Charges
	V	E	82	7,332	3,652	4,294	642
			83	7,411	2,544	3,190	646
			84	911,568	226,379	275,151	48,772
			85	490,964	142,913	178,555	35,642
			86	228,374	75,025	94,370	19,345
	V	W	84	119,049	30,627	38,116	7,489
JAPAN	V	E	83	563	572	651	79
			86	71,429	17,550	20,482	2,932
	V	W	83	843	395	425	30
KOR REP	V	E	85	13,492	7,916	8,580	664
	V	W	81	1,800	1,217	1,321	104
			85	4,497	2,500	2,719	219
MEXICO	O	E	81	318,321	44,368	44,368	
			82	670,863	79,671	79,671	
			83	102,600	9,050	9,050	
			84	438,448	38,312	38,312	
			85	1,466,049	126,011	126,011	
			86	1,405,596	167,932	167,932	
	O	W	86	5,040	1,320	1,320	
N ZEAL	V	E	84	567,563	155,993	206,147	50,154
	V	W	84	254,680	75,673	94,961	19,288
NAMIBIA	V	E	84	39,160	10,270	12,012	1,742
NETHLDS	V	E	83	450	490	511	21
			84	169,680	46,460	51,492	5,032
			85	190,285	63,710	83,142	19,432
			86	125,355	49,326	64,123	14,797
PORTUGL	V	E	82	1,323	575	659	84
			84	1,320	1,260	1,550	290
			85	37,699	9,332	11,678	2,346
REP SAF	N	E	84	3,565,182	1,053,040	1,231,278	178,238
	V	E	81	113,743	42,027	49,528	7,501
			83	485,718	164,676	189,855	25,179
			84	22,786,909	7,381,556	8,573,451	1,191,895
			85	11,508,647	3,504,371	4,089,259	584,888
			86	5,866,778	1,297,541	1,591,196	293,655
	V	W	81	3,267	1,620	1,639	19
			84	337,975	112,426	137,453	25,027
			85	2,040,911	488,182	616,375	128,193
			86	579,768	110,176	146,865	36,689
ROMANIA	V	E	84	39,683	11,250	12,960	1,710
			85	103,683	27,240	31,481	4,241
S ARAB	V	E	84	34,011	11,498	13,137	1,639
			85	84,174	25,274	31,157	5,883
SINGAPR	V	E	86	175	4,010	4,340	330
SOMALIA	V	E	85	312,650	100,896	117,090	16,194
SPAIN	N	E	84	11,367,231	3,041,646	3,695,138	653,492
			85	3,055,855	652,348	812,361	160,013
	O	E	85	62,223	19,356	23,241	3,885
			86	24,715	6,215	7,704	1,489
	V	E	81	7,609	3,800	4,339	539
			82	675	300	300	
			83	7,093,704	1,931,137	2,285,648	354,511
			84	7,851,759	2,035,258	2,481,430	446,172
			85	20,275,294	5,111,135	6,349,089	1,237,954
			86	2,424,812	658,734	800,489	141,755
	V	W	84	238,753	68,296	83,993	15,697
			85	147,516	43,434	55,601	12,167
SWAZLND	V	E	84	31,729	11,769	13,888	2,119
SWITZLD	V	E	81	1,445	565	749	184
			82	2,969	3,597	4,519	922
			83	3,508	3,543	3,768	225
			84	26,675	11,336	14,142	2,806
			85	215,655	59,600	68,302	8,702
			86	782,581	194,199	225,058	30,859
	V	W	84	476	553	591	38
THAILND	V	W	82	5,846	2,905	3,235	330
			84	1,380	759	828	69
TOKELAU	V	W	84	35,715	10,575	11,977	1,402
TURKEY	V	E	83	450	286	316	30
U KING	O	E	84	905	1,927	2,005	78
			85	3,086	5,976	6,301	325
	V	E	82	6,997	9,314	10,001	687
			83	12,697	12,724	13,991	1,267
			84	7,854	7,749	8,790	1,041
			85	221,514	69,115	80,021	10,906
			86	396,931	103,213	126,180	22,967
	V	W	82	157	314	342	28
USSR	V	E	82	3,571	1,264	1,514	250
VENEZ	V	E	85	80,296	17,799	21,799	4,000
			86	24,189	1,461	1,461	
YUGOSLV	O	E	85	42,000	5,845	8,716	2,871
			86	26,002	4,383	6,219	1,836

Crop
Product
TSUSA commodity number, description, and unit of quantity

Peanut

Peanut butter
1454840 PEANUT BUTTER (LB)

Country	Mode	Reg	Yr	Quantity	F.A.S.	C.I.F.	Charges
TOTAL			81	7,770,194	4,824,818	5,238,626	413,808
			82	471,722	189,167	189,335	168
			83	47,287	39,494	39,748	254
			84	18,257	17,326	18,019	693
			85	114,171	62,751	66,586	3,835
			86	954,218	415,218	462,052	46,834
ARGENT	V	E	85	44,712	23,375	27,210	3,835
			86	789,152	310,514	354,432	43,918
AUSTRAL	V	E	81	75,552	46,875	52,921	6,046
	V	W	81	136,842	177,644	193,466	15,822
CANADA	A	E	82	125	259	365	106
	N	E	81	391	1,410	1,442	32
	O	E	81	1,313	1,905	1,905	
			82	443,690	174,221	174,261	40
			83	45,614	37,729	37,729	
			84	15,537	13,060	13,160	100
			85	9,295	5,861	5,861	
			86	8,209	4,209	4,209	
	O	W	85	60,164	33,515	33,515	
			86	119,348	80,505	80,505	
CHINA M	V	E	83	360	350	382	32
CHINA T	O	E	82	27,444	14,391	14,391	
FR GERM	V	E	86	2,381	1,688	1,962	274
FRANCE	V	E	84	2,076	3,383	3,897	514
HG KONG	V	E	86	360	380	409	29
INDIA	O	E	84	181	517	517	
ISRAEL	V	E	83	1,313	1,415	1,637	222
JAPAN	V	W	81	88,272	61,271	73,273	12,002
LEBANON	V	E	86	240	1,118	1,135	17
MALAWI	V	E	86	30,644	13,654	15,832	2,178
NETHLDS	O	E	84	463	366	445	79
			82	463	296	318	22
REP SAF	O	E	81	1,666,686	562,573	601,643	39,070
	V	E	81	5,624,234	3,842,833	4,160,214	317,381
	V	W	81	176,544	129,927	153,353	23,426
U KING	V	E	86	2,330	1,733	1,968	235
	V	W	86	1,914	1,797	2,009	212

Peanut, nut, shelled
1454880 PEANUTS SHELLED ETC QUOTA (LB)

Country	Mode	Reg	Yr	Quantity	F.A.S.	C.I.F.	Charges
TOTAL			81	303,866,961	286,507,508	301,664,150	15,147,415
			82	1,991,192	1,887,903	1,998,307	110,404
			83	2,382,018	873,309	1,002,432	129,123
			84	2,142,617	938,732	1,043,289	104,557
			85	356,233	161,959	190,657	28,698
			86	2,312,639	814,688	946,481	131,793
ARGENT	A	E	81	551	325	575	250
	N	E	81	19,644,776	16,700,307	17,672,456	972,149
	O	E	81	4,931,003	5,050,453	5,068,053	17,600
			84	797,397	482,932	523,884	40,952
			86	755,472	250,512	290,756	40,244
	V	E	81	1,030,583	764,215	815,013	50,798
			83	2,063,762	620,953	725,291	104,338
			84	727,606	211,444	249,451	38,007
			85	237,325	62,019	74,928	12,909
			86	1,292,115	350,286	417,952	67,666
AUSTRAL	O	E	81	132,386	105,909	121,174	15,265
	V	E	81	74,956	66,728	74,417	7,689
BRAZIL	O	E	81	550	447	513	66
	V	E	81	3,556,747	2,738,947	2,966,141	227,194
	V	W	81	1,102	1,000	1,128	128
CANADA	O	E	81	102,245	94,831	95,006	175
			82	9,715	19,198	20,766	1,568
			83	22,956	26,748	26,800	52
			84	61,992	4,632	4,632	
			86	8,008	4,641	4,641	
	O	W	81	196	387	387	
CHINA M	A	E	81	2,941	3,350	9,374	6,024
	A	W	81	2,028	5,988	9,653	3,665
	N	E	83	62,298	44,868	55,082	10,214
	N	W	81	1,257,705	1,212,969	1,274,860	61,891
	O	E	81	7,608,094	8,205,351	8,374,813	163,778
			82	66,216	56,026	63,552	7,526
			83	44,092	15,968	15,968	

Crop
Product
TSUSA commodity number, description, and unit of quantity

Country	Mode	Reg	Yr	Quantity	F.A.S.	C.I.F.	Charges
			84	523,299	204,122	224,449	20,327
			85	54,662	38,488	45,901	7,413
	O	W	81	5,158,828	5,072,970	5,380,355	307,385
			85	11,115	10,001	11,333	1,332
	V	E	81	98,125,071	95,546,336	99,340,842	3,790,963
			82	5,425	3,161	3,773	612
			83	528	414	450	36
			85	15,998	12,072	14,049	1,977
			86	43,583	37,622	43,672	6,050
	V	H	81	329	275	288	13
	V	W	81	46,282,759	41,766,191	43,996,012	2,229,821
			82	1,368,152	1,271,300	1,342,669	71,369
			83	43,555	25,267	27,291	2,024
			84	2,791	3,849	4,435	586
			86	32,415	14,953	16,325	1,372
CHINA T	N	W	81	822,748	769,716	806,370	36,654
	O	E	81	132,277	131,000	138,000	7,000
			82	4,409	6,000	6,693	693
			84	6,700	7,772	9,114	1,342
			85	10,009	11,600	13,603	2,003
	V	E	81	881,041	577,301	611,298	33,997
			82	1,170	1,274	1,439	165
	V	H	81	2,625	3,300	3,674	374
			86	5,002	6,388	7,116	728
	V	W	81	1,973,725	1,810,007	1,878,775	68,768
			82	5,375	5,550	5,731	181
			83	11,253	15,579	16,412	833
			85	1,282	1,210	1,394	184
			86	20,400	21,810	22,477	667
EGYPT	V	E	81	551,150	390,329	413,362	23,033
FR GERM	O	E	81	230	362	387	25
			83	1,190	1,652	1,781	129
			84	2,748	3,811	4,108	297
	V	E	81	7,144	11,356	12,054	698
			82	10,577	13,030	13,947	917
			83	5,291	6,284	6,961	677
FRANCE	V	E	85	953	1,258	1,346	88
	V	H	83	596	726	983	257
HG KONG	O	E	81	1,504	1,716	1,821	105
			82	3,586	3,310	3,627	317
			83	452	500	576	76
			84	5,785	7,148	7,736	588
	O	W	86	20,503	8,882	8,882	
	V	E	81	788,439	851,345	890,904	39,559
			82	6,750	11,145	11,857	712
			83	7,470	10,110	10,991	881
			85	2,536	5,097	5,343	246
			86	15,135	12,133	14,813	2,680
	V	W	81	209,331	201,053	210,110	9,057
			83	214	256	273	17
			84	1,080	589	625	36
			86	10,439	8,485	9,487	1,002
ICELAND	V	E	81	1,886,142	1,955,320	2,006,212	50,892
INDIA	O	E	81	2,468,131	2,648,785	2,709,489	60,704
			82	418,874	412,978	426,978	14,000
	V	E	81	52,194,436	49,558,337	52,832,624	3,274,287
	V	W	82	110	306	352	46
INDNSIA	V	E	81	566,428	431,399	509,878	78,479
	V	W	81	1,500	1,801	1,880	79
ISRAEL	V	E	81	99,207	78,792	85,972	7,180
			86	11,660	6,721	6,841	120
JAPAN	V	E	83	281	420	466	46
			84	590	924	1,147	223
	V	H	81	2,407	4,350	5,228	878
			82	944	3,635	4,309	674
			83	281	1,103	1,404	301
			84	57	280	306	26
	V	W	83	1,525	2,584	2,716	132
MACAO	V	W	83	2,750	1,562	1,619	57
MALAWI	O	E	81	3,540,069	4,112,300	4,200,300	88,000
	V	E	81	934,554	898,369	923,977	25,608
MALAYSA	O	E	82	5,000	5,981	6,896	915
			86	29,950	29,309	32,380	3,071
	V	E	82	57,000	56,263	62,052	5,789
	V	W	81	573,196	550,252	568,473	18,221
MEXICO	O	E	83	44,000	7,480	7,480	
NETHLDS	A	E	83	3,748	5,215	7,528	2,313
	V	E	81	351,601	280,618	293,721	13,103
			83	44,222	70,647	75,009	4,362
PHIL R	V	W	82	440	881	993	112
			83	8,326	4,468	5,460	992
			84	992	1,101	1,255	154
REP SAF	O	E	81	659,192	833,637	834,122	485
	V	E	81	2,333,473	2,376,909	2,475,121	98,212

Country	Mode	Reg	Yr	Quantity	F.A.S.	C.I.F.	Charges
	V	W	81	119,048	94,644	108,000	13,356
SALVADR	V	W	83	1,941	2,219	2,464	245
SENEGAL	V	E	82	8,818	3,517	5,302	1,785
SINGAPR	N	W	81	609,046	657,777	688,311	30,534
	O	E	84	10,000	8,508	10,420	1,912
	V	E	82	12,500	11,206	13,820	2,614
			85	15,150	14,521	16,065	1,544
			86	59,173	54,176	61,409	7,233
	V	W	81	150,823	134,078	138,878	4,800
			83	7,500	6,020	6,340	320
SPAIN	V	E	82	231	476	508	32
SRI LKA	V	E	81	55,115	35,496	42,500	7,004
SUDAN	A	E	81	708	675	1,555	880
	O	E	81	1,037,816	971,002	1,036,907	65,905
	V	E	81	42,339,925	38,264,510	41,467,938	3,203,428
THAILND	V	E	81	10,000	5,963	6,164	201
	V	W	81	369,690	257,370	278,408	21,038
			82	5,900	2,666	3,043	377
			83	2,815	1,474	1,629	155
			84	1,580	1,620	1,727	107
			85	7,203	5,693	6,695	1,002
			86	8,784	8,770	9,730	960
TURKEY	V	E	81	130,512	128,886	132,717	3,831
VENEZ	A	E	83	972	792	1,458	666
ZMBABWE	V	E	81	150,878	141,774	147,960	6,186

Peanut, nut, unshelled

1452000 PEANUTS NOT SHELLED (LB)

Country	Mode	Reg	Yr	Quantity	F.A.S.	C.I.F.	Charges
TOTAL			81	1,454,810	1,143,355	1,199,189	55,834
			82	55,687	15,728	17,313	1,585
			83	298,113	99,234	110,967	11,733
			84	33,526	10,273	11,286	1,013
			85	74,138	30,452	33,298	2,846
			86	716,488	134,752	137,749	2,997
ARGENT	O	E	81	49,988	55,787	55,787	
CANADA	O	E	81	450	699	699	
			84	23,307	3,030	3,030	
	O	W	81	265	524	632	108
CHINA M	O	E	84	513	266	310	44
	O	W	85	33,882	9,826	11,180	1,354
	V	E	81	649,592	548,389	573,783	25,394
			82	13,370	5,698	6,648	950
			83	92,858	60,358	69,388	9,030
			84	1,129	807	916	109
	V	W	81	1,470	1,428	1,612	184
			83	2,267	2,747	2,948	201
CR N AN	A	E	81	1,200	1,080	1,270	190
EGYPT	V	E	81	551,150	390,329	413,362	23,033
HG KONG	O	E	82	550	498	558	60
	O	W	84	5,250	2,833	2,900	67
	V	E	81	2,000	2,028	2,201	173
			82	31,450	4,824	5,127	303
			83	2,070	1,892	2,168	276
INDNSIA	V	W	82	1,575	1,449	1,558	109
ISRAEL	V	E	81	97,157	93,875	99,795	5,920
JAPAN	V	W	81	264	980	1,052	72
KOR REP	V	W	83	254	455	487	32
MALAYSA	O	E	82	1,000	926	1,020	94
			84	3,327	3,337	4,130	793
			85	12,250	11,902	13,292	1,390
	V	E	85	800	1,176	1,278	102
	V	W	81	1,000	930	1,102	172
				30,900	3,445	4,271	826
MEXICO	A	E	83	1,102	444	762	318
	O	E	81	89,274	38,897	38,897	
			82	6,975	1,875	1,875	
			83	44,662	17,552	17,552	
			85	27,206	7,548	7,548	
			86	295,523	70,800	70,800	
	O	W	86	20,834	8,334	8,334	
NETHLDS	O	E	86	400,131	55,618	58,615	2,997
SINGAPR	V	E	83	124,000	12,341	13,391	1,050
	V	W	81	1,000	2,090	2,197	107
THAILND	V	W	81	10,000	6,319	6,800	481
			82	767	458	527	69

1454850 PEANUTS NT SHELLED QUOTA (LB)

Country	Mode	Reg	Yr	Quantity	F.A.S.	C.I.F.	Charges
TOTAL			81	1,608,106	1,508,835	1,607,936	99,101
			82	164,911	129,363	149,623	20,260
			83	579,536	486,900	538,895	51,995
			84	34,679	29,640	32,761	3,121

Crop Product TSUSA commodity number, description, and unit of quantity Country	Mode	Reg	Yr	Quantity	F.A.S.	C.I.F.	Charges
			85	302,553	240,561	275,227	34,666
			86	638,649	484,944	529,169	44,225
CANADA	O	E	81	1,600	2,336	2,336	
	O	W	86	2,400	4,086	4,336	250
CHINA M	N	E	83	14,332	8,402	9,772	1,370
	O	E	82	6,563	3,090	3,521	431
			84	2,640	2,000	2,256	256
	O	W	81	73,260	119,218	119,218	
			82	1,100	747	808	61
	V	E	81	36,788	24,412	27,075	2,663
			82	38,691	23,802	28,316	4,514
			85	4,725	3,405	3,812	407
	V	H	81	1,000	720	798	78
	V	W	81	670,229	585,094	625,278	40,184
			82	16,529	7,983	10,400	2,417
			83	79,548	47,349	52,786	5,437
			84	2,976	1,469	1,584	115
			86	38,971	20,803	22,912	2,109
CHINA T	O	H	82	921	1,105	1,173	68
			83	750	780	845	65
			84	6,563	7,525	8,050	525
	V	E	81	2,502	1,750	2,009	259
			83	780	850	934	84
			85	14,438	11,891	13,620	1,729
	V	H	81	26,037	31,494	34,287	2,793
			82	17,439	20,895	23,198	2,303
			83	77,627	71,710	77,449	5,739
			85	14,126	15,905	17,968	2,063
			86	29,883	38,685	43,584	4,899
	V	W	81	24,292	27,720	29,327	1,607
			83	22,300	23,618	25,086	1,468
			85	1,000	1,020	1,059	39
			86	59,260	54,326	58,753	4,427
EGYPT	V	E	81	66,072	54,840	58,359	3,519
HG KONG	V	E	81	19,630	15,564	18,306	2,742
			82	2,000	2,152	2,278	126
			83	2,375	1,947	2,225	278
			85	4,000	4,823	5,259	436
	V	H	82	8,438	9,675	10,579	904
			83	525	357	385	28
	V	W	81	2,450	2,537	2,672	135
			82	3,000	2,368	2,463	95
			83	22,563	14,825	16,254	1,429
			85	28,000	16,632	18,357	1,725
			86	2,577	1,250	1,456	206
INDNSIA	V	E	81	1,250	1,165	1,332	167
	V	H	81	263	274	291	17
	V	W	81	5,713	5,602	5,926	324
			82	11,350	8,145	8,837	692
			83	6,807	6,493	7,225	732
			86	2,625	2,420	2,541	121
ITALY	A	E	81	48	293	368	75
MALAYSA	N	E	82	20,125	16,642	19,548	2,906
	O	E	81	1,100	910	1,161	251
			84	9,000	7,452	9,409	1,957
			85	30,000	26,368	31,724	5,356
	O	W	85	30,600	26,176	29,936	3,760
	V	E	81	42,650	37,376	45,379	8,003
			83	29,738	24,686	29,584	4,898
			84	13,500	11,194	11,462	268
			85	58,295	51,285	61,225	9,940
			86	14,250	12,329	14,969	2,640
	V	H	83	3,875	4,080	5,014	934
	V	W	81	89,470	80,360	88,219	7,859
			83	129,318	112,075	123,132	11,057
			85	45,170	38,774	43,318	4,544
			86	75,100	69,227	73,913	4,686
REP SAF	O	E	81	65,962	73,304	77,552	4,248
	V	E	81	209,525	161,093	171,008	9,915
SINGAPR	O	E	81	770	601	699	98
			82	23,155	19,650	22,450	2,800
	O	W	81	350	313	349	36
			82	1,750	1,324	1,416	92
			85	1,825	2,041	2,492	451
	V	E	81	10,850	11,547	13,047	1,500
			82	13,850	11,785	14,636	2,851
			83	43,600	38,760	45,620	6,860
			85	31,074	28,635	32,851	4,216
			86	69,352	64,268	71,893	7,625
	V	W	81	43,205	38,000	40,858	2,858
			83	141,430	127,180	137,350	10,170
			86	186,100	149,836	160,753	10,917
THAILND	O	W	85	39,300	13,606	13,606	

Crop Product TSUSA commodity number, description, and unit of quantity Country	Mode	Reg	Yr	Quantity	F.A.S.	C.I.F.	Charges
	V	W	86	158,131	67,714	74,059	6,345
TURKEY	V	E	81	213,090	232,312	242,082	9,770
			83	3,968	3,788	5,234	1,446

Peanut, vegetable oil
1763800 PEANUT OIL (LB)

Country	Mode	Reg	Yr	Quantity	F.A.S.	C.I.F.	Charges
TOTAL			81	84,294	62,592	69,505	6,913
			82	158,855	112,345	124,070	11,725
			83	3,873,551	876,781	964,024	87,243
			84	2,048,553	1,103,796	1,181,137	77,341
			85	892,535	666,710	717,216	50,506
			86	2,388,952	667,794	717,139	49,345
ARGENT	V	E	84	1,286,534	571,897	597,241	25,344
			86	2,096,001	466,623	499,899	33,276
BRAZIL	V	E	83	3,467,754	647,762	715,698	67,936
CHINA M	N	W	84	264,792	166,110	174,627	8,517
	V	E	81	51,411	36,159	40,960	4,801
			82	38,166	24,927	28,302	3,375
			83	58,045	41,200	45,428	4,228
			84	78,537	45,863	52,127	6,264
			85	77,116	64,947	71,047	6,100
			86	76,013	49,320	54,304	4,984
	V	H	81	1,712	1,456	1,571	115
			82	2,491	2,532	2,722	190
			83	2,750	2,344	2,576	232
			84	3,598	3,344	3,795	451
	V	W	81	2,110	1,181	1,254	73
			82	49,831	36,558	39,230	2,672
			83	163,953	84,366	89,424	5,058
			84	25,545	16,273	17,731	1,458
			85	97,621	71,795	75,613	3,818
			86	43,645	29,755	30,958	1,203
CHINA T	V	W	83	788	472	497	25
			84	3,769	3,119	3,375	256
FRANCE	O	E	84	2,028	2,605	2,874	269
	V	E	81	13,978	11,345	12,271	926
			82	8,639	5,426	5,998	572
			83	6,664	4,183	4,660	477
			84	6,386	7,153	8,152	999
			85	3,262	5,074	7,535	2,461
			86	3,696	3,832	4,082	250
	V	W	81	1,360	1,076	1,229	153
			82	3,786	3,292	3,575	283
			83	3,386	1,954	2,112	158
			84	5,881	6,383	6,978	595
			85	4,614	4,086	4,667	581
			86	6,591	5,632	5,901	269
HG KONG	V	E	81	8,135	6,055	6,554	499
			82	50,662	35,650	39,891	4,241
			83	25,449	15,006	17,212	2,206
			84	237,606	181,748	208,159	26,411
			85	177,096	125,710	140,924	15,214
			86	140,895	95,104	103,198	8,094
	V	H	81	5,288	4,824	5,134	310
			82	2,640	2,245	2,453	208
			83	8,637	6,466	7,110	644
			84	8,530	7,196	8,041	845
			85	4,694	3,942	4,383	441
			86	8,107	6,520	7,134	614
	V	W	82	880	492	527	35
			83	48,323	27,033	29,078	2,045
			84	124,394	90,124	95,856	5,732
			85	528,132	391,156	413,047	21,891
			86	14,004	11,008	11,663	655
INDIA	V	E	83	1,631	953	1,000	47
JAPAN	V	E	84	613	503	591	88
MALAYSA	V	E	83	3,600	1,950	2,348	398
	V	H	81	300	496	532	36
REP SAF	V	W	83	37,200	24,120	25,364	1,244
SENEGAL	O	E	83	4,115	2,338	2,530	192
SINGAPR	V	W	82	1,760	1,223	1,372	149
SPAIN	V	E	83	41,256	16,634	18,987	2,353
U KING	V	E	84	340	1,478	1,590	112

Crop / Product / TSUSA commodity number, description, and unit of quantity							
Country	Mode	Reg	Yr	Quantity	F.A.S.	C.I.F.	Charges

Pear

Pear, dried
1488300 PEARS, DRIED (LB)

Country	Mode	Reg	Yr	Quantity	F.A.S.	C.I.F.	Charges
TOTAL			81	24,153	20,600	22,197	1,597
			82	32,246	51,531	54,282	2,751
			83	17,589	20,303	22,016	1,713
			84	9,822	13,069	13,913	844
			85	570,041	140,472	204,757	64,285
			86	292,778	94,329	125,476	31,147
ARGENT	V	E	85	21,208	22,497	24,614	2,117
	V	W	81	13,007	4,024	4,990	966
AUSTRAL	V	E	82	1,102	1,925	2,027	102
			83	220	430	454	24
			84	200	886	921	35
			85	661	1,680	1,749	69
			86	160,773	63,962	84,416	20,454
	V	W	81	7,271	15,062	15,588	526
			82	20,574	41,621	43,170	1,549
			83	2,866	5,696	5,909	213
			84	661	1,338	1,379	41
			85	3,307	5,017	5,184	167
			86	3,528	7,087	7,265	178
CHINA M	V	E	81	3,050	1,016	1,089	73
			82	6,247	3,863	4,468	605
	V	W	82	4,217	3,750	3,984	234
			83	7,457	4,877	5,311	434
			84	1,720	2,530	2,739	209
CYPRUS	V	E	84	2,750	3,195	3,340	145
FRANCE	V	E	85	486,413	98,093	151,409	53,316
GUATMAL	V	E	86	111,120	17,760	26,295	8,535
HAITI	A	E	85	54,600	8,873	17,105	8,232
			86	13,982	4,320	6,120	1,800
HG KONG	V	E	83	450	648	735	87
	V	W	81	825	498	530	32
ITALY	A	E	82	106	372	633	261
	V	E	83	1,190	2,036	2,153	117
PANAMA	A	E	83	1,006	1,705	2,262	557
REP SAF	V	E	83	4,400	4,911	5,192	281
			84	4,125	4,673	5,031	358
			85	2,202	2,475	2,683	208
SINGAPR	V	E	86	3,375	1,200	1,380	180
SOMALIA	V	E	85	1,650	1,837	2,013	176
SPAIN	V	E	84	366	447	503	56

Pear, fresh or in brine
1488100 PEARS, FRESH, APR 1-JUNE 30 (LB)

Country	Mode	Reg	Yr	Quantity	F.A.S.	C.I.F.	Charges
TOTAL			81	14,649,390	4,772,700	6,928,925	2,156,225
			82	5,719,865	2,101,691	2,758,671	656,980
			83	9,494,484	3,280,975	4,523,339	1,242,364
			84	9,514,876	2,984,531	4,154,003	1,169,472
			85	17,566,223	5,439,466	7,559,000	2,119,534
			86	24,228,610	7,233,112	9,539,448	2,306,336
ARGENT	O	E	86	60,288	26,670	26,670	
	V	E	85	600,133	91,402	173,210	81,808
			86	2,348,869	490,521	742,557	252,036
	V	W	85	53,334	25,301	32,443	7,142
AUSTRAL	O	E	84	106,468	65,733	65,733	
	V	E	81	10,459,149	3,259,744	5,151,486	1,891,742
			82	3,083,796	1,030,722	1,606,278	575,556
			83	4,172,996	1,355,900	2,067,920	712,020
			84	5,913,532	1,886,832	2,800,387	913,555
			85	7,049,320	2,385,908	3,511,251	1,125,343
			86	4,901,716	1,692,777	2,559,201	866,424
	V	H	84	53,760	18,262	28,224	9,962
			85	80,440	25,072	37,882	12,810
	V	W	81	77,860	22,849	37,226	14,377
			82	27,204	9,672	14,112	4,440
			83	1,437,680	492,761	737,786	245,025
			84	543,604	199,104	278,580	79,476
			85	3,498,361	1,070,369	1,618,666	548,297
			86	2,376,306	776,479	1,128,128	351,649
C RICA	O	E	81	5,000	1,875	1,929	54
CANADA	O	E	81	160,341	91,060	91,060	
			82	79,344	44,290	44,290	
			83	51,581	25,376	25,376	
			84	39,684	21,057	21,057	
			85	130,294	64,389	64,389	

Crop / Product / TSUSA commodity number, description, and unit of quantity							
Country	Mode	Reg	Yr	Quantity	F.A.S.	C.I.F.	Charges
			86	79,200	40,286	40,286	
	O	W	81	23,281	9,504	9,504	
			82	133,380	29,646	29,646	
			86	36,630	11,177	11,177	
CHILE	A	E	84	3,960	950	3,173	2,223
	O	E	82	70,438	20,985	23,080	2,095
	O	W	81	31,847	12,960	12,960	
	V	E	81	1,894,977	296,604	546,656	250,052
			82	634,354	102,832	164,924	62,092
			83	1,593,060	401,361	619,986	218,625
			84	1,677,209	294,189	437,372	143,183
			85	2,565,079	520,698	728,120	207,422
			86	4,807,866	877,449	1,203,527	326,078
	V	W	82	86,455	18,576	31,373	12,797
			83	568,973	99,263	163,432	64,169
			84	52,275	8,885	14,126	5,241
			85	118,625	19,066	31,391	12,325
			86	668,492	137,966	208,060	70,094
MAURITN	O	E	86	39,600	23,500	23,500	
N ZEAL	N	W	86	11,567	26,207	35,287	9,080
	V	E	85	274,724	90,368	106,050	15,682
			86	770,958	694,734	905,953	211,219
	V	H	83	15,240	4,333	6,858	2,525
			84	88,054	25,757	40,959	15,202
			85	119,050	34,179	54,269	20,090
			86	117,706	45,126	53,792	8,666
	V	W	85	79,869	16,736	27,716	10,980
			86	5,139	2,137	2,772	635
REP SAF	O	E	81	1,960,569	1,061,086	1,061,086	
			82	1,604,894	844,968	844,968	
			83	1,654,954	901,981	901,981	
			84	1,030,378	462,210	462,302	92
			85	1,721,268	753,411	765,157	11,746
			86	5,875,094	1,876,585	2,037,844	161,259
	V	E	85	788,984	183,416	221,158	37,742
			86	2,114,560	509,442	556,366	46,924
	V	W	85	447,058	141,331	169,478	28,147
S ARAB	O	E	85	39,684	17,820	17,820	
SPAIN	V	E	84	5,952	1,552	2,090	538
SWITZLD	V	E	86	14,619	2,056	4,328	2,272
ZMBABWE	O	E	81	36,366	17,018	17,018	

1488200 PEARS, FRESH, JULY 1-MAR 31 (LB)

Country	Mode	Reg	Yr	Quantity	F.A.S.	C.I.F.	Charges
TOTAL			81	6,199,917	1,529,862	2,323,152	793,290
			82	15,451,200	3,576,658	5,496,356	1,919,698
			83	11,967,276	3,262,034	4,866,330	1,604,296
			84	20,279,614	5,211,919	6,723,916	1,511,997
			85	27,092,728	7,453,332	9,967,669	2,514,337
			86	31,626,845	13,430,901	16,783,979	3,353,078
ARGENT	O	E	86	167,208	83,455	83,455	
AUSTRAL	V	E	81	1,679,212	435,159	711,074	275,915
			82	1,447,089	360,674	601,103	240,429
			83	1,740,639	515,343	816,903	301,560
			84	189,637	52,056	75,133	23,077
			85	922,835	243,203	359,575	116,372
			86	1,851,009	585,142	759,117	173,975
	V	H	83	53,547	12,796	21,236	8,440
			84	26,040	5,696	9,602	3,906
			85	80,640	20,972	31,047	10,075
			86	107,306	26,160	41,294	15,134
	V	W	81	53,334	12,685	21,975	9,290
			82	53,334	13,092	21,840	8,748
			83	1,004,517	239,815	394,833	155,018
			84	442,028	105,351	167,107	61,756
			85	1,824,741	487,689	721,798	234,109
			86	2,546,843	750,906	1,053,763	302,857
AUSTRIA	O	W	85	53,334	11,656	18,682	7,026
BELGIUM	A	E	85	3,351	1,177	2,421	1,244
	O	E	84	3,750	1,012	1,387	375
	V	E	81	39,683	10,220	11,657	1,437
CANADA	A	H	85	17,463	6,826	8,612	1,786
	O	E	81	3,731	924	924	
			82	9,475	1,383	1,383	
			83	95,721	24,901	24,901	
			84	25,185	10,323	10,323	
			85	586,270	58,268	58,268	
			86	26,675	7,893	7,893	
	O	W	81	298,320	83,049	83,049	
			82	652,228	176,356	176,356	
			83	211,475	59,126	59,126	
			84	156,245	32,504	32,504	
			85	764,791	136,721	136,721	
			86	518,877	176,414	176,414	

Crop
Product
TSUSA commodity number, description, and unit of quantity

Country	Mode	Reg	Yr	Quantity	F.A.S.	C.I.F.	Charges
	V	W	81	46,297	30,800	39,962	9,162
CHILE	N	W	84	1,720,098	338,257	480,436	142,179
	V	E	81	3,490,645	619,286	998,761	379,475
			82	11,959,228	2,295,907	3,725,888	1,429,981
			83	6,902,498	1,411,370	2,230,911	819,541
			84	11,238,186	1,851,737	2,702,577	850,840
			85	11,494,036	1,871,547	2,815,086	943,539
			86	13,679,934	2,633,849	3,694,765	1,060,916
	V	W	82	64,339	13,824	23,347	9,523
			83	230,884	56,064	85,640	29,576
			85	1,696,858	304,932	459,940	155,008
			86	3,059,702	562,756	865,412	302,656
CHINA M	V	W	81	550	333	351	18
FRANCE	V	E	82	60,602	20,212	25,963	5,751
			83	345,265	108,650	143,985	35,335
			84	883,586	292,232	347,702	55,470
			85	1,565,585	536,472	674,755	138,283
			86	1,331,701	574,286	701,869	127,583
ITALY	V	E	82	1,140	572	845	273
			85	79,246	21,696	26,624	4,928
JAPAN	N	H	84	1,103,125	606,154	839,475	233,321
			85	1,268,695	756,008	992,855	236,847
			86	1,224,737	942,408	1,221,901	279,493
	O	E	84	11,911	10,632	10,632	
			85	7,937	8,640	8,640	
	V	E	85	31,416	23,181	29,925	6,744
	V	H	81	367,359	230,836	309,664	78,828
			82	677,083	402,955	549,293	146,338
			83	914,671	545,563	739,139	193,576
	V	W	81	104,168	71,400	91,624	20,224
			82	384,924	250,637	306,360	55,723
			83	414,685	263,340	315,979	52,639
			84	703,282	456,932	571,669	114,737
			85	2,775,674	2,056,135	2,441,919	385,784
			86	6,099,220	6,656,178	7,658,763	1,002,585
KOR REP	V	H	86	103,175	78,972	98,032	19,060
	V	W	84	59,524	38,023	46,800	8,777
			86	160,782	129,138	143,138	14,000
MEXICO	A	E	85	6,833	20,500	21,574	1,074
	O	E	86	32,176	2,890	2,890	
N ZEAL	A	H	86	1,120	4,226	5,446	1,220
	A	W	81	2,708	3,755	5,234	1,479
			83	506	820	1,154	334
			86	3,086	2,547	4,217	1,670
	V	E	84	144,000	45,776	55,252	9,476
	V	H	81	113,910	31,415	48,877	17,462
			82	141,240	40,059	62,929	22,870
			83	45,760	13,834	21,164	7,330
			86	95,064	27,031	43,786	16,755
	V	W	85	53,334	6,786	6,996	210
			86	64,094	13,008	20,496	7,488
PHIL R	V	W	82	518	987	1,049	62
PORTUGL	V	E	84	33,952	6,160	11,727	5,567
			86	40,018	10,892	15,159	4,267
REP SAF	O	E	84	713,650	274,066	274,498	432
			85	289,396	70,174	85,716	15,542
			86	81,360	33,067	33,067	
	V	E	84	2,825,415	1,085,008	1,087,092	2,084
			85	3,271,847	702,743	933,687	230,944
			86	82,905	19,615	20,568	953
SPAIN	V	E	85	260,394	97,486	119,258	21,772
			86	349,853	110,068	132,534	22,466
	V	W	85	38,052	10,520	13,570	3,050
U KING	V	E	83	7,108	10,412	11,359	947

Pear, juice**
1651500 APLE A PEAR JC N OV 1 PC AL (GAL)
   (See Apple, juice under Apple)

Pear, paste and pulp
1527800 PEAR PASTE AND PULP (LB)

Country	Mode	Reg	Yr	Quantity	F.A.S.	C.I.F.	Charges
TOTAL			82	430,040	69,385	82,785	13,400
			83	402,787	126,023	158,640	32,617
			84	1,310,969	485,483	566,435	80,952
			85	2,215,261	641,838	786,923	145,085
			86	1,191,854	341,829	413,337	71,508
ARGENT	A	E	83	1,096	351	1,646	1,295
	V	E	83	31,973	12,163	14,295	2,132
			84	28,820	22,325	25,962	3,637
			85	112,623	28,163	33,878	5,715

Country	Mode	Reg	Yr	Quantity	F.A.S.	C.I.F.	Charges
			86	160,732	51,964	59,894	7,930
AUSTRAL	A	E	82	510	306	861	555
	A	W	83	1,100	462	2,373	1,911
	V	E	86	78,730	16,165	20,964	4,799
	V	W	86	157,460	54,012	59,834	5,822
AUSTRIA	O	E	83	1,087	353	353	
FR GERM	V	E	84	2,153	278	333	55
FRANCE	V	E	82	178	269	283	14
			84	2,929	1,508	1,678	170
			86	4,170	5,400	6,137	737
HONDURA	V	E	82	353,423	46,151	52,071	5,920
ITALY	V	E	83	205	425	455	30
			85	25,053	6,494	10,100	3,606
REP SAF	V	E	82	75,929	22,659	29,570	6,911
			83	367,326	112,269	139,518	27,249
			84	1,277,067	461,372	538,462	77,090
			85	2,077,585	607,181	742,945	135,764
			86	746,008	204,334	254,505	50,171
SPAIN	V	E	86	44,754	9,954	12,003	2,049

Pear, prepared or preserved
1488600 PEARS, PREP OR PRES, NSPF (LB)

Country	Mode	Reg	Yr	Quantity	F.A.S.	C.I.F.	Charges
TOTAL			81	34,246	31,280	34,140	2,860
			82	60,021	39,544	42,762	3,218
			83	139,643	55,002	64,993	9,991
			84	5,532,283	1,609,469	1,888,705	279,236
			85	40,366,352	12,071,478	14,414,603	2,343,125
			86	12,577,422	3,409,544	4,075,519	665,975
ARGENT	V	E	85	1,217,870	240,800	289,091	48,291
			86	35,417	9,500	11,523	2,023
AUSTRAL	V	E	85	3,601,006	1,292,073	1,514,668	222,595
			86	823,209	252,846	289,813	36,967
	V	W	85	3,537,259	1,375,566	1,523,554	147,988
AUSTRIA	V	E	85	39,683	10,350	12,870	2,520
CANADA	O	E	85	140,365	55,225	55,225	
			86	89,250	3,718	3,718	
	O	W	82	3,000	1,777	1,777	
			84	1,278,900	388,528	388,528	
			85	48,160	12,764	12,764	
CHILE	V	E	85	782,275	220,427	249,527	29,100
			86	306,391	72,322	84,985	12,663
CHINA M	N	W	86	377,644	105,319	117,751	12,432
	V	E	81	6,560	3,502	3,950	448
			82	4,985	4,265	4,871	606
			83	23,520	14,139	16,981	2,842
			84	1,102	927	1,072	145
			86	28,169	13,090	15,759	2,669
	V	H	83	882	537	576	39
			84	250	320	366	46
	V	W	81	18,283	19,413	20,997	1,584
			82	39,396	20,003	21,649	1,646
			83	50,207	15,100	16,267	1,167
			84	23,401	12,783	13,571	788
			85	500,096	122,173	160,251	38,078
			86	12,085	13,045	13,794	749
CHINA T	V	H	86	1,320	1,376	1,491	115
	V	W	83	375	528	550	22
DOM REP	V	E	83	29,750	5,175	6,880	1,705
FR GERM	V	E	84	37,371	18,539	22,648	4,109
			85	113,486	46,672	56,799	10,127
FRANCE	A	E	84	1,502	1,967	2,587	620
	N	E	84	1,566	2,688	3,200	512
	O	E	81	2,511	2,996	3,246	250
			86	720	1,233	1,256	23
	V	E	81	1,454	2,453	2,622	169
			82	2,469	4,532	4,792	260
			83	2,396	2,857	3,049	192
			84	1,530	1,567	1,812	245
			85	117,580	57,247	67,541	10,294
			86	19,434	12,098	13,429	1,331
	V	W	83	952	1,297	1,440	143
			84	678	322	473	151
GREECE	V	E	81	1,175	1,263	1,445	182
			82	591	575	663	88
			86	130,302	32,552	38,402	5,850
	V	W	82	300	300	332	32
HG KONG	V	E	82	860	604	681	77
			83	3,000	2,176	2,405	229
			84	1,641	2,201	2,465	264
			85	2,600	2,447	2,678	231
			86	2,572	1,591	1,789	198

Crop Product TSUSA commodity number, description, and unit of quantity Country	Mode	Reg	Yr	Quantity	F.A.S.	C.I.F.	Charges
	V	H	81	880	296	319	23
			83	300	265	292	27
	V	W	82	4,550	5,353	5,732	379
			83	2,125	1,600	1,727	127
			84	486	367	394	27
			85	2,895	2,972	3,200	228
			86	134,478	36,869	39,672	2,803
HONDURA	V	E	86	159	1,800	2,130	330
HUNGARY	N	E	85	21,800	8,053	14,656	6,603
	V	E	86	10,828	3,119	3,648	529
	V	W	85	9,259	2,729	3,360	631
ISRAEL	V	E	82	2,550	1,200	1,268	68
			85	243,603	101,232	118,193	16,961
			86	294,625	97,814	123,031	25,217
ITALY	V	E	83	2,910	4,562	5,244	682
			84	27,977	8,207	8,763	556
			85	3,045,841	853,957	1,029,029	175,072
			86	463,800	136,647	166,975	30,328
	V	W	83	114	368	382	14
			84	213	621	662	41
			85	580,112	148,722	183,300	34,578
			86	75,900	24,674	29,172	4,498
N ZEAL	V	E	84	968,766	273,733	361,411	87,678
			85	1,064,493	264,948	383,250	118,302
	V	W	84	162,903	48,403	55,473	7,070
			85	69,445	19,615	24,106	4,491
NETHLDS	V	E	85	59,249	20,417	25,922	5,505
			86	76,502	41,077	49,373	8,296
POLAND	V	E	86	4,583	1,600	2,120	520
PORTUGL	V	E	81	309	252	291	39
			84	1,235	812	988	176
			86	5,401	3,158	3,626	468
REP SAF	V	E	84	1,803,289	529,010	620,576	91,566
			85	9,104,223	2,819,205	3,298,356	479,151
			86	1,984,454	472,108	566,273	94,165
	V	W	81	1,090	540	547	7
			85	900,298	271,743	328,803	57,060
			86	34,011	9,093	11,274	2,181
ROMANIA	V	E	85	33,069	6,182	7,562	1,380
SOMALIA	V	E	85	85,376	28,690	32,959	4,269
SPAIN	N	E	85	1,916,906	504,910	621,793	116,883
	O	E	85	25,245	6,640	8,164	1,524
			86	42,900	10,660	13,239	2,579
	V	E	81	1,984	565	723	158
			83	22,752	5,994	8,757	2,763
			84	1,219,473	318,474	403,716	85,242
			85	12,947,135	3,531,169	4,331,062	799,893
			86	7,533,316	2,039,826	2,455,736	415,910
	V	W	85	104,273	30,764	37,196	6,432
SWITZLD	V	E	83	360	404	443	39
			85	3,910	5,694	6,164	470
THAILND	V	W	82	1,320	935	997	62
U KING	V	E	86	2,055	1,973	2,218	245
YUGOSLV	O	E	86	45,948	3,238	3,238	
	V	E	85	48,840	8,092	12,560	4,468
			86	41,949	7,198	10,084	2,886

Pearl Onion

Pearl onion, fresh or frozen
1369200 PEARL ONIONS NOV 10/16IN FR (LB)

Country	Mode	Reg	Yr	Quantity	F.A.S.	C.I.F.	Charges
TOTAL			81	228,621	87,110	124,937	37,827
			82	136,133	76,189	104,403	28,214
			83	83,704	45,696	57,641	11,945
			84	1,492,175	486,358	593,809	107,451
			85	605,431	242,629	299,103	56,474
			86	1,037,697	436,543	531,673	95,130
AUSTRIA	A	E	82	944	545	1,491	946
BELGIUM	A	E	81	106,270	55,960	77,796	21,836
			82	59,125	38,912	57,591	18,679
			83	6,292	4,082	5,522	1,440
	A	W	81	8,906	6,163	9,249	3,086
	V	E	85	147,262	54,937	66,446	11,509
			86	69,097	25,984	31,626	5,642
	V	W	85	44,101	16,703	22,783	6,080
CANADA	O	E	84	320	648	648	
			85	7,500	1,050	1,050	
			86	9,720	6,651	6,651	
FRANCE	A	E	81	19,876	12,069	22,878	10,809

Country	Mode	Reg	Yr	Quantity	F.A.S.	C.I.F.	Charges
			82	15,561	6,158	11,046	4,888
			83	9,540	4,550	7,965	3,415
			84	1,511	2,320	2,721	401
	A	W	81	2,877	840	2,463	1,623
			83	6,614	2,337	6,110	3,773
GUATMAL	V	E	81	5,806	2,248	2,682	434
ISRAEL	O	E	82	21,600	12,741	12,741	
	V	E	81	2,976	1,100	1,139	39
			82	11,905	5,000	6,048	1,048
			84	209,976	79,091	102,991	23,900
			85	125,424	45,290	56,297	11,007
			86	231,066	80,126	109,343	29,217
	V	W	84	39,732	13,745	19,469	5,724
			85	39,793	13,426	18,685	5,259
ITALY	V	E	83	714	455	508	53
			84	1,133	510	513	3
			85	2,428	1,296	1,487	191
MEXICO	O	E	81	61,200	4,555	4,555	
	O	W	81	20,710	4,175	4,175	
			85	27,692	8,886	8,886	
			86	53,740	16,710	16,710	
NETHLDS	A	E	82	3,188	762	1,290	528
	N	W	86	88,000	41,671	45,760	4,089
	O	E	83	60,544	34,272	37,536	3,264
	V	E	84	1,107,504	328,514	377,771	49,257
			85	121,055	65,739	75,756	10,017
			86	353,260	152,524	183,482	30,958
	V	W	82	23,810	12,071	14,196	2,125
			84	131,999	61,530	89,696	28,166
			85	44,000	19,102	25,212	6,110
			86	232,814	112,877	138,101	25,224
U KING	V	E	85	46,176	16,200	22,501	6,301

Pecan

Pecan, nut, shelled, prepared or preserved
1455000 PECANS, SHELLED, BLAND, ETC (LB)

Country	Mode	Reg	Yr	Quantity	F.A.S.	C.I.F.	Charges
TOTAL			81	131,400	58,616	58,689	73
			82	38,631	29,184	29,376	192
			83	268,008	443,156	444,650	1,494
			84	2,430,496	4,103,962	4,313,441	209,479
			85	1,897,358	2,533,740	2,658,147	124,407
			86	1,291,406	2,498,039	2,536,732	38,693
AUSTRAL	V	E	84	1,027,211	1,753,750	1,935,278	181,528
			85	125,060	273,843	286,872	13,029
			86	124,289	271,858	288,455	16,597
	V	H	82	88	394	436	42
	V	W	84	179,933	375,203	403,080	27,877
			85	1,547,928	1,844,006	1,953,664	109,658
			86	93,765	254,742	262,488	7,746
CANADA	O	E	81	123,018	53,371	53,371	
			82	25,150	9,660	9,660	
			84	1,041	2,544	2,544	
			85	580	1,241	1,241	
			86	75,502	13,877	13,877	
	O	W	81	4,400	3,600	3,600	
			84	11,200	15,395	15,395	
			85	1,924	1,094	1,094	
CHINA M	V	E	84	660	1,204	1,278	74
	V	W	85	500	1,400	1,569	169
			86	500	1,038	1,058	20
HG KONG	V	E	83	5,512	13,731	14,193	462
			85	11,000	28,000	29,044	1,044
ISRAEL	A	E	81	60	325	398	73
			82	99	336	486	150
	V	E	85	16,500	8,021	8,528	507
ITALY	V	E	86	307	1,469	1,481	12
MEXICO	O	E	82	13,294	18,794	18,794	
			83	251,902	411,975	411,975	
			84	1,210,451	1,955,866	1,955,866	
			85	183,226	374,188	374,188	
			86	939,431	1,866,594	1,866,594	
	O	W	81	3,922	1,320	1,320	
			83	8,174	12,269	12,269	
			85	10,640	1,947	1,947	
MONSRAT	O	E	86	7,745	5,809	5,809	
N ZEAL	A	W	83	2,420	5,181	6,213	1,032
			86	5,422	11,996	14,864	2,868
REP SAF	V	E	86	44,445	70,656	82,106	11,450

Crop Product TSUSA commodity number, description, and unit of quantity Country	Mode	Reg	Yr	Quantity	F.A.S.	C.I.F.	Charges

Pecan, nut, unshelled
1452200 PECANS NOT SHELLED (LB)

Country	Mode	Reg	Yr	Quantity	F.A.S.	C.I.F.	Charges
TOTAL			81	1,437,073	1,482,671	1,483,376	705
			82	2,918,929	2,282,783	2,287,570	4,787
			83	2,554,679	1,367,868	1,367,868	
			84	6,590,770	3,653,941	3,653,941	
			85	13,756,006	9,239,191	9,245,098	5,907
			86	25,863,037	17,969,520	17,994,579	25,059
AUSTRAL	V	W	81	1,436,511	1,479,881	1,479,881	
			82	2,122,900	1,680,649	1,680,649	
			86	184,940	183,714	208,714	25,000
BRAZIL	V	E	82	22,000	36,221	39,536	3,315
			85	15,400	13,090	15,182	2,092
CHINA M	V	E	86	550	1,154	1,213	59
FRANCE	O	W	85	256,478	102,591	102,591	
ISRAEL	A	E	81	562	2,790	3,495	705
			82	463	890	2,362	1,472
MEXICO	O	E	82	773,566	565,023	565,023	
			83	2,552,687	1,367,328	1,367,328	
			84	6,587,800	3,649,783	3,649,783	
			85	12,638,946	8,714,973	8,714,977	4
			86	24,601,359	17,299,376	17,299,376	
	O	W	83	1,992	540	540	
			85	805,982	348,529	348,529	
			86	1,076,188	485,276	485,276	
PERU	O	W	84	2,970	4,158	4,158	
TURKEY	V	E	85	39,200	60,008	63,819	3,811

Pepper

Black pepper, oleoresin
4502015 BLACK PEPPER (LB)

Country	Mode	Reg	Yr	Quantity	F.A.S.	C.I.F.	Charges
TOTAL			81	232,729	1,854,266	1,909,827	55,561
			82	324,050	2,213,912	2,280,755	66,843
			83	271,782	1,809,536	1,868,571	59,035
			84	243,743	1,745,457	1,795,837	50,380
			85	348,348	3,137,968	3,208,620	70,652
			86	397,192	4,681,827	4,759,123	77,296
CANADA	A	E	82	2,400	16,680	16,973	293
			84	529	3,518	4,240	722
	O	E	82	22,212	168,194	168,194	
			83	9,840	64,944	64,944	
			84	16,179	124,628	124,628	
			85	13,118	121,877	121,877	
			86	21,713	297,397	297,397	
ETHIOP	A	E	86	4,409	66,342	71,266	4,924
HG KONG	V	W	81	10,229	91,771	93,130	1,359
INDIA	A	E	81	942	9,498	12,296	2,798
			82	661	7,209	8,475	1,266
			83	220	2,480	3,150	670
			85	7,408	96,189	107,620	11,431
			86	214	3,000	3,215	215
	N	E	81	96,545	752,026	779,414	27,388
			82	121,489	832,594	867,651	35,057
			83	119,047	788,294	818,485	30,191
			84	117,070	848,165	881,555	33,390
			86	160,349	1,872,796	1,906,061	33,265
	O	E	85	550	5,523	5,523	
	V	E	81	4,205	27,934	32,200	4,266
			82	3,087	18,567	19,002	435
			83	2,220	14,697	15,281	584
			84	2,220	14,626	15,058	432
			85	181,546	1,611,693	1,645,129	33,436
			86	4,409	46,935	47,541	606
	V	W	81	9,228	67,610	70,106	2,496
			82	38,711	279,961	290,349	10,388
			84	1,360	7,665	8,087	422
			85	5,200	39,230	40,995	1,765
			86	25,763	313,310	321,690	8,380
MALAYSA	V	E	81	8,056	55,993	57,389	1,396
NETHLDS	A	E	85	1,124	25,140	26,152	1,012
SINGAPR	A	E	81	44	357	559	202
			82	50	280	471	191
	N	W	81	14,506	117,782	119,946	2,164
			82	16,358	123,937	127,189	3,252
	V	E	81	55,326	444,623	452,750	8,127
			82	95,782	606,948	619,083	12,135

Country	Mode	Reg	Yr	Quantity	F.A.S.	C.I.F.	Charges
			83	138,893	926,937	953,892	26,955
			84	104,180	743,930	758,931	15,001
			85	134,083	1,215,067	1,236,768	21,701
			86	167,685	2,073,757	2,102,682	28,925
	V	W	81	29,248	266,858	271,976	5,118
			82	22,640	134,862	138,092	3,230
SPAIN	V	E	83	1,210	1,710	1,956	246
			84	2,205	2,925	3,338	413
			85	5,319	23,249	24,556	1,307
			86	12,650	8,290	9,271	981
U KING	A	E	81	4,400	19,814	20,061	247
			82	660	24,680	25,276	596
			83	352	10,474	10,863	389

Black pepper, spice
1617720 PEPPER UNGROUND BLACK (LB)

Country	Mode	Reg	Yr	Quantity	F.A.S.	C.I.F.	Charges
TOTAL			81	62,970,370	36,320,185	41,422,448	5,102,263
			82	61,311,754	30,504,496	35,519,813	5,015,317
			83	62,491,478	29,296,948	34,155,084	4,858,136
			84	76,070,197	56,704,417	62,804,852	6,100,435
			85	60,452,740	73,414,357	78,392,558	4,978,201
			86	83,431,535	151,994,510	157,664,585	5,670,075
AFGHAN	V	E	81	66,138	41,160	46,228	5,068
			85	33,069	120,000	123,110	3,110
			86	5,513	9,903	10,196	293
BELGIUM	V	E	84	33,069	27,000	29,400	2,400
			86	66,138	125,250	130,591	5,341
BRAZIL	N	E	82	31,526,530	14,923,043	17,206,378	2,283,335
			83	26,270,485	11,573,558	13,460,761	1,887,203
	O	E	82	1,100	772	772	
			83	35,090	22,215	22,215	
	V	E	81	32,117,235	18,425,788	20,708,369	2,282,581
			82	1,292,826	603,841	700,790	96,949
			83	1,278,943	561,553	655,102	93,549
			84	22,858,994	19,053,467	20,800,526	1,747,059
			85	26,647,546	31,222,955	33,484,586	2,261,631
			86	20,688,679	39,120,920	40,701,196	1,580,276
	V	W	81	260,144	162,089	183,707	21,618
			83	1,177,751	518,890	626,696	107,806
			84	496	5,254	6,177	923
			85	308,644	294,458	320,933	26,475
BURMA	V	E	82	525	607	698	91
C RICA	V	E	84	436	1,617	1,747	130
			85	45,251	54,887	60,949	6,062
			86	125,670	208,347	217,417	9,070
CANADA	O	E	81	848	943	943	
			82	500	353	353	
			83	3,971	4,293	4,293	
			84	5,629	4,380	4,380	
			86	34,125	85,744	87,790	2,046
	O	W	81	329	605	605	
CHINA M	V	E	81	45,953	35,379	42,313	6,934
			82	2,689	4,086	4,460	374
			83	4,500	9,281	9,952	671
			84	922,399	723,984	781,892	57,908
			85	485,118	750,203	780,588	30,385
			86	219,256	389,146	400,159	11,013
	V	W	81	1,001	1,464	1,550	86
			82	3,337	5,660	6,084	424
			83	3,019	3,693	4,031	338
			84	95,149	86,713	90,740	4,027
			85	348,592	432,566	456,201	23,635
			86	285,765	482,314	496,235	13,921
CHINA T	V	E	81	2,879	1,020	1,612	592
			82	1,418	4,416	4,820	404
			83	249	1,585	1,730	145
			84	28,550	23,710	26,042	2,332
			85	25,937	23,527	25,827	2,300
			86	132,410	278,488	288,297	9,809
	V	W	86	2,625	5,887	6,204	317
COLOMB	A	E	83	301	555	686	131
	V	E	85	40,320	36,441	41,436	4,995
DOM REP	V	E	84	33,069	15,849	18,404	2,555
			86	33,069	60,842	64,154	3,312
DOMINCA	V	E	85	33,069	37,387	40,546	3,159
FR GERM	A	E	82	528	3,402	3,690	288
			85	231	2,624	2,874	250
			86	331	1,260	1,608	348
	V	E	86	2,928	8,483	9,647	1,164
	V	W	84	2,300	360	377	17
			85	2,489	9,463	9,926	463

Crop Product TSUSA commodity number, description, and unit of quantity Country	Mode	Reg	Yr	Quantity	F.A.S.	C.I.F.	Charges
FRANCE	A	E	81	1,137	3,613	3,687	74
			83	143	1,199	1,494	295
	N	E	85	2,335	15,471	15,999	528
	O	E	82	10	379	404	25
			84	105	352	374	22
	V	E	81	424	1,495	1,589	94
			82	956	3,079	3,248	169
			83	2,559	7,191	7,781	590
			84	1,212	2,286	2,448	162
			85	1,532	9,090	9,999	909
			86	2,319	13,375	14,214	839
	V	W	83	994	3,385	3,550	165
			84	1,431	7,866	8,364	498
			85	1,505	8,510	9,757	1,247
GREECE	V	E	81	22,400	20,160	22,971	2,811
			82	33,180	19,482	22,414	2,932
GUATMAL	V	E	85	22,500	17,738	19,227	1,489
HG KONG	N	E	82	11,072	7,685	8,158	473
	V	E	81	1,380	1,562	1,743	181
			85	181,720	220,582	238,934	18,352
	V	W	81	375	652	729	77
			83	250	422	450	28
			84	68,448	48,337	50,517	2,180
			86	500	1,535	1,587	52
INDIA	A	E	84	40	323	492	169
			86	2,485	26,948	30,641	3,693
	N	E	81	1,037,273	742,091	828,330	86,239
			82	1,568,848	898,162	1,027,661	129,499
			84	10,028,901	8,310,347	8,973,263	662,916
			85	7,297,168	10,640,229	11,128,959	488,730
			86	36,273,132	63,523,859	65,782,167	2,258,308
	O	E	86	55,017	114,248	114,248	
	V	E	81	111,094	62,401	72,983	10,582
			82	11,662	7,409	8,396	987
			83	5,119,269	2,690,269	3,003,773	313,504
			84	399,897	352,620	373,881	21,261
			85	378,277	497,366	521,412	24,046
			86	4,500,547	8,183,205	8,431,518	248,313
	V	W	81	83,246	58,960	66,694	7,734
			82	290,032	187,000	213,076	26,076
			83	386,766	218,103	253,842	35,739
			84	331,174	253,946	284,259	30,313
			85	1,195,159	1,842,868	1,931,373	88,505
			86	5,409,658	9,908,206	10,264,748	356,542
INDNSIA	N	E	81	16,625,096	9,414,968	11,055,533	1,640,565
			82	14,476,155	7,661,332	9,098,346	1,437,014
			83	19,033,648	8,969,204	10,605,760	1,636,556
			84	26,808,686	18,124,591	20,496,640	2,372,049
			86	6,966,748	13,397,374	13,913,154	515,780
	V	E	81	2,511,240	1,382,466	1,625,822	243,356
			82	2,469,152	1,266,904	1,514,351	247,447
			83	1,818,134	903,355	1,054,995	151,640
			84	3,326,341	1,612,270	1,894,024	281,754
			85	14,287,946	17,277,731	18,545,072	1,267,341
			86	794,538	1,497,788	1,557,440	59,652
	V	W	81	8,675,237	4,991,610	5,662,528	670,918
			82	8,672,586	4,323,216	5,061,730	738,514
			83	6,324,782	3,051,844	3,612,674	560,830
			84	9,600,842	6,773,085	7,563,558	790,473
			85	7,347,478	7,610,036	8,186,054	576,018
			86	5,102,927	9,219,176	9,595,154	375,978
ITALY	A	E	81	1	519	559	40
	V	E	85	237	1,306	1,469	163
			86	148	1,253	1,495	242
IVY CST	V	E	82	2,138	4,536	6,472	1,936
			83	2,213	7,340	7,624	284
JAMAICA	V	E	84	231	328	385	57
JAPAN	A	E	82	150	263	898	635
	N	E	84	488	1,959	2,208	249
	V	W	84	12	354	370	16
			85	45,639	33,736	37,239	3,503
KIRIBAT	A	H	82	188	1,200	1,697	497
KOR REP	O	E	85	13,216	17,846	18,917	1,071
	V	W	83	2,376	2,760	2,905	145
			86	405	2,370	2,565	195
LAOS	V	E	86	33,179	48,157	50,101	1,944
MADAGAS	V	E	86	33,069	66,138	68,308	2,170
MALAYSA	V	E	84	22,284	17,518	18,822	1,304
			85	167,528	190,035	203,602	13,567
			86	1,306,106	2,601,402	2,688,865	87,463
	V	W	81	601,824	389,067	424,150	35,083
			82	380,076	238,012	258,331	20,319
			83	55,068	25,360	30,107	4,747
			84	374,784	328,014	353,229	25,215

Crop Product TSUSA commodity number, description, and unit of quantity Country	Mode	Reg	Yr	Quantity	F.A.S.	C.I.F.	Charges
			85	121,154	128,180	138,527	10,347
			86	47,656	132,222	142,306	10,084
MEXICO	O	E	83	242	493	493	
	O	W	81	69,309	49,445	49,445	
			85	6,226	5,173	5,173	
	V	E	82	22,046	15,981	17,034	1,053
MOROC	V	E	83	132,276	56,681	68,281	11,600
NETHLDS	V	E	83	3,334	17,835	20,100	2,265
			84	231	515	540	25
			86	33,069	57,300	59,400	2,100
	V	W	81	370	872	967	95
			82	1,333	2,965	3,139	174
			84	1,663	2,921	3,113	192
			85	3,542	6,073	6,893	820
PAKISTN	V	E	82	22,134	8,854	9,315	461
PHIL R	V	W	82	975	2,834	3,163	329
ROMANIA	V	W	82	63	647	685	38
S HELNA	V	E	84	22,046	20,528	23,028	2,500
SINGAPR	O	E	85	462,966	576,297	622,055	45,758
	V	E	82	113,770	57,274	63,371	6,097
			83	255,734	218,276	227,016	8,740
			84	22,359	30,407	32,420	2,013
			85	94,168	127,962	137,227	9,265
			86	265,475	459,096	480,864	21,768
	V	W	81	81,626	137,785	144,474	6,689
			82	24,251	12,679	14,084	1,405
			83	9,098	6,332	6,856	524
			84	198,945	161,865	175,367	13,502
			85	152,435	186,020	196,126	10,106
SPAIN	O	E	85	74,800	49,368	56,260	6,892
	V	E	84	48,485	28,111	31,945	3,834
			86	2,100	10,901	11,107	206
SRI LKA	N	E	84	221,120	165,728	175,693	9,965
	V	E	81	650,032	384,061	463,169	79,108
			82	377,415	232,802	249,178	16,376
			83	564,170	408,514	448,589	40,075
			84	440,188	353,396	399,034	45,638
			85	343,538	589,436	617,815	28,379
			86	464,446	977,646	1,030,024	52,378
	V	W	82	900	468	599	131
			84	98,325	77,295	84,869	7,574
			85	5,731	27,801	29,801	2,000
			86	97,002	213,725	224,323	10,598
SURINAM	V	E	85	196,072	249,503	260,839	11,336
			86	236,866	400,919	413,063	12,144
SWITZLD	V	W	86	2,500	3,550	3,723	173
SYRIA	V	E	81	500	386	412	26
T PAC I	A	H	82	78	580	961	381
	O	W	83	1,385	7,375	7,601	226
			84	1,100	11,822	15,588	3,766
			85	150	1,875	2,239	364
THAILND	V	E	83	2,140	2,032	2,266	234
			84	95	532	632	100
			85	35,470	49,377	51,777	2,400
			86	35,088	73,177	75,092	1,915
	V	W	81	2,930	8,502	10,153	1,651
			82	2,654	3,491	3,904	413
			83	844	1,332	1,377	45
			84	3,586	4,960	5,272	312
			86	37,313	69,724	72,380	2,656
TUNISIA	V	E	85	43,982	50,237	52,837	2,600
			86	132,564	213,312	221,284	7,972
U KING	N	E	84	33,529	39,291	42,104	2,813
	O	E	81	278	629	671	42
			84	470	1,397	1,517	120
			86	169	1,320	1,320	
	V	E	81	71	493	512	19
			82	601	1,729	1,838	109
			83	1,744	2,023	2,084	61
YEMEN A	V	E	84	33,025	28,472	30,526	2,054

1617900 PEPPER, BLACK OR WHITE, GRND (LB)

Country	Mode	Reg	Yr	Quantity	F.A.S.	C.I.F.	Charges
TOTAL			81	111,695	153,412	167,903	14,491
			82	179,814	217,976	231,606	13,630
			83	365,110	360,332	379,733	19,401
			84	379,130	510,468	536,906	26,438
			85	148,782	179,949	190,506	10,557
			86	867,400	1,507,310	1,590,812	83,502
BERMUDA	A	E	84	50	436	468	32
BRAZIL	O	W	85	2,600	5,408	5,408	
	V	E	82	8,995	8,031	9,080	1,049
			83	25,683	12,007	15,148	3,141
			84	11,189	5,843	6,900	1,057

Crop
Product
TSUSA commodity number, description, and unit of quantity

Country	Mode	Reg	Yr	Quantity	F.A.S.	C.I.F.	Charges
			85	41,533	34,567	37,866	3,299
C RICA	V	E	86	12,433	3,760	5,082	1,322
	V	W	84	635	1,312	1,480	168
CANADA	A	E	83	165	355	496	141
			84	60	389	430	41
	O	E	81	8,674	12,564	12,564	
			82	45,140	38,910	38,910	
			83	153,431	123,022	123,022	
			84	15,644	15,418	15,579	161
			85	11,000	7,217	7,217	
	O	W	81	6,536	10,222	10,222	
			82	400	319	319	
CHINA M	O	W	84	253	653	703	50
	V	E	82	540	1,062	1,134	72
			83	12,614	8,212	9,558	1,346
			84	1,889	2,611	2,960	349
			86	4,250	4,999	5,521	522
	V	H	81	350	582	614	32
			82	250	396	419	23
			83	250	358	392	34
	V	W	81	2,838	3,274	3,476	202
			82	1,735	3,516	3,787	271
			83	2,495	4,838	5,220	382
			84	15,895	24,840	26,419	1,579
			85	8,850	11,672	12,427	755
			86	63,179	77,993	82,784	4,791
CHINA T	V	E	83	3,124	5,094	5,493	399
			84	319	1,623	1,653	30
			85	661	1,711	2,587	876
			86	650	3,676	3,951	275
	V	W	81	689	4,081	4,270	189
			82	1,575	3,371	3,590	219
			83	1,264	4,279	4,475	196
			84	1,164	6,094	6,451	357
			85	621	3,572	3,751	179
			86	3,179	16,600	17,065	465
DENMARK	V	E	84	33	273	288	15
FINLAND	A	E	83	250	731	758	27
FR GERM	A	E	81	1,300	2,727	3,084	357
	V	E	81	2,056	19,429	20,172	743
			82	22,207	76,376	78,837	2,461
			83	8,576	69,513	71,215	1,702
			84	2,063	12,150	12,835	685
			86	996	2,832	3,157	325
FRANCE	A	E	81	166	1,796	1,841	45
			83	220	255	392	137
	A	W	86	165	1,087	1,354	267
	N	E	86	915	5,439	6,055	616
	V	E	81	1,383	2,182	2,344	162
			82	2,499	2,892	3,230	338
			83	173	862	918	56
			84	827	2,391	2,425	34
	V	W	82	97	478	544	66
GUATMAL	V	W	83	45	384	455	71
HG KONG	N	W	81	1,063	1,628	1,657	29
	V	E	83	638	1,371	1,540	169
			85	3,080	4,700	5,211	511
			86	22,955	37,157	39,841	2,684
	V	H	83	500	668	724	56
	V	W	81	17,240	14,302	15,719	1,417
			82	4,048	7,451	7,901	450
			84	500	825	883	58
			85	382	1,160	1,208	48
			86	16,961	26,350	27,613	1,263
INDIA	N	E	83	67,060	34,638	39,508	4,870
	O	E	82	2,000	1,801	1,801	
			83	5,000	4,575	4,575	
			84	77	282	289	7
			86	550	1,086	1,086	
	V	E	81	220	261	304	43
			82	317	899	943	44
			83	330	321	508	187
			84	14,272	11,247	12,191	944
			86	100,800	168,458	173,545	5,087
	V	W	81	524	364	448	84
			82	1,538	1,030	1,199	169
			83	573	319	350	31
			86	552,897	1,029,005	1,087,181	58,176
INDNSIA	V	E	81	55,115	47,399	49,692	2,293
			84	297,621	385,175	402,467	17,292
	V	W	82	66,138	31,378	37,036	5,658
			83	66,138	44,595	47,915	3,320
			85	44,092	64,662	64,846	184
ISRAEL	V	E	86	37,478	64,655	68,000	3,345

Crop
Product
TSUSA commodity number, description, and unit of quantity

Country	Mode	Reg	Yr	Quantity	F.A.S.	C.I.F.	Charges
ITALY	A	E	84	264	459	489	30
	V	E	82	92	612	674	62
			83	1,913	8,167	8,791	624
			84	3,540	4,144	4,571	427
			86	392	5,938	6,222	284
JAMAICA	V	E	83	17	483	490	7
			86	1,982	1,350	1,458	108
JAPAN	V	E	81	89	1,431	1,599	168
			82	111	1,585	1,703	118
			83	68	1,710	1,842	132
			84	567	3,256	3,735	479
			85	1,074	4,466	4,779	313
	V	W	81	952	6,233	6,508	275
			82	1,526	12,911	13,562	651
			83	569	9,930	10,415	485
			84	896	9,437	9,901	464
			85	288	5,163	5,488	325
			86	595	8,107	8,403	296
KOR REP	V	E	82	240	661	723	62
			83	220	802	843	41
			86	1,890	3,944	4,242	298
	V	W	82	8,818	11,158	11,158	
			85	8,800	10,077	10,725	648
			86	6,614	6,768	7,200	432
MALAYSA	O	E	84	352	519	730	211
	V	W	85	5,890	6,443	6,775	332
MEXICO	A	E	84	1	604	609	5
	O	E	83	2	1,104	1,104	
NETHLDS	A	E	81	7,398	14,343	21,827	7,484
			83	44	296	371	75
	N	E	84	476	920	994	74
	O	E	83	390	1,738	1,821	83
			84	374	1,291	1,394	103
	V	E	81	1,442	2,014	2,214	200
	V	W	86	169	1,056	1,158	102
PAKISTN	V	E	86	22,046	8,042	9,459	1,417
PHIL R	V	E	81	724	419	523	104
PORTUGL	V	E	82	303	499	917	418
			85	6,600	3,186	4,418	1,232
S ARAB	A	E	84	88	531	641	110
SINGAPR	V	H	81	95	363	413	50
	V	W	82	2,756	2,130	2,406	276
			85	794	1,590	1,915	325
SPAIN	O	E	81	435	500	530	30
	V	E	84	3,652	3,642	4,162	520
SRI LKA	V	W	82	600	399	567	168
			83	4,400	2,516	3,134	618
SWITZLD	V	W	85	2,500	1,500	1,575	75
T PAC I	V	W	81	330	912	987	75
THAILND	N	W	82	387	642	723	81
	V	E	82	496	1,318	1,491	173
			83	796	1,509	1,648	139
			84	159	818	916	98
	V	W	81	1,147	3,850	4,161	311
			82	6,837	7,503	8,215	712
			83	7,952	13,785	14,585	800
			84	5,649	11,209	12,049	840
			85	5,032	5,882	6,121	239
			86	10,732	20,155	21,042	887
TRINID	V	E	85	313	2,290	3,140	850
TURKEY	A	W	85	1,100	1,190	1,265	75
	V	W	86	4,409	1,729	1,960	231
U KING	N	E	84	293	684	816	132
	O	E	81	704	1,509	1,634	125
			82	75	371	396	25
			83	198	1,025	1,145	120
			84	328	1,392	1,478	86
			85	3,572	3,493	3,784	291
			86	1,099	6,111	6,376	265
	V	E	81	210	729	774	45
			82	94	277	341	64
			83	12	870	882	12
			86	64	1,013	1,057	44
	V	W	81	15	298	326	28

Capsicum pepper, spice

1618300 PEPPER CAPSICUM ETC UNGROUND (LB)

Country	Mode	Reg	Yr	Quantity	F.A.S.	C.I.F.	Charges
TOTAL			81	9,591,854	5,352,432	6,517,693	1,165,261
			82	9,976,171	6,049,340	7,245,709	1,196,426
			83	13,117,459	6,915,612	8,338,901	1,423,289
			84	14,777,177	7,879,473	9,515,493	1,636,020
			85	13,645,796	7,084,052	8,572,850	1,488,798

Crop
Product
TSUSA commodity number, description, and unit of quantity

Country	Mode	Reg	Yr	Quantity	F.A.S.	C.I.F.	Charges
			86	14,388,681	6,403,697	7,762,391	1,358,694
ALBANIA	V	E	86	41,998	83,930	90,160	6,230
BELGIUM	V	E	86	6,394	28,436	28,793	357
BRAZIL	V	E	85	11,023	7,500	8,156	656
	V	W	83	2,980	3,406	3,572	166
BURUNDI	V	E	82	36,199	14,730	25,657	10,927
C RICA	V	E	81	2,100	400	474	74
CANADA	A	E	81	46	282	363	81
			84	1,600	2,080	2,248	168
	O	E	81	288	320	320	
			82	500	1,095	1,095	
			83	900	1,498	1,498	
			84	7,575	5,775	5,775	
	V	E	85	13,035	37,802	40,826	3,024
CHILE	V	E	86	6,735	17,000	18,200	1,200
CHINA M	N	E	81	1,161,931	740,986	888,031	147,045
			82	1,894,388	1,011,541	1,279,967	268,426
			83	1,346,425	808,988	986,673	177,685
			85	3,658,212	2,167,745	2,658,038	490,293
			86	2,226,792	1,102,738	1,397,825	295,087
	O	E	85	33,066	30,072	34,983	4,911
	V	E	81	440,311	258,156	303,973	45,817
			82	435,735	223,500	284,781	61,281
			83	122,135	83,087	95,471	12,384
			84	2,166,121	1,217,718	1,538,646	320,928
			85	584,186	268,152	352,724	84,572
			86	542,382	256,112	325,409	69,297
	V	W	81	1,554,526	850,816	1,040,564	189,748
			82	1,781,446	967,002	1,187,597	220,595
			83	1,293,595	840,315	970,767	130,452
			84	2,072,099	1,195,467	1,448,763	253,296
			85	1,731,681	1,012,778	1,223,259	210,481
			86	1,273,944	694,513	862,062	167,549
CHINA T	O	E	86	55,115	40,730	46,461	5,731
	V	E	81	1,200	900	1,021	121
			83	11,615	25,916	27,260	1,344
			84	9,828	10,746	11,854	1,108
			85	4,500	3,580	4,040	460
			86	34,259	17,608	21,413	3,805
	V	W	82	22,046	13,376	15,844	2,468
			83	360	407	435	28
			84	11,650	15,286	16,658	1,372
			86	2,648	2,178	2,310	132
COLOMB	A	E	83	301	268	399	131
DENMARK	A	E	84	88	293	343	50
			85	5,748	11,536	12,082	546
			86	220	2,143	2,442	299
	A	W	86	1,830	12,527	13,491	964
DOM REP	A	E	84	300	360	471	111
			85	9,190	5,055	6,865	1,810
			86	5,708	1,018	1,739	721
	V	E	85	75,305	8,287	13,111	4,824
			86	82,250	8,466	14,225	5,759
EGYPT	V	E	81	20,988	10,093	11,959	1,866
			82	53,640	30,701	35,896	5,195
			83	4,409	6,086	6,361	275
			85	33,060	8,498	11,629	3,131
ETHIOP	V	E	83	22,046	18,678	22,110	3,432
FR GERM	A	E	81	44	543	587	44
			84	473	2,168	2,238	70
			85	558	6,352	6,981	629
			86	28,605	49,654	54,563	4,909
	A	W	85	99	1,054	1,203	149
	V	E	81	180	2,215	2,429	214
			82	4,981	42,875	43,932	1,057
			83	34,418	38,071	39,024	953
			84	144	1,603	1,742	139
			86	218	3,370	3,452	82
FRANCE	A	E	82	331	1,191	1,554	363
			83	220	1,644	1,770	126
	A	W	84	343	844	1,252	408
	N	E	81	42,598	34,930	40,769	5,839
			85	1,191	6,576	6,895	319
	V	E	81	86,624	53,182	57,665	4,483
			82	1,601	1,455	1,657	202
			83	441	1,218	1,322	104
			84	1,247	3,891	4,083	192
			86	5,769	24,775	25,826	1,051
	V	W	84	3	430	455	25
			86	1,561	10,355	10,850	495
GUATMAL	A	W	81	439	472	567	95
			83	1,586	1,654	2,137	483
HG KONG	O	E	86	55,116	40,730	46,482	5,752

Crop
Product
TSUSA commodity number, description, and unit of quantity

Country	Mode	Reg	Yr	Quantity	F.A.S.	C.I.F.	Charges
	V	E	81	3,595	3,536	3,778	242
			82	5,348	7,521	8,456	935
			83	5,068	9,856	10,961	1,105
			84	33,255	20,141	25,108	4,967
			85	42,425	34,093	39,860	5,767
			86	98,330	69,301	81,772	12,471
	V	W	82	89,534	49,036	60,393	11,357
			83	15,550	14,718	15,917	1,199
			84	134,675	71,655	86,841	15,186
			85	34,171	14,050	18,329	4,279
INDIA	A	E	86	2,191	19,283	22,661	3,378
	N	E	81	1,455,469	642,522	847,382	204,860
			83	106,769	56,910	70,865	13,955
	O	E	81	19,427	15,143	15,336	193
			82	1,550	1,238	1,277	39
	V	E	82	2,520,495	1,436,538	1,768,368	331,830
			83	5,970,262	2,964,843	3,726,466	761,623
			84	4,608,633	2,423,687	2,958,406	534,719
			85	126,635	83,924	92,948	9,024
			86	1,792,507	892,646	1,076,224	183,578
	V	W	81	154,321	82,460	104,816	22,356
			82	480,137	283,292	350,056	66,764
			83	1,497,154	756,241	948,867	192,626
			84	772	581	655	74
			85	10,912	2,571	2,711	140
			86	248,017	127,395	155,229	27,834
INDNSIA	V	E	84	33,069	19,180	23,483	4,303
ITALY	N	E	82	18,346	38,549	42,498	3,949
	V	E	81	56	1,314	1,435	121
			83	479	2,353	2,651	298
			84	6,633	19,264	21,577	2,313
			85	1,555	5,761	6,376	615
			86	11,093	45,590	50,734	5,144
	V	W	82	56	367	367	57
IVY CST	V	E	85	27,447	10,406	14,506	4,100
JAMAICA	A	E	81	790	1,338	1,826	488
			84	5,132	6,675	11,876	5,201
			85	350	1,050	1,473	423
			86	871	1,822	2,094	272
	V	E	82	885	1,280	1,363	83
			84	524	720	785	65
			85	6,150	3,240	3,558	318
JAPAN	V	E	81	4,845	10,006	11,990	1,984
			82	1,502	4,997	5,416	419
			83	4,000	8,574	9,877	1,303
			84	3,717	11,245	12,664	1,419
			85	27,618	36,114	39,359	3,245
			86	22,756	17,091	19,367	2,276
	V	H	84	150	365	437	72
	V	W	81	35,835	27,600	32,809	5,209
			82	2,153	7,527	8,079	552
			83	2,468	8,255	8,818	563
			84	1,699	6,633	7,014	381
			85	912	2,856	3,091	235
			86	74,950	34,794	45,298	10,504
JORDAN	V	E	85	55,097	32,484	33,212	728
KENYA	V	E	81	9,544	6,801	7,626	825
			82	22,046	9,571	12,408	2,837
			84	8,818	6,944	8,442	1,498
			85	13,344	12,800	14,279	1,479
KOR REP	V	E	81	1,547	5,485	5,697	212
			83	1,024	2,348	2,617	269
			84	10,000	12,815	14,478	1,663
	V	W	81	6,708	11,281	12,250	969
			82	643	3,793	4,034	241
			83	5,380	8,450	9,104	654
			84	15,425	20,692	22,080	1,388
			85	125	1,344	1,432	88
			86	13,228	17,421	18,830	1,409
MALAYSA	V	E	81	1,250	1,430	1,612	182
			82	1,750	2,100	2,400	300
	V	W	81	250	391	450	59
			82	330	287	313	26
			83	864	710	749	39
MEXICO	O	E	81	475,551	533,320	533,320	
			82	605,893	449,101	450,881	1,780
			83	1,149,815	443,121	443,121	
			84	842,426	741,699	741,699	
			85	777,972	1,024,314	1,025,815	1,501
			86	835,672	517,507	517,507	
	O	W	81	483,644	666,908	666,908	
			82	569,187	832,058	832,058	
			83	486,716	288,915	290,245	1,330
			84	596,887	476,488	476,488	

Crop
Product
TSUSA commodity number, description, and unit of quantity

Country	Mode	Reg	Yr	Quantity	F.A.S.	C.I.F.	Charges
			85	288,238	329,767	329,767	
			86	588,119	331,458	331,458	
	V	E	85	741	1,796	2,101	305
MOROC	V	E	86	20,796	5,924	11,080	5,156
NETHLDS	A	E	82	26,881	29,140	36,862	7,722
			83	3,858	4,840	6,270	1,430
			84	5,699	6,697	9,112	2,415
			85	9,805	18,429	23,129	4,700
			86	6,178	14,047	17,586	3,539
	A	W	84	3,858	5,990	9,335	3,345
			85	4,960	1,660	5,940	4,280
	O	E	85	1,020	2,826	3,130	304
	V	E	84	10,836	14,991	15,682	691
			85	3,260	7,031	7,136	105
	V	W	81	185	803	845	42
			83	694	1,539	1,630	91
			86	2,014	5,254	5,520	266
NEW GUI	O	E	81	156,764	65,141	88,788	23,647
	V	E	81	23,387	15,189	19,062	3,873
	V	W	81	103,834	141,625	152,201	10,576
NICARAG	V	E	84	11,022	5,099	6,546	1,447
NIGERIA	V	E	84	138,387	47,522	54,640	7,118
			85	130,039	53,459	60,785	7,326
PAKISTN	N	E	81	2,149,325	663,047	1,000,772	337,725
	V	E	82	1,237,444	456,409	631,199	174,790
			83	863,321	303,430	402,822	99,392
			84	3,730,175	1,275,483	1,706,603	431,120
			85	5,456,493	1,625,333	2,206,995	581,662
			86	5,640,243	1,606,288	2,064,989	458,701
	V	W	81	1,065,352	349,888	491,312	141,424
			82	22,046	8,190	11,999	3,809
			84	98,105	41,752	58,802	17,050
			85	283,172	68,586	101,247	32,661
			86	273,013	77,040	101,518	24,478
PANAMA	V	E	85	4,400	1,987	2,200	213
PERU	V	E	85	2,778	3,499	3,499	
PHIL R	V	E	81	7,380	5,857	6,672	815
			82	2,484	2,034	2,279	245
			83	1,710	1,404	1,700	296
			84	7,473	8,654	9,308	654
	V	W	81	1,440	1,309	1,473	164
			82	2,860	2,106	2,374	268
			83	4,348	3,898	4,347	449
			84	4,644	4,102	4,650	548
PORTUGL	V	E	85	1,663	1,939	2,118	179
REP SAF	V	E	85	11,023	16,243	18,500	2,257
			86	39,550	21,402	26,802	5,400
ROMANIA	V	W	84	1,650	593	639	46
S HELNA	V	E	84	33,069	16,256	20,106	3,850
SINGAPR	V	E	86	750	1,305	1,539	234
SWITZLD	A	E	84	1,984	3,105	4,205	1,100
SYRIA	V	E	81	150	1,340	1,642	302
			83	3,308	5,810	6,108	298
			84	1,984	3,710	3,839	129
THAILND	N	E	81	1,875	4,562	4,943	381
	N	W	84	8,942	9,765	10,536	771
	O	E	84	441	760	874	114
	O	W	85	1,036	1,057	1,134	77
	V	E	81	32,184	42,732	46,655	3,923
			82	19,202	23,356	26,200	2,844
			83	45,665	74,414	81,717	7,303
			84	50,727	54,073	60,367	6,294
			85	42,297	34,059	39,946	5,887
			86	93,977	45,989	56,555	10,566
	V	H	83	970	1,628	1,784	156
			84	331	533	597	64
	V	W	81	54,745	74,757	81,791	7,034
			82	48,989	61,235	67,290	6,055
			83	62,487	98,207	105,718	7,511
			84	27,108	44,151	48,070	3,919
			85	56,304	56,187	62,181	5,994
			86	29,404	34,434	37,182	2,748
TURKEY	O	E	84	990	1,452	1,452	
	V	E	82	65,477	31,430	40,417	8,987
			83	44,092	23,645	27,473	3,828
			84	59,524	31,250	35,265	4,015
			86	222,728	120,227	151,476	31,249
U KING	V	E	81	11,023	8,503	9,103	600
			82	66	719	742	23
			83	26	267	275	8
			84	6,832	7,830	8,006	176
			85	63,000	20,200	25,301	5,101
			86	750	1,196	1,267	71
	V	W	81	4	272	279	7
			84	110	260	298	38
UGANDA	V	E	81	19,070	14,265	15,886	1,621
YUGOSLV	O	W	81	1,029	312	312	

1618400 PEPPER CAPSICUM ETC GROUND (LB)

Country	Mode	Reg	Yr	Quantity	F.A.S.	C.I.F.	Charges
TOTAL			81	378,445	383,752	425,464	41,718
			82	344,408	358,131	398,807	40,676
			83	1,020,903	1,015,299	1,101,314	86,015
			84	678,460	724,771	782,296	57,525
			85	845,112	836,493	925,420	88,927
			86	1,445,435	1,348,368	1,442,007	93,639
AUSTRIA	V	E	84	5,920	5,056	5,725	669
BRAZIL	V	E	83	2,160	420	540	120
C RICA	V	W	83	2,506	1,347	1,562	215
CANADA	A	E	84	600	930	1,228	298
	O	E	81	4,200	5,080	5,164	90
			82	9,940	11,447	11,447	
			83	23,725	21,233	21,233	
			84	3,219	5,682	5,682	
			85	1,000	1,450	1,450	
			86	100	1,452	1,452	
	O	W	81	454	1,443	1,443	
			82	5,000	5,424	5,424	
	V	E	86	1,000	1,450	1,510	60
	V	W	82	3,300	2,310	2,551	241
CHINA M	N	E	82	2,976	3,353	3,676	323
	V	E	81	3,750	3,218	3,611	393
			83	12,255	12,800	13,918	1,118
			84	1,352	3,262	3,562	300
			85	3,700	4,010	4,393	383
			86	2,840	3,718	4,325	607
	V	W	81	11,273	3,749	6,197	2,448
			82	22,666	9,237	10,296	1,059
			83	36,013	24,894	28,970	4,076
			84	15,178	7,774	9,340	1,566
			85	1,100	1,760	1,889	129
			86	35,860	28,439	30,169	1,730
CHINA T	N	W	83	7,215	6,209	6,542	333
	V	E	81	900	1,850	2,154	304
			83	916	2,071	2,165	94
			84	2,368	3,882	4,046	164
			86	34,100	31,924	34,383	2,459
	V	W	81	1,611	3,571	3,718	147
			84	593	2,220	2,365	145
			86	190	1,200	1,228	28
EGYPT	V	E	81	2,314	1,333	1,530	197
ETHIOP	O	E	86	13,228	24,075	25,544	1,469
FR GERM	A	E	82	330	802	974	172
	O	E	86	1,518	4,554	4,765	211
	V	E	82	4,442	6,441	6,985	544
			83	4,298	3,344	3,434	90
			84	2,634	3,356	3,650	294
			86	7,243	13,948	14,908	960
FRANCE	V	E	83	56	879	893	14
			84	119	398	421	23
			85	847	2,091	2,230	139
HG KONG	A	W	85	1,102	1,525	3,072	1,547
	V	E	82	1,360	1,398	1,578	180
			83	250	288	333	45
			84	500	884	1,076	192
			85	27,750	25,468	27,772	2,304
			86	78,100	76,141	81,606	5,465
	V	W	82	1,060	1,179	1,265	86
			83	750	744	816	72
			84	8,818	11,474	12,026	552
			85	18,637	18,978	21,165	2,187
			86	128,257	119,624	127,276	7,652
INDIA	N	E	81	7,759	4,455	5,520	1,065
			82	14,854	13,418	15,235	1,817
			83	22,765	17,426	19,541	2,115
			84	16,626	14,368	16,069	1,701
			85	86,579	89,048	98,652	9,604
			86	13,157	8,527	10,159	1,632
	O	E	81	909	684	755	71
			82	540	513	569	56
			83	9,351	4,733	4,828	95
			84	2,646	1,314	1,542	228
			85	1,764	1,165	1,371	206
	O	W	84	2,205	1,550	1,956	406
	V	E	81	3,967	2,554	3,165	611
			82	6,915	4,893	5,957	1,064
			83	52,252	24,484	29,332	4,848
			84	83,521	36,538	42,816	6,278

Crop Product TSUSA commodity number, description, and unit of quantity Country	Mode	Reg	Yr	Quantity	F.A.S.	C.I.F.	Charges
			85	15,431	8,970	10,295	1,325
			86	53,885	41,207	46,668	5,461
	V	W	82	25,363	13,498	16,046	2,548
			83	32,138	20,751	23,872	3,121
			84	9,682	6,795	7,852	1,057
			85	11,515	8,118	9,318	1,200
			86	7,362	11,333	12,509	1,176
ISRAEL	V	E	85	2,550	1,600	1,748	148
			86	8,378	5,369	5,911	542
ITALY	V	E	83	136	849	959	110
			85	1,102	1,526	1,749	223
JAMAICA	V	E	84	477	876	957	81
			85	7,224	6,209	6,630	421
			86	75	2,700	2,792	92
JAPAN	V	E	81	1,157	5,075	5,455	380
			82	2,537	9,509	10,230	721
			83	649	3,271	3,555	284
			84	2,951	12,027	13,014	987
			85	4,822	7,485	8,102	617
			86	2,246	5,076	5,595	519
	V	H	81	7,191	14,864	16,225	1,361
			82	5,582	9,562	11,320	1,758
			83	5,714	11,221	12,375	1,154
			84	7,746	15,603	17,377	1,774
	V	W	81	10,592	25,012	26,524	1,512
			82	4,743	21,784	22,967	1,183
			83	22,621	50,060	53,013	2,953
			84	40,560	73,056	77,255	4,199
			85	10,941	27,988	30,164	2,176
			86	32,042	42,469	44,418	1,949
KENYA	O	E	82	5,512	2,900	3,467	567
	V	E	82	11,551	5,300	6,301	1,001
KOR REP	A	E	83	4,410	8,600	13,040	4,440
	A	H	83	450	1,049	1,600	551
	N	H	81	4,817	6,800	8,295	1,495
			82	1,350	2,729	3,652	923
	O	E	83	24,156	42,273	42,273	
	V	E	81	729	1,041	1,052	11
			82	33,801	41,370	47,372	6,002
			83	62,149	60,059	64,054	3,995
			84	30,878	37,635	40,827	3,192
			85	126,729	131,294	143,481	12,187
			86	211,846	201,862	216,381	14,519
	V	H	83	13,554	21,135	24,267	3,132
			84	12,983	14,559	16,082	1,523
	V	W	81	150,869	165,538	176,026	10,488
			82	114,396	115,949	126,371	10,422
			83	500,624	545,655	583,259	37,604
			84	310,216	355,657	375,736	20,079
			85	356,197	412,495	452,188	39,693
			86	483,616	534,051	566,440	32,389
LEBANON	O	E	82	220	330	330	
MALAWI	O	E	84	669	1,429	1,567	138
MALAYSA	V	E	81	1,750	2,273	2,627	354
			82	500	736	804	68
			83	243	743	802	59
MEXICO	O	E	82	2,545	1,773	1,773	
			83	11,574	2,919	2,919	
			84	2,313	3,318	3,318	
			85	1,936	3,388	3,388	
			86	105,321	91,433	91,433	
	O	W	81	3,099	2,845	2,845	
			82	2,651	3,114	3,114	
			83	10,111	4,484	4,484	
			84	19,427	6,400	6,400	
			85	7,080	4,956	4,956	
			86	23,023	13,384	13,384	
NETHLDS	A	E	84	260	423	457	34
	O	E	83	1,424	2,807	3,179	372
			84	365	704	760	56
	V	E	81	3,887	5,612	6,377	765
			82	3,263	2,979	3,394	415
			85	4,409	2,119	2,200	81
			86	4,409	1,864	2,210	346
	V	W	81	8,724	14,149	15,491	1,342
			82	1,971	3,213	3,475	262
			83	5,455	7,995	8,607	612
			84	4,178	3,591	3,853	262
			85	4,409	5,280	5,596	316
PAKISTN	N	E	81	55,122	22,552	29,489	6,937
	O	E	81	16,137	8,824	9,758	934
			82	4,010	3,019	3,309	290
			84	881	572	618	46
			86	1,764	1,083	1,207	124

Crop Product TSUSA commodity number, description, and unit of quantity Country	Mode	Reg	Yr	Quantity	F.A.S.	C.I.F.	Charges
	V	E	81	7,821	3,694	5,019	1,325
			83	105,790	50,714	58,980	8,266
			84	1,102	2,600	3,221	621
			85	61,864	22,698	28,622	5,924
			86	155,024	49,844	60,857	11,013
	V	W	81	13,228	4,900	6,790	1,890
			82	6,614	3,000	4,510	1,510
			83	2,205	1,700	2,232	532
			84	4,409	2,396	3,000	604
			85	70,560	24,130	29,651	5,521
PERU	V	E	81	441	400	434	34
PHIL R	V	E	83	360	335	400	65
			84	4,500	3,638	4,082	444
	V	W	83	540	405	468	63
			84	777	375	413	38
PORTUGL	V	E	81	106	301	504	203
			84	1,488	877	964	87
SINGAPR	V	W	81	160	930	977	47
SPAIN	A	E	84	800	3,230	4,174	944
SURINAM	V	E	83	660	400	638	238
THAILND	V	E	81	15,491	20,870	22,992	2,122
			82	13,900	19,262	21,410	2,148
			83	14,114	22,372	24,721	2,349
			84	40,042	52,743	57,238	4,495
			85	7,349	10,549	11,899	1,350
			86	9,395	9,418	10,659	1,241
	V	H	82	598	1,406	1,617	211
	V	W	81	28,221	42,567	47,068	4,501
			82	22,889	29,372	33,427	4,055
			83	20,359	29,257	31,308	2,051
			84	13,367	14,817	16,592	1,775
			85	8,515	12,193	13,439	1,246
			86	18,228	14,992	16,164	1,172
TURKEY	O	E	83	385	270	270	
	V	E	84	2,205	1,500	1,842	342
	V	W	83	5,512	3,136	3,824	688
			84	19,688	10,491	12,377	1,886
			86	6,614	3,750	4,180	430
U KING	O	E	81	11,766	7,568	8,259	691
			82	6,977	6,437	7,013	576
			83	905	1,111	1,225	114
			84	197	771	816	45
	O	W	86	6,614	3,481	3,874	393
	V	E	82	52	474	948	474
			83	153	856	883	27

Chili pepper, fresh or frozen
1371010 PEPPERS,CHILI,FR/CHLD/FROZ (LB)

Country	Mode	Reg	Yr	Quantity	F.A.S.	C.I.F.	Charges
TOTAL			85	25,114,887	5,596,016	5,736,868	140,852
			86	59,846,080	13,762,205	13,910,726	148,521
BELGIUM	A	W	86	3,036	5,411	8,480	3,069
CHINA M	V	E	86	22,046	7,482	13,700	6,218
	V	W	86	143,086	75,536	84,871	9,335
DOM REP	A	E	86	44,400	6,458	11,172	4,714
	N	E	85	1,565,833	226,446	362,704	136,258
			86	527,328	67,975	107,028	39,053
HG KONG	V	E	86	8,800	7,120	7,911	791
	V	W	86	33,069	16,220	18,770	2,550
JAMAICA	A	E	85	6,520	3,000	4,100	1,100
			86	3,388	9,137	9,830	693
MEXICO	O	E	85	11,567,051	1,543,594	1,543,594	
			86	18,202,112	2,135,800	2,139,055	3,255
	O	W	85	11,898,937	3,806,463	3,806,463	
			86	40,631,460	11,222,532	11,223,723	1,191
MONSRAT	O	E	85	34,521	4,650	4,650	
MOZAMBQ	O	E	85	25,496	2,239	2,239	
NETHLDS	A	E	85	3,579	3,951	6,070	2,119
	A	W	86	56,576	139,732	200,877	61,145
	V	E	85	9,000	1,260	1,756	496
PAKISTN	V	E	86	63,374	21,587	25,371	3,784
	V	W	86	99,207	37,225	48,375	11,150
PERU	V	E	85	950	1,800	2,160	360
			86	2,249	4,925	5,275	350
PHIL R	V	W	86	2,700	1,947	2,175	228
THAILND	V	W	85	3,000	2,613	3,132	519
			86	2,159	1,483	1,622	139
TRINID	A	E	86	1,090	1,635	2,491	856

Crop Product TSUSA commodity number, description, and unit of quantity Country	Mode	Reg	Yr	Quantity	F.A.S.	C.I.F.	Charges

Chili pepper, spice
1618000 PEPPR, ANAHEIM ETC UNGROUND (LB)

Country	Mode	Reg	Yr	Quantity	F.A.S.	C.I.F.	Charges
TOTAL			81	1,754,949	1,543,486	1,549,931	6,445
			82	2,689,916	1,772,227	1,772,236	9
			83	1,869,196	705,352	705,957	605
			84	1,850,863	1,036,083	1,042,801	6,718
			85	1,975,176	1,361,748	1,361,895	147
			86	2,148,939	1,033,164	1,033,317	153
CHINA M	V	E	84	750	1,174	1,268	94
	V	W	84	46,296	25,315	30,711	5,396
			86	750	1,242	1,302	60
CHINA T	V	E	86	1,200	1,140	1,233	93
FR GERM	A	E	85	99	1,127	1,272	145
FRANCE	A	E	81	110	1,796	1,865	69
HG KONG	V	W	84	11,574	6,647	7,875	1,228
MEXICO	O	E	81	379,305	337,018	337,018	
			82	976,866	631,532	631,532	
			83	724,426	283,448	283,448	
			84	986,884	504,995	504,995	
			85	1,243,911	947,140	947,140	
			86	1,183,699	515,914	515,914	
	O	W	81	1,331,178	1,188,582	1,188,582	
			82	1,713,050	1,140,695	1,140,704	9
			83	1,144,770	421,904	422,509	605
			84	805,359	497,952	497,952	
			85	731,166	413,481	413,483	2
			86	963,290	514,868	514,868	
PAKISTN	V	E	81	44,356	16,090	22,466	6,376

Paprika, oleoresin
4502010 PAPRIKA (LB)

Country	Mode	Reg	Yr	Quantity	F.A.S.	C.I.F.	Charges
TOTAL			81	616,320	6,154,882	6,225,490	70,613
			82	233,328	4,720,195	4,774,549	54,354
			83	416,044	5,471,050	5,541,016	69,966
			84	555,084	4,947,736	5,042,762	95,026
			85	737,305	6,828,310	7,089,868	261,558
			86	742,646	9,438,796	9,665,073	226,277
BELGIUM	O	E	86	3,207	10,380	11,080	700
	V	E	85	49,764	73,971	88,639	14,668
BULGAR	V	E	85	12,366	22,152	23,331	1,179
CANADA	A	W	84	500	1,463	1,763	300
	O	W	83	22	741	741	
			85	529	1,668	1,668	
	V	E	84	110	2,768	2,993	225
DENMARK	V	E	84	110	367	390	23
ETHIOP	A	E	84	26,064	295,268	324,620	29,352
			85	103,986	1,076,658	1,183,495	106,837
			86	103,918	1,402,890	1,502,327	99,437
	V	E	86	1,290	19,076	20,926	1,850
FR GERM	O	W	86	430	1,424	1,424	
FRANCE	N	E	85	53,354	72,375	82,213	9,838
			86	14,355	129,382	132,576	3,194
HUNGARY	V	E	81	5,419	88,650	93,780	5,130
			82	1,103	13,598	13,898	300
			86	1,489	20,126	20,950	824
INDIA	V	E	81	4,403	35,645	36,825	1,180
			83	31,900	216,602	222,754	6,152
			84	12,133	88,780	90,972	2,192
			85	13,238	109,093	111,567	2,474
ITALY	V	E	83	1,012	6,471	6,618	147
			86	2,998	11,604	11,825	221
MOROC	A	E	85	2,493	28,890	30,993	2,103
	V	E	81	13,492	212,677	215,986	3,309
			82	43,252	710,182	729,397	19,215
			83	63,243	585,605	596,701	11,096
			84	94,049	827,189	840,401	13,212
			85	76,248	649,333	671,455	22,122
			86	137,354	1,324,036	1,354,407	30,371
	V	W	85	2,381	29,162	30,458	1,296
NETHLDS	A	E	83	221	542	624	82
PERU	O	E	81	3,351	15,221	18,542	3,321
	V	E	81	27,079	52,575	55,267	2,692
REP SAF	N	E	85	7,493	66,352	69,715	3,363
			86	2,756	28,801	29,762	961
SPAIN	A	E	85	4,409	60,584	63,750	3,166
	N	E	81	443,661	4,407,231	4,446,507	39,276
			82	146,740	3,214,789	3,240,652	25,863
			83	241,393	3,322,472	3,359,568	37,096
			84	248,603	2,688,983	2,726,546	37,563

Crop Product TSUSA commodity number, description, and unit of quantity Country	Mode	Reg	Yr	Quantity	F.A.S.	C.I.F.	Charges
			85	335,337	3,734,261	3,817,110	82,849
			86	237,353	3,489,305	3,535,829	46,524
	O	E	81	12,672	208,182	210,570	2,393
			82	1,984	27,774	28,061	287
			84	1,971	20,009	20,197	188
			85	882	11,100	11,214	114
	V	E	81	106,243	1,134,701	1,148,013	13,312
			82	40,011	752,916	761,579	8,663
			83	78,253	1,338,617	1,354,010	15,393
			84	170,928	1,015,424	1,027,309	11,885
			85	66,779	782,054	792,006	9,952
			86	202,265	2,550,833	2,585,461	34,628
	V	W	84	550	6,872	6,913	41
			85	8,046	110,657	112,254	1,597
			86	35,231	450,939	458,506	7,567
SWITZLD	V	E	82	238	936	962	26
U KING	O	E	84	66	613	658	45

Paprika, spice
1617100 PAPRIKA, GROUND OR UNGROUND (LB)

Country	Mode	Reg	Yr	Quantity	F.A.S.	C.I.F.	Charges
TOTAL			81	9,919,497	7,673,354	8,348,860	675,506
			82	9,014,795	6,748,669	7,359,710	611,041
			83	11,111,247	7,444,130	8,168,548	724,418
			84	14,726,303	8,912,272	9,990,501	1,078,229
			85	19,061,759	11,550,551	12,967,664	1,417,113
			86	14,056,006	9,493,285	10,635,932	1,142,647
AUSTRIA	V	E	85	1,100	1,600	1,919	319
BELGIUM	A	W	85	4,629	5,817	8,987	3,170
	V	E	85	1,408	5,131	5,531	400
BRAZIL	V	E	86	36,300	24,684	28,004	3,320
	V	W	84	22,543	25,628	28,441	2,813
			85	132,276	124,712	137,872	13,160
			86	297,621	243,139	266,101	22,962
BULGAR	O	E	82	28,660	19,035	21,017	1,982
	V	E	81	85,920	71,148	77,740	6,592
			83	85,920	59,000	63,618	4,618
			86	68,640	42,214	45,217	3,003
	V	W	81	28,660	20,118	26,598	6,480
BURMA	V	E	85	34,320	22,624	24,024	1,400
CANADA	A	E	84	220	595	672	77
	O	E	81	2,893	2,696	2,719	23
			82	2,602	2,569	2,569	
			83	7,241	7,123	7,123	
			84	5,966	6,749	6,882	133
			85	1,099	1,415	1,415	
	O	W	81	1,139	2,160	2,160	
	V	E	86	2,530	3,647	3,795	148
CHINA M	O	E	84	36,300	21,381	24,341	2,960
	V	E	85	37,403	26,930	30,216	3,286
	V	W	85	44,092	23,320	26,434	3,114
DENMARK	A	E	81	80	280	387	107
	V	E	85	38,502	26,567	30,013	3,446
FR GERM	O	E	81	68,640	53,025	59,031	6,006
			83	882	608	646	38
	V	E	81	144,069	132,284	142,347	10,063
			82	12,557	62,503	65,856	3,353
			83	76,388	77,526	80,518	2,992
			84	38,119	28,322	31,752	3,430
			85	400	1,047	1,111	64
			86	8,721	22,059	23,941	1,882
	V	W	81	34,320	27,456	29,832	2,376
			83	34,320	26,208	29,172	2,964
			84	34,620	21,089	24,011	2,922
FRANCE	A	E	85	1,045	1,198	1,752	554
	V	E	83	105	411	432	21
			86	73,820	54,317	61,496	7,179
HG KONG	V	W	82	2,579	4,138	4,378	240
HUNGARY	O	E	81	91,960	72,180	77,862	5,682
			82	342,980	245,614	270,926	25,312
			84	229	507	713	206
	V	E	81	1,372,492	861,623	968,603	106,980
			82	1,235,921	737,608	833,821	96,213
			83	514,806	358,587	394,525	35,938
			84	517,007	294,517	339,178	44,661
			85	1,063,443	662,911	710,413	47,502
			86	1,166,885	766,477	828,564	62,087
	V	W	81	274,560	208,588	230,676	22,088
			82	274,479	237,207	263,003	25,796
			83	34,320	29,172	32,711	3,539
			84	34,320	25,740	28,858	3,118
			85	661	1,410	1,860	450

Crop Product TSUSA commodity number, description, and unit of quantity Country	Mode	Reg	Yr	Quantity	F.A.S.	C.I.F.	Charges
			86	34,320	24,638	26,426	1,788
INDIA	O	E	82	550	327	327	
			84	794	619	689	70
	V	E	84	606	433	489	56
			86	38,500	32,552	36,684	4,132
	V	W	82	794	284	317	33
INDNSIA	V	E	83	176,368	81,078	96,575	15,497
ISRAEL	V	E	85	2,903	2,910	4,373	1,463
ITALY	A	E	84	152	265	277	12
	V	E	81	353	1,866	2,010	144
			82	353	2,340	2,442	102
			83	776	5,265	5,620	355
			85	37,400	20,252	23,264	3,012
			86	26,874	18,758	19,349	591
JAPAN	V	E	84	1,325	1,267	1,674	407
MEXICO	O	E	83	24,336	9,580	9,580	
			84	62,155	19,877	19,877	
			85	12,400	2,852	2,852	
NETHLDS	A	E	86	2,250	10,070	11,474	1,404
PAKISTN	V	E	83	55,115	21,683	28,735	7,052
PERU	N	E	83	11,133	1,263	2,006	743
PHIL R	V	H	82	250	300	366	66
	V	W	81	1,323	900	1,065	165
			83	823	508	586	78
PORTUGL	V	E	85	31,200	16,929	19,656	2,727
REP SAF	V	E	85	63,827	29,900	36,837	6,937
			86	22,000	16,720	19,700	2,980
ROMANIA	V	E	85	34,323	25,938	27,456	1,518
			86	34,319	21,263	24,024	2,761
SPAIN	A	E	86	100	1,320	1,450	130
	N	E	81	4,782,177	3,723,361	4,021,980	298,619
			82	4,633,492	3,447,198	3,732,409	285,211
			83	6,650,959	4,416,574	4,825,741	409,167
			85	9,657,910	6,063,686	6,803,403	739,717
			86	4,800,497	3,360,060	3,785,185	425,125
	O	E	81	1,606,205	1,295,428	1,400,101	104,673
			82	1,456,289	1,129,642	1,229,515	99,873
			83	965,633	639,083	699,760	60,677
			84	739,054	456,188	511,351	55,163
			85	404,511	262,792	275,698	12,906
			86	153,716	108,988	122,357	13,369
	V	E	81	1,211,536	1,037,013	1,122,964	85,951
			82	737,345	615,241	668,440	53,199
			83	1,786,764	1,217,001	1,349,780	132,779
			84	10,492,294	6,354,247	7,129,873	775,626
			85	3,081,516	1,918,943	2,175,054	256,111
			86	5,449,411	3,576,948	4,024,045	447,097
	V	W	81	195,571	152,775	170,352	17,577
			82	285,877	244,276	263,924	19,648
			83	677,560	486,193	533,423	47,230
			84	2,739,074	1,650,768	1,836,830	186,062
			85	4,291,315	2,254,715	2,564,865	310,150
			86	1,806,533	1,129,530	1,266,500	136,970
SWITZLD	V	E	85	72,580	38,170	42,191	4,021
			86	22,000	16,720	19,700	2,980
THAILND	V	E	84	216	1,296	1,540	244
	V	W	86	397	1,082	1,134	52
TURKEY	V	E	84	441	270	331	61
U KING	A	E	86	2,127	5,176	5,690	514
	O	E	81	2,243	791	907	116
			83	75	347	387	40
			84	744	1,130	1,230	100
			85	1,093	1,022	1,124	102
			86	178	1,146	1,146	
	V	E	81	79	512	574	62
			82	67	387	400	13
			83	51	407	412	5
			84	124	1,384	1,492	108
YUGOSLV	V	E	81	15,277	9,150	10,952	1,802
			83	7,672	6,513	7,198	685
			85	10,403	7,760	9,344	1,584
			86	8,267	11,777	13,950	2,173

Pepper (not specified), fresh or frozen
1371000 PEPPERS, FRSH, CHLD, OR FROZ (LB)

Country	Mode	Reg	Yr	Quantity	F.A.S.	C.I.F.	Charges
TOTAL			81	126,967,710	55,985,105	56,582,168	597,985
			82	168,807,296	60,015,324	60,650,889	635,565
			83	153,881,617	49,284,625	50,428,928	1,144,303
			84	217,281,285	85,402,098	87,820,377	2,418,279
			85	191,448,630	83,719,000	86,017,043	2,298,043
ANTIGUA	A	E	82	7,845	4,720	8,177	3,457

Crop Product TSUSA commodity number, description, and unit of quantity Country	Mode	Reg	Yr	Quantity	F.A.S.	C.I.F.	Charges
			83	872	524	914	390
AUSTRIA	A	E	85	298	1,091	1,424	333
BAHAMAS	A	E	81	9,830	4,320	4,678	358
	N	E	82	44,474	7,640	9,912	2,272
			84	109,775	17,050	18,879	1,829
	V	E	83	172,670	24,636	30,008	5,372
			85	74,820	10,440	12,533	2,093
BARBADO	A	E	81	4,460	2,871	3,844	973
BELGIUM	A	E	83	13,411	15,082	19,176	4,094
			84	101,363	131,966	174,524	42,558
			85	298,454	342,242	502,142	159,900
	A	W	84	35,233	46,276	59,590	13,314
			85	34,785	51,687	71,873	20,186
	O	E	85	2,073	3,181	4,663	1,482
BRAZIL	A	W	85	3,616	3,587	6,275	2,688
BULGAR	A	W	85	1,929	2,065	3,222	1,157
C RICA	A	E	83	5,094	585	1,045	460
	N	E	84	11,046	2,680	3,613	933
	V	E	82	5,275	2,894	3,547	653
			83	1,904	850	1,008	158
			84	13,738	4,771	5,689	918
CANADA	O	E	81	549,427	122,880	122,880	
			82	1,314,119	272,526	272,526	
			83	1,051,650	214,764	214,764	
			84	1,548,348	275,538	275,538	
			85	16,803	11,309	11,309	
	O	W	81	59,235	17,395	17,395	
			82	63,061	29,262	29,262	
			83	112,292	18,466	18,466	
			84	116,154	55,944	55,944	
CHILE	A	E	81	6,304	805	1,884	1,079
			83	1,740	366	676	310
CHINA M	N	W	84	99,207	95,994	106,600	10,606
	O	E	84	1,681	3,553	3,601	48
	V	E	83	500	477	540	63
	V	W	81	33,069	16,764	20,853	4,089
			82	54,672	33,893	39,700	5,807
			83	142,162	91,642	106,257	14,615
CHINA T	V	W	82	22,046	11,853	14,500	2,647
			83	88,184	47,351	47,473	122
			84	804	460	483	23
			85	3,424	1,832	1,924	92
DENMARK	A	E	85	5,918	11,685	12,830	1,145
DOM REP	A	E	81	100,447	22,608	34,900	12,301
			82	1,176	420	543	123
			83	42,524	9,074	14,316	5,242
			84	16,773	2,976	5,637	2,661
	N	E	81	4,715,591	810,505	1,357,750	548,211
			82	5,287,822	850,531	1,397,985	547,454
			83	6,097,644	987,136	1,592,880	605,744
			84	8,856,330	1,537,175	2,340,064	802,889
			85	5,336,597	861,987	1,295,222	433,235
	V	E	81	38,510	5,402	7,223	1,821
			82	89,597	36,790	44,919	8,129
			83	31,174	8,754	11,551	2,797
			84	107,127	18,313	29,255	10,942
			85	91,267	15,856	24,238	8,382
EGYPT	A	E	85	4,700	6,104	6,491	387
F W IND	A	E	81	1,500	1,050	1,850	800
FR GERM	A	E	84	1,929	2,253	3,215	962
			85	5,984	9,353	12,318	2,965
	A	W	85	15,876	18,286	27,884	9,598
FRANCE	A	E	81	7,890	1,084	1,914	830
			82	3,041	1,490	2,347	857
			83	14,583	20,476	27,134	6,658
			84	6,061	5,547	9,787	4,240
			85	15,376	26,306	35,877	9,571
	A	W	84	132	750	1,052	302
	N	E	84	24,774	21,988	34,470	12,482
	O	W	84	1,770	311	311	
			85	92,916	44,857	44,858	1
	V	E	82	420	1,633	1,700	67
			83	933	2,380	2,464	84
GREECE	O	E	81	1,387	1,630	1,630	
	V	E	81	12,677	4,995	5,666	671
			82	136,950	35,693	49,654	13,961
			83	224,076	56,222	71,902	15,680
			84	52,414	16,132	22,324	6,192
			85	31,800	7,700	10,773	3,073
	V	W	81	29,040	9,020	12,565	3,545
GUATMAL	A	E	83	14,040	4,914	5,281	367
GUYANA	A	E	82	500	625	1,175	550
HAITI	A	E	81	1,403	2,669	3,089	420
			82	4,137	7,256	9,960	2,704

Crop Product TSUSA commodity number, description, and unit of quantity Country	Mode	Reg	Yr	Quantity	F.A.S.	C.I.F.	Charges
			83	84,481	21,277	30,396	9,119
	N	E	84	9,388	3,213	4,399	1,186
HG KONG	V	W	81	602	457	457	
			82	1,000	400	448	48
			85	10,995	15,000	16,080	1,080
HUNGARY	V	E	83	31,680	7,600	8,900	1,300
INDIA	O	E	82	1,100	629	629	
	V	W	82	44,092	22,283	28,227	5,944
			83	275,574	113,318	148,678	35,360
			84	33,308	14,356	19,336	4,980
ISRAEL	V	E	82	2,426	2,175	2,380	205
			83	86,367	25,587	30,340	4,753
			84	337,804	91,810	108,664	16,854
			85	192,452	43,405	51,830	8,425
ITALY	A	E	84	3,759	14,629	17,294	2,665
			85	7,771	9,713	13,834	4,121
	A	W	84	3,138	5,096	6,446	1,350
	N	E	83	2,837	1,916	2,940	1,024
			84	25,284	22,904	27,138	4,234
	V	E	81	2,722	6,391	7,548	1,157
			84	471	444	536	92
JAMAICA	A	E	81	28,834	33,892	41,263	7,371
			82	2,483	2,317	2,861	544
			83	440,408	276,607	393,495	116,888
			84	301,542	232,817	302,452	69,635
			85	22,130	12,463	16,087	3,624
	N	E	82	58,347	27,317	40,385	13,068
			83	25,278	12,221	14,948	2,727
			84	585,252	178,905	241,376	62,471
			85	2,814,839	1,593,221	1,959,812	366,591
	V	E	81	264,629	137,659	140,709	3,032
			82	302,145	90,865	93,995	3,130
			84	25,000	13,630	14,789	1,159
JAPAN	A	W	85	4,686	7,675	10,546	2,871
	O	E	84	11	627	637	10
	V	W	83	80	325	330	5
KENYA	V	W	82	167	338	378	40
KOR REP	A	E	81	9,150	1,218	2,194	976
	V	E	83	16	977	1,059	82
	V	W	82	1,058	3,822	3,990	168
			83	4,409	5,579	5,816	237
MALI	A	E	85	7,322	13,549	17,303	3,754
	A	W	85	4,960	10,375	13,435	3,060
MEXICO	A	E	81	110	1,500	1,502	2
			84	16,960	1,724	4,223	2,499
	A	W	84	9,921	614	2,054	1,440
			85	3,950	1,025	1,394	369
	O	E	81	9,818,345	3,056,043	3,056,043	
			82	17,266,539	2,877,710	2,877,710	
			83	25,848,256	3,170,963	3,171,215	252
			84	32,866,100	4,597,384	4,597,384	
			85	12,936,274	1,605,876	1,605,878	2
	O	H	83	14,574	4,161	4,161	
	O	W	81	111,242,054	51,681,964	51,682,866	876
			82	144,006,188	55,633,185	55,635,602	2,417
			83	117,966,909	43,256,628	43,257,942	1,314
			84	168,691,383	74,418,765	74,418,768	3
			85	166,816,774	75,544,596	75,544,742	146
MONSRAT	O	W	85	3,744	1,456	1,456	
MOZAMBQ	O	W	85	18,966	7,252	7,252	
N ANTIL	A	E	85	6,000	9,044	10,288	1,244
N ZEAL	A	H	81	12,489	4,515	9,294	4,779
	A	W	84	6,990	10,526	15,637	5,111
	O	W	85	2,524	2,209	2,209	
NETHLDS	A	E	82	5,533	2,936	5,181	2,245
			83	898,548	807,999	1,101,243	293,244
			84	73,676	86,827	121,240	34,413
			85	2,146,786	2,831,405	3,844,514	1,013,109
	A	W	84	330,801	371,067	594,054	222,987
			85	342,886	478,535	695,297	216,762
	N	E	84	2,616,637	2,918,854	3,943,526	1,024,672
	N	W	84	40,883	54,244	73,390	19,146
			85	21,128	28,769	36,124	7,355
	O	E	83	150	752	777	25
			84	33,999	35,311	36,205	894
			85	23,089	37,302	37,302	
NIGER	A	W	85	2,271	3,514	4,944	1,430
PAKISTN	V	E	84	33,069	11,451	15,900	4,449
	V	W	82	44,092	15,733	23,219	7,486
PHIL R	V	W	83	904	631	701	70
			84	1,348	1,096	1,210	114
SINGAPR	V	E	83	132,901	13,917	14,857	940
	V	W	82	18,012	13,481	17,817	4,336
			84	2,372	2,351	2,468	117

Crop Product TSUSA commodity number, description, and unit of quantity Country	Mode	Reg	Yr	Quantity	F.A.S.	C.I.F.	Charges
SPAIN	A	E	83	5,369	3,968	5,760	1,792
			84	2,752	2,209	3,657	1,448
			85	3,857	6,054	7,646	1,592
	V	E	84	21,164	6,080	8,637	2,557
SURINAM	V	E	84	547	1,050	1,209	159
SWITZLD	A	E	83	1,929	1,238	1,897	659
			84	6,327	4,373	7,476	3,103
			85	1,166	2,343	3,162	819
THAILND	V	W	81	12,159	29,431	32,318	2,887
			82	5,300	12,901	14,096	1,195
			83	879	1,590	1,705	115
			84	14,682	7,034	8,396	1,362
			85	1,746	1,141	1,258	117
TRINID	A	E	81	5,846	8,037	9,844	1,807
			82	13,679	12,006	18,064	6,058
			83	2,536	2,742	3,661	919
			84	11,445	11,873	16,737	4,864
TURKEY	O	E	83	715	501	501	
	V	E	83	4,431	10,579	11,079	500
	V	W	83	2,813	1,970	2,484	514
U KING	A	E	83	26,854	34,184	43,808	9,624
			84	21,680	17,674	22,306	4,632
			85	8,917	18,754	22,628	3,874
	A	W	84	11,014	18,104	23,913	5,809
	V	W	84	37,919	5,379	8,344	2,965
VENEZ				6,761	4,756	6,166	1,410
YUGOSLV	V	W	83	7,266	3,696	4,380	684

1371020 PEPPERS NSPF FRS/CHLD/FROZ (LB)

Country	Mode	Reg	Yr	Quantity	F.A.S.	C.I.F.	Charges
TOTAL			85	23,258,868	9,734,315	12,944,064	3,209,749
			86	180,086,584	66,045,310	72,801,479	6,756,169
AUSTRIA	A	E	86	5,512	4,178	5,981	1,803
BAHAMAS	V	E	86	476,225	66,450	71,568	5,118
BELGIUM	A	E	85	382,097	357,404	553,950	196,546
			86	616,469	839,119	1,158,848	319,729
	A	W	85	272,808	273,996	453,913	179,917
			86	217,849	380,102	595,780	215,678
	N	E	85	14,527	23,828	32,097	8,269
BRAZIL	A	W	85	1,320	1,424	2,442	1,018
			86	3,197	6,428	7,528	1,100
	V	E	85	8,818	12,600	14,186	1,586
C RICA	V	E	85	9,219	3,938	4,670	732
CANADA	A	E	86	4,916	5,758	11,094	5,336
	O	E	85	870,744	149,349	149,349	
			86	1,031,102	286,334	286,334	
	O	W	85	10,035	3,599	3,599	
			86	102,455	101,474	101,474	
CHILE	A	E	86	3,828	3,454	6,272	2,818
	V	E	85	22,500	57,072	60,415	3,343
CHINA T	V	E	85	4,390	2,106	2,637	531
			86	80,000	17,600	26,082	8,482
DENMARK	N	E	86	8,875	18,125	18,183	58
DOM REP	A	E	85	40,000	29,998	36,602	6,604
			86	46,835	12,468	23,599	11,131
	N	E	85	3,457,470	482,894	678,983	196,089
			86	6,916,306	1,400,975	1,803,888	402,913
	V	E	85	118,580	18,121	25,355	7,234
			86	680,247	134,844	190,149	55,305
EGYPT	V	E	86	2,381	1,512	1,861	349
FINLAND	A	E	86	1,084	2,166	2,858	692
FR GERM	A	E	85	3,134	4,996	7,049	2,053
			86	3,347	6,202	8,346	2,144
	A	W	85	7,152	12,551	20,766	8,215
			86	3,031	4,220	6,142	1,922
	V	E	86	556	1,061	1,209	148
FRANCE	A	E	85	117,628	119,259	192,129	72,870
			86	250,683	378,655	561,179	182,524
	A	W	85	16,240	14,393	22,070	7,677
	O	E	86	4,307	1,507	1,507	
	O	W	86	24,882	8,580	8,580	
	V	E	86	1,729	6,686	6,960	274
GREECE	V	E	85	58,201	11,660	18,681	7,021
			86	42,351	10,008	12,835	2,827
	V	W	86	121,694	14,973	24,621	9,648
HAITI	V	E	86	37,044	5,211	8,823	3,612
HG KONG	V	E	86	12,500	11,048	12,520	1,472
	V	W	86	13,365	13,021	14,130	1,109
ISRAEL	V	E	85	502,344	164,512	187,100	22,588
			86	1,021,514	251,852	310,612	58,760
ITALY	A	E	86	1,800	5,868	9,447	3,579
	A	W	86	3,432	1,475	3,008	1,533
	N	E	86	18,019	29,440	39,245	9,805
	V	E	85	1,435	5,988	7,124	1,136

Crop Product TSUSA commodity number, description, and unit of quantity Country	Mode	Reg	Yr	Quantity	F.A.S.	C.I.F.	Charges
JAMAICA	A	E	85	117,128	94,143	124,629	30,486
			86	161,674	203,016	254,392	51,376
	N	E	86	6,744,680	1,331,605	1,734,094	402,489
	V	E	86	2,076	2,247	2,590	343
JAPAN	A	E	85	4,119	5,715	6,618	903
	V	E	86	87	1,039	1,094	55
	V	W	86	789	2,155	2,237	82
MALAYSA	O	W	85	21,672	8,514	8,514	
			86	40,716	14,040	14,040	
MALI	A	E	85	4,101	5,011	8,476	3,465
			86	4,056	7,155	9,871	2,716
MAURIT	A	E	85	4,290	2,659	4,409	1,750
			86	1,389	2,219	4,237	2,018
	A	W	86	7,959	7,669	11,857	4,188
MEXICO	O	E	85	3,749,435	573,552	573,552	
			86	6,416,072	619,764	619,766	2
	O	W	85	8,811,758	2,787,077	2,787,077	
			86	146,574,041	48,500,873	48,506,937	6,064
MONGOLA	A	E	85	1,874	1,215	2,900	1,685
MONSRAT	O	W	85	9,000	1,980	1,980	
MOZAMBQ	O	W	85	24,418	11,788	11,788	
			86	48,053	16,570	16,570	
N ZEAL	A	W	86	5,787	2,512	12,423	9,911
NETHLDS	A	E	85	1,199,278	1,096,710	1,706,800	610,090
			86	766,808	1,150,646	1,818,210	667,564
	A	W	85	399,894	418,265	705,766	287,501
			86	169,404	327,277	415,983	88,706
	N	E	85	2,825,862	2,841,020	4,352,966	1,511,946
			86	5,828,914	8,044,483	11,314,097	3,269,614
	N	W	85	4,239	3,686	4,446	760
			86	1,035,402	1,412,876	2,266,940	854,064
	O	E	85	30,830	47,719	47,719	
NIGER	A	E	86	11,597	23,748	28,945	5,197
PAKISTN	V	E	85	33,069	12,897	16,637	3,740
PANAMA	A	E	85	19,990	11,375	16,214	4,839
PERU	V	E	86	1,102	3,600	3,816	216
SPAIN	A	E	85	1,984	2,529	3,480	951
			86	7,055	12,136	16,696	4,560
	O	E	85	27,117	5,867	8,570	2,703
			86	14,238	3,425	4,847	1,422
SWEDEN	A	E	85	4,910	5,895	6,895	1,000
			86	13,613	31,294	33,902	2,608
SWITZLD	A	E	85	5,291	5,891	8,250	2,359
			86	6,063	13,125	16,418	3,293
TRINID	A	E	86	41,658	46,697	61,470	14,773
TURKEY	A	E	85	7,958	9,033	12,308	3,275
			86	3,300	2,745	3,477	732
U KING	A	E	85	15,816	25,213	40,189	14,976
			86	44,600	71,509	92,372	20,863
	A	W	85	5,170	4,873	8,116	3,243
	O	E	86	1,705	3,954	3,954	
VENEZ	N	E	86	376,211	156,137	189,581	33,444
YUGOSLV	V	E	85	11,023	2,000	2,648	648

Pepper (not specified), prepared or preserved
1419820 PEPPERS PREPARED/PRES, NSPF (LB)

Country	Mode	Reg	Yr	Quantity	F.A.S.	C.I.F.	Charges
TOTAL			85	7,441,310	2,081,811	2,417,779	335,968
			86	8,647,381	2,523,737	2,980,082	456,345
AUSTRIA	V	W	85	11,205	4,232	6,344	2,112
BELGIUM	V	E	85	11,100	2,002	2,584	582
			86	44,733	12,937	15,049	2,112
C RICA	V	E	85	62,885	28,086	32,528	4,442
			86	18,255	8,910	10,307	1,397
CANADA	O	E	85	1,680	1,999	1,999	
CHINA M	O	E	85	3,200	4,432	4,889	457
	V	E	85	60,320	17,829	22,720	4,891
			86	12,263	12,597	13,611	1,014
	V	W	85	15,840	6,765	7,560	795
			86	22,025	7,755	8,077	322
CHINA T	O	W	85	17,640	4,324	5,179	855
	V	E	85	78,422	47,832	54,087	6,255
			86	15,873	6,160	7,460	1,300
	V	W	85	42,033	35,600	38,064	2,464
			86	79,271	48,163	50,617	2,454
DOM REP	V	E	85	37,197	5,241	6,469	1,228
ECUADOR	V	E	85	1,048	1,140	1,252	112
FR GERM	V	E	86	1,684	1,065	1,237	172
FRANCE	V	E	85	33,542	29,800	33,992	4,192
			86	6,285	3,936	4,772	836
	V	W	85	21,550	18,549	22,081	3,532
GREECE	V	E	85	161,418	31,908	48,817	16,909

Country	Mode	Reg	Yr	Quantity	F.A.S.	C.I.F.	Charges
			86	404,334	78,964	122,441	43,477
	V	W	85	38,423	3,910	6,606	2,696
			86	60,847	10,120	16,653	6,533
HAITI	V	E	85	105,610	29,531	33,792	4,261
HG KONG	V	E	85	9,400	5,161	5,769	608
			86	8,860	5,612	6,017	405
	V	W	85	14,990	13,370	14,134	764
			86	3,600	1,170	1,309	139
HUNGARY	V	E	85	43,275	12,674	17,077	4,403
			86	321,943	60,717	79,002	18,285
ICELAND	V	E	85	319,976	83,820	99,120	15,300
INDIA	O	E	85	30,893	13,748	16,449	2,701
	V	E	85	4,630	3,324	3,931	607
			86	1,844	1,200	1,320	120
	V	W	85	8,818	4,623	5,810	1,187
ISRAEL	O	E	86	81,570	20,120	20,120	
	V	E	85	3,525,607	908,364	1,118,250	209,886
			86	5,181,011	1,333,869	1,604,535	270,666
ITALY	O	E	86	1,675	1,046	1,155	109
	V	E	85	18,927	10,952	12,662	1,710
			86	22,267	27,121	29,257	2,136
	V	W	85	5,282	5,166	5,658	492
			86	37,027	19,352	23,290	3,938
JAMAICA	V	E	85	16,818	12,994	14,220	1,226
JAPAN	V	E	85	27,119	23,093	25,595	2,502
			86	83,069	62,566	71,552	8,986
	V	W	85	84,865	71,079	76,947	5,868
			86	51,599	53,804	57,224	3,420
KOR REP	N	W	86	22,245	15,498	16,639	1,141
	V	E	85	48,241	40,874	45,945	5,071
			86	63,099	75,149	82,542	7,393
	V	W	85	35,180	27,924	29,805	1,881
			86	18,062	37,938	41,163	3,225
MEXICO	O	E	85	624,946	71,093	71,093	
			86	97,144	16,758	16,758	
	O	W	85	1,518,733	395,678	395,678	
			86	788,280	297,033	297,033	
PAKISTN	V	E	86	26,947	12,344	13,999	1,655
PHIL R	V	E	85	2,970	2,302	2,717	415
			86	2,250	1,904	2,044	140
	V	W	85	5,800	2,780	3,133	353
			86	8,556	4,576	5,296	720
POLAND	V	E	85	18,959	3,171	4,250	1,079
PORTUGL	V	E	85	21,110	5,537	6,750	1,213
			86	50,191	26,590	29,604	3,014
REP SAF	V	E	85	35,216	11,006	13,593	2,587
ROMANIA	V	E	85	210,986	50,485	62,868	12,383
			86	138,151	25,837	32,926	7,089
SPAIN	V	E	85	116,865	20,034	26,930	6,896
			86	452,418	77,744	100,510	22,766
	V	W	85	3,880	1,172	2,579	1,407
SWITZLD	V	E	86	1,865	1,339	1,681	342
THAILND	V	E	85	15,360	8,550	9,475	925
			86	79,049	22,762	26,739	3,977
	V	W	85	11,590	8,190	9,205	1,015
			86	53,431	19,263	21,346	2,083
TURKEY	V	E	85	1,933	2,162	2,488	326
	V	W	86	10,000	4,608	5,118	510
U KING	O	E	85	1,678	1,497	1,678	181
			86	1,830	2,640	2,871	231
	V	E	86	1,852	1,363	1,602	239
YUGOSLV	V	E	85	17,143	6,608	8,660	2,052
			86	308,983	84,407	113,553	29,146

Pepper (not specified), seed
1267100 PEPPER SEED (LB)

Country	Mode	Reg	Yr	Quantity	F.A.S.	C.I.F.	Charges
TOTAL			81	143,996	1,781,112	1,810,835	29,703
			82	75,904	1,136,759	1,150,423	13,664
			83	83,812	1,700,205	1,733,009	32,804
			84	92,877	1,192,181	1,223,034	30,853
			85	221,895	2,614,998	2,668,259	53,261
			86	183,045	2,378,063	2,412,048	33,985
ARGENT	A	W	84	84	494	750	256
AUSTRAL	A	W	84	22	1,150	1,193	43
			85	150	1,868	1,985	117
C RICA	A	E	81	12	3,694	3,721	27
			83	17	2,223	2,389	166
	A	W	85	46	15,280	15,471	191
			86	22	5,523	5,620	97
	O	E	82	4	273	288	15
CANADA	O	E	82	17	516	516	

Crop Product TSUSA commodity number, description, and unit of quantity Country	Mode	Reg	Yr	Quantity	F.A.S.	C.I.F.	Charges
			83	35	1,499	1,499	
			84	34	2,061	2,061	
			85	349	13,724	13,753	29
			86	59	1,100	1,100	
	O	W	85	7,920	15,840	15,840	
CHILE	A	E	81	9,652	49,780	54,363	4,583
			84	10,121	53,582	59,457	5,875
			85	9,654	61,328	67,036	5,708
	A	W	85	9,921	50,125	56,412	6,287
	V	W	81	2,239	13,747	14,120	373
			83	13,590	34,991	35,620	629
			84	6,519	28,934	29,704	770
			85	17,235	157,505	160,056	2,551
			86	74,504	506,128	519,038	12,910
CHINA M	A	E	81	529	85,440	86,487	1,047
	A	W	81	17	713	743	30
			82	309	21,962	22,863	901
			83	132	2,990	3,084	94
			84	48	4,840	5,020	180
CHINA T	A	E	81	1,868	296,375	302,124	5,749
			82	966	166,762	169,762	3,000
			83	567	70,054	71,706	1,652
			84	4,088	328,873	335,981	7,108
			85	1,110	118,739	122,929	4,190
	A	H	86	12,828	21,680	22,259	579
	A	W	81	3,479	376,501	388,597	12,096
			82	1,760	197,567	201,204	3,637
			83	4,193	507,924	524,041	16,117
			84	66	11,222	11,582	360
			85	5,752	805,629	827,284	21,655
	N	W	81	941	53,749	55,790	2,041
			82	1,238	141,611	144,981	3,370
			83	2,460	284,037	290,396	6,359
			84	7,626	275,153	284,739	9,586
			86	16,996	891,469	902,294	10,825
DENMARK	O	E	86	1	2,053	2,062	9
FR GERM	A	E	85	22	30,000	30,294	294
			86	28	29,800	29,974	174
FRANCE	A	E	81	35	353	398	45
			82	20	6,621	6,752	131
			84	1,002	35,312	35,776	464
			86	22	9,500	9,670	170
	A	W	81	4	2,030	2,287	257
			82	89	1,269	1,679	410
			83	22	7,055	7,153	98
	N	E	83	220	75,656	76,128	472
	V	W	81	2,205	13,863	14,296	433
			82	553	2,569	2,622	53
GUATMAL	A	E	81	483	37,274	37,560	286
			82	120	8,398	8,446	48
			83	5	342	345	3
	A	W	81	51	3,942	3,961	19
			82	235	16,071	16,181	110
			83	21	1,387	1,397	10
			84	5	750	805	55
ISRAEL	A	E	83	157	1,578	2,835	1,257
			84	63	24,453	24,904	451
	A	W	85	121	66,550	66,975	425
			86	301	92,318	94,100	1,782
	N	W	84	8,338	64,046	65,756	1,710
			86	2,424	13,200	13,666	466
	V	E	81	2,223	13,845	14,105	260
	V	W	81	1,180	7,375	7,586	211
			82	2,196	16,612	17,095	483
			83	2,480	18,081	18,533	452
			84	12,339	79,140	80,988	1,848
			85	27,210	130,040	131,512	1,472
			86	1,102	5,500	5,663	163
ITALY	A	W	84	49	2,426	2,521	95
	N	E	85	101	2,408	2,612	204
	N	W	81	588	8,125	8,409	284
			83	314	42,407	42,943	536
	V	E	85	661	4,164	4,317	153
			86	259	1,731	1,870	139
	V	W	83	1,484	11,473	11,740	267
			84	3,425	34,216	34,571	355
			85	2,265	32,667	33,349	682
JAPAN	A	E	81	152	24,276	25,446	1,170
			82	7	851	947	96
			83	1	309	385	76
			84	15	3,000	3,068	68
			85	39	10,625	11,157	532
			86	27	5,520	5,596	76
	A	H	83	2	611	742	131

Crop Product TSUSA commodity number, description, and unit of quantity Country	Mode	Reg	Yr	Quantity	F.A.S.	C.I.F.	Charges
	A	W	81	61	11,412	11,706	294
			82	88	16,840	17,233	393
			83	80	16,960	17,315	355
	N	E	82	37	7,349	7,494	145
			84	43	8,245	8,396	151
	N	W	84	2,050	17,610	17,922	312
			86	71	14,773	15,089	316
	O	E	81	19	4,341	4,413	52
			83	8	2,538	2,601	63
			84	1	314	333	19
	V	E	83	30	7,948	8,554	606
	V	W	82	5	551	583	32
			83	4	691	714	23
			84	261	2,084	2,246	162
			85	38	6,917	6,967	50
KENYA	A	E	82	13	881	887	6
	A	W	85	293	25,023	26,203	1,180
	V	E	85	2,800	10,589	11,330	741
KOR REP	A	W	86	50	7,827	8,000	173
	V	E	85	48	4,194	4,278	84
			86	200	3,473	3,497	24
MEXICO	O	E	81	70	2,100	2,100	
	O	W	81	116,992	759,462	759,462	
			82	67,958	442,660	442,660	
			83	50,701	340,449	340,449	
			84	31,407	178,034	178,034	
			85	86,681	498,776	498,776	
			86	53,927	310,165	310,165	
NETHLDS	A	E	82	39	3,828	3,991	163
			83	5,023	2,400	2,458	58
			84	1	1,389	1,631	242
			85	68	60,402	61,308	906
			86	10	12,408	12,712	304
	A	W	83	4	1,229	1,229	
			84	5,264	33,477	34,131	654
			86	18,263	434,487	439,592	5,105
	N	W	82	250	83,568	84,239	671
			83	1,332	257,238	260,117	2,879
			85	50,039	494,967	500,821	5,854
	O	E	81	900	8,340	8,494	154
	V	E	83	128	1,264	1,437	173
			86	380	3,609	3,776	167
	V	W	83	112	724	810	86
THAILND	A	W	85	33	1,802	1,911	109
			81	286	2,236	2,449	213
TURKEY	V	W	86	1,540	4,190	4,675	485
U KING	A	W	81	3	718	764	46
	N	E	83	29	1,983	2,072	89
			84	6	1,376	1,465	89
	O	E	86	31	1,609	1,630	21
	O	W	81	7	1,421	1,454	33

White pepper, spice
1617740 PEPPER, UNGROUND, WHITE (LB)

Country	Mode	Reg	Yr	Quantity	F.A.S.	C.I.F.	Charges
TOTAL			81	5,518,299	4,456,331	4,966,528	510,197
			82	5,998,459	4,282,076	4,779,680	497,604
			83	6,899,296	4,514,846	5,071,300	556,454
			84	8,030,375	9,240,805	9,804,803	563,998
			85	10,498,644	15,911,764	16,607,696	695,932
			86	7,660,357	17,794,767	18,294,246	499,479
B IND O	V	E	85	22,046	30,645	31,967	1,322
BRAZIL	A	E	86	4,409	12,740	16,889	4,149
	V	E	81	1,682,113	1,311,815	1,436,146	124,331
			82	933,160	660,955	735,156	74,201
			83	1,241,281	829,877	918,044	88,167
			84	1,190,466	1,489,423	1,582,075	92,652
			85	543,164	783,484	828,391	44,907
			86	290,976	741,926	768,261	26,335
	V	W	83	17,636	11,252	13,088	1,836
C RICA	V	E	86	5,071	10,243	11,040	797
CANADA	O	E	83	4,000	3,220	3,220	
CHAD	V	E	85	1,100	1,410	1,410	
CHINA M	V	E	82	500	556	616	60
			83	35,109	22,979	25,481	2,502
			84	380,399	479,265	504,725	25,460
			85	573,967	935,288	968,548	33,260
			86	338,740	826,236	843,989	17,753
	V	W	81	1,125	2,525	2,661	136
			82	953	1,857	2,013	156
			83	1,440	1,797	1,883	86
			84	64,456	87,487	91,138	3,651

Crop Product TSUSA commodity number, description, and unit of quantity Country	Mode	Reg	Yr	Quantity	F.A.S.	C.I.F.	Charges
			86	37,195	47,295	48,350	1,055
CHINA T	V	E	81	121,000	99,697	109,322	9,625
			83	128	649	659	10
			84	1,777	2,082	2,307	225
			86	255	1,298	1,418	120
	V	W	84	1,066	925	971	46
			85	33,069	46,634	48,002	1,368
COLOMB	A	E	83	335	317	535	218
FR GERM	A	E	82	220	439	566	127
	N	E	82	9,842	16,599	18,151	1,552
	V	E	83	13,892	15,872	16,406	534
			84	38,204	46,830	49,719	2,889
			85	22,046	32,253	33,584	1,331
			86	15,007	55,365	59,596	4,231
FRANCE	N	E	81	656	1,467	1,770	303
			83	669	944	1,122	178
	N	W	84	1,352	5,788	6,799	1,011
	V	E	83	842	3,824	4,026	202
			84	1,112	8,516	8,827	311
			85	2,456	7,254	7,993	739
			86	110	1,254	1,264	10
	V	W	81	1,069	2,865	3,042	177
			82	339	2,680	2,844	164
			83	264	517	549	32
			85	607	5,905	6,858	953
			86	546	2,306	2,531	225
HG KONG	A	W	81	5,911	8,730	10,230	1,500
	V	E	83	250	416	439	23
			84	37,390	49,377	52,270	2,893
			85	236,448	376,931	391,549	14,618
	V	W	86	33,044	39,500	41,118	1,618
INDIA	V	E	84	133,489	116,701	126,040	9,339
			85	154,363	226,398	238,989	12,591
			86	276,078	567,289	599,315	32,026
	V	W	82	540	366	403	37
			85	44,092	59,528	61,688	2,160
INDNSIA	N	E	81	2,583,498	2,121,266	2,381,863	260,597
	O	E	84	34,953	48,827	48,827	
	V	E	81	220,460	198,199	228,737	30,538
			82	3,788,870	2,642,966	2,962,025	319,059
			83	4,641,313	2,983,447	3,387,890	404,443
			84	4,930,826	5,555,447	5,901,111	345,664
			85	7,474,246	11,319,094	11,816,384	497,290
			86	5,279,431	12,341,511	12,659,221	317,710
	V	W	81	636,968	499,584	550,472	50,888
			82	1,047,186	788,243	875,691	87,448
			83	782,633	514,645	565,725	51,080
			84	734,436	829,147	871,220	42,073
			85	914,909	1,348,912	1,402,966	53,996
			86	808,902	1,722,947	1,780,370	57,423
ITALY	V	E	83	6,270	7,523	7,664	141
			84	3,203	3,546	3,669	123
JAPAN	N	E	84	66,160	87,064	90,750	3,686
	V	E	86	33,069	79,483	81,465	1,982
	V	W	81	35	308	332	24
			86	50	1,444	1,486	42
KOR REP	V	E	84	22,046	30,158	31,456	1,298
MALAYSA	O	E	84	175	258	364	106
	V	E	84	112,243	143,939	150,705	6,766
			85	220,460	357,050	370,370	13,320
			86	108,800	240,780	246,400	5,620
	V	W	81	95,197	69,482	77,105	7,623
			84	17,743	24,604	25,960	1,356
			86	34,377	96,622	99,064	2,442
NETHLDS	A	E	84	650	1,151	1,473	322
	V	W	81	1,941	4,449	4,643	194
			83	2,488	6,394	6,809	415
			84	2,509	6,773	7,275	502
NIGER	V	E	85	33,069	45,000	48,023	3,023
SINGAPR	V	E	81	165,345	127,487	151,087	23,600
			82	153,842	106,951	119,226	12,275
			83	121,253	82,082	86,471	4,389
			84	199,122	181,463	199,784	18,321
			85	181,345	293,316	306,307	12,991
			86	275,566	677,643	696,904	19,261
	V	W	82	55,115	42,171	43,155	984
			83	22,046	16,001	16,101	100
			84	10,080	9,324	10,808	1,484
			85	40,000	40,022	41,907	1,885
SPAIN	V	E	84	38,619	17,982	20,297	2,315
SWITZLD	V	E	82	1,320	4,042	4,220	178
THAILND	N	W	84	4,273	7,249	7,768	519
	O	E	84	187	297	342	45
	V	E	81	1,494	4,610	4,994	384
			82	770	1,648	1,868	220
			83	1,822	3,419	4,672	1,253
			84	1,697	4,442	5,156	714
			85	882	1,328	1,403	75
			86	112,435	310,451	315,638	5,187
	V	W	81	1,487	3,847	4,124	277
			82	5,087	10,020	11,038	1,018
			83	5,625	9,671	10,516	845
			84	1,742	2,740	2,967	227
			85	375	1,254	1,357	103
			86	6,296	18,434	19,927	1,493
U KING	O	E	82	238	949	979	30
	V	E	82	477	1,634	1,729	95

1617900 PEPPER, BLACK OR WHITE, GRND (LB)
(See Black pepper, spice under Pepper)

Peppermint

Menthol
4376400 MENTHOL (LB)

Country	Mode	Reg	Yr	Quantity	F.A.S.	C.I.F.	Charges
TOTAL			81	3,296,298	18,737,713	19,700,521	962,808
			82	1,367,734	6,564,592	6,918,077	353,485
			83	2,548,720	11,408,535	12,036,296	627,761
			84	3,226,607	18,776,885	19,607,063	830,178
			85	1,941,269	13,353,706	13,936,043	582,337
			86	2,556,051	15,424,065	16,207,115	783,050
AUSTRAL	N	E	82	15,630	60,996	67,208	6,212
	V	E	81	17,053	52,266	55,400	3,134
			83	17,902	77,278	80,609	3,331
			84	19,015	94,458	97,651	3,193
			85	12,236	51,649	53,643	1,994
			86	6,900	26,342	27,256	914
	V	W	86	1,190	1,798	1,936	138
BRAZIL	N	E	82	129,807	668,952	720,715	51,763
			84	313,137	1,444,825	1,530,070	85,245
			85	368,005	2,727,047	2,863,458	136,411
	O	E	81	1,035,000	6,854,096	7,162,498	308,402
			82	7,050	20,107	22,793	2,686
			83	27,400	126,218	137,316	11,098
			84	22,766	120,839	122,082	1,243
			85	600	3,750	3,995	245
	V	E	81	766,470	4,024,565	4,265,912	241,347
			82	408,077	2,185,080	2,283,289	98,209
			83	777,208	4,025,008	4,290,665	265,657
			84	460,708	2,987,682	3,131,827	144,145
			85	421,214	4,409,003	4,557,406	148,403
			86	1,140,051	7,206,530	7,599,026	392,496
	V	W	82	6,400	35,123	37,045	1,922
			83	18,800	80,340	85,624	5,284
			84	32,753	145,736	153,049	7,313
			85	2,200	14,960	16,393	1,433
CANADA	O	E	81	414	1,829	1,829	
			82	1,958	8,274	8,274	
			83	790	3,410	3,410	
			84	212	1,167	1,247	80
			85	100	1,280	1,280	
	V	E	85	516	1,641	1,705	64
			86	1,120	3,527	3,630	103
CHINA M	N	E	81	160,700	781,848	820,530	38,682
			86	542,851	3,650,391	3,779,213	128,822
	O	E	81	800,616	4,441,090	4,669,813	228,723
			82	105,750	496,863	523,635	26,772
			83	286,050	1,423,816	1,497,342	73,526
			84	193,200	937,572	984,221	46,649
			85	108,500	718,562	740,476	21,914
			86	34,700	197,480	206,367	8,887
	V	E	81	2,200	11,108	11,376	268
			82	217,566	997,250	1,055,412	58,162
			83	897,494	3,259,857	3,426,317	166,460
			84	1,589,545	9,128,281	9,519,608	391,327
			85	577,032	2,940,971	3,102,869	161,898
			86	245,000	1,384,662	1,452,657	67,995
	V	W	81	354,350	1,760,599	1,863,908	103,309
			82	310,200	1,400,315	1,475,079	74,764
			83	305,600	1,494,531	1,559,189	64,658
			84	75,700	338,427	354,581	16,154
			85	32,900	243,308	251,743	8,435
			86	10,000	57,165	59,750	2,585
CHINA T	O	E	81	18,580	101,687	105,133	3,446

Crop
Product
TSUSA commodity number, description, and unit of quantity

Country	Mode	Reg	Yr	Quantity	F.A.S.	C.I.F.	Charges
	V	E	82	15,000	68,229	72,417	4,188
			84	17,000	194,632	198,999	4,367
			85	40,900	283,860	288,546	4,686
			86	27,609	164,597	170,161	5,564
	V	W	82	10,000	45,865	48,278	2,413
			84	4,000	48,712	50,250	1,538
FR GERM	V	E	84	22,046	100,279	104,086	3,807
			85	23,810	100,101	103,828	3,727
			86	17,638	108,350	113,492	5,142
FRANCE	A	E	81	440	1,707	1,831	124
			83	178	1,430	1,442	12
			84	330	1,347	1,372	25
	N	E	82	1,410	6,789	7,033	244
			86	1,102	6,098	6,552	454
	V	E	84	5,269	10,615	11,715	1,100
			85	441	3,181	3,250	69
HG KONG	A	W	81	60	293	482	189
	O	E	81	16,000	120,800	123,994	3,194
			84	99,000	636,716	656,025	19,309
	V	E	84	20,248	158,590	164,874	6,284
	V	W	82	10,115	50,812	52,626	1,814
ITALY	A	E	84	110	2,950	3,063	113
	V	E	83	47	1,560	1,661	101
			86	2,200	12,192	12,429	237
	V	W	83	40	1,170	1,224	54
JAPAN	N	E	84	265,105	1,558,048	1,633,144	75,096
			85	282,439	1,423,364	1,507,798	84,434
	O	E	83	5,000	19,500	19,500	
	V	E	81	15,964	56,255	58,016	1,761
			82	99,323	355,702	369,044	13,342
			83	199,186	811,473	844,780	33,307
			85	53,650	325,185	331,554	6,369
			86	378,477	2,031,726	2,164,311	132,585
	V	W	85	12,580	76,263	77,744	1,481
MEXICO	O	E	84	8,818	48,000	51,029	3,029
N CALDN	V	E	85	2,205	17,717	18,057	340
N ZEAL	A	W	82	15,741	93,270	100,439	7,169
NETHLDS	V	E	84	50	2,500	2,643	143
PARAGUA	V	E	81	101,400	496,337	523,967	27,630
			82	13,200	67,320	70,921	3,601
			84	6,614	36,080	37,481	1,401
			85	1,323	8,928	9,329	401
			86	6,614	33,649	34,884	1,235
	V	W	81	6,500	29,719	31,408	1,689
SINGAPR	O	E	83	12,000	78,240	82,080	3,840
			84	6,200	69,738	70,223	485
	V	E	84	55,945	653,413	668,613	15,200
SPAIN	A	E	81	441	2,800	3,685	885
	V	E	81	110	714	739	25
			82	441	2,485	2,560	75
			83	441	2,447	2,600	153
			84	2,205	24,435	25,607	1,172
SWITZLD	A	E	86	15	4,753	4,795	42
	V	E	86	75,600	458,361	480,435	22,074
U KING	A	E	83	584	2,257	2,537	280
	N	E	82	66	1,160	1,309	149
			84	6,631	31,843	33,603	1,760
	V	E	85	618	2,936	2,969	33
			86	58,846	69,944	77,270	7,326
VENEZ	A	E	86	6,138	6,500	12,951	6,451

Peppermint, essential oil**
4522200 CORNMINT OIL & PEP OIL NSPF (LB)
   (See Corn mint, essential oil under Corn Mint)
4525400 PEPERMT OIL OF MENT PIPRITA (LB)

Country	Mode	Reg	Yr	Quantity	F.A.S.	C.I.F.	Charges
TOTAL			81	6,709	105,327	108,254	2,927
			82	8,956	94,527	98,270	3,743
			83	17,856	145,380	149,259	3,879
			84	13,609	223,291	230,184	6,893
			85	9,925	171,965	177,745	5,780
			86	104,115	437,462	465,059	27,597
BRAZIL	V	E	86	86,110	260,324	280,651	20,327
CANADA	A	E	82	108	1,599	1,649	50
			86	238	5,029	5,699	670
	A	W	81	107	1,454	1,512	58
			82	147	1,986	2,070	84
			83	100	1,260	1,442	182
	O	E	82	27	459	459	
			84	400	4,270	4,270	
			86	187	1,422	1,422	
CHINA M	V	E	83	6,559	36,203	37,375	1,172

Crop
Product
TSUSA commodity number, description, and unit of quantity

Country	Mode	Reg	Yr	Quantity	F.A.S.	C.I.F.	Charges
			84	772	5,240	5,390	150
FR GERM	A	W	83	45	1,453	1,475	22
	V	E	84	1,433	22,013	22,183	170
			85	401	5,749	5,978	229
FRANCE	A	E	85	3,242	66,805	70,008	3,203
			86	3,445	77,721	80,875	3,154
	N	E	81	3,439	75,883	77,131	1,248
			84	2,898	56,217	57,001	784
	O	E	84	220	4,333	4,600	267
	V	E	82	1,720	34,249	34,499	250
			83	3,440	38,727	39,008	281
HG KONG	V	W	86	11,905	53,931	56,741	2,810
ISRAEL	A	E	82	572	2,298	3,825	1,527
			83	165	1,325	1,855	530
			84	110	513	728	215
	V	E	81	220	930	1,037	107
ITALY	V	E	86	1,720	35,968	36,375	407
JAMAICA	V	E	86	113	1,044	1,099	55
JAPAN	A	E	81	33	263	381	118
NETHLDS	A	E	82	44	263	268	5
	N	E	84	742	32,944	34,886	1,942
	V	E	81	2,205	17,344	18,188	844
			82	4,410	36,132	37,630	1,498
			84	2,205	19,473	20,450	977
			85	2,205	22,585	22,743	158
U KING	A	E	81	397	4,043	4,501	458
			82	55	914	927	13
			83	55	645	698	53
			84	462	5,411	5,743	332
			85	110	1,713	1,887	174
			86	397	2,023	2,197	174
	N	E	81	308	5,410	5,504	94
	V	E	82	1,873	16,627	16,943	316
			83	7,492	65,767	67,406	1,639
			84	4,367	72,877	74,933	2,056
			85	3,967	75,113	77,129	2,016

Perilla

Perilla, fatty acid**
4902200 FATTY ACIDS DRVD HMP KPK ETC (LB)
   (See Hempseed, fatty acid under Hemp)

Perilla, fatty salt**
4904600 FATTY SALTS OF SESAME ETC (LB)
   (See Hempseed, fatty salt under Hemp)

Perilla, seed
1753300 PERILLA SEED (LB)

Country	Mode	Reg	Yr	Quantity	F.A.S.	C.I.F.	Charges
TOTAL			81	480	878	930	52
			82	240	385	407	22
			83	600	760	794	34
			84	28	324	353	29
			85	210	1,470	1,672	202
			86	40,998	10,935	13,551	2,616
CHINA M	V	W	86	40,745	9,555	12,013	2,458
KOR REP	V	E	85	210	1,470	1,672	202
	V	W	81	480	878	930	52
			82	240	385	407	22
			83	600	760	794	34
			84	28	324	353	29
			86	253	1,380	1,538	158

Perilla, vegetable oil
1764000 PERILLA OIL (LB)

Country	Mode	Reg	Yr	Quantity	F.A.S.	C.I.F.	Charges
TOTAL			82	634	1,552	1,942	390
			84	79,935	21,910	24,315	2,405
			86	566,350	149,347	149,664	317
BRAZIL	V	E	86	551,150	139,849	139,849	
FRANCE	O	E	86	15,200	9,498	9,815	317
	V	E	84	73,795	18,338	20,376	2,038
ITALY	O	E	82	634	1,552	1,942	390
			84	140	335	406	71
JAPAN	A	E	84	6,000	3,237	3,533	296

Crop Product TSUSA commodity number, description, and unit of quantity Country	Mode	Reg	Yr	Quantity	F.A.S.	C.I.F.	Charges

Pigeon Pea

Pigeon pea, fresh
1369400 PIGEON PEAS FR CH, 7/1-9/30 (LB)

Country	Mode	Reg	Yr	Quantity	F.A.S.	C.I.F.	Charges
TOTAL			81	46,225	21,267	25,334	4,067
			82	266,378	128,753	147,693	18,940
			83	196,427	85,098	109,563	24,465
			84	44,280	19,579	23,949	4,370
			85	202,678	77,546	100,609	23,063
			86	633,142	274,509	307,214	32,705
BELGIUM	V	E	85	28,656	6,479	9,440	2,961
CANADA	O	E	84	1,100	847	847	
DOM REP	A	E	81	34,225	16,642	20,292	3,650
			82	2,082	1,042	1,483	441
			83	18,883	9,480	13,451	3,971
			85	35,135	17,567	32,661	15,094
			86	94,088	55,667	70,199	14,532
	N	E	82	252,296	122,961	141,111	18,150
			83	137,544	68,771	85,201	16,430
			84	13,190	4,375	7,770	3,395
			86	31,412	14,363	16,016	1,653
	V	E	82	12,000	4,750	5,099	349
			84	29,660	14,100	15,075	975
			85	97,000	45,900	48,674	2,774
			86	459,002	191,175	204,164	12,989
GUATMAL	A	E	86	8,640	2,592	4,260	1,668
INDIA	O	E	84	330	257	257	
KENYA	V	E	83	40,000	6,847	10,911	4,064
PANAMA	V	E	81	12,000	4,625	5,042	417
PERU	V	E	85	41,887	7,600	9,834	2,234
			86	40,000	10,712	12,575	1,863

1370220 PIGEON PEAS FR CH 10/1-6/30 (LB)

Country	Mode	Reg	Yr	Quantity	F.A.S.	C.I.F.	Charges
TOTAL			81	1,138,287	549,016	691,247	142,231
			82	884,771	459,858	577,634	117,776
			83	1,390,207	671,673	842,113	170,440
			84	1,495,025	741,022	1,045,348	304,326
			85	975,950	493,095	699,105	206,010
			86	1,193,569	568,787	692,250	123,463
CANADA	O	E	82	440	272	272	
			83	45,450	6,151	6,151	
	O	W	86	43,900	3,740	3,740	
CHILE	A	E	84	2,665	1,678	3,213	1,535
DOM REP	A	E	81	94,617	36,912	52,936	16,024
			82	444,824	223,069	270,648	47,579
			83	139,935	65,882	95,297	29,415
			84	159,376	65,322	124,930	59,608
			85	78,045	42,948	57,859	14,911
			86	5,095	2,547	3,300	753
	N	E	81	1,004,970	503,328	627,850	124,522
			82	424,813	229,797	296,553	66,756
			83	1,077,877	553,000	689,818	136,818
			84	875,291	439,636	614,592	174,956
			85	832,528	424,445	606,024	181,579
			86	815,934	422,493	532,082	109,589
	V	E	81	35,000	7,000	8,306	1,306
			84	3,235	1,313	2,057	744
			85	2,083	2,642	2,830	188
			86	281,950	121,600	130,250	8,650
FRANCE	A	E	81	2,150	1,032	1,256	224
GUATMAL	A	E	84	5,500	1,375	2,541	1,166
			85	22,835	7,610	14,330	6,720
			86	9,040	2,866	5,537	2,671
	A	W	82	14,694	6,720	10,161	3,441
	N	E	84	380,372	203,158	262,114	58,956
	V	E	83	24,770	14,862	17,273	2,411
			84	15,000	9,000	11,727	2,727
KENYA	V	E	83	40,000	11,882	13,678	1,796
KOR REP	A	E	81	1,550	744	899	155
MEXICO	O	W	83	62,175	19,896	19,896	
			86	1,650	3,571	3,571	
NEPAL	V	E	85	40,459	15,450	18,062	2,612
PANAMA	A	E	84	1,640	656	1,174	518
PERU	V	E	84	51,946	18,884	23,000	4,116
			86	36,000	11,970	13,770	1,800

Pigeon pea, frozen
1369600 PIGEON PEAS FROZEN 7/1-9/30 (LB)

Country	Mode	Reg	Yr	Quantity	F.A.S.	C.I.F.	Charges
TOTAL			81	148,075	58,587	61,499	2,912
			82	45,710	36,881	41,158	4,277
			83	127,890	84,625	89,725	5,100
			84	553,470	194,738	221,769	27,031
			85	302,589	60,522	64,590	4,068
			86	253,032	102,544	111,061	8,517
C RICA	V	E	85	3,465	1,733	2,355	622
			86	7,875	5,907	6,620	713
CANADA	O	E	81	750	265	265	
			85	55,200	5,379	5,379	
			86	80,400	13,278	13,278	
CHINA T	V	W	86	36,000	30,903	34,026	3,123
DOM REP	A	E	82	10,010	4,751	6,296	1,545
	N	E	83	37,600	33,080	35,495	2,415
	V	E	81	81,000	38,880	41,792	2,912
			82	35,700	32,130	34,862	2,732
			83	35,700	32,130	34,701	2,571
			84	223,518	131,672	143,736	12,064
			85	53,066	26,358	29,804	3,446
			86	42,310	18,473	20,051	1,578
FRANCE	A	E	84	3,000	952	2,220	1,268
JAPAN	V	W	86	36,000	30,017	33,120	3,103
MEXICO	O	E	84	132,330	8,633	8,633	
			85	44,090	1,985	1,985	
	O	W	81	66,325	19,442	19,442	
			83	54,088	18,953	18,953	
			84	11,640	3,880	3,880	
			85	146,768	25,067	25,067	
			86	50,447	3,966	3,966	
N ZEAL	V	H	84	182,982	49,601	63,300	13,699
TRINID	A	E	83	502	462	576	114

1370240 PIGEON PEAS FROZN 10/1-6/30 (LB)

Country	Mode	Reg	Yr	Quantity	F.A.S.	C.I.F.	Charges
TOTAL			81	784,810	499,774	545,476	45,702
			82	1,006,098	662,347	725,833	63,486
			83	1,627,851	1,236,909	1,337,429	100,520
			84	1,527,149	1,175,703	1,349,193	173,490
			85	1,599,606	1,251,924	1,360,515	108,591
			86	1,582,962	1,298,963	1,429,299	130,336
C RICA	V	E	84	2,625	1,182	1,388	206
			85	14,595	7,807	9,562	1,755
CANADA	O	E	85	82,500	30,070	30,070	
CHINA M	V	W	86	16,200	14,176	15,963	1,787
CHINA T	V	E	82	15,600	12,435	15,195	2,760
	V	W	81	27,600	24,665	27,047	2,382
			82	27,600	23,561	26,540	2,979
			83	15,900	12,027	13,810	1,783
			84	41,250	36,274	40,465	4,191
			86	4,470	2,830	3,039	209
DOM REP	A	E	84	750	375	560	185
	N	E	81	165,335	115,995	126,935	10,940
			82	316,370	242,161	264,370	22,209
			83	471,487	236,245	248,863	12,618
			84	469,199	405,271	445,190	39,919
	V	E	81	589,891	358,330	389,629	31,299
			82	639,528	381,165	415,247	34,082
			83	1,070,928	940,112	1,012,190	72,078
			84	821,734	575,675	646,211	70,536
			85	1,331,382	1,088,280	1,183,277	94,997
			86	1,502,292	1,267,486	1,390,361	122,875
	V	W	84	18,060	12,642	16,297	3,655
DOMINCA	V	E	85	123,375	108,570	117,825	9,255
FRANCE	A	E	81	1,984	784	1,865	1,081
			86	60,000	14,471	19,936	5,465
GERM DR	V	E	85	8,190	7,207	8,147	940
GUATMAL	A	E	82	7,000	3,025	4,481	1,456
			84	10,280	5,140	7,833	2,693
	A	W	83	30,074	26,888	38,426	11,538
			84	162,905	138,790	190,895	52,105
	N	E	83	19,952	16,957	19,460	2,503
MEXICO	O	W	83	19,500	4,680	4,680	
			84	346	354	354	
PERU	V	E	85	39,564	9,990	11,634	1,644

Crop Product TSUSA commodity number, description, and unit of quantity Country	Mode	Reg	Yr	Quantity	F.A.S.	C.I.F.	Charges

Pimento

Pimento, canned
1416020 PIMIENTOS IN CNTRS NOV 8 OZ (LB)

Country	Mode	Reg	Yr	Quantity	F.A.S.	C.I.F.	Charges
TOTAL			81	4,434,807	4,335,250	4,723,992	388,742
			82	4,814,587	3,547,041	3,977,237	430,196
			83	4,901,798	2,582,665	3,005,864	423,199
			84	6,492,062	3,307,304	3,858,653	551,349
			85	6,956,961	3,952,937	4,633,916	680,979
			86	6,689,561	4,004,265	4,575,783	571,518
AUSTRIA	V	W	83	8,190	3,712	4,266	554
BRAZIL	V	E	82	38,581	17,734	20,507	2,773
CANADA	O	E	83	495	304	304	
DOM REP	V	E	82	6,741	2,568	3,094	526
GUATMAL	V	W	82	475	404	471	67
ITALY	V	E	82	12,763	13,156	14,450	1,294
			85	32,920	12,907	17,244	4,337
JAPAN	V	E	81	223	704	799	95
ROMANIA	V	E	84	11,772	4,680	5,176	496
SPAIN	N	E	83	68,012	30,303	34,523	4,220
			85	2,548,236	1,261,846	1,510,669	248,823
			86	23,100	11,519	13,755	2,236
	N	W	81	27,825	19,162	21,436	2,274
			82	11,419	9,011	10,055	1,044
			85	8,400	3,832	4,607	775
	V	E	81	4,280,710	4,198,264	4,573,016	374,752
			82	4,559,292	3,383,595	3,791,622	408,027
			83	4,539,713	2,418,457	2,815,204	396,747
			84	6,212,123	3,176,809	3,707,032	530,223
			85	4,170,956	2,575,254	2,983,832	408,578
			86	6,402,913	3,871,099	4,416,837	545,738
	V	W	81	126,049	117,120	128,741	11,621
			82	185,316	120,573	137,038	16,465
			83	284,848	129,219	150,805	21,586
			84	268,167	125,815	146,445	20,630
			85	196,449	99,098	117,564	18,466
			86	263,548	121,647	145,191	23,544
THAILND	V	W	83	540	670	762	92

1416040 PIMIENTOS IN CONTRS OV 8 OZ (LB)

Country	Mode	Reg	Yr	Quantity	F.A.S.	C.I.F.	Charges
TOTAL			81	9,474,754	6,331,596	6,923,644	592,048
			82	7,985,946	4,367,857	4,893,807	525,950
			83	7,976,773	2,735,083	3,227,849	492,766
			84	10,543,487	3,550,770	4,255,276	704,506
			85	9,892,107	3,330,545	4,038,764	708,219
			86	15,136,123	5,836,259	6,789,160	952,901
AUSTRIA	V	W	84	10,140	4,283	4,995	712
BRAZIL	V	E	82	321	309	809	500
C RICA	V	E	82	3,520	1,360	1,611	251
CANADA	O	E	81	600	390	390	
			83	51	510	510	
CHINA M	V	E	85.	44,230	10,421	13,300	2,879
DOM REP	V	E	82	20,130	7,160	7,836	676
FRANCE	V	E	81	242	484	516	32
			84	6,510	1,792	2,230	438
GREECE	V	E	84	108,643	32,702	44,649	11,947
			86	3,650	1,712	2,117	405
ISRAEL	V	E	83	142,682	46,270	55,428	9,158
	V	W	85	22,050	9,103	10,830	1,727
ITALY	V	E	81	31,500	18,456	20,286	1,830
			82	9,005	7,443	8,189	746
			84	83,216	17,714	22,785	5,071
			85	25,200	7,653	9,511	1,858
			86	80,688	18,000	23,080	5,080
JAPAN	V	E	83	29,983	10,880	12,580	1,700
MEXICO	O	W	83	41,800	5,000	5,000	
PHIL R	V	E	83	18,000	9,720	10,774	1,054
	V	W	82	1,976	1,526	1,716	190
PORTUGL	V	E	81	195,199	102,535	114,684	12,149
			82	4,850	3,000	3,720	720
			84	8,026	1,758	2,040	282
			86	3,719	1,181	1,428	247
	V	W	81	65,280	27,099	32,822	5,723
ROMANIA	V	E	86	29,101	5,070	6,535	1,465
SPAIN	N	E	81	63,975	42,835	47,294	4,459
			85	1,224,334	478,759	560,085	81,326
			86	59,115	21,840	25,998	4,158
	N	W	81	28,980	24,517	27,561	3,044
			82	42,628	23,760	26,401	2,641
			84	520,003	185,414	225,330	39,916

Crop Product TSUSA commodity number, description, and unit of quantity Country	Mode	Reg	Yr	Quantity	F.A.S.	C.I.F.	Charges
			86	17,047	7,242	8,358	1,116
	O	E	81	13,125	8,644	9,505	861
			84	8,052	5,877	7,006	1,129
	V	E	81	8,835,826	5,926,876	6,472,250	545,374
			82	7,668,426	4,192,497	4,692,706	500,209
			83	7,261,425	2,477,232	2,924,629	447,397
			84	9,392,274	3,160,987	3,778,260	617,273
			85	7,843,323	2,512,368	3,070,608	558,240
			86	14,276,464	5,519,924	6,411,016	891,092
	V	W	81	240,027	179,760	198,336	18,576
			82	235,090	130,802	150,819	20,017
			83	482,652	185,216	218,638	33,422
			84	368,823	129,755	155,092	25,337
			85	732,970	312,241	374,430	62,189
			86	666,339	261,290	310,628	49,338
THAILND	V	E	83	180	255	290	35
YUGOSLV	V	E	84	37,800	10,488	12,889	2,401

Pimento, spice
1618600 PIMENTO UNGROUND (LB)

Country	Mode	Reg	Yr	Quantity	F.A.S.	C.I.F.	Charges
TOTAL			81	1,874,127	1,495,177	1,626,628	131,451
			82	1,157,204	1,129,212	1,208,037	78,825
			83	1,666,383	1,600,403	1,708,499	108,096
			84	1,881,306	1,960,675	2,075,924	115,249
			85	1,533,224	1,561,821	1,656,805	94,984
			86	1,704,298	1,469,593	1,569,129	99,536
BRAZIL	V	E	83	33,040	33,205	35,494	2,289
CANADA	O	E	81	1,420	425	425	
CHINA M	V	W	85	44,092	38,569	44,231	5,662
CYPRUS	V	E	82	123	462	481	19
			83	22	300	303	3
FRANCE	A	E	82	237	644	746	102
	V	E	83	45	411	411	
	V	W	83	264	451	479	28
GUATMAL	V	E	81	287,839	220,734	245,331	24,597
			82	42,038	36,059	39,522	3,463
			83	33,200	30,934	33,588	2,654
			84	171,600	152,777	165,248	12,471
			85	166,299	142,081	152,029	9,948
			86	476,483	347,870	380,218	32,348
	V	W	81	10,000	8,000	8,952	952
			84	17,636	17,800	19,782	1,982
			85	6,614	5,700	6,505	805
			86	11,000	7,906	8,689	783
GUYANA	V	W	86	8,951	4,800	5,722	922
HONDURA	N	E	81	172,000	101,261	110,426	9,165
	V	E	81	277,669	209,373	227,710	18,337
			82	164,454	130,728	141,700	10,972
			83	209,932	192,494	209,307	16,813
			84	428,257	430,499	458,443	27,944
			85	225,987	219,792	233,244	13,452
			86	156,178	145,061	159,688	14,627
JAMAICA	A	E	81	119	420	444	24
	N	E	83	747,219	776,585	829,197	52,612
			86	682,969	662,525	702,634	40,109
	V	E	81	611,779	591,236	641,504	50,268
			82	858,874	905,186	966,457	61,271
			83	135,544	135,145	145,913	10,768
			84	894,336	1,024,087	1,081,171	57,084
			85	755,658	866,190	914,173	47,983
			86	59,524	57,097	61,167	4,070
	V	W	81	32,032	29,470	33,054	3,584
			83	33,600	33,750	36,081	2,331
			86	38,080	36,550	38,786	2,236
MEXICO	O	E	82	44,092	18,391	18,391	
			83	22,081	17,638	17,638	
			85	88,975	77,263	77,263	
			86	233,100	183,296	183,296	
	O	W	83	66,138	54,662	54,662	
			84	64,815	62,994	62,994	
			86	8,013	4,014	4,014	
	V	E	81	331,699	227,211	243,106	15,895
			82	44,092	31,706	34,036	2,330
			83	385,298	324,828	345,426	20,598
			84	260,570	244,318	257,013	12,695
			85	245,599	212,226	229,360	17,134
			86	30,000	20,474	24,915	4,441
	V	W	81	67,020	48,718	52,011	3,293
PHIL R	V	W	81	1,800	1,400	1,500	100
SPAIN	V	E	81	80,750	56,929	62,165	5,236
	V	W	82	3,294	6,036	6,704	668

Crop Product TSUSA commodity number, description, and unit of quantity Country	Mode	Reg	Yr	Quantity	F.A.S.	C.I.F.	Charges
			84	44,092	28,200	31,273	3,073

1618800 PIMENTO GROUND (LB)

Country	Mode	Reg	Yr	Quantity	F.A.S.	C.I.F.	Charges
TOTAL			**81**	**4,409**	**4,074**	**4,074**	
			82	**1,000**	**1,240**	**1,240**	
			83	**9,463**	**12,482**	**12,525**	**43**
			84	**33,600**	**40,740**	**42,606**	**1,866**
			85	**7,165**	**6,010**	**7,019**	**1,009**
CANADA	O	E	82	1,000	1,240	1,240	
			83	8,520	11,084	11,084	
FRANCE	V	E	83	173	823	866	43
JAMAICA	V	E	84	33,600	40,740	42,606	1,866
MEXICO	O	E	81	4,409	4,074	4,074	
	O	W	83	770	575	575	
SPAIN	V	E	85	7,165	6,010	7,019	1,009

Pine

Pignolia, nut, shelled, prepared or preserved
1455200 PIGNOLIA NUTS, SHELLED, ETC (LB)

Country	Mode	Reg	Yr	Quantity	F.A.S.	C.I.F.	Charges
TOTAL			**81**	**567,751**	**1,567,515**	**1,652,036**	**84,521**
			82	**908,023**	**2,660,797**	**2,797,446**	**136,649**
			83	**988,015**	**2,770,135**	**2,878,011**	**107,876**
			84	**1,259,396**	**3,628,814**	**3,775,433**	**146,619**
			85	**1,196,926**	**3,373,385**	**3,540,997**	**167,612**
			86	**2,796,488**	**6,260,318**	**6,562,409**	**302,091**
BELGIUM	A	W	86	5,000	15,505	19,505	4,000
	V	E	86	7,500	27,216	29,553	2,337
CHINA M	O	E	81	14,881	38,691	38,691	
			86	1,543	4,356	4,356	
	V	E	81	163,107	403,106	419,074	15,968
			82	288,953	708,518	737,266	28,748
			83	525,522	1,134,640	1,179,277	44,637
			84	419,430	968,977	1,009,206	40,229
			85	259,002	619,650	648,703	29,053
			86	1,306,145	2,765,621	2,900,401	134,780
	V	W	81	14,331	36,469	37,724	1,255
			82	140,540	353,401	364,066	10,665
			83	169,888	366,054	377,567	11,513
			84	445,499	1,034,350	1,074,499	40,149
			85	458,160	1,065,056	1,117,108	52,052
			86	920,580	1,929,496	2,015,670	86,174
CHINA T	V	E	83	22,047	47,719	51,964	4,245
			84	420	1,612	1,686	74
	V	W	82	13,200	35,606	36,872	1,266
			83	2,592	1,224	1,275	51
			85	2,200	5,059	5,380	321
			86	11,024	20,817	21,400	583
FR GERM	V	W	85	2,498	8,667	9,630	963
FRANCE	V	E	84	8,109	3,500	4,602	1,102
HG KONG	V	E	81	18,167	45,344	47,722	2,378
			82	48,259	116,126	120,220	4,094
			83	8,267	23,551	24,252	701
			84	132,210	298,850	313,661	14,811
			85	51,919	114,993	120,432	5,439
			86	177,445	367,319	384,787	17,468
	V	W	82	6,050	15,571	16,033	462
			83	27,448	59,141	62,425	3,284
			84	36,376	89,647	91,705	2,058
			85	104,455	241,270	259,861	18,591
			86	94,512	209,082	219,288	10,206
INDIA	V	E	84	5,512	11,759	12,372	613
	V	W	85	265	1,107	1,225	118
IRAN	V	E	85	46,297	69,300	71,300	2,000
ITALY	V	E	81	2,756	9,177	9,625	448
			82	441	2,074	2,173	99
			83	3,050	4,882	4,950	68
			84	4,419	27,721	28,411	690
			85	11,023	48,655	50,987	2,332
			86	184	1,658	1,746	88
	V	W	83	52	292	352	60
			85	619	4,088	5,567	1,479
IVY CST	V	W	86	19,401	45,000	50,000	5,000
JAPAN	V	E	81	5,511	14,330	14,728	398
			85	11,023	25,834	26,999	1,165
	V	W	86	17,637	38,475	40,033	1,558
MEXICO	O	E	82	1,043	294	294	
NETHLDS	V	W	85	2,248	12,247	13,608	1,361

Crop Product TSUSA commodity number, description, and unit of quantity Country	Mode	Reg	Yr	Quantity	F.A.S.	C.I.F.	Charges
PAKISTN	V	E	84	1,102	2,716	2,875	159
PORTUGL	V	E	81	180,013	527,149	561,818	34,669
			82	217,174	793,777	834,012	40,235
			83	127,521	633,349	653,861	20,512
			84	115,978	674,643	701,366	26,723
			85	152,161	652,133	683,550	31,417
			86	183,555	653,450	687,780	34,330
	V	W	81	27,500	77,839	81,250	3,411
			82	10,000	35,974	37,422	1,448
			83	11,003	53,705	54,900	1,195
			84	15,000	83,583	85,617	2,034
			85	17,500	75,158	78,172	3,014
			86	23,732	93,421	96,613	3,192
SPAIN	N	E	85	73,956	412,714	430,012	17,298
	O	E	81	588	3,515	3,515	
	V	E	81	136,763	398,546	423,406	24,860
			82	180,162	592,775	641,817	49,042
			83	90,625	445,578	467,188	21,610
			84	74,680	430,436	448,341	17,905
			85	2,500	14,229	14,754	525
			86	15,000	63,353	64,834	1,481
	V	W	81	4,134	13,349	14,483	1,134
			82	1,650	5,181	5,654	473
SWITZLD	V	W	86	13,230	25,549	26,443	894
TURKEY	V	E	82	551	1,500	1,617	117
			84	661	1,020	1,092	72
			85	1,100	3,225	3,709	484

Pignolia, nut, unshelled
1452400 PIGNOLIA NUTS, NOT SHELLED (LB)

Country	Mode	Reg	Yr	Quantity	F.A.S.	C.I.F.	Charges
TOTAL			**81**	**31,538**	**72,639**	**79,013**	**6,374**
			82	**52,052**	**125,767**	**131,975**	**6,208**
			83	**96,549**	**74,547**	**82,734**	**8,187**
			84	**68,027**	**71,592**	**76,718**	**5,126**
			85	**1,629,038**	**1,980,776**	**2,056,363**	**75,587**
			86	**160,708**	**253,171**	**262,503**	**9,332**
BRAZIL	V	E	83	7,500	9,450	9,975	525
CANADA	O	E	84	110	274	274	
CHINA M	O	E	84	757	1,249	1,279	30
	V	E	81	550	1,762	1,856	94
			82	2,200	4,945	5,146	201
			85	22,046	50,389	55,070	4,681
	V	W	82	8,267	22,322	22,759	437
			83	25,318	33,949	35,498	1,549
			84	33,114	33,776	36,163	2,387
			85	32,355	79,081	84,632	5,551
			86	476	1,043	1,059	16
CHINA T	V	E	84	12,000	27,000	28,481	1,481
FINLAND	V	W	81	16,519	27,782	30,580	2,798
			83	8,377	12,020	15,200	3,180
FRANCE	A	E	85	2,776	3,823	4,568	745
HG KONG	V	E	81	2,756	7,727	8,153	426
	V	W	84	22,046	9,293	10,521	1,228
			86	2,204	4,000	4,648	648
IRAN	V	E	85	1,149,742	1,552,543	1,598,743	46,200
			86	116,530	181,920	186,320	4,400
ITALY	V	E	82	66	566	623	57
			85	355,505	184,735	198,936	14,201
MEXICO	O	E	82	5,081	1,747	1,747	
	O	W	85	6,614	1,539	1,539	
PORTUGL	V	E	82	5,512	17,929	18,843	914
			84	10,000	56,579	59,434	2,855
			86	15,000	18,458	20,048	1,590
SPAIN	V	E	81	4,134	13,862	14,927	1,065
			82	18,562	37,377	39,424	2,047
			83	54,858	18,808	21,723	2,915
			84	12,500	14,187	14,773	586
			86	26,498	47,750	50,428	2,678
	V	W	81	7,579	21,506	23,497	1,991
			82	12,364	40,881	43,433	2,552
			85	37,500	37,900	38,668	768
SWITZLD	V	E	83	496	320	338	18

Pine, essential oil
4528025 PINE OIL (LB)

Country	Mode	Reg	Yr	Quantity	F.A.S.	C.I.F.	Charges
TOTAL			**81**	**1,322**	**12,825**	**13,077**	**252**
			82	**363**	**2,617**	**2,692**	**75**
			83	**640,614**	**265,120**	**266,476**	**1,356**
			84	**891,988**	**326,459**	**326,853**	**394**

Crop
Product
TSUSA commodity number, description, and unit of quantity

Country	Mode	Reg	Yr	Quantity	F.A.S.	C.I.F.	Charges
			85	159,937	68,653	73,543	4,890
			86	350,158	152,740	153,544	804
BRAZIL	V	W	85	4,762	2,267	2,587	320
			86	9,524	3,615	4,255	640
CANADA	O	E	85	688	1,058	1,087	29
CHINA M	V	W	83	8,730	4,221	4,554	333
CHINA T	V	W	84	26	338	360	22
FINLAND	V	E	85	37,897	5,329	7,001	1,672
FR GERM	V	E	83	400	2,185	2,215	30
			84	772	12,705	12,910	205
			85	400	1,439	1,521	82
FRANCE	A	E	82	33	319	324	5
	V	E	84	441	4,902	4,981	79
			85	2,315	19,612	22,399	2,787
ITALY	V	E	83	750	15,076	15,351	275
JAPAN	V	E	86	600	4,365	4,529	164
	V	W	83	66	808	837	29
			84	116	1,640	1,728	88
MEXICO	A	E	81	220	9,150	9,302	152
	O	E	83	627,602	237,290	237,290	
			84	890,633	306,874	306,874	
			85	113,875	38,948	38,948	
			86	340,034	144,760	144,760	
SPAIN	V	E	83	2,094	1,600	2,152	552
SWITZLD	V	E	81	1,102	3,675	3,775	100
USSR	A	E	82	330	2,298	2,368	70
	V	E	83	972	3,940	4,077	137

Pine, lumber

2020620 EAST WHITE,RED PINE LBR RUGH (MBF)

Country	Mode	Reg	Yr	Quantity	F.A.S.	C.I.F.	Charges
TOTAL			81	10,132	2,530,529	2,584,572	57,461
			82	14,237	3,348,437	3,706,472	358,035
			83	13,608	3,430,297	3,819,667	389,370
			84	21,987	4,480,881	4,904,978	424,097
			85	18,359	4,723,058	5,378,082	655,024
			86	24,429	6,146,476	6,759,238	612,762
BELGIUM	V	E	81	28	3,360	6,394	3,034
BELIZE	V	E	83	1	300	300	
BRAZIL	V	E	84	93	87,001	107,103	20,102
CANADA	N	E	85	4,278	966,954	1,342,609	375,655
	O	E	81	9,061	2,278,505	2,277,130	2,043
			82	9,193	2,224,234	2,226,120	1,886
			83	5,841	1,622,636	1,622,636	
			84	7,227	2,280,764	2,280,764	
			85	7,775	2,536,894	2,536,894	
			86	9,238	3,098,795	3,098,795	
	O	W	81	3	649	649	
			83	25	7,459	7,459	
			84	184	57,831	57,831	
			85	50	12,370	12,370	
	V	E	82	2,050	386,159	544,744	158,585
			83	2,560	560,233	747,603	187,370
			84	11,533	1,453,262	1,684,555	231,293
			85	2,664	670,662	855,709	185,047
			86	12,108	2,574,181	3,024,266	450,085
	V	W	85	17	1,961	2,770	809
CHILE	V	E	81	27	8,100	11,016	2,916
			83	45	9,943	12,056	2,113
			84	205	32,530	43,173	10,643
			85	481	90,175	119,837	29,662
			86	1,711	227,449	359,750	132,301
FINLAND	V	E	82	75	37,348	48,799	11,451
HG KONG	O	E	84	13	17,810	17,810	
HONDURA	V	E	81	703	183,728	230,345	46,617
			82	2,788	638,689	824,802	186,113
			83	2,358	608,501	801,622	193,121
			84	2,051	466,692	628,242	161,550
			85	478	145,706	189,824	44,118
			86	367	119,208	149,584	30,376
MEXICO	O	E	81	214	36,117	36,117	
			82	131	62,007	62,007	
			83	2,722	588,322	588,322	
			84	478	40,556	40,556	
			85	1,910	206,596	206,596	
			86	984	118,836	118,836	
	O	W	81	87	12,852	12,852	
			83	20	2,425	2,425	
			84	200	40,080	40,080	
			85	488	17,875	17,875	
MOROC	O	E	86	21	8,007	8,007	

Crop
Product
TSUSA commodity number, description, and unit of quantity

Country	Mode	Reg	Yr	Quantity	F.A.S.	C.I.F.	Charges
N ZEAL	V	E	81	9	7,218	10,069	2,851
			83	36	30,478	37,244	6,766
			85	46	40,244	49,203	8,959
SWEDEN	A	E	85	2	1,843	2,020	177
	V	E	84	3	4,355	4,864	509
SWITZLD	V	E	85	170	31,778	42,375	10,597

2020640 EAST WHITE A RED PINE LBR,DR (MBF)

Country	Mode	Reg	Yr	Quantity	F.A.S.	C.I.F.	Charges
TOTAL			81	205,369	44,889,608	44,910,576	21,957
			82	229,346	49,775,980	50,027,042	251,062
			83	273,720	60,031,688	61,013,322	981,634
			84	303,366	66,933,331	67,215,130	281,799
			85	352,641	81,355,174	81,662,795	307,621
			86	204,281	52,761,492	53,357,173	595,681
AUSTRAL	V	E	81	34	2,885	3,432	547
BRAZIL	V	E	82	48	71,716	74,267	2,551
			84	24	12,745	14,887	2,142
			85	111	43,204	49,846	6,642
			86	116	42,408	47,817	5,409
C RICA	V	E	85	33	9,765	11,011	1,246
CANADA	N	E	82	*	722	722	
			85	93,195	20,096,559	20,096,563	4
			86	25,333	10,891,244	10,891,259	15
	N	W	84	319	50,841	51,570	729
	O	E	81	204,382	44,746,770	44,746,075	294
			82	226,162	48,908,176	49,007,199	99,023
			83	261,762	57,457,700	57,679,695	221,995
			84	298,544	65,909,708	65,909,708	
			85	254,038	59,864,094	59,864,096	2
			86	168,389	39,760,841	39,760,844	3
	O	W	81	228	40,315	40,315	
			82	400	73,421	73,684	263
			83	166	47,580	47,580	
			84	422	95,520	95,520	
			85	793	145,451	145,451	
			86	290	66,849	66,849	
	V	E	81	70	12,631	17,055	4,424
			82	791	170,285	232,235	61,950
			83	10,290	2,245,707	2,943,140	697,433
			84	2,688	572,943	793,266	220,323
			85	1,379	407,861	514,785	106,924
			86	2,857	667,658	894,120	226,462
	V	W	83	477	91,609	122,819	31,210
			84	262	47,862	73,167	25,305
CHILE	V	E	81	2	1,680	2,295	615
			83	148	38,219	46,341	8,122
			84	130	4,213	5,609	1,396
			85	1,865	418,879	561,059	142,180
			86	6,303	1,179,391	1,535,874	356,483
CHINA T	V	W	83	127	35,982	42,432	6,450
FRANCE	A	E	84	100	2,973	3,548	575
	V	E	84	102	30,655	37,219	6,564
GUATMAL	V	E	84	30	5,930	8,441	2,511
			86	60	13,800	17,669	3,869
HONDURA	V	E	81	616	47,355	56,249	8,894
			82	1,766	480,426	548,164	67,738
			84	34	10,515	13,342	2,827
			85	710	81,431	88,871	7,440
			86	33	9,895	10,695	800
INDNSIA	V	W	85	11	5,989	8,961	2,972
ITALY	A	E	85	2	3,550	4,193	643
JAPAN	V	W	85	1	2,634	4,188	1,554
MALAYSA	V	E	85	134	3,999	4,815	816
MEXICO	O	E	83	327	47,307	47,307	
			84	574	86,205	86,205	
			85	108	34,754	34,754	
			86	782	97,517	97,517	
	O	W	81	4	977	977	
			83	9	5,263	5,263	
			85	5	3,120	3,120	
			86	28	5,571	5,571	
N ZEAL	V	E	81	14	15,395	18,359	2,964
			82	165	65,197	82,752	17,555
			83	403	53,215	67,464	14,249
			84	44	41,229	51,083	9,854
			85	65	65,611	79,016	13,405
	V	W	82	14	6,037	8,019	1,982
			83	9	7,129	8,839	1,710
			84	81	43,024	51,224	8,200
			85	40	46,600	56,219	9,619
NORWAY	V	W	83	2	1,977	2,442	465
REP SAF	V	E	81	18	20,947	25,166	4,219
SPAIN	V	E	86	67	1,088	1,143	55

Country	Mode	Reg	Yr	Quantity	F.A.S.	C.I.F.	Charges
Crop							
Product							
TSUSA commodity number, description, and unit of quantity							
SWEDEN	V	E	84	11	18,169	19,413	1,244
			85	106	114,549	126,397	11,848
			86	23	25,230	27,815	2,585
SWITZLD	V	E	84	1	799	928	129
			85	45	7,124	9,450	2,326
U KING	O	E	81	1	653	653	
2020925 LODGEPOLE PINE LUMBER ROUGH (MBF)							
TOTAL			81	1,996	424,742	424,742	
			82	2,992	387,306	413,144	25,838
			83	3,152	409,995	430,175	20,180
			84	3,100	441,207	445,042	3,835
			85	1,372	294,983	350,200	55,217
			86	1,727	361,058	400,854	39,796
CANADA	N	W	83	395	83,922	85,746	1,824
	O	E	81	1,375	334,589	334,589	
			82	331	94,070	94,070	
			83	635	107,745	107,745	
			84	605	143,712	143,712	
			85	639	128,154	128,154	
			86	249	48,666	48,666	
	O	W	81	621	90,153	90,153	
			82	2,135	194,727	194,727	
			83	1,806	157,668	157,668	
			84	2,433	287,087	287,087	
			85	116	27,200	27,200	
			86	737	185,342	185,342	
	V	E	82	487	68,119	93,957	25,838
			85	614	136,213	191,158	54,945
			86	644	115,735	153,731	37,996
	V	W	84	62	10,408	14,243	3,835
CHILE	V	E	83	300	58,054	76,410	18,356
FRANCE	V	E	85	3	3,416	3,688	272
			86	97	11,315	13,115	1,800
JAPAN	O	W	83	16	2,606	2,606	
MEXICO	O	E	82	39	30,390	30,390	
2020945 LODGEPOLE PINE LBR, DRESSED (MBF)							
TOTAL			81	438,621	76,605,101	77,346,100	732,773
			82	325,282	45,285,002	45,427,834	142,832
			83	368,383	69,212,725	69,441,545	228,820
			84	262,475	44,309,049	44,415,046	105,997
			85	169,808	26,338,176	26,362,456	24,280
			86	121,712	20,313,624	20,351,151	37,527
CANADA	N	W	81	159,459	25,220,114	25,952,248	732,134
			82	30,539	3,659,556	3,784,376	124,820
			83	24,025	3,796,274	3,984,016	187,742
			84	16,004	2,511,665	2,537,773	26,108
			85	14,390	2,519,886	2,526,263	6,377
	O	E	81	220,744	41,422,119	41,430,345	
			82	240,266	32,989,751	32,997,144	7,393
			83	272,608	51,623,816	51,633,624	9,808
			84	179,612	30,025,018	30,025,029	11
			85	126,096	18,752,758	18,752,760	2
			86	77,455	11,952,486	11,976,496	24,010
	O	W	81	58,257	9,929,766	9,929,766	
			82	54,338	8,591,649	8,591,649	
			83	71,231	13,694,714	13,694,744	30
			84	62,833	11,354,497	11,354,497	
			85	27,561	4,924,220	4,924,220	
			86	43,931	8,323,209	8,333,763	10,554
	V	E	81	12	1,968	2,607	639
			82	116	23,437	34,056	10,619
			83	40	6,687	9,773	3,086
			84	3,549	271,168	319,708	48,540
			85	95	26,218	34,280	8,062
			86	46	7,459	10,422	2,963
	V	W	84	369	69,295	94,240	24,945
			85	632	18,348	25,648	7,300
CHILE	V	E	83	459	89,040	117,194	28,154
CHINA M	O	E	85	61	11,357	11,357	
COLOMB	V	E	84	51	10,296	10,296	
HONDURA	V	E	84	40	52,622	59,015	6,393
JAPAN	V	E	85	754	27,033	29,572	2,539
MEXICO	O	E	81	54	18,434	18,434	
			82	23	20,609	20,609	
			83	20	2,194	2,194	
			84	17	14,488	14,488	
			85	146	51,397	51,397	
			86	41	11,966	11,966	
	O	W	81	73	10,173	10,173	
			86	232	16,237	16,237	

Country	Mode	Reg	Yr	Quantity	F.A.S.	C.I.F.	Charges
Crop							
Product							
TSUSA commodity number, description, and unit of quantity							
MOROC	O	E	86	7	2,267	2,267	
U KING	O	W	81	22	2,527	2,527	
USSR	O	E	85	73	6,959	6,959	
2020965 PINE LBR, NES, RGH (MBF)							
TOTAL			81	16,213	3,003,032	3,150,283	147,251
			82	20,273	3,712,359	3,953,149	240,790
			83	24,921	6,054,079	6,730,080	676,001
			84	21,304	4,987,030	5,618,392	631,362
			85	34,697	6,186,644	7,412,175	1,225,531
			86	33,778	9,607,378	10,648,969	1,041,591
BELIZE	V	E	83	2	855	1,053	198
BRAZIL	V	E	85	14	9,828	21,209	11,381
			86	455	213,509	264,135	50,626
	V	W	86	2	1,829	2,213	384
C RICA	V	E	81	91	29,633	33,671	4,038
CANADA	N	W	84	1,039	218,445	218,571	126
	O	E	81	11,181	1,840,274	1,840,369	95
			82	10,735	1,886,384	1,886,384	
			83	8,677	1,811,950	1,811,950	
			84	3,650	818,597	818,597	
			85	1,790	520,190	520,190	
			86	3,238	825,587	829,250	3,663
	O	W	81	1,651	213,484	213,484	
			82	3,644	401,559	401,559	
			83	1,458	184,495	184,495	
			84	1,474	450,822	450,822	
			85	2,964	790,479	790,481	2
			86	2,957	865,654	870,587	4,933
	V	E	81	38	10,589	13,265	2,676
			82	2,925	607,244	706,213	98,969
			83	9,858	2,238,414	2,758,728	520,314
			84	6,516	1,249,591	1,503,108	253,517
			85	7,223	1,335,083	1,703,974	368,891
			86	1,866	489,628	512,202	22,574
	V	W	81	2	407	524	117
			84	68	13,657	15,091	1,434
			85	14	12,719	14,401	1,682
CHILE	V	E	83	50	10,408	12,872	2,464
			84	4,631	671,723	964,150	292,427
			85	16,999	1,577,970	2,338,262	760,292
			86	12,673	2,168,474	2,970,109	801,635
ECUADOR	V	E	85	65	30,251	36,733	6,482
FR GERM	V	E	84	1	627	655	28
GUATMAL	V	E	85	65	13,404	18,776	5,372
	V	W	86	120	36,000	47,520	11,520
GUYANA	V	E	81	11	300	357	57
HONDURA	V	E	81	3,041	813,751	940,094	126,343
			82	2,418	598,393	719,946	121,553
			83	1,488	283,401	393,115	109,714
			84	504	92,639	126,627	33,988
			85	719	84,510	120,797	36,287
			86	2,461	501,917	548,025	46,108
INDIA	V	E	86	140	2,592	3,352	760
	V	W	86	167	1,864	2,373	509
MEXICO	O	E	81	74	48,890	48,890	
			82	283	152,394	152,394	
			83	3,088	1,339,323	1,339,323	
			84	2,791	1,249,280	1,249,280	
			85	3,119	1,548,748	1,548,748	
			86	8,907	4,136,623	4,136,625	2
	O	W	81	27	1,023	1,023	
			83	117	24,401	24,401	
			84	8	1,158	1,158	
			85	1,431	60,713	60,713	
			86	118	55,233	55,233	
	V	W	86	368	92,012	154,982	62,970
MONSRAT	O	E	86	17	15,721	15,721	
N ZEAL	V	E	81	22	16,652	21,661	5,009
			82	58	50,840	66,052	15,212
			83	182	159,781	202,903	43,122
			84	591	199,567	243,455	43,888
			85	138	112,910	131,295	18,385
			86	192	149,726	173,321	23,595
	V	W	81	75	28,029	36,945	8,916
			82	210	15,545	20,601	5,056
			84	22	19,629	23,420	3,791
			85	146	82,828	98,448	15,620
			86	91	47,692	59,211	11,519
PHIL R	V	E	86	6	3,317	4,110	793
	V	W	85	10	7,011	8,148	1,137
PORTUGL	V	E	84	9	1,295	3,458	2,163
SWEDEN	V	E	83	1	1,051	1,240	189

Crop Product TSUSA commodity number, description, and unit of quantity Country	Mode	Reg	Yr	Quantity	F.A.S.	C.I.F.	Charges
2020985 PINE LUMBER, NSPF, DRESSED (MBF)							
TOTAL			81	267,032	52,281,972	52,971,038	688,539
			82	206,671	35,400,737	36,031,703	630,966
			83	234,428	49,332,590	50,643,210	1,310,620
			84	287,486	56,334,571	57,195,174	860,603
			85	240,106	48,394,901	50,196,844	1,801,943
			86	282,742	64,474,428	66,441,200	1,966,772
AUSTRAL	V	E	86	50	20,876	25,238	4,362
AUSTRIA	V	E	82	1	848	918	70
BELIZE	V	E	83	10	5,879	7,866	1,987
BRAZIL	V	E	82	11	11,277	13,291	2,014
			84	1	610	878	268
			85	263	181,078	224,231	43,153
			86	13	16,213	18,623	2,410
	V	W	85	2	1,820	2,245	425
C RICA	V	E	82	10	3,100	4,620	1,520
			83	29	14,680	17,504	2,824
CANADA	N	E	82	1,447	277,857	366,262	88,405
			83	59,827	11,400,637	11,405,736	5,099
			84	2,075	683,071	746,496	63,425
			85	186,128	34,653,873	34,734,628	80,755
			86	207,230	42,097,319	42,260,607	163,288
	N	W	83	250	50,069	68,071	18,002
			84	331	56,554	78,543	21,989
	O	E	81	254,971	46,872,881	46,873,408	
			82	193,245	32,002,689	32,007,535	4,846
			83	145,088	31,110,171	31,117,515	7,344
			84	258,424	49,937,469	49,944,276	6,807
			85	14,299	4,419,186	4,419,188	2
			86	18,102	7,190,097	7,190,097	
	O	H	86	31	5,381	5,381	
	O	W	81	3,723	922,342	922,342	
			82	5,622	1,089,721	1,089,721	
			83	8,770	1,734,312	1,734,312	
			84	8,407	1,992,668	1,992,668	
			85	7,843	2,432,129	2,432,129	
			86	11,792	4,207,616	4,327,816	120,200
	V	E	81	1,596	294,952	377,474	82,522
			82	3,750	660,423	956,693	296,270
			83	12,539	2,867,824	3,839,800	971,976
			84	2,748	454,270	692,484	238,214
			85	2,673	417,368	668,048	250,680
			86	2,568	503,205	735,917	232,712
	V	W	81	9	1,829	2,354	525
			83	15	2,709	3,685	976
			85	184	29,638	40,171	10,533
			86	238	38,150	53,304	15,154
CHILE	V	E	83	144	37,918	46,897	8,979
			84	6,190	1,260,867	1,603,744	342,877
			85	20,700	3,685,086	4,748,542	1,063,456
			86	17,758	3,049,265	3,967,505	918,240
	V	W	83	4	819	1,753	934
			85	265	22,340	28,263	5,923
			86	305	138,085	177,323	39,238
CHINA M	O	E	85	21	17,600	17,600	
	V	E	86	92	13,073	20,655	7,582
CHINA T	V	W	83	29	17,910	21,210	3,300
COLOMB	V	E	85	90	7,895	15,661	7,766
CZECHO	O	E	85	22	4,295	4,295	
			86	43	9,965	9,965	
DENMARK	V	E	83	1	273	292	19
			84	11	3,972	4,241	269
			86	1	1,022	1,965	943
ECUADOR	O	W	83	4	660	660	
FIJI	V	E	83	18	14,251	18,067	3,816
FINLAND	V	E	82	7	3,776	5,115	1,339
FR GERM	V	E	82	1	4,860	5,168	308
			85	4	8,933	11,124	2,191
			86	15	8,823	9,481	658
	V	W	81	1	260	448	188
FRANCE	O	E	81	6	10,010	11,425	1,415
	V	E	85	4	3,765	4,474	709
			86	4	2,301	4,289	1,988
GABON	O	E	85	59	9,850	9,850	
GUATMAL	V	E	84	1,177	253,433	355,849	102,416
			85	1,448	415,491	543,250	127,759
			86	1,338	410,541	529,421	118,880
HG KONG	V	E	85	8	22,085	24,158	2,073
HONDURA	N	E	81	2,480	1,136,962	1,360,459	223,497
	V	E	81	2,216	1,496,891	1,699,579	202,688
			82	393	510,390	576,166	65,776
			83	2,144	1,001,088	1,262,584	261,496

Crop Product TSUSA commodity number, description, and unit of quantity Country	Mode	Reg	Yr	Quantity	F.A.S.	C.I.F.	Charges
			84	105	134,320	151,552	17,232
			85	739	392,932	460,359	67,427
			86	979	331,344	392,571	61,227
	V	W	81	1	1,325	1,524	199
ISRAEL	O	E	84	3	484	484	
ITALY	O	E	85	37	4,666	4,666	
			86	30	6,858	6,858	
JAPAN	O	E	82	21	10,113	10,113	
	V	E	84	50	73,926	79,141	5,215
			85	4	4,029	4,461	432
	V	W	85	1	2,827	3,041	214
KOR REP	V	H	82	2	1,800	2,428	628
MALAYSA	V	W	81	46	35,540	46,043	10,503
MEXICO	O	E	81	661	781,943	781,943	
			82	382	201,006	201,006	
			83	5,082	969,133	969,133	
			84	7,411	1,210,764	1,210,764	
			85	4,582	1,093,318	1,093,318	
			86	5,931	1,423,386	1,423,386	
	O	W	81	116	44,375	44,375	
			82	258	82,831	82,831	
			83	107	14,788	14,788	
			84	135	57,654	57,654	
			86	13,347	3,872,511	3,872,517	6
N CALDN	O	E	86	16	3,470	3,470	
N ZEAL	N	W	81	49	33,917	37,911	3,994
	V	E	81	21	19,751	24,400	4,649
			82	132	33,765	41,390	7,625
			83	67	30,842	36,979	6,137
			85	371	320,302	392,218	71,916
			86	556	432,922	517,801	84,879
	V	W	81	843	572,322	729,671	157,349
			82	1,268	414,724	550,306	135,582
			83	195	50,124	66,455	16,331
			84	107	38,309	45,404	7,095
			85	356	239,675	302,714	63,039
			86	541	343,841	419,945	76,104
NAURU	V	E	86	73	13,211	16,209	2,998
NETHLDS	V	E	84	35	3,750	4,170	420
PANAMA	V	E	83	90	5,400	6,800	1,400
PERU	V	E	82	118	86,854	112,837	25,983
REP SAF	V	E	84	120	122,424	161,351	38,927
			85	1	2,325	5,087	2,762
			86	1,609	301,485	410,234	108,749
SIER LN	V	E	86	19	4,257	7,602	3,345
SPAIN	V	E	84	96	12,711	21,123	8,412
			86	15	1,150	1,311	161
SWEDEN	V	E	81	4	4,491	5,090	599
			82	3	4,703	5,303	600
			84	60	37,315	44,352	7,037
			85	2	2,395	3,123	728
			86	46	28,061	31,709	3,648
U KING	O	E	81	152	27,156	27,156	
			83	15	3,103	3,103	
	V	E	81	14	3,467	3,878	411
YEMEN A	O	E	81	123	21,558	21,558	
2021220 LMBR, PARANA PINE, ROUGH (MBF)							
TOTAL			81	154	176,820	209,320	32,500
			82	108	87,770	102,755	14,985
			83	364	327,311	392,197	64,886
			84	524	424,979	518,714	93,735
			85	1,241	495,837	576,415	80,578
			86	911	527,552	607,620	80,068
BRAZIL	V	E	81	154	176,820	209,320	32,500
			82	108	87,770	102,755	14,985
			83	364	327,311	392,197	64,886
			84	524	424,979	518,714	93,735
			85	1,241	495,837	576,415	80,578
			86	911	527,552	607,620	80,068
2021240 PAR PINE,D/W LBR,FLRG X SD,M (MBF)							
TOTAL			81	2,137	1,766,074	2,031,860	265,786
			82	2,702	1,813,232	2,135,232	322,000
			83	1,190	920,529	1,114,117	193,588
			84	1,359	937,506	1,131,438	193,932
			85	349	241,404	285,786	44,382
			86	2,974	1,066,918	1,313,458	246,540
BRAZIL	O	E	81	23	12,946	12,946	
	O	W	82	75	23,053	23,053	
	V	E	81	2,114	1,753,128	2,018,914	265,786
			82	2,519	1,734,716	2,045,201	310,485

Crop Product TSUSA commodity number, description, and unit of quantity Country	Mode	Reg	Yr	Quantity	F.A.S.	C.I.F.	Charges
			83	1,190	920,529	1,114,117	193,588
			84	1,359	937,506	1,131,438	193,932
			85	324	237,132	280,140	43,008
			86	683	471,208	529,279	58,071
	V	W	82	108	55,463	66,978	11,515
			85	25	4,272	5,646	1,374
			86	199	92,130	103,544	11,414
CANADA	V	E	86	2,092	503,580	680,635	177,055

Pine, molding
2026200 WOOD MOLDING, STANDARD, PINE (MLF)

Country	Mode	Reg	Yr	Quantity	F.A.S.	C.I.F.	Charges
TOTAL			81	259,496	25,225,875	25,246,454	29,579
			82	274,442	28,475,488	28,572,659	97,171
			83	374,333	42,087,528	42,295,843	208,315
			84	384,155	40,174,774	40,408,813	234,039
			85	369,079	38,137,665	38,380,516	242,851
			86	384,747	41,041,673	41,176,071	134,398
BOLIVIA	V	E	82	6	1,080	3,580	2,500
BRAZIL	N	E	85	6,786	310,789	361,488	50,699
	V	E	83	3,295	138,336	163,658	25,322
			84	5,393	290,900	343,183	52,283
			85	1,139	114,906	186,021	71,115
			86	6,965	336,358	377,268	40,910
C RICA	V	E	84	569	33,990	37,464	3,474
CANADA	A	H	82	1	261	331	70
	A	W	85	6	1,376	2,013	637
	O	E	81	333	68,608	68,609	
			82	716	172,800	172,800	
			83	2,170	330,485	330,485	
			84	720	167,552	167,552	
			85	193	70,016	70,016	
			86	1,782	127,659	127,659	
	O	W	81	190	30,519	30,519	
			82	6	2,085	2,085	
			83	1	489	489	
			84	4	3,019	3,019	
			85	94	20,004	20,004	
			86	268	51,409	51,409	
CHILE	V	W	86	27	3,525	4,604	1,079
CHINA T	V	E	85	16	7,432	8,102	670
			86	509	3,429	3,635	206
	V	W	81	23	9,525	9,825	300
			82	73	20,653	21,653	1,000
			83	16	5,989	6,280	291
			84	31	12,049	12,732	683
			85	60	26,698	28,524	1,826
			86	74	8,826	9,717	891
COLOMB	O	E	84	325	33,229	33,229	
DENMARK	A	E	84	35	2,569	4,660	2,091
FINLAND	N	E	86	*	2,782	2,988	206
FR GERM	A	E	86	48	26,581	27,689	1,108
FRANCE	A	E	83	3	20,511	22,130	1,619
	O	E	85	3	3,423	3,623	200
			86	3	4,240	4,376	136
	V	E	85	7	9,130	9,410	280
			86	9	16,543	16,890	347
GUATMAL	V	E	84	375	20,860	28,474	7,614
			86	1	2,632	2,846	214
HONDURA	V	E	81	1,271	69,401	79,911	10,510
			82	108	10,341	12,263	1,922
			83	71	877	1,040	163
			84	1,612	88,581	100,704	12,123
			85	84	11,067	12,783	1,716
			86	70	14,453	17,953	3,500
ITALY	N	E	86	852	21,556	22,146	590
	V	E	86	155	15,431	15,854	423
MALAYSA	V	E	81	112	5,181	7,023	1,842
			86	11	11,255	12,780	1,525
MEXICO	O	E	81	218,111	20,839,074	20,830,073	
			82	242,538	24,375,109	24,375,109	
			83	337,627	37,463,760	37,464,892	1,132
			84	346,166	35,770,830	35,770,830	
			85	343,873	35,760,844	35,760,846	2
			86	360,561	38,512,886	38,517,819	4,933
	O	W	81	39,320	4,144,023	4,144,023	
			82	27,011	3,512,323	3,512,323	
			83	24,699	3,391,151	3,391,151	
			84	23,463	2,878,218	2,878,218	
			85	6,344	924,944	924,944	
			86	7,852	1,408,548	1,408,548	
MOZAMBQ	O	E	85	340	30,068	30,068	

Country	Mode	Reg	Yr	Quantity	F.A.S.	C.I.F.	Charges
N ZEAL	V	E	82	4	3,336	4,527	1,191
			83	42	14,416	16,962	2,546
			84	48	7,092	10,398	3,306
			86	1,522	28,814	35,859	7,045
	V	W	81	132	57,098	73,918	16,820
			82	3,947	350,931	438,766	87,835
			83	6,234	711,262	887,422	176,160
			84	2,501	553,346	673,728	120,382
			85	2,473	391,340	466,498	75,158
			86	700	182,362	219,856	37,494
PORTUGL	V	E	86	153	8,795	11,554	2,759
SPAIN	A	E	85	106	2,866	4,614	1,748
	V	E	85	108	72,874	78,745	5,871
			86	2,936	102,170	110,391	8,221
	V	W	82	2	696	949	253
SWEDEN	A	E	84	284	106,437	115,539	9,102
			85	401	139,279	153,910	14,631
			86	51	41,252	47,503	6,251
	A	W	84	393	24,661	29,178	4,517
			85	4,022	58,260	64,362	6,102
			86	34	29,961	40,314	10,353
	N	E	84	1,957	76,311	85,988	9,677
	V	E	83	53	8,708	9,481	773
			84	136	82,737	87,088	4,351
			85	331	161,787	172,457	10,670
			86	130	72,134	76,409	4,275
U KING	A	E	82	29	6,382	7,027	645
			84	45	562	2,056	1,494
			85	1	2,649	3,648	999
	A	W	82	1	19,491	21,246	1,755
			84	74	12,054	14,824	2,770
			85	4	4,309	4,567	258
	N	E	83	122	1,544	1,853	309
	O	E	84	4	938	1,051	113
			85	9	1,344	1,457	113
	V	E	81	4	2,446	2,553	107
			84	20	8,839	8,898	59
			85	2,679	12,260	12,416	156
			86	12	3,007	3,339	332
	V	W	86	22	5,065	6,665	1,600

Pine needle, essential oil
4525800 PINE NEEDLE OIL (LB)

Country	Mode	Reg	Yr	Quantity	F.A.S.	C.I.F.	Charges
TOTAL			81	13,498	87,246	87,707	445
			82	36,858	213,782	215,842	2,060
			83	61,422	451,149	455,118	3,969
			84	833,521	695,270	704,630	9,360
			85	201,074	322,686	342,881	20,195
			86	206,915	375,107	380,188	5,081
AUSTRAL	A	E	84	441	3,371	3,716	345
AUSTRIA	N	E	84	28,124	78,352	82,594	4,242
			85	17,683	64,717	81,376	16,659
	V	E	82	2,867	16,158	16,522	364
			83	2,778	7,654	8,136	482
			86	2,381	16,443	17,078	635
CANADA	O	E	81	12,065	72,497	72,497	
			82	22,272	130,468	130,468	
			83	36,469	298,095	298,095	
			84	29,510	267,883	267,883	
			85	10,004	84,760	84,760	
			86	15,302	115,296	115,296	
CHINA M	N	E	85	10,594	35,421	36,918	1,497
			86	13,492	50,693	52,372	1,679
	O	E	82	1,874	7,449	7,676	227
	V	E	83	5,622	18,600	19,182	582
			84	12,401	49,199	50,911	1,712
	V	W	83	5,622	13,460	14,339	879
			84	11,244	31,226	33,163	1,937
			85	9,921	4,732	5,400	668
FR GERM	A	E	81	275	2,643	2,793	150
	N	E	86	4,312	20,944	21,740	796
	V	E	82	400	1,853	1,917	64
			83	800	3,919	4,008	89
			84	800	3,423	3,495	72
			85	797	5,399	5,531	132
			86	4,762	20,742	21,096	354
FRANCE	N	E	82	7,442	41,575	42,676	1,101
			86	4,739	46,331	47,104	773
	V	E	83	6,570	71,099	72,438	1,339
			84	3,969	50,281	50,946	665
			85	6,833	64,624	65,651	1,027

Crop Product TSUSA commodity number, description, and unit of quantity — Country	Mode	Reg	Yr	Quantity	F.A.S.	C.I.F.	Charges
ITALY	A	E	86	110	2,588	2,668	80
	V	E	81	375	7,024	7,107	83
			82	761	10,431	10,607	176
			83	750	15,135	15,351	216
JAPAN	V	W	86	562	2,159	2,277	118
MEXICO	O	E	84	745,290	197,786	197,786	
			85	144,051	53,093	53,093	
			86	157,849	59,858	59,858	
NETHLDS	V	E	83	2,039	16,448	16,675	227
			84	1,158	11,153	11,417	264
			85	419	3,649	3,752	103
			86	3,858	40,711	41,458	747
U KING	V	E	82	1,190	5,323	5,423	100
USSR	V	E	81	783	5,082	5,310	212
			82	52	525	553	28
			83	772	6,739	6,894	155
			84	22	437	442	5
			85	772	6,291	6,400	109
			86	110	1,501	1,518	17

Pine, plywood
2401200 PLYWD, FACE PLY, PARA PINE (MSF)

Country	Mode	Reg	Yr	Quantity	F.A.S.	C.I.F.	Charges
TOTAL			81	264	97,063	117,879	20,816
			82	416	157,516	185,568	28,052
			83	2,764	607,596	728,395	120,799
			84	3,748	890,783	1,111,808	221,025
			85	12,229	2,172,312	2,688,711	516,399
			86	11,947	2,911,396	3,519,087	607,691
BRAZIL	N	E	84	1,997	495,207	611,145	115,938
			85	7,506	1,322,363	1,621,275	298,912
	V	E	81	226	86,052	104,999	18,947
			82	204	92,129	109,438	17,309
			83	1,440	442,651	560,195	117,544
			84	1,558	316,888	420,176	103,288
			85	4,695	835,219	1,050,639	215,420
			86	11,698	2,844,595	3,440,500	595,905
	V	W	81	16	5,678	7,122	1,444
			82	93	28,987	38,981	9,994
			84	15	4,909	6,601	1,692
			86	32	8,119	12,001	3,882
C RICA	V	E	81	22	5,333	5,758	425
			86	74	19,443	21,988	2,545
CANADA	O	E	82	12	3,566	3,566	
			85	4	3,259	3,259	
DOM REP	V	E	86	5	1,139	1,139	
HONDURA	V	E	82	21	8,816	9,565	749
			85	24	11,471	13,538	2,067
			86	51	14,446	16,670	2,224
MEXICO	O	E	83	34	10,264	10,264	
			84	116	52,815	52,815	
	O	W	82	86	24,018	24,018	
			83	1,135	129,079	129,079	
			84	60	18,266	18,266	
NORWAY	V	W	84	2	2,698	2,805	107
PHIL R	V	E	86	87	23,654	26,789	3,135
	V	W	83	146	22,777	25,806	3,029
U KING	A	E	83	9	2,825	3,051	226

2401600 PLYWD, FACE PLY EU RED PINE (MSF)

Country	Mode	Reg	Yr	Quantity	F.A.S.	C.I.F.	Charges
TOTAL			83	1	376	392	16
			84	67	14,394	15,107	713
			85	1,316	41,478	45,663	4,185
			86	792	168,971	200,182	31,211
BELGIUM	V	W	86	18	9,810	11,496	1,686
BRAZIL	V	E	85	4	1,350	1,631	281
			86	4	1,750	2,087	337
CHINA T	V	E	84	67	14,394	15,107	713
			85	170	26,318	28,319	2,001
FINLAND	V	E	85	1,142	13,810	15,713	1,903
FR GERM	V	W	86	33	24,305	27,425	3,120
HG KONG	V	W	83	1	376	392	16
HONDURA	V	E	86	26	5,841	6,780	939
INDNSIA	V	E	86	117	15,167	16,359	1,192
MEXICO	O	E	86	18	3,994	3,994	
SINGAPR	V	E	86	268	40,448	45,076	4,628
USSR	V	E	86	308	67,656	86,965	19,309

Pine, pulpwood, logs
2003557 PINE PULPWOOD LOGS (CD)

Country	Mode	Reg	Yr	Quantity	F.A.S.	C.I.F.	Charges
TOTAL			81	5,719	390,692	403,966	13,274
			82	1,540	88,299	88,299	
			83	732	27,367	27,367	
			84	218	8,258	8,258	
			86	307	30,273	37,749	7,476
CANADA	O	E	81	4,714	287,905	287,905	
			82	1,540	88,299	88,299	
			83	732	27,367	27,367	
			84	218	8,258	8,258	
			86	42	5,434	5,434	
	O	W	86	5	1,002	1,002	
	V	W	81	1,005	102,787	116,061	13,274
FR GERM	V	E	86	130	11,424	12,688	1,264
N ZEAL	V	E	86	130	12,413	18,625	6,212

Pine, veneer
2403200 WOOD-VNER PANEL PARANA PINE (MSF)

Country	Mode	Reg	Yr	Quantity	F.A.S.	C.I.F.	Charges
TOTAL			81	2	11,750	16,325	4,575
			82	154	14,182	15,840	1,658
			83	435	31,587	31,587	
			84	391	91,478	101,173	9,695
			85	221	95,804	115,041	19,237
			86	6,367	145,540	159,247	13,707
AUSTRAL	V	W	81	2	11,750	16,325	4,575
BRAZIL	V	E	84	44	40,319	49,019	8,700
			85	98	41,223	47,513	6,290
			86	1,343	41,785	47,100	5,315
	V	W	85	11	8,986	11,728	2,742
CANADA	N	E	82	*	293	293	
	O	E	83	435	31,587	31,587	
			84	182	30,568	30,568	
			86	416	65,288	65,288	
ECUADOR	V	E	85	112	45,595	55,800	10,205
			86	3,204	8,340	9,840	1,500
FR GERM	V	E	84	156	19,742	20,737	995
INDNSIA	V	E	86	404	25,714	32,514	6,800
IVY CST	O	E	84	9	849	849	
PANAMA	V	E	82	154	13,889	15,547	1,658
U KING	V	E	86	1,000	4,413	4,505	92

2403600 WOOD-VNER PANEL EUR RED PINE (MSF)

Country	Mode	Reg	Yr	Quantity	F.A.S.	C.I.F.	Charges
TOTAL			83	7	2,383	3,178	795
			84	2	566	735	169
			85	37	13,451	15,360	1,909
BRAZIL	V	E	84	2	566	735	169
FINLAND	V	E	85	37	13,451	15,360	1,909
SWEDEN	V	E	83	7	2,383	3,178	795

2405200 WD-VNER PANLS,1 SDE PARA PIN (MSF)

Country	Mode	Reg	Yr	Quantity	F.A.S.	C.I.F.	Charges
TOTAL			81	*	797	797	
			83	1,757	243,777	296,900	53,123
			84	49	32,032	39,817	7,785
			86	42	10,816	11,481	665
BRAZIL	V	E	83	1,757	243,777	296,900	53,123
			84	49	32,032	39,817	7,785
			86	42	10,816	11,481	665
CANADA	N	E	81	*	797	797	

2405600 WD-VNER PANLS, 1 SIDE, EU RD (MSF)

Country	Mode	Reg	Yr	Quantity	F.A.S.	C.I.F.	Charges
TOTAL			81	30	1,523	1,523	
			83	4	10,716	11,466	750
			84	8	340	574	234
			85	6	6,355	6,355	
			86	479	57,341	59,015	1,674
CANADA	O	E	81	30	1,523	1,523	
			85	6	6,355	6,355	
CHINA T	V	E	84	8	340	574	234
U KING	A	E	83	4	10,716	11,466	750
	V	E	86	479	57,341	59,015	1,674

Crop
Product
TSUSA commodity number, description, and unit of quantity

Country	Mode	Reg	Yr	Quantity	F.A.S.	C.I.F.	Charges

Terpineol
4607500 TERPINEOL NOT ARTIFICIAL MIX (LB)

Country	Mode	Reg	Yr	Quantity	F.A.S.	C.I.F.	Charges
TOTAL			81	715,835	639,732	708,000	68,256
			82	653,471	736,096	805,885	69,789
			83	645,051	590,377	641,172	50,795
			84	873,739	615,790	687,198	71,408
			85	489,523	351,350	397,900	46,550
			86	278,182	256,633	284,513	27,880
AUSTRAL	A	E	83	408	5,918	6,379	461
			84	408	6,289	6,956	667
			86	255	5,683	6,223	540
BRAZIL	V	E	84	28,572	13,443	16,869	3,426
CHINA M	V	E	81	192,467	110,544	123,629	13,085
			83	123,579	78,475	91,562	13,087
			84	311,103	159,759	192,016	32,257
			85	14,587	6,863	8,346	1,483
	V	W	81	33,852	19,712	22,478	2,766
			82	34,260	27,526	30,731	3,205
CHINA T	N	E	85	1,600	27,112	28,403	1,291
	V	E	82	882	6,053	6,261	208
			83	400	5,316	5,495	179
			84	2,000	31,473	32,211	738
			86	2,400	39,932	40,894	962
F W IND	V	E	85	2,866	2,655	2,730	75
FR GERM	A	E	85	55	1,339	1,395	56
			86	55	1,561	1,639	78
	N	E	82	1,988	59,149	60,013	864
	V	E	81	400	9,598	9,756	146
			83	39,683	26,420	28,271	1,851
FRANCE	N	E	81	362,872	366,878	399,834	32,956
			82	476,954	515,307	556,138	40,831
			83	343,258	302,081	317,716	15,635
			84	424,583	283,220	305,866	22,646
	V	E	81	882	3,830	3,912	82
			83	4,409	5,322	5,941	619
			84	4,409	4,591	5,009	418
			85	282,106	180,911	201,410	20,499
			86	116,535	81,428	88,442	7,014
HG KONG	V	E	84	10,417	2,550	4,017	1,467
			85	6,208	2,618	3,379	761
NETHLDS	N	E	82	2,934	6,449	7,109	660
			83	2,646	1,977	2,302	325
			84	23,690	13,732	15,326	1,594
	V	E	85	73,445	55,320	57,614	2,294
			86	10,804	8,154	8,341	187
PORTUGL	V	E	81	11,023	11,434	13,315	1,881
			82	13,603	15,144	16,887	1,743
			83	28,221	21,899	26,372	4,473
			84	22,046	18,926	23,007	4,081
			85	54,532	39,564	49,605	10,041
			86	69,666	58,059	68,707	10,648
SPAIN	V	E	81	81,932	92,329	104,139	11,810
			82	6,614	6,246	7,450	1,204
			83	63,823	49,478	56,525	7,047
			84	4,431	3,884	4,316	432
			85	51,367	28,059	37,941	9,882
			86	78,467	61,816	70,267	8,451
SWITZLD	V	E	84	30,479	54,889	57,243	2,354
U KING	A	E	82	295	1,026	1,380	354
			84	999	8,169	8,820	651
	N	E	81	32,407	25,407	30,937	5,530
			82	115,941	99,196	119,916	20,720
			83	38,624	93,491	100,609	7,118
			84	10,602	14,865	15,542	677
	V	E	85	2,757	6,909	7,077	168

Pineapple

Pineapple, candied
1544500 PINEAPPLES CANDIED ETC (LB)

Country	Mode	Reg	Yr	Quantity	F.A.S.	C.I.F.	Charges
TOTAL			81	6,310,559	5,575,203	5,939,530	364,327
			82	3,811,733	3,358,529	3,585,219	226,690
			83	4,334,929	3,694,330	3,909,377	215,047
			84	3,884,764	3,511,218	3,860,399	349,181
			85	7,714,922	6,326,211	6,795,277	469,066
			86	5,650,298	4,245,098	4,491,054	245,956
AUSTRAL	N	W	83	970	1,490	1,699	209
	V	E	81	220	419	594	175
			82	694	1,278	1,421	143
			83	7,035	12,136	12,729	593
			84	3,019	3,963	4,100	137
			85	18,654	29,314	30,598	1,284
			86	5,556	9,266	9,615	349
	V	W	81	1,389	2,505	2,589	84
			82	1,389	2,718	2,841	123
			84	611	1,082	1,122	40
			85	2,180	5,794	5,938	144
			86	1,323	2,105	2,161	56
CANADA	O	E	84	231	257	257	
			86	40,800	15,846	15,846	
CHINA M	O	W	84	338	397	421	24
	V	E	83	37,674	32,674	34,613	1,939
	V	W	84	224	502	542	40
CHINA T	N	E	83	507,519	447,699	480,741	33,042
	N	W	81	770,587	784,660	828,977	44,317
			82	513,369	456,148	479,721	23,573
			84	397,428	348,480	386,563	38,083
	O	E	81	26,400	13,137	15,739	2,602
	O	W	82	6,614	6,086	6,451	365
	V	E	81	2,333,674	2,075,639	2,216,354	140,715
			82	1,094,736	968,743	1,044,508	75,765
			83	46,737	39,297	41,625	2,328
			84	585,689	489,309	531,518	42,209
			85	804,562	601,940	652,734	50,794
			86	249,595	184,782	201,613	16,831
	V	H	81	200	256	275	19
			82	1,250	1,506	1,656	150
	V	W	81	1,804,849	1,684,444	1,783,956	99,512
			82	944,652	933,773	986,815	53,042
			83	926,630	862,781	902,171	39,390
			84	364,084	359,437	380,178	20,741
			85	1,117,879	984,685	1,036,354	51,669
			86	1,128,108	903,209	947,771	44,562
DOM REP	A	E	84	2,200	330	477	147
FR GERM	A	E	86	1,230	4,233	5,384	1,151
	V	E	81	145	592	615	23
			83	476	943	982	39
FRANCE	V	E	81	43,201	25,730	29,333	3,603
			85	530	1,075	1,113	38
HG KONG	V	E	81	70,474	57,495	61,469	3,974
	V	W	83	4,400	3,652	4,096	444
			84	35,274	31,350	33,165	1,815
			85	721,474	649,468	694,002	44,534
			86	174,164	126,837	134,274	7,437
INDIA	V	W	86	39,683	33,840	35,563	1,723
ITALY	V	E	86	1,732	4,446	5,144	698
JAPAN	V	E	81	22,046	14,431	18,137	3,706
			83	35,273	28,746	30,800	2,054
	V	W	84	176,369	162,900	173,032	10,132
KOR REP	V	E	81	13,228	6,263	7,334	1,071
PHIL R	N	W	84	71,868	57,105	61,255	4,150
	V	E	81	121,033	75,762	84,067	8,305
			82	66,977	40,346	44,933	4,587
			83	97,884	75,560	80,387	4,827
			84	60,845	51,060	54,753	3,693
			85	35,274	25,600	28,070	2,470
	V	W	81	174,801	118,628	129,425	10,797
			82	17,637	14,080	14,689	609
			83	95,172	72,058	76,286	4,228
			85	99,507	89,608	96,687	7,079
			86	163,455	105,603	118,073	12,470
REP SAF	V	E	82	1,500	988	1,125	137
			83	7,200	4,555	5,400	845
SINGAPR	V	E	83	35,274	28,847	30,600	1,753
			86	220,460	132,419	142,789	10,370
	V	W	83	13,228	12,257	12,847	590
			85	19,842	14,760	16,158	1,398
SWEDEN	V	E	86	529	1,310	1,355	45
SWITZLD	V	E	82	802	1,683	1,773	90
			83	2,956	6,603	6,867	264
			84	1,849	4,291	4,443	152
			85	792	2,384	2,447	63
			86	529	1,251	1,377	126
	V	W	82	185	399	427	28
			83	740	1,628	1,758	130
			84	979	2,172	2,357	185
			85	3,704	7,172	7,800	628
			86	538	1,901	2,005	104
THAILND	A	E	84	35,274	32,960	73,331	40,371
	N	E	82	976,066	771,977	830,647	58,670
			85	2,456,744	1,860,048	2,005,650	145,602

Crop
Product
TSUSA commodity number, description, and unit of quantity

Country	Mode	Reg	Yr	Quantity	F.A.S.	C.I.F.	Charges
	N	W	84	228,410	269,852	351,520	81,668
			85	897,250	722,485	796,957	74,472
			86	945,840	782,663	823,110	40,447
	V	E	81	688,939	503,423	540,133	36,710
			82	91,930	75,550	81,065	5,515
			83	1,718,078	1,396,403	1,487,023	90,620
			84	1,135,428	978,283	1,043,422	65,139
			85	77,601	60,073	64,907	4,834
			86	1,103,510	707,254	756,519	49,265
	V	W	81	309,847	269,314	282,002	12,688
			82	93,932	83,254	87,147	3,893
			83	780,046	651,791	682,069	30,278
			84	784,644	717,488	757,943	40,455
			85	1,388,455	1,214,310	1,294,393	80,083
			86	1,561,958	1,226,133	1,285,255	59,122
TURKEY	V	E	83	17,637	15,210	16,684	1,474
VENEZ	A	E	86	11,288	2,000	3,200	1,200

Pineapple, canned
1489820 PINEAPPLES, CANNED (LB)

Country	Mode	Reg	Yr	Quantity	F.A.S.	C.I.F.	Charges
TOTAL			81	429,725,836	117,220,499	148,318,914	27,753,791
			82	427,803,566	118,911,150	148,236,845	29,325,695
			83	404,913,319	114,675,527	137,709,841	23,034,314
			84	418,096,146	120,826,764	145,626,506	24,799,742
			85	526,627,312	148,960,335	179,468,995	30,508,660
			86	553,186,664	153,048,150	181,093,829	28,045,679
ARGENT	V	E	86	2,480	3,437	3,554	117
AUSTRAL	V	E	85	34,506	9,286	11,436	2,150
	V	W	86	53,334	12,853	20,496	7,643
BELGIUM	V	E	84	68,212	19,836	23,264	3,428
BRAZIL	V	E	82	33,705	9,042	10,542	1,500
			84	432,685	121,166	150,255	29,089
			85	1,287,575	375,114	451,757	76,643
			86	177,595	49,832	56,014	6,182
	V	W	83	1,283	6,460	6,752	292
			85	248,647	70,359	86,604	16,245
BURMA	V	W	82	36,288	6,990	8,614	1,624
C RICA	V	E	82	2,465	835	993	158
			83	4,343	2,440	3,047	607
			85	43,111	26,090	29,020	2,930
CANADA	O	E	81	970	10,972	10,972	
			82	7,518	14,515	14,515	
			83	7,790	3,632	3,632	
			84	4,660	5,877	5,877	
			85	35,059	39,626	39,626	
			86	57,931	61,367	61,367	
	O	H	86	814,710	427,723	427,723	
	O	W	82	690	822	822	
	V	E	86	67,200	17,269	19,669	2,400
CHINA M	O	W	85	36,542	10,200	11,258	1,058
	V	E	81	316,490	65,051	87,150	22,099
			82	3,000	733	935	202
			83	255,843	65,873	83,636	17,763
			84	1,374,596	350,170	421,273	71,103
			85	853,662	207,668	265,968	58,300
			86	513,028	112,073	135,836	23,763
	V	W	81	694,827	150,421	183,924	33,503
			82	98,763	15,332	19,822	4,490
			83	510,172	119,760	139,054	19,294
			84	1,331,652	312,536	379,122	66,586
			85	549,180	133,784	155,540	21,756
			86	352,853	76,384	87,653	11,269
CHINA T	N	E	81	205,294	58,178	68,359	10,181
			82	51,600	12,202	15,531	3,329
	N	W	86	264,810	71,283	78,198	6,915
	O	E	81	4,013	1,230	1,323	93
			83	618	775	1,423	648
	O	W	81	8,989	1,824	2,424	600
			82	2,528	548	593	45
	V	E	81	5,390,722	1,478,290	1,741,768	263,478
			82	1,851,486	565,039	682,355	117,316
			83	887,664	285,340	331,854	46,514
			84	1,821,171	611,347	719,619	108,272
			85	3,509,883	1,237,932	1,448,922	210,990
			86	4,264,068	1,107,502	1,294,099	186,597
	V	W	81	5,454,612	1,583,648	1,812,312	228,664
			82	4,859,451	1,467,544	1,703,415	235,871
			83	1,676,421	512,549	579,050	66,501
			84	1,799,654	663,004	743,468	80,464
			85	5,444,473	1,719,327	1,958,200	238,873
			86	3,941,427	1,057,280	1,186,572	129,292
COLOMB	V	E	85	2,195	1,270	1,486	216
			86	4,495	2,400	2,640	240
CYPRUS	V	E	81	34,019	9,341	11,088	1,747
			82	68,832	17,325	20,437	3,112
			84	166,939	54,057	62,317	8,260
DOM REP	A	E	81	560	1,540	1,971	431
	V	E	82	3,690	2,918	3,232	314
			83	35,295	9,736	11,401	1,665
			84	34,016	13,732	15,168	1,436
			85	223,866	94,172	104,374	10,202
			86	142,501	61,773	67,069	5,296
ECUADOR	V	E	84	31,848	10,638	12,279	1,641
FRANCE	N	E	84	7,220	6,049	7,694	1,645
	O	E	86	12,680	3,677	3,677	
	V	E	81	587	441	506	65
			82	38,065	6,662	9,503	2,841
			84	825	323	375	52
			86	1,748	1,511	1,684	173
	V	W	81	37,642	8,434	10,185	1,751
			82	173	692	740	48
GREECE	O	E	83	397	498	915	417
GUATMAL	O	E	86	34,800	10,440	10,440	
	V	E	81	29,738	14,293	17,668	3,375
			84	10,391	3,977	4,860	883
			85	20,048	3,731	5,045	1,314
			86	46,987	10,078	14,426	4,348
	V	W	85	23,040	8,064	10,172	2,108
HG KONG	V	E	81	610,504	157,538	187,798	30,260
			82	32,481	7,845	10,023	2,178
			83	164,860	48,598	56,781	8,183
			84	1,131,816	331,491	394,771	63,280
			85	1,121,938	335,566	381,536	45,970
			86	1,560,635	409,407	482,887	73,480
	V	W	81	127,892	33,302	38,536	5,234
			82	399,014	108,069	125,741	17,672
			83	1,073,592	390,532	431,365	40,833
			84	352,214	148,473	165,819	17,346
			85	248,281	73,139	82,207	9,068
			86	437,877	120,437	137,910	17,473
HONDURA	V	E	84	7,530	3,200	3,668	468
			85	40,400	2,020	4,898	2,878
			86	58,071	7,240	12,049	4,809
HUNGARY	V	E	85	33,561	6,246	7,592	1,346
INDIA	V	E	84	33,468	10,182	11,946	1,764
			85	33,600	9,566	11,934	2,368
			86	45,836	15,678	19,197	3,519
	V	W	86	38,119	9,345	10,545	1,200
INDNSIA	V	E	85	3,794,111	1,135,401	1,406,746	271,345
			86	9,730,506	2,403,159	2,946,714	543,555
	V	W	85	1,990,255	764,759	905,621	140,862
			86	2,285,796	563,916	683,665	119,749
ISRAEL	O	E	83	286	429	454	25
	V	E	86	107,144	23,985	29,296	5,311
ITALY	V	E	84	2,498	5,080	5,412	332
			86	90,000	20,700	25,345	4,645
	V	W	81	67,500	17,072	19,946	2,874
			82	29,401	7,791	9,727	1,936
IVY CST	O	E	81	5,100	1,669	1,669	
	V	E	81	3,538,341	795,065	1,022,376	227,311
			82	1,156,301	246,188	305,714	59,526
			83	136,553	30,221	36,804	6,583
			85	262,200	105,758	120,519	14,761
			86	196,650	67,186	82,936	15,750
	V	W	81	37,478	15,716	18,095	2,379
			82	57,376	33,578	37,360	3,782
JAMAICA	V	E	81	2,977	1,479	1,695	216
			83	1,763	2,557	2,930	373
			86	1,062	1,288	1,485	197
JAPAN	V	E	81	237,493	54,537	66,607	12,070
			82	300,998	77,194	93,868	16,674
			83	168,666	47,848	56,967	9,119
			84	792,019	239,445	296,705	57,260
			85	68,175	20,715	25,051	4,336
			86	98,190	33,478	39,079	5,601
	V	W	81	138,710	34,517	40,742	6,225
			82	244,606	60,672	71,252	10,580
			83	36,952	11,330	12,879	1,549
			84	169,674	73,587	84,156	10,569
			85	34,500	10,638	12,238	1,600
			86	69,001	17,020	20,648	3,628
KIRIBAT	V	E	84	38,966	9,613	10,811	1,198
			85	65,550	26,704	30,933	4,229
KOR REP	V	E	82	67,305	18,337	21,740	3,403
			83	271,832	73,256	84,756	11,500

Crop
Product
TSUSA commodity number, description, and unit of quantity

Country	Mode	Reg	Yr	Quantity	F.A.S.	C.I.F.	Charges
			84	32,724	9,430	11,608	2,178
			85	35,328	10,824	13,624	2,800
	V	W	85	33,332	10,147	11,647	1,500
LESOTHO	V	E	83	33,075	7,694	9,194	1,500
MACAO	V	E	81	36,288	8,916	11,313	2,397
MALAYSA	N	W	85	4,576,405	1,323,116	1,543,778	220,662
	V	E	81	3,960,019	1,019,671	1,271,554	251,883
			82	3,021,045	798,771	998,167	199,396
			83	2,344,671	645,675	782,155	136,480
			84	1,739,009	520,832	628,509	107,677
			85	1,736,234	551,197	666,469	115,272
			86	2,281,961	626,245	732,577	106,332
	V	W	81	2,539,101	620,105	753,880	127,434
			82	6,603,275	1,684,780	2,009,989	325,209
			83	7,175,343	2,137,743	2,438,881	301,138
			84	5,840,046	1,681,028	1,965,036	284,008
			85	3,089,671	749,088	863,151	114,063
			86	9,050,750	2,355,759	2,707,584	351,825
MAURITN	V	E	83	101,892	27,173	32,012	4,839
MEXICO	O	E	81	9,530,831	2,629,222	2,629,222	
			82	7,710,680	2,403,037	2,403,037	
			83	6,383,220	1,899,190	1,899,190	
			84	6,445,464	1,892,664	1,892,664	
			85	8,956,458	2,432,683	2,432,683	
			86	12,481,998	3,150,564	3,150,729	165
	O	W	81	87,000	25,635	27,385	1,750
			83	952	306	306	
			86	32,853	10,985	10,985	
	V	E	81	1,500,272	507,516	564,893	57,377
			85	68,860	23,078	26,253	3,175
			86	1,029,217	282,898	312,140	29,242
	V	W	84	119,000	41,736	47,292	5,556
			85	133,920	57,286	63,050	5,764
			86	169,920	54,374	63,493	9,119
NAMIBIA	V	E	81	205,081	46,293	55,207	8,914
			82	60,085	17,173	21,708	4,535
			84	34,019	12,079	14,034	1,955
NETHLDS	V	E	84	38,966	9,851	11,506	1,655
			86	1,895	2,327	2,553	226
PAKISTN	V	W	86	152,013	40,541	50,191	9,650
PHIL R	N	W	81	106,069,780	29,151,876	39,787,169	7,526,202
			83	102,367,967	27,937,362	34,774,242	6,836,880
	V	E	81	75,091,220	22,474,466	29,491,272	6,896,091
			82	82,841,905	24,813,818	32,235,076	7,421,258
			83	98,574,434	29,804,884	36,247,172	6,442,288
			84	61,396,386	18,384,958	23,010,388	4,625,430
			85	112,012,555	30,945,534	38,673,787	7,728,253
			86	89,707,628	26,884,652	33,510,090	6,625,438
	V	H	81	6,293,220	1,798,330	2,320,425	522,095
			82	34,740	10,977	14,083	3,106
			83	65,430	17,862	20,954	3,092
			84	1,890	2,144	2,613	469
			85	97,200	25,800	30,557	4,757
			86	669,600	192,592	213,332	20,740
	V	W	81	4,459,812	1,285,509	1,748,717	355,501
			82	123,164,419	34,253,301	43,417,516	9,164,215
			83	3,737,897	1,007,209	1,249,667	242,458
			84	143,834,563	37,267,340	45,661,818	8,394,478
			85	159,750,198	42,751,708	52,183,444	9,431,736
			86	146,890,323	41,214,668	49,242,632	8,027,964
PORTUGL	V	E	82	550	1,320	1,610	290
			83	34,020	8,194	9,751	1,557
REP SAF	N	E	81	712,137	167,014	204,301	37,287
			83	1,416,074	369,172	436,151	66,979
			85	13,673,374	4,316,338	4,984,907	668,569
			86	666,650	151,268	183,186	31,918
	O	E	81	69,776	22,452	25,367	2,915
	V	E	81	17,389,709	4,186,914	5,118,907	931,993
			82	25,782,706	6,561,993	7,822,486	1,260,493
			83	30,438,686	8,256,690	9,721,169	1,464,479
			84	24,409,283	7,833,699	9,039,771	1,206,072
			85	14,880,114	4,454,791	5,196,397	741,606
			86	16,897,292	4,190,807	5,015,729	824,922
	V	W	81	33,999	5,997	8,270	2,273
			82	34,019	5,709	9,217	3,508
			84	273,022	83,855	95,063	11,208
			85	137,618	44,877	47,918	3,041
			86	37,422	11,935	14,035	2,100
RWANDA	V	W	85	5,216	1,465	1,566	101
S ARAB	V	E	85	34,000	10,653	12,390	1,737
			86	37,075	7,921	9,571	1,650
SINGAPR	N	E	85	1,245,881	388,485	458,307	69,822
	O	E	86	45,903	10,316	12,342	2,026
	V	E	81	2,732,305	686,165	848,074	161,909
			82	3,996,788	1,062,579	1,337,303	274,724
			83	3,602,301	1,030,914	1,226,992	196,078
			84	3,721,734	1,211,490	1,435,937	224,447
			85	3,288,083	1,026,738	1,216,838	190,100
			86	7,997,733	2,019,878	2,405,796	385,918
	V	W	81	8,153,434	2,019,438	2,409,413	389,779
			82	6,598,679	1,725,897	2,121,311	395,414
			83	4,856,500	1,343,994	1,552,529	208,535
			84	5,453,113	1,595,707	1,859,954	264,247
			85	3,567,548	1,094,760	1,264,672	169,912
			86	3,232,736	892,916	1,011,646	118,730
SOMALIA	N	E	85	366,087	115,108	133,854	18,746
SPAIN	V	E	84	116,624	31,762	38,601	6,839
			85	578,744	167,721	197,232	29,511
SRI LKA	V	E	83	34,106	7,552	9,152	1,600
SWAZLND	N	E	85	132,300	41,527	48,824	7,297
	O	E	86	34,010	8,497	10,920	2,423
	V	E	84	34,020	10,512	12,165	1,653
			85	465,550	148,921	173,402	24,481
			86	342,666	96,343	114,206	17,863
SWITZLD	V	E	82	138,211	37,580	44,447	6,867
			85	39,411	9,550	11,270	1,720
			86	34,010	9,371	11,021	1,650
THAILND	A	E	84	220	287	1,164	877
	N	E	83	1,452,139	380,247	449,930	69,683
			84	32,845,487	9,766,388	11,789,289	2,022,901
			85	40,878,236	11,230,579	13,493,451	2,262,872
			86	32,882,767	8,525,298	10,176,845	1,651,547
	N	W	81	17,046,388	4,143,184	4,874,366	731,182
			82	15,871,674	4,214,944	4,891,178	676,234
			83	13,064,990	3,540,950	4,064,475	523,525
			84	10,692,629	3,207,963	3,695,681	487,718
			85	12,562,638	3,946,451	4,499,980	553,529
			86	9,340,112	2,215,888	2,550,995	335,107
	O	E	83	4,508	4,174	4,174	
	O	W	86	2,161	2,543	2,785	242
	V	E	81	104,075,106	27,770,044	33,926,800	6,156,184
			82	99,419,662	27,066,781	33,569,510	6,502,729
			83	93,918,619	26,142,396	31,084,727	4,942,331
			84	73,636,567	21,976,826	26,709,020	4,732,194
			85	79,916,001	23,072,136	28,047,736	4,975,600
			86	118,370,224	32,662,068	38,230,225	5,568,157
	V	H	81	1,278,098	361,435	476,928	115,493
			86	3,087,543	893,016	1,033,529	140,513
	V	W	81	51,317,005	13,746,465	16,358,226	2,611,759
			82	42,684,479	11,448,302	14,027,370	2,579,068
			83	29,322,092	8,300,502	9,624,487	1,323,985
			84	37,095,186	12,062,673	13,920,789	1,858,116
			85	43,846,438	13,420,423	15,413,450	1,993,027
			86	72,048,577	19,714,820	22,300,103	2,585,283
TUNISIA	V	E	85	210,189	65,397	78,258	12,861
			86	35,971	9,022	10,568	1,546
	V	W	84	103,452	30,390	36,484	6,094
U KING	V	E	81	200,797	49,294	60,111	10,817
			82	457,435	115,481	137,529	22,048
			83	682,048	174,908	206,497	31,589
			84	620,688	199,367	228,261	28,894
			85	305,365	96,819	111,417	14,598
			86	154,120	30,917	41,148	10,231
YUGOSLV	O	E	82	37,478	7,834	7,834	
	V	E	83	68,025	18,902	22,334	3,432

Pineapple, fresh

1489000 PINEAPPLES, FRESH, IN BULK (LB)

Country	Mode	Reg	Yr	Quantity	F.A.S.	C.I.F.	Charges
TOTAL			81	63,059,941	4,087,447	4,088,713	1,266
			82	46,623,870	2,340,213	2,358,008	17,795
			83	62,181,448	2,003,802	2,008,208	4,406
			84	34,224,561	1,180,459	1,261,134	80,675
			85	13,227,900	533,415	614,637	81,222
			86	6,400,262	365,937	444,739	78,802
C RICA	V	E	85	114,789	24,460	35,211	10,751
			86	336,194	30,161	40,499	10,338
	V	W	86	157,602	24,200	42,954	18,754
CANADA	O	E	83	121,838	4,424	4,424	
			84	32,893	2,387	2,387	
			86	31,200	2,600	2,600	
COLOMB	A	E	85	23,042	2,321	2,393	72
	N	E	82	21,750	2,545	4,126	1,581
	V	E	85	17,053	6,375	7,475	1,100
			86	15,928	2,720	2,920	200
DOM REP	N	E	82	90,638	33,186	46,735	13,549

Crop
Product
TSUSA commodity number, description, and unit of quantity

Country	Mode	Reg	Yr	Quantity	F.A.S.	C.I.F.	Charges
			84	753,332	60,898	100,364	39,466
	V	E	82	8,000	600	1,148	548
			83	788	367	429	62
			84	71,368	9,155	13,253	4,098
			85	917,163	73,074	134,317	61,243
			86	284,334	29,826	44,903	15,077
F W IND	A	E	84	2,514	1,151	1,705	554
FRANCE	A	E	85	8,124	2,976	4,708	1,732
GUATMAL	A	E	81	17,637	2,400	3,666	1,266
	V	E	82	10,917	5,304	5,347	43
			84	33,440	2,956	5,413	2,457
			86	373,984	45,457	72,924	27,467
HONDURA	V	E	85	25,534	4,634	7,456	2,822
ITALY	V	E	84	2,134	3,522	3,749	227
IVY CST	A	E	83	2,167	2,060	3,060	1,000
			84	52,194	14,599	23,973	9,374
			85	30,277	13,614	15,134	1,520
JAPAN	V	W	84	495	1,124	1,229	105
MEXICO	O	E	81	62,783,419	4,050,988	4,050,988	
			82	46,131,071	2,243,144	2,243,144	
			83	61,399,190	1,920,861	1,920,861	
			84	33,049,418	1,019,634	1,019,635	1
			85	12,071,715	399,851	399,855	4
			86	5,106,219	200,825	200,825	
	O	W	81	258,885	34,059	34,059	
			82	313,754	48,457	48,457	
			83	645,040	72,424	72,424	
			84	89,851	8,140	8,140	
			86	37,100	8,495	8,495	
PANAMA	V	E	86	13,376	4,013	5,064	1,051
	V	W	86	32,885	15,300	19,655	4,355
REP SAF	A	E	83	12,425	3,666	7,010	3,344
			84	25,883	7,645	10,390	2,745
			85	15,564	5,030	6,397	1,367
SENEGAL	A	E	84	16,893	9,096	14,765	5,669
VENEZ	A	E	84	94,146	40,152	56,131	15,979
			85	4,639	1,080	1,691	611
			86	11,440	2,340	3,900	1,560
	V	E	82	47,740	6,977	9,051	2,074

1489300 PINEAPPLES, FRESH, IN CRATES (LB)

Country	Mode	Reg	Yr	Quantity	F.A.S.	C.I.F.	Charges
TOTAL			81	518,213	75,080	95,388	20,308
			82	1,317,657	196,973	300,686	103,713
			83	2,057,915	231,527	314,319	82,792
			84	1,459,375	164,442	249,940	85,498
			85	1,036,475	119,896	190,361	70,465
			86	1,534,965	162,283	234,618	72,335
C RICA	N	E	84	65,715	8,626	12,042	3,416
	V	E	81	287,234	49,901	62,489	12,588
			82	963,581	145,454	234,837	89,383
			83	32,738	6,270	10,073	3,803
			84	36,439	4,980	6,527	1,547
			85	366,733	43,886	68,243	24,357
			86	335,317	29,975	56,715	26,740
COLOMB	A	E	84	91,171	25,796	39,838	14,042
			85	10,584	3,120	3,436	316
	V	E	86	28,681	11,960	15,543	3,583
DOM REP	A	E	82	350	500	892	392
			84	2,397	770	1,058	288
	N	E	81	39,155	4,555	7,380	2,825
			83	170,349	39,305	48,595	9,290
			84	85,470	16,448	23,498	7,050
	O	E	84	6,106	970	1,324	354
	V	E	81	54,365	6,150	8,920	2,770
			82	203,995	14,752	19,941	5,189
			83	415,302	65,316	88,318	23,002
			84	684,911	56,985	90,339	33,354
			85	374,895	31,605	56,388	24,783
			86	244,828	18,992	34,200	15,208
DOMINCA	V	E	85	37,170	5,310	7,819	2,509
ECUADOR	V	E	85	39,640	3,369	3,473	104
F W IND	V	E	82	15,432	4,760	6,560	1,800
FRANCE	V	E	85	29,840	2,052	3,778	1,726
GUATMAL	A	E	81	26,279	4,011	6,136	2,125
	V	E	84	247,166	28,147	47,054	18,907
			85	148,843	25,759	38,929	13,170
			86	197,320	18,952	34,025	15,073
	V	W	85	28,770	4,795	8,295	3,500
HONDURA	N	E	82	30,070	4,005	10,410	6,405
	V	E	83	1,359,640	106,392	150,241	43,849
			84	240,000	21,720	28,260	6,540
			86	68,800	13,768	19,848	6,080
MEXICO	O	E	81	89,736	5,791	5,791	

Crop
Product
TSUSA commodity number, description, and unit of quantity

Country	Mode	Reg	Yr	Quantity	F.A.S.	C.I.F.	Charges
			83	6,944	1,838	1,838	
	O	W	81	21,444	4,672	4,672	
			82	103,501	26,891	26,891	
			83	34,060	3,226	3,226	
			86	559,381	51,444	51,444	
PANAMA	V	E	86	34,775	6,762	9,851	3,089
PORTUGL	A	E	82	728	611	1,155	544
			83	663	288	670	382
	N	E	86	41,995	2,950	4,616	1,666
THAILND	V	W	86	23,868	7,480	8,376	896
VENEZ	A	E	83	38,219	8,892	11,358	2,466

1489600 PINEAPPLES EX CRATED OR BULK (LB)

Country	Mode	Reg	Yr	Quantity	F.A.S.	C.I.F.	Charges
TOTAL			81	74,912,231	6,383,938	8,651,131	2,267,193
			82	82,309,836	6,968,192	10,012,533	3,044,341
			83	86,435,249	7,817,646	11,063,140	3,245,494
			84	98,730,457	9,728,995	13,708,378	3,979,383
			85	104,700,035	10,774,604	15,209,408	4,434,804
			86	156,367,251	17,825,416	23,974,971	6,149,555
BRAZIL	V	E	83	42,099	6,165	11,892	5,727
			84	1,125,064	124,286	225,089	100,803
C RICA	N	E	81	1,896,663	370,891	521,607	150,716
			83	5,058,272	570,564	903,597	333,033
			84	7,165,518	968,287	1,574,382	606,095
			85	9,667,993	1,261,846	2,053,389	791,543
			86	15,190,229	1,973,615	3,090,246	1,116,631
	V	E	81	318,918	59,454	67,568	8,114
			82	3,327,413	351,382	624,937	273,555
			83	3,070,293	490,465	581,404	90,939
			84	13,666,712	2,030,982	2,464,246	433,264
			85	17,221,511	2,515,342	3,106,957	591,615
			86	56,561,695	8,207,245	10,006,327	1,799,082
	V	W	83	31,200	3,510	9,010	5,500
CANADA	O	E	85	12,180	3,780	5,310	1,530
CHILE	V	E	83	1,079,760	84,491	119,313	34,822
COLOMB	A	E	83	156,031	34,406	52,591	18,185
			84	302,243	65,984	121,929	55,945
	N	E	85	409,427	127,871	180,242	52,371
	V	E	85	13,900	1,738	3,665	1,927
			86	364,296	40,726	58,486	17,760
DENMARK	V	E	84	32,574	3,977	5,857	1,880
DOM REP	N	E	81	430,460	32,701	55,248	22,547
			82	1,492,396	117,135	195,206	78,071
			83	2,819,503	228,583	403,405	174,822
			84	8,303,297	855,297	1,416,842	561,545
			85	9,494,111	854,744	1,511,690	656,946
	O	E	83	68,628	4,853	5,348	495
	V	E	81	4,635,440	346,710	626,455	279,745
			82	10,608,702	1,090,355	1,696,326	605,971
			83	9,605,578	888,600	1,454,165	565,565
			84	1,344,022	127,320	214,591	87,271
			85	2,156,762	201,553	335,926	134,373
			86	24,858,325	2,023,882	3,388,470	1,364,588
ECUADOR	A	E	83	31,800	3,051	4,090	1,039
			85	19,000	3,272	3,370	98
			86	37,794	11,114	16,273	5,159
	N	E	85	463,829	40,759	45,893	5,134
	V	E	81	74,407	7,000	8,101	1,101
F W IND	A	E	83	3,000	3,010	3,770	760
			85	7,810	3,226	4,735	1,509
	V	E	83	30,284	7,117	10,781	3,664
FRANCE	V	E	81	11,280	1,128	1,345	217
			84	31,476	2,932	5,223	2,291
GUATMAL	A	W	83	3,058	361	1,388	1,027
	N	E	81	321,609	45,554	68,788	23,234
			82	607,808	45,999	86,350	40,351
			85	1,010,031	154,924	249,097	94,173
	V	E	81	42,260	6,339	8,693	2,354
			82	84,375	5,800	9,255	3,455
			83	426,246	30,838	57,845	27,007
			84	43,000	4,100	6,328	2,228
			86	2,776,185	379,257	500,332	121,075
HAITI	V	E	82	41,740	5,440	8,949	3,509
HONDURA	V	E	81	63,519,645	5,195,277	6,928,390	1,733,113
			82	65,830,750	5,333,816	7,373,245	2,039,429
			83	62,655,244	5,353,945	7,332,871	1,978,926
			84	66,616,608	5,530,376	7,649,704	2,119,328
			85	64,016,210	5,540,958	7,611,064	2,070,106
			86	53,507,300	4,542,792	6,206,083	1,663,291
ITALY	V	E	84	2,975	391	409	18
IVY CST	A	E	81	301,054	58,811	104,863	46,052
			83	5,467	855	1,855	1,000
			85	10,626	3,835	3,835	

Crop Product TSUSA commodity number, description, and unit of quantity Country	Mode	Reg	Yr	Quantity	F.A.S.	C.I.F.	Charges
			86	14,301	3,614	6,721	3,107
	V	E	86	1,468,386	399,883	403,821	3,938
MACAO	A	E	85	4,000	1,788	2,271	483
MEXICO	O	E	81	3,360,495	260,073	260,073	
			82	300,652	16,025	16,025	
			83	1,258,284	58,147	58,147	
			86	931,260	56,667	56,667	
	O	W	82	16,000	2,240	2,240	
			83	59,980	44,985	44,985	
			84	3,060	765	765	
			86	5,963	7,459	7,459	
	V	E	85	88,200	18,900	22,365	3,465
PANAMA	A	E	85	82,738	20,443	29,220	8,777
	N	E	86	494,112	130,084	171,529	41,445
	V	E	84	80,170	11,000	18,166	7,166
			86	31,027	13,490	15,851	2,361
	V	W	86	41,964	15,040	17,089	2,049
PORTUGL	A	E	86	14,030	2,162	3,160	998
	V	E	85	3,131	1,700	2,179	479
REP SAF	A	E	85	272	10,425	11,527	1,102
THAILND	V	E	86	35,287	8,114	9,455	1,341
VENEZ	A	E	83	30,522	3,700	6,683	2,983
			84	13,738	3,298	4,847	1,549
			85	18,298	7,500	26,673	19,173
			86	35,097	10,272	17,002	6,730

Pineapple, jelly or jam
1532400 PINEAPPLE JELLY, JAM ETC (LB)

Country	Mode	Reg	Yr	Quantity	F.A.S.	C.I.F.	Charges
TOTAL			81	10,806	5,790	6,403	613
			82	17,300	10,692	11,686	994
			83	40,776	24,450	27,427	2,977
			84	178,950	78,118	88,802	10,684
			85	106,065	39,664	47,357	7,693
			86	132,296	65,827	73,129	7,302
BELGIUM	V	E	84	1,065	556	639	83
C RICA	V	E	83	9,000	6,138	6,521	383
			84	10,542	7,161	7,694	533
			85	22,939	5,837	7,163	1,326
			86	56,126	21,208	24,448	3,240
CHINA T	V	W	82	1,653	1,202	1,305	103
COLOMB	N	E	84	9,099	4,518	5,643	1,125
DENMARK	V	W	86	8,640	4,114	4,692	578
DOM REP	V	E	81	6,975	1,940	2,159	219
			84	105,851	26,683	31,041	4,358
			85	45,245	10,393	12,259	1,866
			86	24,516	10,468	11,426	958
FR GERM	V	E	86	1,111	1,358	1,414	56
	V	W	82	520	289	327	38
			83	360	281	316	35
FRANCE	V	E	81	1,076	812	901	89
			82	1,677	1,592	1,784	192
			83	3,868	2,189	2,654	465
			84	9,145	7,242	8,317	1,075
			85	1,031	1,180	1,352	172
	V	W	82	1,566	1,057	1,235	178
			83	17,218	11,561	13,025	1,464
			84	4,810	3,472	3,883	411
			85	1,950	1,394	1,606	212
GUATMAL	V	E	83	4,093	312	584	272
			85	3,325	1,285	1,435	150
IRELAND	V	E	83	3,672	2,429	2,692	263
ISRAEL	V	E	84	28,169	19,358	21,472	2,114
			85	30,226	17,905	20,974	3,069
			86	21,488	13,623	15,376	1,753
JAMAICA	V	E	86	3,991	2,159	2,366	207
MEXICO	O	E	82	6,600	2,445	2,445	
			86	8,532	7,338	7,338	
	O	W	83	1,397	410	410	
NETHLDS	V	E	86	3,691	1,323	1,551	228
PHIL R	V	E	82	502	508	541	33
			83	360	344	400	56
			84	2,436	1,632	1,905	273
	V	W	81	815	518	594	76
			82	3,972	2,666	3,058	392
			84	440	609	680	71
			86	1,884	1,540	1,654	114
SWITZLD	O	E	84	551	424	451	27
	V	E	83	556	513	533	20
			84	2,833	2,241	2,416	175
			86	2,317	2,696	2,864	168
	V	W	84	1,653	1,219	1,310	91

Crop Product TSUSA commodity number, description, and unit of quantity Country	Mode	Reg	Yr	Quantity	F.A.S.	C.I.F.	Charges
THAILND	V	W	81	525	476	525	49
U KING	V	E	81	1,415	2,044	2,224	180
			82	810	933	991	58
			83	252	273	292	19
			84	2,356	3,003	3,351	348
	V	W	85	1,349	1,670	2,568	898

Pineapple, juice, concentrated
1654600 PNAPPLE JUICE CONCENTRATED (GAL)

Country	Mode	Reg	Yr	Quantity	F.A.S.	C.I.F.	Charges
TOTAL			81	27,533,306	15,355,710	19,021,458	3,527,771
			82	29,795,625	17,497,576	22,173,027	4,675,451
			83	27,815,597	15,867,330	19,739,539	3,872,209
			84	33,147,400	23,037,271	27,737,588	4,700,317
			85	51,192,175	37,792,148	45,604,480	7,812,332
			86	57,440,598	39,897,664	47,569,038	7,671,374
BELGIUM	V	E	84	1,918	4,991	6,635	1,644
			85	458	4,005	4,805	800
			86	254	1,002	1,129	127
BRAZIL	N	E	84	676,787	664,551	729,232	64,681
			85	1,766,020	1,570,335	1,763,233	192,898
	O	E	83	64,688	54,067	62,084	8,017
			84	1,147,886	992,700	1,084,575	91,875
			85	3,355,297	2,895,728	3,181,140	285,412
			86	3,599,675	2,962,270	3,284,852	322,582
	V	E	81	1,467	789	898	109
			82	1,968	1,955	2,981	1,026
			83	345,801	342,859	376,967	34,108
			84	1,446,082	1,293,729	1,476,226	182,497
			85	340,089	304,924	342,623	37,699
			86	1,736,429	1,301,740	1,518,801	217,061
	V	W	84	40,883	27,788	35,412	7,624
			86	53,950	36,895	43,564	6,669
C RICA	V	E	86	272,160	136,080	148,880	12,800
CANADA	A	W	83	85	339	401	62
	O	E	81	3,005	4,201	4,201	
			82	6,209	16,469	16,469	
			83	152	270	270	
			84	1,040	1,414	1,414	
			85	23,660	35,133	35,133	
			86	33,170	32,138	32,138	
CHINA M	V	E	81	177	473	534	61
			83	8,220	1,666	2,309	643
	V	W	84	4,855	10,053	11,198	1,145
CHINA T	V	E	81	84,500	36,351	43,219	6,868
			84	130,523	77,585	91,008	13,423
			85	2,137,280	1,592,483	1,781,682	189,199
			86	994,591	646,661	745,984	99,323
	V	W	84	42,120	20,474	23,396	2,922
			85	56,515	33,348	37,084	3,736
			86	110,028	70,415	78,813	8,398
COLOMB	A	E	84	86	256	496	240
			85	37,277	21,300	30,592	9,292
	V	E	81	736	1,430	1,560	130
			82	2,286	4,200	4,607	407
DENMARK	O	E	84	127	676	860	184
DOM REP	N	E	83	83,066	75,328	84,983	9,655
	V	E	82	83,221	108,588	121,563	12,975
			83	164,722	70,122	78,122	8,000
			84	130,907	128,513	145,490	16,977
			85	170,384	115,409	130,998	15,589
			86	40,487	14,287	15,240	953
FR GERM	V	E	81	388	1,224	1,754	530
			83	250	415	436	21
			84	414	2,482	3,040	558
	V	W	83	37,800	50,598	52,920	2,322
			84	2,461	1,373	1,895	522
FR POLY	V	W	86	13,650	10,576	12,926	2,350
FRANCE	V	E	85	848	3,567	5,509	1,942
	V	W	84	2	258	295	37
GUATMAL	V	E	82	480	1,428	1,628	200
			83	432	676	743	67
			86	873	1,164	1,609	445
HG KONG	V	E	81	21,125	9,854	11,317	1,463
			84	198,575	138,876	152,728	13,852
			85	160,713	106,882	131,305	24,423
			86	213,046	153,789	167,586	13,797
	V	W	86	11,700	42,553	51,123	8,570
HONDURA	O	E	82	45,607	38,082	38,082	
			83	7,540	28,201	32,460	4,259
			84	12,548	11,025	13,025	2,000
			85	21,840	23,443	23,443	

Crop Product TSUSA commodity number, description, and unit of quantity Country	Mode	Reg	Yr	Quantity	F.A.S.	C.I.F.	Charges
	V	E	81	1,465,776	779,729	958,228	178,499
			82	1,130,922	596,478	757,738	161,260
			83	1,496,668	612,846	701,894	89,048
			84	556,239	647,586	703,209	55,623
			85	1,491,883	1,323,707	1,487,875	164,168
			86	1,814,734	1,144,632	1,269,763	125,131
ISRAEL	V	E	86	15,994	6,303	7,862	1,559
ITALY	V	E	83	1,489	6,166	6,636	470
			84	2,282	4,128	5,928	1,800
JAPAN	V	E	85	380	1,562	1,862	300
	V	W	83	35	511	549	38
			84	45	1,015	1,075	60
KOR REP	V	E	85	232,572	178,401	188,909	10,508
MALAYSA	V	E	86	258,278	150,840	192,677	41,837
MEXICO	A	E	81	5,144	3,858	5,011	1,153
			84	555	1,000	2,172	1,172
	N	E	85	5,179	15,779	19,236	3,457
	O	E	81	557,677	622,145	622,145	
			82	33,392	18,302	18,302	
			83	28,706	30,680	30,680	
			84	411,817	415,033	415,033	
			85	802,105	812,413	812,413	
			86	838,675	698,197	698,197	
	O	W	81	2,273	6,384	6,384	
			82	27,507	31,398	31,398	
			83	33,520	45,351	45,351	
			84	1,312	1,932	1,932	
	V	E	81	1,283	3,223	3,813	590
			85	125,000	120,750	140,295	19,545
			86	102,642	128,613	145,122	16,509
NETHLDS	V	E	84	19,800	32,670	36,590	3,920
			86	39,825	66,983	76,020	9,037
PERU	V	E	81	113	290	373	83
PHIL R	V	E	81	5,473,268	3,778,563	5,044,691	1,239,151
			82	3,832,118	2,746,262	3,626,100	879,838
			83	3,703,914	2,679,663	3,376,824	697,161
			84	3,275,852	2,304,132	2,910,973	606,841
			85	4,333,339	3,214,616	4,153,625	939,009
			86	3,990,931	2,970,392	3,830,144	859,752
	V	H	81	214,102	156,679	206,840	50,161
	V	W	81	5,013,744	2,462,462	3,251,852	678,390
			82	11,378,713	6,962,595	8,874,252	1,911,657
			83	8,117,421	4,404,132	5,584,106	1,179,974
			84	13,163,144	8,822,396	10,993,382	2,170,986
			85	17,469,031	12,729,899	16,243,241	3,513,342
			86	20,043,049	13,568,321	16,357,828	2,789,507
PORTUGL	V	E	81	1,200	4,357	7,307	2,950
			82	113	441	505	64
REP SAF	V	E	81	59,815	37,894	42,935	5,041
			82	186,269	124,590	161,580	36,990
			83	808,144	444,719	571,180	126,461
			84	700,940	510,359	575,363	65,004
			85	1,634,707	1,256,555	1,447,769	191,214
			86	488,204	359,154	444,581	85,427
SINGAPR	V	E	82	252,330	121,854	155,834	33,980
			84	20,625	10,705	12,878	2,173
			85	1,311,462	970,884	1,082,238	111,354
			86	1,617,042	1,032,783	1,206,375	173,592
	V	W	85	238,009	174,667	196,968	22,301
			86	11,700	38,223	48,512	10,289
SPAIN	V	E	85	2,631	7,725	9,427	1,702
			86	516	1,672	1,921	249
SWITZLD	V	E	83	207	900	1,086	186
			85	42,250	32,750	36,816	4,066
THAILND	O	E	86	18,525	23,390	23,390	
	V	E	81	7,584,799	3,842,720	4,636,258	793,538
			82	9,482,210	4,993,454	6,232,177	1,238,723
			83	10,439,015	5,738,924	7,129,312	1,390,388
			84	7,688,553	4,730,346	5,802,359	1,072,013
			85	9,533,843	6,321,962	7,708,069	1,386,107
			86	11,688,931	7,410,252	9,061,918	1,651,666
	V	H	81	63,180	39,366	48,369	9,003
			82	58,320	39,366	48,603	9,237
			83	124,200	111,780	140,602	28,822
			84	235,680	179,091	221,230	42,139
			85	530,505	278,190	322,574	44,384
			86	948,632	559,338	700,263	140,925
	V	W	81	6,979,534	3,563,718	4,123,769	560,051
			82	3,105,090	1,616,137	1,992,046	375,909
			83	2,313,510	1,132,652	1,418,363	285,711
			84	3,275,462	2,020,608	2,301,935	281,327
			85	5,102,011	3,483,044	4,100,894	617,850
			86	8,461,782	6,317,501	7,388,417	1,070,916
TUNISIA	V	E	86	21,125	11,500	13,403	1,903

Crop Product TSUSA commodity number, description, and unit of quantity Country	Mode	Reg	Yr	Quantity	F.A.S.	C.I.F.	Charges
U KING	V	E	82	126,750	55,503	65,766	10,263
			83	36,012	34,465	41,261	6,796
			85	266,887	162,687	184,722	22,035

Pineapple, juice, not concentrated
1654400 PNAPL JUICE NOT CONCENTRATED (GAL)

Country	Mode	Reg	Yr	Quantity	F.A.S.	C.I.F.	Charges
TOTAL			81	9,796,413	10,757,969	15,825,930	4,776,242
			82	8,157,194	8,944,867	11,888,044	2,943,177
			83	4,799,896	5,493,312	7,172,158	1,678,846
			84	4,575,064	5,284,851	6,516,561	1,231,710
			85	5,420,472	6,195,523	7,497,325	1,301,802
			86	7,380,079	8,508,231	10,652,256	2,144,025
BELGIUM	O	E	84	244	740	893	153
	V	E	83	412	809	915	106
			84	5,462	15,825	20,454	4,629
			85	2,564	6,443	7,973	1,530
			86	2,465	7,092	8,075	983
BRAZIL	O	E	85	6,289	3,766	4,253	487
			86	18,497	13,196	15,325	2,129
	V	E	83	111	658	769	111
			85	209	1,468	1,698	230
			86	50,278	94,256	106,783	12,527
C RICA	V	E	84	7,400	2,210	2,554	344
CANADA	O	E	81	21,695	48,674	48,674	
			82	17,643	43,784	43,784	
			83	8,713	22,565	22,565	
			84	4,100	8,036	8,036	
CHINA M	V	E	84	3,823	7,528	9,496	1,968
	V	W	84	4,442	10,068	11,065	997
CHINA T	V	W	82	169	405	419	14
			86	4,762	1,350	1,542	192
DENMARK	V	E	82	1,444	3,572	4,208	636
			83	15,887	3,334	4,515	1,181
	V	W	83	1,682	4,459	4,970	511
DOM REP	V	E	86	86	1,454	1,591	137
FRANCE	V	E	84	519	2,146	2,744	598
GUATMAL	V	E	85	770	1,704	1,932	228
			86	550	1,350	1,409	59
HG KONG	V	E	84	3,609	7,700	9,782	2,082
			86	51,750	57,600	60,681	3,081
INDIA	V	E	86	12,500	35,709	36,557	848
ITALY	O	E	85	15,058	45,112	55,609	10,497
			86	33,664	87,463	112,696	25,233
	V	E	83	898	3,283	3,763	480
			84	74,499	230,550	272,255	41,705
			85	13,797	22,553	28,935	6,382
			86	5,914	18,567	23,193	4,626
	V	W	84	4,032	12,324	14,457	2,133
			85	20,330	60,062	73,084	13,022
JAMAICA	V	E	82	338	1,308	1,415	107
			83	224	1,073	1,274	201
JAPAN	V	E	85	3,152	1,530	1,814	284
MEXICO	A	E	85	317	1,018	1,555	537
	O	E	81	7,058	18,960	18,960	
			82	15,765	43,575	43,575	
			83	19,327	41,611	41,611	
			84	43,951	98,169	98,169	
			85	29,836	87,392	87,392	
			86	32,394	80,981	80,981	
	O	W	81	2,272	6,201	6,201	
			82	1,324	2,116	2,116	
			83	6,165	13,416	13,416	
			84	26,304	44,478	44,478	
			85	25,060	56,732	56,732	
			86	3,218	9,223	9,223	
	V	E	82	1,951	6,130	6,667	537
PHIL R	N	W	81	160,512	179,018	245,085	66,067
	V	E	81	7,397,169	8,124,924	12,013,573	3,738,691
			82	5,182,548	5,702,322	7,716,884	2,014,562
			83	4,405,075	5,067,136	6,608,242	1,541,106
			84	4,025,770	4,442,748	5,516,755	1,074,007
			85	4,808,739	5,369,394	6,486,404	1,117,010
			86	6,591,225	7,410,453	9,351,099	1,940,646
	V	H	81	173,505	193,118	253,580	60,465
	V	W	81	2,034,041	2,186,738	3,238,563	910,061
			82	2,935,862	3,141,025	4,068,266	927,241
			83	247,365	275,328	401,445	126,117
			85	413,310	436,152	543,855	107,703
			86	549,620	625,832	771,963	146,131
PORTUGL	V	E	83	437	1,320	1,859	539
			84	4,480	5,200	6,983	1,783

Crop Product TSUSA commodity number, description, and unit of quantity Country	Mode	Reg	Yr	Quantity	F.A.S.	C.I.F.	Charges
	V	W	84	191	300	524	224
REP SAF	V	E	86	9,772	10,261	11,999	1,738
S ARAB	V	W	84	167	841	1,671	830
SPAIN	V	E	85	9,281	22,325	27,911	5,586
			86	6,784	20,399	23,694	3,295
THAILND	V	E	82	150	630	710	80
			83	93,600	58,320	66,814	8,494
			84	366,071	395,988	496,245	100,257
			85	71,760	79,872	118,178	38,306
	V	W	86	6,600	33,045	35,445	2,400
U KING	A	E	81	161	336	1,294	958

Pineapple, prepared or preserved
1489840 PINEAPPLES PREPARED EXC CND (LB)

Country	Mode	Reg	Yr	Quantity	F.A.S.	C.I.F.	Charges
TOTAL			81	5,282,800	1,704,462	1,785,089	80,627
			82	7,427,913	2,355,925	2,506,663	150,738
			83	12,356,307	4,349,261	4,719,981	370,720
			84	17,222,214	6,146,447	6,980,330	833,883
			85	15,987,055	5,182,681	5,979,574	796,893
			86	12,313,791	4,800,171	5,209,926	409,755
AUSTRAL	V	E	84	1,962	3,727	3,871	144
	V	W	81	414	1,093	1,121	28
			84	595	1,125	1,159	34
			85	3,969	5,409	5,631	222
			86	11,323	3,557	4,148	591
BRAZIL	A	E	83	330	1,539	2,431	892
			84	308	1,347	2,152	805
	V	E	83	6,614	5,587	5,969	382
			84	156,719	40,192	50,254	10,062
	V	W	83	7,170	3,608	3,993	385
			84	12,080	6,083	7,186	1,103
C RICA	V	E	81	17,867	7,540	10,548	3,008
			82	15,039	5,124	6,312	1,188
			83	22,110	12,004	14,899	2,895
			84	46,511	13,295	17,117	3,822
			86	331,650	124,004	152,330	28,326
	V	W	83	7,600	2,128	2,806	678
			84	292,966	67,126	92,963	25,837
			86	42,410	14,700	18,191	3,491
CANADA	A	E	81	150	1,575	1,611	36
			82	351	4,085	4,225	140
	N	E	84	52,990	59,634	59,634	
	O	E	83	9,741	10,100	10,100	
			84	39,230	39,586	39,586	
			85	103,419	69,466	69,466	
			86	32,651	38,836	38,836	
	O	W	84	12,866	14,011	14,011	
			85	79,069	45,805	45,805	
			86	66,460	39,784	39,784	
CHILE	V	W	84	33,750	7,425	9,393	1,968
CHINA M	V	E	84	68,085	17,531	23,264	5,733
			85	157,140	46,948	55,008	8,060
			86	106,920	27,984	31,734	3,750
	V	H	82	200	296	324	28
	V	W	83	12,102	7,125	7,714	589
			84	1,374	1,757	1,909	152
			86	1,750	1,022	1,123	101
CHINA T	A	E	82	1,000	1,050	2,225	1,175
	N	E	84	472,897	403,551	441,802	38,251
			86	341,490	246,865	259,120	12,255
	N	W	85	121,461	75,661	83,981	8,320
	O	E	81	13,244	12,306	12,306	
			82	25,348	28,257	28,787	530
			84	265	314	314	
	V	E	81	51,743	37,980	42,651	4,671
			82	48,548	35,443	39,192	3,749
			83	534,712	472,321	504,383	32,062
			84	304,697	208,345	226,756	18,411
			85	469,670	385,441	409,268	23,827
			86	79,120	37,454	41,460	4,006
	V	H	82	250	320	358	38
			85	1,764	1,732	1,852	120
	V	W	81	306,828	211,174	229,017	17,843
			82	166,881	130,142	142,017	11,875
			83	141,780	158,959	167,000	8,041
			84	205,883	198,259	208,355	10,096
			85	108,468	88,484	95,460	6,976
			86	200,169	139,663	147,388	7,725
DOM REP	N	E	81	8,684	3,206	3,664	458
	V	E	83	22,634	3,714	4,508	794
FRANCE	A	W	85	59	1,355	1,505	150
	O	E	85	45,000	8,750	8,750	
	V	E	86	1,190	1,631	1,890	259
GUATMAL	V	E	81	185,779	91,197	115,958	24,761
			82	32,291	11,007	13,058	2,051
			83	30,092	8,703	10,794	2,091
			84	31,180	10,161	13,832	3,671
			85	41,300	19,806	23,732	3,926
			86	43,773	7,953	10,303	2,350
HG KONG	V	E	83	34,500	8,529	10,229	1,700
			84	1,862	2,023	2,199	176
			85	576,300	176,290	206,290	30,000
			86	150	1,057	1,121	64
	V	W	83	1,814	2,300	2,427	127
			84	37,598	37,006	37,324	318
			85	1,650	2,106	2,226	120
			86	40,778	40,868	42,546	1,678
HONDURA	V	E	85	44,112	19,440	22,083	2,643
			86	26,519	4,523	6,881	2,358
INDIA	V	W	86	11,572	2,027	2,252	225
ITALY	V	E	84	97	261	283	22
IVY CST	V	E	85	65,550	24,510	27,948	3,438
JAPAN	V	E	86	39,375	10,800	12,274	1,474
KOR REP	V	E	83	70,548	61,500	65,326	3,826
			85	4,290	2,049	2,526	477
MALAYSA	V	E	82	68,040	17,951	21,792	3,841
			84	34,020	9,598	11,624	2,026
	V	W	81	220,002	54,886	63,689	8,803
MEXICO	O	E	81	4,046,226	1,046,125	1,046,125	
			82	4,445,932	1,366,500	1,366,500	
			83	5,378,248	1,664,414	1,664,414	
			84	5,128,740	1,501,870	1,501,870	
			85	3,689,340	1,091,960	1,091,960	
			86	3,902,551	1,099,403	1,099,403	
	O	H	83	45,000	7,250	7,250	
	O	W	83	17,280	2,726	2,726	
			86	4,200	1,600	1,600	
	V	E	86	71,428	20,004	24,170	4,166
PERU	V	W	84	20,850	4,587	6,312	1,725
PHIL R	N	E	82	268,245	81,523	97,304	15,781
	O	E	81	2,200	2,944	2,944	
	V	E	83	126,984	96,740	102,828	6,088
			84	6,055,232	1,798,761	2,260,446	461,685
			85	2,540,356	679,001	857,800	178,799
	V	W	81	54,203	34,371	38,121	3,750
			82	1,115	978	1,092	114
			83	900	518	569	51
			84	18,561	13,894	15,080	1,186
			85	4,180	4,891	5,418	527
			86	1,320	1,544	1,732	188
REP SAF	V	E	81	34,019	6,510	8,460	1,950
			82	136,080	38,696	44,925	6,229
			83	166,950	43,139	50,940	7,801
			84	202,525	67,727	77,332	9,605
			85	68,921	19,734	23,128	3,394
			86	11,567	10,710	12,447	1,737
SINGAPR	V	E	82	79,512	20,066	25,441	5,375
			83	66,000	17,084	21,086	4,002
			85	378,039	129,247	149,773	20,526
			86	313,719	67,321	79,906	12,585
	V	W	81	72,433	14,807	17,518	2,711
			82	36,552	8,929	11,810	2,881
SWITZLD	O	E	84	550	2,109	2,200	91
THAILND	O	E	82	8,818	8,377	8,377	
	V	E	81	201,008	121,406	131,022	9,616
			82	1,779,573	512,947	592,092	79,145
			83	5,399,630	1,645,317	1,932,703	287,386
			84	2,011,989	697,438	829,218	131,780
			85	6,008,573	1,758,569	2,161,139	402,570
			86	3,368,674	1,400,298	1,574,591	174,293
	V	W	81	68,000	57,342	60,334	2,992
			82	314,138	84,234	100,832	16,598
			83	200,007	100,566	109,498	8,932
			84	1,975,832	917,704	1,022,884	105,180
			85	1,474,425	526,027	628,825	102,798
			86	3,263,032	1,456,563	1,604,696	148,133
TURKEY	V	E	83	22,046	4,317	4,736	419
U KING	V	E	83	31,515	9,073	10,652	1,579

Crop Product TSUSA commodity number, description, and unit of quantity Country	Mode	Reg	Yr	Quantity	F.A.S.	C.I.F.	Charges

Pistachio

Pistachio, nut, shelled, prepared or preserved
1455300 PISTACHE NUTS, SHELLED, ETC (LB)

Country	Mode	Reg	Yr	Quantity	F.A.S.	C.I.F.	Charges
TOTAL			81	143,279	582,434	600,369	17,935
			82	207,413	660,301	686,974	26,673
			83	597,391	1,020,927	1,087,499	66,572
			84	264,449	827,952	857,361	29,409
			85	1,088,386	1,708,354	1,768,832	60,478
			86	4,371,821	6,484,590	6,751,440	266,850
AFGHAN	O	E	84	509	2,356	2,356	
	V	E	82	4,784	18,988	19,426	438
ARAB EM	V	E	83	197,884	332,112	343,576	11,464
AUSTRAL	V	E	86	4,188	6,518	9,359	2,841
BELGIUM	A	E	84	238	544	550	6
BRAZIL	O	E	86	32,890	38,669	42,809	4,140
CANADA	A	W	85	1,250	2,549	2,658	109
	O	E	85	440	1,760	1,760	
			86	26,200	30,963	30,963	
CHINA M	V	W	81	26,300	84,150	85,505	1,355
			82	5,900	11,798	12,118	320
			83	260,553	303,338	346,276	42,938
			85	60,000	35,116	39,119	4,003
			86	125,605	117,508	125,211	7,703
CHINA T	V	W	82	6,600	6,534	6,993	459
FR GERM	O	E	86	468,698	271,580	292,680	21,100
	V	E	86	382,545	564,854	590,368	25,514
FRANCE	A	E	86	500	1,736	2,157	421
	N	E	83	4,726	4,259	4,446	187
	N	W	84	111	975	1,003	28
	O	E	84	42	275	483	208
	V	E	81	79	491	494	3
			82	117	644	656	12
			84	828	1,504	1,610	106
			86	40	1,323	1,333	10
	V	W	82	4,830	9,008	9,195	187
HG KONG	V	E	84	1,260	917	1,048	131
	V	W	83	20,000	68,523	69,600	1,077
			84	1,092	3,467	3,709	242
			85	103,044	199,591	203,331	3,740
			86	77,010	45,452	49,052	3,600
IRAN	N	E	83	50,741	86,674	89,842	3,168
			86	2,177,256	3,612,900	3,746,171	133,271
	O	E	85	625	1,344	1,344	
			86	156,563	218,863	224,142	5,279
	V	E	84	91,196	229,975	237,255	7,280
			85	662,859	958,940	987,121	28,181
			86	115,743	219,300	230,203	10,903
	V	W	85	36,596	40,890	44,250	3,360
ITALY	A	E	82	97	276	469	193
			83	370	986	1,300	314
	A	W	84	441	2,600	3,345	745
	V	E	85	713	1,447	1,645	198
KOR REP	V	E	84	26,455	76,800	79,309	2,509
LEBANON	A	E	86	3,527	10,880	13,680	2,800
	O	E	85	550	2,090	2,090	
	V	E	85	15,735	11,770	12,909	1,139
MEXICO	O	W	86	2,534	2,222	2,222	
SPAIN	O	E	81	54	277	277	
	V	E	85	529	1,644	1,851	207
SWITZLD	V	W	86	27,563	47,580	50,000	2,420
TOKELAU	V	E	85	15,959	37,500	39,582	2,082
TURKEY	A	W	84	275	1,581	1,724	143
			85	930	5,220	5,346	126
	N	E	84	11,356	41,711	44,336	2,625
	O	E	82	6,600	21,740	23,640	1,900
			83	3,632	8,095	8,289	194
			84	1,413	4,704	4,812	108
			85	12,525	37,886	37,886	
			86	7,406	12,518	12,518	
	V	E	81	93,796	452,801	466,527	13,726
			82	178,326	591,010	614,128	23,118
			83	59,485	216,940	224,170	7,230
			84	128,175	457,106	471,908	14,802
			85	153,829	323,344	337,290	13,946
			86	748,892	1,236,674	1,281,056	44,382
	V	W	81	16,050	40,125	42,901	2,776
			82	159	303	349	46
			85	14,411	31,978	33,872	1,894
			86	14,661	45,050	47,516	2,466
U KING	O	E	81	7,000	4,590	4,665	75

Crop Product TSUSA commodity number, description, and unit of quantity Country	Mode	Reg	Yr	Quantity	F.A.S.	C.I.F.	Charges
			84	1,058	3,437	3,913	476
	V	W	85	6,738	11,700	12,821	1,121
YUGOSLV	V	E	85	1,653	3,585	3,957	372

Pistachio, nut, unshelled
1452600 PISTACHE NUTS NOT SHELLED (LB)

Country	Mode	Reg	Yr	Quantity	F.A.S.	C.I.F.	Charges
TOTAL			81	3,144,172	7,566,944	7,907,130	340,186
			82	6,232,610	13,223,221	13,799,080	575,859
			83	5,712,897	12,377,411	12,698,710	321,299
			84	21,775,906	41,138,582	42,233,519	1,094,937
			85	26,677,861	35,027,605	36,441,091	1,413,486
			86	9,693,145	12,409,825	12,899,560	489,735
AFGHAN	A	E	83	2,315	3,150	3,850	700
	V	E	82	17,230	68,600	72,600	4,000
			86	1,159,970	1,379,218	1,423,559	44,341
ARAB EM	V	E	82	125,926	297,694	306,242	8,548
			84	150,597	276,243	284,178	7,935
			85	431,425	597,348	615,869	18,521
			86	86,883	156,850	160,150	3,300
BELGIUM	A	E	84	568	1,300	1,315	15
CANADA	O	E	83	249	1,038	1,069	31
			86	6,875	13,377	13,974	597
CHINA M	V	E	85	12,504	17,506	18,443	937
	V	W	86	38,217	33,000	35,406	2,406
CHINA T	V	E	86	73,920	111,704	135,744	24,040
DENMARK	V	E	82	39,683	67,950	72,329	4,379
FR GERM	V	E	82	91,341	193,255	198,714	5,459
			83	141,827	275,894	283,253	7,359
			84	169,701	263,303	274,502	11,199
			85	127,663	219,496	228,004	8,508
			86	231,485	338,068	350,726	12,658
FRANCE	V	E	84	110	515	531	16
GREECE	A	E	86	2,313	7,935	8,516	581
	V	E	85	1,350	1,320	1,456	136
	V	W	85	2,249	4,955	5,781	826
HG KONG	V	W	85	29,491	25,362	26,422	1,060
INDIA	O	E	86	1,250	2,000	2,000	
IRAN	N	E	83	4,978,136	11,039,852	11,302,915	263,063
			84	7,888,315	14,555,214	14,951,387	296,173
			85	25,465,861	33,376,485	34,718,396	1,341,911
			86	3,338,743	4,145,654	4,350,435	204,781
	O	E	81	141,977	288,992	291,338	2,346
			82	299,983	283,272	283,800	528
			83	28,087	61,152	63,032	1,880
			85	3,375	7,304	7,304	
			86	908,345	1,141,839	1,161,228	19,389
	V	E	81	2,539,887	6,153,347	6,434,048	280,701
			82	3,822,546	9,185,286	9,601,293	416,007
			84	13,228,338	25,411,746	26,063,833	652,087
			85	362,438	468,359	489,255	20,896
			86	1,460,372	1,878,151	1,955,684	77,533
	V	W	81	393,524	953,400	1,003,314	49,914
			83	1,323	3,170	3,716	546
			84	191,976	322,196	336,688	14,492
			85	9,083	15,540	18,440	2,900
ISRAEL	V	E	81	46,297	113,400	118,817	5,417
			83	50,199	87,627	90,578	2,951
ITALY	A	W	85	794	1,274	1,956	682
	V	E	85	107,342	132,846	142,851	10,005
			86	30,000	72,000	74,189	2,189
LEBANON	V	E	83	633	1,630	1,692	62
			86	3,404	3,746	4,150	404
MEXICO	O	W	86	902,000	744,150	744,150	
S ARAB	V	E	83	48,016	119,790	122,840	3,050
TURKEY	A	W	85	378	1,760	1,790	30
	O	E	81	441	2,805	2,962	157
			82	207,233	351,830	361,634	9,804
			83	1,760	6,178	6,661	483
			84	550	1,596	1,596	
			85	9,538	22,418	22,418	
			86	73,980	133,215	136,344	3,129
	V	E	81	22,046	55,000	56,651	1,651
			82	1,628,668	2,775,334	2,902,468	127,134
			83	460,132	777,245	818,288	41,043
			84	144,649	304,469	317,145	12,676
			85	10,405	11,470	12,219	749
			86	1,393,763	2,246,543	2,340,124	93,581
	V	W	83	220	685	816	131
			84	1,102	2,000	2,344	344
			85	7,717	12,400	13,407	1,007
			86	19,842	35,375	38,587	3,212

Crop Product TSUSA commodity number, description, and unit of quantity Country	Mode	Reg	Yr	Quantity	F.A.S.	C.I.F.	Charges
U KING	N	E	85	55,826	76,702	79,400	2,698
YUGOSLV	V	E	85	2,205	2,060	2,274	214

Plantain

*Plantain, flour***

1520000 BANANA AND PLANTAIN FLOUR (LB)
   (See Banana, flour under Banana)

Plantain, fresh

1491000 PLANTAINS, FRESH (LB)

Country	Mode	Reg	Yr	Quantity	F.A.S.	C.I.F.	Charges
TOTAL			81	166,674,461	16,355,735	22,254,989	5,923,222
			82	180,431,569	20,389,821	28,161,589	7,771,768
			83	187,670,853	23,000,900	30,479,443	7,478,543
			84	192,644,701	23,606,253	32,095,970	8,489,717
			85	211,167,213	25,511,684	33,595,633	8,083,949
			86	234,250,890	25,627,036	35,083,788	9,456,752
AFGHAN	A	E	84	12,500	550	2,050	1,500
	V	E	83	140,000	11,200	23,550	12,350
			84	1,745,640	305,487	323,298	17,811
AUSTRAL	V	W	85	21,164	4,976	6,625	1,649
BERMUDA	V	E	82	80,250	6,048	9,079	3,031
BRAZIL	A	E	83	21,826	1,800	2,669	869
			86	24,900	5,850	8,850	3,000
	V	E	82	416,360	32,570	40,424	7,854
			83	2,085,800	240,132	251,240	11,108
			84	551,360	96,488	103,893	7,405
			85	1,005,920	156,527	159,064	2,537
C RICA	N	E	81	17,997,646	1,945,981	2,875,452	929,471
			83	21,099,504	2,011,544	3,257,559	1,246,015
			85	5,345,644	489,045	816,138	327,093
	O	E	81	318,400	54,773	59,694	4,921
			82	65,460	12,428	12,428	
	V	E	81	9,602,829	969,709	1,276,369	321,038
			82	39,967,293	4,448,623	6,447,925	1,999,302
			83	14,829,830	2,030,543	2,530,436	499,893
			84	11,543,275	1,249,343	1,815,399	566,056
			85	2,422,886	352,491	435,519	83,028
			86	7,391,661	1,057,813	1,399,363	341,550
	V	W	81	102,860	6,011	13,444	7,433
			82	497,305	80,880	120,094	39,214
			83	466,552	56,152	92,524	36,372
			84	166,025	29,946	44,793	14,847
			85	212,604	24,050	38,836	14,786
			86	12,000	2,250	3,753	1,503
CANADA	A	E	85	71,000	18,400	23,493	5,093
	O	E	81	70,700	13,137	13,137	
	O	W	84	74,920	18,730	18,730	
			86	40,950	18,900	18,900	
	V	E	85	27,460	2,984	4,541	1,557
CAYMAN	V	E	82	45,396	3,600	5,338	1,738
CHILE	V	E	85	28,334	10,282	13,433	3,151
COLOMB	N	E	82	28,701,291	3,425,254	4,712,051	1,286,797
			83	25,107,492	4,285,372	5,453,420	1,168,048
			84	51,572,176	6,326,695	8,140,720	1,814,025
			85	31,010,947	3,156,618	3,827,321	670,703
	V	E	81	52,762,298	5,247,616	6,615,112	1,377,086
			82	18,617,230	2,210,095	2,599,271	389,176
			83	39,306,253	4,213,800	4,899,374	685,574
			84	30,289,289	3,265,107	3,586,757	321,650
			85	50,137,650	5,533,238	7,113,403	1,580,165
			86	93,242,531	9,480,348	12,055,828	2,575,480
COOK IS	V	E	85	43,932	4,773	5,444	671
DENMARK	V	E	86	16,020	2,403	2,842	439
DOM REP	N	E	81	13,582,780	1,977,639	2,740,748	763,109
			82	21,363,953	3,361,940	4,485,647	1,123,707
			83	7,768,659	1,343,293	1,794,313	451,020
			84	8,568,075	1,128,172	1,603,184	475,012
			86	878,919	113,030	162,479	49,449
	V	E	81	1,820,857	208,550	301,767	93,217
			82	2,000,179	197,925	286,640	88,715
			83	304,340	54,260	79,354	25,094
			84	930,025	87,596	139,696	52,100
			85	4,594,722	863,080	1,124,016	260,936
			86	2,285,096	402,615	513,234	110,619
DOMINCA	V	E	81	4,800	300	361	61
			83	2,400	3,600	3,645	45
ECUADOR	A	E	81	18,000	2,000	3,730	1,730

Country	Mode	Reg	Yr	Quantity	F.A.S.	C.I.F.	Charges
			82	39,000	4,000	7,454	3,454
	N	E	81	8,805,907	980,727	1,686,533	705,806
			82	62,350,244	6,002,413	8,451,366	2,448,953
			83	60,321,665	6,259,891	8,611,757	2,351,866
			84	55,702,237	7,068,200	10,190,285	3,122,085
			85	50,380,139	6,220,474	7,860,291	1,639,817
			86	66,293,098	7,038,608	9,488,371	2,449,763
	N	W	81	3,704,990	281,294	394,619	113,325
			82	1,328,829	91,739	118,756	27,017
			83	2,758,021	184,558	247,213	62,655
			85	13,306,011	1,487,908	2,111,556	623,648
	V	E	81	55,294,767	4,424,948	5,859,102	1,434,154
			82	659,444	76,716	120,193	43,477
			83	388,670	36,289	63,314	27,025
			84	3,195,163	275,247	465,534	190,287
			85	12,379,470	1,767,858	2,017,102	249,244
			86	486,101	71,015	102,372	31,357
	V	W	84	7,487,042	514,122	686,127	172,005
			86	6,352,220	485,978	645,712	159,734
EGYPT	V	E	86	20,688	1,224	1,875	651
F W IND	A	E	84	24,450	4,625	5,425	800
FRANCE	V	E	81	33,600	1,960	2,391	431
			83	38,334	8,043	11,570	3,527
			84	11,600	967	1,814	847
GERM DR	V	E	86	34,963	20,625	22,807	2,182
GUATMAL	A	E	82	35,016	2,169	5,280	3,111
	A	W	81	84,919	6,590	19,817	13,227
			82	71,574	7,909	21,736	13,827
			84	84,391	13,483	30,639	17,156
			86	16,000	1,397	7,203	5,806
	N	E	81	282,302	23,543	50,378	26,835
			83	47,142	4,206	9,162	4,956
	N	W	83	370,381	32,312	83,579	51,267
	O	W	83	135,000	10,800	10,800	
	V	E	83	66,140	8,783	12,504	3,721
			84	935,092	88,573	158,337	69,764
			85	3,114,954	279,554	503,506	223,952
			86	3,544,538	371,270	587,097	215,827
	V	W	83	12,000	800	1,181	381
HEARD I	V	E	86	31,500	3,850	5,957	2,107
HONDURA	A	E	81	12,000	1,055	3,765	2,710
			84	10,020	358	1,636	1,278
	N	E	83	98,537	11,500	19,588	8,088
			84	590,956	47,350	89,156	41,806
			85	12,870,800	1,330,758	1,425,858	95,100
	V	E	81	38,000	3,763	3,763	
			82	940,026	76,499	141,019	64,520
			83	278,000	27,941	30,964	3,023
			84	880,954	93,286	100,439	7,153
			85	9,996,711	1,207,775	1,815,112	607,337
			86	29,916,176	2,867,750	3,998,703	1,130,953
	V	W	86	40,839	3,542	6,741	3,199
JAMAICA	A	E	82	4,500	2,681	4,120	1,439
			84	16,254	4,791	8,193	3,402
	N	E	83	110,400	26,245	29,390	3,145
			84	16,450	2,607	4,081	1,474
			85	15,835	6,692	10,433	3,741
	V	E	85	13,456	2,000	2,537	537
			86	30,319	4,815	6,793	1,978
KIRIBAT	V	E	85	97,600	13,860	18,801	4,941
			86	37,000	3,750	6,195	2,445
MEXICO	O	E	82	40,000	3,960	3,960	
			83	11,680	612	612	
			84	81,438	12,272	12,272	
			85	18,000	2,100	2,100	
	O	W	81	536,315	53,634	53,634	
			82	137,403	14,134	14,134	
			83	655,495	72,055	72,055	
			84	336,109	34,018	34,018	
			85	74,250	8,235	8,235	
			86	254,350	30,643	30,643	
N ANTIL	O	E	83	7,600	1,710	2,543	833
N ZEAL	A	W	81	2,492	1,549	3,217	1,668
NICARAG	V	W	84	6,726	1,062	1,416	354
PANAMA	N	E	81	1,275,931	115,032	218,149	103,117
			82	228,528	25,242	40,695	15,453
			83	388,632	49,658	78,867	29,209
	N	W	82	2,373,088	255,202	440,151	184,949
	V	E	82	427,500	41,250	63,424	22,174
			83	38,250	3,563	5,251	1,688
			84	100,092	8,435	14,606	6,171
	V	W	81	321,668	35,644	59,500	23,856
			82	37,500	4,050	7,334	3,284
			83	1,581,400	166,702	293,653	126,951

Crop Product TSUSA commodity number, description, and unit of quantity Country	Mode	Reg	Yr	Quantity	F.A.S.	C.I.F.	Charges
			84	394,600	40,647	69,712	29,065
			85	19,522	1,589	2,594	1,005
PHIL R	V	W	81	400	280	307	27
			82	4,200	2,494	3,070	576
			83	5,280	2,376	2,704	328
			84	1,800	604	738	134
			85	1,260	1,175	1,368	193
SALVADR	V	E	83	63,000	9,800	16,074	6,274
	V	W	86	199,950	15,810	15,810	
SPAIN	V	E	86	4,377,584	440,939	548,668	107,729
SWITZLD	A	E	84	3,000	284	494	210
	V	E	84	62,958	5,996	12,472	6,476
			85	54,000	9,000	10,863	1,863
TRINID	V	E	83	7,500	1,125	1,425	300
TURKEY	V	E	84	34,000	1,360	3,621	2,261
U KING	V	E	85	31,040	1,280	3,758	2,478
VENEZ	A	E	83	9,135,570	1,825,135	2,479,053	653,918
			84	60,406	10,140	15,069	4,929
			85	757,862	148,051	253,849	105,798
			86	18,723,487	3,182,611	5,443,592	2,260,981
	N	E	84	17,155,678	2,869,712	4,411,366	1,541,654
			85	13,114,040	2,406,911	3,979,837	1,572,926
	V	E	83	19,500	5,100	8,100	3,000

Plantain, paste and pulp**
1527200 BANANA, PLNTAIN PASTE, PULP (LB)
   (See Banana, paste and pulp under Banana)

Plantain, prepared or preserved
1491500 PLANTAINS, PREP OR PRES (LB)

Country	Mode	Reg	Yr	Quantity	F.A.S.	C.I.F.	Charges
TOTAL			81	5,433,644	648,878	955,748	306,870
			82	5,219,360	675,170	1,025,781	384,625
			83	5,189,205	841,904	1,213,423	371,519
			84	4,470,258	558,983	841,367	282,384
			85	4,874,336	872,592	1,196,091	323,499
			86	5,219,040	936,820	1,332,016	395,196
C RICA	N	E	83	3,490,159	379,068	581,467	202,399
	V	E	81	1,665,615	159,329	255,148	95,819
			82	2,018,314	192,893	307,913	115,020
			83	98,703	105,914	127,086	21,172
			84	2,971,397	323,592	503,376	179,784
			85	1,652,399	358,215	468,333	110,118
			86	671,396	237,165	299,093	61,928
	V	W	83	33,236	5,986	8,982	2,996
			85	19,842	3,480	4,506	1,026
CANADA	O	E	86	928	2,252	2,252	
CHILE	V	E	86	11,111	1,513	2,489	976
COLOMB	V	E	84	18,633	6,947	7,543	596
DOM REP	A	E	82	5,745	1,200	1,785	585
			86	43,162	32,475	36,570	4,095
	N	E	82	66,236	99,657	117,040	17,383
			83	177,559	168,409	190,282	21,873
			84	32,948	50,068	55,740	5,672
	V	E	81	118,899	136,888	153,065	16,177
			82	5,655	10,685	12,581	1,896
			83	62,400	23,400	24,892	1,492
			84	15,944	25,157	28,248	3,091
			85	36,418	22,255	25,077	2,822
			86	82,964	28,473	33,371	4,898
ECUADOR	V	E	83	4,380	639	676	37
			85	78,040	6,069	6,226	157
			86	2,500	1,500	1,772	272
GUATMAL	N	E	81	1,202,060	53,346	121,224	67,878
	V	E	82	1,246,600	60,600	143,083	82,483
			83	33,000	3,600	6,092	2,492
			84	1,824	1,140	1,270	130
			85	415,990	42,828	72,289	29,461
			86	960,930	92,389	164,509	72,120
HONDURA	N	E	81	1,052,099	108,918	178,169	69,251
			82	1,229,040	119,496	212,785	93,289
			83	1,215,100	125,350	228,852	103,502
			84	1,168,650	127,463	206,122	78,659
	V	E	84	257,300	21,000	34,647	13,647
			85	2,400,144	253,504	411,467	157,963
			86	2,580,650	304,772	490,732	185,960
JAMAICA	A	E	83	1,025	2,288	2,540	252
JAPAN	V	E	86	1,326	5,730	6,180	450
KIRIBAT	V	E	85	35,400	3,600	6,161	2,561
			86	497,700	79,310	114,843	35,533
PANAMA	N	E	81	1,394,126	189,391	246,852	57,461

Crop Product TSUSA commodity number, description, and unit of quantity Country	Mode	Reg	Yr	Quantity	F.A.S.	C.I.F.	Charges
	V	E	82	605,674	164,647	201,284	36,637
			83	41,400	4,550	6,708	2,158
PHIL R	V	E	83	750	422	527	105
			86	713	1,066	1,276	210
	V	W	82	723	855	963	108
			83	5,440	2,458	3,227	769
			84	1,882	1,617	2,010	393
SALVADR	V	E	82	29,453	16,698	16,698	34,014
	V	W	81	845	1,006	1,290	284
			82	11,206	7,911	11,024	3,113
			83	17,995	16,060	22,556	6,496
			84	1,680	1,999	2,411	412
THAILND	V	E	82	714	528	625	97
	V	W	83	718	1,443	1,578	135
			85	5,401	20,400	21,952	1,552
			86	26,350	2,561	2,799	238
VENEZ	A	E	83	7,340	2,317	7,958	5,641
			86	28,883	5,870	8,840	2,970
	V	E	85	230,702	162,241	180,080	17,839
			86	310,427	141,744	167,290	25,546

Plum

Plum, candied**
1544300 KUMQUATS, ETC, CANDIED, ETC (LB)
   (See Kumquat, candied under Kumquat)

Plum, canned
1492820 PLUMS, PRUNES, PREP, CANNED (LB)

Country	Mode	Reg	Yr	Quantity	F.A.S.	C.I.F.	Charges
TOTAL			81	733,404	1,098,801	1,163,904	65,103
			82	670,343	958,272	1,022,176	63,904
			83	922,696	1,121,088	1,202,708	81,620
			84	881,878	1,141,483	1,226,730	85,247
			85	962,672	1,218,947	1,309,485	90,538
			86	770,579	1,074,694	1,155,216	80,522
BELGIUM	V	E	81	263	739	760	21
			83	1,740	1,179	1,325	146
			84	22,107	9,469	10,726	1,257
			85	14,501	6,385	7,483	1,098
			86	13,465	6,963	8,099	1,136
CANADA	O	W	83	18,309	11,171	11,171	
			84	8,752	7,300	7,300	
			85	1,069	1,450	1,450	
	V	E	85	3,399	1,986	2,256	270
			86	2,112	1,292	1,450	158
CHINA M	V	E	81	1,100	1,924	2,057	133
			82	970	1,297	1,431	134
			83	9,334	7,148	8,132	984
			84	2,503	1,617	1,993	376
			85	10,220	12,822	15,069	2,247
	V	H	81	15,455	19,482	20,585	1,103
			82	37,111	27,042	29,893	2,851
			83	69,727	89,486	98,259	8,773
			84	14,144	18,974	20,246	1,272
			85	4,853	6,916	7,269	353
			86	12,750	24,395	26,620	2,225
	V	W	81	2,273	2,572	2,797	225
			82	6,302	5,674	6,067	393
			83	31,703	31,945	34,614	2,669
			84	40,103	35,039	37,917	2,878
			85	81,931	106,955	116,181	9,226
			86	134,037	177,955	192,996	15,041
CHINA T	N	E	84	4,890	9,534	10,315	781
	N	H	85	68,244	94,521	104,712	10,191
	O	E	84	391	967	967	
	V	E	81	6,625	12,070	12,992	922
			82	37,329	26,839	29,697	2,858
			83	4,726	5,129	5,764	635
			84	2,969	5,509	6,433	924
			85	9,782	13,184	15,112	1,928
			86	2,251	3,922	4,286	364
	V	H	81	25,023	48,955	52,717	3,762
			82	16,350	27,554	29,779	2,225
			83	22,226	38,033	41,377	3,344
			84	17,000	26,565	28,442	1,877
			86	40,750	47,225	51,366	4,141
	V	W	81	20,907	13,174	14,225	1,051
			82	27,853	21,262	23,262	2,000

Crop Product TSUSA commodity number, description, and unit of quantity Country	Mode	Reg	Yr	Quantity	F.A.S.	C.I.F.	Charges
			83	182,947	106,622	111,914	5,292
			84	63,301	45,989	51,001	5,012
			85	175,612	180,293	191,590	11,297
			86	110,973	116,508	124,757	8,249
FR GERM	A	E	81	68	307	313	6
	V	E	83	3,136	1,625	1,855	230
			84	22,970	5,883	7,830	1,947
	V	W	81	1,200	884	1,055	171
			83	324	304	358	54
FRANCE	A	E	82	106	380	464	84
			84	7,111	2,774	2,823	49
	N	E	83	4,386	6,079	6,632	553
			84	24,121	19,555	21,937	2,382
	N	W	86	588	3,356	4,111	755
	O	E	81	1,362	1,640	1,765	125
			84	1,560	817	889	72
	V	E	81	7,128	4,811	5,407	596
			82	15,155	9,301	10,632	1,331
			83	31,653	31,411	34,273	2,862
			84	14,709	7,273	8,188	915
			85	34,167	18,037	20,614	2,577
			86	71,353	73,259	81,746	8,487
	V	W	81	486	1,141	1,235	94
			82	1,800	1,581	1,606	25
			83	10,758	7,809	8,422	613
			84	19,310	16,385	17,904	1,519
			85	918	1,137	1,257	120
GREECE	V	E	85	3,926	4,680	5,062	382
HG KONG	N	H	82	378,307	608,386	641,729	33,343
	V	E	81	27,481	60,079	62,903	2,824
			82	13,325	28,738	30,610	1,872
			83	17,180	26,996	29,211	2,215
			84	11,323	20,091	22,463	2,372
			85	36,024	29,062	33,232	4,170
			86	6,226	12,419	13,516	1,097
	V	H	81	511,891	734,967	773,005	38,038
			83	336,771	499,584	528,334	28,750
			84	442,262	643,354	678,593	35,239
			85	336,314	469,157	493,250	24,093
			86	171,362	261,957	277,434	15,477
	V	W	81	33,663	56,067	59,198	3,131
			82	35,289	52,653	56,241	3,588
			83	37,959	63,153	67,468	4,315
			84	22,001	37,169	39,326	2,157
			85	82,926	116,672	125,939	9,267
			86	78,432	101,709	107,367	5,658
ISRAEL	V	E	81	3,672	2,550	3,027	477
			82	6,426	4,498	5,111	613
			83	13,612	9,412	10,431	1,019
			84	13,770	10,633	11,842	1,209
ITALY	A	E	81	77	299	389	90
JAMAICA	A	E	84	518	390	499	109
	V	E	83	1,774	2,746	3,123	377
JAPAN	N	H	81	12,025	28,949	33,488	4,539
	N	W	84	14,153	27,669	29,659	1,990
	O	E	81	794	1,521	1,720	199
			82	265	552	623	71
	O	W	86	378	2,459	2,557	98
	V	E	81	8,699	13,898	15,250	1,352
			82	9,322	18,136	20,521	2,385
			83	10,740	22,327	24,508	2,181
			84	18,495	33,538	36,995	3,457
			85	10,568	26,095	28,422	2,327
			86	12,107	38,944	40,666	1,722
	V	H	82	8,514	16,675	18,714	2,039
			83	21,854	43,681	49,524	5,843
			84	26,715	53,333	61,092	7,759
			85	20,875	42,876	46,809	3,933
			86	24,975	67,567	74,596	7,029
	V	W	81	44,593	84,532	89,917	5,385
			82	42,776	81,039	86,371	5,332
			83	53,518	93,445	99,425	5,980
			84	33,473	77,226	84,359	7,133
			85	35,210	68,252	72,986	4,734
			86	42,390	113,175	118,660	5,485
KOR REP	V	W	81	225	427	492	65
MEXICO	O	E	85	8,854	2,797	2,797	
	O	W	84	750	600	600	
NETHLDS	V	E	83	678	727	758	31
POLAND	V	E	83	21,989	8,627	10,643	2,016
			84	16,853	6,361	7,286	925
			85	10,148	4,289	5,073	784
SINGAPR	V	W	82	1,410	2,388	2,580	192
SWITZLD	V	E	81	5,145	3,679	4,075	396

Crop Product TSUSA commodity number, description, and unit of quantity Country	Mode	Reg	Yr	Quantity	F.A.S.	C.I.F.	Charges
			82	3,868	4,346	4,731	385
			83	6,180	4,948	5,281	333
			84	4,234	3,928	4,149	221
			86	9,770	9,800	10,611	811
	V	W	84	476	492	527	35
			85	3,527	5,299	5,611	312
			86	1,313	1,162	1,238	76
THAILND	V	E	82	11,100	7,053	8,060	1,007
			84	4,745	4,745	5,353	608
	V	W	82	10,639	8,173	8,922	749
			86	4,680	2,462	2,688	226
U KING	O	E	81	720	871	971	100
			83	114	284	312	28
			85	788	1,050	1,313	263
	V	E	81	2,304	2,821	3,075	254
			82	4,438	4,213	4,524	311
			83	9,133	6,923	9,266	2,343
			84	6,169	8,304	9,076	772
			85	417	1,182	1,284	102
			86	2,247	2,267	2,418	151
	V	W	81	225	442	486	44
			83	225	294	328	34
USSR	V	E	82	1,688	492	608	116
YUGOSLV	V	E	85	8,399	3,850	4,714	864
			86	28,420	5,898	8,034	2,136

Plum, dried

1492600 PRUNES PLUMS DRIED (LB)

Country	Mode	Reg	Yr	Quantity	F.A.S.	C.I.F.	Charges
TOTAL			**81**	**158,328**	**237,947**	**251,549**	**13,602**
			82	**297,061**	**331,290**	**356,744**	**25,454**
			83	**929,234**	**483,263**	**542,825**	**59,562**
			84	**1,414,113**	**521,122**	**607,916**	**86,794**
			85	**1,825,823**	**609,791**	**720,821**	**111,030**
			86	**3,162,657**	**1,052,849**	**1,221,680**	**168,831**
AFGHAN	V	W	84	10,675	5,326	6,190	864
			86	14,337	12,160	14,717	2,557
ARAB EM	V	W	84	523	870	929	59
ARGENT	V	E	83	235,385	35,271	47,066	11,795
			84	35,057	15,050	17,128	2,078
			85	550,795	143,953	173,390	29,437
			86	311,913	77,252	93,211	15,959
CANADA	O	W	83	5	311	311	
	V	E	85	39,683	8,100	9,940	1,840
CHILE	O	E	86	30,865	9,325	10,027	702
	V	E	82	83,775	16,589	21,495	4,906
			83	163,141	37,561	47,041	9,480
			85	735,715	174,191	207,730	33,539
			86	1,568,707	408,024	481,579	73,555
	V	W	86	39,683	10,468	13,068	2,600
CHINA M	O	E	83	250	466	504	38
	V	E	81	9,136	10,918	12,104	1,186
			82	7,463	7,738	8,383	645
			83	25,963	26,778	29,585	2,807
			84	20,253	16,018	18,333	2,315
			85	11,220	7,675	8,970	1,295
	V	W	81	9,450	14,357	15,277	920
			82	33,152	49,121	51,657	2,536
			83	21,056	25,547	27,373	1,826
			84	34,057	39,435	43,010	3,575
			85	8,548	15,168	15,970	802
CHINA T	O	H	83	13,300	21,500	22,550	1,050
	V	E	82	1,625	2,945	3,344	399
			83	6,765	13,626	14,852	1,226
			84	11,897	24,072	26,147	2,075
			85	16,568	29,277	32,197	2,920
			86	7,605	16,430	18,826	2,396
	V	H	82	51,794	76,125	81,231	5,106
			83	8,000	11,890	12,910	1,020
			84	2,646	1,650	1,798	148
	V	W	81	102,433	132,137	138,273	6,136
			82	66,783	77,959	82,010	4,051
			83	139,440	160,124	167,092	6,968
			84	47,985	67,403	71,908	4,505
			85	71,652	71,861	75,554	3,693
			86	179,170	188,595	194,342	5,747
FR GERM	V	E	85	52,360	11,240	14,108	2,868
FRANCE	N	E	83	1,093	3,489	3,794	305
	O	E	82	154	273	311	38
	V	E	81	2,645	4,179	4,545	366
			83	265	465	511	46
			84	1,788	4,456	4,624	168

Crop
Product
TSUSA commodity number, description, and unit of quantity

Country	Mode	Reg	Yr	Quantity	F.A.S.	C.I.F.	Charges
			85	254,793	83,138	102,472	19,334
			86	928,532	209,907	267,560	57,653
	V	W	84	106	337	354	17
HG KONG	O	W	82	1,562	2,196	2,340	144
	V	E	81	11,406	30,430	32,789	2,359
			82	12,299	27,421	29,725	2,304
			83	15,353	22,972	25,512	2,540
			84	14,500	29,467	32,314	2,847
			85	3,073	6,567	7,337	770
			86	34,988	64,927	70,996	6,069
	V	W	81	18,088	34,383	35,985	1,602
			82	31,128	55,971	59,601	3,630
			83	16,373	26,841	28,853	2,012
			84	14,697	10,179	10,659	480
			85	24,952	8,677	10,258	1,581
			86	2,350	1,175	1,273	98
IRAN	A	W	84	104	470	717	247
	V	W	85	35,696	37,895	48,293	10,398
ITALY	V	W	85	13,867	1,384	2,824	1,440
JAPAN	O	E	81	284	461	527	66
	V	E	81	1,625	5,289	5,599	310
			82	415	773	913	140
			83	480	918	997	79
			84	3,674	10,273	11,031	758
			85	720	1,493	1,606	113
			86	480	1,266	1,342	76
	V	W	81	1,694	3,479	3,835	356
			82	1,293	3,326	3,625	299
			83	1,192	2,784	2,879	95
			84	6,569	19,254	20,087	833
			85	2,875	7,728	8,086	358
			86	8,114	28,329	29,458	1,129
KOR REP	V	E	84	1,500	4,916	5,301	385
MADAGAS	V	E	84	573	936	973	37
MEXICO	O	W	86	6,327	1,028	1,028	
NETHLDS	A	E	84	794	1,701	2,531	830
REP SAF	V	E	83	231,483	70,649	85,649	15,000
SWITZLD	O	E	83	2,035	5,939	6,105	166
THAILND	A	W	82	211	950	1,308	358
	V	E	82	220	461	477	16
	V	W	81	1,567	2,314	2,615	301
			82	2,982	7,442	8,207	765
			83	1,520	3,163	3,406	243
			84	197	439	480	41
TURKEY	N	E	83	5,020	3,907	4,322	415
	V	E	82	2,205	2,000	2,117	117
			83	1,102	900	1,113	213
			84	20,944	10,039	11,241	1,202
	V	W	84	7,716	6,610	7,241	631
			86	29,586	23,963	24,253	290
YUGOSLV	O	E	84	181,255	34,880	44,550	9,670
	V	E	83	40,013	8,162	10,400	2,238
			84	996,603	217,341	270,370	53,029
			85	3,306	1,444	2,086	642

Plum, fresh

1491800 PRUNES ETC, FRESH, 1/1-5/31 (LB)

Country	Mode	Reg	Yr	Quantity	F.A.S.	C.I.F.	Charges
TOTAL			81	3,299,486	1,174,394	1,744,009	569,615
			82	3,426,133	1,633,479	2,146,193	512,714
			83	8,023,466	3,406,942	4,528,751	1,121,809
			84	12,897,210	4,496,281	6,118,040	1,621,759
			85	28,814,417	10,096,031	13,444,794	3,348,763
			86	31,286,810	8,449,439	11,541,655	3,092,216
AUSTRAL	A	W	82	1,151	977	1,500	523
BELGIUM	V	E	83	2,820	640	1,059	419
CANADA	O	E	84	35,715	10,139	10,139	
CHILE	A	E	81	30,494	12,068	13,396	1,328
			82	86,549	58,421	101,821	43,400
			83	3,182	1,998	4,998	3,000
			85	38,130	15,760	38,306	22,546
	N	E	81	74,796	36,399	70,245	33,846
			83	4,326	1,918	2,209	291
			84	42,607	16,873	24,644	7,771
			86	3,683,211	815,760	1,127,999	312,239
	N	W	81	35,559	15,329	15,887	558
			83	448,922	178,297	246,289	67,992
			86	4,118,036	1,028,414	1,417,223	388,809
	O	W	84	12,614	8,904	8,904	
	V	E	81	3,054,246	1,067,697	1,576,966	509,269
			82	3,117,817	1,445,252	1,868,735	423,483
			83	7,522,598	3,183,556	4,218,707	1,035,151

Crop
Product
TSUSA commodity number, description, and unit of quantity

Country	Mode	Reg	Yr	Quantity	F.A.S.	C.I.F.	Charges
			84	10,574,656	3,639,211	4,990,384	1,351,173
			85	23,877,739	8,334,756	11,052,000	2,717,244
			86	20,158,012	5,701,291	7,814,172	2,112,881
	V	W	81	76,588	25,399	36,797	11,398
			82	181,288	86,512	112,417	25,905
			83	15,675	7,584	9,708	2,124
			84	2,100,269	755,375	990,623	235,248
			85	4,873,052	1,732,393	2,336,917	604,524
			86	3,304,696	896,932	1,173,002	276,070
COOK IS	V	E	86	22,855	7,042	9,259	2,217
HG KONG	V	W	83	13,228	9,465	10,565	1,100
ITALY	V	E	84	92	380	398	18
JAPAN	A	H	84	1,017	632	1,102	470
N ZEAL	A	E	82	5,367	10,699	13,909	3,210
			83	2,310	4,621	7,355	2,734
			84	2,750	1,764	4,394	2,630
	A	H	81	2,728	1,498	2,432	934
			82	2,907	2,903	4,064	1,161
			83	243	266	436	170
			84	10,838	6,650	10,945	4,295
			85	3,405	3,102	4,145	1,043
	A	W	81	25,075	16,004	28,286	12,282
			82	20,893	24,461	37,868	13,407
			83	10,162	18,597	27,425	8,828
			84	16,270	18,496	29,901	11,405
PERU	V	E	82	10,161	4,254	5,879	1,625
REP SAF	V	E	84	64,667	27,143	35,892	8,749
SWITZLD	V	E	85	22,091	10,020	13,426	3,406
YUGOSLV	O	E	84	35,715	10,714	10,714	

1492100 PLUMS ETC, FR, JUN 1-DEC 31 (LB)

Country	Mode	Reg	Yr	Quantity	F.A.S.	C.I.F.	Charges
TOTAL			81	206,142	36,735	59,566	22,831
			82	86,225	61,882	92,137	30,255
			83	369,048	178,191	294,387	116,196
			84	397,105	169,441	331,962	162,521
			85	1,544,450	495,798	729,571	233,773
			86	2,359,592	808,387	1,230,044	421,657
ARGENT	A	E	84	10,626	5,972	14,462	8,490
BOLIVIA	A	E	83	5,276	1,114	1,950	836
C RICA	V	E	81	164,417	17,168	22,727	5,559
CANADA	O	E	81	3,065	1,630	1,630	
			82	17,150	9,960	9,960	
			83	143	1,498	1,498	
			85	40,544	11,684	11,684	
			86	328	5,402	5,402	
	O	W	84	10,081	1,246	1,246	
			85	126,975	11,947	11,947	
			86	60,661	1,517	1,517	
CHILE	A	E	81	25,505	12,429	27,497	15,068
			82	67,842	51,341	81,446	30,105
			83	213,945	121,506	213,374	91,868
			84	226,509	95,686	231,491	135,805
			85	139,934	50,697	112,146	61,449
			86	260,468	173,634	368,422	194,788
	N	W	83	149,684	54,073	77,565	23,492
	O	W	84	18,006	8,993	8,993	
	V	E	81	13,155	5,508	7,712	2,204
			84	93,502	42,639	56,235	13,596
			85	1,224,596	417,570	587,621	170,051
			86	2,032,072	621,434	838,865	217,431
	V	W	84	12,343	4,989	6,625	1,636
ECUADOR	A	E	84	11,924	4,496	4,976	480
FR GERM	O	E	82	858	321	429	108
INDIA	V	E	85	12,401	3,900	6,173	2,273
JAPAN	V	W	84	126	333	347	14
N ZEAL	A	H	84	873	810	1,172	362
	A	W	84	1,210	1,277	2,007	730
PHIL R	V	W	82	375	260	302	42
SWITZLD	A	E	86	6,063	6,400	15,838	9,438
VENEZ	A	E	84	11,905	3,000	4,408	1,408

Plum, in brine

1492400 PRUNES PLUMS IN BRINE (LB)

Country	Mode	Reg	Yr	Quantity	F.A.S.	C.I.F.	Charges
TOTAL			81	91,061	161,032	176,462	15,430
			82	217,537	199,374	220,462	21,088
			83	92,211	127,159	137,676	10,517
			84	124,580	116,525	128,662	12,137
			85	76,147	60,641	68,580	7,939
			86	94,654	67,277	74,528	7,251
BELGIUM	V	E	84	1,389	724	792	68

Crop Product TSUSA commodity number, description, and unit of quantity Country	Mode	Reg	Yr	Quantity	F.A.S.	C.I.F.	Charges
CHINA M	V	W	81	360	431	456	25
			82	540	698	745	47
			83	720	340	374	34
CHINA T	V	H	82	113,603	55,665	61,398	5,733
			83	23,265	15,980	17,490	1,510
			84	62,501	28,350	33,327	4,977
			85	49,601	28,801	32,714	3,913
			86	59,634	29,890	34,081	4,191
	V	W	82	27,584	12,504	13,847	1,343
			83	15,347	10,391	11,083	692
			84	14,991	6,400	7,135	735
			85	10,771	5,126	6,055	929
			86	17,895	9,136	10,243	1,107
FR GERM	O	E	85	4,500	1,341	1,860	519
	V	E	84	3,450	1,034	1,146	112
FRANCE	V	E	83	3,793	1,797	1,899	102
			84	5,258	2,673	2,896	223
HG KONG	V	E	81	1,200	984	1,106	122
			82	990	1,218	1,387	169
			83	4,055	6,334	6,939	605
			84	1,755	1,598	1,771	173
			86	1,870	1,780	2,230	450
	V	W	81	7,650	7,838	8,238	400
			82	6,990	7,243	7,767	524
			83	6,921	12,752	13,621	869
			84	1,230	1,004	1,289	285
			85	540	1,169	1,268	99
ITALY	V	E	84	263	455	486	31
JAPAN	N	E	83	921	1,887	2,072	185
	O	E	81	2,847	4,763	5,063	300
			82	1,488	2,973	3,273	300
			84	758	1,381	1,525	144
	V	E	81	10,818	19,076	20,583	1,507
			82	11,828	24,160	26,511	2,351
			83	17,184	37,815	41,166	3,351
			84	17,643	39,419	42,759	3,340
			85	5,303	13,097	14,523	1,426
			86	2,865	10,246	10,969	723
	V	H	81	43,363	81,446	91,467	10,021
			82	32,400	55,676	63,428	7,752
			83	1,954	3,382	3,997	615
	V	W	81	24,823	46,494	49,549	3,055
			82	22,114	39,237	42,106	2,869
			83	18,051	36,481	39,035	2,554
			84	15,342	33,487	35,536	2,049
			85	5,432	11,107	12,160	1,053
			86	12,390	16,225	17,005	780

Plum, prepared or preserved
1492840 PLUMS PRUNE PREP,NOT CANNED (LB)

Country	Mode	Reg	Yr	Quantity	F.A.S.	C.I.F.	Charges
TOTAL			81	836,318	1,391,375	1,470,451	79,076
			82	1,041,718	1,659,299	1,767,765	108,466
			83	1,244,123	1,815,103	1,944,677	129,574
			84	1,588,023	2,061,678	2,229,945	168,267
			85	1,668,823	1,957,986	2,128,935	170,949
			86	1,239,708	1,560,705	1,662,497	101,792
AUSTRAL	V	E	84	1,219	4,087	4,537	450
CHINA M	N	H	85	94,113	137,416	150,417	13,001
	N	W	82	49,930	65,071	69,901	4,830
			83	1,900	2,787	2,923	136
	O	E	84	5,256	5,109	5,983	874
			85	5,380	3,881	4,426	545
	O	W	84	10,397	15,581	16,634	1,053
	V	E	81	47,413	48,174	53,606	5,432
			82	50,767	52,438	57,895	5,457
			83	91,463	103,667	112,792	9,125
			84	141,433	115,137	133,821	18,684
			85	202,968	159,731	182,817	23,086
			86	56,723	45,189	51,393	6,204
	V	H	81	7,196	12,077	12,928	851
			82	28,776	50,368	54,640	4,272
			83	27,735	47,720	51,693	3,973
			84	54,530	84,232	90,845	6,613
			86	54,504	86,556	92,942	6,386
	V	W	81	64,112	86,983	92,895	5,912
			82	62,345	86,337	92,109	5,772
			83	146,485	190,211	206,673	16,462
			84	253,863	306,710	333,071	26,361
			85	167,668	241,677	256,793	15,116
			86	134,491	182,409	190,850	8,441
CHINA T	N	H	85	115,086	149,569	165,115	15,546
	N	W	83	176,060	204,378	213,971	9,593
	O	E	85	2,139	4,515	5,069	554
	O	H	85	2,500	3,255	3,646	391
			86	22,035	23,170	24,440	1,270
	O	W	81	5,000	8,073	8,400	327
			82	12,500	16,842	17,550	708
			83	7,500	9,689	10,125	436
	V	E	81	13,236	29,132	30,954	1,822
			82	15,098	32,968	34,913	1,945
			83	31,999	52,326	56,314	3,988
			84	14,858	31,381	33,539	2,158
			85	36,829	66,576	71,295	4,719
			86	71,522	106,347	116,330	9,983
	V	H	81	21,201	36,968	39,803	2,835
			82	47,770	78,204	84,512	6,308
			83	55,631	92,947	100,110	7,163
			84	71,988	112,735	119,327	6,592
			86	117,159	139,667	150,794	11,127
	V	W	81	202,357	290,791	301,482	10,691
			82	274,224	347,215	362,999	15,784
			83	95,548	147,390	155,452	8,062
			84	485,022	565,832	600,790	34,958
			85	580,053	524,409	561,415	37,006
			86	416,017	378,935	400,255	21,320
FR GERM	V	E	84	14,312	4,858	5,848	990
FRANCE	V	E	82	534	553	609	56
			83	978	673	716	43
			84	40,354	17,273	19,637	2,364
			85	7,508	3,874	4,486	612
			86	338	4,320	4,569	249
	V	W	81	392	327	356	29
			85	3,306	3,229	4,491	1,262
GUATMAL	V	E	85	5,496	1,086	1,900	814
			86	3,343	1,504	1,775	271
HG KONG	N	H	85	99,478	131,066	144,336	13,270
	O	E	86	946	1,417	1,489	72
	V	E	81	98,209	218,481	231,391	12,910
			82	89,789	192,094	205,213	13,119
			83	100,740	192,562	206,021	13,459
			84	104,262	159,515	174,658	15,143
			85	129,226	168,305	184,940	16,635
			86	84,827	120,694	130,757	10,063
	V	H	81	63,208	98,588	104,898	6,310
			82	128,440	204,007	216,990	12,983
			83	156,992	214,743	233,834	19,091
			84	107,294	164,715	178,116	13,401
			86	78,009	124,253	133,222	8,969
	V	W	81	258,206	480,874	506,660	25,786
			82	217,064	431,022	459,348	28,326
			83	226,055	355,156	377,212	22,056
			84	179,449	275,346	293,236	17,890
			85	132,609	201,579	209,573	7,994
			86	125,805	194,721	201,123	6,402
ISRAEL	V	E	81	18,027	9,632	11,309	1,677
			82	1,587	1,400	1,479	79
			83	5,400	3,750	4,230	480
ITALY	V	E	83	2,400	1,744	1,835	91
			84	189	507	550	43
JAMAICA	V	E	85	4,560	2,342	2,459	117
JAPAN	N	H	82	12,850	24,029	25,616	1,587
	N	W	84	17,030	40,619	42,807	2,188
	V	E	81	15,106	28,502	30,153	1,651
			82	15,064	27,845	31,515	3,670
			83	8,030	19,101	20,845	1,744
			84	22,167	52,787	58,063	5,276
			85	10,525	24,561	26,988	2,427
			86	3,700	10,330	10,918	588
	V	H	81	9,291	18,496	19,606	1,110
			83	33,624	60,423	66,345	5,922
			84	32,379	57,400	64,720	7,320
			85	45,614	85,910	100,153	14,243
			86	22,618	58,720	65,479	6,759
	V	W	81	11,599	23,064	24,618	1,554
			82	18,011	37,023	39,408	2,385
			83	28,472	60,503	64,327	3,824
			84	7,232	18,115	19,110	995
			85	17,546	37,386	40,319	2,933
			86	34,002	77,001	80,292	3,291
KOR REP	V	E	83	1,366	1,701	1,824	123
	V	W	82	154	341	359	18
MACAO	V	E	83	2,500	2,760	3,108	348
			86	1,250	1,340	1,561	221
	V	H	83	8,825	10,390	11,286	896
MALAYSA	V	E	85	1,075	1,135	1,278	143

384   Table 1. U.S. Import Statistics for Crop-Specific Commodities by Crop Name

Crop
Product
TSUSA commodity number, description, and unit of quantity

Country	Mode	Reg	Yr	Quantity	F.A.S.	C.I.F.	Charges
	V	H	84	4,750	6,060	6,544	484
MEXICO	O	E	86	10,919	1,993	1,993	
POLAND	V	E	82	8,422	3,920	4,368	448
PORTUGL	A	E	84	2,112	5,808	8,150	2,342
SINGAPR	V	E	86	1,500	2,139	2,315	176
	V	H	82	1,650	3,065	3,177	112
			83	750	1,303	1,375	72
	V	W	83	20,437	24,340	25,546	1,206
THAILND	O	W	83	1,202	745	805	60
	V	E	81	1,500	900	1,044	144
	V	H	84	2,359	3,492	3,841	349
	V	W	81	265	313	348	35
			82	6,743	4,557	5,164	607
			83	2,848	2,784	3,148	364
			84	743	1,106	1,164	58
U KING	V	E	83	9,214	11,310	12,167	857
			84	14,825	13,273	14,954	1,681
			85	5,144	6,484	7,019	535

Prune, juice
1655000 PRUNE JUICE NOV 1% ALCOLOL (GAL)

Country	Mode	Reg	Yr	Quantity	F.A.S.	C.I.F.	Charges
TOTAL			81	856,548	1,006,185	1,032,960	26,775
			82	841,589	924,889	970,666	45,777
			83	1,448,668	1,564,663	1,656,599	91,936
			84	1,063,477	1,154,219	1,227,727	73,508
			85	1,739,673	1,636,166	1,784,397	148,231
			86	1,609,669	1,409,822	1,540,905	131,083
ARGENT	V	E	83	47,880	28,420	32,790	4,370
			84	75,046	24,015	27,745	3,730
AUSTRAL	A	W	81	15	502	1,140	638
	O	E	82	9,853	12,642	12,642	
BELGIUM	O	E	85	28,590	37,516	38,716	1,200
			86	128,440	122,154	135,304	13,150
	V	E	85	122,616	111,693	123,942	12,249
			86	141,588	147,501	159,291	11,790
BRAZIL	V	E	83	32,198	102,751	124,463	21,712
	V	W	82	20,723	13,160	15,700	2,540
CANADA	O	E	81	587,949	751,859	751,859	
			82	432,074	565,918	565,918	
			83	603,554	795,970	795,970	
			84	402,174	539,127	539,127	
			85	217,492	281,900	281,900	
			86	390,995	297,718	299,718	2,000
	O	W	85	16,200	34,028	34,028	
			86	16,200	36,903	36,903	
CHINA M	V	E	81	734	1,790	2,112	322
	V	W	82	113	442	477	35
CHINA T	V	E	81	71	330	358	28
			82	107	501	550	49
			86	994	2,430	2,702	272
	V	W	81	914	6,579	7,179	600
			82	2,850	2,422	2,614	192
			83	4,148	9,605	10,139	534
			86	3,810	4,531	4,866	335
DOM REP	V	E	83	29,594	14,798	16,510	1,712
EGYPT	O	E	83	94	550	550	
FIJI	V	W	85	2,700	2,480	3,217	737
FR GERM	V	E	81	164	505	552	47
			84	77,011	86,510	97,773	11,263
			85	276,727	218,832	240,167	21,335
			86	156,199	174,889	187,362	12,473
	V	W	84	106	564	614	50
			85	41,040	73,136	75,635	2,499
FRANCE	N	E	81	60,000	53,816	60,269	6,453
	V	E	81	174,712	141,980	159,404	17,424
			82	357,959	298,532	337,602	39,070
			83	413,494	383,094	424,208	41,114
			84	320,929	349,692	389,131	39,439
			85	131,018	135,162	153,266	18,104
			86	367,128	289,755	338,854	49,099
	V	W	82	79	1,125	1,186	61
			86	17,523	16,444	20,744	4,300
GREECE	V	E	86	89	2,000	2,020	20
INDIA	V	W	86	46,080	30,643	35,232	4,589
ISRAEL	O	E	81	4,605	3,666	3,666	
ITALY	V	E	81	94	282	355	73
			82	281	875	3,432	2,557
			85	140	2,043	2,269	226
			86	2,220	1,754	2,212	458
JAMAICA	A	E	83	450	2,666	3,330	664
JAPAN	V	E	85	18,145	26,203	28,340	2,137
			86	310	1,641	1,768	127
	V	W	83	158	3,527	3,733	206
			84	1,486	12,088	12,847	759
			86	165	2,254	2,375	121
MEXICO	O	E	84	731	738	738	
			85	337	1,065	1,065	
	O	W	81	675	1,896	1,896	
			82	1,800	4,800	4,800	
			83	686	1,350	1,350	
			84	3,819	6,015	6,015	
			85	1,958	2,677	2,677	
NETHLDS	N	E	85	294,898	275,757	305,079	29,322
	O	E	85	116,929	70,190	72,520	2,330
			86	51,350	33,404	36,569	3,165
	V	E	81	15,000	29,010	30,200	1,190
			82	15,750	24,472	25,745	1,273
			83	221,312	154,692	166,218	11,526
			84	38,720	31,091	35,702	4,611
			85	143,558	136,132	148,773	12,641
			86	127,160	112,991	124,128	11,137
NORWAY	V	W	86	428	3,620	4,106	486
PERU	A	E	84	10,725	5,850	6,786	936
PHIL R	V	W	86	2,400	1,662	1,842	180
REP SAF	V	E	83	95,100	67,240	77,338	10,098
			84	110,950	81,040	91,620	10,580
			85	248,656	176,742	205,789	29,047
			86	137,649	114,423	130,612	16,189
SWEDEN	V	E	85	238	1,354	1,630	276
THAILND	V	W	85	28,152	13,300	24,556	11,256
			86	18,941	13,105	14,297	1,192
TURKEY	O	E	81	11,615	13,970	13,970	
YUGOSLV	O	E	85	50,279	35,956	40,828	4,872
	V	E	84	21,780	17,489	19,629	2,140

Prune, wine
1672000 PRUNE WINE (GAL)

Country	Mode	Reg	Yr	Quantity	F.A.S.	C.I.F.	Charges
TOTAL			81	27,025	156,079	188,426	32,347
			82	21,913	90,647	100,181	9,534
			83	69,201	275,593	300,408	24,815
			84	16,169	86,315	92,303	5,988
			85	16,150	31,184	37,562	6,378
			86	2,139	15,865	19,599	3,734
CANADA	O	E	85	648	1,241	1,241	
FRANCE	O	E	81	11,891	62,342	75,488	13,146
			82	1,426	7,434	8,880	1,446
			83	863	4,378	5,967	1,589
	V	E	81	2,615	14,525	17,202	2,677
ITALY	O	E	83	119	1,435	1,539	104
JAPAN	V	E	82	357	2,053	2,671	618
			86	2,139	15,865	19,599	3,734
	V	W	83	47	308	383	75
			84	2,813	23,816	25,550	1,734
SPAIN	O	E	81	10,083	63,350	76,817	13,467
			82	309	2,010	2,377	367
			83	240	1,802	2,148	346
	V	E	81	2,436	15,862	18,919	3,057
			83	944	7,290	8,175	885
U KING	O	E	82	13,560	59,389	62,939	3,550
			83	238	1,625	1,811	186
	V	E	83	66,750	258,755	280,385	21,630
			84	13,356	62,499	66,753	4,254
			85	9,205	15,297	18,387	3,090
	V	W	82	6,261	19,761	23,314	3,553
			85	6,297	14,646	17,934	3,288

Potato

Potato, dried
1405000 POTATOES, DRIED, DEHYDRATED (LB)

Country	Mode	Reg	Yr	Quantity	F.A.S.	C.I.F.	Charges
TOTAL			81	2,374,463	951,884	971,636	19,752
			82	1,514,763	577,036	594,331	17,295
			83	417,186	163,585	172,748	9,163
			84	3,171,523	1,320,966	1,386,086	65,120
			85	2,571,400	1,081,622	1,159,833	78,211
			86	4,225,550	1,430,611	1,489,823	59,212
BELGIUM	O	E	84	34,480	21,343	22,993	1,650
CANADA	A	E	81	4,961	1,860	3,529	1,669

Crop Product TSUSA commodity number, description, and unit of quantity Country	Mode	Reg	Yr	Quantity	F.A.S.	C.I.F.	Charges
	O	E	81	2,160,636	845,998	854,058	8,060
			82	1,433,080	520,385	533,288	12,903
			83	366,131	122,987	126,388	3,401
			84	2,452,706	871,553	871,553	
			85	1,638,193	558,065	558,065	
			86	2,349,583	730,855	730,855	
	O	W	81	120,440	35,521	35,521	
			82	40,000	14,017	14,017	
			83	432	544	544	
			85	87,617	29,571	29,571	
			86	929,965	309,069	309,069	
CHINA M	O	W	83	500	277	290	13
	V	E	81	8,463	5,519	6,341	822
			82	2,125	4,439	4,719	280
			83	2,090	1,790	4,049	2,259
			84	3,371	2,971	3,448	477
			86	10,200	6,883	7,768	885
	V	W	81	6,775	4,795	5,182	387
			82	6,573	3,821	4,107	286
			83	8,830	5,157	5,438	281
			84	3,005	2,119	2,232	113
			85	9,127	6,210	8,010	1,800
			86	21,921	11,702	12,346	644
CHINA T	V	E	85	476	1,200	1,249	49
			86	375	1,230	1,253	23
	V	W	83	328	447	485	38
			84	656	924	1,013	89
			85	1,190	1,206	1,292	86
COLOMB	V	E	84	11,975	7,680	9,608	1,928
FR GERM	A	E	81	1,606	848	919	71
			84	463	267	477	210
	V	E	81	5,284	7,632	8,157	525
			82	349	453	493	40
			86	7,709	3,295	4,911	1,616
	V	W	83	22,873	16,843	18,602	1,759
FRANCE	A	E	81	287	380	503	123
	V	E	82	5,000	6,725	7,366	641
HG KONG	A	W	84	841	2,820	4,074	1,254
	V	E	81	2,750	2,076	2,327	251
	V	W	84	1,575	1,358	1,491	133
			85	4,850	3,630	3,748	118
			86	1,000	1,056	1,092	36
INDNSIA	V	E	84	49,714	68,101	73,879	5,778
IRELAND	V	E	83	706	1,748	1,848	100
ISRAEL	V	E	84	11,162	4,893	6,092	1,199
			85	26,832	32,608	36,235	3,627
			86	3,850	1,340	1,694	354
	V	W	81	22,046	11,923	14,329	2,406
JAPAN	V	E	83	114	2,535	2,847	312
	V	W	82	488	782	837	55
			83	258	600	647	47
			84	236	406	451	45
			86	421	1,365	1,454	89
KOR REP	V	E	81	1,684	6,819	7,493	674
			82	2,344	9,815	10,921	1,106
			83	815	4,763	5,189	426
			84	1,301	5,651	6,127	476
			85	500	1,868	2,067	199
			86	567	1,641	1,782	141
	V	W	81	1,324	4,096	4,277	181
			82	1,033	4,657	5,065	408
			83	131	645	675	30
			84	3,850	4,669	5,191	522
			85	225	1,440	1,618	178
			86	3,541	3,467	4,063	596
MEXICO	O	W	81	6,790	1,540	1,540	
			83	7,000	1,647	1,647	
			84	53,468	7,976	7,976	
			86	7,744	1,936	1,936	
NETHLDS	O	E	81	20,725	14,229	17,517	3,288
	V	E	84	34,645	17,000	20,696	3,696
			86	83,774	35,444	41,235	5,791
PERU	V	E	81	8,799	5,510	6,112	602
			82	671	600	659	59
			83	6,427	2,970	3,326	356
			84	10,547	5,800	6,618	818
			85	18,821	10,045	10,712	667
			86	41,152	29,926	32,026	2,100
	V	W	81	1,389	2,602	2,799	197
PHIL R	V	W	86	1,989	1,550	1,763	213
SPAIN	V	E	82	23,100	11,342	12,859	1,517
SWITZLD	V	E	84	1,967	3,487	3,661	174
U KING	A	E	81	504	536	1,032	496
			84	1,629	1,182	2,207	1,025

Crop Product TSUSA commodity number, description, and unit of quantity Country	Mode	Reg	Yr	Quantity	F.A.S.	C.I.F.	Charges
	N	W	84	144,938	88,393	103,141	14,748
	O	E	84	112,577	69,691	78,632	8,941
	V	E	84	236,417	132,682	154,526	21,844
			85	783,569	435,779	507,266	71,487
			86	714,891	270,441	314,317	43,876
	V	W	83	551	632	773	141
			86	46,868	19,411	22,259	2,848

1418620 POTATOES, DEHYDRATED (LB)

Country	Mode	Reg	Yr	Quantity	F.A.S.	C.I.F.	Charges
TOTAL			81	135,564	66,880	66,880	
			82	44,016	25,886	26,344	458
			83	135,080	68,292	78,179	9,887
			84	363,843	172,756	192,312	19,556
			85	2,825,820	1,537,393	1,759,510	222,117
			86	1,193,931	529,354	550,404	21,050
CANADA	O	E	81	135,564	66,880	66,880	
			82	41,400	23,886	23,886	
			83	83,520	31,983	31,983	
			84	238,554	95,521	95,521	
			85	250,333	124,453	124,453	
			86	997,305	418,846	418,846	
CHINA M	V	W	83	1,160	1,477	1,569	92
ISRAEL	V	E	86	4,409	1,541	2,117	576
NETHLDS	A	E	85	2,700	1,381	3,785	2,404
	A	H	86	1,500	1,335	4,543	3,208
	A	W	86	1,900	1,412	3,454	2,042
	V	E	85	12,212	12,413	13,145	732
			86	85,800	41,210	43,984	2,774
	V	W	83	50,400	34,832	44,627	9,795
			84	85,500	52,418	65,804	13,386
			85	30,000	15,733	21,356	5,623
			86	60,027	50,125	59,875	9,750
SPAIN	V	E	84	250	253	358	105
U KING	A	E	84	562	323	775	452
	A	W	82	411	478	593	115
	O	E	84	35,229	21,807	25,431	3,624
			85	1,695,056	850,710	992,486	141,776
	V	E	82	2,205	1,522	1,865	343
			85	653,073	420,188	468,824	48,636
	V	W	84	3,748	2,434	4,423	1,989
			85	182,446	112,515	135,461	22,946
			86	42,990	14,885	17,585	2,700

Potato, flour
1407000 POTATO FLOUR (LB)

Country	Mode	Reg	Yr	Quantity	F.A.S.	C.I.F.	Charges
TOTAL			81	602,144	96,775	97,500	725
			82	699,789	224,567	225,853	1,286
			83	775,086	257,792	267,202	9,410
			84	1,007,035	320,510	327,834	7,324
			85	1,141,663	357,725	365,371	7,646
			86	1,304,789	402,468	413,230	10,762
CANADA	O	E	81	594,800	88,272	88,272	
			82	677,290	215,638	215,638	
			83	655,846	199,162	199,162	
			84	918,670	270,543	270,543	
			85	995,330	291,714	291,714	
			86	1,112,210	328,314	328,314	
	V	E	83	53,955	29,000	31,700	2,700
CHINA M	V	E	81	4,963	3,701	4,099	398
			82	109	385	399	14
			83	2,500	558	852	294
			84	9,605	3,656	4,685	1,029
	V	W	82	7,563	1,801	1,929	128
			83	5,788	3,377	3,798	421
			84	14,305	3,219	3,446	227
			85	5,500	1,073	1,215	142
CHINA T	V	E	83	5,313	2,954	3,367	413
			84	24,343	10,646	12,903	2,257
			85	40,494	22,746	23,681	935
			86	2,502	1,250	1,505	255
	V	W	81	1,310	471	487	16
			83	56	562	601	39
			84	25,994	25,551	28,083	2,532
			86	13,227	3,773	4,018	245
FR GERM	O	E	86	3,413	3,423	3,850	427
	V	E	85	2,205	1,003	1,203	200
HG KONG	V	E	83	5,578	1,422	2,016	594
			84	5,025	1,278	1,620	342
			86	16,535	6,201	6,698	497
	V	W	82	3,724	1,093	1,244	151

Crop
Product
TSUSA commodity number, description, and unit of quantity

Country	Mode	Reg	Yr	Quantity	F.A.S.	C.I.F.	Charges
			83	3,334	812	1,211	399
IRAN	V	E	82	1,640	458	562	104
ISRAEL	V	E	85	13,774	14,850	16,530	1,680
JAPAN	V	E	81	490	2,813	2,998	185
			83	750	2,519	2,735	216
	V	W	81	150	361	380	19
			82	656	383	441	58
			83	5,237	3,768	3,998	230
			84	2,625	1,316	1,511	195
			85	5,512	2,287	2,485	198
			86	4,931	6,230	6,575	345
KOR REP	V	E	84	210	451	524	73
	V	W	82	1,200	578	662	84
MEXICO	O	W	81	146	307	307	
N ANTIL	V	E	83	11,000	1,495	2,851	1,356
NETHLDS	V	E	82	6,000	2,536	2,904	368
			83	9,100	6,737	9,012	2,275
			84	2,101	654	981	327
			85	37,385	6,321	8,702	2,381
	V	W	83	14,556	2,991	3,214	223
			86	19,250	3,043	3,736	693
PERU	V	E	82	895	800	879	79
			84	3,307	2,350	2,556	206
PHIL R	V	W	81	285	850	957	107
			82	251	595	663	68
			83	2,073	2,435	2,685	250
			84	600	538	642	104
			86	2,912	2,398	2,806	408
PORTUGL	V	E	82	461	300	532	232
SWITZLD	V	E	85	807	1,253	1,324	71
THAILND	V	W	84	250	308	340	32
U KING	V	E	85	40,656	16,478	18,517	2,039
			86	129,809	47,836	55,728	7,892

Potato, fresh

1372000 POTATOES, WHITE, CERT SEED (CWT)

Country	Mode	Reg	Yr	Quantity	F.A.S.	C.I.F.	Charges
TOTAL			81	982,905	8,614,628	8,614,628	
			82	1,023,298	5,681,956	5,689,764	7,808
CANADA	O	E	81	932,462	8,143,494	8,143,494	
			82	947,571	4,996,928	5,004,736	7,808
	O	W	81	50,443	471,134	471,134	
			82	75,727	685,028	685,028	

1372020 POTATO WH CRT SD NOV CWT QUOTA (CWT)

Country	Mode	Reg	Yr	Quantity	F.A.S.	C.I.F.	Charges
TOTAL			83	470,586	2,175,995	2,175,995	
			84	406,185	3,449,720	3,459,236	9,516
			85	541,311	3,132,182	3,132,182	
			86	232,390	1,165,142	1,165,142	
CANADA	O	E	83	427,311	1,862,278	1,862,278	
			84	361,776	3,058,684	3,063,883	5,199
			85	494,881	2,718,117	2,718,117	
			86	202,521	947,936	947,936	
	O	W	83	43,275	313,717	313,717	
			84	42,994	376,806	376,806	
			85	45,930	412,015	412,015	
			86	29,869	217,206	217,206	
DOM REP	V	E	84	1,415	14,230	18,547	4,317
ITALY	O	E	85	500	2,050	2,050	

1372040 POTATO WH CRT SEED OV CWT QUOTA (CWT)

Country	Mode	Reg	Yr	Quantity	F.A.S.	C.I.F.	Charges
TOTAL			83	221,680	1,377,389	1,377,389	
			84	303,697	2,646,376	2,665,752	19,376
			85	488,808	3,828,608	3,828,614	6
			86	402,018	3,041,341	3,041,341	
CANADA	O	E	83	124,956	596,985	596,985	
			84	118,081	1,051,043	1,051,043	
			85	224,753	1,244,891	1,244,893	2
			86	99,949	437,292	437,292	
	O	H	85	1,040	8,322	8,322	
	O	W	83	96,724	780,404	780,404	
			84	179,435	1,534,476	1,534,476	
			85	262,616	2,571,962	2,571,966	4
			86	301,657	2,602,091	2,602,091	
DOM REP	V	E	84	6,181	60,857	80,233	19,376
JAPAN	O	E	86	412	1,958	1,958	
MOROC	O	W	85	399	3,433	3,433	

1372100 WHITE SEED POTATO ABV QUOTA (CWT)

Country	Mode	Reg	Yr	Quantity	F.A.S.	C.I.F.	Charges
TOTAL			81	470,783	4,323,132	4,323,253	156
			82	277,463	1,511,836	1,511,836	
CANADA	O	E	81	405,268	3,760,330	3,760,295	
			82	264,043	1,385,740	1,385,740	
	O	W	81	65,515	562,802	562,958	156
			82	12,919	122,598	122,598	
MEXICO	O	E	82	501	3,498	3,498	

1372120 POTATO WH CRT SD NOV CWT X QOTA (CWT)

Country	Mode	Reg	Yr	Quantity	F.A.S.	C.I.F.	Charges
TOTAL			83	954	6,407	7,587	1,180
			84	3,371	28,666	30,511	1,845
			85	10,615	55,970	56,520	550
			86	1,406	11,425	11,976	551
CANADA	O	E	83	724	3,024	3,024	
			84	2,869	23,936	23,936	
			85	10,015	49,970	49,970	
			86	866	4,945	4,945	
	O	W	85	460	4,600	4,600	
	V	E	86	540	6,480	7,031	551
DOM REP	V	E	83	230	3,383	4,563	1,180
			84	502	4,730	6,575	1,845
			85	140	1,400	1,950	550

1372140 POTATO WH CERT SD OV CWT EX QTA (CWT)

Country	Mode	Reg	Yr	Quantity	F.A.S.	C.I.F.	Charges
TOTAL			83	2,069	16,591	20,586	3,995
			84	2,450	19,580	19,980	400
			85	13,298	63,808	63,808	
			86	637	2,570	2,570	
CANADA	O	E	83	798	4,938	4,938	
			84	1,794	13,028	13,028	
			85	12,858	59,628	59,628	
			86	637	2,570	2,570	
	O	W	84	440	3,960	3,960	
			85	440	4,180	4,180	
DOM REP	V	E	83	1,271	11,653	15,648	3,995
			84	216	2,592	2,992	400

1372500 POTATOES, EXC SEED, WTHN QUO (CWT)

Country	Mode	Reg	Yr	Quantity	F.A.S.	C.I.F.	Charges
TOTAL			81	470,456	2,979,432	2,979,243	
			82	423,638	2,472,412	2,474,574	2,162
CANADA	O	E	81	470,406	2,978,972	2,978,783	
			82	423,638	2,472,412	2,474,574	2,162
	O	W	81	50	460	460	

1372510 RUSSET POT N CRT SD NOV CWT QU (CWT)

Country	Mode	Reg	Yr	Quantity	F.A.S.	C.I.F.	Charges
TOTAL			83	198,441	2,175,790	2,175,790	
			84	31,538	317,725	327,725	10,000
			85	247,295	1,450,628	1,454,857	4,229
			86	54,317	557,391	560,822	3,431
CANADA	O	E	83	198,001	2,170,327	2,170,327	
			84	31,118	314,365	324,365	10,000
			85	246,970	1,446,410	1,447,512	1,102
			86	53,967	553,897	557,328	3,431
	O	W	83	440	5,463	5,463	
			84	420	3,360	3,360	
			86	350	3,494	3,494	
	V	H	85	325	4,218	7,345	3,127

1372520 POTATO NSPF N CRT SD NOV CWT QU (CWT)

Country	Mode	Reg	Yr	Quantity	F.A.S.	C.I.F.	Charges
TOTAL			83	147,785	1,291,675	1,310,848	19,173
			84	197,493	1,210,900	1,246,589	35,689
			85	100,848	574,923	609,374	34,451
			86	164,412	1,367,415	1,370,551	3,136
CANADA	O	E	83	131,691	1,112,074	1,112,074	
			84	182,780	1,071,688	1,071,688	
			85	74,820	364,280	364,280	
			86	162,509	1,346,031	1,346,031	
	O	W	83	420	3,213	3,213	
			85	950	8,372	8,372	
			86	900	9,028	9,028	
	V	E	83	15,674	176,388	195,561	19,173
			84	11,239	104,892	117,051	12,159
			85	24,958	197,987	232,167	34,180
DOM REP	V	E	84	3,373	33,305	55,946	22,641
FRANCE	V	E	84	101	1,015	1,904	889
			85	120	4,284	4,555	271
			86	343	11,205	14,224	3,019
JAPAN	V	E	86	660	1,151	1,268	117

Crop
Product
TSUSA commodity number, description, and unit of quantity

1372530 RUSSET POT N CRT SD OV CWT QOTA (CWT)

Country	Mode	Reg	Yr	Quantity	F.A.S.	C.I.F.	Charges
TOTAL			83	93,930	428,295	428,295	
			84	74,785	277,490	277,490	
			85	108,807	406,265	406,265	
			86	59,856	222,119	222,119	
CANADA	O	E	83	93,450	424,695	424,695	
			84	74,785	277,490	277,490	
			85	108,807	406,265	406,265	
			86	59,856	222,119	222,119	
	O	W	83	480	3,600	3,600	

1372540 POTS NSPF NT CRT SEED OV CWT QU (CWT)

Country	Mode	Reg	Yr	Quantity	F.A.S.	C.I.F.	Charges
TOTAL			83	39,169	157,777	157,777	
			84	178,456	701,235	701,339	104
			85	7,415	29,217	29,217	
			86	36,539	191,852	193,584	1,732
CANADA	A	W	84	288	869	973	104
	O	E	83	39,169	157,777	157,777	
			84	178,168	700,366	700,366	
			85	7,415	29,217	29,217	
			86	35,533	181,449	181,449	
	O	W	86	430	4,300	4,300	
	V	E	86	576	6,103	7,835	1,732

1372800 POTATO, EXC SEED, ABV QUOTA (CWT)

Country	Mode	Reg	Yr	Quantity	F.A.S.	C.I.F.	Charges
TOTAL			81	1,999,384	16,873,669	16,873,676	6
			82	3,060,104	21,130,479	21,387,616	257,137
CANADA	O	E	81	1,927,814	16,483,536	16,483,543	6
			82	2,970,682	19,939,224	19,944,656	5,432
	O	W	81	71,395	388,208	388,208	
			82	8	1,382	1,382	
	V	E	82	89,414	1,189,873	1,441,578	251,705
YEMEN A	O	E	81	175	1,925	1,925	

1372810 RUSSET POT N CRT NOV CWT EX QTA (CWT)

Country	Mode	Reg	Yr	Quantity	F.A.S.	C.I.F.	Charges
TOTAL			83	684,539	5,629,786	5,637,340	7,554
			84	807,471	10,943,061	10,949,670	6,609
			85	983,363	9,444,215	9,517,456	73,241
			86	1,397,325	9,987,711	9,992,201	4,490
CANADA	A	H	83	565	2,600	9,748	7,148
			85	200	3,217	5,939	2,722
	O	E	83	683,493	5,621,016	5,621,016	
			84	804,309	10,909,527	10,909,527	
			85	938,871	8,995,649	8,995,651	2
			86	1,396,725	9,979,311	9,981,615	2,304
	O	W	83	420	5,524	5,524	
			84	1,422	15,349	15,349	
			85	132	2,301	2,301	
	V	E	85	43,585	436,148	504,791	68,643
			86	600	8,400	10,586	2,186
DOM REP	V	E	83	61	646	1,052	406
			84	1,740	18,185	24,794	6,609
			85	575	6,900	8,774	1,874

1372820 POTATO NSPF N CRT NOV CWT X QTA (CWT)

Country	Mode	Reg	Yr	Quantity	F.A.S.	C.I.F.	Charges
TOTAL			83	872,157	6,041,357	6,180,620	139,263
			84	681,311	5,414,302	5,566,964	152,662
			85	804,902	4,828,879	4,922,240	93,361
			86	669,851	4,310,735	4,520,767	210,032
BAHAMAS	V	E	84	48	1,088	1,120	32
CANADA	N	E	83	62,421	705,961	845,224	139,263
	O	E	83	809,461	5,331,858	5,331,858	
			84	628,561	4,884,856	4,884,867	11
			85	766,610	4,455,052	4,455,058	6
			86	594,831	3,662,995	3,665,885	2,890
	O	W	83	275	3,538	3,538	
			84	1,694	24,707	24,707	
			85	1,600	23,015	23,015	
	V	E	84	8,847	125,798	135,142	9,344
			85	19,539	186,025	224,893	38,868
			86	74,796	638,893	843,818	204,925
DOM REP	N	E	84	40,601	365,294	498,806	133,512
	V	E	84	1,560	12,559	22,322	9,763
			85	16,653	162,074	216,561	54,487
			86	98	3,360	3,954	594
FRANCE	V	E	86	126	5,487	7,110	1,623
MOROC	O	E	85	500	2,713	2,713	

1372830 RUSSET POT N CRT OV CWT EX QUTA (CWT)

Country	Mode	Reg	Yr	Quantity	F.A.S.	C.I.F.	Charges
TOTAL			83	460,446	1,445,787	1,445,907	120
			84	325,863	1,565,778	1,567,477	1,699
			85	482,093	2,040,505	2,040,509	4
			86	347,355	1,237,101	1,237,101	
CANADA	A	H	83	375	2,005	2,125	120
	O	E	83	460,071	1,443,782	1,443,782	
			84	325,023	1,556,782	1,558,481	1,699
			85	482,093	2,040,505	2,040,509	4
			86	347,355	1,237,101	1,237,101	
	O	W	84	840	8,996	8,996	

1372840 POTATO NSPF NT CRT OV CWT X QTA (CWT)

Country	Mode	Reg	Yr	Quantity	F.A.S.	C.I.F.	Charges
TOTAL			83	299,106	1,285,624	1,289,035	3,411
			84	238,876	1,092,305	1,092,305	
			85	269,962	1,262,018	1,264,970	2,952
			86	78,472	393,712	396,435	2,723
CANADA	A	E	86	22	1,050	1,297	247
	N	E	85	39,177	259,704	259,704	
	O	E	83	298,210	1,272,099	1,272,099	
			84	238,426	1,089,833	1,089,833	
			85	229,929	991,693	991,693	
			86	72,597	376,130	376,130	
	O	W	83	200	2,900	2,900	
			84	450	2,472	2,472	
			86	941	4,581	4,581	
DOM REP	V	E	83	696	10,625	14,036	3,411
			85	775	9,300	11,710	2,410
			86	230	2,768	3,221	453
FRANCE	V	E	85	81	1,321	1,863	542
			86	4,682	9,183	11,206	2,023

Potato, frozen

1418610 POTATOES, FROZEN (LB)

Country	Mode	Reg	Yr	Quantity	F.A.S.	C.I.F.	Charges
TOTAL			81	14,989,135	2,944,539	2,947,128	2,589
			82	22,164,380	4,398,970	4,411,419	12,449
			83	26,557,461	5,248,890	5,368,585	119,695
			84	49,732,382	10,362,688	10,921,114	558,426
			85	69,080,904	13,444,130	14,633,652	1,189,522
			86	73,526,953	15,529,827	16,345,874	816,047
BELGIUM	V	W	84	39,683	11,855	12,006	151
CANADA	N	E	84	4,647,545	992,466	1,507,129	514,663
			85	9,273,953	1,672,363	2,697,545	1,025,182
			86	2,494,505	461,405	641,298	179,893
	O	E	81	14,989,135	2,944,539	2,947,128	2,589
			82	22,074,442	4,374,637	4,377,736	3,099
			83	25,377,200	5,019,706	5,019,706	
			84	44,603,934	9,273,821	9,273,821	
			85	57,754,467	11,391,556	11,391,561	5
			86	64,116,270	13,880,955	13,887,720	6,765
	O	W	83	42,120	13,233	13,288	55
			84	39,390	5,872	5,872	
			85	20,520	6,293	6,293	
	V	E	83	1,049,521	192,322	305,606	113,284
			84	316,740	58,044	92,136	34,092
			85	603,111	119,188	158,934	39,746
			86	5,175,685	806,722	1,311,727	505,005
FRANCE	O	E	85	5,291	2,952	3,432	480
	V	E	86	3,603	1,263	1,584	321
GABON	O	E	86	41,250	4,984	4,984	
GUINEA	V	E	86	77,572	24,147	30,892	6,745
JAPAN	V	E	82	438	1,107	1,243	136
	V	W	82	440	439	468	29
			84	880	947	995	48
KOR REP	V	E	84	510	774	903	129
NETHLDS	V	E	83	88,620	23,629	29,985	6,356
			84	44,100	7,029	11,028	3,999
			85	1,378,941	238,313	356,817	118,504
			86	1,580,248	339,469	449,713	110,244
	V	W	82	89,060	22,787	31,972	9,185
			84	39,600	11,880	17,224	5,344
			85	44,621	13,465	19,070	5,605
PHIL R	V	W	86	2,108	1,227	1,456	229
U KING	V	E	86	35,712	9,655	16,500	6,845

Potato, prepared or preserved
1418630 POTATOES PREP OR PRES NSPF (LB)

Country	Mode	Reg	Yr	Quantity	F.A.S.	C.I.F.	Charges
TOTAL			81	1,528,592	323,859	334,019	10,160
			82	1,343,579	323,749	346,166	22,417
			83	1,138,151	290,560	312,196	21,636
			84	1,822,334	389,313	426,339	37,026
			85	1,152,260	308,512	338,435	29,923
			86	1,964,687	578,329	633,122	54,793
ARGENT	V	E	81	16,875	9,758	11,023	1,265
			82	16,875	7,491	8,874	1,383
			86	12,042	5,880	6,727	847
BELGIUM	V	E	81	3,750	1,069	1,247	178
			82	141,066	34,750	40,985	6,235
			83	44,447	11,632	13,377	1,745
			84	284,639	58,023	73,120	15,097
			85	254,888	55,323	69,650	14,327
			86	328,672	104,296	121,220	16,924
	V	W	83	16,875	3,995	4,957	962
			84	33,750	7,042	9,556	2,514
			85	10,125	8,175	9,029	854
			86	108,583	41,207	47,013	5,806
BRAZIL	O	E	81	2,063	1,106	1,106	
	V	E	81	32,175	10,725	12,707	1,982
			82	33,495	11,165	14,305	3,140
			83	33,000	11,000	13,293	2,293
			85	30,937	8,460	10,708	2,248
C RICA	V	E	83	20,268	20,151	26,783	6,632
CANADA	A	W	84	100	268	280	12
	O	E	81	1,423,573	249,096	250,596	1,500
			82	1,051,536	204,495	206,897	2,402
			83	910,939	166,594	166,594	
			84	1,320,603	207,166	207,166	
			85	707,949	143,033	143,033	
			86	951,779	199,253	199,253	
	O	W	84	3,440	4,462	4,462	
			85	26,066	27,040	27,565	525
			86	2,726	3,160	3,160	
	V	E	86	84,315	29,142	36,175	7,033
CHINA M	V	E	81	2,470	791	871	80
	V	W	82	5,937	2,697	2,874	177
			83	3,000	1,378	1,466	88
CHINA T	V	E	82	1,246	1,325	1,504	179
			84	580	816	979	163
COLOMB	A	E	85	8,416	3,681	5,709	2,028
	N	E	84	33,650	20,415	27,486	7,071
	V	E	81	5,400	2,736	3,232	496
			82	23,448	13,497	16,603	3,106
			83	57,479	41,473	46,115	4,642
			84	34,659	19,901	22,486	2,585
			85	3,000	2,040	2,230	190
			86	3,865	2,822	3,103	281
DENMARK	V	E	84	2,963	3,749	4,368	619
DOM REP	V	E	81	1,968	410	517	107
FR GERM	O	E	83	2,960	3,340	3,953	613
	V	E	81	12,454	19,834	21,679	1,845
			83	863	1,102	1,218	116
			85	4,034	6,264	6,440	176
			86	61,021	10,562	11,600	1,038
	V	W	83	3,200	2,378	2,916	538
			84	600	252	313	61
FRANCE	N	E	82	11,723	3,847	4,653	806
			83	8,050	3,237	4,312	1,075
	V	E	81	11,729	3,057	3,824	767
			84	5,063	1,084	1,191	107
			86	3,672	1,286	1,477	191
	V	W	83	1,488	566	624	58
HG KONG	V	E	81	2,250	749	851	102
	V	W	82	1,500	540	583	43
			84	750	471	477	6
INDIA	V	E	83	1,237	852	1,592	740
ITALY	V	E	84	952	811	1,068	257
JAPAN	V	E	81	281	494	537	43
			83	143	301	326	25
			84	158	266	294	28
			85	1,589	3,873	4,295	422
	V	H	81	394	824	1,024	200
			82	261	342	448	106
			83	704	944	1,165	221
			84	881	1,381	1,596	215
	V	W	81	2,957	15,696	16,358	662
			82	479	997	1,076	79

Country	Mode	Reg	Yr	Quantity	F.A.S.	C.I.F.	Charges
			83	3,776	5,446	5,781	335
			84	6,202	9,695	10,606	911
			85	2,628	3,377	3,638	261
			86	422	1,490	1,588	98
KOR REP	V	E	81	1,555	1,054	1,210	156
NETHLDS	O	E	82	54,013	41,753	46,397	4,644
	V	E	84	36,000	4,266	6,039	1,773
PERU	V	E	86	34,074	21,275	22,975	1,700
PHIL R	V	W	81	31	337	393	56
			82	2,000	850	967	117
			83	1,300	1,411	1,605	194
			84	12,620	9,192	10,519	1,327
			85	7,980	5,610	6,319	709
			86	15,849	10,389	11,437	1,048
S HELNA	O	E	86	9,259	5,310	6,241	931
SINGAPR	V	E	84	7,875	17,222	17,806	584
SPAIN	V	E	85	37,831	5,180	5,430	250
SWEDEN	V	E	81	2,676	1,988	2,250	262
			83	1,008	573	633	60
			85	3,111	1,462	1,582	120
	V	W	81	1,008	599	663	64
			84	1,050	578	618	40
SWITZLD	V	E	81	3,783	2,865	3,162	297
			84	569	446	475	29
THAILND	V	W	81	1,200	671	769	98
			86	4,670	3,602	3,995	393
U KING	O	E	84	35,230	21,807	25,434	3,627
	V	E	83	27,414	14,187	15,486	1,299
			86	343,738	138,655	157,158	18,503
	V	W	85	53,706	34,994	42,807	7,813

Potato, seed, eyes
1256700 SEED POTATO EYES (LB)

Country	Mode	Reg	Yr	Quantity	F.A.S.	C.I.F.	Charges
TOTAL			81	47,400	4,029	4,029	
			85	5,000	2,398	2,398	
			86	300	2,934	2,934	
CANADA	O	E	81	47,400	4,029	4,029	
			85	5,000	2,398	2,398	
			86	300	2,934	2,934	

Potato, starch
1325000 POTATO STARCH (LB)

Country	Mode	Reg	Yr	Quantity	F.A.S.	C.I.F.	Charges
TOTAL			81	41,409,838	5,597,419	7,185,958	1,556,923
			82	26,788,865	4,147,564	5,141,774	994,210
			83	21,795,153	2,788,180	3,498,769	710,589
			84	30,083,742	5,231,868	6,415,786	1,183,918
			85	61,080,632	11,828,453	14,552,848	2,724,395
			86	47,422,463	11,085,145	13,558,076	2,472,931
BELGIUM	O	E	81	39,326	4,863	6,723	1,860
			82	237,912	32,329	41,731	9,402
			85	39,021	5,612	7,501	1,889
	V	E	82	57,292	8,129	10,185	2,056
			83	157,621	16,366	21,126	4,760
			85	73,072	34,026	50,808	16,782
			86	385,920	56,459	73,710	17,251
BRAZIL	V	W	86	17,636	1,792	2,908	1,116
CANADA	A	E	84	1,573	13,117	13,393	276
			85	27,826	30,458	31,194	736
			86	3,647	21,947	23,376	1,429
	O	E	81	1,940,140	306,461	320,527	14,066
			82	673,289	159,814	161,974	2,160
			83	1,684,045	309,081	309,081	
			84	978,841	198,329	201,293	2,964
			85	457,687	98,651	100,251	1,600
			86	1,629,411	271,047	272,972	1,925
CHINA M	V	E	81	9,619	4,242	4,546	304
			82	20,311	5,155	6,641	1,486
			83	14,650	3,909	7,784	3,875
			84	33,840	9,598	12,705	3,107
			85	6,581	2,262	2,693	431
			86	44,431	3,770	4,069	299
	V	W	82	9,191	2,116	2,287	171
			83	1,406	427	483	56
			86	5,500	2,488	2,691	203
CHINA T	V	E	85	3,900	1,710	1,946	236
	V	W	83	6,000	4,282	4,576	294
			84	7,518	5,108	5,511	403
			85	4,400	2,309	2,500	191

Crop Product TSUSA commodity number, description, and unit of quantity Country	Mode	Reg	Yr	Quantity	F.A.S.	C.I.F.	Charges
DENMARK	N	E	81	648,583	88,204	123,876	35,672
	O	E	85	1,721,499	231,063	319,289	88,226
			86	2,819,840	381,473	528,906	147,433
	V	E	81	104,025	15,952	23,556	4,358
			82	45,534	6,467	8,368	1,901
			84	97,223	14,076	19,833	5,757
			85	96,544	14,079	19,836	5,757
			86	512,543	64,154	95,654	31,500
FINLAND	O	E	84	45,745	13,563	16,646	3,083
			85	1,154,115	341,287	418,894	77,607
			86	504,976	141,268	168,798	27,530
	V	E	81	493,230	155,184	178,134	22,950
			84	45,745	16,646	18,144	1,498
			85	2,348,111	706,516	844,495	137,979
			86	158,744	44,302	53,332	9,030
FR GERM	A	E	82	2,178	832	1,835	1,003
	N	E	84	831,634	182,925	224,239	41,314
			85	1,302,089	379,392	455,580	76,188
			86	561,890	148,636	190,463	41,827
	O	E	81	2,681,380	309,258	371,825	62,567
			82	39,683	3,999	5,950	1,951
			83	1,099,631	290,815	360,807	69,992
			84	2,313,647	393,809	480,302	86,493
			85	2,485,490	662,682	740,506	77,824
			86	3,029,261	723,613	889,063	165,450
	V	E	81	127,291	17,641	23,679	6,038
			82	670,679	130,997	155,306	24,309
			83	363,547	100,630	117,184	16,554
			84	1,176,332	293,750	355,381	61,631
			85	8,358,541	1,096,332	1,232,653	136,321
			86	1,560,487	502,911	579,368	76,457
	V	W	81	2,253	1,353	1,600	247
			83	85,744	35,773	40,172	4,399
			84	137,443	48,529	59,282	10,753
			85	264,518	81,694	101,964	20,270
			86	398,591	170,717	202,893	32,176
FRANCE	N	E	84	626,208	75,254	104,839	29,585
			85	2,510,485	433,419	558,709	125,290
	O	E	81	161,713	22,501	27,378	4,877
			83	61,864	9,312	12,593	3,281
			84	43,543	4,150	5,980	1,830
			86	1,873,910	555,256	654,733	99,477
	V	E	81	818,484	333,231	368,134	34,903
			82	1,362,713	573,184	633,983	60,799
			83	1,531,776	187,468	247,236	59,768
			84	1,910,681	717,047	816,255	99,208
			85	4,122,558	1,373,870	1,586,073	212,203
			86	7,689,322	2,500,604	2,968,841	468,237
	V	W	81	87,302	150,315	155,643	5,328
			82	41,668	63,882	63,882	
			84	87,284	9,188	15,163	5,975
			86	396,828	65,340	95,340	30,000
HG KONG	O	E	83	2,000	489	533	44
	V	E	81	5,100	2,007	2,400	393
			82	8,745	2,202	2,702	500
			83	13,813	5,181	5,770	589
			84	5,250	1,155	1,551	396
			85	31,781	9,102	11,114	2,012
			86	15,020	3,316	3,876	560
	V	W	82	4,306	1,148	1,230	82
			83	6,800	1,414	1,579	165
			84	1,496	963	1,013	50
			85	126	2,151	2,339	188
IRELAND	O	E	82	236,430	26,244	38,994	12,750
ITALY	V	E	81	43,542	5,835	7,600	1,765
JAPAN	N	W	84	9,239	6,417	6,793	376
	V	E	81	17,972	12,161	13,466	1,305
			82	13,830	8,585	9,451	866
			83	33,662	22,064	24,161	2,097
			84	57,819	32,366	35,809	3,443
			85	14,370	10,464	11,480	1,016
			86	12,644	11,956	12,729	773
	V	H	82	1,515	565	743	178
			83	1,422	903	1,083	180
	V	W	81	46,757	25,044	26,655	1,611
			82	55,176	28,800	30,849	2,049
			83	63,028	33,742	35,839	2,097
			84	69,073	33,858	37,540	3,682
			85	48,894	26,258	27,591	1,333
			86	45,060	38,506	41,133	2,627
KOR REP	V	E	82	4,409	1,050	1,158	108
			83	938	556	622	66
			84	1,800	1,326	1,495	169
	V	W	81	1,200	649	700	51

Crop Product TSUSA commodity number, description, and unit of quantity Country	Mode	Reg	Yr	Quantity	F.A.S.	C.I.F.	Charges
MEXICO	O	W	83	5,952	750	750	
			85	10,882	2,298	2,298	
NETHLDS	A	E	82	1,433	322	1,288	966
	N	E	81	2,057,213	231,677	314,185	82,508
			82	3,475,144	382,706	519,744	137,038
			83	1,693,782	167,616	215,113	47,497
			84	3,276,948	378,437	508,790	130,353
			85	3,333,245	991,516	1,156,022	164,506
			86	3,062,729	512,220	685,453	173,233
	N	W	85	66,246	19,128	25,613	6,485
	O	E	81	14,401,475	1,678,637	2,278,641	600,004
			82	9,535,889	1,068,501	1,423,672	355,171
			83	7,969,642	830,643	1,089,964	259,321
			84	8,875,122	1,366,698	1,646,983	280,285
			85	14,939,945	2,322,949	2,921,549	598,600
			86	4,317,108	657,776	841,532	183,756
	O	W	84	2,205	455	618	163
	V	E	81	17,116,865	2,143,493	2,820,444	648,581
			82	10,027,804	1,521,177	1,882,825	361,648
			83	6,356,600	678,593	890,775	212,182
			84	8,025,954	1,078,929	1,404,633	325,704
			85	16,347,360	2,653,719	3,534,637	880,918
			86	10,367,795	1,651,036	2,107,727	456,691
	V	W	81	41,471	5,986	7,940	1,954
			84	97,082	26,814	32,751	5,937
			86	324,079	41,156	59,091	17,935
NIGER	V	E	85	27,778	4,644	5,629	985
PERU	A	W	83	298	407	914	507
POLAND	V	E	86	39,682	5,263	5,474	211
SPAIN	V	W	85	4,409	1,300	1,477	177
SWEDEN	N	E	86	819,450	346,320	418,820	72,500
	O	E	84	419,276	92,420	111,026	18,606
			85	178,511	38,217	44,617	6,400
			86	6,213,629	1,969,350	2,353,854	384,504
	V	E	81	89,069	33,619	40,021	6,402
			82	263,734	119,360	136,976	17,616
			83	99,208	18,566	23,166	4,600
			84	667,441	177,634	232,258	54,624
			85	568,786	145,315	200,918	55,603
			86	525,218	158,852	181,452	22,600
SWITZLD	V	E	83	236,430	21,510	29,637	8,127
			86	1,190	1,178	1,229	51
THAILND	V	E	83	36,900	6,495	8,386	1,891
	V	W	85	3,600	1,400	1,519	119
U KING	N	E	81	475,828	49,106	68,285	19,179
	O	E	83	156,796	20,306	24,636	4,330
			84	198,097	33,819	38,489	4,670
			85	356,394	54,331	69,713	15,382
	V	E	83	111,598	20,882	24,799	3,917
			84	39,683	5,488	7,071	1,583
			85	171,868	50,299	61,440	11,141
			86	85,922	32,439	38,589	6,150

Psyllium

Psyllium, seed husk, natural drug
4391070 PSYLLIUM SEED HUSKS (LB)

Country	Mode	Reg	Yr	Quantity	F.A.S.	C.I.F.	Charges
TOTAL			81	11,088,347	9,080,185	10,237,715	1,157,530
			82	8,571,710	7,988,442	8,848,605	860,163
			83	8,874,018	10,475,046	11,331,685	856,639
			84	17,812,060	27,576,103	29,276,707	1,700,604
			85	29,038,552	34,554,253	37,420,819	2,866,566
			86	12,169,601	13,770,136	14,891,034	1,120,898
ARGENT	V	E	81	11,023	6,898	8,445	1,547
BRAZIL	V	W	84	8,809	4,660	5,630	970
BULGAR	V	W	84	17,500	6,272	10,400	4,128
CANADA	A	E	81	500	2,000	2,234	234
CHILE	V	W	84	66,077	32,288	33,170	882
CHINA M	A	W	86	460	11,566	12,206	640
	V	E	84	88	11,257	11,665	408
CHINA T	V	W	81	251,322	171,000	193,800	22,800
			83	44,092	41,755	45,472	3,717
			84	1,587	7,343	7,858	515
EGYPT	V	E	83	220	4,850	4,972	122
FR GERM	V	E	81	529	1,678	1,870	192
	V	W	84	7,247	5,537	6,411	874
HG KONG	V	E	83	1,000	830	898	68
			86	3,486	6,211	7,005	794
INDIA	N	E	86	260,605	229,100	256,629	27,529

Crop
Product
TSUSA commodity number, description, and unit of quantity

Country	Mode	Reg	Yr	Quantity	F.A.S.	C.I.F.	Charges
	O	E	82	44,000	42,838	45,738	2,900
			85	44,533	62,620	67,657	5,037
	V	E	81	3,353,824	2,391,414	2,835,713	444,299
			82	1,972,037	1,649,337	1,903,133	253,796
			83	2,180,585	2,466,825	2,712,146	245,321
			84	3,182,403	5,082,054	5,426,338	344,284
			85	3,465,678	3,859,097	4,201,739	342,642
			86	2,128,430	2,344,169	2,539,730	195,561
	V	W	81	7,470,917	6,506,774	7,195,002	688,228
			82	6,555,589	6,296,012	6,899,464	603,452
			83	6,565,617	7,861,516	8,461,771	600,255
			84	14,351,151	22,180,911	23,507,388	1,326,477
			85	25,486,453	30,587,886	33,102,374	2,514,488
			86	9,776,620	11,179,090	12,075,464	896,374
JAPAN	A	E	81	232	421	651	230
	V	E	83	5,512	5,355	5,919	564
KOR REP	V	W	83	44,092	71,621	74,957	3,336
PHIL R	V	W	85	41,888	44,650	49,049	4,399
S HELNA	V	E	84	118,400	176,405	190,503	14,098
SPAIN	V	W	84	8,774	3,800	4,928	1,128
SWITZLD	V	E	82	84	255	270	15
U KING	V	E	84	50,024	65,576	72,416	6,840
	V	W	83	32,900	22,294	25,550	3,256

Pumpkin

Pumpkin, fresh or frozen**
1379300 PUMPKIN, BREADFRUIT, FR, CH, FZ (LB)
   (See Breadfruit, fresh or frozen under Breadfruit)

Q

Quebracho

Quebracho, tannin
4705030 QUEBRACHO WOOD (LB)

Country	Mode	Reg	Yr	Quantity	F.A.S.	C.I.F.	Charges
TOTAL			81	2,886,626	824,316	969,259	144,943
			82	1,084,980	355,868	413,062	57,194
			83	1,404,085	489,580	560,597	71,017
			84	418,874	158,420	181,607	23,187
			85	2,876,850	1,128,572	1,290,000	161,428
			86	3,107,563	971,031	1,107,638	136,607
ARGENT	O	E	86	103,042	41,937	41,937	
	V	E	81	2,732,304	783,866	921,824	137,958
			82	599,968	189,406	218,539	29,133
			83	864,520	315,966	360,152	44,186
			84	286,598	108,940	123,903	14,963
			85	2,022,388	828,792	942,855	114,063
			86	2,399,798	742,893	859,968	117,075
	V	W	81	22,046	6,010	6,199	189
			82	308,644	111,342	131,017	19,675
			83	197,967	73,052	85,986	12,934
			84	110,230	41,100	48,221	7,121
			85	268,452	99,996	117,428	17,432
			86	128,184	55,952	64,488	8,536
BRAZIL	V	E	83	198,414	66,640	76,344	9,704
			84	22,046	8,380	9,483	1,103
			85	176,372	62,417	71,663	9,246
			86	88,184	32,000	36,499	4,499
CANADA	O	E	86	256,079	59,249	59,249	
MEXICO	O	E	83	55,000	6,362	6,362	
PARAGUA	V	E	81	132,276	34,440	41,236	6,796
			82	176,368	55,120	63,506	8,386
			83	88,184	27,560	31,753	4,193
			85	387,592	128,987	148,571	19,584
			86	132,276	39,000	45,497	6,497
VENEZ	V	E	85	22,046	8,380	9,483	1,103

4705740 QUEBRACHO NOT CRUDE OR PROC (LB)

Country	Mode	Reg	Yr	Quantity	F.A.S.	C.I.F.	Charges
TOTAL			81	33,338,786	8,678,995	10,398,209	1,719,214
			82	14,604,615	4,548,336	5,305,853	757,517
			83	15,439,235	5,009,969	5,766,514	756,545
			84	12,063,018	3,823,900	4,395,746	571,846
			85	7,892,002	2,297,752	2,709,798	412,046
			86	8,570,263	2,810,904	3,231,310	420,406
ARGENT	N	E	84	2,342,916	792,241	912,208	119,967
	N	W	85	225,899	82,320	100,122	17,802
	O	W	81	14,903	5,365	5,365	
	V	E	81	27,169,388	7,050,438	8,429,192	1,378,754
			82	10,127,513	3,119,022	3,630,029	511,007
			83	14,350,085	4,604,951	5,296,549	691,598
			84	6,749,550	2,092,886	2,386,503	293,617
			85	6,709,018	1,861,801	2,201,522	339,721
			86	7,466,677	2,446,479	2,804,423	357,944
	V	W	81	2,112,284	646,378	785,175	138,797
			82	1,443,541	496,917	587,802	90,885
			83	582,092	230,548	270,594	40,046
			84	449,575	182,780	213,411	30,631
			85	286,296	111,876	130,304	18,428
			86	174,201	65,240	76,539	11,299
AUSTRIA	V	E	86	157,774	67,545	80,115	12,570
BRAZIL	V	E	81	50,706	14,090	17,420	3,330
			82	127,558	45,870	54,726	8,856
			83	110,230	41,630	47,292	5,662
			84	81,570	29,289	33,345	4,056
			85	161,834	58,762	66,661	7,899
			86	39,683	15,840	17,868	2,028
FR GERM	V	E	84	40,000	15,160	17,257	2,097
FRANCE	V	E	81	2,205	2,457	2,650	193
			82	4,630	7,607	7,637	30
			85	46,297	14,182	16,391	2,209
ISRAEL	V	E	83	88,184	28,920	33,194	4,274
PANAMA	V	E	86	220,460	65,000	76,160	11,160
PARAGUA	V	E	81	3,504,284	857,459	1,030,281	172,822
			82	2,460,453	773,974	897,664	123,690
			83	308,644	103,920	118,885	14,965
			84	2,399,407	711,544	833,022	121,478
			85	334,791	126,517	144,605	18,088
			86	511,468	150,800	176,205	25,405
REP SAF	V	E	81	485,016	102,808	128,126	25,318
			82	440,920	104,946	127,995	23,049
			85	127,867	42,294	50,193	7,899

Quince

Quince, jelly or jam
1532800 QUINCE JELLY, JAM, ETC. (LB)

Country	Mode	Reg	Yr	Quantity	F.A.S.	C.I.F.	Charges
TOTAL			81	59,591	42,008	48,331	6,323
			82	128,947	73,041	83,425	10,384
			83	194,906	90,952	105,278	14,326
			84	155,872	77,046	93,800	16,754
			85	81,954	31,181	37,138	5,957
			86	326,576	151,630	173,066	21,436
ARGENT	O	E	81	20	805	805	
	V	E	82	9,557	3,629	4,452	823
			83	12,428	5,011	5,980	969
			84	3,712	1,468	1,815	347
			86	40,958	19,911	22,235	2,324
	V	W	83	5,682	2,598	3,199	601
			84	3,385	929	1,269	340
			85	3,704	1,420	1,837	417
BRAZIL	V	E	82	33,000	16,300	20,096	3,796
			83	7,838	3,871	4,721	850
			86	65,128	25,965	30,484	4,519
CANADA	O	E	82	420	261	261	
	V	E	83	600	1,102	1,170	68
CHINA T	V	W	83	462	449	511	62
EGYPT	V	E	83	3,571	1,890	2,227	337
FR GERM	V	E	81	1,095	949	1,007	58
			82	1,165	894	983	89
			84	1,080	999	1,146	147
	V	W	82	520	357	403	46
FRANCE	N	E	84	1,161	712	840	128
	O	E	81	1,620	1,888	2,113	225
	V	E	81	5,029	4,277	4,779	502

Crop Product TSUSA commodity number, description, and unit of quantity Country	Mode	Reg	Yr	Quantity	F.A.S.	C.I.F.	Charges
			82	9,456	7,756	8,544	788
			83	14,022	7,445	8,557	1,112
			84	11,869	6,340	7,179	839
			85	1,617	1,097	1,265	168
			86	3,791	6,181	7,206	1,025
	V	W	81	1,562	1,089	1,187	98
			82	2,574	1,957	2,150	193
			84	8,480	6,312	7,109	797
G BISAU	V	E	81	2,117	1,560	1,752	192
GREECE	O	E	82	360	274	274	
	V	E	81	6,478	6,030	7,242	1,212
			83	7,139	5,495	6,623	1,128
			84	3,600	3,600	4,399	799
			85	3,600	1,995	2,324	329
			86	14,571	12,103	13,824	1,721
	V	W	82	1,914	1,900	2,124	224
			83	1,186	1,150	1,290	140
			84	3,586	3,300	3,771	471
GUATMAL	V	E	84	675	433	486	53
HUNGARY	V	E	83	25,206	7,613	9,451	1,838
ISRAEL	V	E	81	2,698	1,475	1,785	310
			82	4,500	3,126	3,444	318
			83	1,800	1,250	1,417	167
			84	2,700	1,637	1,817	180
LEBANON	N	E	84	6,481	4,148	4,570	422
	O	E	81	525	498	498	
			84	1,058	631	699	68
	V	E	81	3,846	3,300	3,710	410
			83	4,521	4,449	4,770	321
			84	1,323	950	1,022	72
	V	W	83	1,323	862	966	104
			86	3,469	1,183	1,354	171
MEXICO	O	W	82	14,848	2,696	2,696	
			83	4,850	703	703	
			84	6,700	1,891	1,891	
			85	22,000	4,201	4,201	
			86	54,048	7,404	7,404	
NETHLDS	V	E	83	450	399	421	22
PERU	V	E	86	2,780	3,341	3,602	261
PORTUGL	V	E	81	19,161	8,200	9,766	1,566
			82	14,620	7,650	8,623	973
			83	86,586	35,718	41,029	5,311
			84	48,671	19,275	25,366	6,091
			85	20,921	8,491	9,526	1,035
			86	63,404	27,280	32,399	5,119
	V	W	82	4,233	2,880	3,305	425
			84	4,233	2,304	2,991	687
			86	4,233	2,304	3,209	905
REP SAF	V	W	83	225	292	345	53
			84	238	292	374	82
ROMANIA	V	E	84	18,851	7,858	8,914	1,056
			85	3,000	1,125	1,288	163
			86	13,227	3,146	3,828	682
S HELNA	O	E	86	13,750	7,395	8,676	1,281
SPAIN	A	W	84	970	294	1,334	1,040
	V	E	81	397	261	282	21
			82	12,772	4,371	5,544	1,173
			83	9,839	2,178	2,783	605
			84	10,770	2,448	4,072	1,624
			85	22,000	10,100	13,588	3,488
			86	28,578	18,327	20,076	1,749
SWITZLD	V	E	81	7,796	5,202	6,156	954
			82	10,925	9,350	10,150	800
			83	7,152	5,604	6,050	446
			84	5,251	3,292	3,610	318
			85	2,159	1,451	1,609	158
			86	9,791	11,680	12,309	629
	V	W	81	1,035	853	965	112
			82	1,530	1,915	2,174	259
			83	720	870	979	109
			86	1,574	1,603	1,734	131
TURKEY	V	E	84	5,972	3,772	4,356	584
U KING	O	E	84	1,173	2,488	2,614	126
	V	E	81	2,641	3,731	4,057	326
			82	6,553	7,725	8,202	477
			83	2,877	3,893	4,313	420
			84	450	508	592	84
			86	899	1,140	1,216	76
YUGOSLV	V	E	84	3,483	1,165	1,564	399
			85	2,953	1,301	1,500	199
			86	6,375	2,667	3,510	843

Quince, paste and pulp**
1524000 APPLE AND QUINCE PASTE AND PULP (LB)
(See Apple, paste and pulp under Apple)

R

Radish

Radish, fresh or frozen
1374000 RADISHES, FRSH, CHLD, FROZEN (LB)

Country	Mode	Reg	Yr	Quantity	F.A.S.	C.I.F.	Charges
TOTAL			81	6,370,014	838,436	868,520	30,104
			82	7,799,502	1,224,818	1,265,524	40,706
			83	10,749,355	2,126,567	2,157,631	31,064
			84	15,889,060	2,825,393	2,871,428	46,035
			85	14,690,945	2,716,809	2,742,224	25,415
			86	18,757,834	4,008,013	4,023,793	15,780
BELGIUM	A	E	83	198	387	470	83
			84	4,148	4,923	7,451	2,528
			86	1,270	3,027	3,557	530
CANADA	O	E	81	603,757	113,291	113,291	
			82	1,218,465	114,391	114,391	
			83	828,308	171,969	171,969	
			84	986,165	107,397	107,397	
			85	522,402	71,070	71,070	
			86	732,943	194,362	194,362	
	O	W	81	16,790	3,268	3,268	
			82	24,140	5,165	5,165	
			83	3	489	489	
			84	40,000	3,600	3,600	
			85	223,790	39,509	39,509	
			86	49,380	8,318	8,318	
CHINA M	V	E	83	1,000	362	446	84
	V	W	82	500	259	275	16
			83	1,250	462	508	46
			84	21,000	1,755	2,065	310
CHINA T	N	W	83	26,471	14,775	17,422	2,647
			84	7,881	7,319	8,704	1,385
	V	E	83	8,640	1,260	1,351	91
			84	1,078	870	1,056	186
	V	W	82	20,040	20,693	22,151	1,458
			85	7,625	6,602	7,002	400
			86	12,540	9,188	9,588	400
COLOMB	O	W	81	5,000	519	519	
DOM REP	A	E	81	29,300	3,000	8,999	5,999
			82	5,723	384	674	290
	N	E	83	72,096	3,288	8,367	5,079
			85	218,178	8,800	15,549	6,749
	V	E	81	355,134	20,336	44,343	24,007
			82	492,783	24,639	62,278	37,639
			83	208,518	8,669	22,592	13,923
			84	600,179	28,005	64,567	36,562
			85	275,230	37,920	53,754	15,834
			86	239,362	33,934	46,343	12,409
GUATMAL	A	E	83	14,142	3,193	6,373	3,180
HAITI	V	E	83	89,100	4,500	8,820	4,320
			84	45,000	2,250	2,250	
			85	45,000	1,800	1,953	153
HG KONG	V	E	82	7,200	1,295	1,427	132
			83	14,400	1,570	1,604	34
	V	W	81	109	327	366	39
			84	1,260	627	701	74
			85	4,896	1,420	1,660	240
ITALY	O	E	82	238	2,000	2,200	200
JAMAICA	V	E	82	11,316	3,822	3,942	120
JAPAN	A	H	81	11	312	371	59
	N	E	84	2,567	4,050	5,848	1,798
	V	E	82	310	653	694	41
			83	5,975	7,241	8,566	1,325
			84	2,007	7,098	7,593	495
			85	3,003	2,839	3,027	188
			86	44	1,039	1,130	91

Country	Mode	Reg	Yr	Quantity	F.A.S.	C.I.F.	Charges
	V	H	83	1,584	563	781	218
			84	2,454	1,122	2,185	1,063
			85	5,368	2,477	3,519	1,042
			86	6,490	3,519	5,070	1,551
	V	W	82	3,086	2,665	2,858	193
			83	1,800	322	356	34
			84	3,929	3,745	4,383	638
			86	722	1,023	1,085	62
KOR REP	V	E	85	28,750	5,809	6,148	339
			86	276	1,012	1,093	81
	V	W	84	375	777	839	62
MEXICO	O	E	81	15,893	1,802	1,802	
			85	9,450	2,205	2,205	
			86	31,743	9,345	9,345	
	O	W	81	5,344,020	695,581	695,561	
			82	6,012,265	1,046,912	1,047,343	431
			83	9,475,870	1,907,517	1,907,517	
			84	14,122,383	2,646,033	2,646,040	7
			85	13,312,991	2,527,988	2,527,989	1
			86	17,656,190	3,737,661	3,738,317	656
MONSRAT	O	W	86	22,674	3,338	3,338	
MOZAMBQ	O	W	85	33,622	6,146	6,146	
			86	4,200	2,247	2,247	
NETHLDS	A	E	84	2,436	2,741	3,612	871
			85	640	2,224	2,693	469
PANAMA	V	E	84	45,000	2,250	2,250	
THAILND	V	W	82	3,436	1,940	2,126	186
			84	1,198	831	887	56

Radish, seed
1267300 RADISH SEED (LB)

Country	Mode	Reg	Yr	Quantity	F.A.S.	C.I.F.	Charges
TOTAL			81	14,627	63,915	75,711	11,796
			82	26,481	93,558	115,153	21,595
			83	66,321	171,026	211,870	40,844
			84	52,195	145,889	189,178	43,289
			85	24,611	139,356	145,442	6,086
			86	27,534	154,715	172,834	18,119
AUSTRAL	V	H	84	1,323	1,290	1,440	150
			86	3,370	2,062	2,320	258
BRAZIL	V	W	82	4,409	3,000	3,088	88
CANADA	O	W	83	198	395	395	
CHINA M	V	W	84	200	823	871	48
DENMARK	A	W	83	550	330	944	614
	V	E	85	539	11,984	12,233	249
FR GERM	A	E	82	500	910	1,291	381
			84	165	352	541	189
	N	E	81	1,098	1,429	1,869	440
	V	E	84	20	366	389	23
			86	562	1,233	1,449	216
FRANCE	A	E	81	661	678	1,745	1,067
			82	785	958	1,794	836
			83	639	1,799	2,418	619
	A	W	84	447	487	894	407
	V	E	84	44	285	304	19
	V	W	81	150	371	384	13
			83	1,102	1,229	1,555	326
HG KONG	O	E	83	60	300	450	150
	V	E	82	150	497	508	11
	V	W	81	100	282	284	2
ITALY	N	W	84	641	1,710	3,488	1,778
	V	W	85	500	1,700	1,865	165
			86	619	1,950	2,163	213
JAPAN	A	E	81	107	743	898	155
			82	331	6,264	7,485	1,221
			83	236	3,097	4,113	1,016
			84	4,690	16,480	18,542	2,062
			85	661	11,676	12,412	736
	A	W	81	1,546	2,137	6,476	4,339
			82	2,141	3,094	7,669	4,575
			83	3,486	4,679	12,803	8,124
			84	9,010	13,041	32,097	19,056
	N	E	84	1,404	6,849	7,570	721
			85	260	9,050	10,064	1,014
	N	H	81	393	4,617	5,102	485
			82	1,430	11,684	12,172	488
			84	2,146	7,438	8,507	1,069
			86	345	3,306	3,751	445
	N	W	81	3,408	26,633	29,650	3,017
			82	14,705	48,146	60,716	12,570
			83	19,654	73,660	95,601	21,941
			84	19,970	63,883	77,518	13,635

Country	Mode	Reg	Yr	Quantity	F.A.S.	C.I.F.	Charges
			86	11,140	44,993	56,023	11,030
	O	E	82	5	345	519	174
			83	30	746	932	186
	V	E	81	4,370	11,697	11,957	260
			82	875	15,599	15,721	122
			83	900	16,448	17,701	1,253
			84	10	266	309	43
	V	H	83	5,792	11,218	12,280	1,062
			85	1,148	9,629	10,044	415
	V	W	81	1,724	5,103	5,488	385
			83	19,265	14,308	16,655	2,347
			84	7,664	7,866	8,991	1,125
			85	5,763	50,473	52,805	2,332
			86	2,050	1,764	2,153	389
KOR REP	A	E	81	239	6,523	7,277	754
	A	W	81	7	368	403	35
	N	E	85	15,225	39,415	40,412	997
	O	W	82	15	300	335	35
			83	20	347	469	122
	V	E	86	4,620	34,747	34,998	251
	V	W	86	1,761	15,220	15,399	179
MEXICO	O	W	82	200	350	350	
			83	10,142	11,374	11,374	
NETHLDS	A	E	81	127	275	525	250
			82	100	417	493	76
			83	831	2,401	3,230	829
			86	1,213	1,092	2,550	1,458
	A	W	82	395	458	1,217	759
			83	176	300	420	120
			84	733	1,115	1,837	722
	N	W	82	218	600	825	225
	O	E	82	200	400	400	
			83	1,578	3,099	3,099	
			84	200	450	450	
	V	E	81	540	1,567	1,898	331
			84	200	520	730	210
	V	W	81	113	323	495	172
SWITZLD	O	E	81	44	1,169	1,260	91
	V	E	82	22	536	570	34
U KING	A	E	83	1,252	23,472	25,465	1,993
			84	3,328	22,668	24,700	2,032
			85	175	3,107	3,129	22
			86	1,810	46,819	50,478	3,659
	N	E	85	340	2,322	2,478	156
	O	E	86	44	1,529	1,550	21
	V	E	83	410	1,824	1,966	142

Raffia Palm

Palm leaf, basket**
2224200 BASKTS A BAGS, RATTN, PLM LF (NO)

Country	Mode	Reg	Yr	Quantity	F.A.S.	C.I.F.	Charges
TOTAL			81	23,083,306	14,247,880	16,854,904	2,606,299
			82	23,582,124	13,543,445	16,097,488	2,554,043
			83	27,920,528	13,784,046	16,935,108	3,151,062
			84	28,384,245	16,487,278	20,922,909	4,435,631
			85	27,915,341	18,143,737	22,889,753	4,746,016
			86	33,488,195	24,708,011	30,846,462	6,138,451
BARBADO	A	E	85	192	1,509	1,614	105
BELGIUM	V	E	86	1,500	7,543	9,893	2,350
BNGLDSH	A	E	81	3,780	2,751	4,776	2,025
			82	1,000	686	1,120	434
	V	E	81	11,803	30,665	40,642	9,977
			82	11,699	32,624	50,627	18,003
			83	6,740	16,781	24,725	7,944
			84	2,053	13,015	20,420	7,405
			85	812	6,196	9,086	2,890
	V	W	81	14,345	27,396	34,879	7,483
			82	8,674	12,251	16,778	4,527
			83	7,863	8,828	10,553	1,725
			84	6,054	8,490	10,342	1,852
			85	1,609	5,021	7,134	2,113
			86	866	3,197	3,925	728
BOTSWAN	O	W	82	150	1,632	1,837	205
BRAZIL	A	E	81	480	1,361	1,524	163
	V	E	84	34,992	13,997	24,995	10,998
	V	W	84	9,936	3,974	9,672	5,698
C RICA	V	E	83	150	375	417	42
			84	206	482	564	82
CAMROON	V	W	85	5,472	3,064	3,327	263

Crop
Product
TSUSA commodity number, description, and unit of quantity

Country	Mode	Reg	Yr	Quantity	F.A.S.	C.I.F.	Charges
CANADA	A	E	82	11	330	385	55
	O	E	81	1,356	1,163	1,263	100
			82	2,582	3,959	3,959	
			83	191	336	336	
	V	E	84	2,630	3,286	4,589	1,303
CHILE	V	E	85	2,832	2,212	3,193	981
			86	2,012	3,400	4,080	680
CHINA M	A	E	83	1,217	2,058	5,214	3,156
			84	4,586	3,582	4,890	1,308
			86	6,000	1,080	1,953	873
	A	W	83	5,740	8,721	21,817	13,096
	N	E	84	959,416	927,282	1,190,872	263,590
			86	137,275	120,412	149,421	29,009
	N	W	83	328,699	364,097	464,583	100,486
	O	E	81	1,440	610	787	177
			82	5,421	7,515	9,542	2,027
			83	13,762	18,182	23,014	4,832
			84	3,052	5,808	8,839	3,031
			85	39,120	33,890	45,000	11,110
			86	27,162	15,632	19,526	3,894
	O	W	81	181	910	965	55
			82	1,116	1,243	1,502	259
	V	E	81	1,272,082	879,854	1,087,715	209,096
			82	2,286,998	1,478,139	1,903,819	425,680
			83	2,127,457	1,401,777	1,760,121	358,344
			84	786,012	878,941	1,146,141	267,200
			85	1,180,972	1,235,006	1,563,963	328,957
			86	1,277,832	1,206,832	1,486,730	279,898
	V	H	81	3,163	4,999	5,453	454
			83	544	1,963	2,454	491
			84	859	3,327	4,543	1,216
			86	1,668	3,124	4,248	1,124
	V	W	81	1,664,700	1,227,676	1,462,599	234,923
			82	1,398,572	1,127,112	1,378,556	251,444
			83	2,031,062	1,394,629	1,691,361	296,732
			84	2,170,225	2,405,368	2,934,779	529,411
			85	2,296,786	2,066,841	2,560,754	493,913
			86	4,569,749	3,468,441	4,277,808	809,367
CHINA T	A	E	81	288	630	1,175	545
			83	73	420	620	200
	A	W	84	84	479	1,866	1,387
			86	6,000	1,320	1,414	94
	N	E	82	121,838	137,849	165,368	27,519
			83	100,529	78,250	98,682	20,432
			85	55,611	27,157	46,908	19,751
			86	43,100	8,866	14,877	6,011
	N	W	82	204,682	225,997	253,730	27,733
			84	56,117	96,003	109,493	13,490
			85	62,397	51,722	66,824	15,102
	O	E	82	700	3,420	4,578	1,158
			83	1,824	4,127	4,669	542
			84	522	2,890	4,311	1,421
			86	209,491	42,128	45,133	3,005
	O	H	86	480	2,490	2,865	375
	V	E	81	347,853	396,552	458,561	62,009
			82	89,398	131,385	160,149	28,764
			83	93,910	107,473	128,174	20,701
			84	164,526	267,161	323,921	56,760
			85	131,587	186,037	225,487	39,450
			86	383,695	378,628	448,766	70,138
	V	H	81	4,408	4,958	5,709	751
			82	678	3,960	4,628	668
			83	2,133	12,443	15,700	3,257
			84	3,408	10,706	12,695	1,989
			85	3,508	11,603	13,292	1,689
			86	2,788	9,076	10,450	1,374
	V	W	81	856,981	856,466	972,720	114,294
			82	275,221	328,745	394,641	65,896
			83	479,048	530,566	604,164	73,598
			84	952,056	589,753	705,496	115,743
			85	499,660	474,101	553,674	79,573
			86	613,490	486,483	550,751	64,268
COLOMB	A	E	81	136,522	131,455	152,314	20,859
			82	99,112	82,497	96,169	13,672
			83	46,969	36,278	40,786	4,508
			84	70,354	86,502	98,501	11,999
			85	246,244	121,633	150,644	29,011
			86	284,279	119,760	149,485	29,725
	A	W	81	1,538	3,538	4,607	1,069
			82	3,092	1,593	1,653	60
			83	47,606	24,791	29,218	4,427
			84	90,995	48,583	59,972	11,389
	N	E	81	1,149	938	1,168	230
DOM REP	A	E	86	864	1,160	1,979	819

Crop
Product
TSUSA commodity number, description, and unit of quantity

Country	Mode	Reg	Yr	Quantity	F.A.S.	C.I.F.	Charges
	V	E	81	4,230	3,412	5,494	2,082
			82	3,686	9,758	11,951	2,193
ECUADOR	A	E	83	60	296	319	23
			84	94	473	509	36
EGYPT	A	E	86	50,000	25,000	31,913	6,913
F W IND	V	W	81	21,446	6,029	8,626	2,597
			84	7,228	6,936	9,571	2,635
FINLAND	V	W	86	4,400	3,478	5,058	1,580
FR GERM	A	E	83	187	617	669	52
			85	100,000	2,286	2,780	494
	A	W	84	11	403	526	123
	N	E	82	166	1,856	2,048	192
			84	436	6,312	7,922	1,610
	O	E	84	79	2,165	2,615	450
	O	W	83	94	797	797	
	V	E	81	94	4,999	5,451	452
			83	56	261	273	12
			84	123	2,095	2,337	242
			85	27	1,204	1,552	348
			86	31	2,162	2,342	180
	V	W	85	85	4,064	5,013	949
FRANCE	A	E	81	79	1,473	1,645	172
			83	213	3,303	3,830	527
			84	26	439	834	395
			85	2	1,143	1,162	19
			86	93	3,693	4,376	683
	A	W	83	418	419	498	79
	N	E	82	1,640	32,588	35,507	2,919
	O	E	82	500	2,963	3,259	296
	V	E	81	944	19,400	23,252	3,852
			82	532	9,841	10,251	410
			83	1,997	32,280	35,794	3,514
			84	2,899	12,655	14,750	2,095
			85	3,301	14,229	16,024	1,795
			86	2,862	10,814	12,049	1,235
	V	W	81	1,920	889	972	83
			83	395	527	565	38
			85	3	1,356	1,437	81
GHANA	V	E	83	240	1,403	2,780	1,377
GREECE	V	E	82	802	5,282	6,303	1,021
	V	W	81	220	2,550	3,302	752
GUATMAL	A	E	82	225	421	463	42
			83	4,400	2,919	3,491	572
			84	35,424	1,290	1,554	264
	A	W	81	318	2,420	3,171	751
			84	9,509	346	460	114
	N	E	81	18,201	104,944	139,249	34,305
	O	E	82	120	691	691	
			84	209	414	664	250
	V	E	82	12,673	64,506	85,385	20,879
			83	10,434	8,783	9,145	362
			84	1,944	1,546	1,698	152
HAITI	A	E	82	142	712	802	90
			84	2,000	1,500	2,242	742
	N	E	81	847,579	732,623	869,445	136,822
			82	191,448	257,355	302,951	45,596
			83	4,093	7,959	9,676	1,717
			84	54,556	47,699	57,797	10,098
	N	W	81	9,226	10,724	14,888	4,164
	O	E	81	468	312	362	50
	V	E	81	225,236	224,711	277,225	52,514
			82	303,676	258,356	315,076	56,720
			83	302,878	209,392	256,042	46,650
			84	238,505	130,309	163,613	33,304
			85	108,886	206,099	242,185	36,086
			86	72,567	226,272	237,054	10,782
	V	W	82	419	2,095	3,576	1,481
			83	4,651	7,512	9,748	2,236
			84	13,642	15,861	20,142	4,281
			85	16,682	17,703	22,546	4,843
HG KONG	A	E	82	2,600	3,256	4,599	1,343
			83	1,368	2,411	3,037	626
			84	2,122	1,188	3,203	2,015
	A	W	84	320	2,044	3,440	1,396
	N	E	82	128,931	177,173	216,184	39,011
			83	6,293	39,408	49,187	9,779
			84	90,610	142,775	194,373	51,598
			86	111,252	180,708	223,722	43,014
	N	W	81	91,488	56,872	68,323	11,451
			82	51,347	42,609	51,514	8,905
			84	220,826	197,015	236,271	39,256
			85	141,107	144,216	180,655	36,439
	O	E	81	4,672	4,186	5,103	917
			82	200	490	519	29

Crop
Product
TSUSA commodity number, description, and unit of quantity

Country	Mode	Reg	Yr	Quantity	F.A.S.	C.I.F.	Charges
			83	1,340	7,207	7,758	551
			84	732	6,529	6,896	367
			85	6,970	7,078	7,306	228
			86	63,868	13,767	16,730	2,963
	V	E	81	486,856	535,743	639,739	103,996
			82	446,495	502,560	613,427	110,867
			83	348,341	359,145	450,576	91,431
			84	495,991	504,467	667,355	162,888
			85	319,040	401,525	504,949	103,424
			86	321,712	286,381	365,920	79,539
	V	H	81	36	301	320	19
			82	3,345	2,773	3,217	444
			83	1,020	8,574	9,835	1,261
			84	1,857	8,007	9,569	1,562
			85	1,984	13,650	14,768	1,118
			86	1,996	23,311	26,097	2,786
	V	W	81	641,622	570,042	656,327	86,285
			82	586,735	542,696	637,877	95,181
			83	594,569	486,147	589,744	103,597
			84	616,141	616,377	743,747	127,370
			85	396,494	506,657	611,984	105,327
			86	649,271	833,640	1,002,387	168,747
HONDURA	A	E	85	3,095	4,297	5,033	736
	N	E	82	314	1,849	2,071	222
			83	836	4,128	4,509	381
	V	E	84	2,044	7,245	7,973	728
			85	595	1,907	2,134	227
			86	2,067	1,198	1,472	274
INDIA	A	E	83	15,658	7,376	12,375	4,999
			84	941	10,408	14,448	4,040
	A	W	81	1,233	7,340	9,758	2,418
			82	898	7,448	10,715	3,267
	N	E	82	3,675	4,418	5,923	1,505
	N	W	81	25,090	62,557	75,473	12,916
	V	E	81	29,345	13,529	25,755	12,226
			82	3,518	5,561	9,229	3,668
			83	8,825	15,668	19,932	4,264
			84	11,847	32,416	45,826	13,410
			85	6,214	28,855	34,364	5,509
	V	W	81	21,671	59,322	77,461	18,139
			82	45,390	82,445	108,804	26,359
			83	28,345	117,445	164,529	47,084
			84	30,610	128,768	168,244	39,476
			85	20,239	79,790	119,786	39,996
			86	9,132	50,851	62,534	11,683
INDNSIA	A	W	83	280	966	1,839	873
			84	790	1,928	3,879	1,951
			85	555	1,943	3,257	1,314
	N	W	81	16,752	33,606	43,351	9,745
			82	18,276	56,205	75,038	18,833
			83	16,524	40,875	56,261	15,386
			84	31,132	83,889	120,906	37,017
			85	44,919	158,398	201,923	43,525
			86	227,837	585,094	775,560	190,466
	V	E	81	78	343	381	38
			82	51,390	21,066	28,125	7,059
			83	1,200	6,922	9,881	2,959
			84	9,343	29,798	44,410	14,612
			85	24,740	67,950	100,485	32,535
			86	73,732	153,217	218,546	65,329
	V	H	86	631	1,623	2,634	1,011
	V	W	81	6,394	22,317	26,712	4,395
			82	4,820	30,110	42,306	12,196
			83	49,068	290,914	357,585	66,671
			84	78,626	355,735	495,711	139,976
			85	90,261	342,222	466,778	124,556
			86	143,583	321,000	443,149	122,149
ISRAEL	A	E	83	72	720	1,120	400
	V	W	84	7,200	1,675	2,250	575
ITALY	A	E	86	450	6,478	6,681	203
	N	E	82	12,222	13,151	13,838	687
	V	E	81	7,957	18,942	19,445	503
			82	2,160	4,000	4,889	889
			83	7,435	7,333	8,201	868
			84	1,425	2,473	3,279	806
			86	2,979	6,627	7,766	1,139
	V	W	81	7,131	18,284	20,792	2,508
			84	48	532	759	227
IVY CST	V	W	86	5,246	45,013	47,582	2,569
JAMAICA	A	E	81	4,250	5,215	7,035	1,820
			82	600	1,405	2,077	672
	V	E	85	171	1,934	3,544	1,610
			86	1,892	16,455	18,949	2,494
JAPAN	A	H	82	320	1,058	2,239	1,181
	A	W	81	110	1,954	2,686	732
			83	50	419	632	213
			84	40	293	367	74
	N	W	84	8,576	6,195	7,678	1,483
	V	E	81	27	1,911	2,318	407
			82	4,410	6,618	8,808	2,190
			83	277	2,356	2,995	639
			84	44,964	13,802	17,222	3,420
			85	3,600	6,504	8,946	2,442
			86	2,000	1,707	1,889	182
	V	H	81	1,540	3,211	3,982	771
			83	1,035	1,564	1,725	161
			84	500	255	290	35
			85	671	5,362	6,343	981
			86	28	1,248	1,361	113
	V	W	81	593	2,694	3,294	600
			82	7,200	10,175	10,510	335
			83	54,211	17,175	22,383	5,208
			84	11,837	7,697	11,003	3,306
			85	2,727	5,963	7,429	1,466
			86	12,097	19,146	24,085	4,939
KENYA	A	E	82	850	4,208	7,221	3,013
			84	287	2,386	2,948	562
			85	500	16,065	17,898	1,833
	A	W	81	272	1,141	1,897	756
			86	230	1,233	1,333	100
	V	E	81	237	269	306	37
KOR REP	A	W	84	500	488	1,850	1,362
	O	E	83	3,200	3,772	5,069	1,297
			86	2,520	1,080	1,080	
	V	E	82	840	3,829	3,903	74
			83	972	4,602	5,541	939
			84	15,648	8,937	11,663	2,726
	V	W	81	10,000	23,416	27,145	3,729
			82	11,520	2,784	2,856	72
			83	19,368	17,476	20,403	2,927
			84	7,196	16,879	20,646	3,767
			85	5,522	14,181	16,542	2,361
			86	20,903	43,448	47,215	3,767
MACAO	V	E	81	26,236	25,145	29,146	4,001
			82	13,314	11,012	13,571	2,559
			83	42,661	25,979	39,603	13,624
			84	112,793	68,210	85,581	17,371
			85	47,792	45,920	54,641	8,721
			86	68,804	72,650	85,930	13,280
	V	H	81	7,556	3,264	3,727	463
			82	700	406	511	105
			83	4,896	1,858	2,315	457
	V	W	81	47,914	33,819	38,149	4,330
			82	100,448	72,941	85,716	12,775
			83	110,926	67,033	76,615	9,582
			84	127,397	150,218	173,307	23,089
			85	103,016	128,598	143,520	14,922
			86	222,224	186,220	209,379	23,159
MALAYSA	V	E	81	108	1,078	1,294	216
			83	172	863	2,788	1,925
	V	W	81	16	282	331	49
			84	312	798	984	186
MAURITN	V	E	83	1,737	7,862	9,862	2,000
MEXICO	A	E	81	43,526	13,798	19,458	5,660
			83	150	280	430	150
			84	2,437	9,939	11,077	1,138
	A	W	81	13,077	35,252	39,661	4,409
			83	365	519	907	388
			84	767	1,845	2,247	402
	N	E	81	5,077,889	1,972,006	1,977,833	5,827
			82	8,218	8,518	9,589	1,071
			84	28,597	13,442	16,291	2,849
	N	W	82	102,015	39,027	40,057	1,030
	O	E	81	1,602,729	667,071	667,500	429
			82	10,052,038	3,514,716	3,519,595	4,879
			83	9,968,001	2,176,369	2,176,816	447
			84	11,299,024	3,049,136	3,052,584	3,448
			85	11,694,941	2,959,919	2,960,078	159
			86	12,489,623	2,951,128	2,951,477	349
	O	H	85	50,000	11,500	11,500	
	O	W	81	1,710,233	595,972	596,082	110
			82	675,808	225,746	225,746	
			83	1,368,550	284,755	284,755	
			84	170,967	52,534	52,534	
			85	474,120	86,080	86,080	
			86	204,087	32,777	32,777	
	V	E	81	83,680	22,816	26,499	3,683
			82	82,266	84,925	89,771	4,846

R 395

Crop Product TSUSA commodity number, description, and unit of quantity Country	Mode	Reg	Yr	Quantity	F.A.S.	C.I.F.	Charges
			83	10,205	11,059	13,373	2,314
			84	20,900	11,591	15,164	3,573
			85	49,530	15,076	17,446	2,370
			86	15,240	5,119	6,549	1,430
	V	W	81	2,529	6,021	6,021	
			83	152	303	507	204
MOROC	A	E	81	55	440	947	507
			82	36	266	283	17
			84	400	468	1,350	882
	N	E	81	2,260	5,465	6,631	1,166
			84	35,050	18,806	24,406	5,600
	V	E	81	10,088	27,210	35,203	7,993
			83	44,013	105,893	118,366	12,473
			84	44,655	84,463	100,026	15,563
			85	73,390	124,548	146,161	21,613
			86	16,042	30,032	35,103	5,071
	V	W	81	1,884	4,745	5,508	763
			82	1,500	10,500	10,792	292
NETHLDS	A	E	84	2,586	1,389	1,771	382
PANAMA	V	W	86	695	2,231	2,689	458
PERU	A	E	81	360	288	304	16
			83	586	3,236	3,822	586
			84	1,038	4,280	5,673	1,393
			86	940	2,303	3,046	743
	A	W	82	100	300	449	149
			83	1,798	1,600	3,375	1,775
			84	700	1,400	1,942	542
	N	W	81	828	2,483	3,186	703
	V	E	81	1,242	3,230	4,231	1,001
			85	3,148	9,044	13,985	4,941
PHIL R	A	E	83	350	680	2,172	1,492
	N	E	81	270,568	162,741	218,440	55,699
			83	363,318	313,152	420,621	107,469
			85	679,459	1,007,331	1,451,764	444,433
			86	1,148,373	1,674,398	2,266,692	592,294
	N	W	81	1,178	2,199	2,671	472
			82	3,100,572	1,491,314	1,896,429	405,115
			83	2,186,445	1,596,122	2,166,390	570,268
			84	3,812,133	2,056,972	2,846,956	789,984
			85	1,103,789	1,321,265	1,736,382	415,117
			86	4,193,211	4,209,694	5,387,163	1,177,469
	O	E	81	36,868	22,252	27,405	5,153
			82	27,264	16,372	20,503	4,131
			83	3,785	19,506	23,269	3,763
			84	1,934	4,176	5,743	1,567
			85	4,700	1,317	2,302	985
			86	31,229	17,353	24,591	7,238
	O	W	81	120	338	529	191
			84	346	1,647	2,031	384
	V	E	81	1,044,688	578,042	776,143	198,101
			82	1,208,602	894,969	1,210,568	315,599
			83	1,182,619	724,928	974,592	249,664
			84	2,110,883	1,125,336	1,726,573	601,237
			85	1,747,594	1,136,468	1,646,791	510,323
			86	1,316,047	1,349,400	1,806,384	456,984
	V	H	81	36,510	28,579	38,261	9,682
			82	45,014	47,703	62,639	14,936
			83	71,601	99,580	131,614	32,034
			84	80,089	78,769	117,980	39,211
			85	103,255	99,128	141,808	42,680
			86	72,187	90,086	125,060	34,974
	V	W	81	6,076,833	3,539,643	4,543,978	1,004,335
			82	1,589,266	1,047,428	1,392,593	345,165
			83	5,657,728	2,351,400	3,084,196	732,796
			84	3,044,911	1,657,775	2,482,962	825,187
			85	5,738,839	4,348,786	5,887,170	1,538,384
			86	3,903,444	4,249,893	5,722,281	1,472,388
PITCARN	V	W	86	10,957	19,941	25,293	5,352
POLAND	V	E	84	3,966	7,688	8,844	1,156
PORTUGL	V	E	81	2,664	8,225	9,840	1,615
			82	5,424	3,978	6,101	2,123
			84	5,432	12,428	18,127	5,699
			86	686	1,254	1,314	60
	V	W	85	4,456	3,177	9,926	6,749
			86	2,268	1,915	2,984	1,069
REP SAF	A	E	82	65	576	660	84
			86	383	3,145	3,947	802
ROMANIA	V	E	85	2,593	16,103	21,932	5,829
SALVADR	A	E	84	2,200	7,611	7,947	336
			85	863	6,338	7,975	1,637
	A	W	81	1,375	900	1,329	429
	N	E	81	19,475	10,744	20,541	9,797
			82	24,900	9,070	19,247	10,177
	V	E	81	11,795	5,420	9,650	4,230

Crop Product TSUSA commodity number, description, and unit of quantity Country	Mode	Reg	Yr	Quantity	F.A.S.	C.I.F.	Charges
			82	1,500	800	1,155	355
SINGAPR	V	E	81	160	1,117	1,707	590
			82	1,440	7,245	8,610	1,365
			83	6,032	14,306	21,448	7,142
			84	13,812	17,367	20,443	3,076
			85	31,341	76,500	100,292	23,792
			86	300	1,650	2,279	629
	V	W	81	15,921	9,239	11,606	2,367
			82	206	1,132	1,332	200
			83	33,856	16,166	20,348	4,182
			84	15,117	9,001	12,643	3,642
			85	6,020	18,350	22,993	4,643
			86	1,862	12,747	16,794	4,047
SOLMN I	V	E	85	100	1,098	1,286	188
SPAIN	A	E	82	25	257	329	72
			84	52	1,063	1,198	135
	V	E	81	749	1,462	1,929	467
			82	349	1,617	2,183	566
			83	815	3,065	4,055	990
			84	21,795	42,679	53,897	11,218
			85	14,477	51,229	59,872	8,643
	V	W	83	60	259	390	131
SRI LKA	V	E	81	2,768	4,699	6,499	1,800
	V	W	81	1,238	2,798	3,208	410
			82	853	1,177	1,333	156
			83	2,263	7,484	9,806	2,322
			84	525	1,729	1,924	195
SWITZLD	A	E	86	24	1,371	1,642	271
	V	E	86	9,692	10,829	13,589	2,760
	V	W	85	27,219	14,954	19,095	4,141
			86	6,652	21,165	23,680	2,515
THAILND	A	E	84	37	283	2,722	2,439
	N	E	86	283,520	560,537	748,619	188,082
	N	W	82	22,342	56,329	73,477	17,148
			83	2,032	8,364	11,194	2,830
			84	2,297	6,973	8,500	1,527
			86	43,774	82,736	95,461	12,725
	V	E	81	10,835	18,245	24,557	6,312
			82	34,118	52,090	62,262	10,172
			83	11,546	40,829	54,671	13,842
			84	2,938	21,764	28,853	7,089
			85	93,240	168,414	219,999	51,585
			86	2,918	13,762	20,322	6,560
	V	H	81	33	291	330	39
			83	515	3,526	4,017	491
			85	1,230	10,229	13,242	3,013
			86	486	4,422	6,560	2,138
	V	W	81	105,672	289,295	371,575	82,280
			82	57,344	182,616	240,366	57,750
			83	50,651	161,108	198,519	37,411
			84	28,742	168,272	210,654	42,382
			85	33,272	192,567	247,504	54,937
			86	77,503	306,775	395,195	88,420
U KING	A	E	81	36	1,420	2,035	615
	V	E	81	66	2,004	2,055	51
			83	100	665	977	312
			84	116	311	327	16
			85	10	1,602	1,613	11
	V	W	81	55	2,162	2,251	89
			82	90	3,249	5,642	2,393
			83	72	1,817	2,052	235
VENEZ	A	E	85	1,755	5,623	6,673	1,050
			86	2,190	27,535	29,147	1,612
WALLIS	V	W	82	10,368	731	948	217
YUGOSLV	V	E	82	910	1,187	1,838	651
			83	6,358	2,031	5,253	3,222
			84	12,376	6,642	9,307	2,665
			86	11,204	20,727	27,727	7,000
	V	W	81	96	574	946	372
ZMBABWE	A	E	83	250	283	638	355
	V	E	81	2,009	5,503	8,166	2,663

Raffia, webbing
2223400 WOV MATL,RAFFIA,F/BLINDS,ETC (NULL)

Country	Mode	Reg	Yr	Quantity	F.A.S.	C.I.F.	Charges
TOTAL			81	-	48,994	53,989	4,995
			82	-	33,373	34,884	1,511
			83	-	9,886	13,064	3,178
			84	-	11,807	22,739	10,932
			85	-	11,350	12,428	1,078
			86	-	4,334	4,980	646
CANADA	N	E	86	-	2,197	2,197	

Crop Product TSUSA commodity number, description, and unit of quantity Country	Mode	Reg	Yr	Quantity	F.A.S.	C.I.F.	Charges
CHINA T	N	H	82	-	23,741	23,987	246
	N	W	86	-	2,137	2,783	646
FR GERM	N	E	81	-	16,261	17,939	1,678
			82	-	4,331	4,400	69
FRANCE	N	E	81	-	2,748	2,874	126
HG KONG	N	E	81	-	533	1,361	828
ITALY	N	E	81	-	21,966	23,880	1,914
			82	-	3,348	4,495	1,147
			83	-	9,580	12,695	3,115
			85	-	3,979	3,979	
MADAGAS	N	E	81	-	7,486	7,935	449
			84	-	11,807	22,739	10,932
			85	-	7,371	8,449	1,078
SWITZLD	N	E	82	-	1,953	2,002	49
VENEZ	N	E	83	-	306	369	63

Ramie

Ramie, fiber, processed
3044400 RAMIE FIBERS PROCESSED ETC (LB)

Country	Mode	Reg	Yr	Quantity	F.A.S.	C.I.F.	Charges
TOTAL			81	52,135	98,850	110,441	11,591
			82	35,419	67,202	71,780	4,578
			83	111	1,249	1,534	285
			84	15,586	26,735	29,665	2,930
			85	33,818	78,148	83,635	5,487
			86	4,563	10,583	11,119	536
ARGENT	V	E	84	15,432	26,320	28,952	2,632
BRAZIL	A	E	84	154	415	713	298
			85	461	1,235	2,030	795
	V	E	81	51,365	96,092	105,468	9,376
			82	30,864	62,300	66,530	4,230
			85	30,865	69,600	73,886	4,286
CHINA M	V	E	85	2,183	5,689	6,010	321
			86	4,365	9,938	10,395	457
	V	W	82	2,315	3,346	3,543	197
CHINA T	A	W	83	65	775	1,022	247
FRANCE	V	W	86	198	645	724	79
ITALY	A	E	83	46	474	512	38
PHIL R	A	W	81	770	2,758	4,973	2,215
			85	99	479	564	85
	V	W	82	2,240	1,556	1,707	151
U KING	O	E	85	210	1,145	1,145	

Ramie, fiber, raw and waste
3044200 RAMIE RAW AND WASTES (LTN)

Country	Mode	Reg	Yr	Quantity	F.A.S.	C.I.F.	Charges
TOTAL			82	2	1,502	3,004	1,502
			86	1	2,273	2,558	285
BRAZIL	A	E	82	2	1,502	3,004	1,502
PHIL R	V	E	86	1	2,273	2,558	285

Rape

Rapeseed
1753900 RAPESEED (LB)

Country	Mode	Reg	Yr	Quantity	F.A.S.	C.I.F.	Charges
TOTAL			81	585,258	77,390	77,390	
			82	927,832	132,939	133,550	611
			83	1,180,134	159,696	159,856	160
			84	2,308,163	282,003	282,003	
			85	1,346,609	277,445	281,867	4,422
			86	1,760,952	253,014	253,420	406
CANADA	A	E	82	3,957	1,504	1,634	130
	N	E	84	10,768	4,111	4,111	
	O	E	81	462,595	70,017	70,017	
			82	812,423	106,020	106,020	
			83	1,070,232	141,228	141,228	
			84	1,791,325	239,618	239,618	
			85	1,152,657	213,569	213,569	
			86	1,654,496	224,550	224,550	
	O	W	81	122,663	7,373	7,373	
			82	101,565	18,642	18,664	22
			83	109,075	18,095	18,095	
			84	506,070	38,274	38,274	

Crop Product TSUSA commodity number, description, and unit of quantity Country	Mode	Reg	Yr	Quantity	F.A.S.	C.I.F.	Charges
			85	91,261	23,572	23,572	
			86	78,240	19,437	19,437	
FR GERM	A	E	85	500	2,530	3,212	682
	A	W	85	62,280	8,611	8,757	146
	V	W	86	716	2,511	2,646	135
POLAND	V	E	82	9,887	6,773	7,232	459
			85	35,337	24,375	26,455	2,080
SWEDEN	V	E	83	827	373	533	160
	V	W	86	27,500	6,516	6,787	271
U KING	A	E	85	4,574	4,788	6,302	1,514

Rapeseed, fatty acid**
4902200 FATTY ACIDS DRVD HMP KPK ETC (LB)
(See Hempseed, fatty acid under Hemp)

Rapeseed, fatty salt**
4904600 FATTY SALTS OF SESAME ETC (LB)
(See Hempseed, fatty salt under Hemp)

Rapeseed, oil cake and oil-cake meal
1845100 RAPESEED OIL CAKE AND MEAL (LB)

Country	Mode	Reg	Yr	Quantity	F.A.S.	C.I.F.	Charges
TOTAL			81	89,090,021	7,827,874	7,828,352	478
			82	57,561,444	4,111,914	4,122,116	10,202
			83	147,815,608	11,618,120	11,626,694	8,574
			84	238,413,781	16,995,307	16,995,307	
			85	307,458,794	13,475,288	13,475,312	24
			86	280,726,517	13,953,741	13,960,532	6,791
CANADA	N	E	85	10,900,604	491,113	491,113	
	O	E	81	35,661,399	3,339,488	3,339,488	
			82	27,187,229	2,057,262	2,057,262	
			83	38,999,142	3,108,807	3,115,033	6,226
			84	53,451,181	3,946,552	3,946,552	
			85	38,303,460	2,131,834	2,131,838	4
			86	59,207,570	3,612,112	3,618,903	6,791
	O	H	85	37,630	2,070	2,070	
			86	57,700	3,549	3,549	
	O	W	81	53,426,417	4,487,236	4,487,236	
			82	30,374,215	2,054,652	2,064,854	10,202
			83	108,669,992	8,500,628	8,502,976	2,348
			84	184,962,600	13,048,755	13,048,755	
			85	258,176,900	10,848,274	10,848,294	20
			86	221,399,077	10,334,817	10,334,817	
JAPAN	V	W	81	2,205	1,150	1,628	478
MEXICO	O	W	83	146,474	8,685	8,685	
			86	62,170	3,263	3,263	
MOROC	O	E	85	40,200	1,997	1,997	

Rapeseed, oil, hydrogenated
1781500 RAPESEED OIL, HYDROGENATED (LB)

Country	Mode	Reg	Yr	Quantity	F.A.S.	C.I.F.	Charges
TOTAL			84	135,420	55,701	55,701	
			85	161,438	96,330	96,330	
			86	513,696	232,985	236,334	3,349
CANADA	O	E	84	135,420	55,701	55,701	
			85	161,438	96,330	96,330	
			86	470,618	217,087	217,087	
SWEDEN	O	E	86	43,078	15,898	19,247	3,349

Rapeseed, vegetable oil, edible
1764600 RAPESEED OIL EDIBLE FOR MFR (LB)

Country	Mode	Reg	Yr	Quantity	F.A.S.	C.I.F.	Charges
TOTAL			81	22,518	6,540	6,540	
			82	222,425	59,642	59,642	
			84	886,143	357,960	367,640	9,680
			86	102,495	20,201	20,643	442
CANADA	O	E	81	838	337	337	
			82	222,425	59,642	59,642	
			86	93,453	11,912	11,912	
FRANCE	V	E	86	2,711	7,276	7,612	336
HG KONG	V	E	84	48	1,448	1,464	16
MEXICO	O	W	81	21,680	6,203	6,203	
NETHLDS	V	E	84	886,095	356,512	366,176	9,664
SWITZLD	A	E	86	6,331	1,013	1,119	106

1764700 RAPESEED OIL, EDIBLE, NSPF (LB)

Country	Mode	Reg	Yr	Quantity	F.A.S.	C.I.F.	Charges
TOTAL			81	2,900,559	811,840	812,282	442

Crop Product TSUSA commodity number, description, and unit of quantity Country	Mode	Reg	Yr	Quantity	F.A.S.	C.I.F.	Charges
			82	4,031,957	1,010,639	1,010,639	
			83	3,449,240	989,221	989,221	
			84	3,421,871	1,217,785	1,217,828	43
			85	16,012,597	4,190,222	4,190,222	
			86	99,246,573	14,736,211	14,738,763	2,552
CANADA	A	W	83	700	568	568	
	O	E	81	2,887,238	809,840	809,840	
			82	4,031,957	1,010,639	1,010,639	
			83	3,448,540	988,653	988,653	
			84	3,421,756	1,217,033	1,217,033	
			85	15,833,055	4,130,950	4,130,950	
			86	90,458,276	13,531,841	13,531,841	
	O	W	81	13,321	2,000	2,442	442
			85	179,542	59,272	59,272	
			86	8,785,395	1,200,967	1,200,967	
FRANCE	A	E	86	1,359	1,142	2,312	1,170
JAPAN	V	E	84	115	752	795	43
SWEDEN	A	E	86	1,543	2,261	3,643	1,382

Rapeseed, vegetable oil, inedible
1764400 RAPESEED OIL INEDBL FOR MFR (LB)

Country	Mode	Reg	Yr	Quantity	F.A.S.	C.I.F.	Charges
TOTAL			81	10,901,695	3,572,732	3,697,536	124,804
			82	10,905,470	3,302,541	3,372,270	69,729
			83	8,268,124	2,522,534	2,551,959	29,425
			84	6,925,467	2,481,261	2,504,190	22,929
			85	12,053,846	4,115,753	4,131,984	16,231
			86	7,978,824	1,900,560	1,900,560	
CANADA	O	E	81	4,438,229	1,531,525	1,531,525	
			82	5,525,685	1,657,016	1,657,016	
			83	6,465,892	1,997,925	1,997,925	
			84	5,578,554	1,996,665	1,996,665	
			85	10,990,788	3,679,362	3,679,362	
			86	7,978,824	1,900,560	1,900,560	
FR GERM	O	E	82	925,932	286,020	300,706	14,686
			85	1,063,058	436,391	452,622	16,231
HG KONG	V	E	84	48	993	1,005	12
JAPAN	V	E	83	728	399	452	53
NETHLDS	O	E	84	463,032	231,033	239,264	8,231
	V	E	82	1,020,811	324,470	337,089	12,619
POLAND	O	E	81	3,314,364	957,669	1,011,614	53,945
			82	1,656,554	429,805	452,229	22,424
	V	E	81	345,100	89,695	93,676	3,981
SWITZLD	O	E	81	2,804,002	993,843	1,060,721	66,878
			82	1,776,488	605,230	625,230	20,000
			83	1,801,504	524,210	553,582	29,372
			84	883,833	252,570	267,256	14,686

1764500 RAPESEED OIL INEDIBLE, NSPF (LB)

Country	Mode	Reg	Yr	Quantity	F.A.S.	C.I.F.	Charges
TOTAL			81	33,910	17,381	17,381	
			82	32,000	10,159	10,159	
			83	67,950	26,802	26,802	
			84	224,913	68,701	68,701	
			85	5,572,519	1,482,347	1,482,347	
			86	11,300,134	2,364,216	2,396,984	32,768
CANADA	O	E	81	910	401	401	
			82	32,000	10,159	10,159	
			83	45,000	15,283	15,283	
			85	5,537,069	1,476,320	1,476,320	
			86	8,220,640	1,561,294	1,561,294	
	O	W	83	450	269	269	
			84	134,913	27,301	27,301	
			85	35,450	6,027	6,027	
			86	52,450	4,462	4,462	
MEXICO	O	W	81	33,000	16,980	16,980	
			83	22,500	11,250	11,250	
			84	90,000	41,400	41,400	
			86	55,000	18,792	18,792	
POLAND	V	E	86	1,455,036	371,580	387,567	15,987
SWITZLD	V	E	86	1,517,008	408,088	424,869	16,781

Raspberry

Raspberry, fresh or in brine**
1465400 RASPBERRIES AND LOGANBERRIES, 7/1-8/31 (LB)
(See Loganberry, fresh or in brine under Loganberry)

Crop Product TSUSA commodity number, description, and unit of quantity Country	Mode	Reg	Yr	Quantity	F.A.S.	C.I.F.	Charges

1465600 RASPBERRIES AND LOGANBERRIES, 9/1-6/30 (LB)
(See Loganberry, fresh or in brine under Loganberry)

Raspberry, frozen
1467400 RASPBERRIES, FROZEN (LB)

Country	Mode	Reg	Yr	Quantity	F.A.S.	C.I.F.	Charges
TOTAL			81	1,413,237	767,923	814,838	46,915
			82	1,633,990	953,302	1,036,057	82,755
			83	1,103,210	571,569	659,836	88,267
			84	4,787,895	2,441,344	2,640,457	199,113
			85	4,390,888	2,517,310	2,993,053	475,743
			86	14,135,142	7,913,405	9,509,570	1,596,165
BRAZIL	V	E	82	2,200	2,002	2,568	566
CANADA	O	E	82	91,275	62,260	66,340	4,080
			84	372,560	207,181	207,181	
			85	12,212	7,439	7,439	
			86	176,281	119,652	119,652	
	O	W	81	984,740	520,136	520,136	
			82	744,820	442,605	442,605	
			83	369,114	252,696	252,696	
			84	2,539,567	1,440,962	1,440,962	
			85	996,046	661,443	667,702	6,259
			86	1,178,888	800,794	800,794	
	V	E	83	31,310	28,489	35,140	6,651
			85	637	2,689	4,011	1,322
CHILE	A	E	83	13,316	16,777	31,034	14,257
			84	1,217	814	3,016	2,202
			86	8,236	10,747	19,875	9,128
	N	E	84	101,095	47,404	61,655	14,251
			85	206,724	85,777	111,627	25,850
	O	E	84	12,610	4,845	6,091	1,246
			85	15,015	8,982	8,982	
			86	43,989	24,137	24,137	
	V	E	83	45,371	17,262	22,229	4,967
			85	17,636	6,456	6,972	516
			86	909,683	453,819	586,261	132,442
	V	W	84	30,800	13,599	18,480	4,881
FR GERM	A	E	84	99	937	999	62
	V	E	82	83,259	45,707	52,372	6,665
			83	44,191	16,277	19,002	2,725
			84	272,904	113,552	131,939	18,387
			85	36,300	11,746	16,441	4,695
			86	35,274	8,581	14,080	5,499
FRANCE	V	E	83	2,789	2,382	2,683	301
			84	45,015	26,572	29,634	3,062
			86	29,277	31,430	35,407	3,977
HUNGARY	V	E	85	110,936	36,198	49,740	13,542
			86	278,214	98,426	137,432	39,006
	V	W	86	1,191,307	623,859	729,525	105,666
ITALY	V	E	85	1,584	1,960	2,332	372
N ZEAL	A	W	82	130	331	443	112
			84	1,524	4,116	6,402	2,286
	N	W	84	68,491	29,309	38,409	9,100
	V	E	82	249,876	131,957	162,422	30,465
			83	375,841	121,419	161,072	39,653
			84	584,053	207,058	262,776	55,718
			85	716,394	378,936	456,861	77,925
			86	888,436	417,340	513,138	95,798
	V	W	83	52,847	32,203	40,436	8,233
			84	21,200	15,022	17,578	2,556
			85	309,213	200,758	243,098	42,340
			86	607,474	316,566	400,436	83,870
NETHLDS	O	E	82	720	581	581	
			86	38,603	18,541	18,541	
	V	E	81	428,497	247,787	294,702	46,915
			82	92,594	42,885	53,696	10,811
			83	47,619	16,626	22,857	6,231
			84	46,263	16,493	19,576	3,083
			86	514,468	274,663	320,650	45,987
	V	W	86	434,878	264,163	300,436	36,273
POLAND	V	E	84	254,252	80,881	116,550	35,669
			85	370,302	129,496	198,665	69,169
			86	290,400	102,663	174,178	71,515
SPAIN	V	E	86	12,125	11,274	12,838	1,564
U KING	O	E	82	368,547	224,353	254,372	30,019
			83	120,812	67,438	72,687	5,249
			84	81,702	44,120	50,656	6,536
			86	112,436	52,380	65,846	13,466
	V	E	82	567	621	658	37
			84	317,065	152,875	189,087	36,212
			85	735,869	361,273	445,678	84,405
			86	483,462	279,212	334,866	55,654

Crop
Product
TSUSA commodity number, description, and unit of quantity

Country	Mode	Reg	Yr	Quantity	F.A.S.	C.I.F.	Charges
	V	W	86	245,769	153,525	172,669	19,144
YUGOSLV	N	E	86	146,253	127,488	146,162	18,674
	O	E	86	34,480	31,183	33,283	2,100
	V	E	84	37,478	35,604	39,466	3,862
			85	760,520	556,798	686,265	129,467
			86	5,643,861	3,266,385	4,037,630	771,245
	V	W	85	101,500	67,359	87,240	19,881
			86	831,348	426,577	511,734	85,157

Raspberry, prepared or preserved
1468400 RASPBERRIES PREP, PRES NSPF (LB)

Country	Mode	Reg	Yr	Quantity	F.A.S.	C.I.F.	Charges
TOTAL			81	186,075	97,675	107,184	9,509
			82	71,649	68,483	77,044	8,561
			83	187,271	212,880	232,766	19,886
			84	288,482	253,932	281,587	27,655
			85	764,250	579,243	623,160	43,917
			86	748,622	698,716	773,931	75,215
AUSTRIA	V	E	82	488	1,602	1,661	59
			83	1,093	3,142	3,352	210
			84	1,840	3,535	3,959	424
			85	992	1,053	1,209	156
BELGIUM	V	E	84	2,053	1,771	2,014	243
CANADA	O	E	85	148,941	77,523	77,523	
	O	W	81	84,954	45,041	45,041	
			82	7,750	3,715	3,715	
			83	1,700	752	752	
			84	29,200	18,104	18,104	
			85	259,532	225,088	225,088	
			86	154,395	129,628	129,628	
	V	E	86	20,420	14,351	15,987	1,636
CHILE	A	E	84	1,756	2,341	4,613	2,272
			86	4,345	5,242	10,792	5,550
COLOMB	V	E	82	5,400	5,008	5,568	560
DENMARK	V	E	83	1,323	15,356	15,600	244
			85	28,334	20,948	22,962	2,014
			86	85,200	48,101	55,938	7,837
	V	W	86	7,125	3,157	5,671	2,514
FR GERM	A	E	84	33	291	331	40
			85	795	6,404	7,054	650
	N	E	85	103,041	67,940	78,012	10,072
	O	E	86	2,526	2,207	3,588	1,381
	V	E	81	594	565	619	54
			83	3,045	2,209	2,549	340
			84	21,108	14,346	16,153	1,807
			85	3,295	2,412	2,845	433
			86	73,487	50,608	57,540	6,932
	V	W	83	432	496	584	88
			85	5,113	3,037	4,153	1,116
FRANCE	A	W	84	71	264	307	43
	N	E	83	89,041	93,273	102,179	8,906
			84	40,963	32,667	36,190	3,523
	O	E	81	263	272	296	24
			84	8,502	5,980	7,053	1,073
			85	3,965	3,867	4,453	586
			86	720	1,037	1,111	74
	V	E	81	8,045	8,751	9,987	1,236
			82	28,975	30,387	34,276	3,889
			83	800	1,469	1,678	209
			84	9,428	8,759	9,382	623
			85	21,131	20,090	22,607	2,517
			86	255,495	291,806	326,854	35,048
	V	W	81	525	2,103	2,204	101
			82	581	2,631	2,861	230
			83	8,196	7,402	8,090	688
			84	6,220	7,642	8,404	762
			85	13,214	1,339	3,718	2,379
			86	3,025	4,389	4,981	592
HUNGARY	V	E	84	5,833	1,648	2,274	626
			86	6,342	4,178	4,514	336
IRELAND	V	E	82	255	355	360	5
ITALY	V	E	82	3,797	2,679	3,047	368
			84	816	558	649	91
			85	455	1,952	2,212	260
N ZEAL	A	E	83	398	3,516	4,248	732
	V	W	86	20,543	13,077	16,434	3,357
NETHLDS	A	E	86	1,548	3,955	4,975	1,020
	N	E	85	10,513	11,315	13,583	2,268
	O	E	81	29,844	17,606	18,656	1,050
			82	1,008	832	832	
	V	E	85	42,020	25,611	29,722	4,111
POLAND	O	E	82	12,830	8,190	10,357	2,167
	V	E	81	58,217	19,065	25,451	6,386
			82	3,480	1,620	1,805	185
			83	9,900	3,640	4,380	740
			84	23,287	8,615	10,481	1,866
			85	38,867	12,998	15,862	2,864
ROMANIA	V	E	84	2,400	1,397	1,525	128
SWEDEN	O	E	81	348	817	895	78
			84	297	312	340	28
	V	E	82	1,553	1,371	1,562	191
SWITZLD	V	E	82	810	1,662	1,733	71
			84	8,637	9,548	10,132	584
			85	7,023	8,467	9,202	735
			86	5,174	7,493	8,137	644
	V	W	84	476	553	591	38
U KING	O	E	84	1,800	927	1,036	109
	V	E	81	1,434	2,048	2,303	255
			82	4,223	6,972	7,692	720
			83	71,148	81,268	88,968	7,700
			84	115,247	131,166	143,945	12,779
			85	73,384	80,200	92,454	12,254
			86	73,003	89,782	98,076	8,294
	V	W	81	323	772	889	117
			82	499	1,459	1,575	116
			83	195	357	386	29
			84	8,515	3,508	4,104	596
			85	3,635	8,999	10,501	1,502
YUGOSLV	O	E	86	35,274	29,705	29,705	
	V	W	81	1,528	635	843	208

Rattan

Rattan
2221040 RATTAN EXCEPT WEBBING (NULL)

Country	Mode	Reg	Yr	Quantity	F.A.S.	C.I.F.	Charges
TOTAL			81	-	6,364,524	6,975,322	610,798
			82	-	5,518,850	6,014,604	495,754
			83	-	5,788,748	6,369,265	580,517
			84	-	7,412,134	8,352,570	940,436
			85	-	5,493,357	6,137,449	644,092
			86	-	6,428,506	6,999,911	571,405
BELIZE	N	E	86	-	4,445	5,253	808
CANADA	N	E	84	-	24,600	27,200	2,600
			86	-	2,079	2,079	
CHINA M	N	E	81	-	825	882	57
			82	-	70,688	71,686	998
			83	-	7,810	9,280	1,470
			84	-	46,504	49,548	3,044
			85	-	26,041	28,304	2,263
	N	H	84	-	1,928	2,124	196
	N	W	81	-	6,726	7,275	549
			82	-	796	916	120
			83	-	8,836	10,164	1,328
			84	-	541	670	129
			85	-	25,297	27,108	1,811
			86	-	1,959	2,137	178
CHINA T	N	E	82	-	1,286	1,418	132
			83	-	31,966	39,339	7,373
			84	-	11,023	12,134	1,111
			85	-	20,265	24,534	4,269
			86	-	24,178	29,465	5,287
	N	W	81	-	993	1,187	194
			82	-	66,170	77,422	11,252
			83	-	63,778	68,990	5,212
			84	-	27,213	30,706	3,493
			85	-	20,383	22,284	1,901
			86	-	19,644	21,079	1,435
FINLAND	N	E	83	-	372	386	14
			84	-	1,092	1,183	91
FR GERM	N	E	82	-	401	422	21
			84	-	47,503	51,163	3,660
			85	-	222,734	238,199	15,465
			86	-	126,584	136,134	9,550
FRANCE	N	E	81	-	1,405	1,682	277
HG KONG	N	E	81	-	1,677,966	1,788,283	110,317
			82	-	1,565,654	1,683,745	118,091
			83	-	1,281,129	1,399,663	118,534
			84	-	2,034,300	2,279,549	245,249
			85	-	1,623,165	1,781,756	158,591
			86	-	2,443,108	2,616,561	173,453
	N	H	82	-	322	397	75

Crop
Product
TSUSA commodity number, description, and unit of quantity

Country	Mode	Reg	Yr	Quantity	F.A.S.	C.I.F.	Charges
			85	-	1,450	1,566	116
	N W		81	-	704,026	771,656	67,630
			82	-	641,152	709,855	68,703
			83	-	630,108	691,857	61,749
			84	-	555,986	617,072	61,086
			85	-	628,354	689,033	60,679
			86	-	949,564	990,120	40,556
INDIA	N E		85	-	7,121	7,776	655
INDNSIA	N E		81	-	861,146	970,805	109,659
			82	-	836,734	939,722	102,988
			83	-	1,006,462	1,131,576	125,114
			84	-	1,837,188	2,110,008	272,820
			85	-	1,117,948	1,294,778	176,830
			86	-	942,277	1,055,493	113,216
	N W		81	-	425,395	463,914	38,519
			82	-	101,582	114,924	13,342
			83	-	62,192	68,244	6,052
			84	-	127,368	144,194	16,826
			85	-	42,849	46,373	3,524
			86	-	9,684	11,816	2,132
ITALY	N E		81	-	14,905	15,880	975
JAPAN	N E		81	-	130,501	133,518	3,017
			83	-	376	398	22
			84	-	14,108	16,193	2,085
	N W		83	-	15,811	17,611	1,800
			84	-	18,425	20,111	1,686
			85	-	1,040	1,223	183
KOR REP	N E		83	-	5,050	5,779	729
	N W		81	-	621	778	157
MACAO	N E		81	-	14,759	16,894	2,135
MALAYSA	N E		81	-	21,250	23,106	1,856
			82	-	39,984	43,899	3,915
			83	-	37,138	43,375	6,237
			84	-	958	1,300	342
	N W		81	-	1,860	1,970	110
			83	-	8,940	9,119	179
			84	-	21,112	23,851	2,739
			85	-	6,771	10,065	3,294
MEXICO	N E		81	-	1,505	1,505	
			82	-	7,226	7,226	
			83	-	3,735	3,735	
			84	-	56,979	58,016	1,037
			85	-	5,949	5,949	
			86	-	1,294	1,294	
PHIL R	N E		81	-	41,692	50,096	8,404
			82	-	34,061	43,274	9,213
			83	-	36,163	41,077	4,914
			84	-	52,978	66,608	13,630
			85	-	17,837	22,626	4,789
			86	-	106,027	125,122	19,095
	N H		82	-	2,277	2,827	550
			83	-	5,245	6,661	1,416
			84	-	4,606	5,761	1,155
			85	-	2,717	3,408	691
	N W		81	-	75,977	93,104	17,127
			82	-	7,267	12,368	5,101
			83	-	37,860	42,154	4,294
			84	-	30,700	35,082	4,382
			86	-	3,396	5,509	2,113
SINGAPR	N E		81	-	1,393,708	1,514,075	120,367
			82	-	1,802,698	1,939,673	136,975
			83	-	2,201,843	2,410,285	208,442
			84	-	2,126,242	2,371,720	245,478
			85	-	1,499,871	1,684,152	184,281
			86	-	1,532,641	1,708,547	175,906
	N W		81	-	971,943	1,095,372	123,429
			82	-	339,814	363,581	23,767
			83	-	340,004	365,188	25,184
			84	-	358,376	405,464	47,088
			85	-	210,666	231,256	20,590
			86	-	259,209	286,367	27,158
SPAIN	N E		81	-	393	591	198
			83	-	528	803	275
			84	-	966	1,025	59
			85	-	2,899	3,431	532
			86	-	2,417	2,935	518
T PAC I	N W		85	-	10,000	13,628	3,628
THAILND	N W		81	-	16,928	22,749	5,821
			82	-	738	1,249	511
U KING	N E		83	-	3,402	3,581	179
			84	-	11,438	21,888	10,450

Rattan, basket**

2224200 BASKTS A BAGS, RATTN, PLM LF (NO)
(See Palm leaf, basket under Raffia Palm)

Rattan, stick**

2220505 RATTAN STICKS 4 METERS LONG (NO)

Country	Mode	Reg	Yr	Quantity	F.A.S.	C.I.F.	Charges
TOTAL			82	213,928	97,371	123,257	25,886
			83	820,241	756,778	866,685	109,907
			84	2,885,503	599,694	733,901	134,207
			85	4,560,055	749,774	947,692	197,918
			86	5,035,666	840,343	985,967	145,624
CANADA	O E		86	30	1,084	1,084	
CHINA M	V E		82	2,000	3,509	5,390	1,881
			83	10,175	7,743	13,914	6,171
			84	232,000	5,475	7,128	1,653
			85	611,300	55,938	81,785	25,847
			86	3,344,540	78,205	91,274	13,069
	V W		82	1,074	698	850	152
			83	12,882	12,882	19,770	6,888
			84	909,900	56,674	74,435	17,761
			85	1,492,050	33,444	45,869	12,425
			86	395,800	19,325	25,270	5,945
CHINA T	A E		86	20,000	1,300	3,517	2,217
	N W		84	14,500	10,132	13,069	2,937
	V E		82	86,950	36,136	45,306	9,170
			83	17,295	8,545	10,108	1,563
			84	1,203,950	39,497	52,039	12,542
			85	1,179,112	40,422	50,214	9,792
	V H		83	1,800	1,411	1,845	434
	V W		82	82,500	18,808	26,952	8,144
			83	122,123	19,443	26,216	6,773
			84	112,300	41,624	57,111	15,487
			85	26,400	15,807	20,363	4,556
			86	324,174	59,288	64,503	5,215
FRANCE	O E		82	54	828	963	135
GUATMAL	V E		82	13,430	6,971	10,661	3,690
			83	10,250	4,200	6,363	2,163
HAITI	V E		83	71,216	105,000	114,678	9,678
HG KONG	A W		84	16,000	2,786	3,025	239
	V E		82	4,320	4,080	4,735	655
			83	26,000	10,301	14,316	4,015
			84	92,590	101,868	126,834	24,966
			85	222,976	256,578	311,866	55,288
			86	466,881	214,639	249,206	34,567
	V W		83	47,000	48,370	65,064	16,694
			84	17,290	27,218	33,832	6,614
			85	658,880	56,582	67,552	10,970
			86	17,162	20,542	24,265	3,723
INDIA	V E		85	11,240	25,840	39,087	13,247
INDNSIA	O E		85	7,000	14,580	18,053	3,473
	V E		82	15,000	12,286	13,324	1,038
			83	13,857	38,157	44,070	5,913
			84	72,565	127,292	148,314	21,022
			85	87,372	96,661	132,277	35,616
			86	149,436	87,276	125,243	37,967
	V W		83	4,089	11,040	14,135	3,095
			84	18,635	32,489	39,735	7,246
			85	3,000	5,270	7,770	2,500
ITALY	A E		86	42	1,134	1,191	57
JAPAN	V E		83	146,200	83,062	103,258	20,196
			84	37,263	20,515	24,695	4,180
			85	140,300	83,189	102,374	19,185
			86	90,400	62,074	73,966	11,892
	V H		82	200	463	482	19
	V W		83	52,024	42,489	49,264	6,775
			84	141,550	98,542	114,736	16,194
			86	53,300	55,263	60,721	5,458
MALAYSA	V E		83	4,900	10,196	11,007	811
			84	3,100	6,450	6,974	524
MEXICO	O W		83	110	290	290	
PANAMA	V W		86	24,294	3,329	4,527	1,198
PHIL R	V W		84	25	880	1,330	450
			86	33,806	6,372	8,834	2,462
SINGAPR	O E		86	6,465	11,187	12,271	1,084
	V E		82	8,400	13,592	14,594	1,002
			83	67,640	126,241	137,126	10,885
			84	10,150	15,161	16,014	853
			85	8,100	5,114	5,943	829
			86	72,070	117,939	131,560	13,621
	V W		83	182,180	222,575	227,728	5,153

Crop
Product
TSUSA commodity number, description, and unit of quantity

Country	Mode	Reg	Yr	Quantity	F.A.S.	C.I.F.	Charges
			84	3,685	13,091	14,630	1,539
			85	112,325	60,349	64,539	4,190
			86	37,266	101,386	108,535	7,149
THAILND	V	E	83	30,500	4,833	7,533	2,700

2220590 BAMBOO/RAT STICKS ROUGH/CUT (NULL)
   (See Bamboo, stick under Bamboo)

Rattan, webbing**
2221020 RATTAN WEBBING (SFT)

Country	Mode	Reg	Yr	Quantity	F.A.S.	C.I.F.	Charges
TOTAL			81	14,997,168	8,763,165	9,095,205	332,040
			82	7,178,238	3,653,474	3,849,044	195,570
			83	11,927,370	5,362,315	5,653,003	290,688
			84	11,340,711	4,639,697	4,994,180	354,483
			85	6,785,709	2,695,896	2,894,230	198,334
			86	7,622,785	2,695,058	2,856,006	160,948
BURMA	V	W	85	14,000	6,160	6,645	485
			86	9,000	3,960	4,142	182
CANADA	O	E	84	1,000	2,498	2,526	28
CHINA M	N	W	81	3,060	15,605	18,080	2,475
	V	E	81	1,417,336	931,588	954,840	23,252
			82	365,332	214,081	219,970	5,889
			83	397,250	180,431	187,997	7,566
			84	195,000	55,508	62,898	7,390
			85	456,414	196,241	207,693	11,452
			86	6,100	6,548	8,956	2,408
	V	H	84	4,639	3,218	4,059	841
	V	W	81	335,435	235,885	246,001	10,116
			82	203,581	122,885	128,076	5,191
			83	93,416	64,018	65,890	1,872
			85	183,667	81,109	84,725	3,616
CHINA T	A	E	83	2,377	950	2,156	1,206
	N	E	84	112,104	35,905	38,543	2,638
	V	E	81	110,917	67,505	69,170	1,665
			83	91,835	45,190	47,009	1,819
			84	246,002	98,900	105,406	6,506
			86	248,858	56,374	59,349	2,975
	V	W	81	57	6,327	6,580	253
			82	2,250	278	300	22
			83	78,832	40,559	41,914	1,355
			84	15,152	6,288	6,715	427
			85	5,050	1,587	1,738	151
			86	148,500	37,086	37,742	656
FR GERM	V	E	86	80,032	115,738	122,909	7,171
HAITI	V	E	81	968	400	407	7
HG KONG	A	E	81	4,125	1,842	3,265	1,423
			82	9,165	5,275	9,758	4,483
	A	W	85	12,450	6,180	8,630	2,450
	N	E	81	4,411,147	2,767,657	2,854,395	86,738
			82	2,039,623	1,129,997	1,191,102	61,105
			83	3,087,803	1,349,597	1,423,352	73,755
			84	3,290,451	1,478,407	1,578,623	100,216
			85	2,185,580	844,685	910,320	65,635
	N	W	81	956,921	556,658	577,326	20,668
			84	10,977	5,409	6,173	764
	O	E	82	60,000	34,045	35,400	1,355
			83	7,083	3,148	3,289	141
			84	27,500	15,125	16,280	1,155
	V	E	81	6,007,249	3,310,531	3,453,829	143,298
			82	2,696,874	1,143,214	1,214,879	71,665
			83	5,025,131	2,205,100	2,326,260	121,160
			84	6,131,804	2,305,266	2,495,129	189,863
			85	2,815,213	1,072,839	1,150,395	77,556
			86	5,843,016	2,036,451	2,144,534	108,083
	V	H	82	450	358	439	81
			83	6,000	3,300	3,623	323
			85	7,167	3,508	3,641	133
	V	W	81	1,563,589	790,771	827,786	37,015
			82	1,715,880	961,745	1,005,010	43,265
			83	2,823,143	1,343,746	1,414,144	70,398
			84	971,091	473,550	504,051	30,501
			85	717,498	291,569	307,511	15,942
			86	924,024	330,322	357,301	26,979
INDNSIA	N	E	84	*	22,119	26,289	4,170
	V	E	81	166,666	64,738	69,055	4,317
			82	81,249	38,039	40,164	2,125
			83	109,040	63,070	66,836	3,766
			84	178,373	76,426	81,693	5,267
			85	35,083	7,697	9,149	1,452
			86	59,140	16,045	20,658	4,613
	V	W	81	11,667	8,038	8,614	576
			82	3,750	1,943	2,133	190

Crop
Product
TSUSA commodity number, description, and unit of quantity

Country	Mode	Reg	Yr	Quantity	F.A.S.	C.I.F.	Charges
			83	32,400	5,720	7,383	1,663
			84	9,600	4,630	5,779	1,149
JAPAN	V	E	81	5,085	2,441	2,497	56
			84	47,000	22,555	23,682	1,127
			85	38,416	13,585	14,643	1,058
	V	W	83	16,667	9,202	9,667	465
PHIL R	A	W	83	1,000	430	1,361	931
	V	E	86	99,434	24,858	27,648	2,790
	V	W	83	7,076	3,892	4,575	683
SINGAPR	N	E	85	120,580	63,642	71,941	8,299
	O	E	86	6,768	7,960	8,726	766
	V	E	83	8,500	4,679	5,196	517
			84	21,952	8,890	9,949	1,059
			85	194,591	107,094	117,199	10,105
			86	25,189	15,452	16,483	1,031
	V	W	81	2,946	3,179	3,360	181
			82	84	1,614	1,813	199
			84	875	461	525	64
			86	172,716	44,264	47,558	3,294
SPAIN	V	E	84	74,516	21,587	22,772	1,185
U KING	V	E	83	139,817	39,283	42,351	3,068
			84	2,675	2,955	3,088	133

2223000 WOV MTL BMBO RATN ETC F/BLDS (NULL)
   (See Bamboo, webbing under Bamboo)

Rice

Rice, hulled
1305600 BASMATI BROWN RICE, HULLED (LB)

Country	Mode	Reg	Yr	Quantity	F.A.S.	C.I.F.	Charges
TOTAL			81	1,773,141	672,916	800,252	127,336
			82	1,455,814	552,838	651,998	99,160
			83	2,739,728	1,073,441	1,234,327	160,886
			84	1,591,939	591,463	682,412	90,949
			85	5,225,946	1,990,806	2,282,013	291,207
			86	5,788,647	2,742,183	3,001,328	259,145
AFGHAN	V	E	86	6,891	2,311	2,711	400
ARAB EM	V	W	84	52,360	19,399	22,833	3,434
BELGIUM	V	E	83	1,800	1,461	2,985	1,524
CANADA	A	E	84	550	319	319	
	O	E	82	1,650	1,133	1,133	
			83	77,504	39,011	39,011	
			84	180,512	104,423	104,423	
			85	226,206	136,961	136,965	4
			86	269,247	176,858	176,858	
	O	W	85	5,500	3,300	3,300	
			86	2,710	1,788	1,788	
CHINA M	O	E	86	1,650	1,023	1,023	
CHINA T	O	E	82	40,774	15,073	17,104	2,031
	V	W	84	41,237	13,729	16,825	3,096
			85	39,683	13,760	16,560	2,800
			86	44,092	20,560	22,937	2,377
HG KONG	V	W	83	39,167	7,437	8,502	1,065
INDIA	A	E	84	550	297	297	
	N	E	82	197,314	73,413	89,357	15,944
			85	1,150,681	454,765	508,905	54,140
	N	W	81	183,192	74,648	86,459	11,811
			86	302,911	134,703	149,084	14,381
	O	E	81	6,325	3,961	3,961	
			82	24,200	13,715	13,715	
			83	490,643	202,489	227,362	24,873
			84	32,002	17,220	17,243	23
			85	25,057	9,922	9,922	
			86	238,605	113,482	113,482	
	V	E	81	837,488	299,930	360,438	60,508
			82	429,413	162,325	192,587	30,262
			83	1,097,126	446,404	519,129	72,725
			84	455,860	168,208	198,949	30,741
			85	48,501	14,628	18,793	4,165
			86	1,554,082	680,491	764,832	84,341
	V	W	81	674,190	264,110	312,905	48,795
			82	740,217	280,116	329,811	49,695
			83	577,439	231,983	266,551	34,568
			84	639,808	210,649	250,507	39,858
			85	3,207,644	1,228,370	1,434,882	206,512
			86	2,926,882	1,485,553	1,624,577	139,024
JAPAN	V	E	85	7,430	10,942	12,802	1,860
KOR REP	V	W	84	5,858	1,485	1,609	124
NETHLDS	V	E	86	77,000	43,650	49,161	5,511
PAKISTN	O	E	83	27,820	12,761	13,651	890

Crop Product TSUSA commodity number, description, and unit of quantity Country	Mode	Reg	Yr	Quantity	F.A.S.	C.I.F.	Charges
			84	24,409	10,547	12,114	1,567
			85	40,050	12,792	12,792	
			86	22,000	14,128	14,128	
	V	E	81	360	453	487	34
			83	396,829	123,580	148,588	25,008
			84	39,827	15,460	18,432	2,972
			85	127,990	45,892	55,350	9,458
			86	4,950	2,058	2,300	242
	V	W	81	40,924	15,500	19,695	4,195
			82	2,300	2,080	2,327	247
			84	79,366	23,040	30,634	7,594
SINGAPR	V	W	81	29,762	13,410	15,300	1,890
SWITZLD	O	E	86	9,515	6,045	6,045	
THAILND	V	E	85	15,000	2,404	3,160	756
			86	119,857	17,904	24,193	6,289
	V	W	82	19,046	4,190	4,918	728
			84	39,600	6,687	8,227	1,540
			85	304,693	42,568	52,662	10,094
			86	208,255	41,629	48,209	6,580
U KING	O	E	85	23,102	12,711	13,701	990
	V	E	81	900	904	1,007	103
			82	900	793	1,046	253
			83	20,400	2,020	2,253	233
	V	W	85	4,409	1,791	2,219	428
VENEZ	O	E	83	11,000	6,295	6,295	

1305800 BROWN RICE, NSPF, HULLED (LB)

TOTAL			**81**	**493,264**	**157,156**	**178,411**	**21,255**
			82	**147,048**	**45,186**	**52,783**	**7,597**
			83	**98,624**	**41,161**	**50,992**	**9,831**
			84	**662,158**	**180,435**	**210,438**	**30,003**
			85	**894,613**	**160,381**	**186,821**	**26,440**
			86	**810,770**	**175,748**	**199,418**	**23,670**
AUSTRAL	A	E	82	1,102	255	1,437	1,182
CANADA	O	E	81	1,352	710	710	
			82	3,523	1,854	1,854	
			83	600	387	387	
			85	3,300	1,459	1,459	
			86	44,110	11,660	11,660	
CHINA M	V	E	83	1,913	428	486	58
			84	5,548	1,230	1,645	415
			86	4,405	1,041	1,153	112
	V	W	85	11,357	4,833	4,833	
CHINA T	V	E	86	42,998	8,374	9,999	1,625
	V	W	84	513	806	883	77
FRANCE	V	W	85	39,683	10,561	10,761	200
HG KONG	V	E	83	500	464	496	32
			85	12,500	5,720	6,549	829
			86	409	1,619	1,793	174
	V	W	83	1,000	499	570	71
			84	750	586	887	301
INDIA	N	E	85	22,109	10,426	10,717	291
	O	E	81	2,420	1,532	1,532	
			82	1,430	797	797	
			83	11,880	7,323	7,323	
			84	75,194	31,628	31,628	
			85	8,250	2,762	2,762	
			86	10,593	2,090	2,090	
	V	E	83	2,205	520	666	146
			84	9,303	2,573	2,932	359
			85	24,251	8,603	10,635	2,032
	V	W	81	512	257	324	67
			82	3,748	1,373	1,696	323
			83	18,794	5,555	7,444	1,889
			84	158,952	57,894	68,324	10,430
			86	14,220	4,227	4,735	508
ITALY	N	E	83	5,268	2,819	3,495	676
	O	E	84	2,205	776	932	156
	V	E	81	25,000	19,900	21,771	1,871
			82	2,495	3,269	3,508	239
			83	1,047	631	740	109
			84	12,880	6,737	7,595	858
			85	26,764	13,504	15,579	2,075
			86	2,204	1,100	1,191	91
	V	W	82	720	730	888	158
			84	3,000	1,138	1,508	370
			86	5,369	3,752	4,124	372
JAPAN	A	E	82	40	260	273	13
	V	E	82	538	655	707	52
			83	2,412	2,665	2,942	277
			84	3,217	3,750	4,249	499
			85	36,082	10,525	12,186	1,661
			86	2,503	2,705	2,869	164

Crop Product TSUSA commodity number, description, and unit of quantity Country	Mode	Reg	Yr	Quantity	F.A.S.	C.I.F.	Charges
	V	W	81	5,159	10,734	11,717	983
			84	4,238	3,743	3,933	190
			86	4,126	8,464	9,005	541
KENYA	O	E	83	3,580	1,787	1,787	
KOR REP	V	E	86	8,503	7,530	8,588	1,058
NETHLDS	V	E	82	327	1,691	1,725	34
			86	2,397	1,140	1,254	114
	V	W	83	242	365	387	22
PAKISTN	O	E	83	39,683	11,970	17,191	5,221
PERU	V	E	85	221,670	12,000	13,146	1,146
PHIL R	V	W	81	4,108	2,566	2,990	424
			83	750	791	876	85
			85	183	1,900	2,115	215
SINGAPR	V	W	81	39,685	9,360	11,610	2,250
SPAIN	V	E	83	1,323	357	535	178
SWEDEN	A	E	82	988	367	1,062	695
	V	E	82	726	527	546	19
THAILND	O	E	85	46,200	5,198	5,198	
	V	E	81	16,575	4,560	5,188	628
			82	8,750	1,927	2,448	521
			83	7,427	4,600	5,667	1,067
			84	122,323	20,911	27,466	6,555
			85	159,857	26,388	34,403	8,015
	V	W	81	398,453	107,537	122,569	15,032
			82	122,661	31,481	35,842	4,361
			84	262,933	48,354	57,775	9,421
			85	279,943	45,227	55,203	9,976
			86	550,640	95,475	110,010	14,535
TURKEY	O	E	85	2,464	1,275	1,275	
U KING	V	W	84	1,102	309	681	372
			86	2,464	1,605	1,911	306
VENEZ	V	E	86	115,829	24,966	29,036	4,070

Rice, meal and flour
1313500 RICE MEAL AND FLOUR, EDIBLE (LB)

TOTAL			**81**	**3,356,059**	**920,516**	**1,021,069**	**100,552**
			82	**2,090,119**	**620,158**	**712,691**	**92,533**
			83	**3,944,739**	**991,744**	**1,135,507**	**143,763**
			84	**2,834,878**	**845,652**	**951,276**	**105,624**
			85	**4,945,154**	**1,280,269**	**1,469,474**	**189,205**
			86	**3,776,086**	**989,192**	**1,127,706**	**138,514**
BRAZIL	A	E	83	5,280	1,680	7,773	6,093
	V	E	81	2,200	650	725	75
			83	3,307	600	705	105
			85	8,554	4,268	4,885	617
CANADA	O	E	81	940,400	127,104	127,105	
			82	96,000	12,892	12,892	
			83	336,000	50,538	50,538	
			84	201,713	45,514	45,514	
			85	88,431	36,909	36,909	
			86	50,850	23,293	23,293	
	O	W	82	2,200	478	478	
CHINA M	O	E	84	1,323	354	415	61
	V	E	81	247,280	53,512	64,871	11,359
			82	64,407	16,101	20,129	4,028
			83	8,820	2,590	3,228	638
			84	4,620	922	1,055	133
			85	2,500	1,199	1,304	105
	V	H	81	8,607	2,739	2,943	204
			82	2,646	523	576	53
			83	13,859	3,181	3,425	244
			84	2,594	641	739	98
	V	W	81	162,099	46,413	51,330	4,917
			82	97,383	27,297	29,212	1,915
			83	289,659	75,977	82,689	6,712
			84	322,920	81,809	90,508	8,699
			85	611,613	143,329	165,439	22,110
			86	182,867	36,167	42,695	6,528
CHINA T	A	E	82	3,076	808	5,411	4,603
	A	W	83	2,998	966	5,546	4,580
	O	E	83	11,892	5,472	5,585	113
	V	E	81	5,030	4,195	4,716	521
			82	750	685	735	50
			83	31,599	5,309	7,030	1,721
			84	4,632	1,822	2,444	622
			85	15,162	7,355	9,553	2,198
			86	16,646	12,861	15,016	2,155
	V	W	81	6,638	3,069	3,339	270
			82	13,485	3,618	4,180	562
			83	2,721	2,279	2,647	368
			84	1,439	880	934	54

Crop
Product
TSUSA commodity number, description, and unit of quantity

Country	Mode	Reg	Yr	Quantity	F.A.S.	C.I.F.	Charges
			85	80,602	20,575	23,135	2,560
			86	76,266	36,175	39,623	3,448
COLOMB	A E		86	2,115	3,840	4,243	403
	V E		85	5,723	2,200	2,451	251
ECUADOR	V E		83	2,000	600	752	152
			84	5,000	2,000	2,374	374
FIJI	A E		83	8,100	1,226	2,445	1,219
	V W		81	15,246	8,690	11,087	2,397
FR GERM	V E		86	139,390	65,787	79,897	14,110
FRANCE	V E		83	307	392	434	42
G BISAU	V E		81	661	1,605	1,987	382
GUATMAL	A W		81	1,944	2,165	2,664	499
			83	981	356	567	211
	V E		85	6,012	4,889	5,290	401
HG KONG	O E		83	10,940	1,981	2,193	212
	V E		81	100,920	53,530	58,987	5,457
			82	79,100	34,496	40,531	6,035
			83	90,269	27,822	34,270	6,448
			84	102,923	22,135	27,032	4,897
			85	19,000	3,622	3,965	343
	V H		81	10,713	5,547	5,878	331
			82	3,450	936	1,055	119
			84	1,575	297	337	40
	V W		81	180,601	87,304	92,550	5,246
			82	87,090	41,557	44,342	2,785
			83	138,115	59,372	63,953	4,581
			84	116,693	61,906	65,031	3,125
			85	169,850	70,932	79,385	8,453
			86	56,844	24,211	25,231	1,020
ICELAND	V E		86	16,535	20,000	22,200	2,200
INDIA	A E		81	26,268	12,814	15,930	3,116
	O E		82	344	328	348	20
			83	6,548	2,805	3,322	517
			84	3,792	5,282	6,008	726
	V E		81	4,842	2,006	2,491	485
			82	2,172	2,840	3,275	435
			83	27,763	10,062	12,177	2,115
			84	8,598	5,087	5,985	898
			85	1,847	1,270	1,520	250
	V W		81	11,023	4,590	5,525	935
			82	11,673	3,233	4,259	1,026
			83	624	613	718	105
			84	1,984	480	592	112
INDNSIA	V W		84	753	1,232	1,304	72
ITALY	V E		86	19,841	3,613	3,790	177
JAPAN	A E		82	893	405	1,858	1,453
	N H		81	3,194	8,425	9,450	1,025
	N W		84	8,166	14,334	15,792	1,458
	V E		81	7,484	8,678	9,648	970
			82	13,911	16,097	17,820	1,723
			83	12,500	22,445	24,573	2,128
			84	27,617	48,173	53,666	5,493
			85	23,281	39,703	43,680	3,977
			86	10,123	18,862	20,135	1,273
	V H		82	2,550	5,817	6,346	529
			83	2,062	3,834	4,194	360
			84	1,583	2,881	3,188	307
			85	540	1,160	1,276	116
			86	1,080	2,913	3,145	232
	V W		81	7,884	16,690	17,990	1,300
			82	5,651	10,599	11,326	727
			83	23,660	27,437	29,804	2,367
			84	17,663	25,419	26,874	1,455
			85	16,796	15,290	16,298	1,008
			86	38,978	22,678	24,918	2,240
KOR REP	N E		84	5,820	5,204	7,211	2,007
	N W		84	822	3,150	4,175	1,025
	V E		81	2,646	790	913	123
			82	1,441	1,838	1,942	104
			83	1,649	838	918	80
			85	3,300	3,347	4,344	997
			86	6,600	7,119	7,881	762
	V H		81	206	300	341	41
	V W		81	528	1,103	1,161	58
			82	1,200	2,061	2,244	183
			83	66,452	13,152	15,442	2,290
			84	19,237	8,869	9,400	531
			85	1,920	1,830	1,939	109
			86	2,058	2,227	2,487	260
MALAYSA	V W		82	6,613	1,028	1,112	84
MEXICO	O E		81	7,550	4,632	4,632	
			82	5,280	390	390	
			83	3,624	484	484	
			85	9,750	5,460	5,460	
	O W		81	111,239	58,391	58,391	
			82	109,671	35,038	35,038	
			83	130,853	18,574	18,574	
			84	107,653	21,207	21,207	
			85	46,198	13,274	13,276	2
			86	40,854	14,425	14,425	
NETHLDS	V E		82	353	389	432	43
PHIL R	V E		83	3,003	2,700	3,227	527
			84	350	275	332	57
			85	1,077	1,184	1,451	267
	V W		84	2,375	1,752	1,993	241
PORTUGL	V E		85	3,307	1,650	1,896	246
SALVADR	V E		86	4,008	1,005	1,560	555
	V W		83	3,810	1,280	1,281	1
			84	16,055	5,809	8,288	2,479
			85	22,500	9,000	11,781	2,781
SINGAPR	V W		81	53,056	14,992	17,933	2,941
SWITZLD	V W		85	6,481	1,338	1,666	328
THAILND	N E		83	287,377	66,772	82,129	15,357
	N W		83	5,302	1,556	1,787	231
	O W		84	14,800	2,940	3,340	400
	V E		81	349,688	80,932	97,914	16,982
			82	395,890	91,179	109,515	18,336
			83	239,270	60,857	71,556	10,699
			84	155,835	40,012	48,166	8,154
			85	348,123	88,015	110,155	22,140
			86	470,537	105,134	123,435	18,301
	V H		81	10,251	2,735	3,096	361
			84	2,500	515	589	74
	V W		81	1,077,861	306,915	347,472	40,557
			82	1,082,010	309,145	356,810	47,665
			83	2,173,395	517,994	591,541	73,547
			84	1,657,245	428,010	489,031	61,021
			85	3,452,587	802,470	922,416	119,946
			86	2,640,494	588,882	673,732	84,850
U KING	O E		82	880	380	435	55
			84	3,977	1,408	1,551	143
	V E		84	7,287	3,105	3,586	481
	V W		84	5,334	2,228	2,615	387

Rice, milled for humans
1313000   RICE MILLD EDIBL BRAN REMOVD (LB)

Country	Mode	Reg	Yr	Quantity	F.A.S.	C.I.F.	Charges
TOTAL			81	12,297,464	3,412,408	3,984,494	572,086
			82	35,904,288	8,438,282	9,880,248	1,441,966
			83	42,619,929	10,141,988	11,797,969	1,655,981
			84	59,744,006	12,541,946	15,029,690	2,487,744
			85	122,797,587	21,631,135	26,442,987	4,811,852
			86	162,207,241	29,564,438	34,611,800	5,047,362
ARAB EM	V E		85	85,428	29,150	34,271	5,121
	V W		85	44,092	15,065	17,914	2,849
BRAZIL	V E		86	2,018,173	490,978	590,844	99,866
BURMA	V E		82	3,120	852	976	124
CANADA	O E		81	22,395	11,685	12,189	504
			82	44,630	25,570	25,570	
			83	12,978	8,135	8,143	8
			84	34,992	18,048	18,119	71
			85	11,290	6,166	6,166	
			86	19,266	24,266	24,266	
	O W		81	1,045	735	735	
			82	16,500	4,650	4,650	
			83	55	356	356	
CHINA M	N W		82	160,917	44,916	50,409	5,493
	O W		81	13,750	4,400	4,400	
	V E		81	247,228	55,792	66,575	10,783
			82	120,013	27,678	33,302	5,624
			83	79,991	13,523	17,342	3,819
			84	2,000	1,506	1,720	214
	V W		81	263,765	64,284	75,924	11,640
			82	993,471	233,460	270,650	37,190
			83	18,660	4,929	6,007	1,078
			86	126,183	19,432	24,380	4,948
CHINA T	N W		81	53,785	17,451	20,117	2,666
	V E		81	78,070	17,789	21,450	3,661
			82	42,529	17,000	19,296	2,296
			83	8,500	4,575	5,519	944
			84	634	624	684	60
			85	637,421	105,168	138,332	33,164
			86	645,944	96,058	124,462	28,404
	V W		82	79,283	23,824	25,160	1,336
			83	201,829	44,467	50,721	6,254
			84	954	961	1,058	97

Crop
Product
TSUSA commodity number, description, and unit of quantity

Country	Mode	Reg	Yr	Quantity	F.A.S.	C.I.F.	Charges
			85	1,977,630	352,287	418,413	66,126
			86	3,504,954	621,437	730,558	109,121
CZECHO	V	E	83	39,683	11,826	14,144	2,318
ECUADOR	V	E	84	80,909	26,791	31,935	5,144
FINLAND	V	E	84	101,250	19,093	24,893	5,800
FR GERM	A	E	84	1,102	458	1,339	881
FRANCE	A	E	82	3,358	8,555	9,029	474
			84	130	416	494	78
	V	E	83	6,837	3,568	3,726	158
			85	8,113	5,428	6,519	1,091
			86	12,750	6,518	7,158	640
GHANA	V	E	86	40,071	5,063	6,594	1,531
HG KONG	O	E	84	18,108	20,300	20,597	297
	V	E	81	38,250	11,734	13,334	1,600
			82	40,500	63,527	65,705	2,178
			83	10,594	3,878	4,745	867
			84	3,736	1,283	1,612	329
			85	5,100	1,264	1,646	382
			86	46,081	9,298	11,198	1,900
	V	W	81	2,500	1,512	1,562	50
			82	40,911	12,519	15,395	2,876
			83	156,163	35,271	39,846	4,575
			84	152,823	29,084	33,914	4,830
			85	517,633	90,016	111,342	21,326
			86	182,041	22,913	24,367	1,454
INDIA	N	E	81	530,566	203,037	243,322	40,285
			82	1,340,280	517,519	608,091	90,572
			83	2,019,632	781,173	902,751	121,578
			84	3,053,972	1,052,389	1,252,533	200,144
			85	4,831,174	1,893,987	2,190,575	296,588
			86	132,798	55,753	63,885	8,132
	O	E	81	2,600	1,452	1,452	
			82	35	372	372	
			83	107,751	45,449	51,561	6,112
			84	56,423	23,507	23,507	
			85	88,998	34,810	34,810	
			86	208,374	94,194	100,572	6,378
	O	W	81	1,045	630	630	
			86	5,566	3,026	3,026	
	V	E	81	110,276	44,278	53,748	9,470
			82	233,609	94,617	111,174	16,557
			83	1,751,911	698,728	817,092	118,364
			84	1,383,756	460,306	549,963	89,657
			85	1,824,665	722,666	845,441	122,775
			86	6,158,984	2,878,685	3,204,562	325,877
	V	W	81	265,992	98,639	114,550	15,911
			82	1,179,157	491,238	572,055	80,817
			83	3,223,035	1,358,416	1,557,199	198,783
			84	1,937,127	771,602	908,390	136,788
			85	4,239,734	1,558,375	1,844,400	286,025
			86	4,430,451	2,122,013	2,367,705	245,692
INDNSIA	V	E	82	40,000	8,000	10,400	2,400
			86	46,296	15,749	20,049	4,300
IRAN	V	E	83	13,228	5,403	6,114	711
	V	W	83	30,864	8,120	9,457	1,337
ITALY	A	E	82	33	300	310	10
	N	E	85	322,035	170,324	192,300	21,976
	O	E	81	26,628	17,323	17,323	
			82	30,696	19,365	19,365	
			83	49,200	24,078	24,078	
			84	51,168	31,780	31,780	
			85	15,096	8,898	8,898	
			86	11,064	6,879	7,174	295
	O	W	86	6,063	2,449	2,907	458
	V	E	81	209,207	102,940	119,210	16,270
			82	340,961	196,334	217,015	20,681
			83	313,341	196,557	216,511	19,954
			84	351,966	184,761	206,710	21,949
			85	40,275	19,861	23,739	3,878
			86	432,836	268,819	302,337	33,518
	V	W	83	39,589	22,581	25,860	3,279
			84	68,059	28,463	32,975	4,512
			85	12,526	10,098	10,886	788
			86	110,634	66,838	73,963	7,125
JAPAN	A	E	82	5	3,000	3,026	26
	V	E	81	40,000	9,500	11,658	2,158
			82	701	895	1,195	300
			84	220	518	556	38
			86	3,008	3,346	3,806	460
	V	H	84	39,670	7,220	8,777	1,557
	V	W	81	357	845	902	57
			82	119,049	33,957	38,945	4,988
			83	1,324	3,203	3,500	297
			84	196,236	41,308	46,765	5,457

Crop
Product
TSUSA commodity number, description, and unit of quantity

Country	Mode	Reg	Yr	Quantity	F.A.S.	C.I.F.	Charges
			85	39,683	13,475	16,172	2,697
			86	116,065	30,627	35,277	4,650
KENYA	O	E	84	990	561	561	
KOR REP	V	E	86	1,398	1,900	2,122	222
	V	W	81	40,000	8,800	10,504	1,704
			84	80,071	14,732	17,442	2,710
			85	1,200	1,082	1,153	71
			86	1,236	3,577	3,688	111
MALAYSA	V	W	81	500	267	297	30
MEXICO	O	E	85	90,000	14,220	14,220	
	O	W	81	1,250	625	625	
NETHLDS	V	E	81	1,194	638	733	95
			82	1,204	661	743	82
	V	W	81	6,080	3,763	4,041	278
			82	597	308	343	35
			83	2,413	1,638	1,755	117
			84	1,382	555	691	136
PAKISTN	N	E	81	1,153,505	404,734	486,173	81,439
			82	389,628	135,490	162,052	26,562
			83	255,712	84,241	99,228	14,987
			85	21,605	10,603	12,018	1,415
			86	256,343	105,146	119,008	13,862
	O	E	83	15,201	5,745	6,319	574
			84	71,345	25,105	30,174	5,069
			85	4,409	2,052	2,303	251
			86	4,846	2,795	3,166	371
	V	E	81	90,223	30,260	36,820	6,560
			82	5,000	2,377	3,023	646
			83	287,224	107,043	124,118	17,075
			84	95,377	42,600	48,392	5,792
			85	24,637	11,146	13,841	2,695
			86	42,108	17,258	19,785	2,527
	V	W	81	180,486	65,343	77,807	12,464
			82	5,000	2,256	2,594	338
			83	84,878	26,685	32,781	6,096
			84	580	1,824	2,234	410
			85	91,376	14,962	18,510	3,548
PERU	N	E	85	57,320	24,850	27,860	3,010
	V	E	86	56,192	30,592	33,276	2,684
PHIL R	V	E	83	226,512	25,394	35,356	9,962
			84	328,431	26,934	40,950	14,016
			85	1,770	1,301	1,496	195
			86	30	1,163	1,326	163
	V	H	81	990	688	773	85
			82	1,020	677	801	124
			83	1,645	1,225	1,347	122
			84	1,760	1,040	1,238	198
			85	79,335	12,235	15,659	3,424
	V	W	83	370,153	46,800	59,903	13,103
			84	169,778	21,259	27,049	5,790
			85	85,460	14,525	17,696	3,171
SINGAPR	O	W	81	5,510	1,680	1,680	
	V	E	83	158,541	28,898	36,299	7,401
			84	79,400	15,140	18,720	3,580
			85	80,142	7,130	12,201	5,071
			86	41,250	7,321	10,113	2,792
	V	W	81	2,500	1,835	2,183	348
			82	500	293	325	32
			83	500	386	425	39
			84	571,991	124,557	141,628	17,071
			86	125,000	17,551	21,032	3,481
SPAIN	V	E	81	43,651	10,296	14,432	4,136
SWEDEN	A	E	83	1,323	460	1,785	1,325
THAILND	N	E	85	4,373,180	661,240	883,077	221,837
			86	1,936,983	287,754	372,294	84,540
	N	H	84	612,907	119,148	144,059	24,911
	N	W	82	10,016,017	2,262,764	2,636,545	373,781
			84	26,713,014	5,010,547	5,987,106	976,559
			85	21,095,258	3,249,406	3,917,870	668,464
	O	E	81	120,052	40,311	44,379	4,068
	O	W	85	7,502	1,455	1,542	87
			86	205,752	23,548	25,219	1,671
	V	E	81	1,023,699	262,804	320,926	58,122
			82	2,666,249	571,366	714,574	143,208
			83	4,462,904	856,668	1,056,425	199,757
			84	7,272,263	1,389,978	1,762,447	372,469
			85	11,206,253	1,685,066	2,291,174	606,108
			86	22,560,657	3,476,042	4,326,559	850,517
	V	H	81	39,021	12,094	13,389	1,295
			82	272,816	61,453	71,267	9,814
			83	434,884	84,125	100,181	16,056
			85	1,362,806	213,592	269,197	55,605
			86	1,678,809	267,614	337,913	70,299
	V	W	81	7,654,954	1,891,645	2,176,625	284,980

Crop Product TSUSA commodity number, description, and unit of quantity Country	Mode	Reg	Yr	Quantity	F.A.S.	C.I.F.	Charges
			82	17,716,499	3,572,489	4,185,891	613,402
			83	28,221,874	5,592,720	6,465,928	873,208
			84	16,061,966	2,965,698	3,538,193	572,495
			85	69,461,363	10,645,697	13,015,023	2,369,326
			86	116,944,102	18,459,929	21,586,073	3,126,144
TURKEY	O	E	83	11,000	5,724	11,447	5,723
	V	E	84	12,200	5,500	6,509	1,009
U KING	O	E	81	25,400	11,352	12,554	1,202
			84	43,210	17,352	20,005	2,653
			85	48,950	21,182	23,632	2,450
	V	E	81	990	1,247	1,472	225
			84	92,106	38,998	43,971	4,973
			85	4,128	2,353	2,691	338
			86	7,790	5,043	5,935	892
VENEZ	V	E	86	87,143	12,864	15,201	2,337

1313300 RICE, BROKEN, EDIBLE (LB)

	Mode	Reg	Yr	Quantity	F.A.S.	C.I.F.	Charges
TOTAL			81	44,538	14,196	17,954	3,758
			82	262,502	51,873	64,040	12,167
			83	43,361	13,823	17,160	3,337
			84	55,425	9,048	12,333	3,285
			85	493,322	53,306	67,292	13,986
			86	245,927	34,887	41,678	6,791
CANADA	O	E	84	4,650	1,953	1,953	
			85	156,868	11,547	11,547	
CHINA T	V	E	82	39,683	10,080	12,558	2,478
COLOMB	V	E	82	11,023	450	700	250
HG KONG	V	W	83	1,500	776	846	70
INDIA	O	E	82	1,100	314	314	
			86	2,750	1,221	1,221	
	V	W	81	39,578	12,659	15,831	3,172
JAPAN	V	E	83	308	256	286	30
MEXICO	O	E	83	783	281	289	8
PAKISTN	V	E	83	39,690	12,000	15,158	3,158
	V	W	82	22,046	1,900	4,695	2,795
THAILND	V	E	82	39,670	8,367	10,611	2,244
			84	50,775	7,095	10,380	3,285
			85	90,142	12,394	17,501	5,107
			86	7,010	2,727	3,002	275
	V	W	81	4,960	1,537	2,123	586
			82	148,980	30,762	35,162	4,400
			83	1,080	510	581	71
			85	246,312	29,365	38,244	8,879
			86	236,167	30,939	37,455	6,516

1313700 RICE, PATNA, CLEANED F SOUPS (LB)

	Mode	Reg	Yr	Quantity	F.A.S.	C.I.F.	Charges
TOTAL			81	3,082	2,310	2,670	360
			83	249	475	510	35
			84	500	599	626	27
CHINA M	V	W	84	500	599	626	27
CHINA T	V	W	83	249	475	510	35
THAILND	V	E	81	3,082	2,310	2,670	360

Rice, milled not for humans
1316700 RICE NFIT HUMAN CONSUMPTION (CWT)

	Mode	Reg	Yr	Quantity	F.A.S.	C.I.F.	Charges
TOTAL			82	121	978	978	
			84	1,150	594	594	
			85	8,338	4,496	4,496	
CANADA	O	E	82	121	978	978	
			84	1,150	594	594	
			85	8,338	4,496	4,496	

Rice, paddy
1305000 RICE, PADDY OR ROUGH (LB)

	Mode	Reg	Yr	Quantity	F.A.S.	C.I.F.	Charges
TOTAL			81	41,504	20,745	22,996	2,251
			82	258,637	77,158	88,352	11,194
			83	315,476	81,779	96,021	14,242
			84	265,388	56,172	67,704	11,532
			85	597,218	117,967	145,200	27,233
			86	1,583,642	282,494	342,485	59,991
CANADA	O	E	82	4,441	9,345	9,345	
			83	60	508	508	
			84	40,480	8,242	8,242	
			85	7,977	4,462	4,462	
			86	6,985	5,621	5,621	
CHINA M	V	W	82	39,683	9,118	10,584	1,466

	Mode	Reg	Yr	Quantity	F.A.S.	C.I.F.	Charges
			86	5,742	1,487	1,619	132
CHINA T	V	E	82	39,683	7,101	9,407	2,306
	V	W	81	250	380	408	28
			86	40,000	5,443	6,738	1,295
HG KONG	V	W	85	301	1,080	1,106	26
INDIA	O	E	82	2,750	1,390	1,390	
			83	41,250	19,566	19,566	
			84	28,195	12,674	12,674	
			85	58,046	27,662	29,302	1,640
			86	7,354	8,264	8,264	
	V	E	81	3,465	1,247	1,442	195
			82	2,684	951	1,165	214
			83	15,477	7,140	8,707	1,567
	V	W	83	880	368	410	42
ITALY	V	E	85	14,899	8,240	8,730	490
			86	10,300	6,781	7,537	756
	V	W	86	4,409	2,181	3,256	1,075
JAPAN	V	E	82	218	380	432	52
	V	W	83	600	442	466	24
			84	900	663	733	70
PAKISTN	O	E	81	28,812	15,999	17,639	1,640
			82	21,200	10,412	11,606	1,194
			83	15,000	7,514	9,410	1,896
			84	20,000	8,572	9,540	968
			86	30,512	18,020	18,020	
PHIL R	V	E	83	108,665	17,333	23,325	5,992
			84	17,500	1,015	1,443	428
	V	W	81	8,977	3,119	3,507	388
			82	2,540	2,219	2,510	291
			83	4,840	3,805	4,237	432
			84	1,038	1,069	1,204	135
SINGAPR	V	E	85	80,000	12,702	16,606	3,904
SWEDEN	V	E	83	49,604	9,283	11,189	1,906
THAILND	O	E	84	50	750	750	
	V	E	82	79,366	20,160	22,679	2,519
			83	39,600	8,176	8,217	41
			84	77,083	14,019	18,226	4,207
			85	277,620	40,993	55,866	14,873
			86	382,599	62,197	74,920	12,723
	V	W	82	66,072	16,082	19,234	3,152
			83	39,500	7,644	9,986	2,342
			84	80,142	9,168	14,892	5,724
			85	158,375	22,828	29,128	6,300
			86	1,045,741	159,985	201,982	41,997
TUNISIA	V	W	86	40,000	5,843	7,076	1,233
U KING	O	E	86	10,000	6,672	7,452	780

Rice, straw and fiber
1927500 RICE STRAW AND RICE FIBER (STN)

	Mode	Reg	Yr	Quantity	F.A.S.	C.I.F.	Charges
TOTAL			81	1	1,278	1,591	313
			82	7	322	322	
			83	25	1,315	1,622	307
			84	3	7,182	11,342	4,160
			85	1	1,500	1,710	210
CANADA	O	E	82	7	322	322	
CHINA T	A	W	81	1	1,278	1,591	313
	V	E	84	1	825	1,311	486
HG KONG	V	E	83	25	1,315	1,622	307
JAPAN	A	E	85	1	1,500	1,710	210
	V	W	84	1	1,357	1,621	264
VENEZ	A	E	84	1	5,000	8,410	3,410

Rice, wine
1672500 RICE WINE OR SAKE (GAL)

	Mode	Reg	Yr	Quantity	F.A.S.	C.I.F.	Charges
TOTAL			81	515,639	3,359,516	3,941,622	584,764
			82	566,113	3,615,715	4,222,602	606,887
			83	693,341	4,404,904	5,102,557	697,653
			84	754,324	4,919,970	5,811,757	891,787
			85	926,779	6,415,329	7,469,951	1,054,622
			86	800,436	6,271,545	7,102,039	830,494
CANADA	O	E	82	420	2,367	2,367	
CHINA M	O	W	82	278	598	662	64
	V	E	83	2,971	13,813	19,241	5,428
			84	10,044	65,081	83,786	18,705
			85	11,920	87,638	111,253	23,615
			86	634	3,921	5,100	1,179
	V	W	81	12,547	98,560	116,548	17,988
			82	8,530	78,989	90,847	11,858

Crop Product TSUSA commodity number, description, and unit of quantity Country	Mode	Reg	Yr	Quantity	F.A.S.	C.I.F.	Charges
			83	11,537	114,824	122,758	7,934
			84	7,640	80,095	87,627	7,532
			85	24,945	196,329	224,597	28,268
			86	17,365	127,995	143,576	15,581
CHINA T	O	W	85	1,141	10,993	11,615	622
	V	E	81	12,307	120,080	136,753	16,673
			82	9,272	90,563	104,848	14,285
			83	15,692	119,406	138,543	19,137
			84	13,314	115,680	136,700	21,020
			85	1,450	13,950	15,884	1,934
			86	2,329	22,766	25,511	2,745
	V	W	81	14,142	114,486	129,842	15,356
			82	26,828	254,040	276,362	22,322
			83	21,883	187,165	200,669	13,504
			84	38,925	87,158	93,299	6,141
			85	20,231	217,170	234,419	17,249
			86	14,948	176,415	193,152	16,737
FR GERM	O	E	82	1,141	6,295	8,219	1,924
FRANCE	V	E	83	357	2,490	3,047	557
			84	209	905	1,147	242
GERM DR	O	E	81	1,484	7,866	10,362	2,496
HG KONG	O	E	85	213	4,840	5,718	878
	O	W	85	128	3,036	3,271	235
	V	E	81	3,141	16,658	19,111	2,453
			82	2,219	10,944	13,666	2,722
			85	4,157	35,755	43,345	7,590
			86	9,039	60,102	78,563	18,461
	V	W	81	2,288	48,031	49,774	1,743
			84	294	3,987	4,436	449
			85	13,350	111,004	120,301	9,297
			86	20,932	182,350	192,639	10,289
ITALY	V	E	84	369	1,190	1,470	280
			86	3,300	10,904	13,390	2,486
JAPAN	A	E	82	20	490	1,065	575
			83	2	252	349	97
			84	190	1,592	2,680	1,088
	N	E	81	78,849	477,005	568,466	91,461
			82	86,333	527,763	624,684	96,921
			83	102,131	626,734	730,548	103,814
			84	174,205	1,107,059	1,316,701	209,642
			85	163,870	1,153,012	1,387,367	234,355
			86	19,459	150,867	174,354	23,487
	N	H	82	22,053	142,448	171,951	29,503
	N	W	81	212,778	1,340,367	1,523,453	185,853
			83	134,999	874,680	997,177	122,497
			84	241,031	1,689,864	1,891,040	201,176
	O	E	81	53,208	311,289	398,523	87,234
			82	70,570	422,228	532,373	110,145
			83	99,984	655,156	806,425	151,269
			84	57,156	375,931	473,561	97,630
			85	119,525	705,053	891,417	186,364
			86	47,921	321,633	387,858	66,225
	O	W	81	15,163	73,552	85,502	11,950
			82	17,029	101,283	112,099	10,816
			83	1,464	7,005	7,947	942
			85	1,229	7,572	8,403	831
			86	238	3,318	3,451	133
	V	E	81	46,497	318,280	387,334	68,945
			82	44,619	315,914	383,022	67,108
			83	55,544	355,916	426,332	70,416
			84	60,424	409,335	510,707	101,372
			85	64,356	511,205	620,521	109,316
			86	280,795	2,103,072	2,461,530	358,458
	V	H	81	24,021	174,700	209,472	34,772
			83	24,829	187,538	217,477	29,939
			84	21,465	162,995	192,509	29,514
			85	25,474	209,400	247,087	37,687
			86	29,586	294,426	344,138	49,712
	V	W	81	35,195	232,814	275,230	42,416
			82	273,400	1,627,508	1,859,579	232,071
			83	217,430	1,245,960	1,415,080	169,120
			84	119,763	786,987	976,701	189,714
			85	460,070	3,064,208	3,446,245	382,037
			86	341,677	2,730,342	2,986,424	256,082
KOR REP	O	W	85	3,239	19,466	20,871	1,405
	V	E	84	1,733	10,756	12,901	2,145
			85	1,984	14,467	16,696	2,229
			86	2,225	14,241	16,588	2,347
	V	W	81	225	11,124	12,393	1,269
			82	1,118	20,709	23,066	2,357
			85	2,055	16,640	17,520	880
			86	9,288	58,068	62,645	4,577
SPAIN	O	E	81	1,254	6,699	8,909	2,210
			82	2,283	13,576	17,792	4,216

Crop Product TSUSA commodity number, description, and unit of quantity Country	Mode	Reg	Yr	Quantity	F.A.S.	C.I.F.	Charges
			83	4,518	13,965	16,964	2,999
	V	E	81	2,540	8,005	9,950	1,945
			84	7,562	21,355	26,492	5,137
			85	3,962	12,130	15,232	3,102
THAILND	V	E	86	700	11,125	13,120	1,995
U KING	O	E	85	3,480	21,461	28,189	6,728

Rose

Rose, essential oil
4526000 ROSE OIL OR ATTAR OF ROSES (OZ)

Country	Mode	Reg	Yr	Quantity	F.A.S.	C.I.F.	Charges
TOTAL			**81**	**35,622**	**2,318,662**	**2,336,736**	**18,084**
			82	**43,678**	**3,552,233**	**3,572,211**	**19,978**
			83	**40,515**	**3,425,168**	**3,451,982**	**26,814**
			84	**63,508**	**3,431,493**	**3,477,658**	**46,165**
			85	**93,412**	**6,811,203**	**6,930,456**	**119,253**
			86	**97,870**	**7,676,352**	**7,736,886**	**60,534**
BELGIUM	A	E	83	704	64,050	64,392	342
BRAZIL	V	E	83	2,381	21,941	23,731	1,790
			84	12,559	183,199	199,450	16,251
			85	3,968	17,706	19,171	1,465
			86	29,586	104,695	113,728	9,033
BULGAR	A	E	81	10,130	595,346	598,336	2,990
			82	10,056	991,790	994,683	2,893
			86	176	2,342	2,450	108
	N	E	83	7,375	856,189	858,511	2,322
			84	8,895	658,308	661,828	3,520
			85	1,631	218,573	219,538	965
			86	677	88,350	89,032	682
BURMA	A	E	86	416	24,000	24,331	331
CANADA	N	E	82	3,412	34,468	34,784	316
	O	E	81	253	23,124	23,124	
CHILE	V	W	86	388	16,500	16,970	470
CHINA M	O	E	81	441	10,293	10,416	123
	V	W	85	97	3,145	3,440	295
CHINA T	A	E	85	1,760	210,000	210,231	231
	V	W	84	281	3,971	4,506	535
			85	186	4,937	5,497	560
FR GERM	A	E	84	68	5,544	5,692	148
			85	71	1,787	1,820	33
			86	1,109	14,734	15,016	282
FRANCE	A	E	82	400	21,037	21,238	201
			83	144	6,261	6,376	115
	A	W	84	176	708	721	13
	N	E	81	19,823	1,271,052	1,283,035	11,983
			82	25,568	2,106,265	2,120,653	14,388
			83	12,105	1,202,256	1,216,764	14,508
			84	22,293	1,485,805	1,503,893	18,088
			85	48,463	3,090,114	3,187,288	97,174
			86	40,522	3,789,230	3,814,776	25,546
	V	E	81	400	421	430	9
HAITI	A	E	83	450	8,663	8,865	202
HG KONG	A	E	86	353	12,607	12,671	64
INDIA	A	E	81	353	32,000	32,256	256
			83	661	30,900	31,908	1,008
			85	1,234	50,622	51,202	580
	V	W	82	122	424	560	136
INDNSIA	O	E	85	4,409	211,254	213,253	1,999
IRELAND	A	E	82	565	90,732	91,339	607
ITALY	A	E	84	176	2,905	2,913	8
			86	128	1,798	2,057	259
JAPAN	A	E	83	37	5,150	5,310	160
MOROC	A	E	83	135	4,915	4,919	4
			85	2,032	64,888	65,079	191
MOZAMBQ	A	E	86	13	24,349	24,412	63
NETHLDS	A	E	81	2,218	254,414	255,847	1,433
			82	2,625	238,502	239,215	713
			83	2,668	426,002	426,751	749
			84	836	278,371	279,239	868
			85	10,223	1,080,626	1,088,702	8,076
			86	5,113	631,000	634,541	3,541
REP SAF	A	E	81	352	6,200	6,325	125
S ARAB	A	E	83	96	800	912	112
SPAIN	A	E	86	1,940	6,875	7,278	403
	V	E	85	43	21,483	21,784	301
SWITZLD	A	E	81	553	49,637	49,780	143
			82	388	26,915	27,211	296
			83	858	87,393	88,179	786
			85	1,136	104,504	105,509	1,005

Crop Product TSUSA commodity number, description, and unit of quantity Country	Mode	Reg	Yr	Quantity	F.A.S.	C.I.F.	Charges
	A	W	86	456	12,757	13,409	652
	N	E	84	9,205	72,932	73,670	738
			86	863	55,933	56,595	662
TURKEY	A	E	82	538	41,723	42,149	426
			83	12,883	709,411	714,064	4,653
			84	9,019	739,750	745,746	5,996
			85	13,860	1,650,541	1,656,522	5,981
			86	12,548	2,849,042	2,867,080	18,038
	N	E	81	1,099	76,175	77,187	1,022
U KING	A	E	83	18	1,237	1,300	63
			85	4,213	79,752	80,102	350
	N	E	82	4	377	379	2
			86	3,582	42,140	42,540	400
	O	E	85	86	1,271	1,318	47

Rose, fresh
1921800 ROSES, FRESH (NO)

Country	Mode	Reg	Yr	Quantity	F.A.S.	C.I.F.	Charges
TOTAL			**81**	**67,525,602**	**11,683,624**	**14,478,505**	**2,115,242**
			82	**94,140,752**	**18,839,841**	**21,043,073**	**2,203,232**
ALGERIA	A	E	82	43,575	6,260	7,266	1,006
BRAZIL	A	E	81	450,048	73,081	100,099	27,018
			82	339,140	42,222	66,756	24,534
C RICA	A	E	82	78,050	8,264	10,531	2,267
CANADA	A	E	82	2,000	1,000	1,278	278
	A	W	81	500	690	714	24
	O	E	81	495,301	188,188	188,188	
			82	882,189	365,379	365,379	
	O	W	81	101,510	27,804	27,804	
CHILE	A	E	81	6,350	1,016	1,351	335
			82	113,050	16,729	22,415	5,686
COLOMB	A	E	81	638,775	142,398	176,889	29,993
			82	853,880	236,182	274,264	38,082
	A	W	81	8,900	4,744	4,956	212
			82	4,800	1,025	1,088	63
	N	E	81	52,283,290	9,500,557	11,647,105	1,473,579
			82	74,576,572	15,811,533	17,294,121	1,482,588
DOM REP	A	E	81	189,940	19,273	24,486	5,213
			82	2,612,523	264,060	324,099	60,039
	N	E	81	1,538,025	120,031	153,521	33,490
EGYPT	A	E	81	5,200	260	936	676
FR GERM	A	E	82	1,500	375	459	84
FRANCE	A	E	81	3,760	892	992	100
GUATMAL	A	E	81	1,686,972	323,711	362,363	37,751
			82	2,579,074	391,838	443,801	51,963
	A	W	81	1,920	528	584	56
HG KONG	V	W	82	109	2,644	2,865	221
INDNSIA	V	E	82	274	12,282	12,345	63
ISRAEL	A	E	81	6,172,129	320,465	707,324	385,588
			82	5,279,626	295,184	595,114	299,930
MEXICO	A	E	82	267,954	39,204	45,302	6,098
	A	W	82	4,000	542	1,140	598
	O	W	81	372,535	50,883	50,883	
			82	736,217	87,966	87,966	
N ZEAL	A	W	81	14,884	31,226	35,403	4,177
NETHLDS	A	E	81	2,962,696	792,863	887,160	94,297
			82	1,332,900	314,152	380,214	66,062
	A	W	81	266,986	46,132	52,964	6,832
			82	73,040	21,390	27,181	5,791
	N	E	82	3,750,712	822,123	951,439	129,316
PORTUGL	A	E	82	1,480	342	418	76
REP SAF	A	E	82	960	269	385	116
SPAIN	A	E	81	220,780	25,744	39,150	13,406
			82	551,868	92,251	118,802	26,551
U KING	A	E	81	102,361	12,730	15,156	2,426
			82	36,599	3,672	4,727	1,055
	A	W	82	14,900	2,061	2,726	665
VENEZ	A	E	81	6,500	1,300	1,469	169

1921810 ROSES, SWEETHEART, FRESH (NO)

Country	Mode	Reg	Yr	Quantity	F.A.S.	C.I.F.	Charges
TOTAL			**83**	**1,931,261**	**437,524**	**469,833**	**32,309**
			84	**2,669,648**	**530,076**	**592,675**	**62,599**
			85	**2,310,635**	**433,244**	**554,679**	**121,435**
			86	**2,469,142**	**599,151**	**703,722**	**104,571**
C RICA	A	E	84	22,900	2,471	2,889	418
			85	74,400	8,890	11,311	2,421
			86	62,325	17,580	20,532	2,952
	A	W	84	92,560	10,403	12,170	1,767
			85	272,688	42,763	48,488	5,725
			86	339,770	51,477	57,857	6,380
	N	E	86	564,623	97,721	109,444	11,723

Crop Product TSUSA commodity number, description, and unit of quantity Country	Mode	Reg	Yr	Quantity	F.A.S.	C.I.F.	Charges
CANADA	O	E	83	514,273	175,762	175,762	
			84	535,980	212,497	212,497	
			85	122,721	65,298	65,298	
			86	205,573	131,729	131,729	
	O	W	83	9,600	2,853	2,853	
			84	816	298	298	
CHILE	A	E	83	3,300	602	835	233
COLOMB	A	E	83	919,238	172,564	193,461	20,897
			85	516,350	101,678	123,455	21,777
			86	573,560	92,511	113,448	20,937
	N	E	84	1,464,275	213,794	244,280	30,486
ECUADOR	A	E	84	19,158	4,633	5,353	720
FRANCE	A	E	83	3,400	458	566	108
INDIA	A	W	85	23,680	3,728	5,888	2,160
			86	36,200	4,670	4,738	68
IRAN	A	W	85	44,020	3,363	8,175	4,812
ISRAEL	A	E	83	31,000	3,503	5,476	1,973
			84	224,240	21,064	36,199	15,135
			85	545,230	105,362	145,305	39,943
			86	22,084	10,009	15,257	5,248
	A	W	85	425,020	35,722	63,558	27,836
			86	382,520	28,726	63,397	34,671
ITALY	A	E	83	19,800	2,652	3,145	493
MEXICO	A	E	85	88,086	14,836	16,322	1,486
	O	W	85	103,450	11,230	11,230	
NETHLDS	A	E	83	280,080	56,854	64,229	7,375
			84	274,089	55,831	67,218	11,387
			85	166,240	42,004	52,274	10,270
			86	274,107	162,522	185,046	22,524
	A	W	83	860	257	330	73
	N	E	83	44,600	8,545	9,639	1,094
	O	E	83	520	1,891	1,891	
			86	4,820	1,140	1,208	68
	O	W	86	3,560	1,066	1,066	
	V	E	84	35,630	9,085	11,771	2,686
SPAIN	A	E	83	1,140	353	416	63
VENEZ	A	E	85	32,200	9,600	14,605	5,005

1921890 ROSES, NSPF, FRESH (NO)

Country	Mode	Reg	Yr	Quantity	F.A.S.	C.I.F.	Charges
TOTAL			**83**	**124,164,232**	**30,287,979**	**33,213,705**	**2,925,726**
			84	**156,130,060**	**37,280,296**	**41,694,316**	**4,414,020**
			85	**166,342,543**	**41,941,786**	**47,818,216**	**5,876,430**
			86	**209,511,826**	**45,831,840**	**53,042,911**	**7,211,071**
ARGENT	A	E	83	81,700	3,268	8,867	5,599
BELGIUM	A	E	84	900	278	307	29
BOLIVIA	A	E	83	9,000	1,025	1,866	841
			86	5,250	280	630	350
			86	15,375	1,230	1,770	540
BRAZIL	A	E	83	77,140	9,177	15,223	6,046
			84	147,700	14,020	23,038	9,018
			85	263,760	36,146	52,683	16,537
			86	276,660	46,266	68,231	21,965
	A	W	86	90,012	4,501	9,191	4,690
C AF RP	A	E	86	14,700	3,272	3,851	579
C RICA	A	E	83	301,375	35,692	44,307	8,615
			84	667,290	95,477	112,855	17,378
			85	1,995,630	306,585	334,554	27,969
			86	201,285	69,468	77,174	7,706
	A	W	84	13,000	1,085	1,310	225
			85	11,250	3,308	3,660	352
			86	74,068	29,376	32,922	3,546
	N	E	86	722,918	234,816	254,389	19,573
CANADA	A	E	83	14,400	2,761	3,039	278
			85	317,850	100,232	109,690	9,458
			86	62,828	10,362	12,044	1,682
	A	W	86	17,500	2,625	2,973	348
	O	E	83	508,622	242,831	242,831	
			84	714,165	375,380	375,380	
			85	227,614	142,321	144,759	2,438
			86	343,999	230,838	230,838	
	O	W	83	52,121	41,188	41,188	
			84	14,580	43,108	43,108	
			85	135,037	22,891	22,891	
			86	276,595	40,251	40,251	
	V	E	84	18,800	4,478	4,839	361
CHILE	A	E	83	72,500	10,418	15,017	4,599
			84	106,225	14,948	20,373	5,425
			85	179,650	28,745	47,908	19,163
			86	256,000	25,595	43,951	18,356
CHINA T	A	W	86	6,500	1,495	3,261	1,766
COCOS I	A	E	85	5,100	1,215	1,355	140
			86	13,800	3,696	4,189	493
COLOMB	A	E	83	1,155,271	301,464	350,489	49,025

Crop Product TSUSA commodity number, description, and unit of quantity Country	Mode	Reg	Yr	Quantity	F.A.S.	C.I.F.	Charges
			84	863,150	240,144	277,146	37,002
			85	1,033,997	401,145	439,317	38,172
			86	953,655	215,306	252,282	36,976
	A	H	85	21,400	8,400	8,953	553
			86	16,200	3,240	3,818	578
	A	W	83	3,003	749	986	237
			84	7,800	2,393	2,732	339
			85	86,317	32,762	37,690	4,928
			86	98,501	47,756	52,930	5,174
	N	E	83	96,628,440	25,524,946	27,474,953	1,950,007
			84	119,187,007	30,119,636	33,047,408	2,927,772
			85	131,557,889	34,825,002	38,834,235	4,009,233
			86	167,018,108	37,259,909	42,514,225	5,254,316
	O	E	85	35,900	14,368	15,589	1,221
DENMARK	A	E	85	10,500	2,415	2,695	280
DOM REP	A	E	83	2,484,384	202,864	254,856	51,992
			84	2,919,611	274,556	357,423	82,867
			85	291,804	29,006	42,030	13,024
			86	1,958,884	288,365	402,933	114,568
	N	E	85	1,510,015	175,945	250,097	74,152
ECUADOR	A	E	83	3,000	300	494	194
			84	870	783	1,256	473
			85	378,240	75,337	94,692	19,355
			86	3,985,049	596,628	774,022	177,394
	N	E	84	1,075,447	135,969	163,253	27,284
EGYPT	A	E	86	14,700	1,250	1,806	556
FR GERM	A	E	83	13,560	3,393	3,993	600
			84	4,580	1,168	1,354	186
			86	2,680	6,710	7,120	410
FRANCE	A	E	83	20,822	6,155	7,539	1,384
			84	25,162	13,764	19,682	5,918
			85	39,440	15,719	18,211	2,492
			86	65,550	45,862	52,960	7,098
	A	W	83	15,860	8,245	9,973	1,728
			84	1,694	5,624	6,962	1,338
			86	3,960	1,774	2,293	519
	N	E	85	22,705	7,000	14,284	7,284
GERM DR	A	E	86	5,600	1,120	1,345	225
GREECE	A	E	84	29,584	13,870	16,767	2,897
			85	11,540	4,095	4,772	677
			86	40,152	31,050	35,727	4,677
GUATMAL	A	E	83	4,410,790	609,367	710,985	101,618
			84	688,573	97,918	113,248	15,330
			85	6,738,754	737,721	944,990	207,269
			86	6,334,456	793,195	999,590	206,395
	N	E	84	5,562,646	822,481	947,122	124,641
			85	391,585	68,807	82,764	13,957
			86	2,889,625	420,435	522,630	102,195
HG KONG	A	W	83	5,200	425	620	195
HONDURA	A	E	84	30,800	7,130	7,662	532
IRAN	A	W	86	40,500	2,835	5,339	2,504
ISRAEL	A	E	83	4,297,751	437,424	705,825	268,401
			84	5,262,165	777,325	1,182,732	405,407
			85	790,006	154,499	265,504	111,005
			86	2,263,329	408,386	659,554	251,168
	A	W	84	25,600	3,958	6,315	2,357
			85	1,423,101	266,081	403,142	137,061
			86	880,750	119,526	219,699	100,173
	N	E	85	3,348,109	542,005	1,001,181	459,176
ITALY	A	E	83	41,700	17,789	20,054	2,265
			84	57,530	29,888	34,622	4,734
			85	26,962	18,796	21,225	2,429
			86	55,965	24,038	28,584	4,546
	A	W	84	14,990	2,639	3,187	548
IVY CST	A	E	85	5,768	5,191	8,136	2,945
JAMAICA	A	E	83	2,500	645	681	36
			84	83,491	20,891	27,749	6,858
			85	125,195	37,199	40,216	3,017
			86	530,872	178,987	208,607	29,620
JAPAN	A	E	84	9,100	1,820	1,972	152
			86	6,010	1,366	1,902	536
KIRIBAT	A	E	85	471,473	56,278	70,102	13,824
			86	222,585	25,581	32,896	7,315
LAOS	A	E	85	8,700	1,044	1,915	871
MACAO	A	E	86	10,360	2,441	4,882	2,441
MALI	A	E	85	11,470	3,026	4,036	1,010
MEXICO	A	E	83	2,382,550	575,666	624,558	48,892
			84	3,624,486	956,182	1,016,881	60,699
			85	1,541,940	483,873	520,365	36,492
			86	8,250,227	1,430,128	1,608,816	178,688
	A	W	83	18,094	2,700	3,943	1,243
			84	55,099	20,961	25,215	4,254
			85	34,980	18,328	20,652	2,324
			86	234,828	47,958	59,103	11,145
	N	E	83	747,251	134,500	148,136	13,636
			84	715,856	219,374	236,613	17,239
			85	4,541,146	1,160,947	1,226,786	65,839
			86	3,807,882	1,038,466	1,091,273	52,807
	O	E	83	28,750	7,500	7,500	
	O	W	83	1,629,250	209,156	209,606	450
			84	2,717,434	328,908	328,908	
			85	1,683,016	164,574	164,574	
			86	1,156,133	102,848	102,848	
MONSRAT	A	E	85	13,400	5,561	5,972	411
MOROC	A	W	85	3,200	1,808	2,084	276
	A	E	83	3,200	931	1,250	319
			84	18,376	5,913	8,505	2,592
			85	22,780	6,068	7,342	1,274
			86	31,974	12,692	16,498	3,806
	A	W	85	15,560	2,704	5,617	2,913
	V	W	86	11,000	13,831	26,436	12,605
N ANTIL	A	E	85	6,220	3,537	4,937	1,400
			86	6,240	1,404	1,685	281
N CALDN	A	E	85	24,290	4,396	5,167	771
N ZEAL	A	E	84	963	867	1,087	220
	A	H	83	1,402	485	674	189
	A	W	86	1,950	1,043	1,101	58
NETHLDS	A	E	83	5,802,418	1,445,384	1,698,611	253,227
			84	8,015,302	1,997,474	2,459,479	462,005
			85	1,421,218	375,976	448,010	72,034
			86	1,596,271	629,124	749,017	119,893
	A	W	83	748,016	136,808	181,710	44,902
			84	888,957	231,435	289,266	57,831
			85	336,791	100,014	130,530	30,516
			86	124,904	70,241	87,578	17,337
	N	E	83	284,820	68,517	74,049	5,532
			84	125,360	23,258	27,872	4,614
			85	4,333,735	1,263,787	1,605,834	342,047
			86	3,751,389	1,109,442	1,462,612	353,170
	O	E	83	224	374	374	
	V	E	84	1,580	681	821	140
NIGER	A	E	85	7,940	3,219	3,960	741
PANAMA	A	E	83	720	305	368	63
			84	20,000	1,475	1,788	313
			85	6,000	2,890	2,998	108
			86	50,165	6,727	8,420	1,693
PERU	A	E	83	56,870	14,685	16,619	1,934
			84	237,200	65,223	71,232	6,009
			85	80,000	9,600	12,140	2,540
			86	57,100	10,250	12,402	2,152
	A	W	86	7,500	6,400	6,654	254
POLAND	A	E	83	50,225	4,981	5,874	893
REP SAF	A	E	84	2,990	2,388	2,845	457
			86	3,672	3,305	4,284	979
SINGAPR	A	E	83	6,460	1,038	1,256	218
	A	W	84	500	264	327	63
			86	49,600	9,656	10,083	427
SPAIN	A	E	83	2,189,102	221,011	320,990	99,979
			84	1,969,986	264,389	370,249	105,860
			85	501,418	131,300	164,414	33,114
			86	423,753	84,613	119,853	35,240
	A	W	84	107,300	15,755	21,162	5,407
			85	7,200	1,730	2,195	465
			86	139,287	56,902	76,838	19,936
SWITZLD	A	E	84	2,300	348	555	207
			85	5,400	1,068	1,597	529
			86	220	1,544	2,164	620
THAILND	A	E	83	4,480	1,156	1,343	187
			84	27,460	6,412	8,090	1,678
			85	24,310	7,331	12,786	5,455
U KING	A	E	83	11,261	2,656	3,058	402
			84	47,366	11,996	15,146	3,150
	A	W	84	13,835	5,982	7,843	1,861
VENEZ	A	E	85	247,058	68,171	144,952	76,781
			86	20,000	13,200	21,752	8,552
ZMBABWE	A	E	85	8,200	1,620	2,028	408
			86	18,000	2,515	3,315	800

Rose, plant
1256500 ROSE PLANTS ON OWN ROOTS (NO)

			Yr	Quantity	F.A.S.	C.I.F.	Charges
TOTAL			81	81,987	149,938	150,813	875
			82	44,249	126,836	127,842	1,006
			83	96,083	129,636	130,378	742
			84	122,970	207,852	212,803	4,951
			85	171,740	241,360	242,253	893
			86	197,636	416,826	418,529	1,703

Crop
Product
TSUSA commodity number, description, and unit of quantity

Country	Mode	Reg	Yr	Quantity	F.A.S.	C.I.F.	Charges
BOLIVIA	V	E	84	2,505	2,505	4,509	2,004
CANADA	A	E	82	364	632	824	192
			83	607	1,672	1,974	302
			84	1,471	4,439	4,921	482
			85	226	1,038	1,038	
			86	765	1,574	2,108	534
	A	W	83	90	270	270	
			84	1,568	3,996	4,867	871
			86	620	2,243	2,756	513
	O	E	81	56,312	139,982	139,982	
			82	43,635	124,626	124,626	
			83	69,369	112,592	112,592	
			84	102,861	172,355	172,355	
			85	145,616	230,214	230,214	
			86	108,766	256,244	256,244	
	O	W	83	21,887	11,666	11,666	
			84	8,474	20,571	20,571	
			85	2,538	6,813	6,813	
			86	62,485	155,265	155,265	
FR GERM	A	W	83	385	662	829	167
FRANCE	A	E	84	562	562	773	211
	A	W	83	1,440	771	820	49
			84	850	850	1,004	154
HAITI	A	E	83	1,805	660	710	50
ISRAEL	A	E	86	25,000	1,500	2,156	656
JAMAICA	A	E	81	700	1,050	1,191	141
JAPAN	A	W	82	250	1,578	2,392	814
NETHLDS	A	E	81	1,350	1,367	1,532	165
			83	500	1,343	1,517	174
			84	1,800	1,398	2,409	1,011
	V	E	81	23,625	7,539	8,108	569
U KING	A	E	84	2,800	903	959	56
	A	W	84	79	273	435	162
			85	23,360	3,295	4,188	893

Rose, seedling
1256000 SEEDLINGS, CUT, ROSE STOCK (NO)

Country	Mode	Reg	Yr	Quantity	F.A.S.	C.I.F.	Charges
TOTAL			81	64,007	7,988	10,048	2,060
			82	164,055	9,284	10,202	918
			83	279,814	9,065	12,184	3,119
			84	24,265	2,108	2,410	302
			85	54,405	5,873	6,491	618
			86	5,300	1,484	1,484	
C RICA	V	E	83	9,380	1,688	4,398	2,710
CANADA	A	E	81	18,500	2,775	4,007	1,232
	A	W	85	24,200	3,612	4,012	400
	O	E	81	34,500	3,806	3,806	
			82	34,650	4,414	4,414	
			83	239,660	5,398	5,398	
			85	30,165	1,203	1,203	
			86	5,300	1,484	1,484	
	O	W	83	2,270	553	553	
DOM REP	A	E	81	307	700	1,249	549
			82	64,000	1,968	2,365	397
FRANCE	A	E	81	10,700	707	986	279
			82	64,000	2,047	2,301	254
			83	28,500	1,158	1,365	207
			84	23,625	1,802	2,009	207
			85	40	1,058	1,276	218
	N	E	83	4	268	470	202
GUATMAL	A	E	84	640	306	401	95
NETHLDS	A	W	82	1,405	855	1,122	267

Rosemary

Rosemary, essential oil
4526200 ROSEMARY OIL (LB)

Country	Mode	Reg	Yr	Quantity	F.A.S.	C.I.F.	Charges
TOTAL			81	121,115	650,012	678,979	28,937
			82	70,939	333,726	350,538	16,812
			83	136,987	616,653	640,756	24,103
			84	179,719	679,913	707,165	27,252
			85	74,076	307,850	316,705	8,855
			86	112,803	649,129	672,245	23,116
CHINA T	V	E	86	882	4,090	4,378	288
FRANCE	N	E	81	44,796	227,831	236,553	8,722
			82	20,393	105,167	109,220	4,053

Crop
Product
TSUSA commodity number, description, and unit of quantity

Country	Mode	Reg	Yr	Quantity	F.A.S.	C.I.F.	Charges
			83	27,498	110,119	114,977	4,858
			84	40,206	133,650	139,698	6,048
			85	40,379	187,701	191,920	4,219
			86	23,514	182,262	186,712	4,450
INDIA	A	E	83	220	9,900	10,384	484
ITALY	V	E	81	1,323	7,913	8,051	138
MOROC	V	E	81	15,432	90,850	94,907	4,057
NETHLDS	N	E	84	8,819	42,359	44,098	1,739
	V	E	85	6,615	28,411	28,859	448
SPAIN	N	E	81	55,997	304,143	319,507	15,334
			83	95,932	441,027	457,186	16,159
			84	123,076	472,691	491,240	18,549
			85	24,221	79,559	83,126	3,567
	V	E	81	1,322	6,869	7,190	321
			82	50,345	227,043	239,757	12,714
			83	882	2,281	2,487	206
			85	441	1,421	1,500	79
			86	64,156	264,264	274,990	10,726
SWITZLD	A	E	81	40	956	1,001	45
TUNISIA	V	E	81	2,205	11,450	11,770	320
			83	11,023	45,867	47,989	2,122
			84	4,851	23,851	24,549	698
			86	23,975	197,171	204,789	7,618
U KING	N	E	84	2,767	7,362	7,580	218
			85	2,420	10,758	11,300	542
	O	E	83	991	5,635	5,830	195
	V	E	82	201	1,516	1,561	45
			83	441	1,824	1,903	79
			86	276	1,342	1,376	34

Rosemary, spice
1619000 ROSEMARY, EXCEPT MANUFACTURD (LB)

Country	Mode	Reg	Yr	Quantity	F.A.S.	C.I.F.	Charges
TOTAL			81	588,631	184,992	245,170	60,178
			82	606,366	183,781	263,827	80,102
			83	1,028,182	272,668	374,233	101,565
			84	671,497	133,184	183,099	49,915
			85	979,078	230,832	310,155	79,323
			86	1,013,245	291,908	380,385	88,477
ALBANIA	V	E	81	108,143	35,535	50,120	14,585
			82	10,975	4,925	5,433	508
			83	119,869	32,350	45,316	12,966
			86	28,025	9,228	12,369	3,141
CANADA	O	E	81	22,222	1,400	1,400	
			83	1,132	1,977	1,977	
			84	478	2,631	2,631	
FR GERM	O	E	82	51	5,266	5,432	166
	V	E	84	22	1,993	2,032	39
FRANCE	V	E	82	11,034	3,138	4,214	1,076
			83	171,733	52,704	67,597	14,893
			84	11,178	2,995	5,121	2,126
			85	84,307	27,693	34,352	6,659
			86	137,486	49,391	62,238	12,847
	V	W	84	11	942	1,020	78
			85	4,486	1,482	1,802	320
INDIA	O	E	81	16,000	1,000	1,060	60
INDNSIA	V	W	85	3,307	1,124	1,285	161
ITALY	V	E	81	20,943	8,111	10,260	2,149
			82	92	506	557	51
			83	177	1,584	1,656	72
	V	W	82	56	303	303	56
JAMAICA	A	E	83	20,000	4,550	4,570	20
N ZEAL	A	E	85	53	1,616	2,616	1,000
			86	474	5,688	7,951	2,263
	A	W	83	296	2,013	2,393	380
			84	520	3,562	4,237	675
NETHLDS	A	E	85	18,630	6,602	6,762	160
	O	E	85	40,000	5,005	5,059	54
PORTUGL	N	E	85	48,501	14,070	16,282	2,212
	O	E	84	6,160	2,212	2,212	
	V	E	81	94,398	29,046	37,789	8,743
			82	205,926	49,385	78,423	29,038
			83	162,652	36,392	55,436	19,044
			84	112,968	22,508	35,061	12,553
			85	85,876	16,089	26,425	10,336
			86	199,410	62,489	80,856	18,367
SPAIN	V	E	81	247,480	76,194	102,467	26,273
			82	193,899	52,497	75,194	22,697
			83	311,419	67,661	101,689	34,028
			84	431,126	59,103	82,541	23,438
			85	435,492	76,861	106,556	29,695
			86	396,904	99,817	132,067	32,250

Crop Product TSUSA commodity number, description, and unit of quantity Country	Mode	Reg	Yr	Quantity	F.A.S.	C.I.F.	Charges
	V	W	81	2,161	700	825	125
			82	4,385	1,800	2,475	675
			85	3,911	1,506	2,014	508
			86	15,400	4,884	5,687	803
U KING	O	E	82	27	1,279	1,304	25
YUGOSLV	V	E	81	75,761	32,318	40,336	8,018
			82	179,921	64,682	90,492	25,810
			83	200,904	68,432	88,540	20,108
			84	109,034	37,238	48,244	11,006
			85	294,515	83,789	112,061	28,272
			86	235,546	60,411	79,217	18,806
	V	W	81	1,523	688	913	225

1619200 ROSEMARY, MANUFACTURED (LB)

Country	Mode	Reg	Yr	Quantity	F.A.S.	C.I.F.	Charges
TOTAL			81	4,074	8,858	9,698	840
			82	845	4,293	4,459	166
			83	34,047	14,940	18,637	3,697
			84	27,810	9,797	13,045	3,248
			85	60,690	45,713	50,819	5,106
			86	28,096	32,450	35,529	3,079
BRAZIL	V	W	84	655	362	410	48
CANADA	O	E	81	480	406	406	
COLOMB	A	E	84	28	330	357	27
FR GERM	A	E	81	4	673	686	13
	O	E	81	1,063	618	665	47
			82	695	353	421	68
			83	1,984	1,012	1,033	21
	V	E	83	2,203	1,281	1,472	191
			84	691	575	621	46
			85	2,204	3,716	3,974	258
			86	22,690	25,482	27,819	2,337
	V	W	83	635	338	393	55
FRANCE	A	E	81	11	1,917	2,028	111
	A	W	82	18	251	262	11
	N	E	81	238	3,586	3,842	256
	V	E	82	51	967	1,004	37
			83	167	4,511	4,599	88
			84	354	1,400	1,554	154
GREECE	V	E	84	532	298	339	41
	V	W	84	220	298	333	35
JAPAN	V	E	84	285	561	591	30
N ZEAL	V	E	86	94	1,124	1,510	386
PORTUGL	V	E	84	24,255	4,185	6,885	2,700
SPAIN	V	E	83	28,729	6,795	10,073	3,278
			85	17,600	10,736	11,677	941
	V	W	84	666	405	464	59
			85	18,157	19,081	21,784	2,703
SWEDEN	V	E	85	551	7,220	7,749	529
			86	5,312	5,844	6,200	356
SWITZLD	A	E	85	132	1,860	2,225	365
U KING	O	E	81	38	274	289	15
			82	81	2,722	2,772	50
	V	E	81	35	424	449	25
			83	329	1,003	1,067	64
			84	124	1,383	1,491	108
			85	22,046	3,100	3,410	310
YUGOSLV	V	W	81	2,205	960	1,333	373

Rosewood

Bois de rose, essential oil**
4524000 LIGNALOE OIL OR BOIS DE ROSE (LB)
(See Lignaloe, essential oil under Agalloch)

Rosha Grass

Palmarosa, essential oil
4525000 PALMAROSA OIL (LB)

Country	Mode	Reg	Yr	Quantity	F.A.S.	C.I.F.	Charges
TOTAL			81	21,033	219,343	236,726	17,383
			82	21,417	288,809	301,698	12,889
			83	29,071	467,603	484,059	16,456
			84	37,853	617,758	640,482	22,724
			85	17,026	273,842	285,032	11,190
			86	35,747	511,830	526,499	14,669
BRAZIL	N	E	84	9,814	156,926	162,567	5,641
	V	E	81	2,326	25,966	26,907	941

Country	Mode	Reg	Yr	Quantity	F.A.S.	C.I.F.	Charges
			82	5,644	69,530	72,133	2,603
			83	2,315	28,309	29,656	1,347
			85	1,555	24,913	25,818	905
			86	4,244	57,215	59,462	2,247
CHINA M	V	E	84	4,409	53,206	54,302	1,096
FRANCE	A	E	81	71	2,209	2,236	27
			82	35	369	373	4
			83	531	7,813	8,068	255
			84	44	668	681	13
	A	W	84	22	418	509	91
	N	E	85	317	8,595	9,194	599
GUATMAL	N	E	86	5,805	53,095	54,838	1,743
	V	E	85	560	8,025	8,257	232
HG KONG	A	E	84	22	429	487	58
INDIA	N	E	81	17,016	173,410	188,926	15,516
			82	8,333	113,553	119,343	5,790
			83	22,432	371,883	385,022	13,139
			84	18,248	314,237	326,436	12,199
			86	21,226	346,827	354,005	7,178
	V	E	85	11,816	189,992	197,113	7,121
			86	3,281	37,413	39,332	1,919
	V	W	81	1,587	17,147	18,035	888
			82	7,405	105,357	109,849	4,492
			83	1,588	24,692	25,696	1,004
			84	4,719	77,092	80,291	3,199
			85	1,984	29,227	30,678	1,451
INDNSIA	V	E	83	2,205	34,906	35,617	711
ITALY	A	E	84	275	14,531	14,951	420
PARAGUA	V	E	85	794	13,090	13,972	882
			86	1,191	17,280	18,862	1,582
SWITZLD	A	E	81	33	611	622	11
			84	300	251	258	7

Rubber-Tree

Rubber, latex
4460540 RUBBER MILK OR LATEX (CLB)

Country	Mode	Reg	Yr	Quantity	F.A.S.	C.I.F.	Charges
TOTAL			81	135,168,856	79,380,031	88,825,014	9,524,983
			82	111,415,989	53,513,997	63,426,182	9,912,185
			83	132,214,621	68,371,309	80,244,772	11,873,463
			84	142,647,579	80,518,344	93,529,688	13,011,344
			85	137,554,572	63,718,909	74,901,939	11,183,030
			86	158,940,881	70,816,289	81,308,730	10,492,441
BELGIUM	V	E	82	4,519	2,369	2,864	495
BRAZIL	A	E	86	19,253	12,870	14,452	1,582
	V	E	84	170,129	66,251	72,020	5,769
			85	1,389,023	711,848	847,715	135,867
			86	1,419,640	640,891	755,314	114,423
CANADA	A	E	83	18	500	526	26
			84	829	258	332	74
	O	E	81	51,003	27,822	27,822	
			82	39,702	21,165	21,165	
			84	249,255	139,120	139,120	
			85	40,395	29,535	29,535	
			86	9,920	7,113	8,331	1,218
	O	W	82	1,340	816	816	
CHINA M	V	E	82	8,964	3,200	4,258	1,058
CHINA T	N	E	86	27,998	13,650	16,424	2,774
	V	E	82	7,062,386	3,088,376	3,696,724	608,348
			85	6,175,811	2,590,588	2,892,021	301,433
			86	723,764	205,598	246,287	40,689
	V	W	86	53,780	17,655	19,313	1,658
FR GERM	A	E	84	51,588	2,307	2,411	104
FRANCE	V	E	82	97	534	547	13
GUATMAL	V	E	83	1,100	495	548	53
			86	1,783,156	719,138	811,802	92,664
INDIA	V	E	83	302,596	164,402	182,004	17,602
			84	958,985	346,262	385,180	38,918
			85	941,028	421,110	430,510	9,400
			86	1,160,131	362,824	425,660	62,836
	V	W	85	28,046	11,249	12,989	1,740
			86	25,396	10,719	12,158	1,439
INDNSIA	A	E	81	25	2,205	2,339	134
	N	E	85	20,448,545	9,118,693	10,775,255	1,656,562
	V	E	81	36,172,551	15,641,552	17,774,761	2,213,209
			82	18,580,679	7,734,195	9,324,240	1,590,045
			83	28,604,883	15,013,466	17,775,411	2,761,945
			84	30,983,496	17,196,248	20,446,062	3,249,814
			85	11,308,641	4,669,962	5,688,211	1,018,249

Crop
Product
TSUSA commodity number, description, and unit of quantity

Country	Mode	Reg	Yr	Quantity	F.A.S.	C.I.F.	Charges
			86	35,015,010	15,289,963	17,393,496	2,103,533
	V W		81	286,348	173,874	199,023	25,149
			82	43,004	16,678	20,798	4,120
			83	282,462	157,181	178,909	21,728
			84	479,860	265,046	291,373	26,327
			85	1,201,250	515,633	619,755	104,122
			86	1,061,250	515,365	608,919	93,554
ITALY	A E		81	6,000	1,698	4,940	3,242
			83	9,523	3,149	3,738	589
JAPAN	A E		83	666	551	853	302
			86	13	4,445	4,528	83
	V E		83	11,012	10,966	12,056	1,090
			84	12,346	10,637	11,934	1,297
			85	11,025	13,214	14,428	1,214
			86	42,404	28,339	31,322	2,983
	V W		82	3,527	2,844	3,102	258
			84	3,461	2,730	3,069	339
			85	4,916	3,298	3,411	113
LIBERIA	A E		84	84	1,000	1,844	844
	V E		81	52,508,349	34,566,263	38,300,981	3,734,718
			82	39,928,703	20,336,199	23,625,314	3,289,115
			83	42,117,195	23,821,053	27,586,285	3,765,232
			84	54,053,006	34,782,439	39,926,895	5,144,456
			85	49,776,896	24,789,803	29,097,117	4,307,314
			86	63,327,869	29,568,995	33,420,257	3,851,262
MALAYSA	A E		81	1,799	1,465	1,802	337
			83	492	292	2,073	1,781
	A W		83	529	400	547	147
	O E		82	141,120	56,095	64,840	8,745
			83	49,340	5,060	5,060	
	V E		81	39,291,006	24,646,881	27,646,196	2,999,315
			82	39,285,789	19,129,592	22,997,627	3,868,035
			83	46,959,271	22,886,196	27,077,925	4,191,729
			84	48,839,886	23,850,484	27,906,075	4,055,591
			85	39,356,931	17,730,452	20,923,635	3,193,183
			86	46,753,449	20,054,407	23,664,934	3,610,527
	V W		81	4,059,490	2,554,958	2,881,914	326,956
			82	3,787,874	1,782,473	2,108,184	325,711
			83	3,131,473	1,741,246	2,018,678	277,432
			84	3,378,005	1,942,986	2,173,378	230,392
			85	5,031,261	2,262,122	2,561,714	299,592
			86	5,452,445	2,572,124	2,971,102	398,978
NETHLDS	V E		84	4,024	10,856	11,351	495
PERU	V E		83	4,630	1,063	1,677	614
PHIL R	V E		82	165,375	56,110	75,246	19,136
SINGAPR	V E		81	705,154	432,160	491,089	58,929
			82	564,921	308,872	356,242	47,370
			83	8,231,755	3,505,812	4,161,882	656,070
			84	459,771	255,355	304,342	48,987
			85	37,199	22,159	24,243	2,084
			86	782,053	395,572	436,729	41,157
	V W		81	311,764	227,439	242,588	15,149
			82	87,196	45,660	46,188	528
			83	130,229	58,988	63,530	4,542
			84	279,492	168,900	181,984	13,084
			85	142,995	63,965	70,410	6,445
			86	116,806	52,058	67,017	14,959
SRI LKA	V E		81	1,775,367	1,103,714	1,251,559	147,845
			82	1,671,110	912,158	1,057,902	145,744
			83	1,575,850	659,570	783,210	123,640
			84	1,590,385	914,605	1,042,602	127,997
			85	1,531,189	727,071	855,003	127,932
			86	836,955	240,362	273,796	33,434
THAILND	N E		85	129,421	38,207	55,987	17,780
	V E		82	39,683	16,661	20,125	3,464
			83	801,597	340,919	389,860	48,941
			84	110,230	49,570	56,095	6,525
			86	278,222	82,057	101,772	19,715
	V W		86	51,367	22,144	25,117	2,973
U KING	N E		84	1,022,747	513,290	573,621	60,331

Rubber, natural
4460544 RIBBED SMOKED SHEETS GRDE 1 (LB)

Country	Mode	Reg	Yr	Quantity	F.A.S.	C.I.F.	Charges
TOTAL			81	65,905,610	39,158,347	42,484,289	3,325,942
			82	121,565,773	50,043,963	56,024,222	5,980,259
			83	105,814,598	50,073,692	55,444,151	5,370,459
			84	117,758,700	59,209,692	65,004,967	5,795,275
			85	116,394,880	44,359,497	50,107,792	5,748,295
			86	92,683,472	34,629,641	38,544,084	3,914,443
BELGIUM	V E		84	517,017	212,205	239,892	27,687
			85	441,370	164,945	187,414	22,469

Crop
Product
TSUSA commodity number, description, and unit of quantity

Country	Mode	Reg	Yr	Quantity	F.A.S.	C.I.F.	Charges
			86	663,917	236,100	267,946	31,846
CANADA	O E		81	4,410	2,720	2,720	
CHINA M	V W		84	88,200	34,398	37,998	3,600
CHINA T	V E		84	110,230	61,950	67,200	5,250
FR GERM	V E		84	323,336	174,084	193,444	19,360
GREECE	V E		84	224,208	118,830	129,892	11,062
INDIA	V E		82	41,667	16,171	19,588	3,417
			85	440,765	164,848	186,814	21,966
			86	48,578	16,578	18,461	1,883
	V W		84	147,840	65,050	77,631	12,581
INDNSIA	N E		83	38,952,268	17,264,313	19,298,125	2,033,812
	V E		81	31,781,073	19,121,794	20,660,760	1,538,966
			82	41,698,849	16,473,120	18,668,456	2,195,336
			83	6,055,212	2,621,982	2,938,884	316,902
			84	51,394,931	25,142,155	27,735,164	2,593,009
			85	66,348,789	24,692,900	28,219,783	3,526,883
			86	51,601,744	18,884,380	21,271,168	2,386,788
	V W		81	1,180,859	633,696	683,705	50,009
			82	1,426,960	559,385	614,266	54,881
			83	3,164,270	1,507,922	1,660,343	152,421
			84	5,631,547	3,011,564	3,338,984	327,420
			85	5,400,386	2,448,356	2,725,746	277,390
			86	5,948,137	2,178,079	2,409,886	231,807
ITALY	V E		85	115,742	51,062	56,717	5,655
JAPAN	V E		81	40,234	28,287	30,307	2,020
			82	17,688	9,402	10,429	1,027
			85	228,692	82,805	107,446	24,641
			86	43,496	17,612	19,601	1,989
LIBERIA	V E		81	318,949	180,896	195,458	14,562
MACAO	V E		84	66,138	44,916	51,177	6,261
	V W		86	22,721	8,924	10,022	1,098
MALAYSA	A E		81	220,460	118,214	128,988	10,774
	N W		85	1,036,194	410,413	458,858	48,445
	O E		82	141,120	65,621	74,738	9,117
			84	141,120	74,088	83,144	9,056
			86	136,308	88,649	114,263	25,614
	V E		81	25,901,107	15,235,022	16,584,995	1,349,973
			82	39,821,884	17,366,424	19,344,950	1,978,526
			83	43,822,269	21,797,635	23,812,721	2,015,086
			84	47,027,474	23,964,877	25,973,057	2,008,180
			85	36,979,649	14,347,005	15,883,290	1,536,285
			86	25,112,490	9,491,886	10,349,784	857,898
	V W		81	4,359,812	2,566,852	2,801,584	234,732
			82	30,806,854	12,173,063	13,497,491	1,324,428
			83	7,930,457	3,963,189	4,425,777	462,588
			84	6,320,880	3,255,922	3,668,382	412,460
			85	454,501	168,028	186,588	18,560
			86	803,500	312,458	342,361	29,903
MALI	N E		86	1,507,798	570,222	615,527	45,305
MAURIT	V E		86	91,857	18,373	20,530	2,157
MEXICO	O E		86	33,727	16,325	16,325	
PHIL R	V E		84	224,208	115,679	127,659	11,980
SIER LN	V W		86	111,112	47,060	47,779	719
SINGAPR	V E		81	371,916	203,881	222,089	18,208
			82	5,427,145	2,374,302	2,649,405	275,103
			83	2,549,523	1,319,837	1,437,005	117,168
			84	1,419,051	719,880	795,567	75,687
			85	1,737,707	655,933	726,297	70,364
			86	1,665,249	868,922	941,856	72,934
	V W		81	471,465	331,023	355,298	24,275
			82	297,792	124,113	140,950	16,837
			83	1,523,399	797,223	964,572	167,349
			84	1,057,754	512,694	582,492	69,798
			85	110,360	37,845	43,458	5,613
			86	121,892	51,847	58,205	6,358
SRI LKA	V E		81	671,083	402,103	456,704	54,601
			82	1,614,979	787,197	895,278	108,081
			83	527,349	274,853	314,699	39,846
			84	1,403,086	803,643	913,915	110,272
			85	851,975	332,434	405,785	73,351
			86	2,227,917	885,401	996,139	110,738
	V W		81	110,250	48,976	56,881	7,905
			86	291,118	115,651	127,078	11,427
THAILND	V E		81	363,762	218,794	234,171	15,377
			82	270,835	95,165	108,671	13,506
			83	1,289,851	526,738	592,025	65,287
			84	990,503	494,007	549,829	55,822
			85	1,977,584	704,210	811,435	107,225
			86	869,204	312,069	348,509	36,440
	V W		81	110,230	66,089	70,629	4,540
			85	271,166	98,713	108,161	9,448
			86	1,179,019	421,113	466,915	45,802
U KING	V E		84	671,177	403,750	439,540	35,790
			86	203,688	87,992	101,729	13,737

Crop Product TSUSA commodity number, description, and unit of quantity Country	Mode	Reg	Yr	Quantity	F.A.S.	C.I.F.	Charges

4460548 RIBBED SMOKED SHEETS GRDE 2 (LB)

Country	Mode	Reg	Yr	Quantity	F.A.S.	C.I.F.	Charges
TOTAL			81	51,209,243	28,871,357	31,382,718	2,511,361
			82	52,460,764	21,000,923	23,730,643	2,729,720
			83	60,949,205	28,304,705	31,240,997	2,936,292
			84	63,688,345	31,137,166	34,262,085	3,124,919
			85	61,006,407	21,855,189	24,832,517	2,977,328
			86	56,127,774	20,186,563	22,603,859	2,417,296
BELGIUM	V	E	86	143,243	51,020	58,367	7,347
BRAZIL	V	E	83	330,690	129,995	146,602	16,607
			84	275,576	149,188	162,970	13,782
CHINA M	V	E	84	110,250	113,558	119,868	6,310
CHINA T	V	E	86	79,366	29,306	31,876	2,570
INDIA	V	E	85	242,506	90,020	102,199	12,179
INDNSIA	V	E	81	4,382,357	2,237,334	2,466,802	229,468
			82	7,043,996	2,581,237	2,977,155	395,918
			83	9,632,090	3,820,815	4,303,197	482,382
			84	10,160,693	4,750,709	5,263,545	512,836
			85	4,562,414	1,552,467	1,783,448	230,981
			86	6,886,142	2,422,739	2,745,996	323,257
	V	W	81	178,581	93,009	100,620	7,611
			82	210,187	73,775	81,817	8,042
			83	78,814	28,530	31,571	3,041
			86	330,750	123,775	140,988	17,213
JAPAN	V	E	82	120,371	66,744	72,368	5,624
LIBERIA	V	E	85	81,000	28,148	31,739	3,591
MALAYSA	N	E	83	4,991,408	2,428,358	2,666,429	238,071
	N	W	82	774,128	290,517	320,063	29,546
	V	E	81	34,649,651	19,868,247	21,518,813	1,650,566
			82	31,697,733	13,194,256	14,799,147	1,604,891
			83	30,809,265	14,983,701	16,430,618	1,446,917
			84	38,424,614	19,423,581	21,223,695	1,800,114
			85	33,938,445	12,499,714	13,979,130	1,479,416
			86	23,820,784	8,735,962	9,647,190	911,228
	V	W	81	3,535,862	2,085,432	2,268,917	183,485
			82	1,777,937	761,926	856,458	94,532
			83	810,908	388,201	421,513	33,312
			84	929,180	449,781	499,667	49,886
			85	379,231	136,431	160,566	24,135
			86	46,305	16,008	17,983	1,975
MALI	V	E	86	3,183,903	1,124,315	1,254,086	129,771
MAURIT	V	E	86	174,406	55,360	61,140	5,780
NETHLDS	V	E	86	470,391	207,340	233,324	25,984
SINGAPR	V	E	81	731,113	449,198	486,984	37,786
			82	4,576,938	1,738,890	1,990,599	251,709
			83	1,554,240	789,894	867,060	77,166
			84	2,723,008	1,157,419	1,308,365	150,946
			85	1,862,734	632,309	729,507	97,198
			86	1,190,032	453,941	500,367	46,426
	V	W	81	253,984	150,279	163,371	13,092
			82	152,849	61,993	69,993	8,000
			83	874,190	423,609	459,348	35,739
			85	661,500	225,939	261,223	35,284
			86	661,500	216,867	251,854	34,987
SRI LKA	V	E	81	369,271	176,999	205,879	28,880
			82	539,920	222,566	261,197	38,631
			83	110,230	39,143	46,305	7,162
			84	33,069	13,062	15,291	2,229
			86	518,081	197,499	223,827	26,328
SWEDEN	V	E	81	88,200	38,588	42,795	4,207
THAILND	V	E	81	6,841,651	3,686,774	4,035,509	348,735
			82	5,566,705	2,009,019	2,301,846	292,827
			83	11,757,370	5,272,459	5,868,354	595,895
			84	11,031,955	5,079,868	5,668,684	588,816
			85	18,219,416	6,269,403	7,299,264	1,029,861
			86	16,875,619	5,960,356	6,751,078	790,722
	V	W	81	178,573	85,497	93,028	7,531
			85	1,059,161	420,758	485,441	64,683
			86	1,653,750	551,486	638,394	86,908
U KING	V	E	86	93,502	40,589	47,389	6,800

4460552 RIBBED SMOKED SHEETS GRDE 3 (LB)

Country	Mode	Reg	Yr	Quantity	F.A.S.	C.I.F.	Charges
TOTAL			81	28,962,386	15,584,857	17,019,559	1,435,702
			82	59,880,602	21,461,049	24,438,079	2,977,030
			83	34,249,346	14,806,943	16,586,313	1,779,370
			84	35,894,923	16,756,349	18,624,763	1,868,414
			85	52,767,294	18,565,906	21,114,059	2,548,153
			86	45,659,233	16,134,759	17,945,096	1,810,337
BELGIUM	V	E	86	33,133	11,845	13,651	1,806
INDNSIA	V	E	81	2,494,901	1,254,260	1,383,015	128,755
			82	3,444,982	1,212,347	1,409,579	197,232
			83	5,515,632	2,075,358	2,359,750	284,392
			84	3,844,201	1,805,613	2,015,164	209,551
			85	2,949,665	1,005,558	1,167,373	161,815
			86	3,822,543	1,335,147	1,506,075	170,928
	V	W	81	242,550	119,346	128,408	9,062
			82	179,695	75,498	82,143	6,645
			85	88,184	31,091	34,691	3,600
			86	175,437	64,091	70,469	6,378
JAPAN	V	E	82	60,749	26,580	29,483	2,903
			85	1,166,232	390,116	452,437	62,321
			86	242,506	77,000	87,885	10,885
MACAO	V	E	83	44,974	15,117	15,792	675
MALAYSA	V	E	81	16,458,277	8,881,675	9,692,668	811,993
			82	24,320,649	8,870,259	10,180,414	1,310,155
			83	11,579,597	5,607,846	6,214,550	606,704
			84	12,007,459	5,631,258	6,219,424	588,166
			85	28,737,304	10,312,102	11,571,078	1,258,976
			86	20,828,042	7,522,833	8,274,352	751,519
	V	W	81	374,846	184,071	198,902	14,831
			82	18,551,875	6,535,217	7,280,541	745,324
			83	1,533,682	591,052	656,333	65,281
			84	79,378	34,630	38,198	3,568
			85	110,250	38,698	43,204	4,506
			86	88,192	34,508	37,928	3,420
MALI	V	E	86	727,506	270,222	295,972	25,750
MAURIT	V	E	86	255,240	80,067	88,859	8,792
NIGERIA	V	E	82	66,138	9,185	14,196	5,011
SINGAPR	V	E	81	1,869,639	966,759	1,046,688	79,929
			82	2,010,700	713,439	812,063	98,624
			83	686,597	350,631	382,047	31,416
			84	749,621	314,627	353,798	39,171
			85	2,206,134	789,494	891,379	101,885
			86	1,498,016	591,972	650,496	58,524
	V	W	82	220,500	80,196	91,236	11,040
			83	132,280	47,353	52,651	5,298
			86	119,048	40,179	46,194	6,015
SRI LKA	V	E	81	859,794	378,704	445,510	66,806
			82	2,669,751	996,078	1,180,806	184,728
			83	1,323,478	455,743	542,613	86,870
			84	119,048	58,280	66,545	8,265
			86	2,669,498	969,703	1,104,354	134,651
THAILND	V	E	81	6,239,099	3,555,362	3,859,974	304,612
			82	8,355,563	2,942,250	3,357,618	415,368
			83	13,208,237	5,552,153	6,234,087	681,934
			84	19,095,216	8,911,941	9,931,634	1,019,693
			85	17,509,525	5,998,847	6,953,897	955,050
			86	15,144,957	5,115,422	5,744,766	629,344
	V	W	81	423,280	244,680	264,394	19,714
			83	224,869	111,690	128,490	16,800
			86	55,115	21,770	24,095	2,325

4460556 RIBBED SMOKED SHEETS, NSPOF (LB)

Country	Mode	Reg	Yr	Quantity	F.A.S.	C.I.F.	Charges
TOTAL			81	131,297,478	69,510,603	75,818,758	6,308,155
			82	29,967,236	10,677,361	12,101,703	1,424,342
			83	26,375,201	10,892,262	12,099,899	1,207,637
			84	22,558,098	10,424,493	11,640,342	1,215,849
			85	23,363,141	8,268,330	9,542,735	1,274,405
			86	34,990,178	12,535,308	14,018,375	1,483,067
BRAZIL	V	E	83	110,230	37,000	42,441	5,441
CANADA	O	E	81	10,000	14,466	14,466	
CHINA M	V	E	83	363,759	134,447	151,383	16,936
	V	W	82	443,856	159,200	173,969	14,769
INDNSIA	V	E	81	69,721,235	36,814,258	40,203,965	3,389,707
			82	2,650,269	909,411	1,038,640	129,229
			83	3,458,177	1,390,461	1,563,145	172,684
			84	3,752,919	1,654,695	1,833,035	178,340
			85	472,536	162,373	186,249	23,876
			86	2,633,549	930,308	1,047,605	117,297
	V	W	81	2,550,352	1,270,340	1,373,688	103,348
			82	1,718,140	635,171	702,391	67,220
			83	687,284	319,307	345,842	26,535
			84	405,522	187,542	204,604	17,062
			85	1,046,950	392,026	437,015	44,989
			86	440,309	148,309	166,042	17,733
JAPAN	V	E	85	229,278	86,112	98,662	12,550
			86	136,685	46,799	53,039	6,240
LIBERIA	V	E	83	488,250	41,759	46,076	4,317
			84	1,349,215	558,000	614,022	56,022
			85	674,608	243,000	269,644	26,644
			86	206,134	81,346	81,346	
MALAYSA	N	E	81	1,962,290	1,085,131	1,180,830	95,699
	O	E	85	475,662	196,372	196,372	
			86	39,683	17,469	17,469	
	V	E	81	14,480,956	7,391,175	8,098,335	707,160

Crop
Product
TSUSA commodity number, description, and unit of quantity

Country	Mode	Reg	Yr	Quantity	F.A.S.	C.I.F.	Charges
			82	6,517,203	2,293,436	2,660,991	367,555
			83	7,717,824	3,423,170	3,774,080	350,910
			84	8,542,375	4,111,371	4,668,359	556,988
			85	7,397,837	2,634,589	2,994,768	360,179
			86	10,317,187	3,856,942	4,300,215	443,273
	V W		81	10,729,575	5,444,049	5,876,101	432,052
			82	13,668,909	4,915,152	5,491,514	576,362
			83	4,911,949	1,980,460	2,165,630	185,170
			84	2,649,837	1,174,403	1,272,005	97,602
			85	819,612	294,244	325,520	31,276
			86	1,101,424	400,345	446,098	45,753
PHIL R	V E		86	222,224	81,557	92,765	11,208
SINGAPR	V E		81	10,782,853	5,966,987	6,439,565	472,578
			82	149,913	50,679	57,756	7,077
			83	1,315,967	657,930	725,942	68,012
			84	1,082,477	488,798	547,695	58,897
			85	1,477,117	511,549	583,494	71,945
			86	2,183,838	786,210	892,975	106,765
	V W		81	500,805	345,514	371,742	26,228
			82	445,324	155,781	172,871	17,090
			83	507,066	278,267	300,154	21,887
			84	396,828	198,328	213,558	15,230
			86	40,953	22,273	23,857	1,584
SRI LKA	V E		81	399,915	240,200	270,198	29,998
			82	380,955	174,042	206,470	32,428
			83	598,770	205,096	242,684	37,588
			84	120,286	72,094	82,581	10,487
			85	82,011	35,366	41,147	5,781
			86	1,061,288	397,359	451,016	53,657
	V W		83	22,046	12,655	14,564	1,909
			86	90,301	38,556	46,980	8,424
THAILND	V E		81	19,322,452	10,523,992	11,539,311	1,015,319
			82	3,955,917	1,369,238	1,579,806	210,568
			83	6,193,879	2,411,710	2,727,958	316,248
			84	4,087,783	1,907,815	2,125,745	217,930
			85	10,645,202	3,698,011	4,393,692	695,681
			86	16,220,575	5,634,822	6,300,566	665,744
	V W		81	396,826	194,220	209,507	15,287
			82	36,750	15,251	17,295	2,044
			84	55,115	24,722	27,272	2,550
			85	42,328	14,688	16,172	1,484
			86	295,416	93,013	98,402	5,389
U KING	V E		84	115,741	46,725	51,466	4,741
ZAIRE	V E		81	440,219	220,271	241,050	20,779

4460560 TECH SPECIFIED RUBBR GRDE 5 (LB)

Country	Mode	Reg	Yr	Quantity	F.A.S.	C.I.F.	Charges
TOTAL			81	68,720,524	38,206,988	41,514,122	3,307,134
			82	90,181,321	35,703,437	40,012,450	4,309,013
			83	73,464,075	32,824,371	36,273,844	3,449,473
			84	81,987,355	39,612,721	43,646,320	4,033,599
			85	85,456,617	31,750,828	35,658,797	3,907,969
			86	77,624,645	29,114,062	32,323,382	3,209,320
CHINA M	V E		84	480,690	253,762	278,116	24,354
INDIA	V E		83	110,230	40,510	45,914	5,404
			85	250,001	86,383	98,371	11,988
INDNSIA	N E		83	15,067,042	6,715,101	7,410,517	695,416
	O E		85	125,837	50,335	50,335	
	V E		81	24,165,123	13,483,602	14,675,271	1,191,669
			82	23,668,545	9,055,167	10,235,449	1,180,282
			83	10,212,840	4,292,274	4,832,201	539,927
			84	36,150,503	17,346,355	19,202,018	1,855,663
			85	30,730,213	11,236,116	12,740,922	1,504,806
			86	37,642,434	14,222,883	15,822,743	1,599,860
	V W		81	6,653,504	3,472,710	3,731,516	258,806
			82	4,814,347	1,792,254	1,973,332	181,078
			83	3,033,421	1,242,125	1,355,580	113,455
			84	1,818,129	888,453	965,405	76,952
			85	4,158,748	1,692,485	1,872,488	180,003
			86	4,679,608	1,860,845	2,014,148	153,303
IVY CST	V E		85	39,577	15,138	16,923	1,785
			86	409,715	170,800	189,408	18,608
JAPAN	V E		85	112,415	47,106	53,714	6,608
LIBERIA	V E		81	2,113,623	1,157,331	1,240,362	83,031
			82	2,402,981	991,568	1,080,823	89,255
			83	2,150,584	796,313	898,775	102,462
			84	5,290,511	2,389,107	2,565,515	176,408
			85	8,612,802	3,273,023	3,612,649	339,626
			86	9,450,253	3,580,307	3,984,961	404,654
MALAYSA	N E		86	8,184,594	2,990,138	3,315,028	324,890
	N W		84	754,068	364,157	384,056	19,899
			86	530,745	161,420	171,362	9,942
	V E		81	31,262,358	17,736,319	19,276,787	1,540,468
			82	55,098,570	22,177,537	24,828,903	2,651,366

Country	Mode	Reg	Yr	Quantity	F.A.S.	C.I.F.	Charges
			83	39,152,982	18,077,249	19,915,324	1,838,075
			84	34,177,953	16,579,705	18,305,545	1,725,840
			85	35,169,450	12,951,560	14,562,937	1,611,377
			86	12,110,106	4,480,225	4,997,295	517,070
	V W		81	2,709,269	1,373,042	1,475,735	102,693
			82	1,938,485	760,727	834,820	74,093
			83	2,120,967	911,205	992,176	80,971
			84	1,292,861	603,807	655,293	51,486
			85	2,045,025	784,447	831,380	46,933
			86	214,752	79,788	87,743	7,955
MEXICO	O E		86	76,705	37,969	37,969	
PHIL R	V E		81	502,598	250,633	286,511	35,878
			82	276,024	109,386	133,292	23,906
			83	55,125	26,460	29,460	3,000
			84	136,692	51,363	61,527	10,164
			86	55,155	16,603	19,569	2,966
	V W		81	529,186	294,802	339,685	44,883
			82	157,712	52,279	65,372	13,093
			83	143,299	46,214	51,589	5,375
			86	70,548	23,768	26,872	3,104
SINGAPR	V E		81	143,299	86,498	93,917	7,419
			82	1,661,516	701,776	787,347	85,571
			83	544,563	293,772	316,670	22,898
			84	785,797	431,983	473,090	41,107
			85	1,422,849	498,356	566,354	67,998
			86	1,393,528	499,441	550,774	51,333
	V W		85	110,230	40,500	45,000	4,500
SPAIN	A E		86	46	4,400	4,695	295
SRI LKA	V E		81	399,034	227,498	257,067	29,569
			82	123,458	45,310	53,758	8,448
			83	24,251	12,961	14,813	1,852
			84	233,688	116,818	125,339	8,521
			85	39,683	16,434	19,530	3,096
			86	251,325	91,978	102,632	10,654
THAILND	V E		81	242,530	124,553	137,271	12,718
			82	39,683	17,433	19,354	1,921
			83	590,833	257,757	287,175	29,418
			84	787,097	552,471	591,590	39,119
			85	2,639,787	1,058,945	1,188,194	129,249
			86	2,555,131	893,497	998,183	104,686
	V W		83	257,938	112,430	123,650	11,220
U KING	V E		84	79,366	34,740	38,826	4,086

4460564 TECH SPECIFIED RUBBR GRD CV (LB)

Country	Mode	Reg	Yr	Quantity	F.A.S.	C.I.F.	Charges
TOTAL			81	54,683,093	31,811,060	34,369,199	2,558,139
			82	21,884,879	8,811,010	9,850,923	1,039,913
			83	48,266,292	25,563,744	27,725,853	2,162,109
			84	63,898,642	32,886,445	35,883,251	2,996,806
			85	68,374,648	26,508,778	29,684,304	3,175,526
			86	64,465,352	25,951,636	28,675,027	2,723,391
CANADA	O E		81	70,548	55,945	55,945	
CHINA M	V E		81	39,683	24,455	26,373	1,918
			82	110,230	47,933	53,608	5,675
			84	354,975	197,359	215,728	18,369
	V W		84	123,478	59,931	65,109	5,178
HG KONG	V E		86	79,366	32,265	35,425	3,160
INDNSIA	N W		83	4,195,661	1,944,049	2,078,697	134,648
			85	5,841,751	2,232,388	2,454,986	222,598
	O E		86	230,160	98,969	108,021	9,052
	V E		81	3,886,919	2,200,623	2,391,866	191,243
			82	2,782,235	1,156,243	1,297,829	141,586
			83	2,762,045	1,269,242	1,401,352	132,110
			84	5,608,043	3,017,373	3,282,705	265,332
			85	4,668,498	1,742,860	2,071,637	328,777
			86	4,617,815	1,738,290	1,935,561	197,271
	V W		81	1,432,992	649,022	704,748	55,726
			82	1,984,140	728,000	802,671	74,671
			84	4,049,749	2,150,652	2,326,053	175,401
			85	399,033	152,344	168,962	16,618
			86	7,370,607	3,032,799	3,322,389	289,590
IRELAND	V W		86	126,985	57,096	61,416	4,320
ITALY	V W		85	55,115	20,313	22,637	2,324
IVY CST	V E		86	26,986	10,220	11,495	1,275
JAPAN	V E		86	66,138	28,604	31,244	2,640
LIBERIA	V E		81	10,757,528	6,003,179	6,437,632	434,453
			83	423,000	186,628	205,616	18,988
			85	2,199,555	1,095,612	1,135,639	40,027
			86	655,810	248,093	289,833	41,740
MALAYSA	N E		83	917,114	538,997	578,935	39,938
			86	37,416,922	15,117,923	16,753,494	1,635,571
	N W		83	4,137,881	2,324,764	2,486,401	161,637
	O E		86	39,683	18,558	18,558	
	V E		81	32,224,756	19,010,284	20,625,232	1,614,948

Crop Product TSUSA commodity number, description, and unit of quantity Country	Mode	Reg	Yr	Quantity	F.A.S.	C.I.F.	Charges
			82	13,727,819	5,577,551	6,259,888	682,337
			83	30,671,327	16,615,396	18,073,616	1,458,220
			84	41,240,383	21,269,696	23,253,397	1,983,701
			85	44,114,126	17,012,857	19,110,983	2,098,126
			86	4,531,332	1,844,320	2,037,679	193,359
	V W		81	4,803,941	3,047,033	3,240,809	193,776
			82	3,099,678	1,220,704	1,347,406	126,702
			83	2,936,889	1,500,622	1,616,033	115,411
			84	9,084,278	4,538,041	4,918,040	379,999
			85	7,905,360	2,913,588	3,230,589	317,001
			86	7,217,717	2,893,942	3,154,182	260,240
MALI	V E		86	84,657	33,796	36,896	3,100
MALTA	V E		85	22,046	8,875	10,025	1,150
MAURIT	V E		86	121,693	43,264	47,804	4,540
NAMIBIA	V E		86	141,154	54,696	61,642	6,946
NORFOLK	V E		81	71,958	38,687	43,469	4,782
SINGAPR	V E		81	984,712	522,836	564,556	41,720
			82	180,777	80,579	89,521	8,942
			83	1,697,680	908,773	986,760	77,987
			84	2,172,282	1,066,871	1,171,141	104,270
			85	1,387,136	635,401	698,270	62,869
			86	286,818	104,306	116,255	11,949
	V W		83	341,713	194,298	207,808	13,510
			85	485,902	168,561	187,259	18,698
			86	543,214	218,629	234,858	16,229
SRI LKA	V E		83	22,046	12,423	14,169	1,746
THAILND	V E		81	410,056	258,996	278,569	19,573
			83	160,936	68,552	76,466	7,914
			84	1,265,454	586,522	651,078	64,556
			85	1,135,367	467,259	528,310	61,051
			86	781,310	327,525	364,097	36,572
	V W		85	160,759	58,720	65,007	6,287
URUGUAY	V E		86	126,985	48,341	54,178	5,837

4460568 TECH SPECIFIED RUBBR GRDE 1 (LB)

Country	Mode	Reg	Yr	Quantity	F.A.S.	C.I.F.	Charges
TOTAL			81	14,047,525	8,054,355	8,808,399	750,010
			82	13,149,211	5,155,445	5,779,624	624,179
			83	29,047,027	14,609,948	15,951,787	1,341,839
			84	41,481,725	21,377,733	23,248,214	1,870,481
			85	58,293,357	22,386,752	25,063,208	2,676,456
			86	52,059,768	21,389,860	23,652,488	2,262,628
BELGIUM	V E		84	74,956	36,375	40,247	3,872
CHINA M	V E		84	297,667	169,276	184,989	15,713
HG KONG	V E		86	39,683	16,682	18,264	1,582
INDIA	V E		85	110,484	45,890	51,952	6,062
INDNSIA	N E		86	6,271,737	2,351,997	2,621,037	269,640
	V E		81	868,796	465,333	509,142	43,809
			82	1,706,363	651,068	736,979	85,911
			83	1,469,628	577,734	646,818	69,084
			84	1,005,298	588,433	635,328	46,895
			85	5,387,878	1,917,827	2,187,501	269,674
			86	762,480	291,423	387,625	96,202
	V W		81	112,435	49,735	54,103	4,368
			82	297,621	103,033	106,281	3,248
			83	679,016	327,648	353,545	25,897
			84	240,301	120,935	130,486	9,551
			85	44,975	16,337	17,889	1,552
			86	707,238	262,124	288,107	25,983
ITALY	V E		85	39,683	14,724	16,809	2,085
IVY CST	V E		84	196,739	91,665	102,375	10,710
			85	107,937	44,262	49,617	5,355
			86	541,487	175,526	198,707	23,181
JAPAN	V E		82	55,115	20,913	23,523	2,610
			86	66,138	27,392	30,232	2,840
LIBERIA	V E		83	56,014	27,695	33,857	6,162
			85	1,407,483	556,885	617,103	60,218
			86	1,453,234	542,704	609,998	67,294
MALAYSA	V E		81	11,203,972	6,431,775	7,030,676	594,867
			82	9,441,028	3,721,722	4,187,278	465,556
			83	20,915,124	10,772,552	11,770,446	997,894
			84	33,521,651	17,190,091	18,726,549	1,536,458
			85	45,801,857	17,764,931	19,867,000	2,102,069
			86	38,922,708	16,486,638	18,128,981	1,642,343
	V W		81	1,039,995	591,892	633,256	41,364
			82	1,468,307	591,919	649,887	57,968
			83	4,613,283	2,265,161	2,447,400	182,239
			84	4,924,149	2,524,820	2,712,188	187,368
			85	2,715,333	1,070,927	1,174,904	103,977
			86	2,670,293	991,342	1,096,350	105,008
MALTA	V E		85	110,250	41,308	47,101	5,793
MAURIT	V E		85	39,683	14,652	15,945	1,293
			86	79,380	31,629	35,820	4,191
NAMIBIA	V E		86	80,660	30,641	34,610	3,969

Country	Mode	Reg	Yr	Quantity	F.A.S.	C.I.F.	Charges
SINGAPR	V E		83	44,092	23,814	25,834	2,020
			84	828,545	397,803	437,964	40,161
			85	1,925,057	734,047	823,978	89,931
			86	39,683	14,261	15,985	1,724
	V W		83	359,351	209,736	223,785	14,049
SRI LKA	V E		81	767,202	481,220	543,958	62,738
			83	33,069	18,039	20,670	2,631
THAILND	V E		81	55,125	34,400	37,264	2,864
			82	180,777	66,790	75,676	8,886
			83	877,450	387,569	429,432	41,863
			84	392,419	258,335	278,088	19,753
			85	602,737	164,962	193,409	28,447
			86	313,935	125,609	139,171	13,562
URUGUAY	V E		86	111,112	42,492	47,601	5,109

4460572 TECH SPECIFIED RUBBR GRD 10 (LB)

Country	Mode	Reg	Yr	Quantity	F.A.S.	C.I.F.	Charges
TOTAL			81	46,379,558	22,336,743	24,502,566	2,165,883
			82	47,564,762	16,490,219	18,586,763	2,096,544
			83	57,341,710	22,980,529	25,439,895	2,459,366
			84	99,960,296	43,999,735	48,602,954	4,603,219
			85	102,299,757	34,369,837	39,274,983	4,905,146
			86	83,401,783	27,229,540	30,853,792	3,624,252
BELGIUM	V E		86	39,683	13,393	15,018	1,625
CANADA	O W		82	41,888	15,080	15,080	
INDIA	V E		82	23,809	9,972	12,065	2,093
			84	120,371	57,778	62,987	5,209
			85	258,379	81,306	92,939	11,633
	V W		86	458,557	158,687	177,124	18,437
INDNSIA	N W		81	14,971,237	7,086,509	7,660,245	573,736
			82	11,036,400	3,802,127	4,212,395	410,268
			85	12,915,472	4,543,276	5,048,756	505,480
	O E		84	115,742	50,783	50,783	
	V E		81	23,120,254	10,995,290	12,120,533	1,125,303
			82	26,562,225	9,187,810	10,471,743	1,283,933
			83	28,410,060	11,065,432	12,381,149	1,315,717
			84	40,752,082	17,939,120	19,948,660	2,009,540
			85	43,117,828	14,418,668	16,494,984	2,076,316
			86	46,362,774	14,902,995	16,819,688	1,916,693
	V W		81	1,050,051	504,675	544,385	39,710
			82	3,094,158	1,026,832	1,145,273	118,441
			83	17,583,203	7,000,441	7,633,001	632,560
			84	23,201,878	10,368,596	11,291,668	923,072
			85	4,945,909	1,616,956	1,817,847	200,891
			86	9,576,970	3,110,040	3,442,211	332,171
IVY CST	V E		86	29,234	9,245	10,779	1,534
LIBERIA	V E		81	1,331,677	667,213	805,147	137,934
			82	247,500	75,150	82,056	6,906
			83	1,716,300	763,819	852,528	88,709
			84	22,400,362	9,820,961	10,912,357	1,091,396
			85	31,109,676	10,021,262	11,679,584	1,658,322
			86	24,111,782	8,055,683	9,290,651	1,234,968
MACAO	V E		84	119,048	52,084	57,515	5,431
MALAYSA	N W		84	3,502,430	1,519,969	1,653,259	133,290
	V E		81	3,280,486	1,737,558	1,923,331	185,773
			82	2,308,220	815,659	926,833	111,174
			83	4,898,771	2,068,118	2,299,939	231,821
			84	8,658,958	3,750,803	4,135,531	384,728
			85	6,141,179	2,332,088	2,602,233	270,145
			86	2,510,612	881,614	988,430	106,816
	V W		81	2,436,257	1,244,309	1,337,935	93,626
			82	3,793,768	1,392,446	1,538,243	145,797
			83	3,425,718	1,493,149	1,628,984	135,835
			84	110,250	48,786	53,424	4,638
			85	817,468	267,127	298,455	31,328
			86	238,096	74,186	83,157	8,971
PHIL R	V E		84	237,215	83,974	95,230	11,256
			85	171,958	53,212	61,896	8,684
SINGAPR	V E		81	189,596	101,189	110,990	9,801
			82	123,458	48,391	54,371	5,980
			83	271,126	132,505	144,767	12,262
			86	74,075	23,697	26,734	3,037
	V W		82	333,336	116,752	128,704	11,952
			83	834,991	378,026	409,459	31,433
			84	153,991	70,482	76,024	5,542
			85	370,042	122,723	137,641	14,918
SRI LKA	V E		83	2,205	1,109	1,282	173
THAILND	V E		83	199,296	77,930	88,786	10,856
			84	587,969	236,399	265,516	29,117
			85	2,451,846	913,219	1,040,648	127,429

4460576 TECH SPECIFIED RUBBR GRD 20 (LB)

Country	Mode	Reg	Yr	Quantity	F.A.S.	C.I.F.	Charges
TOTAL			81	682,275,711	328,275,852	360,384,514	32,104,810
			82	658,633,373	231,717,510	262,238,233	30,520,723

414   Table 1. U.S. Import Statistics for Crop-Specific Commodities by Crop Name

Crop
Product
TSUSA commodity number, description, and unit of quantity

Country	Mode	Reg	Yr	Quantity	F.A.S.	C.I.F.	Charges
			83	722,185,492	291,578,522	324,365,817	32,787,295
			84	867,957,243	380,063,416	420,667,074	40,603,658
			85	896,850,531	304,669,505	347,078,807	42,409,302
			86	813,330,867	269,990,653	303,299,668	33,309,015
BURKINA	V	E	85	562,716	205,111	234,420	29,309
CANADA	O	E	81	31,482	15,777	15,777	
			83	33,730	11,047	11,047	
	O	W	83	113,209	39,525	39,525	
CHINA M	V	E	81	22,010	8,572	9,710	1,138
			83	604,061	244,008	272,286	28,278
			86	277,780	84,722	95,499	10,777
	V	W	82	551,170	185,530	206,721	21,191
			83	120,371	52,109	56,371	4,262
CHINA T	V	E	83	317,462	171,861	184,725	12,864
	V	W	84	925,932	420,584	462,740	42,156
			85	962,969	325,818	378,280	52,462
FRANCE	V	E	86	40,476	10,417	12,913	2,496
GREECE	V	E	84	112,435	49,471	54,618	5,147
HG KONG	V	E	85	263,891	71,757	84,949	13,192
INDIA	V	E	81	899,477	372,185	418,686	46,501
			82	790,348	262,145	299,508	37,363
			83	715,086	282,456	316,398	33,942
			85	5,324,950	1,811,970	2,053,980	242,010
			86	511,114	170,001	190,627	20,626
	V	W	85	277,779	95,139	104,976	9,837
			86	88,889	30,389	33,429	3,040
INDNSIA	N	E	83	214,330,830	86,935,918	97,480,238	10,544,320
			84	37,535,804	16,525,774	18,343,006	1,817,232
			85	273,530,301	94,306,896	108,051,777	13,744,881
			86	43,458,404	13,969,167	15,748,143	1,778,976
	N	W	81	117,235,078	55,098,054	59,599,997	4,501,943
			82	118,179,837	41,294,274	45,654,947	4,360,673
			83	134,306,267	54,647,219	59,591,820	4,944,601
			84	173,106,084	76,712,354	83,498,405	6,786,051
			85	138,386,759	47,259,808	52,612,533	5,352,725
			86	118,412,416	41,199,392	45,246,676	4,047,284
	O	E	82	373,349	155,667	155,667	
			83	752,738	323,781	323,781	
	V	E	81	391,145,022	188,519,578	207,922,866	19,396,386
			82	378,330,662	130,688,706	149,529,400	18,840,694
			83	184,131,462	72,253,310	81,012,907	8,759,597
			84	540,033,870	236,730,304	263,018,918	26,288,614
			85	350,252,727	117,696,647	134,494,941	16,798,294
			86	521,661,607	169,520,932	191,205,005	21,684,073
	V	W	81	5,734,834	2,668,124	2,887,517	219,393
			82	4,885,110	1,701,846	1,892,266	190,420
			83	5,427,311	2,107,461	2,310,124	202,663
			84	5,161,752	2,251,752	2,457,488	205,736
			85	13,423,988	4,642,803	5,175,571	532,768
			86	9,835,617	3,333,444	3,683,588	350,144
IRELAND	V	E	85	578,710	204,250	231,000	26,750
ITALY	V	E	86	41,657	13,646	15,345	1,699
	V	W	85	110,230	37,751	42,390	4,639
JAPAN	V	E	82	233,688	80,882	91,875	10,993
			84	120,372	55,070	60,378	5,308
			85	925,932	373,120	423,220	50,100
	V	W	86	69,445	20,088	22,743	2,655
KOR REP	V	W	84	250,001	100,625	110,709	10,084
LEBANON	V	E	85	97,020	26,758	26,816	58
LIBERIA	N	E	82	9,376,446	3,241,339	3,710,157	468,818
	V	E	81	29,939,725	14,161,192	15,740,848	1,579,676
			82	15,627,091	5,621,685	6,504,061	882,376
			83	33,591,444	13,051,082	14,733,310	1,682,228
			84	18,520,836	7,751,437	8,729,115	977,678
			85	15,116,387	4,680,884	5,457,348	776,464
			86	18,162,133	5,756,931	6,680,845	923,914
MACAO	V	E	81	496,035	249,057	278,364	29,307
			85	597,227	228,899	257,802	28,903
	V	W	82	472,422	164,294	181,980	17,686
			83	231,484	100,732	108,932	8,200
			84	340,742	137,165	151,841	14,676
MALAYSA	N	W	82	39,398,639	14,694,787	16,191,311	1,496,524
			83	25,339,968	10,546,472	11,497,543	951,071
	V	E	81	39,361,964	18,796,844	20,641,569	1,844,725
			82	25,659,507	9,601,638	10,840,590	1,238,952
			83	34,792,775	14,242,814	15,802,575	1,559,761
			84	33,635,271	14,611,549	16,135,108	1,523,559
			85	22,421,851	7,578,533	8,608,542	1,030,009
			86	29,452,813	10,255,895	11,349,117	1,093,222
	V	W	81	30,637,544	14,416,824	15,608,060	1,194,266
			82	826,761	320,688	353,486	32,798
			83	621,696	263,116	287,018	23,902
			84	20,571,272	8,551,215	9,319,089	767,874
			85	5,297,068	1,873,659	2,084,367	210,708
			86	4,184,246	1,348,639	1,519,639	171,000
MALI	V	E	86	1,197,889	428,047	466,677	38,630
MAURIT	V	E	86	42,328	15,400	16,950	1,550
MONSRAT	V	E	86	126,985	44,080	48,730	4,650
MOROC	V	E	86	211,633	79,216	92,041	12,825
NAMIBIA	V	E	86	268,868	84,150	97,380	13,230
NETHLDS	V	E	82	224,869	113,559	125,105	11,546
NIGERIA	V	E	81	220,460	72,240	89,261	17,021
			86	317,463	99,395	115,599	16,204
PHIL R	N	E	83	780,430	316,717	353,697	36,980
	V	E	81	4,353,534	1,995,555	2,303,093	307,538
			82	771,610	257,592	317,160	59,568
			84	644,536	243,322	278,011	34,689
			85	5,216,617	1,543,399	1,801,461	258,062
			86	3,215,812	791,092	963,103	172,011
	V	W	81	584,219	244,143	285,311	41,168
			82	1,375,932	458,768	535,883	77,115
			83	1,230,357	415,131	475,528	60,397
			84	275,576	117,265	129,593	12,328
			85	301,036	93,775	109,813	16,038
			86	347,887	128,406	139,395	10,989
SINGAPR	N	W	82	6,777,157	2,425,990	2,684,818	258,828
	V	E	81	25,037,125	12,847,606	13,946,829	1,099,223
			82	13,513,561	5,194,765	5,824,560	629,795
			83	23,209,196	9,928,847	11,071,491	1,142,644
			84	5,583,707	2,436,585	2,701,079	264,494
			85	3,753,410	1,321,949	1,505,896	183,947
			86	3,786,134	1,626,405	1,785,865	159,460
	V	W	81	3,869,758	2,260,349	2,403,413	143,064
			82	311,621	107,605	119,306	11,701
			83	12,384,563	5,296,780	5,734,758	437,978
			84	5,652,810	2,527,222	2,756,863	229,641
			85	11,367,771	3,905,415	4,360,234	454,819
			86	6,242,854	3,046,265	3,326,578	280,313
SRI LKA	V	E	84	243,057	93,365	113,475	20,110
			85	695,551	256,331	301,684	45,353
THAILND	V	E	81	32,389,982	16,377,891	18,048,488	1,670,597
			82	34,780,713	13,005,839	14,615,189	1,609,350
			83	24,298,666	9,450,526	10,741,372	1,290,846
			84	24,934,541	10,612,120	12,195,690	1,583,570
			85	34,531,014	11,660,444	13,647,085	1,986,641
			86	32,985,291	11,158,567	12,795,000	1,636,433
	V	W	82	6,172,880	2,139,911	2,404,243	264,332
			83	25,169,848	11,069,471	12,145,096	1,075,625
			85	12,854,627	4,468,389	5,029,722	561,333
			86	18,168,892	6,706,113	7,571,098	864,985
U KING	V	E	84	308,645	136,237	150,948	14,711
			86	222,224	69,854	77,683	7,829

4460580 TECH SPECIFIED RUBBER NSPF (LB)

Country	Mode	Reg	Yr	Quantity	F.A.S.	C.I.F.	Charges
TOTAL			81	113,228,006	55,553,205	61,268,239	5,691,569
			82	156,489,531	57,210,693	64,917,823	7,707,130
			83	171,174,135	69,249,377	77,355,190	8,105,813
			84	195,880,018	85,845,893	95,779,709	9,933,816
			85	166,438,681	60,448,937	68,891,490	8,442,553
			86	188,735,025	66,963,659	75,593,014	8,629,355
BRAZIL	V	E	82	7,275	3,638	4,192	554
BURKINA	V	E	85	97,020	27,728	32,765	5,037
CANADA	O	E	83	121,319	49,500	49,500	
			85	41,887	18,430	18,430	
CHINA M	V	E	83	121,253	47,537	53,212	5,675
			84	55,115	35,000	38,058	3,058
	V	W	83	119,048	68,751	73,206	4,455
CHINA T	V	E	81	1,312,178	657,792	711,495	53,703
			82	169,344	70,769	77,857	7,088
			85	187,832	61,344	69,724	8,380
COLOMB	V	E	84	66,138	34,525	39,684	5,159
GUATMAL	V	E	85	43,133	12,894	15,510	2,616
INDIA	V	E	85	575,069	188,129	216,514	28,385
			86	111,112	48,258	51,356	3,098
INDNSIA	N	E	86	9,368,493	3,015,477	3,422,483	407,006
	N	W	81	8,138,314	3,905,670	4,214,836	309,166
	O	E	85	274,965	106,707	106,707	
	V	E	81	40,416,325	19,202,431	21,199,560	1,973,664
			82	90,178,143	32,561,181	37,059,637	4,498,456
			83	74,672,650	30,315,519	33,921,647	3,606,128
			84	104,387,503	45,514,508	50,911,236	5,396,728
			85	39,556,615	13,962,549	15,949,212	1,986,663
			86	20,939,725	7,201,771	8,119,262	917,491
	V	W	81	1,355,342	562,556	628,424	65,868
			82	3,509,919	1,329,616	1,463,444	133,828
			83	3,304,514	1,346,286	1,467,616	121,330

Crop Product TSUSA commodity number, description, and unit of quantity Country	Mode	Reg	Yr	Quantity	F.A.S.	C.I.F.	Charges
			84	2,474,451	1,150,444	1,256,824	106,380
			85	2,610,776	951,126	1,056,289	105,163
			86	1,222,979	470,107	517,243	47,136
IRAN	V	W	84	88,204	48,622	54,241	5,619
ITALY	V	E	85	242,506	80,330	94,017	13,687
IVY CST	V	E	81	215,874	118,329	128,791	10,462
			84	219,472	87,244	97,884	10,640
			85	79,154	30,139	33,539	3,400
			86	2,666,095	1,040,545	1,167,818	127,273
JAPAN	A	E	81	3,440	3,685	4,530	845
	V	E	85	423,283	153,832	172,131	18,299
			86	1,481,493	524,335	568,523	44,188
	V	W	86	37,037	20,007	21,717	1,710
LIBERIA	N	E	82	1,725,055	534,715	618,220	83,505
	V	E	81	10,917,410	5,713,541	6,420,775	707,234
			82	88,752	22,660	26,934	4,274
			83	11,938,258	4,211,743	4,712,661	500,918
			84	15,870,723	5,094,431	5,827,385	732,954
			85	6,355,374	2,139,389	2,474,032	334,643
			86	11,601,660	3,383,190	3,919,104	535,914
MALAYSA	N	W	81	7,708,756	4,339,257	4,636,240	296,983
			84	1,468,512	612,794	673,137	60,343
	V	E	81	7,533,975	4,132,707	4,661,432	528,725
			82	11,960,074	4,638,128	5,206,231	568,103
			83	25,200,556	10,484,884	11,709,790	1,224,906
			84	27,555,752	13,186,439	14,668,386	1,481,947
			85	45,540,958	15,671,476	17,870,555	2,199,079
			86	89,378,547	32,427,622	36,588,534	4,160,912
	V	W	81	1,336,007	726,352	781,159	54,807
			82	5,835,239	2,288,648	2,516,269	227,621
			83	2,235,372	979,784	1,073,194	93,410
			84	672,582	302,941	333,898	30,957
			85	1,637,281	567,029	630,887	63,858
			86	3,131,243	1,212,052	1,331,471	119,419
MALI	V	E	86	931,222	317,103	350,513	33,410
MALTA	V	W	86	100,530	34,930	38,552	3,622
MAURIT	V	E	86	2,947,441	1,029,555	1,175,805	146,250
MEXICO	O	E	85	70,547	30,864	34,544	3,680
			86	594,492	263,806	263,806	
N ZEAL	V	E	83	119,048	44,345	49,975	5,630
NAMIBIA	V	E	86	31,500	10,755	12,254	1,499
NETHLDS	V	E	82	2,258	1,420	1,573	153
NIGERIA	V	E	82	66,138	25,343	26,358	1,015
PHIL R	O	E	85	222,224	83,775	99,794	16,019
	V	E	81	2,022,307	920,688	1,050,142	129,454
			82	1,236,606	501,669	580,720	79,051
			83	1,550,599	734,385	820,382	85,997
			85	955,032	358,836	406,626	47,790
			86	4,584,957	1,510,879	1,694,869	183,990
	V	W	81	654,813	304,904	343,155	38,251
			82	345,970	127,433	166,437	39,004
			85	576,724	220,541	259,844	39,303
			86	292,772	105,927	116,019	10,092
SIER LN	V	E	85	39,683	13,951	16,928	2,977
SINGAPR	N	W	81	3,040,636	1,508,041	1,622,812	114,771
	V	E	81	12,443,775	6,180,583	6,684,303	503,720
			82	13,722,469	5,207,102	5,773,780	566,678
			83	17,338,353	7,299,362	8,012,304	712,942
			84	10,531,481	4,924,362	5,391,546	467,184
			85	11,953,118	4,237,722	4,814,228	576,506
			86	10,441,672	3,627,901	4,072,618	444,717
	V	W	81	33,069	17,775	19,084	1,309
			82	55,115	19,955	22,137	2,182
			83	3,485,315	1,617,805	1,773,532	155,727
			84	203,956	95,545	104,816	9,271
			85	45,362	17,408	20,626	3,218
			86	150,359	72,890	79,605	6,715
SPAIN	A	E	83	69	2,675	2,853	178
SRI LKA	V	E	81	1,318,350	679,982	788,480	108,498
			82	1,836,914	788,078	943,466	155,388
			83	2,035,707	881,401	1,040,841	159,440
			84	2,027,362	1,111,873	1,275,383	163,510
			85	3,108,215	1,229,882	1,446,682	216,800
			86	5,457,378	2,306,073	2,581,124	275,051
	V	W	82	185,277	78,480	94,739	16,259
			84	23,810	13,889	15,210	1,321
			85	92,593	39,347	44,332	4,985
			86	51,588	28,766	31,210	2,444
THAILND	V	E	81	14,777,435	6,578,912	7,373,021	794,109
			82	25,529,709	9,002,689	10,325,044	1,322,355
			83	28,932,074	11,165,400	12,594,477	1,429,077
			84	29,731,242	13,436,524	14,872,636	1,436,112
			85	48,761,889	19,215,954	21,831,769	2,615,815
			86	26,119,456	9,324,572	10,626,508	1,301,936
	V	W	84	11,034	5,449	6,184	735
			86	40,715	16,693	18,425	1,732
U KING	V	E	85	35,274	9,169	10,785	1,616
			84	492,681	191,303	213,201	21,898

4460584 NAT RUB N CONT FIL ETC NSPF (LB)

Country	Mode	Reg	Yr	Quantity	F.A.S.	C.I.F.	Charges
TOTAL			81	91,922,293	52,891,108	57,505,063	4,613,956
			82	46,092,922	17,770,632	20,073,915	2,303,283
			83	38,860,180	18,101,195	20,217,826	2,116,631
			84	27,433,442	13,425,335	14,784,288	1,358,953
			85	24,814,219	9,293,274	10,509,226	1,215,952
			86	27,774,414	10,150,474	11,245,150	1,094,676
ARGENT	V	E	81	220,460	85,174	95,785	10,611
AUSTRAL	N	W	84	8,237	15,508	17,075	1,567
AUSTRIA	V	E	84	2,205	2,568	2,767	199
BELGIUM	V	E	85	110,230	44,368	50,013	5,645
BRAZIL	A	E	81	1,129	650	669	19
	V	E	81	14,231	10,422	12,145	1,723
			82	32,785	30,549	33,696	3,147
			83	3,097	2,013	2,389	376
			84	272,936	413,067	441,723	28,656
			85	125,218	172,179	179,849	7,670
			86	6,898	4,139	4,689	550
CANADA	O	E	81	14,774	9,284	9,284	
			82	51,554	21,112	21,833	721
			83	5,799	3,088	3,088	
			84	43,449	18,781	18,781	
			85	95,841	58,580	58,782	202
			86	93,403	64,958	64,958	
	O	W	81	258,750	141,078	141,078	
			82	165,225	73,992	113,481	39,489
			83	112,500	49,922	49,922	
			84	34,723	16,580	16,580	
			86	24,255	10,187	10,187	
CHINA M	V	E	81	209,445	128,868	139,250	10,382
			82	33,069	12,153	13,919	1,766
CHiNA T	A	E	84	463	367	1,914	1,547
FR GERM	A	E	81	53	902	1,171	269
			83	5,426	4,133	8,391	4,258
			86	7,505	11,775	19,085	7,310
	A	W	81	129	1,604	1,832	228
	V	E	85	5,027	8,162	8,913	751
			86	18,677	28,135	29,979	1,844
	V	W	81	2,205	4,245	4,388	143
			84	2,429	4,381	4,900	519
FRANCE	A	E	84	581	1,289	1,628	339
	V	E	81	39,683	29,732	31,539	1,807
			82	882	920	1,041	121
			85	5,565	6,437	6,489	52
GUATMAL	V	E	82	44,000	17,600	20,677	3,077
			83	90,400	47,121	51,802	4,681
			84	390,938	223,333	244,076	20,743
			85	1,029,707	386,836	425,132	38,296
			86	343,171	110,653	131,565	20,912
HAITI	V	E	81	108,192	32,458	41,407	8,949
HG KONG	V	E	86	39,683	20,938	22,928	1,990
	V	W	82	420	264	270	6
			83	1,051	2,154	2,277	123
INDIA	V	W	85	506,001	174,653	194,941	20,288
INDNSIA	N	E	83	2,106,685	770,133	881,291	111,158
			84	155,951	72,537	80,078	7,541
	N	W	81	7,311,190	3,906,802	4,159,003	252,201
			82	619,908	246,404	259,035	12,631
			83	945,211	502,621	532,545	29,924
			84	353,476	192,607	201,619	9,012
			85	704,919	260,243	266,765	6,522
			86	127,426	50,398	52,318	1,920
	O	E	82	390,932	138,017	138,017	
			83	75,472	33,208	33,208	
	V	E	81	23,264,744	12,022,607	13,156,833	1,134,226
			82	14,905,415	5,410,482	6,176,429	765,947
			83	6,771,064	2,520,944	2,848,920	327,976
			84	4,077,567	1,761,566	1,971,784	210,218
			85	3,212,258	1,026,096	1,173,956	147,860
			86	6,587,171	2,137,874	2,384,419	246,545
	V	W	81	1,106,321	498,868	543,288	44,420
			82	2,476,754	821,657	938,967	117,310
			83	3,208,856	1,263,983	1,402,795	138,812
			84	4,585,660	2,063,760	2,248,229	184,469
			85	2,568,638	926,439	1,025,878	99,439
			86	1,605,468	538,850	601,081	62,231
IRELAND	A	E	84	584	455	823	368
ISRAEL	V	E	86	142,718	142,779	150,661	7,882

Crop
Product
TSUSA commodity number, description, and unit of quantity

Country	Mode	Reg	Yr	Quantity	F.A.S.	C.I.F.	Charges
ITALY	O	E	83	2,636	7,215	7,423	208
	V	E	81	28,660	21,520	23,400	1,880
			82	1,292	2,307	2,531	224
IVY CST	V	E	81	1,115,349	699,385	769,301	69,916
			83	35,979	19,873	21,485	1,612
			84	406,301	198,480	218,055	19,575
			85	31,200	12,678	15,678	3,000
JAPAN	V	E	83	1,175,944	2,119,006	2,140,398	21,392
	V	W	84	1,546	2,209	2,489	280
			86	43,587	18,857	21,027	2,170
KOR REP	V	W	84	35,274	79,234	87,950	8,716
LIBERIA	N	E	82	4,460,702	1,538,015	1,676,047	138,032
	V	E	81	5,315,412	2,556,523	2,829,028	272,505
			82	1,218,021	452,743	531,294	78,551
			83	5,762,036	1,916,977	2,265,675	348,698
			84	2,840,007	1,133,477	1,227,824	94,347
			85	2,905,500	1,060,848	1,145,405	84,557
			86	7,413,530	2,617,919	2,867,420	249,501
MACAO	V	E	83	120,371	40,368	46,596	6,228
MALAYSA	A	E	81	734	528	2,978	2,450
			83	251	519	829	310
			86	7,095	9,673	21,346	11,673
	N	E	83	275,890	163,975	175,044	11,069
	N	W	81	1,259,099	766,006	817,617	51,611
			82	1,176,493	469,467	493,213	23,746
			83	435,753	196,834	202,541	5,707
			84	558,115	368,382	384,813	16,431
	O	E	81	150,674	109,184	109,184	
			82	83,790	37,706	37,706	
			83	32,665	15,830	15,830	
			84	136,840	83,879	83,879	
			85	244,720	119,338	119,338	
			86	305,504	134,900	134,900	
	O	W	86	83,790	35,192	35,192	
	V	E	81	35,007,156	21,910,179	23,694,649	1,784,471
			82	13,356,477	5,679,429	6,372,300	692,871
			83	8,478,842	4,073,092	4,537,458	464,366
			84	6,866,649	3,269,706	3,607,590	337,884
			85	6,243,543	2,371,159	2,796,432	425,273
			86	4,559,180	1,736,044	1,919,714	183,670
	V	W	81	3,605,221	1,931,965	2,095,309	163,344
			82	2,368,055	757,052	851,736	94,684
			83	3,080,263	1,191,139	1,326,834	135,695
			84	1,375,795	618,211	680,731	62,520
			85	1,647,503	512,300	574,784	62,484
			86	1,541,428	570,863	626,567	55,704
MALTA	V	W	86	111,112	25,012	28,847	3,835
MAURIT	V	E	85	55,115	22,235	25,263	3,028
MEXICO	O	E	86	10,582	5,604	5,604	
MOROC	V	E	85	76,719	24,479	27,830	3,351
NETHLDS	V	E	82	1,728	1,214	1,314	100
			84	2,645	7,773	8,059	286
			85	3,728	5,077	5,771	694
			86	43,167	17,877	20,216	2,339
NEW GUI	V	E	86	347,225	118,109	131,534	13,425
NIGERIA	V	E	81	220,460	77,704	94,554	16,850
			82	440,938	154,057	180,952	26,895
NORFOLK	V	E	81	364,377	172,234	192,157	19,923
PHIL R	V	E	81	863,973	432,729	490,897	58,168
			82	503,403	174,991	212,187	37,196
			84	178,591	73,157	81,922	8,765
			85	299,743	121,921	139,596	17,675
			86	656,970	196,588	230,005	33,417
	V	W	81	88,188	37,538	42,749	5,211
			82	110,240	40,963	50,256	9,293
			84	224,890	95,630	104,310	8,680
			85	35,840	11,443	12,992	1,549
REP SAF	V	E	81	143,916	93,158	102,999	9,841
			82	5,470	4,422	5,802	1,380
	V	W	82	145,503	50,210	55,865	5,655
ROMANIA	V	E	81	542,140	229,061	250,831	21,770
SINGAPR	V	E	81	3,463,454	2,570,456	2,738,231	167,775
			82	757,440	324,096	361,538	37,442
			83	488,400	253,147	282,651	29,504
			84	443,669	223,638	244,000	20,362
			85	275,046	96,545	106,285	9,740
			86	852,833	373,351	424,622	51,271
	V	W	81	1,031,357	562,180	603,477	41,297
			82	259,592	81,458	92,153	10,695
			83	1,884,482	625,411	785,544	160,133
			84	115,741	54,230	58,750	4,520
			85	52,911	18,736	20,621	1,885
			86	107,091	38,851	42,176	3,325
SPAIN	A	E	85	2,403	3,500	3,500	
			86	8,541	13,500	13,707	207
	V	E	85	223,252	137,782	150,256	12,474
SRI LKA	N	E	83	1,211,576	1,093,187	1,199,708	106,521
	V	E	81	4,646,479	3,037,862	3,408,376	370,514
			82	2,307,686	1,163,569	1,351,795	188,226
			83	2,185,219	1,015,401	1,199,153	183,752
			84	3,109,039	1,842,665	2,091,210	248,545
			85	2,047,413	941,495	1,100,285	158,790
			86	1,514,784	702,953	782,907	79,954
	V	W	81	216,048	92,879	112,137	19,258
			82	39,684	15,834	20,961	5,127
			83	147,709	71,653	84,159	12,506
			84	80,248	43,907	48,255	4,348
			85	651,729	232,220	262,517	30,297
			86	24,251	11,615	12,827	1,212
SWEDEN	A	E	82	64	362	374	12
SWITZLD	A	E	81	165	739	874	135
			83	9	452	514	62
	V	E	81	6,945	3,894	4,285	391
			86	496	1,450	1,651	201
THAILND	V	E	81	1,047,170	587,619	641,927	54,308
			83	261,245	103,623	116,881	13,258
			84	1,113,240	532,353	587,748	55,395
			85	1,648,041	533,137	606,366	73,229
			86	921,081	313,033	352,039	39,006
	V	W	81	110,230	58,246	64,346	6,100
			83	75,956	27,501	31,145	3,644
			86	225,792	85,350	97,530	12,180
U KING	A	E	83	1,764	7,040	7,926	886
	N	E	81	29,442	15,917	19,109	3,192
			86	*	3,047	3,449	402
	O	E	81	8,818	6,741	7,799	1,058
			82	2,006	1,482	1,789	307
			84	13,228	9,319	11,932	2,613
	V	E	82	13,023	7,737	10,141	2,404
			84	2,425	2,286	2,794	508
			85	6,409	4,388	5,589	1,201
ZAIRE	V	E	81	105,520	44,167	51,177	7,010

4461000 NAT RUBBER CONT FILLERS ETC (LB)

Country	Mode	Reg	Yr	Quantity	F.A.S.	C.I.F.	Charges
TOTAL			81	1,214,774	850,701	914,478	63,777
			82	454,557	267,134	294,092	26,958
			83	818,304	479,848	536,825	56,977
			84	7,708,532	4,877,525	4,933,519	55,994
			85	10,982,491	6,311,436	6,421,309	109,873
			86	1,346,680	808,086	886,621	78,535
BRAZIL	V	E	83	116,564	27,530	34,199	6,669
CANADA	O	E	81	805	2,369	2,369	
			82	410	458	458	
			83	34,419	35,515	35,515	
			84	6,979,497	4,418,591	4,418,591	
			85	9,348,492	5,594,892	5,595,394	502
			86	15,217	21,893	21,893	
	O	W	86	4,064	2,460	2,460	
DOM REP	A	E	82	2,228	712	947	235
FR GERM	A	E	81	3,925	1,671	3,402	1,731
			83	345	2,387	2,685	298
			84	80	1,571	1,585	14
			86	524	1,230	1,545	315
	N	E	83	20,880	23,081	26,797	3,716
	O	E	83	8,992	8,428	8,428	
	V	E	81	6,017	4,041	5,199	1,158
			82	16,830	13,098	14,432	1,334
			83	39,683	16,950	18,883	1,933
			84	49,244	35,730	40,589	4,859
			85	57,491	45,497	50,693	5,196
			86	42,996	44,452	46,662	2,210
	V	W	81	11,965	16,548	17,946	1,398
			82	23,678	29,538	32,235	2,697
			83	23,161	23,942	26,065	2,123
			84	25,745	25,434	28,498	3,064
			85	8,302	7,600	8,461	861
			86	30,679	39,241	45,244	6,003
FRANCE	A	E	83	9	274	281	7
	V	E	83	1,234	3,085	3,235	150
			84	77	662	699	37
	V	W	83	404	1,343	1,474	131
INDNSIA	V	E	85	46,561	21,481	26,491	5,010
	V	W	81	22,046	13,443	14,330	887
ITALY	A	E	83	8,002	9,978	14,519	4,541
			84	1,090	593	1,265	672
	V	W	83	34,171	8,058	10,495	2,437
JAPAN	A	W	82	50	1,148	1,396	248

Crop Product TSUSA commodity number, description, and unit of quantity Country	Mode	Reg	Yr	Quantity	F.A.S.	C.I.F.	Charges
			86	2,204	5,800	14,023	8,223
	V	E	86	26,900	34,188	35,351	1,163
	V	W	81	377	1,606	1,732	126
			83	432	2,497	2,607	110
			84	1,121	7,993	8,184	191
			85	407,414	153,003	171,039	18,036
			86	568,767	302,941	330,920	27,979
KOR REP	V	E	86	40,853	18,270	21,805	3,535
MALAYSA	V	E	81	411,249	319,517	344,709	25,192
			82	242,516	131,261	148,298	17,037
			83	481,956	288,573	320,455	31,882
			84	535,913	315,333	353,611	38,278
			85	646,430	325,116	371,911	46,795
			86	388,008	184,920	203,541	18,621
	V	W	81	720,906	463,145	493,935	30,790
			82	110,230	57,671	62,023	4,352
			83	22,046	11,050	11,880	830
			84	68,784	33,735	40,560	6,825
			85	169,201	73,456	90,505	17,049
MEXICO	O	E	82	32,899	19,250	19,250	
			85	2,600	1,482	1,482	
NETHLDS	O	E	83	7,370	4,895	5,568	673
	V	E	81	3	544	550	6
			82	3,670	2,579	2,804	225
			86	19,345	14,641	15,016	375
PORTUGL	V	E	84	5,247	1,380	2,054	674
SINGAPR	V	E	84	36,668	27,260	27,596	336
	V	W	81	33,000	17,235	18,554	1,319
			82	22,046	11,419	12,249	830
			83	1,000	1,179	1,240	61
			85	33,069	11,588	13,298	1,710
SPAIN	V	E	84	3,412	3,902	4,320	418
			86	40,420	52,744	54,944	2,200
	V	W	85	53,230	35,294	39,425	4,131
			86	39,123	43,527	45,677	2,150
SRI LKA	V	E	83	17,636	11,083	12,499	1,416
SWITZLD	V	E	85	175,706	33,324	41,873	8,549
U KING	V	E	81	4,481	10,582	11,752	1,170
			84	1,654	5,341	5,967	626
			85	33,995	8,703	10,737	2,034
			86	127,580	41,779	47,540	5,761

4461200 CHLORINATED NATURAL RUBBER (LB)

Country	Mode	Reg	Yr	Quantity	F.A.S.	C.I.F.	Charges
TOTAL			81	123,555	174,813	185,540	10,727
			82	163,835	211,510	234,157	22,647
			83	1,171,939	1,438,562	1,535,147	96,585
			84	706,014	870,664	946,320	75,656
			85	624,632	722,848	782,684	59,836
			86	252,565	295,146	322,299	27,153
CANADA	O	E	83	146,006	161,316	161,316	
	O	W	84	22,000	12,070	12,070	
CHINA T	A	W	83	336	300	1,073	773
DOM REP	V	E	84	38,450	41,480	42,846	1,366
FR GERM	V	E	81	46,755	58,931	62,660	3,729
GERM DR	V	E	85	11,023	3,199	3,518	319
			86	22,046	14,600	16,000	1,400
ITALY	V	E	83	44,092	39,149	41,709	2,560
			84	132,276	131,279	139,433	8,154
			85	264,552	265,696	283,504	17,808
			86	35,273	35,571	38,400	2,829
JAPAN	O	E	83	97,002	103,125	103,125	
	V	E	82	116,708	166,101	183,718	17,617
			83	477,655	662,960	726,449	63,489
			84	37,422	75,967	83,479	7,512
			85	172,493	241,996	264,813	22,817
			86	137,790	136,723	147,947	11,224
	V	W	83	82,597	123,085	132,391	9,306
			84	449,254	588,955	645,038	56,083
			85	175,176	209,342	228,132	18,790
			86	54,861	107,035	118,468	11,433
NETHLDS	V	E	84	17,090	12,857	14,747	1,890
SWEDEN	V	E	83	26,455	30,312	46,583	16,271
U KING	O	E	83	271,265	287,850	287,850	
	V	E	81	76,800	115,882	122,880	6,998
			82	47,127	45,409	50,439	5,030
			83	26,531	30,465	34,651	4,186
			84	9,522	8,056	8,707	651
			86	2,595	1,217	1,484	267
	V	W	85	1,388	2,615	2,717	102

Rubber, seed
1754200 RUBBER SEED (LB)

Rutabaga

Rutabaga, fresh
1383020 RUTABAGAS FR CUT SLICED ETC (LB)

Country	Mode	Reg	Yr	Quantity	F.A.S.	C.I.F.	Charges
TOTAL			81	81,720	15,433	15,433	
			82	138,920	30,291	30,291	
			83	194,064	43,340	43,340	
			84	102,400	18,359	18,359	
			85	12,000	2,686	2,686	
			86	48,000	1,097	1,097	
CANADA	O	E	81	81,720	15,433	15,433	
			82	138,920	30,291	30,291	
			83	194,064	43,340	43,340	
			84	102,400	18,359	18,359	
			85	12,000	2,686	2,686	
			86	48,000	1,097	1,097	

Rutabaga, fresh or frozen**
1376600 TURNIPS OR RUTABAGAS (CWT)

Country	Mode	Reg	Yr	Quantity	F.A.S.	C.I.F.	Charges
TOTAL			81	760,725	6,611,801	6,611,901	100
			82	727,743	6,167,880	6,168,372	492
			83	700,835	5,952,084	5,954,070	1,986
			84	693,458	6,185,970	6,186,199	229
			85	597,064	4,656,519	4,656,637	118
			86	549,743	4,820,978	4,821,152	174
CANADA	N	E	81	368,285	3,126,324	3,126,424	100
			85	286,958	2,172,133	2,172,133	
	O	E	81	386,489	3,454,211	3,454,211	
			82	725,665	6,157,057	6,157,057	
			83	698,502	5,933,100	5,933,120	20
			84	689,602	6,130,711	6,130,711	
			85	306,519	2,413,814	2,413,816	2
			86	547,935	4,778,711	4,778,711	
	O	W	82	425	3,825	3,825	
			84	65	1,559	1,559	
			85	278	5,841	5,841	
			86	100	1,784	1,784	
	V	E	83	370	8,000	9,500	1,500
CHINA M	V	W	82	45	2,690	3,015	325
CHINA T	V	W	82	5	430	452	22
			83	49	2,814	3,048	234
			84	11	1,185	1,291	106
GREECE	O	E	84	88	875	875	
HG KONG	V	E	86	42	2,193	2,367	174
	V	W	82	1,508	1,331	1,476	145
			83	1,500	861	927	66
			84	324	1,045	1,168	123
JAPAN	O	E	84	438	3,867	3,867	
	V	H	83	35	300	382	82
MEXICO	O	W	81	5,651	28,466	28,466	
			82	95	2,547	2,547	
			83	378	6,432	6,432	
			84	2,930	46,728	46,728	
			85	3,282	63,406	63,406	
			86	1,666	38,290	38,290	
THAILND	V	W	83	1	577	661	84
			85	27	1,325	1,441	116
YEMEN A	O	E	81	300	2,800	2,800	

Rutabaga, frozen
1383040 RUTABAGAS, FROZEN (LB)

Country	Mode	Reg	Yr	Quantity	F.A.S.	C.I.F.	Charges
TOTAL			81	135,300	19,926	19,926	
			82	141,100	40,832	40,832	
			83	47,120	10,887	10,887	
			84	187,886	40,625	40,625	
			85	62,028	39,176	39,886	710
			86	271,661	59,756	59,756	
CANADA	O	E	81	135,300	19,926	19,926	
			82	141,100	40,832	40,832	
			83	47,120	10,887	10,887	

Crop Product TSUSA commodity number, description, and unit of quantity Country	Mode	Reg	Yr	Quantity	F.A.S.	C.I.F.	Charges
			84	187,886	40,625	40,625	
			85	60,341	32,444	32,444	
			86	271,661	59,756	59,756	
THAILND	V	E	85	1,687	6,732	7,442	710

Rutabaga, seed**
1268900 RUTABAGA AND TURNIP SEED (LB)

Country	Mode	Reg	Yr	Quantity	F.A.S.	C.I.F.	Charges
TOTAL			81	4,351	89,127	94,586	5,459
			82	7,502	121,743	126,594	4,851
			83	8,532	59,959	66,676	6,717
			84	9,437	93,413	97,176	3,763
			85	92,507	218,770	227,199	8,429
			86	18,939	16,792	17,138	346
CANADA	O	W	83	2,000	510	510	
			84	1,000	511	511	
HG KONG	V	W	82	110	344	371	27
JAPAN	A	E	81	500	8,155	9,944	1,789
			82	225	6,254	7,365	1,111
			83	100	405	780	375
			84	378	10,140	11,265	1,125
			85	154	4,407	4,685	278
	A	W	83	977	3,344	5,293	1,949
			85	90	1,350	1,638	288
	N	E	81	290	7,242	8,427	1,185
	N	W	81	1,990	47,543	49,273	1,730
			82	1,520	31,862	34,221	2,359
			83	1,650	35,102	38,458	3,356
			84	1,896	41,747	43,128	1,381
			86	16,931	13,326	13,475	149
	O	E	81	115	2,864	3,177	313
			82	10	305	333	28
			83	15	456	557	101
	O	W	83	25	730	730	
	V	E	81	1,282	19,079	19,467	388
			82	1,459	37,367	37,854	487
			83	200	840	930	90
			85	250	1,375	1,387	12
	V	H	82	53	690	727	37
			83	44	702	742	40
			84	22	350	367	17
	V	W	81	174	4,244	4,298	54
			82	1,849	43,482	44,145	663
			83	849	15,518	15,754	236
			84	1,260	30,934	31,247	313
			85	5,954	125,743	126,722	979
N ZEAL	V	W	83	2,205	1,054	1,393	339
			85	4,409	1,871	2,655	784
NETHLDS	A	W	82	2,205	866	966	100
			83	467	1,298	1,529	231
	N	W	84	4,563	7,064	7,695	631
	V	E	85	22,046	35,164	36,180	1,016
	V	W	85	59,478	46,244	51,140	4,896
			86	2,000	2,000	2,075	75
U KING	A	E	82	71	573	612	39
			86	8	1,466	1,588	122
	A	W	84	198	284	530	246
	V	E	84	120	2,383	2,433	50
			85	126	2,616	2,792	176

Rye

Ergot, natural drug
4355000 ERGOT (LB)

Country	Mode	Reg	Yr	Quantity	F.A.S.	C.I.F.	Charges
TOTAL			82	4,410	9,946	10,925	979
			83	4,630	12,962	13,960	998
			84	5,006	17,308	19,264	1,956
			85	17	1,174	1,273	99
			86	2	3,750	3,774	24
CZECHO	A	E	86	2	3,750	3,774	24
JAPAN	A	W	85	17	1,174	1,273	99
PORTUGL	A	E	84	5,006	17,308	19,264	1,956
	V	E	82	4,410	9,946	10,925	979
			83	4,630	12,962	13,960	998

Ergotamine, alkaloid
4371200 ERGOTAMINE COMPOUNDS (LB)

Country	Mode	Reg	Yr	Quantity	F.A.S.	C.I.F.	Charges
TOTAL			81	468	4,060,468	4,071,168	10,740
			82	791	12,341,206	12,368,186	26,980
			83	592	9,501,737	9,529,224	27,487
			84	10,767	11,817,963	11,845,644	27,681
			85	616	10,895,048	10,922,070	27,022
			86	1,456	18,667,975	18,701,286	33,311
BELGIUM	V	E	86	8	9,439	10,000	561
CANADA	O	E	85	7	6,347	6,347	
CZECHO	A	E	81	2	10,508	10,600	92
			84	11	19,062	19,152	90
			85	17	27,169	27,405	236
FR GERM	A	E	81	13	15,961	16,120	159
			82	54	17,868	18,072	204
			83	20	26,536	26,720	184
			84	33	43,575	44,128	553
			85	31	42,115	42,618	503
			86	17	38,621	38,890	269
	N	E	81	*	1,286	1,303	17
	O	E	84	1	457	471	14
HUNGARY	A	E	81	47	78,569	79,439	870
			83	15	13,158	13,320	162
			84	33	18,150	18,400	250
			85	13	7,392	7,500	108
			86	22	12,304	12,504	200
ITALY	A	E	81	1	1,735	2,110	375
			85	4	2,445	2,501	56
			86	2	1,861	2,000	139
	V	E	83	3	781	833	52
	V	W	83	4	1,238	1,295	57
SWITZLD	A	E	81	364	3,910,718	3,919,638	8,960
			82	703	12,312,268	12,338,738	26,470
			83	3	18,093	18,189	96
			84	10,685	11,733,199	11,759,951	26,752
			85	524	10,781,800	10,807,794	25,994
			86	1,188	18,486,496	18,517,646	31,150
	N	E	82	*	309	324	15
			83	497	9,415,132	9,441,607	26,475
	O	E	83	2	575	650	75
U KING	A	E	81	3	15,757	15,830	73
			86	15	1,466	1,516	50
YUGOSLV	A	E	81	38	25,934	26,128	194
			82	34	10,761	11,052	291
			83	48	26,224	26,610	386
			84	4	3,520	3,542	22
			85	20	27,780	27,905	125
			86	204	117,788	118,730	942

Rye, grain
1306000 RYE IN GRAIN (BU)

Country	Mode	Reg	Yr	Quantity	F.A.S.	C.I.F.	Charges
TOTAL			81	42,610	141,022	141,022	
			82	2,277,218	6,648,580	6,648,580	
			83	2,597,704	6,089,286	6,089,923	637
			84	408,705	873,502	874,337	835
			85	1,490,076	3,272,434	3,272,434	
			86	1,839,079	3,671,110	3,674,009	2,899
CANADA	O	E	81	42,610	141,022	141,022	
			82	2,256,700	6,577,583	6,577,583	
			83	2,559,306	5,955,098	5,955,098	
			84	407,850	866,794	866,794	
			85	1,098,543	2,388,754	2,388,754	
			86	917,273	2,009,655	2,012,552	2,897
	O	W	82	20,518	70,997	70,997	
			83	38,049	131,842	131,842	
			84	776	2,678	2,678	
			85	391,533	883,680	883,680	
			86	921,806	1,661,455	1,661,457	2
DOM REP	V	E	83	349	2,346	2,983	637
POLAND	V	E	84	79	4,030	4,865	835

Rye, malt
1321500 RYE MALT (CWT)

Country	Mode	Reg	Yr	Quantity	F.A.S.	C.I.F.	Charges
TOTAL			81	5	650	748	98
			85	58	2,793	5,924	3,131
CHINA M	V	E	81	5	650	748	98

Crop
Product
TSUSA commodity number, description, and unit of quantity

Country	Mode	Reg	Yr	Quantity	F.A.S.	C.I.F.	Charges
U KING	A E		85	51	1,518	4,507	2,989
	V W		85	7	1,275	1,417	142

Rye, milled for humans
1313800 RYE, MILLED, EDIBLE (CWT)

Country	Mode	Reg	Yr	Quantity	F.A.S.	C.I.F.	Charges
TOTAL			81	5,015	1,581	1,713	132
			82	1,320	9,490	9,490	
			83	1,096	10,976	13,226	2,250
			84	968	7,162	8,839	1,677
			85	7,216	44,629	44,629	
			86	7,137	65,640	65,640	
CANADA	O E		81	15	295	295	
			82	1,320	9,490	9,490	
			83	683	4,924	4,924	
			84	562	2,056	2,056	
			85	7,216	44,629	44,629	
			86	7,104	62,891	62,891	
CHINA M	V W		81	5,000	1,286	1,418	132
FR GERM	V E		83	413	6,052	8,302	2,250
			84	406	5,106	6,783	1,677
	V W		86	33	2,749	2,749	

Rye, milled not for humans
1317000 RYE NT FIT HUMAN CONSUMPTION (CWT)

Country	Mode	Reg	Yr	Quantity	F.A.S.	C.I.F.	Charges
TOTAL			82	169	1,413	1,413	
			83	648	3,053	3,053	
			84	5,041	18,000	18,000	
			86	1,197	4,063	4,063	
CANADA	O E		82	121	1,117	1,117	
			83	648	3,053	3,053	
			84	5,041	18,000	18,000	
	O W		82	48	296	296	
			86	1,197	4,063	4,063	

Ryegrass

Ryegrass, seed
1267700 RYE GRASS SEED (LB)

Country	Mode	Reg	Yr	Quantity	F.A.S.	C.I.F.	Charges
TOTAL			81	774,614	326,993	384,627	57,634
			82	1,156,197	471,009	548,825	77,816
			83	323,495	156,268	203,032	46,764
			84	284,114	155,658	187,546	31,888
			85	2,078,950	645,859	758,983	113,124
			86	6,849,402	2,805,252	3,279,150	473,898
ARGENT	V E		85	44,136	20,744	23,536	2,792
			86	39,683	12,150	16,258	4,108
AUSTRAL	V E		81	53,176	18,199	22,308	4,109
			85	262,016	79,825	98,158	18,333
			86	52,910	24,497	27,114	2,617
	V W		81	162,457	48,227	61,194	12,967
			82	169,842	57,205	65,563	8,358
			85	646,907	184,701	228,044	43,343
			86	1,370,014	350,772	417,747	66,975
AUSTRIA	V W		86	85,000	32,959	36,821	3,862
BELGIUM	V W		83	14,857	39,758	41,400	1,642
			84	2,535	2,393	2,536	143
			85	1,100	1,265	1,502	237
			86	1,984	2,843	3,098	255
CANADA	O E		81	96,583	42,651	42,651	
			82	149,144	41,039	41,039	
			83	105,888	10,071	10,071	
			84	15,000	33,000	33,000	
			85	585,689	40,147	40,147	
			86	13,076	16,025	16,025	
	O W		81	220	1,060	1,060	
			83	60,620	27,304	27,304	
			84	38,051	45,846	45,846	
			85	42,543	101,011	101,011	
			86	90,508	176,446	176,446	
DENMARK	A E		81	440	260	850	590
	O E		81	85,145	30,984	37,903	6,919
			82	541,626	209,554	245,261	35,707
	V E		81	22,240	8,840	10,123	1,283
			83	22,000	14,740	17,140	2,400

Crop
Product
TSUSA commodity number, description, and unit of quantity

Country	Mode	Reg	Yr	Quantity	F.A.S.	C.I.F.	Charges
			86	154,322	53,167	64,381	11,214
	V W		81	880	968	1,115	147
			82	93,475	34,081	40,349	6,268
			84	14,520	12,755	14,520	1,765
			85	130,686	42,411	52,908	10,497
			86	2,860	3,819	4,290	471
FR GERM	A E		82	3,417	3,631	5,813	2,182
	A W		84	1,080	1,100	1,760	660
	O E		81	44,052	13,005	18,942	5,937
	V E		81	43,480	16,371	18,954	2,583
			82	36,773	37,887	41,204	3,317
	V W		81	2,640	3,960	4,434	474
			82	7,534	10,019	11,411	1,392
			83	5,070	3,770	4,310	540
			84	31,800	10,135	14,310	4,175
			85	58,953	20,021	24,759	4,738
FRANCE	V W		81	2,500	2,750	3,140	390
JAPAN	A W		82	528	264	1,519	1,255
			83	7,342	3,250	16,989	13,739
			84	1,200	442	2,631	2,189
	N W		81	5,168	1,281	5,609	4,328
			83	18,376	4,201	22,997	18,796
			84	8,970	3,459	11,286	7,827
	V W		81	18,926	6,376	8,925	2,549
			82	36,280	9,503	14,802	5,299
			83	15,929	5,737	6,932	1,195
			84	156,930	34,840	46,070	11,230
			85	38,052	11,081	15,079	3,998
			86	20,424	8,372	10,808	2,436
KOR REP	A W		81	270	419	1,079	660
N ZEAL	A W		81	1,873	841	2,090	1,249
			82	2,032	1,874	3,290	1,416
	V E		81	2,343	1,737	1,913	176
			82	198	385	398	13
			83	25,133	6,512	9,300	2,788
			86	129,515	58,541	67,344	8,803
	V H		85	9,921	5,393	7,143	1,750
			86	14,977	6,472	9,264	2,792
	V W		85	4,409	1,060	2,723	1,663
			86	4,517,637	1,853,639	2,187,534	333,895
NETHLDS	A E		81	775	1,005	1,402	397
			82	1,712	1,758	2,646	888
			83	486	1,213	1,507	294
			85	1,102	2,059	2,838	779
	A W		82	1,047	1,532	2,104	572
	N W		82	74,588	36,733	44,207	7,474
			83	40,152	32,036	35,887	3,851
			84	5,625	4,330	6,712	2,382
			85	162,286	99,543	115,294	15,751
			86	102,801	82,136	91,287	9,151
	O E		81	44,100	19,885	22,050	2,165
	V E		83	330	330	413	83
			86	6,508	13,262	14,360	1,098
	V W		81	52,248	37,055	42,750	5,695
			82	37,591	24,582	27,959	3,377
			83	3,812	3,231	3,774	543
			84	6,601	4,241	4,899	658
			85	4,971	3,137	4,018	881
			86	240,570	101,088	121,311	20,223
POLAND	V E		84	298	292	424	132
SWITZLD	V W		83	2,000	1,987	2,191	204
			86	1,543	2,222	2,369	147
U KING	A E		81	600	1,195	1,760	565
			86	5,070	6,842	12,693	5,851
	A W		81	221	787	1,007	220
			82	110	340	524	184
	N E		81	128,858	62,032	65,526	3,494
	O W		83	1,500	2,128	2,817	689
			84	1,504	2,825	3,552	727
	V E		85	200	4,875	5,425	550
	V W		81	5,419	7,105	7,842	737
			82	300	622	736	114
			85	85,979	28,586	36,398	7,812

Crop
Product
TSUSA commodity number, description, and unit of quantity

S

Sage

Sage, spice
1619400 SAGE UNGROUND (LB)

Country	Mode	Reg	Yr	Quantity	F.A.S.	C.I.F.	Charges
TOTAL			81	3,266,580	4,822,406	5,255,777	433,371
			82	3,184,230	3,613,033	4,047,283	434,306
			83	3,334,782	3,223,148	3,653,767	430,619
			84	4,169,910	3,716,547	4,243,613	527,066
			85	4,301,669	4,601,606	5,219,864	618,258
			86	4,621,128	5,617,866	6,178,615	560,749
ALBANIA	N	E	85	1,759,259	1,821,910	2,113,900	291,990
	O	E	84	6,614	7,143	7,143	
	V	E	81	1,784,819	2,603,454	2,869,982	266,528
			82	1,956,767	2,098,522	2,379,826	281,304
			83	1,731,971	1,546,756	1,768,213	221,457
			84	2,585,089	2,100,294	2,432,049	331,755
			85	302,525	270,792	300,793	30,001
			86	2,558,481	3,010,372	3,321,663	311,291
	V	W	85	35,169	40,307	44,670	4,363
BELGIUM	V	E	85	18,430	17,280	18,880	1,600
	V	W	85	20,126	22,393	23,735	1,342
CANADA	O	E	81	17,500	27,376	27,376	
			85	12,125	17,581	17,581	
CHINA M	V	E	84	152	331	361	30
CZECHO	V	E	86	95,794	103,444	111,144	7,700
FR GERM	V	E	83	288	375	402	27
			85	164,748	162,911	177,444	14,533
			86	266,854	326,350	350,596	24,246
	V	W	86	19,114	25,143	27,033	1,890
FRANCE	A	E	81	33	654	692	38
			82	148	2,396	2,527	131
			83	120	2,236	2,375	139
	A	W	82	69	279	322	43
	N	E	81	22,239	30,241	34,209	3,968
	O	E	81	3,000	4,510	4,555	45
			83	2,000	2,674	2,699	25
			84	100	1,260	1,273	13
	V	E	82	41,913	47,371	51,985	4,614
			83	29,397	27,236	30,011	2,775
			84	38,537	29,270	32,133	2,863
			85	55,249	51,679	57,910	6,231
			86	20,062	22,698	25,203	2,505
	V	W	84	110	565	612	47
GREECE	V	E	81	11,512	6,808	7,577	769
			82	4,669	8,405	10,473	2,068
			83	135,861	117,243	128,462	11,219
			84	13,438	11,200	12,874	1,674
INDIA	O	E	81	668	500	530	30
	V	E	84	1,102	293	352	59
INDNSIA	V	E	84	22,487	16,865	19,175	2,310
ISRAEL	V	E	82	26,160	31,945	36,696	4,751
ITALY	V	E	81	20,159	29,988	33,799	3,811
			82	20,159	23,120	26,338	3,218
			83	21,244	20,606	22,726	2,120
	V	W	82	56	303	303	56
MEXICO	O	W	82	4,302	2,925	2,925	
NETHLDS	A	E	83	48	646	657	11
	O	E	81	3,000	4,050	4,095	45
			82	200	2,500	2,540	40
			84	250	3,086	3,125	39
	V	E	84	165	2,107	2,224	117
			85	800	7,606	7,744	138
			86	17,922	19,476	21,757	2,281
SALVADR	A	E	83	705	1,603	1,904	301
SPAIN	V	E	82	8,818	5,263	6,432	1,169
TURKEY	V	E	81	202,828	92,257	110,373	18,116
			82	171,528	110,446	126,193	15,747
			83	212,966	95,705	117,745	22,040
			84	245,735	109,827	132,297	22,470
			85	206,101	104,804	132,110	27,306
			86	84,998	63,605	75,535	11,930
	V	W	82	19,842	14,900	16,330	1,430
			85	4,000	2,678	3,414	736
			86	5,512	3,026	4,089	1,063
U KING	V	E	84	124	1,383	1,491	108
URUGUAY	V	E	85	66,019	80,041	88,895	8,854
USSR	V	E	82	2,416	1,294	1,955	661
YUGOSLV	N	E	81	1,131,890	1,929,334	2,064,624	135,290
			83	1,200,182	1,408,068	1,578,573	170,505
			85	1,646,095	1,987,883	2,219,047	231,164
			86	1,504,069	1,958,866	2,156,309	197,443
	O	E	81	30,864	50,111	50,111	
			84	33,069	53,705	53,705	
			85	11,023	13,741	13,741	
			86	48,322	84,886	85,286	400
	V	E	81	37,008	41,624	46,273	4,649
			82	927,183	1,263,364	1,382,438	119,074
			84	1,222,938	1,379,218	1,544,799	165,581
	V	W	81	1,060	1,499	1,581	82

1619600 SAGE GROUND OR RUBBED (LB)

Country	Mode	Reg	Yr	Quantity	F.A.S.	C.I.F.	Charges
TOTAL			81	32,701	56,312	60,028	3,716
			82	25,850	34,701	35,730	1,029
			83	41,114	37,073	39,593	2,520
			84	12,105	19,051	19,275	224
			85	102,998	101,134	113,121	11,987
			86	22,175	26,102	29,259	3,157
ALBANIA	V	E	85	67,858	68,151	75,455	7,304
	V	W	85	17,471	19,020	22,297	3,277
ALGERIA	A	E	86	116	1,389	1,589	200
CANADA	O	E	81	704	865	865	
			82	18,275	27,256	27,256	
			83	18,640	23,951	23,951	
			84	11,452	16,486	16,486	
			85	32	1,232	1,232	
	O	W	81	542	1,609	1,609	
COLOMB	A	E	84	28	330	357	27
CZECHO	V	E	86	21,587	23,500	26,000	2,500
FR GERM	V	E	81	72	403	417	14
			84	242	286	308	22
	V	W	81	1,792	1,289	1,311	22
			82	1,761	1,257	1,361	104
FRANCE	V	E	81	153	2,423	2,537	114
			82	39	1,045	1,084	39
			83	120	2,478	2,551	73
			84	171	1,416	1,459	43
			85	2,205	2,716	2,881	165
			86	472	1,213	1,670	457
GREECE	V	E	82	3,000	3,800	4,458	658
INDIA	V	E	82	2,205	602	770	168
ITALY	V	E	84	184	277	389	112
ROMANIA	O	E	82	570	741	801	60
TURKEY	V	E	83	22,046	9,977	12,408	2,431
			85	15,432	10,015	11,256	1,241
U KING	O	E	81	75	310	360	50
			84	28	256	276	20
	V	E	81	141	467	507	40
			83	308	667	683	16
USSR	V	E	81	2,222	608	916	308
YUGOSLV	V	E	81	27,000	48,338	51,506	3,168

Sago Palm

Sago, flour and starch**
1323540 ARROWRT A SAGO FLOUR A STRCH (LB)
(See Arrowroot, flour and starch under Arrowroot)

Sandalwood

Sandalwood, essential oil
4526400 SANDALWOOD OIL (LB)

Country	Mode	Reg	Yr	Quantity	F.A.S.	C.I.F.	Charges
TOTAL			81	52,767	1,762,946	1,813,435	50,489
			82	59,103	2,218,471	2,306,864	88,393
			83	52,500	1,980,258	2,030,303	50,045
			84	71,728	2,885,592	2,951,265	65,673
			85	55,715	2,754,007	2,811,704	57,697
			86	41,961	3,123,177	3,197,327	74,150
CANADA	O	E	83	739	8,441	8,441	
	O	W	84	8	600	620	20
FR GERM	A	E	85	22	1,058	1,114	56
FRANCE	A	E	82	18	318	339	21
	N	E	81	5,536	148,384	152,423	4,039

Crop Product TSUSA commodity number, description, and unit of quantity Country	Mode	Reg	Yr	Quantity	F.A.S.	C.I.F.	Charges
			82	2,545	75,409	77,438	2,029
			83	5,408	155,048	158,784	3,736
			84	9,612	317,679	326,489	8,810
			85	6,122	246,366	251,504	5,138
			86	5,180	262,019	268,672	6,653
INDIA	A	E	81	18,133	719,668	754,473	34,805
			82	25,474	1,085,685	1,151,415	65,730
			83	551	27,195	28,140	945
			85	4,409	278,371	285,219	6,848
			86	31,559	2,600,665	2,657,589	56,924
	N	E	83	16,788	772,473	803,598	31,125
			84	21,826	1,070,087	1,101,134	31,047
			85	20,290	1,144,645	1,173,792	29,147
	V	W	82	5	650	775	125
			85	2,205	69,374	70,189	815
INDNSIA	A	E	86	2,418	125,652	131,244	5,592
	N	E	82	30,621	1,041,819	1,059,314	17,495
			83	14,437	512,648	519,932	7,284
			84	26,112	947,523	965,286	17,763
			85	21,804	978,710	992,336	13,626
	V	E	81	23,587	712,694	721,566	8,872
			83	1,323	48,587	49,236	649
	V	W	81	4,409	152,418	154,755	2,337
			83	5,731	173,095	176,591	3,496
			84	12,126	476,795	483,008	6,213
			86	1,102	54,608	55,470	862
JAPAN	A	E	85	265	8,219	9,320	1,101
			86	106	2,499	3,120	621
NETHLDS	A	E	83	22	1,081	1,141	60
	V	E	84	441	3,933	3,984	51
PHIL R	V	E	81	1,102	29,782	30,218	436
SINGAPR	A	E	82	440	14,590	17,583	2,993
	V	E	83	7,054	266,160	268,076	1,916
			84	439	18,824	18,977	153
SRI LKA	A	E	83	278	11,780	12,500	720
			84	220	9,829	10,241	412
			85	143	5,200	5,450	250
SWITZLD	A	E	84	33	2,016	2,075	59
			86	53	3,750	3,867	117
	N	E	83	22	746	760	14
U KING	A	E	84	705	36,564	37,660	1,096
			86	1,543	73,984	77,365	3,381
	N	E	85	455	22,064	22,780	716
	O	E	83	147	3,004	3,104	100
			84	206	1,742	1,791	49

Sapodilla

Chicle, gum
1883200 CHICLE CRUDE (LB)

Country	Mode	Reg	Yr	Quantity	F.A.S.	C.I.F.	Charges
TOTAL			81	971,167	2,485,827	2,545,359	59,532
			82	81,856	156,090	160,593	4,503
			83	532,918	676,649	686,617	9,968
			84	391,855	1,020,516	1,040,828	20,312
			85	682,926	879,552	937,952	58,400
			86	1,212,950	1,180,825	1,234,958	54,133
BELIZE	N	E	84	371,545	999,609	1,018,115	18,506
	V	E	82	38,133	110,586	114,231	3,645
			83	120,863	349,824	358,607	8,783
CANADA	O	E	82	38,000	29,775	30,133	358
COLOMB	V	E	81	11,023	5,000	5,791	791
DENMARK	V	E	85	44,090	28,991	29,736	745
DOM REP	V	E	86	127,502	19,850	20,648	798
FINLAND	V	E	84	15,130	7,205	8,052	847
FRANCE	A	E	83	2,178	1,294	2,479	1,185
			84	110	967	1,726	759
	V	E	81	1,075	821	983	162
IRELAND	V	E	85	500,693	645,154	695,654	50,500
			86	426,845	517,721	552,763	35,042
ITALY	V	E	81	661	372	508	136
MALAYSA	V	E	85	1,000	3,408	3,577	169
MEXICO	O	E	82	5,291	14,889	15,389	500
			83	409,877	325,531	325,531	
			84	4,960	12,400	12,400	
			85	42,398	124,929	124,929	
			86	101,036	278,526	278,526	
	O	W	82	432	840	840	
	V	E	81	921,253	2,454,369	2,511,074	56,705
SPAIN	V	E	85	82,540	65,520	71,367	5,847

Crop Product TSUSA commodity number, description, and unit of quantity Country	Mode	Reg	Yr	Quantity	F.A.S.	C.I.F.	Charges
			86	557,567	364,728	383,021	18,293
U KING	A	E	84	110	335	535	200
			85	12,205	11,550	12,689	1,139
VENEZ	V	E	81	37,155	25,265	27,003	1,738

1883400 CHICLE REFINED OR ADVANCED (LB)

Country	Mode	Reg	Yr	Quantity	F.A.S.	C.I.F.	Charges
TOTAL			81	2,863	9,424	15,810	6,386
			82	26,933	20,596	23,266	2,670
			83	11,163	20,653	21,358	705
			84	106,064	34,487	41,117	6,630
			85	190,639	92,575	103,766	11,191
			86	132,654	141,089	149,700	8,611
ARGENT	V	E	85	37,928	18,700	20,400	1,700
AUSTRIA	A	E	86	8,380	5,112	6,109	997
BELGIUM	V	E	86	30,099	47,232	47,500	268
BRAZIL	V	E	84	6,259	4,458	5,360	902
			85	25,887	8,552	9,698	1,146
CANADA	A	W	82	1	300	349	49
	O	E	83	2,150	575	575	
			84	248	574	574	
CHINA M	V	E	82	26,455	16,777	19,200	2,423
DOM REP	V	E	85	450	1,650	2,453	803
FR GERM	A	W	81	76	2,128	2,206	78
	O	E	83	1,411	3,696	3,696	
	V	E	85	85,516	59,384	64,099	4,715
			86	2,205	4,505	4,709	204
FRANCE	A	E	81	362	3,508	3,653	145
			82	55	2,151	2,171	20
	V	E	83	66	2,729	2,853	124
GUATMAL	A	E	83	133	541	636	95
	V	E	83	2,904	6,300	6,498	198
			86	12,839	6,000	6,964	964
IRELAND	O	E	84	1,323	1,838	1,838	
ITALY	V	E	84	871	738	804	66
JAPAN	A	E	81	2,425	3,788	9,951	6,163
			82	44	612	790	178
			83	55	765	780	15
			84	93	897	1,084	187
	V	E	86	570	1,627	1,712	85
	V	W	86	531	2,031	2,084	53
KOR REP	V	W	83	4,444	6,047	6,320	273
MEXICO	O	E	86	3,541	4,950	4,950	
	O	W	82	378	756	756	
			84	4,486	7,487	7,487	
PORTUGL	V	E	84	92,594	18,208	23,478	5,270
U KING	A	E	84	190	287	492	205
			85	276	1,276	1,470	194
	O	E	85	40,582	3,013	5,646	2,633
	V	E	86	74,489	69,632	75,672	6,040

Sapodilla, fresh or prepared or preserved**
1468700 CASHEW APPLES,ETC FR OR PRES (LB)
(See Cashew apple, fresh or prepared or preserved under Cashew)

Sapodilla, jelly or jam**
1530200 CASHEW APPLE, MANGO JELLY (LB)
(See Cashew apple, jelly or jam under Cashew)

Sapodilla, paste and pulp**
1524300 FRUIT PASTE, CASHEW APPL ETC (LB)
(See Cashew apple, paste and pulp under Cashew)

Sassafras

Safrol
4607000 SAFROL NOT IN ARTIFICIAL MIX (LB)

Country	Mode	Reg	Yr	Quantity	F.A.S.	C.I.F.	Charges
TOTAL			85	1	3,380	3,530	150
			86	992	20,258	21,068	810
FRANCE	A	E	85	1	3,380	3,530	150
SWITZLD	A	E	86	992	20,258	21,068	810

Sassofras, essential oil
4528030 SASSOFRAS, OCOTEA CYMBARUM (LB)

Country	Mode	Reg	Yr	Quantity	F.A.S.	C.I.F.	Charges
TOTAL			81	578,353	1,006,999	1,091,356	84,357

Crop Product TSUSA commodity number, description, and unit of quantity							
Country	Mode	Reg	Yr	Quantity	F.A.S.	C.I.F.	Charges
			82	1,076,315	1,669,699	1,830,134	160,435
			83	472,334	756,541	829,323	72,782
			84	1,082,387	2,780,569	2,970,550	189,981
			85	1,011,046	1,718,267	1,864,980	146,713
			86	513,231	861,938	927,251	65,313
BRAZIL	N	E	85	1,011,046	1,718,267	1,864,980	146,713
	V	E	81	489,729	816,343	890,786	74,443
			82	1,009,648	1,553,177	1,704,943	151,766
			83	392,241	614,992	676,825	61,833
			84	1,053,793	2,699,499	2,886,228	186,729
			86	481,330	789,815	851,883	62,068
CHINA M	V	E	81	33,069	71,999	74,819	2,820
			82	22,222	38,841	41,731	2,890
			83	80,093	141,549	152,498	10,949
			84	6,548	17,015	17,869	854
			86	21,759	41,822	44,185	2,363
	V	W	81	55,555	118,657	125,751	7,094
			82	44,445	77,681	83,460	5,779
			84	22,046	64,055	66,453	2,398
CHINA T	V	E	86	7,937	3,132	3,600	468
INDNSIA	V	E	86	2,205	27,169	27,583	414

Savory

Savory, spice
1620100 SAVORY, EXCEPT MANUFACTURED (LB)

Country	Mode	Reg	Yr	Quantity	F.A.S.	C.I.F.	Charges
TOTAL			81	119,367	60,467	77,183	16,716
			82	130,297	43,444	54,845	11,401
			83	212,556	69,797	94,904	25,107
			84	159,043	67,182	84,352	17,170
			85	268,882	117,510	147,603	30,093
			86	252,757	100,450	122,695	22,245
ALBANIA	V	E	81	32,241	14,552	19,594	5,042
			82	11,030	4,949	5,460	511
			83	11,023	4,307	6,007	1,700
CHINA M	V	W	81	251	505	543	38
FRANCE	A	E	82	45	366	381	15
	A	W	82	69	282	325	43
	O	E	83	150	420	440	20
	V	E	83	67,308	27,670	33,996	6,326
			84	105,829	44,835	56,357	11,522
			85	164,175	73,569	91,818	18,249
			86	60,499	30,436	34,120	3,684
	V	W	84	300	828	1,103	275
INDIA	V	E	86	11,023	7,452	8,452	1,000
ITALY	V	E	83	22,399	8,589	11,130	2,541
NETHLDS	A	E	81	125	284	404	120
			83	180	540	682	142
	O	E	82	100	252	267	15
			83	300	887	920	33
			84	150	606	662	56
	V	W	81	200	453	528	75
U KING	O	E	84	276	295	355	60
YUGOSLV	V	E	81	86,550	44,673	56,114	11,441
			82	119,053	37,595	48,412	10,817
			83	111,196	27,384	41,729	14,345
			84	52,488	20,618	25,875	5,257
			85	104,707	43,941	55,785	11,844
			86	181,235	62,562	80,123	17,561

1620300 SAVORY, MANUFACTURED (LB)

Country	Mode	Reg	Yr	Quantity	F.A.S.	C.I.F.	Charges
TOTAL			81	527	931	951	20
			82	92	1,264	1,375	111
			83	333	1,460	1,708	248
			84	170	646	1,938	1,292
CANADA	O	E	81	480	406	406	
FR GERM	A	W	84	170	646	1,938	1,292
	V	E	81	47	525	545	20
			82	92	1,264	1,375	111
			83	63	767	805	38
FRANCE	V	E	83	32	283	300	17
ITALY	V	E	83	238	410	603	193

Sen

Sen, plywood
2402320 PLYWD, FACE PLY SEN (MSF)

Country	Mode	Reg	Yr	Quantity	F.A.S.	C.I.F.	Charges
TOTAL			81	73,587	27,946,342	30,487,748	2,543,357
			82	56,993	20,930,869	22,993,917	2,063,048
			83	90,704	30,631,659	33,424,957	2,793,298
			84	93,382	32,016,663	34,832,700	2,816,037
			85	78,052	24,328,373	26,714,827	2,386,454
			86	58,160	18,069,738	19,742,965	1,673,227
CHINA T	V	E	81	13,390	3,152,103	3,418,668	266,565
			82	15,861	3,730,209	4,058,776	328,567
			83	33,897	7,517,361	8,107,205	589,844
			84	38,526	9,039,862	9,711,013	671,151
			85	34,168	6,827,645	7,463,227	635,582
			86	32,078	6,636,975	7,275,148	638,173
	V	W	81	741	203,499	217,696	14,197
			82	671	179,319	191,454	12,135
			83	1,390	325,180	346,736	21,556
			84	1,541	366,818	388,152	21,334
			85	3,093	598,998	641,319	42,321
			86	1,767	382,827	408,670	25,843
JAPAN	N	E	85	2,636	654,934	709,756	54,822
	N	W	84	8,252	2,475,402	2,619,473	144,071
			85	1,461	366,150	394,459	28,309
	V	E	81	38,421	17,900,823	19,695,875	1,797,210
			82	30,518	13,922,336	15,417,452	1,495,116
			83	39,481	18,191,096	20,071,884	1,880,788
			84	41,086	18,817,702	20,697,189	1,879,487
			85	24,936	12,519,456	13,917,481	1,398,025
			86	15,643	8,536,416	9,394,019	857,603
	V	W	81	20,310	6,569,241	7,019,316	449,868
			82	9,713	3,056,849	3,280,144	223,295
			83	15,067	4,453,065	4,744,063	290,998
			84	3,686	1,208,051	1,298,205	90,154
			85	11,582	3,330,263	3,555,681	225,418
			86	8,672	2,513,520	2,665,128	151,608
KOR REP	V	E	81	709	115,127	130,259	15,132
			82	230	42,156	46,091	3,935
			83	508	114,821	123,277	8,456
			84	121	70,200	77,264	7,064
			85	48	12,111	12,828	717
	V	W	81	16	5,549	5,934	385
			83	361	30,136	31,792	1,656
			84	170	38,628	41,404	2,776
			85	128	18,816	20,076	1,260

Sesame

Sesame, fatty acid**
4902200 FATTY ACIDS DRVD HMP KPK ETC (LB)
(See Hempseed, fatty acid under Hemp)

Sesame, fatty salt**
4904600 FATTY SALTS OF SESAME ETC (LB)
(See Hempseed, fatty salt under Hemp)

Sesame, seed
1754500 SESAME SEED (LB)

Country	Mode	Reg	Yr	Quantity	F.A.S.	C.I.F.	Charges
TOTAL			81	83,672,943	35,159,272	36,076,950	917,678
			82	73,220,927	32,454,447	33,206,706	752,259
			83	94,332,842	39,962,784	42,143,315	2,180,531
			84	81,038,267	32,985,977	33,996,200	1,010,223
			85	82,306,507	31,013,564	32,385,653	1,372,089
			86	76,155,272	24,957,286	25,695,642	738,356
AUSTRAL	V	E	84	66,000	31,039	36,300	5,261
BELIZE	V	E	84	88,000	50,600	52,682	2,082
BRAZIL	V	E	85	211,520	99,925	111,068	11,143
C RICA	V	E	85	44,000	21,287	23,657	2,370
CANADA	O	E	82	4,286	4,498	4,498	
			83	1,334	1,988	1,988	
			84	48,357	13,521	13,521	
			86	39,061	24,226	24,305	79
	O	W	81	48,000	25,738	25,738	

Crop
Product
TSUSA commodity number, description, and unit of quantity

Country	Mode	Reg	Yr	Quantity	F.A.S.	C.I.F.	Charges
			82	5,115	3,683	3,683	
			83	22,000	11,000	11,000	
			85	45,000	20,475	20,475	
			86	44,000	17,600	17,600	
CHINA M	N	W	84	53,617	25,584	28,810	3,226
			85	5,750	4,129	4,418	289
	O	E	83	900	583	636	53
	O	W	84	158,875	60,535	60,535	
	V	E	81	3,499	3,164	3,404	240
			82	1,876	1,039	1,264	225
			83	6,283,660	2,155,052	2,479,727	324,675
			84	1,627,310	486,572	581,412	94,840
			85	1,058,258	533,895	632,174	98,279
			86	2,105,715	560,001	660,117	100,116
	V	W	81	16,830	11,175	11,880	705
			82	24,512	16,922	18,313	1,391
			83	11,936,689	3,816,849	4,516,573	699,724
			84	314,983	124,763	126,715	1,952
			85	770,867	219,440	227,243	7,803
			86	39,320	14,739	16,491	1,752
CHINA T	V	E	82	120	260	298	38
			83	4,900	1,615	1,794	179
			84	2,250	1,478	1,861	383
			85	1,252	1,090	1,181	91
	V	W	81	1,160	1,148	1,195	47
			83	191	1,388	1,459	71
			84	240	500	532	32
			86	7,500	6,300	6,425	125
COLOMB	A	E	84	4,405	2,600	3,323	723
	V	E	81	36,764	11,658	13,671	2,013
			83	129,782	50,919	58,145	7,226
			85	136,998	67,835	75,945	8,110
DENMARK	V	W	85	37,506	14,438	16,038	1,600
DOM REP	A	E	84	600	840	1,570	730
	N	E	82	11,850	1,677	2,149	472
			84	6,300	1,395	1,690	295
	V	E	81	5,400	1,600	1,668	68
			83	6,338	684	909	225
			85	44,000	14,960	16,460	1,500
			86	44,000	19,800	21,500	1,700
ECUADOR	V	W	85	37,500	15,000	16,600	1,600
EGYPT	V	E	83	2,547,088	992,819	1,080,846	88,027
			84	771,830	293,368	325,789	32,421
ETHIOP	V	W	81	1,250	1,973	2,083	110
FR GERM	O	W	82	1,000	837	1,424	587
FRANCE	O	W	85	44,000	18,480	18,480	
	V	E	84	661	1,274	1,558	284
GREECE	N	E	82	11,421	7,365	8,459	1,094
	O	E	83	4,290	3,425	3,425	
	V	E	81	1,031	2,240	2,340	100
			85	9,270	6,518	8,302	1,784
			86	10,801	6,970	8,237	1,267
GUATMAL	N	E	83	8,740,284	3,871,954	4,302,457	430,503
	N	W	81	77,300	33,313	35,596	2,283
			82	44,506	23,284	25,813	2,529
			84	177,836	76,296	87,060	10,764
	O	E	85	44,000	20,406	22,880	2,474
	V	E	81	13,647,662	5,180,117	5,751,967	571,850
			82	15,123,260	6,322,000	6,876,555	554,555
			83	6,363,456	2,706,124	3,029,385	323,261
			84	13,648,404	5,806,709	6,346,224	539,515
			85	13,052,423	4,873,949	5,379,217	505,268
			86	7,347,049	2,875,941	3,158,369	282,428
	V	W	81	1,579,000	501,353	597,182	95,829
			82	44,000	22,880	25,370	2,490
			83	679,531	357,389	396,578	39,189
			84	76,000	35,652	39,600	3,948
			85	1,036,500	443,852	500,078	56,226
			86	809,000	334,432	367,224	32,792
GUYANA	V	E	85	44,835	16,141	18,489	2,348
HG KONG	V	E	82	1,000	677	734	57
			84	2,000	1,507	1,773	266
			86	714,290	170,400	194,400	24,000
	V	W	81	3,400	2,641	2,835	194
			82	3,903	2,938	3,165	227
			83	5,080	3,422	3,634	212
			84	17,110	14,776	16,552	1,776
			85	7,560	8,270	8,758	488
			86	214,917	96,862	101,751	4,889
HONDURA	N	E	81	1,643,690	533,840	611,291	77,451
	V	E	81	171,000	77,426	83,358	5,932
			82	1,188,000	508,440	547,015	38,575
			83	747,908	350,722	386,639	35,917
			84	705,403	316,964	351,325	34,361

Crop
Product
TSUSA commodity number, description, and unit of quantity

Country	Mode	Reg	Yr	Quantity	F.A.S.	C.I.F.	Charges
			85	854,000	373,673	415,682	42,009
			86	908,410	298,902	339,520	40,618
INDIA	V	E	84	1,279	805	924	119
ISRAEL	V	E	85	4,406	6,000	7,102	1,102
			86	3,339	4,813	5,538	725
JAPAN	V	E	81	2,053	6,207	6,663	456
			82	6,551	10,950	11,982	1,032
			83	3,836	6,207	7,329	1,122
			84	22,137	27,723	31,299	3,576
			85	46,933	52,170	56,446	4,276
			86	67,820	95,184	104,184	9,000
	V	H	81	9,856	12,317	13,973	1,656
			82	12,731	14,548	16,443	1,895
			83	10,309	11,216	12,575	1,359
			84	16,131	18,146	20,650	2,504
			85	14,200	14,842	16,807	1,965
			86	5,970	9,737	11,046	1,309
	V	W	81	75,754	99,218	105,447	6,229
			82	53,005	69,325	73,531	4,206
			83	79,267	90,070	95,521	5,451
			84	110,781	120,950	131,442	10,492
			85	96,866	111,826	119,747	7,921
			86	118,341	158,612	168,592	9,980
KIRIBAT	V	E	85	44,000	20,240	21,767	1,527
			86	92,160	35,776	39,171	3,395
KOR REP	V	E	84	240	324	347	23
	V	W	82	704	620	654	34
			83	18,315	5,423	6,000	577
			85	4,718	4,357	4,600	243
LEBANON	V	E	83	13,713	12,595	13,356	761
			86	58,076	38,082	43,941	5,859
MALAYSA	O	W	86	26,000	10,400	10,400	
MEXICO	N	E	83	148,202	64,316	66,197	1,881
	N	W	82	1,556,447	524,114	525,459	1,345
			83	145,998	82,116	86,466	4,350
			84	1,601,146	450,661	451,761	1,100
	O	E	81	20,871,697	6,985,449	6,991,554	6,105
			82	20,682,796	6,845,204	6,846,940	1,736
			83	6,375,538	2,171,854	2,208,621	36,767
			84	7,768,323	2,429,546	2,429,546	
			85	5,528,881	1,563,121	1,563,121	
			86	11,680,781	2,955,710	2,955,710	
	O	W	81	41,679,360	20,026,666	20,028,991	2,325
			82	31,372,921	16,516,463	16,516,463	
			83	46,298,826	21,436,427	21,436,427	
			84	48,790,440	20,767,646	20,767,646	
			85	46,597,155	18,340,935	18,342,409	1,474
			86	46,072,805	15,417,883	15,417,907	24
	V	E	81	400	323	360	37
			82	44,000	22,660	23,762	1,102
			84	37,478	11,942	13,492	1,550
			86	96,000	40,320	43,720	3,400
	V	W	82	35,935	19,560	20,955	1,395
MONGOLA	V	E	86	40,000	12,760	14,405	1,645
NETHLDS	V	E	83	77,600	35,800	38,950	3,150
NICARAG	N	E	81	308,000	157,763	180,549	22,786
	V	E	81	1,716,000	843,690	899,786	56,096
			82	1,488,800	817,960	867,716	49,756
			83	1,231,120	647,920	690,414	42,494
			84	528,000	249,040	284,972	35,932
			85	792,000	331,960	381,275	49,315
	V	W	81	365,601	177,618	197,949	20,331
			82	677,600	345,197	383,558	38,361
			83	320,000	181,875	199,315	17,440
			84	247,000	112,450	124,331	11,881
			85	299,000	122,430	137,114	14,684
PHIL R	V	E	83	206,791	66,789	80,138	13,349
SALVADR	N	E	81	481,000	159,911	176,991	17,080
	O	E	83	500	310	342	32
	V	E	81	841,912	262,400	284,989	22,589
			82	793,256	328,182	372,802	44,620
			83	1,079,584	484,666	543,445	58,759
			84	3,523,960	1,169,930	1,349,688	179,758
			85	6,557,620	2,283,345	2,608,457	325,112
			86	5,197,053	1,607,916	1,802,969	195,053
	V	W	81	59,950	25,604	28,906	3,302
			83	117,400	53,585	60,170	6,585
			84	529,000	226,800	252,318	25,518
			85	567,462	229,640	258,892	29,252
			86	292,007	89,917	101,803	11,886
SINGAPR	V	E	86	1,518	1,275	1,388	113
	V	W	86	570	1,455	1,750	295
SYRIA	O	E	84	440	475	505	30
	V	E	86	30,559	18,720	20,572	1,852

Crop
Product
TSUSA commodity number, description, and unit of quantity

Country	Mode	Reg	Yr	Quantity	F.A.S.	C.I.F.	Charges
THAILND	O W		84	1,279	1,523	1,651	128
	V E		81	15,447	9,073	9,982	909
			82	2,500	1,125	1,241	116
			83	11,998	6,922	7,767	845
			84	12,556	11,257	12,567	1,310
			85	2,500	1,408	1,574	166
	V H		84	426	270	304	34
	V W		81	9,927	5,647	6,602	955
			82	28,832	22,039	26,460	4,421
			83	41,864	25,468	27,658	2,190
			84	77,470	40,516	43,925	3,409
			85	31,107	18,415	20,085	1,670
			86	42,209	20,503	22,738	2,235
USSR	V E		86	46,001	12,050	13,869	1,819
VENEZ	V E		83	678,550	253,292	287,429	34,137
			85	4,234,420	1,139,112	1,329,112	190,000

Sesame, vegetable oil, edible
1765000 SESAME OIL, EDIBLE (LB)

Country	Mode	Reg	Yr	Quantity	F.A.S.	C.I.F.	Charges
TOTAL			81	5,304,111	6,715,253	7,114,717	399,464
			82	5,799,456	6,719,510	7,154,544	435,034
			83	5,869,291	6,800,480	7,256,224	455,744
			84	6,763,247	7,182,885	7,720,856	537,971
			85	7,887,552	8,455,618	9,171,351	715,733
			86	8,030,820	9,469,233	10,092,050	622,817
BELGIUM	O E		86	675	1,243	1,312	69
	V E		85	595	1,096	1,188	92
CANADA	O E		81	7,000	4,210	4,210	
			82	1,250	716	716	
			83	2,381	3,060	3,060	
			84	1,500	930	930	
			85	2,174	1,100	1,100	
			86	8,428	11,116	11,116	
CHINA M	O E		81	441	331	387	56
	V E		81	170,450	171,289	184,413	13,124
			82	335,179	313,356	340,507	27,151
			83	199,947	192,474	208,192	15,718
			84	312,599	246,381	273,133	26,752
			85	224,995	170,170	190,232	20,062
			86	304,771	210,040	236,082	26,042
	V H		81	13,307	16,368	17,300	932
			82	1,630	1,848	2,022	174
			83	1,093	936	1,054	118
			84	2,442	2,567	2,828	261
			85	2,650	3,259	3,711	452
			86	1,429	1,480	1,601	121
	V W		81	51,760	47,293	52,837	5,544
			82	80,611	69,363	72,427	3,064
			83	350,106	265,070	279,711	14,641
			84	255,548	178,969	191,623	12,654
			85	582,941	437,292	467,247	29,955
			86	565,914	408,317	430,063	21,746
CHINA T	V E		81	24,304	38,302	38,609	307
			82	126,009	171,631	185,529	13,898
			83	34,255	38,770	43,083	4,313
			84	53,309	66,846	74,687	7,841
			85	24,798	31,933	34,849	2,916
			86	39,018	49,591	53,493	3,902
	V H		81	2,646	3,900	4,076	176
			82	3,174	4,680	5,123	443
			86	9,309	10,136	10,938	802
	V W		81	14,047	9,405	10,307	902
			82	56,002	55,054	59,637	4,583
			83	10,904	14,664	16,441	1,777
			84	17,072	24,270	27,088	2,818
			85	114,140	89,951	96,676	6,725
			86	148,654	127,010	135,134	8,124
DENMARK	V E		81	419,856	393,140	411,612	18,472
			82	582,066	551,204	579,102	27,898
			83	388,044	332,535	352,824	20,289
			84	420,381	328,231	347,880	19,649
			85	323,420	222,777	241,073	18,296
			86	128,497	119,073	125,904	6,831
EGYPT	O E		83	7,500	6,468	6,468	
FR GERM	N E		85	34,645	28,369	30,409	2,040
	O E		82	38,945	37,590	39,713	2,123
			83	65,344	56,538	59,232	2,694
			85	32,672	23,993	25,608	1,615
	V E		81	44,574	39,801	41,671	1,870
			82	152,884	130,930	140,392	9,462
			83	15,873	13,042	13,764	722
			84	98,016	74,679	79,068	4,389
			85	49,427	33,148	41,751	8,603
			86	161,428	127,568	135,096	7,528
	V W		83	32,672	27,861	29,494	1,633
			84	57,804	80,764	87,224	6,460
			85	232,056	163,227	182,304	19,077
			86	32,672	24,804	26,566	1,762
FRANCE	A E		83	529	598	598	
	V E		81	128	260	277	17
			82	181	313	352	39
			84	769	5,199	5,609	410
			85	3,931	7,437	8,240	803
GREECE	V E		82	31,482	20,135	23,564	3,429
			83	79,366	51,566	58,167	6,601
HG KONG	O E		83	480	442	482	40
	V E		81	393,135	382,852	407,470	24,618
			82	229,992	213,535	231,279	17,744
			83	44,450	75,464	83,285	7,821
			84	9,160	7,452	8,853	1,401
			85	106,894	72,333	80,216	7,883
			86	82,424	83,225	92,061	8,836
	V H		81	7,878	9,631	10,354	723
			82	330	500	519	19
			83	4,995	3,195	3,568	373
			84	7,639	5,126	5,826	700
			86	1,111	1,183	1,259	76
	V W		81	50,926	50,438	54,764	4,326
			82	9,369	13,086	15,402	2,316
			83	62,244	45,814	48,591	2,777
			84	164,322	135,013	142,775	7,762
			85	225,286	212,386	223,761	11,375
			86	388,164	293,090	306,530	13,440
ISRAEL	V E		83	339	275	294	19
			86	38,259	26,874	29,083	2,209
ITALY	V E		82	33,510	32,800	34,521	1,721
			83	134,052	121,293	127,869	6,576
			84	119,754	111,823	117,862	6,039
			85	316,923	219,853	252,954	33,101
			86	420,705	295,775	325,584	29,809
	V W		85	341,560	260,742	296,355	35,613
			86	286,908	189,839	218,157	28,318
IVY CST	V W		86	25,485	21,980	22,560	580
JAPAN	N E		85	138,119	179,855	197,831	17,976
			86	446,345	580,561	621,918	41,357
	N W		84	467,473	564,473	596,488	32,015
	O E		83	50,211	74,400	74,400	
			84	20,132	31,844	32,187	343
			85	8,036	10,244	10,244	
			86	1,200	2,407	2,520	113
	O W		85	578	1,794	1,885	91
	V E		81	1,479,749	1,889,718	2,025,838	136,120
			82	1,811,633	2,165,309	2,309,460	144,151
			83	1,636,398	2,152,663	2,321,087	168,424
			84	1,765,371	2,273,213	2,464,225	191,012
			85	1,996,950	2,535,137	2,782,431	247,294
			86	1,934,192	2,784,166	2,979,859	195,693
	V H		81	173,518	278,361	310,176	31,815
			82	182,942	282,614	312,446	29,832
			83	272,289	400,962	441,335	40,373
			84	191,972	294,290	330,020	35,730
			85	197,234	287,196	325,269	38,073
			86	202,895	360,291	400,138	39,847
	V W		81	1,461,183	2,014,085	2,123,349	109,264
			82	1,358,392	1,883,601	1,993,380	109,779
			83	1,793,078	2,350,978	2,475,778	124,800
			84	1,463,691	1,919,543	2,029,601	110,058
			85	2,426,117	2,981,884	3,153,621	171,737
			86	2,125,820	3,186,421	3,328,647	142,226
KOR REP	V E		81	40,906	71,700	74,699	2,999
			85	23,583	32,748	34,669	1,921
			86	700	1,059	1,144	85
	V W		81	461,956	817,496	842,910	25,414
			82	211,010	301,654	313,466	11,812
			83	179,369	220,007	229,143	9,136
			84	122,846	87,446	92,158	4,712
			85	39,804	40,850	44,135	3,285
LEBANON	O E		81	5,479	6,009	6,009	
			82	5,637	1,217	1,217	
			83	8,823	8,013	8,013	
			84	31,553	18,948	21,452	2,504
			85	24,850	19,651	20,644	993
	V E		82	57,582	48,025	52,241	4,216
			83	120,019	69,351	73,825	4,474
			84	14,270	15,180	16,247	1,067

Crop Product TSUSA commodity number, description, and unit of quantity Country	Mode	Reg	Yr	Quantity	F.A.S.	C.I.F.	Charges
			85	105,629	71,734	78,218	6,484
			86	144,528	100,196	113,286	13,090
	V	W	86	46,164	26,844	29,353	2,509
MEXICO	O	E	82	154,454	70,060	70,060	
			83	146,826	59,772	59,772	
			84	331,912	137,961	137,961	
	O	W	81	306,373	291,837	294,215	2,378
			82	149,891	147,147	147,181	34
			86	12,668	8,561	8,561	
NETHLDS	V	E	81	11,023	9,672	10,923	1,251
PHIL R	V	E	84	8,438	17,052	18,513	1,461
S ARAB	V	E	86	9,724	10,725	11,731	1,006
SINGAPR	O	W	81	270	537	537	
	V	E	82	288	524	556	32
			86	713	1,425	1,647	222
	V	W	81	48,939	56,770	62,327	5,557
			82	65,963	88,618	94,162	5,544
			83	78,689	93,695	98,457	4,762
			84	111,263	130,064	136,761	6,697
			85	9,776	11,111	12,925	1,814
			86	15,114	17,772	20,808	3,036
SPAIN	V	W	85	42,262	26,838	29,838	3,000
SRI LKA	V	E	85	4,409	10,339	11,072	733
SYRIA	V	E	81	2,250	4,035	4,837	802
			84	10,035	4,500	5,524	1,024
THAILND	N	E	85	55,325	59,530	64,048	4,518
	V	E	86	82,463	97,694	104,244	6,550
	V	W	81	112,013	107,813	120,610	12,797
			82	119,050	114,000	129,570	15,570
			83	103,176	101,120	115,234	14,114
			84	163,063	168,336	185,254	16,918
			85	177,479	194,000	212,114	18,114
			86	134,920	151,200	159,670	8,470
TURKEY	O	E	85	1,980	1,440	1,440	
	V	E	86	7,750	5,907	6,375	468
	V	W	85	16,314	12,201	13,293	1,092
VENEZ	A	E	83	2,839	2,054	2,472	418
	V	E	83	43,000	17,400	20,531	3,131
			84	317,009	147,069	163,098	16,029
			86	133,391	79,852	84,702	4,850
	V	W	84	223,904	104,716	125,981	21,265
			86	88,382	51,808	54,908	3,100

Sesame, vegetable oil, inedible
1764900 SESAME OIL, INEDIBLE (LB)

Country	Mode	Reg	Yr	Quantity	F.A.S.	C.I.F.	Charges
TOTAL			82	33,510	34,462	35,809	1,347
			83	246,362	185,224	187,799	2,575
			84	3,322	2,183	3,505	1,322
			85	38,614	12,122	12,854	732
			86	35,644	29,136	31,139	2,003
CHINA M	V	W	84	3,031	1,930	2,312	382
			86	31,746	23,600	25,258	1,658
CHINA T	V	E	85	4,227	4,300	4,592	292
	V	W	83	353	633	758	125
HG KONG	V	E	85	1,715	1,267	1,369	102
ITALY	V	E	82	33,510	34,462	35,809	1,347
	V	W	85	32,672	6,555	6,893	338
JAPAN	A	E	84	291	253	1,193	940
	V	E	83	245	407	443	36
			86	3,898	5,536	5,881	345
	V	W	83	35,423	33,959	36,373	2,414
MEXICO	O	E	83	210,341	150,225	150,225	

Sesbania

Sesbania, seed
1267900 SESBANIA SEED (LB)

Country	Mode	Reg	Yr	Quantity	F.A.S.	C.I.F.	Charges
TOTAL			82	21,410	3,520	3,520	
MEXICO	O	W	82	21,410	3,520	3,520	

Sisal

Sisal, fiber, processed**
3044800 SISAL A HENEQUEN FIB PROCESS (LB)
    (See Henequen, fiber, processed under Henequen)

Sisal, fiber, raw and waste**
3044600 SISAL A HENEQ RAW A WASTES (LTN)
    (See Henequen, fiber, raw and waste under Henequen)

Snow Pea

Snow pea, fresh
1370405 SNOW PEAS FRS/CH 10/1-6/30 (LB)

Country	Mode	Reg	Yr	Quantity	F.A.S.	C.I.F.	Charges
TOTAL			85	2,051,085	839,140	1,301,721	462,581
			86	12,360,518	5,403,392	7,142,414	1,739,022
CHINA T	V	E	85	36,800	23,960	28,988	5,028
COLOMB	V	E	86	2,750	1,017	1,291	274
DENMARK	A	E	86	5,000	1,300	1,902	602
DOM REP	A	E	85	332,507	146,288	211,569	65,281
			86	1,733,701	749,520	1,109,505	359,985
GREECE	A	E	86	3,000	1,350	2,126	776
GUATMAL	A	E	85	69,807	23,904	39,332	15,428
			86	26,778	22,115	27,020	4,905
	A	H	85	7,000	2,800	4,250	1,450
	A	W	85	72,919	29,350	54,757	25,407
			86	105,622	26,836	61,800	34,964
	N	E	85	1,353,997	524,366	840,427	316,061
			86	7,286,630	2,715,949	3,937,253	1,221,304
	N	W	86	267,031	70,801	151,263	80,462
	O	E	85	5,401	1,125	2,725	1,600
	V	E	86	199,350	61,953	77,625	15,672
	V	W	86	25,000	6,250	9,420	3,170
HONDURA	A	E	85	4,040	9,690	11,938	2,248
			86	65,987	34,740	45,830	11,090
JAPAN	V	W	86	327	2,074	2,170	96
KIRIBAT	A	E	85	137,300	46,536	76,614	30,078
			86	11,350	3,309	5,964	2,655
MEXICO	O	E	86	35,208	9,755	9,755	
	O	W	85	31,314	31,121	31,121	
			86	2,580,784	1,691,623	1,691,623	
U KING	A	E	86	12,000	4,800	7,867	3,067

Sorghum

Sorghum, grain
1304000 GRAIN SORGHUM (LB)

Country	Mode	Reg	Yr	Quantity	F.A.S.	C.I.F.	Charges
TOTAL			81	156,333	18,117	29,070	10,953
			82	3,779,950	664,271	899,130	234,859
			83	6,008	3,478	3,784	306
			84	14,708,194	1,501,818	1,573,498	71,680
			85	80,000	13,200	13,200	
			86	436,187	24,404	25,600	1,196
ARGENT	A	E	81	2,204	2,204	6,289	4,085
			82	20,592	6,362	38,380	32,018
			84	521	313	1,311	998
	V	E	82	2,235,751	457,013	590,708	133,695
			84	14,693,808	1,497,195	1,567,771	70,576
AUSTRAL	V	E	84	2,293	518	624	106
	V	W	81	9,369	2,881	3,400	519
BELGIUM	V	E	82	116,249	14,520	21,572	7,052
CANADA	O	E	84	11,572	3,792	3,792	
			86	44,634	1,495	1,495	
FR GERM	A	E	81	882	1,192	1,513	321
FRANCE	V	E	82	993,478	126,103	187,684	61,581
GUATMAL	V	E	81	143,000	11,440	17,367	5,927
INDIA	V	W	86	35,274	3,885	4,894	1,009
INDNSIA	O	E	81	878	400	501	101
KOR REP	V	E	83	1,624	1,571	1,740	169
	V	W	82	8,145	7,155	7,668	513
			83	4,384	1,907	2,044	137
			86	3,279	3,139	3,326	187

Crop
Product
TSUSA commodity number, description, and unit of quantity

Country	Mode	Reg	Yr	Quantity	F.A.S.	C.I.F.	Charges
MEXICO	O E		82	405,735	53,118	53,118	
			85	80,000	13,200	13,200	
			86	353,000	15,885	15,885	

Soursop

Soursop, fresh or prepared or preserved**
1468700 CASHEW APPLES,ETC FR OR PRES (LB)
  (See Cashew apple, fresh or prepared or preserved under Cashew)

Soursop, jelly or jam**
1530200 CASHEW APPLE, MANGO JELLY (LB)
  (See Cashew apple, jelly or jam under Cashew)

Soursop, paste and pulp**
1524300 FRUIT PASTE, CASHEW APPL ETC (LB)
  (See Cashew apple, paste and pulp under Cashew)

Soybean

Soy sauce
1824500 SOY SAUCE, THIN (LB)

Country	Mode	Reg	Yr	Quantity	F.A.S.	C.I.F.	Charges
TOTAL			81	20,893,292	7,410,039	8,436,634	1,026,590
			82	21,391,609	7,728,229	8,946,172	1,217,943
			83	24,317,486	8,424,082	9,694,694	1,270,612
			84	24,563,372	8,792,032	10,238,185	1,446,153
			85	29,688,958	9,845,694	11,530,433	1,684,739
			86	32,459,014	12,402,726	13,943,037	1,540,311
AUSTRAL	V E		84	7,875	2,260	2,509	249
BELGIUM	V E		86	13,228	6,503	7,378	875
	V W		85	74,207	60,945	67,320	6,375
CAMROON	V E		86	4,200	1,063	1,269	206
CANADA	O E		81	1,000	498	498	
			82	45,000	22,301	22,301	
			83	3,472	4,571	4,571	
			84	740	846	846	
			86	582,752	96,400	96,400	
CHINA M	N E		82	1,218,802	317,705	419,699	101,994
	N W		84	838,006	250,394	290,981	40,587
			85	162,586	42,839	53,760	10,921
			86	893,100	199,350	223,925	24,575
	O E		81	6,000	1,250	1,425	175
			83	3,590	742	790	48
			84	34,094	14,804	20,434	5,630
	O W		82	794	254	299	45
			83	4,200	921	964	43
			86	3,330	1,435	1,527	92
	V E		81	1,860,763	604,101	712,318	108,217
			82	46,869	12,552	14,833	2,281
			83	1,933,982	409,325	533,950	124,625
			84	1,779,049	419,121	553,889	134,768
			85	3,559,069	722,273	949,509	227,236
			86	1,108,892	245,646	302,671	57,025
	V H		81	34,262	9,458	11,071	1,613
			82	68,077	16,016	19,954	3,938
			83	16,796	10,051	11,174	1,123
			84	56,884	16,152	19,586	3,434
			85	64,216	19,343	21,688	2,345
			86	64,134	14,978	16,571	1,593
	V W		81	1,638,048	401,841	467,839	65,998
			82	2,131,673	528,080	640,686	112,606
			83	2,377,296	591,454	672,724	81,270
			84	1,493,271	358,877	426,943	68,066
			85	2,349,032	578,666	687,299	108,633
			86	2,104,133	478,451	568,625	90,174
CHINA T	A W		82	330	360	756	396
	N E		84	367,294	97,642	126,115	28,473
			85	499,655	116,181	149,436	33,255
	N W		82	912,438	208,682	261,162	52,480
	O E		82	29,915	4,715	5,165	450
	V E		81	373,783	104,707	124,012	19,311
			82	342,587	105,321	127,380	22,059
			83	426,190	106,019	132,292	26,273
			84	46,335	12,703	17,966	5,263
			85	33,401	10,172	12,700	2,528
			86	936,390	207,567	260,859	53,292
	V H		81	600	450	482	32
			82	750	444	490	46
	V W		81	631,911	164,660	194,190	29,530
			82	323,956	79,636	97,003	17,367
			83	970,167	205,617	236,799	31,182
			84	1,706,043	328,120	406,249	78,129
			85	2,322,601	310,338	394,574	84,236
			86	2,972,712	420,889	518,880	97,991
DENMARK	V W		85	48,615	18,339	22,164	3,825
FR GERM	V E		82	20,832	26,594	30,168	3,574
			84	3,083	2,027	2,358	331
	V W		82	825	2,070	2,583	513
			85	8,217	3,703	4,627	924
			86	17,600	16,322	18,890	2,568
FRANCE	V E		83	615	447	508	61
			85	33,747	31,504	34,987	3,483
	V W		83	26,504	31,616	34,343	2,727
			85	24,091	21,792	24,791	2,999
			86	39,325	29,392	31,511	2,119
GAZA ST	V W		84	1,950	622	654	32
GERM DR	V W		85	11,455	7,488	9,130	1,642
			86	7,814	6,401	7,903	1,502
GUYANA	V E		81	3,240	3,642	6,304	2,662
HG KONG	N E		84	140,846	50,936	62,687	11,751
			85	2,964,465	875,749	1,075,387	199,638
	N W		83	122,821	38,013	41,024	3,011
			84	597,970	218,064	237,183	19,119
	O E		83	32,850	14,235	14,235	
			84	68,400	24,651	24,651	
			85	110,940	19,450	29,154	9,704
	O W		81	1,050	410	410	
			85	18,900	4,221	4,703	482
	V E		81	5,521,196	1,966,119	2,215,511	249,392
			82	4,979,468	1,774,197	2,066,841	292,644
			83	4,896,414	1,528,047	1,807,996	279,949
			84	3,173,219	1,003,529	1,232,401	228,872
			85	1,135,520	309,968	377,661	67,693
			86	5,011,765	1,509,220	1,760,248	251,028
	V H		81	60,635	17,482	19,270	1,788
			82	47,818	15,656	19,986	4,330
			83	142,933	46,396	53,058	6,662
			84	45,083	13,624	15,437	1,813
			85	10,500	2,467	2,800	333
			86	12,300	3,228	3,798	570
	V W		81	1,777,355	642,306	690,623	48,317
			82	1,632,158	602,703	658,200	55,497
			83	2,288,276	740,696	813,210	72,514
			84	2,457,299	783,926	883,520	99,594
			85	2,421,652	781,012	881,059	100,047
			86	3,711,946	1,149,025	1,261,907	112,882
INDNSIA	V W		82	5,621	5,785	7,201	1,416
			83	2,977	1,969	2,196	227
			84	2,143	1,121	1,255	134
			85	1,640	1,425	1,573	148
			86	1,649	2,482	2,858	376
ISRAEL	V E		83	15,622	4,984	5,877	893
ITALY	V E		82	3,788	2,063	2,350	287
JAMAICA	V E		86	1,117	1,034	1,090	56
JAPAN	A E		82	846	601	3,142	2,541
			83	1,102	2,535	4,835	2,300
			84	1,627	3,884	6,701	2,817
			85	551	1,191	1,577	386
			86	1,659	4,952	5,754	802
	A W		84	2,786	4,875	5,810	935
	N E		83	1,869,642	763,800	899,773	135,973
			85	2,042,595	850,675	1,007,622	156,947
	N H		82	1,074,889	350,470	430,667	80,197
			83	866,133	313,865	383,930	70,065
			84	1,045,198	386,498	475,777	89,279
	N W		82	2,777,599	1,150,980	1,289,666	138,686
			83	68,303	46,659	54,433	7,774
			84	5,202,034	2,398,185	2,638,866	240,681
			85	2,444,797	1,263,957	1,362,472	98,515
			86	2,315,290	1,511,674	1,609,461	97,787
	O E		81	184,047	66,822	74,410	7,588
			82	75,858	24,799	27,972	3,173
			84	140,718	47,704	52,934	5,230
			85	5,952	1,438	1,561	123
			86	35,722	18,217	19,073	856
	O H		81	186,485	47,245	62,672	15,436
			82	33,102	5,857	7,737	1,880
			84	7,616	2,520	3,197	677
	V E		81	1,585,616	631,576	738,250	106,654

Crop
Product
TSUSA commodity number, description, and unit of quantity

Country	Mode	Reg	Yr	Quantity	F.A.S.	C.I.F.	Charges
			82	1,827,950	762,034	899,022	136,988
			83	819,674	345,085	407,883	62,798
			84	3,184,164	1,387,413	1,643,423	256,010
			85	892,952	419,838	495,354	75,516
			86	3,470,352	1,902,953	2,146,960	244,007
	V	H	81	944,162	309,192	377,395	68,203
			83	30,920	8,321	10,576	2,255
			85	1,004,990	338,868	412,418	73,550
			86	1,060,623	425,710	510,935	85,225
	V	W	81	5,323,049	2,114,314	2,368,232	253,918
			82	2,797,078	1,246,553	1,365,349	118,796
			83	6,034,772	2,616,543	2,888,135	271,592
			84	777,435	377,173	421,095	43,922
			85	5,500,232	2,269,495	2,564,214	294,719
			86	5,754,715	3,046,248	3,328,649	282,401
KOR REP	O	E	83	615	276	278	2
	V	E	81	62,816	18,619	21,425	2,806
			82	41,433	15,015	17,151	2,136
			83	126,678	34,728	42,060	7,332
			84	84,038	23,799	29,477	5,678
			85	65,924	21,791	26,466	4,675
			86	63,627	22,177	25,766	3,589
	V	H	83	9,728	3,601	4,179	578
			84	2,680	790	1,078	288
			85	2,200	2,143	2,420	277
	V	W	81	243,151	76,695	87,500	10,805
			82	289,153	105,582	116,611	11,029
			83	311,296	107,095	120,045	12,950
			84	321,862	117,135	131,893	14,758
			85	697,216	206,342	240,797	34,455
			86	678,197	199,775	225,152	25,377
MALAYSA	V	E	86	7,575	2,082	2,443	361
MEXICO	O	E	81	8,400	11,680	11,680	
			84	43,490	43,832	43,832	
	O	W	83	675	356	356	
	V	E	84	3,600	806	866	60
NETHLDS	O	W	84	3,300	460	487	27
	V	E	81	17,029	18,827	20,629	1,802
			82	21,755	19,700	21,615	1,915
			83	11,043	6,608	8,361	1,753
			84	18,175	8,140	9,396	1,256
			85	25,318	16,344	19,256	2,912
			86	74,603	72,751	78,283	5,532
	V	W	81	18,735	16,694	18,916	2,222
			82	18,874	15,619	17,346	1,727
			83	41,980	31,154	33,503	2,349
			84	36,378	26,258	28,230	1,972
			85	188,351	134,201	146,734	12,533
			86	389,834	344,296	370,127	25,831
NIGERIA	A	E	84	9	652	1,002	350
PHIL R	N	W	83	5,896	2,328	2,862	534
	O	W	85	4,946	2,165	2,386	221
	V	E	81	39,944	15,870	20,563	4,693
			82	78,641	28,642	35,917	7,275
			83	63,027	21,470	26,376	4,906
			84	71,642	25,433	31,204	5,771
			85	62,354	25,371	32,014	6,643
			86	76,208	41,732	49,862	8,130
	V	H	85	317	1,240	1,293	53
	V	W	81	195,906	76,327	92,923	16,596
			82	272,009	106,383	127,330	20,947
			83	345,486	129,836	152,385	22,549
			84	334,071	113,659	135,707	22,048
			85	427,929	160,367	188,690	28,323
			86	435,070	159,257	185,889	26,632
SINGAPR	V	E	81	3,713	2,879	3,354	475
			83	35,405	17,999	24,228	6,229
			84	1,870	1,327	1,495	168
			86	4,375	1,666	1,814	148
	V	W	81	17,088	6,443	7,287	844
			82	31,811	18,031	19,700	1,669
			83	9,859	5,544	6,731	1,187
			84	8,219	2,880	3,380	500
			85	54,000	21,960	24,558	2,598
			86	61,700	20,553	23,678	3,125
SPAIN	V	E	86	23,750	33,704	34,466	762
SWAZLND	V	E	81	160	252	275	23
SWITZLD	V	E	82	1,300	1,760	1,973	213
			85	43,707	16,291	21,410	5,119
			86	82,541	15,185	23,526	8,341
	V	W	81	6,320	12,848	13,525	677
			82	26,346	28,019	30,002	1,983
			84	7,114	3,749	4,096	347
			86	8,580	1,826	2,010	184
SYRIA	V	E	81	5,850	4,432	4,715	283
THAILND	O	E	81	2,160	590	590	
	V	E	81	38,970	14,127	16,113	1,986
			82	21,642	10,581	12,262	1,681
			83	81,760	36,437	43,937	7,500
			84	91,085	34,583	42,736	8,153
			85	38,595	18,770	22,470	3,700
			86	46,297	29,792	36,031	6,239
	V	H	82	2,326	922	1,044	122
			83	1,857	706	814	108
			84	899	394	448	54
	V	W	81	99,642	47,323	51,839	4,516
			82	185,551	110,595	122,791	12,196
			83	316,446	193,717	212,849	19,132
			84	295,168	162,159	177,795	15,636
			85	296,514	133,656	148,683	15,027
			86	312,159	147,145	163,785	16,640
TRINID	A	E	82	1,400	620	1,030	410
U KING	A	W	82	345	332	788	456
	O	E	84	33,180	9,606	11,060	1,454
	V	E	81	206	360	388	28
			84	25,430	8,699	10,536	1,837
			85	35,009	1,716	3,716	2,000
	V	W	83	484	316	454	138
VENEZ	V	E	86	69,750	11,645	13,063	1,418

Soybean

1755000 SOYBEANS (LB)

Country	Mode	Reg	Yr	Quantity	F.A.S.	C.I.F.	Charges
TOTAL			81	18,734,828	2,595,748	2,602,047	6,299
			82	14,195,175	1,461,466	1,464,984	3,518
			83	5,523,221	758,304	762,961	4,657
			84	24,135,394	3,218,980	3,227,736	8,756
			85	9,058,347	968,917	976,002	7,085
			86	39,453,665	5,679,948	5,682,557	2,609
AUSTRAL	V	W	83	1,545	1,918	2,117	199
BELIZE	A	E	82	5,529	2,779	4,806	2,027
	N	E	81	1,554	777	1,388	611
	V	E	83	1,823	925	1,053	128
CANADA	O	E	81	18,611,597	2,546,252	2,546,252	
			82	14,043,421	1,428,757	1,428,763	6
			83	5,467,082	710,266	710,266	
			84	24,036,084	3,169,598	3,169,598	
			85	8,869,569	902,257	902,257	
			86	39,406,812	5,637,994	5,637,994	
	O	W	81	2,500	750	750	
			84	2,520	336	336	
			85	45,953	9,865	9,865	
	V	E	84	44,000	16,409	19,501	3,092
CHILE	A	E	86	10,968	2,488	2,503	15
CHINA M	V	H	84	325	748	876	128
	V	W	84	420	700	763	63
			85	80,366	16,993	18,993	2,000
CHINA T	V	E	85	40,020	18,258	20,841	2,583
	V	H	81	1,500	1,125	1,216	91
			82	3,000	3,020	3,244	224
			83	5,000	3,250	3,708	458
			84	1,000	635	701	66
			86	3,000	1,590	1,744	154
	V	W	84	24,000	10,000	12,550	2,550
			85	3,900	1,950	2,252	302
FR GERM	A	E	83	1,085	316	836	520
			84	22	490	640	150
	O	E	84	2,355	654	875	221
FRANCE	V	E	86	4,806	6,013	6,299	286
HG KONG	V	W	81	5,000	3,210	3,479	269
			82	8,571	3,983	4,227	244
			83	4,258	2,239	2,398	159
			84	11,297	5,490	6,303	813
			85	5,910	2,303	2,609	306
INDIA	V	E	81	44,092	19,795	24,700	4,905
JAPAN	V	E	83	27,125	23,433	24,898	1,465
			86	20,106	22,320	23,628	1,308
	V	H	81	2,094	3,459	3,882	423
			82	5,641	8,923	9,940	1,017
			83	10,011	11,431	12,830	1,399
			84	8,371	12,170	13,642	1,472
			85	10,016	15,024	16,660	1,636
			86	4,500	6,818	7,338	520
	V	W	85	948	1,077	1,210	133
			86	794	1,550	1,706	156
KOR REP	V	E	83	1,452	1,412	1,540	128

Crop Product TSUSA commodity number, description, and unit of quantity Country	Mode	Reg	Yr	Quantity	F.A.S.	C.I.F.	Charges
	V	W	83	1,440	1,939	2,028	89
			85	1,665	1,190	1,315	125
MEXICO	O	E	81	66,491	20,380	20,380	
			82	129,013	14,004	14,004	
SINGAPR	V	W	83	2,400	1,175	1,287	112
			86	2,679	1,175	1,345	170
THAILND	V	E	84	5,000	1,750	1,951	201

Soybean, oil cake and oil-cake meal**
1845200 SOYA,COTTONSD OIL CAKE/MEAL (LB)
(See Cottonseed, oil cake and oil-cake meal under Cotton)

Soybean, prepared or preserved
1410500 SOYBEANS ETC PREP OR PRES (LB)

Country	Mode	Reg	Yr	Quantity	F.A.S.	C.I.F.	Charges
TOTAL			81	737,724	431,469	481,403	49,934
			82	1,062,445	671,290	743,548	72,258
			83	1,116,948	718,611	803,105	84,494
			84	732,467	503,086	566,750	63,664
			85	1,220,421	677,109	767,153	90,044
			86	2,158,818	1,109,326	1,236,008	126,682
BELGIUM	V	E	84	3,086	3,821	4,954	1,133
CANADA	O	E	81	117,000	13,480	13,480	
			82	54,793	4,500	4,500	
			83	19,140	11,817	11,817	
			84	1,675	1,030	1,030	
			86	366,072	40,055	40,055	
CHILE	V	E	83	2,640	1,749	1,981	232
CHINA M	V	E	81	17,695	7,187	8,345	1,158
			82	49,677	24,685	29,803	5,118
			83	36,195	20,282	23,843	3,561
			84	18,917	14,581	17,581	3,000
			85	115,251	43,563	52,076	8,513
			86	349,673	186,151	211,985	25,834
	V	H	82	4,891	2,860	3,144	284
			83	1,190	795	889	94
			84	750	295	321	26
	V	W	81	14,187	7,038	7,513	475
			82	25,906	15,016	16,309	1,293
			83	36,662	19,116	20,436	1,320
			84	18,236	9,980	11,090	1,110
			85	8,925	4,172	4,708	536
			86	6,562	2,017	2,122	105
CHINA T	O	E	84	408	2,110	2,110	
	O	W	85	19,489	5,515	6,497	982
	V	E	81	1,450	1,980	2,138	158
			82	14,872	9,796	10,464	668
			83	51,956	25,325	27,591	2,266
			84	24,400	13,436	14,415	979
			85	50,829	23,791	25,184	1,393
			86	7,978	6,894	7,863	969
	V	H	83	10,899	6,722	8,419	1,697
	V	W	81	121,071	55,106	60,551	5,445
			82	277,936	145,550	166,453	20,903
			83	269,572	134,567	159,186	24,619
			84	63,689	28,474	34,490	6,016
			85	337,288	142,627	170,115	27,488
			86	366,712	183,133	206,286	23,153
DOM REP	A	E	81	308	300	354	54
FR GERM	A	E	84	9,271	7,102	8,030	928
HG KONG	N	E	84	4,903	4,551	5,012	461
	O	E	83	5,600	2,387	2,643	256
	V	E	81	107,025	55,825	63,121	7,296
			82	99,499	53,510	61,606	8,096
			83	87,365	45,058	51,590	6,532
			84	53,430	25,540	30,132	4,592
			85	38,470	19,929	22,872	2,943
			86	117,796	74,414	83,754	9,340
	V	H	81	14,836	7,096	7,546	450
			82	7,350	3,765	4,061	296
			83	19,021	8,076	8,801	725
			84	8,430	3,829	4,301	472
	V	W	81	56,485	26,481	28,251	1,770
			82	87,916	44,190	47,767	3,577
			83	85,371	38,171	40,510	2,339
			84	49,384	21,980	23,645	1,665
			85	34,380	16,158	17,597	1,439
			86	47,740	22,887	24,657	1,770
INDIA	V	W	85	1,411	1,768	2,270	502
INDNSIA	V	W	83	1,538	1,820	2,097	277
ISRAEL	V	E	86	3,864	1,333	1,708	375

Country	Mode	Reg	Yr	Quantity	F.A.S.	C.I.F.	Charges
	V	W	82	44,092	66,777	70,452	3,675
			83	41,888	61,662	64,885	3,223
JAPAN	A	E	81	5	2,500	2,521	21
	N	H	81	17,857	20,204	23,743	3,539
			83	21,901	24,318	28,532	4,214
	O	W	86	1,680	2,946	2,946	
	V	E	81	54,874	69,654	83,280	13,626
			82	79,376	73,931	82,960	9,029
			83	64,492	64,837	74,141	9,304
			84	91,867	77,812	89,155	11,343
			85	61,086	58,084	65,120	7,036
			86	49,325	73,268	80,542	7,274
	V	H	82	19,436	21,585	24,501	2,916
			84	25,601	28,964	33,778	4,814
			85	17,179	19,604	22,054	2,450
			86	19,913	29,131	33,372	4,241
	V	W	81	102,888	115,311	126,249	10,938
			82	151,310	144,878	154,793	9,915
			83	165,556	171,664	185,305	13,641
			84	173,680	174,205	188,727	14,522
			85	221,140	199,907	217,100	17,193
			86	263,373	284,997	302,500	17,503
KOR REP	N	W	86	77,171	22,943	25,575	2,632
	V	E	81	2,450	1,255	1,461	206
			82	9,950	4,625	4,980	355
			83	2,250	1,109	1,198	89
			84	3,011	2,806	3,160	354
			85	2,250	1,151	1,286	135
	V	W	81	17,648	12,479	13,825	1,346
			82	33,673	9,097	10,427	1,330
			83	133,803	46,715	52,535	5,820
			84	61,047	24,284	28,430	4,146
			85	89,117	28,981	31,789	2,808
NETHLDS	O	E	85	11,023	2,806	4,173	1,367
			86	120,000	40,800	47,279	6,479
	V	E	83	2,646	3,358	3,786	428
			84	10,030	8,428	9,663	1,235
			85	77,988	50,464	56,830	6,366
			86	226,448	77,850	96,638	18,788
	V	W	82	794	625	793	168
PHIL R	V	E	85	30	1,029	1,149	120
	V	H	81	640	474	529	55
			83	2,492	1,923	2,209	286
			84	2,826	1,964	2,249	285
	V	W	81	4,259	2,493	2,835	342
			82	5,507	4,649	5,215	566
			83	4,368	2,707	3,170	463
			84	5,447	4,755	5,398	643
			85	1,230	3,794	4,181	387
			86	7,516	7,946	9,251	1,305
PORTUGL	V	E	86	1,368	1,800	2,052	252
SINGAPR	V	E	81	1,078	652	747	95
			82	7,148	4,084	4,544	460
			83	16,045	9,279	10,762	1,483
			84	16,921	11,887	13,305	1,418
			85	12,413	8,001	9,131	1,130
			86	6,303	2,375	2,734	359
	V	W	81	85,968	31,954	34,914	2,960
			82	87,419	36,842	40,418	3,576
			83	20,307	10,560	11,635	1,075
			84	83,803	30,577	35,016	4,439
			85	113,722	42,165	48,680	6,515
			86	85,503	35,419	40,110	4,691
SOLMN I	V	E	85	7,200	3,600	4,341	741
THAILND	V	E	83	12,550	4,222	4,702	480
	V	W	82	900	325	358	33
			83	1,501	372	442	70
			84	1,655	675	758	83
			86	33,821	12,967	14,579	1,612

Soybean, vegetable oil
1765200 SOYBEAN OIL (LB)

Country	Mode	Reg	Yr	Quantity	F.A.S.	C.I.F.	Charges
TOTAL			81	11,081	170,633	174,971	4,338
			82	114,232	25,672	30,211	4,539
			83	69,673	15,911	16,664	753
			84	162,815	72,546	82,477	9,931
			85	26,170,540	6,820,707	7,007,095	186,388
			86	1,870,031	378,082	387,624	9,542
ARGENT	O	E	85	5,337,337	1,399,704	1,448,124	48,420
BRAZIL	O	E	85	8,001,470	2,029,969	2,108,360	78,391
	V	E	84	7,579	1,895	2,623	728

Crop Product TSUSA commodity number, description, and unit of quantity Country	Mode	Reg	Yr	Quantity	F.A.S.	C.I.F.	Charges
			85	39,683	11,176	13,083	1,907
CANADA	O	E	81	1,680	605	726	121
			82	64,065	11,568	11,568	
			83	65,445	10,943	10,943	
			84	40,476	14,065	14,065	
			85	6,495,128	1,841,340	1,841,340	
			86	1,828,968	348,180	348,180	
CHINA M	V	E	83	1,500	2,200	2,341	141
			84	960	1,064	1,147	83
			86	26,270	17,625	19,158	1,533
COLOMB	A	E	86	66	1,051	1,077	26
DENMARK	V	E	84	42,549	16,864	20,287	3,423
DOM REP	A	W	84	767	384	1,097	713
FR GERM	A	E	82	15	1,784	1,866	82
	A	W	82	388	267	620	353
FRANCE	A	E	82	18,885	3,513	6,365	2,852
			83	4	959	1,357	398
			84	154	752	827	75
	V	E	83	443	740	774	34
			85	4,208,028	1,023,380	1,060,490	37,110
HG KONG	V	E	84	14,925	8,300	10,091	1,791
			85	35,913	17,612	20,171	2,559
	V	H	86	5,040	3,658	3,963	305
JAPAN	V	E	81	884	708	879	171
			82	1,346	930	1,035	105
			84	800	650	694	44
			86	441	1,421	1,509	88
	V	H	82	873	478	698	220
			83	315	426	511	85
			84	1,654	1,390	1,863	473
			86	1,089	1,263	1,416	153
	V	W	83	1,966	643	738	95
			84	52,951	27,182	29,783	2,601
KOR REP	V	W	85	1,429	1,528	1,615	87
NETHLDS	V	E	82	28,660	7,132	8,059	927
			85	2,051,552	495,998	513,912	17,914
SWEDEN	A	E	86	8,157	4,884	12,321	7,437
	V	E	81	7,937	168,087	171,646	3,559
SWITZLD	A	E	81	580	1,233	1,720	487

Spearmint

Spearmint, essential oil
4528035 SPEARMINT (LB)

Country	Mode	Reg	Yr	Quantity	F.A.S.	C.I.F.	Charges
TOTAL			81	61,796	418,207	427,741	9,534
			82	104,811	618,212	631,927	13,715
			83	57,393	330,063	338,210	8,147
			84	166,093	901,973	933,121	31,148
			85	26,823	163,438	167,539	4,101
			86	25,074	172,114	175,079	2,965
CANADA	O	E	84	385	830	830	
CHINA M	N	E	83	33,874	157,206	162,492	5,286
			85	13,393	80,419	83,585	3,166
	V	E	81	4,277	21,134	21,840	706
			82	23,776	109,501	113,208	3,707
			84	139,739	697,226	722,987	25,761
			85	11,138	69,020	69,570	550
			86	9,027	48,260	49,164	904
	V	W	81	56,133	393,537	401,949	8,412
			82	81,035	508,711	518,719	10,008
			83	20,491	132,301	134,482	2,181
			84	19,414	144,132	146,823	2,691
			85	418	3,228	3,277	49
			86	16,047	123,854	125,915	2,061
FR GERM	A	E	84	2,410	33,035	34,952	1,917
HG KONG	V	W	84	2,183	16,916	17,198	282
IRELAND	V	E	83	2,028	31,252	31,393	141
JAPAN	V	E	83	200	2,104	2,211	107
	V	W	84	1,874	8,287	8,543	256
			85	1,874	10,771	11,107	336
SINGAPR	V	W	81	1,386	3,536	3,952	416
U KING	A	E	84	88	1,547	1,788	241
	O	E	83	800	7,200	7,632	432

Spinach

Spinach, seed
1268100 SPINACH SEED (LB)

Country	Mode	Reg	Yr	Quantity	F.A.S.	C.I.F.	Charges
TOTAL			81	35,108	41,733	47,964	6,231
			82	41,149	48,481	57,253	8,772
			83	237,391	235,270	252,507	17,237
			84	400,248	585,180	622,204	37,024
			85	370,486	538,046	574,068	36,022
			86	430,881	627,996	653,958	25,962
BELGIUM	V	E	82	2,500	2,912	3,254	342
			83	2,000	4,777	5,222	445
CANADA	O	W	83	129,880	40,084	40,084	
			84	118,840	41,978	41,978	
			85	104,700	31,410	31,410	
			86	58,000	24,360	24,360	
CHINA M	V	E	83	90	551	558	7
	V	W	81	150	313	325	12
			83	50	266	275	9
			85	550	1,059	1,096	37
CHINA T	V	W	83	2,180	2,720	2,777	57
DENMARK	A	E	86	1,000	1,380	1,859	479
	A	W	84	1,286	1,019	2,124	1,105
	V	E	81	2,900	3,004	3,354	350
			82	1,500	1,508	1,704	196
			85	1,500	1,642	2,212	570
	V	W	84	6,750	4,006	4,822	816
			86	21,025	26,560	28,349	1,789
FR GERM	V	E	85	1,500	6,430	6,860	430
	V	W	82	8,500	5,260	6,644	1,384
FRANCE	V	E	81	1,000	1,541	1,695	154
			82	4,543	2,662	2,851	189
	V	W	82	1,101	1,673	1,934	261
			83	2,200	2,941	3,214	273
HG KONG	V	W	81	390	633	675	42
			82	481	352	367	15
			83	440	3,097	3,143	46
INDIA	A	E	81	125	500	565	65
			83	100	650	989	339
JAPAN	A	W	82	806	1,531	3,308	1,777
			83	1,564	3,044	6,310	3,266
			84	132	258	677	419
			85	543	1,011	2,371	1,360
	V	W	81	5,120	4,608	5,688	1,080
			82	581	527	610	83
			84	2,297	4,384	4,958	574
N ZEAL	V	E	82	1,100	1,528	1,821	293
NETHLDS	A	E	81	1,090	2,772	3,464	692
			82	2,042	2,633	3,706	1,073
			83	1,000	2,109	2,531	422
			84	3,527	5,218	7,357	2,139
	A	W	84	132	397	685	288
	N	E	81	2,094	2,099	2,798	699
			85	1,365	3,724	4,342	618
	N	W	84	150,553	299,660	319,856	20,196
			85	151,816	295,802	316,976	21,174
	O	E	81	1,123	3,014	3,182	168
			82	5,500	7,220	7,953	733
			83	12,160	18,228	19,889	1,661
			84	23,100	38,649	41,996	3,347
			86	113,400	66,250	66,450	200
	V	E	81	3,000	4,429	4,965	536
			82	4,900	9,941	10,917	976
			83	45,525	97,422	102,643	5,221
			84	72,827	175,523	181,113	5,590
			85	77,110	174,656	182,299	7,643
			86	30,479	82,622	86,634	4,012
	V	W	81	15,150	15,927	17,872	1,945
			82	7,595	10,734	12,184	1,450
			83	36,290	55,304	60,228	4,924
			84	14,716	10,190	12,114	1,924
			85	31,402	22,312	26,502	4,190
			86	206,857	416,878	435,743	18,865
REP SAF	V	E	83	220	600	608	8
SINGAPR	V	E	81	90	319	325	6
SPAIN	V	E	81	2,240	873	1,040	167
SWEDEN	V	W	84	6,000	3,598	4,173	575
U KING	A	E	81	35	318	433	115
			86	98	8,628	9,224	596
	N	E	81	601	1,383	1,583	200
	O	E	84	88	300	351	51

Crop
Product
TSUSA commodity number, description, and unit of quantity

Country	Mode	Reg	Yr	Quantity	F.A.S.	C.I.F.	Charges
	V	E	86	22	1,318	1,339	21
	V	E	83	3,692	3,477	4,036	559

Spruce

Spruce, lumber

2020320 LUMBER, SPRUCE, ROUGH ETC. (MBF)

Country	Mode	Reg	Yr	Quantity	F.A.S.	C.I.F.	Charges
TOTAL			81	59,485	13,044,481	13,074,606	30,151
			82	69,558	14,079,244	14,379,554	300,310
			83	65,293	14,122,075	14,795,035	672,960
			84	82,037	16,932,159	17,783,890	851,731
			85	95,016	19,482,843	21,440,700	1,957,857
			86	121,965	23,912,286	26,518,723	2,606,437
ANTIGUA	V	E	86	78	19,322	24,598	5,276
BELGIUM	V	E	86	6	8,540	9,287	747
BRAZIL	N	W	82	*	400	1,078	678
	V	E	81	39	18,500	25,330	6,830
			84	443	30,914	34,999	4,085
			85	153	61,550	87,424	25,874
			86	984	515,915	677,785	161,870
CANADA	N	E	85	10,492	2,071,083	2,757,905	686,822
	N	W	82	10,808	3,108,604	3,108,976	372
			83	16,117	3,750,985	3,751,084	99
			84	17,986	4,906,005	4,906,258	253
			86	32,191	7,092,029	7,173,626	81,597
	O	E	81	42,717	8,505,663	8,505,637	
			82	48,235	8,823,473	8,828,948	5,475
			83	37,532	7,566,466	7,566,466	
			84	36,036	7,436,757	7,436,777	20
			85	36,683	7,371,600	7,374,715	3,115
			86	42,940	8,686,522	8,686,522	
	O	W	81	15,569	4,392,211	4,392,211	
			82	812	140,514	140,514	
			83	640	120,425	120,425	
			84	4,056	584,505	584,505	
			85	26,886	5,148,947	5,149,798	851
			86	864	83,628	83,884	256
	V	E	81	69	14,599	18,845	4,246
			82	9,133	1,911,398	2,165,333	253,935
			83	10,857	2,615,436	3,281,837	666,401
			84	23,213	3,872,664	4,689,986	817,322
			85	19,454	4,424,511	5,573,114	1,148,603
			86	44,295	7,365,699	9,716,247	2,350,548
	V	W	81	704	79,063	93,909	14,846
			82	281	33,734	37,059	3,325
			83	106	13,829	15,023	1,194
			84	102	19,259	21,459	2,200
			85	197	28,881	30,860	1,979
CHINA T	V	E	84	59	16,819	23,699	6,880
COLOMB	V	E	85	175	50,301	55,839	5,538
ECUADOR	V	E	82	10	7,196	8,129	933
	V	W	82	100	6,900	8,562	1,662
FR GERM	A	E	81	1	391	396	5
			82	1	554	566	12
			83	1	390	399	9
	N	E	86	*	1,400	1,574	174
	N	W	81	*	3,688	4,111	423
			84	*	432	469	37
			85	*	2,191	2,272	81
	O	E	83	2	1,259	1,793	534
			84	4	7,756	8,740	984
	V	E	81	177	2,598	2,670	72
			83	2	1,388	1,528	140
			84	1	1,536	1,868	332
			85	15	45,333	48,594	3,261
			86	318	67,226	70,761	3,535
	V	W	81	158	4,938	6,680	1,742
			84	1	1,933	2,578	645
FRANCE	O	E	81	18	3,090	3,090	
GABON	O	E	85	17	4,752	4,752	
	V	E	85	887	167,547	213,321	45,774
			86	277	66,006	67,640	1,634
GUATMAL	V	E	86	12	5,999	6,799	800
HG KONG	V	E	84	8	1,917	4,388	2,471
	V	W	83	7	13,897	14,897	1,000
INDNSIA	V	E	84	128	51,662	68,164	16,502
	V	W	83	18	10,783	12,815	2,032
JAPAN	V	W	81	17	10,558	11,214	656
MEXICO	O	E	83	2	829	829	

Country	Mode	Reg	Yr	Quantity	F.A.S.	C.I.F.	Charges
PERU	V	E	85	57	106,147	142,106	35,959
REP SAF	V	W	82	102	36,389	68,522	32,133
SINGAPR	V	W	83	9	26,388	27,939	1,551
SWITZLD	V	E	82	76	10,082	11,867	1,785
U KING	V	E	81	16	9,182	10,513	1,331

2020340 LUMBER SPRUCE, DRESSED ETC. (MBF)

Country	Mode	Reg	Yr	Quantity	F.A.S.	C.I.F.	Charges
TOTAL			81	5,951,255	1,112,497,543	1,114,471,341	1,954,774
			82	6,271,635	1,020,517,968	1,023,758,259	3,240,291
			83	8,289,080	1,611,123,708	1,616,180,844	5,057,136
			84	9,389,388	1,730,684,142	1,735,634,656	4,950,514
			85	10,298,342	1,864,865,396	1,872,848,900	7,983,504
			86	10,267,108	1,949,877,853	1,968,343,479	18,465,626
ANTIGUA	V	E	86	49	13,922	17,242	3,320
AUSTRIA	V	E	83	1	455	491	36
BELGIUM	O	E	81	120	30,000	30,000	
			84	25	4,737	4,737	
BRAZIL	V	E	81	69	52,277	65,908	13,631
			82	37	30,072	38,680	8,608
			83	63	4,327	5,599	1,272
			85	11	6,302	7,791	1,489
			86	98	50,536	59,340	8,804
CANADA	N	E	81	1,162	223,869	245,691	21,822
			82	1,348,664	249,114,890	249,700,718	585,828
			83	545,854	109,463,497	110,778,313	1,314,816
			84	3,470,474	728,669,812	728,843,395	173,583
			85	4,175,630	881,968,087	887,316,113	5,348,026
			86	3,565,181	755,043,608	758,823,997	3,780,389
	N	H	83	390	156,994	172,516	15,522
	N	W	81	588,652	91,302,906	92,627,855	1,303,022
			82	526,227	76,315,895	77,499,135	1,183,240
			83	673,760	118,849,902	121,346,632	2,496,730
			84	758,834	125,343,453	126,837,158	1,493,705
			85	1,022,848	164,527,351	165,369,380	842,029
			86	904,191	157,711,258	163,715,149	6,003,891
	O	E	81	5,270,936	1,004,161,157	1,004,479,537	321,283
			82	4,256,229	673,282,352	673,380,329	97,977
			83	6,914,006	1,354,060,662	1,354,867,935	807,273
			84	4,817,291	815,814,035	815,849,936	35,901
			85	4,717,314	749,312,812	749,430,190	117,378
			86	5,351,342	955,820,544	958,968,167	3,147,623
	O	H	82	106	19,679	19,679	
			86	21	3,587	3,587	
	O	W	81	81,865	15,341,701	15,341,701	
			82	120,414	17,967,559	17,980,353	12,794
			83	148,802	27,306,740	27,306,740	
			84	252,360	45,776,523	45,776,523	
			85	329,018	57,262,462	57,262,472	10
			86	322,674	58,636,559	58,718,736	82,177
	V	E	81	7,036	1,052,419	1,340,491	288,072
			82	18,806	3,463,351	4,808,118	1,344,767
			83	5,226	1,032,306	1,437,209	404,903
			84	85,016	13,880,114	17,010,425	3,130,311
			85	42,222	9,506,233	11,116,334	1,610,101
			86	119,635	21,837,467	27,267,931	5,430,464
	V	W	83	82	17,997	19,469	1,472
			84	182	3,094	3,094	
			85	559	89,863	92,876	3,013
CHILE	V	E	85	270	129,233	162,131	32,898
			86	46	23,985	27,883	3,898
CHINA M	O	E	84	159	31,375	31,375	
			85	6,348	1,150,701	1,150,701	
			86	819	132,787	132,787	
CHINA T	O	E	81	32	6,509	6,509	
			82	53	8,138	8,138	
	V	W	86	3	8,812	9,819	1,007
COCOS I	O	E	86	26	7,231	7,231	
COLOMB	O	E	84	769	108,289	108,289	
			85	420	102,424	102,424	
	V	E	85	90	7,894	15,660	7,766
CZECHO	O	E	85	66	13,050	13,050	
			86	5	1,172	1,172	
DENMARK	V	E	81	53	57,109	63,630	6,521
			83	18	27,628	30,727	3,099
			84	38	56,873	63,752	6,879
ECUADOR	O	W	83	63	10,797	10,797	
FINLAND	V	E	84	3,029	545,190	568,646	23,456
			86	114	15,624	17,658	2,034
FR GERM	A	W	82	1	739	843	104
	N	E	81	*	844	1,015	171
			83	*	1,327	1,391	64
	O	E	81	82	18,758	18,889	131
			82	87	23,753	23,939	186

Crop
Product
TSUSA commodity number, description, and unit of quantity

Country	Mode	Reg	Yr	Quantity	F.A.S.	C.I.F.	Charges
			83	24	5,980	5,980	
			84	15	38,220	39,108	888
			85	25	4,500	4,500	
			86	53	53,236	54,508	1,272
	O	W	82	27	6,353	6,353	
	V	E	81	1	20,975	21,096	121
			82	3	1,850	2,467	617
			83	1	1,876	1,940	64
			84	190	85,017	102,442	17,425
			85	1	1,082	1,164	82
			86	314	5,238	5,673	435
	V	W	82	1	566	619	53
			83	3	2,902	2,991	89
FRANCE	O	E	81	130	23,406	23,406	
			82	110	19,539	19,539	
			83	27	8,064	8,064	
			85	26	7,006	7,006	
			86	27	6,880	6,880	
GABON	O	E	85	94	20,090	20,090	
			86	279	56,966	56,966	
	O	W	85	57	10,103	10,103	
GHANA	V	W	84	291	120,202	168,879	48,677
HONDURA	V	E	82	65	26,574	32,691	6,117
			83	72	28,644	36,992	8,348
			84	60	22,521	30,022	7,501
			85	139	140,392	157,892	17,500
INDIA	O	E	82	110	35,835	35,835	
			85	27	6,720	6,720	
			86	111	25,963	25,963	
INDNSIA	V	W	84	58	50,557	54,333	3,776
ISRAEL	A	W	86	1	1,382	1,694	312
	O	E	84	26	4,353	4,353	
ITALY	O	E	81	132	23,316	23,316	
			82	22	3,613	3,613	
			85	201	45,377	45,377	
			86	286	66,615	66,615	
	O	W	86	65	9,974	9,974	
IVY CST	O	E	83	8	12,392	12,392	
JAPAN	A	H	85	1	5,623	6,851	1,228
	O	E	81	99	15,611	15,611	
			82	34	10,501	10,501	
			83	21	2,566	2,566	
			85	28	5,210	5,210	
			86	119	23,442	23,442	
KIRIBAT	O	E	85	27	7,585	7,585	
			86	25	4,164	4,164	
KOR REP	O	E	81	149	27,087	27,087	
			83	45	4,692	4,692	
LAOS	O	E	86	316	55,325	55,325	
MALAYSA	V	W	83	7	7,071	7,196	125
MEXICO	O	E	82	30	10,153	10,153	
			83	421	61,366	61,366	
			84	54	10,836	10,836	
			85	32	4,057	4,057	
			86	28	4,706	4,706	
	O	W	84	44	9,351	9,351	
			86	10	2,408	2,408	
MOROC	O	E	85	886	152,286	152,286	
			86	329	72,980	72,980	
N CALDN	O	E	85	168	28,304	28,304	
			86	44	9,575	9,575	
N ZEAL	V	E	83	8	12,885	15,948	3,063
NETHLDS	O	E	82	23	2,761	2,761	
			83	61	15,064	15,064	
			85	26	7,711	7,711	
PANAMA	O	E	85	83	15,872	15,872	
			86	105	18,330	18,330	
PHIL R	V	E	85	15	7,969	9,953	1,984
REP SAF	O	E	81	279	53,803	53,803	
			82	557	166,505	166,505	
			83	99	21,582	21,582	
			84	164	38,180	38,180	
			85	102	23,493	23,493	
			86	225	52,494	52,494	
ROMANIA	O	E	81	53	12,137	12,137	
S ARAB	O	E	85	30	5,925	5,925	
SINGAPR	O	E	86	84	19,000	19,000	
SPAIN	O	E	81	27	5,425	5,425	
			85	22	1,979	1,979	
	V	E	84	96	12,712	21,124	8,412
SRI LKA	O	E	86	24	4,125	4,125	
SWEDEN	O	E	81	47	8,682	8,682	
SWITZLD	A	E	83	1	341	601	260
	O	E	81	27	5,480	5,480	
			85	68	5,413	5,413	
U KING	O	E	81	201	35,320	35,320	
			82	29	7,290	7,290	
			83	17	5,651	5,651	
			84	25	4,000	4,000	
			85	277	46,570	46,570	
			86	224	28,725	28,725	
	O	W	84	99	26,605	26,605	
USSR	O	E	85	1,211	235,717	235,717	
			86	145	26,568	26,568	
	O	W	84	89	28,093	28,093	
			86	90	22,665	22,665	
YEMEN A	O	E	81	103	18,752	18,752	

Spruce, pulpwood, logs
2003553 SPRUCE PULPWOOD LOGS (CD)

Country	Mode	Reg	Yr	Quantity	F.A.S.	C.I.F.	Charges
TOTAL			81	33,485	1,965,139	1,985,337	20,180
			82	15,992	722,489	722,849	360
			83	25,568	1,176,344	1,176,344	
			84	52,662	2,406,448	2,406,451	3
			85	5,102	241,717	241,717	
			86	5,630	436,075	436,075	
CANADA	O	E	81	32,474	1,862,555	1,868,552	5,979
			82	15,969	719,571	719,931	360
			83	25,568	1,176,344	1,176,344	
			84	52,646	2,405,488	2,405,491	3
			85	4,287	193,142	193,142	
			86	5,630	436,075	436,075	
	O	W	84	16	960	960	
	V	W	81	1,011	102,584	116,785	14,201
			82	23	2,918	2,918	
			85	815	48,575	48,575	

Squash

Squash, fresh or frozen
1375000 SQUASH, FRSH, CHILLED, FROZN (LB)

Country	Mode	Reg	Yr	Quantity	F.A.S.	C.I.F.	Charges
TOTAL			81	80,795,451	22,169,841	22,196,807	28,117
			82	104,209,429	24,353,058	24,383,967	30,909
			83	114,615,705	26,974,856	27,005,048	30,192
			84	133,208,518	24,130,206	24,450,017	319,811
			85	122,055,330	23,077,228	23,401,344	324,116
			86	126,193,772	20,512,134	20,930,008	417,874
BAHAMAS	A	E	82	3,000	480	844	364
	N	E	81	33,700	4,525	5,895	1,370
BELIZE	A	E	86	108,760	66,028	80,858	14,830
C RICA	N	E	83	53,022	6,391	8,465	2,074
	V	E	82	30,479	2,400	4,296	1,896
			83	38,512	3,745	6,006	2,261
			84	233,538	28,904	42,910	14,006
			85	544,183	79,675	114,056	34,381
			86	882,337	103,272	165,425	62,153
	V	W	81	110,374	35,690	45,964	10,274
			85	39,657	10,842	17,223	6,381
CANADA	O	E	81	220,486	26,119	26,119	
			82	130,690	29,498	29,498	
			83	61,000	15,817	15,817	
			84	246,941	45,462	45,462	
			85	59,285	8,213	8,213	
			86	8,000	2,103	2,103	
	O	W	81	16,575	1,658	1,658	
			83	35,680	10,996	10,996	
			84	30,059	6,201	6,201	
			86	32,664	7,934	7,934	
	V	E	85	5,952	1,200	2,100	900
CHILE	A	E	86	36,900	31,458	59,393	27,935
	A	W	86	12,480	10,992	20,052	9,060
	V	W	82	7,302	994	2,816	1,822
CHINA M	V	E	82	2,625	4,462	4,932	470
DOM REP	A	E	81	49,742	5,799	10,666	4,867
			83	10,040	1,430	2,410	980
	A	W	82	575	1,260	1,518	258
	N	E	82	237,241	28,765	45,667	16,902
			83	248,568	29,295	45,760	16,465
			84	3,652,926	635,752	857,207	221,455
			85	1,995,953	318,172	439,341	121,169
			86	529,250	66,774	93,908	27,134

Crop
Product
TSUSA commodity number, description, and unit of quantity

Country	Mode	Reg	Yr	Quantity	F.A.S.	C.I.F.	Charges
	V	E	82	7,042	1,200	1,624	424
			83	14,100	1,410	2,079	669
			84	414,740	54,157	76,461	22,304
			85	305,846	43,009	58,220	15,211
			86	552,195	81,568	112,942	31,374
	V	W	84	7,600	1,444	1,838	394
DOMINCA	A	E	85	11,200	1,656	3,018	1,362
	V	E	86	166,450	23,308	35,721	12,413
FRANCE	A	E	82	5,410	979	1,756	777
	O	W	83	7,380	2,340	2,340	
			85	112,158	20,851	20,851	
			86	17,712	2,160	2,160	
	V	E	81	35,000	3,500	5,043	1,543
GUATMAL	V	E	83	3,894	1,324	1,477	153
			84	19,940	14,058	15,014	956
GUYANA	V	E	82	11,000	1,695	2,445	750
HAITI	V	E	86	14,880	2,605	3,471	866
HG KONG	O	W	86	63,779	11,080	11,080	
	V	E	83	384	630	665	35
HONDURA	A	E	81	6,738	597	1,397	800
	V	E	85	21,560	8,624	11,321	2,697
			86	15,200	1,600	2,900	1,300
ISRAEL	V	E	86	14,550	5,700	7,070	1,370
JAMAICA	A	E	81	647	355	518	163
			82	43,550	3,000	6,960	3,960
			85	177,405	29,434	36,382	6,948
			86	16,732	10,351	13,548	3,197
	N	E	83	116,386	11,067	18,622	7,555
			84	427,058	94,301	149,694	55,393
			85	770,593	294,785	411,201	116,416
			86	1,438,160	300,194	463,120	162,926
	V	E	81	50,000	11,517	16,250	4,733
JAPAN	V	W	81	656	639	674	35
			82	438	344	357	13
			84	1,094	790	889	99
MALAYSA	O	W	85	8,080	2,020	2,020	
			86	89,110	13,875	13,875	
MEXICO	O	E	81	6,089,114	483,851	483,851	
			82	4,134,474	271,201	271,201	
			83	8,266,831	516,314	516,314	
			84	10,401,280	659,560	659,841	281
			85	4,440,774	345,301	345,481	180
			86	7,662,370	513,337	513,337	
	O	W	81	74,181,729	21,595,009	21,597,938	4,080
			82	99,593,168	24,006,015	24,008,751	2,736
			83	105,759,908	26,374,097	26,374,097	
			84	117,734,119	22,582,652	22,582,659	7
			85	113,011,208	21,856,953	21,856,968	15
			86	113,935,914	19,117,147	19,123,707	6,560
MOZAMBQ	O	W	85	47,784	12,022	12,022	
			86	67,256	10,593	10,593	
N ZEAL	A	W	81	690	582	834	252
	V	H	84	37,038	5,925	10,752	4,827
			85	503,692	44,471	62,927	18,456
			86	432,903	101,472	149,744	48,272
NETHLDS	A	E	86	2,314	2,850	3,278	428
PANAMA	N	E	86	65,695	17,571	23,678	6,107
S VN GR	V	E	86	1,122	1,112	1,741	629
THAILND	V	W	82	75	269	280	11
			84	2,185	1,000	1,089	89
			86	2,094	1,050	1,121	71
TRINID	A	E	82	2,360	496	1,022	526
	V	E	86	24,945	6,000	7,249	1,249

Strawberry

Strawberry, fresh or in brine

1465800 STRAWBERRY, 6/15-9/15, INCL (LB)

Country	Mode	Reg	Yr	Quantity	F.A.S.	C.I.F.	Charges
TOTAL			81	1,281,931	629,027	629,189	162
			82	1,509,842	898,115	898,620	505
			83	806,974	218,099	218,713	614
			84	469,627	202,173	205,846	3,673
			85	690,276	316,641	323,744	7,103
			86	234,544	149,430	149,430	
BELGIUM	A	E	84	176	338	404	66
	V	E	83	540	353	404	51
BRAZIL	O	W	82	121,200	83,022	83,022	
CANADA	A	E	81	386	1,085	1,247	162
	O	E	81	675,745	274,962	274,962	

Country	Mode	Reg	Yr	Quantity	F.A.S.	C.I.F.	Charges
			82	620,369	285,749	285,749	
			83	757,643	194,479	194,479	
			84	463,810	196,203	196,203	
			85	392,034	164,203	164,203	
			86	125,780	73,078	73,078	
	O	W	81	605,800	352,980	352,980	
			82	763,500	523,358	523,358	
			83	43,200	18,576	18,576	
			85	263,945	129,022	129,022	
			86	100,800	70,560	70,560	
CHILE	A	E	84	1,978	1,814	4,229	2,415
ECUADOR	A	E	83	2,205	900	1,203	303
			84	1,386	630	904	274
			85	25,473	16,015	20,783	4,768
FRANCE	A	E	84	616	388	573	185
GUATMAL	A	E	84	1,000	1,000	1,280	280
MEXICO	A	W	85	7,143	4,212	5,352	1,140
	O	W	86	7,964	5,792	5,792	
N ZEAL	A	W	84	661	1,800	2,253	453
			85	647	1,050	1,645	595
NETHLDS	A	E	82	60	353	395	42
SPAIN	A	E	85	1,034	2,139	2,739	600
SWITZLD	V	E	83	3,386	3,791	4,051	260
U KING	V	E	82	4,713	5,633	6,096	463

1466000 STRAWBERRIES, FRSH O IN BRNE (LB)

Country	Mode	Reg	Yr	Quantity	F.A.S.	C.I.F.	Charges
TOTAL			**81**	**5,385,680**	**3,741,153**	**4,164,601**	**423,448**
			82	**2,950,741**	**3,007,667**	**3,828,571**	**820,904**
			83	**4,311,891**	**3,962,734**	**4,816,374**	**853,640**
			84	**8,327,247**	**6,598,859**	**8,252,443**	**1,653,584**
			85	**9,433,278**	**6,947,225**	**8,819,496**	**1,872,271**
			86	**12,589,213**	**7,042,734**	**8,275,272**	**1,232,538**
ARGENT	A	E	84	3,897	2,752	5,616	2,864
			85	2,427	3,103	5,112	2,009
			86	2,006	1,644	2,646	1,002
	A	W	86	8,185	1,500	4,278	2,778
AUSTRAL	A	E	82	1,515	3,888	5,752	1,864
			84	1,510	3,144	5,200	2,056
	A	H	82	3,735	5,433	9,790	4,357
			85	1,143	3,657	5,387	1,730
	A	W	82	2,258	3,290	4,364	1,074
			83	1,799	10,012	11,212	1,200
			84	4,595	13,085	14,709	1,624
			85	20,213	29,454	46,009	16,555
			86	2,352	6,934	9,446	2,512
AUSTRIA	A	E	84	2,000	7,410	10,998	3,588
	A	W	84	2,480	4,082	5,390	1,308
BELGIUM	A	E	83	665	1,596	1,845	249
	A	W	83	2,856	6,535	8,090	1,555
C RICA	A	E	83	1,995	1,390	2,072	682
			84	6,454	5,258	6,689	1,431
			85	10,852	12,841	15,209	2,368
			86	193,853	157,063	205,806	48,743
	A	W	84	6,001	6,457	9,039	2,582
			85	915	1,300	1,558	258
	V	E	83	59,520	14,880	15,980	1,100
CANADA	A	E	81	129	726	947	221
	A	W	86	8,700	3,910	4,468	558
	O	E	81	2,400	1,133	1,133	
			82	790	316	316	
			83	14,858	6,842	6,842	
			84	166,400	122,800	122,800	
			85	6,600	3,174	3,174	
			86	44,160	43,800	43,800	
	O	W	82	595	1,573	1,573	
			83	425	1,229	1,229	
			85	123,516	38,408	38,408	
			86	43,200	27,945	27,945	
CHILE	A	E	82	11,890	11,945	19,721	7,776
			83	52,116	45,435	94,553	49,118
			84	47,046	39,290	81,629	42,339
			85	36,861	28,508	57,930	29,422
			86	6,570	4,476	10,274	5,798
	A	W	83	1,488	998	1,943	945
			84	3,998	3,878	7,153	3,275
	O	E	83	3,720	8,928	8,928	
CHINA T	V	E	84	220	298	359	61
COLOMB	A	E	85	1,323	1,500	1,790	290
	V	E	84	105,847	25,382	34,135	8,753
DOM REP	V	E	86	9,600	2,835	3,540	705
ECUADOR	A	E	83	42,814	21,729	29,969	8,240
			84	82,841	55,990	74,678	18,688
			85	449,073	323,710	430,067	106,357

Crop / Product / TSUSA commodity number, description, and unit of quantity Country	Mode	Reg	Yr	Quantity	F.A.S.	C.I.F.	Charges
			86	97,985	101,205	116,425	15,220
	V	W	85	215,002	15,000	20,070	5,070
FRANCE	A	E	81	35	646	750	104
			82	258	1,174	1,318	144
			83	658	8,300	8,822	522
			84	88	280	313	33
			86	88	1,429	1,530	101
	V	E	83	9,259	7,241	9,045	1,804
			84	41,667	29,410	36,684	7,274
GUATMAL	A	E	81	52,710	30,902	46,823	15,921
			82	3,405	3,565	4,880	1,315
			84	5,102	4,889	5,736	847
			85	40,683	6,840	16,617	9,777
			86	137,933	32,346	78,494	46,148
	A	W	86	59,192	10,848	31,854	21,006
ISRAEL	A	E	82	5,292	3,600	16,207	12,607
			83	3,885	2,979	11,325	8,346
			84	32,918	33,240	135,208	101,968
			85	57,058	45,110	176,935	131,825
	V	E	81	2,754	1,667	1,986	319
JAPAN	A	H	84	153	340	687	347
	A	W	82	1,457	2,666	3,888	1,222
MEXICO	A	E	81	13,308	5,128	9,048	3,920
			82	31,159	16,331	27,387	11,056
			83	29,117	14,757	19,529	4,772
			84	180,305	153,084	189,871	36,787
			85	147,621	77,734	120,981	43,247
			86	174,772	178,380	215,099	36,719
	A	W	81	74,935	83,467	91,849	8,382
			82	14,847	18,624	21,594	2,970
			83	445	324	799	475
			84	29,686	22,510	27,781	5,271
			85	186,466	93,995	120,430	26,435
			86	96,858	27,825	43,240	15,415
	O	E	81	4,455,853	2,082,269	2,082,269	
			82	1,708,898	675,060	683,938	8,878
			83	2,967,729	1,485,337	1,485,337	
			84	5,757,528	2,482,357	2,482,357	
			85	5,380,386	2,075,388	2,075,390	2
			86	3,898,215	1,024,076	1,024,076	
	O	W	81	69,195	48,608	48,608	
			82	19,635	8,004	8,004	
			83	20,974	13,824	13,824	
			84	123,970	64,278	64,278	
			85	994,457	505,849	505,849	
			86	6,528,847	3,004,456	3,004,456	
MOZAMBQ	A	H	86	1,361	2,600	5,250	2,650
	A	W	85	5,227	1,728	2,488	760
N ZEAL	A	E	81	49,899	109,350	149,578	40,228
			82	167,529	363,644	499,148	135,504
			83	158,962	333,796	470,476	136,680
			84	227,564	386,801	561,438	174,637
			85	57,739	128,056	193,203	65,147
			86	20,722	38,098	63,567	25,469
	A	H	81	39,298	76,239	94,310	18,071
			82	45,505	90,274	113,254	22,980
			83	40,471	79,378	102,974	23,596
			84	53,814	101,836	133,785	31,949
			85	72,035	146,960	209,366	62,406
			86	128,161	232,703	359,721	127,018
	A	W	81	617,224	1,275,490	1,611,772	336,282
			82	765,089	1,452,443	1,954,697	502,254
			83	807,790	1,727,628	2,297,814	570,186
			84	1,399,384	2,928,992	4,111,291	1,182,299
			85	1,597,337	3,324,648	4,685,384	1,360,736
			86	1,053,590	2,070,358	2,936,171	865,813
	N	W	82	148,817	294,426	400,323	105,897
			83	79,652	155,712	197,788	42,076
			84	29,233	72,212	93,880	21,668
	O	W	81	7,940	25,528	25,528	
			82	15,044	45,488	45,488	
			84	8,689	15,894	15,894	
			85	11,306	33,073	34,572	1,499
			86	330	1,205	1,205	
NAMIBIA	A	H	85	1,416	2,509	3,950	1,441
NETHLDS	A	E	86	2,503	5,723	8,000	2,277
	A	W	84	3,263	12,046	13,621	1,575
			86	4,296	10,841	15,222	4,381
PANAMA	A	E	86	11,783	22,220	23,089	869
PERU	A	E	85	1,808	2,952	4,337	1,385
PHIL R	V	W	83	650	508	569	61
REP SAF	A	E	82	1,044	2,106	2,948	842
SPAIN	A	E	84	594	864	1,224	360
			85	3,026	25,808	28,340	2,532

Crop / Product / TSUSA commodity number, description, and unit of quantity Country	Mode	Reg	Yr	Quantity	F.A.S.	C.I.F.	Charges
			86	3,972	7,185	10,003	2,818
	V	E	86	44,000	18,329	22,440	4,111
SWITZLD	V	E	82	1,979	3,817	3,981	164
THAILND	V	E	85	8,788	15,920	16,940	1,020
			86	5,979	2,800	3,227	427
	V	W	83	2,998	2,250	2,404	154
U KING	V	E	83	7,000	11,126	13,005	1,879

Strawberry, frozen
1467625 STRAWBERRIES FROZN NOV 40OZ (LB)

Country	Mode	Reg	Yr	Quantity	F.A.S.	C.I.F.	Charges
TOTAL			81	3,425,412	1,595,747	1,651,123	55,376
			82	633,476	269,450	277,267	7,817
			83	1,579,121	596,198	629,063	32,865
			84	1,826,532	618,325	629,815	11,490
			85	2,326,420	686,802	771,981	85,179
			86	2,002,605	794,044	1,011,926	217,882
BRAZIL	V	E	85	19,841	6,349	8,446	2,097
C RICA	A	E	84	2,086	2,525	3,051	526
CANADA	O	E	82	450	362	362	
	O	W	84	35,625	2,795	2,795	
			85	90,690	43,602	43,602	
			86	25,980	12,475	12,475	
CHILE	V	E	83	42,960	19,684	26,252	6,568
			85	213,311	85,109	108,955	23,846
			86	81,150	26,566	36,566	10,000
ECUADOR	V	E	85	505,638	140,631	190,077	49,446
			86	1,345,895	507,787	670,704	162,917
FR GERM	V	E	82	39,198	19,800	23,458	3,658
FRANCE	V	E	81	21,535	16,821	18,844	2,023
			82	39,698	29,918	34,077	4,159
			83	44,152	34,178	37,297	3,119
			84	22,866	9,450	10,348	898
			86	58,271	56,869	62,683	5,814
GUATMAL	A	E	84	1,400	300	661	361
	V	E	83	8,050	5,595	6,370	775
			86	78,940	5,715	11,805	6,090
MEXICO	O	E	81	2,908,931	1,389,244	1,389,244	
			82	554,130	219,370	219,370	
			83	1,278,777	448,021	448,021	
			84	1,643,724	560,302	560,302	
			85	1,424,640	386,732	386,732	
			86	147,080	30,545	30,545	
	O	W	86	39,750	9,142	9,142	
N ZEAL	A	W	84	493	943	1,350	407
PANAMA	A	E	86	1,124	2,800	2,972	172
POLAND	V	E	81	492,009	187,648	240,629	52,981
			85	72,300	24,379	34,169	9,790
SPAIN	V	E	84	37,708	14,489	19,011	4,522
SWITZLD	V	E	81	2,937	2,034	2,406	372
U KING	V	E	86	43,717	23,591	27,660	4,069
YUGOSLV	V	E	83	205,182	88,720	111,123	22,403
			84	42,880	18,379	23,155	4,776
			86	220,448	127,696	156,516	28,820

1467630 STRAWBERRIES FRZN OVER 40OZ (LB)

Country	Mode	Reg	Yr	Quantity	F.A.S.	C.I.F.	Charges
TOTAL			81	56,696,918	25,158,997	25,843,200	684,760
			82	34,224,300	17,238,736	17,854,411	615,675
			83	40,956,486	16,235,074	17,270,108	1,035,034
			84	49,103,929	16,399,433	17,416,021	1,016,588
			85	57,364,073	15,686,093	17,146,189	1,460,096
			86	48,744,767	16,255,412	18,105,589	1,850,177
BRAZIL	V	E	84	174,218	50,140	78,308	28,168
			85	119,004	29,165	42,291	13,126
C RICA	A	E	86	2,622	3,960	4,827	867
	V	E	86	38,955	9,428	12,540	3,112
CANADA	O	E	82	176,095	87,711	87,711	
			83	5,880	3,787	3,787	
			84	42,306	12,875	12,875	
			85	130,820	63,674	63,674	
			86	210,408	97,622	97,622	
	O	W	81	80,000	48,000	48,000	
			82	37,500	21,310	21,310	
			83	33,555	5,526	5,526	
			84	189,170	84,203	84,203	
			85	229,140	98,143	98,143	
			86	345,700	167,754	167,754	
	V	E	86	12,041	4,096	5,505	1,409
CHILE	O	E	83	25,557	6,967	9,478	2,511
			84	9,008	3,910	4,860	950
			86	16,723	6,400	7,938	1,538

Crop
Product
TSUSA commodity number, description, and unit of quantity

Country	Mode	Reg	Yr	Quantity	F.A.S.	C.I.F.	Charges
	V	E	83	1,645,909	708,481	887,906	179,425
			84	2,373,249	836,155	1,071,974	235,819
			85	699,230	220,574	292,974	72,400
			86	990,511	342,167	459,590	117,423
	V	W	84	128,045	34,819	52,025	17,206
			86	46,541	24,008	29,908	5,900
DENMARK	O	E	83	45,000	20,700	20,700	
ECUADOR	V	E	86	289,062	117,293	149,267	31,974
FR GERM	V	E	86	36,000	9,992	14,429	4,437
FRANCE	N	E	83	4,922	5,996	6,602	606
	V	W	86	331	1,190	1,266	76
GUATMAL	V	E	84	1,890	1,219	1,408	189
			86	600,420	50,493	98,217	47,724
HUNGARY	V	E	86	39,000	17,550	21,387	3,837
ISRAEL	A	E	82	2,684	1,692	8,924	7,232
	V	E	83	46,250	19,953	23,318	3,365
IVY CST	V	E	85	44,322	6,172	11,524	5,352
MALAYSA	O	E	85	48,990	12,248	12,248	
MEXICO	O	E	81	51,320,360	23,098,841	23,099,616	1,332
			82	29,383,846	15,002,236	15,004,482	2,246
			83	32,568,124	12,845,170	12,845,253	83
			84	40,386,925	13,432,870	13,433,018	148
			85	47,035,806	12,684,283	12,684,289	6
			86	38,420,523	12,828,155	12,828,359	204
	O	W	84	26,768	5,354	5,354	
			85	53,200	7,980	7,980	
MONSRAT	O	E	85	39,000	12,480	12,480	
N ZEAL	A	W	82	1,102	2,346	2,880	534
	V	W	85	33,267	11,300	14,970	3,670
			86	171,475	63,078	85,159	22,081
NETHLDS	V	E	82	47,619	27,796	30,972	3,176
			83	44,040	18,378	24,882	6,504
POLAND	N	E	82	3,137,306	1,394,945	1,788,809	393,864
	O	E	84	12,210	2,824	2,824	
	V	E	81	5,255,308	1,995,959	2,673,967	678,008
			82	1,358,782	604,220	805,214	200,994
			83	6,537,229	2,600,116	3,442,656	842,540
			84	5,760,140	1,935,064	2,669,172	734,108
			85	8,862,722	2,515,896	3,867,064	1,351,168
			86	6,560,820	2,020,158	3,487,839	1,467,681
	V	W	85	34,485	12,832	23,450	10,618
			86	72,600	28,840	45,795	16,955
PORTUGL	O	E	82	79,366	96,480	104,109	7,629
SPAIN	V	E	86	44,092	17,261	19,260	1,999
TURKEY	V	E	86	41,005	22,334	29,114	6,780
YUGOSLV	V	E	81	41,250	16,197	21,617	5,420
			85	22,046	7,250	9,597	2,347
			86	817,979	427,729	545,318	117,589

Strawberry, jelly or jam
1530300 STRAWBERRY JELLY, JAM, ETC. (LB)

Country	Mode	Reg	Yr	Quantity	F.A.S.	C.I.F.	Charges
TOTAL			81	1,112,596	1,070,228	1,123,785	53,592
			82	1,147,091	966,289	1,027,920	61,631
			83	1,649,429	1,319,501	1,431,506	112,005
			84	3,058,240	2,193,600	2,443,153	249,553
			85	6,545,365	3,638,190	4,184,026	545,836
			86	11,146,560	5,880,165	6,665,301	785,136
ARGENT	V	E	83	600	347	437	90
AUSTRAL	V	E	85	8,005	13,942	15,645	1,703
AUSTRIA	V	E	82	752	960	1,052	92
			83	6,500	8,886	9,463	577
			84	1,161	1,489	1,671	182
			85	1,542	2,056	2,588	532
			86	5,208	8,625	9,332	707
	V	W	86	6,702	8,877	9,652	775
BELGIUM	N	E	84	20,783	15,056	19,870	4,814
	O	E	84	27,346	14,892	17,996	3,104
			85	27,914	14,543	19,174	4,631
			86	1,658	1,956	2,203	247
	V	E	81	3,439	1,014	1,365	351
			84	82,060	45,693	53,309	7,616
			85	60,301	33,003	39,797	6,794
			86	76,011	47,571	53,508	5,937
	V	W	84	10,251	5,409	6,124	715
BRAZIL	V	E	83	660	758	840	82
BULGAR	V	E	86	3,610	1,016	1,224	208
C RICA	A	E	86	9,801	8,400	10,572	2,172
	V	E	83	7,500	6,738	7,146	408
			84	14,010	11,797	12,674	877
			85	17,324	7,384	9,012	1,628
CANADA	A	H	85	748	1,452	1,609	157

Crop
Product
TSUSA commodity number, description, and unit of quantity

Country	Mode	Reg	Yr	Quantity	F.A.S.	C.I.F.	Charges
	N	W	84	269,166	234,145	234,145	
	O	E	81	39,731	62,417	62,382	
			82	11,331	12,381	12,381	
			83	59,842	33,596	33,596	
			84	28,134	29,394	29,414	20
			85	267,877	99,807	99,807	
			86	729,329	363,117	363,117	
	O	W	81	536,603	471,979	471,979	
			82	500,451	392,300	392,300	
			83	293,455	244,796	245,286	490
			85	196,272	161,544	161,544	
			86	263,616	203,759	203,759	
	V	E	85	14,594	10,889	12,394	1,505
			86	11,700	8,305	9,323	1,018
CHILE	A	E	84	1,122	1,500	3,263	1,763
	V	E	85	8,290	6,719	7,347	628
CHINA M	O	E	84	317	330	342	12
DENMARK	A	E	85	1,377	1,260	2,478	1,218
	N	W	86	1,547,151	726,097	828,713	102,616
	V	E	82	841	780	920	140
			83	10,309	15,057	15,991	934
			84	10,118	14,280	15,240	960
			85	11,741	7,333	8,169	836
			86	494,861	272,786	310,264	37,478
	V	W	85	61,243	26,872	31,922	5,050
			86	510,313	258,844	296,136	37,292
DOM REP	V	E	85	2,700	2,025	2,155	130
EGYPT	V	E	86	12,667	6,941	7,654	713
FR GERM	N	E	85	567,196	381,746	425,600	43,854
	O	E	82	392	280	399	119
			83	2,808	2,369	2,530	161
			84	554,075	356,607	398,737	42,130
			86	85,654	56,642	63,260	6,618
	V	E	81	3,390	3,235	3,454	219
			82	36,134	28,884	32,065	3,181
			83	284,179	181,260	197,737	16,477
			84	459,841	300,660	338,618	37,958
			85	1,351,107	862,585	970,165	107,580
			86	2,275,064	1,552,252	1,701,371	149,119
	V	W	82	520	324	366	42
			83	2,880	2,598	2,864	266
			84	1,200	988	1,160	172
			85	28,248	18,641	21,762	3,121
			86	3,600	2,968	3,592	624
FRANCE	A	E	84	864	295	300	5
	N	E	81	78,698	84,010	93,752	9,742
			82	39,519	49,583	55,868	6,285
			83	49,426	57,469	65,571	8,102
			84	202,414	132,090	152,666	20,576
			85	154,606	169,220	191,409	22,189
			86	63,966	94,459	106,247	11,788
	N	W	86	3,514	4,638	6,568	1,930
	O	E	81	1,242	1,290	1,419	129
			82	2,005	1,814	2,080	266
			83	7,792	8,240	9,138	898
			84	1,380	1,099	1,099	
			86	7,800	10,655	10,688	33
	V	E	81	7,543	9,275	9,995	720
			82	76,226	63,591	72,154	8,563
			83	56,034	49,284	55,555	6,271
			84	102,735	79,612	90,576	10,964
			85	316,095	249,918	283,495	33,577
			86	141,350	145,616	163,116	17,500
	V	W	81	13,916	12,167	13,302	1,135
			82	24,799	21,961	24,882	2,921
			83	97,122	79,579	90,746	11,167
			84	158,917	118,686	134,268	15,582
			85	82,099	68,776	81,472	12,696
			86	44,876	54,917	58,770	3,853
GREECE	V	E	86	28,039	35,728	40,233	4,505
GUATMAL	A	E	84	441	336	634	298
HUNGARY	O	E	85	103,296	33,628	33,888	260
	V	E	81	23,809	7,821	9,900	2,079
			82	7,920	2,860	3,690	830
			83	25,206	8,917	11,070	2,153
			84	115,523	35,190	49,765	14,575
			85	1,029,055	212,297	306,919	94,622
			86	1,787,991	356,450	525,487	169,037
	V	W	85	270,749	46,542	80,023	33,481
			86	918,073	219,600	270,806	51,206
IRELAND	O	E	81	450	1,343	1,488	145
	V	E	81	15,587	13,890	15,137	1,247
			82	7,678	7,115	7,875	760
			83	11,460	10,625	11,859	1,234

Crop
Product
TSUSA commodity number, description, and unit of quantity

Country	Mode	Reg	Yr	Quantity	F.A.S.	C.I.F.	Charges
			84	8,781	6,478	7,626	1,148
			85	4,912	3,072	3,626	554
			86	5,931	4,220	4,694	474
ISRAEL	N	E	84	266,283	147,029	166,155	19,126
			85	282,693	144,379	163,363	18,984
	V	E	81	24,921	14,143	15,899	1,756
			82	96,586	67,185	75,053	7,868
			83	209,275	144,873	162,278	17,405
			84	147,251	88,390	97,999	9,609
			85	535,234	231,981	273,306	41,325
			86	679,532	356,454	407,423	50,969
	V	W	83	7,210	12,175	13,498	1,323
ITALY	O	E	84	9,630	4,524	4,872	348
	V	E	81	2,376	1,640	1,650	10
			82	9,583	7,234	8,321	1,087
			83	15,027	9,205	10,654	1,449
			84	17,204	15,266	17,253	1,987
			85	13,478	15,005	16,243	1,238
			86	2,231	3,966	4,317	351
	V	W	83	328	645	718	73
JAMAICA	A	E	82	1,750	320	466	146
	O	E	84	11,895	5,355	5,355	
			85	28,158	19,146	19,146	
JAPAN	V	H	81	208	252	323	71
	V	W	82	458	678	721	43
			83	2,925	2,658	3,011	353
			84	3,200	1,780	2,655	875
LEBANON	V	E	84	1,058	1,034	1,092	58
MADAGAS	V	E	84	661	632	674	42
MEXICO	O	E	83	60,000	13,800	13,800	
			84	123	863	863	
			85	5,000	15,681	15,681	
			86	14,160	13,027	13,027	
NETHLDS	O	E	85	208,053	79,565	92,014	12,449
			86	368,595	197,682	232,994	35,312
	V	E	82	2,756	2,393	2,455	62
			84	10,610	4,953	5,835	882
			85	3,373	6,120	6,772	652
			86	10,537	11,836	13,133	1,297
	V	W	84	973	281	305	24
			85	27,564	13,081	15,296	2,215
			86	14,779	10,260	11,784	1,524
NIUE	V	E	85	45,952	10,488	17,488	7,000
NORWAY	V	E	84	48	563	629	66
			86	16,606	25,272	26,016	744
PAKISTN	V	E	85	13,437	14,932	16,870	1,938
POLAND	N	E	82	23,712	10,670	13,102	2,432
			83	9,600	3,600	4,419	819
	O	E	81	6,000	4,958	6,151	1,193
			82	38,299	17,280	20,834	3,554
			84	6,375	2,700	2,970	270
	V	E	81	13,244	4,644	6,132	1,488
			83	24,000	9,000	10,950	1,950
			84	44,024	16,651	19,943	3,292
			85	37,456	15,344	19,138	3,794
			86	20,403	6,800	9,145	2,345
PORTUGL	V	E	82	1,058	452	518	66
			83	4,401	374	1,305	931
REP SAF	V	W	83	675	1,009	1,191	182
			84	536	757	970	213
ROMANIA	V	E	83	19,920	8,883	10,096	1,213
			84	86,507	42,235	47,830	5,595
			85	87,602	35,818	40,792	4,974
			86	291,582	73,473	89,122	15,649
SPAIN	V	E	82	904	900	1,173	273
			84	975	771	871	100
			85	5,767	3,509	3,882	373
SWEDEN	V	E	86	912	1,316	1,459	143
SWITZLD	A	E	86	3,840	2,581	2,661	80
	N	W	82	2,673	3,210	3,874	664
	O	E	81	2,402	1,465	1,559	94
			82	3,292	2,517	3,129	612
			83	3,031	1,876	2,166	290
			84	2,861	2,455	2,676	221
			85	8,730	6,496	7,289	793
			86	11,324	15,183	16,490	1,307
	O	W	85	2,204	1,043	1,182	139
	V	E	81	99,486	104,790	115,164	10,374
			82	124,103	124,798	133,138	8,340
			83	128,789	121,963	129,355	7,392
			84	88,555	108,201	114,346	6,145
			85	149,877	142,383	154,339	11,956
			86	182,350	251,868	268,785	16,917
	V	W	81	34,440	23,788	25,927	2,139

Crop
Product
TSUSA commodity number, description, and unit of quantity

Country	Mode	Reg	Yr	Quantity	F.A.S.	C.I.F.	Charges
			82	2,945	2,894	3,406	512
			83	33,036	31,825	34,176	2,351
			84	37,801	32,432	35,144	2,712
			85	50,159	57,636	62,191	4,555
			86	66,187	79,128	83,170	4,042
TURKEY	V	E	83	595	351	444	93
			84	7,808	5,918	6,604	686
			86	2,605	1,365	1,543	178
U KING	A	E	83	154	273	281	8
			84	251	310	408	98
	N	E	81	122,684	186,167	198,077	11,910
			82	52,165	71,010	75,542	4,532
			83	49,034	56,941	66,783	9,842
			84	72,303	108,126	122,405	14,279
			85	195,214	225,266	249,527	24,261
	N	W	83	25,613	22,740	25,556	2,816
			84	40,318	47,100	51,997	4,897
			86	22,655	27,366	30,577	3,211
	O	E	81	11,918	20,828	22,263	1,435
			82	4,631	5,964	6,560	596
			83	50,380	62,590	67,368	4,778
			84	83,978	79,582	85,522	5,940
			85	8,926	13,232	15,018	1,786
			86	105,761	109,680	117,254	7,574
	O	W	82	210	400	400	
	V	E	81	13,455	16,788	19,276	2,488
			82	34,888	39,429	44,356	4,927
			83	84,476	99,382	108,043	8,661
			84	32,154	55,449	61,612	6,163
			85	26,502	36,924	41,285	4,361
			86	113,462	158,116	174,361	16,245
	V	H	85	843	1,530	1,719	189
	V	W	81	2,711	3,187	3,610	423
			82	21,229	19,522	21,449	1,927
			83	3,699	4,369	4,936	567
			84	4,795	9,442	10,728	1,286
			85	58,375	62,628	71,335	8,707
			86	35,302	28,616	32,534	3,918
USSR	O	E	82	5,026	1,500	1,765	265
	V	E	81	54,343	19,137	23,581	4,444
			82	12,255	5,100	5,626	526
			85	7,870	1,942	2,520	578
	V	W	83	1,488	450	649	199
YUGOSLV	V	E	84	9,424	4,775	5,943	1,168
			85	155,607	48,807	65,630	16,823
			86	139,017	49,557	66,440	16,883
	V	W	86	6,235	2,180	2,777	597

Strawberry, paste and pulp
1528820 STRAWBERRY PASTE AND PULP (LB)

Country	Mode	Reg	Yr	Quantity	F.A.S.	C.I.F.	Charges
TOTAL			81	3,846,993	1,313,357	1,313,448	91
			82	1,392,791	554,841	554,870	29
			83	529,323	148,242	148,287	45
			84	779,562	201,537	203,222	1,685
			85	1,464,560	286,705	286,964	259
			86	479,864	136,364	140,172	3,808
BRAZIL	V	E	84	300	2,472	2,749	277
CANADA	O	E	82	119	308	337	29
			84	450	357	357	
	O	W	82	16,800	8,400	8,400	
FR GERM	A	E	84	110	256	338	82
	V	E	84	800	328	392	64
FRANCE	A	E	84	212	279	368	89
	V	E	81	921	1,507	1,598	91
			84	10,466	9,186	10,359	1,173
			86	10,353	11,607	13,309	1,702
	V	W	86	992	1,045	1,138	93
ITALY	V	E	83	279	640	685	45
			85	717	1,280	1,539	259
JAMAICA	V	E	86	21,649	8,540	9,679	1,139
MEXICO	O	E	81	3,846,072	1,311,850	1,311,850	
			82	1,374,402	545,125	545,125	
			83	529,044	147,602	147,602	
			84	767,224	188,659	188,659	
			85	1,463,843	285,425	285,425	
			86	445,700	112,877	112,877	
	O	W	82	1,470	1,008	1,008	
SPAIN	A	E	86	337	1,150	1,977	827
SWITZLD	V	E	86	833	1,145	1,192	47

Strawberry, prepared or preserved
1468500 STRAWBERRIES PREP PRES NSPF (LB)

Country	Mode	Reg	Yr	Quantity	F.A.S.	C.I.F.	Charges
TOTAL			81	661,565	355,108	398,833	43,313
			82	595,749	444,632	505,487	60,855
			83	789,520	522,571	559,011	36,440
			84	1,120,301	668,178	726,276	58,098
			85	4,148,318	1,815,386	1,890,927	75,541
			86	1,813,251	1,196,504	1,278,887	82,383
AUSTRIA	V	E	82	804	1,000	1,101	101
			83	288	379	428	49
			84	4,602	5,130	5,758	628
			85	4,090	3,572	4,099	527
BELGIUM	V	E	82	11,286	8,313	9,416	1,103
			83	17,743	14,144	15,907	1,763
			84	17,242	9,321	10,308	987
	V	W	83	2,808	1,835	2,062	227
			84	4,248	2,775	3,259	484
BRAZIL	V	E	82	19,500	16,865	19,376	2,511
CANADA	O	E	82	36,000	15,207	15,207	
			83	4,402	5,556	5,556	
			84	1,330	4,960	4,960	
			85	115,561	55,020	65,119	10,099
			86	29,845	18,503	18,503	
	O	W	81	16,700	12,589	12,589	
			82	23,120	13,590	13,590	
			83	43,900	22,937	22,937	
			85	2,083,320	927,577	927,577	
			86	443,951	232,294	232,294	
	V	E	85	3,885	2,788	3,166	378
CHILE	O	E	86	9,536	2,857	2,857	
CHINA T	V	W	83	3,556	3,659	4,136	477
DENMARK	V	E	81	1,204	634	837	203
			86	94,080	53,108	61,786	8,678
	V	W	86	8,572	5,268	7,642	2,374
FR GERM	O	E	85	3,576	2,593	2,593	
			86	8,631	7,123	8,968	1,845
	V	E	83	460	570	626	56
			84	27,251	18,307	20,070	1,763
			85	107,389	75,955	86,578	10,623
			86	11,561	19,330	20,559	1,229
	V	W	83	540	525	618	93
FRANCE	N	E	83	115,100	106,769	117,729	10,960
			84	285,015	167,249	191,304	24,055
	O	E	81	11,789	15,460	16,660	1,200
			82	3,022	4,048	4,398	350
			84	10,899	8,306	9,558	1,252
			85	4,561	3,983	4,587	604
			86	7,212	12,959	14,240	1,281
	V	E	81	33,250	29,200	33,089	3,477
			82	54,636	58,522	65,789	7,267
			83	25,774	23,164	25,536	2,372
			84	14,711	14,170	15,970	1,800
			85	138,622	99,929	114,150	14,221
			86	278,529	293,139	329,556	36,417
	V	W	81	5,547	6,605	7,178	573
			82	656	2,479	2,617	138
			83	201	423	452	29
			86	2,010	2,707	3,080	373
GREECE	V	E	83	601	825	927	102
			85	5,214	6,216	6,724	508
HUNGARY	V	E	86	9,117	5,942	6,485	543
IRELAND	V	E	82	277	385	390	5
ISRAEL	V	E	81	41,588	12,532	15,117	2,585
			82	9,180	7,446	8,461	1,015
			83	36,948	27,933	30,988	3,055
			84	15,606	14,223	15,823	1,600
			85	13,890	10,677	11,665	988
			86	2,724	2,080	2,206	126
ITALY	O	E	85	412	2,773	3,300	527
	V	E	82	5,106	3,589	4,088	499
			84	6,772	7,763	8,869	1,106
			85	2,197	4,439	5,128	689
			86	2,112	3,636	4,063	427
	V	W	84	423	841	911	70
JAMAICA	V	E	84	4,375	2,363	2,888	525
JAPAN	V	E	86	4,740	3,546	4,034	488
	V	W	83	664	820	930	110
LEBANON	A	W	84	840	700	734	34
MEXICO	A	E	84	2,465	2,160	2,968	808
	O	E	81	252,951	128,261	128,261	
			83	328,975	81,230	81,230	
			84	469,129	113,394	113,394	
			85	1,296,247	288,873	290,349	1,476
			86	668,021	192,863	192,863	
N ZEAL	A	E	85	5,052	8,872	13,733	4,861
NETHLDS	O	E	85	107,323	31,564	31,564	
	V	E	83	8,211	7,009	7,622	613
			84	1,574	1,717	1,827	110
			85	10,100	10,479	11,894	1,415
POLAND	O	E	82	257,215	105,651	136,074	30,423
	V	E	81	255,202	91,864	123,233	31,369
			82	3,480	1,620	1,805	185
			83	11,137	4,095	5,002	907
			84	7,312	2,715	3,331	616
			85	4,507	1,818	2,367	549
ROMANIA	V	E	84	2,400	1,287	1,415	128
SPAIN	V	E	86	4,500	2,039	2,388	349
SWEDEN	V	E	82	1,553	1,338	1,524	186
SWITZLD	N	E	84	18,059	20,889	22,472	1,583
	O	E	82	220	841	989	148
	V	E	81	5,864	3,389	3,836	447
			82	25,241	24,703	26,699	1,996
			83	28,390	29,707	32,061	2,354
			84	4,294	4,481	4,717	236
			85	11,511	10,672	11,538	866
			86	20,132	25,606	27,308	1,702
	V	W	84	476	553	591	38
U KING	N	E	81	24,246	35,419	37,493	2,074
			82	111,844	133,641	142,046	8,405
	O	E	81	2,400	4,000	4,400	400
			82	4,729	8,645	9,310	665
			83	9,386	17,398	18,586	1,188
			84	53,469	81,152	85,216	4,064
			85	91,032	107,220	113,267	6,047
			86	61,938	123,674	129,947	6,273
	V	E	81	10,560	14,155	15,093	938
			82	27,275	35,040	40,765	5,725
			83	150,006	172,732	184,652	11,920
			84	160,192	179,990	195,576	15,586
			85	131,617	146,597	165,206	18,609
			86	144,484	188,444	207,818	19,374
	V	W	81	264	1,000	1,047	47
			82	605	1,709	1,842	133
			83	430	861	1,026	165
			84	6,897	3,051	3,570	519
			85	8,212	13,769	16,323	2,554
VENEZ	O	E	86	1,556	1,386	2,290	904
YUGOSLV	V	E	84	720	681	787	106

Strychnine Tree

Brucine, alkaloid
4370000 BRUCINE AND ITS COMPOUNDS (AOZ)

Country	Mode	Reg	Yr	Quantity	F.A.S.	C.I.F.	Charges
TOTAL			81	635,084	1,409,704	1,507,866	98,162
			82	629,250	1,601,252	1,686,643	85,391
			83	673,316	954,153	1,022,903	68,750
			84	626,597	737,640	785,340	47,700
			85	1,059,277	1,409,525	1,460,803	51,278
			86	720,764	1,311,460	1,354,108	42,648
CANADA	O	E	82	484	1,041	1,116	75
CHINA M	V	E	85	5,512	16,938	17,053	115
FR GERM	A	E	86	144	10,438	10,466	28
	V	E	85	400,000	91,426	92,000	574
FRANCE	N	E	81	13,168	24,214	25,334	1,120
INDIA	A	E	81	39,000	123,339	131,305	7,966
			82	43,816	113,727	120,228	6,501
			83	105,000	136,687	166,304	29,617
			84	49,429	73,884	81,333	7,449
	A	W	84	7,600	15,776	20,069	4,293
			85	9,500	21,410	23,222	1,812
	N	E	81	576,789	1,246,999	1,335,696	88,697
			82	584,100	1,484,770	1,563,585	78,815
			83	546,316	789,621	827,786	38,165
			84	407,820	606,238	640,382	34,144
			85	512,536	1,006,968	1,042,857	35,889
			86	543,722	1,136,235	1,172,004	35,769
	O	E	82	850	1,714	1,714	
	O	W	83	2,000	3,300	3,812	512
			86	14,650	18,313	18,433	120
	V	E	83	20,000	24,545	25,001	456

Crop Product TSUSA commodity number, description, and unit of quantity Country	Mode	Reg	Yr	Quantity	F.A.S.	C.I.F.	Charges
			86	25,008	54,250	55,035	785
	V	W	84	151,748	26,553	27,556	1,003
			85	70,000	135,711	145,273	9,562
			86	135,000	85,548	91,080	5,532
ITALY	A	E	81	1,600	3,240	3,290	50
	V	E	85	61,729	137,072	140,398	3,326
S HELNA	V	E	84	10,000	15,189	16,000	811
SWITZLD	A	E	86	2,240	6,676	7,090	414
U KING	A	E	81	4,527	11,912	12,241	329

Nux Vomica
4356500 NUX VOMICA (LB)

Strychnine, alkaloid
4371600 STRYCHNINE AND SALT OF (AOZ)

Country	Mode	Reg	Yr	Quantity	F.A.S.	C.I.F.	Charges
TOTAL			81	372,008	446,880	490,874	43,994
			82	153,442	161,780	175,922	14,142
			83	270,967	223,395	245,969	22,574
			84	208,353	206,129	218,742	12,613
			85	189,020	206,759	219,835	13,076
			86	204,948	255,351	272,756	17,405
FINLAND	A	E	86	2,760	3,375	3,474	99
INDIA	A	E	82	386	1,306	1,600	294
			83	247	392	490	98
			84	337	2,102	2,475	373
			86	11,500	13,382	15,245	1,863
	N	E	81	335,008	402,566	445,411	42,845
			82	123,056	131,390	144,322	12,932
			83	179,720	146,172	165,590	19,418
			84	88,016	108,414	115,521	7,107
			85	106,828	120,507	129,012	8,505
			86	150,400	189,898	203,657	13,759
	V	E	81	12,000	14,900	15,445	545
			83	40,000	28,000	28,892	892
			84	70,000	49,000	50,749	1,749
	V	W	81	25,000	29,414	30,018	604
			82	30,000	29,084	30,000	916
			83	51,000	48,831	50,997	2,166
			84	50,000	46,613	49,997	3,384
			85	82,192	86,252	90,823	4,571
			86	40,000	46,970	48,369	1,399
JAPAN	A	E	86	288	1,726	2,011	285

Styrax

Styrax, balsam
1882000 BALSAMS, STYRAX (LB)

Country	Mode	Reg	Yr	Quantity	F.A.S.	C.I.F.	Charges
TOTAL			81	61,148	162,183	167,919	5,736
			82	95,095	216,809	226,708	9,899
			83	93,894	226,539	237,487	10,948
			84	67,762	176,921	183,470	6,549
			85	143,144	523,232	537,672	14,440
			86	134,782	331,987	349,962	17,975
ARAB EM	V	E	84	2,205	8,640	9,091	451
DENMARK	V	E	86	22,000	20,326	23,826	3,500
FR GERM	A	E	83	66	1,560	1,741	181
			84	110	2,506	2,617	111
			85	55	1,226	1,308	82
	V	E	81	55	983	1,012	29
FRANCE	A	E	81	130	768	776	8
	N	E	86	760	9,815	10,296	481
	V	E	85	30,450	25,344	27,934	2,590
HONDURA	N	E	82	73,912	173,195	181,188	7,993
	V	E	81	60,081	156,136	161,611	5,475
			82	15,213	32,164	33,536	1,372
			83	93,387	221,717	232,341	10,624
			84	65,046	163,277	169,230	5,953
			85	111,687	491,122	502,728	11,606
			86	98,844	268,760	280,529	11,769
JAPAN	V	W	82	458	545	600	55
MEXICO	V	E	82	5,071	8,050	8,458	408
NETHLDS	N	E	86	458	4,340	4,443	103
	V	E	84	401	2,498	2,532	34
			85	247	1,955	2,004	49
			86	220	1,857	1,906	49
SALVADR	V	E	86	2,500	12,470	12,988	518

Crop Product TSUSA commodity number, description, and unit of quantity Country	Mode	Reg	Yr	Quantity	F.A.S.	C.I.F.	Charges
SWITZLD	A	E	83	441	3,262	3,405	143
	V	E	82	441	2,855	2,926	71
TURKEY	V	E	85	705	3,585	3,698	113
U KING	V	E	81	882	4,296	4,520	224
			86	10,000	14,419	15,974	1,555

Sugar Beet

Sugar beet**
1551000 BEETS, SUGAR, NATURAL STATE (STN)

Country	Mode	Reg	Yr	Quantity	F.A.S.	C.I.F.	Charges
TOTAL			84	19	4,933	7,363	2,430
			86	1,470	3,059	3,206	147
FR GERM	V	E	84	19	4,933	7,363	2,430
U KING	V	E	86	1,470	3,059	3,206	147

1551500 SUGAR BEET A CANE NT NATURAL (CLB)

Country	Mode	Reg	Yr	Quantity	F.A.S.	C.I.F.	Charges
TOTAL			82	3,969	1,324	1,559	235
			83	1,109	1,056	1,216	160
			84	469	2,563	3,062	499
			85	11	3,593	3,630	37
FR GERM	A	E	85	11	3,593	3,630	37
HG KONG	V	W	83	1,102	700	822	122
			84	50	950	1,035	85
ITALY	A	E	83	7	356	394	38
			84	375	450	839	389
SWITZLD	O	E	84	1	902	909	7
THAILND	V	E	82	3,969	1,324	1,559	235
U KING	A	E	84	43	261	279	18

Sugar beet, processed**
1552025 CANE SUGAR IMMEDITE CNSMPTN (LB)

Country	Mode	Reg	Yr	Quantity	F.A.S.	C.I.F.	Charges
TOTAL			81	9,736,129	2,541,576	2,731,217	189,641
			82	65,595,318	11,753,933	11,898,003	144,070
			83	38,119,529	6,542,907	7,455,969	913,062
			84	49,993,852	11,369,255	12,031,526	662,271
			85	60,197,391	13,329,204	14,004,101	674,897
			86	39,752,292	9,278,389	9,600,768	322,379
AUSTRAL	V	E	81	661,380	134,928	166,500	31,572
AUSTRIA	V	E	81	1,781	1,822	2,031	209
B VIRGN	O	E	81	97	700	750	50
	V	E	83	38,000	8,850	9,350	500
BAHAMAS	V	E	84	39,750	7,076	8,576	1,500
BELGIUM	V	E	81	3,920	8,561	9,029	468
			83	1,444	4,398	4,599	201
			84	2,000	3,438	3,666	228
			85	28,027	10,373	12,199	1,826
			86	40,833	13,928	16,007	2,079
	V	W	81	37,478	21,626	24,489	2,863
BRAZIL	O	E	83	2,112,007	210,760	306,908	96,148
	V	E	81	344,468	92,126	118,430	26,304
			82	564,173	86,291	106,313	20,022
			83	11,749,967	1,166,971	1,713,372	546,401
			84	9,780	1,761	2,276	515
C RICA	O	E	84	36,376	26,000	27,906	1,906
	V	E	84	39,919	18,108	20,741	2,633
			85	10,837	2,362	3,366	1,004
			86	86,921	29,206	35,492	6,286
	V	W	86	48,533	16,762	21,066	4,304
CANADA	A	E	83	44,000	9,384	11,724	2,340
	N	E	83	269,990	60,759	77,932	17,173
			85	18,569,082	3,989,225	4,009,482	20,257
			86	117,201	16,436	20,320	3,884
	N	W	86	1,747,810	435,065	435,065	
	O	E	81	5,301,097	1,086,934	1,087,336	402
			82	56,160,663	9,868,500	9,874,617	6,117
			83	17,559,013	3,765,974	3,767,433	1,459
			84	21,858,068	4,648,086	4,665,942	17,856
			85	9,597,788	2,284,816	2,288,837	4,021
			86	24,643,522	5,757,037	5,766,170	9,133
	O	W	82	6,295,333	1,218,188	1,218,188	
			83	946,560	185,214	185,214	
			84	949,723	185,397	185,397	
			85	365,500	70,245	70,245	
	V	E	81	78,500	23,256	27,606	4,350
			82	108,893	25,340	32,091	6,751
			83	163,799	23,836	33,737	9,901

Crop Product TSUSA commodity number, description, and unit of quantity Country	Mode	Reg	Yr	Quantity	F.A.S.	C.I.F.	Charges
			85	117,644	18,494	24,057	5,563
			86	118,305	25,796	33,340	7,544
CHINA M	O E		84	24,802	6,288	8,098	1,810
			86	64,400	19,250	22,660	3,410
	O W		83	45,350	12,931	14,193	1,262
			84	252,891	78,099	86,256	8,157
			86	35,000	9,307	9,607	300
	V E		81	16,050	7,926	8,788	862
			82	17,450	7,227	8,037	810
			86	42,000	12,875	14,994	2,119
	V H		81	12,400	5,711	6,284	573
	V W		81	428,559	168,220	181,712	13,492
			82	145,304	42,889	47,406	4,517
			83	28,340	6,087	6,766	679
			84	307,417	87,808	96,510	8,702
CHINA T	A E		83	992	311	352	41
	V E		82	661,380	132,737	166,500	33,763
			83	1,000	415	468	53
			85	86,692	17,150	23,456	6,306
			86	73,935	15,150	18,817	3,667
	V W		83	4,125	1,140	1,190	50
			84	20,976	11,860	12,746	886
COLOMB	A E		85	7,316	1,463	1,465	2
	N E		84	192,630	59,409	70,577	11,168
			85	125,442	46,831	62,675	15,844
			86	182,233	62,775	80,595	17,820
	O E		85	22,530	6,526	7,066	540
	V E		81	635,536	227,083	239,419	12,336
			82	38,581	8,400	10,420	2,020
			83	115,742	27,916	34,098	6,182
			85	91,577	59,052	64,629	5,577
			86	174,418	55,628	65,899	10,271
	V W		86	115,264	26,135	30,508	4,373
CR N AN	V E		81	5,604	4,463	4,563	100
DOM REP	O E		82	56,200	7,868	9,428	1,560
			84	490,000	118,825	134,609	15,784
	V E		81	150,000	35,100	39,484	4,384
			82	43,800	6,132	7,692	1,560
			83	1,704,830	327,328	366,811	39,483
			84	19,846,662	4,638,295	5,041,644	403,349
			85	22,804,368	4,930,187	5,271,537	341,350
			86	10,468,740	2,346,912	2,494,970	148,058
FR GERM	N E		86	39,683	4,175	6,984	2,809
	N W		82	4,705	5,991	6,832	841
	V E		83	275,199	35,802	53,642	17,840
			84	758,583	94,124	147,792	53,668
			85	476,196	37,042	70,137	33,095
			86	970,522	97,696	165,862	68,166
	V W		81	1,407	1,362	1,565	203
			85	5,930	2,980	3,023	43
FRANCE	A E		82	1,328	370	792	422
	N E		82	9,030	4,553	4,986	433
			83	5,177	1,897	2,837	940
	N W		86	8,884	4,892	7,603	2,711
	O E		83	21,341	8,190	8,456	266
			86	1,384	1,030	1,030	
	O W		86	812	2,913	3,083	170
	V E		81	6,261	2,484	2,622	138
			82	63,693	8,647	11,549	2,902
			83	71,420	12,293	16,005	3,712
			84	15,648	9,801	10,196	395
			85	5,606	1,970	2,456	486
	V W		82	286	361	411	50
			84	3,386	1,090	1,272	182
			85	3,386	1,067	1,175	108
GABON	V E		85	6,687,323	1,492,127	1,671,831	179,704
GUATMAL	A E		84	2,000	422	929	507
	V E		81	880,000	366,520	400,206	33,686
			82	608,960	107,633	135,235	27,602
			83	88,000	19,932	23,150	3,218
			84	2,204,587	493,547	521,012	27,465
	V W		81	132,200	56,760	65,346	8,586
			82	44,000	7,040	10,940	3,900
			85	22,325	6,698	8,105	1,407
GUYANA	O E		81	7,700	4,610	5,364	754
	V E		82	27,085	10,290	12,155	1,865
HG KONG	O E		85	37,500	8,400	10,293	1,893
			86	51,005	16,670	16,900	230
	O W		84	10,141	1,305	1,445	140
			86	7,500	2,527	2,769	242
	V E		82	10,000	4,382	5,279	897
			83	5,000	2,209	2,397	188
			84	2,500	1,084	1,241	157
			85	85,500	25,760	30,960	5,200
			86	6,000	2,420	2,790	370
	V H		81	2,750	1,522	1,620	98
			82	750	414	449	35
	V W		81	108,321	44,893	47,789	2,896
			82	38,250	23,037	24,678	1,641
			83	28,000	9,821	10,327	506
			84	157,343	47,636	51,412	3,776
			85	26,400	4,864	6,163	1,299
			86	60,500	14,043	15,114	1,071
INDIA	N E		86	50,096	46,923	50,212	3,289
	O E		81	6,614	2,523	2,649	126
			84	1,800	1,286	1,382	96
			85	2,205	2,104	2,342	238
	V E		81	59,505	20,042	24,297	4,255
			82	194,723	47,399	60,395	12,996
			83	20,000	4,054	5,835	1,781
			84	101,063	23,966	29,156	5,190
			85	83,775	43,067	48,830	5,763
	V W		81	17,790	4,939	6,678	1,739
			83	1,083	899	1,108	209
			84	2,310	514	579	65
ITALY	V E		83	44,092	18,400	20,450	2,050
			84	160,363	60,100	69,296	9,196
JAMAICA	V E		83	440,763	121,061	133,341	12,280
JAPAN	N W		83	28,700	7,567	9,406	1,839
	V H		81	661	880	970	90
	V W		82	2,671	6,298	7,261	963
			84	2,430	1,155	1,203	48
KOR REP	V E		81	661,380	134,292	165,000	30,708
	V W		82	3,500	1,624	1,786	162
MALAWI	O E		82	6,169	2,784	2,951	167
	V E		85	7,875	3,680	3,781	101
			86	8,553	4,092	4,747	655
MALAYSA	V W		81	500	282	295	13
MAURIT	O E		81	11,000	6,322	7,355	1,033
	V E		82	189,637	30,199	39,900	9,701
			83	2,022,967	446,848	585,542	138,694
			84	2,258,732	630,927	701,705	70,778
MEXICO	O E		81	12,389	4,713	5,331	618
			82	84,985	17,728	17,728	
			83	2,220	361	361	
			84	4,451	717	717	
			85	39,837	8,697	8,697	
			86	365,634	52,592	52,592	
	O W		81	97,666	37,537	37,537	
			82	200,922	58,824	58,824	
N ANTIL	N E		84	141,696	45,709	52,102	6,393
	V E		84	13,000	1,274	1,404	130
			84	41,580	11,708	13,808	2,100
			85	10,000	3,089	3,339	250
NETHLDS	A E		82	492	669	1,285	616
			84	179	356	581	225
	V E		83	39,600	8,123	9,123	1,000
	V W		81	183	520	563	43
PHIL R	N W		84	4,141	29,239	33,058	3,819
			85	40,252	46,099	52,888	6,789
			86	56,385	58,228	64,859	6,631
	O E		85	37,500	7,125	8,081	956
			86	9,650	2,254	2,434	180
	V E		83	1,590	981	1,087	106
			85	376,500	92,137	108,984	16,847
	V W		81	1,200	1,134	1,214	80
			83	165,824	8,542	9,557	1,015
			84	1,000	580	659	79
			85	1,243	6,866	7,680	814
			86	10,591	6,629	7,219	590
REP SAF	V E		85	231,483	35,435	44,135	8,700
	V W		83	3,600	4,374	5,164	790
S ARAB	A E		84	441	531	1,006	475
SALVADR	V E		83	39,035	6,551	9,725	3,174
			86	4,959	1,200	1,619	419
SWEDEN	N E		84	2,205	1,090	1,441	351
			86	4,416	2,631	3,421	790
	V E		81	11,155	6,683	8,290	1,607
			82	4,762	3,121	3,793	672
			83	3,334	2,983	3,543	560
			86	6,755	5,652	6,680	1,028
	V W		81	794	465	574	109
			84	2,222	989	1,008	19
			86	1,581	1,615	1,796	181
SWITZLD	A E		81	238	359	603	244
			82	181	281	730	449
	O E		86	108	3,064	3,119	55
	V E		86	819	15,765	16,080	315

Crop Product TSUSA commodity number, description, and unit of quantity Country	Mode	Reg	Yr	Quantity	F.A.S.	C.I.F.	Charges
THAILND	V	E	85	112,500	28,515	34,405	5,890
TRINID	A	E	85	800	1,700	1,770	70
U KING	N	E	81	3,526	2,775	3,498	723
			86	106,176	79,515	88,120	8,605
	O	E	81	11,185	14,725	16,086	1,361
			82	1,623	2,004	2,248	244
			83	12,000	1,567	1,926	359
			84	12,000	1,837	1,924	87
	V	E	81	11,834	5,504	7,940	2,436
			82	5,348	6,382	6,725	343
			83	15,425	8,178	8,840	662
			84	32,057	19,092	21,658	2,566
			85	61,206	25,758	28,044	2,286
	V	W	82	441	330	379	49
VENEZ	O	E	85	15,246	7,300	7,968	668
	V	E	86	21,164	9,601	10,225	624

1552045 CANE, BEET SUGAR, ETC, NSPF (LB)

Country	Mode	Reg	Yr	Quantity	F.A.S.	C.I.F.	Charges
TOTAL			81	10,098,887,938	2,139,729,031	2,292,585,011	152,855,980
			82	5,166,580,791	786,216,090	851,828,801	65,612,711
			83	5,791,679,449	1,019,024,387	1,083,066,083	64,041,696
			84	5,844,655,279	1,097,405,785	1,157,784,298	60,378,513
			85	4,785,020,974	798,532,743	852,299,415	53,766,672
			86	3,787,036,987	615,134,476	657,042,752	41,908,276
ARGENT	O	E	82	50,397,608	5,253,537	6,410,211	1,156,674
			83	154,305,215	19,566,225	21,467,512	1,901,287
			84	64,149,865	5,462,746	6,233,035	770,289
			85	29,176,260	2,200,819	2,340,881	140,062
			86	36,789,300	4,554,341	4,836,209	281,868
	V	E	81	878,616,828	209,715,259	230,124,832	20,409,573
			82	288,969,358	36,122,221	40,350,386	4,228,165
			83	275,217,845	32,418,701	37,701,765	5,283,064
			84	369,868,852	60,205,696	66,611,865	6,406,169
			85	286,464,102	46,375,330	51,498,441	5,123,111
			86	72,368,158	11,211,941	12,706,597	1,494,656
AUSTRAL	O	E	82	44,632,805	8,429,462	9,042,009	612,547
	V	E	81	1,607,046,133	297,255,670	324,389,353	27,133,683
			82	291,672,683	45,034,407	47,913,593	2,879,186
			83	434,789,978	79,982,906	82,997,713	3,014,807
			84	496,363,437	97,688,356	100,524,290	2,835,934
			85	258,579,460	48,272,990	50,956,936	2,683,946
			86	208,920,442	38,600,148	40,900,277	2,300,129
	V	W	81	141,013,800	33,309,197	35,224,081	1,914,884
BARBADO	V	E	81	21,280,000	8,964,200	9,190,960	226,760
			82	52,773,049	9,147,878	9,992,270	844,392
			83	29,629,824	6,210,499	6,532,090	321,591
			84	12,768,000	2,824,282	3,012,517	188,235
			85	34,357,488	7,222,270	7,402,571	180,301
BELIZE	O	E	82	16,273,248	2,966,798	3,116,061	149,263
			83	1,125,098	225,132	241,662	16,530
	V	E	81	95,262,530	19,500,142	20,381,305	881,163
			82	77,406,947	12,990,237	13,655,767	665,530
			83	61,042,152	11,406,729	11,922,117	515,388
			84	56,313,960	12,223,680	12,645,912	422,232
			85	26,910,890	5,440,415	5,668,426	228,011
			86	109,049,749	11,110,293	12,242,060	1,131,767
BOLIVIA	O	E	82	4,447,061	787,056	856,046	68,990
			83	15,587,472	1,095,799	1,422,807	327,008
	V	E	81	21,560,832	8,115,968	8,544,754	428,786
			82	66,905,920	10,927,731	12,343,534	1,415,803
			83	86,119,660	13,573,815	15,361,667	1,787,852
			84	18,628,302	3,602,101	4,139,327	537,226
			85	35,948,976	6,847,038	7,686,616	839,578
			86	13,081,600	2,254,260	2,569,247	314,987
BRAZIL	O	E	82	46,598,780	4,832,089	5,447,713	615,624
			83	41,250,441	5,011,869	5,201,700	189,831
			85	103,250,858	16,357,470	17,337,364	979,894
			86	91,019,126	28,343,686	31,306,997	2,963,311
	V	E	81	2,107,270,937	387,718,361	416,345,377	28,627,016
			82	497,064,577	83,938,391	92,123,303	8,184,912
			83	672,443,849	112,644,836	123,639,963	10,995,127
			84	662,315,644	129,068,914	136,737,401	7,668,487
			85	554,558,476	110,102,774	117,045,024	6,942,250
			86	343,618,746	65,872,542	69,565,757	3,693,215
C RICA	O	E	82	19,322,696	3,092,295	3,285,273	192,978
			84	70,307,275	14,729,196	15,904,711	1,175,515
			85	6,488,311	1,312,125	1,387,329	75,204
			86	63,015,385	10,938,777	11,978,518	1,039,741
	V	E	81	124,499,702	33,439,656	35,189,673	1,750,017
			82	93,462,193	14,122,012	15,420,009	1,297,997
			83	126,933,778	26,561,481	27,790,606	1,229,125
			84	108,640,235	20,538,282	21,842,010	1,303,728
			86	75,187,093	3,362,949	4,211,831	848,882
CAMROON	V	E	81	10,930,114	3,560,594	3,839,332	278,738
CANADA	O	E	82	2,206,955	321,879	321,879	
			83	4,847,699	853,973	853,973	
			84	5,103,542	869,259	869,259	
	V	E	85	7,352,032	1,240,839	1,314,722	73,883
CHINA M	V	W	81	4,975	1,748	1,913	165
			82	4,653	1,522	1,617	95
CHINA T	O	E	82	9,758,360	2,049,255	2,235,409	186,154
	V	E	82	110,219,000	14,952,945	16,441,521	1,488,576
			83	66,834,668	11,989,167	12,634,195	645,028
			84	68,453,740	13,863,686	14,512,193	648,507
			85	50,917,440	10,388,498	10,567,557	179,059
	V	W	86	39,790,825	7,138,474	7,174,166	35,692
CO BRAZ	V	E	84	16,000,000	3,448,000	3,678,627	230,627
			85	16,534,493	3,289,292	3,534,094	244,802
			86	23,919,840	4,286,402	4,591,162	304,760
COLOMB	O	E	82	39,087,234	4,683,577	5,303,285	619,708
			85	40,644,366	1,544,716	1,734,901	190,185
			86	37,146,439	1,902,092	2,284,783	382,691
	V	E	81	420,926,786	100,120,350	105,444,512	5,324,162
			82	31,290,125	5,688,208	5,957,606	269,398
			83	145,539,042	29,783,645	31,111,546	1,327,901
			84	128,260,716	24,675,029	25,502,601	827,572
			85	309,577,860	23,460,549	26,634,056	3,173,507
			86	210,623,428	21,234,841	23,047,785	1,812,944
CR N AN	O	E	82	6,262,790	1,223,040	1,261,431	38,391
	V	E	81	20,069,524	3,766,311	4,048,907	282,596
			82	11,710,093	2,400,000	2,469,219	69,219
			83	37,206,940	8,146,209	8,323,183	176,974
			84	29,035,328	6,114,490	6,291,407	176,917
			85	10,061,200	2,054,382	2,160,001	105,619
			86	18,285,130	3,810,647	3,982,935	172,288
DOM REP	O	E	82	196,337,740	34,087,555	36,049,790	1,962,235
			83	87,798,222	15,717,217	16,591,282	874,065
			84	56,055,632	10,542,680	10,934,439	391,759
			85	4,402,457	468,280	488,989	20,709
			86	39,122,387	2,455,971	2,569,609	113,638
	V	E	81	1,474,249,787	333,198,935	347,283,624	14,084,689
			82	520,163,206	72,882,404	77,252,189	4,369,785
			83	815,812,712	150,104,811	157,010,293	6,905,482
			84	960,093,590	186,354,469	193,198,640	6,844,171
			85	888,335,961	138,086,723	144,381,667	6,294,944
			86	562,564,560	94,480,109	99,329,919	4,849,810
ECUADOR	O	E	81	14,496,325	2,342,606	2,407,260	64,654
			85	17,251,218	2,846,451	2,977,560	131,109
	V	E	81	67,625,224	15,805,617	16,794,948	989,331
			82	51,109,115	7,847,613	8,344,117	496,504
			84	37,326,974	8,172,496	8,559,738	387,242
			85	36,859,577	7,347,644	7,713,310	365,666
			86	36,685,523	7,211,746	7,617,922	406,176
FIJI	O	E	82	8,742,418	1,835,908	1,997,787	161,879
	V	E	81	86,056,320	13,084,829	15,345,342	2,260,513
			82	29,764,222	6,250,487	6,808,777	558,290
			83	70,337,750	14,153,989	14,967,075	813,086
			84	62,012,960	8,960,917	9,940,920	980,003
			86	30,864,960	6,088,763	6,453,241	364,478
FR GERM	V	E	85	212	1,323	1,470	147
	V	W	81	2,277	6,569	7,097	528
GUATMAL	N	E	83	70,121,678	15,018,179	15,644,040	625,861
	O	E	82	39,906,944	6,967,478	7,344,820	377,342
			83	47,899,916	6,910,251	7,270,345	360,094
			84	17,307,694	3,146,205	3,236,205	90,000
			85	47,143,384	6,923,840	7,451,723	527,883
			86	120,132,928	21,693,914	22,577,035	883,121
	V	E	81	416,000,626	85,521,347	91,187,577	5,666,230
			82	79,279,343	12,108,314	12,974,098	865,784
			83	177,759,769	34,919,246	36,512,634	1,593,388
			84	274,517,363	51,750,885	54,289,790	2,538,905
			85	147,004,777	22,407,159	23,741,207	1,334,048
			86	136,027,604	21,340,147	22,727,739	1,387,592
	V	W	82	250,000	47,500	65,638	18,138
			85	24,960,320	4,850,464	5,234,343	383,879
			86	25,635	6,409	6,868	459
GUYANA	O	E	82	5,269,140	1,040,655	1,079,167	38,512
	V	E	81	148,780,620	33,778,641	35,895,900	2,117,259
			82	89,984,750	15,824,807	16,585,190	760,383
			83	63,657,534	11,974,885	12,474,718	499,833
			84	71,311,950	14,835,562	15,323,655	488,093
			85	11,706,240	2,434,499	2,537,435	102,936
			86	39,771,963	7,792,824	8,230,006	437,182
HAITI	V	E	82	13,133,989	2,612,767	2,670,649	57,882
			83	29,785,342	4,587,998	4,842,858	254,860
			84	33,405,120	7,061,894	7,327,258	265,364
HG KONG	V	W	81	4,500	2,172	2,357	185

Crop
Product
TSUSA commodity number, description, and unit of quantity

Country	Mode	Reg	Yr	Quantity	F.A.S.	C.I.F.	Charges
HONDURA	O E		82	22,979,740	3,073,591	3,255,329	181,738
			83	98,084,109	8,430,569	9,517,905	1,087,336
			84	4,802,470	375,553	409,170	33,617
			85	15,285,972	443,293	498,284	54,991
			86	15,307,696	447,855	503,200	55,345
	V E		81	183,300,714	46,317,395	48,461,296	2,143,901
			82	121,977,349	17,772,996	18,915,764	1,142,768
			83	113,196,841	18,353,239	19,460,970	1,107,731
			84	170,552,166	29,327,747	31,832,663	2,504,916
			85	80,821,320	10,326,737	11,310,648	983,911
			86	46,432,880	5,395,050	5,910,009	514,959
INDIA	V E		81	2,161	902	1,061	159
			83	57,815,635	10,995,640	11,898,845	903,205
			84	2,370	579	653	74
			85	39,020,800	7,564,544	8,114,154	549,610
	V W		82	22,032	5,497	5,746	249
IVY CST	O E		83	20,160,384	2,139,858	2,407,968	268,110
			86	493,131	73,571	73,571	
	V E		83	97,512,974	12,210,790	13,170,235	959,445
			85	23,781,387	3,728,922	3,989,147	260,225
			86	23,479,680	4,635,592	4,912,314	276,722
JAMAICA	O E		82	3,891,200	591,943	682,178	90,235
			83	22,294,720	4,319,069	4,624,861	305,792
	V E		82	14,611,276	2,781,383	2,939,403	158,020
			83	48,540,974	9,471,284	10,157,736	686,452
			84	64,225,488	13,616,052	14,379,710	763,658
			85	43,558,368	8,643,866	9,004,960	361,094
			86	11,200,000	2,280,457	2,346,400	65,943
MADAGAS	V E		81	24,028,480	7,824,478	8,428,134	603,656
			83	31,958,800	6,300,769	6,792,677	491,908
			84	31,499,070	6,919,758	7,408,482	488,724
			85	23,912,379	4,776,819	5,239,228	462,409
			86	24,030,720	4,347,531	4,700,664	353,133
MALAWI	O E		82	2,561,060	270,704	303,998	33,294
			83	10,881,602	1,150,186	1,291,647	141,461
			85	23,977,600	3,922,004	4,377,665	455,661
	V E		81	149,876,525	36,386,546	39,215,512	2,828,966
			82	53,719,710	8,863,687	9,992,018	1,128,331
			84	71,631,008	10,372,730	11,542,656	1,169,926
			85	54,201,280	9,792,551	10,679,584	887,033
MALAYSA	V E		81	765	1,007	1,109	102
MAURIT	O E		82	8,653,055	1,471,396	1,513,029	41,633
	V E		82	30,136,074	5,919,320	6,318,870	399,550
			83	57,959,146	12,348,652	12,876,944	528,292
			84	64,910,669	13,605,329	14,240,393	635,064
			85	21,547,086	4,312,194	4,648,875	336,681
			86	58,583,617	10,692,625	11,336,578	643,953
MEXICO	V E		83	64,234,945	13,678,682	14,077,885	399,203
			85	33,907,860	5,096,681	5,402,828	306,147
			86	220,642,457	21,847,671	23,551,919	1,704,248
MOZAMBQ	O E		82	369,600	65,338	72,884	7,546
	V E		82	101,534,990	32,823,077	34,426,449	1,603,372
			82	43,479,694	6,587,459	7,145,498	558,039
			83	56,530,073	11,551,492	12,316,083	764,591
			84	55,157,760	10,442,264	11,329,603	887,339
			85	19,012,960	3,692,039	4,020,283	328,244
			86	42,877,030	8,615,560	9,265,170	649,610
N ANTIL	V E		81	9,856,000	2,365,440	2,448,898	83,458
			82	6,137,600	1,313,446	1,369,333	55,887
NEW GUI	V E		85	24,250,200	4,595,094	5,098,577	503,483
	V W		86	23,765,588	3,700,295	4,171,860	471,565
NICARAG	O E		83	6,284,880	743,731	834,896	91,165
	V E		81	135,559,194	33,129,276	35,132,063	2,002,787
			82	101,433,927	15,645,923	17,247,616	1,601,693
			83	115,430,189	23,753,692	24,841,306	1,087,614
			84	11,650,500	2,067,964	2,173,198	105,234
			85	11,650,487	2,297,320	2,447,887	150,567
PANAMA	O E		82	51,018,330	6,343,257	7,053,773	710,516
			83	65,766,047	9,946,865	10,939,838	992,973
			84	740,182	165,488	177,481	11,993
			85	6,312,658	304,192	339,961	35,769
	V E		81	228,402,639	56,969,724	60,954,880	3,985,156
			82	131,589,825	19,256,079	20,960,758	1,704,679
			83	226,461,195	38,104,406	41,338,918	3,234,512
			84	117,889,585	25,590,833	27,106,717	1,515,884
			85	124,619,831	20,825,290	22,580,408	1,755,118
			86	70,604,993	10,504,003	11,570,470	1,066,467
PARAGUA	V E		81	31,064,912	9,105,495	9,859,117	753,622
			82	7,559,586	1,247,279	1,497,962	250,683
			83	21,459,508	4,724,626	4,939,321	214,695
			86	22,523,200	4,261,002	4,702,844	441,842
PERU	O E		82	995,600	160,541	172,110	11,569
			83	22,437,374	4,670,000	4,942,476	272,476
	V E		82	150,864,239	28,451,891	29,837,641	1,385,750
			83	155,574,596	31,971,224	33,410,664	1,439,440
			84	209,348,969	43,772,232	45,608,200	1,835,968
			85	192,862,033	39,528,240	42,389,024	2,860,784
			86	111,328,155	21,809,548	23,178,480	1,368,932
PHIL R	O E		82	168,722,630	21,766,384	23,381,374	1,614,990
			83	21,981,120	4,596,178	4,824,201	228,023
			85	102,144,000	19,945,833	21,164,382	1,218,549
	V E		81	498,130,537	126,536,885	136,168,364	9,631,479
			82	236,134,080	31,566,161	34,376,525	2,810,364
			83	501,635,839	97,435,090	102,960,531	5,525,441
			84	808,142,429	130,557,304	138,121,522	7,564,218
			85	568,438,660	104,086,175	111,053,839	6,967,664
			86	406,907,362	76,868,083	82,093,081	5,224,998
	V W		86	47,002,072	8,236,982	8,278,166	41,184
REP SAF	O E		82	49,441,280	4,996,819	5,179,021	182,202
			86	27,926,484	610,580	715,985	105,405
	V E		82	23,517,772	3,819,055	3,999,908	180,853
			83	94,782,942	11,047,579	11,459,154	411,575
			84	162,093,101	30,869,176	32,354,707	1,485,531
			85	111,275,720	17,585,813	18,652,908	1,067,095
			86	46,892,160	8,802,944	9,308,237	505,293
SALVADR	O E		82	1,593,056	282,402	402,858	120,456
			83	6,364,730	1,126,557	1,188,295	61,738
	V E		81	56,208,342	13,405,749	14,144,254	738,505
			82	132,432,540	21,992,698	23,347,607	1,354,909
			83	147,423,018	30,446,972	31,516,839	1,069,867
			84	134,593,710	28,765,404	30,185,251	1,419,847
			85	148,761,638	24,673,449	26,698,741	2,025,292
			86	91,383,991	10,432,468	11,194,274	761,806
SWAZLND	O E		82	33,245,470	5,219,538	5,506,261	286,723
			84	44,243,536	9,826,489	10,171,589	345,100
	V E		81	334,562,088	63,015,489	68,715,709	5,700,220
			82	130,583,472	22,023,512	23,308,951	1,285,439
			83	80,034,984	12,160,858	12,777,837	616,979
			84	50,708,161	11,000,656	11,392,684	392,028
			85	35,163,520	6,785,118	7,232,332	447,214
			86	53,382,887	10,497,111	11,105,839	608,728
THAILND	O E		82	43,286,657	6,008,437	6,537,117	528,680
	V E		81	502,881,280	87,225,243	94,904,146	7,678,903
			82	570,331,470	82,911,788	91,318,872	8,407,084
			83	32,627,840	5,831,536	6,465,431	633,895
			84	82,286,557	16,810,097	18,140,153	1,330,056
			85	71,878,817	12,358,093	13,096,077	737,984
			86	46,422,703	8,934,679	9,732,844	798,165
	V H		82	27,778,212	3,214,771	3,574,396	359,625
TRINID	V E		84	41,524,354	8,276,166	8,701,418	425,252
			85	20,107,120	4,067,487	4,173,108	105,621
			86	24,469,760	4,938,026	5,077,619	139,593
U KING	V E		81	129	294	346	52
			82	1,357	878	1,139	261
URUGUAY	O E		84	1,234,215	296,381	337,053	40,672
	V E		83	30,861,760	6,358,952	6,713,174	354,222
			84	14,660,800	2,830,831	3,133,353	302,522
			85	9,479,680	1,831,467	2,024,772	193,305
			86	23,587,200	4,352,642	4,674,436	321,794
ZMBABWE	N E		82	27,642,860	5,003,358	5,334,708	331,350
	O E		82	31,285,462	5,437,413	5,657,586	220,173
			84	82,994,000	15,447,219	17,356,082	1,908,863
	V E		81	187,781,342	35,413,859	38,074,569	2,660,710
			82	144,177,574	21,681,118	25,498,204	3,817,086
			83	67,336,640	12,298,329	12,803,702	505,373
			84	1,524,000	330,708	365,760	35,052
			85	30,563,240	5,873,632	6,265,120	391,488
			86	39,782,400	7,158,925	7,728,129	569,204

1553000 SUGARS, ETC NOV 6% NON SUGAR (CLB)

Country	Mode	Reg	Yr	Quantity	F.A.S.	C.I.F.	Charges
TOTAL			81	299,493	83,508	86,614	3,106
			82	5,268,850	920,280	922,790	2,510
			83	4,572,100	933,739	937,324	3,585
			84	13,363,284	2,789,192	2,790,149	957
			85	14,123,753	2,910,978	2,911,340	362
			86	8,604,067	1,873,951	1,877,422	3,471
BRAZIL	V E		83	37,779	9,853	12,481	2,628
CANADA	O E		81	283,603	66,870	66,870	
			82	5,087,392	873,174	874,131	957
			83	2,144,143	465,950	466,907	957
			84	6,961,528	1,500,738	1,500,738	
			85	6,723,966	1,441,406	1,441,406	
			86	4,055,823	930,848	931,283	435
	O W		82	171,380	34,568	34,568	
			83	2,314,496	436,738	436,738	
			84	6,281,234	1,266,108	1,267,065	957
			85	7,163,818	1,428,060	1,428,062	2

Crop Product TSUSA commodity number, description, and unit of quantity Country	Mode	Reg	Yr	Quantity	F.A.S.	C.I.F.	Charges
			86	4,374,301	886,117	886,117	
FR GERM	V	E	81	3,030	1,442	1,849	407
			82	1,356	765	838	73
JAMAICA	V	E	85	7,200	7,200	7,560	360
MEXICO	O	W	81	1,256	356	356	
			83	75,682	21,198	21,198	
			84	120,522	22,346	22,346	
			85	228,769	34,312	34,312	
			86	142,625	38,637	38,637	
PHIL R	V	W	86	3,748	1,429	1,721	292
U KING	A	E	81	2,082	3,788	4,818	1,030
	O	E	82	2,122	3,838	4,774	936
	V	E	81	1,800	1,447	1,649	202
			82	6,600	7,935	8,479	544
			86	27,570	16,920	19,664	2,744
	V	W	81	7,722	9,605	11,072	1,467

1553500 SUGARS, N SGR SLDS OV 6 PCT (GAL)

Country	Mode	Reg	Yr	Quantity	F.A.S.	C.I.F.	Charges
TOTAL			81	2,037,997	5,519,435	5,712,080	192,645
			82	2,566,147	4,202,420	4,324,390	121,970
			83	2,336,217	3,762,334	3,914,940	152,606
			84	3,494,729	4,968,851	5,120,869	152,018
			85	4,164,140	5,248,650	5,567,447	318,797
			86	8,097,310	7,059,478	7,611,099	551,621
AUSTRAL	N	W	85	133	3,238	3,833	595
BARBADO	O	E	81	295,453	1,302,910	1,302,910	
			82	301,903	1,326,336	1,326,336	
			83	275,747	1,212,583	1,212,583	
			84	290,357	1,309,131	1,309,131	
			85	267,347	1,132,032	1,132,888	856
			86	300,206	1,201,529	1,201,529	
	V	E	81	656,316	2,297,106	2,382,292	85,186
			82	646,467	1,096,257	1,121,274	25,017
			84	465,368	756,223	763,785	7,562
			85	408,454	663,738	670,338	6,600
			86	203,416	244,099	268,509	24,410
BELGIUM	V	E	86	489	6,055	6,689	634
BRAZIL	A	E	82	364	453	3,057	2,604
	O	E	82	74,512	56,600	65,706	9,106
			86	10,546	10,726	10,726	
	V	E	84	1,500	788	1,657	869
			86	1,570,507	673,329	819,352	146,023
C RICA	V	E	86	753,238	159,900	220,900	61,000
CANADA	O	E	81	19,184	74,380	74,380	
			82	17,811	62,010	62,010	
			83	25,440	82,982	82,982	
			84	12,414	26,996	26,996	
			85	63,093	114,685	114,685	
			86	967,150	1,045,458	1,045,458	
	O	W	83	4,406	11,730	11,730	
			84	43,388	119,629	119,629	
			85	91,085	250,526	250,526	
			86	110,173	286,211	286,211	
	V	E	86	2,308	5,980	8,580	2,600
CHINA M	V	E	81	1,875	4,075	4,964	889
			82	375	751	992	241
	V	W	81	773	1,472	1,617	145
			82	1,883	4,265	4,541	276
			83	1,876	3,185	3,486	301
			84	2,888	7,882	8,767	885
CHINA T	V	E	81	225	740	802	62
	V	W	81	745	2,545	2,686	141
			82	367	1,030	1,087	57
			83	475	897	914	17
			84	4	259	272	13
DOM REP	V	E	81	975,838	1,590,616	1,689,891	99,275
			82	1,498,275	1,522,359	1,605,674	83,315
			83	2,024,149	2,424,927	2,576,567	151,640
			84	2,599,312	2,615,320	2,752,845	137,525
			85	2,582,830	2,501,648	2,704,692	203,044
			86	3,882,956	3,207,091	3,489,696	282,605
F W IND	O	E	81	17,434	96,537	96,537	
			82	20,454	123,150	123,150	
			83	2,859	18,736	18,736	
			84	2,578	16,839	16,839	
FR GERM	O	E	82	202	525	551	26
	O	W	84	270	562	706	144
	V	E	81	470	2,640	2,803	163
			82	645	4,099	4,562	463
			83	1,170	6,604	7,092	488
			84	1,275	3,682	4,045	363
			86	378	3,056	3,324	268
	V	W	81	83	694	834	140

Crop Product TSUSA commodity number, description, and unit of quantity Country	Mode	Reg	Yr	Quantity	F.A.S.	C.I.F.	Charges
			84	270	1,130	1,362	232
FRANCE	A	E	84	111	936	1,348	412
	V	E	84	234	710	960	250
	V	W	84	11,887	3,003	3,225	222
			85	11,888	5,306	6,029	723
INDNSIA	V	W	84	21	285	302	17
JAMAICA	V	E	86	2,369	10,925	11,878	953
JAPAN	V	E	84	15	369	392	23
LEBANON	V	E	82	2,249	2,550	2,699	149
NETHLDS	A	E	83	5	276	390	114
	V	W	81	68	605	661	56
PERU	V	E	81	66,138	124,500	130,880	6,380
REP SAF	V	E	85	738,890	573,680	680,659	106,979
			86	291,000	185,817	218,800	32,983
SINGAPR	V	E	84	61,729	103,138	106,400	3,262
	V	W	84	113	658	691	33
THAILND	V	E	86	300	1,200	1,345	145
	V	W	84	5	254	267	13
TRINID	O	E	81	3,057	18,611	18,611	
U KING	O	E	85	420	3,797	3,797	
			86	2,274	18,102	18,102	
	V	E	81	338	2,004	2,212	208
			82	640	2,035	2,751	716
			83	90	414	460	46
			84	990	1,057	1,250	193

1554000 MOLASSES INEDIBLE N SUGAR (CLB)

Country	Mode	Reg	Yr	Quantity	F.A.S.	C.I.F.	Charges
TOTAL			81	1,200,814,166	112,208,424	133,526,527	21,318,103
			82	1,334,891,595	59,539,403	75,357,888	15,818,485
			83	1,726,722,619	79,938,813	102,306,261	22,367,448
			84	1,765,654,280	94,029,351	118,282,280	24,252,929
			85	2,098,580,233	89,528,702	114,481,646	24,952,944
			86	1,573,222,405	84,316,546	104,323,116	20,006,570
AUSTRAL	A	W	84	364	548	580	32
	V	E	81	90,657,433	10,302,258	13,126,014	2,823,756
			82	129,384,970	3,109,199	5,384,243	2,275,044
			83	54,668,389	2,125,073	2,840,750	715,677
			84	264,114,551	9,878,705	14,434,791	4,556,086
			85	300,189,697	7,370,854	9,661,582	2,290,728
			86	151,831,613	6,319,809	9,116,213	2,796,404
BAHAMAS	V	E	83	261,394	15,098	34,899	19,801
BARBADO	O	E	83	85,453	6,488	6,488	
			84	230,128	21,376	21,376	
			85	44,853	4,004	4,004	
			86	24,253	2,493	2,493	
	V	E	81	5,474,412	515,858	605,975	90,117
			82	16,233,932	646,347	863,565	217,218
			83	30,960,075	1,614,830	1,904,020	289,190
			84	49,538,426	2,348,302	2,583,423	235,121
			85	28,391,108	1,618,188	1,832,008	213,820
			86	574,182	31,679	40,254	8,575
BELIZE	V	E	81	24,334,860	2,139,536	2,630,007	490,471
			82	45,526,909	1,107,585	1,452,688	345,103
			83	41,987,565	1,472,395	2,014,898	542,503
			84	24,739,852	1,340,121	1,588,866	248,745
BRAZIL	V	E	81	130,746,160	14,184,661	16,648,929	2,464,268
			82	3,300	404	600	196
			83	25,603,657	1,585,053	2,112,443	527,390
			84	79,713,813	4,803,265	6,056,935	1,253,670
			85	299,876,384	18,572,350	22,400,540	3,828,190
			86	424,029,973	26,295,235	31,643,606	5,348,371
C RICA	V	E	81	6,581,735	631,539	764,267	132,728
			83	3,325,192	135,225	161,229	26,004
			84	10,202,678	535,802	658,756	122,954
			85	5,812,207	199,758	296,696	96,938
	V	W	81	10,777,890	547,973	618,313	70,340
CANADA	O	E	81	66,565	8,229	8,229	
			82	122,932	10,438	10,438	
			83	840,161	96,859	96,859	
			84	1,770,527	176,725	176,725	
			85	10,118,008	803,701	803,701	
			86	8,475,896	1,172,989	1,172,991	2
	O	W	82	1,162,196	41,934	41,934	
			83	90,219	2,978	2,978	
			86	3,291,790	120,500	120,502	2
CHILE	V	E	86	13,511,173	462,171	595,238	133,067
	V	W	83	6,878,773	342,595	578,515	235,920
CHINA M	V	W	81	3,600	5,705	5,990	285
			82	11,950	5,731	6,097	366
COLOMB	N	E	82	92,292,881	3,020,077	3,805,420	785,343
	V	E	81	161,804,064	10,500,268	11,782,877	1,282,609
			82	45,791,864	3,020,123	3,685,667	665,544
			83	162,960,596	6,850,218	9,523,460	2,673,242

Crop
Product
TSUSA commodity number, description, and unit of quantity

Country	Mode	Reg	Yr	Quantity	F.A.S.	C.I.F.	Charges
			84	55,754,125	2,641,685	3,360,383	718,698
			85	53,989,603	1,976,079	2,585,760	609,681
			86	118,755,043	7,142,569	8,323,896	1,181,327
CR N AN	V	E	82	8,959,275	483,934	602,591	118,657
			86	7,777,123	413,824	529,966	116,142
DOM REP	O	E	82	15,662,292	430,713	545,188	114,475
	V	E	81	174,237,608	19,989,670	21,987,830	1,998,160
			82	211,023,476	13,737,606	15,131,890	1,394,284
			83	211,031,235	9,517,738	11,437,917	1,920,179
			84	202,852,269	12,554,084	14,218,418	1,664,334
			85	124,184,969	6,426,288	7,527,025	1,100,737
			86	200,505,532	9,597,486	11,538,217	1,940,731
ECUADOR	V	E	81	63,496,817	4,196,281	5,561,977	1,365,696
			82	7,427,357	375,375	528,153	152,778
			83	4,938,113	247,500	279,000	31,500
			84	37,131,932	1,508,912	1,887,443	378,531
			85	58,596,982	1,634,252	2,225,126	590,874
EGYPT	V	E	84	38,068,915	1,876,802	2,495,866	619,064
F W IND	O	E	84	929	353	353	
FIJI	V	E	81	51,319,268	4,970,122	6,240,624	1,270,502
			82	47,242,613	1,600,221	2,875,835	1,275,624
			83	39,933,610	1,310,111	2,085,158	775,047
			85	51,731,308	1,926,044	3,066,028	1,139,984
	V	W	83	16,510,837	471,976	652,372	180,396
			84	22,186,917	1,026,450	1,507,689	481,239
			85	13,037,204	459,172	695,266	236,094
FR GERM	O	E	81	720	415	537	122
			83	1,080	609	706	97
FRANCE	V	E	81	19,779,239	3,065,717	3,375,867	310,150
			82	48,360,292	5,264,585	5,657,710	393,125
			83	126,447,402	14,818,362	16,516,051	1,697,689
			84	84,103,920	7,305,020	8,409,830	1,104,810
			85	37,848,394	3,137,278	3,663,238	525,960
GREECE	V	E	83	12,928,127	369,442	652,719	283,277
GUATMAL	V	E	81	108,480,993	10,663,324	13,371,317	2,707,993
			82	46,130,015	1,933,124	2,505,082	571,958
			83	126,903,797	4,566,702	6,662,022	2,095,320
			84	145,976,168	9,471,541	11,802,866	2,331,325
			85	145,365,347	5,925,075	7,809,815	1,884,740
			86	126,961,435	5,285,793	6,883,508	1,597,715
	V	W	82	6,041,861	189,350	287,818	98,468
			83	53,294,327	1,474,723	2,092,568	617,845
			84	23,230,703	2,826,274	3,016,899	190,625
			85	51,307,670	1,629,855	2,204,329	574,474
			86	56,998,028	1,601,155	2,091,219	490,064
GUYANA	V	E	81	25,755,643	2,386,641	2,851,838	465,197
			82	25,666,111	1,588,562	1,955,470	366,908
			83	39,592,481	1,619,105	2,075,811	456,706
			84	18,682,002	1,212,189	1,264,903	52,714
			86	10,804,093	752,578	808,393	55,815
HAITI	V	E	81	11,559,047	750,694	840,618	89,924
			82	13,543,035	345,351	541,146	195,795
			83	18,763,946	356,190	464,106	107,916
			84	17,084,828	649,890	928,107	278,217
			86	37,660,282	1,555,122	1,996,135	441,013
HG KONG	V	E	86	4,959	1,101	1,169	68
HONDURA	V	E	81	26,543,035	2,454,817	2,952,223	497,406
			82	59,767,193	2,010,432	2,543,552	533,120
			83	56,702,296	2,492,792	2,963,638	470,846
			84	48,294,073	3,089,289	3,683,740	594,451
			86	37,724,827	2,093,309	2,562,040	468,731
	V	W	81	15,834,364	1,092,568	1,248,825	156,257
			82	60,428,894	1,151,988	1,637,406	485,418
			83	7,803,403	392,558	555,685	163,127
			85	9,171,220	440,000	571,360	131,360
INDIA	V	E	84	11,294,955	549,107	810,555	261,448
INDNSIA	V	E	84	25,463,361	1,449,000	1,629,000	180,000
			86	11,581,998	654,169	957,259	303,090
	V	W	81	25,748,739	1,006,661	1,495,227	488,566
			82	27,914,133	784,627	1,169,743	385,116
			83	19,725,266	204,481	409,773	205,292
ITALY	V	E	81	17,819,977	1,283,748	1,652,459	368,711
			85	17,837,309	602,847	788,371	185,524
			86	15,895,332	1,010,420	1,265,667	255,247
JAMAICA	V	E	83	24,500,105	951,002	1,276,363	325,361
			84	4,683	1,529	1,770	241
			86	3,412	2,975	3,133	158
JAPAN	V	E	81	3,591,176	73,303	239,712	166,409
KENYA	V	E	84	5,123,939	254,790	363,724	108,934
MALAYSA	V	W	84	6,696,581	185,667	276,790	91,123
MAURIT	V	E	81	10,168,711	915,049	1,177,896	262,847
			82	25,897,932	1,402,235	1,933,110	530,875
			83	46,091,079	2,058,863	2,292,255	233,392
			84	32,780,175	958,364	1,529,699	571,335
			85	33,750,079	1,164,360	1,666,637	502,277
			86	12,513,832	604,738	904,923	300,185
MEXICO	O	E	81	4,073,027	80,798	80,798	
			83	13,834,708	462,625	462,625	
			84	571,581	21,896	21,896	
			85	906,047	28,473	28,473	
			86	694,350	32,997	32,997	
	V	E	81	26,954,280	2,838,305	3,445,357	607,052
			82	118,607,026	4,933,470	5,595,994	662,524
			83	94,468,896	4,022,513	4,643,513	621,000
			84	130,931,814	6,570,594	7,783,059	1,212,465
			85	205,508,885	9,426,162	11,143,167	1,717,005
			86	103,027,262	6,572,906	7,626,628	1,053,722
	V	W	81	8,826,129	785,904	919,086	133,182
			82	20,381,325	1,065,956	1,328,705	262,749
MOZAMBQ	V	E	82	8,587,623	374,550	562,645	188,095
			83	309,526	225,000	337,500	112,500
			84	10,459,893	399,000	604,390	205,390
			85	20,950,213	420,000	656,200	236,200
NETHLDS	V	E	81	48,559,049	6,511,449	7,135,401	623,952
			82	38,079,615	4,205,949	4,579,121	373,172
			83	40,211,904	2,879,857	3,295,670	415,813
			84	15,873,120	1,282,080	1,506,637	224,557
			85	58,085,037	4,793,712	5,463,763	670,051
			86	20,000,131	2,334,080	2,565,038	230,958
NICARAG	V	E	81	54,496,442	4,798,973	5,902,420	1,103,447
			83	34,466,267	1,290,743	1,753,704	462,961
			84	26,308,894	1,590,211	1,953,556	363,345
			85	13,831,581	509,459	668,863	159,404
	V	W	84	15,335,168	588,865	737,724	148,859
PANAMA	V	E	81	37,670,746	2,518,435	3,160,421	641,986
			82	19,255,455	892,446	1,155,841	263,395
			83	112,242,114	4,447,980	5,657,705	1,209,725
			84	61,290,485	3,911,995	4,571,414	659,419
			85	37,940,117	1,723,038	2,117,892	394,854
			86	46,134,190	2,506,236	2,949,685	443,449
PERU	V	E	82	79,779,654	2,238,861	3,191,150	952,289
			83	149,118,559	5,565,089	7,685,668	2,120,579
			84	102,342,617	3,961,258	5,419,615	1,458,357
			85	83,232,049	2,753,838	3,548,877	795,039
			86	7,921,073	202,668	311,559	108,891
PHIL R	V	W	83	11,725,379	547,001	876,600	329,599
			85	16,067,746	336,006	548,523	212,517
REP SAF	V	E	81	21,091,500	1,069,644	1,529,736	460,092
			82	47,833,745	995,221	2,042,530	1,047,309
			83	95,937,952	3,956,441	5,821,702	1,865,261
			84	61,267,542	2,496,148	3,839,401	1,343,253
			85	219,081,361	9,300,572	12,875,030	3,574,458
			86	98,209,628	5,358,924	7,143,241	1,784,317
S ARAB	V	E	85	47,455,052	1,538,055	2,351,696	813,641
SALVADR	V	E	83	8,783,958	520,903	727,269	206,366
SOMALIA	V	E	84	8,576,760	553,700	746,467	192,767
			85	10,783,306	470,315	707,831	237,516
SUDAN	V	E	82	23,638,415	1,285,731	1,741,509	455,778
			84	38,538,113	1,789,609	2,680,936	891,327
SWAZLND	V	E	84	3,966,516	173,000	259,050	86,050
			85	34,412,042	1,102,207	1,530,188	427,981
			86	46,605,341	1,373,127	2,256,480	883,353
THAILND	V	E	82	1,080	1,248	1,411	163
			83	919,318	149,953	161,861	11,908
			84	17,466,437	753,115	1,003,780	250,665
			85	48,184,177	1,357,943	2,119,719	761,776
	V	W	82	43,573,798	1,251,524	1,959,120	707,596
			83	26,303,973	538,030	893,668	355,638
			84	39,555,975	1,699,771	2,398,835	699,064
			85	30,507,425	917,044	1,463,772	546,728
TNZANIA	V	E	84	8,265,155	432,583	613,493	180,910
			85	12,561,989	229,269	439,012	209,743
			86	11,705,654	815,493	880,666	65,173
TRINID	O	E	81	445,056	55,879	55,879	
			82	558,446	34,516	34,516	
			83	252,199	19,112	19,112	
			84	14,560	1,561	1,561	
			85	14,560	1,508	1,508	
	V	E	81	13,915,881	1,864,000	2,109,878	245,878
			83	5,319,288	214,600	276,981	62,381
			84	14,301,431	844,776	995,378	150,602
U KING	V	E	85	17,806,304	730,996	1,015,646	284,650
URUGUAY	V	E	84	5,547,405	293,399	435,601	142,202

Crop Product TSUSA commodity number, description, and unit of quantity Country	Mode	Reg	Yr	Quantity	F.A.S.	C.I.F.	Charges

Sugar beet, seed
1260300 SUGAR BEET SEED (LB)

Country	Mode	Reg	Yr	Quantity	F.A.S.	C.I.F.	Charges
TOTAL			81	269,659	2,173,648	2,223,325	49,677
			82	361,750	3,300,852	3,427,124	126,272
			83	341,803	1,987,333	2,042,546	55,213
			84	61,942	392,666	415,873	23,207
			85	136,338	1,871,791	1,884,073	12,282
			86	149,604	2,977,404	3,014,098	36,694
BELGIUM	A	W	81	132	1,409	1,550	141
CANADA	O	E	83	35,690	92,794	95,385	2,591
	O	W	81	58,601	66,934	66,934	
			82	32,901	13,050	13,050	
DENMARK	A	E	81	3,372	2,022	4,904	2,882
			82	4,353	2,310	5,286	2,976
			86	3,605	2,022	3,857	1,835
	A	W	83	5,657	2,537	5,828	3,291
			84	4,597	2,036	5,624	3,588
			85	3,827	1,710	5,246	3,536
	N	E	85	15,187	136,660	136,660	
	V	E	86	5,015	45,500	45,975	475
FR GERM	A	E	81	555	4,437	4,544	107
			82	522	4,184	4,599	415
			83	874	5,891	6,433	542
			84	363	2,905	3,163	258
			85	1,137	5,123	6,128	1,005
			86	1,438	11,527	13,640	2,113
	A	W	84	6,926	39,721	46,067	6,346
	N	W	83	383	548	653	105
	O	E	82	35	286	396	110
	V	E	82	930	930	1,025	95
			85	1,473	4,005	4,578	573
	V	W	81	3,855	4,551	5,254	703
			82	845	3,062	3,290	228
			83	382	3,060	3,165	105
			86	663	5,178	5,405	227
FRANCE	A	E	82	39	584	858	274
	A	W	81	33	495	608	113
ITALY	A	E	82	496	263	602	339
JAPAN	A	W	81	223	4,429	5,020	591
			82	904	15,440	17,538	2,098
			83	110	2,885	3,050	165
			84	254	3,858	4,569	711
			86	466	204,463	207,505	3,042
	V	W	85	2,213	79,220	79,681	461
			86	1,582	661,648	662,593	945
N ZEAL	A	W	81	12,375	12,881	20,325	7,444
NETHLDS	A	E	81	666	749	1,751	1,002
			83	220	400	809	409
	A	W	84	811	468	929	461
REP SAF	V	E	85	462	9,188	9,379	191
SWEDEN	A	E	81	7,473	107,040	113,574	6,534
			82	7,883	123,980	129,194	5,214
			84	4,275	60,203	64,844	4,641
			85	2,724	38,985	41,490	2,505
			86	2,613	20,839	24,646	3,807
	A	W	81	443	6,631	8,412	1,781
			83	12,079	181,780	193,347	11,567
			85	2,800	36,406	38,917	2,511
			86	4,685	88,411	96,394	7,983
	V	E	82	152,600	1,179,790	1,274,153	94,363
			83	61,127	529,376	543,802	14,426
			84	15,450	212,693	218,156	5,463
			85	105,534	1,547,067	1,548,567	1,500
			86	125,072	1,871,400	1,886,112	14,712
U KING	A	E	81	2,034	3,535	5,653	2,118
			82	364	287	578	291
			83	10,340	21,847	26,939	5,092
			86	794	15,549	17,104	1,555
	A	W	81	307	490	583	93
	O	E	81	179,590	1,958,045	1,984,213	26,168
			82	158,097	1,955,268	1,974,818	19,550
			83	210,100	1,135,350	1,151,294	15,944
			84	26,647	69,282	70,682	1,400
			85	981	13,427	13,427	
			86	3,671	50,867	50,867	
	V	W	82	1,781	1,418	1,737	319
			83	4,841	10,865	11,841	976
			84	2,619	1,500	1,839	339

Sugarcane

Sugarcane**
1551200 SUGARCANE, NATURAL (STN)

Country	Mode	Reg	Yr	Quantity	F.A.S.	C.I.F.	Charges
TOTAL			81	2	764	808	44
			82	*	708	792	84
			83	*	280	316	36
			84	2	1,349	1,419	70
			85	50	6,179	7,465	1,286
			86	55,517	380,477	385,429	4,952
C RICA	V	E	85	45	2,707	3,600	893
			86	565	4,532	5,720	1,188
	V	W	86	6	4,410	6,155	1,745
CHINA T	N	W	83	*	280	316	36
	V	W	81	1	462	483	21
			84	2	1,349	1,419	70
COLOMB	O	E	86	54,894	356,846	357,900	1,054
CR N AN	V	E	86	35	1,149	1,169	20
INDIA	N	W	82	*	708	792	84
PERU	V	E	81	1	302	325	23
THAILND	V	W	85	5	3,472	3,865	393
			86	17	13,540	14,485	945

1551500 SUGAR BEET A CANE NT NATURAL (CLB)
(See Sugar beet under Sugar Beet)

Sugarcane, processed**
1552025 CANE SUGAR IMMEDITE CNSMPTN (LB)
(See Sugar beet, processed under Sugar Beet)
1552045 CANE, BEET SUGAR, ETC, NSPF (LB)
(See Sugar beet, processed under Sugar Beet)
1553000 SUGARS, ETC NOV 6% NON SUGAR (CLB)
(See Sugar beet, processed under Sugar Beet)
1553500 SUGARS, N SGR SLDS OV 6 PCT (GAL)
(See Sugar beet, processed under Sugar Beet)
1554000 MOLASSES INEDIBLE N SUGAR (CLB)
(See Sugar beet, processed under Sugar Beet)

Sumac

Japan wax
4941400 JAPAN WAX (LB)

Country	Mode	Reg	Yr	Quantity	F.A.S.	C.I.F.	Charges
TOTAL			81	107,415	433,172	441,410	8,238
			82	93,656	290,049	298,750	8,701
			83	111,302	288,123	301,422	13,299
			84	140,492	352,426	371,107	18,681
			85	181,712	385,086	405,198	20,112
			86	57,799	225,134	232,586	7,452
BRAZIL	V	E	85	44,023	38,144	42,205	4,061
FR GERM	V	W	83	4,000	2,699	3,078	379
JAPAN	O	E	84	39	369	384	15
	V	E	81	107,415	433,172	441,410	8,238
			82	93,656	290,049	298,750	8,701
			83	107,302	285,424	298,344	12,920
			84	139,953	350,330	368,848	18,518
			85	115,702	310,072	325,272	15,200
			86	33,600	128,484	132,468	3,984
	V	W	84	500	1,727	1,875	148
			85	21,987	36,870	37,721	851
			86	24,199	96,650	100,118	3,468

Sumac, dye or tannin**
4705500 MYROBALAN AND SUMAC (LB)
(See Myrobalan, tannin under Myrobalan)

Sunflower

Sunflower, oil, fatty acid**
4902200 FATTY ACIDS DRVD HMP KPK ETC (LB)
(See Hempseed, fatty acid under Hemp)

Sunflower, oil, fatty salt**

4904600 FATTY SALTS OF SESAME ETC (LB)

(See Hempseed, fatty salt under Hemp)

Sunflower, seed

1755100 SUNFLOWER SEED (LB)

Country	Mode	Reg	Yr	Quantity	F.A.S.	C.I.F.	Charges
TOTAL			81	80,351,202	9,766,845	9,924,765	157,920
			82	70,123,212	7,194,614	7,280,449	85,835
			83	85,156,721	9,570,855	9,716,256	145,401
			84	53,940,981	7,826,239	8,072,640	246,401
			85	50,571,634	6,158,027	6,314,199	156,172
			86	45,573,991	3,513,732	3,696,606	182,874
ARGENT	A	E	82	1,313	1,313	3,185	1,872
			83	6,778	9,794	22,955	13,161
			84	2,981	1,681	5,718	4,037
			85	30,966	12,506	40,626	28,120
	V	E	83	4,225,579	243,833	316,668	72,835
			86	24,824,524	1,261,248	1,324,310	63,062
AUSTRAL	V	W	86	13,439	6,409	7,001	592
CANADA	N	E	85	1,677,740	304,135	304,135	
	O	E	81	78,181,021	9,143,564	9,143,564	
			82	68,535,070	6,902,883	6,918,761	15,878
			83	79,314,762	9,030,202	9,035,142	4,940
			84	48,178,526	6,814,863	6,814,863	
			85	46,842,431	5,464,236	5,464,936	700
			86	18,921,323	1,890,095	1,890,358	263
	O	W	81	468,540	47,993	47,993	
			82	490,470	65,406	65,406	
			83	767,418	104,678	104,678	
			84	295,777	56,995	56,995	
			85	170,400	35,203	35,203	
			86	207,357	30,327	30,327	
	V	E	82	39,996	8,799	9,024	225
CHILE	A	E	82	696	947	1,986	1,039
			83	8,551	8,551	15,001	6,450
			84	26,131	6,519	23,114	16,595
			85	11,357	7,512	8,905	1,393
			86	17,173	8,861	22,634	13,773
	O	E	86	13,175	6,335	6,575	240
CHINA M	O	E	84	224,449	49,669	50,069	400
			85	38,742	8,100	8,100	
	O	W	81	375	312	326	14
	V	E	81	38,580	5,586	10,288	4,702
			82	83,702	13,047	19,865	6,818
			83	39,683	5,540	9,090	3,550
			84	1,190,406	221,124	276,194	55,070
			85	149,215	23,831	35,989	12,158
			86	311,246	49,021	66,346	17,325
	V	W	81	137,636	27,509	33,595	6,086
			82	607,146	111,721	142,328	30,607
			83	613,391	117,416	151,281	33,865
			84	2,937,638	541,846	690,134	148,288
			85	1,338,090	206,136	286,919	80,783
			86	989,723	143,967	202,373	58,406
CHINA T	O	E	84	674,608	32,603	32,603	
	V	E	82	44,000	10,711	13,975	3,264
			83	22,490	4,437	5,110	673
	V	W	82	1,125	792	869	77
			83	375	253	264	11
			84	3,575	425	455	30
EGYPT	V	E	82	22,046	5,500	7,397	1,897
			84	8,907	7,615	8,078	463
FR GERM	O	E	82	4,000	1,581	1,581	
	V	E	83	44,092	14,001	15,581	1,580
FRANCE	A	E	83	1,082	2,426	3,179	753
			84	231	671	949	278
	O	E	84	780	422	555	133
	V	E	83	154	1,718	1,785	67
GREECE	V	E	86	1,764	1,024	1,167	143
HG KONG	V	E	84	215,836	40,871	51,283	10,412
ICELAND	V	E	85	22,859	9,096	12,096	3,000
ISRAEL	V	E	81	326,743	70,801	94,689	23,888
			82	46,805	8,346	12,177	3,831
			83	108,177	26,330	33,846	7,516
			84	23,728	15,959	18,989	3,030
			85	84,060	40,223	48,422	8,199
			86	109,007	62,008	76,397	14,389
JAPAN	V	W	81	38,581	7,294	10,238	2,944
			82	43,561	10,508	12,483	1,975
			85	121,764	19,442	25,959	6,517
KENYA	V	E	84	2,246	553	701	148
MALAWI	V	E	81	97,122	17,205	27,194	9,989
MEXICO	O	E	81	71,313	81,259	81,259	
			83	4,189	1,676	1,676	
MONGOLA	O	E	85	37,130	3,991	3,991	
MOZAMBQ	V	E	81	71,193	10,692	16,969	6,277
	V	W	81	383,741	68,064	111,506	43,442
NETHLDS	A	E	82	3,200	2,363	3,626	1,263
	V	E	81	47,463	29,344	33,855	4,511
PHIL R	V	W	82	82	441	454	13
REP SAF	A	E	84	5,070	4,327	7,900	3,573
	N	E	81	135,792	158,683	188,378	29,695
	V	E	81	352,000	97,262	123,618	26,356
			82	200,000	50,256	67,332	17,076
			86	52,951	33,800	41,236	7,436
SPAIN	V	E	85	46,880	23,616	38,918	15,302
SWITZLD	V	E	86	112,309	20,637	27,882	7,245
U KING	V	W	84	150,092	30,096	34,040	3,944
YUGOSLV	V	W	81	1,102	1,277	1,293	16

Sunflower, vegetable oil, edible

1765500 SUNFLOWER OIL, EDIBLE (LB)

Country	Mode	Reg	Yr	Quantity	F.A.S.	C.I.F.	Charges
TOTAL			81	245,971	91,423	98,475	7,052
			82	507,937	168,771	175,540	6,769
			83	108,361	43,572	45,725	2,153
			84	156,416	82,935	89,053	6,118
			85	89,332	104,439	111,079	6,640
			86	220,163	141,770	159,738	17,968
BELGIUM	A	E	81	1,014	394	405	11
CANADA	A	E	84	6,160	5,972	6,497	525
			85	24,619	74,269	78,184	3,915
			86	87,837	74,929	81,189	6,260
	O	E	81	169,678	50,765	50,765	
			82	295,646	78,530	78,530	
			83	47,860	13,611	13,611	
			84	10,104	6,914	6,914	
			85	33,204	7,060	7,060	
	O	W	82	162,699	65,653	65,653	
			83	37,600	19,787	19,787	
			84	87,268	45,575	45,575	
CHINA M	A	E	86	12,240	11,349	12,167	818
FR GERM	A	E	84	13,647	6,271	6,830	559
FRANCE	N	E	83	5,585	3,182	3,504	322
			84	1,940	2,830	3,743	913
	V	E	81	1,832	1,274	1,424	150
			86	110	2,499	2,583	84
IRELAND	V	E	81	36,708	21,340	25,771	4,431
			82	40,789	21,625	27,866	6,241
			84	12,236	6,118	7,630	1,512
ISRAEL	A	E	86	82,396	40,000	45,160	5,160
ITALY	A	E	81	47	445	507	62
JAPAN	V	W	85	1,350	2,790	3,022	232
TURKEY	V	E	86	1,625	1,042	1,208	166
U KING	O	E	83	15,906	6,475	8,093	1,618
	V	E	81	12,336	6,899	8,373	1,474
			85	30,159	20,320	22,813	2,493
			86	16,755	7,735	9,215	1,480
USSR	O	E	81	4,409	954	1,100	146
			82	4,982	1,344	1,491	147
			84	22,575	8,246	10,328	2,082
	V	E	81	19,947	9,352	10,130	778
			82	2,487	1,063	1,171	108
			83	1,410	517	730	213
			86	19,200	4,216	8,216	4,000
	V	W	82	1,334	556	829	273
			84	2,486	1,009	1,536	527

Sunflower, vegetable oil, inedible

1765400 SUNFLOWER OIL INEDIBLE (LB)

Country	Mode	Reg	Yr	Quantity	F.A.S.	C.I.F.	Charges
TOTAL			86	11,023	59,151	61,179	2,028
FRANCE	V	E	86	11,023	59,151	61,179	2,028

Crop Product TSUSA commodity number, description, and unit of quantity Country	Mode	Reg	Yr	Quantity	F.A.S.	C.I.F.	Charges

Sunn Hemp

Sunn hemp, fiber, processed
3045200 SUNN FIBERS PROCESSED ETC (LB)

TOTAL			86	26,947	15,870	18,299	2,429
JAPAN	V	E	86	3,247	11,592	12,639	1,047
VENEZ	V	E	86	23,700	4,278	5,660	1,382

Sunn hemp, fiber, raw and waste
3045000 SUNN, RAW AND WASTES (LTN)

TOTAL			84	3	349	356	7
U KING	A	E	84	3	349	356	7

Sweet Potato

Sweet potato, fresh or frozen
1378930 SWEET POTATOES, FRSH, CH FZ (LB)

TOTAL			81	7,896,956	665,950	894,820	228,870
			82	10,305,137	886,272	1,216,690	330,418
			83	16,727,010	1,389,026	1,875,095	486,069
			84	17,414,908	1,454,896	1,972,579	517,683
			85	21,551,656	1,805,570	2,457,968	652,398
			86	16,928,303	1,725,049	2,318,158	593,109
CHINA T	V	E	84	315	348	389	41
COLOMB	V	E	86	9,450	1,512	2,369	857
DENMARK	V	E	86	10,500	1,680	1,987	307
DOM REP	N	E	81	7,888,011	662,629	890,617	227,988
			82	10,273,002	882,560	1,210,594	328,034
			83	16,641,795	1,378,496	1,860,980	482,484
			84	16,286,150	1,353,665	1,835,964	482,299
			85	20,569,157	1,712,733	2,335,154	622,421
			86	15,534,742	1,507,156	2,039,167	532,011
	V	E	81	800	875	1,352	477
			82	31,000	2,480	4,767	2,287
			83	63,970	5,730	8,710	2,980
			84	1,088,030	90,766	120,144	29,378
			85	981,005	91,550	121,342	29,792
			86	1,373,611	214,701	274,635	59,934
FRANCE	V	E	84	4,000	341	629	288
GUATMAL	V	E	81	8,145	2,446	2,851	405
HAITI	V	E	84	27,498	2,500	7,200	4,700
JAMAICA	A	E	83	15,593	2,550	2,804	254
			84	1,560	2,902	3,397	495
JAPAN	V	E	85	1,494	1,287	1,472	185
	V	W	82	435	655	686	31
			83	652	991	1,044	53
			84	5,500	3,025	3,293	268
PHIL R	V	W	82	700	577	643	66
			83	1,750	869	1,073	204
			84	1,605	553	720	167
ROMANIA	V	W	84	250	796	843	47
TRINID	V	E	83	3,250	390	484	94

Sweetsop

*Sweetsop, fresh or prepaerd or preserved***
1468700 CASHEW APPLES,ETC FR OR PRES (LB)
(See Cashew apple, fresh or prepared or preserved under Cashew)

*Sweetsop, jelly or jam***
1530200 CASHEW APPLE, MANGO JELLY (LB)
(See Cashew apple, jelly or jam under Cashew)

*Sweetsop, paste and pulp***
1524300 FRUIT PASTE, CASHEW APPL ETC (LB)
(See Cashew apple, paste and pulp under Cashew)

Crop Product TSUSA commodity number, description, and unit of quantity Country	Mode	Reg	Yr	Quantity	F.A.S.	C.I.F.	Charges

T

Tall Meadow Oat Grass

Tall oat, seed
1268300 TALL OAT SEED (LB)

TOTAL			81	2,750	435	435	
			82	13,669	2,257	2,257	
CANADA	O	E	81	2,750	435	435	
			82	13,669	2,257	2,257	

Tamarind

Tamarind, fresh or prepared or preserved
1494000 TAMARINOS FRESH PREP OR PRES (LB)

TOTAL			81	1,549,591	569,905	665,963	96,128
			82	1,091,631	446,559	495,438	48,879
			83	3,091,159	796,260	946,351	150,091
			84	2,053,409	575,436	638,518	63,082
			85	1,708,290	565,929	664,439	98,510
			86	1,819,485	587,554	671,957	84,403
BURMA	V	E	82	1,000	788	905	117
C RICA	V	E	81	43,488	7,248	8,754	1,506
			82	22,752	3,792	4,580	788
			84	7,293	1,692	2,162	470
			85	51,011	7,708	11,643	3,935
CANADA	O	E	83	360	658	658	
CHINA M	V	W	84	396	1,800	1,860	60
CHINA T	V	E	82	1,250	363	494	131
			83	7,872	3,292	3,913	621
	V	W	81	500	528	600	72
COLOMB	V	E	82	15,000	1,512	2,202	690
			83	1,051,724	104,826	159,634	54,808
			84	429,670	51,540	51,540	
DOM REP	N	E	81	517,391	154,455	202,184	47,729
			82	45,565	7,843	9,991	2,148
			83	415,357	79,272	105,635	26,363
			84	297,136	48,726	65,965	17,239
	V	E	81	127,484	19,265	24,506	5,241
			82	61,330	17,852	21,316	3,464
			83	135,690	16,777	22,207	5,430
			84	122,975	15,206	19,336	4,130
			85	431,368	124,554	144,512	19,958
			86	336,973	73,951	91,635	17,684
	V	W	84	4,500	1,710	2,204	494
ECUADOR	V	E	83	139,672	10,744	16,788	6,044
	V	W	85	198,336	14,462	29,230	14,768
FR GERM	V	W	82	42	322	402	80
GUATMAL	V	E	85	180,000	35,500	45,000	9,500
HAITI	V	E	81	7,039	1,852	2,346	494
			83	1,000	398	449	51
			84	11,800	1,628	1,918	290
HG KONG	V	E	82	1,250	338	407	69
	V	W	85	5,688	5,530	5,977	447
			86	804	2,009	2,232	223
INDIA	N	E	82	50,989	31,326	37,718	6,392
			83	6,073	3,837	4,496	659
			84	32,497	26,005	30,301	4,296
			85	39,979	20,299	22,021	1,722
			86	4,782	4,343	4,914	571
	N	W	84	19,691	14,712	16,980	2,268
	O	E	82	3,616	2,209	2,209	
			83	1,045	1,088	1,238	150
			84	5,459	2,557	2,733	176
			85	1,430	1,198	1,412	214
	V	E	81	90,222	56,237	70,565	14,328
			82	6,582	5,250	6,547	1,297
			83	92,713	48,701	60,522	11,821
			84	125,204	62,718	74,647	11,929
			85	97,918	53,686	62,281	8,595
			86	182,061	96,653	112,450	15,797
	V	W	81	3,472	3,441	4,017	576
			82	28,182	20,739	24,306	3,567
			83	38,010	28,759	33,738	4,979

Crop Product TSUSA commodity number, description, and unit of quantity Country Mode Reg Yr	Quantity	F.A.S.	C.I.F.	Charges
84	12,867	9,304	11,356	2,052
85	60,984	25,125	28,608	3,483
86	31,516	20,420	22,696	2,276
INDNSIA O E 81	5,000	1,100	1,240	140
V W 81	1,279	554	600	46
83	232	300	339	39
85	8,818	1,054	1,180	126
JAPAN V E 81	800	440	501	61
V W 81	1,896	2,077	2,234	157
LEBANON A W 84	350	360	378	18
MALAYSA V E 81	5,000	1,016	1,213	197
MEXICO A W 85	4,655	1,056	2,262	1,206
O E 81	103,978	20,275	20,275	
82	48,559	9,606	9,606	
83	58,886	9,268	10,268	1,000
84	70,839	49,497	49,497	
85	21,708	20,459	20,459	
86	36,706	40,137	40,137	
O W 81	332,971	94,648	94,648	
82	518,557	128,705	128,705	
83	678,341	185,420	185,420	
84	689,422	161,694	161,694	
85	292,163	73,583	73,583	
86	595,120	123,490	123,490	
N ZEAL A E 81	10,409	7,701	8,616	915
82	3,611	5,003	6,222	1,219
85	4,996	6,797	12,397	5,600
A W 81	2,819	3,238	4,885	1,647
82	3,423	4,132	5,637	1,505
83	300	278	464	186
85	5,445	7,747	13,167	5,420
V E 83	16,561	10,191	13,156	2,965
NETHLDS V E 81	197	285	316	31
V W 86	20,100	1,493	1,713	220
PANAMA A E 86	12,000	1,800	4,308	2,508
PHIL R O W 83	433	606	655	49
V E 81	17,517	15,545	18,041	2,496
82	32,282	26,550	30,992	4,442
83	55,824	31,984	36,791	4,807
84	35,107	25,520	30,819	5,299
85	12,154	10,569	12,548	1,979
86	10,956	11,928	13,182	1,254
V H 81	6,164	6,227	7,561	1,404
82	15,968	14,083	16,520	2,437
83	59,341	52,645	61,846	9,201
84	8,813	6,638	7,664	1,026
85	7,838	7,577	8,686	1,109
86	28,638	30,569	34,182	3,613
V W 81	83,314	72,718	81,354	8,636
82	92,972	88,244	99,280	11,036
83	75,862	62,947	70,058	7,111
84	43,787	28,681	32,146	3,465
85	21,941	28,761	32,444	3,683
86	35,982	38,781	42,330	3,549
SINGAPR V E 82	5,000	1,000	1,240	240
83	5,000	1,050	1,240	190
V W 81	1,742	646	699	53
SPAIN V E 86	180,303	44,610	61,262	16,652
THAILND N E 81	32,002	17,594	19,628	2,034
O E 86	2,502	1,383	1,506	123
O W 85	5,809	2,755	2,955	200
86	4,685	1,990	2,179	189
V E 81	4,850	2,725	3,141	416
82	34,906	20,990	23,943	2,953
83	50,119	26,406	30,231	3,825
84	24,571	17,911	19,992	2,081
85	59,328	22,610	26,232	3,622
86	52,061	26,345	30,010	3,665
V H 81	588	449	504	55
82	350	256	295	39
83	2,989	2,675	2,911	236
84	1,499	1,157	1,294	137
V W 81	149,469	79,641	87,535	7,894
82	98,445	55,656	61,921	6,265
83	197,755	114,138	123,694	9,556
84	66,801	38,846	42,642	3,796
85	196,721	94,899	107,842	12,943
86	237,184	58,404	67,374	8,970
VENEZ A E 84	42,902	7,534	11,390	3,856
86	47,112	9,248	16,357	7,109

Tamarind, paste and pulp
1526000 TAMARIND PASTE AND PULP (LB)

Crop Product TSUSA commodity number, description, and unit of quantity Country Mode Reg Yr	Quantity	F.A.S.	C.I.F.	Charges
TOTAL 81	469,544	196,708	218,535	21,827
82	694,528	217,148	238,524	21,376
83	704,692	288,981	317,919	28,938
84	430,443	131,714	143,714	12,000
85	220,192	124,812	135,956	11,144
86	582,553	244,823	269,776	24,953
COLOMB V E 86	22,050	15,000	15,350	350
DOM REP V E 81	288,252	88,100	98,649	10,549
82	383,739	62,494	76,169	13,675
83	444,917	161,950	179,140	17,190
84	164,102	19,247	24,045	4,798
85	78,406	18,411	22,606	4,195
86	355,510	95,202	108,533	13,331
GUATMAL A W 82	1,440	455	721	266
84	2,200	562	1,069	507
V W 84	482	665	754	89
HAITI V E 82	2,612	1,306	1,538	232
INDIA O E 81	8,913	7,182	8,152	970
82	360	389	389	
83	12,263	7,368	8,446	1,078
84	16,115	7,783	8,786	1,003
V E 81	47,579	33,865	41,576	7,711
82	31,648	21,430	25,066	3,636
83	67,619	54,401	61,247	6,846
84	38,219	25,884	29,797	3,913
85	51,170	62,782	68,976	6,194
86	83,612	75,545	83,242	7,697
V W 81	13,242	9,842	11,746	1,904
82	24,344	14,328	17,007	2,679
83	31,577	14,633	18,014	3,381
84	14,826	6,386	7,621	1,235
86	27,333	12,565	14,519	1,954
ITALY V E 86	5,348	1,180	1,652	472
MEXICO O E 81	8,024	3,584	3,584	
82	1,874	647	647	
84	33,700	9,394	9,394	
86	4,224	1,277	1,277	
O W 81	98,178	50,145	50,145	
82	232,325	109,176	109,176	
83	137,916	44,672	44,672	
84	155,043	56,858	56,858	
85	88,075	38,861	38,861	
86	67,137	31,933	31,933	
PAKISTN O E 86	3,552	2,442	2,765	323
PHIL R V E 81	639	1,167	1,467	300
82	2,178	1,184	1,340	156
85	72	2,678	3,194	516
V W 81	967	570	655	85
86	13,787	9,679	10,505	826
SINGAPR O E 82	362	451	490	39
SWITZLD V E 85	2,469	2,080	2,319	239
THAILND V W 81	3,750	2,253	2,561	308
82	13,646	5,288	5,981	693
83	10,400	5,957	6,400	443
84	5,756	4,935	5,390	455

Tangerine

Tangerine, canned
1472900 ORANGES, MANDARIN, CANNED (LB)

Country Mode Reg Yr	Quantity	F.A.S.	C.I.F.	Charges
TOTAL 81	78,478,286	35,561,588	39,444,210	3,883,162
82	65,292,235	28,833,522	32,348,093	3,514,571
83	79,991,656	33,902,187	38,419,778	4,517,591
84	97,081,764	39,653,980	45,820,387	6,166,407
85	98,989,619	36,690,338	43,130,477	6,440,139
86	95,388,758	39,401,149	44,778,201	5,377,052
ARGENT V E 85	41,138	10,520	12,703	2,183
BELGIUM N E 83	2,832	2,583	3,778	1,195
V E 84	23,704	19,977	23,348	3,371
85	10,505	9,281	10,181	900
V W 83	1,369	1,385	1,556	171
84	1,054	1,067	1,253	186
85	2,525	2,434	2,927	493
CANADA O E 85	39,683	9,926	9,926	
O W 86	46,640	10,500	10,500	

Crop
Product
TSUSA commodity number, description, and unit of quantity

Country	Mode	Reg	Yr	Quantity	F.A.S.	C.I.F.	Charges
CHINA M	N	E	83	1,011,490	328,367	405,249	76,882
	N	W	83	2,761,187	825,424	943,343	117,919
	V	E	81	1,839,872	613,320	726,388	113,068
			82	1,006,843	351,936	423,536	71,600
			83	705,861	235,833	287,962	52,129
			84	1,490,626	514,163	617,418	103,255
			85	1,123,279	413,131	482,032	68,901
			86	1,872,602	618,532	757,426	138,894
	V	H	81	28,793	12,215	13,605	1,390
			84	8,250	3,230	3,842	612
			85	29,700	10,373	11,790	1,417
			86	52,553	17,428	20,232	2,804
	V	W	81	1,557,274	589,231	661,989	72,758
			82	2,387,421	798,906	918,420	119,514
			83	2,633,636	979,940	1,122,847	142,907
			84	4,048,120	1,376,631	1,598,834	222,203
			85	2,150,452	738,917	841,762	102,845
			86	2,152,113	678,361	784,286	105,925
CHINA T	N	E	82	2,295,141	707,266	855,172	147,906
			84	376,654	170,881	204,130	33,249
			86	456,674	101,960	120,678	18,718
	O	E	81	9,900	3,553	4,221	668
			82	1,209	2,640	3,116	476
			83	4,013	1,420	1,699	279
			86	6,200	2,167	2,167	
	O	W	82	2,849	959	1,037	78
	V	E	81	7,722,903	2,663,019	3,083,015	419,996
			82	4,313,683	1,468,936	1,746,736	277,800
			83	3,401,675	1,158,132	1,358,619	200,487
			84	1,790,536	597,738	723,529	125,791
			85	667,852	193,229	239,962	46,733
			86	811,832	270,143	305,893	35,750
	V	H	81	80,683	31,895	34,994	3,099
			83	30,159	10,210	11,955	1,745
			84	28,088	9,100	11,011	1,911
			85	15,912	4,208	5,120	912
			86	10,031	3,200	3,996	796
	V	W	81	17,031,223	6,516,810	7,190,335	673,525
			82	10,356,371	3,369,706	3,775,647	405,941
			83	7,100,322	2,576,602	2,863,507	286,905
			84	6,692,039	2,296,441	2,584,222	287,781
			85	4,137,045	1,214,124	1,386,066	171,942
			86	2,870,054	1,039,509	1,136,090	96,581
COLOMB	V	E	84	39,286	9,293	11,488	2,195
			86	3,070	3,360	3,695	335
	V	W	86	7,425	3,038	3,437	399
DENMARK	V	E	83	31,350	12,186	13,903	1,717
DOM REP	V	E	84	86,728	8,507	12,789	4,282
ECUADOR	V	E	85	8,700	7,540	8,387	847
FR GERM	V	E	84	1,380	826	1,007	181
FRANCE	V	E	83	1,550	2,257	2,575	318
GREECE	V	E	84	31,350	11,020	13,020	2,000
			85	14,300	13,723	16,310	2,587
HG KONG	V	E	81	99,000	40,227	45,694	5,467
			82	178,023	76,261	86,235	9,974
			83	263,375	91,071	110,455	19,384
			84	167,058	59,353	70,600	11,247
			85	90,000	61,110	72,768	11,658
			86	267,200	87,684	108,669	20,985
	V	W	81	305,122	111,998	127,151	15,153
			83	89,858	31,975	35,179	3,204
			84	161,083	58,883	67,206	8,323
			85	183,091	61,039	72,251	11,212
			86	61,050	21,162	23,767	2,605
ISRAEL	V	W	84	125,831	55,245	60,600	5,355
ITALY	V	E	81	281	763	845	82
			83	62,698	22,800	26,682	3,882
			84	38,119	12,184	14,427	2,243
			85	95,349	20,876	31,737	10,861
			86	5,490	8,036	8,708	672
	V	W	85	66,717	21,195	25,008	3,813
JAMAICA	V	W	84	31,365	75,522	78,866	3,344
JAPAN	N	E	84	5,113,976	2,507,792	2,936,952	429,160
	N	H	81	511,207	278,387	322,334	43,947
			82	501,621	287,645	335,146	47,501
			83	583,952	293,471	343,880	50,409
			84	571,900	312,471	367,163	54,692
	N	W	84	3,712,525	1,833,334	2,040,302	206,968
			85	7,321,940	3,862,704	4,279,272	416,568
	O	E	81	8,588	4,320	4,547	227
			82	60,713	29,814	31,994	2,180
			83	72,601	34,070	36,040	1,970
			85	7,920	3,734	4,085	351
	O	W	84	12,563	6,141	6,371	230
	V	E	81	15,156,917	7,866,097	8,739,009	873,452
			82	14,172,871	7,194,371	8,058,559	864,188
			83	17,269,007	8,413,200	9,644,767	1,231,567
			84	10,021,058	4,982,493	5,838,867	856,374
			85	14,203,328	7,337,256	8,501,309	1,164,053
			86	13,070,917	6,968,626	7,914,344	945,718
	V	H	85	392,367	208,971	242,352	33,381
			86	334,370	180,234	210,698	30,464
	V	W	81	25,837,955	13,409,821	14,637,017	1,227,196
			82	21,829,072	11,124,829	12,288,843	1,164,014
			83	25,110,895	12,402,575	13,704,599	1,302,024
			84	22,791,491	11,397,009	12,830,417	1,433,408
			85	14,143,677	7,371,567	8,166,768	795,201
			86	14,879,646	8,095,688	8,810,569	714,881
JORDAN	V	W	86	33,000	17,504	18,560	1,056
KOR REP	N	E	85	1,162,573	528,074	605,077	77,003
	V	E	81	470,584	245,766	272,244	26,478
			82	583,497	282,194	316,771	34,577
			83	1,690,115	768,727	875,933	107,206
			84	4,690,267	2,132,178	2,448,047	315,869
			85	1,311,610	602,075	722,081	120,006
			86	4,226,731	2,005,841	2,259,278	253,437
	V	H	84	62,700	28,500	33,391	4,891
			85	62,700	27,360	32,711	5,351
			86	156,749	73,150	81,150	8,000
	V	W	81	1,589,423	791,732	864,664	72,932
			82	4,491,479	1,887,835	2,061,700	173,865
			83	3,843,576	1,672,043	1,886,198	214,155
			84	7,079,970	2,804,095	3,100,292	296,197
			85	4,035,376	1,841,701	2,024,099	182,398
			86	8,888,816	4,085,942	4,420,852	334,910
LAOS	V	W	85	39,888	8,550	11,631	3,081
MACAO	V	E	81	12,038	4,290	4,906	616
			82	62,850	27,126	31,457	4,331
			83	31,560	15,340	17,604	2,264
MALAYSA	V	E	83	31,350	15,200	17,753	2,553
	V	W	82	31,350	15,105	17,026	1,921
MEXICO	O	E	85	63,301	5,645	5,645	
NETHLDS	V	E	86	2,906	2,749	2,846	97
PHIL R	V	E	82	2,250	1,170	1,256	86
	V	W	81	271,717	142,413	154,195	11,782
			82	67,948	34,163	38,379	4,216
			86	320,320	158,687	172,167	13,480
PORTUGL	V	E	83	33,000	13,978	16,311	2,333
ROMANIA	V	E	85	30,525	15,725	18,399	2,674
SPAIN	N	E	85	21,774,727	5,226,481	6,649,764	1,423,283
			86	1,571,446	559,818	666,620	106,802
	N	W	84	496,765	122,644	157,600	34,956
			86	572,489	229,616	272,404	42,788
	O	E	85	64,350	18,231	18,231	
			86	45,580	11,656	14,856	3,200
	V	E	81	5,447,446	1,989,920	2,281,517	291,597
			82	2,312,159	892,281	1,032,938	140,657
			83	12,906,161	3,891,553	4,563,205	671,652
			84	26,489,357	7,929,465	9,584,640	1,655,175
			85	19,780,098	5,161,744	6,452,419	1,290,675
			86	38,141,705	12,461,408	14,629,226	2,167,818
	V	W	81	113,460	58,345	69,194	10,849
			82	117,750	45,810	56,017	10,207
			83	255,004	71,340	88,449	17,109
			84	274,764	71,382	92,248	20,866
			85	5,700,696	1,569,233	2,046,730	477,497
			86	3,773,349	1,318,493	1,602,353	283,860
SWEDEN	V	E	86	370,292	179,216	197,492	18,276
THAILND	O	W	84	11,220	5,426	5,800	374
	V	E	81	383,900	187,466	206,346	18,880
			82	517,135	234,569	268,108	33,539
			83	63,060	30,505	35,730	5,225
			84	597,086	235,409	274,648	39,239
			85	218,295	109,661	120,974	11,313
			86	302,456	164,099	188,407	24,308
	V	W	84	14,851	5,580	6,059	479
			86	41,025	14,275	15,350	1,075
U KING	V	E	86	1,027	1,067	1,199	132
YUGOSLV	V	E	86	33,000	8,000	10,286	2,286

Tangerine, fresh

1473120 MANDARINS, TANGERINES, FRSH (LB)

Country	Mode	Reg	Yr	Quantity	F.A.S.	C.I.F.	Charges
TOTAL			81	38,394,223	5,544,168	5,646,718	102,550
			82	33,085,089	4,973,416	5,826,737	853,321
			83	43,179,168	4,612,248	5,032,281	420,033
			84	18,657,747	2,421,906	2,714,729	292,823

Crop
Product
TSUSA commodity number, description, and unit of quantity

Country	Mode	Reg	Yr	Quantity	F.A.S.	C.I.F.	Charges
			85	15,981,448	3,179,670	3,644,705	465,035
			86	29,007,908	6,852,545	8,054,303	1,201,758
AUSTRAL	O	W	83	27,937	6,559	11,114	4,555
	V	W	82	27,937	7,187	12,109	4,922
			83	23,352	6,418	10,497	4,079
			84	28,746	6,799	11,582	4,783
CANADA	O	E	82	18,650	772	772	
CHINA M	V	E	84	293	299	350	51
DOM REP	N	E	83	31,810	1,522	2,940	1,418
			84	12,805	2,803	4,103	1,300
			85	98,400	14,076	18,359	4,283
	V	E	84	65,280	7,122	9,603	2,481
			86	161,701	31,272	41,426	10,154
EGYPT	V	E	86	96,032	27,720	32,994	5,274
GREECE	V	E	84	1,800	882	948	66
ISRAEL	V	E	85	17,250	6,875	7,815	940
ITALY	V	E	84	42,108	10,504	18,991	8,487
JAPAN	V	E	86	30,690	17,632	20,163	2,531
	V	W	81	1,543,320	682,717	775,868	93,151
			82	1,506,204	681,524	867,130	185,606
			83	2,576,916	1,067,285	1,341,315	274,030
			84	1,154,376	478,618	629,641	151,023
			85	2,873,692	1,534,494	1,832,091	297,597
			86	3,471,052	2,241,332	2,545,869	304,537
KOR REP	V	W	86	35,063	15,003	15,983	980
MEXICO	O	E	81	36,745,632	4,828,546	4,828,546	
			82	25,967,667	2,416,099	2,419,441	3,342
			83	39,084,229	3,070,736	3,070,736	
			84	16,175,522	1,548,070	1,548,070	
			85	10,248,251	870,242	870,242	
			86	16,229,888	1,572,194	1,572,194	
	O	W	86	43,546	3,456	3,456	
PERU	V	E	86	43,729	17,550	31,969	14,419
SPAIN	N	E	83	1,434,924	459,728	595,679	135,951
			84	1,176,817	366,809	491,441	124,632
	O	E	85	35,640	17,760	17,760	
			86	436,271	225,175	225,175	
	V	E	81	105,271	32,905	42,304	9,399
			82	5,564,631	1,867,834	2,527,285	659,451
			85	2,662,580	726,247	885,240	158,993
			86	8,459,936	2,701,211	3,565,074	863,863
	V	W	85	45,635	9,976	13,198	3,222

Tarragon

Tarragon, spice
1620500 TARRAGON CRUDE NOT MFRD (LB)

Country	Mode	Reg	Yr	Quantity	F.A.S.	C.I.F.	Charges
TOTAL			81	65,326	286,506	307,390	20,884
			82	132,597	408,410	432,550	24,140
			83	102,221	278,143	295,210	17,067
			84	121,974	386,961	420,761	33,800
			85	103,050	344,070	397,056	52,986
			86	97,417	429,831	478,274	48,443
AUSTRAL	A	E	84	132	1,237	2,187	950
			85	100	1,484	1,784	300
	A	W	84	811	5,429	6,475	1,046
CANADA	A	W	85	425	2,965	3,563	598
	O	E	82	20	288	309	21
			83	37	1,209	1,209	
			85	733	1,140	1,140	
CHINA M	V	W	81	490	498	518	20
COLOMB	A	E	81	1,170	4,950	5,574	624
			84	35	300	322	22
DENMARK	V	E	82	166	298	305	7
FR GERM	V	E	84	4	362	370	8
FRANCE	A	W	82	175	1,899	2,008	109
			83	77	321	485	164
	N	E	81	49,056	234,862	250,956	16,094
			82	75,970	323,699	341,551	17,852
			83	67,296	245,036	256,985	11,949
	V	E	81	5,074	25,231	26,215	984
			82	2,205	9,415	9,702	287
			83	2,231	8,321	8,674	353
			84	101,749	315,201	336,810	21,609
			85	76,299	241,116	259,100	17,984
			86	72,319	294,113	314,117	20,004
	V	W	81	450	382	468	86
			82	2,205	9,240	9,813	573

Country	Mode	Reg	Yr	Quantity	F.A.S.	C.I.F.	Charges
			84	111	253	304	51
INDNSIA	V	W	85	2,381	8,572	9,798	1,226
ISRAEL	V	E	81	3,307	8,729	11,203	2,474
			82	7,712	25,439	28,360	2,921
			84	4,410	8,306	9,042	736
MEXICO	O	E	81	307	1,000	1,000	
	V	E	82	44,092	35,000	37,139	2,139
N ANTIL	V	E	86	854	2,448	2,632	184
N ZEAL	A	E	84	402	3,444	4,051	607
			85	1,763	26,740	47,241	20,501
			86	7,757	56,783	66,308	9,525
	A	W	83	1,030	2,482	3,126	644
			84	8,089	44,742	52,870	8,128
			85	7,639	52,700	64,455	11,755
			86	13,601	73,729	92,358	18,629
NETHLDS	A	E	82	52	3,132	3,363	231
			83	10	1,902	1,909	7
	N	E	81	5,472	10,854	11,456	602
	V	E	83	2,060	3,690	3,879	189
			84	2,183	4,109	4,342	233
			86	786	1,658	1,709	51
	V	W	85	1,310	1,945	2,159	214
SINGAPR	V	E	85	12,400	7,408	7,816	408
SPAIN	V	E	83	29,480	15,182	18,943	3,761
THAILND	V	E	84	4,048	3,578	3,988	410
YUGOSLV	V	E	86	2,100	1,100	1,150	50

1620700 TARRAGON, MANUFACTURED (LB)

Country	Mode	Reg	Yr	Quantity	F.A.S.	C.I.F.	Charges
TOTAL			81	15,171	35,129	37,463	2,334
			82	14,297	30,606	32,483	1,877
			83	46,111	59,497	64,833	5,336
			84	22,112	40,740	44,715	3,975
			85	39,821	64,878	73,267	8,389
			86	89,778	129,991	138,715	8,724
BELGIUM	A	W	83	576	558	969	411
	V	E	86	4,548	1,641	1,818	177
CANADA	O	E	81	505	1,046	1,046	
			82	25	834	834	
			83	373	1,244	1,244	
			84	150	2,062	2,062	
			85	90	2,077	2,077	
DENMARK	V	E	84	7	294	311	17
			85	1,702	3,006	3,312	306
			86	19,400	5,135	5,332	197
FR GERM	O	E	81	2,125	2,446	2,756	310
			85	1,543	1,373	1,497	124
	V	E	83	450	2,629	2,633	4
			86	999	2,228	2,388	160
FRANCE	N	E	81	224	1,464	1,724	260
	N	W	84	1,037	2,745	3,132	387
	O	E	81	238	3,263	3,263	
	V	E	81	158	282	316	34
			82	3,356	7,554	7,938	384
			83	27,634	20,056	21,671	1,615
			84	6,719	6,051	6,829	778
			85	9,512	19,208	20,632	1,424
			86	33,726	68,478	72,876	4,398
	V	W	81	1,155	2,339	2,518	179
			82	2,191	6,558	7,127	569
			83	2,044	5,243	5,852	609
			84	871	2,151	2,298	147
			86	416	1,871	2,168	297
GIBRALT	O	E	81	225	1,079	1,079	
IRAN	V	W	82	1,102	1,316	1,365	49
ISRAEL	V	E	83	4,415	8,830	10,017	1,187
N ZEAL	A	E	85	287	1,500	1,800	300
	A	W	84	1,092	6,228	7,163	935
			85	282	2,092	2,813	721
NETHLDS	A	E	81	4	673	686	13
	O	E	82	925	1,691	1,754	63
			83	926	1,630	1,695	65
			84	873	1,489	1,544	55
			85	873	1,328	1,509	181
			86	1,310	2,993	3,072	79
	V	E	81	8,180	15,680	16,585	905
			82	5,317	10,084	10,747	663
			83	6,856	13,118	14,227	1,109
			84	7,504	12,775	13,959	1,184
			85	19,994	23,321	25,044	1,723
			86	28,281	44,237	47,533	3,296
	V	W	81	423	1,830	1,927	97
			82	1,381	2,569	2,718	149
			83	2,533	4,568	4,843	275

Crop Product TSUSA commodity number, description, and unit of quantity Country	Mode	Reg	Yr	Quantity	F.A.S.	C.I.F.	Charges
			84	3,740	6,633	7,066	433
			85	3,666	5,644	6,167	523
			86	1,048	2,387	2,507	120
U KING	N	E	81	1,727	3,843	4,289	446
	O	E	81	207	1,184	1,274	90
			83	16	278	308	30
			85	126	2,092	2,204	112
			86	50	1,021	1,021	
	V	E	83	288	1,343	1,374	31
			84	119	312	351	39
			85	1,746	3,237	6,212	2,975

Tea

Tea

1605000 TEA, CRUDE OR PREPARED (LB)

Country	Mode	Reg	Yr	Quantity	F.A.S.	C.I.F.	Charges
TOTAL			81	190,253,504	132,947,350	152,787,245	19,984,667
			82	182,613,081	128,714,273	147,553,891	18,839,618
			83	170,451,456	131,371,711	147,554,735	16,183,024
			84	194,565,040	202,475,983	221,973,885	19,497,902
			85	174,617,454	165,865,227	183,216,294	17,351,067
			86	197,963,356	132,617,537	150,707,399	18,089,862
ALGERIA	V	E	85	85,891	47,119	54,669	7,550
			86	39,154	23,088	26,838	3,750
ANTIGUA	V	E	85	259,840	184,548	210,350	25,802
			86	23,148	4,620	6,830	2,210
ARAB EM	A	W	82	190	412	781	369
	V	W	83	12,021	23,527	24,192	665
			85	4,247	56,810	58,537	1,727
ARGENT	N	E	81	1,730,131	765,651	925,518	159,867
			82	10,015,646	3,937,377	4,816,651	879,274
			83	6,905,417	2,808,178	3,491,451	683,273
			84	4,038,797	2,262,307	2,696,018	433,711
	O	E	81	20,087	6,973	6,973	
			82	8,888	8,080	8,080	
			83	230,161	134,677	134,677	
			84	205,115	148,581	157,466	8,885
			85	144,571	105,587	108,777	3,190
	V	E	81	20,288,809	8,134,641	10,140,395	2,005,754
			82	16,903,632	7,374,420	9,011,068	1,636,648
			83	26,165,396	10,278,251	12,832,965	2,554,714
			84	35,584,041	21,645,766	25,254,106	3,608,340
			85	33,263,493	16,647,233	19,903,334	3,256,101
			86	35,789,971	8,803,106	12,159,203	3,356,097
	V	W	81	30,071	15,686	19,583	3,897
			82	40,000	26,450	29,387	2,937
			83	18,750	7,910	10,462	2,552
			84	167,894	141,199	163,629	22,430
			85	176,367	164,000	186,136	22,136
AUSTRAL	A	E	84	98	535	656	121
	A	W	84	869	3,779	5,488	1,709
			85	364	1,428	1,664	236
	V	E	83	61,112	28,919	36,302	7,383
			86	189	1,586	1,761	175
	V	W	81	3,968	6,301	7,668	1,367
			82	3,968	4,660	5,438	778
			83	7,936	10,331	12,134	1,803
			84	3,968	8,140	9,031	891
			85	7,900	12,147	13,716	1,569
			86	8,871	17,392	19,334	1,942
AUSTRIA	A	E	82	44,900	167,030	198,508	31,478
			83	400	1,917	2,173	256
			85	633	3,155	4,720	1,565
	A	W	84	3,040	8,323	8,410	87
BELGIUM	O	E	82	85,538	55,551	59,925	4,374
	V	E	81	270,764	183,123	207,215	24,092
			82	196,788	122,414	131,200	8,786
			83	24,818	23,266	24,626	1,360
			84	51,588	51,480	52,780	1,300
			85	40,123	85,668	90,158	4,490
			86	45,903	36,718	43,314	6,596
	V	W	86	27,055	209,769	216,041	6,272
BERMUDA	A	E	83	107	255	334	79
BNGLDSH	V	E	81	5,000	3,742	4,992	1,250
			82	200,696	129,257	176,990	47,733
			83	74,880	54,022	63,812	9,790
			84	45,236	56,670	63,281	6,611
			85	31,069	37,472	41,909	4,437
			86	72,135	42,307	52,205	9,898
BRAZIL	A	E	81	3,671	12,500	16,662	4,162
			82	288	2,122	2,789	667
			83	71	570	836	266
			84	351	5,017	6,685	1,668
			85	949	4,926	6,056	1,130
	A	W	81	1,301	3,500	4,896	1,396
	N	E	81	1,771,962	961,377	1,161,215	199,838
			83	1,257,717	862,843	1,002,628	139,785
			86	1,186,820	627,508	723,505	95,997
	N	W	81	522,816	393,781	473,879	80,098
			82	104,115	106,441	125,634	19,193
			85	123,144	116,901	145,226	28,325
			86	126,593	131,590	148,573	16,983
	O	E	82	20,964	20,395	20,395	
			83	4,541	4,017	4,017	
			84	65,785	76,072	77,047	975
			85	12,557	10,480	10,480	
			86	166,034	102,536	110,379	7,843
	V	E	81	5,497,835	3,324,362	3,900,219	575,857
			82	7,081,790	3,859,028	4,696,018	836,990
			83	6,754,763	4,459,587	5,249,739	790,152
			84	7,403,269	7,678,011	8,514,782	836,771
			85	8,751,447	6,938,405	7,890,474	952,069
			86	10,108,322	4,511,576	5,499,065	987,489
	V	W	82	432,439	271,744	334,001	62,257
			83	638,659	507,397	607,440	100,043
			84	488,841	525,159	621,145	95,986
			85	549,161	543,115	628,987	85,872
			86	655,400	340,450	416,627	76,177
BULGAR	V	E	83	34,130	15,907	17,495	1,588
	V	W	81	6,536	3,261	3,308	47
C RICA	V	W	82	241	330	354	24
CAMROON	V	W	85	1,447	3,477	3,663	186
CANADA	A	E	82	84	273	359	86
			83	587	3,408	4,098	690
	N	E	82	970,039	1,479,589	1,480,871	1,282
	N	W	83	46,886	72,374	72,599	225
			84	80,364	124,077	126,389	2,312
	O	E	81	3,619,060	5,191,352	5,192,666	1,315
			82	3,558,826	5,882,742	5,882,742	
			83	4,607,100	7,488,780	7,497,406	8,626
			84	4,254,384	8,106,530	8,106,530	
			85	3,889,459	8,580,794	8,584,449	3,655
			86	3,435,688	5,259,716	5,262,064	2,348
	O	W	81	103,856	141,912	143,721	1,809
			82	115,430	184,271	186,899	2,628
			85	148,878	218,196	218,556	360
			86	67,125	144,352	148,038	3,686
	V	E	81	104,058	55,654	65,740	10,086
			84	318,485	171,088	196,351	25,263
	V	W	84	22,068	21,172	22,523	1,351
CAYMAN	V	E	86	89,425	66,062	71,912	5,850
CHINA M	A	E	81	443	3,000	4,769	1,769
			82	100	270	462	192
	A	H	81	129	350	370	20
	A	W	83	230	777	1,411	634
			85	331	5,865	7,500	1,635
	N	E	81	2,263,589	1,669,632	1,967,890	298,258
			82	2,014,737	1,446,115	1,723,621	277,506
			83	1,466,233	990,217	1,160,661	170,444
			84	2,484,004	2,233,291	2,518,945	285,654
			85	4,857,343	5,232,537	5,817,131	584,594
	N	H	82	13,217	35,057	37,850	2,793
	N	W	81	555,140	367,504	422,963	55,459
			82	46,847	55,266	62,090	6,824
			83	1,834,343	2,152,032	2,369,607	217,575
			84	1,211,013	1,562,547	1,692,476	129,929
			86	1,079,855	1,555,743	1,665,516	109,773
	O	E	81	4,787	4,413	4,533	120
			83	59,983	33,616	33,650	34
			84	89,898	83,538	86,622	3,084
			85	2,970	11,106	12,549	1,443
			86	73	2,318	2,588	270
	O	H	82	5,291	26,720	27,781	1,061
	O	W	81	1,188	9,387	9,800	413
			83	2,391	9,152	9,583	431
			86	3,112	2,920	3,172	252
	V	E	81	4,335,957	2,660,401	3,085,694	425,293
			82	6,659,948	3,491,597	4,162,496	670,899
			83	5,593,713	3,316,339	3,880,532	564,193
			84	9,282,517	7,416,830	8,412,872	996,042
			85	6,712,612	4,795,433	5,491,155	695,722
			86	16,161,134	7,525,583	9,201,044	1,675,461
	V	H	81	5,808	15,833	16,965	1,132

Crop
Product
TSUSA commodity number, description, and unit of quantity

Country	Mode	Reg	Yr	Quantity	F.A.S.	C.I.F.	Charges
			82	4,519	8,411	9,891	1,480
			83	968	2,790	3,047	257
			84	5,720	14,216	15,642	1,426
			85	2,944	7,082	7,867	785
			86	2,084	6,070	6,678	608
	V	W	81	8,580,284	5,988,756	6,819,833	831,077
			82	6,529,074	4,931,312	5,616,398	685,086
			83	5,148,264	3,429,647	3,962,494	532,847
			84	8,140,446	6,927,286	7,822,788	895,502
			85	12,403,736	8,216,590	9,530,800	1,314,210
			86	19,254,872	7,376,547	9,444,119	2,067,572
CHINA T	A	E	84	966	2,852	5,346	2,494
	A	W	82	264	409	1,029	620
			85	332	4,630	5,385	755
	N	E	82	666,907	993,927	1,070,950	77,023
			83	611,494	519,739	592,898	73,159
			84	1,681,755	1,324,164	1,484,429	160,265
			86	716,242	709,873	784,959	75,086
	N	H	84	21,143	41,551	45,420	3,869
			85	22,813	55,148	64,056	8,908
	N	W	82	186,297	206,564	227,239	20,675
			83	464,106	694,914	751,994	57,080
			84	773,161	2,448,266	2,561,410	113,144
			85	96,821	83,475	92,710	9,235
			86	461,839	742,035	900,055	158,020
	O	E	82	44,000	23,320	24,270	950
			83	176	270	270	
			84	60,832	53,516	53,554	38
			85	3,969	5,159	5,159	
	O	W	81	1,875	3,372	3,715	343
			83	90,000	47,250	51,570	4,320
	V	E	81	5,898,565	3,145,353	3,622,517	474,395
			82	5,719,943	2,720,966	3,198,747	477,781
			83	5,397,297	2,424,698	2,836,269	411,571
			84	8,097,365	4,833,472	5,539,247	705,775
			85	1,591,380	1,273,969	1,474,229	200,260
			86	469,870	327,326	378,414	51,088
	V	H	81	36,105	43,980	48,085	4,105
			82	48,332	56,526	63,295	6,769
			83	29,884	35,537	39,621	4,084
			86	12,235	18,623	20,328	1,705
	V	W	81	3,391,950	1,951,495	2,268,409	316,914
			82	1,664,385	1,002,970	1,163,468	160,498
			83	1,190,768	719,163	824,323	105,160
			84	3,266,076	1,970,618	2,290,994	320,376
			85	2,742,682	3,122,929	3,423,094	300,165
			86	1,557,412	1,264,904	1,406,062	141,158
COLOMB	O	E	85	22,046	21,100	22,356	1,256
	V	E	85	165,782	86,480	103,278	16,798
	V	W	81	78,178	71,567	82,583	12,387
			82	41,270	30,607	34,267	3,660
CR N AN	V	E	85	620	2,897	3,124	227
DENMARK	V	W	85	4,806	10,441	11,457	1,016
DOM REP	A	E	82	1,560	624	1,038	414
	V	E	81	156,312	115,212	123,006	6,412
ECUADOR	V	E	81	1,312,409	712,162	832,642	120,480
			82	594,038	328,982	394,006	65,024
			83	834,047	427,910	511,193	83,283
			84	897,009	638,150	740,599	102,449
			85	425,641	202,270	239,005	36,735
			86	998,881	374,211	444,424	70,213
	V	W	81	33,952	20,711	22,978	2,267
			84	39,241	30,976	35,183	4,207
FINLAND	V	W	86	2,200	5,413	5,803	390
FR GERM	A	E	81	3,408	10,685	13,333	2,648
			82	6,007	17,511	23,982	6,471
			83	295	1,268	1,517	249
			84	51,708	172,862	209,350	36,488
			86	2,423	8,877	9,601	724
	A	W	86	2,425	5,358	7,540	2,182
	N	E	81	385,886	934,634	995,478	60,844
			82	255,976	840,167	895,055	54,888
			83	1,130,044	3,665,306	3,777,366	112,060
			84	1,022,785	3,219,037	3,426,217	207,180
			85	1,057,061	2,218,672	2,443,352	224,680
			86	598,473	2,048,099	2,115,119	67,020
	N	W	82	6,853	24,611	25,697	1,086
			84	16,002	41,547	46,175	4,628
			85	44,761	138,060	149,309	11,249
			86	25,531	42,020	46,911	4,891
	O	E	81	188	609	609	
			82	1,262	3,171	3,386	215
			83	2,706	12,079	12,424	345
			84	4,386	12,888	12,888	

Crop
Product
TSUSA commodity number, description, and unit of quantity

Country	Mode	Reg	Yr	Quantity	F.A.S.	C.I.F.	Charges
			85	8,766	20,717	20,717	
			86	4,640	11,671	11,671	
	V	E	81	225,513	672,534	698,088	25,554
			82	772,107	1,523,916	1,579,934	56,018
			83	281,223	616,832	641,838	25,006
			84	1,457,132	2,512,877	2,664,655	151,778
			85	5,602,057	12,278,256	12,762,307	484,051
			86	4,944,890	6,605,384	6,904,576	299,192
	V	W	81	23,162	59,067	62,733	3,666
			82	6,526	14,003	15,460	1,457
			83	10,918	33,738	37,417	3,679
			84	6,479	15,366	16,203	837
			85	3,461	8,629	8,991	362
			86	10,188	26,902	29,615	2,713
FRANCE	A	E	83	585	2,279	2,677	398
			84	714	2,205	3,032	827
			85	112	1,285	1,570	285
	N	E	81	13,537	40,920	44,983	4,063
			82	9,810	40,838	44,573	3,735
			83	7,815	31,747	34,001	2,254
			84	12,772	51,108	59,240	8,132
			85	7,561	35,224	37,782	2,558
			86	5,600	32,352	36,072	3,720
	N	W	83	1,312	5,025	6,156	1,131
			84	1,906	7,916	9,707	1,791
	O	E	81	665	5,366	6,013	647
			82	1,405	4,030	4,625	595
			83	772	497	587	90
	V	E	81	85	389	428	39
			82	2,632	10,663	11,230	567
			83	1,731	6,691	7,128	437
			84	365	1,412	1,466	54
			85	3,032	10,855	11,625	770
			86	25,532	19,666	22,615	2,949
	V	W	81	320	2,182	2,429	247
			82	568	7,382	7,858	476
			83	991	5,797	6,097	300
			84	551	3,192	4,197	1,005
			86	926	3,630	3,780	150
GERM DR	V	E	83	289,472	545,832	564,615	18,783
			86	88,184	41,229	45,800	4,571
GREECE	V	E	82	1,772	1,000	1,168	168
			84	500	1,000	1,224	224
	V	W	85	287	1,417	1,591	174
GUATMAL	A	E	84	864	400	565	165
	V	E	83	35,200	18,480	20,752	2,272
			84	21,120	12,672	15,108	2,436
			85	127,911	54,715	63,618	8,903
			86	555,763	409,690	488,978	79,288
GUINEA	V	E	81	43,524	35,722	37,401	1,679
	V	W	86	42,746	25,389	29,113	3,724
HAITI	A	E	82	604	1,879	2,378	499
	V	E	82	378	1,584	1,656	72
			83	43,079	34,120	37,870	3,750
			84	3,010	6,720	7,197	477
			85	3,388	10,500	11,340	840
HEARD I	A	W	85	225	4,875	5,475	600
HG KONG	A	E	83	42	327	345	18
			85	220	6,188	6,695	507
	A	W	81	1,200	4,861	7,319	2,458
	N	E	82	69,674	154,290	172,730	18,440
			83	56,647	151,542	164,673	13,131
			84	60,704	148,403	164,121	15,718
			86	169,296	233,645	251,962	18,317
	N	W	83	87,160	172,628	182,877	10,249
			85	138,030	260,301	278,958	18,657
	O	E	81	2,106	2,570	2,776	206
			85	41,667	29,278	29,794	516
			86	707	3,400	3,958	558
	O	W	82	500	1,155	1,231	76
			84	3,335	8,911	9,435	524
			86	5,250	3,759	3,944	185
	V	E	81	299,234	363,575	404,506	40,931
			82	42,444	32,410	37,101	4,691
			83	149,325	107,576	124,333	16,757
			84	420,625	287,679	322,567	34,888
			85	904,152	886,488	987,442	100,954
			86	1,269,020	400,430	489,294	88,864
	V	H	81	4,452	10,874	11,578	704
			82	3,572	8,569	9,194	625
			83	3,293	5,935	6,845	910
			84	1,083	2,611	2,951	340
			85	1,829	5,004	5,417	413
			86	1,923	4,983	5,503	520

Crop
Product
TSUSA commodity number, description, and unit of quantity

Country	Mode	Reg	Yr	Quantity	F.A.S.	C.I.F.	Charges
	V	W	81	334,619	434,006	478,413	44,407
			82	196,193	323,036	349,445	26,409
			83	144,648	184,382	200,647	16,265
			84	559,005	724,595	768,873	44,278
			85	826,205	629,940	718,590	88,650
			86	2,341,029	1,383,358	1,564,125	180,767
HONDURA	V	E	86	724,900	57,663	70,349	12,686
INDIA	A	E	82	578	2,352	2,577	225
			83	1,480	5,427	8,010	2,583
			84	48,205	168,617	231,724	63,107
			85	10,296	152,717	183,630	30,913
			86	63,143	146,234	221,735	75,501
	N	E	81	1,294,563	1,760,055	1,974,195	214,140
			82	980,789	1,464,585	1,642,842	178,257
			83	414,556	918,919	993,133	74,214
			84	629,717	898,533	972,043	73,510
			85	822,012	906,571	1,011,957	105,386
			86	1,106,856	1,458,679	1,595,271	136,592
	N	W	83	424,572	635,462	706,293	70,831
			86	151,224	235,971	259,800	23,829
	O	E	81	467,395	464,231	493,662	29,431
			82	392,158	344,316	365,898	21,582
			83	61,286	78,443	85,971	7,528
			84	917,600	1,217,344	1,260,148	42,804
			85	898,119	1,314,461	1,337,875	23,414
			86	901,834	995,442	995,442	
	O	W	85	48,500	76,145	76,145	
	V	E	81	4,200,878	5,410,521	6,143,545	740,835
			82	2,909,596	4,025,063	4,489,867	464,804
			83	3,480,577	4,369,818	4,856,241	486,423
			84	3,408,933	5,558,915	6,016,504	457,589
			85	3,056,142	6,088,709	6,487,973	399,264
			86	2,566,527	4,051,796	4,360,137	308,341
	V	W	81	4,452,392	3,736,957	4,356,150	623,913
			82	2,034,299	2,019,094	2,320,960	301,866
			83	1,998,699	3,077,647	3,350,017	272,370
			84	3,279,916	6,347,206	6,827,602	480,396
			85	1,652,161	2,238,293	2,501,731	263,438
			86	3,749,814	5,756,776	6,189,674	432,898
INDNSIA	N	E	81	6,280,315	3,545,745	4,347,228	801,483
			82	2,271,279	1,387,268	1,555,130	167,862
			83	751,501	567,430	636,513	69,083
			84	203,616	289,521	312,632	23,111
			85	1,384,848	1,398,428	1,532,086	133,658
	O	E	81	121,952	64,561	73,272	8,711
			84	162,296	243,872	243,872	
			85	64,528	94,719	94,719	
			86	68,806	54,744	54,744	
	V	E	81	9,012,184	6,150,539	7,238,008	1,087,469
			82	14,568,894	8,828,134	10,332,183	1,504,049
			83	17,084,845	12,734,455	14,314,877	1,580,422
			84	20,488,381	22,406,010	24,513,123	2,107,113
			85	14,628,480	11,378,537	12,724,080	1,345,543
			86	22,858,194	16,772,102	18,510,417	1,738,315
	V	W	81	16,939,446	11,134,305	13,089,200	1,955,031
			82	13,919,986	8,695,746	10,203,667	1,507,921
			83	13,803,634	11,931,600	13,294,341	1,362,741
			84	13,319,035	16,504,823	17,964,007	1,459,184
			85	12,236,996	10,823,590	12,030,990	1,207,400
			86	12,872,934	8,042,726	9,126,223	1,083,497
IRAN	O	E	82	24,251	12,368	12,368	
	V	E	81	88,184	36,252	39,362	3,110
			82	25,764	14,078	18,237	4,159
			83	33,438	17,190	19,388	2,198
			84	217,900	220,708	233,044	12,336
			85	32,960	24,001	26,619	2,618
			86	65,341	31,345	36,205	4,860
	V	W	83	9,921	16,552	17,675	1,123
IRELAND	A	E	82	252	812	1,241	429
			83	640	1,624	2,149	525
	A	W	82	900	637	1,344	707
	N	E	81	9,871	27,998	31,370	3,372
			82	700	2,948	3,733	785
			83	14,199	32,014	36,986	4,972
			84	7,150	14,624	16,837	2,213
			86	18,825	77,982	86,685	8,703
	O	E	81	265	937	1,038	101
			84	1,885	2,971	3,647	676
			85	764	2,058	2,618	560
	V	E	82	9,420	21,844	23,706	1,862
			84	2,147	8,002	9,120	1,118
			85	11,800	42,235	46,163	3,928
			86	5,347	11,226	13,689	2,463
	V	W	81	5,176	12,168	13,273	1,105

Crop
Product
TSUSA commodity number, description, and unit of quantity

Country	Mode	Reg	Yr	Quantity	F.A.S.	C.I.F.	Charges
ISRAEL	O	E	82	8,841	13,266	14,334	1,068
	V	E	81	42,372	61,891	70,769	8,878
			82	68,071	92,314	104,416	12,102
			83	85,296	141,737	154,286	12,549
			84	55,041	92,136	101,515	9,379
			85	73,451	129,013	147,092	18,079
			86	49,698	89,997	101,378	11,381
ITALY	O	E	86	194	1,346	1,730	384
	V	E	81	42,328	21,940	23,703	1,763
			82	1,881	10,797	12,238	1,441
			83	1,116	7,057	7,429	372
			84	3,036	17,258	19,217	1,959
			85	225	1,996	2,120	124
			86	18,163	25,314	28,666	3,352
	V	W	82	989	1,887	2,086	199
IVY CST	V	E	85	19,239	18,979	21,721	2,742
JAMAICA	A	E	83	575	906	1,556	650
			84	710	729	804	75
JAPAN	A	E	82	53	1,227	1,593	366
			83	10	388	879	491
			84	157	3,223	4,018	795
			85	1,076	9,542	13,733	4,191
	N	E	81	72,055	91,618	102,998	11,380
			82	56,102	104,479	116,596	12,117
			83	74,350	123,556	142,453	18,897
			84	90,106	192,391	218,338	25,947
			85	5,262	20,753	22,569	1,816
			86	80,430	192,093	206,605	14,512
	N	H	81	27,666	87,018	97,702	10,684
			82	33,048	92,691	104,239	11,548
			83	27,561	79,710	89,013	9,303
			84	25,511	82,008	92,870	10,862
			86	13,769	66,598	74,752	8,154
	N	W	81	62,401	206,317	218,943	12,626
			82	64,495	195,056	207,667	12,611
			83	128,463	289,354	308,014	18,660
			84	130,522	328,288	357,895	29,607
			85	43,920	131,160	138,695	7,535
			86	68,118	210,807	221,262	10,455
	O	E	81	1,138	3,000	3,244	244
			82	246	724	995	271
			83	394	1,034	1,133	99
			84	7,561	11,111	12,473	1,362
			86	790	3,612	3,781	169
	O	W	85	570	1,608	1,687	79
	V	E	81	610,173	229,575	289,021	59,446
			82	935,939	345,393	439,423	94,030
			83	2,181,790	565,900	748,602	182,702
			84	1,526,888	524,271	645,061	120,790
			85	2,662,087	1,081,369	1,317,356	235,987
			86	710,711	251,195	301,791	50,596
	V	H	85	14,925	44,161	50,274	6,113
	V	W	81	4,706,062	1,628,081	1,939,808	311,727
			82	4,248,628	1,513,977	1,806,262	292,285
			83	1,454,225	536,556	658,102	121,546
			84	2,915,645	1,058,172	1,306,596	248,424
			85	1,888,390	821,943	1,010,905	188,962
			86	1,670,799	788,948	913,222	124,274
KENYA	A	E	84	423	846	996	150
			85	463	1,680	1,727	47
	N	E	82	1,305,200	1,231,212	1,384,699	153,487
			83	813,363	770,836	847,422	76,586
			84	3,447,243	5,924,040	6,254,273	330,233
			85	871,354	1,192,193	1,268,943	76,750
	O	E	81	42,946	47,117	47,117	
			82	46,870	39,781	40,053	272
			83	24,000	31,439	31,439	
			84	632,152	771,234	792,770	21,536
			85	25,637	47,412	47,412	
	V	E	81	11,901,703	11,509,939	12,905,534	1,411,478
			82	13,226,657	12,927,312	14,397,829	1,470,517
			83	8,917,110	9,149,774	10,058,524	908,750
			84	4,327,910	6,864,729	7,265,602	400,873
			85	8,040,239	11,703,384	12,346,002	642,618
			86	8,883,577	10,119,751	10,869,157	749,406
	V	W	81	177,149	163,772	194,488	30,716
			82	740,171	1,222,485	1,322,800	100,315
			83	244,758	243,258	281,127	37,869
			84	259,798	369,976	396,258	26,282
			85	215,503	298,371	318,827	20,456
			86	506,236	533,878	564,687	30,809
KOR REP	A	E	84	107	1,278	1,488	210
	A	W	83	106	1,623	1,723	100
	N	E	81	8,197	14,417	17,215	2,798

Crop
Product
TSUSA commodity number, description, and unit of quantity

Country	Mode	Reg	Yr	Quantity	F.A.S.	C.I.F.	Charges
			82	2,037	9,596	12,912	3,316
			83	11,407	26,592	31,331	4,739
			84	10,207	14,252	15,603	1,351
	O	E	86	44	1,142	1,142	
	V	E	81	82,853	38,011	43,737	5,726
			82	1,000	7,398	7,697	299
			83	42,683	20,780	24,678	3,898
			84	661	4,600	4,930	330
			85	12,138	33,073	36,528	3,455
			86	152,173	190,631	209,918	19,287
	V	W	81	2,526	2,908	3,329	421
			82	7,791	11,392	12,558	1,166
			83	2,395	5,252	5,786	534
			84	14,172	35,576	37,876	2,300
			85	18,986	52,006	57,840	5,834
			86	96,482	138,889	153,348	14,459
LESOTHO	O	E	85	18,344	32,705	32,705	
	V	E	84	100,309	139,387	147,279	7,892
MACAO	V	E	83	24,251	17,387	19,741	2,354
			84	28,109	36,542	39,142	2,600
			86	26,455	12,002	16,802	4,800
	V	H	82	95	317	342	25
MALAWI	O	E	81	23,426	18,083	18,083	
			82	125,332	108,981	110,816	1,835
			83	23,368	20,788	21,066	278
			84	57,100	81,401	81,401	
			85	10,560	19,625	19,625	
	V	E	81	5,171,647	3,308,863	3,864,288	562,749
			82	2,981,832	2,126,227	2,426,960	300,733
			83	2,816,329	2,448,375	2,682,358	233,983
			84	1,959,786	2,965,082	3,126,192	161,110
			85	2,050,275	2,171,514	2,360,324	188,810
			86	2,656,945	1,841,389	2,060,066	218,677
MALAYSA	V	E	83	162,138	63,505	79,215	15,710
	V	H	81	206	715	751	36
			84	815	2,399	2,601	202
	V	W	81	22,090	12,758	15,135	2,377
			84	153	390	409	19
MALI	V	E	85	21,623	38,705	40,337	1,632
MAURIT	N	E	83	114,905	89,524	100,112	10,588
	O	E	84	56,864	81,557	81,557	
	V	E	81	18,519	16,563	17,560	997
			82	39,417	26,784	34,552	7,768
			83	454,517	374,462	425,424	50,962
			84	418,078	511,477	551,095	39,618
			85	386,954	183,865	220,052	36,187
			86	388,950	176,097	210,399	34,302
	V	W	84	21,385	30,628	32,814	2,186
MAURITN	V	E	83	59,877	47,624	54,383	6,759
MEXICO	A	E	84	2	342	345	3
	O	W	86	5,511	3,000	3,000	
MOROC	A	E	86	114	1,313	1,601	288
	O	E	85	14,904	34,222	34,222	
	V	E	81	25,781	33,939	38,655	4,716
MOZAMBQ	N	E	81	378,570	257,577	285,512	27,935
	O	E	81	78,338	50,911	55,009	4,098
	V	E	81	8,802,593	4,684,794	5,231,107	546,313
			82	8,752,310	4,646,406	5,383,230	736,824
			83	7,765,944	4,331,636	4,782,299	450,663
			84	4,943,331	3,714,411	4,025,899	311,488
			85	1,527,964	1,127,364	1,236,860	109,496
			86	612,715	242,870	278,902	36,032
	V	W	81	28,947	20,427	24,256	3,829
			83	38,815	25,177	31,773	6,596
N ANTIL	V	E	81	29,101	15,180	17,778	2,598
			86	88,184	51,091	57,887	6,796
N CALDN	V	E	86	19,400	7,040	8,548	1,508
N ZEAL	A	W	85	1,833	7,063	9,253	2,190
	V	E	83	45,856	31,336	36,612	5,276
	V	H	83	135	542	581	39
NETHLDS	A	E	85	254	1,527	1,693	166
	N	E	81	2,647,712	1,511,117	1,653,329	142,212
			82	907,945	527,919	577,942	50,023
			83	5,131,705	2,888,204	3,104,879	216,675
			84	641,090	571,512	612,904	41,392
	O	E	81	84,656	45,056	50,145	5,089
			83	91,022	64,514	68,848	4,334
			84	90,278	85,388	91,231	5,843
			85	134,101	127,504	138,120	10,616
			86	22,782	13,951	16,019	2,068
	V	E	81	14,125,132	7,467,544	8,183,145	715,601
			82	12,532,976	6,781,675	7,456,958	675,283
			83	4,988,910	3,285,181	3,562,686	277,505
			84	9,757,102	8,056,909	8,587,123	530,214
			85	9,153,562	7,070,394	7,586,915	516,521
			86	8,849,795	5,240,622	5,732,252	491,630
	V	W	81	47,105	35,164	42,079	6,915
			82	28,652	18,794	21,860	3,066
			83	55,195	47,766	52,773	5,007
			84	74,818	83,718	93,779	10,061
			85	1,090	2,976	3,215	239
			86	62,117	43,090	49,007	5,917
NEW GUI	V	E	81	76,861	45,565	52,447	6,882
			82	94,256	66,587	74,653	8,066
			83	55,822	39,663	46,439	6,776
			84	168,254	223,231	235,901	12,670
			85	137,061	79,506	89,736	10,230
	V	W	81	45,459	20,407	23,384	2,977
			86	30,314	18,416	19,102	686
NORFOLK	V	E	82	21,826	15,447	16,770	1,323
			84	173,182	248,957	268,157	19,200
PAKISTN	O	E	84	19,841	26,934	26,934	
PARAGUA	A	E	84	475	480	1,358	878
PERU	A	E	83	1,698	8,050	8,905	855
	V	E	81	36,702	17,767	19,442	1,675
			83	15,873	12,600	14,410	1,810
			85	20,923	18,000	19,764	1,764
PHIL R	V	W	85	47,950	46,818	53,616	6,798
PORTUGL	V	E	81	335	1,600	1,674	74
			83	9,321	34,727	35,581	854
			85	4,992	6,084	8,648	2,564
			86	446	1,419	1,544	125
REP SAF	N	E	83	132,545	112,108	119,636	7,528
	O	E	81	6,490	7,867	7,867	
			82	16,094	16,416	16,416	
			83	44,974	45,292	47,166	1,874
	V	E	81	433,677	573,973	609,674	35,701
			82	522,749	393,367	444,565	51,198
			83	329,505	271,318	293,621	22,303
			84	650,779	944,326	995,060	50,734
			85	391,494	599,326	631,738	32,412
			86	671,990	332,614	379,101	46,487
	V	H	82	249	872	922	50
	V	W	81	21,339	15,497	19,133	3,636
ROMANIA	V	E	84	110	328	346	18
	V	W	84	501	2,521	2,686	165
RWANDA	O	E	84	351,228	387,728	397,028	9,300
			85	2,513	4,480	4,480	
	V	E	81	1,041,077	935,657	1,047,931	112,274
			82	1,572,060	1,453,424	1,611,820	158,396
			83	1,471,858	1,416,672	1,532,515	115,843
			84	1,218,066	1,911,005	2,015,825	104,820
			85	2,162,273	2,513,863	2,671,080	157,217
			86	2,559,955	2,456,504	2,769,385	312,881
	V	W	82	116,314	101,380	120,182	18,802
			83	20,723	16,544	18,321	1,777
			85	23,810	34,560	38,505	3,945
			86	45,973	43,407	47,638	4,231
SIER LN	V	E	86	1,988	17,320	18,228	908
SINGAPR	N	E	83	62	1,258	1,366	108
	V	E	82	4,343	1,360	1,639	279
			83	118,075	86,056	96,036	9,980
			84	922,452	967,421	1,075,973	108,552
			85	389,136	314,303	342,683	28,380
			86	71,330	23,539	25,417	1,878
	V	W	81	389,168	228,613	277,540	48,927
			82	50,221	31,085	38,062	6,977
			83	290,995	195,037	224,574	29,537
			84	203,084	218,961	236,397	17,436
			85	13,398	5,000	5,742	742
			86	79,921	142,969	149,547	6,578
SPAIN	A	E	84	397	3,600	4,178	578
	N	E	84	1,054	6,625	8,242	1,617
	O	E	84	12,218	29,978	30,410	432
	V	E	82	97,857	108,787	119,632	10,845
			85	35,300	84,747	93,792	9,045
			86	30,632	85,090	93,984	8,894
SRI LKA	A	E	82	516	999	1,574	575
			85	3,249	6,612	7,412	800
	N	E	82	1,184,669	835,992	1,043,346	207,354
			84	2,038,117	3,194,215	3,415,724	221,509
			85	470,498	587,335	664,087	76,752
			86	370,878	539,636	555,676	16,040
	N	W	81	12,398	11,253	12,984	1,731
			82	1,461,227	1,157,633	1,359,093	201,460
			84	31,789	44,212	50,512	6,300
			85	4,821	7,118	7,727	609
	O	E	81	507,498	373,108	397,487	24,379

Crop
Product
TSUSA commodity number, description, and unit of quantity

Country	Mode	Reg	Yr	Quantity	F.A.S.	C.I.F.	Charges
			82	1,182,015	847,713	947,542	99,829
			83	1,747,253	2,008,124	2,128,857	120,733
			84	2,077,410	2,715,032	2,861,135	146,103
			85	1,614,469	1,532,382	1,645,294	112,912
			86	855,768	506,549	582,740	76,191
	O	W	86	430	2,015	2,015	
	V	E	81	17,218,982	14,690,326	17,084,807	2,486,308
			82	13,577,164	10,924,219	12,883,273	1,959,054
			83	6,610,312	6,777,197	7,636,336	859,139
			84	3,763,920	5,059,282	5,538,209	478,927
			85	7,027,687	7,689,683	8,474,772	785,089
			86	4,767,784	3,561,029	4,053,643	492,614
	V	W	81	10,901,211	8,231,949	9,753,055	1,540,956
			82	9,969,020	7,150,225	8,556,149	1,405,924
			83	9,512,155	8,724,650	9,918,548	1,193,898
			84	12,773,491	17,364,542	18,907,521	1,542,979
			85	12,475,302	14,115,399	15,816,958	1,701,559
			86	11,019,946	8,756,260	9,945,789	1,189,529
SUDAN	V	W	86	11,555	11,327	14,438	3,111
SURINAM	V	W	86	33,620	33,542	38,358	4,816
SWITZLD	A	E	81	220	1,542	2,328	786
			83	540	1,470	2,054	584
			86	450	1,224	1,974	750
	A	W	82	458	575	1,343	768
			85	560	14,400	14,919	519
			86	5,240	41,025	41,707	682
	O	E	84	2,580	3,996	4,415	419
	V	E	81	1,060	826	940	114
			82	31,892	93,241	105,470	12,229
			83	693	3,188	3,335	147
			84	972	1,510	1,624	114
			85	195,000	160,718	184,059	23,341
			86	10,438	25,685	26,486	801
	V	W	81	43,417	38,645	45,395	6,750
			84	952	1,431	1,503	72
			85	44,881	21,674	26,487	4,813
			86	138,402	46,341	50,974	4,633
THAILND	V	E	81	55,398	60,202	68,404	8,202
			82	2,017	4,076	4,347	271
			83	600	530	580	50
			84	1,146	4,000	4,433	433
			85	1,190	3,440	3,646	206
			86	26,403	62,835	66,008	3,173
	V	W	81	5,073	8,618	9,617	999
			82	4,502	4,891	7,540	2,649
			83	13,444	14,618	15,384	766
			84	13,665	11,924	12,741	817
			85	8,452	10,040	10,910	870
			86	21,164	6,250	6,809	559
TNZANIA	O	E	81	22,046	18,940	20,900	1,960
			84	103,130	105,184	109,184	4,000
	V	E	81	2,150,404	1,837,806	2,096,123	258,317
			82	1,188,893	971,823	1,117,415	145,592
			83	568,225	494,682	555,909	61,227
			84	657,915	941,229	1,002,610	61,381
			85	588,432	495,651	554,263	58,612
			86	1,181,296	924,633	1,018,308	93,675
	V	W	81	21,219	19,097	20,839	1,742
			84	19,621	27,590	31,090	3,500
TUNISIA	V	W	86	22,045	12,500	15,389	2,889
TURKEY	A	E	82	104	261	609	348
	V	E	83	656	2,187	2,572	385
			84	375	490	525	35
			85	1,825	1,808	1,973	165
			86	1,593	1,022	1,184	162
U KING	A	E	81	3,525	16,041	17,377	1,336
			83	263	562	848	286
			84	1,517	8,361	9,754	1,393
			85	9,051	80,032	86,434	6,402
			86	3,268	24,154	32,567	8,413
	A	H	86	1,016	8,434	11,548	3,114
	A	W	83	508	2,193	2,728	535
	N	E	81	468,699	1,222,320	1,302,399	80,079
			82	394,899	1,076,436	1,140,160	63,724
			83	394,592	772,223	831,105	58,882
			84	237,646	695,245	751,508	56,263
			85	142,574	590,554	626,196	35,642
			86	228,536	664,770	708,467	43,697
	N	W	81	68,085	136,310	150,089	13,779
			82	73,870	203,658	223,696	20,038
			83	46,865	137,464	150,973	13,509
			84	73,077	276,879	312,270	35,391
			85	69,512	261,837	295,362	33,525
			86	50,001	171,476	199,905	28,429

Crop
Product
TSUSA commodity number, description, and unit of quantity

Country	Mode	Reg	Yr	Quantity	F.A.S.	C.I.F.	Charges
	O	E	81	126,604	99,901	110,538	10,637
			82	2,272	21,457	23,457	2,000
			83	56,046	85,795	87,538	1,743
			84	123,109	259,321	262,103	2,782
			85	98,492	265,052	268,755	3,703
			86	23,428	149,931	158,088	8,157
	V	E	81	1,333,012	1,348,478	1,466,198	117,720
			82	1,049,583	1,704,096	1,812,478	108,382
			83	1,093,754	1,533,998	1,674,494	140,496
			84	807,687	1,449,789	1,603,817	154,028
			85	557,069	751,343	825,496	74,153
			86	1,052,494	886,831	998,176	111,345
	V	H	83	908	2,206	2,401	195
	V	W	81	977	7,798	8,474	676
			82	2,438	9,693	10,658	965
			83	9,167	17,122	19,511	2,389
			84	9,291	27,782	31,700	3,918
			85	258,157	735,878	765,623	29,745
			86	657,283	2,919,170	3,058,536	139,366
UGANDA	V	E	82	21,517	19,150	21,700	2,550
			83	21,449	16,325	18,969	2,644
			84	46,678	49,948	55,172	5,224
			85	22,046	30,900	33,000	2,100
USSR	O	E	82	5,754	3,775	4,382	607
	V	E	81	1,006,367	364,370	401,349	36,979
			82	995,399	393,670	444,034	50,364
			83	1,412,542	605,377	688,752	83,375
			84	819,465	365,412	414,733	49,321
			85	36,502	13,027	16,122	3,095
			86	271,563	74,849	101,789	26,940
	V	W	81	220	560	685	125
			82	3,804	2,815	4,198	1,383
VENEZ	A	E	86	577	2,855	3,685	830
YUGOSLV	V	E	81	4,470	7,395	8,161	766
			82	10,843	8,077	9,113	1,036
			83	12,019	12,497	13,560	1,063
			84	6,944	13,211	14,046	835
			85	1,924	10,074	10,900	826
			86	725	6,244	6,567	323
ZAIRE	V	E	83	268,353	194,178	217,901	23,723
			86	217,199	113,401	136,660	23,259
ZAMBIA	V	E	83	42,726	38,272	40,112	1,840
			86	282,103	226,977	245,717	18,740
ZMBABWE	A	E	86	2,550	3,068	5,160	2,092
	O	E	81	61,197	47,873	50,793	2,920
			85	30,219	40,175	41,100	925
	V	E	81	79,806	63,544	66,979	3,435
			82	295,338	211,294	239,152	27,858
			83	468,411	376,906	417,183	40,277
			84	518,666	496,316	539,389	43,073
			85	345,064	287,861	314,388	26,527
			86	418,967	229,090	269,769	40,679

Theophylline, alkaloid
4372040 THEOPHYLLINE A DERIVATIVES (LB)

Country	Mode	Reg	Yr	Quantity	F.A.S.	C.I.F.	Charges
TOTAL			81	1,488,314	6,672,021	6,913,811	157,503
			82	1,476,250	6,146,392	6,307,799	161,407
			83	1,899,337	7,554,703	7,754,239	199,536
			84	1,960,007	8,041,309	8,274,563	233,254
			85	1,920,396	7,003,975	7,189,153	185,178
			86	2,476,680	11,417,866	11,680,039	262,173
AUSTRAL	A	E	81	1,700	79,226	82,285	3,059
BELGIUM	V	E	86	39,683	182,885	185,647	2,762
BRAZIL	A	E	85	22	12,500	12,592	92
CHINA M	A	E	82	551	1,835	2,125	290
	N	E	81	9,647	42,713	44,692	1,979
			82	28,716	110,724	117,935	7,211
			85	82,671	271,475	282,420	10,945
	V	E	83	53,654	197,302	205,188	7,886
			84	69,207	237,082	244,365	7,283
			86	83,775	249,349	262,875	13,526
FR GERM	A	E	81	321	6,875	7,354	479
			82	90	1,123	1,168	45
			83	3,967	15,783	17,936	2,153
			84	110	830	925	95
	N	E	81	1,453,277	6,435,005	6,667,705	148,413
			82	1,443,456	5,997,957	6,149,369	151,412
			83	1,764,790	7,031,996	7,212,012	180,016
			84	1,875,820	7,725,806	7,949,560	223,754
			85	1,831,023	6,661,276	6,834,058	172,782
			86	1,991,508	9,226,919	9,429,726	202,807

Crop
Product
TSUSA commodity number, description, and unit of quantity

Country	Mode	Reg	Yr	Quantity	F.A.S.	C.I.F.	Charges
	O	E	83	440	2,146	2,216	70
			85	3,153	37,952	38,716	764
			86	551	2,816	2,893	77
	V	E	84	8,667	36,176	37,395	1,219
			86	352,781	1,643,274	1,684,508	41,234
	V	W	81	22,046	99,659	103,100	3,441
FRANCE	V	E	86	2,205	9,925	10,150	225
HUNGARY	A	E	86	44	46,110	46,554	444
IRELAND	A	E	83	198	475	735	260
NETHLDS	A	E	84	246	4,777	4,907	130
	O	E	83	1	600	662	62
	V	E	83	30,870	133,272	136,779	3,507
SWITZLD	N	E	84	5,957	36,638	37,411	773
			86	4,535	43,523	44,424	901
	V	E	81	1,323	8,543	8,675	132
			83	2,205	14,071	14,245	174
			85	2,205	14,393	14,711	318
			86	1,543	11,432	11,610	178
U KING	A	E	82	3,115	31,837	33,952	2,115
			83	3,527	17,496	20,137	2,641
			86	55	1,633	1,652	19
	A	W	82	322	2,916	3,250	334
	O	E	83	2	267	287	20
	V	E	83	39,683	141,295	144,042	2,747
			85	1,322	6,379	6,656	277

Teak

Teak, lumber**

2023200 BALSA/TEAK LUMBER ROUGH (MBF)
(See Balsa, lumber under Balsa)
2023215 TEAK LUMBER, ROUGH (MBF)

Country	Mode	Reg	Yr	Quantity	F.A.S.	C.I.F.	Charges
TOTAL			84	18,125	16,945,147	18,678,395	1,733,248
			85	14,357	18,473,734	20,273,866	1,800,132
			86	13,949	19,904,247	21,716,049	1,811,802
AUSTRIA	V	E	86	11	32,145	34,781	2,636
BOLIVIA	V	W	85	8	23,556	24,956	1,400
BRAZIL	V	E	84	4	4,800	5,769	969
			85	2	1,840	2,406	566
			86	12	25,023	29,208	4,185
	V	W	86	11	36,227	37,827	1,600
BRUNEI	V	E	85	36	116,966	125,708	8,742
BURMA	N	W	84	821	1,552,756	1,739,902	187,146
			86	527	1,353,395	1,472,421	119,026
	O	E	85	3	9,158	9,158	
	V	E	84	3,482	1,900,567	2,137,090	236,523
			85	759	1,536,441	1,703,855	167,414
			86	923	1,628,732	1,770,136	141,404
	V	H	84	3	8,289	9,224	935
			85	3	7,330	8,367	1,037
	V	W	84	175	409,989	467,589	57,600
			85	734	1,515,836	1,698,664	182,828
			86	78	245,865	261,579	15,714
C RICA	V	E	86	2	5,400	5,925	525
	V	W	84	16	13,481	15,308	1,827
CANADA	N	E	84	*	1,951	1,951	
	O	E	84	18	4,023	4,023	
	O	W	84	1	3,293	3,293	
	V	E	85	1,115	308,550	380,359	71,809
CHINA M	V	E	84	80	162,356	178,088	15,732
			86	24	58,630	65,387	6,757
	V	W	84	88	148,410	168,028	19,618
			85	66	133,320	148,769	15,449
			86	8	15,277	16,889	1,612
CHINA T	V	E	84	1,081	1,505,738	1,600,676	94,938
			85	401	1,064,424	1,125,580	61,156
			86	184	456,584	486,964	30,380
	V	H	84	2	4,983	5,657	674
	V	W	84	210	465,152	485,412	20,260
			85	86	226,231	235,410	9,179
			86	44	121,310	128,878	7,568
FR GERM	V	E	84	8	14,123	16,607	2,484
			85	276	264,197	307,732	43,535
			86	151	244,638	296,660	52,022
HG KONG	N	W	84	278	642,472	688,594	46,122
	V	E	84	5,854	2,160,832	2,483,067	322,235
			85	160	436,770	493,104	56,334
			86	196	483,136	535,672	52,536
	V	W	84	207	275,763	300,829	25,066
			85	1,091	836,501	901,238	64,737
			86	1,129	355,863	380,029	24,166
HONDURA	V	E	85	1	2,633	2,747	114
INDIA	V	E	85	46	60,360	66,381	6,021
			86	49	99,917	109,597	9,680
	V	W	85	12	27,005	29,200	2,195
			86	16	34,315	36,487	2,172
INDNSIA	V	E	84	3,150	2,269,472	2,508,920	239,448
			85	2,995	3,389,013	3,771,947	382,934
			86	2,336	2,699,506	3,015,882	316,376
	V	W	84	656	725,200	799,885	74,685
			85	729	1,160,113	1,262,850	102,737
			86	992	907,999	983,952	75,953
JAPAN	V	E	85	37	24,425	30,581	6,156
			86	3	7,575	8,742	1,167
	V	W	85	24	50,591	55,851	5,260
KOR REP	V	E	84	15	32,758	39,058	6,300
			85	47	28,226	30,686	2,460
	V	W	86	24	65,215	69,341	4,126
MACAO	V	E	85	8	13,044	15,833	2,789
MALAYSA	V	E	86	6	12,027	14,677	2,650
	V	W	84	14	32,755	34,505	1,750
			85	4	8,199	8,917	718
			86	12	35,660	38,435	2,775
MAURIT	V	E	85	53	115,562	126,825	11,263
PHIL R	V	E	84	4	10,649	11,261	612
			85	132	285,566	305,246	19,680
			86	132	211,410	230,084	18,674
SENEGAL	V	E	86	12	42,829	45,694	2,865
SINGAPR	O	E	84	10	24,075	26,993	2,918
	V	E	84	1,302	2,960,498	3,191,359	230,861
			85	1,853	3,391,520	3,661,752	270,232
			86	3,355	4,403,711	4,792,349	388,638
	V	H	85	14	44,942	48,442	3,500
			86	13	42,305	45,663	3,358
	V	W	84	597	1,563,076	1,696,176	133,100
			85	235	675,872	715,723	39,851
			86	786	538,234	574,083	35,849
SPAIN	V	E	85	12	39,767	40,730	963
SURINAM	V	E	84	25	14,826	19,344	4,518
			85	97	59,952	79,595	19,643
			86	79	46,224	60,507	14,283
SWEDEN	V	E	84	6	5,103	5,577	474
THAILND	N	W	85	74	173,684	182,388	8,704
	O	E	84	1	961	961	
	V	E	84	2,962	1,678,759	1,837,828	159,069
			86	1,959	3,647,704	3,948,076	300,372
	V	W	85	251	679,794	737,356	57,562
			86	875	2,047,391	2,220,124	172,733
TRINID	O	E	84	1	598	598	
	V	E	85	8	40,378	44,815	4,437
U KING	V	E	84	3	3,614	5,137	1,523
YUGOSLV	V	E	84	13	22,584	27,514	4,930
			85	23	43,209	52,867	9,658

2023300 BALSA/TEAK LBR DSD EX SIDNG (MBF)
(See Balsa, lumber under Balsa)
2023315 TEAK LUMBER DRESSED EXCL SIDING (MBF)

Country	Mode	Reg	Yr	Quantity	F.A.S.	C.I.F.	Charges
TOTAL			84	1,233	1,876,327	2,085,264	208,937
			85	1,910	2,405,961	2,588,589	182,628
			86	721	1,697,677	1,806,451	108,774
ARAB EM	V	E	85	3	4,026	5,826	1,800
AUSTRAL	V	E	85	16	21,600	25,970	4,370
			86	15	17,922	22,226	4,304
BRAZIL	V	E	85	64	21,440	26,526	5,086
BURMA	N	E	84	*	950	950	
	N	W	85	6	17,061	17,990	929
	O	E	86	2	6,443	6,443	
	V	E	84	68	205,798	226,492	20,694
			85	38	104,364	114,839	10,475
			86	21	49,892	54,978	5,086
	V	W	84	81	129,452	140,574	11,122
			85	38	76,678	83,382	6,704
			86	20	84,860	87,953	3,093
C RICA	A	E	84	2	386	868	482
	V	H	84	1	2,080	2,704	624
CANADA	O	E	85	1	4,862	4,862	
			86	2	4,571	4,571	
CHINA M	V	W	84	9	14,499	16,372	1,873
CHINA T	A	E	85	1	1,320	1,618	298
	V	E	84	59	176,369	193,439	17,070
			85	70	195,370	209,487	14,117
			86	12	33,185	34,600	1,415

Crop Product TSUSA commodity number, description, and unit of quantity Country	Mode	Reg	Yr	Quantity	F.A.S.	C.I.F.	Charges
	V	W	84	12	40,764	43,744	2,980
			85	348	957,741	995,832	38,091
			86	185	630,526	653,762	23,236
DENMARK	N	E	85	*	3,373	3,709	336
FR GERM	V	E	84	1	3,827	4,169	342
			85	15	27,673	31,502	3,829
			86	14	19,943	20,647	704
FRANCE	V	E	84	24	4,253	6,477	2,224
			85	6	13,992	15,985	1,993
			86	1	1,502	1,969	467
HG KONG	V	E	84	178	332,748	385,816	53,068
			85	167	162,436	182,398	19,962
	V	W	84	12	31,069	33,066	1,997
			85	23	64,197	68,522	4,325
HUNGARY	V	W	86	12	23,856	26,083	2,227
INDIA	V	E	84	18	20,645	21,780	1,135
INDNSIA	V	E	84	144	243,776	273,328	29,552
			85	607	122,870	139,794	16,924
	V	W	84	143	85,584	92,530	6,946
			85	111	247,766	269,079	21,313
			86	151	117,911	128,432	10,521
MEXICO	V	E	86	5	11,078	12,593	1,515
NETHLDS	V	E	84	67	28,979	36,019	7,040
			86	3	18,879	19,772	893
NORWAY	V	E	85	12	33,267	37,475	4,208
	V	W	85	1	1,037	1,852	815
PERU	V	E	84	5	8,400	9,124	724
PHIL R	V	E	85	22	68,799	73,918	5,119
SINGAPR	V	E	84	199	224,589	252,024	27,435
			85	34	71,271	76,007	4,736
			86	52	93,449	104,990	11,541
	V	W	84	101	309,095	327,607	18,512
			85	215	120,364	131,714	11,350
			86	3	5,992	6,607	615
THAILND	V	E	84	109	13,064	18,181	5,117
			85	15	55,311	60,049	4,738
			86	171	420,724	452,493	31,769
	V	W	86	52	156,944	168,332	11,388
U KING	O	E	85	96	4,703	4,893	190
	V	E	85	1	4,440	5,360	920

Teasel

Teasel
1929000 TEASELS (LB)

Country	Mode	Reg	Yr	Quantity	F.A.S.	C.I.F.	Charges
TOTAL			84	229	1,662	1,822	160
FRANCE	V	E	84	229	1,662	1,822	160

Thyme

Thyme, essential oil
4526600 THYME OIL (LB)

Country	Mode	Reg	Yr	Quantity	F.A.S.	C.I.F.	Charges
TOTAL			81	15,471	211,409	218,411	7,002
			82	19,800	258,158	264,356	6,198
			83	31,720	291,749	300,170	8,421
			84	18,614	182,717	188,537	5,820
			85	26,165	194,433	199,700	5,267
			86	22,585	195,553	202,161	6,608
CANADA	O	E	81	44	831	831	
FRANCE	A	E	82	220	3,214	3,237	23
			86	441	2,762	2,943	181
	A	W	81	23	320	349	29
	N	E	81	3,489	59,097	61,148	2,051
			82	4,870	54,761	56,636	1,875
			83	9,365	65,557	68,009	2,452
			84	8,575	80,042	82,935	2,893
			85	5,712	47,455	48,909	1,454
			86	10,700	80,578	82,514	1,936
INDNSIA	V	W	82	2,205	59,234	60,442	1,208
ISRAEL	V	E	82	247	2,536	2,563	27
			85	1,282	11,401	11,585	184
NETHLDS	A	E	86	529	5,824	6,376	552
	N	E	83	882	8,806	9,075	269
			85	5,282	10,533	10,753	220
	V	E	84	882	7,977	8,135	158

Country	Mode	Reg	Yr	Quantity	F.A.S.	C.I.F.	Charges
SPAIN	N	E	81	11,906	150,902	155,819	4,917
			83	21,330	215,362	221,006	5,644
			84	9,038	92,604	95,326	2,722
			85	13,889	125,044	128,453	3,409
			86	10,474	103,007	106,395	3,388
	V	E	82	12,126	136,601	139,575	2,974
SWITZLD	A	E	81	9	259	264	5
			83	33	863	888	25
			84	86	1,842	1,881	39
U KING	A	E	82	132	1,812	1,903	91
			86	441	3,382	3,933	551
	V	E	83	110	1,161	1,192	31
			84	33	252	260	8

Thyme, spice
1620900 THYME,CRUDE,NOT MANUFACTURED (LB)

Country	Mode	Reg	Yr	Quantity	F.A.S.	C.I.F.	Charges
TOTAL			81	1,273,995	1,044,365	1,193,568	149,203
			82	1,548,295	1,137,458	1,332,525	195,123
			83	1,970,341	1,297,108	1,553,323	256,215
			84	1,569,568	946,371	1,154,112	207,741
			85	2,051,291	1,018,313	1,225,164	206,851
			86	2,282,244	1,419,031	1,653,294	234,263
CANADA	O	E	81	640	684	684	
			83	2,386	3,558	3,558	
			84	50	550	550	
			85	733	1,043	1,043	
DENMARK	V	E	82	32,257	22,392	26,512	4,120
DOM REP	A	E	83	120	460	492	32
			84	1,125	4,459	4,771	312
			85	288	1,056	1,132	76
			86	723	2,410	2,602	192
FR GERM	O	E	81	1,053	1,158	1,246	88
			82	1,026	1,139	1,280	141
			83	1,984	1,627	1,648	21
	V	E	84	28	1,177	1,200	23
FRANCE	N	E	81	101,404	119,296	130,985	11,689
			85	80,597	45,409	51,207	5,798
	O	E	84	25	961	964	3
	V	E	82	13,865	16,909	18,324	1,415
			83	121,805	163,646	177,916	14,270
			84	34,092	26,687	30,936	4,249
			85	7,275	3,531	4,147	616
			86	24,455	9,502	11,407	1,905
	V	W	85	4,497	1,932	2,350	418
GREECE	V	E	83	28,660	18,179	21,850	3,671
INDNSIA	V	W	85	8,818	5,644	6,451	807
ITALY	V	E	83	58	495	508	13
	V	W	82	56	303	303	56
JAMAICA	A	E	81	312	996	1,536	540
			82	4,924	11,032	13,245	2,213
			83	4,211	10,787	12,559	1,772
			84	23,020	51,872	61,916	10,044
			85	17,765	45,667	49,811	4,144
			86	38,590	98,701	127,532	28,831
	N	E	81	3,434	13,183	15,228	2,045
JAPAN	A	E	85	411	1,507	1,616	109
			86	360	1,200	1,330	130
LEBANON	V	E	83	922	888	925	37
			84	20	350	352	2
MOROC	V	E	83	6,173	2,167	3,095	928
			85	11,000	3,018	4,166	1,148
			86	66,398	23,328	30,532	7,204
NETHLDS	A	E	81	40	1,401	1,471	70
			83	50	1,381	1,478	97
SPAIN	N	E	86	1,706,132	966,108	1,116,336	150,228
	V	E	81	1,154,363	897,348	1,030,607	133,259
			82	1,493,962	1,083,746	1,270,755	187,009
			83	1,789,640	1,078,243	1,312,361	234,118
			84	1,461,476	813,580	1,004,592	191,012
			85	1,911,642	905,307	1,097,735	192,428
			86	406,651	277,205	319,688	42,483
	V	W	81	6,691	6,925	8,214	1,289
			83	2,204	1,706	2,029	323
			85	7,935	3,056	4,088	1,032
			86	15,400	9,267	10,791	1,524
SWITZLD	A	E	85	330	1,143	1,418	275
SYRIA	V	E	81	6,058	3,374	3,597	223
			82	2,205	1,937	2,106	169
			83	11,928	13,586	14,424	838
			84	45,323	45,315	47,088	1,773
			86	23,535	31,310	33,076	1,766

Crop
Product
TSUSA commodity number, description, and unit of quantity

Country	Mode	Reg	Yr	Quantity	F.A.S.	C.I.F.	Charges
TRINID	A E		83	200	385	480	95
TURKEY	V E		84	4,409	1,420	1,743	323

1621100 THYME, MANUFACTURED (LB)

Country	Mode	Reg	Yr	Quantity	F.A.S.	C.I.F.	Charges
TOTAL			81	22,803	25,404	27,653	2,249
			82	5,304	8,517	9,011	494
			83	26,891	30,492	40,770	10,278
			84	8,823	17,754	20,805	3,051
			85	6,874	9,302	10,115	813
			86	12,351	13,578	15,931	2,353
CANADA	O E		81	705	876	876	
			82	1,000	1,520	1,520	
			83	3,200	3,759	3,759	
			84	1,835	4,916	4,916	
COLOMB	A E		83	335	317	535	218
DENMARK	V E		85	2,384	2,962	3,384	422
			86	146	2,847	2,956	109
FR GERM	V E		84	380	631	681	50
FRANCE	V E		81	176	3,408	3,507	99
			82	120	2,138	2,222	84
			83	200	2,802	2,896	94
			84	1,167	1,123	1,162	39
			85	1,697	2,170	2,357	187
	V W		83	264	403	428	25
GREECE	V E		84	531	298	339	41
	V W		84	220	298	333	35
INDIA	O E		84	20	360	360	
JAMAICA	A E		82	580	724	857	133
			83	5,316	12,321	20,315	7,994
			84	1,767	7,337	8,744	1,407
			86	48	2,300	2,641	341
	N E		81	362	1,262	1,808	546
JORDAN	V E		83	9,921	5,000	5,750	750
LEBANON	A E		84	343	385	722	337
	O E		82	420	435	435	
	V E		84	980	463	586	123
			85	2,793	4,170	4,374	204
			86	1,171	1,284	1,365	81
SYRIA	V E		81	19,830	17,465	18,886	1,421
			82	2,205	1,800	1,895	95
			83	866	1,000	1,119	119
	V W		81	1,521	1,389	1,512	123
			82	979	1,900	2,082	182
TURKEY	V E		83	1,213	864	1,114	250
			86	10,986	7,147	8,969	1,822
	V W		83	5,512	3,742	4,563	821
U KING	O E		81	29	329	344	15
	V E		81	180	675	720	45
			83	64	284	291	7
			84	124	1,383	1,491	108
VENEZ	A E		84	1,456	560	1,471	911

Thymol
4377200 THYMOL (LB)

Country	Mode	Reg	Yr	Quantity	F.A.S.	C.I.F.	Charges
TOTAL			82	86	5,395	5,447	52
			83	3,549	11,918	12,620	702
			84	3,863	11,663	12,433	770
			85	1,265	6,630	7,183	553
			86	2,637	12,162	12,822	660
DENMARK	A E		82	86	5,395	5,447	52
			83	30	1,152	1,170	18
			85	65	3,475	3,529	54
			86	68	3,786	3,871	85
FR GERM	A E		85	649	1,828	2,248	420
			86	360	1,086	1,350	264
	A W		86	4	1,102	1,163	61
	V E		83	2,204	7,144	7,500	356
			84	2,205	7,093	7,500	407
FRANCE	V E		83	1,315	3,622	3,950	328
			84	1,653	4,083	4,407	324
			85	551	1,327	1,406	79
			86	2,205	6,188	6,438	250
U KING	A E		84	5	487	526	39

Crop
Product
TSUSA commodity number, description, and unit of quantity

Timothy

Timothy, seed
1268500 TIMOTHY SEED (LB)

Country	Mode	Reg	Yr	Quantity	F.A.S.	C.I.F.	Charges
TOTAL			81	2,635,887	1,063,606	1,064,981	1,375
			82	1,865,714	490,709	493,314	2,605
			83	1,491,013	452,031	452,314	283
			84	1,759,131	492,224	494,780	2,556
			85	1,948,410	554,647	555,007	360
			86	2,490,961	903,997	905,183	1,186
CANADA	O E		81	2,165,634	938,654	938,654	
			82	1,403,876	396,050	396,050	
			83	862,894	327,275	327,275	
			84	1,045,514	351,898	351,898	
			85	1,222,519	416,198	416,198	
			86	1,223,882	577,500	577,500	
	O W		81	462,747	108,817	108,817	
			82	453,730	80,962	80,962	
			83	626,326	123,467	123,467	
			84	705,168	129,687	129,687	
			85	722,100	132,159	132,159	
			86	1,257,690	306,011	306,011	
ITALY	O E		84	2,469	4,939	4,939	
JAPAN	N W		84	1,781	1,760	3,575	1,815
	V W		81	3,881	5,704	6,167	463
			82	1,070	834	1,006	172
			83	1,370	631	746	115
			84	2,780	1,792	2,085	293
			85	2,535	4,201	4,384	183
			86	2,138	7,532	7,844	312
MALI	V W		85	661	1,012	1,189	177
NETHLDS	A E		82	5,698	10,181	12,401	2,220
			84	500	791	1,161	370
			86	1,188	3,488	3,798	310
	O E		81	895	1,312	1,522	210
			84	324	632	632	
			85	595	1,077	1,077	
			86	1,102	2,149	2,330	181
	V E		81	1,978	4,514	4,759	245
			82	536	1,090	1,206	116
			86	882	1,977	2,140	163
	V W		82	804	1,592	1,689	97
			83	423	658	826	168
			84	595	725	803	78
SWEDEN	V W		86	4,079	5,340	5,560	220
U KING	A E		81	110	803	908	105
	A W		81	220	1,298	1,528	230
	O E		81	422	2,504	2,626	122

Tobacco

Nicotine, alkaloid
4371300 NICOTINE AND COMPOUNDS (LB)

Country	Mode	Reg	Yr	Quantity	F.A.S.	C.I.F.	Charges
TOTAL			81	15,432	52,791	56,910	4,119
			82	47,438	168,586	178,362	9,776
			83	26,116	101,506	122,418	20,912
			84	485,537	2,510,030	2,666,069	156,039
			85	445,451	2,477,925	2,579,582	101,657
			86	94,243	657,415	703,668	46,253
CHINA M	O E		86	24	2,000	2,500	500
DENMARK	A E		84	197,753	1,050,754	1,152,275	101,521
			85	52,943	293,386	313,503	20,117
			86	1,115	24,728	51,327	26,599
	V E		82	4,310	49,000	51,022	2,022
			84	172,684	1,190,128	1,229,542	39,414
			85	361,586	2,075,393	2,152,964	77,571
			86	25,793	232,253	232,648	395
FR GERM	A E		85	1	2,584	2,585	1
	O E		83	1	1,060	1,110	50
FRANCE	A E		83	110	2,350	2,550	200
INDIA	N E		81	1,378	12,334	12,900	566
	V E		81	12,885	30,372	32,976	2,604
			82	43,128	119,586	127,340	7,754
			83	25,083	89,552	109,856	20,304
			84	93,030	221,253	234,975	13,722
			85	1,761	16,224	16,750	526

Crop Product TSUSA commodity number, description, and unit of quantity Country	Mode	Reg	Yr	Quantity	F.A.S.	C.I.F.	Charges
			86	37,479	146,768	156,832	10,064
	V	W	86	441	5,000	5,175	175
ITALY	V	E	83	20	450	480	30
	V	W	83	20	450	471	21
JAPAN	V	W	84	9	400	466	66
SPAIN	V	E	84	22,046	45,000	46,261	1,261
SWEDEN	A	E	81	286	1,163	1,892	729
	V	E	86	27,591	219,789	227,604	7,815
SWITZLD	A	E	85	6	5,500	5,675	175
	V	E	81	882	8,585	8,800	215
U KING	A	E	81	1	337	342	5
			84	15	2,171	2,221	50
			85	53	8,710	8,787	77
			86	36	3,472	3,566	94
	N	E	84	*	324	329	5
	O	E	85	26,455	40,055	42,240	2,185
	V	E	83	882	7,644	7,951	307
			85	2,646	36,073	37,078	1,005
			86	1,764	23,405	24,016	611

Tobacco, filler, mixed or unmixed, under 35% wrapper tobacco

1702800 CIG LEAF NT STEM, NOV 8.5IN (LB)

Country	Mode	Reg	Yr	Quantity	F.A.S.	C.I.F.	Charges
TOTAL			81	178,498,643	243,700,991	255,135,430	11,431,999
			82	174,042,647	252,855,924	265,153,312	12,297,388
			83	184,037,259	293,592,963	307,170,026	13,577,063
			84	168,910,539	278,328,767	290,941,466	12,612,699
			85	171,459,973	277,933,235	290,592,815	12,659,580
			86	177,234,811	281,846,118	296,194,576	14,348,458
ARGENT	O	E	81	295	332	364	32
			85	139,066	286,911	306,180	19,269
BELGIUM	O	E	81	1,128	1,900	2,012	112
			82	713	1,187	1,256	69
BOLIVIA	O	E	86	167,906	226,532	239,998	13,466
BRAZIL	O	E	81	3,840	6,282	6,685	403
			83	220,460	349,345	372,165	22,820
BRUNEI	O	E	81	10,552	11,818	12,920	1,102
BULGAR	N	E	81	35,566	56,163	59,133	2,970
	O	E	81	12,618,123	18,149,921	19,223,036	1,073,115
			82	12,226,080	17,658,554	18,764,944	1,106,390
			83	14,485,260	21,280,822	22,743,494	1,462,672
			84	11,686,242	18,549,025	19,741,503	1,192,478
			85	10,179,570	16,399,983	17,261,701	861,718
			86	10,997,920	17,802,750	18,706,063	903,313
	V	E	81	1,237	1,850	1,988	138
			83	2,645,520	4,554,500	4,779,469	224,969
CANADA	O	E	86	952	1,380	1,380	
CHINA T	A	E	83	661	807	1,525	718
CYPRUS	O	E	81	5,917	6,745	7,026	281
			82	3,921	6,506	6,722	216
			83	28,930	48,550	50,776	2,226
			84	1,108	2,016	2,079	63
			85	3,657	6,652	6,860	208
			86	7,541	13,711	14,147	436
	V	E	82	67,473	138,031	144,171	6,140
			83	19,242	31,172	32,549	1,377
			84	6,884	15,115	15,986	871
			85	68,376	109,270	114,854	5,584
			86	25,054	39,528	41,939	2,411
	V	W	84	44,156	71,504	74,787	3,283
			85	38,543	62,415	64,992	2,577
DENMARK	O	E	81	56,048	49,829	53,112	3,283
FR GERM	O	E	85	68,984	130,868	136,352	5,484
GIBRALT	O	E	81	28,998	31,536	38,534	6,998
GREECE	N	E	81	220,661	431,443	446,905	15,462
			83	3,906,794	6,436,343	6,713,595	277,252
	O	E	81	24,701,238	41,074,949	42,448,153	1,373,204
			82	23,772,104	45,206,533	46,888,059	1,681,526
			83	27,156,001	50,823,203	52,768,835	1,945,632
			84	28,635,274	52,241,315	54,343,486	2,102,171
			85	28,422,093	47,395,118	49,456,978	2,061,860
			86	31,273,232	46,244,346	48,480,900	2,236,554
	V	E	81	597,290	1,137,902	1,182,267	44,365
			82	1,188,223	2,992,707	3,089,619	96,912
			83	3,572	6,817	7,587	770
			85	1,089,041	1,346,874	1,426,452	79,578
			86	487,779	266,643	305,688	39,045
GUATMAL	O	E	82	305,649	505,717	522,654	16,937
HG KONG	O	E	81	11,717	21,694	22,504	810
HUNGARY	O	E	81	73,134	116,198	123,457	7,259
INDIA	O	E	81	108,312	92,330	115,585	23,255
			82	770	707	863	156
INDNSIA	O	E	82	126,642	146,836	162,472	15,636
			85	40,983	56,975	62,648	5,673
IRELAND	O	E	81	38,579	63,619	65,576	1,957
ITALY	N	E	83	761,300	836,078	916,620	80,542
	O	E	81	8,458,786	6,667,846	7,455,885	788,039
			82	7,521,847	4,948,271	5,476,567	528,296
			83	1,714,141	1,352,634	1,496,609	143,975
			84	1,570,408	1,568,923	1,734,408	165,485
			85	665,879	585,263	654,770	69,507
LEBANON	O	E	81	7,678,786	12,182,792	12,866,607	683,815
			82	6,484,109	11,710,140	12,414,072	703,932
			83	2,478,063	4,504,325	4,751,760	247,435
			84	2,415,346	4,551,489	4,771,408	219,919
			85	3,345,364	5,983,142	6,245,591	262,449
			86	1,524,862	3,024,853	3,155,449	130,596
	V	E	81	306,889	565,287	599,770	34,483
			83	440,920	980,000	1,017,016	37,016
MEXICO	O	E	83	437	2,115	5,085	2,970
PHIL R	O	E	83	27,317	19,522	21,571	2,049
ROMANIA	O	E	81	33,654	66,958	69,529	2,571
SINGAPR	O	E	81	721	684	776	92
SPAIN	O	E	81	1,253	1,268	1,348	80
SRI LKA	O	E	81	53,559	59,569	65,551	5,982
SYRIA	O	E	81	4,337,374	7,333,567	7,669,751	336,184
			82	2,935,926	5,100,393	5,387,171	286,778
			83	1,667,600	3,117,102	3,283,849	166,747
			85	199,520	362,204	377,369	15,165
			86	461,392	837,597	872,665	35,068
	V	E	82	1,102	1,500	1,647	147
			84	1,213	7,300	7,684	384
			85	196,007	373,414	388,726	15,312
THAILND	O	E	81	5,633,692	6,590,441	7,208,220	617,779
			82	5,037,732	6,205,391	6,743,504	538,113
			83	5,302,576	6,787,836	7,368,120	580,284
			84	4,738,867	6,459,809	7,011,709	551,900
			85	4,793,765	6,374,345	6,941,118	566,773
			86	4,639,478	5,839,099	6,477,459	638,360
	V	E	81	29,871	5,420	8,886	3,466
			82	1,090,158	1,329,583	1,449,111	119,528
			83	65,000	14,742	21,316	6,574
			84	35,559	12,904	18,089	5,185
			85	3,281	4,500	4,988	488
			86	37,481	23,384	26,835	3,451
	V	W	83	222,305	151,256	179,852	28,596
TURKEY	A	E	84	392	837	1,859	1,022
	N	E	81	2,825,447	3,753,002	3,924,796	171,794
			82	4,040,737	4,808,974	5,081,388	272,414
			83	7,231,959	13,821,010	14,314,789	493,779
	O	E	81	96,562,624	123,595,574	128,978,078	5,380,064
			82	98,748,877	134,869,392	141,061,003	6,191,611
			83	104,957,258	159,992,697	167,001,165	7,008,468
			84	106,627,265	171,462,061	178,782,782	7,320,721
			85	107,907,358	171,967,941	179,476,088	7,508,147
			86	109,511,466	175,436,315	184,250,486	8,814,171
	V	E	81	1,121,308	1,591,987	1,667,182	75,195
			82	12,015	16,028	18,246	2,218
			83	456,633	824,518	859,915	35,397
			84	18,519	25,500	27,184	1,684
			85	881	1,840	2,054	214
			86	3,400,827	5,273,634	5,497,607	223,973
U KING	O	E	85	11,686	25,546	26,534	988
			86	763,998	1,192,079	1,252,781	60,702
USSR	O	E	81	573,732	707,365	752,446	45,081
			82	25,546	29,544	32,298	2,754
			83	2,366	3,007	3,328	321
			84	1,894	2,255	2,496	241
YUGOSLV	O	E	81	12,588,973	19,756,163	20,504,253	748,090
			82	9,791,442	16,013,227	16,669,973	656,746
			83	10,242,944	17,654,562	18,459,036	804,474
			84	13,042,932	23,311,145	24,350,645	1,039,500
			85	14,274,039	26,454,834	27,632,548	1,177,714
			86	13,934,923	25,624,267	26,871,179	1,246,912
	V	E	82	440,920	735,260	790,667	55,407
ZMBABWE	O	E	84	84,480	47,569	55,361	7,792
			85	11,880	5,140	6,012	872

1703210 CIG LEAF NT STMD FLUE-CURED (LB)

Country	Mode	Reg	Yr	Quantity	F.A.S.	C.I.F.	Charges
TOTAL			81	14,962,767	12,880,985	14,244,470	1,363,485
			82	9,708,280	12,454,720	12,892,536	437,816
			83	14,880,540	18,924,461	19,799,911	875,450
			84	22,324,726	24,378,150	25,819,790	1,441,640
			85	24,357,044	23,643,441	25,255,411	1,611,970

Crop Product TSUSA commodity number, description, and unit of quantity Country	Mode	Reg	Yr	Quantity	F.A.S.	C.I.F.	Charges
			86	32,278,777	31,614,329	32,760,357	1,146,028
ARGENT	A	E	84	298	298	498	200
	O	E	81	1,982,435	1,369,759	1,570,803	201,044
			82	49,383	67,088	72,648	5,560
			83	656,089	891,312	965,186	73,874
			85	198,000	172,700	194,421	21,721
			86	1,135,059	1,091,565	1,149,310	57,745
	V	E	81	69,224	78,500	86,346	7,846
			82	15,712	26,096	27,903	1,807
			85	94,187	85,504	104,084	18,580
			86	713,495	722,306	797,215	74,909
BRAZIL	A	E	84	959	279	1,403	1,124
	N	E	82	106,055	111,679	123,546	11,867
			84	5,059,957	4,529,325	5,095,445	566,120
	O	E	81	5,537,131	4,488,090	5,026,109	538,019
			82	1,483,151	1,754,186	1,930,180	175,994
			83	189,425	188,145	209,458	21,313
			84	548,309	591,147	623,834	32,687
			85	8,631,003	7,633,092	8,484,798	851,706
			86	904,777	892,001	1,070,558	178,557
	V	E	81	515,191	462,779	519,953	57,174
			82	981,857	1,075,691	1,191,373	115,682
			83	5,123,325	5,592,502	6,168,493	575,991
			84	4,415,693	4,715,432	5,224,424	508,992
			85	4,056,980	3,424,649	3,848,943	424,294
			86	4,024,799	3,488,625	3,852,022	363,397
CANADA	A	E	81	176	396	467	71
	N	E	85	3,542,352	4,299,197	4,299,197	
	O	E	81	1,876,734	2,663,060	2,663,060	
			82	5,674,776	7,989,564	7,993,193	3,629
			83	6,959,112	10,022,497	10,022,497	
			84	8,615,775	10,754,114	10,756,803	2,689
			85	4,910,429	6,436,511	6,441,126	4,615
			86	17,440,306	17,865,277	17,865,277	
	V	E	81	3,145,800	3,845,051	3,908,430	63,379
CHINA M	V	E	86	70,386	53,453	60,700	7,247
CHINA T	A	W	83	408	408	1,884	1,476
			84	264	455	888	433
	V	E	85	281,040	90,238	142,663	52,425
HONDURA	A	E	84	287	431	869	438
INDNSIA	O	E	84	84,196	18,430	27,160	8,730
			85	110,019	24,083	35,491	11,408
ITALY	O	E	86	42,250	7,723	10,370	2,647
	V	E	82	161,366	196,529	209,016	12,487
			83	360,963	549,572	567,306	17,734
			84	346,863	339,776	355,605	15,829
	V	W	85	109,774	15,738	22,615	6,877
JAPAN	A	E	83	218	910	1,274	364
			84	185	259	451	192
	V	E	81	1,521	5,510	5,581	71
			83	1,455	8,015	8,608	593
KOR REP	A	E	84	177	354	541	187
	O	E	84	13,230	18,631	20,226	1,595
			86	33,073	1,764	1,764	
	V	E	84	113,757	138,979	152,465	13,486
			85	241,624	317,526	337,327	19,801
			86	2,205	4,789	5,079	290
MALAWI	O	E	81	700,040	438,477	541,215	102,738
			83	339,217	206,842	243,617	36,775
			85	10,516	1,527	2,186	659
			86	427,866	62,411	89,210	26,799
	V	E	81	333,137	211,296	255,230	43,934
			86	882	2,203	2,281	78
	V	W	85	378,772	60,807	84,534	23,727
MEXICO	O	E	81	13,271	8,209	8,209	
			82	11,497	7,114	7,114	
PERU	V	E	85	132,717	163,790	177,020	13,230
PHIL R	O	E	82	112,435	116,620	129,286	12,666
			83	55,949	52,118	56,115	3,997
			84	519,255	637,693	666,674	28,981
POLAND	O	E	81	132,276	96,000	112,313	16,313
			83	639,834	649,719	722,267	72,548
	V	E	84	740,932	816,077	919,494	103,417
			85	348,333	274,253	313,322	39,069
			86	1,062,864	946,648	1,083,877	137,229
PORTUGL	V	E	86	490,303	396,425	430,547	34,122
REP SAF	O	E	81	1,008,977	505,182	608,422	103,240
			82	315,228	297,220	323,611	26,391
			83	169,386	136,556	149,010	12,454
			84	473,655	568,386	610,410	42,024
			85	442,459	345,038	398,688	53,650
			86	35,611	22,344	26,471	4,127
	V	E	81	609,638	596,739	656,203	59,464

Crop Product TSUSA commodity number, description, and unit of quantity Country	Mode	Reg	Yr	Quantity	F.A.S.	C.I.F.	Charges
			82	255,496	189,192	207,977	18,785
			83	203,350	210,463	230,062	19,599
			85	502,649	142,021	185,403	43,382
			86	853,662	380,416	445,808	65,392
SWITZLD	A	E	84	883	418	768	350
THAILND	O	E	81	490,425	528,277	573,123	44,846
			82	159,676	209,003	223,092	14,089
			83	16,607	12,694	14,495	1,801
			86	5,292	4,800	5,263	463
	V	E	81	24,162	21,113	23,898	2,785
	V	W	82	221,452	301,350	328,825	27,475
			86	1,369,060	1,300,607	1,369,927	69,320
YUGOSLV	V	W	83	125,602	357,146	390,859	33,713
			84	551,150	475,000	517,599	42,599
ZAMBIA	O	E	81	2,205	1,818	1,920	102
ZMBABWE	O	E	81	1,250,403	973,819	1,119,557	145,738
			82	28,600	32,906	35,230	2,324
			83	39,600	45,562	48,780	3,218
			84	379,211	226,053	253,684	27,631
			85	366,186	156,767	183,593	26,826
			86	302,832	186,687	222,544	35,857
	V	E	81	415,821	431,961	472,061	40,100
			82	131,596	80,482	89,542	9,060
			84	459,690	546,613	590,549	43,936
			86	218,255	339,234	363,704	24,470

1703230 CIG LEAF NOT STEMMED BURLEY (LB)

Country	Mode	Reg	Yr	Quantity	F.A.S.	C.I.F.	Charges
TOTAL			81	32,358,508	26,848,693	29,512,770	2,664,077
			82	6,907,704	8,069,278	8,828,568	759,290
			83	12,273,388	13,641,247	14,731,285	1,090,038
			84	19,853,627	18,955,849	20,536,899	1,581,050
			85	19,411,118	18,787,798	20,372,160	1,584,362
			86	8,852,571	7,331,105	8,026,347	695,242
ARGENT	A	E	82	305	305	984	679
	O	E	81	88,837	45,401	53,923	8,522
			83	180,984	185,532	204,304	18,772
			84	102,830	81,160	92,505	11,345
			85	461,601	541,943	541,943	
	V	E	85	164,728	215,167	238,372	23,205
			86	750,490	723,710	799,549	75,839
BRAZIL	A	E	81	529	290	1,230	940
			83	997	1,126	1,714	588
	N	E	83	3,057,761	3,478,543	3,821,778	343,235
	O	E	81	4,661,164	3,362,448	3,809,738	447,290
			82	4,491,868	5,299,540	5,814,511	514,971
			83	3,715,320	4,059,806	4,480,180	420,374
			84	1,417,995	1,425,735	1,588,464	162,729
			85	1,272,811	1,323,179	1,475,078	151,899
			86	369,290	437,030	488,523	51,493
	V	E	82	892,934	1,161,884	1,266,573	104,689
			84	3,645,842	3,000,275	3,410,306	410,031
			85	3,979,387	3,206,977	3,635,486	428,509
			86	110,170	97,273	109,135	11,862
BURMA	O	E	84	55,115	56,500	58,986	2,486
C RICA	V	E	81	43,719	77,289	81,908	4,619
CANADA	O	E	81	297,372	352,827	352,827	
			83	1,559,513	1,849,725	1,849,725	
			84	147,097	71,780	71,780	
			85	7,996	3,358	3,358	
CHILE	A	E	81	369	369	1,425	1,056
CHINA M	A	E	84	683	934	1,503	569
	O	E	82	40,455	47,844	50,449	2,605
			83	131,192	148,804	159,043	10,239
			84	434,639	493,903	525,351	31,448
			85	330,470	322,033	350,512	28,479
			86	110,000	81,685	81,685	
	V	E	81	129,101	87,975	95,125	7,150
COLOMB	A	E	81	57,914	39,324	46,631	7,307
			83	144,362	124,991	142,842	17,851
			84	108,021	88,308	102,758	14,450
	O	E	81	75,260	60,603	68,886	8,283
			84	39,690	54,082	61,468	7,386
			85	43,274	59,835	65,352	5,517
			86	103,739	137,927	158,122	20,195
	V	E	85	171,873	156,114	176,843	20,729
DENMARK	V	E	82	6,600	4,064	5,055	991
DOM REP	O	E	83	14,256	19,502	21,302	1,800
	V	E	84	137,497	87,609	99,381	11,772
			85	78,066	44,393	49,423	5,030
			86	260,780	215,646	229,349	13,703
ECUADOR	O	E	83	39,874	34,090	38,502	4,412
FR GERM	O	E	85	10,809	17,018	18,153	1,135
			86	6,485	10,210	10,932	722

Crop
Product
TSUSA commodity number, description, and unit of quantity

Country	Mode	Reg	Yr	Quantity	F.A.S.	C.I.F.	Charges
FRANCE	O	E	84	126,350	111,145	122,342	11,197
			85	230,879	254,233	254,233	
			86	64,961	50,786	52,738	1,952
GREECE	O	E	81	6,014,443	5,237,072	5,568,359	331,287
			84	89,080	46,672	54,104	7,432
			85	43,969	24,503	28,405	3,902
GUATMAL	O	E	81	382,043	385,785	400,037	14,252
			82	66,392	140,868	145,058	4,190
			84	284,680	217,728	240,555	22,827
	V	E	81	61,760	44,857	48,033	3,176
			82	30,997	19,166	21,201	2,035
			83	127,331	127,794	136,716	8,922
			84	5,281,891	5,353,502	5,765,881	412,379
			85	7,114,458	6,924,368	7,538,836	614,468
			86	3,343,576	2,058,927	2,263,173	204,246
HAITI	V	E	84	81,531	44,842	51,173	6,331
			85	530,114	344,689	379,875	35,186
			86	221,855	142,317	159,123	16,806
HONDURA	A	E	83	1,701	1,956	2,224	268
			85	989	1,005	1,372	367
	N	E	84	2,492,443	2,287,389	2,492,623	205,234
	O	E	81	245,024	219,140	228,333	9,193
			82	22,800	14,022	15,196	1,174
			83	115,078	123,245	130,213	6,968
			84	222,781	251,789	265,722	13,933
	V	E	81	259,150	293,381	305,204	11,823
			82	118,949	120,648	126,372	5,724
			83	84,384	86,138	92,350	6,212
			84	264,100	246,259	268,314	22,055
			85	2,294,365	2,681,020	2,856,094	175,074
			86	763,715	641,877	694,807	52,930
INDIA	O	E	81	453,571	319,753	392,998	73,245
			85	5,230	5,836	7,028	1,192
ITALY	A	E	82	6,173	2,439	5,845	3,406
	O	E	81	8,545,218	5,012,615	5,745,296	732,681
			82	209,321	86,368	104,464	18,096
			83	296,279	158,114	178,993	20,879
			84	177,397	98,982	112,750	13,768
			85	198,414	114,687	133,026	18,339
			86	37,289	177,697	214,813	37,116
	V	E	81	1,200,080	681,911	791,612	109,701
			82	466,478	307,458	342,590	35,132
			83	4,581	1,981	2,603	622
			84	65,064	61,900	66,578	4,678
			86	72,891	24,331	30,527	6,196
JAMAICA	V	E	85	66,552	43,259	48,314	5,055
JAPAN	A	E	84	284	336	403	67
			85	1,213	1,100	4,907	3,807
	O	E	81	401,819	352,797	402,041	49,244
			84	1,521	2,979	3,596	617
KOR REP	O	E	81	1,810,726	1,658,713	1,887,427	228,714
			86	218,241	291,491	291,491	
	V	E	83	35,730	37,372	41,067	3,695
			84	873,180	1,244,272	1,335,279	91,007
			85	220,500	275,210	299,726	24,516
			86	349,272	458,964	483,265	24,301
	V	W	83	449,820	563,285	609,499	46,214
MALAWI	O	E	81	1,714,889	1,271,241	1,512,758	241,517
			82	124,803	204,550	217,889	13,339
			84	47,619	96,833	104,055	7,222
			86	955,310	851,690	942,103	90,413
	V	E	81	608,704	504,514	584,794	80,280
			82	16,865	27,332	30,479	3,147
MEXICO	O	E	81	2,159,022	4,786,403	4,800,079	13,676
			82	91,071	154,600	167,781	13,181
			83	778,838	1,250,659	1,280,163	29,504
			84	2,759,867	2,820,275	2,829,190	8,915
			85	1,809,046	1,835,704	1,848,498	12,794
			86	286,774	395,037	420,366	25,329
	O	W	85	150,925	145,371	145,371	
	V	E	86	419	1,142	1,183	41
NETHLDS	V	E	82	83,429	84,788	90,636	5,848
PARAGUA	V	E	81	33,415	23,493	28,928	5,435
			84	42,864	32,031	36,456	4,425
			85	66,138	41,250	49,109	7,859
PHIL R	O	E	81	186,442	132,421	152,764	20,343
PORTUGL	V	E	81	287,015	276,326	319,288	42,962
REP SAF	O	E	81	53,900	35,709	43,355	7,646
	V	E	82	237,303	391,379	421,327	29,948
			83	201,866	192,574	212,173	19,599
ROMANIA	O	E	81	471,564	334,506	375,661	41,155
			84	392,165	317,376	365,219	47,843
	V	E	81	435,944	309,947	347,975	38,028
			83	775,315	715,654	795,755	80,101
			84	96,405	78,712	89,677	10,965
SALVADR	V	E	85	152,819	202,580	219,326	16,746
			86	149,785	86,221	100,850	14,629
SPAIN	A	E	84	487	717	1,390	673
SWITZLD	V	E	86	166,689	100,244	114,183	13,939
THAILND	O	E	81	164,895	97,073	111,012	13,939
			83	425,930	405,356	444,414	39,058
			84	464,509	281,824	319,090	37,266
			85	4,492	2,966	3,520	554
	V	E	81	35,274	16,000	19,514	3,514
			83	132,276	75,000	85,725	10,725
	V	W	86	510,840	346,900	380,430	33,530
VENEZ	A	E	82	961	2,023	2,158	135
	V	E	81	407,635	166,412	189,683	23,271
YUGOSLV	O	E	81	1,062,892	650,635	733,008	82,373
ZMBABWE	V	E	81	8,818	11,463	12,918	1,455

1703240 CIG LEAF NOT STEMMED, NSPF (LB)

Country	Mode	Reg	Yr	Quantity	F.A.S.	C.I.F.	Charges
TOTAL			81	3,194,867	2,581,997	2,852,140	270,143
			82	2,029,722	2,185,278	2,354,126	168,848
			83	1,723,309	2,024,415	2,167,466	143,051
			84	2,813,908	2,653,012	2,882,168	229,156
			85	1,519,926	1,711,481	1,742,641	31,160
			86	2,823,881	3,080,707	3,160,870	80,163
AUSTRAL	A	E	83	265	421	2,296	1,875
	V	E	82	1,543	2,651	3,818	1,167
AUSTRIA	V	E	84	13,252	28,553	30,409	1,856
BELGIUM	V	E	82	66,843	65,493	70,038	4,545
			83	67,163	60,093	65,067	4,974
BRAZIL	A	E	81	622	292	492	200
			82	291	291	840	549
			83	314	369	1,081	712
			84	333	521	1,232	711
	O	E	81	900,633	752,036	846,146	94,110
			82	28,589	38,864	41,605	2,741
			84	89,364	53,707	62,906	9,199
			85	178,164	114,736	119,180	4,444
			86	141,390	64,200	79,555	15,355
	V	E	83	4,950	5,655	7,681	2,026
			84	52,377	15,443	21,484	6,041
BULGAR	O	E	82	3,220	1,936	2,128	192
CANADA	A	E	81	200	335	440	105
			82	22	406	515	109
	O	E	81	332,559	368,651	368,651	
			82	178,430	157,509	157,509	
			83	451,700	470,508	470,508	
			84	383,579	476,892	476,892	
			85	1,201,578	1,422,441	1,422,441	
			86	2,176,550	2,451,227	2,451,227	
CHILE	A	W	81	661	331	353	22
CYPRUS	V	E	82	4,008	7,554	7,908	354
			86	11,634	24,274	25,341	1,067
FR GERM	A	E	84	395	656	1,323	667
			86	1,112	2,599	3,978	1,379
GREECE	A	E	83	83	1,002	1,122	120
	O	E	83	69,747	5,611	6,333	722
			84	179,184	16,557	21,892	5,335
			85	64	1,050	1,055	5
			86	20,085	1,648	3,700	2,052
	V	E	82	417	287	328	41
			84	306,476	56,482	87,239	30,757
HAITI	V	E	85	61,311	39,852	43,366	3,514
INDIA	A	E	82	220	378	1,034	656
	V	E	81	198,414	149,700	177,273	27,573
INDNSIA	V	E	84	370,373	527,160	572,663	45,503
ITALY	O	E	81	503,518	248,570	281,827	33,257
	V	E	81	78,954	64,275	68,433	4,158
			82	632,943	772,251	817,909	45,658
			83	104,474	116,580	125,170	8,590
			84	1,101,721	1,058,488	1,144,443	85,955
JAPAN	A	E	83	2,550	12,851	14,308	1,457
			85	2,072	7,660	14,689	7,029
	A	W	83	672	494	511	17
	V	W	83	610,491	944,858	1,026,364	81,506
LEBANON	O	E	81	628,495	465,243	511,351	46,108
			82	316,212	189,635	208,212	18,577
	V	E	86	3,808	8,612	9,259	647
MALAWI	A	E	85	838	1,307	1,905	598
	O	E	81	8,400	4,514	5,100	586
			82	2,520	1,354	1,530	176
			83	3,659	2,031	2,286	255
			86	3,352	3,350	3,350	
	V	E	81	252,000	250,614	284,866	34,252

Crop Product TSUSA commodity number, description, and unit of quantity Country	Mode	Reg	Yr	Quantity	F.A.S.	C.I.F.	Charges
			82	420,000	538,184	597,684	59,500
			84	96,600	179,763	185,970	6,207
MALAYSA	A	W	81	3,126	1,804	1,874	70
			84	615	1,755	3,913	2,158
MEXICO	O	E	81	37,058	24,866	24,866	
			82	57,473	38,568	38,568	
			86	5,028	5,024	5,024	
N ANTIL	A	E	82	538	269	282	13
NETHLDS	V	E	83	55,439	56,496	60,835	4,339
PARAGUA	V	E	81	65,810	45,101	54,898	9,797
PHIL R	A	E	84	2,414	1,207	7,683	6,476
			85	441	1,015	2,324	1,309
	V	E	84	63,629	52,686	59,317	6,631
SPAIN	A	E	82	441	1,140	1,159	19
			86	573	1,700	2,680	980
SWEDEN	A	E	84	165	645	709	64
SWITZLD	A	E	81	882	1,000	1,538	538
			82	529	1,142	1,489	347
			85	789	1,651	3,141	1,490
			86	970	3,913	5,667	1,754
	V	E	84	1,852	1,895	2,145	250
SYRIA	V	E	82	1,102	2,800	2,882	82
			84	1,102	7,168	7,571	403
THAILND	O	E	81	4,765	2,961	3,234	273
			82	5,020	3,780	4,268	488
			83	13,785	11,736	13,281	1,545
USSR	O	E	81	177,787	200,899	219,626	18,727
			82	309,361	360,786	394,420	33,634
			83	338,689	336,204	371,134	34,930
			84	118,653	155,595	174,235	18,640
			85	74,669	121,769	134,540	12,771
			86	319,019	452,912	499,139	46,227
ZMBABWE	A	E	81	311	311	661	350
	O	E	84	31,824	17,839	20,142	2,303
			86	140,360	61,248	71,950	10,702

1703500 TOBAC, NOV 35% WRAP, STEMMD (LB)

Country	Mode	Reg	Yr	Quantity	F.A.S.	C.I.F.	Charges
TOTAL			**81**	**258,902**	**367,048**	**318,570**	**11,522**
			82	**75,420**	**142,016**	**151,025**	**9,009**
			83	**16,588,421**	**24,356,335**	**25,789,684**	**1,433,349**
			84	**92,198,190**	**147,373,607**	**155,675,044**	**8,301,437**
			85	**53,037,736**	**77,791,210**	**83,376,392**	**5,585,182**
ARGENT	O	E	83	3,489	4,280	4,633	353
			84	3,256,637	5,958,590	6,332,687	374,097
			85	4,472,638	7,249,120	7,794,045	544,925
	V	E	83	442,407	498,436	545,717	47,281
			84	248,039	284,830	314,244	29,414
			85	1,185,799	1,320,890	1,546,997	226,107
BRAZIL	A	E	84	876	738	1,668	930
	N	E	84	1,259,611	2,072,818	2,229,763	156,945
			85	972,518	1,668,739	1,779,711	110,972
	O	E	83	6,054,745	8,422,051	9,052,360	630,309
			84	28,538,713	45,205,137	48,486,766	3,281,629
			85	22,034,320	34,889,084	37,478,354	2,589,270
	V	E	83	1,123,729	1,296,481	1,416,442	119,961
			84	2,843,499	3,097,534	3,398,584	301,050
			85	2,203,158	2,304,499	2,548,891	244,392
C RICA	O	E	83	1,580	2,789	2,876	87
			84	138,433	220,955	232,093	11,138
CANADA	O	E	81	148,311	194,982	194,982	
			83	1,584,362	3,276,083	3,276,329	246
			84	4,150,827	7,399,460	7,400,698	1,238
			85	121,040	215,255	215,255	
	V	E	83	552	2,597	2,700	103
CHILE	O	E	84	1,138,319	1,555,458	1,643,687	88,229
			85	9,296	14,107	14,825	718
	V	E	84	2,646	4,149	4,357	208
CHINA M	O	E	84	11,166	14,840	15,493	653
CHINA T	V	E	85	38,113	16,583	26,217	9,634
COLOMB	O	E	83	251,313	383,360	392,937	9,577
			84	251,388	247,914	277,294	29,380
DENMARK	V	E	83	11,200	6,816	7,374	558
DOM REP	O	E	83	46,083	84,657	86,464	1,807
	V	E	83	17,600	10,912	11,522	610
			84	33,335	88,559	93,768	5,209
ECUADOR	O	E	84	55,115	111,750	114,556	2,806
FR GERM	O	E	83	6,600	7,579	8,034	455
			84	865,877	1,150,210	1,238,114	87,904
			85	220,460	314,000	343,704	29,704
GREECE	O	E	84	996,728	1,311,064	1,387,938	76,874
			85	1,865,140	2,570,478	2,714,262	143,784
	V	E	84	600,982	871,443	916,011	44,568
			85	10,433	8,919	9,062	143
GUATMAL	O	E	83	773,967	1,378,566	1,423,640	45,074
			84	5,405,951	9,562,159	9,847,940	285,781
	V	E	84	4,147,271	7,772,117	8,105,714	333,597
			85	812,168	1,076,249	1,138,427	62,178
HONDURA	A	E	84	1,963	5,889	6,232	343
	O	E	84	947,964	1,422,403	1,504,839	82,436
			84	2,595,562	4,770,944	4,916,157	145,213
	V	E	84	1,471,693	3,048,642	3,160,402	111,760
			85	792,230	1,550,798	1,611,350	60,552
HUNGARY	O	E	84	58,824	73,184	75,721	2,537
			85	92,787	117,490	125,839	8,349
INDIA	O	E	83	397	450	505	55
			84	10,719	12,085	13,557	1,472
			85	1,588	1,798	2,020	222
	V	E	84	104,167	110,883	122,147	11,264
INDNSIA	O	E	85	509,131	692,820	761,127	68,307
ITALY	A	E	84	440	317	917	600
	N	E	85	220,958	30,861	51,258	20,397
	O	E	83	20,764	16,067	17,519	1,452
			84	2,354,652	3,486,913	3,669,172	182,259
			85	2,057,998	2,598,462	2,750,728	152,266
	V	E	84	115,522	78,600	88,680	10,080
JAPAN	A	W	84	304	531	783	252
	O	E	84	510,681	691,231	733,086	41,855
	V	E	84	226,147	355,988	386,694	30,706
	V	W	83	70,925	91,417	98,434	7,017
			85	335,805	520,934	568,026	47,092
KOR REP	O	E	83	2,995,430	5,206,604	5,518,841	312,237
			84	9,374,182	16,255,620	17,238,523	982,903
			85	2,346,743	4,240,254	4,440,938	200,684
	V	E	81	106,845	168,809	119,653	10,844
			82	75,420	142,016	151,025	9,009
			83	112,455	139,735	151,101	11,366
			84	339,390	736,827	785,239	48,412
			85	229,279	420,462	446,288	25,826
MALAWI	O	E	84	3,963,649	4,796,676	5,214,647	417,971
			85	5,183,893	6,396,811	6,926,837	530,026
	V	E	83	538,902	989,820	1,035,193	45,373
			84	681,026	999,271	1,056,609	57,338
			85	966,229	1,414,396	1,501,731	87,335
MEXICO	A	E	83	768	2,667	3,340	673
	O	E	84	3,388,279	3,908,162	3,915,635	7,473
			85	1,327,797	1,092,605	1,107,766	15,161
NICARAG	O	E	83	4,150	7,321	7,548	227
			84	372,686	881,704	905,755	24,051
	V	E	84	400,862	636,253	673,655	37,402
PANAMA	A	E	85	1,058	2,116	2,116	
	O	E	83	64,231	120,486	124,176	3,690
			84	2,847,723	6,333,431	6,538,155	204,724
	V	E	84	953,496	1,716,293	1,757,336	41,043
			85	1,046,022	1,882,838	1,940,431	57,593
PARAGUA	A	E	85	1,365	2,023	2,883	860
	V	E	84	40,000	28,000	32,627	4,627
PERU	A	E	81	578	1,003	1,681	678
PHIL R	O	E	81	3,168	2,254	2,254	
POLAND	O	E	85	2,000	2,882	3,122	240
	V	E	85	30,439	65,956	68,487	2,531
REP SAF	O	E	84	249,273	259,136	278,562	19,426
			85	410,787	498,951	532,859	33,908
	V	E	84	2,800	420	1,110	690
			85	17,504	2,626	3,573	947
SALVADR	O	E	83	66,236	145,519	149,864	4,345
			84	232,023	502,514	517,354	14,840
	V	E	84	303,105	672,727	706,703	33,976
SPAIN	A	E	84	291	584	584	
	O	E	85	3,770	3,129	3,129	
	V	E	85	134,593	202,030	202,030	
SRI LKA	V	E	83	36,518	40,820	48,829	8,009
THAILND	O	E	83	330,078	292,073	326,240	34,167
			84	3,981,573	6,296,861	6,686,151	389,290
			85	1,942,712	3,315,746	3,501,828	186,082
	V	E	84	121,716	159,596	175,694	16,098
	V	W	84	699,522	986,638	1,085,961	99,323
TNZANIA	O	E	84	653,975	225,871	298,402	72,531
			85	573,439	189,644	252,498	62,854
VENEZ	O	E	83	1,081,986	506,346	572,227	65,881
			84	1,076,473	553,092	618,590	65,498
			85	401,400	206,432	230,881	24,449
YUGOSLV	O	E	85	2,190	2,881	2,881	
ZMBABWE	O	E	84	195,424	410,373	442,538	32,165
			85	460,936	688,342	726,016	37,674
	V	E	84	924,635	1,448,626	1,530,291	81,665

Crop Product TSUSA commodity number, description, and unit of quantity Country	Mode	Reg	Yr	Quantity	F.A.S.	C.I.F.	Charges

1703510 TOB STM FLU-CRD NOV35% WPR (LB)

Country	Mode	Reg	Yr	Quantity	F.A.S.	C.I.F.	Charges
TOTAL			85	35,533,577	56,306,703	59,929,607	3,622,904
			86	63,063,104	92,472,550	98,848,672	6,376,122
ARGENT	O	E	85	66,218	71,348	74,847	3,499
			86	4,492,516	7,326,149	7,841,966	515,817
	V	E	85	939,583	903,524	1,005,727	102,203
			86	741,019	777,458	855,188	77,730
AUSTRAL	O	E	85	80,289	18,670	30,442	11,772
BRAZIL	O	E	85	23,445,581	39,529,414	42,187,477	2,658,063
			86	39,786,874	61,394,440	65,742,462	4,348,022
	V	E	85	2,582,801	3,016,859	3,327,532	310,673
			86	5,080,320	5,604,565	6,089,874	485,309
CANADA	N	E	86	507,524	924,088	931,396	7,308
	O	E	85	2,560,715	4,243,032	4,243,032	
			86	4,435,862	7,092,731	7,092,731	
CHILE	O	E	86	117,770	186,141	195,325	9,184
CHINA T	V	E	85	185,627	64,759	84,083	19,324
DOM REP	V	E	86	323,349	308,152	326,293	18,141
ECUADOR	O	E	86	7,920	10,771	11,969	1,198
FRANCE	V	E	86	516,169	631,811	673,358	41,547
ITALY	O	E	86	347,580	262,988	279,109	16,121
JAPAN	O	E	86	21,208	25,450	25,450	
	V	E	86	337,326	498,864	550,784	51,920
	V	W	85	29,233	38,852	43,238	4,386
			86	58,466	77,704	86,595	8,891
KOR REP	O	E	85	891,652	1,561,344	1,595,185	33,841
			86	1,043,817	1,685,069	1,885,887	200,818
	V	E	85	354,941	729,330	760,077	30,747
MALAWI	O	E	85	433,155	527,932	563,634	35,702
			86	850,351	1,141,124	1,216,470	75,346
	V	E	86	22,050	41,387	43,602	2,215
MEXICO	O	E	85	6,750	2,239	2,303	64
PHIL R	V	E	86	29,101	2,904	5,769	2,865
POLAND	O	E	86	472,400	680,798	737,482	56,684
REP SAF	O	E	85	1,177,074	1,770,814	1,886,203	115,389
			86	740,561	728,456	810,168	81,712
	V	E	85	431,184	581,885	620,658	38,773
			86	516,520	280,451	323,138	42,687
THAILND	O	E	85	600,227	664,677	748,529	83,852
			86	277,985	134,709	189,508	54,799
	V	E	85	3,160	3,881	3,943	62
	V	W	85	127,710	16,219	38,462	22,243
TNZANIA	O	E	85	45,992	11,927	18,240	6,313
			86	427,442	200,053	241,577	41,524
TURK IS	O	E	85	515,876	996,930	1,049,041	52,111
YUGOSLV	O	E	85	407,340	535,732	561,536	25,804
			86	477,250	627,778	666,384	38,606
ZMBABWE	O	E	85	275,824	238,656	268,135	29,479
			86	900,165	1,165,652	1,302,684	137,032
	V	E	85	375,805	782,560	821,226	38,666
			86	528,399	658,976	719,560	60,584

1703520 TOB STMMD NSPF NOV 35% WPR (LB)

Country	Mode	Reg	Yr	Quantity	F.A.S.	C.I.F.	Charges
TOTAL			85	35,551,305	54,784,099	58,245,128	3,461,029
			86	80,604,764	126,067,746	133,643,732	7,575,986
ARGENT	O	E	85	2,857,132	4,459,318	4,782,552	323,234
			86	5,245,809	7,719,877	8,291,352	571,475
	V	E	85	474,717	559,273	613,755	54,482
			86	42,335	59,248	61,974	2,726
BELGIUM	V	E	86	92,593	165,900	176,400	10,500
BRAZIL	N	E	86	704,103	517,464	586,840	69,376
	O	E	85	12,199,058	17,548,248	18,769,584	1,221,336
			86	19,000,492	31,964,034	34,025,928	2,061,894
	V	E	85	3,647,709	5,001,180	5,440,877	439,697
			86	3,529,938	3,930,666	4,266,308	335,642
C RICA	O	E	85	6,432	5,027	5,329	302
CANADA	O	E	85	173,887	261,071	261,071	
			86	519,974	881,820	881,820	
CHILE	O	E	85	238,652	361,374	381,046	19,672
			86	161,652	335,266	347,483	12,217
	V	E	85	3,086	4,840	5,076	236
			86	256,310	401,889	418,898	17,009
CHINA M	O	E	86	756,853	772,544	861,977	89,433
COLOMB	O	E	85	21,743	22,433	25,135	2,702
			86	992,978	1,270,388	1,465,492	195,104
DOM REP	V	E	86	30,810	28,653	30,669	2,016
ECUADOR	O	E	86	55,115	111,750	114,558	2,808
FR GERM	V	E	86	2,204	6,430	7,365	935
GREECE	V	E	85	718,820	1,031,725	1,085,408	53,683
			86	2,606,832	3,911,526	4,100,397	188,871
GUATMAL	V	E	85	1,028,760	1,868,235	1,931,168	62,933
			86	3,098,120	4,837,537	5,024,597	187,060
HONDURA	O	E	86	1,264,804	1,618,154	1,646,938	28,784
	V	E	85	928,425	1,756,464	1,832,446	75,982
			86	1,500,949	2,898,274	2,977,965	79,691
INDIA	O	E	85	15,082	16,590	18,546	1,956
			86	188,693	198,468	219,841	21,373
ITALY	O	E	85	402,348	497,050	523,191	26,141
			86	5,356,302	6,708,089	7,108,883	400,794
	V	E	85	123,328	89,602	97,852	8,250
			86	818,823	487,929	550,451	62,522
KOR REP	O	E	85	6,889,991	13,025,334	13,713,545	688,211
			86	10,314,944	20,119,714	21,264,565	1,144,851
	V	E	85	125,662	208,230	219,960	11,730
			86	619,984	989,298	1,038,182	48,884
MALAWI	O	E	85	1,271,971	2,074,452	2,240,180	165,728
			86	5,792,365	11,830,116	12,610,020	779,904
	V	E	86	281,497	255,833	286,114	30,281
MALAYSA	A	E	86	1,268	4,955	8,355	3,400
MEXICO	O	E	85	892,278	678,173	685,547	7,374
			86	4,741,591	6,972,097	7,001,952	29,855
	V	E	86	2,932	8,595	8,812	217
PANAMA	O	E	86	929,072	1,672,330	1,716,671	44,341
PARAGUA	O	E	86	38,809	80,198	84,877	4,679
POLAND	O	E	86	71,200	102,610	111,153	8,543
REP SAF	O	E	85	72,000	108,630	114,455	5,825
			86	28,840	31,946	32,913	967
	V	E	85	10,500	1,575	1,754	179
SALVADR	V	E	86	67,650	108,235	113,476	5,241
SURINAM	V	E	86	2,205	3,015	3,195	180
THAILND	O	E	85	3,088,731	4,694,474	4,948,347	253,873
			86	6,232,291	9,222,491	9,847,994	625,503
	V	E	86	574,834	581,948	691,190	109,242
	V	W	85	19,550	2,933	3,483	550
			86	246,000	260,244	279,868	19,624
TNZANIA	O	E	85	37,279	8,361	12,610	4,249
			86	393,920	139,833	183,353	43,520
TURKEY	O	E	85	275,631	480,741	511,658	30,917
U KING	V	E	86	84,672	129,063	133,108	4,045
VENEZ	V	E	86	224,785	115,548	129,317	13,769
YUGOSLV	V	E	85	10,533	1,580	1,705	125
ZMBABWE	O	E	85	18,000	17,186	18,848	1,662
			86	3,720,295	4,595,941	4,913,634	317,693
	V	E	86	9,921	17,830	18,847	1,017

1704000 FILER TBCO LEAF N STMD NSPF (LB)

Country	Mode	Reg	Yr	Quantity	F.A.S.	C.I.F.	Charges
TOTAL			81	4,339,313	4,474,162	4,802,669	328,537
			82	1,670,602	2,647,443	2,795,645	148,202
			83	2,388,722	3,828,787	4,069,304	240,517
			84	8,005,732	8,937,681	9,588,766	651,085
			85	4,693,980	4,244,246	4,684,259	440,013
			86	5,439,889	4,647,096	5,056,976	409,880
ARGENT	O	E	81	11,935	5,875	7,049	1,174
			82	5,236	3,487	3,779	292
			86	26,910	15,541	19,185	3,644
BELGIUM	O	E	84	7,854	3,184	4,003	819
BRAZIL	O	E	81	17,200	13,398	14,988	1,590
			84	2,453	3,209	3,452	243
			86	72,442	77,241	85,220	7,979
	V	E	81	403,666	426,229	460,913	34,684
			82	111	1,644	1,834	190
			85	9,330	25,003	26,150	1,147
			86	147,119	172,038	184,899	12,861
	V	W	84	26,032	23,616	26,714	3,098
C AF RP	O	E	83	2,423	11,518	11,847	329
			84	3,532	8,754	9,204	450
			85	3,562	14,978	15,271	293
CAMROON	N	E	83	14,883	213,806	219,668	5,862
	O	E	81	65,726	351,133	360,298	9,165
			82	28,574	284,938	291,824	6,886
			83	61,544	505,679	535,702	30,023
			84	83,506	578,569	618,538	39,969
			85	94,150	458,616	487,207	28,591
			86	32,701	227,826	232,673	4,847
CANADA	O	E	81	2,130	1,426	1,426	
			82	32,199	11,713	11,713	
			83	115,332	153,875	153,875	
			86	40,722	41,734	41,734	
CHINA T	O	E	84	6,614	3,435	3,921	486
COLOMB	O	E	81	31,808	24,966	27,122	2,156
			82	8,989	10,202	10,931	729
			83	118,820	145,303	153,959	8,656
			84	16,450	15,654	18,196	2,542
			86	118,662	130,859	143,661	12,802

Crop
Product
TSUSA commodity number, description, and unit of quantity

Country	Mode	Reg	Yr	Quantity	F.A.S.	C.I.F.	Charges
DENMARK	O	E	83	12,366	13,125	13,923	798
DOM REP	N	E	85	196,971	233,487	246,399	12,912
	O	E	81	203,176	188,467	204,261	15,824
			82	195,714	166,310	185,979	19,669
			83	195,010	230,462	250,212	19,750
			84	2,858,865	2,577,138	2,753,371	176,233
			85	1,103,466	692,138	818,239	126,101
			86	1,545,711	1,303,984	1,390,221	86,237
	V	E	81	361,905	290,264	307,068	16,804
			82	2,785	2,697	3,303	606
			83	4,548	11,608	11,932	324
			84	2,163,428	2,129,447	2,264,490	135,043
			85	1,035,527	989,700	1,039,766	50,066
			86	1,947,372	1,632,007	1,732,360	100,353
ECUADOR	A	E	81	1,140	2,868	3,825	957
	N	E	82	5,482	10,031	10,845	814
			85	5,080	11,562	13,121	1,559
	O	E	81	84,655	152,043	161,676	9,633
			82	45,550	75,997	80,932	4,935
			83	31,871	33,155	36,087	2,932
			84	27,770	32,769	34,956	2,187
			85	73,648	97,884	103,387	5,503
			86	28,178	57,918	60,781	2,863
	V	E	83	7,304	13,293	13,993	700
			84	4,065	8,130	8,830	700
FR GERM	O	E	83	22,574	13,606	14,624	1,018
			84	299,699	174,842	206,927	32,085
			86	285,808	155,705	199,070	43,365
	O	W	84	4,900	4,541	5,203	662
	V	E	82	234,657	147,171	165,800	18,629
FRANCE	O	E	81	797	7,165	7,235	70
			85	64,108	27,234	34,760	7,526
			86	71,709	38,394	46,575	8,181
HONDURA	A	E	83	9,042	15,848	17,266	1,418
	N	E	81	5,772	7,513	8,441	928
			82	13,279	20,645	22,050	1,405
	O	E	81	292,039	428,234	443,908	15,674
			82	121,215	215,873	225,804	9,931
			83	217,159	543,480	564,618	21,138
			84	343,829	719,681	749,423	29,742
			85	32,641	81,567	85,003	3,436
			86	1,486	1,863	1,949	86
	V	E	81	61,967	93,408	97,342	3,934
			82	5,939	13,775	14,934	1,159
			83	36,064	28,851	30,565	1,714
			84	18,709	15,799	17,800	2,001
			85	1,106	10,792	10,963	171
			86	82,202	103,200	109,856	6,656
INDIA	O	E	81	25,261	5,817	8,390	2,573
			82	17,064	2,285	4,028	1,743
	V	E	86	38,801	40,906	45,284	4,378
INDNSIA	O	E	81	3,759	1,632	2,184	552
			85	91,335	99,285	110,561	11,276
			86	9,947	3,645	4,864	1,219
	V	E	85	199,957	46,711	67,141	20,430
IRELAND	O	E	82	15,098	9,814	11,168	1,354
ISRAEL	A	E	86	3,997	4,996	5,433	437
ITALY	O	E	81	51,631	8,901	12,914	4,013
			83	32,613	16,004	19,470	3,466
			84	150,173	37,981	57,601	19,620
			85	277,476	70,822	100,996	30,174
			86	42,793	12,217	16,917	4,700
	V	E	84	790,426	1,073,665	1,176,281	102,616
			85	252,815	180,845	200,986	20,141
			86	647,306	162,957	239,707	76,750
	V	W	85	196,591	32,074	55,286	23,212
JAMAICA	O	E	81	9,780	4,823	5,342	519
			85	123,977	49,591	55,681	6,090
MALAWI	O	E	81	2,646	1,440	1,584	144
	V	E	86	105,821	35,632	45,489	9,857
MEXICO	N	E	83	8,749	32,187	32,975	788
	O	E	81	1,105,379	1,225,608	1,282,499	56,891
			82	666,515	1,052,074	1,099,732	47,658
			83	681,557	933,285	985,399	52,114
			84	931,774	1,268,006	1,341,864	73,858
			85	145,881	415,838	434,124	18,286
			86	66,161	229,803	234,492	4,689
	V	E	81	53,406	112,007	115,367	3,360
			82	15,166	33,946	36,946	3,000
			83	1,437	7,188	7,873	685
			85	60,042	219,834	228,243	8,409
			86	8,345	26,212	27,064	852
NETHLDS	V	E	82	198	643	800	157
NICARAG	A	E	83	2,642	4,634	5,186	552
			84	6,477	9,068	10,387	1,319
	N	E	82	3,994	5,368	5,834	466
	O	E	81	372,528	570,270	595,957	25,687
			82	157,783	327,121	349,196	22,075
			83	212,210	498,574	524,123	25,549
			84	104,751	134,473	142,902	8,429
			85	41,706	55,313	59,863	4,550
			86	19,598	24,229	25,620	1,391
	V	E	81	46,566	43,427	45,341	1,914
			82	64,610	236,547	240,055	3,508
PANAMA	O	E	84	7,517	17,285	18,138	853
			85	58,201	47,429	54,437	7,008
			86	38,274	109,538	119,479	9,941
	V	E	86	5,605	5,207	5,489	282
PARAGUA	O	E	83	3,582	1,716	2,086	370
			85	17,614	16,525	19,351	2,826
			86	3,080	2,068	2,390	322
	V	E	81	853,797	439,174	529,137	89,963
			85	300,000	160,125	178,215	18,090
	V	W	82	6,541	4,406	5,251	845
			85	308,796	206,893	239,109	32,216
PHIL R	O	E	81	39,502	9,516	14,664	5,148
			82	23,903	10,756	12,907	2,151
			83	103,609	59,949	69,053	9,104
			84	102,643	73,899	84,680	10,781
			86	49,139	31,376	36,564	5,188
	V	E	83	441,514	322,305	368,505	46,200
SPAIN	O	E	81	230,613	58,196	82,927	24,731
			83	51,318	16,336	22,888	6,552
			84	43,204	18,051	25,202	7,151
SWITZLD	A	E	81	529	362	811	449
	A	W	84	69	485	532	47
SYRIA	V	E	81	551	3,000	3,475	475
			84	992	6,000	6,151	151

1704500 FILLER TOBACCO, STEMD, NSPF (LB)

Country	Mode	Reg	Yr	Quantity	F.A.S.	C.I.F.	Charges
TOTAL			81	2,051,778	4,230,790	4,385,748	154,958
			82	1,796,834	4,085,025	4,222,306	137,281
			83	1,533,560	3,633,588	3,751,695	118,107
			84	5,091,850	10,745,479	11,141,809	396,330
			85	3,173,831	5,856,844	6,089,505	232,661
			86	1,888,571	4,036,297	4,155,157	118,860
ARGENT	O	E	81	4,821	9,406	10,013	607
BRAZIL	O	E	81	219,823	336,947	357,607	20,660
			82	145,137	265,006	282,588	17,582
			83	119,417	231,795	245,538	13,743
			84	107,586	208,579	219,941	11,362
			85	87,769	159,670	168,476	8,806
			86	59,820	108,839	115,608	6,769
	V	E	81	189,386	434,159	452,051	17,892
			82	53,996	108,490	114,510	6,020
			83	45,368	97,560	104,537	6,977
			84	31,851	74,203	78,393	4,190
			85	19,693	48,753	51,893	3,140
			86	26,483	52,081	55,355	3,274
C RICA	N	E	81	4,663	7,760	8,769	1,009
	V	E	86	2,599	7,797	8,089	292
CAMROON	O	E	85	3,963	10,351	10,712	361
CANADA	O	E	83	29,613	17,063	20,285	3,222
			84	44,183	32,868	32,868	
			85	39,245	57,419	57,419	
			86	177,529	192,220	192,220	
COLOMB	O	E	84	5,501	11,169	11,673	504
			85	12,402	32,647	33,650	1,003
			86	6,850	12,678	13,277	599
	V	E	83	225	416	502	86
			84	7,619	13,714	14,633	919
			86	8,799	16,278	17,082	804
DOM REP	N	E	85	56,787	159,749	171,003	11,254
	O	E	81	770,548	1,700,181	1,751,200	51,019
			82	670,955	1,617,081	1,658,595	41,514
			83	551,715	1,398,134	1,432,176	34,042
			84	1,252,840	3,030,387	3,111,567	81,180
			85	653,872	1,605,528	1,644,931	39,403
			86	311,795	808,312	826,215	17,903
	V	E	81	100,521	212,077	216,586	4,550
			82	243,582	567,725	583,086	15,361
			83	185,946	496,855	504,624	7,769
			84	1,016,671	2,954,662	3,041,169	86,507
			85	846,219	1,319,267	1,370,906	51,639
			86	802,296	1,813,864	1,868,089	54,225
ECUADOR	N	E	82	6,600	12,012	13,008	996
			85	6,136	12,272	13,963	1,691

Country	Mode	Reg	Yr	Quantity	F.A.S.	C.I.F.	Charges
	O	E	81	11,330	15,704	16,589	885
			82	9,845	17,720	18,576	856
			83	3,987	7,253	7,684	431
			84	8,914	17,227	18,069	842
			85	13,680	23,870	25,375	1,505
			86	16,175	30,477	31,894	1,417
	V	E	83	6,601	12,014	12,647	633
			84	2,365	4,730	5,137	407
			86	6,486	12,383	13,268	885
FR GERM	O	E	86	87,517	100,581	105,953	5,372
	V	E	81	573	1,650	1,993	343
FRANCE	O	E	81	1,140	2,205	2,245	40
HONDURA	A	E	83	5,850	16,416	17,379	963
	N	E	81	59,716	145,804	155,938	10,134
			82	21,870	52,999	55,035	2,036
			85	12,977	36,364	37,980	1,616
	O	E	81	289,164	665,444	687,048	21,604
			82	241,758	595,902	616,486	20,584
			83	183,683	464,027	480,040	16,013
			84	233,610	594,157	609,479	15,322
			85	81,928	228,604	234,797	6,193
			86	98,432	262,159	269,246	7,087
	V	E	82	6,823	17,299	17,689	390
			83	4,500	2,250	2,490	240
			84	5,813	16,607	17,069	462
			86	1,619	5,666	5,785	119
INDNSIA	A	E	81	455	1,405	2,498	1,093
	O	E	85	34,549	38,374	42,135	3,761
ISRAEL	A	E	86	2,524	4,403	4,677	274
ITALY	O	E	85	22,050	13,230	14,815	1,585
JAMAICA	V	E	85	748	1,142	1,244	102
MALAWI	O	E	84	1,153,975	2,034,671	2,133,625	98,954
			85	720,747	1,185,223	1,242,489	57,266
	V	E	84	296,352	308,894	331,350	22,456
MEXICO	O	E	81	333,489	575,608	595,967	20,359
			82	329,820	693,466	718,176	24,710
			83	343,069	787,442	816,739	29,297
			84	310,581	706,855	729,120	22,265
			85	214,545	495,096	511,217	16,121
			86	172,016	401,507	413,569	12,062
	V	E	81	22,096	48,562	49,886	1,324
			82	11,410	24,874	26,924	2,050
			84	20,250	28,973	30,721	1,748
			85	6,675	16,020	16,798	778
			86	14,984	35,275	36,837	1,562
NETHLDS	O	E	83	499	1,239	1,349	110
			84	657	1,651	1,826	175
NICARAG	A	E	81	176	520	653	133
			84	4,561	7,798	8,990	1,192
	O	E	81	37,187	60,234	62,939	2,705
			82	44,624	95,688	99,540	3,852
			83	49,411	92,853	96,987	4,134
			84	30,831	50,703	53,696	2,993
			85	17,346	40,577	41,970	1,393
			86	23,260	56,316	57,926	1,610
	V	E	81	6,690	13,124	13,766	642
			82	10,110	16,275	16,885	610
			83	3,676	8,271	8,718	447
			84	8,517	21,024	21,569	545
			85	11,784	28,855	29,599	744
PANAMA	O	E	86	42,830	95,471	98,126	2,655
	V	E	84	11,374	25,003	26,301	1,298
			86	4,507	6,760	7,126	366
PHIL R	A	E	82	304	488	1,208	720
REP SAF	O	E	84	537,799	601,604	644,613	43,009
			85	332,216	355,127	380,984	25,857
SWEDEN	V	E	85	550	1,936	1,964	28

Tobacco, filler, mixed, over 35% wrapper tobacco
1702000 FILLER TOBACCO MIXED N STEMD (LB)

Country	Mode	Reg	Yr	Quantity	F.A.S.	C.I.F.	Charges
TOTAL			81	220,394	453,625	504,178	50,553
			82	2,694	20,124	20,454	330
			83	280,017	285,093	302,334	17,241
			84	32,914	38,879	39,928	1,049
			85	275,120	358,157	374,513	16,356
BRAZIL	V	E	81	213,946	424,865	474,817	49,952
			83	199,957	87,897	97,956	10,059
C AF RP	O	E	81	829	9,884	9,983	99
CANADA	O	E	83	3,176	8,103	9,090	987
			84	19,400	3,006	3,006	
DOM REP	V	E	83	278	2,100	2,126	26

Country	Mode	Reg	Yr	Quantity	F.A.S.	C.I.F.	Charges
ECUADOR	O	E	81	1,649	7,085	7,271	186
			83	485	2,068	2,118	50
GREECE	O	E	83	52,241	93,984	97,315	3,331
			84	11,025	25,396	26,247	851
HONDURA	A	E	81	208	624	763	139
	O	E	81	1,516	6,970	7,057	87
			82	54	300	310	10
			83	1,517	278	410	132
			84	1,388	6,345	6,462	117
MEXICO	O	E	81	1,036	2,269	2,302	33
			82	1,914	19,141	19,367	226
			84	923	3,301	3,344	43
			85	806	3,306	3,353	47
	V	E	83	21,670	90,125	92,721	2,596
NETHLDS	V	E	85	4,548	3,370	3,611	241
NICARAG	V	E	83	693	538	598	60
SWEDEN	V	W	84	178	831	869	38
THAILND	O	E	82	726	683	777	94
TURKEY	O	E	85	269,766	351,481	367,549	16,068
YUGOSLV	O	E	81	1,210	1,928	1,985	57

1702500 TOBACCO OV35 PCT WRAPER STEM (LB)

Country	Mode	Reg	Yr	Quantity	F.A.S.	C.I.F.	Charges
TOTAL			81	95,453	165,076	170,415	5,339
			82	175,015	209,928	221,957	12,029
			83	57,595	112,651	117,397	4,746
			84	102,131	175,635	181,189	5,554
			86	2,767	3,604	3,815	211
AUSTRIA	A	E	84	1	2,000	2,005	5
GREECE	O	E	81	93,344	162,153	167,349	5,196
			82	7,558	15,923	16,463	540
			83	22,375	51,141	52,846	1,705
			84	48,894	96,352	99,883	3,531
			86	2,767	3,604	3,815	211
HONDURA	O	E	84	53,236	77,283	79,301	2,018
SYRIA	O	E	81	2,109	2,923	3,066	143
			82	1,245	1,754	1,839	85
TURKEY	O	E	82	166,212	192,251	203,655	11,404
YUGOSLV	O	E	83	35,220	61,510	64,551	3,041

Tobacco, leaf
1700100 LF TOBAC, UNSTM, 2 CTRY MIX (LB)

Country	Mode	Reg	Yr	Quantity	F.A.S.	C.I.F.	Charges
TOTAL			81	2,000	2,170	2,433	263
			83	3,360	12,901	13,182	281
			84	14,727	59,491	60,835	1,344
			85	1,972	8,333	8,441	108
HONDURA	O	E	83	1,682	6,258	6,408	150
			84	8,207	38,173	39,221	1,048
MALAYSA	V	W	81	2,000	2,170	2,433	263
MEXICO	O	E	83	1,678	6,643	6,774	131
			84	6,520	21,318	21,614	296
			85	1,972	8,333	8,441	108

1700500 LF TOBAC, STEM, 2 CTRY MIXD (LB)

Country	Mode	Reg	Yr	Quantity	F.A.S.	C.I.F.	Charges
TOTAL			82	71,728	158,655	206,374	47,719
			83	317,520	261,900	296,586	34,686
			84	10,828	98,709	100,590	1,881
			86	3,902	97,095	99,642	2,547
BRAZIL	O	E	82	67,356	114,508	159,552	45,044
	V	E	83	317,520	261,900	296,586	34,686
CAMROON	V	E	84	220	2,148	2,245	97
DOM REP	V	E	82	1,372	4,802	4,910	108
HONDURA	V	E	84	3,108	32,164	32,669	505
			86	3,902	97,095	99,642	2,547
MEXICO	V	E	84	6,655	57,334	58,411	1,077
NICARAG	V	E	84	845	7,063	7,265	202
U KING	V	E	82	3,000	39,345	41,912	2,567

Tobacco, manufactured or not manufactured
1708050 TOB EXC SMOKNG, FLUE-CURED (LB)

Country	Mode	Reg	Yr	Quantity	F.A.S.	C.I.F.	Charges
TOTAL			85	602,870	988,412	1,078,811	90,399
			86	792,281	1,356,131	1,464,175	108,044
DENMARK	N	E	86	465	18,820	19,300	480
	O	E	86	14,752	12,855	14,475	1,620
	V	E	85	602,870	988,412	1,078,811	90,399
			86	582,777	979,780	1,060,646	80,866
FR GERM	V	E	86	194,026	338,497	363,000	24,503

Crop / Product / TSUSA commodity number, description, and unit of quantity / Country	Mode	Reg	Yr	Quantity	F.A.S.	C.I.F.	Charges
INDIA	A	E	86	261	6,179	6,754	575
1708070 TOBACCO, MFG OR NOT, NSPF (LB)							
TOTAL			81	101,516,842	137,817,683	146,711,959	8,894,176
			82	110,829,511	161,692,268	171,827,069	10,134,801
			83	210,050,555	329,735,282	349,501,476	19,766,194
			84	7,004,181	10,488,212	11,094,244	606,032
			85	2,217,555	3,775,243	4,050,546	275,303
			86	1,453,452	3,290,468	3,561,377	270,909
ARGENT	N	E	81	140,328	140,310	155,435	15,125
	O	E	81	1,242,552	1,583,511	1,667,113	83,602
			82	1,294,014	1,298,155	1,421,696	123,541
			83	5,796,264	8,427,106	9,071,268	644,162
			85	120,393	135,430	146,855	11,425
	V	E	82	160,301	240,607	257,213	16,606
			83	3,371,506	4,383,241	4,764,214	380,973
AUSTRAL	V	H	84	264	1,294	1,397	103
BAHAMAS	A	E	81	308	300	367	67
BARBADO	O	E	84	79,189	62,559	66,518	3,959
BELGIUM	A	E	85	331	1,017	1,531	514
	O	E	82	16,673	67,256	80,105	12,849
	V	E	81	9,237	11,313	15,855	4,542
			84	12,000	26,400	28,299	1,899
BRAZIL	A	E	81	908	454	555	101
			83	4,558	4,046	11,452	7,406
	N	E	81	8,736,423	12,137,934	13,160,651	1,022,717
			82	1,553,140	2,557,479	2,737,425	179,946
			83	9,759,746	15,708,156	16,862,107	1,153,951
	O	E	81	24,482,528	30,526,066	32,831,453	2,305,287
			82	29,895,735	42,418,875	45,657,100	3,238,225
			83	62,529,450	98,815,777	106,222,174	7,406,397
			84	979,345	1,797,150	1,908,468	111,318
	V	E	81	814,732	1,236,572	1,334,997	98,425
			82	7,143,729	12,447,985	13,284,436	836,451
			83	9,992,116	15,563,083	17,045,908	1,482,825
			85	79,295	75,901	85,960	10,059
C RICA	O	E	82	279,836	436,769	455,157	18,388
			83	31,922	62,043	64,878	2,835
	V	E	82	179,586	233,582	246,993	13,411
			83	3,278	4,387	4,877	490
CAMROON	A	E	83	1,909	18,314	19,230	916
CANADA	A	E	84	109	709	900	191
			86	800	5,139	5,519	380
	N	W	82	898	2,130	2,541	411
			84	8,465	30,137	41,628	11,491
	O	E	81	4,185,438	7,137,911	7,139,668	1,757
			82	6,795,584	13,588,967	13,588,967	
			83	4,580,156	8,501,885	8,502,472	587
			84	7,488	24,880	25,017	137
			85	3,492	9,896	9,896	
			86	57,923	39,560	39,560	
	O	W	81	1,444	3,752	6,101	2,349
			82	890	2,609	3,399	790
			83	4,201	13,287	15,824	2,537
			84	284	820	890	70
			85	2,106	5,561	7,742	2,181
			86	5,417	14,061	19,402	5,341
	V	W	85	300	1,095	1,416	321
CHILE	O	E	82	1,716	2,607	2,740	133
			83	523,672	770,249	811,994	41,745
	V	E	82	1,413,664	1,667,461	1,785,542	118,081
			83	1,543,220	2,351,800	2,466,441	114,641
CHINA M	O	E	83	91,971	123,576	135,313	11,737
CHINA T	V	W	84	463	600	630	30
COLOMB	O	E	81	188,137	201,295	251,444	50,149
			82	382,670	374,155	431,498	57,343
			83	252,656	324,181	381,462	57,281
DENMARK	A	E	81	1,156	2,323	3,452	1,129
			82	463	1,040	1,599	559
			83	17,677	48,627	55,051	6,424
			84	5,875	16,812	19,429	2,617
			85	8,806	31,245	35,332	4,087
			86	4,233	12,668	17,811	5,143
	N	E	81	1,705,082	2,621,319	2,874,181	252,862
			82	1,447,238	2,278,040	2,498,636	220,596
			84	301,014	644,672	682,624	37,952
			85	164,358	327,863	344,522	16,659
			86	4,544	17,628	19,430	1,802
	N	W	82	62,426	147,737	160,539	12,802
			83	334,196	756,105	831,143	75,038
			84	108,437	258,001	282,173	24,172
			85	24,795	66,172	76,711	10,539
	O	E	83	444,673	885,285	928,286	43,001

Crop / Product / TSUSA commodity number, description, and unit of quantity / Country	Mode	Reg	Yr	Quantity	F.A.S.	C.I.F.	Charges
			84	14,837	18,917	21,728	2,811
			85	47,046	45,760	51,020	5,260
			86	52,318	136,114	148,321	12,207
	V	E	81	77,025	122,654	131,031	8,377
			82	130,242	223,989	240,166	16,177
			83	2,177,591	3,506,579	3,736,862	230,283
			84	1,433,077	2,319,175	2,471,348	152,173
			85	874,606	1,559,102	1,677,531	118,429
			86	524,822	1,262,141	1,353,546	91,405
	V	W	81	358	11,504	11,801	297
			82	17,677	16,410	18,625	2,215
			85	13,222	41,034	45,668	4,634
			86	207,467	541,343	569,878	28,535
DOM REP	A	E	81	112	958	1,080	122
			84	1,027	1,477	1,757	280
	V	E	82	7,540	15,695	16,195	500
			83	7,773	10,890	12,110	1,220
			85	435,507	274,760	300,436	25,676
ECUADOR	O	E	81	396,203	551,324	566,737	15,413
			82	97,163	127,751	131,615	3,864
FR GERM	A	E	81	4,691	6,776	10,104	3,328
	O	E	81	207,082	125,114	145,524	20,410
			82	36,299	42,628	45,280	2,652
			83	38,285	50,503	53,302	2,799
			84	20,600	38,379	41,774	3,395
			85	5,952	12,902	14,650	1,748
	V	E	81	59,322	72,533	84,744	12,211
			82	30,480	48,926	51,907	2,981
			83	22,217	40,357	40,856	499
			84	7,141	19,848	21,309	1,461
			85	84,561	177,483	190,457	12,974
			86	341,039	591,225	639,225	48,000
	V	W	82	22,320	48,103	52,600	4,497
			84	2,750	9,135	9,386	251
			85	16,402	26,520	27,957	1,437
FRANCE	A	E	85	219	1,149	1,338	189
	N	E	84	5,196	24,461	26,844	2,383
	O	E	82	69,836	41,169	46,243	5,074
	V	E	81	175	750	796	46
			82	2,427	8,721	10,029	1,308
			83	3,919	13,041	14,303	1,262
GREECE	O	E	81	1,007,319	1,325,136	1,413,548	88,412
			82	4,947,376	7,276,576	7,670,473	393,897
			83	6,587,747	11,453,037	12,014,463	561,426
	V	W	81	5,309	12,040	12,467	427
GUATMAL	O	E	81	4,607,405	7,649,810	7,885,338	235,528
			82	2,776,681	4,738,055	4,870,252	132,197
			83	6,992,163	12,594,096	13,072,982	478,886
	V	E	81	123,174	218,476	225,358	6,882
			82	28,968	39,463	41,617	2,154
			85	80,262	140,626	145,529	4,903
HG KONG	O	E	82	27,558	26,916	30,144	3,228
	V	W	82	80	374	414	40
HONDURA	O	E	81	4,113,450	5,431,970	5,681,518	249,548
			82	1,748,223	2,188,346	2,306,389	118,043
			83	6,165,869	10,784,277	11,189,657	405,380
			84	2,238,904	2,371,807	2,539,960	168,153
	V	E	81	134,064	230,590	237,035	6,445
			82	151,861	196,754	204,331	7,577
			83	36,418	57,020	58,833	1,813
HUNGARY	O	E	83	88,184	115,000	118,768	3,768
	V	E	83	196,430	294,030	307,179	13,149
INDIA	A	E	82	8,636	58,625	71,337	12,712
			83	1,682	30,809	40,651	9,842
			84	26,103	133,180	150,796	17,616
			85	7,128	109,429	123,165	13,736
			86	5,850	139,486	149,108	9,622
	A	W	83	1,362	6,513	8,059	1,546
			85	546	5,751	7,196	1,445
	N	E	81	272	5,882	7,323	1,441
			82	727	5,928	6,500	572
			83	7,141	46,150	55,649	9,499
			86	5,720	106,764	115,667	8,903
	N	W	81	722	26,095	31,403	5,308
			82	325	9,018	11,621	2,603
			83	2,022	10,578	13,167	2,589
			84	781	4,706	5,892	1,186
	O	E	81	1,238,560	1,729,001	2,016,380	287,379
			82	1,326,545	2,037,878	2,420,472	382,594
			83	163,617	185,861	208,597	22,736
			84	100	378	378	
	V	E	81	131,494	51,309	69,545	18,236
			82	356,934	391,620	420,763	29,143
			83	265	4,379	4,734	355

Crop
Product
TSUSA commodity number, description, and unit of quantity

Country	Mode	Reg	Yr	Quantity	F.A.S.	C.I.F.	Charges
			84	496	2,509	2,734	225
	V	W	81	11,401	12,016	14,169	2,153
			82	31,933	21,962	26,475	4,513
			83	10,547	2,933	5,935	3,002
			84	2,205	2,976	3,990	1,014
			85	17,277	31,715	33,624	1,909
INDNSIA	A	E	84	220	500	800	300
	O	E	82	9,091	7,835	9,225	1,390
	V	W	81	100,502	114,795	125,950	11,155
IRAN	V	E	86	159	1,193	1,238	45
IRELAND	A	E	86	602	4,431	4,983	552
	O	E	83	72	568	584	16
	V	E	81	22,086	77,588	82,447	4,859
			82	21,960	81,183	86,014	4,831
			84	29,110	51,974	55,880	3,906
	V	W	83	21	253	268	15
ITALY	A	E	81	4,535	2,061	4,783	2,722
			82	13	523	580	57
			83	882	441	1,303	862
	N	E	81	199,979	158,624	175,204	16,580
			82	653,423	754,184	802,906	48,722
			83	231,474	163,050	178,860	15,810
	O	E	81	1,274,755	1,208,521	1,312,539	104,018
			82	1,273,245	1,472,736	1,572,150	99,414
			83	14,140,563	14,941,915	16,007,976	1,066,061
			86	11,020	6,534	7,367	833
	V	E	81	317,463	192,060	217,093	25,033
			82	1,562,463	2,352,679	2,475,997	123,318
			83	301,825	368,349	391,799	23,450
KOR REP	N	E	81	1,440,475	2,006,081	2,128,967	122,886
	O	E	81	21,492,948	30,821,131	32,690,829	1,869,698
			82	17,292,554	26,266,058	27,858,347	1,592,289
			83	23,368,453	40,321,433	42,720,407	2,398,974
	V	E	81	361,250	624,312	662,223	37,911
			82	31,425	59,173	62,927	3,754
			83	1,086,776	2,085,076	2,209,354	124,278
	V	W	83	489,990	773,131	826,886	53,755
LEBANON	O	E	81	3,120	846	1,342	496
			82	426	301	336	35
MALAWI	A	E	83	2,646	4,583	4,764	181
	N	E	83	70,125	190,073	200,559	10,486
	O	E	81	837,432	819,179	951,133	131,954
			82	2,875,460	4,822,848	5,199,389	376,541
			83	7,792,888	15,139,144	16,152,739	1,013,595
			84	169,344	336,005	361,541	25,536
	V	E	81	317,169	357,163	406,874	49,711
			82	440,686	1,001,318	1,072,316	70,998
			83	1,189,225	1,956,083	2,093,606	137,523
MEXICO	O	E	81	4,477,009	5,749,087	5,760,246	11,159
			82	6,028,879	10,231,818	10,246,606	14,788
			83	20,701,404	30,448,352	30,470,433	22,081
			84	1,267,528	2,006,011	2,006,223	212
			85	172,603	406,996	407,179	183
			86	2,439	1,384	1,534	150
NETHLDS	A	E	81	1,852	6,480	7,934	1,454
			82	2,169	6,142	7,352	1,210
	N	E	81	2,000	8,305	9,672	1,367
			83	5,210	12,200	13,564	1,364
	N	W	86	2,794	8,881	12,093	3,212
	O	E	81	18,135	75,682	78,415	2,733
			82	71,887	298,998	311,239	12,241
			83	261	1,034	1,089	55
			84	1,276	6,150	6,545	395
			86	105,270	60,190	79,557	19,367
	V	E	81	52,197	52,797	57,052	4,255
			82	4,756	15,077	16,703	1,626
			83	1,902	728	1,834	1,106
			84	3,081	5,476	5,519	43
			85	3,103	11,364	11,552	188
			86	2,425	1,753	1,797	44
	V	W	81	1,885	9,089	10,007	918
			82	24,093	52,197	55,571	3,374
			84	6,433	19,788	21,587	1,799
			85	6,984	15,502	17,060	1,558
NICARAG	O	E	81	182,800	355,143	370,151	15,008
			82	23,940	42,237	43,545	1,308
			83	1,056,403	2,006,214	2,080,818	74,604
NORWAY	O	E	81	741	3,825	4,240	415
			82	538	5,144	5,267	123
			83	53	286	304	18
			84	142	352	423	71
	V	E	82	2,261	5,560	6,102	542
			83	1,541	3,754	4,124	370
			84	3,042	7,350	8,242	892

Crop
Product
TSUSA commodity number, description, and unit of quantity

Country	Mode	Reg	Yr	Quantity	F.A.S.	C.I.F.	Charges
	V	W	81	2,614	6,760	7,536	776
OMAN	V	W	83	251	907	1,063	156
PAKISTN	O	E	81	2,553	1,914	2,115	201
	V	W	81	41	393	662	269
			82	992	496	596	100
PANAMA	A	E	83	232	252	477	225
	O	E	81	1,700,690	3,083,089	3,161,956	78,867
			82	550,469	1,140,738	1,169,186	28,448
			83	2,008,770	3,478,350	3,605,938	127,588
	V	E	81	116,815	171,651	176,654	5,003
PHIL R	O	E	81	512,596	486,723	554,588	67,865
			82	742,824	901,243	979,717	78,474
			83	4,212,116	5,314,579	5,736,183	421,604
	V	E	82	593,168	770,136	857,806	87,670
			83	60,350	102,595	109,526	6,931
			86	9,698	9,460	12,460	3,000
	V	W	83	230,711	88,952	108,218	19,266
			85	573	2,577	2,778	201
			86	819	5,319	6,147	828
POLAND	O	E	83	110,230	186,500	205,575	19,075
REP SAF	A	E	82	441	368	1,454	1,086
	O	E	81	123,850	118,255	131,567	13,312
			82	370	559	624	65
			83	2,623,025	3,697,015	3,937,735	240,720
			84	4,417	7,068	7,213	145
			85	6,625	10,601	10,817	216
	V	E	81	2,323,890	3,708,216	3,896,519	188,303
			82	947,125	1,183,676	1,253,269	69,593
			83	185,240	310,879	325,870	14,991
ROMANIA	O	E	82	163,094	234,502	254,450	19,948
			83	341,275	614,295	650,639	36,344
S ARAB	A	E	81	260	280	283	3
SALVADR	O	E	81	441,014	879,450	901,363	21,913
			82	560,551	887,153	917,793	30,640
			83	771,025	1,335,287	1,387,650	52,363
	V	E	81	32,966	64,108	65,942	1,834
SINGAPR	V	W	85	1,780	1,901	2,097	196
SPAIN	V	E	82	42,328	42,336	50,727	8,391
			86	16,402	73,880	76,980	3,100
SRI LKA	V	E	83	10,428	11,659	14,365	2,706
SWEDEN	A	E	84	108	267	435	168
			85	4,500	21,140	27,092	5,952
	A	W	84	114	629	672	43
	O	E	81	78	583	622	39
			83	469	2,401	2,678	277
	V	E	81	385,112	1,362,290	1,445,364	83,074
			84	8,712	27,915	28,729	814
			85	1,131	1,033	1,974	941
SWITZLD	A	E	81	2,596	3,083	4,820	1,737
			82	517	613	999	386
			84	6,305	4,516	7,785	3,269
			86	992	3,071	4,166	1,095
	A	W	84	147	992	1,042	50
			85	586	9,292	9,843	551
	V	E	83	6,173	4,638	6,112	1,474
THAILND	O	E	81	4,973,346	4,030,801	4,519,262	488,461
			82	10,225,529	8,434,186	9,528,665	1,094,479
			83	1,770,798	2,297,615	2,469,946	172,331
	V	E	81	53,045	74,477	83,261	8,784
			83	550,709	899,280	949,276	49,996
			86	547	1,250	1,383	133
	V	W	81	926,621	1,325,273	1,415,081	89,808
			82	1,393,338	2,365,943	2,516,256	150,313
			83	100,492	151,471	162,039	10,568
			84	18,121	39,437	42,576	3,139
			85	2,866	9,241	9,718	477
			86	2,402	6,560	6,974	414
TNZANIA	O	E	81	26,579	17,725	20,000	2,275
			82	47,214	32,654	36,478	3,824
			83	279,778	245,358	278,979	33,621
TURKEY	O	E	81	462,654	170,968	207,996	37,028
			82	903,747	331,441	394,108	62,667
			83	1,329,576	357,910	441,980	84,070
			84	218,317	82,611	96,852	14,241
U KING	A	E	81	1,523	8,875	10,415	1,540
			84	234	1,636	2,141	505
			85	2,340	5,922	6,929	1,007
			86	5,040	13,104	16,933	3,829
	A	W	85	5,910	19,482	22,255	2,773
	N	E	81	10,643	78,137	82,072	3,935
			82	2,774	23,643	25,482	1,839
			84	9,672	69,968	73,901	3,933
			85	20,905	173,581	185,766	12,185
	N	W	84	1,069	7,665	8,474	809

Crop
Product
TSUSA commodity number, description, and unit of quantity

Country	Mode	Reg	Yr	Quantity	F.A.S.	C.I.F.	Charges
			85	1,045	6,200	6,950	750
	O	E	81	286	2,806	2,901	95
			82	352	3,040	3,198	158
			83	1,131	1,283	1,384	101
			84	44	380	403	23
			86	33,000	25,075	32,238	7,163
	V	E	81	22,707	84,704	88,789	4,085
			82	1,209	2,990	3,293	303
			83	12,016	96,725	100,490	3,765
			86	46,200	193,128	207,098	13,970
	V	W	82	3,240	18,266	19,233	967
			83	2,122	11,540	12,270	730
			86	3,510	9,126	10,962	1,836
VENEZ	A	E	84	595	540	1,392	852
	O	E	81	798,956	952,028	1,114,085	162,057
			82	981,776	1,292,625	1,363,643	71,018
			83	900	463	518	55
YUGOSLV	O	E	83	612	819	1,102	283
ZAMBIA	O	E	81	2,205	1,720	1,865	145
			83	267,894	386,455	421,655	35,200
ZMBABWE	O	E	81	793,889	938,530	1,021,984	83,454
			82	682,910	724,036	790,497	66,461
			83	2,538,063	4,985,848	5,238,820	252,972
	V	E	81	3,064,569	4,415,077	4,749,983	334,906
			82	217,880	495,252	517,989	22,737
			83	408,052	768,338	819,516	51,178

Tobacco, scrap

1706020 CIGAR LEAF SCRAP TOBACCO (LB)

Country	Mode	Reg	Yr	Quantity	F.A.S.	C.I.F.	Charges
TOTAL			81	41,795,570	32,959,914	37,186,156	4,199,585
			82	39,410,560	31,886,557	35,816,936	3,930,379
			83	35,297,772	29,138,035	32,822,722	3,684,687
			84	40,055,363	33,021,693	36,994,501	3,972,808
			85	31,836,679	26,946,260	30,566,868	3,620,608
			86	25,401,712	19,666,544	22,301,119	2,634,575
ARGENT	O	E	81	1,054,694	366,816	474,656	107,840
			82	1,274,190	516,593	655,169	138,576
			83	2,822,723	1,468,420	1,815,498	347,078
			84	1,118,200	450,564	557,879	107,315
			85	1,017,771	426,645	531,450	104,805
			86	507,384	227,531	283,321	55,790
	O	W	84	3,705	1,277	1,992	715
BAHAMAS	V	E	81	4,634	4,402	4,518	116
BELGIUM	O	E	81	147,054	72,449	91,600	19,151
			82	22,996	2,773	5,062	2,289
			83	64,540	25,740	31,640	5,900
			85	12,871	5,028	6,257	1,229
	V	E	81	1,866	1,312	1,329	17
BRAZIL	O	E	81	2,824,478	3,478,374	3,773,199	294,825
			82	3,499,431	5,003,704	5,458,141	454,437
			83	2,808,417	4,171,106	4,517,356	346,250
			84	3,239,792	4,947,411	5,335,275	387,864
			85	3,094,952	4,416,460	4,756,350	339,890
			86	2,070,994	2,811,786	3,034,239	222,453
	O	W	84	28,204	45,162	49,785	4,623
			85	7,074	6,923	7,845	922
			86	105,077	141,288	154,904	13,616
	V	E	81	626,437	821,011	889,119	68,108
			82	246,198	333,650	361,796	28,146
			83	12,447	14,192	15,948	1,756
			84	531,160	580,808	645,783	64,975
			85	165,118	197,987	217,469	19,482
			86	200,426	264,149	282,181	18,032
C AF RP	O	E	81	245,711	345,494	380,804	35,310
			83	35,382	43,982	51,896	7,914
			84	24,324	28,190	40,932	12,742
			85	203,527	276,671	299,310	22,639
			86	28,288	42,257	45,512	3,255
C RICA	A	E	83	6,718	3,360	5,051	1,691
			84	2,675	1,982	2,598	616
	O	E	81	8,246	7,417	8,042	625
	V	E	81	1,736	1,736	2,116	380
			85	21,600	8,640	10,664	2,024
CAMROON	O	E	81	455,929	626,664	682,052	55,388
			82	580,873	710,246	785,874	75,628
			83	600,852	859,299	930,543	71,244
			84	671,818	978,433	1,066,665	88,232
			85	841,290	1,185,203	1,280,774	95,571
			86	257,395	363,244	384,123	20,879
	V	E	81	33,679	25,259	29,882	4,623
			82	196,166	265,733	286,467	20,734

Crop
Product
TSUSA commodity number, description, and unit of quantity

Country	Mode	Reg	Yr	Quantity	F.A.S.	C.I.F.	Charges
			83	6,090	8,657	8,826	169
			84	103,793	145,949	156,695	10,746
CANADA	O	E	81	108,276	43,793	46,682	2,889
			82	41,312	8,686	8,686	
			83	1,914	7,563	8,933	1,370
			85	45,811	8,624	11,894	3,270
			86	29,988	44,481	44,481	
CHINA T	O	E	84	3,419	1,252	1,592	340
COLOMB	O	E	81	1,706,578	1,699,478	1,838,667	139,189
			82	1,439,449	1,560,463	1,685,884	125,421
			83	1,526,878	1,856,280	2,011,464	155,184
			84	1,646,236	2,226,399	2,392,606	166,207
			85	1,367,238	1,770,535	1,907,468	136,933
			86	1,021,464	1,178,295	1,299,206	120,911
	O	W	83	37,445	57,377	60,728	3,351
			85	9,313	18,304	19,568	1,264
CYPRUS	O	E	81	3,540	6,086	6,392	306
			82	590	1,019	1,070	51
			83	3,777	6,491	6,818	327
DENMARK	O	E	83	9,546	8,022	8,510	488
	V	E	83	2,205	700	821	121
DOM REP	A	E	81	1,458	6,928	7,904	976
			82	1,279	780	1,120	340
			83	2,668	2,008	2,785	777
			84	8	252	308	56
	N	E	81	758,511	528,008	608,096	53,441
			83	165,425	157,319	168,634	11,315
			84	227,523	191,236	209,736	18,500
			85	16,790	22,998	24,198	1,200
			86	6,085	15,447	16,114	667
	O	E	81	5,850,681	5,857,479	6,248,734	391,245
			82	4,651,508	5,202,749	5,546,141	343,392
			83	3,850,892	4,738,787	5,083,815	345,028
			84	4,761,027	4,255,436	4,520,028	264,592
			85	802,648	891,895	973,463	81,568
			86	2,096,540	1,410,233	1,534,797	124,564
	V	E	81	17,477	18,619	19,101	482
			82	468,563	380,321	415,427	35,106
			83	51,995	57,381	59,574	2,193
			84	1,242,740	1,286,754	1,363,297	76,543
			85	2,556,704	2,734,498	2,897,400	162,902
			86	955,774	933,368	992,195	58,827
ECUADOR	O	E	82	6,289	3,890	4,679	789
			83	989	411	483	72
			85	23,770	27,378	34,485	7,107
			86	3,106	7,881	8,381	500
FR GERM	O	E	81	1,590,287	1,004,950	1,185,632	180,682
			82	2,051,653	1,319,271	1,506,410	187,139
			83	1,158,944	842,941	909,840	66,899
			84	2,192,065	1,476,364	1,657,442	181,078
			85	818,798	734,282	814,896	80,614
			86	904,370	605,790	689,906	84,116
	V	W	82	75,340	24,605	32,749	8,144
FRANCE	O	E	82	20,320	24,089	25,139	1,050
			83	160,500	118,707	127,282	8,575
			84	260,949	92,694	126,897	34,203
			85	700,052	569,139	678,381	109,242
			86	1,550,370	618,568	823,610	205,042
	V	E	85	5,672	1,872	2,583	711
GREECE	O	E	81	297,780	153,912	184,457	30,545
			82	162,533	120,014	135,311	15,297
			83	121,559	94,780	109,469	14,689
			84	48,610	39,351	46,374	7,023
			85	71,132	54,398	64,150	9,752
			86	431,612	178,272	223,538	45,266
HAITI	O	E	82	1,061	1,015	1,063	48
HG KONG	O	E	85	5,040	3,549	4,080	531
HONDURA	N	E	81	11,383	9,140	9,932	792
			82	39,476	44,387	47,561	3,174
			83	4,964	3,775	4,551	776
			86	6,891	13,983	15,641	1,658
	O	E	81	214,012	180,124	195,251	15,127
			82	369,058	327,200	358,934	31,734
			83	146,265	112,487	124,715	12,228
			84	345,545	146,081	193,777	47,696
			85	56,206	40,272	42,094	1,822
			86	71,900	57,453	63,538	6,085
	O	W	83	3,867	4,091	4,471	380
	V	E	81	89,307	89,140	95,893	6,753
			82	16,249	17,730	18,307	577
			83	86,467	96,695	99,811	3,116
			84	168,399	149,277	163,936	14,659
			85	233,299	156,612	177,750	21,138
			86	207,307	193,338	211,410	18,072

Crop Product TSUSA commodity number, description, and unit of quantity Country	Mode	Reg	Yr	Quantity	F.A.S.	C.I.F.	Charges
INDIA	O	E	81	17,086	2,708	3,962	1,254
			83	156,968	20,598	36,305	15,707
			86	30,569	34,494	38,074	3,580
INDNSIA	N	E	84	60,178	46,903	55,751	8,848
	O	E	81	5,565,268	3,248,446	3,991,996	743,550
			82	5,115,556	3,063,007	3,704,094	641,087
			83	5,610,021	3,670,300	4,363,386	693,086
			84	5,903,478	4,671,280	5,400,902	729,622
			85	4,607,444	3,972,291	4,576,690	604,399
			86	3,781,096	3,639,125	4,113,405	474,280
	O	W	84	13,990	9,241	11,021	1,780
			86	7,000	8,159	9,175	1,016
	V	E	81	1,198,090	1,396,511	1,554,137	157,626
			82	1,302,943	1,248,958	1,405,163	156,205
			83	260,918	314,177	348,774	34,597
			85	502,435	487,372	551,409	64,037
			86	149,912	188,888	202,648	13,760
	V	W	81	466,494	585,661	635,948	50,287
			85	81,744	92,372	103,750	11,378
ITALY	O	E	81	1,902,626	357,451	511,340	153,889
			82	3,133,064	668,364	899,749	231,385
			83	5,324,500	1,529,260	2,078,588	549,328
			84	7,319,079	1,990,475	2,625,060	634,585
			85	6,315,953	1,922,139	2,668,194	746,055
			86	5,644,861	1,584,692	2,122,763	538,071
	V	E	82	1,594	506	628	122
			84	933,659	167,958	248,228	80,270
			85	274,908	57,939	86,889	28,950
	V	W	85	75,113	11,243	19,335	8,092
IVY CST	O	E	81	96,017	92,597	101,089	8,492
JAMAICA	A	E	86	1,131	12,908	13,952	1,044
	O	E	81	123,013	52,313	75,194	22,881
			82	28,328	11,557	14,468	2,911
			83	29,058	14,400	19,658	5,258
			84	52,457	21,632	27,204	5,572
	V	E	82	14,100	5,820	7,344	1,524
			84	44,908	21,847	27,137	5,290
			85	251,300	104,166	120,493	16,327
			86	147,100	121,256	138,151	16,895
MACAO	O	E	83	3,770	1,319	1,740	421
			86	1,166	2,145	2,273	128
MALAWI	O	E	84	887,608	933,841	1,034,663	100,822
MALI	O	E	86	71,894	98,037	106,018	7,981
MEXICO	O	E	81	3,576,457	3,722,572	3,997,217	274,645
			82	3,070,238	3,298,523	3,544,613	246,090
			83	2,322,320	2,676,746	2,861,682	184,936
			84	1,976,332	2,210,451	2,400,256	189,805
			85	909,540	1,015,142	1,104,759	89,617
			86	694,564	703,617	770,581	66,964
	V	E	81	462,480	306,254	336,679	30,425
			82	21,948	20,939	24,246	3,307
NAMIBIA	O	E	81	39,639	43,461	48,338	4,877
NETHLDS	O	E	81	274,362	174,324	198,918	24,594
			85	41,203	30,882	44,864	13,982
NICARAG	A	E	84	2,154	3,299	3,731	432
	O	E	81	89,381	91,678	99,981	8,303
			82	182,216	135,283	149,794	14,511
			83	141,041	117,722	127,338	9,616
			84	53,273	43,380	50,768	7,388
			85	29,153	22,265	25,303	3,038
			86	73,016	75,906	82,932	7,026
	V	E	81	21,180	15,249	17,098	1,849
			82	30,591	26,982	28,619	1,637
			83	33,718	25,011	27,751	2,740
			84	5,134	8,773	9,082	309
			85	7,335	5,868	6,270	402
NIGERIA	O	E	81	6,668	18,529	19,645	1,116
PANAMA	O	E	85	4,208	2,104	2,328	224
	V	E	86	3,777	2,266	2,389	123
PARAGUA	O	E	81	2,462,768	1,724,905	1,982,397	257,492
			82	1,806,544	1,552,378	1,768,229	215,851
			83	1,290,159	1,196,359	1,337,946	141,587
			84	1,135,403	1,405,739	1,550,721	144,982
			85	939,279	1,051,645	1,219,326	167,681
			86	913,093	882,464	1,020,612	138,148
	O	W	84	34,657	35,054	38,739	3,685
	V	E	86	47,412	8,602	13,824	5,222
PHIL R	O	E	81	8,415,481	5,268,131	6,229,084	960,953
			82	7,367,977	5,127,318	5,888,501	761,183
			83	5,035,907	4,272,288	4,771,443	499,155
			84	4,322,636	4,034,755	4,520,046	485,291
			85	3,999,596	3,099,972	3,574,400	474,428
			86	2,978,315	2,712,783	3,031,786	319,003
	O	W	84	15,055	11,252	12,697	1,445

Crop Product TSUSA commodity number, description, and unit of quantity Country	Mode	Reg	Yr	Quantity	F.A.S.	C.I.F.	Charges
	V	E	82	518,322	287,998	336,147	48,149
			84	350,167	216,764	252,404	35,640
			85	1,691,504	1,487,983	1,653,847	165,864
			86	139,772	115,161	127,811	12,650
	V	W	81	39,683	24,093	28,469	4,376
			83	119,049	122,024	133,975	11,951
			86	39,683	38,889	42,483	3,594
REP SAF	O	E	81	49,874	68,543	75,612	7,069
			84	18,233	26,909	28,931	2,022
			85	1,548	1,301	1,380	79
			86	222,380	329,788	355,145	25,357
ROMANIA	O	E	81	73,312	32,256	38,062	5,806
			82	45,002	19,800	23,365	3,565
SPAIN	O	E	81	689,897	263,725	323,959	60,234
			82	1,251,479	460,637	581,417	120,780
			83	793,616	274,505	367,638	93,133
			84	306,770	117,268	163,563	46,295
	V	E	82	209,124	63,289	65,867	2,578
			83	288,108	73,968	103,352	29,384
TNZANIA	O	E	85	12,785	4,521	6,818	2,297
TRINID	O	E	83	8,693	6,936	7,808	872
TURKEY	O	E	81	166,601	114,745	123,175	8,430
			82	147,000	26,280	33,702	7,422
			83	64,543	5,950	7,006	1,056
U KING	A	E	81	4,839	7,171	9,798	2,627
	O	E	85	14,955	19,142	38,284	19,142
URUGUAY	O	E	83	31,474	24,406	26,475	2,069
VENEZ	V	E	83	90,440	31,495	32,395	900

1706040 SCRAP TOBACCO NT CIGAR LEAF (LB)

Country	Mode	Reg	Yr	Quantity	F.A.S.	C.I.F.	Charges
TOTAL			81	18,445,012	12,196,776	13,444,467	1,247,691
			82	19,189,200	10,169,807	11,596,252	1,426,445
			83	12,186,070	7,150,954	8,124,270	973,316
			84	12,838,227	7,732,710	8,816,999	1,084,289
			85	11,734,396	6,213,128	7,310,792	1,097,664
			86	17,200,919	8,507,303	10,051,671	1,544,368
ARGENT	O	E	81	70,137	42,384	49,827	7,443
			82	1,736	705	796	91
			83	157,034	69,027	81,607	12,580
			84	665	907	973	66
			85	46,693	42,324	46,859	4,535
	V	E	82	7,825	2,739	3,110	371
			83	20,000	3,045	3,323	278
			84	594	594	1,307	713
AUSTRAL	V	E	82	661	992	1,419	427
BARBADO	O	E	84	2,595	2,050	2,153	103
BELGIUM	V	E	82	90	1,466	1,716	250
			85	34,191	4,445	7,140	2,695
BRAZIL	O	E	81	2,125,323	2,831,781	3,040,298	208,517
			82	849,388	993,198	1,075,400	82,202
			83	541,223	603,352	663,044	59,692
			84	227,731	208,945	232,621	23,676
			85	167,946	191,520	212,764	21,244
			86	877,775	1,076,577	1,209,838	133,261
	O	W	85	4,001	4,865	5,392	527
			86	7,290	8,500	9,340	840
	V	E	81	527,968	479,303	530,764	51,461
			82	428,569	421,880	467,238	45,358
			83	630,629	622,788	702,773	79,985
			84	352,804	472,757	515,503	42,746
			85	101,504	128,910	138,070	9,160
	V	W	85	156,583	19,177	36,316	17,139
BULGAR	O	E	82	34,344	5,625	7,050	1,425
C RICA	O	E	81	16,222	19,738	20,545	807
	V	E	82	10,412	5,206	6,116	910
CAMROON	O	E	81	406,119	471,628	520,499	48,871
			82	683,518	900,814	991,509	90,695
			83	866,543	1,224,079	1,323,468	99,389
			84	555,215	792,695	849,729	57,034
			85	557,757	771,064	827,371	56,307
			86	1,323,870	1,397,899	1,504,322	106,423
	V	E	82	28,188	38,358	41,370	3,012
			83	45,637	64,173	69,009	4,906
CANADA	O	E	81	12,681	2,111	2,111	
			82	221,445	39,548	39,548	
			83	321,044	99,946	99,946	
			84	249,050	50,990	50,990	
			85	31,202	23,318	23,318	
CHILE	V	E	83	2,646	383	402	19
CHINA T	V	E	82	2,800	504	560	56
COLOMB	O	E	81	394,439	330,562	351,382	20,820
			82	125,785	114,961	126,452	11,491
			83	17,777	12,071	13,463	1,392

Crop
Product
TSUSA commodity number, description, and unit of quantity

Country	Mode	Reg	Yr	Quantity	F.A.S.	C.I.F.	Charges
			85	51,229	74,522	79,467	4,945
			86	575,397	711,166	808,166	97,000
	V	E	81	242,884	291,461	308,479	17,018
			82	99,355	122,969	138,965	15,996
			83	100,071	134,133	142,463	8,330
			84	49,992	67,008	71,760	4,752
			85	49,991	61,497	65,470	3,973
			86	34,385	41,254	43,564	2,310
DENMARK	O	E	83	9,196	7,728	8,198	470
			84	8,595	6,098	6,694	596
	V	E	81	17,961	8,654	12,232	3,578
			82	18,400	10,719	12,172	1,453
			83	17,196	11,954	14,016	2,062
			84	34,829	29,362	33,407	4,045
			85	19,600	12,814	15,591	2,777
DOM REP	A	E	82	1,061	578	862	284
			84	1,389	1,400	1,811	411
	O	E	81	97,819	98,480	107,356	8,876
			82	4,624	3,367	3,759	392
	V	E	81	6,536	4,881	5,024	143
			82	32,411	34,732	37,427	2,695
			83	3,358	3,816	3,987	171
			84	56,651	46,597	51,125	4,528
			85	80,344	63,076	67,482	4,406
ECUADOR	V	E	85	21,600	25,488	28,028	2,540
			86	21,600	25,488	28,215	2,727
FR GERM	O	E	83	16,905	14,109	15,646	1,537
			85	3,059	1,807	2,034	227
	V	E	82	36,089	4,692	7,871	3,179
			83	36,760	4,779	8,244	3,465
			85	61,160	10,467	16,320	5,853
			86	29,178	3,793	7,134	3,341
FRANCE	V	E	84	23,508	16,617	19,017	2,400
GREECE	O	E	81	245,450	127,098	135,580	8,482
			82	126,364	28,401	31,016	2,615
			84	65,570	11,287	16,231	4,944
			85	149,987	27,164	37,611	10,447
			86	213,909	36,821	52,951	16,130
	V	E	82	679	616	838	222
			84	4,409	800	1,436	636
			86	13,228	2,400	4,426	2,026
GUATMAL	O	E	81	412,224	691,688	710,577	18,889
			82	347,786	604,381	618,367	13,986
			83	85,722	28,871	30,004	1,133
			84	50,270	49,679	52,031	2,352
	V	E	81	170,636	27,302	34,567	7,265
HG KONG	A	E	81	42	546	771	225
HONDURA	O	E	81	290,489	533,369	545,684	12,315
			82	225,812	349,300	361,314	12,014
			83	13,635	4,458	5,248	790
			84	324,608	321,380	343,623	22,243
	V	E	81	2,074	2,074	2,520	446
			83	1,592	1,831	1,852	21
			84	37,213	37,213	40,365	3,152
INDIA	O	E	81	19,035	3,748	5,671	1,923
			82	10,649	2,545	2,698	153
			85	21,457	16,320	21,180	4,860
			86	6,614	4,080	5,295	1,215
	V	E	83	12,346	4,410	6,132	1,722
			84	24,471	14,934	18,859	3,925
INDNSIA	O	E	81	1,270,376	1,299,471	1,459,446	159,975
			82	1,726,675	1,823,718	2,023,916	200,198
			83	1,610,576	1,865,052	2,040,644	175,592
			84	1,981,147	2,346,840	2,557,904	211,064
			85	1,632,967	2,030,771	2,246,115	215,344
			86	1,510,458	1,849,057	2,085,078	236,021
	O	W	84	12,842	9,969	11,609	1,640
	V	E	81	419,265	289,480	332,136	42,656
			82	151,671	102,543	123,005	20,462
			83	634,559	516,188	576,725	60,537
			84	310,227	232,727	267,823	35,096
			85	330,028	379,274	421,143	41,869
			86	478,397	501,985	550,385	48,400
	V	W	81	44,092	38,570	43,402	4,832
			83	88,151	68,071	77,675	9,604
ITALY	O	E	81	51,408	9,244	13,175	3,931
			82	177,283	70,226	84,007	13,781
			83	315,304	195,172	219,738	24,566
			84	19,608	3,806	5,677	1,871
			85	179,501	32,932	46,921	13,989
			86	164,036	44,314	58,774	14,460
	V	E	86	29,866	5,731	8,490	2,759
KOR REP	O	E	81	65,050	3,982	9,972	5,990
			82	82,725	19,657	28,362	8,705

Crop
Product
TSUSA commodity number, description, and unit of quantity

Country	Mode	Reg	Yr	Quantity	F.A.S.	C.I.F.	Charges
			83	5,292	4,080	4,539	459
			84	2,205	1,700	1,891	191
			85	7,442	5,739	5,739	
	V	E	83	107,984	5,518	15,853	10,335
	V	W	81	42,082	1,965	5,623	3,658
LEBANON	O	E	82	1,267,042	289,408	413,852	124,444
			83	312,394	80,102	102,244	22,142
			84	961,280	241,552	327,853	86,301
			85	739,461	225,726	306,163	80,437
			86	324,810	109,794	139,123	29,329
	V	E	81	355,141	91,436	127,273	35,837
			82	330,690	64,500	97,652	33,152
MALAWI	O	E	81	119,980	88,773	106,659	17,886
			82	30,450	13,151	17,747	4,596
			86	60,720	45,815	50,611	4,796
MEXICO	N	E	81	67,735	70,109	71,273	1,164
	O	E	81	549,786	535,604	538,289	2,685
			82	472,380	396,442	417,617	21,175
			83	194,319	104,889	107,326	2,437
			84	40,396	42,866	45,667	2,801
			85	11,248	8,464	8,464	
	O	W	81	98,227	5,874	5,874	
	V	E	82	88,961	76,932	82,306	5,374
			83	120,041	114,449	118,779	4,330
			84	67,708	55,920	60,310	4,390
			86	167,526	196,722	208,750	12,028
MOZAMBQ	O	E	81	13,464	8,628	9,516	888
			82	6,732	4,314	4,758	444
NETHLDS	V	E	82	16,795	3,504	6,197	2,693
			83	25,340	968	3,089	2,121
			84	23,594	912	2,373	1,461
			86	26,863	1,001	2,895	1,894
NICARAG	O	E	81	49,936	43,011	45,124	2,113
			84	9,240	9,446	10,117	671
	V	E	81	8,850	6,372	7,066	694
			85	68,496	68,496	73,060	4,564
PANAMA	O	E	81	617,939	1,205,536	1,232,406	26,870
			82	184,551	366,879	375,010	8,131
			84	23,570	37,297	38,846	1,549
PARAGUA	O	E	83	18,000	18,161	21,376	3,215
PHIL R	O	E	81	1,475,949	768,767	910,480	141,713
			82	440,033	237,669	281,961	44,292
			83	15,517	6,332	7,179	847
	V	E	81	455,446	332,196	370,985	38,789
			82	189,596	170,559	186,912	16,353
			83	118,545	118,545	124,838	6,293
			84	736,176	738,955	849,918	110,963
			85	39,683	40,080	44,390	4,310
			86	278,472	297,965	321,801	23,836
REP SAF	O	E	81	3,742	3,742	4,171	429
			83	51,608	81,412	86,696	5,284
			84	505,822	739,471	793,488	54,017
			85	351,912	510,466	549,112	38,646
			86	8,448	1,282	2,265	983
	V	E	82	2,100	378	432	54
			83	17,150	2,687	4,113	1,426
			84	4,409	4,400	5,165	765
			85	19,180	16,086	18,091	2,005
ROMANIA	O	E	81	4,684	1,171	1,271	100
			82	6,500	13,975	14,618	643
			83	16,250	6,500	8,385	1,885
S ARAB	O	E	86	2,205	1,521	1,841	320
SALVADR	O	E	81	93,498	174,509	178,720	4,211
			82	539,240	1,071,983	1,095,733	23,750
			84	16,316	27,428	28,466	1,038
SUDAN	A	E	86	1,323	1,350	1,789	439
SWITZLD	A	E	81	794	388	867	479
			82	1,193	2,053	2,802	749
SYRIA	O	E	81	242,506	46,175	61,490	15,315
THAILND	O	E	81	171,414	87,366	109,955	22,589
			82	807,056	161,757	253,985	92,228
			83	385,644	127,360	175,058	47,698
			84	468,455	84,580	145,422	60,842
			85	638,107	129,553	237,185	107,632
			86	789,364	153,118	264,623	111,505
	V	E	85	6,650	3,857	5,179	1,322
	V	W	85	118,800	14,553	36,650	22,097
TNZANIA	O	E	83	59,500	8,925	16,507	7,582
TURKEY	N	E	85	518,263	106,535	137,897	31,362
	O	E	81	6,722,180	1,015,309	1,280,341	265,032
			82	8,295,334	1,391,604	1,832,194	440,590
			83	4,292,239	719,402	962,921	243,519
			84	5,464,654	1,002,331	1,319,492	317,161
			85	5,502,621	1,159,653	1,540,355	380,702

Crop / Product / TSUSA commodity number, description, and unit of quantity Country	Mode	Reg	Yr	Quantity	F.A.S.	C.I.F.	Charges
			86	10,147,530	1,955,295	2,644,292	688,997
	O	W	83	26,712	2,996	5,176	2,180
	V	E	83	712,086	161,500	206,939	45,439
			85	11,933	2,165	3,915	1,750
	V	W	82	849,004	154,042	209,250	55,208
U KING	V	E	81	209,504	44,627	64,258	19,631
			82	183,961	35,734	49,175	13,441
			83	96,394	14,802	25,768	10,966
			84	120,419	21,197	35,343	14,146
			86	107,655	34,375	37,703	3,328
VENEZ	O	E	81	54,918	28,230	31,575	3,345
YUGOSLV	V	E	81	882	720	841	121
ZMBABWE	O	E	81	97,909	26,619	31,360	4,741
			82	37,037	9,727	16,241	6,514
	V	E	81	80,216	2,094	7,032	4,938
			82	4,200	756	947	191
			83	63,151	12,890	19,807	6,917

Tobacco, stem
1705000 TOBACCO STEMS, NOT CUT, ETC (LB)

Country	Mode	Reg	Yr	Quantity	F.A.S.	C.I.F.	Charges
TOTAL			81	38,186,894	5,745,101	7,920,444	2,151,192
			82	39,002,347	7,018,512	10,090,577	2,992,106
			83	33,426,907	5,907,074	8,465,686	2,558,612
			84	34,505,900	4,572,730	7,426,447	2,853,717
			85	35,376,059	5,606,152	8,386,806	2,780,654
			86	40,854,789	6,083,996	8,913,371	2,829,375
ARGENT	N	E	81	260,576	31,664	52,857	21,193
			82	5,899,561	868,449	1,436,552	568,103
	O	E	81	22,719	1,429	2,164	735
			82	43,053	4,722	7,080	2,358
			83	61,184	4,034	5,517	1,483
			84	70,251	13,379	15,927	2,548
			85	4,360	3,410	4,058	648
	V	E	81	1,693,638	237,194	378,225	141,031
			83	2,690,477	406,557	639,681	233,124
			84	3,667,682	501,650	867,408	365,758
			85	1,885,961	271,955	445,010	173,055
			86	4,960,676	711,810	1,053,185	341,375
AUSTRAL	V	E	82	441	662	946	284
BELGIUM	O	E	81	38,696	1,366	1,989	623
			83	5,717	450	661	211
			86	9,335	3,812	5,464	1,652
BRAZIL	N	E	81	9,090,764	1,236,322	1,879,268	642,946
			82	13,064,225	2,167,595	3,587,119	1,419,524
			83	7,160,322	1,015,613	1,777,205	761,592
	O	E	81	78,361	8,363	12,519	4,156
			82	590,906	73,799	124,467	50,668
			83	338,545	486,600	524,014	37,414
			84	102,921	11,019	18,250	7,231
			85	223,398	26,841	43,980	17,139
			86	335,276	63,874	90,895	27,021
	V	E	81	1,146,735	128,232	225,198	96,966
			82	1,546,082	182,061	342,183	160,122
			83	2,802,977	395,223	640,138	244,915
			84	10,899,531	1,660,001	2,782,978	1,122,977
			85	17,734,458	3,027,550	4,678,062	1,650,512
			86	18,397,049	2,996,668	4,439,156	1,442,488
	V	W	85	22,220	2,721	5,010	2,289
C RICA	V	E	82	87,914	8,791	15,827	7,036
CAMROON	O	E	83	1,640	1,222	1,553	331
			84	34	450	561	111
CANADA	O	E	81	1,501,594	189,790	189,790	
			82	3,142,087	628,091	629,208	1,117
			83	3,167,428	726,297	726,508	211
			84	2,346,083	388,249	388,249	
			85	4,223,856	950,127	950,127	
			86	3,029,374	499,374	499,374	
CHINA M	O	E	83	72,314	19,886	21,775	1,889
			86	83,725	4,329	4,893	564
	V	E	84	31,867	4,012	4,133	121
	V	W	84	344,281	54,915	74,959	20,044
CHINA T	V	E	82	57,688	5,049	8,707	3,658
			84	2,197	2,660	2,923	263
COLOMB	O	E	81	138,265	34,679	39,688	5,009
			82	17,964	2,985	3,909	924
			83	70,690	7,142	9,130	1,988
			84	66,115	12,847	15,166	2,319
			85	218,206	9,754	11,027	1,273
			86	4,514	2,771	3,225	454
DOM REP	N	E	81	676,993	65,217	131,304	41,936
			82	447,497	50,809	78,406	27,597

Country	Mode	Reg	Yr	Quantity	F.A.S.	C.I.F.	Charges
			84	161,912	16,285	28,987	12,702
	O	E	81	288,790	27,432	37,946	10,514
			82	153,406	15,595	22,390	6,795
			83	354,639	37,151	49,634	12,483
			84	58,770	8,375	13,081	4,706
			85	21,185	2,542	4,217	1,675
			86	27,355	3,281	4,649	1,368
	V	E	81	103,217	6,709	13,575	6,866
			82	64,723	7,593	11,756	4,163
			83	384,608	40,118	58,701	18,583
			84	369,850	163,434	181,407	17,973
			85	229,816	19,278	33,335	14,057
			86	128,433	16,389	25,916	9,527
FR GERM	O	E	81	345,691	12,696	21,591	8,895
			82	495,110	20,648	35,329	14,681
			83	221,006	11,944	22,472	10,528
			84	73,094	18,048	24,003	5,955
			85	49,087	42,409	50,048	7,639
			86	15,397	2,309	3,541	1,232
	V	E	83	194,446	22,050	54,045	31,995
			84	390,864	25,784	59,927	34,143
			85	552,063	24,521	61,271	36,750
			86	753,345	40,736	93,366	52,630
	V	W	83	987,180	32,457	79,900	47,443
			84	716,705	93,915	161,913	67,998
FRANCE	O	E	83	121,725	4,043	5,318	1,275
			84	125,624	11,879	14,132	2,253
			85	19,921	18,876	22,277	3,401
	V	E	86	75,675	3,784	3,784	
GIBRALT	O	E	82	6,739	522	522	222
GREECE	O	E	81	1,429,721	169,844	181,500	11,656
			82	565,545	106,724	109,838	3,114
			83	27,536	1,400	1,923	523
			84	14,472	900	1,213	313
			85	2,172	1,866	2,194	328
	V	E	82	1,358,871	108,852	251,209	62,398
	V	W	82	287,597	32,105	53,194	21,089
GUATMAL	O	E	81	61,960	3,296	4,642	1,346
			83	20,680	3,633	3,851	218
	V	E	81	1,547,877	108,831	179,045	70,214
			84	79,380	6,204	9,209	3,005
			85	39,683	3,520	5,588	2,068
HG KONG	V	E	81	204,000	15,810	33,176	17,366
			85	456,352	46,575	84,575	38,000
			86	982,370	102,777	211,526	108,749
HONDURA	O	E	81	500,316	150,918	172,095	21,177
			82	362,363	180,101	195,879	15,778
			83	294,446	13,444	34,843	21,399
	V	E	81	546,570	28,702	47,968	19,266
HUNGARY	O	E	81	10,688	762	769	7
INDIA	O	E	81	2,270	459	660	201
			82	18,117	2,899	4,202	1,303
			83	10,971	827	909	82
	V	E	83	507,057	89,700	154,620	64,920
			85	2,315	3,550	5,586	2,036
	V	W	81	2,200	3,684	4,625	941
INDNSIA	O	E	81	18,079	1,972	2,554	582
			82	76,667	12,608	17,230	4,622
			83	212,666	20,880	27,554	6,674
			84	143,944	30,792	40,517	9,725
			85	22,737	7,165	9,948	2,783
			86	107	1,289	1,735	446
	V	E	83	11,283	2,354	3,739	1,385
ITALY	N	E	81	1,221,027	69,929	159,663	89,734
	O	E	81	1,581	309	507	198
			82	83,342	7,330	10,076	2,746
			83	335,611	13,873	18,261	4,388
			84	378,268	50,922	66,212	15,290
			85	47,518	20,794	30,550	9,756
			86	127,043	19,123	30,672	11,549
	V	E	81	649,095	36,456	83,150	46,694
			82	1,561,621	89,628	207,267	117,639
			83	270,285	46,635	68,748	22,113
			84	90,557	12,222	21,661	9,439
			85	470,812	20,145	45,539	25,394
	V	W	84	1,808,926	161,544	275,467	113,923
JAMAICA	O	E	81	21,200	5,896	7,989	2,093
			83	12,740	500	859	359
	V	E	81	3,300	344	695	351
			84	8,700	889	1,874	985
JAPAN	V	E	81	312,042	26,936	52,757	25,821
			82	128,418	13,104	24,240	11,136
			85	864,541	150,168	251,596	101,428
	V	W	83	2,205,151	540,135	773,485	233,350

Crop Product TSUSA commodity number, description, and unit of quantity Country	Mode	Reg	Yr	Quantity	F.A.S.	C.I.F.	Charges
			86	900	2,073	2,147	74
KOR REP	N	E	81	2,722,111	226,846	408,971	182,125
	O	E	82	535,925	86,135	121,465	35,330
			83	86,083	3,867	4,261	394
	V	E	81	4,272,991	228,402	469,808	241,406
			82	169,774	15,177	30,020	14,843
			83	391,658	31,587	53,570	21,983
			84	332,345	34,435	58,617	24,182
			85	176,809	15,220	28,748	13,528
			86	607,431	74,943	140,380	65,437
	V	W	81	1,057,339	79,052	169,079	90,027
			84	118,735	13,534	25,843	12,309
			85	232,522	23,717	44,173	20,456
LEBANON	O	E	82	8,880	1,955	2,922	967
			84	2,508	502	781	279
MACAO	O	E	82	3,448	400	611	211
			83	174	300	398	98
MALAWI	N	E	82	32,454	4,542	6,302	1,760
	V	E	81	107,314	20,813	33,812	12,999
			82	2,600	519	834	315
			83	383,379	45,274	92,279	47,005
			86	295,680	69,080	96,400	27,320
MEXICO	O	E	81	2,537,736	1,986,736	2,003,681	16,945
			82	3,281,824	1,820,219	1,830,656	10,437
			83	1,890,957	863,518	887,410	23,892
			84	629,708	72,661	86,321	13,660
			85	227,210	12,772	12,981	209
			86	2,586,319	441,443	446,105	4,662
	O	W	81	111,979	163,489	163,489	
	V	E	84	2,221	2,332	2,750	418
NETHLDS	A	E	84	1,764	3,384	4,183	799
	O	E	81	132,020	4,787	6,968	2,181
	V	E	83	17,821	565	2,486	1,921
			84	775,662	28,169	71,169	43,000
			85	286,494	10,014	28,239	18,225
			86	222,224	11,639	24,974	13,335
NICARAG	O	E	81	3,046	299	400	101
NIGERIA	O	E	81	2,019	333	431	98
PANAMA	V	E	81	336,112	16,806	29,219	12,413
PARAGUA	O	E	81	240,369	9,327	23,539	14,212
			82	138,789	9,238	25,504	16,266
			83	161,394	17,709	29,467	11,758
			84	231,730	24,907	43,738	18,831
			85	6,395	8,131	9,273	1,142
			86	84,766	16,604	25,605	9,001
PERU	O	E	84	14,441	1,459	1,549	90
PHIL R	N	E	85	2,919,641	354,651	610,911	256,260
	O	E	81	452,244	19,651	40,593	20,942
			82	310,513	14,574	36,929	22,355
			83	451,585	26,997	46,888	19,891
			84	510,707	50,584	87,099	36,515
			86	81,718	12,255	19,515	7,260
	V	E	81	903,225	88,222	178,950	90,728
			82	2,424,399	263,910	477,610	213,700
			83	4,191,143	444,877	785,384	340,507
			84	5,219,486	544,249	1,009,663	465,414
			85	224,849	24,480	43,730	19,250
			86	3,054,650	370,058	654,538	284,480
	V	W	86	47,658	5,190	10,950	5,760
POLAND	O	E	84	157,727	23,375	26,283	2,908
	V	E	82	165,527	14,814	36,273	21,459
			83	543,439	92,172	153,592	61,420
			84	435,686	46,333	98,095	51,762
	V	W	83	117,462	27,016	43,451	16,435
PORTUGL	V	E	86	11,560	2,890	2,890	
REP SAF	O	E	81	57,417	3,445	3,809	364
			84	287,978	67,723	75,320	7,597
			85	334,109	29,480	47,110	17,630
	V	E	82	13,800	690	788	98
			83	95,586	8,577	15,787	7,210
			84	244,170	22,597	40,992	18,395
			85	830,653	73,633	121,934	48,301
			86	43,225	2,161	2,161	
ROMANIA	O	E	81	47,710	7,517	8,156	639
			82	52,101	5,210	5,450	240
			83	103,807	5,191	16,679	11,488
	V	E	83	9,518	441	484	43
	V	W	82	178,701	21,457	33,410	11,953
SALVADR	V	E	81	126,766	6,338	10,839	4,501
SINGAPR	O	E	82	4,200	441	738	297
	V	E	81	175,366	13,018	25,390	12,372
SPAIN	O	E	81	49,481	3,239	4,388	1,149
			82	157,998	12,786	18,177	5,391
			83	151,995	8,776	11,728	2,952
SRI LKA	V	E	84	115,249	5,300	7,017	1,717
	V	E	83	461,202	123,786	174,745	50,959
	V	W	81	38,977	26,879	32,488	5,609
SWITZLD	V	E	84	195,301	8,554	10,773	2,219
	V	W	84	940,747	58,540	119,625	61,085
THAILND	O	E	81	224,869	19,441	34,652	15,211
			82	4,440	978	1,461	483
			84	42,778	8,716	14,681	5,965
	V	E	81	637,083	55,486	102,477	46,991
			82	500,091	50,455	85,814	35,359
			83	149,913	22,440	39,135	16,695
			84	956,088	117,433	232,534	115,101
			85	1,750,635	245,792	421,786	175,994
			86	4,655,426	577,248	973,888	396,640
	V	W	81	837,638	75,391	148,789	73,398
			82	789,579	71,823	151,677	79,854
			83	1,067,347	145,426	249,795	104,369
			84	1,330,726	186,546	338,077	151,531
			85	1,119,063	132,735	243,946	111,211
			86	74,100	3,705	3,705	
TNZANIA	O	E	83	6,606	330	366	36
TURKEY	O	E	82	11,346	2,498	3,733	1,235
U KING	O	E	83	37,992	4,939	5,519	580
			85	317	1,270	1,302	32
			86	198	1,431	1,496	65
	V	E	83	2,078	769	1,181	412
URUGUAY	O	E	83	6,903	450	561	111
VENEZ	O	E	81	1,000,378	64,447	72,559	8,112
YUGOSLV	V	E	85	100,915	5,046	5,444	398
ZMBABWE	O	E	81	45,862	2,131	2,318	187
	V	E	81	41,616	5,571	9,788	4,217
			82	156,021	30,191	42,667	12,476
			83	552,241	87,555	144,781	57,226
			84	8,115	1,022	1,180	158
			85	75,786	15,444	23,231	7,787
			86	159,260	20,950	37,236	16,286
	V	W	81	110,561	12,538	18,637	6,099

1705500 TOBACCO STEMS,CUT,GROUND,ETC (LB)

			Yr	Quantity	F.A.S.	C.I.F.	Charges
TOTAL			81	**45,863**	**26,460**	**27,548**	**1,088**
			82	**24,722**	**3,225**	**3,225**	
			83	**241,682**	**38,862**	**45,923**	**7,061**
			84	**189,091**	**36,963**	**40,913**	**3,950**
			85	**105,406**	**3,812**	**6,262**	**2,450**
			86	**104,555**	**13,700**	**23,077**	**9,377**
CANADA	O	E	81	42,638	24,460	24,460	
			82	2,676	916	916	
			83	17,738	8,687	8,687	
			84	40,909	22,091	22,091	
			85	70,000	1,040	1,040	
DOM REP	A	E	86	535	2,677	2,815	138
FR GERM	V	E	81	3,225	2,000	3,088	1,088
INDNSIA	O	E	82	22,046	2,309	2,309	
			83	187,658	25,458	31,769	6,311
			84	148,182	14,872	18,822	3,950
			85	35,406	2,772	5,222	2,450
			86	104,020	11,023	20,262	9,239
ITALY	O	E	83	36,286	4,717	5,467	750

Tobacco, wrapper
1701000 WRPPR TOB MIX OR NT, NT STEM (LB)

			Yr	Quantity	F.A.S.	C.I.F.	Charges
TOTAL			81	**1,396,853**	**7,121,290**	**7,297,740**	**176,450**
			82	**1,405,580**	**7,784,357**	**8,003,278**	**218,921**
			83	**1,872,224**	**10,331,257**	**10,634,031**	**302,774**
			84	**2,110,954**	**9,960,995**	**10,275,526**	**314,531**
			85	**2,044,320**	**10,227,552**	**10,554,416**	**326,864**
			86	**1,636,578**	**8,772,761**	**8,968,969**	**196,208**
BELGIUM	V	E	83	3,408	25,452	25,994	542
BRAZIL	O	E	85	708	1,468	1,521	53
			86	7,988	22,424	23,315	891
	V	E	82	4,978	44,729	46,584	1,855
			83	3,395	17,373	17,873	500
			84	9,717	37,448	38,549	1,101
			85	57,333	299,079	306,817	7,738
			86	25,254	222,122	227,307	5,185
C AF RP	O	E	81	14,102	169,539	173,485	3,946
			82	8,451	105,265	106,831	1,566
			83	9,934	118,004	119,325	1,321
			84	21,808	115,348	115,753	405
			85	717	3,585	3,646	61

Crop
Product
TSUSA commodity number, description, and unit of quantity

Country	Mode	Reg	Yr	Quantity	F.A.S.	C.I.F.	Charges
	V	E	82	5,167	26,093	27,125	1,032
			83	6,825	73,454	74,631	1,177
			84	4,809	86,433	86,929	496
C RICA	A	E	86	9,138	48,788	50,795	2,007
	N	E	86	19,846	100,857	105,649	4,792
CAMROON	A	E	81	913	10,176	10,553	377
			83	339	3,785	4,089	304
	N	E	83	6,238	40,403	41,426	1,023
	O	E	81	251,059	2,123,075	2,164,911	41,836
			82	224,170	2,053,302	2,095,442	42,140
			83	185,514	1,779,003	1,863,824	84,821
			84	208,168	1,737,236	1,820,101	82,865
			85	162,851	1,306,031	1,380,625	74,594
			86	119,527	1,064,901	1,083,218	18,317
	V	E	82	6,878	79,796	82,010	2,214
			83	182,232	1,041,470	1,052,233	10,763
			84	40,345	705,694	712,477	6,783
			85	28,360	582,514	588,014	5,500
			86	48,530	958,184	971,212	13,028
CANADA	A	E	81	15	750	777	27
	O	E	83	45	862	862	
CHINA M	V	E	85	569	5,494	5,637	143
			86	842	11,999	12,310	311
COLOMB	O	E	83	110	400	412	12
			84	4,416	13,891	14,313	422
			85	3,243	10,817	11,109	292
DOM REP	A	E	81	33	300	460	160
	N	E	81	2,868	4,395	4,627	232
			82	8,994	7,426	7,716	290
			83	9,440	24,538	24,876	338
			84	22,882	58,023	62,537	4,514
			85	13,839	75,246	76,436	1,190
	O	E	81	7,790	41,868	42,813	945
			82	22,364	63,376	65,311	1,935
			83	44,023	193,092	196,775	3,683
			84	126,019	132,842	138,276	5,434
			86	250,286	702,958	720,095	17,137
	V	E	81	20,289	58,666	59,854	1,188
			82	103,072	562,346	591,452	29,106
			83	29,211	163,878	170,049	6,171
			84	68,667	307,079	316,078	8,999
			85	41,011	258,761	263,629	4,868
			86	12,658	38,212	40,136	1,924
DOMINCA	V	E	85	4,587	34,403	34,665	262
ECUADOR	N	E	82	8,760	50,580	52,012	1,432
			84	6,268	33,623	34,899	1,276
			85	6,662	26,381	29,340	2,959
	O	E	81	58,951	211,496	218,821	7,325
			82	88,679	248,347	256,148	7,801
			83	126,462	359,355	368,840	9,485
			84	86,866	298,399	309,421	11,022
			85	132,561	497,900	509,012	11,112
			86	120,408	388,344	400,517	12,173
	V	E	81	21,276	88,355	90,866	2,511
			83	14,925	75,077	77,401	2,324
			86	13,587	48,204	50,446	2,242
FR GERM	V	E	82	593	3,231	3,331	100
FRANCE	O	E	81	561	5,043	5,092	49
GIBRALT	O	E	83	2,607	30,997	31,206	209
HONDURA	A	E	82	2,302	2,302	2,691	389
			84	23,812	45,568	48,520	2,952
			86	1,168	1,460	1,664	204
	N	E	81	9,179	28,931	29,552	621
			83	45,888	169,260	173,627	4,367
			84	176,530	1,421,708	1,457,412	35,704
			85	314,220	1,435,798	1,484,779	48,981
			86	83,914	688,384	701,171	12,787
	O	E	81	409,737	1,626,989	1,676,178	49,189
			82	257,175	1,100,911	1,133,503	32,592
			83	332,979	1,215,123	1,254,743	39,620
			84	461,662	1,896,122	1,948,781	52,659
			85	496,585	2,296,503	2,358,205	61,702
			86	302,985	1,417,715	1,461,511	43,796
	V	E	81	111,161	469,191	487,183	17,992
			82	39,559	327,165	343,854	16,689
			83	142,427	1,187,523	1,211,235	23,712
			84	6,963	19,472	19,959	487
			85	43,194	371,691	381,013	9,322
			86	77,357	620,395	631,901	11,506
INDNSIA	V	E	84	6,284	31,355	32,310	955
ISRAEL	A	E	86	17,318	52,368	53,857	1,489
JAMAICA	A	E	83	2,054	25,303	25,806	503
MALI	O	E	81	867	11,592	11,713	121
MEXICO	A	E	82	302	3,624	3,773	149
			84	2,475	2,588	2,756	168
			85	28,298	245,517	254,123	8,606
	N	E	81	2,677	16,478	17,050	572
			83	7,338	47,143	48,047	904
			86	140,952	230,717	239,768	9,051
	O	E	81	132,146	865,325	870,320	4,995
			82	57,021	288,872	295,665	6,793
			83	47,884	220,670	225,579	4,909
			84	28,268	130,627	132,382	1,755
			85	51,232	334,067	337,452	3,385
			86	28,510	144,257	147,179	2,922
	V	E	81	2,537	15,729	15,963	234
			82	112,183	894,385	907,453	13,068
			83	113,229	1,076,021	1,089,888	13,867
			84	151,675	966,828	978,479	11,651
			85	88,961	540,550	547,687	7,137
			86	222,549	1,597,570	1,616,047	18,477
N CALDN	A	E	85	28,342	82,511	89,023	6,512
	N	E	85	47,961	138,712	147,840	9,128
NETHLDS	O	E	81	459	5,658	5,773	115
			85	6,498	63,626	66,044	2,418
	V	E	83	172	952	1,111	159
			85	29,527	168,391	170,988	2,597
NICARAG	A	E	81	174	300	397	97
			82	1,211	3,269	3,447	178
	N	E	81	55,303	123,142	126,818	3,676
			82	142,829	629,965	648,148	18,183
			83	73,389	190,174	198,337	8,163
			84	373,441	852,012	900,918	48,906
			85	280,221	806,218	842,879	36,661
	O	E	81	294,756	1,244,292	1,284,534	40,242
			82	271,567	1,051,675	1,088,151	36,476
			83	385,546	1,642,293	1,708,678	66,385
			84	248,228	945,785	976,462	30,677
			85	87,266	313,969	326,107	12,138
			86	12,122	45,856	47,602	1,746
	V	E	82	38,976	232,659	237,511	4,852
			83	96,544	609,138	626,427	17,289
			84	5,474	42,596	44,374	1,778
			85	7,397	21,663	22,166	503
PANAMA	O	E	84	7,057	31,175	32,142	967
			85	81,757	304,977	313,704	8,727
			86	30,294	111,147	114,781	3,634
	V	E	84	19,020	48,643	50,972	2,329
			86	91,345	255,899	268,488	12,589
REP SAF	A	E	84	100	500	726	226
	O	E	82	349	5,039	5,120	81
U KING	A	E	81	66	514	737	223
	A	W	85	420	1,680	1,955	275

1701500 WRPPR TOB, MIX OR NOT, STEM (LB)

Country	Mode	Reg	Yr	Quantity	F.A.S.	C.I.F.	Charges
TOTAL			81	68,750	552,687	582,442	29,643
			82	299,156	2,306,255	2,384,072	77,817
			83	129,134	549,492	574,363	24,871
			84	68,738	539,897	567,300	27,403
			85	162,522	950,491	988,545	38,054
			86	270,564	2,892,714	2,970,937	78,223
BRAZIL	V	E	85	49,964	150,058	155,738	5,680
CAMROON	A	E	81	1,867	17,658	18,018	360
			82	9,027	85,220	89,724	4,504
			83	10,883	86,764	92,076	5,312
			85	2,288	17,361	18,764	1,403
	N	E	84	35,720	341,350	352,506	11,156
			86	95,183	1,170,218	1,188,117	17,899
	V	E	81	1,343	20,287	20,493	206
			82	74,451	992,899	1,005,236	12,337
			83	26,291	260,622	264,686	4,064
			84	8,549	70,957	75,092	4,135
			85	13,553	175,815	179,251	3,436
			86	876	9,765	9,923	158
CANADA	A	E	85	3,016	3,385	4,085	700
CHINA M	V	E	86	2,968	38,998	39,564	566
DOM REP	A	E	81	16	380	464	84
			85	1,150	1,150	1,730	580
	N	E	81	1,253	4,744	4,975	164
	O	E	81	880	436	437	1
			82	3,289	5,903	6,051	148
			85	6,019	16,070	16,481	411
	V	E	81	7,852	117,581	118,833	1,207
			82	71,447	409,630	430,068	20,438
			83	6,613	54,737	55,636	899
			84	17,043	116,194	126,926	10,732
			85	63,909	411,770	432,313	20,543

Crop
Product
TSUSA commodity number, description, and unit of quantity

Country	Mode	Reg	Yr	Quantity	F.A.S.	C.I.F.	Charges
			86	94,285	553,452	576,785	23,333
ECUADOR	V	E	82	5,580	31,693	31,950	257
HONDURA	A	E	81	3,822	7,879	9,358	1,479
			82	49,314	62,434	71,633	9,199
			83	6,713	21,195	22,645	1,450
			84	2,443	4,109	4,661	552
	N	E	83	59,013	57,272	67,674	10,402
	O	E	82	5,421	16,827	19,393	2,566
			83	13,778	41,647	43,194	1,547
	V	E	81	35,566	313,304	335,779	22,475
			82	35,426	594,498	617,229	22,731
			83	3,314	6,909	7,147	238
			85	6,148	50,989	52,302	1,313
			86	32,212	441,790	450,941	9,151
INDNSIA	V	W	81	5,952	29,700	30,498	798
			82	3,307	18,199	18,677	478
MEXICO	A	E	86	1,286	13,606	15,103	1,497
	O	E	82	7,455	30,726	31,638	912
			83	732	3,113	3,175	62
			84	925	2,311	2,348	37
	V	E	82	274	2,740	3,082	342
			85	14,814	114,371	116,782	2,411
			86	308	2,414	2,864	450
NETHLDS	A	E	81	3,466	30,619	32,826	2,207
			82	1,835	17,902	19,413	1,511
			83	1,797	17,233	18,130	897
			85	1,218	6,330	7,815	1,485
			86	413	4,575	6,333	1,758
	V	E	86	26,316	592,900	612,396	19,496
NICARAG	A	E	81	3,243	2,595	2,898	303
			82	137	421	550	129
			84	96	816	861	45
	N	E	82	28,535	21,180	21,884	704
	V	E	81	3,490	7,504	7,863	359
			82	3,658	15,983	17,544	1,561
			84	3,962	4,160	4,906	746
			85	443	3,192	3,284	92
PANAMA	V	E	86	13,525	16,925	20,233	3,308
SWITZLD	V	E	86	3,192	48,071	48,678	607

Tolu Balsam

Tolu, balsam
1882200 BALSAMS, TOLU (LB)

Country	Mode	Reg	Yr	Quantity	F.A.S.	C.I.F.	Charges
TOTAL			81	17,207	90,608	94,666	4,058
			82	30,876	152,262	158,465	6,203
			83	46,242	208,855	217,580	8,725
			84	50,845	213,327	222,150	8,823
			85	17,166	82,916	86,418	3,502
			86	51,575	251,880	261,765	9,885
ARAB EM	V	E	84	2,205	9,141	9,141	
FR GERM	A	E	85	1,102	3,143	4,011	868
	V	E	82	2,205	8,265	8,429	164
			84	7,716	27,654	28,888	1,234
			86	7,054	31,056	32,096	1,040
FRANCE	A	E	81	11	349	361	12
			84	52	1,202	1,225	23
			85	717	9,633	9,838	205
	N	E	82	342	1,577	1,763	186
	V	E	86	441	3,331	3,382	51
HONDURA	V	E	83	7,606	18,830	19,893	1,063
			84	8,620	27,238	28,044	806
NETHLDS	V	E	86	234	2,268	2,299	31
SALVADR	V	E	86	5,512	12,048	12,560	512
SINGAPR	V	E	81	1,102	4,960	5,088	128
U KING	A	E	86	4,162	14,818	16,172	1,354
	N	E	81	16,094	85,299	89,217	3,918
			84	32,252	148,092	154,852	6,760
			86	34,172	188,359	195,256	6,897
	V	E	82	28,329	142,420	148,273	5,853
			83	38,636	190,025	197,687	7,662
			85	15,347	70,140	72,569	2,429

Crop
Product
TSUSA commodity number, description, and unit of quantity

Tomato

Tomato, flour
1407400 TOMATO FLOUR (LB)

Country	Mode	Reg	Yr	Quantity	F.A.S.	C.I.F.	Charges
TOTAL			82	2,625,041	3,322,151	3,569,358	247,207
			83	5,311,651	6,785,723	7,412,186	626,463
			84	7,411,293	9,244,780	10,008,834	764,054
			85	7,639,306	9,160,292	9,931,647	771,355
			86	8,336,660	9,395,681	10,229,238	833,557
ALBANIA	O	E	86	39,683	36,954	39,896	2,942
ARGENT	V	E	85	3,563	4,227	4,575	348
BELGIUM	O	E	85	59,400	74,122	89,100	14,978
CANADA	O	E	82	22,170	32,873	32,873	
			83	40,853	58,479	58,479	
			84	61,105	52,609	52,609	
FR GERM	A	W	86	2,214	4,287	6,642	2,355
	N	E	84	5,455	6,507	7,090	583
FRANCE	N	E	85	25,741	32,588	39,124	6,536
	O	E	83	79,366	96,300	100,701	4,401
			84	595,245	694,291	738,530	44,239
			85	680,562	741,039	791,766	50,727
			86	198,415	203,866	217,903	14,037
	V	E	83	40,463	52,049	54,673	2,624
			84	1,764	6,286	6,480	194
			85	22,046	42,552	44,052	1,500
			86	44,145	51,941	56,663	4,722
HUNGARY	O	E	86	186,285	181,393	190,826	9,433
	V	E	83	17,637	22,781	23,986	1,205
			85	72,752	69,641	78,509	8,868
			86	55,115	54,398	56,813	2,415
ISRAEL	A	E	84	198	307	924	617
	O	E	84	3,025	4,481	4,481	
	V	E	84	32,408	48,444	50,232	1,788
			85	29,533	32,999	35,190	2,191
ITALY	A	E	82	132	304	500	196
			83	242	1,010	1,144	134
			84	520	1,545	1,855	310
			86	330	1,110	1,482	372
	N	W	85	1,852	3,762	5,949	2,187
	O	E	86	9,198	24,507	26,073	1,566
	V	E	82	353	2,340	2,444	104
			83	5,538	6,560	6,923	363
			84	3,918	9,161	9,737	576
			85	11,019	13,465	16,028	2,563
			86	17,958	36,472	38,770	2,298
	V	W	83	331	760	833	73
			84	2,315	5,173	5,711	538
			86	1,609	2,749	2,909	160
JAPAN	O	E	84	39,683	47,497	50,488	2,991
MEXICO	A	E	84	529	1,210	1,867	657
	O	W	82	370	756	756	
MOROC	V	E	82	328,316	409,445	441,606	32,161
			83	909,368	1,139,447	1,237,446	97,999
			84	874,290	1,110,996	1,197,795	86,799
			85	1,774,716	2,022,240	2,205,569	183,329
			86	1,363,612	1,566,389	1,688,079	121,690
NETHLDS	N	E	85	54,453	55,626	59,386	3,760
	O	E	86	88,360	79,366	86,834	7,468
	V	W	83	1,815	3,852	4,538	686
			85	29,700	36,788	38,876	2,088
PORTUGL	N	E	84	677,964	890,785	936,983	46,198
			85	52,911	55,780	59,740	3,960
	O	E	82	480,693	549,810	595,349	45,539
			83	1,686,539	2,028,453	2,185,922	157,469
			84	1,587,871	1,837,586	1,980,426	142,840
			85	917,206	986,913	1,068,982	82,069
			86	1,424,351	1,374,729	1,483,032	108,303
	V	E	82	343,918	454,800	481,336	26,536
			83	478,398	618,150	659,788	41,638
			84	18,000	53,100	54,866	1,766
			85	529,045	668,050	705,605	37,555
			86	935,724	975,636	1,045,665	70,029
SINGAPR	O	E	85	36,850	52,092	64,488	12,396
SPAIN	A	E	86	1,102	1,285	3,046	1,761
	N	E	83	122,311	172,372	183,453	11,081
			85	335,274	431,325	462,700	31,375
	V	E	82	1,372,089	1,765,068	1,892,982	127,914
			83	818,989	995,594	1,072,107	76,513
			84	1,860,046	2,254,183	2,436,620	182,437
			85	1,466,383	1,796,957	1,940,707	143,750
			86	2,020,802	2,382,135	2,555,566	173,431

Crop Product TSUSA commodity number, description, and unit of quantity Country	Mode	Reg	Yr	Quantity	F.A.S.	C.I.F.	Charges
	V	W	82	40,150	51,794	57,025	5,231
			84	120,450	106,768	120,625	13,857
SWEDEN	O	E	85	305,347	408,850	452,330	43,480
SWITZLD	N	E	84	1,016,107	1,445,188	1,627,077	181,889
			85	633,663	855,316	939,215	83,899
	O	E	83	962,715	1,405,175	1,622,521	217,346
			86	268,675	356,974	533,418	176,444
	V	E	82	36,850	54,961	64,487	9,526
			84	320,650	424,740	460,946	36,206
			85	417,450	563,073	597,340	34,267
			86	1,234,178	1,530,299	1,633,383	103,084
	V	W	83	147,086	184,741	199,672	14,931
			84	189,750	243,923	263,492	19,569
			85	179,840	212,887	232,416	19,529
			86	248,316	295,680	310,435	14,755
U KING	V	E	86	196,586	235,511	251,803	16,292

Tomato, fresh or frozen
1376000 TOMATOE, FRSH, CHLD, OR FROZ (LB)

Country	Mode	Reg	Yr	Quantity	F.A.S.	C.I.F.	Charges
TOTAL			81	349,775,862	177,887,669	178,158,691	248,079
			82	335,309,052	97,902,836	98,182,700	279,864
			83	508,300,542	169,673,037	170,063,310	390,273
			84	461,295,563	98,236,615	99,026,972	790,357
			85	488,763,159	99,031,041	100,582,184	1,551,143
			86	528,657,730	177,084,673	179,192,071	2,107,398
ARGENT	V	E	83	140,365	280,730	291,863	11,133
BAHAMAS	A	E	82	336,383	49,696	56,188	6,492
	N	E	81	289,310	24,046	33,562	9,516
	V	E	85	47,600	18,200	18,890	690
BELGIUM	A	E	82	660	498	721	223
			83	24,173	16,854	25,225	8,371
			84	94,133	53,170	96,970	43,800
			85	191,121	130,944	214,070	83,126
			86	127,894	104,625	172,777	68,152
	A	W	84	926	714	1,031	317
			85	265	3,017	4,892	1,875
			86	44,041	48,087	83,470	35,383
BELIZE	A	W	86	2,700	1,200	1,800	600
	O	E	86	66,025	31,926	31,926	
BULGAR	A	E	85	1,653	1,372	2,321	949
CANADA	O	E	81	278,663	102,931	102,931	
			82	433,879	200,694	200,694	
			83	358,331	196,668	196,668	
			84	538,981	310,317	310,317	
			85	731,884	420,236	420,236	
			86	1,133,476	647,981	647,981	
	O	W	81	132,063	82,769	82,769	
			82	137,142	38,414	38,414	
			83	187,990	61,256	61,256	
			84	397,919	97,228	97,228	
			85	529,507	163,811	163,811	
			86	800,872	313,228	313,228	
CHINA T	O	W	81	16,380	11,182	11,182	
COLOMB	A	E	84	32,780	14,498	23,940	9,442
			85	2,090	1,235	1,735	500
DENMARK	O	E	86	2,475	4,941	4,941	
DOM REP	A	E	81	22,428	5,836	10,395	4,559
			82	3,888	862	1,817	955
			84	5,430	543	1,659	1,116
	N	E	81	1,985,707	353,955	448,814	94,859
			82	400,575	36,471	57,196	20,725
			83	1,519,092	143,072	213,290	70,218
			84	939,231	109,435	151,547	42,112
			85	2,157,805	310,100	415,855	105,755
			86	1,265,718	172,551	229,682	57,131
	V	E	81	30,120	8,534	10,223	1,689
			83	13,530	3,453	4,616	1,163
			84	336,666	32,327	44,023	11,696
			85	1,399,072	149,218	224,882	75,664
			86	15,970,125	1,859,077	2,849,265	990,188
FR GERM	A	E	86	528	1,457	2,078	621
FRANCE	A	E	83	4,640	2,962	6,411	3,449
			84	6,727	3,702	5,845	2,143
			85	80,293	44,594	82,212	37,618
			86	169,527	144,140	255,431	111,291
	O	E	85	28,488	1,351	1,351	
	O	W	84	41,877	9,693	9,693	
			85	52,614	10,925	10,925	
GUATMAL	A	E	83	3,000	1,050	1,741	691
	V	E	84	93,275	50,184	57,107	6,923
			85	27,645	15,268	18,953	3,685

Crop Product TSUSA commodity number, description, and unit of quantity Country	Mode	Reg	Yr	Quantity	F.A.S.	C.I.F.	Charges

Country	Mode	Reg	Yr	Quantity	F.A.S.	C.I.F.	Charges
ISRAEL	A	E	81	59,483	69,919	157,548	86,629
			82	114,980	39,892	252,115	212,223
			83	117,954	30,155	177,815	147,660
			84	134,486	30,320	136,865	106,545
			85	430,925	108,731	557,703	448,972
			86	59,763	13,967	74,770	60,803
	N	E	86	183,815	49,566	55,624	6,058
ITALY	A	E	83	466	282	506	224
			84	10,526	16,220	22,282	6,062
			85	1,720	1,459	2,063	604
	A	W	84	506	1,950	2,377	427
	N	E	81	952	3,541	3,894	353
	V	E	81	32,031	8,026	12,735	4,709
			82	202,823	38,400	62,580	24,180
			84	141,096	46,195	65,067	18,872
			86	160,055	39,480	70,060	30,580
JAMAICA	A	E	83	425,108	188,835	296,326	107,491
			84	14,740	7,501	7,643	142
			85	20,620	14,645	17,241	2,596
			86	3,175	1,911	3,822	1,911
	N	E	84	146,488	98,352	132,280	33,928
	V	E	82	133,820	46,560	61,624	15,064
			84	25,000	21,560	23,393	1,833
			86	44,728	4,704	7,217	2,513
JAPAN	V	W	83	980	392	405	13
MALI	A	E	86	1,157	1,158	1,598	440
MEXICO	A	E	85	190,373	28,836	52,786	23,950
	A	W	81	34,894	13,190	18,030	4,840
	O	E	81	9,892,110	1,769,216	1,769,216	
			82	4,154,330	412,729	412,729	
			83	9,633,235	1,024,616	1,024,618	2
			84	10,635,761	991,333	991,339	6
			85	8,000,535	1,049,011	1,049,015	4
			86	7,523,298	761,684	761,684	
	O	W	81	336,979,004	175,417,333	175,473,334	34,058
			82	329,390,572	97,038,620	97,038,622	2
			83	495,703,188	167,622,014	167,622,016	2
			84	445,876,070	95,216,311	95,216,329	18
			85	472,534,986	94,921,622	94,921,648	26
			86	499,491,580	171,593,454	171,697,095	103,641
MONSRAT	O	W	85	79,600	17,100	17,100	
MOROC	A	E	83	50,469	36,656	45,465	8,809
			85	4,209	1,500	2,643	1,143
	O	W	86	25,973	11,640	11,640	
MOZAMBQ	O	W	85	184,193	36,850	36,850	
			86	98,998	44,640	44,640	
N ZEAL	A	H	84	2,116	1,637	2,631	994
	A	W	81	6,566	7,656	10,296	2,640
			84	5,068	3,723	6,642	2,919
			85	10,591	11,518	16,285	4,767
NETHLDS	A	E	83	103,923	61,451	88,929	27,478
			84	1,229,472	784,023	1,171,891	387,868
			85	1,682,820	1,338,914	1,978,921	640,007
			86	1,348,363	1,085,029	1,606,727	521,698
	A	W	84	53,812	30,905	60,728	29,823
			85	85,353	63,598	122,468	58,870
			86	95,363	108,814	176,451	67,637
	N	E	86	5,787	7,338	9,638	2,300
	N	W	84	25,952	24,852	26,752	1,900
			85	20,102	18,392	26,314	7,922
	O	E	84	64,246	32,558	32,558	
			85	21,619	23,952	23,952	
NIGER	A	E	86	11,188	12,167	54,191	42,024
PANAMA	V	E	85	26,600	11,712	14,124	2,412
SPAIN	A	E	81	16,151	9,535	13,762	4,227
			84	103,913	63,281	109,391	46,110
			85	28,093	21,269	32,846	11,577
			86	4,762	4,969	6,710	1,741
	O	E	85	2,698	2,913	2,913	
	V	E	85	27,000	4,481	6,719	2,238
SWEDEN	A	E	86	5,486	6,474	7,022	548
SWITZLD	A	E	83	1,978	773	1,442	669
			84	10,754	4,992	8,372	3,380
U KING	A	E	84	12,933	9,370	10,843	1,473
			85	17,856	31,500	39,767	8,267
			86	6,558	7,115	8,715	1,600
VENEZ	A	E	83	12,120	1,818	4,718	2,900
			84	314,679	169,721	200,229	30,508
			85	143,229	52,767	80,693	27,926
			86	4,300	1,350	1,888	538

1376200 TOMATO, JUL 15-AUG 31, INCL (LB)

Country	Mode	Reg	Yr	Quantity	F.A.S.	C.I.F.	Charges
TOTAL			81	15,713,600	4,067,802	4,081,137	13,334
			82	8,996,423	2,064,513	2,065,179	666

Crop Product TSUSA commodity number, description, and unit of quantity Country	Mode	Reg	Yr	Quantity	F.A.S.	C.I.F.	Charges
			83	17,210,946	2,492,609	2,495,113	2,504
			84	33,348,925	8,783,439	8,867,555	84,116
			85	38,884,738	6,453,376	6,614,564	161,188
			86	50,365,809	7,364,936	7,510,423	145,487
BELGIUM	A	E	83	1,320	280	599	319
			84	8,607	6,168	8,931	2,763
			85	48,893	21,334	42,819	21,485
			86	32,498	18,855	29,848	10,993
	A	W	84	397	323	398	75
			86	1,984	1,185	1,998	813
BELIZE	O	E	86	23,750	3,563	3,563	
CANADA	O	E	81	445,958	96,884	96,885	
			82	647,080	120,674	120,674	
			83	282,690	82,452	82,452	
			84	1,294,251	511,626	511,626	
			85	295,160	129,461	129,461	
			86	515,282	238,928	238,928	
	O	W	83	3,000	1,800	1,800	
			84	13,960	9,877	9,877	
			85	102,520	32,714	32,714	
			86	279,920	80,586	80,586	
DOM REP	A	E	82	8,640	1,048	1,559	511
	V	E	81	110,400	15,682	21,531	5,849
			82	1,500	346	501	155
			83	18,060	2,269	2,866	597
			84	49,650	5,390	7,102	1,712
			85	41,790	5,442	7,702	2,260
			86	6,432	1,106	1,487	381
FINLAND	A	E	86	585	1,170	1,544	374
FRANCE	A	E	85	11,017	4,218	9,295	5,077
			86	39,060	26,943	56,250	29,307
	O	W	86	42,768	5,664	5,664	
ISRAEL	A	E	83	2,315	315	946	631
	V	E	84	35,604	8,500	10,286	1,786
			85	40,948	7,340	9,025	1,685
ITALY	A	E	84	2,006	1,071	1,847	776
			86	4,351	2,063	4,206	2,143
	V	E	81	37,460	8,687	13,830	5,143
MEXICO	O	E	81	27,459	5,708	5,708	
			82	67,914	20,692	20,692	
			83	26,388	1,852	1,852	
			84	23,944	4,484	4,484	
			86	237,645	28,018	28,018	
	O	W	81	15,049,797	3,933,285	3,933,285	
			82	8,271,289	1,921,753	1,921,753	
			83	16,874,446	2,401,163	2,401,163	
			84	31,607,482	8,006,652	8,006,652	
			85	37,969,908	6,035,335	6,035,341	6
			86	48,865,492	6,749,038	6,749,038	
MOZAMBQ	O	W	85	43,659	7,422	7,422	
N ZEAL	A	W	81	1,232	1,478	1,774	296
			84	2,630	2,463	4,002	1,539
NETHLDS	A	E	83	2,727	2,478	3,435	957
			84	204,085	154,232	214,487	60,255
			85	33,195	17,546	29,740	12,194
			86	301,286	196,554	292,071	95,517
	A	W	84	23,215	14,072	25,088	11,016
			86	13,886	10,248	16,146	5,898
	N	E	85	290,046	185,064	303,545	118,481
	O	E	84	44,947	34,160	34,307	147
			85	7,602	7,500	7,500	
	O	W	84	38,147	24,421	28,468	4,047
SPAIN	V	E	81	41,294	6,078	8,124	2,046
TRINID	A	E	86	870	1,015	1,076	61

1376300 TOMATOES, FRESH OR FROZEN (LB)

Crop Product TSUSA commodity number, description, and unit of quantity Country	Mode	Reg	Yr	Quantity	F.A.S.	C.I.F.	Charges
TOTAL			81	160,395,825	56,889,505	56,905,299	25,753
			82	248,313,317	74,157,165	74,334,244	177,079
			83	212,683,787	56,704,483	57,024,678	320,195
			84	329,649,901	67,809,166	68,504,177	695,011
			85	323,339,452	67,572,777	68,397,480	824,703
			86	402,078,037	150,329,246	151,366,992	1,037,746
AUSTRIA	A	E	86	1,429	1,245	1,782	537
BAHAMAS	A	E	86	155,614	33,250	47,074	13,824
	N	E	81	250,396	35,734	43,594	7,860
			82	408,828	62,480	81,795	19,315
	V	E	85	5,260	2,630	3,014	384
BELGIUM	A	E	83	2,450	2,507	3,337	830
			84	4,135	4,097	7,033	2,936
			85	101,450	69,292	107,541	38,249
			86	24,691	24,335	41,080	16,745
	A	W	86	4,758	7,390	11,648	4,258

Crop Product TSUSA commodity number, description, and unit of quantity Country	Mode	Reg	Yr	Quantity	F.A.S.	C.I.F.	Charges
C RICA	A	E	84	1,500	300	446	146
CANADA	O	E	81	4,110	1,242	1,242	
			82	24,815	9,600	9,600	
			83	3,020	1,074	1,074	
			84	61,638	10,759	10,787	28
			85	31,397	2,482	2,482	
			86	12,320	7,040	7,040	
	O	W	81	127,285	47,836	47,836	
			83	903,536	272,832	272,832	
			84	87,550	19,825	19,825	
			86	38,480	10,301	11,197	896
CHILE	A	E	86	2,398	1,635	2,969	1,334
COLOMB	A	E	84	10,626	4,515	7,609	3,094
			85	36,839	30,988	44,736	13,748
			86	7,282	4,966	8,320	3,354
DENMARK	A	W	85	2,355	1,576	4,272	2,696
DOM REP	A	E	83	5,450	1,051	2,074	1,023
			84	3,000	500	1,000	500
	N	E	82	337,874	35,486	52,391	16,905
			83	163,440	11,706	20,590	8,884
			84	1,007,365	123,963	167,125	43,162
			85	975,229	113,042	158,125	45,083
			86	727,835	108,872	140,750	31,878
	V	E	81	335,760	48,602	63,557	14,955
			82	24,390	2,602	3,882	1,280
			83	1,100	280	427	147
			84	108,870	14,971	20,234	5,263
			85	105,999	16,384	22,608	6,224
			86	4,051,391	559,257	818,992	259,735
FRANCE	A	E	84	9,740	5,890	10,523	4,633
			85	14,776	10,891	18,451	7,560
			86	70,872	53,866	95,202	41,336
	O	W	85	100,838	24,170	24,170	
			86	106,160	37,310	37,310	
GREECE	A	E	85	2,169	1,279	1,928	649
GUATMAL	V	E	85	44,620	10,000	16,176	6,176
HAITI	A	E	84	21,033	3,335	5,536	2,201
ISRAEL	A	E	82	69,137	21,676	138,229	116,553
			83	130,140	37,140	230,669	193,529
			84	504,982	135,445	579,549	444,104
			85	633,235	151,943	608,161	456,218
			86	951,072	213,861	563,221	349,360
	V	E	85	80,924	11,532	15,714	4,182
			86	115,742	21,858	27,518	5,660
ITALY	A	E	83	210	750	910	160
			84	3,306	4,088	5,235	1,147
	A	W	84	79	280	339	59
	V	E	82	31,500	7,500	10,464	2,964
			85	228,683	45,132	52,342	7,210
			86	707,305	136,800	183,066	46,266
JAMAICA	A	E	82	61,625	5,456	14,425	8,969
			83	441,107	222,627	333,523	110,896
			84	334,516	161,690	196,708	35,018
			85	48,549	16,207	21,686	5,479
	N	E	84	228,223	134,989	169,296	34,307
			85	317,448	221,272	251,284	30,012
	V	E	82	54,600	21,840	27,786	5,946
MALAYSA	O	W	86	459,351	179,000	179,000	
MEXICO	O	E	81	13,601,376	2,372,278	2,372,278	
			82	22,708,936	2,436,065	2,436,065	
			83	20,530,956	1,838,426	1,838,426	
			84	23,127,856	1,887,508	1,887,508	
			85	26,221,089	1,932,329	1,932,331	2
			86	20,775,378	1,618,295	1,618,295	
	O	W	81	146,012,130	54,376,605	54,366,646	
			82	224,525,672	71,542,915	71,544,551	1,636
			83	190,472,475	54,300,814	54,300,814	
			84	303,538,667	65,046,466	65,046,466	
			85	293,498,050	64,478,047	64,478,764	717
			86	373,136,366	146,923,558	146,993,586	70,028
	V	E	83	12,857	3,450	3,515	65
MONGOLA	O	W	85	31,828	7,020	7,020	
MONSRAT	O	W	85	104,338	22,800	22,800	
			86	31,360	12,800	12,800	
MOROC	A	E	85	32,731	13,575	19,670	6,095
MOZAMBQ	O	E	86	58,503	4,624	4,624	
	O	W	85	133,527	28,050	28,050	
			86	33,935	14,240	14,240	
N ZEAL	A	H	85	19,008	11,358	16,645	5,287
	A	W	81	378	414	482	68
NETHLDS	A	E	82	5,940	5,738	7,189	1,451
			83	9,387	6,116	8,975	2,859
			84	64,261	44,837	67,067	22,230
			85	257,453	205,485	299,532	94,047

Crop Product TSUSA commodity number, description, and unit of quantity Country	Mode	Reg	Yr	Quantity	F.A.S.	C.I.F.	Charges
			86	198,101	150,084	238,888	88,804
	A	W	84	1,402	395	943	548
			85	15,658	12,375	26,735	14,360
			86	64,506	31,637	61,607	29,970
	O	E	84	4,368	4,513	4,513	
			85	11,592	12,782	12,782	
PAKISTN	A	E	86	10,053	1,643	2,103	460
PANAMA	N	E	81	64,390	6,794	9,664	2,870
PORTUGL	A	E	85	13,078	7,513	12,891	5,378
			86	3,175	2,292	3,369	1,077
SPAIN	A	E	83	7,659	5,710	7,512	1,802
			84	7,296	7,464	10,697	3,233
			85	122,391	63,781	106,505	42,724
			86	95,917	47,784	73,239	25,455
	A	W	86	9,009	5,028	10,926	5,898
	N	E	84	66,368	22,688	43,872	21,184
			86	67,293	26,317	41,587	15,270
	O	W	85	4,227	3,390	3,390	
	V	E	82	60,000	5,807	7,867	2,060
			86	19,709	20,060	21,110	1,050
TURKEY	A	E	85	4,244	2,550	3,645	1,095
VENEZ	A	E	84	297,506	137,398	194,792	57,394
			85	140,467	42,902	74,030	31,128
			86	292,138	102,022	139,682	37,660
W SAMOA	A	E	86	1,508	1,126	1,841	715

Tomato, paste

1416520 TOMATO PASTE (LB)

Country	Mode	Reg	Yr	Quantity	F.A.S.	C.I.F.	Charges
TOTAL			81	65,202,175	22,826,372	25,606,474	2,780,102
			82	198,029,353	74,575,485	83,011,542	8,436,057
			83	160,742,004	52,666,268	58,998,045	6,331,777
			84	151,045,139	45,728,574	51,403,721	5,675,147
			85	111,399,767	28,297,587	33,867,383	5,569,796
			86	130,625,270	32,518,392	38,084,641	5,566,249
ARGENT	V	E	83	203,819	70,931	85,175	14,244
			85	635,399	126,816	165,480	38,664
BELGIUM	V	E	82	161,967	83,997	94,987	10,990
			83	111,352	41,670	47,278	5,608
			84	8,147	7,662	9,181	1,519
			86	196,739	41,751	49,830	8,079
BRAZIL	N	E	82	1,762,688	747,017	860,399	113,382
	O	E	85	1,584,332	656,350	660,217	3,867
			86	479,479	103,543	119,869	16,326
	V	E	81	2,731,304	1,045,053	1,287,258	242,205
			82	2,830,464	1,030,207	1,197,822	167,615
			83	4,347,396	1,500,270	1,759,129	258,859
			84	3,128,051	1,111,793	1,304,913	193,120
			85	1,214,655	439,353	516,424	77,071
			86	1,139,723	361,147	422,283	61,136
	V	W	84	9,348	3,150	3,783	633
BULGAR	V	E	86	36,656	10,742	12,199	1,457
CANADA	O	E	81	156,542	38,234	38,234	
			82	521,766	145,871	145,871	
			83	268,600	70,431	70,431	
			84	118,698	28,096	30,739	2,643
			85	79,888	27,567	27,567	
			86	2,478,341	478,935	478,935	
CHILE	V	E	81	1,954,007	654,509	749,889	95,380
			82	2,992,673	1,111,131	1,250,992	139,861
			83	3,274,135	1,112,642	1,254,354	141,712
			84	2,465,327	808,271	913,636	105,365
			85	3,006,966	847,319	952,573	105,254
			86	2,930,200	639,440	754,156	114,716
	V	W	82	35,938	12,019	14,790	2,771
CHINA M	A	E	81	34,127	10,449	12,520	2,071
	O	W	84	618,209	215,934	228,945	13,011
			85	160,894	56,181	58,179	1,998
	V	E	82	178,573	67,852	80,250	12,398
	V	W	82	31,894	10,576	12,247	1,671
			83	363,768	127,020	137,332	10,312
			84	33,731	11,050	12,990	1,940
CHINA T	N	W	84	426,250	147,067	162,421	15,354
	O	W	83	36,365	12,702	15,693	2,991
			84	171,013	59,714	70,306	10,592
			85	213,745	74,636	80,484	5,848
	V	E	81	1,230,090	363,443	441,162	77,719
			82	12,004,809	4,215,890	4,935,784	719,894
			83	3,519,930	1,232,622	1,421,899	189,277
			84	2,361,979	787,261	937,514	150,253
			86	33,994	5,824	7,341	1,517
	V	H	83	29,260	10,150	10,994	844
	V	W	81	7,154,639	2,099,704	2,343,851	244,147
			82	39,025,044	13,819,784	15,231,104	1,411,320
			83	17,626,679	6,127,696	6,724,558	596,862
			84	8,942,138	2,869,408	3,195,735	326,327
			85	2,660,390	744,855	851,791	106,936
			86	2,098,613	588,135	648,641	60,506
DOM REP	N	E	86	298,395	139,599	152,348	12,749
	V	E	84	2,921,888	925,643	1,032,197	106,554
			85	721,166	278,389	309,790	31,401
			86	463,722	270,634	286,008	15,374
FR GERM	V	E	82	164	632	720	88
			83	151,943	45,028	54,977	9,949
			84	97,866	29,430	33,956	4,526
			85	239,816	54,564	68,205	13,641
			86	155,908	30,300	39,100	8,800
FRANCE	O	E	83	243,057	82,362	95,254	12,892
	V	E	81	478,220	203,944	232,181	28,237
			82	3,550,173	1,240,993	1,427,720	186,727
			83	2,389,965	723,555	833,188	109,633
			84	1,087,251	350,791	404,673	53,882
			85	33,039	16,066	17,863	1,797
			86	245,750	52,912	64,958	12,046
	V	W	81	12,124	8,555	8,996	441
			82	49,171	16,798	20,251	3,453
GREECE	O	E	83	690	385	385	
	V	E	81	20,529	6,647	8,258	1,611
			82	2,163,983	731,389	854,458	123,069
			83	977,551	328,153	395,258	67,105
			84	6,124	2,830	3,607	777
			85	169,499	51,114	58,562	7,448
			86	3,175	1,260	1,432	172
	V	W	82	19,876	5,400	6,994	1,594
HUNGARY	V	E	85	40,034	10,815	14,446	3,631
			86	469,053	125,933	154,920	28,987
ICELAND	V	E	85	73,016	14,239	17,339	3,100
			86	37,800	8,465	10,615	2,150
IRAN	V	E	86	85,979	18,915	22,306	3,391
IRELAND	V	E	86	39,021	7,033	8,803	1,770
ISRAEL	N	E	81	4,495,241	1,507,832	1,726,903	219,071
			84	7,144,494	1,953,789	2,256,378	302,589
			85	10,728,601	2,120,459	2,551,837	431,378
	O	E	81	166,793	54,296	59,525	5,229
			82	85,594	39,804	43,499	3,695
			83	135,800	55,000	61,792	6,792
			85	155,902	29,968	38,175	8,207
			86	532,591	157,005	165,882	8,877
	V	E	81	6,292,154	2,098,367	2,421,354	322,987
			82	24,780,304	8,468,254	9,695,123	1,226,869
			83	16,518,284	5,525,503	6,299,564	774,061
			84	5,453,506	1,580,698	1,809,101	228,403
			85	14,306,425	2,973,648	3,590,255	616,607
			86	26,831,287	5,699,505	6,925,935	1,226,430
	V	W	82	183,076	91,085	112,679	21,594
			83	44,645	16,295	18,207	1,912
ITALY	A	E	83	7,486	5,526	12,524	6,998
	N	E	81	66,739	17,963	22,180	4,217
			82	101,889	42,826	48,749	5,923
			83	10,102,097	3,811,898	4,425,171	613,273
			84	7,315,854	2,631,073	3,088,615	457,542
			86	28,540	7,000	8,440	1,440
	N	W	83	85,870	49,112	57,954	8,842
			84	329,593	75,624	99,825	24,201
	O	E	83	42,787	20,525	20,525	
			84	104,763	30,797	36,160	5,363
			85	424,447	103,356	146,586	43,230
			86	176,730	39,374	47,339	7,965
	V	E	81	5,228,567	1,974,701	2,245,617	270,916
			82	19,265,963	7,614,160	8,751,708	1,137,548
			83	13,746,849	2,425,451	2,838,908	413,457
			84	4,437,334	1,482,463	1,791,183	308,720
			85	9,936,770	3,150,152	3,762,494	612,342
			86	9,324,190	3,041,333	3,639,639	598,306
	V	W	82	3,561,447	1,410,598	1,705,709	295,111
			83	93,372	27,770	34,430	6,660
			84	7,572	6,961	8,968	2,007
			85	94,742	25,026	33,596	8,570
			86	35,285	16,610	20,928	4,318
JAPAN	V	W	83	53,552	20,848	22,515	1,667
KOR REP	V	W	82	70,763	25,731	29,785	4,054
MEXICO	A	E	81	110	286	328	42
	N	E	85	374,550	97,756	131,042	33,286
			86	249,700	62,175	77,960	15,785
	O	E	81	16,658,346	6,507,763	6,507,763	
			82	34,145,770	15,290,661	15,290,661	

Crop
Product
TSUSA commodity number, description, and unit of quantity

Country	Mode	Reg	Yr	Quantity	F.A.S.	C.I.F.	Charges
			83	27,368,049	8,941,220	8,941,220	
			84	38,314,488	9,136,339	9,136,339	
			85	12,309,750	3,218,648	3,218,648	
			86	22,427,820	5,679,868	5,679,870	2
	O	W	81	1,499	650	650	
			82	1,947,477	782,560	812,110	29,550
			83	4,480,772	1,430,659	1,430,659	
			84	5,343,175	1,788,150	1,788,150	
			85	576,617	159,075	159,075	
			86	5,292,952	1,994,293	1,994,293	
	V	E	85	1,960,200	504,544	675,201	170,657
			86	1,498,201	382,033	497,659	115,626
NETHLDS	V	E	82	235,461	79,570	91,318	11,748
			83	79,544	28,783	32,439	3,656
			84	268,688	72,137	84,154	12,017
			85	14,400	9,540	9,769	229
			86	1,734,289	380,329	460,272	79,943
	V	W	83	70,199	25,182	31,212	6,030
PANAMA	V	E	82	48,501	14,060	17,313	3,253
PERU	N	E	82	675,899	292,519	333,706	41,187
			83	534,361	161,603	190,096	28,493
	O	E	82	195,556	84,216	97,988	13,772
			83	1,207,931	419,041	482,914	63,873
			84	458,733	155,281	171,237	15,956
			85	221,712	44,013	51,285	7,272
	V	E	82	2,009,259	872,781	1,022,510	149,729
			83	622,885	249,754	278,421	28,667
			84	1,198,325	365,969	414,308	48,339
			85	952,226	196,397	228,378	31,981
POLAND	V	E	85	41,072	9,540	11,588	2,048
			86	122,850	38,665	45,480	6,815
PORTUGL	N	E	84	8,806,167	2,769,094	3,185,346	416,252
			85	13,736,518	3,643,343	4,466,422	823,079
	N	W	84	934,051	345,224	423,580	78,356
	O	E	81	34,615	13,223	16,731	3,508
			82	953,411	411,552	413,474	1,922
			83	842,139	332,514	371,911	39,397
			84	630,354	200,697	226,169	25,472
			85	404,434	113,872	135,735	21,863
			86	46,736	9,637	11,637	2,000
	V	E	81	10,150,555	3,655,413	4,434,217	778,804
			82	25,157,894	9,390,888	10,817,847	1,426,959
			83	29,672,952	10,326,736	12,113,090	1,786,354
			84	35,326,814	11,641,750	13,716,921	2,075,171
			85	15,744,335	3,766,608	5,110,783	1,344,175
			86	34,979,206	8,071,007	10,431,287	2,360,280
	V	W	82	144,000	49,888	62,035	12,147
			83	211,294	78,061	95,248	17,187
			84	187,726	62,326	71,149	8,823
			86	694,456	144,215	190,163	45,948
REP SAF	V	E	83	39,052	10,300	12,265	1,965
ROMANIA	O	E	82	107,929	51,670	56,892	5,222
	V	E	81	364,702	94,300	116,295	21,995
			82	662,187	186,436	223,422	36,986
			83	1,057,343	285,600	330,380	44,780
			85	153,660	32,594	38,240	5,646
			86	35,924	11,895	12,906	1,011
SPAIN	O	E	82	116,932	34,505	41,183	6,678
	V	E	81	6,614,599	2,041,072	2,421,366	380,294
			82	10,961,890	3,835,481	4,511,156	675,675
			83	13,275,936	4,799,051	5,504,712	705,661
			84	9,884,366	3,419,572	4,027,204	607,632
			85	14,592,376	3,677,799	4,506,284	828,485
			86	7,041,787	1,881,782	2,274,772	392,990
SWEDEN	V	E	85	315,344	69,312	97,956	28,644
			86	45,892	10,832	13,973	3,141
SWITZLD	V	E	82	33,750	12,805	15,300	2,495
			83	131,137	45,088	50,740	5,652
			85	36,289	11,977	13,657	1,680
			86	116,590	26,600	30,931	4,331
TUNISIA	V	E	82	83,424	27,808	32,494	4,686
			85	84,260	23,800	27,120	3,320
			86	163,705	41,889	48,712	6,823
TURKEY	N	E	86	829,339	198,096	241,007	42,911
	O	E	82	5,248	1,663	1,663	
			83	7,367	2,415	2,415	
			84	348	687	687	
			86	745,000	183,632	209,750	26,118
	V	E	81	1,356,673	429,968	511,196	81,228
			82	6,232,495	1,879,184	2,225,249	346,065
			83	6,556,492	2,024,998	2,362,372	337,374
			84	3,268,488	945,475	1,088,152	142,677
			85	3,222,672	875,266	1,009,099	133,833
			86	6,274,387	1,506,283	1,764,562	258,279

Crop
Product
TSUSA commodity number, description, and unit of quantity

Country	Mode	Reg	Yr	Quantity	F.A.S.	C.I.F.	Charges
	V	W	83	167,196	50,270	57,658	7,388
			84	167,918	50,980	58,415	7,435
			85	72,752	20,631	27,749	7,118
U KING	O	E	84	413	612	664	52
	V	E	83	42,103	11,448	12,798	1,350
			85	106,874	21,999	27,489	5,490
			86	204,725	49,766	57,500	7,734

Tomato, prepared or preserved
1416600 TOMATOES PREPARED EXC SAUCE (LB)

Country	Mode	Reg	Yr	Quantity	F.A.S.	C.I.F.	Charges
TOTAL			81	97,227,954	18,965,796	24,630,800	5,669,395
			82	167,017,976	32,905,022	42,391,372	9,486,350
			83	186,708,619	40,026,094	49,464,250	9,438,156
			84	233,567,191	49,918,931	62,645,280	12,726,349
			85	220,027,730	41,566,020	54,279,904	12,713,884
			86	197,558,779	36,304,169	46,973,420	10,669,251
ARGENT	A	E	84	1,733	399	681	282
	V	E	83	45,000	8,996	11,815	2,819
			84	209,160	47,310	60,051	12,741
AUSTRIA	V	E	85	3,562	4,415	6,683	2,268
BELGIUM	V	E	83	5,100	972	1,099	127
BRAZIL	V	E	81	696	270	304	34
			82	37,200	15,500	19,308	3,808
			83	19,320	8,050	9,491	1,441
			84	19,920	8,300	10,023	1,723
			85	1,389	4,050	4,930	880
CANADA	O	E	81	406,079	97,467	97,467	
			82	1,093,123	230,933	230,933	
			83	8,872,073	3,344,772	3,344,822	50
			84	1,647,927	410,121	410,121	
			85	1,194,072	278,938	278,938	
			86	1,797,212	404,029	404,029	
CHINA M	V	E	82	427,437	73,589	103,598	30,009
			84	94,980	21,103	28,108	7,005
			85	512,012	112,066	142,005	29,939
	V	W	81	440,956	94,388	111,330	16,942
			82	503,802	103,653	122,417	18,764
			83	16,992	6,298	7,161	863
CHINA T	N	W	84	13,542,517	2,986,506	3,464,675	478,169
	V	E	81	98,812	20,039	27,225	7,186
			82	851,608	180,471	234,590	54,119
			83	1,502,040	327,537	404,346	76,809
			84	5,548,484	1,184,897	1,537,102	352,205
			85	1,857,054	421,038	532,934	111,896
			86	8,545,372	1,544,664	1,912,346	367,682
	V	W	81	853,030	202,323	230,206	27,883
			82	3,200,532	681,452	794,931	113,479
			83	5,013,461	1,122,367	1,305,383	183,016
			84	11,472,731	2,515,935	2,926,633	410,698
			85	11,759,021	2,495,421	2,924,966	429,545
			86	2,906,438	551,719	629,834	78,115
COLOMB	V	E	82	4,849	3,592	3,857	265
			84	2,100	1,590	1,759	169
			85	38,445	5,728	8,198	2,470
DENMARK	A	E	82	65	303	366	63
	V	E	82	39,683	6,360	8,106	1,746
			83	129,704	22,528	29,466	6,938
			85	151,200	18,368	28,800	10,432
DOM REP	V	E	82	1,500	400	535	135
			84	95,848	29,476	35,696	6,220
			85	47,170	13,488	16,030	2,542
FR GERM	A	E	81	645	645	700	55
			83	10,024	25,886	29,872	3,986
	V	E	84	19,003	3,997	4,723	726
			85	120,079	16,222	22,246	6,024
			86	31,429	13,219	14,766	1,547
	V	W	86	368	2,740	2,859	119
FRANCE	V	E	81	394	994	1,049	55
			82	114,725	24,802	31,910	7,108
			83	573	748	798	50
			84	89,793	28,636	29,873	1,237
			85	46,414	25,427	28,241	2,814
			86	175,769	20,836	29,539	8,703
	V	W	83	574	373	446	73
			84	165	758	822	64
			85	44,907	13,695	14,917	1,222
			86	675	2,855	3,158	303
GREECE	O	E	83	1,140	311	311	
	V	E	81	12,820	6,670	8,037	1,367
			82	1,653	653	706	53
			83	2,925	1,125	1,270	145

Crop Product TSUSA commodity number, description, and unit of quantity Country	Mode	Reg	Yr	Quantity	F.A.S.	C.I.F.	Charges
			84	41,006	9,300	11,400	2,100
			85	182,325	39,100	53,232	14,132
			86	86,619	15,280	21,998	6,718
GUATMAL	V	E	86	7,200	2,700	3,188	488
ICELAND	V	E	85	828,802	151,025	193,252	42,227
			86	192,005	50,524	64,175	13,651
INDIA	O	E	85	2,381	2,768	3,163	395
	V	E	81	1,825	1,978	2,441	463
			82	4,764	5,197	6,571	1,374
			83	1,351	1,666	1,932	266
			84	1,905	2,289	2,592	303
			86	2,357	2,795	3,163	368
	V	W	82	2,064	2,274	2,795	521
			85	1,787	2,028	2,530	502
			86	2,381	2,795	3,163	368
ISRAEL	N	E	82	490,733	102,192	126,869	24,677
			83	21,292,613	4,983,171	6,064,235	1,081,064
			84	13,269,622	3,128,436	3,783,905	655,469
			85	14,108,977	2,911,458	3,602,661	691,203
	O	E	82	39,000	7,500	9,264	1,764
	V	E	81	14,355,621	2,893,520	3,597,538	708,409
			82	23,754,482	5,295,786	6,517,081	1,221,295
			83	26,365,580	5,881,957	7,147,460	1,265,503
			84	20,969,237	4,621,575	5,635,340	1,013,765
			85	19,642,230	4,039,441	5,019,758	980,317
			86	24,423,195	4,629,534	5,821,536	1,192,002
	V	W	82	429,589	92,650	119,143	26,493
			83	1,114,249	273,924	349,350	75,426
			84	690,980	167,580	208,180	40,600
			85	194,663	39,348	51,445	12,097
			86	1,758,514	375,206	467,327	92,121
ITALY	A	E	83	951	1,875	2,524	649
			84	787	1,807	2,298	491
	N	E	81	54,297,586	10,733,642	14,169,835	3,436,193
			82	70,585,830	14,327,501	18,648,873	4,321,372
			83	55,697,232	12,094,331	15,278,985	3,184,654
			84	81,955,962	19,098,032	23,935,704	4,837,672
			85	83,660,432	16,569,808	21,431,401	4,861,593
			86	94,041,772	17,776,756	22,758,146	4,981,390
	N	W	84	2,033,828	625,335	801,005	175,670
	O	E	81	410	2,007	2,007	
			82	33,000	8,626	9,160	534
			83	69,817	22,468	26,140	3,672
			84	90,804	21,348	24,337	2,989
			85	2,399,027	675,815	1,015,006	339,191
			86	2,991,427	917,392	1,341,171	423,779
	O	W	83	31,500	8,715	12,952	4,237
	V	E	81	2,675,783	544,360	716,945	172,585
			82	6,120,221	1,302,588	1,703,139	400,551
			83	4,555,822	1,119,620	1,427,614	307,994
			84	7,291,898	1,869,075	2,366,315	497,240
			85	5,977,394	1,277,415	1,675,131	397,716
			86	9,313,164	1,776,120	2,341,029	564,909
	V	W	81	142,153	28,805	43,442	14,637
			82	476,693	128,263	174,959	46,696
			83	501,149	142,609	182,199	39,590
			84	37,790	13,976	16,720	2,744
			85	4,895,674	1,271,121	1,646,605	375,484
			86	1,242,580	415,304	502,906	87,602
JAPAN	V	E	82	70,470	13,092	17,311	4,219
			83	311,114	74,998	90,713	15,715
			86	44,753	4,756	7,024	2,268
	V	W	83	16,762	3,860	4,223	363
			84	76,830	14,365	16,445	2,080
MEXICO	O	E	81	6,253	5,067	5,067	
			82	25,080	4,628	4,628	
			83	102,794	13,792	13,792	
			85	214,661	57,161	57,161	
			86	3,872	1,680	1,680	
	O	W	81	296,864	110,535	110,535	
			82	67,369	28,438	28,438	
			84	1,522	406	406	
			85	50,745	12,935	12,935	
	V	W	81	6,698	2,886	2,891	5
NETHLDS	V	E	84	8,961	2,284	2,873	589
			85	47,210	8,337	11,531	3,194
			86	260,287	40,310	53,847	13,537
NORWAY	V	E	82	242,859	49,664	62,366	12,702
PERU	V	E	84	34,722	6,580	7,710	1,130
			85	812,982	189,700	231,095	41,395
			86	802,133	173,075	212,275	39,200
PHIL R	V	E	82	40,278	6,415	8,531	2,116
	V	W	82	720	452	506	54
POLAND	V	E	85	34,105	5,150	7,050	1,900

Crop Product TSUSA commodity number, description, and unit of quantity Country	Mode	Reg	Yr	Quantity	F.A.S.	C.I.F.	Charges
			86	37,919	5,595	7,500	1,905
PORTUGL	N	E	85	209,447	36,425	46,145	9,720
	O	E	84	13,795	700	718	18
	V	E	82	1,004,401	249,968	312,682	62,714
			83	186,101	45,221	51,620	6,399
			84	504,226	105,414	127,935	22,521
			85	388,423	72,631	92,584	19,953
			86	768,884	141,863	184,212	42,349
REP SAF	V	E	82	84,000	11,598	15,962	4,364
			86	27,000	5,500	7,513	2,013
SPAIN	A	E	86	41,072	5,850	5,960	110
	N	E	81	12,399,264	2,174,132	2,831,578	657,446
			82	2,060,976	335,225	437,711	102,486
			83	24,279,346	4,269,853	5,552,189	1,282,336
			84	35,549,810	6,427,709	8,424,738	1,997,029
			85	36,801,290	6,059,322	8,350,923	2,291,601
			86	7,433,484	1,175,451	1,620,712	445,261
	O	E	83	135,372	77,661	77,661	
			86	102,103	11,364	16,339	4,975
	V	E	81	11,187,664	2,038,585	2,662,398	623,813
			82	54,712,787	9,523,048	12,512,249	2,989,201
			83	35,807,002	6,035,228	7,892,051	1,856,823
			84	35,916,445	6,166,862	8,224,567	2,057,705
			85	32,966,392	4,634,478	6,607,219	1,972,741
			86	40,310,788	6,199,779	8,482,407	2,282,628
	V	W	82	493,851	84,606	116,804	32,198
			83	582,629	97,620	132,701	35,081
			84	2,142,387	346,840	481,339	134,499
			85	624,582	75,936	118,502	42,566
			86	165,150	28,114	41,905	13,791
SWITZLD	A	E	82	2,632	3,603	5,073	1,470
THAILND	V	E	84	2,403	1,886	2,202	316
	V	W	84	68,652	17,300	22,409	5,109
TURKEY	V	E	81	39,375	6,413	8,574	2,161
			84	82,540	17,472	21,341	3,869
U KING	V	E	83	36,540	5,407	7,026	1,619
			84	550	312	397	85
			85	75,226	11,803	16,116	4,313
	V	W	83	1,769	2,155	2,603	448
			85	1,650	1,470	1,664	194
USSR	V	E	81	5,026	1,070	1,231	161
VENEZ	V	E	84	36,168	13,020	14,137	1,117
			86	42,857	6,364	7,713	1,349
YUGOSLV	O	E	85	132,000	12,489	23,907	11,418

Tomato, sauce

1416540 TOMATO SAUCE (INCLUDE PULP) (LB)

Country	Mode	Reg	Yr	Quantity	F.A.S.	C.I.F.	Charges
TOTAL			81	9,116,339	2,071,773	2,570,097	498,324
			82	21,824,299	5,398,795	6,531,856	1,133,061
			83	23,626,127	5,617,463	6,708,661	1,091,198
			84	28,000,486	7,143,404	8,551,662	1,408,258
			85	33,585,701	8,446,930	10,715,367	2,268,437
			86	31,589,972	7,337,643	9,298,488	1,960,845
ARGENT	V	E	85	16,067	4,338	4,986	648
AUSTRAL	A	W	84	296	429	804	375
BRAZIL	V	E	82	66,773	15,346	22,046	6,700
			83	31,482	12,676	14,872	2,196
			84	31,500	13,528	15,681	2,153
			85	31,500	13,528	15,466	1,938
CANADA	O	E	81	43,424	10,125	10,125	
			82	407,295	102,312	102,312	
			83	761,796	169,483	169,483	
			84	337,430	76,703	76,703	
			85	22,950	5,598	5,598	
			86	337,859	77,574	77,574	
CHILE	V	E	82	32,356	12,862	14,592	1,730
			83	72,500	23,490	26,821	3,331
CHINA M	V	W	84	441	284	311	27
CHINA T	O	E	83	362,964	127,020	144,942	17,922
	V	E	81	569	428	452	24
			82	35,496	12,070	14,523	2,453
			83	201,292	45,241	55,940	10,699
			84	34,111	7,350	9,055	1,705
	V	W	83	1,101,310	240,011	275,233	35,222
			84	91,800	28,900	32,700	3,800
			85	133,813	37,235	42,418	5,183
			86	150,099	26,452	30,248	3,796
DOM REP	V	E	81	375	325	337	12
			84	169,892	66,417	74,231	7,814
			85	54,686	15,639	17,502	1,863
			86	25,760	11,650	13,505	1,855

Crop
Product
TSUSA commodity number, description, and unit of quantity

Country	Mode	Reg	Yr	Quantity	F.A.S.	C.I.F.	Charges
DOMINCA	V	E	85	1,440	1,400	1,528	128
			86	5,300	4,050	4,730	680
FR GERM	V	E	84	153,003	37,492	43,652	6,160
			85	40,000	6,463	7,992	1,529
FRANCE	A	E	84	634	948	1,836	888
	V	E	81	1,790	1,015	1,210	195
			83	1,539	905	1,054	149
			84	794	1,040	1,114	74
			86	1,101	3,002	3,126	124
	V	W	83	3,273	4,935	5,211	276
GREECE	V	E	83	40,500	9,000	11,629	2,629
			86	9,520	2,550	2,867	317
HG KONG	O	E	85	83,809	23,989	25,154	1,165
	V	E	85	245,080	70,151	93,559	23,408
HUNGARY	V	E	84	4,448	646	960	314
ICELAND	V	E	85	120,300	21,036	26,807	5,771
			86	116,027	28,934	34,961	6,027
ISRAEL	A	E	83	922	270	1,398	1,128
	N	E	85	8,341,601	1,549,974	1,939,854	389,880
	O	E	85	36,150	5,035	7,286	2,251
	V	E	81	8,008,791	1,686,414	2,094,182	407,768
			82	18,954,172	4,474,219	5,441,821	967,602
			83	16,439,988	3,896,996	4,667,533	770,537
			84	18,200,994	4,242,274	5,079,460	837,186
			85	5,702,813	1,030,899	1,316,424	285,525
			86	12,888,636	2,305,008	2,872,517	567,509
	V	W	83	35,715	9,444	11,460	2,016
			84	75,601	17,344	21,811	4,467
ITALY	A	W	86	220	1,123	1,782	659
	N	E	84	2,760,343	1,096,504	1,297,995	201,491
			86	4,882,679	1,245,093	1,573,679	328,586
	O	E	82	7,040	1,990	2,035	45
			84	41,905	16,012	19,112	3,100
			85	2,435,772	657,685	867,150	209,465
			86	4,412,938	1,666,789	2,193,430	526,641
	V	E	81	107,298	25,196	31,237	6,041
			82	790,900	288,304	338,241	49,937
			83	2,632,511	637,327	787,384	150,057
			84	41,871	13,260	16,654	3,394
			85	8,745,522	3,088,130	3,959,248	871,118
			86	1,401,609	303,291	383,360	80,069
	V	W	84	5,743	3,109	3,776	667
			85	1,053,472	423,257	498,018	74,761
			86	143,348	36,061	43,758	7,697
JAPAN	V	E	82	78,042	17,350	21,355	4,005
			83	39,683	8,601	10,780	2,179
			85	78,829	16,136	20,420	4,284
	V	W	85	625,010	140,000	174,973	34,973
MEXICO	O	E	83	44,000	8,000	8,000	
			84	272,500	98,236	98,236	
	O	W	82	3,557	732	732	
			86	23,115	4,974	4,974	
NETHLDS	A	E	84	6,159	348	415	67
	V	E	83	19,842	4,081	4,725	644
			85	39,332	6,552	8,387	1,835
PERU	A	E	82	1,186	485	668	183
PHIL R	V	W	82	131	330	379	49
			84	3,600	1,720	2,000	280
PORTUGL	O	E	84	12,150	2,800	2,872	72
	V	E	81	857,052	329,540	405,249	75,709
			82	1,374,169	461,391	557,897	96,506
			83	806,857	211,183	247,585	36,402
			84	852,042	179,063	218,341	39,278
			85	1,359,638	248,039	320,310	72,271
			86	1,696,888	305,673	395,989	90,316
	V	W	84	35,100	7,796	10,080	2,284
REP SAF	V	E	85	41,888	14,745	19,490	4,745
ROMANIA	V	E	81	96,500	18,450	26,992	8,542
SALVADR	V	E	85	10,625	5,000	6,047	1,047
SPAIN	V	E	82	73,182	11,404	15,255	3,851
			83	826,044	151,572	196,639	45,067
			84	4,868,129	1,231,201	1,523,863	292,662
			85	4,279,887	1,047,710	1,317,799	270,089
			86	5,413,376	1,300,729	1,643,585	342,856
	V	W	85	43,652	4,570	7,416	2,846
SWITZLD	V	E	83	41,072	25,547	29,687	4,140
THAILND	V	E	81	540	280	313	33
TURKEY	V	E	83	162,837	31,681	38,285	6,604
			86	81,497	14,690	18,403	3,713
U KING	V	E	85	40,068	6,854	8,479	1,625
YUGOSLV	V	E	85	1,797	2,967	3,056	89

Crop
Product
TSUSA commodity number, description, and unit of quantity

Tonka Bean

Coumarin
4133200 COUMARIN (LB)

Country	Mode	Reg	Yr	Quantity	F.A.S.	C.I.F.	Charges
TOTAL			81	338,758	1,407,029	1,464,735	57,706
			82	180,454	801,673	832,204	30,531
			83	360,238	1,420,057	1,479,853	59,796
			84	190,151	765,632	792,323	26,691
			85	432,493	1,838,546	1,903,273	64,727
			86	230,324	936,456	965,444	28,988
CHINA M	N	E	84	124,559	495,159	512,787	17,628
	O	E	81	66,028	256,917	268,334	11,417
			82	61,329	268,076	277,839	9,763
			83	104,056	394,317	411,431	17,114
			84	55,776	223,130	230,161	7,031
			85	188,793	797,116	826,948	29,832
	V	E	81	69,224	270,275	281,952	11,677
			82	8,818	40,916	42,210	1,294
			83	205,027	813,724	846,925	33,201
			85	210,532	853,742	883,508	29,766
			86	227,152	915,424	942,458	27,034
	V	W	81	132,276	519,324	540,262	20,938
			82	94,797	404,738	421,417	16,679
			83	45,855	182,908	190,860	7,952
			84	4,409	19,875	20,602	727
CHINA T	O	E	81	22,046	104,718	107,726	3,008
FR GERM	A	E	81	1	1,815	1,830	15
			82	100	13,722	13,820	98
			83	9	3,262	3,275	13
			84	6	1,401	1,413	12
			86	528	2,555	2,880	325
	N	E	83	1,323	6,016	6,409	393
	V	E	85	1,984	9,327	9,480	153
FRANCE	O	E	86	882	4,434	4,534	100
	V	E	81	441	3,064	3,344	280
			82	991	6,111	6,416	305
			83	3,968	19,830	20,953	1,123
			84	5,401	26,067	27,360	1,293
			85	17,957	83,936	86,615	2,679
			86	1,101	10,743	11,222	479
HG KONG	A	E	86	661	3,300	4,350	1,050
JAPAN	O	E	82	14,330	66,330	68,591	2,261
	V	W	81	4,286	47,086	48,392	1,306
MALAYSA	O	E	85	2,204	50,600	51,493	893
NETHLDS	V	E	81	44,092	200,873	209,642	8,769
SWITZLD	A	E	82	88	1,517	1,645	128
	O	E	82	1	263	266	3
	V	E	85	11,023	43,825	45,229	1,404
U KING	A	E	81	364	2,957	3,253	296

Tonka bean
1931000 TONKA BEANS (LB)

Country	Mode	Reg	Yr	Quantity	F.A.S.	C.I.F.	Charges
TOTAL			81	42,974	126,301	133,872	7,571
			82	48,925	188,868	195,846	6,978
			83	93,946	328,667	342,937	14,270
			84	78,926	266,443	276,658	10,215
			85	11,111	32,848	34,284	1,436
			86	34,148	108,310	111,962	3,652
BRAZIL	V	E	81	9,558	41,210	43,034	1,824
			82	42,695	173,133	179,647	6,514
			83	48,494	193,224	201,478	8,254
			84	35,582	134,469	139,288	4,819
			86	2,205	7,743	8,045	302
BULGAR	V	E	83	8,642	1,420	3,142	1,722
ITALY	V	E	84	2,183	8,941	9,452	511
			85	4,409	12,671	13,440	769
			86	3,438	14,468	15,238	770
JAPAN	V	E	82	395	307	344	37
TRINID	V	E	81	14,330	36,130	38,643	2,513
			84	3,000	8,190	9,869	1,679
VENEZ	N	E	83	19,137	57,485	59,826	2,341
	V	E	81	19,086	48,961	52,195	3,234
			82	5,835	15,428	15,855	427
			83	17,673	76,538	78,491	1,953
			84	38,161	114,843	118,049	3,206
			85	6,702	20,177	20,844	667
			86	28,505	86,099	88,679	2,580

Crop Product TSUSA commodity number, description, and unit of quantity Country	Mode	Reg	Yr	Quantity	F.A.S.	C.I.F.	Charges

Tragacanth

Tragacanth, gum
1883840 TRAGACANTH GUM, NATURAL (LB)

Country	Mode	Reg	Yr	Quantity	F.A.S.	C.I.F.	Charges
TOTAL			81	641,325	1,988,355	2,144,255	155,900
			82	293,453	1,810,836	1,850,304	39,468
			83	219,594	1,957,524	2,010,630	53,106
			84	260,807	2,041,958	2,083,698	41,740
			85	387,115	2,255,616	2,314,078	58,462
			86	343,747	2,029,401	2,093,087	63,686
BRAZIL	V	E	81	470,823	693,005	811,848	118,843
			82	143,299	214,949	229,231	14,282
			85	17,837	26,528	28,550	2,022
			86	110,245	152,403	162,104	9,701
FR GERM	N	E	85	36,850	161,633	166,438	4,805
			86	60,352	663,852	671,235	7,383
	V	E	84	10,679	88,827	89,477	650
FRANCE	A	E	82	55	397	465	68
			85	1,900	15,170	15,631	461
	O	E	83	2,750	20,913	21,999	1,086
			84	2,090	17,138	18,307	1,169
	V	E	83	2,200	16,700	17,599	899
			84	1,650	13,006	13,846	840
			86	3,758	29,625	30,469	844
INDIA	V	E	81	21,332	19,714	21,362	1,648
IRAN	N	E	81	55,132	719,395	731,753	12,358
			83	173,024	1,563,911	1,603,360	39,449
			86	94,428	883,684	917,153	33,469
	V	E	81	17,600	138,600	142,603	4,003
			82	139,175	1,522,092	1,544,562	22,470
			84	126,915	1,358,970	1,384,400	25,430
			85	159,759	1,725,941	1,760,749	34,808
JAPAN	V	E	82	6,482	32,458	34,104	1,646
			85	2,205	55,105	56,095	990
	V	W	86	17,600	21,120	22,719	1,599
PAKISTN	V	E	84	40,000	11,700	14,391	2,691
			85	114,000	38,783	47,084	8,301
TUNISIA	V	E	85	3,704	26,158	26,681	523
TURKEY	O	E	84	107	1,285	1,285	
	V	E	81	76,438	417,641	436,689	19,048
			82	4,442	40,940	41,942	1,002
			83	41,620	356,000	367,672	11,672
			84	79,366	551,032	561,992	10,960
			85	50,860	206,298	212,850	6,552
			86	57,364	278,717	289,407	10,690

Truffle

Truffle, fresh or dried or prepared or preserved
1443000 TRUFFLES FRESH DRIED ETC (LB)

Country	Mode	Reg	Yr	Quantity	F.A.S.	C.I.F.	Charges
TOTAL			81	27,336	1,432,672	1,487,026	54,354
			82	23,861	1,096,911	1,142,882	45,971
			83	40,711	1,332,665	1,403,957	71,292
			84	55,367	2,251,115	2,354,482	103,367
			85	68,013	2,728,783	2,837,436	108,653
			86	68,193	3,017,253	3,151,003	133,750
AUSTRAL	A	H	86	462	1,155	1,468	313
BELGIUM	A	W	84	4	380	420	40
	O	E	86	945	2,147	2,147	
CANADA	A	E	81	4	831	925	94
	A	W	84	1,235	2,223	2,683	460
			85	1,500	3,380	3,661	281
	O	E	81	33	7,870	7,870	
CHILE	A	W	83	3,300	15,657	18,150	2,493
CHINA M	V	W	81	100	9,828	12,111	2,283
			85	6,959	25,981	29,349	3,368
CHINA T	A	E	86	6	2,139	2,673	534
	V	W	86	3,908	16,904	17,678	774
FR GERM	A	W	84	18	1,896	2,015	119
	V	E	83	3	361	362	1
FRANCE	A	E	81	1,325	60,208	63,026	2,818
			82	1,817	82,977	87,634	4,657
			83	3,279	129,050	139,101	10,051
			84	3,625	134,708	145,761	11,053
			85	3,384	129,490	138,119	8,629
			86	3,619	246,858	253,397	6,539

Country	Mode	Reg	Yr	Quantity	F.A.S.	C.I.F.	Charges
	A	W	81	34	4,769	5,067	298
			83	35	3,494	3,843	349
			84	55	4,973	5,397	424
			85	259	12,165	14,264	2,099
			86	1,153	34,263	36,080	1,817
	N	E	81	12,628	542,407	560,943	18,536
			82	7,439	250,661	260,537	9,876
			83	15,742	534,760	558,183	23,423
			84	16,963	587,176	608,641	21,465
			85	18,902	473,785	496,728	22,943
			86	7,744	498,064	521,652	23,588
	N	W	81	5,960	320,193	334,314	14,121
			82	6,451	247,684	259,242	11,558
			83	6,749	205,704	218,237	12,533
			84	9,598	273,579	288,668	15,089
			85	9,499	252,532	263,452	10,920
			86	7,416	267,575	278,257	10,682
	O	E	81	28	6,703	6,703	
			82	862	27,306	28,192	886
			84	222	6,374	7,024	650
	V	E	81	35	6,669	6,925	256
			82	1,467	70,384	72,653	2,269
			83	3,277	32,821	34,261	1,440
			84	3,499	23,654	25,841	2,187
			85	1,358	46,574	47,892	1,318
			86	4,284	97,854	100,887	3,033
	V	W	81	775	33,703	35,458	1,755
			82	286	11,138	11,687	549
			83	38	1,983	2,096	113
			84	271	2,407	2,613	206
			85	252	11,380	12,109	729
GREECE	A	E	85	106	9,120	9,364	244
ITALY	A	E	81	250	30,499	32,250	1,751
			82	249	44,296	45,855	1,559
			83	399	27,666	28,767	1,101
			84	10,917	924,148	960,836	36,688
			85	588	36,491	38,624	2,133
			86	17,580	1,329,429	1,396,951	67,522
	A	W	82	188	24,974	26,037	1,063
			83	328	26,046	28,036	1,990
			84	2,504	132,381	140,647	8,266
			85	1,349	197,126	200,179	3,053
			86	279	23,840	25,197	1,357
	N	E	81	5,853	396,334	407,468	11,134
			82	4,574	331,413	344,565	13,152
			83	4,027	301,659	315,702	14,043
			85	14,011	1,028,233	1,070,198	41,965
	N	W	83	129	11,739	12,959	1,220
			86	2,474	147,312	150,835	3,523
	O	E	81	147	9,441	10,366	925
	V	E	81	10	1,289	1,482	193
			82	13	1,115	1,196	81
			84	670	2,198	2,400	202
			85	1,261	1,948	2,054	106
JAPAN	A	W	86	159	20,008	20,400	392
	V	W	81	44	262	290	28
			83	151	665	709	44
			84	1,980	3,235	3,376	141
KOR REP	V	W	86	1,304	11,878	14,528	2,650
LEBANON	V	E	83	1,403	9,365	9,938	573
			84	1,799	8,976	9,477	501
			85	992	5,097	5,459	362
			86	1,316	6,944	8,727	1,783
MEXICO	O	W	83	172	258	258	
NETHLDS	A	E	81	1	393	395	2
			82	98	1,784	1,958	174
			83	6	1,019	1,125	106
			84	25	3,533	3,595	62
	V	E	82	361	2,074	2,151	77
			83	477	2,797	2,873	76
	V	W	83	244	1,424	1,505	81
PHIL R	V	W	81	109	1,273	1,433	160
			82	56	1,105	1,175	70
			83	289	1,187	1,312	125
PORTUGL	A	E	84	29	3,750	3,893	143
SENEGAL	A	E	84	26	2,786	3,461	675
			86	6	1,202	1,208	6
SPAIN	A	E	83	162	9,979	10,150	171
			84	1,617	128,871	133,658	4,787
			85	6,298	445,707	454,148	8,441
			86	823	159,743	160,923	1,180
	N	W	85	947	31,144	32,804	1,660
			86	1,487	48,748	50,801	2,053
	V	E	86	13,228	101,190	107,194	6,004

Crop Product TSUSA commodity number, description, and unit of quantity Country	Mode	Reg	Yr	Quantity	F.A.S.	C.I.F.	Charges
SWITZLD	A	E	84	286	1,854	1,998	144
			85	176	9,850	10,168	318
	N	E	83	501	15,031	16,390	1,359
U KING	A	E	84	24	2,013	2,078	65
	V	E	85	172	8,780	8,864	84

Tulip

Tulip, bulbs
1250100 TULIP BULBS (NO)

Country	Mode	Reg	Yr	Quantity	F.A.S.	C.I.F.	Charges
TOTAL			81	180,607,689	14,638,138	15,941,839	1,298,087
			82	186,206,178	15,106,608	16,559,275	1,452,667
			83	204,997,835	15,374,041	16,870,579	1,496,538
			84	246,714,819	17,953,328	20,082,048	2,128,720
			85	287,893,116	19,743,684	22,173,544	2,429,860
			86	287,375,810	21,994,145	24,453,438	2,459,293
ALBANIA	V	E	85	170,000	10,016	12,220	2,204
AUSTRAL	A	E	86	35,000	9,828	11,656	1,828
BELGIUM	V	E	83	243,225	34,231	35,633	1,402
			84	283,165	9,975	11,304	1,329
CANADA	O	E	81	28,000	1,860	1,860	
			82	8,123	4,291	4,291	
			84	144	313	313	
			85	60,538	26,512	26,512	
			86	18,014	8,674	8,674	
	O	W	85	170,430	8,777	8,777	
			86	19,000	12,621	12,942	321
CHINA T	V	E	85	15,840	1,535	1,707	172
FR GERM	V	E	85	2,224,280	169,764	201,866	32,102
FRANCE	V	E	81	10,200	552	594	42
			82	82,480	6,558	7,313	755
			84	165,596	15,004	16,721	1,717
ISRAEL	V	E	81	231,590	20,504	22,540	2,036
			82	1,098,993	83,970	92,162	8,192
			83	1,347,360	105,478	123,614	18,136
			84	1,006,000	91,940	101,032	9,092
			85	2,679,888	245,640	262,093	16,453
	V	W	84	119,814	11,523	13,520	1,997
JAPAN	N	W	85	276,250	14,603	16,173	1,570
			86	282,628	21,070	22,693	1,623
	O	W	83	197,150	10,158	11,502	1,344
	V	E	81	198,000	12,590	14,060	1,470
			82	300,000	11,050	12,751	1,701
			83	573,000	23,163	27,225	4,062
			85	1,107,000	40,752	51,427	10,675
			86	1,245,000	55,680	65,598	9,918
	V	W	81	1,915,050	120,274	128,435	12,447
			82	1,181,950	83,471	94,143	10,672
			83	1,277,900	50,193	58,392	8,199
			84	1,682,050	71,891	84,952	13,061
			85	1,833,500	76,247	88,490	12,243
			86	1,252,300	57,276	66,687	9,411
KOR REP	V	E	83	93,150	9,466	10,352	886
	V	W	85	14,100	9,179	9,742	563
MALI	V	E	85	730,200	39,287	46,496	7,209
			86	1,074,867	49,391	58,609	9,218
NETHLDS	A	E	81	88,600	7,214	8,281	1,067
			82	542,127	48,438	65,401	16,963
			83	311,682	22,453	29,447	6,994
			84	247,579	13,639	20,138	6,499
			85	52,658	12,687	22,852	10,165
			86	110,248	11,277	15,097	3,820
	A	W	83	52,650	4,290	6,978	2,688
			84	42,050	6,772	8,323	1,551
	N	E	81	133,436,228	11,186,505	12,155,861	959,456
			82	138,722,579	11,417,884	12,468,332	1,050,448
			83	151,783,441	11,823,518	12,909,487	1,085,969
			84	178,354,312	13,670,377	15,234,829	1,564,452
			85	212,936,578	14,791,242	16,517,433	1,726,191
			86	210,757,331	16,678,943	18,469,066	1,790,123
	N	W	82	5,675,577	395,799	467,988	72,189
			83	8,759,867	600,244	690,269	90,025
			84	13,399,387	830,533	987,740	157,207
			85	12,586,363	692,747	833,442	140,695
			86	4,801,749	372,566	429,088	56,522
	O	E	81	153,877	19,478	19,478	
			82	206,947	21,857	22,220	363
			83	215,657	19,762	20,967	1,205
			84	304,963	15,984	17,319	1,335

Crop Product TSUSA commodity number, description, and unit of quantity Country	Mode	Reg	Yr	Quantity	F.A.S.	C.I.F.	Charges
			85	1,018,988	77,885	78,719	834
			86	635,565	57,888	57,888	
	V	E	81	33,050,654	2,480,114	2,699,578	219,464
			82	33,377,745	2,698,825	2,943,676	244,851
			83	38,702,209	2,579,221	2,841,601	262,380
			84	49,460,446	3,116,642	3,468,662	352,020
			85	49,235,734	3,360,373	3,796,865	436,492
			86	53,135,893	3,673,026	4,117,899	444,873
	V	W	81	10,661,908	741,637	838,530	96,893
			82	4,155,207	271,974	311,012	39,038
			83	1,157,594	71,928	83,539	11,611
			84	997,324	64,959	76,905	11,946
			85	2,780,769	166,438	198,730	32,292
			86	14,008,215	985,905	1,117,541	131,636
NORFOLK	V	E	81	569,800	28,447	31,974	3,527
U KING	A	E	84	163,450	9,579	13,885	4,306
	A	W	82	15,000	1,189	1,647	458
	V	E	81	171,000	9,933	11,222	1,289
			82	426,000	29,069	32,069	3,000
			83	282,950	19,936	21,573	1,637
			84	488,539	24,197	26,405	2,208
	V	W	81	92,782	9,030	9,426	396
YEMEN S	V	E	82	413,450	32,233	36,270	4,037

Tung

Tung, nut
1755400 TUNG NUTS (LB)

Country	Mode	Reg	Yr	Quantity	F.A.S.	C.I.F.	Charges
TOTAL			85	43,530	3,504	3,504	
CANADA	O	E	85	43,530	3,504	3,504	

Tung, vegetable oil
1766000 TUNG OIL (LB)

Country	Mode	Reg	Yr	Quantity	F.A.S.	C.I.F.	Charges
TOTAL			81	15,032,617	8,039,043	8,524,080	485,037
			82	14,399,199	8,016,469	8,542,513	526,044
			83	13,634,967	7,795,878	8,227,221	431,343
			84	13,928,118	12,461,220	12,889,282	428,062
			85	15,297,688	6,581,462	7,075,055	493,593
			86	11,690,086	3,733,518	4,124,935	391,417
ARGENT	O	E	84	45,000	55,029	55,029	
	V	E	81	8,879,217	4,676,902	4,937,250	260,348
			82	9,525,579	4,789,820	5,140,956	351,136
			83	8,278,073	4,502,664	4,740,697	238,033
			84	7,015,154	6,085,569	6,231,187	145,618
			85	11,428,611	4,902,159	5,243,309	341,150
			86	9,376,805	3,003,205	3,269,956	266,751
	V	W	81	412,208	225,024	244,080	19,056
			82	108,766	76,010	87,067	11,057
			83	74,655	43,596	49,653	6,057
			85	88,720	62,861	70,189	7,328
AUSTRAL	V	E	86	95,370	14,472	19,827	5,355
BRAZIL	O	E	83	4,200	4,724	4,724	
	V	E	81	2,579	2,046	2,203	157
			82	275,707	178,865	183,595	4,730
			83	1,477,012	587,629	630,135	42,506
	V	W	82	424,180	270,801	288,442	17,641
CANADA	O	E	84	2,379	2,540	2,540	
			86	5,254	1,893	1,893	
CHINA M	V	E	83	207,387	187,902	208,219	20,317
			84	602,084	661,703	699,863	38,160
			85	130,688	80,394	93,957	13,563
			86	192,276	85,832	99,941	14,109
	V	W	81	110,230	62,491	71,321	8,830
			82	132,277	72,659	89,084	16,425
			83	196,808	140,599	156,672	16,073
			84	865,819	867,818	938,218	70,400
			85	163,372	85,621	99,145	13,524
			86	686,166	270,739	326,856	56,117
CHINA T	V	E	84	100,234	112,156	119,076	6,920
	V	W	82	36,050	23,669	24,026	357
			84	236,111	247,988	264,285	16,297
HG KONG	V	W	84	418	655	742	87
MALAWI	V	E	81	312,541	148,376	168,054	19,678
MOZAMBQ	V	E	81	34,727	14,098	16,974	2,876
N ZEAL	A	H	86	891	1,452	2,261	809
NETHLDS	V	E	83	880,501	790,590	819,706	29,116
			85	68,784	33,815	38,688	4,873

Crop Product TSUSA commodity number, description, and unit of quantity Country	Mode	Reg	Yr	Quantity	F.A.S.	C.I.F.	Charges
NORWAY	V E		84	670	685	740	55
PARAGUA	V E		81	5,070,797	2,811,266	2,970,354	159,088
			82	3,832,173	2,568,883	2,688,240	119,357
			83	2,516,331	1,538,174	1,617,415	79,241
			84	5,059,746	4,426,726	4,577,211	150,485
			85	3,353,095	1,381,494	1,489,116	107,622
			86	1,214,276	277,517	317,613	40,096
	V W		81	30,864	17,260	19,673	2,413
			82	64,467	35,762	41,103	5,341
			85	31,746	19,467	21,904	2,437
SPAIN	V E		86	119,048	78,408	86,588	8,180
SWITZLD	V W		85	32,672	15,651	18,747	3,096
U KING	O E		84	503	351	391	40
ZAMBIA	V E		81	110,000	57,889	65,282	7,393
ZMBABWE	V E		81	69,454	23,691	28,889	5,198

Turmeric

Tumeric, spice
1621300 TURMERIC (LB)

Country	Mode	Reg	Yr	Quantity	F.A.S.	C.I.F.	Charges
TOTAL			81	4,105,955	1,130,657	1,466,991	336,334
			82	3,536,514	946,759	1,235,539	288,780
			83	3,527,523	1,368,647	1,602,330	233,683
			84	3,944,130	2,155,036	2,437,201	282,165
			85	4,630,200	2,661,140	2,963,740	302,600
			86	4,285,304	2,576,430	2,850,354	273,924
AUSTRAL	O W		84	25	1,031	1,162	131
AUSTRIA	V E		84	825	866	981	115
BRAZIL	V E		83	28,665	14,300	15,821	1,521
			84	199,201	84,466	102,369	17,903
			85	128,396	65,945	76,479	10,534
			86	50,970	24,364	27,832	3,468
C RICA	V E		85	207,322	110,247	127,105	16,858
			86	170,583	92,794	104,403	11,609
CANADA	O E		81	480	559	559	
			83	53,146	40,221	40,221	
			84	22,525	19,455	19,455	
	O W		85	5,500	3,300	3,300	
CHINA M	O E		83	1,100	2,526	2,674	148
	V E		82	33,069	7,773	9,375	1,602
			83	475,265	118,776	148,846	30,070
			84	77,161	30,984	36,503	5,519
			85	142,708	52,910	61,971	9,061
			86	162,562	70,874	91,527	20,653
	V W		81	250	306	326	20
			82	44,092	8,529	11,780	3,251
			83	70,690	16,823	21,373	4,550
CHINA T	V E		86	1,679	1,482	1,603	121
FIJI	A E		82	1,900	712	1,373	661
			83	4,872	2,237	4,295	2,058
			86	21,091	9,041	18,312	9,271
	A H		81	600	363	537	174
			82	2,679	1,353	1,977	624
			83	6,124	2,628	4,057	1,429
			84	14,981	6,809	12,478	5,669
			85	2,685	1,940	2,668	728
			86	4,830	2,198	3,628	1,430
	A W		81	1,500	699	1,469	770
			82	4,345	2,868	5,824	2,956
			83	2,340	1,128	2,230	1,102
			84	3,070	1,190	2,290	1,100
			85	5,588	3,545	5,745	2,200
			86	4,500	2,085	4,423	2,338
	N W		81	26,263	10,231	13,861	3,630
			82	15,022	7,144	12,679	5,535
			83	28,225	25,555	34,254	8,699
			84	49,187	21,917	32,636	10,719
			85	22,201	8,941	12,660	3,719
			86	21,900	9,247	13,248	4,001
	V W		81	6,250	2,998	4,155	1,157
FRANCE	V E		83	113	323	340	17
GREECE	V E		86	39,899	21,899	24,399	2,500
HAITI	V E		81	22,046	2,683	4,423	1,740
			83	34,000	20,400	23,771	3,371
			84	112,131	24,711	35,581	10,870
HG KONG	V E		83	104,092	23,332	32,254	8,922
	V W		82	708	574	631	57
INDIA	N E		81	3,019,864	834,000	1,073,908	239,908
			82	2,058,378	534,125	701,006	166,881

Country	Mode	Reg	Yr	Quantity	F.A.S.	C.I.F.	Charges
			83	1,757,754	707,399	816,265	108,866
			84	2,102,417	1,366,559	1,507,052	140,493
			85	2,599,041	1,711,708	1,871,934	160,226
			86	2,535,812	1,586,313	1,726,890	140,577
	O E		81	2,860	1,558	1,621	63
			82	120,878	29,789	40,399	10,610
			83	2,234	1,566	1,788	222
			84	46,623	15,953	20,475	4,522
			85	1,500	1,800	1,800	
			86	132,277	84,657	92,441	7,784
	V E		81	483,409	118,444	159,611	41,167
			82	749,030	183,994	239,149	55,155
			83	718,304	276,975	317,542	40,567
			84	347,025	186,421	210,747	24,326
			85	457,965	312,378	339,757	27,379
			86	564,658	378,516	410,218	31,702
	V W		81	510,276	131,313	175,149	43,836
			82	295,336	79,535	105,599	26,064
			83	134,843	73,178	85,575	12,397
			84	122,383	70,808	81,648	10,840
			85	123,758	82,465	93,227	10,762
			86	156,334	99,267	110,070	10,803
INDNSIA	V E		82	77,094	29,252	35,655	6,403
			83	16,534	11,255	13,521	2,266
	V W		85	22,046	7,562	9,756	2,194
IVY CST	V E		85	108,666	17,256	21,756	4,500
JAMAICA	A E		84	2,223	333	983	650
	V E		81	19,855	11,042	13,119	2,077
			82	77,100	40,610	45,306	4,696
			83	2,970	1,188	1,429	241
			84	6,650	2,911	3,325	414
			85	183,851	78,243	90,230	11,987
JAPAN	V E		82	2,205	600	705	105
	V W		83	1,102	485	554	69
			86	6,201	2,877	3,427	550
KENYA	V W		85	1,764	1,176	1,325	149
N ZEAL	A H		81	642	458	681	223
NETHLDS	V E		84	39,000	25,750	27,429	1,679
NIGERIA	V E		85	218,196	33,600	45,150	11,550
PAKISTN	O E		84	46,279	24,381	26,597	2,216
			86	1,103	1,142	1,293	151
	V E		86	8,358	6,671	7,524	853
	V W		85	3,251	3,786	4,411	625
PERU	V E		82	44,048	6,911	9,525	2,614
			83	66,226	14,904	19,674	4,770
			84	603,050	164,369	199,416	35,047
			85	342,227	138,072	164,529	26,457
			86	370,170	159,311	183,548	24,237
PHIL R	A E		82	1,580	590	671	81
S HELNA	V E		84	145,277	100,458	109,847	9,389
SINGAPR	V W		82	2,205	841	950	109
SPAIN	V E		86	30,780	22,222	24,022	1,800
T PAC I	V W		83	6,309	2,461	3,382	921
THAILND	V E		81	1,251	3,140	3,553	413
			82	873	2,011	2,201	190
			83	2,024	3,711	4,057	346
			84	1,718	2,084	2,341	257
			85	53,535	26,266	29,937	3,671
	V W		81	2,285	5,624	6,081	457
			82	2,844	5,630	6,239	609
			83	2,997	3,294	3,528	234
			84	2,159	3,275	3,550	275
			86	1,597	1,470	1,546	76
TRINID	A E		83	125	260	300	40
TURKEY	O E		83	1,650	598	1,195	597
U KING	O E		81	8,124	7,239	7,938	699
			82	3,128	3,918	4,495	577
			83	5,819	3,124	3,384	260
			84	220	305	336	31

Turnip

Turnip, fresh or frozen**
1376600 TURNIPS OR RUTABAGAS (CWT)
   (See Rutabaga, fresh or frozen under Rutabaga)

Turnip, seed**
1268900 RUTABAGA AND TURNIP SEED (LB)
   (See Rutabaga, seed under Rutabaga)

Crop / Product / TSUSA commodity number, description, and unit of quantity — Country	Mode	Reg	Yr	Quantity	F.A.S.	C.I.F.	Charges

V

Vanilla

Vanilla, bean
1931500 VANILLA BEANS (LB)

Country	Mode	Reg	Yr	Quantity	F.A.S.	C.I.F.	Charges
TOTAL			81	1,411,417	30,952,234	31,779,127	826,893
			82	1,948,389	45,196,087	46,510,536	1,314,449
			83	2,154,780	50,811,567	52,628,576	1,817,009
			84	1,854,894	49,933,773	51,404,602	1,470,829
			85	1,638,274	47,578,308	49,159,688	1,581,380
			86	2,206,576	58,563,670	60,278,626	1,714,956
ARGENT	V	E	86	4,453	136,394	137,360	966
AUSTRAL	V	E	81	88,184	1,800,000	1,826,738	26,738
CANADA	O	E	82	99	2,976	2,976	
			83	148	4,095	4,095	
			84	55	2,061	2,061	
COMOROS	A	E	82	27,260	413,841	430,328	16,487
			83	128,831	3,417,515	3,571,896	154,381
			84	74,954	1,907,689	1,976,494	68,805
			86	37,754	1,054,017	1,109,446	55,429
	N	E	81	141,853	3,308,261	3,488,987	180,726
			82	191,164	5,101,450	5,295,392	193,942
			85	189,983	5,867,754	6,154,836	287,082
	V	E	83	1,653	46,875	47,427	552
			85	1,460	48,008	48,622	614
			86	69,914	2,186,731	2,211,202	24,471
F IND O	N	E	86	1,653	52,013	54,647	2,634
FIJI	A	H	86	2,200	63,800	66,660	2,860
FR GERM	O	E	82	40	1,508	1,836	328
	V	E	81	234	3,978	4,505	527
			82	31,901	724,305	727,248	2,943
FR POLY	A	W	82	97	3,840	3,915	75
			84	650	17,900	18,325	425
			85	1,547	27,098	30,107	3,009
			86	1,546	40,735	42,121	1,386
	V	E	81	198	7,600	7,601	1
			82	264	11,443	11,610	167
			83	1,141	40,284	41,125	841
			84	176	5,674	5,813	139
			85	751	26,992	27,919	927
			86	1,289	58,031	59,240	1,209
FRANCE	N	E	81	9,392	245,566	251,414	5,848
			82	48,998	1,238,604	1,261,054	22,450
			83	3,392	92,923	94,311	1,388
	V	E	82	1,523	38,671	39,064	393
			83	394	866	923	57
INDNSIA	A	E	81	2,347	59,075	64,559	5,484
			86	7,715	148,752	158,999	10,247
	A	H	83	1,102	15,000	17,422	2,422
	A	W	81	23,586	479,244	508,690	29,446
			82	28,151	230,359	282,346	51,987
			83	12,762	298,683	324,782	26,099
			84	11,239	230,675	252,706	22,031
			85	33,274	770,750	840,443	69,693
			86	42,438	795,578	878,470	82,892
	N	E	81	144,143	1,890,963	2,054,910	163,947
			82	142,702	1,372,653	1,601,536	228,883
			83	496,582	6,177,314	6,931,872	754,558
			84	365,824	6,911,877	7,584,402	672,525
			85	371,691	8,412,463	9,071,117	658,654
			86	553,200	9,038,492	9,993,844	955,352
	N	W	83	3,925	87,791	93,772	5,981
			86	17,227	448,647	468,432	19,785
	V	E	81	66,412	1,164,693	1,193,803	29,110
			82	55,040	599,788	611,390	11,602
			83	14,927	205,962	210,572	4,610
			84	46,638	1,135,905	1,155,178	19,273
	V	W	81	35,274	714,432	720,000	5,568
			86	4,275	120,703	121,220	517
ITALY	V	E	83	22,046	574,275	577,960	3,685
MADAGAS	A	E	84	44	2,065	2,908	843
			85	1,234	40,245	41,986	1,741
			86	6,037	169,510	174,749	5,239
	A	H	84	3,092	90,978	94,014	3,036
	A	W	86	33	1,134	1,189	55
	N	E	81	730,289	17,367,656	17,663,885	296,229
			82	917,185	22,590,782	23,191,117	600,335
			83	1,153,626	31,457,123	32,154,596	697,473
			84	1,157,723	33,930,507	34,538,907	608,400
			85	644,127	19,694,970	20,043,418	348,448
			86	824,070	24,340,659	24,582,984	242,325
	O	E	81	16,567	458,179	458,179	
			82	167	4,820	4,820	
			83	160	2,458	2,486	28
			84	220	9,127	9,127	
			86	3,364	104,113	104,113	
	V	E	81	130,071	2,950,297	2,995,227	44,930
			82	361,734	9,149,850	9,287,631	137,781
			83	281,303	7,560,546	7,705,616	145,070
			84	167,140	4,873,265	4,939,735	66,470
			85	373,214	11,981,118	12,178,433	197,315
			86	596,783	18,845,624	19,129,730	284,106
	V	W	84	22	767	1,182	415
			85	40	1,181	1,278	97
			86	1,765	4,465	4,882	417
MALAYSA	V	E	82	122,483	3,249,769	3,273,591	23,822
			83	26,455	684,000	699,011	15,011
MEXICO	A	E	83	224	4,468	4,958	490
	O	E	82	1,338	84,231	84,231	
			84	14,025	426,540	426,540	
			85	91	4,586	4,586	
			86	3,510	182,560	182,560	
	V	E	85	6,046	224,511	226,353	1,842
N CALDN	V	E	84	1,146	43,643	44,532	889
SINGAPR	A	E	83	90	1,237	1,456	219
	A	W	81	11,023	237,500	250,428	12,928
T PAC I	A	W	86	112	4,099	4,370	271
TONGA	A	E	86	15,951	466,320	482,815	16,495
	A	H	81	3,708	89,731	96,677	6,946
			82	7,520	134,076	143,267	9,191
			83	3,382	80,620	82,684	2,064
			84	3,652	118,200	121,581	3,381
			86	5,000	145,000	150,833	5,833
	A	W	81	8,136	175,059	193,524	18,465
			82	10,723	243,121	257,184	14,063
			83	2,637	59,532	61,612	2,080
			84	1,901	50,000	53,500	3,500
			85	14,816	478,632	490,590	11,958
			86	6,287	156,293	158,760	2,467
	V	E	84	6,393	176,900	177,597	697

Vanillin, aldehyde
4134000 VANILLIN (LB)

Country	Mode	Reg	Yr	Quantity	F.A.S.	C.I.F.	Charges
TOTAL			81	4,388,724	17,147,194	17,377,185	229,991
			82	3,949,703	16,207,003	16,502,903	295,900
			83	3,351,552	14,499,315	14,776,828	277,513
			84	3,464,728	15,110,667	15,417,103	306,436
			85	3,756,715	17,847,010	18,194,943	347,933
			86	3,278,419	14,989,082	15,192,686	203,604
BELGIUM	V	W	84	238	1,080	1,170	90
CANADA	A	E	83	11,023	36,700	37,731	1,031
	N	E	83	22,046	62,650	64,906	2,256
			84	1,821,648	8,708,890	8,877,279	168,389
			85	1,836,535	9,305,239	9,467,873	162,634
	O	E	81	3,737,965	15,037,595	15,183,252	145,657
			82	2,901,286	12,886,594	13,038,698	152,104
			83	2,684,927	12,110,453	12,295,666	185,213
			84	794,467	3,260,776	3,266,345	5,569
			85	641,088	2,833,897	2,835,668	1,771
			86	2,329,076	10,958,415	11,028,658	70,243
	O	W	81	2,620	2,260	2,260	
	V	E	84	46,648	217,925	222,977	5,052
			85	383,337	1,948,345	1,981,848	33,503
			86	42,593	216,343	220,206	3,863
CHINA M	N	E	85	582,009	2,432,110	2,536,973	104,863
	O	E	81	104,829	348,230	367,153	18,923
			82	191,463	406,084	425,386	19,302
			83	65,587	218,321	229,878	11,557
			84	56,215	188,115	199,914	11,799
			85	82,452	295,553	309,679	14,126
			86	2,205	8,878	9,123	245
	V	E	81	112,434	380,420	395,521	15,101
			82	112,434	376,238	395,065	18,827
			83	317,460	1,072,821	1,119,018	46,197
			84	564,374	1,965,664	2,060,815	95,151
			86	616,183	2,534,949	2,634,392	99,443
	V	W	81	205,027	689,776	721,237	31,461
			82	363,760	1,204,358	1,269,432	65,074

Crop Product TSUSA commodity number, description, and unit of quantity Country	Mode	Reg	Yr	Quantity	F.A.S.	C.I.F.	Charges
			83	59,524	198,139	208,594	10,455
			84	159	580	664	84
			85	19,841	84,024	87,546	3,522
DOM REP	A	E	86	990	3,404	3,565	161
	V	E	83	320	864	974	110
			86	1,394	1,150	1,250	100
FR GERM	A	E	86	4,410	30,800	31,387	587
	O	E	81	32	2,922	3,055	133
			82	310	1,824	2,030	206
			83	17	912	998	86
			84	729	4,104	4,490	386
			85	200	1,023	1,158	135
FRANCE	N	E	81	162,809	526,159	540,390	14,231
			85	167,550	670,048	687,299	17,251
	O	E	86	39,682	167,000	171,828	4,828
	V	E	82	283,176	978,936	1,002,752	23,816
			83	160,935	580,443	593,039	12,596
			84	159,564	596,267	610,692	14,425
			86	208,556	886,949	905,142	18,193
	V	W	86	11,023	47,063	48,300	1,237
HG KONG	O	E	86	4,630	18,643	19,157	514
ISRAEL	V	E	85	3,142	2,070	3,160	1,090
ITALY	V	E	83	55	1,041	1,095	54
JAPAN	N	E	83	24,806	197,966	204,867	6,901
			86	9,411	70,731	73,738	3,007
	O	E	82	24,251	87,657	90,952	3,295
			84	2,205	17,429	18,090	661
			85	3,858	29,721	30,840	1,119
	V	E	81	13,228	106,934	109,545	2,611
			82	72,751	258,538	271,384	12,846
			84	15,435	121,670	125,663	3,993
			85	20,943	161,422	167,241	5,819
			86	3,306	24,732	25,628	896
	V	W	81	49,780	52,898	54,772	1,874
NETHLDS	O	E	86	4,960	20,025	20,312	287
	V	E	85	4,410	18,100	18,504	404
U KING	A	E	84	841	20,362	21,054	692
			85	326	9,368	9,733	365
	A	W	82	22	505	582	77
	N	E	82	250	6,269	6,622	353
			83	4,739	16,197	17,046	849
	V	E	83	113	2,808	3,016	208
			84	2,205	7,805	7,950	145
			85	11,024	56,090	57,421	1,331

Vetch

Hairy vetch, seed
1269100 VETCH SEED, HAIRY (LB)

Country	Mode	Reg	Yr	Quantity	F.A.S.	C.I.F.	Charges
TOTAL			84	2,200	1,496	1,795	299
			85	600	4,214	4,303	89
FR GERM	V	W	84	2,200	1,496	1,795	299
NETHLDS	V	E	85	600	4,214	4,303	89

Vetch (not Hairy), seed
1269300 VETCH SEED, NSPF (LB)

Country	Mode	Reg	Yr	Quantity	F.A.S.	C.I.F.	Charges
TOTAL			82	412,771	96,049	135,108	39,059
			83	4,296	5,762	5,863	101
			84	17,041	7,510	7,836	326
			85	1,100	2,000	2,000	
			86	16,968	7,961	8,133	172
BELGIUM	A	E	84	660	296	396	100
C RICA	A	E	83	10	1,588	1,633	45
CANADA	O	W	82	3,575	17,080	17,080	
			84	1,100	2,310	2,310	
			85	1,100	2,000	2,000	
			86	1,047	1,986	1,986	
FRANCE	V	E	82	407,851	77,948	116,755	38,807
JAPAN	A	W	82	20	628	772	144
	V	W	83	86	1,711	1,767	56
KOR REP	A	W	84	55	512	738	226
MEXICO	O	W	83	4,200	2,463	2,463	
			84	15,226	4,392	4,392	
			86	15,917	3,109	3,109	
NETHLDS	A	E	86	4	2,866	3,038	172
	V	E	82	1,325	393	501	108

Vetiver

Vetiver, essential oil
4526800 VETIVERT OIL (LB)

Country	Mode	Reg	Yr	Quantity	F.A.S.	C.I.F.	Charges
TOTAL			81	132,760	2,081,723	2,156,559	74,442
			82	236,642	3,623,431	3,695,996	72,565
			83	179,213	3,196,270	3,270,948	74,678
			84	167,874	3,346,614	3,402,613	55,999
			85	155,782	2,864,695	2,939,390	74,695
			86	165,968	3,483,120	3,542,361	59,241
BRAZIL	V	E	81	330	3,128	3,299	171
			82	882	13,156	13,523	367
CHINA M	O	E	82	772	14,235	14,692	457
	V	E	82	59,083	496,984	508,458	11,474
			83	17,858	217,617	221,903	4,286
			84	21,606	288,146	293,016	4,870
			85	2,205	27,627	28,130	503
			86	8,818	99,452	101,420	1,968
	V	W	82	45,305	474,474	484,303	9,829
			84	1,102	15,475	15,976	501
COMOROS	A	E	84	110	3,700	3,829	129
F IND O	A	E	82	220	7,519	7,927	408
			83	1,102	36,500	37,686	1,186
			84	1,102	36,025	37,142	1,117
			85	551	22,050	22,791	741
			86	441	21,013	21,727	714
	N	E	81	1,785	41,343	42,924	1,581
FR GERM	V	E	84	135	1,180	1,212	32
FRANCE	N	E	81	17,392	509,529	544,522	34,993
			82	9,956	321,917	329,415	7,498
			83	20,086	449,365	458,615	9,250
			84	15,476	451,232	458,979	7,747
			85	11,160	273,192	279,032	5,840
			86	10,754	392,412	401,119	8,707
HAITI	A	E	82	450	8,182	8,365	183
			83	31,950	569,271	581,473	12,202
			84	900	18,137	18,541	404
	N	E	81	89,284	1,304,219	1,336,911	32,692
			82	101,777	1,952,912	1,990,232	37,320
			83	91,360	1,644,925	1,687,558	42,633
			84	97,780	2,057,539	2,091,703	34,164
			85	93,442	1,807,783	1,860,058	52,275
			86	119,646	2,617,588	2,659,470	41,882
HG KONG	V	E	81	6	267	282	15
INDIA	A	E	83	114	5,750	6,084	334
			85	1,102	108,533	111,995	3,462
INDNSIA	N	E	82	12,245	197,622	200,464	2,842
			85	31,305	410,520	418,336	7,816
			86	19,402	255,572	259,251	3,679
	V	E	81	23,172	204,908	209,806	4,504
			83	2,767	46,873	47,423	550
			84	14,992	221,733	224,356	2,623
	V	W	82	3,968	64,558	65,928	1,370
			83	10,143	138,608	141,781	3,173
			84	9,700	155,424	157,932	2,508
			85	13,228	190,832	194,142	3,310
			86	6,614	90,156	92,154	1,998
JAPAN	V	W	84	220	8,094	8,221	127
NETHLDS	A	E	84	22	443	553	110
	N	E	81	15	1,079	1,121	42
			83	947	39,105	39,499	394
	V	E	85	2,205	10,219	10,515	296
SINGAPR	V	E	83	2,205	36,528	37,046	518
			84	4,410	72,900	74,460	1,560
SRI LKA	A	E	85	110	4,956	5,275	319
SWITZLD	A	E	86	293	6,927	7,220	293
	N	E	81	771	16,867	17,305	438
			83	53	3,000	3,026	26
			84	319	16,586	16,693	107
			85	474	8,983	9,116	133
	V	E	82	1,543	59,060	59,578	518
U KING	N	E	83	628	8,728	8,854	126
	V	E	81	5	383	389	6
USSR	V	E	82	441	12,812	13,111	299

W

Walnut

Walnut, nut, pickled
1455400 WALNUTS PICKLED IMMATURE (LB)

Country	Mode	Reg	Yr	Quantity	F.A.S.	C.I.F.	Charges
TOTAL			81	5,496	9,925	11,217	1,292
			82	8,621	15,564	18,199	2,635
			83	4,267	6,021	7,052	1,031
			84	641	919	1,051	132
			85	124,423	85,120	85,870	750
			86	8,848	16,819	18,226	1,407
CANADA	O	W	85	122,288	81,228	81,228	
			86	1,200	2,174	2,174	
HG KONG	V	W	86	5,512	10,134	10,472	338
U KING	N	E	81	4,730	8,434	9,467	1,033
	O	E	82	1,141	1,720	2,166	446
			84	285	474	548	74
			85	1,497	2,813	3,390	577
	V	E	81	143	270	313	43
			82	6,939	12,832	14,886	2,054
			83	3,911	5,336	6,294	958
			84	356	445	503	58
			85	638	1,079	1,252	173
			86	2,136	4,511	5,580	1,069
	V	W	81	623	1,221	1,437	216
			82	541	1,012	1,147	135
			83	356	685	758	73

Walnut, nut, shelled, prepared or preserved
1455500 WALNUTS, SHELLED, NOT PICKLD (LB)

Country	Mode	Reg	Yr	Quantity	F.A.S.	C.I.F.	Charges
TOTAL			81	5,942	7,522	8,366	844
			82	103,454	173,651	177,061	3,410
			83	216,756	339,802	345,255	5,453
			84	98,747	119,785	122,926	3,141
			85	329,554	399,518	410,477	10,959
			86	238,776	363,259	371,225	7,966
BRAZIL	O	E	84	138	411	435	24
	V	E	86	35,000	103,425	107,657	4,232
CANADA	O	E	82	41,735	68,344	68,344	
			84	18,712	21,705	21,705	
			86	48,774	55,158	55,158	
CHINA M	N	E	83	23,532	26,176	29,917	3,741
	N	W	84	55,912	69,023	71,262	2,239
			85	93,236	122,873	127,665	4,792
	O	E	86	60,960	86,230	86,230	
	O	W	83	176,352	281,431	281,431	
			85	170,670	228,760	228,760	
	V	E	81	3,120	3,157	3,609	452
			82	1,557	2,187	2,427	240
			84	1,307	2,715	2,972	257
			85	15,437	13,866	15,724	1,858
			86	11,023	14,119	14,254	135
	V	W	81	900	1,060	1,150	90
			82	25,005	46,988	49,513	2,525
			83	510	969	1,040	71
			84	498	988	1,046	58
			85	992	1,215	1,348	133
			86	35,185	30,058	30,707	649
CHINA T	O	E	84	374	654	654	
	O	W	82	28,600	51,292	51,292	
	V	E	83	5,250	2,875	3,088	213
			85	641	1,301	1,499	198
FRANCE	A	E	81	48	307	362	55
	V	E	86	974	3,843	4,169	326
HG KONG	V	E	81	1,763	2,645	2,864	219
			84	300	556	630	74
			85	2,995	4,029	4,377	348
	V	W	82	761	859	959	100
			83	1,000	1,249	1,302	53
			85	17,554	15,489	17,119	1,630
INDIA	O	E	84	16,231	18,017	18,017	
ITALY	V	E	82	397	654	684	30
			83	212	372	397	25
NETHLDS	V	E	84	1,777	1,908	2,022	114

Country	Mode	Reg	Yr	Quantity	F.A.S.	C.I.F.	Charges
PHIL R	V	E	84	200	320	387	67
SPAIN	V	E	81	111	353	381	28
			82	79	272	290	18
THAILND	V	E	84	3,000	2,950	3,164	214
TURKEY	V	E	86	46,297	69,300	71,805	2,505
	V	W	82	99	258	298	40
U KING	V	E	83	9,900	26,730	28,080	1,350
			84	298	538	632	94
			86	563	1,126	1,245	119
USSR	V	E	82	5,221	2,797	3,254	457
			85	28,029	11,985	13,985	2,000

Walnut, nut, unshelled
1452800 WALNUTS NOT SHELLED (LB)

Country	Mode	Reg	Yr	Quantity	F.A.S.	C.I.F.	Charges
TOTAL			81	1,113	1,903	2,066	163
			82	4,674	4,883	5,612	729
			83	9,366	10,108	12,325	2,217
			84	639	1,397	1,644	247
			86	34,969	7,677	8,607	930
CANADA	O	E	82	265	450	516	66
CHINA M	O	E	83	440	642	1,104	462
	V	E	82	4,409	4,433	5,096	663
			83	8,818	9,163	10,819	1,656
	V	W	81	450	600	626	26
			86	900	1,495	1,583	88
FRANCE	V	E	84	95	624	684	60
			86	938	2,884	3,581	697
HG KONG	V	W	81	492	667	734	67
ITALY	A	W	83	108	303	402	99
JAPAN	A	W	84	44	452	631	179
MEXICO	O	W	86	32,060	1,603	1,603	
SPAIN	V	E	81	171	636	706	70
SWITZLD	V	E	86	1,071	1,695	1,840	145
U KING	V	E	84	500	321	329	8

Walnut, plywood
2401900 PLYWD, FACE PLY WALNUT (MSF)

Country	Mode	Reg	Yr	Quantity	F.A.S.	C.I.F.	Charges
TOTAL			81	4,413	1,593,579	1,693,894	100,315
			82	2,640	1,121,509	1,188,259	66,750
			83	2,723	1,140,538	1,212,594	72,056
			84	6,111	2,239,470	2,450,857	211,387
			85	3,643	1,302,468	1,407,174	104,706
			86	4,271	1,258,767	1,389,362	130,595
BRAZIL	V	E	84	7	1,847	2,140	293
			86	32	9,911	11,466	1,555
CANADA	O	E	81	5	9,164	9,164	
			82	9	16,684	16,684	
			83	68	72,920	72,920	
			84	45	50,312	50,312	
			85	336	77,465	77,465	
			86	95	44,734	44,734	
	O	W	81	12	15,919	15,919	
			82	4	4,959	4,959	
			83	6	5,026	5,026	
			84	9	11,834	11,834	
			86	5	7,646	7,646	
CHINA T	N	W	81	29	15,060	15,969	909
	O	W	84	4	4,445	4,445	
	V	E	81	2,655	831,635	888,407	56,772
			82	1,346	520,416	553,607	33,191
			83	1,169	480,312	512,604	32,292
			84	1,361	609,617	646,689	37,072
			85	990	399,626	425,474	25,848
			86	1,051	454,015	487,619	33,604
	V	H	86	16	12,464	15,166	2,702
	V	W	81	1,254	488,468	517,521	29,053
			82	987	425,642	450,335	24,693
			83	860	403,863	425,160	21,297
			84	1,290	600,676	639,442	38,766
			85	1,372	507,532	541,972	34,440
			86	1,247	504,974	538,423	33,449
COLOMB	N	E	86	1,768	181,342	236,646	55,304
	V	E	83	288	47,700	53,366	5,666
			84	3,069	837,732	961,262	123,530
			85	777	263,045	302,912	39,867
INDNSIA	V	E	83	19	14,464	15,489	1,025
			85	100	12,678	14,381	1,703
ITALY	V	E	84	5	9,750	10,340	590

Crop Product TSUSA commodity number, description, and unit of quantity Country	Mode	Reg	Yr	Quantity	F.A.S.	C.I.F.	Charges
JAPAN	V	E	81	30	23,624	25,980	2,356
			82	20	11,490	12,332	842
			83	10	8,030	8,805	775
			86	3	1,845	2,079	234
	V	W	81	234	148,749	155,767	7,018
			82	205	126,142	132,551	6,409
			83	153	57,388	62,300	4,912
			84	101	64,477	67,619	3,142
			85	68	42,122	44,970	2,848
			86	43	31,865	34,406	2,541
KOR REP	V	E	81	114	28,522	31,070	2,548
			82	66	15,120	16,674	1,554
			83	73	15,456	16,963	1,507
	V	W	81	80	32,438	34,097	1,659
			82	3	1,056	1,117	61
			84	16	5,600	5,905	305
PERU	V	E	86	11	9,971	11,177	1,206
PHIL R	V	E	83	75	33,779	38,235	4,456
			84	197	39,559	46,643	7,084
	V	W	83	2	1,600	1,726	126
SINGAPR	V	E	84	4	2,085	2,378	293
	V	H	84	3	1,536	1,848	312

Waterchestnut

Waterchestnut, frozen**
1378400 WATER CHESTNUTS, FROZEN (LB)

Country	Mode	Reg	Yr	Quantity	F.A.S.	C.I.F.	Charges
TOTAL			**82**	**1,612**	**1,213**	**1,763**	**550**
			83	**81,268**	**42,494**	**48,558**	**6,064**
			84	**634,922**	**360,394**	**410,494**	**50,100**
			85	**302,846**	**158,643**	**202,113**	**43,470**
			86	**294,812**	**163,468**	**189,442**	**25,974**
CHINA M	V	E	86	33,716	10,268	12,063	1,795
	V	W	86	3,510	1,770	2,107	337
CHINA T	V	E	84	20,000	16,687	18,335	1,648
			85	109,994	76,995	88,698	11,703
			86	170,000	116,673	134,493	17,820
	V	W	83	81,008	42,243	48,307	6,064
			84	531,220	322,909	361,997	39,088
			86	25,599	6,902	9,188	2,286
GUATMAL	A	W	82	1,612	1,213	1,763	550
			84	450	425	679	254
HG KONG	V	E	84	75,992	18,344	27,454	9,110
			86	28,200	15,530	18,066	2,536
	V	W	86	33,787	12,325	13,525	1,200
JAMAICA	A	E	85	192,412	80,309	112,076	31,767
JAPAN	V	E	85	440	1,339	1,339	
MEXICO	O	W	83	260	251	251	
			84	7,260	2,029	2,029	

1384000 BAMBOO SHOOTS, CHESTNUTS FZ (LB)
   (See Bamboo shoot, frozen under Bamboo)
1384100 MIX PEA POD/WATER CHSTNT FZ (LB)
   (See Pea, pod, frozen under Pea)

Waterchestnut, prepared or preserved
1417000 WATERCHESTNUTS, PREP OR PRES (LB)

Country	Mode	Reg	Yr	Quantity	F.A.S.	C.I.F.	Charges
TOTAL			**81**	**36,645,247**	**15,551,315**	**17,404,067**	**1,852,752**
			82	**46,154,519**	**19,359,850**	**21,909,653**	**2,549,803**
			83	**44,180,989**	**17,954,463**	**20,094,179**	**2,139,716**
			84	**47,688,430**	**17,906,485**	**20,747,044**	**2,840,559**
ARAB EM	V	W	84	49,500	19,005	21,993	2,988
CANADA	A	E	84	60	1,086	1,126	40
	O	E	84	9,250	3,578	4,769	1,191
CHINA M	N	E	81	5,154,992	1,603,335	1,870,431	267,096
			83	44,341	13,755	15,764	2,009
	N	W	82	1,161,941	479,017	539,459	60,442
			84	1,405,968	464,365	528,827	64,462
	O	E	81	76,449	35,977	37,161	1,184
			83	106,145	32,126	38,097	5,971
			84	30,650	10,607	10,607	
	V	E	81	2,405,690	731,772	874,347	142,575
			82	13,213,111	4,425,980	5,228,310	802,330
			83	7,971,928	2,536,168	3,009,543	473,375
			84	16,884,373	5,252,129	6,480,563	1,228,434
	V	H	81	231,227	94,210	104,618	10,408
			82	256,696	111,964	125,868	13,904
			83	176,885	81,591	93,867	12,276
			84	235,766	120,200	134,989	14,789
	V	W	81	12,469,623	4,139,734	4,750,177	610,443
			82	11,476,167	4,221,706	4,765,509	543,803
			83	10,810,671	3,639,648	4,100,464	460,816
			84	14,340,333	4,947,992	5,648,475	700,483
CHINA T	A	W	83	20	260	2,198	1,938
	N	H	82	134,201	91,243	100,951	9,708
	N	W	81	1,276,104	758,841	818,095	59,254
			82	1,915,061	923,753	1,015,475	91,722
			83	1,113,037	557,628	600,012	42,384
	O	E	82	14,820	7,318	8,626	1,308
			84	95,800	23,600	23,600	
	O	W	82	3,360	1,848	2,267	419
	V	E	81	3,438,803	2,086,049	2,310,842	224,793
			82	4,791,063	2,562,264	2,933,288	371,024
			83	4,783,747	2,197,107	2,526,673	329,566
			84	3,829,262	1,949,885	2,278,044	328,159
	V	H	81	131,242	96,685	105,305	8,620
			82	9,306	8,835	9,707	872
			83	159,211	100,755	111,977	11,222
			84	60,315	38,949	42,605	3,656
	V	W	81	8,321,931	4,816,045	5,197,015	380,970
			82	10,728,368	5,595,407	6,111,623	516,216
			83	15,592,104	7,627,785	8,252,565	624,780
			84	7,567,214	3,949,152	4,266,652	317,500
FRANCE	A	E	84	119	870	1,028	158
	V	E	83	750	1,254	2,281	1,027
GAZA ST	V	E	84	1,500	545	573	28
GREECE	V	E	83	29,101	7,260	10,240	2,980
HG KONG	V	E	81	1,191,428	377,331	440,431	63,100
			82	628,846	228,449	261,734	33,285
			83	1,551,490	521,704	617,974	96,270
			84	1,097,716	412,370	505,578	93,208
	V	H	81	15,000	13,200	14,500	1,300
			82	20,075	7,154	8,142	988
			83	17,328	6,537	7,421	884
	V	W	81	1,459,055	534,295	590,784	56,489
			82	1,584,796	578,560	666,036	87,476
			83	1,647,599	552,242	616,530	64,288
			84	1,982,719	676,546	753,556	77,010
INDNSIA	V	W	82	9,000	4,500	5,103	603
ITALY	V	W	81	300	252	265	13
JAPAN	V	E	81	31,500	30,450	34,072	3,622
			82	19,500	13,780	16,497	2,717
			83	22,715	11,440	13,097	1,657
			84	73,545	20,090	26,504	6,414
	V	H	84	105	279	311	32
	V	W	81	336,099	179,047	196,301	17,254
			82	44,719	31,094	34,486	3,392
			83	64,260	35,962	39,746	3,784
			84	4,713	4,113	4,699	586
KOR REP	V	E	81	7,500	5,490	6,241	751
			82	22,894	13,491	15,648	2,157
			83	979	1,518	1,648	130
			84	1,958	2,420	2,714	294
	V	H	83	7,950	2,883	3,376	493
	V	W	81	13,405	12,312	12,984	672
			82	2,310	3,212	3,407	195
			83	3,720	5,906	6,449	543
MACAO	V	E	81	29,552	11,330	12,777	1,447
	V	W	81	43,350	18,700	20,834	2,134
PHIL R	V	W	84	2,337	886	1,053	167
ROMANIA	V	W	84	587	843	921	78
SPAIN	V	E	83	43,322	6,490	8,034	1,544
THAILND	V	E	81	8,250	3,985	4,338	353
			82	96,887	42,173	48,286	6,113
			83	3,293	1,770	1,996	226
			84	10,503	4,934	5,638	704
	V	W	81	3,747	2,275	2,549	274
			82	21,398	8,102	9,231	1,129
			83	30,393	12,674	14,227	1,553
			84	4,137	2,041	2,219	178

1417010 WATER CHESTNUTS SLICED PREP (LB)

Country	Mode	Reg	Yr	Quantity	F.A.S.	C.I.F.	Charges
TOTAL			**85**	**45,515,772**	**17,233,987**	**19,837,907**	**2,603,920**
			86	**58,345,678**	**21,524,456**	**24,102,188**	**2,577,732**
CHILE	V	W	86	9,000	3,929	4,229	300
CHINA M	N	E	85	10,592,570	3,355,966	4,020,189	664,223
			86	566,324	162,006	199,644	37,638
	N	W	85	1,803,304	721,104	813,385	92,281
			86	2,661,721	1,041,389	1,170,695	129,306
	V	E	85	3,293,393	1,069,872	1,293,494	223,622

Crop
Product
TSUSA commodity number, description, and unit of quantity

Country	Mode	Reg	Yr	Quantity	F.A.S.	C.I.F.	Charges
			86	16,373,276	5,009,987	5,794,085	784,098
	V	H	85	146,000	58,421	65,013	6,592
			86	110,870	44,428	49,062	4,634
	V	W	85	12,947,033	4,544,292	5,199,365	655,073
			86	15,496,253	5,503,467	6,083,872	580,405
CHINA T	N	E	85	1,143,979	546,233	650,713	104,480
			86	147,556	62,943	71,089	8,146
	O	E	85	9,600	7,296	8,281	985
	V	E	85	4,147,095	1,731,570	2,018,350	286,780
			86	6,123,649	2,979,168	3,351,181	372,013
	V	H	85	64,912	33,408	37,632	4,224
			86	56,776	28,540	31,755	3,215
	V	W	85	7,929,977	3,827,020	4,175,902	348,882
			86	7,405,183	3,518,434	3,795,726	277,292
COOK IS	V	E	86	10,803	3,761	4,340	579
CYPRUS	V	E	86	17,100	7,572	8,983	1,411
HG KONG	V	E	85	1,330,779	530,796	631,064	100,268
			86	4,329,144	1,511,230	1,694,944	183,714
	V	H	85	33,787	11,888	13,443	1,555
	V	W	85	1,281,573	469,042	532,678	63,636
			86	4,556,120	1,488,624	1,656,507	167,883
JAPAN	V	E	85	56,473	28,763	33,603	4,840
	V	W	85	85,856	30,560	36,237	5,677
			86	309	1,535	1,584	49
KOR REP	V	E	86	93,858	27,066	29,976	2,910
	V	W	85	153,000	80,580	87,780	7,200
			86	2,963	4,240	4,552	312
RWANDA	V	E	85	119,049	26,678	33,924	7,246
SWITZLD	V	E	85	188,058	74,781	89,047	14,266
			86	204,673	66,503	83,125	16,622
	V	W	85	25,470	10,197	12,297	2,100
			86	177,400	57,834	64,782	6,948
THAILND	V	E	85	37,831	11,660	14,038	2,378
			86	2,700	1,800	2,057	257
	V	W	85	98,893	49,600	54,771	5,171
U KING	V	E	85	27,140	14,260	16,701	2,441

1417020 WATER CHESTNUTS WHOLE, PREP (LB)

Country	Mode	Reg	Yr	Quantity	F.A.S.	C.I.F.	Charges
TOTAL			85	17,217,075	7,086,743	8,035,002	948,259
			86	13,361,593	5,328,125	5,943,112	614,987
CANADA	V	W	85	445,200	124,088	148,960	24,872
CHINA M	V	E	85	2,262,194	794,196	960,795	166,599
			86	1,645,800	435,964	520,548	84,584
	V	H	85	86,990	49,455	54,747	5,292
			86	85,223	36,851	41,567	4,716
	V	W	85	4,592,454	1,603,923	1,834,911	230,988
			86	3,158,825	1,135,034	1,257,307	122,273
CHINA T	N	E	85	636,770	327,667	385,506	57,839
			86	23,411	10,184	11,447	1,263
	N	W	85	22,875	17,643	20,616	2,973
	O	W	85	220	2,189	2,189	
	V	E	85	1,669,817	777,880	907,153	129,273
			86	1,822,390	848,716	976,651	127,935
	V	H	85	140,085	74,688	83,436	8,748
			86	88,578	45,163	50,381	5,218
	V	W	85	5,669,863	2,710,806	2,956,866	246,060
			86	4,053,562	1,878,110	2,031,421	153,311
COOK IS	V	E	86	23,148	7,929	9,150	1,221
FR GERM	V	E	86	79,200	31,152	37,452	6,300
FRANCE	V	E	86	4,500	3,648	4,217	569
HG KONG	O	W	85	5,850	1,900	2,135	235
	V	E	85	289,029	108,047	124,426	16,379
			86	645,927	345,056	393,908	48,852
	V	H	86	43,933	12,662	14,767	2,105
	V	W	85	1,170,111	414,018	461,907	47,889
			86	1,449,424	458,834	497,760	38,926
INDIA	V	E	86	160,982	41,143	54,999	13,856
KOR REP	V	E	85	3,500	2,400	2,683	283
			86	28,200	13,133	14,360	1,227
	V	W	85	27,609	16,795	18,547	1,752
SINGAPR	V	E	86	6,501	3,705	4,033	328
SPAIN	V	E	85	28,836	5,004	6,554	1,550
SWITZLD	V	E	85	26,400	11,218	13,512	2,294
	V	W	85	139,272	44,826	50,059	5,233
			86	6,000	1,780	1,870	90
THAILND	V	E	86	10,500	7,560	8,871	1,311
	V	W	86	25,489	11,501	12,403	902

Crop
Product
TSUSA commodity number, description, and unit of quantity

Country	Mode	Reg	Yr	Quantity	F.A.S.	C.I.F.	Charges

Watermelon

Watermelon, fresh

1482500 WATERMELONS FR DEC 1-MAR 31 (LB)

Country	Mode	Reg	Yr	Quantity	F.A.S.	C.I.F.	Charges
TOTAL			81	1,185,413	183,712	209,158	25,446
			82	93,799,069	5,174,716	5,203,798	29,082
			83	42,911,070	2,275,828	2,289,163	13,335
			84	75,136,704	3,876,349	3,964,041	87,692
			85	81,207,035	4,935,976	5,223,220	287,244
			86	83,905,657	4,503,922	5,163,556	659,634
AUSTRAL	V	E	82	80,640	28,957	33,466	4,509
C RICA	V	E	84	42,950	1,575	3,675	2,100
			85	238,844	45,190	62,718	17,528
CANADA	O	E	83	22	924	924	
			85	50	5,899	5,899	
			86	20	2,264	2,264	
	O	W	85	32,360	2,248	2,248	
CHILE	V	E	84	28,520	2,352	2,652	300
DOM REP	V	E	84	2,024	552	740	188
			85	401,978	32,655	56,097	23,442
			86	2,028,310	87,362	175,763	88,401
DOMINCA	V	E	86	15,743	4,390	4,830	440
ECUADOR	V	E	85	38,360	6,713	9,590	2,877
GUATMAL	V	E	81	28,240	4,236	6,358	2,122
			84	125,649	4,553	12,665	8,112
			85	601,420	22,674	52,831	30,157
			86	2,660,493	169,422	345,049	175,627
	V	W	86	37,728	1,048	4,208	3,160
HONDURA	V	E	82	66,985	9,289	10,508	1,219
			83	17,471	1,682	3,015	1,333
			84	339,175	40,390	52,745	12,355
			85	373,163	53,647	62,379	8,732
			86	1,719,218	261,348	296,235	34,887
JAMAICA	A	E	84	80,000	20,800	35,733	14,933
	N	E	84	315,029	15,973	27,094	11,121
	V	E	83	233,800	23,020	32,952	9,932
MEXICO	O	E	81	479,621	49,962	49,962	
			82	59,397,739	3,461,700	3,484,004	22,304
			83	22,545,456	1,336,452	1,336,452	
			84	45,004,550	2,257,703	2,257,703	
			85	60,545,371	3,713,589	3,714,789	1,200
			86	45,909,620	2,105,129	2,105,129	
	O	H	84	33,223	844	844	
	O	W	81	405,054	33,276	33,276	
			82	34,252,605	1,674,113	1,675,063	950
			83	20,103,132	898,048	898,048	
			84	28,861,866	1,468,841	1,468,841	
			85	16,102,893	726,069	726,069	
			86	26,329,340	1,320,965	1,320,965	
MOROC	V	E	83	10,439	14,235	15,702	1,467
NETHLDS	A	E	83	750	1,467	2,070	603
NICARAG	V	E	81	159,152	36,608	45,527	8,919
PANAMA	N	E	85	859,134	122,542	190,398	67,856
	V	E	84	271,252	40,100	61,879	21,779
			85	555,616	99,552	141,019	41,467
			86	1,564,405	221,500	329,218	107,718
	V	W	86	576,105	131,982	176,478	44,496
S VN GR	V	E	86	104,494	26,640	39,895	13,255
SALVADR	O	E	85	55,628	2,332	2,332	
	V	E	85	513,071	25,172	62,602	37,430
			86	2,960,181	171,872	363,522	191,650
	V	H	85	56,000	1,936	7,512	5,576
	V	W	85	389,000	34,338	70,115	35,777
SWEDEN	V	E	84	17,066	7,658	10,800	3,142
THAILND	V	W	82	1,100	657	757	100
VENEZ	A	E	81	113,346	59,630	74,035	14,405
			84	15,400	15,008	28,670	13,662
	V	E	85	444,147	41,420	56,622	15,202

1482800 WATERMELONS FR APR 1-NOV 30 (LB)

Country	Mode	Reg	Yr	Quantity	F.A.S.	C.I.F.	Charges
TOTAL			81	82,843,699	6,889,326	6,889,136	
			82	143,636,636	6,518,663	6,522,038	3,375
			83	143,322,660	10,182,854	10,190,351	7,497
			84	208,308,702	8,788,064	8,801,627	13,563
			85	138,813,538	9,349,587	9,433,908	84,321
			86	113,509,948	6,888,228	7,491,537	603,309
BRAZIL	A	E	84	327	966	1,857	891
C RICA	V	E	83	21,517	1,573	2,538	965
CANADA	O	E	84	28,250	1,513	1,513	
			85	87,490	5,175	5,175	

Crop
Product
TSUSA commodity number, description, and unit of quantity

Country	Mode	Reg	Yr	Quantity	F.A.S.	C.I.F.	Charges
	O	W	81	23,589	1,651	1,651	
CHILE	V	E	85	52,910	8,496	14,854	6,358
DOM REP	V	E	82	45,000	2,250	5,145	2,895
			83	15,500	1,685	2,285	600
			84	63,888	4,670	7,086	2,416
			85	193,059	13,587	23,161	9,574
			86	644,952	31,084	58,818	27,734
FRANCE	O	W	85	29,720	1,189	1,189	
GUATMAL	O	E	85	449,400	15,313	15,313	
	V	E	84	5,570	1,114	1,407	293
			85	497,814	20,072	29,393	9,321
			86	1,651,699	89,669	210,472	120,803
HG KONG	O	W	85	37,420	2,619	2,619	
	V	E	86	901	1,793	2,099	306
HONDURA	V	E	84	42,000	7,875	10,710	2,835
			86	38,400	1,200	4,220	3,020
JAPAN	V	W	83	177	389	412	23
MEXICO	O	E	81	40,619,435	3,882,739	3,882,649	
			82	58,145,340	2,474,040	2,474,040	
			83	40,089,886	2,844,327	2,844,327	
			84	75,853,672	3,716,971	3,716,971	
			85	66,152,348	4,667,750	4,667,756	6
			86	45,195,478	3,124,310	3,124,310	
	O	W	81	42,200,675	3,004,936	3,004,836	
			82	85,437,478	4,037,382	4,037,382	
			83	103,122,601	7,332,797	7,332,803	6
			84	132,223,484	5,045,086	5,045,086	
			85	70,506,323	4,466,639	4,466,643	4
			86	59,719,139	2,605,575	2,605,575	
NETHLDS	O	W	84	47,750	3,813	3,813	
PANAMA	V	E	83	71,885	1,536	7,423	5,887
			85	595,529	107,826	154,302	46,476
			86	4,754,669	870,246	1,209,210	338,964
	V	W	85	152,416	28,683	37,557	8,874
			86	267,094	59,675	79,709	20,034
S VN GR	V	E	86	146,867	41,940	51,525	9,585
SALVADR	V	E	86	1,090,749	62,736	145,599	82,863
SPAIN	V	E	85	30,450	9,372	11,566	2,194
THAILND	V	W	82	8,818	4,991	5,471	480
			83	1,094	547	563	16
			84	1,201	656	713	57
VENEZ	A	E	84	42,560	5,400	12,471	7,071
	V	E	85	28,659	2,866	4,380	1,514

Watermelon, seed, prepared or preserved
1826000 WATERMELON SEEDS PREP, PRES (LB)

Country	Mode	Reg	Yr	Quantity	F.A.S.	C.I.F.	Charges
TOTAL	.		81	271,638	266,186	287,415	21,229
			82	385,451	330,217	363,834	33,617
			83	358,631	344,227	375,401	31,174
			84	447,975	347,376	379,822	32,446
			85	385,502	327,456	350,259	22,803
			86	513,815	430,103	462,760	32,657
CANADA	O	E	85	17,985	17,877	17,877	
	V	W	85	5,050	5,438	5,835	397
CHINA M	N	E	82	101,946	55,107	61,717	6,610
	N	W	84	30,246	26,375	27,987	1,612
			85	55,424	51,831	55,066	3,235
			86	23,453	24,934	28,376	3,442
	O	W	81	600	1,308	1,366	58
	V	E	81	8,150	10,449	11,098	649
			82	750	912	1,007	95
			83	91,364	54,196	61,737	7,541
			84	156,682	108,626	120,762	12,136
			85	61,480	32,380	35,372	2,992
			86	42,363	22,164	25,404	3,240
	V	H	81	310	579	612	33
			82	500	757	848	91
			83	853	913	988	75
			84	7,632	1,804	1,974	170
			85	1,797	1,845	1,948	103
			86	3,720	4,063	4,429	366
	V	W	81	35,995	37,718	40,824	3,106
			82	33,662	37,815	40,579	2,764
			83	96,196	84,282	89,749	5,467
			84	95,984	78,182	85,277	7,095
			85	47,700	44,139	46,981	2,842
			86	125,575	73,519	78,458	4,939
CHINA T	A	E	85	8,600	7,395	7,820	425
	N	W	82	15,253	34,946	37,133	2,187
	V	E	81	29,246	57,400	60,655	3,255
			82	60,811	80,637	86,814	6,177
			83	13,929	31,884	33,034	1,150
			84	5,898	9,475	10,291	816
			85	4,249	10,097	10,725	628
			86	11,562	19,903	21,347	1,444
	V	H	82	800	1,520	1,653	133
			83	1,600	3,040	3,254	214
			84	249	575	633	58
			86	904	1,602	1,739	137
	V	W	81	17,146	18,518	19,326	808
			82	5,064	9,295	9,983	688
			83	19,452	41,366	43,693	2,327
			84	3,917	4,667	5,010	343
			85	9,575	9,602	10,195	593
			86	8,383	9,340	9,833	493
DENMARK	V	E	81	17,280	26,193	27,922	1,729
DOM REP	A	E	84	180	251	365	114
EGYPT	V	E	82	6,614	4,981	5,550	569
FR GERM	O	E	84	232	1,075	1,250	175
GREECE	V	E	84	780	442	523	81
HG KONG	O	W	84	4,000	8,209	8,636	427
	V	E	81	1,694	2,015	2,323	308
			82	11,186	12,945	13,964	1,019
			83	21,050	20,112	22,352	2,240
			84	23,405	21,718	23,768	2,050
			85	12,830	12,029	13,067	1,038
			86	26,515	24,789	26,743	1,954
	V	W	81	24,645	29,100	30,800	1,700
			82	17,301	20,220	21,613	1,393
			83	56,066	51,946	55,276	3,330
			84	58,402	55,388	58,838	3,450
			85	127,532	112,891	121,152	8,261
			86	223,725	197,086	208,214	11,128
INDIA	A	E	86	3,850	13,722	14,881	1,159
	V	E	83	4,500	1,720	2,139	419
ISRAEL	A	E	81	11	1,950	2,010	60
	A	W	86	970	4,275	5,597	1,322
	V	E	82	2,205	1,256	1,598	342
			86	4,365	2,528	2,942	414
JAPAN	V	E	83	9,493	17,887	21,453	3,566
LEBANON	V	E	81	16,204	9,544	10,454	910
			83	8,862	4,020	4,527	507
			84	8,003	3,267	3,449	182
MEXICO	O	E	85	1,235	1,046	1,046	
	O	W	86	5,221	2,316	2,316	
NETHLDS	A	E	81	15	285	347	62
	V	E	85	800	3,456	3,875	419
PAKISTN	V	W	84	1,102	522	660	138
PHIL R	V	W	83	900	760	836	76
			86	5,245	7,427	8,161	734
SUDAN	V	W	83	6,614	16,500	19,000	2,500
SWITZLD	V	W	85	6,500	6,139	6,431	292
SYRIA	V	W	81	17,409	16,654	18,461	1,807
THAILND	O	W	84	882	438	477	39
	V	E	81	2,500	1,538	1,700	162
			82	5,984	3,190	3,648	458
			83	6,232	3,206	3,647	441
			84	10,363	5,065	6,015	950
			85	2,205	1,062	1,214	152
			86	9,409	13,050	13,828	778
	V	H	82	750	358	428	70
	V	W	81	61,713	36,316	40,239	3,923
			82	81,542	45,779	50,638	4,859
			83	21,520	12,395	13,716	1,321
			84	40,018	21,297	23,907	2,610
			85	22,540	10,229	11,655	1,426
			86	15,655	6,251	6,756	505
U KING	O	E	81	38,720	16,619	19,278	2,659
			82	41,083	20,499	26,661	6,162
	V	E	86	2,900	3,134	3,736	602

Wattle

Wattle, dye or tannin
4705040 WATTLE (LB)

Country	Mode	Reg	Yr	Quantity	F.A.S.	C.I.F.	Charges
TOTAL			81	4,479,088	632,249	838,765	206,516
			82	4,390,432	836,780	1,058,386	221,606
			83	5,604,004	1,412,353	1,679,787	267,434
			84	2,447,706	734,546	874,859	140,313
			85	3,548,165	1,011,008	1,186,772	175,764
			86	7,818,319	1,936,739	2,215,037	278,298

Crop Product TSUSA commodity number, description, and unit of quantity Country	Mode	Reg	Yr	Quantity	F.A.S.	C.I.F.	Charges
ARGENT	V	E	82	88,184	25,906	30,099	4,193
			86	22,880	8,380	9,483	1,103
BRAZIL	N	E	81	162,039	40,725	46,999	6,274
	O	E	82	2,557	1,144	1,144	
			83	108,377	7,260	7,260	
			86	39,683	14,286	14,286	
	V	E	82	594,138	187,825	216,448	28,623
			83	1,226,108	374,688	429,358	54,670
			84	1,720,185	492,206	589,871	97,665
			85	2,891,192	791,264	925,967	134,703
			86	2,627,185	875,541	978,314	102,773
HG KONG	V	E	86	85,538	30,000	30,332	332
NAMIBIA	V	E	83	44,092	15,960	18,196	2,236
PARAGUA	V	E	86	282,189	102,400	116,954	14,554
REP SAF	N	E	83	487,768	145,611	175,820	30,209
	O	E	85	79,366	24,948	29,788	4,840
			86	79,366	24,948	29,998	5,050
	V	E	81	4,317,049	591,524	791,766	200,242
			82	3,705,553	621,905	810,695	188,790
			83	3,696,203	853,900	1,031,272	177,372
			84	705,475	234,360	275,468	41,108
			85	520,287	174,048	206,303	32,255
			86	4,408,108	782,232	916,100	133,868
	V	W	83	41,456	14,934	17,881	2,947
			84	22,046	7,980	9,520	1,540
			85	57,320	20,748	24,714	3,966
			86	273,370	98,952	119,570	20,618

4705760 WATTLE NOT CRUDE OR PROC (LB)

			Yr	Quantity	F.A.S.	C.I.F.	Charges
TOTAL			81	26,240,520	6,358,327	7,656,497	1,298,170
			82	14,583,104	4,276,472	5,006,549	730,077
			83	14,969,638	4,954,530	5,748,949	794,419
			84	18,991,795	5,538,001	6,509,367	971,366
			85	14,393,028	4,590,232	5,321,137	730,905
			86	15,346,350	5,228,509	6,005,480	776,971
ARGENT	V	E	81	220,460	52,546	63,873	11,327
			82	22,046	8,380	9,546	1,166
			83	179,164	66,202	75,108	8,906
			84	401,237	152,516	173,240	20,724
			85	251,468	88,440	101,844	13,404
			86	276,904	117,844	133,088	15,244
BELGIUM	V	E	84	137,972	45,826	53,082	7,256
BELIZE	V	E	85	666,549	191,000	219,816	28,816
BRAZIL	N	E	82	360,011	125,400	143,640	18,240
	O	E	83	10,932	5,847	5,847	
	V	E	81	9,151,639	2,140,273	2,529,974	389,701
			82	4,768,478	1,488,829	1,696,899	208,070
			83	7,677,621	2,458,302	2,858,510	400,208
			84	13,017,486	3,485,329	4,118,922	633,593
			85	7,854,759	2,366,813	2,723,103	356,290
			86	7,879,475	2,507,356	2,826,819	319,463
	V	W	83	69,136	22,080	27,359	5,279
			84	285,187	78,736	96,758	18,022
			85	104,410	31,840	38,730	6,890
			86	35,274	12,000	13,899	1,899
CHILE	V	E	86	401,992	164,368	194,257	29,889
CYPRUS	V	E	84	43,292	16,560	18,893	2,333
FRANCE	V	E	83	88,184	37,654	39,906	2,252
			84	37,478	11,368	13,492	2,124
			85	44,000	17,390	19,763	2,373
KOR REP	V	E	83	220,460	76,000	87,615	11,615
MAURITN	V	E	83	44,092	15,960	20,321	4,361
NETHLDS	V	E	84	138,890	46,094	52,987	6,893
PARAGUA	V	E	82	88,184	27,560	31,753	4,193
			86	44,092	16,000	18,205	2,205
REP SAF	A	E	81	937	551	3,160	2,609
	N	E	81	4,819,234	1,175,104	1,429,251	254,147
	V	E	81	11,662,445	2,890,701	3,503,152	612,451
			82	8,936,522	2,486,930	2,957,481	470,551
			83	6,530,773	2,219,361	2,570,566	351,205
			84	4,930,253	1,701,572	1,981,993	280,421
			85	5,163,898	1,784,379	2,090,209	305,830
			86	6,547,708	2,361,736	2,760,426	398,690
	V	W	81	385,805	99,152	127,087	27,935
			82	352,748	121,600	146,404	24,804
			83	149,276	53,124	63,717	10,593
			86	66,548	24,000	28,028	4,028
SPAIN	V	E	85	273,370	97,602	113,205	15,603
SWITZLD	V	E	86	94,357	25,205	30,758	5,553
TURKEY	V	E	82	22,046	6,208	7,961	1,753
U KING	V	E	82	33,069	11,565	12,865	1,300
			85	34,574	12,768	14,467	1,699

Wheat

Wheat, for humans
1307040 WHEAT EXC SEED, EDIBLE (BU)

Crop Product TSUSA commodity number, description, and unit of quantity Country	Mode	Reg	Yr	Quantity	F.A.S.	C.I.F.	Charges
TOTAL			81	6,807	42,642	42,642	
			82	2,002,290	5,968,227	6,355,280	387,053
			83	1,935,245	5,692,673	5,692,838	165
			84	3,692,743	14,998,412	15,050,724	52,312
			85	9,962,793	36,759,644	36,902,246	142,602
			86	9,342,543	25,532,705	26,294,160	761,455
CANADA	N	E	85	9,727,469	36,054,861	36,196,289	141,428
			86	6,011,617	16,210,074	16,968,162	758,088
	O	E	81	6,057	36,044	36,044	
			82	966,572	2,793,412	2,793,412	
			83	1,934,194	5,685,965	5,685,965	
			84	87,158	307,999	307,999	
			85	233,335	687,139	687,139	
			86	3,321,482	9,270,534	9,270,542	8
	O	W	81	750	6,598	6,598	
			82	750	5,763	5,763	
			83	1,035	4,629	4,629	
			84	1,018	5,105	5,105	
			86	8,254	29,361	29,361	
	V	E	82	1,034,857	3,162,528	3,549,217	386,689
			84	3,604,426	14,677,434	14,729,100	51,666
CHINA M	V	W	86	808	5,328	7,382	2,054
JAPAN	V	W	83	16	2,079	2,244	165
			84	11	1,217	1,374	157
KOR REP	V	W	82	111	6,524	6,888	364
			84	105	5,542	5,896	354
			85	1,916	16,314	17,422	1,108
			86	382	17,408	18,713	1,305
MEXICO	A	W	84	7	400	500	100
TURKEY	A	W	84	18	715	750	35
	V	E	85	73	1,330	1,396	66

Wheat, gluten
1829600 WHEAT GLUTEN (LB)

			Yr	Quantity	F.A.S.	C.I.F.	Charges
TOTAL			81	45,349,853	22,162,154	24,015,540	1,847,514
			82	43,931,281	17,906,043	19,664,595	1,758,552
			83	49,026,289	24,102,703	25,900,275	1,797,572
			84	53,560,943	26,416,613	28,415,232	1,998,619
			85	56,324,748	24,725,170	26,682,606	1,957,436
			86	59,056,004	29,482,572	31,383,590	1,901,018
ARGENT	V	E	82	177,325	41,179	53,907	12,728
			83	2,114,036	783,437	979,906	196,469
			84	1,260,003	549,462	667,412	117,950
			85	2,536,119	995,645	1,197,237	201,592
			86	3,066,038	1,350,470	1,495,259	144,789
AUSTRAL	A	W	82	1,001	1,031	1,393	362
			83	385	270	1,642	1,372
	N	E	82	7,659,683	2,833,787	3,252,067	418,280
			84	240,001	118,118	131,001	12,883
			85	2,239,200	882,291	965,240	82,949
			86	2,040,000	939,201	1,020,032	80,831
	N	W	84	6,633,689	3,128,283	3,455,297	327,014
			86	4,311,563	2,002,871	2,194,232	191,361
	O	E	81	35,000	17,161	19,250	2,089
	V	E	81	19,577,301	8,831,537	9,977,676	1,146,139
			82	13,006,485	4,848,473	5,516,751	668,278
			83	16,436,985	7,727,442	8,484,546	757,104
			84	18,158,088	8,522,459	9,346,321	823,862
			85	15,743,260	6,599,254	7,240,190	640,936
			86	13,493,773	6,030,208	6,593,786	563,578
	V	H	81	360,000	166,473	184,772	18,299
			82	520,000	197,938	224,455	26,517
			83	400,000	176,124	196,999	20,875
			84	441,550	212,814	234,497	21,683
			85	639,900	266,577	294,484	27,907
			86	400,900	191,808	207,677	15,869
	V	W	81	11,728,729	5,443,332	6,009,353	566,021
			82	10,925,199	4,143,532	4,700,545	557,013
			83	11,122,751	5,177,531	5,737,745	560,214
			84	6,557,343	3,059,984	3,376,981	316,997
			85	15,806,122	6,314,239	7,092,997	778,758
			86	11,843,111	5,464,450	5,987,649	523,199
AUSTRIA	O	E	84	154,002	68,632	76,513	7,881
	V	E	81	240,000	102,726	117,225	14,499

Crop
Product
TSUSA commodity number, description, and unit of quantity

Country	Mode	Reg	Yr	Quantity	F.A.S.	C.I.F.	Charges
			82	40,000	18,000	19,741	1,741
			83	80,000	40,000	43,751	3,751
			84	348,003	157,659	171,031	13,372
	V	W	84	40,000	20,000	21,575	1,575
			86	80,000	36,000	39,990	3,990
BELGIUM	N	E	86	4,001	8,894	9,360	466
	V	E	85	22,221	11,352	13,513	2,161
			86	205,453	86,016	100,486	14,470
CANADA	A	E	81	380	293	301	8
	O	E	81	11,306,654	6,529,012	6,536,822	1,938
			82	10,245,332	5,189,893	5,189,893	
			83	12,522,068	7,371,514	7,371,514	
			84	12,469,925	7,316,951	7,316,951	
			85	15,417,307	7,932,536	7,932,536	
			86	16,110,543	9,420,182	9,420,182	
	O	W	81	220,800	137,000	137,000	
	V	W	81	40,800	24,480	26,194	1,714
			82	299,500	149,585	162,457	12,872
			83	498,900	255,962	273,349	17,387
			84	200,000	117,376	125,156	7,780
CHINA M	V	E	83	1,873	659	716	57
			85	5,291	1,046	1,313	267
	V	W	81	3,051	1,502	1,659	157
			82	7,470	951	1,077	126
			83	3,448	1,912	2,030	118
			84	1,795	2,667	2,836	169
CHINA T	O	E	86	3,000	2,600	2,787	187
	V	E	81	22,818	12,925	14,151	1,226
			82	48,180	41,612	46,273	4,661
			83	12,586	9,057	10,449	1,392
			84	37,575	31,183	35,320	4,137
			85	72,062	64,825	72,523	7,698
			86	87,867	80,764	89,764	9,000
	V	H	81	2,400	1,920	2,102	182
			82	11,400	9,763	10,683	920
			84	1,515	1,285	1,544	259
	V	W	81	107,173	86,477	92,385	5,908
			82	85,967	67,361	73,253	5,892
			83	122,085	100,404	106,783	6,379
			84	153,872	116,010	125,045	9,035
			85	282,843	224,893	242,657	17,764
			86	335,421	257,546	271,235	13,689
CZECHO	O	E	81	159,331	75,256	83,254	7,998
FINLAND	V	E	82	88,228	31,665	36,675	5,010
			83	826,167	355,881	408,070	52,189
			84	1,959,678	860,569	996,415	135,846
			85	880,014	341,338	404,144	62,806
			86	168,728	87,188	96,220	9,032
FR GERM	O	E	83	471,958	227,772	247,622	19,850
			84	39,683	17,759	19,489	1,730
			86	12,676	7,707	7,707	
	V	E	82	120,000	44,400	50,989	6,589
			83	2,217,911	1,027,674	1,104,757	77,083
			84	2,719,759	1,160,674	1,254,115	93,441
			85	181,275	88,586	96,292	7,706
			86	2,483,563	1,515,334	1,617,076	101,742
FRANCE	A	E	81	100	1,919	1,991	72
	N	E	85	305,559	126,630	142,505	15,875
	O	E	85	148,150	49,056	55,212	6,156
			86	158,334	35,338	40,338	5,000
	V	E	83	238,098	99,792	107,712	7,920
			84	5,582	8,667	9,166	499
			85	357,807	132,603	153,882	21,279
			86	2,004,371	963,313	1,088,388	125,075
	V	W	83	1,653	4,875	4,945	70
			85	1,929	6,773	7,452	679
GERM DR	V	E	86	79,000	46,275	50,975	4,700
HG KONG	V	E	81	1,350	1,256	1,379	123
			83	366	434	468	34
			85	7,300	3,350	4,023	673
	V	W	81	1,100	949	1,086	137
			83	1,684	2,920	3,502	582
			84	1,886	3,020	3,175	155
			85	600	1,428	1,533	105
HUNGARY	O	E	82	270,675	81,420	95,869	14,449
			83	1,157,307	368,426	406,980	38,554
			84	688,192	262,793	294,353	31,560
			85	1,190,260	451,759	507,065	55,306
			86	1,078,006	425,412	459,634	34,222
	V	E	81	1,071,577	486,951	547,009	60,058
			82	115,500	52,640	58,645	6,005
			84	154,002	68,147	72,992	4,845
			86	154,350	80,361	86,061	5,700
INDIA	A	E	81	1,376	2,193	4,862	2,669
ITALY	V	E	83	6,264	5,801	6,510	709
	O	E	86	42,857	26,859	26,859	
	V	E	85	2,712	3,577	3,791	214
			86	34,244	4,854	7,287	2,433
JAPAN	O	E	82	11	368	399	31
	V	E	81	2,085	2,047	2,360	313
			82	1,063	2,489	2,684	195
			83	3,014	8,629	9,307	678
			84	4,567	12,551	13,468	917
			85	5,392	9,799	10,829	1,030
			86	1,557	4,931	5,223	292
	V	H	81	235	1,581	1,716	135
			82	440	1,767	2,103	336
	V	W	81	952	4,567	4,817	250
			82	1,220	3,770	4,005	235
			83	582	2,425	2,580	155
			84	3,784	7,231	7,973	742
			85	3,307	3,395	3,565	170
			86	291	2,706	2,801	95
KOR REP	V	E	83	3,750	3,500	3,866	366
NETHLDS	A	E	81	434	358	505	147
	V	E	81	1,869	2,195	2,476	281
			84	44,250	19,837	21,951	2,114
			86	240,000	104,532	120,497	15,965
	V	W	83	211,642	83,547	95,212	11,665
			86	74,000	38,953	41,810	2,857
NORFOLK	V	E	82	80,000	25,600	29,566	3,966
PHIL R	V	E	81	7,646	5,880	6,516	636
			82	8,704	7,058	7,857	799
			83	5,342	4,770	5,233	463
			84	1,060	1,002	1,052	50
	V	W	81	20,412	13,425	15,162	1,737
			82	59,199	37,770	42,386	4,616
			83	23,878	14,186	15,641	1,455
			84	63,125	37,218	41,259	4,041
			85	50,387	29,835	33,107	3,272
			86	26,548	21,141	23,873	2,732
ROMANIA	V	E	81	436,280	208,739	223,517	14,778
			82	158,699	73,991	80,922	6,931
			83	277,063	124,696	134,865	10,169
			84	474,428	216,029	233,271	17,242
			85	312,931	130,909	146,549	15,640
			86	428,952	185,325	209,870	24,545
SPAIN	V	W	83	44,092	17,706	20,500	2,794
SWEDEN	O	E	84	39,959	18,299	20,579	2,280
	V	E	84	439,920	194,702	224,360	29,658
			85	40,000	14,800	16,235	1,435
			86	40,500	23,352	25,110	1,758
SWITZLD	V	E	86	899	1,868	1,919	51
THAILND	V	E	85	720	1,425	1,626	201
	V	W	84	795	797	858	61
			85	22,558	16,419	18,419	2,000
			86	2,909	1,680	1,850	170
U KING	O	E	86	42,549	34,433	37,653	3,220
	V	E	83	220,401	105,357	113,075	7,718
			84	222,912	104,435	113,276	8,841
			85	49,522	20,830	23,687	2,857

1845800 WHEAT GLUTEN AS ANIMAL FEED (LB)

Country	Mode	Reg	Yr	Quantity	F.A.S.	C.I.F.	Charges
TOTAL			81	2,702,767	1,451,839	1,461,112	9,273
			82	2,511,413	1,031,268	1,086,903	55,635
			83	1,388,483	662,354	698,520	36,166
			84	2,477,599	1,099,692	1,131,611	31,919
			85	1,758,202	884,212	962,190	77,978
			86	1,898,624	992,475	1,101,559	109,084
AUSTRAL	V	E	82	480,000	191,522	221,840	30,318
			83	160,000	62,835	72,381	9,546
	V	W	81	160,000	76,231	84,800	8,569
			82	480,000	196,478	221,795	25,317
			83	40,000	15,684	17,702	2,018
			84	40,080	15,820	17,800	1,980
			85	56,966	5,460	10,169	4,709
AUSTRIA	V	E	83	80,000	32,718	38,480	5,762
CANADA	O	E	81	2,502,600	1,353,413	1,353,413	
			82	1,481,513	633,412	633,412	
			83	877,000	456,324	456,324	
			84	1,963,020	838,014	838,014	
			85	917,000	429,744	429,744	
			86	360,000	228,343	228,343	
	O	W	81	485	1,476	1,476	
			82	69,900	9,856	9,856	
			86	6,173	5,113	5,113	
	V	E	84	276,000	147,399	162,974	15,575

Crop Product TSUSA commodity number, description, and unit of quantity Country	Mode	Reg	Yr	Quantity	F.A.S.	C.I.F.	Charges
FINLAND	O	E	85	120,000	59,332	69,600	10,268
			86	852,001	418,251	479,771	61,520
	V	E	83	220,460	89,243	106,353	17,110
			84	78,704	38,985	44,426	5,441
			86	40,000	19,925	23,154	3,229
FR GERM	O	E	84	39,958	18,811	21,796	2,985
			85	80,000	39,568	45,968	6,400
			86	201,130	106,331	119,644	13,313
	V	E	86	126,720	74,201	81,101	6,900
GREECE	V	E	85	12,236	16,914	17,443	529
HUNGARY	V	E	86	36,300	24,321	27,121	2,800
JAPAN	V	E	84	86	2,600	2,742	142
ROMANIA	V	E	81	39,682	20,719	21,423	704
SWEDEN	O	E	85	452,000	276,713	322,772	46,059
			86	160,000	62,386	75,303	12,917
	V	E	84	79,751	38,063	43,859	5,796
			85	120,000	56,481	66,494	10,013
			86	80,000	31,738	37,688	5,950
U KING	V	E	83	11,023	5,550	7,280	1,730
			86	36,300	21,866	24,321	2,455

Wheat, milled for humans
1314000 WHEAT, MILLED, EDIBLE (CWT)

Country	Mode	Reg	Yr	Quantity	F.A.S.	C.I.F.	Charges
TOTAL			81	157,298	3,048,556	3,089,834	41,278
			82	265,960	3,038,217	3,062,654	24,437
			83	157,827	2,105,837	2,179,869	74,032
			84	142,693	2,124,286	2,204,320	80,034
			85	156,266	2,024,654	2,094,838	70,184
			86	198,202	2,382,492	2,488,285	105,793
AUSTRAL	A	H	86	76	4,138	9,483	5,345
	O	E	82	18	915	915	
	V	E	84	35	2,039	2,166	127
			85	35	1,919	2,057	138
AUSTRIA	V	E	81	44	3,066	3,291	225
			82	44	2,547	2,745	198
			85	35	1,675	1,930	255
			86	3,535	5,547	5,914	367
BELGIUM	O	E	81	2,456	30,422	32,622	2,200
	V	E	83	307	698	1,092	394
			84	3	275	294	19
			86	1,345	45,832	51,582	5,750
BRAZIL	A	E	84	44	301	1,564	1,263
CANADA	A	E	82	11	952	1,387	435
			83	14	312	312	
	N	E	82	386	2,629	2,929	300
			83	26,700	436,906	438,230	1,324
			85	133,168	1,617,865	1,617,865	
	O	E	81	130,882	2,677,710	2,677,710	
			82	217,434	2,641,384	2,641,384	
			83	107,713	1,240,864	1,240,864	
			84	122,816	1,701,692	1,701,692	
			85	2,432	31,583	31,954	371
			86	132,059	1,741,675	1,742,105	430
	O	W	81	259	5,746	5,746	
			82	880	13,236	13,236	
			83	292	5,896	5,896	
			84	97	1,581	1,581	
			86	3,367	15,589	15,589	
CHINA M	O	E	84	25	623	715	92
	V	E	81	80	2,769	3,371	602
			82	87	2,316	3,038	722
			83	589	14,509	21,792	7,283
			84	1,028	24,517	36,537	12,020
			85	185	5,240	6,569	1,329
			86	190	6,863	7,957	1,094
	V	W	81	268	10,831	11,615	784
			82	251	8,521	9,280	759
			83	882	12,713	14,186	1,473
			84	615	17,859	20,755	2,896
			85	126	3,150	3,624	474
CHINA T	A	E	82	22	396	3,492	3,096
	A	W	82	22	364	2,092	1,728
COLOMB	V	E	86	21,429	17,550	19,574	2,024
EGYPT	V	E	81	1,482	15,887	22,591	6,704
FR GERM	A	E	86	35	1,109	1,175	66
	O	E	86	434	18,550	24,018	5,468
	V	E	81	99	7,857	8,503	646
			82	37	2,177	2,431	254
			83	1,456	10,381	11,511	1,130
			84	21	1,193	1,331	138
			85	229	9,016	9,830	814

Country	Mode	Reg	Yr	Quantity	F.A.S.	C.I.F.	Charges
			86	983	21,454	23,538	2,084
	V	W	86	1,986	57,606	69,055	11,449
FRANCE	A	E	84	30	867	2,016	1,149
			86	534	12,862	18,271	5,409
	N	E	84	2,382	56,491	67,739	11,248
			86	4,367	125,426	143,243	17,817
	V	E	81	3,543	118,022	140,556	22,534
			82	1,551	42,026	48,686	6,660
			83	6,363	161,318	191,911	30,593
			84	5,168	133,023	156,401	23,378
			85	7,587	170,080	207,975	37,895
			86	3,330	103,851	115,673	11,822
	V	W	81	55	2,003	2,505	502
			82	462	15,505	17,805	2,300
			83	769	23,147	30,415	7,268
			84	421	10,179	13,645	3,466
			85	755	19,815	26,222	6,407
			86	891	31,063	37,623	6,560
GREECE	V	E	86	88	2,230	2,534	304
HG KONG	O	E	83	30	735	801	66
	O	W	84	36	767	848	81
	V	E	81	37	451	530	79
			82	15	499	693	194
			83	928	19,788	25,169	5,381
			84	590	13,461	19,355	5,894
			85	610	20,123	24,769	4,646
			86	75	3,088	3,696	608
	V	H	82	10	270	304	34
			84	27	613	677	64
	V	W	82	155	5,201	5,533	332
			83	53	2,180	2,329	149
			84	91	2,318	2,541	223
INDIA	O	E	81	48	2,948	3,140	192
			82	59	4,485	4,937	452
			83	30	2,437	2,560	123
			84	397	8,672	8,871	199
			85	2	1,325	1,463	138
			86	2	1,881	2,063	182
	O	W	83	2	305	325	20
	V	E	83	19	1,294	1,468	174
			85	18	1,416	1,533	117
	V	W	83	11	330	378	48
IRAN	V	W	83	3	1,234	1,446	212
ITALY	A	E	84	3	825	1,218	393
	V	E	83	15	317	428	111
	V	W	81	30	1,440	1,700	260
			83	43	1,593	1,932	339
JAPAN	N	E	86	6,383	28,779	38,890	10,111
	N	W	84	2,060	55,213	61,028	5,815
	V	E	81	1,361	5,473	6,061	588
			82	179	8,559	9,340	781
			83	320	12,080	13,038	958
			84	2,652	33,913	37,143	3,230
			85	6,046	8,122	9,064	942
	V	H	82	6	650	856	206
			84	16	1,058	1,388	330
	V	W	81	1,720	65,377	70,068	4,691
			82	2,006	71,863	76,495	4,632
			83	2,579	74,337	80,625	6,288
			84	2,057	17,219	18,267	1,048
			85	3,552	111,047	122,633	11,586
			86	7,252	92,625	98,828	6,203
KENYA	O	E	84	18	603	603	
KOR REP	V	E	85	1,218	6,855	7,698	843
			86	5,744	12,618	16,526	3,908
LEBANON	V	E	86	220	2,708	3,234	526
MALAWI	O	E	81	220	400	400	
			82	898	15,750	15,750	
			83	491	7,536	7,536	
			84	308	4,522	4,522	
MEXICO	O	E	81	6,668	26,043	26,043	
			82	30,840	113,383	113,383	
			83	7,459	50,247	50,247	
			84	811	8,350	8,350	
			86	120	1,200	1,200	
	O	W	81	7,501	65,478	65,478	
			82	10,436	76,537	76,537	
			86	250	2,500	2,500	
NEPAL	O	E	83	44	920	920	
NETHLDS	V	E	81	7	280	337	57
			83	55	802	1,191	389
PERU	V	E	84	11	612	674	62
			86	2,507	3,351	3,551	200
PORTUGL	V	E	82	24	880	983	103

Crop Product TSUSA commodity number, description, and unit of quantity Country	Mode	Reg	Yr	Quantity	F.A.S.	C.I.F.	Charges
			83	176	12,687	19,451	6,764
			84	66	1,520	1,833	313
			85	113	4,721	6,442	1,721
			86	192	6,312	7,242	930
SINGAPR	V	W	81	12	1,150	1,265	115
SPAIN	V	W	85	44	1,674	1,765	91
SWEDEN	A	E	83	12	328	1,486	1,158
SWITZLD	O	E	86	554	11,624	17,671	6,047
	V	E	83	44	2,593	2,855	262
THAILND	V	W	82	5	429	451	22
			83	154	2,851	3,069	218
TUNISIA	A	W	86	31	1,678	2,028	350
TURKEY	O	E	83	8	400	400	
			84	66	1,683	1,683	
			85	53	3,739	3,739	
	V	E	81	110	4,250	5,050	800
			82	109	5,900	6,950	1,050
			83	110	2,948	4,774	1,826
			84	566	15,069	17,439	2,370
			86	223	2,783	3,522	739
U KING	A	E	81	2	308	481	173
			84	35	365	2,146	1,781
			85	45	3,094	5,195	2,101
	O	E	82	4	390	424	34
			83	6	398	398	
			84	5	936	1,061	125
	V	E	81	14	345	370	25
			82	9	453	598	145
			83	150	753	834	81
			84	44	1,148	1,692	544
			85	13	2,195	2,511	316
	V	W	81	400	300	401	101
VENEZ	A	E	84	149	4,779	6,545	1,766

Wheat, milled not for humans
1317200 WHEAT FLOUR NOT FIT HUM CONS (CWT)

Country	Mode	Reg	Yr	Quantity	F.A.S.	C.I.F.	Charges
TOTAL			81	10,299	72,461	76,329	3,868
			82	12,157	41,949	44,879	2,930
			83	5,756	30,847	32,264	1,417
			84	11,702	36,045	38,575	2,530
			85	80,260	136,033	142,287	6,254
			86	51,978	149,784	156,019	6,235
ARGENT	A	E	82	6	253	1,468	1,215
BELGIUM	V	E	86	29	2,148	2,330	182
CANADA	O	E	81	1,025	24,145	24,145	
			82	2,161	29,728	29,728	
			83	1,232	17,991	17,991	
			84	862	11,584	11,584	
			85	38,199	76,717	76,717	
			86	43,050	74,104	74,104	
	O	W	81	5,167	32,338	32,338	
			86	7,715	7,715	7,715	
CHINA M	N	W	82	2,500	600	661	61
	V	E	82	354	2,224	2,782	558
			83	250	609	666	57
	V	W	83	25	634	708	74
			84	535	2,087	2,227	140
			85	40	1,051	1,133	82
			86	200	8,289	8,837	548
CHINA T	V	W	85	3	1,087	1,139	52
FR GERM	V	E	86	22	4,247	5,563	1,316
FRANCE	V	E	83	6	722	771	49
HG KONG	V	E	81	3,265	1,462	1,590	128
	V	H	82	2,000	499	670	171
	V	W	81	15	505	532	27
			84	1,065	3,377	3,520	143
			85	45	6,216	6,597	381
			86	65	2,049	2,168	119
ITALY	A	E	82	1	307	522	215
JAPAN	A	W	81	20	2,105	2,533	428
	V	E	81	271	1,772	1,933	161
			82	573	2,038	2,350	312
			83	51	2,744	3,118	374
			84	8,888	8,357	9,504	1,147
			85	20,092	27,065	29,796	2,731
			86	666	35,789	37,753	1,964
	V	W	81	207	7,632	8,270	638
			82	4,562	6,300	6,698	398
			83	3,456	5,666	6,091	425
			84	352	10,640	11,740	1,100
			85	20,403	14,878	16,439	1,561

Crop Product TSUSA commodity number, description, and unit of quantity Country	Mode	Reg	Yr	Quantity	F.A.S.	C.I.F.	Charges
			86	112	9,305	9,722	417
KOR REP	V	E	86	66	3,663	3,857	194
MEXICO	O	W	83	66	308	308	
PORTUGL	V	E	83	20	704	788	84
THAILND	V	W	83	646	984	1,134	150
U KING	A	E	83	4	485	689	204
	O	E	85	198	2,094	2,134	40
	V	E	81	329	2,502	4,988	2,486
	V	W	85	1,280	6,925	8,332	1,407
			86	53	2,475	3,970	1,495

1317500 WHEAT, MILLD, EX FLR, INEDIB (CWT)

Country	Mode	Reg	Yr	Quantity	F.A.S.	C.I.F.	Charges
TOTAL			81	868	8,280	9,144	864
			82	25	2,174	2,407	233
			83	574	5,267	6,083	816
			84	941	9,799	9,950	151
			85	11	2,393	2,586	193
			86	42,160	132,385	138,327	5,942
AUSTRAL	A	W	84	6	605	734	129
BELGIUM	V	E	85	5	1,151	1,278	127
CANADA	O	E	81	839	7,481	7,481	
			83	545	1,639	1,639	
			84	933	8,800	8,800	
			86	29,634	97,774	97,774	
CHINA T	V	E	83	3	500	654	154
			86	24	2,080	2,436	356
F W IND	V	E	86	12,502	32,531	38,117	5,586
ITALY	V	E	83	26	3,043	3,833	790
JAPAN	V	E	82	5	303	352	49
	V	W	83	3	585	611	26
			84	2	394	416	22
			85	6	1,242	1,308	66
NETHLDS	V	E	82	20	1,871	2,055	184
U KING	A	E	81	26	299	1,009	710

Wheat, not for humans
1306600 WHEAT,EXCEPT SEED, INEDIBLE (BU)

Country	Mode	Reg	Yr	Quantity	F.A.S.	C.I.F.	Charges
TOTAL			81	3,355	13,345	13,345	
			82	16,701	54,864	75,654	20,790
			83	6,318	25,123	25,123	
			84	1,124	2,149	2,265	116
			85	7,108	20,491	20,491	
			86	266,217	586,017	586,017	
AUSTRAL	V	W	82	742	4,035	23,104	19,069
CANADA	O	E	81	3,355	13,345	13,345	
			82	15,938	49,639	49,639	
			83	4,508	16,005	16,005	
			84	132	675	675	
			85	5,529	15,789	15,789	
			86	203,785	449,080	449,080	
	O	W	83	1,810	9,118	9,118	
			85	1,579	4,702	4,702	
			86	62,432	136,937	136,937	
JAPAN	V	E	84	992	1,474	1,590	116
SWEDEN	A	W	82	21	1,190	2,911	1,721

Wheat, seed, for humans
1307020 SEED WHEAT, EDIBLE (BU)

Country	Mode	Reg	Yr	Quantity	F.A.S.	C.I.F.	Charges
TOTAL			81	10,249	83,777	83,777	
			82	57,948	382,555	382,555	
			83	9,420	62,528	62,528	
			84	13,469	65,244	65,244	
			85	27,308	142,946	142,946	
			86	166,558	499,942	499,942	
CANADA	O	E	81	4,323	26,829	26,829	
			82	53,511	358,017	358,017	
			83	5,144	39,671	39,671	
			84	12,530	60,275	60,275	
			85	19,129	98,412	98,412	
			86	154,542	441,844	441,844	
	O	W	81	3,333	25,802	25,802	
			82	4,437	24,538	24,538	
			83	4,276	22,857	22,857	
			84	939	4,969	4,969	
			85	8,179	44,534	44,534	
			86	12,016	58,098	58,098	
FR GERM	O	E	81	367	9,253	9,253	

Crop Product TSUSA commodity number, description, and unit of quantity Country	Mode	Reg	Yr	Quantity	F.A.S.	C.I.F.	Charges
MEXICO	O	W	81	2,226	21,893	21,893	

Wheat, seed, not for humans
1306300 SEED WHEAT, INEDIBLE (BU)

Country	Mode	Reg	Yr	Quantity	F.A.S.	C.I.F.	Charges
TOTAL			81	13,602	103,391	103,391	
			82	16,893	70,269	70,269	
			83	8,056	57,903	57,903	
			84	2,036	14,352	14,615	263
			85	761	5,171	5,171	
			86	5,082	31,513	31,513	
CANADA	O	E	81	13,027	99,397	99,397	
			82	15,611	61,334	61,334	
			83	7,891	55,540	55,540	
			84	2,025	13,952	13,952	
			85	761	5,171	5,171	
			86	5,082	31,513	31,513	
	O	W	81	575	3,994	3,994	
			83	62	543	543	
FR GERM	O	E	83	103	1,820	1,820	
MEXICO	O	W	82	1,282	8,935	8,935	
U KING	O	E	84	11	400	663	263

Wheatgrass

Wheatgrass, seed
1269500 WHEAT GRASS SEED (LB)

Country	Mode	Reg	Yr	Quantity	F.A.S.	C.I.F.	Charges
TOTAL			81	1,404,814	878,928	884,511	5,583
			82	763,813	497,216	500,638	3,422
			83	1,625,291	972,956	972,956	
			84	723,575	509,097	509,480	383
			85	319,955	396,120	396,120	
			86	2,218,862	2,950,702	2,976,008	25,306
ARGENT	O	E	81	25,022	18,804	18,804	
	V	E	81	60,685	25,099	30,682	5,583
			82	44,092	17,000	20,422	3,422
			86	200,860	78,014	96,867	18,853
AUSTRAL	V	W	86	69,421	44,237	50,140	5,903
CANADA	O	E	81	257,649	162,547	162,547	
			82	250,858	132,674	132,674	
			83	231,065	137,304	137,304	
			84	135,150	116,605	116,605	
			85	111,520	124,382	124,382	
			86	485,804	545,073	545,073	
	O	W	81	1,061,458	672,478	672,478	
			82	442,408	346,836	346,836	
			83	1,379,235	830,230	830,230	
			84	586,154	389,938	389,938	
			85	208,435	271,738	271,738	
			86	1,457,552	2,275,306	2,275,306	
FR GERM	O	E	83	14,991	5,422	5,422	
HUNGARY	V	E	86	5,225	8,072	8,622	550
INDIA	V	E	84	265	304	342	38
MEXICO	O	E	82	26,455	706	706	
POLAND	V	E	84	2,006	2,250	2,595	345

Wild Rice

Wild rice
1827000 WILD RICE (LB)

Country	Mode	Reg	Yr	Quantity	F.A.S.	C.I.F.	Charges
TOTAL			81	1,417,283	2,637,326	2,639,322	1,996
			82	678,434	1,326,997	1,328,773	1,776
			83	683,051	1,233,328	1,235,728	2,400
			84	1,133,771	1,714,809	1,735,022	20,213
			85	1,155,089	1,071,144	1,096,286	25,142
			86	805,192	584,638	608,296	23,658
CANADA	A	H	83	200	907	1,034	127
			84	100	432	540	108
	O	E	81	1,402,079	2,629,481	2,629,481	
			82	668,526	1,314,291	1,314,291	
			83	610,239	1,189,024	1,189,024	
			84	698,407	1,619,252	1,621,162	1,910
			85	432,034	874,793	874,793	

Country	Mode	Reg	Yr	Quantity	F.A.S.	C.I.F.	Charges
			86	309,710	486,426	486,426	
	O	W	81	550	357	430	73
			82	500	2,250	2,265	15
			84	600	3,411	3,411	
			85	41,385	92,015	92,015	
			86	661	2,430	2,430	
CHINA M	V	E	83	11,916	2,622	3,379	757
CHINA T	V	E	84	3,960	2,755	3,369	614
			85	3,219	2,200	2,639	439
	V	W	81	358	375	443	68
			83	10,315	11,559	12,659	1,100
			84	40,036	6,941	9,860	2,919
			85	41,746	6,768	9,831	3,063
FRANCE	V	E	82	7,810	6,258	7,809	1,551
			83	3,842	5,100	5,261	161
HG KONG	V	E	83	600	456	532	76
	V	W	81	1,800	907	981	74
			84	80,000	14,841	15,583	742
			85	40,036	7,366	7,734	368
INDIA	O	E	83	41,471	21,365	21,365	
			84	29,370	10,497	10,497	
			85	11,275	3,186	3,186	
			86	23,972	12,170	13,422	1,252
	V	E	86	2,205	1,040	1,409	369
	V	W	82	1,102	298	360	62
			83	1,190	556	556	
JAPAN	V	E	83	22	718	776	58
			84	1,960	2,551	2,779	228
	V	H	82	496	3,900	4,048	148
	V	W	84	36,191	7,060	7,413	353
PAKISTN	V	W	81	10,911	5,163	6,620	1,457
PHIL R	V	W	81	482	400	509	109
			83	500	396	442	46
			84	1,050	399	454	55
PORTUGL	V	E	83	2,756	625	700	75
SINGAPR	V	W	84	120,067	22,641	28,770	6,129
THAILND	V	E	84	80,142	15,904	19,935	4,031
	V	W	81	1,103	643	858	215
			84	40,036	7,378	10,297	2,919
			85	585,394	84,816	106,088	21,272
			86	458,146	71,750	91,017	19,267
U KING	V	E	84	1,852	747	952	205
			86	10,498	10,822	13,592	2,770

Willow

Willow, basket
2224100 BASKETS AND BAGS WILLOW (NO)

Country	Mode	Reg	Yr	Quantity	F.A.S.	C.I.F.	Charges
TOTAL			81	11,014,683	9,331,124	11,876,341	2,545,217
			82	11,383,686	8,726,726	11,759,189	3,032,463
			83	18,408,727	12,710,317	17,502,551	4,792,234
			84	24,482,904	17,685,807	24,909,895	7,224,088
			85	25,509,062	18,365,698	25,162,593	6,796,895
			86	27,653,514	18,440,239	24,718,310	6,278,071
AUSTRIA	V	E	81	50	500	505	5
			83	31	467	500	33
			84	74	775	829	54
BELGIUM	A	E	81	1,008	966	1,166	200
	V	E	85	728	9,560	11,905	2,345
BRAZIL	V	E	82	6,000	4,272	6,014	1,742
CAMROON	V	W	85	88,778	30,196	49,390	19,194
CANADA	O	E	81	193	1,199	1,199	
			82	691	5,325	6,544	1,219
			84	32	296	296	
			85	354	2,645	2,645	
	V	E	85	1,988	2,174	3,960	1,786
CHILE	A	E	81	3,000	8,100	9,319	1,219
	O	E	86	4,590	17,332	17,332	
	V	E	85	3,184	3,893	4,922	1,029
CHINA M	A	E	82	240	594	3,952	3,358
			83	6,888	448	1,333	885
			86	2,000	1,767	11,893	10,126
	A	H	86	5,240	4,416	14,636	10,220
	N	E	81	496,263	342,845	477,100	134,255
			83	2,826,896	1,209,099	1,859,075	649,976
			84	4,504,739	2,218,514	3,604,186	1,385,672
			85	23,244	29,488	44,024	14,536
			86	921,234	434,152	616,134	181,982
	N	W	82	1,452,805	866,773	1,185,592	318,819

Crop Product TSUSA commodity number, description, and unit of quantity Country	Mode	Reg	Yr	Quantity	F.A.S.	C.I.F.	Charges
			83	1,638,066	995,530	1,347,500	351,970
			85	4,332,296	2,600,691	3,315,268	714,577
			86	43,482	46,590	61,553	14,963
	O	E	81	18,946	8,658	10,260	1,602
			82	765	7,925	7,925	
			83	49,802	28,014	40,900	12,886
			84	111,439	73,753	89,546	15,793
			85	29,245	21,092	27,510	6,418
			86	220,224	78,582	95,371	16,789
	V	E	81	895,533	472,092	631,076	158,984
			82	2,169,440	1,236,607	1,707,002	470,395
			83	2,688,467	1,728,245	2,388,237	659,992
			84	4,921,679	3,515,304	5,060,655	1,545,351
			85	8,616,346	5,021,356	7,368,658	2,347,302
			86	7,361,476	4,500,692	6,140,606	1,639,914
	V	H	81	640	275	336	61
			84	1,060	1,437	2,036	599
			85	2,750	5,798	7,481	1,683
			86	1,992	2,240	3,694	1,454
	V	W	81	4,597,699	3,197,374	4,064,212	866,838
			82	3,421,388	2,208,881	3,015,137	806,256
			83	5,305,229	3,320,402	4,497,306	1,176,904
			84	8,463,522	5,616,475	7,742,643	2,126,168
			85	6,504,872	4,627,985	6,278,659	1,650,674
			86	13,122,730	7,662,572	10,145,266	2,482,694
CHINA T	A	E	82	88	434	1,259	825
	V	E	81	391	792	985	193
			82	40,634	38,208	51,136	12,928
			83	76,570	61,592	87,035	25,443
			84	114,126	108,054	125,492	17,438
			85	45,970	45,607	57,444	11,837
			86	46,864	49,185	60,936	11,751
	V	H	84	69	400	444	44
	V	W	81	33,952	25,575	32,651	7,076
			82	18,191	23,470	29,266	5,796
			83	55,263	40,813	48,304	7,491
			84	110,887	104,131	128,607	24,476
			85	174,793	61,230	80,053	18,823
			86	41,487	75,521	94,018	18,497
COLOMB	A	E	81	1,086	3,317	3,946	629
			85	8,915	5,032	6,367	1,335
CRIST I	A	E	86	748	2,296	2,296	
CZECHO	V	E	86	800	4,120	4,399	279
DOM REP	V	E	86	240	1,847	2,730	883
ECUADOR	A	E	81	31	400	432	32
			83	2,880	480	715	235
FR GERM	A	E	83	56	321	801	480
	O	E	81	122	2,633	2,723	90
			84	9	503	552	49
	V	E	81	925	10,938	12,392	1,454
			82	1,232	10,668	12,901	2,233
			83	309	3,018	3,236	218
			84	20,643	25,703	33,685	7,982
			85	6,510	20,590	24,264	3,674
			86	5,174	5,989	8,296	2,307
	V	W	81	2,923	21,490	28,112	6,622
			82	486	4,063	4,886	823
			85	77	4,402	5,371	969
FRANCE	A	E	84	9	306	434	128
	N	E	81	2,245	2,622	2,942	320
			83	550	7,492	10,263	2,771
			84	2,198	9,106	11,264	2,158
			86	528	5,985	6,387	402
	N	W	84	621	4,504	6,018	1,514
	O	E	84	280	5,257	8,257	3,000
	V	E	82	7,778	10,412	11,602	1,190
			83	9,481	32,530	36,125	3,595
			84	462	5,364	6,418	1,054
			85	5,478	20,711	24,699	3,988
	V	W	81	807	5,930	7,452	1,522
			82	24	433	484	51
			83	180	2,197	2,460	263
			84	92	790	875	85
			85	241	3,491	4,038	547
G BISAU	V	E	82	7,824	4,317	6,396	2,079
GERM DR	V	E	83	5,303	6,065	9,635	3,570
HAITI	N	E	86	19,194	43,105	53,968	10,863
	V	E	85	855	1,767	2,333	566
HG KONG	A	E	81	3,804	11,332	21,179	9,847
			84	279	278	2,040	1,762
	N	E	84	4,806	5,702	7,947	2,245
	N	W	81	2,874	7,993	9,430	1,437
			84	191,458	110,136	143,521	33,385
	O	E	84	19,582	19,031	19,606	575

Crop Product TSUSA commodity number, description, and unit of quantity Country	Mode	Reg	Yr	Quantity	F.A.S.	C.I.F.	Charges
	V	E	81	49,524	20,772	25,364	4,592
			82	38,886	34,530	42,726	8,196
			83	160,331	89,922	123,157	33,235
			84	210,289	206,740	295,727	88,987
			85	253,037	325,248	429,462	104,214
			86	576,655	474,927	643,680	168,753
	V	H	83	2,076	616	899	283
	V	W	81	426,681	135,609	155,189	19,580
			82	126,045	73,513	92,411	18,898
			83	475,261	298,065	382,364	84,299
			84	743,563	511,469	673,813	162,344
			85	895,603	555,387	711,155	155,768
			86	1,383,569	841,016	1,105,140	264,124
HUNGARY	N	E	82	1,584	5,877	9,311	3,434
	O	E	86	7,414	22,243	33,613	11,370
	V	E	81	3,392	10,350	13,535	3,185
			83	3,505	17,725	25,015	7,290
			84	4,408	17,276	20,688	3,412
			85	1,500	5,533	9,000	3,467
			86	15,016	59,082	83,753	24,671
	V	W	86	1,936	14,828	22,922	8,094
INDIA	A	W	81	961	9,699	12,768	3,069
			84	500	1,771	2,155	384
	V	E	81	14,629	7,372	9,966	2,594
			85	2,166	9,163	12,824	3,661
	V	W	81	14,020	28,491	38,970	10,479
			82	3,392	6,248	7,738	1,490
			83	2,300	9,975	14,777	4,802
			84	6,899	25,839	34,086	8,247
			85	5,128	10,415	15,504	5,089
			86	1,300	7,334	12,868	5,534
INDNSIA	V	W	83	1,320	15,576	20,411	4,835
			84	2,917	15,476	23,009	7,533
			85	3,148	6,905	10,374	3,469
			86	20,354	43,060	58,096	15,036
IRAN	V	W	84	2,169	4,827	8,760	3,933
IRELAND	N	E	81	562	8,350	9,754	1,404
	O	E	81	50	1,952	3,059	1,107
			82	50	636	984	348
			83	84	757	1,032	275
	V	E	81	120	2,988	3,341	353
ISRAEL	V	E	81	979	3,924	4,635	711
			82	1,040	3,967	4,743	776
			83	534	2,867	3,081	214
ITALY	A	E	83	17	536	553	17
	V	E	81	38,710	161,983	194,621	32,638
			82	32,665	46,444	61,211	14,767
			83	27,936	45,157	56,875	11,718
			84	15,117	22,359	28,141	5,782
			85	10,634	31,786	42,388	10,602
			86	1,714	14,120	18,070	3,950
	V	W	81	6,499	17,973	25,061	7,088
			82	501	3,803	4,861	1,058
			83	154	1,688	1,882	194
			84	432	6,358	6,732	374
			86	528	3,682	6,386	2,704
JAMAICA	A	E	85	600	1,100	1,200	100
JAPAN	V	E	81	30,514	9,902	12,955	3,053
			82	714	1,321	1,395	74
			83	2,880	6,827	8,476	1,649
			84	1,344	2,517	3,076	559
			85	59,608	22,779	47,880	25,101
			86	35,501	18,427	30,336	11,909
	V	H	83	205	742	901	159
	V	W	81	280	268	347	79
			82	357	624	742	118
			83	67,000	22,342	38,527	16,185
			84	4,272	7,096	13,020	5,924
			85	15,524	14,703	21,446	6,743
			86	3,754	3,117	3,974	857
KOR REP	A	E	84	960	350	537	187
	V	E	81	928	6,525	8,481	1,956
			83	11,336	4,939	5,772	833
			84	21,508	22,899	26,810	3,911
			86	11,567	7,184	8,843	1,659
	V	W	83	3,072	1,221	1,304	83
			84	7,200	1,860	2,116	256
			86	3,900	4,255	6,269	2,014
MACAO	V	E	84	1,176	871	1,044	173
	V	W	86	39,588	19,784	24,565	4,781
MEXICO	O	E	81	8,715	16,751	16,751	
			82	10,092	14,862	14,862	
			83	17,406	44,285	44,285	
			84	11,600	24,144	24,743	599

Crop
Product
TSUSA commodity number, description, and unit of quantity

Country	Mode	Reg	Yr	Quantity	F.A.S.	C.I.F.	Charges
			85	11,032	5,051	5,051	
			86	20,749	6,975	9,438	2,463
	O	W	81	7,419	11,394	11,394	
			82	3,200	2,706	2,706	
			84	3,441	2,284	2,284	
			85	8,000	4,832	4,939	107
NETHLDS	A	E	86	1,372	1,303	1,394	91
	V	E	85	5,511	12,330	14,621	2,291
			86	8,724	12,739	16,274	3,535
	V	W	81	300	510	609	99
PHIL R	O	E	84	144	480	652	172
	V	E	81	36,737	44,282	64,260	19,978
			82	20,205	9,209	11,716	2,507
			83	195,348	105,094	137,739	32,645
			84	174,132	131,789	186,576	54,787
			85	128,746	107,321	144,656	37,335
			86	158,575	163,088	209,673	46,585
	V	W	81	137,314	109,555	142,549	32,994
			82	50,329	65,916	79,265	13,349
			83	94,267	49,401	64,681	15,280
			84	132,654	79,266	129,842	50,576
			85	99,973	116,412	156,934	40,522
			86	95,301	162,330	209,176	46,846
PITCARN	V	E	85	7,160	8,918	10,628	1,710
POLAND	N	E	82	169,358	335,816	403,065	67,249
	O	E	82	47,414	79,555	91,684	12,129
			86	9,562	11,227	13,177	1,950
	V	E	81	415,750	780,452	941,060	160,608
			82	45,233	79,007	95,693	16,686
			83	246,575	410,151	496,259	86,108
			84	224,615	435,664	522,176	86,512
			85	159,665	302,021	379,311	77,290
			86	142,756	180,824	254,930	74,106
	V	W	81	20,295	53,373	71,609	18,236
			82	57,043	49,136	73,347	24,211
PORTUGL	A	E	82	126	1,096	1,758	662
			84	1,084	2,217	4,790	2,573
			85	15,582	3,564	4,535	971
	N	E	84	1,574,874	975,205	1,262,956	287,751
	N	W	84	110,085	87,362	119,144	31,782
	O	E	81	2,246	7,363	8,163	800
			82	892	7,157	10,205	3,048
	V	E	81	2,374,970	1,626,398	1,992,664	366,266
			82	2,439,210	1,508,269	1,942,425	434,156
			83	2,675,757	1,393,043	1,818,009	424,966
			84	1,256,314	668,733	919,933	251,200
			85	2,225,233	1,586,206	2,132,912	546,706
			86	1,776,088	1,359,835	1,735,819	375,984
	V	W	81	87,647	120,034	155,839	35,805
			82	50,758	70,475	100,341	29,866
			83	87,929	108,702	157,062	48,360
			84	4,615	13,396	25,883	12,487
			85	152,177	149,423	198,206	48,783
			86	6,682	26,597	32,249	5,652
ROMANIA	N	E	86	2,484	13,820	14,704	884
	V	E	81	47,592	156,581	214,814	58,233
			82	47,457	170,034	251,180	81,146
			83	48,618	188,211	247,629	59,418
			84	51,720	222,490	321,987	99,497
			85	28,162	196,225	272,771	76,546
			86	43,003	213,337	305,680	92,343
	V	W	81	43,133	113,562	187,432	73,870
			82	47,202	109,977	190,219	80,242
			83	58,536	83,413	134,724	51,311
			84	16,633	44,285	74,274	29,989
			85	11,453	33,434	50,440	17,006
			86	8,740	29,045	44,033	14,988
S HELNA	V	E	86	1,106	7,174	9,274	2,100
SPAIN	A	E	83	124	256	759	503
			84	138	333	1,011	678
	N	E	82	13,970	51,305	61,538	10,233
			84	37,234	124,250	159,148	34,898
	N	W	84	5,601	25,593	36,249	10,656
	O	E	81	581	4,343	6,643	2,300
			82	118	435	435	
	O	W	81	2,380	6,784	8,445	1,661
	V	E	81	78,596	287,896	347,726	59,830
			82	69,217	264,375	332,433	68,058
			83	115,673	411,368	519,468	108,100
			84	191,360	631,679	807,148	175,469
			85	281,101	870,560	1,079,975	209,415
			86	121,600	450,772	548,368	97,596
	V	W	81	23,107	69,540	85,149	15,609
			82	23,702	66,236	85,200	18,964
			83	37,450	103,711	131,960	28,249
			84	9,418	34,433	57,356	22,923
			85	23,916	35,088	59,411	24,323
			86	3,070	16,497	20,987	4,490
SRI LKA	V	W	85	1,310	1,547	2,153	606
SWITZLD	A	E	85	6,000	1,140	1,599	459
	V	E	85	27,100	24,277	40,049	15,772
			86	23,477	17,490	29,850	12,360
	V	W	85	228,464	62,543	80,882	18,339
			86	206,514	53,055	64,346	11,291
THAILND	V	E	81	2	400	422	22
			86	226	2,930	3,329	399
U KING	A	E	82	120	1,549	1,818	269
			83	65	787	852	65
			84	56	1,761	1,907	146
			85	35	2,340	2,895	555
			86	1,579	15,433	18,348	2,915
	N	E	81	1,207	7,485	9,116	1,631
			82	2,762	23,367	26,795	3,428
			83	797	15,155	16,933	1,778
			84	18,142	29,693	33,752	4,059
			85	9,175	92,924	106,440	13,516
			86	25,417	80,895	87,900	7,005
	N	W	83	764	9,099	10,012	913
	O	E	81	20	432	449	17
			82	244	2,480	3,149	669
	V	E	81	83	742	855	113
			82	1,991	12,456	14,266	1,810
			83	142	2,865	3,239	374
			84	2,197	26,504	30,777	4,273
			85	6,065	30,524	34,863	4,339
			86	1,816	8,741	9,688	947
	V	W	81	816	8,782	9,558	776
			82	946	11,403	12,222	819
			83	53	1,093	1,238	145
			84	474	6,265	7,480	1,215
			85	170	2,073	2,479	406
URUGUAY	V	E	85	1,668	10,221	17,287	7,066
YUGOSLV	N	E	81	34,182	33,827	46,805	12,978
			82	18,465	28,511	42,114	13,603
			83	5,479	21,460	31,143	9,683
			84	32,878	62,118	78,500	16,382
			85	39,288	75,622	101,334	25,712
	O	E	83	329	878	988	110
			84	238	719	827	108
			86	7,203	9,340	13,142	3,802
	V	E	81	909,069	1,108,938	1,408,205	299,267
			82	828,239	1,021,782	1,403,775	381,993
			83	1,170,155	1,578,113	2,273,247	695,134
			84	1,065,793	1,275,384	1,796,246	520,862
			85	880,253	1,022,383	1,460,219	437,836
			86	1,053,403	1,060,218	1,566,179	505,961
	V	W	81	132,181	210,511	310,361	99,850
			82	102,573	140,267	230,760	90,493
			83	229,278	227,564	393,873	166,309
			84	66,644	106,233	169,189	62,956
			85	58,251	107,992	177,779	69,787
			86	33,268	67,124	102,322	35,198

Willow, prepared

2222000 WILLOW PREP FOR BSKT MAKERS (LB)

Country	Mode	Reg	Yr	Quantity	F.A.S.	C.I.F.	Charges
TOTAL			81	54,437	52,146	60,887	8,741
			82	3,491	12,370	13,933	1,563
			83	86,633	44,355	52,986	8,631
			84	96,608	57,087	70,014	12,927
			85	41,369	34,174	40,760	6,586
			86	935	8,370	9,957	1,587
BELGIUM	V	E	81	2,204	1,840	2,137	297
CHINA T	V	W	85	4,945	3,900	4,642	742
HG KONG	A	E	82	90	310	462	152
			86	313	1,199	1,714	515
ITALY	V	E	81	6,504	649	2,125	1,476
			82	319	446	494	48
KOR REP	A	W	84	204	2,927	3,568	641
NETHLDS	V	E	82	1,360	1,248	1,596	348
PORTUGL	V	E	81	21,301	14,898	17,548	2,650
			83	62,104	22,772	28,032	5,260
			84	94,150	44,626	55,561	10,935
			85	16,700	12,005	13,895	1,890
	V	W	81	22,733	15,399	18,970	3,571
			83	22,606	14,394	16,956	2,562

Crop Product TSUSA commodity number, description, and unit of quantity Country	Mode	Reg	Yr	Quantity	F.A.S.	C.I.F.	Charges
SINGAPR	V	E	82	138	313	428	115
SPAIN	A	E	81	93	719	946	227
			82	120	880	1,130	250
			83	260	1,481	1,753	272
			86	114	1,171	1,713	542
	V	E	81	1,602	18,641	19,161	520
			82	1,464	9,173	9,823	650
			83	1,663	5,708	6,245	537
			84	2,254	9,534	10,885	1,351
			85	925	6,720	7,331	611
			86	508	6,000	6,530	530
	V	W	85	18,799	11,549	14,892	3,343

2222500 WILLOW,EX PRE F BASKET MAKER (LB)

	Mode	Reg	Yr	Quantity	F.A.S.	C.I.F.	Charges
TOTAL			81	9,615	16,800	20,789	3,989
			82	5,988	11,615	14,410	2,795
			83	12,621	14,369	18,229	3,860
			84	22,990	24,584	30,595	6,011
			85	12,607	25,369	29,010	3,641
			86	1,652	12,132	13,749	1,617
CHINA M	A	E	86	168	3,406	3,706	300
	V	E	83	716	547	793	246
	V	W	81	970	1,407	1,883	476
			83	1,034	1,204	2,084	880
			85	4,694	5,480	6,338	858
FR GERM	O	E	84	1,894	1,588	2,431	843
	V	E	83	1,102	700	779	79
HG KONG	V	W	84	180	585	700	115
ITALY	V	W	81	330	444	515	71
			82	220	318	346	28
SPAIN	A	E	81	40	719	895	176
			82	185	1,531	1,931	400
			83	429	2,271	2,953	682
			84	291	1,856	2,502	646
	V	E	81	4,961	10,250	12,677	2,427
			82	3,336	7,048	8,485	1,437
			83	2,115	2,901	3,279	378
			84	11,704	18,340	22,156	3,816
			85	3,724	4,811	5,496	685
			86	1,334	3,384	4,039	655
	V	W	81	3,314	3,980	4,819	839
			82	2,247	2,718	3,648	930
			83	7,144	6,382	7,872	1,490
			84	8,921	2,215	2,806	591
U KING	V	E	83	81	364	469	105
	V	W	86	150	5,342	6,004	662
YUGOSLV	V	E	85	4,189	15,078	17,176	2,098

Willow, webbing**
2223000 WOV MTL BMBO RATN ETC F/BLDS (NULL)
(See Bamboo, webbing under Bamboo)

Wormwood

Santonin
4376600 SANTONIN AND SALTS (LB)

	Mode	Reg	Yr	Quantity	F.A.S.	C.I.F.	Charges
TOTAL			81	78	3,523	3,611	88
			82	7	561	675	114
			84	61	619	619	
			85	285	1,653	1,653	
CANADA	O	E	81	63	650	650	
			84	61	619	619	
			85	285	1,653	1,653	
DENMARK	A	E	81	1	1,200	1,250	50
INDIA	A	E	82	7	561	675	114
PAKISTN	A	E	81	14	1,673	1,711	38

Y

Yam

Yam, fresh
1378800 YAMS, FRESH OR CHILLED (LB)

	Mode	Reg	Yr	Quantity	F.A.S.	C.I.F.	Charges
TOTAL			81	9,931,349	2,342,885	3,077,984	705,764
			82	16,315,650	3,638,126	4,713,695	1,075,569
			83	18,389,264	4,902,697	6,332,602	1,429,905
			84	21,580,212	5,363,995	7,205,267	1,841,272
			85	25,038,016	6,215,230	8,434,976	2,219,746
			86	28,829,015	7,368,332	9,494,202	2,125,870
BNGLDSH	V	E	81	72,000	8,867	14,400	5,533
BRAZIL	A	E	85	5,512	1,300	4,215	2,915
	N	E	83	4,807,297	1,312,483	1,592,120	279,637
			84	5,181,913	1,388,324	1,732,787	344,463
			85	4,892,078	1,160,661	1,476,714	316,053
			86	3,069,483	710,048	881,377	171,329
	V	E	81	2,583,243	546,657	744,267	197,610
			82	3,030,017	812,030	1,023,288	211,258
			83	706,813	185,451	234,888	49,437
			84	225,982	57,173	67,937	10,764
			85	283,171	66,437	82,660	16,223
			86	1,079,757	248,760	307,678	58,918
C RICA	N	E	84	41,480	10,495	14,136	3,641
			86	371,581	59,000	85,793	26,793
	V	E	81	44,500	9,640	14,882	5,242
			83	8,427	1,900	2,573	673
			83	185,981	52,079	65,611	13,532
			84	435,297	70,690	97,872	27,182
			85	263,567	36,879	56,295	19,416
	V	W	81	3,750	394	874	480
			83	5,227	2,810	3,259	449
			84	7,747	1,405	2,385	980
			85	37,672	8,463	12,391	3,928
			86	7,606	1,350	2,368	1,018
CANADA	O	E	84	6,000	4,065	5,256	1,191
CHINA M	N	W	84	9,605	3,811	5,107	1,296
	V	E	84	250	864	983	119
	V	H	86	3,110	1,128	1,571	443
	V	W	82	41,189	10,731	13,945	3,214
			83	54,007	12,197	16,098	3,901
			84	44,064	9,383	12,589	3,206
COLOMB	N	E	81	3,495,432	473,744	619,226	145,482
			82	5,165,489	644,857	834,844	189,987
			83	3,268,324	669,768	881,144	211,376
			84	5,137,498	991,757	1,273,568	281,811
			85	187,956	36,075	63,502	27,427
	V	E	81	1,468,650	257,148	332,424	45,941
			82	3,727,556	558,143	717,115	158,972
			83	2,547,210	466,734	567,924	101,190
			84	2,743,552	554,440	597,281	42,841
			85	9,261,291	1,630,251	2,097,376	467,125
			86	14,348,187	2,384,787	3,055,027	670,240
DOM REP	A	E	81	7,700	770	1,571	801
			82	5,900	590	860	270
			84	11,250	6,250	8,750	2,500
			85	147,175	62,314	93,965	31,651
			86	116,590	60,560	84,807	24,247
	N	E	81	78,560	29,326	37,247	7,921
			82	123,920	22,406	30,103	7,697
			83	603,980	100,521	131,917	31,396
			84	779,256	186,501	255,315	68,814
	V	E	81	21,910	3,130	4,148	1,018
			82	42,400	5,600	7,322	1,722
			83	75,340	17,620	21,826	4,206
			84	18,863	2,668	5,034	2,366
			85	735,200	140,994	166,865	25,871
			86	8,615	3,760	4,537	777
DOMINCA	V	E	83	489	450	508	58
			86	30,329	13,372	15,952	2,580
ECUADOR	V	E	81	44,092	11,000	14,905	3,905
			86	35,000	1,002	2,947	1,945
FIJI	A	H	81	2,202	1,163	1,720	557
			84	950	528	1,005	477
	V	W	81	2,714	1,137	1,585	448
			82	4,867	1,677	2,276	599
			83	7,610	2,594	3,247	653
			84	2,239	711	886	175

Crop
Product
TSUSA commodity number, description, and unit of quantity

Country	Mode	Reg	Yr	Quantity	F.A.S.	C.I.F.	Charges
HAITI	A	E	82	8,325	1,903	2,893	990
			84	10,000	2,000	5,742	3,742
	N	E	83	34,620	6,650	11,249	4,599
HG KONG	V	W	82	5,460	1,265	1,856	591
			84	17,670	3,497	4,613	1,116
INDIA	V	E	84	55,115	11,200	15,004	3,804
ISRAEL	A	E	85	12,147	1,539	5,976	4,437
ITALY	A	E	83	4,464	1,000	2,030	1,030
JAMAICA	A	E	81	99,035	57,928	76,366	18,438
			82	28,115	14,940	19,690	4,750
			83	27,720	11,564	14,272	2,708
			84	88,184	39,112	49,316	10,204
			85	1,821,723	551,625	817,956	266,331
			86	47,617	17,029	22,514	5,485
	N	E	81	1,889,422	854,752	1,111,565	256,813
			82	4,021,063	1,459,809	1,941,646	481,837
			83	5,875,707	1,919,780	2,624,008	704,228
			84	6,633,200	1,882,405	2,895,339	1,012,934
			85	7,099,341	2,358,841	3,367,139	1,008,298
			86	9,454,482	3,746,836	4,878,738	1,131,902
	V	E	83	28,980	8,694	10,812	2,118
JAPAN	N	E	83	4,400	5,045	7,703	2,658
			84	9,086	10,602	13,045	2,443
			85	103,741	41,120	53,309	12,189
			86	76,957	42,511	55,515	13,004
	N	H	83	36,499	38,828	46,384	7,556
			84	41,507	41,731	49,940	8,209
	N	W	84	45,784	55,857	60,171	4,314
	V	E	81	2,200	2,387	2,592	205
			82	7,920	9,897	11,465	1,568
			85	40,000	10,968	13,305	2,337
			86	6,614	7,725	8,357	632
	V	H	81	22,836	23,001	27,213	4,212
			82	20,986	25,164	30,520	5,356
			85	21,103	20,892	25,901	5,009
			86	32,296	28,785	33,391	4,606
	V	W	81	53,728	55,373	60,179	4,806
			82	57,820	63,929	68,423	4,494
			83	80,104	78,318	84,140	5,822
			84	23,122	24,592	26,474	1,882
			85	101,339	80,621	89,644	9,023
			86	18,384	14,335	16,320	1,985
MEXICO	O	W	83	5,310	990	990	
NIGERIA	A	E	86	7,123	1,299	6,300	5,001
PANAMA	A	E	81	12,500	2,500	4,844	2,344
			82	14,696	3,030	4,549	1,519
PHIL R	V	E	84	1,968	571	830	259
	V	W	83	1,617	1,406	1,565	159
			84	6,814	2,977	3,426	449
S LUCIA	A	E	84	1,816	386	476	90
SURINAM	V	E	85	25,000	6,250	7,763	1,513
TONGA	V	W	81	26,875	3,968	7,976	4,008
			82	1,500	255	327	72
TRINID	V	E	83	1,550	341	451	110
VENEZ	A	E	83	26,015	7,374	10,456	3,082
	V	E	86	115,284	26,045	31,010	4,965

Yam, frozen
1378910 YAMS, FROZEN (LB)

Country	Mode	Reg	Yr	Quantity	F.A.S.	C.I.F.	Charges
TOTAL			81	38,460	5,945	8,244	2,299
			82	110,485	23,968	32,431	8,463
			83	223,395	56,801	71,033	14,232
			84	458,878	112,723	132,876	20,153
			85	69,948	34,536	39,572	5,036
			86	237,193	80,450	105,674	25,224
BRAZIL	V	E	83	65,710	16,335	23,200	6,865
			86	110,230	25,000	40,662	15,662
C RICA	V	E	86	3,330	1,232	1,296	64
	V	W	86	3,600	1,368	1,909	541
DOM REP	A	E	82	5,250	525	814	289
	N	E	81	35,150	4,595	6,628	2,033
			82	98,465	14,163	20,857	6,694
			84	387,800	71,708	83,713	12,005
	V	E	81	3,310	1,350	1,616	266
			83	137,262	28,862	35,385	6,523
			84	45,812	19,107	22,614	3,507
			85	40,230	20,163	23,067	2,904
			86	85,872	34,450	39,181	4,731
	V	W	84	4,680	2,387	3,077	690
DOMINCA	V	E	85	7,632	3,816	4,272	456
JAMAICA	A	E	86	19,493	9,822	11,979	2,157

Crop
Product
TSUSA commodity number, description, and unit of quantity

Country	Mode	Reg	Yr	Quantity	F.A.S.	C.I.F.	Charges
	V	E	83	19,935	10,890	11,702	812
JAPAN	N	H	84	880	1,932	2,921	989
	V	E	82	176	363	422	59
			84	2,759	5,518	6,988	1,470
	V	H	82	5,494	7,599	8,963	1,364
	V	W	82	1,100	1,318	1,375	57
			83	488	714	746	32
			84	6,600	5,610	6,037	427
PHIL R	V	E	86	11,528	7,136	8,815	1,679
	V	W	84	10,347	6,461	7,526	1,065
			85	22,086	10,557	12,233	1,676
			86	3,140	1,442	1,832	390

Ylang-Ylang

Ylang-ylang, essential oil
4527000 CANANGA OR YLANG YLANG OIL (LB)

Country	Mode	Reg	Yr	Quantity	F.A.S.	C.I.F.	Charges
TOTAL			**81**	**96,815**	**2,469,721**	**2,528,243**	**58,505**
			82	**99,730**	**1,996,838**	**2,047,149**	**50,311**
			83	**71,343**	**1,345,466**	**1,379,962**	**34,496**
			84	**82,503**	**1,724,925**	**1,769,538**	**44,613**
			85	**93,065**	**1,448,414**	**1,493,314**	**44,900**
			86	**71,111**	**1,755,476**	**1,795,778**	**40,302**
BELGIUM	V	E	82	165	2,659	2,716	57
BULGAR	A	E	81	220	9,400	9,585	185
CANADA	O	E	82	30	463	463	
COMOROS	N	E	81	10,036	206,460	210,800	4,340
			83	776	10,942	11,266	324
			85	3,109	57,958	59,310	1,352
	V	E	82	2,260	32,746	33,448	702
			86	1,984	40,051	40,503	452
F IND O	A	E	81	728	20,174	20,599	425
			84	880	9,377	9,744	367
FR GERM	A	E	82	6	323	329	6
			83	24	347	359	12
	V	E	84	55	997	1,007	10
			85	220	3,140	3,167	27
FRANCE	N	E	81	57,358	1,644,005	1,682,827	38,823
			82	77,675	1,652,462	1,695,397	42,935
			83	59,115	1,075,686	1,104,525	28,839
			84	64,097	1,396,095	1,431,624	35,529
			85	66,759	1,174,385	1,211,877	37,492
			86	53,874	1,526,710	1,561,945	35,235
HUNGARY	V	E	81	110	1,658	1,699	23
INDNSIA	N	E	81	16,864	228,578	236,216	7,638
			84	2,689	49,823	52,999	3,176
			85	11,353	92,898	95,235	2,337
	V	E	82	16,671	249,485	254,552	5,067
			83	1,422	28,539	29,049	510
			86	5,346	37,257	37,816	559
	V	W	82	1,543	23,862	24,403	541
			83	6,327	123,314	125,657	2,343
			84	12,312	214,229	218,209	3,980
			85	5,556	51,920	53,307	1,387
			86	4,894	33,180	33,968	788
ISRAEL	V	E	83	661	8,217	8,433	216
ITALY	A	E	82	154	1,829	1,884	55
			83	200	13,349	13,548	199
			85	50	1,207	1,250	43
JAPAN	V	W	84	1,190	20,345	20,836	491
MADAGAS	A	E	81	3,527	121,212	123,912	2,700
MOROC	A	E	86	440	47,530	47,967	437
NETHLDS	A	E	83	55	613	646	33
			84	99	1,131	1,271	140
	V	E	86	661	11,687	12,945	1,258
REP SAF	A	E	81	220	4,082	4,123	41
SINGAPR	V	E	81	271	3,647	3,763	116
SPAIN	V	E	83	882	26,275	26,564	289
SWITZLD	A	E	81	55	1,550	1,608	58
			82	626	20,873	21,460	587
			85	451	9,847	10,249	402
			86	826	25,027	25,845	818
	N	E	81	813	23,084	23,685	601
			83	1,670	54,269	55,820	1,551
			84	1,181	32,928	33,848	920
U KING	N	E	83	211	3,915	4,095	180
			85	5,567	57,059	58,919	1,860
			86	3,086	34,034	34,789	755
	V	E	82	600	12,136	12,497	361

Country	Mode	Reg	Yr	Quantity	F.A.S.	C.I.F.	Charges
USSR	V	E	81	6,613	205,871	209,426	3,555

Yucca

Yucca, fresh or frozen
1383500 YUCCA FR FZ REDUCED IN SIZE (LB)

Country	Mode	Reg	Yr	Quantity	F.A.S.	C.I.F.	Charges
TOTAL			81	10,856,289	1,928,565	2,767,580	839,015
			82	11,392,175	2,021,962	2,973,197	951,235
			83	12,436,508	2,170,731	3,182,866	1,012,135
			84	12,824,965	2,351,593	3,366,666	1,015,073
			85	13,587,928	2,674,109	3,802,629	1,128,520
			86	14,693,150	3,332,625	4,535,868	1,203,243
C AF RP	V	W	85	15,378	3,146	4,754	1,608
C RICA	A	E	85	2,129	1,088	1,510	422
	N	E	81	2,487,579	399,827	632,797	232,970
			84	3,663,624	657,183	893,231	236,048
			85	834,258	168,097	237,587	69,490
	N	W	84	386,428	60,793	89,701	28,908
	V	E	81	6,804,712	1,212,305	1,679,373	467,068
			82	10,118,927	1,808,113	2,619,212	811,099
			83	10,012,884	1,793,328	2,578,825	785,497
			84	5,715,455	1,190,611	1,716,886	526,275
			85	10,007,178	1,994,436	2,845,224	850,788
			86	12,166,180	2,773,532	3,781,244	1,007,712
	V	W	81	156,402	26,241	47,402	21,161
			82	183,486	33,695	51,660	17,965
			83	429,713	77,029	117,259	40,230
			84	609,749	109,077	168,924	59,847
			85	1,230,460	228,643	342,526	113,883
			86	1,200,153	286,137	409,319	123,182
DOM REP	A	E	81	26,528	4,528	6,908	2,380
	N	E	81	389,967	129,632	154,649	25,017
			82	270,828	69,048	86,260	17,212
			83	327,950	42,964	56,828	13,864
			84	660,555	86,078	122,627	36,549
			86	88,520	11,408	14,384	2,976
	V	E	81	413,008	76,837	93,634	16,797
			82	271,875	54,692	69,018	14,326
			83	849,224	174,531	227,674	53,143
			84	1,380,682	204,651	286,815	82,164
			85	1,337,585	252,511	333,968	81,457
			86	729,727	180,733	221,331	40,598
ECUADOR	A	E	82	7,365	1,200	1,882	682
	V	E	82	15,932	1,707	3,983	2,276
			83	72,031	14,752	16,421	1,669
			86	184,530	35,227	45,864	10,637
	V	W	85	13,390	1,545	2,592	1,047
F W IND	V	E	83	36,512	3,912	6,539	2,627
FIJI	A	H	84	2,882	1,590	3,615	2,025
GREECE	V	E	86	42,000	10,006	13,230	3,224
GUATMAL	A	E	82	25,092	984	5,348	4,364
			83	37,128	1,456	8,343	6,887
	A	W	81	356,824	29,184	88,516	59,332
			82	292,358	22,447	74,691	52,244
			83	470,883	18,472	108,607	90,135
			84	227,662	12,811	37,898	25,087
	V	E	81	176,456	31,213	41,938	10,725
			82	8,442	2,111	2,533	422
			83	28,112	3,959	7,280	3,321
			84	20,000	1,000	2,232	1,232
			85	39,600	3,960	7,547	3,587
			86	195,822	15,748	21,742	5,994
	V	W	85	70,000	6,300	9,621	3,321
HG KONG	V	W	81	12,813	7,438	8,483	1,045
HONDURA	V	E	82	161,580	15,551	43,372	27,821
			83	62,609	7,025	12,431	5,406
			85	6,000	1,600	2,004	404
			86	51,780	7,210	11,267	4,057
LIBERIA	V	E	81	2,900	1,112	1,808	696
			82	3,300	1,430	2,247	817
MEXICO	A	W	84	91,568	3,730	9,204	5,474
PHIL R	V	E	81	29,100	10,248	12,072	1,824
			82	29,390	10,087	11,955	1,868
			83	70,850	27,712	34,018	6,306
			84	47,700	15,550	23,820	8,270
			85	10,700	3,745	5,167	1,422
			86	17,050	5,084	6,590	1,506
	V	W	82	3,600	897	1,036	139
			84	18,660	8,519	11,713	3,194

Country	Mode	Reg	Yr	Quantity	F.A.S.	C.I.F.	Charges
			85	21,250	9,038	10,129	1,091
			86	4,700	1,740	2,088	348
SALVADR	V	E	83	38,612	5,591	8,641	3,050
SIER LN	V	E	86	12,688	5,800	8,809	3,009

Table 2

U.S. Import Statistics for Non-Crop Specific Commodities

by

End-Use

Product TSUSA commodity number, description, and unit of quantity Country	Mode	Reg	Yr	Quantity	F.A.S.	C.I.F.	Charges

Animal feed

Bran
1841000 BRAN, SHORTS,ETC FRM MILLNG (STN)

Country	Mode	Reg	Yr	Quantity	F.A.S.	C.I.F.	Charges
TOTAL			81	143,153	16,602,055	18,043,474	1,442,419
			82	118,454	11,285,631	12,643,221	1,357,590
			83	129,224	13,219,986	14,554,210	1,334,224
			84	176,941	17,023,295	18,531,806	1,508,511
			85	178,666	13,248,214	14,760,822	1,512,608
			86	118,004	8,741,306	9,693,211	951,905
ARGENT	V	E	81	4,538	651,411	708,055	56,644
			82	450	48,248	72,821	24,573
			83	231	37,820	55,035	17,215
			84	19,628	2,083,411	2,324,263	240,852
			85	12,461	799,578	928,341	128,763
			86	25,452	1,785,507	2,185,877	400,370
BELIZE	V	E	86	55	2,750	2,750	
BRAZIL	V	E	84	13,758	1,185,387	1,472,739	287,352
			85	20,016	1,179,684	1,492,561	312,877
			86	2,205	140,000	186,000	46,000
CANADA	N	E	84	61,358	6,240,405	6,240,405	
			85	76,622	5,798,263	5,798,265	2
	N	W	86	35	43,299	50,634	7,335
	O	E	81	86,671	9,995,404	9,994,404	
			82	57,882	5,232,861	5,253,714	20,853
			83	66,147	7,092,456	7,092,456	
			84	24,327	2,026,119	2,026,119	
			85	3,493	274,181	274,181	
			86	61,870	4,914,560	4,914,562	2
	O	H	82	28	2,606	2,606	
	O	W	81	1,476	193,505	193,505	
			82	463	56,794	56,794	
			83	518	66,142	66,142	
			84	6,057	586,741	586,741	
			85	3,049	235,233	235,233	
			86	403	37,148	37,148	
	V	W	85	69	4,058	4,256	198
			86	286	25,261	45,697	20,436
CHILE	V	E	81	7,066	755,990	1,040,233	284,243
			82	18,300	1,767,743	2,158,150	390,407
			83	17,019	1,517,104	1,893,974	376,870
CHINA M	V	E	84	5	998	1,136	138
CHINA T	V	E	84	1	415	564	149
	V	W	83	1	356	368	12
DENMARK	O	E	84	12	2,200	2,200	
DOM REP	V	E	81	2,543	300,914	354,601	53,687
			82	1,669	180,039	215,502	35,463
F W IND	V	E	81	1,097	145,791	162,356	16,565
			82	408	49,580	53,546	3,966
			85	1,736	138,499	169,178	30,679
GHANA	V	E	83	4,000	360,000	452,000	92,000
HAITI	V	E	81	16,930	1,691,920	2,079,461	387,541
			82	29,130	2,911,479	3,563,768	652,289
			83	33,957	3,371,210	4,051,050	679,840
			84	30,934	2,928,871	3,474,243	545,372
			85	40,812	3,213,248	3,955,802	742,554
			86	10,394	681,291	834,871	153,580
	V	W	81	812	81,200	99,876	18,676
ITALY	O	E	85	243	20,144	20,144	
JAMAICA	V	E	84	1,212	108,086	118,776	10,690
			85	13,221	1,213,626	1,396,261	182,635
			86	6,495	553,531	626,373	72,842
JAPAN	V	E	81	2	612	733	121
			82	1	306	398	92
			83	1	881	968	87
LAOS	O	W	86	29	2,659	2,659	
LIBERIA	V	E	82	1,064	109,975	130,005	20,030
			84	10,093	944,171	1,163,171	219,000
MEXICO	O	W	84	2	302	302	
N ANTIL	V	E	82	194	24,289	29,889	5,600
NIGERIA	V	E	81	18,168	2,334,740	2,912,792	578,052
			82	4,322	431,255	521,427	90,172
			83	4,000	462,966	554,966	92,000
PERU	V	E	84	5,508	531,158	651,111	119,953
REP SAF	V	E	81	2,212	277,015	291,015	14,000
			82	1,687	181,244	219,639	38,395
S VN GR	V	E	81	1,385	143,000	175,890	32,890
SIER LN	V	E	84	551	54,500	67,000	12,500
SWEDEN	N	E	82	*	4,000	4,150	150
SWITZLD	A	W	84	1	792	847	55
U KING	O	E	81	253	30,553	30,553	

Country	Mode	Reg	Yr	Quantity	F.A.S.	C.I.F.	Charges
			82	82	8,012	8,012	
			83	43	4,451	6,251	1,800
			84	22	2,139	2,139	
ZAIRE	V	E	82	2,774	277,200	352,800	75,600
			83	3,307	306,600	381,000	74,400
			84	3,472	327,600	400,050	72,450
			85	6,944	371,700	486,600	114,900
			86	10,780	555,300	806,640	251,340

Grain and malt, sprout
1842500 BREWERS GRAINS, MALT SPROUT (STN)

Country	Mode	Reg	Yr	Quantity	F.A.S.	C.I.F.	Charges
TOTAL			81	137,615	15,291,444	15,287,118	1,765
			82	129,369	10,776,203	10,778,120	1,917
			83	137,842	12,101,046	12,101,571	525
			84	149,418	13,118,771	13,127,389	8,618
			85	79,700	7,543,363	7,555,598	12,235
			86	70,365	7,549,656	7,550,961	1,305
CANADA	N	E	84	34,907	2,895,161	2,895,161	
			85	14,219	1,248,249	1,248,249	
	O	E	81	127,645	13,854,615	13,850,289	1,765
			82	122,266	9,806,468	9,807,948	1,480
			83	128,467	10,879,842	10,879,902	60
			84	93,593	8,338,605	8,344,399	5,794
			85	47,021	4,144,228	4,144,232	4
			86	48,611	5,529,772	5,529,772	
	O	W	81	9,767	1,410,195	1,410,195	
			82	7,061	967,185	967,185	
			83	9,374	1,219,923	1,219,923	
			84	20,895	1,882,553	1,885,249	2,696
			85	18,330	2,123,461	2,123,561	100
			86	21,637	2,002,737	2,002,741	4
FR GERM	V	E	85	22	8,605	11,348	2,743
GABON	O	E	86	25	2,827	2,827	
INDIA	O	E	86	21	1,700	1,700	
ITALY	O	E	85	46	5,508	5,508	
JAPAN	N	W	83	*	716	776	60
KOR REP	O	E	86	25	2,659	2,659	
	V	W	85	1	1,260	2,520	1,260
NETHLDS	A	E	84	3	252	380	128
REP SAF	O	E	81	68	10,488	10,488	
			82	40	1,340	1,340	
			84	20	2,200	2,200	
			86	21	1,425	1,425	
U KING	A	E	82	1	610	1,012	402
	O	E	81	135	16,146	16,146	
	V	E	85	61	12,052	20,180	8,128
			86	25	8,536	9,837	1,301
YUGOSLV	A	E	83	1	565	970	405
	V	E	82	1	600	635	35

Grain, hulled
1844000 GRAIN HULLS (CWT)

Country	Mode	Reg	Yr	Quantity	F.A.S.	C.I.F.	Charges
TOTAL			81	255,122	633,577	633,577	
			82	297,326	572,074	573,205	1,131
			83	271,622	467,954	468,273	319
			84	280,105	536,920	558,586	21,666
			85	146,252	351,472	453,041	101,569
			86	104,883	299,189	304,823	5,634
ARGENT	V	E	84	440	5,890	8,289	2,399
AUSTRAL	V	E	84	981	2,226	2,471	245
	V	H	84	8,145	20,944	30,162	9,218
CANADA	N	E	84	94,725	156,708	156,708	
	O	E	81	255,012	632,548	632,548	
			82	297,324	571,643	571,643	
			83	268,692	461,237	461,237	
			84	150,537	297,597	297,597	
			85	38,278	104,095	104,095	
			86	93,846	242,241	242,243	2
	O	W	81	110	1,029	1,029	
			83	450	4,763	4,763	
			85	24	1,125	1,125	
FR GERM	O	E	83	2,480	1,954	2,273	319
HAITI	V	E	84	25,277	53,555	63,359	9,804
			85	107,950	246,252	347,821	101,569
			86	11,037	56,948	62,580	5,632
JAPAN	A	E	82	2	431	1,562	1,131

Product
TSUSA commodity number, description, and unit of quantity

Grain or seed, screening or chaff
1844700 SCREENNGS, SCALPNG ETC NSPF (STN)

Country	Mode	Reg	Yr	Quantity	F.A.S.	C.I.F.	Charges
TOTAL			81	47,008	4,479,584	4,555,481	70,511
			82	66,787	5,411,038	5,481,339	70,301
			83	92,181	7,025,788	7,074,260	48,472
			84	114,744	10,435,846	10,610,368	174,522
			85	69,780	5,111,581	5,238,867	127,286
			86	87,680	5,779,610	6,318,623	539,013
ARGENT	V	E	84	13,887	1,716,654	1,864,207	147,553
AUSTRAL	V	H	85	1,467	64,342	116,209	51,867
			86	6,106	560,731	1,087,236	526,505
BRAZIL	V	E	85	3,638	137,663	206,069	68,406
			86	507	19,320	29,900	10,580
CANADA	N	W	81	1,021	80,252	141,789	61,537
			82	1,022	80,819	135,923	55,104
			83	1,040	81,700	118,000	36,300
			85	294	24,091	31,091	7,000
	O	E	81	11,621	955,481	955,481	
			82	12,880	1,064,613	1,065,911	1,298
			83	12,959	1,014,892	1,014,892	
			84	23,429	1,670,444	1,670,444	
			85	6,787	412,753	412,753	
			86	5,018	347,741	347,741	
	O	H	86	30	1,628	1,628	
	O	W	81	34,325	3,423,353	3,433,911	5,172
			82	52,732	4,196,675	4,199,015	2,340
			83	77,634	5,816,573	5,816,573	
			84	76,599	6,968,342	6,968,342	
			85	57,571	4,471,617	4,471,617	
			86	75,936	4,830,397	4,830,403	6
	V	W	84	807	78,117	105,086	26,969
CHINA T	V	W	81	2	880	1,162	282
			82	1	312	602	290
DOM REP	V	E	83	45	6,750	8,299	1,549
ETHIOP	V	E	82	13	13,467	15,325	1,858
FR GERM	O	E	82	102	9,169	9,169	
FRANCE	V	E	81	14	15,905	18,855	2,950
HAITI	V	E	81	25	3,713	4,283	570
INDIA	V	E	82	37	45,983	55,394	9,411
	V	W	86	19	15,375	17,068	1,693
ITALY	O	E	83	34	2,617	2,617	
JAPAN	V	E	86	64	4,418	4,647	229
MEXICO	V	W	83	61	3,847	3,847	
NETHLDS	A	E	85	23	1,115	1,128	13
SPAIN	V	E	83	353	35,056	37,860	2,804
U KING	O	E	84	22	2,289	2,289	
	V	E	83	55	64,353	72,172	7,819

Hay
1843000 HAY (STN)

Country	Mode	Reg	Yr	Quantity	F.A.S.	C.I.F.	Charges
TOTAL			81	100,338	5,974,640	5,977,447	2,807
			82	99,008	6,919,697	6,932,159	12,462
			83	63,340	4,898,205	4,903,477	5,272
			84	111,013	8,434,811	8,444,700	9,889
			85	53,046	4,875,494	4,893,917	18,423
			86	64,925	6,010,189	6,020,855	10,666
CANADA	N	E	84	28,817	2,058,849	2,058,849	
			85	5,028	759,354	759,356	2
	N	W	86	62	7,238	9,238	2,000
	O	E	81	98,850	5,838,919	5,838,919	
			82	98,119	6,835,923	6,846,707	10,784
			83	62,555	4,816,151	4,816,151	
			84	76,640	5,912,018	5,919,807	7,789
			85	45,085	3,836,465	3,837,115	650
			86	45,252	4,064,531	4,064,535	4
	O	W	81	1,268	116,053	116,053	
			82	812	77,936	79,614	1,678
			83	664	62,312	62,312	
			84	5,482	451,169	451,169	
			85	2,645	244,296	244,296	
			86	19,322	1,894,019	1,894,019	
	V	E	81	40	4,125	4,476	351
DENMARK	O	E	82	31	2,785	2,785	
FR GERM	O	E	82	25	1,944	1,944	
ITALY	O	E	81	16	873	873	
			86	19	1,225	1,225	
JAPAN	O	E	83	11	666	666	
	V	E	86	66	11,985	12,647	662
	V	W	81	45	8,335	10,791	2,456
			83	96	18,361	23,633	5,272
			84	74	12,775	14,875	2,100
			85	251	32,818	50,589	17,771
			86	166	26,876	34,876	8,000
KOR REP	O	E	82	5	300	300	
MEXICO	O	W	83	14	715	715	
			86	5	1,712	1,712	
MOROC	O	E	85	20	1,200	1,200	
			86	18	1,028	1,028	
REP SAF	O	E	81	112	5,859	5,859	
			86	15	1,575	1,575	
SPAIN	O	E	82	16	809	809	
U KING	O	E	81	7	476	476	
			85	17	1,361	1,361	

Straw
1843500 STRAW EXCEPT FLAX OR RICE (STN)

Country	Mode	Reg	Yr	Quantity	F.A.S.	C.I.F.	Charges
TOTAL			81	10,894	547,813	547,813	
			82	12,981	714,558	714,560	2
			83	12,153	686,680	687,479	799
			84	12,519	729,881	730,623	742
			85	3,185	293,103	295,576	2,473
			86	2,566	232,200	232,200	
CANADA	O	E	81	10,894	547,813	547,813	
			82	12,944	712,568	712,570	2
			83	12,144	686,195	686,994	799
			84	12,494	728,822	728,827	5
			85	3,163	283,167	283,167	
			86	2,366	213,931	213,931	
	O	W	82	21	1,190	1,190	
			83	9	485	485	
			86	200	18,269	18,269	
CHINA T	V	W	85	22	9,936	12,409	2,473
DENMARK	O	E	82	16	800	800	
ITALY	N	E	84	*	312	1,049	737
U KING	O	E	84	25	747	747	

Vegetable, oil cake and oil-cake meal
1845300 VEG OIL CAKE AND MEAL, NSPF (LB)

Country	Mode	Reg	Yr	Quantity	F.A.S.	C.I.F.	Charges
TOTAL			81	3,962,012	374,283	416,601	42,318
			82	18,323,388	1,133,996	1,352,014	218,018
			83	6,148,738	489,926	607,213	117,287
			84	6,279,313	546,504	670,763	124,259
			85	15,285,866	687,675	938,278	250,603
			86	12,757,262	778,245	826,931	48,686
ARGENT	V	E	82	12,121,090	702,062	813,555	111,493
			84	2,054,708	218,088	226,812	8,724
			85	8,918,004	334,202	394,393	60,191
			86	11,023,010	661,525	709,944	48,419
AUSTRAL	V	H	83	463,852	24,380	45,293	20,913
			84	2,310,221	148,251	224,387	76,136
			85	2,955,826	145,164	261,357	116,193
BELGIUM	A	E	84	2,205	264	1,465	1,201
CANADA	O	E	81	1,838,054	202,993	202,993	
			82	32,850	4,311	4,311	
			83	370,638	33,745	33,745	
			84	164,968	15,738	15,738	
			85	109,043	5,731	5,731	
			86	1,131,680	86,502	86,502	
	O	W	82	120,000	14,643	14,643	
			83	121,900	15,855	15,855	
			84	53,000	3,818	3,818	
			85	212,154	10,894	10,894	
			86	600,797	28,601	28,601	
CHINA M	V	E	85	4,284	1,755	2,063	308
FR GERM	V	E	83	42,500	6,615	8,133	1,518
			84	25,000	4,016	4,912	896
	V	W	83	67,528	7,500	8,874	1,374
FRANCE	A	E	83	110	359	407	48
	V	E	81	4,408	6,602	7,075	473
			82	50,400	6,953	7,544	591
			83	56,984	10,867	11,742	875
			84	57,423	22,295	27,007	4,712
			85	122,172	27,684	29,035	1,351
HAITI	V	E	82	2,289,000	143,063	169,387	26,324
			83	264,554	17,196	23,218	6,022
			84	42,240	5,970	7,433	1,463
INDNSIA	V	W	83	521	700	819	119
ITALY	V	E	82	392	1,254	1,386	132
JAPAN	A	E	84	158	2,160	2,439	279

Product TSUSA commodity number, description, and unit of quantity Country	Mode	Reg	Yr	Quantity	F.A.S.	C.I.F.	Charges
	V	W	83	1,443	1,935	2,188	253
KOR REP	V	W	83	1,300	2,423	2,800	377
			85	2,423	1,580	1,785	205
MEXICO	A	E	83	378	3,091	3,527	436
NETHLDS	V	W	85	1,764	1,265	1,733	468
			86	1,775	1,617	1,884	267
PHIL R	V	W	85	4,976	2,459	2,818	359
T PAC I	V	H	81	2,119,010	163,644	204,839	41,195
			82	3,709,656	261,710	341,188	79,478
			83	4,757,140	365,619	451,019	85,400
			84	1,569,280	125,545	156,345	30,800
			85	2,955,220	156,941	228,469	71,528
U KING	A	E	81	540	1,044	1,694	650

Beverage

Fermented alcoholic beverages

1671500 CIDER,FERMENTED,STILL,SPRKNG (GAL)

Country	Mode	Reg	Yr	Quantity	F.A.S.	C.I.F.	Charges
TOTAL			81	221,608	952,980	1,187,728	234,748
			82	371,694	698,178	873,864	175,686
			83	299,264	928,899	1,178,223	249,324
			84	319,600	934,506	1,201,507	267,001
			85	200,077	780,091	934,046	153,955
			86	382,512	1,243,953	1,383,667	139,714
ARGENT	O	E	85	4,965	13,675	19,056	5,381
	O	W	81	2,700	12,878	15,766	2,888
	V	E	81	7,350	37,600	52,186	14,586
			82	193,470	154,692	180,040	25,348
			83	15,050	55,415	78,174	22,759
			84	4,652	17,547	24,170	6,623
			85	12,462	40,334	54,003	13,669
			86	21,813	55,282	69,597	14,315
	V	W	81	1,902	9,000	11,542	2,542
			83	4,783	18,960	24,884	5,924
			85	3,939	17,864	23,530	5,666
AUSTRAL	A	E	81	24	700	775	75
BELGIUM	V	E	86	666	1,884	2,581	697
CANADA	O	E	81	263	1,266	1,266	
			82	18,129	40,127	40,127	
			83	2,875	16,185	16,185	
			84	1,553	3,151	3,151	
			85	14,186	34,900	34,900	
	O	W	84	2,854	10,973	10,973	
			85	37,930	180,201	180,201	
			86	125,272	571,594	571,594	
CHINA M	V	W	81	95	1,051	1,089	38
			83	1,188	13,325	14,655	1,330
DENMARK	O	E	82	447	2,027	2,553	526
	V	E	82	538	3,005	3,755	750
FINLAND	O	E	83	33	453	480	27
FR GERM	O	E	82	618	1,500	1,590	90
	V	E	84	35,280	86,240	106,015	19,775
			86	26,352	19,106	20,551	1,445
	V	W	81	683	2,337	3,540	1,203
			84	417	1,621	2,045	424
			85	685	1,422	2,484	1,062
FRANCE	O	E	83	2,735	14,818	17,420	2,602
			84	2,246	11,923	14,669	2,746
	O	W	86	361	1,563	1,655	92
	V	E	81	17,154	69,694	87,012	17,318
			82	28,744	77,765	92,628	14,863
			83	31,623	113,342	136,839	23,497
			84	21,302	69,066	87,746	18,680
			85	11,968	48,418	61,337	12,919
			86	22,750	126,872	153,599	26,727
	V	W	81	3,646	13,763	16,468	2,705
			82	7,714	24,973	28,262	3,289
			83	9,495	32,672	39,186	6,514
			84	23,869	90,362	114,440	24,078
			85	3,726	11,767	13,936	2,169
			86	28,641	99,916	120,963	21,047
ITALY	V	E	85	9,510	15,493	15,493	
JAMAICA	V	E	81	1,225	1,450	1,583	133
JAPAN	V	W	83	793	2,483	2,860	377

Product TSUSA commodity number, description, and unit of quantity Country	Mode	Reg	Yr	Quantity	F.A.S.	C.I.F.	Charges
MEXICO	O	E	84	3,474	13,632	13,632	
	O	W	84	634	3,265	3,265	
NETHLDS	V	E	81	6,974	32,252	36,820	4,568
			83	13,230	37,885	44,571	6,686
			85	3,465	9,922	11,673	1,751
REP SAF	A	E	82	55	387	588	201
SALVADR	V	E	84	4,453	27,600	31,800	4,200
SPAIN	O	E	82	108	300	418	118
			83	108	300	418	118
			84	5,508	17,629	20,304	2,675
	V	E	81	137,483	572,048	716,434	144,386
			82	81,625	330,864	422,970	92,106
			83	181,109	550,008	690,405	140,397
			84	162,554	479,826	653,809	173,983
			85	64,217	248,021	310,867	62,846
			86	131,570	274,873	331,755	56,882
	V	W	81	4,313	17,000	23,573	6,573
			84	1,754	5,253	7,240	1,987
			85	16,480	69,005	91,227	22,222
SWEDEN	V	E	86	2,205	8,339	9,808	1,469
U KING	N	E	83	3,077	19,634	24,003	4,369
	O	E	85	2,409	10,997	13,337	2,340
			86	919	2,970	2,970	
	V	E	81	33,355	157,868	190,252	32,384
			82	36,950	45,413	81,509	36,096
			83	33,165	53,419	88,143	34,724
			84	49,684	99,683	111,513	11,830
			85	11,538	64,442	84,787	20,345
			86	16,936	58,406	70,679	12,273
	V	W	81	4,441	24,073	29,422	5,349
			82	2,662	13,860	16,159	2,299
			85	2,597	13,630	17,215	3,585
			86	4,847	23,148	27,915	4,767

1675000 FERMENTED ALCHL BEVRGS NSPF (GAL)

Country	Mode	Reg	Yr	Quantity	F.A.S.	C.I.F.	Charges
TOTAL			81	3,082,531	12,777,255	15,399,389	2,625,389
			82	3,120,780	12,588,302	15,351,003	2,762,701
			83	2,630,037	10,594,628	12,792,624	2,197,996
			84	2,620,441	10,715,113	13,061,744	2,346,631
			85	2,776,745	12,736,021	15,544,523	2,808,502
			86	1,422,995	7,202,434	8,589,544	1,387,110
BELGIUM	O	E	82	11,888	40,000	52,000	12,000
	V	E	85	4,594	15,803	20,609	4,806
			86	12,630	55,280	64,814	9,534
BERMUDA	A	E	81	4	1,240	1,350	110
	V	E	84	18,172	52,201	65,224	13,023
BRAZIL	V	E	83	1,904	6,532	7,991	1,459
			85	1,684	5,212	7,002	1,790
	V	W	86	2,932	9,470	12,886	3,416
CANADA	A	E	86	1,189	10,645	10,645	
	O	E	81	1,348	9,247	9,247	
			82	2,739	21,583	22,723	1,140
			83	9,955	60,973	61,473	500
			84	10,850	77,475	77,475	
			85	27,229	175,879	175,879	
			86	7,147	37,934	39,000	1,066
	O	W	85	2,475	7,752	7,752	
			86	6,933	20,380	20,380	
	V	E	81	2,853	8,898	9,173	275
CHINA M	V	E	84	118	882	980	98
			85	2,756	8,638	10,946	2,308
	V	W	81	476	3,028	3,372	344
			82	2,221	26,527	29,569	3,042
			83	793	9,517	9,954	437
			84	873	11,934	14,138	2,204
			85	1,070	8,893	11,880	2,987
			86	2,377	17,736	20,623	2,887
CHINA T	O	E	81	38	300	324	24
	V	E	81	67	423	471	48
			82	333	3,044	4,047	1,003
			86	285	1,990	2,166	176
	V	W	81	3,627	24,681	28,266	3,585
			82	3,734	29,609	32,592	2,983
			83	3,370	24,141	25,922	1,781
			84	6,273	7,268	7,779	511
			85	1,437	10,229	11,047	818
CZECHO	O	E	82	485	325	733	408
			84	1,966	13,027	14,237	1,210
			85	974	6,720	7,502	782
DENMARK	N	E	83	24,224	161,970	183,022	21,052
			84	10,104	75,151	86,711	11,560
			85	29,634	314,312	350,887	36,575
	O	E	81	10,951	79,320	91,280	11,960
			82	21,992	158,125	179,351	21,226

Product
TSUSA commodity number, description, and unit of quantity

Country	Mode	Reg	Yr	Quantity	F.A.S.	C.I.F.	Charges
			83	24,803	223,949	249,497	25,548
			84	21,210	137,364	161,354	23,990
			85	18,464	117,170	137,773	20,603
			86	12,888	112,948	129,545	16,597
	V	E	81	138,411	998,769	1,152,264	153,495
			82	131,157	876,103	1,011,952	135,849
			83	79,679	592,294	683,112	90,818
			84	101,483	679,440	798,695	119,255
			85	47,983	313,014	379,586	66,572
			86	30,372	300,154	345,241	45,087
	V	W	81	35,798	240,701	277,357	36,656
			82	20,570	140,593	162,898	22,305
			83	27,985	181,556	200,959	19,403
			84	22,076	136,746	163,242	26,496
			85	42,488	289,321	328,786	39,465
			86	5,229	92,181	100,640	8,459
DOM REP	V	E	82	750	2,079	3,619	1,540
			85	1,860	1,984	2,460	476
FINLAND	O	E	83	29	510	540	30
FR GERM	N	E	85	7,979	22,438	32,536	10,098
	N	W	82	425	2,516	2,986	470
	O	E	81	3,637	20,373	23,665	3,292
			82	9,924	43,241	53,573	10,332
			83	7,091	34,705	41,291	6,586
			84	4,120	16,822	20,844	4,022
			85	8,912	48,501	60,571	12,070
	V	E	81	3,922	16,499	20,491	3,992
			82	4,101	16,225	19,513	3,288
			83	14,731	73,790	87,905	14,115
			84	11,295	64,619	80,159	15,540
			85	112,951	445,564	595,128	149,564
			86	27,051	113,014	133,396	20,382
	V	W	81	821	4,961	5,963	1,002
			82	2,721	24,320	27,345	3,025
			83	4,534	29,129	34,140	5,011
			84	17,024	61,773	73,979	12,206
			85	10,060	48,379	60,997	12,618
			86	1,922	17,616	21,092	3,476
FRANCE	N	E	81	4,224	20,926	23,448	2,522
	O	E	81	6,511	24,223	31,656	7,433
			82	4,658	15,088	19,425	4,337
			83	3,263	13,021	15,904	2,883
			84	3,895	40,682	58,565	17,883
			85	10,018	56,446	68,984	12,538
			86	3,818	26,083	30,933	4,850
	V	E	81	1,166	12,312	13,235	923
			82	3,130	10,333	12,733	2,400
			83	5,495	26,528	31,884	5,356
			84	951	7,929	9,416	1,487
			85	380,799	2,133,789	2,486,235	352,446
			86	453,820	2,217,754	2,676,903	459,149
	V	W	81	6,024	66,500	71,890	5,390
			82	870	7,682	8,523	841
			83	119	504	574	70
			85	2,257	17,551	20,729	3,178
			86	31,278	111,441	153,192	41,751
GREECE	V	E	84	711	2,550	3,222	672
	V	W	84	1,743	6,600	8,229	1,629
HG KONG	V	W	81	476	6,437	6,866	429
			82	1,902	12,000	24,757	12,757
ICELAND	O	E	86	237	1,567	1,967	400
ISRAEL	N	E	81	2,457	10,807	13,089	2,282
	O	E	81	1,642	7,227	8,315	1,088
			82	383	1,691	1,808	117
	V	E	81	368	1,628	1,977	349
			85	772	3,030	3,579	549
ITALY	N	E	86	39,805	156,613	190,330	33,717
	O	E	81	19,827	76,747	94,312	17,565
			82	20,675	63,713	79,639	15,926
			83	9,071	28,292	36,152	7,860
			84	3,325	13,204	16,337	3,133
			85	1,620	10,909	13,590	2,681
	O	W	82	594	5,125	5,602	477
	V	E	81	11,154	41,545	49,866	8,321
			82	121,140	376,952	541,984	165,032
			83	10,800	38,863	49,132	10,269
			84	21,442	76,947	97,511	20,564
			85	135,952	355,722	478,734	123,012
			86	10,502	41,891	49,032	7,141
	V	W	83	3,804	17,955	22,153	4,198
			84	3,138	23,760	27,045	3,285
			85	2,813	7,182	10,269	3,087
			86	1,070	9,882	11,109	1,227
IVY CST	V	E	84	5,268	20,160	28,839	8,679
			85	3,512	13,440	27,247	13,807

Product
TSUSA commodity number, description, and unit of quantity

Country	Mode	Reg	Yr	Quantity	F.A.S.	C.I.F.	Charges
JAMAICA	V	E	81	1,759	10,661	11,930	1,269
			82	892	7,218	8,123	905
			83	936	8,021	9,544	1,523
			84	786	6,300	7,782	1,482
			85	238	1,900	2,174	274
			86	476	3,866	4,683	817
JAPAN	A	E	84	60	537	2,358	1,821
	N	E	81	64,835	457,895	540,598	82,703
			86	14,382	140,899	156,059	15,160
	O	E	81	33,101	196,270	253,407	57,137
			82	42,531	301,768	366,734	64,966
			83	39,609	253,049	319,512	66,463
			84	27,470	181,356	231,264	49,908
			85	33,169	233,064	291,149	58,085
			86	12,653	110,797	135,045	24,248
	O	W	81	56	416	416	
			82	238	1,450	1,611	161
			83	2,996	22,108	24,722	2,614
			84	48	290	324	34
			85	593	4,500	4,856	356
	V	E	81	59,903	449,106	527,926	78,820
			82	121,788	937,100	1,100,087	162,987
			83	150,976	1,174,219	1,364,119	189,900
			84	198,319	1,601,484	1,880,618	279,134
			85	178,630	1,466,199	1,746,957	280,758
			86	112,382	928,003	1,095,047	167,044
	V	H	81	818	5,850	7,035	1,185
			82	654	4,268	5,172	904
			83	822	5,523	6,381	858
			84	292	1,998	2,286	288
			86	878	8,272	9,336	1,064
	V	W	81	90,890	673,945	749,686	75,741
			82	78,603	564,502	630,786	66,284
			83	92,051	656,869	735,371	78,502
			84	142,546	1,025,847	1,150,107	124,260
			85	132,481	955,671	1,058,746	103,075
			86	70,434	529,245	574,550	45,305
KOR REP	V	E	85	6,063	31,850	36,205	4,355
MEXICO	A	E	84	225	612	1,509	897
	O	E	81	119	595	784	189
			82	1,197	3,964	4,930	966
			84	80,338	235,908	235,908	
			85	11,341	39,627	39,627	
			86	29,801	88,550	88,550	
N ZEAL	V	E	86	228	2,342	2,847	505
	V	H	83	24	264	292	28
	V	W	81	2,297	33,507	36,266	2,759
			82	2,325	48,965	51,642	2,677
			83	11,485	177,020	190,656	13,636
			85	6,773	44,495	52,589	8,094
			86	4,602	41,618	46,971	5,353
NETHLDS	A	E	86	1,600	8,027	8,631	604
	O	E	81	416	2,530	2,948	418
			82	178	3,378	3,657	279
			83	2,139	15,303	17,728	2,425
			84	4,279	28,816	35,131	6,315
			85	6,939	49,205	56,827	7,622
	V	E	81	9,645	49,494	58,781	9,287
			82	3,611	14,274	19,006	4,732
			83	3,348	16,297	20,838	4,541
			84	1,450	9,681	11,295	1,614
			85	36,847	222,530	257,553	35,023
			86	36,639	261,935	292,340	30,405
	V	W	85	5,208	40,232	44,703	4,471
			86	2,596	23,564	25,156	1,592
POLAND	O	E	81	1,462	12,391	14,861	2,470
			82	1,665	13,739	17,336	3,597
			83	2,852	21,793	26,766	4,973
			84	356	3,300	3,924	624
			85	354	3,300	3,924	624
	V	E	81	4,347	33,806	41,467	7,661
			82	3,461	37,210	42,588	5,378
			83	1,189	8,441	10,436	1,995
			84	3,992	27,633	35,144	7,511
			85	5,646	52,263	60,112	7,849
			86	475	5,000	7,200	2,200
	V	W	81	713	8,900	9,838	938
PORTUGL	O	E	81	1,071	4,458	5,548	1,090
			82	1,129	6,286	7,246	960
			84	2,414	7,562	9,491	1,929
	V	E	81	17,769	57,227	72,278	15,051
			82	8,322	26,216	32,546	6,330
			83	1,466	4,673	6,591	1,918
			84	2,575	7,370	8,852	1,482
			85	8,549	25,214	33,029	7,815

Product TSUSA commodity number, description, and unit of quantity Country	Mode	Reg	Yr	Quantity	F.A.S.	C.I.F.	Charges
			86	1,497	4,609	6,068	1,459
	V	W	81	88	1,487	1,746	259
REP SAF	A	E	81	11	291	478	187
SPAIN	N	E	81	704,299	2,494,753	3,058,012	563,259
			82	112,053	376,054	485,516	109,462
			83	156,336	473,562	597,413	123,851
			84	66,739	216,168	271,345	55,177
			85	267,621	886,131	1,138,389	252,258
			86	21,639	64,723	77,518	12,795
	O	E	81	240,444	702,304	892,273	189,969
			82	223,628	773,480	952,590	179,110
			83	209,893	633,626	782,837	149,211
			84	93,721	326,071	400,504	74,433
			85	107,850	342,327	439,398	97,071
			86	43,919	154,041	187,880	33,839
	O	W	81	3,218	9,350	10,727	1,377
	V	E	81	1,540,028	5,664,373	6,877,143	1,216,025
			82	2,101,374	7,377,552	9,053,316	1,675,764
			83	1,678,258	5,416,298	6,706,969	1,290,671
			84	1,671,210	5,179,238	6,544,781	1,365,543
			85	969,076	3,067,005	3,957,287	890,282
			86	389,289	1,299,001	1,657,655	358,654
	V	W	81	27,822	89,060	120,542	31,482
			82	28,679	102,373	137,687	35,314
			83	24,363	77,177	107,951	30,774
			84	15,830	47,056	66,037	18,981
			85	22,149	65,146	93,155	28,009
			86	8,191	30,885	40,838	9,953
SWEDEN	V	E	81	2,996	22,839	25,960	3,121
	V	W	86	2,853	24,528	24,885	357
U KING	A	E	84	61	413	1,163	750
	N	E	83	5,888	39,838	43,817	3,979
	O	E	81	10,988	52,404	67,458	15,054
			82	13,874	57,067	71,077	14,010
			83	9,148	47,291	54,778	7,487
			84	4,338	22,098	26,449	4,351
			85	6,298	41,935	52,112	10,177
			86	1,187	8,070	9,184	1,114
	V	E	81	6,024	49,175	54,231	5,056
			82	7,711	48,343	55,149	6,806
			83	3,899	15,399	19,338	3,939
			84	36,939	255,304	317,361	62,057
			85	96,192	626,591	738,484	111,893
			86	15,789	109,880	125,207	15,327
	V	W	81	1,190	15,026	16,452	1,426
			82	475	6,221	6,832	611
			83	238	2,473	3,087	614
			84	237	2,562	2,854	292
			85	14,435	98,958	126,539	27,581
YUGOSLV	A	E	83	388	700	914	214
	O	W	81	420	2,350	2,721	371
			83	83	455	959	504
			84	179	975	1,276	301

1675005 FERMNTD ALC BEV NSPF OV 14% ALC (GAL)

Country	Mode	Reg	Yr	Quantity	F.A.S.	C.I.F.	Charges
TOTAL			86	225,026	1,537,696	1,757,238	219,542
AUSTRAL	V	E	86	173	2,835	5,666	2,831
DENMARK	N	E	86	8,150	117,854	125,164	7,310
	O	E	86	18,762	179,152	208,557	29,405
	V	E	86	36,952	391,996	439,234	47,238
	V	W	86	3,175	42,169	44,658	2,489
FR GERM	V	E	86	2,589	18,366	21,038	2,672
FRANCE	O	E	86	61	1,246	1,926	680
	V	E	86	4,573	28,427	35,432	7,005
ITALY	V	E	86	102,861	388,017	460,333	72,316
JAPAN	V	E	86	14,042	129,423	145,026	15,603
	V	W	86	7,475	78,882	84,384	5,502
N ZEAL	V	W	86	2,296	22,218	24,894	2,676
NETHLDS	O	E	86	2,483	22,835	25,698	2,863
SPAIN	V	E	86	16,502	60,646	74,813	14,167
SWEDEN	O	E	86	1,604	15,043	17,843	2,800
U KING	V	E	86	3,328	38,587	42,572	3,985

1675025 FER ALC BEV NSPF 7 TO 14% ALCH (GAL)

Country	Mode	Reg	Yr	Quantity	F.A.S.	C.I.F.	Charges
TOTAL			86	995,038	4,871,772	5,794,964	923,192
BELGIUM	V	E	86	8,383	30,945	36,631	5,686
CANADA	O	E	86	1,237	10,645	10,645	
DENMARK	O	E	86	476	4,573	5,089	516
	V	E	86	1,545	8,112	11,222	3,110
FR GERM	V	E	86	369	4,642	5,680	1,038
	V	W	86	678	1,667	2,063	396
FRANCE	A	E	86	7	1,172	1,404	232
	O	E	86	832	5,821	6,795	974
	V	E	86	21,862	132,070	157,304	25,234
	V	W	86	5,492	11,270	12,270	1,000
ITALY	O	E	86	5,586	34,052	38,894	4,842
	V	E	86	307,322	1,665,957	1,963,481	297,524
JAPAN	V	E	86	3,979	34,686	40,624	5,938
	V	E	86	52,883	486,457	564,083	77,626
	V	H	86	712	8,946	10,198	1,252
	V	W	86	68,071	546,021	602,598	56,577
JORDAN	O	E	86	951	6,850	8,180	1,330
MEXICO	O	E	86	8,598	30,560	30,560	
N ZEAL	V	W	86	2,674	27,086	30,172	3,086
NETHLDS	V	E	86	6,300	23,297	26,485	3,188
	V	E	86	11,381	24,174	30,324	6,150
POLAND	V	E	86	713	9,000	10,972	1,972
SPAIN	N	E	86	7,489	22,448	32,432	9,984
	O	E	86	37,201	116,777	147,600	30,823
	V	E	86	402,703	1,476,688	1,829,001	352,313
	V	W	86	15,897	39,754	49,476	9,722
SWEDEN	V	E	86	2,095	6,484	9,549	3,065
U KING	O	E	86	948	6,272	9,269	2,997
	V	E	86	18,417	91,647	107,836	16,193
	V	W	86	237	3,703	4,127	424

1675050 FERMNTD ALC BEV NSPF UN 7% ALCH (GAL)

Country	Mode	Reg	Yr	Quantity	F.A.S.	C.I.F.	Charges
TOTAL			86	2,666,331	12,074,337	14,432,461	2,358,124
CANADA	O	E	86	54,804	161,891	161,891	
	O	W	86	6,342	27,425	27,425	
DENMARK	O	E	86	2,401	22,088	25,022	2,934
	V	E	86	1,509	21,699	23,669	1,970
FR GERM	V	E	86	2,156	26,551	27,975	1,424
FRANCE	V	E	86	262,794	1,615,183	1,947,853	332,670
	V	W	86	2,596	16,667	19,656	2,989
ITALY	O	E	86	7,302	27,095	32,888	5,793
	V	E	86	2,057,794	8,425,032	10,217,727	1,792,695
	V	H	86	6,485	23,108	35,708	12,600
	V	W	86	170,178	1,037,965	1,172,619	134,654
JAMAICA	V	E	86	356	2,856	3,526	670
JAPAN	O	E	86	2,186	19,500	21,933	2,433
	V	E	86	14,264	147,972	163,330	15,358
	V	W	86	1,060	6,627	7,294	667
MEXICO	O	E	86	2,971	10,560	10,560	
NETHLDS	V	E	86	6,097	61,079	65,400	4,321
	V	W	86	15,047	265,639	276,830	11,191
PORTUGL	V	E	86	2,247	6,824	9,714	2,890
SPAIN	O	E	86	1,069	3,425	3,596	171
	V	E	86	45,353	139,385	170,373	30,988
	V	W	86	1,201	3,576	5,117	1,541
U KING	V	E	86	119	2,190	2,355	165

1679000 IMITATIONS OF WINES (PFG)

Country	Mode	Reg	Yr	Quantity	F.A.S.	C.I.F.	Charges
TOTAL			83	79	639	737	98
			86	2,596	19,247	22,821	3,574
FRANCE	V	E	86	2,596	19,247	22,821	3,574
	V	W	83	79	639	737	98

Fruit, juice, concentrated

1653570 CITRUS FRT JUICE NSPF CONCT (GAL)

Country	Mode	Reg	Yr	Quantity	F.A.S.	C.I.F.	Charges
TOTAL			81	1,296,041	1,337,955	1,457,484	119,529
			82	9,701,674	9,180,457	10,175,765	995,308
			83	3,616,740	2,894,795	3,366,020	471,225
ARGENT	N	E	83	779,982	273,960	374,746	100,786
	O	E	82	371,420	188,822	237,636	48,814
			83	346,378	120,514	165,319	44,805
	V	E	81	371,420	180,962	231,717	50,755
			83	25,300	11,040	13,851	2,811
	V	W	83	22,050	7,638	11,527	3,889
AUSTRAL	O	W	83	339,500	796,038	940,861	144,823
	V	E	81	176	1,270	1,378	108
	V	W	81	131,750	143,938	176,100	32,162
AUSTRIA	O	E	83	104	1,930	2,067	137
BELGIUM	A	E	82	85	541	1,425	884
BRAZIL	O	E	82	2,903,574	2,047,970	2,309,465	261,495
			83	141,038	47,025	59,110	12,085
	V	E	82	5,592,674	4,618,305	5,124,429	506,124
			83	1,342,635	457,053	556,749	99,696
CANADA	A	E	82	90	1,226	1,484	258
	O	E	81	857	3,261	3,261	
			82	373	2,453	2,453	
			83	220	279	279	
	O	W	81	264	640	931	291

Product
TSUSA commodity number, description, and unit of quantity

Country	Mode	Reg	Yr	Quantity	F.A.S.	C.I.F.	Charges
CHINA M	V	E	81	248	516	576	60
			82	17,537	8,593	9,232	639
	V	W	83	506	1,086	1,189	103
COLOMB	A	E	82	74	433	493	60
	V	E	81	1,867	3,467	3,777	310
DENMARK	V	E	82	187	330	391	61
DOM REP	V	E	83	80	855	1,064	209
EGYPT	O	E	81	850	2,740	3,129	389
FR GERM	A	E	81	3,832	11,618	13,448	1,830
			82	10,021	36,624	54,086	17,462
	V	E	81	168,895	450,660	478,073	27,413
			82	484,075	1,731,899	1,856,807	124,908
			83	201,254	686,188	714,429	28,241
	V	W	82	78,653	278,032	303,971	25,939
			83	97,956	345,646	371,388	25,742
FRANCE	V	E	83	13,381	25,245	29,451	4,206
GERM DR	V	E	82	18,038	64,143	69,067	4,924
GREECE	V	E	82	928	1,800	2,249	449
			83	180	780	880	100
HG KONG	V	E	81	1,148	306	346	40
			82	8,658	7,682	8,504	822
			83	76	1,718	1,928	210
	V	W	82	180	291	300	9
			83	990	2,362	2,461	99
INDIA	O	E	81	18	291	291	
			83	20	288	343	55
ISRAEL	V	E	81	19,733	8,935	11,156	2,221
			82	7,322	4,272	5,317	1,045
ITALY	O	E	83	5	1,035	1,035	
JAMAICA	A	E	82	12	469	594	125
JAPAN	V	E	81	4	666	709	43
			83	24	2,369	3,869	1,500
MEXICO	A	E	82	221	1,200	1,432	232
	A	W	82	655	3,150	4,269	1,119
	O	E	81	514,012	437,069	437,069	
			82	206,895	182,274	182,274	
			83	303,558	105,188	105,188	
	O	W	81	80,174	83,692	85,617	1,925
			83	605	740	740	
	V	E	82	121	349	380	31
PHIL R	V	W	82	75	758	817	59
			83	150	907	1,004	97
SINGAPR	V	W	81	111	725	825	100
THAILND	V	W	82	233	1,450	1,604	154
U KING	A	W	82	228	541	1,355	814
	N	E	83	197	2,411	2,854	443
	V	E	81	27	4,049	4,812	763
	V	W	83	551	2,500	3,688	1,188

1653580 CITRUS FRT JUICE NSPF, CONCENTD (GAL)

Country	Mode	Reg	Yr	Quantity	F.A.S.	C.I.F.	Charges
TOTAL			84	3,046,497	3,457,565	3,674,523	216,958
AUSTRIA	O	E	84	955	5,377	5,993	616
BELIZE	V	E	84	1,021,965	910,882	973,761	62,879
BRAZIL	O	E	84	237,931	299,352	323,309	23,957
	V	E	84	938,015	1,133,457	1,204,474	71,017
CANADA	O	E	84	1,716	4,300	4,300	
	O	W	84	100	688	688	
CR N AN	V	E	84	230	995	1,095	100
DOM REP	V	E	84	390	3,539	3,867	328
DOMINCA	N	E	84	120	1,089	1,283	194
	V	E	84	90	816	930	114
FR GERM	A	E	84	3,099	16,330	19,236	2,906
	N	W	84	35,264	123,433	133,778	10,345
	V	E	84	57,079	221,810	228,212	6,402
FRANCE	V	E	84	55,163	86,033	101,751	15,718
JAMAICA	A	E	84	688	4,300	9,126	4,826
	N	E	84	203	1,014	1,062	48
	V	E	84	107,173	115,620	129,236	13,616
JAPAN	A	E	84	25	267	1,253	986
	V	E	84	1,800	3,124	3,623	499
	V	W	84	185	537	580	43
MEXICO	O	E	84	570,823	491,967	491,967	
N ANTIL	V	E	84	46	270	334	64
NETHLDS	A	W	84	124	2,994	3,847	853
	V	E	84	13,312	29,120	30,530	1,410
	V	W	84	1	251	288	37

1653680 CITRUS FRT JUICE NSPF, CONCENTD (GAL)

Country	Mode	Reg	Yr	Quantity	F.A.S.	C.I.F.	Charges
TOTAL			85	6,362,412	6,884,307	7,302,602	418,295
			86	17,995,291	17,360,319	18,833,373	1,473,054
ARGENT	O	E	86	103,768	71,710	72,325	615
AUSTRAL	O	E	86	142,192	85,813	112,854	27,041
	V	E	86	204,602	148,385	186,597	38,212

Product
TSUSA commodity number, description, and unit of quantity

Country	Mode	Reg	Yr	Quantity	F.A.S.	C.I.F.	Charges
	V	W	86	340,419	246,835	297,911	51,076
AUSTRIA	A	E	85	3,961	7,287	23,628	16,341
BELGIUM	O	E	85	852	1,321	1,858	537
BELIZE	V	E	85	1,619,642	1,854,482	1,947,149	92,667
			86	3,449,800	4,068,550	4,281,504	212,954
BRAZIL	O	E	85	3,223,729	3,362,668	3,580,083	217,415
			86	3,136,921	3,229,542	3,506,212	276,670
	V	E	85	9,045	8,765	9,328	563
			86	555,818	386,557	419,422	32,865
CANADA	O	E	85	22,433	18,678	18,678	
COLOMB	V	E	86	22,731	30,232	33,732	3,500
CYPRUS	V	E	86	10	1,092	1,168	76
DOM REP	V	E	85	12,166	98,580	105,989	7,409
			86	20,198	141,891	152,112	10,221
DOMINCA	V	E	85	14,252	25,867	28,269	2,402
			86	57,932	129,071	144,597	15,526
FR GERM	A	E	85	4,200	10,085	10,615	530
			86	15,829	73,710	107,614	33,904
	A	W	86	482,160	919,548	1,113,465	193,917
	N	E	85	186,468	674,676	713,043	38,367
	O	E	85	955	5,377	5,993	616
	V	E	86	58,590	223,480	230,480	7,000
FRANCE	V	E	85	87,946	147,502	168,272	20,770
			86	39,440	133,313	144,414	11,101
HG KONG	V	E	85	155	1,396	1,520	124
HONDURA	O	E	85	33,358	35,758	35,758	
	V	E	85	284,351	305,443	339,746	34,303
			86	232,292	204,686	242,875	38,189
ISRAEL	O	E	86	1,271,605	931,165	1,149,630	218,465
	V	E	86	385,275	348,727	398,340	49,613
ITALY	V	E	86	873	1,986	2,370	384
JAMAICA	A	E	85	461	4,305	5,555	1,250
			86	413	2,000	2,660	660
	V	E	85	347,024	210,978	230,389	19,411
			86	367,170	743,732	804,574	60,842
JAPAN	V	E	86	77	1,023	1,464	441
	V	W	85	315	1,404	1,626	222
MEXICO	O	E	85	691,755	759,218	759,218	
			86	5,955,056	3,838,852	3,838,854	2
N ZEAL	O	E	86	343,332	210,330	268,610	58,280
NETHLDS	A	E	85	812	2,193	3,105	912
PANAMA	V	E	86	546,000	456,300	540,595	84,295
VENEZ	V	E	85	5,000	23,000	25,823	2,823
			86	76,320	57,113	65,951	8,838

Fruit, juice, not concentrated
1653000 CIT FRT JUICE NOT CON, NSPF (GAL)

Country	Mode	Reg	Yr	Quantity	F.A.S.	C.I.F.	Charges
TOTAL			81	10,096,688	15,464,384	16,566,126	1,101,742
			82	3,102,118	6,116,651	6,195,276	78,625
			83	5,596,984	7,969,227	8,057,937	88,710
ARAB EM	V	E	83	27	270	301	31
BELGIUM	A	E	83	162	670	1,408	738
	V	E	83	996	1,883	2,129	246
BRAZIL	A	E	83	530	1,080	5,473	4,393
	O	E	81	5,649,611	8,024,945	9,014,207	989,262
			82	258	387	394	7
	O	W	82	2,885	7,023	7,023	
	V	E	83	8,441	6,890	11,053	4,163
CANADA	A	E	82	463	1,518	3,810	2,292
	O	E	81	204,976	476,860	476,860	
			82	435,330	1,048,746	1,048,746	
			83	665,321	1,721,557	1,721,557	
	O	W	81	13,092	34,466	34,466	
			82	10,873	28,129	28,129	
			83	20,581	90,095	90,095	
CHINA M	V	W	81	90	338	357	19
CHINA T	V	W	82	338	920	1,003	83
			83	79	367	385	18
CYPRUS	V	E	81	195	1,200	1,558	358
			82	145	900	1,105	205
			83	375	1,820	1,865	45
DENMARK	V	E	82	15,191	40,472	47,973	7,501
			83	17,409	39,732	48,229	8,497
	V	W	83	7,503	16,836	19,189	2,353
DOM REP	V	E	82	931	1,740	2,377	637
			83	400	1,000	1,346	346
DOMINCA	V	E	82	59	357	398	41
FR GERM	A	E	82	119	460	1,979	1,519
	V	W	82	16,800	36,093	39,057	2,964
			83	102	464	577	113
FRANCE	V	E	83	7,642	26,747	38,618	11,871
	V	W	83	159	382	528	146

Product TSUSA commodity number, description, and unit of quantity Country	Mode	Reg	Yr	Quantity	F.A.S.	C.I.F.	Charges
HG KONG	V	E	82	132	320	369	49
	V	W	83	2,138	3,827	4,277	450
HONDURA	A	E	83	10	315	737	422
ISRAEL	V	E	81	2,250	11,250	13,704	2,454
			82	563	2,250	2,646	396
ITALY	N	E	81	85,262	383,689	451,397	67,708
			82	61,477	334,129	373,098	38,969
	O	E	82	1,348	3,069	3,119	50
	V	E	81	26,552	167,982	201,282	33,300
			82	17,251	117,087	130,287	13,200
			83	68,137	303,120	351,302	48,182
	V	W	81	3,000	17,581	23,636	6,055
			83	4,109	14,733	17,157	2,424
JAMAICA	V	E	83	1,875	6,989	7,315	326
JAPAN	V	E	81	8	514	567	53
			82	664	3,182	3,507	325
	V	H	81	504	3,361	4,000	639
			82	235	1,474	1,696	222
			83	819	4,563	5,191	628
	V	W	81	619	2,902	3,092	190
			82	1,799	9,504	10,112	608
			83	6,828	32,494	34,717	2,223
KOR REP	V	W	81	3	737	798	61
			82	6,300	29,894	32,340	2,446
MEXICO	O	E	81	4,105,144	6,323,743	6,323,743	
			82	2,517,163	4,399,123	4,399,123	
			83	4,780,147	5,685,760	5,685,760	
	O	W	81	2,431	6,384	6,384	
			82	3,724	10,339	10,339	
			83	3,044	6,659	6,659	
N ZEAL	A	W	82	20	538	1,122	584
NETHLDS	V	E	82	1,255	2,040	2,550	510
NORWAY	V	W	83	33	310	361	51
PORTUGL	V	E	82	674	1,396	1,692	296
SPAIN	V	E	82	3,938	26,726	30,827	4,101
			83	87	391	631	240
SWEDEN	O	W	81	71	265	265	
SWITZLD	V	E	82	2,180	8,505	9,977	1,472
THAILND	V	W	81	40	395	429	34
TRINID	A	E	83	30	273	1,077	804
U KING	O	E	81	103	334	334	
	V	W	82	3	330	478	148
YUGOSLV	V	E	81	2,737	7,438	9,047	1,609

1653080 CITRUS FRT JUICE NT CNCTRD NSPF (GAL)

Country	Mode	Reg	Yr	Quantity	F.A.S.	C.I.F.	Charges
TOTAL			84	1,114,156	2,143,996	2,237,586	93,590
BELGIUM	O	E	84	349	717	828	111
	V	E	84	5,894	13,338	17,776	4,438
CANADA	O	E	84	936,751	1,554,700	1,554,700	
CYPRUS	V	E	84	608	6,792	7,663	871
DENMARK	V	E	84	116	350	430	80
DOM REP	V	E	84	29,344	27,393	31,275	3,882
FR GERM	O	E	84	24,021	120,581	131,332	10,751
	O	W	84	111	430	647	217
FRANCE	V	E	84	2,997	10,115	12,400	2,285
GAZA ST	O	E	84	406	540	540	
HG KONG	V	W	84	3,123	6,472	7,408	936
ITALY	O	E	84	3,041	13,800	16,063	2,263
	V	E	84	77,260	253,562	307,172	53,610
JAMAICA	N	E	84	1,040	4,110	4,476	366
JAPAN	V	E	84	1,641	8,334	9,600	1,266
	V	W	84	2,067	6,900	7,790	890
MEXICO	O	E	84	9,195	17,627	17,821	194
	O	W	84	3,570	8,725	8,725	
N ZEAL	V	H	84	405	2,632	3,551	919
NETHLDS	V	E	84	343	1,616	1,793	177
PANAMA	O	E	84	765	4,481	4,838	357
PHIL R	V	W	84	47	452	563	111
SPAIN	V	E	84	533	1,352	3,024	1,672
SWITZLD	V	E	84	10,354	77,715	85,829	8,114
U KING	V	E	84	20	972	1,052	80
ZAIRE	O	E	84	155	290	290	

1653200 CITRUS FRT JUICE NT CNCTRD NSPF (GAL)

Country	Mode	Reg	Yr	Quantity	F.A.S.	C.I.F.	Charges
TOTAL			85	1,181,941	2,328,350	2,512,190	183,840
			86	2,075,090	3,564,496	3,699,665	135,169
AUSTRIA	A	E	86	805	1,637	9,127	7,490
BELGIUM	V	E	85	1,552	4,071	5,236	1,165
			86	589	1,540	1,918	378
C RICA	O	E	86	491	1,358	1,467	109
CANADA	N	E	85	3,564	14,490	14,490	
	O	E	85	377,454	866,753	866,753	
			86	360,365	675,382	675,383	1

Country	Mode	Reg	Yr	Quantity	F.A.S.	C.I.F.	Charges
CHINA T	V	W	86	8,100	17,200	18,791	1,591
CYPRUS	V	E	85	497	2,409	2,685	276
			86	763	4,481	4,868	387
DOM REP	V	E	85	18,052	15,343	17,343	2,000
			86	9,626	8,183	9,191	1,008
FR GERM	V	E	85	563	1,236	1,454	218
	V	W	86	2,362	20,442	21,579	1,137
FRANCE	V	E	85	45,874	162,293	181,484	19,191
			86	32,219	147,428	160,550	13,122
GUATMAL	V	E	86	1,375	1,750	2,165	415
HG KONG	V	W	85	1,076	2,677	3,012	335
ISRAEL	V	E	85	4,845	19,884	24,503	4,619
			86	43,645	120,851	148,123	27,272
	V	W	85	2,278	9,121	11,880	2,759
ITALY	O	E	85	126,711	363,950	435,165	71,215
			86	41,720	89,088	120,381	31,293
	V	E	85	74,893	243,024	305,947	62,923
			86	35,616	145,968	180,498	34,530
	V	W	86	2,625	17,103	20,401	3,298
JAMAICA	V	E	85	546	5,026	5,531	505
			86	18,225	43,032	51,210	8,178
JAPAN	V	W	85	594	2,601	2,828	227
MEXICO	O	E	85	504,609	525,819	525,819	
			86	1,511,293	2,235,325	2,235,325	
SINGAPR	A	E	85	2	1,397	2,357	960
SPAIN	V	E	85	2,758	13,012	15,912	2,900
SWITZLD	V	E	85	16,073	75,244	89,791	14,547
			86	5,175	29,240	33,900	4,660
U KING	O	E	86	96	4,488	4,788	300

Fruit, juice, with alcohol
1655500 FRUIT JCES N MXD NOV 1% ACHL (GAL)

Country	Mode	Reg	Yr	Quantity	F.A.S.	C.I.F.	Charges
TOTAL			81	2,657,603	5,956,225	6,302,836	346,481
			82	3,419,386	8,144,736	8,700,878	556,142
			83	4,363,014	11,434,484	12,159,855	725,371
			84	6,483,175	18,193,500	19,168,877	975,377
			85	7,200,400	21,796,928	22,959,415	1,162,487
			86	8,623,390	26,223,507	27,512,582	1,289,075
ARGENT	V	E	81	3,422	13,688	16,363	2,675
			83	87,463	109,388	126,716	17,328
			84	14,400	8,700	10,630	1,930
			85	25,880	25,490	30,254	4,764
			86	105,600	70,400	84,972	14,572
	V	W	82	53,606	63,367	74,097	10,730
			86	17,110	73,978	87,773	13,795
AUSTRAL	O	E	82	5,936	18,066	18,066	
			84	6,784	28,393	28,393	
	V	E	82	6,402	21,355	22,191	836
			83	21,944	70,358	76,087	5,729
			85	2,083	8,153	8,291	138
			86	196,986	774,047	811,875	37,828
	V	H	86	46,977	67,942	101,916	33,974
	V	W	81	78	1,103	1,156	53
			82	51,877	188,073	192,311	4,238
			83	32,104	161,573	166,031	4,458
			86	25,272	24,486	25,855	1,369
AUSTRIA	A	E	84	3,888	11,310	14,246	2,936
			85	7,465	26,904	32,227	5,323
	A	W	86	108	1,812	2,813	1,001
	N	E	82	536,466	1,714,819	1,755,370	40,551
			84	116,452	515,816	535,365	19,549
			85	215,117	834,300	852,510	18,210
	O	E	81	244	1,781	2,225	444
	V	E	81	703,987	2,178,676	2,237,706	59,030
			82	73,052	129,300	133,273	3,973
			83	130,086	320,982	328,310	7,328
			84	36,234	146,365	149,679	3,314
			85	209,102	855,988	885,902	29,914
			86	624,761	2,954,543	3,065,703	111,160
	V	W	81	28,080	114,018	117,625	3,607
			82	73,868	258,973	262,838	3,865
			83	24,192	106,487	108,864	2,377
			84	32,130	138,381	142,201	3,820
			85	42,660	155,431	160,952	5,521
			86	231,396	1,198,042	1,240,418	42,376
BELGIUM	A	E	84	300	340	357	17
	N	E	85	140,152	184,558	218,795	34,237
	O	E	81	63,450	51,850	58,455	6,605
			82	81,675	50,665	59,385	8,720
			83	15,825	10,248	11,568	1,320
			84	1,354	3,467	3,718	251
			85	3,673	6,840	9,636	2,796

Product
TSUSA commodity number, description, and unit of quantity

Country	Mode	Reg	Yr	Quantity	F.A.S.	C.I.F.	Charges
	O	W	84	19,968	22,131	22,231	100
	V	E	82	3,000	11,798	13,004	1,206
			83	16,504	11,387	14,410	3,023
			84	166,105	209,104	247,705	38,601
			85	11,259	39,756	47,540	7,784
			86	329,191	922,260	988,361	66,101
	V	W	86	11,247	30,867	36,603	5,736
BELIZE	V	E	86	18,452	67,903	71,711	3,808
BRAZIL	A	E	82	32,400	4,500	4,812	312
			86	100	1,500	1,571	71
	O	E	85	75,864	139,659	146,160	6,501
			86	59,493	77,185	82,178	4,993
	V	E	83	35,329	43,810	56,298	12,488
			84	123,195	299,520	330,091	30,571
			85	153,715	379,507	414,910	35,403
			86	122,324	267,835	283,512	15,677
	V	W	84	446	1,330	1,475	145
			86	2,685	10,621	13,417	2,796
BULGAR	V	E	86	1,145	2,065	2,933	868
C RICA	V	E	81	159,448	235,758	284,702	48,944
			82	85,891	177,188	210,482	33,294
			83	97,897	107,510	127,543	20,033
			84	42,484	27,374	34,148	6,774
CANADA	A	H	84	188	423	516	93
			85	6,168	12,600	14,775	2,175
			86	3,412	6,300	7,538	1,238
	A	W	86	398	1,700	2,183	483
	O	E	81	81,903	246,263	246,263	
			82	27,927	102,169	102,169	
			83	140,605	280,500	280,500	
			84	146,526	346,308	346,360	52
			85	67,855	136,743	136,743	
			86	3,451	13,687	13,687	
	O	W	81	36,087	104,197	104,197	
			82	5,924	13,236	13,236	
			83	27,326	58,769	58,769	
			84	349,355	2,511,075	2,511,075	
			85	711,674	2,768,157	2,768,159	2
			86	577,915	3,510,158	3,510,158	
	V	E	86	25,410	17,096	19,304	2,208
CHILE	V	E	83	44,900	120,469	129,888	9,419
			84	137,289	133,727	142,878	9,151
			85	164,450	157,060	171,747	14,687
			86	72,629	127,188	136,777	9,589
	V	W	83	1,120	863	989	126
			86	64,590	64,169	76,847	12,678
CHINA M	N	W	86	18,988	50,471	56,668	6,197
	O	E	82	557	1,217	1,449	232
			85	483	3,377	3,744	367
	V	E	81	15,951	37,277	43,867	6,590
			82	16,565	46,773	54,183	7,410
			83	34,917	69,921	79,854	9,933
			84	1,673	5,678	6,220	542
			85	8,117	28,283	30,189	1,906
			86	10,987	16,468	19,099	2,631
	V	W	81	12,610	30,598	36,340	5,742
			82	14,111	58,167	63,224	5,057
			83	27,020	58,980	67,585	8,605
			84	104,564	257,787	289,215	31,428
			85	19,986	48,920	54,902	5,982
			86	54,606	121,970	136,912	14,942
CHINA T	N	W	82	*	1,140	1,190	50
	O	E	83	42	417	458	41
	V	E	81	9,129	5,169	5,822	653
			82	9,309	15,415	17,181	1,766
			83	22,847	28,083	32,640	4,557
			84	103,010	107,338	124,323	16,985
			85	61,181	82,368	94,873	12,505
			86	21,988	54,947	62,462	7,515
	V	H	82	8,000	49,777	56,000	6,223
	V	W	81	107,973	192,051	207,585	15,534
			82	35,530	205,095	214,047	8,952
			83	53,457	172,466	183,989	11,523
			84	22,003	55,037	60,747	5,710
			85	46,541	128,840	145,914	17,074
			86	119,004	262,621	285,958	23,337
COLOMB	A	E	83	295,625	1,305,420	1,351,396	45,976
			84	1,587	11,984	16,226	4,242
			86	5,385	59,850	67,822	7,972
	A	W	85	347	2,109	3,829	1,720
			86	668	2,869	6,760	3,891
	N	E	84	773,450	1,718,317	1,803,655	85,338
			85	385,900	537,286	575,555	38,269
			86	65,852	285,122	291,985	6,863
	V	E	81	5,299	9,504	10,365	861
			82	5,910	23,626	25,892	2,266
			83	53,330	41,420	44,986	3,566
			84	110,027	327,770	363,979	36,209
			85	17,039	81,339	89,229	7,890
			86	21,245	68,578	74,872	6,294
	V	W	82	22,000	155,760	162,223	6,463
			86	10,375	33,160	40,000	6,840
DENMARK	V	E	81	30,700	123,382	129,833	6,451
			82	80,571	255,358	263,556	8,198
			83	45,254	125,022	132,243	7,221
			84	114,348	271,613	287,730	16,117
			85	25,272	57,001	59,707	2,706
			86	11,942	22,632	23,090	458
	V	W	81	89	348	394	46
			84	51,694	130,226	135,020	4,794
			85	12,733	27,721	31,770	4,049
DOM REP	A	E	84	125	475	711	236
	V	E	81	137,470	146,294	159,856	13,562
			82	85,701	198,929	209,344	10,415
			83	20,724	82,436	89,637	7,201
			84	4,737	32,530	35,213	2,683
			85	26,319	87,756	93,845	6,089
			86	5,919	32,173	38,992	6,819
DOMINCA	V	E	86	175	4,363	4,483	120
ECUADOR	A	E	83	594	288	386	98
	V	E	82	45,054	88,191	107,885	19,694
			83	29,741	22,247	30,858	8,611
			84	29,691	51,431	64,059	12,628
			85	29,749	32,419	40,883	8,464
			86	74,602	37,079	46,631	9,552
	V	W	82	215,887	427,900	485,795	57,895
			83	18,540	59,772	66,137	6,365
			85	2,158	28,354	30,240	1,886
			86	26,522	85,172	90,816	5,644
EGYPT	O	E	81	95	733	733	
			83	938	3,667	3,667	
			84	97	574	574	
	V	E	81	18,105	74,422	84,170	9,748
			82	12,225	70,050	75,588	5,538
			83	66,929	102,380	113,244	10,864
			84	50,371	31,150	33,819	2,669
			85	2,250	11,230	12,132	902
			86	11,060	35,953	43,835	7,882
	V	W	84	2,239	10,223	11,600	1,377
			85	10,750	32,500	38,148	5,648
			86	1,631	6,784	8,093	1,309
F W IND	V	E	81	16	265	274	9
			82	73	632	778	146
FIJI	V	W	82	6,864	38,057	43,202	5,145
			85	204	1,644	2,063	419
FR GERM	A	E	84	123	401	1,229	828
			85	826	10,085	14,162	4,077
			86	1,491	1,620	3,808	2,188
	A	W	85	4,400	15,128	20,627	5,499
	N	E	81	236,631	653,880	675,749	21,869
			82	275,815	607,734	628,678	20,944
			83	595,116	1,367,267	1,432,844	65,577
			84	843,582	2,048,696	2,140,490	91,794
			85	753,058	1,736,465	1,828,980	92,515
			86	1,510,190	3,996,421	4,143,792	147,371
	O	E	81	1,023	5,305	6,298	993
			82	36,750	53,025	54,950	1,925
			83	38,447	55,210	57,140	1,930
			84	32,571	88,093	88,302	209
			85	4,309	22,612	23,601	989
			86	1,050	3,410	3,410	
	O	W	85	3,794	1,419	1,419	
	V	E	81	70	267	294	27
			82	36,225	52,612	55,372	2,760
			83	206,008	728,389	759,408	31,019
			84	482,218	1,382,737	1,445,745	63,008
			85	418,038	1,515,679	1,600,304	84,625
			86	884,557	1,682,551	1,744,947	62,396
	V	H	86	6,615	29,165	36,321	7,156
	V	W	81	2,226	2,716	2,895	179
			82	889	4,541	6,751	2,210
			83	177,353	470,445	481,517	11,072
			84	287,347	1,502,050	1,538,088	36,038
			85	1,081,196	3,728,597	3,845,736	117,139
			86	1,008,505	2,888,576	2,993,060	104,484
FRANCE	A	E	82	38	534	727	193
			86	679	8,017	8,929	912
	N	E	83	19,996	28,538	30,517	1,979
			84	41,466	37,444	43,312	5,868
			85	6,202	35,990	40,065	4,075

Product TSUSA commodity number, description, and unit of quantity Country	Mode	Reg	Yr	Quantity	F.A.S.	C.I.F.	Charges
			86	19,636	165,443	180,658	15,215
	O	E	82	270	3,017	3,041	24
			85	443	2,013	2,270	257
			86	51	2,834	2,834	
	V	E	81	595	4,085	4,141	56
			82	124,546	96,141	106,289	10,148
			83	392	849	1,228	379
			84	190	767	964	197
			85	1,379	4,023	4,624	601
			86	1,416	28,515	32,132	3,617
	V	W	81	349	4,950	5,160	210
			82	119	1,450	1,570	120
			85	4,619	15,541	17,094	1,553
			86	1,788	6,961	8,157	1,196
GERM DR	V	W	85	128,520	592,742	604,799	12,057
GREECE	V	E	81	79	546	611	65
			82	79	600	692	92
			83	158	1,050	1,231	181
			84	79	500	561	61
			85	1,584	2,500	2,739	239
			86	1,425	4,548	4,979	431
	V	W	82	120	1,100	1,282	182
			83	159	1,200	1,355	155
			86	1,846	12,500	13,994	1,494
GUATMAL	N	E	82	1,412	4,366	5,166	800
			83	2,820	5,313	6,492	1,179
	V	E	84	4,906	5,802	10,419	4,617
			85	2,453	5,428	6,129	701
			86	10,279	22,340	26,188	3,848
HAITI	V	E	81	1,700	2,200	2,431	231
HG KONG	V	E	81	2,885	8,812	9,842	1,030
			82	643	1,553	1,686	133
			83	4,708	12,650	14,639	1,989
			84	7,523	20,444	25,453	5,009
			85	8,984	27,418	31,654	4,236
			86	27,950	11,081	13,991	2,910
	V	W	81	1,369	25,250	25,850	600
			82	2,342	6,986	7,884	898
			83	3,488	6,245	6,945	700
			84	18,279	51,688	56,604	4,916
			85	34,329	76,911	87,659	10,748
			86	63,759	130,533	143,831	13,298
HONDURA	O	E	85	9,620	12,685	12,685	
	V	E	85	45,746	49,994	54,168	4,174
HUNGARY	V	E	82	6,498	3,400	4,061	661
			83	70,707	44,548	47,841	3,293
			86	3,481	14,059	16,463	2,404
	V	W	84	20,706	55,160	60,360	5,200
			85	2,708	7,008	11,385	4,377
			86	2,215	8,350	8,486	136
INDIA	O	E	83	103	488	537	49
			85	6	1,072	1,215	143
	V	E	82	216	1,635	1,838	203
			83	5,352	18,176	21,209	3,033
			84	6,754	10,874	13,187	2,313
			86	4,024	12,345	16,345	4,000
	V	W	81	2,319	8,554	10,745	2,191
			82	5,951	4,963	5,912	949
			83	2,926	4,984	5,702	718
			84	10,230	19,812	24,448	4,636
			85	6,477	8,742	12,547	3,805
			86	26,442	64,410	74,131	9,721
INDNSIA	V	E	83	150	750	1,093	343
	V	W	86	331	1,650	1,855	205
IRAN	V	E	82	309	934	1,058	124
IRAQ	O	E	86	58	1,326	1,326	
	V	E	86	21,000	23,667	26,772	3,105
IRELAND	V	E	84	24,422	19,136	24,205	5,069
			86	50	4,406	6,050	1,644
ISRAEL	O	E	81	100	283	283	
	V	E	81	35,833	20,995	26,595	5,600
			82	10,812	12,998	16,100	3,102
			83	64,733	104,878	114,178	9,300
			86	9,784	10,388	15,394	5,006
	V	W	82	16,500	78,469	88,943	10,474
			85	9,990	4,650	6,244	1,594
ITALY	O	E	82	1,013	3,111	3,311	200
			83	1,271	3,499	4,100	601
			84	721	1,792	2,677	885
			86	25,137	54,020	75,320	21,300
	V	E	81	29,920	63,336	85,594	22,258
			82	36,116	75,134	90,916	15,782
			83	31,252	74,666	94,734	20,070
			84	146,226	443,131	534,717	91,586
			85	56,181	223,986	274,734	50,748

Product TSUSA commodity number, description, and unit of quantity Country	Mode	Reg	Yr	Quantity	F.A.S.	C.I.F.	Charges
			86	77,144	274,377	328,736	54,359
	V	W	83	117	2,719	4,438	1,719
			84	11,743	35,837	46,991	11,154
			85	7,794	18,857	24,327	5,470
			86	13,426	14,274	18,361	4,087
JAMAICA	A	E	81	58	675	1,191	516
			82	1,569	6,919	10,516	3,597
	N	E	82	3,498	8,272	9,843	1,571
			83	5,883	31,048	34,106	3,058
			85	2,793	2,474	3,276	802
			86	1,718	5,514	5,927	413
	V	E	81	6,317	13,849	19,405	5,556
			83	2,303	8,523	10,129	1,606
			84	381	2,337	2,675	338
			85	2,814	10,653	12,490	1,837
			86	42,417	44,463	49,453	4,990
	V	W	84	3,750	1,263	1,963	700
JAPAN	A	E	84	2	2,091	2,321	230
	N	W	84	323	2,333	2,567	234
	V	E	81	130	1,761	1,888	127
			82	75	3,044	3,382	338
			83	105	2,335	2,621	286
			84	77	1,762	1,944	182
			85	961	3,568	3,809	241
			86	3,238	15,320	17,405	2,085
	V	H	83	42	515	574	59
	V	W	81	2,717	34,866	38,682	3,816
			82	7,744	93,450	100,936	7,486
			83	8,345	91,453	98,319	6,866
			84	10,974	112,182	114,901	2,719
			85	16,789	181,788	187,432	5,644
			86	15,075	207,087	210,936	3,849
KENYA	V	E	83	47	254	271	17
KOR REP	V	E	83	26,786	6,480	7,981	1,501
			86	3,198	22,154	24,316	2,162
	V	H	86	413	1,293	2,056	763
	V	W	81	99	350	405	55
			83	80	1,060	1,130	70
			86	22,517	45,179	49,801	4,622
LEBANON	N	E	84	2,782	21,616	26,261	4,645
	O	E	81	38	320	320	
	V	E	81	6,619	30,407	34,320	3,913
			82	8,162	34,200	37,812	3,612
			83	4,717	22,725	25,132	2,407
			84	76	370	422	52
			85	761	5,258	5,863	605
			86	463	3,560	3,921	361
	V	W	85	715	3,974	4,182	208
MALAYSA	V	W	85	4,720	18,076	19,238	1,162
			86	6,929	8,772	9,494	722
MEXICO	A	E	82	292	4,500	5,035	535
	A	W	82	58	657	889	232
	N	E	82	12,220	38,595	42,668	4,073
	O	E	81	11,162	22,194	22,194	
			82	3,214	9,697	9,697	
			83	13,606	25,206	25,206	
			84	73,825	57,129	57,129	
			85	8,394	29,277	30,011	734
			86	9,736	26,287	26,287	
	O	W	81	18,003	55,063	55,063	
			82	65,961	139,037	139,037	
			83	155,037	314,396	314,396	
			84	326,074	735,000	735,000	
			85	48,331	141,344	141,344	
	V	E	81	2,284	5,737	6,786	1,049
			86	528	1,753	1,898	145
	V	W	82	376	961	1,041	80
			86	192	2,280	2,699	419
N ZEAL	A	W	86	1,064	1,427	2,146	719
	O	E	85	21,983	76,698	78,813	2,115
	V	E	82	106	2,476	2,746	270
			83	26,880	108,862	115,493	6,631
			84	90,403	396,724	415,880	19,156
			85	55,804	226,828	245,684	18,856
			86	81,344	423,556	455,009	31,453
	V	H	82	3,429	18,245	23,400	5,155
	V	W	82	1,420	35,364	37,065	1,701
			83	53,288	209,962	220,996	11,034
			84	9,482	39,383	41,807	2,424
			85	63,447	492,246	509,451	17,205
			86	35,647	300,693	311,253	10,560
NETHLDS	A	E	82	101	1,000	1,501	501
			84	20	500	1,144	644
			85	100	2,500	2,950	450
	N	E	81	322,715	910,807	943,326	32,519

Product
TSUSA commodity number, description, and unit of quantity

Country	Mode	Reg	Yr	Quantity	F.A.S.	C.I.F.	Charges
			82	193,645	526,606	545,332	18,726
			83	372,298	1,200,171	1,240,024	39,853
			84	367,097	965,437	994,303	28,866
			85	653,140	2,144,815	2,216,711	71,896
			86	222,051	674,373	697,115	22,742
	N	W	84	22,154	66,255	75,697	9,442
	O	E	83	59,904	87,967	91,454	3,487
			84	43,645	124,071	130,142	6,071
	V	E	81	7,284	30,672	32,232	1,560
			82	90,769	375,559	385,915	10,356
			83	290,355	1,059,703	1,087,766	28,063
			84	389,467	1,102,182	1,130,455	28,273
			85	365,127	1,508,472	1,578,118	69,646
			86	450,558	1,738,299	1,774,486	36,187
	V	W	81	3,622	13,719	14,517	798
			82	2,000	7,466	7,801	335
			83	76	471	501	30
			84	27,275	122,588	125,572	2,984
			85	32,280	63,753	68,862	5,109
NORWAY	V	W	84	50	538	716	178
			85	284	2,409	2,946	537
			86	171	1,509	1,766	257
PANAMA	A	E	85	863	3,580	3,661	81
	O	E	84	3,741	21,898	21,898	
	V	E	82	39,021	24,780	26,748	1,968
			83	31,138	120,187	139,969	19,782
			84	10,746	38,062	44,332	6,270
	V	H	82	14,640	87,206	106,788	19,582
			83	4,586	20,241	25,939	5,698
	V	W	82	20,159	116,064	127,656	11,592
			83	36,518	174,874	200,486	25,612
PERU	A	E	82	1,046	4,239	6,652	2,413
			83	26,896	104,733	168,146	63,413
			84	37,042	58,768	92,490	33,722
	N	E	85	29,879	70,769	88,061	17,292
	V	E	81	28,621	52,394	61,870	9,476
			83	13,073	45,819	54,724	8,905
			84	23,973	39,583	45,897	6,314
			85	58,033	116,467	132,500	16,033
			86	52,474	99,971	125,137	25,166
	V	W	82	23,464	8,077	9,860	1,783
			84	48,649	198,255	213,766	15,511
			85	93,673	299,335	327,993	28,658
			86	61,438	125,253	133,416	8,163
PHIL R	O	W	86	2,250	1,545	1,545	
	V	E	82	311	2,862	3,094	232
			83	195	1,540	1,805	265
			84	438	856	1,232	376
			85	3,825	15,895	16,594	699
			86	25	1,035	1,180	145
	V	H	84	663	821	1,205	384
	V	W	81	7,313	22,674	26,522	3,848
			82	39,274	22,040	26,748	4,708
			83	6,448	23,162	27,141	3,979
			84	8,493	24,525	28,305	3,780
			85	36,031	62,224	70,919	8,695
			86	44,230	67,443	77,217	9,774
POLAND	V	E	81	625	1,885	2,720	835
			83	1,237	3,800	5,913	2,113
			84	1,832	6,120	7,515	1,395
			86	975	3,168	4,042	874
PORTUGL	V	E	82	35,468	99,283	103,236	3,953
			83	1,613	7,567	9,191	1,624
			84	321	818	1,138	320
			86	6,398	17,698	21,263	3,565
REP SAF	A	E	81	176	850	7,090	6,240
	N	E	83	502,544	1,006,064	1,095,685	89,621
	O	E	83	1,652	12,306	12,306	
	V	E	82	443,596	839,579	917,540	77,961
			83	23,035	55,910	61,690	5,780
			84	193,236	299,007	337,829	38,822
			85	3,542	14,169	16,136	1,967
			86	52,630	21,863	27,418	5,555
	V	W	82	9,600	17,074	19,803	2,729
			83	26,866	37,991	44,102	6,111
			85	26,866	32,218	37,404	5,186
S ARAB	V	E	85	9,720	42,450	48,920	6,470
			86	7,293	35,810	43,210	7,400
	V	W	84	167	841	1,671	830
			85	6,480	30,240	32,740	2,500
S VN GR	V	E	83	138	1,242	1,475	233
SINGAPR	O	W	86	175	1,123	1,184	61
	V	E	81	84,500	36,281	43,115	6,834
			83	190	660	719	59
			84	1,173	1,311	1,573	262

Product
TSUSA commodity number, description, and unit of quantity

Country	Mode	Reg	Yr	Quantity	F.A.S.	C.I.F.	Charges
			85	3,289	8,571	10,380	1,809
			86	2,504	8,678	9,615	937
	V	W	81	243,654	54,435	67,635	13,200
			82	216	645	715	70
			83	1,204	3,063	3,478	415
			84	1,065	12,732	14,321	1,589
			86	21,223	44,919	50,436	5,517
SPAIN	V	E	81	2,400	8,000	9,500	1,500
			83	2,682	5,408	6,532	1,124
			84	5,762	12,002	12,135	133
			85	89,734	189,715	233,940	44,225
			86	25,655	56,694	67,257	10,563
SRI LKA	V	W	86	512	3,039	3,496	457
SWEDEN	A	E	83	439	962	3,266	2,304
	O	E	84	387	333	357	24
	V	E	85	901	6,112	6,561	449
			86	367	3,016	3,547	531
	V	W	81	5,600	17,210	19,867	2,657
			82	1,050	2,757	3,237	480
			84	2,100	5,513	6,690	1,177
SWITZLD	A	E	84	15	605	757	152
	V	E	81	67,903	126,099	131,043	4,944
			83	1,036	4,126	5,453	1,327
			84	40,950	49,956	52,000	2,044
			85	146,527	221,447	230,278	8,831
			86	207,905	467,041	477,402	10,361
	V	W	82	337	2,931	3,083	152
			85	28,486	94,456	99,091	4,635
SYRIA	V	E	83	243	1,890	2,001	111
THAILND	N	E	86	9,167	44,850	52,692	7,842
	V	E	81	84,500	36,560	43,115	6,555
			82	190,125	83,535	116,400	32,865
			85	31,396	137,481	179,800	42,319
			86	1,575	5,629	6,190	561
	V	W	81	39	635	693	58
			82	15,262	19,965	21,858	1,893
			83	8,516	36,066	40,691	4,625
			84	8,591	41,642	45,998	4,356
			85	95,116	153,237	168,455	15,218
			86	111,615	230,913	256,775	25,862
TRINID	V	E	85	121	1,488	1,726	238
TURKEY	A	W	84	428	3,106	17,278	14,172
	V	E	82	1,375	3,417	3,687	270
			83	70,046	121,750	128,414	6,664
			84	131,150	264,385	286,088	21,703
			85	16,008	36,685	38,292	1,607
			86	86,760	87,383	96,320	8,937
U KING	A	E	81	12	323	673	350
	N	E	81	9,438	39,837	40,663	826
			83	173	966	1,017	51
			84	1,032	7,464	8,440	976
			85	4,865	30,474	34,326	3,852
			86	15,665	36,896	43,239	6,343
	O	E	84	302	8,677	9,743	1,066
	V	E	82	27,385	54,767	62,596	7,829
			83	1,677	6,596	7,629	1,033
			84	581	730	779	49
			85	4,438	24,080	29,916	5,836
			86	14,291	62,914	64,694	1,780
	V	W	81	140	1,748	1,837	89
			82	77	857	921	64
			83	808	22,886	25,620	2,734
			84	82	754	795	41
			86	2,472	11,895	14,126	2,231
VENEZ	V	E	86	124,070	109,207	139,282	30,075
W SAMOA	V	W	84	25,595	87,055	111,869	24,814
			85	38,374	96,241	132,692	36,451
YUGOSLV	V	E	81	8,119	49,318	51,707	2,259
			82	9,297	44,711	46,642	1,931
			83	9,800	36,817	40,161	3,344
			84	35,889	78,788	88,483	9,695
			85	83,170	139,552	153,935	14,383
			86	100,010	141,122	156,483	15,361
	V	W	81	4,280	19,000	20,038	1,038
			84	25,031	34,581	41,193	6,612
			85	31,818	14,071	19,124	5,053
			86	48,522	67,100	72,595	5,495
ZAIRE	O	E	84	84	290	290	

1656500 FRUIT JUICE,MIXD,ALCOL 1 PCT (GAL)

Country	Mode	Reg	Yr	Quantity	F.A.S.	C.I.F.	Charges
TOTAL			81	125,129	446,268	483,858	37,590
			82	390,565	1,380,577	1,473,546	92,969
			83	362,545	1,222,505	1,274,949	52,444
			84	322,451	991,080	1,084,862	93,782
			85	399,477	785,408	878,010	92,602

Product TSUSA commodity number, description, and unit of quantity Country	Mode	Reg	Yr	Quantity	F.A.S.	C.I.F.	Charges
			86	508,596	994,842	1,128,565	133,723
AUSTRAL	A	W	84	982	9,702	10,882	1,180
AUSTRIA	A	E	85	2,496	4,561	13,882	9,321
			86	687	1,397	7,789	6,392
	V	E	84	32,130	140,327	142,590	2,263
			86	27,596	56,233	84,625	28,392
BELGIUM	O	E	84	1,185	3,240	3,820	580
			85	871	2,200	3,093	893
	V	E	84	16,310	46,010	59,939	13,929
			85	29,214	74,024	95,556	21,532
			86	18,046	50,803	61,484	10,681
	V	W	86	2,914	8,426	9,998	1,572
BRAZIL	V	E	85	2,938	8,082	10,070	1,988
BULGAR	V	E	86	702	1,266	1,798	532
CANADA	A	E	83	190	740	1,478	738
			84	228	722	1,140	418
	N	W	86	61	4,863	4,967	104
	O	E	81	815	5,104	5,104	
			82	127,468	359,487	359,487	
			83	66,195	257,691	257,691	
			84	59,916	193,982	193,982	
			85	99,656	260,150	260,150	
			86	158,332	404,417	404,417	
	O	W	85	24,487	36,005	36,005	
			86	1,496	9,266	9,266	
CHINA M	V	E	83	113	340	425	85
	V	W	83	1,575	3,717	4,037	320
CHINA T	V	W	84	39	320	345	25
			85	3,668	9,198	10,448	1,250
			86	21,356	51,267	57,071	5,804
COLOMB	N	E	86	4,927	36,507	39,060	2,553
DENMARK	V	E	82	2,151	4,986	6,266	1,280
			83	963	2,275	2,631	356
			86	2,168	9,639	10,088	449
	V	W	83	3,362	8,918	9,940	1,022
DOM REP	V	E	83	225	750	793	43
			85	1,125	3,750	4,052	302
			86	1,072	2,600	2,709	109
ECUADOR	A	E	85	99	1,668	1,851	183
FR GERM	A	E	84	70	754	1,287	533
	N	E	85	20,427	74,395	77,818	3,423
	V	E	81	103,015	382,634	407,666	25,032
			82	154,912	602,784	655,676	52,892
			83	197,258	700,849	733,854	33,005
			84	40,974	132,257	139,147	6,890
			85	844	4,118	4,171	53
			86	26,628	47,048	51,558	4,510
	V	W	82	45,090	176,393	195,815	19,422
			83	35,470	138,635	148,633	9,998
			86	605	4,363	4,786	423
FRANCE	A	E	84	399	699	3,060	2,361
	O	E	82	76	1,551	1,551	
			83	85	442	531	89
	V	E	81	44	342	420	78
			83	227	897	985	88
			84	9,400	19,848	26,265	6,417
			85	5,390	22,884	27,922	5,038
			86	1,980	14,247	16,790	2,543
GERM DR	V	E	82	24,151	95,300	101,519	6,219
HG KONG	V	E	81	1,426	3,143	3,885	742
			83	53	447	491	44
HUNGARY	V	E	85	139,920	92,042	102,049	10,007
ISRAEL	V	E	86	856	1,948	2,430	482
ITALY	O	E	85	20,017	42,221	54,022	11,801
			86	51,057	125,240	162,490	37,250
	V	E	83	751	2,883	3,323	440
			84	101,006	309,935	361,306	51,371
			85	3,861	18,004	20,533	2,529
			86	8,007	28,751	35,502	6,751
	V	W	84	10,125	30,948	36,306	5,358
			85	35,642	104,971	127,906	22,935
JAMAICA	N	E	83	678	2,750	2,940	190
			86	203	4,150	4,447	297
	V	E	83	600	313	363	50
			84	40	3,496	3,754	258
			85	1,788	3,410	3,637	227
			86	2,779	8,752	9,592	840
JAPAN	A	E	84	50	267	942	675
	O	H	86	32,573	6,184	6,555	371
	V	W	86	1,615	3,524	4,699	1,175
MEXICO	O	E	82	558	1,785	1,920	135
			83	169	383	383	
			84	3,598	8,717	8,813	96
			85	1,745	8,207	8,207	

Product TSUSA commodity number, description, and unit of quantity Country	Mode	Reg	Yr	Quantity	F.A.S.	C.I.F.	Charges
			86	644	1,845	1,845	
	O	W	81	1,575	3,980	3,980	
			82	15,306	39,429	39,429	
			83	28,293	58,992	58,992	
			84	44,557	81,399	81,399	
			85	4,318	12,822	12,822	
N ZEAL	V	W	82	3,125	12,801	13,692	891
NETHLDS	V	E	83	5,085	11,491	12,258	767
			85	987	2,696	3,816	1,120
PANAMA	A	E	81	1,040	3,328	4,944	1,616
	V	E	82	2,652	46,410	47,736	1,326
PHIL R	V	W	84	58	445	562	117
REP SAF	V	W	83	18,003	14,268	17,488	3,220
SINGAPR	V	W	81	1,460	2,319	2,579	260
SRI LKA	V	W	86	713	1,183	1,455	272
SWEDEN	V	E	83	689	3,395	4,264	869
			84	689	3,318	4,206	888
THAILND	V	E	86	95,063	54,990	70,641	15,651
	V	W	86	6,417	3,570	3,956	386
U KING	V	E	83	2,417	12,014	13,134	1,120
VENEZ	V	E	86	37,455	46,526	50,833	4,307
YUGOSLV	O	E	83	144	315	315	
			84	90	331	331	
	V	E	81	15,754	45,418	55,280	9,862
			82	15,076	39,651	50,455	10,804
			86	3,249	10,200	12,500	2,300

1657000 FRUIT JUICES OV 1 PCT ALCHL (GAL)

Country	Mode	Reg	Yr	Quantity	F.A.S.	C.I.F.	Charges
TOTAL			81	38,815	144,878	156,969	12,091
			82	567	1,491	1,491	
			83	74,236	34,784	38,822	4,038
			85	8,722	42,286	49,786	7,500
			86	43,101	13,865	14,646	781
ARGENT	V	E	83	74,011	34,415	38,453	4,038
CANADA	O	E	82	567	1,491	1,491	
FR GERM	V	E	81	37,578	142,058	153,776	11,718
	V	W	85	3,778	14,206	15,854	1,648
FRANCE	V	E	85	4,944	28,080	33,932	5,852
			86	828	1,853	2,634	781
ITALY	V	W	81	1,237	2,820	3,193	373
MEXICO	O	W	83	225	369	369	
			86	42,273	12,012	12,012	

Non-alcoholic beverages

1662000 GINGER ALE,GINGER BEER ETC (GAL)

Country	Mode	Reg	Yr	Quantity	F.A.S.	C.I.F.	Charges
TOTAL			81	385,376	828,892	856,256	27,364
			82	430,622	883,696	920,444	36,748
			83	501,838	1,124,820	1,174,473	49,653
			84	630,287	1,101,058	1,140,791	39,733
			85	376,533	720,088	766,607	46,519
			86	150,829	352,883	390,798	37,915
BAHAMAS	V	E	81	20,619	48,430	56,836	8,406
			82	26,776	63,723	75,759	12,036
			83	47,840	117,012	135,590	18,578
			84	21,066	49,628	58,567	8,939
			85	12,188	29,494	33,931	4,437
			86	4,212	11,479	13,045	1,566
BELGIUM	V	E	84	2,831	5,289	6,940	1,651
			85	2,557	5,541	8,526	2,985
BRAZIL	V	W	81	2,160	3,168	4,062	894
			82	2,160	3,168	5,311	2,143
			83	1,440	2,207	3,694	1,487
CANADA	O	E	81	322,759	634,764	634,764	
			82	360,805	719,319	721,534	2,215
			83	408,059	845,297	845,297	
			84	422,400	791,956	795,611	3,655
			85	319,916	572,408	572,500	92
			86	89,403	174,547	174,547	
	O	W	81	5,905	14,902	14,902	
			82	13,820	32,170	32,170	
			83	3,313	8,074	8,074	
			84	21,003	43,426	43,426	
	V	E	83	2,543	6,780	9,005	2,225
CHINA M	V	W	81	25	720	959	239
			83	486	2,076	3,198	1,122
DENMARK	V	E	82	788	1,203	1,755	552
ECUADOR	V	E	84	99,207	99,701	106,118	6,417
F W IND	A	E	86	107	300	455	155
FR GERM	O	E	84	2,016	5,159	7,759	2,600
			85	1,319	1,644	2,727	1,083
	V	E	82	1,003	2,916	3,139	223

Product
TSUSA commodity number, description, and unit of quantity

Country	Mode	Reg	Yr	Quantity	F.A.S.	C.I.F.	Charges
			84	157	382	511	129
			85	1,961	3,814	6,309	2,495
			86	6,014	17,427	22,257	4,830
	V	W	82	157	711	907	196
			83	2,520	6,006	7,813	1,807
FRANCE	V	E	86	4,067	5,729	7,516	1,787
	V	W	84	6,020	11,576	15,996	4,420
			85	3,013	5,255	8,101	2,846
			86	2,970	8,640	10,866	2,226
HG KONG	V	E	81	16,596	46,510	51,693	5,183
INDIA	V	E	84	125	366	403	37
	V	W	85	652	1,082	1,222	140
IRELAND	V	E	85	2,970	9,280	11,075	1,795
			86	773	6,333	6,752	419
ITALY	V	E	81	6,431	24,707	29,017	4,310
			82	1,705	1,503	2,465	962
			83	23,133	97,892	114,470	16,578
			84	4,115	14,312	19,429	5,117
			85	10,959	46,374	63,352	16,978
			86	6,817	29,751	37,234	7,483
	V	W	82	216	507	847	340
			84	164	698	943	245
			85	324	1,886	2,361	475
IVY CST	V	E	84	39,683	52,200	54,000	1,800
JAMAICA	A	E	82	2,065	7,875	11,566	3,691
			83	1,929	8,267	11,427	3,160
	V	E	82	1,671	7,889	8,940	1,051
			83	1,006	10,723	11,231	508
			85	2,025	5,400	6,406	1,006
			86	1,500	3,600	4,050	450
JAPAN	V	E	81	609	2,647	2,930	283
			82	1,364	2,415	2,693	278
			83	5,277	6,822	7,659	837
			84	5,717	11,525	12,421	896
			85	164	1,239	1,354	115
			86	1,495	3,241	3,477	236
	V	W	82	242	1,213	1,287	74
			83	160	833	880	47
			84	973	3,007	3,191	184
MEXICO	O	E	83	364	930	930	
			86	48	1,147	1,147	
N ZEAL	O	W	85	3,600	3,355	3,556	201
NETHLDS	O	E	82	167	400	424	24
	V	E	86	13,543	33,437	39,037	5,600
NORWAY	O	E	81	2,240	6,704	8,612	1,908
			82	278	846	1,286	440
			83	139	380	470	90
			84	507	1,368	1,613	245
			85	1,779	4,673	6,467	1,794
			86	611	2,912	4,093	1,181
	V	E	85	900	1,483	2,351	868
	V	W	81	254	801	951	150
			82	1,232	3,364	4,103	739
			83	510	1,470	2,085	615
			84	1,466	3,254	4,148	894
			85	763	2,351	3,531	1,180
			86	2,489	9,339	11,396	2,057
PORTUGL	V	E	82	6,885	15,317	22,159	6,842
			84	1,806	3,863	5,713	1,850
			85	739	2,448	3,010	562
SWEDEN	O	W	82	644	2,580	2,880	300
SWITZLD	V	E	85	7,845	15,390	22,368	6,978
			86	8,039	27,489	32,135	4,646
	V	W	84	188	727	802	75
U KING	A	E	81	565	2,949	3,599	650
	N	E	81	3,877	27,212	30,676	3,464
	O	E	81	2,925	13,038	14,639	1,601
			82	5,428	9,546	11,632	2,086
			83	984	3,335	4,002	667
			84	225	690	716	26
	V	E	81	411	2,340	2,616	276
			82	3,044	6,445	8,803	2,358
			83	1,935	6,231	8,138	1,907
			84	360	1,096	1,527	431
			85	2,859	6,971	7,460	489
			86	8,848	17,812	23,246	5,434
	V	W	82	65	286	329	43
			83	200	485	510	25
			84	258	835	957	122

1664040 BEVERAGES NSPF UN 1/2% ALCO (GAL)

Country	Mode	Reg	Yr	Quantity	F.A.S.	C.I.F.	Charges
TOTAL			81	6,073,286	11,400,332	12,241,300	847,541
			82	13,627,982	19,526,295	21,007,930	1,481,635
			83	8,034,712	14,798,900	16,670,040	1,871,140
			84	10,372,175	24,074,441	27,436,117	3,361,676

Product
TSUSA commodity number, description, and unit of quantity

Country	Mode	Reg	Yr	Quantity	F.A.S.	C.I.F.	Charges
			85	30,781,915	53,296,632	57,715,130	4,418,498
			86	16,725,956	43,435,458	48,960,839	5,525,381
ARGENT	V	E	83	3,533	2,229	4,161	1,932
AUSTRAL	N	W	82	20,380	121,934	139,515	17,581
	V	E	81	19,465	114,925	139,055	24,130
			84	1,575	2,045	2,483	438
			85	3,578	26,535	28,643	2,108
	V	H	81	2,857	15,490	17,549	2,059
			85	4,541	26,724	30,137	3,413
	V	W	81	40,354	253,500	295,951	42,451
			82	56,750	369,279	422,614	53,335
			83	4,629	27,331	34,011	6,680
			84	16,299	83,472	96,077	12,605
			85	38,135	189,863	218,325	28,462
			86	32,066	155,046	180,739	25,693
AUSTRIA	O	E	85	9,671	20,856	30,916	10,060
			86	3,043	9,252	12,252	3,000
	V	E	81	920	325	375	50
			84	238	2,601	2,945	344
			85	9,268	19,451	27,210	7,759
			86	110	2,292	2,570	278
	V	W	85	2,742	5,583	7,593	2,010
BARBADO	V	E	84	11	409	421	12
BELGIUM	O	E	86	15,627	38,802	44,549	5,747
	V	E	84	5,184	15,032	15,492	460
			85	164,321	376,056	488,053	111,997
			86	144,109	307,015	394,195	87,180
	V	W	81	230	501	606	105
			84	16,434	36,529	47,518	10,989
			85	23,788	55,205	72,954	17,749
			86	52,555	167,406	199,348	31,942
BELIZE	O	E	81	339,554	381,429	389,090	7,661
			82	257,298	270,374	275,380	5,006
BRAZIL	A	E	82	12	575	753	178
			83	53	275	284	9
	A	W	82	6	260	456	196
	O	E	81	1,784,689	1,963,123	2,012,211	49,088
			82	6,294,805	6,321,664	6,489,998	168,334
			83	1,389,149	1,089,407	1,252,693	163,286
	V	E	81	4,725	7,875	12,033	4,158
			82	75	300	351	51
			83	25,938	47,158	70,800	23,642
			84	13,636	31,853	42,843	10,990
			85	19,844	45,077	60,087	15,010
			86	3,420	4,104	5,827	1,723
	V	W	84	3,938	6,125	8,529	2,404
C RICA	V	E	85	18,469	35,812	43,717	7,905
			86	478	2,880	3,137	257
CANADA	A	E	82	216	855	1,428	573
	A	H	84	184	811	1,226	415
			85	274	1,102	2,061	959
	A	W	82	5	389	702	313
			85	27	1,820	1,889	69
			86	120	1,100	1,413	313
	N	E	81	1,828	11,027	13,412	2,385
	O	E	81	1,799,160	3,397,372	3,394,128	
			82	2,840,229	4,080,161	4,131,303	51,142
			83	1,954,174	3,306,491	3,353,021	46,530
			84	1,933,809	3,467,269	3,471,887	4,618
			85	2,536,141	4,795,906	4,798,418	2,512
			86	3,343,025	6,676,455	6,676,455	
	O	W	81	16,031	77,768	77,768	
			82	29,176	143,173	143,173	
			83	115,556	367,960	368,698	738
			84	193,241	484,624	484,624	
			85	116,685	270,976	270,976	
			86	29,047	84,613	84,613	
CHINA M	O	E	82	1,856	4,056	4,830	774
	V	E	81	59,745	142,251	168,573	26,322
			82	82,178	105,753	135,467	29,714
			83	121,134	253,796	309,788	55,992
			84	116,902	228,351	290,443	62,092
			85	79,945	171,882	209,415	37,533
			86	48,549	127,544	149,931	22,387
	V	H	81	83	266	284	18
			82	116	282	303	21
			83	166	487	522	35
			84	55	718	844	126
			85	133	1,376	1,579	203
	V	W	81	14,089	30,147	34,616	4,469
			82	29,192	70,384	81,525	11,141
			83	28,661	77,539	86,827	9,288
			84	48,772	136,091	163,066	26,975
			85	62,048	283,234	300,558	17,324

Product TSUSA commodity number, description, and unit of quantity Country	Mode	Reg	Yr	Quantity	F.A.S.	C.I.F.	Charges
			86	73,085	227,581	244,104	16,523
CHINA T	O	W	85	3,297	4,913	6,194	1,281
	V	E	81	22,837	29,796	33,400	3,604
			82	16,526	35,900	42,188	6,288
			83	143,935	116,452	131,210	14,758
			84	135,458	192,347	238,306	45,959
			85	99,590	73,958	88,957	14,999
			86	130,674	201,909	240,430	38,521
	V	H	82	225	780	927	147
			83	12,382	24,870	30,540	5,670
			84	238	638	781	143
			86	827	1,650	1,902	252
	V	W	81	11,026	18,296	20,002	1,706
			82	12,218	18,943	20,933	1,990
			83	9,059	24,628	26,692	2,064
			84	183,705	188,310	216,008	27,698
			85	152,030	238,143	268,682	30,539
			86	661,033	1,129,542	1,235,697	106,155
COLOMB	V	E	81	24,273	63,091	80,611	17,520
			83	3,235	28,500	30,953	2,453
			84	41,676	73,492	79,736	6,244
			85	14,992	78,734	85,155	6,421
			86	102,912	294,467	324,175	29,708
CYPRUS	V	E	83	206	1,534	1,700	166
			85	200	1,278	1,429	151
CZECHO	V	E	82	89	420	425	5
DENMARK	A	E	86	1,430	1,872	1,874	2
	N	E	83	239,898	455,708	664,015	208,307
			85	11,558	26,720	38,244	11,524
	O	E	83	29,190	73,867	88,864	14,997
			85	19,226	46,551	66,133	19,582
	O	W	83	4,190	8,378	11,045	2,667
	V	E	81	301,396	616,455	847,263	230,808
			82	235,754	485,736	713,834	228,098
			83	119,873	179,538	226,870	47,332
			84	233,185	478,789	681,222	202,433
			85	259,669	530,210	762,057	231,847
			86	248,812	651,333	865,238	213,905
	V	W	83	25,705	83,728	98,189	14,461
			84	26,721	69,209	93,971	24,762
			85	9,513	3,718	5,903	2,185
			86	3,170	12,353	14,538	2,185
DOM REP	N	E	84	7,382	21,328	31,085	9,757
	V	E	81	46,481	63,575	77,567	13,992
			82	7,898	14,360	18,665	4,305
			83	8,669	44,832	49,348	4,516
			84	381,545	274,511	330,476	55,965
			85	10,422	39,850	45,039	5,189
			86	35,616	161,187	173,855	12,668
	V	W	82	4,679	20,930	22,756	1,826
ECUADOR	V	E	85	3,150	13,776	16,235	2,459
EGYPT	O	E	84	188	1,000	1,000	
			85	537	4,458	5,017	559
	V	E	84	3,741	18,700	20,137	1,437
			85	16,543	63,435	68,185	4,750
	V	W	85	1,638	21,142	22,153	1,011
F W IND	V	E	84	8,409	18,426	30,970	12,544
FR GERM	A	E	84	34	409	1,351	942
	N	E	83	37,600	124,735	145,584	20,849
			84	137,087	386,539	478,361	91,822
			85	274,121	499,517	667,108	167,591
			86	923	4,285	5,218	933
	N	W	84	24,477	87,028	102,785	15,757
	O	E	81	5,162	10,452	12,619	2,167
			82	6,119	14,672	19,132	4,460
			83	11,555	25,977	32,795	6,818
			84	67,447	135,446	158,197	22,751
			85	31,484	62,322	62,322	
			86	4,418	17,515	22,721	5,206
	V	E	81	15,198	51,281	62,241	10,960
			82	1,034,969	2,091,673	2,485,304	393,631
			83	26,263	62,190	75,037	12,847
			84	250,586	698,651	833,132	134,481
			85	634,569	2,001,009	2,460,004	458,995
			86	478,261	1,487,511	1,800,036	312,525
	V	W	81	6,989	68,228	72,969	8,070
			82	4,086	12,058	14,908	2,850
			83	685,353	1,439,332	1,665,080	225,748
			84	16,418	55,406	70,029	14,623
			85	182,983	393,460	547,236	153,776
			86	89,071	298,865	387,913	89,048
FRANCE	N	E	84	43,487	97,138	118,321	21,183
	O	E	83	3,241	6,547	7,975	1,428
			84	505	1,145	1,329	184
	V	E	81	4,257	10,241	14,048	3,807

Product TSUSA commodity number, description, and unit of quantity Country	Mode	Reg	Yr	Quantity	F.A.S.	C.I.F.	Charges
			82	18,200	47,649	58,413	10,764
			83	25,999	48,060	58,987	10,927
			84	37,046	77,865	92,127	14,262
			85	195,400	422,145	501,767	79,622
			86	199,372	501,558	609,202	107,644
	V	W	81	13,255	44,317	56,120	11,803
			82	2,765	7,584	9,549	1,965
			83	24,906	91,358	108,886	17,528
			84	24,819	84,334	104,150	19,816
			85	48,093	125,246	158,498	33,252
			86	14,656	32,681	42,156	9,475
GERM DR	V	E	86	3,240	5,286	7,711	2,425
GREECE	V	E	82	139	1,450	1,690	240
GUATMAL	A	W	82	12	530	559	29
			84	416	1,675	1,992	317
	V	E	85	7,696	8,664	10,996	2,332
			86	3,300	9,736	11,075	1,339
GUYANA	O	E	81	8,112	21,888	21,888	
HAITI	A	E	83	1,406	671	712	41
	V	E	82	1,375	3,781	4,499	718
HG KONG	N	W	81	69,000	161,502	180,462	18,960
			84	319,289	642,957	747,530	104,573
			85	243,100	370,232	422,670	52,438
			86	243,248	534,462	598,316	63,854
	V	E	81	156,196	439,187	495,650	56,463
			82	149,869	384,973	454,767	69,794
			83	204,998	511,332	601,087	89,755
			84	195,057	514,310	623,729	109,419
			85	257,074	710,550	838,243	127,693
			86	380,952	940,444	1,068,747	128,303
	V	H	82	8,246	20,760	24,520	3,760
			83	34,765	21,214	25,189	3,975
			85	1,498	3,175	3,826	651
	V	W	81	63,378	131,414	146,134	14,720
			82	118,798	296,553	342,754	46,201
			83	240,410	489,302	549,614	60,312
			84	92,052	229,788	260,104	30,316
			85	154,763	332,804	371,866	39,062
			86	153,777	365,501	404,484	38,983
HUNGARY	O	E	86	475	2,200	2,747	547
INDIA	O	E	81	5	400	400	
	V	E	81	526	4,176	5,105	929
			82	173	1,584	1,872	288
			85	331	3,794	4,510	716
			86	3,554	2,371	2,668	297
	V	W	81	200	1,293	1,570	277
			82	231	538	604	66
			83	35	575	685	110
			84	666	5,042	5,705	663
			85	1,616	15,600	23,603	8,003
IRAN	V	E	82	148	411	520	109
			85	6,194	18,560	22,958	4,398
	V	W	86	7,290	22,778	35,742	12,964
IRELAND	N	E	85	11,880	42,340	49,771	7,431
			86	17,240	53,547	64,150	10,603
	V	E	84	554	5,488	5,698	210
			85	316,067	1,003,050	1,187,850	184,800
			86	1,105,471	3,453,218	4,094,850	641,632
	V	W	86	306,045	957,469	1,197,049	239,580
ISRAEL	A	E	83	12	270	657	387
	O	E	84	4,055	21,539	24,066	2,527
	V	E	81	5,982	15,722	20,822	5,100
			82	30,946	9,320	11,820	2,500
			83	27,844	17,790	22,590	4,800
			84	25,942	77,919	98,438	20,519
			85	73,291	77,664	101,827	24,163
			86	17,025	51,699	66,384	14,685
	V	W	81	3,300	9,770	12,608	2,838
			84	6,188	8,250	10,458	2,208
			85	27,117	14,052	19,760	5,708
			86	1,050	3,720	5,398	1,678
ITALY	N	E	83	6,715	22,579	30,115	7,536
	V	E	81	48,838	161,685	199,973	38,288
			82	43,704	139,110	180,698	41,588
			83	39,833	116,566	155,548	38,982
			84	175,207	302,103	400,773	98,670
			85	173,064	454,914	592,789	137,875
			86	190,745	508,609	700,398	191,789
	V	W	81	4,207	19,119	24,955	5,836
			82	17,480	73,579	93,391	19,812
			83	7,929	31,268	40,032	8,764
			84	12,577	49,354	61,686	12,332
			85	27,564	111,792	147,029	35,237
			86	7,992	32,568	43,516	10,948
JAMAICA	A	E	82	178	500	1,145	645

Product
TSUSA commodity number, description, and unit of quantity

Country	Mode	Reg	Yr	Quantity	F.A.S.	C.I.F.	Charges
			83	4	276	363	87
			84	30	328	412	84
	N	E	83	4,497	10,886	12,558	1,672
			84	4,369	17,726	20,638	2,912
			85	1,408	10,914	12,432	1,518
			86	4,742	23,614	26,509	2,895
	O	E	84	998	4,357	4,357	
			85	1,207	5,387	5,387	
	V	E	81	1,374	4,982	5,424	442
			82	1,708	6,819	7,399	580
			83	11,128	13,265	16,010	2,745
			84	12,816	52,048	59,756	7,708
			85	807	4,300	5,035	735
			86	57,915	99,448	117,290	17,842
	V	W	81	37	1,105	1,680	575
			84	3,300	905	1,521	616
			86	1,191	3,710	4,882	1,172
JAPAN	A	W	86	1,650	16,220	17,842	1,622
	N	E	83	30,077	92,410	106,291	13,881
	N	H	83	29,963	125,567	154,043	28,476
	N	W	83	50,258	183,592	218,393	34,801
			84	108,120	428,514	473,298	44,784
	O	E	84	13,895	71,053	81,945	10,892
	O	W	85	399	1,211	1,310	99
	V	E	81	3,014	13,025	15,299	2,274
			82	13,117	51,197	58,425	7,228
			83	10,766	14,081	16,471	2,390
			84	150,091	497,884	573,282	75,398
			85	221,364	727,073	858,379	131,306
			86	596,548	1,387,359	1,587,065	199,706
	V	H	81	9,271	46,494	53,962	7,468
			82	59,252	159,768	182,534	22,766
			84	49,046	203,267	242,391	39,124
			85	27,650	117,004	142,056	25,052
			86	61,741	294,423	352,321	57,898
	V	W	81	55,319	192,337	211,502	19,165
			82	36,573	162,913	177,427	14,514
			83	103,477	384,583	423,340	38,757
			84	211,334	962,071	1,075,191	113,120
			85	998,647	2,837,177	3,154,813	317,636
			86	1,367,860	4,209,946	4,570,353	360,407
KOR REP	N	W	84	36,432	197,470	210,550	13,080
	O	E	86	1,234	8,012	8,985	973
	V	E	81	1,560	17,982	19,800	1,818
			82	32,269	139,927	151,807	11,880
			83	20,826	111,338	124,491	13,153
			84	38,529	175,859	197,477	21,618
			85	119,777	285,480	330,830	45,350
			86	92,564	344,198	390,559	46,361
	V	H	82	1,727	16,750	19,078	2,328
			83	4,936	53,429	58,937	5,508
			84	2,650	19,479	22,972	3,493
			85	5,260	32,492	39,824	7,332
			86	18,677	29,612	33,954	4,342
	V	W	81	22,742	158,242	170,575	12,333
			82	48,062	279,254	302,583	23,329
			83	59,387	330,552	359,883	29,331
			84	19,342	153,328	168,691	15,363
			85	74,588	522,701	574,392	51,691
			86	141,444	770,023	838,424	68,401
LEBANON	V	E	84	673	5,412	6,111	699
			85	74,407	45,944	52,339	6,395
			86	7,472	17,833	19,722	1,889
	V	W	84	750	11,500	12,026	526
			85	8,451	10,902	13,647	2,745
			86	947	8,450	8,881	431
MALAYSA	O	E	85	7,289	9,150	9,150	
	V	E	85	3,750	12,584	14,160	1,576
			86	7,970	22,230	26,033	3,803
	V	W	81	533	2,491	2,666	175
			84	112	1,154	1,224	70
			85	2,265	7,622	8,527	905
			86	156,666	258,549	288,753	30,204
MAURIT	V	E	85	79	1,178	1,227	49
MEXICO	A	E	84	5	1,000	1,083	83
			86	211	2,000	3,124	1,124
	A	W	81	7	4,848	4,968	120
			82	199	959	1,599	640
	O	E	81	279,404	621,046	633,440	12,394
			82	1,282,722	1,811,196	1,870,034	58,838
			83	798,112	1,105,658	1,136,024	30,366
			84	1,200,279	2,285,184	2,295,984	10,800
			85	18,509,459	24,134,082	24,135,082	1,000
			86	711,109	1,720,695	1,720,695	
	O	W	81	388,516	983,567	983,567	
			82	308,828	756,798	756,798	
			83	221,386	304,659	304,659	
			84	114,403	172,183	172,183	
			85	300,821	758,822	758,822	
			86	541,669	1,176,038	1,176,263	225
	V	E	82	9,480	27,600	33,280	5,680
			83	66,523	91,571	131,331	39,760
			85	26,792	43,303	48,263	4,960
	V	W	81	55,022	144,194	163,652	19,458
MOZAMBQ	O	E	85	7,398	25,093	28,376	3,283
N ANTIL	V	E	83	946	6,133	6,603	470
			85	141	4,463	4,963	500
			86	3,780	6,240	8,127	1,887
N ZEAL	V	E	81	248	899	1,035	136
			84	2,813	7,092	9,284	2,192
NETHLDS	V	E	81	4,013	9,847	13,632	3,785
			82	6,940	29,048	35,133	6,085
			83	12,645	35,717	48,830	13,113
			84	24,269	202,017	221,686	19,669
			85	96,451	229,616	286,295	56,679
			86	27,122	96,499	109,612	13,113
	V	W	84	5,063	8,968	12,968	4,000
			85	5,963	15,300	20,142	4,842
			86	4,505	10,210	10,410	200
NORWAY	A	E	82	16	320	470	150
	O	E	81	736	2,449	2,596	147
	O	W	82	140	456	1,197	741
	V	E	86	9,624	20,744	27,698	6,954
	V	W	81	507	1,634	2,195	561
			82	255	893	1,052	159
PAKISTN	V	E	83	179	1,245	1,394	149
	V	W	85	49	3,400	3,400	
PANAMA	A	E	84	1,032	3,000	4,186	1,186
	V	E	81	1,312	3,600	5,136	1,536
			82	2,193	7,225	9,798	2,573
			83	1,314	4,350	6,618	2,268
PERU	V	E	84	47,700	49,423	53,547	4,124
			85	1,897	3,642	3,982	340
			86	8,767	6,730	7,230	500
PHIL R	V	E	81	2,344	14,140	16,510	2,370
			83	1,443	9,237	11,122	1,885
			84	788	5,352	7,009	1,657
	V	W	81	3,637	4,534	5,374	840
			82	14,839	29,376	32,930	3,554
			83	1,437	6,632	7,014	382
			84	830	5,895	7,075	1,180
			85	3,475	21,058	24,231	3,173
			86	1,764	11,682	12,961	1,279
POLAND	V	E	84	1,725	5,120	6,710	1,590
			85	2,363	3,413	5,988	2,575
PORTUGL	O	E	84	131	300	300	
	V	E	81	46,254	145,115	193,280	48,165
			82	31,622	93,908	118,253	24,345
			83	28,154	61,960	83,786	21,826
			84	21,641	41,539	55,171	13,632
			85	21,038	47,055	72,214	25,159
			86	23,011	71,179	96,557	25,378
REP SAF	A	E	84	888	1,220	3,512	2,292
	V	E	83	342	583	786	203
ROMANIA	V	W	84	930	10,267	10,856	589
RWANDA	V	W	85	2,571	11,250	14,140	2,890
SALVADR	A	E	83	136	310	650	340
	A	W	84	860	2,000	4,413	2,413
SINGAPR	O	E	83	148	864	864	
	V	E	81	23,933	56,635	67,973	11,338
			82	51,117	81,539	95,213	13,674
			83	32,535	66,120	77,563	11,443
			84	186,067	146,586	175,317	28,731
			85	147,257	158,766	189,436	30,670
			86	176,446	299,069	351,809	52,740
	V	H	82	3,652	7,700	8,588	888
	V	W	81	252,572	531,478	605,571	74,093
			82	346,518	524,284	602,989	78,705
			83	315,308	690,159	782,393	92,234
			84	433,331	945,676	1,094,082	148,406
			85	1,057,191	1,145,012	1,350,908	205,896
			86	1,058,073	1,320,484	1,521,765	201,281
SOLMN I	V	E	85	19,013	7,813	9,422	1,609
SPAIN	N	E	86	97,558	307,590	378,690	71,100
	V	E	82	1,097	4,275	5,585	1,310
			83	16,528	50,728	59,573	8,845
			84	140,481	332,416	428,852	96,436
			85	229,785	549,206	704,844	155,638
			86	186,410	541,149	656,643	115,494
	V	W	85	2,432	7,450	10,361	2,911

Product TSUSA commodity number, description, and unit of quantity Country	Mode	Reg	Yr	Quantity	F.A.S.	C.I.F.	Charges
			86	4,323	12,750	17,234	4,484
SWAZLND	V	E	85	2,355	7,764	7,788	24
SWEDEN	A	E	82	134	363	1,357	994
	O	E	86	6,390	29,792	29,792	
	V	E	82	8,526	43,000	43,000	
			83	75,564	220,736	223,538	2,802
			84	25,394	82,886	107,413	24,527
			85	7,383	18,801	24,759	5,958
			86	31,470	84,019	124,016	39,997
	V	W	85	1,350	3,553	6,203	2,650
			86	53,053	187,374	219,806	32,432
SWITZLD	N	E	84	32,976	104,147	121,694	17,547
			86	17,349	56,545	72,444	15,899
	O	E	82	10	791	891	100
			83	6,718	20,907	26,354	5,447
			84	27,000	81,230	100,381	19,151
			85	64,726	232,863	303,756	70,893
			86	45,151	158,006	192,817	34,811
	V	E	81	8,562	24,172	28,352	4,180
			82	11,459	32,622	38,097	5,475
			83	447,123	1,358,081	1,652,948	294,867
			84	2,104,709	6,344,582	7,480,274	1,135,692
			85	1,829,227	5,598,832	6,470,424	871,592
			86	1,642,265	5,896,228	6,736,644	840,416
	V	W	83	7,533	23,129	29,519	6,390
			84	424,292	709,216	885,023	175,807
			85	163,369	500,287	573,526	73,239
			86	443,323	1,650,721	1,944,806	294,085
THAILND	N	W	84	12,279	34,844	37,606	2,762
	O	E	82	47	2,100	2,719	619
	O	W	82	648	533	602	69
	V	E	81	2,100	1,537	1,759	222
			82	124	626	685	59
			83	1,490	6,592	7,392	800
			84	8,876	44,674	48,905	4,231
			85	79,942	70,130	80,047	9,917
			86	127,473	138,702	156,920	18,218
	V	W	81	9,566	46,269	52,178	5,909
			82	16,652	32,265	35,436	3,171
			83	19,282	59,095	63,862	4,767
			84	29,973	99,583	110,305	10,722
			85	78,233	256,524	281,402	24,878
			86	150,355	388,642	417,499	28,857
TRINID	A	E	81	77	1,112	1,427	315
			84	21	478	618	140
	V	E	83	3,375	9,171	11,700	2,529
			85	3,804	12,221	14,522	2,301
			86	6,883	16,937	18,209	1,272
TURKEY	A	W	84	55	660	2,124	1,464
U KING	A	E	81	90	501	1,088	587
			82	792	2,235	2,748	513
			83	27	297	399	102
			84	517	3,862	7,231	3,369
			85	6	2,186	2,322	136
	N	E	81	488	2,132	2,627	495
			83	7,120	33,883	40,717	6,834
			84	14,967	80,685	93,927	13,242
			85	58,903	184,382	226,653	42,271
			86	183,457	615,443	731,770	116,327
	N	W	82	443	4,929	5,731	802
			83	1,640	3,452	3,762	310
			85	29,211	95,043	123,692	28,649
	O	E	81	484	3,747	4,204	457
			82	3,113	13,424	15,409	1,985
			83	3,765	12,464	13,493	1,029
			84	2,903	16,740	19,406	2,666
			85	4,792	26,483	27,963	1,480
			86	8,233	20,296	24,796	4,500
	V	E	81	1,286	8,609	11,154	2,545
			82	3,598	20,973	25,805	4,832
			83	5,433	26,256	31,957	5,701
			84	7,510	20,042	24,470	4,428
			85	69,842	205,225	244,424	39,199
			86	367,375	1,205,587	1,436,780	231,193
	V	H	86	2,970	9,280	10,613	1,333
	V	W	81	605	6,172	6,915	743
			82	412	1,039	1,147	108
			83	91	1,701	1,894	193
			84	4,935	42,057	47,422	5,365
			85	20,735	99,773	119,027	19,254
			86	99,216	315,067	404,319	89,252
USSR	O	E	81	102	427	491	64
VENEZ	A	E	82	30	300	578	278
			83	862	1,642	2,175	533
	V	E	84	9,375	14,950	17,071	2,121

Product TSUSA commodity number, description, and unit of quantity Country	Mode	Reg	Yr	Quantity	F.A.S.	C.I.F.	Charges
			85	22,256	29,604	36,652	7,048
			86	1,200	2,860	3,047	187
YUGOSLV	O	E	83	3,337	8,788	9,836	1,048
			85	420	1,585	1,585	
			86	8,987	18,847	18,847	
	V	E	81	3,223	7,123	9,210	2,087
			82	2,547	5,657	7,882	2,225
			83	10,698	32,327	39,700	7,373
			84	24,235	51,146	64,136	12,990
			85	4,037	6,279	9,461	3,182

Vegetable, juice
1663000 VEG JUICE, NOV 1/2% ALCOHOL (GAL)

Country	Mode	Reg	Yr	Quantity	F.A.S.	C.I.F.	Charges
TOTAL			81	239,739	510,547	576,564	66,017
			82	182,966	390,026	435,494	45,468
			83	163,983	316,289	366,734	50,445
			84	506,593	1,443,262	1,609,245	165,983
			85	832,218	2,129,132	2,376,603	247,471
			86	1,705,838	3,510,640	3,670,612	159,972
BELGIUM	O	E	84	349	628	725	97
			85	770	1,111	1,562	451
	V	E	84	5,086	14,442	18,003	3,561
			85	1,527	2,397	3,372	975
			86	936	2,455	2,776	321
BRAZIL	A	E	86	13	2,610	2,880	270
CANADA	A	W	83	193	634	868	234
	O	E	81	38,241	66,792	66,792	
			82	71,476	81,656	81,656	
			83	53,618	73,207	73,385	178
			84	174,017	308,507	308,507	
			85	454,097	752,358	752,358	
			86	1,307,852	2,191,066	2,191,066	
	O	W	82	120	607	607	
			83	408	2,390	2,390	
			84	2,627	13,289	13,289	
			85	420	1,919	1,919	
CHINA M	V	E	82	4,508	20,364	21,024	660
			83	43	265	305	40
			84	88	1,257	1,323	66
			85	70	1,558	1,824	266
			86	243	2,663	2,906	243
	V	W	82	647	2,197	2,311	114
			83	1,125	1,781	1,939	158
			84	1,193	3,292	3,567	275
			85	172	1,232	1,367	135
CHINA T	A	E	86	15	1,212	1,711	499
	V	E	81	420	2,079	2,241	162
			82	837	2,120	2,613	493
			84	950	2,136	2,637	501
	V	W	81	8,163	15,035	16,410	1,375
			82	3,236	3,902	4,302	400
			83	8,827	10,861	11,748	887
			84	3,421	3,056	3,434	378
			85	661	1,700	3,597	1,897
			86	11,640	26,696	30,518	3,822
COLOMB	V	E	85	1,540	2,322	2,337	15
			86	2,116	3,360	3,560	200
CYPRUS	V	E	83	70	464	2,075	1,611
			84	36	267	309	42
DOM REP	V	E	86	1,388	1,361	1,647	286
FR GERM	A	W	86	13	1,410	1,834	424
	N	E	83	131	2,505	3,267	762
			84	359	3,767	4,729	962
	V	E	81	3,012	6,224	8,531	2,307
			82	2,180	8,589	10,040	1,451
	V	H	86	1,433	4,565	6,121	1,556
	V	W	85	1,517	4,011	4,854	843
			86	1,348	7,288	8,123	835
FRANCE	A	E	81	56	9,231	9,622	391
			82	15	1,582	1,677	95
			83	2,056	9,174	10,039	865
			86	2,125	24,442	25,591	1,149
	A	W	84	84	1,569	2,609	1,040
	N	E	84	1,772	21,409	22,149	740
			85	1,252	15,074	27,560	12,486
	O	E	84	3	435	477	42
			86	31	2,686	3,846	1,160
	V	E	84	36	482	495	13
			84	319	4,236	4,580	344
			85	790	12,083	12,299	216
			86	85	2,700	2,764	64
HG KONG	V	W	81	57,556	108,229	123,118	14,889

Country	Mode	Reg	Yr	Quantity	F.A.S.	C.I.F.	Charges
			82	47,873	89,724	104,709	14,985
			83	25,894	6,225	7,397	1,172
INDIA	V	W	82	60	913	1,046	133
INDNSIA	V	W	84	349	1,080	1,143	63
ISRAEL	A	E	86	6,280	7,536	8,300	764
	N	E	86	55,699	67,743	86,468	18,725
	O	E	81	14,316	22,642	26,281	3,639
	V	E	81	50,003	62,457	81,048	18,591
			82	15,414	24,970	31,244	6,274
			84	67,245	92,403	123,945	31,542
			85	94,151	133,801	186,147	52,346
			86	18,931	28,132	38,853	10,721
ITALY	V	E	82	100	439	501	62
			83	26,240	45,320	62,991	17,671
			84	13,554	22,198	28,065	5,867
			85	353	1,489	1,863	374
			86	5,867	19,998	23,163	3,165
JAMAICA	N	E	82	5,507	25,769	30,926	5,157
			83	1,208	5,235	5,533	298
	O	E	84	1,101	5,246	5,246	
			85	685	3,052	3,052	
			86	514	2,644	2,644	
	V	E	81	9,606	32,984	38,408	5,424
			82	6,640	26,385	28,890	2,505
			83	3,570	9,143	10,041	898
			84	51,600	43,437	48,187	4,750
			85	1,781	5,519	6,012	493
			86	23,611	46,861	51,333	4,472
JAPAN	A	W	83	117	444	2,141	1,697
	O	E	84	20,250	98,807	112,911	14,104
	V	E	82	1,190	4,260	4,550	290
			83	7,164	36,007	43,308	7,301
			84	20,975	114,188	130,577	16,389
			85	74,486	331,700	383,954	52,254
			86	32,219	166,447	186,703	20,256
	V	H	84	1,688	16,189	19,454	3,265
			85	647	2,863	3,562	699
	V	W	81	16	593	680	87
			83	7,810	36,807	41,671	4,864
			84	86,568	450,378	497,176	46,798
			85	149,537	679,283	771,280	91,997
			86	127,169	669,565	729,041	59,476
KOR REP	V	E	84	3,375	16,189	18,626	2,437
			86	2,405	3,041	3,531	490
	V	W	85	360	4,280	5,009	729
			86	446	1,709	1,993	284
LEBANON	V	W	84	338	6,000	6,300	300
MALAYSA	V	W	86	5,614	11,540	12,320	780
MEXICO	O	E	81	22,639	56,795	56,795	
			82	4,810	21,964	22,369	405
			83	553	7,855	7,855	
			84	6,338	41,522	41,522	
			85	4,485	20,026	20,026	
	O	W	81	203	502	502	
NETHLDS	V	E	85	115	1,021	1,445	424
PANAMA	O	E	86	3,387	6,585	9,085	2,500
PHIL R	V	W	84	50	1,027	1,099	72
			86	8,067	13,752	15,987	2,235
PORTUGL	V	E	84	1,638	3,175	4,845	1,670
			85	3,017	13,167	17,874	4,707
SINGAPR	V	E	81	7,500	2,119	2,519	400
			83	7,832	3,241	3,750	509
	V	W	81	3,424	11,340	13,910	2,570
			82	3,043	10,560	12,898	2,338
			84	14,942	50,125	58,611	8,486
			85	7,299	29,120	33,092	3,972
			86	42,419	53,884	61,958	8,074
SPAIN	V	E	85	500	2,500	3,693	1,193
			86	1,716	4,671	5,521	850
SWEDEN	A	E	82	50	262	338	76
SWITZLD	N	E	86	18,522	105,124	118,377	13,253
	V	E	81	24,208	111,264	127,187	15,923
			82	15,260	63,763	73,793	10,030
			83	15,580	62,484	73,641	11,157
			84	23,897	96,348	117,515	21,167
			85	20,981	84,391	102,324	17,933
			86	2,295	10,551	12,151	1,600
THAILND	V	E	85	3,675	9,100	10,736	1,636
	V	W	81	263	1,686	1,845	159
			83	1,508	1,765	1,895	130
			84	1,146	2,644	2,862	218
			85	7,330	12,055	13,485	1,430
			86	21,439	16,343	17,841	1,498
U KING	A	E	81	113	575	675	100
	O	E	84	476	2,085	2,085	

Country	Mode	Reg	Yr	Quantity	F.A.S.	C.I.F.	Charges
	V	E	84	34	375	706	331
YUGOSLV	V	E	84	504	1,018	1,382	364
	V	W	84	221	538	650	112

Confectionery

Confectionery products without chocolate
1571010 CONFECTRY, NT CON CHOC NSPF (LB)

Country	Mode	Reg	Yr	Quantity	F.A.S.	C.I.F.	Charges
TOTAL			86	104,788,624	75,346,744	83,033,771	7,687,027
AFGHAN	V	E	86	960	12,854	14,746	1,892
ANTIGUA	V	E	86	114,413	121,955	137,088	15,133
ARGENT	V	E	86	6,041,802	2,970,987	3,389,952	418,965
	V	W	86	72,448	47,406	53,481	6,075
AUSTRAL	A	E	86	800	2,034	2,589	555
	A	H	86	1,221	4,166	5,489	1,323
	A	W	86	1,682	7,570	8,550	980
	V	E	86	131,463	93,500	102,994	9,494
	V	W	86	325,298	352,770	391,479	38,709
AUSTRIA	N	E	86	35,296	22,418	26,290	3,872
	V	E	86	240,171	211,943	237,297	25,354
BELGIUM	A	E	86	615	2,342	2,912	570
	N	E	86	1,295,112	912,896	1,029,614	116,718
	O	E	86	206,489	154,584	169,390	14,806
	V	E	86	775,558	613,558	672,974	59,416
	V	W	86	67,444	43,203	54,931	11,728
BELIZE	V	E	86	33,422	8,508	11,280	2,772
BRAZIL	N	E	86	15,361,866	5,712,992	6,614,184	901,192
	O	E	86	6,944	3,056	3,372	316
	V	E	86	7,394,036	3,179,579	3,670,938	491,359
	V	W	86	821,614	488,211	592,585	104,374
C RICA	V	E	86	35,284	20,880	22,580	1,700
	V	W	86	21,218	6,675	8,552	1,877
CANADA	A	E	86	459	1,106	1,686	580
	O	E	86	8,322,921	7,559,031	7,559,153	122
	O	W	86	78,785	72,440	72,440	
	V	E	86	2,500	1,990	2,187	197
CHILE	A	E	86	11,585	9,246	15,261	6,015
	V	E	86	480,979	250,288	281,813	31,525
CHINA M	O	E	86	3,762	3,728	3,986	258
	O	W	86	5,050	3,883	4,015	132
	V	E	86	29,515	17,880	19,782	1,902
	V	H	86	1,500	1,252	1,392	140
	V	W	86	455,470	209,057	228,236	19,179
CHINA T	A	E	86	341	1,075	1,188	113
	V	E	86	429,225	491,202	529,254	38,052
	V	W	86	575,024	766,695	839,345	72,650
COLOMB	N	E	86	30,135	28,746	35,056	6,310
	V	E	86	4,598,493	1,902,376	2,256,603	354,227
CZECHO	V	E	86	8,024	6,434	7,632	1,198
DENMARK	A	W	86	460	1,129	2,037	908
	V	E	86	195,630	139,822	154,456	14,634
DOM REP	V	E	86	348,786	165,827	182,014	16,187
DOMINCA	V	E	86	10,645	8,290	9,308	1,018
ECUADOR	A	E	86	63,740	46,356	58,802	12,446
FINLAND	A	E	86	6,279	12,629	19,756	7,127
	V	E	86	72,799	82,311	91,051	8,740
FR GERM	A	E	86	125	1,419	1,501	82
	N	E	86	11,959,260	9,563,686	10,494,487	930,801
	N	W	86	469,610	417,504	460,208	42,704
	O	E	86	634,760	536,196	581,642	45,446
	V	E	86	7,620,203	6,162,699	6,774,190	611,491
	V	W	86	421,926	357,058	403,891	46,833
FRANCE	A	E	86	366	2,422	3,378	956
	N	E	86	596,088	771,137	826,006	54,869
	O	E	86	9,169	23,788	25,633	1,845
	V	E	86	208,676	299,469	325,231	25,762
	V	W	86	53,901	72,047	79,188	7,141
GERM DR	V	E	86	36,000	14,693	16,943	2,250
GREECE	V	E	86	71,833	60,311	70,144	9,833
GUATMAL	V	E	86	9,414	6,835	7,469	634
HG KONG	O	E	86	1,000	2,430	2,494	64
	V	E	86	240,206	281,485	304,041	22,556
	V	H	86	2,442	3,245	3,647	402
	V	W	86	999,003	1,014,180	1,072,718	58,538

Product TSUSA commodity number, description, and unit of quantity Country	Mode	Reg	Yr	Quantity	F.A.S.	C.I.F.	Charges
HUNGARY	V	E	86	112,567	71,283	83,699	12,416
ICELAND	V	E	86	1,946	2,766	3,257	491
INDIA	V	E	86	1,146	1,026	1,138	112
	V	W	86	2,200	2,305	2,526	221
INDNSIA	V	E	86	1,200	1,540	1,727	187
	V	W	86	11,580	12,939	13,697	758
IRELAND	V	E	86	48,628	46,788	53,815	7,027
ISRAEL	O	E	86	39,619	22,272	24,518	2,246
	V	E	86	1,040,917	649,281	744,111	94,830
	V	W	86	88,422	29,030	36,215	7,185
ITALY	N	E	86	34,754	43,387	49,624	6,237
	N	W	86	18,660	41,835	46,358	4,523
	O	E	86	12,923	24,120	24,120	
	V	E	86	3,262,696	3,034,729	3,361,321	326,592
	V	W	86	73,084	91,507	98,990	7,483
JAMAICA	V	E	86	924,396	480,632	539,163	58,531
JAPAN	A	E	86	1,138	10,815	12,000	1,185
	N	H	86	14,564	23,178	28,988	5,810
	O	E	86	50	1,007	1,007	
	O	W	86	637	1,546	1,608	62
	V	E	86	59,046	157,038	170,103	13,065
	V	H	86	1,585	2,422	2,701	279
	V	W	86	435,214	567,584	602,031	34,447
KENYA	V	W	86	1,471	1,471	1,640	169
KOR REP	A	E	86	3,410	2,035	6,000	3,965
	N	W	86	136,082	123,578	138,335	14,757
	V	E	86	23,115	52,219	55,983	3,764
	V	W	86	10,295	28,632	30,960	2,328
LEBANON	V	E	86	158,777	121,925	135,837	13,912
	V	W	86	23,927	19,869	21,410	1,541
MAURIT	A	E	86	547	6,197	7,064	867
MEXICO	N	E	86	606,997	329,852	330,445	593
	O	E	86	35,541	16,443	16,902	459
	O	W	86	1,221,116	597,139	597,139	
	V	E	86	110,414	159,105	163,650	4,545
MOZAMBQ	O	W	86	4,420	1,660	1,660	
N ZEAL	O	W	86	1,500	1,260	2,760	1,500
	V	E	86	105,014	59,175	68,641	9,466
	V	W	86	481,331	260,351	326,856	66,505
NETHLDS	N	E	86	3,854,903	2,947,483	3,167,551	220,068
	N	W	86	271,075	206,018	245,063	39,045
	O	E	86	897,438	655,690	731,903	76,213
	V	E	86	3,077,275	3,572,570	3,870,725	298,155
	V	W	86	213,305	154,409	168,852	14,443
PERU	V	E	86	3,159	3,644	3,784	140
PHIL R	O	W	86	1,302	2,557	2,557	
	V	E	86	5,345	5,039	5,693	654
	V	W	86	21,904	23,263	25,589	2,326
POLAND	V	E	86	156,835	84,189	95,391	11,202
PORTUGL	V	E	86	114,635	83,885	93,126	9,241
REP SAF	V	E	86	219,800	93,287	110,944	17,657
	V	W	86	34,257	51,023	53,872	2,849
SPAIN	V	E	86	1,695,373	2,301,172	2,531,151	229,979
	V	W	86	236,042	288,385	317,673	29,288
SWEDEN	V	E	86	1,004,978	721,036	783,050	62,014
	V	W	86	47,507	39,708	47,213	7,505
SWITZLD	A	E	86	1,975	10,165	12,928	2,763
	A	W	86	895	10,748	11,818	1,070
	N	E	86	23,247	102,487	107,643	5,156
	N	W	86	1,628	4,848	5,291	443
	O	E	86	47,271	65,930	70,210	4,280
	V	E	86	146,436	184,739	198,502	13,763
	V	W	86	35,582	37,323	39,289	1,966
THAILND	O	W	86	2,425	2,028	2,221	193
	V	E	86	24,224	20,723	22,803	2,080
	V	W	86	7,710	8,998	9,572	574
TURKEY	N	W	86	12,897	8,516	10,243	1,727
	V	E	86	457,118	327,361	359,321	31,960
U KING	A	E	86	1,277	3,647	4,412	765
	N	E	86	6,747,960	7,514,188	8,248,606	734,418
	N	W	86	225,989	181,295	209,150	27,855
	O	E	86	195,442	141,002	153,371	12,369
	O	W	86	220	1,378	1,534	156
	V	E	86	1,500,262	1,039,262	1,206,849	167,587
	V	W	86	627,805	449,404	517,637	68,233
URUGUAY	V	E	86	24,974	7,171	9,140	1,969
USSR	O	E	86	2,988	2,928	2,928	
	V	E	86	9,266	8,500	9,245	745
VENEZ	A	E	86	1,912	2,112	2,397	285
	V	E	86	3,265	2,993	3,133	140
YUGOSLV	V	E	86	1,590,721	475,207	650,715	175,508
	V	W	86	77,828	33,008	50,146	17,138

1571020 CONFECTRY, NT CON CHOC NSPF (LB)

TOTAL		81		89,298,523	83,790,276	90,279,897	6,528,518

Product TSUSA commodity number, description, and unit of quantity Country	Mode	Reg	Yr	Quantity	F.A.S.	C.I.F.	Charges
			82	90,990,943	81,914,260	88,859,867	6,945,607
			83	111,688,587	95,135,115	103,496,995	8,361,880
			84	150,690,132	116,603,774	129,904,587	13,300,813
			85	210,641,638	156,648,903	175,204,968	18,556,065
ANTIGUA	V	E	85	542,224	308,038	347,760	39,722
ARAB EM	N	E	84	60,636	39,420	44,021	4,601
ARGENT	N	E	84	24,309	11,386	13,391	2,005
			85	368,467	178,494	207,316	28,822
	O	E	81	493	516	516	
	V	E	81	1,160,025	765,137	857,599	92,462
			82	4,077,332	2,389,533	2,721,970	332,437
			83	6,290,786	3,051,481	3,538,742	487,261
			84	9,796,396	4,484,334	5,186,777	702,443
			85	8,734,656	4,451,455	5,099,444	647,989
	V	W	81	109,597	63,207	73,646	10,439
			82	387,381	234,475	270,244	35,769
			83	281,216	128,962	154,288	25,326
			84	238,111	118,497	141,487	22,990
			85	251,996	104,057	126,051	21,994
AUSTRAL	A	E	84	206	1,134	1,388	254
	A	W	82	737	3,377	4,015	638
			84	894	3,720	5,073	1,353
			85	1,204	5,558	6,506	948
	N	E	82	68,204	48,368	52,634	4,266
	N	H	82	21,500	41,022	52,179	11,157
			83	19,301	37,124	47,240	10,116
	N	W	84	28,972	21,594	24,943	3,349
			85	34,054	43,146	52,430	9,284
	V	E	81	247,343	164,396	196,083	31,687
			82	628	769	859	90
			84	57,807	38,729	43,286	4,557
			85	226,010	123,801	140,779	16,978
	V	H	84	7,997	25,745	31,009	5,264
			85	14,406	25,225	30,322	5,097
	V	W	81	317,469	229,079	256,596	27,517
			82	234,616	177,496	200,762	23,266
			83	93,915	64,206	74,436	10,230
			84	4,803	7,338	7,808	470
			85	303,187	235,870	257,203	21,333
AUSTRIA	N	E	83	5,185	4,301	5,634	1,333
			84	80,727	100,970	117,061	16,091
			85	1,452,583	946,082	1,068,011	121,929
	N	W	85	28,411	40,546	46,707	6,161
	O	E	81	59,129	43,927	47,265	3,338
			82	29,678	23,884	25,886	2,002
			84	40,036	15,133	18,034	2,901
	V	E	81	17,908	26,277	30,388	4,111
			82	16,437	18,305	19,658	1,353
			83	29,521	30,315	32,815	2,500
			84	14,393	13,053	15,683	2,630
			85	1,468,024	1,053,613	1,196,821	143,208
	V	W	81	25,984	23,406	27,754	4,348
			82	8,317	6,654	7,878	1,224
			83	20,742	27,110	31,131	4,021
			84	13,614	12,633	15,008	2,375
			85	49,048	31,722	38,936	7,214
B VIRGN	V	E	82	30	264	267	3
BAHAMAS	V	E	84	378	920	958	38
BELGIUM	A	E	81	71	278	347	69
			82	362	1,126	1,408	282
			83	271	612	774	162
			84	195	579	802	223
			85	8,785	87,801	96,041	8,240
	A	W	84	156	455	675	220
	N	E	81	550,114	396,119	434,066	37,947
			82	879,337	588,331	642,480	54,149
			83	1,222,934	878,398	952,138	73,740
			84	2,058,879	1,319,906	1,503,108	183,202
			85	4,701,143	2,842,833	3,256,612	413,779
	N	W	83	71,548	47,409	55,101	7,692
			84	36,451	26,605	34,350	7,745
			85	84,383	53,447	63,418	9,971
	O	E	81	54,541	37,962	40,224	2,262
			82	99,299	79,341	85,179	5,838
			83	245,576	221,935	232,870	10,935
			84	40,309	96,077	98,619	2,542
			85	313,852	216,063	241,974	25,911
	V	E	81	179,353	132,571	151,024	18,453
			82	54,997	103,734	107,274	3,540
			83	242,637	148,498	161,176	12,678
			84	658,619	442,161	483,754	41,593
			85	1,817,514	1,492,856	1,656,095	163,239
	V	W	81	56,420	38,788	43,431	4,643
			82	41,167	24,146	28,247	4,101

Product
TSUSA commodity number, description, and unit of quantity

Country	Mode	Reg	Yr	Quantity	F.A.S.	C.I.F.	Charges
			83	9,365	4,872	5,725	853
			84	10,039	4,677	6,198	1,521
			85	65,386	36,066	42,685	6,619
BRAZIL	A	E	82	6,132	5,547	16,966	11,419
			83	3,855	2,679	8,040	5,361
	A	W	83	439	299	824	525
	N	E	81	719,629	414,352	468,989	54,637
			82	6,226,373	2,751,242	3,255,014	503,772
			83	451,257	134,769	171,808	37,039
			84	9,843,153	3,678,335	4,415,868	737,533
			85	18,093,783	6,516,349	7,684,850	1,168,501
	O	E	82	400	320	320	
	V	E	81	10,784,904	5,279,138	6,127,528	848,389
			82	3,984,421	1,821,360	2,149,889	328,529
			83	15,188,707	6,866,315	8,065,122	1,198,807
			84	10,809,602	4,562,410	5,396,208	833,798
			85	15,957,287	5,558,883	6,633,424	1,074,541
	V	W	81	439,841	211,940	254,104	42,164
			82	252,536	136,277	159,630	23,353
			83	259,166	113,259	139,232	25,973
			84	599,032	226,031	284,367	58,336
			85	597,271	222,450	272,727	50,277
BULGAR	V	E	85	83,556	61,908	66,208	4,300
C RICA	A	E	84	48	295	392	97
			85	2,284	12,938	13,195	257
	N	E	83	64,001	55,432	60,528	5,096
	V	E	81	199,688	147,563	162,692	15,129
			82	282,016	120,497	140,610	20,113
			83	355,649	183,878	206,217	22,339
			84	295,646	189,109	208,098	18,989
			85	129,010	48,315	54,936	6,621
	V	W	84	3,485	872	1,453	581
CANADA	A	E	81	947	2,338	2,681	343
			82	989	3,612	3,818	206
			83	350	1,611	1,737	126
			84	1,076	1,601	1,794	193
	A	W	82	992	1,574	1,814	240
			83	50	417	498	81
			84	462	554	739	185
			85	5,051	8,763	9,686	923
	N	E	81	2,310,078	1,874,043	1,874,219	176
			82	4,536,940	3,342,271	3,349,200	6,929
			83	1,615,633	1,312,394	1,313,271	877
			84	7,871,876	5,752,140	5,755,230	3,090
			85	10,389,595	7,831,019	7,831,077	58
	N	W	81	1,115	913	1,298	385
			82	6,360	9,556	9,790	234
			85	247,276	209,518	210,503	985
	O	E	81	2,458,694	1,831,065	1,831,444	88
			82	829,135	815,816	815,916	100
			83	4,247,423	3,091,212	3,105,876	14,664
			84	397,996	353,483	355,374	1,891
			85	452,196	360,744	360,929	185
	O	W	81	54,019	77,648	77,648	
			82	74,378	81,972	81,972	
			83	8,009	24,805	25,065	260
			84	47,331	56,617	56,617	
			85	4,133	1,502	1,502	
	V	E	83	1,505	1,234	1,434	200
CHILE	A	E	84	2,025	1,243	2,337	1,094
	V	E	84	144,708	71,093	80,656	9,563
			85	155,941	70,632	81,780	11,148
	V	W	83	1,252	544	699	155
CHINA M	N	E	82	170,303	104,457	119,847	15,390
	N	W	85	512,618	257,636	276,603	18,967
	O	E	83	1,600	808	882	74
			84	6,960	9,294	10,139	845
			85	4,850	4,620	4,620	
	O	W	83	2,500	1,047	1,095	48
			84	3,900	2,576	2,980	404
			85	5,500	3,522	3,869	347
	V	E	81	145,507	106,688	119,920	13,232
			82	16,858	6,284	7,152	868
			83	396,683	162,677	193,205	30,528
			84	445,559	239,718	285,876	46,158
			85	234,971	160,962	190,154	29,192
	V	H	81	9,658	7,868	8,403	535
			82	17,392	12,251	13,196	945
			83	43,351	30,985	34,308	3,323
			84	30,622	27,821	30,227	2,406
			85	5,272	6,486	7,051	565
	V	W	81	339,369	255,404	275,389	19,985
			82	485,533	319,011	344,383	25,372
			83	704,461	385,407	418,215	32,808
			84	784,142	443,569	488,828	45,259
			85	299,455	196,766	213,258	16,492
CHINA T	A	E	84	745	1,664	2,547	883
	A	W	84	466	414	1,100	686
	N	E	83	6,711	11,401	21,049	9,648
			84	12,170	24,868	44,603	19,735
			85	37,276	74,492	87,997	13,505
	N	W	84	254,467	246,291	271,113	24,822
			85	292,558	395,532	427,773	32,241
	O	E	81	4,436	2,614	2,984	370
			82	3,218	1,629	1,826	197
			84	5,004	2,200	2,580	380
	O	W	81	103	380	380	
			85	7,200	5,150	5,150	
	V	E	81	104,227	161,261	173,762	12,501
			82	102,799	132,917	144,177	11,260
			83	106,751	103,891	116,161	12,270
			84	58,069	73,210	81,824	8,614
			85	214,446	266,380	298,974	32,594
	V	H	81	22,507	28,452	30,855	2,403
			82	23,957	31,345	34,235	2,890
			83	35,100	46,871	50,829	3,958
			84	31,323	41,959	46,641	4,682
			85	35,963	45,481	50,600	5,119
	V	W	81	268,394	358,934	387,196	28,262
			82	235,042	297,337	332,141	34,804
			83	447,275	574,654	628,114	53,460
			84	987,654	1,323,915	1,493,399	169,484
			85	597,788	1,091,797	1,231,267	139,470
COLOMB	A	E	83	7,830	7,258	12,368	5,110
			84	1,890	416	514	98
			85	800	1,680	1,861	181
	N	E	83	2,064,487	867,517	1,043,727	176,210
			84	1,441,516	644,324	761,215	116,891
			85	1,842,477	823,058	978,502	155,444
	V	E	81	5,557,608	2,603,310	3,016,494	413,184
			82	5,537,227	2,176,994	2,559,721	382,727
			83	2,793,056	1,274,527	1,498,494	223,967
			84	2,908,087	1,339,648	1,586,095	246,447
			85	3,716,759	1,746,906	2,062,197	315,291
	V	W	81	384,732	175,388	204,960	29,572
			82	241,209	110,694	130,606	19,912
			83	27,837	11,942	14,196	2,254
CYPRUS	V	E	81	448	1,028	1,120	92
			82	7,337	12,328	13,968	1,640
			83	364	358	406	48
			84	4,128	8,302	8,983	681
			85	3,090	5,069	5,618	549
CZECHO	V	E	81	7,394	11,082	13,562	2,480
			82	14,414	39,437	42,821	3,384
			83	14,775	14,604	17,508	2,904
			84	1,998	1,981	2,218	237
			85	19,419	41,339	50,489	9,150
DENMARK	A	E	83	1,437	2,594	4,594	2,000
			84	1,185	1,469	2,711	1,242
	A	W	81	264	722	1,046	324
	N	E	81	1,773,637	1,533,251	1,658,706	125,455
			82	1,678,841	1,801,705	1,949,788	148,083
			83	2,549,045	2,388,057	2,595,684	207,627
			84	2,118,419	1,637,024	1,806,918	169,894
	N	W	81	55,890	134,303	145,624	11,321
	O	E	81	230	265	297	32
			82	14,603	24,222	26,787	2,565
			83	3,360	4,714	4,920	206
			84	2,808	3,716	3,854	138
	V	E	81	7,376	8,237	9,061	824
			82	26,004	26,614	29,085	2,471
			83	39,771	40,963	43,313	2,350
			84	400	1,948	1,980	32
			85	1,813,499	1,632,932	1,794,344	161,412
	V	W	82	7,180	13,363	15,369	2,006
			83	18,298	35,082	38,949	3,867
			84	15,137	27,112	32,046	4,934
			85	8,241	16,130	18,198	2,068
DOM REP	A	E	82	1,518	700	1,144	444
			84	180	360	707	347
	N	E	81	467,986	223,896	252,643	28,747
			82	337,115	166,961	200,372	33,411
			83	228,321	98,461	127,429	28,968
			84	274,849	109,542	133,453	23,911
			85	24,299	15,101	19,072	3,971
	V	E	81	18,893	30,715	31,594	879
			82	2,436	1,362	1,978	616
			84	18,787	7,788	9,903	2,115
			85	539,697	215,101	235,137	20,036
DOMINCA	V	E	85	7,790	4,979	5,770	791

Product TSUSA commodity number, description, and unit of quantity Country	Mode	Reg	Yr	Quantity	F.A.S.	C.I.F.	Charges
ECUADOR	A	E	83	2,004	1,313	1,595	282
			84	350	400	766	366
			85	13,823	10,022	12,722	2,700
EGYPT	A	E	85	4,630	3,280	4,200	920
	V	E	83	3,968	4,860	5,738	878
F W IND	A	E	85	2,627	7,018	9,625	2,607
FIJI	V	H	85	1,720	2,544	2,945	401
FINLAND	A	E	85	1,217	4,416	6,030	1,614
	N	E	82	565,053	649,520	714,270	64,750
			84	642,938	687,962	767,203	79,241
	V	E	81	1,175,880	1,211,436	1,344,054	132,618
			82	185,813	195,414	213,836	18,422
			83	1,039,884	960,194	1,085,140	124,946
			84	157,458	166,295	189,590	23,295
			85	805,290	836,165	928,537	92,372
	V	W	82	19,360	24,876	28,248	3,372
			84	71,429	62,080	72,189	10,109
			85	103,185	106,030	119,254	13,224
FR GERM	A	E	82	108,286	80,521	105,954	25,433
			83	892	1,699	2,401	702
			84	132	333	493	160
	A	W	82	282	922	1,159	237
			83	319	665	1,150	485
	N	E	81	9,978,418	12,843,502	13,493,045	649,807
			82	9,950,686	12,589,395	13,229,134	639,739
			83	15,861,873	17,696,494	18,805,690	1,109,196
			84	25,533,076	24,270,654	26,972,432	2,701,778
			85	35,839,598	29,932,012	33,393,864	3,461,852
	N	W	81	28,365	29,127	32,492	3,365
			82	1,972,881	1,961,613	2,116,797	155,184
			83	1,603,339	1,935,165	2,167,973	232,808
			84	2,251,418	2,210,471	2,620,739	410,268
			85	5,293,823	4,130,191	4,828,586	698,395
	O	E	82	1,440	1,244	1,291	47
			83	42,760	34,553	37,077	2,524
			84	329,901	329,408	356,013	26,605
			85	621,180	435,832	510,307	74,475
	V	E	81	3,989,000	5,730,053	5,967,585	267,550
			82	3,892,609	5,348,513	5,594,997	246,484
			83	2,527,886	3,262,070	3,421,664	159,594
			84	4,259,590	3,860,430	4,180,830	320,400
			85	16,085,628	12,905,201	14,501,086	1,595,885
	V	W	81	1,558,556	2,147,192	2,289,567	142,375
			83	251,697	357,911	386,871	28,960
			84	143,831	109,129	109,220	91
FRANCE	A	E	81	10,725	29,676	36,472	6,796
			82	118,967	146,231	214,586	68,355
			83	32,276	40,533	56,676	16,143
			84	20,418	13,535	15,827	2,292
			85	1,237	16,199	17,306	1,107
	A	W	85	200	1,097	1,495	398
	N	E	81	988,917	1,599,597	1,691,632	92,035
			82	919,477	1,311,755	1,390,231	78,476
			83	1,319,083	1,874,661	2,000,032	125,371
			84	1,783,522	2,123,221	2,295,489	172,268
			85	2,050,558	2,597,088	2,852,786	255,698
	N	W	81	69,748	70,728	80,776	10,048
			82	118,410	138,664	178,183	39,519
			83	93,392	118,552	139,410	20,858
			84	58,429	171,406	192,662	21,256
			85	102,471	80,701	108,363	27,662
	O	E	81	4,489	14,017	14,982	965
			82	54,456	56,203	60,281	4,078
			84	75,946	55,995	58,272	2,277
			85	50,770	49,441	56,711	7,270
	O	W	85	519	1,119	1,346	227
	V	E	81	67,505	77,977	85,430	7,453
			82	44,661	93,443	101,262	7,819
			83	410,642	428,909	470,134	41,225
			84	741,777	523,829	568,559	44,730
			85	312,547	266,132	303,169	37,037
	V	H	83	210	287	387	100
	V	W	83	1,788	3,279	3,751	472
GAZA ST	V	E	83	4,762	5,093	5,689	596
GERM DR	A	W	82	95	463	554	91
	V	E	83	39,635	16,026	17,292	1,266
			84	449,442	263,181	299,665	36,484
	V	W	83	4,365	2,925	3,792	867
			85	46,200	22,410	30,221	7,811
GIBRAT	V	E	84	19,515	22,027	25,227	3,200
GREECE	A	E	83	733	387	992	605
	N	E	82	96,818	81,933	94,408	12,475
			83	116,332	85,091	102,046	16,955
			85	86,778	74,175	88,180	14,005
	O	E	82	1,440	1,097	1,097	
			83	400	278	278	
			84	7,849	6,042	7,345	1,303
	V	E	81	265,056	216,088	242,484	26,396
			82	4,308	2,100	2,438	338
			83	28,878	21,677	24,529	2,852
			84	206,268	161,380	187,030	25,650
			85	57,085	39,814	46,517	6,703
	V	W	81	26,011	23,219	25,595	2,376
			84	3,525	3,077	3,948	871
			85	3,909	2,526	2,904	378
GRENADA	V	E	85	18,792	15,863	18,837	2,974
GUATMAL	A	W	81	833	351	441	90
	N	W	84	4,785	4,398	4,920	522
	V	E	81	293,204	124,826	139,479	14,653
			84	7,497	3,415	3,686	271
			85	116,364	104,599	110,263	5,664
HG KONG	N	E	81	527,660	568,011	614,042	46,031
			83	674,171	725,910	817,140	91,230
			84	196,660	126,640	146,630	19,990
	O	E	81	357	719	762	43
			82	113	412	437	25
			84	6,000	3,102	3,614	512
	O	W	82	7,703	4,395	4,682	287
			83	2,400	2,200	2,304	104
			84	4,475	3,958	4,606	648
	V	E	81	31,900	38,004	41,957	3,953
			82	563,637	685,891	751,332	65,441
			83	65,699	86,206	95,917	9,711
			84	554,109	872,530	966,569	94,039
			85	792,303	963,449	1,076,232	112,783
	V	H	81	21,742	32,354	33,862	1,508
			82	31,266	48,139	50,695	2,556
			83	27,601	28,330	31,019	2,689
			84	24,431	30,650	33,947	3,297
			85	10,835	12,934	14,353	1,419
	V	W	81	743,621	702,384	749,737	47,353
			82	693,948	766,515	820,408	53,893
			83	1,329,206	1,405,028	1,510,131	105,103
			84	1,894,456	1,792,470	1,934,638	142,168
			85	1,863,171	1,966,804	2,109,944	143,140
HONDURA	A	E	82	238	550	819	269
			84	292	295	328	33
	V	E	83	3,006	1,314	1,548	234
HUNGARY	V	E	81	92,070	55,383	64,266	8,883
			82	25,160	11,497	14,539	3,042
			83	25,948	14,071	16,737	2,666
			84	38,071	28,377	32,212	3,835
			85	21,785	36,026	42,830	6,804
ICELAND	V	E	83	55,406	112,146	116,212	4,066
INDIA	N	E	81	15,482	15,783	20,706	4,923
			84	12,889	15,334	17,607	2,273
	O	E	81	1,675	1,601	1,808	207
			83	946	1,355	1,532	177
			84	1,378	756	856	100
			85	1,360	9,030	9,030	
	O	W	84	330	495	579	84
	V	E	81	7,020	5,275	6,405	1,130
			82	8,691	10,312	12,268	1,956
			83	18,768	19,717	22,032	2,315
			84	510	313	352	39
			85	5,545	16,513	18,200	1,687
	V	W	81	15,082	12,561	14,871	2,310
			82	7,261	7,664	9,102	1,438
			83	3,478	3,472	4,063	591
			84	2,895	2,843	3,224	381
			85	4,408	2,200	3,193	993
INDNSIA	V	E	81	6,558	7,752	8,358	606
			82	2,476	3,127	3,502	375
			83	3,000	3,653	4,033	380
			84	6,899	7,510	8,285	775
			85	1,200	2,920	3,196	276
	V	W	81	51,222	63,230	65,840	2,610
			83	1,220	1,314	1,395	81
			84	47,881	35,054	39,251	4,197
			85	11,741	10,962	12,285	1,323
IRAN	A	E	82	579	1,425	3,210	1,785
IRELAND	A	E	81	200	632	961	329
	N	E	81	267,167	622,553	651,566	29,013
			82	474,431	1,023,519	1,072,802	49,283
			83	281	675	971	296
	O	W	82	324	261	261	
			85	111,588	67,359	67,359	
	V	E	81	33,869	25,169	30,399	5,230
			82	23,409	18,272	20,841	2,569
			83	138,573	360,366	383,370	23,004

Product
TSUSA commodity number, description, and unit of quantity

Country	Mode	Reg	Yr	Quantity	F.A.S.	C.I.F.	Charges
			84	322,926	234,969	271,399	36,430
			85	184,604	107,804	132,173	24,369
	V	W	81	27,866	22,750	26,834	4,084
			82	21,101	17,399	21,267	3,868
			83	20,496	37,533	41,659	4,126
			84	45,072	50,830	58,771	7,941
			85	54,490	30,100	35,959	5,859
ISRAEL	N	E	82	230,766	141,034	160,505	19,471
			84	1,187,109	674,187	767,013	92,826
	O	E	81	81,600	49,675	54,825	5,150
			83	558	2,130	2,130	
			84	23,651	18,733	20,551	1,818
	V	E	81	1,260,697	685,663	780,977	95,314
			82	1,369,231	823,299	936,141	112,842
			83	1,401,559	836,746	954,856	118,110
			84	860,675	492,699	561,409	68,710
			85	1,822,325	968,104	1,126,023	157,919
	V	W	81	83,751	38,859	45,631	6,772
			85	52,221	18,309	21,455	3,146
ITALY	A	E	81	1,485	3,325	4,794	1,469
			82	5,492	20,589	23,783	3,194
			83	2,463	3,603	6,044	2,441
			84	966	2,627	3,124	497
	N	E	81	2,979,530	3,104,491	3,388,128	284,537
			82	1,123,619	1,271,963	1,383,811	111,848
			83	1,142,517	1,144,279	1,231,623	87,344
			84	5,315,503	4,591,159	5,192,295	601,136
			85	5,322,727	4,531,312	5,075,913	544,601
	N	W	81	273,505	247,850	279,985	32,135
			82	6,591	13,088	15,244	2,156
			84	135,886	203,559	228,169	24,610
			85	61,081	116,646	130,021	13,375
	O	E	81	24,074	19,737	21,651	1,914
			83	618	1,313	1,313	
			84	8,268	8,004	8,461	457
			85	47,135	39,742	45,125	5,383
	V	E	81	1,289,458	1,114,981	1,232,677	117,696
			82	2,773,498	2,428,132	2,653,398	225,266
			83	3,784,809	3,349,110	3,635,416	286,306
			84	446,263	446,249	496,963	50,714
			85	817,510	762,643	852,325	89,682
	V	W	81	31,856	27,936	31,586	3,650
			82	139,998	157,087	176,624	19,537
			83	254,096	229,494	259,834	30,340
			85	242,188	202,577	224,066	21,489
JAMAICA	A	E	83	280	662	789	127
			84	335	594	844	250
			85	7,287	10,940	12,275	1,335
	V	E	83	385	752	1,023	271
			84	40,047	19,196	21,456	2,260
			85	1,076,005	485,021	559,064	74,043
JAPAN	A	E	81	1,799	9,493	14,061	4,568
			83	75	286	535	249
			85	2,098	5,597	9,662	4,065
	A	H	83	20,752	51,949	76,133	24,184
	A	W	83	30	374	463	89
			84	290	769	1,538	769
			85	472	1,147	2,245	1,098
	N	E	81	71,985	118,950	131,125	12,175
			82	145,333	340,673	372,228	31,555
			83	155,977	304,811	335,834	31,023
			84	332,972	774,094	862,581	88,487
			85	8,575	17,771	28,180	10,409
	N	H	82	112,379	233,665	271,943	38,278
			83	119,153	263,611	305,207	41,596
			84	184,368	443,784	517,139	73,355
	N	W	81	459,447	1,093,325	1,147,357	54,032
			82	120,262	253,698	267,146	13,448
			83	561,955	1,108,681	1,194,513	85,832
			84	631,544	1,268,103	1,357,463	89,360
			85	1,654,286	3,932,544	4,274,154	341,619
	O	E	81	3,521	8,500	9,014	514
			82	1,164	2,496	2,747	251
			83	595	1,576	1,727	151
			84	2,165	6,873	7,554	681
			85	2,438	4,851	5,422	571
	O	H	82	212	984	1,200	216
			84	423	1,503	1,907	404
	O	W	85	2,681	8,309	8,906	597
	V	E	81	19,326	42,805	46,141	3,336
			82	41,691	95,737	104,009	8,272
			83	46,387	91,448	100,241	8,793
			84	87,236	138,101	152,191	14,090
			85	343,342	769,610	861,878	92,268
	V	H	81	97,945	208,097	235,998	27,901

Product
TSUSA commodity number, description, and unit of quantity

Country	Mode	Reg	Yr	Quantity	F.A.S.	C.I.F.	Charges
			85	119,098	252,129	288,084	35,955
	V	W	81	65,716	159,251	170,787	11,536
			82	233,750	471,312	502,175	30,863
			83	70,139	146,633	157,383	10,750
			84	217,462	586,127	628,410	42,283
			85	103,042	261,910	291,229	29,319
KENYA	O	E	82	600	467	467	
	V	E	85	300	4,536	4,758	222
KOR REP	V	E	83	7,534	7,482	8,157	675
			84	131,171	61,936	74,218	12,282
			85	5,724	34,117	37,246	3,129
	V	W	81	27,936	30,817	32,395	1,578
			82	24,907	23,965	27,035	3,070
			83	8,078	4,616	4,912	296
			84	24,731	25,057	27,469	2,412
			85	107,622	102,204	112,649	10,445
LEBANON	A	E	83	361	334	434	100
	A	W	84	375	585	614	29
	N	E	81	29,233	37,042	43,413	6,371
			84	61,250	65,335	70,468	5,133
	N	W	85	40,423	22,942	25,459	2,517
	O	E	81	4,036	3,800	3,800	
			82	2,770	3,189	3,189	
			83	1,616	2,559	2,559	
	V	E	81	13,704	22,098	24,190	2,092
			82	17,749	23,213	25,604	2,391
			83	127,522	171,554	182,052	10,498
			84	42,494	23,273	25,267	1,994
			85	206,279	167,604	185,211	17,607
	V	W	82	4,497	6,931	7,681	750
MACAO	V	W	83	899	880	961	81
MALAYSA	V	W	82	860	731	791	60
MALI	V	E	85	199,877	165,903	180,587	14,684
MAURIT	A	E	85	661	6,577	7,943	1,366
	V	E	81	820	4,540	6,075	1,535
			85	3,150	3,652	4,586	934
MEXICO	A	W	82	3,383	596	1,155	559
	N	E	84	44,930	20,327	24,121	3,794
	O	E	81	874,508	683,636	690,078	6,442
			82	929,130	583,295	596,110	12,815
			83	264,585	157,503	157,503	
			84	105,298	88,589	88,589	
			85	241,872	239,375	239,375	
	O	W	81	664,951	496,574	496,574	
			82	1,115,821	669,589	672,010	2,421
			83	856,129	408,428	409,055	627
			84	1,124,371	653,193	653,193	
			85	1,198,077	776,374	776,375	1
	V	E	82	299,564	166,184	188,887	22,703
			83	182,522	147,220	154,661	7,441
			84	47,164	17,265	19,061	1,796
			85	2,170	2,160	2,310	150
	V	W	84	6,114	22,460	23,460	1,000
N ZEAL	A	H	85	999	5,351	6,688	1,337
	V	E	81	17,716	10,482	13,820	3,338
			82	16,130	8,305	10,945	2,640
			83	16,765	8,644	11,134	2,490
			84	40,973	22,322	30,027	7,705
			85	59,853	25,059	34,912	9,853
	V	W	81	154,924	76,492	83,867	7,375
			82	186,082	112,557	126,341	13,784
			83	285,703	186,451	198,649	12,198
			84	503,570	279,890	310,983	31,093
			85	331,532	204,003	247,172	43,169
NAURU	V	E	85	58,188	20,112	24,730	4,618
NETHLDS	A	E	81	250	316	351	35
			83	1,397	1,065	1,974	909
			84	1,294	1,840	2,792	952
	A	W	84	446	268	530	262
	N	E	81	2,269,789	2,012,699	2,142,031	129,332
			82	2,106,285	2,017,346	2,142,299	124,953
			83	1,830,253	1,129,053	1,209,912	80,859
			84	6,710,499	5,276,485	5,711,700	435,215
			85	7,150,742	5,647,687	6,230,865	583,178
	N	W	84	65,371	54,129	60,509	6,380
	O	E	81	1,504,813	1,033,580	1,090,522	54,999
			82	2,019,620	1,306,600	1,374,877	68,277
			83	138,318	126,422	127,882	1,460
			84	173,293	180,259	182,451	2,192
			85	1,428,960	917,992	997,162	79,170
	O	W	83	179	331	331	
			84	4,878	2,936	2,936	
	V	E	81	1,976,004	2,057,634	2,185,322	127,688
			82	2,306,451	2,199,807	2,360,272	160,465
			83	6,201,454	5,437,066	5,850,282	413,216

Product
TSUSA commodity number, description, and unit of quantity

Country	Mode	Reg	Yr	Quantity	F.A.S.	C.I.F.	Charges
			84	2,877,038	2,519,508	2,853,612	334,104
			85	3,035,630	2,520,819	2,789,592	268,773
	V	W	81	337,846	323,125	359,905	36,780
			82	423,146	379,022	418,638	39,616
			83	691,445	651,012	702,276	51,264
			84	836,565	706,934	788,456	81,522
			85	878,505	739,219	826,099	86,880
NIGER	V	E	85	244,229	192,564	209,942	17,378
NORFOLK	V	E	85	40,476	24,488	26,973	2,485
NORWAY	A	E	85	2,894	7,001	8,969	1,968
	V	E	81	1,058	1,396	1,505	109
			82	92,578	84,140	94,767	10,627
			83	4,392	9,625	10,732	1,107
			84	85,186	73,310	80,301	6,991
			85	92,975	41,961	49,426	7,465
	V	W	81	400	990	1,069	79
			82	839	587	821	234
			83	496	622	732	110
			84	575	999	1,182	183
			85	1,642	2,670	3,144	474
OMAN	V	E	84	50,443	23,875	27,451	3,576
PAKISTN	O	E	83	1,102	649	704	55
	V	E	83	714	1,254	1,408	154
			84	1,102	575	712	137
PERU	V	E	84	896	1,295	1,540	245
			85	6,600	6,593	7,102	509
PHIL R	N	E	82	9,349	17,497	19,763	2,266
	N	W	83	23,022	17,456	20,031	2,575
	O	E	84	40,000	7,600	7,600	
	V	E	81	24,177	29,669	33,808	4,139
			82	898	1,224	1,443	219
			83	6,716	8,821	9,977	1,156
			84	5,626	6,311	7,075	764
			85	796	1,106	1,294	188
	V	H	81	1,413	1,114	1,284	170
			82	2,344	2,697	3,185	488
			83	6,354	4,187	5,115	928
			84	2,718	1,323	1,596	273
			85	2,521	2,241	2,612	371
	V	W	81	43,118	43,956	48,531	4,575
			82	74,174	64,666	71,318	6,652
			83	31,077	35,296	38,911	3,615
			84	25,370	37,581	41,591	4,010
			85	11,911	14,212	15,719	1,507
POLAND	N	E	82	198,239	149,808	170,398	20,590
			84	46,160	23,850	27,455	3,605
	N	W	81	54,918	44,742	47,082	2,340
			82	87,746	72,117	78,467	6,350
	O	E	81	38,880	21,384	24,094	2,710
			82	191,918	111,502	126,121	14,619
			83	38,373	21,158	23,799	2,641
			84	13	389	389	
			85	110	1,349	1,349	
	O	W	85	18,222	20,125	20,125	
	V	E	81	984,600	473,940	575,084	101,144
			82	135,127	69,713	81,170	11,457
			83	84,306	40,554	47,631	7,077
			84	298,514	149,139	169,573	20,434
			85	191,391	115,086	130,239	15,153
PORTUGL	A	E	84	3,500	3,600	4,354	754
	N	E	82	30,935	32,866	39,402	6,536
	O	E	82	850	896	896	
	V	E	81	21,828	16,880	20,087	3,207
			82	1,550	8,256	8,383	127
			83	80,075	44,000	53,012	9,012
			84	187,021	101,066	116,021	14,955
			85	677,384	365,741	419,443	53,702
REP SAF	A	E	83	443	362	1,209	847
	N	E	84	1,758,886	867,388	999,785	132,397
	O	E	81	42,746	28,837	34,586	5,749
			82	221,477	169,310	185,908	16,598
			83	76,326	52,420	58,725	6,305
			84	175,829	112,432	124,976	12,544
			85	138,659	76,936	86,233	9,297
	V	E	81	2,272,503	1,298,990	1,479,011	180,021
			82	1,643,901	815,905	964,838	148,933
			83	2,327,607	1,141,609	1,331,685	190,076
			84	148,843	71,818	84,580	12,762
			85	1,478,498	630,220	743,706	113,486
	V	W	82	420	916	953	37
			83	29,261	14,510	17,403	2,893
			85	66,008	68,147	73,984	5,837
ROMANIA	V	E	81	29,994	28,255	31,382	3,127
SALVADR	V	E	82	10,559	7,140	9,240	2,100
			83	8,910	6,067	7,920	1,853
			85	3,245	1,015	1,484	469
	V	W	81	30,644	19,013	23,542	4,529
			82	13,538	9,276	12,014	2,738
			83	7,439	7,342	8,583	1,241
			84	2,344	3,212	3,580	368
			85	1,800	1,750	2,160	410
SINGAPR	N	E	83	1,560	3,822	3,982	160
	O	W	81	300	646	646	
	V	H	83	1,000	937	1,007	70
	V	W	81	215	274	302	28
			82	18	271	295	24
			83	17,102	20,570	21,592	1,022
			84	33,134	23,320	25,152	1,832
			85	11,309	29,631	31,572	1,941
SPAIN	A	E	83	2,650	2,627	3,986	1,359
			84	444	294	900	606
	N	E	82	1,677,402	2,678,929	2,819,166	140,237
			83	809,215	1,478,436	1,561,577	83,141
			84	3,833,309	4,637,461	5,073,173	435,712
			85	117,236	80,892	90,933	10,041
	N	W	83	83,075	139,633	147,243	7,610
			84	23,497	17,722	21,696	3,974
	O	E	82	7,935	5,736	6,428	692
			83	3,600	4,440	4,440	
			85	99,422	72,581	79,125	6,544
	V	E	81	3,717,166	7,185,486	7,592,195	406,709
			82	5,293,606	7,919,041	8,534,939	615,898
			83	5,145,271	7,810,656	8,244,291	433,635
			84	4,733,613	5,813,270	6,239,019	425,749
			85	7,980,660	10,950,017	11,788,467	838,450
	V	W	81	9,215	23,629	24,797	1,168
			82	9,736	25,997	27,790	1,793
			83	63,188	112,300	116,500	4,200
			84	274,347	422,430	449,005	26,575
			85	436,747	653,887	707,339	53,452
SUDAN	O	E	82	1,102	671	757	86
SWAZLND	V	E	81	534	1,696	1,824	128
SWEDEN	A	E	81	1,520	6,336	7,759	1,423
			82	503	2,010	2,596	586
			85	1,130	3,076	4,997	1,921
	N	W	84	2,052	4,627	5,519	892
	V	E	81	4,157,593	3,490,066	3,784,814	294,748
			82	4,229,931	3,129,460	3,540,865	411,405
			83	5,096,530	3,810,948	4,116,530	305,582
			84	4,607,686	3,453,480	3,805,674	352,194
			85	4,911,596	3,664,054	4,095,451	431,397
	V	W	81	190,441	195,379	220,117	24,738
			82	86,105	105,388	122,103	16,715
			83	85,134	65,206	79,768	14,562
			84	89,149	66,156	79,651	13,495
			85	75,422	72,531	83,204	10,673
SWITZLD	A	E	82	512	2,598	3,179	581
			83	12,134	65,048	71,423	6,375
			84	2,376	10,744	13,340	2,596
			85	6,320	29,530	34,728	5,198
	N	E	81	169,183	277,686	304,774	27,088
			82	268,334	354,544	380,521	25,977
			83	383,896	708,242	751,515	43,273
			84	345,064	617,172	664,978	47,806
			85	217,970	468,171	504,899	36,728
	N	W	82	80,874	98,477	105,433	6,956
			83	74,837	111,236	121,838	10,602
			84	133,406	200,429	221,346	20,917
	O	E	81	3,038	4,669	4,936	267
			83	11,096	10,503	11,065	562
			84	11,322	13,573	14,227	654
			85	36,868	37,700	40,918	3,218
	O	W	84	59,665	43,489	49,976	6,487
			85	31,872	41,924	43,362	1,438
	V	E	81	121,187	185,024	199,439	14,415
			82	14,462	86,718	90,719	4,001
			83	78,342	169,525	182,007	12,483
			84	60,659	189,388	204,005	14,617
			85	127,132	245,720	271,248	25,528
	V	H	82	204	624	687	63
			83	120	314	342	28
			84	156	300	339	39
	V	W	81	72,101	77,051	83,203	6,152
			83	1,823	3,488	3,860	372
			84	630	1,470	1,689	219
			85	24,446	60,753	65,495	4,742
SYRIA	V	E	81	638	450	528	78
			84	532	822	892	70
			85	7,143	5,502	6,081	579
	V	W	85	25,610	8,062	9,294	1,232

Product TSUSA commodity number, description, and unit of quantity Country	Mode	Reg	Yr	Quantity	F.A.S.	C.I.F.	Charges
THAILND	N	E	83	2,330	1,700	1,943	243
	O	E	84	811	499	574	75
	V	E	81	14,342	9,635	10,985	1,350
			82	8,274	6,781	7,594	813
			83	103,735	44,682	51,732	7,050
			84	7,815	5,887	6,926	1,039
			85	5,314	3,973	4,615	642
	V	W	81	69,860	52,667	58,649	5,982
			82	181,286	127,131	140,339	13,208
			83	283,841	160,997	177,993	16,996
			84	118,774	89,456	97,439	7,983
			85	183,813	96,635	106,605	9,970
TNZANIA	V	W	84	63	347	350	3
TRINID	V	E	85	43,000	81,411	86,749	5,338
TURKEY	N	W	82	878	830	943	113
	V	E	81	27,413	24,829	27,084	2,255
			82	43,160	30,227	33,786	3,559
			83	127,153	78,209	88,240	10,031
			84	554,088	288,017	334,282	46,265
			85	405,306	249,909	284,065	34,156
	V	W	83	1,958	2,168	2,581	413
			85	35,024	28,617	32,100	3,483
U KING	A	E	81	400	1,234	1,700	466
			82	15,338	17,370	24,341	6,971
			83	19,735	27,720	36,442	8,722
			84	9,661	14,627	18,555	3,928
			85	5,168	5,202	8,790	3,588
	A	W	81	126	396	625	229
			82	494	1,271	1,696	425
			84	200	373	596	223
	N	E	81	9,575,028	9,397,958	10,068,312	680,305
			82	6,949,639	6,500,083	7,005,635	505,552
			83	9,393,108	8,594,470	9,258,500	664,030
			84	11,746,613	9,745,367	10,923,431	1,178,064
			85	17,266,886	15,330,009	17,113,885	1,783,876
	N	W	81	731,509	693,836	758,194	64,357
			82	935,944	817,540	920,830	103,290
			83	1,208,947	1,113,420	1,252,848	139,428
			84	1,169,458	943,931	1,095,579	151,648
			85	733,565	615,704	701,587	85,883
	O	E	81	281,523	275,165	292,877	17,712
			82	94,546	84,239	90,194	5,955
			83	49,440	88,823	93,140	4,317
			84	381,315	286,372	300,787	14,415
			85	535,527	390,344	421,429	31,085
	V	E	81	1,723,494	1,791,520	1,921,803	130,283
			82	373,456	426,314	460,846	34,532
			83	697,683	544,674	604,149	59,475
			84	2,039,471	1,588,428	1,824,725	236,297
			85	1,301,736	1,000,734	1,184,332	183,598
	V	H	81	180	385	408	23
			83	118	416	470	54
			84	668	2,015	2,242	227
			85	601	1,159	1,328	169
	V	W	81	123,585	256,823	284,477	27,654
			82	132,217	256,104	283,307	27,203
			83	36,571	26,232	30,224	3,992
			84	2,401	1,811	2,399	588
			85	671,231	518,509	615,227	96,718
USSR	O	E	81	1,102	465	534	69
	V	E	81	4,409	2,781	3,013	232
			82	15,626	19,109	19,902	793
			85	4,206	3,290	3,624	334
VENEZ	A	E	82	1,437	3,488	4,075	587
			83	665	961	1,644	683
			84	5,985	9,299	10,455	1,156
	V	E	83	22,559	8,562	10,454	1,892
			85	37,500	12,096	16,536	4,440
YUGOSLV	O	E	82	655	914	914	
			83	1,064	1,247	1,247	
			84	1,334	1,502	1,502	
			85	80,862	21,614	27,153	5,539
	O	W	85	11,000	11,924	11,924	
	V	E	81	917,698	402,840	467,811	64,971
			82	1,130,787	444,560	524,279	79,719
			83	984,763	385,092	468,810	83,718
			84	1,973,393	544,325	720,723	176,398
			85	4,056,473	1,178,485	1,646,696	468,211
	V	W	84	832,703	228,820	297,099	68,279
			85	44,364	43,479	80,184	36,705

Fruit, candied

1545300 FRUIT, CANDIED, ETC, NSPF (LB)

Product TSUSA commodity number, description, and unit of quantity Country	Mode	Reg	Yr	Quantity	F.A.S.	C.I.F.	Charges
TOTAL			81	2,410,866	2,677,175	2,836,789	159,614
			82	2,686,465	2,907,307	3,081,072	173,765
			83	3,032,351	3,014,483	3,200,275	185,792
			84	2,996,221	2,842,956	3,023,526	180,570
			85	3,625,188	3,176,367	3,403,997	227,630
			86	2,758,275	2,482,467	2,622,385	139,918
AUSTRAL	N	E	85	168,396	296,672	321,924	25,252
	N	W	83	145,558	273,055	284,172	11,117
			84	119,926	235,740	245,099	9,359
			85	148,857	258,747	269,298	10,551
	V	E	81	301,825	594,593	622,826	28,233
			82	225,289	466,411	486,943	20,532
			83	250,652	519,712	542,591	22,879
			84	527,717	501,478	519,521	18,043
			85	57,901	137,114	139,944	2,830
			86	165,195	269,491	285,552	16,061
	V	H	84	1,102	2,261	2,367	106
			86	1,102	1,991	2,074	83
	V	W	81	203,436	396,420	411,210	14,790
			82	170,363	362,476	375,823	13,347
			83	97,317	214,855	222,608	7,753
			84	206,077	454,374	468,749	14,375
			85	247,357	486,881	503,108	16,227
			86	506,093	741,650	765,495	23,845
BRAZIL	V	E	83	4,409	1,080	1,395	315
			84	21,165	6,914	8,783	1,869
			85	68,942	24,109	28,979	4,870
C RICA	V	E	83	2,205	1,533	1,696	163
			84	2,205	1,533	1,730	197
CANADA	O	E	83	3,253	1,001	1,625	624
			84	808	902	902	
			85	5,310	4,334	4,334	
	O	W	84	386	920	920	
	V	W	86	4,576	2,746	2,746	
CHINA M	O	E	81	688	611	611	
	V	E	81	3,374	4,069	4,465	396
			82	2,640	5,231	5,399	168
			83	19,118	16,230	18,237	2,007
			84	43,268	15,167	20,234	5,067
			85	20,629	17,759	22,099	4,340
			86	18,136	7,498	8,912	1,414
	V	W	81	77,247	66,960	72,238	5,278
			82	40,006	36,171	39,059	2,888
			83	55,677	41,999	45,524	3,525
			84	46,523	37,118	40,344	3,226
			85	9,850	8,838	9,465	627
CHINA T	N	E	85	854,701	511,175	568,808	57,633
	N	W	81	140,026	131,346	138,904	7,558
			82	109,311	130,409	137,327	6,918
	O	E	82	68,305	65,200	69,091	3,891
	V	E	81	711,323	595,512	637,483	41,971
			82	1,030,562	909,336	975,183	65,847
			83	1,330,704	988,150	1,064,083	75,933
			84	901,580	640,178	701,028	60,850
			85	329,313	213,511	230,132	16,621
			86	414,587	242,765	264,108	21,343
	V	H	84	441	420	530	110
	V	W	81	650,690	606,271	645,774	39,503
			82	631,857	588,754	621,229	32,475
			83	756,680	644,229	679,112	34,883
			84	701,794	567,073	598,584	31,511
			85	1,086,736	761,672	797,494	35,822
			86	902,192	696,365	728,485	32,120
COLOMB	A	E	84	10,892	14,456	15,788	1,332
			85	1,490	2,130	2,556	426
DENMARK	V	W	85	845	2,492	2,946	454
DOM REP	V	E	84	28,823	27,535	28,635	1,100
F W IND	V	E	84	22,284	10,510	12,180	1,670
FR GERM	A	E	85	1,122	1,617	2,170	553
	V	E	81	2,710	11,096	11,522	426
			84	121	265	289	24
			86	1,307	5,000	5,068	68
FRANCE	A	E	81	189	655	986	331
			82	130	967	1,150	183
			83	503	1,625	2,082	457
			84	970	3,659	4,946	1,287
			85	679	4,657	5,225	568
			86	16,479	15,510	16,423	913
	A	W	84	64	477	547	70
			86	565	2,737	3,783	1,046

Product TSUSA commodity number, description, and unit of quantity							
Country	Mode	Reg	Yr	Quantity	F.A.S.	C.I.F.	Charges
	N	E	81	22,852	12,862	14,894	2,032
			82	13,063	13,099	14,615	1,516
			83	17,373	36,428	39,059	2,631
			84	222	1,112	1,437	325
			86	8,877	8,884	9,744	860
	V	E	81	2,557	6,432	7,204	772
			82	298	2,121	2,181	60
			84	1,460	2,220	2,487	267
			85	290	1,096	1,188	92
	V	W	81	3	1,133	1,134	1
			82	250	555	579	24
GREECE	A	E	83	648	1,371	1,944	573
	V	E	83	875	1,047	1,177	130
HG KONG	V	E	81	24,164	45,935	47,162	1,227
			82	1,500	962	1,018	56
			83	3,494	2,655	3,142	487
			84	3,626	7,527	7,978	451
			85	10,878	13,418	14,626	1,208
			86	7,088	5,821	6,603	782
	V	W	81	1,122	1,799	1,905	106
			82	5,720	7,776	8,372	596
			83	10,673	11,661	12,199	538
			84	3,536	2,065	2,239	174
			85	9,470	8,383	8,752	369
			86	50,706	40,674	42,683	2,009
INDIA	V	W	83	984	524	644	120
INDNSIA	V	W	81	438	459	511	52
ITALY	A	E	86	5,035	16,387	21,471	5,084
	V	E	81	1,323	963	1,081	118
			82	3,951	3,569	4,231	662
			83	220	624	722	98
			84	1,318	1,569	2,059	490
			85	1,763	1,393	1,494	101
			86	9,228	13,716	14,561	845
JAPAN	A	E	84	139	267	837	570
	V	E	82	7,626	15,220	15,613	393
			83	1,000	1,900	1,981	81
			84	1,000	1,980	2,061	81
	V	W	83	17,420	11,475	12,491	1,016
			84	2,500	4,848	5,239	391
			85	1,250	2,375	2,761	386
			86	44	1,665	1,689	24
KOR REP	V	E	81	8,818	2,920	3,419	499
MALAYSA	V	W	86	2,500	3,166	3,416	250
N ZEAL	A	W	83	299	642	934	292
			84	3,375	8,997	11,229	2,232
	V	E	86	3,334	7,714	8,230	516
	V	W	86	3,794	7,807	8,730	923
NETHLDS	V	E	82	1,400	1,012	1,103	91
PHIL R	V	E	81	26,777	19,292	20,945	1,653
			82	89,551	55,218	60,888	5,670
			83	21,420	11,995	13,678	1,683
			84	32,884	17,010	19,375	2,365
			85	73,607	43,120	48,881	5,761
	V	W	81	92,308	58,046	64,158	6,112
			82	66,593	51,014	54,438	3,424
			83	29,172	16,660	18,629	1,969
			84	86,551	51,703	55,458	3,755
			85	291,739	166,989	182,778	15,789
			86	121,283	58,258	67,845	9,587
PORTUGL	A	E	85	5,190	15,049	18,961	3,912
	A	W	83	1,344	3,288	4,659	1,371
	V	E	81	4,310	3,852	4,651	799
			83	5,621	4,527	5,092	565
			84	500	502	553	51
			86	2,976	2,700	3,167	467
REP SAF	A	E	83	432	583	1,337	754
SINGAPR	V	W	85	15,432	10,430	11,418	988
SPAIN	A	W	84	2,509	1,698	4,624	2,926
	V	E	81	2,028	3,233	3,390	157
			82	5,592	7,129	7,851	722
			83	29,536	18,040	20,347	2,307
			84	2,196	2,917	3,135	218
	V	W	85	491	1,003	1,048	45
SWITZLD	A	E	83	345	1,360	1,574	214
			84	150	689	834	145
	O	E	82	1,902	3,357	3,731	374
			84	1,326	1,897	1,938	41
	V	E	81	2,136	4,147	4,381	234
			82	1,124	2,213	2,361	148
			83	18,749	11,691	12,175	484
			84	20,495	12,371	14,004	1,633
			85	9,525	9,157	9,984	827
			86	23,990	22,409	24,792	2,383
	V	W	85	1,587	2,914	3,156	242

Product TSUSA commodity number, description, and unit of quantity							
Country	Mode	Reg	Yr	Quantity	F.A.S.	C.I.F.	Charges
			86	421	1,328	1,379	51
SYRIA	V	E	86	3,968	1,620	1,913	293
THAILND	A	W	85	13,200	11,100	23,257	12,157
	N	E	82	150,342	126,622	136,405	9,783
	O	E	81	12,434	11,011	11,261	250
	O	W	81	1,354	1,205	1,464	259
	V	E	81	96,120	78,586	84,447	5,861
			82	49,912	45,746	49,082	3,336
			83	102,291	82,789	88,184	5,395
			84	107,364	122,788	132,762	9,974
			85	52,910	35,268	37,975	2,707
			86	316,973	177,767	191,867	14,100
	V	W	81	20,614	17,767	18,763	996
			82	9,178	6,739	7,400	661
			83	93,356	83,379	87,882	4,503
			84	88,059	79,490	83,742	4,252
			85	135,728	122,964	129,236	6,272
			86	167,826	126,798	131,649	4,851
TURKEY	V	E	83	11,023	8,375	9,300	925
U KING	O	E	84	865	326	359	33

Fruit, peel, candied
1543500 FRUIT PEEL CANDIED ETC NSPF (LB)

Country	Mode	Reg	Yr	Quantity	F.A.S.	C.I.F.	Charges
TOTAL			81	3,390	3,685	4,116	431
			82	4,464	10,753	11,478	725
			83	8,778	13,458	14,859	1,401
			84	21,855	27,331	30,731	3,400
			85	195	1,160	1,207	47
			86	4,889	8,910	9,455	545
BRAZIL	V	E	83	2,100	1,400	1,859	459
CHINA M	V	W	82	500	972	1,025	53
FR GERM	V	E	82	1,721	6,393	6,642	249
			83	1,905	6,342	6,874	532
			84	18,551	23,969	26,821	2,852
			85	195	1,160	1,207	47
			86	992	1,392	1,490	98
FRANCE	A	E	82	330	700	866	166
	V	E	83	660	1,414	1,476	62
			84	752	1,436	1,736	300
HG KONG	V	W	81	1,200	622	656	34
N ZEAL	V	E	86	1,693	4,791	5,095	304
PORTUGL	A	E	81	301	289	443	154
SPAIN	V	E	81	996	1,554	1,710	156
			82	1,473	2,271	2,453	182
			83	1,329	1,780	1,900	120
			84	248	304	320	16
SWITZLD	V	E	82	440	417	492	75
			83	2,158	1,774	1,946	172
			84	1,863	1,302	1,508	206
			86	1,102	1,289	1,347	58
	V	W	83	626	748	804	56
			84	441	320	346	26
			86	1,102	1,438	1,523	85
THAILND	V	E	81	893	1,220	1,307	87

Nut, candied
1545000 CANDIED, CRYSTALD,GLACE NUTS (LB)

Country	Mode	Reg	Yr	Quantity	F.A.S.	C.I.F.	Charges
TOTAL			81	66,827	119,641	128,862	9,221
			82	86,588	181,671	190,465	8,794
			83	72,927	98,793	108,256	9,463
			84	447,925	475,442	492,613	17,171
			85	369,618	436,213	453,609	17,396
			86	414,059	414,870	428,404	13,534
ARGENT	V	E	85	27,028	14,664	16,723	2,059
AUSTRAL	V	E	81	2,645	4,974	5,149	175
			83	110	340	440	100
	V	W	86	5,319	8,162	8,599	437
BELGIUM	A	E	84	276	353	475	122
	V	E	82	309	399	445	46
C RICA	V	E	84	22,000	4,500	5,320	820
CANADA	O	E	81	500	505	505	
			82	9,340	7,487	7,487	
			83	20,750	21,936	21,939	3
			84	300,744	333,008	333,008	
			85	226,392	212,705	212,705	
			86	267,731	273,412	274,777	1,365
CHINA M	O	E	85	2,268	2,266	2,266	
			86	2,500	1,950	1,950	
	V	E	81	1,250	2,551	2,741	190

Product
TSUSA commodity number, description, and unit of quantity

Country	Mode	Reg	Yr	Quantity	F.A.S.	C.I.F.	Charges
			83	4,800	3,114	3,583	469
			84	12,639	17,439	20,079	2,640
			85	9,080	11,292	12,319	1,027
			86	5,881	5,847	6,363	516
	V	H	86	750	1,029	1,237	208
	V	W	81	10,202	17,537	18,037	500
			82	54,635	110,134	115,671	5,537
			83	2,625	2,437	2,625	188
			84	16,976	21,289	22,414	1,125
			85	15,655	13,389	14,181	792
			86	2,500	1,056	1,097	41
CHINA T	V	E	83	1,043	330	411	81
			85	2,500	1,140	1,264	124
			86	35,274	21,685	23,360	1,675
	V	W	84	691	1,064	1,179	115
			86	1,117	1,584	1,722	138
COLOMB	V	E	84	212	782	796	14
CYPRUS	V	E	82	485	1,200	1,289	89
			84	240	600	627	27
DENMARK	O	E	85	5,000	3,528	3,528	
DOM REP	V	E	81	3,000	1,250	1,669	419
FR GERM	V	E	81	15,432	22,511	24,500	1,989
			83	12,743	19,107	20,568	1,461
			85	2,004	1,231	1,468	237
	V	W	85	32,738	94,065	100,065	6,000
FRANCE	A	E	83	161	993	1,099	106
			84	355	1,384	1,472	88
	A	W	84	66	494	566	72
	N	E	81	1,689	6,078	6,780	702
			84	11,494	11,469	12,482	1,013
	O	E	81	1,527	6,531	6,831	300
			82	794	3,235	3,335	100
	V	E	81	371	958	1,161	203
			83	464	599	631	32
			84	880	3,582	4,126	544
			85	5,991	16,615	17,998	1,383
			86	8,967	18,743	20,849	2,106
	V	W	81	334	1,962	2,037	75
			82	180	505	527	22
GREECE	V	E	81	7,029	8,237	8,956	719
			84	2,996	899	941	42
HG KONG	V	E	82	4,938	10,357	10,887	530
			83	2,000	3,679	4,251	572
			84	2,200	4,015	4,388	373
			85	4,750	7,177	7,721	544
	V	W	81	975	1,637	1,756	119
			82	2,417	4,608	4,853	245
			83	6,750	12,168	12,956	788
			84	2,750	3,296	3,563	267
			86	1,350	2,276	2,386	110
INDIA	V	E	84	617	1,838	2,052	214
ITALY	A	E	83	287	993	1,136	143
			84	337	1,410	1,859	449
			85	1,891	5,511	7,962	2,451
			86	1,000	2,298	2,817	519
	A	W	84	400	1,650	2,415	765
	N	E	83	1,302	2,012	2,452	440
	V	E	81	6,050	11,553	12,913	1,360
			82	213	407	431	24
			83	12,787	14,794	18,303	3,509
			84	159	620	679	59
			85	5,567	15,020	15,537	517
			86	463	1,093	1,404	311
	V	W	82	7,703	31,853	32,779	926
JAPAN	A	H	81	24	314	512	198
	V	W	83	146	266	294	28
			84	915	1,595	1,693	98
LEBANON	O	E	85	3,288	5,126	5,126	
	V	E	85	1,845	2,184	2,340	156
MEXICO	O	E	84	1,895	5,534	5,534	
			85	1,347	5,322	5,322	
	O	W	82	360	369	369	
NETHLDS	V	E	82	180	255	274	19
	V	W	81	273	340	369	29
			85	1,502	1,401	1,583	182
PHIL R	V	W	81	243	907	994	87
			83	591	1,212	1,311	99
			84	5,077	5,750	6,473	723
			85	9,441	11,056	12,138	1,082
			86	17,145	19,864	21,308	1,444
PORTUGL	A	E	84	4,385	4,183	5,482	1,299
	V	E	81	6,600	7,500	8,075	575
			84	16,556	14,136	15,610	1,474
SPAIN	V	E	81	8,019	22,966	24,398	1,432
			82	2,866	7,823	8,347	524

Product
TSUSA commodity number, description, and unit of quantity

Country	Mode	Reg	Yr	Quantity	F.A.S.	C.I.F.	Charges
			83	4,027	10,367	11,123	756
			84	2,271	5,403	5,933	530
			85	4,758	8,717	9,275	558
			86	2,302	5,582	6,127	545
SWITZLD	A	E	83	1,018	3,946	4,594	648
			84	100	459	556	97
	O	E	84	223	747	798	51
	V	E	81	226	710	806	96
			84	37,148	22,318	25,780	3,462
THAILND	V	W	81	438	620	673	53
			83	1,323	500	540	40
			84	1,986	1,690	1,857	167
TURKEY	O	E	84	176	449	449	
	V	E	82	551	1,250	1,347	97
			84	209	427	466	39
			86	5,106	5,080	5,601	521
U KING	A	E	82	1,617	1,789	2,424	635
			84	190	512	679	167
	A	W	84	762	2,547	2,862	315
	O	E	85	6,573	3,804	4,088	284
			86	55,520	37,061	39,570	2,509
	V	E	86	1,134	8,148	9,237	1,089

Nut, fruit, and vegetable, candied
1549000 MXTRE CANDIED FRUIT,NUTS,ETC (LB)

Country	Mode	Reg	Yr	Quantity	F.A.S.	C.I.F.	Charges
TOTAL			81	15,437	18,816	20,342	1,526
			82	6,868	11,172	12,735	1,563
			83	87,541	49,166	57,217	8,051
			84	63,526	25,255	30,284	5,029
			85	99,186	87,465	96,730	9,265
			86	24,403	29,911	31,430	1,519
AUSTRAL	N	W	83	518	879	1,129	250
	V	E	83	2,400	7,176	7,584	408
	V	W	81	529	832	861	29
			84	397	544	566	22
			85	1,323	4,669	4,778	109
BRAZIL	V	E	83	12,125	2,684	3,466	782
			84	51,368	12,885	16,565	3,680
			85	38,140	8,849	11,473	2,624
CANADA	A	E	82	210	455	485	30
	O	E	81	4,460	2,351	2,351	
			84	3,449	2,515	2,531	16
	O	W	86	11,975	13,846	13,846	
CHINA M	V	E	86	1,980	2,677	2,911	234
	V	W	85	16,590	17,283	19,090	1,807
			86	1,980	2,085	2,085	
COLOMB	V	E	85	6,000	10,500	10,841	341
FR GERM	V	E	82	476	1,986	2,045	59
			83	1,094	3,872	4,650	778
			84	1,128	2,106	2,235	129
FRANCE	A	E	86	286	1,824	2,248	424
	O	E	82	132	590	643	53
	V	E	81	713	2,857	3,041	184
			82	195	320	337	17
			83	179	828	944	116
			84	1,011	2,166	2,771	605
GREECE	V	E	81	993	1,805	2,020	215
HG KONG	V	W	86	1,980	2,085	2,206	121
ITALY	A	E	81	397	1,572	1,715	143
			82	242	2,100	2,425	325
	A	W	86	337	1,048	1,412	364
	V	E	81	4,531	4,903	5,290	387
			82	5,296	5,321	6,349	1,028
			83	1,988	2,221	2,569	348
			84	4,740	3,915	4,280	365
JAPAN	V	W	83	3,720	4,665	4,897	232
PHIL R	V	W	83	900	1,025	1,143	118
PORTUGL	V	E	81	1,653	1,262	1,604	342
			84	992	810	986	176
			86	3,545	2,450	2,698	248
REP SAF	V	E	83	63,369	23,881	28,657	4,776
SPAIN	V	E	81	2,161	3,234	3,460	226
			82	317	400	451	51
			83	490	616	655	39
			85	14,633	21,393	24,988	3,595
SWITZLD	V	W	83	441	301	329	28
			84	441	314	350	36
THAILND	V	W	85	22,500	24,771	25,560	789
U KING	A	E	83	317	1,018	1,194	176
	V	E	86	2,320	3,896	4,024	128

Product TSUSA commodity number, description, and unit of quantity Country	Mode	Reg	Yr	Quantity	F.A.S.	C.I.F.	Charges

Vegetable, candied
1546000 CANDIED GLACE VEG SUBS NSPF (LB)

Country	Mode	Reg	Yr	Quantity	F.A.S.	C.I.F.	Charges
TOTAL			81	240,872	239,297	256,470	17,173
			82	295,945	322,855	344,097	21,242
			83	240,632	283,004	305,382	22,378
			84	484,198	457,911	496,747	38,836
			85	704,832	440,581	484,532	43,951
			86	924,904	720,763	757,857	37,094
ARGENT	V	E	84	18,059	9,978	11,622	1,644
			85	42,758	18,560	21,914	3,354
			86	37,441	15,368	16,228	860
	V	W	84	3,471	6,459	6,577	118
AUSTRAL	V	E	82	4,340	13,572	13,955	383
			83	2,400	7,176	7,584	408
			84	4,400	8,253	8,561	308
	V	W	81	1,200	3,666	3,798	132
			83	19,841	35,289	36,982	1,693
			84	10,035	17,001	17,805	804
			86	4,177	7,740	7,757	17
BELGIUM	V	E	85	3,089	7,010	7,562	552
BRAZIL	V	E	85	64,057	25,835	30,230	4,395
C RICA	V	E	84	1,404	6,776	6,969	193
			85	2,205	1,429	1,623	194
CANADA	O	E	83	400	255	272	17
			84	2,780	4,361	4,361	
			85	3,430	4,816	4,816	
			86	100	1,014	1,014	
CHINA M	V	E	81	10,220	9,315	10,086	771
			82	2,001	1,611	1,801	190
			83	8,540	4,898	5,837	939
			84	8,900	9,754	11,329	1,575
			85	12,775	15,619	17,195	1,576
	V	H	84	1,500	2,477	2,683	206
			86	5,550	4,220	5,050	830
	V	W	81	13,356	12,325	13,108	783
			82	7,088	3,742	4,146	404
			83	10,540	10,707	11,427	720
			84	37,948	37,571	39,563	1,992
			85	71,075	49,113	54,096	4,983
			86	36,437	24,644	26,238	1,594
CHINA T	O	E	82	11,023	11,000	11,711	711
			84	331	405	445	40
	V	E	81	4,410	3,220	3,461	241
			82	40,053	38,030	40,520	2,490
			83	9,568	8,314	8,974	660
			84	449	1,001	1,053	52
			85	102,404	67,062	72,377	5,315
			86	1,763	10,561	11,130	569
	V	W	81	113,364	92,780	97,724	4,944
			82	139,232	137,238	144,897	7,659
			83	80,472	86,062	92,756	6,694
			84	78,065	58,194	61,624	3,430
			85	120,021	91,353	94,949	3,596
			86	9,758	11,447	12,195	748
COLOMB	A	E	84	14,459	22,304	24,682	2,378
			85	3,306	1,990	2,388	398
DOM REP	A	E	84	250	1,000	1,058	58
F W IND	A	E	81	220	257	321	64
FR GERM	A	E	83	112	456	509	53
			84	182	663	807	144
			86	99	1,079	1,184	105
	V	E	84	5,762	6,197	6,732	535
FRANCE	A	W	84	2,234	635	1,902	1,267
	N	E	81	5,392	25,319	26,813	1,494
			84	3,233	2,614	2,947	333
	N	W	84	6,255	11,176	11,806	630
			85	3,681	9,801	11,514	1,713
	O	E	82	657	2,091	2,196	105
			86	287	1,356	1,456	100
	V	E	82	1,678	4,805	5,241	436
			83	1,583	4,784	5,319	535
			84	439	2,048	2,126	78
			85	4,474	5,619	5,969	350
			86	1,850	10,363	11,123	760
	V	W	81	2,404	12,362	13,891	1,529
			82	5,790	20,592	21,736	1,144
			83	1,100	5,080	5,323	243
			86	1,162	8,726	8,994	268
GREECE	V	E	81	476	440	523	83
HG KONG	V	E	81	6,200	6,746	7,199	453
			82	15,560	19,645	20,781	1,136
			83	15,351	21,800	22,439	639

Country	Mode	Reg	Yr	Quantity	F.A.S.	C.I.F.	Charges
			84	840	1,185	1,305	120
			86	16,578	16,687	18,254	1,567
	V	W	81	8,730	13,765	14,895	1,130
			82	7,877	11,816	12,818	1,002
			83	41,538	44,393	47,730	3,337
			84	9,606	7,049	7,668	619
			85	4,101	1,199	1,415	216
			86	46,727	37,019	38,943	1,924
HUNGARY	O	E	86	10,032	18,679	18,679	
INDIA	N	W	84	887	899	977	78
	V	E	82	810	464	525	61
	V	W	82	9,418	6,267	7,025	758
			83	563	285	369	84
			85	1,480	1,080	1,195	115
			86	39,683	31,500	33,104	1,604
ISRAEL	V	W	85	30,679	19,805	22,329	2,524
ITALY	V	E	83	193	465	498	33
JAMAICA	V	E	82	2,126	1,059	1,121	62
JAPAN	V	E	81	2,500	4,750	4,865	115
	V	H	82	400	807	1,054	247
			83	934	1,767	2,299	532
			84	798	1,368	1,874	506
	V	W	81	393	744	791	47
			82	1,139	2,282	2,532	250
			83	1,168	2,067	2,217	150
			84	410	813	890	77
			85	5,892	7,719	8,056	337
KOR REP	V	W	86	97	3,250	3,337	87
LEBANON	V	E	86	1,979	1,376	1,514	138
MEXICO	O	E	82	718	334	334	
	O	W	83	2,245	4,320	4,320	
N ZEAL	A	W	85	529	1,201	1,977	776
NETHLDS	V	E	84	200,000	191,601	200,000	8,399
PERU	A	W	84	490	2,094	2,644	550
PHIL R	A	E	82	500	989	1,701	712
	V	E	84	16,648	10,253	11,963	1,710
	V	W	81	62,012	41,780	45,918	4,138
			82	956	1,492	1,732	240
			83	27,419	21,547	23,653	2,106
			84	4,382	3,914	4,340	426
			85	6,023	3,455	3,743	288
			86	26,295	11,380	12,870	1,490
PORTUGL	V	E	81	904	738	876	138
			86	2,778	2,167	2,311	144
SINGAPR	V	W	81	4,078	6,090	6,699	609
SPAIN	V	E	84	462	664	703	39
	V	W	85	76,500	15,794	21,783	5,989
SWITZLD	V	E	82	440	927	1,095	168
			83	1,068	1,666	1,828	162
			84	1,666	3,132	3,318	186
			85	14,846	13,703	14,661	958
			86	14,992	19,127	20,570	1,443
	V	W	82	176	323	352	29
			83	265	489	510	21
			84	618	1,092	1,172	80
SYRIA	V	E	81	1,433	1,381	1,406	25
			83	11,464	15,551	18,367	2,816
			84	2,866	2,447	2,589	142
THAILND	V	E	82	287	423	488	65
			84	24,790	18,677	25,927	7,250
			86	102,293	55,966	59,874	3,908
	V	W	82	43,164	39,240	41,382	2,142
			83	441	531	550	19
			84	976	550	602	52
			85	79,366	66,940	69,455	2,515
			86	557,692	421,431	439,138	17,707
TURKEY	V	E	83	2,205	1,703	1,809	106
			86	7,134	5,663	6,894	1,231
U KING	A	E	84	103	256	373	117
			85	590	1,808	1,903	95
	N	E	81	3,580	3,619	4,096	477
	V	E	82	512	4,106	4,954	848
			83	1,222	3,399	3,810	411
			85	232	1,622	1,882	260
YUGOSLV	V	E	84	18,500	3,050	5,750	2,700
			85	51,319	8,048	11,500	3,452

Essential Oil

Citrus, essential oil
4528010 CITRUS, NSPF (LB)

Country	Mode	Reg	Yr	Quantity	F.A.S.	C.I.F.	Charges
TOTAL			81	10,192	145,248	151,040	5,792
			82	3,456	55,250	57,285	2,035
			83	2,204	39,617	41,447	1,830
			84	35,117	317,066	318,577	1,511
			86	92,161	150,332	157,487	7,155
ARGENT	V	E	81	1,554	20,128	21,119	991
BRAZIL	A	E	83	750	8,003	8,840	837
	V	E	81	1,157	3,693	3,943	250
			86	48,651	61,093	68,161	7,068
FR GERM	V	E	86	500	1,140	1,227	87
FRANCE	A	E	83	13	765	786	21
			84	44	13,425	13,533	108
HAITI	A	E	84	1,200	14,503	15,000	497
ITALY	N	E	81	7,481	121,427	125,978	4,551
	V	E	82	3,086	31,275	32,864	1,589
			83	1,190	20,038	20,428	390
MEXICO	O	E	84	33,565	266,780	266,780	
			86	43,010	88,099	88,099	
SPAIN	A	W	83	172	3,119	3,508	389
SWITZLD	A	E	82	370	23,975	24,421	446
			83	79	7,692	7,885	193
			84	220	20,896	21,526	630
U KING	A	E	84	88	1,462	1,738	276

Essential oil (not specified)
4528042 OILS DIST OR ESSENT, NSPF (LB)

Country	Mode	Reg	Yr	Quantity	F.A.S.	C.I.F.	Charges
TOTAL			81	2,431,178	17,463,154	18,015,229	550,113
			82	2,113,609	13,261,585	13,727,685	466,100
			83	2,901,325	19,030,994	19,635,306	604,312
			84	2,983,297	21,505,178	22,298,118	792,940
			85	3,013,053	25,469,974	26,257,263	787,289
			86	3,049,318	24,720,143	25,481,839	761,696
ALGERIA	V	E	81	441	1,337	1,486	149
ANTIGUA	V	E	85	600	23,197	23,334	137
ARGENT	A	E	85	132	6,000	6,456	456
	N	E	86	2,039	24,160	25,182	1,022
	V	E	81	653	289	342	53
			82	4,409	5,841	6,711	870
			83	4,719	45,440	46,944	1,504
			84	2,315	33,510	34,432	922
AUSTRAL	A	E	86	1,578	25,354	31,461	6,107
	A	W	82	2	1,020	1,076	56
			84	320	3,737	4,422	685
			85	1,066	17,457	18,879	1,422
			86	53	3,912	4,110	198
	N	E	82	11,221	92,527	95,108	2,581
			83	4,506	46,107	47,489	1,382
			84	3,442	38,614	40,009	1,395
			85	2,021	40,460	41,473	1,013
	N	W	84	1,748	17,480	20,386	2,906
	V	E	81	8,332	65,080	67,049	1,969
			85	1,119	18,344	18,595	251
	V	W	81	4,464	472	1,080	608
			85	16,636	299,376	302,758	3,382
			86	3,354	26,444	27,737	1,293
AUSTRIA	A	W	81	50	439	649	210
	N	E	81	8,432	226,778	229,227	2,449
			82	8,915	224,327	228,305	3,978
			83	20,437	284,361	289,851	5,490
			84	25,611	262,473	268,884	6,411
			85	37,031	448,836	458,121	9,285
			86	61,066	597,109	607,986	10,877
	V	E	84	71,958	34,212	38,183	3,971
			86	315	5,393	5,522	129
BAHAMAS	A	E	84	210	7,455	7,575	120
	V	E	83	538	1,244	1,248	4
			85	1,000	15,500	15,559	59
BELGIUM	A	E	83	35	1,120	1,176	56
			84	99	2,711	2,800	89
			85	17	1,146	1,249	103
			86	33	5,578	5,710	132
	N	E	81	551	57,239	58,302	1,063
			82	486	50,215	51,194	979
			83	1,979	55,564	56,791	1,227
			84	8,466	39,735	41,338	1,603
			85	1,027	103,985	105,032	1,047
			86	931	51,944	52,920	976
BRAZIL	A	E	81	36	495	638	143
			83	750	3,910	4,690	780
	N	E	83	48,585	160,065	174,262	14,197
			84	282,914	529,230	578,246	49,016
			85	313,964	759,073	818,817	59,744
			86	175,329	497,030	528,944	31,914
	V	E	81	73,551	276,868	293,843	16,945
			82	41,454	133,899	143,532	9,633
			83	17,102	61,622	65,458	3,836
			84	7,628	53,610	55,320	1,710
			85	16,018	154,332	158,785	4,453
			86	9,535	10,813	11,378	565
CANADA	O	E	81	49,336	365,882	365,882	
			82	44,226	256,900	256,990	90
			83	33,259	268,761	268,761	
			84	37,008	264,788	264,788	
			85	3,906	64,910	64,910	
			86	61,824	337,534	337,534	
	O	W	83	43	1,982	2,921	939
CHILE	A	E	86	121	1,650	1,833	183
CHINA M	N	E	81	51,543	167,521	181,915	14,286
			82	127,485	363,958	386,373	22,415
			84	239,940	895,206	929,957	34,751
			85	525,509	1,783,963	1,869,350	85,387
			86	755,796	1,809,846	1,903,423	93,577
	O	E	81	130,512	326,866	346,295	19,429
			82	360,727	786,046	847,618	61,572
			83	45,513	108,784	115,797	7,013
			84	2,205	24,369	24,759	390
	V	E	83	570,355	1,453,210	1,547,321	94,111
			84	28,550	59,838	64,116	4,278
			85	28,572	70,439	74,779	4,340
	V	W	81	531,207	1,273,545	1,333,813	60,268
			82	226,942	621,599	657,282	35,683
			83	14,827	74,196	77,267	3,071
			84	45,982	120,507	126,169	5,662
			85	12,170	35,144	37,387	2,243
			86	55,556	98,529	107,258	8,729
CHINA T	A	E	83	220	4,513	5,126	613
			85	915	18,794	19,856	1,062
	O	E	81	220	7,375	7,484	109
	V	E	81	11,706	79,819	80,814	995
			83	26,411	31,065	34,410	3,345
			84	7,543	41,034	42,124	1,090
			85	3,968	14,052	14,620	568
			86	8,934	46,052	47,596	1,544
	V	W	81	2,381	11,765	11,987	222
			83	5,758	14,612	15,531	919
			85	1,065	12,799	13,078	279
COMOROS	A	E	81	220	7,984	8,016	32
			82	121	3,935	3,995	60
			84	110	4,116	4,186	70
CR N AN	V	E	81	3,584	33,200	34,490	1,290
DENMARK	N	E	84	368	1,733	1,938	205
	V	E	82	912	1,082	1,126	44
			84	276	654	708	54
			85	280	4,579	4,790	211
DOM REP	A	E	81	2,688	23,848	24,597	749
	N	E	81	6,016	52,331	54,052	1,721
			83	14,968	135,721	138,365	2,644
	V	E	82	8,064	72,793	75,453	2,660
			83	8,554	78,650	79,612	962
			84	32,356	307,726	318,433	10,707
			85	10,770	97,641	102,214	4,573
DOMINCA	N	E	82	19,160	171,963	178,427	6,464
			86	30,150	285,803	295,915	10,112
	O	E	82	1,344	12,297	12,794	497
			85	9,000	86,067	88,971	2,904
	V	E	81	7,168	65,584	67,739	2,155
			83	4,480	41,464	42,762	1,298
EGYPT	A	E	81	891	27,181	27,780	599
			84	110	6,250	6,395	145
			85	99	5,828	6,112	284
			86	2,874	196,323	202,968	6,645
	A	W	82	80	1,240	1,490	250
	N	E	81	2,722	235,494	239,445	3,951
			82	4,045	158,838	161,399	2,561
			83	1,873	279,987	283,240	3,253
			84	3,737	509,650	520,285	10,635
			85	5,514	247,525	252,796	5,271
	O	E	83	4	1,400	1,450	50
FR GERM	A	E	83	51	478	509	31

Product
TSUSA commodity number, description, and unit of quantity

Country	Mode	Reg	Yr	Quantity	F.A.S.	C.I.F.	Charges
			84	375	18,279	19,594	1,315
			85	1,321	29,159	31,269	2,110
			86	110	1,063	1,211	148
	A	W	83	390	10,485	10,693	208
			84	2,182	35,104	37,426	2,322
			85	2,355	34,996	38,060	3,064
	N	E	81	9,025	141,936	145,607	3,671
			82	2,334	86,962	89,458	2,496
			83	27,842	194,017	197,549	3,532
			84	33,386	234,395	239,962	5,567
			85	8,010	90,871	93,449	2,578
			86	11,063	181,920	185,852	3,932
	N	W	82	32	659	737	78
	V	E	81	1,675	11,335	11,724	389
			85	2,200	34,100	34,159	59
FRANCE	A	E	81	144	2,615	3,307	692
			82	335	4,816	5,244	428
			83	153	14,718	15,194	476
			84	1,460	34,390	36,841	2,451
			85	2,147	80,287	85,877	5,590
			86	428	24,223	25,816	1,593
	A	W	82	210	485	631	146
			84	1,022	4,881	6,033	1,152
			86	180	2,959	3,218	259
	N	E	81	967,339	8,280,340	8,514,588	233,785
			82	645,058	5,623,512	5,780,334	156,822
			83	996,790	7,548,660	7,744,545	195,885
			84	1,214,164	8,546,144	8,906,317	360,173
			85	878,767	7,675,743	7,892,228	216,485
			86	975,407	10,357,574	10,672,010	314,436
	N	W	81	205	3,870	4,175	305
			83	89,869	34,896	41,354	6,458
			86	408	6,498	7,046	548
	O	E	81	194	316	327	11
			82	23,496	49,073	52,939	3,866
			83	9,700	23,481	24,795	1,314
			84	1,190	8,268	8,575	307
	V	E	82	2,481	7,723	8,348	625
			83	300	4,650	4,669	19
			84	1,114	15,122	15,495	373
			85	7,733	58,268	59,529	1,261
			86	3,500	54,250	54,406	156
	V	W	86	1,511	4,301	4,649	348
GABON	A	E	86	53	4,665	4,756	91
GHANA	V	E	85	115	9,391	9,464	73
GIBRAT	V	E	83	1,466	6,876	7,200	324
GREECE	A	E	81	22	254	284	30
			84	444	1,203	1,672	469
	V	E	86	661	1,933	2,070	137
GUATMAL	A	E	81	157	12,320	12,626	306
			82	1,289	55,356	56,607	1,251
			83	510	28,275	28,765	490
			84	1,441	177,134	178,912	1,778
	N	E	81	2,152	144,280	146,639	2,359
			82	860	34,000	34,968	968
			83	2,217	163,618	166,133	2,515
			84	2,055	289,722	292,449	2,727
			85	5,047	433,808	440,540	6,732
			86	1,963	136,452	138,871	2,419
	V	E	84	441	36,300	37,224	924
			86	22	3,044	3,072	28
HAITI	A	E	83	8,800	60,108	63,108	3,000
			84	83,162	655,169	695,484	40,315
	N	E	82	100,571	702,460	727,845	25,385
			83	172,953	1,306,346	1,361,354	55,008
			84	1,310	87,004	87,452	448
			85	85,584	595,713	629,981	34,268
			86	95,858	663,459	682,324	18,865
	V	E	81	76,742	585,681	603,756	18,075
			83	2,200	21,338	21,950	612
HG KONG	A	E	86	441	13,968	14,979	1,011
	N	E	85	3,167	84,902	85,936	1,034
	O	E	84	364	6,763	6,845	82
	V	E	81	49,603	44,417	51,128	6,711
			84	9,865	24,454	25,954	1,500
			86	29,375	27,245	29,664	2,419
	V	W	81	6,738	9,769	10,335	566
			82	23,292	25,165	27,147	1,982
			83	10,133	40,944	43,007	2,063
			84	50	1,620	1,745	125
HONDURA	N	E	86	1,543	15,370	16,077	707
	V	E	81	14,266	62,698	64,199	1,501
			82	1,014	8,280	8,567	287
			83	7,252	64,161	65,578	1,417
			84	19,819	88,300	90,356	2,056
			85	4,133	39,166	39,882	716
			86	518	5,155	5,356	201
HUNGARY	A	E	82	33	2,769	2,791	22
			86	55	2,069	2,125	56
	N	E	81	3,382	39,902	40,809	907
			83	4,275	4,125	4,858	733
			84	816	30,362	31,186	824
	O	E	84	3,307	38,027	38,027	
	V	E	85	338	11,185	11,458	273
INDIA	A	E	81	441	2,999	4,213	1,214
			82	344	6,852	8,006	1,154
			83	282	4,904	5,833	929
			84	887	27,401	29,048	1,647
			85	88	17,600	17,857	257
			86	3,950	131,834	136,753	4,919
	A	W	82	14	287	304	17
	N	E	81	10,290	219,544	235,058	15,514
			82	8,567	191,130	201,680	10,550
			83	15,907	582,524	603,215	20,691
			84	22,276	786,810	810,801	23,991
			85	61,565	2,717,330	2,773,144	55,814
			86	40,608	1,477,924	1,509,175	31,251
	O	W	84	7	270	300	30
	V	E	82	350	570	764	194
			83	2,205	19,000	20,017	1,017
			86	4,400	36,866	38,236	1,370
	V	W	81	10	992	1,044	52
			82	529	15,500	16,144	644
			84	8	647	664	17
			85	1,984	18,156	18,917	761
INDNSIA	A	E	82	110	2,230	2,580	350
	N	E	81	43,664	229,807	240,902	10,971
			83	88,052	501,591	517,216	15,625
			84	132,711	959,941	992,214	32,273
			85	105,112	783,663	817,215	33,552
			86	129,706	1,421,795	1,458,458	36,663
	V	E	82	55,950	319,044	332,418	13,374
			83	10,935	48,255	50,320	2,065
			84	3,968	27,117	28,101	984
	V	W	82	8,731	52,528	54,954	2,426
			83	330	8,249	8,599	350
			84	6,173	48,254	49,138	884
			86	4,078	35,538	36,322	784
IRELAND	A	E	83	696	16,618	18,894	2,276
			84	45	12,685	12,756	71
	N	E	82	133	10,949	11,185	236
ISRAEL	A	E	83	93	964	1,094	130
	N	E	86	10,587	11,546	13,841	2,295
	V	E	82	276	6,876	7,008	132
			83	31,570	155,833	157,481	1,648
			84	254	9,150	9,235	85
			85	3,178	62,912	64,347	1,435
ITALY	A	E	83	22	1,512	1,577	65
			85	114	7,794	8,233	439
	A	W	85	114	8,250	8,900	650
	N	E	81	74,329	1,295,624	1,325,849	30,190
			82	49,892	755,826	767,323	11,497
			83	66,585	884,653	902,549	17,896
			84	75,513	1,122,910	1,148,220	25,310
			85	63,346	875,895	896,080	20,185
			86	62,148	724,043	746,798	22,755
	V	E	82	1,984	26,370	27,098	728
JAMAICA	A	E	85	160	5,600	6,267	667
	N	E	81	45,523	394,223	406,916	12,693
			82	23,636	223,650	228,559	4,909
			83	55,358	698,555	715,427	16,872
			84	62,741	804,060	829,355	25,295
			85	60,003	808,698	826,722	18,024
			86	35,761	353,363	371,591	18,228
	O	E	81	2,425	22,220	22,553	333
			82	500	6,770	6,770	
	V	E	82	2,475	29,353	29,584	231
			83	2,400	25,551	26,624	1,073
			84	15,099	201,067	206,774	5,707
			85	1,004	13,180	13,848	668
			86	5,835	65,304	67,560	2,256
JAPAN	A	E	83	55	9,209	9,779	570
			85	250	5,479	5,917	438
			86	40	9,302	10,026	724
	A	W	86	140	1,365	1,943	578
	N	E	81	3,160	27,664	29,054	1,390
			82	588	11,792	12,866	1,074
			84	190	6,268	6,904	636
	N	W	84	1,526	6,329	6,688	359
			85	3,092	4,762	5,146	384

Table 2. U.S. Import Statistics for Non Crop-Specific Commodities by End-Use

Product
TSUSA commodity number, description, and unit of quantity

Country	Mode	Reg	Yr	Quantity	F.A.S.	C.I.F.	Charges
	V	W	81	2,104	7,375	7,819	444
			82	785	2,765	2,861	96
			83	1,522	2,693	2,849	156
			86	132	1,419	1,528	109
KOR REP	V	E	82	165	1,811	1,947	136
			84	1,453	2,838	3,279	441
			86	63	1,265	1,279	14
LAOS	A	E	84	10	2,310	2,384	74
LEBANON	O	E	84	1,500	2,040	2,040	
	V	E	86	4,950	4,895	5,407	512
LIBERIA	V	E	81	551	258	353	95
MACAO	A	E	86	881	22,822	23,500	678
	V	W	81	674	648	687	39
			83	13	540	576	36
MADAGAS	N	E	83	253	6,852	7,004	152
			85	1,455	12,906	14,160	1,254
	V	E	84	243	7,490	7,835	345
			86	500	6,258	6,413	155
MALAYSA	A	E	83	441	820	1,753	933
			84	220	545	1,176	631
MEXICO	A	E	81	4,432	225,626	229,023	3,397
			82	2,226	53,103	55,365	2,262
			83	9,244	268,197	274,803	6,606
			84	14,182	430,287	442,341	12,054
			85	10,817	258,653	266,754	8,101
	N	E	82	577	16,990	17,469	479
			83	419	14,407	14,968	561
			86	10,668	293,020	302,531	9,511
	O	E	82	2,205	14,900	14,900	
			83	25,160	30,702	30,702	
			84	121,692	652,800	652,800	
			85	75,838	412,800	412,800	
			86	88,313	407,848	407,988	140
	O	W	83	430	1,218	1,218	
			84	1,330	1,452	1,452	
	V	E	86	1,000	45,000	45,155	155
MOROC	A	E	83	3,525	80,920	85,978	5,058
			84	2,620	104,230	105,922	1,692
	N	E	81	3,583	44,246	45,384	1,138
			82	2,127	27,082	28,383	1,301
			83	318	4,943	5,083	140
			85	2,480	38,480	40,598	2,118
	V	E	81	4,410	55,718	56,736	1,018
			82	2,205	29,345	30,168	823
			83	4,189	1,384	2,375	991
			85	661	5,860	5,976	116
			86	3,814	85,234	86,921	1,687
N ZEAL	A	E	82	10	1,057	1,310	253
NETHLDS	A	E	81	123	3,398	3,620	222
			82	77	436	520	84
			84	59	2,220	2,507	287
			86	1	1,003	2,006	1,003
	N	E	81	9,309	303,218	306,738	3,227
			82	9,046	225,011	228,528	3,517
			83	62,728	622,067	637,758	15,691
			84	38,382	672,073	687,069	14,996
			85	38,609	659,532	672,847	13,315
			86	90,799	1,255,763	1,278,652	22,889
	V	E	82	77	434	538	104
			83	4,400	2,500	2,690	190
NIGERIA	V	E	81	276	4,545	4,670	125
			82	534	7,400	7,402	2
NORWAY	V	E	82	284	689	729	40
PAKISTN	A	E	85	431	13,062	13,317	255
			86	805	23,381	25,184	1,803
	N	E	81	1,264	22,847	23,539	692
	V	E	81	816	7,168	7,456	288
			82	408	3,332	3,729	397
	V	W	84	419	3,636	3,830	194
PANAMA	A	E	83	104	199,975	200,048	73
PARAGUA	V	E	81	11,023	18,480	20,799	2,319
			82	108,027	148,440	167,984	19,544
			83	102,561	135,196	156,360	21,164
			84	132,277	253,805	280,860	27,055
			85	229,432	462,580	513,298	50,718
			86	33,598	88,370	96,013	7,643
PERU	A	E	81	441	6,452	6,540	88
PHIL R	V	E	81	3,373	1,326	1,649	323
			82	1,124	408	567	159
POLAND	A	E	81	2,323	36,639	40,068	3,429
			82	1,160	17,766	19,462	1,696
PORTUGL	V	E	82	4,233	9,165	10,250	1,085
REP SAF	A	E	86	1,362	55,525	56,932	1,407
	N	E	81	12,484	140,470	147,146	6,676
			82	2,013	146,181	148,886	2,705
			83	9,971	108,998	112,741	3,743
			84	33,089	188,424	193,551	5,127
			85	12,544	119,763	123,542	3,779
			86	6,684	32,074	33,608	1,534
	V	E	82	67,020	139,840	145,030	5,190
			83	95,503	160,284	166,884	6,600
			86	32,725	28,203	30,879	2,676
	V	W	83	29,270	49,125	53,375	4,250
S ARAB	A	E	86	161	13,831	14,202	371
S HELNA	V	E	84	441	14,794	15,208	414
SALVADR	V	E	81	1,500	12,750	13,085	335
			82	1,500	8,250	8,461	211
			86	1,500	7,500	7,781	281
SENEGAL	A	E	86	4,409	22,975	25,760	2,785
SINGAPR	A	E	81	771	17,091	17,803	712
	V	E	83	2,205	13,095	13,379	284
			86	2,380	19,381	19,817	436
	V	W	81	5,140	3,832	4,121	289
			82	1,865	2,379	2,549	170
			83	3,894	12,720	13,914	1,194
			84	80	1,040	1,090	50
SPAIN	A	E	83	207	2,892	3,147	255
			84	18	351	438	87
			85	132	2,869	3,219	350
	A	W	83	573	9,333	10,521	1,188
			84	57	1,063	1,301	238
	N	E	81	49,951	213,133	229,748	16,615
			82	37,921	267,166	279,579	12,413
			83	52,765	273,029	285,779	12,750
			84	44,194	258,870	275,454	16,584
			85	72,609	306,676	325,532	18,856
			86	47,276	409,525	425,501	15,976
	O	E	82	2,177	1,341	1,341	
	V	E	82	12	557	669	112
			85	441	1,728	1,904	176
			86	6,654	19,337	20,019	682
SRI LKA	A	E	81	882	78,800	81,031	2,231
			82	529	41,066	41,760	694
			83	220	12,125	12,691	566
			85	154	6,300	6,635	335
			86	52	6,402	6,480	78
	A	W	82	22	2,150	2,239	89
	N	E	82	154	13,702	13,953	251
			84	198	39,035	39,801	766
	V	E	81	55	6,391	6,556	165
			83	849	10,144	10,312	168
SWITZLD	A	E	81	18	278	288	10
			82	68	1,459	1,577	118
			84	392	24,145	26,096	1,951
			85	77	9,874	10,134	260
			86	275	17,207	17,754	547
	N	E	81	13,855	250,013	255,794	5,527
			82	16,514	326,603	335,036	8,433
			83	8,563	667,008	673,299	6,291
			84	28,620	587,023	600,884	13,861
			85	20,694	480,456	504,289	23,833
			86	18,683	531,398	549,238	17,840
	V	E	86	2,386	41,032	41,781	749
THAILND	V	W	81	30	504	570	66
			82	288	4,266	4,752	486
			83	63	850	908	58
TRINID	A	E	83	2,332	1,568	2,376	808
			84	937	1,617	3,554	1,937
TUNISIA	A	E	85	11	4,060	4,110	50
TURKEY	V	E	85	397	11,325	11,596	271
U KING	A	E	81	788	10,600	11,032	432
			82	2,368	88,043	89,626	1,583
			83	379	3,569	4,051	482
			84	99	2,929	3,132	203
			85	108	1,321	1,681	360
	A	W	81	12	5,738	5,797	59
			82	24	439	521	82
			83	11	1,061	1,124	63
			84	66	3,647	3,767	120
	N	E	81	7,346	239,936	243,724	3,788
			82	4,805	173,936	177,416	3,480
			83	7,325	243,319	247,731	4,412
			84	36,388	408,511	418,320	9,809
			85	111,345	3,320,723	3,369,532	48,809
			86	39,261	881,082	892,404	11,322
	N	W	84	606	1,975	2,090	115
			85	96,213	177,807	187,611	9,804
	O	E	81	6,213	4,932	5,429	497
			82	2,025	1,346	1,514	168
			83	7,990	19,048	19,687	639

Product TSUSA commodity number, description, and unit of quantity Country	Mode	Reg	Yr	Quantity	F.A.S.	C.I.F.	Charges
			84	1,683	13,712	14,172	460
			85	5,269	8,742	9,178	436
			86	6,929	12,268	13,154	886
	O	W	83	7	750	803	53
	V	E	81	1,960	30,106	30,524	418
			83	4,551	145,240	147,164	1,924
			84	3,815	57,266	58,391	1,125
			85	34,003	178,093	183,348	5,255
			86	42,716	434,130	444,617	10,487
	V	W	81	641	12,112	12,372	260
			82	2,436	1,228	1,360	132
			83	1,238	804	965	161
USSR	N	E	83	1,030	29,282	29,750	468
	V	E	81	12,653	165,864	169,352	3,217
			82	1,993	32,371	33,325	954
			84	550	16,744	16,867	123
			85	452	10,098	10,203	105
			86	495	19,898	20,034	136
YUGOSLV	N	E	81	63,987	692,462	713,758	20,912
			82	19,928	229,661	234,247	4,586
			83	22,265	245,464	249,556	4,092
			84	14,416	127,337	130,221	2,884
			85	4,755	116,017	118,477	2,460
			86	9,127	107,783	110,540	2,757
	V	E	83	500	10,500	10,626	126
			84	1,000	16,781	17,086	305
			85	800	13,894	14,176	282
			86	882	25,812	27,079	1,267

Fiber

Istle, fiber
1926600 ISTLE OR TAMPICO FIBERS (LB)

Country	Mode	Reg	Yr	Quantity	F.A.S.	C.I.F.	Charges
TOTAL			81	4,955,681	4,280,095	4,280,095	
			82	5,538,682	5,842,574	5,842,663	89
			83	5,769,570	6,273,745	6,273,745	
			84	5,388,011	6,272,750	6,272,750	
			85	4,851,943	5,068,924	5,068,924	
			86	5,336,287	5,501,598	5,501,598	
CANADA	O	E	81	48,479	63,739	63,739	
			85	54,014	59,083	59,083	
MEXICO	O	E	81	4,906,761	4,216,086	4,216,086	
			82	5,538,682	5,842,574	5,842,663	89
			83	5,769,570	6,273,745	6,273,745	
			84	5,388,011	6,272,750	6,272,750	
			85	4,797,929	5,009,841	5,009,841	
			86	5,336,287	5,501,598	5,501,598	
	O	W	81	441	270	270	

Straw and vegetable, fiber
1928000 CRUDE STRAW A VEG FIBER NSPF (LB)

Country	Mode	Reg	Yr	Quantity	F.A.S.	C.I.F.	Charges
TOTAL			81	678,071	314,540	370,066	55,526
			82	543,578	261,109	347,053	85,944
			83	613,973	245,429	308,336	62,907
			84	1,134,883	175,741	253,540	77,799
			85	619,976	188,119	238,931	50,812
			86	804,192	360,860	482,792	121,932
ARGENT	A	E	82	6,978	1,000	10,637	9,637
BRAZIL	V	E	86	5,048	2,778	3,400	622
CANADA	O	E	81	38,472	1,375	1,375	
			82	4,190	4,465	5,205	740
			84	49,100	1,330	1,330	
	O	W	83	551	606	606	
CHINA M	V	E	83	224	448	459	11
			84	1,082	1,371	1,598	227
	V	W	81	2,201	3,143	3,363	220
			82	62,829	79,066	82,698	3,632
			83	1,530	676	720	44
			84	93,110	26,548	36,420	9,872
			85	12,430	6,914	8,431	1,517
CHINA T	V	E	81	5,000	9,600	10,410	810

Product TSUSA commodity number, description, and unit of quantity Country	Mode	Reg	Yr	Quantity	F.A.S.	C.I.F.	Charges
			84	560,000	17,920	19,754	1,834
			86	4,650	7,666	8,225	559
	V	W	81	250	384	409	25
			82	250	386	430	44
			83	529	345	369	24
ECUADOR	V	E	81	4,352	1,958	2,793	835
FRANCE	V	E	81	35,053	19,853	26,853	7,000
			82	53,571	19,016	30,036	11,020
			84	33,310	16,293	21,840	5,547
	V	W	82	33,069	22,633	27,266	4,633
			83	61,200	108,018	116,541	8,523
HG KONG	V	E	84	6,000	1,650	2,305	655
INDIA	V	E	81	17,401	6,148	8,702	2,554
			82	10,024	4,214	6,173	1,959
			84	25,760	3,766	4,909	1,143
			85	55,436	31,865	37,584	5,719
			86	92,831	49,408	57,290	7,882
	V	W	85	132,957	38,955	46,405	7,450
JAPAN	V	E	83	5,000	3,652	4,041	389
	V	W	81	6,000	3,837	4,097	260
KOR REP	V	W	81	1,748	4,861	5,061	200
			83	400	900	1,005	105
MADAGAS	O	E	81	109,285	68,739	69,368	629
	V	E	81	313,548	132,753	168,584	35,831
			82	282,005	100,349	145,106	44,757
			83	338,380	106,633	147,385	40,752
			84	282,124	83,618	134,624	51,006
			85	311,253	75,558	103,168	27,610
			86	164,288	82,871	106,949	24,078
	V	H	85	33,145	18,162	20,174	2,012
			86	66,521	48,957	71,111	22,154
MEXICO	O	E	82	24,446	1,113	1,113	
			83	147,392	5,126	5,126	
			84	47,382	6,536	6,536	
			85	29,074	4,489	4,489	
			86	8,400	4,148	4,148	
	O	W	81	44,869	7,825	7,825	
			84	2,137	748	748	
	V	E	81	6,733	13,954	14,454	500
			82	6,229	18,274	18,786	512
			84	6,377	8,245	9,490	1,245
			86	3,338	4,263	4,565	302
NETHLDS	A	E	82	2,940	712	909	197
	O	E	86	36,363	20,614	23,900	3,286
PHIL R	V	E	83	2,113	4,601	6,308	1,707
			84	1,206	1,731	2,795	1,064
			85	290	1,042	1,543	501
	V	W	81	620	2,850	3,136	286
			82	2,840	1,276	1,468	192
			83	4,508	2,796	3,217	421
			84	824	625	695	70
			85	281	1,085	1,714	629
			86	2,720	2,282	2,564	282
REP SAF	V	E	81	69,875	32,590	38,355	5,765
			84	15,278	2,433	4,433	2,000
			86	179,190	49,384	72,985	23,601
SIER LN	N	E	82	33,600	6,578	12,768	6,190
	V	E	81	22,399	3,841	4,404	563
			86	232,947	84,850	123,974	39,124
SINGAPR	V	E	84	425	960	1,488	528
SPAIN	A	E	83	111	500	705	205
	V	E	81	265	829	877	48
SRI LKA	V	E	82	19,489	1,359	3,689	2,330
THAILND	V	W	82	1,118	668	769	101
U KING	V	E	83	43,791	8,907	16,398	7,491
			85	36,292	7,847	10,718	2,871
	V	W	83	8,244	2,221	5,456	3,235
			84	10,768	1,967	4,575	2,608
			85	8,818	2,202	4,705	2,503
			86	7,896	3,639	3,681	42

Vegetable, fiber, processed
3045800 OT VEG FIB PROCES NSPF, ETC (LB)

Country	Mode	Reg	Yr	Quantity	F.A.S.	C.I.F.	Charges
TOTAL			81	1,861	683	764	81
			82	4,060	2,518	3,027	509
			83	103,408	17,999	18,990	991
			84	376,882	72,107	86,653	14,546
			85	196,387	86,812	99,617	12,805
			86	52,639	15,229	21,373	6,144
AFGHAN	V	E	84	7,504	2,830	3,530	700
CANADA	O	E	81	1,800	329	329	
INDIA	O	E	84	85,592	43,753	43,753	

Product
TSUSA commodity number, description, and unit of quantity

Country	Mode	Reg	Yr	Quantity	F.A.S.	C.I.F.	Charges
	V	E	85	196,089	86,329	98,829	12,500
	V	E	82	4,000	1,880	2,389	509
			86	16,704	9,251	11,462	2,211
	V	W	83	6,720	2,350	3,256	906
ITALY	A	E	83	65	309	394	85
KENYA	A	E	81	61	354	435	81
MEXICO	O	E	82	60	638	638	
	O	W	83	96,623	15,340	15,340	
			84	47,100	7,479	7,479	
NETHLDS	V	E	85	298	483	788	305
SRI LKA	V	E	84	19,401	1,908	4,078	2,170
			86	35,935	5,978	9,911	3,933
THAILND	V	E	84	217,285	16,137	27,813	11,676

Vegetable, fiber, raw and waste
3045600 OTH VEG FIB NSPF, RAW WASTE (LTN)

Country	Mode	Reg	Yr	Quantity	F.A.S.	C.I.F.	Charges
TOTAL			81	1,973	285,369	487,356	201,987
			82	4	3,688	4,779	1,091
			83	106	48,066	60,513	12,447
			84	581	122,695	184,608	61,913
			85	21	16,318	22,721	6,403
			86	42	19,725	25,567	5,842
ARGENT	A	E	84	1	800	1,913	1,113
BNGLDSH	V	E	81	300	21,566	26,568	5,002
CANADA	O	E	81	11	10,082	10,082	
COLOMB	A	E	85	1	447	2,453	2,006
INDIA	V	E	81	26	21,582	29,486	7,904
			82	4	3,688	4,779	1,091
			85	15	13,608	16,676	3,068
			86	8	7,769	9,508	1,739
JAPAN	N	W	85	*	624	739	115
LESOTHO	V	E	81	50	24,294	33,123	8,829
SRI LKA	V	E	83	25	5,606	6,201	595
			84	18	5,933	9,861	3,928
			85	5	1,639	2,853	1,214
			86	34	11,956	16,059	4,103
THAILND	V	E	81	1,586	207,845	388,097	180,252
			84	502	85,956	139,468	53,512
U KING	O	E	83	20	9,286	10,606	1,320
			84	60	30,006	33,366	3,360
	V	E	83	61	33,174	43,706	10,532

Fruit

Fruit, canned
1500200 FRUIT MIX CND NO APRCOT ETC (LB)

Country	Mode	Reg	Yr	Quantity	F.A.S.	C.I.F.	Charges
TOTAL			81	6,056,315	2,045,638	2,499,187	352,248
			82	9,347,545	3,138,328	3,765,411	627,083
			83	1,261,733	486,850	580,696	93,846
			84	9,315,750	3,016,741	3,617,725	600,984
			85	12,186,307	4,654,570	5,451,572	797,002
			86	9,284,064	3,671,684	4,209,582	537,898
AUSTRAL	V	E	85	339,955	261,819	304,545	42,726
			86	96,756	12,301	14,689	2,388
AUSTRIA	V	E	85	875	1,051	1,206	155
BELGIUM	V	E	83	4,428	3,000	3,385	385
			84	63,274	33,426	40,044	6,618
			85	67,038	33,876	39,856	5,980
	V	W	85	10,514	5,330	6,467	1,137
C RICA	A	E	83	4,464	2,837	4,457	1,620
CANADA	A	H	84	130	862	940	78
			85	1,457	1,101	1,250	149
CHINA M	V	E	85	2,500	4,913	5,658	745
	V	W	81	840	291	328	37
CHINA T	V	E	81	5,625	1,868	2,211	343
			82	4,650	2,729	3,063	334
			83	2,250	911	1,056	145
			84	1,688	692	794	102
			85	3,000	1,875	2,172	297
	V	W	85	33,730	12,572	14,127	1,555
DENMARK	V	E	81	1,561	766	1,007	241
DOM REP	V	E	82	6,705	2,346	2,628	282
			84	5,805	900	1,123	223
			86	17,600	5,198	6,623	1,425
FR GERM	V	E	81	544	631	674	43
			83	210	534	565	31
			84	48,333	24,416	29,405	4,989
			85	141,015	152,197	188,497	36,300
FRANCE	V	E	81	8,684	8,575	9,372	797
			82	10,783	9,754	10,677	923
			83	20,348	16,799	19,638	2,839
			84	75,530	46,207	55,373	9,166
			85	34,927	24,421	28,069	3,648
			86	116,094	117,418	130,479	13,061
GREECE	V	E	85	2,355	2,808	3,037	229
HG KONG	O	W	85	3,000	1,600	1,798	198
	V	E	81	1,218	2,761	2,914	153
			84	813	978	1,113	135
	V	W	81	122	259	289	30
			82	406	768	822	54
			83	525	1,766	1,872	106
			86	820	1,750	1,844	94
INDIA	V	E	83	2,436	2,393	2,752	359
			84	5,007	3,700	4,178	478
	V	W	81	545	259	326	67
			82	1,145	1,150	1,371	221
			83	884	886	1,445	559
IRELAND	V	E	83	270	552	719	167
ISRAEL	V	E	85	84,216	27,700	32,509	4,809
			86	3,450	1,257	1,450	193
ITALY	V	E	83	1,058	1,362	1,436	74
			84	68,784	26,400	30,806	4,406
			85	39,682	10,800	12,969	2,169
			86	873	1,906	1,978	72
JAPAN	V	E	81	16,508	9,994	10,120	126
			83	678	604	649	45
			84	1,527	1,243	1,446	203
			86	1,690	1,331	1,514	183
	V	W	81	7,275	6,375	6,683	308
			82	894	773	806	33
			83	8,851	8,356	8,728	372
			84	1,962	1,734	1,828	94
			85	2,812	3,082	3,232	150
MEXICO	O	E	81	20,340	7,379	7,379	
NETHLDS	V	E	83	899	1,123	1,171	48
PHIL R	V	E	81	746,747	308,392	391,656	56,012
			82	491,231	174,584	205,902	31,318
			83	28,461	14,749	17,069	2,320
			84	382,436	126,750	160,598	33,848
			85	567,721	236,659	283,091	46,432
			86	608,268	241,193	282,927	41,734
	V	H	81	1,872	2,080	2,477	397
			82	1,296	1,404	1,658	254
			85	4,878	5,282	5,932	650
	V	W	81	5,178,803	1,645,809	2,008,172	288,314
			82	8,792,597	2,914,657	3,505,174	590,517
			83	1,089,552	365,952	445,800	79,848
			84	8,204,592	2,596,686	3,118,191	521,505
			85	5,551,829	2,026,298	2,373,771	347,473
			86	8,083,513	3,139,535	3,601,937	462,402
REP SAF	V	E	84	293,032	66,510	74,611	8,101
			85	3,604,269	1,225,080	1,425,494	200,414
			86	37,412	10,062	11,747	1,685
	V	W	85	1,328,532	463,192	548,022	84,830
SPAIN	V	E	85	7,110	2,826	2,968	142
			86	53,460	16,666	19,505	2,839
SWITZLD	V	E	82	8,095	8,553	9,496	943
			83	7,421	7,755	8,301	546
			84	5,112	4,923	5,200	277
			85	2,248	2,019	2,130	111
			86	2,023	2,662	2,797	135
THAILND	V	E	81	31,140	24,151	26,408	2,257
			82	10,487	7,868	8,892	1,024
			83	6,299	4,196	4,753	557
			84	12,227	8,591	9,549	958
			85	28,148	16,069	18,137	2,068
			86	55,951	26,821	30,112	3,291
	V	W	81	34,362	25,539	28,605	3,066
			82	18,028	12,076	13,128	1,052
			83	74,640	42,823	46,112	3,289
			84	134,696	62,985	71,724	8,739
			85	317,735	124,562	138,611	14,049
			86	185,925	83,919	91,242	7,323
U KING	V	E	81	129	509	566	57
			82	864	979	1,042	63
			83	7,179	9,220	9,652	432

Product / TSUSA commodity number, description, and unit of quantity Country	Mode	Reg	Yr	Quantity	F.A.S.	C.I.F.	Charges
			84	10,262	9,194	10,178	984
			85	6,761	7,438	8,024	586
			86	2,829	2,865	3,161	296
	V	W	82	364	687	752	65
			83	880	1,032	1,136	104
VENEZ	V	E	86	17,400	6,800	7,577	777
YUGOSLV	V	E	84	540	544	624	80

Fruit, dried
1466600 OTH BERRIES DRIED EVAP NSPF (LB)

Country	Mode	Reg	Yr	Quantity	F.A.S.	C.I.F.	Charges
TOTAL			81	75,489	65,830	66,756	926
			82	148,366	84,182	91,146	6,964
			83	76,225	68,259	77,972	9,713
			84	67,647	46,736	54,420	7,684
			85	84,547	65,368	76,893	11,525
			86	169,651	119,197	123,748	4,551
ALBANIA	V	W	82	4,147	1,751	1,853	102
AUSTRAL	O	E	82	38,445	27,758	27,758	
BELGIUM	V	E	84	12,564	7,540	9,028	1,488
BRAZIL	A	E	83	15,178	7,340	10,048	2,708
			84	100	931	1,299	368
	N	W	83	424	4,224	4,658	434
			84	3,310	3,300	3,440	140
BULGAR	V	W	81	2,308	882	886	4
CANADA	O	E	81	70,090	57,045	57,045	
			82	745	14,140	14,140	
			83	7,145	14,444	14,444	
			85	45,000	15,750	15,750	
CHILE	A	E	85	1,259	2,285	3,827	1,542
CHINA M	A	E	81	132	920	1,144	224
	V	E	82	500	6,687	7,254	567
			83	125	984	993	9
			84	300	2,282	2,597	315
			85	500	1,216	1,359	143
	V	W	81	1,350	3,628	3,776	148
			82	587	4,405	4,435	30
			83	330	1,287	1,366	79
CHINA T	V	W	84	500	1,730	1,862	132
CZECHO	V	E	83	520	280	318	38
FR GERM	A	E	84	33	333	406	73
			85	510	3,706	4,055	349
			86	24,099	19,473	20,659	1,186
	V	E	84	5,071	4,828	5,192	364
			85	12,998	21,810	22,719	909
			86	126,096	88,621	90,967	2,346
	V	W	81	601	692	903	211
			82	1,239	1,388	1,790	402
			83	6,191	3,510	4,202	692
			84	1,001	1,025	1,410	385
			86	1,001	1,136	1,327	191
FRANCE	O	W	81	22	548	699	151
	V	E	81	486	1,555	1,633	78
			84	694	2,070	2,189	119
			86	380	2,905	2,935	30
	V	W	83	211	1,026	1,133	107
HG KONG	A	E	82	179	2,092	2,355	263
	V	E	83	1,850	958	1,124	166
	V	W	83	125	462	481	19
INDNSIA	A	W	83	120	285	327	42
IRAN	V	E	83	14,550	12,439	14,075	1,636
ISRAEL	O	E	83	440	2,454	2,595	141
JAPAN	A	W	83	88	350	700	350
KOR REP	V	E	83	600	1,922	2,010	88
MEXICO	A	E	83	88	281	335	54
	O	E	85	13,651	3,456	3,456	
N ZEAL	A	E	85	50	1,425	2,875	1,450
	A	W	85	4,926	12,007	18,212	6,205
NETHLDS	A	E	86	15,500	5,502	6,107	605
PAKISTN	N	E	82	993	995	1,206	211
	V	E	85	1,653	1,200	1,560	360
	V	W	82	573	325	389	64
			83	1,279	435	710	275
PHIL R	V	W	81	500	560	670	110
PORTUGL	V	E	82	6,063	3,174	4,090	916
			83	8,377	3,844	4,806	962
	V	W	85	4,000	2,513	3,080	567
ROMANIA	V	E	84	2,206	1,291	1,502	211
SPAIN	V	E	82	87,302	12,962	16,766	3,804
SWITZLD	A	E	84	12,100	3,538	4,841	1,303
TURKEY	V	E	82	7,487	7,622	8,196	574
			83	11,484	6,358	7,564	1,206
			84	14,014	8,700	9,642	942

Product / TSUSA commodity number, description, and unit of quantity Country	Mode	Reg	Yr	Quantity	F.A.S.	C.I.F.	Charges
			86	2,575	1,560	1,753	193
	V	W	84	15,432	8,620	10,384	1,764
U KING	V	E	82	106	883	914	31
			83	42	265	284	19
YUGOSLV	V	E	83	7,058	5,111	5,799	688
	V	W	84	322	548	628	80

Fruit, flour
1520500 FRUIT FLR NT BANANA PLANTAIN (LB)

Country	Mode	Reg	Yr	Quantity	F.A.S.	C.I.F.	Charges
TOTAL			81	5,105,627	1,213,390	1,552,584	339,194
			82	4,031,879	869,854	1,125,892	256,038
			83	4,863,779	1,131,579	1,390,588	259,009
			84	4,262,178	1,118,917	1,381,850	262,933
			85	3,331,390	1,031,448	1,264,601	233,153
			86	2,819,440	742,696	918,662	175,966
BRAZIL	V	E	83	10,128	23,886	29,857	5,971
			84	26,832	49,402	55,304	5,902
			85	49,769	170,453	185,594	15,141
CANADA	O	E	83	950	5,000	5,000	
CHINA M	V	E	83	9,406	8,418	9,252	834
	V	W	83	11,613	7,675	8,489	814
CHINA T	V	E	86	43,999	10,064	15,096	5,032
	V	W	84	713	1,528	1,666	138
CYPRUS	V	E	81	472,473	115,897	137,074	21,177
			82	1,401,700	303,561	375,632	72,071
			83	2,013,250	428,982	513,514	84,532
			84	1,437,850	320,610	372,251	51,641
			85	1,147,405	245,014	293,128	48,114
			86	1,616,556	379,169	460,609	81,440
	V	W	81	657,800	138,138	186,782	48,644
			82	94,000	19,740	26,566	6,826
			84	60,000	14,520	20,159	5,639
			85	171,750	38,943	48,289	9,346
DENMARK	N	E	84	165	2,513	2,784	271
	V	E	86	660	7,548	8,373	825
FR GERM	A	E	82	182	2,717	2,840	123
	O	E	83	1	572	652	80
	V	E	83	47,000	12,455	15,215	2,760
			85	2,750	5,009	6,325	1,316
			86	1,828	2,715	3,898	1,183
	V	W	82	754	1,310	1,435	125
FRANCE	A	W	84	24	501	558	57
	O	E	81	11,023	5,488	5,603	115
			85	4,401	10,668	12,544	1,876
			86	1,461	3,905	4,041	136
	V	E	81	11,023	5,488	5,603	115
			85	11,023	23,570	24,401	831
			86	398	1,177	1,260	83
	V	W	81	17	254	270	16
			82	33	547	573	26
			83	64	846	909	63
GREECE	V	E	81	512,750	124,696	150,943	26,247
			82	214,500	39,944	53,502	13,558
			83	612,130	136,575	167,808	31,233
			84	260,400	61,762	75,423	13,661
			85	306,600	51,708	70,182	18,474
HG KONG	V	W	84	250	513	557	44
INDIA	A	E	84	2,051	8,899	11,298	2,399
			85	8,914	12,813	17,473	4,660
	N	E	84	2,975	1,868	2,236	368
	O	E	83	396	596	681	85
	V	E	81	4,635	3,554	4,208	654
			82	3,213	3,275	3,826	551
			83	14,536	11,598	13,132	1,534
			84	9,921	4,255	5,200	945
			85	6,219	9,982	10,904	922
			86	3,516	3,558	4,063	505
	V	W	81	770	581	666	85
			82	46,872	13,768	17,188	3,420
			83	4,304	5,142	5,723	581
			84	1,554	5,920	7,811	1,891
			85	1,371	7,296	7,669	373
			86	8,234	7,470	8,363	893
IRELAND	V	W	81	44,092	10,502	13,553	3,051
ISRAEL	V	E	83	2,728	6,073	6,536	463
			85	2,205	3,723	4,294	571
	V	W	86	57,250	12,881	16,661	3,780
ITALY	A	E	83	276	312	312	
	V	E	81	1,839,505	406,949	531,927	124,978
			82	798,726	158,943	213,068	54,125
			83	767,135	153,442	194,371	40,929
			84	959,965	192,475	251,805	59,330

Product
TSUSA commodity number, description, and unit of quantity

Country	Mode	Reg	Yr	Quantity	F.A.S.	C.I.F.	Charges
			85	790,815	166,614	222,224	55,610
			86	200,861	41,168	52,803	11,635
	V	W	82	27,500	7,655	10,872	3,217
			83	75,001	15,504	22,065	6,561
			84	75,601	15,445	23,524	8,079
NETHLDS	A	E	86	716	2,234	3,006	772
	V	E	85	264	3,249	3,349	100
PHIL R	V	W	81	234	645	675	30
			82	2,025	1,093	1,256	163
PORTUGL	V	E	82	4,960	2,788	3,294	506
SPAIN	N	W	83	589,502	127,072	164,063	36,991
	V	E	81	443,028	103,975	133,068	29,093
			82	117,023	24,686	33,086	8,400
			83	358,251	84,066	104,145	20,079
			84	508,155	112,215	151,687	39,472
			85	110,592	23,309	32,597	9,288
			86	216,280	44,353	54,452	10,099
	V	W	81	1,105,087	261,491	345,589	84,098
			82	1,315,111	275,834	366,754	90,920
			83	334,875	77,880	99,039	21,159
			84	851,934	178,387	234,964	56,577
			85	649,733	121,757	171,678	49,921
			86	576,319	111,517	158,243	46,726
SWEDEN	O	E	85	9,460	22,218	27,321	5,103
SWITZLD	A	E	83	220	1,308	1,715	407
			84	27,623	67,755	79,463	11,708
			85	16,869	39,151	45,759	6,608
			86	8,895	24,409	29,289	4,880
	A	W	84	110	583	816	233
	N	E	82	5,280	13,993	16,000	2,007
			83	12,013	24,177	28,110	3,933
			84	7,645	25,592	26,457	865
			85	41,250	75,971	80,870	4,899
	O	E	81	220	518	602	84
			86	16,526	38,132	40,507	2,375
	V	E	81	2,249	34,794	35,460	666
			84	8,981	17,603	18,825	1,222
			86	28,022	50,121	54,203	4,082
	V	W	84	19,250	35,953	38,372	2,419
THAILND	V	W	81	721	420	561	141
			86	37,919	2,275	3,795	1,520
U KING	O	E	84	179	618	690	72

Fruit, fresh

1473300 CITRUS FRUIT, FRESH, NSPF (LB)

Country	Mode	Reg	Yr	Quantity	F.A.S.	C.I.F.	Charges
TOTAL			81	115,523	19,224	29,559	10,335
			82	854,975	111,761	213,126	101,365
			83	1,121,223	290,405	431,395	140,990
			84	884,754	211,274	302,954	91,680
			85	1,222,713	280,005	389,714	109,709
			86	2,675,083	561,556	763,204	201,648
BAHAMAS	V	E	85	63,650	2,850	3,304	454
			86	236,210	8,970	11,134	2,164
C RICA	V	E	81	12,346	1,292	1,720	428
CHILE	A	E	83	20,463	5,500	6,458	958
			84	1,878	607	1,800	1,193
			85	13,811	7,634	18,629	10,995
	O	E	85	4,920	2,624	2,624	
	V	W	84	20,741	5,880	8,100	2,220
			86	1,130,124	229,845	326,462	96,617
DOM REP	A	E	81	2,700	270	558	288
			84	14,822	1,835	3,307	1,472
	N	E	84	35,970	8,174	11,300	3,126
	V	E	82	30,940	2,730	6,321	3,591
			83	10,400	2,755	3,681	926
			85	1,080	2,710	2,813	103
			86	58,350	2,580	5,943	3,363
FRANCE	A	E	81	51	351	391	40
HAITI	A	E	85	38,210	7,247	12,305	5,058
JAMAICA	V	E	81	92,140	8,496	12,918	4,422
			82	821,050	103,631	199,590	95,959
			83	1,089,589	281,449	420,043	138,594
			84	795,336	190,136	269,807	79,671
			85	1,089,290	244,785	331,432	86,647
			86	1,247,640	316,966	416,242	99,276
JAPAN	A	E	84	110	280	1,208	928
	V	W	84	164	1,225	1,285	60
MEXICO	A	W	84	14,109	2,400	4,448	2,048
N ZEAL	A	E	82	2,985	5,400	7,215	1,815
	A	W	81	8,286	8,815	13,972	5,157
			83	771	701	1,213	512
			84	1,624	737	1,699	962

Product
TSUSA commodity number, description, and unit of quantity

Country	Mode	Reg	Yr	Quantity	F.A.S.	C.I.F.	Charges
			85	9,526	9,801	14,790	4,989
PERU	V	E	86	2,759	3,195	3,423	228
SWITZLD	A	E	85	2,226	2,354	3,817	1,463

1483000 MELONS NES DEC 1 TO MAY 31 (LB)

Country	Mode	Reg	Yr	Quantity	F.A.S.	C.I.F.	Charges
TOTAL			81	19,202,174	2,895,257	3,379,126	483,869
			82	56,165,822	7,929,735	9,979,897	2,050,162
			83	54,653,438	6,700,665	9,135,073	2,434,408
			84	96,173,896	11,720,796	15,513,659	3,792,863
			85	94,188,981	11,959,561	16,235,255	4,275,694
			86	135,270,662	18,912,929	26,283,672	7,370,743
ANTIGUA	A	E	86	8,818	2,000	2,000	
BAHAMAS	V	E	84	98,336	10,904	22,996	12,092
BELGIUM	A	E	84	194	480	543	63
BRAZIL	V	E	84	327,686	88,150	145,412	57,262
			85	1,794,597	262,389	519,029	256,640
			86	163,661	29,405	55,941	26,536
C RICA	V	E	81	30,000	6,250	9,364	3,114
			82	1,220,991	323,900	431,953	108,053
			83	762,953	188,236	261,073	72,837
			84	1,202,207	338,348	433,615	95,267
			85	1,731,401	235,153	323,004	87,851
			86	741,149	123,365	183,747	60,382
	V	W	83	105,900	28,614	40,016	11,402
			84	45,494	19,602	24,514	4,912
CANADA	A	E	85	25,847	2,534	5,189	2,655
	O	E	85	82,420	6,498	6,498	
			86	64,800	4,131	4,131	
	O	W	83	76,020	21,720	21,720	
CHILE	N	E	84	13,642,292	2,004,031	3,135,182	1,131,151
	N	W	84	3,411,762	560,177	800,603	240,426
	O	E	82	19,712	5,632	7,477	1,845
	V	E	81	461,053	62,467	110,365	47,898
			82	3,527,017	682,149	981,776	299,627
			83	9,760,202	1,874,937	2,726,074	851,137
			84	531,439	76,124	129,258	53,134
			85	9,082,227	1,225,529	2,016,241	790,712
			86	8,061,487	1,156,767	2,086,021	929,254
	V	W	83	1,652,858	306,336	486,412	180,076
			84	75,822	9,712	17,867	8,155
			85	1,806,434	215,887	444,805	228,918
			86	2,240,543	303,512	580,447	276,935
CHINA M	V	W	83	1,425	675	776	101
			84	2,850	890	996	106
COLOMB	A	E	85	9,717	3,270	6,457	3,187
	N	E	86	164,775	19,338	23,650	4,312
	V	E	82	154,900	38,725	59,618	20,893
			85	30,874	6,712	11,572	4,860
DOM REP	A	E	82	1,600	275	485	210
			83	17,520	2,455	4,206	1,751
			84	11,680	1,216	2,685	1,469
			85	6,026	1,572	2,882	1,310
	N	E	82	746,321	37,668	80,999	43,331
			84	1,392,993	130,037	227,979	97,942
			85	231,725	23,296	44,028	20,732
			86	2,376,385	250,402	445,798	195,396
	V	E	82	177,060	16,095	26,119	10,024
			83	620,374	74,702	110,144	35,442
			84	706,904	101,553	143,817	42,264
			85	1,509,122	138,850	265,788	126,938
			86	6,463,100	537,511	999,910	462,399
ECUADOR	A	E	84	57,740	11,810	23,141	11,331
	N	E	84	879,773	116,743	194,807	78,064
	V	E	81	301,992	34,965	61,064	26,099
			82	4,462,460	451,943	882,691	430,748
			83	1,194,293	128,266	277,911	149,645
			84	1,761,973	163,255	371,252	207,997
			85	4,115,622	514,970	986,838	471,868
			86	3,866,869	524,139	843,281	319,142
F W IND	A	E	84	185	581	770	189
FRANCE	A	E	81	380	1,071	1,211	140
			82	1,396	4,823	5,698	875
			83	712	2,012	2,386	374
			84	3,496	5,552	7,383	1,831
	O	E	85	35,430	5,964	5,964	
GUATMAL	N	E	81	4,607,172	478,616	817,502	338,886
			86	20,603,079	2,266,422	3,915,191	1,648,769
	O	E	84	233,945	16,746	24,506	7,760
			85	454,020	19,931	19,931	
			86	279,370	20,673	20,673	
	V	E	81	38,532	3,705	6,666	2,961
			82	8,740,335	934,560	1,570,219	635,659
			83	7,780,876	720,260	1,249,792	529,532
			84	17,735,373	1,310,531	2,071,385	760,854

Product TSUSA commodity number, description, and unit of quantity Country	Mode	Reg	Yr	Quantity	F.A.S.	C.I.F.	Charges
			85	10,807,644	1,126,706	1,919,935	793,229
			86	6,546,912	756,629	1,235,117	478,488
	V	W	81	64,526	19,290	24,165	4,875
			82	220,107	34,979	53,079	18,100
			85	103,968	6,240	16,987	10,747
			86	186,313	26,900	46,168	19,268
HAITI	A	E	82	10,389	2,160	3,395	1,235
			84	81,543	18,032	30,348	12,316
			86	15,000	2,850	5,627	2,777
	V	E	86	27,600	6,900	6,900	
HG KONG	V	W	82	1,000	779	806	27
HONDURA	N	E	82	1,025,680	166,962	265,219	98,257
			86	3,954,965	505,869	861,619	355,750
	V	E	82	185,610	25,703	27,753	2,050
			83	1,385,039	184,374	339,393	155,019
			84	3,328,692	491,409	597,470	106,061
			85	1,335,127	212,272	268,080	55,808
			86	780,432	101,808	148,436	46,628
ISRAEL	A	E	82	524	280	546	266
			84	18,288	4,374	19,256	14,882
			85	12,538	3,309	33,398	30,089
			86	11,991	3,267	18,290	15,023
	N	E	84	40,358	7,487	11,970	4,483
ITALY	N	E	83	15,742	2,809	7,977	5,168
JAMAICA	A	E	84	123,657	146,790	191,066	44,276
			86	21,981	5,833	9,531	3,698
	N	E	84	457,309	43,301	65,508	22,207
			85	1,260,397	650,046	847,111	197,065
			86	2,232,709	446,548	583,192	136,644
	V	E	83	27,600	2,760	4,063	1,303
			84	36,453	35,013	40,920	5,907
			85	36,667	21,245	31,928	10,683
JAPAN	V	W	83	240	471	497	26
KENYA	A	E	86	2,242	5,851	6,560	709
KIRIBAT	V	E	86	45,064	2,417	8,457	6,040
MEXICO	A	E	85	19,467	4,326	9,229	4,903
	O	E	81	11,478,586	1,769,372	1,769,372	
			82	29,271,326	3,371,094	3,371,094	
			83	24,010,627	1,546,517	1,546,517	
			84	35,238,508	2,560,234	2,560,234	
			85	40,665,191	3,325,795	3,325,799	4
			86	34,169,128	2,698,109	2,698,109	
	O	W	81	1,770,474	380,321	380,321	
			82	4,360,987	710,805	710,805	
			83	3,101,097	328,894	328,894	
			84	7,447,375	1,456,829	1,456,829	
			85	7,428,752	1,330,686	1,330,686	
			86	21,745,853	4,048,087	4,048,088	1
MOZAMBQ	O	W	86	10,580	2,673	2,673	
N ZEAL	A	E	84	1,937	3,820	6,048	2,228
			86	3,455	3,031	6,543	3,512
	A	H	86	7,937	8,461	15,462	7,001
	A	W	82	3,778	3,765	5,324	1,559
			83	9,101	9,327	17,206	7,879
			84	4,832	6,059	9,225	3,166
			85	2,384	2,638	4,438	1,800
			86	5,937	11,804	18,552	6,748
NETHLDS	A	E	82	136	863	949	86
			83	414	1,057	1,357	300
NICARAG	A	E	81	7,500	750	1,531	781
	V	E	81	31,625	2,732	5,816	3,084
NORWAY	A	E	85	15,000	3,242	5,429	2,187
PANAMA	A	E	85	22,367	7,050	9,569	2,519
			86	18,148	5,933	8,094	2,161
	N	E	83	321,407	72,659	103,063	30,404
			85	1,183,673	298,871	411,790	112,919
			86	1,673,428	588,874	720,355	131,481
	N	W	84	285,728	84,069	107,894	23,825
			86	984,898	270,341	351,566	81,225
	V	E	84	362,875	95,114	120,910	25,796
			85	51,225	8,816	12,820	4,004
			86	881,588	233,157	303,175	70,018
	V	W	84	94,378	25,901	33,359	7,458
			85	8,000	3,160	4,104	944
			86	724,258	195,983	252,917	56,934
PERU	V	E	85	88,661	14,624	31,816	17,192
PHIL R	V	W	83	400	350	383	33
SALVADR	O	E	85	69,400	5,500	5,500	
			86	231,000	14,401	14,401	
	O	W	83	40,320	11,520	11,520	
	V	E	83	1,793,835	278,950	424,874	145,924
			84	3,705,810	475,068	815,195	340,127
			85	6,157,335	587,954	1,039,836	451,882
			86	9,591,638	1,343,349	2,234,085	890,736
	V	W	83	306,478	41,175	74,916	33,741

Product TSUSA commodity number, description, and unit of quantity Country	Mode	Reg	Yr	Quantity	F.A.S.	C.I.F.	Charges
			84	564,515	61,577	121,927	60,350
			85	92,614	12,705	22,000	9,295
			86	52,910	7,200	13,650	6,450
SENEGAL	A	E	82	44	256	356	100
			84	354	940	1,188	248
SPAIN	N	E	84	680,588	150,268	253,134	102,866
	V	E	81	410,334	135,718	191,749	56,031
			82	202,903	50,034	78,568	28,534
			83	221,058	47,834	70,577	22,743
			85	1,008,786	211,601	272,601	61,000
			86	253,082	53,590	76,919	23,329
THAILND	V	E	84	2,565	990	1,059	69
	V	W	83	5,140	1,943	2,174	231
U KING	O	E	83	1,100	1,234	1,357	123
VENEZ	A	E	82	1,831,546	1,066,285	1,414,968	348,683
			83	1,440,707	820,578	1,019,795	199,217
			84	1,575,987	1,087,079	1,291,408	204,329
			85	154,852	58,763	75,820	17,057
			86	21,206	6,600	9,993	3,393
	N	E	85	2,749,471	1,401,457	1,898,153	496,696
			86	3,988,370	1,635,789	2,410,692	774,903
	V	E	86	2,048,001	683,010	1,007,711	324,701

1483200 MELONS NSPF, FRESH 6/1-11/30 (LB)

Country	Mode	Reg	Yr	Quantity	F.A.S.	C.I.F.	Charges
TOTAL			81	121,340	33,180	48,535	15,355
			82	348,062	70,861	101,793	30,932
			83	237,766	42,255	64,127	21,872
			84	1,959,000	193,834	230,354	36,520
			85	4,838,621	337,652	348,788	11,136
			86	8,455,470	910,261	1,185,665	275,404
ANTIGUA	V	E	86	315,000	61,141	80,981	19,840
BELGIUM	A	E	84	1,074	558	856	298
BRAZIL	A	E	84	6,460	1,365	4,074	2,709
	V	E	86	31,879	2,892	3,042	150
CANADA	O	E	82	1,460	292	292	
			85	3,780	1,134	1,134	
			86	34,848	6,727	6,727	
DOM REP	N	E	84	23,200	4,047	5,592	1,545
			85	27,080	2,708	6,238	3,530
	V	E	82	26,400	1,320	2,528	1,208
			83	29,412	1,596	3,038	1,442
			84	16,112	4,677	5,305	628
			86	28,525	13,040	14,523	1,483
ECUADOR	V	E	86	1,386,256	135,189	175,152	39,963
FR GERM	V	E	82	1	1,500	2,449	949
FRANCE	A	E	81	309	508	589	81
			82	3,753	5,079	6,134	1,055
			83	11,239	13,653	18,405	4,752
			84	17,950	16,493	24,523	8,030
			85	701	1,021	1,463	442
			86	2,656	1,236	2,451	1,215
	A	W	82	326	265	413	148
	O	E	81	137	538	538	
GREECE	A	E	84	1,509	1,000	2,011	1,011
GUATMAL	A	E	82	3,044	457	557	100
	V	E	83	151,683	21,855	37,086	15,231
			84	53,440	10,688	13,498	2,810
			86	2,866,486	303,982	481,235	177,253
HONDURA	V	E	85	17,975	2,356	3,032	676
ISRAEL	A	E	84	1,507	2,589	3,252	663
			86	29,839	6,213	6,718	505
	V	E	82	33,422	4,548	9,048	4,500
ITALY	A	E	83	1,313	1,199	1,616	417
JAMAICA	N	E	86	116,000	33,618	45,487	11,869
	V	E	81	16,000	2,000	3,385	1,385
			84	40,000	6,544	9,646	3,102
			85	115,034	2,673	2,755	82
JAPAN	V	W	83	131	416	446	30
MEXICO	O	E	82	54,278	4,973	4,973	
			83	24,980	1,412	1,412	
			84	293,140	17,792	17,792	
			85	801,970	54,677	54,677	
			86	883,700	49,925	49,925	
	O	W	82	70,080	6,675	6,675	
			83	19,008	2,124	2,124	
			84	1,434,918	115,467	115,467	
			85	3,856,241	271,826	271,826	
			86	2,389,067	238,721	238,721	
N ZEAL	A	H	86	695	1,424	2,382	958
	A	W	86	374	1,050	1,263	213
NETHLDS	A	E	82	1,031	1,434	1,605	171
			84	3,805	2,307	3,647	1,340
PANAMA	A	E	86	890	1,706	2,000	294
	V	E	86	5,376	3,360	3,948	588

Product
TSUSA commodity number, description, and unit of quantity

Country	Mode	Reg	Yr	Quantity	F.A.S.	C.I.F.	Charges
SALVADR	V	E	86	242,275	29,073	31,223	2,150
SPAIN	A	E	85	15,840	1,257	7,663	6,406
	N	E	84	55,391	5,127	16,511	11,384
	V	E	81	104,894	30,134	44,023	13,889
			82	154,267	44,318	67,119	22,801
			86	121,604	20,964	39,887	18,923
VENEZ	A	E	84	10,494	5,180	8,180	3,000

1495000 FRUITS, NSPF, FRESH (LB)

Country	Mode	Reg	Yr	Quantity	F.A.S.	C.I.F.	Charges
TOTAL			81	7,098,321	1,796,060	1,965,122	169,062
			82	7,463,202	1,939,873	2,101,003	161,130
			83	8,811,181	2,122,788	2,432,422	309,634
			84	12,210,127	2,543,002	3,065,652	522,650
			85	9,968,243	2,475,110	3,192,642	717,532
			86	13,598,943	4,106,460	4,942,502	836,042
ARGENT	A	E	84	39,204	15,261	43,945	28,684
			85	5,617	2,548	6,664	4,116
AUSTRAL	A	E	83	3,000	4,941	8,203	3,262
BELGIUM	A	W	83	1,083	1,174	1,692	518
			85	1,984	4,140	4,246	106
C RICA	A	E	84	1,102	863	1,122	259
	A	W	86	8,500	2,875	5,162	2,287
CANADA	A	W	85	591	1,233	1,669	436
			86	580	1,456	1,818	362
	O	E	81	180,370	19,747	19,747	
			83	19,270	5,242	5,242	
			84	15,040	3,960	3,960	
			85	94,274	30,764	30,764	
			86	51,980	7,380	7,380	
	O	W	81	297,704	37,001	37,001	
CHILE	A	E	81	14,025	5,300	6,014	714
			82	21,560	9,543	18,492	8,949
			83	183,363	100,757	200,423	99,666
			84	120,463	38,778	110,193	71,415
			85	388,446	181,385	441,273	259,888
			86	64,919	24,540	55,558	31,018
	N	E	84	369,364	148,517	278,792	130,275
	N	W	86	559,322	165,033	235,262	70,229
	O	W	81	89,604	57,397	57,397	
			84	1,312	680	1,598	918
	V	E	84	131,378	45,877	64,552	18,675
			85	417,474	106,907	153,946	47,039
			86	491,425	214,928	316,455	101,527
	V	W	81	132,930	46,263	70,275	24,012
			83	118,791	27,163	40,573	13,410
			84	49,728	16,838	23,342	6,504
			85	384,735	107,365	150,184	42,819
CHINA M	V	E	81	750	315	364	49
	V	W	84	750	796	826	30
			85	6,358	6,045	6,545	500
			86	5,600	3,713	3,899	186
CHINA T	O	E	84	26,905	9,080	9,080	
	V	W	83	2,249	1,280	1,447	167
			84	1,600	1,235	1,423	188
COLOMB	A	E	86	551	1,062	1,259	197
DOM REP	A	E	81	18,401	1,818	3,066	1,248
			82	99,545	10,045	19,726	9,681
			83	198,173	21,113	59,090	37,977
			84	45,856	5,196	10,781	5,585
			85	24,223	4,464	9,159	4,695
			86	3,320	2,795	3,281	486
	N	E	81	456,032	50,273	127,546	77,273
			82	291,882	33,652	92,617	58,965
			84	342,260	50,430	114,399	63,969
	V	E	81	3,200	500	675	175
			82	4,050	675	935	260
			85	10,245	2,920	3,558	638
			86	69,300	18,414	23,480	5,066
ECUADOR	V	E	86	77,005	8,194	12,974	4,780
FRANCE	A	E	81	218	3,179	3,563	384
			82	3,435	6,214	7,907	1,693
			84	4,071	5,390	7,048	1,658
	A	W	83	340	625	825	200
	O	W	85	17,600	2,319	2,319	
GUATMAL	A	E	84	16,430	31,180	34,393	3,213
	V	E	82	34,800	1,050	3,111	2,061
			83	38,800	1,334	3,766	2,432
	V	W	86	35,000	2,450	2,513	63
HAITI	A	E	81	114,535	15,797	27,557	11,760
			83	58,867	8,409	15,113	6,704
			84	28,642	2,981	6,943	3,962
			85	10,095	2,307	4,251	1,944
			86	14,287	3,193	4,552	1,359
	N	E	82	47,848	9,521	16,097	6,576
			84	127,499	15,939	31,813	15,874
			86	48,440	9,420	16,262	6,842
HG KONG	A	E	86	9,487	9,816	10,386	570
	A	W	86	362	1,145	1,499	354
	V	E	81	533	943	1,000	57
	V	W	84	3,200	3,590	3,783	193
HONDURA	A	E	83	16,371	5,037	6,919	1,882
ISRAEL	A	E	85	7,914	2,872	4,732	1,860
	N	E	85	418,731	93,426	220,488	127,062
			86	108,111	43,173	99,518	56,345
ITALY	A	W	82	948	1,244	1,777	533
	N	E	86	31,305	16,745	27,131	10,386
JAMAICA	A	E	81	5,570	2,194	3,340	1,146
			83	25,149	4,539	6,484	1,945
			86	5,048	2,798	3,126	328
MEXICO	A	E	83	23,338	7,738	13,123	5,385
			84	13,189	4,038	5,981	1,943
			85	19,712	5,376	8,652	3,276
			86	31,586	7,050	11,489	4,439
	A	W	84	32,118	5,670	9,772	4,102
			85	14,160	4,155	6,343	2,188
			86	19,676	9,335	13,482	4,147
	O	E	81	72,104	7,997	7,997	
			82	55,872	6,554	6,554	
			83	522,374	53,963	53,963	
			84	2,260,299	214,099	214,099	
			85	637,457	103,336	103,336	
			86	928,478	198,827	198,827	
	O	W	81	5,525,318	1,402,026	1,402,026	
			82	6,738,270	1,635,254	1,636,784	1,530
			83	7,295,086	1,517,030	1,517,030	
			84	8,278,071	1,521,453	1,521,453	
			85	7,043,018	1,119,651	1,119,661	10
			86	10,045,374	1,836,080	1,836,082	2
	V	E	83	5,060	2,822	3,351	529
MONSRAT	O	W	86	7,050	1,270	1,270	
N ZEAL	A	E	81	19,577	20,194	32,441	12,247
			82	57,683	63,928	86,326	22,398
			83	40,822	52,081	78,604	26,523
			84	58,694	70,644	119,136	48,492
			85	9,534	11,353	21,058	9,705
			86	89,966	34,177	70,121	35,944
	A	H	82	1,669	2,997	4,286	1,289
			83	1,874	4,037	5,121	1,084
			85	1,414	2,410	4,055	1,645
			86	2,095	4,077	6,370	2,293
	A	W	81	75,363	82,006	104,046	22,040
			82	76,825	102,734	138,729	35,995
			83	97,498	121,110	182,019	60,909
			84	24,834	32,923	55,686	22,763
			85	4,625	5,851	7,891	2,040
			86	526,332	854,991	1,265,752	410,761
	N	E	81	46,788	19,758	24,333	4,575
	N	W	83	6,230	7,627	11,269	3,642
			84	123,623	157,994	222,855	64,861
			85	204,647	313,989	462,936	148,947
	O	E	85	63,775	30,764	30,764	
			86	25,344	18,432	18,432	
	O	W	84	697	1,894	1,894	
			86	1,200	4,200	4,200	
	V	E	81	15,660	6,776	13,155	6,379
			83	105,344	82,279	102,606	20,327
	V	W	81	20,004	7,066	12,625	5,559
NETHLDS	A	E	84	1,904	2,175	2,879	704
			86	21,781	13,284	29,295	16,011
	A	W	84	1,985	3,291	3,714	423
			86	24,774	24,655	44,102	19,447
PHIL R	A	E	82	1,112	1,291	3,664	2,373
	V	E	83	1,200	728	886	158
	V	W	82	1,134	1,565	1,783	218
			83	10,832	8,244	9,291	1,047
			84	540	251	287	36
			86	1,960	1,070	1,214	144
SALVADR	A	W	84	17,124	5,825	15,574	9,749
SINGAPR	V	E	82	1,216	995	1,103	108
	V	W	83	4,623	2,010	2,163	153
SWITZLD	A	E	85	19,081	5,284	10,648	5,364
			86	10,148	5,683	7,874	2,191
THAILND	A	E	81	128	966	1,121	155
	N	E	86	53,523	89,126	98,726	9,600
	N	W	82	10,363	16,701	22,147	5,446
			83	25,985	73,430	94,628	21,198
			84	51,968	102,004	116,550	14,546
			85	126,272	224,938	261,746	36,808
			86	215,115	460,465	498,683	38,218

Product TSUSA commodity number, description, and unit of quantity Country	Mode	Reg	Yr	Quantity	F.A.S.	C.I.F.	Charges
	V	E	81	976	1,385	1,518	133
			82	481	1,920	2,142	222
			83	1,495	1,075	1,279	204
			84	7,682	8,796	10,907	2,111
			85	25,056	81,658	95,699	14,041
	V	W	81	7,820	6,393	7,185	792
			82	14,509	33,990	36,823	2,833
			83	3,964	7,000	7,312	312
			84	12,595	15,354	16,872	1,518
			85	11,205	17,650	20,055	2,405
			86	9,999	4,608	5,068	460
U KING	A	W	81	711	766	1,130	364

Fruit, fresh or in brine
1466200 BERRIES NSPF FRSH O IN BRNE (LB)

Country	Mode	Reg	Yr	Quantity	F.A.S.	C.I.F.	Charges
TOTAL			81	16,205,304	4,414,368	4,436,426	22,058
			82	14,628,999	4,100,334	4,121,923	21,589
			83	19,073,760	5,606,703	5,699,314	92,611
			84	13,493,123	4,201,822	4,359,264	157,442
			85	17,560,521	5,052,605	5,181,228	128,623
			86	17,628,371	5,113,793	5,225,246	111,453
ARGENT	A	E	84	954	1,260	2,163	903
AUSTRAL	V	E	85	7,511	3,004	3,181	177
AUSTRIA	A	W	84	141	842	1,112	270
BELGIUM	V	E	84	463	603	660	57
CANADA	A	W	85	264	1,208	1,458	250
			86	542	1,852	2,313	461
	O	E	84	7,325	2,842	2,842	
			85	45,000	15,714	15,714	
	O	W	81	16,158,998	4,344,601	4,344,601	
			82	14,571,136	4,021,647	4,021,648	1
			83	18,751,121	5,361,027	5,361,027	
			84	13,276,298	3,869,012	3,869,012	
			85	17,221,802	4,669,202	4,669,202	
			86	17,486,985	4,748,127	4,748,127	
CHILE	A	E	81	4,466	2,805	3,114	309
			82	2,269	2,716	4,195	1,479
			83	37,777	25,135	42,734	17,599
			84	114,549	110,149	200,101	89,952
			85	8,592	8,552	12,731	4,179
			86	26,979	45,180	75,723	30,543
	A	W	81	419	2,160	3,043	883
			83	1,243	1,410	2,347	937
			85	1,105	3,400	4,016	616
	N	E	85	52,696	27,658	41,967	14,309
CHINA M	V	E	83	3,000	616	668	52
	V	W	81	188	1,245	1,302	57
			82	750	6,299	6,551	252
CHINA T	V	E	84	10,612	5,400	5,894	494
COLOMB	A	E	82	9,219	12,680	14,823	2,143
			83	7,089	4,306	7,258	2,952
			84	378	783	1,313	530
			85	622	2,052	2,752	700
DENMARK	A	W	86	480	1,344	1,786	442
	V	W	85	761	1,934	2,146	212
DOM REP	V	E	83	2,650	265	428	163
ECUADOR	A	E	83	1,102	500	650	150
FR GERM	O	E	83	2,220	2,164	2,252	88
	V	E	83	9,342	3,793	4,097	304
			85	4,400	5,738	6,381	643
FRANCE	V	E	84	2,551	3,372	3,589	217
			85	1,369	1,727	1,965	238
GUATMAL	A	E	84	900	840	1,455	615
HAITI	A	E	83	87,925	10,350	18,724	8,374
INDIA	V	E	84	1,125	591	843	252
			85	2,812	1,362	1,739	377
	V	W	84	456	316	437	121
ITALY	V	E	83	3,042	3,902	4,299	397
			85	7,804	9,478	10,528	1,050
			86	11,111	15,523	16,273	750
N ZEAL	A	E	81	2,508	5,551	6,518	967
			82	4,372	8,238	10,718	2,480
			83	8,936	19,719	28,050	8,331
			84	13,193	30,935	43,487	12,552
			86	16,460	14,660	26,485	11,825
	A	H	82	319	725	850	125
			84	2,262	5,972	8,009	2,037
			86	530	3,658	4,350	692
	A	W	81	20,457	37,885	51,790	13,905
			82	29,563	38,793	52,673	13,880
			83	100,898	139,972	183,762	43,790
			84	57,492	165,644	214,767	49,123

Product TSUSA commodity number, description, and unit of quantity Country	Mode	Reg	Yr	Quantity	F.A.S.	C.I.F.	Charges
			85	87,243	256,943	340,454	83,511
			86	74,136	267,959	332,541	64,582
	N	W	81	18,268	20,121	26,058	5,937
	O	W	82	118	288	288	
			83	155	679	679	
	V	E	83	32,619	18,230	25,012	6,782
			85	106,660	34,040	51,744	17,704
NETHLDS	A	E	83	158	444	617	173
SEYCHEL	A	E	85	1,340	3,402	6,609	3,207
SINGAPR	V	E	83	1,510	1,100	1,374	274
SWEDEN	V	W	85	698	1,163	1,280	117
THAILND	O	W	84	525	438	465	27
	V	E	82	10,052	7,975	9,130	1,155
			83	20,995	11,880	13,026	1,146
			84	3,000	1,800	2,041	241
	V	W	82	1,201	973	1,047	74
TURKEY	V	E	86	10,534	11,290	12,448	1,158
U KING	O	E	84	899	1,023	1,074	51
VENEZ	A	E	83	1,978	1,211	2,310	1,099
YUGOSLV	V	E	85	9,842	6,028	7,361	1,333
			86	614	4,200	5,200	1,000

Fruit, frozen
1467800 BERRIES, FROZEN, NSPF (LB)

Country	Mode	Reg	Yr	Quantity	F.A.S.	C.I.F.	Charges
TOTAL			82	8,405	9,673	9,758	85
			83	97,570	33,830	45,340	11,510
			84	1,476,229	472,259	569,774	97,515
			85	2,337,519	969,521	1,226,840	257,319
			86	2,153,165	1,158,063	1,395,495	237,432
BARBADO	V	E	83	20,089	9,370	10,417	1,047
CANADA	O	E	82	8,055	9,373	9,373	
			85	3,200	1,157	1,157	
			86	2,400	1,099	1,099	
	O	W	86	16,020	8,088	8,088	
CHILE	V	E	85	389,826	112,918	143,368	30,450
			86	780,927	311,188	400,664	89,476
COLOMB	A	E	82	350	300	385	85
			83	1,251	2,473	2,737	264
DOM REP	V	E	85	15,939	11,954	13,406	1,452
FRANCE	A	E	84	710	810	1,154	344
	V	E	84	42,343	17,129	27,022	9,893
GUATMAL	V	E	84	1,815	545	611	66
N ZEAL	V	E	85	129,994	50,868	69,152	18,284
			86	153,424	78,612	97,628	19,016
	V	W	83	75,556	17,963	26,066	8,103
			84	65,358	19,443	29,313	9,870
			85	201,927	104,993	128,658	23,665
			86	315,171	177,473	211,296	33,823
NETHLDS	V	E	85	37,693	15,433	19,231	3,798
REP SAF	V	W	84	798,677	214,059	219,972	5,913
SPAIN	V	E	85	30,556	6,558	7,901	1,343
SWEDEN	A	W	85	776	1,425	2,020	595
	N	W	85	2,764	2,872	3,479	607
THAILND	A	E	83	674	4,024	6,120	2,096
			84	2,022	4,878	11,844	6,966
	V	W	86	16,000	11,800	12,832	1,032
YUGOSLV	V	E	84	485,939	188,086	241,709	53,623
			85	1,359,154	597,615	752,093	154,478
			86	825,131	537,408	627,292	89,884
	V	W	84	79,365	27,309	38,149	10,840
			85	165,690	63,728	86,375	22,647
			86	44,092	32,395	36,596	4,201

Fruit, jelly or jam
1530440 BERRY NSPF JELLY, JAMS, ETC (LB)

Country	Mode	Reg	Yr	Quantity	F.A.S.	C.I.F.	Charges
TOTAL			81	1,908,377	1,916,187	2,032,850	116,668
			82	409,989	418,587	438,552	19,965
AUSTRIA	V	E	81	398	505	536	31
CANADA	O	E	81	177,485	285,775	285,770	
			82	11,936	21,057	21,057	
	O	W	81	666,081	621,542	621,542	
			82	174,806	138,271	138,271	
F W IND	A	E	81	2,756	2,828	3,659	831
	V	E	82	3,803	5,111	5,310	199
FR GERM	O	E	81	360	290	311	21
	V	E	81	11,160	10,171	10,704	533
			82	13,042	11,458	12,343	885
	V	W	81	3,352	2,188	2,692	504
FRANCE	N	E	81	174,427	193,865	215,724	21,859

Product TSUSA commodity number, description, and unit of quantity Country	Mode	Reg	Yr	Quantity	F.A.S.	C.I.F.	Charges
			82	23,278	25,680	28,354	2,674
	O	E	81	18,620	27,122	29,114	1,992
			82	4,516	6,448	6,798	350
	V	E	81	54,954	49,799	54,874	5,075
			82	21,404	25,478	27,858	2,380
	V	W	81	39,005	40,395	44,209	3,814
			82	5,829	5,685	6,204	519
GREECE	V	E	81	3,350	4,700	5,485	785
HUNGARY	V	E	81	27,778	8,711	11,025	2,314
INDIA	V	W	82	476	475	552	77
IRELAND	N	E	81	43,847	40,075	44,574	4,499
	V	E	82	2,318	2,196	2,558	362
ITALY	V	E	81	9,541	7,741	8,688	947
JAPAN	A	W	81	84	309	709	400
	V	W	81	347	615	655	40
			82	190	389	408	19
NETHLDS	V	E	82	4,956	5,666	5,857	191
NORWAY	V	E	82	567	722	767	45
	V	W	81	1,190	1,592	1,891	299
POLAND	O	E	81	24,021	9,915	12,300	2,385
	V	E	81	141,318	52,022	69,224	17,202
PORTUGL	V	E	82	1,695	8,640	8,869	229
SWITZLD	A	W	82	452	533	752	219
	O	E	81	1,301	1,012	1,074	62
			82	2,417	2,321	2,637	316
	V	E	81	102,006	98,193	108,857	10,664
			82	27,087	31,852	33,742	1,890
	V	W	81	26,515	24,304	26,721	2,417
U KING	N	E	81	222,056	280,971	302,645	21,674
			82	69,390	84,714	90,159	5,445
	O	E	81	27,916	50,231	53,615	3,384
	V	E	81	47,260	51,200	57,843	6,643
			82	17,109	19,387	21,225	1,838
	V	W	81	38,333	35,672	40,251	4,579
			82	24,718	22,504	24,831	2,327
USSR	O	E	81	5,291	1,620	2,100	480
	V	E	81	37,625	12,824	16,058	3,234

1530600 BERRY NSPF JELLY, JAMS, ETC (LB)

Country	Mode	Reg	Yr	Quantity	F.A.S.	C.I.F.	Charges
TOTAL			82	1,623,088	1,293,443	1,405,739	112,296
			83	842,800	618,261	680,622	62,361
AUSTRIA	V	E	82	1,880	2,363	2,581	218
			83	2,532	3,336	3,766	430
BELGIUM	V	E	82	9,692	7,096	8,038	942
CANADA	O	E	82	14,681	10,412	10,412	
			83	10,344	2,874	2,874	
	O	W	82	529,640	421,646	421,646	
			83	111,638	99,650	99,650	
DENMARK	V	E	82	2,562	2,376	2,801	425
FINLAND	V	E	83	12	381	451	70
FR GERM	N	E	82	6,834	5,731	7,493	1,762
	V	E	82	62,936	53,045	58,956	5,911
			83	182,675	114,861	125,550	10,689
	V	W	82	7,081	4,631	5,455	824
FRANCE	A	W	82	474	847	1,393	546
	N	E	82	71,846	77,277	85,650	8,373
			83	40,823	48,315	52,056	3,741
	N	W	82	19,818	22,184	24,698	2,514
	O	E	82	8,094	8,267	9,471	1,204
			83	7,157	10,738	12,080	1,342
	V	E	82	153,837	140,676	158,653	17,977
			83	19,840	16,797	19,032	2,235
	V	W	82	53,054	47,984	53,867	5,883
			83	95,218	75,544	85,556	10,012
HUNGARY	V	E	82	115,056	39,080	49,465	10,385
			83	128,017	43,567	54,120	10,553
IRELAND	V	E	82	2,340	2,013	2,168	155
			83	6,129	6,658	7,495	837
ITALY	N	E	82	8,393	5,923	6,870	947
	V	E	82	3,544	2,460	2,801	341
			83	1,994	1,230	1,487	257
	V	W	82	252	476	548	72
			83	108	278	294	16
NETHLDS	V	W	83	368	304	323	19
NORWAY	V	W	82	450	771	908	137
			83	939	1,434	1,554	120
POLAND	N	E	82	144,000	64,166	78,385	14,219
	O	E	82	53,510	24,170	29,262	5,092
			83	16,000	10,800	13,140	2,340
	V	E	83	48,000	22,000	26,233	4,233
PORTUGL	V	E	83	2,679	5,500	5,707	207
ROMANIA	V	E	83	9,960	4,605	5,198	593
SWITZLD	N	E	82	3,342	2,572	2,824	252
	N	W	82	5,352	7,327	8,547	1,220

Product TSUSA commodity number, description, and unit of quantity Country	Mode	Reg	Yr	Quantity	F.A.S.	C.I.F.	Charges
	V	E	82	107,751	113,211	121,998	8,787
			83	58,057	57,221	61,042	3,821
	V	W	82	6,780	6,341	7,344	1,003
			83	8,696	7,332	7,974	642
U KING	N	E	82	79,897	92,200	98,790	6,590
	N	W	83	6,770	4,981	6,477	1,496
	O	E	82	10,476	13,096	14,430	1,334
			83	180	274	349	75
	O	W	82	420	799	799	
	V	E	82	55,962	74,323	80,539	6,216
			83	70,680	69,885	77,284	7,399
	V	W	82	39,588	26,094	29,671	3,577
			83	13,984	9,696	10,930	1,234
USSR	V	E	82	43,546	13,886	19,276	5,390

1530700 BERRY NSPF JELLY, JAMS, ETC (LB)

Country	Mode	Reg	Yr	Quantity	F.A.S.	C.I.F.	Charges
TOTAL			83	1,559,493	1,344,953	1,460,403	115,450
			84	4,064,162	3,052,030	3,419,197	367,167
			85	6,762,268	4,226,304	4,835,269	608,965
			86	9,686,794	5,976,709	6,774,149	797,440
AUSTRAL	O	E	84	210	305	305	
	V	E	85	5,182	8,277	9,292	1,015
AUSTRIA	V	E	83	5,103	6,514	6,945	431
			84	6,511	7,678	8,630	952
			85	7,324	9,487	11,556	2,069
			86	9,642	16,401	17,746	1,345
	V	W	83	1,824	1,314	1,358	44
			86	9,536	13,142	14,290	1,148
BELGIUM	N	E	84	11,013	8,051	9,250	1,199
	O	E	84	21,898	11,573	13,769	2,196
			85	56,450	30,260	36,453	6,193
			86	6,630	8,767	9,753	986
	V	E	83	16,888	16,759	18,449	1,690
			84	87,358	63,962	74,170	10,208
			85	98,420	66,786	77,559	10,773
			86	84,584	69,403	78,425	9,022
	V	W	83	2,808	1,835	2,062	227
			84	12,728	6,888	7,837	949
			85	10,809	6,137	7,464	1,327
			86	7,619	4,948	5,608	660
BULGAR	V	E	86	14,489	4,076	4,912	836
CANADA	A	H	85	819	1,567	1,737	170
	N	W	84	389,796	328,512	328,512	
	O	E	83	30,732	16,988	16,988	
			84	53,217	54,747	54,747	
			85	439,980	154,220	155,373	1,153
			86	89,963	80,765	80,765	
	O	W	83	281,472	244,719	245,209	490
			85	248,165	176,419	176,419	
			86	289,253	225,935	225,935	
	V	E	85	14,102	13,729	15,635	1,906
CHILE	V	E	85	14,145	11,424	12,568	1,144
CHINA M	V	E	84	364	623	676	53
			85	1,890	2,838	3,248	410
DENMARK	A	E	86	135	1,872	1,874	2
	N	W	86	1,528,202	761,922	864,195	102,273
	V	E	83	20,500	29,950	31,355	1,405
			84	15,179	21,420	23,818	2,398
			85	32,005	18,226	21,216	2,990
			86	310,830	166,070	190,930	24,860
	V	W	85	98,578	57,808	67,383	9,575
			86	448,382	229,283	261,519	32,236
FR GERM	N	E	85	615,594	366,115	411,636	45,521
			86	40,062	27,051	29,699	2,648
	O	E	83	6,680	6,154	6,580	426
			84	316,520	178,543	203,650	25,107
	V	E	83	129,932	93,541	99,165	5,624
			84	684,516	424,505	476,589	52,084
			85	1,205,359	726,782	824,756	97,974
			86	1,844,225	1,159,239	1,283,835	124,596
	V	W	83	3,680	2,951	3,938	987
			84	9,408	7,608	8,918	1,310
			85	131,395	88,218	104,957	16,739
			86	39,632	34,373	38,749	4,376
FRANCE	A	E	84	248	398	672	274
	N	E	83	104,100	97,172	108,727	11,555
			84	562,119	423,297	486,582	63,285
			85	360,119	326,576	377,762	51,186
			86	274,694	323,382	356,730	33,348
	N	W	84	235,939	179,806	203,788	23,982
	O	E	83	1,080	1,544	1,544	
			84	12,936	10,459	10,995	536
			85	844	1,227	1,872	645
			86	19,900	32,033	34,202	2,169

Country	Mode	Reg	Yr	Quantity	F.A.S.	C.I.F.	Charges
	V	E	83	146,645	127,052	142,756	15,704
			84	189,865	151,740	174,729	22,989
			85	489,214	388,235	443,630	55,395
			86	412,299	512,494	577,799	65,305
	V	W	83	130,648	124,751	140,501	15,750
			84	72,329	82,766	92,106	9,340
			85	190,982	190,917	214,675	23,758
			86	92,178	109,414	119,768	10,354
GREECE	V	E	86	3,262	4,718	5,355	637
HUNGARY	O	E	85	44,400	23,727	23,727	
			86	36,000	9,441	9,441	
	V	E	83	25,206	10,140	12,000	1,860
			84	280,026	112,749	157,492	44,743
			85	848,787	172,575	255,767	83,192
			86	1,541,565	309,844	448,509	138,665
	V	W	85	165,480	33,778	53,175	19,397
			86	698,470	167,796	207,469	39,673
INDIA	O	E	84	350	468	468	
	V	W	83	440	500	602	102
			84	440	500	675	175
IRELAND	N	E	83	10,584	8,094	8,944	850
	V	E	83	820	573	711	138
			84	33,097	23,616	29,160	5,544
			85	18,808	12,802	15,059	2,257
			86	17,221	12,312	13,810	1,498
ISRAEL	V	E	85	9,997	4,973	6,000	1,027
			86	27,395	26,486	30,481	3,995
ITALY	V	E	83	11,672	13,165	14,399	1,234
			84	22,556	24,315	27,870	3,555
			85	15,785	25,711	27,750	2,039
			86	14,883	14,981	16,951	1,970
	V	W	83	722	1,688	1,880	192
			86	1,658	3,146	3,329	183
JAPAN	V	E	86	12,539	7,199	8,190	991
	V	W	83	5,850	6,600	7,477	877
MADAGAS	V	E	84	1,166	1,352	1,425	73
MEXICO	O	E	85	50	1,278	1,278	
	O	W	85	3,936	3,057	3,057	
NETHLDS	O	E	85	13,800	5,025	5,025	
			86	287,187	147,198	176,306	29,108
	V	E	83	11,158	9,151	9,985	834
			84	17,253	19,385	21,477	2,092
			85	4,959	5,695	6,336	641
			86	1,687	3,420	3,735	315
	V	W	84	3,906	2,066	2,232	166
			85	2,640	1,738	2,126	388
			86	26,038	22,196	25,513	3,317
NIUE	V	E	85	18,519	4,227	7,048	2,821
NORWAY	V	E	83	1,330	1,689	1,978	289
			84	692	2,413	2,684	271
			86	7,996	12,168	12,526	358
	V	W	83	7,843	8,768	10,244	1,476
			84	1,925	2,179	2,899	720
			85	1,809	2,024	2,468	444
			86	6,908	11,076	12,548	1,472
PAKISTN	V	E	85	11,306	12,565	14,196	1,631
POLAND	N	E	83	21,600	8,100	9,951	1,851
			84	80,977	41,354	46,995	5,641
	V	E	83	75,400	29,358	34,918	5,560
			84	104,700	41,635	49,372	7,737
			85	156,470	59,511	74,167	14,656
			86	75,945	25,550	33,295	7,745
PORTUGL	V	E	84	924	745	1,000	255
REP SAF	V	W	83	1,013	2,018	2,383	365
			84	417	673	862	189
ROMANIA	V	E	83	12,000	5,142	5,895	753
			84	149,108	67,589	76,501	8,912
			85	134,172	54,155	61,964	7,809
			86	44,614	11,191	13,791	2,600
SPAIN	V	E	85	11,532	7,387	8,171	784
SWEDEN	A	E	86	2,370	9,150	13,191	4,041
	N	E	86	11,722	28,199	36,707	8,508
	V	E	83	611	786	852	66
			84	1,714	2,791	3,141	350
			85	26,221	16,543	18,021	1,478
			86	55,063	101,865	110,509	8,644
	V	W	83	1,744	2,175	2,706	531
			84	349	414	443	29
			85	4,021	4,578	5,226	648
			86	9,049	11,443	11,732	289
SWITZLD	A	E	86	2,410	1,777	1,832	55
	O	E	83	1,378	1,096	1,228	132
			84	8,420	7,000	7,716	716
			85	20,435	17,172	20,039	2,867
			86	22,217	30,348	33,050	2,702

Country	Mode	Reg	Yr	Quantity	F.A.S.	C.I.F.	Charges
	O	W	85	1,232	1,100	1,172	72
	V	E	83	139,220	131,486	139,724	8,238
			84	135,533	115,646	123,594	7,948
			85	189,186	174,097	190,324	16,227
			86	276,586	339,681	361,987	22,306
	V	W	83	41,456	39,413	42,276	2,863
			84	29,100	27,896	30,225	2,329
			85	83,580	70,304	77,703	7,399
			86	50,162	52,267	55,370	3,103
TURKEY	V	E	83	281	323	341	18
			84	595	648	735	87
			86	3,333	2,074	2,441	367
U KING	A	E	83	262	515	530	15
			84	2,249	3,635	5,321	1,686
			85	648	1,016	1,957	941
			86	569	1,081	1,422	341
	N	E	83	140,038	105,872	121,676	15,804
			84	167,288	199,972	223,009	23,037
			85	520,292	482,962	541,449	58,487
			86	199,720	186,093	209,818	23,725
	N	W	85	142,047	138,885	160,640	21,755
			86	53,794	66,941	75,868	8,927
	O	E	83	31,568	44,104	46,915	2,811
			84	180,931	217,506	230,855	13,349
			85	70,252	134,909	142,410	7,501
			86	258,164	329,024	349,136	20,112
	O	W	85	5,292	3,604	4,246	642
	V	E	83	76,860	94,560	102,907	8,347
			84	48,696	68,602	76,780	8,178
			85	12,678	15,069	16,620	1,551
			86	93,085	101,573	114,239	12,666
	V	H	85	1,124	2,040	2,292	252
	V	W	83	58,345	48,393	54,304	5,911
			84	83,358	92,329	101,605	9,276
			85	40,271	40,077	45,679	5,602
			86	90,857	77,504	87,868	10,364
YUGOSLV	O	E	86	4,356	1,317	1,317	
	V	E	84	25,797	11,354	14,457	3,103
			85	161,163	48,472	64,986	16,514
			86	215,350	62,757	84,172	21,415
	V	W	84	441	317	461	144
			86	12,364	4,323	5,507	1,184

1533200 JELLIES, JAMS, ETC, NSPF (LB)

Country	Mode	Reg	Yr	Quantity	F.A.S.	C.I.F.	Charges
TOTAL			81	1,923,039	1,575,911	1,725,473	149,634
			82	2,589,953	2,023,778	2,215,244	191,466
			83	3,063,923	2,367,055	2,627,307	260,252
			84	5,655,652	3,879,690	4,395,869	516,179
			85	9,854,920	5,038,168	5,902,175	864,007
			86	12,918,363	6,775,207	7,766,347	991,140
ARGENT	O	E	81	912	1,188	1,188	
	V	E	82	20,606	8,289	10,149	1,860
			83	56,121	19,848	24,121	4,273
			84	18,408	9,234	11,015	1,781
			85	3,225	1,106	1,367	261
			86	1,190	1,082	1,179	97
	V	W	83	9,271	4,021	4,922	901
			84	924	270	369	99
			85	1,166	1,470	2,033	563
AUSTRAL	A	W	84	50	495	556	61
	N	W	83	6,021	6,843	7,644	801
	V	E	81	400	272	345	73
			85	4,252	6,732	7,568	836
			86	4,033	7,501	8,322	821
	V	W	86	1,533	1,180	1,310	130
AUSTRIA	O	E	85	16,535	5,466	6,996	1,530
	V	E	81	1,424	1,716	1,820	104
			83	8,120	11,972	12,815	843
			84	7,117	8,701	9,747	1,046
			85	3,588	4,056	4,864	808
			86	2,676	4,432	4,795	363
	V	W	83	482	347	358	11
			86	4,886	6,471	7,036	565
BELGIUM	A	E	82	450	298	582	284
			84	2,896	1,430	3,157	1,727
	A	W	83	2,314	1,210	2,468	1,258
			84	3,172	2,046	4,754	2,708
	N	E	83	7,031	9,704	10,770	1,066
			84	10,622	7,681	10,398	2,717
	O	E	84	58,637	35,960	41,802	5,842
			85	59,810	25,804	32,917	7,113
			86	6,552	7,392	8,367	975
	V	E	81	27,789	7,563	10,184	2,621
			82	18,861	11,799	13,207	1,408

Product
TSUSA commodity number, description, and unit of quantity

Country	Mode	Reg	Yr	Quantity	F.A.S.	C.I.F.	Charges
			84	121,811	86,748	100,421	13,673
			85	86,947	43,462	51,212	7,750
			86	150,037	108,440	123,423	14,983
	V	W	83	1,404	917	1,030	113
			84	24,285	16,045	19,382	3,337
			85	3,780	1,888	2,312	424
			86	60,510	37,575	40,412	2,837
BRAZIL	V	E	83	11,153	2,039	2,540	501
			84	2,006	1,250	1,443	193
			85	792	1,402	1,588	186
	V	W	81	1,320	440	552	112
			85	1,693	1,237	1,484	247
BULGAR	O	W	81	450	343	343	
			82	1,690	1,100	1,100	
	V	E	86	50,104	10,580	17,569	6,989
C RICA	V	E	86	4,320	2,409	2,802	393
	V	W	86	8,952	6,530	6,530	
CANADA	N	E	84	863	901	968	67
	N	W	84	72,825	60,986	60,986	
	O	E	81	221,458	123,669	123,597	
			82	189,953	84,375	85,773	1,398
			83	178,946	86,468	86,496	28
			84	382,565	274,048	274,658	610
			85	205,083	113,570	114,435	865
			86	930,644	442,715	442,715	
	O	W	81	134,557	106,841	106,841	
			82	313,179	230,611	230,611	
			83	130,340	103,260	103,260	
			85	39,143	29,986	29,986	
			86	37,062	24,772	24,772	
	V	E	83	12,714	13,593	14,748	1,155
			85	6,926	5,947	6,794	847
			86	39,717	25,378	28,221	2,843
CHILE	V	E	85	17,258	14,144	15,408	1,264
CHINA M	A	W	83	22	823	950	127
	N	W	82	2,271	1,617	1,852	235
			83	8,745	4,860	5,343	483
			84	1,196	1,707	1,863	156
			86	57,149	19,300	21,366	2,066
	V	E	81	80	1,327	1,331	4
			82	219	1,125	1,148	23
			83	12,810	2,539	4,165	1,626
			84	60,179	14,644	20,176	5,532
			85	120	1,466	1,482	16
			86	14,062	8,772	10,160	1,388
	V	W	81	5,658	2,667	2,918	251
			82	14,820	3,340	3,714	374
			84	5,700	1,150	1,551	401
			85	78,654	11,646	13,225	1,579
			86	4,984	2,096	2,301	205
CHINA T	A	E	81	4,433	4,490	4,776	286
	A	W	81	3,300	2,680	2,768	88
	N	W	84	15,812	15,349	16,580	1,231
			86	325,414	93,537	102,378	8,841
	O	E	81	4,275	1,200	1,296	96
	V	E	81	15,124	5,801	6,578	777
			82	3,206	900	1,011	111
			83	2,620	1,120	1,313	193
			84	52,593	17,640	23,134	5,494
			85	29,796	11,186	14,338	3,152
			86	19,153	17,315	18,851	1,536
	V	W	81	11,698	2,857	3,444	587
			82	9,714	3,587	4,231	644
			83	24,849	9,029	9,667	638
			84	28,638	7,870	8,925	1,055
			85	9,130	8,080	8,671	591
			86	20,164	7,916	8,561	645
COLOMB	A	E	85	1,554	3,320	3,984	664
			86	3,800	4,172	4,381	209
	N	E	84	21,075	4,706	5,985	1,279
	V	E	85	15,554	12,000	12,784	784
DENMARK	O	E	84	1,250	1,170	1,250	80
	V	E	84	16,309	22,499	24,987	2,488
			85	34,242	25,982	29,096	3,114
			86	118,478	57,614	67,286	9,672
	V	W	83	1,425	702	791	89
			85	95,358	45,170	52,942	7,772
			86	577,991	260,833	297,698	36,865
DOM REP	A	E	82	3,000	555	1,381	826
	N	E	86	23,057	11,370	12,573	1,203
	V	E	81	6,615	1,853	2,049	196
			82	35,631	13,695	14,545	850
			83	42,334	14,465	16,739	2,274
			84	80,699	20,176	26,956	6,780
			85	166,180	33,317	38,061	4,744

Product
TSUSA commodity number, description, and unit of quantity

Country	Mode	Reg	Yr	Quantity	F.A.S.	C.I.F.	Charges
			86	35,533	10,285	11,221	936
ECUADOR	V	E	86	39,636	7,340	9,540	2,200
EGYPT	O	E	83	2,900	3,150	3,400	250
	V	E	81	18,806	8,985	10,707	1,722
			86	54,267	28,114	31,536	3,422
	V	W	84	9,971	4,186	4,750	564
			86	8,333	4,950	5,772	822
F W IND	A	E	81	2,756	3,614	4,445	831
	V	E	82	9,425	9,703	10,268	565
FR GERM	N	E	81	28,542	23,372	25,059	1,687
			82	3,805	2,981	3,883	902
			85	1,190,493	626,891	710,997	84,106
	N	W	85	61,402	47,126	53,935	6,809
	O	E	81	751	732	867	135
			82	2,812	1,865	2,137	272
			83	13,908	9,622	10,606	984
			84	522,858	257,138	295,229	38,091
			86	51,389	29,173	32,689	3,516
	V	E	82	107,492	86,530	94,259	7,729
			83	224,534	143,103	157,162	14,059
			84	545,092	330,980	373,009	42,029
			85	250,983	138,630	159,414	20,784
			86	1,170,031	722,009	797,733	75,724
	V	W	81	6,435	3,747	4,573	826
			82	11,601	6,801	7,919	1,118
			83	8,942	7,496	9,255	1,759
			84	12,951	9,543	11,045	1,502
			85	24,226	17,057	20,843	3,786
			86	47,003	30,832	36,583	5,751
FRANCE	A	E	82	260	747	901	154
			83	1,175	1,259	2,116	857
			84	1,071	1,296	1,950	654
			85	5,071	9,043	12,541	3,498
	A	W	82	474	758	1,246	488
	N	E	81	109,648	114,928	130,917	15,989
			82	126,041	124,563	138,005	13,442
			83	150,751	125,492	141,651	16,159
			84	370,231	316,832	367,962	51,130
			85	240,966	213,711	258,286	44,575
			86	101,654	146,872	164,097	17,225
	N	W	82	22,993	30,125	33,697	3,572
			84	309,402	233,440	264,941	31,501
			85	125,001	128,727	144,303	15,576
	O	E	81	10,870	14,070	15,020	950
			82	10,490	10,449	11,570	1,121
			83	19,079	17,903	19,978	2,075
			84	7,950	6,280	6,410	130
			86	96,702	76,359	76,945	586
	O	W	81	16	721	742	21
	V	E	81	32,735	43,592	46,550	2,958
			82	109,039	104,963	116,680	11,717
			83	127,664	104,460	116,814	12,354
			84	204,393	174,313	197,228	22,915
			85	493,546	396,242	443,878	47,636
			86	446,404	483,001	547,744	64,743
	V	H	81	1,125	941	1,077	136
			83	562	481	682	201
	V	W	81	33,829	31,464	34,369	2,905
			82	66,518	54,676	61,334	6,658
			83	210,446	182,150	205,684	23,534
			84	5,228	4,646	5,515	869
			85	53,857	45,481	52,972	7,491
			86	68,187	96,673	109,224	12,551
GREECE	A	E	83	705	568	1,033	465
	A	W	85	3,924	4,725	4,965	240
	N	W	84	1,824	2,567	2,806	239
	O	E	81	228	270	270	
			82	4,017	3,502	3,717	215
			83	2,969	3,435	3,435	
			84	804	747	747	
	V	E	81	14,402	15,220	17,718	2,498
			83	9,607	8,662	9,891	1,229
			84	3,135	4,010	4,529	519
			85	18,840	8,000	10,796	2,796
			86	46,918	49,667	56,686	7,019
	V	W	82	4,796	1,380	1,837	457
			83	2,936	2,745	3,124	379
GUYANA	O	E	82	5,525	505	505	
	V	E	81	177	575	653	78
HG KONG	A	W	85	6,110	5,009	5,650	641
	N	E	82	812	1,087	1,399	312
	N	W	86	44,860	13,420	14,820	1,400
	V	E	81	600	1,178	1,253	75
			82	250	436	472	36
			84	6,240	6,048	6,709	661

Product TSUSA commodity number, description, and unit of quantity Country	Mode	Reg	Yr	Quantity	F.A.S.	C.I.F.	Charges
			85	1,950	1,443	1,689	246
	V	W	81	1,138	676	728	52
			82	247	256	269	13
			83	6,000	4,392	4,895	503
			84	1,909	1,793	1,912	119
			85	1,350	1,401	1,503	102
			86	5,700	1,090	1,170	80
HONDURA	V	E	84	38,059	11,663	14,225	2,562
HUNGARY	O	E	85	281,334	92,632	93,372	740
			86	123,970	21,173	21,173	
	V	E	81	52,650	14,873	18,826	3,953
			82	132,180	40,099	51,470	11,371
			83	50,411	19,780	24,000	4,220
			84	444,157	170,533	221,100	50,567
			85	2,234,296	496,306	685,044	188,738
			86	2,944,030	574,004	857,108	283,104
	V	W	85	634,351	120,292	195,495	75,203
			86	1,564,828	355,160	440,439	85,279
INDIA	O	E	81	551	402	441	39
			84	2,576	1,285	1,433	148
	V	E	82	127	269	296	27
			83	2,646	2,284	2,600	316
			85	1,058	1,242	1,418	176
	V	W	82	550	390	443	53
			83	1,852	1,435	1,675	240
			84	212	795	948	153
INDNSIA	V	W	82	209	335	364	29
			83	544	1,429	1,542	113
IRELAND	N	E	81	6,761	6,887	7,645	758
			83	7,429	7,886	9,125	1,239
	O	E	81	3,874	7,318	8,108	790
	V	E	82	3,943	3,652	4,088	436
			84	13,807	11,644	13,361	1,717
			85	22,879	11,417	13,809	2,392
			86	12,510	12,979	14,770	1,791
ISRAEL	N	E	83	41,897	28,974	34,206	5,232
			85	20,757	11,117	12,967	1,850
	V	E	81	68,391	35,657	41,017	5,360
			82	107,674	76,124	85,477	9,353
			83	245,253	156,488	176,015	19,527
			84	226,157	155,018	171,989	16,971
			85	231,078	144,530	163,582	19,052
			86	349,610	208,916	235,493	26,577
ITALY	A	E	83	3,072	6,171	9,316	3,145
			84	1,481	2,488	4,242	1,754
	N	E	81	12,801	10,463	12,033	1,570
			82	20,363	16,588	19,203	2,615
			84	21,754	22,339	25,457	3,118
	N	W	86	2,044	4,351	4,592	241
	O	E	83	630	552	635	83
			84	14,074	6,612	7,120	508
	V	E	82	9,824	7,072	7,994	922
			83	25,070	23,343	26,209	2,866
			84	65	420	462	42
			85	31,566	34,492	37,920	3,428
			86	10,924	26,894	29,056	2,162
	V	W	82	372	744	867	123
			83	4,988	8,689	10,197	1,508
			84	10,008	5,859	6,242	383
			86	565	1,642	1,670	28
JAMAICA	A	E	84	600	438	1,040	602
	O	E	85	3,593	2,402	2,523	121
	V	E	82	1,746	602	674	72
			83	1,800	1,348	1,610	262
			84	2,055	942	1,056	114
JAPAN	A	W	81	108	289	662	373
	N	H	82	709	718	965	247
	N	W	84	9,367	8,445	9,179	734
			85	9,734	24,707	25,856	1,149
	V	E	81	2,520	6,129	6,636	507
			82	14,112	15,362	16,966	1,604
			83	16,210	26,059	28,989	2,930
			84	30,834	38,383	42,745	4,362
			85	30,011	22,543	26,505	3,962
			86	70,913	49,769	54,352	4,583
	V	H	81	347	326	441	115
			83	1,124	924	1,178	254
			84	1,485	866	985	119
	V	W	81	9,500	15,261	16,525	1,264
			82	12,209	18,048	19,656	1,608
			83	31,038	46,098	49,581	3,483
			84	13,900	20,007	21,828	1,821
			85	4,447	5,117	5,749	632
			86	84,876	76,885	82,418	5,533
KOR REP	V	E	82	1,982	4,589	4,879	290

Product TSUSA commodity number, description, and unit of quantity Country	Mode	Reg	Yr	Quantity	F.A.S.	C.I.F.	Charges
			86	1,713	9,679	9,867	188
	V	W	82	3,072	3,727	4,090	363
			83	5,238	3,746	3,934	188
			84	1,914	3,438	3,710	272
			85	5,776	1,812	3,094	1,282
			86	8,306	3,855	4,114	259
LEBANON	N	E	84	34,798	24,014	26,197	2,183
	O	E	81	63	500	500	
			82	336	336	336	
			83	18,240	5,601	5,601	
			85	1,100	4,202	4,202	
	V	E	81	13,232	10,470	11,401	931
			82	11,211	8,096	9,112	1,016
			83	24,852	20,500	22,436	1,936
			84	4,891	3,520	3,883	363
			85	49,987	30,779	34,863	4,084
			86	31,465	21,284	23,285	2,001
	V	W	83	3,968	3,000	3,363	363
			84	2,117	1,640	1,722	82
			85	7,189	4,590	4,924	334
			86	33,301	17,419	19,795	2,376
LESOTHO	V	E	85	58	1,496	1,609	113
MADAGAS	V	E	84	1,026	957	1,021	64
MALAYSA	V	E	81	1,500	1,953	2,207	254
			83	630	1,170	1,259	89
			85	2,325	1,461	1,570	109
			86	1,800	3,223	3,424	201
	V	W	83	259	318	334	16
			84	1,012	713	821	108
			85	4,687	4,326	4,625	299
			86	3,519	2,686	2,904	218
MEXICO	A	E	86	1,791	2,160	3,408	1,248
	O	E	83	876	572	572	
			84	50	628	628	
			85	10,000	8,250	8,250	
			86	2,381	1,775	1,775	
MOROC	O	E	81	1,512	1,641	1,641	
			82	1,470	1,280	1,280	
N ZEAL	V	W	85	630	1,051	1,164	113
			86	2,970	1,264	1,588	324
NETHLDS	A	E	83	794	432	1,032	600
	A	W	82	1,120	499	813	314
	O	E	81	476	269	276	7
			82	1,190	639	709	70
			83	4,259	840	903	63
			84	2,346	1,510	1,697	187
			85	304,164	109,852	124,612	14,760
			86	248,660	149,475	175,367	25,892
	V	E	81	2,143	1,213	1,386	173
			82	5,061	3,686	3,952	266
			83	8,297	10,093	10,924	831
			84	36,019	17,117	19,960	2,843
			85	24,347	22,958	25,857	2,899
			86	19,559	7,372	8,681	1,309
	V	W	81	1,560	1,092	1,210	118
			82	393	376	406	30
			83	736	260	277	17
			84	3,302	1,612	1,777	165
			86	7,879	5,079	5,834	755
NIUE	V	E	85	218,255	29,888	49,832	19,944
NORWAY	V	E	82	185	878	1,029	151
			86	37,130	56,504	58,168	1,664
PAKISTN	V	E	85	2,696	2,995	3,384	389
PERU	V	E	86	8,279	17,089	18,402	1,313
PHIL R	O	W	83	450	436	487	51
	V	E	81	1,260	1,155	1,380	225
			82	3,435	3,596	4,271	675
			83	2,760	2,654	3,043	389
			84	7,941	6,684	7,972	1,288
			85	1,346	2,026	2,416	390
			86	108	1,743	1,743	
	V	H	81	2,970	3,465	3,944	479
			82	360	400	457	57
			84	992	967	1,103	136
	V	W	81	27,315	9,603	10,877	1,274
			82	9,951	7,653	8,386	733
			83	18,558	12,784	14,640	1,856
			84	34,709	21,641	27,684	6,043
			85	41,870	32,366	37,685	5,319
			86	23,397	20,079	22,329	2,250
POLAND	N	E	84	60,210	25,476	29,473	3,997
	O	E	81	6,000	4,958	6,151	1,193
			82	34,367	19,615	23,867	4,252
	V	E	81	75,550	29,061	37,131	8,070
			82	24,000	14,000	16,259	2,259

Product
TSUSA commodity number, description, and unit of quantity

Country	Mode	Reg	Yr	Quantity	F.A.S.	C.I.F.	Charges
			83	51,400	19,390	23,797	4,407
			84	90,750	33,890	41,332	7,442
			85	112,314	43,425	55,586	12,161
			86	49,684	16,960	22,074	5,114
PORTUGL	V	E	81	809	482	547	65
			82	25,451	10,723	12,340	1,617
			83	5,067	3,302	3,858	556
			84	14,587	11,188	14,544	3,356
			85	18,487	6,300	7,763	1,463
REP SAF	N	W	83	1,852	2,286	4,629	2,343
	V	E	86	81,359	47,535	54,562	7,027
	V	W	84	2,107	2,625	3,364	739
ROMANIA	V	E	83	20,520	7,842	8,852	1,010
			84	75,699	30,875	35,103	4,228
			85	113,605	42,272	48,376	6,104
			86	196,197	46,849	57,340	10,491
SALVADR	V	W	83	2,083	1,885	2,218	333
			84	2,895	2,126	2,411	285
SINGAPR	V	E	83	708	561	642	81
			84	644	362	421	59
	V	W	81	44,218	27,869	30,419	2,550
			82	3,464	3,151	3,394	243
			83	3,776	3,146	3,468	322
			84	423	707	766	59
			85	3,095	1,610	1,929	319
			86	2,222	1,470	1,617	147
SPAIN	A	E	82	973	908	1,774	866
	V	E	82	1,446	1,368	1,697	329
			84	4,225	2,428	3,031	603
			85	156,465	41,124	54,557	13,433
			86	2,625	1,265	1,470	205
SRI LKA	V	E	82	310	287	324	37
SWEDEN	A	E	83	103	310	332	22
			84	60	287	452	165
	V	E	84	2,031	3,266	3,593	327
			86	6,695	4,600	4,758	158
SWITZLD	N	E	82	13,221	7,451	8,102	651
			84	15,171	8,432	9,891	1,459
	N	W	82	6,130	7,757	9,148	1,391
	O	E	81	8,023	7,597	8,478	881
			82	11,798	12,938	16,032	3,094
			83	11,989	7,323	8,282	959
			84	15,344	9,746	10,748	1,002
			85	51,905	34,189	39,472	5,283
			86	44,086	47,691	51,748	4,057
	O	W	85	3,289	1,887	2,139	252
	V	E	81	105,081	93,746	103,094	9,348
			82	177,969	159,689	171,047	11,358
			83	227,590	206,467	219,586	13,119
			84	172,157	155,573	164,590	9,017
			85	359,955	268,102	291,280	23,178
			86	311,347	363,510	390,542	27,032
	V	W	81	50,079	42,445	46,754	4,309
			82	22,794	23,080	25,510	2,430
			83	97,824	77,782	83,225	5,443
			84	119,373	89,626	97,112	7,486
			85	96,720	85,040	93,267	8,227
			86	108,945	120,315	127,088	6,773
THAILND	O	E	86	1,874	2,493	2,714	221
	V	E	82	2,040	1,746	1,874	128
			84	180	262	319	57
	V	W	81	3,445	963	1,028	65
			82	2,123	2,016	2,564	548
			83	543	683	754	71
			85	13,379	10,435	11,439	1,004
			86	22,327	19,252	21,042	1,790
TRINID	V	E	83	4,382	7,350	7,607	257
TUNISIA	V	E	86	7,158	5,340	5,924	584
TURKEY	V	E	82	270	400	593	193
			83	28,165	17,870	22,100	4,230
			84	15,850	10,144	11,620	1,476
			86	76,810	47,894	53,886	5,992
	V	W	85	7,738	4,500	5,234	734
U KING	A	E	81	289	1,035	1,285	250
			82	1,137	1,430	1,616	186
			83	629	1,426	1,663	237
			84	5,243	7,341	10,371	3,030
			85	1,337	3,801	7,323	3,522
	N	E	81	337,476	373,767	404,087	30,320
			82	357,115	383,893	415,643	31,750
			83	275,749	279,271	310,637	31,366
			84	330,114	352,307	398,707	46,400
			85	697,564	626,524	706,322	79,798
			86	683,024	712,903	783,879	70,976
	N	W	82	35,582	35,019	40,610	5,591

Product
TSUSA commodity number, description, and unit of quantity

Country	Mode	Reg	Yr	Quantity	F.A.S.	C.I.F.	Charges
			83	110,508	82,682	93,291	10,609
			84	210,173	188,460	210,200	21,740
			86	16,799	19,734	22,307	2,573
	O	E	81	148,327	136,786	149,933	13,147
			82	176,805	150,382	166,672	16,290
			83	115,374	97,414	108,170	10,756
			84	224,888	194,379	210,697	16,318
			85	112,882	181,386	193,262	11,876
			86	108,466	196,576	206,456	9,880
	O	W	85	7,749	4,998	5,890	892
	V	E	81	95,745	97,282	108,555	11,273
			82	60,091	52,337	57,694	5,357
			83	198,405	204,195	224,217	20,022
			84	159,591	134,574	153,774	19,200
			85	70,402	77,689	88,356	10,667
			86	155,746	166,509	186,826	20,317
	V	W	81	93,878	83,351	94,787	11,436
			82	71,990	62,369	70,230	7,861
			83	4,290	4,705	5,371	666
			84	47,145	47,584	53,208	5,624
			85	285,395	256,691	289,402	32,711
			86	193,145	234,546	258,787	24,241
USSR	O	E	81	9,214	2,745	3,159	414
			82	24,616	6,626	6,979	353
			83	2,048	720	720	
	V	E	81	8,201	3,022	3,242	220
			82	19,534	7,476	8,363	887
			83	34,183	11,342	17,893	6,551
			86	19,581	10,385	12,440	2,055
VENEZ	A	E	84	2,752	600	1,110	510
	V	E	86	3,000	1,175	1,274	99
YUGOSLV	O	E	84	3,910	2,121	2,712	591
			86	19,200	5,522	5,522	
	O	W	81	950	498	498	
			84	4,233	1,989	1,989	
	V	E	81	21,438	10,165	11,963	1,798
			82	72,746	40,741	45,327	4,586
			83	43,954	26,559	30,446	3,887
			84	117,860	52,956	64,521	11,565
			85	204,600	71,423	92,932	21,509
			86	509,758	174,518	225,238	50,720
	V	W	81	3,231	2,181	2,228	47
			84	3,638	1,663	2,418	755
			86	18,702	6,539	8,330	1,791

Fruit, paste and pulp
1527640 FRUIT PASTES AND PULP, NSPF (LB)

Country	Mode	Reg	Yr	Quantity	F.A.S.	C.I.F.	Charges
TOTAL			81	**573,643**	**258,546**	**289,042**	**30,496**
			82	**131,230**	**51,422**	**62,070**	**10,648**
ARGENT	V	E	81	24,275	17,240	19,500	2,260
			82	16,543	8,783	10,383	1,600
BOLIVIA	V	E	81	5,247	1,250	1,654	404
BRAZIL	O	E	81	1,125	655	655	
	V	W	81	3,704	1,295	1,562	267
C RICA	V	E	81	42,098	13,490	15,836	2,346
CANADA	O	E	82	810	454	454	
CHINA M	V	E	81	3,400	1,902	2,286	384
	V	W	81	133	582	602	20
COLOMB	V	E	81	8,200	5,490	6,533	1,043
DOM REP	V	E	81	10,350	3,301	3,921	620
			82	1,984	735	834	99
FR GERM	V	E	81	912	2,499	2,735	236
			82	98	273	291	18
FRANCE	A	E	81	145	628	740	112
			82	265	600	791	191
	N	E	81	2,862	6,324	6,983	659
	O	E	81	175	568	637	69
	V	E	82	758	1,813	1,998	185
HG KONG	V	E	81	3,390	685	859	174
	V	W	81	5,080	4,538	5,114	576
			82	450	502	529	27
INDIA	V	W	81	1,090	947	1,182	235
JAPAN	O	E	81	2,779	4,018	4,280	262
			82	2,015	2,965	3,421	456
	V	E	81	2,301	3,175	3,411	236
	V	W	81	4,603	10,998	11,842	844
			82	442	3,264	3,525	261
MALAYSA	V	W	81	1,313	3,449	3,801	352
MEXICO	O	W	81	246,413	69,966	69,966	
			82	58,020	15,391	15,391	
NETHLDS	A	E	82	159	318	352	34
	V	E	81	74,015	42,696	48,646	5,950

Product TSUSA commodity number, description, and unit of quantity Country	Mode	Reg	Yr	Quantity	F.A.S.	C.I.F.	Charges
PHIL R	V	E	81	330	419	495	76
	V	W	81	28,028	20,557	22,818	2,261
			82	7,287	2,930	3,490	560
PORTUGL	V	E	81	64,152	28,128	36,090	7,962
			82	5,291	2,788	3,781	993
REP SAF	A	E	81	9,080	2,322	2,586	264
	V	E	81	6,724	2,060	2,866	806
			82	36,673	9,700	15,873	6,173
SPAIN	V	E	81	8,061	4,599	5,332	733
THAILND	V	E	81	2,800	1,736	2,054	318
			82	435	906	957	51
U KING	A	E	81	298	515	775	260
URUGUAY	V	E	81	10,560	2,514	3,281	767

1528140 FRUIT PASTES AND PULP, NSPF (LB)

Country	Mode	Reg	Yr	Quantity	F.A.S.	C.I.F.	Charges
TOTAL			82	700,033	271,594	319,136	47,542
			83	270,644	100,720	114,898	14,178
ARGENT	V	E	82	38,204	15,083	17,953	2,870
			83	95,253	38,251	43,428	5,177
AUSTRAL	A	E	82	525	315	888	573
BRAZIL	V	E	83	4,075	1,409	1,735	326
	V	W	82	3,684	1,140	1,406	266
CANADA	O	E	82	3,021	4,173	4,470	297
CHINA M	V	W	82	383	943	1,011	68
COLOMB	A	E	82	400	900	1,125	225
CYPRUS	V	E	82	581	1,105	1,181	76
DENMARK	V	E	82	322	504	524	20
DOM REP	V	E	82	26,947	8,930	11,438	2,508
FRANCE	A	E	82	96	645	753	108
			83	1,087	1,882	2,557	675
	N	E	82	2,871	8,893	10,050	1,157
	O	E	82	522	617	673	56
	V	W	82	875	2,035	2,214	179
			83	212	1,043	1,077	34
HG KONG	V	E	82	1,863	1,370	1,498	128
			83	600	1,092	1,200	108
	V	W	82	500	586	620	34
ITALY	A	E	82	415	1,330	1,955	625
	A	W	83	746	1,666	2,209	543
	V	E	82	2,110	3,606	3,788	182
			83	1,538	3,796	4,082	286
	V	W	83	2,728	3,791	4,084	293
JAMAICA	V	E	83	492	788	804	16
JAPAN	V	E	82	1,491	3,053	3,335	282
			83	456	985	1,164	179
	V	W	82	2,660	8,573	9,642	1,069
			83	1,534	2,931	3,161	230
LEBANON	V	E	82	8,267	8,600	9,448	848
	V	W	82	8,267	8,600	9,800	1,200
MEXICO	O	E	82	14,100	4,667	4,667	
			83	2,800	560	560	
	O	W	82	237,707	41,959	41,959	
			83	86,022	10,888	10,888	
N ZEAL	V	E	82	36,129	10,154	16,390	6,236
	V	H	82	6,071	1,351	1,800	449
	V	W	82	70,911	23,517	31,279	7,762
NETHLDS	A	E	82	132	285	336	51
	V	E	82	395	317	369	52
PHIL R	V	W	82	8,984	5,762	6,948	1,186
			83	5,335	2,840	3,441	601
PORTUGL	V	E	82	22,177	11,923	14,950	3,027
			83	3,930	1,886	2,425	539
REP SAF	V	E	82	122,392	44,520	52,837	8,317
			83	61,885	24,772	29,614	4,842
SINGAPR	V	W	82	2,778	4,786	5,266	480
SWITZLD	V	E	83	228	297	297	
THAILND	V	E	82	1,320	980	1,122	142
			83	1,323	943	1,047	104
U KING	V	E	82	73,333	41,272	48,566	7,294

1528840 FRUIT PASTES AND PULP, NSPF (LB)

Country	Mode	Reg	Yr	Quantity	F.A.S.	C.I.F.	Charges
TOTAL			83	441,656	194,980	230,455	35,475
			84	2,610,364	855,569	1,018,934	163,365
			85	3,780,638	1,442,241	1,690,531	248,290
			86	4,044,786	1,752,920	2,004,168	251,248
ARGENT	O	E	83	37,498	7,144	9,909	2,765
			84	524,965	100,012	138,724	38,712
			85	258,235	71,687	79,313	7,626
	V	E	83	167,315	54,122	63,891	9,769
			84	242,352	71,862	85,041	13,179
			85	953,932	297,000	346,166	49,166
			86	652,334	220,461	259,832	39,371
	V	W	83	15,000	7,480	9,230	1,750

Product TSUSA commodity number, description, and unit of quantity Country	Mode	Reg	Yr	Quantity	F.A.S.	C.I.F.	Charges
			84	39,144	10,635	12,048	1,413
			85	4,630	2,215	2,706	491
AUSTRAL	A	W	83	570	283	1,456	1,173
	V	E	86	157,460	53,087	65,840	12,753
BELGIUM	N	E	83	16,767	15,208	18,735	3,527
	V	E	84	3,348	4,690	5,561	871
	V	W	83	1,888	1,003	1,127	124
			84	2,017	1,072	1,259	187
BRAZIL	O	E	86	25,080	10,260	16,096	5,836
	V	E	83	2,045	684	868	184
			84	1,790	481	618	137
			86	1,560	1,052	1,181	129
	V	W	83	7,356	1,938	2,500	562
CANADA	O	E	85	85,511	50,394	50,394	
	O	W	84	2,800	1,908	1,908	
			85	75,520	52,388	52,388	
			86	358,520	254,366	254,366	
CHILE	A	E	83	1,102	500	968	468
	V	E	85	77,439	20,728	24,998	4,270
CHINA M	N	E	85	10,100	6,086	7,660	1,574
	O	E	85	1,950	1,334	1,528	194
CHINA T	V	E	85	375	1,200	1,409	209
	V	W	83	2,294	1,650	1,764	114
			84	3,716	3,176	3,594	418
			85	4,257	5,895	6,393	498
			86	7,018	11,655	12,191	536
COLOMB	A	E	84	7,078	6,167	7,540	1,373
			85	112,593	62,296	91,983	29,687
DOM REP	V	E	83	27,570	17,939	20,310	2,371
			84	151,210	39,313	46,746	7,433
			85	93,070	30,880	36,109	5,229
			86	167,060	78,303	91,496	13,193
FR GERM	A	E	84	660	1,920	2,535	615
			86	1,051	1,801	2,235	434
	V	E	83	1,347	4,192	4,761	569
			84	2,724	4,219	4,393	174
			86	35,274	12,083	17,600	5,517
	V	W	84	132	371	411	40
FRANCE	A	E	83	1,065	1,989	2,438	449
			84	3,142	7,571	9,712	2,141
			86	2,508	5,041	7,557	2,516
	A	W	86	1,543	1,702	3,254	1,552
	N	E	83	1,950	5,350	6,046	696
			84	13,324	23,796	28,779	4,983
			85	8,576	9,156	13,500	4,344
			86	54,843	68,740	81,412	12,672
	N	W	84	2,151	4,082	4,914	832
			85	3,188	3,770	5,438	1,668
			86	29,791	32,695	36,122	3,427
	O	W	86	4,340	5,054	5,145	91
	V	E	83	724	1,957	2,088	131
			84	23,014	15,943	17,788	1,845
			85	2,192	6,334	7,133	799
			86	15,525	22,684	25,696	3,012
	V	W	83	238	767	801	34
			86	275	1,149	1,198	49
GERM DR	V	E	85	5,250	3,675	4,154	479
GHANA	A	E	85	6,000	1,052	1,052	
GUATMAL	V	E	84	7,980	5,199	5,790	591
			85	5,720	12,680	14,275	1,595
			86	150,206	65,469	78,395	12,926
HG KONG	V	E	84	1,703	1,409	1,674	265
HONDURA	V	E	84	44,112	29,672	32,593	2,921
			86	39,000	1,900	4,433	2,533
HUNGARY	V	E	84	17,000	3,172	3,704	532
INDIA	V	W	84	4,464	1,908	2,265	357
ISRAEL	V	E	85	4,219	3,881	4,607	726
ITALY	A	W	85	2,832	5,376	8,150	2,774
	N	E	84	6,735	9,192	10,541	1,349
	V	E	83	2,017	5,424	5,894	470
			84	6,228	5,440	7,091	1,651
			85	7,544	20,256	22,107	1,851
			86	46,011	30,269	34,992	4,723
	V	W	83	196	264	294	30
			84	169	269	310	41
			86	188	1,928	2,003	75
IVY CST	V	E	85	1,833	1,055	1,667	612
JAMAICA	A	E	86	2,604	1,088	1,239	151
JAPAN	A	H	84	26	771	1,025	254
			85	90	1,576	1,846	270
	N	E	83	424	849	931	82
	O	E	84	1,336	2,382	2,632	250
			86	741	2,307	2,415	108
	V	E	83	1,321	4,191	4,499	308
			84	32,497	29,252	31,358	2,106

Product
TSUSA commodity number, description, and unit of quantity

Country	Mode	Reg	Yr	Quantity	F.A.S.	C.I.F.	Charges
			85	9,019	14,338	15,879	1,541
			86	5,046	13,136	13,847	711
	V	H	86	97	2,917	3,079	162
	V	W	83	5,989	14,319	15,295	976
			84	9,204	24,737	26,314	1,577
			85	7,590	21,031	23,073	2,042
			86	15,796	41,999	44,285	2,286
KIRIBAT	V	E	86	17,322	6,622	7,757	1,135
LEBANON	V	E	85	1,905	1,650	1,958	308
	V	W	83	1,853	3,900	4,269	369
			85	1,852	4,000	4,585	585
			86	4,762	1,890	2,148	258
MAURIT	V	E	86	37,037	13,832	19,426	5,594
MEXICO	O	E	83	4,335	1,733	1,733	
			84	95,969	8,913	8,913	
			85	166,193	52,950	52,950	
			86	335,099	64,384	64,384	
	O	W	83	62,975	10,380	10,380	
			84	25,141	2,675	2,675	
N ZEAL	V	E	83	49,989	18,138	23,994	5,856
			84	112,303	49,275	64,574	15,299
			85	131,924	35,868	54,598	18,730
			86	67,506	16,035	24,011	7,976
	V	W	85	38,735	10,775	15,177	4,402
			86	37,477	14,620	19,097	4,477
NETHLDS	A	E	83	172	355	384	29
			84	529	1,280	1,495	215
	V	E	86	169,309	92,551	109,180	16,629
	V	W	84	1,834	1,681	2,217	536
PERU	V	E	83	441	323	345	22
PHIL R	V	W	83	910	856	958	102
			84	5,347	5,175	6,059	884
			85	8,414	3,350	4,234	884
PORTUGL	V	E	83	5,467	2,422	3,031	609
REP SAF	V	E	83	1,146	381	459	78
			84	1,217,052	365,159	422,825	57,666
			85	1,351,122	453,754	526,630	72,876
			86	1,166,405	428,905	490,091	61,186
	V	W	85	36,672	13,738	16,319	2,581
			86	147,832	54,861	63,966	9,105
SENEGAL	A	E	84	184	510	667	157
SPAIN	V	E	84	1,609	2,429	3,063	634
			86	3,055	2,515	2,861	346
SWITZLD	V	E	83	17,990	7,344	8,864	1,520
			85	1,944	1,942	2,267	325
			86	2,917	4,190	4,531	341
THAILND	V	E	83	750	922	1,062	140
			85	2,880	1,689	2,132	443
	V	W	84	7,544	6,050	6,601	551
			85	19,536	13,535	14,529	994
TURKEY	A	W	84	110	1,210	1,269	59
	V	E	83	952	973	1,171	198
	V	W	84	2,709	1,987	3,356	1,369
U KING	A	E	84	249	303	419	116
	O	E	84	1,763	1,473	1,637	164
			85	22,046	10,582	10,582	
	V	E	85	255,750	132,125	160,642	28,517
			86	53,607	34,422	39,494	5,072
VENEZ	V	E	86	165,214	46,827	53,756	6,929
YUGOSLV	V	E	86	46,373	26,948	33,853	6,905

Fruit, peel
1522200 FRUIT PEEL, OTHER, CRUDE ETC (LB)

Country	Mode	Reg	Yr	Quantity	F.A.S.	C.I.F.	Charges
TOTAL			81	24,528	37,505	39,804	2,299
			82	16,666	14,074	15,236	1,162
			83	15,561	8,894	10,126	1,232
			84	112,100	96,541	125,117	28,576
			85	25,879	31,846	34,587	2,741
			86	44,589	20,915	24,312	3,397
BELGIUM	V	E	84	78,396	65,123	72,898	7,775
CHILE	V	W	85	24,640	29,344	31,844	2,500
CHINA M	V	E	81	1,375	4,342	4,459	117
CHINA T	V	W	83	3,931	1,417	1,918	501
			86	1,369	2,700	2,742	42
DOM REP	A	E	81	900	390	600	210
FRANCE	V	E	81	100	1,749	1,907	158
			84	4,330	2,743	3,031	288
GREECE	V	E	86	1,080	1,020	1,164	144
HG KONG	O	E	83	1,510	1,769	1,929	160
	V	E	81	2,700	1,644	1,769	125
			82	945	1,845	1,986	141
INDIA	O	E	82	423	393	419	26

Product
TSUSA commodity number, description, and unit of quantity

Country	Mode	Reg	Yr	Quantity	F.A.S.	C.I.F.	Charges
			83	954	1,292	1,417	125
	V	E	83	1,350	573	710	137
			83	6,300	2,345	2,656	311
JAPAN	V	E	82	526	1,426	1,641	215
			85	39	1,269	1,414	145
KOR REP	V	W	81	805	727	858	131
MEXICO	A	E	84	1,642	5,658	6,524	866
	O	E	84	5,456	1,909	1,909	
	V	E	86	41,140	15,395	18,412	3,017
PAKISTN	O	E	82	288	421	437	16
PHIL R	V	E	81	410	1,304	1,541	237
			82	575	2,337	2,377	40
			86	1,000	1,800	1,994	194
SPAIN	V	E	82	1,350	1,256	1,546	290
SWITZLD	V	E	82	1,764	1,222	1,291	69
			83	2,866	2,071	2,206	135
			84	1,984	1,577	1,640	63
THAILND	A	E	84	19,973	18,664	38,165	19,501
	V	E	84	414	1,300	1,461	161
			82	451	270	308	38
	V	W	81	63	265	285	20
			84	319	867	950	83
TURKEY	V	E	81	15,800	24,381	25,322	941
			82	10,119	4,536	4,849	313
U KING	N	E	81	611	830	892	62
	O	E	82	225	368	382	14
			85	1,200	1,233	1,329	96

1523800 FRUIT PEEL PRES O PREP NSPF (LB)

Country	Mode	Reg	Yr	Quantity	F.A.S.	C.I.F.	Charges
TOTAL			81	17,540	14,832	16,187	1,355
			82	57,624	54,741	64,968	10,227
			83	10,898	10,418	11,601	1,183
			84	24,240	21,816	24,446	2,630
			85	21,279	7,764	9,609	1,845
			86	15,825	14,506	16,771	2,265
AUSTRAL	V	E	82	1,433	2,766	2,885	119
BRAZIL	V	W	82	2,368	1,250	1,542	292
CHINA M	V	E	81	281	680	696	16
			84	500	928	1,012	84
	V	W	81	880	797	883	86
			83	270	394	448	54
			84	1,649	2,922	3,168	246
			85	330	1,826	1,861	35
COLOMB	V	W	82	51,298	48,000	57,600	9,600
DENMARK	A	E	85	1,818	1,229	1,819	590
DOM REP	V	E	82	1,176	700	738	38
			84	2,760	828	985	157
			85	17,128	2,714	3,760	1,046
FR GERM	O	E	82	120	373	481	108
	V	E	84	344	697	733	36
FRANCE	N	E	84	706	2,364	3,058	694
	V	E	84	149	1,133	1,230	97
GREECE	V	E	81	3,600	3,856	4,305	449
HG KONG	V	E	81	2,400	1,411	1,530	119
			82	500	596	616	20
			83	1,200	900	969	69
	V	W	81	8,516	5,696	6,004	308
			83	1,980	1,183	1,241	58
			84	2,070	2,748	2,849	101
			85	2,003	1,995	2,169	174
HONDURA	V	E	81	1,200	657	709	52
ITALY	V	E	84	291	725	757	32
JAPAN	V	W	81	38	310	340	30
			83	95	277	300	23
KOR REP	V	W	81	625	1,425	1,720	295
PHIL R	V	E	83	600	310	363	53
	V	W	84	5,025	1,763	2,024	261
PORTUGL	V	E	86	12,433	8,039	9,887	1,848
SWITZLD	A	E	83	440	1,896	2,172	276
	V	E	82	440	300	300	
			83	3,087	2,351	2,507	156
	V	W	86	330	1,158	1,184	26
THAILND	V	E	83	189	330	376	46
			84	8,968	6,772	7,599	827
	V	W	82	289	756	806	50
			83	3,037	2,777	3,225	448
U KING	V	E	84	1,778	936	1,031	95
			86	3,062	5,309	5,700	391

Fruit, prepared or preserved
1468600 BERRIES, PRES OR PRES, NSPF (LB)

Country	Mode	Reg	Yr	Quantity	F.A.S.	C.I.F.	Charges
TOTAL			81	84,154	61,183	70,628	9,445

Product TSUSA commodity number, description, and unit of quantity Country	Mode	Reg	Yr	Quantity	F.A.S.	C.I.F.	Charges
			82	56,382	52,651	57,746	5,095
			83	79,645	67,143	74,878	7,735
			84	232,802	140,069	164,873	24,804
			85	351,626	182,682	206,439	23,757
			86	165,249	117,639	131,852	14,213
AUSTRIA	V	E	82	202	587	612	25
			83	605	1,770	1,887	117
			84	1,520	1,934	2,171	237
			85	997	1,199	1,376	177
BELGIUM	V	E	84	1,653	1,301	1,451	150
CANADA	O	E	84	342	845	845	
	O	W	81	5,775	3,074	3,074	
			82	10,450	5,975	5,975	
			83	6,410	2,708	2,708	
			85	80,640	36,990	36,990	
CHILE	V	E	85	20,766	33,028	37,393	4,365
CHINA M	V	W	82	2,940	627	821	194
CHINA T	V	H	84	1,124	1,012	1,020	8
	V	W	84	6,000	1,550	1,694	144
COLOMB	A	E	83	1,204	1,260	1,855	595
	V	E	81	5,325	5,668	6,286	618
			82	4,967	4,890	5,336	446
			85	13,623	6,586	7,929	1,343
DOM REP	V	E	84	1,995	1,396	1,529	133
FR GERM	O	E	81	307	752	936	184
			82	972	700	786	86
			86	8,360	7,557	8,896	1,339
	V	E	82	3,810	4,968	5,589	621
			83	1,800	1,652	1,854	202
			84	5,287	3,793	4,187	394
			85	4,002	3,742	4,085	343
			86	7,912	8,523	9,220	697
	V	W	83	994	1,030	1,213	183
FRANCE	N	E	83	16,920	19,528	22,738	3,210
	N	W	84	4,195	5,802	6,408	606
	O	E	81	2,922	3,714	4,037	323
			82	2,489	3,127	3,327	200
			86	360	1,322	1,417	95
	V	E	81	3,253	5,283	5,602	319
			82	4,533	5,960	6,507	547
			83	329	305	352	47
			84	9,761	6,750	7,547	797
			85	3,011	3,066	3,422	356
			86	17,364	22,916	26,521	3,605
	V	W	81	225	308	322	14
HUNGARY	V	E	84	52,878	16,632	22,803	6,171
INDIA	O	E	84	1,651	908	1,111	203
	V	E	81	1,685	908	1,088	180
			83	635	429	494	65
	V	W	81	952	416	505	89
			82	360	309	364	55
			84	466	260	313	53
ITALY	V	E	82	7,242	5,118	5,804	686
			83	7,872	3,713	4,487	774
			84	26,481	22,130	25,535	3,405
			85	42,637	12,130	13,792	1,662
N ZEAL	A	W	84	252	574	785	211
	V	E	84	37,778	10,507	16,245	5,738
			85	9,180	3,574	4,609	1,035
	V	W	85	58,492	21,888	28,412	6,524
NETHLDS	V	E	83	1,799	2,029	2,116	87
			84	2,923	2,980	3,180	200
POLAND	O	E	84	2,200	2,002	2,402	400
	V	E	81	39,150	12,815	17,641	4,826
			83	12,771	5,515	6,083	568
			84	6,188	2,275	2,738	463
			85	13,478	5,720	7,861	2,141
			86	8,197	4,634	5,357	723
REP SAF	V	E	86	37,421	9,666	11,387	1,721
ROMANIA	V	E	83	4,800	2,318	2,619	301
			84	20,432	10,744	12,106	1,362
			85	3,307	1,366	1,538	172
SPAIN	V	E	85	40,565	11,127	12,552	1,425
			86	40,880	10,436	12,829	2,393
SWEDEN	N	E	86	6,922	9,915	10,909	994
	O	E	85	3,000	1,462	1,559	97
			86	3,170	4,768	5,149	381
	V	E	81	13,368	19,007	20,886	1,879
			83	349	1,056	1,094	38
			84	2,444	3,401	3,762	361
	V	W	81	233	538	595	57
			84	582	1,907	2,040	133
SWITZLD	V	E	81	3,816	2,414	2,740	326
			82	14,724	16,360	17,935	1,575

Product TSUSA commodity number, description, and unit of quantity Country	Mode	Reg	Yr	Quantity	F.A.S.	C.I.F.	Charges
			83	15,706	16,118	17,258	1,140
			84	19,118	19,220	20,462	1,242
			85	13,489	12,384	13,564	1,180
			86	21,284	21,964	23,142	1,178
THAILND	V	E	81	1,200	764	857	93
			82	600	912	1,137	225
			83	507	678	774	96
	V	W	84	2,682	1,741	1,903	162
			85	29,045	15,212	16,520	1,308
			86	6,000	3,590	3,988	398
TURKEY	V	E	86	957	1,026	1,131	105
U KING	N	E	83	2,256	2,969	3,187	218
	O	E	84	5,345	10,832	11,511	672
			85	3,544	7,792	8,195	403
			86	3,303	8,069	8,433	364
	V	E	81	4,650	3,699	3,987	288
			82	3,093	3,118	3,553	435
			83	1,657	2,238	2,307	69
			84	10,471	5,478	6,342	864
			86	3,119	3,253	3,473	220
	V	W	81	1,293	1,823	2,072	249
			83	165	266	291	25
			84	8,313	3,425	4,007	582
USSR	O	E	83	2,866	1,561	1,561	
YUGOSLV	V	E	84	721	670	776	106
			85	11,850	5,416	6,642	1,226

1473600 CITRUS FRUIT PREP PRES NSPF (LB)

Country	Mode	Reg	Yr	Quantity	F.A.S.	C.I.F.	Charges
TOTAL			81	4,749	4,807	5,546	739
			82	37,526	32,285	36,193	3,908
			83	20,651	14,215	15,191	976
			84	113,688	92,695	101,640	8,945
			85	48,232	27,444	34,104	6,660
			86	152,569	66,042	72,511	6,469
BOTSWAN	V	E	86	21,450	4,565	6,006	1,441
CHILE	V	E	85	6,614	2,668	3,466	798
CHINA T	V	E	82	600	420	521	101
			85	13,500	7,025	8,289	1,264
	V	W	81	1,790	1,080	1,300	220
			85	2,990	2,240	2,398	158
COLOMB	V	E	82	2,338	2,790	3,273	483
			86	18,168	10,185	10,580	395
DOM REP	V	E	82	12,512	8,465	8,703	238
			84	2,944	874	934	60
ECUADOR	V	E	83	1,968	2,500	2,641	141
FR GERM	V	E	85	992	2,554	2,759	205
			86	529	1,943	2,013	70
FRANCE	N	E	84	6,319	6,357	7,296	939
	V	E	82	500	1,121	1,194	73
			83	397	918	985	67
	V	W	81	507	2,114	2,259	145
			82	129	517	553	36
GREECE	O	E	82	300	276	276	
HAITI	V	E	83	17,207	9,366	10,054	688
HG KONG	V	W	86	33,730	11,250	12,046	796
HONDURA	V	E	85	3,918	1,866	4,821	2,955
INDIA	O	E	84	476	608	608	
	V	E	81	882	574	676	102
			82	1,003	1,102	1,250	148
			86	625	1,123	1,281	158
	V	W	81	1,124	709	948	239
ISRAEL	N	E	86	18,975	6,655	7,898	1,243
	O	E	83	550	727	769	42
	V	E	85	13,800	5,225	5,969	744
			86	5,175	1,785	2,057	272
JAPAN	V	E	85	39	1,296	1,411	115
MALAYSA	V	E	82	420	780	876	96
PHIL R	V	E	82	4,500	5,849	6,739	890
	V	W	83	308	297	329	32
			84	16,891	16,717	19,440	2,723
			85	1,249	1,185	1,335	150
SINGAPR	V	W	81	446	330	363	33
THAILND	O	W	84	1,793	1,344	1,457	113
	V	W	82	15,224	10,965	12,808	1,843
			83	221	407	413	6
			84	85,265	66,795	71,905	5,110
			85	5,130	3,385	3,656	271
			86	46,055	21,785	23,188	1,403
U KING	V	E	86	7,862	6,751	7,442	691

1483500 MELONS, PREP OR PRES (LB)

Country	Mode	Reg	Yr	Quantity	F.A.S.	C.I.F.	Charges
TOTAL			81	405,338	141,595	170,125	28,709
			82	159,470	71,473	89,597	18,124
			83	104,334	36,150	39,675	3,525

Product
TSUSA commodity number, description, and unit of quantity

Country	Mode	Reg	Yr	Quantity	F.A.S.	C.I.F.	Charges
			84	635,575	127,238	168,342	41,104
			85	873,676	201,892	251,507	49,615
			86	2,834,019	834,429	999,714	165,285
ARAB EM	V	W	85	11,023	2,400	2,979	579
C RICA	V	E	82	2,319	696	899	203
			84	40,880	8,176	11,105	2,929
			86	41,040	9,850	12,850	3,000
	V	W	82	52,150	26,331	38,051	11,720
CANADA	O	E	84	10	366	366	
CHILE	V	E	86	63,525	16,828	24,549	7,721
	V	W	85	119,049	16,000	25,455	9,455
CHINA M	V	E	84	9,122	3,611	4,529	918
			86	13,850	7,372	8,163	791
	V	W	81	18,731	6,156	7,076	920
			82	11,489	6,902	7,481	579
			83	21,097	6,049	6,530	481
			84	8,445	1,612	1,703	91
			86	19,659	7,729	8,117	388
CHINA T	O	E	84	485	336	369	33
	V	E	81	1,032	786	837	51
			84	2,742	3,038	3,363	325
			85	900	1,430	1,887	457
			86	3,085	6,074	6,437	363
	V	W	81	3,439	2,120	2,239	119
			82	11,850	7,280	7,751	471
			83	7,520	4,160	4,619	459
			84	3,930	2,247	2,438	191
DOM REP	N	E	84	353,871	63,522	90,376	26,854
	V	E	86	49,240	4,280	7,494	3,214
FRANCE	V	W	84	2,700	4,261	4,483	222
GUATMAL	N	E	81	127,320	43,144	55,424	12,280
	O	E	86	32,666	2,475	2,475	
	V	E	81	146,988	49,123	62,591	13,647
			82	42,383	11,035	14,274	3,239
			84	49,000	9,800	12,877	3,077
			85	251,187	110,323	133,196	22,873
			86	1,359,964	463,132	579,253	116,121
	V	W	86	338,230	103,661	129,299	25,638
HG KONG	V	E	85	19,489	10,256	11,627	1,371
	V	W	84	500	417	462	45
			85	11,400	1,880	2,081	201
			86	5,700	1,300	1,386	86
HONDURA	V	E	85	138,000	24,470	36,915	12,445
INDIA	V	E	83	889	374	445	71
	V	W	83	2,116	958	1,186	228
			84	635	275	333	58
ISRAEL	V	E	81	17,100	7,500	9,098	1,598
			83	23,418	9,497	10,610	1,113
JAPAN	A	E	85	61	1,079	1,145	66
	V	E	81	113	289	313	24
			83	349	764	820	56
			84	286	419	450	31
			86	704	1,548	1,635	87
	V	W	81	285	615	661	46
			82	132	514	545	31
			83	4,768	9,795	10,658	863
			84	2,185	4,357	4,816	459
MEXICO	O	E	81	89,970	31,541	31,541	
			83	39,690	1,836	1,836	
			84	36,250	2,132	2,132	
	O	W	85	298,809	31,645	31,645	
			86	819,988	166,492	166,492	
PANAMA	V	E	85	23,758	2,409	4,577	2,168
			86	35,312	22,133	25,200	3,067
PHIL R	V	W	84	6,504	1,799	2,006	207
			86	5,536	4,260	5,031	771
SALVADR	V	E	86	42,770	15,975	20,013	4,038
SURINAM	V	E	84	661	1,080	1,195	115
SWITZLD	O	E	86	2,750	1,320	1,320	
THAILND	O	E	82	1,501	902	992	90
	V	E	82	875	512	560	48
			83	4,100	2,091	2,325	234
	V	W	81	360	321	345	24
			82	36,771	17,301	19,044	1,743
			83	387	626	646	20
			84	481	350	394	44
TURKEY	V	E	84	116,888	19,440	24,945	5,505

1496000 FRUITS, NSPF, PREP OR PRES (LB)

Country	Mode	Reg	Yr	Quantity	F.A.S.	C.I.F.	Charges
TOTAL			81	2,313,742	1,842,681	2,045,241	202,590
			82	3,764,448	2,651,361	2,943,521	292,160
			83	5,516,119	3,923,199	4,299,595	376,396
			84	4,924,379	3,496,425	3,895,397	398,972
			85	5,716,282	4,023,299	4,449,907	426,608

Product
TSUSA commodity number, description, and unit of quantity

Country	Mode	Reg	Yr	Quantity	F.A.S.	C.I.F.	Charges
			86	10,683,693	6,969,634	7,628,081	658,447
ARGENT	V	E	81	18,519	3,125	3,370	245
AUSTRAL	V	E	82	347	368	446	78
			83	1,720	1,004	1,121	117
			84	1,543	3,240	3,365	125
			85	441	1,072	1,116	44
	V	H	82	276	251	278	27
	V	W	82	220	455	470	15
AUSTRIA	V	E	83	293	431	463	32
BAHAMAS	A	E	82	4,500	2,025	2,525	500
BELGIUM	A	E	85	5,255	6,569	10,261	3,692
	V	E	84	3,699	3,022	3,608	586
BRAZIL	V	E	83	3,914	2,337	2,847	510
	V	W	83	772	2,155	2,758	603
C RICA	A	W	85	933	2,000	2,358	358
			86	858	4,125	4,388	263
	O	E	84	2,795	2,645	2,839	194
	V	E	81	105,010	24,008	29,847	5,839
			82	2,124	4,932	5,170	238
			83	58,344	75,159	82,639	7,480
			84	89,676	48,210	56,259	8,049
			85	2,467	13,995	14,415	420
	V	W	82	11,207	3,979	6,166	2,187
			83	32,491	5,836	9,440	3,604
CANADA	O	E	82	12,540	6,177	6,177	
			86	1,500	1,235	1,235	
	O	W	82	28,000	6,720	6,720	
CHILE	A	E	84	231	500	826	326
			85	581	1,896	2,646	750
	V	E	84	3,611	819	1,308	489
			85	20,800	14,153	16,948	2,795
CHINA M	N	E	81	100,618	73,984	82,479	8,495
	O	E	84	1,600	1,173	1,373	200
	O	W	84	1,350	1,182	1,273	91
			86	114	2,198	2,388	190
	V	E	82	165,680	100,119	116,433	16,314
			83	205,026	115,487	132,910	17,423
			84	149,278	131,759	145,137	13,378
			85	124,356	108,445	119,413	10,968
			86	424,181	307,581	339,031	31,450
	V	H	81	3,067	4,874	5,171	297
			82	2,790	2,546	2,811	265
			83	5,422	3,781	4,129	348
			84	3,159	3,464	3,808	344
			85	1,202	1,369	1,541	172
			86	13,229	9,198	10,460	1,262
	V	W	81	142,201	96,529	104,345	7,816
			82	106,289	85,936	92,078	6,142
			83	209,783	141,306	150,834	9,528
			84	275,061	193,329	209,566	16,237
			85	241,524	200,783	215,407	14,624
			86	358,124	234,730	256,007	21,277
CHINA T	O	E	81	4,500	2,700	2,917	217
	V	E	81	138,942	88,514	98,265	9,751
			82	79,825	60,485	66,532	6,047
			83	110,912	90,859	100,613	9,754
			84	111,709	80,493	90,078	9,585
			85	147,295	107,769	120,742	12,973
			86	259,042	163,918	185,847	21,929
	V	H	81	12,942	18,336	19,902	1,566
			82	8,200	13,036	14,152	1,116
			83	23,127	34,538	37,095	2,557
			84	11,873	14,687	15,710	1,023
			85	3,702	6,661	7,126	465
			86	12,556	18,315	19,790	1,475
	V	W	81	158,804	94,023	99,917	5,894
			82	140,310	80,946	88,640	7,694
			83	198,720	130,396	139,184	8,788
			84	263,900	156,671	171,329	14,658
			85	541,647	262,785	287,753	24,968
			86	533,651	361,013	387,840	26,827
COLOMB	A	E	82	4,845	9,488	10,891	1,403
			83	22,858	23,853	26,466	2,613
			84	58,918	108,701	121,850	13,149
			85	44,243	68,642	78,223	9,581
			86	55,510	60,168	65,011	4,843
	V	E	81	14,055	12,593	14,246	1,653
			82	71,932	57,707	64,331	6,624
			83	18,860	14,837	16,667	1,830
			84	12,750	3,666	3,868	202
			85	4,200	3,300	3,608	308
DOM REP	N	E	81	44,690	27,560	32,750	5,190
			82	4,200	1,840	2,500	660
			83	24,380	9,710	18,107	8,397

Product
TSUSA commodity number, description, and unit of quantity

Country	Mode	Reg	Yr	Quantity	F.A.S.	C.I.F.	Charges
			86	208,000	65,678	84,853	19,175
	V	E	81	103,919	48,487	57,986	9,499
			82	34,646	14,373	16,468	2,095
			83	36,892	17,951	21,784	3,833
			84	123,115	40,888	49,890	9,002
			85	149,140	53,999	62,385	8,386
	V	W	84	5,200	2,652	3,419	767
DOMINCA	V	E	85	608	1,145	1,370	225
ECUADOR	A	E	84	3,746	5,626	6,344	718
	V	E	81	14,003	8,740	9,789	1,049
			82	26,265	22,800	24,770	1,970
			83	28,027	24,440	26,474	2,034
			84	9,000	6,600	7,405	805
			86	33,587	23,130	26,293	3,163
FR GERM	V	E	83	13,459	6,092	6,321	229
			84	150,493	69,209	82,870	13,661
			85	6,327	3,847	4,559	712
FRANCE	A	E	83	865	1,680	2,104	424
			85	3,581	10,695	13,441	2,746
			86	330	1,016	1,300	284
	N	E	82	2,165	3,417	3,908	491
			84	380	801	1,015	214
			86	18,359	60,410	65,823	5,413
	O	E	81	249	315	390	75
			84	62	270	320	50
			85	6,162	7,830	8,739	909
	V	E	81	959	634	722	88
			82	978	499	558	59
			83	9,819	7,252	8,122	870
			84	1,460	1,022	1,137	115
			85	593	1,322	1,476	154
			86	4,166	5,256	5,675	419
	V	W	82	298	605	649	44
			83	476	649	720	71
			84	595	537	681	144
GREECE	V	E	81	8,666	6,917	8,040	1,123
			82	2,265	2,357	2,773	416
			83	7,901	6,040	6,745	705
			84	10,251	6,768	7,874	1,106
			85	2,215	2,640	2,856	216
			86	11,002	8,567	10,394	1,827
GUATMAL	A	E	84	20,187	2,894	7,485	4,591
	A	W	84	11,442	3,909	6,814	2,905
	N	E	82	45,638	32,474	36,565	4,091
	V	E	81	4,440	4,440	5,070	630
			82	17,400	10,660	12,185	1,525
			84	18,559	1,688	4,311	2,623
			85	68,272	23,956	31,438	7,482
			86	38,160	12,680	16,527	3,847
	V	W	85	33,922	2,444	6,179	3,735
			86	71,533	11,738	16,068	4,330
HAITI	A	E	83	50	800	906	106
	V	E	82	27,829	8,824	11,488	2,664
HG KONG	O	E	86	2,769	1,660	1,953	293
	O	W	85	5,850	2,475	2,781	306
	V	E	81	24,899	29,637	32,130	2,493
			82	51,103	45,673	50,429	4,756
			83	56,940	62,316	68,854	6,538
			84	72,317	101,236	109,582	8,346
			85	73,589	53,471	62,181	8,710
			86	222,316	181,531	200,615	19,084
	V	H	81	4,441	4,896	5,205	309
			82	9,052	10,979	11,993	1,014
			83	9,209	8,032	8,749	717
			84	6,032	5,947	6,498	551
			85	2,400	3,195	3,507	312
			86	2,650	2,602	2,805	203
	V	W	81	37,262	40,355	42,536	2,181
			82	74,222	62,580	67,246	4,666
			83	70,686	65,455	69,800	4,345
			84	98,905	79,036	84,622	5,586
			85	60,368	59,067	63,600	4,533
			86	175,987	120,453	128,997	8,544
INDIA	V	E	81	1,447	2,402	2,750	348
			82	855	988	1,177	189
			83	18,312	17,874	20,281	2,407
			84	7,253	6,947	8,247	1,300
			85	3,024	3,619	4,032	413
	V	W	81	2,627	3,085	4,067	982
			82	1,217	1,574	1,870	296
			83	1,959	1,237	1,530	293
			84	24,346	16,449	18,963	2,514
INDNSIA	V	E	84	1,250	560	819	259
	V	W	81	1,060	993	1,105	112
			83	1,432	1,315	1,408	93
			84	387	990	1,060	70
			86	4,986	8,626	9,508	882
ISRAEL	V	E	83	4,500	3,000	3,366	366
			84	2,646	847	1,063	216
ITALY	A	E	84	143	1,625	1,723	98
	V	E	82	258	333	369	36
			83	1,800	1,308	1,381	73
			84	2,485	3,036	3,295	259
			85	1,762	5,420	6,137	717
			86	565	3,316	3,554	238
	V	W	82	127	456	515	59
			83	2,920	4,754	5,246	492
			84	22,072	3,031	3,184	153
			86	1,387	2,252	2,304	52
JAMAICA	N	E	83	28,684	12,959	14,121	1,162
JAPAN	A	H	82	2,852	15,524	24,275	8,751
	N	H	81	8,073	41,810	59,136	17,326
			83	5,600	28,542	38,589	10,047
			84	8,675	35,339	46,811	11,472
			85	5,066	28,015	38,824	10,809
			86	8,100	49,091	67,703	18,612
	V	E	81	1,695	1,483	1,608	125
			82	1,768	1,500	1,681	181
			83	5,085	3,814	4,183	369
			84	1,466	3,243	3,576	333
			85	3,300	3,416	3,717	301
			86	12,252	24,112	26,563	2,451
	V	H	86	210	1,444	1,562	118
	V	W	81	3,347	3,560	3,727	167
			83	4,024	5,136	5,515	379
			84	433	1,237	1,347	110
			85	7,754	11,206	12,047	841
			86	3,240	2,456	2,740	284
KOR REP	V	E	83	720	2,260	2,412	152
			84	1,365	4,029	4,415	386
			86	1,779	3,108	3,286	178
	V	H	83	720	1,723	1,874	151
	V	W	82	310	530	573	43
			83	1,401	3,602	3,983	381
			84	7,916	10,634	12,433	1,799
			85	21,697	51,356	54,133	2,777
			86	41,647	86,125	90,900	4,775
LEBANON	A	W	84	700	720	755	35
	O	E	85	720	1,410	1,410	
MACAO	V	H	83	1,200	618	671	53
MALAYSA	V	E	81	675	453	507	54
			82	7,979	6,291	6,690	399
			83	4,642	3,326	3,500	174
			84	630	947	1,088	141
			85	10,862	10,310	10,956	646
			86	10,270	4,437	5,344	907
	V	W	81	11,550	7,057	8,396	1,339
			82	2,669	2,458	2,688	230
			83	1,604	1,163	1,232	69
			84	2,325	1,384	1,600	216
			85	34,800	22,871	24,541	1,670
			86	149,040	81,736	86,885	5,149
MEXICO	O	E	84	2,039	926	926	
			85	183,721	39,175	39,175	
			86	980,397	251,377	251,377	
	O	W	81	42,778	65,168	65,168	
			82	311,981	228,426	228,426	
			83	1,006,693	307,363	307,363	
			84	386,764	117,352	117,352	
			85	170,250	61,905	61,905	
			86	500,289	87,605	87,605	
	V	W	82	413	300	331	31
N ZEAL	A	W	84	2,342	3,899	5,707	1,808
	V	E	81	10,148	8,287	9,897	1,610
			83	6,000	4,630	5,528	898
			84	9,543	13,710	15,088	1,378
			85	13,946	12,075	14,172	2,097
			86	134,634	41,807	55,342	13,535
	V	W	86	172,209	84,196	95,985	11,789
NETHLDS	A	E	83	106	300	340	40
	O	E	86	2,116	1,702	2,079	377
PAKISTN	V	E	84	441	400	450	50
			85	900	1,110	1,387	277
PHIL R	N	W	83	2,059	2,217	2,531	314
	O	W	85	1,080	1,116	1,230	114
	V	E	81	169,107	153,839	171,363	17,524
			82	136,338	127,136	143,382	16,246
			83	126,886	125,647	142,447	16,800
			84	156,570	132,107	153,145	21,038
			85	116,413	101,222	117,673	16,451

Product TSUSA commodity number, description, and unit of quantity Country	Mode	Reg	Yr	Quantity	F.A.S.	C.I.F.	Charges
			86	114,970	110,569	128,063	17,494
	V	H	81	19,751	21,346	25,565	4,219
			82	19,572	23,128	26,864	3,736
			83	24,494	28,435	33,251	4,816
			84	29,446	31,029	37,538	6,509
			85	36,648	41,328	48,667	7,339
			86	29,454	30,805	35,175	4,370
	V	W	81	374,222	347,228	386,168	38,970
			82	515,951	477,980	535,763	57,783
			83	481,582	418,924	471,498	52,574
			84	664,086	486,308	556,835	70,527
			85	588,056	482,833	542,198	59,365
			86	502,665	427,481	477,009	49,528
PORTUGL	V	E	81	3,963	4,439	5,039	600
			83	782	825	883	58
			84	675	360	398	38
			85	2,975	6,020	6,495	475
			86	3,009	1,774	1,892	118
REP SAF	V	E	84	4,126	4,714	5,032	318
SALVADR	A	W	84	1,018	349	1,196	847
SINGAPR	O	W	81	1,800	1,735	1,735	
	V	E	81	7,202	6,367	7,153	786
			82	8,770	10,077	10,715	638
			83	20,296	16,580	19,337	2,757
			84	1,138	988	1,312	324
			86	28,500	13,650	15,698	2,048
	V	H	82	450	398	440	42
	V	W	81	26,322	23,680	25,441	1,761
			82	52,114	34,628	37,712	3,084
			83	21,332	23,279	25,251	1,972
			84	24,991	20,019	21,575	1,556
			85	16,482	23,380	25,816	2,436
			86	87,539	60,803	63,785	2,982
SPAIN	V	E	84	43,121	10,749	12,739	1,990
			86	5,212	3,822	4,584	762
	V	W	81	2,205	405	638	233
			82	33,069	7,883	9,960	2,077
			83	33,069	7,889	9,960	2,071
			86	24,700	7,010	8,515	1,505
SRI LKA	V	W	85	1,228	1,395	1,563	168
SWITZLD	V	E	82	3,085	4,033	4,106	73
			83	1,542	811	867	56
			84	4,296	6,542	7,048	506
			85	7,074	9,560	10,445	885
THAILND	A	H	81	420	420	1,517	1,097
	N	E	81	103,050	84,112	93,352	9,240
			82	94,537	88,072	102,192	14,120
			83	254,098	234,731	262,078	27,347
			84	210,199	118,679	133,649	14,970
			86	16,995	19,140	20,738	1,598
	N	H	82	2,324	4,326	8,494	4,168
			84	2,047	1,602	1,815	213
	N	W	81	361,172	297,424	323,196	25,772
			82	1,346,120	738,846	812,131	73,285
			84	595,682	460,911	494,542	33,631
			86	3,090,129	1,991,150	2,155,959	164,809
	O	E	83	897	600	655	55
			85	4,742	4,649	5,871	1,222
	O	W	83	10,767	4,532	4,842	310
	V	E	81	7,848	8,670	9,702	1,032
			82	63,087	47,121	55,244	8,123
			83	51,496	37,931	41,959	4,028
			84	225,704	197,239	220,546	23,307
			85	440,205	267,670	302,567	34,897
			86	915,758	679,336	758,196	78,860
	V	H	81	4,667	4,076	4,582	506
			82	9,730	13,830	16,335	2,505
			83	9,783	8,205	9,309	1,104
			84	1,345	816	918	102
			85	7,700	16,852	19,426	2,574
			86	6,453	15,461	17,673	2,212
	V	W	81	205,908	162,328	176,581	14,253
			82	211,684	160,327	182,952	22,625
			83	2,206,796	1,732,083	1,881,718	149,635
			84	931,514	695,470	763,878	68,408
			85	2,444,507	1,767,102	1,921,442	154,340
			86	1,348,976	1,178,112	1,269,259	91,147
TUNISIA	A	W	86	1,682	5,600	6,360	760
TURKEY	V	E	86	10,248	4,238	4,959	721
U KING	O	E	84	433	324	357	33
	V	E	81	519	1,647	1,771	124
			82	2,042	2,945	3,284	339
			83	14,727	19,287	20,731	1,444
			84	13,113	16,511	17,885	1,374
			85	10,098	10,313	12,026	1,713

Product TSUSA commodity number, description, and unit of quantity Country	Mode	Reg	Yr	Quantity	F.A.S.	C.I.F.	Charges
			86	26,658	30,091	34,179	4,088
	V	W	85	3,607	4,217	4,934	717
USSR	O	E	83	7,165	3,903	3,903	
VENEZ	A	E	84	6,757	1,759	2,623	864
	V	E	85	25,992	8,229	11,049	2,820

1500500 FRUIT MIXTURES PREPARED (LB)

Country	Mode	Reg	Yr	Quantity	F.A.S.	C.I.F.	Charges
TOTAL			81	8,329,175	3,203,392	3,264,996	61,604
			82	10,656,037	3,200,362	3,252,671	52,309
			83	14,108,363	3,238,185	3,295,316	57,131
			84	30,088,002	9,511,345	10,297,059	785,714
			85	49,838,856	16,618,088	18,615,081	1,996,993
			86	35,422,007	10,270,152	11,098,816	828,664
ANTIGUA	V	E	85	38,700	10,452	12,642	2,190
ARGENT	V	E	84	1,924,432	563,228	670,448	107,220
			85	1,357,107	348,454	418,861	70,407
AUSTRAL	A	E	85	2,116	2,819	4,492	1,673
	A	H	82	441	328	987	659
	N	E	85	425,880	132,929	161,599	28,670
	V	E	85	905,063	301,041	370,465	69,424
			86	1,810,425	594,279	693,875	99,596
	V	W	82	237	582	603	21
			85	172,743	69,675	80,699	11,024
			86	84,851	69,664	83,184	13,520
AUSTRIA	V	E	82	2,367	5,158	5,448	290
			83	853	1,629	1,786	157
BELGIUM	V	E	83	15,771	12,307	14,075	1,768
			84	17,993	8,863	10,443	1,580
			85	50,695	19,084	21,921	2,837
			86	1,858	1,346	1,526	180
	V	W	83	1,888	980	1,101	121
			84	2,514	1,305	1,532	227
			85	2,832	1,393	1,675	282
CANADA	A	H	83	2,322	2,723	2,958	235
			84	5,792	6,278	6,969	691
			85	6,535	6,769	7,648	879
			86	1,050	1,247	1,247	
	N	W	85	38,030	34,638	34,638	
	O	E	81	3,306	3,118	3,118	
			82	18,082	10,920	11,481	561
			83	109,827	77,105	78,553	1,448
			84	400,263	345,208	345,208	
			85	413,070	443,835	443,835	
			86	702,214	641,281	641,281	
	O	W	82	10,704	14,245	14,245	
			83	4,497	14,308	14,308	
			84	22,456	20,686	20,686	
			86	620,788	492,668	492,668	
	V	E	86	37,696	11,400	12,787	1,387
CHILE	O	E	86	37,400	11,189	12,704	1,515
	V	E	84	758,739	250,736	286,010	35,274
			85	2,050,009	697,914	782,676	84,762
			86	2,311,905	703,781	799,164	95,383
CHINA M	V	E	82	6,241	6,792	7,496	704
			85	13,650	8,763	9,732	969
	V	W	81	969	2,686	2,832	146
			82	4,912	5,507	5,834	327
			83	3,314	5,280	5,582	302
			85	129,159	53,415	62,993	9,578
CHINA T	O	E	84	265	332	332	
	V	E	81	41,250	17,500	20,226	2,726
			86	5,250	8,780	9,428	648
	V	W	81	204,286	86,667	96,583	9,916
			86	992	1,850	2,164	314
COLOMB	V	E	81	3,135	1,725	2,071	346
			82	2,250	1,731	1,933	202
DOM REP	A	E	81	1,741	725	1,066	341
			82	7,033	3,955	7,873	3,918
			83	5,000	920	2,134	1,214
	N	E	84	4,722	2,360	2,742	382
			86	157,220	57,925	68,565	10,640
	V	E	81	16,368	5,782	6,574	792
			82	16,980	8,425	9,280	855
			83	2,755	1,740	1,906	166
			84	1,966	1,200	1,340	140
			85	2,730	1,638	1,839	201
			86	721,091	248,733	298,055	49,322
FR GERM	A	E	81	68	307	313	6
	N	E	83	1,156	1,011	1,130	119
			84	1,169	910	2,220	1,310
	O	E	85	6,918	8,025	9,180	1,155
			86	4,896	4,394	4,394	
	V	E	84	30,327	19,128	23,473	4,345
			85	142,085	74,819	89,756	14,937

Product TSUSA commodity number, description, and unit of quantity — Country	Mode	Reg	Yr	Quantity	F.A.S.	C.I.F.	Charges
			86	35,534	26,477	30,126	3,649
FRANCE	A	E	83	700	756	1,376	620
	A	W	85	545	1,729	2,448	719
	N	E	84	65,091	88,334	97,321	8,987
	N	W	83	1,819	7,226	7,902	676
	O	E	84	1,251	891	1,039	148
	V	E	82	1,967	3,404	3,616	212
			83	10,160	14,443	15,777	1,334
			84	9,186	8,169	9,075	906
			85	181,934	167,648	181,863	14,215
			86	62,847	46,446	52,500	6,054
	V	W	81	1,555	4,058	4,338	280
			82	2,858	6,686	7,053	367
			83	2,004	8,128	9,007	879
			84	305	941	1,010	69
GREECE	V	E	84	2,646	1,134	1,320	186
			85	1,824,658	648,254	765,058	116,804
			86	3,237,107	1,076,272	1,256,961	180,689
	V	W	81	1,400	2,660	3,052	392
GUATMAL	V	E	85	40,000	10,000	12,696	2,696
			86	25,755	2,327	3,794	1,467
HG KONG	V	E	81	4,240	7,598	8,039	441
			82	7,790	12,518	13,738	1,220
			86	4,824	2,754	3,010	256
	V	W	81	1,386	2,178	2,304	126
			82	556	794	842	48
			83	23,224	17,575	18,773	1,198
			84	813	1,711	1,851	140
			85	3,270	2,734	2,895	161
HONDURA	V	E	84	32,504	1,912	4,070	2,158
			85	36,800	1,900	4,778	2,878
			86	563,900	29,900	73,234	43,334
HUNGARY	V	E	82	43,500	10,083	12,615	2,532
INDIA	V	E	82	1,058	550	730	180
			83	410	374	442	68
			84	1,166	683	813	130
	V	W	81	1,552	2,129	2,586	457
			82	3,725	1,501	1,807	306
			83	1,218	1,242	1,432	190
			84	6,289	748	911	163
			85	10,347	7,163	8,520	1,357
INDNSIA	V	W	82	110	265	297	32
ISRAEL	V	E	81	195,599	72,634	83,192	10,558
			82	114,295	48,617	55,284	6,667
			83	45,029	19,229	22,231	3,002
			85	364,942	146,319	163,547	17,228
			86	698,491	260,799	311,499	50,700
	V	W	81	14,835	5,646	6,435	789
			82	12,075	4,685	5,634	949
			83	5,175	1,963	2,390	427
ITALY	N	E	82	10,639	19,659	25,304	5,645
			85	3,814,809	1,292,484	1,516,902	224,418
	O	E	84	29,763	9,694	11,510	1,816
			85	40,881	12,338	14,874	2,536
			86	17,250	6,495	7,585	1,090
	V	E	81	6,577	6,650	7,940	1,290
			82	164	324	359	35
			83	2,823	2,364	2,498	134
			84	3,129,389	1,121,423	1,304,436	183,013
			85	9,177,304	3,105,233	3,671,084	565,851
			86	86,096	33,373	39,653	6,280
	V	W	82	767	1,513	1,618	105
			84	483,211	159,824	191,952	32,128
			85	1,600,426	511,475	612,365	100,890
			86	753	1,624	1,624	
JAMAICA	V	E	81	1,810	1,000	2,094	1,094
JAPAN	V	E	81	308,848	167,765	185,923	18,158
			82	118,028	60,998	67,473	6,475
			83	255,372	130,487	149,395	18,908
			84	153,507	81,848	96,128	14,280
			85	1,773	3,475	3,847	372
			86	2,183	4,256	4,425	169
	V	W	81	89,320	48,270	53,682	5,412
			82	200,595	97,533	108,452	10,919
			83	175,464	86,996	98,697	11,701
			84	184,288	98,228	114,442	16,214
			85	5,771	4,267	4,446	179
			86	3,394	3,167	3,254	87
KOR REP	V	W	81	156,750	81,225	88,182	6,957
MEXICO	O	E	81	7,242,570	2,663,181	2,663,181	
			82	9,955,933	2,835,591	2,835,595	4
			83	13,339,359	2,783,411	2,784,374	963
			84	16,081,515	4,122,777	4,122,777	
			85	15,504,117	4,354,471	4,354,471	
			86	19,189,846	4,320,215	4,320,315	100
	O	W	81	16,480	5,919	5,919	
			84	24,000	7,125	7,125	
			86	20,096	5,652	5,652	
NETHLDS	V	E	85	50,963	28,478	33,272	4,794
			86	97,059	54,858	68,874	14,016
PHIL R	V	E	81	540	531	569	38
			83	900	1,013	1,216	203
			86	4,956	3,735	4,805	1,070
	V	H	84	1,692	1,360	1,554	194
	V	W	81	2,998	3,712	4,101	389
			82	1,620	1,853	2,108	255
			83	2,520	2,554	2,826	272
			84	3,877	3,071	3,619	548
			86	1,620	1,940	2,088	148
REP SAF	A	E	83	114	350	1,239	889
	N	E	85	690,963	238,334	275,584	37,250
	V	E	84	5,848,946	2,282,165	2,593,037	310,872
			85	6,753,658	2,447,238	2,801,263	354,025
			86	2,247,068	669,477	780,943	111,466
	V	W	84	102,898	35,406	41,647	6,241
S ARAB	V	E	85	11,336	3,830	4,539	709
SOMALIA	V	E	85	502,688	189,672	216,194	26,522
SPAIN	O	E	86	42,465	11,860	14,239	2,379
	V	E	83	71,597	19,383	27,352	7,969
			84	727,611	244,289	298,915	54,626
			85	3,221,714	1,124,392	1,335,748	211,356
			86	1,865,513	631,585	733,499	101,914
	V	W	82	89,365	19,059	25,861	6,802
			86	4,050	1,590	1,872	282
SWITZLD	V	E	85	80,950	24,259	27,360	3,101
			86	532,510	151,648	172,526	20,878
THAILND	O	E	85	1,217	1,336	1,687	351
	V	E	81	1,801	1,066	1,259	193
			82	6,295	4,605	5,167	562
			83	3,000	2,230	2,460	230
			84	2,400	1,828	2,027	199
			85	66,336	24,650	28,759	4,109
			86	33,168	12,325	13,763	1,438
	V	W	81	9,162	7,304	7,958	654
			82	13,080	8,710	9,759	1,049
			83	11,497	10,164	11,402	1,238
			84	19,223	11,368	12,082	714
			85	32,987	14,904	16,933	2,029
			86	24,816	8,964	9,726	762
TURKEY	V	E	86	7,937	2,448	2,992	544
U KING	N	E	83	5,351	4,742	5,171	429
			85	4,914	6,310	6,804	494
	O	E	81	375	560	622	62
			82	135	596	653	57
			85	7,825	10,307	10,806	499
			86	12,813	18,493	19,876	1,383
	V	E	82	1,920	2,149	2,425	276
			83	2,240	4,073	4,192	119
			84	5,602	5,875	6,638	763
			85	48,406	19,225	21,687	2,462
			86	102,320	32,935	38,939	6,004
	V	W	81	254	796	837	41
			82	315	1,026	1,101	75
			83	1,004	1,479	1,631	152
			84	191	307	357	50

Grain

Malt extract

1322500 MALT EXTRACT, FLUID (GAL)

Country	Mode	Reg	Yr	Quantity	F.A.S.	C.I.F.	Charges
TOTAL			81	80,040	523,340	596,244	72,905
			82	194,220	1,059,912	1,165,098	105,186
			83	456,481	2,328,443	2,537,734	209,291
			84	678,332	2,898,811	3,178,890	280,079
			85	753,803	3,166,232	3,525,636	359,404
			86	419,582	2,130,047	2,358,271	228,224
AUSTRAL	V	W	81	1,980	9,744	12,486	2,742
			82	1,100	5,369	6,492	1,123
			83	4,734	21,975	25,468	3,493

548   Table 2. U.S. Import Statistics for Non Crop-Specific Commodities by End-Use

Product
TSUSA commodity number, description, and unit of quantity

Country	Mode	Reg	Yr	Quantity	F.A.S.	C.I.F.	Charges
			84	4,686	30,711	34,181	3,470
			85	3,064	12,162	14,362	2,200
			86	6,466	32,138	35,901	3,763
CANADA	A	E	81	55	322	495	173
	A	W	83	5	340	514	174
	O	E	81	12,876	57,862	61,745	3,884
			82	48,835	201,601	201,601	
			83	100,604	435,623	435,623	
			84	216,048	950,209	952,079	1,870
			85	216,107	1,121,034	1,123,734	2,700
			86	107,917	524,257	527,517	3,260
	O	W	81	1,438	16,123	16,123	
			82	3,283	31,441	31,441	
			83	1,532	21,017	21,017	
			84	482	5,631	5,631	
			85	333	3,360	3,360	
			86	918	3,300	3,300	
CHINA M	V	E	81	1,685	17,038	18,377	1,339
	V	E	82	478	1,278	1,518	240
			83	11	350	386	36
			84	442	2,659	3,100	441
	V	W	83	296	859	910	51
DENMARK	V	E	82	314	590	875	285
			83	3,528	7,861	10,453	2,592
DOM REP	V	E	83	2,801	5,087	7,827	2,740
			84	3,482	11,533	14,887	3,354
			85	690	6,454	6,711	257
FINLAND	A	E	84	5,230	20,210	23,990	3,780
			85	2,860	11,879	13,299	1,420
	N	E	86	5,466	26,651	28,352	1,701
	V	E	85	6,600	15,680	19,128	3,448
			86	1,850	8,077	8,315	238
FR GERM	N	E	86	2,807	23,637	29,034	5,397
	O	W	82	27	315	315	
			83	129	1,505	1,505	
			84	30	350	350	
	V	E	84	2,098	22,813	24,539	1,726
			85	687	3,856	5,355	1,499
	V	W	82	413	551	682	131
			83	1,073	6,947	8,264	1,317
			84	440	2,467	4,144	1,677
FRANCE	V	E	84	3,373	8,446	10,046	1,600
GREECE	V	E	85	2,871	19,538	22,736	3,198
HG KONG	V	E	84	25	591	704	113
			86	474	8,146	8,614	468
IRAN	V	E	86	3,248	28,071	34,058	5,987
IRELAND	O	W	83	27	315	315	
	V	E	81	495	3,133	3,966	833
			82	1,080	6,630	8,158	1,528
			83	6,081	21,418	25,736	4,318
			84	5,298	14,934	17,390	2,456
			85	1,320	9,976	12,345	2,369
ITALY	O	E	85	3,100	12,976	12,976	
	V	E	82	8,066	23,581	29,919	6,338
			83	6,160	19,940	23,183	3,243
			84	39,984	124,539	145,939	21,400
			85	56,024	189,579	239,953	50,374
			86	44,442	155,211	187,211	32,000
JAPAN	O	W	83	39	374	374	
	V	H	82	120	390	487	97
			83	265	1,068	1,226	158
			84	90	271	376	105
	V	W	86	361	4,982	5,038	56
KOR REP	V	E	84	150	1,325	1,500	175
	V	W	83	180	430	473	43
			84	513	1,130	1,217	87
			86	214	1,666	1,792	126
MEXICO	O	E	82	550	3,509	4,461	952
	V	E	83	2,160	8,187	9,018	831
NETHLDS	O	E	84	113	2,100	2,331	231
			86	481	6,528	7,178	650
	V	E	83	1,885	22,675	24,399	1,724
			85	8,486	61,703	67,296	5,593
SWITZLD	V	E	83	1,157	3,704	4,704	1,000
U KING	N	E	81	21,930	144,189	161,481	17,292
			82	54,621	358,546	387,971	29,425
			83	180,094	946,122	1,040,834	94,712
			84	143,828	499,985	568,239	68,254
			85	264,629	955,974	1,103,068	147,094
			86	122,544	601,152	672,648	71,496
	N	W	81	5,475	30,768	38,225	7,457
	O	E	81	19,541	167,148	185,953	18,805
			82	14,402	117,733	131,002	13,269
			83	22,446	161,014	174,777	13,763
			84	14,582	108,224	122,926	14,702
			85	3,402	14,205	16,097	1,892
			86	16,458	66,820	79,071	12,251
	O	W	85	2,891	16,420	17,806	1,386
			86	40	1,751	1,751	
	V	E	81	5,290	33,240	40,710	7,470
			82	46,672	226,774	264,710	37,936
			83	103,370	548,321	615,670	67,349
			84	219,184	990,617	1,129,208	138,591
			85	168,291	656,931	778,042	121,111
			86	97,960	587,129	671,527	84,398
	V	W	81	9,275	43,773	56,683	12,910
			82	14,259	81,604	95,466	13,862
			83	17,904	93,311	105,058	11,747
			84	18,254	100,066	116,113	16,047
			85	12,448	54,505	69,368	14,863
			86	7,936	50,531	56,964	6,433

1323000 MALT EXTRACT, SOLID, CONDNSD (LB)

Country	Mode	Reg	Yr	Quantity	F.A.S.	C.I.F.	Charges
TOTAL			81	112,020	74,750	86,266	11,516
			82	216,418	127,671	140,002	12,331
			83	476,207	174,586	189,688	15,102
			84	694,538	290,284	324,198	33,914
			85	801,921	368,501	421,369	52,868
			86	1,557,640	755,701	893,020	137,319
AUSTRAL	A	H	85	3,212	1,702	1,767	65
			86	2,000	1,360	2,570	1,210
	A	W	86	20,000	19,077	26,981	7,904
	V	E	86	30,027	10,644	12,701	2,057
	V	W	81	7,951	4,618	5,878	1,260
			82	5,255	4,802	5,741	939
			83	6,843	5,679	6,731	1,052
			84	58,768	33,546	37,350	3,804
			85	154,102	70,995	81,804	10,809
			86	473,984	228,708	285,990	57,282
AUSTRIA	V	W	84	30,864	12,691	14,352	1,661
CANADA	A	W	83	71	319	371	52
	O	E	81	2,098	881	881	
			82	1,279	536	536	
			83	3,197	1,375	1,375	
			84	38,226	26,860	26,860	
			86	8,960	3,200	3,200	
	O	W	83	148,800	19,784	19,784	
	V	E	81	11,209	7,443	8,027	584
CHINA M	V	W	83	2,841	691	745	54
			84	4,097	1,061	1,103	42
			85	7,480	1,337	1,410	73
CHINA T	V	W	82	1,190	252	324	72
DENMARK	V	E	84	2,000	3,076	3,572	496
			85	8,818	12,302	13,622	1,320
DOM REP	V	E	83	12,000	3,360	3,558	198
FRANCE	V	E	83	15,873	4,612	5,544	932
HG KONG	V	W	85	3,961	1,213	1,286	73
IRELAND	V	E	82	18,519	12,964	15,750	2,786
			84	72	1,200	1,397	197
ITALY	V	E	85	37,037	10,535	12,157	1,622
	V	W	86	87,264	37,641	49,570	11,929
JAPAN	V	W	85	4,286	3,102	3,248	146
			86	16,313	12,252	12,929	677
KOR REP	N	W	81	1,672	4,086	5,193	1,107
	V	E	85	2,998	2,881	3,200	319
	V	W	81	3,227	1,586	1,743	157
			86	2,998	1,846	2,079	233
MEXICO	A	E	86	45,040	21,463	22,473	1,010
	O	E	82	89,010	46,715	47,511	796
			83	33,069	14,639	15,449	810
			84	33,069	14,700	14,700	
			85	262,507	124,308	131,018	6,710
			86	269,291	126,194	131,467	5,273
	V	E	83	10,053	4,677	5,046	369
			84	104,250	47,513	52,053	4,540
NETHLDS	N	E	85	24,013	11,592	13,525	1,933
	V	E	84	92,594	14,274	17,919	3,645
			85	9,000	3,114	4,079	965
			86	66,136	34,811	43,891	9,080
SWITZLD	A	E	85	353	4,335	4,640	305
	V	E	84	24,978	25,412	26,683	1,271
THAILND	V	W	84	1,498	1,530	1,682	152
U KING	A	E	83	551	380	781	401
			85	3,031	1,803	2,099	296
	N	E	81	18,419	12,709	14,639	1,930
			83	88,622	46,841	50,505	3,664
			86	11,299	7,480	8,176	696
	O	E	81	44,487	30,042	32,838	2,796
			82	38,018	22,873	25,417	2,544

Product TSUSA commodity number, description, and unit of quantity Country	Mode	Reg	Yr	Quantity	F.A.S.	C.I.F.	Charges
			83	13,976	5,667	6,722	1,055
			84	2,692	1,833	1,943	110
			85	99,877	46,059	57,621	11,562
			86	93,337	41,378	50,928	9,550
	O	W	81	4,630	3,344	3,947	603
	V	E	81	7,815	3,453	4,982	1,529
			82	33,731	18,496	20,220	1,724
			83	75,622	42,141	45,059	2,918
			84	138,079	57,311	61,671	4,360
			85	160,377	67,007	78,952	11,945
			86	322,474	158,866	180,816	21,950
	V	W	81	10,512	6,588	8,138	1,550
			82	29,416	21,033	24,503	3,470
			83	27,652	13,886	15,861	1,975
			84	163,351	49,277	62,913	13,636
			85	57,906	16,751	23,098	6,347
			86	108,517	50,781	59,249	8,468

Milled grain, edible
1314500 MILD GRAIN PROD NSPF EDIBLE (LB)

Country	Mode	Reg	Yr	Quantity	F.A.S.	C.I.F.	Charges
TOTAL			81	34,557	25,654	26,941	1,287
			82	62,983	36,226	40,024	3,798
			83	84,241	37,458	40,505	3,047
			84	120,004	47,801	53,477	5,676
			85	128,193	34,380	39,177	4,797
			86	214,861	67,820	79,313	11,493
AUSTRAL	O	E	81	1,045	575	575	
	V	W	86	44,092	6,620	7,996	1,376
BELGIUM	A	E	84	200	316	468	152
CANADA	O	E	81	8,511	10,377	10,377	
			82	17,979	5,217	5,217	
			83	47,508	7,039	7,039	
			84	43,334	15,222	15,222	
			85	75,053	8,792	8,792	
			86	712	2,428	2,428	
	O	W	81	790	360	434	74
			86	2,704	1,780	1,780	
	V	E	86	19,500	2,684	3,784	1,100
CHINA M	V	W	81	3,489	1,615	1,723	108
			82	422	320	348	28
			83	2,450	965	1,044	79
CHINA T	V	W	81	278	265	284	19
FR GERM	O	E	86	14,716	5,698	7,081	1,383
	V	E	86	25,408	12,258	13,729	1,471
FRANCE	O	E	81	600	254	282	28
	V	E	84	3,300	825	1,132	307
HG KONG	V	E	85	1,111	1,134	1,247	113
HONDURA	V	E	82	461	465	516	51
INDIA	A	E	84	220	550	666	116
	O	E	81	1,008	555	610	55
			82	570	281	312	31
	V	E	84	440	363	417	54
			86	6,600	1,425	1,634	209
	V	W	81	1,053	721	793	72
ITALY	V	E	84	23,349	2,550	3,324	774
			86	24,600	6,396	8,319	1,923
JAPAN	V	E	81	790	600	657	57
			82	639	1,072	1,186	114
			83	2,782	7,636	8,256	620
			84	1,761	3,629	3,884	255
			86	3,332	2,280	2,481	201
	V	H	84	210	414	463	49
	V	W	82	4,142	4,163	4,643	480
			83	209	619	661	42
			84	1,905	1,288	1,367	79
			85	3,000	1,321	1,386	65
KENYA	O	E	82	1,058	430	477	47
	V	E	84	6,085	2,201	2,531	330
KOR REP	V	E	81	719	280	297	17
			82	7,246	5,657	6,169	512
			83	2,112	825	947	122
			85	5,178	5,889	6,630	741
			86	1,440	1,817	1,956	139
	V	W	81	6,681	5,543	5,965	422
			82	8,520	9,236	9,733	497
			83	12,298	10,203	10,857	654
			84	4,159	4,731	4,988	257
			85	7,200	5,781	6,484	703
			86	14,929	13,910	14,758	848
MALAWI	O	E	82	3,065	1,390	1,390	
	V	E	84	3,968	2,849	3,276	427
N ZEAL	V	W	85	4,971	1,008	1,218	210

Country	Mode	Reg	Yr	Quantity	F.A.S.	C.I.F.	Charges
PERU	A	E	84	1,065	450	1,643	1,193
			85	11,023	4,000	6,094	2,094
PHIL R	V	E	82	392	494	592	98
THAILND	V	W	83	2,866	4,087	4,317	230
			84	145	370	407	37
			85	15,013	3,950	4,223	273
			86	37,950	2,858	4,328	1,470
TURKEY	V	E	84	2,778	842	968	126
U KING	A	E	83	1,798	291	1,010	719
	O	E	81	4,717	2,225	2,428	203
			82	14,456	5,445	6,120	675
			83	12,218	5,793	6,374	581
			84	19,413	7,858	8,697	839
			86	6,389	2,273	2,522	249
	V	E	81	2,760	1,233	1,349	116
			84	7,672	3,343	4,024	681
			86	12,489	5,393	6,517	1,124
	V	W	81	2,116	1,051	1,167	116
			82	2,517	1,575	2,787	1,212
			85	5,644	2,505	3,103	598
USSR	O	E	82	1,516	481	534	53

1318500 MILLED GRAINS MIXED, EDIBLE (LB)

Country	Mode	Reg	Yr	Quantity	F.A.S.	C.I.F.	Charges
TOTAL			81	2,016	3,456	4,272	816
			82	1,676	423	423	
			83	2,436	3,359	3,720	361
			84	167,300	29,422	34,948	5,526
			85	66,073	19,024	21,744	2,720
			86	29,308	24,681	26,408	1,727
BELGIUM	V	E	85	25,000	3,869	4,334	465
CANADA	O	E	82	1,676	423	423	
			84	94,114	17,494	17,494	
			85	20,547	5,293	5,293	
			86	19,100	9,930	9,930	
FR GERM	V	E	83	440	277	368	91
			84	70,000	10,019	13,127	3,108
FRANCE	V	E	83	496	2,104	2,186	82
			85	12,131	7,539	8,626	1,087
			86	7,532	12,005	13,422	1,417
ITALY	V	E	85	8,395	2,323	3,491	1,168
KOR REP	V	E	86	1,371	1,225	1,362	137
	V	W	81	1,200	1,593	1,716	123
			86	1,305	1,521	1,694	173
NETHLDS	A	E	84	1,102	256	1,343	1,087
PHIL R	V	W	83	1,500	978	1,166	188
PORTUGL	V	E	81	110	643	844	201
SWITZLD	A	E	81	706	1,220	1,712	492
U KING	A	E	84	1,800	1,332	2,461	1,129
	A	W	84	284	321	523	202

Milled grain, inedible
1318000 MILLED GRAIN NT EDIBLE NSPF (CWT)

Country	Mode	Reg	Yr	Quantity	F.A.S.	C.I.F.	Charges
TOTAL			81	1,857	23,109	23,558	449
			82	1,621	16,462	18,482	2,020
			83	434	10,710	11,181	471
			84	2,922	55,348	57,247	1,899
			85	1,712	33,629	38,071	4,442
			86	2,988	22,230	25,353	3,123
AUSTRAL	A	W	82	4	296	1,433	1,137
BELGIUM	A	E	86	2	1,900	2,097	197
BRAZIL	V	E	84	66	1,500	1,784	284
			85	312	8,185	10,199	2,014
			86	336	2,416	3,793	1,377
CANADA	O	E	81	1,183	18,996	18,996	
			83	420	6,526	6,526	
			84	1,972	41,573	41,573	
	O	W	84	647	5,268	5,268	
			85	1,198	9,066	9,066	
CHINA T	V	W	84	118	2,282	2,472	190
DENMARK	A	E	84	11	845	1,882	1,037
FR GERM	A	E	81	3	1,192	1,322	130
INDIA	V	E	86	40	1,216	1,826	610
JAPAN	A	E	82	43	725	1,125	400
	N	E	84	*	268	297	29
	V	E	81	4	610	677	67
			82	14	2,378	2,640	262
			83	7	3,524	3,912	388
			84	7	2,374	2,629	255
			85	20	1,825	2,109	284
	V	W	81	665	1,928	2,097	169
			82	660	1,500	1,632	132

Product
TSUSA commodity number, description, and unit of quantity

Country	Mode	Reg	Yr	Quantity	F.A.S.	C.I.F.	Charges
KOR REP	V	E	83	7	660	743	83
			84	62	759	811	52
			85	106	9,658	11,258	1,600
			86	1,786	8,300	9,121	821
	V	W	86	11	1,202	1,320	118
MEXICO	O	W	86	813	7,196	7,196	
PHIL R	V	W	81	2	383	466	83
REP SAF	O	E	82	180	10,581	10,581	
THAILND	V	E	84	39	479	531	52
	V	W	82	720	982	1,071	89
			85	10	1,140	1,260	120
U KING	V	E	85	66	3,755	4,179	424

1319000 MILLED GRAIN MIXTURE, INEDIB (CWT)

Country	Mode	Reg	Yr	Quantity	F.A.S.	C.I.F.	Charges
TOTAL			82	35	274	274	
			83	70	460	460	
			84	49	968	1,803	835
			85	380	2,465	2,465	
CANADA	A	E	84	34	611	1,446	835
	O	E	82	35	274	274	
			83	70	460	460	
	O	W	85	380	2,465	2,465	
INDIA	O	E	84	15	357	357	

Miscellaneous

Argol

4267400 ARGOLS ETC U90% POT BITART (LB)

Country	Mode	Reg	Yr	Quantity	F.A.S.	C.I.F.	Charges
TOTAL			84	1,543	933	1,612	679
			85	9,741	20,574	22,685	2,111
			86	115,743	62,758	67,220	4,462
CHINA M	V	W	86	115,743	62,758	67,220	4,462
FRANCE	A	E	84	1,543	933	1,612	679
PANAMA	V	E	85	9,741	20,574	22,685	2,111

Fatty acid

4902650 FATTY ACIDS OF VEG ORIG ETC (LB)

Country	Mode	Reg	Yr	Quantity	F.A.S.	C.I.F.	Charges
TOTAL			81	2,248,447	1,334,284	1,474,056	139,772
			82	2,027,131	1,014,767	1,127,366	112,599
			83	1,762,676	1,027,440	1,125,299	97,859
			84	4,444,918	3,125,732	3,348,940	223,208
			85	10,695,935	3,734,759	3,975,596	240,837
			86	8,601,543	3,690,716	3,946,717	256,001
BELGIUM	V	E	85	28,483	17,771	20,522	2,751
BRAZIL	V	E	81	1,844,538	1,073,553	1,184,263	110,710
			82	1,865,811	915,825	1,019,845	104,020
			83	1,679,950	976,001	1,070,587	94,586
			84	4,146,581	2,958,438	3,172,054	213,616
			85	7,351,297	2,190,344	2,420,474	230,130
			86	4,934,372	2,407,107	2,660,154	253,047
CANADA	A	W	82	1	700	750	50
	N	E	85	2,735,662	1,240,315	1,240,315	
	O	E	82	40,000	5,709	5,709	
			84	182,297	68,191	68,191	
			85	491,234	225,652	225,652	
			86	3,620,830	1,225,290	1,225,290	
CHINA M	V	E	82	38,084	58,735	62,000	3,265
			86	39,683	46,560	48,600	2,040
FR GERM	O	E	85	40,036	12,873	16,161	3,288
	V	E	81	236,731	163,963	183,562	19,599
			82	39,683	15,242	17,100	1,858
			83	39,683	19,826	21,060	1,234
INDIA	A	E	84	15	1,970	2,085	115
			85	22	2,105	2,200	95
			86	44	6,531	6,870	339
	O	E	81	35,274	23,634	23,634	
	V	E	81	90,044	43,946	51,017	7,071
ISRAEL	N	E	84	*	4,855	4,873	18
JAPAN	A	W	84	3	3,774	3,784	10
NAURU	V	E	85	9,523	6,279	6,955	676

Product
TSUSA commodity number, description, and unit of quantity

Country	Mode	Reg	Yr	Quantity	F.A.S.	C.I.F.	Charges
NETHLDS	O	E	81	41,599	28,707	31,099	2,392
			83	38,744	27,407	29,446	2,039
			84	40,783	29,295	30,995	1,700
			85	32,627	31,371	34,258	2,887
	V	E	84	75,239	59,209	66,958	7,749
SWITZLD	N	E	86	*	1,378	1,453	75
U KING	O	E	81	276	481	481	
			82	3,472	4,943	4,943	
			83	4,299	4,206	4,206	
	V	E	82	40,080	13,613	17,019	3,406
			85	438	5,149	5,159	10
	V	W	85	6,613	2,900	3,900	1,000
			86	6,614	3,850	4,350	500

4902670 FATTY ACID O VEG ORIG, NSPF (LB)

Country	Mode	Reg	Yr	Quantity	F.A.S.	C.I.F.	Charges
TOTAL			81	5,399,220	2,761,778	3,032,749	270,971
			82	4,552,510	2,249,916	2,513,114	263,198
			83	4,507,221	2,617,415	2,821,813	204,398
			84	7,085,925	3,963,303	4,286,784	323,481
			85	5,055,029	2,144,669	2,404,449	259,780
			86	5,854,669	1,957,438	2,144,180	186,742
BRAZIL	N	E	82	279,991	134,985	151,368	16,383
	V	E	81	3,464,096	1,928,179	2,127,701	199,522
			82	3,324,728	1,600,521	1,814,013	213,492
			83	2,920,596	1,494,570	1,637,252	142,682
			84	5,258,837	2,887,969	3,143,741	255,772
			85	2,832,599	1,147,722	1,289,384	141,662
			86	3,438,731	1,267,592	1,422,475	154,883
CANADA	A	W	84	95	35,000	35,124	124
	O	E	81	642,078	136,912	136,912	
			82	456,265	122,168	122,229	61
			83	722,924	243,123	243,123	
			84	1,171,701	491,031	491,031	
			85	890,871	344,859	344,862	3
			86	1,182,948	297,276	297,636	360
CHINA M	V	E	82	39,021	62,791	65,500	2,709
			83	423,283	525,181	562,464	37,283
			84	99,207	135,461	145,794	10,333
			86	38,500	17,150	19,291	2,141
DENMARK	V	E	83	928	2,390	2,495	105
			84	883	1,767	1,860	93
			85	8,818	3,163	4,454	1,291
			86	8,818	16,195	17,215	1,020
FINLAND	V	E	84	276	763	835	72
FR GERM	A	E	86	2,204	4,012	4,012	
	N	E	81	141,673	100,588	111,471	10,883
			82	213,141	159,412	168,568	9,156
			83	99,604	78,442	85,523	7,081
			84	47,504	40,782	46,222	5,440
			85	41,138	47,175	50,593	3,418
			86	17,090	37,384	40,292	2,908
	O	E	85	1,633	2,664	2,821	157
	V	E	84	43,475	48,449	53,965	5,516
			85	37,699	26,464	29,730	3,266
			86	18,254	23,147	25,041	1,894
	V	W	86	13,030	22,121	23,752	1,631
FRANCE	A	E	82	11	587	592	5
	V	E	81	63,051	117,846	125,107	7,261
			86	11,791	22,312	22,855	543
HG KONG	V	E	84	102,000	135,691	145,569	9,878
INDIA	A	E	81	6	330	355	25
			82	8	1,435	1,575	140
			83	31	5,097	5,590	493
			84	90	9,674	10,486	812
			85	22	1,094	1,185	91
			86	24	4,241	4,478	237
	A	W	81	7	1,245	1,350	105
	O	E	81	264,555	178,207	178,207	
			83	123,456	71,055	71,055	
	V	E	81	493,439	101,662	130,591	28,929
			82	91,792	42,300	48,976	6,676
			84	72,364	43,280	49,976	6,696
ITALY	V	E	85	400	2,768	3,048	280
JAPAN	A	E	83	529	812	2,480	1,668
			84	2,127	2,672	6,332	3,660
	A	W	84	826	3,405	5,530	2,125
	N	W	85	37,000	5,550	9,750	4,200
	V	E	81	11,905	12,931	14,202	1,271
			82	12,499	6,672	7,600	928
	V	W	81	661	1,950	2,095	145
			83	13,507	60,181	64,210	4,029
			85	74,000	11,100	19,500	8,400
MEXICO	O	E	85	150,100	11,980	11,980	
			86	808,420	46,383	46,383	

Product TSUSA commodity number, description, and unit of quantity Country	Mode	Reg	Yr	Quantity	F.A.S.	C.I.F.	Charges
NETHLDS	O	E	81	105,221	66,400	73,946	7,546
			83	78,270	50,403	55,360	4,957
			84	12,596	9,539	10,057	518
			85	256,448	182,334	206,602	24,268
			86	100,176	72,893	80,535	7,642
	V	E	81	212,528	115,528	130,812	15,284
			82	94,137	64,733	70,365	5,632
			83	120,587	81,683	87,203	5,520
			84	75,690	52,276	56,712	4,436
			85	185,433	115,919	129,191	13,272
			86	4,078	3,909	4,167	258
	V	W	82	40,745	51,811	59,770	7,959
			86	95,437	77,574	83,789	6,215
NORWAY	V	E	84	186,866	54,312	65,762	11,450
			85	222,223	68,151	81,649	13,498
SPAIN	V	E	82	172	2,501	2,558	57
SWEDEN	O	E	84	2	275	281	6
SWITZLD	N	E	83	*	407	409	2
	V	E	85	10,790	51,689	52,391	702
THAILND	V	E	86	114,639	31,481	37,672	6,191
U KING	A	E	83	7	339	395	56
			84	11,386	7,462	13,887	6,425
			85	220	5,120	5,300	180
			86	529	12,498	13,292	794
	N	E	83	3,499	3,732	4,254	522
			84	*	3,495	3,620	125
			85	*	1,049	1,054	5
			86	*	1,270	1,295	25
	O	E	85	178,140	68,956	96,394	27,438
	V	E	85	127,495	46,912	64,561	17,649

Fatty ester
4909400 OTHER FATTY ESTERS VEG ORIG (LB)

Country	Mode	Reg	Yr	Quantity	F.A.S.	C.I.F.	Charges
TOTAL			81	288,070	281,213	302,975	21,762
			82	1,114,633	863,799	947,772	83,973
			83	1,000,124	1,212,280	1,273,496	61,216
			84	2,500,092	2,018,810	2,175,077	156,267
			85	2,628,528	1,522,315	1,721,568	199,253
			86	2,976,544	1,787,245	2,034,243	246,998
ARGENT	V	E	85	1,102	1,200	1,292	92
BELGIUM	V	E	85	42,328	50,294	52,978	2,684
			86	28,483	33,971	35,889	1,918
BRAZIL	V	E	81	109,604	67,738	73,460	5,722
			82	143,812	82,836	91,055	8,219
			83	115,393	85,453	91,472	6,019
			84	1,230,368	843,766	907,456	63,690
			85	1,751,164	744,260	871,198	126,938
			86	1,639,875	499,769	632,533	132,764
CANADA	A	E	83	21	5,737	5,781	44
	O	E	82	110	251	251	
			84	9,318	4,302	4,302	
			85	13,020	12,011	12,011	
			86	76,870	53,626	53,712	86
	O	W	82	7,600	4,099	4,099	
			84	600	914	914	
FR GERM	A	E	83	12	1,036	1,043	7
			84	7,441	8,002	14,921	6,919
			86	5,818	7,760	12,316	4,556
	N	E	83	22,621	308,708	310,370	1,662
			84	19,155	22,239	23,549	1,310
	O	E	81	1,984	11,134	11,468	334
			85	4,409	2,554	2,800	246
	V	E	81	6,481	24,347	24,877	530
			82	143,234	80,258	87,718	7,460
			83	59,259	74,162	77,629	3,467
			84	109,788	117,596	125,432	7,836
			85	360,605	295,986	326,225	30,239
			86	840,220	828,946	893,946	65,113
	V	W	84	78,922	93,373	97,948	4,575
			85	60,230	49,944	53,645	3,701
FRANCE	A	E	85	220	6,500	6,819	319
	N	E	84	684,822	653,818	708,565	54,747
			85	86,741	101,523	108,363	6,840
	V	E	82	604,170	505,112	562,095	56,983
			83	697,948	646,187	684,377	38,190
			86	1,874	9,289	9,537	248
INDIA	A	E	81	24	1,443	1,755	312
			82	19	1,160	1,335	175
			83	209	2,563	2,864	301
			84	20	1,351	1,555	204
			85	66	3,375	3,791	416
	V	E	81	421	624	764	140

Country	Mode	Reg	Yr	Quantity	F.A.S.	C.I.F.	Charges
ITALY	O	E	85	427	27,778	27,778	
	V	W	84	1,735	2,040	2,583	543
JAPAN	A	E	81	12	592	650	58
			83	109	2,850	6,030	3,180
			85	33	1,524	1,706	182
	A	W	85	33	1,552	1,833	281
	N	E	86	12,769	41,141	44,604	3,463
	V	E	81	3,308	6,300	7,119	819
			84	45,789	26,779	29,840	3,061
			85	18,426	18,264	19,818	1,554
			86	891	22,715	23,411	696
	V	W	83	8,818	22,806	25,200	2,394
			84	43,605	26,936	30,488	3,552
			85	228	2,621	2,732	111
			86	2,205	13,684	14,100	416
MEXICO	O	E	82	4,850	3,476	3,476	
			83	5,004	3,609	3,609	
NETHLDS	A	W	82	110	3,141	3,246	105
	N	E	83	41,953	22,436	24,483	2,047
	O	E	81	14,220	14,494	15,017	523
			82	14,219	15,288	16,107	819
			83	23,314	23,339	25,201	1,862
			84	53,351	35,687	38,484	2,797
			85	36,588	39,688	41,761	2,073
	V	E	81	78,991	82,702	89,294	6,592
			82	82,088	84,195	88,044	3,849
			84	202,623	167,065	173,327	6,262
			85	172,617	106,805	124,014	17,209
			86	366,999	272,957	310,554	37,597
	V	W	82	47,510	50,013	52,580	2,567
NORWAY	V	E	83	25,463	13,394	15,437	2,043
SPAIN	V	E	84	11,023	10,750	11,289	539
SWEDEN	O	E	81	1	603	615	12
			82	1	582	602	20
	V	E	81	20,007	14,272	16,103	1,831
SWITZLD	A	E	84	1,531	2,671	2,871	200
	A	W	81	110	619	828	209
	N	E	84	*	743	756	13
	O	E	82	22	517	627	110
	V	E	82	66,888	32,871	36,537	3,666
			85	40,476	33,450	35,896	2,446
U KING	A	E	81	2,632	5,788	7,735	1,947
			86	540	3,500	3,641	141
	O	E	84	1	778	797	19
	V	E	81	50,275	50,557	53,290	2,733
			85	39,815	22,986	26,908	3,922

Fatty salt
4905000 OTHER FATTY SALTS VEG ORIGIN (LB)

Country	Mode	Reg	Yr	Quantity	F.A.S.	C.I.F.	Charges
TOTAL			81	3,015	6,404	7,268	864
			82	81,890	62,863	71,544	8,681
			83	150,728	93,908	101,922	8,014
			84	628,000	370,295	416,296	46,001
			85	1,401,072	857,194	943,770	86,576
			86	883,899	434,825	461,407	26,582
BELGIUM	V	E	85	24,118	7,725	8,287	562
			86	16,534	4,386	5,018	632
BRAZIL	V	E	82	728	675	774	99
			85	910,719	562,827	625,897	63,070
CANADA	O	E	81	25	2,190	2,190	
			82	400	450	450	
			85	29,822	20,581	20,581	
			86	1,760	1,149	1,149	
	O	W	82	25	2,114	2,114	
			84	31	2,184	2,184	
CHINA T	V	E	82	37,500	19,259	23,133	3,874
	V	W	84	38,000	22,800	27,023	4,223
DENMARK	V	W	86	2,500	1,021	1,083	62
FR GERM	N	E	84	78,771	59,692	62,424	2,732
	V	E	81	2,974	3,700	4,425	725
			82	2,204	2,634	3,622	988
			83	40,126	21,958	23,335	1,377
			84	134,481	80,078	89,842	9,764
			85	124,339	74,769	83,146	8,377
			86	104,938	69,835	74,966	5,131
	V	W	84	38,578	12,101	13,650	1,549
			86	8,819	9,045	9,600	555
FRANCE	A	E	84	207	483	596	113
	V	E	82	22	305	352	47
			83	19,886	11,133	13,460	2,327
	V	W	83	4,444	510	578	68
ITALY	V	E	83	41,870	56,525	60,149	3,624

Product
TSUSA commodity number, description, and unit of quantity

Country	Mode	Reg	Yr	Quantity	F.A.S.	C.I.F.	Charges
	V	W	86	87,928	80,912	86,796	5,884
JAPAN	A	E	81	16	514	653	139
			82	1	756	779	23
			86	18,523	5,557	5,649	92
	A	W	86	397	1,993	3,543	1,550
	V	E	83	1,684	773	834	61
			84	5,989	1,919	2,042	123
MEXICO	O	E	84	34,061	19,975	22,960	2,985
			85	191,789	124,931	126,513	1,582
			86	487,946	173,324	173,324	
	V	E	84	22,046	16,535	18,439	1,904
			85	44,092	29,261	33,069	3,808
NETHLDS	A	E	82	275	303	498	195
			84	2,205	1,245	2,300	1,055
	V	E	83	1,650	1,041	1,247	206
			84	202,911	123,608	138,991	15,383
			85	37,681	20,344	25,358	5,014
			86	77,161	40,796	46,611	5,815
	V	W	86	16,535	9,625	11,250	1,625
SPAIN	V	E	82	130	1,198	1,249	51
			83	39,506	846	1,047	201
			84	22,222	7,636	10,080	2,444
			85	33,334	11,484	15,271	3,787
	V	W	84	44,445	17,116	20,463	3,347
			86	46,032	20,082	23,184	3,102
SWEDEN	V	W	86	14,815	12,565	14,515	1,950
SWITZLD	A	E	82	18	17,877	18,097	220
			86	11	1,683	1,811	128
	N	E	86	*	2,852	2,908	56
	O	E	82	40,565	16,192	19,297	3,105
			83	1	431	436	5
			84	3,183	2,360	2,628	268
U KING	A	E	82	22	1,100	1,179	79
	O	E	84	270	300	338	38
	V	E	84	600	2,263	2,336	73
	V	W	83	1,561	691	836	145
			85	5,178	5,272	5,648	376

Fruit, juice, inedible
1921500 CITRUS FRUIT JUICE UNFIT BEV (LB)

Country	Mode	Reg	Yr	Quantity	F.A.S.	C.I.F.	Charges
TOTAL			81	3,323,132	3,333,007	3,412,822	79,815
			82	816,442	582,690	601,358	18,668
			83	2,301,725	1,057,803	1,098,086	40,283
			84	1,211,039	874,382	914,622	40,240
			85	1,854,066	1,330,682	1,371,097	40,415
			86	2,004,758	1,223,415	1,244,478	21,063
BRAZIL	V	E	83	4,189	1,368	1,600	232
C RICA	A	E	86	3,599	3,890	5,716	1,826
CANADA	O	E	81	2,395,984	2,070,649	2,070,649	
			82	120,962	103,067	103,067	
CHINA T	V	W	82	1,125	725	809	84
GHANA	V	E	81	909,917	1,246,376	1,324,937	78,561
GREECE	A	E	83	1,700	780	5,823	5,043
HG KONG	V	W	84	1,400	2,392	2,583	191
INDIA	V	W	83	85	544	641	97
IRAN	V	E	84	19,841	21,690	25,119	3,429
JAMAICA	V	E	81	17,231	15,982	17,236	1,254
JAPAN	V	W	84	244	490	506	16
MALAYSA	V	W	86	68,796	39,228	41,878	2,650
MEXICO	N	W	86	115,618	85,788	89,792	4,004
	O	E	82	579,515	311,466	311,466	
			83	620,513	347,470	347,470	
			85	966,317	576,619	577,682	1,063
			86	1,504,560	893,410	893,410	
	V	W	83	1,675,238	707,641	742,552	34,911
			84	1,188,793	849,150	885,703	36,553
			85	860,162	708,847	746,375	37,528
			86	269,709	178,344	187,846	9,502
PERU	V	W	86	42,476	22,755	25,836	3,081
SPAIN	V	W	85	27,587	45,216	47,040	1,824
THAILND	V	W	84	761	660	711	51
U KING	V	E	82	42,840	55,811	61,264	5,453
	V	W	82	72,000	111,621	124,752	13,131

Monosodium glutamate
4253000 MONSODIUM GLUTAMATE (LB)

Country	Mode	Reg	Yr	Quantity	F.A.S.	C.I.F.	Charges
TOTAL			81	32,401,990	28,363,381	30,098,674	1,661,625
			82	33,257,994	22,788,592	24,692,186	1,903,594
			83	42,055,894	22,055,864	24,338,685	2,282,821
			84	64,689,465	34,669,114	38,261,694	3,592,580
			85	81,553,496	44,787,065	49,197,631	4,410,566
			86	83,192,127	46,508,483	50,532,704	4,024,221
AFGHAN	V	E	84	37,000	18,084	20,249	2,165
			85	108,000	55,326	61,559	6,233
ARGENT	V	E	83	193,000	95,886	107,549	11,663
			85	288,000	147,286	157,132	9,846
	V	W	83	36,000	18,189	20,772	2,583
BELGIUM	O	E	84	74,956	34,490	38,680	4,190
			85	150,001	174,245	190,492	16,247
	V	E	84	40,000	21,400	23,701	2,301
			85	150,001	87,133	92,805	5,672
			86	195,000	103,210	111,704	8,494
BHUTAN	V	E	86	40,000	21,968	23,868	1,900
BRAZIL	A	E	84	500	300	1,152	852
	N	E	85	11,920,000	6,231,289	6,938,950	707,661
	O	E	84	24,467	18,717	18,717	
			85	39,683	21,133	23,579	2,446
			86	72,752	47,123	47,123	
	O	H	82	78,000	47,551	56,357	8,806
			83	17,000	8,284	9,809	1,525
			86	72,000	35,480	42,480	7,000
	V	E	81	6,053,205	5,125,089	5,585,823	460,734
			82	11,114,495	6,965,239	7,737,611	772,372
			83	17,216,280	8,487,975	9,566,819	1,078,844
			84	26,686,716	13,333,808	14,887,597	1,553,789
			85	23,576,973	12,310,995	13,666,669	1,355,674
			86	34,090,865	18,917,570	20,568,585	1,651,015
	V	W	81	550,500	516,498	576,042	48,675
			82	792,000	483,199	549,885	66,686
			83	3,060,850	1,540,932	1,767,816	226,884
			84	2,659,270	1,302,680	1,490,659	187,979
			85	3,728,200	1,929,558	2,145,584	216,026
			86	5,442,781	2,861,574	3,142,301	280,727
CANADA	O	E	81	1,000	710	710	
			82	5,990	6,493	6,493	
			83	425	1,223	1,223	
			84	30	1,412	1,412	
			86	164,468	106,049	106,049	
	O	W	83	275	365	365	
CHINA M	O	E	84	500	509	587	78
	V	E	81	25,420	23,269	25,027	1,758
			82	80,750	64,659	68,387	3,728
			83	18,329	15,269	16,992	1,723
			86	11,923	35,621	37,990	2,369
	V	W	81	129,500	126,201	129,795	3,594
			82	8,000	7,539	8,217	678
			83	6,750	4,253	4,589	336
			86	4,905	4,299	4,466	167
CHINA T	N	E	81	2,419,102	2,353,395	2,468,482	115,087
	N	W	85	8,026,207	4,429,542	4,690,999	261,457
	O	E	86	56,552	35,597	37,397	1,800
	V	E	81	319,955	300,635	315,307	14,672
			82	2,650,540	1,812,707	1,966,999	154,292
			83	1,987,087	1,120,536	1,234,757	114,221
			84	2,661,517	1,160,593	1,310,108	149,515
			85	4,147,820	2,467,420	2,749,313	281,893
			86	5,266,624	3,129,474	3,446,500	317,026
	V	H	81	29,685	30,550	32,392	1,842
			82	40,250	35,304	37,844	2,540
			83	26,706	18,849	20,180	1,331
			84	13,500	9,253	9,896	643
			85	33,000	23,080	25,202	2,122
			86	22,500	15,450	17,141	1,691
	V	W	81	5,432,000	5,087,866	5,295,736	184,870
			82	6,724,982	4,862,087	5,155,018	292,931
			83	7,891,643	4,585,567	4,852,330	266,763
			84	8,883,142	5,387,468	5,740,223	352,755
			85	6,724,758	4,023,317	4,315,308	291,991
			86	16,784,458	9,616,822	10,303,453	686,631
ECUADOR	V	E	81	39,683	36,000	38,674	2,674
FR GERM	V	E	81	99,483	80,542	85,964	5,422
			85	51,030	65,323	70,805	5,482
	V	W	85	10,000	7,440	8,165	725
FRANCE	N	E	85	2,789,256	1,676,622	1,790,773	114,151
	V	E	83	38,581	22,836	23,706	870
			84	1,924,860	1,100,565	1,174,643	74,078
			85	342,463	195,651	212,708	17,057
			86	2,810,259	1,543,047	1,649,583	106,536
	V	W	82	33,320	20,558	21,658	1,100
HG KONG	O	E	81	250	297	297	
	V	E	81	11,147	8,976	9,887	911
			82	41,788	36,697	38,775	2,078
			83	746	1,378	1,468	90
			85	4,490	8,423	9,099	676

Product
TSUSA commodity number, description, and unit of quantity

Country	Mode	Reg	Yr	Quantity	F.A.S.	C.I.F.	Charges
			86	46,379	34,693	36,941	2,248
	V	H	81	11,020	10,168	10,896	728
			82	6,888	6,471	6,875	404
	V	W	81	81,147	43,132	44,821	1,689
			82	13,650	14,305	15,038	733
			83	38,581	27,201	28,437	1,236
			84	94,863	65,337	69,899	4,562
			85	40,478	21,593	23,843	2,250
			86	123,238	67,700	71,275	3,575
INDIA	V	W	86	72,750	39,700	41,300	1,600
INDNSIA	V	E	81	80,000	65,766	73,164	7,398
			82	409,000	296,088	325,126	29,038
			86	188,580	92,425	109,170	16,745
	V	H	81	1,650	1,968	2,052	84
	V	W	81	15,000	15,150	15,825	675
			82	8,100	5,670	5,996	326
			85	38,600	18,710	22,237	3,527
			86	10,283	60,000	65,000	5,000
ITALY	N	E	86	156,566	84,367	92,115	7,748
	V	E	86	251,402	130,662	146,507	15,845
JAPAN	A	E	86	79	1,050	1,218	168
	N	W	84	533,774	333,884	364,342	30,458
	O	E	82	68,751	56,074	58,875	2,801
	O	H	81	281,786	261,431	292,087	30,656
			82	229,112	182,739	209,333	26,594
			83	46,458	86,539	95,721	9,182
			84	233,630	152,165	182,591	30,426
			85	386,300	248,706	300,536	51,830
			86	157,728	110,471	135,146	24,675
	V	E	81	2,732,290	2,166,588	2,287,597	121,009
			82	1,735,276	1,247,440	1,331,998	84,558
			83	599,172	255,061	283,440	28,379
			84	4,376,307	2,471,295	2,765,591	294,296
			85	1,873,497	859,621	961,991	102,370
			86	1,196,859	492,880	547,969	55,089
	V	H	81	184,616	177,972	199,039	21,067
			82	62,947	48,130	54,944	6,814
			83	263	1,158	1,199	41
			84	33,053	19,016	22,819	3,803
			85	112,000	63,677	77,344	13,667
			86	330	1,452	1,634	182
	V	W	81	4,952,548	4,430,404	4,687,583	217,380
			82	1,948,402	1,545,807	1,632,487	86,680
			83	464,827	314,315	335,951	21,636
			84	2,911,962	1,710,151	1,875,318	165,167
			85	2,985,606	1,731,269	1,923,398	192,129
			86	1,159,745	738,057	830,855	92,798
KENYA	V	W	86	3,740	3,104	3,460	356
KOR REP	N	E	86	2,981,414	1,622,046	1,799,122	177,076
	N	W	85	11,000	13,534	14,800	1,266
			86	43,500	22,732	23,029	297
	O	E	81	116,600	92,050	100,039	7,989
			85	40,000	22,254	22,254	
			86	20,465	12,993	12,993	
	V	E	81	4,006,678	3,413,544	3,587,733	174,189
			82	3,448,352	2,468,969	2,633,948	164,979
			83	5,447,735	2,852,216	3,114,749	262,533
			84	5,209,447	3,001,411	3,309,260	307,849
			85	5,235,463	3,037,228	3,352,828	315,600
			86	1,610,156	884,914	976,888	91,974
	V	H	82	8,200	5,769	6,433	664
	V	W	81	4,822,852	3,987,598	4,225,412	237,814
			82	3,724,916	2,539,281	2,731,243	191,962
			83	4,246,411	2,208,480	2,428,354	219,874
			84	6,419,420	3,568,502	3,894,808	326,306
			85	8,259,869	4,639,373	5,043,352	403,979
			86	9,401,876	5,219,395	5,654,152	434,757
MALAYSA	V	W	81	1,157	860	911	51
N ZEAL	V	E	84	37,000	18,104	20,238	2,134
NAURU	V	E	85	40,000	21,400	23,594	2,194
PERU	V	E	84	115,742	55,991	63,572	7,581
	V	W	84	38,581	17,454	21,087	3,633
PHIL R	V	W	81	12	565	643	78
			86	2,826	1,546	1,683	137
SINGAPR	V	W	86	38,000	23,180	24,080	900
SPAIN	N	E	84	337,303	156,108	173,411	17,303
	V	E	82	3,500	4,181	4,608	427
			83	411,535	207,240	228,830	21,590
			84	683,424	313,375	345,846	32,471
	V	W	84	37,478	17,209	19,594	2,385
SWITZLD	V	W	84	120	359	395	36
THAILND	V	E	83	39,067	21,660	23,552	1,892
			84	274,162	164,198	180,459	16,261
			85	394,725	227,007	250,592	23,585
			86	520,501	296,363	316,374	20,011

Product
TSUSA commodity number, description, and unit of quantity

Country	Mode	Reg	Yr	Quantity	F.A.S.	C.I.F.	Charges
	V	W	81	3,704	6,157	6,736	579
			82	20,785	25,635	28,038	2,403
			83	268,173	160,452	170,077	9,625
			84	346,741	215,276	234,840	19,564
			85	46,076	28,910	31,720	2,810
			86	170,623	95,469	103,153	7,684

4934200 PREP CONTG 50% MONOSM GLUTAM (NULL)

Country	Mode	Reg	Yr	Quantity	F.A.S.	C.I.F.	Charges
TOTAL			81	-	152,504	162,324	9,820
			82	-	110,010	118,540	8,530
			83	-	117,336	122,629	5,293
			84	-	119,088	126,637	7,549
			85	-	56,451	58,666	2,215
			86	-	47,931	52,914	4,983
BRAZIL	N	E	81	-	72,000	77,528	5,528
			84	-	7,246	7,246	
CANADA	N	W	81	-	1,043	1,043	
CHINA M	N	E	82	-	7,177	7,936	759
			83	-	9,800	10,879	1,079
			84	-	2,770	3,035	265
	N	W	81	-	331	346	15
			82	-	392	426	34
			83	-	330	360	30
CHINA T	N	E	82	-	4,730	5,186	456
			83	-	460	500	40
			84	-	879	1,070	191
	N	W	81	-	4,000	4,224	224
			82	-	15,085	16,032	947
			84	-	33,122	36,112	2,990
			85	-	5,100	5,709	609
FR GERM	N	E	81	-	26,172	26,942	770
			82	-	50,535	54,380	3,845
			83	-	55,080	56,211	1,131
			84	-	63,266	65,399	2,133
HG KONG	N	E	83	-	4,728	5,240	512
	N	W	81	-	1,358	1,431	73
			82	-	717	750	33
			83	-	854	898	44
			84	-	1,653	1,739	86
			86	-	1,375	1,448	73
JAPAN	N	E	81	-	398	401	3
			82	-	6,836	7,544	708
			83	-	381	402	21
			84	-	1,657	1,882	225
			86	-	4,299	5,098	799
	N	H	81	-	12,691	13,384	693
			82	-	4,351	4,520	169
			83	-	7,782	8,086	304
			84	-	4,850	5,424	574
			85	-	10,962	11,639	677
			86	-	8,556	9,300	744
	N	W	81	-	34,511	37,025	2,514
			82	-	20,187	21,766	1,579
			83	-	3,219	3,719	500
			84	-	2,125	3,044	919
			85	-	40,389	41,318	929
			86	-	29,393	32,298	2,905
KOR REP	N	W	83	-	21,657	22,877	1,220
THAILND	N	E	86	-	3,000	3,355	355
	N	W	86	-	1,308	1,415	107
U KING	N	E	83	-	13,045	13,457	412
			84	-	1,520	1,686	166

Palmetic acid
4902402 PALMETIC ACID (LB)

Country	Mode	Reg	Yr	Quantity	F.A.S.	C.I.F.	Charges
TOTAL			86	6,234,557	588,532	658,059	69,527
FR GERM	V	E	86	37,699	11,998	15,939	3,941
MALAYSA	V	E	86	2,628,732	352,175	389,787	37,612
	V	W	86	3,568,126	224,359	252,333	27,974

Pectin
4550400 PECTIN (LB)

Country	Mode	Reg	Yr	Quantity	F.A.S.	C.I.F.	Charges
TOTAL			81	3,344,648	12,821,636	13,235,106	413,470
			82	3,938,340	16,601,157	16,930,270	329,113
			83	2,469,014	8,790,503	8,964,776	174,273
			84	4,180,602	12,725,402	13,068,307	342,905
			85	4,390,976	14,085,752	14,472,880	387,128
			86	4,580,138	15,779,055	16,177,607	398,552

Product TSUSA commodity number, description, and unit of quantity Country	Mode	Reg	Yr	Quantity	F.A.S.	C.I.F.	Charges
AUSTRIA	V	W	81	600	310	371	61
BELGIUM	O	E	84	54,453	151,336	157,454	6,118
	V	E	83	992	4,013	4,248	235
CANADA	O	E	82	150	649	649	
			86	1,013	4,536	4,536	
DENMARK	A	E	84	2,708	7,529	9,696	2,167
			85	661	3,378	3,922	544
			86	1,216	5,487	6,488	1,001
	N	E	81	115,741	390,453	405,327	14,874
			82	356,034	1,541,278	1,581,248	39,970
			83	93,149	275,648	282,356	6,708
			84	1,130,858	3,346,584	3,423,940	77,356
			85	174,384	557,980	580,789	22,809
			86	359,571	1,297,052	1,318,054	21,002
	O	E	84	7,165	29,409	30,105	696
	V	E	81	1,497,109	5,303,858	5,561,989	258,131
			82	1,688,019	7,037,457	7,156,186	118,729
			83	827,936	3,106,114	3,162,772	56,658
			84	718,371	2,230,687	2,294,001	63,314
			85	1,228,416	4,378,648	4,484,667	106,019
			86	1,765,785	6,253,728	6,403,417	149,689
	V	W	81	68,343	293,919	304,778	10,859
			83	25,904	123,123	125,463	2,340
			84	295,748	937,182	966,213	29,031
			85	175,047	606,230	623,845	17,615
			86	84,129	493,575	500,173	6,598
DOMINCA	V	E	85	23,810	57,407	57,866	459
FR GERM	A	E	82	882	6,240	6,400	160
			83	1,322	5,262	6,035	773
			85	110	1,585	1,790	205
			86	331	1,251	1,630	379
	A	W	85	2,976	13,221	16,378	3,157
	N	E	81	7,763	21,313	23,230	1,917
			82	4,407	27,006	28,903	1,897
			83	29,269	83,476	86,751	3,275
			84	70,548	170,880	180,248	9,368
			85	422,080	1,663,152	1,690,702	27,550
			86	34,171	98,293	102,583	4,290
	O	E	82	110	388	388	
	V	E	81	42,581	158,716	162,802	4,086
			82	39,297	98,716	103,807	5,091
			84	34,833	86,558	90,798	4,240
			85	524,659	1,660,328	1,715,062	54,734
			86	595,738	2,381,410	2,431,350	49,940
	V	W	81	2,205	7,969	8,583	614
			82	1,322	3,771	4,010	239
			85	114,419	272,765	282,256	9,491
FRANCE	A	E	83	331	1,523	1,658	135
			84	551	2,075	2,484	409
			85	8,863	13,516	16,242	2,726
			86	5,827	16,262	20,250	3,988
	A	W	81	110	583	634	51
	N	E	84	2,776	10,811	12,261	1,450
			85	40,631	131,145	140,593	9,448
	O	E	86	7,000	3,000	3,201	201
	V	E	83	1,653	5,619	6,144	525
			85	26,235	77,991	81,212	3,221
			86	69,843	265,395	273,305	7,910
	V	W	83	1,102	3,218	3,450	232
			84	1,102	3,293	3,450	157
GREECE	V	E	85	22,216	45,358	47,702	2,344
ISRAEL	V	E	81	94,985	278,537	291,879	13,342
			82	31,458	92,777	97,799	5,022
			83	38,736	107,641	114,075	6,434
			84	23,149	54,819	58,733	3,914
			85	43,017	101,448	108,884	7,436
			86	40,841	97,151	103,943	6,792
ITALY	N	E	84	141,366	558,048	569,327	11,279
	V	E	81	181,879	698,233	711,347	13,114
			82	66,799	266,046	270,251	4,205
			83	271,054	1,091,932	1,108,207	16,275
			84	216,604	893,872	911,122	17,250
			85	81,774	304,128	312,239	8,111
	V	W	84	25,904	103,567	105,772	2,205
JAPAN	V	W	82	2,756	11,013	11,951	938
MEXICO	O	E	83	278,106	846,953	846,953	
			84	484,895	1,259,475	1,259,475	
			85	656,050	1,719,730	1,720,889	1,159
			86	525,492	1,409,910	1,409,910	
	O	W	81	497,802	2,161,347	2,161,347	
			82	461,421	2,273,335	2,273,335	
			83	172,178	767,567	767,567	
	V	E	86	41,061	108,681	110,994	2,313
	V	W	84	132,276	396,355	401,635	5,280
NETHLDS	V	E	82	51,808	314,306	321,382	7,076

Product TSUSA commodity number, description, and unit of quantity Country	Mode	Reg	Yr	Quantity	F.A.S.	C.I.F.	Charges
NORWAY	V	W	86	15,538	48,168	51,222	3,054
SPAIN	N	E	82	5,005	15,040	16,859	1,819
			83	7,276	17,131	20,156	3,025
	V	E	81	3,307	6,783	7,850	1,067
			84	1,102	2,707	2,950	243
			85	13,227	7,372	7,907	535
			86	2,645	7,715	7,960	245
SWEDEN	A	W	82	148	462	663	201
SWITZLD	A	E	81	1,101	3,902	4,824	922
			82	220	1,220	1,328	108
			84	22	317	322	5
			85	3,307	13,815	18,320	4,505
			86	419	2,136	2,536	400
	A	W	85	441	1,200	1,591	391
	N	E	84	7,224	29,805	31,654	1,849
	N	W	84	838	4,235	4,925	690
	V	W	86	2,535	9,692	10,257	565
U KING	A	E	81	6,614	55,890	58,631	2,741
			82	43,916	204,824	217,967	13,143
			83	220	680	840	160
			84	2,348	6,221	7,494	1,273
	N	E	81	267,911	865,785	906,291	40,506
			82	330,473	1,051,365	1,096,643	45,278
			83	245,417	727,609	759,211	31,602
			84	234,570	704,677	732,854	28,177
			86	390,938	1,207,205	1,256,448	49,243
	N	W	82	80,800	264,257	275,419	11,162
			83	82,302	254,213	260,345	6,132
			84	324,323	982,943	1,034,274	51,331
			86	321,018	1,082,699	1,139,470	56,771
	O	E	83	9,480	27,993	29,068	1,075
			85	33,550	90,255	95,922	5,667
	V	E	81	448,637	2,143,995	2,182,735	38,740
			82	654,797	2,939,134	2,998,137	59,003
			83	312,041	1,133,058	1,163,147	30,089
			84	266,868	752,017	777,120	25,103
			85	457,872	1,339,686	1,391,025	51,339
			86	262,337	830,555	858,147	27,592
	V	W	81	107,960	430,043	442,488	12,445
			82	118,518	451,873	466,945	15,072
			83	70,546	207,730	216,330	8,600
			85	337,231	1,025,414	1,073,077	47,663
			86	52,690	155,154	161,733	6,579

Plants, seeds, and planting materials for USDA or USBG
8350000 PLANTS ETC FOR USDA OR USBG (NULL)

Country	Mode	Reg	Yr	Quantity	F.A.S.	C.I.F.	Charges
TOTAL			81	-	6,958	7,107	149
			82	-	55,806	55,966	160
			84	-	3,330	3,570	240
			86	-	42,000	51,457	9,457
CANADA	N	E	82	-	824	824	
			84	-	340	401	61
	N	W	81	-	5,387	5,387	
			82	-	44,790	44,790	
HG KONG	N	W	86	-	42,000	51,457	9,457
JAPAN	N	W	84	-	2,990	3,169	179
NETHLDS	N	E	82	-	497	550	53
U KING	N	E	82	-	9,695	9,802	107
	N	W	81	-	1,571	1,720	149

Pyrethrum
4935500 PYRETHRUM OR INSCT FLS CRUDE (LB)

Country	Mode	Reg	Yr	Quantity	F.A.S.	C.I.F.	Charges
TOTAL			81	209,437	117,440	138,680	21,240
			82	413,044	1,087,878	1,158,546	70,668
			83	243,792	1,221,248	1,302,187	80,939
			84	162,559	2,212,566	2,474,890	262,324
			85	406,701	3,073,276	3,204,734	131,458
			86	692,302	3,386,912	3,555,853	168,941
ECUADOR	A	E	83	1,801	14,101	15,396	1,295
			84	2,732	91,365	93,012	1,647
			85	2,290	89,318	90,683	1,365
FR GERM	V	E	86	50,706	12,612	17,997	5,385
KENYA	A	E	84	26,631	647,600	676,006	28,406
			86	11,023	449,200	462,480	13,280
	V	E	81	88,184	39,730	48,665	8,935
			82	132,276	63,230	80,550	17,320
			83	80,538	47,883	57,098	9,215
			86	33,073	20,600	29,459	8,859
NETHLDS	V	E	84	31,747	8,921	10,522	1,601

Country	Mode	Reg	Yr	Quantity	F.A.S.	C.I.F.	Charges
NEW GUI	A E		82	1,697	36,349	37,144	795
	O E		86	8,664	151,261	152,256	995
	V W		82	7,760	154,596	156,596	2,000
			83	21,082	456,302	458,320	2,018
			85	37,844	662,799	666,628	3,829
			86	107,651	323,669	325,604	1,935
REP SAF	V E		81	88,184	43,350	52,304	8,954
RWANDA	A E		83	5,750	85,882	107,585	21,703
			84	47,000	594,836	633,374	38,538
			85	292,500	1,096,488	1,147,773	51,285
			86	68,738	704,558	737,817	33,259
	V E		86	22,500	272,940	275,562	2,622
SWEDEN	A E		83	1	1,861	1,907	46
TNZANIA	A E		82	271,311	833,703	884,256	50,553
			83	134,620	615,219	661,881	46,662
			84	54,449	869,844	1,061,976	192,132
			85	67,453	1,021,886	1,093,392	71,506
			86	389,947	1,452,072	1,554,678	102,606
	V E		81	33,069	34,360	37,711	3,351
U KING	A E		85	6,614	202,785	206,258	3,473

4935600 PYRETHRUM INSECT FLOWERS ADV (LB)

Country	Mode	Reg	Yr	Quantity	F.A.S.	C.I.F.	Charges
TOTAL			81	150,778	7,263,190	7,411,508	148,318
			82	431,217	16,539,573	16,910,076	370,503
			83	282,788	10,004,817	10,337,630	332,813
			84	326,054	11,773,674	12,048,900	275,226
			85	355,870	11,826,497	12,150,691	324,194
			86	273,811	9,788,791	10,020,677	231,886
AUSTRAL	A E		84	377	7,831	9,278	1,447
	A W		81	66	5,428	5,722	294
BELGIUM	A E		84	9,000	125,282	133,591	8,309
CANADA	A E		81	3,042	155,304	157,228	1,924
ECUADOR	A E		81	10,724	421,373	429,461	8,088
			82	11,948	426,749	434,280	7,531
			83	3,277	114,148	116,500	2,352
			84	1,490	16,782	17,916	1,134
FR GERM	A E		84	1	416	492	76
			85	6,614	255,000	316,059	61,059
JAPAN	A E		85	543	1,122	2,719	1,597
KENYA	A E		81	71,211	4,446,798	4,538,649	91,851
			82	75,985	4,243,090	4,331,363	88,273
			83	60,982	2,919,066	3,003,219	84,153
			84	50,388	2,305,155	2,386,803	81,648
			85	100,604	3,914,588	3,969,048	54,460
			86	214,104	7,854,579	8,024,072	169,493
	A W		84	2,205	126,236	130,455	4,219
	N E		81	11,788	752,163	768,981	16,818
			82	161,219	6,179,361	6,329,770	150,409
			83	51,025	1,659,631	1,730,495	70,864
			84	166,856	6,639,304	6,742,176	102,872
			85	130,965	4,619,630	4,759,043	139,413
			86	13,229	599,386	624,271	24,885
	O E		81	31,916	758,006	765,638	7,632
			82	56,507	3,359,920	3,373,055	13,135
			83	73,664	3,522,002	3,534,427	12,425
	V E		83	2,050	13,100	17,934	4,834
			85	30,147	1,088,935	1,095,649	6,714
KOR REP	A E		86	8,818	351,200	359,734	8,534
NETHLDS	A E		83	15	961	984	23
NEW GUI	A E		82	3,087	70,000	77,290	7,290
	V W		81	3,516	113,756	113,977	221
			83	10,185	213,058	216,986	3,928
			84	15,328	325,104	326,464	1,360
NIGERIA	A E		86	10,069	320,000	328,549	8,549
PHIL R	V W		82	265	5,858	5,990	132
REP SAF	A E		81	3,307	218,400	222,229	3,829
			85	10,693	844,584	862,342	17,758
			86	10,075	334,900	343,232	8,332
	V E		85	4,610	29,420	42,974	13,554
RWANDA	A E		82	6,946	128,587	139,975	11,388
			83	26,423	424,687	506,708	82,021
			84	27,500	372,460	406,448	33,988
			85	22,500	274,122	277,191	3,069
			86	1,102	40,000	44,082	4,082
SPAIN	A E		84	22,046	963,005	984,324	21,319
TNZANIA	A E		81	15,208	391,962	409,623	17,661
			82	75,805	1,476,437	1,546,380	69,943
			83	41,938	768,245	834,830	66,585
			85	22,487	340,068	353,299	13,231
	V E		82	11,023	11,360	12,500	1,140
U KING	A E		82	28,432	638,211	659,473	21,262
			83	8,228	268,349	272,786	4,437
			84	26,454	817,815	835,459	17,644
			86	4,409	192,000	193,696	1,696

Country	Mode	Reg	Yr	Quantity	F.A.S.	C.I.F.	Charges
	N E		85	26,707	459,028	472,367	13,339
	V E		83	5,001	101,570	102,761	1,191
			84	4,409	74,284	75,494	1,210
			86	12,005	96,726	103,041	6,315

Starch (not specified)
1325500 STARCHES, NSPF (LB)

Country	Mode	Reg	Yr	Quantity	F.A.S.	C.I.F.	Charges
TOTAL			81	14,205,267	3,210,992	3,290,570	79,562
			82	26,235,796	5,330,902	5,435,077	104,175
			83	42,386,803	6,320,008	6,445,823	125,815
			84	36,723,651	5,895,428	6,106,704	211,276
			85	36,751,537	5,340,370	5,537,079	196,709
			86	63,974,461	7,607,041	7,906,659	299,618
AUSTRAL	V E		83	2,000	585	2,355	1,770
	V W		81	10,000	2,070	2,247	177
			84	1,102	726	832	106
			86	35,274	3,085	4,516	1,431
AUSTRIA	V E		81	714	560	624	64
BELGIUM	N E		84	407,850	119,257	142,889	23,632
			85	830,961	283,912	325,128	41,216
	O E		84	79,366	11,491	15,944	4,453
	V E		81	38,581	10,970	13,345	2,375
			82	99,204	30,843	34,949	4,106
			83	507,082	40,655	46,954	6,299
			85	44,092	15,483	17,660	2,177
			86	1,282,661	440,158	511,996	71,838
	V W		85	44,092	16,029	19,801	3,772
			86	176,368	70,156	79,200	9,044
BRAZIL	V E		84	727	300	332	32
			85	3,681	1,296	1,450	154
			86	3,307	4,660	5,497	837
CANADA	A E		86	15,160	16,980	17,335	355
	N E		81	19,444	25,578	26,366	788
			82	26,262	27,737	31,102	3,365
			85	5,237	16,216	17,196	980
	N W		85	48,432	14,217	14,370	153
	O E		81	12,470,257	2,372,902	2,372,975	57
			82	22,987,915	4,050,829	4,051,041	212
			83	36,525,698	5,069,136	5,069,508	372
			84	26,519,398	3,988,333	3,989,173	840
			85	26,021,331	3,115,053	3,115,053	
			86	44,571,460	4,491,195	4,492,097	902
	O W		81	42,000	8,810	8,810	
			85	23,281	3,467	3,467	
	V E		85	1,746	2,831	3,499	668
	V W		83	194,128	48,334	57,971	9,637
CHILE	O E		83	1,200	864	864	
	V E		86	263,653	49,319	70,919	21,600
CHINA M	N W		82	155,394	45,952	49,631	3,679
			85	190,250	63,731	72,337	8,606
	O E		83	9,000	2,576	2,808	232
			84	1,500	429	500	71
			86	3,000	4,257	4,446	189
	O W		83	3,000	1,166	1,220	54
			86	7,620	4,137	4,377	240
	V E		81	194,588	71,080	83,822	12,742
			82	119,415	39,988	48,217	8,229
			83	120,198	47,490	57,993	10,503
			84	131,915	49,221	61,345	12,124
			85	196,893	53,710	69,553	15,843
			86	179,061	107,381	120,747	13,366
	V H		82	2,400	899	962	63
			83	1,000	265	288	23
			84	9,000	2,944	3,245	301
			86	8,600	2,837	3,180	343
	V W		81	125,438	46,991	50,331	3,340
			82	171,681	78,084	86,472	8,388
			83	369,253	150,179	160,889	10,710
			84	263,049	94,450	102,337	7,887
			85	184,573	62,508	68,205	5,697
			86	629,497	195,702	215,241	19,539
CHINA T	A W		84	110	312	607	295
	V E		83	625	575	653	78
			85	5,500	2,311	2,778	467
			86	1,250	1,150	1,269	119
	V W		81	9,488	11,890	12,455	565
			82	5,005	2,851	3,185	334
			83	65,410	31,259	33,652	2,393
			84	13,663	9,554	10,307	753
			85	18,200	13,813	14,692	879
			86	3,042	1,580	1,637	57
COLOMB	A E		86	6,930	6,779	8,523	1,744

Product
TSUSA commodity number, description, and unit of quantity

Country	Mode	Reg	Yr	Quantity	F.A.S.	C.I.F.	Charges
	N	E	84	48,068	17,546	20,197	2,651
DENMARK	A	E	82	1,203	915	2,036	1,121
	O	E	83	4,700	3,225	3,636	411
DOM REP	V	E	84	10,410	4,800	6,283	1,483
			85	9,900	6,000	6,256	256
			86	9,900	6,000	6,337	337
FINLAND	A	W	86	3,102	1,060	1,900	840
	O	E	82	163,692	32,885	42,300	9,415
			83	41,060	8,815	10,915	2,100
			84	141,557	32,254	37,722	5,468
			85	99,207	31,846	37,619	5,773
	V	E	83	201,168	36,937	48,374	11,437
			84	52,910	11,708	11,931	223
			86	39,991	7,652	9,514	1,862
FR GERM	A	E	84	13	4,890	4,935	45
			85	3,969	10,299	12,355	2,056
	N	E	82	10,685	8,735	9,388	653
			84	3,993	3,154	3,455	301
	O	E	81	2,494	1,068	1,240	172
			82	225	908	908	
			83	43,367	21,618	24,113	2,495
			84	1,269	3,535	3,889	354
	V	E	81	22,542	22,844	23,982	1,138
			82	40,828	9,855	12,230	2,375
			83	104,194	26,939	32,732	5,793
			84	875	447	530	83
			86	2,530	4,100	4,466	366
	V	W	81	4,668	6,087	6,309	222
			82	1,400	1,173	1,252	79
			83	1,166	733	948	215
			84	551	356	391	35
			86	1,764	3,116	3,770	654
FRANCE	A	E	84	3,969	1,057	3,391	2,334
	A	W	86	4,375	1,664	1,735	71
	O	E	81	39,600	5,600	5,600	
	V	E	81	6,614	3,450	4,111	661
			84	12,734	6,205	7,020	815
			85	6,012	4,822	5,562	740
			86	544,345	213,125	249,970	36,845
GREECE	V	E	81	4,566	3,550	3,928	378
			82	4,620	3,800	4,526	726
			83	529	326	414	88
			84	15,300	8,180	9,064	884
HG KONG	N	E	85	210,575	64,175	75,243	11,068
	O	E	86	11,000	5,168	5,168	
	O	W	83	7,000	4,078	4,270	192
	V	E	81	225,937	94,572	108,492	13,920
			82	181,878	70,773	82,064	11,291
			83	233,151	75,617	94,014	18,397
			84	149,287	49,085	61,466	12,381
			85	2,500	1,166	1,351	185
			86	494,862	175,755	199,172	23,417
	V	H	81	37,450	12,925	13,794	869
			82	54,801	18,211	19,856	1,645
			83	50,420	15,368	16,917	1,549
			84	42,300	13,759	15,480	1,721
			85	35,400	12,197	13,445	1,248
			86	43,600	14,863	16,564	1,701
	V	W	81	239,729	86,594	92,333	5,739
			82	231,269	82,389	88,690	6,301
			83	258,862	83,498	89,480	5,982
			84	171,583	76,492	82,307	5,815
			85	261,337	94,624	105,029	10,405
			86	174,306	59,277	65,678	6,401
INDIA	V	E	85	5,070	2,153	2,399	246
INDNSIA	V	W	86	661	1,421	1,477	56
ITALY	A	E	82	639	251	349	98
	V	E	82	655	374	406	32
			83	1,091	624	677	53
			84	5,254	2,074	2,273	199
			86	192,131	56,373	67,572	11,199
JAPAN	A	E	82	217	2,830	3,702	872
			83	238	3,408	4,328	920
			84	441	1,300	2,850	1,550
	N	E	83	211	1,022	1,121	99
			85	1,051	2,768	3,256	488
	O	E	81	517	1,431	1,618	187
			84	3,129	9,554	10,510	956
			86	456	2,097	2,195	98
	V	E	81	3,244	3,009	3,311	302
			82	3,881	4,267	4,992	725
			83	6,980	57,762	59,091	1,329
			84	8,260	12,327	13,462	1,135
			85	1,995	5,633	6,178	545
			86	4,297	12,815	13,403	588
	V	H	82	11,023	2,173	3,027	854
			84	6,272	2,339	3,028	689
	V	W	81	21,387	27,057	31,426	4,369
			82	5,211	13,240	14,553	1,313
			83	10,022	15,270	16,583	1,313
			84	8,871	17,281	18,869	1,588
			85	8,577	16,558	17,933	1,375
			86	35,248	60,521	65,036	4,515
KOR REP	N	W	82	3,600	1,164	1,496	332
			84	16,347	22,892	24,229	1,337
	V	E	81	1,938	4,533	5,072	539
			82	2,930	8,024	8,803	779
			83	3,577	6,597	7,073	476
			84	5,829	10,302	11,229	927
			85	13,622	8,729	9,623	894
			86	66,235	17,391	18,626	1,235
	V	H	81	588	2,377	2,758	381
			82	360	1,033	1,202	169
	V	W	81	10,505	30,437	32,243	1,806
			82	18,054	50,900	54,651	3,751
			83	18,046	16,579	17,898	1,319
			84	6,135	6,262	7,013	751
			85	20,627	31,299	34,339	3,040
			86	21,046	31,955	34,055	2,100
MALAYSA	V	E	85	27,383	6,728	7,526	798
	V	W	85	20,005	3,582	3,800	218
MEXICO	O	E	82	196	392	392	
			83	757,762	76,058	76,955	897
			84	1,660,411	185,836	185,836	
			85	242,453	104,267	104,267	
			86	2,679,027	258,642	258,642	
	O	W	81	249,810	157,321	157,321	
			82	1,489,171	455,262	455,262	
			83	2,337,826	311,415	311,572	157
			84	5,165,805	788,544	788,544	
			85	7,026,984	992,392	992,392	
			86	11,514,819	967,171	967,171	
	V	E	84	1,385,504	160,298	246,418	86,120
			85	432,000	37,640	62,640	25,000
	V	W	84	330	285	294	9
			86	79,401	4,483	6,903	2,420
MOROC	O	E	85	38,608	4,232	4,232	
NETHLDS	A	W	83	13,228	1,571	2,654	1,083
	N	E	84	34,925	14,218	17,141	2,923
			85	56,050	24,063	27,377	3,314
	O	E	81	196,149	78,566	90,942	12,376
			82	166,147	68,653	80,068	11,415
			83	140,124	54,169	59,724	5,555
			84	84,074	32,801	35,689	2,888
			85	84,075	31,051	35,851	4,800
			86	31,677	12,086	13,386	1,300
	V	E	81	28,000	9,316	10,750	1,434
			82	66,606	100,553	106,810	6,257
			83	56,050	21,199	24,078	2,879
			84	28,000	12,250	14,838	2,588
			85	89,280	31,354	39,851	8,497
			86	189,061	71,031	85,202	14,171
	V	W	83	28,025	11,850	13,632	1,782
			84	5,650	1,921	2,497	576
			85	28,000	11,813	15,842	4,029
PANAMA	A	E	86	2,973	2,880	3,969	1,089
PHIL R	V	W	81	1,800	358	628	270
			84	125	817	899	82
			85	2,955	2,128	2,352	224
			86	1,193	1,335	1,521	186
PORTUGL	O	E	86	22,928	4,949	4,949	
	V	E	82	661	267	327	60
REP SAF	V	E	81	2,000	640	897	257
	V	W	83	2,002	291	393	102
ROMANIA	V	W	84	99	303	321	18
SINGAPR	V	E	86	38,000	6,080	8,228	2,148
SPAIN	N	W	86	61,575	22,101	37,552	15,451
	V	E	85	96,115	46,238	57,723	11,485
SWEDEN	V	E	83	148,812	28,071	38,187	10,116
SWITZLD	A	E	82	220	338	522	184
	V	E	81	22,124	4,380	5,878	1,498
			85	1,650	3,118	3,701	583
	V	W	85	7,607	2,429	2,571	142
			86	3,190	2,248	2,593	345
THAILND	V	E	81	14,961	4,422	4,980	558
			82	195	824	931	107
			83	3,254	1,087	1,234	147
			84	16,875	3,225	4,162	937
			85	113,340	21,120	27,837	6,717
	V	W	81	69,956	19,314	21,932	2,618

Product TSUSA commodity number, description, and unit of quantity Country	Mode	Reg	Yr	Quantity	F.A.S.	C.I.F.	Charges
			82	91,450	31,390	35,321	3,931
			83	73,405	20,195	22,885	2,690
			84	29,792	7,314	7,977	663
			85	44,988	7,210	7,861	651
			86	205,070	31,036	34,437	3,401
U KING	A	E	86	2,866	1,232	2,925	1,693
	N	E	81	88,178	80,290	90,050	9,760
			82	114,203	81,559	92,839	11,280
			84	168,024	92,448	112,687	20,239
	O	E	83	41,939	22,602	26,770	4,168
	V	E	85	141,933	54,159	65,479	11,320
			86	166,086	83,809	100,534	16,725
	V	W	82	2,500	581	615	34
			84	1,000	352	366	14
VENEZ	V	E	86	139,863	64,229	71,029	6,800

Tea for manufacturing chemical products
8670000 TEA FOR MFG OF CHEM PROD ETC (NULL)

Country	Mode	Reg	Yr	Quantity	F.A.S.	C.I.F.	Charges
TOTAL			85	-	10,629	10,629	
			86	-	101,383	109,686	8,303
CANADA	N	E	85	-	10,629	10,629	
KOR REP	N	E	86	-	101,383	109,686	8,303

Vegetable, glue
4553000 VEG GLUE UNDER 4O CENTS LB (LB)

Country	Mode	Reg	Yr	Quantity	F.A.S.	C.I.F.	Charges
TOTAL			81	6,624	1,349	1,583	234
			83	40,565	6,770	8,587	1,817
			84	452,574	87,805	114,720	26,915
			85	763,128	163,970	199,695	35,725
			86	578,331	181,799	208,020	26,221
BRAZIL	V	E	84	1,935	350	440	90
CANADA	O	E	85	11,360	5,040	5,040	
CHINA M	V	E	84	74,956	14,321	18,862	4,541
CHINA T	V	E	84	374,681	71,874	94,016	22,142
			85	751,768	158,930	194,655	35,725
			86	482,259	151,328	173,625	22,297
	V	W	84	1,002	1,260	1,402	142
			86	77,760	25,193	28,829	3,636
ITALY	V	E	81	6,624	1,349	1,583	234
			86	5,952	2,188	2,386	198
KOR REP	V	W	86	12,360	3,090	3,180	90
SWITZLD	V	E	83	39,683	6,464	7,678	1,214
U KING	A	E	83	882	306	909	603

4553200 VEG GLUE NOT UN 4O CENTS LB (LB)

Country	Mode	Reg	Yr	Quantity	F.A.S.	C.I.F.	Charges
TOTAL			81	98,625	143,407	160,306	16,899
			82	75,133	116,133	127,052	10,919
			83	59,921	90,549	97,887	7,338
			84	75,050	145,322	176,914	31,592
			85	120,568	163,531	188,422	24,891
			86	258,326	333,857	371,116	37,259
AUSTRIA	A	E	81	825	699	997	298
BRAZIL	V	E	84	3,061	6,325	7,686	1,361
CANADA	O	E	81	15,182	12,989	13,501	512
			82	14,553	15,799	15,799	
			83	32,905	35,285	35,285	
			84	20,101	17,836	17,836	
			85	39,969	25,645	25,645	
			86	53,462	33,032	33,032	
	V	E	85	4,410	14,108	14,108	
CHINA M	V	E	82	500	1,485	1,600	115
			83	10	261	265	4
			84	340	532	562	30
CHINA T	N	E	85	4,498	7,588	8,953	1,365
			86	6,356	22,783	24,387	1,604
	O	E	86	2,134	1,901	2,358	457
	V	E	81	8,642	10,901	15,792	4,891
			82	2,382	3,475	3,859	384
			83	2,224	2,881	3,132	251
			84	7,169	7,828	9,392	1,564
			85	2,094	2,400	2,655	255
			86	3,858	8,373	9,944	1,571
	V	W	82	386	620	663	43
			84	3,941	6,032	6,631	599
			85	3,721	12,292	13,180	888
			86	81,614	104,268	113,572	9,304
FR GERM	A	E	81	33	1,078	1,218	140
			82	78	1,245	1,296	51

Product TSUSA commodity number, description, and unit of quantity Country	Mode	Reg	Yr	Quantity	F.A.S.	C.I.F.	Charges
			83	66	1,120	1,142	22
			84	95	454	505	51
			85	3,307	6,253	7,796	1,543
	A	W	84	45	295	347	52
	N	E	82	448	647	667	20
			83	223	2,302	2,386	84
			84	11,684	21,463	33,476	12,013
	V	E	81	42,158	70,547	73,424	2,877
			82	27,482	44,079	46,390	2,311
			83	9,582	16,176	16,939	763
			84	1,623	4,514	4,861	347
			85	27,339	49,575	53,563	3,988
			86	16,058	37,087	39,831	2,744
	V	W	84	827	361	404	43
			85	19,839	11,984	13,769	1,785
			86	42,108	29,178	32,337	3,159
FRANCE	A	E	81	1,148	1,962	2,138	176
			82	276	319	653	334
			86	220	2,391	2,602	211
	N	E	82	28	643	659	16
	O	W	84	209	868	868	
	V	E	81	1,175	4,544	4,616	72
			82	882	636	767	131
			83	303	647	680	33
			84	1,146	2,086	2,750	664
			85	2,349	4,084	4,515	431
			86	720	2,943	2,971	28
	V	W	86	1,270	2,187	2,419	232
GERM DR	V	E	82	2,205	14,374	14,645	271
GREECE	V	W	86	1,102	1,097	1,538	441
HG KONG	A	E	84	1,002	4,155	4,628	473
			85	165	1,280	1,600	320
	V	E	83	854	2,002	2,184	182
			86	1,862	1,676	1,704	28
	V	W	83	156	316	343	27
ITALY	A	E	84	416	3,254	3,981	727
			86	584	1,726	2,885	1,159
	V	E	81	419	1,342	1,504	162
			83	82	272	291	19
			85	882	2,067	2,188	121
	V	W	81	8,761	13,561	15,765	2,204
			83	7,403	10,678	13,264	2,586
			84	11,778	17,391	17,974	583
			85	2,006	2,861	3,254	393
			86	12,589	15,075	19,110	4,035
JAPAN	A	E	82	529	2,560	2,812	252
	A	H	82	71	418	537	119
	A	W	83	668	6,201	7,368	1,167
	N	E	84	4,040	28,011	34,814	6,803
			86	1,817	23,648	25,680	2,032
	N	W	81	489	5,946	7,014	1,068
			82	1,815	9,349	11,344	1,995
			84	2,265	4,355	9,173	4,818
			85	8,441	14,612	27,948	13,336
	V	E	81	443	2,362	2,467	105
			85	372	2,164	2,264	100
			86	626	2,602	2,732	130
	V	H	81	155	380	396	16
			82	26	822	849	27
	V	W	81	35	380	398	18
			84	1,438	11,140	11,736	596
			86	2,633	6,735	7,024	289
KOR REP	V	W	85	550	1,772	1,867	95
			86	1,201	5,436	5,729	293
N ZEAL	V	W	81	11,905	8,692	11,058	2,366
NETHLDS	A	E	82	56	690	720	30
	O	E	84	2,005	1,149	1,149	
	V	E	82	2,524	4,600	4,909	309
			83	190	1,211	1,253	42
			84	851	1,284	1,306	22
			85	393	1,143	1,278	135
			86	9,656	8,368	9,095	727
	V	W	83	728	949	1,014	65
SPAIN	V	E	81	461	935	1,023	88
			86	926	3,836	4,046	210
SWEDEN	A	E	83	94	919	1,030	111
	V	E	82	551	601	652	51
SWITZLD	A	E	84	300	3,445	3,756	311
			85	4	1,012	1,063	51
			86	8,543	8,738	16,515	7,777
	A	W	84	32	260	268	8
	V	E	81	5,500	3,603	3,905	302
			82	90	1,802	1,841	39
			83	134	1,313	1,338	25
			85	229	2,691	2,776	85

Product TSUSA commodity number, description, and unit of quantity — Country	Mode	Reg	Yr	Quantity	F.A.S.	C.I.F.	Charges
			86	6,607	9,548	10,269	721
U KING	A	E	81	1,294	3,486	5,090	1,604
			82	2,073	2,373	4,528	2,155
			83	3,603	2,879	4,469	1,590
			84	441	374	738	364
	V	E	82	18,178	9,596	11,862	2,266
			83	696	5,137	5,504	367
			84	241	1,910	2,073	163
			86	2,380	1,229	1,336	107

Vegetable substance
1932560 VEG SUBSTANCE, CRUDE, NSPF (NULL)

Country	Mode	Reg	Yr	Quantity	F.A.S.	C.I.F.	Charges
TOTAL			81	-	8,118,694	9,624,103	1,505,409
			82	-	10,048,520	11,285,296	1,236,776
			83	-	10,286,017	11,686,161	1,400,144
			84	-	9,940,327	11,638,921	1,698,594
			85	-	9,453,573	10,945,631	1,492,058
			86	-	9,792,896	11,351,404	1,558,508
ALBANIA	N	E	81	-	5,014	5,463	449
	N	W	81	-	5,386	5,548	162
			82	-	883	883	
ARGENT	N	E	83	-	2,000	2,609	609
			85	-	1,188	1,491	303
			86	-	15,675	18,676	3,001
	N	W	83	-	8,818	10,682	1,864
			84	-	21,689	27,890	6,201
			85	-	9,954	12,651	2,697
			86	-	13,879	18,223	4,344
AUSTRAL	N	E	84	-	10,411	10,986	575
			85	-	8,421	8,809	388
			86	-	2,580	2,754	174
	N	H	81	-	5,141	5,962	821
			82	-	19,733	26,026	6,293
	N	W	81	-	87,121	93,281	6,160
			82	-	60,092	66,348	6,256
			83	-	55,229	56,882	1,653
			84	-	39,160	42,162	3,002
			85	-	27,931	31,489	3,558
			86	-	10,624	11,497	873
AUSTRIA	N	E	82	-	4,992	5,306	314
			83	-	129,440	134,710	5,270
			84	-	68,250	69,948	1,698
	N	W	81	-	28,264	30,117	1,853
B VIRGN	N	E	84	-	253	258	5
BAHAMAS	N	E	81	-	34,000	34,436	436
BELGIUM	N	E	82	-	1,088	1,481	393
			83	-	6,973	7,838	865
			85	-	9,063	9,884	821
			86	-	8,084	8,704	620
	N	W	81	-	396	624	228
			82	-	400	622	222
			84	-	4,696	6,732	2,036
BELIZE	N	E	81	-	1,345	2,602	1,257
BRAZIL	N	E	81	-	637	773	136
			82	-	8,520	10,712	2,192
			83	-	6,479	8,047	1,568
			84	-	1,830	2,613	783
			85	-	2,145	2,600	455
			86	-	6,483	7,530	1,047
	N	W	83	-	49,446	52,996	3,550
			84	-	3,451	5,209	1,758
			85	-	4,505	6,000	1,495
			86	-	15,058	16,356	1,298
BULGAR	N	E	81	-	1,092	1,230	138
			82	-	692	850	158
			83	-	20,052	27,329	7,277
			84	-	6,097	8,438	2,341
			85	-	7,860	9,600	1,740
	N	W	82	-	639	834	195
			83	-	1,177	1,594	417
BURKINA	N	E	84	-	280	283	3
C RICA	N	E	81	-	9,079	13,798	4,719
			82	-	38,619	52,188	13,569
			83	-	8,320	12,825	4,505
			84	-	15,349	20,669	5,320
			86	-	28,250	30,652	2,402
	N	W	82	-	750	1,372	622
			86	-	8,120	10,620	2,500
CANADA	N	E	81	-	162,510	162,510	
			82	-	263,094	263,125	31
			83	-	501,639	501,639	
			84	-	385,541	388,308	2,767

Country	Mode	Reg	Yr	Quantity	F.A.S.	C.I.F.	Charges
			85	-	443,429	444,126	697
			86	-	425,231	429,932	4,701
	N	W	81	-	109,972	110,384	412
			82	-	158,963	159,124	161
			83	-	197,409	197,690	281
			84	-	529,081	529,081	
			85	-	455,239	455,239	
			86	-	444,242	444,242	
CHILE	N	E	81	-	411,385	471,783	60,398
			82	-	221,385	253,771	32,386
			83	-	639,961	709,766	69,805
			84	-	422,796	470,951	48,155
			85	-	238,626	279,020	40,394
			86	-	255,855	306,227	50,372
	N	W	82	-	34,452	39,558	5,106
			84	-	44,201	51,655	7,454
			85	-	4,536	5,210	674
			86	-	27,759	30,687	2,928
CHINA M	N	E	81	-	898,590	948,034	49,444
			82	-	1,619,001	1,727,923	108,922
			83	-	945,984	1,006,101	60,117
			84	-	395,728	428,660	32,932
			85	-	843,227	922,928	79,701
			86	-	757,629	856,306	98,677
	N	H	83	-	1,059	1,182	123
			84	-	808	918	110
	N	W	81	-	414,832	440,263	25,431
			82	-	916,924	997,922	80,998
			83	-	1,192,373	1,276,806	84,433
			84	-	748,294	837,219	88,925
			85	-	1,225,734	1,331,170	105,436
			86	-	1,297,799	1,442,874	145,075
CHINA T	N	E	81	-	120,279	137,235	16,956
			82	-	222,520	246,276	23,756
			83	-	157,845	166,200	8,355
			84	-	127,304	139,656	12,352
			85	-	99,888	110,524	10,636
			86	-	149,190	163,246	14,056
	N	H	81	-	2,096	2,321	225
			82	-	2,568	2,802	234
			83	-	1,550	1,748	198
			84	-	3,629	4,131	502
			86	-	2,293	2,512	219
	N	W	81	-	121,105	129,471	8,366
			82	-	122,363	131,418	9,055
			83	-	170,600	178,867	8,267
			84	-	147,251	160,891	13,640
			85	-	198,956	213,206	14,250
			86	-	332,586	353,142	20,556
COLOMB	N	E	81	-	3,982	4,198	216
			82	-	28,932	29,059	127
			83	-	91,216	93,073	1,857
			84	-	37,400	38,888	1,488
			85	-	75,646	78,766	3,120
			86	-	8,100	8,562	462
CYPRUS	N	E	81	-	132,932	188,637	55,705
			82	-	79,114	125,446	46,332
			83	-	87,807	124,315	36,508
			84	-	152,845	206,782	53,937
			85	-	67,209	103,762	36,553
			86	-	42,311	59,373	17,062
DENMARK	N	E	83	-	906	1,173	267
			85	-	10,040	10,640	600
			86	-	9,857	10,507	650
DOM REP	N	E	81	-	1,526,669	2,140,187	613,518
			82	-	1,561,131	2,034,845	473,714
			83	-	1,924,421	2,511,254	586,833
			84	-	2,234,567	3,046,520	811,953
			85	-	2,229,655	2,959,845	730,190
			86	-	1,842,927	2,456,991	614,064
	N	W	84	-	1,224	1,597	373
ECUADOR	N	E	81	-	3,647	4,718	1,071
			82	-	1,500	3,234	1,734
			83	-	1,200	2,477	1,277
			84	-	3,022	3,884	862
			85	-	2,200	3,166	966
	N	W	84	-	515	728	213
EGYPT	N	E	81	-	16,859	19,145	2,286
			82	-	16,437	17,837	1,400
			83	-	9,599	10,102	503
			84	-	440	1,894	1,454
			85	-	27,350	34,821	7,471
			86	-	35,009	54,226	19,217
	N	W	81	-	1,498	1,506	8
			83	-	1,675	1,909	234

Product
TSUSA commodity number, description, and unit of quantity

Country	Mode	Reg	Yr	Quantity	F.A.S.	C.I.F.	Charges
			85	-	2,450	3,065	615
ETHIOP	N	E	81	-	1,099	1,451	352
FIJI	N	E	81	-	1,440	1,627	187
	N	H	82	-	5,853	6,088	235
	N	W	84	-	36,300	40,284	3,984
			85	-	45,500	48,007	2,507
			86	-	4,326	4,567	241
FR GERM	N	E	81	-	6,445	7,312	867
			82	-	99,513	110,451	10,938
			83	-	79,474	89,699	10,225
			84	-	19,371	22,250	2,879
			85	-	33,611	38,475	4,864
			86	-	3,922	4,784	862
	N	W	81	-	23,960	24,406	446
			82	-	125,658	135,334	9,676
			83	-	83,907	93,037	9,130
			84	-	57,246	61,212	3,966
			85	-	127,481	142,653	15,172
			86	-	85,808	88,331	2,523
FRANCE	N	E	81	-	172,989	182,592	9,603
			82	-	56,258	60,995	4,737
			83	-	128,086	135,652	7,566
			84	-	206,649	226,490	19,841
			85	-	7,951	9,039	1,088
			86	-	29,073	31,304	2,231
	N	W	81	-	3,985	4,204	219
			83	-	14,671	16,179	1,508
			84	-	10,531	11,958	1,427
			85	-	42,194	46,800	4,606
			86	-	99,990	100,309	319
GHANA	N	E	86	-	2,000	2,028	28
GREECE	N	E	81	-	116,854	131,061	14,207
			82	-	31,103	36,606	5,503
			83	-	55,970	71,838	15,868
			84	-	48,746	67,664	18,918
			85	-	58,987	77,483	18,496
			86	-	148,762	191,000	42,238
	N	W	86	-	13,549	16,049	2,500
GUATMAL	N	E	81	-	320,315	453,595	133,280
			82	-	85,253	129,830	44,577
			83	-	136,711	211,959	75,248
			84	-	456,728	613,387	156,659
			85	-	73,270	81,347	8,077
			86	-	113,982	129,341	15,359
	N	W	81	-	104,197	131,316	27,119
			82	-	45,460	57,005	11,545
			83	-	32,170	40,308	8,138
			84	-	49,010	66,674	17,664
			85	-	82,757	104,056	21,299
			86	-	68,191	84,166	15,975
HAITI	N	E	81	-	6,712	8,175	1,463
			82	-	38,676	45,917	7,241
			83	-	69,856	80,665	10,809
			84	-	21,195	23,605	2,410
			85	-	4,356	5,134	778
			86	-	6,424	8,183	1,759
	N	W	83	-	2,548	3,305	757
HG KONG	N	E	81	-	237,467	252,069	14,602
			82	-	111,874	122,360	10,486
			83	-	183,317	195,385	12,068
			84	-	69,077	75,960	6,883
			85	-	77,448	85,583	8,135
			86	-	166,012	177,712	11,700
	N	H	83	-	342	395	53
	N	W	81	-	2,337	2,474	137
			82	-	158,416	170,258	11,842
			83	-	44,217	47,019	2,802
			84	-	57,180	62,561	5,381
			85	-	104,828	114,230	9,402
			86	-	800,445	889,305	88,860
HONDURA	N	E	81	-	330	571	241
ICELAND	N	E	82	-	689	831	142
INDIA	N	E	81	-	24,696	33,937	9,241
			82	-	61,514	80,618	19,104
			83	-	33,409	39,141	5,732
			84	-	148,668	167,471	18,803
			85	-	18,311	21,698	3,387
			86	-	16,817	19,655	2,838
	N	W	81	-	37,767	45,270	7,503
			82	-	55,209	64,538	9,329
			83	-	85,277	101,721	16,444
			84	-	33,580	37,672	4,092
			85	-	60,782	70,267	9,485
			86	-	49,565	55,760	6,195
INDNSIA	N	E	81	-	353	391	38
	N	W	81	-	919	964	45
			82	-	3,255	3,456	201
			83	-	884	1,006	122
			84	-	1,160	1,336	176
			85	-	10,545	12,498	1,953
IRELAND	N	E	86	-	303,053	333,917	30,864
ISRAEL	N	E	81	-	9,428	11,512	2,084
			82	-	18,552	21,892	3,340
			83	-	35,621	47,434	11,813
			84	-	13,450	15,548	2,098
			85	-	11,033	13,833	2,800
			86	-	27,595	33,038	5,443
ITALY	N	E	81	-	304,840	331,555	26,715
			82	-	325,463	354,479	29,016
			83	-	302,964	331,043	28,079
			84	-	321,702	345,921	24,219
			85	-	180,082	195,077	14,995
			86	-	201,674	218,383	16,709
	N	W	81	-	16,632	18,144	1,512
			83	-	981	1,101	120
JAMAICA	N	E	83	-	1,109	1,858	749
			84	-	10,365	13,116	2,751
			85	-	14,773	19,362	4,589
			86	-	3,600	4,680	1,080
JAPAN	N	E	81	-	129,512	135,120	5,608
			82	-	225,724	231,646	5,922
			83	-	136,635	141,502	4,867
			84	-	58,191	60,656	2,465
			85	-	27,153	28,240	1,087
			86	-	32,761	33,915	1,154
	N	H	82	-	372	633	261
			83	-	1,709	2,317	608
	N	W	81	-	76,987	80,494	3,507
			82	-	7,143	7,590	447
			83	-	24,302	24,956	654
			84	-	8,823	9,620	797
			85	-	51,717	53,485	1,768
			86	-	23,738	25,224	1,486
JORDAN	N	E	83	-	1,167	1,325	158
KENYA	N	W	83	-	500	571	71
KOR REP	N	E	81	-	8,077	8,675	598
			82	-	28,419	30,975	2,556
			83	-	31,312	34,307	2,995
			84	-	19,536	21,561	2,025
			85	-	8,032	8,986	954
			86	-	6,906	7,432	526
	N	W	81	-	68,607	71,703	3,096
			82	-	41,071	43,077	2,006
			83	-	5,599	6,266	667
			84	-	45,561	48,750	3,189
			85	-	13,504	14,501	997
			86	-	118,648	123,967	5,319
LIBERIA	N	E	82	-	2,807	4,916	2,109
MADAGAS	N	E	81	-	29,881	30,176	295
MALAYSA	N	E	81	-	2,684	3,239	555
			82	-	12,799	15,376	2,577
			83	-	1,430	1,531	101
			84	-	1,808	2,080	272
			85	-	11,182	11,279	97
	N	W	81	-	2,842	3,105	263
			82	-	1,206	1,400	194
			83	-	791	980	189
MEXICO	N	E	81	-	721,176	758,649	37,473
			82	-	1,633,778	1,656,666	22,888
			83	-	646,469	656,297	9,828
			84	-	692,395	695,344	2,949
			85	-	509,894	511,666	1,772
			86	-	140,312	140,730	418
	N	W	81	-	212,744	212,894	150
			82	-	219,719	223,107	3,388
			83	-	215,848	215,927	79
			84	-	333,477	344,575	11,098
			85	-	238,039	308,589	70,550
			86	-	450,888	479,268	28,380
MOROC	N	E	81	-	6,571	17,219	10,648
			82	-	15,266	20,870	5,604
			83	-	132,862	166,804	33,942
			84	-	91,514	113,613	22,099
			85	-	47,922	67,367	19,445
	N	W	81	-	2,066	2,071	5
			82	-	2,613	2,844	231
N ZEAL	N	H	83	-	7,904	11,057	3,153
			84	-	6,613	8,536	1,923
			85	-	15,948	21,424	5,476
			86	-	40,629	51,346	10,717

Product
TSUSA commodity number, description, and unit of quantity

Country	Mode	Reg	Yr	Quantity	F.A.S.	C.I.F.	Charges
	N	W	82	-	540	788	248
NETHLDS	N	E	81	-	6,000	6,052	52
			83	-	7,604	8,552	948
			84	-	29,624	33,712	4,088
			85	-	3,600	3,709	109
			86	-	23,907	28,526	4,619
	N	W	81	-	262	293	31
			83	-	3,405	3,564	159
NIGERIA	N	E	81	-	9,921	11,671	1,750
NORWAY	N	E	84	-	21,731	24,619	2,888
PAKISTN	N	E	81	-	4,337	6,646	2,309
			83	-	26,875	36,748	9,873
			84	-	22,520	25,330	2,810
	N	W	82	-	12,435	13,922	1,487
			83	-	13,418	14,819	1,401
			84	-	10,327	17,052	6,725
			85	-	7,275	7,323	48
PARAGUA	N	E	82	-	2,591	3,691	1,100
PERU	N	E	82	-	975	1,428	453
			83	-	3,224	3,943	719
			84	-	5,436	6,603	1,167
			86	-	8,185	9,056	871
PHIL R	N	E	81	-	5,166	6,238	1,072
			82	-	8,332	9,271	939
			83	-	5,183	5,804	621
			84	-	32,909	43,151	10,242
			85	-	12,690	15,820	3,130
			86	-	41,284	54,497	13,213
	N	H	81	-	50,507	169,682	119,175
	N	W	81	-	10,310	11,826	1,516
			82	-	7,442	8,417	975
			83	-	33,343	38,713	5,370
			84	-	48,809	63,718	14,909
			85	-	31,465	41,997	10,532
			86	-	32,093	42,018	9,925
POLAND	N	E	82	-	8,715	9,498	783
			83	-	3,060	3,318	258
			84	-	8,999	9,554	555
			86	-	1,749	1,888	139
PORTUGL	N	E	81	-	93,995	143,604	49,609
			82	-	65,999	116,636	50,637
			83	-	39,793	66,458	26,665
			84	-	14,892	22,914	8,022
			85	-	4,960	8,004	3,044
			86	-	16,856	22,844	5,988
REP SAF	N	E	81	-	15,501	16,513	1,012
			82	-	11,225	12,071	846
			83	-	6,003	6,429	426
	N	W	81	-	5,879	6,459	580
ROMANIA	N	E	81	-	15,374	19,955	4,581
			82	-	15,115	20,121	5,006
			83	-	5,930	6,753	823
			84	-	8,705	9,490	785
S VN GR	N	E	85	-	18,711	19,310	599
SALVADR	N	E	83	-	318	394	76
SINGAPR	N	W	81	-	1,850	2,226	376
			85	-	38,560	41,843	3,283
SPAIN	N	E	81	-	676,513	793,047	116,534
			82	-	836,376	945,413	109,037
			83	-	1,017,746	1,151,476	133,730
			84	-	1,170,287	1,331,470	161,183
			85	-	652,195	776,032	123,837
			86	-	535,622	657,421	121,799
	N	W	81	-	170,087	183,720	13,633
			82	-	80,954	86,030	5,076
			83	-	142,771	159,923	17,152
			84	-	112,831	123,339	10,508
			85	-	279,230	302,429	23,199
			86	-	116,983	127,135	10,152
SUDAN	N	E	81	-	27,744	29,026	1,282
			86	-	41,666	45,600	3,934
	N	W	82	-	19,539	19,734	195
			83	-	12,660	14,809	2,149
SWEDEN	N	E	81	-	92,286	93,195	909
			82	-	31,456	31,830	374
			83	-	915	970	55
	N	W	82	-	336	356	20
SWITZLD	N	E	81	-	268	406	138
			84	-	734	734	
			85	-	1,845	1,845	
	N	W	83	-	2,332	2,741	409
			85	-	88,380	95,580	7,200
SYRIA	N	E	81	-	442	478	36
			84	-	390	478	88
THAILND	N	E	81	-	16,045	18,107	2,062

Product
TSUSA commodity number, description, and unit of quantity

Country	Mode	Reg	Yr	Quantity	F.A.S.	C.I.F.	Charges
			82	-	10,474	11,867	1,393
			83	-	10,703	12,531	1,828
			84	-	20,793	24,066	3,273
			85	-	27,824	31,701	3,877
			86	-	12,748	14,438	1,690
	N	W	81	-	11,746	12,972	1,226
			82	-	14,747	16,424	1,677
			83	-	30,385	33,444	3,059
			84	-	33,717	37,660	3,943
			85	-	81,519	92,041	10,522
			86	-	91,917	107,713	15,796
TRINID	N	E	81	-	963	1,742	779
			84	-	12,340	16,449	4,109
			86	-	2,288	2,521	233
TUNISIA	N	E	86	-	74,045	102,290	28,245
TURKEY	N	E	83	-	7,314	7,975	661
			86	-	3,216	4,171	955
	N	W	84	-	760	975	215
U KING	N	E	81	-	23,900	24,705	805
			83	-	11,643	12,386	743
			84	-	309	407	98
			85	-	194,093	194,129	36
			86	-	37,327	65,704	28,377
	N	W	83	-	454	470	16
			86	-	3,450	4,708	1,258
USSR	N	E	83	-	8,591	9,271	680
			85	-	2,914	3,254	340
	N	W	82	-	1,097	1,176	79
VENEZ	N	E	81	-	4,147	4,354	207
			82	-	14,436	15,370	934
W SAMOA	N	W	86	-	8,466	10,159	1,693
YUGOSLV	N	E	81	-	117,028	140,087	23,059
			82	-	98,972	111,562	12,590
			83	-	178,012	208,769	30,757
			84	-	156,855	179,647	22,792
			85	-	131,657	157,300	25,643
			86	-	41,613	51,000	9,387
	N	W	81	-	680	902	222
			82	-	8,309	10,971	2,662
			83	-	3,115	3,502	387
			84	-	2,371	2,758	387
			85	-	4,103	4,223	120
			86	-	1,270	1,482	212

Vegetable, tallow
1769000 VEGETABLE TALLOW (LB)

Country	Mode	Reg	Yr	Quantity	F.A.S.	C.I.F.	Charges
TOTAL			81	1,422	3,038	3,191	153
			82	13,496	6,222	6,767	545
			83	721	1,823	1,934	111
			84	800	623	703	80
			85	43,668	17,709	17,883	174
			86	56,580	19,631	19,799	168
CANADA	O	E	85	24,200	6,547	6,547	
			86	51,950	16,144	16,144	
FR GERM	O	E	81	828	1,019	1,049	30
	V	W	82	13,100	5,492	5,992	500
FRANCE	A	E	81	154	1,113	1,152	39
	V	E	85	5,398	3,664	3,838	174
			86	1,984	1,771	1,832	61
INDIA	V	E	82	176	345	376	31
SWEDEN	V	E	86	2,646	1,716	1,823	107
U KING	O	E	82	220	385	399	14
			83	721	1,823	1,934	111
			84	800	623	703	80
	V	E	81	440	906	990	84
	V	W	85	14,070	7,498	7,498	

Vegetable, wax
4941800 VEGETABLE WAXES, NSPF (LB)

Country	Mode	Reg	Yr	Quantity	F.A.S.	C.I.F.	Charges
TOTAL			81	240,650	278,025	298,361	20,436
			82	192,261	361,856	391,648	29,792
			83	458,870	501,558	581,979	80,421
			84	511,859	396,584	462,966	66,382
			85	591,924	346,695	395,721	49,026
			86	490,394	318,737	360,888	42,151
BELGIUM	O	E	84	71,352	31,579	36,984	5,405
BRAZIL	O	E	82	5,133	2,020	2,141	121
			86	2,000	3,380	3,380	
	V	E	84	86,146	77,797	88,850	11,053

Product TSUSA commodity number, description, and unit of quantity Country	Mode	Reg	Yr	Quantity	F.A.S.	C.I.F.	Charges
			85	250,503	103,691	117,700	14,009
			86	177,002	92,310	107,239	14,929
	V	W	85	121,255	94,946	105,436	10,490
			86	97,003	59,928	68,171	8,243
CANADA	O	E	81	39,102	15,565	15,565	
			82	1,109	1,149	1,149	
			83	448	876	876	
			84	38,619	32,384	32,384	
			85	2,000	1,683	1,683	
			86	6,261	6,406	6,406	
COLOMB	V	E	81	24,286	44,445	45,768	1,323
			83	33,157	54,720	58,022	3,302
			84	22,046	17,000	18,354	1,354
DENMARK	A	E	81	26	1,321	1,240	19
			82	23	1,191	1,206	15
			84	22	1,061	1,078	17
	V	E	84	287	394	422	28
FR GERM	A	E	82	125	448	592	144
	N	E	82	3,324	10,342	10,547	205
			83	21,386	19,369	21,744	2,375
			84	23,534	23,803	25,400	1,597
			85	99,995	64,569	79,475	14,906
			86	1,375	2,696	3,331	635
	V	E	81	17,985	35,174	37,985	2,811
			82	5,220	5,641	6,547	906
			83	8,267	24,921	25,609	688
			84	22,218	10,938	13,311	2,373
			85	9,921	9,040	10,267	1,227
			86	20,944	26,570	28,949	2,379
FRANCE	A	E	84	209	565	856	291
	A	W	84	224	679	846	167
	O	W	82	61	390	390	
	V	E	81	2,200	1,059	1,086	27
	V	W	82	174	489	510	21
			83	225	267	330	63
			85	24,251	18,810	20,908	2,098
HUNGARY	V	E	86	39,683	6,582	9,646	3,064
ITALY	A	E	81	360	450	842	392
JAPAN	A	E	82	1,102	1,715	4,413	2,698
			84	14,771	22,048	56,002	33,954
	N	E	82	114,078	111,792	128,823	17,031
			83	69,224	53,315	66,944	13,629
	V	E	81	122,355	103,538	113,594	10,056
			82	6,614	12,532	13,574	1,042
			83	4,409	10,338	10,837	499
			84	2,205	5,465	5,864	399
			85	1,124	3,395	3,670	275
			86	59,763	69,530	79,173	9,643
	V	W	83	198	2,051	2,090	39
			85	700	10,297	10,408	111
JORDAN	A	E	81	1,102	1,785	4,428	2,643
MEXICO	O	W	81	19,570	58,239	58,239	
			82	9,102	142,758	142,758	
			83	21,098	28,199	28,199	
			84	2,145	8,980	8,980	
NETHLDS	A	E	83	47	398	452	54
	N	E	86	80,798	38,983	40,458	1,475
	O	E	83	117,373	55,700	62,278	6,578
			84	112,467	50,703	54,262	3,559
	V	E	83	5,536	3,821	4,568	747
			85	80,632	37,508	43,108	5,600
	V	W	82	2,200	1,557	1,799	242
NORWAY	V	E	84	42,989	43,849	46,347	2,498
SPAIN	V	E	82	1,850	2,625	3,188	563
			84	92	1,101	1,163	62
			86	2,495	5,083	5,905	822
SWEDEN	V	E	81	4,268	600	1,041	441
			82	187	719	869	150
SWITZLD	N	E	81	9,003	12,984	15,082	2,098
			82	30,338	48,382	53,585	5,203
			83	173,723	234,521	286,228	51,707
			84	72,121	65,058	68,481	3,423
	V	E	82	4,409	5,080	5,410	330
			86	1,323	1,550	1,765	215
U KING	A	E	81	303	1,931	2,453	522
			84	338	2,033	2,054	21
			86	424	3,409	3,855	446
	N	E	82	7,212	13,026	14,147	1,121
			83	3,774	12,733	13,360	627
	V	E	81	70	375	390	15
			84	74	1,147	1,328	181
			85	1,543	2,756	3,066	310
			86	1,323	2,310	2,610	300
	V	W	81	20	559	648	89
			83	5	329	442	113

Waffer, inedible
1932000 WAFERS NOT EDIBLE (LB)

Product TSUSA commodity number, description, and unit of quantity Country	Mode	Reg	Yr	Quantity	F.A.S.	C.I.F.	Charges
TOTAL			81	26,067	95,132	101,375	6,243
			82	16,987	72,130	76,306	4,176
			83	39,821	115,294	127,136	11,842
			84	16,611	73,078	77,434	4,356
			85	20,137	82,916	91,835	8,919
			86	20,254	124,719	136,193	11,474
BELGIUM	O	E	85	525	2,907	3,779	872
CANADA	O	E	82	250	421	421	
FR GERM	A	E	84	126	2,475	2,579	104
			86	53	2,014	2,146	132
	V	W	84	75	433	554	121
			86	485	1,208	1,300	92
FRANCE	V	E	83	1,750	3,620	3,692	72
GUATMAL	V	E	83	14,200	13,800	15,915	2,115
HG KONG	V	E	81	75	404	420	16
ITALY	N	E	84	4,242	22,395	23,557	1,162
			85	4,863	22,009	22,726	717
	O	E	81	5,104	31,018	31,553	535
			82	613	4,530	4,753	223
	V	E	81	4,493	25,293	25,832	539
			82	7,433	36,351	37,093	742
			83	9,397	33,816	36,531	2,715
			84	5,364	15,909	16,619	710
			85	4,958	17,963	21,632	3,669
			86	12,228	65,686	72,138	6,452
NETHLDS	A	E	81	90	915	997	82
			83	88	556	665	109
			86	645	5,722	6,699	977
	O	E	81	2,727	4,263	4,734	471
			83	1,052	1,697	2,255	558
			84	1,746	6,765	7,120	355
	V	E	81	13,070	32,824	36,815	3,991
			82	8,691	30,828	34,039	3,211
			83	13,334	61,805	68,078	6,273
			84	3,651	23,267	25,012	1,745
			85	9,791	40,037	43,698	3,661
			86	6,843	50,089	53,910	3,821
U KING	V	E	84	1,407	1,834	1,993	159
YUGOSLV	A	E	81	508	415	1,024	609

Miscellaneous edible preparation

Bakery products
1822000 BAKERY PRODUCTS (LB)

Country	Mode	Reg	Yr	Quantity	F.A.S.	C.I.F.	Charges
TOTAL			81	105,795,581	95,465,510	102,178,745	6,708,653
			82	129,624,851	117,986,283	126,964,900	8,978,617
			83	149,251,181	131,227,502	141,382,813	10,155,311
			84	194,251,095	166,187,754	182,792,179	16,604,425
			85	256,803,497	215,780,411	239,719,564	23,939,153
			86	277,502,202	249,730,394	271,795,114	22,064,720
ALGERIA	V	E	82	27,804	16,215	18,161	1,946
ARAB EM	O	E	81	390	309	309	
	V	E	84	39,736	38,722	42,972	4,250
ARGENT	A	E	82	1,491	573	1,146	573
			83	2,480	1,917	3,829	1,912
			84	9,542	7,845	17,932	10,087
			85	1,984	2,741	5,611	2,870
	N	E	83	124,418	75,144	101,658	26,514
			84	463,133	214,761	285,196	70,435
			85	122,247	49,220	65,304	16,084
			86	14,459	8,715	12,161	3,446
	N	W	84	38,560	33,185	47,636	14,451
	V	E	81	183,012	90,181	105,905	15,724
			82	531,029	233,788	289,438	55,650
			83	525,889	226,482	283,033	56,551
			84	1,003,534	427,866	523,139	95,273
			85	520,470	246,474	304,410	57,936

Table 2. U.S. Import Statistics for Non Crop-Specific Commodities by End-Use

Product
TSUSA commodity number, description, and unit of quantity

Country	Mode	Reg	Yr	Quantity	F.A.S.	C.I.F.	Charges
			86	1,069,565	518,950	653,848	134,898
	V	W	81	7,055	9,600	11,109	1,509
			83	7,410	9,512	11,904	2,392
			85	60,145	41,405	56,910	15,505
			86	47,660	15,901	23,221	7,320
AUSTRAL	A	E	85	11,645	25,590	35,084	9,494
	A	H	82	3,747	8,180	11,979	3,799
			86	1,617	4,804	11,241	6,437
	A	W	82	1,228	1,911	2,905	994
			85	1,071	1,310	2,410	1,100
			86	821	1,024	1,787	763
	N	H	81	4,298	7,270	10,553	3,283
			83	3,558	5,863	8,919	3,056
			84	3,685	7,440	10,577	3,137
			85	27,363	32,177	42,186	10,009
	N	W	81	2,565	5,297	7,229	1,932
			84	1,744	1,841	2,770	929
			85	256,546	308,646	353,098	44,452
			86	122,318	146,205	190,196	43,991
	O	E	85	4,070	2,700	2,700	
	O	W	85	5,512	5,327	5,327	
	V	E	83	25,397	23,040	24,828	1,788
			84	49,109	44,403	50,227	5,824
			85	3,000	5,494	6,025	531
			86	3,420	6,709	7,252	543
	V	H	86	9,552	9,643	12,093	2,450
	V	W	81	2,201	3,585	4,032	447
			82	624	349	399	50
			84	34,990	45,159	52,847	7,688
			86	47,651	69,018	79,718	10,700
AUSTRIA	A	E	82	490	1,289	1,908	619
			84	7,438	14,661	20,023	5,362
			86	440	4,643	5,152	509
	A	W	84	151	334	596	262
	N	E	81	684,514	569,961	645,519	75,558
			82	8,533	8,850	11,072	2,222
			83	1,341,659	841,210	918,028	76,818
			84	1,444,142	1,057,504	1,168,300	110,796
			85	1,089,572	991,577	1,113,319	121,742
			86	1,199,036	1,293,052	1,393,760	100,708
	N	W	82	51,804	51,738	58,895	7,157
			83	133,598	108,518	116,915	8,397
			85	146,520	111,997	129,438	17,441
	O	E	81	7,216	3,098	3,623	525
			83	1,584	1,228	1,228	
			84	30,659	24,435	25,181	746
			85	30,396	22,690	23,312	622
			86	16,862	17,659	18,841	1,182
	O	W	83	417	591	834	243
			84	2,205	2,102	2,102	
			85	3,748	3,603	3,603	
			86	4,350	9,924	11,130	1,206
	V	E	81	2,645	5,468	6,495	1,027
			82	1,592,956	1,582,740	1,775,016	192,276
			83	853,642	738,403	818,964	80,561
			84	221,134	167,022	186,626	19,604
			85	157,370	145,730	162,883	17,153
			86	385,277	366,295	411,097	44,802
	V	W	82	30,006	20,626	27,841	7,215
			83	38,252	31,915	63,431	31,516
			84	262,689	195,854	215,517	19,663
			86	244,968	230,811	260,486	29,675
BELGIUM	A	E	82	3,191	4,958	7,492	2,534
			83	3,713	3,325	5,799	2,474
			84	169,533	154,208	213,305	59,097
			86	6,523	9,284	15,934	6,650
	A	W	82	4,556	5,899	8,653	2,754
			83	141	271	354	83
			86	11,849	24,172	38,056	13,884
	N	E	81	464,743	736,190	803,102	66,912
			82	2,327,789	3,204,006	3,475,820	271,814
			83	2,814,035	3,971,388	4,225,333	253,945
			84	2,417,330	3,054,176	3,371,824	317,648
			85	1,781,481	2,229,733	2,496,845	267,112
			86	2,085,254	3,869,251	4,127,718	258,467
	N	W	84	212,394	253,930	317,285	63,355
			85	730,165	844,469	1,043,166	198,697
			86	1,581,734	2,694,660	3,017,682	323,022
	O	E	81	6,459	8,311	8,897	586
			82	2,339	2,262	2,859	597
			83	294	570	652	82
			84	2,951	2,225	3,407	1,182
			85	224,204	200,326	228,921	28,595
	V	E	81	284,594	230,035	260,697	30,662
			82	377,384	256,989	293,578	36,589
			83	606,417	612,283	683,871	71,588
			84	1,074,605	1,016,083	1,128,890	112,807
			85	285,102	436,363	495,491	59,128
			86	1,103,900	1,624,399	1,778,994	154,595
	V	W	81	136,197	183,055	203,624	20,569
			82	3,968	10,012	11,422	1,410
			83	51,744	103,602	115,896	12,294
			85	238,928	260,715	322,049	61,334
			86	454,421	654,093	770,667	116,574
BNGLDSH	V	W	85	494	1,626	1,744	118
BRAZIL	A	E	86	529	1,275	1,925	650
	A	W	82	1,137	2,064	3,734	1,670
	V	E	82	82,701	57,980	72,688	14,708
			83	170,833	88,700	108,938	20,238
			84	290,508	201,217	243,112	41,895
			85	647,677	301,463	366,640	65,177
			86	1,043,887	545,176	678,583	133,407
	V	W	85	141,736	88,497	113,247	24,750
			86	178,067	89,134	106,745	17,611
BULGAR	V	E	85	19,471	18,805	22,011	3,206
C RICA	N	E	81	381,715	269,589	309,885	40,296
	V	E	81	7,132	5,558	7,051	1,493
			82	682,703	349,019	407,372	58,353
			83	667,676	360,013	415,330	55,317
			84	317,045	145,190	163,778	18,588
			85	538,596	239,428	270,782	31,354
			86	510,309	266,878	301,591	34,713
CANADA	A	E	81	15,697	11,134	16,253	4,870
			82	7,341	4,647	6,183	1,536
			83	1,585	3,351	4,067	716
			84	11,034	14,127	17,188	3,061
			85	4,223	6,285	6,965	680
			86	16,267	21,168	24,875	3,707
	A	H	81	4,341	1,295	1,891	596
			82	62,038	33,764	44,769	11,005
			83	110,114	96,957	113,787	16,830
			84	79,917	61,588	79,433	17,845
			85	65,696	50,934	62,163	11,229
			86	57,644	50,627	62,059	11,432
	A	W	84	3,888	5,229	7,062	1,833
			86	2,380	4,002	4,782	780
	N	E	81	17,510,879	12,975,836	12,983,962	4,936
			82	18,779,441	14,175,644	14,181,286	5,642
			83	21,762,450	16,675,765	16,681,031	5,266
			84	45,558,869	34,227,506	34,232,947	5,441
			85	64,683,431	50,220,766	50,222,476	1,710
			86	45,200,346	33,702,345	33,702,828	483
	N	W	81	4,610,194	2,513,120	2,513,120	
			82	4,399,598	2,550,401	2,564,840	14,439
			84	5,101,590	2,875,179	2,875,195	16
			85	4,021	7,754	8,812	1,058
			86	5,211,893	2,910,271	2,919,459	9,188
	O	E	81	24,593,617	18,905,672	18,909,407	3,900
			82	27,037,314	22,273,695	22,301,787	28,092
			83	26,526,844	22,189,259	22,194,909	5,650
			84	15,810,333	15,049,153	15,062,760	13,607
			85	12,932,412	12,939,531	12,940,157	626
			86	45,068,774	37,508,437	37,517,399	8,962
	O	W	81	301,777	229,172	229,172	
			82	356,684	218,724	218,724	
			83	4,761,463	2,839,009	2,844,027	5,018
			84	9,570	12,076	12,076	
			85	6,305,133	3,558,648	3,558,648	
			86	1,719,882	965,148	965,148	
	V	E	82	24,520	29,545	33,201	3,656
			85	1,324	1,996	2,305	309
			86	220,080	53,329	87,125	33,796
	V	W	81	331	1,126	1,141	15
CHILE	A	W	86	5,974	3,180	10,565	7,385
	V	E	83	845	991	1,318	327
			84	21,572	17,221	20,221	3,000
			85	13,025	13,280	15,613	2,333
			86	9,627	5,780	7,280	1,500
	V	W	82	12,967	9,387	11,877	2,490
			83	43,351	35,438	45,269	9,831
			84	34,287	24,441	31,805	7,364
			85	26,769	15,734	21,089	5,355
			86	35,684	20,889	27,997	7,108
CHINA M	A	E	85	3,806	7,177	8,221	1,044
			86	1,450	2,125	2,453	328
	N	E	81	59,626	51,712	59,633	7,921
			83	120,963	165,976	180,386	14,410
	N	W	81	27,890	31,101	35,512	4,411
			82	16,964	15,063	16,328	1,265
			85	172,412	101,869	113,892	12,023

Product
TSUSA commodity number, description, and unit of quantity

Country	Mode	Reg	Yr	Quantity	F.A.S.	C.I.F.	Charges
			86	248,975	146,005	165,738	19,733
	O E		82	2,000	1,440	1,440	
			83	3,000	2,289	2,320	31
			84	300	679	679	
			85	7,716	7,826	8,693	867
			86	4,125	3,137	3,444	307
	O W		83	1,170	1,145	1,198	53
			86	4,313	6,409	6,725	316
	V E		81	2,181	2,775	3,208	433
			82	34,885	25,114	28,193	3,079
			83	13,156	3,882	5,163	1,281
			84	121,103	68,280	83,147	14,867
			85	82,903	59,135	69,489	10,354
			86	164,578	167,870	191,406	23,536
	V H		82	3,150	2,903	3,468	565
			83	2,000	1,750	2,013	263
			84	3,018	3,436	3,955	519
			85	895	1,426	1,591	165
			86	2,970	2,688	3,011	323
	V W		81	33,844	23,060	25,281	2,221
			82	87,192	51,950	57,350	5,400
			83	209,734	134,083	149,730	15,647
			84	160,488	132,675	144,936	12,261
			85	91,844	82,502	88,489	5,987
			86	173,513	130,140	138,615	8,475
CHINA T	A W		82	6,283	2,480	3,880	1,400
	N W		82	375,288	280,392	318,108	37,716
			83	793,820	764,854	851,438	86,584
			84	1,227,883	1,137,183	1,273,062	135,879
			85	5,510	8,512	10,005	1,493
			86	1,189,981	1,115,136	1,212,472	97,336
	O E		81	1,500	1,050	1,134	84
			84	2,259	1,852	1,964	112
			85	25,383	20,445	23,684	3,239
	O W		81	3,387	7,421	7,421	
			82	113	294	307	13
			86	19,835	23,185	23,185	
	V E		81	141,609	165,391	187,571	22,180
			82	249,924	254,138	293,331	39,193
			83	262,328	297,144	338,246	41,102
			84	411,368	461,354	539,520	78,166
			85	422,645	485,718	554,253	68,535
			86	808,645	890,934	992,812	101,878
	V H		81	327,885	301,372	331,615	30,243
			82	411,756	375,225	421,207	45,982
			83	439,438	423,755	480,943	57,188
			84	447,158	442,012	507,528	65,516
			85	522,243	503,092	579,420	76,328
			86	680,709	682,886	771,940	89,054
	V W		81	345,170	289,193	325,364	36,171
			82	185,508	209,185	228,963	19,778
			83	120,036	126,121	139,116	12,995
			84	206,742	230,336	261,615	31,279
			85	1,716,697	1,665,242	1,839,495	174,253
			86	801,047	916,547	992,277	75,690
COLOMB	A E		84	4,063	2,574	3,267	693
			85	4,657	6,534	9,048	2,514
	N E		84	2,077,294	1,133,586	1,285,228	151,642
			85	505,668	358,457	534,262	175,805
			86	409,570	285,678	363,855	78,177
	V E		81	1,389,818	737,677	825,252	87,575
			82	513,738	254,216	293,804	39,588
			83	568,376	306,767	343,744	36,977
			85	2,479,858	1,308,136	1,526,580	218,444
			86	2,991,858	1,651,033	1,864,908	213,875
CYPRUS	N E		85	5,077	8,187	10,295	2,108
	V E		84	3,107	2,359	2,512	153
			86	4,682	4,234	4,835	601
	V W		86	16,687	14,201	16,801	2,600
DENMARK	A E		81	152	289	610	321
			83	703	1,401	1,506	105
			84	16,770	17,114	31,825	14,711
	N E		81	7,109,307	8,842,212	9,631,467	789,255
			82	9,617,770	11,383,131	12,364,928	981,797
			83	16,234,521	15,553,895	17,089,131	1,535,236
			84	23,518,780	20,029,274	23,249,524	3,220,250
			85	28,451,833	23,555,970	27,352,782	3,796,812
			86	23,390,784	20,868,609	23,918,695	3,050,086
	N W		81	82,563	89,543	102,391	12,848
			82	1,801,959	2,273,044	2,505,647	232,603
			83	72,725	68,526	79,695	11,169
			84	4,419,098	3,917,527	4,639,132	721,605
			85	10,501,272	8,724,330	10,781,001	2,056,671
			86	7,087,493	6,633,900	7,571,410	937,510
	O E		82	35,403	44,177	50,270	6,093
			83	58,695	45,872	50,361	4,489
			84	4,281	5,237	5,237	
			85	147,086	151,736	170,344	18,608
			86	55,648	66,221	66,221	
	O W		84	20,672	19,501	23,049	3,548
	V E		81	4,411,612	5,782,559	6,341,365	558,806
			82	6,849,132	7,512,476	8,226,324	713,848
			83	8,990,031	9,124,564	10,058,301	933,737
			84	14,956,701	13,191,714	15,278,485	2,086,771
			85	21,491,945	18,727,611	21,800,736	3,073,125
			86	25,544,755	24,514,085	27,957,890	3,443,805
	V H		81	29,215	27,788	31,228	3,440
			85	295,309	333,092	410,493	77,401
			86	203,663	261,475	288,935	27,460
	V W		81	1,618,601	2,152,511	2,463,465	310,954
			82	651,572	859,238	968,622	109,384
			83	2,417,442	2,437,580	2,775,084	337,504
			84	708,998	650,454	812,767	162,313
			85	3,835,979	3,279,965	4,022,171	742,206
			86	6,277,939	5,699,143	6,587,489	888,346
DJIBUTI	V E		85	17,295	17,605	20,172	2,567
DOM REP	A E		81	3,535	2,525	2,919	394
			83	2,312	919	1,206	287
	N E		81	169,254	95,433	121,735	26,302
			82	1,415,905	840,317	940,271	99,954
			83	94,752	25,045	33,255	8,210
			84	385,286	143,148	175,053	31,905
			85	63,611	21,933	26,238	4,305
	V E		81	1,215,842	676,752	733,003	56,251
			82	11,325	4,425	6,072	1,647
			83	926,125	441,051	498,182	57,131
			84	847,390	489,700	540,243	50,543
			85	1,556,357	874,150	957,872	83,722
			86	2,076,297	1,129,274	1,231,636	102,362
DOMINCA	V E		85	34,590	27,515	32,542	5,027
ECUADOR	A E		83	100	427	604	177
FALK IS	V E		85	18,016	15,456	19,740	4,284
FIJI	N H		81	10,994	6,819	8,983	2,164
			84	37,376	18,203	23,753	5,550
	V H		81	26,228	16,276	19,503	3,227
			82	21,869	14,200	17,782	3,582
			83	44,748	24,347	31,090	6,743
			84	41,180	20,740	26,106	5,366
			85	54,551	27,792	35,749	7,957
			86	22,659	12,590	15,565	2,975
	V W		81	69,948	47,952	58,748	10,796
			82	109,456	67,255	80,482	13,227
			83	70,974	41,161	49,843	8,682
			84	186,357	102,195	125,580	23,385
			85	154,913	87,263	107,602	20,339
			86	179,366	97,606	119,372	21,766
FINLAND	A H		81	1,000	1,017	1,220	203
	A W		84	944	726	2,217	1,491
	N E		86	91,587	72,230	82,371	10,141
	O W		86	1,033	11,471	13,146	1,675
	V E		81	425,074	397,325	455,257	57,932
			82	336,956	338,305	383,562	45,257
			83	386,484	370,109	420,588	50,479
			84	172,891	135,222	163,542	28,320
			85	194,550	161,211	193,684	32,473
			86	59,918	54,760	63,793	9,033
	V W		81	85,836	67,832	78,190	10,358
			82	102,111	76,176	89,969	13,793
			83	125,141	90,852	105,624	14,772
			84	125,180	106,728	120,958	14,230
			85	128,828	102,040	119,774	17,734
			86	127,868	109,091	125,736	16,645
FR GERM	A E		81	114,949	165,474	243,510	78,036
			82	3,101	6,817	9,287	2,470
			83	11,337	23,940	30,766	6,826
			84	7,037	10,709	15,354	4,645
			85	1,138	3,815	4,818	1,003
			86	21,728	47,309	63,819	16,510
	A W		82	5,836	10,124	13,108	2,984
			83	173	287	409	122
			84	236	652	1,956	1,304
			85	718	2,219	3,123	904
	N E		81	4,204,144	4,174,343	4,696,255	520,912
			82	4,801,901	4,560,105	5,185,098	624,993
			83	6,473,045	6,112,602	6,861,684	749,082
			84	8,785,952	7,478,250	8,715,008	1,236,758
			85	12,835,285	10,337,155	12,344,346	2,007,191
			86	9,484,895	9,726,272	11,120,703	1,394,431
	N W		81	747,168	877,272	1,038,086	160,814
			82	401,273	326,170	410,112	83,942

Product
TSUSA commodity number, description, and unit of quantity

Country	Mode	Reg	Yr	Quantity	F.A.S.	C.I.F.	Charges
			83	1,477,697	1,279,034	1,539,011	259,977
			84	1,779,371	1,403,918	1,726,539	322,621
			85	4,073,687	2,700,139	3,402,665	702,526
			86	3,369,586	2,791,766	3,284,154	492,388
	O	E	81	1,478	1,728	1,866	138
			82	68,348	44,804	53,160	8,356
			83	182,423	126,763	154,713	27,950
			84	221,292	190,966	212,621	21,655
			85	254,135	233,087	265,403	32,316
			86	243,264	275,131	293,492	18,361
	V	E	81	604,161	561,649	639,630	77,981
			82	1,592,429	1,443,454	1,691,923	248,469
			83	1,692,943	1,579,599	1,780,861	201,262
			84	2,295,520	1,831,040	2,132,235	301,195
			85	3,204,961	2,389,649	2,848,102	458,453
			86	7,583,119	6,610,512	7,613,353	1,002,841
	V	H	85	54,388	31,244	40,940	9,696
	V	W	81	132,601	63,573	73,017	9,444
			82	675,521	567,935	678,237	110,302
			83	95,918	65,560	78,209	12,649
			84	41,339	24,316	29,185	4,869
			85	44,555	29,435	39,877	10,442
			86	65,868	42,248	53,963	11,715
FRANCE	A	E	81	4,736	8,992	13,488	4,496
			82	23,318	20,092	38,419	18,327
			83	2,302	8,636	10,643	2,007
			84	6,371	15,044	19,636	4,592
			85	5,843	15,038	20,764	5,726
			86	6,655	15,624	24,219	8,595
	A	W	84	1,651	2,385	3,313	928
	N	E	81	1,176,462	1,393,908	1,553,126	159,218
			82	2,316,527	2,429,875	2,788,548	358,673
			83	3,399,795	3,819,696	4,291,049	471,353
			84	3,773,178	3,844,073	4,528,969	684,896
			85	3,801,089	3,754,160	4,362,260	608,100
			86	3,179,441	3,436,997	3,923,512	486,515
	N	W	82	145,216	177,933	204,168	26,235
			83	269,034	362,556	412,555	49,999
			84	739,537	772,478	950,741	178,263
			85	1,496,295	1,581,057	1,856,338	275,281
			86	1,204,068	1,514,837	1,726,413	211,576
	O	E	82	358	798	942	144
			83	14,659	13,740	17,334	3,594
			84	10,558	7,175	7,939	764
			85	16,185	20,909	24,245	3,336
			86	42,504	68,189	68,743	554
	O	W	81	10	615	632	17
			82	1,113	1,897	2,306	409
			85	2,116	5,512	5,512	
	V	E	81	146,109	191,203	215,892	24,689
			82	188,358	223,099	252,894	29,795
			83	282,962	334,279	378,436	44,157
			84	404,573	390,686	463,546	72,860
			85	638,121	848,480	979,533	131,053
			86	1,292,977	1,424,772	1,621,841	197,069
	V	H	83	799	1,155	1,512	357
	V	W	81	141,075	216,532	240,307	23,775
			82	80,357	112,466	125,188	12,722
			83	18,177	15,537	23,063	7,526
			84	17,740	11,003	15,298	4,295
			85	2,365	10,539	11,442	903
			86	504,213	611,924	687,552	75,628
G BISAU	V	E	81	2,765	1,456	1,708	252
GABON	O	W	85	1,600	1,137	1,137	
GAZA ST	V	W	84	2,025	890	936	46
GERM DR	V	E	83	1,034	1,299	1,581	282
			84	21,618	18,365	20,442	2,077
			85	39,239	28,548	33,298	4,750
			86	21,517	13,615	15,715	2,100
	V	W	85	952	1,143	1,296	153
GREECE	A	E	82	1,587	2,727	4,262	1,535
			83	1,263	937	1,805	868
			85	1,778	2,240	3,450	1,210
	N	E	83	32,613	33,404	40,210	6,806
	O	E	83	1,470	1,167	1,167	
			84	3,343	2,464	2,464	
			85	1,645	1,549	1,549	
			86	6,860	5,352	5,352	
	V	E	81	1,433	1,205	1,375	170
			82	2,591	2,345	2,843	498
			83	29,121	23,654	28,803	5,149
			84	109,103	94,127	108,517	14,390
			85	510,179	392,945	460,052	67,107
			86	988,715	891,498	1,033,549	142,051
	V	W	82	5,300	3,689	4,138	449
			83	2,474	1,975	2,202	227
			86	287,701	311,225	350,797	39,572
GREENLD	V	E	85	54,864	65,266	73,289	8,023
GRENADA	V	W	86	9,788	7,687	11,366	3,679
GUATMAL	A	W	83	370	848	1,293	445
			84	760	1,916	2,344	428
	V	E	81	37,985	21,302	23,948	2,646
			84	1,558	2,386	2,952	566
			85	21,434	15,784	17,071	1,287
GUINEA	O	E	85	7,606	5,405	6,900	1,495
HG KONG	A	E	85	4,822	8,112	15,050	6,938
	A	W	83	3,344	10,694	15,978	5,284
			84	1,971	4,673	7,468	2,795
	N	E	81	347,768	483,474	536,184	52,710
			82	62,581	125,954	150,883	24,929
			83	549,973	678,853	753,504	74,651
			84	93,810	109,429	122,551	13,122
			85	800,099	1,115,818	1,232,342	116,524
			86	793,866	1,050,021	1,160,697	110,676
	N	H	81	11,855	20,569	23,826	3,257
			82	28,298	37,458	43,565	6,107
			83	76,364	76,015	86,400	10,385
			84	50,460	66,127	81,787	15,660
	N	W	81	318,515	455,845	493,218	36,981
			82	860,762	1,050,278	1,142,960	92,682
			83	1,127,103	1,238,996	1,354,399	115,403
			84	902,901	982,422	1,081,182	98,760
			85	1,298,632	1,532,619	1,677,611	144,992
			86	1,730,327	2,104,022	2,245,609	141,587
	O	E	82	29,240	28,614	28,614	
			84	11,265	13,544	15,407	1,863
			85	10,785	9,890	11,106	1,216
	O	W	84	720	1,288	1,348	60
			86	1,798	3,108	3,276	168
	V	E	81	57,405	47,065	54,384	7,319
			82	331,965	467,182	513,197	46,015
			83	4,570	8,513	9,154	641
			84	577,648	825,287	922,540	97,253
			85	27,499	28,867	34,472	5,605
			86	46,189	52,363	57,818	5,455
	V	H	81	8,543	17,744	19,205	1,461
			82	7,756	17,079	18,605	1,526
			83	6,386	13,143	14,370	1,227
			84	3,156	5,146	5,696	550
			85	58,426	77,370	85,633	8,263
			86	79,480	103,560	115,029	11,469
	V	W	81	224,777	281,739	304,654	22,915
			82	42,573	53,893	60,564	6,671
			83	137,804	161,389	177,337	15,948
			84	779,550	825,022	905,213	80,191
			85	396,552	393,820	429,814	35,994
			86	621,912	478,753	522,207	43,454
HONDURA	A	E	81	2,060	850	1,777	927
			82	850	495	797	302
	O	E	86	15,013	40,020	41,413	1,393
	V	E	83	12,436	16,465	17,306	841
HUNGARY	O	E	86	31,400	20,610	20,610	
	V	E	82	440	390	451	61
			84	29,269	16,353	19,383	3,030
			85	202,513	154,122	185,075	30,953
			86	229,433	131,108	157,833	26,725
	V	W	82	6,984	4,815	6,109	1,294
			86	43,192	34,098	37,168	3,070
ICELAND	N	E	85	147,761	124,148	142,824	18,676
	V	E	84	101	1,165	1,975	810
INDIA	N	E	83	2,786	2,592	2,731	139
			84	62,064	50,076	57,607	7,531
			85	56,977	40,202	45,577	5,375
	O	E	81	1,366	1,172	1,292	120
			82	389	1,413	1,514	101
			83	4,890	4,217	4,616	399
			84	5,974	6,286	6,561	275
			85	13,853	5,666	6,347	681
			86	1,058	1,318	1,449	131
	V	E	81	34,466	25,654	31,307	5,653
			82	50,755	34,180	40,613	6,433
			83	56,024	41,380	47,422	6,042
			84	27,004	22,638	26,034	3,396
			85	211,480	143,179	164,472	21,293
			86	311,621	215,630	241,696	26,066
	V	W	81	22,782	15,940	19,587	3,647
			82	95,599	60,205	72,113	11,908
			83	36,969	23,438	30,295	6,857
			84	34,188	28,493	32,806	4,313
			85	131,707	98,442	116,090	17,648

Product
TSUSA commodity number, description, and unit of quantity

Country	Mode	Reg	Yr	Quantity	F.A.S.	C.I.F.	Charges
			86	42,412	36,969	40,495	3,526
INDNSIA	N	W	85	1,208	4,519	5,062	543
	V	H	84	595	549	620	71
	V	W	81	661	823	917	94
			82	7,471	12,092	14,130	2,038
			83	55,990	57,922	70,722	12,800
			84	91,170	134,885	154,840	19,955
			85	75,587	76,828	93,703	16,875
			86	81,623	84,177	98,889	14,712
IRELAND	A	E	82	306	1,292	1,452	160
			84	128	263	569	306
			85	281	1,131	1,222	91
			86	4,340	4,173	9,367	5,194
	A	W	83	185	314	471	157
	N	E	81	55,094	83,915	91,356	7,441
			82	118,775	141,911	155,983	14,072
			83	119,096	150,281	167,518	17,237
			84	126,507	124,203	144,434	20,231
			85	133,314	140,208	170,872	30,664
			86	56,131	63,471	73,768	10,297
	O	E	81	15,079	11,928	14,605	2,677
			86	4,057	8,872	9,650	778
	V	E	81	15,402	16,286	19,323	3,037
			82	26,834	25,662	28,588	2,926
			83	22,462	21,213	22,959	1,746
			84	6,190	9,235	10,509	1,274
			85	37,367	84,338	93,189	8,851
			86	54,504	47,693	59,540	11,847
	V	W	82	41,127	38,220	43,431	5,211
			84	1,943	4,990	5,511	521
			85	11,180	8,015	8,803	788
			86	14,383	15,766	18,908	3,142
ISRAEL	A	E	84	130	270	419	149
			85	2,718	9,199	11,507	2,308
	N	E	84	2,356,945	2,096,734	2,365,880	269,146
			85	2,428,448	2,100,187	2,410,510	310,323
			86	888,398	839,886	967,107	127,221
	O	E	81	7,900	3,776	3,776	
			82	1,715	3,391	3,391	
			83	2,644	1,797	1,797	
			84	10,888	9,747	9,747	
			85	17,691	16,758	19,172	2,414
			86	18,026	15,980	16,908	928
	V	E	81	3,283,762	2,330,675	2,758,356	427,681
			82	3,341,220	2,558,626	2,913,613	354,987
			83	3,611,301	2,766,745	3,151,492	384,747
			84	1,493,276	1,112,885	1,257,835	144,950
			85	670,226	610,059	702,708	92,649
			86	2,118,932	1,724,221	1,981,166	256,945
	V	W	81	285,061	176,759	213,757	36,998
			82	252,124	169,469	202,836	33,367
			83	368,873	274,996	320,100	45,104
			84	649,592	502,692	580,496	77,804
			85	345,410	235,090	260,967	25,877
			86	448,724	296,453	352,960	56,507
ITALY	A	E	81	1,589	3,084	5,403	2,319
			82	4,513	9,743	16,368	6,625
			83	3,482	8,581	12,140	3,559
			84	6,576	18,078	24,638	6,560
			85	11,088	31,930	52,716	20,786
			86	4,914	17,480	24,115	6,635
	N	E	81	1,432,364	2,450,582	2,741,603	291,101
			82	1,944,084	2,623,491	3,003,764	380,273
			83	1,959,917	3,015,278	3,399,555	384,277
			84	2,684,628	4,181,684	4,770,543	588,859
			85	3,341,531	4,893,890	5,686,930	793,040
			86	3,300,924	5,557,984	6,278,022	720,038
	N	W	81	16,275	29,095	35,137	6,042
			82	69,181	113,170	143,536	30,366
			83	47,341	71,820	87,462	15,642
			84	282,727	366,762	441,655	74,893
			85	430,658	582,408	701,117	118,709
			86	79,728	78,985	98,040	19,055
	O	E	81	16,114	40,686	43,426	2,740
			82	2,520	4,483	4,483	
			83	21,479	33,213	36,356	3,143
			84	38,240	39,342	40,277	935
			85	4,342	10,896	11,049	153
			86	18,396	37,178	44,633	7,455
	O	W	81	8,287	39,226	42,981	3,755
			85	5,512	7,092	7,149	57
			86	7,973	12,213	13,332	1,119
	V	E	81	155,128	282,615	319,396	36,781
			82	232,288	379,157	426,596	47,439
			83	211,317	316,518	366,015	49,497

Product
TSUSA commodity number, description, and unit of quantity

Country	Mode	Reg	Yr	Quantity	F.A.S.	C.I.F.	Charges
			84	341,017	529,997	625,880	95,883
			85	588,027	689,248	834,438	145,190
			86	1,127,721	1,432,950	1,664,677	231,727
	V	W	81	95,303	177,247	211,756	34,509
			82	88,991	125,921	152,488	26,567
			83	44,639	70,196	80,153	9,957
			84	23,332	24,824	31,217	6,393
			85	213,595	272,770	323,412	50,642
			86	599,961	994,360	1,130,494	136,134
IVY CST	V	E	86	21,618	21,646	23,796	2,150
	V	W	85	3,300	3,040	3,313	273
JAMAICA	A	E	81	2,000	1,000	1,800	800
			83	6,550	5,116	6,808	1,692
	N	E	81	80,404	50,790	65,717	14,927
			82	242,294	155,410	193,030	37,620
			83	209,132	162,549	198,611	36,062
			84	292,257	210,206	255,015	44,809
			85	304,154	153,978	180,610	26,632
			86	47,809	25,045	28,535	3,490
	O	E	84	15,891	19,072	19,072	
			85	16,235	16,498	16,498	
	V	E	82	1,323	1,416	1,583	167
			83	4,522	3,200	3,618	418
			84	10,659	9,502	10,987	1,485
			85	79,487	46,159	55,261	9,102
			86	453,231	205,741	240,914	35,173
JAPAN	A	E	81	11,244	6,191	6,497	306
			82	693	1,913	4,137	2,224
			84	988	1,207	4,300	3,093
			85	1,962	1,570	4,367	2,797
			86	8,248	3,113	3,998	885
	A	W	81	1,007	6,487	10,064	3,577
	N	E	81	776,771	1,471,945	1,708,977	237,032
			82	1,550,457	3,151,841	3,743,739	591,898
			83	958,392	1,584,085	1,830,580	246,495
			84	1,320,785	2,176,011	2,494,446	318,435
			85	1,625,436	2,488,284	2,854,419	366,135
			86	252,260	380,630	425,767	45,137
	N	H	81	485,146	864,469	1,029,359	164,890
			82	613,051	1,094,573	1,350,168	255,595
			83	729,091	1,396,065	1,685,955	289,890
			84	620,836	1,183,375	1,450,777	267,402
			85	513,627	1,083,369	1,301,879	218,510
			86	365,636	932,804	1,071,954	139,150
	N	W	81	1,179,390	1,611,534	1,749,977	138,447
			82	2,215,546	3,109,356	3,397,089	287,733
			83	2,910,994	3,937,731	4,278,927	341,196
			84	3,339,396	4,730,608	5,168,149	437,541
			85	4,677,974	6,140,589	6,701,146	560,557
			86	3,488,059	5,692,371	6,079,490	387,119
	O	E	81	1,908	6,014	6,278	264
			82	767	2,494	2,734	240
			83	842	3,104	3,402	298
			84	4,662	13,930	15,570	1,640
			85	1,131	2,093	2,219	126
			86	11,612	20,999	20,999	
	O	H	84	572	1,736	2,177	441
			86	536	1,148	1,377	229
	O	W	83	1,332	1,300	1,379	79
			85	4,946	9,367	10,082	715
			86	3,418	7,540	7,660	120
	V	E	81	117,957	222,857	255,700	32,843
			82	229,237	423,910	487,677	63,767
			83	240,514	419,023	487,655	68,632
			84	346,626	556,928	641,700	84,772
			85	186,493	353,542	410,716	57,174
			86	2,018,353	3,551,606	3,866,426	314,820
	V	H	85	948	1,814	2,086	272
			86	65,552	128,337	174,391	46,054
	V	W	81	1,040,837	1,523,513	1,706,821	183,308
			82	333,147	585,913	657,156	71,243
			83	357,011	598,133	659,966	61,833
			84	607,676	938,924	1,052,239	113,315
			85	483,269	728,480	797,156	68,676
			86	2,208,405	3,710,825	3,985,857	275,032
KENYA	V	W	85	1,102	1,114	1,255	141
KOR REP	N	E	86	240,379	237,550	278,663	41,113
	O	H	86	1,382	3,288	4,142	854
	V	E	82	2,440	4,419	4,742	323
			83	11,170	9,856	10,868	1,012
			84	69,712	96,119	112,702	16,583
			85	122,182	131,565	149,803	18,238
			86	49,213	56,773	64,179	7,406
	V	H	81	45,530	54,810	61,960	7,150
			82	17,884	28,909	33,966	5,057

Product
TSUSA commodity number, description, and unit of quantity

Country	Mode	Reg	Yr	Quantity	F.A.S.	C.I.F.	Charges
			83	18,672	31,130	36,332	5,202
			84	31,727	43,287	52,988	9,701
			85	25,483	41,749	50,241	8,492
			86	58,543	85,857	98,277	12,420
	V	W	81	279,836	191,076	213,314	22,238
			82	70,837	109,478	117,885	8,407
			83	83,481	83,425	91,763	8,338
			84	210,758	215,985	242,543	26,558
			85	426,108	334,913	370,281	35,368
			86	752,398	821,499	910,756	89,257
LEBANON	V	E	82	5,167	4,207	4,499	292
			83	4,766	7,300	8,220	920
			85	10,790	11,196	12,179	983
			86	25,789	15,107	16,536	1,429
	V	W	86	244	3,000	3,034	34
MACAO	V	E	81	7,085	7,823	8,279	456
			82	1,746	2,099	2,278	179
			83	7,778	7,177	8,050	873
			84	4,965	5,210	5,909	699
			85	7,230	7,523	8,342	819
			86	2,730	2,405	2,855	450
	V	H	84	276	637	690	53
	V	W	81	3,510	3,964	4,385	421
			82	3,045	4,865	5,279	414
			83	2,005	2,231	2,374	143
			84	2,625	2,342	2,645	303
MALAYSA	O	E	86	22,955	9,856	9,856	
	V	E	81	1,294	3,623	3,868	245
			82	2,188	4,581	5,000	419
			83	538	1,489	1,560	71
			84	3,644	6,011	7,400	1,389
			85	7,989	14,074	15,129	1,055
	V	W	81	394	1,071	1,199	128
			82	480	653	709	56
			83	6,517	8,803	9,930	1,127
MALI	V	E	85	5,394	2,871	3,498	627
MEXICO	A	E	83	5,960	6,174	7,172	998
			85	900	9,120	9,456	336
	N	E	84	735	1,128	1,235	107
	O	E	81	2,394,664	1,744,483	1,745,908	1,425
			82	3,763,365	2,316,085	2,331,122	15,037
			83	4,049,840	1,633,014	1,633,014	
			84	4,144,429	2,132,688	2,132,688	
			85	9,749,253	5,347,646	5,347,646	
			86	11,988,708	6,035,880	6,035,880	
	O	W	81	6,565,624	3,642,024	3,642,024	
			82	7,069,016	3,486,160	3,486,160	
			83	6,021,759	2,210,417	2,210,996	579
			84	7,120,608	3,640,786	3,640,786	
			85	4,499,320	2,295,027	2,295,079	52
			86	4,385,229	1,941,890	1,941,890	
	V	E	84	18,939	6,046	7,018	972
	V	W	85	22,249	11,097	12,197	1,100
N ANTIL	V	E	85	684	1,489	2,134	645
N ZEAL	A	H	81	808	874	1,247	373
			82	826	1,761	2,167	406
			83	2,604	2,524	3,697	1,173
	N	E	84	48,734	32,970	66,209	33,239
			86	37,325	46,487	52,950	6,463
	N	H	81	12,315	12,031	16,436	4,405
			86	42,028	52,823	63,326	10,503
	N	W	82	3,943	4,459	5,846	1,387
			85	251,151	290,224	329,126	38,902
	V	E	84	16,769	26,875	29,911	3,036
			85	248,590	276,874	340,222	63,348
			86	284,945	378,757	434,619	55,862
	V	W	81	2,637	5,547	6,332	785
			82	12,879	18,450	21,885	3,435
			83	37,518	52,376	58,297	5,921
			84	353,121	417,188	473,221	56,033
			85	101,449	122,749	142,718	19,969
			86	494,479	732,777	818,166	85,389
NAURU	V	E	86	7,937	7,812	8,760	948
NETHLDS	A	E	81	14,746	28,018	37,056	9,038
			82	980	963	1,705	742
			83	1,077	2,577	3,447	870
			84	2,665	3,372	4,819	1,447
			85	4,041	4,813	6,679	1,866
	A	W	84	568	585	1,014	429
	N	E	81	1,274,916	1,141,345	1,237,462	96,117
			82	3,663,079	2,993,713	3,258,344	264,631
			83	2,603,776	2,340,782	2,575,705	234,923
			84	2,675,347	2,275,486	2,545,197	269,711
			85	3,425,352	2,464,155	2,858,881	394,726
			86	2,964,012	3,114,199	3,477,995	363,796
	N	W	84	272,645	221,179	257,521	36,342
			85	599,683	412,377	493,598	81,221
	O	E	81	38,644	33,556	35,646	2,090
			82	27,466	30,329	34,159	3,830
			83	18,860	11,770	12,864	1,094
			84	94,440	75,939	85,841	9,902
			85	137,614	106,876	121,580	14,704
			86	27,581	36,972	40,761	3,789
	O	W	83	998	813	813	
			84	217	312	312	
			85	2,481	4,050	4,050	
			86	1,696	2,480	2,480	
	V	E	81	828,294	904,671	975,619	70,948
			82	920,933	1,155,103	1,243,113	88,010
			83	790,582	1,032,752	1,117,063	84,311
			84	950,838	1,415,220	1,527,037	111,817
			85	1,212,941	1,411,491	1,582,635	171,144
			86	1,506,917	1,891,259	2,089,683	198,424
	V	W	81	192,280	201,130	221,043	19,913
			82	130,682	110,431	124,012	13,581
			83	242,937	215,037	239,155	24,118
			84	3,791	4,438	4,940	502
			85	61,726	55,213	73,798	18,585
			86	547,674	723,489	809,453	85,964
NORWAY	N	E	85	681,065	579,637	682,027	102,390
	N	W	82	58,651	44,181	56,016	11,835
			84	154,237	118,701	148,870	30,169
			85	127,293	100,813	129,325	28,512
	O	E	82	14,797	15,604	18,035	2,431
	V	E	81	1,190,018	917,213	1,084,412	167,199
			82	1,180,351	1,007,274	1,177,741	170,467
			83	1,098,346	869,935	1,018,339	148,404
			84	1,198,704	943,050	1,121,107	178,057
			85	203,418	173,338	211,105	37,767
			86	926,658	887,465	1,030,102	142,637
	V	W	81	372,081	308,055	368,405	60,350
			82	81,732	72,442	86,022	13,580
			83	189,030	143,282	174,401	31,119
			84	91,977	70,963	89,737	18,774
			85	156,722	129,390	160,804	31,414
			86	250,041	228,086	278,312	50,226
OMAN	V	E	82	22,456	30,353	32,609	2,256
PAKISTN	O	E	83	1,488	701	752	51
	V	E	86	1,200	2,079	2,547	468
PANAMA	N	E	84	83,219	51,120	54,279	3,159
	V	E	81	67,407	43,200	46,111	2,911
			82	73,420	46,800	49,896	3,096
			83	36,750	25,200	26,728	1,528
			85	56,802	37,008	40,432	3,424
			86	24,532	17,444	20,744	3,300
PERU	A	E	83	2,646	8,832	11,086	2,254
			85	1,539	2,400	3,120	720
	A	W	82	647	1,000	1,506	506
			84	1,000	2,160	2,970	810
			85	5,210	9,365	11,820	2,455
	N	E	84	17,263	29,280	36,395	7,115
			85	11,949	21,630	25,880	4,250
			86	13,214	21,750	28,460	6,710
	N	W	86	3,969	7,200	11,517	4,317
	V	E	82	4,116	10,578	11,523	945
			83	5,320	8,183	9,786	1,603
			85	21,911	40,001	49,412	9,411
			86	1,620	2,400	3,023	623
PHIL R	A	E	86	758	1,121	3,752	2,631
	A	H	82	145	317	439	122
	N	E	84	6,206	4,913	5,952	1,039
	O	E	83	11,000	2,200	2,615	415
	O	W	83	90	551	560	9
			85	1,085	2,065	2,316	251
			86	8,065	10,381	10,381	
	V	E	81	15,668	23,329	27,232	3,903
			82	32,790	40,223	45,781	5,558
			83	66,621	62,890	72,780	9,890
			84	43,542	46,835	54,672	7,837
			85	55,766	63,979	74,335	10,356
			86	70,284	77,704	89,852	12,148
	V	H	81	2,961	5,712	6,773	1,061
			82	18,831	25,438	29,461	4,023
			83	52,432	70,634	83,895	13,261
			84	83,305	83,486	99,441	15,955
			85	45,576	56,955	68,264	11,309
			86	38,005	56,021	64,107	8,086
	V	W	81	125,633	178,383	198,320	19,937
			82	134,262	191,496	216,245	24,749
			83	253,212	263,570	292,037	28,467

Country	Mode	Reg	Yr	Quantity	F.A.S.	C.I.F.	Charges
			84	297,728	312,721	359,805	47,084
			85	415,618	420,259	478,921	58,662
			86	489,963	484,898	540,731	55,833
POLAND	N	E	81	376,071	262,077	321,006	58,929
			82	138,845	105,302	115,869	10,567
	O	E	82	13,943	26,780	29,732	2,952
			83	38,236	57,923	62,260	4,337
			84	21,526	25,806	28,388	2,582
			85	11,957	11,180	11,180	
			86	13,453	10,391	10,391	
	O	W	81	4,444	6,418	6,418	
	V	E	81	22,561	28,513	31,300	2,787
			82	25,327	42,309	47,124	4,815
			83	144,908	173,346	189,623	16,277
			84	140,869	157,083	169,206	12,123
			85	273,198	234,149	266,181	32,032
			86	175,019	183,717	204,557	20,840
	V	W	86	28,699	15,247	18,026	2,779
PORTUGL	A	E	81	1,100	1,750	3,379	1,629
			84	15,819	12,548	18,991	6,443
	N	E	83	223,987	180,005	205,482	25,477
			84	326,276	152,204	179,061	26,857
			85	272,749	124,919	153,193	28,274
	V	E	81	254,991	180,583	224,954	44,371
			82	170,642	101,376	127,493	26,117
			83	96,598	54,813	72,427	17,614
			84	109,555	61,284	79,823	18,539
			85	75,186	47,933	64,620	16,687
			86	367,147	211,594	260,038	48,444
	V	W	82	11,234	9,850	11,043	1,193
			84	11,781	6,180	8,455	2,275
			85	8,944	7,669	10,684	3,015
REP SAF	A	E	83	681	1,360	2,686	1,326
RWANDA	V	W	85	20,496	19,533	21,972	2,439
SALVADR	A	E	83	906	743	1,381	638
	N	E	84	4,202	5,513	6,820	1,307
	V	W	81	3,209	1,832	2,722	890
			82	7,831	5,063	8,264	3,201
			83	13,514	23,086	25,707	2,621
			84	3,646	6,083	6,955	872
			85	34,214	36,758	48,272	11,514
			86	44,725	54,913	63,042	8,129
SINGAPR	O	E	81	488	692	734	42
	O	W	81	6,364	15,129	15,129	
	V	E	81	1,080	1,799	2,075	276
			82	1,692	1,935	2,140	205
			83	19,306	13,051	17,246	4,195
			84	10,203	9,858	12,288	2,430
			85	3,199	9,019	9,868	849
	V	H	83	673	705	782	77
	V	W	81	57,936	68,928	75,810	6,882
			82	64,289	64,904	70,691	5,787
			83	108,502	92,946	100,311	7,365
			84	55,029	70,523	77,113	6,590
			85	159,631	165,737	182,760	17,023
			86	166,658	193,629	213,675	20,046
SOLMN I	V	E	85	5,687	8,871	9,241	370
SPAIN	A	E	81	782	710	1,642	932
			83	530	722	1,269	547
			84	661	2,621	6,261	3,640
	N	E	81	812,674	643,970	727,938	83,968
			82	127,045	130,598	152,240	21,642
			83	8,906	12,727	16,126	3,399
			85	1,079,685	627,614	767,905	140,291
	N	W	84	139,975	97,365	121,679	24,314
	O	E	84	8,985	9,644	9,644	
	V	E	81	152,625	142,204	166,619	24,415
			82	2,192,052	1,423,065	1,614,849	191,784
			83	3,536,024	2,132,932	2,415,463	282,531
			84	3,627,883	2,209,654	2,572,715	363,061
			85	4,758,533	2,670,900	3,098,789	427,889
			86	5,076,071	3,229,483	3,736,096	506,613
	V	W	81	8,192	9,858	12,488	2,630
			82	14,603	17,779	20,897	3,118
			83	8,042	10,843	13,169	2,326
			85	1,631,852	921,765	1,098,883	177,118
			86	2,840,001	1,835,850	2,095,606	259,756
SWEDEN	A	E	82	529	2,160	2,691	531
			84	463	650	1,312	662
	N	E	81	151,335	152,597	181,354	28,757
			82	184,469	154,162	195,256	41,094
			84	454,426	431,012	512,266	81,254
			85	637,808	531,389	626,086	94,697
			86	466,108	409,820	469,472	59,652
	N	W	81	11,210	6,803	8,516	1,713
	O	E	86	29,624	34,553	41,064	6,511
	V	E	81	51,670	67,935	80,904	12,969
			82	125,281	191,241	213,184	21,943
			83	211,534	223,255	261,148	37,893
			84	185,996	148,102	181,231	33,129
			85	101,423	73,176	91,788	18,612
			86	95,099	118,964	144,131	25,167
	V	W	81	23,421	20,772	26,051	5,279
			82	35,638	25,298	34,596	9,298
			83	50,163	40,408	52,244	11,836
			84	12,423	9,154	11,033	1,879
			85	40,324	35,339	49,869	14,530
			86	175,078	218,547	250,323	31,776
SWITZLD	A	E	82	265	549	590	41
			83	229	439	564	125
			84	220	254	515	261
			85	1,038	3,553	4,457	904
	N	E	81	237,922	428,134	455,319	27,185
			82	314,114	460,490	488,041	27,551
			83	290,748	359,439	377,519	18,080
			84	681	853	933	80
			85	621,930	779,242	852,248	73,006
			86	536,630	844,813	905,913	61,100
	N	W	82	25,245	40,703	44,381	3,678
			84	6,216	13,197	16,201	3,004
	O	E	81	110,378	121,683	126,723	5,040
			83	117,702	118,093	122,779	4,686
			84	231	911	911	
			85	395	1,035	1,113	78
			86	4,193	14,982	15,462	480
	O	W	85	461	1,044	1,183	139
	V	E	81	2,931	7,555	7,902	347
			82	10,006	29,153	30,852	1,699
			83	11,574	21,234	22,165	931
			84	608,338	754,335	832,596	78,261
			85	35,294	69,636	76,703	7,067
			86	274,621	462,377	497,707	35,330
	V	W	81	12,244	30,853	35,678	4,825
			83	5,617	16,460	19,258	2,798
			84	35,294	45,904	50,535	4,631
			85	34,340	65,841	78,698	12,857
			86	46,223	49,953	57,125	7,172
THAILND	N	W	85	20,338	16,408	20,359	3,951
	O	E	82	7,876	3,375	4,370	995
			86	877	2,704	2,944	240
	O	W	86	3,949	4,916	5,260	344
	V	E	81	138,870	77,870	95,131	17,261
			82	136,298	89,190	108,800	19,610
			83	150,780	90,192	101,652	11,460
			84	112,660	77,599	84,684	7,085
			85	84,776	53,537	62,612	9,075
			86	60,908	53,872	60,450	6,578
	V	W	81	81,086	54,101	64,711	10,610
			82	16,444	18,252	20,540	2,288
			83	97,810	112,591	123,602	11,011
			84	97,412	121,957	140,442	18,485
			85	99,222	98,374	107,377	9,003
			86	169,211	144,065	158,181	14,116
TONGA	A	H	82	3,690	1,783	3,708	1,925
	V	H	83	6,614	3,180	3,925	745
TRINID	A	E	82	634	567	777	210
			86	7,267	5,092	10,196	5,104
	V	E	82	44,445	29,053	33,256	4,203
			83	9,259	14,677	16,080	1,403
			84	3,400	5,934	8,355	2,421
			86	79,689	110,028	124,169	14,141
TURKEY	V	E	86	61,919	34,056	43,440	9,384
	V	W	85	2,205	1,069	1,139	70
U KING	A	E	81	4,109	3,561	5,370	1,809
			82	3,505	5,064	7,376	2,312
			83	6,173	17,342	20,262	2,920
			84	10,484	27,088	32,014	4,926
			85	16,987	54,587	68,165	13,578
			86	3,556	20,387	24,887	4,500
	A	W	81	2,141	2,952	5,005	2,053
			82	410	461	971	510
			83	529	608	1,115	507
	N	E	81	3,524,306	4,294,044	4,722,542	428,498
			82	3,684,588	4,069,547	4,517,394	447,847
			83	5,394,549	5,384,311	5,982,623	598,312
			84	6,872,466	6,733,901	7,576,891	842,990
			85	8,968,245	8,853,105	10,213,598	1,360,493
			86	6,867,974	7,344,596	8,281,787	937,191
	N	W	81	536,962	733,472	815,922	82,450
			82	634,711	777,041	877,302	100,261

Product
TSUSA commodity number, description, and unit of quantity

Country	Mode	Reg	Yr	Quantity	F.A.S.	C.I.F.	Charges
			83	348,403	349,042	398,565	49,523
			84	921,304	806,972	972,675	165,703
			85	1,026,481	1,193,041	1,398,733	205,692
			86	1,471,160	1,765,550	1,953,793	188,243
	O	E	81	102,710	148,512	158,961	10,449
			82	127,010	132,486	152,132	19,646
			83	307,784	363,212	408,413	45,201
			84	378,279	496,358	532,011	35,653
			85	422,132	613,379	663,936	50,557
			86	393,883	651,584	707,100	55,516
	V	E	81	932,088	1,060,744	1,190,969	130,225
			82	1,161,888	1,375,021	1,545,501	170,480
			83	1,117,331	1,107,826	1,272,245	164,419
			84	1,010,778	1,064,139	1,235,345	171,206
			85	749,936	705,130	855,557	150,427
			86	1,411,441	1,722,409	1,970,452	248,043
	V	H	84	126	324	362	38
	V	W	81	90,642	115,577	135,897	20,320
			83	176,389	244,636	270,605	25,969
			84	10,382	12,605	16,301	3,696
			85	1,536,814	1,251,739	1,576,674	324,935
			86	349,621	359,925	419,666	59,741
URUGUAY	V	E	85	1,903	3,117	3,576	459
USSR	O	E	84	1,182	829	829	
	V	E	84	31,399	20,066	22,776	2,710
VENEZ	A	E	82	3,587	700	2,438	1,738
			83	562	800	864	64
			84	15,008	16,852	19,623	2,771
			85	9,943	11,809	13,231	1,422
	N	E	86	58,098	53,222	59,543	6,321
	V	E	82	86,856	36,810	47,586	10,776
			86	33,016	28,080	30,357	2,277
W SAMOA	A	H	81	750	470	1,037	567
	A	W	81	375	268	759	491
YUGOSLV	A	E	84	3,053	2,142	4,064	1,922
	O	E	84	3,775	2,280	2,280	
			86	17,898	9,194	9,194	
	O	W	82	1,520	2,279	2,279	
			83	1,124	1,128	1,128	
			84	7,750	3,821	3,821	
			85	2,463	3,011	3,011	
			86	2,474	2,860	2,860	
	V	E	81	408,630	297,958	358,442	60,484
			82	486,821	278,493	357,584	79,091
			83	683,774	407,999	550,448	142,449
			84	674,566	357,194	475,052	117,858
			85	618,617	303,737	410,453	106,716
			86	530,399	252,613	327,744	75,131
	V	W	82	37,732	20,934	26,865	5,931

1822520 RYE BREAD, HARD CRISP (LB)

Country	Mode	Reg	Yr	Quantity	F.A.S.	C.I.F.	Charges
TOTAL			81	2,374,798	1,666,941	2,059,583	382,178
			82	3,035,260	2,122,663	2,579,133	456,470
			83	4,159,355	2,861,783	3,484,071	622,288
			84	4,395,813	3,102,889	3,825,480	722,591
			85	3,587,278	2,480,241	3,129,674	649,433
			86	3,138,592	2,497,839	2,979,853	482,014
CANADA	A	E	81	28,004	15,585	24,992	8,934
			82	42,484	26,198	39,406	13,208
			83	212,323	119,776	166,436	46,660
			84	187,395	122,544	164,576	42,032
			85	127,585	83,528	113,384	29,856
			86	99,602	86,552	105,360	18,808
	A	W	84	23,566	21,821	29,443	7,622
			85	3,949	3,157	4,066	909
			86	2,925	2,949	3,426	477
	N	E	81	75,680	47,969	69,204	21,235
			82	85,178	56,370	81,334	24,964
			84	19,509	9,727	12,187	2,460
	O	E	81	1,346	1,364	1,364	
			82	588	253	253	
			83	2,925	1,176	1,176	
			84	5,910	5,086	5,086	
			85	142,454	110,862	110,862	
			86	201,764	178,062	178,062	
	O	W	81	103,597	79,686	79,686	
			82	110,900	93,003	93,003	
			83	81,263	73,242	73,242	
			84	42,080	37,994	37,994	
			85	61,840	52,757	52,757	
			86	102,380	124,849	124,849	
CHINA M	A	E	85	33,858	23,861	29,223	5,362
			86	2,358	1,687	2,336	649
CHINA T	V	W	82	72,222	40,194	44,634	4,440

Product
TSUSA commodity number, description, and unit of quantity

Country	Mode	Reg	Yr	Quantity	F.A.S.	C.I.F.	Charges
DENMARK	O	E	84	2,453	3,509	4,092	583
			85	8,466	9,934	12,960	3,026
	V	E	82	1,350	461	681	220
			85	9,720	12,679	15,552	2,873
	V	W	84	7,893	3,627	4,950	1,323
DOM REP	V	W	83	2,095	2,085	2,297	212
FINLAND	V	E	82	11,523	11,880	13,612	1,732
			84	174,485	191,502	216,695	25,193
	V	W	81	53,875	48,272	57,813	9,541
			82	68,132	62,702	74,796	12,094
			83	12,855	10,816	13,860	3,044
			84	135,717	129,290	150,599	21,309
			85	72,617	70,013	84,324	14,311
			86	114,097	142,259	152,962	10,703
FR GERM	N	E	81	234,926	185,111	218,061	32,950
			82	261,821	190,002	222,921	32,919
			83	296,439	225,759	267,108	41,349
			84	10,980	8,397	10,586	2,189
	N	W	86	28,820	10,774	11,249	475
	O	E	81	42,494	29,011	34,453	5,442
			82	63,335	39,638	47,690	8,052
			83	65,447	40,752	48,972	8,220
			84	18,027	11,864	14,955	3,091
			85	148,531	86,486	114,204	27,718
			86	56,492	36,307	44,188	7,881
	O	W	85	2,635	1,107	1,107	
	V	E	82	9,441	5,953	7,366	1,413
			83	65,350	45,360	53,168	7,808
			84	491,411	367,760	431,283	63,523
			85	178,252	114,910	147,110	32,200
			86	228,110	174,340	205,516	31,176
	V	W	81	166,840	123,090	146,404	23,314
			82	180,671	132,787	159,773	26,986
			83	162,589	122,353	145,388	23,035
			84	305,196	247,996	293,507	45,511
			85	234,489	170,501	221,997	51,496
			86	210,004	172,527	208,322	35,795
FRANCE	A	E	82	515	288	438	150
	O	W	86	847	1,218	1,289	71
	V	E	86	13,656	15,671	16,217	546
	V	W	82	3,395	4,237	4,677	440
			83	18,790	23,165	25,586	2,421
			84	8,666	10,070	10,899	829
			85	8,911	10,226	11,855	1,629
			86	20,217	32,309	33,861	1,552
GERM DR	V	E	85	21,058	11,152	14,744	3,592
GREECE	V	E	83	17,799	15,510	19,418	3,908
			84	20,670	12,950	16,656	3,706
			85	21,526	14,907	19,255	4,348
			86	5,800	4,065	5,639	1,574
INDIA	V	E	83	5,077	4,153	4,766	613
			85	2,834	2,119	2,535	416
ITALY	V	E	83	1,185	971	1,108	137
JAPAN	V	W	84	27	383	403	20
KOR REP	V	E	86	5,787	5,335	5,791	456
N ZEAL	A	W	84	16,667	11,369	22,324	10,955
NETHLDS	A	W	84	8,288	6,336	9,834	3,498
	N	W	85	15,828	12,900	17,824	4,924
	V	E	81	735	418	465	47
			82	13,521	9,774	13,055	3,281
			83	3,600	1,092	1,285	193
			85	11,623	10,660	13,108	2,448
	V	W	81	10,598	3,057	3,376	319
			82	10,507	2,889	3,206	317
			83	5,953	2,504	2,733	229
			84	812	572	615	43
			85	8,549	7,947	9,371	1,424
NORWAY	N	W	83	27,461	21,766	26,724	4,958
	V	E	81	75,890	64,903	74,395	9,492
			82	89,101	108,091	120,606	12,515
			83	122,502	119,263	132,615	13,352
			84	149,826	140,011	159,098	19,087
			85	58,671	50,938	61,986	11,048
			86	9,629	12,232	14,437	2,205
	V	W	81	42,821	42,188	51,021	8,833
			82	70,114	111,785	125,334	13,549
			83	81,751	98,483	113,923	15,440
			84	102,439	128,807	155,477	26,670
			85	78,942	84,958	107,971	23,013
			86	113,428	165,620	173,734	8,114
PHIL R	V	E	86	2,671	3,340	3,620	280
	V	H	83	36	259	312	53
SINGAPR	V	W	81	16,888	10,617	14,175	3,558
SWEDEN	N	E	86	215,472	128,410	200,614	72,204
	O	E	84	19,147	11,112	14,254	3,142

Product
TSUSA commodity number, description, and unit of quantity

Country	Mode	Reg	Yr	Quantity	F.A.S.	C.I.F.	Charges
			85	115,701	73,027	94,690	21,663
			86	18,355	10,901	15,328	4,427
	V	E	81	1,034,255	666,967	851,142	174,184
			82	1,376,939	854,312	1,065,442	211,130
			83	1,894,339	1,205,391	1,493,076	287,685
			84	1,348,625	828,753	1,041,180	212,427
			85	640,258	439,716	557,068	117,352
			86	228,391	153,806	193,178	39,372
	V	W	81	485,812	346,634	430,733	84,099
			82	512,778	327,926	410,635	82,709
			83	1,021,677	657,083	813,017	155,934
			84	1,221,972	738,305	950,965	212,660
			85	1,461,942	894,026	1,163,920	269,894
			86	1,414,896	987,143	1,223,623	236,480
SWITZLD	O	E	83	11,805	21,508	22,916	1,408
			85	44,683	69,735	77,345	7,610
	V	E	82	12,728	14,989	17,108	2,119
			83	32,764	37,180	41,320	4,140
			84	7,196	5,973	7,667	1,694
			86	13,156	18,389	20,897	2,508
THAILND	V	W	86	5,621	5,908	6,644	736
U KING	N	E	86	19,173	15,566	20,655	5,089
	O	E	81	1,037	2,069	2,299	230
			82	12,169	11,845	13,578	1,733
			83	13,105	11,863	13,325	1,462
			84	2,955	2,142	2,623	481
	V	E	82	23,148	14,750	16,674	1,924
			84	11,567	9,940	14,692	4,752
			85	4,656	11,058	13,039	1,981
			86	4,941	7,620	8,056	436
	V	W	82	2,700	2,336	2,911	575
			83	225	273	300	27
			84	52,334	35,049	42,840	7,791
			85	67,700	47,077	57,417	10,340

1822550 BREAD IN LOAF OR ROLL, NSPF (LB)

Country	Mode	Reg	Yr	Quantity	F.A.S.	C.I.F.	Charges
TOTAL			81	2,443,700	1,081,318	1,110,583	29,265
			82	13,112,189	7,686,575	7,730,004	43,429
			83	5,826,657	3,195,880	3,272,377	76,497
			84	3,569,274	1,748,787	1,838,158	89,371
			85	1,336,914	916,089	1,069,396	153,307
			86	2,580,350	1,827,770	2,072,715	244,945
CANADA	A	E	81	383	300	340	40
			82	697	313	513	200
	A	H	81	36,469	35,567	40,088	4,521
			82	18,907	19,409	21,271	1,862
			83	9,875	11,542	13,019	1,477
			84	34,383	30,728	35,876	5,148
			85	2,704	2,095	2,413	318
			86	5,153	4,052	4,587	535
	A	W	84	29,099	35,688	42,423	6,735
			85	21,641	25,052	28,578	3,526
			86	14,112	17,277	37,350	20,073
	N	W	84	5,994	3,552	4,041	489
	O	E	81	2,154,738	824,360	824,484	124
			82	12,707,544	7,344,506	7,345,349	843
			83	5,203,939	2,736,051	2,736,771	720
			84	2,846,905	1,222,000	1,222,000	
			85	299,326	154,309	154,309	
			86	579,264	426,477	426,477	
	O	W	81	27,112	16,931	16,931	
			82	22,157	14,976	14,976	
			83	38,495	36,401	36,401	
			84	101,294	138,600	138,600	
			85	184,246	135,854	135,854	
			86	700,183	448,941	448,941	
CHINA M	O	E	81	890	342	342	
CHINA T	V	W	83	7,951	8,589	10,103	1,514
DENMARK	O	E	86	5,036	7,644	8,861	1,217
DOM REP	A	E	83	4,312	1,219	1,650	431
	V	W	83	1,033	788	868	80
FR GERM	A	E	84	3,938	1,012	2,413	1,401
	N	E	81	22,836	12,976	15,315	2,339
			82	101,166	39,474	44,552	5,078
			85	42,219	21,334	25,842	4,508
	O	E	81	20,756	12,289	14,358	2,069
			82	20,420	12,592	15,030	2,438
			83	36,550	5,510	6,735	1,225
			86	2,370	2,822	2,822	
	O	W	85	3,690	1,284	1,284	
	V	E	81	11,593	9,706	11,473	1,767
			82	6,130	4,362	4,921	559
			83	78,573	55,708	61,197	5,489
			84	118,491	42,564	49,529	6,965

Product
TSUSA commodity number, description, and unit of quantity

Country	Mode	Reg	Yr	Quantity	F.A.S.	C.I.F.	Charges
			85	42,328	13,352	17,541	4,189
			86	180,052	91,528	103,094	11,566
	V	W	81	138,352	133,052	149,421	16,369
			82	2,003	2,057	2,526	469
			83	2,682	1,964	2,403	439
			84	130,618	39,490	49,322	9,832
			85	194,052	69,588	87,575	17,987
			86	234,777	115,969	144,950	28,981
FRANCE	A	E	82	656	886	1,726	840
			84	1,019	1,343	1,982	639
			85	9,829	9,758	15,978	6,220
			86	10,079	15,027	36,768	21,741
	N	E	86	3,543	7,929	9,805	1,876
	O	W	85	2,933	4,335	4,335	
	V	E	82	660	853	910	57
			83	400	523	555	32
			84	400	261	331	70
			85	204,893	180,750	217,260	36,510
			86	504,887	416,625	520,206	103,581
	V	W	81	95	827	860	33
			82	11,569	13,109	13,644	535
			83	31,262	15,655	18,225	2,570
			84	100,102	70,964	85,447	14,483
			85	22,056	17,147	20,658	3,511
GERM DR	V	E	85	7,486	4,236	5,602	1,366
GREECE	V	E	83	17,558	11,635	14,264	2,629
GUATMAL	A	W	82	619	304	397	93
HG KONG	V	W	83	960	1,327	1,445	118
ITALY	N	W	84	2,425	4,104	5,225	1,121
	V	E	83	22,080	32,568	37,814	5,246
			84	3,684	5,221	5,456	235
			85	62,108	88,941	112,786	23,845
			86	51,500	40,479	46,060	5,581
	V	W	83	24,915	35,112	44,828	9,716
			84	48,819	57,573	76,027	18,454
			85	50,417	69,935	91,949	22,014
			86	16,869	36,993	42,914	5,921
JAMAICA	A	E	82	4,231	7,754	8,488	734
			84	6,224	9,929	11,298	1,369
			85	660	1,146	1,665	519
JAPAN	V	E	84	963	644	694	50
			86	7,092	3,365	4,038	673
	V	W	82	264	398	418	20
KOR REP	V	E	86	2,640	3,840	4,369	529
N ZEAL	A	H	83	4,551	1,473	3,315	1,842
NETHLDS	A	E	85	2,655	2,644	5,211	2,567
	O	E	81	714	468	491	23
			84	1,446	631	785	154
			86	8,130	2,773	2,800	27
	V	W	82	1,312	255	277	22
			86	4,572	6,015	6,750	735
NORWAY	V	E	81	29,762	34,500	36,480	1,980
			82	4,457	4,703	5,168	465
PERU	A	W	85	1,128	1,620	2,941	1,321
PHIL R	V	W	84	457	448	514	66
SPAIN	V	E	82	207,417	219,320	247,901	28,581
			83	332,793	236,676	277,845	41,169
			84	122,677	75,409	95,778	20,369
			85	182,543	112,709	137,615	24,906
			86	126,891	113,365	133,915	20,550
SWEDEN	V	E	84	10,106	8,069	9,811	1,742
			86	7,877	4,091	6,332	2,241
	V	W	86	111,941	56,706	75,488	18,782
SWITZLD	V	E	83	8,728	3,139	4,939	1,800
			84	230	557	606	49
U KING	A	E	82	1,980	1,304	1,937	633
			86	3,382	5,852	6,188	336

1822560 BREAD CRUMBS (LB)

Country	Mode	Reg	Yr	Quantity	F.A.S.	C.I.F.	Charges
TOTAL			81	42,401,066	15,307,440	15,710,962	403,521
			82	42,380,851	13,788,091	14,229,401	441,310
			83	50,644,392	18,795,446	19,267,147	471,701
			84	54,041,305	22,120,639	22,832,301	711,662
			85	57,940,516	25,082,601	26,327,046	1,244,445
			86	72,329,632	30,081,770	31,394,263	1,312,493
ARGENT	A	E	86	2,639	3,800	5,526	1,726
	V	E	81	11,905	1,165	1,291	126
	V	W	84	5,610	4,700	7,027	2,327
AUSTRAL	V	W	85	13,100	13,243	13,419	176
AUSTRIA	A	E	84	1,603	2,202	3,610	1,408
BELGIUM	O	E	81	3,424	3,202	3,462	260
			82	3,432	7,192	8,457	1,265
			83	8,457	8,351	10,468	2,117
			86	1,369	7,670	8,081	411

Product
TSUSA commodity number, description, and unit of quantity

Country	Mode	Reg	Yr	Quantity	F.A.S.	C.I.F.	Charges
	V	E	83	335	1,117	1,263	146
			84	443	541	572	31
			85	7,754	16,538	18,670	2,132
			86	25,538	29,584	35,718	6,134
BRAZIL	A	E	81	345	676	1,231	555
	V	E	85	17,330	14,624	19,610	4,986
CANADA	A	E	82	27,500	15,742	23,968	8,226
			83	38,710	19,087	27,896	8,809
			84	5,887	2,894	3,412	518
			85	47,414	18,822	25,296	6,474
			86	7,991	5,116	7,185	2,069
	A	H	82	574	526	601	75
			83	9,679	4,444	4,800	356
	A	W	81	19,376	8,422	10,662	2,240
			82	4,202	3,061	4,378	1,317
			84	9,229	6,215	11,029	4,814
			85	35,729	29,743	39,310	9,567
			86	52,822	47,124	77,890	30,766
	N	E	81	39,572,227	13,192,488	13,192,909	420
			85	37,793,351	15,707,286	15,707,286	
	O	E	81	361,054	102,598	102,598	
			82	39,842,917	11,568,537	11,572,376	3,839
			83	47,735,877	16,500,706	16,500,706	
			84	49,857,038	18,952,965	18,952,973	8
			85	12,988,759	3,944,655	3,944,655	
			86	63,929,453	22,926,528	22,927,008	480
	O	W	81	100,607	40,763	40,763	
			82	11,163	10,653	10,653	
			83	35,580	16,301	16,301	
			86	24,963	18,633	18,633	
CHINA M	V	E	86	3,746	1,479	1,554	75
	V	H	82	275	289	318	29
	V	W	83	1,065	387	433	46
			86	6,913	6,162	7,259	1,097
CHINA T	O	E	82	40	472	472	
	V	E	84	3,000	4,118	4,643	525
			86	1,799	1,400	1,522	122
	V	W	81	723	997	1,048	51
			82	1,095	884	1,018	134
			84	1,649	6,276	6,889	613
COLOMB	A	E	85	2,170	5,466	6,196	730
			86	2,095	5,000	5,510	510
CYPRUS	V	E	86	5,593	5,349	6,603	1,254
DENMARK	A	E	85	6,129	3,809	8,288	4,479
	O	E	86	10,573	20,141	23,566	3,425
	V	E	85	16,876	17,316	20,270	2,954
			86	45,371	45,148	49,034	3,886
DOM REP	A	E	81	9,560	2,297	3,090	793
			82	27,158	7,613	13,728	6,115
	N	E	83	27,975	12,365	15,768	3,403
			85	16,340	8,734	10,123	1,389
	V	E	81	68,287	42,638	47,108	4,470
			82	325	819	869	50
			84	15,811	5,758	7,386	1,628
			85	31,381	6,065	7,563	1,498
			86	58,500	28,433	33,464	5,031
DOMINCA	V	E	85	18,455	11,094	12,806	1,712
			86	37,955	9,596	10,920	1,324
FIJI	V	E	85	9,742	11,568	13,968	2,400
FINLAND	V	E	81	373,274	334,217	388,971	54,754
			82	359,575	357,291	410,734	53,443
			83	359,880	323,851	373,730	49,879
			84	226,300	219,292	263,024	43,732
			85	338,900	325,852	369,675	43,823
			86	271,530	323,352	353,319	29,967
	V	W	81	100,104	89,771	107,139	17,368
			82	37,443	34,922	41,080	6,158
			83	49,594	44,837	52,396	7,559
			84	24,718	23,832	27,481	3,649
FR GERM	A	E	81	200	294	744	450
	N	E	82	138,194	78,092	92,072	13,980
			83	220,027	92,332	107,440	15,108
			84	266,230	121,831	144,799	22,968
			85	435,373	290,886	349,819	58,933
			86	19,867	18,372	21,384	3,012
	N	W	84	227,435	145,287	173,591	28,304
			86	4,121	3,553	5,987	2,434
	O	E	81	14,957	10,260	11,846	1,586
			82	29,480	22,639	26,524	3,885
			83	36,291	25,578	30,163	4,585
			85	108,828	68,575	84,993	16,418
			86	75,220	53,383	65,398	12,015
	V	E	81	46,220	38,587	42,799	4,212
			82	22,155	17,772	20,529	2,757
			83	68,436	27,454	32,936	5,482

Product
TSUSA commodity number, description, and unit of quantity

Country	Mode	Reg	Yr	Quantity	F.A.S.	C.I.F.	Charges
			84	42,063	23,165	30,038	6,873
			85	213,598	158,911	186,993	28,082
			86	502,219	432,671	504,940	72,269
	V	W	81	29,993	20,604	25,454	4,850
			82	42,375	22,987	26,891	3,904
			83	94,063	41,333	52,769	11,436
			85	63,420	52,353	63,548	11,195
			86	18,852	19,561	22,184	2,623
FRANCE	A	E	86	2,205	2,590	4,524	1,934
	A	W	84	100	263	788	525
	N	E	81	285,053	173,847	199,373	25,526
			83	205,161	212,612	243,223	30,611
			84	238,490	219,647	248,069	28,422
			85	885,037	642,411	845,281	202,870
			86	269,177	362,297	411,390	49,093
	O	E	82	2,153	1,872	2,153	281
			83	1,544	946	990	44
			84	192	444	1,973	1,529
	O	W	85	2,063	4,798	5,385	587
	V	E	81	85,061	75,181	93,533	18,352
			82	344,468	315,956	372,136	56,180
			83	97,492	76,390	100,991	24,601
			84	225,992	167,889	217,027	49,138
			85	49,797	48,844	61,898	13,054
			86	1,098,080	459,417	586,499	127,082
	V	W	81	14,634	18,600	20,004	1,404
			82	7,575	7,508	8,027	519
			83	18,389	23,033	26,235	3,202
			84	9,372	11,389	13,001	1,612
			85	18,573	19,211	21,192	1,981
			86	8,644	13,096	14,484	1,388
GREECE	V	E	83	24,138	16,121	19,284	3,163
			84	46,964	33,170	40,138	6,968
			85	46,098	29,103	37,713	8,610
			86	84,451	87,780	100,098	12,318
GUATMAL	A	W	81	721	470	603	133
HG KONG	V	H	83	834	656	736	80
	V	W	85	2,746	1,720	1,812	92
			86	675	1,335	1,522	187
INDIA	V	E	84	2,116	1,582	1,749	167
	V	W	82	638	430	494	64
			83	8,771	5,012	6,599	1,587
IRELAND	V	E	86	3,600	3,217	3,604	387
ISRAEL	N	E	84	26,655	37,538	44,655	7,117
	V	E	82	9,360	11,232	12,606	1,374
			84	8,995	12,240	14,242	2,002
			85	36,906	42,187	52,091	9,904
			86	2,814	2,752	3,180	428
ITALY	A	E	82	750	507	863	356
	A	W	81	357	586	1,273	687
	N	E	82	137,333	115,320	151,780	36,460
			83	253,377	234,246	306,334	72,088
			84	418,340	360,270	455,959	95,689
			86	863,317	1,009,348	1,219,814	210,466
	O	E	81	7,778	8,713	8,713	
			82	41,036	40,230	40,230	
			83	6,000	8,902	10,983	2,081
			84	20,667	22,976	24,573	1,597
			85	3,587	9,628	10,612	984
	V	E	81	98,982	99,607	127,300	27,693
			82	2,921	7,452	8,097	645
			83	17,315	22,997	27,624	4,627
			84	17,065	15,268	18,069	2,801
			85	627,177	593,433	752,949	159,516
			86	27,020	38,368	43,872	5,504
	V	W	83	4,433	8,773	11,230	2,457
			84	18,307	33,515	35,301	1,786
			85	20,322	45,121	52,734	7,613
			86	11,411	12,860	17,433	4,573
JAMAICA	A	E	84	3,495	4,389	6,242	1,853
			85	7,574	9,986	10,732	746
JAPAN	N	H	81	139,584	95,360	112,799	17,439
			83	195,599	132,368	160,212	27,844
			84	230,206	152,310	193,925	41,615
	N	W	84	43,621	28,401	32,494	4,093
	V	E	81	53,610	34,605	38,833	4,228
			82	70,859	43,914	50,584	6,670
			83	84,467	56,207	62,285	6,078
			84	100,243	63,807	70,914	7,107
			85	141,336	73,261	89,875	16,614
			86	131,647	97,814	114,293	16,479
	V	H	82	186,815	121,066	145,574	24,508
			85	212,122	135,447	183,689	48,242
			86	228,161	186,076	242,287	56,211
	V	W	81	118,059	55,845	76,953	21,108

Product
TSUSA commodity number, description, and unit of quantity

Country	Mode	Reg	Yr	Quantity	F.A.S.	C.I.F.	Charges
			82	59,765	45,260	49,597	4,337
			83	71,822	56,184	59,894	3,710
			84	39,446	34,120	37,131	3,011
			85	162,974	95,656	124,780	29,124
			86	99,304	120,443	127,201	6,758
KOR REP	V	E	82	550	417	455	38
			83	20,592	18,497	21,245	2,748
			84	34,979	30,189	34,910	4,721
			85	3,960	4,565	5,239	674
			86	3,075	2,026	2,189	163
	V	H	86	22,046	9,250	12,250	3,000
	V	W	82	14,286	6,175	7,440	1,265
			83	35,441	15,681	19,073	3,392
			84	17,329	12,331	13,718	1,387
			85	71,740	41,779	48,773	6,994
			86	19,818	17,498	19,960	2,462
MEXICO	A	E	81	14,702	9,877	17,744	7,867
	A	W	82	3,913	4,317	5,452	1,135
	O	E	86	25,533	11,572	11,572	
	O	W	81	2,500	1,837	1,837	
			85	1,875	1,470	1,470	
N ANTIL	V	E	83	32,348	4,386	5,257	871
N ZEAL	A	W	81	629	764	1,073	309
	V	W	86	65,004	57,579	69,938	12,359
NAURU	V	E	86	7,052	6,941	7,783	842
NETHLDS	A	E	82	375	375	441	66
	N	E	85	29,542	29,506	33,051	3,545
	N	W	84	7,009	2,193	2,648	455
	O	E	81	33,401	31,690	35,716	4,026
			82	18,144	16,275	19,065	2,790
			83	9,149	10,043	11,846	1,803
			84	32,652	33,748	37,436	3,688
	V	E	81	339,917	336,139	399,255	63,116
			82	339,661	339,843	401,449	61,606
			83	326,180	333,121	390,008	56,887
			84	345,595	287,487	368,896	81,409
			85	333,679	319,885	401,076	81,191
			86	327,619	447,963	540,746	92,783
	V	W	82	948	2,406	2,694	288
			83	2,111	4,505	5,687	1,182
			85	8,730	7,116	8,662	1,546
			86	9,186	8,364	9,600	1,236
NORWAY	O	E	86	14,991	14,128	16,548	2,420
	V	E	81	49,187	41,287	48,264	6,977
			82	44,229	41,763	47,891	6,128
			83	8,068	4,505	7,112	2,607
			84	173,963	164,638	192,593	27,955
			85	221,589	218,970	255,825	36,855
			86	147,873	176,320	194,215	17,895
	V	W	81	31,121	29,845	35,533	5,688
			82	24,238	20,187	22,860	2,673
			85	11,274	10,006	12,822	2,816
PERU	A	W	82	511	565	1,289	724
			85	1,418	2,400	3,870	1,470
	V	E	85	3,017	11,327	12,623	1,296
PHIL R	V	E	83	3,481	5,740	6,617	877
			84	353	588	723	135
			85	500	1,250	1,661	411
	V	H	83	869	1,309	1,576	267
	V	W	82	330	1,530	1,828	298
			83	9,877	4,914	5,469	555
			84	1,563	4,871	5,457	586
			85	7,958	9,620	10,436	816
			86	6,277	7,032	7,769	737
POLAND	A	E	83	7,604	15,027	19,794	4,767
PORTUGL	O	E	83	5,636	2,100	2,100	
	V	E	82	8,777	7,866	9,875	2,009
			83	23,936	21,763	24,403	2,640
			84	34,460	30,498	38,307	7,809
			85	44,395	35,386	44,546	9,160
			86	7,496	5,440	7,040	1,600
S HELNA	V	E	86	10,569	7,366	8,878	1,512
SALVADR	A	E	84	1,944	1,248	2,031	783
SPAIN	V	E	81	269,573	277,491	354,939	77,448
			82	344,820	327,420	414,269	86,849
			83	266,034	186,257	242,325	56,068
			84	414,792	295,553	349,877	54,324
			85	296,106	201,844	253,608	51,764
			86	401,713	391,443	471,522	80,079
	V	W	82	12,699	9,479	12,279	2,800
SWEDEN	A	E	83	1,075	1,191	3,061	1,870
			84	1,667	1,805	2,611	806
	N	E	82	8,085	3,979	6,304	2,325
			85	15,712	6,954	12,254	5,300
			86	17,762	11,028	15,328	4,300

Product
TSUSA commodity number, description, and unit of quantity

Country	Mode	Reg	Yr	Quantity	F.A.S.	C.I.F.	Charges
	N	W	82	8,562	4,335	5,404	1,069
			85	16,140	9,238	14,424	5,186
	O	E	84	7,854	2,942	5,820	2,878
	V	E	81	138,800	122,445	151,101	28,656
			82	74,471	68,846	88,020	19,174
			83	162,208	153,140	188,235	35,095
			84	702,235	446,284	571,020	124,736
			85	2,290,350	1,524,718	1,838,991	314,273
			86	2,496,938	1,695,777	1,981,630	285,853
	V	W	82	7,854	3,510	4,738	1,228
			83	36,322	14,359	19,922	5,563
			84	59,090	17,755	29,106	11,351
			85	7,809	1,145	3,336	2,191
			86	7,870	3,969	6,552	2,583
SWITZLD	O	E	85	11,200	23,520	23,520	
	V	E	82	29,566	39,786	45,040	5,254
			83	1,966	7,446	7,654	208
			84	20,117	30,341	33,189	2,848
			86	56,734	149,904	166,688	16,784
	V	W	82	1,946	4,137	4,410	273
			84	184	371	439	68
			86	1,969	1,463	1,602	139
THAILND	V	W	84	3,152	2,210	2,379	169
U KING	A	E	83	1,394	968	1,491	523
			85	875	2,257	2,311	54
	A	W	85	983	4,413	4,477	64
	N	E	84	27,552	22,707	29,781	7,074
			85	168,631	150,453	169,259	18,806
			86	728,267	630,487	740,916	110,429
	O	E	83	8,389	7,754	9,212	1,458
			84	16,206	12,769	16,609	3,840
	V	E	82	1,690	2,245	2,493	248
			83	2,609	4,167	4,364	197
			84	276	270	295	25
			85	12,072	8,433	11,581	3,148
			86	12,205	16,772	18,651	1,879
	V	W	81	511	792	1,013	221
			82	23,400	21,543	27,548	6,005
			83	3,792	5,983	7,007	1,024
			84	1,051	1,547	1,732	185
USSR	O	E	82	220	854	1,348	494
YUGOSLV	V	E	81	4,630	3,480	3,988	508

Bean, processed products
1821500 BEAN CAKE A STICK, MISO, ETC (LB)

Country	Mode	Reg	Yr	Quantity	F.A.S.	C.I.F.	Charges
TOTAL			81	4,966,559	3,513,271	3,846,524	333,203
			82	5,453,568	3,669,539	4,054,550	385,011
			83	6,453,004	4,480,614	4,950,172	469,558
			84	6,742,449	4,830,610	5,361,914	531,304
			85	8,115,651	5,319,282	5,890,946	571,664
			86	8,731,155	5,974,701	6,512,844	538,143
AUSTRAL	V	W	83	2,550	2,833	3,001	168
BELGIUM	N	E	86	1,938	3,639	3,834	195
CANADA	O	E	83	450	2,059	2,059	
	O	W	82	37,795	16,453	16,453	
			83	615	833	833	
			84	297	416	416	
CHILE	V	E	83	440	477	540	63
CHINA M	A	W	84	2,000	3,308	3,404	96
	N	W	86	10,780	10,299	10,639	340
	O	E	84	2,880	920	1,048	128
			84	3,584	3,951	4,488	537
	V	E	81	106,398	70,966	80,501	9,535
			82	103,063	71,247	81,448	10,201
			83	187,002	131,178	152,465	21,287
			84	94,413	85,045	97,771	12,726
			85	81,626	52,658	61,994	9,336
			86	79,961	46,513	55,354	8,841
	V	H	81	12,830	11,641	12,549	908
			82	7,740	9,622	10,507	885
			83	1,980	284	327	43
			84	1,100	838	985	147
	V	W	81	148,047	118,484	128,290	9,806
			82	173,167	141,274	155,243	13,969
			83	318,673	262,600	288,688	26,088
			84	349,249	328,444	366,995	38,551
			85	480,735	431,697	473,744	42,047
			86	453,946	400,695	440,511	39,816
CHINA T	A	H	82	132	382	752	370
	N	E	84	322,972	271,739	316,248	44,509
	O	E	81	2,940	1,883	2,034	151
			84	1,049	1,911	2,100	189

Product TSUSA commodity number, description, and unit of quantity Country	Mode	Reg	Yr	Quantity	F.A.S.	C.I.F.	Charges
	O	W	85	2,903	1,110	1,306	196
			82	1,268	720	752	32
	V	E	81	255,793	196,397	218,313	21,916
			82	202,369	170,566	192,287	21,721
			83	327,042	223,675	255,752	32,077
			84	69,390	66,167	75,800	9,633
			85	388,376	299,478	342,720	43,242
			86	412,639	334,881	368,971	34,090
	V	H	81	479	560	600	40
			82	2,895	3,291	3,514	223
			83	480	620	639	19
			84	951	926	1,087	161
			85	2,187	2,750	2,967	217
			86	7,979	5,182	5,681	499
	V	W	81	242,405	211,693	230,118	18,425
			82	163,279	127,727	140,003	12,276
			83	292,056	231,907	251,334	19,427
			84	321,582	263,043	290,373	27,330
			85	443,729	348,641	383,887	35,246
			86	489,297	389,176	414,158	24,982
FR GERM	V	E	82	144	1,140	1,243	103
FRANCE	V	E	85	720	1,455	1,664	209
GUATMAL	V	E	85	8,660	7,152	7,543	391
HG KONG	N	W	81	51,223	52,406	55,349	2,943
			84	23,166	17,498	19,326	1,828
			85	468,447	428,451	462,196	33,745
	O	E	81	1,200	820	935	115
			83	2,750	4,358	4,799	441
			84	2,856	3,334	3,334	
			86	12,250	12,836	12,836	
	O	W	81	1,500	913	1,001	88
			82	2,360	481	513	32
	V	E	81	398,567	459,288	498,767	39,481
			82	421,036	471,995	516,130	44,135
			83	408,125	412,992	458,245	45,253
			84	174,013	154,174	175,954	21,780
			85	131,678	92,922	105,576	12,654
			86	130,508	84,019	94,292	10,273
	V	H	81	86,516	103,781	111,473	7,692
			82	69,169	81,720	88,285	6,565
			83	53,805	58,188	63,334	5,146
			84	6,142	8,253	9,247	994
			85	6,800	9,637	10,843	1,206
			86	14,844	22,805	25,858	3,053
	V	W	81	312,936	280,157	298,952	18,795
			82	357,002	353,306	380,266	26,960
			83	469,537	440,608	472,713	32,105
			84	528,696	497,189	527,825	30,636
			85	100,211	93,414	103,538	10,124
			86	542,844	477,819	506,694	28,875
HONDURA	V	E	81	3,120	2,765	2,985	220
INDIA	O	E	83	691	437	469	32
	V	E	81	1,367	1,341	1,620	279
			82	4,414	3,100	3,738	638
			83	1,124	1,567	1,763	196
			84	1,065	1,406	1,689	283
			85	11,924	4,696	5,339	643
	V	W	81	917	631	751	120
			82	584	631	745	114
			83	206	255	302	47
INDNSIA	V	E	82	2,880	963	1,236	273
	V	W	81	525	367	409	42
			84	276	513	553	40
JAMAICA	V	E	85	6,808	11,483	12,525	1,042
JAPAN	A	E	82	29	263	271	8
	N	E	82	712,455	438,624	502,497	63,873
			83	802,403	484,504	548,131	63,627
			84	993,876	625,508	711,532	86,024
			85	99,751	49,936	56,969	7,033
			86	942,397	652,223	724,190	71,967
	N	H	81	224,842	158,092	187,035	28,943
			82	301,038	189,106	229,692	40,586
			83	355,142	243,516	295,091	51,575
			84	359,740	244,591	290,298	45,707
			86	242,606	245,871	283,757	37,886
	N	W	81	977,959	524,060	570,601	46,489
			82	1,312,683	655,802	712,134	56,332
			83	2,137,121	1,294,937	1,396,011	101,074
			84	1,494,116	904,537	977,314	72,777
			86	682,532	570,744	603,811	33,067
	O	E	81	6,683	5,688	6,313	625
			82	1,310	672	759	87
			84	37,903	26,632	29,298	2,666
	O	W	85	2,706	1,905	2,052	147
	V	E	81	396,748	319,630	359,335	39,705

Product TSUSA commodity number, description, and unit of quantity Country	Mode	Reg	Yr	Quantity	F.A.S.	C.I.F.	Charges
			82	124,184	106,146	117,108	10,962
			83	212,277	156,938	178,154	21,216
			84	265,509	210,637	237,812	27,175
			85	1,371,793	778,438	886,478	108,040
			86	370,953	246,494	274,876	28,382
	V	H	82	1,139	893	1,249	356
			85	290,948	216,921	252,341	35,420
			86	26,598	29,425	33,625	4,200
	V	W	81	854,690	619,084	669,504	50,420
			82	821,215	538,635	585,002	46,367
			83	368,813	298,248	323,859	25,611
			84	991,012	709,464	765,837	56,373
			85	3,820,148	2,214,066	2,410,266	196,200
			86	3,407,768	1,901,892	2,052,161	150,269
KENYA	V	W	86	2,195	1,653	1,842	189
KOR REP	O	E	86	9,716	3,590	3,590	
	V	E	81	22,127	13,433	15,478	2,045
			82	49,340	44,220	49,275	5,055
			83	41,605	25,028	27,736	2,708
			84	193,877	135,299	156,445	21,146
			85	201,069	170,266	191,900	21,634
			86	357,685	233,425	257,502	24,077
	V	H	81	14,093	4,389	5,797	1,408
			82	15,548	8,627	9,744	1,117
			83	21,879	12,214	14,867	2,653
			84	11,307	6,727	7,672	945
			85	10,088	5,442	6,468	1,026
			86	10,916	5,257	6,095	838
	V	W	81	794,213	313,872	342,495	28,623
			82	483,667	187,755	204,471	16,716
			83	406,259	157,188	172,657	15,469
			84	433,433	232,157	252,691	20,534
			85	91,473	52,707	58,827	6,120
			86	432,691	228,591	256,618	28,027
LEBANON	V	W	83	14,074	7,140	8,005	865
MACAO	V	W	86	6,000	7,608	8,076	468
MALAYSA	V	E	81	3,000	1,500	1,561	61
	V	H	82	210	295	316	21
	V	W	82	3,777	1,808	1,856	48
MEXICO	V	E	83	730	947	1,052	105
N ZEAL	V	H	83	300	368	394	26
NETHLDS	V	W	81	519	1,100	1,237	137
			84	4,020	2,778	4,402	1,624
PHIL R	V	E	81	6,381	7,754	8,753	999
			82	14,413	9,267	10,405	1,138
			83	918	711	809	98
			84	1,694	855	1,126	271
			85	4,800	2,550	2,934	384
			86	788	1,049	1,196	147
	V	W	81	9,705	9,928	11,388	1,460
			82	8,200	7,758	8,929	1,171
			83	15,494	13,158	14,493	1,335
			84	9,045	7,809	8,887	1,078
			85	24,953	21,385	24,188	2,803
			86	21,662	20,714	24,106	3,392
SINGAPR	V	W	82	8,212	5,220	5,646	426
SWITZLD	O	E	86	3,925	8,898	9,395	497
	V	E	82	2,000	2,691	2,910	219
			85	5,270	2,510	2,778	268
	V	W	83	2,070	1,456	1,512	56
THAILND	V	E	81	882	1,614	1,880	266
			82	1,540	1,689	1,923	234
			83	480	823	939	116
			84	2,783	1,768	2,026	258
			86	9,151	3,963	4,741	778
	V	W	81	25,074	18,114	19,452	1,338
			82	43,311	15,450	17,248	1,798
			83	5,913	8,567	9,199	632
			84	41,333	13,693	18,979	5,286
			85	51,760	13,653	15,598	1,945
			86	46,586	25,440	28,435	2,995
TURKEY	O	E	85	2,756	1,038	1,165	127
U KING	V	E	85	783	1,006	1,125	119
	V	W	85	2,549	1,915	2,015	100

Cereal

1823000 CEREAL FOODS AND PREPS (LB)

Country	Mode	Reg	Yr	Quantity	F.A.S.	C.I.F.	Charges
TOTAL			81	29,105,652	8,992,437	9,261,737	269,250
			82	25,310,452	10,223,962	10,599,344	375,382
			83	14,860,639	7,950,022	8,240,442	290,420
			84	38,941,387	12,287,880	12,791,644	503,764
			85	34,403,095	12,315,941	12,926,858	610,917
			86	21,961,621	14,354,476	14,934,254	579,778

Product TSUSA commodity number, description, and unit of quantity Country	Mode	Reg	Yr	Quantity	F.A.S.	C.I.F.	Charges
ARGENT	V	E	86	38,045	36,156	37,956	1,800
AUSTRAL	A	E	82	13	310	343	33
	A	W	83	1,293	927	2,078	1,151
			85	3,800	1,908	1,989	81
	N	W	85	149,132	89,880	107,409	17,529
	O	E	84	485	579	579	
	V	W	81	161,640	69,068	88,193	19,125
			82	92,228	37,008	49,260	12,252
			83	59,729	23,013	30,646	7,633
			84	127,230	52,644	67,514	14,870
			86	141,456	62,816	84,595	21,779
AUSTRIA	V	E	84	10,856	8,927	10,409	1,482
BAHAMAS	A	W	84	962	348	883	535
BELGIUM	V	E	81	19,336	32,125	40,985	8,860
			82	109,295	135,991	195,450	59,459
			83	35,118	43,896	65,431	21,535
			84	96,704	104,489	150,077	45,588
			85	91,230	82,382	106,947	24,565
			86	116,335	90,779	114,349	23,570
BRAZIL	V	E	84	32,871	10,017	12,477	2,460
C RICA	V	E	82	229,286	128,240	155,561	27,321
			83	104,510	62,092	74,813	12,721
			84	1,107,290	792,595	905,913	113,318
			85	1,186,180	857,674	954,750	97,076
			86	1,188,892	848,351	931,880	83,529
CANADA	A	E	81	4,277	2,852	3,287	435
			83	640	647	1,080	433
	A	W	86	14,624	11,890	13,663	1,773
	N	E	85	4,906,964	1,965,633	1,965,633	
	O	E	81	7,943,371	3,702,397	3,702,397	
			82	9,152,703	4,688,266	4,688,983	717
			83	8,164,425	4,258,097	4,259,738	1,641
			84	6,392,683	3,572,362	3,572,404	42
			85	3,453,738	2,157,775	2,157,775	
			86	13,297,770	8,055,153	8,084,267	29,114
	O	W	81	747,997	343,905	343,905	
			82	565,147	373,190	373,190	
			83	753,861	483,530	483,530	
			84	1,099,584	734,760	734,760	
			85	807,584	548,569	548,569	
			86	921,084	706,366	706,366	
	V	E	86	73,861	58,541	62,856	4,315
CHINA M	V	E	82	125	468	475	7
			85	4,821	2,275	2,475	200
	V	W	83	6,000	2,753	2,910	157
			85	33,442	27,732	30,974	3,242
			86	2,340	1,544	1,641	97
CHINA T	V	E	83	4,900	2,155	2,481	326
	V	W	81	23,820	10,488	12,219	1,731
			82	1,283	300	352	52
			83	7,097	2,293	2,594	301
			84	2,585	2,310	2,541	231
			85	4,754	8,270	9,059	789
			86	22,766	15,814	16,681	867
COLOMB	V	E	81	1,449,087	960,757	1,064,809	104,052
			82	1,726,664	1,188,693	1,308,965	120,272
			83	1,332,060	940,773	1,037,458	96,685
			84	1,496,898	1,014,045	1,120,406	106,361
			85	2,134,284	1,403,848	1,554,028	150,180
			86	1,838,966	1,360,413	1,477,654	117,241
	V	W	83	6,653	6,461	7,331	870
			85	2,910	3,156	3,626	470
DENMARK	V	E	81	12,405	11,863	13,129	1,266
			82	55,837	78,614	86,269	7,655
			83	77,769	82,489	89,846	7,357
	V	W	83	24,435	9,513	12,991	3,478
DOM REP	V	E	85	74,840	69,117	74,622	5,505
ECUADOR	V	E	81	2,000	1,100	1,291	191
			83	7,788	1,891	2,530	639
FR GERM	A	E	84	322	284	338	54
			86	31,030	16,221	33,505	17,284
	N	E	85	81,430	82,054	95,028	12,974
			86	136,845	136,440	156,789	20,349
	N	W	86	43,218	40,071	50,897	10,826
	O	E	82	14,157	13,044	14,923	1,879
			84	7,584	1,881	2,576	695
	V	E	81	651	1,762	1,839	77
			82	22,914	24,307	28,044	3,737
			83	21,479	12,644	14,684	2,040
			84	6,305	5,901	6,438	537
			86	47,950	29,777	40,563	10,786
	V	W	81	1,050	777	901	124
			85	17,064	12,127	15,344	3,217
FRANCE	A	E	83	423	508	677	169

Product TSUSA commodity number, description, and unit of quantity Country	Mode	Reg	Yr	Quantity	F.A.S.	C.I.F.	Charges
			85	915	1,050	2,873	1,823
	N	E	85	5,808	2,052	2,714	662
	O	E	82	8,768	2,608	3,684	1,076
			83	17,558	4,879	6,558	1,679
			84	3,000	1,031	1,317	286
	V	E	81	4,000	2,124	2,280	156
			84	26,168	8,190	10,134	1,944
			86	18,464	16,405	18,891	2,486
	V	W	85	661	1,698	1,942	244
GREECE	O	E	82	2,000	2,800	2,800	
			84	67	306	306	
	V	E	83	700	2,150	2,270	120
			86	1,576	1,205	1,374	169
GUATMAL	A	E	82	638	821	945	124
	A	W	81	34,910	29,520	38,575	9,055
			82	34,283	30,456	40,287	9,831
			83	31,923	27,140	36,454	9,314
			84	14,763	14,760	18,517	3,757
			85	7,368	6,003	7,631	1,628
	O	E	84	179	304	400	96
			85	1,999	1,538	1,869	331
	O	W	85	1,470	1,529	1,529	
	V	E	84	2,903	2,176	4,467	2,291
			85	7,070	6,210	7,771	1,561
HG KONG	V	E	86	2,250	2,446	2,642	196
	V	H	81	1,800	2,070	2,288	218
	V	W	83	4,500	3,771	3,939	168
			85	16,800	5,957	6,473	516
HONDURA	V	E	85	2,649	1,277	1,609	332
INDIA	A	E	84	646	363	418	55
	N	E	84	47,300	12,603	14,861	2,258
			85	8,973	4,562	5,130	568
	O	E	81	7,430	2,279	2,533	254
			82	550	289	321	32
			83	4,860	3,989	4,492	503
			84	7,554	4,888	5,346	458
	O	W	84	1,500	1,095	1,163	68
	V	E	81	242,786	90,248	113,395	23,147
			82	147,145	51,006	63,772	12,766
			83	193,648	77,951	93,453	15,502
			84	344,961	114,685	145,306	30,621
			85	312,742	103,669	128,357	24,688
			86	231,187	77,912	93,565	15,653
	V	W	81	158,635	56,825	72,467	15,642
			82	83,386	37,079	43,708	6,629
			83	146,046	53,717	64,037	10,320
			84	76,685	28,438	36,024	7,586
			85	63,867	19,150	26,148	6,998
			86	65,429	23,007	28,403	5,396
IRAN	V	E	86	3,598	6,230	7,530	1,300
IRELAND	N	E	86	25,106	8,211	10,298	2,087
	V	E	81	12,130	8,741	10,709	1,968
			82	893	2,185	2,639	454
			83	3,705	2,704	3,292	588
			84	21,899	18,038	21,196	3,158
			85	36,682	30,409	33,150	2,741
			86	10,676	10,706	12,418	1,712
ISRAEL	V	E	83	24,920	19,107	22,123	3,016
			84	4,442	972	1,468	496
			86	62,268	60,821	66,767	5,946
ITALY	A	E	85	1,294	1,193	2,753	1,560
	V	E	81	39,054	22,004	26,819	4,815
			82	73,447	26,087	30,606	4,519
			83	13,059	8,121	9,374	1,253
			84	27,337	12,813	15,191	2,378
			85	358,291	183,496	235,647	52,151
			86	121,517	48,153	56,318	8,165
	V	W	83	529	1,340	1,644	304
			86	17,676	5,310	6,584	1,274
JAMAICA	V	E	82	16,485	11,775	13,349	1,574
			84	5,400	5,928	6,338	410
			86	18	1,321	1,448	127
JAPAN	A	H	81	25	267	466	199
	A	W	85	333	2,402	3,344	942
	N	E	84	1,652	2,222	2,589	367
	V	E	81	9,600	3,448	3,818	370
			82	791	2,412	2,570	158
			83	143	294	311	17
			84	328	785	840	55
			85	2,520	3,840	4,306	466
	V	H	83	107	746	884	138
	V	W	81	730	1,996	2,250	254
			82	556	1,550	1,719	169
			83	190	2,038	2,227	189
			84	936	1,561	1,724	163

Product
TSUSA commodity number, description, and unit of quantity

Country	Mode	Reg	Yr	Quantity	F.A.S.	C.I.F.	Charges
			85	12,069	11,709	13,336	1,627
			86	4,361	7,110	7,422	312
KOR REP	V	E	81	899	534	642	108
			82	3,838	2,576	2,799	223
			85	7,373	4,817	5,787	970
			86	4,509	9,001	9,828	827
	V	W	81	7,284	9,672	10,375	703
			82	2,880	6,620	7,063	443
			83	12,880	13,702	14,703	1,001
			84	1,084	1,121	1,242	121
			85	7,377	6,212	6,754	542
			86	18,704	32,340	34,167	1,827
LEBANON	V	E	84	154	490	560	70
			85	4,021	2,303	2,609	306
LIBERIA	V	E	82	1,550	300	531	231
			83	1,950	500	600	100
MALAWI	O	E	86	15,400	4,189	4,189	
MEXICO	A	E	82	380	741	936	195
			83	60	1,477	1,477	
	O	E	81	46,857	27,324	27,324	
			82	3,218,980	553,393	553,393	
			83	500	500	500	
			84	2,400,450	381,556	381,556	
			85	4,875,000	770,250	770,250	
			86	37,871	23,608	23,608	
	O	W	81	16,339,177	2,200,863	2,200,863	
			82	7,781,110	1,219,351	1,219,351	
			83	1,667,188	270,217	270,217	
			84	23,477,926	3,781,737	3,781,737	
			85	13,293,398	2,224,698	2,224,698	
			86	687,995	329,611	329,611	
	V	E	81	69,842	49,157	53,622	4,465
			84	1,893	1,516	1,728	212
MONGOLA	V	E	85	2,987	1,728	2,074	346
NETHLDS	V	E	82	11,594	12,359	13,743	1,384
			83	5,968	2,700	3,220	520
			85	43,761	31,493	39,253	7,760
			86	12,108	5,653	6,319	666
NICARAG	V	W	82	17,000	7,425	10,503	3,078
			83	30,100	13,300	16,313	3,013
			84	7,500	1,500	2,944	1,444
			85	15,000	3,000	5,451	2,451
NORWAY	V	W	82	5,042	2,289	3,469	1,180
			86	571	1,770	2,372	602
PAKISTN	V	E	81	66,130	28,089	32,521	4,432
PERU	V	E	81	5,134	3,196	3,559	363
			85	2,976	1,485	1,761	276
PHIL R	V	E	81	2,640	1,898	2,122	224
			82	5,081	5,377	5,952	575
			83	284	625	665	40
			84	699	331	386	55
			86	4,093	2,408	2,902	494
	V	H	83	560	280	343	63
			84	513	323	391	68
	V	W	81	22,820	28,667	31,506	2,839
			82	20,630	21,709	23,761	2,052
			83	12,269	14,007	15,452	1,445
			84	22,745	19,212	21,733	2,521
			85	114	2,804	3,140	336
			86	2,095	2,724	2,933	209
PORTUGL	O	E	83	450	600	600	
	V	E	81	33,982	32,794	40,965	8,171
			82	66,942	68,411	85,503	17,092
			83	61,208	76,336	83,062	6,726
			84	98,937	88,726	102,292	13,566
			85	172,848	152,336	177,010	24,674
			86	147,719	153,290	171,242	17,952
REP SAF	V	E	82	1,323	1,288	1,681	393
SALVADR	A	E	83	1,301	1,504	2,233	729
			85	1,527	1,700	2,418	718
			86	5,009	1,050	3,267	2,217
	A	W	84	14,721	7,553	16,239	8,686
			86	795	3,000	3,895	895
	V	E	85	11,706	14,035	15,099	1,064
			86	19,213	10,978	12,713	1,735
	V	W	85	4,257	4,255	4,792	537
			86	5,438	1,258	2,392	1,134
SINGAPR	V	W	84	480	1,310	1,449	139
SPAIN	V	E	81	3,840	3,379	3,585	206
			82	31,429	12,085	16,093	4,008
			83	32,663	16,335	20,233	3,898
			84	25,474	18,062	21,415	3,353
			85	69,058	47,161	52,975	5,814
			86	41,515	24,238	26,091	1,853
SWAZLND	A	E	86	2,149	1,016	2,858	1,842

Product
TSUSA commodity number, description, and unit of quantity

Country	Mode	Reg	Yr	Quantity	F.A.S.	C.I.F.	Charges
SWEDEN	V	E	86	946	1,973	2,168	195
SWITZLD	N	E	81	1,408,824	1,166,857	1,211,035	44,128
			82	1,539,757	1,261,185	1,307,502	46,317
			83	1,509,692	1,227,855	1,283,678	55,823
	V	E	81	18,898	12,387	14,305	1,918
			82	8,568	5,815	7,641	1,826
			83	48,687	38,679	42,012	3,333
			84	1,767,440	1,344,564	1,461,683	117,119
			85	1,608,571	1,100,853	1,221,168	120,315
			86	1,621,377	1,568,163	1,681,635	113,472
	V	W	81	121,586	32,640	34,525	1,885
			82	42,423	35,420	45,147	9,727
			83	200	543	588	45
			84	66,896	49,840	57,455	7,615
			85	133,679	102,134	116,740	14,606
			86	206,002	205,565	223,264	17,699
THAILND	V	E	86	2,511	5,941	6,659	718
	V	W	81	44,092	14,547	16,228	1,681
			82	913	2,337	2,594	257
			83	518	1,406	1,518	112
TOKELAU	V	E	82	47,461	34,869	38,255	3,386
TURKEY	V	E	82	4,387	2,000	2,288	288
U KING	A	E	81	2,897	1,589	4,392	2,803
			82	1,349	1,041	2,169	1,128
			83	441	296	644	348
			84	561	502	882	380
			85	2,646	1,347	3,793	2,446
	A	W	82	402	338	610	272
	N	E	82	33,624	49,142	53,637	4,495
	N	W	81	5,698	4,059	4,978	919
	O	E	84	450	516	568	52
	V	E	81	6,749	4,606	4,996	390
			82	3,207	2,294	2,788	494
			83	15,581	8,771	9,810	1,039
			84	17,293	24,892	28,987	4,095
			85	32,234	27,028	32,052	5,024
			86	59,888	54,847	61,009	6,162
	V	W	82	30	324	368	44
VENEZ	A	E	83	13,423	2,990	4,222	1,232
	O	E	85	17,820	4,420	4,825	405
	V	E	81	22,046	13,473	15,500	2,027
			82	121,958	77,774	83,352	5,578
			83	392,848	113,700	124,188	10,488
			84	66,092	31,829	33,477	1,648
			85	303,058	111,738	119,399	7,661
			86	586,405	172,684	193,810	21,126
YUGOSLV	V	E	81	1,323	2,160	2,427	267

Edible preparations (not specified)

1830500 EDIBLE PREP NSPF NOV5.5% BF (LB)

Country	Mode	Reg	Yr	Quantity	F.A.S.	C.I.F.	Charges
TOTAL			81	84,392,284	66,625,956	72,359,980	5,725,916
			82	90,873,363	70,918,442	77,547,797	6,629,355
			83	180,193,404	111,237,176	120,446,271	9,209,095
			84	391,317,134	179,779,643	191,665,497	11,885,854
ANGOLA	V	E	83	6,789	8,226	11,304	3,078
ARGENT	N	E	83	1,557,775	890,458	972,089	81,631
			84	148,511	89,714	106,784	17,070
	O	E	81	4,020	2,519	2,639	120
			82	1,000	1,450	1,450	
	V	E	81	61,765	67,448	74,020	6,572
			82	938,684	468,721	517,901	49,180
			83	539,611	306,443	332,249	25,806
			84	2,171,690	1,565,867	1,681,683	115,816
	V	W	81	2,850	2,218	2,460	242
			82	1,970	1,413	1,604	191
			83	499,890	305,838	341,484	35,646
			84	1,092,492	969,689	1,045,148	75,459
AUSTRAL	A	E	82	3,703	23,520	27,319	3,799
			83	1,060	1,256	2,673	1,417
			84	400	1,728	2,435	707
	A	W	82	1,199	4,520	6,009	1,489
	N	E	83	26,166	46,543	49,246	2,703
	N	W	82	3,127	3,578	4,640	1,062
			84	981	3,622	4,014	392
	V	E	81	222,951	96,661	114,868	18,207
			82	786,110	311,983	371,571	59,588
			83	1,218,673	430,300	502,157	71,857
			84	1,194,025	663,444	733,149	69,705
	V	H	83	550	1,200	1,300	100
	V	W	81	130,016	48,155	56,026	7,871
			82	547,625	184,636	218,737	34,101
			83	463,285	156,440	186,837	30,397

Product
TSUSA commodity number, description, and unit of quantity

Country	Mode	Reg	Yr	Quantity	F.A.S.	C.I.F.	Charges
			84	107,024	37,200	43,842	6,642
AUSTRIA	A	E	81	750	634	719	85
			83	112	286	404	118
	A	W	83	859	3,302	5,088	1,786
			84	4,860	5,423	7,396	1,973
	N	E	84	11,028	11,223	14,117	2,894
	N	W	82	9,020	8,634	10,230	1,596
			84	80,930	86,151	113,685	27,534
	O	E	82	11	704	704	
			83	701	1,025	1,025	
	O	W	83	2,808	5,697	6,123	426
	V	E	81	21,754	20,026	22,244	2,218
			82	2,464	3,186	3,675	489
			83	3,201	1,112	1,347	235
			84	460,039	437,907	491,700	53,793
	V	W	83	4,651	4,750	5,322	572
			84	70	549	620	71
B VIRGN	V	E	82	540	1,440	1,640	200
BAHAMAS	V	E	82	17,196	11,053	12,490	1,437
BARBADO	A	E	84	385	560	607	47
	V	E	82	1,800	2,020	2,245	225
BELGIUM	A	E	81	1,110	1,865	2,861	996
			82	936	1,198	1,512	314
			84	2,156	2,127	3,144	1,017
	N	E	81	110,190	61,524	71,402	9,878
			82	145,785	75,289	85,471	10,182
			83	325,204	216,299	235,798	19,499
			84	619,010	374,707	415,483	40,776
	N	W	84	5,516	7,673	9,347	1,674
	O	E	81	1,596	864	921	57
			83	8,873,604	1,049,334	1,186,494	137,160
			84	1,932,333	213,994	254,302	40,308
	V	E	81	31,008	28,578	32,867	4,289
			82	2,425	2,062	2,208	146
			83	1,510	920	1,232	312
			84	4,981,320	525,461	565,594	40,133
	V	W	81	13,000	18,029	19,320	1,291
			82	1,250	1,691	1,812	121
			84	1,380	3,845	4,406	561
BRAZIL	A	E	82	2,958	3,678	4,426	748
			83	106	468	491	23
	A	W	83	9,656	20,100	27,654	7,554
	N	E	81	2,652	2,328	3,194	866
			83	53,461	30,259	33,602	3,343
	N	W	83	880	4,100	4,666	566
			84	296,938	1,207,849	1,273,305	65,456
	V	E	81	4,145	2,290	3,708	1,418
			82	164,881	128,047	157,528	29,481
			83	97,806	68,337	76,500	8,163
			84	37,206	36,087	43,572	7,485
	V	W	83	8,988,500	1,379,474	2,028,075	648,601
			84	1,894	1,275	1,796	521
BULGAR	O	W	82	1,848	1,879	1,879	
	V	E	82	12,000	4,804	5,999	1,195
			84	2,205	566	752	186
BURKINA	V	E	84	16,928	9,448	10,514	1,066
C RICA	V	E	81	868,291	598,955	679,859	80,904
			82	2,291,121	708,004	879,668	171,664
			83	1,206,544	685,335	827,218	141,883
			84	2,013,430	898,902	1,088,193	189,291
	V	W	81	207,760	128,584	142,752	14,168
			82	238,138	68,045	89,416	21,371
			83	237,420	52,802	71,629	18,827
			84	1,588,929	287,183	417,764	130,581
CANADA	A	E	81	5,911	10,346	11,721	1,375
			82	3,143	7,365	10,623	3,258
			83	74	960	1,135	175
			84	2,292	4,799	5,448	649
	A	H	81	230	1,321	1,486	165
			82	124	379	442	63
			83	246	793	959	166
			84	32,386	25,362	35,147	9,785
	A	W	81	1,354	5,160	6,002	842
			82	7,886	6,950	8,010	1,060
			84	1,020	670	1,237	567
	N	E	81	4,697,446	6,738,200	6,744,645	6,403
			82	3,826,423	2,835,551	2,843,970	8,419
			83	10,906,174	10,239,404	10,239,778	374
			84	149,103,528	34,690,456	34,702,354	11,898
	N	W	81	45,170	66,926	71,164	4,238
			83	6,223,702	1,558,737	1,559,338	601
			84	1,753,766	786,731	790,446	3,715
	O	E	81	5,759,261	2,215,440	2,223,821	2,847
			82	6,217,810	3,171,029	3,172,234	1,205
			83	40,531,020	11,635,312	11,658,406	23,094

Product
TSUSA commodity number, description, and unit of quantity

Country	Mode	Reg	Yr	Quantity	F.A.S.	C.I.F.	Charges
			84	96,643,023	11,709,033	11,711,706	2,673
	O	W	81	962,555	625,576	625,945	286
			82	782,825	708,368	711,592	3,224
			83	60,418	78,413	79,588	1,175
			84	235,628	231,648	231,648	
	V	E	82	390	1,025	1,126	101
			84	74,087	10,580	10,580	
CHILE	A	E	84	481	650	1,117	467
	O	E	84	1,539	1,528	1,528	
	O	W	83	1,632	6,336	6,336	
	V	E	82	4,298	7,915	8,280	365
			84	2,294	1,851	2,111	260
	V	W	83	752	976	1,088	112
			84	37,669	66,637	75,036	8,399
CHINA M	N	E	82	343,509	322,628	354,029	31,401
			83	360,220	422,240	460,036	37,796
			84	367,254	386,645	442,804	56,159
	N	H	81	32,151	37,544	40,307	2,763
	N	W	82	304,028	243,783	267,906	24,123
			83	285,154	262,888	289,662	26,774
			84	453,417	436,203	471,722	35,519
	O	E	83	2,175	4,065	4,432	367
			84	5,328	4,918	4,963	45
	O	W	81	500	536	580	44
			83	528	421	440	19
	V	E	81	492,605	603,628	654,763	51,135
			82	7,904	10,624	12,207	1,583
			83	6,075	13,109	14,311	1,202
			84	20,200	21,552	25,356	3,804
	V	H	82	46,124	38,387	41,600	3,213
			83	7,491	10,184	11,141	957
			84	15,368	18,367	20,044	1,677
	V	W	81	725,607	475,307	520,672	45,365
			82	150,277	224,365	238,712	14,347
			83	273,236	266,356	287,444	21,088
			84	78,738	69,805	76,201	6,396
CHINA T	A	E	82	1,322	12,370	15,421	3,051
			84	440	3,800	3,975	175
	N	E	82	1,528,015	1,281,510	1,482,448	200,938
			84	45,329	62,268	69,819	7,551
	N	H	81	291,571	192,435	214,967	22,532
			82	31,559	15,283	25,047	9,764
	N	W	81	2,211,502	1,734,906	1,913,117	178,211
			82	4,321,585	3,386,743	3,742,008	355,265
			83	2,583,767	2,331,786	2,527,769	195,983
			84	4,820,807	3,480,474	3,886,435	405,961
	O	E	81	4,830	3,950	4,268	318
			83	1,000	593	593	
			84	9,301	10,358	10,602	244
	O	W	82	780	1,263	1,319	56
	V	E	81	1,921,429	1,572,591	1,801,567	228,976
			82	220,251	191,283	224,316	33,033
			83	2,079,985	1,696,593	1,976,370	279,777
			84	2,297,943	1,728,601	2,072,419	343,818
	V	H	82	431,293	326,328	390,574	64,246
			83	738,302	568,695	675,062	106,367
			84	438,780	354,103	438,797	84,694
	V	W	81	2,066,297	1,452,684	1,630,692	178,000
			82	471,758	499,241	545,691	46,450
			83	2,356,715	1,718,385	1,930,645	212,260
			84	990,449	719,348	833,727	114,379
COLOMB	A	E	84	62,776	249,758	267,401	17,643
	N	E	82	29,194	19,200	21,306	2,106
			84	365,048	397,309	437,452	40,143
	O	E	83	878	1,216	1,216	
	V	E	81	374,451	320,284	354,085	33,801
			82	409,812	616,353	664,714	48,361
			83	388,399	409,356	457,106	47,750
			84	65,575	390,513	402,926	12,413
	V	W	82	919	8,173	9,421	1,248
CYPRUS	V	E	81	33,200	16,757	20,314	3,557
			82	2,375	4,020	4,577	557
			83	2,596	6,036	6,813	777
			84	1,742	4,721	5,272	551
DENMARK	A	E	83	2,654	4,875	7,206	2,331
			84	220	300	340	40
	A	W	84	616	687	1,609	922
	N	E	81	25,265	100,513	107,683	7,170
			82	123,495	262,047	278,077	16,030
			83	12,589	35,460	36,924	1,464
			84	26,014	77,278	79,988	2,710
	N	W	83	13,748	17,719	19,298	1,579
			84	3,169	4,464	5,307	843
	O	E	81	66,358	31,241	34,273	3,032
			84	27,558	92,300	94,486	2,186

Product
TSUSA commodity number, description, and unit of quantity

Country	Mode	Reg	Yr	Quantity	F.A.S.	C.I.F.	Charges
	V E		81	286	622	695	73
			82	18,500	56,740	58,297	1,557
			83	170,145	293,343	309,148	15,805
			84	84,171	158,064	171,031	12,967
	V W		81	1,533	2,818	3,204	386
			82	4,389	4,355	4,935	580
			83	24,313	30,947	39,683	8,736
			84	20,309	22,665	25,819	3,154
DOM REP	A E		81	743	300	412	112
			82	1,625	1,219	1,458	239
			83	1,176	290	446	156
	N E		81	2,790,321	1,273,395	1,402,287	128,892
			82	188,150	134,081	140,394	6,313
			83	13,754,650	5,113,633	5,670,986	557,353
			84	1,092,725	426,317	471,044	44,727
	V E		81	19,381,065	5,935,331	6,728,065	792,734
			82	20,935,262	7,639,404	8,527,197	887,793
			83	2,380,187	1,328,587	1,446,062	117,475
			84	15,758,601	6,153,722	6,786,940	633,218
	V W		81	108,192	45,940	58,272	12,332
			82	40,572	22,138	25,240	3,102
			83	6,750	5,665	6,207	542
ECUADOR	V E		82	2,558	1,000	1,210	210
			83	1,999	500	670	170
			84	11,446	7,280	8,216	936
EGYPT	O E		84	770	1,834	1,834	
	V E		83	41,111	16,800	19,403	2,603
			84	11,746	4,800	5,211	411
F W IND	V E		82	110	410	438	28
FIJI	N H		81	2,977	5,616	6,185	569
			82	8,253	22,919	26,951	4,032
	V H		84	5,189	4,785	5,244	459
	V W		81	2,206	2,034	2,220	186
			82	7,018	2,921	3,567	646
			83	754	738	826	88
FINLAND	A E		81	330	981	1,027	46
	O E		84	1,250	1,972	1,972	
FR GERM	A E		81	12,579	30,961	37,790	6,829
			82	1,491	4,426	5,500	1,074
			83	521	3,081	3,130	49
			84	7,487	55,905	61,022	5,117
	A W		81	8,267	22,785	27,468	4,683
			84	238	283	548	265
	N E		81	915,787	1,264,230	1,355,338	91,108
			82	1,212,382	1,637,839	1,755,215	117,376
			83	1,402,598	1,686,548	1,810,333	123,785
			84	2,207,060	1,978,426	2,158,153	179,727
	N W		82	3,401	2,735	3,501	766
			84	211,504	93,854	109,185	15,331
	O E		81	3,177	12,952	12,990	38
			82	5,140	17,499	17,499	
			83	21,099	46,500	49,698	3,198
			84	34,016	18,556	19,796	1,240
	O W		81	1,162	1,250	1,250	
			82	3,010	8,259	8,259	
			83	12,043	15,806	16,405	599
			84	9,428	6,348	6,348	
	V E		81	105,865	133,900	142,282	8,382
			82	228,788	250,977	282,122	31,145
			83	641,915	466,465	507,535	41,070
			84	585,702	365,702	408,937	43,235
	V H		82	1,045	1,157	1,348	191
	V W		81	139,155	241,430	259,693	18,263
			82	120,538	131,760	145,455	13,695
			83	137,954	137,412	148,996	11,584
			84	20,382	25,071	29,387	4,316
FRANCE	A E		81	1,625	3,803	5,723	1,920
			82	5,046	10,115	13,600	3,485
			83	5,662	17,292	22,867	5,575
			84	3,806	2,007	3,337	1,330
	A W		82	31	266	307	41
			84	35	264	480	216
	N E		81	557,005	645,512	706,226	60,714
			82	452,668	523,201	585,120	61,919
			83	441,614	427,489	491,605	64,116
			84	753,382	666,155	737,739	71,584
	N W		81	6,934	18,914	20,310	1,396
			82	86,609	167,034	183,267	16,233
			83	68,988	89,323	108,390	19,067
			84	82,381	87,843	116,067	28,224
	O E		81	3,519	6,335	6,785	450
			82	4,296	7,015	7,515	500
			83	281,553	30,669	35,527	4,858
			84	45	529	529	
	V E		81	13,557	28,048	29,709	1,661

Product
TSUSA commodity number, description, and unit of quantity

Country	Mode	Reg	Yr	Quantity	F.A.S.	C.I.F.	Charges
			82	21,268	70,935	74,689	3,754
			83	183,882	100,387	108,452	8,065
			84	709,690	222,796	244,113	21,317
	V H		83	263	354	472	118
	V W		81	16,493	25,208	26,573	1,365
			83	634	1,284	1,384	100
			84	6,323	8,833	9,829	996
G BISAU	V E		81	402	1,315	1,454	139
GERM DR	V E		81	1,197	1,824	2,220	396
GHANA	V E		82	5,079	3,494	6,412	2,918
GIBRAT	A E		83	1,212	468	608	140
GREECE	N E		82	848,442	678,421	754,332	75,911
			83	1,108,822	756,356	860,499	104,143
	O E		81	17,926	2,363	2,363	
			82	7,645	5,174	5,174	
			83	18,678	13,054	13,054	
			84	9,570	6,474	6,474	
	V E		81	1,096,950	824,522	928,390	103,868
			82	49,940	42,034	45,233	3,199
			83	48,583	39,531	45,299	5,768
			84	1,330,284	874,826	1,004,475	129,649
	V W		81	24,720	19,490	23,715	4,225
			82	38,019	48,148	54,479	6,331
			83	19,535	23,128	25,094	1,966
			84	37,917	35,355	39,007	3,652
GUATMAL	A E		82	1,868	675	1,249	574
			84	1,219	891	1,936	1,045
	A W		81	6,455	2,013	3,632	1,619
			82	1,348	1,253	1,823	570
			83	6,471	5,418	8,105	2,687
			84	3,480	2,957	4,167	1,210
	N W		82	6,617	7,795	9,882	2,087
			83	40,783	47,138	56,343	9,205
	O E		84	1,166,356	86,193	89,108	2,915
	V E		81	33,450	55,952	58,520	2,568
			83	190	392	405	13
			84	2,092,338	161,189	169,335	8,146
	V W		83	5,964	4,788	5,870	1,082
			84	8,521	11,885	13,480	1,595
HAITI	A E		83	432	1,188	1,514	326
			84	200	624	746	122
	V E		83	5,779	8,607	9,617	1,010
HG KONG	N E		81	71,335	72,101	78,534	6,433
			84	129,860	146,202	166,165	19,963
	N W		81	747,901	1,896,681	2,026,639	129,958
			83	378,847	823,150	882,786	59,636
			84	285,522	642,534	678,047	35,513
	O E		83	3,680	4,302	4,688	386
			84	4,436	4,001	4,603	602
	O W		84	5,732	6,266	6,935	669
	V E		81	365,265	305,499	357,815	52,316
			82	390,599	414,224	476,655	62,431
			83	595,426	470,374	550,281	79,907
			84	461,197	424,447	495,514	71,067
	V H		81	101,006	60,431	68,836	8,405
			82	199,145	168,315	194,069	25,754
			83	237,775	145,941	176,554	30,613
			84	172,362	102,862	122,140	19,278
	V W		81	334,679	259,544	295,221	35,677
			82	918,219	1,363,438	1,487,262	123,824
			83	845,988	585,896	657,603	71,707
			84	555,673	424,730	469,877	45,147
HONDURA	V E		84	1,950	1,170	1,479	309
HUNGARY	V E		83	60,252	19,630	24,285	4,655
INDIA	N E		81	3,589	3,513	3,917	404
			82	10,534	12,692	13,993	1,301
			83	45,942	36,483	41,003	4,520
			84	393,266	357,857	404,019	46,162
	N W		84	7,750	4,845	5,295	450
	O E		81	24,093	16,906	20,460	3,554
			82	247	330	330	
			83	3,346	8,138	8,428	290
			84	25,738	23,366	24,908	1,542
	V E		81	413,779	380,679	461,718	81,039
			82	234,718	220,036	261,109	41,073
			83	382,704	336,955	387,134	50,179
			84	158,716	127,020	144,683	17,663
	V W		81	188,475	156,711	193,379	36,668
			82	225,010	177,335	210,870	33,535
			83	136,377	112,110	134,805	22,695
			84	200,370	121,741	145,919	24,178
INDNSIA	V W		81	413	906	1,085	179
			82	17,130	30,041	34,382	4,341
			83	33,252	49,240	55,241	6,001
			84	2,401	2,813	3,151	338

Product
TSUSA commodity number, description, and unit of quantity

Country	Mode	Reg	Yr	Quantity	F.A.S.	C.I.F.	Charges
IRAN	V	E	82	450	499	538	39
IRELAND	A	E	81	84	409	619	210
			82	765	1,530	2,934	1,404
	N	E	81	291,729	249,977	275,251	25,274
	O	E	81	862,662	409,327	448,605	39,278
			82	6	328	389	61
			83	827	3,225	3,225	
			84	17,880	58,080	63,380	5,300
	O	W	81	13	480	502	22
	V	E	81	440,332	197,219	218,049	20,830
			82	137,613	155,737	171,001	15,264
			83	31,081	34,684	37,877	3,193
			84	1,146,551	1,307,647	1,488,180	180,533
	V	W	81	4,088	4,761	5,939	1,178
ISRAEL	A	E	83	1,987	1,196	2,124	928
	N	E	83	353,433	340,507	388,378	47,871
			84	320,725	362,558	406,165	43,607
	O	E	81	12,406	11,204	11,204	
			84	3,164	2,188	2,188	
	V	E	81	403,610	374,568	418,451	43,883
			82	342,240	448,793	485,397	36,604
			83	77,368	97,788	104,681	6,893
			84	32,058	80,002	85,963	5,961
	V	W	82	45,844	11,113	14,185	3,072
			83	4,662	5,382	5,763	381
			84	27,959	16,271	27,544	11,273
ITALY	A	E	81	1,293	2,759	3,710	951
			82	17,220	28,807	40,165	11,358
			83	35,469	48,004	72,474	24,470
			84	3,074	3,755	6,288	2,533
	A	W	82	510	1,223	1,988	765
			84	4,594	5,869	8,244	2,375
	N	E	81	681,971	610,355	674,907	64,552
			82	1,341,447	929,760	1,036,734	106,974
			83	1,625,559	1,776,966	1,978,072	201,106
			84	3,379,700	3,516,245	3,853,009	336,764
	N	W	83	250,100	299,945	334,760	34,815
			84	283,900	399,391	450,110	50,719
	O	E	82	50	261	261	
			83	4,630	5,898	5,898	
			84	722	3,017	3,017	
	O	W	81	132	659	675	16
	V	E	81	20,944	85,656	87,511	1,855
			82	196,159	273,869	297,800	23,931
			83	468,721	479,322	520,362	41,040
			84	302,382	401,785	461,412	59,627
	V	W	81	6,949	13,993	16,306	2,313
			82	114,275	108,863	119,404	10,541
			83	3,882	55,208	57,217	2,009
			84	7,465	17,319	18,266	947
IVY CST	V	E	82	31,746	13,219	17,920	4,701
			84	37,807	19,397	23,164	3,767
JAMAICA	A	E	84	1,141	786	2,800	2,014
	N	E	81	132,289	204,124	219,534	15,410
			82	41,856	69,672	75,521	5,849
			83	5,876	17,404	18,586	1,182
			84	29,416	42,185	45,394	3,209
	O	E	81	5,985	4,039	4,039	
			84	1,306	1,156	1,156	
	V	E	83	157,587	230,010	241,329	11,319
			84	44,033	24,817	27,813	2,996
	V	W	84	3,684	2,021	2,709	688
JAPAN	A	E	81	3,014	13,950	21,878	7,928
			82	3,763	21,288	31,128	9,840
			83	-579	725	3,022	2,297
			84	1,118	5,191	8,813	3,622
	A	W	81	4,786	8,089	8,688	599
			82	2,669	3,408	3,408	
			83	4,209	8,206	12,081	3,875
			84	433	3,087	3,992	905
	N	E	81	2,058,303	2,336,721	2,626,150	289,429
			82	4,943,737	6,763,337	7,315,367	552,030
			83	1,646,769	1,771,332	2,072,914	301,582
			84	2,225,688	2,953,398	3,312,898	359,500
	N	H	81	1,232,038	1,560,502	1,833,568	273,066
			82	1,409,684	1,738,247	2,041,499	303,252
			83	1,378,298	1,835,036	2,142,227	307,191
			84	1,296,556	1,648,207	1,934,505	286,298
	N	W	81	4,837,437	6,307,787	6,794,469	486,618
			82	7,796,008	10,758,454	11,430,407	671,953
			83	16,305,910	22,557,393	24,065,767	1,508,374
			84	23,987,119	36,338,796	38,379,839	2,041,043
	O	E	81	68,550	128,020	135,025	7,005
			82	5,389	11,240	12,266	1,026
			83	25,579	28,340	32,612	4,272

Product
TSUSA commodity number, description, and unit of quantity

Country	Mode	Reg	Yr	Quantity	F.A.S.	C.I.F.	Charges
			84	20,565	38,802	41,682	2,880
	O	H	81	1,714	2,224	2,533	309
			82	1,423	1,798	2,131	333
			83	1,163	1,302	1,608	306
			84	37,884	10,982	15,267	4,285
	O	W	83	1,481	2,863	3,049	186
	V	E	81	1,867,702	2,960,711	3,185,335	224,624
			82	528,966	486,709	553,944	67,235
			83	4,791,326	6,950,650	7,450,983	500,333
			84	16,947,230	25,062,904	26,746,277	1,683,373
	V	H	83	3,728	2,041	2,432	391
			84	3,581	4,715	5,420	705
	V	W	81	846,495	846,730	955,860	109,130
			82	588,310	782,846	857,707	74,861
			83	794,120	1,110,143	1,220,951	110,808
			84	1,184,575	1,746,081	1,891,749	145,668
KENYA	A	E	82	21,605	65,387	66,150	763
			83	2,205	26,933	33,631	6,698
			84	400	4,850	5,944	1,094
	N	E	84	7,991	7,626	10,328	2,702
	O	E	81	264	809	900	91
KOR REP	A	E	81	4,204	32,441	40,076	7,635
	A	W	82	331	810	1,277	467
	N	E	84	692,978	449,507	549,136	99,629
	N	H	81	623,951	303,712	399,871	96,159
	N	W	84	1,492,470	973,455	1,112,523	139,068
	O	E	81	7,182	2,855	3,500	645
			83	800	1,587	1,587	
	V	E	81	581,036	402,794	468,866	66,072
			82	951,043	830,882	937,467	106,585
			83	1,089,315	641,928	786,214	144,286
			84	1,058,363	897,581	1,048,016	150,435
	V	H	82	942,222	440,503	595,328	154,825
			83	927,286	436,614	609,222	172,608
			84	1,087,078	485,381	709,359	223,978
	V	W	81	1,447,742	768,687	881,238	112,551
			82	3,137,959	1,454,509	1,697,685	243,176
			83	3,123,220	1,634,568	1,881,436	246,868
			84	2,701,662	1,274,896	1,516,598	241,702
LEBANON	N	E	84	235,060	202,947	222,223	19,276
	O	E	81	12,036	8,894	10,115	1,221
			82	780	640	640	
			83	5,024	3,732	3,732	
			84	990	760	760	
	V	E	81	121,340	86,007	95,973	9,966
			82	42,831	29,381	32,403	3,022
			83	176,797	184,384	196,394	12,010
			84	80,280	41,707	45,492	3,785
	V	W	82	8,730	7,104	8,266	1,162
MACAO	V	E	83	3,000	2,289	2,706	417
			84	630	1,025	1,092	67
	V	W	81	197	253	285	32
			82	788	1,086	1,228	142
			83	394	511	537	26
			84	1,476	2,829	3,057	228
MALAWI	O	E	84	1,071	1,955	2,143	188
MALAYSA	V	E	81	12,687	9,021	10,800	1,779
			82	3,533	2,794	2,918	124
			83	25,190	30,035	31,736	1,701
			84	9,563	9,007	9,993	986
	V	H	82	212	269	288	19
	V	W	81	27,390	12,467	16,100	3,633
			82	75,125	39,181	45,533	6,352
			83	48,477	22,851	30,691	7,840
			84	56,414	26,960	32,599	5,639
MEXICO	A	E	81	6,614	32,550	35,576	3,026
			82	2,716	1,720	3,130	1,410
			83	39,600	194,520	204,874	10,354
			84	92,581	446,837	469,438	22,601
	A	W	81	29,317	182,148	190,202	8,054
			82	5,671	24,721	27,997	3,276
	N	E	81	5,964,810	3,207,680	3,213,444	5,764
			82	9,597	62,357	71,642	9,285
			84	90,437	414,750	430,663	15,913
	N	W	81	354,197	975,539	1,041,556	66,017
			82	97,474	230,169	240,317	10,148
			83	55,697	27,883	29,255	1,372
			84	106,211	62,872	65,072	2,200
	O	E	81	334,515	175,491	177,248	1,757
			82	3,008,582	1,181,060	1,181,117	57
			83	1,093,583	906,473	932,161	25,688
			84	864,364	544,090	544,108	18
	O	W	81	1,400,089	1,670,047	1,670,047	
			82	2,084,860	1,785,933	1,785,933	
			83	4,354,411	3,847,773	3,847,773	

Product
TSUSA commodity number, description, and unit of quantity

Country	Mode	Reg	Yr	Quantity	F.A.S.	C.I.F.	Charges
			84	5,466,209	5,014,880	5,014,882	2
	V	E	82	4,938	2,681	2,914	233
			83	2,205	16,582	17,424	842
			84	1,013	1,075	1,139	64
	V	W	81	15,432	55,860	61,068	5,208
MOROC	O	E	81	1,590	1,062	1,062	
	V	E	84	22,417	34,705	37,512	2,807
N ANTIL	V	E	83	668	330	396	66
N ZEAL	A	W	83	22	450	581	131
			84	198	677	826	149
	N	H	84	5,308	4,871	5,907	1,036
	V	E	84	12,604	7,409	8,823	1,414
	V	H	81	11,265	6,886	9,397	2,511
			82	6,586	4,267	5,376	1,109
			83	5,292	3,605	4,320	715
	V	W	84	12,346	7,506	8,642	1,136
NETHLDS	A	E	81	3,823	2,946	5,545	2,599
			82	536	1,005	1,376	371
			83	750	559	1,304	745
			84	1,058	1,256	1,870	614
	N	E	81	30,602	30,413	34,916	4,503
			82	394,167	369,410	431,624	62,214
			83	609,011	416,337	455,051	38,714
			84	1,204,927	671,664	767,780	96,116
	N	W	83	39,585	41,637	44,838	3,201
			84	75,622	59,113	68,221	9,108
	O	E	81	1,156	1,675	1,842	167
			82	1,041	1,024	1,024	
			83	3,273,516	364,883	421,731	56,848
			84	30,256	12,799	14,039	1,240
	V	E	81	15,993	13,334	14,649	1,315
			82	39,666	37,829	41,068	3,239
			83	135,160	77,814	87,359	9,545
			84	446,874	212,097	246,836	34,739
	V	W	81	34,957	58,816	62,171	3,355
			82	14,427	11,072	12,452	1,380
			83	744	1,111	1,140	29
NORWAY	N	E	84	18,529	12,925	15,688	2,763
	N	W	81	2,646	2,806	4,199	1,393
			83	540	1,411	1,651	240
	O	E	83	14,554	14,538	15,671	1,133
			84	30,856	29,463	32,835	3,372
	V	E	81	3,383	8,783	9,666	883
			82	34,664	36,703	39,529	2,826
			83	22,487	22,562	23,860	1,298
	V	W	82	4,008	4,257	4,701	444
			83	8,399	7,265	9,701	2,436
PAKISTN	N	E	82	2,058	4,367	4,726	359
	V	E	81	1,378	1,334	1,705	371
			83	10,500	10,563	11,663	1,100
			84	12,598	9,810	13,234	3,424
	V	W	81	99	1,800	2,496	696
			82	5,817	5,049	6,023	974
			84	3,681	4,120	4,986	866
PANAMA	V	E	81	224,698	193,898	212,588	18,690
			82	390,970	545,641	570,725	25,084
			83	267,335	342,943	361,407	18,464
			84	115,599	108,955	122,843	13,888
PERU	A	E	83	749	4,028	5,121	1,093
			84	440	3,440	4,123	683
	A	W	84	3,636	23,040	26,040	3,000
	O	E	84	4,500	1,788	1,788	
	V	E	82	24,576	20,400	22,232	1,832
			84	53,152	206,152	218,804	12,652
	V	W	81	1,656	4,062	4,229	167
PHIL R	A	W	83	666	579	671	92
	N	E	82	238,060	200,970	229,358	28,388
	N	W	81	644,860	480,640	542,756	62,106
			83	78,883	56,074	66,052	9,978
	O	E	81	12,840	8,381	8,381	
			84	40,000	7,600	7,600	
	V	E	81	287,682	234,371	263,144	28,753
			82	57,426	41,458	48,441	6,983
			83	274,187	216,244	248,496	32,252
			84	382,758	273,301	327,405	54,104
	V	H	81	73,339	52,300	61,230	8,930
			82	233,684	176,488	205,481	28,993
			83	192,102	141,732	165,470	23,738
			84	138,598	107,010	129,818	22,808
	V	W	81	607,760	539,336	604,729	65,393
			82	1,779,833	1,365,951	1,545,192	179,241
			83	1,767,126	1,254,111	1,410,031	155,920
			84	2,370,113	1,524,025	1,763,115	239,090
POLAND	V	E	81	44,180	3,905	4,459	554
			83	12,176	4,624	5,643	1,019
			84	4,352	10,472	10,912	440
PORTUGL	V	E	81	14,981	28,049	33,129	5,080
			82	60,779	51,375	58,280	6,905
			83	68,304	31,362	36,119	4,757
			84	127,320	102,708	116,777	14,069
	V	W	81	678	2,475	3,132	657
			84	267	410	696	286
REP SAF	A	E	81	397	587	1,663	1,076
			82	265	342	735	393
			83	406	764	1,371	607
	A	W	82	13,278	27,863	37,671	9,808
	O	E	83	481	275	395	120
	V	E	81	181,931	209,815	236,356	26,541
			82	91,436	108,950	119,110	10,160
			83	49,567	36,047	52,056	16,009
			84	58,422	39,975	56,475	16,500
	V	W	81	6,700	9,516	10,716	1,200
			82	9,260	11,022	14,059	3,037
			84	4,475	2,791	4,345	1,554
ROMANIA	V	E	82	41,876	21,259	22,614	1,355
			84	10,646	6,180	6,772	592
S ARAB	A	E	84	264	531	831	300
SALVADR	A	E	81	485	702	1,058	356
			82	10,079	7,488	9,996	2,508
			84	3,000	1,500	2,599	1,099
	A	W	83	1,074	831	1,948	1,117
			84	3,664	3,720	6,932	3,212
	N	W	84	27,222	22,162	27,945	5,783
	V	E	84	2,730	1,839	2,069	230
	V	W	81	1,727	1,126	1,665	539
			82	7,413	5,808	7,408	1,600
			83	12,038	10,483	13,654	3,171
SIER LN	V	E	81	460	1,080	1,199	119
SINGAPR	O	E	81	10,193	5,738	6,082	344
			83	315	392	428	36
	O	W	81	1,110	1,255	1,255	
			83	210	926	926	
	V	E	81	3,695	2,635	2,980	345
			82	80,286	38,481	43,306	4,825
			83	3,128	2,692	3,585	893
			84	25,066	14,024	18,422	4,398
	V	H	82	2,108	1,973	2,198	225
	V	W	81	274,934	166,238	183,505	17,267
			82	230,697	136,683	153,255	16,572
			83	258,832	124,852	141,144	16,292
			84	149,179	83,948	97,521	13,573
SPAIN	A	E	83	689	1,800	2,696	896
			84	2,310	1,370	3,460	2,090
	N	E	82	1,321,819	1,164,917	1,358,587	193,670
	N	W	84	41,212	18,247	26,755	8,508
	O	E	81	910	909	909	
			82	423	1,564	1,564	
			84	500	681	681	
	V	E	81	1,805,309	1,826,842	2,103,009	276,170
			82	561,022	622,533	725,150	102,617
			83	2,578,836	1,568,160	1,916,338	348,178
			84	3,781,752	2,092,990	2,567,366	474,376
	V	W	81	6,234	8,104	9,316	1,212
			82	10,067	11,934	13,520	1,586
			83	22,452	20,426	23,913	3,487
SRI LKA	V	W	82	8,143	7,630	8,980	1,350
SURINAM	O	E	83	184	259	259	
SWAZLND	O	E	84	718,477	126,938	126,938	
	V	W	84	18,783	11,398	13,551	2,153
SWEDEN	A	E	81	264	1,469	1,787	318
			82	1,697	1,743	2,840	1,097
			83	176	534	815	281
			84	750	533	548	15
	N	E	82	38,384	40,814	45,722	4,908
			83	182,718	156,824	178,240	21,416
			84	121,575	126,237	138,371	12,134
	N	W	81	417,704	405,607	469,436	63,829
			84	333,426	322,058	360,964	38,906
	O	E	83	18,783	13,188	14,713	1,525
	O	W	84	26,473	28,453	32,207	3,754
	V	E	81	638,262	498,523	551,067	52,544
			82	34,722	37,937	42,904	4,967
			83	190,310	205,524	254,455	48,931
			84	153,223	185,218	224,363	39,145
	V	W	81	23,725	26,894	31,658	4,764
			82	251,354	250,577	288,327	37,750
			83	375,032	359,372	407,898	48,526
			84	63,777	49,170	58,570	9,400
SWITZLD	A	E	81	105	317	449	132
			82	1,993	5,156	7,817	2,661

Product TSUSA commodity number, description, and unit of quantity Country	Mode	Reg	Yr	Quantity	F.A.S.	C.I.F.	Charges
			83	55	303	355	52
			84	2,305	5,161	6,658	1,497
	A	W	82	19	1,133	1,245	112
			84	1,455	4,357	5,560	1,203
	N	E	81	515,672	1,087,393	1,138,803	51,189
			82	524,806	958,608	1,014,277	55,669
			83	1,334,588	1,480,292	1,568,460	88,168
			84	1,010,139	1,809,038	1,928,329	119,291
	N	W	81	234,736	392,041	421,843	29,802
			83	346,827	506,276	540,623	34,347
			84	406,371	687,614	744,530	56,916
	O	E	81	51,681	46,987	53,171	6,184
			82	128,962	124,714	135,314	10,600
			83	153,979	167,671	177,694	10,023
			84	143,062	147,948	158,889	10,941
	V	E	81	496,228	659,282	697,482	38,200
			82	796,585	942,983	1,018,340	75,357
			83	1,172,177	1,187,879	1,310,432	122,553
			84	1,096,722	1,202,097	1,306,048	103,951
	V	H	84	240	734	826	92
	V	W	81	32,322	51,398	56,859	3,330
			82	193,539	298,068	318,978	20,910
			83	24,113	33,356	35,268	1,912
			84	174,757	238,274	256,570	18,296
SYRIA	O	E	81	127	303	303	
			82	420	480	480	
	V	E	81	20,116	15,154	16,682	1,528
			82	6,944	3,674	3,997	323
			83	46,521	43,733	46,417	2,684
			84	1,609	6,490	6,867	377
THAILND	N	E	81	12,129	15,362	16,655	1,293
			83	6,338	4,977	5,688	711
			84	1,039,716	862,982	963,469	100,487
	N	H	84	123,997	88,866	102,067	13,201
	N	W	82	4,926	25,876	28,638	2,762
			84	3,238,153	1,783,595	1,951,402	167,807
	O	E	82	7,496	5,000	5,500	500
			84	1,200	408	408	
	O	W	83	9,612	6,350	6,731	381
			84	13,596	9,835	10,740	905
	V	E	81	540,132	453,129	501,923	48,794
			82	620,891	470,726	527,927	57,201
			83	591,696	535,713	600,078	64,365
			84	166,193	95,495	108,228	12,733
	V	H	81	27,750	27,974	30,955	2,981
			82	46,891	44,331	51,967	7,636
			83	76,671	61,549	71,102	9,553
			84	2,099	1,428	1,603	175
	V	W	81	2,092,623	1,687,895	1,838,841	150,946
			82	2,608,379	1,906,328	2,110,626	204,298
			83	4,320,411	3,083,539	3,325,487	241,948
			84	2,283,614	1,565,589	1,717,589	152,000
TONGA	N	H	82	376	1,241	1,557	316
TRINID	A	E	82	286	610	914	304
			84	250	379	489	110
	V	E	81	405,096	228,157	268,117	39,960
			82	219,007	153,364	181,537	28,173
TUNISIA	V	W	82	1,058	1,320	1,430	110
TURKEY	O	E	81	127	346	363	17
			84	770	889	889	
	V	E	81	2,423	1,514	1,804	290
			82	3,466	4,023	5,569	1,546
			83	47,329	36,597	42,972	6,375
			84	1,501	1,035	1,154	119
	V	W	84	16,535	11,475	13,349	1,874
U KING	A	E	81	118,181	808,861	879,044	70,177
			82	12,285	12,423	14,690	2,267
			83	12,724	8,493	14,264	5,771
			84	6,079	4,608	7,342	2,734
	A	W	81	107	756	888	132
			83	1,254	2,556	3,393	837
	N	E	81	344,258	546,142	597,586	51,444
			82	584,904	1,303,849	1,426,550	122,701
			83	800,772	1,186,989	1,374,348	187,359
			84	1,181,159	1,549,200	1,687,465	138,265
	N	W	81	45,689	52,166	58,313	6,147
			82	19,567	24,729	27,763	3,034
			83	663,344	299,354	324,319	24,965
			84	281,757	251,066	282,825	31,759
	O	E	81	58,107	49,658	53,663	4,005
			82	3,539	6,342	6,877	535
			83	6,267,310	846,798	944,950	98,152
			84	82,130	111,545	115,508	3,963
	O	W	84	72,669	80,443	89,380	8,937
	V	E	81	193,270	182,363	201,085	18,722

Product TSUSA commodity number, description, and unit of quantity Country	Mode	Reg	Yr	Quantity	F.A.S.	C.I.F.	Charges
			82	45,719	50,540	56,232	5,692
			83	64,260	58,876	64,148	5,272
			84	150,729	108,696	125,414	16,718
	V	H	81	456	691	738	47
			82	1,422	3,098	3,341	243
			83	615	1,757	1,896	139
			84	1,092	1,522	1,690	168
	V	W	81	929	999	1,142	143
			82	104,357	138,222	151,131	12,909
			83	5,178	6,010	6,762	752
			84	3,987	3,728	4,960	1,232
URUGUAY	A	E	81	48	864	1,049	185
USSR	O	E	81	8,107	3,343	3,851	508
			82	13,889	4,554	5,416	862
	V	E	81	22,928	10,704	11,670	966
VENEZ	A	E	81	5,168	3,644	8,044	4,400
			82	551	571	852	281
			83	30,332	9,846	16,703	6,857
W SAMOA	A	H	81	8,214	7,603	9,117	1,514
			82	20,108	10,290	14,506	4,216
	A	W	81	1,991	2,205	2,777	572
			82	620	1,425	1,984	559
	N	H	82	53,445	37,262	44,626	7,364
	V	H	83	81,210	51,121	55,632	4,511
			84	53,513	42,462	45,469	3,007
	V	W	82	14,854	11,452	12,862	1,410
			83	109,803	83,655	92,722	9,067
			84	114,080	57,806	64,230	6,424
YUGOSLV	O	W	81	2,075	1,673	1,673	
			82	4,115	4,061	4,061	
			83	1,642	1,077	1,077	
			84	1,650	1,880	1,880	
	V	E	81	111,839	116,468	128,919	12,451
			82	126,956	97,469	104,790	7,321
			83	117,458	121,348	138,409	17,061
			84	151,830	153,907	169,457	15,550

Grass jelly
1823300 GRASS JELLY (LB)

Country	Mode	Reg	Yr	Quantity	F.A.S.	C.I.F.	Charges
TOTAL			81	1,190,119	301,388	339,212	37,824
			82	1,087,634	245,313	289,922	44,609
			83	1,351,198	307,720	359,600	51,880
			84	2,103,135	517,663	616,577	98,914
			85	1,235,644	336,117	387,992	51,875
			86	1,891,780	459,629	522,838	63,209
BURKINA	V	W	81	6,150	1,440	1,624	184
CHINA M	V	E	81	56,288	10,352	12,816	2,464
			82	96,631	37,236	42,512	5,276
			83	59,801	13,261	17,324	4,063
			84	174,713	35,844	50,470	14,626
			85	34,971	8,013	10,374	2,361
			86	149,594	28,683	34,589	5,906
	V	H	83	2,166	361	402	41
			84	5,130	920	1,070	150
			85	11,464	2,260	2,558	298
	V	W	81	315,758	49,380	57,855	8,475
			82	438,776	70,386	86,822	16,436
			83	430,954	65,123	79,825	14,702
			84	537,785	103,361	126,400	23,039
			85	232,742	70,038	79,191	9,153
			86	752,285	180,833	201,328	20,495
CHINA T	V	E	81	174,774	44,864	51,383	6,519
			82	95,990	26,179	31,094	4,915
			83	167,900	50,950	60,752	9,802
			84	191,614	53,483	65,216	11,733
			85	75,689	20,949	25,712	4,763
			86	98,485	30,440	36,404	5,964
	V	H	81	7,980	2,162	2,367	205
			83	2,850	800	854	54
			84	9,263	2,486	2,811	325
			85	8,550	2,505	2,743	238
			86	11,905	3,813	4,382	569
	V	W	81	524,685	143,438	158,432	14,994
			82	386,112	99,889	114,128	14,239
			83	578,819	150,653	167,988	17,335
			84	1,065,347	284,254	326,159	41,905
			85	687,455	177,251	201,312	24,061
			86	405,524	104,962	116,914	11,952
HG KONG	V	E	81	3,600	556	657	101
			82	624	1,128	1,210	82
			83	4,650	1,753	2,373	620
			84	250	1,796	1,828	32

Product TSUSA commodity number, description, and unit of quantity Country	Mode	Reg	Yr	Quantity	F.A.S.	C.I.F.	Charges
			85	77,207	20,773	26,814	6,041
			86	111,103	23,492	28,361	4,869
	V	W	81	34,282	4,932	5,852	920
			82	46,643	7,135	9,866	2,731
			83	90,083	19,673	23,938	4,265
			84	101,694	19,279	23,684	4,405
			85	87,973	18,897	21,683	2,786
			86	182,752	32,261	36,423	4,162
ITALY	V	E	81	36,707	17,575	20,427	2,852
			86	85,247	17,412	22,639	5,227
JAPAN	V	E	83	888	1,295	1,440	145
			84	12,074	12,627	14,784	2,157
			85	9,892	10,432	12,258	1,826
			86	7,979	6,080	7,184	1,104
	V	W	84	711	1,147	1,365	218
			86	7,856	12,820	13,407	587
KOR REP	V	E	81	1,707	2,129	2,347	218
			84	163	866	886	20
			86	8,250	2,870	3,376	506
	V	W	82	22,858	3,360	4,290	930
			83	5,688	1,360	1,470	110
MALAYSA	V	W	85	9,701	4,999	5,347	348
			86	46,350	10,193	11,393	1,200
SWITZLD	V	E	81	28,188	24,560	25,452	892
	V	W	86	24,450	5,770	6,438	668
THAILND	V	E	84	2,111	1,200	1,354	154
	V	W	83	1,756	1,669	1,859	190
			84	2,280	400	550	150
U KING	V	E	83	5,643	822	1,375	553

Macaroni

1823500 MACARONI ETC CONTG NO EGGS (LB)

Country	Mode	Reg	Yr	Quantity	F.A.S.	C.I.F.	Charges
TOTAL			81	94,362,433	39,650,789	44,369,637	4,720,474
			82	110,311,163	41,022,011	46,790,503	5,771,928
			83	128,488,143	45,499,870	52,333,831	6,833,961
			84	167,833,355	55,313,412	65,175,612	9,862,200
			85	172,576,982	57,227,972	67,572,784	10,344,812
			86	178,903,667	58,834,780	68,515,373	9,680,593
ARGENT	V	E	83	37,258	11,586	13,700	2,114
AUSTRAL	N	E	83	2,095	1,048	1,350	302
	N	W	85	1,368	2,038	2,412	374
AUSTRIA	V	W	84	438	371	400	29
BELGIUM	V	E	81	25,353	7,273	8,346	1,073
			82	421,300	108,457	136,660	28,203
			85	4,585	7,805	8,663	858
			86	76,659	27,386	32,134	4,748
BRAZIL	O	E	82	4,800	1,493	1,493	
BURMA	V	E	82	1,350	3,580	3,972	392
C RICA	V	E	83	4,365	2,475	2,835	360
			86	7,206	5,094	5,945	851
CANADA	A	E	82	2,970	1,453	1,453	3,436
	A	H	82	7,417	3,591	4,665	1,074
			84	11,604	4,399	8,143	3,744
			85	4,176	2,099	2,696	597
			86	4,418	2,771	4,105	1,334
	N	E	84	139,623	31,059	39,144	8,085
			85	10,277,873	3,964,962	3,964,962	
	N	W	81	3,330,945	1,301,419	1,302,003	584
			82	1,826,448	731,922	731,922	
			83	1,391,396	571,891	571,891	
			84	246,102	160,402	160,402	
	O	E	81	23,091,134	9,857,306	9,863,319	7,878
			82	21,085,121	8,426,118	8,426,118	
			83	20,074,354	8,070,622	8,070,622	
			84	20,976,581	8,426,223	8,426,808	585
			85	10,822,215	4,150,576	4,151,353	777
			86	21,691,932	8,016,906	8,016,906	
	O	W	81	74,063	39,228	39,228	
			82	45,031	21,402	21,402	
			83	12,420	5,510	5,510	
			84	1,000	455	455	
			85	99,483	65,162	65,718	556
			86	94,520	44,529	44,529	
CHILE	V	E	83	6,140	2,686	3,042	356
CHINA M	N	E	85	1,716,860	702,013	916,982	214,969
	N	W	82	2,191,203	510,369	619,826	109,457
			84	3,480,750	1,117,134	1,317,089	199,955
			86	1,913,287	731,711	834,614	102,903
	O	E	81	29,491	27,977	28,086	109
			83	5,554	2,722	3,123	401
			84	14,223	7,072	8,000	928
			85	107,611	43,236	45,162	1,926

Product TSUSA commodity number, description, and unit of quantity Country	Mode	Reg	Yr	Quantity	F.A.S.	C.I.F.	Charges
			86	17,437	6,603	7,742	1,139
	O	W	81	500	528	571	43
			82	12,980	3,953	5,176	1,223
			84	6,450	1,111	1,229	118
			85	16,830	3,748	7,496	3,748
			86	19,637	8,421	8,943	522
	V	E	81	1,676,955	829,510	991,374	161,864
			82	1,130,227	492,553	610,303	117,750
			83	1,575,439	624,749	784,447	159,698
			84	1,321,485	499,653	669,104	169,451
			85	83,525	26,848	33,163	6,315
			86	1,527,176	568,040	698,738	130,698
	V	H	81	57,170	31,694	36,119	4,425
			82	63,651	33,881	39,363	5,482
			83	53,706	24,455	29,756	5,301
			84	139,724	110,491	124,889	14,398
			85	151,228	75,100	90,109	15,009
			86	113,538	56,375	64,498	8,123
	V	W	81	4,242,567	2,008,558	2,364,360	355,802
			82	3,969,562	1,723,152	2,048,155	325,003
			83	6,408,962	2,638,298	3,087,305	449,007
			84	6,154,737	2,169,735	2,592,618	422,883
			85	8,542,537	3,204,004	3,781,171	577,167
			86	6,149,733	1,947,213	2,196,302	249,089
CHINA T	N	E	85	1,078,864	707,360	864,377	157,017
	N	W	85	80,956	31,265	35,545	4,280
			86	224,925	79,988	86,912	6,924
	O	E	81	2,640	535	689	154
			84	7,328	6,371	7,471	1,100
	O	W	81	1,427	842	879	37
			85	8,744	4,959	5,664	705
	V	E	81	565,660	532,708	609,181	76,473
			82	630,406	493,770	578,135	84,365
			83	866,115	604,217	710,468	106,251
			84	804,523	572,548	712,721	140,173
			85	90,685	69,495	83,735	14,240
			86	1,461,497	915,951	1,064,790	148,839
	V	H	81	227,329	140,990	158,478	17,488
			82	261,530	157,246	181,655	24,409
			83	268,565	182,673	210,948	28,275
			84	211,681	199,931	224,115	24,184
			85	240,020	142,475	171,757	29,282
			86	204,016	142,687	167,349	24,662
	V	W	81	1,897,546	1,519,739	1,683,190	163,451
			82	1,807,573	1,291,026	1,458,404	167,378
			83	3,135,072	2,004,317	2,237,494	233,177
			84	2,869,492	1,940,394	2,181,629	241,235
			85	2,851,717	1,771,724	1,986,630	214,906
			86	4,230,970	2,431,785	2,649,296	217,511
CYPRUS	V	E	82	9,299	3,454	3,893	439
			83	990	595	673	78
			84	750	300	386	86
			86	163,065	40,370	49,734	9,364
	V	W	86	52,936	14,721	19,363	4,642
CZECHO	O	E	81	900	549	608	59
FR GERM	N	E	83	2,575	1,876	2,490	614
	N	W	82	5,361	2,834	2,959	125
	O	E	81	6,744	5,288	5,804	516
			84	2,381	2,091	2,171	80
	O	W	85	2,831	2,144	2,144	
	V	E	82	1,167	994	1,069	75
			83	1,947	3,696	3,942	246
			84	18,014	14,060	16,647	2,587
			85	34,882	11,524	13,317	1,793
			86	9,899	9,413	9,869	456
	V	W	81	1,094	954	1,136	182
			83	3,793	2,972	3,334	362
			84	1,100	967	1,028	61
FRANCE	N	E	82	279,632	85,892	101,880	15,988
	O	E	82	9,237	2,560	2,643	83
	V	E	81	439,501	163,301	188,465	25,164
			82	328,518	77,876	96,506	18,630
			83	266,296	99,489	111,504	12,015
			84	262,393	68,400	91,189	22,789
			85	224,973	65,278	79,499	14,221
			86	247,783	89,213	101,049	11,836
	V	W	83	39,683	8,100	9,890	1,790
			84	198,414	42,568	50,715	8,147
			85	272,098	73,538	87,209	13,671
			86	396,915	117,042	139,046	22,004
GREECE	N	E	81	876,838	221,994	287,809	65,815
	O	E	81	2,772	1,759	1,759	
			82	6,916	3,283	3,283	
			83	2,705	2,009	2,009	
			84	1,580	812	812	

Product TSUSA commodity number, description, and unit of quantity Country	Mode	Reg	Yr	Quantity	F.A.S.	C.I.F.	Charges
			85	2,866	1,520	1,614	94
			86	11,539	7,384	7,384	
	V	E	81	92,246	27,950	36,883	8,933
			82	948,947	269,175	346,549	77,374
			83	993,693	262,772	348,176	85,404
			84	1,151,690	281,405	397,314	115,909
			85	928,428	236,764	309,895	73,131
			86	1,219,122	306,762	416,885	110,123
	V	W	85	8,810	4,200	4,856	656
GUATMAL	A	W	82	497	463	597	134
			84	872	1,013	1,503	490
	N	W	85	11,973	12,672	14,495	1,823
	V	E	84	453	580	779	199
			85	26,508	17,919	19,445	1,526
HG KONG	N	E	85	547,435	239,146	295,163	56,017
	N	W	83	108,952	36,200	43,287	7,087
			84	41,639	21,281	24,466	3,185
	O	E	81	4,224	12,736	13,758	1,022
			83	3,080	1,085	1,182	97
			84	7,300	3,326	3,858	532
			85	52,475	17,683	22,216	4,533
			86	4,500	1,452	1,594	142
	O	W	84	11,736	7,980	10,652	2,672
	V	E	81	1,342,177	892,615	1,009,498	115,631
			82	1,078,406	660,073	766,765	106,692
			83	1,418,904	765,057	909,625	144,568
			84	963,473	534,789	648,709	113,920
			85	976,225	518,067	619,751	101,684
			86	2,143,812	1,163,822	1,333,832	170,010
	V	H	81	282,323	357,908	387,251	29,343
			82	299,613	381,711	415,462	33,751
			83	239,054	296,257	331,142	34,885
			84	262,321	343,607	388,103	44,496
			85	251,449	339,057	383,073	44,016
			86	245,218	312,523	352,778	40,255
	V	W	81	1,274,234	971,218	1,055,019	83,801
			82	1,214,210	834,594	923,309	88,715
			83	1,855,578	1,263,879	1,399,600	135,721
			84	2,480,264	1,503,029	1,682,879	179,850
			85	4,285,130	1,821,700	2,064,933	243,233
			86	4,746,194	1,914,525	2,112,717	198,192
HONDURA	V	E	81	7,480	6,348	7,128	780
HUNGARY	V	E	83	15,541	23,000	25,000	2,000
			85	24,342	2,975	4,377	1,402
INDIA	N	E	84	7,093	4,420	5,275	855
	O	E	81	501	1,186	2,071	885
			82	110	890	890	
			83	7,658	3,965	4,404	439
			84	6,041	2,425	2,680	255
	O	W	84	700	470	499	29
	V	E	81	9,345	7,509	9,375	1,866
			82	12,778	7,111	8,996	1,885
			83	25,011	22,489	24,407	1,918
			84	18,109	11,839	14,679	2,840
			85	11,981	5,953	6,728	775
			86	7,302	3,711	4,038	327
	V	W	81	18,866	7,691	9,204	1,513
			82	2,435	1,361	1,528	167
			83	4,349	2,918	3,486	568
			84	33,520	14,255	17,433	3,178
INDNSIA	V	W	82	1,320	343	372	29
			84	3,175	1,650	1,991	341
			85	1,499	4,024	4,262	238
ISRAEL	V	E	81	25,495	24,368	27,824	3,456
			82	13,841	16,812	19,836	3,024
			83	20,617	27,721	33,172	5,451
			84	36,841	38,830	44,894	6,064
			85	40,313	27,936	32,295	4,359
			86	87,048	57,991	66,262	8,271
	V	W	85	11,920	4,214	5,518	1,304
			86	3,003	1,725	1,984	259
ITALY	A	E	84	10,140	4,132	9,042	4,910
	A	H	82	441	473	1,568	1,095
	A	W	85	43,962	12,105	15,237	3,132
	N	E	82	43,600,684	12,039,803	14,673,573	2,633,770
			83	53,097,818	13,079,515	16,219,875	3,140,360
			84	84,705,588	20,626,813	25,945,222	5,318,409
			85	75,367,606	17,634,821	22,308,249	4,673,428
			86	42,531,813	10,264,191	12,799,530	2,535,339
	N	W	85	11,069,067	3,071,852	3,911,152	839,300
			86	1,057,478	363,266	446,940	83,674
	O	E	81	143,725	53,874	62,360	8,486
			82	43,153	16,429	16,556	127
			83	96,343	37,168	47,566	10,398
			84	1,698	703	703	
			85	264,722	71,508	79,104	7,596
			86	1,797,189	313,674	391,490	77,816
	O	W	86	119,828	24,510	24,510	
	V	E	81	38,489,843	12,239,317	14,797,278	2,557,961
			82	6,792,549	2,150,997	2,605,859	454,862
			83	11,820,813	2,992,296	3,763,636	771,340
			84	13,689,959	3,559,573	4,450,232	890,659
			85	17,904,245	4,501,359	5,783,826	1,282,467
			86	50,206,277	11,430,040	14,779,161	3,349,121
	V	W	81	1,235,187	521,409	615,121	93,712
			82	2,506,023	817,723	974,801	157,078
			83	5,169,022	1,445,329	1,748,163	302,834
			84	8,679,045	2,415,440	2,959,249	543,809
			85	389,396	98,546	119,361	20,815
			86	9,119,517	2,432,148	3,102,962	670,814
JAPAN	A	E	82	201	394	784	390
			83	30	265	577	312
	N	E	81	877,658	600,356	673,861	73,505
			82	1,092,790	742,526	839,370	96,844
			83	1,026,157	728,556	822,759	94,203
			85	1,773,529	1,345,323	1,522,376	177,053
			86	15,713	20,670	21,661	991
	N	H	81	396,904	310,115	363,415	53,300
			82	447,721	323,240	392,261	69,021
			83	416,429	360,498	431,341	70,843
			84	375,857	338,603	409,166	70,563
	N	W	81	1,395,319	956,876	1,043,788	87,912
			82	1,730,609	1,136,387	1,232,796	96,409
			83	2,795,591	2,126,758	2,302,854	176,096
			84	2,938,714	2,038,899	2,222,594	183,695
			85	1,777,357	1,200,394	1,295,303	94,909
	O	E	81	21,245	22,439	24,370	1,931
			82	11,433	9,906	10,853	947
			83	2,952	3,930	3,930	
			84	59,895	52,841	57,741	4,900
			85	2,145	1,041	1,262	221
			86	2,972	3,244	3,516	272
	O	W	85	7,226	6,776	7,241	465
			86	2,097	2,387	2,508	121
	V	E	81	427,141	244,997	275,598	30,601
			82	599,929	377,763	437,331	59,568
			83	631,513	508,916	563,946	55,030
			84	1,813,416	1,385,169	1,580,716	195,547
			85	252,786	222,800	246,879	24,079
			86	1,927,845	1,843,163	2,024,026	180,863
	V	H	85	324,978	279,882	335,648	55,766
			86	388,288	376,950	434,683	57,733
	V	W	81	1,554,054	1,022,875	1,119,410	96,535
			82	1,841,302	1,136,805	1,248,775	111,970
			83	977,606	681,155	749,464	68,309
			84	780,800	674,033	729,831	55,798
			85	3,465,009	2,580,196	2,815,027	234,831
			86	4,587,450	4,231,586	4,499,098	267,512
JORDAN	V	H	85	3,150	1,308	1,587	279
KENYA	O	E	82	1,323	751	833	82
	V	W	86	5,967	3,610	4,024	414
KOR REP	N	E	84	711,327	478,436	571,317	92,881
	N	W	85	74,107	42,769	53,499	10,730
	O	E	81	2,100	2,863	3,120	257
			82	4,502	5,972	6,526	554
			86	16,820	7,353	7,353	
	V	E	81	447,455	239,642	279,404	39,762
			82	546,664	343,396	396,185	52,789
			83	895,117	480,518	562,867	82,349
			84	164,740	92,572	114,727	22,155
			85	1,409,829	912,320	1,138,016	225,696
			86	1,642,687	943,378	1,108,768	165,390
	V	H	81	68,430	28,032	32,717	4,685
			82	126,760	46,432	55,780	9,348
			83	227,060	83,021	106,649	23,628
			84	93,388	37,607	50,598	12,991
			85	110,754	37,432	50,508	13,076
			86	214,427	58,240	68,865	10,625
	V	W	81	939,168	655,833	728,744	72,911
			82	1,166,859	698,364	782,156	83,792
			83	2,251,857	1,314,714	1,481,059	166,345
			84	2,191,482	1,368,572	1,581,374	212,802
			85	2,269,066	1,310,706	1,528,595	217,889
			86	2,960,012	1,492,664	1,699,392	206,728
LEBANON	V	E	81	1,100	689	775	86
			83	1,102	959	1,006	47
			84	1,102	648	685	37
MALAYSA	O	E	84	420	315	315	
			86	5,233	1,881	1,881	
	O	W	84	22,589	8,713	8,713	

Product
TSUSA commodity number, description, and unit of quantity

Country	Mode	Reg	Yr	Quantity	F.A.S.	C.I.F.	Charges
	V	E	81	42,400	15,030	20,417	5,387
			82	31,320	12,835	15,430	2,595
			83	14,501	6,518	7,721	1,203
			84	9,600	4,564	5,509	945
			85	40,851	11,042	15,141	4,099
	V	H	82	551	346	371	25
	V	W	81	20,182	5,851	6,649	798
			82	5,644	3,150	3,498	348
			85	3,936	2,298	2,566	268
			86	33,352	18,837	23,929	5,092
MALI	V	E	82	425,440	101,430	129,457	28,027
MAURIT	V	E	85	4,000	1,666	2,538	872
MEXICO	O	E	81	785,132	274,038	274,038	
			82	1,084,766	331,470	331,470	
			83	1,604,899	426,449	426,449	
			84	1,627,147	437,851	437,851	
			85	3,595,343	1,247,136	1,247,136	
			86	3,816,347	1,303,785	1,303,785	
	O	W	81	2,164,386	647,154	647,154	
			82	2,455,264	471,453	471,453	
			83	2,398,264	443,773	444,756	983
			84	2,068,043	698,619	698,619	
			85	1,089,813	354,936	354,936	
			86	1,859,017	567,184	567,184	
	V	E	83	1,125	657	729	72
	V	W	81	36,508	11,178	13,298	2,120
MONSRAT	O	E	85	44,141	15,865	15,865	
NETHLDS	V	E	81	72,439	28,172	36,995	8,823
			82	65,796	22,225	32,006	9,781
			83	15,643	9,251	11,867	2,616
			84	648	397	401	4
			85	36,553	20,591	21,332	741
	V	W	81	2,987	1,852	1,983	131
			82	2,439	1,870	2,069	199
			83	4,988	4,405	4,780	375
			84	8,075	5,095	5,680	585
			85	4,499	2,678	2,902	224
			86	623	1,042	1,169	127
PAKISTN	O	E	82	11,679	6,375	6,884	509
			83	9,253	5,367	5,863	496
			84	9,094	4,130	4,567	437
			85	2,976	1,495	1,682	187
	V	E	81	5,563	2,020	3,347	1,327
			82	1,464	809	945	136
			83	22,338	6,733	9,815	3,082
			84	18,254	5,516	6,779	1,263
			85	11,265	5,427	6,518	1,091
			86	27,678	8,782	10,170	1,388
	V	H	82	315	271	288	17
	V	W	81	24,565	3,027	4,492	1,465
			82	5,926	1,680	2,525	845
			83	60	516	678	162
			84	298	830	913	83
PHIL R	N	W	83	34,047	28,521	34,113	5,592
			85	564,031	434,072	495,059	60,987
	O	E	85	3,560	2,666	3,260	594
	O	H	86	3,000	2,035	2,789	754
	O	W	85	54	4,659	5,134	475
			86	2,500	1,864	1,864	
	V	E	81	243,258	184,138	219,768	35,630
			82	274,749	219,532	264,968	45,436
			83	229,835	189,275	217,617	28,342
			84	182,473	128,864	152,602	23,738
			85	186,401	139,345	172,984	33,639
			86	199,053	151,398	180,156	28,758
	V	H	81	36,926	28,993	35,393	6,400
			82	71,740	57,753	68,786	11,033
			83	94,948	69,775	83,051	13,276
			84	100,936	81,585	101,413	19,828
			85	104,809	84,505	105,012	20,507
			86	119,733	93,870	109,053	15,183
	V	W	81	959,981	698,648	822,779	124,144
			82	1,230,564	913,441	1,070,464	157,023
			83	1,081,919	800,962	923,027	122,065
			84	1,119,989	791,145	938,654	147,509
			85	756,905	527,562	616,671	89,109
			86	1,527,214	927,659	1,051,749	124,090
PORTUGL	V	E	81	122,877	31,555	40,801	9,246
			82	79,022	24,329	30,661	6,332
			83	100,781	31,163	40,123	8,960
			84	154,956	48,448	60,130	11,682
			85	100,869	33,350	40,718	7,368
			86	110,713	38,395	49,948	11,553
ROMANIA	V	E	83	18,823	6,002	7,542	1,540
	V	W	84	6,765	10,882	11,756	874

Product
TSUSA commodity number, description, and unit of quantity

Country	Mode	Reg	Yr	Quantity	F.A.S.	C.I.F.	Charges
SALVADR	V	E	85	5,316	2,615	3,104	489
SINGAPR	O	E	81	10,000	3,660	3,880	220
	O	W	85	3,373	1,800	1,926	126
	V	E	81	1,984	679	779	100
			82	6,503	4,107	4,812	705
			85	137,229	68,295	91,887	23,592
			86	142,901	79,876	100,149	20,273
	V	W	81	338,690	132,878	156,226	23,348
			82	243,699	83,245	100,081	16,836
			83	97,061	37,954	43,702	5,748
			84	186,313	64,241	76,182	11,941
			85	222,177	89,224	102,969	13,745
			86	173,281	76,839	85,014	8,175
SPAIN	N	W	84	135,428	44,585	62,853	18,268
			85	64,155	25,424	31,545	6,121
	V	E	81	46,420	17,149	20,929	3,780
			83	212,300	51,482	62,439	10,957
			84	179,310	67,579	83,150	15,571
			85	63,045	13,219	17,486	4,267
			86	83,860	9,856	12,776	2,920
	V	W	85	10,139	4,476	5,764	1,288
			86	36,428	4,093	5,843	1,750
SURINAM	V	E	85	10,853	4,384	6,408	2,024
SWEDEN	V	E	82	7,718	2,571	3,004	433
			85	11,418	3,144	5,111	1,967
SWITZLD	A	E	83	3,304	3,345	5,018	1,673
	N	E	82	7,370	11,827	14,031	2,204
	V	E	85	47,690	8,772	10,299	1,527
			86	90,223	24,052	31,436	7,384
	V	W	85	49,719	16,692	19,149	2,457
			86	32,668	11,583	13,554	1,971
SYRIA	V	E	81	5,259	5,808	6,745	937
T PAC I	V	W	86	1,350	1,131	1,669	538
THAILND	N	E	81	610,168	281,729	321,362	39,633
			83	10,875	3,894	5,007	1,113
			84	31,781	12,877	16,568	3,691
	N	W	84	1,247,482	652,382	732,992	80,610
	O	E	81	3,198	2,633	2,633	
			82	164	1,600	2,072	472
			83	7,213	4,950	5,407	457
			84	51,550	22,015	22,723	708
			85	29,640	8,892	8,892	
	V	E	81	183,623	82,169	95,434	13,265
			82	1,001,919	400,117	477,946	77,829
			83	883,087	384,213	443,987	59,774
			84	771,468	358,794	416,297	57,503
			85	927,816	690,050	769,589	79,539
			86	1,355,418	634,894	721,734	86,840
	V	H	81	33,503	23,366	26,281	2,915
			82	53,494	21,980	25,053	3,073
			83	27,737	9,559	11,036	1,477
			84	7,601	3,372	3,772	400
	V	W	81	2,984,122	1,258,271	1,446,289	188,018
			82	4,992,833	2,106,677	2,466,447	359,770
			83	3,318,493	1,543,767	1,722,616	178,849
			84	1,742,222	626,908	744,339	117,431
			85	2,631,755	971,396	1,127,134	155,738
			86	5,362,350	1,897,653	2,162,833	265,180
TRINID	V	E	86	27,962	11,520	12,507	987
U KING	N	E	82	45,768	12,182	14,876	2,694
			84	9,215	2,443	3,640	1,197
			85	82,195	54,920	65,054	10,134
	O	E	82	794	408	454	46
			83	595	306	336	30
			84	2,415	1,888	1,888	
			85	211,380	130,842	152,691	21,849
	V	E	83	2,970	1,478	1,641	163
			85	941,349	460,421	558,341	97,920
			86	220,871	127,607	144,586	16,979
	V	W	82	5,811	2,143	2,321	178
			83	1,313	329	352	23
			85	74,510	50,578	54,655	4,077
			86	225	1,756	1,770	14
VENEZ	A	E	83	4,409	1,980	3,066	1,086
YUGOSLV	O	E	84	11,592	4,249	5,132	883
	V	E	81	22,840	10,635	13,468	2,833
			82	10,185	4,590	6,006	1,416
			83	26,085	12,319	15,587	3,268
			84	14,940	3,638	6,098	2,460
			85	98,868	21,214	30,071	8,857

1823600 MACARONI ETC CONTG EGGS (LB)

			Yr	Quantity	F.A.S.	C.I.F.	Charges
TOTAL			81	7,558,866	4,308,237	4,718,755	409,045
			82	8,470,802	4,740,371	5,215,725	475,354
			83	9,793,077	5,254,169	5,791,446	537,277

Product
TSUSA commodity number, description, and unit of quantity

Country	Mode	Reg	Yr	Quantity	F.A.S.	C.I.F.	Charges
			84	11,889,258	5,969,613	6,663,412	693,799
			85	11,515,792	5,491,373	6,185,022	693,649
			86	12,289,244	6,086,547	6,750,024	663,477
AUSTRAL	V	W	82	650	325	502	177
AUSTRIA	V	W	84	547	530	572	42
BAHAMAS	O	E	84	31,905	40,969	42,518	1,549
BELGIUM	O	E	81	1,065	641	692	51
			82	4,708	3,597	4,007	410
			84	33,174	41,209	43,668	2,459
C RICA	V	E	83	25,152	6,048	9,506	3,458
CANADA	A	W	81	200	260	420	160
			82	580	421	549	128
			83	400	359	473	114
	N	W	81	4,144	2,540	2,984	444
			83	113,689	61,009	61,009	
	O	E	81	2,867,138	1,445,723	1,448,387	1,191
			82	3,432,920	1,644,461	1,645,594	1,133
			83	3,420,617	1,701,417	1,703,884	2,467
			84	3,401,407	1,895,848	1,897,353	1,505
			85	3,751,777	1,772,731	1,772,732	1
			86	4,731,859	1,958,922	1,958,941	19
	O	W	81	226,764	131,196	131,196	
			82	278,517	145,125	145,125	
			83	1,700	1,026	1,226	200
			84	64,378	37,509	37,509	
			85	123,791	67,410	67,410	
			86	325,416	209,793	209,793	
	V	E	85	16,712	17,640	18,973	1,333
			86	19,162	21,960	23,898	1,938
CHINA M	O	E	84	750	354	415	61
	V	E	81	28,194	12,723	14,982	2,259
			82	30,291	10,364	13,042	2,678
			83	9,369	4,329	4,897	568
			84	39,223	20,203	25,322	5,119
			85	24,612	8,585	11,820	3,235
			86	23,298	10,643	13,959	3,316
	V	H	81	360	353	383	30
			84	12,823	14,292	16,775	2,483
			86	8,280	2,030	2,380	350
	V	W	81	26,279	14,511	15,637	1,126
			82	48,499	23,628	26,403	2,775
			83	83,312	27,568	32,143	4,575
			84	16,125	8,367	9,099	732
			85	51,455	27,577	30,847	3,270
			86	55,420	19,022	21,850	2,828
CHINA T	V	E	81	13,057	8,090	8,924	834
			82	36,431	24,497	28,363	3,866
			83	84,873	57,455	69,540	12,085
			84	36,851	33,875	38,431	4,556
			85	9,989	6,022	7,067	1,045
			86	14,435	9,921	12,254	2,333
	V	H	86	11,336	8,372	10,737	2,365
	V	W	81	262,616	144,062	166,499	22,437
			82	477,663	276,021	329,108	53,087
			83	280,920	161,198	188,897	27,699
			84	272,750	167,056	192,280	25,224
			85	134,659	91,488	103,879	12,391
			86	195,213	126,372	139,410	13,038
FR GERM	N	E	85	74,452	46,407	51,613	5,206
			86	32,758	37,159	41,367	4,208
	O	E	81	15,821	13,669	14,773	1,104
			82	54,132	42,840	49,344	6,504
			83	65,561	52,939	56,074	3,135
			84	85,190	59,668	65,670	6,002
			85	4,469	4,671	5,570	899
			86	17,626	19,007	19,982	975
	V	E	81	103,362	79,832	90,536	10,704
			82	149,047	117,184	127,892	10,708
			83	150,721	121,574	132,987	11,413
			84	177,763	115,614	133,690	18,076
			85	141,407	102,380	114,429	12,049
			86	129,076	135,061	144,994	9,933
	V	W	81	2,734	2,727	3,179	452
			82	4,594	3,304	3,614	310
			83	4,033	4,225	5,158	933
			84	1,008	1,034	1,174	140
			85	1,094	2,548	2,958	410
			86	5,809	6,918	7,734	816
FRANCE	V	E	82	11,023	1,704	2,919	1,215
			83	36,049	31,468	36,883	5,415
			84	54,154	11,383	14,924	3,541
			86	37,642	19,161	21,782	2,621
G BISAU	V	E	81	2,802	756	1,004	248
GREECE	O	E	81	500	345	345	
			82	1,270	850	850	
			83	1,160	772	772	
			84	1,958	1,095	1,095	
	V	E	81	72,501	26,290	32,066	5,776
			82	110,357	35,921	46,051	10,130
			83	58,460	20,551	27,180	6,629
			84	62,274	25,766	31,818	6,052
			85	17,115	8,654	9,320	666
			86	30,614	14,950	16,961	2,011
GUATMAL	A	E	82	1,064	1,098	1,408	310
			86	3,385	1,500	1,691	191
	A	W	81	21,910	18,433	23,919	5,486
			82	21,140	18,391	24,313	5,922
			83	20,616	18,127	24,160	6,033
			84	17,503	16,519	21,286	4,767
			85	800	1,006	1,238	232
	N	W	83	10,762	10,192	12,429	2,237
			84	12,820	12,768	15,252	2,484
			85	14,159	11,235	13,958	2,723
	O	W	84	1,020	860	860	
			85	17,030	9,187	9,187	
			86	36,000	16,000	16,000	
	V	E	86	8,380	6,715	7,260	545
	V	W	85	1,200	1,221	1,285	64
			86	688	1,004	1,069	65
HG KONG	N	E	84	20,351	12,692	14,641	1,949
	O	E	81	375	429	429	
			84	1,020	510	510	
	V	E	81	212,959	138,316	155,270	16,954
			82	267,924	183,478	207,186	23,708
			83	177,489	114,056	130,463	16,407
			84	122,091	82,259	94,932	12,673
			85	113,855	79,719	93,577	13,858
			86	123,381	75,400	83,820	8,420
	V	H	81	18,088	16,119	17,720	1,601
			82	8,618	6,931	7,947	1,016
			83	11,324	9,290	10,326	1,036
			84	9,720	8,627	9,662	1,035
			85	10,872	8,126	9,180	1,054
			86	7,000	5,765	6,357	592
	V	W	81	768,905	537,207	582,565	45,358
			82	646,187	427,973	468,338	40,365
			83	789,227	561,474	605,150	43,676
			84	569,494	335,207	370,587	35,380
			85	436,769	283,874	311,252	27,378
			86	436,547	255,631	274,357	18,726
HUNGARY	N	E	81	21,274	9,116	9,937	821
	V	E	84	40,313	34,692	37,701	3,009
			85	21,043	21,399	22,859	1,460
			86	73,962	54,564	62,017	7,453
INDIA	O	E	81	881	462	462	
			83	476	284	330	46
	V	E	81	2,328	1,586	1,908	322
			82	1,200	1,093	1,362	269
			83	3,217	2,048	2,453	405
			84	1,980	2,080	2,352	272
	V	W	83	2,540	1,529	1,832	303
INDNSIA	V	W	84	284	465	492	27
ITALY	A	E	83	5,225	9,480	12,225	2,745
	N	E	82	1,544,025	820,151	978,658	158,507
			83	1,099,697	546,808	674,461	127,653
			84	1,263,202	725,949	868,739	142,790
			86	805,279	497,616	595,724	98,108
	N	W	84	351,354	277,447	308,353	30,906
			85	273,674	110,711	140,787	30,076
	O	E	81	6,078	5,933	6,918	985
			82	2,190	2,074	2,074	
			84	3,686	2,499	2,499	
			85	24,967	6,290	8,253	1,963
			86	52,119	17,469	24,354	6,885
	V	E	81	1,838,793	837,757	998,021	160,264
			82	281,719	118,757	144,376	25,619
			83	992,148	305,660	377,916	72,256
			84	1,440,509	581,542	711,314	129,772
			85	3,604,111	1,324,043	1,663,370	339,327
			86	2,901,868	1,063,270	1,329,076	265,806
	V	W	81	71,226	55,261	65,981	10,720
			82	182,084	121,476	142,904	21,428
			83	697,480	248,861	301,080	52,219
			84	2,187,188	525,177	677,636	152,459
			85	807,634	291,536	355,127	63,591
			86	911,553	437,571	541,434	103,863
JAMAICA	A	E	83	450	584	737	153
JAPAN	A	E	81	6,918	18,826	33,329	14,503
			82	60	294	639	345

Product
TSUSA commodity number, description, and unit of quantity

Country	Mode	Reg	Yr	Quantity	F.A.S.	C.I.F.	Charges
	N	E	84	11,283	9,073	12,353	3,280
			85	37,369	32,876	36,149	3,273
	N	W	84	42,453	18,591	21,757	3,166
	O	E	83	2,000	2,750	2,750	
			85	780	1,075	1,075	
	V	E	81	7,440	6,705	7,475	770
			82	8,933	12,556	13,530	974
			83	5,385	2,169	2,354	185
			84	7,002	8,754	9,903	1,149
			85	36,428	10,047	13,057	3,010
			86	26,463	10,607	12,416	1,809
	V	H	81	1,307	1,768	2,016	248
			82	563	532	634	102
	V	W	81	31,293	21,769	24,084	2,315
			82	5,037	4,165	4,557	392
			83	61,011	49,273	58,976	9,703
			84	7,021	6,189	6,892	703
			85	45,902	31,726	35,620	3,894
			86	69,916	77,386	82,613	5,227
KOR REP	V	E	81	12,129	9,517	11,320	1,803
			83	21,963	15,288	18,824	3,536
			84	43,268	21,257	27,961	6,704
			85	68,957	66,631	79,515	12,884
			86	125,435	68,338	84,830	16,492
	V	H	81	10,560	3,632	4,102	470
	V	W	81	44,556	39,682	43,303	3,621
			82	44,963	25,200	29,036	3,836
			83	61,227	31,723	36,981	5,258
			84	51,559	34,706	38,999	4,293
			85	332,495	170,694	201,974	31,280
			86	105,741	83,765	94,103	10,338
LEBANON	V	E	84	3,307	2,005	2,282	277
MACAO	V	W	83	3,822	1,755	1,905	150
MALAYSA	V	W	82	16,787	8,665	10,829	2,164
MEXICO	O	E	81	9,807	3,235	3,235	
			82	15,136	5,502	5,502	
			83	107,926	34,988	34,988	
			84	266,900	67,785	67,785	
			85	195,133	98,240	98,240	
			86	184,939	58,408	58,408	
	O	W	82	198	499	499	
			83	191,874	45,028	45,028	
			84	329,389	80,641	80,641	
			85	4,944	2,255	2,255	
NETHLDS	N	E	84	19,052	24,342	25,324	982
	O	E	81	1,254	1,016	1,041	25
			86	1,294	2,506	2,719	213
	V	E	82	2,595	1,632	1,837	205
			83	9,659	4,172	4,878	706
			84	1,565	900	980	80
			85	7,776	2,863	3,225	362
PAKISTN	V	E	83	712	267	269	2
			84	595	260	263	3
			85	2,976	1,239	1,502	263
			86	27,062	6,851	7,924	1,073
	V	W	84	3,631	1,647	2,082	435
			86	5,181	2,404	2,775	371
PERU	V	W	82	11,023	4,000	5,800	1,800
PHIL R	O	E	85	1,998	1,530	2,791	1,261
	V	E	81	104,272	90,657	107,005	16,348
			82	110,144	91,323	108,484	17,161
			83	66,611	57,489	67,999	10,510
			84	68,612	86,954	98,368	11,414
			85	38,091	33,065	39,073	6,008
			86	26,964	21,451	25,219	3,768
	V	H	81	10,912	9,168	11,080	1,912
			82	28,548	24,703	29,333	4,630
			83	23,304	20,367	24,320	3,953
			84	19,834	17,287	21,411	4,124
			85	21,470	19,308	23,422	4,114
			86	37,410	35,097	40,455	5,358
	V	W	81	248,922	202,357	233,724	31,367
			82	290,981	230,716	269,140	38,424
			83	263,393	189,385	217,579	28,194
			84	256,301	172,215	201,951	29,736
			85	341,286	236,156	276,872	40,716
			86	226,529	160,986	183,079	22,093
PORTUGL	V	E	81	21,935	6,672	8,188	1,516
			82	25,099	6,972	10,187	3,215
			83	56,218	15,603	18,309	2,706
			84	26,855	8,836	10,996	2,160
			85	53,812	18,827	23,424	4,597
			86	41,918	14,233	16,826	2,593
	V	W	82	2,400	630	699	69
			84	3,403	1,003	1,615	612

Product
TSUSA commodity number, description, and unit of quantity

Country	Mode	Reg	Yr	Quantity	F.A.S.	C.I.F.	Charges
ROMANIA	V	E	83	397	255	320	65
SINGAPR	O	W	84	816	555	607	52
	V	W	81	4,266	1,277	1,377	100
			82	1,378	611	660	49
			84	2,249	1,200	1,385	185
			85	21,363	12,540	14,883	2,343
SPAIN	V	E	81	1,367	641	746	105
			83	1,375	813	1,000	187
			84	47,540	16,886	19,010	2,124
			85	112,820	34,880	45,792	10,912
	V	W	86	44,089	8,207	10,396	2,189
SUDAN	V	E	83	440,920	340,000	378,227	38,227
SWEDEN	V	W	85	16,580	3,334	5,367	2,033
SWITZLD	N	E	81	214,827	217,335	237,417	20,082
			82	204,548	234,170	252,867	18,697
			83	109,682	132,108	140,445	8,337
			85	254,240	307,398	331,501	24,103
	O	E	84	151,641	186,686	197,751	11,065
			85	10,318	12,652	13,453	801
	V	E	81	61,380	81,730	87,152	5,422
			83	106,155	133,420	141,382	7,962
			84	37,837	42,401	44,751	2,350
			85	18,840	19,688	20,920	1,232
			86	291,944	466,093	492,864	26,771
	V	W	83	6,283	3,468	3,813	345
THAILND	V	E	81	12,011	4,320	4,786	466
			82	10,172	7,074	8,172	1,098
			83	9,433	5,913	6,755	842
			84	80,825	32,982	38,530	5,548
			85	24,293	10,949	12,381	1,432
			86	16,018	7,435	8,584	1,149
	V	W	81	68,254	47,904	54,576	6,672
			82	43,404	27,379	32,949	5,570
			83	72,285	68,091	75,777	7,686
			84	23,424	10,862	12,183	1,321
			85	44,919	28,065	31,444	3,379
U KING	A	E	84	150	576	734	158
	N	E	81	65,697	22,438	28,617	6,179
	O	E	82	5,500	4,800	5,131	331
	V	E	83	2,798	7,497	9,530	2,033
			85	8,203	2,363	3,133	770
			86	14,642	19,487	20,201	714
VENEZ	A	E	81	1,477	1,500	1,975	475
YUGOSLV	O	W	84	551	349	349	
	V	E	81	27,928	11,751	17,070	5,319
			82	46,500	17,284	23,311	6,027
			83	21,977	12,016	14,846	2,830
			84	47,380	20,606	27,420	6,814
			85	137,153	28,512	41,263	12,751
			86	45,593	11,497	17,411	5,914

Pancake flour, flour mixes, and refrigerated doughs
1830100 PANCAKE FLOUR & FLOUR MIXES (LB)

Country	Mode	Reg	Yr	Quantity	F.A.S.	C.I.F.	Charges
TOTAL			81	12,103,526	3,354,083	3,506,986	152,903
			82	8,661,901	2,907,779	3,107,029	199,250
			83	14,125,776	5,601,395	5,867,540	266,145
			84	19,448,305	8,250,013	8,547,777	297,764
			85	16,067,221	7,037,306	7,524,159	486,853
			86	22,949,503	8,271,179	8,818,142	546,963
AUSTRAL	N	W	85	5,968	6,062	7,175	1,113
	V	W	84	183,236	87,487	106,444	18,957
			85	342,401	194,712	241,774	47,062
			86	156,561	99,706	116,334	16,628
AUSTRIA	V	E	81	10,267	6,617	7,333	716
			82	210	1,471	1,723	252
	V	W	82	946	1,248	1,425	177
			83	1,190	1,355	1,545	190
			84	16,930	9,024	12,447	3,423
BELGIUM	N	E	84	67,416	32,130	41,189	9,059
	O	E	86	206,149	105,014	128,105	23,091
	V	E	82	1,925	4,085	5,143	1,058
			85	650,797	246,649	314,836	68,187
			86	281,587	109,080	143,825	34,745
C RICA	V	E	82	427,328	90,743	128,208	37,465
			83	660,408	91,575	148,968	57,393
	V	W	83	155,392	33,933	45,629	11,696
CANADA	A	E	82	1,800	529	1,169	640
			84	9,000	923	1,300	377
	A	H	85	5,926	2,413	3,230	817
	N	E	81	11,440	3,487	3,827	340
			82	98,525	75,193	75,193	
			83	4,987,051	2,310,666	2,310,666	

Country	Mode	Reg	Yr	Quantity	F.A.S.	C.I.F.	Charges
			86	23,721	9,049	9,684	635
	O	E	81	10,285,607	2,196,427	2,196,602	175
			82	5,935,995	1,383,667	1,383,876	209
			83	4,828,119	1,426,130	1,426,309	179
			84	14,466,707	5,788,955	5,789,157	202
			85	9,040,049	3,833,023	3,836,003	2,980
			86	12,227,798	4,091,061	4,091,061	
	O	W	81	108,912	60,573	60,573	
			82	280,631	80,328	82,839	2,511
			83	1,040,476	234,476	250,306	15,830
			84	1,775,990	656,038	665,805	9,767
			85	1,652,522	481,512	481,960	448
			86	2,324,171	832,644	848,468	15,824
CHINA M	V	E	82	10,573	9,167	10,778	1,611
			83	1,350	1,487	1,627	140
	V	W	83	2,750	2,037	2,124	87
			84	27,019	12,662	15,345	2,683
CHINA T	V	E	82	33,624	30,463	34,444	3,981
			83	51,200	34,524	37,706	3,182
			84	100,057	55,520	73,362	17,842
			85	82,959	88,093	101,175	13,082
			86	119,688	118,195	131,342	13,147
	V	W	81	4,189	2,865	3,078	213
			82	2,495	1,250	1,425	175
			83	59,883	43,794	49,779	5,985
			84	24,651	16,598	20,544	3,946
			85	142,328	85,768	97,402	11,634
			86	421,817	238,697	263,945	25,248
COLOMB	V	E	86	10,375	6,058	6,862	804
DENMARK	O	E	82	1,101	606	664	58
	V	E	84	30,861	16,682	19,772	3,090
	V	W	82	2,205	1,155	1,291	136
			83	1,450	848	941	93
			84	20,106	15,833	20,144	4,311
FR GERM	A	E	82	1,819	709	1,584	875
			86	24,912	4,208	4,338	130
	N	E	86	125,322	20,822	30,158	9,336
	N	W	82	47,384	41,973	46,861	4,888
	O	E	81	30,230	36,493	39,858	3,365
			82	15,258	11,607	12,377	770
			83	6,200	1,043	1,343	300
			84	1,612	1,767	1,990	223
			85	535,043	100,570	121,209	20,639
			86	6,833	7,546	7,546	
	O	W	85	2,965	5,093	5,093	
	V	E	83	19,013	16,297	17,353	1,056
			84	210,820	61,628	68,968	7,340
			85	661,642	143,284	178,767	35,483
			86	2,388,775	388,508	526,715	138,207
	V	W	81	19,451	17,342	17,500	158
			82	45,349	66,995	69,224	2,229
			83	38,356	39,876	43,449	3,573
			84	84,139	43,028	48,957	5,929
			85	33,012	30,609	40,574	9,965
			86	19,376	20,599	22,786	2,187
FRANCE	A	E	84	3,366	5,026	6,600	1,574
			85	5,885	6,662	9,420	2,758
			86	10,450	14,932	24,288	9,356
	N	E	82	5,919	6,050	6,920	870
			84	44,708	33,529	37,087	3,558
			85	68,961	58,681	70,663	11,982
	N	W	83	20,251	18,024	24,583	6,559
			84	69,170	39,149	50,341	11,192
	O	E	86	1,693,117	230,623	231,562	939
	V	E	81	3,307	3,073	3,330	257
			83	32,647	25,179	28,632	3,453
			84	10,088	1,479	1,693	214
			85	124,062	80,192	90,425	10,233
			86	181,684	97,658	119,724	22,066
	V	W	82	17,516	13,117	16,175	3,058
GREECE	V	E	86	37,280	23,065	28,414	5,349
HG KONG	V	E	81	34,388	25,616	30,822	5,206
			82	67,827	51,907	63,346	11,439
			83	67,665	39,841	45,705	5,864
			84	90,232	75,873	89,079	13,206
			85	262,439	234,640	264,380	29,740
			86	142,828	139,167	154,794	15,627
	V	W	82	13,200	5,856	6,093	237
			84	7,500	10,115	11,156	1,041
			85	18,092	12,920	14,185	1,265
			86	21,525	26,692	27,782	1,090
INDIA	O	E	81	12	600	600	
			84	525	673	743	70
	V	E	81	3,698	3,735	4,625	890
			82	12,028	14,168	16,771	2,603

Country	Mode	Reg	Yr	Quantity	F.A.S.	C.I.F.	Charges
			83	13,024	19,536	22,608	3,072
			84	3,489	4,279	5,052	773
			85	5,016	6,487	7,194	707
			86	5,525	5,976	6,499	523
	V	W	82	4,391	6,080	7,374	1,294
			84	992	1,305	1,529	224
			85	5,605	6,421	7,487	1,066
			86	9,066	11,017	11,559	542
IRELAND	A	E	81	8,818	2,459	4,188	1,729
	V	E	83	1,013	489	677	188
			84	11,760	1,871	2,343	472
			85	2,400	1,108	1,257	149
			86	8,995	3,507	4,364	857
ISRAEL	O	E	83	2,646	2,340	2,593	253
	V	E	81	5,292	3,360	3,910	550
			82	5,292	4,020	4,575	555
			83	1,896	1,677	1,862	185
ITALY	A	E	84	441	440	637	197
	V	E	84	25,339	22,960	27,910	4,950
			85	36,885	24,090	29,258	5,168
			86	30,100	24,806	25,595	789
JAPAN	N	E	83	6,729	9,190	11,075	1,885
			85	91,999	48,658	58,099	9,441
	N	W	83	353,213	185,238	199,810	14,572
			84	337,724	198,007	214,693	16,686
	O	W	85	1,425	1,138	1,182	44
			86	2,203	2,016	2,107	91
	V	E	81	19,652	11,317	12,802	1,485
			82	60,850	33,812	39,047	5,235
			83	67,877	37,243	42,871	5,628
			84	88,606	50,973	59,430	8,457
			85	82,751	48,699	59,219	10,520
			86	164,837	109,324	123,652	14,328
	V	H	82	17,562	7,580	9,402	1,822
			83	11,831	4,883	6,950	2,067
			84	5,374	2,480	3,284	804
			85	9,600	4,164	4,825	661
			86	10,450	5,989	6,701	712
	V	W	81	542,481	367,749	397,672	29,923
			82	668,702	422,157	462,594	40,437
			83	575,666	359,461	389,488	30,027
			84	633,155	328,654	357,591	28,937
			85	974,067	529,209	581,470	52,261
			86	831,604	572,793	610,697	37,904
KOR REP	V	E	82	992	794	843	49
			84	5,693	5,536	6,170	634
			85	3,307	1,050	1,142	92
			86	18,452	13,531	14,649	1,118
	V	W	81	240	442	462	20
			82	720	1,735	1,855	120
			84	480	1,159	1,321	162
			85	4,841	4,536	5,659	1,123
			86	7,375	6,161	6,291	130
MEXICO	O	W	81	29,429	18,322	18,322	
			82	77,776	30,098	30,098	
			83	109,899	32,448	32,448	
			84	53,572	25,280	25,280	
			85	77,711	26,065	26,065	
			86	86,155	36,517	36,517	
NETHLDS	A	W	84	882	788	1,477	689
	O	E	81	750	397	421	24
			85	7,175	3,986	3,986	
	V	E	82	6,614	3,271	3,544	273
			83	58,730	26,514	30,386	3,872
			84	45,941	21,635	24,941	3,306
			85	37,500	4,649	5,368	719
			86	60,278	25,093	32,641	7,548
	V	W	81	10,326	6,994	7,727	733
			82	1,521	1,106	1,179	73
			83	7,219	3,187	3,532	345
			85	33,943	14,072	15,717	1,645
			86	16,909	9,575	10,479	904
NORWAY	V	W	82	850	1,255	1,481	226
PHIL R	N	E	85	238,469	155,797	192,445	36,648
	V	E	81	234,340	154,743	182,580	27,837
			82	270,221	181,280	211,704	30,424
			83	274,219	184,233	209,849	25,616
			84	221,477	137,698	170,489	32,791
			85	20,050	15,735	19,650	3,915
			86	230,108	168,249	201,395	33,146
	V	H	85	19,238	7,125	10,376	3,251
			86	13,538	10,071	12,339	2,268
	V	W	81	723,055	410,602	487,372	76,770
			82	457,199	283,301	323,566	40,265
			83	641,699	391,526	449,970	58,444

Product TSUSA commodity number, description, and unit of quantity Country	Mode	Reg	Yr	Quantity	F.A.S.	C.I.F.	Charges
			84	740,471	456,341	533,147	76,806
			85	619,246	402,158	477,312	75,154
			86	929,087	613,660	715,644	101,984
PORTUGL	V	E	83	1,628	579	749	170
			85	3,750	1,920	2,000	80
SALVADR	A	E	85	6,000	4,826	6,136	1,310
SINGAPR	V	E	85	23,854	15,294	19,494	4,200
	V	W	85	22,487	13,904	16,407	2,503
			86	26,455	16,122	18,742	2,620
SPAIN	V	E	85	4,960	2,784	3,106	322
			86	20,032	20,101	22,981	2,880
SWEDEN	V	E	81	4,444	2,429	3,094	665
			83	10,725	6,614	8,849	2,235
SWITZLD	A	W	83	1,102	2,493	3,341	848
	N	E	81	3,012	4,408	4,633	225
	O	E	81	5,142	7,572	8,031	459
			82	3,012	4,543	4,805	262
			86	2,634	2,895	3,182	287
	V	E	81	1,076	1,574	1,642	68
			82	4,303	6,682	7,535	853
			83	3,949	6,265	6,450	185
			84	1,399	2,171	2,274	103
			86	3,025	3,736	4,147	411
THAILND	O	W	86	926	2,170	2,376	206
	V	E	82	3,085	2,704	3,261	557
			84	19,967	16,361	19,193	2,832
			85	6,611	2,179	2,636	457
			86	1,043	1,968	2,190	222
	V	W	82	13,205	7,611	8,235	624
			83	5,139	3,610	3,949	339
			84	1,334	2,241	2,425	184
			85	25,759	17,886	19,691	1,805
			86	36,014	13,763	15,038	1,275
TURKEY	V	W	85	10,582	17,125	18,022	897
U KING	N	E	85	10,716	7,649	10,101	2,452
	V	E	84	2,116	1,593	1,772	179
			86	10,723	8,815	10,624	1,809
	V	W	81	3,968	4,887	5,982	1,095
			82	60	263	302	39
			83	4,171	2,784	3,418	634
			84	3,960	4,122	4,696	574
			85	46,223	37,709	40,584	2,875
VENEZ	V	E	82	41,888	17,200	18,100	900

Sauces

1824600 SAUCES EXCEPT THIN SOY (LB)

Product TSUSA commodity number, description, and unit of quantity Country	Mode	Reg	Yr	Quantity	F.A.S.	C.I.F.	Charges
TOTAL			**81**	**26,423,863**	**20,086,184**	**21,777,588**	**1,683,471**
			82	**39,648,828**	**25,347,435**	**27,351,600**	**2,004,165**
			83	**65,934,044**	**31,080,651**	**33,267,170**	**2,186,519**
			84	**47,545,422**	**29,352,043**	**32,424,511**	**3,072,468**
			85	**46,347,182**	**29,387,847**	**32,424,205**	**3,036,358**
			86	**59,853,728**	**36,044,165**	**39,315,226**	**3,271,061**
ARGENT	V	W	86	2,940	1,934	2,311	377
AUSTRAL	A	H	86	7,921	9,056	14,612	5,556
	A	W	84	1,144	400	667	267
	V	H	85	952	1,946	2,610	664
	V	W	82	500	468	631	163
			83	1,080	960	1,454	494
			84	2,900	1,644	2,260	616
			85	13,017	4,681	6,909	2,228
			86	37,505	57,694	66,480	8,786
AUSTRIA	V	W	83	2,636	2,692	3,016	324
BARBADO	A	E	83	2,250	510	3,325	2,815
			84	202	282	292	10
	V	E	81	36,975	30,170	34,148	3,978
			82	30,675	32,904	37,095	4,191
			83	10,425	12,451	13,257	806
			84	51,347	57,359	61,923	4,564
			85	45,875	57,840	65,732	7,892
			86	40,223	29,550	33,438	3,888
BELGIUM	N	E	84	19,044	33,491	35,859	2,368
			85	182,967	105,109	126,768	21,659
	O	E	81	310	300	317	17
			83	5,419	15,213	15,911	698
			85	17,462	10,016	14,200	4,184
	V	E	83	4,648	5,899	7,898	1,999
			84	26,224	15,096	16,877	1,781
			85	116,271	70,729	79,948	9,219
			86	177,779	106,648	123,674	17,026
	V	W	83	1,133	492	553	61
			84	1,699	739	868	129
			85	52,876	37,285	41,257	3,972
			86	16,258	10,902	12,740	1,838
BELIZE	O	E	86	1,988	2,650	2,650	
	V	E	86	3,375	4,572	4,950	378
BRAZIL	V	E	82	56,382	13,182	16,923	3,741
			83	24,426	12,474	13,942	1,468
			84	22,457	5,084	6,129	1,045
BURMA	V	E	82	2,705	2,630	2,932	302
C RICA	A	E	84	1,478	448	765	317
			85	2,910	2,688	4,168	1,480
	A	W	81	2,253	708	2,114	1,406
	N	E	83	15,209	12,028	13,902	1,874
	V	E	81	229,467	130,882	157,898	27,016
			82	162,678	87,025	103,294	16,269
			83	323,877	157,981	184,848	26,867
			84	162,487	89,012	102,060	13,048
			85	157,508	75,066	88,500	13,434
			86	144,822	66,168	77,803	11,635
	V	W	82	25,873	5,573	9,111	3,538
			83	86,150	27,884	36,314	8,430
			84	42,027	6,621	9,528	2,907
			85	38,382	8,793	12,105	3,312
			86	6,026	2,003	2,003	
CANADA	A	E	82	590	1,135	1,418	283
			83	879	350	665	315
	N	E	85	234,249	154,901	154,901	
	O	E	81	1,358,837	424,094	425,147	1,063
			82	9,871,847	2,356,131	2,357,280	1,149
			83	30,680,816	7,208,613	7,208,663	50
			84	4,120,311	1,193,720	1,193,720	
			85	2,355,590	632,224	632,472	248
			86	3,631,640	1,159,989	1,159,989	
	O	W	81	62,103	66,638	66,638	
			82	70,495	81,330	83,242	1,912
			83	59,461	76,695	77,081	386
			84	9,370	18,193	18,193	
			85	99,050	81,183	81,183	
			86	115,654	116,441	116,554	113
	V	E	83	1,429	2,406	2,544	138
			85	1,310	1,598	1,860	262
CHILE	V	E	86	82,253	18,751	22,486	3,735
	V	W	83	4,339	4,040	5,285	1,245
CHINA M	N	W	83	11,988	10,427	11,286	859
			84	207,375	66,275	74,942	8,667
	O	E	83	3,000	724	790	66
			84	32,492	18,579	23,502	4,923
			85	38,080	63,127	67,180	4,053
	V	E	81	100,696	52,954	59,522	6,568
			82	138,243	53,726	63,005	9,279
			83	210,950	112,094	129,435	17,341
			84	334,392	136,948	167,347	30,399
			85	231,590	94,782	116,347	21,565
			86	321,032	177,723	207,086	29,363
	V	H	81	4,385	2,948	3,146	198
			83	300	325	351	26
			84	2,760	1,235	1,440	205
			85	3,690	2,925	3,178	253
			86	9,600	3,549	4,220	671
	V	W	81	171,883	77,442	85,196	7,754
			82	384,535	144,036	168,961	24,925
			83	357,200	103,499	118,830	15,331
			84	263,527	91,288	107,824	16,536
			85	347,522	122,122	136,714	14,592
			86	593,319	184,655	209,855	25,200
CHINA T	A	W	83	600	334	367	33
	N	E	85	859,545	741,431	832,810	91,379
	N	W	86	26,563	13,759	15,058	1,299
	O	E	81	2,640	3,696	4,711	1,015
			84	1,651	1,943	2,124	181
			86	7,050	6,015	6,448	433
	O	W	82	169	1,368	1,428	60
			85	1,014	1,147	1,288	141
	V	E	81	1,019,556	802,398	882,403	82,005
			82	834,754	743,977	825,014	81,037
			83	960,442	910,487	1,001,915	91,428
			84	1,137,798	947,550	1,084,925	137,375
			85	225,005	104,932	127,577	22,645
			86	1,494,740	1,185,204	1,309,362	124,158
	V	H	81	6,241	7,610	8,334	724
			82	9,663	10,103	10,992	889
			83	6,328	9,352	10,127	775
			84	5,234	8,282	9,247	965
			85	7,087	8,995	9,966	971
			86	7,761	9,754	10,813	1,059
	V	W	81	800,779	654,533	702,898	48,365
			82	1,397,201	1,055,733	1,165,082	109,349

Product
TSUSA commodity number, description, and unit of quantity

Country	Mode	Reg	Yr	Quantity	F.A.S.	C.I.F.	Charges
			83	1,660,705	1,087,672	1,184,062	96,390
			84	1,873,042	1,133,174	1,258,174	125,000
			85	1,221,091	940,505	1,012,832	72,327
			86	2,246,200	1,278,460	1,374,554	96,094
COLOMB	A	E	83	1,983	1,682	2,599	917
			84	1,123	575	593	18
	N	E	86	27,522	30,696	32,409	1,713
	V	E	85	9,687	5,603	6,557	954
DENMARK	A	W	84	250	816	1,114	298
	N	E	83	2,192	2,492	3,490	998
			86	1,161	8,488	9,704	1,216
	V	E	81	5,955	5,841	6,708	867
			82	850	756	1,095	339
			84	701	1,865	2,574	709
			85	2,917	7,605	8,941	1,336
	V	W	81	618	738	1,008	270
			82	322	299	448	149
			83	2,006	1,269	1,594	325
			85	2,791	4,324	5,068	744
DOM REP	A	E	81	18,254	1,558	2,166	608
	N	E	83	2,100	1,792	2,082	290
			84	16,079	5,781	7,139	1,358
	V	E	81	25,965	31,210	33,444	2,234
			84	1,400	860	966	106
			85	116,574	45,634	50,436	4,802
			86	69,963	33,223	37,688	4,465
DOMINCA	V	E	82	14	451	503	52
			84	150	677	725	48
			85	3,523	8,152	8,830	678
			86	3,970	2,083	2,470	387
EGYPT	V	W	85	348	1,682	1,762	80
FR GERM	N	E	82	3,759	5,579	6,298	719
			85	13,267	20,569	22,427	1,858
	O	E	81	1,510	3,010	3,258	248
			83	2,947	5,713	6,139	426
			84	9,807	14,562	16,697	2,135
			85	3,258	7,871	8,872	1,001
	V	E	81	16,641	27,714	29,820	2,106
			82	27,277	54,863	60,336	5,473
			83	29,649	52,216	55,979	3,763
			84	46,726	54,191	57,926	3,735
			85	5,265	9,432	10,345	913
			86	42,513	87,508	93,395	5,887
	V	W	81	53,086	114,561	120,533	5,972
			82	131,974	187,440	204,690	17,250
			83	161,799	172,371	190,290	17,919
			84	52,510	50,573	61,224	10,651
			85	7,279	5,604	6,602	998
			86	7,997	12,276	13,419	1,143
FRANCE	A	E	81	20	310	340	30
			82	30	265	308	43
			84	950	1,668	2,559	891
			86	992	2,873	3,243	370
	A	W	82	348	352	522	170
	N	E	81	45,850	43,303	47,307	4,004
			82	39,393	38,801	43,815	5,014
			83	37,157	48,333	53,404	5,071
			84	57,011	43,563	52,606	9,043
			85	33,028	43,404	54,566	11,162
			86	49,945	80,473	88,876	8,403
	N	W	81	55,296	102,444	108,744	6,300
			86	94,815	50,784	58,474	7,690
	O	E	81	1,156	3,226	3,619	393
			82	580	1,094	1,257	163
			83	1,700	1,136	1,238	102
			85	2,502	4,796	5,158	362
			86	7,170	10,874	11,597	723
	V	E	81	4,412	1,595	1,685	90
			82	14,692	19,024	20,277	1,253
			83	16,922	19,115	21,415	2,300
			84	18,357	23,186	26,327	3,141
			85	37,414	49,305	53,323	4,018
			86	46,486	47,042	53,366	6,324
	V	W	81	3,222	4,254	4,523	269
			82	20,601	29,862	32,006	2,144
			83	26,023	31,187	33,959	2,772
			84	126,029	103,993	121,787	17,794
			85	24,457	30,675	33,283	2,608
			86	17,249	30,680	33,688	3,008
GAZA ST	V	W	84	338	2,612	2,747	135
GREECE	V	E	84	1,984	1,620	1,983	363
GRENADA	V	E	84	1,800	1,670	2,076	406
GUATMAL	A	W	83	719	798	1,072	274
			84	512	325	401	76
	V	E	84	2,830	2,795	3,134	339

Product
TSUSA commodity number, description, and unit of quantity

Country	Mode	Reg	Yr	Quantity	F.A.S.	C.I.F.	Charges
			85	19,625	22,886	24,268	1,382
			86	8,264	12,066	12,426	360
	V	W	83	502	339	402	63
GUYANA	O	E	81	630	1,200	1,200	
			83	3,066	1,400	1,400	
			84	527	1,432	1,432	
			85	4,120	10,385	10,385	
			86	4,320	1,096	1,096	
	V	E	81	5,106	4,605	5,534	929
			82	11,306	6,902	8,666	1,764
HG KONG	N	E	84	131,473	72,263	85,668	13,405
	N	H	85	9,000	7,484	13,237	5,753
	N	W	83	455,226	159,826	176,078	16,252
			84	1,172,842	662,032	723,988	61,956
	O	E	81	600	594	642	48
			84	3,477	1,610	1,735	125
			85	17,160	6,668	7,892	1,224
	O	W	82	4,500	3,016	3,214	198
			86	6,251	7,688	8,140	452
	V	E	81	2,917,191	1,560,072	1,728,428	168,356
			82	3,194,638	1,653,557	1,875,469	221,912
			83	4,145,104	1,863,464	2,139,076	275,612
			84	5,004,076	2,332,570	2,738,382	405,812
			85	5,872,432	2,617,568	3,019,497	401,929
			86	7,508,421	3,273,005	3,677,547	404,542
	V	H	81	131,323	87,450	93,244	5,794
			82	193,278	122,205	132,355	10,150
			83	76,493	54,664	59,866	5,202
			84	105,108	59,342	66,869	7,527
			85	36,478	23,317	25,751	2,434
			86	67,266	50,361	54,389	4,028
	V	W	81	2,696,745	1,517,151	1,616,159	99,008
			82	4,327,811	2,665,798	2,856,344	190,546
			83	4,869,177	3,220,804	3,397,881	177,077
			84	7,639,067	4,046,946	4,378,706	331,760
			85	5,185,179	2,744,169	2,971,286	227,117
			86	7,024,890	3,420,335	3,650,632	230,297
HONDURA	V	E	81	2,165	2,879	3,124	245
			82	1,033	1,665	1,894	229
ICELAND	V	E	85	35,986	7,927	9,677	1,750
			86	23,400	10,101	12,391	2,290
INDIA	N	E	82	284,006	221,859	270,897	49,038
			83	6,351	6,046	6,912	866
	N	W	83	24,604	12,159	13,888	1,729
			84	3,775	4,606	5,082	476
	O	E	81	265	257	299	42
			84	1,683	1,464	1,773	309
			85	13,933	5,251	5,986	735
	O	W	86	18,990	26,846	28,430	1,584
	V	E	81	268,409	240,371	301,768	61,397
			82	2,210	3,302	3,712	410
			83	270,755	199,589	241,066	41,477
			84	208,381	166,161	193,390	27,229
			85	121,021	66,769	75,710	8,941
			86	108,869	67,984	76,610	8,626
	V	W	81	192,188	117,029	145,948	28,919
			82	212,123	110,927	136,715	25,788
			83	134,572	67,377	82,369	14,992
			84	170,108	92,935	117,728	24,793
			85	229,858	126,437	147,145	20,708
			86	207,108	122,578	140,910	18,332
INDNSIA	V	E	83	1,938	608	915	307
	V	W	81	3,130	1,627	2,459	832
			82	1,427	1,700	2,112	412
			83	16,458	7,492	9,906	2,414
			84	5,865	5,931	6,692	761
			85	15,065	5,477	6,306	829
			86	73,613	54,691	63,423	8,732
IRAN	V	E	85	6,563	3,989	4,557	568
			86	6,750	5,475	7,731	2,256
IRELAND	O	E	81	16,200	8,640	13,210	4,570
			84	1,470	1,842	2,370	528
	V	E	82	27,938	60,589	65,299	4,710
			83	28,965	65,832	72,225	6,393
			84	53,422	17,367	23,531	6,164
			85	21,664	11,531	15,664	4,133
			86	51,012	27,682	33,701	6,019
	V	W	81	9,530	4,992	8,480	3,488
			82	8,194	5,472	8,380	2,908
			83	1,350	905	1,467	562
			84	15,095	6,383	7,228	845
			85	6,382	6,110	6,497	387
			86	1,350	1,032	1,041	9
ISRAEL	V	E	81	265,180	60,973	75,784	14,811
			82	382,473	109,225	130,645	21,420

Product
TSUSA commodity number, description, and unit of quantity

Country	Mode	Reg	Yr	Quantity	F.A.S.	C.I.F.	Charges
			83	876,781	264,313	313,115	48,802
			84	1,737,483	535,815	624,416	88,601
			85	4,094,953	877,596	1,077,828	200,232
			86	7,526,029	1,654,086	2,011,956	357,870
	V	W	82	2,475	1,970	2,204	234
			83	1,917	1,953	2,102	149
			84	2,063	1,881	2,019	138
			85	4,532	5,890	6,408	518
			86	16,424	13,127	14,339	1,212
ITALY	N	E	82	248,402	353,200	397,113	43,913
			83	121,671	186,643	215,849	29,206
			84	111,518	276,231	304,416	28,185
	N	W	86	8,474	11,322	12,111	789
	O	E	81	2,649	2,376	2,609	233
			84	1,031	1,297	1,459	162
			85	3,476	3,830	4,541	711
			86	2,786	5,700	6,555	855
	O	W	85	8,818	7,164	7,926	762
	V	E	81	620,621	473,693	561,485	90,792
			82	39,197	36,107	39,957	3,850
			83	7,255	7,896	9,007	1,111
			84	33,266	30,829	35,592	4,763
			85	258,026	491,307	534,627	43,320
			86	383,615	592,866	659,437	66,571
	V	W	81	179,723	110,105	140,269	30,164
			82	165,176	105,673	132,776	27,103
			83	20,551	40,184	44,297	4,113
			84	9,196	25,847	28,230	2,383
			85	12,810	27,368	29,922	2,554
			86	40,331	119,491	125,159	5,668
IVY CST	V	E	83	3,527	1,850	2,310	460
			84	31,746	23,850	25,760	1,910
			86	6,428	4,428	4,926	498
JAMAICA	A	E	81	294	448	473	25
			82	2,549	1,896	2,115	219
			83	125	317	451	134
	N	E	82	161,830	213,803	229,580	15,777
			83	21,558	18,374	19,786	1,412
			84	57,908	86,987	93,647	6,660
			85	81,519	64,810	69,737	4,927
	N	W	84	20,356	36,177	41,146	4,969
	O	E	84	225	425	425	
			85	7,975	6,645	6,788	143
	V	E	81	426,883	549,597	618,822	69,225
			82	314,212	399,162	427,114	27,952
			83	402,400	609,182	657,080	47,898
			84	508,848	678,966	737,847	58,881
			85	575,511	795,351	860,796	65,445
			86	526,213	689,048	749,618	60,570
	V	W	82	55,200	97,313	106,085	8,772
			83	64,260	103,950	108,181	4,231
			84	60,810	98,365	109,490	11,125
			85	101,495	128,930	143,415	14,485
			86	57,381	111,865	123,300	11,435
JAPAN	N	E	81	296,517	344,511	388,398	43,887
			83	634,242	563,746	641,749	78,003
			84	651,950	724,163	818,722	94,559
			85	659,457	666,434	768,151	101,717
			86	988,923	950,227	1,049,106	98,879
	N	H	81	201,387	212,227	248,920	35,693
			83	314,179	320,425	372,002	51,577
			84	328,000	338,216	395,800	57,584
	N	W	83	1,552,989	1,119,500	1,206,480	86,980
			84	664,775	584,227	632,573	48,346
			85	414,964	418,909	450,826	31,917
	O	E	85	1,424	2,659	2,659	
	O	H	81	11,338	6,050	7,908	1,849
			82	10,340	19,932	22,000	2,068
			83	25,618	51,031	57,200	6,169
			84	28,659	55,543	69,291	13,748
			85	2,293	3,883	4,400	517
			86	7,143	14,332	16,500	2,168
	O	W	85	3,071	3,424	3,688	264
			86	7,613	15,213	15,999	786
	V	E	81	41,015	42,128	47,331	5,203
			82	485,348	564,398	629,159	64,761
			83	174,723	169,149	186,045	16,896
			84	264,781	223,470	250,796	27,326
			85	240,910	239,372	267,024	27,652
			86	408,805	394,655	433,748	39,093
	V	H	82	250,790	262,960	306,292	43,332
			85	327,788	395,814	463,359	67,545
			86	326,838	535,212	607,036	71,824
	V	W	81	1,043,943	1,093,583	1,180,360	86,234
			82	1,140,824	1,221,631	1,311,627	89,996

Product
TSUSA commodity number, description, and unit of quantity

Country	Mode	Reg	Yr	Quantity	F.A.S.	C.I.F.	Charges
			83	126,502	131,625	143,432	11,807
			84	649,024	630,319	687,369	57,050
			85	1,864,742	1,740,104	1,889,977	149,873
			86	2,846,569	3,283,268	3,458,976	175,708
JORDAN	V	E	84	7,200	9,254	9,578	324
KOR REP	V	E	81	51,567	23,602	26,994	3,392
			82	168,927	135,315	151,556	16,241
			83	254,831	195,162	214,485	19,323
			84	159,679	99,732	121,649	21,917
			85	238,160	135,358	158,739	23,381
			86	550,459	279,855	325,950	46,095
	V	H	82	1,621	1,175	1,366	191
			83	12,609	7,960	9,103	1,143
			84	6,423	3,335	4,346	1,011
			85	3,496	3,129	3,786	657
			86	7,372	2,031	2,418	387
	V	W	81	39,272	21,696	23,849	2,153
			82	56,527	35,027	38,470	3,443
			83	152,965	134,221	144,740	10,519
			84	214,511	131,253	143,805	12,552
			85	245,832	110,562	128,370	17,808
			86	435,064	193,020	214,514	21,494
LEBANON	O	E	83	1,950	976	976	
	V	E	84	3,782	1,788	2,262	474
			85	7,360	6,171	6,461	290
			86	14,629	7,231	8,301	1,070
	V	W	84	14,231	10,300	10,815	515
MALAYSA	O	W	85	2,963	2,162	2,162	
	V	E	81	2,700	4,334	4,680	346
			82	9,240	8,422	9,660	1,238
			83	6,603	5,112	5,207	95
			84	9,931	6,994	8,063	1,069
			86	10,658	3,913	4,423	510
	V	W	81	6,450	4,608	5,360	752
			82	19,970	16,852	18,537	1,685
			83	19,390	16,886	18,569	1,683
			84	1,012	623	731	108
			85	27,592	23,515	26,254	2,739
			86	29,628	22,160	25,249	3,089
MEXICO	A	W	86	3,264	1,323	2,222	899
	O	E	81	3,459,965	2,417,958	2,417,958	
			82	3,269,976	2,514,377	2,514,377	
			83	3,170,481	1,844,626	1,844,626	
			84	2,150,230	1,180,651	1,180,651	
			85	3,081,086	2,291,941	2,291,941	
			86	2,841,315	1,898,030	1,898,030	
	O	W	81	2,825,187	1,784,943	1,785,373	188
			82	3,253,924	1,717,694	1,717,694	
			83	3,353,442	1,076,569	1,076,605	36
			84	3,727,283	1,397,979	1,397,979	
			85	3,619,545	1,679,188	1,679,188	
			86	4,639,497	2,154,107	2,154,110	3
	V	E	84	26,025	9,387	10,081	694
	V	W	81	29,190	16,958	17,952	994
			82	2,100	1,200	1,374	174
			84	67,337	14,216	16,533	2,317
N ZEAL	V	E	84	656	1,051	1,170	119
NETHLDS	N	E	81	127,028	128,847	149,034	20,187
			86	9,542	19,369	22,529	3,160
	O	E	81	6,255	8,798	9,347	549
			83	2,115	3,812	4,198	386
			85	2,019	1,086	1,258	172
			86	8,840	30,241	32,533	2,292
	O	W	84	4,040	4,423	4,688	265
	V	E	81	2,072	1,978	2,305	327
			82	74,674	76,068	86,045	9,977
			83	58,624	68,444	73,846	5,402
			84	94,353	98,507	109,819	11,312
			85	73,766	65,595	73,081	7,486
			86	7,078	7,330	8,523	1,193
	V	W	81	63,975	124,338	131,217	6,879
			82	15,560	27,220	28,981	1,761
			83	18,092	23,741	25,352	1,611
			84	14,467	10,431	11,912	1,481
			85	259,249	174,505	198,216	23,711
			86	137,804	136,180	148,809	12,629
NORWAY	V	E	83	97	1,462	1,602	140
	V	W	81	842	1,032	1,324	292
			82	337	359	423	64
			83	337	394	394	
			84	674	874	1,105	231
PAKISTN	V	E	81	1,176	972	1,206	234
			83	2,445	3,808	4,257	449
			85	1,058	1,800	2,056	256
			86	1,764	1,410	1,676	266

Product
TSUSA commodity number, description, and unit of quantity

Country	Mode	Reg	Yr	Quantity	F.A.S.	C.I.F.	Charges
	V	W	82	3,830	4,036	4,913	877
			84	2,355	2,000	2,654	654
			85	3,780	5,348	5,644	296
PERU	A	E	82	1,270	2,160	2,833	673
	V	E	85	24,495	24,496	25,692	1,196
			86	55,597	60,148	63,548	3,400
PHIL R	N	W	83	4,151	2,171	2,627	456
	O	H	85	17,280	8,832	11,132	2,300
	V	E	81	33,410	19,782	23,572	3,790
			82	75,243	45,041	54,077	9,036
			83	77,181	36,854	43,629	6,775
			84	96,300	42,581	52,365	9,784
			85	57,952	42,709	50,377	7,668
			86	35,288	26,332	31,567	5,235
	V	H	81	711	652	730	78
			82	1,095	856	991	135
			83	2,145	1,401	1,678	277
			84	8,008	3,693	4,733	1,040
			85	9,928	15,775	18,369	2,594
			86	7,836	8,836	9,722	886
	V	W	81	205,426	100,641	116,717	16,076
			82	280,438	141,539	163,811	22,272
			83	355,163	175,051	197,393	22,342
			84	418,866	182,568	213,059	30,491
			85	364,623	198,924	225,806	26,882
			86	587,285	292,357	329,178	36,821
PORTUGL	V	E	81	6,788	4,510	6,704	2,194
			82	28,381	13,734	16,267	2,533
			83	31,968	8,264	9,726	1,462
			84	14,591	40,536	41,365	829
			85	174,052	30,859	40,982	10,123
			86	476,590	90,440	116,679	26,239
REP SAF	V	E	86	56,591	43,492	48,686	5,194
S VN GR	V	E	84	329	278	308	30
SALVADR	V	E	84	506	379	413	34
SINGAPR	N	W	84	25,129	15,274	16,921	1,647
	O	E	82	8	511	553	42
	O	W	81	624	772	772	
	V	E	81	28,280	28,179	32,141	3,962
			82	28,676	29,778	32,478	2,700
			83	63,963	45,108	53,433	8,325
			84	44,616	41,876	48,133	6,257
			85	50,513	30,945	36,842	5,897
			86	58,352	48,635	55,154	6,519
	V	W	81	218,679	161,883	179,392	17,509
			82	182,019	147,656	160,501	12,845
			83	167,759	107,147	119,492	12,345
			84	266,058	165,523	184,378	18,855
			85	158,546	113,311	131,323	18,012
			86	203,813	142,116	159,485	17,369
SPAIN	N	E	82	978,950	282,054	368,842	86,788
			85	371,604	72,628	113,310	40,682
	V	E	81	2,454,469	722,497	981,956	259,459
			82	2,063,066	542,397	770,547	228,150
			83	3,820,470	796,310	1,142,060	345,750
			84	4,955,872	926,840	1,375,989	449,149
			85	3,674,706	737,670	1,096,938	359,268
			86	4,268,951	1,032,966	1,450,612	417,646
	V	W	81	34,724	10,616	15,585	4,969
			82	54,391	13,672	19,663	5,991
			83	117,936	27,556	38,044	10,488
			84	97,994	22,851	31,636	8,785
			85	152,196	25,845	36,164	10,319
			86	56,819	17,990	24,533	6,543
SRI LKA	O	E	81	86	306	306	
			83	590	324	324	
SURINAM	V	E	84	5,775	1,600	2,203	603
SWAZLND	O	E	85	6,268	10,494	10,990	496
	V	E	86	29,882	5,233	6,739	1,506
SWEDEN	A	E	85	827	1,425	2,311	886
	A	W	84	53	389	463	74
	N	E	83	7,089	10,679	12,396	1,717
	O	E	84	32,081	61,025	64,201	3,176
			86	9,849	6,810	7,899	1,089
	V	E	81	139	276	291	15
			82	4,246	9,792	10,680	888
			84	5,748	10,163	11,892	1,729
			85	47,157	67,221	72,045	4,824
			86	40,169	28,999	32,360	3,361
	V	W	81	11,818	25,871	27,790	1,919
			82	19,048	15,069	19,969	4,900
SWITZLD	A	E	84	5,295	8,696	11,685	2,989
			86	7,829	4,529	11,344	6,815
	N	E	81	588,227	1,194,666	1,256,208	60,977
			82	185,045	398,825	417,518	18,693

Product
TSUSA commodity number, description, and unit of quantity

Country	Mode	Reg	Yr	Quantity	F.A.S.	C.I.F.	Charges
			83	1,182,946	2,259,593	2,374,551	114,958
			84	1,065,632	1,641,320	1,744,799	103,479
			85	2,316,291	3,468,059	3,712,072	244,013
			86	96,013	175,909	188,746	12,837
	N	W	81	466,283	929,165	980,545	51,380
			82	820,875	1,308,918	1,404,512	95,594
			84	1,013,024	1,946,425	2,090,615	144,190
			85	866,732	1,478,095	1,621,968	143,873
			86	39,296	57,841	62,038	4,197
	O	E	81	334,400	771,677	806,084	34,405
			82	27,956	64,794	68,456	3,662
			83	15,831	23,711	26,063	2,352
			84	1,119,133	1,919,280	2,029,778	110,498
			85	5,084	8,572	8,572	
			86	32,709	58,657	64,609	5,952
	V	E	81	374,064	659,449	700,642	41,193
			82	1,509,298	2,856,198	3,003,325	147,127
			83	871,189	1,415,341	1,501,980	86,639
			84	366,882	594,184	617,348	23,164
			85	504,351	840,824	890,003	49,179
			86	2,834,608	4,618,081	4,881,692	263,611
	V	W	81	180,891	300,472	335,264	24,210
			82	49,809	117,494	124,621	7,127
			83	867,222	1,422,107	1,517,445	95,338
			84	571,192	580,513	643,763	63,250
			85	400,552	374,078	421,951	47,873
			86	959,574	1,620,182	1,732,906	112,724
SYRIA	V	E	81	10,350	9,945	10,510	565
THAILND	N	E	85	228,504	204,803	234,342	29,539
			86	408,665	359,905	399,234	39,329
	N	H	84	9,088	8,491	9,552	1,061
	N	W	84	550,386	489,475	528,251	38,776
			85	30,487	10,818	12,561	1,743
	O	E	82	1,747	1,814	1,995	181
			83	1,234	825	901	76
			85	5,970	8,770	8,770	
			86	6,292	4,736	5,490	754
	O	W	82	210	640	640	
			84	2,001	1,649	1,788	139
			85	5,638	6,533	7,129	596
			86	8,280	6,430	7,042	612
	V	E	81	314,103	280,592	315,476	34,884
			82	223,484	199,853	226,960	27,107
			83	256,855	212,139	239,167	27,028
			84	305,519	274,864	308,193	33,329
			85	45,446	32,846	38,174	5,328
			86	200,486	87,466	104,968	17,502
	V	H	81	9,709	9,086	10,097	1,011
			82	6,080	4,094	4,680	586
			83	7,419	6,885	7,778	893
			85	25,065	10,919	12,461	1,542
			86	7,959	5,476	6,706	1,230
	V	W	81	583,157	470,670	519,677	49,007
			82	750,051	637,104	707,694	70,590
			83	938,802	688,310	747,056	58,746
			84	375,630	298,744	329,509	30,765
			85	941,685	635,015	697,834	62,819
			86	1,305,629	769,994	840,058	70,064
TRINID	A	E	81	2,730	1,168	1,588	420
			83	4,450	2,937	4,025	1,088
			84	3,700	2,200	3,510	1,310
	N	E	83	97,061	180,324	188,862	8,538
			84	47,531	86,940	91,261	4,321
	V	E	81	17,204	27,685	29,035	1,350
			82	90,064	155,953	162,845	6,892
			83	11,625	19,600	20,283	683
			84	12,801	19,665	20,992	1,327
			85	150,341	212,447	223,063	10,616
			86	82,265	59,362	64,952	5,590
TURKEY	V	E	86	9,259	4,425	4,576	151
U KING	A	E	82	2,815	2,707	3,142	435
			84	948	859	1,185	326
	N	E	81	206,586	282,674	307,915	25,241
			82	334,699	344,806	383,309	38,503
			83	540,790	545,354	605,575	60,221
			84	712,140	521,125	598,123	76,998
			85	1,001,195	827,340	934,816	107,476
			86	750,938	718,441	793,284	74,843
	N	W	81	57,261	80,882	96,405	15,523
			82	39,746	46,226	52,295	6,069
			84	24,259	20,502	25,109	4,607
	O	E	81	38,375	55,178	59,035	3,857
			82	59,033	60,997	65,707	4,710
			83	24,458	29,204	31,865	2,661
			84	191,451	175,025	193,046	18,021

Product
TSUSA commodity number, description, and unit of quantity

Country	Mode	Reg	Yr	Quantity	F.A.S.	C.I.F.	Charges
			85	34,901	51,149	56,880	5,731
			86	22,544	40,478	43,163	2,685
	V	E	81	239,863	322,418	356,026	33,608
			82	138,501	135,692	150,009	14,317
			83	169,296	160,732	178,294	17,562
			84	215,150	164,184	183,602	19,418
			85	115,973	94,176	113,283	19,107
			86	396,830	302,587	345,091	42,504
	V	W	81	28,685	37,713	42,045	4,332
			82	21,942	24,738	26,165	1,427
			83	127,930	137,496	152,891	15,395
			84	140,136	134,381	150,547	16,166
			85	219,331	127,770	148,284	20,514
			86	163,259	185,534	203,961	18,427
URUGUAY	V	E	82	200	424	514	90
VENEZ	A	E	83	7,485	15,295	21,358	6,063
	V	E	82	36,810	28,923	29,823	900
			86	328,849	85,321	97,269	11,948
YUGOSLV	V	E	82	3,516	2,862	3,095	233
			83	3,309	2,411	2,695	284
			84	1,883	960	1,139	179

Soups

1825200 SOUPS & SOUP PREPS, NSPF (LB)

Country	Mode	Reg	Yr	Quantity	F.A.S.	C.I.F.	Charges
TOTAL			81	11,780,291	20,073,052	21,357,667	1,263,191
			82	13,317,632	23,877,946	25,431,687	1,553,741
			83	15,936,283	26,215,099	27,764,115	1,549,016
			84	17,390,723	25,730,143	27,420,861	1,690,718
			85	20,616,696	28,098,178	30,155,616	2,057,438
			86	21,795,657	32,304,173	34,199,368	1,895,195
ARGENT	A	E	82	1,246	1,130	2,614	1,484
	O	E	81	3,960	1,188	2,168	980
	V	W	82	49,736	149,208	153,914	4,706
			83	153,552	132,769	143,422	10,653
AUSTRAL	A	W	84	2,028	1,122	2,513	1,391
	N	W	85	54,197	37,082	42,170	5,088
			86	118,881	73,941	86,122	12,181
	O	E	84	525	975	1,308	333
			85	578	1,072	1,299	227
	V	W	84	281	690	721	31
AUSTRIA	O	E	81	1,044	1,244	1,244	
			82	1,688	2,925	3,226	301
			83	195	264	264	
			85	735	1,365	1,465	100
	O	W	83	480	975	1,048	73
BAHAMAS	O	E	84	11,430	15,828	16,444	616
BELGIUM	N	E	84	78,651	95,298	99,223	3,925
	O	E	81	1,267	2,467	2,659	192
			83	74,577	113,683	120,270	6,587
			84	13,715	17,860	18,815	955
			85	12,366	26,751	29,511	2,760
			86	1,303	2,400	2,533	133
	V	E	85	2,903	2,763	3,043	280
			86	13,580	29,443	32,598	3,155
BRAZIL	A	E	82	1,343	1,254	3,031	1,777
	V	E	82	11,199	34,720	35,259	539
			84	6,720	18,816	19,193	377
			85	6,720	18,816	19,163	347
	V	W	83	300	850	888	38
BURMA	V	E	82	540	1,620	1,811	191
C RICA	V	E	86	168,748	289,209	309,652	20,443
	V	W	83	660	484	834	350
CANADA	A	E	82	552	1,130	1,290	160
			86	485	1,037	1,186	149
	A	W	84	2,467	5,958	6,193	235
	N	E	82	1,725	2,314	2,857	543
			83	98,909	126,298	126,323	25
	O	E	81	408,788	420,582	420,582	
			82	306,807	494,828	495,513	685
			83	1,487,442	1,402,220	1,406,311	4,091
			84	882,898	916,796	917,123	327
			85	1,577,926	934,008	934,110	102
			86	3,807,377	1,649,882	1,649,882	
	O	W	81	13,857	17,481	17,601	120
			82	8,137	8,338	8,338	
			83	104,761	94,025	94,431	406
			84	145,635	129,740	129,741	1
			85	76,291	75,635	75,761	126
			86	34,073	32,137	32,137	
	V	E	85	3,122	4,198	4,673	475
CHILE	O	E	83	260	1,301	1,301	
	V	W	85	4,050	3,271	3,700	429
CHINA M	N	E	83	219,149	302,725	328,810	26,085
	O	E	81	1,675	1,216	1,420	204
			83	2,028	2,130	2,411	281
			84	1,581	2,448	2,822	374
			85	20,000	3,622	3,911	289
	O	W	86	2,500	1,070	1,070	
	V	E	81	129,418	186,255	202,915	16,660
			82	116,618	148,263	163,539	15,276
			83	5,100	10,115	11,359	1,244
			84	42,444	78,810	87,058	8,248
			85	18,861	24,089	27,167	3,078
			86	38,233	48,997	54,303	5,306
	V	H	81	630	577	619	42
			82	32	269	284	15
			83	132	1,322	1,462	140
			84	259	300	329	29
	V	W	81	174,631	198,318	213,409	15,091
			82	193,279	213,365	228,655	15,290
			83	200,985	280,845	299,092	18,247
			84	198,625	241,945	259,048	17,103
			85	170,418	175,741	187,444	11,703
			86	175,765	165,280	174,217	8,937
CHINA T	O	E	81	641	310	335	25
			84	265	270	297	27
	V	E	81	28,612	21,068	24,127	3,059
			82	12,080	14,407	15,532	1,125
			83	24,200	19,611	21,791	2,180
			84	64,163	44,170	54,508	10,338
			85	12,697	6,921	8,091	1,170
			86	32,166	18,440	20,575	2,135
	V	H	82	62	467	607	140
	V	W	81	19,611	9,393	10,113	720
			82	19,080	11,175	12,060	885
			83	45,757	41,798	44,848	3,050
			84	147,434	94,193	108,856	14,663
			85	85,571	60,423	69,120	8,697
			86	61,367	45,559	48,409	2,850
COLOMB	V	E	82	4,752	3,168	3,609	441
CYPRUS	A	E	85	882	1,600	2,663	1,063
DENMARK	V	E	81	300	419	497	78
			82	525	353	402	49
			85	3,571	3,144	4,275	1,131
			86	11,725	11,177	11,927	750
	V	W	85	337	1,010	1,121	111
DOM REP	A	E	84	3,248	3,918	5,418	1,500
	N	E	83	25,250	9,425	14,407	4,982
			84	77,231	36,981	46,157	9,176
			85	137,999	78,542	88,961	10,419
			86	99,420	89,554	99,596	10,042
	V	E	83	3,150	1,800	2,238	438
			84	875	500	672	172
			85	106,004	46,083	53,385	7,302
			86	206,564	130,453	141,165	10,712
	V	W	83	1,885	780	862	82
ECUADOR	A	E	82	188	400	812	412
	N	E	82	84,332	84,089	88,577	4,488
	V	E	81	155,189	224,556	233,950	9,394
			83	32,094	42,402	44,657	2,255
ETHIOP	O	W	86	1,763	1,452	1,452	
FINLAND	A	W	84	2,846	482	1,210	728
	V	E	85	24,445	7,356	10,056	2,700
	V	W	85	33,592	10,797	15,288	4,491
			86	31,288	9,846	14,284	4,438
FR GERM	A	E	81	420	270	469	199
			84	270	385	625	240
	N	E	85	13,005	9,920	11,251	1,331
	N	W	84	1,037	2,889	3,274	385
	O	E	81	13,037	17,933	19,916	1,983
			82	8,006	7,929	9,146	1,217
			83	10,392	12,029	13,639	1,610
			84	8,331	7,023	8,042	1,019
			86	5,880	2,846	3,294	448
	V	E	81	65,479	109,699	118,983	9,284
			82	131,380	255,525	274,901	19,376
			83	174,707	246,447	260,152	13,705
			84	148,394	143,175	152,560	9,385
			85	158,320	97,871	110,884	13,013
			86	309,060	369,125	398,944	29,819
	V	W	81	98,727	205,948	217,670	11,722
			82	77,232	146,427	154,949	8,522
			83	47,562	93,584	98,379	4,795
			84	8,321	7,007	7,896	889
			85	95,513	95,130	107,941	12,811
			86	13,795	21,167	21,844	677
FRANCE	A	E	82	315	600	671	71

Product
TSUSA commodity number, description, and unit of quantity

Country	Mode	Reg	Yr	Quantity	F.A.S.	C.I.F.	Charges
			83	121	251	351	100
			84	2,479	1,906	4,323	2,417
	N	E	81	12,080	15,614	16,602	988
			82	4,704	8,538	9,037	499
			84	15,550	18,873	20,746	1,873
			86	51,360	100,075	106,161	6,086
	N	W	84	28,222	23,007	24,651	1,644
	O	E	82	63	276	316	40
			84	1,455	1,767	2,223	456
			85	5,502	2,579	3,160	581
			86	525	1,248	1,442	194
	V	E	81	25,151	29,945	32,490	2,545
			82	19,924	23,618	26,030	2,412
			83	46,324	44,825	48,740	3,915
			84	38,417	42,403	47,640	5,237
			85	51,802	66,617	73,276	6,659
			86	41,160	63,816	66,631	2,815
	V	W	81	83,044	140,337	148,416	8,079
			82	79,743	107,618	115,156	7,538
			83	2,840	3,749	4,190	441
			84	551	683	754	71
			85	42,565	53,149	58,584	5,435
			86	74,079	134,904	146,863	11,959
GHANA	N	E	86	7,079	7,120	12,092	4,972
	V	E	81	4,733	4,200	4,869	669
			83	256	960	1,166	206
			86	4,189	5,810	6,748	938
GUATMAL	A	E	82	1,510	2,298	2,908	610
			83	4,639	6,255	7,989	1,734
	A	W	81	41,225	60,620	72,116	11,496
			82	28,212	47,303	57,903	10,600
			83	24,418	40,933	51,414	10,481
			84	16,325	28,780	36,342	7,562
			85	4,380	12,691	15,272	2,581
			86	720	1,329	1,589	260
	N	E	83	125,772	275,334	286,066	10,732
	N	W	82	29,729	46,756	54,187	7,431
			83	29,815	36,034	43,175	7,141
			84	15,312	27,836	33,295	5,459
			85	36,048	51,959	56,574	4,615
			86	2,449	5,723	6,508	785
	O	E	84	2,187	3,695	4,865	1,170
			85	24,867	13,549	13,549	
	O	W	85	185,469	109,623	109,623	
			86	42,000	24,802	24,802	
	V	E	84	50,862	69,076	72,812	3,736
			85	160,935	196,186	214,869	18,683
			86	132,533	168,390	181,792	13,402
	V	W	83	3,731	7,212	9,292	2,080
			85	6,020	16,885	17,648	763
			86	40,540	50,534	54,969	4,435
HG KONG	N	W	82	20,353	24,572	27,172	2,600
	O	E	81	626	1,800	1,944	144
			83	1,010	1,732	1,888	156
			84	563	846	846	
	O	W	85	541	2,391	2,617	226
	V	E	81	21,295	31,179	33,873	2,694
			82	17,729	27,333	29,412	2,079
			83	49,445	63,616	70,101	6,485
			84	33,478	37,570	44,333	6,763
			85	12,618	34,438	37,610	3,172
			86	68,057	62,567	71,411	8,844
	V	H	82	150	294	314	20
	V	W	81	15,031	23,045	24,518	1,473
			82	27,188	28,407	30,583	2,176
			83	41,381	63,669	67,432	3,763
			84	41,629	90,776	95,416	4,640
			85	33,334	37,784	40,171	2,387
			86	36,014	56,149	59,938	3,789
ICELAND	V	E	86	1,777	1,712	1,774	62
INDIA	O	E	81	50	419	419	
	V	W	81	220	444	556	112
INDNSIA	V	W	84	5,420	23,169	24,649	1,480
			86	353	2,707	2,967	260
IRELAND	A	E	82	41	380	849	469
	N	E	86	3,020	5,402	6,950	1,548
	O	E	84	288	376	486	110
	V	E	85	24,030	44,057	47,019	2,962
ISRAEL	A	E	85	2,191	4,476	6,134	1,658
	N	E	82	356,128	552,907	604,475	51,568
			84	36,871	54,532	60,451	5,919
	O	E	81	600	415	415	
			82	231	959	959	
			83	6,530	1,055	1,055	
			84	16,542	21,636	23,554	1,918
			85	2,994	1,504	1,736	232
			86	5,943	6,237	6,823	586
	V	E	81	282,826	389,745	427,407	37,662
			82	93,566	125,159	137,304	12,145
			83	328,858	594,418	634,337	39,919
			84	703,408	922,056	994,037	71,981
			85	1,142,889	1,321,108	1,447,515	126,407
			86	1,085,218	1,553,154	1,688,045	134,891
	V	W	82	9,577	16,674	18,652	1,978
			83	11,622	24,032	26,092	2,060
			84	14,442	25,664	27,504	1,840
			85	33,640	41,737	45,282	3,545
			86	2,636	7,682	8,979	1,297
ITALY	V	E	82	874	807	885	78
			83	135,195	28,103	29,538	1,435
			85	30,359	51,726	57,080	5,354
	V	W	84	5,587	11,904	13,075	1,171
			85	4,889	10,272	10,973	701
IVY CST	V	E	82	37,957	13,704	22,293	8,589
			83	31,746	12,995	15,587	2,592
			84	83,675	44,780	54,995	10,215
JAMAICA	A	E	82	65	385	573	188
			85	6,775	14,750	15,946	1,196
	N	E	82	751	912	1,004	92
			83	16,754	19,849	20,861	1,012
	V	E	83	14,317	31,623	35,628	4,005
			84	1,612	1,520	2,299	779
			85	6,844	3,432	3,826	394
			86	72,605	59,129	63,800	4,671
	V	W	84	450	599	683	84
JAPAN	A	E	82	114	513	929	416
	A	W	81	20,276	41,690	50,096	8,406
			82	1,530	4,274	8,801	4,527
			83	3,616	4,864	13,383	8,519
			84	503	669	2,216	1,547
	N	E	84	200,016	517,061	571,606	54,545
			85	186,296	503,665	548,411	44,746
			86	200,366	651,467	703,374	51,907
	N	H	81	263,278	529,832	570,322	40,490
			82	295,015	563,118	611,990	48,872
			83	273,104	569,166	625,874	56,708
			84	303,262	636,672	703,946	67,274
			86	274,371	674,106	754,487	80,381
	N	W	82	1,095,957	2,044,980	2,199,168	154,188
			83	1,221,114	2,588,924	2,772,216	183,292
			84	1,037,292	2,211,553	2,331,778	120,225
			85	1,741,643	3,212,828	3,384,386	171,558
			86	1,198,714	2,888,407	3,012,630	124,223
	O	H	81	17,193	43,481	47,610	4,129
			82	38,791	122,445	136,086	13,641
			83	71,165	221,100	248,357	27,257
			84	33,545	85,398	97,410	12,012
			85	41,461	74,954	83,110	8,156
			86	41,722	88,147	98,737	10,590
	O	W	85	541	2,391	2,617	226
			86	1,185	4,676	4,913	237
	V	E	81	144,517	419,301	464,639	45,946
			82	222,306	596,366	664,332	67,966
			83	304,515	789,313	865,038	75,725
			84	61,096	138,622	151,174	12,552
			85	8,296	23,867	27,465	3,598
			86	79,744	238,656	259,150	20,494
	V	H	81	7,901	18,876	20,699	1,823
			85	299,672	585,497	647,389	61,892
			86	38,645	74,465	81,059	6,594
	V	W	81	947,804	2,059,046	2,164,546	105,480
			82	195,298	485,060	522,462	37,402
			83	67,886	161,298	176,152	14,854
			84	102,680	217,935	240,130	22,195
			85	216,844	777,462	824,383	46,921
			86	476,818	1,487,537	1,562,934	75,397
JORDAN	V	E	84	975	896	927	31
			85	4,409	5,930	6,224	294
			86	11,023	5,166	5,425	259
KENYA	V	W	86	858	2,414	2,662	248
KIRIBAT	O	W	85	3,417	1,500	1,500	
KOR REP	N	E	84	31,066	35,120	39,693	4,573
	N	W	84	127,631	139,563	157,253	17,690
	V	E	81	10,719	8,994	9,973	979
			82	25,581	26,778	30,764	3,986
			83	125,235	99,608	118,056	18,448
			84	24,965	39,786	42,280	2,494
			85	65,640	113,205	126,311	13,106
			86	104,931	157,230	174,148	16,918
	V	H	82	99	451	519	68

Product TSUSA commodity number, description, and unit of quantity Country	Mode	Reg	Yr	Quantity	F.A.S.	C.I.F.	Charges
			83	330	2,019	2,362	343
			84	496	784	971	187
			85	638	1,356	1,771	415
	V	W	81	211,915	139,953	159,809	19,855
			82	141,417	112,833	127,518	14,685
			83	146,932	116,599	130,246	13,647
			84	45,208	73,895	80,070	6,175
			85	1,012,591	838,323	914,121	75,798
			86	1,032,027	934,927	1,014,134	79,207
LEBANON	V	E	81	4,632	4,515	4,942	427
			83	1,195	1,355	1,525	170
			84	573	689	727	38
			85	714	1,032	1,083	51
			86	11,230	12,734	13,829	1,095
	V	W	83	1,005	880	987	107
MACAO	V	W	82	33,700	1,330	1,403	73
MALAYSA	V	E	84	3,748	10,499	10,852	353
			85	4,649	7,480	8,294	814
			86	9,930	14,769	15,652	883
	V	H	86	360	1,600	1,631	31
	V	W	84	2,325	3,792	3,900	108
			85	36,304	31,615	34,329	2,714
			86	30,796	48,019	49,476	1,457
MEXICO	A	W	82	9,484	3,365	4,980	1,615
	O	E	81	43,880	107,884	107,884	
			82	338,967	606,942	606,942	
			83	265,424	360,840	360,840	
			84	290,221	457,933	457,933	
			85	561,984	721,008	721,008	
			86	394,188	602,237	602,237	
	O	W	81	697,335	1,307,985	1,307,985	
			82	900,764	1,593,504	1,593,602	98
			83	578,249	706,221	706,221	
			84	604,395	657,269	657,269	
			85	869,523	1,304,277	1,304,277	
			86	1,104,171	1,420,589	1,420,589	
N ZEAL	V	E	82	2,414	5,147	5,551	404
			83	1,343	2,186	2,404	218
			84	479	680	767	87
	V	W	83	1,036	1,024	1,157	133
NETHLDS	A	E	86	470	4,829	5,317	488
	N	E	81	31,324	50,320	52,797	2,477
			84	14,344	16,472	17,597	1,125
			86	1,531	7,576	9,005	1,429
	N	W	84	16,533	20,325	22,228	1,903
	O	E	85	6,670	6,411	6,859	448
			86	6,279	15,393	16,477	1,084
	V	E	81	157,315	239,946	260,893	20,947
			82	19,130	34,986	38,500	3,514
			83	58,738	90,525	95,809	5,284
			84	12,990	24,665	27,455	2,790
			85	2,735	5,589	6,187	598
			86	53,329	69,040	71,520	2,480
	V	W	81	97,297	152,233	160,731	8,498
			82	4,836	10,328	11,332	1,004
			83	7,367	15,194	16,319	1,125
			85	19,433	19,203	21,304	2,101
			86	135,810	193,455	208,619	15,164
NORWAY	N	E	82	18,916	41,479	47,109	5,630
			83	40,409	105,158	111,171	6,013
	V	E	81	2,979	5,073	6,641	1,568
			82	292	371	394	23
			83	1,430	983	1,631	648
			84	30,439	82,659	87,549	4,890
			85	94,702	139,112	157,207	18,095
			86	41,654	44,315	52,250	7,935
	V	W	81	13,440	27,231	30,106	2,875
			82	5,375	11,625	13,156	1,531
			83	5,639	13,051	14,327	1,276
			84	9,502	11,684	13,118	1,434
			85	9,535	20,197	22,700	2,503
			86	3,587	8,688	9,042	354
PERU	A	E	82	1,210	1,080	1,417	337
PHIL R	O	W	86	394	1,905	1,905	
	V	E	81	3,524	5,038	5,826	788
			82	8,575	22,728	26,613	3,885
			83	65,484	58,943	67,560	8,617
			84	21,007	38,273	43,846	5,573
			85	18,780	67,926	74,359	6,433
			86	29,810	102,788	113,212	10,424
	V	H	82	1,879	5,809	6,770	961
			83	1,141	4,125	4,869	744
			84	341	2,325	2,782	457
			86	323	1,135	1,362	227
	V	W	81	10,152	27,395	30,857	3,462

Product TSUSA commodity number, description, and unit of quantity Country	Mode	Reg	Yr	Quantity	F.A.S.	C.I.F.	Charges
			82	67,827	92,395	100,993	8,598
			83	67,732	106,182	117,749	11,567
			84	219,487	300,988	335,450	34,462
			85	343,999	457,471	502,603	45,132
			86	294,896	441,398	478,338	36,940
POLAND	N	E	82	20,998	18,106	19,670	1,564
	V	E	81	38,680	39,553	44,498	4,945
			83	23,534	19,242	20,537	1,295
			84	31,747	27,891	29,700	1,809
			85	22,942	19,937	23,410	3,473
			86	25,332	22,231	24,291	2,060
PORTUGL	N	E	85	13,006	19,799	24,306	4,507
	V	E	82	620	1,382	1,442	60
			83	7,155	4,812	5,934	1,122
			84	27,718	17,183	18,376	1,193
			85	2,235	5,179	5,807	628
			86	21,210	26,226	28,738	2,512
REP SAF	V	E	86	21,808	50,854	53,339	2,485
	V	W	81	3,520	432	485	53
ROMANIA	V	W	84	131	457	499	42
SALVADR	A	E	83	491	1,292	1,704	412
	V	W	86	821	1,137	1,239	102
SINGAPR	O	E	81	4,800	7,362	8,300	938
	O	W	85	4,761	5,510	5,686	176
	V	E	81	2,880	4,442	5,023	581
			82	9,555	16,141	17,194	1,053
			83	19,200	31,158	33,752	2,594
			84	24,987	41,844	44,289	2,445
			85	20,400	33,720	35,682	1,962
			86	1,440	7,347	7,536	189
	V	W	81	29,000	34,920	37,335	2,415
			82	47,687	60,907	66,010	5,103
			83	49,198	67,338	71,139	3,801
			84	24,960	32,028	36,743	4,715
			85	80,048	129,863	137,925	8,062
			86	73,324	81,473	86,659	5,186
SPAIN	A	E	82	390	692	1,308	616
			84	331	365	737	372
	N	E	82	164,524	215,625	240,583	24,958
			83	199,407	209,499	235,345	25,846
	V	E	81	23,464	26,433	29,391	2,958
			83	42,252	36,513	41,848	5,335
			84	150,922	120,062	131,184	11,122
			85	236,127	233,096	252,058	18,962
			86	208,997	252,252	269,968	17,716
	V	W	82	792	1,218	1,317	99
SWAZLND	O	E	85	34,528	51,126	53,544	2,418
SWEDEN	N	E	85	2,478	26,799	28,336	1,537
	O	E	84	1,080	2,363	2,486	123
	V	E	81	550	670	705	35
			82	9,237	19,180	20,370	1,190
			83	13,027	30,193	32,288	2,095
			84	21,195	18,484	21,925	3,441
			85	972	1,693	1,693	
			86	14,213	16,077	18,459	2,382
	V	W	81	51,471	75,254	80,500	5,246
			82	24,270	55,509	58,869	3,360
			84	407	730	759	29
SWITZLD	A	E	82	3,547	3,653	5,256	1,603
			83	5,779	10,138	13,582	3,444
			86	2,400	4,013	4,523	510
	A	W	83	1,470	3,534	6,280	2,746
			84	798	1,137	1,824	687
	N	E	81	3,990,344	7,215,390	7,697,329	480,022
			82	3,587,867	7,167,687	7,637,697	470,010
			83	4,518,588	8,239,904	8,640,867	400,963
			84	7,252,425	11,234,644	11,871,961	637,317
			85	6,576,023	9,623,017	10,387,551	764,534
			86	160,253	292,207	318,649	26,442
	N	W	82	1,242,835	2,214,691	2,353,986	139,295
			83	1,332,916	2,240,162	2,374,950	134,788
			84	1,700,287	2,795,740	3,048,751	253,011
			85	1,501,093	2,266,836	2,513,689	246,853
			86	1,144,230	2,199,663	2,357,853	158,190
	O	E	81	256,153	396,177	426,646	30,469
			82	256,564	480,457	508,079	27,622
			83	210,855	460,844	486,283	25,439
			84	46,266	72,938	80,219	7,281
			85	28,478	48,653	49,231	578
			86	2,047	2,210	2,325	115
	O	W	85	12,561	10,189	10,864	675
	V	E	81	1,244,018	2,051,485	2,185,016	133,531
			82	2,372,335	4,103,658	4,376,508	272,850
			83	2,128,953	3,927,757	4,186,522	258,765
			84	777,024	1,159,256	1,222,026	62,770

Product TSUSA commodity number, description, and unit of quantity — Country	Mode	Reg	Yr	Quantity	F.A.S.	C.I.F.	Charges
			85	1,310,405	2,054,420	2,195,125	140,705
			86	6,789,874	12,532,411	13,233,832	701,421
	V	W	81	1,066,861	1,959,636	2,116,553	136,823
			82	137,293	270,666	287,490	16,824
			83	229,307	455,755	479,427	23,672
			84	303,665	508,689	532,605	23,916
			85	228,773	354,994	376,091	21,097
			86	469,600	807,744	858,618	50,874
THAILND	N	W	84	6,035	8,053	8,708	655
	V	E	81	1,295	3,240	3,613	373
			82	1,873	3,599	4,022	423
			83	10,798	15,087	16,625	1,538
			84	3,718	9,892	10,866	974
			85	2,558	4,270	4,897	627
			86	24,393	22,734	28,253	5,519
	V	H	81	473	549	617	68
			83	58	679	733	54
	V	W	81	18,521	24,562	26,723	2,161
			82	39,789	34,216	37,036	2,820
			83	12,228	16,306	17,567	1,261
			84	12,284	14,487	15,906	1,419
			85	43,795	37,169	42,335	5,166
			86	77,477	101,175	108,720	7,545
TURKEY	V	E	83	1,020	1,411	1,697	286
			84	5,703	3,592	4,094	502
			85	1,715	2,346	2,567	221
U KING	A	E	82	1,536	1,237	1,955	718
			83	441	296	1,189	893
			84	1,175	1,186	1,503	317
	N	E	81	93,039	91,491	102,929	11,438
			82	49,213	39,592	46,606	7,014
			83	161,294	123,538	135,231	11,693
			84	725,932	499,464	570,516	71,052
			86	303,550	239,194	277,784	38,590
	N	W	81	14,231	10,794	11,955	1,161
			82	6,415	8,610	9,783	1,173
			84	2,098	2,305	3,182	877
	O	E	81	24,000	54,216	58,110	3,894
			82	13,690	22,886	28,564	5,678
			83	35,045	59,066	61,206	2,140
			84	24,736	9,847	11,627	1,780
	V	E	81	3,109	2,793	3,240	447
			82	2,143	774	1,069	295
			83	1,002	1,706	2,006	300
			84	9,215	13,511	15,769	2,258
			85	305,739	245,084	280,666	35,582
			86	43,781	52,885	62,384	9,499
	V	W	82	1,438	6,230	6,684	454
			83	10,772	24,815	27,060	2,245
			84	10,676	23,425	25,150	1,725
			85	7,644	16,632	17,772	1,140
			86	11,198	53,329	54,451	1,122
USSR	O	E	81	1,929	367	422	55
VENEZ	A	E	81	11,319	19,634	26,415	6,781
			83	145	398	527	129
	V	E	81	577,506	730,021	763,685	33,664
			82	83,400	89,250	92,250	3,000
			86	7,720	20,499	21,908	1,409
YUGOSLV	O	E	85	37,610	27,578	30,358	2,780
			86	1,322	1,504	1,504	
	O	W	81	4,753	6,344	6,384	40
			83	397	437	437	
			84	6,482	7,134	7,134	
			85	1,521	1,706	1,706	
	V	E	81	20,109	5,990	7,193	1,203
			82	50,795	41,269	44,999	3,730
			83	22,561	19,134	21,025	1,891
			84	55,962	54,239	58,525	4,286
			85	143,084	131,277	142,783	11,506
			86	5,275	7,835	8,747	912
	V	W	81	8,618	5,817	5,942	125
			84	2,646	1,957	2,845	888
			85	8,929	6,863	8,719	1,856

Spring roll and dumpling
1825300 SPRING ROLLS/STUFF DUMPLING (LB)

Country			Yr	Quantity	F.A.S.	C.I.F.	Charges
TOTAL			81	151,494	232,170	252,617	20,447
			82	925,343	1,320,041	1,431,094	111,053
			83	1,675,427	2,364,832	2,586,708	221,876
			84	1,818,236	2,451,431	2,679,204	227,773
			85	2,347,040	3,472,533	3,735,053	262,520
			86	2,634,544	4,327,738	4,659,719	331,981

Product TSUSA commodity number, description, and unit of quantity — Country	Mode	Reg	Yr	Quantity	F.A.S.	C.I.F.	Charges
CANADA	O	E	85	25,746	8,767	8,767	
CHINA M	V	E	81	3,989	3,445	4,503	1,058
	V	W	82	5,291	5,558	6,211	653
			83	13,073	8,312	9,073	761
			84	22,622	15,964	19,504	3,540
			85	38,728	18,192	21,476	3,284
			86	35,294	17,603	19,897	2,294
CHINA T	O	W	85	8,045	6,268	7,213	945
	V	E	81	83,475	85,890	95,424	9,534
			82	59,758	57,236	64,653	7,417
			83	1,925	1,663	2,187	524
			84	1,066	1,061	1,381	320
			85	18,867	16,562	18,174	1,612
			86	1,742	4,271	4,662	391
	V	H	83	5,469	5,553	6,523	970
			84	4,238	3,042	3,631	589
			85	11,524	8,151	9,769	1,618
	V	W	81	17,176	20,427	22,614	2,187
			82	27,725	15,350	18,485	3,135
			83	93,398	61,637	74,513	12,876
			84	132,893	94,876	110,720	15,844
			85	157,025	126,666	141,255	14,589
			86	170,168	147,967	160,483	12,516
DENMARK	V	W	85	22,640	21,890	26,883	4,993
			86	54,920	41,827	52,753	10,926
FR GERM	V	E	83	3,848	3,680	4,068	388
			85	3,240	5,022	5,273	251
	V	W	82	613	391	425	34
HG KONG	N	W	84	1,590	3,061	3,794	733
			85	591,493	1,369,786	1,433,979	64,193
	V	E	81	7,851	17,795	18,508	713
			82	30,768	88,845	96,614	7,769
			83	50,160	138,105	149,246	11,141
			84	52,374	128,223	138,741	10,518
			85	28,335	71,308	77,456	6,148
			86	100,881	267,004	303,940	36,936
	V	H	82	17,261	44,363	47,360	2,997
			83	75,935	205,894	219,519	13,625
			84	60,934	163,431	175,449	12,018
			85	72,761	196,209	210,613	14,404
			86	85,561	226,600	244,034	17,434
	V	W	81	37,464	100,344	106,845	6,501
			82	189,935	478,326	507,742	29,416
			83	298,834	636,591	684,920	48,329
			84	350,390	722,126	763,878	41,752
			85	43,306	104,825	117,151	12,326
			86	413,629	1,004,895	1,053,093	48,198
INDNSIA	V	E	86	1,984	1,080	1,219	139
ITALY	V	E	84	23,895	10,000	12,145	2,145
JAPAN	N	H	84	273,447	302,197	333,236	31,039
	N	W	84	200,104	237,702	260,239	22,537
	V	E	82	63,388	69,732	77,108	7,376
			83	384,968	488,203	543,277	55,074
			84	488,874	570,858	634,890	64,032
			85	238,651	267,039	296,356	29,317
			86	196,847	334,947	367,755	32,808
	V	H	82	86,074	94,657	103,194	8,537
			83	396,760	437,483	478,348	40,865
			85	169,356	192,885	211,537	18,652
			86	132,393	177,370	194,943	17,573
	V	W	81	906	1,875	2,020	145
			82	419,079	440,025	480,374	40,349
			83	342,468	367,928	403,656	35,728
			84	70,362	76,394	83,322	6,928
			85	467,633	701,071	748,857	47,786
			86	757,331	1,506,943	1,597,085	90,142
JORDAN	V	W	86	8,100	18,121	19,008	887
KOR REP	V	E	85	71,581	57,260	65,898	8,638
			86	93,835	88,126	101,089	12,963
	V	H	84	1,625	1,958	2,125	167
	V	W	82	2,160	2,288	2,640	352
			84	122,319	107,364	120,080	12,716
			85	340,290	279,375	310,167	30,792
			86	539,867	450,370	494,027	43,657
MACAO	V	E	81	413	927	992	65
			82	215	488	512	24
MALAYSA	V	W	85	23,501	12,467	13,706	1,239
NORWAY	V	W	81	220	1,467	1,711	244
PHIL R	V	W	82	16,725	13,607	15,923	2,316
			83	2,800	1,257	1,392	135
			84	2,375	4,355	5,077	722
			85	8,000	4,140	4,889	749
			86	13,184	7,179	7,708	529
SINGAPR	V	E	83	1,799	2,376	3,140	764
			84	9,128	8,819	10,992	2,173

Product
TSUSA commodity number, description, and unit of quantity

Country	Mode	Reg	Yr	Quantity	F.A.S.	C.I.F.	Charges
	V	W	86	17,762	26,940	30,369	3,429
THAILND	V	E	85	6,318	4,650	5,634	984
			86	11,046	6,495	7,654	1,159
	V	W	82	6,351	9,175	9,853	678
			83	3,990	6,150	6,846	696

Vinegar
1825500 VINEGAR MALT (PFG)

Country	Mode	Reg	Yr	Quantity	F.A.S.	C.I.F.	Charges
TOTAL			81	11,523	43,285	47,822	4,537
			82	37,089	62,722	70,082	7,360
			83	55,439	50,769	55,959	5,190
			84	41,735	51,854	56,420	4,566
			85	84,254	58,146	65,666	7,520
			86	67,946	71,470	75,674	4,204
CANADA	A	E	85	2,731	1,900	2,478	578
	O	E	81	2,009	1,756	1,756	
			82	5,484	8,184	8,184	
			83	650	4,381	4,381	
			84	16,302	25,601	25,601	
			85	1,145	7,117	7,117	
			86	13,469	18,413	18,413	
	O	W	81	4,944	16,188	16,188	
			82	5,265	15,768	15,768	
			83	2,589	11,271	11,271	
			84	13	713	713	
			86	1,112	4,208	4,208	
CHINA M	V	E	82	1,200	1,226	1,388	162
	V	W	81	397	448	543	95
			84	5,061	1,927	2,154	227
FR GERM	A	E	83	275	374	574	200
	V	W	84	87	282	342	60
FRANCE	V	E	83	57	441	467	26
			84	706	4,271	5,214	943
			85	30,287	20,357	21,369	1,012
	V	W	86	1	2,192	2,446	254
HG KONG	V	E	82	6,000	1,957	2,289	332
	V	H	82	1,000	323	372	49
	V	W	81	7	488	516	28
			82	6,235	4,016	4,413	397
			84	129	278	295	17
ISRAEL	V	W	86	9,472	2,349	2,702	353
ITALY	V	E	84	165	836	1,181	345
			85	2,400	1,444	1,743	299
JAPAN	N	E	86	*	20,800	20,800	
	V	E	83	12,581	3,706	4,142	436
			84	14,525	5,262	5,879	617
			86	179	2,468	2,890	422
	V	W	82	401	3,716	4,060	344
			83	768	2,464	2,592	128
			84	4	1,873	1,988	115
			85	73	6,047	6,678	631
			86	39,853	9,018	9,836	818
KOR REP	V	E	81	348	1,555	1,833	278
			83	17,907	11,751	13,213	1,462
			85	18,363	6,571	8,433	1,862
MEXICO	O	W	82	66	269	269	
NETHLDS	V	E	81	203	2,575	2,675	100
PHIL R	V	W	82	2,474	2,054	2,335	281
SPAIN	V	E	81	259	3,612	4,318	706
			85	4,680	4,862	6,926	2,064
	V	W	82	166	840	1,038	198
U KING	N	E	84	11	1,800	1,973	173
	O	E	81	69	1,131	1,290	159
			82	340	2,998	3,732	734
			83	11	651	1,002	351
			84	1,323	2,103	2,576	473
	V	E	81	2,696	13,276	16,081	2,805
			82	8,458	21,371	26,234	4,863
			83	20,601	15,730	18,317	2,587
			84	3,409	6,908	8,504	1,596
			85	24,575	9,848	10,922	1,074
			86	3,860	12,022	14,379	2,357
	V	W	81	591	2,256	2,622	366

1825800 VINEGAR OTHER THAN MALT (PFG)

Country	Mode	Reg	Yr	Quantity	F.A.S.	C.I.F.	Charges
TOTAL			81	958,468	1,831,436	2,166,945	335,519
			82	1,534,941	2,177,302	2,571,136	393,834
			83	2,082,982	2,956,905	3,552,223	595,318
			84	1,994,758	3,566,333	4,308,324	741,991
			85	2,314,082	4,362,356	5,296,553	934,197
			86	2,257,707	6,227,280	7,255,252	1,027,972

Product
TSUSA commodity number, description, and unit of quantity

Country	Mode	Reg	Yr	Quantity	F.A.S.	C.I.F.	Charges
ARGENT	V	W	83	511,271	239,042	318,062	79,020
AUSTRAL	A	W	84	156	4,084	5,865	1,781
	V	E	84	24	333	362	29
	V	W	83	1,902	21,702	21,862	160
AUSTRIA	V	W	83	30	255	285	30
BELGIUM	N	E	85	8,141	15,991	19,695	3,704
	O	E	85	675	1,209	1,552	343
	V	E	82	2,961	5,847	7,098	1,251
			85	3,184	9,072	11,638	2,566
			86	21,573	41,404	50,887	9,483
	V	W	86	968	4,586	5,368	782
BRAZIL	V	E	83	1,150	1,035	1,299	264
			86	634	1,400	1,651	251
CANADA	O	E	81	113,230	29,571	29,571	
			82	636,709	166,525	166,525	
			83	251,994	74,384	74,384	
			84	440,634	72,515	72,515	
			85	389,385	105,905	105,905	
			86	44,065	12,779	12,779	
	O	W	83	1,393	7,064	7,437	373
CHINA M	O	E	85	525	2,382	2,712	330
	O	W	82	8	818	957	139
			83	377	506	530	24
	V	E	81	9,605	34,989	41,721	6,732
			82	10,977	26,956	32,181	5,225
			83	15,326	34,334	43,519	9,185
			84	13,564	28,558	36,790	8,232
			85	13,079	32,673	38,514	5,841
			86	30,318	60,074	67,627	7,553
	V	H	84	84	381	448	67
	V	W	81	13,243	31,606	34,139	2,533
			82	21,808	62,802	71,184	8,382
			83	25,386	61,205	66,481	5,276
			84	19,387	69,309	76,056	6,747
			85	10,371	39,285	41,299	2,014
			86	28,337	48,355	51,888	3,533
CHINA T	V	E	81	182	700	810	110
			82	1,586	5,042	6,222	1,180
			83	974	4,464	4,903	439
			84	2,976	5,720	6,859	1,139
			85	769	1,800	2,352	552
			86	5,083	4,681	5,773	1,092
	V	H	82	82	389	409	20
	V	W	81	460	2,203	2,510	307
			82	1,584	5,092	5,750	658
			83	6,423	7,936	8,980	1,044
			84	9,609	19,361	21,975	2,614
			85	417	4,652	5,193	541
			86	30,034	32,053	35,248	3,195
DENMARK	V	E	83	761	481	498	17
DOM REP	V	E	84	30,163	12,563	15,448	2,885
			85	9,270	17,040	22,765	5,725
	V	W	83	2,457	6,788	7,513	725
F GUIAN	V	E	82	122	748	880	132
FR GERM	N	E	86	1,874	7,348	8,295	947
	O	E	81	1,822	8,743	10,420	1,677
			82	822	3,081	3,538	457
			83	874	2,317	2,483	166
			84	2,174	7,809	9,397	1,588
			85	4,654	14,905	17,265	2,360
	V	E	81	15,118	31,101	34,263	3,162
			82	19,653	40,921	45,504	4,583
			83	18,835	41,107	47,328	6,221
			84	22,030	44,823	52,706	7,883
			85	15,687	28,207	34,112	5,905
			86	21,739	52,295	61,049	8,754
	V	W	81	823	2,560	3,271	711
			82	120	444	472	28
			83	1,265	1,592	1,867	275
			84	659	1,995	2,254	259
FRANCE	A	E	81	16	284	301	17
			83	25	688	1,112	424
			84	5	327	567	240
			85	193	1,097	2,246	1,149
	N	E	81	93,263	307,101	351,666	44,565
			82	104,989	314,156	364,811	50,655
			83	194,545	419,793	494,056	74,263
			84	217,037	474,375	571,921	97,546
			86	273,384	823,613	962,292	138,679
	N	W	81	5,367	30,721	33,296	2,575
			83	34,420	56,384	63,486	7,102
	O	E	81	9,377	45,416	47,729	2,313
			82	1,313	6,914	7,693	779
			83	9,740	12,076	13,512	1,436
			85	579	2,459	2,650	191

Product TSUSA commodity number, description, and unit of quantity Country	Mode	Reg	Yr	Quantity	F.A.S.	C.I.F.	Charges
			86	4,233	24,326	25,569	1,243
	O	W	85	923	2,642	3,238	596
	V	E	81	11,695	30,112	34,960	4,848
			82	25,452	73,467	85,744	12,277
			83	40,312	116,995	139,606	22,611
			84	37,706	171,154	197,088	25,934
			85	248,365	638,833	744,324	105,491
			86	170,577	392,876	446,112	53,236
	V	W	81	15,978	30,091	34,450	4,359
			82	30,612	75,836	81,991	6,155
			83	6,997	24,408	27,694	3,286
			84	40,357	89,839	99,245	9,406
			85	46,297	110,785	135,697	24,912
			86	121,530	150,613	174,346	23,733
GREECE	V	E	82	58	300	318	18
			83	816	722	829	107
			84	280	1,825	2,235	410
			85	386	5,688	8,123	2,435
			86	90	1,635	2,033	398
	V	W	83	1,373	1,214	1,398	184
			86	3,000	2,398	2,948	550
HG KONG	N	E	85	2,140	34,256	42,113	7,857
	O	E	81	10,138	2,497	2,497	
			84	263	1,702	1,997	295
	V	E	81	41,499	72,718	83,606	10,888
			82	26,299	88,435	102,878	14,443
			83	45,688	106,957	125,543	18,586
			84	33,861	86,076	104,269	18,193
			85	16,658	51,412	61,048	9,636
			86	64,613	98,858	111,849	12,991
	V	H	81	745	2,950	3,162	212
			82	3,394	6,473	7,092	619
			83	1,168	5,594	6,385	791
			84	3,306	10,417	11,677	1,260
	V	W	81	19,785	74,418	80,089	5,671
			82	32,871	106,115	115,341	9,226
			83	26,571	94,129	101,149	7,020
			84	41,319	117,525	127,157	9,632
			85	16,409	71,760	77,403	5,643
			86	44,524	99,932	107,459	7,527
HONDURA	V	E	81	271	1,059	1,143	84
INDIA	V	E	81	18,000	11,912	12,379	467
ITALY	A	E	82	32	1,318	1,393	75
			84	1	471	616	145
	A	W	85	25	1,500	1,715	215
	N	E	82	42,887	160,732	188,617	27,885
			86	283,749	1,255,330	1,454,911	199,581
	N	W	83	1,838	6,148	6,819	671
			84	17,724	90,342	104,800	14,458
			86	12,863	52,419	59,187	6,768
	O	E	81	759	2,037	2,236	199
			83	2,344	11,393	13,721	2,328
			84	1,058	6,097	6,356	259
			85	2,961	11,400	11,400	
			86	2,774	10,800	10,800	
	V	E	81	38,745	151,628	179,031	27,403
			82	508	2,885	3,227	342
			83	101,225	313,908	367,482	53,574
			84	122,764	455,085	533,534	78,449
			85	309,307	985,363	1,161,841	176,478
			86	100,984	503,531	570,790	67,259
	V	W	81	11,820	44,449	54,696	10,247
			82	10,413	71,850	83,664	11,814
			83	19,816	110,212	129,431	19,219
			84	1,962	12,845	15,321	2,476
			85	41,422	145,653	163,836	18,183
			86	17,482	108,191	122,207	14,016
JAPAN	N	E	83	81	1,372	1,506	134
	N	H	83	75,088	152,072	217,885	65,813
			84	70,602	150,118	217,129	67,011
	N	W	84	317,207	407,459	514,040	106,581
	O	E	82	29	2,542	2,865	323
			84	339	3,456	3,838	382
	V	E	81	54,914	118,832	139,168	20,346
			82	81,851	139,247	172,881	33,634
			83	106,068	189,107	227,870	38,763
			84	113,490	272,954	335,833	62,879
			85	163,963	304,378	364,994	60,616
			86	123,260	393,521	447,904	54,383
	V	H	81	70,591	128,191	174,820	46,629
			82	64,449	120,056	171,489	51,433
			85	55,850	120,212	166,907	46,695
			86	77,402	174,798	221,479	46,681
	V	W	81	328,193	476,595	587,381	110,786
			82	297,989	443,968	550,281	106,313

Product TSUSA commodity number, description, and unit of quantity Country	Mode	Reg	Yr	Quantity	F.A.S.	C.I.F.	Charges
			83	396,028	544,955	665,109	120,154
			84	140,822	289,520	340,124	50,604
			85	635,109	806,913	1,009,578	202,665
			86	436,202	1,099,833	1,259,190	159,357
KOR REP	O	W	84	39	335	335	
	V	E	81	534	2,256	2,557	301
			82	14,731	26,608	29,935	3,327
			83	13,094	15,361	17,179	1,818
			84	13,385	23,578	27,904	4,326
			85	11,423	15,326	17,433	2,107
			86	19,466	23,542	26,158	2,616
	V	W	81	14,344	45,622	49,550	3,928
			82	20,361	63,961	70,184	6,223
			83	12,742	27,116	29,258	2,142
			84	14,160	27,937	32,020	4,083
			85	22,017	42,794	47,167	4,373
			86	26,943	59,978	67,015	7,037
MADAGAS	V	E	84	1,003	3,700	4,140	440
MALAYSA	V	E	86	281	1,043	1,249	206
MAURIT	V	E	85	1,223	2,008	3,198	1,190
			86	286	1,908	2,039	131
MEXICO	O	E	86	3,100	5,580	5,580	
NETHLDS	O	E	81	357	767	1,152	385
			83	9	556	599	43
	V	E	81	252	510	948	438
			82	744	1,349	1,511	162
			83	13,717	21,677	24,572	2,895
			84	3,793	24,445	28,941	4,496
			85	3,192	29,542	33,265	3,723
			86	4,522	24,961	27,486	2,525
	V	W	81	372	1,011	1,071	60
			82	234	431	480	49
			83	1,084	1,758	1,898	140
			84	1,190	2,017	2,224	207
NORWAY	V	E	83	918	741	812	71
PHIL R	N	W	82	26,550	29,667	36,911	7,244
	V	E	81	2,155	2,597	3,266	669
			82	3,453	7,554	9,567	2,013
			83	3,064	4,418	5,549	1,131
			84	11,462	9,493	11,413	1,920
			85	9,218	13,673	18,856	5,183
			86	2,715	4,545	6,396	1,851
	V	H	82	179	605	805	200
			84	539	691	905	214
			85	488	15,727	17,377	1,650
	V	W	81	37,010	43,324	51,200	7,876
			82	21,993	35,944	42,326	6,382
			83	83,523	98,302	116,783	18,481
			84	61,312	88,394	101,514	13,120
			85	38,890	58,340	69,954	11,614
			86	73,229	87,956	102,712	14,756
PORTUGL	V	E	84	3,662	1,204	1,479	275
			85	2,996	4,622	6,760	2,138
			86	5,445	4,731	6,981	2,250
ROMANIA	V	W	84	254	1,747	1,909	162
SINGAPR	V	W	82	244	715	782	67
			83	7,781	2,532	2,695	163
			84	9,600	13,103	14,028	925
SPAIN	N	E	81	357	2,879	3,340	461
	V	E	81	9,899	41,706	54,057	12,351
			82	12,143	45,221	56,418	11,197
			83	19,801	65,364	83,964	18,600
			84	17,636	93,821	116,334	22,513
			85	17,089	70,751	88,306	17,555
			86	18,780	90,383	114,465	24,082
	V	W	81	464	2,162	2,445	283
			82	8,103	18,439	25,689	7,250
			83	15,836	29,154	37,959	8,805
			84	144,077	329,263	432,788	103,525
			85	198,030	506,776	692,919	186,143
			86	170,254	416,910	563,536	146,626
SWEDEN	N	E	86	3,697	5,304	5,881	577
	V	E	81	1,848	3,280	3,884	604
			82	3,333	3,278	4,070	792
			83	1,867	1,554	1,667	113
			84	1,609	2,076	2,308	232
	V	W	81	344	465	574	109
			82	310	415	500	85
			84	145	584	712	128
SWITZLD	V	E	84	27	2,045	2,147	102
	V	W	84	22	875	926	51
			85	342	1,069	1,209	140
			86	355	4,018	4,228	210
SYRIA	V	E	81	2,419	2,166	2,314	148
THAILND	V	E	81	1,106	1,569	1,808	239

Product
TSUSA commodity number, description, and unit of quantity

Country	Mode	Reg	Yr	Quantity	F.A.S.	C.I.F.	Charges
			82	960	1,038	1,190	152
			83	1,653	1,465	1,704	239
			84	2,830	2,619	2,980	361
			86	2,950	3,315	3,690	375
	V	W	81	413	1,478	1,747	269
			82	1,416	2,922	3,201	279
			83	2,284	2,825	3,035	210
			84	490	1,876	2,109	233
			85	296	1,058	1,122	64
			86	828	1,100	1,100	
TRINID	V	E	86	1,913	12,012	13,041	1,029
U KING	A	E	84	13	2,317	4,350	2,033
			85	792	1,878	2,800	922
	N	E	83	762	9,419	10,021	602
			84	4,233	22,562	25,215	2,653
			85	1,951	6,850	8,646	1,796
	O	E	83	64	1,733	1,824	91
			84	34	652	739	87
			85	172	3,100	3,503	403
			86	627	14,480	15,195	715
	V	E	81	688	6,650	7,127	477
			82	609	6,196	6,562	366
			85	8,701	13,998	15,869	1,871
			86	1,024	7,865	8,859	994
	V	W	84	1,680	1,961	2,482	521
			85	512	7,372	8,054	682
YUGOSLV	V	E	81	267	510	590	80
			83	222	591	680	89

Yeast extract

1824000 NON-ALCHL PREP OF YEAST EXT (LB)

Country	Mode	Reg	Yr	Quantity	F.A.S.	C.I.F.	Charges
TOTAL			81	2,777,329	4,751,594	4,917,233	165,639
			82	2,039,030	3,174,133	3,304,988	130,855
			83	3,055,506	4,241,638	4,466,457	224,819
			84	5,019,028	5,670,725	5,974,851	304,126
			85	3,596,613	4,704,906	4,977,684	272,778
			86	3,553,449	4,500,007	4,845,096	345,089
AUSTRAL	N	W	82	27,252	28,077	33,628	5,551
			83	15,730	23,253	33,813	10,560
			84	4,387	8,051	9,060	1,009
BELGIUM	O	E	83	2,205	1,261	1,660	399
	V	E	83	34,612	27,169	29,374	2,205
			84	181,254	136,060	146,194	10,134
			85	29,246	21,993	24,113	2,120
			86	2,813	1,808	1,971	163
C RICA	V	E	83	21,377	19,472	22,558	3,086
CANADA	A	E	83	110	303	378	75
	A	W	83	20	490	530	40
	N	E	84	13,612	17,896	17,896	
			85	60,448	90,883	90,883	
	O	E	81	637,741	952,727	952,727	
			82	485,016	726,741	726,741	
			83	280,998	454,615	454,626	11
			84	429,472	587,326	587,326	
			85	184,284	229,129	229,129	
			86	383,032	502,198	502,478	280
	O	W	81	18,488	28,347	28,347	
			85	9,480	8,326	8,326	
CHINA M	O	W	86	69	1,176	1,259	83
	V	E	82	500	641	676	35
	V	W	84	1,170	460	513	53
CHINA T	V	E	82	6,720	1,060	1,191	131
			86	6,543	6,523	7,010	487
	V	W	81	3,000	2,400	2,563	163
			85	7,011	4,940	5,237	297
			86	29,772	4,730	5,448	718
DENMARK	V	W	86	587	1,010	1,123	113
DOM REP	V	E	84	2,725	1,813	2,078	265
FINLAND	O	E	85	11,905	2,466	2,847	381
FR GERM	A	E	82	4,180	7,742	11,093	3,351
			83	2,996	7,051	8,663	1,612
	N	E	81	91,210	148,040	157,910	9,870
			82	194,710	335,713	356,808	21,095
			83	514,322	834,525	873,096	38,571
			84	646,469	895,970	946,406	50,436
			85	466,154	801,902	846,398	44,496
			86	43,144	93,882	103,209	9,327
	V	E	82	25,353	49,954	51,379	1,425
			83	18,673	8,006	9,746	1,740
			84	89,309	139,318	145,823	6,505
			85	2,756	1,658	2,158	500
			86	1,323	1,053	1,290	237

Product
TSUSA commodity number, description, and unit of quantity

Country	Mode	Reg	Yr	Quantity	F.A.S.	C.I.F.	Charges
	V	W	84	428	366	450	84
FRANCE	A	E	82	54	288	424	136
			84	99	290	497	207
			86	4,002	7,120	10,765	3,645
	N	E	83	1,338,153	2,295,693	2,410,408	114,715
			84	1,620,401	2,711,761	2,826,541	114,780
			85	1,692,263	2,699,195	2,834,569	135,374
	O	E	82	121,394	59,428	67,597	8,169
			83	435,225	206,204	232,524	26,320
			84	161,403	84,589	94,480	9,891
			86	43,807	29,853	32,989	3,136
	V	E	81	1,923,157	3,511,545	3,654,927	143,382
			82	1,096,524	1,856,279	1,936,325	80,046
			83	39,683	20,680	23,183	2,503
			84	539,313	246,737	289,645	42,908
			85	506,652	300,042	339,884	39,842
			86	2,449,799	3,368,707	3,619,143	250,436
	V	W	82	10,000	19,349	21,149	1,800
			83	31,200	49,602	53,045	3,443
GERM DR	V	E	85	25,353	45,374	47,914	2,540
HG KONG	V	E	81	4,605	2,982	3,160	178
			83	200	631	736	105
			84	35,630	18,521	21,223	2,702
	V	W	82	675	1,187	1,300	113
			84	825	670	727	57
			85	5,775	4,710	5,106	396
INDIA	V	E	83	6,131	5,842	6,828	986
IRELAND	A	E	85	957	1,402	2,149	747
	V	E	82	8,250	6,600	7,909	1,309
ISRAEL	V	E	86	39,682	7,157	8,852	1,695
ITALY	A	E	84	1,318	3,250	4,016	766
	N	E	84	12,147	16,064	17,564	1,500
	V	E	81	1,038	3,727	4,086	359
			83	1,539	4,977	5,193	216
			84	3,289	7,515	7,828	313
			85	45,913	60,149	63,887	3,738
			86	35,450	44,483	45,000	517
JAMAICA	A	E	83	112	448	460	12
	V	E	82	96	274	348	74
JAPAN	A	E	86	12,015	19,952	42,936	22,984
	N	W	81	4,920	4,503	8,388	3,885
	V	E	81	600	1,454	1,644	190
			82	1,968	1,400	1,511	111
			83	1,855	2,930	3,172	242
			84	5,408	5,500	5,816	316
	V	H	84	63	387	406	19
	V	W	81	973	1,475	1,532	57
			82	51	712	739	27
			83	1,192	1,083	1,134	51
			84	1,930	6,129	6,472	343
			85	4,153	11,102	12,065	963
KOR REP	V	E	83	4,250	2,544	2,776	232
			84	6,751	15,409	16,344	935
			85	7,170	6,958	7,568	610
			86	1,850	6,578	6,891	313
	V	W	83	1,920	930	1,160	230
MEXICO	O	W	81	1,190	725	725	
			83	3,726	3,474	3,474	
			86	4,189	1,293	1,293	
NETHLDS	A	E	81	110	399	406	7
			83	238	584	629	45
			84	110	323	484	161
			86	881	2,539	3,311	772
	V	E	81	74,603	81,081	86,716	5,635
			86	73,267	72,098	76,297	4,199
PHIL R	V	E	81	5,198	2,466	2,837	371
			82	904	2,428	2,585	157
			86	2,015	6,029	6,503	474
	V	W	83	4,298	9,616	10,151	535
			84	472	379	469	90
			86	5,945	14,536	16,757	2,221
PORTUGL	V	E	84	2,367	789	872	83
SINGAPR	V	W	85	1,048	1,491	1,510	19
SPAIN	V	E	86	23,810	6,000	9,243	3,243
SWEDEN	V	E	85	39,683	23,964	25,794	1,830
SWITZLD	N	E	84	198,415	109,687	119,843	10,156
			85	158,732	100,390	106,521	6,131
	O	E	83	114,087	68,261	71,321	3,060
			84	674,795	390,002	422,163	32,161
			85	77,162	36,918	41,293	4,375
	V	E	82	19,500	30,383	32,056	1,673
			83	176,236	206,954	220,654	13,700
			84	311,676	205,842	220,077	14,235
			85	109,366	93,662	101,390	7,728
			86	198,415	115,922	130,347	14,425

Product TSUSA commodity number, description, and unit of quantity Country	Mode	Reg	Yr	Quantity	F.A.S.	C.I.F.	Charges
THAILND	V	E	81	350	280	336	56
			82	210	354	390	36
			83	1,874	1,025	1,043	18
			86	3,425	11,690	12,909	1,219
	V	W	82	759	1,933	2,097	164
			83	12,285	6,103	6,702	599
			84	1,484	1,445	1,540	95
			85	6,688	4,247	4,617	370
U KING	N	E	84	41,873	27,945	30,054	2,109
			86	108,496	118,450	132,436	13,986
	O	E	84	6,063	4,628	4,628	
			85	527	1,815	1,815	
	V	E	81	225	963	1,067	104
			82	5,325	2,506	3,217	711
			83	1,225	3,446	3,917	471
			84	1,391	845	985	140
			85	100,782	82,372	97,866	15,494
			86	10,731	22,373	25,144	2,771
	V	W	81	9,921	8,480	9,862	1,382
			82	23,810	38,841	43,200	4,359
			83	12,037	20,763	22,151	1,388
			84	11,905	20,506	21,600	1,094
			85	11,905	20,216	21,600	1,384
			86	68,387	32,847	40,492	7,645
YUGOSLV	N	E	82	5,779	2,243	2,625	382
	V	E	83	8,197	3,305	4,397	1,092
			84	11,074	4,252	4,831	579

Nut

Nut, mixed
1459000 NUT EDIBLE MIX 2ORMORE KINDS (LB)

Country	Mode	Reg	Yr	Quantity	F.A.S.	C.I.F.	Charges
TOTAL			81	33,113	81,765	84,725	2,960
			82	22,602	53,438	55,538	2,100
			83	12,995	24,576	28,707	4,131
			84	87,995	211,066	226,548	15,482
			85	82,647	111,172	115,158	3,986
			86	187,281	232,429	246,845	14,416
CANADA	A	E	81	91	282	312	30
			82	465	388	543	155
	O	E	82	200	375	421	46
			83	6,722	10,076	12,988	2,912
			84	1,107	3,318	3,445	127
			85	43,760	52,048	52,048	
			86	44,470	19,071	19,071	
	O	W	81	8,803	26,817	26,817	
			82	10,537	32,344	32,344	
			83	4,588	11,417	11,417	
			84	4,862	14,520	14,520	
CHINA M	V	H	81	11,095	24,465	25,885	1,420
	V	W	81	11,060	27,300	28,420	1,120
			82	7,936	15,887	16,975	1,088
			83	774	596	641	45
			84	2,088	2,717	2,996	279
FRANCE	A	E	82	427	983	1,223	240
	V	E	81	264	531	566	35
	V	W	84	238	912	1,068	156
GREECE	O	E	83	241	481	734	253
HG KONG	V	W	86	900	1,188	1,249	61
ISRAEL	N	E	86	23,347	42,740	45,661	2,921
	O	E	85	4,302	10,038	10,038	
	V	E	84	67,113	172,838	185,418	12,580
			85	4,050	9,935	10,439	504
			86	59,983	108,302	116,294	7,992
ITALY	A	E	82	226	601	962	361
			83	175	449	1,047	598
			84	329	1,121	1,561	440
LEBANON	V	W	86	2,116	6,109	6,250	141
MEXICO	O	E	84	1,500	370	370	
PAKISTN	V	E	86	110	1,105	1,479	374
PHIL R	V	E	81	1,800	2,370	2,725	355
	V	W	82	1,440	1,407	1,501	94
			86	2,520	2,470	2,685	215
SINGAPR	V	W	82	1,153	962	1,046	84

Product TSUSA commodity number, description, and unit of quantity Country	Mode	Reg	Yr	Quantity	F.A.S.	C.I.F.	Charges
SPAIN	V	E	82	218	491	523	32
			84	10,758	15,270	17,170	1,900
			85	21,313	26,402	28,959	2,557
			86	4,034	6,918	7,661	743
SWITZLD	V	E	85	2	2,004	2,357	353
	V	W	85	661	1,330	1,415	85
THAILND	V	W	83	232	891	957	66
U KING	O	E	85	7,920	6,559	6,953	394
			86	47,124	38,282	38,282	
	V	E	83	263	666	923	257
			85	639	2,856	2,949	93
			86	2,677	6,244	8,213	1,969

Nut, shelled
1455820 NUTS, EDIBLE, NSPF, SHELLED (LB)

Country	Mode	Reg	Yr	Quantity	F.A.S.	C.I.F.	Charges
TOTAL			82	109,002	147,113	156,737	9,624
			83	145,288	160,890	180,438	19,548
			84	460,448	580,636	623,357	42,721
			85	200,522	326,239	357,250	31,011
			86	128,922	194,885	206,707	11,822
CHINA M	O	W	84	6,295	4,212	5,802	1,590
			86	4,200	1,363	1,430	67
	V	E	82	5,948	5,287	6,058	771
			83	11,155	11,363	12,894	1,531
			84	19,773	35,699	37,874	2,175
			85	77,358	92,829	101,721	8,892
			86	8,818	3,047	3,943	896
	V	H	82	390	477	504	27
			84	972	1,091	1,226	135
	V	W	82	34,229	78,692	81,915	3,223
			83	32,001	33,072	35,831	2,759
			84	61,062	86,318	89,796	3,478
			85	20,294	32,305	33,827	1,522
			86	40,984	43,245	45,892	2,647
CHINA T	N	E	84	5,451	10,866	11,509	643
	V	E	83	4,250	7,420	8,250	830
			85	1,781	5,242	5,479	237
	V	H	85	500	1,300	1,428	128
	V	W	83	500	1,400	1,468	68
			86	4,200	1,867	1,996	129
FR GERM	V	E	82	220	507	553	46
			85	1,058	1,837	1,972	135
GUATMAL	V	W	85	68,775	137,550	144,550	7,000
HG KONG	V	E	82	2,100	3,931	3,943	12
			84	2,550	1,776	2,042	266
			86	2,100	1,316	1,414	98
	V	H	82	4,500	2,420	2,646	226
			85	1,609	4,725	4,980	255
			86	5,842	18,954	20,000	1,046
	V	W	82	10,814	18,443	19,070	627
			83	4,958	10,005	10,430	425
			84	2,160	1,898	2,039	141
			85	4,066	5,261	5,841	580
			86	22,182	32,322	33,421	1,099
INDIA	V	E	82	996	2,161	2,561	400
			83	927	1,930	2,175	245
			84	168	1,122	1,244	122
			86	1,560	5,591	5,990	399
	V	W	83	167	263	313	50
INDNSIA	V	W	82	840	829	900	71
			85	915	1,178	1,300	122
			86	390	1,255	1,370	115
ITALY	A	E	84	3,527	4,026	6,868	2,842
	A	W	83	327	838	1,117	279
	V	E	82	44,974	23,731	27,089	3,358
			84	220,579	289,927	306,851	16,924
			85	2,145	4,641	5,028	387
			86	5,800	24,093	26,043	1,950
	V	W	82	60	403	490	87
			84	1,094	1,488	1,660	172
JAPAN	N	E	84	212	862	1,211	349
	V	E	82	190	610	643	33
			83	521	1,234	1,342	108
	V	H	82	602	3,811	4,058	247
			86	864	2,023	2,360	337
	V	W	82	66	253	263	10
			83	381	1,237	1,342	105
			84	190	655	688	33
			86	567	2,240	2,299	59
KOR REP	V	W	83	1,800	3,150	3,406	256
			84	540	1,039	1,119	80
MALAYSA	V	W	84	551	599	655	56

Product TSUSA commodity number, description, and unit of quantity Country	Mode	Reg	Yr	Quantity	F.A.S.	C.I.F.	Charges
NETHLDS	V	E	83	15	340	411	71
	V	W	83	688	634	684	50
PHIL R	V	E	82	317	620	667	47
			83	375	800	935	135
	V	W	84	656	1,049	1,174	125
SINGAPR	V	W	83	1,671	2,340	2,521	181
			84	3,875	4,309	4,829	520
			85	1,100	1,156	1,339	183
SPAIN	N	E	83	85,394	84,394	96,823	12,429
	V	E	82	2,756	4,938	5,377	439
SWITZLD	V	W	86	2,755	5,569	5,745	176
THAILND	V	E	84	300	650	800	150
TURKEY	A	E	85	1,968	5,000	9,006	4,006
	V	E	84	130,493	133,050	145,970	12,920
			86	28,660	52,000	54,804	2,804
U KING	A	E	83	158	470	496	26
			85	6,255	8,972	14,085	5,113
	V	W	85	1,124	1,888	2,015	127
YUGOSLV	V	E	85	11,574	22,355	24,679	2,324

Nut, shelled, prepared or preserved
1457020 NUTS, PICKED, PREPARED,NSPF (LB)

Country	Mode	Reg	Yr	Quantity	F.A.S.	C.I.F.	Charges
TOTAL			82	234,487	251,683	275,344	23,661
			83	371,821	435,483	466,135	30,652
			84	556,909	533,444	587,994	54,550
			85	629,951	564,887	612,663	47,776
			86	891,941	734,254	800,067	65,813
AUSTRIA	A	W	82	367	938	1,344	406
BELGIUM	A	W	84	529	467	677	210
	V	E	83	1,147	1,119	1,226	107
			84	1,680	2,711	2,877	166
BRAZIL	V	E	83	3,307	525	657	132
CANADA	O	E	83	5,621	3,429	3,511	82
			85	23,760	19,280	19,280	
			86	1,980	1,547	1,547	
CHINA M	N	E	83	38,440	28,739	32,230	3,491
	N	W	84	47,165	41,597	44,299	2,702
	O	E	83	213	589	600	11
	O	W	83	4,080	1,528	1,600	72
			86	70	1,643	1,760	117
	V	E	82	33,039	23,849	27,031	3,182
			83	1,550	2,159	2,390	231
			84	23,383	24,436	27,225	2,789
			85	25,963	18,235	21,147	2,912
			86	58,333	41,715	44,865	3,150
	V	H	82	3,612	4,192	4,576	384
			83	2,936	2,090	2,284	194
			84	3,390	2,471	2,745	274
	V	W	82	58,105	57,663	62,411	4,748
			83	101,870	97,333	102,371	5,038
			84	71,728	51,539	54,357	2,818
			85	57,460	54,558	57,786	3,228
			86	108,951	68,079	73,372	5,293
CHINA T	N	E	84	74,816	44,617	56,777	12,160
	O	W	82	150	582	582	
	V	E	82	2,300	4,120	4,400	280
			83	10,058	31,118	33,063	1,945
			84	2,700	1,160	1,272	112
			85	41,259	38,325	43,038	4,713
			86	49,518	46,053	50,633	4,580
	V	H	85	438	1,050	1,175	125
	V	W	82	22,515	47,288	49,513	2,225
			83	37,740	102,836	108,132	5,296
			84	45,549	111,369	116,758	5,389
			85	117,491	159,659	170,425	10,766
			86	165,351	174,434	188,950	14,516
DOM REP	V	E	82	37,440	13,260	15,824	2,564
			83	78,468	26,154	27,806	1,652
			85	36,450	12,150	13,453	1,303
			86	52,016	18,756	20,662	1,906
FR GERM	V	E	82	176	353	381	28
	V	W	83	1,323	1,678	1,920	242
			85	673	1,535	1,920	385
FRANCE	N	E	83	1,426	2,545	3,229	684
	V	E	83	1,795	3,565	3,783	218
HAITI	V	E	82	14,250	5,750	6,760	1,010
HG KONG	O	W	84	2,100	1,366	1,462	96
			85	3,000	1,400	1,573	173
	V	E	82	8,694	5,535	6,233	698
			83	250	528	561	33
			84	1,300	2,502	2,796	294
			85	7,308	5,297	5,945	648

Country	Mode	Reg	Yr	Quantity	F.A.S.	C.I.F.	Charges
			86	5,995	2,726	3,062	336
	V	H	83	965	976	1,070	94
	V	W	82	13,172	15,158	16,180	1,022
			83	15,754	16,989	18,446	1,457
			84	33,985	29,516	31,515	1,999
			85	16,845	15,528	16,258	730
			86	76,897	44,523	46,538	2,015
INDIA	O	E	83	1,874	2,625	2,933	308
			84	3,007	3,301	3,772	471
	V	E	82	1,860	3,223	3,605	382
			83	1,637	4,693	5,235	542
			84	2,558	3,363	3,507	144
			85	437	1,001	1,156	155
	V	W	82	1,938	4,842	5,759	917
			83	458	1,308	1,498	190
			84	874	603	679	76
INDNSIA	V	W	82	1,028	1,083	1,179	96
			83	992	1,254	1,354	100
			86	2,337	3,000	3,315	315
IRAQ	A	E	86	8,818	20,400	26,900	6,500
ITALY	A	E	86	1,102	2,820	4,408	1,588
	V	E	86	617	1,940	2,018	78
	V	W	82	265	2,262	2,262	
			83	1,103	5,289	5,795	506
			86	110	2,199	2,219	20
IVY CST	V	E	86	9,894	8,858	12,358	3,500
JAPAN	V	E	82	1,462	5,010	5,488	478
			83	1,079	4,740	5,276	536
			84	2,448	8,709	9,443	734
			85	760	2,581	2,757	176
			86	1,615	5,855	6,161	306
	V	H	82	2,072	6,648	7,282	634
			83	758	2,711	2,923	212
			84	987	3,437	3,902	465
			85	857	2,858	3,123	265
			86	762	3,162	3,493	331
	V	W	82	4,480	15,931	16,941	1,010
			83	3,201	9,773	10,362	589
			84	2,702	9,015	9,695	680
			85	8,975	10,701	11,138	437
			86	919	3,797	3,928	131
KOR REP	A	E	84	480	718	802	84
	V	E	82	94	314	355	41
			86	260	1,003	1,084	81
	V	W	82	544	3,091	3,304	213
			85	27,523	26,314	28,790	2,476
			86	24,519	18,237	20,147	1,910
LEBANON	V	E	83	447	701	974	273
			85	3,003	3,400	3,588	188
			86	2,593	2,855	3,163	308
MALAYSA	V	W	82	551	569	630	61
			85	2,000	1,580	1,664	84
MEXICO	A	E	85	1,146	1,800	2,507	707
	A	W	82	4,287	6,957	7,873	916
	O	W	85	48,649	16,308	16,308	
NETHLDS	V	E	83	728	759	933	174
PAKISTN	V	W	86	1,102	1,288	1,500	212
PHIL R	V	E	82	1,834	3,212	3,744	532
			84	15,336	9,149	11,186	2,037
			86	1,242	1,035	1,191	156
	V	H	83	28	710	833	123
			84	1,080	960	1,209	249
	V	W	82	567	1,400	1,542	142
			83	6,989	6,454	7,160	706
			84	12,295	7,611	8,511	900
			85	3,033	2,262	2,507	245
PORTUGL	V	E	84	5,391	35,265	36,575	1,310
REP SAF	V	E	84	66,055	17,362	20,665	3,303
ROMANIA	V	E	85	4,762	2,761	3,101	340
	V	W	84	206	433	473	40
SINGAPR	V	W	82	840	799	900	101
			83	500	623	685	62
SWITZLD	V	E	82	3,127	4,681	4,986	305
			83	7,418	11,006	11,673	667
			84	5,533	8,596	9,160	564
	V	W	83	4,078	6,612	6,988	376
			84	220	365	387	22
THAILND	N	W	84	24,966	24,499	26,718	2,219
	O	W	83	2,340	2,496	2,496	
	V	E	82	3,000	1,970	2,270	300
			83	5,400	4,885	5,459	574
			84	57,990	49,785	58,691	8,906
			85	17,585	24,980	30,766	5,786
	V	H	84	598	356	400	44
	V	W	82	12,894	11,356	12,370	1,014

Country	Mode	Reg	Yr	Quantity	F.A.S.	C.I.F.	Charges
			83	25,672	44,591	48,298	3,707
			84	45,858	36,166	39,459	3,293
			85	153,098	121,010	132,657	11,647
			86	214,566	171,873	187,784	15,911
TURKEY	A E		86	2,756	1,175	1,233	58
	O E		86	25,794	14,310	15,621	1,311
	V E		86	6,614	19,400	20,584	1,184
U KING	O E		85	27,476	20,314	20,601	287
			86	67,210	51,571	51,571	

Nut, unshelled
1453020 NUTS, EDBLE NSPF NT SHELLED (LB)

Country	Mode	Reg	Yr	Quantity	F.A.S.	C.I.F.	Charges
TOTAL			82	239,021	248,378	268,481	20,103
			83	282,139	334,168	359,538	25,370
			84	422,838	363,999	389,423	25,424
			85	165,733	165,931	181,062	15,131
			86	230,203	268,144	299,972	31,828
BRAZIL	O E		82	93,750	46,875	46,875	
CANADA	O E		85	5,232	5,499	5,499	
			86	720	2,576	2,576	
CHINA M	N W		84	7,015	11,232	13,425	2,193
	V E		82	9,320	21,299	22,824	1,525
			83	17,992	19,403	21,656	2,253
			84	14,036	20,317	23,304	2,987
			85	9,586	9,339	10,343	1,004
			86	2,800	2,716	3,037	321
	V H		82	1,964	3,382	3,643	261
			83	700	1,603	1,770	167
			84	500	875	982	107
			85	3,900	4,190	5,392	1,202
			86	2,798	3,009	3,588	579
	V W		82	47,163	62,016	70,375	8,359
			83	54,636	59,169	67,401	8,232
			84	37,194	50,833	55,192	4,359
			85	88,556	81,466	89,736	8,270
			86	52,228	62,181	66,677	4,496
CHINA T	O E		84	258,293	162,488	162,576	88
	V E		82	22,950	35,616	39,123	3,507
			83	10,809	25,211	27,629	2,418
			84	12,875	17,617	20,200	2,583
			85	1,355	1,150	1,313	163
			86	45,522	33,853	37,482	3,629
	V H		82	625	1,350	1,462	112
	V W		82	1,750	7,255	7,833	578
			83	16,964	32,281	34,151	1,870
			84	8,395	17,057	18,287	1,230
			85	5,719	10,619	11,333	714
			86	630	1,481	1,509	28
HG KONG	V E		82	600	460	526	66
			83	2,234	1,141	1,209	68
			84	500	500	569	69
			85	1,393	1,406	1,583	177
			86	1,641	5,042	5,431	389
	V H		84	780	1,803	1,944	141
	V W		82	3,144	4,920	5,186	266
			83	15,092	15,835	17,004	1,169
			84	10,078	11,598	12,995	1,397
			85	4,605	3,214	3,556	342
			86	52,574	34,760	38,696	3,936
INDIA	O E		82	110	255	261	6
			84	896	666	788	122
	V E		82	1,263	3,913	4,131	218
			83	4,805	5,505	5,887	382
			84	794	1,459	1,698	239
INDNSIA	V W		83	110	255	273	18
			84	425	693	733	40
IRAN	V E		85	7,151	13,700	14,432	732
			86	42,219	70,695	74,571	3,876
IRAQ	A E		86	17,637	40,800	53,704	12,904
ITALY	A E		82	262	396	565	169
			84	119	277	445	168
	V E		86	291	1,194	1,237	43
JAPAN	V E		84	246	844	876	32
	V W		83	95	329	354	25
			84	137	612	656	44
			86	378	1,179	1,212	33
KOR REP	V W		84	2,783	4,863	5,076	213
MACAO	V W		85	3,360	3,830	3,972	142
MALAYSA	V W		82	2,266	1,892	2,065	173
MEXICO	A E		83	16,209	11,375	13,373	1,998
			84	23,166	18,954	24,542	5,588
	O W		83	42,518	50,464	50,464	

Country	Mode	Reg	Yr	Quantity	F.A.S.	C.I.F.	Charges
NIGERIA	V E		84	1,579	2,302	2,468	166
PHIL R	V E		83	150	432	462	30
			84	494	930	1,118	188
			86	3,528	2,318	2,590	272
	V W		82	1,894	2,217	2,394	177
			83	360	410	443	33
			84	2,710	1,652	1,866	214
			86	5,364	2,317	2,861	544
SPAIN	V E		82	159	510	544	34
			83	258	805	888	83
THAILND	V W		82	18,732	25,272	28,070	2,798
			84	38,721	35,087	37,999	2,912
TURKEY	O E		83	66,138	79,200	83,970	4,770
	V E		82	33,069	30,750	32,604	1,854
			83	33,069	30,750	32,604	1,854
			85	32,672	29,316	31,516	2,200
			86	1,000	2,075	2,239	164
	V W		84	1,102	1,340	1,684	344
U KING	V E		85	2,204	2,202	2,387	185
			86	873	1,948	2,562	614

Oil

Hardening oils, fats, and greases
1782000 HYDROGENATED OILS, ETC NSPF (LB)

Country	Mode	Reg	Yr	Quantity	F.A.S.	C.I.F.	Charges
TOTAL			81	10,807,524	5,137,033	5,789,137	652,104
			82	9,561,958	4,058,447	4,674,051	615,604
			83	9,162,688	3,705,341	4,138,283	432,942
			84	11,842,481	6,935,766	7,561,632	625,866
			85	11,313,881	4,576,640	5,153,256	576,616
			86	13,714,556	4,964,330	5,637,585	673,255
ARGENT	V E		81	79,983	37,474	42,085	4,611
BELGIUM	V E		84	5,456	4,725	6,275	1,550
			85	3,086	1,010	1,085	75
BRAZIL	N E		84	2,951,144	1,571,572	1,718,713	147,141
			85	1,939,369	652,428	745,991	93,563
	V E		81	8,168,445	3,787,313	4,253,601	466,288
			82	7,998,616	3,004,663	3,515,453	510,790
			83	7,878,747	3,012,961	3,363,100	350,139
			84	7,677,990	4,407,209	4,802,298	395,089
			85	7,837,932	2,843,472	3,224,112	380,640
			86	10,356,815	2,857,102	3,328,062	470,960
	V W		86	80,000	20,626	26,199	5,573
CANADA	O E		81	186,905	73,781	73,781	
			82	4,016	4,832	5,017	185
			83	20,286	8,396	8,396	
			84	43,464	20,647	20,647	
			85	15,840	8,380	8,380	
			86	167,816	83,614	83,614	
	O W		82	6,204	6,951	7,263	312
DENMARK	V E		83	45,000	32,166	34,468	2,302
			84	20,614	16,860	18,084	1,224
			85	23,841	19,216	20,742	1,526
			86	13,227	10,272	11,068	796
FR GERM	O E		81	553	2,321	2,513	192
			82	1,764	1,361	1,478	117
			86	3,410	9,922	10,857	935
	V E		81	316,964	103,907	120,675	16,768
			82	281,262	99,778	113,072	13,294
			83	7,657	7,046	7,520	474
			84	10,881	12,480	13,623	1,143
			85	5,508	6,232	7,143	911
			86	162,812	73,875	85,654	11,779
	V W		82	1,184	1,228	1,502	274
			83	1,149	1,236	1,941	705
			84	2,412	1,075	1,375	300
FRANCE	A E		82	1,998	6,287	7,072	785
			85	5,159	31,713	33,723	2,010
	N E		81	3,033	19,158	20,482	1,324
			83	1,177	2,400	2,574	174
			84	2,513	6,056	8,317	2,261
	O E		81	2,680	2,432	2,432	
			82	4,487	4,858	4,858	
	V E		86	774	1,839	3,057	1,218

Product TSUSA commodity number, description, and unit of quantity							
Country	Mode	Reg	Yr	Quantity	F.A.S.	C.I.F.	Charges
GREECE	O	E	86	2,920	1,756	1,756	
	V	E	81	170,339	164,033	181,891	17,858
			82	119,632	110,531	124,606	14,075
			83	104,219	83,485	94,166	10,681
			85	41,607	27,189	30,317	3,128
			86	116,552	70,877	86,129	15,252
INDIA	V	E	81	1,356,326	585,702	690,663	104,961
			82	295,356	123,273	145,232	21,959
			83	372,876	129,993	153,525	23,532
IRAN	V	W	84	6,572	4,339	4,870	531
IRELAND	A	E	81	106	313	557	244
ISRAEL	V	E	86	47,707	24,686	28,190	3,504
ITALY	A	E	81	448	381	413	32
	N	E	81	54,343	31,212	37,970	6,758
	V	E	85	14,357	27,858	28,669	811
JAPAN	V	E	81	54,056	91,774	98,194	6,420
			82	229,931	396,411	415,591	19,180
			83	251,450	117,520	135,213	17,693
			84	88,477	106,952	116,192	9,240
			85	3,333	10,159	11,082	923
			86	25,800	41,466	43,292	1,826
	V	W	83	22,090	47,620	51,646	4,026
			84	22,090	47,320	51,646	4,326
			86	5,926	24,325	25,598	1,273
LEBANON	O	E	81	204	326	351	25
	V	E	81	2,381	1,573	2,508	935
LIBERIA	V	E	81	144	400	485	85
MALAYSA	V	E	81	4,500	1,388	1,410	22
N ZEAL	V	E	86	50,389	43,571	45,729	2,158
NETHLDS	N	E	81	178,478	118,646	132,316	13,670
			82	170,914	90,452	99,721	9,269
			84	347,501	219,213	239,302	20,089
			85	487,614	293,155	322,859	29,704
			86	464,032	229,238	252,499	23,261
	O	E	82	1,080	748	748	
			85	4,743	5,458	5,458	
			86	17,959	11,271	11,271	
	V	E	81	208,012	105,223	114,850	9,627
			82	255,441	115,124	127,522	12,398
			83	392,468	226,871	247,567	20,696
			84	481,264	380,575	405,064	24,489
			85	583,077	371,207	405,870	34,663
			86	1,330,175	835,861	901,349	65,488
	V	W	81	2,486	1,573	1,809	236
			84	1,102	1,399	1,547	148
			85	2,480	2,864	3,151	287
PHIL R	V	W	86	12	1,848	2,265	417
SPAIN	V	E	82	72,000	25,776	30,050	4,274
SWEDEN	O	E	86	63,095	27,121	31,885	4,764
	V	E	86	198,050	113,235	128,517	15,282
SWITZLD	A	E	86	1,026	2,047	3,654	1,607
	V	E	86	809	1,507	1,573	66
U KING	A	E	84	220	398	525	127
	A	W	86	9,000	28,000	28,856	856
	N	E	82	90,204	42,910	49,828	6,918
			83	56,278	31,306	33,627	2,321
			84	99,593	76,912	89,866	12,954
			85	311,155	253,558	279,263	25,705
	O	E	81	1,680	1,189	1,189	
			82	26,309	22,535	24,131	1,596
			83	8,691	4,087	4,240	153
			84	41,148	28,776	32,105	3,329
	V	E	81	15,458	6,914	8,962	2,048
			82	1,560	729	907	178
			83	600	254	300	46
			84	40,040	29,258	31,183	1,925
			85	34,780	22,741	25,411	2,670
			86	596,250	450,271	496,511	46,240

Nut, oil
1766400 NUT OILS, NSPF (LB)

TOTAL			81	1,856,004	864,874	952,324	87,450
			82	1,164,365	767,872	827,178	59,306
			83	477,208	834,384	877,549	43,165
			84	1,777,463	1,083,920	1,140,921	57,001
			85	990,577	1,021,990	1,101,520	79,530
			86	1,307,651	1,919,547	2,072,699	153,152
ARGENT	V	E	85	552,825	208,377	227,791	19,414
AUSTRIA	V	E	83	8,051	14,200	15,000	800
	V	W	83	9,120	14,000	15,360	1,360
			85	7,103	14,200	15,400	1,200
BELGIUM	V	W	84	1,224	1,859	2,099	240

Product TSUSA commodity number, description, and unit of quantity							
Country	Mode	Reg	Yr	Quantity	F.A.S.	C.I.F.	Charges
BRAZIL	N	E	82	1,014,121	375,742	412,618	36,876
	V	E	81	1,724,880	564,926	637,774	72,848
			83	180,778	183,402	201,617	18,215
			84	1,455,036	468,258	493,725	25,467
			86	476,194	148,080	157,191	9,111
CANADA	O	E	81	9,101	10,367	10,367	
			85	6,300	2,107	2,107	
FR GERM	N	E	84	767	1,986	2,083	97
	O	E	82	3,029	337	514	177
	V	E	83	906	1,399	1,493	94
	V	W	85	10,670	14,880	16,560	1,680
FRANCE	A	E	85	721	1,735	2,258	523
	A	W	81	15	699	1,133	434
			82	16	408	507	99
	N	E	81	71,209	138,508	146,744	8,236
			82	101,478	163,674	178,113	14,439
			83	113,838	205,706	219,048	13,342
			84	126,706	232,051	250,912	18,861
			85	156,787	331,574	362,900	31,326
			86	160,046	454,691	484,406	29,715
	N	W	82	21,935	41,167	45,060	3,893
			83	36,234	62,936	68,552	5,616
			85	69,185	110,155	128,660	18,505
	O	E	81	5,176	9,128	9,865	737
			82	547	875	945	70
			83	3,933	4,967	5,340	373
			85	4,962	9,388	10,144	756
			86	6,879	18,443	21,882	3,439
	O	W	86	2,380	4,761	5,086	325
	V	E	81	1,642	3,667	4,091	424
			82	7,608	18,924	19,997	1,073
			83	18,878	35,508	37,822	2,314
			84	20,112	42,848	47,402	4,554
			85	29,755	56,228	60,516	4,288
			86	57,804	157,500	169,222	11,722
	V	H	86	475	1,105	1,140	35
	V	W	81	15,616	36,571	38,960	2,389
			82	960	2,758	2,977	219
			83	3,312	10,549	11,045	496
			84	48,056	79,474	86,706	7,232
			85	7,438	16,244	17,789	1,545
			86	59,215	142,457	154,884	12,427
GHANA	V	E	86	10,465	2,374	3,445	1,071
GUYANA	V	E	81	14,000	5,120	7,133	2,013
HG KONG	O	E	83	255	731	786	55
	V	E	81	2,040	1,380	1,490	110
			86	1,796	1,102	1,167	65
	V	W	83	4,360	1,731	1,921	190
			84	3,830	1,394	1,795	401
			86	14,363	7,320	7,694	374
INDIA	A	E	82	794	811	2,602	1,791
	O	E	82	392	847	945	98
	V	W	83	467	709	767	58
INDNSIA	V	E	86	2,380	20,210	20,736	526
ITALY	V	E	81	86	544	594	50
			86	817	3,518	4,079	561
IVY CST	V	E	86	11,076	12,249	13,403	1,154
MEXICO	O	W	81	12,231	93,303	93,303	
			82	10,321	156,418	156,418	
			83	96,563	295,991	295,991	
			84	121,250	255,156	255,156	
			85	140,549	251,808	251,808	
			86	138,534	186,527	186,527	
NETHLDS	O	E	81	8	661	870	209
	V	E	82	49	1,253	1,407	154
			83	63	1,805	2,003	198
SWEDEN	V	E	82	1,913	3,180	3,406	226
SWITZLD	A	E	86	6,614	115,209	115,510	301
U KING	O	E	82	1,202	1,478	1,669	191
			84	482	894	1,043	149
	V	E	83	450	750	804	54
			85	4,282	5,294	5,587	293
			86	358,150	642,800	725,018	82,218
	V	W	86	463	1,201	1,309	108

Oil bearing nut and seed
1755700 OIL BEARNG NUTS & SEED NSPF (LB)

TOTAL			81	590,763	187,497	194,643	7,146
			82	1,253,518	339,159	360,801	21,642
			83	3,165,170	1,165,192	1,319,099	153,907
			84	10,806,744	3,121,840	3,781,407	659,567
			85	9,555,466	2,245,730	2,498,203	252,473
			86	5,268,281	963,713	1,086,865	123,152

Product TSUSA commodity number, description, and unit of quantity Country	Mode	Reg	Yr	Quantity	F.A.S.	C.I.F.	Charges
AUSTRAL	O	E	86	297,387	52,777	52,777	
	V	E	86	103,087	17,855	20,828	2,973
	V	W	85	4,410	7,012	7,288	276
			86	225,495	36,087	48,717	12,630
AUSTRIA	V	E	86	32,755	4,951	6,821	1,870
BELGIUM	V	W	84	31,000	18,628	20,414	1,786
BELIZE	A	E	84	416	261	517	256
	V	E	82	4,488	449	553	104
BRAZIL	A	E	81	200	4,000	4,393	393
C RICA	V	E	82	4,500	2,025	2,318	293
CANADA	N	E	85	255,011	41,642	41,773	131
	O	E	81	377,840	73,720	73,720	
			82	533,949	101,738	101,738	
			83	761,114	114,727	114,727	
			84	764,384	135,733	135,733	
			85	2,254,829	335,562	336,062	500
			86	1,585,570	174,926	176,926	2,000
	O	W	81	40,750	3,607	3,607	
			82	162,630	13,692	13,692	
			83	25,860	2,147	2,147	
			84	257,983	24,521	24,521	
			85	3,649,318	463,066	463,066	
			86	1,438,906	144,460	144,460	
CHINA M	V	E	81	700	835	959	124
			83	28,660	11,384	12,832	1,448
			84	3,540	4,351	4,852	501
			85	2,500	2,040	2,358	318
			86	274,772	44,874	64,064	19,190
	V	H	81	90	308	326	18
			82	150	317	374	57
			83	50	275	289	14
	V	W	81	5,811	11,536	12,044	508
			82	7,708	13,183	13,835	652
			83	2,184	1,817	2,010	193
			84	5,161	4,544	4,828	284
			85	14,442	36,255	39,160	2,905
			86	511,531	107,646	137,988	30,342
CHINA T	A	E	85	270	1,728	1,763	35
	O	E	84	763	1,342	1,342	
	V	E	84	2,500	3,141	3,354	213
	V	W	81	270	732	758	26
			82	1,000	3,800	4,015	215
ETHIOP	V	E	83	1,993,577	676,686	823,401	146,715
			84	7,458,013	2,027,893	2,518,783	490,890
			85	2,095,898	809,648	967,446	157,798
			86	43,211	14,935	18,575	3,640
	V	W	84	433,866	141,633	173,500	31,867
FR GERM	O	E	84	490	534	684	150
	V	E	84	38,140	14,693	16,435	1,742
FRANCE	A	E	81	53	277	278	1
	A	W	81	1,323	6,477	6,944	467
	O	E	86	1,275	2,875	3,089	214
	V	E	81	450	1,483	2,195	712
			82	1,744	5,173	5,674	501
			83	4,631	8,683	9,389	706
			84	4,490	15,732	17,972	2,240
			86	2,553	5,829	6,394	565
GUATMAL	A	W	81	6,600	1,236	1,688	452
			82	700	715	998	283
			83	662	577	742	165
			84	480	519	633	114
	V	E	84	33,100	19,860	22,630	2,770
	V	W	86	10,000	4,422	5,500	1,078
HG KONG	V	E	83	5,793	7,851	8,670	819
			84	5,804	6,766	7,361	595
			85	1,250	1,232	1,439	207
			86	8,000	8,612	9,426	814
	V	W	84	500	466	501	35
			86	7,000	4,524	4,848	324
INDIA	A	E	86	178	1,002	1,147	145
	O	E	83	331	477	519	42
	V	E	81	57,860	30,063	32,180	2,117
			82	203,858	121,616	139,347	17,731
			83	1,391	2,913	3,235	322
			84	1,550,697	548,277	665,310	117,033
			85	714,290	278,360	330,107	51,747
	V	W	81	2,083	2,665	3,106	441
			82	212	266	326	60
			83	309	436	516	80
ISRAEL	V	E	82	11,023	2,251	2,916	665
			84	51,015	17,448	21,770	4,322
ITALY	V	E	83	2,167	1,475	1,745	270
			84	8,112	3,916	4,126	210
			85	216,050	75,208	93,500	18,292

Product TSUSA commodity number, description, and unit of quantity Country	Mode	Reg	Yr	Quantity	F.A.S.	C.I.F.	Charges
IVY CST	V	E	86	337,740	69,280	95,728	26,448
JAPAN	V	E	85	224,869	86,700	104,157	17,457
LEBANON	V	E	81	11,023	6,000	6,654	654
MEXICO	A	E	84	64	482	602	120
	O	E	81	1,323	587	587	
	O	W	81	19,339	25,172	25,172	
			82	310,050	65,825	65,825	
			83	294,228	310,334	310,334	
			84	81,472	86,795	86,795	
			85	48,011	67,600	67,600	
			86	85,448	36,560	36,560	
N ZEAL	V	W	86	44,092	3,754	6,300	2,546
NETHLDS	V	E	82	331	424	565	141
			86	198,415	209,780	222,080	12,300
	V	W	83	31,235	15,928	17,610	1,682
			84	61,800	36,620	39,890	3,270
			85	20,384	15,600	17,400	1,800
NIGERIA	O	E	81	44,835	11,743	11,743	
PAKISTN	V	E	83	5,540	5,135	6,079	944
	V	W	81	1,926	1,855	2,119	264
			84	2,205	1,730	2,118	388
PERU	V	E	81	11,111	847	1,512	665
			82	11,023	2,179	2,925	746
PHIL R	V	W	81	375	442	487	45
PORTUGL	N	E	85	132	1,253	1,308	55
	O	E	86	275	1,306	1,306	
REP SAF	V	E	86	2,094	4,188	4,511	323
SENEGAL	V	E	86	12,200	4,880	7,130	2,250
SWITZLD	V	E	84	500	671	840	169
SYRIA	V	E	81	6,613	3,581	3,795	214
THAILND	V	E	81	188	331	376	45
			83	2,407	1,455	1,637	182
			84	2,375	1,367	1,551	184
	V	W	82	90	634	690	56
			83	5,031	2,892	3,217	325
			84	7,550	3,284	3,672	388
			85	12,737	5,956	6,824	868
U KING	A	E	82	62	4,872	5,010	138
	O	E	85	39,815	15,636	15,636	
	V	E	85	1,250	1,232	1,316	84
			86	46,297	8,190	11,690	3,500
YUGOSLV	V	E	84	324	633	673	40

Oil mixtures

1783000 OIL MIXTURES, NSPF (LB)

Country	Mode	Reg	Yr	Quantity	F.A.S.	C.I.F.	Charges
TOTAL			81	887,446	1,397,874	1,464,218	66,344
			82	360,274	595,463	632,870	37,407
			83	1,081,717	913,483	990,976	77,493
			84	882,854	779,959	857,542	77,583
			85	2,249,943	920,898	974,777	53,879
			86	2,964,792	1,068,526	1,113,753	45,227
CANADA	A	E	82	662	774	1,122	348
	A	W	83	936	711	842	131
	O	E	81	13,581	5,813	5,813	
			82	6,997	2,512	2,512	
			83	44,322	13,955	13,955	
			84	84,293	20,054	20,054	
			85	1,486,418	383,198	384,629	1,431
			86	1,972,050	441,023	441,023	
	O	W	84	20,021	25,935	25,935	
			85	122,660	20,805	20,805	
			86	337,560	50,610	50,610	
CHINA M	V	E	82	2,160	931	1,030	99
			83	82,828	64,848	71,140	6,292
			84	33,950	22,795	25,220	2,425
			85	41,330	23,386	26,738	3,352
			86	103,165	69,659	74,585	4,926
	V	H	82	6,705	7,034	7,550	516
			83	2,400	2,201	2,349	148
			84	11,820	11,267	12,517	1,250
			85	2,880	3,214	3,401	187
			86	2,880	3,206	3,611	405
	V	W	83	3,139	3,428	3,816	388
			84	18,207	12,451	13,871	1,420
CHINA T	V	E	86	88,506	63,807	69,646	5,839
	V	W	83	9,211	12,266	13,142	876
FR GERM	N	E	83	194	2,041	2,105	64
FRANCE	O	E	86	406	1,035	1,098	63
GREECE	V	E	83	33,863	23,040	27,440	4,400
			84	169,050	122,469	144,169	21,700
			85	7,350	6,723	7,937	1,214
HG KONG	V	E	83	215,103	159,771	173,146	13,375

Product
TSUSA commodity number, description, and unit of quantity

Country	Mode	Reg	Yr	Quantity	F.A.S.	C.I.F.	Charges
			84	50,960	36,683	40,599	3,916
			85	176,721	111,283	122,816	11,533
			86	147,698	118,456	126,605	8,149
	V	H	82	5,040	5,883	6,328	445
			83	4,320	4,032	4,443	411
			84	3,240	3,425	3,924	499
			85	2,160	1,579	1,759	180
			86	2,160	1,568	1,602	34
	V	W	83	102,550	70,533	76,584	6,051
INDIA	V	E	83	250	1,000	1,153	153
ISRAEL	V	E	84	65,800	57,941	62,790	4,849
ITALY	V	E	82	158	744	1,043	299
JAPAN	V	E	81	2,118	3,449	3,745	296
			83	512,571	450,437	485,695	35,258
			84	354,488	359,167	388,783	29,616
			85	361,186	309,481	335,927	26,446
			86	278,994	277,050	296,065	19,015
	V	H	81	21,477	31,458	36,126	4,668
			82	34,117	54,716	64,140	9,424
			83	36,942	50,699	57,244	6,545
			84	33,888	49,380	57,372	7,992
			85	42,854	54,509	63,623	9,114
			86	23,398	40,198	46,422	6,224
	V	W	81	138	1,008	1,044	36
			82	23,674	30,764	32,691	1,927
			83	33,088	54,521	57,922	3,401
			84	28,715	48,135	51,098	2,963
			85	4,560	5,516	5,938	422
MEXICO	O	E	85	1,824	1,204	1,204	
	O	W	81	7,920	1,998	1,998	
NETHLDS	V	E	81	201,600	279,816	293,452	13,636
			82	41,587	54,531	57,971	3,440
	V	W	81	40,320	53,466	56,226	2,760
PANAMA	V	E	86	7,975	1,914	2,486	572
PHIL R	V	E	84	8,203	9,210	9,999	789
SWITZLD	A	E	84	219	1,047	1,211	164
U KING	A	E	82	1,592	1,428	1,634	206
	N	E	81	479,332	848,037	888,037	39,936
	V	E	81	120,960	172,765	177,777	5,012
			82	197,262	381,615	398,877	17,262
	V	W	82	40,320	54,531	57,972	3,441

Vegetable, oil
1767000 OTHER VEGETABLE OILS NSPF (LB)

Country	Mode	Reg	Yr	Quantity	F.A.S.	C.I.F.	Charges
TOTAL			81	467,564	603,134	654,813	51,679
			82	840,213	745,185	825,059	79,874
			83	945,560	825,337	900,453	75,116
			84	384,571	690,390	751,229	60,839
			85	694,152	1,182,327	1,275,773	93,446
			86	4,932,911	3,388,337	3,579,071	190,734
ARGENT	V	E	84	1,643	681	992	311
			86	2,199,089	687,750	748,650	60,900
AUSTRAL	V	E	86	2,381	27,000	27,401	401
	V	H	86	396	4,778	4,858	80
	V	W	86	2,133,125	1,304,226	1,338,334	34,108
AUSTRIA	V	E	81	413	2,790	3,164	374
			82	6,778	16,005	17,612	1,607
			83	2,152	8,780	9,860	1,080
			84	3,801	8,600	9,800	1,200
			85	1,651	5,320	6,169	849
	V	W	82	917	3,040	3,239	199
BELGIUM	A	E	84	110	2,993	3,096	103
			85	110	3,000	3,085	85
	V	E	82	8,799	3,520	4,102	582
	V	W	85	1,953	1,148	1,298	150
BRAZIL	A	E	84	348	1,418	2,286	868
			86	220	1,016	1,409	393
	V	E	83	6,274	770	855	85
			84	3,292	856	1,021	165
			85	105,239	66,350	80,893	14,543
			86	37,497	13,140	16,225	3,085
	V	W	81	22,876	53,608	58,899	5,291
			82	8,973	21,571	23,660	2,089
CANADA	A	E	83	2,049	11,134	11,345	211
			84	1,554	7,874	8,136	262
	A	W	84	1,761	61,360	63,500	2,140
	N	E	86	11,073	38,644	40,020	1,376
	O	E	81	26,167	11,905	12,851	946
			82	39,897	9,084	9,084	
			83	25,538	7,866	7,866	
			84	5,661	5,928	5,954	26
			85	45,240	15,606	15,606	

Product
TSUSA commodity number, description, and unit of quantity

Country	Mode	Reg	Yr	Quantity	F.A.S.	C.I.F.	Charges
			86	22,508	13,165	13,165	
CHINA M	O	W	83	1,902	562	562	
	O	E	84	600	326	383	57
	V	E	81	1,050	1,050	1,180	130
			84	400	255	295	40
	V	W	81	1,058	1,722	1,823	101
			83	27,840	22,005	22,853	848
			84	8,466	5,050	5,453	403
			85	2,375	1,395	1,499	104
CHINA T	V	E	82	390	300	330	30
			83	2,025	2,525	2,870	345
			84	2,025	3,142	3,468	326
			85	944	1,216	1,335	119
			86	6,674	4,458	5,138	680
	V	W	81	20,060	24,164	25,487	1,323
			82	945	2,940	3,160	220
			83	2,315	7,031	7,370	339
			84	5,323	8,106	8,765	659
			85	6,008	6,126	7,327	1,201
			86	2,872	7,541	8,007	466
COLOMB	A	E	83	4,003	6,328	6,788	460
			85	165	1,109	1,139	30
			86	2,517	7,448	7,925	477
DENMARK	V	E	83	1,675	4,498	4,632	134
FR GERM	A	E	83	332	1,328	1,418	90
			86	419	1,001	1,319	318
	N	E	82	538	1,577	1,774	197
			86	12,940	55,446	57,324	1,878
	O	W	84	1	336	370	34
	V	E	81	1,239	3,057	3,434	377
			82	2,955	5,350	5,950	600
			83	911	1,780	2,020	240
			84	12,874	22,076	23,363	1,287
			85	10,476	17,604	18,252	648
			86	8,959	14,548	15,280	732
	V	W	82	904	3,324	3,695	371
			86	2,094	5,530	5,934	404
FRANCE	A	E	83	1,764	9,212	10,598	1,386
			86	6	3,325	3,408	83
	N	E	81	76,177	74,396	85,418	11,022
			82	162,912	88,307	106,398	18,091
			83	83,093	66,476	73,368	6,892
			84	44,671	37,447	43,890	6,443
			86	47,979	40,510	47,580	7,070
	N	W	81	5,748	3,547	4,205	658
	V	E	82	49,286	20,320	23,730	3,410
			83	50,271	19,114	22,206	3,092
			84	4,053	7,987	9,101	1,114
			85	95,009	79,386	88,753	9,367
			86	45,993	26,155	30,261	4,106
	V	W	81	3,430	5,575	5,826	251
			82	34,645	17,392	19,980	2,588
			83	335,298	133,350	154,182	20,832
			84	1,235	2,316	2,692	376
			85	2,066	2,658	3,128	470
			86	44,876	27,744	32,895	5,151
GREECE	O	E	81	1,596	2,163	2,163	
			82	300	474	474	
GUATMAL	A	W	85	121	6,075	6,280	205
HG KONG	V	E	81	165	294	306	12
			83	472	397	448	51
			86	36,631	14,990	16,699	1,709
	V	W	81	3,361	2,029	2,239	210
			83	2,419	3,448	3,926	478
			84	8,380	4,533	4,830	297
			85	64,644	34,560	36,751	2,191
HONDURA	V	E	81	1,223	14,637	15,219	582
HUNGARY	A	E	84	44	2,960	3,017	57
ICELAND	A	E	84	700	768	1,036	268
INDIA	A	W	86	11	1,685	1,750	65
	O	E	84	425	383	417	34
	O	W	81	900	270	283	13
	V	E	82	439,001	466,361	507,233	40,872
			83	158,676	164,804	179,925	15,121
	V	W	81	394	257	312	55
			82	698	1,078	1,254	176
			85	1,976	1,066	1,321	255
ITALY	A	E	83	110	1,600	1,836	236
			84	2,581	3,888	5,942	2,054
	O	E	86	2,006	6,000	6,781	781
	V	E	81	605	264	285	21
			83	143	559	634	75
			84	4,909	4,795	6,099	1,304
			85	2,416	2,334	2,731	397
	V	W	86	3,651	1,927	2,187	260

Product / Country	Mode	Reg	Yr	Quantity	F.A.S.	C.I.F.	Charges
JAMAICA	V	E	84	280	673	709	36
			85	3,278	32,629	33,250	621
			86	5,792	45,174	45,692	518
JAPAN	A	E	84	341	836	1,463	627
	N	E	81	37,582	36,264	40,358	4,094
	V	E	82	19,725	11,751	14,005	2,254
			83	31,070	21,385	24,584	3,199
			84	31,066	21,943	25,055	3,112
			85	38,320	29,654	33,848	4,194
			86	56,879	46,518	54,444	7,926
	V	H	81	7,770	10,937	12,176	1,239
			83	1,943	1,465	1,714	249
			85	3,630	1,837	2,187	350
			86	4,653	4,426	5,084	658
	V	W	81	71,845	75,147	83,761	8,614
			82	11,620	19,793	21,101	1,308
			83	54,868	69,573	73,275	3,702
			84	63,455	64,715	68,680	3,965
			85	28,015	28,975	31,661	2,686
			86	24,982	43,154	46,159	3,005
KENYA	V	E	84	1,449	763	840	77
KOR REP	V	E	85	432	1,200	1,252	52
	V	W	85	1,268	3,526	3,856	330
LEBANON	O	E	84	19,021	15,424	16,821	1,397
	V	E	86	3,175	2,800	3,111	311
MEXICO	A	E	82	336	8,595	8,945	350
			85	44	1,493	1,543	50
	O	E	84	64,088	24,703	24,703	
	O	W	81	51,200	20,000	20,000	
			82	812	10,361	10,361	
			85	30,000	28,500	28,500	
			86	4,019	9,200	9,200	
N ZEAL	V	E	83	13,333	5,619	7,378	1,759
	V	W	83	1,400	6,821	7,000	179
NETHLDS	N	E	82	7,244	3,773	4,467	694
			83	11,072	4,775	5,365	590
	V	E	81	9,022	5,226	5,792	566
			84	3,744	2,924	3,394	470
			85	36,255	18,206	20,265	2,059
			86	15,100	7,544	8,796	1,252
NORWAY	O	E	85	41,116	12,046	16,536	4,490
PAKISTN	V	E	86	8,300	4,080	4,588	508
PORTUGL	V	E	84	2,003	1,060	1,203	143
			85	4,565	1,857	2,869	1,012
REP SAF	V	E	83	63,669	103,968	108,968	5,000
			85	80,875	77,038	83,638	6,600
			86	65,406	60,073	64,859	4,786
	V	W	81	91,998	229,493	242,136	12,643
			86	7,121	5,976	6,656	680
SINGAPR	V	W	81	186	2,966	3,291	325
			82	496	1,766	1,917	151
			83	1,312	1,297	1,372	75
			84	153	959	1,036	77
SWEDEN	A	E	85	100	2,610	2,799	189
			86	2,235	74,025	75,829	1,804
	A	W	86	3,968	50,350	55,552	5,202
SWITZLD	A	E	86	3,100	113,152	121,889	8,737
THAILND	V	W	81	137	361	377	16
			86	9,916	4,671	5,052	381
U KING	A	E	82	397	2,830	3,098	268
			83	6,567	44,806	46,205	1,399
			84	3,191	59,239	60,624	1,385
			85	496	25,875	26,163	288
			86	21,710	342,645	357,809	15,164
	A	W	83	990	4,383	4,525	142
	N	E	81	13,871	9,446	10,935	1,489
			82	33,020	18,548	21,691	3,143
			83	37,924	73,486	78,442	4,956
			84	53,126	274,040	300,874	26,834
			85	74,932	659,882	698,695	38,813
			86	58,159	258,941	273,071	14,130
	O	E	81	9,276	6,848	7,483	635
			82	5,420	2,857	3,196	339
			83	16	1,020	1,020	
			84	11,662	7,443	8,097	654
			85	4,800	7,673	8,345	672
	O	W	86	1,913	1,255	1,427	172
	V	E	81	264	254	278	24
			82	337	255	294	39
			83	1,450	1,234	1,313	79
			84	7,423	4,742	5,554	812
			86	12,566	6,326	7,303	977
	V	W	81	750	719	798	79
			82	2,848	2,403	2,699	296
			83	2,481	1,156	1,354	198

Product / Country	Mode	Reg	Yr	Quantity	F.A.S.	C.I.F.	Charges
			84	2,431	2,929	3,401	472
			85	5,633	4,373	4,799	426
YUGOSLV	O	E	82	20	1,610	1,610	
			83	380	678	678	
	V	E	81	7,201	3,745	4,334	589
			83	7,823	10,104	11,698	1,594
			84	5,906	13,185	13,802	617
	V	W	84	375	734	1,067	333

Ornamental

Bulbs, roots, corms, and tubers
1253270 BULBS, ETC, NSPF, WITH SOIL (NO)

Country	Mode	Reg	Yr	Quantity	F.A.S.	C.I.F.	Charges
TOTAL			81	46,789	45,851	51,614	5,763
			82	84,663	139,270	140,082	812
			83	383,178	166,660	173,423	6,763
			84	966,408	628,293	635,941	7,648
			85	1,417,907	740,305	748,559	8,254
			86	9,895,093	1,306,297	1,309,652	3,355
BELGIUM	V	E	82	8,900	1,986	2,131	145
CANADA	A	E	81	474	1,459	1,525	66
			86	5,400	1,910	1,945	35
	A	W	83	4,000	800	836	36
	N	E	85	22,778	54,873	54,873	
	O	E	81	8,631	20,219	20,219	
			82	64,638	134,805	134,805	
			83	101,037	116,432	116,432	
			84	235,123	480,620	481,335	715
			85	1,316,379	626,012	626,014	2
			86	9,793,168	1,278,081	1,278,081	
	O	W	81	15	304	304	
			83	4,400	13,333	13,333	
			84	83,046	23,223	23,223	
FIJI	A	W	86	6,408	3,533	4,863	1,330
ISRAEL	V	E	86	32,900	9,400	9,495	95
JAPAN	A	E	81	344	784	1,311	527
	A	W	83	26,000	5,538	9,712	4,174
			86	460	1,104	1,841	737
	V	W	84	6,200	4,641	4,988	347
			85	13,000	1,996	2,405	409
N ZEAL	A	E	86	53	1,333	1,333	
	A	H	85	1,950	1,303	1,384	81
NETHLDS	A	E	82	11,125	2,479	3,146	667
			86	900	1,677	1,765	88
	A	W	86	25,200	5,918	6,768	850
	O	E	83	14,300	1,271	1,271	
			84	235,299	9,395	9,395	
			86	30,604	3,341	3,561	220
	V	E	83	233,441	29,286	31,839	2,553
			84	406,710	110,068	116,535	6,467
	V	W	81	36,825	13,987	15,567	1,580
REP SAF	A	E	81	205	1,723	1,926	203
			85	49,800	54,603	62,303	7,700
U KING	A	W	85	14,000	1,518	1,580	62
	N	E	84	30	346	465	119
	O	E	81	45	329	350	21
W SAMOA	A	W	81	250	7,046	10,412	3,366

1253470 BULBS, ROOTS, ETC, NSPF (NO)

Country	Mode	Reg	Yr	Quantity	F.A.S.	C.I.F.	Charges
TOTAL			81	109,124,539	7,806,021	8,662,077	854,755
			82	92,933,970	7,653,019	8,443,787	790,768
			83	134,121,373	8,650,673	9,634,121	983,448
			84	157,695,131	11,736,650	12,996,086	1,258,004
			85	189,357,288	13,623,480	15,211,453	1,587,973
			86	230,009,705	16,190,873	18,155,164	1,964,291
ARGENT	O	E	83	5,000	300	350	50
AUSTRAL	A	E	86	35,000	5,159	6,119	960
	A	W	86	30	1,426	1,497	71
BELGIUM	A	E	81	199,550	60,803	71,112	10,309
			84	37,875	12,158	14,918	2,760
			86	19,000	1,955	2,803	848
	A	W	85	38,650	6,488	7,903	1,415
	N	E	81	327,358	97,669	106,419	8,750

Product
TSUSA commodity number, description, and unit of quantity

Country	Mode	Reg	Yr	Quantity	F.A.S.	C.I.F.	Charges
			82	771,469	83,892	92,687	8,795
			83	294,399	29,371	33,527	4,156
			84	602,748	97,819	108,151	10,332
			85	2,260,865	306,173	329,335	23,162
			86	79,288	33,605	40,050	6,445
	N	W	81	144,800	62,575	70,642	8,067
			83	56,075	7,628	8,798	1,170
	O	E	85	6,250	1,675	2,353	678
	V	E	81	430,582	63,270	67,213	3,943
			82	370,076	44,221	48,963	4,742
			83	82,225	20,814	22,666	1,852
			84	259,224	44,508	48,855	4,347
			85	72,100	15,538	16,919	1,381
			86	164,965	33,502	36,792	3,290
	V	W	81	10,650	4,133	4,504	371
			82	20,360	7,896	8,146	250
			83	1,580	402	442	40
			84	15,070	5,133	5,326	193
			85	17,425	5,240	5,590	350
BELIZE	A	E	82	450	450	571	121
BRAZIL	A	E	84	4,290	1,073	2,129	1,056
	V	W	81	1,578	3,240	3,631	391
CANADA	A	E	82	4,700	1,231	1,318	87
			83	3,800	3,772	4,110	338
	O	E	81	3,000	1,542	1,542	
			82	5,700	2,185	2,185	
			83	195,000	12,599	12,599	
			85	150,000	4,050	4,050	
	O	W	81	396	739	739	
			82	19,046	12,935	12,935	
			83	32,974	27,721	27,721	
			84	59,439	38,378	38,378	
			85	27,484	44,555	44,555	
			86	60,215	60,218	60,218	
CHINA M	A	E	82	150	403	450	47
	A	W	81	1,435	3,187	3,686	499
CHINA T	V	E	85	9,130	6,567	6,744	177
	V	W	83	2,500	1,125	1,244	119
			84	7,000	2,100	2,467	367
			85	8,000	2,400	2,534	134
			86	6,000	1,860	2,069	209
COLOMB	A	E	84	628,995	229,002	261,648	32,646
DOM REP	V	E	84	49,300	1,479	2,922	1,443
FR GERM	A	E	82	80,800	21,327	21,754	427
			83	51,500	13,795	14,010	215
			86	50,000	18,458	18,630	172
	V	E	83	2,700	3,715	4,036	321
			85	9,239	7,668	8,875	1,207
			86	115,200	9,441	9,908	467
FRANCE	V	E	81	7,035	4,876	5,401	525
			82	141,548	7,411	8,241	830
			83	314,177	39,667	41,271	1,604
			84	387,517	28,047	29,220	1,173
GUATMAL	V	E	81	8,000	2,400	2,561	161
			82	18,000	5,040	5,767	727
GUINEA	A	W	85	4,200	3,156	3,259	103
HG KONG	V	E	86	5,643	4,009	6,830	2,821
INDIA	A	E	82	4,250	2,101	2,755	654
			83	329,092	5,808	11,142	5,334
			84	25,197	2,421	4,014	1,593
			85	848,917	22,043	34,788	12,745
			86	90,500	2,803	4,340	1,537
	A	W	81	45,950	3,031	6,464	3,433
			82	66,021	4,008	7,254	3,246
			83	78,000	3,505	6,566	3,061
			84	82,100	4,098	7,042	2,944
			86	297,500	7,436	11,899	4,463
	N	E	81	61,100	1,104	1,822	718
			82	696,800	11,381	15,252	3,871
			83	400,580	7,311	9,063	1,752
			84	478,000	13,420	17,028	3,608
	V	E	86	377,500	12,808	13,265	457
ISRAEL	A	E	86	1,020,300	14,121	18,624	4,503
	N	E	81	82,614	19,404	25,057	5,653
			85	798,891	133,923	152,654	18,731
	N	W	83	208,140	133,776	137,704	3,928
	V	E	81	1,145,539	75,739	82,339	6,600
			82	988,825	120,760	134,955	14,195
			83	3,652,424	271,340	290,562	19,222
			84	2,101,827	192,499	213,150	20,651
			85	1,000,724	82,485	89,621	7,136
			86	616,679	94,278	102,194	7,916
	V	W	81	78,898	12,153	13,229	1,076
			82	1,054,720	46,905	50,641	3,736
			83	149,368	8,339	9,698	1,359
ITALY	V	E	86	45,700	2,143	2,192	49
JAPAN	A	E	81	4,600	1,671	2,868	1,197
			83	12,000	3,280	3,954	674
			84	13,000	3,210	5,170	1,960
			86	16,000	4,065	4,474	409
	A	W	82	12,345	3,215	3,694	479
			85	3,557	3,695	5,038	1,343
	N	E	81	188,000	46,557	53,019	6,462
			82	127,985	30,035	32,949	2,914
			83	175,763	30,646	43,758	13,112
			84	142,785	49,235	54,386	5,151
			85	282,845	104,920	119,620	14,700
			86	69,090	32,526	34,371	1,845
	N	W	81	1,428,276	299,828	391,138	91,705
			82	230,954	75,512	98,040	22,528
			83	149,012	37,025	44,526	7,501
			84	219,555	56,819	63,617	6,798
	V	E	81	10,500	1,774	2,039	265
			84	8,925	1,532	1,704	172
			86	159,800	44,424	48,176	3,752
	V	W	82	150,150	26,668	29,112	2,444
			83	101,700	21,237	23,177	1,940
			84	189,750	39,545	43,022	3,477
			85	1,433,915	147,366	163,764	16,398
			86	486,980	131,196	143,562	12,366
MALI	V	E	85	64,800	1,671	1,820	149
			86	653,675	84,827	99,125	14,298
MAURIT	A	W	85	19,500	6,042	6,891	849
MEXICO	O	W	83	3,111,023	27,039	27,039	
N ANTIL	A	E	86	2,839	2,129	2,264	135
N ZEAL	A	H	86	19,620	12,514	13,869	1,355
	A	W	84	34,770	31,059	31,693	634
			85	34,114	19,990	20,668	678
			86	2,756	2,843	2,968	125
NETHLDS	A	E	81	11,450	2,423	2,746	323
			82	728,882	13,146	16,188	3,042
			83	1,634,490	25,108	29,312	4,204
			84	470,491	19,576	26,543	6,967
			85	911,658	37,345	48,838	11,493
			86	237,008	28,701	33,560	4,859
	A	W	84	10,425	2,731	3,216	485
			85	17,500	1,077	1,276	199
	N	E	81	84,242,896	4,524,932	4,872,611	347,077
			82	63,277,779	4,512,885	4,907,558	394,673
			83	96,053,819	5,007,019	5,506,481	499,462
			84	115,057,509	6,762,698	7,396,190	633,492
			85	135,817,032	8,329,710	9,216,674	886,964
			86	161,558,314	10,588,841	11,729,881	1,141,040
	N	W	81	152,932	42,755	45,073	2,318
			82	590,846	60,329	70,554	10,225
			83	3,855,013	247,569	279,233	31,664
			84	5,678,371	400,675	480,444	79,769
			85	11,972,555	551,669	650,503	98,834
			86	16,862,592	818,024	951,251	133,227
	O	E	81	37,945	4,098	4,098	
			82	29,101	2,968	3,033	65
			83	17,695	2,546	2,783	237
			84	293,330	41,288	45,229	3,941
			85	23,556	1,666	1,666	
			86	180,543	60,475	62,875	
	V	E	81	13,588,343	1,436,287	1,578,256	140,875
			82	12,598,488	1,297,743	1,438,634	140,891
			83	16,974,156	1,323,918	1,485,020	161,102
			84	23,575,339	2,092,020	2,345,481	252,029
			85	27,259,996	1,792,651	2,032,383	239,732
			86	32,892,969	2,465,579	2,776,534	310,955
	V	W	81	3,262,965	323,221	357,711	34,490
			82	6,828,674	392,492	432,179	39,687
			83	1,652,025	94,824	106,783	11,959
			84	1,777,209	85,238	102,083	16,845
			85	836,142	47,132	55,712	8,580
			86	3,123,744	102,280	120,550	18,270
NICARAG	A	E	86	500	1,413	1,534	121
PERU	A	E	81	14,000	350	435	85
REP SAF	A	E	84	345	837	1,004	167
			85	1,295,421	1,805,874	2,029,086	223,212
			86	130,000	3,726	4,373	647
	A	W	85	1,692,000	25,974	27,508	1,534
	N	E	81	1,086,561	607,872	777,395	169,523
			82	1,661,538	791,319	916,646	125,327
			83	1,156,952	1,120,182	1,316,432	196,250
			84	1,797,130	1,272,539	1,413,781	141,242
			86	4,108,555	1,341,918	1,615,284	273,366
	O	E	83	6,000	5,966	7,089	1,123
	V	E	81	354,206	14,640	16,310	1,670

Product TSUSA commodity number, description, and unit of quantity Country	Mode	Reg	Yr	Quantity	F.A.S.	C.I.F.	Charges
			82	576,425	24,023	25,426	1,403
			83	2,127,732	59,798	64,128	4,330
			84	1,769,149	93,857	104,023	10,166
			85	1,455,481	48,624	55,592	6,968
			86	3,326,000	72,010	73,903	1,893
	V	W	81	966,680	38,288	40,211	1,923
			82	478,024	20,241	21,667	1,426
			84	28,229	1,142	1,326	184
SINGAPR	A	E	81	21,400	1,100	2,050	950
SPAIN	V	E	85	13,081	13,440	14,498	1,058
SRI LKA	A	E	81	79,000	815	2,399	1,584
SURINAM	A	E	83	500	500	553	53
SWEDEN	V	E	82	11,625	1,496	1,691	195
THAILND	A	E	82	23,905	4,265	5,909	1,644
			83	500	500	850	350
			84	1,500	1,500	2,493	993
TURKEY	V	E	81	221,800	5,845	7,131	1,286
			82	410,750	8,731	9,052	321
			83	591,700	13,595	14,810	1,215
			84	574,050	11,916	13,400	1,484
			85	500,250	8,687	11,018	2,331
			86	584,462	46,291	48,091	1,800
U KING	A	E	84	100,905	3,130	3,762	632
			85	1,080	1,550	1,590	40
			86	1,054	3,795	4,458	663
	A	W	82	15,200	573	794	221
			84	5,000	1,402	1,630	228
			85	10,500	1,050	1,170	120
	N	E	84	1,202,890	84,576	90,772	6,196
			85	305,905	21,680	24,938	3,258
	V	E	81	745,687	28,261	30,324	2,063
			82	929,959	14,882	16,411	1,529
			83	600,657	31,596	33,993	2,397
			85	72,900	5,112	6,271	1,159
			86	2,243,609	34,331	39,569	5,238
	V	W	81	158,813	9,439	9,902	463
			85	81,625	4,594	5,749	1,155
			86	363,075	4,693	5,517	824
VENEZ	A	W	86	3,000	1,050	1,545	495
W SAMOA	V	W	83	28,080	6,000	7,233	1,233
			84	5,892	7,990	9,869	1,879
YEMEN S	V	E	82	8,425	350	376	26
			83	13,022	1,337	1,458	121

Cut flowers
1922100 CUT FLOWERS, FRESH (NULL)

Country	Mode	Reg	Yr	Quantity	F.A.S.	C.I.F.	Charges
TOTAL			81	-	85,188,752	106,900,871	21,027,413
			82	-	106,453,599	128,138,997	21,685,398
ALGERIA	N	E	82	-	243,358	303,414	60,056
AUSTRAL	N	E	81	-	151,127	184,913	33,786
			82	-	162,622	201,599	38,977
	N	H	81	-	726	949	223
			82	-	1,145	2,283	1,138
	N	W	81	-	258,106	312,691	54,585
			82	-	334,045	421,836	87,791
AUSTRIA	N	W	81	-	2,733	3,455	722
BELGIUM	N	E	82	-	7,191	9,137	1,946
BRAZIL	N	E	81	-	11,548	20,116	8,568
			82	-	19,118	32,478	13,360
	N	W	82	-	600	690	90
C AF RP	N	E	81	-	371	415	44
C RICA	N	E	81	-	306,398	377,566	71,168
			82	-	448,977	614,799	165,822
	N	W	81	-	963	1,402	439
CANADA	N	E	81	-	1,165,305	1,167,308	2,003
			82	-	1,356,820	1,356,943	123
	N	W	81	-	92,673	92,830	157
			82	-	102,590	103,163	573
CHINA T	N	E	82	-	450	500	50
COLOMB	N	E	81	-	66,556,631	84,171,838	16,927,341
			82	-	76,764,278	91,026,079	14,261,801
	N	W	81	-	7,029	9,188	1,197
			82	-	9,776	11,795	2,019
COOK IS	N	H	81	-	18,521	24,059	5,538
			82	-	28,594	37,301	8,707
DENMARK	N	W	81	-	582	952	370
DOM REP	N	E	81	-	194,737	244,104	49,367
			82	-	122,693	175,308	52,615
DOMINCA	N	E	82	-	252	532	280
ECUADOR	N	E	81	-	135,727	179,771	44,044
			82	-	53,537	70,705	17,168
	N	W	82	-	640	1,047	407

Country	Mode	Reg	Yr	Quantity	F.A.S.	C.I.F.	Charges
F W IND	N	E	81	-	2,070	2,757	687
FR GERM	N	E	81	-	23,190	28,412	5,222
			82	-	10,254	12,432	2,178
	N	W	82	-	654	1,081	427
FRANCE	N	E	81	-	2,005	2,321	316
			82	-	10,132	12,045	1,913
	N	W	82	-	2,360	3,433	1,073
GUATMAL	N	E	81	-	228,439	282,236	53,797
			82	-	271,471	335,662	64,191
	N	W	81	-	7,129	8,801	1,672
			82	-	845	1,505	660
HAITI	N	E	81	-	425	451	26
			82	-	2,686	3,218	532
HG KONG	N	W	82	-	909	956	47
INDIA	N	E	82	-	1,171	1,680	509
ISRAEL	N	E	81	-	308,485	737,527	428,042
			82	-	334,394	914,801	580,407
ITALY	N	E	81	-	82,313	121,840	39,527
			82	-	287,192	366,451	79,259
IVY CST	N	E	81	-	7,587	16,916	9,329
			82	-	6,372	18,486	12,114
JAMAICA	N	E	81	-	55,063	74,442	19,379
			82	-	66,829	83,702	16,873
JAPAN	N	W	81	-	1,128	1,667	539
			82	-	1,943	3,388	1,445
KENYA	N	E	82	-	6,286	17,420	11,134
LIBERIA	N	E	81	-	3,668	4,521	853
MALAYSA	N	E	82	-	324	645	321
MEXICO	N	E	81	-	567,024	652,497	85,473
			82	-	923,412	1,054,587	131,175
	N	W	81	-	1,154,857	1,184,808	29,951
			82	-	1,838,177	1,850,832	12,655
N ANTIL	N	W	82	-	14,620	23,316	8,696
N ZEAL	N	E	81	-	116,191	140,456	24,265
			82	-	63,565	79,729	16,164
	N	H	81	-	9,140	10,854	1,714
			82	-	34,074	42,704	8,630
	N	W	81	-	130,600	148,188	17,588
			82	-	93,005	118,413	25,408
NETHLDS	N	E	81	-	11,303,261	13,463,144	2,159,883
			82	-	18,923,144	23,211,790	4,288,646
	N	H	81	-	539	893	354
	N	W	81	-	221,138	295,714	74,576
			82	-	947,320	1,304,458	357,138
NICARAG	N	E	82	-	10,283	12,203	1,920
NORWAY	N	E	82	-	1,213	1,665	452
PANAMA	N	E	81	-	132,845	150,881	18,036
	N	W	81	-	600	641	41
PERU	N	E	81	-	889,785	1,228,339	339,424
			82	-	1,449,915	1,981,626	531,711
	N	W	81	-	141,273	218,126	77,727
			82	-	96,020	148,861	52,841
PORTUGL	N	E	82	-	7,772	9,312	1,540
REP SAF	N	E	81	-	65,296	111,606	46,312
			82	-	278,858	397,276	118,418
	N	W	82	-	10,038	18,332	8,294
SINGAPR	N	E	81	-	54,878	87,597	32,719
			82	-	44,987	66,108	21,121
	N	W	81	-	55,811	81,890	26,079
			82	-	151,775	218,888	67,113
SPAIN	N	E	81	-	34,123	44,079	9,956
			82	-	50,492	80,605	30,113
SWEDEN	N	E	82	-	7,304	8,741	1,437
SWITZLD	N	E	81	-	18,073	23,367	5,294
			82	-	11,937	19,440	7,503
THAILND	N	E	81	-	37,547	78,876	41,329
			82	-	161,119	314,722	153,603
	N	H	81	-	420	895	475
			82	-	1,942	3,928	1,986
	N	W	81	-	324,518	529,869	205,727
			82	-	386,610	657,003	270,393
TONGA	N	E	81	-	1,524	2,046	522
U KING	N	E	81	-	287,174	353,098	65,924
			82	-	276,787	355,815	79,028
	N	W	82	-	7,468	10,778	3,310
USSR	N	E	82	-	1,425	1,987	562
VENEZ	N	E	81	-	16,285	17,879	4,594
W SAMOA	N	H	82	-	1,000	1,044	44

1922190 CUT FLOWERS, FRESH (NULL)

Country	Mode	Reg	Yr	Quantity	F.A.S.	C.I.F.	Charges
TOTAL			83	-	45,536,009	56,795,890	11,259,881
			84	-	65,655,466	84,603,891	18,948,425
			85	-	78,156,952	103,737,164	25,580,212
ALGERIA	N	E	83	-	11,588	13,265	1,677

Product
TSUSA commodity number, description, and unit of quantity

Country	Mode	Reg	Yr	Quantity	F.A.S.	C.I.F.	Charges
ARGENT	N E		83	-	5,422	14,007	8,585
AUSTRAL	N E		83	-	127,591	165,571	37,980
			84	-	238,059	331,394	93,335
			85	-	95,651	118,178	22,527
	N W		83	-	309,230	343,425	34,195
			84	-	356,100	502,769	146,669
			85	-	361,342	517,859	156,517
AUSTRIA	N E		83	-	10,006	11,969	1,963
			84	-	452	894	442
	N W		83	-	596	1,484	888
			84	-	5,571	8,985	3,414
BELGIUM	N E		83	-	9,849	11,080	1,231
			84	-	6,926	8,184	1,258
			85	-	37,839	42,291	4,452
BOLIVIA	N E		84	-	336	876	540
BOTSWAN	N E		84	-	7,940	8,084	144
BRAZIL	N E		83	-	19,358	37,679	18,321
			84	-	44,727	88,726	43,999
			85	-	118,155	167,790	49,635
	N W		83	-	300	397	97
C RICA	N E		83	-	45,494	56,693	11,199
			84	-	159,082	198,705	39,623
			85	-	354,487	454,322	99,835
	N W		83	-	1,120	1,845	725
			84	-	5,721	8,817	3,096
			85	-	11,907	16,468	4,561
CANADA	N E		83	-	1,132,440	1,132,756	316
			84	-	1,604,779	1,605,869	1,090
			85	-	1,422,312	1,423,648	1,336
	N W		83	-	223,234	223,931	697
			84	-	520,167	521,389	1,222
			85	-	583,698	585,153	1,455
CHILE	N E		83	-	2,522	4,258	1,736
			84	-	7,403	16,145	8,742
			85	-	5,889	9,547	3,658
CHINA M	N E		84	-	403	550	147
	N W		83	-	1,978	2,111	133
			85	-	8,877	9,456	579
CHINA T	N E		84	-	1,100	1,630	530
			85	-	6,664	9,841	3,177
	N W		83	-	5,058	5,933	875
			84	-	5,318	5,888	570
			85	-	10,470	10,670	200
COLOMB	N E		83	-	7,954,970	9,216,314	1,261,344
			84	-	8,759,869	10,299,432	1,539,563
			85	-	8,089,167	9,790,006	1,700,839
	N W		84	-	439	558	119
			85	-	23,280	27,082	3,802
COOK IS	N H		83	-	5,577	7,941	2,364
			84	-	6,622	9,339	2,717
CZECHO	N E		85	-	2,775	4,181	1,406
DENMARK	N E		84	-	4,142	5,104	962
			85	-	2,844	3,191	347
	N W		84	-	2,304	2,518	214
			85	-	1,157	2,036	879
DOM REP	N E		83	-	27,746	38,964	11,218
			84	-	12,954	18,704	5,750
			85	-	5,895	7,821	1,926
DOMINCA	N E		84	-	2,638	5,655	3,017
ECUADOR	N E		83	-	13,331	16,829	3,498
			84	-	57,131	76,030	18,899
			85	-	57,282	77,782	20,500
	N W		83	-	2,405	5,167	2,762
ETHIOP	N W		85	-	6,050	7,094	1,044
F W IND	N E		84	-	12,942	18,934	5,992
			85	-	4,292	5,845	1,553
FR GERM	N E		83	-	105,685	128,678	22,993
			84	-	71,521	89,469	17,948
			85	-	10,807	13,303	2,496
	N W		84	-	750	900	150
FRANCE	N E		83	-	218,937	290,680	71,743
			84	-	427,406	547,436	120,030
			85	-	928,541	1,147,326	218,785
	N W		83	-	9,004	11,501	2,497
			84	-	68,962	90,575	21,613
			85	-	90,905	116,717	25,812
GABON	N E		85	-	1,500	2,546	1,046
GERM DR	N E		85	-	1,497	2,262	765
GREECE	N E		83	-	2,652	3,947	1,295
			84	-	3,346	4,746	1,400
			85	-	1,075	1,489	414
GUATMAL	N E		83	-	46,482	72,246	25,764
			84	-	105,403	161,517	56,114
			85	-	1,980	2,790	810
	N W		83	-	325	709	384

Product
TSUSA commodity number, description, and unit of quantity

Country	Mode	Reg	Yr	Quantity	F.A.S.	C.I.F.	Charges
HAITI	N E		83	-	3,078	3,703	625
			84	-	3,831	5,501	1,670
			85	-	3,000	3,296	296
HG KONG	N E		83	-	12,446	14,553	2,107
	N W		83	-	2,126	3,101	975
HONDURA	N E		84	-	6,731	8,229	1,498
			85	-	5,564	6,125	561
ICELAND	N E		85	-	17,544	23,734	6,190
IRAN	N W		85	-	2,458	5,240	2,782
ISRAEL	N E		83	-	519,610	1,193,848	674,238
			84	-	1,379,502	2,788,905	1,409,403
			85	-	2,730,300	4,957,379	2,227,079
	N W		84	-	30,595	54,857	24,262
			85	-	407,595	701,620	294,025
ITALY	N E		83	-	352,738	426,530	73,792
			84	-	655,350	865,365	210,015
			85	-	725,644	928,992	203,348
	N W		83	-	4,263	5,295	1,032
			84	-	13,718	17,351	3,633
			85	-	21,998	27,482	5,484
IVY CST	N E		83	-	339	841	502
			84	-	55,399	113,443	58,044
			85	-	165,604	246,389	80,785
	N W		83	-	637	1,121	484
			84	-	406	917	511
JAMAICA	N E		83	-	62,777	69,944	7,167
			84	-	143,030	186,490	43,460
			85	-	103,103	117,852	14,749
	N W		83	-	260	295	35
JAPAN	N E		83	-	400	600	200
			84	-	6,297	9,428	3,131
			85	-	13,794	16,685	2,891
	N W		83	-	800	1,392	592
			85	-	2,171	3,279	1,108
KENYA	N E		83	-	32,966	49,343	16,377
			84	-	23,431	33,587	10,156
			85	-	24,322	38,421	14,099
	N W		85	-	11,809	15,950	4,141
KIRIBAT	N E		85	-	95,269	129,413	34,144
KOR REP	N E		84	-	50,299	81,266	30,967
			85	-	6,287	10,587	4,300
	N W		85	-	13,560	15,560	2,000
LIBERIA	N E		83	-	3,141	3,484	343
MALI	N E		85	-	68,654	95,850	27,196
	N W		85	-	12,113	16,300	4,187
MALTA	N E		85	-	5,231	6,108	877
MAURIT	N E		85	-	1,790	1,994	204
MAURITN	N E		84	-	4,088	5,090	1,002
MEXICO	N E		83	-	137,742	156,042	18,300
			84	-	245,858	348,496	102,638
			85	-	193,367	274,319	80,952
	N W		83	-	628,170	630,731	2,561
			84	-	373,649	392,335	18,686
			85	-	454,345	474,494	20,149
MONSRAT	N W		85	-	1,380	1,591	211
MOZAMBQ	N E		85	-	21,074	24,815	3,741
N ANTIL	N E		85	-	849,852	1,007,199	157,347
N CALDN	N E		85	-	16,662	22,187	5,525
N ZEAL	N E		85	-	163,054	222,082	59,028
			84	-	258,675	345,804	87,129
			85	-	207,032	261,176	54,144
	N H		83	-	64,955	83,543	18,588
			84	-	28,523	35,613	7,090
			85	-	5,345	8,273	2,928
	N W		83	-	203,135	245,610	42,475
			84	-	383,181	478,923	95,742
			85	-	255,211	333,906	78,695
NAMIBIA	N E		85	-	10,323	11,324	1,001
NETHLDS	N E		83	-	27,490,862	34,038,130	6,547,268
			84	-	39,961,800	51,028,867	11,067,067
			85	-	46,501,039	61,474,483	14,973,444
	N W		83	-	2,595,552	3,392,774	797,222
			84	-	4,805,303	6,236,866	1,431,563
			85	-	5,446,870	7,526,364	2,079,494
NIGER	N E		85	-	79,528	97,545	18,017
NORWAY	N E		83	-	2,019	3,910	1,891
			85	-	25,683	32,602	6,919
PANAMA	N E		85	-	1,005	1,215	210
PERU	N E		83	-	458,099	659,926	201,827
			84	-	1,165,464	1,645,619	480,155
			85	-	1,907,181	2,691,350	784,169
	N W		85	-	511,339	576,366	65,027
PHIL R	N W		85	-	738	837	99
POLAND	N E		83	-	13,912	16,433	2,521
PORTUGL	N E		83	-	11,237	15,676	4,439

Product TSUSA commodity number, description, and unit of quantity Country	Mode	Reg	Yr	Quantity	F.A.S.	C.I.F.	Charges
			84	-	79,920	102,275	22,355
			85	-	109,625	157,718	48,093
REP SAF	N	E	83	-	750,842	977,606	226,764
			84	-	997,215	1,322,278	325,063
			85	-	1,744,660	2,301,309	556,649
	N	W	83	-	9,587	18,018	8,431
			84	-	34,584	43,764	9,180
			85	-	43,893	55,553	11,660
S ARAB	N	E	85	-	5,279	6,962	1,683
SINGAPR	N	E	83	-	121,688	166,783	45,095
			84	-	210,287	271,712	61,425
			85	-	876,243	1,169,253	293,010
	N	W	83	-	243,084	350,777	107,693
			84	-	287,574	443,003	155,429
			85	-	188,283	278,154	89,871
SPAIN	N	E	83	-	123,048	199,716	76,668
			84	-	146,818	250,035	103,217
			85	-	223,366	335,299	111,933
	N	W	83	-	6,440	7,051	611
			84	-	4,255	5,029	774
SRI LKA	N	E	85	-	1,112	1,942	830
SWEDEN	N	E	84	-	3,457	5,236	1,779
			85	-	22,820	32,673	9,853
	N	W	83	-	1,484	2,231	747
SWITZLD	N	E	83	-	17,770	30,966	13,196
			84	-	16,785	23,733	6,948
			85	-	12,742	17,991	5,249
THAILND	N	E	83	-	448,960	828,030	379,070
			84	-	829,374	1,444,689	615,315
			85	-	738,365	1,210,370	472,005
	N	H	83	-	788	1,495	707
	N	W	83	-	458,468	759,796	301,328
			84	-	478,936	760,889	281,953
			85	-	470,514	667,328	196,814
TURK IS	N	E	84	-	10,734	11,609	875
TURKEY	N	E	84	-	326	389	63
U KING	N	E	83	-	271,514	361,991	90,477
			84	-	427,029	552,629	125,600
			85	-	534,971	719,240	184,269
	N	W	83	-	24,380	32,306	7,926
			84	-	30,124	40,567	10,443
			85	-	11,128	15,183	4,055
URUGUAY	N	E	85	-	1,320	2,181	861
YEMEN S	N	E	84	-	2,405	3,280	875
ZAIRE	N	E	85	-	1,247	1,849	602

1922192 CUT FLOWERS, FRESH (NULL)

Country	Mode	Reg	Yr	Quantity	F.A.S.	C.I.F.	Charges
TOTAL			86	-	89,021,499	117,217,272	28,195,773
ALBANIA	N	E	86	-	9,941	19,271	9,330
ARGENT	N	E	86	-	1,340	2,527	1,187
AUSTRAL	N	E	86	-	43,993	77,119	33,126
	N	W	86	-	212,155	342,540	130,385
AUSTRIA	N	E	86	-	8,035	8,716	681
BELGIUM	N	E	86	-	13,153	16,391	3,238
BRAZIL	N	E	86	-	43,312	86,397	43,085
BULGAR	N	E	86	-	51,546	53,546	2,000
C RICA	N	E	86	-	864,776	1,081,845	217,069
	N	W	86	-	103,567	132,320	28,753
CANADA	N	E	86	-	1,859,307	1,866,071	6,764
	N	W	86	-	793,377	793,377	
CAYMAN	N	E	86	-	4,450	8,920	4,470
CHILE	N	E	86	-	22,409	34,500	12,091
	N	W	86	-	4,614	6,878	2,264
CHINA T	N	W	86	-	1,875	1,899	24
COLOMB	N	E	86	-	14,957,448	18,665,953	3,708,505
DENMARK	N	E	86	-	8,106	9,019	913
DOM REP	N	E	86	-	47,036	66,694	19,658
ECUADOR	N	E	86	-	113,738	163,252	49,514
	N	W	86	-	11,904	16,319	4,415
ETHIOP	N	E	86	-	111,252	143,243	31,991
F W IND	N	E	86	-	13,572	19,435	5,863
FALK IS	N	E	86	-	2,267	3,073	806
FR GERM	N	E	86	-	54,458	93,209	38,751
FRANCE	N	E	86	-	1,428,662	1,781,377	352,715
	N	W	86	-	122,245	167,281	45,036
GERM DR	N	E	86	-	2,146	3,056	910
GUATMAL	N	E	86	-	10,546	16,927	6,381
HONDURA	N	E	86	-	9,490	12,675	3,185
ICELAND	N	E	86	-	10,441	14,218	3,777
ISRAEL	N	E	86	-	3,200,921	5,367,855	2,166,934
	N	W	86	-	166,167	272,429	106,262
ITALY	N	E	86	-	641,334	829,862	188,528
	N	W	86	-	1,977	2,033	56
IVY CST	N	E	86	-	176,935	258,006	81,071
JAMAICA	N	E	86	-	160,154	195,347	35,193
JAPAN	N	E	86	-	28,607	42,338	13,731
KENYA	N	E	86	-	110,815	150,669	39,854
	N	W	86	-	4,704	7,520	2,816
KIRIBAT	N	E	86	-	13,793	18,875	5,082
KOR REP	N	E	86	-	1,980	2,385	405
	N	W	86	-	21,272	24,254	2,982
MACAO	N	E	86	-	2,426	4,794	2,368
MALI	N	E	86	-	13,099	16,375	3,276
MAURIT	N	W	86	-	18,986	22,698	3,712
MEXICO	N	E	86	-	129,665	185,930	56,265
	N	W	86	-	1,899,735	1,946,079	46,344
MOROC	N	E	86	-	1,690	2,125	435
MOZAMBQ	N	E	86	-	1,577	1,627	50
N ANTIL	N	E	86	-	419,926	504,237	84,311
N CALDN	N	E	86	-	13,275	19,390	6,115
	N	W	86	-	2,500	2,825	325
N ZEAL	N	E	86	-	32,492	47,867	15,375
	N	H	86	-	1,187	1,400	213
	N	W	86	-	151,368	198,202	46,834
NAMIBIA	N	E	86	-	3,293	4,007	714
NETHLDS	N	E	86	-	50,387,844	66,749,991	16,362,147
	N	W	86	-	5,258,121	7,090,172	1,832,051
NIGER	N	W	86	-	139,745	146,863	7,118
PANAMA	N	E	86	-	12,492	13,716	1,224
PERU	N	E	86	-	1,430,286	2,229,724	799,438
	N	W	86	-	22,513	35,780	13,267
PHIL R	N	W	86	-	2,000	3,070	1,070
PORTUGL	N	E	86	-	271,226	366,884	95,658
REP SAF	N	E	86	-	1,697,781	2,335,900	638,119
	N	W	86	-	5,509	7,878	2,369
S ARAB	N	E	86	-	23,854	30,689	6,835
SEYCHEL	N	E	86	-	1,814	5,861	4,047
SINGAPR	N	E	86	-	54,365	72,956	18,591
	N	W	86	-	101,977	153,278	51,301
SPAIN	N	E	86	-	320,047	476,816	156,769
	N	W	86	-	44,999	49,210	4,211
SUDAN	N	W	86	-	2,149	3,156	1,007
SWAZLND	N	E	86	-	171,582	292,996	121,414
	N	W	86	-	1,606	2,764	1,158
SWITZLD	N	E	86	-	3,098	9,748	6,650
THAILND	N	E	86	-	523,271	768,232	244,961
	N	W	86	-	204,544	300,671	96,127
TUNISIA	N	E	86	-	3,398	6,146	2,748
U KING	N	E	86	-	148,379	189,963	41,584
	N	W	86	-	9,295	12,197	2,902
ZMBABWE	N	E	86	-	18,565	25,434	6,869

Fruit trees

1254000 FRT TREE SEEDLINGS CUTS ETC (NO)

Country	Mode	Reg	Yr	Quantity	F.A.S.	C.I.F.	Charges
TOTAL			81	1,876,540	465,378	510,766	45,388
			82	2,074,180	459,128	506,844	47,716
			83	1,121,258	272,525	298,329	25,804
			84	1,435,557	422,572	468,224	45,652
			85	1,021,816	224,504	250,216	25,712
			86	813,364	257,710	299,698	41,988
AUSTRAL	A	H	81	1,400	413	639	226
	A	W	81	2,000	2,200	2,408	208
BELGIUM	A	E	81	50,000	21,498	25,125	3,627
			82	339,000	100,213	118,763	18,550
			83	195,000	64,554	73,207	8,653
			85	5,000	2,000	2,575	575
	A	W	82	15,000	4,460	6,521	2,061
			84	632,633	218,286	248,411	30,125
			85	66,400	29,713	29,833	120
			86	51,600	28,190	38,258	10,068
CANADA	A	E	81	136,500	5,597	6,273	676
			82	3,500	1,475	1,667	192
			85	14,000	2,251	2,626	375
	A	W	82	13,450	905	1,084	179
			83	2,850	285	325	40
	N	W	81	225,636	54,735	54,735	
			82	460,569	80,390	80,390	
			83	270,350	63,294	63,294	
	O	E	81	82,066	12,567	12,567	
			82	8,000	3,002	3,002	
			83	30,178	8,943	8,943	
			84	43,910	12,549	12,549	
			85	570	1,643	1,643	
			86	62,535	60,236	60,236	
	O	W	84	141,159	46,443	46,443	
			85	233,208	45,035	45,037	

Product TSUSA commodity number, description, and unit of quantity Country	Mode	Reg	Yr	Quantity	F.A.S.	C.I.F.	Charges
			86	115,239	44,188	44,188	
CHINA T	A	W	83	800	1,750	2,311	561
FR GERM	A	E	82	1,110,113	229,829	252,369	22,540
			84	129,680	29,200	38,213	9,013
FRANCE	A	E	81	77,038	9,476	11,183	1,707
			82	26,544	17,457	18,350	893
			84	4,850	3,438	3,738	300
	V	E	85	8,850	10,373	17,565	7,192
			86	1,900	3,559	3,762	203
HAITI	A	E	86	5,000	1,565	1,679	114
ITALY	N	W	82	4	612	811	199
JAMAICA	A	E	83	50	389	424	35
JAPAN	A	W	83	200	840	984	144
KOR REP	V	W	85	22,000	20,625	23,339	2,714
N ZEAL	A	H	86	3,500	3,500	3,922	422
	A	W	83	107,060	21,418	22,751	1,333
			84	27,650	7,497	8,275	778
			86	540	1,200	1,808	608
NETHLDS	A	E	82	98,000	20,785	23,887	3,102
			84	297,375	40,478	44,843	4,365
			86	417,550	105,397	133,227	27,830
	N	E	81	1,302,900	360,782	399,725	38,943
			83	514,050	110,457	125,117	14,660
			85	671,788	112,864	127,598	14,734
PHIL R	A	H	83	120	285	487	202
SINGAPR	A	H	84	600	3,800	4,082	282
SPAIN	A	W	86	153,500	7,675	10,210	2,535
U KING	A	E	81	1,000	310	519	209
	A	W	83	600	310	486	176
			84	157,700	60,881	61,670	789

1255000 FRT TREE GRFD FRT PLANT CUTS (NO)

Country	Mode	Reg	Yr	Quantity	F.A.S.	C.I.F.	Charges
TOTAL			81	4,495,556	558,260	576,227	17,967
			82	4,849,032	295,736	300,959	5,223
			83	8,259,008	409,658	414,781	5,123
			84	9,055,135	918,644	942,753	24,109
			85	13,547,474	1,482,340	1,538,949	56,609
			86	24,120,506	1,749,688	1,823,161	73,473
BAHAMAS	V	E	82	5,000	800	890	90
			83	10,000	1,600	1,881	281
CANADA	A	E	81	16,000	756	1,012	256
			82	192,500	7,861	9,790	1,929
			83	20,189	12,420	16,254	3,834
			84	7,500	2,863	3,404	541
			85	6,900	1,664	2,054	390
			86	123,256	5,842	6,849	1,007
	A	W	82	170	726	871	145
			83	194	903	903	
			84	510	973	1,164	191
			85	333	1,168	1,168	
			86	330	1,149	1,149	
	N	E	83	550,201	24,459	24,483	24
			84	7,499,800	305,400	305,437	37
	O	E	81	4,371,765	301,779	301,779	
			82	4,597,966	240,694	240,694	
			83	7,608,419	315,833	315,833	
			84	997,468	464,225	464,225	
			85	13,183,700	725,055	725,055	
			86	23,412,368	1,260,412	1,260,412	
	O	W	81	4,130	19,434	19,434	
			82	2,996	8,486	8,486	
			83	3,243	12,029	12,029	
			84	9,306	3,347	3,347	
			85	17,110	26,218	26,218	
			86	365,535	78,506	78,506	
DOM REP	V	E	84	480,000	3,600	15,069	11,469
FR GERM	O	E	83	30,000	30,000	30,000	
FRANCE	V	W	86	9,400	13,426	18,640	5,214
ISRAEL	A	E	84	12,700	1,223	1,690	467
N ZEAL	A	H	81	22,000	48,967	51,700	2,733
			85	1,485	3,931	4,448	517
	A	W	81	81,661	187,324	202,302	14,978
			82	42,000	36,490	39,378	2,888
			83	3,233	9,376	9,968	592
			84	47,851	137,013	148,417	11,404
			85	282,876	641,883	682,665	40,782
			86	197,536	388,181	455,253	67,072
	N	W	85	36,870	79,994	94,401	14,407
NETHLDS	A	W	85	18,200	2,427	2,940	513
	V	E	83	33,350	2,284	2,437	153
			86	12,081	2,172	2,352	180
SINGAPR	A	H	83	179	754	993	239
U KING	A	E	82	8,400	679	850	171

Herbaceous perennials

1253290 HERBACEOUS PERENNIAL & SOIL (NO)

Country	Mode	Reg	Yr	Quantity	F.A.S.	C.I.F.	Charges
TOTAL			81	3,337,829	5,277,342	5,279,481	2,139
			82	5,651,396	7,597,849	7,604,501	6,652
			83	5,955,088	9,299,425	9,301,374	1,949
			84	6,685,179	11,184,569	11,185,341	772
			85	12,281,050	12,053,423	12,063,956	10,533
			86	13,300,303	13,757,505	13,763,890	6,385
BELGIUM	A	E	85	72,260	10,456	14,386	3,930
CANADA	A	E	82	1,200	409	512	103
			84	1,800	3,600	3,644	44
			85	4,500	3,375	4,024	649
	N	E	82	437,685	702,600	702,885	285
			85	7,172,924	11,801,640	11,801,670	30
	N	W	81	9,192	3,137	3,714	577
	O	E	81	3,289,352	5,267,536	5,268,146	610
			82	5,183,104	6,878,769	6,878,909	140
			83	5,820,887	9,278,820	9,278,820	
			84	6,662,850	11,176,733	11,176,733	
			85	971,169	181,405	181,405	
			86	13,167,685	13,682,574	13,685,778	3,204
	O	W	83	1,520	2,788	2,788	
			84	7,489	1,880	1,880	
			85	18,190	2,867	2,867	
			86	17,594	14,647	14,647	
CHINA M	V	E	81	1,000	1,400	1,484	84
GUATMAL	A	E	81	1,090	2,686	3,224	538
			82	8,925	3,471	4,377	906
			83	1,120	2,096	2,296	200
	N	E	82	15,460	11,172	15,086	3,914
INDIA	A	E	84	375	453	594	141
ISRAEL	A	E	84	8,200	1,066	1,542	476
			85	100,820	13,389	15,581	2,192
	A	W	83	1,190	466	645	179
			86	81,602	27,281	28,009	728
JAPAN	V	W	86	15,600	24,312	26,520	2,208
MAURIT	A	E	82	904	1,130	2,419	1,289
MEXICO	O	E	86	2,286	5,680	5,680	
NETHLDS	A	E	83	5,100	950	1,128	178
			85	6,070	1,167	1,322	155
			86	536	1,511	1,726	215
	A	W	81	22,850	1,252	1,574	322
			85	1,055	1,740	2,528	788
	O	E	81	14,345	1,331	1,339	8
			82	4,118	298	313	15
			83	26,771	2,977	2,977	
			84	4,000	379	379	
			85	25,000	1,063	1,063	
	V	E	85	3,866,006	30,736	33,164	2,428
SPAIN	A	E	83	98,500	11,328	12,720	1,392
U KING	A	W	84	465	458	569	111
			85	43,056	5,585	5,946	361
			86	15,000	1,500	1,530	30

1253490 HERBACEOUS PERENNIALS, NSPF (NO)

Country	Mode	Reg	Yr	Quantity	F.A.S.	C.I.F.	Charges
TOTAL			81	2,490,961	478,188	523,777	45,588
			82	6,044,680	737,074	875,444	138,370
			83	4,803,823	759,119	847,485	88,366
			84	9,586,551	1,359,276	1,617,252	257,976
			85	11,842,689	1,699,957	1,977,625	277,668
			86	11,691,985	1,570,705	1,848,301	277,596
AUSTRAL	A	E	84	8,033	3,092	3,656	564
			86	4,100	1,370	1,776	406
BELGIUM	A	E	82	48,155	13,645	15,838	2,193
			83	22,175	6,288	7,903	1,615
			86	40,200	6,580	8,141	1,561
	V	W	81	6,500	2,874	2,997	123
BRAZIL	A	E	83	16,100	3,380	3,844	464
			84	8,670	6,720	7,062	342
			86	397	1,230	1,530	300
	A	W	83	10,000	700	1,881	1,181
	V	W	81	2,538	6,680	7,617	937
			82	1,433	3,340	3,944	604
			84	2,400	3,180	5,120	1,940
BULGAR	V	E	85	2,984	2,141	2,939	798
C RICA	A	E	82	563	437	706	269
			85	7,020	1,140	1,244	104
			86	10,000	1,650	2,268	618
	A	W	84	30,000	10,000	11,132	1,132
CANADA	A	E	85	1,460	1,222	1,540	318
			86	8,000	1,600	3,092	1,492

Product
TSUSA commodity number, description, and unit of quantity

Country	Mode	Reg	Yr	Quantity	F.A.S.	C.I.F.	Charges
	A	W	81	19,600	5,292	6,902	1,610
			84	300	800	918	118
	O	E	81	288,157	221,745	221,746	
			82	356,463	215,252	215,252	
			83	1,400,045	93,378	93,378	
			84	2,657,858	130,539	130,539	
			85	1,073,400	57,566	57,566	
			86	951,577	74,116	74,556	440
	O	W	81	50,095	42,859	42,859	
			82	117,204	134,369	134,369	
			83	169,018	256,575	256,931	356
			84	334,608	468,617	468,623	6
			85	164,856	207,220	207,220	
			86	174,718	278,474	278,474	
CHINA M	A	E	86	1,020	2,383	3,535	1,152
CHINA T	A	E	86	7,000	1,050	1,277	227
	A	W	83	1,102	1,280	2,240	960
			84	1,000	350	508	158
			86	2,500	2,425	4,275	1,850
	V	W	86	19,000	25,857	28,079	2,222
COLOMB	A	E	84	19,020	9,536	10,443	907
EGYPT	V	E	83	8,000	8,000	10,915	2,915
FIJI	A	W	86	1,893	1,530	2,219	689
FR GERM	A	E	81	67,080	27,718	31,011	3,293
			82	1,000	750	868	118
			83	1,200	345	436	91
			85	90,000	1,418	1,667	249
	A	W	81	3,500	252	394	142
			84	3,000	417	665	248
FRANCE	A	E	84	6,000	1,234	1,521	287
			85	350,000	1,050	1,324	274
GUATMAL	A	E	81	51,702	19,115	20,462	1,347
			84	805	300	536	236
	A	W	83	8,275	264	816	552
			84	48,632	7,791	10,164	2,373
	V	E	84	307,026	111,210	156,242	45,032
			85	144,025	31,349	41,470	10,121
			86	23,023	16,315	18,415	2,100
HONDURA	A	E	82	93,500	2,805	4,465	1,660
			83	54,432	4,168	6,528	2,360
			84	22,777	4,335	5,430	1,095
INDIA	A	E	81	3,601	1,585	4,024	2,439
			82	53,000	1,480	1,984	504
			83	50,280	1,913	6,450	4,537
			84	975	395	571	176
			85	8,700	2,193	3,053	860
			86	38,220	4,695	4,878	183
	A	W	81	186,150	3,895	7,057	3,162
			82	79,000	805	2,157	1,352
			83	38,500	474	876	402
ISRAEL	A	E	81	3,972	644	2,737	2,093
			82	30,860	3,350	15,615	12,265
			83	374,712	22,620	38,977	16,357
			84	1,290,037	113,633	135,943	22,310
			85	2,816,787	418,755	503,647	84,892
			86	2,413,202	349,297	447,904	98,607
	V	E	84	14,000	3,577	3,930	353
JAMAICA	A	E	83	19,600	402	527	125
			84	10,540	1,169	2,023	854
JAPAN	A	E	81	5,000	1,125	1,547	422
			84	13,200	3,411	5,647	2,236
			85	24,580	12,180	14,118	1,938
			86	19,798	5,294	6,821	1,527
	A	W	81	40,000	3,002	6,075	3,073
			83	5,000	2,300	3,699	1,399
			84	327,670	127,624	211,097	83,473
			85	12,406	5,787	6,512	725
			86	2,100	2,109	2,854	745
	N	W	82	320,112	185,768	261,853	76,085
			83	340,700	119,460	123,848	4,388
			85	333,915	69,807	76,617	6,810
			86	1,145,270	42,858	49,264	6,406
	O	E	83	13,000	2,480	2,530	50
	V	E	82	16,400	2,780	3,089	309
			83	10,250	2,028	2,198	170
			84	9,500	1,915	2,069	154
			85	18,800	2,500	2,647	147
	V	H	84	12,000	5,054	5,418	364
	V	W	81	43,000	9,822	10,917	1,095
			83	112,510	47,859	51,705	3,846
			84	37,000	34,451	41,841	7,390
			85	373,500	264,747	302,975	38,228
			86	2,175	3,780	4,307	527
MADAGAS	A	E	81	2,545	983	1,325	342
			82	9,700	2,861	3,510	649
			83	1,800	574	834	260
MEXICO	N	W	84	29,483	8,284	11,405	3,121
	O	E	82	1,008	4,421	4,421	
			84	2,000	400	400	
N ANTIL	A	E	85	1,500	1,225	1,459	234
N ZEAL	A	H	84	4,280	5,535	5,980	445
			86	9,000	7,130	8,468	1,338
	A	W	83	4,330	3,130	3,843	713
			84	1,550	1,685	1,890	205
			85	64,948	61,894	68,538	6,644
			86	46,717	38,154	41,712	3,558
NETHLDS	A	E	81	99,350	6,503	7,417	914
			82	2,704,851	80,999	94,590	13,591
			83	259,263	15,025	19,168	4,143
			84	143,350	8,158	9,996	1,838
			85	345,894	42,058	56,787	14,729
			86	1,721,240	85,492	105,332	19,840
	A	H	86	250	1,250	1,641	391
	A	W	81	268,100	59,827	65,981	6,154
			82	763,078	32,286	41,486	9,200
			83	77,575	3,755	4,708	953
			84	185,645	11,431	18,008	6,577
			85	460,230	27,520	35,859	8,339
			86	232,071	68,565	82,640	14,075
	N	E	84	665,237	24,610	30,561	5,951
	N	W	83	1,455,285	138,439	169,099	30,660
			84	2,785,241	181,481	239,341	57,860
			85	5,073,800	269,165	339,450	70,285
			86	4,041,898	509,461	618,902	109,441
	O	E	81	1,950	400	400	
			82	22,000	2,168	2,168	
			84	34,848	3,750	3,750	
	V	E	81	96,342	16,373	17,615	1,242
			82	325,600	17,720	21,615	3,895
			84	354,504	40,646	44,335	3,689
			85	100,368	197,798	225,759	27,961
			86	640,830	20,192	24,958	4,766
	V	W	81	3,320	1,701	1,863	162
			84	4,400	1,003	1,187	184
PERU	A	E	81	42,136	6,140	7,226	1,086
			82	35,853	5,850	6,612	762
			83	14,258	3,475	4,033	558
			84	76,475	2,820	4,293	1,473
			85	456	1,080	1,321	241
	A	W	85	8,311	1,031	1,610	579
REP SAF	A	E	81	23,545	19,916	29,624	9,708
			83	58	733	883	150
	A	W	81	1,030,000	16,463	18,857	2,394
			82	690,000	14,146	16,879	2,733
			83	120	296	770	474
			84	22,507	11,902	13,991	2,089
			85	150,750	4,398	5,914	1,516
			86	1,100	2,609	3,780	1,171
SINGAPR	A	E	81	278	291	531	240
			82	173,100	8,012	14,993	6,981
			83	42,035	5,273	9,634	4,361
			84	83,000	5,001	7,547	2,546
SPAIN	A	E	83	104,000	11,961	13,280	1,319
SRI LKA	A	E	81	50,500	488	1,551	1,063
			82	91,800	865	2,439	1,574
			83	4,200	416	1,002	586
			86	9,600	1,715	2,438	723
	A	W	81	100,000	495	1,563	1,068
			82	100,000	495	1,900	1,405
			83	170,000	880	2,925	2,045
THAILND	A	E	81	2,000	2,000	3,479	1,479
			82	4,000	1,800	3,928	2,128
	A	W	83	5,000	255	392	137
U KING	A	E	83	1,000	536	595	59
			84	3,980	2,798	2,968	170
			85	150,000	2,532	2,778	246
			86	100,220	5,707	6,100	393
	A	W	82	6,000	670	763	93
			83	10,000	457	637	180
			85	46,799	5,768	6,628	860
			86	14,766	5,004	5,111	107
	N	E	85	17,200	6,413	6,983	570
	O	E	84	25,000	422	502	80
			86	10,100	2,813	3,554	741

Live plants

1258200 LIVE PLANTS, SOIL ATTACHED (NO)

TOTAL			81	10,812,088	5,711,776	5,830,218	118,440

Product
TSUSA commodity number, description, and unit of quantity

Country	Mode	Reg	Yr	Quantity	F.A.S.	C.I.F.	Charges
			82	10,209,886	5,290,085	5,379,485	89,400
			83	13,797,055	6,020,647	6,110,301	89,654
			84	20,555,771	8,054,122	8,203,459	149,337
			85	20,038,364	9,501,846	9,591,602	89,756
			86	20,871,196	11,326,541	11,444,811	118,270
AUSTRAL	A	H	85	14,174	10,071	10,287	216
	A	W	81	936	643	781	138
			84	1,146	1,944	2,228	284
			85	1,000	9,182	9,366	184
			86	2,217	1,778	1,954	176
	N	W	86	16,190	21,384	23,521	2,137
BELGIUM	A	W	84	15,330	5,689	6,440	751
BOLIVIA	A	W	84	1,580	485	1,255	770
BRAZIL	V	E	85	53,250	10,370	13,469	3,099
C RICA	A	E	86	505,459	20,267	24,017	3,750
	A	W	81	3,241,411	368,390	430,199	61,809
			82	4,076,243	311,918	370,410	58,492
			83	5,841,284	427,003	489,297	62,294
			84	10,266,103	474,293	559,717	85,424
			85	396,608	22,697	25,819	3,122
	N	W	85	1,944,228	101,549	117,546	15,997
	V	E	84	66,926	18,927	29,033	10,106
	V	W	85	1,230	11,392	15,606	4,214
			86	91,288	7,842	9,582	1,740
CANADA	A	E	81	20,000	2,242	3,347	1,105
			82	40,150	9,042	10,639	1,597
			83	123,289	24,214	26,775	2,561
			84	111,413	43,306	50,295	6,989
			85	1,728	1,016	1,170	154
			86	19,800	9,734	12,516	2,782
	A	H	84	14,792	15,242	20,911	5,669
			85	12,446	14,074	18,573	4,499
			86	15,954	25,195	30,373	5,178
	A	W	81	4,200	1,134	1,520	386
			83	4,608	3,767	4,831	1,064
			84	12,240	6,767	8,851	2,084
			85	9,050	4,302	5,044	742
	N	E	81	4,270,199	4,029,066	4,030,496	1,430
			82	5,052,578	4,570,796	4,570,853	57
			85	5,493,473	7,937,042	7,937,046	4
			86	87,617	37,116	37,492	376
	N	W	81	158,119	262,054	262,381	327
			82	30,494	83,181	84,147	966
	O	E	81	1,836,444	791,558	791,560	
			82	338,949	206,445	206,772	327
			83	6,506,494	5,315,162	5,315,162	
			84	9,277,358	7,008,396	7,008,396	
			85	5,669,286	446,394	446,394	
			86	10,176,354	10,095,238	10,095,981	743
	O	W	82	3,395	10,171	10,171	
			83	49,495	156,083	156,083	
			84	46,920	284,984	284,984	
			85	155,484	578,102	578,102	
			86	105,592	596,675	596,675	
CHILE	O	E	84	2,344	6,907	6,907	
CHINA T	A	W	86	26,508	29,954	31,186	1,232
	O	E	82	144	489	489	
FR GERM	A	E	85	2,000	1,849	2,258	409
	A	W	81	280	975	1,624	649
	O	W	81	5,600	1,420	1,420	
FRANCE	A	E	83	210	663	703	40
	A	W	81	1,715	890	2,256	1,366
			82	256	2,683	3,083	400
GUATMAL	A	E	83	84,170	6,592	7,075	483
			86	30,000	1,771	2,204	433
	A	W	81	13,075	1,716	3,365	1,649
			82	17,297	1,672	2,857	1,185
			83	219,080	10,016	12,798	2,782
			84	96,282	3,419	4,171	752
	V	E	81	934,440	142,046	167,262	25,216
			82	499,109	57,973	71,113	13,140
HONDURA	A	E	83	312,805	8,005	8,679	674
	V	E	82	9,283	2,664	4,052	1,388
ISRAEL	A	E	82	10,300	4,406	5,919	1,513
			84	176	3,180	4,062	882
	A	W	81	10,200	4,802	6,438	1,636
			84	3,975	1,193	1,702	509
			86	21,018	2,572	2,572	
JAMAICA	A	E	83	6,550	1,245	1,480	235
			84	1,485	5,409	7,996	2,587
JAPAN	A	E	81	19,250	5,025	8,910	3,885
			83	560	3,264	4,896	1,632
	A	W	81	53,769	18,116	27,090	8,974
			82	34,767	11,615	19,618	8,003

Product
TSUSA commodity number, description, and unit of quantity

Country	Mode	Reg	Yr	Quantity	F.A.S.	C.I.F.	Charges
			83	53,268	12,757	22,778	10,021
			84	110,285	28,281	44,010	15,729
			85	7,110	2,702	3,211	509
	N	W	85	16,030	20,947	24,500	3,553
			86	11,100	7,098	8,825	1,727
	V	W	85	19,200	10,128	10,944	816
KOR REP	A	W	85	248,989	6,007	6,927	920
	V	W	84	15,500	30,000	32,091	2,091
MADAGAS	A	W	82	141	1,749	2,109	360
MEXICO	A	W	83	564,400	22,657	26,916	4,259
			84	354,545	39,994	45,315	5,321
			85	5,772,928	272,738	319,213	46,475
			86	9,254,174	398,603	481,855	83,252
	O	E	84	1,175	4,534	4,534	
N ANTIL	A	E	85	115	1,269	1,626	357
N ZEAL	A	W	81	9,900	3,238	3,839	601
			83	9,255	21,287	23,895	2,608
			84	44,104	57,503	64,102	6,599
NETHLDS	A	E	81	159,410	24,877	29,639	4,762
			82	35,170	4,401	4,920	519
			83	19,004	2,996	3,342	346
			84	47,500	4,575	5,152	577
			85	14,000	1,422	1,784	362
			86	104,423	27,220	30,908	3,688
	A	W	81	3,920	2,919	3,681	762
			82	56,410	6,554	7,830	1,276
			84	32,400	4,292	6,143	1,851
			85	143,777	28,227	30,977	2,750
			86	239,615	30,968	40,019	9,051
	N	W	83	2,173	4,156	4,586	430
	O	E	84	1,190	2,051	2,051	
			86	4,387	5,151	5,151	
PANAMA	A	W	85	62,258	10,366	11,740	1,374
PERU	A	W	81	8,240	3,590	6,226	2,636
SPAIN	A	E	84	31,000	2,480	2,834	354
	A	W	86	159,500	7,975	9,980	2,005
THAILND	A	E	83	210	260	485	225
U KING	A	W	81	60,980	47,075	48,184	1,109
			82	5,200	4,326	4,503	177
	O	E	83	200	520	520	
	V	E	84	2	271	279	8

1258400 LIVE PLANTS F PLANTING NSPF (NO)

Country	Mode	Reg	Yr	Quantity	F.A.S.	C.I.F.	Charges
TOTAL			81	143,208,566	13,670,051	16,292,576	2,635,411
			82	152,971,368	12,915,277	15,676,387	2,761,110
			83	172,297,438	12,372,751	15,192,397	2,819,646
			84	217,652,946	17,929,184	21,897,181	3,967,997
			85	162,780,575	18,554,284	22,689,552	4,135,268
			86	189,457,639	20,876,312	25,477,172	4,600,860
ALGERIA	A	E	82	21,050	3,468	3,729	261
ARGENT	A	W	82	10,641	2,632	4,802	2,170
			84	12,000	1,400	2,934	1,534
			86	118,000	13,466	19,161	5,695
AUSTRAL	A	E	84	155	1,700	1,856	156
			86	30,089	26,688	29,198	2,510
	A	H	81	14,800	6,807	7,152	345
			82	1,000	321	362	41
			83	10,000	2,774	3,085	311
			84	48,700	47,550	49,122	1,572
			85	212,648	152,172	159,635	7,463
			86	193,875	129,463	135,833	6,370
	A	W	81	18	861	978	117
			82	7,810	2,928	3,443	515
			83	360	300	325	25
			84	5,299	19,230	21,795	2,565
			85	565,942	72,622	79,935	7,313
			86	34,580	35,588	39,048	3,460
BAHAMAS	A	E	82	3,470	252	302	50
	N	E	81	143,650	2,643	3,143	500
	O	E	83	7,000	320	425	105
BARBADO	A	E	85	2,800	2,800	3,216	416
			86	40,000	4,000	5,483	1,483
	A	W	86	24,750	13,572	14,828	1,256
BELGIUM	A	E	81	35,128	44,992	39,809	5,293
			82	28,906	22,479	27,376	4,897
			83	161,709	46,509	56,974	10,465
			84	1,029,256	240,277	280,145	39,868
			85	502,966	107,489	130,827	23,338
			86	743,630	169,079	195,907	26,828
	A	W	82	6,000	3,400	3,719	319
			83	19,737	10,551	12,266	1,715
			84	22,450	6,408	7,199	791
			85	14,527	12,176	14,592	2,416
			86	92,232	20,654	22,337	1,683

Product
TSUSA commodity number, description, and unit of quantity

Country	Mode	Reg	Yr	Quantity	F.A.S.	C.I.F.	Charges
BELIZE	A	E	81	174,000	3,845	4,255	410
			82	1,752,958	62,494	73,479	10,985
			83	1,292,970	64,807	78,333	13,526
			84	760,755	38,163	43,851	5,688
			85	377,260	22,671	26,036	3,365
			86	535,715	46,050	50,493	4,443
	N	E	81	2,527,034	93,945	105,315	11,370
			84	15,980	2,112	2,380	268
BERMUDA	A	E	85	5,000	1,500	2,205	705
BOLIVIA	A	E	83	1,800	450	609	159
			84	96,840	5,489	7,129	1,640
BRAZIL	A	E	81	565,292	161,350	199,795	38,445
			82	229,184	60,147	76,655	16,508
			83	1,309,254	211,359	262,943	51,584
			84	294,887	80,621	112,081	31,460
			85	1,540,912	243,817	309,259	65,442
			86	656,533	143,893	190,447	46,554
	A	H	81	4,000	3,000	4,021	1,021
	A	W	81	1,778	2,025	2,985	960
			82	18,000	1,260	2,636	1,376
			83	1,138	1,190	3,168	1,978
			84	19,130	2,415	4,274	1,859
			86	5,000	1,500	2,149	649
	N	E	82	376,350	94,425	118,643	24,218
			84	1,542,655	171,526	216,938	45,412
			86	182,362	36,483	48,324	11,841
	V	E	86	9,210	6,448	9,128	2,680
BRUNEI	A	E	86	597	6,523	7,288	765
BULGAR	A	E	85	38,500	4,316	5,211	895
C AF RP	A	E	84	515	306	415	109
C RICA	A	E	81	514,041	114,028	139,196	25,168
			82	247,425	19,738	28,660	8,922
			83	987,196	37,338	55,886	18,548
			84	385,484	23,821	30,634	6,813
			86	274,432	19,435	26,017	6,582
	A	W	81	140,485	21,849	25,242	3,393
			82	6,772	5,631	8,450	2,819
			83	9,500	5,315	6,673	1,358
			84	6,310	2,156	3,247	1,091
			85	1,520	1,637	3,355	1,718
			86	512,650	22,468	27,501	5,033
	N	E	81	24,767,499	2,170,491	2,796,970	626,479
			82	36,087,472	2,275,839	3,051,956	776,117
			83	48,796,232	2,231,616	3,034,023	802,407
			84	61,922,978	4,409,719	5,576,032	1,166,313
			85	53,161,677	4,875,013	6,114,955	1,239,942
			86	73,110,406	5,391,765	6,954,777	1,563,012
	N	W	84	520,058	146,179	181,048	34,869
			85	727,417	89,521	118,358	28,837
			86	931,664	138,568	181,071	42,503
	O	E	84	380,560	15,239	15,239	
			85	527,643	62,140	62,140	
			86	516,620	38,126	38,126	
	V	E	83	7,880	5,497	7,776	2,279
			84	52,200	15,201	22,136	6,935
			85	2,600	9,690	13,243	3,553
			86	12,325	10,742	14,217	3,475
	V	H	85	27,568	49,111	65,811	16,700
			86	28,600	25,540	36,940	11,400
	V	W	84	52,948	15,958	21,398	5,440
			85	41,480	26,957	33,857	6,900
CANADA	A	E	81	157,258	8,958	11,021	2,063
			82	209,747	11,633	13,694	2,061
			83	340,300	20,357	23,930	3,573
			84	218,409	17,840	21,974	4,134
			85	132,175	21,134	23,576	2,442
			86	244,892	11,949	16,236	4,287
	A	H	81	444	499	835	336
	A	W	81	5,582	1,352	1,428	76
			82	7,000	381	436	55
			84	2,057	2,875	3,166	291
	N	E	82	642	1,808	1,852	44
			84	5,010	3,214	3,457	243
			86	6	3,270	3,666	396
	N	W	81	301,651	245,131	246,392	1,261
			82	272,844	389,189	389,229	40
			83	860,053	694,461	694,727	266
			84	1,846,283	1,965,079	1,965,650	571
			85	1,537,405	1,556,544	1,556,546	2
	O	E	81	1,385,175	906,735	906,737	
			82	813,256	337,617	337,617	
			83	204,189	126,521	126,521	
			84	566,044	172,014	172,014	
			85	400,243	155,601	155,601	
			86	1,020,461	309,014	309,014	

Product
TSUSA commodity number, description, and unit of quantity

Country	Mode	Reg	Yr	Quantity	F.A.S.	C.I.F.	Charges
	O	W	83	240	317	317	
			84	6,273	7,459	7,459	
			86	1,803,500	1,835,758	1,835,758	
CAYMAN	A	E	81	2,047,660	35,123	38,930	3,807
	V	E	82	2,100	650	1,099	449
CHILE	A	H	85	11,600	1,016	1,174	158
	A	W	83	2,750	800	4,565	3,765
CHINA M	A	E	82	275	1,657	1,850	193
			83	270	2,878	3,330	452
	A	W	81	225	3,987	5,345	1,358
	O	W	85	790	11,318	12,367	1,049
CHINA T	A	E	81	5,400	1,176	1,587	411
			84	294	2,962	4,081	1,119
			85	476	3,350	4,705	1,355
			86	207	2,905	5,516	2,611
	A	H	81	26,000	4,973	5,386	413
			83	2,000	1,395	2,250	855
			84	21,505	8,813	10,027	1,214
			85	178,300	81,637	94,479	12,842
			86	80,300	12,680	16,294	3,614
	A	W	81	42,000	9,660	10,279	619
			82	24,770	24,205	24,852	647
			83	3,576	1,982	2,582	600
			84	670	5,470	6,135	665
			85	20,139	6,729	7,485	756
			86	1,596	17,563	18,863	1,300
	O	W	83	20,000	4,600	4,700	100
	V	W	82	900	540	961	421
COLOMB	A	E	81	13,535,490	1,426,208	1,662,842	238,027
			82	6,800	2,476	2,783	307
			83	12,863	888	1,160	272
			84	64,556	949	1,799	850
			85	5,070,785	262,265	364,443	102,178
			86	551,504	133,369	167,523	34,154
	N	E	82	12,134,180	1,409,755	1,599,384	189,629
			83	8,990,848	587,554	702,389	114,835
			84	6,622,421	309,028	408,739	99,711
COMOROS	A	E	83	364,975	14,117	16,196	2,079
DENMARK	A	E	81	884,460	114,283	129,011	14,728
			82	154,363	18,949	21,966	3,017
			83	88,350	14,386	19,556	5,170
			84	36,489	68,590	88,297	19,707
			85	174,860	44,188	50,900	6,712
			86	56,360	7,552	8,641	1,089
	A	W	81	206,081	16,378	19,492	3,114
			82	218,700	31,822	37,108	5,286
			83	152,600	25,968	28,836	2,868
			84	172,190	18,247	26,078	7,831
			85	367,879	15,246	19,881	4,635
			86	635,721	26,683	33,097	6,414
	N	E	84	139,597	8,780	10,382	1,602
	N	W	85	6	1,399	2,212	813
DOM REP	A	E	82	12,393	5,356	6,470	1,114
	N	E	81	3,356,507	358,830	534,604	175,594
			82	2,334,470	299,464	453,050	153,586
			83	2,372,205	306,006	484,919	178,913
			84	2,641,221	400,296	705,793	305,497
			85	3,562,364	501,229	971,522	470,293
			86	4,452,361	744,743	1,214,233	469,490
	V	E	82	461,829	158,965	222,751	63,786
			83	677,262	184,020	256,649	72,629
			84	50,000	400	1,768	1,368
ECUADOR	A	E	81	34,850	3,851	4,168	317
	A	W	81	7,000	5,250	7,825	2,575
			82	10,210	7,350	10,261	2,911
			83	10,425	6,675	10,207	3,532
			84	14,782	13,660	19,488	5,828
FR GERM	A	E	81	690,074	79,862	86,597	6,735
			82	480,185	58,992	65,722	6,730
			83	480,368	23,184	31,342	8,158
			84	75,956	13,000	16,918	3,918
			85	1,196,825	104,224	114,119	9,895
			86	1,269,911	126,038	142,131	16,093
	A	W	81	2,180	1,895	2,693	798
			82	19,984	9,495	12,274	2,779
			83	22,000	6,361	6,579	218
			84	10,132	7,991	9,048	1,057
			85	595	2,340	2,731	391
			86	27,595	15,122	18,030	2,908
	N	E	82	959,960	57,037	68,406	11,369
	N	W	83	13,000	5,200	5,257	57
	O	E	83	300	2,677	2,703	26
FRANCE	A	E	81	14	485	552	67
			83	22,707	2,389	2,721	332
			84	228,511	89,608	121,642	32,034

Product
TSUSA commodity number, description, and unit of quantity

Country	Mode	Reg	Yr	Quantity	F.A.S.	C.I.F.	Charges
			85	31,000	19,874	23,324	3,450
			86	4,300	1,075	1,374	299
	A	W	81	13,450	4,098	5,484	1,386
			82	157	1,661	2,196	535
			84	875	1,058	1,246	188
	N	E	84	1,752,286	36,528	47,257	10,729
	V	E	82	400,000	38,397	41,897	3,500
			83	1,100,000	156,986	160,186	3,200
GERM DR	A	E	81	1,940	876	1,106	230
			85	26,200	5,213	5,655	442
			86	34,500	2,806	3,196	390
GREECE	A	E	85	12,450	1,202	1,432	230
GUATMAL	A	E	81	260,840	58,540	63,447	4,907
			82	383,405	39,583	47,262	7,679
			83	4,341	2,218	3,004	786
			84	207,570	12,509	15,071	2,562
			85	573,978	19,923	26,512	6,589
			86	3,171,319	121,103	146,775	25,672
	A	W	81	1,406,480	239,585	342,886	103,301
			82	2,089,372	184,927	250,275	65,348
			83	353,781	69,151	95,966	26,815
			84	1,071,914	67,949	99,793	31,844
			85	42,450	2,606	4,299	1,693
			86	540,370	36,940	54,669	17,729
	N	E	81	20,086,927	2,214,164	2,624,739	410,575
			82	24,981,717	1,982,713	2,313,292	330,579
			83	29,040,693	1,884,996	2,269,492	384,496
			84	37,459,517	2,315,948	2,959,800	643,852
			85	34,231,429	1,891,207	2,419,245	528,038
			86	42,271,924	1,589,860	2,015,584	425,724
	N	W	83	1,183,950	71,606	111,402	39,796
			85	3,416,237	72,444	111,798	39,354
	V	E	81	32,000	16,000	16,990	990
			82	32,000	14,400	16,469	2,069
			83	1,700	19,320	20,627	1,307
			86	75,959	29,395	35,646	6,251
GUYANA	A	E	81	3,000	10,325	11,396	1,071
			85	753,155	16,581	21,130	4,549
			86	3,500	1,200	1,200	
	A	W	85	28,150	1,086	1,936	850
HAITI	A	E	81	11,805	13,329	15,127	1,798
			82	495,878	53,533	62,614	9,081
			83	1,054,021	136,410	156,685	20,275
			84	13,338	3,640	3,896	256
			85	661	4,900	5,081	181
			86	121,100	6,504	7,259	755
	N	E	84	1,805,862	210,599	249,779	39,180
			85	3,292,912	243,691	292,456	48,765
			86	3,553,366	234,267	277,709	43,442
	V	E	85	35,120	5,970	9,677	3,707
HG KONG	A	E	86	21,432	8,445	11,231	2,786
	A	H	86	44,000	4,000	4,919	919
	A	W	81	1,000	4,000	4,359	359
			83	1,700	5,100	7,161	2,061
			85	1,000	2,200	3,583	1,383
	V	E	86	384	4,228	5,132	904
HONDURA	A	E	81	655,277	43,467	48,051	4,584
			82	33,248	5,283	5,956	673
			83	1,188,550	40,403	48,636	8,233
			84	793,827	79,315	96,171	16,856
			85	157,139	25,888	29,943	4,055
			86	587,633	61,785	69,167	7,382
	A	W		400	423	511	88
	N	E	81	19,754,821	1,616,550	1,885,674	269,124
			82	21,271,605	1,463,988	1,718,857	254,869
			83	27,304,925	1,203,073	1,458,340	255,267
			84	34,619,685	1,596,193	1,899,958	303,765
			85	12,982,667	1,282,808	1,511,138	228,330
			86	7,411,918	758,561	949,996	191,435
	N	W	83	3	460	595	135
HUNGARY	A	E	86	5,580	1,596	2,032	436
INDIA	A	E	81	2,893	1,451	2,219	768
INDNSIA	A	W	82	25	625	721	96
IRAN	A	E	84	265,825	8,804	10,226	1,422
ISRAEL	A	E	81	67,625	20,940	30,597	9,657
			82	224,383	43,997	70,491	26,494
			83	159,279	12,061	17,031	4,970
			84	863,890	122,223	158,726	36,503
			85	3,282,799	526,572	616,020	89,448
			86	3,729,911	763,822	923,712	159,890
	A	W	81	38,628	18,584	27,943	9,359
			82	6,000	2,126	2,639	513
			83	58,939	18,055	25,426	7,371
			84	97,231	18,221	27,040	8,819
			85	20,340	4,181	7,922	3,741

Product
TSUSA commodity number, description, and unit of quantity

Country	Mode	Reg	Yr	Quantity	F.A.S.	C.I.F.	Charges
			86	400,325	55,819	65,908	10,089
ITALY	A	E	81	64,300	24,790	32,419	7,629
			82	6,000	1,850	2,924	1,074
			83	1,000	297	612	315
			84	104,100	9,628	11,473	1,845
			85	79,600	9,800	10,853	1,053
			86	13,050	3,462	5,394	1,932
	A	W	83	200	328	1,012	684
			84	2,685	319	676	357
IVY CST	A	E	84	280	300	450	150
JAMAICA	A	E	81	16,772	5,322	6,056	734
			82	33,534,152	951,340	1,070,427	119,087
			83	27,511,716	954,164	1,094,704	140,540
			84	1,504,023	128,511	173,305	44,794
			85	7,810,105	808,268	949,356	141,088
			86	7,177,023	1,053,350	1,191,815	138,465
	N	E	81	37,370,605	922,150	1,034,727	112,577
			83	357,310	18,308	21,257	2,949
			84	30,856,447	847,074	987,032	139,958
			85	987,883	111,333	127,792	16,459
JAPAN	A	E	81	62,258	14,098	20,365	6,267
			83	150	975	1,418	443
			84	213	1,906	2,719	813
			85	2,000	1,300	2,032	732
			86	22,500	9,475	12,531	3,056
	A	H	81	10,000	3,000	4,315	1,315
			84	7,000	9,600	13,047	3,447
	A	W	81	119,367	37,497	56,710	19,213
			82	789,720	31,866	52,931	21,065
			83	76,950	23,313	36,237	12,924
			84	1,231,315	262,150	432,975	170,825
			85	968,821	196,600	305,489	108,889
			86	854,806	280,801	392,410	111,609
	N	E	81	396,132	145,359	186,594	41,235
			82	269,622	158,366	193,894	35,528
			83	311,323	209,042	255,880	46,838
			84	321,911	203,420	263,472	60,052
			85	155,836	117,210	148,256	31,046
			86	172,366	122,347	173,561	51,214
	N	W	81	1,517,805	450,399	661,348	210,949
			82	1,270,927	431,759	629,596	197,837
			83	1,137,939	285,932	413,144	127,212
			84	160,221	81,248	107,410	26,162
			85	132,336	58,919	72,152	13,233
			86	995,830	743,648	782,415	38,767
	O	E	81	700	1,496	1,516	20
	V	E	86	209,863	184,632	202,331	17,699
	V	H	81	10,500	12,537	17,526	4,989
			85	27,700	12,000	14,752	2,752
	V	W	81	6,145	20,990	22,469	1,479
			82	21,900	18,787	20,325	1,538
			83	1,900	3,662	4,005	343
			84	6	303	339	36
			85	25,053	26,397	30,095	3,698
			86	22,516	28,875	33,122	4,247
KIRIBAT	A	E	85	880	10,450	15,215	4,765
			86	200,114	9,165	10,071	906
	A	W	85	103,500	10,298	12,682	2,384
	N	E	86	475,405	43,348	50,189	6,841
KOR REP	A	E	84	22,000	10,000	11,174	1,174
			85	83	1,561	1,874	313
	A	H	86	25,000	7,929	9,500	1,571
	A	W	86	20,000	6,049	7,600	1,551
	V	E	82	400,000	26,662	27,324	662
MADAGAS	A	E	82	5,200	875	1,387	512
			83	1,000	330	656	326
			84	2,000	490	645	155
			86	693	4,404	5,488	1,084
	A	W	81	574	3,425	4,130	705
			82	375	4,260	5,118	858
			83	1,338	6,702	9,018	2,316
			84	410	1,250	1,639	389
MALAYSA	A	E	85	14,025	1,019	1,629	610
			86	15,276	2,037	2,800	763
MEXICO	A	E	81	15,000	1,950	2,270	320
			82	6,800	1,846	1,987	141
			83	248,473	6,457	7,708	1,251
			84	51,319	7,431	8,122	691
			86	3,267,850	212,449	221,121	8,672
	A	W	81	1,500	400	1,060	660
			82	3,462	1,030	2,219	1,189
			83	99,259	12,270	19,000	6,730
			84	264,536	26,054	34,579	8,525
			85	180,080	8,050	10,476	2,426
			86	113,408	9,425	11,331	1,906

Product TSUSA commodity number, description, and unit of quantity Country	Mode	Reg	Yr	Quantity	F.A.S.	C.I.F.	Charges
	O	E	81	4,373,452	68,962	67,963	200
			82	2,417,628	63,612	63,612	
			83	2,676,906	62,566	62,566	
			84	3,360,953	91,700	91,700	
			85	3,135,997	69,259	69,259	
			86	4,018,018	89,896	89,896	
	O	W	82	4,000	280	280	
			83	160,350	8,610	8,610	
			84	5,915,655	22,837	22,837	
	V	E	81	4,200	1,785	2,445	660
			82	10,415	18,130	19,094	964
			83	1,008	1,866	2,040	174
MONGOLA	N	E	86	47,452	3,274	3,989	715
MONSRAT	A	E	84	67,000	1,625	2,012	387
N ANTIL	A	E	81	13,406	10,011	13,123	3,112
			85	410,698	49,644	57,883	8,239
			86	72,397	8,416	10,394	1,978
N ZEAL	A	E	82	6,500	4,275	4,409	134
	A	H	81	3,045	2,219	2,810	591
			82	7,200	3,700	4,183	483
			83	2,320	3,876	4,284	408
			84	750	818	900	82
			86	999	11,335	12,083	748
	A	W	81	49,706	38,323	42,936	4,613
			82	47,398	27,131	32,085	4,954
			83	35,542	63,588	67,898	4,310
			84	12,239	14,883	16,689	1,806
			85	180,772	201,609	223,308	21,699
			86	43,520	218,983	249,894	30,911
NETHLDS	A	E	81	1,666,001	306,988	357,546	50,558
			82	2,492,319	533,152	663,683	130,531
			83	3,895,044	694,921	830,409	135,488
			84	852,814	129,745	148,980	19,235
			85	3,577,803	855,703	1,000,628	144,925
			86	2,774,670	828,939	1,001,241	172,302
	A	H	81	600	300	367	67
	A	W	81	1,048,533	283,025	333,319	50,294
			82	1,625,583	322,251	392,422	70,171
			83	1,062,231	264,864	307,904	43,040
			84	1,421,881	409,330	489,197	79,867
			85	1,734,773	781,029	988,176	207,147
			86	2,374,465	1,500,055	1,823,688	323,633
	N	E	81	1,757,307	694,844	761,482	66,638
			82	2,061,472	773,286	878,541	105,255
			83	2,161,811	799,019	913,151	114,132
			84	5,743,826	1,708,134	1,978,359	270,225
			85	3,087,790	1,314,434	1,573,905	259,471
			86	2,885,100	1,484,585	1,762,531	277,946
	N	W	81	161,246	360,563	380,181	19,618
			82	85,948	142,705	152,235	9,530
			83	423,335	212,612	241,594	28,982
			84	1,373,780	255,789	318,051	62,262
			85	266,148	160,688	173,785	13,097
			86	183,291	52,743	64,637	11,894
	O	W	82	400	550	550	
NICARAG	V	E	81	15,800	8,208	12,613	4,405
			82	30,600	6,120	8,803	2,683
	V	W	84	570	257	393	136
NIGER	A	E	86	1,700	8,925	10,174	1,249
NORWAY	A	E	81	200	338	372	34
PANAMA	A	E	81	14,100	6,155	7,177	1,022
			82	930	2,585	2,749	164
			84	15,731	3,977	4,905	928
			85	29,362	6,118	7,043	925
	A	W	81	77,130	5,070	8,560	3,490
			82	203,100	11,063	14,379	3,316
	N	E	83	22,030	11,213	15,330	4,117
PARAGUA	A	W	86	12,000	1,200	4,225	3,025
PERU	A	E	81	1,150	1,250	2,286	1,036
			82	5,593	800	1,600	800
			84	350	525	1,125	600
	A	W	81	3,000	750	1,375	625
			82	19,100	5,225	8,258	3,033
			83	320	260	309	49
			84	1,208	2,272	3,448	1,176
			86	3,000	1,050	2,048	998
PHIL R	A	E	85	20	1,495	2,027	532
			86	1,035	2,538	3,039	501
REP SAF	A	E	81	2,403	3,286	7,022	3,736
			82	1,399	2,331	3,329	998
			83	236	461	739	278
			84	79,927	137,957	152,979	15,022
	A	W	81	180	416	817	401
			82	309	267	757	490
			83	645	902	1,944	1,042

Product TSUSA commodity number, description, and unit of quantity Country	Mode	Reg	Yr	Quantity	F.A.S.	C.I.F.	Charges
			84	95	2,289	2,537	248
			86	1,437	3,957	3,957	
S LUCIA	A	E	84	9,000	795	994	199
SALVADR	N	E	81	278,735	19,534	35,153	15,619
			82	282,152	61,203	95,090	33,887
			83	426,618	143,586	187,773	44,187
			84	129,607	53,052	68,926	15,874
	V	E	81	16,635	1,680	3,828	2,148
			85	72,421	18,414	26,761	8,347
			86	105,305	33,795	41,465	7,670
SINGAPR	A	E	81	10,000	468	802	334
			83	72,000	5,787	9,758	3,971
			84	147,838	40,788	55,461	14,673
			85	111,500	7,452	11,772	4,320
			86	50,093	4,898	7,313	2,415
	A	H	81	4,500	1,117	2,226	1,109
			82	4,048	2,120	4,006	1,886
			84	103	340	492	152
	A	W	81	50	313	371	58
SPAIN	A	E	82	251,000	20,072	22,771	2,699
			83	1,855,858	237,088	260,234	23,146
			84	4,354,571	432,574	500,627	68,053
			85	9,167,190	772,159	887,322	115,163
			86	9,982,650	467,232	614,455	147,223
	A	W	81	32,400	13,297	17,089	3,792
			82	19,200	5,760	9,288	3,528
			83	422	2,485	3,217	732
			84	90,000	13,170	14,072	902
			86	2,869,065	84,247	114,267	30,020
	N	W	84	517,500	63,413	69,440	6,027
			85	917,452	138,154	155,027	16,873
SRI LKA	A	E	82	64,700	625	1,189	564
			83	8,380	867	1,916	1,049
			86	11,140	3,442	5,057	1,615
SUDAN	A	E	85	18,800	1,128	2,041	913
	N	E	85	36,195	12,935	16,032	3,097
SURINAM	A	E	81	1,800	306	601	295
			86	98,000	6,399	7,815	1,416
SWEDEN	A	E	82	62,626	8,126	9,052	926
SWITZLD	A	E	81	255	637	694	57
			82	1,900	3,524	3,942	418
			83	794,250	17,909	24,871	6,962
			86	4,150	1,311	1,473	162
THAILND	A	E	81	451	1,320	1,812	492
			83	1,725	2,686	3,689	1,003
			84	1,400	849	999	150
			85	825	2,754	3,518	764
			86	2,264	1,128	1,979	851
	N	E	84	3	430	676	246
U KING	A	E	81	11,700	2,520	2,819	299
			82	115,498	52,483	61,078	8,595
			83	232,810	43,738	49,538	5,800
			84	130,688	104,275	114,061	9,786
			85	211,938	151,026	162,335	11,309
			86	154,869	107,400	115,608	8,208
	A	W	81	40,250	22,522	24,165	1,643
			82	2,356	1,249	1,713	464
			83	17,100	1,466	1,499	33
			84	53,611	12,944	15,533	2,589
			85	40,700	8,880	10,550	1,670
			86	114	1,065	1,481	416
	N	E	81	104,211	57,667	63,854	6,187
VENEZ	A	E	81	12,000	383	660	277

Vegetable substance, ornamental
1932520 VEG SUB, CRUDE, ORNAMENTAL (NULL)

Country	Mode	Reg	Yr	Quantity	F.A.S.	C.I.F.	Charges
TOTAL			81	-	6,346,805	6,888,098	541,293
			82	-	6,723,731	7,400,095	676,364
			83	-	5,078,933	5,659,675	580,742
			84	-	5,400,218	5,998,997	598,779
			85	-	6,154,267	6,615,073	460,806
			86	-	6,154,110	6,735,394	581,284
AUSTRIA	N	E	83	-	436	593	157
BELGIUM	N	E	85	-	5,002	5,670	668
BELIZE	N	E	81	-	276	758	482
			83	-	35,108	38,316	3,208
BRAZIL	N	E	83	-	551	1,531	980
BULGAR	N	E	83	-	4,631	6,264	1,633
			85	-	2,760	5,469	2,709
C RICA	N	E	81	-	34,949	46,207	11,258
			82	-	40,960	49,721	8,761
			83	-	560	938	378

Product
TSUSA commodity number, description, and unit of quantity

Country	Mode	Reg	Yr	Quantity	F.A.S.	C.I.F.	Charges
			84	-	125,980	169,187	43,207
			85	-	145,451	197,832	52,381
			86	-	218,415	310,181	91,766
CANADA	N	E	81	-	835,506	835,506	
			82	-	795,886	795,886	
			83	-	517,482	517,482	
			84	-	692,464	692,464	
			85	-	737,072	737,072	
			86	-	894,169	894,169	
	N	W	81	-	769,557	769,557	
			82	-	572,601	572,980	379
			83	-	606,149	606,499	350
			84	-	291,516	294,061	2,545
			85	-	146,709	146,709	
			86	-	310,667	310,667	
CHINA M	N	E	82	-	240,302	255,263	14,961
			83	-	7,948	8,357	409
			84	-	152,400	162,300	9,900
			85	-	139,216	155,713	16,497
			86	-	74,888	78,998	4,110
	N	W	81	-	24,579	26,909	2,330
			82	-	1,725	1,782	57
			83	-	52,451	55,563	3,112
			84	-	2,817	3,116	299
			86	-	69,180	94,752	25,572
CHINA T	N	H	81	-	1,620	1,799	179
			82	-	360	383	23
			83	-	658	708	50
			84	-	360	411	51
	N	W	81	-	5,806	6,468	662
			82	-	9,146	9,962	816
			83	-	9,530	10,061	531
			84	-	10,090	10,801	711
			85	-	15,103	16,046	943
			86	-	19,296	21,004	1,708
COLOMB	N	E	81	-	2,080	2,903	823
			82	-	258	569	311
			84	-	2,279	3,783	1,504
			85	-	6,424	8,423	1,999
DOM REP	N	E	84	-	5,892	8,912	3,020
			85	-	2,028	3,460	1,432
			86	-	2,565	3,839	1,274
ECUADOR	N	E	83	-	271	298	27
			86	-	27,600	28,685	1,085
EGYPT	N	E	86	-	12,175	13,390	1,215
FIJI	N	H	81	-	2,140	2,304	164
			82	-	1,071	1,152	81
FR GERM	N	E	81	-	4,472	4,472	
			82	-	399,915	408,355	8,440
			83	-	4,509	4,897	388
FRANCE	N	E	81	-	3,515	4,124	609
			84	-	14,829	15,139	310
			85	-	25,356	26,877	1,521
			86	-	11,859	12,624	765
	N	W	84	-	7,984	8,643	659
GIBRALT	N	E	86	-	3,500	5,297	1,797
GREECE	N	E	81	-	23,935	26,400	2,465
			85	-	1,807	2,034	227
GUATMAL	N	E	81	-	1,904,891	2,416,827	511,936
			82	-	1,772,057	2,358,139	586,082
			83	-	1,091,125	1,647,090	555,965
			84	-	1,372,900	1,874,138	501,238
			85	-	1,943,169	2,288,728	345,559
			86	-	1,918,545	2,319,104	400,559
GUINEA	N	E	85	-	17,122	19,791	2,669
GUYANA	N	E	86	-	24,920	29,748	4,828
HAITI	N	E	81	-	10,411	12,225	1,814
			83	-	3,456	4,077	621
			84	-	15,750	16,664	914
			85	-	42,618	50,332	7,714
			86	-	36,978	52,455	15,477
HG KONG	N	E	85	-	32,574	36,083	3,509
	N	W	83	-	6,960	7,679	719
			86	-	4,020	5,770	1,750
HONDURA	N	E	84	-	75,253	87,474	12,221
			85	-	19,976	23,654	3,678
			86	-	4,376	7,308	2,932
INDIA	N	E	83	-	912	1,286	374
	N	W	82	-	1,465	3,293	1,828
			85	-	4,204	5,029	825
			86	-	3,285	3,860	575
ISRAEL	N	E	82	-	45,541	48,052	2,511
ITALY	N	E	83	-	475	1,810	1,335
			84	-	11,156	14,275	3,119
			85	-	15,704	17,809	2,105

Product
TSUSA commodity number, description, and unit of quantity

Country	Mode	Reg	Yr	Quantity	F.A.S.	C.I.F.	Charges
			86	-	8,613	9,528	915
JAMAICA	N	E	86	-	13,177	14,859	1,682
JAPAN	N	E	84	-	12,592	13,316	724
	N	H	81	-	619	765	146
			82	-	547	690	143
	N	W	81	-	892	968	76
			82	-	630	686	56
			83	-	288	305	17
			84	-	3,188	3,382	194
			86	-	2,146	2,214	68
KENYA	N	W	82	-	374	395	21
KIRIBAT	N	E	85	-	19,609	20,040	431
			86	-	9,263	12,002	2,739
MALAYSA	N	E	85	-	14,211	14,211	
MEXICO	N	E	81	-	2,679,813	2,684,693	4,880
			82	-	2,733,196	2,736,904	3,708
			83	-	2,706,999	2,710,352	3,353
			84	-	2,507,719	2,508,963	1,244
			85	-	2,732,404	2,734,465	2,061
			86	-	2,384,818	2,391,676	6,858
	N	W	83	-	6,258	6,258	
			84	-	7,727	7,727	
			85	-	13,863	13,863	
			86	-	28,751	28,751	
MOROC	N	E	82	-	34,375	73,385	39,010
NETHLDS	N	E	82	-	279	365	86
			86	-	4,549	6,231	1,682
PAKISTN	N	W	82	-	4,460	4,998	538
			85	-	3,800	4,236	436
PERU	N	E	81	-	2,263	2,406	143
			82	-	1,133	1,236	103
			83	-	3,306	4,401	1,095
			84	-	252	352	100
			86	-	1,209	1,209	
	N	W	84	-	300	416	116
PHIL R	N	E	81	-	682	999	317
			82	-	9,331	12,824	3,493
			83	-	2,055	2,555	500
			84	-	355	523	168
			85	-	6,240	7,675	1,435
	N	W	82	-	638	755	117
			83	-	778	862	84
REP SAF	N	E	81	-	1,952	1,952	
ROMANIA	N	E	83	-	3,451	4,507	1,056
			86	-	10,873	12,816	1,943
SAO T P	N	E	86	-	3,500	6,410	2,910
SPAIN	N	E	81	-	26,357	28,658	2,301
			82	-	42,772	46,465	3,693
			83	-	3,307	5,426	2,119
			85	-	10,256	15,525	5,269
			86	-	7,895	8,972	1,077
	N	W	81	-	8,506	8,992	486
			82	-	8,666	9,131	465
SRI LKA	N	E	81	-	265	430	165
SWITZLD	N	E	81	-	1,275	1,275	
THAILND	N	E	81	-	444	501	57
			84	-	450	537	87
			85	-	4,080	4,440	360
	N	W	82	-	5,683	6,334	651
			83	-	3,200	3,430	230
			84	-	1,504	1,612	108
			85	-	1,323	1,441	118
TURKEY	N	E	83	-	2,175	2,690	515
U KING	N	E	84	-	346	346	
			85	-	3,621	4,151	530
			86	-	7,880	7,880	
	N	W	82	-	360	390	30
VENEZ	N	E	82	-	6,920	7,770	850
			85	-	10,000	10,608	608
YUGOSLV	N	E	83	-	3,904	5,440	1,536
			84	-	77,195	92,685	15,490
			85	-	32,565	37,687	5,122
			86	-	34,998	40,995	5,997

Seed

Flower, seed
1264100 FLOWER SEEDS (LB)

Country	Mode	Reg	Yr	Quantity	F.A.S.	C.I.F.	Charges
TOTAL			81	235,272	9,316,736	9,451,939	137,331
			82	259,978	11,746,258	11,905,283	159,025
			83	199,963	10,217,345	10,365,015	147,670
			84	319,003	17,535,018	17,790,278	255,260
			85	343,051	17,485,444	17,739,868	254,424
			86	357,149	18,091,882	18,382,820	290,938
AUSTRAL	A	H	85	422	9,025	9,516	491
			86	1,755	9,000	9,837	837
	A	W	82	73	2,492	2,851	359
			84	1,167	15,107	16,687	1,580
			85	39	17,071	18,000	929
	V	E	86	1,442	8,992	9,926	934
	V	W	82	6,614	1,886	2,654	768
AUSTRIA	A	E	86	18	1,480	1,538	58
	A	W	83	26	4,723	4,810	87
BELGIUM	A	E	81	15	1,480	1,566	86
			82	102	1,241	1,429	188
			83	11	740	809	69
			84	174	298,338	303,581	5,243
			85	5	54,600	55,015	415
			86	68	3,982	4,104	122
	O	E	81	353	2,233	2,289	56
			82	8	837	847	10
			83	21	1,607	1,655	48
	V	E	81	190	595	685	90
			82	453	6,409	6,555	146
	V	W	85	620	8,180	8,534	354
BRAZIL	A	E	81	114	1,657	1,916	259
	A	W	84	53	851	1,119	268
			85	26	2,211	2,670	459
	N	E	81	16	800	853	53
	V	E	81	1,409	2,400	3,083	683
C RICA	A	E	81	4,502	2,280,793	2,304,503	23,710
			82	4,014	2,473,813	2,495,924	22,111
			83	1,724	869,024	872,715	3,691
			84	1,208	1,217,537	1,220,935	3,398
			85	1,170	1,142,714	1,145,570	2,856
			86	3,470	2,390,313	2,397,718	7,405
	A	W	81	410	118,470	119,477	1,007
			82	426	301,077	302,947	1,870
			83	1,414	291,807	295,235	3,428
			84	428	589,743	595,138	5,395
			85	719	455,273	459,956	4,683
			86	329	341,638	343,445	1,807
	N	E	82	125	7,841	8,038	197
			83	882	990,274	992,872	2,598
			84	2,153	2,183,580	2,189,479	5,899
			85	3,513	2,371,387	2,379,155	7,768
	N	W	81	902	256,570	258,500	1,930
			82	*	561	562	1
	O	E	81	5	2,120	2,145	25
			82	22	3,606	3,752	146
			83	31	17,271	17,448	177
			84	1,192	7,225	7,284	59
CANADA	A	E	84	96	1,828	1,984	156
			85	197	4,248	4,414	166
	A	W	82	48	8,351	8,439	88
			83	26	4,666	4,724	58
	N	E	86	304	32,637	32,731	94
	O	E	81	6,376	112,955	113,913	
			82	5,556	171,112	171,148	36
			83	4,642	226,603	226,681	78
			84	1,360	87,632	87,726	94
			85	1,299	81,923	82,125	202
			86	10,221	71,210	71,210	
	O	W	81	35	1,074	1,113	39
			83	24	1,011	1,077	66
			84	3	300	330	30
			86	1,140	4,008	4,008	
CHILE	A	E	84	299	2,674	3,009	335
	V	W	84	5,979	14,595	15,828	1,233
			85	16,175	29,208	33,569	4,361
			86	4,433	12,045	17,008	4,963
CHINA M	V	E	86	2,761	4,200	6,300	2,100
CHINA T	A	E	83	80	11,052	11,372	320
	A	H	84	429	10,797	12,513	1,716
	A	W	81	262	4,294	4,894	600
			82	232	4,554	5,601	1,047
			84	691	11,562	14,426	2,864
	N	W	81	1,252	22,144	23,981	1,837
			82	694	3,369	3,763	394
			83	2,997	24,720	26,127	1,407
			84	3,337	24,850	25,726	876
			85	4,019	63,219	70,320	7,101
			86	1,893	17,832	18,390	558
	V	W	81	88	360	441	81
COLOMB	A	W	86	409	5,000	5,500	500
DENMARK	A	E	81	200	4,657	5,164	507
			82	157	14,356	16,072	1,716
			83	1,162	45,389	47,922	2,533
			84	1,487	96,269	99,682	3,413
			85	2,948	25,089	25,648	559
			86	11,265	84,213	92,964	8,751
	A	W	83	11	610	610	
			84	112	1,260	1,545	285
			85	5,643	5,765	6,264	499
			86	547	4,887	5,457	570
	N	E	81	70	5,437	5,681	244
			82	151	26,928	27,155	227
			83	874	24,065	24,357	292
			84	143	53,716	54,093	377
			85	147	45,869	46,619	750
			86	124	34,415	35,151	736
	N	W	81	2,512	10,465	11,498	1,033
			82	1,268	5,791	5,998	207
			83	580	1,580	2,154	574
			84	1,049	12,143	12,744	601
			85	4,072	45,684	46,933	1,249
			86	13,165	60,549	64,890	4,341
	O	E	81	98	19,423	19,657	234
			82	60	29,948	30,143	195
			83	48	5,605	5,779	174
			84	11	1,825	1,866	41
			86	13	1,117	1,173	56
	V	E	81	360	7,223	7,545	322
			82	500	8,716	9,256	540
			83	180	3,248	3,433	185
			84	100	7,692	7,852	160
			85	308	8,041	8,435	394
			86	2,230	10,012	10,459	447
	V	W	82	1,200	2,100	2,335	235
			84	1,000	3,167	3,371	204
			85	1,531	8,636	9,111	475
EGYPT	V	E	81	5,510	3,081	3,488	407
FR GERM	A	E	81	388	37,715	38,341	626
			82	234	41,225	41,735	510
			83	180	30,256	30,985	729
			84	1,137	134,990	137,103	2,113
			85	957	120,793	123,233	2,440
			86	1,511	339,430	343,961	4,531
	A	W	82	18	12,154	12,224	70
			83	14	8,985	9,128	143
			85	8	10,197	10,405	208
	N	E	81	120	50,543	50,759	216
			82	901	165,419	167,037	1,618
			83	559	128,468	130,391	1,923
			84	1,305	351,659	356,113	4,454
			85	4,612	393,518	398,612	5,094
			86	1,309	228,888	231,935	3,047
	N	W	82	105	9,804	10,001	197
			84	2,430	17,589	19,911	2,322
			85	4,476	50,475	54,148	3,673
			86	3,091	56,137	60,199	4,062
	O	E	81	537	134,577	136,318	1,741
			82	696	49,591	50,782	1,191
			83	340	122,364	124,077	1,713
			84	430	134,423	136,111	1,688
			85	74	34,340	34,733	393
			86	181	29,927	30,404	477
	O	W	81	69	3,738	3,824	86
			82	1	285	295	10
			83	94	6,985	7,287	302
			84	15	2,759	2,855	96
	V	E	81	541	2,225	2,648	423
			83	355	880	1,039	159
			84	705	3,470	3,670	200
			85	511	1,520	1,765	245
			86	13,162	116,149	119,720	3,571
	V	W	84	638	4,417	4,837	420
			86	6,487	59,190	60,951	1,761
FRANCE	A	E	81	2,975	52,169	58,103	5,934
			82	2,516	68,180	71,470	3,290

Product
TSUSA commodity number, description, and unit of quantity

Country	Mode	Reg	Yr	Quantity	F.A.S.	C.I.F.	Charges
			83	4,022	149,826	154,169	4,343
			84	8,125	117,324	130,259	12,935
			85	9,465	99,841	105,781	5,940
			86	16,097	314,614	334,244	19,630
	A	W	82	200	8,584	9,463	879
	N	E	81	8,243	114,813	117,278	5,562
			82	9,171	152,355	160,062	7,707
			83	11,649	184,644	193,282	8,638
			84	7,032	208,088	216,599	8,511
			85	10,288	314,440	317,617	3,177
			86	2,402	178,985	183,135	4,150
	N	W	81	10,633	106,114	110,113	3,999
			82	17,896	119,339	123,089	3,750
			83	10,353	84,129	86,700	2,571
			84	14,931	127,663	137,517	9,854
			85	25,795	228,383	239,584	11,201
			86	13,971	124,291	132,502	8,211
	O	E	81	12,316	138,892	140,687	1,795
			82	15,502	140,852	143,075	2,223
			83	13,311	137,985	139,867	1,882
			84	11,702	156,342	158,370	2,028
			86	1,202	28,986	29,814	828
	O	W	81	11	409	409	
	V	E	81	5,222	53,427	55,771	2,344
			82	3,760	47,197	48,713	1,516
			83	4,215	37,444	40,056	2,612
			84	3,895	81,340	83,913	2,573
			85	8,289	108,289	111,743	3,454
			86	2,421	17,699	18,658	959
	V	W	81	601	4,424	4,562	138
			82	2,200	12,064	12,853	789
			83	3,832	34,011	35,748	1,737
			84	351	3,338	3,630	292
			85	3,301	28,690	29,918	1,228
			86	3,773	25,098	26,315	1,217
GERM DR	A	E	84	2	3,430	3,540	110
	O	E	82	40	702	727	25
GREECE	A	E	85	22	33,588	33,675	87
GUATMAL	A	E	81	3,036	1,227,854	1,233,493	5,639
			82	1,721	738,039	741,213	3,174
			83	161	73,038	73,577	539
			84	991	447,196	453,137	5,941
			85	1,296	186,518	189,473	2,955
	A	W	81	428	127,543	128,158	615
			82	2,543	1,000,566	1,006,016	5,450
			83	2,206	1,111,736	1,120,095	8,359
			84	4,294	2,076,759	2,102,035	25,276
			85	3,111	1,580,565	1,601,630	21,065
			86	8,434	2,742,717	2,777,450	34,733
HONDURA	A	E	81	75	111,764	112,557	793
			82	180	208,550	210,662	2,112
			83	59	84,405	84,524	119
			84	40	31,892	32,197	305
			85	185	84,474	85,013	539
			86	487	91,755	92,751	996
	A	W	84	60	1,600	1,723	123
			85	116	3,868	4,164	296
			86	36	1,280	1,361	81
HUNGARY	A	E	82	220	723	918	195
	A	W	85	5	1,258	1,408	150
INDIA	A	E	81	5	1,125	1,195	70
			82	132	4,383	4,781	398
			83	60	2,042	2,271	229
			84	563	30,218	31,237	1,019
			86	859	44,008	51,782	7,774
	O	E	81	81	74,261	74,614	353
			82	84	2,691	2,714	23
	V	W	81	20,918	7,927	10,105	2,178
INDNSIA	A	W	83	1	1,350	1,374	24
ISRAEL	A	E	81	50	523	683	160
			84	12	1,125	1,185	60
			85	58	1,629	1,714	85
	V	E	84	26	2,507	2,754	247
	V	W	85	1,621	17,375	18,027	652
			86	53	2,261	2,449	188
ITALY	A	E	81	1,387	80,537	82,830	2,293
			82	1,274	108,497	110,840	2,343
			83	1,107	59,539	61,336	1,797
			84	1,036	25,802	27,346	1,544
			85	1,051	108,701	110,652	1,951
			86	1,896	122,620	127,243	4,623
	A	W	83	75	1,314	1,657	343
			86	450	17,040	18,464	1,424
	N	E	81	493	18,896	19,450	554
			84	683	112,562	113,792	1,230
			85	843	34,104	35,072	968
	N	W	81	722	12,989	13,666	677
			84	1,940	47,582	50,126	2,544
			85	4,500	100,043	104,113	4,070
			86	1,919	35,633	36,901	1,268
	O	E	82	13	3,058	3,227	169
			83	179	5,416	5,628	212
			84	8	870	920	50
	V	E	82	618	19,746	20,051	305
	V	W	82	1,588	33,874	34,425	551
			83	641	11,679	12,183	504
JAPAN	A	E	81	600	239,694	244,259	4,565
			82	532	241,957	245,516	3,559
			83	515	203,559	207,006	3,447
			84	342	138,119	140,412	2,293
			85	420	219,250	223,378	4,128
			86	1,303	285,904	293,585	7,681
	A	H	82	12	195,000	195,116	116
			86	3	20,387	20,412	25
	A	W	81	512	307,910	312,095	4,185
			82	759	319,905	323,949	4,044
			83	850	187,410	190,722	3,312
			84	265	173,694	175,782	2,088
			85	318	235,282	237,879	2,597
			86	3,879	2,122,529	2,153,544	31,015
	N	E	81	435	117,267	119,717	2,450
			82	1,385	493,644	500,017	6,373
			83	1,195	963,243	972,214	8,971
			84	7,901	1,779,440	1,793,843	14,403
			85	8,447	1,656,230	1,668,907	12,677
			86	949	941,132	948,791	7,659
	N	W	81	904	225,729	227,823	2,094
			82	316	61,161	63,403	2,242
			83	134	98,665	100,067	1,402
			84	569	188,306	191,740	3,434
			85	1,664	469,667	478,504	8,837
			86	5,314	36,579	38,462	1,883
	O	E	82	6	9,798	9,883	85
			83	3	3,793	3,830	37
			84	16	36,996	37,196	200
			85	8	9,105	9,193	88
			86	4	1,320	1,372	52
	V	E	81	250	5,873	6,136	263
			82	951	14,105	14,416	311
			83	700	4,300	4,641	341
			84	224	6,096	6,252	156
			85	345	10,185	10,351	166
			86	1,165	15,158	15,548	390
	V	W	81	1,295	24,225	24,596	371
			82	400	9,100	9,205	105
			83	300	6,000	6,095	95
			84	750	5,684	5,973	289
			85	800	6,000	6,165	165
KENYA	A	E	82	197	73,236	74,010	774
	A	W	83	114	51,000	51,935	935
			84	451	283,128	286,700	3,572
			85	855	700,000	706,232	6,232
			86	726	480,000	484,973	4,973
KIRIBAT	A	W	86	110	20,000	20,251	251
KOR REP	A	E	82	2	7,171	7,253	82
			83	32	17,727	18,108	381
			84	46	13,712	14,112	400
	O	E	83	4	948	985	37
MALI	V	W	85	165	3,731	3,819	88
MEXICO	A	W	85	22	20,000	20,297	297
	N	W	83	*	3,300	3,300	
	O	E	84	15	500	500	
	O	W	81	16,250	209,385	209,385	
			82	11,320	157,226	157,226	
			83	8,246	282,930	282,930	
			84	18,598	243,607	243,607	
			85	51,815	773,034	773,034	
			86	51,669	771,960	771,960	
N ZEAL	A	H	86	875	5,916	6,836	920
	A	W	82	833	1,873	2,575	702
			84	1,302	8,355	9,552	1,197
			86	409	2,180	3,070	890
	N	W	85	4,926	16,651	18,112	1,461
	O	E	81	1	1,947	1,957	10
	V	W	81	392	1,046	1,149	103
			82	882	1,995	2,216	221
			83	425	1,791	1,891	100
			86	1,457	8,748	9,148	400
NETHLDS	A	E	81	10,873	381,493	392,622	11,128
			82	7,643	426,544	436,125	9,581

Product TSUSA commodity number, description, and unit of quantity Country	Mode	Reg	Yr	Quantity	F.A.S.	C.I.F.	Charges
			83	5,159	554,139	562,975	8,836
			84	50,943	915,542	945,623	30,081
			85	20,226	1,001,981	1,020,900	18,919
			86	26,738	1,403,795	1,431,196	27,401
	A	W	81	20	1,899	1,958	59
			84	437	20,077	20,729	652
			85	146	1,921	2,014	93
			86	648	27,433	28,468	1,035
	N	E	81	60,994	2,095,721	2,120,787	25,056
			82	27,853	2,782,400	2,809,628	27,228
			83	31,004	2,215,922	2,248,664	32,742
			84	41,606	3,887,759	3,916,878	29,119
			85	34,332	3,408,967	3,457,944	48,977
			86	17,149	3,084,428	3,105,392	20,964
	N	W	81	33,180	222,647	229,486	6,839
			82	41,832	296,782	313,983	17,201
			83	28,628	239,135	256,124	16,989
			84	44,529	402,311	422,804	20,493
			85	60,486	573,713	594,215	20,502
			86	50,784	475,703	493,716	18,013
	O	E	81	1,769	10,927	11,221	294
			82	37,415	304,589	310,904	6,315
			83	27,322	260,151	264,095	3,944
			84	23	8,153	8,226	73
			85	1,389	22,638	23,053	415
			86	34	4,166	4,191	25
	O	W	84	5	541	565	24
	V	E	81	23,557	130,882	136,645	5,763
			82	15,610	170,132	174,984	4,852
			83	9,019	97,263	99,893	2,630
			84	23,735	259,628	266,864	7,236
			85	6,997	32,099	33,689	1,590
			86	36,035	291,647	301,011	9,364
	V	W	83	4,409	10,652	11,926	1,274
			84	670	2,128	2,393	265
			86	647	6,491	6,868	377
NIGER	A	E	85	12	29,415	29,469	54
			86	1	3,709	3,764	55
NORWAY	A	E	85	220	30,751	31,041	290
REP SAF	A	E	82	19	18,770	18,840	70
			85	190	3,504	4,286	782
	A	W	84	46	20,000	20,284	284
			86	100	2,030	2,135	105
	O	H	81	37	943	974	31
	V	E	84	133	8,042	8,209	167
SPAIN	A	E	81	66	1,782	1,989	207
			82	51	1,339	1,473	134
			83	42	1,011	1,109	98
	A	W	84	61	1,435	1,510	75
SWEDEN	A	E	84	661	12,858	13,804	946
	A	W	84	20	403	738	335
	O	E	82	6	2,088	2,094	6
	V	E	82	303	4,032	4,175	143
			83	200	1,606	1,738	132
			84	4,937	16,339	16,961	622
			86	2,700	10,068	10,341	273
	V	W	83	950	3,057	3,251	194
SWITZLD	A	E	84	1,001	22,569	24,172	1,603
			85	369	15,213	16,401	1,188
			86	521	19,668	20,657	989
	A	W	83	26	13,793	14,038	245
			84	39	12,664	12,896	232
			85	33	1,731	1,803	72
	N	E	81	50	30,006	30,505	499
			82	7	17,967	18,135	168
			84	17	2,873	2,984	111
	N	W	82	24	7,982	8,291	309
	O	E	81	20	5,424	5,539	115
			82	23	2,428	2,453	25
			83	6	15,709	15,753	44
			84	47	13,225	13,329	104
			86	3	6,529	6,618	89
	O	W	81	22	1,935	1,967	32
			83	10	582	587	5
			84	11	494	518	24
	V	E	82	52	8,514	9,048	534
			85	604	7,516	7,654	138
			86	1,322	11,696	12,674	978
U KING	A	E	81	1,064	10,368	11,203	835
			82	45	2,482	2,566	84
			83	255	18,116	19,705	1,589
			84	1,539	37,341	40,249	2,908
			85	1,935	79,795	84,833	5,038
			86	5,234	139,895	148,702	8,807
	A	W	81	31	6,314	6,824	510
			82	100	753	755	2
			83	348	3,639	4,264	625
			85	93	19,491	20,250	759
			86	606	75,221	79,335	4,114
	N	E	81	3,272	40,803	43,630	2,827
			82	1,247	39,515	41,044	1,529
			83	1,448	83,030	86,258	3,228
			84	2,141	62,396	65,876	3,480
			85	1,675	188,103	200,694	12,591
			86	329	38,329	39,731	1,402
	N	W	84	197	23,791	24,247	456
			85	164	17,092	17,509	417
	O	E	81	23	3,972	4,042	70
			82	34	2,247	2,403	156
			83	11	3,553	3,592	39
			84	85	9,331	9,556	225
			86	669	78,256	79,680	1,424
	O	W	81	43	4,275	4,434	159
			82	115	8,083	8,207	124
	V	E	82	88	3,574	3,998	424
	V	W	84	1,319	2,345	2,525	180
URUGUAY	V	E	82	22,000	19,800	21,450	1,650
VENEZ	V	W	81	7,000	21,500	23,145	1,645
			82	4,600	17,200	18,100	900
			83	10,357	61,280	62,276	996
			84	29,500	147,500	154,871	7,371
ZAMBIA	A	E	85	40	3,700	3,803	103
ZMBABWE	A	E	83	105	9,550	9,889	339
			86	61	5,601	5,721	120
	V	W	86	10,377	21,166	22,620	1,454

Garden seed

1271000 GARDEN SEED NSPF EX GRAS SD (LB)

Country	Mode	Reg	Yr	Quantity	F.A.S.	C.I.F.	Charges
TOTAL			81	13,203,621	17,205,527	18,437,153	1,230,244
			82	21,805,507	25,326,552	27,149,574	1,823,022
			83	20,431,470	24,451,513	26,009,817	1,558,304
			84	18,212,187	25,280,749	26,936,397	1,655,648
			85	20,235,099	26,631,935	28,492,053	1,860,118
			86	28,898,943	32,826,281	34,652,755	1,826,474
ANTIGUA	A	E	86	225	2,600	2,927	327
ARGENT	A	E	81	1,210	1,210	3,115	1,905
			84	11,461	12,115	25,655	13,540
			85	12,500	2,835	19,556	16,721
			86	2,915	1,325	4,360	3,035
	A	W	86	4,409	1,560	6,809	5,249
	V	E	82	8,687	8,182	8,746	564
			85	357,145	93,960	112,882	18,922
	V	W	83	4,464	1,438	2,230	792
AUSTRAL	A	E	85	150	5,109	7,079	1,970
			86	100	1,074	1,074	
	A	H	84	959	8,532	9,800	1,268
			85	10,876	97,074	101,264	4,190
			86	796	10,652	11,790	1,138
	A	W	82	2,833	30,947	35,191	4,244
			83	1,981	14,910	17,873	2,963
			85	735	7,691	8,874	1,183
			86	5,438	41,983	44,770	2,787
	N	H	81	1,223	3,373	3,782	409
	N	W	81	100,363	420,815	461,374	40,559
			82	38,235	190,198	209,473	19,275
			83	76,908	300,637	322,549	21,912
			84	384,293	297,473	330,910	33,437
			85	135,371	500,776	525,167	24,391
			86	34,907	282,838	308,413	25,575
	O	W	83	10	268	277	9
	V	E	81	12,925	4,994	5,167	173
			84	88,184	29,515	33,200	3,685
			86	1,206	3,942	4,329	387
	V	W	83	1,212	379	476	97
			86	34,921	3,851	4,274	423
AUSTRIA	A	E	81	388	1,500	1,924	424
	A	W	86	188	2,503	2,720	217
BAHAMAS	V	E	82	1,224	1,728	1,850	122
BELGIUM	A	E	82	27	363	412	49
			83	7	637	692	55
			85	300	1,524	1,709	185
	A	W	84	1,123	10,534	11,189	655
			85	21	4,365	4,429	64
	N	E	83	17,637	4,395	5,895	1,500
	V	E	84	87,794	40,502	44,753	4,251
BELIZE	A	E	84	2,600	1,400	1,400	
BNGLDSH	A	W	83	55	643	920	277

618   Table 2. U.S. Import Statistics for Non Crop-Specific Commodities by End-Use

Product TSUSA commodity number, description, and unit of quantity Country	Mode	Reg	Yr	Quantity	F.A.S.	C.I.F.	Charges
BOLIVIA	A	E	83	1,480	621	1,476	855
BRAZIL	A	E	81	1,957	6,370	8,870	2,500
			82	165	450	729	279
			84	624	1,400	2,096	696
			86	2,178	9,500	11,389	1,889
	A	W	81	3,746	5,793	7,672	1,879
			83	9	348	398	50
			84	55	650	839	189
			85	576	3,823	5,539	1,716
	N	E	82	17	3,600	3,646	46
	N	W	81	6,333	26,879	30,461	3,582
			85	1,455	11,526	12,750	1,224
	O	E	81	4	3,150	3,167	17
			84	100	9,680	9,749	69
	V	E	83	2,205	900	1,028	128
			84	23,427	15,875	18,094	2,219
			85	4,190	19,059	19,819	760
			86	216,051	72,500	88,156	15,656
	V	W	82	49,843	269,982	281,718	11,736
			85	5,855	36,955	40,009	3,054
			86	1,102	8,887	9,290	403
C RICA	A	E	81	2,402	42,710	46,313	3,603
			82	2,920	55,196	58,133	2,937
			83	3,487	139,725	143,663	3,938
			84	2,985	93,669	98,090	4,421
			85	2,198	88,978	92,134	3,156
			86	1,722	111,410	113,467	2,057
	A	W	81	523	17,818	18,547	729
			82	713	19,314	20,245	931
			83	383	13,248	13,907	659
			84	355	28,056	29,073	1,017
			85	1,078	35,327	36,901	1,574
			86	753	29,857	31,208	1,351
	N	E	83	39	732	839	107
			84	634	11,102	12,204	1,102
	N	W	85	155	72,817	73,476	659
	O	E	83	14	1,358	1,397	39
			84	60	1,745	1,810	65
	V	W	83	50	3,250	3,366	116
CANADA	A	E	81	1,200	13,352	13,979	627
			82	298	17,214	17,497	283
			83	35	1,225	1,264	39
			84	28	1,386	1,597	211
			85	904	26,216	26,589	373
			86	6,477	23,850	27,237	3,387
	A	W	81	117	6,500	6,699	199
			84	242	301	637	336
			85	1,177	2,172	3,077	905
			86	106	20,136	20,171	35
	N	W	82	1,773	1,098	1,667	569
			84	49,067	50,765	51,510	745
	O	E	81	744,741	559,159	560,517	146
			82	369,301	427,849	427,849	
			83	863,479	518,496	518,513	17
			84	972,549	399,548	400,085	537
			85	319,055	237,157	237,157	
			86	979,776	381,454	381,454	
	O	W	81	235,673	40,977	40,994	17
			82	167,542	27,647	27,647	
			83	16,996	8,482	8,982	500
			84	34,975	10,858	10,868	10
			85	145,801	41,093	41,093	
			86	82,992	75,681	75,681	
CHILE	A	E	81	16,455	83,090	92,276	9,186
			83	11,987	39,769	46,345	6,576
			84	7,436	32,329	38,755	6,426
			85	109,705	259,863	317,755	57,892
			86	32,872	379,663	400,204	20,541
	A	W	81	2,433	30,041	32,159	2,118
			82	2,560	199,622	201,213	1,591
			83	5,169	15,156	17,706	2,550
			84	1,327	4,020	5,165	1,145
			86	666	6,759	7,580	821
	N	E	81	18,878	77,142	85,939	8,797
	N	W	81	268,337	1,637,510	1,680,814	43,304
			82	263,127	1,733,842	1,783,945	50,103
			83	241,747	1,640,801	1,684,082	43,281
			84	235,457	1,956,525	2,030,599	74,074
			85	855,278	4,232,381	4,353,773	121,392
			86	868,469	5,751,625	5,880,358	128,733
	V	E	85	14,671	18,552	20,447	1,895
			86	126,269	50,000	55,850	5,850
	V	W	82	72,678	533,289	543,237	9,948
			85	117,405	123,256	138,037	14,781
			86	52,503	168,989	176,147	7,158
CHINA M	A	E	81	175	1,960	2,499	539
			86	671	24,464	25,662	1,198
	A	H	86	2,643	81,859	86,816	4,957
	A	W	82	101	5,290	5,348	58
			83	392	1,370	3,009	1,639
			86	31,255	832,867	882,207	49,340
	N	E	81	713,735	720,773	779,617	58,844
	N	W	81	657	16,439	18,280	1,841
			82	22,552	33,329	34,044	715
			83	5,125	301,660	311,397	9,737
			84	17,067	863,633	894,289	30,656
			85	18,301	486,237	516,298	30,061
			86	7,939	265,213	275,492	10,279
	O	E	82	44,864	39,682	39,682	
	V	E	81	66,138	51,114	53,148	2,034
			82	931,684	855,489	917,665	62,176
			83	397,558	419,829	444,206	24,377
			84	204,689	204,906	220,603	15,697
			85	567,840	393,961	436,326	42,365
			86	236,465	140,058	156,135	16,077
	V	H	83	100	680	782	102
	V	W	81	21,958	24,268	25,378	1,110
			82	327,287	277,659	300,963	23,304
			84	31,074	13,758	15,920	2,162
			85	72,751	36,667	41,622	4,955
CHINA T	A	E	81	1,992	91,658	96,767	5,109
			82	3,731	195,643	203,945	8,302
			83	2,906	130,014	138,082	8,068
			84	5,265	256,740	268,737	11,997
			85	1,637	112,582	117,420	4,838
			86	1,582	111,464	116,441	4,977
	A	H	81	51	322	483	161
			82	802	52,166	52,561	395
			83	2,739	140,143	144,576	4,433
			84	1,751	114,547	118,754	4,207
			85	1,286	87,955	91,168	3,213
			86	4,406	348,260	358,588	10,328
	A	W	81	475	18,645	19,119	474
			82	18,720	1,069,274	1,113,482	44,208
			83	644	45,625	51,991	6,366
			84	9,155	544,372	561,982	17,610
			85	2,094	141,856	147,167	5,311
			86	10,584	797,653	829,587	31,934
	N	E	81	791	7,500	7,926	426
	N	W	81	59,771	2,773,332	2,893,638	120,306
			82	47,143	2,751,126	2,821,304	70,178
			83	109,427	4,996,115	5,161,736	165,621
			84	120,808	7,463,954	7,662,452	198,498
			85	121,950	5,039,133	5,211,417	172,284
			86	68,849	4,097,243	4,195,436	98,193
	O	E	86	140	7,630	7,630	
	V	E	81	416	20,844	20,943	99
			86	4,409	1,827	2,354	527
	V	H	82	1,899	3,865	3,948	83
			83	218	2,178	2,293	115
			84	4,698	6,025	6,448	423
	V	W	81	3,166	32,706	33,102	396
			82	1,715	55,615	55,980	365
			83	5,087	58,481	59,213	732
			84	2,467	990	1,100	110
			86	1,031	86,819	87,083	264
DENMARK	A	E	81	603	6,786	8,094	1,308
			82	100	1,094	1,448	354
			83	375	5,316	5,790	474
			84	198	3,055	4,100	1,045
			86	380	6,750	7,399	649
	A	W	81	195	878	1,184	306
			82	62	255	377	122
			85	2,890	30,523	33,033	2,510
			86	1,001	12,270	13,911	1,641
	N	E	81	4,367	29,220	30,625	1,405
			82	28,865	37,928	42,059	4,131
	N	W	81	1,439	5,207	5,583	376
			82	651	6,570	7,011	441
			83	1,794	71,972	73,889	1,917
	O	E	84	3	255	255	
			85	375	1,199	1,303	104
			86	13	2,818	2,818	
	V	E	81	166	998	1,128	130
			83	807	2,254	2,647	393
			84	175	4,028	4,153	125
			86	2,826	8,871	9,533	662
	V	W	81	8,865	29,382	30,907	1,525
			82	1,446	10,694	11,019	325
			83	220	2,952	3,175	223

Product
TSUSA commodity number, description, and unit of quantity

Country	Mode	Reg	Yr	Quantity	F.A.S.	C.I.F.	Charges
			84	13,228	83,407	85,492	2,085
			86	15,537	120,527	123,356	2,829
DJIBUTI	V	E	84	229,014	49,665	64,295	14,630
DOM REP	A	E	81	4,260	1,710	2,643	933
			83	1,050	9,450	10,500	1,050
			84	525	4,988	5,483	495
			86	6,000	3,000	3,740	740
	N	E	84	3,008	588	909	321
EGYPT	A	E	84	220	1,750	2,108	358
	A	W	81	54	887	1,105	218
			83	220	400	984	584
	V	E	82	882	1,000	1,525	525
	V	W	85	1,102	9,750	10,156	406
			86	15,232	16,266	19,156	2,890
ETHIOP	N	E	84	5,107,688	1,659,247	2,016,172	356,925
			85	3,446,110	1,593,980	1,797,694	203,714
			86	5,500,846	2,309,473	2,604,923	295,450
	O	E	82	172,844	101,880	111,979	10,099
	V	E	82	6,034,128	3,330,468	3,742,090	411,622
			83	8,616,683	3,285,171	3,821,562	536,391
			84	4,140,156	1,288,645	1,487,588	198,943
			85	5,589,355	2,225,450	2,684,183	458,733
			86	1,945,271	771,572	852,412	80,840
	V	W	82	86,859	48,719	55,487	6,768
FR GERM	A	E	81	47	1,109	1,160	51
			82	38	8,522	8,666	144
			83	382	3,761	4,144	383
			84	2,341	8,251	10,292	2,041
			85	3,497	25,648	30,127	4,479
			86	666	99,773	100,634	861
	A	W	81	16	447	485	38
			82	200	12,446	12,769	323
			83	5	7,240	7,358	118
			84	509	17,988	19,012	1,024
			86	300	4,264	6,534	2,270
	N	E	82	561	3,893	4,297	404
			84	766	9,659	10,275	616
			85	42,445	51,773	54,227	2,454
	N	W	83	2,502	21,908	23,677	1,769
			86	12,082	41,942	45,974	4,032
	O	E	81	38	1,543	1,612	69
			82	31	2,037	2,053	16
			83	33	293	357	64
			84	71	13,056	13,188	132
			85	4	1,455	1,475	20
			86	2,055	28,266	28,481	215
	O	W	81	15	1,598	1,640	42
	V	E	81	3,307	8,365	8,496	131
			82	1,052	7,649	7,978	329
			83	690	5,305	5,477	172
			84	22,008	33,867	38,043	4,176
			85	26,148	29,642	31,841	2,199
			86	80,302	107,108	115,032	7,924
	V	W	81	40,790	9,311	12,530	3,219
			82	7,825	1,639	3,503	1,864
			83	171,518	33,446	45,150	11,704
			84	551	992	1,148	156
			85	9,370	5,693	6,569	876
FRANCE	A	E	81	5,828	54,755	60,374	5,619
			82	8,576	60,281	65,833	5,552
			83	1,825	12,104	14,480	2,376
			84	1,011	31,055	32,425	1,370
			85	7,202	24,770	29,335	4,565
			86	9,658	24,447	36,146	11,699
	A	W	81	4	430	487	57
			82	600	1,859	2,639	780
			83	563	10,764	11,375	611
			84	34	384	500	116
			85	1,346	19,106	20,945	1,839
			86	772	4,537	5,949	1,412
	N	E	81	2,933	13,117	14,781	1,664
			82	637	1,775	2,026	251
			83	14,380	58,853	60,270	1,417
			84	3,461	21,547	22,863	1,316
			85	41,856	33,464	38,240	4,776
			86	860	9,242	10,069	827
	N	W	81	14,485	30,325	34,368	4,043
			82	15,070	31,149	34,671	3,522
			83	17,079	26,853	35,891	9,038
			84	7,002	23,163	26,026	2,863
			85	12,345	13,339	15,746	2,407
			86	21,432	32,681	44,590	11,909
	O	E	81	79,806	18,914	20,854	1,940
			83	26	1,804	1,839	35
			84	2	560	573	13
			86	88,185	26,400	31,420	5,020
	V	E	81	10,172	18,883	21,288	2,405
			82	22,142	74,313	77,259	2,946
			83	1,812	12,782	13,435	653
			84	80,128	50,328	60,426	10,098
			85	441	2,798	3,032	234
			86	11,386	28,927	31,098	2,171
	V	W	81	22,156	83,027	85,295	2,268
			83	11,528	12,042	13,636	1,594
			84	661	3,190	3,549	359
			86	4,341	6,136	6,622	486
GERM DR	A	E	85	4	77,346	77,413	67
GHANA	A	E	81	44	600	789	189
GREECE	A	E	85	7	6,539	6,571	32
	V	E	81	82,174	62,230	72,100	9,870
			82	33,069	23,250	26,005	2,755
			86	7,975	29,425	30,895	1,470
GUATMAL	A	E	81	671	32,263	32,682	419
			82	117	8,450	8,508	58
			83	35	2,176	2,192	16
			84	300	300	636	336
	A	W	81	24	1,341	1,348	7
			82	571	23,688	24,171	483
			83	199	12,417	12,736	319
			84	346	9,960	10,754	794
	N	E	84	3,223	3,900	4,735	835
	V	E	81	132,750	65,685	72,542	6,857
			82	2,205	2,820	3,087	267
			83	980	686	884	198
			84	107,388	36,227	43,298	7,071
			85	44,000	12,116	14,720	2,604
			86	6,011	6,500	7,258	758
HAITI	A	E	83	1,999	375	565	190
HG KONG	A	H	86	463	23,286	24,695	1,409
	A	W	81	249	4,953	5,598	645
	N	E	83	30,815	43,229	46,048	2,819
	N	W	81	2,384	4,921	7,978	3,057
			82	330	713	917	204
			83	1,321	68,336	70,820	2,484
	O	E	86	7,500	6,186	6,186	
	V	E	83	30,861	21,734	24,976	3,242
			84	213,640	211,372	228,798	17,426
			85	59,391	36,284	40,979	4,695
			86	119,050	102,625	107,824	5,199
	V	W	81	203	1,018	1,090	72
			82	2,678	4,655	4,850	195
			85	7,000	7,063	7,321	258
			86	125,001	36,300	41,300	5,000
HONDURA	A	E	81	120	28,438	29,290	852
			82	308	10,020	11,047	1,027
			83	181	4,646	5,033	387
			84	188	21,403	21,891	488
			85	327	241,904	242,552	648
	A	W	85	12	16,132	16,227	95
			86	39	8,021	8,131	110
HUNGARY	V	W	85	5,214	26,091	27,884	1,793
ICELAND	V	W	85	551	2,067	2,077	10
INDIA	A	E	81	61	1,875	2,179	304
			82	22	320	325	5
			83	269	6,289	7,122	833
			84	2,266	38,096	43,350	5,254
			85	3,077	96,783	104,614	7,831
			86	14,284	315,591	347,507	31,916
	A	W	81	2,529	67,167	76,445	9,278
			82	7,614	257,298	280,515	23,217
			83	19,317	834,494	878,483	43,989
			84	3,773	131,726	141,283	9,557
			85	17,825	558,793	605,775	46,982
			86	33	1,395	1,525	130
	N	E	83	5,768,865	2,448,348	2,704,555	256,207
			84	2,645,766	892,208	1,074,118	181,910
			85	4,469,592	1,805,247	2,025,797	220,550
	N	W	81	417,381	241,834	273,733	31,899
			84	54,834	295,396	315,842	20,446
			85	241,790	158,001	173,767	15,766
			86	110,384	67,642	73,695	6,053
	O	E	81	8	2,811	2,845	34
			83	78,740	52,709	52,709	
			84	1,037	1,032	1,135	103
	V	E	81	5,195,870	2,545,246	2,967,288	422,042
			82	9,701,205	5,039,259	5,750,541	711,282
			83	660,763	285,943	332,286	46,343
			84	163,964	41,347	52,865	11,518
			85	678,218	253,770	298,306	44,536
			86	15,059,919	6,861,381	7,450,908	589,527

Product
TSUSA commodity number, description, and unit of quantity

Country	Mode	Reg	Yr	Quantity	F.A.S.	C.I.F.	Charges
	V	W	81	2,350,049	1,083,913	1,255,151	171,238
			82	1,148,978	652,657	749,066	96,409
			83	514,217	209,072	228,606	19,534
			86	5,777	6,368	7,429	1,061
INDNSIA	V	E	85	37,478	18,177	21,588	3,411
IRAN	V	E	85	10,703	20,500	21,596	1,096
			86	140	1,118	1,252	134
IRELAND	A	E	84	140	2,590	2,907	317
ISRAEL	A	E	81	157	3,200	3,565	365
			82	297	3,141	3,881	740
			83	1,110	5,315	7,000	1,685
			84	991	15,158	16,404	1,246
			86	108	49,930	50,381	451
	A	W	82	70	11,718	12,142	424
			84	220	12,413	13,365	952
			85	11	1,496	1,582	86
			86	3,167	141,995	146,618	4,623
	N	E	83	44,654	28,701	33,081	4,380
	N	W	81	10,442	55,358	56,883	1,525
			82	1,884	11,281	12,370	1,089
			83	22,531	129,926	133,330	3,404
			84	61,913	302,022	334,215	32,193
			85	98,986	482,544	502,873	20,329
	V	E	81	35,621	205,482	209,931	4,449
			82	39,560	295,472	300,506	5,034
			83	51,203	281,637	290,203	8,566
			84	6,668	34,840	35,957	1,117
			85	668	21,822	22,241	419
			86	590	3,373	3,688	315
	V	W	81	11,764	47,331	48,999	1,668
			82	21,535	100,517	103,351	2,834
			83	51,548	205,380	212,347	6,967
			84	529	1,926	2,273	347
			85	17,825	99,484	102,062	2,578
			86	8,529	95,346	97,490	2,144
ITALY	A	E	81	4,140	48,657	53,484	4,827
			82	10,013	23,082	27,442	4,360
			83	1,269	8,514	10,493	1,979
			84	5,054	25,361	29,784	4,423
			85	2,733	6,293	9,603	3,310
			86	200	4,039	4,604	565
	A	W	84	110	808	952	144
	N	E	83	2,306	27,188	29,691	2,503
			84	984	13,282	13,589	307
			86	220,422	91,485	98,924	7,439
	N	W	81	10,322	71,726	78,680	6,954
			82	113,147	647,698	669,882	22,184
			83	53,830	342,859	356,619	13,760
			84	97,686	612,566	639,025	26,459
			85	207,496	1,012,627	1,044,901	32,274
			86	58,193	404,973	425,458	20,485
	O	E	84	6	430	458	28
	V	E	81	21,246	119,827	122,803	2,976
			82	8,603	64,188	66,133	1,945
			83	19,912	37,824	39,247	1,423
			84	220	264	294	30
			85	8,933	56,196	57,041	845
	V	W	81	77,223	430,874	443,266	12,392
			82	37,589	27,386	32,190	4,804
			83	7,815	48,575	49,563	988
			84	441	2,832	2,983	151
			86	47,224	287,130	294,680	7,550
JAMAICA	A	E	84	880	392	392	
	V	E	81	6,276	3,260	4,995	1,735
			83	2,395	992	1,362	370
JAPAN	A	E	81	1,304	78,717	84,796	6,079
			82	1,541	58,196	63,164	4,968
			83	857	67,258	70,681	3,423
			84	1,216	70,422	76,152	5,730
			85	2,782	180,952	187,184	6,232
			86	2,108	63,321	70,531	7,210
	A	H	81	386	20,519	21,823	1,304
			85	22	1,896	1,937	41
	A	W	81	2,793	71,766	76,443	4,677
			82	5,086	77,979	86,874	8,895
			83	1,810	68,479	74,278	5,799
			84	1,422	46,028	48,336	2,308
			85	2,871	96,956	107,353	10,397
			86	764	38,144	40,871	2,727
	N	E	81	4,339	286,212	294,208	7,996
			82	3,467	170,964	176,282	5,318
			83	2,222	143,637	150,957	7,320
			84	3,435	148,009	154,654	6,645
			86	220	13,848	14,435	587
	N	H	81	705	4,870	5,341	471

Product
TSUSA commodity number, description, and unit of quantity

Country	Mode	Reg	Yr	Quantity	F.A.S.	C.I.F.	Charges
			83	2,299	14,119	14,820	701
			84	2,691	17,314	18,529	1,215
			85	385	4,316	4,494	178
	N	W	81	19,554	230,095	247,414	17,319
			82	50,470	599,173	623,233	24,060
			83	20,016	872,363	894,015	21,652
			84	31,329	952,328	973,071	20,743
			85	24,163	640,379	654,905	14,526
			86	30,348	921,131	968,710	47,579
	O	E	81	422	12,114	12,920	796
			82	186	6,798	7,321	523
			83	95	4,612	5,001	389
			84	758	5,595	6,064	469
			85	11	1,460	1,601	141
	O	W	81	15	675	759	84
			82	40	1,650	1,788	138
			84	1,863	39,559	45,994	6,435
	V	E	82	661	469	504	35
			83	4,250	124,365	125,530	1,165
			84	2,472	33,637	34,824	1,187
			85	469	20,412	20,724	312
			86	16,832	70,162	73,014	2,852
	V	H	82	8,674	111,977	113,440	1,463
			86	413	3,822	4,416	594
	V	W	81	4,335	87,180	88,670	1,490
			82	8,390	85,388	86,948	1,560
			83	510	50,330	50,588	258
			84	1,545	51,976	53,017	1,041
			85	23,206	113,563	115,397	1,834
			86	10,321	77,990	78,775	785
JORDAN	A	W	84	110	945	1,170	225
			85	419	6,641	6,928	287
KENYA	A	E	82	8	884	890	6
	A	W	83	220	500	1,573	1,073
			84	97	4,215	4,694	479
			85	62	3,571	3,739	168
	V	E	83	57,790	27,448	30,759	3,311
			85	11,875	59,176	63,475	4,299
KIRIBAT	V	E	85	39,683	16,300	19,897	3,597
KOR REP	A	E	84	259	16,501	17,576	1,075
			85	163	4,262	4,757	495
			86	202	2,665	3,209	544
	A	W	82	232	15,680	16,341	661
			83	68	4,620	4,786	166
	O	W	81	20	481	519	38
	V	E	82	8,818	32,120	32,917	797
			83	264	4,717	4,885	168
			84	119	3,680	3,806	126
			85	588	11,784	12,020	236
	V	W	81	73	1,542	1,650	108
			83	5,188	172,905	173,774	869
			84	4,409	5,001	5,318	317
			86	477	8,100	8,234	134
LEBANON	V	E	81	42,990	15,081	17,040	1,959
			82	31,690	17,179	19,413	2,234
			83	6,089	1,869	2,011	142
MEXICO	A	E	82	2,164	9,006	9,522	516
			83	1,000	1,000	1,210	210
	A	W	81	7,481	48,873	52,544	3,671
			82	6,302	63,020	65,409	2,389
			83	7,986	79,229	81,732	2,503
			84	7,672	83,574	86,362	2,788
			85	6,814	71,110	74,109	2,999
			86	6,757	56,859	59,658	2,799
	N	E	82	22,528	40,426	40,518	92
			85	6,658	84,078	84,078	
	N	W	81	164,574	1,262,128	1,262,151	23
	O	E	81	1,100	5,609	5,609	
			82	42,530	24,074	24,074	
			83	27,522	4,745	4,745	
			84	357,600	126,519	126,519	
			85	40,035	43,760	43,760	
			86	565,966	642,191	642,191	
	O	H	81	361	2,160	2,583	423
	O	W	81	268,061	427,979	428,149	170
			82	637,509	2,176,781	2,176,966	185
			83	391,777	1,821,697	1,821,697	
			84	643,078	1,551,898	1,551,898	
			85	562,915	1,620,248	1,620,248	
			86	329,431	1,081,253	1,081,253	
	V	E	81	626,646	889,024	920,993	31,969
			82	68,023	85,998	89,053	3,055
			83	140,050	161,250	186,672	25,600
MOROC	V	E	84	22,046	4,750	6,550	1,800
	V	W	84	80,104	23,360	36,464	13,104

Product
TSUSA commodity number, description, and unit of quantity

Country	Mode	Reg	Yr	Quantity	F.A.S.	C.I.F.	Charges
			86	99,206	25,223	31,126	5,903
N ZEAL	A	W	81	2,815	4,192	6,427	2,235
			82	453	4,052	5,095	1,043
			83	891	5,225	6,518	1,293
			84	301	12,793	13,277	484
			85	110	2,459	2,596	137
	N	W	84	5,801	2,685	3,614	929
			86	291,058	82,999	104,186	21,187
	V	E	82	36,000	9,630	10,428	798
			85	12,894	32,716	40,969	8,253
	V	W	81	295,908	83,757	109,956	26,199
			82	136,373	40,806	48,941	8,135
			83	614,779	188,287	239,858	51,571
			84	369,384	68,155	95,167	27,012
			85	507,696	82,838	115,791	32,953
			86	405,375	72,927	96,847	23,920
NEPAL	A	W	84	79	2,586	2,840	254
	O	E	81	10,977	7,073	8,174	1,101
	V	E	81	21,760	9,020	11,493	2,473
			83	45,856	21,708	26,730	5,022
			84	64,815	22,050	29,212	7,162
			86	466,519	187,453	225,266	37,813
NETHLDS	A	E	81	1,441	125,197	128,599	3,402
			82	1,788	276,046	279,189	3,143
			83	2,142	225,009	227,768	2,759
			84	2,319	151,163	155,004	3,841
			85	2,605	173,588	177,596	4,008
			86	3,705	581,337	589,278	7,941
	A	W	81	55	1,125	1,345	220
			82	293	5,980	6,564	584
			83	400	4,105	4,388	283
			84	1,142	12,343	14,446	2,103
			85	458	8,103	8,660	557
			86	2,998	177,724	183,414	5,690
	N	E	81	6,666	158,227	160,630	2,243
			82	13,613	86,198	90,382	4,184
			83	2,866	31,632	33,507	1,875
			84	9,862	203,465	208,418	4,953
			86	1,217	63,794	64,902	1,108
	N	W	81	10,787	490,445	498,673	8,228
			82	31,086	630,905	647,230	16,325
			83	85,445	691,199	710,961	19,762
			84	116,840	1,398,605	1,432,356	33,751
			85	154,480	1,002,396	1,030,952	28,556
			86	99,393	1,249,491	1,275,621	26,130
	O	E	81	610	6,642	6,780	138
			82	40,033	23,879	25,761	1,882
			83	400	15,112	15,229	117
			84	265	4,303	4,421	118
			86	205	7,029	7,029	
	O	W	81	17	1,566	1,566	
			82	1	434	441	7
			84	6	1,873	1,893	20
	V	E	81	42,053	37,559	40,864	3,305
			82	5,443	12,599	13,997	1,398
			83	57,128	39,512	46,163	6,651
			84	12,681	36,847	40,620	3,773
			85	14,293	26,203	30,066	3,863
			86	28,831	15,883	17,780	1,897
	V	W	81	1,102	2,755	2,988	233
			82	17,008	7,092	8,398	1,306
			83	9,749	10,132	11,291	1,159
			84	28,944	33,347	39,285	5,938
			85	10,273	62,758	64,339	1,581
			86	14,150	12,197	13,775	1,578
NICARAG	V	W	83	11,500	4,715	5,637	922
NIGERIA	A	E	84	826	413	695	282
NORFOLK	A	W	86	94	3,450	3,597	147
PAKISTN	V	E	85	3,307	1,798	2,269	471
			86	14,330	12,069	13,718	1,649
	V	W	83	2,205	692	920	228
			84	8,800	1,112	1,963	851
PANAMA	A	E	85	27,000	17,727	27,923	10,196
PERU	A	E	82	11,023	10,500	18,138	7,638
	V	E	82	9,852	2,041	2,694	653
			86	39,948	11,440	12,349	909
	V	W	85	220	2,800	2,966	166
PHIL R	A	W	81	508	15,756	16,924	1,168
			83	293	2,750	3,578	828
	N	W	84	1,513	10,520	11,236	716
			85	790	41,479	41,912	433
	V	W	81	457	460	508	48
			82	1,025	24,420	24,744	324
			83	1,681	2,030	2,248	218
PORTUGL	A	W	82	457	123,521	124,703	1,182

Product
TSUSA commodity number, description, and unit of quantity

Country	Mode	Reg	Yr	Quantity	F.A.S.	C.I.F.	Charges
	V	E	81	9,811	5,414	6,108	694
			82	3,350	3,579	4,080	501
			83	1,543	1,246	1,434	188
	V	W	82	39,683	18,600	21,600	3,000
			84	110	555	705	150
			85	79,366	25,883	32,497	6,614
REP SAF	A	E	82	777	4,121	5,709	1,588
			83	1,532	5,838	8,802	2,964
			84	836	15,020	16,960	1,940
			86	9	1,292	1,339	47
	A	W	81	616	4,995	6,798	1,803
			82	462	5,982	6,876	894
			83	679	8,835	9,405	570
			85	83	6,783	6,935	152
			86	595	1,622	2,410	788
	O	W	82	7	1,050	1,070	20
	V	E	81	46,614	13,652	17,453	3,801
			82	1,845	7,311	7,663	352
			83	715	3,639	3,689	50
			84	1,891	27,972	28,818	846
			85	39,600	23,166	25,397	2,231
	V	W	86	3,042	5,197	5,563	366
ROMANIA	A	W	81	584	33,076	34,856	1,780
	V	E	85	272	1,804	1,858	54
S ARAB	A	W	86	1,376	5,781	8,278	2,497
SALVADR	A	E	81	8,600	4,300	6,730	2,430
			82	3,400	2,040	2,937	897
			83	4,554	2,760	3,726	966
			84	1,086	272	677	405
	V	E	84	288,808	108,014	127,574	19,560
			85	220,000	103,120	119,680	16,560
	V	W	83	2,583	2,337	2,780	443
			85	4,000	1,335	2,137	802
SINGAPR	V	W	83	198	666	780	114
SOMALIA	A	W	85	17	4,400	4,480	80
SPAIN	A	E	81	53	921	1,070	149
			82	50	1,307	1,464	157
			85	187	4,389	4,718	329
	A	W	84	703	4,237	6,023	1,786
	N	W	81	943	2,343	3,523	1,180
			83	164,695	61,846	74,557	12,711
	V	E	81	110	880	994	114
			82	551	565	673	108
	V	W	81	331	2,213	2,331	118
			82	15,178	26,861	28,777	1,916
			83	17,637	13,650	14,969	1,319
			85	16	2,021	2,171	150
SUDAN	O	E	81	8,100	5,569	5,569	
	V	E	81	233,328	81,266	99,133	17,867
			82	194,820	103,928	121,635	17,707
			83	421,043	736,450	754,625	18,175
			84	79,366	21,600	26,000	4,400
			85	141,094	52,800	58,722	5,922
			86	68,136	26,817	31,351	4,534
SWEDEN	A	E	84	3,153	7,335	9,005	1,670
	A	W	83	213	384	566	182
	O	E	84	39,683	11,880	13,880	2,000
	V	E	81	4,409	856	1,766	910
			82	400	386	514	128
			84	403	3,477	3,910	433
	V	W	81	330	495	604	109
SWITZLD	A	E	83	100	267	447	180
			84	220	1,218	1,528	310
			86	415	5,702	6,335	633
	A	W	81	17	9,734	9,944	210
			82	30	3,389	3,457	68
			84	121	740	1,002	262
	V	E	82	3,633	8,111	8,928	817
			83	1,543	2,148	2,410	262
			85	1,102	2,563	2,937	374
SYRIA	V	E	83	1,323	1,200	1,270	70
THAILND	A	E	84	18	860	1,024	164
	A	W	82	1,930	118,209	121,233	3,024
			83	13,516	787,458	804,584	17,126
			84	19,660	997,958	1,029,103	31,145
			85	1,432	62,846	65,331	2,485
			86	6,003	341,778	351,625	9,847
	N	W	81	264,355	54,741	59,822	5,081
			82	2,714	14,264	16,025	1,761
			85	85,003	268,286	281,467	13,181
			86	12,145	374,282	390,628	16,346
	V	E	81	2,325	2,182	2,423	241
			82	22,046	8,000	9,712	1,712
			84	61	262	295	33
	V	W	81	33,069	13,250	15,765	2,515

Country	Mode	Reg	Yr	Quantity	F.A.S.	C.I.F.	Charges
			83	2,728	2,374	3,128	754
			84	79,366	18,926	22,122	3,196
TURKEY	V	E	84	2,204	749	1,055	306
			86	3,000	1,868	2,160	292
	V	W	85	2,998	8,160	9,018	858
			86	5,827	17,180	19,167	1,987
U KING	A	E	81	338	12,048	12,858	810
			82	3,398	49,484	52,368	2,884
			83	4,271	75,942	77,547	1,605
			84	12,746	77,172	83,048	5,876
			85	1,075	17,046	18,527	1,481
			86	1,660	58,596	62,332	3,736
	A	W	81	654	6,480	7,996	1,516
			83	348	89,070	90,114	1,044
			84	6,620	3,456	6,852	3,396
			85	97	1,612	1,753	141
	N	E	81	16,364	104,235	113,825	9,590
			82	905	5,308	5,794	486
			83	9,186	85,765	90,585	4,820
			84	227,148	102,846	130,983	28,137
			85	21,640	69,318	78,547	9,229
			86	3,096	10,488	14,693	4,205
	N	W	81	445	1,648	1,860	212
			82	12,793	10,148	12,773	2,625
			83	9,584	3,831	5,679	1,848
			84	69,920	52,187	59,195	7,008
			85	15,363	110,147	118,252	8,105
	O	E	81	70	2,389	2,524	135
			82	3	463	483	20
			83	251	1,784	1,901	117
			84	4,056	5,609	6,724	1,115
			86	592	22,645	23,086	441
	O	W	81	14	740	831	91
			82	35	438	511	73
			84	21	1,979	1,995	16
			85	21,909	4,249	4,249	
	V	E	82	142,636	53,180	65,014	11,834
			83	46,087	9,082	12,024	2,942
			84	1,243	1,316	1,505	189
			85	22,141	4,755	5,159	404
			86	2,646	3,641	4,005	364
	V	W	82	772	1,139	1,155	16
			84	2,000	326	731	405
			85	18,739	35,009	35,485	476
			86	16,600	16,875	18,811	1,936
URUGUAY	V	E	81	44,092	93,762	97,114	3,352
USSR	A	E	81	1,124	7,650	10,586	2,936
	O	W	81	1,000	1,090	1,240	150
VENEZ	A	E	85	200	1,250	2,295	1,045
			86	1,764	2,640	3,453	813
	A	W	83	22	297	390	93
YUGOSLV	A	E	82	364	2,402	2,582	180
	O	E	81	26,455	26,455	26,455	
	V	E	81	107,463	134,806	144,544	9,738
			82	256,153	228,979	251,441	22,462
			83	239,799	192,537	214,065	21,528
			84	296,905	162,788	191,697	28,909
			85	122,731	78,499	91,463	12,964

Grass and forage crop, seed
1270100 GRASS & FOR CROP SEEDS NSPF (LB)

Country	Mode	Reg	Yr	Quantity	F.A.S.	C.I.F.	Charges
TOTAL			81	1,533,253	2,012,451	2,117,582	105,131
			82	2,340,027	1,401,155	1,529,415	128,260
			83	1,901,564	2,530,574	2,591,862	61,288
			84	2,962,345	1,837,817	1,967,549	129,732
			85	3,412,922	2,836,395	2,962,293	125,898
			86	4,249,824	6,179,214	6,350,117	170,903
ANTIGUA	V	E	86	39,683	18,195	20,700	2,505
ARGENT	A	E	81	564	510	1,451	941
			85	9,048	3,456	9,366	5,910
	V	E	81	22,046	31,000	32,900	1,900
			82	824,419	244,170	266,432	22,262
			83	12,125	14,575	15,391	816
			84	169,754	61,600	71,883	10,283
			85	1,563,590	404,892	409,522	4,630
			86	458,464	372,735	401,221	28,486
	V	W	86	30,864	20,080	22,400	2,320
AUSTRAL	A	E	86	400	1,488	1,939	451
	A	H	85	7,652	20,755	24,364	3,609
			86	440	1,940	2,379	439
	A	W	83	122	4,011	4,687	676
			84	187	1,804	1,982	178

Country	Mode	Reg	Yr	Quantity	F.A.S.	C.I.F.	Charges
			86	1,305	4,978	5,340	362
	N	H	81	8,804	29,492	32,955	3,463
			84	29,530	46,057	50,337	4,280
			86	21,664	36,184	41,620	5,436
	N	W	84	4,546	4,920	5,992	1,072
	V	E	81	296,433	327,746	370,438	42,692
			82	450,411	369,699	421,115	51,416
			83	213,637	211,184	236,580	25,396
			84	277,911	268,196	288,893	20,697
			85	425,686	355,859	388,677	32,818
			86	396,762	403,565	426,749	23,184
	V	H	82	5,911	10,485	11,746	1,261
			83	3,000	7,143	7,819	676
			85	4,919	9,435	9,946	511
	V	W	81	4,409	7,937	8,648	711
			82	18,026	29,131	32,103	2,972
			84	74,690	36,429	45,046	8,617
			85	98,005	30,866	39,216	8,350
			86	105,624	70,779	77,010	6,231
AUSTRIA	A	W	86	140	1,610	1,766	156
BELGIUM	O	E	82	313,867	78,364	99,360	20,996
BRAZIL	A	E	81	2,799	1,825	5,690	3,865
			82	35	270	363	93
			85	2,000	8,500	9,900	1,400
	A	W	84	33	555	730	175
			85	120	1,626	1,806	180
	V	E	83	22,000	55,500	57,664	2,164
			84	18,695	9,752	13,217	3,465
			85	22,046	29,266	31,900	2,634
C RICA	A	E	81	67	2,146	2,286	140
			84	9,796	2,181	2,425	244
			85	853	10,884	11,820	936
			86	1,553	18,376	19,664	1,288
CANADA	N	W	82	74,595	7,438	7,571	133
			84	21,251	7,415	7,959	544
	O	E	81	428,212	819,709	819,709	
			82	331,485	367,086	367,086	
			83	857,238	864,619	864,619	
			84	954,875	775,455	776,351	896
			85	490,484	521,164	521,164	
			86	1,590,293	2,130,685	2,130,685	
	O	W	81	116,566	107,850	107,850	
			82	40,000	45,600	45,600	
			83	478,766	143,810	144,278	468
			84	258,852	134,898	134,898	
			85	62,800	54,695	54,695	
			86	588,182	820,432	820,432	
CHILE	V	W	83	110,512	1,014,979	1,028,895	13,916
			86	108,903	46,928	57,362	10,434
CHINA M	A	E	86	915	101,548	104,272	2,724
	V	W	83	500	746	883	137
CHINA T	A	E	85	1,317	94,074	97,837	3,763
			86	4,099	288,909	298,430	9,521
	A	W	81	97	4,818	5,132	314
			82	227	6,788	7,474	686
			84	2,000	10,875	11,671	796
			85	245	14,737	15,230	493
DENMARK	A	E	86	435	34,247	34,901	654
	N	E	85	11,342	12,011	13,025	1,014
	O	E	81	54,480	27,902	29,482	1,580
			83	9,998	5,406	6,356	950
			84	22,046	11,073	12,887	1,814
			85	17,096	20,177	22,800	2,623
			86	44,092	57,967	59,888	1,921
	V	E	82	10,824	7,326	7,830	504
			84	11,023	5,550	6,718	1,168
			85	149,780	58,415	66,815	8,400
	V	W	82	530	583	733	150
			83	11,000	6,545	7,952	1,407
			86	132,300	35,244	45,644	10,400
ETHIOP	V	E	86	43,210	20,200	23,866	3,666
FR GERM	A	E	81	210	2,310	2,585	275
			83	580	1,769	2,043	274
			84	6,834	4,165	7,676	3,511
			86	188	45,532	48,432	2,900
	A	W	82	209	13,149	13,489	340
			83	164	310	444	134
	N	E	85	148	17,163	17,470	307
	O	E	82	1,500	2,060	2,060	
			85	22,046	25,324	26,455	1,131
	V	E	84	452,602	131,170	147,879	16,709
			85	8,700	15,955	18,749	2,794
			86	116,844	181,643	188,524	6,881
	V	W	82	220	740	850	110
FRANCE	A	E	82	3,118	7,931	11,550	3,619

Product TSUSA commodity number, description, and unit of quantity Country	Mode	Reg	Yr	Quantity	F.A.S.	C.I.F.	Charges
			85	1,358	35,109	37,521	2,412
			86	1,507	35,348	37,872	2,524
	A	W	81	110	436	716	280
	V	E	82	5,457	8,592	8,902	310
			86	7,835	1,892	3,544	1,652
	V	W	85	500	1,477	1,606	129
GERM DR	V	E	84	66,139	112,104	117,283	5,179
GUATMAL	A	E	84	1,000	256	560	304
	N	E	81	140,000	60,617	67,801	7,184
HUNGARY	V	E	86	22,190	29,085	31,066	1,981
	V	W	86	46,775	40,745	43,283	2,538
INDIA	O	E	83	46,600	41,365	44,565	3,200
	V	E	81	89,588	43,500	51,905	8,405
			82	58,863	31,105	36,017	4,912
			85	22,000	7,483	9,243	1,760
	V	W	81	43,809	21,053	23,972	2,919
			82	24,467	9,566	11,218	1,652
			83	11,220	4,178	4,966	788
			85	59,650	23,988	29,353	5,365
ISRAEL	A	E	86	395	50,316	51,343	1,027
	V	W	81	6,614	44,602	45,328	726
			84	265	2,980	3,140	160
ITALY	A	E	81	92	400	617	217
			84	313	1,890	2,267	377
			85	478	48,304	48,465	161
			86	65	1,614	1,629	15
	V	E	85	42,329	21,657	24,000	2,343
			86	52,498	22,498	24,908	2,410
	V	W	83	13,020	78,452	80,766	2,314
JAMAICA	V	E	84	21,436	12,300	13,761	1,461
JAPAN	A	E	81	2,658	23,928	26,198	2,270
			82	250	12,718	13,773	1,055
			86	288	35,175	36,618	1,443
	A	W	84	64	4,200	4,479	279
			85	117	11,565	12,182	617
	N	E	85	21,701	255,450	261,533	6,083
	N	W	84	4,629	1,353	3,029	1,676
	O	E	81	25	3,013	3,159	146
	O	H	84	18	1,208	1,294	86
	V	E	86	2,207	1,530	1,887	357
KOR REP	V	W	81	2,205	17,671	18,088	417
			83	4,409	51,300	52,060	760
			86	3,307	41,742	42,210	468
MEXICO	A	E	84	49	600	634	34
	O	E	83	22,485	8,969	8,969	
			84	6,352	6,459	6,459	
			86	2,250	5,490	5,490	
	O	W	84	4,153	2,040	2,040	
MOROC	V	E	84	30,864	5,640	7,280	1,640
N ZEAL	A	H	82	134	871	1,285	414
	A	W	86	124	1,775	2,195	420
	O	W	81	50	500	530	30
	V	E	81	313	618	681	63
			83	78,886	9,959	16,380	6,421
			84	4,431	7,210	7,910	700
	V	H	81	1,602	2,402	2,677	275
			84	171	292	345	53
	V	W	82	1,929	1,555	2,026	471
			84	3,858	1,269	2,054	785
			86	88,184	57,154	62,700	5,546
NETHLDS	A	E	81	769	4,487	5,076	589
			82	1,533	6,632	7,573	941
			83	22	602	622	20
			84	684	6,594	6,783	189
			85	94,949	552,366	554,710	2,344
			86	5,448	889,774	895,678	5,904
	A	W	82	22	2,380	2,522	142
			86	650	1,985	2,644	659
	O	E	81	12	3,173	3,240	67
	V	E	82	22,040	14,495	16,530	2,035
			84	30	308	317	9
			85	39,240	32,971	36,989	4,018
			86	74,957	77,021	81,318	4,297
	V	W	81	2,629	1,088	1,354	266
			82	7,123	5,914	6,770	856
			83	4,365	1,792	2,263	471
			84	13,687	6,485	7,654	1,169
			85	2,205	1,258	3,530	2,272
NIGERIA	O	E	86	18,000	12,240	12,240	
POLAND	V	E	85	4,409	4,000	4,100	100
REP SAF	N	E	85	22,479	13,337	15,794	2,457
	V	E	81	243,683	248,120	269,578	21,458
			84	92,594	46,930	52,222	5,292
			85	118,883	61,210	69,515	8,305
			86	79,365	51,321	54,899	3,578

Product TSUSA commodity number, description, and unit of quantity Country	Mode	Reg	Yr	Quantity	F.A.S.	C.I.F.	Charges
	V	W	84	39,683	20,385	23,015	2,630
			85	39,300	22,410	25,186	2,776
SALVADR	A	E	81	1,300	1,105	1,345	240
SPAIN	V	E	86	39,683	19,800	22,600	2,800
	V	W	82	552	5,099	5,316	217
SUDAN	V	E	81	330,000	50,802	80,025	29,223
			86	37,037	13,115	14,565	1,450
SWEDEN	V	E	85	44,203	29,750	32,545	2,795
	V	W	84	6,614	5,949	6,878	929
SWITZLD	A	E	82	110	754	779	25
			84	220	416	582	166
			85	188	2,176	2,415	239
			86	59	4,603	4,960	357
	V	E	82	2,213	4,466	4,746	280
THAILND	A	W	86	105	25,000	26,500	1,500
	V	E	81	375	1,050	1,180	130
	V	W	81	175	1,366	1,496	130
U KING	A	E	82	1,543	2,429	3,997	1,568
			83	906	2,607	2,871	264
	A	W	82	21	1,505	1,574	69
			84	238	1,342	1,410	68
	O	E	83	9	753	789	36
	V	E	82	39,683	18,988	20,606	1,618
			84	7,000	7,000	8,975	1,975
	V	W	85	1,056	2,630	2,849	219
			86	80,535	46,726	56,744	10,018
URUGUAY	V	E	81	33,069	69,825	72,750	2,925
			82	98,710	83,266	90,419	7,153
YUGOSLV	V	E	81	29,488	100,252	100,765	513
			84	13,228	19,710	20,609	899

Tree and shrub, seed
1268700 TREE AND SHRUB SEEDS (LB)

Country	Mode	Reg	Yr	Quantity	F.A.S.	C.I.F.	Charges
TOTAL			81	443,215	1,073,618	1,146,120	72,702
			82	296,329	718,514	782,383	63,869
			83	237,925	893,253	974,045	80,792
			84	298,271	1,088,668	1,163,906	75,238
			85	496,513	1,394,103	1,503,982	109,879
			86	413,726	1,382,925	1,485,374	102,449
ARAB EM	A	W	85	121	1,670	1,948	278
ARGENT	A	E	83	10,780	20,200	32,415	12,215
AUSTRAL	A	E	81	939	7,630	9,056	1,426
			82	352	4,088	5,317	1,229
			84	146	5,748	6,464	716
			86	2,000	17,880	17,946	66
	A	H	83	24	739	871	132
			84	2,327	64,130	66,525	2,395
			85	1,533	26,151	28,231	2,080
			86	440	8,713	10,169	1,456
	A	W	81	1,393	21,327	23,328	2,001
			82	66	3,959	4,301	342
			83	1,123	8,188	9,245	1,057
			85	1,069	12,531	13,757	1,226
			86	3,663	54,002	56,875	2,873
	N	W	81	2,466	22,163	25,491	3,328
			82	705	12,194	12,561	367
	O	W	83	5	311	316	5
	V	E	86	20,202	23,666	25,471	1,805
	V	W	84	247	1,354	1,604	250
AUSTRIA	A	W	83	520	5,106	5,250	144
BELGIUM	A	E	81	99	3,600	3,746	146
			82	537	19,193	19,583	390
			83	506	16,867	17,139	272
			85	502	15,925	16,438	513
	V	E	86	22,044	18,718	20,281	1,563
BRAZIL	A	E	83	1,980	27,000	29,164	2,164
			85	33	7,000	7,363	363
	A	W	85	1,129	1,024	3,550	2,526
	O	E	81	52	20,350	20,477	127
	V	W	83	1,187	3,180	3,519	339
BULGAR	A	E	83	551	4,750	5,178	428
	A	W	84	112	1,025	1,140	115
			85	220	1,850	2,053	203
			86	243	1,940	2,183	243
C RICA	A	E	81	233	2,768	2,995	227
			82	506	750	779	29
	A	W	84	17	425	485	60
CANADA	A	E	83	439	15,303	15,762	459
			84	64	1,725	1,816	91
			85	100	2,800	2,921	121
			86	250	7,876	8,139	263
	A	W	81	7	1,500	1,529	29

Product
TSUSA commodity number, description, and unit of quantity

Country	Mode	Reg	Yr	Quantity	F.A.S.	C.I.F.	Charges
			83	69	3,770	3,962	192
			85	756	19,265	19,489	224
			86	175	16,925	17,144	219
		N W	83	292	16,606	16,676	70
		O E	81	1,523	27,377	27,377	
			82	1,515	21,711	21,886	175
			83	446	9,965	10,053	88
			84	574	18,057	18,340	283
			85	417	17,348	17,348	
			86	610	13,272	13,272	
		O W	82	112	9,100	9,131	31
			83	100	350	350	
			84	255	4,854	4,854	
			85	28	2,332	2,332	
			86	423	21,121	21,121	
CHILE	A E		81	500	5,301	5,751	450
	A W		82	223	923	1,471	548
	V W		81	694	1,291	1,413	122
			82	2,163	5,179	5,590	411
CHINA M	A W		84	588	10,063	11,386	1,323
			86	3,990	88,673	94,647	5,974
	V E		85	8,128	12,500	13,438	938
CHINA T	A E		81	1,044	1,000	1,236	236
			84	1,000	12,000	12,468	468
	A H		81	2,209	8,828	11,181	2,353
			82	838	6,450	9,311	2,861
			84	6,977	18,682	26,572	7,890
			85	12,719	50,588	66,288	15,700
			86	478	4,410	6,152	1,742
	A W		82	55	825	1,061	236
			83	438	5,250	5,543	293
			84	1,347	31,890	33,521	1,631
			85	486	24,910	26,172	1,262
			86	38	2,800	2,926	126
	N E		86	*	2,500	2,906	406
	N H		83	4,786	13,822	20,744	6,922
	V W		81	5,080	6,800	7,755	955
DENMARK	A E		82	268	2,759	3,012	253
			83	809	4,215	4,557	342
			84	228	2,350	2,623	273
			85	1,400	12,422	13,533	1,111
	O E		81	39	548	640	92
DOM REP	V E		82	351	350	486	136
FR GERM	A E		81	1,061	31,776	32,461	685
			82	5,540	32,442	36,259	3,817
			83	866	9,668	10,137	469
			84	264	2,913	3,317	404
			85	16,019	26,541	36,507	9,966
			86	79	4,904	5,180	276
	A H		83	41	737	800	63
	A W		81	1,030	18,633	19,787	1,154
			83	136	6,667	6,908	241
			84	5,625	59,137	65,077	5,940
			85	6,947	69,192	73,846	4,654
			86	5,445	88,627	94,190	5,563
	N E		81	65,216	178,516	189,403	10,887
			82	107,474	101,405	116,713	15,308
			83	40,745	82,719	87,178	4,459
			84	65,949	87,285	93,646	6,361
			85	43,982	58,638	63,236	4,598
			86	81,259	119,258	124,272	5,014
	N H		84	132	4,569	5,054	485
	N W		81	10,212	50,990	53,742	2,752
			82	1,845	11,059	11,627	568
			84	593	7,205	7,738	533
	O E		81	6	2,106	2,132	26
	O W		81	40	649	680	31
			82	5	1,475	1,475	
FRANCE	A E		81	3,034	29,252	31,600	2,348
			82	550	10,708	11,028	320
			83	793	16,805	17,543	738
			84	494	10,078	10,658	580
			85	305	4,804	5,038	234
	A W		81	1,691	9,993	12,269	2,276
			82	2,202	15,832	16,763	931
			83	348	4,508	4,905	397
			84	278	4,430	4,989	559
			85	821	11,149	12,780	1,631
			86	220	4,233	4,438	205
GUATMAL	A E		81	1,722	49,675	50,334	659
			82	1,340	31,538	32,796	1,258
			83	7,022	156,682	159,823	3,141
			84	2,474	49,880	50,855	975
			85	64	2,870	2,970	100
			86	10,987	235,340	241,623	6,283

Product
TSUSA commodity number, description, and unit of quantity

Country	Mode	Reg	Yr	Quantity	F.A.S.	C.I.F.	Charges
	N E		85	10,205	191,080	194,364	3,284
HAITI	A E		81	2	500	590	90
			84	4,566	26,724	27,902	1,178
			85	1,642	8,602	9,248	646
HG KONG	A W		86	1,100	1,921	3,580	1,659
HONDURA	A E		81	1,233	43,616	44,231	615
			82	1,060	53,792	54,310	518
			84	866	36,360	36,770	410
HUNGARY	A E		84	117	1,460	1,557	97
	A W		83	1,464	5,761	6,876	1,115
			84	290	879	1,120	241
			86	469	6,129	6,571	442
	O W		85	547	3,844	4,239	395
	V W		81	1,693	4,248	4,412	164
INDIA	A E		81	661	2,735	4,698	1,963
			83	231	1,290	1,988	698
			84	521	3,718	4,953	1,235
	A W		82	140	330	926	596
			84	125	425	775	350
	N E		81	1,457	3,537	5,197	1,660
			83	1,352	3,339	4,114	775
			84	653	2,068	3,007	939
			86	1,805	2,643	3,956	1,313
	V E		82	1,653	1,705	2,092	387
			85	1,035	1,995	2,193	198
	V W		82	2,205	4,750	5,700	950
			84	1,565	3,190	3,355	165
ISRAEL	A E		81	88	2,180	2,540	360
	A H		83	66	1,571	1,955	384
	A W		82	415	2,004	2,990	986
	N W		85	287	5,105	5,437	332
	O E		84	3	600	629	29
	V W		81	110	600	736	136
			83	132	1,560	1,721	161
ITALY	A E		81	414	3,301	3,814	513
			82	3,202	25,041	28,124	3,083
			83	162	746	839	93
			84	4,249	10,902	14,036	3,134
			85	1,286	8,181	9,390	1,209
			86	2,683	19,984	23,855	3,871
	A W		81	825	9,280	10,725	1,445
			82	100	1,273	1,594	321
			83	210	3,148	3,898	750
			84	854	4,332	5,673	1,341
			85	390	3,334	4,020	686
	N E		81	5,766	32,089	36,495	4,406
			83	3,675	23,709	26,368	2,659
	N W		83	6,525	11,780	13,715	1,935
	O W		81	25	450	520	70
	V E		82	568	3,098	3,348	250
	V W		81	8,000	11,820	13,264	1,444
			82	6,000	8,160	9,281	1,121
			84	2,500	4,158	4,539	381
			85	6,961	13,995	15,540	1,545
			86	5,497	10,590	11,075	485
JAMAICA	V E		81	150,476	56,628	63,653	7,025
			82	4,288	2,240	3,425	1,185
JAPAN	A E		81	512	8,634	10,670	2,036
			83	550	9,737	11,542	1,805
			84	1,455	28,127	32,829	4,702
			85	2,504	54,185	61,044	6,859
			86	1,161	13,083	15,547	2,464
	A W		81	107	3,528	4,023	495
			82	460	9,293	11,031	1,738
			83	304	7,887	9,051	1,164
			84	88	4,641	5,004	363
			85	45	1,361	1,510	149
			86	33	1,387	1,551	164
	N E		81	1,853	28,485	33,229	4,744
			82	1,966	23,382	27,983	4,601
			83	2,724	44,193	49,856	5,663
	N W		81	15,958	18,032	20,232	2,200
			82	26,890	32,278	39,993	7,715
			83	27,793	28,345	32,381	4,036
			84	25,525	24,877	30,754	5,877
			86	41,233	130,265	135,129	4,864
	O E		81	224	4,603	5,484	881
			82	280	5,205	5,719	514
			83	3	1,308	1,335	27
	O W		82	40	485	572	87
	V E		82	1,055	22,527	23,143	616
	V H		81	3,956	3,474	3,956	482
			82	2,134	1,709	1,895	186
			83	3,241	2,499	2,771	272
			84	1,433	1,395	1,650	255

Product TSUSA commodity number, description, and unit of quantity Country	Mode	Reg	Yr	Quantity	F.A.S.	C.I.F.	Charges
			85	50,105	55,660	63,315	7,655
	V	W	81	1,411	32,466	32,926	460
			82	500	10,822	11,000	178
			83	326	6,000	6,113	113
			84	4,528	12,647	13,294	647
			85	41,876	46,376	51,784	5,408
			86	200	4,286	4,400	114
KENYA	A	W	82	9	5,430	5,567	137
KOR REP	A	E	84	93	2,501	2,851	350
			85	1,567	11,261	13,988	2,727
			86	675	8,379	9,287	908
	A	W	85	232	4,781	5,482	701
			86	50	1,429	1,651	222
	N	E	83	560	10,391	11,178	787
	V	E	81	738	9,284	9,449	165
	V	W	82	509	8,832	9,144	312
LEBANON	V	E	86	2,001	1,391	1,531	140
MADAGAS	A	E	86	30,393	106,087	144,118	38,031
	A	W	83	1,210	1,100	1,392	292
			84	1,710	6,190	7,420	1,230
			85	395	4,000	4,160	160
MEXICO	A	W	81	99	1,000	1,089	89
			82	88	856	995	139
			84	1,527	5,497	6,533	1,036
	N	H	82	1,030	7,233	8,835	1,602
	O	E	81	104,804	160,073	159,873	
			82	102,104	92,364	92,364	
			83	82,832	81,222	81,222	
			84	122,013	221,229	221,369	140
			85	151,741	288,365	288,365	
			86	142,881	212,348	212,348	
	O	H	83	10,100	64,000	75,574	11,574
	O	W	81	16,694	33,103	33,103	
			82	1,047	3,394	3,394	
			83	8,850	3,876	3,876	
			84	8,175	16,965	16,965	
			85	11,605	17,715	17,715	
			86	15,299	14,464	14,464	
N ZEAL	A	H	81	52	2,507	2,677	170
			82	55	4,214	4,419	205
			83	998	17,278	18,647	1,369
			85	1,332	31,467	32,865	1,398
			86	494	9,431	10,279	848
	A	W	81	146	1,568	1,891	323
			82	13	505	544	39
			84	220	2,375	3,339	964
			85	245	4,387	4,759	372
			86	24	1,595	1,691	96
	N	E	81	500	4,550	5,133	583
	N	H	84	1,999	26,353	27,322	969
NETHLDS	A	E	83	33	300	413	113
			86	228	6,659	7,227	568
	A	H	83	69	861	1,200	339
			85	238	4,400	4,674	274
	A	W	82	489	5,365	6,279	914
			83	1,112	22,306	23,694	1,388
			84	3,183	15,273	18,103	2,830
			85	13,229	25,616	35,567	9,951
	O	E	82	275	898	898	
			85	3	1,687	1,717	30
	V	E	85	79,497	54,919	60,166	5,247
	V	W	86	2,000	4,060	4,600	540
NICARAG	A	E	82	1,500	30,000	30,879	879
PAKISTN	A	E	81	66	900	1,223	323
			86	110	1,913	2,186	273
	O	E	84	353	953	1,035	82
PERU	V	E	81	11,111	878	1,512	634
PHIL R	V	W	82	975	798	855	57
POLAND	A	E	81	149	6,744	7,226	482
PORTUGL	V	E	81	485	374	457	83
REP SAF	A	E	81	661	11,550	13,477	1,927
			84	14,866	158,377	167,423	9,046
	A	W	81	1,199	876	1,352	476
			82	243	2,533	3,225	692
			83	4,577	56,818	60,980	4,162
			84	683	1,916	2,395	479
			85	12,015	70,310	78,312	8,002
			86	2,315	20,394	23,544	3,150
SEYCHEL	A	W	81	212	1,169	1,469	300
SINGAPR	A	H	81	91	4,132	4,445	313
			82	106	3,664	4,111	447
			83	42	619	814	195
			84	53	3,645	3,841	196
	A	W	84	375	6,184	7,178	994
			86	900	2,450	4,440	1,990
SPAIN	A	E	81	198	2,988	3,334	346
			82	737	8,340	8,810	470
			83	533	10,285	11,245	960
			84	323	5,955	6,361	406
			85	299	4,968	5,385	417
			86	243	4,226	4,335	109
	A	W	82	845	1,782	2,754	972
			83	220	3,970	4,259	289
			84	443	4,729	5,582	853
			85	308	5,955	6,692	737
	N	E	81	1,254	15,442	16,546	1,104
	N	W	83	1,351	1,984	2,422	438
	O	E	81	2,940	9,906	9,906	
			82	3,069	11,939	11,939	
			83	330	1,738	1,738	
	V	E	81	3,307	5,100	5,567	467
	V	W	81	683	6,659	6,784	125
			82	518	2,244	2,385	141
			85	4,322	6,600	7,004	404
			86	3,804	6,825	7,693	868
SWITZLD	A	E	86	792	3,907	4,669	762
THAILND	A	H	84	35	1,501	1,600	99
			85	265	2,400	2,906	506
	A	W	83	37	802	964	162
TURKEY	A	E	82	59	630	1,051	421
			84	392	4,960	5,476	516
			85	270	2,766	3,066	300
	A	W	81	46	400	591	191
			83	30	1,052	1,105	53
			85	120	2,999	3,218	219
			86	67	1,106	1,324	218
	O	E	82	220	890	890	
U KING	A	E	85	842	43,776	44,899	1,123
			86	239	16,806	17,195	389
	A	W	82	75	4,142	4,492	350
			85	536	4,215	4,479	264
	N	E	82	215	5,197	5,482	285
			83	471	3,727	4,557	830
			84	23	2,005	2,266	261
	O	E	84	75	2,300	2,413	113
	V	E	81	456	4,735	4,982	247
USSR	A	E	82	552	5,928	6,349	421
			83	1,352	19,443	20,532	1,089
			86	110	1,161	1,500	339
	A	W	84	765	17,145	17,828	683
			85	364	3,355	3,590	235
	N	E	82	1,541	4,939	5,642	703
	N	W	82	397	5,738	6,054	316
	V	E	81	2,170	14,470	15,179	709
YUGOSLV	A	E	83	176	1,670	1,898	228
			84	596	7,987	8,290	303
	A	W	83	278	3,530	3,774	244
			84	1,340	10,325	11,337	1,012
			85	2,875	17,750	18,100	350
			86	4,374	33,148	36,693	3,545
ZMBABWE	A	E	81	93	2,931	3,077	146
			82	55	625	750	125
	A	W	85	551	5,183	5,551	368

Spice and Flavoring

Curry, spice
1612900 CURRY AND CURRY POWDER (LB)

Country	Mode	Reg	Yr	Quantity	F.A.S.	C.I.F.	Charges
TOTAL			81	487,207	748,691	834,023	85,332
			82	612,437	976,912	1,084,967	108,055
			83	863,621	1,306,137	1,423,437	117,300
			84	676,251	1,042,897	1,155,471	112,574
			85	609,052	737,452	821,093	83,641
			86	610,623	836,069	910,259	74,190
AUSTRAL	V	E	81	120	1,455	1,565	110
BELGIUM	V	E	83	390	871	1,285	414
	V	W	85	938	1,184	1,339	155
CANADA	O	E	81	1,269	2,058	2,058	
			83	8,414	11,225	11,225	

Product
TSUSA commodity number, description, and unit of quantity

Country	Mode	Reg	Yr	Quantity	F.A.S.	C.I.F.	Charges
			84	5,533	10,347	10,347	
			85	6,070	9,269	9,269	
			86	9,138	21,183	21,183	
	O	W	81	248	373	373	
CHINA M	V	E	82	1,500	2,232	2,408	176
			83	3,750	5,618	6,030	412
	V	W	81	1,360	1,519	1,630	111
			82	983	1,585	1,802	217
			83	2,026	2,674	2,883	209
			84	2,120	1,959	2,089	130
			85	1,611	2,521	2,664	143
			86	2,520	4,626	4,777	151
CHINA T	V	E	82	750	1,688	1,770	82
	V	W	81	356	1,936	2,005	69
			82	1,556	1,599	1,725	126
			83	1,418	1,035	1,114	79
			84	7,183	10,846	11,692	846
			86	1,645	3,413	3,528	115
COLOMB	A	E	83	335	317	535	218
DOM REP	A	E	81	2,500	332	429	97
			84	1,000	3,163	3,367	204
	V	E	86	1,345	2,667	2,755	88
F W IND	A	E	81	188	371	570	199
FIJI	A	H	84	505	1,916	2,356	440
	V	W	81	318	1,155	1,250	95
FR GERM	N	E	82	5,216	3,537	4,043	506
	O	E	81	3,346	1,873	2,015	142
			83	6,358	3,052	3,290	238
	V	E	81	1,208	12,369	12,998	629
			82	7,369	53,371	54,793	1,422
			83	12,130	44,361	45,493	1,132
			84	2,559	4,661	5,072	411
			85	306	1,308	1,410	102
			86	12,046	20,498	22,380	1,882
	V	W	84	200	360	377	17
FRANCE	V	E	83	84	323	340	17
GUYANA	N	E	82	64,070	95,785	106,314	10,529
			83	22,955	39,177	42,312	3,135
	O	E	83	930	1,686	1,686	
			84	1,156	2,781	2,781	
	V	E	81	27,463	19,420	21,221	1,801
			84	26,250	54,965	59,849	4,884
			85	3,000	9,030	9,592	562
HG KONG	V	E	81	500	598	663	65
			84	540	581	633	52
			86	599	1,119	1,168	49
	V	H	81	315	816	869	53
	V	W	81	1,560	4,501	4,733	232
			82	2,939	5,074	5,367	293
			83	960	885	958	73
			84	5,169	4,633	4,963	330
			85	2,989	4,425	4,739	314
INDIA	N	E	81	49,535	45,070	55,506	10,436
			82	65,899	66,968	81,035	14,067
			83	104,854	84,235	105,789	21,554
			84	116,926	122,007	145,947	23,940
			85	159,552	116,394	141,594	25,200
			86	90,941	77,349	87,512	10,163
	N	W	84	9,881	8,417	9,287	870
	O	E	81	1,224	6,884	7,008	124
			83	16,009	27,750	28,118	368
			84	17,764	19,137	20,457	1,320
			85	6,226	5,157	5,459	302
			86	39,588	21,609	22,835	1,226
	O	W	86	536	1,741	1,938	197
	V	E	81	8,623	9,154	11,716	2,562
			82	17,745	25,689	30,449	4,760
			83	48,233	47,602	57,465	9,863
			84	10,907	6,574	7,782	1,208
			85	18,914	16,398	20,022	3,624
			86	13,278	17,022	21,824	4,802
	V	W	81	90,641	70,851	84,130	13,279
			82	33,837	38,648	46,664	8,016
			83	41,270	32,004	37,409	5,405
			84	27,131	43,111	49,355	6,244
			85	23,334	30,680	35,474	4,794
			86	95,850	84,908	96,559	11,651
INDNSIA	V	W	84	145	293	376	83
ITALY	V	E	85	2,713	4,846	5,188	342
JAMAICA	A	E	81	1,263	4,315	4,640	325
			83	40	1,800	2,000	200
			84	100	311	371	60
	V	E	83	1,980	8,642	9,292	650
JAPAN	N	W	86	50,364	94,693	102,620	7,927
	O	E	84	2,403	3,234	3,234	

Product
TSUSA commodity number, description, and unit of quantity

Country	Mode	Reg	Yr	Quantity	F.A.S.	C.I.F.	Charges
	V	E	81	10,022	29,036	31,436	2,400
			82	36,707	67,942	75,226	7,284
			83	30,029	60,011	65,720	5,709
			84	57,207	105,163	115,463	10,300
			85	54,630	101,198	110,947	9,749
			86	75,296	156,618	167,197	10,579
	V	H	81	49,786	97,774	111,242	13,468
			82	68,936	128,237	146,203	17,966
			83	76,656	132,724	149,434	16,710
			84	54,729	114,397	130,469	16,072
			85	4,986	6,488	7,487	999
			86	7,323	15,583	17,381	1,798
	V	W	81	67,281	138,677	146,620	7,943
			82	115,803	212,633	225,808	13,175
			83	334,857	558,689	589,239	30,550
			84	108,230	205,134	217,782	12,648
			85	118,252	184,719	198,423	13,704
			86	32,343	75,911	80,843	4,932
KENYA	O	E	82	5,400	791	878	87
KOR REP	V	E	81	2,528	4,483	4,964	481
			82	6,438	8,642	9,428	786
			83	4,857	8,120	8,414	294
			84	440	735	811	76
			85	2,200	4,514	4,956	442
			86	3,279	5,139	5,526	387
	V	H	82	440	824	949	125
			83	992	1,183	1,309	126
	V	W	81	10,176	17,860	18,870	1,010
			82	12,731	20,221	21,360	1,139
			83	23,630	32,508	34,544	2,036
			84	10,408	15,031	16,508	1,477
			85	8,541	14,867	15,826	959
			86	16,741	27,575	29,496	1,921
MALAYSA	O	E	84	614	1,355	1,355	
	V	E	81	2,040	2,452	2,797	345
			82	9,743	11,168	12,033	865
			83	4,948	6,950	7,374	424
			84	2,160	2,350	2,701	351
			85	3,320	3,957	4,562	605
			86	4,800	5,309	5,640	331
	V	W	81	5,808	6,152	6,928	776
			82	14,361	15,980	17,629	1,649
			83	2,520	2,600	3,540	940
			84	6,432	8,019	8,848	829
			85	9,440	12,688	13,724	1,036
			86	11,904	14,184	15,164	980
MOROC	V	E	85	6,008	2,189	2,610	421
NETHLDS	V	E	82	5,610	4,901	5,405	504
PAKISTN	O	E	83	794	1,806	1,965	159
			84	5,330	936	1,030	94
	V	E	85	1,587	1,653	1,890	237
			86	476	1,420	1,665	245
	V	W	85	2,518	3,587	4,086	499
PHIL R	V	E	84	180	611	671	60
REP SAF	V	E	85	870	1,320	1,370	50
ROMANIA	V	W	84	1,285	1,012	1,106	94
S LUCIA	V	E	82	1,676	2,018	2,138	120
			83	545	1,421	1,741	320
			84	230	815	905	90
SALVADR	V	E	83	2,400	4,080	4,608	528
SINGAPR	N	W	81	1,425	1,219	1,262	43
	V	E	81	877	5,380	6,141	761
			82	2,331	7,178	7,959	781
			83	288	1,011	1,160	149
			84	7,613	9,295	10,284	989
			85	959	1,209	1,563	354
			86	386	2,293	2,332	39
	V	H	81	67	263	300	37
			82	1,549	2,088	2,328	240
	V	W	81	38,998	74,776	82,147	7,371
			82	13,267	15,436	16,642	1,206
			83	3,010	4,860	5,378	518
			84	22,007	27,845	30,798	2,953
			85	7,376	13,770	15,912	2,142
			86	28,328	27,480	31,091	3,611
SYRIA	V	E	81	500	765	850	85
THAILND	N	H	84	5,033	6,032	6,755	723
	O	E	84	600	800	800	
	O	W	86	450	1,203	1,317	114
	V	E	81	19,614	25,310	28,231	2,921
			82	9,882	24,707	27,444	2,737
			83	27,018	54,787	58,447	3,660
			84	27,365	41,147	44,351	3,204
			85	21,554	23,182	25,493	2,311
			86	11,237	17,475	19,026	1,551

Product TSUSA commodity number, description, and unit of quantity Country	Mode	Reg	Yr	Quantity	F.A.S.	C.I.F.	Charges
	V	H	81	1,459	3,281	3,654	373
			82	3,921	6,323	7,265	942
			83	1,967	4,830	5,527	697
			85	2,403	2,701	3,072	371
	V	W	81	63,623	105,087	114,443	9,356
			82	62,794	90,157	99,675	9,518
			83	55,151	77,917	83,769	5,852
			84	79,908	119,333	127,786	8,453
			85	50,304	63,594	69,093	5,499
			86	60,426	68,755	73,846	5,091
TRINID	A	E	81	3,513	14,231	17,839	3,608
			82	12,782	19,591	23,632	4,041
			83	5,601	11,654	13,724	2,070
			84	1,541	3,476	4,670	1,194
			86	3,120	7,890	8,451	561
	N	E	84	16,718	46,451	54,704	8,253
	O	E	84	204	345	345	
	V	E	84	794	1,961	2,076	115
			85	33,049	47,283	50,729	3,446
			86	977	2,692	3,086	394
TURKEY	O	E	82	265	751	838	87
	V	E	84	970	2,511	3,092	581
			86	19,851	30,375	31,409	1,034
U KING	A	E	83	22	288	317	29
	N	E	81	6,377	12,894	14,088	1,194
			82	19,478	24,671	27,149	2,478
			83	12,649	19,275	21,162	1,887
			84	14,789	13,884	15,402	1,518
	O	E	81	8,385	14,480	15,831	1,351
			82	2,948	8,035	9,408	1,373
			83	1,059	2,269	2,465	196
			84	7,359	5,638	6,228	590
			85	672	1,190	1,283	93
	V	E	81	905	2,653	2,989	336
			82	1,633	4,713	5,120	407
			83	2,128	3,608	3,893	285
			84	4,867	6,201	6,705	504
			85	450	1,037	1,206	169
			86	15,003	22,868	25,055	2,187
	V	W	81	1,786	6,868	8,012	1,144
			82	1,878	3,729	4,080	351
			83	364	2,289	2,483	194
			84	1,766	3,124	3,491	367
			85	54,280	45,094	50,111	5,017
			86	833	2,471	2,655	184

Flavoring extracts

4501000 FLAV EXT ETC NO ALCO, PILLS (NULL)

Country	Mode	Reg	Yr	Quantity	F.A.S.	C.I.F.	Charges
TOTAL			81	-	44,532	50,061	5,529
			82	-	66,430	68,348	1,918
			83	-	361,210	382,103	20,893
			84	-	55,733	64,525	8,792
			85	-	124,164	137,770	13,606
			86	-	346,558	371,404	24,846
ARGENT	N	E	84	-	3,177	3,591	414
			86	-	6,300	7,148	848
AUSTRAL	N	E	85	-	2,543	2,899	356
AUSTRIA	N	E	82	-	532	645	113
			85	-	2,583	3,019	436
			86	-	5,465	6,204	739
	N	W	84	-	3,767	4,258	491
BARBADO	N	E	83	-	2,134	2,293	159
CANADA	N	E	81	-	2,962	2,962	
			83	-	16,659	16,659	
			84	-	15,361	15,763	402
			85	-	13,950	14,960	1,010
	N	W	86	-	1,318	1,393	75
DOM REP	N	E	84	-	2,258	4,287	2,029
			85	-	1,267	1,395	128
FR GERM	N	E	81	-	13,474	15,661	2,187
			82	-	2,288	2,446	158
			83	-	134,270	139,238	4,968
			84	-	6,036	6,315	279
			85	-	5,559	6,493	934
			86	-	21,294	22,867	1,573
	N	W	83	-	156,454	167,001	10,547
			85	-	26,794	29,886	3,092
			86	-	4,392	7,009	2,617
FRANCE	N	E	81	-	681	767	86
			84	-	1,320	1,467	147
			85	-	14,032	15,729	1,697
			86	-	2,549	2,556	7

Product TSUSA commodity number, description, and unit of quantity Country	Mode	Reg	Yr	Quantity	F.A.S.	C.I.F.	Charges
	N	W	81	-	272	289	17
			83	-	256	283	27
			85	-	6,806	7,527	721
GUYANA	N	E	83	-	667	1,037	370
HAITI	N	E	86	-	3,015	3,793	778
HG KONG	N	W	84	-	1,358	1,465	107
HONDURA	N	E	81	-	25,679	28,725	3,046
			85	-	1,503	1,528	25
INDIA	N	E	83	-	463	528	65
ITALY	N	E	83	-	15,058	15,660	602
			84	-	750	1,330	580
			85	-	7,332	10,361	3,029
			86	-	7,195	8,454	1,259
	N	W	81	-	517	610	93
JAMAICA	N	E	83	-	328	354	26
			86	-	10,475	11,345	870
JAPAN	N	E	84	-	9,737	11,592	1,855
	N	W	82	-	730	780	50
			83	-	8,218	9,101	883
			84	-	701	766	65
			86	-	25,409	27,348	1,939
MAURIT	N	W	86	-	6,138	10,200	4,062
NETHLDS	N	E	83	-	1,073	1,152	79
			85	-	13,580	14,027	447
			86	-	1,013	2,647	1,634
	N	W	84	-	2,418	3,450	1,032
			86	-	1,180	1,323	143
PHIL R	N	W	83	-	600	600	
SINGAPR	N	E	82	-	50,000	51,270	1,270
SPAIN	N	E	84	-	500	571	71
SWITZLD	N	E	82	-	450	499	49
			84	-	4,450	5,514	1,064
			86	-	4,839	5,852	1,013
THAILND	N	E	82	-	999	1,086	87
	N	W	81	-	947	1,047	100
			82	-	8,290	8,441	151
			84	-	3,900	4,156	256
			85	-	2,859	3,329	470
U KING	N	E	82	-	3,141	3,181	40
			83	-	21,507	24,547	3,040
			85	-	25,356	26,617	1,261
			86	-	245,976	253,265	7,289
VENEZ	N	E	83	-	3,523	3,650	127

4502025 SPICE OLEORESINS NSPF (LB)

Country	Mode	Reg	Yr	Quantity	F.A.S.	C.I.F.	Charges
TOTAL			81	173,995	1,664,553	1,699,664	35,121
			82	215,314	1,722,622	1,764,839	42,217
			83	207,249	1,857,782	1,948,151	90,369
			84	195,895	1,786,136	1,846,644	60,508
			85	325,682	2,685,203	2,741,200	55,997
			86	359,893	2,866,728	2,935,863	69,135
ARGENT	V	W	82	1,200	1,428	1,699	271
BELGIUM	A	E	86	110	2,627	2,732	105
CANADA	A	E	81	10	262	290	28
			83	449	5,126	5,345	219
			86	1,106	23,280	25,515	2,235
	A	W	84	434	280	325	45
	O	E	81	36,538	309,042	309,042	
			82	27,507	268,312	268,312	
			83	28,931	237,118	237,118	
			84	25,699	256,557	256,609	52
			85	30,542	279,694	279,694	
			86	44,154	278,555	279,374	819
	O	W	83	850	14,290	14,290	
CHINA M	V	E	86	220	2,548	2,613	65
CHINA T	V	W	81	308	1,464	1,549	95
			82	441	750	864	114
DENMARK	V	E	82	4,166	2,675	2,921	246
DOM REP	V	E	83	541	900	1,007	107
EGYPT	A	E	82	2	2,059	2,100	41
ETHIOP	A	E	83	41,844	454,408	505,006	50,598
			84	24,170	239,876	264,949	25,073
	V	E	81	42,131	567,302	577,558	10,256
			82	39,021	536,517	544,690	8,173
FR GERM	A	E	81	132	533	661	128
			82	17	443	474	31
			83	10	731	803	72
			84	440	1,092	1,283	191
	N	W	85	4,375	13,691	15,028	1,337
	O	E	82	908	537	640	103
			84	15	484	609	125
			86	338	1,313	2,134	821
	O	W	86	18	4,168	4,641	473
	V	E	81	4,674	2,988	3,652	664

Product
TSUSA commodity number, description, and unit of quantity

Country	Mode	Reg	Yr	Quantity	F.A.S.	C.I.F.	Charges
			83	12,152	6,905	8,237	1,332
FRANCE	A	E	82	220	4,514	4,548	34
			86	366	27,622	28,046	424
	N	E	81	698	4,861	5,361	500
			84	2,714	19,268	19,639	371
			85	147	3,206	3,240	34
	V	E	86	152	8,736	8,772	36
	V	W	83	600	1,932	2,016	84
HG KONG	V	W	81	9,127	45,705	46,374	669
			86	882	4,200	4,247	47
INDIA	A	E	81	220	5,070	5,818	748
			82	590	9,188	10,224	1,036
			83	1,062	17,933	20,794	2,861
			84	441	15,000	15,649	649
			86	291	2,587	3,139	552
	N	E	81	21,927	243,500	252,549	9,049
			82	45,634	429,265	444,879	15,614
			83	73,049	618,832	636,971	18,139
			84	55,206	730,056	752,273	22,217
			85	71,069	836,461	854,712	18,251
			86	105,831	901,353	929,455	28,102
	O	E	83	1,352	40,657	40,657	
			84	3,144	22,728	22,728	
			85	6,720	2,055	2,055	
	V	E	81	3,385	59,224	61,400	2,176
			83	8,066	123,928	127,088	3,160
			84	2,817	34,745	35,330	585
			85	2,799	22,492	24,978	2,486
			86	17,671	211,908	217,580	5,672
	V	W	82	2,260	45,167	46,016	849
			83	4,447	19,549	20,432	883
			84	2,210	12,187	12,591	404
			85	2,997	33,796	34,525	729
			86	18,131	122,604	127,938	5,334
INDNSIA	V	E	83	2,205	33,828	35,175	1,347
			84	2,205	33,839	35,175	1,336
			85	1,378	42,923	43,341	418
ITALY	A	E	85	5,780	10,451	15,604	5,153
			86	132	1,560	2,025	465
	A	W	85	220	1,800	1,827	27
JAMAICA	V	E	84	7,050	9,665	9,956	291
			85	120	1,081	1,331	250
JAPAN	A	E	81	683	11,034	13,775	2,741
			83	113	2,425	2,909	484
			86	397	12,420	14,028	1,608
	A	W	85	110	3,235	3,551	316
			86	22	3,000	3,199	199
	N	E	82	1,430	30,256	34,725	4,469
	V	E	85	794	23,046	23,364	318
			86	397	11,577	11,700	123
	V	W	81	79	805	882	77
			85	28,828	79,662	82,835	3,173
			86	397	11,534	13,165	1,631
LEBANON	V	E	84	2,116	1,620	1,850	230
			85	1,905	2,898	3,169	271
N ZEAL	V	E	81	1,402	771	924	153
	V	W	82	32,704	23,325	26,925	3,600
NETHLDS	A	E	82	1	326	384	58
			83	132	564	642	78
	V	E	84	4,409	2,930	3,130	200
NIGERIA	A	E	85	132	1,860	2,033	173
PHIL R	V	W	81	500	450	504	54
			83	1,380	1,877	2,117	240
REP SAF	N	E	86	*	2,369	2,676	307
SINGAPR	V	E	81	16,925	110,260	112,520	2,260
			82	58,685	348,802	355,750	6,948
			83	26,599	254,341	264,595	10,254
			84	52,863	381,918	389,576	7,658
			85	126,759	1,254,277	1,274,968	20,691
			86	134,274	1,153,385	1,170,260	16,875
	V	W	81	34,462	274,878	279,316	4,438
SPAIN	V	E	83	661	4,481	4,615	134
			86	2,204	16,463	16,870	407
	V	W	84	9,920	23,160	24,183	1,023
			85	40,787	64,851	67,002	2,151
			86	30,865	26,186	27,830	1,644
SWEDEN	V	E	86	1,212	17,366	17,874	508
SWITZLD	A	E	86	250	2,828	3,026	198
THAILND	V	W	81	123	402	433	31
			82	32	355	390	35
			83	2,425	1,127	1,217	90
U KING	A	E	81	671	26,002	27,056	1,054
			82	496	18,703	19,298	595
			83	381	16,830	17,117	287
			84	42	731	789	58

Product
TSUSA commodity number, description, and unit of quantity

Country	Mode	Reg	Yr	Quantity	F.A.S.	C.I.F.	Charges
			86	253	5,155	5,342	187
	V	E	85	220	7,724	7,943	219
			86	220	11,384	11,682	298

4502040 OTH FLAV EXTR NO ALCO ETC (LB)

Country	Mode	Reg	Yr	Quantity	F.A.S.	C.I.F.	Charges
TOTAL			81	2,819,098	9,875,603	10,359,256	483,259
			82	3,544,416	10,618,793	11,132,777	513,984
			83	4,161,721	14,771,134	15,368,316	597,182
			84	7,706,164	21,093,781	22,202,961	1,109,180
			85	8,254,007	19,674,451	21,011,685	1,337,234
			86	8,595,337	23,570,920	25,003,090	1,432,170
ARGENT	A	E	84	116	550	748	198
	N	E	84	62,948	49,382	59,109	9,727
	O	E	81	279,100	76,821	76,821	
			82	421,655	274,701	274,701	
			83	208,520	130,512	130,512	
			84	4,080	1,993	1,993	
	V	E	81	142,982	74,105	84,126	10,021
			82	47,016	42,555	47,400	4,845
			83	9,045	28,867	29,343	476
			84	26,311	11,591	14,614	3,023
			85	88,661	55,191	62,414	7,223
			86	39,637	21,300	24,671	3,371
	V	W	82	23,512	17,547	19,170	1,623
			84	1,970	607	761	154
			85	246,573	86,287	103,933	17,646
			86	317,784	142,712	168,119	25,407
AUSTRAL	A	E	81	3	305	821	516
			84	71	655	905	250
	A	W	83	7	1,140	1,196	56
			84	7	10,958	11,011	53
			85	4	3,755	3,793	38
	N	W	82	*	374	426	52
	V	E	81	1,951	19,125	19,566	441
			82	332	999	1,038	39
			83	2,537	14,684	15,333	649
			86	1,134	1,620	1,665	45
	V	H	83	392	1,527	1,741	214
	V	W	85	799	7,828	8,407	579
AUSTRIA	A	E	81	159	680	823	143
	O	E	82	54,388	39,117	41,377	2,260
			83	35,965	23,319	23,319	
			84	35,979	18,364	21,544	3,180
			85	1,764	1,208	1,208	
	V	E	81	35,274	18,203	20,072	1,869
			82	198	473	495	22
			83	337,359	175,700	189,525	13,825
			84	701,383	396,554	430,295	33,741
			85	251,642	205,927	220,102	14,175
			86	50,848	27,204	29,791	2,587
	V	W	82	2,205	7,567	8,003	436
			83	88,335	64,779	70,288	5,509
			84	421,664	200,081	227,877	27,796
			85	560,120	222,182	260,379	38,197
BARBADO	V	E	82	20,375	26,642	30,111	3,469
			83	5,400	7,272	7,743	471
			85	7,350	8,530	9,235	705
			86	8,101	9,974	12,248	2,274
BELGIUM	A	E	81	673	3,083	3,319	236
			82	100	2,565	2,689	124
			83	1,816	10,630	11,271	641
			84	445	9,204	9,686	482
			85	2,340	37,081	38,854	1,773
			86	2,635	17,931	19,669	1,738
	N	E	81	3,080	19,616	21,107	1,491
			82	701	4,169	4,410	241
			83	2,393	14,822	15,764	942
	V	E	84	1,149	2,666	2,733	67
	V	W	84	1,921	5,230	5,874	644
			86	38,708	21,262	23,472	2,210
BELIZE	V	E	85	11,598	8,338	9,015	677
			86	5,038	1,504	1,697	193
BRAZIL	A	E	81	66	770	985	215
			82	55	3,750	3,997	.247
			86	2	1,685	1,735	50
	A	W	82	132	9,000	9,508	508
			83	55	3,750	4,005	255
			85	110	3,500	3,647	147
	N	E	82	80,008	109,066	119,801	10,735
			83	45,032	137,611	145,839	8,228
			84	20,367	53,486	59,078	5,592
			85	526,776	471,311	515,661	44,350
			86	1,080,988	496,352	568,650	72,298
	O	E	84	11,000	5,867	5,867	

Product TSUSA commodity number, description, and unit of quantity Country	Mode	Reg	Yr	Quantity	F.A.S.	C.I.F.	Charges
			86	179,738	82,019	91,198	9,179
	V	E	81	157,463	143,138	183,214	40,076
			82	673,547	160,657	203,282	42,625
			83	397,015	127,337	150,733	23,396
			84	1,379,254	534,820	622,273	87,453
			85	1,409,113	816,598	920,752	104,154
			86	1,987,909	1,089,145	1,203,370	114,225
	V	W	86	286	3,474	3,474	
BULGAR	A	E	82	3,031	20,905	25,500	4,595
			83	1,984	13,545	15,276	1,731
C RICA	V	E	85	39,683	19,800	21,317	1,517
CANADA	A	E	81	46	400	400	
			83	978	2,585	3,414	829
	A	H	84	1,368	1,459	2,923	1,464
	A	W	82	145	1,494	1,594	100
			84	3,582	38,247	39,899	1,652
			85	1,175	25,148	26,144	996
	N	E	84	103	3,180	3,327	147
			86	5,181	14,533	15,771	1,238
	N	W	81	169	673	704	31
			83	1,489	9,181	9,871	690
	O	E	81	150,431	156,250	156,250	
			82	75,200	136,005	137,430	1,425
			83	314,120	305,567	305,684	117
			84	309,940	286,000	286,621	621
			85	457,143	306,991	307,103	112
			86	604,069	384,854	385,906	1,052
	O	W	81	181	1,083	1,113	30
			82	6,344	6,525	6,525	
			83	8,343	110,898	110,898	
			84	14,075	53,352	53,931	579
			85	28,047	113,412	113,412	
			86	25,315	161,512	161,512	
	V	E	82	7,979	10,977	11,526	549
			85	75,244	6,085	6,510	425
			86	39,900	18,993	22,708	3,715
CHILE	V	E	81	5,767	2,766	3,226	460
			82	56,737	36,123	38,678	2,555
			83	14,137	8,073	9,386	1,313
			86	85,521	73,026	77,886	4,860
	V	W	83	536	264	303	39
CHINA M	A	W	84	44	295	438	143
	V	E	85	3,307	22,146	22,742	596
	V	W	82	500	783	920	137
			85	9,484	13,262	14,068	806
CHINA T	V	E	81	3,000	14,256	15,365	1,109
			83	6,911	1,950	2,339	389
	V	W	82	200	3,500	3,937	437
			84	1,535	15,263	17,107	1,844
			85	3,738	6,302	6,928	626
			86	4,598	10,747	11,693	946
COLOMB	A	E	85	2,172	4,012	5,099	1,087
	V	E	82	300	816	876	60
			83	1,082	4,435	4,759	324
			85	485	3,180	3,316	136
DENMARK	A	E	81	1,385	18,670	20,000	1,330
			82	3,710	14,401	19,597	5,196
			83	6,704	32,540	39,822	7,282
			84	91,562	109,487	125,285	15,798
			85	385	12,187	13,241	1,054
			86	555	6,911	8,275	1,364
	A	W	81	800	3,849	5,160	1,311
	N	E	81	854	6,763	7,183	420
			85	33,853	20,242	21,877	1,635
	N	W	83	9,283	7,072	8,170	1,098
	O	E	81	11,202	147,227	152,118	4,891
			82	10,101	143,174	146,877	3,703
			83	4,102	11,898	12,256	358
	V	E	81	7,444	119,554	122,188	2,634
			82	28,513	287,034	298,099	11,065
			83	34,506	233,865	244,750	10,885
			84	66,506	251,701	261,843	10,142
			85	31,676	135,826	141,653	5,827
	V	W	82	435	501	751	250
			83	450	910	1,247	337
			84	37,335	16,440	19,312	2,872
			85	32,000	11,647	14,040	2,393
DOM REP	A	E	82	1,750	272	764	492
			83	1,305	3,581	3,901	320
	N	E	83	23,293	5,751	8,680	2,929
			84	48,599	20,197	27,308	7,111
			86	38,548	28,091	32,020	3,929
	V	E	82	2,150	543	614	71
			84	12,406	8,549	10,389	1,840
			85	36,368	22,695	25,260	2,565
			86	6,550	5,078	7,350	2,272
DOMINCA	V	E	81	900	8,251	8,548	297
EGYPT	A	E	81	3	3,078	3,171	93
			82	6	4,795	4,923	128
ETHIOP	A	E	84	2,200	20,961	22,000	1,039
			85	6,615	64,813	74,952	10,139
			86	24,251	298,599	323,006	24,407
	V	E	82	14,109	201,118	204,192	3,074
F W IND	N	E	82	39,343	36,198	40,128	3,930
	V	E	85	441	2,424	2,493	69
FIJI	V	W	82	2,205	1,699	1,850	151
FR GERM	A	E	81	5,779	38,386	44,469	6,083
			82	123	2,302	2,561	259
			83	747	16,276	16,965	689
			84	12,507	166,473	177,236	10,763
			85	42,225	154,202	198,448	44,246
			86	14,274	170,915	193,818	22,903
	A	H	85	715	23,462	24,257	795
	A	W	82	900	7,608	8,953	1,345
			83	761	10,234	11,018	784
			84	1,790	16,186	18,136	1,950
			85	3,371	51,712	57,563	5,851
			86	10,818	122,954	138,222	15,268
	N	E	81	38,842	280,359	290,202	9,556
			82	24,968	156,233	161,164	4,931
			83	43,445	275,808	283,919	8,111
			84	211,507	575,599	602,455	26,856
			85	739,969	1,693,177	1,833,255	140,078
			86	226,782	906,455	1,000,337	93,882
	N	W	81	1,779	8,560	10,229	1,669
			82	56,650	184,955	195,686	10,731
			83	61,215	402,855	427,773	24,918
			84	246,393	898,722	951,306	52,584
			85	118,687	380,275	424,838	44,563
			86	63,003	449,087	488,050	38,963
	O	E	81	1,033	733	1,107	374
			82	537	2,239	2,239	
			84	17,109	9,012	9,012	
			85	209	2,615	2,817	202
			86	261	6,721	6,721	
	V	E	81	198,076	912,976	962,575	49,599
			82	225,433	747,929	791,758	43,829
			83	420,120	1,994,345	2,057,816	63,471
			84	1,032,355	2,620,278	2,717,497	97,219
			85	54,956	116,230	120,109	3,879
			86	514,324	1,257,807	1,345,530	87,723
	V	W	81	62	5,439	5,561	122
			83	1,042	691	773	82
			84	18,474	10,396	11,882	1,486
			86	16,279	26,848	30,209	3,361
FR POLY	O	W	83	9	376	380	4
FRANCE	A	E	81	3,646	9,295	12,847	3,552
			82	4,017	14,846	18,220	3,374
			83	4,109	26,689	31,938	5,249
			84	13,211	38,426	46,423	7,997
			85	6,583	127,862	136,810	8,948
			86	3,869	130,851	141,801	10,950
	A	W	82	77	1,054	1,151	97
			83	265	4,183	4,263	80
	N	E	81	109,539	777,183	813,314	35,994
			82	123,816	762,372	801,878	39,506
			83	154,707	754,918	799,254	44,336
			84	257,379	1,053,459	1,160,796	107,337
			85	228,578	1,306,614	1,373,971	67,357
			86	258,505	1,480,578	1,561,977	81,399
	N	W	83	467	10,740	11,908	1,168
	O	E	81	45,450	28,624	30,179	1,555
			82	10,009	33,763	35,000	1,237
			83	1,855	6,467	6,801	334
			84	160	1,300	1,300	
			86	300	2,150	2,150	
	V	E	81	61,478	66,504	79,359	12,855
			82	47,805	27,670	31,307	3,637
			83	21,954	17,175	18,664	1,489
			84	2,062	3,151	3,428	277
			85	12,349	15,194	17,557	2,363
			86	42,203	25,319	30,334	5,015
	V	W	81	54,103	83,547	91,564	8,017
			82	16,882	12,258	13,308	1,050
			83	357	1,539	1,699	160
			84	2,640	5,981	6,639	658
			85	1,850	2,699	2,945	246
			86	5,232	13,327	13,471	144
GREECE	A	E	81	902	68,047	69,712	1,665
			83	4	4,750	4,843	93

Product
TSUSA commodity number, description, and unit of quantity

Country	Mode	Reg	Yr	Quantity	F.A.S.	C.I.F.	Charges
			86	22	2,350	2,468	118
	O	E	83	51	341	394	53
	V	E	84	37,908	41,028	44,125	3,097
			85	80,475	299,207	311,097	11,890
GUATMAL	A	E	84	788	334	739	405
	A	W	81	1,226	995	1,348	353
			82	1,100	946	1,404	458
			83	2,975	1,731	2,632	901
			84	10,741	7,074	9,723	2,649
GUYANA	V	E	81	2,584	1,905	2,000	95
			82	13,859	11,707	12,934	1,227
			83	7,775	17,617	18,135	518
			84	298	330	335	5
HAITI	V	E	81	8,800	10,450	11,130	680
			82	2,640	2,970	3,534	564
			83	15,581	20,249	22,900	2,651
			84	5,720	6,075	7,097	1,022
			85	66,381	6,600	7,128	528
			86	10,103	8,158	9,430	1,272
HG KONG	A	E	85	1,124	2,270	2,560	290
	O	W	86	225	1,634	1,906	272
	V	E	83	4,975	11,625	12,275	650
	V	W	84	806	3,145	3,235	90
HONDURA	V	E	82	1,084	3,146	3,412	266
			83	7,718	3,401	3,783	382
			84	3,006	1,803	2,003	200
			85	1,670	1,002	1,179	177
HUNGARY	V	E	81	2,205	1,474	1,716	242
			84	4,427	2,432	2,701	269
			86	1,480	6,748	8,285	1,537
INDIA	A	E	81	1,057	20,805	23,674	2,869
			83	231	1,050	1,647	597
			84	7,793	115,101	120,578	5,477
			85	3,306	104,582	109,682	5,100
			86	4,551	22,970	30,673	7,703
	N	E	81	71,425	548,381	572,607	24,226
			82	42,035	343,684	357,641	13,957
			83	24,302	274,692	280,605	5,913
			84	112,855	1,097,368	1,141,800	44,432
			85	80,178	1,062,599	1,091,974	29,375
			86	45,590	312,104	325,165	13,061
	O	E	81	28	318	318	
			84	2,880	58,997	59,074	77
	V	E	81	23,946	112,546	115,081	2,535
			82	608	14,171	14,495	324
			83	12,825	46,588	49,836	3,248
			84	1,255	2,899	3,125	226
			85	13,095	79,458	80,601	1,143
			86	3,307	77,070	77,801	731
	V	W	81	9,168	73,483	76,116	2,633
			82	16,012	147,098	151,122	4,024
			83	3,495	70,665	71,857	1,192
			84	2,930	3,120	3,795	675
			85	13,823	32,728	34,957	2,229
			86	48,655	83,227	90,756	7,529
INDNSIA	A	E	82	165	2,407	3,177	770
	V	W	84	211	344	364	20
IRAN	V	W	84	2,646	1,100	1,347	247
IRELAND	A	E	83	3,304	11,864	13,821	1,957
			86	5,817	764,334	770,136	5,802
	N	E	81	6,903	18,181	19,627	1,446
			84	318	3,008	3,335	327
	O	E	81	308	924	924	
			85	138	1,421	1,421	
			86	748	2,760	2,945	185
	V	E	81	28,006	61,474	70,543	9,069
			82	23,282	56,586	61,946	5,360
			83	33,157	62,870	67,805	4,935
			84	9,680	19,162	22,075	2,913
			85	772	2,210	2,519	309
			86	4,002	17,972	18,674	702
ISRAEL	N	E	81	1,052	27,225	28,146	921
			82	1,020	19,774	21,373	1,599
			84	3,909	68,814	72,969	4,155
			85	4,073	87,587	89,465	1,878
			86	3,752	87,514	90,027	2,513
	V	E	83	3,775	3,134	3,370	236
			85	968	18,789	19,250	461
			86	441	6,136	6,375	239
	V	W	86	4,105	1,503	1,967	464
ITALY	A	E	81	1,236	4,007	5,391	1,384
			82	1,951	3,934	6,871	2,937
			83	1,712	4,448	7,259	2,811
			84	1,897	7,167	9,686	2,519
			85	9,213	26,784	35,123	8,339

Product
TSUSA commodity number, description, and unit of quantity

Country	Mode	Reg	Yr	Quantity	F.A.S.	C.I.F.	Charges
	A	W	84	158	275	448	173
	N	E	81	5,300	12,644	13,987	1,343
			82	3,788	14,186	15,601	1,415
			83	55,541	91,212	102,085	10,873
			84	188,483	333,133	363,971	30,838
			85	106,193	150,895	184,003	33,108
			86	111,238	267,561	286,700	19,139
	N	W	82	12,584	13,257	16,282	3,025
			83	16,399	12,978	15,659	2,681
			84	23,772	48,584	58,749	10,165
	O	E	81	45	1,252	1,252	
			84	977	9,575	9,575	
			85	13,367	60,087	61,093	1,006
	V	E	81	17,468	47,773	50,842	3,069
			82	4,081	8,822	9,526	704
			83	9,655	46,434	50,226	3,792
			84	68,459	137,752	144,715	6,963
			85	32,466	65,622	72,416	6,794
			86	179,737	160,031	178,307	18,276
	V	W	81	23,475	16,000	17,551	1,551
			83	14,949	19,305	22,110	2,805
			85	39,642	51,758	56,586	4,828
			86	112,202	154,676	162,873	8,197
JAMAICA	A	E	81	2,000	3,314	3,514	200
			83	110	1,020	1,287	267
	N	E	81	30,558	48,899	53,177	4,278
			85	15,557	23,210	25,126	1,916
	V	E	81	1,392	1,371	1,473	102
			82	6,072	19,363	20,872	1,509
			83	50,713	63,783	67,277	3,494
			84	36,633	53,340	57,253	3,913
			85	47,873	53,498	56,783	3,285
			86	21,704	19,674	20,777	1,103
JAPAN	A	E	81	55	530	804	274
			82	2,304	33,928	40,589	6,661
			83	3,710	22,728	32,200	9,472
			84	354	2,628	4,160	1,532
			85	397	28,620	30,721	2,101
			86	4,317	105,700	123,595	17,895
	A	H	82	16	344	435	91
	A	W	81	165	1,590	2,439	849
			82	1,157	35,421	38,460	3,039
			83	710	18,543	20,244	1,701
			84	606	17,219	19,313	2,094
			85	2,911	123,072	131,856	8,784
			86	10,520	345,291	384,848	39,557
	N	E	81	117,378	951,805	986,284	34,479
			82	111,419	1,117,544	1,155,664	38,120
			83	126,569	1,212,090	1,263,624	51,534
			84	116,554	1,076,664	1,132,210	55,546
			85	124,972	1,104,017	1,147,569	43,552
			86	280,504	1,917,629	2,015,744	98,115
	N	W	81	8,832	7,759	9,326	1,567
			82	4,332	77,321	78,765	1,444
			84	16,376	36,331	44,029	7,698
			85	60,840	184,199	226,822	42,623
			86	220,160	903,449	976,729	73,280
	O	E	81	28	1,327	1,382	55
			82	1,128	16,534	17,064	530
			83	11,904	61,626	63,727	2,101
			84	24,007	187,159	191,459	4,300
			85	3,968	19,950	20,475	525
	V	E	81	5,329	172,377	174,183	1,806
			82	2,595	79,053	80,306	1,253
			83	6,612	213,708	216,000	2,292
			84	7,281	239,689	242,391	2,702
			85	19,897	341,632	346,933	5,301
			86	6,010	225,479	228,344	2,865
	V	W	82	39,967	35,326	38,375	3,049
			83	59,592	74,007	78,904	4,897
			84	39,251	681,101	691,883	10,782
			85	4,299	36,870	37,532	662
			86	54,540	619,979	634,713	14,734
KENYA	V	E	84	7,216	6,912	8,264	1,352
			85	63,196	55,365	59,145	3,780
KOR REP	V	E	82	450	578	615	37
			83	5,806	1,638	2,017	379
			85	586	20,459	21,609	1,150
			86	1,623	58,457	59,376	919
	V	W	84	5,510	8,460	9,065	605
			86	3,000	3,140	3,323	183
LEBANON	N	E	84	5,714	6,378	7,017	639
	O	E	81	108	313	313	
			82	180	299	299	
	V	E	81	7,937	12,100	14,359	2,259

Product
TSUSA commodity number, description, and unit of quantity

Country	Mode	Reg	Yr	Quantity	F.A.S.	C.I.F.	Charges
			82	5,511	5,836	6,421	585
			83	9,376	9,742	10,385	643
			84	7,582	8,250	8,675	425
			85	16,688	15,761	17,288	1,527
			86	11,883	14,882	17,125	2,243
	V	W	86	3,174	3,900	4,420	520
MEXICO	A	E	81	10,395	32,002	37,778	5,776
			82	14,139	52,525	60,663	8,138
			83	5,960	20,542	24,433	3,891
			84	26,444	40,615	49,887	9,272
			85	39,670	62,501	78,353	15,852
			86	13,307	39,127	48,527	9,400
	A	W	81	15,699	9,906	12,997	3,091
			83	4,637	3,241	4,933	1,692
			84	13,849	6,826	9,119	2,293
			85	4,960	3,400	4,282	882
			86	24,562	19,400	26,050	6,650
	N	E	81	8,384	46,180	47,974	1,794
			86	8,932	10,521	12,426	1,905
	N	W	81	21,982	36,050	36,069	19
			82	22,001	4,361	5,717	1,356
	O	E	81	1,266	15,864	15,925	61
			82	70,664	159,437	162,789	3,352
			83	247,043	307,218	308,069	851
			84	189,852	94,900	94,900	
			85	166,679	113,126	113,126	
			86	52,923	80,008	80,218	210
	O	W	81	4,224	1,542	1,542	
			82	334	1,080	1,080	
			83	617	286	286	
			84	25,875	31,785	31,785	
			85	24,222	48,114	48,114	
			86	14,134	6,308	6,308	
MOROC	V	E	85	2,094	6,183	7,161	978
N ZEAL	V	E	81	107,905	50,976	60,604	9,628
			82	117,965	78,677	88,925	10,248
			83	1,870	1,230	1,300	70
			84	75,613	40,555	46,142	5,587
	V	W	81	70,106	33,977	41,139	7,162
			82	94,093	69,939	80,809	10,870
			83	2,804	1,703	1,982	279
			84	19,628	10,286	12,093	1,807
			85	42,950	23,155	26,541	3,386
			86	17,543	12,121	13,824	1,703
NETHLDS	A	E	81	1,360	21,381	22,811	1,430
			82	275	11,676	12,459	783
			83	468	2,689	3,029	340
			84	558	19,355	20,724	1,369
			85	638	40,303	41,477	1,174
			86	7,804	113,443	115,135	1,692
	A	W	82	77	1,538	1,553	15
	N	E	81	98,941	676,858	693,842	17,014
			82	65,868	533,712	547,909	14,197
			83	266,403	1,556,811	1,614,877	58,066
			84	351,268	2,014,060	2,089,534	75,474
			85	304,643	2,206,243	2,311,711	105,468
			86	260,711	2,660,422	2,743,772	83,350
	O	E	81	9,168	60,737	61,958	1,221
			82	19,984	172,112	178,973	6,861
			84	16,266	106,516	108,089	1,573
			85	40,313	23,767	23,823	56
	V	E	81	3,954	11,177	12,415	1,238
			82	8,524	10,271	11,191	920
			83	31,523	115,807	121,487	5,680
			84	18,880	72,200	74,269	2,069
			85	43,392	146,499	150,927	4,428
			86	47,998	152,112	154,676	2,564
	V	W	84	60,421	195,099	199,883	4,784
			86	31,940	44,173	47,600	3,427
NIGERIA	O	E	81	3,215	21,698	21,698	
	V	E	82	441	4,640	4,752	112
NORWAY	A	E	81	212	1,089	1,297	208
			83	1,344	7,400	8,595	1,195
			84	556	2,477	2,863	386
			85	3,386	12,585	14,879	2,294
	V	E	82	3,527	27,496	28,458	962
			83	344	1,572	1,872	300
			84	2,779	12,897	13,679	782
PERU	A	E	81	96	6,525	6,758	233
			82	141	7,125	7,383	258
			83	93,676	68,585	70,018	1,433
PHIL R	A	E	84	127	1,181	1,616	435
	V	W	83	900	405	513	108
			84	39,934	13,875	24,033	10,158
			85	69,536	15,003	16,638	1,635
			86	63,277	22,066	30,035	7,969
PORTUGL	V	E	81	12,807	174,655	177,873	3,218
			82	22,355	13,949	15,499	1,550
			83	11,569	10,316	10,889	573
			84	24,958	13,087	14,406	1,319
			86	96,944	39,152	43,892	4,740
REP SAF	A	E	82	66	5,886	6,153	267
			84	8	375	435	60
	N	E	81	173,472	206,863	222,400	15,537
	O	E	82	3,968	24,661	25,613	952
			83	1,266	1,689	1,689	
			84	2,464	843	843	
	V	E	81	255,525	142,916	156,545	13,629
			82	204,790	175,945	188,369	12,424
			83	169,669	126,499	135,339	8,840
			84	99,177	180,535	188,470	7,935
			85	129,164	203,116	213,718	10,602
			86	52,101	147,671	153,690	6,019
	V	W	81	20,072	11,483	13,363	1,880
			83	94,915	47,305	51,785	4,480
			84	72,114	34,727	39,647	4,920
			85	141,982	46,730	54,894	8,164
ROMANIA	V	E	84	165,345	532,267	541,200	8,933
			85	165,345	229,811	241,200	11,389
			86	295,725	408,388	431,395	23,007
S HELNA	V	E	84	2,205	9,708	10,117	409
SALVADR	A	E	81	25	674	723	49
SINGAPR	A	W	86	1,120	34,074	34,200	126
	V	E	81	18,033	88,037	89,560	1,523
			82	15,535	110,623	112,560	1,937
			83	36,209	144,959	149,005	4,046
			84	43,765	246,594	251,941	5,347
			86	33,730	259,834	263,896	4,062
	V	W	81	44,163	232,525	236,620	4,095
			82	53,742	314,591	320,199	5,608
			85	675	3,315	3,526	211
SPAIN	A	E	82	1,102	974	1,224	250
			84	33	523	574	51
			85	10	2,081	2,200	119
	A	W	83	50	799	903	104
			85	44	1,600	1,900	300
	N	E	81	5,131	46,148	48,087	1,939
			82	15,702	92,390	94,459	2,069
			83	21,708	899,695	906,524	6,829
			84	12,846	67,325	73,581	6,256
			85	7,913	65,916	72,405	6,489
			86	37,308	158,269	169,006	10,737
	N	W	84	44,008	70,532	88,556	18,024
			85	347,540	281,238	316,336	35,098
	V	E	82	104,537	64,552	70,251	5,699
			84	26,455	18,189	21,600	3,411
			86	71,509	31,831	36,913	5,082
	V	W	82	2,023	1,246	1,421	175
			83	8,818	6,926	8,525	1,599
			86	54,593	71,507	75,691	4,184
SURINAM	A	E	86	202	5,304	5,704	400
SWAZLND	A	E	86	84	12,142	12,336	194
SWEDEN	N	E	85	904	5,237	5,460	223
	V	E	81	5,512	3,340	4,018	678
			82	11,376	7,583	9,502	1,919
			84	1,406	2,891	3,178	287
			85	370	1,053	1,103	50
			86	1,772	20,576	21,240	664
	V	W	84	867	1,970	2,452	482
SWITZLD	A	E	81	120,159	2,287,522	2,345,978	58,456
			82	19,832	71,118	81,005	9,887
			83	13,593	93,974	102,321	8,347
			84	17,534	140,691	152,962	12,271
			85	23,231	187,766	205,410	17,644
			86	19,132	171,473	190,796	19,323
	N	E	82	140,230	2,547,626	2,608,730	61,104
			83	157,680	3,264,651	3,339,284	74,633
			84	258,162	4,610,308	4,745,720	135,412
			85	321,618	4,302,914	4,529,344	226,430
			86	225,679	3,820,598	4,014,615	194,017
	O	E	83	300	885	885	
			84	88	1,007	1,007	
	V	E	81	6,451	7,051	7,430	379
			82	11,437	16,391	17,475	1,084
			83	32,330	20,542	23,304	2,762
			84	2,648	10,492	11,274	782
			85	741	3,396	3,577	181
			86	16,240	170,066	174,187	4,121
	V	W	82	159	666	691	25
			83	504	1,098	1,166	68

Table 2. U.S. Import Statistics for Non Crop-Specific Commodities by End-Use

Product
TSUSA commodity number, description, and unit of quantity

Country	Mode	Reg	Yr	Quantity	F.A.S.	C.I.F.	Charges
			84	72,181	31,243	35,951	4,708
			85	33,582	64,235	66,342	2,107
SYRIA	O	E	85	525	1,012	1,012	
THAILND	V	E	81	1,981	11,373	12,015	642
			82	1,173	8,976	9,840	864
			83	1,043	1,769	2,032	263
			84	1,025	1,652	1,932	280
			85	173	1,280	1,375	95
			86	1,250	4,750	5,265	515
	V	H	82	25	281	330	49
			83	173	1,284	1,412	128
	V	W	81	11,469	58,861	63,929	5,068
			82	9,407	32,714	35,931	3,217
			83	10,590	24,247	26,055	1,808
			84	3,193	12,338	13,453	1,115
			85	44,045	29,661	32,642	2,981
			86	37,455	27,318	30,150	2,832
TRINID	A	E	81	11,829	6,926	9,375	2,449
			82	14,641	6,392	9,226	2,834
			83	7,150	4,800	7,050	2,250
			84	5,072	3,150	4,190	1,040
	N	E	84	13,574	9,137	10,857	1,720
	V	E	85	3,300	4,681	5,023	342
TURKEY	V	E	81	6,614	43,200	44,987	1,787
			82	19,842	134,100	136,146	2,046
			83	30,314	201,900	206,508	4,608
			84	57,505	220,793	225,993	5,200
			85	163,507	472,014	489,638	17,624
			86	57,379	385,383	398,370	12,987
U KING	A	E	81	22	343	542	199
			82	172	1,789	2,179	390
			83	2,301	1,499	2,660	1,161
			84	689	14,395	15,181	786
			85	4,026	34,286	40,858	6,572
			86	1,359	80,158	82,922	2,764
	A	W	81	8,796	98,357	104,568	6,211
			82	231	4,429	4,673	244
			84	300	3,245	3,535	290
			86	22	4,407	4,481	74
	N	E	81	19,393	77,286	85,942	8,656
			82	73,408	201,083	227,560	26,477
			83	120,035	394,289	434,448	40,159
			84	80,351	318,514	351,861	33,347
			85	117,526	306,126	350,954	44,828
			86	157,632	786,546	821,929	35,383
	O	E	81	886	9,188	10,091	903
			83	3,696	3,846	4,330	484
			84	10,323	15,516	16,704	1,188
			85	2,205	1,146	1,621	475
	V	E	81	26,910	45,741	52,125	6,384
			83	2,006	10,593	11,009	416
			84	3,315	8,298	8,476	178
			85	18,506	31,128	31,657	529
			86	20,046	34,457	36,894	2,437
	V	W	82	638	454	521	67
			84	124	1,084	1,169	85
USSR	V	E	86	441	15,400	16,709	1,309
VENEZ	A	E	81	11,129	17,102	20,334	3,232
			82	11,130	16,876	22,599	5,723
			83	11,938	19,866	22,468	2,602
			84	7,434	15,196	18,113	2,917
			85	6,364	10,194	13,078	2,884
			86	5,046	8,232	9,538	1,306
YUGOSLV	A	E	82	1,323	5,400	6,363	963
			85	44	2,237	2,700	463
	V	E	81	176	509	1,039	530
			83	995	14,836	15,649	813
			84	44	834	1,059	225
			86	882	1,600	1,732	132
	V	W	85	71,958	29,197	33,642	4,445
			86	7,938	3,423	4,159	736
ZAIRE	A	E	86	61	2,794	2,821	27

4503000 FLAV EXTR ETC NOT OV 20% ALC (LB)

Country	Mode	Reg	Yr	Quantity	F.A.S.	C.I.F.	Charges
TOTAL			81	6,769,044	3,026,511	3,323,507	296,522
			82	8,067,447	3,897,338	4,331,009	433,671
			83	9,504,058	5,295,249	5,893,685	598,436
			84	12,350,982	6,366,400	7,148,016	781,616
			85	14,321,519	8,377,778	9,274,160	896,382
			86	23,766,446	17,314,339	19,151,503	1,837,164
AFGHAN	A	E	86	20,200	35,310	50,606	15,296
ARGENT	A	E	86	3,635	2,310	6,439	4,129
	N	E	86	270,712	144,246	165,418	21,172
	O	E	81	150,877	111,109	122,566	11,457

Country	Mode	Reg	Yr	Quantity	F.A.S.	C.I.F.	Charges
	V	E	81	1,070,748	579,165	656,802	77,637
			82	945,873	815,844	892,155	76,311
			83	1,317,646	963,184	1,059,504	96,320
			84	1,176,695	621,966	706,320	84,354
			85	731,907	338,041	387,072	49,031
			86	607,766	374,955	415,374	40,419
	V	W	81	177,165	105,317	118,838	13,521
			82	143,571	86,396	100,121	13,725
			83	220,969	117,739	135,676	17,937
			84	1,362	2,724	3,259	535
			85	80,226	35,722	42,241	6,519
			86	49,775	31,969	36,196	4,227
AUSTRAL	A	E	84	24	402	533	131
			86	75	1,646	2,296	650
	A	W	84	33	331	386	55
	V	E	85	4,320	12,908	14,574	1,666
			86	662,112	353,075	385,715	32,640
	V	W	81	35,622	35,899	37,672	1,773
			82	41,891	41,107	44,053	2,946
			86	35,979	12,757	14,816	2,059
AUSTRIA	A	E	81	100	560	863	303
			82	541	2,292	3,409	1,117
	N	E	81	237,548	161,943	173,708	11,765
			83	57,472	29,806	31,333	1,527
			84	208,784	80,571	91,218	10,647
			86	6,178	5,535	6,142	607
	O	E	81	441	439	439	
			83	16,653	9,418	10,653	1,235
			84	82,936	37,028	42,514	5,486
			85	35,850	14,033	15,462	1,429
	V	E	82	136,396	80,958	87,840	6,882
			82	340,853	256,675	273,928	17,253
			83	473,356	237,881	258,518	20,637
			84	970,110	486,676	536,446	49,770
			85	347,849	167,194	185,308	18,114
			86	1,683,064	842,563	924,839	82,276
	V	W	81	16,834	15,895	16,816	921
			82	79,413	61,440	65,138	3,698
			83	54,375	25,332	28,069	2,737
			84	374,012	232,466	257,907	25,441
			85	389,003	158,744	181,885	23,141
			86	478,053	245,392	271,677	26,285
BAHRAIN	V	E	85	6,638	16,423	16,807	384
BARBADO	V	E	84	234	807	827	20
BELGIUM	A	E	81	97	570	904	334
			83	147	924	1,208	284
	O	E	86	304,762	161,152	176,952	15,800
	V	E	86	214,093	210,977	226,139	15,162
BRAZIL	N	E	83	1,864,364	300,947	381,431	80,484
	O	E	81	190,881	19,273	20,970	1,697
			83	4,409	1,217	1,725	508
			84	41,887	10,487	13,272	2,785
			86	1,114,913	582,673	647,145	64,472
	V	E	81	3,077,314	393,837	438,543	44,706
			82	4,706,502	613,414	725,793	112,379
			83	1,144,380	138,765	194,406	55,641
			84	5,103,318	1,289,114	1,522,360	233,246
			85	7,463,568	2,013,240	2,299,427	286,187
			86	12,406,076	5,952,231	6,591,745	639,514
	V	W	81	80,850	5,704	6,494	790
			82	289,481	18,723	42,770	24,047
			83	453,985	33,198	65,605	32,407
			84	587,525	55,328	91,180	35,852
			85	37,963	5,194	7,587	2,393
C RICA	A	E	84	362	714	1,211	497
CANADA	O	E	81	5,366	6,300	6,300	
			82	8,569	9,821	9,821	
			83	4,319	13,673	13,673	
			84	5,216	14,539	14,671	132
			85	1,246	10,373	10,373	
			86	2,103	31,585	31,585	
	O	W	83	2,200	2,038	2,248	210
			84	84	8,815	8,815	
			86	1,653	5,795	5,795	
CHILE	V	E	82	25,132	12,468	13,420	952
			83	230,169	137,947	146,484	8,537
			84	288,802	158,937	169,640	10,703
			85	184,674	82,198	89,186	6,988
			86	146,493	84,567	90,413	5,846
	V	W	82	15,168	8,444	9,650	1,206
			83	30,985	17,683	19,950	2,267
CHINA M	V	E	85	41,182	17,304	21,004	3,700
CHINA T	V	E	85	3,528	18,687	20,800	2,113
COLOMB	A	E	85	661	3,585	3,748	163
	N	E	84	1,190	5,715	6,118	403

Product
TSUSA commodity number, description, and unit of quantity

Country	Mode	Reg	Yr	Quantity	F.A.S.	C.I.F.	Charges
	V	E	82	277	1,130	1,400	270
			83	220	1,012	1,049	37
DENMARK	A	E	83	909	451	801	350
	V	E	83	8,334	4,571	5,086	515
	V	W	85	22,802	20,937	23,192	2,255
DOM REP	A	E	81	492	295	428	133
			82	7,283	22,928	25,242	2,314
	N	E	82	54,480	10,146	14,489	4,343
			83	25,313	7,836	9,647	1,811
			84	5,860	1,166	1,563	397
	V	E	81	33,207	9,569	11,354	1,785
FR GERM	A	E	81	70	4,861	5,128	267
			82	2,002	33,106	35,371	2,265
			83	13,179	182,486	190,834	8,348
			84	333	1,720	2,166	446
	A	W	85	3,132	56,425	60,499	4,074
			86	5,211	60,664	69,110	8,446
	N	E	81	186,758	147,020	158,610	11,590
			82	45,919	45,265	47,866	2,601
			83	153,393	271,790	282,000	10,210
			84	597,420	451,360	486,561	35,201
			85	874,830	792,140	844,158	52,018
			86	496,091	648,910	677,786	28,876
	N	W	85	118,651	198,377	207,936	9,559
			86	280,555	208,772	236,509	27,737
	O	E	81	8,450	7,444	7,444	
			84	7,975	5,605	6,105	500
			85	97,498	34,101	38,977	4,876
			86	54,631	24,299	26,359	2,060
	V	E	81	153,140	91,137	99,780	8,643
			82	1,870	1,061	1,353	292
			83	812,651	448,887	522,969	74,082
			84	383,340	231,428	255,277	23,849
			85	568,382	521,065	550,155	29,090
			86	760,729	367,263	394,109	26,846
	V	W	81	12,550	26,863	29,260	2,397
			82	8,866	18,418	19,245	827
			83	127,130	92,021	99,297	7,276
			84	84,281	51,668	56,485	4,817
			85	263,052	179,322	197,919	18,597
			86	299,424	225,332	241,670	16,338
FRANCE	A	E	81	2,042	33,896	35,112	1,216
			82	4,214	65,580	67,877	2,297
			83	6,353	73,918	78,024	4,106
			84	1,498	12,031	13,361	1,330
			85	3,870	49,638	53,209	3,571
			86	2,174	37,800	40,205	2,405
	N	E	81	66,688	208,596	221,892	13,155
			82	270,408	709,622	783,989	74,367
			83	460,418	740,902	806,166	65,264
			84	660,698	1,041,431	1,166,607	125,176
			85	681,951	1,286,001	1,498,223	212,222
			86	1,884,052	3,018,625	3,615,650	597,025
	O	E	81	73,752	49,866	51,741	1,874
			82	35,013	20,275	22,587	2,312
			86	1,795	2,096	2,096	
	V	E	81	970	558	622	64
			82	34,392	19,637	21,494	1,857
			83	170,003	84,885	96,141	11,256
			84	107,767	54,125	60,320	6,195
			85	50,953	30,122	33,318	3,196
			86	337,462	132,046	147,348	15,302
	V	W	82	77,811	38,837	50,252	11,415
			83	194,049	105,404	114,040	8,636
			86	32,452	16,683	19,056	2,373
GREECE	V	E	84	66,314	74,765	79,551	4,786
GUYANA	V	E	81	1,200	3,870	4,021	151
HAITI	V	E	85	4,363	3,920	4,735	815
HUNGARY	V	E	81	30,032	12,817	15,949	3,132
			82	2,205	1,143	1,358	215
			83	4,408	2,306	2,638	332
INDIA	A	E	84	5	505	938	433
IRELAND	A	E	85	88	1,360	1,490	130
			86	788	49,875	50,047	172
ISRAEL	V	E	82	1,210	1,232	1,354	122
			83	1,272	868	942	74
ITALY	A	E	83	121	440	678	238
			84	264	666	681	15
	N	W	84	23,327	26,260	27,951	1,691
	O	E	86	35,261	15,132	17,292	2,160
	V	E	81	114,688	74,322	79,278	4,956
			83	146,965	54,223	60,465	6,242
			84	141,084	55,916	62,630	6,714
			85	3,130	5,835	6,510	675
			86	36,369	19,559	21,051	1,492

Product
TSUSA commodity number, description, and unit of quantity

Country	Mode	Reg	Yr	Quantity	F.A.S.	C.I.F.	Charges
	V	W	82	5,459	6,555	7,401	846
			83	19,461	26,848	28,792	1,944
			84	32,593	14,144	16,490	2,346
			85	5,122	4,733	5,253	520
			86	763	1,543	2,123	580
JAMAICA	V	E	81	900	787	1,077	290
			82	890	1,734	1,858	124
			85	1,831	6,500	6,807	307
JAPAN	A	E	82	66	279	311	32
			83	471	6,084	7,646	1,562
			84	110	440	1,376	936
	V	E	83	4,762	32,082	32,852	770
			84	3,175	22,096	22,807	711
	V	W	81	881	5,865	6,120	255
			82	11,746	76,746	78,208	1,462
			83	20,238	131,176	134,763	3,587
			84	11,829	79,474	82,770	3,296
			85	7,898	45,967	47,629	1,662
			86	15,031	110,270	148,273	38,003
MEXICO	A	E	82	2,425	20,257	22,781	2,524
	A	W	81	382	734	1,069	335
			85	13	7,000	8,870	1,870
	O	E	83	29,603	17,212	17,212	
			84	18,732	30,456	30,456	
			85	29,015	42,606	42,606	
			86	11,200	5,585	5,585	
	O	W	81	838	427	427	
			84	16,203	10,284	10,284	
N ZEAL	V	E	86	1,685	3,805	4,064	259
NETHLDS	A	E	81	117	3,829	3,991	162
			82	689	1,885	2,027	142
			84	90	448	704	256
			86	1,400	27,683	30,240	2,557
	N	E	82	29,981	133,811	139,438	5,627
			83	30,307	128,842	135,176	6,334
			85	601,912	819,145	858,424	39,279
			86	633,106	1,162,978	1,205,001	42,023
	O	E	84	44,272	24,996	29,971	4,975
			85	76,190	41,173	43,773	2,600
	V	E	81	285,402	216,857	232,682	15,493
			82	512,404	359,258	391,942	32,684
			83	804,261	472,451	502,540	30,089
			84	825,897	746,166	798,398	52,232
			85	633,055	333,295	369,200	35,905
			86	123,850	58,836	62,103	3,267
	V	W	81	116,403	72,506	78,349	5,843
			82	111,094	119,628	126,043	6,415
			83	189,079	124,215	133,960	9,745
			84	116,403	77,711	82,822	5,111
			85	222,302	328,063	346,349	18,286
			86	65,520	258,254	265,471	7,217
NORWAY	A	W	86	5,187	20,601	25,839	5,238
PORTUGL	N	E	86	39,027	1,481,275	1,487,119	5,844
	V	E	83	36,707	18,934	20,470	1,536
			84	35,200	21,466	22,969	1,503
			85	108,160	245,620	250,104	4,484
	V	W	85	36,000	12,369	15,162	2,793
REP SAF	V	E	81	189,596	122,355	136,102	13,747
			82	37,760	24,694	27,580	2,886
			83	36,756	12,884	14,456	1,572
			84	3,213	1,197	1,534	337
			85	118,784	46,121	51,515	5,394
			86	114,241	45,902	52,933	7,031
	V	W	81	31,438	17,113	20,118	3,005
			84	7,572	3,011	4,357	1,346
			86	36,715	14,210	15,830	1,620
SPAIN	A	W	83	221	1,800	3,428	1,628
	O	E	82	82	345	345	
	V	E	81	145,795	88,753	100,008	11,255
			82	166,418	109,066	119,327	10,261
			83	209,048	116,458	127,981	11,523
			84	108,171	67,628	75,043	7,415
			85	204,354	103,624	122,196	18,572
			86	132,330	55,588	63,274	7,686
	V	W	82	36,480	23,576	25,601	2,025
			84	189,918	99,146	114,096	14,950
SWEDEN	A	E	83	11	257	322	65
	V	E	82	1,100	3,250	3,712	462
			83	1,100	3,450	4,009	559
			86	12,777	4,530	6,246	1,716
SWITZLD	A	E	82	397	7,141	7,668	527
			83	1,086	10,049	10,892	843
			84	385	3,678	3,980	302
			85	440	4,180	4,560	380
	N	E	84	6,477	81,291	85,996	4,705

Product
TSUSA commodity number, description, and unit of quantity

Country	Mode	Reg	Yr	Quantity	F.A.S.	C.I.F.	Charges
			85	60,122	108,444	116,564	8,120
	V	E	82	1,436	11,696	12,073	377
			84	133	2,301	2,426	125
			86	15,631	32,072	32,538	466
	V	W	81	35,280	22,274	26,634	4,360
			85	450	2,050	2,110	60
THAILND	V	E	81	940	9,437	10,289	852
			82	457	5,081	5,898	817
			83	174	2,861	3,145	284
			84	30	418	462	44
	V	W	81	144	5,895	6,047	152
			85	564	2,637	2,878	241
TURKEY	V	E	85	186,390	49,013	58,990	9,977
			86	188,595	44,279	50,617	6,338
U KING	A	E	83	255	2,569	2,815	246
	N	E	84	5,695	51,079	59,435	8,356
			86	61,712	46,267	47,290	1,023
	V	E	81	95,766	256,850	275,313	18,463
			82	5,619	77,332	84,661	7,329
			83	79,390	68,334	72,956	4,622
			85	7,360	97,349	100,055	2,706
			86	37,584	17,025	19,123	2,098
	V	W	81	884	14,746	15,907	1,161
			84	895	13,149	14,155	1,006
			86	447	6,397	6,777	380
YUGOSLV	O	E	83	6,295	5,034	5,034	
	V	E	83	4,774	2,048	2,382	334
			84	1,249	555	612	57
			86	35,009	11,445	13,477	2,032
	V	W	83	29,912	9,909	11,594	1,685
ZAIRE	A	E	85	240	5,000	5,320	320

4504000 FLAV EXTR ETC 20 TO 50% ALCH (LB)

Country	Mode	Reg	Yr	Quantity	F.A.S.	C.I.F.	Charges
TOTAL			81	396,836	618,944	672,465	53,521
			82	235,351	793,650	841,908	48,258
			83	291,817	916,189	975,917	59,728
			84	255,256	1,132,205	1,184,943	52,738
			85	289,173	1,589,985	1,655,658	65,673
			86	363,050	4,086,447	4,145,570	59,123
ARGENT	N	E	81	102,831	228,555	245,806	17,251
	V	E	82	79,102	182,988	193,510	10,522
BELGIUM	A	E	84	237	477	738	261
BERMUDA	V	E	83	542	2,708	2,947	239
			84	410	3,266	3,426	160
BRAZIL	V	E	81	126,927	9,414	18,605	9,191
CANADA	N	E	85	136	3,552	3,638	86
			86	140	3,653	3,735	82
	O	E	81	474	15,705	15,705	
			82	812	25,879	25,879	
			83	3,531	92,682	92,692	10
			84	36,408	413,381	413,532	151
			85	46,802	886,447	886,447	
			86	140,536	1,175,992	1,176,009	17
CHINA T	V	W	85	2,117	9,607	9,900	293
DENMARK	A	E	81	1,500	23,250	25,131	1,881
	V	E	83	33	11,053	11,440	387
DOM REP	V	E	82	1,105	685	914	229
			83	2,875	1,410	2,270	860
			84	2,643	1,570	2,214	644
FR GERM	A	E	84	22	1,642	1,756	114
	A	W	81	743	1,052	1,697	645
			83	498	669	1,228	559
	N	E	81	5,328	43,112	44,411	1,299
			82	1,399	15,428	16,400	972
			84	899	12,892	13,561	669
			85	8,772	42,939	45,320	2,381
			86	33,301	185,597	196,848	11,251
	O	E	83	1,151	5,656	6,565	909
			84	1,567	7,714	8,515	801
			85	260	1,462	1,655	193
			86	1,523	8,955	9,004	49
	V	E	83	3,733	31,728	32,883	1,155
			85	1,166	1,775	1,958	183
			86	9,083	19,289	20,502	1,213
	V	W	82	4,848	10,476	10,863	387
			85	7,925	9,360	9,990	630
FRANCE	A	E	81	90	286	480	194
			84	784	4,438	5,195	757
	A	W	83	44	1,086	1,280	194
			86	172	3,980	4,634	654
	N	E	81	459	2,849	3,084	235
			82	4,821	15,577	16,772	1,195
			83	3,803	17,893	19,109	1,216
			84	14,236	109,133	114,167	5,034

Product
TSUSA commodity number, description, and unit of quantity

Country	Mode	Reg	Yr	Quantity	F.A.S.	C.I.F.	Charges
			85	18,298	99,453	106,452	6,999
			86	41,008	168,871	181,471	12,600
	O	W	82	829	1,264	1,314	50
	V	E	85	12,292	30,614	33,240	2,626
HAITI	V	E	86	11,683	15,840	17,086	1,246
IRELAND	A	E	86	8,037	2,137,661	2,144,994	7,333
ITALY	N	W	83	59,847	59,770	74,587	14,817
	V	E	81	73,606	94,212	102,938	8,726
			82	35,263	52,195	54,976	2,781
			83	89,593	128,516	134,411	5,895
			84	76,501	105,525	112,286	6,761
			85	68,400	94,829	102,770	7,941
			86	27,040	39,832	43,492	3,660
	V	W	81	45,106	54,300	59,087	4,787
			84	2,963	7,700	7,995	295
JAPAN	N	W	82	23,261	85,826	92,634	6,808
	V	E	82	154	1,183	1,286	103
	V	W	81	17,816	53,193	56,147	2,954
			83	24,134	107,673	112,279	4,606
			84	16,455	71,224	76,025	4,801
			85	25,843	111,263	116,498	5,235
			86	27,976	143,076	147,553	4,477
MADAGAS	V	E	84	20,703	121,928	126,680	4,752
MEXICO	O	E	82	1,944	1,960	1,960	
			85	529	3,000	3,000	
	O	W	83	1,885	2,605	2,822	217
			84	70	3,125	3,125	
			85	1,100	5,980	5,980	
NETHLDS	A	E	82	1,984	7,635	8,127	492
			84	1,885	7,818	8,379	561
			85	13,655	51,425	58,735	7,310
			86	1,009	65,945	73,505	7,560
	N	E	82	5,743	26,549	28,756	2,207
	V	E	81	110	685	761	76
			82	331	446	525	79
			83	4,645	19,607	19,929	322
			84	33,061	28,986	31,560	2,574
			85	51,274	63,026	71,008	7,982
			86	50,372	58,522	64,924	6,402
NORWAY	A	E	83	1,765	8,288	9,984	1,696
			84	18,931	50,842	67,174	16,332
			85	18,973	52,398	69,920	17,522
SINGAPR	V	E	85	5	1,307	1,348	41
SWEDEN	V	E	81	1,693	3,467	4,035	568
SWITZLD	A	E	83	264	1,141	1,486	345
			84	176	1,428	1,571	143
			85	2,480	15,188	17,538	2,350
			86	121	1,007	1,069	62
	V	E	81	209	3,563	3,704	141
			83	15,979	145,516	147,872	2,356
			84	21,929	139,923	145,243	5,320
			85	5,511	73,645	74,480	835
THAILND	V	W	84	635	3,388	3,425	37
U KING	A	W	83	1,045	5,313	6,061	748
			84	1,082	6,897	7,746	849
	N	E	83	4,253	22,023	23,680	1,657
			84	2,952	20,386	21,244	858
			86	3,541	30,557	31,447	890
	V	E	81	8,888	47,746	50,245	2,499
			82	73,755	365,559	387,992	22,433
			83	71,749	249,770	271,163	21,393
			84	121	2,178	2,254	76
			85	1,847	19,229	21,264	2,035
	V	W	81	11,056	37,555	40,629	3,074
			83	448	1,082	1,229	147
			84	586	6,344	7,132	788
			85	1,788	13,486	14,517	1,031
			86	1,788	25,156	26,651	1,495
VENEZ	V	E	86	5,720	2,514	2,646	132

4505000 FLAV EXTR ETC OV 50 PCT ALCO (LB)

Country	Mode	Reg	Yr	Quantity	F.A.S.	C.I.F.	Charges
TOTAL			81	199,911	634,647	692,988	58,067
			82	332,615	877,130	937,738	60,608
			83	321,850	964,498	1,016,282	51,784
			84	262,164	799,963	828,447	28,484
			85	336,090	1,173,462	1,269,889	96,427
			86	462,771	1,471,781	1,540,628	68,847
BELGIUM	A	E	84	780	2,036	3,113	1,077
			86	746	2,679	3,440	761
	V	E	84	3,999	683	1,255	572
CANADA	O	E	82	24	2,000	2,000	
			83	751	14,615	14,615	
			84	481	5,568	5,568	
			85	6,941	33,310	33,310	

Product
TSUSA commodity number, description, and unit of quantity

Country	Mode	Reg	Yr	Quantity	F.A.S.	C.I.F.	Charges
			86	147,856	58,643	58,643	
	O	W	84	37	2,836	2,836	
COLOMB	A	E	85	992	9,255	10,112	857
			86	1,703	10,447	11,937	1,490
	N	E	84	506	3,930	4,438	508
	V	E	83	66	538	557	19
DENMARK	A	W	81	231	1,263	2,071	534
FR GERM	N	E	85	16,073	46,547	50,154	3,607
			86	24,344	110,811	122,378	11,567
	V	E	86	2,300	9,332	9,612	280
FRANCE	A	E	81	98	286	480	194
			82	230	2,165	2,719	554
			83	330	3,015	3,497	482
			86	1,212	4,833	4,956	123
	A	H	83	320	4,275	4,653	378
	A	W	83	95	2,596	2,880	284
			85	17	1,374	2,922	1,548
	N	E	81	3,272	86,067	88,171	2,104
			82	11,250	44,007	45,379	1,372
			83	15,800	89,624	98,126	8,502
			84	16,731	126,470	131,472	5,002
			85	10,708	58,140	61,008	2,868
			86	1,818	9,399	10,661	1,262
	V	E	84	9,576	7,783	9,824	2,041
			85	13,626	12,016	13,538	1,522
			86	1,703	8,587	9,156	569
	V	W	82	317	768	868	100
GERM DR	V	W	85	5,503	31,166	31,800	634
IRAN	A	E	86	1,052	3,250	4,293	1,043
IRELAND	A	E	83	1,199	7,341	8,800	1,459
			84	801	6,525	7,598	1,073
	V	E	86	4,489	14,564	15,094	530
ITALY	N	E	86	29,093	57,281	62,180	4,899
	V	E	85	1,111	2,434	2,664	230
			86	1,389	2,723	2,880	157
	V	W	81	12,275	20,400	22,377	1,977
			82	13,503	22,440	24,754	2,314
			83	10,448	17,340	19,988	2,648
JAMAICA	V	E	81	376	404	530	126
JAPAN	A	E	83	55	2,250	2,546	296
	V	W	81	66	251	283	32
			82	430	1,465	1,583	118
			83	496	1,885	2,027	142
			84	364	1,835	1,878	43
			85	496	1,845	1,881	36
			86	496	2,222	2,254	32
MEXICO	A	E	81	2,452	4,200	5,056	856
	A	W	81	23,753	55,350	63,304	7,954
			84	1,544	3,600	3,986	386
			86	4,082	12,800	14,802	2,002
	N	W	82	36,239	112,475	121,654	9,179
	O	E	82	115,394	263,800	263,800	
			83	142,453	389,622	389,622	
			84	137,102	374,000	374,000	
			85	120,351	310,000	310,000	
			86	37,772	92,000	92,000	
	O	W	85	880	5,530	5,530	
NETHLDS	A	E	81	65	1,089	1,303	214
			82	26	535	564	29
			83	23	806	921	115
			84	2,393	300	345	45
			86	10	1,349	1,405	56
	N	E	85	21,677	92,861	101,350	8,489
			86	46,822	292,959	308,755	15,796
	V	E	82	165	7,746	7,941	195
			83	8,613	12,859	13,572	713
			84	1,790	14,333	14,683	350
			85	2,000	157,868	191,000	33,132
			86	4,489	14,567	14,920	353
SPAIN	A	E	86	1,631	10,180	11,531	1,351
SWITZLD	A	E	83	1,157	13,585	14,280	695
			84	2,259	18,106	19,925	1,819
			85	2,413	14,310	16,113	1,803
			86	2,503	19,624	22,472	2,848
	N	E	86	7,604	105,322	109,435	4,113
	V	E	82	335	1,702	1,809	107
			83	53	336	351	15
			84	185	1,176	1,224	48
	V	W	82	53	336	348	12
			83	53	336	355	19
			84	476	1,600	1,659	59
U KING	A	E	84	90	748	899	151
	N	E	84	55,778	156,141	163,509	7,368
			86	117,302	552,274	567,375	15,101
	V	E	81	130,771	366,617	402,178	35,561
			82	154,649	417,691	464,319	46,628
			83	139,938	403,475	439,492	36,017
			85	84,474	245,859	275,619	29,760
	V	W	81	26,552	98,720	107,235	8,515
			84	27,272	72,293	80,235	7,942
			85	48,828	150,947	162,888	11,941
			86	22,355	75,935	80,449	4,514

Spice and spice seed

1621500 MIXED SPICES SPCE SEEDS NSPF (LB)

Country	Mode	Reg	Yr	Quantity	F.A.S.	C.I.F.	Charges
TOTAL			81	1,867,279	1,863,725	2,100,889	245,067
			82	2,768,057	2,397,727	2,706,878	309,151
			83	2,943,826	3,270,284	3,626,744	356,460
			84	3,333,685	3,290,270	3,683,623	393,353
			85	3,319,886	3,404,195	3,815,646	411,451
			86	4,470,041	4,437,763	4,885,833	448,070
ARGENT	A	E	82	794	1,080	3,085	2,005
	V	E	84	8,818	6,000	7,395	1,395
AUSTRAL	A	W	84	785	2,283	3,204	921
	O	E	84	153	2,461	2,461	
	O	W	84	25	825	930	105
	V	E	84	135	352	452	100
AUSTRIA	A	E	81	220	1,258	1,754	496
			86	200	1,175	1,375	200
	O	E	81	55	1,104	1,222	118
			82	198	628	628	
			83	167	643	643	
			84	88	321	321	
	O	W	84	225	1,138	1,271	133
	V	E	82	133	1,167	1,278	111
			84	426	766	867	101
	V	W	83	560	571	639	68
B VIRGN	A	E	85	184	1,504	1,713	209
	V	E	81	450	288	344	56
			82	600	1,440	1,628	188
			84	86	2,081	2,152	71
BELGIUM	A	E	86	2,800	1,325	2,275	950
	N	E	84	14,024	20,033	21,301	1,268
	O	E	81	634	616	652	36
			82	2,150	2,072	2,072	
			83	3,732	1,107	1,943	836
			84	156	310	310	
	V	E	81	394	2,508	2,631	123
			83	33,639	33,329	36,950	3,621
			84	13,602	2,988	3,403	415
			85	17,989	16,056	18,242	2,186
			86	66,396	56,387	61,362	4,975
	V	W	85	5,856	4,043	5,539	1,496
			86	483	1,245	1,262	17
BNGLDSH	V	E	83	10,912	3,093	3,929	836
BRAZIL	N	E	85	6,693	13,287	16,013	2,726
	V	E	81	25	338	358	20
			83	11,122	6,650	8,243	1,593
			84	9,142	7,566	8,869	1,303
			85	17,648	9,531	11,806	2,275
			86	2,872	2,449	2,737	288
	V	W	83	13,214	52,918	54,748	1,830
			84	22,046	79,514	82,744	3,230
			85	4,707	21,189	22,696	1,507
BURMA	A	W	84	268	515	1,104	589
	V	E	82	217	787	896	109
C RICA	A	E	84	1,919	2,429	4,164	1,735
	V	E	85	44,900	22,800	26,264	3,464
CANADA	A	E	81	496	1,210	1,405	195
			82	405	1,033	1,433	400
			83	220	643	993	350
			84	1,509	4,886	5,663	777
	A	H	81	146	458	514	56
	A	W	83	374	616	754	138
			84	380	2,253	2,568	315
	N	E	84	5,348	6,416	6,684	268
	N	W	83	1,309	4,327	4,386	59
	O	E	81	47,601	44,045	44,416	371
			82	24,064	33,969	34,511	542
			83	69,175	87,422	87,918	496
			84	43,465	75,167	75,269	102
			85	56,512	108,071	108,245	174
			86	32,615	39,938	39,938	
	O	W	81	4,930	6,820	7,150	330
			82	319	758	758	
			83	356	591	591	
			84	4,056	3,747	3,747	

Product
TSUSA commodity number, description, and unit of quantity

Country	Mode	Reg	Yr	Quantity	F.A.S.	C.I.F.	Charges
			86	5,346	3,225	3,225	
	V	E	85	1,100	1,100	1,183	83
CHILE	V	E	86	70,455	46,942	54,942	8,000
	V	W	84	20,124	10,983	11,206	223
CHINA M	N	E	81	17,092	21,192	24,868	3,676
			82	30,068	43,417	48,208	4,791
			83	83,935	77,687	85,669	7,982
			84	53,643	58,467	65,568	7,101
	N	W	81	32,102	41,441	44,351	2,910
			83	45,465	44,286	47,779	3,493
			84	91,665	88,553	100,574	12,021
	O	E	83	500	412	450	38
			84	125	875	875	
	O	W	84	1,000	501	530	29
	V	E	81	500	1,417	1,607	190
			82	4,259	6,077	6,810	733
			83	30,510	15,503	17,195	1,692
			84	2,949	3,897	4,275	378
			85	29,265	43,807	50,020	6,213
			86	59,875	52,045	58,551	6,506
	V	H	81	3,800	4,808	5,057	249
			82	5,200	6,427	6,823	396
			83	10,153	12,147	13,195	1,048
			84	4,465	7,764	8,384	620
			85	4,600	5,792	6,481	689
			86	3,444	5,147	5,622	475
	V	W	81	39,327	49,704	53,165	3,461
			82	66,281	82,210	89,596	7,386
			83	68,744	81,086	86,933	5,847
			84	65,110	101,034	107,483	6,449
			85	81,198	117,076	120,777	3,701
			86	40,410	43,763	47,753	3,990
CHINA T	A	W	83	500	450	495	45
	V	E	82	845	3,240	3,571	331
			83	17,556	16,713	18,286	1,573
			84	40,540	45,270	49,317	4,047
			85	39,612	41,804	45,580	3,776
			86	15,243	33,212	36,386	3,174
	V	W	81	4,227	5,981	6,375	394
			82	3,083	5,954	6,402	448
			83	9,060	9,525	10,160	635
			84	11,280	16,949	17,926	977
			85	6,921	16,890	17,826	936
			86	31,215	63,681	67,506	3,825
COLOMB	A	E	83	4,329	5,749	7,793	2,044
			84	2,199	7,646	8,968	1,322
			85	186	1,569	1,803	234
CYPRUS	V	E	83	85	932	1,009	77
DENMARK	A	E	81	500	1,355	1,440	85
			82	160	766	984	218
			83	200	2,310	2,529	219
			84	700	7,771	11,236	3,465
	V	E	81	2,200	5,053	5,258	205
			82	612	1,373	1,393	20
			83	2,486	24,066	26,344	2,278
			86	3,504	58,428	60,828	2,400
DOM REP	A	E	81	5,600	1,115	2,024	909
			82	13,100	2,327	4,192	1,865
			84	906	1,347	1,619	272
	N	E	82	22,100	9,279	13,595	4,316
			83	31,918	4,251	9,884	5,633
	V	E	81	2,200	1,000	1,697	697
			82	2,476	3,000	3,086	86
			83	5,967	4,248	4,864	616
			84	7,006	3,417	4,056	639
			85	23,043	4,192	5,363	1,171
			86	6,200	5,650	5,924	274
ECUADOR	A	E	82	463	4,800	5,155	355
EGYPT	O	E	82	488	1,378	1,426	48
			83	100	990	990	
			84	2,680	2,025	2,025	
	V	E	82	2,205	2,954	3,166	212
			84	10,500	9,843	11,032	1,189
			86	28,253	17,190	20,774	3,584
	V	W	86	6,000	1,554	1,595	41
FIJI	A	W	81	2,400	1,200	1,324	124
			84	2,000	2,683	3,254	571
			86	13,995	3,919	6,425	2,506
	V	W	81	540	2,133	2,161	28
FR GERM	A	E	82	937	2,659	3,364	705
			83	446	1,228	1,770	542
			84	136	739	1,489	750
			86	1,651	20,461	23,871	3,410
	A	W	81	154	254	389	135
			83	121	483	650	167

Product
TSUSA commodity number, description, and unit of quantity

Country	Mode	Reg	Yr	Quantity	F.A.S.	C.I.F.	Charges
			85	568	10,694	11,395	701
			86	33	4,440	4,527	87
	N	E	81	3,521	15,573	16,437	864
			82	8,833	9,382	10,365	983
			83	82,527	209,214	218,110	8,896
			84	65,203	101,326	110,190	8,864
			85	4,308	14,379	15,578	1,199
	N	W	81	1,834	2,809	3,623	814
			82	9,695	12,072	14,764	2,692
			84	6,779	14,214	15,642	1,428
			85	4,984	8,014	10,243	2,229
	O	E	81	21,189	33,799	36,495	2,696
			82	60,449	67,061	72,298	5,237
			83	28,083	29,291	31,925	2,634
			84	8,501	8,194	8,889	695
			85	19,941	19,436	22,117	2,681
			86	31,171	27,921	30,329	2,408
	O	W	83	270	1,214	1,287	73
	V	E	81	3,290	9,414	10,702	1,288
			82	14,284	47,460	49,660	2,200
			83	6,599	37,711	39,200	1,489
			84	26,054	59,508	66,415	6,907
			85	39,038	61,506	67,401	5,895
			86	41,336	83,551	92,613	9,062
	V	W	83	69,929	60,810	68,766	7,956
			84	2,393	7,284	8,386	1,102
			86	631	3,617	4,217	600
FRANCE	A	E	81	2,326	4,451	6,303	1,852
			82	750	2,161	2,608	447
			83	1,473	3,827	4,950	1,123
			84	1,195	15,191	16,886	1,695
			85	1,274	10,028	11,154	1,126
			86	3,102	7,981	11,055	3,074
	A	W	84	235	266	469	203
	N	E	81	40,262	164,300	177,771	13,471
			82	34,519	154,356	165,475	11,119
			83	43,077	130,121	140,879	10,758
			84	62,188	205,360	220,244	14,884
			85	143,033	155,327	168,062	12,735
			86	97,200	224,868	242,955	18,087
	N	W	81	11,891	47,557	53,659	6,102
			82	27,549	66,647	71,673	5,026
			83	41,856	91,178	99,701	8,523
			84	16,916	34,759	40,132	5,373
			85	31,689	47,211	55,968	8,757
			86	22,675	15,760	18,036	2,276
	O	E	81	199	1,450	1,816	366
			82	400	2,189	2,395	206
			84	514	2,164	2,436	272
			85	654	4,797	5,367	570
			86	1,716	7,024	8,595	1,571
	V	E	81	3,138	8,012	8,561	549
			82	8,054	17,548	18,906	1,358
			83	5,583	26,242	27,361	1,119
			84	11,428	31,753	34,955	3,202
			85	10,926	34,199	37,552	3,353
			86	12,888	63,847	69,004	5,157
	V	W	82	261	930	1,004	74
			83	13,650	17,162	18,487	1,325
			84	6,349	14,750	16,880	2,130
			86	27,612	101,474	109,067	7,593
GREECE	O	E	83	376	1,172	1,194	22
	V	E	81	14,922	4,692	5,344	652
			83	400	400	485	85
			84	300	690	773	83
GUATMAL	A	W	81	376	259	352	93
			82	3,279	2,566	3,370	804
			83	510	1,067	1,574	507
			84	150	297	348	51
	N	E	82	14,726	21,654	22,931	1,277
	N	W	81	2,078	2,474	2,793	319
	O	W	86	8,818	6,690	7,337	647
	V	E	81	64,000	45,300	48,282	2,982
			82	67,000	45,600	49,388	3,788
			85	20,282	13,630	17,548	3,918
			86	3,938	3,200	3,553	353
	V	W	81	1,000	850	884	34
			82	44,202	6,000	7,382	1,382
			84	130	1,700	1,995	295
			85	4,000	3,400	3,853	453
GUYANA	O	E	83	216	345	345	
			84	180	374	374	
HAITI	V	E	81	2,715	1,629	1,735	106
			83	7,657	2,084	2,523	439
			85	11,193	2,600	3,300	700

Product
TSUSA commodity number, description, and unit of quantity

Country	Mode	Reg	Yr	Quantity	F.A.S.	C.I.F.	Charges
HG KONG	A	E	81	221	2,670	2,976	306
			86	990	24,503	26,181	1,678
	N	E	81	8,849	12,421	13,464	1,043
			82	4,199	8,913	10,065	1,152
			83	15,555	17,625	25,753	8,128
			84	13,756	17,465	19,719	2,254
	N	W	81	4,038	9,607	12,736	3,129
	O	E	85	2,880	2,000	2,460	460
	O	W	82	563	1,690	1,801	111
	V	E	81	4,120	7,003	7,402	399
			82	4,035	11,526	12,374	848
			83	4,540	9,137	10,262	1,125
			84	12,564	20,038	23,027	2,989
			85	33,369	46,841	53,333	6,492
			86	40,048	56,043	62,612	6,569
	V	H	81	1,000	1,262	1,341	79
			82	1,000	1,293	1,367	74
			83	500	885	980	95
			85	2,600	3,492	3,960	468
			86	2,161	3,700	4,171	471
	V	W	81	14,107	16,779	18,116	1,337
			82	23,614	31,641	34,144	2,503
			83	30,175	39,713	44,325	4,612
			84	20,924	27,727	29,863	2,136
			85	48,165	69,013	74,540	5,527
			86	132,378	177,882	187,539	9,657
HONDURA	V	E	82	17,528	37,506	38,642	1,136
			84	60,954	60,482	64,433	3,951
HUNGARY	V	E	83	9,531	7,505	8,489	984
	V	W	84	646	388	452	64
INDIA	A	E	83	220	1,221	1,777	556
			84	2,045	1,149	1,321	172
			85	2,916	12,468	15,664	3,196
			86	950	6,052	7,751	1,699
	A	W	83	330	550	869	319
	N	E	81	13,948	21,495	24,790	3,295
			82	312,104	179,940	217,963	38,023
			83	18,272	28,568	31,151	2,583
			84	99,169	103,395	115,545	12,150
			85	202,296	151,129	174,951	23,822
			86	557,271	255,383	300,764	45,381
	N	W	83	16,930	6,590	7,882	1,292
			84	8,723	8,703	10,568	1,865
	O	E	81	6,378	3,335	3,335	
			82	14,155	18,211	19,252	1,041
			83	10,609	25,475	26,456	981
			84	24,411	32,287	32,287	
			85	36,771	31,683	34,041	2,358
			86	83,094	78,095	79,963	1,868
	O	W	86	1,834	1,224	1,224	
	V	E	81	301,773	173,042	217,408	44,366
			82	88,762	68,275	80,109	11,834
			83	318,182	290,709	333,405	42,696
			84	236,677	227,832	263,550	35,718
			85	286,034	236,270	280,464	44,194
			86	169,091	136,715	155,556	18,841
	V	W	81	192,603	100,078	122,989	22,911
			82	216,973	131,213	153,541	22,328
			83	154,475	131,315	151,887	20,572
			84	160,808	105,296	125,798	20,502
			85	159,662	87,205	104,534	17,329
			86	181,361	108,369	124,593	16,224
INDNSIA	V	W	81	720	892	1,056	164
			82	474	1,103	1,343	240
			83	3,640	4,879	5,430	551
			84	4,786	8,216	8,966	750
			85	9,595	12,037	13,690	1,653
			86	24,565	16,610	19,391	2,781
IRAN	A	E	81	229	32,036	32,376	340
	A	W	83	4,820	5,694	12,256	6,562
	V	E	85	32,710	25,765	28,747	2,982
	V	W	82	1,102	1,020	1,058	38
			84	6,939	6,060	7,708	1,648
			85	7,048	6,922	9,134	2,212
IRELAND	A	E	83	314	345	810	465
			84	550	549	1,305	756
	V	W	85	6,925	12,288	13,065	777
ISRAEL	O	E	84	4,840	6,331	6,899	568
	V	E	81	186,983	47,857	62,331	14,474
			82	576,392	130,887	165,264	34,377
			83	127,147	188,936	200,046	11,110
			85	21,847	18,077	20,720	2,643
			86	31,587	56,100	60,669	4,569
ITALY	A	W	82	192	5,410	5,999	589
			84	110	375	691	316

Product
TSUSA commodity number, description, and unit of quantity

Country	Mode	Reg	Yr	Quantity	F.A.S.	C.I.F.	Charges
	N	E	84	1,327	5,016	5,588	572
			85	3,502	14,514	15,355	841
			86	6,527	48,972	54,972	6,000
	V	E	81	4,689	14,726	15,735	1,009
			82	5,446	17,818	19,771	1,953
			83	7,964	41,772	44,656	2,884
			84	446	598	617	19
			85	1,861	4,112	4,498	386
			86	8,107	20,762	21,930	1,168
	V	W	81	396	1,542	1,802	260
			82	34	303	303	
			83	79	443	534	91
			86	1,392	10,202	10,772	570
JAMAICA	A	E	81	1,811	3,358	4,262	904
			82	354	636	861	225
			83	5,165	5,686	8,081	2,395
			84	1,100	3,327	4,132	805
	V	E	82	1,415	2,550	2,772	222
			85	956	1,649	1,784	135
JAPAN	A	E	81	12	355	413	58
			82	1,696	15,365	18,791	3,426
			83	832	3,202	5,295	2,093
			84	445	1,818	2,151	333
	N	E	83	8,089	19,775	24,106	4,331
			84	6,881	23,931	25,944	2,013
			86	53,656	166,913	175,613	8,700
	N	W	82	14,474	48,525	51,835	3,310
			84	6,294	44,960	47,161	2,201
			86	4,347	13,089	15,061	1,972
	O	E	83	55	287	314	27
			84	2,474	4,794	5,264	470
	V	E	81	1,455	3,101	3,323	222
			82	14,558	32,921	36,218	3,297
			83	16,422	46,811	50,621	3,810
			84	35,501	68,841	74,130	5,289
			85	46,743	94,289	104,196	9,907
			86	27,960	70,959	74,541	3,582
	V	H	81	30	311	316	5
			82	139	281	317	36
	V	W	81	9,378	30,484	32,476	1,992
			82	10,407	55,087	58,447	3,360
			83	58,694	95,201	101,741	6,540
			84	24,152	55,473	60,730	5,257
			85	63,104	177,765	188,439	10,674
			86	68,910	217,690	228,922	11,232
JORDAN	V	E	85	1,102	1,400	1,571	171
			86	11,023	5,438	5,710	272
KENYA	O	E	82	1,623	2,924	3,245	321
			83	11,015	3,906	4,026	120
			86	3,079	1,578	1,813	235
	V	E	84	32,900	7,704	9,987	2,283
			85	80,933	35,274	41,556	6,282
KOR REP	V	E	81	910	1,840	2,017	177
			82	1,653	2,700	2,775	75
			83	10,522	4,996	5,470	474
			84	5,574	4,518	5,314	796
			85	5,373	7,864	8,703	839
			86	26,250	35,759	39,166	3,407
	V	W	81	465	668	803	135
			82	16,841	17,015	20,274	3,259
			83	5,690	12,396	14,097	1,701
			84	12,844	15,261	17,621	2,360
			85	18,347	45,962	50,696	4,734
			86	51,061	79,290	86,054	6,764
LEBANON	A	E	81	328	4,616	5,586	970
	O	E	84	8,480	8,650	8,650	
			85	5,850	2,600	2,600	
	V	E	81	5,622	8,644	9,323	679
			82	2,925	2,994	3,205	211
			83	882	940	1,058	118
			84	551	1,935	2,209	274
			85	2,602	4,153	4,351	198
			86	51,176	46,722	51,094	4,372
	V	W	85	981	3,041	3,041	
			86	49,059	31,126	32,704	1,578
LIBERIA	V	E	81	2,740	1,051	1,709	658
MACAO	V	E	85	16,755	28,520	31,191	2,671
MADAGAS	V	E	81	37,676	44,975	54,123	9,148
			82	14,488	52,635	55,668	3,033
			83	5,291	2,767	3,801	1,034
			84	29,000	7,163	10,863	3,700
			85	83,757	66,683	81,333	14,650
			86	47,183	14,158	17,158	3,000
MALAWI	O	E	82	90	1,189	1,287	98
	V	E	83	88	291	297	6

Product
TSUSA commodity number, description, and unit of quantity

Country	Mode	Reg	Yr	Quantity	F.A.S.	C.I.F.	Charges
			84	678	614	653	39
MALAYSA	O E	84	247	425	425		
	V E	81	8,429	17,186	18,379	1,193
		82	18,295	36,571	39,980	3,409
		83	14,504	37,179	40,670	3,491
		84	17,515	44,154	48,869	4,715
		85	26,434	62,585	69,004	6,419
		86	51,749	116,480	128,749	12,269
	V H	81	1,380	1,782	1,892	110
	V W	82	7,734	7,173	7,884	711
		83	8,891	17,167	18,750	1,583
		84	30,896	65,728	71,661	5,933
		85	28,681	64,724	71,273	6,549
		86	9,028	17,936	19,877	1,941
MEXICO	A E	84	67	771	861	90
	N E	83	4,099	2,561	2,762	201
	O E	81	8,031	19,328	19,328	
		82	14,143	18,157	18,157	
		83	162	1,024	1,024	
		84	185	392	392	
		86	352,895	92,199	92,199	
	O W	84	132	257	257	
		86	17,380	9,543	9,543	
	V E	81	44,092	31,962	34,393	2,431
		83	2,455	2,178	2,352	174
		86	11,457	8,579	9,405	826
MOROC	N E	83	531,121	106,487	133,860	27,373
		86	34,613	28,330	34,194	5,864
	O E	83	290	320	320	
		86	300	5,685	6,685	1,000
	V E	82	162,700	35,277	43,235	7,958
		83	39,683	8,612	10,627	2,015
		84	1,087,838	212,682	266,268	53,586
		85	410,946	115,921	138,048	22,127
		86	487,943	207,943	236,659	28,716
N ANTIL	V E	86	1,473	4,222	4,539	317
N ZEAL	A W	84	444	323	623	300
NETHLDS	A E	83	82	4,444	4,598	154
		84	253	932	1,040	108
	A W	86	825	2,521	3,576	1,055
	N E	84	9,046	21,038	23,823	2,785
		85	19,395	50,741	57,302	6,561
	N W	81	31,882	37,905	42,216	4,311
		84	78,812	54,804	59,978	5,174
	O E	83	588	3,705	3,781	76
		84	1,164	2,224	2,369	145
		86	244	1,149	1,254	105
	V E	81	34,937	46,614	52,544	5,930
		82	57,954	85,684	91,842	6,158
		83	35,049	107,666	118,593	10,927
		84	7,726	16,064	17,121	1,057
		85	75,048	45,798	50,288	4,490
		86	41,554	77,772	87,392	9,620
	V W	81	665	1,346	1,544	198
		82	24,067	19,483	21,434	1,951
		83	87,057	61,102	65,690	4,588
		84	2,500	1,540	1,663	123
		85	48,989	42,583	47,135	4,552
		86	33,069	48,119	52,526	4,407
PAKISTN	A E	86	1,047	1,265	3,911	2,646
	N W	84	1,176	2,584	2,895	311
	O E	81	2,666	1,264	1,287	23
		82	110	273	295	22
		83	2,110	2,704	3,003	299
		84	11,168	11,780	12,905	1,125
	V E	81	244,802	47,381	61,208	21,730
		82	243,090	44,408	63,984	19,576
		83	66,865	19,936	26,384	6,448
		84	18,485	12,847	15,326	2,479
		85	40,752	31,912	37,636	5,724
		86	46,252	42,908	47,031	4,123
	V W	81	2,465	1,053	1,383	330
		82	2,205	320	481	161
		83	2,135	2,463	2,596	133
		84	3,772	2,648	3,436	788
		85	69,565	37,512	43,581	6,069
		86	11,133	3,858	4,441	583
PERU	A E	86	500	4,154	5,793	1,639
	N E	82	13,712	52,470	64,303	11,833
		83	20,441	73,600	83,511	9,911
	V E	85	490	1,549	1,734	185
		86	17,195	11,593	13,001	1,408
	V W	85	11,023	4,250	4,362	112
PHIL R	V E	81	2,288	1,065	1,305	240
		82	5,071	4,859	5,534	675

Product
TSUSA commodity number, description, and unit of quantity

Country	Mode	Reg	Yr	Quantity	F.A.S.	C.I.F.	Charges
			83	5,926	6,436	7,729	1,293
			84	9,811	14,144	17,378	3,234
			85	21,050	37,016	42,920	5,904
			86	22,120	28,349	32,848	4,499
	V H	84	2,084	1,112	1,310	198
	V W	81	2,502	3,551	4,018	467
		82	12,854	13,777	15,226	1,449
		83	9,006	8,610	9,485	875
		84	13,753	17,410	19,344	1,934
		85	13,458	17,040	19,532	2,492
		86	25,988	28,759	32,311	3,552
POLAND	V E	84	506	2,902	3,055	153
PORTUGL	V E	82	12,479	8,152	9,550	1,398
		83	12,418	8,974	10,049	1,075
		84	21,413	10,891	13,865	2,974
		85	949	3,313	4,033	720
		86	727	2,867	3,526	659
REP SAF	V E	81	330	300	482	182
ROMANIA	A E	83	225	589	718	129
S LUCIA	V E	84	30	883	908	25
S VN GR	V E	82	230	350	476	126
SALVADR	A E	83	165	360	428	68
		84	50	260	327	67
	V E	81	20,000	32,200	33,569	1,369
SIER LN	V E	84	220	660	768	108
SINGAPR	A W	83	18	262	294	32
	N E	86	2,235	12,830	14,307	1,477
	V E	81	2,638	1,862	1,899	37
		82	2,509	1,000	1,025	25
		83	2,260	3,190	3,565	375
		85	7,842	25,000	26,378	1,378
		86	2,734	2,078	2,255	177
	V H	81	319	1,223	1,393	170
	V W	81	2,087	5,954	6,549	595
		82	9,042	11,933	13,590	1,657
		83	6,567	9,790	10,838	1,048
		84	2,685	6,527	7,120	593
		85	1,181	5,629	6,162	533
SPAIN	A E	81	10	4,001	4,100	99
		83	87	10,145	10,552	407
		84	3,267	17,400	19,402	2,002
		85	19	4,852	5,050	198
		86	530	22,949	24,963	2,014
	A W	83	1,400	4,451	4,616	165
		85	7	2,175	2,416	241
		86	3,351	14,505	15,665	1,160
	N E	83	17,292	109,819	117,771	7,952
		84	64,342	211,324	241,067	29,743
		85	75,040	296,832	327,499	30,667
		86	48,018	226,463	252,360	25,897
	O E	81	7	3,183	3,220	37
		82	10	2,797	2,827	30
		83	2	766	861	95
		84	2	762	762	
		85	36	1,025	1,185	160
		86	605	1,080	1,110	30
	V E	81	6,938	23,529	26,408	2,879
		82	881	2,134	3,008	874
		83	1,157	762	830	68
		85	6,173	26,270	29,253	2,983
SRI LKA	V E	84	1,106	7,184	8,255	1,071
	V W	83	3,067	10,686	12,514	1,828
		85	1,530	1,117	1,567	450
SWEDEN	A E	81	269	1,121	1,421	300
	A W	81	300	1,126	1,414	288
	N E	81	1,135	26,453	26,780	327
SWITZLD	A E	81	1,013	2,257	3,032	775
		83	1,047	2,068	2,834	766
		84	123	373	594	221
		86	2,154	3,966	5,775	1,809
	N E	82	2,101	7,630	8,565	935
		84	4,281	7,934	9,151	1,217
		86	26,665	42,426	44,231	1,805
	N W	82	18,345	35,620	38,172	2,552
	O E	85	2,501	3,767	3,930	163
	V E	81	313	655	728	73
		82	31,469	9,102	10,029	927
		83	100,636	55,513	61,614	6,101
		84	67,728	50,461	54,852	4,391
		85	30,845	53,102	57,256	4,154
		86	12,311	20,737	22,137	1,400
	V W	81	15,261	32,572	34,718	2,146
		82	998	2,241	2,518	277
		83	4,953	8,597	9,445	848
		84	480	628	720	92

Product TSUSA commodity number, description, and unit of quantity Country	Mode	Reg	Yr	Quantity	F.A.S.	C.I.F.	Charges
SYRIA	O	E	82	990	1,253	1,253	
			84	1,210	2,468	2,625	157
	V	E	81	5,070	8,372	8,937	565
			83	6,464	5,905	6,422	517
	V	W	81	9,048	12,364	13,660	1,296
			82	1,082	2,100	2,302	202
THAILND	A	W	81	360	1,309	2,752	1,443
	N	E	84	7,486	11,216	12,555	1,339
			86	46,495	45,203	51,923	6,720
	N	W	81	92,066	183,800	198,934	15,134
			83	492	1,015	1,057	42
			84	157,397	206,921	222,284	15,363
	O	E	82	277	625	809	184
			83	7,213	7,675	8,383	708
			84	300	310	310	
	O	W	82	524	666	753	87
			84	278	421	456	35
			85	2,183	4,354	4,671	317
	V	E	81	20,165	34,378	38,160	3,782
			82	72,038	84,723	95,930	11,207
			83	72,054	84,916	96,454	11,538
			84	58,535	73,835	83,577	9,742
			85	44,950	52,562	59,761	7,199
			86	4,269	8,774	9,810	1,036
	V	H	81	337	1,525	1,705	180
			82	95	429	495	66
			83	883	2,132	2,400	268
			84	294	706	798	92
	V	W	81	37,808	76,957	84,406	7,449
			82	186,059	245,430	271,598	26,168
			83	180,126	240,739	263,615	22,876
			84	91,095	107,502	119,880	12,378
			85	135,964	146,814	160,962	14,148
			86	255,318	289,113	305,830	16,717
TRINID	A	E	81	628	829	899	70
			83	888	3,853	4,173	320
			84	235	565	620	55
	V	E	85	2,204	5,324	5,771	447
TURKEY	A	E	85	4,796	2,615	3,178	563
	A	W	84	990	1,514	1,671	157
	O	E	81	560	1,666	1,666	
			82	495	380	380	
			83	1,487	1,649	2,462	813
			84	760	4,434	4,640	206
			85	3,802	5,221	5,221	
			86	3,850	10,450	10,450	
	V	E	81	82,122	14,120	17,238	3,118
			82	15,510	10,601	12,777	2,176
			83	5,014	7,420	9,442	2,022
			84	2,753	9,649	10,707	1,058
			85	48,483	10,994	13,489	2,495
			86	417,446	92,458	110,713	18,255
	V	W	83	5,512	2,002	2,441	439
			84	9,370	5,076	5,785	709
			85	18,768	34,894	37,056	2,162
			86	11,023	5,250	5,952	702
U KING	A	E	81	2,489	4,373	5,262	889
			82	1,304	2,160	2,607	447
			84	2,194	5,303	6,225	922
			86	2,452	13,560	16,126	2,566
	A	W	81	229	2,887	3,191	304
			85	1,480	9,194	9,468	274
			86	54	1,512	1,928	416
	N	E	81	8,238	44,889	48,751	3,862
			82	19,416	73,187	78,626	5,439
			83	13,589	44,265	47,767	3,502
			84	30,409	52,394	59,613	7,219
			85	111,394	72,340	82,278	9,938
			86	15,888	35,804	38,233	2,429
	N	W	82	1,404	5,537	5,758	221
			84	1,906	4,446	5,251	805
			86	2,490	7,799	8,268	469
	O	E	81	14,837	31,558	34,588	3,030
			82	2,382	8,258	8,812	554
			83	23,509	27,569	29,431	1,862
			84	846	6,070	6,236	166
			85	250	3,028	3,103	75
			86	18,031	20,581	22,467	1,886
	O	W	83	55	484	489	5
	V	E	82	658	1,909	2,204	295
			83	19,992	33,269	35,356	2,087
			84	24,117	22,501	26,325	3,824
			85	8,081	8,856	9,769	913
			86	34,514	42,385	47,171	4,786
	V	W	81	16,463	14,611	16,785	2,174

Product TSUSA commodity number, description, and unit of quantity Country	Mode	Reg	Yr	Quantity	F.A.S.	C.I.F.	Charges
			82	2,110	3,555	3,978	423
			83	2,555	6,151	7,392	1,241
			84	132	822	891	69
			86	753	6,062	7,093	1,031
W SAMOA	V	W	85	170,543	68,238	81,781	13,543
			86	33,030	15,272	18,419	3,147
YUGOSLV	O	E	85	3,000	2,400	2,400	
	O	W	82	1,320	1,511	1,511	
			83	660	1,094	1,094	
			84	1,323	1,528	1,528	
	V	E	83	14,303	3,445	3,886	441
			85	2,469	3,131	3,488	357
			86	81,196	60,832	69,624	8,792
	V	W	81	3,285	1,199	1,618	419
			83	2,183	1,101	1,422	321
			85	52,577	22,569	28,000	5,431

Sweetener

Dextrose
1556000 DEXTROSE (LB)

Country	Mode	Reg	Yr	Quantity	F.A.S.	C.I.F.	Charges
TOTAL			81	933,515	188,623	228,102	39,479
			82	624,977	243,931	274,319	30,388
			83	6,996,935	1,110,524	1,368,328	257,804
			84	22,478,386	3,603,497	4,764,019	1,160,522
			85	25,112,854	4,374,944	5,816,197	1,441,253
			86	16,195,138	2,962,020	3,707,496	745,476
AUSTRIA	V	W	85	39,683	13,597	13,952	355
BAHAMAS	O	E	85	184,000	23,920	24,270	350
BELGIUM	O	E	81	31,967	7,502	9,362	1,860
			84	74,956	12,959	16,490	3,531
			85	149,912	25,999	33,567	7,568
	V	E	86	44,379	7,227	8,078	851
	V	W	84	110,616	17,674	22,378	4,704
CANADA	A	E	83	1,240	494	594	100
	O	E	81	110	475	475	
			82	43,476	8,724	8,724	
			83	346,661	80,337	80,337	
			84	519,942	112,844	113,156	312
			85	51,955	13,969	13,969	
			86	271,446	38,396	38,396	
	O	W	81	200	278	278	
			82	400	615	615	
			85	601	1,378	1,485	107
CHINA M	V	E	82	16,400	11,195	12,096	901
			83	2,664	1,445	1,642	197
			85	5,500	1,222	1,434	212
			86	40,894	10,181	12,031	1,850
	V	H	82	288	474	514	40
	V	W	81	3,850	943	1,061	118
			82	11,552	3,496	3,832	336
			83	11,482	2,948	3,195	247
			84	2,047	839	902	63
			86	5,512	1,230	1,371	141
DENMARK	V	E	81	2,315	1,267	1,435	168
FINLAND	V	W	84	20,668	5,428	7,219	1,791
			86	107,798	55,780	56,350	570
FR GERM	A	E	82	1,162	29,279	31,350	2,071
			83	24,755	24,145	25,001	856
			84	23,327	17,530	18,718	1,188
	N	E	82	53,025	11,360	12,398	1,038
			83	620,598	127,352	143,315	15,963
			85	562,070	107,940	130,285	22,345
	O	E	81	6,546	6,243	7,420	1,177
			82	855	1,164	1,311	147
			84	524,992	93,819	113,911	20,092
			85	88,086	43,796	48,117	4,321
			86	3,525	4,413	5,290	877
	V	E	81	2,271	1,318	1,451	133
			82	3,306	1,966	1,966	
			83	3,645	2,499	3,052	553
			84	39,881	7,453	9,488	2,035
			85	42,000	5,542	6,192	650
			86	461,915	86,440	106,847	20,407

Product
TSUSA commodity number, description, and unit of quantity

Country	Mode	Reg	Yr	Quantity	F.A.S.	C.I.F.	Charges
	V	W	81	700	946	1,056	110
			83	5,919	4,561	5,324	763
			86	115,742	56,970	57,570	600
FRANCE	A	E	81	5	640	715	75
	N	E	83	246,000	34,953	43,300	8,347
			84	5,433,304	845,213	1,123,081	277,868
			85	14,573,120	2,297,852	3,163,653	865,801
	O	E	82	4,630	1,302	1,882	580
			83	441,003	51,010	69,790	18,780
			84	112,400	22,156	24,356	2,200
			86	262,805	36,188	47,601	11,413
	V	E	82	38,015	6,370	8,346	1,976
			83	4,537,732	585,003	755,652	170,649
			84	14,116,408	2,121,656	2,904,201	782,545
			85	6,971,929	1,116,456	1,530,063	413,607
			86	11,885,410	2,095,125	2,752,601	657,476
	V	W	86	39,601	3,565	6,413	2,848
GAZA ST	V	E	82	1,350	1,654	1,826	172
GIBRAT	V	E	83	166,900	19,305	25,035	5,730
HG KONG	O	E	83	1,260	2,273	2,477	204
			84	1,080	1,233	1,447	214
			85	4,960	1,108	1,197	89
	V	E	82	7,705	3,846	4,588	742
			83	7,732	6,542	7,062	520
			84	5,654	10,285	11,673	1,388
			85	4,357	3,005	3,400	395
	V	W	82	7,500	8,566	9,340	774
			83	21,270	23,879	25,213	1,334
			84	480	764	819	55
			85	15,120	15,053	16,084	1,031
INDIA	O	E	82	2,645	1,289	1,418	129
	V	W	82	4,405	1,221	1,570	349
ISRAEL	V	E	84	6,205	1,479	2,387	908
			85	11,508	1,462	2,360	898
ITALY	A	E	85	20	2,017	2,072	55
	O	E	84	39,352	10,605	10,605	
			86	2,028,399	223,318	223,318	
	V	E	81	571,432	72,775	96,628	23,853
			83	712	1,558	1,666	108
			84	475,294	76,240	96,627	20,387
			85	126,000	20,004	26,854	6,850
			86	84,000	10,742	12,002	1,260
JAPAN	A	E	84	441	1,380	2,502	1,122
	A	W	84	7,110	4,962	5,359	397
	V	W	82	720	1,017	1,037	20
			85	7,980	5,242	5,340	98
			86	10,053	10,238	11,076	838
KOR REP	V	E	82	1,323	450	530	80
	V	W	82	4,762	1,907	2,160	253
MALAYSA	V	E	81	2,072	2,562	2,710	148
			82	520	560	617	57
			85	36,960	38,640	41,979	3,339
	V	W	82	7,200	8,150	9,150	1,000
MEXICO	O	E	86	39,681	6,678	6,678	
	O	W	86	22,046	3,020	3,020	
	V	E	86	18,849	2,736	4,020	1,284
N ANTIL	V	E	83	10,000	2,224	2,666	442
NETHLDS	A	E	86	2,205	7,250	9,196	1,946
	N	E	83	32,166	16,443	26,778	10,335
	O	E	81	246,143	57,612	65,162	7,550
			82	219,448	49,116	60,126	11,010
			84	315,516	59,629	68,291	8,662
			85	774,475	269,736	299,492	29,756
			86	132,496	29,731	36,731	7,000
	V	E	81	2,200	472	550	78
			82	1,512	900	1,058	158
			83	220,157	28,772	38,661	9,889
			84	84,917	16,800	21,553	4,753
			85	67,240	14,394	18,063	3,669
			86	217,814	70,700	80,099	9,399
	V	W	83	105,839	14,341	16,765	2,424
REP SAF	O	E	85	15,984	3,996	3,996	
	V	E	85	154,322	21,540	29,540	8,000
SPAIN	O	E	84	41,667	11,229	11,229	
	V	E	85	433,494	74,517	94,746	20,229
SWITZLD	O	E	82	112,434	21,913	23,049	1,136
			83	37,478	6,442	7,871	1,429
			84	114,659	42,221	46,626	4,405
			85	39,683	26,360	30,960	4,600
	V	E	82	3,197	2,018	2,157	139
			83	8,832	9,662	10,094	432
			84	6,668	3,424	3,578	154
			85	87,743	49,200	53,746	4,546
			86	231,480	126,000	140,730	14,730
	V	W	83	12,236	6,950	7,507	557
			84	4,960	2,769	2,915	146
			85	87,302	65,578	74,878	9,300
THAILND	V	E	81	450	706	813	107
	V	W	82	1,276	310	409	99
			83	1,410	1,163	1,268	105
			84	599	287	311	24
U KING	N	E	81	29,581	16,222	18,162	1,940
			84	72,470	50,920	56,950	6,030
	O	E	81	31,967	16,423	18,288	1,865
	V	E	82	71,896	58,489	64,981	6,492
			83	41,377	31,648	35,446	3,798
			84	125,700	15,681	20,772	5,091
			85	57,699	35,966	40,852	4,886
			86	169,088	76,092	88,078	11,986
	V	W	81	1,706	2,239	2,536	297
			82	3,975	6,580	7,269	689
			83	8,501	11,725	12,643	918
			84	4,611	6,322	7,935	1,613
			85	2,640	3,632	4,265	633
YUGOSLV	V	E	85	39,683	3,505	5,642	2,137
	V	W	83	79,366	12,850	15,974	3,124
			84	192,462	29,696	38,540	8,844
			85	476,828	68,318	93,744	25,426

1556500 DEXTROSE SIRUP (LB)

Country	Mode	Reg	Yr	Quantity	F.A.S.	C.I.F.	Charges
TOTAL			81	47,748	7,528	7,936	408
			82	97,281	23,474	27,720	4,246
			83	3,613,538	434,776	451,109	16,333
			84	1,760,882	241,777	252,690	10,913
			85	1,109,168	209,449	265,894	56,445
			86	6,744,991	1,279,173	1,650,503	371,330
AUSTRAL	V	E	84	2,205	764	885	121
BRAZIL	V	E	85	212,967	37,146	52,205	15,059
			86	137,568	21,033	29,515	8,482
CANADA	O	E	81	41,055	5,644	5,644	
			82	40,000	2,547	2,547	
			83	3,264,029	324,695	324,695	
			84	1,261,041	169,800	172,660	2,860
			85	47,575	7,900	7,900	
			86	129,432	11,690	11,690	
CHINA M	V	E	82	9,480	2,606	3,317	711
	V	W	82	5,039	1,224	1,463	239
			83	25,229	4,999	5,615	616
			84	44,156	11,124	11,999	875
			85	19,939	4,510	4,843	333
			86	30,878	8,347	8,902	555
CHINA T	V	W	84	4,762	2,186	2,400	214
FRANCE	O	E	85	263,670	50,112	65,109	14,997
	V	E	84	1,392	954	1,075	121
			85	529,106	94,511	118,010	23,499
			86	6,322,877	1,222,520	1,583,952	361,432
	V	W	84	794	933	1,027	94
GREECE	O	E	84	396	322	322	
HG KONG	V	W	84	2,378	824	885	61
			86	21,164	5,728	6,214	486
ITALY	V	E	84	397	1,647	1,706	59
JAMAICA	V	E	86	3,525	1,672	1,904	232
JAPAN	A	E	84	9,640	3,115	4,927	1,812
	V	E	83	5,512	1,297	1,825	528
	V	W	82	24,751	9,081	11,020	1,939
			83	30,260	9,032	9,660	628
KOR REP	V	E	82	1,190	426	540	114
			83	21,808	8,792	9,911	1,119
			86	3,150	1,116	1,200	84
	V	H	83	926	415	480	65
	V	W	82	5,167	2,441	2,623	182
			83	11,507	4,600	5,051	451
			84	11,344	3,773	4,256	483
			85	31,320	9,457	10,258	801
LEBANON	O	E	81	300	339	339	
MEXICO	O	E	84	348,000	23,012	23,012	
	O	W	86	96,000	5,420	5,420	
NETHLDS	A	E	83	3,830	2,040	3,038	998
	O	E	83	194,446	62,628	71,541	8,913
			84	42,461	6,790	8,990	2,200
	V	E	81	6,393	1,545	1,953	408
			82	6,614	1,288	1,725	437
NORWAY	A	E	84	6	300	360	60
SINGAPR	O	E	84	195	256	282	26
THAILND	V	W	82	5,040	3,861	4,485	624
			84	9,686	3,750	4,158	408
			85	1,570	1,216	2,116	900
U KING	N	E	83	55,991	16,278	19,293	3,015
	V	E	84	16,926	12,361	13,818	1,457

Product TSUSA commodity number, description, and unit of quantity Country	Mode		Reg	Yr	Quantity	F.A.S.	C.I.F.	Charges
				85	3,021	4,597	5,453	856
	V	W		84	5,500	1,513	1,634	121

Fructose from starches
1557520 HIGH FRUCTSE SIRUP F/STACH (LB)

Country	Mode		Reg	Yr	Quantity	F.A.S.	C.I.F.	Charges
TOTAL				85	493,902,317	48,619,990	48,634,917	14,927
				86	598,826,959	62,766,954	62,801,471	34,517
BRAZIL	O	E		85	740,746	57,778	57,778	
CANADA	O	E		85	491,330,035	48,447,237	48,447,255	18
				86	554,838,014	60,569,837	60,569,841	4
	O	W		86	902,979	183,442	183,442	
DOM REP	V	E		85	2,176	1,088	2,103	1,015
FR GERM	V	E		86	252	3,443	3,646	203
GABON	O	E		86	4,041,344	222,921	229,246	6,325
GUATMAL	O	E		85	1,691,206	59,193	60,847	1,654
				86	31,499,375	1,356,372	1,375,808	19,436
HG KONG	V	E		85	22,260	6,654	8,315	1,661
	V	W		85	3,150	2,000	2,190	190
HONDURA	O	E		86	7,409,137	377,740	377,740	
HUNGARY	V	E		85	40,839	11,681	13,821	2,140
INDIA	V	W		85	1,323	2,100	2,394	294
ITALY	V	E		86	1,468	1,444	2,894	1,450
JAMAICA	V	E		85	30,520	14,077	19,117	5,040
JAPAN	V	W		86	71,113	40,287	46,339	6,052
KIRIBAT	V	E		86	47,774	5,183	5,183	
LEBANON	V	W		86	13,688	4,667	5,343	676
SWITZLD	V	E		85	8,769	6,727	7,131	404
U KING	V	E		86	1,815	1,618	1,989	371
	V	W		85	3,436	1,810	2,221	411
YUGOSLV	O	E		85	27,857	9,645	11,745	2,100

Levulose
4936600 LEVULOSE (LB)

Country	Mode		Reg	Yr	Quantity	F.A.S.	C.I.F.	Charges
TOTAL				81	7,511,051	5,709,192	6,204,986	495,794
				82	8,561,281	6,479,925	6,986,894	506,969
				83	3,322,098	1,673,859	1,807,917	134,058
				84	3,962,362	2,445,363	2,703,051	257,688
				85	4,306,782	2,444,125	2,696,396	252,271
				86	7,015,088	3,426,547	3,788,728	362,181
AUSTRIA	V	E		84	79,366	51,352	57,600	6,248
BELGIUM	O	E		82	44,644	34,585	37,260	2,675
	V	E		83	76,719	37,360	40,487	3,127
				84	212,049	145,929	157,761	11,832
				85	352,431	147,837	164,710	16,873
				86	42,527	15,617	16,917	1,300
	V	W		83	211,642	131,840	146,814	14,974
				84	220,460	140,062	153,800	13,738
				86	39,683	19,100	21,600	2,500
CANADA	O	E		81	214,160	161,520	161,520	
				82	142,300	12,705	12,705	
				83	961,834	139,199	139,199	
				84	19,817	13,778	13,778	
				85	3,960	2,725	2,725	
				86	29,469	18,335	18,335	
	V	W		85	43,651	24,308	28,708	4,400
FINLAND	O	E		82	29,211	13,250	13,250	
	V	E		81	5,174,216	3,935,947	4,272,747	336,800
				82	1,516,024	1,169,565	1,261,901	92,336
				83	176,368	124,091	136,000	11,909
				85	44,092	30,845	33,400	2,555
				86	231,483	110,647	123,900	13,253
	V	W		81	1,940,048	1,471,527	1,616,028	144,501
				82	3,631,090	2,776,568	3,025,245	248,677
				83	257,938	186,827	204,000	17,173
				84	467,376	326,550	354,797	28,247
				85	88,184	62,900	66,800	3,900
				86	132,276	94,100	100,200	6,100
FR GERM	A	W		83	1,100	842	2,292	1,450
	N	E		82	618,068	483,832	515,844	32,012
	O	E		84	11,904	8,600	8,600	
				85	6,613	4,401	4,401	
	O	W		83	119,049	75,441	82,332	6,891
	V	E		81	3,660	6,510	6,834	324
				82	2,372,931	1,852,062	1,971,227	119,165
				83	559,882	374,357	396,912	22,555
				84	765,705	403,326	450,361	47,035
				85	832,129	446,085	496,613	50,528
				86	1,495,757	710,503	809,662	99,159
	V	W		81	132,276	101,888	111,600	9,712

Product TSUSA commodity number, description, and unit of quantity Country	Mode		Reg	Yr	Quantity	F.A.S.	C.I.F.	Charges
				82	158,732	99,650	109,689	10,039
				83	833,343	524,937	574,560	49,623
				84	1,432,723	870,708	964,327	93,619
				85	168,850	88,845	102,295	13,450
				86	407,191	222,698	251,598	28,900
FRANCE	A	E		84	441	270	540	270
	N	E		85	210,320	119,148	137,037	17,889
	O	E		83	2,866	1,913	2,100	187
				84	22,046	13,500	14,790	1,290
	V	E		81	24,691	16,800	19,806	3,006
				82	4,630	3,150	3,341	191
				83	80,887	49,532	52,491	2,959
				84	80,579	45,418	48,636	3,218
				86	1,454,778	653,573	748,092	94,519
	V	W		81	22,000	15,000	16,451	1,451
				84	39,683	22,320	25,200	2,880
				85	194,538	98,685	113,179	14,494
				86	522,300	172,971	201,656	28,685
JAPAN	A	E		83	710	849	2,244	1,395
	N	E		84	35,277	20,258	23,916	3,658
	V	E		86	35,274	15,000	17,990	2,990
	V	W		84	530,309	344,999	388,044	43,045
				85	1,915,480	1,152,065	1,243,571	91,506
				86	2,620,550	1,372,274	1,455,779	83,505
KOR REP	V	W		85	33,175	17,807	19,047	1,240
NETHLDS	V	E		83	39,683	25,802	27,504	1,702
				85	35,274	18,548	21,028	2,480
SWITZLD	A	E		83	77	869	982	113
				84	976	9,189	9,797	608
				86	3,800	21,729	22,999	1,270
	N	E		85	80,697	57,705	65,164	7,459
	O	E		85	174,604	95,900	109,717	13,817
	V	E		82	43,651	34,558	36,432	1,874
				84	43,651	29,104	31,104	2,000
	V	W		85	122,784	76,321	88,001	11,680

Sugar, sirup, and molasses, blends
1557500 SUGARS SIRUPS ETC BLENDS (LB)

Country	Mode		Reg	Yr	Quantity	F.A.S.	C.I.F.	Charges
TOTAL				81	7,259,194	1,986,104	2,205,202	219,439
				82	28,933,900	5,524,433	5,732,758	208,325
				83	322,360,203	37,933,407	38,178,890	245,483
				84	401,925,183	46,965,159	47,271,304	306,145
ARGENT	V	E		83	111,257	44,441	52,798	8,357
AUSTRAL	O	E		82	4	459	466	7
				84	4,498	1,336	1,547	211
AUSTRIA	O	E		83	4,687	4,819	5,133	314
	O	W		83	1,348	2,736	2,941	205
BAHAMAS	O	E		84	1,776,000	332,112	335,722	3,610
	V	E		84	896,000	167,552	167,598	46
BARBADO	V	E		82	13,275	13,435	15,195	1,760
				83	2,925	3,375	3,593	218
BELGIUM	O	E		81	741	386	414	28
				84	960,000	98,285	106,619	8,334
	V	E		83	88,933	26,222	31,287	5,065
				84	138,934	37,286	42,920	5,634
BRAZIL	V	E		83	276	630	787	157
				84	1,978	1,548	1,551	3
CANADA	A	H		83	2,296	2,525	2,731	206
	N	E		81	26,044	85,676	88,012	2,336
				82	17,273	63,218	66,325	3,107
				83	16,086	48,336	49,246	910
				84	247,263,937	27,569,703	27,569,703	
	O	E		81	36,857	25,860	25,860	
				82	24,921,349	3,776,989	3,777,436	447
				83	289,931,880	32,377,318	32,377,519	201
				84	146,926,239	16,976,062	16,978,641	2,579
	O	W		81	5,770	5,138	5,138	
				82	193,858	26,227	26,227	
				83	29,066,720	3,740,937	3,740,937	
				84	236,620	41,024	41,024	
CHINA M	O	E		81	975	1,150	1,325	175
				84	731	1,172	1,367	195
	V	E		81	186,590	69,686	86,106	16,420
				82	110,967	30,377	36,914	6,537
				83	40,831	29,123	33,234	4,111
				84	11,937	3,692	4,615	923
	V	H		81	600	386	404	18
				82	1,200	777	831	54
				83	600	367	400	33
				84	1,485	1,182	1,300	118
	V	W		81	48,690	30,528	33,287	2,759
				82	80,920	30,261	33,338	3,077

Product
TSUSA commodity number, description, and unit of quantity

Country	Mode	Reg	Yr	Quantity	F.A.S.	C.I.F.	Charges
			83	25,999	14,314	15,485	1,171
			84	6,742	3,317	3,925	608
CHINA T	V	E	81	3,375	1,757	1,908	151
			83	11,938	8,782	9,688	906
			84	13,955	8,417	9,663	1,246
	V	W	81	7,167	5,800	6,164	364
			82	8,403	4,820	5,188	368
			83	16,693	10,261	11,170	909
			84	17,738	18,169	19,707	1,538
COLOMB	A	E	83	432	350	530	180
CYPRUS	V	E	82	3,030	2,612	3,334	722
			83	3,674	3,688	4,212	524
			84	703	700	805	105
CZECHO	V	E	81	15,873	9,005	11,507	2,502
DOM REP	A	E	81	1,000	292	389	97
	V	E	81	126,394	22,249	26,153	3,904
			82	119,554	26,711	29,732	3,021
			83	214,410	35,818	41,925	6,107
			84	258,206	42,727	51,501	8,774
DOMINCA	V	E	84	2,200	6,067	6,628	561
FR GERM	N	E	81	36,148	49,591	54,956	5,365
			82	61,102	63,743	69,589	5,846
			83	77,548	99,262	108,553	9,291
			84	34,898	51,174	55,468	4,294
	O	E	81	1,485	2,233	2,468	235
			83	526	2,128	2,489	361
			84	12,242	5,230	5,674	444
	V	E	82	12,958	9,862	10,692	830
			83	11,197	7,489	8,202	713
			84	262,248	123,565	143,143	19,578
	V	W	81	5,052	7,433	7,751	318
			82	2,617	2,557	2,743	186
			83	7,173	6,553	7,434	881
			84	911	807	957	150
FRANCE	A	E	82	2,976	3,254	5,088	1,834
	N	E	81	710	1,916	2,414	498
			84	24,627	29,498	35,211	5,713
	N	W	83	22,360	13,755	15,349	1,594
	O	E	81	37,781	53,908	58,838	4,930
			82	9,249	12,084	12,826	742
			83	1,405	1,902	2,280	378
			84	2,596	2,988	4,285	1,297
	O	W	83	5,910	2,670	3,181	511
	V	E	81	28,069	30,752	34,380	3,628
			82	46,344	45,591	50,874	5,283
			83	23,814	31,339	34,793	3,454
			84	56,688	24,657	28,922	4,265
	V	W	81	2,547	2,623	2,843	220
			82	61,351	39,466	44,059	4,593
			83	18,987	9,962	11,705	1,743
			84	57,556	38,734	45,444	6,710
GREECE	O	E	83	450	527	527	
	V	E	81	8,342	5,616	6,459	843
			82	17,702	15,125	18,920	3,795
			83	5,042	4,832	6,892	2,060
			84	14,803	8,086	9,275	1,189
GUATMAL	V	E	82	63,192	34,681	39,580	4,899
HAITI	A	E	83	290	504	595	91
	V	E	83	1,500	675	761	86
HG KONG	N	W	83	50,814	17,712	18,771	1,059
	V	E	81	667,221	262,894	291,279	28,385
			82	386,967	146,653	168,813	22,160
			83	674,011	235,382	272,556	37,174
			84	869,621	278,938	338,409	59,471
	V	H	81	1,800	1,457	1,557	100
			82	780	657	711	54
			83	1,200	764	843	79
			84	1,200	780	868	88
	V	W	81	143,294	45,078	47,935	2,857
			82	98,827	40,325	43,300	2,975
			83	130,060	62,388	68,237	5,849
			84	254,504	88,610	100,602	11,992
HUNGARY	V	E	81	15,873	4,076	5,159	1,083
			82	41,862	16,048	20,640	4,592
			83	15,750	9,618	10,740	1,122
INDIA	N	E	84	14,821	10,593	12,025	1,432
	O	E	83	5,911	3,980	4,421	441
	V	E	81	4,808	2,818	3,528	710
			82	17,883	15,284	18,213	2,929
			83	42,499	31,715	36,555	4,840
			84	6,220	7,497	8,596	1,099
	V	W	81	19,561	9,958	12,765	2,807
			82	3,762	3,787	4,373	586
			83	17,802	8,950	11,082	2,132
INDNSIA	V	W	82	354	304	330	26
			83	1,567	1,156	1,242	86
			84	32,305	4,222	4,550	328
IRAQ	O	E	83	42,990	34,466	37,912	3,446
	V	E	83	26,400	13,000	17,100	4,100
IRELAND	V	E	81	15,820	10,218	12,436	2,218
			83	224	260	269	9
			84	47	533	730	197
ISRAEL	O	E	83	308	350	370	20
	V	E	84	86,933	33,655	42,069	8,414
	V	W	82	2,149	2,677	2,810	133
ITALY	A	E	82	106	256	321	65
			84	254	253	416	163
	N	E	83	104,130	59,397	70,220	10,823
			84	84,372	66,437	77,412	10,975
	O	E	81	925	950	950	
	V	E	81	31,878	18,347	26,826	8,479
			82	58,142	44,299	48,725	4,426
			83	2,967	2,584	3,057	473
			84	5,520	6,446	8,347	1,901
	V	W	82	20,503	9,643	10,887	1,244
			83	767	583	707	124
			84	8,810	6,534	7,452	918
JAMAICA	A	E	81	600	288	298	10
			82	1,689	1,300	1,596	296
			83	188	345	645	300
			84	1,810	837	1,157	320
	N	E	82	1,271	2,497	2,774	277
			83	149,513	66,247	70,384	4,137
			84	6,000	2,166	3,026	860
	O	E	84	5,083	3,311	3,311	
	V	E	81	374,447	187,042	211,990	24,948
			82	210,286	143,089	162,121	19,032
			83	325,427	185,743	213,959	28,216
			84	354,199	150,893	171,599	20,706
	V	W	84	2,438	1,198	1,676	478
JAPAN	N	E	84	7,547	6,050	6,674	624
	V	E	81	8,315	6,497	7,111	614
			82	7,757	6,424	7,282	858
			83	9,747	7,661	8,262	601
			84	10,594	9,994	11,265	1,271
	V	H	81	517	451	511	60
			82	1,217	1,061	1,467	406
			83	8,274	7,908	9,224	1,316
			84	1,442	1,456	1,665	209
	V	W	81	4,693	5,247	5,504	257
			82	11,138	16,799	18,041	1,242
			83	19,718	15,223	17,070	1,847
			84	37,286	33,525	36,503	2,978
KOR REP	V	E	83	5,337	3,034	3,268	234
			84	1,980	649	938	289
	V	W	81	323	710	787	77
			82	7,496	1,717	1,886	169
			83	5,098	2,902	3,202	300
			84	5,736	2,062	2,382	320
LEBANON	N	E	84	11,957	16,273	17,493	1,220
	O	E	81	750	1,068	1,068	
			82	3,337	5,323	5,323	
			83	4,403	4,561	4,561	
			84	400	470	470	
	V	E	81	4,101	5,052	5,554	502
			82	24,420	29,408	31,995	2,587
			83	74,553	46,598	50,013	3,415
			84	2,043	1,790	1,981	191
MALAYSA	V	W	84	1,320	1,700	1,800	100
MEXICO	A	E	83	623	342	474	132
	O	E	81	3,924,800	390,559	390,559	
			82	1,477,700	238,267	238,267	
			83	88,125	19,848	19,848	
	V	E	84	1,890	484	520	36
N ANTIL	V	E	84	951	3,600	4,246	646
NETHLDS	O	E	81	1,455	702	713	11
			82	2,033	1,884	1,935	51
			84	456	362	390	28
	V	E	81	14,615	8,547	9,984	1,437
			82	2,568	2,143	2,401	258
			83	7,579	5,345	6,036	691
			84	6,813	5,362	6,303	941
	V	W	81	1,561	820	889	69
			82	1,693	858	925	67
			83	4,107	2,654	2,857	203
			84	6,725	3,670	4,060	390
NORWAY	A	E	82	4,540	12,614	17,175	4,561
			83	19,472	19,971	24,043	4,072
	V	E	81	375	841	909	68
			83	185	361	389	28

Product TSUSA commodity number, description, and unit of quantity							
Country	Mode	Reg	Yr	Quantity	F.A.S.	C.I.F.	Charges
	V	W	81	1,819	1,383	2,282	899
			82	1,764	2,282	2,769	487
			83	463	938	1,032	94
PAKISTN	O	E	82	229	450	450	
	V	E	81	10,500	6,625	9,847	3,222
			83	34,223	24,144	28,355	4,211
			84	25,132	15,518	18,017	2,499
	V	W	81	8,643	7,550	9,728	2,178
			82	13,228	8,315	10,868	2,553
			83	1,950	1,698	2,443	745
			84	3,196	4,900	5,945	1,045
PERU	V	E	84	530	1,056	1,109	53
PHIL R	V	E	81	1,060	1,140	1,282	142
			82	720	780	902	122
			83	1,800	1,815	2,004	189
	V	W	81	100,058	17,085	21,975	4,890
			82	752	406	466	60
			83	3,472	2,365	2,718	353
			84	572	349	397	48
POLAND	N	E	82	37,737	38,932	47,257	8,325
			84	30,304	17,753	21,986	4,233
	O	E	81	31,746	18,936	23,616	4,680
			82	47,619	31,230	37,610	6,380
			83	31,746	19,920	24,020	4,100
	V	E	81	69,219	46,514	58,456	11,942
			82	26,581	20,602	23,886	3,284
			83	26,100	24,040	28,462	4,422
			84	68,556	53,950	64,325	10,375
ROMANIA	V	W	84	739	315	334	19
SALVADR	V	E	83	41,667	15,120	17,827	2,707
			84	88,444	28,728	33,398	4,670
SINGAPR	O	E	83	273	326	359	33
	V	E	83	6,715	1,825	2,575	750
			84	37,406	14,327	16,686	2,359
	V	W	81	1,124	878	987	109
			82	2,100	1,072	1,176	104
			83	704	302	330	28
			84	674	304	330	26
SWEDEN	A	E	83	4,645	3,683	6,621	2,938
	N	E	81	12,222	671	680	9
	O	E	84	1,110	528	724	196
	V	E	81	10,790	10,926	11,734	808
			82	3,692	3,914	4,696	782
			83	26,823	39,260	41,506	2,246
			84	30,568	23,765	26,607	2,842
	V	W	84	1,724	2,032	2,117	85
SWITZLD	N	E	84	87,302	46,868	54,677	7,809
	O	E	81	3	447	454	7
	V	E	81	135,432	147,460	158,596	11,477
			82	67,994	93,878	101,170	7,292
			83	79,556	78,756	83,260	4,504
			84	45,122	31,854	34,293	2,439
	V	W	81	5,933	5,377	6,134	757
			82	8,512	10,565	12,074	1,509
			83	38,349	28,774	31,054	2,280
			84	3,439	3,012	3,542	530
SYRIA	O	E	81	270	342	342	
			82	945	1,813	1,813	
	V	E	82	5,558	13,680	14,401	721
			83	1,075	1,150	1,847	697
	V	W	81	3,129	3,666	3,992	326
THAILND	V	E	81	32,063	20,147	23,040	2,893
			82	44,994	27,796	31,654	3,858
			83	29,638	14,838	16,828	1,990
			84	27,724	17,420	20,014	2,594
	V	H	81	2,969	2,140	2,407	267
			83	1,772	981	1,100	119
	V	W	81	733,921	145,436	177,183	31,747
			82	64,903	48,310	53,820	5,510
			83	49,896	27,740	30,058	2,318
			84	46,688	33,364	36,068	2,704
TRINID	A	E	84	1,675	3,000	3,675	675
	N	E	84	24,485	29,149	30,986	1,837
	V	E	81	40,128	34,485	37,104	2,619
			82	18,135	18,600	22,296	3,696
			83	11,700	13,554	14,401	847
			84	10,238	11,860	12,387	527
TURKEY	V	E	81	12,959	13,744	15,468	1,724
			82	10,847	9,375	10,328	953
			83	431	338	373	35
			84	4,209	2,600	2,953	353
U KING	A	E	81	198	381	503	122
	N	E	81	14,862	18,570	20,404	1,834
			82	35,466	43,355	49,375	6,020
			83	74,206	62,946	71,062	8,116

Product TSUSA commodity number, description, and unit of quantity							
Country	Mode	Reg	Yr	Quantity	F.A.S.	C.I.F.	Charges
			84	93,691	69,524	76,522	6,998
	N	W	82	6,189	5,050	6,031	981
	O	E	81	3,460	4,028	4,414	386
			82	20,071	19,858	22,318	2,460
			83	12,496	16,875	19,210	2,335
			84	59,739	38,977	44,723	5,746
	O	W	84	10,885	8,641	9,893	1,252
	V	E	81	1,716	681	736	55
			82	6,735	9,686	11,560	1,874
			84	28,760	13,281	16,682	3,401
	V	W	81	15,065	15,053	17,824	2,771
			82	38,825	22,691	26,678	3,987
			83	38,017	17,946	21,462	3,516
			84	8,766	5,828	7,643	1,815
YUGOSLV	N	E	84	41,153	20,883	24,807	3,924
	O	W	81	13,912	5,850	6,689	839
			82	7,800	5,636	6,415	779
			83	11,981	8,473	10,551	2,078
			84	16,381	11,219	11,530	311
	V	E	81	165,865	72,758	85,835	13,077
			82	297,599	126,062	152,086	26,024
			83	253,966	108,805	131,763	22,958
			84	257,558	87,590	110,596	23,006
	V	W	81	12,186	8,226	8,402	176
			82	29,101	14,529	18,991	4,462
			83	19,603	10,107	12,975	2,868
			84	52,664	21,124	26,188	5,064

1557540 SUGAR SIRUP MOLASSES, BLEND (LB)

Country	Mode	Reg	Yr	Quantity	F.A.S.	C.I.F.	Charges
TOTAL			85	36,034,824	5,019,120	5,285,854	266,734
			86	43,932,515	8,430,050	8,880,043	449,993
AUSTRIA	V	E	85	9,454	3,482	4,556	1,074
B IND O	V	E	86	31,747	13,440	21,355	7,915
BARBADO	V	E	85	1,950	2,159	2,337	178
BELGIUM	V	E	85	4,895	7,680	8,402	722
			86	331	1,271	1,404	133
BRAZIL	O	E	85	4,974,300	406,514	406,514	
			86	61,920	23,714	23,714	
	V	E	85	91,270	17,098	23,846	6,748
CANADA	N	E	85	10,329,703	1,406,617	1,406,617	
			86	1,239	3,063	3,301	238
	O	E	85	12,288,130	1,467,614	1,468,358	744
			86	18,454,755	4,184,128	4,184,128	
	O	W	85	3,113	2,847	2,847	
			86	4,219	2,023	2,023	
CHINA M	V	E	85	600	1,160	1,413	253
			86	10,673	2,628	2,941	313
	V	W	85	17,849	9,975	10,935	960
CHINA T	O	E	86	7,716	4,850	5,728	878
	V	E	86	23,302	8,078	9,376	1,298
	V	W	85	27,697	19,734	21,364	1,630
			86	31,976	22,868	24,602	1,734
DENMARK	V	W	85	2,150	1,429	1,585	156
DOM REP	N	E	85	1,032,090	365,490	404,874	39,384
	V	E	85	198,045	51,752	61,394	9,642
			86	4,000,473	1,368,987	1,519,548	150,561
DOMINCA	V	E	85	2,100	3,560	3,787	227
FR GERM	O	E	86	7,000	6,051	7,051	1,000
	O	W	85	1,200	1,123	1,123	
	V	E	85	73,939	86,874	96,237	9,363
			86	56,933	61,118	65,954	4,836
	V	W	85	4,182	4,575	5,398	823
			86	126,510	72,479	75,521	3,042
FRANCE	O	E	85	1,920	1,075	1,075	
			86	3,202	7,650	8,187	537
	V	E	85	59,788	50,061	56,879	6,818
			86	31,847	36,959	41,175	4,216
	V	W	85	42,056	19,653	23,566	3,913
			86	74,097	28,225	31,874	3,649
GABON	O	E	86	3,451,556	147,120	147,120	
GREECE	V	E	86	1,100	1,725	1,827	102
GUATMAL	O	E	85	5,378,042	196,298	199,590	3,292
			86	10,399,343	449,358	449,358	
HG KONG	V	E	85	330,056	124,030	147,378	23,348
			86	398,544	127,481	146,373	18,892
	V	W	85	180,552	93,938	99,813	5,875
			86	202,168	60,207	69,847	9,640
HONDURA	O	E	86	3,334,445	170,000	170,000	
HUNGARY	V	E	86	21,600	8,324	9,769	1,445
INDIA	V	E	85	11,009	7,013	8,446	1,433
			86	21,218	13,086	15,293	2,207
	V	W	86	2,700	1,841	1,858	17
INDNSIA	V	W	85	5,745	5,682	6,351	669
			86	21,055	12,789	15,272	2,483

Product
TSUSA commodity number, description, and unit of quantity

Country	Mode		Reg	Yr	Quantity	F.A.S.	C.I.F.	Charges
IRAQ	N	W	86	29,240	8,088	12,130	4,042
	O	E	86	47,021	25,781	25,781	
	V	E	86	27,846	18,995	22,981	3,986
	V	W	85	23,450	5,869	8,869	3,000
ISRAEL	V	E	86	20,721	5,714	7,909	2,195
ITALY	N	E	85	108,212	50,021	59,864	9,843
	N	W	86	9,159	10,678	16,945	6,267
	O	E	85	1,984	1,150	1,150	
	V	E	85	40,566	17,854	22,158	4,304
			86	80,283	64,778	73,610	8,832
JAMAICA	N	E	85	90,608	36,954	41,513	4,559
			86	135,796	112,368	141,720	29,352
	O	E	85	14,625	6,000	6,715	715
	V	E	85	240,096	94,409	108,854	14,445
			86	342,549	135,900	152,751	16,851
JAPAN	V	E	85	50,027	22,628	25,443	2,815
			86	48,307	36,220	39,653	3,433
	V	W	85	39,693	28,562	30,917	2,355
			86	112,601	117,216	124,570	7,354
KOR REP	V	E	86	4,233	1,280	1,389	109
LEBANON	N	E	85	32,482	26,563	29,080	2,517
	V	E	85	125,493	84,496	95,868	11,372
			86	46,275	46,096	51,688	5,592
	V	W	85	25,056	20,271	24,382	4,111
			86	72,677	54,710	62,095	7,385
MEXICO	O	W	85	3,038	1,116	1,116	
NETHLDS	V	E	85	3,990	1,437	1,645	208
	V	W	86	7,889	4,924	5,413	489
NORWAY	V	W	86	463	1,046	1,060	14
PAKISTN	V	E	85	72,694	30,117	36,621	6,504
			86	65,028	37,331	43,865	6,534
	V	W	85	1,488	1,297	1,427	130
			86	1,072	1,045	1,340	295
POLAND	O	E	85	15,873	9,410	10,919	1,509
	O	W	85	44	2,399	2,849	450
	V	E	85	79,365	49,800	59,500	9,700
			86	144,041	92,277	111,640	19,363
SINGAPR	V	E	85	975	1,033	1,163	130
SWEDEN	V	E	85	1,558	2,587	2,743	156
			86	1,301	2,811	3,058	247
SWITZLD	N	E	85	9,731	11,979	12,914	935
	V	E	85	11,177	9,749	10,756	1,007
			86	22,492	23,642	25,157	1,515
	V	W	85	6,878	5,695	6,392	697
			86	61,871	63,939	67,989	4,050
SYRIA	V	E	86	2,646	1,995	2,210	215
THAILND	V	E	85	13,282	9,895	10,456	561
			86	14,586	8,277	9,749	1,472
	V	W	85	62,906	37,424	40,993	3,569
			86	120,358	60,710	66,512	5,802
TRINID	V	E	85	18,570	21,359	22,422	1,063
			86	22,425	16,100	17,478	1,378
U KING	N	E	85	27,907	21,159	23,761	2,602
	O	E	85	377,163	202,980	243,896	40,916
			86	33,720	19,321	22,456	3,135
	V	E	85	105,172	62,463	75,155	12,692
			86	77,462	45,931	50,654	4,723
	V	W	85	48,035	17,630	23,892	6,262
			86	67,893	48,808	56,099	7,291
YUGOSLV	O	W	85	7,804	2,637	2,637	
			86	28,405	11,914	14,161	2,247
	V	E	85	171,953	86,611	106,202	19,591
			86	431,816	140,981	182,061	41,080
	V	W	85	163,184	43,623	63,771	20,148
			86	38,580	6,221	6,446	225

Vegetable

Vegetable, dried

1405600 VEG, DRIED, DHYDRATED, NSPF (LB)

		Yr	Quantity	F.A.S.	C.I.F.	Charges
TOTAL		81	3,820,397	8,294,565	8,985,660	691,387
		82	5,266,627	11,078,088	11,928,527	850,439
		83	5,055,337	10,910,775	11,711,103	800,328
		84	6,091,695	12,088,879	12,989,228	900,349
		85	6,147,933	12,408,120	13,384,477	976,357

Product
TSUSA commodity number, description, and unit of quantity

Country	Mode		Reg	Yr	Quantity	F.A.S.	C.I.F.	Charges
				86	7,731,425	14,219,219	15,374,850	1,155,631
ARGENT	V	E	83	4,409	12,246	12,861	615
			84	8,000	20,000	21,207	1,207
			85	10,800	27,000	29,062	2,062
			86	51,766	50,279	57,633	7,354
	V	W	83	3,372	5,307	5,820	513
AUSTRIA	V	E	84	573	1,570	1,774	204
BELGIUM	A	E	83	442	2,097	2,292	195
	A	W	84	792	1,743	2,176	433
			85	2,015	7,620	9,303	1,683
	V	E	84	3,108	1,685	2,054	369
			85	1,587	3,460	3,761	301
BRAZIL	V	E	83	1,196	2,712	3,381	669
			84	2,977	7,292	9,384	2,092
			85	16,535	14,625	17,471	2,846
			86	6,986	27,071	29,915	2,844
C RICA	V	E	86	19,934	25,744	29,719	3,975
	V	W	84	9,090	2,198	2,735	537
CANADA	N	E	82	39,758	129,717	129,945	228
			84	2,617	13,658	13,729	71
	N	W	82	34,080	87,249	92,239	4,990
	O	E	81	140,243	460,352	461,845	1,493
			82	204,795	600,544	611,068	10,524
			83	237,611	561,514	561,514	
			84	225,569	234,402	234,402	
			85	86,480	148,141	148,141	
			86	81,898	152,413	153,557	1,144
	O	W	81	446	1,128	1,283	155
			82	1,803	7,422	7,422	
			83	5,234	14,277	14,277	
			86	8,725	17,450	17,450	
	V	E	84	10,320	25,189	29,710	4,521
			86	4,398	11,012	11,705	693
	V	W	85	1,250	2,132	2,288	156
CHILE	A	E	84	4,409	10,298	13,054	2,756
	N	E	84	39,156	98,741	107,484	8,743
	N	W	86	498,503	1,100,968	1,237,585	136,617
	O	E	81	11,023	30,265	31,457	1,192
	V	E	81	11,051	26,422	27,626	1,204
			82	43,466	17,987	20,367	2,380
			83	14,359	18,236	23,387	5,151
			84	13,051	33,280	35,641	2,361
			85	214,089	572,646	611,906	39,260
			86	137,763	285,601	310,229	24,628
	V	W	81	233,298	611,985	702,832	90,847
			82	64,150	197,438	226,502	29,064
			83	199,525	573,743	646,739	72,996
			84	296,888	738,994	819,095	80,101
			85	446,706	962,740	1,070,754	108,014
			86	838,838	1,904,874	2,059,709	154,835
CHINA M	N	E	81	453,079	835,832	910,083	74,251
			83	437,877	599,679	662,202	62,523
	N	W	82	181,368	298,427	320,561	22,134
			83	18,767	13,924	15,191	1,267
			84	1,149,513	1,870,125	1,958,324	88,199
	O	E	81	375	700	819	119
			84	9,683	7,411	8,251	840
			85	12,000	5,080	5,960	880
			86	5,300	3,815	4,293	478
	O	W	84	1,050	1,243	1,338	95
			86	9,677	7,483	8,001	518
	V	E	81	3,069	10,879	11,944	1,065
			82	450,035	700,058	767,572	67,514
			83	7,559	13,545	14,826	1,281
			84	441,616	559,848	629,264	69,416
			85	542,428	527,083	607,962	80,879
			86	350,079	322,754	363,250	40,496
	V	H	81	11,509	39,317	41,885	2,568
			82	10,487	27,663	30,119	2,456
			83	8,497	21,801	23,931	2,130
			84	11,074	17,559	19,745	2,186
			85	3,054	4,324	4,818	494
			86	7,786	9,040	9,945	905
	V	W	81	295,897	486,160	517,863	31,703
			82	301,416	376,711	416,289	39,578
			83	500,775	685,972	742,094	56,122
			84	139,230	120,541	147,295	26,754
			85	501,129	745,861	792,553	46,692
			86	501,292	497,246	523,421	26,175
CHINA T	A	E	86	1,600	3,557	15,944	12,387
	A	W	83	250	503	553	50
	N	E	81	94,203	215,187	236,263	21,076
			82	13,605	65,515	74,817	9,302
	N	W	85	376,057	924,533	979,140	54,607

Product
TSUSA commodity number, description, and unit of quantity

Country	Mode	Reg	Yr	Quantity	F.A.S.	C.I.F.	Charges
	O	E	84	750	1,100	1,290	190
			85	5,016	3,612	3,612	
	O	W	82	480	1,459	1,523	64
			85	809	5,284	5,394	110
			86	10,000	5,399	5,399	
	V	E	81	14,970	49,586	55,210	5,624
			82	82,521	264,074	286,726	22,652
			83	108,610	236,045	260,795	24,750
			84	112,523	301,305	332,366	31,061
			85	72,866	193,549	211,563	18,014
			86	136,599	410,330	439,513	29,183
	V	H	81	4,923	18,878	20,648	1,770
			82	5,354	16,950	18,825	1,875
			83	2,182	7,788	8,752	964
			84	2,611	6,813	7,690	877
			85	3,641	10,229	11,398	1,169
			86	4,946	17,299	18,894	1,595
	V	W	81	140,767	390,542	418,630	28,088
			82	287,438	791,496	843,301	51,805
			83	349,955	849,907	911,326	61,419
			84	485,712	1,009,505	1,091,784	82,279
			85	216,531	524,635	564,584	39,949
			86	590,779	1,576,374	1,657,669	81,295
DENMARK	A	E	82	1,953	21,791	27,531	5,740
	N	E	85	11,426	49,667	57,988	8,321
	O	E	82	2,502	32,306	34,402	2,096
			83	2,340	32,095	33,498	1,403
	V	E	83	1,740	23,264	25,197	1,933
			84	35	1,172	1,238	66
			86	11,676	112,591	123,148	10,557
EGYPT	O	E	81	1,042	1,631	1,631	
			82	914	1,925	1,925	
			83	990	1,522	1,522	
			84	946	1,975	2,107	132
	V	E	81	18,038	23,350	24,838	1,488
			82	14,509	15,704	17,335	1,631
			83	14,573	18,658	19,837	1,179
			84	8,925	6,002	7,006	1,004
			85	12,744	10,678	12,477	1,799
			86	3,306	2,925	3,254	329
FIJI	A	H	86	3,102	1,045	1,895	850
	O	W	83	986	4,141	4,391	250
FINLAND	A	H	86	3,102	1,045	1,895	850
FR GERM	A	E	82	540	1,472	2,025	553
			83	2,240	7,651	7,678	27
			85	1,871	20,838	23,926	3,088
			86	2,304	15,010	17,359	2,349
	A	W	83	50	490	563	73
			85	500	1,230	1,838	608
			86	319	2,049	2,405	356
	N	E	81	59,722	135,186	153,003	17,817
			82	17,104	49,499	53,102	3,603
			83	86,691	205,196	226,458	21,262
			84	54,946	115,662	132,266	16,604
			85	310,839	619,682	690,726	71,044
			86	284,200	525,162	593,987	68,825
	N	W	84	5,861	18,004	20,461	2,457
			86	13,764	29,717	36,155	6,438
	O	E	83	52,944	72,250	76,001	3,751
			85	27,841	31,926	35,173	3,247
			86	23,430	40,393	42,393	2,000
	V	E	81	65,404	167,022	183,902	16,880
			82	108,474	273,020	293,584	20,564
			83	119,737	261,373	281,429	20,056
			84	136,487	287,999	316,227	28,228
			85	49,432	136,188	146,937	10,749
			86	160,141	277,990	322,920	44,930
	V	W	81	26,145	59,771	70,377	10,606
			82	26,815	70,813	86,215	15,402
			83	9,914	26,760	30,975	4,215
			84	23,645	61,130	67,217	6,087
FRANCE	A	E	81	6,613	7,606	10,811	3,205
			82	36	345	516	171
			84	223	575	683	108
	N	E	86	10,332	25,735	27,535	1,800
	O	E	81	160	882	957	75
	O	W	81	438	1,273	1,623	350
	V	E	81	71	2,180	2,381	201
			82	1,125	420	510	90
			83	45	411	432	21
			84	3,338	5,681	6,151	470
			85	10,039	36,064	37,464	1,400
	V	W	83	265	469	498	29
GREECE	O	E	83	9,680	36,973	37,136	163
	V	E	84	3,000	1,796	2,167	371
			86	2,920	7,040	7,408	368
HAITI	V	E	82	8,260	9,408	10,945	1,537
HG KONG	N	W	81	31,074	47,392	51,039	3,647
			86	11,018	13,089	13,556	467
	O	E	81	1,980	2,200	2,360	160
			86	3,000	3,184	3,184	
	O	W	81	661	1,006	1,103	97
			82	2,019	1,102	1,174	72
	V	E	81	58,748	65,616	72,274	6,658
			82	83,603	119,451	131,858	12,407
			83	141,515	292,998	310,158	17,160
			84	63,709	87,494	99,886	12,392
			85	169,501	162,383	181,976	19,593
			86	90,218	78,491	86,990	8,499
	V	H	81	4,961	12,727	13,762	1,035
			82	9,318	16,636	18,010	1,374
			83	4,823	4,813	5,290	477
			84	1,350	2,173	2,362	189
	V	W	81	19,325	32,461	34,418	1,957
			82	101,373	175,057	183,671	8,614
			83	126,768	241,863	251,819	9,956
			84	170,027	271,576	287,372	15,796
			85	60,692	70,505	74,786	4,281
			86	207,790	153,698	163,516	9,818
HUNGARY	O	E	85	17,141	16,814	17,578	764
			86	144,070	140,853	148,238	7,385
	V	W	83	33,245	93,087	95,762	2,675
			85	740	1,393	1,494	101
INDIA	A	E	82	185	1,553	1,951	398
			85	1,323	8,432	9,304	872
			86	1,480	12,250	13,955	1,705
	N	E	81	1,331	3,773	6,219	2,446
			83	2,324	2,799	3,443	644
			84	25,769	30,631	35,658	5,027
	O	E	82	881	296	326	30
	O	W	81	16,060	7,050	7,379	329
	V	E	81	177	355	409	54
			82	705	773	985	212
			84	41,337	26,938	33,364	6,426
	V	W	81	240	267	372	105
			82	3,573	15,385	19,243	3,858
			83	2,410	1,466	1,830	364
			84	14,454	7,260	8,165	905
			86	1,653	5,865	6,063	198
INDNSIA	V	E	82	1,500	522	666	144
	V	W	81	400	4,184	4,347	163
			82	600	1,502	1,630	128
			83	350	598	632	34
IRAN	V	E	83	4,400	5,250	6,587	1,337
	V	W	84	5,268	2,400	3,311	911
ISRAEL	A	E	82	205	444	892	448
			83	210	347	1,099	752
			84	15,400	47,046	59,290	12,244
	A	W	84	4,400	11,892	16,601	4,709
	N	E	84	58,888	125,249	145,178	19,929
			85	71,126	215,054	242,538	27,484
			86	92,351	172,113	187,153	15,040
	O	E	81	4,990	13,157	13,157	
			82	28,644	60,859	62,221	1,362
			83	172,729	501,054	531,646	30,592
			84	1,800	6,061	6,061	
			86	2,154	2,995	2,995	
	V	E	81	271,493	695,022	738,260	43,238
			82	424,212	1,015,232	1,097,987	82,755
			83	301,044	691,549	740,598	49,049
			84	476,958	1,370,254	1,450,829	80,575
			85	642,249	1,930,481	2,043,530	113,049
			86	573,424	1,209,845	1,294,964	85,119
	V	W	81	58,228	114,843	122,814	7,971
			82	87,642	166,318	178,820	12,502
			83	71,116	84,042	93,767	9,725
			84	44,144	77,799	84,656	6,857
			85	15,840	59,439	62,568	3,129
			86	9,061	22,249	24,660	2,411
ITALY	A	E	82	110	458	558	100
			83	35,980	108,243	120,343	12,100
			84	2,295	8,274	10,029	1,755
			86	561	2,222	2,383	161
	A	W	84	4,795	9,486	12,101	2,615
	N	E	82	15,337	30,114	33,057	2,943
			83	18,928	43,998	50,615	6,617
			84	81,395	90,871	109,091	18,220
			85	85,642	183,564	208,300	24,736
			86	86,956	207,353	222,451	15,098
	N	W	84	1,906	6,222	7,566	1,344

Product
TSUSA commodity number, description, and unit of quantity

Country	Mode	Reg	Yr	Quantity	F.A.S.	C.I.F.	Charges
			86	6,177	16,421	18,301	1,880
	O	E	84	25	359	359	
	V	E	81	2,205	3,794	4,211	417
			83	28,724	91,257	96,716	5,459
			84	29,488	90,432	97,377	6,945
			85	36,167	111,830	120,184	8,354
			86	19,066	29,787	34,123	4,336
	V	W	81	26,460	91,287	96,466	5,179
			83	3,613	8,544	9,000	456
			85	3,571	7,715	8,746	1,031
IVY CST	V	W	85	7,095	2,946	3,490	544
JAPAN	A	W	81	132	416	729	313
	N	E	83	23,556	57,572	73,043	15,471
	N	H	82	36,127	139,217	158,063	18,846
			83	33,755	139,587	154,611	15,024
			84	34,998	110,519	125,387	14,868
	N	W	81	31,345	120,606	127,162	6,556
			84	25,360	75,064	80,065	5,001
			85	144,413	195,679	206,239	10,560
	O	E	81	2,222	2,983	3,326	343
			84	783	1,537	1,624	87
	V	E	81	21,111	84,323	90,778	6,455
			82	13,958	53,952	59,739	5,787
			83	2,171	12,021	13,378	1,357
			84	25,942	90,336	98,805	8,469
			85	35,977	53,880	60,814	6,934
			86	70,796	91,059	97,316	6,257
	V	H	81	35,357	147,105	164,420	17,315
			85	18,944	71,641	80,047	8,406
			86	25,839	129,161	144,233	15,072
	V	W	81	48,967	118,716	128,622	9,906
			82	69,366	178,468	192,281	13,813
			83	71,563	254,109	278,100	23,991
			84	32,217	105,681	112,987	7,306
			85	40,666	74,337	80,270	5,933
			86	118,193	277,672	292,173	14,501
KENYA	A	E	84	2,200	6,600	7,260	660
	O	E	83	79,366	12,226	15,742	3,516
			84	5,563	4,067	4,474	407
	V	E	84	18,542	5,733	6,382	649
			86	8,818	2,360	3,210	850
	V	W	85	1,540	2,210	2,441	231
			86	294	3,873	4,321	448
KOR REP	A	E	85	29,280	18,089	20,379	2,290
	N	E	83	41,903	103,335	114,997	11,662
	N	W	82	1,491	2,808	2,942	134
			84	81,224	183,600	195,314	11,714
	O	E	86	250	1,520	1,520	
	O	W	86	225	1,575	1,575	
	V	E	81	58,396	113,355	125,613	12,258
			82	35,794	137,038	150,670	13,632
			83	15,509	52,758	59,497	6,739
			84	78,498	235,546	254,719	19,173
			85	96,517	145,064	159,740	14,676
			86	96,261	212,766	228,864	16,098
	V	H	81	4,943	11,302	14,145	2,843
			82	3,632	13,102	15,360	2,258
			83	2,344	10,506	12,305	1,799
			84	3,115	9,823	11,636	1,813
			85	8,529	14,772	16,923	2,151
			86	3,177	9,519	10,526	1,007
	V	W	81	114,926	366,607	390,450	24,143
			82	85,291	302,704	324,165	21,461
			83	68,164	237,348	254,098	16,750
			84	39,600	100,105	109,329	9,224
			85	169,760	381,203	407,810	26,607
			86	243,832	469,791	499,691	29,900
LEBANON	V	E	81	2,010	1,300	1,434	134
			82	617	670	865	195
			84	3,142	4,680	5,344	664
MACAO	V	E	85	16,343	75,718	78,237	2,519
	V	H	82	500	1,086	1,337	251
MALAWI	O	E	84	6,944	2,882	3,129	247
MALAYSA	V	E	82	510	391	427	36
			83	550	720	768	48
	V	H	81	250	469	503	34
	V	W	82	770	1,993	2,156	163
MEXICO	A	E	84	10,778	3,733	5,895	2,162
			85	2,315	5,292	7,799	2,507
	O	E	81	52,167	154,328	154,328	
			82	166,652	441,795	441,795	
			83	101,572	254,630	254,630	
			84	186,737	412,096	412,096	
			85	173,108	215,748	218,478	2,730
			86	415,049	454,951	454,951	
	O	W	81	108,001	423,301	423,301	
			82	180,494	583,621	583,621	
			83	345,234	940,837	940,837	
			84	463,543	1,040,203	1,040,203	
			85	195,370	477,164	477,164	
			86	249,326	491,360	491,360	
MOROC	A	E	84	9,359	16,890	21,747	4,857
	N	E	83	10,028	17,510	20,389	2,879
	O	E	83	660	990	990	
			86	20,363	64,001	66,795	2,794
	V	E	81	11,000	24,328	29,151	4,823
			82	22,000	57,476	60,500	3,024
			83	49,787	127,691	137,998	10,307
			84	108,234	191,986	221,821	29,835
			85	20,580	32,973	38,291	5,318
			86	73,354	124,107	145,992	21,885
	V	W	81	89,704	186,115	225,593	39,478
			82	11,023	26,031	30,800	4,769
			83	43,336	115,608	125,412	9,804
			86	19,224	11,429	16,874	5,445
N ZEAL	A	H	84	126	601	700	99
NETHLDS	O	E	81	940	350	367	17
			82	181	781	899	118
			84	4,633	6,938	8,143	1,205
	V	E	81	1,589	5,847	6,303	456
			82	2,331	7,249	8,031	782
			83	426	1,474	1,491	17
			84	1,240	8,367	8,518	151
			85	2,094	3,416	3,788	372
			86	29,354	55,580	61,205	5,625
	V	W	81	79	259	289	30
			82	602	1,112	1,212	100
			83	393	593	643	50
			84	7,575	33,408	38,055	4,647
			85	2,293	1,032	1,151	119
			86	970	2,695	3,017	322
NIGERIA	A	E	86	898	1,859	2,273	414
	V	E	81	920	920	1,277	357
PAKISTN	V	E	81	278	252	312	60
			86	2,664	1,519	1,940	421
	V	W	86	35,274	9,681	11,325	1,644
PERU	A	E	81	103	1,150	1,214	64
			82	98	324	345	21
			84	542	3,816	4,101	285
			86	1,521	12,627	18,371	5,744
	A	W	86	63	1,678	1,783	105
	V	E	81	9,390	4,000	4,714	714
			82	10,502	7,760	8,489	729
			83	6,816	3,150	3,527	377
			84	26,860	53,634	65,091	11,457
			85	37,914	267,860	276,341	8,481
			86	121,685	117,134	124,720	7,586
PHIL R	V	E	83	750	1,954	2,057	103
			84	750	1,954	2,033	79
	V	W	81	5,088	16,091	18,292	2,193
			82	3,875	6,563	7,308	745
			83	9,346	21,435	24,816	3,381
			84	7,772	7,401	8,189	788
			85	26,570	15,240	17,797	2,557
POLAND	V	E	85	11,023	10,000	11,573	1,573
			86	20,766	13,632	15,211	1,579
PORTUGL	A	E	82	980	1,505	2,038	533
	N	E	84	37,086	105,345	116,116	10,771
	O	E	81	16,470	45,128	47,762	2,634
			84	6,176	17,940	17,940	
			86	26,455	28,200	30,141	1,941
	V	E	81	103,919	255,381	296,326	40,945
			82	291,634	868,887	950,322	81,435
			83	211,628	572,684	630,211	57,527
			84	48,291	111,408	126,449	15,041
			85	157,347	344,112	366,792	22,680
			86	90,227	183,884	196,684	12,800
	V	W	81	3,605	11,023	13,458	2,435
			82	25,840	76,610	82,837	6,227
			83	7,000	9,569	14,700	5,131
			85	21,000	47,193	51,450	4,257
REP SAF	A	E	81	12	392	658	266
			86	15,440	25,583	34,320	8,737
	N	E	83	134,504	284,765	309,200	24,435
			85	66,573	119,696	133,003	13,307
	O	E	83	506	1,894	1,894	
	V	E	81	8,620	23,136	25,017	1,881
			82	64,910	166,962	184,492	17,530
			83	35,195	71,372	76,107	4,735
			85	5,099	4,576	6,124	1,548

Country	Mode	Reg	Yr	Quantity	F.A.S.	C.I.F.	Charges
			86	102,282	143,768	160,851	17,083
SINGAPR	V	E	83	28,900	31,250	33,364	2,114
	V	W	83	250	800	865	65
			84	140	800	840	40
SPAIN	A	E	83	100	472	1,635	1,163
	N	E	86	103,179	188,330	225,385	37,055
	V	E	85	1,111	3,738	4,283	545
			86	13,560	19,842	22,783	2,941
	V	W	84	440	386	409	23
			85	34,458	8,592	11,233	2,641
SWEDEN	V	E	81	44,092	28,231	33,951	5,720
			85	204	2,570	2,870	300
SWITZLD	A	E	82	220	693	778	85
			85	95	1,390	1,445	55
	N	E	81	744,040	1,064,161	1,155,734	91,573
			82	1,294,095	1,852,790	2,030,579	177,789
			83	161,700	223,116	255,448	32,332
			86	19,208	41,874	45,162	3,288
	V	E	81	36,850	55,139	64,487	9,348
			85	2,829	1,998	2,227	229
			86	6,162	7,686	9,863	2,177
	V	W	82	87,686	116,358	127,882	11,524
			83	30,000	37,784	39,589	1,805
			85	5,178	17,231	18,092	861
SYRIA	O	E	82	105	328	328	
THAILND	O	W	83	248	480	480	
			84	2,867	4,219	4,574	355
			85	1,283	1,052	1,169	117
	V	E	81	7,513	10,522	11,533	1,011
			82	5,055	10,738	11,569	831
			83	17,066	13,939	15,865	1,926
			84	10,544	10,671	12,221	1,550
			85	351	1,400	1,460	60
			86	10,356	9,423	10,329	906
	V	H	81	3,619	4,861	5,697	836
			82	2,650	3,588	4,162	574
			83	2,500	3,233	3,605	372
			84	4,160	5,058	5,643	585
	V	W	81	40,046	68,000	72,619	4,619
			82	66,270	95,218	103,711	8,493
			83	78,222	82,240	89,166	6,926
			84	95,113	136,639	148,602	11,963
			85	101,432	75,715	83,978	8,263
			86	85,106	85,808	92,997	7,189
TUNISIA	A	E	86	661	1,650	2,164	514
TURKEY	A	E	84	1,073	4,586	5,015	429
			86	2,400	4,585	7,010	2,425
	N	E	85	177,115	357,696	388,015	30,319
			86	35,769	77,557	83,459	5,902
	O	E	81	8,873	27,965	29,649	1,684
			82	110	301	301	
			83	400	660	660	
			84	6,451	6,305	6,875	570
			86	830	1,045	1,045	
	V	E	81	96,466	237,652	251,601	13,949
			82	65,290	148,146	159,621	11,475
			83	288,895	728,006	774,124	46,118
			84	438,282	1,101,647	1,166,417	64,770
			85	381,176	853,590	923,528	69,938
			86	442,960	987,008	1,061,142	74,134
	V	W	82	4,092	14,735	16,163	1,428
			84	3,300	7,639	8,250	611
			85	44,469	122,081	131,305	9,224
			86	105,822	223,649	236,593	12,944
U KING	A	E	86	1,071	2,000	2,702	702
	O	E	81	16,535	7,583	8,344	761
			82	48,501	90,993	93,123	2,130
			86	22,052	44,609	47,870	3,261
	V	E	84	369	2,123	2,259	136
			85	2,857	1,550	1,550	
			86	30,285	33,062	37,669	4,607
W SAMOA	V	W	82	480	980	1,201	221
			85	60,339	20,372	26,471	6,099
			86	24,960	8,281	10,718	2,437
YUGOSLV	V	E	85	3,009	2,867	3,507	640

Vegetable, flour

1407500 VEG REDUCED TO FLOUR, NSPF (LB)

Country	Mode	Reg	Yr	Quantity	F.A.S.	C.I.F.	Charges
TOTAL			**81**	**5,629,231**	**6,306,881**	**6,922,926**	**615,893**
			82	**2,185,184**	**2,576,987**	**2,823,252**	**246,265**
ARGENT	O	E	82	2,205	2,832	3,099	267
AUSTRAL	V	W	81	24,960	9,719	11,125	1,406
CANADA	O	E	81	89,412	73,400	73,737	337
			82	94,661	68,945	69,270	325
	O	W	82	1,750	1,100	1,158	58
CHINA M	V	E	81	20,460	24,211	26,135	1,924
			82	1,760	2,169	2,417	248
	V	W	81	29,229	30,875	32,527	1,652
			82	6,854	7,218	7,746	528
CHINA T	V	E	81	500	1,330	1,384	54
			82	3,755	3,554	3,857	303
	V	W	81	24,519	31,824	33,634	1,810
			82	6,033	7,934	8,336	402
FR GERM	A	E	82	132	389	512	123
	N	E	81	4,431	10,400	11,450	1,050
	N	W	81	4,890	7,015	8,829	1,814
	O	E	81	151,151	41,191	49,457	8,266
	V	E	81	46,472	72,983	79,193	6,210
			82	36,669	50,676	54,551	3,875
	V	W	82	2,508	3,175	3,840	665
FRANCE	O	E	81	882	1,455	1,735	280
	V	E	81	8,837	12,695	14,032	1,337
HG KONG	V	E	81	34,355	31,321	34,241	2,920
			82	11,300	9,844	10,402	558
	V	H	82	250	337	367	30
	V	W	81	16,509	14,720	15,644	924
			82	2,260	1,942	2,068	126
INDIA	O	E	81	20,828	11,635	12,699	1,064
	O	W	81	8,250	3,600	3,913	313
	V	E	82	1,473	1,725	1,964	239
	V	W	81	1,974	1,296	1,701	405
			82	12,191	7,645	8,660	1,015
ISRAEL	O	E	81	32,750	31,988	31,988	
			82	16,000	17,976	17,976	
	V	E	81	218,054	134,295	164,944	30,649
			82	119,989	80,946	93,275	12,329
	V	W	81	1,000	770	952	182
ITALY	N	E	81	749	1,839	2,584	745
	V	E	81	88,200	18,577	23,901	5,324
JAPAN	N	E	81	6,713	15,291	16,606	1,315
	N	W	81	105,679	296,881	313,118	16,237
			82	47,024	121,715	128,003	6,288
	O	E	81	6,666	8,548	9,637	1,089
	V	E	81	55,251	127,463	135,740	8,277
			82	7,004	28,164	30,145	1,981
	V	H	81	22,203	94,597	102,939	8,342
			82	3,397	11,699	13,070	1,371
	V	W	81	34,315	120,843	128,859	8,016
			82	13,609	43,583	46,050	2,467
KENYA	O	E	81	31,760	13,498	16,152	2,654
			82	26,374	12,964	15,099	2,135
	V	E	81	51,200	24,300	27,947	3,647
	V	W	81	926	478	695	217
KOR REP	O	E	82	1,125	1,116	1,232	116
	V	E	81	4,142	6,328	6,815	487
			82	5,190	4,753	5,049	296
	V	H	81	2,951	1,953	2,465	512
	V	W	81	73,455	65,616	70,030	4,262
			82	35,989	44,162	46,606	2,444
MALAWI	O	E	81	15,800	6,138	6,666	528
			82	2,205	795	795	
MOROC	V	E	81	70,272	85,378	92,900	7,522
			82	88,674	107,690	116,980	9,290
NETHLDS	V	E	81	6,750	810	958	148
NIGERIA	V	E	81	7,300	4,320	5,996	1,676
PHIL R	V	E	81	4,865	10,955	13,021	2,066
			82	750	2,394	2,848	454
	V	W	81	17,031	41,217	45,065	3,848
			82	2,736	3,540	3,906	366
PORTUGL	O	E	81	992,075	1,163,700	1,267,476	103,776
			82	436,513	513,720	557,016	43,296
	V	E	81	473,736	630,600	671,015	40,415
			82	167,550	216,000	229,028	13,028
SINGAPR	V	W	82	397	451	500	49
SPAIN	V	E	81	1,656,852	1,983,608	2,164,804	181,196
			82	558,318	720,742	778,747	58,005
	V	W	81	40,150	38,946	47,002	8,056
SWITZLD	N	E	81	501,600	732,015	843,723	111,708
	O	E	82	255,640	392,991	465,850	72,859
THAILND	O	E	81	11,100	3,762	3,762	
	V	H	81	331	714	802	88
			82	170	295	340	45
	V	W	81	3,625	4,943	5,107	164
			82	41,976	11,244	14,052	2,808
U KING	N	E	81	351,810	160,529	176,738	16,209
	O	E	81	238,889	88,700	102,722	14,022
			82	116,623	48,676	53,511	4,835

Product
TSUSA commodity number, description, and unit of quantity

Country	Mode	Reg	Yr	Quantity	F.A.S.	C.I.F.	Charges
	O	W	82	1,235	549	604	55
	V	E	81	10,729	6,083	6,574	491
			82	26,455	10,320	11,688	1,368
	V	W	81	2,643	1,528	1,787	259
			82	26,440	11,017	12,635	1,618

1407600 VEG REDUCED TO FLOUR, NSPF (LB)

Country	Mode	Reg	Yr	Quantity	F.A.S.	C.I.F.	Charges
TOTAL			82	3,078,533	3,390,319	3,774,197	383,878
			83	3,082,302	3,539,138	3,832,769	293,631
			84	3,824,920	3,774,357	4,135,383	361,026
			85	3,850,953	4,328,439	4,701,676	373,237
			86	4,483,096	4,841,470	5,235,561	394,091
ARGENT	V	E	83	8,817	11,864	14,564	2,700
			86	22,046	15,000	17,421	2,421
AUSTRAL	O	W	84	35	1,500	1,690	190
	V	E	82	12,897	3,435	4,147	712
	V	W	86	172,961	76,090	85,432	9,342
BELGIUM	A	E	84	542	2,033	2,228	195
			85	2,032	6,174	10,388	4,214
			86	445	2,189	2,365	176
	V	E	84	34,832	12,880	14,094	1,214
	V	W	85	2,646	2,328	2,632	304
BRAZIL	V	E	82	8,000	3,400	4,262	862
			83	5,550	1,363	2,062	699
			84	4,409	7,457	8,000	543
			85	39,600	63,672	72,972	9,300
			86	11,885	22,049	24,056	2,007
BULGAR	V	E	86	1,102	2,229	3,149	920
C RICA	V	E	86	2,205	2,907	3,242	335
CANADA	A	E	84	1,000	4,867	6,428	1,561
	O	E	82	49,310	41,576	41,576	
			83	300,872	176,101	176,101	
			84	245,761	86,567	86,567	
			85	258,007	99,790	99,790	
			86	273,273	124,072	124,168	96
	V	W	82	29,875	8,500	9,387	887
CHILE	A	E	86	540	1,319	1,693	374
	N	E	86	148,568	206,077	232,855	26,778
	V	E	82	2,205	4,851	5,074	223
			84	16,296	43,402	46,939	3,537
			85	61,999	111,613	122,048	10,435
			86	105,388	169,670	180,532	10,862
	V	W	83	2,205	2,171	2,525	354
			84	1,543	1,290	1,560	270
			85	28,526	51,447	57,366	5,919
			86	56,484	79,186	87,363	8,177
CHINA M	O	E	85	7,200	7,881	8,511	630
	V	E	82	11,360	10,641	11,499	858
			83	28,145	31,054	34,052	2,998
			84	26,540	27,055	30,686	3,631
			85	46,803	46,111	51,540	5,429
			86	64,917	62,259	69,042	6,783
	V	H	83	620	807	897	90
	V	W	82	19,261	22,610	24,109	1,499
			83	51,204	51,865	55,858	3,993
			84	33,626	40,158	42,881	2,723
			85	28,413	28,132	29,833	1,701
			86	70,394	65,578	69,751	4,173
CHINA T	N	E	82	2,541	10,762	14,498	3,736
			85	10,703	66,540	68,789	2,249
	N	W	83	23,661	29,691	35,250	5,559
			85	118,821	224,684	234,577	9,893
	O	E	83	1,102	2,835	3,005	170
	V	E	82	5,750	5,135	6,040	905
			83	21,409	26,014	29,100	3,086
			84	4,002	6,965	7,692	727
			85	750	2,160	2,441	281
			86	22,801	59,387	62,638	3,251
	V	W	82	65,938	270,224	276,425	6,201
			83	172,684	466,128	479,268	13,140
			84	188,234	279,040	296,248	17,208
			85	69,449	103,139	111,064	7,925
			86	269,182	369,598	387,422	17,824
COLOMB	A	E	83	31,967	9,925	13,550	3,625
			84	8,819	2,956	4,899	1,943
	V	E	85	4,720	7,490	7,990	500
CYPRUS	V	W	84	35,850	10,953	13,535	2,582
ECUADOR	V	E	83	2,999	797	1,022	225
			84	2,000	2,500	2,916	416
			86	18,000	2,700	4,248	1,548
FIJI	A	W	86	2,695	5,734	7,939	2,205
FR GERM	A	E	86	6,248	10,626	15,739	5,113
	N	E	82	47,415	39,588	44,022	4,434
			83	143,282	143,360	162,056	18,696
			84	185,308	263,398	294,608	31,210
			85	294,656	420,070	451,077	31,007
			86	291,515	511,498	537,597	26,099
	O	E	84	2,205	9,607	9,782	175
			85	528	2,376	2,376	
			86	69,412	53,648	59,493	5,845
	V	E	82	80,236	51,754	57,977	6,223
			83	92,496	130,846	146,357	15,511
			84	87,904	113,261	127,337	14,076
			85	39,777	60,973	68,278	7,305
			86	190,059	213,144	235,470	22,326
	V	W	82	3,404	3,128	3,450	322
			83	5,978	9,111	10,296	1,185
			84	18,350	25,554	28,652	3,098
FRANCE	A	E	82	331	274	512	238
			85	970	2,010	2,812	802
	N	E	84	19,289	28,688	32,275	3,587
	O	E	83	1,102	2,602	2,673	71
			85	550	2,201	2,475	274
	V	E	83	2,318	3,247	3,640	393
			85	35,982	64,367	67,821	3,454
			86	16,369	35,538	38,787	3,249
GHANA	V	E	86	1,425	5,267	6,161	894
GUATMAL	O	E	84	18,488	6,594	7,158	564
HG KONG	V	E	82	18,370	23,464	24,885	1,421
			83	56,785	47,544	52,665	5,121
			84	53,901	45,119	49,578	4,459
			85	40,016	44,514	48,098	3,584
			86	26,910	27,946	30,349	2,403
	V	H	82	500	669	705	36
	V	W	82	8,460	15,654	16,194	540
			83	25,140	19,350	21,258	1,908
			84	9,003	6,177	6,567	390
			85	23,185	20,942	21,762	820
			86	133,837	185,088	192,623	7,535
HONDURA	V	E	86	24,000	5,892	7,288	1,396
HUNGARY	V	E	85	6,614	7,093	7,871	778
			86	2,275	3,632	3,891	259
INDIA	N	E	84	15,208	8,018	9,160	1,142
	O	E	82	735	493	493	
			83	6,649	4,679	4,941	262
			84	35,391	12,949	14,187	1,238
			86	17,765	7,276	8,081	805
	V	E	82	4,037	6,076	6,843	767
			83	19,402	13,578	15,428	1,850
			84	8,102	7,227	8,269	1,042
			85	33,668	16,716	19,634	2,918
			86	72,568	39,302	47,388	8,086
	V	W	82	28,938	12,713	14,770	2,057
			83	2,576	4,344	5,001	657
			85	609	2,885	3,577	692
			86	4,141	3,873	4,318	445
INDNSIA	N	W	84	39,640	29,258	41,154	11,896
	V	W	82	336	300	362	62
			83	441	666	803	137
			85	12,213	31,282	33,002	1,720
			86	5,182	8,973	9,532	559
IRAN	V	W	84	14,374	7,006	7,864	858
IRELAND	V	W	85	2,705	13,167	14,995	1,828
ISRAEL	O	E	82	157,610	138,907	149,128	10,221
			83	123,210	113,578	123,166	9,588
			84	98,342	85,192	91,656	6,464
			86	6,300	7,923	7,923	
	V	E	82	170,885	134,999	152,820	17,821
			83	158,868	168,667	187,192	18,525
			84	655,272	675,434	732,047	56,613
			85	614,571	705,922	782,666	76,744
			86	110,495	85,417	95,207	9,790
	V	W	83	19,391	37,264	39,803	2,539
			84	30,997	19,305	22,853	3,548
			85	57,600	56,598	63,362	6,764
ITALY	A	E	82	595	950	1,561	611
	V	E	84	2,205	4,329	4,663	334
	V	W	82	1,984	3,169	3,456	287
			83	9,700	17,759	19,894	2,135
			84	1,654	3,285	3,585	300
			85	1,102	2,108	2,286	178
IVY CST	A	E	86	5,652	10,300	13,500	3,200
JAPAN	A	E	86	66	1,044	1,520	476
	N	E	82	45,095	112,038	121,319	9,281
			85	88,446	193,582	211,714	18,132
	N	H	83	20,805	115,135	122,953	7,818
			84	39,651	149,790	160,299	10,509
			85	11,463	83,891	88,417	4,526
			86	10,778	25,808	27,294	1,486

Product TSUSA commodity number, description, and unit of quantity Country	Mode	Reg	Yr	Quantity	F.A.S.	C.I.F.	Charges
	N	W	82	57,216	140,844	148,602	7,758
			83	19,872	34,577	36,356	1,779
			84	204,475	514,863	537,108	22,245
			86	104,722	249,542	259,941	10,399
	O	E	85	420	1,181	1,318	137
	O	W	85	185	1,361	1,382	21
	V	E	82	18,489	28,870	31,714	2,844
			83	92,900	217,572	235,501	17,929
			84	96,599	229,730	249,978	20,248
			85	5,866	23,276	25,787	2,511
			86	88,068	244,700	262,188	17,488
	V	H	82	18,501	75,419	81,926	6,507
			86	21,698	124,878	137,073	12,195
	V	W	82	33,704	99,329	105,352	6,023
			83	244,897	614,989	641,361	26,372
			84	21,109	51,650	55,746	4,096
			85	360,830	724,708	762,034	37,326
			86	117,041	309,652	323,243	13,591
KENYA	N	E	84	137,545	47,320	57,568	10,248
	O	E	82	1,828	3,448	3,793	345
			84	2,685	1,916	2,170	254
			85	49,258	16,913	20,562	3,649
	V	E	82	338,570	125,375	151,068	25,693
			83	166,268	59,420	71,456	12,036
			84	105,847	34,740	42,078	7,338
			85	74,006	27,340	32,217	4,877
	V	W	84	18,109	6,700	7,903	1,203
			85	16,830	5,473	6,165	692
			86	36,608	12,730	15,726	2,996
KOR REP	O	E	86	1,126	4,200	4,200	
	O	W	84	2,304	1,728	1,728	
	V	E	82	23,110	29,338	32,273	2,935
			83	37,182	48,911	53,011	4,100
			84	7,797	6,387	7,309	922
			85	38,629	39,435	44,339	4,904
			86	64,051	100,640	110,930	10,290
	V	H	83	2,956	2,266	2,618	352
			84	1,143	910	1,155	245
	V	W	82	39,490	42,362	45,784	3,422
			83	64,015	60,883	66,723	5,840
			84	81,465	75,901	80,964	5,063
			85	85,128	84,449	90,111	5,662
			86	225,213	219,918	233,376	13,458
LEBANON	V	W	85	4,021	2,800	3,209	409
MACAO	V	W	83	2,000	2,474	2,565	91
MALAWI	O	E	82	14,374	5,922	5,922	
			83	1,984	838	838	
			84	27,998	10,478	11,151	673
			85	3,307	1,102	1,102	
MEXICO	O	E	84	10,271	13,211	13,211	
			85	60,141	35,566	35,629	63
			86	24,460	47,907	47,907	
	O	W	83	11,300	25,010	25,010	
			84	180	885	885	
			86	12,012	6,921	6,921	
	V	E	86	24,431	7,264	9,157	1,893
	V	W	83	250	343	353	10
MOROC	O	E	85	3,968	12,276	12,890	614
	V	E	82	40,234	48,682	52,842	4,160
			86	5,216	9,933	10,282	349
	V	W	83	40,150	52,195	56,430	4,235
NETHLDS	A	E	82	1,213	299	1,196	897
	O	E	84	9,000	6,124	6,892	768
			85	5,060	21,758	23,656	1,898
	V	E	84	11,023	15,000	17,370	2,370
			85	23,328	30,446	32,132	1,686
			86	1,375	2,120	2,306	186
NIGERIA	A	E	84	1,213	1,600	2,789	1,189
			86	2,192	1,790	1,790	
PAKISTN	O	E	84	2,625	1,824	2,035	211
	V	E	85	8,708	2,531	3,042	511
			86	6,669	2,068	2,432	364
PERU	V	E	84	1,861	3,900	4,097	197
			85	36,111	18,675	20,016	1,341
			86	20,888	10,784	11,434	650
PHIL R	V	E	82	1,680	2,680	3,135	455
			83	8,908	9,363	10,646	1,283
			84	4,623	10,263	12,055	1,792
			85	9,086	8,745	10,712	1,967
			86	7,505	7,807	8,905	1,098
	V	H	83	120	437	518	81
			85	380	1,270	1,554	284
	V	W	82	4,025	8,229	9,149	920
			83	30,559	45,313	49,784	4,471
			84	17,579	25,021	27,776	2,755

Product TSUSA commodity number, description, and unit of quantity Country	Mode	Reg	Yr	Quantity	F.A.S.	C.I.F.	Charges
			85	22,123	40,288	42,518	2,230
			86	21,580	28,518	31,510	2,992
POLAND	V	E	86	16,711	9,928	11,629	1,701
PORTUGL	O	E	82	198,415	242,280	261,525	19,245
			84	10,560	14,950	14,950	
			86	26,455	28,180	30,140	1,960
	V	E	82	39,683	47,700	51,673	3,973
			85	39,200	92,120	97,647	5,527
REP SAF	A	E	85	2,645	1,409	2,595	1,186
	V	E	83	4,505	3,471	4,042	571
SALVADR	V	E	85	4,812	1,960	3,025	1,065
SINGAPR	V	W	82	397	444	500	56
			83	5,000	1,250	1,257	7
SPAIN	V	E	82	40,150	51,794	56,029	4,235
			83	80,300	103,588	112,058	8,470
			86	40,150	48,180	53,457	5,277
	V	W	82	80,300	103,588	112,516	8,928
			85	8,729	1,051	1,553	502
SWITZLD	A	E	82	55	322	361	39
			86	3,058	10,796	13,572	2,776
	N	E	82	779,914	1,141,976	1,326,492	184,516
			84	101,228	177,779	205,204	27,425
			86	9,694	11,710	15,439	3,729
	O	E	83	169,950	241,165	275,299	34,134
			86	35,546	16,265	17,373	1,108
	V	E	83	73,700	110,666	128,974	18,308
			84	59,400	74,076	79,471	5,395
			86	117,150	141,132	150,359	9,227
	V	W	82	29,700	49,926	51,976	2,050
THAILND	O	E	84	5,512	2,077	2,273	196
	V	E	82	1,771	1,979	2,256	277
			83	1,027	2,499	2,879	380
			84	2,542	1,719	1,975	256
			85	3,574	4,874	5,506	632
			86	3,000	1,360	1,514	154
	V	H	83	265	326	362	36
	V	W	82	94,182	25,980	30,720	4,740
			83	10,632	7,003	7,553	550
			84	7,101	6,868	7,488	620
			85	46,479	28,964	31,010	2,046
			86	29,533	19,808	21,284	1,476
TNZANIA	V	E	82	10,882	7,290	8,920	1,630
TUNISIA	A	E	86	1,560	2,877	4,232	1,355
TURKEY	A	E	84	3,201	6,521	13,218	6,697
	V	E	83	3,630	5,967	6,312	345
			84	1,192	2,157	2,332	175
			85	64,603	161,377	173,886	12,509
			86	88,922	207,186	222,576	15,390
	V	W	84	15,432	4,550	4,622	72
U KING	A	E	84	7,039	3,929	4,847	918
	N	E	83	269,543	108,782	118,972	10,190
			84	827,031	359,598	403,276	43,678
			85	707,103	301,469	348,694	47,225
			86	336,163	124,048	140,794	16,746
	O	E	82	363,693	147,744	165,531	17,787
			83	210,744	78,449	87,077	8,628
			84	680	340	340	
			86	111,756	54,825	62,560	7,735
	O	W	86	61,649	25,392	27,564	2,172
	V	E	82	17,528	9,457	10,712	1,255
			83	58,999	23,170	25,538	2,368
			84	53,741	19,825	22,360	2,535
			85	53,998	22,742	25,952	3,210
			86	490,492	188,753	220,832	32,079
	V	W	82	53,361	23,732	26,716	2,984
			83	33,112	18,371	22,126	3,755
			84	26,637	10,003	13,002	2,999
			85	168,101	61,022	69,269	8,247
			86	88,519	51,419	57,438	6,019
VENEZ	N	E	83	70,984	12,715	16,120	3,405
	V	E	83	26,455	4,000	4,762	762
YUGOSLV	V	E	83	717	780	888	108

Vegetable, fresh

1379575 VEGS, FRESH, CHILLED, NSPF (LB)

Country	Mode	Reg	Yr	Quantity	F.A.S.	C.I.F.	Charges
TOTAL			81	9,194,979	1,218,392	1,966,703	751,311
			82	14,576,395	1,840,443	3,001,028	1,160,585
			83	7,795,919	999,286	1,528,115	528,829
BELGIUM	A	E	81	2,463	2,379	3,225	846
			82	2,574	4,422	5,865	1,443
			83	250	362	552	190
	A	W	81	92	737	1,150	413

Table 2. U.S. Import Statistics for Non Crop-Specific Commodities by End-Use

Product
TSUSA commodity number, description, and unit of quantity

Country	Mode	Reg	Yr	Quantity	F.A.S.	C.I.F.	Charges
			82	3,558	5,171	7,529	2,358
			83	10,676	9,607	15,021	5,414
	N	E	82	13,411	6,762	8,723	1,961
	V	E	83	1,763	705	885	180
BRAZIL	N	E	81	28,005	1,377	3,218	1,841
C RICA	V	E	81	53	612	745	133
			82	61,026	4,246	8,394	4,148
			83	44,023	4,450	7,454	3,004
CANADA	A	E	81	467	300	904	604
	O	E	81	1,340,485	132,953	132,953	
			82	1,108,017	65,958	65,958	
			83	4,265	1,237	1,237	
	O	W	82	1,300	312	312	
CHILE	A	E	82	1,250	1,000	1,470	470
CHINA M	A	E	81	2,490	780	4,287	3,507
	N	E	82	212,898	78,153	118,241	40,088
	V	E	82	750	296	326	30
			83	56,110	16,889	24,318	7,429
	V	W	81	183,547	43,363	57,065	13,702
			82	420,690	98,540	133,507	34,967
			83	296,540	74,965	98,315	23,350
CHINA T	A	E	81	1,557	826	2,772	1,946
	N	E	82	40,584	14,301	22,307	8,006
COLOMB	A	E	83	6,425	465	1,565	1,100
CR N AN	A	E	81	2,500	450	450	3,000
DOM REP	A	E	81	3,956	307	1,157	850
			83	10,000	1,300	2,223	923
	N	E	81	4,794,383	593,774	1,262,963	669,189
			82	8,651,923	1,044,145	2,038,825	994,680
			83	4,231,706	528,131	989,862	461,731
	V	E	81	801,639	85,391	123,565	38,174
			82	501,940	61,540	81,823	20,283
			83	112,150	13,654	18,151	4,497
DOMINCA	V	E	83	300	300	340	40
ETHIOP	A	E	82	105	637	854	217
FRANCE	A	E	81	27,440	1,680	4,203	2,523
			82	4,689	1,076	1,644	568
			83	79	282	329	47
	N	E	82	1,337	711	941	230
			83	1,476	855	1,210	355
GUATMAL	A	E	82	4,200	377	477	100
			83	4,605	339	839	500
	V	E	81	9,232	2,348	3,138	790
HG KONG	N	E	82	35,390	11,454	19,572	8,118
	V	E	81	17,500	9,316	12,020	2,704
			82	13,100	6,606	8,816	2,210
	V	H	81	2,400	1,643	1,775	132
			82	4,225	3,091	3,395	304
			83	1,300	931	1,022	91
	V	W	81	29,891	6,199	8,404	2,205
			82	49,717	20,815	28,014	7,199
			83	106,658	20,671	28,647	7,976
HONDURA	V	E	82	136,775	6,675	15,514	8,839
ITALY	A	W	83	1,584	1,192	2,175	983
JAMAICA	A	E	83	39,409	3,284	6,599	3,315
	N	E		60,820	6,582	11,389	4,807
			82	102,675	13,577	24,918	11,341
			83	48,000	3,016	7,491	4,475
	V	E	83	44,050	2,643	3,843	1,200
JAPAN	N	H	82	8,580	9,132	12,172	3,040
	V	E	82	600	375	432	57
	V	H	81	2,200	2,371	2,749	378
	V	W	83	32,364	18,073	19,668	1,595
MEXICO	O	E	81	1,684,258	263,775	263,775	
			82	2,401,791	236,949	236,949	
			83	823,864	55,888	55,888	
	O	W	81	147,489	38,979	38,979	
			82	655,661	96,336	96,336	
			83	1,916,358	239,663	239,663	
MOROC	N	E	81	46,207	20,929	23,919	2,990
			82	122,304	43,631	51,693	8,062
N ZEAL	A	H	81	530	442	577	135
NETHLDS	A	E	82	375	346	381	35
PHIL R	V	E	81	625	404	410	6
			82	4,670	2,729	3,082	353
PORTUGL	A	E	83	1,964	384	818	434
TRINID	A	E	81	4,750	475	911	436
			82	10,280	1,080	2,558	1,478

1379775 VEGS, FRESH, CHILLED, NSPF (LB)

Country	Mode	Reg	Yr	Quantity	F.A.S.	C.I.F.	Charges
TOTAL			83	6,715,366	857,040	1,529,427	672,387
			84	15,084,709	2,357,939	3,772,099	1,414,160
			85	10,007,951	3,085,063	3,972,935	887,872
			86	10,632,059	2,873,685	3,982,102	1,108,417

Product
TSUSA commodity number, description, and unit of quantity

Country	Mode	Reg	Yr	Quantity	F.A.S.	C.I.F.	Charges
ARGENT	N	E	85	4,960	2,250	5,799	3,549
BARBADO	A	W	84	132	340	390	50
BELGIUM	A	E	83	1,254	1,438	2,245	807
			84	8,854	9,982	14,000	4,018
			85	43,974	53,534	77,075	23,541
			86	17,696	13,147	24,989	11,842
	A	W	83	17,153	16,448	23,525	7,077
			84	23,110	28,210	41,583	13,373
			85	77,962	76,407	123,172	46,765
			86	93,018	74,330	133,952	59,622
	N	E	83	5,994	2,485	3,278	793
			86	23,774	23,901	38,184	14,283
BRAZIL	A	W	85	788	1,428	2,310	882
	V	E	86	21,551	6,526	9,896	3,370
C RICA	V	E	83	5,000	500	640	140
			84	17,700	1,782	2,537	755
			85	35,050	4,403	6,904	2,501
CANADA	A	E	86	88,426	26,429	39,876	13,447
	N	E	86	161,390	41,153	74,663	33,510
	O	E	83	1,761,675	164,026	164,026	
			84	2,832,823	207,595	207,595	
			85	1,894,401	254,503	254,503	
			86	1,621,350	180,947	180,947	
	O	W	85	41,220	29,634	29,634	
			86	26,761	8,238	8,238	
CHILE	A	E	83	136,030	55,338	138,195	82,857
			84	9,014	3,500	9,426	5,926
			85	127,159	59,025	150,385	91,360
			86	11,155	4,000	12,250	8,250
	A	W	85	2,152	1,171	2,482	1,311
	N	E	84	219,993	109,341	226,721	117,380
	N	W	85	27,777	12,180	19,262	7,082
	V	E	84	60,370	17,880	27,534	9,654
			85	191,145	62,342	90,888	28,546
CHINA M	A	E	84	6,820	3,312	11,952	8,640
			85	29,750	12,346	16,340	3,994
			86	123,540	35,927	76,724	40,797
	N	E	83	30,240	9,838	18,154	8,316
	N	W	84	17,810	7,046	7,161	115
	O	E	83	32,169	14,990	14,990	
			84	45,966	13,107	13,107	
			85	38,541	10,364	10,364	
			86	84,606	21,988	21,988	
	V	E	84	18,850	4,327	6,947	2,620
	V	H	85	38,005	12,780	16,703	3,923
			86	58,285	20,721	27,778	7,057
	V	W	83	168,475	39,009	56,395	17,386
			84	361,883	83,988	119,233	35,245
			85	646,209	138,614	196,891	58,277
			86	865,068	203,819	277,329	73,510
CHINA T	A	E	85	8,100	2,835	4,993	2,158
			86	7,000	4,050	4,650	600
	O	E	84	13,020	2,515	2,515	
			85	78,417	24,762	24,762	
			86	14,355	5,093	5,093	
	V	W	86	18,000	11,470	12,600	1,130
COLOMB	V	E	86	6,530	1,018	1,548	530
DENMARK	V	E	86	6,400	1,116	1,320	204
DOM REP	A	E	85	45,385	4,745	10,522	5,777
			86	38,246	3,360	9,819	6,459
	N	E	83	2,609,761	272,832	761,684	488,852
			84	5,145,497	493,927	1,548,139	1,054,212
			85	341,558	51,368	104,909	53,541
			86	136,265	22,596	43,758	21,162
	V	E	83	323,792	33,559	47,180	13,621
			84	17,055	2,747	3,935	1,188
			85	235,055	41,666	47,348	5,682
			86	289,544	72,379	82,279	9,900
DOMINCA	O	E	85	1,372	1,144	1,144	
ECUADOR	A	E	85	4,400	2,405	4,820	2,415
	V	E	85	21,587	6,936	11,436	4,500
FR GERM	A	E	84	485	578	1,386	808
			85	1,860	3,629	4,110	481
	A	W	83	1,576	2,094	3,035	941
			84	1,572	1,395	2,483	1,088
FRANCE	A	E	83	14,220	9,512	13,945	4,433
			84	3,545	329	1,111	782
	A	W	83	441	1,511	1,785	274
			84	1,958	2,464	3,895	1,431
			85	661	1,050	1,414	364
			86	2,698	1,714	3,141	1,427
	O	W	85	13,910	5,651	5,651	
GRENADA	A	E	85	3,274	3,738	4,973	1,235
GUATMAL	A	E	86	4,300	2,064	3,729	1,665
HG KONG	A	E	83	3,840	2,000	7,324	5,324

Product TSUSA commodity number, description, and unit of quantity Country	Mode	Reg	Yr	Quantity	F.A.S.	C.I.F.	Charges
			84	6,195	3,089	7,614	4,525
	O	E	84	3,195	533	533	
	V	H	83	2,860	2,156	2,430	274
			84	1,625	980	1,173	193
	V	W	84	65,380	14,857	20,550	5,693
			85	74,549	16,269	20,100	3,831
			86	35,282	9,751	11,354	1,603
ITALY	A	E	84	2,105	3,212	4,726	1,514
			85	402,274	344,692	681,780	337,088
			86	73,506	60,621	128,731	68,110
	A	W	83	46,246	47,573	77,369	29,796
			84	184,461	186,416	299,085	112,669
			85	180,128	192,508	303,388	110,880
			86	32,625	20,218	32,246	12,028
	N	E	86	628,419	532,739	1,064,601	531,862
	N	W	86	227,732	199,960	354,848	154,888
IVY CST	A	E	86	22,400	7,840	13,714	5,874
	V	W	86	29,300	7,025	8,625	1,600
JAMAICA	A	E	83	41,251	3,701	8,180	4,479
			84	14,550	2,183	5,209	3,026
			86	27,199	15,721	26,596	10,875
	N	E	84	63,214	24,315	32,889	8,574
			85	96,870	35,442	51,715	16,273
	V	E	83	10,149	1,435	1,669	234
JAPAN	A	E	85	6,300	1,953	3,528	1,575
	N	W	84	4,532	3,577	4,011	434
	V	E	86	7,110	8,645	9,417	772
	V	H	84	12,577	16,428	19,788	3,360
			85	5,512	7,280	8,378	1,098
			86	1,895	2,054	2,959	905
	V	W	83	3,410	2,122	2,277	155
			84	7,370	4,994	5,386	392
			85	20,872	18,001	19,461	1,460
			86	48,077	47,789	50,403	2,614
MAURIT	A	W	86	1,700	1,157	1,926	769
MAURITN	A	E	84	441	850	1,512	662
MEXICO	A	E	83	1,329	680	911	231
			85	19,163	18,095	24,211	6,116
			86	3,867	3,483	5,183	1,700
	A	W	85	3,661	1,120	1,786	666
	O	E	83	1,172,734	101,249	101,269	20
			84	476,066	36,774	36,774	
			85	526,072	163,698	163,698	
			86	102,760	28,895	28,895	
	O	W	83	258,167	45,104	45,104	
			84	5,330,032	1,024,765	1,024,765	
			85	4,476,983	1,313,126	1,313,127	1
			86	5,629,939	1,097,559	1,098,025	466
MOROC	A	E	85	13,402	5,786	8,380	2,594
			86	16,534	8,801	14,801	6,000
	N	E	83	64,686	25,533	30,817	5,284
			84	82,557	25,015	33,229	8,214
N ZEAL	A	W	83	1,314	1,331	2,157	826
			84	66	295	545	250
			85	7,359	4,211	7,205	2,994
NETHLDS	A	E	83	220	300	520	220
			84	10,582	4,042	5,172	1,130
			85	9,087	10,634	13,901	3,267
			86	3,064	2,524	3,904	1,380
	A	W	84	5,704	10,489	16,378	5,889
			85	46,818	26,291	41,888	15,597
			86	3,264	3,921	6,769	2,848
	N	W	86	28,135	23,175	43,420	20,245
NIGER	A	E	85	1,441	1,248	2,408	1,160
PHIL R	V	E	83	1,380	276	323	47
S VN GR	A	E	86	4,921	3,553	4,450	897
	V	E	84	7,600	760	1,110	350
SWITZLD	V	W	86	100,765	27,501	32,524	5,023
THAILND	V	W	86	28,572	12,420	13,605	1,185
U KING	A	W	85	1,398	2,646	4,524	1,878
W SAMOA	V	W	86	16,425	3,500	5,018	1,518

1384210 VEGS NSPF, FR, CHLD, SLICED (LB)

Country	Mode	Reg	Yr	Quantity	F.A.S.	C.I.F.	Charges
TOTAL			81	344,680	121,563	130,581	9,018
			82	277,684	76,209	100,388	24,179
CANADA	O	E	81	107,670	30,318	30,318	
	O	W	81	126,093	27,476	27,476	
			82	44,100	8,644	8,644	
CHINA M	V	W	81	70,690	28,489	36,278	7,789
			82	204,067	58,869	80,781	21,912
GUATMAL	V	E	81	18,000	4,986	5,760	774
			82	25,003	6,881	8,473	1,592
JAMAICA	A	E	82	3,650	511	897	386
JAPAN	V	E	81	2,035	3,810	4,097	287

Product TSUSA commodity number, description, and unit of quantity Country	Mode	Reg	Yr	Quantity	F.A.S.	C.I.F.	Charges
	V	W	82	210	944	987	43
LIBERIA	V	E	81	630	315	483	168
MEXICO	O	E	81	19,562	26,169	26,169	
THAILND	V	W	82	654	360	606	246

1384610 VEGS NSPF, FR, CHLD, SLICED (LB)

Country	Mode	Reg	Yr	Quantity	F.A.S.	C.I.F.	Charges
TOTAL			82	330,862	111,471	126,513	15,042
			83	765,951	194,558	241,332	46,774
			84	1,710,865	343,369	419,081	75,712
			85	1,131,069	361,996	475,263	113,267
			86	1,450,705	369,457	448,024	78,567
ARGENT	A	E	84	9,558	2,001	8,277	6,276
AUSTRAL	A	E	85	2,341	4,233	5,575	1,342
BELGIUM	A	E	82	176	282	344	62
			83	242	274	511	237
			85	2,837	2,978	3,623	645
			86	4,116	5,822	9,687	3,865
	A	W	82	1,597	1,537	1,591	54
			83	440	308	423	115
			84	264	264	345	81
	O	E	85	1,111	1,148	1,472	324
C RICA	V	E	85	22,500	2,607	3,967	1,360
CANADA	A	E	85	9,484	3,183	5,406	2,223
			86	4,836	2,194	3,157	963
	N	W	84	71,920	13,346	13,346	
	O	E	82	152,432	41,041	41,041	
			83	148,030	21,770	21,770	
			84	203,400	29,699	29,699	
			85	119,740	28,825	28,825	
			86	103,292	20,426	20,426	
	O	W	82	67,060	13,743	13,743	
			83	162,955	29,009	29,009	
			86	20,000	5,550	5,550	
CHILE	A	E	84	9,578	4,819	12,003	7,184
	A	W	82	832	643	1,007	364
			84	2,970	1,350	3,651	2,301
			85	6,100	1,524	3,224	1,700
CHINA M	N	E	84	23,770	13,014	16,996	3,982
	N	W	82	71,126	26,887	36,148	9,261
			84	341,465	116,180	156,479	40,299
	O	E	83	3,250	1,950	1,950	
	V	E	83	79,165	27,841	37,399	9,558
			86	85,604	20,803	33,557	12,754
	V	W	83	168,456	51,359	69,956	18,597
			84	81,201	14,096	23,823	9,727
			85	635,559	142,403	214,921	72,518
			86	436,091	89,567	118,675	29,108
CHINA T	A	W	84	1,900	665	665	
	O	E	85	11,220	2,369	2,369	
COLOMB	A	E	84	600	413	436	23
DOM REP	A	E	84	7,486	1,276	2,942	1,666
			85	20,157	4,457	9,085	4,628
	N	E	83	12,885	2,425	3,185	760
	V	E	83	39,000	6,330	8,595	2,265
			84	4,975	495	1,039	544
FIJI	V	W	86	53,400	21,894	29,935	8,041
FRANCE	A	E	83	4,048	4,452	5,189	737
			84	2,285	4,413	5,445	1,032
			86	220	1,005	1,319	314
	V	E	85	5,762	2,083	2,305	222
	V	E	86	24,235	8,961	10,572	1,611
GUATMAL	V	E	83	32,504	11,135	13,001	1,866
			86	25,400	1,910	4,340	2,430
HG KONG	O	E	84	6,000	319	319	
	V	E	86	37,400	6,749	10,740	3,991
	V	W	82	13,150	5,052	6,851	1,799
			83	108,665	32,418	44,718	12,300
			85	35,873	8,178	11,620	3,442
			86	6,726	2,861	3,219	358
ITALY	V	W	86	3,131	1,105	1,329	224
JAMAICA	A	E	86	5,869	9,247	10,709	1,462
	V	E	84	4,017	2,058	2,276	218
JAPAN	A	E	82	30	377	496	119
	V	E	84	7,184	7,764	8,754	990
			85	18,705	14,622	17,794	3,172
			86	2,922	4,015	4,313	298
	V	H	82	283	1,385	1,470	85
			84	616	539	603	64
	V	W	82	493	592	635	43
			83	2,798	3,262	3,471	209
			84	3,807	3,514	3,647	133
			85	127,813	92,045	105,184	13,139
			86	164,096	163,030	176,178	13,148
MALAYSA	V	E	83	838	650	702	52

Product TSUSA commodity number, description, and unit of quantity Country	Mode	Reg	Yr	Quantity	F.A.S.	C.I.F.	Charges
			85	4,261	2,733	3,558	825
MALI	A	E	85	1,984	3,000	3,630	630
MEXICO	O	E	84	874,530	96,172	96,172	
			86	493,367	9,868	9,868	
	O	W	82	1,300	416	416	
			83	1,875	720	720	
			84	47,764	26,687	26,687	
			85	37,128	23,136	23,136	
N ZEAL	A	W	82	2,283	1,915	2,872	957
NETHLDS	A	E	84	1,433	994	1,508	514
			85	225	1,060	1,166	106
	V	W	82	20,100	17,601	19,899	2,298
PHIL R	V	E	84	2,500	1,500	1,879	379
	V	W	83	800	655	733	78
			84	1,525	1,008	1,163	155
SWITZLD	V	E	85	44,974	14,600	20,863	6,263
THAILND	V	E	85	3,295	1,262	1,990	728
	V	W	84	117	783	927	144

Vegetable, frozen
1379580 VEGETABLES, FROZEN, NSPF (LB)

Country	Mode	Reg	Yr	Quantity	F.A.S.	C.I.F.	Charges
TOTAL			81	173,153	46,945	50,193	3,248
			82	33,188	5,666	7,114	1,448
			83	4,400	1,775	1,903	128
BELGIUM	A	W	82	155	255	385	130
CANADA	O	E	81	133,514	35,901	35,901	
			82	560	297	297	
			83	1,440	608	608	
CHINA M	V	W	81	19,775	3,797	5,754	1,957
DOM REP	N	E	82	18,950	1,100	1,783	683
	V	E	81	7,400	1,036	1,346	310
			82	4,980	1,107	1,501	394
			83	1,550	885	978	93
GUATMAL	A	W	82	449	313	381	68
JAPAN	V	E	81	2,749	3,380	3,927	547
	V	H	82	660	1,080	1,206	126
MEXICO	O	W	82	5,450	811	811	
PHIL R	V	E	81	8,465	2,411	2,779	368
			83	1,410	282	317	35
	V	W	81	1,250	420	486	66
THAILND	V	W	82	1,984	703	750	47

1379780 VEGETABLES, FROZEN, NSPF (LB)

Country	Mode	Reg	Yr	Quantity	F.A.S.	C.I.F.	Charges
TOTAL			83	79,825	15,377	20,035	4,658
			84	169,468	68,670	81,175	12,505
CANADA	O	E	83	35,380	9,378	9,378	
			84	81,054	25,408	25,408	
CHILE	A	E	84	6,195	2,464	6,194	3,730
CHINA M	V	W	84	21,495	4,639	7,234	2,595
CHINA T	O	E	84	680	466	466	
DOM REP	A	E	83	7,475	1,122	2,729	1,607
	V	E	83	2,500	325	422	97
EGYPT	O	E	84	4,641	4,131	4,131	
GUATMAL	V	E	84	1,200	347	420	73
ITALY	A	W	84	3,149	3,452	5,542	2,090
JAMAICA	A	E	83	22,000	1,125	3,225	2,100
	V	E	84	20,867	8,925	9,907	982
JAPAN	V	E	84	33	264	298	34
	V	W	84	6,480	4,567	4,900	333
NETHLDS	O	W	84	1,100	2,299	2,299	
PHIL R	V	E	83	12,470	3,427	4,281	854
			84	14,960	4,652	6,158	1,506
	V	W	84	7,614	7,056	8,218	1,162

1379785 VEGETABLES FROZEN, NSPF (LB)

Country	Mode	Reg	Yr	Quantity	F.A.S.	C.I.F.	Charges
TOTAL			85	173,799	83,101	91,659	8,558
			86	208,936	118,212	143,897	25,685
BELGIUM	V	E	85	15,608	3,972	5,869	1,897
CANADA	O	E	86	25,540	8,360	8,360	
CHINA M	V	W	86	24,450	10,438	11,857	1,419
CHINA T	V	W	86	12,000	8,767	9,384	617
DOM REP	V	E	86	6,090	4,263	4,879	616
EGYPT	O	E	85	25,076	35,098	35,098	
GUATMAL	A	E	85	43,615	13,085	17,318	4,233
	V	E	86	36,050	24,324	26,935	2,611
ISRAEL	V	E	86	59,325	37,392	51,493	14,101
ITALY	A	E	85	1,222	1,218	2,083	865
			86	6,181	9,836	14,984	5,148
JAMAICA	A	E	86	4,680	3,309	3,482	173
JAPAN	V	H	85	988	1,452	2,063	611

Product TSUSA commodity number, description, and unit of quantity Country	Mode	Reg	Yr	Quantity	F.A.S.	C.I.F.	Charges
MEXICO	O	E	85	75,200	26,400	26,400	
			86	17,645	5,933	5,933	
THAILND	V	W	86	16,975	5,590	6,590	1,000
U KING	V	E	85	12,090	1,876	2,828	952

1384250 VEG NSPF FZ REDUCED IN SIZE (LB)

Country	Mode	Reg	Yr	Quantity	F.A.S.	C.I.F.	Charges
TOTAL			81	9,599,322	2,598,833	2,676,910	78,074
			82	3,310,763	996,058	1,035,076	39,018
BELGIUM	A	E	81	287	611	739	128
C RICA	V	E	81	39,900	10,123	16,704	6,581
CANADA	O	E	81	5,212,464	1,156,606	1,156,609	
			82	2,087,664	472,417	472,417	
	O	W	81	80,000	31,800	31,800	
CHINA M	V	W	81	960	414	468	54
CHINA T	V	E	81	149,697	123,113	144,698	21,585
			82	23,034	20,279	22,606	2,327
	V	W	81	284,526	151,780	174,893	23,113
			82	145,875	99,173	108,513	9,340
DOM REP	N	E	81	76,820	39,719	43,623	3,904
	V	E	81	30,225	14,768	16,042	1,274
			82	128,616	46,291	51,830	5,539
GUATMAL	V	E	81	13,604	3,676	4,773	1,097
			82	50,000	11,869	14,721	2,852
HG KONG	V	W	81	900	297	317	20
ITALY	V	E	81	27,381	6,554	11,683	5,129
			82	78,264	20,900	31,837	10,937
JAPAN	V	E	81	9,702	9,960	11,212	1,252
			82	2,793	3,348	4,002	654
	V	H	81	160	937	1,105	168
	V	W	81	308	256	282	26
LIBERIA	V	E	81	8,484	2,171	4,713	2,542
MEXICO	O	E	81	3,450,728	963,513	963,513	
			82	630,703	245,213	245,213	
	O	W	81	110,000	33,215	33,215	
			82	102,624	29,258	29,258	
NETHLDS	A	E	81	218	447	564	117
	V	W	81	36,600	28,430	33,284	4,854
			82	59,265	46,317	53,574	7,257
NICARAG	V	E	81	56,000	15,800	20,165	4,365
PHIL R	V	E	81	1,200	940	1,076	136
	V	W	81	6,710	2,223	3,022	799
			82	1,925	993	1,105	112
PORTUGL	V	E	81	835	725	939	214
REP SAF	A	E	81	245	400	1,022	622
SALVADR	V	E	81	1,368	355	449	94

1384650 VEG NSPF FZ REDUCED IN SIZE (LB)

Country	Mode	Reg	Yr	Quantity	F.A.S.	C.I.F.	Charges
TOTAL			82	7,051,121	2,235,009	2,312,230	77,221
			83	11,332,993	3,323,514	3,424,906	101,392
			84	20,476,690	4,970,723	5,078,838	108,115
			85	30,983,245	7,412,537	7,571,428	158,891
			86	32,456,197	8,155,650	8,440,154	284,504
BELGIUM	A	E	83	170	300	365	65
			84	887	876	1,401	525
	A	W	83	5,263	2,202	4,831	2,629
			84	6,448	4,248	6,031	1,783
	N	E	85	11,095	4,340	5,798	1,458
	O	E	84	19,320	4,121	4,121	
			86	25,212	6,027	8,546	2,519
	V	E	85	164,938	48,839	65,100	16,261
			86	126,000	32,346	42,848	10,502
	V	W	86	40,346	37,591	42,570	4,979
C RICA	V	E	82	113,400	19,563	26,011	6,448
			83	43,389	9,546	13,912	4,366
			84	33,757	20,108	21,849	1,741
			85	11,646	3,494	4,693	1,199
			86	34,240	11,314	14,573	3,259
	V	W	86	140,760	33,923	47,237	13,314
CANADA	A	E	84	97	270	300	30
			85	10,282	4,599	8,036	3,437
	A	W	82	3,726	1,227	1,717	490
			86	5,300	3,290	4,004	714
	N	E	85	726,399	209,708	209,708	
	O	E	82	3,819,419	1,056,267	1,056,267	
			83	8,088,025	1,943,570	1,946,408	2,838
			84	18,117,642	3,776,435	3,777,603	1,168
			85	23,562,002	5,264,016	5,269,200	5,184
			86	23,141,194	5,469,796	5,469,801	5
	O	W	82	2,890	518	518	
			83	14,459	5,439	5,439	
			85	7,620	2,580	2,580	
			86	172,749	27,061	27,061	
	V	E	82	40,500	3,196	4,222	1,026

Product TSUSA commodity number, description, and unit of quantity Country	Mode	Reg	Yr	Quantity	F.A.S.	C.I.F.	Charges
			84	36,000	11,520	11,520	
	V	H	86	36,240	11,944	11,944	
CHILE	A	E	85	3,647	1,845	4,395	2,550
	V	E	85	43,238	11,825	16,425	4,600
			86	487,249	85,425	145,800	60,375
CHINA M	A	E	85	7,660	2,441	5,057	2,616
	N	E	84	25,320	13,384	17,604	4,220
	V	E	83	42,455	9,861	14,522	4,661
			85	64,006	12,080	21,437	9,357
			86	18,739	5,845	7,576	1,731
	V	H	83	397	314	405	91
	V	W	84	36,388	12,347	20,018	7,671
			85	59,581	9,705	13,532	3,827
CHINA T	O	E	85	10,758	3,722	3,722	
	V	E	82	30,900	21,894	31,599	9,705
			83	74,824	46,255	52,988	6,733
			84	1,444	1,995	2,421	426
			85	40,000	27,210	31,477	4,267
			86	1,500	1,342	1,500	158
	V	W	82	159,330	43,816	57,035	13,219
			83	1,200	735	823	88
			84	14,530	4,151	4,449	298
			85	10,000	3,494	4,200	706
			86	314,080	205,473	220,304	14,831
DENMARK	V	E	85	41,998	6,651	10,356	3,705
DOM REP	A	E	83	600	2,400	2,740	340
	N	E	82	45,444	23,055	26,747	3,692
	V	E	82	114,525	45,964	51,751	5,787
			83	65,724	28,063	32,816	4,753
			84	106,613	50,041	57,176	7,135
			85	180,018	90,167	102,117	11,950
			86	276,095	130,004	149,708	19,704
ECUADOR	V	E	83	3,000	300	345	45
EGYPT	A	W	84	7,846	9,683	10,743	1,060
	N	W	86	83,544	41,775	56,450	14,675
	O	E	85	2,550	2,400	2,400	
			86	16,363	11,147	11,147	
	V	E	84	1,500	1,200	1,410	210
			85	18,739	10,500	10,923	423
			86	52,911	17,100	25,621	8,521
	V	W	85	26,455	13,000	18,184	5,184
FR GERM	V	E	82	8,325	7,326	8,499	1,173
			83	396	577	713	136
FRANCE	A	E	82	637	1,443	2,003	560
			83	508	1,230	1,392	162
	V	E	85	35,204	5,986	7,456	1,470
			86	121,304	45,385	55,921	10,536
GUATMAL	N	E	82	128,518	24,740	32,190	7,450
	V	E	82	1,200	258	342	84
			83	153,758	35,821	43,935	8,114
			84	185,081	78,781	86,937	8,156
			85	322,250	100,172	120,611	20,439
			86	849,590	208,861	264,438	55,577
HG KONG	A	E	83	4,405	1,299	7,252	5,953
	V	E	84	3,927	461	702	241
			85	41,116	4,448	7,051	2,603
			86	16,402	4,131	6,342	2,211
	V	H	84	975	636	756	120
	V	W	86	23,940	3,045	5,549	2,504
HONDURA	V	E	84	28,000	28,492	30,830	2,338
INDNSIA	O	E	85	16,137	5,871	5,871	
ISRAEL	V	E	84	28,800	11,274	15,552	4,278
			86	149,454	44,877	63,678	18,801
ITALY	A	W	85	2,183	2,080	3,903	1,823
	V	E	82	62,831	14,955	23,408	8,453
			85	73,713	17,807	30,847	13,040
JAMAICA	A	E	84	678	1,092	1,332	240
			86	2,141	1,330	1,430	100
	V	E	84	25	1,990	2,159	169
JAPAN	V	E	82	9,773	10,289	11,838	1,549
			83	15,340	17,404	19,698	2,294
			84	18,416	19,574	22,401	2,827
			85	8,800	9,120	10,760	1,640
			86	8,800	8,289	9,182	893
	V	H	82	160	799	879	80
			84	2,112	2,563	2,860	297
	V	W	82	1,912	3,833	4,074	241
			83	1,355	1,417	1,507	90
			84	7,497	6,403	6,887	484
			85	11,000	9,009	10,070	1,061
KOR REP	V	E	83	3,075	3,432	3,891	459
			84	300	516	609	93
			86	2,957	4,500	4,742	242
	V	W	85	42,516	18,561	20,567	2,006
			86	57,445	22,397	23,787	1,390

Product TSUSA commodity number, description, and unit of quantity Country	Mode	Reg	Yr	Quantity	F.A.S.	C.I.F.	Charges
LAOS	O	E	86	23,865	6,657	6,657	
LIBERIA	V	E	82	3,000	1,305	2,051	746
MEXICO	A	E	83	1,980	266	606	340
	O	E	82	2,224,571	811,752	811,752	
			83	2,279,036	819,361	819,361	
			84	1,281,095	564,978	564,978	
			85	4,876,018	1,284,167	1,284,168	1
			86	5,852,275	1,475,552	1,475,556	4
	O	W	82	140,010	44,658	44,658	
			85	162,560	48,404	48,404	
N ZEAL	A	E	82	1,800	1,849	2,402	553
	A	W	84	1,562	405	898	493
	O	E	85	28,333	4,942	4,942	
NETHLDS	A	E	85	4,459	8,750	9,900	1,150
	A	W	84	507	400	550	150
	N	W	86	119,561	112,291	126,172	13,881
	V	E	83	44,092	15,322	18,894	3,572
			84	178,297	56,650	72,757	16,107
			85	119,055	16,207	27,512	11,305
			86	11,287	3,656	4,741	1,085
	V	W	82	95,723	81,338	93,764	12,426
			83	312,925	271,409	306,648	35,239
			84	256,012	236,594	273,351	36,757
			85	121,029	90,265	106,845	16,580
PERU	V	E	86	21,528	8,238	12,738	4,500
PHIL R	V	E	82	2,582	2,205	2,653	448
			83	1,400	750	858	108
			84	3,000	935	1,343	408
			85	10,730	3,222	4,535	1,313
			86	29,260	13,877	18,646	4,769
	V	H	84	1,001	576	685	109
	V	W	82	12,950	6,211	7,242	1,031
			83	21,890	10,708	13,250	2,542
			84	33,269	13,933	18,683	4,750
			85	12,405	5,115	7,401	2,286
			86	14,360	5,745	6,984	1,239
PORTUGL	V	E	82	19,250	333	495	162
REP SAF	O	E	86	7,412	2,059	2,059	
SALVADR	V	E	85	10,512	4,765	5,733	968
SINGAPR	V	W	83	4,255	1,159	2,261	1,102
SPAIN	O	E	86	69,647	13,502	18,598	5,096
	V	E	82	8,100	4,501	5,318	817
THAILND	N	W	84	30,093	25,769	28,842	3,073
	O	E	83	10,197	1,842	1,842	
	V	E	82	3,459	1,268	2,546	1,278
			83	7,240	3,438	5,910	2,472
			84	3,251	2,030	2,517	487
			85	13,014	8,936	11,961	3,025
	V	W	82	4,286	4,947	5,567	620
			83	79,611	73,508	84,673	11,165
			84	5,000	6,292	6,563	271
			85	19,919	22,086	23,543	1,457
			86	62,697	32,875	36,061	3,186
TRINID	A	E	83	9,200	384	478	94
U KING	A	E	85	40,300	6,387	6,387	
	O	E	83	34,000	9,459	9,459	
	V	W	83	724	1,242	1,366	124
W SAMOA	V	W	86	39,750	6,980	10,183	3,203
YEMAN S	O	E	86	9,360	3,621	3,621	

1418900 VEGETABLES, FROZEN, NSPF (LB)

	Mode	Reg	Yr	Quantity	F.A.S.	C.I.F.	Charges
TOTAL			81	237,997	109,002	109,677	675
			82	737,943	301,668	304,442	2,774
			83	1,498,868	590,678	593,243	2,565
			84	1,880,536	740,678	801,312	60,634
			85	1,905,471	708,613	786,626	78,013
			86	4,781,129	1,743,652	1,863,522	119,870
ALBANIA	V	E	85	42,664	8,533	11,529	2,996
CANADA	O	E	81	5,028	2,664	2,664	
			82	21,252	15,259	15,259	
			83	93,393	43,039	43,039	
			84	237,110	140,254	140,254	
			85	259,026	190,689	190,689	
			86	517,086	451,746	451,746	
	O	W	81	9,578	7,653	7,653	
			82	78,999	24,499	24,499	
			83	752,700	248,560	248,560	
			84	167,200	53,309	53,309	
			86	1,661,075	546,429	546,429	
CHINA M	V	E	81	2,984	1,297	1,465	168
	V	W	84	2,000	951	1,020	69
DOM REP	V	E	83	2,000	1,000	1,139	139
			84	30,650	15,636	18,390	2,754
			85	63,110	32,134	38,558	6,424

Product
TSUSA commodity number, description, and unit of quantity

Country	Mode	Reg	Yr	Quantity	F.A.S.	C.I.F.	Charges
			86	152,100	43,800	59,719	15,919
FR GERM	V	E	84	74,074	14,880	18,480	3,600
FRANCE	V	E	82	31,875	16,531	18,067	1,536
			86	18,016	7,853	10,151	2,298
GUATMAL	V	E	84	800,164	257,662	304,473	46,811
			85	1,180,550	318,768	384,809	66,041
			86	1,723,152	373,485	468,358	94,873
HUNGARY	V	E	84	20,250	4,748	8,240	3,492
INDNSIA	O	E	85	1,824	1,558	1,558	
ISRAEL	V	E	86	45,999	12,872	17,902	5,030
JAPAN	V	E	82	4,408	5,070	6,002	932
			83	669	780	876	96
			84	1,585	1,703	1,936	233
	V	H	84	660	636	681	45
	V	W	81	2,957	2,502	2,778	276
			82	2,979	3,266	3,572	306
			83	444	1,049	1,172	123
			84	372	856	967	111
KOR REP	V	H	81	1,200	965	1,196	231
	V	W	84	6,072	6,211	6,696	485
			86	1,200	2,200	2,320	120
MEXICO	O	E	81	216,250	93,921	93,921	
			82	521,030	209,953	209,953	
			83	630,150	283,566	283,566	
			84	480,875	223,010	223,010	
			85	305,258	141,770	141,770	
			86	651,501	293,871	293,871	
	O	W	82	77,400	27,090	27,090	
NETHLDS	V	E	84	44,134	9,592	11,217	1,625
			85	44,134	9,592	11,542	1,950
PHIL R	V	W	83	1,000	439	504	65
			84	8,740	4,447	5,169	722
			85	2,145	1,179	1,262	83
THAILND	V	E	85	1,371	1,035	1,218	183
			86	9,721	8,210	9,657	1,447
	V	W	83	18,512	12,245	14,387	2,142
			84	6,650	6,783	7,470	687
			85	5,389	3,355	3,691	336
			86	1,279	3,186	3,369	183

Vegetable, in brine or pickled

1417760 VEG NSPF IN SALT, BRINE ETC (LB)

Country	Mode	Reg	Yr	Quantity	F.A.S.	C.I.F.	Charges
TOTAL			81	72,776,556	26,384,862	28,295,231	1,917,847
			82	76,748,337	25,881,431	27,646,806	1,765,375
			83	83,169,474	21,619,392	23,812,157	2,192,765
			84	90,907,088	26,827,126	29,689,193	2,862,067
			85	102,505,047	30,223,970	32,895,769	2,671,799
			86	108,046,642	28,537,626	31,367,000	2,829,374
AUSTRIA	O	E	84	22,487	5,200	6,800	1,600
	V	E	81	24,172	7,345	9,658	2,313
			82	14,172	6,534	6,932	398
			83	51,411	19,714	24,663	4,949
			84	32,006	16,908	19,003	2,095
			85	55,409	18,305	22,042	3,737
			86	122,677	35,421	42,718	7,297
BELGIUM	O	E	81	2,072	2,736	3,102	366
	V	E	81	32,888	9,151	10,663	1,512
			82	121,320	38,370	46,566	8,196
			83	196,112	39,497	46,380	6,883
			84	140,049	24,510	29,069	4,559
			85	591,166	119,377	145,527	26,150
			86	655,549	170,279	206,958	36,679
	V	W	85	7,020	1,879	3,062	1,183
			86	59,040	27,090	30,041	2,951
BRAZIL	V	E	84	2,216	1,462	1,746	284
			85	60,847	8,050	13,210	5,160
			86	102,025	17,290	24,852	7,562
	V	W	82	17,460	25,500	29,607	4,107
			83	17,460	21,750	25,995	4,245
BULGAR	V	E	84	91,447	17,641	24,264	6,623
BURKINA	V	W	81	6,920	3,264	3,523	259
C RICA	A	E	83	3,333	1,453	2,163	710
	N	E	84	2,374	2,403	3,194	791
	V	E	81	117,592	19,878	27,246	7,368
			82	24,057	9,537	11,329	1,792
			83	49,874	25,421	29,739	4,318
			84	119,660	20,426	26,666	6,240
			85	123,526	71,529	79,944	8,415
			86	202,548	41,046	50,855	9,809
	V	W	83	4,174	2,585	3,360	775
CANADA	O	E	81	214,042	33,561	33,561	
			82	4,864	3,122	3,122	
			83	328,537	62,200	64,750	2,550
			84	218,741	96,030	96,030	
			85	729,481	411,032	411,032	
			86	1,359,543	574,414	574,491	77
	O	W	81	300	333	401	68
			84	17,299	5,469	5,469	
			85	1,350	2,044	2,044	
	V	E	84	7,031	2,906	3,324	418
CHILE	V	E	86	69,663	39,703	44,227	4,524
CHINA M	N	W	84	246,961	90,700	100,755	10,055
	O	E	86	3,843	1,400	1,400	
	O	W	85	16,314	5,262	5,549	287
	V	E	81	45,970	24,453	29,596	5,143
			82	136,083	48,387	60,491	12,104
			83	41,424	14,305	16,495	2,190
			84	79,127	36,151	42,818	6,667
			85	28,330	10,190	12,376	2,186
			86	55,347	17,589	21,227	3,638
	V	H	82	12,236	5,695	6,089	394
			84	813	276	335	59
	V	W	81	283,726	120,865	134,384	13,519
			82	481,240	190,158	214,404	24,246
			83	400,081	129,107	145,696	16,589
			84	81,224	37,170	40,797	3,627
			85	179,193	58,311	65,545	7,234
			86	172,672	54,035	59,881	5,846
CHINA T	O	E	84	2,954	1,616	1,776	160
	V	E	81	243,625	120,300	134,657	14,357
			82	135,019	92,687	104,892	12,205
			83	163,259	89,157	101,787	12,630
			84	157,503	127,789	152,188	24,399
			85	197,786	156,092	179,914	23,822
			86	298,053	227,609	256,302	28,693
	V	H	81	2,475	1,510	1,608	98
			82	4,154	2,686	2,959	273
			83	1,585	925	996	71
			84	4,623	2,569	3,049	480
			85	2,205	1,150	1,346	196
			86	2,200	1,150	1,324	174
	V	W	81	1,759,958	487,908	550,222	62,314
			82	323,808	166,541	182,776	16,235
			83	494,803	273,962	295,796	21,834
			84	453,836	261,562	289,631	28,069
			85	435,966	256,822	278,467	21,645
			86	866,675	494,200	534,263	40,063
COLOMB	A	E	83	17,860	9,595	11,701	2,106
	V	E	81	4,251,102	2,406,421	2,673,263	266,842
			82	713,856	409,102	495,809	86,707
			83	1,906,444	1,121,427	1,240,080	118,653
			84	2,747,089	1,549,819	1,764,856	215,037
			85	1,263,764	755,956	868,624	112,668
			86	2,301,017	1,355,650	1,548,615	192,965
	V	W	85	163,753	96,578	110,197	13,619
CYPRUS	V	E	85	1,031	1,410	1,587	177
DOM REP	V	E	82	52,801	11,308	16,572	5,264
			85	209,713	20,974	42,020	21,046
EGYPT	O	E	81	390	393	393	
FIJI	V	W	81	463	272	420	148
FINLAND	V	E	86	95,238	17,280	24,777	7,497
FR GERM	N	E	81	47,561	44,374	48,215	3,841
	O	E	81	7,033	6,970	7,953	983
			82	21,263	11,858	13,503	1,645
			83	20,695	6,557	7,197	640
			84	57,599	21,592	24,853	3,261
			85	89,117	29,620	38,073	8,453
			86	7,468	5,430	6,845	1,415
	V	E	81	19,183	10,020	11,969	1,949
			82	56,627	45,929	51,256	5,327
			83	69,215	62,426	71,304	8,878
			84	153,177	90,523	105,077	14,554
			85	221,411	101,632	120,371	18,739
			86	327,799	142,206	179,821	37,615
	V	W	81	5,182	17,663	19,638	1,975
			82	4,619	2,032	2,286	254
			83	2,818	6,615	8,791	2,176
			84	1,144	2,352	2,761	409
			85	12,314	12,981	15,761	2,780
			86	10,393	8,659	9,657	998
FRANCE	A	W	85	473	1,050	1,242	192
	N	E	82	24,746	21,839	24,807	2,968
			83	73,797	69,143	74,835	5,692
			84	111,351	111,241	123,875	12,634
			86	202,450	266,501	290,094	23,593
	O	E	82	600	944	1,029	85
			83	4,915	7,347	8,874	1,527

Product
TSUSA commodity number, description, and unit of quantity

Country	Mode	Reg	Yr	Quantity	F.A.S.	C.I.F.	Charges
			84	2,191	2,453	2,770	317
			85	56,336	26,658	26,827	169
	O	W	85	4,365	1,598	1,958	360
	V	E	81	16,692	20,153	22,510	2,357
			82	9,976	12,026	13,940	1,914
			83	3,585	4,115	4,510	395
			84	217,590	36,801	46,830	10,029
			85	386,298	307,905	349,053	41,148
			86	140,584	109,823	121,873	12,050
	V	W	81	42,610	54,582	59,782	5,200
			82	8,845	3,573	3,863	290
			83	76,833	25,084	28,740	3,656
			84	85,521	30,124	33,984	3,860
			85	64,057	48,010	56,197	8,187
			86	88,351	73,137	79,383	6,246
GIBRAT	V	E	86	902,010	125,466	184,844	59,378
GREECE	N	E	81	1,323,114	380,270	479,391	99,121
			83	4,860,006	950,967	1,354,905	403,938
			84	487,710	138,505	184,349	45,844
			86	90,147	11,500	18,583	7,083
	N	W	84	1,881,742	464,874	625,864	160,990
	O	E	81	90,162	30,625	39,519	8,894
			82	4,272	2,401	2,401	
			86	24,341	9,234	11,677	2,443
	V	E	81	9,771,160	2,957,837	3,753,174	802,815
			82	9,442,501	2,288,744	3,048,138	759,394
			83	9,094,436	1,810,087	2,505,308	695,221
			84	16,289,893	3,937,866	5,389,847	1,451,981
			85	11,734,310	2,148,566	3,114,357	965,791
			86	14,354,251	2,093,231	3,208,884	1,115,653
	V	W	81	2,615,228	761,276	999,428	238,152
			82	3,752,384	867,840	1,220,104	352,264
			83	4,945,596	1,008,636	1,425,472	416,836
			84	2,562,258	803,629	1,056,986	253,357
			85	5,824,689	1,217,292	1,786,398	569,106
			86	5,587,720	845,977	1,318,374	472,397
GUATMAL	V	E	81	29,477	8,472	11,794	3,322
			82	118,503	40,173	52,142	11,969
			84	69,169	24,987	29,753	4,766
			86	6,490	4,240	5,006	766
	V	W	82	459	271	316	45
			83	4,445	2,989	3,540	551
			85	29,100	5,520	8,250	2,730
HAITI	V	E	84	263,757	74,145	94,973	20,828
			85	176,020	53,814	63,704	9,890
			86	344,001	51,600	82,056	30,456
HG KONG	N	W	84	3,230	1,116	1,201	85
	V	E	81	6,030	4,850	5,284	434
			82	45,945	18,889	22,261	3,372
			83	35,977	11,225	13,815	2,590
			84	600	278	336	58
			85	61,565	19,305	24,694	5,389
			86	112,822	40,515	48,188	7,673
	V	H	81	1,558	1,494	1,587	93
			82	2,175	1,521	1,636	115
			83	1,572	1,049	1,159	110
			84	4,403	2,695	3,024	329
	V	W	81	32,667	29,694	31,391	1,697
			82	43,548	36,398	39,067	2,669
			83	115,745	45,695	49,980	4,285
			84	41,624	15,620	17,372	1,752
			85	57,253	19,816	22,098	2,282
			86	38,769	15,214	16,366	1,152
HONDURA	N	E	81	973,008	469,511	521,159	51,648
	V	E	81	101,497	41,828	45,904	4,076
			82	1,546,237	913,949	1,027,898	113,949
			83	1,813,225	814,546	932,261	117,715
			84	1,274,410	445,900	510,148	64,248
			85	2,028,713	895,392	1,048,460	153,068
			86	1,090,025	412,524	459,067	46,543
HUNGARY	N	E	85	389,069	79,938	122,936	42,998
	V	E	81	162,032	25,339	32,059	6,720
			82	296,203	63,939	77,503	13,564
			84	334,774	67,240	101,298	34,058
			85	144,787	30,536	42,379	11,843
			86	483,012	107,761	164,784	57,023
	V	W	84	43,362	8,653	12,712	4,059
			85	418,701	71,989	107,081	35,092
			86	161,511	29,970	44,520	14,550
INDIA	N	E	84	22,445	15,071	16,643	1,572
			85	25,867	13,976	16,065	2,089
	O	E	81	317	320	350	30
			83	91,270	6,426	6,459	33
			84	13,491	5,530	6,083	553
			85	23,589	12,257	14,028	1,771
			86	4,003	3,095	3,439	344
	V	E	81	68,989	36,876	48,549	11,673
			82	61,908	42,854	51,618	8,764
			83	78,285	48,708	57,179	8,471
			84	84,725	65,540	73,498	7,958
			85	166,659	95,888	110,392	14,504
			86	121,277	70,688	79,795	9,107
	V	W	81	32,975	17,482	22,525	5,043
			82	78,767	41,865	51,630	9,765
			83	66,742	40,200	48,941	8,741
			84	87,170	33,829	43,679	9,850
			85	23,931	16,277	25,959	9,682
			86	31,614	16,939	18,960	2,021
ISRAEL	A	E	83	74,956	19,105	22,176	3,071
	N	E	81	30,385	8,701	10,859	2,158
			83	9,517	4,115	4,591	476
	V	E	81	1,336,604	368,164	443,056	74,892
			82	1,451,400	440,388	520,304	79,916
			83	769,195	263,001	311,445	48,444
			84	1,898,783	594,594	693,653	99,059
			85	2,137,609	609,700	740,207	130,507
			86	2,061,358	593,228	708,132	114,904
	V	W	83	67,078	22,746	28,134	5,388
			85	4,896	2,880	3,571	691
			86	65,249	24,268	27,443	3,175
ITALY	A	E	82	317	1,490	2,107	617
			83	309	492	492	
	N	E	83	218,972	131,637	151,460	19,823
			85	26,728	8,515	11,042	2,527
			86	43,952	15,433	18,261	2,828
	O	E	81	90,562	22,470	31,012	8,542
			83	12,346	5,600	7,464	1,864
			84	14,228	7,868	9,646	1,778
			85	35,096	13,022	17,659	4,637
	V	E	81	345,824	179,831	207,539	27,708
			82	378,648	145,327	171,728	26,401
			83	185,718	56,431	67,030	10,599
			84	451,473	183,910	220,084	36,174
			85	374,316	182,370	218,707	36,337
			86	331,785	196,854	222,055	25,201
	V	W	81	261,847	125,294	155,232	29,938
			82	291,793	121,516	147,782	26,266
			83	282,138	110,098	133,164	23,066
			84	215,362	99,201	119,052	19,851
			85	225,341	102,845	125,633	22,788
			86	180,950	105,311	123,395	18,084
IVY CST	V	E	86	192,792	24,558	37,482	12,924
JAMAICA	A	E	83	1,988	284	771	487
	N	E	83	33,402	32,150	35,857	3,707
	O	E	85	1,960	1,196	1,196	
	V	E	81	109,467	72,854	82,334	9,480
			82	57,000	58,408	63,925	5,517
			83	17,189	14,260	15,376	1,116
			84	39,460	37,514	40,099	2,585
			85	58,809	29,902	34,222	4,320
			86	89,002	18,200	24,151	5,951
JAPAN	N	E	81	43,688	44,790	51,457	6,667
			82	32,282	32,330	36,540	4,210
			83	424	743	816	73
			84	84,931	105,117	119,042	13,925
	N	H	84	85,053	65,402	77,361	11,959
	N	W	84	87,431	57,628	63,142	5,514
	O	E	81	78	560	604	44
			84	2,614	5,453	5,987	534
			85	1,384	2,784	3,023	239
			86	5,454	2,214	2,267	53
	V	E	81	24,940	31,671	34,193	2,522
			82	46,632	45,547	50,796	5,249
			83	67,344	93,329	107,013	13,684
			84	25,259	32,497	36,378	3,881
			85	90,473	94,064	103,829	9,765
			86	396,864	467,483	507,953	40,470
	V	H	81	44,242	31,538	37,744	6,206
			82	57,584	42,084	50,657	8,573
			83	75,082	64,327	75,828	11,501
			85	30,025	23,961	27,861	3,900
			86	88,917	94,836	106,846	12,010
	V	W	81	161,022	164,305	177,922	13,617
			82	222,622	205,142	223,065	17,923
			83	533,412	402,973	438,567	35,594
			84	231,993	226,071	245,921	19,850
			85	488,614	362,717	401,545	38,828
			86	545,754	543,003	587,290	44,287
JORDAN	V	E	85	21,164	8,000	8,978	978
KENYA	O	E	84	638	1,552	1,739	187

Table 2. U.S. Import Statistics for Non Crop-Specific Commodities by End-Use

Product
TSUSA commodity number, description, and unit of quantity

Country	Mode	Reg	Yr	Quantity	F.A.S.	C.I.F.	Charges
KOR REP	O	W	84	1,584	1,901	1,901	
	V	E	81	18,493	7,782	8,665	883
			82	1,200	600	645	45
			83	36,012	7,787	10,897	3,110
			84	46,982	14,825	17,373	2,548
			85	31,349	27,066	30,683	3,617
			86	78,382	61,321	68,746	7,425
	V	H	86	3,900	2,978	3,316	338
	V	W	81	16,377	8,015	8,646	631
			82	164,769	57,986	64,200	6,214
			83	42,747	36,306	39,276	2,970
			84	39,752	22,023	24,155	2,132
			85	126,045	83,426	91,794	8,368
			86	382,490	220,449	244,912	24,463
LEBANON	V	E	82	5,200	3,600	4,054	454
			85	20,068	11,825	13,002	1,177
			86	20,700	13,743	15,602	1,859
MACAO	V	E	86	16,370	8,942	10,785	1,843
MALAYSA	O	W	85	30,428	14,548	14,548	
	V	E	81	1,575	4,830	5,090	260
			82	431	435	475	40
			83	3,587	6,591	7,143	552
			84	1,576	3,810	4,200	390
MEXICO	O	E	81	35,119,339	11,196,544	11,205,884	9,340
			82	42,948,064	13,731,542	13,731,542	
			83	38,645,097	8,544,879	8,544,879	
			84	41,144,231	10,128,741	10,133,546	4,805
			85	48,887,980	13,614,231	13,614,549	318
			86	50,173,680	11,918,638	11,919,727	1,089
	O	W	81	11,666,725	5,092,892	5,094,236	1,344
			82	12,002,391	4,730,095	4,730,095	
			83	15,459,409	4,170,458	4,178,559	8,101
			84	15,149,616	5,052,470	5,053,570	1,100
			85	20,571,182	6,468,900	6,469,180	280
			86	19,123,507	4,876,172	4,876,174	2
	V	E	81	703	520	601	81
			84	39,683	5,940	8,450	2,510
			86	6,613	1,527	1,896	369
	V	W	81	166,727	83,487	90,769	7,282
			82	140,003	69,731	81,498	11,767
			83	88,522	17,070	19,460	2,390
			84	93,472	16,309	19,147	2,838
MONGOLA	V	E	86	64,320	26,640	29,752	3,112
MOROC	V	E	81	16,314	8,510	10,453	1,943
			83	992	491	608	117
			84	60,106	35,785	43,440	7,655
			85	58,731	23,310	27,895	4,585
			86	119,533	77,094	86,858	9,764
NETHLDS	O	E	86	21,420	6,737	6,905	168
	V	E	81	678	566	610	44
			82	3,670	2,604	2,750	146
			83	5,292	13,025	14,772	1,747
			84	90,439	33,251	38,289	5,038
			85	172,664	73,435	84,920	11,485
			86	114,652	64,419	76,123	11,704
	V	W	82	794	571	629	58
			83	2,223	1,277	1,458	181
			84	1,964	796	1,039	243
			85	28,380	7,098	7,495	397
PAKISTN	V	E	83	3,336	3,538	3,911	373
			84	1,260	1,260	1,591	331
			85	4,853	4,402	4,928	526
			86	12,493	6,027	7,698	1,671
	V	W	84	6,025	9,301	10,708	1,407
			86	3,095	3,123	3,600	477
PHIL R	V	E	81	10,120	8,563	11,596	3,033
			82	6,381	5,366	6,214	848
			83	6,470	6,042	6,819	777
			84	9,630	7,679	9,124	1,445
	V	H	83	300	255	302	47
	V	W	81	50,957	44,359	49,997	5,638
			82	29,924	26,086	29,289	3,203
			83	23,454	18,217	20,511	2,294
			84	24,193	18,136	20,713	2,577
			85	8,478	5,808	6,549	741
			86	25,428	23,516	26,153	2,637
POLAND	N	E	82	22,230	6,685	9,042	2,357
			83	130,203	28,426	38,137	9,711
			84	33,787	7,762	10,298	2,536
	O	E	81	22,487	4,824	7,649	2,825
			82	61,967	15,900	22,109	6,209
			85	45,000	10,700	15,350	4,650
	V	E	81	18,150	4,095	5,565	1,470
			82	6,085	1,280	1,575	295
			83	171,969	42,948	57,524	14,576

Product
TSUSA commodity number, description, and unit of quantity

Country	Mode	Reg	Yr	Quantity	F.A.S.	C.I.F.	Charges
			84	59,374	15,080	19,710	4,630
			85	157,862	42,914	60,191	17,277
			86	35,182	8,925	12,082	3,157
	V	W	82	45,000	11,200	17,114	5,914
PORTUGL	V	E	81	11,704	3,960	5,423	1,463
			82	48,025	17,818	21,705	3,887
			84	19,006	8,257	9,944	1,687
			85	8,412	1,666	1,826	160
			86	5,539	3,124	3,651	527
ROMANIA	V	E	81	44,000	10,780	13,037	2,257
			84	15,644	8,032	8,889	857
			85	29,101	4,730	7,973	3,243
SALVADR	V	E	83	34,677	26,550	27,767	1,217
SINGAPR	V	W	81	255	253	283	30
			82	3,783	1,983	2,186	203
			84	1,099	820	861	41
			86	2,575	1,034	1,141	107
SPAIN	O	E	82	53,969	14,908	18,488	3,580
			84	22,705	19,736	22,284	2,548
	V	E	81	501,593	469,178	513,311	44,133
			82	553,397	341,298	381,149	39,851
			83	475,376	319,043	357,293	38,250
			84	1,198,619	656,715	747,691	90,976
			85	1,064,638	462,355	543,246	80,891
			86	558,672	337,082	381,777	44,695
	V	W	82	60,847	13,214	18,221	5,007
			84	29,101	5,869	8,334	2,465
			86	148,394	56,954	67,248	10,294
SWEDEN	V	E	81	15,894	11,418	12,648	1,230
			82	5,971	4,969	5,739	770
			83	13,211	7,744	8,339	595
			84	1,666	1,122	1,213	91
	V	W	84	1,164	977	1,094	117
SWITZLD	O	E	84	6,235	3,922	4,340	418
	V	E	82	8,729	8,339	8,824	485
			83	35,855	16,576	18,501	1,925
			84	3,929	2,471	2,627	156
			86	329,562	185,989	200,088	14,099
	V	W	81	1,588	1,461	1,609	148
			83	2,625	2,666	2,859	193
			84	4,470	4,762	5,123	361
			85	1,984	1,491	1,603	112
SYRIA	O	E	84	1,102	775	834	59
	V	E	81	960	720	844	124
			84	736	330	405	75
THAILND	O	E	82	360	331	364	33
	V	E	81	52,815	36,895	43,666	6,771
			82	125,851	76,716	89,240	12,524
			83	246,479	132,652	147,551	14,899
			84	444,565	259,859	296,442	36,583
			85	402,314	225,673	252,220	26,547
			86	570,549	307,809	344,700	36,891
	V	H	81	960	901	1,005	104
			83	456	318	373	55
	V	W	81	162,341	93,617	104,833	11,216
			82	251,057	138,176	154,452	16,276
			83	171,282	118,726	129,326	10,600
			84	333,216	230,978	253,738	22,760
			85	306,118	166,451	182,062	15,611
			86	822,206	416,348	456,914	40,566
TUNISIA	V	E	86	2,087	1,557	1,727	170
	V	W	86	2,723	1,418	1,538	120
TURKEY	O	E	83	840	453	453	
			85	1,265	1,391	1,391	
	V	E	85	15,697	4,405	6,335	1,930
			86	35,733	14,491	17,312	2,821
	V	W	84	10,100	4,999	5,969	970
U KING	N	E	81	3,707	4,198	4,864	666
			82	10,592	12,819	14,467	1,648
			83	6,610	6,203	7,216	1,013
			84	16,508	15,007	18,145	3,138
			85	6,902	4,712	8,022	3,310
	O	E	81	31,727	44,802	48,643	3,841
			82	40,610	43,357	47,403	4,046
			83	23,664	28,684	31,059	2,375
			84	26,219	20,615	23,406	2,791
			86	4,234	2,442	2,766	324
	V	E	81	4,846	6,055	6,744	689
			82	7,170	8,400	9,361	961
			83	23,948	31,081	34,698	3,617
			84	2,741	1,895	2,233	338
			85	392,011	73,964	108,178	34,214
			86	316,378	65,549	92,693	27,144
	V	W	81	2,850	3,876	4,271	395
			82	617	810	932	122

Product TSUSA commodity number, description, and unit of quantity Country	Mode	Reg	Yr	Quantity	F.A.S.	C.I.F.	Charges
			83	1,120	853	1,100	247
			84	2,435	2,268	2,495	227
			85	92,868	22,262	31,019	8,757
			86	1,938	1,416	1,470	54
USSR	V	E	82	2,857	950	1,150	200
	V	W	81	810	318	389	71
VENEZ	V	E	84	186,174	39,172	48,648	9,476
			85	359,279	139,983	158,676	18,693
			86	235,177	147,186	166,358	19,172
YUGOSLV	O	E	84	7,090	2,794	3,120	326
			86	4,939	1,404	1,404	
	O	W	82	2,438	1,343	1,343	
			83	1,523	2,151	2,151	
			84	5,113	6,340	6,340	
	V	E	81	51,032	23,239	27,070	3,831
			82	35,029	13,415	16,701	3,286
			83	113,078	62,658	72,510	9,852
			84	105,776	36,364	45,974	9,610
			85	179,581	80,287	95,892	15,605
			86	306,966	70,318	96,462	26,144
	V	W	83	14,533	11,520	13,650	2,130

Vegetable, prepared or preserved
1418500 PALM HEARTS, PREP OR PRES (LB)

Country	Mode	Reg	Yr	Quantity	F.A.S.	C.I.F.	Charges
TOTAL			81	1,302,368	1,296,957	1,448,812	151,855
			82	2,170,217	1,977,486	2,300,546	323,060
			83	2,400,849	2,050,828	2,381,790	330,962
			84	4,245,240	3,718,313	4,180,184	461,871
			85	4,372,711	2,832,121	3,280,891	448,770
			86	4,595,834	3,617,930	4,003,353	385,423
ARGENT	V	E	82	21,000	16,900	19,640	2,740
			85	4,500	2,907	2,999	92
BELGIUM	V	E	83	34,920	51,150	55,795	4,645
			84	70,040	60,429	66,276	5,847
BELIZE	V	E	83	2,646	3,000	3,575	575
			85	106,425	83,290	97,664	14,374
BRAZIL	A	E	84	1,990	3,344	4,012	668
	N	E	82	28,234	22,341	25,755	3,414
			85	1,256,320	752,396	884,413	132,017
			86	144,042	108,554	121,584	13,030
	V	E	81	1,116,643	1,124,345	1,252,736	128,391
			82	1,727,942	1,556,440	1,818,178	261,738
			83	1,848,283	1,547,917	1,815,992	268,075
			84	2,943,187	2,636,616	2,980,553	343,937
			85	1,570,608	1,064,534	1,236,140	171,606
			86	3,030,624	2,668,462	2,952,594	284,132
	V	W	81	43,702	54,838	60,438	5,600
			82	181,957	185,112	217,265	32,153
			83	347,191	329,266	374,266	45,000
			84	361,967	363,549	414,930	51,381
			85	767,200	526,513	615,258	88,745
			86	802,723	463,748	515,744	51,996
C RICA	O	E	85	35,509	18,780	18,780	
	V	E	81	62,745	54,927	65,075	10,148
			82	116,575	92,371	102,376	10,005
			83	118,974	85,275	94,577	9,302
			84	384,751	314,806	343,928	29,122
			85	395,156	240,392	264,836	24,444
			86	346,821	223,418	246,104	22,686
	V	W	81	75,657	59,447	66,805	7,358
			82	14,525	8,350	10,247	1,897
			83	6,513	3,125	3,901	776
			84	215,800	139,133	155,005	15,872
			85	191,063	115,578	129,722	14,144
			86	120,593	87,580	95,151	7,571
CHINA M	V	E	82	1,313	916	1,002	86
CHINA T	V	E	84	450	270	325	55
			86	1,864	1,650	1,796	146
	V	H	83	2,250	1,075	1,155	80
ECUADOR	V	E	84	60,881	45,220	49,625	4,405
	V	W	84	31,238	22,610	24,502	1,892
			85	29,400	18,200	20,330	2,130
FRANCE	V	E	84	1,579	1,722	1,944	222
	V	W	85	556	1,013	1,076	63
GUATMAL	V	E	82	43,000	35,822	38,500	2,678
			83	6,652	5,693	6,147	454
HG KONG	V	W	83	1,200	531	627	96
			84	2,955	2,150	2,305	155
JAPAN	V	E	81	689	1,318	1,408	90
			83	134	320	349	29
			84	263	261	277	16
PERU	V	E	83	6,349	5,495	5,950	455

Product TSUSA commodity number, description, and unit of quantity Country	Mode	Reg	Yr	Quantity	F.A.S.	C.I.F.	Charges
PHIL R	V	W	81	2,932	2,082	2,350	268
			82	14,002	13,450	15,295	1,845
			83	1,900	1,582	1,657	75
			84	3,275	1,933	2,209	276
			85	3,825	2,567	2,833	266
SALVADR	N	E	83	10,405	8,385	8,982	597
	V	W	84	1,200	1,659	1,854	195
SPAIN	V	E	85	2,249	1,635	1,927	292
THAILND	V	E	83	2,098	1,201	1,450	249
			86	4,497	2,000	2,243	243
	V	W	82	2,200	5,784	7,221	1,437
			83	13,303	7,594	8,300	706
			84	37,566	22,530	24,453	1,923
			85	9,900	4,316	4,913	597
			86	43,420	15,268	17,005	1,737
VENEZ	A	E	83	129	420	517	97
	V	E	82	19,469	40,000	45,067	5,067
			84	126,000	100,880	106,536	5,656
			86	101,250	47,250	51,132	3,882

1419800 VEGETABLES, PREP, PRES, NES (LB)

Country	Mode	Reg	Yr	Quantity	F.A.S.	C.I.F.	Charges
TOTAL			81	12,818,126	7,230,293	7,749,961	521,022
			82	20,539,509	12,054,227	13,059,712	1,005,485
			83	22,594,347	11,858,944	12,874,858	1,015,914
			84	28,959,097	13,753,858	15,121,076	1,367,218
ARGENT	V	E	81	73,264	20,457	22,392	1,935
			82	39,639	15,080	18,004	2,924
			83	13,760	5,391	6,499	1,108
			84	45,026	17,278	20,868	3,590
	V	W	82	25,926	11,225	13,726	2,501
			83	17,756	6,580	8,120	1,540
			84	5,544	1,925	2,878	953
AUSTRAL	V	E	82	4,198	5,834	6,436	602
	V	W	81	2,535	2,865	3,109	244
			82	5,578	6,440	7,035	595
			83	3,440	3,072	3,391	319
AUSTRIA	V	E	81	233,535	95,150	111,759	16,609
			82	259,921	118,655	130,482	11,827
			83	203,278	114,975	122,007	7,032
			84	150,869	46,627	50,104	3,477
	V	W	81	1,659	857	1,247	390
			83	39,923	13,949	16,015	2,066
			84	49,230	16,835	19,876	3,041
BELGIUM	A	E	84	112	270	386	116
	N	E	81	84,800	46,317	52,725	6,408
			82	332,556	148,687	163,927	15,240
			83	457,806	141,315	163,898	22,583
	N	W	83	162,265	44,718	52,381	7,663
	O	E	81	4,160	937	1,094	157
			82	8,535	2,304	2,718	414
			83	10,049	2,847	3,173	326
	V	E	81	50,272	20,640	23,633	2,993
			82	51,575	24,521	27,587	3,066
			83	92,615	35,204	39,498	4,294
			84	1,174,729	289,821	348,685	58,864
	V	W	81	41,124	12,089	14,427	2,338
			82	139,230	44,914	51,204	6,290
			83	80	368	500	132
			84	180,219	38,465	48,017	9,552
BERMUDA	A	E	83	45	531	563	32
BRAZIL	V	E	82	3,361	1,305	1,571	266
			83	3,240	1,946	2,284	338
			84	1,050	279	363	84
	V	W	82	238	705	861	156
			83	10,672	2,899	3,750	851
BULGAR	V	E	84	48,775	13,373	15,750	2,377
C RICA	V	E	81	8,905	9,504	11,883	2,379
			82	11,702	3,981	5,179	1,198
			83	803	1,012	1,295	283
			84	10,015	5,219	6,270	1,051
	V	W	82	1,288	450	482	32
			83	4,266	2,765	3,594	829
CANADA	A	H	82	360	360	386	26
	O	E	81	1,018,099	160,149	160,149	
			82	335,795	118,456	118,456	
			83	111,771	63,033	63,088	55
			84	180,114	66,449	66,449	
	O	W	82	358,292	114,423	114,423	
			83	716,400	361,556	361,556	
			84	58,468	8,283	8,283	
CHINA M	N	E	81	694,191	284,423	338,786	54,363
	N	W	82	794,023	322,374	355,951	33,577
			83	730,121	245,730	266,326	20,596
			84	438,962	166,639	184,844	18,205

658   Table 2. U.S. Import Statistics for Non Crop-Specific Commodities by End-Use

Product
TSUSA commodity number, description, and unit of quantity

Country	Mode	Reg	Yr	Quantity	F.A.S.	C.I.F.	Charges
	O	E	81	1,800	582	680	98
			83	1,000	466	508	42
			84	6,392	2,589	2,950	361
	O	W	81	4,294	1,772	1,917	145
			84	7,384	3,434	3,723	289
	V	E	81	475,365	193,498	226,116	32,588
			82	931,520	388,581	456,343	67,762
			83	27,617	8,224	9,805	1,581
			84	657,918	243,328	309,038	65,710
	V	H	81	5,236	3,166	3,391	225
			82	54,792	25,066	27,498	2,432
			83	14,128	7,292	8,041	749
			84	19,111	10,112	11,673	1,561
	V	W	81	696,053	293,197	321,021	29,108
			82	602,697	276,937	305,038	28,101
			83	653,921	251,072	279,131	28,059
			84	916,972	343,775	385,114	41,339
CHINA T	N	E	81	19,440	11,140	12,303	1,163
	O	E	81	6,798	5,633	7,200	1,567
	O	W	82	794	1,308	1,366	58
			84	28,800	7,058	8,423	1,365
	V	E	81	357,334	233,231	257,226	23,995
			82	677,607	446,837	501,468	54,631
			83	807,316	529,446	596,261	66,815
			84	892,490	557,642	647,446	89,804
	V	H	81	10,351	7,932	8,927	995
			82	33,448	27,115	29,915	2,800
			83	16,112	16,919	18,191	1,272
			84	21,264	20,168	22,693	2,525
	V	W	81	612,808	395,427	427,088	31,661
			82	959,360	628,337	681,324	52,987
			83	1,120,979	743,302	804,504	61,202
			84	1,110,973	727,346	800,399	73,053
COLOMB	A	E	83	301	298	429	131
	V	E	82	21,235	10,940	12,476	1,536
			84	1,100	3,900	4,603	703
CYPRUS	V	E	81	34,800	13,917	16,000	2,083
			82	975	793	847	54
			83	599	915	990	75
			84	2,750	1,399	1,543	144
DENMARK	V	E	84	122	3,242	3,286	44
	V	W	84	675	747	832	85
DOM REP	A	E	83	2,107	505	670	165
	N	E	82	103,559	32,231	36,203	3,972
			84	134,280	36,657	41,622	4,965
	V	E	81	25,780	10,243	11,334	1,091
			82	5,973	3,091	3,246	155
			83	124,217	32,487	40,343	7,856
			84	282,162	89,386	120,389	31,003
ECUADOR	V	E	83	6,402	2,800	3,399	599
EGYPT	V	E	81	1,212	500	597	97
FIJI	V	W	81	8,800	10,331	10,445	114
FR GERM	N	E	83	9,067	18,446	20,528	2,082
	O	E	81	143	259	279	20
			83	2,133	1,201	1,358	157
	V	E	81	13,311	5,778	6,487	709
			82	77,348	74,637	80,692	6,055
			83	42,808	15,110	16,799	1,689
			84	62,126	35,165	40,138	4,973
	V	W	81	1,355	940	1,172	232
			82	7,359	6,422	7,108	686
			83	1,430	1,876	2,081	205
			84	4,399	1,683	1,830	147
FRANCE	A	E	81	66	1,427	1,654	227
	N	E	81	108,387	45,177	51,825	6,648
			82	147,978	61,652	72,270	10,618
			83	199,847	80,547	90,280	9,733
			84	3,843	2,134	2,256	122
	O	E	81	617	1,845	2,051	206
			83	2,444	1,822	2,226	404
	O	W	84	700	493	744	251
	V	E	81	371	784	845	61
			82	15,201	12,144	13,453	1,309
			83	63,993	26,689	32,328	5,639
			84	1,250,813	374,280	462,623	88,343
	V	W	81	55,402	32,518	34,684	2,166
			82	85,765	89,167	95,887	6,720
			83	80,232	76,687	84,283	7,596
			84	105,324	76,792	84,174	7,382
GHANA	V	E	82	13,050	5,896	10,819	4,923
GREECE	N	E	82	17,807	11,540	13,634	2,094
			84	85,016	43,838	54,817	10,979
	O	E	81	900	380	380	
			83	8,017	3,789	3,789	
			84	8,328	3,439	3,439	
	V	E	81	65,069	36,025	41,904	5,879
			82	55,114	94,038	99,489	5,451
			83	120,682	67,809	80,167	12,358
			84	103,265	48,318	57,749	9,431
	V	W	82	242,662	55,492	79,013	23,521
			83	55,422	10,999	15,622	4,623
			84	1,304	1,161	1,298	137
GUATMAL	A	E	84	375	399	547	148
	A	W	82	541	811	1,129	318
			84	1,573	2,151	2,958	807
	V	E	82	5,760	2,304	2,765	461
HAITI	V	E	82	12,000	5,750	6,226	476
			84	24,132	7,537	9,562	2,025
HG KONG	N	E	83	332,564	148,472	173,756	25,284
	N	W	83	9,817	5,793	6,172	379
			84	49,940	27,139	29,577	2,438
	O	E	83	1,230	422	460	38
			84	2,500	2,279	2,606	327
	O	W	81	1,720	969	1,063	94
			84	5,535	1,900	2,058	158
	V	E	81	205,632	134,494	151,531	17,037
			82	291,354	170,873	194,882	24,009
			83	155,125	106,497	119,940	13,443
			84	240,457	126,976	153,498	26,522
	V	H	81	24,862	22,005	23,444	1,439
			82	35,886	29,599	31,875	2,276
			83	26,748	21,902	24,216	2,314
			84	24,195	18,226	20,214	1,988
	V	W	81	228,705	172,776	184,598	11,822
			82	379,442	262,348	283,743	21,395
			83	472,976	281,340	304,655	23,315
			84	464,584	236,871	256,554	19,683
HONDURA	V	E	81	720	918	991	73
HUNGARY	V	E	81	26,454	3,982	5,039	1,057
			82	38,438	8,093	10,376	2,283
			83	168,014	116,811	133,440	16,629
			84	52,222	22,070	28,281	6,211
	V	W	83	14,754	3,476	5,580	2,104
INDIA	N	E	81	2,805	1,602	2,034	432
			84	64,830	33,808	40,753	6,945
	O	E	81	17,787	9,585	11,021	1,436
			82	63,847	32,829	37,663	4,834
			83	7,498	4,664	5,105	441
			84	6,063	4,697	4,919	222
	V	E	81	156,028	82,239	107,510	25,271
			82	289,917	161,013	201,356	40,343
			83	296,995	167,244	194,406	27,162
			84	303,414	168,302	193,648	25,346
	V	W	81	23,381	15,208	20,542	5,334
			82	176,561	114,186	139,663	25,477
			83	48,248	28,968	35,257	6,289
			84	54,880	30,360	36,407	6,047
INDNSIA	V	W	83	4,500	2,267	2,495	228
ISRAEL	V	E	81	235,795	86,203	102,709	16,506
			82	1,451,340	407,330	492,583	85,253
			83	1,913,674	583,927	690,251	106,324
			84	2,908,654	896,766	1,059,386	162,620
	V	W	84	194,447	51,990	67,279	15,289
ITALY	A	E	83	386	1,075	1,392	317
			84	320	805	1,668	863
	N	E	82	84,442	91,727	102,208	10,481
			83	96,241	86,763	98,718	11,955
	O	E	81	2,239	2,774	3,046	272
			83	833	265	265	
			84	4,346	1,901	2,139	238
	V	E	81	247,484	154,164	173,785	19,621
			82	76,794	51,174	59,204	8,030
			83	74,281	22,275	28,884	6,609
			84	109,966	120,816	134,536	13,720
	V	W	82	794	3,810	4,155	345
			83	9,903	7,382	8,473	1,091
			84	5,351	3,665	4,321	656
JAMAICA	A	E	81	3,550	1,612	2,012	400
			82	7,351	4,808	5,936	1,128
	N	E	84	21,762	12,433	13,544	1,111
	V	E	81	14,250	7,000	8,230	1,230
			82	105,793	60,832	67,119	6,287
			83	92,032	50,223	56,287	6,064
			84	35,925	18,043	19,350	1,307
	V	W	84	3,113	1,705	2,293	588
JAPAN	N	E	82	551,214	518,751	585,878	67,127
			84	602,109	668,935	762,864	93,929
	N	H	82	450,250	521,909	619,118	97,209
			83	408,065	481,363	563,559	82,196
			84	461,566	559,494	660,332	100,838

Product
TSUSA commodity number, description, and unit of quantity

Country	Mode	Reg	Yr	Quantity	F.A.S.	C.I.F.	Charges
	N	W	83	1,527,545	1,556,831	1,668,893	112,062
			84	958,894	942,594	1,010,775	68,181
	V	E	81	396,637	395,451	447,398	51,947
			82	161,169	142,350	163,187	20,837
			83	650,850	646,591	727,220	80,629
			84	315,003	217,738	253,890	36,152
	V	H	81	275,825	337,025	398,186	61,161
			82	4,950	4,228	5,603	1,375
			83	1,225	1,115	1,231	116
	V	W	81	974,586	1,065,700	1,133,399	67,699
			82	1,593,815	1,610,663	1,730,243	119,580
			83	98,565	109,814	118,709	8,895
			84	612,321	695,791	751,327	55,536
KOR REP	N	E	84	70,603	54,086	61,509	7,423
	V	E	81	56,223	34,901	39,320	4,419
			82	55,308	43,007	47,705	4,698
			83	82,543	70,475	77,784	7,309
			84	42,126	26,533	30,749	4,216
	V	H	81	15,052	10,805	13,162	2,357
			82	4,860	5,365	6,294	929
			83	14,984	8,250	10,067	1,817
			84	7,111	5,411	6,493	1,082
	V	W	81	114,966	84,140	90,890	6,750
			82	170,600	134,171	143,767	9,596
			83	188,259	146,995	157,885	10,890
			84	231,872	161,056	174,224	13,168
LEBANON	O	E	82	870	1,233	1,233	
			84	1,490	1,307	1,340	33
	V	E	81	1,556	2,886	3,232	346
			82	13,819	8,081	9,062	981
			83	14,262	8,320	9,251	931
			84	15,302	9,381	10,141	760
	V	W	83	6,032	4,875	5,426	551
MACAO	V	H	83	700	981	1,066	85
MALAWI	O	E	84	446	620	679	59
MALAYSA	V	E	82	4,532	4,878	5,163	285
			83	1,200	900	959	59
			84	2,645	2,171	2,399	228
	V	W	83	600	500	527	27
MEXICO	A	E	83	220	335	575	240
			84	184	440	691	251
	O	E	81	1,518,632	725,280	725,180	
			82	2,190,143	1,205,352	1,205,352	
			83	1,770,434	845,047	845,047	
			84	2,019,860	742,968	744,368	1,400
	O	W	81	3,578,526	1,844,978	1,844,978	
			82	4,985,125	2,669,777	2,688,527	18,750
			83	6,292,848	2,351,092	2,351,092	
			84	8,785,414	3,309,328	3,309,328	
	V	W	81	73,022	18,412	21,753	3,341
			83	50,148	11,354	12,945	1,591
			84	41,449	8,933	10,285	1,352
MOROC	V	E	82	13,051	7,400	8,326	926
			84	19,048	11,664	13,146	1,482
N ZEAL	V	W	84	75	398	495	97
NETHLDS	A	E	82	500	380	919	539
	O	E	83	775	281	309	28
	V	E	81	5,022	10,662	11,094	432
			82	9,423	4,341	4,835	494
			83	2,587	947	1,176	229
			84	562	666	694	28
	V	W	81	25,794	18,603	23,918	5,315
			82	41,000	29,581	37,156	7,575
			83	8,141	4,358	4,812	454
			84	2,955	2,219	2,497	278
NORFOLK	V	E	84	25,500	11,692	13,485	1,793
NORWAY	A	E	83	331	332	658	326
PAKISTN	O	E	84	5,707	1,687	1,886	199
	V	E	83	2,629	2,570	2,886	316
			84	1,140	1,260	1,591	331
	V	W	82	2,270	2,397	2,920	523
			84	954	1,000	1,327	327
PERU	N	E	83	41,842	85,719	108,338	22,619
	V	E	83	4,317	8,640	9,495	855
			84	7,976	16,051	16,863	812
	V	W	83	4,365	1,600	2,077	477
PHIL R	V	E	81	13,763	7,856	8,952	1,096
			82	25,227	12,050	14,500	2,450
			83	10,753	7,081	8,207	1,126
			84	39,128	21,340	26,975	5,635
	V	H	82	486	408	477	69
	V	W	81	46,852	31,187	34,785	3,598
			82	62,584	45,905	51,525	5,620
			83	119,386	67,581	75,782	8,201
			84	94,614	49,838	56,628	6,790
POLAND	N	E	82	33,600	9,130	13,286	4,156
	O	E	83	22,486	5,200	7,500	2,300
	V	E	83	32,325	9,725	12,876	3,151
			84	4,344	1,231	1,625	394
	V	W	83	22,500	5,200	8,191	2,991
			84	22,500	5,200	8,191	2,991
PORTUGL	V	E	81	2,866	1,828	3,060	1,232
			82	1,478	733	996	263
			83	10,816	9,261	11,819	2,558
			84	11,148	5,217	6,415	1,198
REP SAF	V	E	83	20,875	63,250	67,126	3,876
ROMANIA	V	E	84	107,069	29,774	36,339	6,565
	V	W	84	1,858	1,718	1,871	153
S HELNA	V	E	84	30,688	11,073	13,301	2,228
SALVADR	A	E	83	1,000	750	1,000	250
	V	E	82	10,670	8,063	10,063	2,000
			84	1,800	3,455	3,884	429
	V	W	82	2,991	2,775	3,226	451
			83	2,907	3,171	3,767	596
			84	600	955	1,067	112
SINGAPR	V	E	81	1,164	467	536	69
			82	1,707	1,544	1,665	121
	V	W	81	931	323	372	49
			82	6,045	4,486	4,930	444
			83	1,819	3,807	4,422	615
			84	1,029	768	806	38
SPAIN	V	E	81	126,018	53,515	60,821	7,306
			82	110,689	64,488	72,821	8,333
			83	71,156	19,574	25,257	5,683
			84	274,849	117,949	141,070	23,121
	V	W	82	11,025	5,364	6,196	832
			83	17,850	7,467	8,786	1,319
			84	27,108	13,113	15,843	2,730
SURINAM	O	E	83	22	423	423	
	V	E	84	3,269	900	1,110	210
SWAZLND	V	E	84	18,452	6,999	7,728	729
SWEDEN	V	E	81	1,442	1,894	1,990	96
			83	777	1,805	1,940	135
SWITZLD	N	E	82	18,868	23,940	25,071	1,131
	V	E	81	2,249	1,603	1,862	259
			83	86,229	47,253	59,043	11,790
			84	482,911	300,739	319,386	18,647
SYRIA	V	E	83	110	260	278	18
THAILND	N	W	84	368,221	271,959	302,827	30,868
	O	E	82	2,028	780	858	78
			83	2,400	1,650	1,905	255
	O	W	83	2,705	1,350	1,459	109
			84	2,990	2,150	2,331	181
	V	E	81	131,900	69,805	78,325	8,520
			82	66,893	46,697	53,417	6,720
			83	68,869	54,798	61,936	7,138
			84	130,433	85,904	98,578	12,674
	V	H	81	850	966	1,078	112
			82	1,168	780	877	97
			83	2,984	1,972	2,202	230
			84	5,046	3,385	3,832	447
	V	W	81	154,350	101,743	111,227	9,484
			82	279,639	248,438	270,272	21,834
			83	396,256	283,820	316,638	32,818
			84	299,062	199,249	220,276	21,027
TNZANIA	V	E	81	221	1,109	1,276	167
TURKEY	O	E	83	306	288	288	
	V	E	82	132,276	38,812	45,439	6,627
			83	1,652	743	820	77
			84	59,332	28,384	33,355	4,971
	V	W	83	14,160	8,086	10,195	2,109
U KING	N	E	81	6,744	4,875	5,558	683
			82	2,425	3,166	3,543	377
	N	W	82	570	652	860	208
	O	E	81	270	716	716	
			82	3,348	2,137	2,296	159
			83	188	273	293	20
			84	4,817	3,921	4,329	408
	V	E	81	531	614	896	282
			83	10,819	12,113	12,631	518
			84	9,988	6,778	7,482	704
	V	W	81	3,299	2,250	2,705	455
			82	1,373	856	856	
			84	4,660	2,048	2,180	132
USSR	O	E	81	4,409	1,031	1,337	306
	V	E	81	10,767	4,625	6,058	1,433
			82	46,351	14,502	16,809	2,307
			84	85,105	19,481	21,444	1,963
	V	W	82	1,764	338	504	166
VENEZ	A	E	82	400	270	973	703

Product
TSUSA commodity number, description, and unit of quantity

Country	Mode	Reg	Yr	Quantity	F.A.S.	C.I.F.	Charges
	V	E	83	125,091	14,392	20,494	6,102
W SAMOA	A	W	82	1,995	735	1,607	872
	V	H	83	2,309	1,626	1,749	123
			84	1,998	1,585	1,696	111
	V	W	83	1,427	1,580	1,826	246
YUGOSLV	O	W	82	1,023	357	357	
			83	200	1,045	1,045	
	V	E	81	58,202	24,845	30,398	5,553
			82	13,266	3,532	3,600	68
			83	11,429	3,334	4,764	1,430
			84	4,585	4,934	5,456	522

1419840 VEGETABLES, PREP, PRES, NES (LB)

Country	Mode	Reg	Yr	Quantity	F.A.S.	C.I.F.	Charges
TOTAL			85	27,604,449	13,503,153	14,800,501	1,297,348
			86	29,739,506	15,600,441	16,996,427	1,395,986
ARGENT	V	E	86	216,611	134,209	155,395	21,186
	V	W	85	47,940	17,310	21,453	4,143
AUSTRAL	V	W	86	3,527	2,745	2,980	235
AUSTRIA	N	E	85	17,289	7,821	9,497	1,676
	V	E	85	39,021	12,013	14,221	2,208
			86	54,942	17,037	21,309	4,272
BELGIUM	N	E	85	878,868	197,334	244,782	47,448
	O	E	86	6,368	2,678	2,710	32
	V	E	85	435,365	179,606	211,378	31,772
			86	1,035,592	470,899	541,126	70,227
	V	W	85	147,075	42,946	54,900	11,954
			86	218,124	81,569	93,812	12,243
BELIZE	V	E	86	9,200	2,300	2,663	363
BRAZIL	V	E	85	3,544	1,781	2,130	349
			86	6,328	2,813	3,279	466
BULGAR	V	E	85	106,171	30,089	36,650	6,561
			86	21,164	5,000	6,400	1,400
C RICA	V	E	85	211,532	102,808	115,255	12,447
			86	91,667	49,368	57,879	8,511
	V	W	85	2,369	1,183	1,399	216
CANADA	O	E	85	911,548	198,050	198,050	
			86	1,107,231	219,468	219,468	
	O	W	85	432,330	23,778	23,779	1
	V	W	85	1,980	1,004	1,077	73
CHINA M	N	E	85	458,130	199,697	243,724	44,027
	O	E	85	20,755	11,375	13,112	1,737
			86	5,500	3,186	3,578	392
	O	W	85	12,390	3,157	3,328	171
			86	4,536	1,260	1,260	
	V	E	86	956,903	359,704	418,461	58,757
	V	H	85	8,711	4,413	4,916	503
			86	23,284	11,370	12,721	1,351
	V	W	85	735,421	313,029	341,477	28,448
			86	967,286	354,149	380,226	26,077
CHINA T	N	E	85	766,268	478,016	549,322	71,306
	O	E	85	5,483	3,611	4,195	584
			86	2,093	2,010	2,154	144
	O	W	85	30,900	4,196	4,824	628
	V	E	85	66,521	57,042	64,851	7,809
			86	879,097	549,387	618,262	68,875
	V	H	85	27,299	29,843	32,555	2,712
			86	26,866	26,500	29,048	2,548
	V	W	85	1,454,641	947,619	1,037,599	89,980
			86	2,037,082	1,192,860	1,293,258	100,398
COLOMB	V	E	85	4,964	2,400	2,890	490
			86	3,968	1,728	2,111	383
DOM REP	V	E	85	681,197	258,206	338,368	80,162
			86	1,163,112	370,556	489,761	119,205
	V	W	86	87,300	31,500	38,303	6,803
ECUADOR	V	E	85	5,000	3,000	3,337	337
EGYPT	O	E	85	1,122	1,114	1,114	
	V	E	86	2,756	3,250	4,000	750
FR GERM	V	E	85	19,262	17,053	20,304	3,251
			86	74,401	31,250	34,396	3,146
	V	W	85	8,352	8,538	10,542	2,004
			86	2,588	5,531	6,033	502
FRANCE	N	E	85	34,539	6,665	8,844	2,179
	O	W	85	4,233	4,261	5,222	961
	V	E	85	1,420,515	366,928	449,330	82,402
			86	1,044,363	254,228	307,443	53,215
	V	W	85	187,363	70,197	81,883	11,686
			86	35,107	42,775	45,838	3,063
GHANA	V	E	86	7,000	1,800	2,950	1,150
GREECE	O	E	85	2,196	1,192	1,192	
	V	E	85	295,521	93,453	115,682	22,229
			86	341,671	134,546	164,594	30,048
	V	W	85	34,157	35,934	41,849	5,915
HG KONG	O	E	85	13,266	3,281	4,069	788
			86	4,551	1,768	2,080	312
	V	E	85	185,546	125,492	142,749	17,257
			86	509,414	218,512	248,391	29,879
	V	H	85	10,886	9,271	10,102	831
			86	8,465	7,421	8,004	583
	V	W	85	396,716	181,271	195,719	14,448
			86	527,475	249,301	265,998	16,697
HONDURA	V	E	85	41,520	9,544	11,466	1,922
HUNGARY	V	E	85	1,260	3,276	3,331	55
			86	262,864	69,646	86,712	17,066
ICELAND	V	E	86	8,000	5,289	6,267	978
INDIA	N	E	85	103,328	52,997	62,901	9,904
	O	E	85	29,525	11,693	13,774	2,081
			86	2,200	1,027	1,027	
	V	E	85	306,484	161,771	186,812	25,041
			86	256,712	144,338	164,450	20,112
	V	W	85	111,614	58,495	69,546	11,051
			86	90,657	54,341	63,158	8,817
ISRAEL	V	E	85	1,017,469	292,421	355,203	62,782
			86	1,944,388	500,455	611,528	111,073
	V	W	85	51,019	14,971	18,346	3,375
			86	9,942	4,552	5,295	743
ITALY	A	W	86	543	1,845	2,927	1,082
	N	E	86	514,145	616,698	665,475	48,777
	N	W	85	9,720	8,220	11,328	3,108
	O	E	85	4,749	4,933	5,521	588
	V	E	85	262,654	258,217	282,879	24,662
			86	101,494	116,602	126,430	9,828
	V	W	85	16,436	20,880	22,558	1,678
			86	36,006	17,028	20,003	2,975
JAMAICA	O	E	85	3,900	1,383	1,383	
	V	E	85	98,605	50,594	56,570	5,976
			86	37,437	14,189	16,051	1,862
JAPAN	N	E	85	841,091	718,265	815,359	97,094
	N	H	86	49,203	76,037	87,895	11,858
	N	W	85	566,534	600,989	642,285	41,296
	O	E	85	9,010	6,280	7,018	738
	O	W	85	7,833	7,233	7,736	503
			86	1,164	1,781	1,852	71
	V	E	85	25,793	22,038	25,110	3,072
			86	672,292	743,616	815,773	72,157
	V	H	85	384,503	439,652	513,536	73,884
			86	276,964	459,420	522,333	62,913
	V	W	85	1,404,950	1,246,255	1,348,277	102,022
			86	1,303,507	1,825,801	1,922,423	96,622
KENYA	V	W	85	3,270	2,626	2,927	301
KOR REP	N	E	86	84,837	76,496	86,460	9,964
	N	W	85	3,258	6,379	7,139	760
	V	E	85	127,063	118,923	136,494	17,571
			86	70,449	43,012	49,390	6,378
	V	H	85	48,885	25,514	30,878	5,364
			86	29,396	20,330	22,712	2,382
	V	W	85	201,723	155,012	169,611	14,599
			86	487,905	362,691	392,847	30,156
LEBANON	V	E	85	50,650	27,526	31,526	4,000
			86	29,817	14,112	15,825	1,713
	V	W	86	18,801	9,204	10,308	1,104
LESOTHO	V	E	85	248	2,329	2,425	96
MALAWI	V	E	86	6,179	3,523	3,898	375
MALAYSA	V	E	86	11,894	3,548	4,276	728
	V	W	86	11,500	6,516	6,884	368
MEXICO	O	E	85	2,189,805	908,510	908,510	
			86	1,926,162	787,325	787,325	
	O	W	85	7,326,162	3,061,694	3,061,694	
			86	6,992,758	3,125,672	3,125,672	
MOROC	V	E	85	3,660	2,158	3,116	958
			86	19,841	14,400	16,635	2,235
NETHLDS	O	E	86	12,811	4,101	4,208	107
	V	E	85	318,585	84,245	113,207	28,962
			86	646,302	402,921	483,499	80,578
	V	W	85	21,334	6,217	7,027	810
PAKISTN	V	E	85	15,998	11,667	13,592	1,925
			86	51,918	18,658	22,439	3,781
	V	W	85	4,320	2,677	2,825	148
PERU	N	E	85	14,082	25,129	29,885	4,756
			86	5,761	10,506	12,094	1,588
	V	E	85	3,307	3,888	4,162	274
PHIL R	V	E	85	121,068	50,894	63,965	13,071
			86	54,826	29,136	34,895	5,759
	V	H	86	1,983	1,507	1,781	274
	V	W	85	121,477	61,341	71,714	10,373
			86	124,471	63,327	75,090	11,763
POLAND	V	E	85	27,376	6,433	7,603	1,170
			86	52,307	11,144	15,340	4,196
REP SAF	V	E	86	8,055	13,825	17,197	3,372
ROMANIA	V	E	86	30,211	7,350	8,750	1,400

Product TSUSA commodity number, description, and unit of quantity Country	Mode	Reg	Yr	Quantity	F.A.S.	C.I.F.	Charges
SALVADR	V	W	85	6,900	7,276	8,612	1,336
SINGAPR	V	E	86	15,084	11,982	15,258	3,276
	V	W	85	2,500	1,400	1,544	144
			86	18,566	7,609	8,415	806
SPAIN	V	E	85	263,301	118,210	137,733	19,523
			86	18,875	10,134	11,780	1,646
	V	W	85	37,170	21,240	23,851	2,611
			86	34,272	15,844	17,783	1,939
SRI LKA	V	W	86	1,327	1,305	1,508	203
SWEDEN	V	E	86	82,666	43,413	48,204	4,791
SWITZLD	V	E	85	515,633	289,683	320,387	30,704
			86	111,723	58,291	62,576	4,285
	V	W	86	13,337	6,844	7,198	354
THAILND	A	E	86	400	1,474	2,160	686
	N	E	86	260,909	145,075	166,155	21,080
	O	E	85	4,176	2,175	2,747	572
	O	W	85	5,778	5,502	6,086	584
			86	2,403	1,330	1,456	126
	V	E	85	110,291	70,525	81,604	11,079
			86	21,782	12,475	13,846	1,371
	V	W	85	613,704	366,243	406,736	40,493
			86	1,249,934	634,196	693,045	58,849
TUNISIA	V	E	86	1,479	1,104	1,224	120
TURKEY	O	E	85	2,022	1,065	1,065	
	V	E	85	14,561	4,300	4,901	601
			86	25,724	11,665	13,091	1,426
U KING	N	E	86	46,183	34,824	40,338	5,514
	O	E	85	9,869	11,556	12,667	1,111
			86	3,876	5,298	5,903	605
	V	E	85	2,429	2,401	2,765	364
			86	27,199	20,481	22,453	1,972
	V	W	85	15,844	23,247	26,567	3,320
VENEZ	V	E	86	4,303	3,260	3,904	644
W SAMOA	V	H	85	1,649	1,134	1,250	116
	V	W	86	1,479	1,106	1,200	94
YUGOSLV	V	E	85	8,441	5,265	5,938	673
			86	5,754	2,115	2,920	805
	V	W	85	24,484	8,654	12,134	3,480

Product TSUSA commodity number, description, and unit of quantity Country	Mode	Reg	Yr	Quantity	F.A.S.	C.I.F.	Charges

Appendix A

Abbreviations of Countries

Abbreviation	Name	Includes
AFGHAN	Afghanistan	
ALBANIA	Albania	
ALGERIA	Algeria	
AM SAM	American Samoa	Tutuila Island and dependencies
ANGOLA	Angola	Cabinda
ANTIGUA	Antigua	Barbuda and Redonda Islands
ARAB EM	United Arab Emirates	
ARGENT	Argentina	
AUSTRAL	Australia	Tasmania, Lord Howe, Macquarie, Ashmore, and Cartier Islands
AUSTRIA	Austria	
B IND O	British Indian Ocean Territory	Chagos Archipelago and Diego Garcia Island
B VIRGN	British Virgin Islands	Anegada, Jost Van Dyke, Tortola, and Virgin Gorda Islands
BAHAMAS	Bahamas	Grand Bahama, Great Abaco, Harbour Island, Eleuthera, New Providence, Andros, Great Exuma, Long Island, Great Inagua, and associated small islands
BAHRAIN	Bahrain	
BARBADO	Barbados	
BELGIUM	Belgium and Luxembourg	
BELIZE	Belize	
BENIN	Benin	(formerly Dahomey)
BERMUDA	Bermuda	
BHUTAN	Bhutan	
BNGLDSH	Bangladesh	
BOLIVIA	Bolivia	
BOTSWAN	Botswana	
BRAZIL	Brazil	Penedos de Sao Pedro e Sao Paulo, Fernando de Noronha, and Ilha da Trinidade (in South Atlantic)
BRUNEI	Brunei	
BULGAR	Bulgaria	
BURKINA	Burkina	
BURMA	Burma	
BURUNDI	Burundi	
C AF RP	Central African Republic	(formerly Central African Empire)
C RICA	Costa Rica	
C VERDE	Cape Verde	
CAMBOD	Cambodia	
CAMROON	Cameroon	
CANADA	Canada	
CAYMAN	Cayman Islands	
CHAD	Chad	
CHILE	Chile	Isla Sala y Gomez, Islas San Felix, Islas San Ambrosio, Islas Juan Fernandez, and Easter Island
CHINA M	China (Mainland)	
CHINA T	China (Taiwan)	Pescadores
CO BRAZ	Congo (Brazzaville)	
COCOS I	Cocos (Keeling) Islands	
COLOMB	Colombia	
COMOROS	Comoros	
COOK IS	Cook Islands	
CR N AN	St. Christopher-Nevis-Anguilla	Sombrero Island.
CRIST I	Christmas Island (in the Indian Ocean)	
CUBA	Cuba	Isla de Pinos
CYPRUS	Cyprus	
CZECHO	Czechoslovakia	
DENMARK	Denmark	Bornholm Island and Faeroe Islands(port = Torshavn)
DJIBUTI	Djibouti	(formerly Afars and Issas)
DOM REP	Dominican Republic	
DOMINCA	Dominica	
ECUADOR	Ecuador	Galapagos Islands
EGYPT	Egypt	

Abbreviation	Name	Includes
EQ GUIN	Equatorial Guinea	Rio Muni, Macias Nguema Biyogo (Fernando Po), Pagalu (Annobon), Corisco, and Elobey Islands
ETHIOP	Ethiopia	
F GUIAN	French Guiana	
F IND O	French Indian Ocean Areas	Reunion Island; French Southern and Antarctic Lands
F W IND	French West Indies	Guadeloupe (including Grande-Terre, Basse-Terre, Iles des Saintes, Iles de la Petite-Terre, La Desirade, Ile Saint-Barthelemy, Marie-Galante, and Northern St. Martin) and Martinique
FALK IS	Falkland Islands (Islas Malvinas)	Falkland Islands and South Georgia, South Orkney, South Shetland, South Sandwich Islands
FIJI	Fiji	
FINLAND	Finland	Aland Islands
FR GERM	Federal Republic of Germany (West Germany)	Western Sectors of Berlin
FR POLY	French Polynesia	Society Islands, Tuamotu and Gambier, Marquesas Islands, Iles Australes, and Clipperton Island
FRANCE	France	Corsica, Andorra(port = Barcelona), and Monaco(port = Monaco)
G BISAU	Guinea-Bissau	
GABON	Gabon	
GAMBIA	The Gambia	
GAZA ST	Gaza Strip	
GERM DR	German Democratic Republic (East Germany)	Eastern Sectors of Berlin
GHANA	Ghana	
GIBRALT	Gibraltar	
GREECE	Greece	Crete, Ionian Islands, and Grecian Archipelago, with the Aegean Islands of Limnos, Samothraki, Khios, Samos, Lesvos, and the Dodecanese (including Rhodes Island)
GREENLD	Greenland	
GRENADA	Grenada	Southern Grenadine Islands
GUAM	Guam	
GUATMAL	Guatemala	
GUINEA	Guinea	
GUYANA	Guyana	
HAITI	Haiti	Ile de la Gonave and Tortuga Island
HAWAII	Hawaii	
HEARD I	Heard Island and McDonald Islands	
HG KONG	Hong Kong	
HONDURA	Honduras	Islas de la Bahia and Swan Islands
HUNGARY	Hungary	
ICELAND	Iceland	
INDIA	India	Andaman, Nicobar, and Laccadive Islands
INDNSIA	Indonesia	(including former Portuguese Timor)
IRAN	Iran	
IRAQ	Iraq	
IRELAND	Ireland	excludes Northern Ireland
ISRAEL	Israel	
ITALY	Italy	Islands of Sicily, Sardinia, Elba, Pantelleria, and Lampedusa; Vatican City; and San Marino
IVY CST	Ivory Coast	
JAMAICA	Jamaica	Morant Cays and Pedro Cays
JAPAN	Japan	Four main Islands of Honshu, Kyushu, Shikoku, and Hokkaido and islands adjacent thereto; Ryukyus,(including Okinawa, Sakishima, and all other Ryukyu Islands), and the following islands: Nansei-Shoto, Nampo-Shoto, Bonin, Nishino-Shima (Rosario), Volcano, Daito-Jima, Okino-Tori-Shima (Parece Vela), and Minami-Tori-Shima (Marcus)
JORDAN	Jordan	
KENYA	Kenya	
KIRIBAT	Kiribati	Gilbert Islands, Banaba (Ocean Island), Phoenix Islands, including Canton and Enderbury Islands, and Washington,

Abbreviation	Name	Includes
		Fanning, Christmas, Malden, Starbuck, Caroline, Vostok, and Flint in the Line Islands
KOR REP	Korea, Republic of	
KUWAIT	Kuwait	
LAOS	Laos	
LEBANON	Lebanon	
LESOTHO	Lesotho	
LIBERIA	Liberia	
LIBYA	Libya	
MACAO	Macao (Macau)	
MADAGAS	Madagascar	
MALAWI	Malawi	
MALAYSA	Malaysia	(including former Federation of Malaya, Sarawak, and Sabah)
MALDIVE	Maldive Islands	
MALI	Mali	
MALTA	Malta and Gozo	
MAURIT	Mauritius	Rodrigues Island, Agalega Islands, and Cargados Carajos Shoals
MAURITN	Mauritania	
MEXICO	Mexico	Isla de Cozumel and Islas Revillagigedo
MID IS	Midway Islands	
MONGOLA	Mongolia	
MONSRAT	Montserrat	
MOROC	Morocco	Ifni
MOZAMBQ	Mozambique	
N ANTIL	Netherlands Antilles	Curacao, Aruba, Bonaire, Saba, St. Eustatius, and St. Martin (southern part)
N CALDN	New Caledonia	Loyalty Islands, Isle of Pines, and Walpole Island
N ZEAL	New Zealand	Antipodes, Auckland, Bounty, Campbell, Kermadec, Chatham, Three Kings and Snares Islands, and associated small islands
NAMIBIA	Namibia	(formerly South-West Africa)
NAURU	Nauru	
NEPAL	Nepal	
NETHLDS	Netherlands	
NEW GUI	Papua New Guinea	Eastern New Guinea, Bismarck, and Louisiade Archipelagos, Admiralty, d'Entrecasteaux, Northern Solomon (Bougainville, Buka, etc.). and islands of New Britain, New Ireland, and associated small islands
NICARAG	Nicaragua	
NIGER	Niger	
NIGERIA	Nigeria	
NIUE	Niue	
NO KOR	North Korea	
NORFOLK	Norfolk Island	
NORWAY	Norway	Svalbard, Bjornoya, (Bear Island) and Jan Mayen Island
OMAN	Oman	
P RICO	Puerto Rico	
PAKISTN	Pakistan	
PANAMA	Panama	
PARAGUA	Paraguay	
PERU	Peru	
PHIL R	Philippines	
PITCARN	Pitcairn Island	
POLAND	Poland	
PORTUGL	Portugal	Azores and Madeira Islands
QATAR	Qatar	
REP SAF	Republic of South Africa	
ROMANIA	Romania	
RWANDA	Rwanda	
S ARAB	Saudi Arabia	
S HELNA	St. Helena	Islands of Ascension, Gough, Inaccessible, Nightingale, and Tristan da Cunha

Abbreviation	Name	Includes
S LUCIA	St. Lucia	
S VN GR	St. Vincent and the Grenadines	excluding the Southern Grenadines
SALVADR	El Salvador	
SAO T P	Sao Tome and Principe	
SENEGAL	Senegal	
SEYCHEL	Seychelles	Aldabra Islands, Alphonse, Bijoutier, and St. Francois Islands, Amirante Isles, Cosmoledo Group, Farquhar Group, Ile Desroches, and St. Pierre Island
SIER LN	Sierra Leone	
SINGAPR	Singapore	
SOLMN I	Solomon Islands	Southern Solomon Islands, primarily Guadalcanal, Malaita, San Cristobal, Santa Isabel, and Choiseul
SOMALIA	Somalia	
SP MQEL	St. Pierre and Miquelon	
SPAIN	Spain	Balearic and Canary Islands, Ceuta, Melilla, Islas Chafarinas, Penon de Alhucemas and Penon de Velez de la Gomera
SRI LKA	Sri Lanka (Ceylon)	
SUDAN	Sudan	
SURINAM	Suriname	
SWAZLND	Swaziland	
SWEDEN	Sweden	Islands of Oland and Gotland (Gothland)
SWITZLD	Switzerland	Liechtenstein(port = Rotterdam)
SYRIA	Syria	
T PAC I	Trust Territory of the Pacific Islands	Caroline, Marshall and Mariana Islands (except Guam) under U.S. Administration
THAILND	Thailand	
TNZANIA	Tanzania	
TOGO	Togo	
TOKELAU	Tokelau Islands	
TONGA	Tonga	
TRINID	Trinidad and Tobago	
TUNISIA	Tunisia	
TURK IS	Turks and Caicos Islands	
TURKEY	Turkey	(in Europe and Asia)
TUVALU	Tuvalu	(including former Ellice Islands)
U KING	United Kingdom of Great Britain and Northern Ireland	England, Wales, Channel Islands, Isles of Wight and Man(port = Douglas), and Scilly Islands; Scotland, Hebrides, Orkney and Shetland Islands; and Northern Ireland
UGANDA	Uganda	
URUGUAY	Uruguay	
USA	United States of America	
USSR	Union of Soviet Socialist Republics	(in Europe and Asia) Sakhalin and Kuril Islands, Estonia, Latvia and Lithuania
VANUATA	Vanuatu	(formerly New Hebrides)
VENEZ	Venezuela	
VIETNAM	Vietnam	
VIRG IS	Virgin Islands of the United States	
W SAHAR	Western Sahara	
W SAMOA	Western Samoa	
WAKE IS	Wake Island	
WALLIS	Wallis and Futuna	
YEMEN S	Yemen (Sana)	
YEMEN A	Yemen (Aden)	(formerly Southern Yemen) islands of Kamaran, Perim, and Socotra
YUGOSLV	Yugoslavia	Otok Lastovo (Lagosta)
ZAIRE	Zaire	
ZAMBIA	Zambia	
ZMBABWE	Zimbabwe	(formerly Rhodesia)

Appendix B

Abbreviations for Units of Quantity

Abbreviation	Description	Abbreviation	Description
ADJ	Adjustments	JWL	Jewel
AOZ	Avoirdupois ounce	LB	Pound
BBL	Barrel	LF	Leaf
BFT	Board feet	LFT	Linear foot
BRU	Brushes	LTN	Long ton (2240 pounds)
BU	Bushel	LYD	Linear yard
C	Hundred	M	Thousand (1000)
CAR	Carat	MBF	M (1000) board feet
CD	Cord	MC	Millicurie
CFT	Cubic feet	MCF	M (1000) cubic feet
CLB	Content pound	MFT	M (1000) feet
CRT	Crate	MLF	M (1000) linear feet
CTN	Content ton	MSF	M (1000) square feet
CUR.	Curie	MYD	M (1000) yards
CWT	Hundredweight (100 pounds)	NO	Number
CYD	Cubic yard	OZ	Ounce
DOZ	Dozen	PC(s)	Piece(s)
DPC	Dozen pieces	PFG	Proof gallon
DPR	Dozen pair	PK	Pack
FT	Foot	PR	Pair
GAL	Gallon	SFT	Square foot
GBL	Gross pound	SQ	Squares
GBX	Gross boxes (gross containers)	SQI	Square inch
GR	Gross	STN	Short ton (2000 pounds)
GRL	Gross lines	SYD	Square yard
GRM	Gram	TOZ	Troy ounce
GTN	Gross ton	YD	Yard
HLB	100 pounds		

Appendix C

Abbreviations of TSUSA Commodity Descriptions

Abbreviation	Description
A	AND
ABV	ABOVE
ACHL	ALCOHOL
AD	ADDED
	ADVANCED
ADD	ADDITIVE
ADV	ADVANCED
AIRTITE	AIRTIGHT
AL	ALCOHOL
ALC	ALCOHOL
ALCH	ALCOHOL
ALCHL	ALCOHOL
ALCO	ALCOHOL
ALCOLOL	ALCOHOL
ALHL	ALCOHOL
ALKAS	ALKALOIDS
AOV	ABOVE
APLE	APPLE
APPL	APPLE
APRCOT	APRICOT
ARB#	ARBITRARY NUMBER
ARROWRT	ARROWROOT
ART	ARTICLES
ARTIFIC	ARTIFICIAL
ARTS	ARTICLES
ASSEM	ASSEMBLED
ATTACHD	ATTACHED
BALSA/TEAK	BALSA OR TEAK
BAMBOO/RAT	BAMBOO OR RATTAN
BASKTS	BASKETS
BCKD	BACKED
BD	BOARD
BEV	BEVERAGES
BEVRGS	BEVERAGES
BF	BUTTERFAT
BFT/MILK	BUTTERFAT OR OTHER MILK
BITART	BITARTRATE
BKD	BACKED
	BAKED
BLCH	BLEACHED
BLCKS	BLOCKS
BLDG	BUILDING
BLDGBOARD	BUILDING BOARDS
BLDGS	BUILDINGS
BLHDS	BARRELHEADS
BLUEBERYS	BLUEBERRIES
BMB	BAMBOO
BMBO	BAMBOO
BOXWD	BOXWOOD
BRCH	BIRCH
BRD	BOARD
BRDS	BOARDS
BRM	BROOM
BRNE	BRINE
BSKT	BASKETS
BUCKWHT	BUCKWHEAT
BVL/RD	BEVEL OR RED
BXES	BOXES
C	CARD
CAKE/MEAL	CAKE AND OIL-CAKE MEAL
CAN	CANADIAN

Abbreviation	Description
CANDY-CONFECTON	CANDY-CONFECTION
CAS	CASSIA
CAULIFLOWR	CAULIFLOWER
CD	CARD
CDR	CEDAR
CEDR	CEDAR
CERT	CERTIFIED
CERTIFD	CERTIFIED
CFT	CUBIC FOOT
CH	CHILLED
CHEM	CHEMICAL
CHLD	CHILLED
CHLLD	CHILLED
CHOC	CHOCOLATE
CHP	CHIP
CHSTNT	CHESTNUT
CIG	CIGARETTE
CINN	CINNAMON
CIT	CITRUS
CITRN	CITRON
CL	CLEAR
CLR	CLEAR
CNCNTRT	CONCENTRATE
CNCTRD	CONCENTRATED
CND	CANNED
CNSMPTN	CONSUMPTION
CNTR	CONTAINER
CNTRS	CONTAINERS
COM	COMPOUNDS
COMB	COMBED
COMP	COMPOSITION
	COMPRESSED
COMPRESSD	COMPRESSED
CON	CONCENTRATED
	CONFECTIONERY
CONCENTD	CONCENTRATED
CONCENTRATD	CONCENTRATED
CONCNTRTD	CONCENTRATED
CONCT	CONCENTRATED
COND	CONDITION
CONDNSD	CONDENSED
CONFECTRY	CONFECTIONARY
CONS	CONSUMPTION
CONT	CONTAINERS
	CONTAINING
CONTAINR	CONTAINERS
CONTG	CONTAINING
CONTRS	CONTAINERS
CORK-RUB	CORK-RUBBER
COT	COTTON
COTTONSD	COTTONSEED
COV	COVERINGS
CPDS	COMPOUNDS
CR	CRUDE
CRD	CARDED
CRT	CERTIFIED
CRU	CRUDE
CRYSTALD	CRYSTALLIZED
CT	CENTS
CTRY	COUNTRY
CTS	CENTS

Abbreviation	Description	Abbreviation	Description
CURRNT	CURRANT		FLOUR
CURTNS	CURTAINS	FLRG	FLOORING
CWT	HUNDREDWEIGHT (100 pounds)	FLRING	FLOORING
D/W	DRESSED OR WORKED	FLRNG	FLOORING
DEHYD	DEHYDRATED	FLS	FLOWERS
DEHYDRATD	DEHYDRATED	FLU-CRD	FLUE-CURED
DEHYDRTD	DEHYDRATED	FR	FRESH
DIM	DIMENSION	FR/CH	FRESH OR CHILLED
DIMS	DIMENSIONS	FRES	FRESH
DIST	DISTILLED	FRM	FROM
DM	DIMENSION	FROZ	FROZEN
DOUG	DOUGLAS	FROZN	FROZEN
DR	DRESSED	FRS/CH	FRESH OR CHILLED
DRD	DRIED	FRS/CHLD/FROZ	FRESH OR CHILLED OR
DRESSD	DRESSED		FROZEN
DRILL/TREAT	DRILLED OR TREATED	FRSH	FRESH
DRL/TRD	DRILLED OR TREATED	FRT	FRUIT
DRLD/TRD/RSWN	DRILLED OR TREATED OR	FRUCTSE	FRUCTOSE
	RESAWN	FRZ	FROZEN
DRSD	DRESSED	FRZN	FROZEN
DRVD	DERIVED	FT	FOOT
DSD	DRESSED	FZ	FROZEN
DSKS	DISKS	FZN	FROZEN
EDBLE	EDIBLE	GAL	GALLON
EDIBL	EDIBLE	GL	GALLON
ESSENT	ESSENTIAL	GLUTAM	GLUTAMATE
ESTR	ESTERS	GOOSEBERY	GOOSEBERRY
ET	EXCEPT	GR	GRAINED
EU	EUROPEAN	GRANLTD	GRANULATED
EUR	EUROPEAN	GRAS	GRASS
EVAP	EVAPORATED	GRD	GRADE
EVRGRN	EVERGREEN	GRDE	GRADE
EX	EXCEED	GRFD	GRAFTED
	EXCEPT	GRND	GROUND
EX/CUT	EXCLUDE CUT	GRP	GRAPE
EXC	EXCEEDING	GUNSTK	GUNSTOCKS
	EXCEPT	HAR	HARSH
EXCD	EXCEEDED	HARDBORD	HARDBOARD
EXCDG	EXCEEDING	HARDWD	HARDWOOD
EXCL	EXCLUDE	HBD	HARDBOARD
EXCPT	EXCEPT	HCK	HACKLED
EXT	EXTRACTS	HDBOARD	HARDBOARD
EXTR	EXTRACTS	HDLS	HANDLES
F	FOR	HDRD	HARDBOARD
	FROM	HDWD	HARDWOOD
F/BLDS	FOR BLINDS	HEM	HEMLOCK
F/BLIND	FOR BLINDS	HENEQ	HENEQUEN
F/STACH	FROM STARCHES	HHLD	HOUSEHOLD
FAB	FABRICATED	HLW	HOLLOW
FACE/FNSH	FACE FINISHED	HMP	HEMPSEED
FC	FACE	HOR	HORMONES
FER	FERMENTED	HRD/SWD	HARDWOOD AND SOFTWOOD
FERMNTD	FERMENTED	HRDWD	HARDWOOD
FIB	FIBERS	HULLD	HULLED
	FIBROUS	HUM	HUMAN
FIL	FILLER	IMMEDITE	IMMEDIATE
FILER	FILLER	IN	INCHES
FIN	FINISHED	INCL	INCLUDING
FLAV	FLAVORING		INCLUSIVE
FLG	FLOORING	INEDBL	INEDIBLE
FLR	FLOOR	INEDIB	INEDIBLE

Abbreviation	Description	Abbreviation	Description
INSCT	INSECT	N/CRDE	OTHER THAN CRUDE
INST	INSTANT	N/HLW	NOT HOLLOW
JAP	JAPANESE	N/REINF	NOT REINFORCED
JC	JUICE	NA	NATURAL
JCE	JUICE	NAT	NATURAL
JCES	JUICES	NATRL	NATURAL
JUC	JUICE	NES	NOT SPECIALLY PROVIDED FOR
KERNL	KERNEL	NFIT	NOT FIT
KIDNY	KIDNEY	NO	NOT OVER
KPK	KAPOK	NO.	NUMBER
KRNL	KERNEL	NON-ALCHL	NON-ALCOHOL
KRNLS	KERNELS	NOV	NOT OVER
LAMNATD	LAMINATED		NOVEMBER
LAVENDR	LAVENDER	NSPF	NOT SPECIALLY PROVIDED FOR
LB	POUND	NSPOF	NOT SPECIALLY PROVIDED FOR
LBR	LUMBER	NT	NOT
LBR/SIDING	LUMBER AND SIDING	NUN	NOT UNDER
LBS	POUNDS	O	OF
LEMN	LEMON		OR
LF	LEAF	OM	OR MORE
LGTH	LENGTH	ORIG	ORIGIN
LIN	LINSEED	ORNGE	ORANGE
LMBR	LUMBER	OT	OTHER
LOG/TIMBER	LOGS AND TIMBER	OTH	OTHER
LUAN	LAUAN	OTWS	OTHERWISE
LUMBR	LUMBER	OV	OVER
M	MOLDING	OZ	OUNCE
MAH	MAHOGANY	P	POTASSIUM
MAHOG	MAHOGANY	P/MAHG	PHILIPPINE MAHOGANY
MAHOGNSPF	MAHOGANY NOT SPECIALLY	P/MHG	PHILIPPINE MAHOGANY
	PROVIDED FOR	PANLS	PANELS
MAHOGNY	MAHOGANY	PAR	PARANA
MANGRVE	MANGROVE	PARA	PARANA
MANUFACTURD	MANUFACTURED	PATTRN	PATTERN
MAP	MAPLE	PC	PERCENT
MAT	MATERIAL	PCKNG	PACKING
MENT	MENTHA	PCT	PERCENT
MFG	MANUFACTURING	PEP	PEPPERMINT
MFR	MANUFACTURE	PEPERMT	PEPPERMINT
MFRD	MANUFACTURED	PEPPR	PEPPER
MIL	MILLED	PER	PERFORATED
MILD	MILLED	PERF	PERFORATED
MILLD	MILLED	PHIL	PHILIPPINE
MILLNG	MILLING	PICKED	PICKLED
MIX/FZ	MIXED OR FROZEN	PICKLD	PICKLED
MIXD	MIXED	PIN	PINE
MIXT	MIXTURES	PIPRITA	PIPERITA
MIXTUR	MIXTURE	PKG	PACKAGE
MLD	MILLED	PLM	PALM
	MOLDING	PLNKS	PLANKS
MLDGS	MOLDINGS	PLNTAIN	PLANTAIN
MONOSM	MONOSODIUM	PLPWD	PULPWOOD
MT	MEAT	PLY	PLYWOOD
MTL	MATERIAL	PLYWD	PLYWOOD
MUSHRM	MUSHROOM	PM	PALM
MUSHROM	MUSHROOM	PNAPL	PINEAPPLE
MXD	MIXED	PNAPPLE	PINEAPPLE
MXTRE	MIXTURE	POT	POTATO
N	IN	POTS	POTATOES
	NOT	PRCSD	PROCESSED
N/ADV	NOT ADVANCED	PRE	PREPARED

Abbreviation	Description	Abbreviation	Description
PREFAB	PREFABRICATED	SMOKNG	SMOKING
PREP	PREPARED	SOFTWD	SOFTWOOD
PREP/PRES	PREPARED OR PRESERVED	SOLBL	SOLUBLE
PREPS	PRESERVATIVES	SOYA	SOYBEAN
PRES	PRESERVED	SP	SPECIFIED
PRESS	PRESSED	SPAN	SPANISH
PRO	PROCESSED	SPCE	SPICE
PROC	PROCESSED	SPEC	SPECIFIED
PROCD	PROCESSED	SPN	SPANISH
PROCES	PROCESSES	SPRKNG	SPARKLING
PROCESD	PROCESSED	SQI	SQUARE INCH
PROCESS	PROCESSED	ST	STAPLE
PROCSED	PROCESSED	STCK	STICK
PROD	PRODUCTS	STD	STANDARD
PRP	PREPARED	STEMD	STEMMED
PULPWD	PULPWOOD	STEMMD	STEMMED
PURF	PURIFIED	STM	STEMMED
QOTA	QUOTA	STMD	STEMMED
QTA	QUOTA	STMMD	STEMMED
QU	QUOTA	STMS	STEMS
QUO	QUOTA	STN	SHORT TON
QUTA	QUOTA	STOP	STOPPERS
R	RAW	STP	STAPLE
RAT	RATTAN	STPL	STAPLE
RATN	RATTAN	STPRS	STOPPERS
RATTN	RATTAN	STPS	STRIPS
RD	RED	STRCH	STARCH
REDUCE	REDUCED	STRIP/PLANK	STRIPS AND PLANKS
REINF	REINFORCED	STRP	STRIPS
REINF/BCKD	REINFORCED OR BACKED	STRPS	STRIPS
REINF/BKD	REINFORCED OR BACKED	STUFD	STUFFED
REINS/BKD	REINFORCED OR BACKED	SUB	SUBSTANCES
REMOVD	REMOVED	SUBS	SUBSTANCES
RGH	ROUGH	SUG	SUGAR
ROLLS/STUFF	ROLLS AND STUFFED	SULF	SULFONATED OR SULFATED
ROV	ROVING	SULPH	SULFATED
RR	RAILROAD		SULFONATED
RSWN	RESAWN	SWT	SWEETENED
RTN	RATTAN	SYN	SYNTHETIC
RUB	RUBBER	SYNT	SYNTHETIC
RUBBR	RUBBER	SYNTH	SYNTHETIC
RUGH	ROUGH	TAN	TANNING
S	SODIUM	TAPERD	TAPERED
	SOFT	TBCO	TOBACCO
SALTD	SALTED	TECH	TECHNICALLY
SAUKRT	SAUERKRAUT	TEX	TEXTILE
SCREENNGS	SCREENINGS	THRD	THREAD
SD	SEED	TOB	TOBACCO
	SIDING	TOBAC	TOBACCO
SDE	SIDE	TREATD	TREATED
SDG	SIDINGS	TRTD	TREATED
SFT	SOFT	TXTR	TEXTURE
SFTWD	SOFTWOOD	U	UNDER
SFWD	SOFTWOOD	UN	UNDER
SGR	SUGAR	UNASS	UNASSEMBLED
SHELL/BLANCH	SHELLED OR BLANCHED	UND	UNDER
SHPD	SHAPED	UNGD	UNGROUND
SIDNG	SIDING	UNGRD	UNGROUND
SL	SLIVER	UNGRND	UNGROUND
SLDS	SOLIDS	UNITS/SASH	UNITS AND SASH
SLIV	SLIVER	UNMFD	UNMANUFACTURED

Abbreviation	Description	Abbreviation	Description
UNMXD	UNMIXED	W/SRFC	WITH SURFACE
UNSP	UNSPUN	WD	WOOD
UNSPN	UNSPUN	WD-VENR	WOOD-VENEER
UNSTM	UNSTEMMED	WD-VNER	WOOD-VENEER
UNSWEET	UNSWEETENED	WH	WHITE
USBG	UNITED STATES BOTANIC GARDEN	WIL	WILLOW
		WKD	WORKED
USDA	UNITED STATES DEPT. OF AGRICULTURE	WNE	WINE
		WOOD-VNER	WOOD-VENEER
UTNSL	UTENSIL	WOV	WOVEN
VEG	VEGETABLE	WOVN	WOVEN
VEGS	VEGETABLES	WPR	WRAPPER
VEN	VENEER	WRAPER	WRAPPER
VENR	VENEER	WRKD	WORKED
VENRS	VENEERS	WRPPR	WRAPPER
VIT	VITAMIN	WSTE	WASTE
VNER	VENEER	WTHN	WITHIN
VUL	VULCANIZED	X	EXCEED
W.	WESTERN		EXCEPT
W/LOUVER	WITH LOUVER	XMAS	CHRISTMAS
W/RED	WESTERN RED		

Appendix D

Reference Sources

1. Bailey, Liberty H., and Ethel Z. Bailey. *Hortus Third: A Concise Dictionary of Plants Cultivated in the United States and Canada.* New York: Macmillan Publishing Co., Inc., 1976.
2. Boutelje, Julius B. *Encyclopedia of World Timbers.* Stockholm: Swedish Forest Products Research Laboratory, 1980.
3. Considine, Douglas M. *Foods and Food Production Encyclopedia.* New York: Van Nostrand Reinhold Company, Inc., 1982.
4. Duke, James A. *CRC Handbook of Medicinal Herbs.* Boca Raton, Florida: CRC Press, Inc., 1985.
5. Duke, James A. *Handbook of Legumes of World Economic Importance.* New York: Plenum Press, 1981.
6. Everett, Thomas H. *The New York Botanical Garden Illustrated Encyclopedia of Horticulture*, Vol. 6. New York: Garland Publishing Co., 1981.
7. Gennaro, Alfonso R., ed. *Remington's Pharmaceutical Sciences.* Easton, Pennsylvania: Mack Publishing Company, 1985.
8. Graf, Alfred Byrd. *Tropica: Color Cyclopedia of Exotic Plants and Trees from the Tropics and Subtropics for Warm-Region Horticulture--in Cool Climate the Sheltered Indoors.* New Jersey: Roehrs Company, 1978.
9. Hillier, H.G. *Hillier's Manual of Trees and Shrubs.* Newton Abbot: David and Charles Ltd., 1981.
10. Martin, Franklin W. *CRC Handbook of Tropical Food Crops.* Boca Raton, Florida: CRC Press, Inc., 1984.
11. McCurrach, James C. *Palms of the World.* Gainesville: University Presses of Florida, 1976.
12. Roecklein, John C., and PingSun Leung. *A Profile of Economic Plants.* New Brunswick, New Jersey: Transaction, Inc., 1987.
13. Rosengarten, Frederic Jr. *The Book of Edible Nuts.* New York: Walker and Company, 1984.
14. Schauenberg, Paul, and Ferdinand Paris. *Guide to Medicinal Plants.* New Canaan, Connecticut: Keats, 1977.
15. Stuart, Malcolm. *The Encyclopedia of Herbs and Herbalism.* New York: Grosset and Dunlap, 1979.
16. Terrel, Edward E. *A Checklist of Names for 3,000 Vascular Plants of Economic Importance.* Agricultural Research Service, USDA, Agricultural Handbook No. 505, 1977.
17. *The American Heritage Dictionary of the English Language.* Boston, Massachusetts: Houghton Mifflin Company, 1981.
18. *The Random House Dictionary of the English Language, Unabridged.* New York: Random House, Inc., 1979.
19. Titmuss, F. H. *Commercial Timbers of the World.* London: The Technical Press Ltd., 1965.
20. Turner, David, and Ken Muir. *Handbook of Soft Fruit Growing.* Dover, New Hampshire: Croom Helm Ltd., 1985.
21. U.S. Department of Commerce, Bureau of the Census. *Census Catalogue and Guide 1987.* Washington, D.C.: U.S. Government Printing Office, 1987.
22. U.S. Department of Commerce, Bureau of the Census. *Guide to Foreign Trade Statistics 1983.* Washington D.C.: U.S. Government Printing Office, 1984.
23. U.S. Department of Commerce, Bureau of the Census. *U.S. Foreign Trade Statistics Classifications and Cross-Classifications, 1980.* Washington, D.C.: U.S. Government Printing Office, 1981.
24. U.S. Department of Commerce, Bureau of the Census. *U.S. General Imports: World Area and Country of Origin By Schedule A Commodity Groupings.* Report FT155/Annual 1985. Washington, D.C.: U.S. Government Printing Office, 1986.
25. U.S. Department of Commerce, Bureau of the Census. *U.S. Imports for Comsumption and General Imports.* Report FT246/Annual 1981-1985. Washington, D.C.: U.S. Government Printing Office, 1982-1986.
26. U.S. International Trade Commission. *Tariff Schedules of the United States Annotated 1981-1986.* Washington, D.C.: U.S. Government Printing Office, 1980-1985.
27. Usher, George. *A Dictionary of Plants Used by Man.* New York: Hafner Press, 1974.
28. *Webster's Third New International Dictionary, Unabridged.* Springfield, Massachusetts: Merriam-Webster Inc., 1986.
29. Yamaguchi, Mas. *World Vegetables, Principles, Production, and Nutritive Values.* Westport, Connecticut: AVI Publishing Company, Inc., 1983.

Index A

Alphabetical Listing of Products by Crop, Table 1

Index B

Alphabetical Listing of Products by End-Use, Table 2

Index C

Alphabetical Listing of Products by Country

Country/Territory Product	Page
Paprika, spice	356
Partridgeberry, prepared or perserved	335
Pear, fresh or in brine	347
Pear, juice	348
Pear, paste and pulp	348
Pear, prepared or preserved	348
Pearl onion, fresh or frozen	349
Pectin	553
Pepper (not specified), fresh or frozen	357
Pepper (not specified), prepared or preserved	359
Pimento, canned	364
Pine, lumber	366
Pine needle, essential oil	369
Poppy, seed	320
Poppy, straw extract, natural drug	320
Quebracho, tannin	390
Raisin	221
Raspberry, fresh or in brine	397
Raspberry, prepared or preserved	398
Rubber, natural	410
Ryegrass, seed	419
Sauces	586
Sauerkraut	65
Soups	590
Spice and spice seed	635
Spruce, lumber	430
Starch (not specified)	555
Strawberry, fresh or in brine	432
Strawberry, jelly or jam	434
Strawberry, prepared or preserved	436
Sugar beet, processed	437
Sugar, sirup, and molasses, blends	641
Sugarcane, processed	443
Tea	449
Teak, lumber	454
Tobacco, filler, mixed or unmixed, under 35% wrapper tobacco	457
Tobacco, filler, mixed, over 35% wrapper tobacco	463
Tomato, fresh or frozen	473
Tomato, prepared or preserved	476
Tree and shrub, seed	623
Tumeric, spice	481
Vegetable, dried	644
Vegetable, glue	557
Vegetable, in brine or pickled	654
Vegetable, oil	602
Vegetable, prepared or preserved	657
Vegetable substance	558
Vegetable substance, ornamental	613
Vinegar	594
Wheat, gluten	488
Wheat, milled for humans	490
Willow, basket	492
Azores	
See Portugal	
Bahamas	
Avocado, fresh or prepared or preserved	22
Banana, fresh	31
Bean (not specified), fresh or frozen	42

Country/Territory Product	Page
Beer	231
Breadfruit, fresh or frozen	60
Cabbage, fresh or frozen	63
Cassia, essential oil	82
Cereal	572
Cinchona, alkaloid	101
Cocoa, confectionery	121
Coconut, in shell	129
Confectionery products without chocolate	516
Cucumber, fresh or frozen	162
Dextrose	639
Edible preparations (not specified)	574
Essential oil (not specified)	526
Fruit, fresh	532
Fruit, prepared or preserved	542
Fruit trees	607
Garden seed	617
Grape, wine	201
Grapefruit, fresh	223
Grapefruit, prepared or preserved	224
Lemon, fresh	251
Lime, essential oil	258
Lime, fresh or in brine	259
Linseed, oil, fatty acid	182
Live plants	609
Macaroni	580
Mango, fresh	270
Non-alcoholic beverages	511
Nutmeg, essential oil	297
Orange, essential oil	321
Orange, fresh	322
Papaya, fresh	332
Papaya, jelly or jam	332
Papaya, prepared or preserved	333
Pea, prepared or preserved	340
Pepper (not specified), fresh or frozen	357
Potato, fresh	386
Pumpkin, fresh or frozen	390
Soups	590
Squash, fresh or frozen	431
Sugar beet, processed	437
Sugar, sirup, and molasses, blends	641
Sugarcane, processed	443
Tobacco, manufactured or not manufactured	463
Tobacco, scrap	466
Tomato, fresh or frozen	473
Vegetable substance	558
Bahia, Islas de la	
See Honduras	
Bahrain	
Apple, juice	10
Cocoa, powder	126
Flavoring extracts	627
Orange, juice, concentrated	322
Pear, juice	348
Balearic Islands	
See Spain	
Banaba	
See Kiribati	

Country/Territory Product	Page
Tobacco, filler, mixed or unmixed, under 35% wrapper tobacco	457
Tobacco, filler, mixed, over 35% wrapper tobacco	463
Tobacco, leaf	463
Tobacco, manufactured or not manufactured	463
Tobacco, scrap	466
Tobacco, stem	469
Tobacco, wrapper	470
Tomato, fresh or frozen	473
Tomato, paste	475
Tomato, prepared or preserved	476
Tomato, sauce	477
Tree and shrub, seed	623
Valonia, dye or tannin	300
Vanillin, aldehyde	482
Vegetable, candied	525
Vegetable, fresh	649
Vegetable, frozen	652
Vegetable, in brine or pickled	654
Vegetable, juice	515
Vegetable, prepared or preserved	657
Vegetable substance	558
Vegetable substance, ornamental	613
Vinegar	594
Waterchestnut, frozen	485
Watermelon, fresh	486
Watermelon, seed, prepared or preserved	487
Willow, basket	492
Yam, fresh	495
Yam, frozen	496
Yeast extract	596
Yucca, fresh or frozen	497

East Germany
See German Democratic Republic (East Germany)

Easter Island
See Chile

Eastern Sectors of Berlin
See German Democratic Republic (East Germany)

Ecuador

Country/Territory Product	Page
Abaca, fiber, processed	3
Abaca, fiber, raw and waste	3
Anise, spice	8
Apple, fresh	9
Apple, juice	10
Apricot, fresh or in brine	15
Asparagus, fresh	19
Avocado, fresh or prepared or preserved	22
Bakery products	561
Balsa, lumber	22
Bamboo, basket	25
Bamboo, stick	29
Banana, dried	31
Banana, flour	31
Banana, fresh	31
Banana, paste and pulp	33
Banana, prepared or preserved	33
Barley, milled for humans	36
Basil, spice	37
Bean (not specified), in brine or pickled	43
Beer	231
Birch, plywood	54
Birch, veneer	56
Black currant, prepared or perserved	167
Blueberry, fresh or in brine	57
Blueberry, prepared or preserved	58
Brazil nut, nut, shelled, prepared or preserved	59
Breadfruit, fresh or frozen	60
Cabbage, fresh or frozen	63
Cantaloupe, fresh	67
Cardamom, spice	70
Carnation, fresh	71
Carrot, fresh or frozen	75
Cashew apple, fresh or prepared or preserved	76
Cashew apple, paste and pulp	77
Cashew, nut, shelled, prepared or preserved	78
Castor bean, vegetable oil, edible	84
Cauliflower, fresh or frozen	84
Cereal	572
Cherry, fresh	92
Chocolate, sweetened	109
Chocolate, unsweetened	115
Chrysanthemum, fresh	100
Cinchona, natural drug	101
Cocoa, bean	116
Cocoa, bean shell	118
Cocoa, bean waste	118
Cocoa butter	119
Cocoa, confectionery	121
Cocoa, powder	126
Cocoa, sweetened	128
Coconut, in shell	129
Coconut, meat, prepared or preserved	130
Coffee, crude	137
Coffee, instant	143
Coffee, roasted or ground	145
Confectionery products without chocolate	516
Corn, milled for humans	268
Corn, milled not for humans	268
Corn, seed	268
Cut flowers	605
Edible preparations (not specified)	574
Fennel, spice	175
Fig, prepared or preserved	179
Fruit, fresh	532
Fruit, fresh or in brine	535
Fruit, jelly or jam	535
Fruit, juice, with alcohol	507
Fruit, prepared or preserved	542
Ginger, root, spice	187
Gooseberry, prepared or perserved	193
Grape, fresh	197
Grape, wine	201
Grapefruit, fresh	223
Grapefruit, prepared or preserved	224
Guava, paste and pulp	227
Hemp, fiber, processed	230
Henequen, fiber, raw and waste	231
Kidney bean, dried	46

Country/Territory Product	Page
Pine, lumber	366
Pine, molding	369
Pine, plywood	370
Pine, veneer	370
Potato, starch	388
Rattan	398
Rattan, basket	399
Rice, milled for humans	402
Sago, flour and starch	420
Soups	590
Spruce, lumber	430
Starch (not specified)	555
Strychnine, alkaloid	437
Tea	449
Teak, lumber	454
Tomato, fresh or frozen	473
Vegetable, dried	644
Vegetable, in brine or pickled	654
Wheat, gluten	488
White pepper, spice	360
Yeast extract	596
Flint Island	
See Kiribati	
France	
Abaca, fiber, raw and waste	3
Aconite, natural drug	278
Alfalfa, seed	3
Alizarin, dye	264
Almond, nut, shelled	4
Almond, nut, shelled, prepared or preserved	4
Almond, nut, unshelled	5
Almond, vegetable oil, edible	6
Aloe, natural drug	6
Anise, essential oil	7
Anise, spice	8
Apple, fresh	9
Apple, juice	10
Apple, paste and pulp	13
Apple, prepared or preserved	13
Apricot, dried	14
Apricot, kernel	15
Apricot, paste and pulp	16
Apricot, prepared or preserved	16
Argol	550
Arrowroot, flour and starch	17
Artichoke, in brine or pickled	18
Artichoke, prepared or preserved	18
Asafetida, natural drug	19
Asparagus, fresh	19
Asparagus, frozen	20
Asparagus, prepared or preserved	21
Avocado, fresh or prepared or preserved	22
Babassu, vegetable oil, edible	22
Bakery products	561
Bamboo, basket	25
Bamboo shoot, canned	27
Bamboo, stick	29
Banana, fresh	31
Barbasco, root	34

Country/Territory Product	Page
Barberry, dried	35
Barley, milled for humans	36
Basil, spice	37
Bay, rum or water	38
Bean (not specified), dried	38
Bean (not specified), fresh or frozen	42
Bean (not specified), in brine or pickled	43
Bean (not specified), prepared or preserved	44
Bean, processed products	571
Beech, lumber	51
Beer	231
Beet, fresh or frozen	51
Beet, seed	52
Bergamot, essential oil	53
Birch, lumber	54
Birch, veneer	56
Bitter almond, essential oil	6
Black currant, frozen	167
Black currant, prepared or perserved	167
Black pepper, spice	350
Blueberry, fresh or in brine	57
Blueberry, frozen	57
Blueberry, prepared or preserved	58
Bluegrass (not Kentucky), seed	58
Bois de rose, essential oil	409
Boxwood, lumber	59
Boysenberry, frozen	59
Brazil nut, nut, unshelled	60
Breadfruit, fresh or frozen	60
Brierroot	225
Broccoli, frozen	61
Broomcorn	61
Brucine, alkaloid	436
Brussels sprouts, fresh	62
Brussels sprouts, frozen	62
Buchu, leaf, natural drug	62
Bulbs, roots, corms, and tubers	603
Cabbage, fresh or frozen	63
Cabbage, prepared or preserved	64
Cabbage, seed	65
Camphor	66
Camphor, essential oil	66
Cantaloupe, fresh	67
Caper, spice	68
Capsicum pepper, spice	352
Caraway, essential oil	69
Caraway, spice	70
Cardamom, spice	70
Carnation, fresh	71
Carob, gum	73
Carrot, canned	74
Carrot, fresh or frozen	75
Carrot, seed	76
Cashew apple, jelly or jam	77
Cashew, nut, shelled, prepared or preserved	78
Cassava, flour and starch	80
Cassia, essential oil	82
Cassia, spice	82
Castor bean, soap	84

Country/Territory Product	Page
Live plants	609
Nutmeg, spice	297
Orchid, plant	328
Peppermint, essential oil	362
Plum, dried	381
Raffia, webbing	395
Spice and spice seed	635
Straw and vegetable, fiber	529
Strawberry, jelly or jam	434
Sugar beet, processed	437
Sugarcane, processed	443
Tree and shrub, seed	623
Vanilla, bean	482
Vegetable substance	558
Vinegar	594
Ylang-ylang, essential oil	496
Madeira Islands	
See Portugal	
Malaita Island	
See Solomon Islands	
Malawi	
Bean (not specified), dried	38
Bean (not specified), prepared or preserved	44
Capsicum pepper, spice	352
Cereal	572
Chickpea, dried	96
Chickpea, prepared or preserved	98
Coffee, crude	137
Coriander, spice	148
Cowpea, dried	160
Cummin, spice	166
Edible preparations (not specified)	574
Guar, gum	225
Guar, seed	226
Lentil, dried	254
Lima bean, dried	47
Macadamia, nut, shelled or blanched	263
Mango, prepared or preserved	272
Milled grain, edible	549
Mung bean, dried	48
Pea, dried	336
Pea, prepared or preserved	340
Peanut butter	344
Peanut, nut, shelled	344
Spice and spice seed	635
Sugar beet, processed	437
Sugarcane, processed	443
Sunflower, seed	444
Tea	449
Tobacco, filler, mixed or unmixed, under 35% wrapper tobacco	457
Tobacco, manufactured or not manufactured	463
Tobacco, scrap	466
Tobacco, stem	469
Tung, vegetable oil	480
Vegetable, dried	644
Vegetable, flour	647
Vegetable, prepared or preserved	657
Wheat, milled for humans	490

Country/Territory Product	Page
Malaya	
See Malaysia	
Malaysia	
Almond, nut, shelled	4
Anise, spice	8
Apple, fresh	9
Arrowroot, flour and starch	17
Bakery products	561
Balsa, lumber	22
Bamboo, basket	25
Bamboo shoot, canned	27
Bamboo, stick	29
Banana, fresh	31
Banana, prepared or preserved	33
Bean (not specified), fresh or frozen	42
Bean, processed products	571
Beech, hardwood flooring	50
Beer	231
Beet, fresh or frozen	51
Birch, hardwood flooring	53
Birch, lumber	54
Birch, plywood	54
Black pepper, oleoresin	350
Black pepper, spice	350
Brazil nut, nut, shelled, prepared or preserved	59
Broccoli, fresh	61
Brussels sprouts, frozen	62
Camphor	66
Cantaloupe, fresh	67
Capsicum pepper, spice	352
Carrot, fresh or frozen	75
Cashew, nut, shelled, prepared or preserved	78
Cashew, nut, unshelled	80
Cassava, flour and starch	80
Cassia, spice	82
Cedar, woodsiding	89
Chicle, gum	421
Clove, essential oil	105
Clove, spice	106
Cocoa, bean	116
Cocoa, bean waste	118
Cocoa butter	119
Cocoa, powder	126
Coconut, meat, prepared or preserved	130
Coconut, oil, fatty acid	133
Coconut, surface-active agent	134
Coconut, vegetable oil	135
Coffee, crude	137
Coffee, roasted or ground	145
Confectionery products without chocolate	516
Corn, canned	267
Coumarin	478
Cucumber, fresh or frozen	162
Curry, spice	625
Cut flowers	605
Dextrose	639
Edible preparations (not specified)	574
Eggplant, fresh or frozen	172
Essential oil (not specified)	526

Country/Territory Product	Page
Corn, seed	268
Cotton, fiber, linters	156
Cotton, fiber, raw	157
Cottonseed, oil cake and oil-cake meal	159
Cowpea, dried	160
Cowpea, fresh or frozen	161
Creosote oil	51
Cucumber, fresh or frozen	162
Cucumber, in brine or pickled	164
Cummin, spice	166
Cut flowers	605
Dasheen, fresh or frozen	167
Date, fresh or dried	168
Dendrobium orchid, fresh	328
Dextrose	639
Digitalis (Lanata), natural drug	171
Dill, spice	171
Douglas fir, lumber	172
Ebony, lumber	172
Edible preparations (not specified)	574
Eggplant, fresh or frozen	172
Endive, fresh or frozen	173
Essential oil (not specified)	526
Eucalyptus, essential oil	174
Fatty acid	550
Fatty ester	551
Fatty salt	551
Fennel, spice	175
Fermented alcoholic beverages	503
Fescue (not Red or Meadow), seed	176
Ficin	177
Fiddlehead fern, fresh or frozen	176
Fig, fresh or in brine	178
Fig, paste and pulp	179
Fig, prepared or preserved	179
Filbert, nut, shelled, prepared or preserved	179
Flavoring extracts	627
Flax, straw	181
Flower, seed	615
Fruit, canned	530
Fruit, dried	531
Fruit, fresh	532
Fruit, jelly or jam	535
Fruit, juice, concentrated	505
Fruit, juice, inedible	552
Fruit, juice, not concentrated	506
Fruit, juice, with alcohol	507
Fruit, paste and pulp	540
Fruit, peel	542
Fruit, prepared or preserved	542
Galia melon, fresh	183
Garden seed	617
Garlic, dried	183
Garlic, essential oil	184
Garlic, flour	184
Garlic, fresh or frozen	185
Ginger, root, candied	186
Ginger, root, spice	187
Ginseng, crude	190

Country/Territory Product	Page
Gooseberry, prepared or perserved	193
Grain or seed, screening or chaff	502
Grape, fresh	197
Grape, juice, concentrated	199
Grape, juice, not concentrated	199
Grape, prepared or preserved	200
Grape, wine	201
Grapefruit, essential oil	223
Grapefruit, fresh	223
Grapefruit, prepared or preserved	224
Grass and forage crop, seed	622
Guar, gum	225
Guar, seed	226
Guava, jelly or jam	226
Guava, paste and pulp	227
Guava, prepared or preserved	227
Gum arabic, gum	228
Hay	502
Henequen, fiber, processed	231
Henequen, fiber, raw and waste	231
Herbaceous perennials	608
Hop, extract	240
Hops	241
Horseradish, fresh or frozen	241
Ipecac, natural drug	243
Istle, fiber	529
Jalap, natural drug	244
Jicama, fresh	244
Kidney bean, frozen	47
Kumquat, candied	248
Kumquat, canned	248
Lancewood, lumber	248
Laurel, leaf, spice	249
Lauric acid	137
Lemon, essential oil	250
Lemon, fresh	251
Lemon grass, essential oil	253
Lemon, juice, concentrated	251
Lemon, prepared or preserved	252
Lentil, dried	254
Lentil, fresh or frozen	255
Lettuce, fresh or frozen	255
Lignum vitae, lumber	257
Lima bean, dried	47
Lima bean, fresh or frozen	47
Lime, essential oil	258
Lime, fresh or in brine	259
Lime, juice, concentrated	260
Lime, juice, not concentrated	260
Lime, prepared or preserved	260
Lingonberry, prepared or perserved	160
Linseed, oil	182
Linseed, vegetable oil	182
Litchi, nut, canned	261
Live plants	609
Loganberry, fresh or in brine	261
Loganberry, prepared or perserved	262
Logwood, dye	262
Longan, canned	262

Index D

Numerical Listing of TSUSA Commodities
with Crop or End-Use

TSUSA commodity		Crop/End-Use	Page
1250100	TULIP BULBS	Tulip	480
1250500	HYACINTH BULBS	Hyacinth	242
1251000	LILY BULBS	Lily	257
1251500	NARCISSUS BULBS	Narcissus	295
1252000	CROCUS CORMS	Crocus	162
1252500	LILY OF THE VALLEY PIPS	Lily	258
1253220	IRIS BULBS, SOIL ATTACHED	Iris	243
1253240	GLADIOLUS CORMS, WITH SOIL	Gladiolus	192
1253260	BEGONIA TUBERS SOIL ATTACHD	Begonia	52
1253270	BULBS, ETC, NSPF, WITH SOIL	Ornamental	603
1253290	HERBACEOUS PERENNIAL & SOIL	Ornamental	608
1253420	IRIS BULBS, NSPF	Iris	243
1253440	GLADIOLUS CORMS, NSPF	Gladiolus	192
1253460	BEGONIA TUBERS, NSPF	Begonia	52
1253470	BULBS, ROOTS, ETC, NSPF	Ornamental	603
1253490	HERBACEOUS PERENNIALS, NSPF	Ornamental	608
1254000	FRT TREE SEEDLINGS CUTS ETC	Ornamental	607
1255000	FRT TREE GRFD FRT PLANT CUTS	Ornamental	608
1256000	SEEDLINGS, CUT, ROSE STOCK	Rose	408
1256500	ROSE PLANTS ON OWN ROOTS	Rose	407
1256700	SEED POTATO EYES	Potato	388
1257000	ORCHID PLANTS	Orchid	328
1258200	LIVE PLANTS, SOIL ATTACHED	Ornamental	609
1258400	LIVE PLANTS F PLANTING NSPF	Ornamental	610
1260100	ALFALFA SEEDS	Alfalfa	3
1260300	SUGAR BEET SEED	Sugar Beet	443
1260500	BEET SEED EXCEPT SUGAR BEET	Beet	52
1260700	BENT GRASS SEED	Bent Grass	53
1260900	BLUEGRASS SEED KENTUCKY	Bluegrass	58
1261100	BLUEGRASS SEED, NSPF	Bluegrass	58
1261500	CABBAGE SEED	Cabbage	65
1261700	CARROT SEED	Carrot	76
1261900	CAULIFLOWER SEED	Cauliflower	85
1262100	CELERY SEEDS	Celery	90
1262300	CLOVER SEED ALSIKE	Clover	107
1262500	CLOVER SEED, CRIMSON	Clover	108
1262700	CLOVER SEED, RED	Clover	108
1262900	CLOVER SEED, SWEET	Clover	108
1263100	CLOVER SEED, WHITE A LADINO	Clover	108
1263300	CLOVER SEED, NSPF	Clover	107
1263500	CREEPING RED FESCUE SEED	Fescue	176
1263700	MEADOW FESCUE SEED	Fescue	177
1263900	FESCUE SEED, NSPF	Fescue	176
1264100	FLOWER SEEDS	Seed	615
1265100	KALE GARDEN SEEDS	Kale	246
1265300	KOHLRABI SEEDS	Kohlrabi	247
1265500	MANGELWURZEL SEED	Mangel Beet	270
1265700	MILLET SEED	Millet	277
1265900	MUSHROOM SPAWN SEED	Mushroom	292
1266100	ONION SEED	Onion	318
1266300	ORCHARD GRASS SEED	Orchard Grass	328
1266500	PARSLEY SEED	Parsley	334
1266700	PARSNIP SEED	Parsnip	335
1267100	PEPPER SEED	Pepper	359
1267300	RADISH SEED	Radish	392
1267700	RYE GRASS SEED	Ryegrass	419
1267900	SESBANIA SEED	Sesbania	425
1268100	SPINACH SEED	Spinach	429
1268300	TALL OAT SEED	Tall Meadow Oat Grass	445
1268500	TIMOTHY SEED	Timothy	456
1268700	TREE AND SHRUB SEEDS	Seed	623

TSUSA commodity		Crop/End-Use	Page
1268900	RUTABAGA AND TURNIP SEED	Rutabaga	418
		Turnip	481
1269100	VETCH SEED, HAIRY	Vetch	483
1269300	VETCH SEED, NSPF	Vetch	483
1269500	WHEAT GRASS SEED	Wheatgrass	492
1270100	GRASS & FOR CROP SEEDS NSPF	Seed	622
1271000	GARDEN SEED NSPF EX GRAS SD	Seed	617
1300800	BARLEY FOR MALTING PURPOSES	Barley	35
1301100	BARLEY, NSPF	Barley	35
1301500	BUCKWHEAT, HULLD OR NT HULLD	Buckwheat	63
1302000	CANARY SEED	Canary-grass	67
1303000	CORN OR MAIZE CERTFIED SEED	Maize	268
1303200	YELLOW DENT CORN EX CERTIFD	Maize	269
1303700	CORN EX CERTIFIED SEED NSPF	Maize	269
1304000	GRAIN SORGHUM	Sorghum	425
1304500	OATS, HULLED OR UNHULLED	Oat	300
1305000	RICE, PADDY OR ROUGH	Rice	404
1305600	BASMATI BROWN RICE, HULLED	Rice	400
1305800	BROWN RICE, NSPF, HULLED	Rice	401
1306000	RYE IN GRAIN	Rye	418
1306300	SEED WHEAT, INEDIBLE	Wheat	492
1306600	WHEAT,EXCEPT SEED, INEDIBLE	Wheat	491
1307020	SEED WHEAT, EDIBLE	Wheat	491
1307040	WHEAT EXC SEED, EDIBLE	Wheat	488
1311000	PEARL BARLEY, EDIBLE	Barley	37
1311200	BARLEY MILLED EDIBL EX PEARL	Barley	36
1311500	BUCKWHEAT, MILLED, EDIBLE	Buckwheat	63
1312000	CORN, MILLED, EDIBLE	Maize	268
1312500	OATS, MILLD, EDBLE NOV $8CWT	Oat	300
1312700	OATS, MILLD, EDBLE OV $8 CWT	Oat	300
1313000	RICE MILLD EDIBL BRAN REMOVD	Rice	402
1313300	RICE, BROKEN, EDIBLE	Rice	404
1313500	RICE MEAL AND FLOUR, EDIBLE	Rice	401
1313700	RICE, PATNA, CLEANED F SOUPS	Rice	404
1313800	RYE, MILLED, EDIBLE	Rye	419
1314000	WHEAT, MILLED, EDIBLE	Wheat	490
1314500	MILD GRAIN PROD NSPF EDIBLE	Grain	549
1315000	BARLEY, MIL N FOR HUMAN CONS	Barley	36
1315700	BUCKWHT MLD NOT FOR HUM CONS	Buckwheat	63
1316000	CORN NFIT HUMAN CONSUMPTION	Maize	268
1316500	OATS MILLED N FIT HUM CONS	Oat	301
1316700	RICE NFIT HUMAN CONSUMPTION	Rice	404
1317000	RYE NT FIT HUMAN CONSUMPTION	Rye	419
1317200	WHEAT FLOUR NOT FIT HUM CONS	Wheat	491
1317500	WHEAT, MILLD, EX FLR, INEDIB	Wheat	491
1318000	MILLED GRAIN NT EDIBLE NSPF	Grain	549
1318500	MILLED GRAINS MIXED, EDIBLE	Grain	549
1319000	MILLED GRAIN MIXTURE, INEDIB	Grain	550
1321500	RYE MALT	Rye	418
1322000	BARLEY AND OTHER MALTS, NSPF	Barley	35
1322500	MALT EXTRACT, FLUID	Grain	547
1323000	MALT EXTRACT, SOLID, CONDNSD	Grain	548
1323520	TAPIOCA CASSAVA FLR A STARCH	Cassava	80
1323540	ARROWRT A SAGO FLOUR A STRCH	Arrowroot	17
		Sago Palm	420
1325000	POTATO STARCH	Potato	388
1325500	STARCHES, NSPF	Miscellaneous	555
1350300	ASPARAGUS, 9/15-11/15, AIR	Asparagus	19
1350520	ASPARAGUS, FRESH OR CHILLED	Asparagus	19
1350540	ASPARAGUS, FROZEN	Asparagus	20
1351000	BEANS, LIMA, JUN1-OCT31 INCL	Bean	47

TSUSA commodity		Crop/End-Use	Page
1374000	RADISHES, FRSH, CHLD, FROZEN	Radish	391
1375000	SQUASH, FRSH, CHILLED, FROZN	Squash	431
1376000	TOMATOE, FRSH, CHLD, OR FROZ	Tomato	473
1376200	TOMATO, JUL 15-AUG 31, INCL	Tomato	473
1376300	TOMATOES, FRESH OR FROZEN	Tomato	474
1376600	TURNIPS OR RUTABAGAS	Rutabaga	417
		Turnip	481
1377120	BRUSSEL SPROUTS, FRSH, CHLD	Brussels Sprouts	62
1377140	BRUSSELS SPROUTS, FROZEN	Brussels Sprouts	62
1377500	CHAYOTE, FRSH, CHLD OR FRZN	Chayote	91
1377800	FIDDLEHEAD FERNS FR, CH, FZ	Fern	176
1377900	JICAMAS, FRESH OR CHILLED	Jicama	244
1378000	PARSNIPS, FRSH, CHLD OR FRZ	Parsnip	335
1378400	WATER CHESTNUTS, FROZEN	Waterchestnut	485
1378800	YAMS, FRESH OR CHILLED	Yam	495
1378910	YAMS, FROZEN	Yam	496
1378930	SWEET POTATOES, FRSH, CH FZ	Sweet Potato	445
1379300	PUMPKIN, BREADFRUIT, FR, CH, FZ	Breadfruit	60
		Pumpkin	390
1379575	VEGS, FRESH, CHILLED, NSPF	Vegetable	649
1379580	VEGETABLES, FROZEN, NSPF	Vegetable	652
1379730	BROCCOLI, FRESH OR CHILLED	Broccoli	61
1379775	VEGS, FRESH, CHILLED, NSPF	Vegetable	650
1379780	VEGETABLES, FROZEN, NSPF	Vegetable	652
1379785	VEGETABLES FROZEN, NSPF	Vegetable	652
1380520	BROCCOLI ETC FR, CUT SLICED	Broccoli	61
		Cauliflower	84
		Okra	304
1380540	BROCCOLI FZ REDUCE IN SIZE	Broccoli	61
1380560	CAULIFLOWER FZ, CUT, SLICED	Cauliflower	85
1380580	OKRA, FRZN, REDUCED IN SIZE	Okra	304
1382500	KIDNEY BEANS, FROZEN	Bean	47
1383020	RUTABAGAS FR CUT SLICED ETC	Rutabaga	417
1383040	RUTABAGAS, FROZEN	Rutabaga	417
1383500	YUCCA FR FZ REDUCED IN SIZE	Yucca	497
1384000	BAMBOO SHOOTS, CHESTNUTS FZ	Bamboo	28
		Waterchestnut	485
1384100	MIX PEA POD/WATER CHSTNT FZ	Pea	340
		Waterchestnut	485
1384210	VEGS NSPF, FR, CHLD, SLICED	Vegetable	651
1384250	VEG NSPF FZ REDUCED IN SIZE	Vegetable	652
1384610	VEGS NSPF, FR, CHLD, SLICED	Vegetable	651
1384640	ASPARAGUS, FRZ, CUT, SLICED	Asparagus	20
1384650	VEG NSPF FZ REDUCED IN SIZE	Vegetable	652
1400900	MUNG BEANS, DRIED, DEHYDRATD	Bean	48
1401000	RED KIDNEY BEANS DRIED DEHYD	Bean	46
1401120	LIMA BEANS DRY MAY 1-AUG 31	Bean	47
1401140	DRIED BEANS, NSPF	Bean	38
1401400	MUNG BEANS, 9/1-4/30, INCL	Bean	49
1401620	LIMA BEANS, DRIED, 9/1-4/30	Bean	47
1401640	RED KIDNY BEAN DRY 9/1-4/30	Bean	47
1401660	BEANS, DRY, NSPF, 9/1-4/30	Bean	40
1402000	CHICKPEAS OR GARBANZOS SPLIT	Chickpea	96
1402100	CHICKPEAS OR GARBANZOS, NSPF	Chickpea	97
1402500	COWPEAS, BLACK-EYE, DRIED ETC	Cowpea	160
1402600	COWPEAS, EXCEPT BLACKEYE DRD	Cowpea	161
1403000	GARLIC, DRIED, DEHYDRATED	Garlic	183
1403500	LENTILS, DRIED, DEHYDRATED	Lentil	254
1403800	LUPINES, DRIED, DEHYDRATED	Lupine	262
1404000	ONIONS, DRIED, DEHYDRATED	Onion	313
1404500	PEAS,SPLIT,DRIED, DEHYDRATED	Pea	336

TSUSA commodity	Crop/End-Use	Page
1450200 CHESTNUTS, PREP, PRES, NSPF	Chestnut	95
1450400 COCONUTS IN SHELL	Coconut Palm	129
1450700 COCONUT MT FZN NOV10% SUG AD	Coconut Palm	130
1450800 COCONUT MEAT, SHREDDED, ETC	Coconut Palm	130
1450900 COCONUT MEAT NSPF PREP PRES	Coconut Palm	131
1451200 ALMONDS NOT SHELLED	Almond	5
1451400 BRAZIL NUTS NOT SHELLED	Brazil Nut	60
1451600 CASHEW NUTS NOT SHELLED	Cashew	80
1451800 FILBERTS NOT SHELLED	Filbert	180
1452000 PEANUTS NOT SHELLED	Peanut	345
1452200 PECANS NOT SHELLED	Pecan	350
1452400 PIGNOLIA NUTS, NOT SHELLED	Pine	365
1452600 PISTACHE NUTS NOT SHELLED	Pistachio	378
1452800 WALNUTS NOT SHELLED	Walnut	484
1453010 MACADAMIA NUTS, NOT SHELLED	Macadamia	264
1453020 NUTS, EDBLE NSPF NT SHELLED	Nut	599
1454000 ALMONDS, SHELLED	Almond	4
1454100 ALMONDS BLANCHED ROASTED ETC	Almond	4
1454200 BRAZIL NUTS, SHELLED	Brazil Nut	59
1454400 CASHEW NUTS SHELLED ETC	Cashew	78
1454600 FILBERT NUTS, SHELLED, ETC	Filbert	179
1454840 PEANUT BUTTER	Peanut	344
1454850 PEANUTS NT SHELLED QUOTA	Peanut	345
1454880 PEANUTS SHELLED ETC QUOTA	Peanut	344
1455000 PECANS, SHELLED, BLAND, ETC	Pecan	349
1455200 PIGNOLIA NUTS, SHELLED, ETC	Pine	365
1455300 PISTACHE NUTS, SHELLED, ETC	Pistachio	378
1455400 WALNUTS PICKLED IMMATURE	Walnut	484
1455500 WALNUTS, SHELLED, NOT PICKLD	Walnut	484
1455810 MACADAMIA NUTS SHELL/BLANCH	Macadamia	263
1455820 NUTS, EDIBLE, NSPF, SHELLED	Nut	597
1456500 LITCHI OR LONGAN, CANNED	Litchi	261
	Longan	262
1457010 MACADAMIA NUTS PICKLED,PREP	Macadamia	263
1457020 NUTS, PICKED, PREPARED,NSPF	Nut	598
1459000 NUT EDIBLE MIX 2ORMORE KINDS	Nut	597
1461000 APPLES, FRESH	Apple	9
1461200 APPLES, DRIED	Apple	9
1461400 APPLES, PREP OR PRES, NSPF	Apple	13
1462000 APRICOTS, FRESH OR IN BRINE	Apricot	15
1462200 APRICOTS, DRIED	Apricot	14
1462400 APRICOTS, PREP OR PRES, NSPF	Apricot	16
1463000 AVOCADOS,FRESH PREP OR PRES	Avocado	22
1464000 BANANAS, FRESH	Banana	31
1464200 BANANAS, DRIED	Banana	31
1464400 BANANAS, NSPF, PREP OR PRES	Banana	33
1465000 BLUEBERRIES, FRESH O IN BRNE	Blueberry	57
1465200 LINGON OR PARTRIDGE BERRIES	Cowberry	159
	Partridgeberry	335
1465400 RASPBERRIES AND LOGANBERRIES, 7/1-8/31	Loganberry	261
	Raspberry	397
1465600 RASPBERRIES AND LOGANBERRIES, 9/1-6/30	Loganberry	262
	Raspberry	397
1465800 STRAWBERRY, 6/15-9/15, INCL	Strawberry	432
1466000 STRAWBERRIES, FRSH O IN BRNE	Strawberry	432
1466200 BERRIES NSPF FRSH O IN BRNE	Fruit	535
1466400 BARBERRIES, DRIED	Barberry	35
1466600 OTH BERRIES DRIED EVAP NSPF	Fruit	531
1466800 BLUEBERRIES , FROZEN	Blueberry	57
1466900 BLACK CURRANTS, ETC, FROZEN	Cowberry	159
	Currant	167

TSUSA commodity		Crop/End-Use	Page
1476100	FR GRAPE NSPF FEB 15-MAR 31	Grape	197
1476300	FR GRAPE NSPF APR 1-JUNE 30	Grape	198
1476400	FRSH GRAPE EX HOTHOUSE NSPF	Grape	198
1476600	CURRANTS, RAISINS, NO SEEDS	Grape	221
1476800	SULTANA RAISINS, NO SEEDS	Grape	221
1477000	RAISINS FR SEEDLESS GRAPES	Grape	221
1477200	RAISINS MADE FRM SEED GRAPES	Grape	221
1477500	DRIED GRAPES EXCEPT RAISINS	Grape	197
1477700	GRAPES, PREP OR PRES	Grape	200
1478000	GUAVAS,FR,DRD,PCKLD,IN BRINE	Guava	226
1478500	GUAVAS,PREP AND PRES, NSPF	Guava	227
1479800	MANGOES, FRESH NOV 1-APR 30	Mango	270
1480000	MANGOES, FRESH MAY 1-OCT 31	Mango	270
1480300	MANGOES FRESH SEPT 1-MAY 31	Mango	270
1480600	MANGOES FRESH JUNE 1-AUG 31	Mango	271
1480800	MANGOES, PREPARED PRESERVED	Mango	272
1481000	CANTALOUP,FR,8-1 TO 9-15	Cantaloupe	67
1481200	CANTALOUPES FRESH 12/1-3/31	Cantaloupe	67
1481700	CANTALOUPES, FRESH, NSPF	Cantaloupe	68
1481900	OGEN/GALIA MELONS 12/1-5/31	Galia Melon	183
		Ogen Melon	301
1482200	OGEN/GALIA MELONS 6/1-11/30	Galia Melon	183
		Ogen Melon	301
1482500	WATERMELONS FR DEC 1-MAR 31	Watermelon	486
1482800	WATERMELONS FR APR 1-NOV 30	Watermelon	486
1483000	MELONS NES DEC 1 TO MAY 31	Fruit	532
1483200	MELONS NSPF, FRSH 6/1-11/30	Fruit	533
1483500	MELONS, PREP OR PRES	Fruit	543
1484000	OLIVES FRESH	Olive	305
1484200	OLIVES IN BRINE NT RIPE ETC	Olive	305
1484420	OLIVES N BRINE NT OV 0.3GAL	Olive	306
1484440	OLIVES IN BRINE OVER 0.3GAL	Olive	306
1484600	OLIVES IN BRINE RIPE ETC	Olive	307
1484800	OLIVES IN BRINE RIPE, NSPF	Olive	307
1485020	OLIVES, PITTED NT OV 0.3GAL	Olive	308
1485040	OLIVES, PITTED, OVER 0.3GAL	Olive	308
1485065	OLIVES STUFFED NT OV 0.3GAL	Olive	309
1485070	OLIVES STUFD NSPF NOV0.3GAL	Olive	309
1485080	OLIVES, STUFFED OVER 0.3GAL	Olive	310
1485200	OLIVES, DRIED, NOT RIPE	Olive	304
1485400	OLIVES, DRIED, RIPE	Olive	304
1485600	OLIVES PREP OR PRES, NSPF	Olive	310
1486000	PAPAYAS, FRESH	Papaya	332
1486500	PAPAYAS, PREP OR PRES	Papaya	333
1487000	PEACHES IMPORTED JUN1-NOV30	Peach	342
1487200	PEACHES FRESH IN BRINE NSPF	Peach	342
1487400	PEACHES, DRIED	Peach	341
1487700	WHITE FLESHED PEACHES, PREP	Peach	343
1487800	PEACHES, PREP OR PRES, NSPF	Peach	343
1488100	PEARS, FRESH, APR 1-JUNE 30	Pear	347
1488200	PEARS, FRESH, JULY 1-MAR 31	Pear	347
1488300	PEARS, DRIED	Pear	347
1488600	PEARS, PREP OR PRES, NSPF	Pear	348
1489000	PINEAPPLES, FRESH, IN BULK	Pineapple	373
1489300	PINEAPPLES, FRESH, IN CRATES	Pineapple	374
1489600	PINEAPPLES EX CRATED OR BULK	Pineapple	374
1489820	PINEAPPLES, CANNED	Pineapple	372
1489840	PINEAPPLES PREPARED EXC CND	Pineapple	377
1491000	PLANTAINS, FRESH	Plantain	379
1491500	PLANTAINS, PREP OR PRES	Plantain	380
1491800	PRUNES ETC, FRESH, 1/1-5/31	Plum	382

TSUSA commodity		Crop/End-Use	Page
1492100	PLUMS ETC, FR, JUN 1-DEC 31	Plum	382
1492400	PRUNES PLUMS IN BRINE	Plum	382
1492600	PRUNES PLUMS DRIED	Plum	381
1492820	PLUMS, PRUNES, PREP, CANNED	Plum	380
1492840	PLUMS PRUNE PREP,NOT CANNED	Plum	383
1494000	TAMARINOS FRESH PREP OR PRES	Tamarind	445
1494800	CHINESE GOOSEBERY (KIWI FRT) FR	Kiwi	247
1495000	FRUITS, NSPF, FRESH	Fruit	534
1496000	FRUITS, NSPF, PREP OR PRES	Fruit	544
1500200	FRUIT MIX CND NO APRCOT ETC	Fruit	530
1500500	FRUIT MIXTURES PREPARED	Fruit	546
1520000	BANANA AND PLANTAIN FLOUR	Banana	31
		Plantain	379
1520500	FRUIT FLR NT BANANA PLANTAIN	Fruit	531
1521000	CITRON PEEL CRUDE, DRIED ETC	Citron	104
1521400	ORANGE PEEL CRUDE, DRIED ETC	Orange	325
1521800	LEMN PEEL, CRUDE, DRIED BRNE	Lemon	251
1522200	FRUIT PEEL, OTHER, CRUDE ETC	Fruit	542
1522600	CITRN PEEL PRES O PREP NSPF	Citron	104
1523000	ORNGE PEEL PRES O PREP NSPF	Orange	326
1523400	LEMON PEEL PRES O PREP NSPF	Lemon	252
1523800	FRUIT PEEL PRES O PREP NSPF	Fruit	542
1524000	APPLE AND QUINCE PASTE AND PULP	Apple	13
		Quince	391
1524200	APRICOT PASTE AND PULP	Apricot	16
1524300	FRUIT PASTE, CASHEW APPL ETC	Cashew	77
		Mamey Colorado	270
		Sapodilla	421
		Soursop	426
		Sweetsop	445
1525000	FIG PASTE AND PULP	Fig	179
1525400	GUAVA PASTE AND PULP	Guava	227
1525800	MANGO PASTE AND PULP	Mango	271
1526000	TAMARIND PASTE AND PULP	Tamarind	446
1526200	ORANGE PASTE AND PULP	Orange	325
1526500	PAPAYA PASTE AND PULP	Papaya	332
1527200	BANANA, PLNTAIN PASTE, PULP	Banana	33
		Plantain	380
1527640	FRUIT PASTES AND PULP, NSPF	Fruit	540
1527800	PEAR PASTE AND PULP	Pear	348
1528140	FRUIT PASTES AND PULP, NSPF	Fruit	541
1528820	STRAWBERRY PASTE AND PULP	Strawberry	435
1528840	FRUIT PASTES AND PULP, NSPF	Fruit	541
1530200	CASHEW APPLE, MANGO JELLY	Cashew	77
		Mamey Colorado	270
		Mango	271
		Sapodilla	421
		Soursop	426
		Sweetsop	445
1530300	STRAWBERRY JELLY, JAM, ETC.	Strawberry	434
1530440	BERRY NSPF JELLY, JAMS, ETC	Fruit	535
1530500	MULBERRY JAM,MARMALADE,ETC	Mulberry	278
1530600	BERRY NSPF JELLY, JAMS, ETC	Fruit	536
1530700	BERRY NSPF JELLY, JAMS, ETC	Fruit	536
1530800	GUAVA JELLY, JAM, ETC	Guava	226
1531600	ORANGE MARMALADE	Orange	324
1532000	PAPAYA JELLY, JAM, ETC	Papaya	332
1532400	PINEAPPLE JELLY, JAM ETC	Pineapple	375
1532800	QUINCE JELLY, JAM, ETC.	Quince	390
1533200	JELLIES, JAMS, ETC, NSPF	Fruit	537
1540500	CHERRIES, CANDIED,GLACE,ETC	Cherry	91

TSUSA commodity		Crop/End-Use	Page
1541000	CHESTNUTS,CANDIED, PREP, ETC	Chestnut	94
1541500	CITRONS, CANDIED, GLACE, ETC	Citron	104
1542000	CITRON PEEL CANDIED ETC	Citron	105
1542500	LEMON PEEL, CANDIED ETC	Lemon	252
1543000	ORANGE PEEL, CANDIED ETC	Orange	326
1543500	FRUIT PEEL CANDIED ETC NSPF	Confectionery	523
1544000	GINGER ROOT, CANDIED ETC	Ginger	186
1544300	KUMQUATS, ETC, CANDIED, ETC	Kumquat	248
		Mango	270
		Plum	380
1544500	PINEAPPLES CANDIED ETC	Pineapple	371
1545000	CANDIED, CRYSTALD,GLACE NUTS	Confectionery	523
1545300	FRUIT, CANDIED, ETC, NSPF	Confectionery	522
1546000	CANDIED GLACE VEG SUBS NSPF	Confectionery	525
1549000	MXTRE CANDIED FRUIT,NUTS,ETC	Confectionery	524
1551000	BEETS, SUGAR, NATURAL STATE	Sugar Beet	437
1551200	SUGARCANE, NATURAL	Sugarcane	443
1551500	SUGAR BEET A CANE NT NATURAL	Sugar Beet	437
		Sugarcane	443
1552025	CANE SUGAR IMMEDITE CNSMPTN	Sugar Beet	437
		Sugarcane	443
1552045	CANE, BEET SUGAR, ETC, NSPF	Sugar Beet	439
		Sugarcane	443
1553000	SUGARS, ETC NOV 6% NON SUGAR	Sugar Beet	440
		Sugarcane	443
1553500	SUGARS, N SGR SLDS OV 6 PCT	Sugar Beet	441
		Sugarcane	443
1554000	MOLASSES INEDIBLE N SUGAR	Sugar Beet	441
		Sugarcane	443
1555000	MAPLE SUGAR	Maple	275
1555500	MAPLE SIRUP	Maple	275
1556000	DEXTROSE	Sweetener	639
1556500	DEXTROSE SIRUP	Sweetener	640
1557500	SUGARS SIRUPS ETC BLENDS	Sweetener	641
1557520	HIGH FRUCTSE SIRUP F/STACH	Sweetener	641
1557540	SUGAR SIRUP MOLASSES, BLEND	Sweetener	643
1561000	COCOA BEANS	Cocoa	116
1562000	CHOCOLATE, UNSWEETENED	Cocoa	115
1562500	CHOC,SWEET,BARS NOT UND 10LB	Cocoa	109
1563020	CHOC SWEET, CANDY-CONFECTON	Cocoa	110
1563045	CHOC SWT, NO BFT/MILK SOLID	Cocoa	113
1563050	CHOC SWEET OV 5.5% BF QUOTA	Cocoa	115
1563065	CHOC SWT NOV 5.5% BF QUOTA	Cocoa	115
1563500	COCOA BUTTER	Cocoa	119
1564000	COCOA UNSWEET AND COCOA CAKE	Cocoa	126
1564500	COCOA, SWEETENED	Cocoa	128
1564700	CONFECTIONERS COATINGS,ETC	Cocoa	121
1565000	COCOA BEAN SHELLS	Cocoa	118
1565500	COCOA BEAN WASTES EX SHELLS	Cocoa	118
1571010	CONFECTRY, NT CON CHOC NSPF	Confectionery	516
1571020	CONFECTRY, NT CON CHOC NSPF	Confectionery	517
1571040	CONFECTIONERY CON CHOC NSPF	Cocoa	121
1571050	CONFECTIONERY CON CHOC NSPF	Cocoa	126
1601020	COFFEE, CRUDE	Coffee	137
1601040	COFFEE ROASTED OR GROUND	Coffee	145
1602000	SOLBL OR INST COFFEE NO ADD	Coffee	143
1602100	COFFEE ESSENCE, EXTRACT ETC	Coffee	142
1603000	CHICORY ROOTS, CRUDE	Chicory	99
1603500	CHICORY, GROUND OR OTWS PREP	Chicory	99
1604000	COFFEE SUBSTITUTES, NSPF	Coffee	145
1605000	TEA, CRUDE OR PREPARED	Tea	449

TSUSA commodity	Crop/End-Use	Page
1606000 MATE, CRUDE	Mate	276
1606500 MATE, PREPARED	Mate	276
1610100 ANISE	Anise	8
1610300 BASIL, CRUDE OR NOT MFRD	Basil	37
1610500 BASIL, MANUFACTURED	Basil	38
1610600 CAPERS IN CONTAINR OV 7.5LB	Caper	68
1610700 CAPERS	Caper	69
1610800 CAPERS, NSPF	Caper	69
1610900 CARAWAY	Caraway	70
1611100 CARDAMON	Cardamom	70
1611300 CASSIA, CAS BUD A VERA UNGRD	Cassia	82
1611500 CASSIA AND BUDS VERA GROUND	Cassia	83
1611700 CINNAMON AND CHIPS UNGROUND	Cinnamon	103
1611900 CINNAMON A CINN CHIPS GROUND	Cinnamon	103
1612100 CLOVES AND CLOVE STMS, UNGD	Clove	106
1612300 CLOVES A CLOVE STEMS, GROUND	Clove	107
1612500 CORIANDER	Coriander	148
1612700 CUMMIN	Cummin	166
1612900 CURRY AND CURRY POWDER	Spice and Flavoring	625
1613100 DILL	Dill	171
1613300 FENNEL	Fennel	175
1613500 GINGER ROOT, UNGROUND	Ginger	187
1613700 GINGER ROOT, GRND, N CANDIED	Ginger	189
1613900 LAUREL LEAVES, CRUDE	Laurel	249
1614100 LAUREL LEAVES, EXCEPT CRUDE	Laurel	249
1614300 MACE, BOMBAY OR WILD, UNGRND	Nutmeg	296
1614500 MACE, BOMBAY OR WILD, GROUND	Nutmeg	296
1614700 MACE, UNGROUND, NSPF	Nutmeg	296
1614900 MACE, NSPF, GROUND	Nutmeg	297
1615100 MARJORAM, CRUDE OR NOT MFRD	Marjoram	275
1615300 MARJORAM, OTHER THAN CRUDE	Marjoram	276
1615500 MINT LEAVES, CRUDE NOT MFRD	Mint	277
1615700 MINT LEAVES, MANUFACTURED	Mint	278
1615800 MUSTARD, GROUND	Mustard	293
1616000 MUSTARD, PREPARED	Mustard	294
1616100 MUSTARD SEEDS WHOLE	Mustard	293
1616300 NUTMEGS, UNGROUND	Nutmeg	297
1616500 NUTMEGS, GROUND	Nutmeg	298
1616700 ORIGANUM, CRUDE OR NOT MFRD	Oregano	330
1616900 ORIGANUM, EXCEPT CRUDE	Oregano	331
1617100 PAPRIKA, GROUND OR UNGROUND	Pepper	356
1617300 PARSLEY, CRUDE N MANUFACTURD	Parsley	334
1617500 PARSLEY, MANUFACTURED	Parsley	334
1617720 PEPPER UNGROUND BLACK	Pepper	350
1617740 PEPPER, UNGROUND, WHITE	Pepper	360
1617900 PEPPER, BLACK OR WHITE, GRND	Pepper	351
	Pepper	361
1618000 PEPPR, ANAHEIM ETC UNGROUND	Pepper	356
1618300 PEPPER CAPSICUM ETC UNGROUND	Pepper	352
1618400 PEPPER CAPSICUM ETC GROUND	Pepper	354
1618600 PIMENTO UNGROUND	Pimento	364
1618800 PIMENTO GROUND	Pimento	365
1619000 ROSEMARY, EXCEPT MANUFACTURD	Rosemary	408
1619200 ROSEMARY, MANUFACTURED	Rosemary	409
1619400 SAGE UNGROUND	Sage	420
1619600 SAGE GROUND OR RUBBED	Sage	420
1620100 SAVORY, EXCEPT MANUFACTURED	Savory	422
1620300 SAVORY, MANUFACTURED	Savory	422
1620500 TARRAGON CRUDE NOT MFRD	Tarragon	448
1620700 TARRAGON, MANUFACTURED	Tarragon	448
1620900 THYME,CRUDE,NOT MANUFACTURED	Thyme	455

TSUSA commodity		Crop/End-Use	Page
1621100	THYME, MANUFACTURED	Thyme	456
1621300	TURMERIC	Turmeric	481
1621500	MIXED SPICES SPCE SEEDS NSPF	Spice and Flavoring	635
1651500	APLE A PEAR JC N OV 1 PC AL	Apple	10
		Pear	348
1652520	LIME JCE UNMXD N CONCENTRATD	Lime	260
1652540	LIME-JUICE UNMXD CONCNTRTD	Lime	260
1652700	ORANGE JUICE UNMXD NOT CONCENTD	Orange	323
1652900	ORANGE JUICE CONCENTRATED	Orange	322
1653000	CIT FRT JUICE NOT CON, NSPF	Beverage	506
1653080	CITRUS FRT JUICE NT CNCTRD NSPF	Beverage	507
1653200	CITRUS FRT JUICE NT CNCTRD NSPF	Beverage	507
1653570	CITRUS FRT JUICE NSPF CONCT	Beverage	505
1653580	CITRUS FRT JUICE NSPF, CONCENTD	Beverage	506
1653650	LEMON JUICE UNMIXED CONCENTRATD	Lemon	251
1653680	CITRUS FRT JUICE NSPF, CONCENTD	Beverage	506
1654020	GRAPE JUC NT CNCNTRT NT MIX	Grape	199
1654040	GRAPE JUC CNCNTRT FZ,NT MIX	Grape	199
1654060	GRAPE JUC CNCNTRT NT MIX/FZ	Grape	199
1654400	PNAPL JUICE NOT CONCENTRATED	Pineapple	376
1654600	PNAPPLE JUICE CONCENTRATED	Pineapple	375
1655000	PRUNE JUICE NOV 1% ALCOLOL	Plum	384
1655500	FRUIT JCES N MXD NOV 1% ACHL	Beverage	507
1656500	FRUIT JUICE,MIXD,ALCOL 1 PCT	Beverage	510
1657000	FRUIT JUICES OV 1 PCT ALCHL	Beverage	511
1662000	GINGER ALE,GINGER BEER ETC	Beverage	511
1663000	VEG JUICE, NOV 1/2% ALCOHOL	Beverage	515
1664040	BEVERAGES NSPF UN 1/2% ALCO	Beverage	512
1670515	BEER, ETC NOV1GL,GLASS CNTR	Hop	231
1670530	BEER, ETC NT OV 1 GAL, NSPF	Hop	237
1670540	ALE,PORTER,STOUT,BEER,OV GAL	Hop	239
1671020	CHAMPAGNE WINE NOV $6 GAL	Grape	193
1671040	CHAMPAGNE AND WNE OV $6 GAL	Grape	194
1671500	CIDER,FERMENTED,STILL,SPRKNG	Beverage	503
1672000	PRUNE WINE	Plum	384
1672500	RICE WINE OR SAKE	Rice	404
1673005	WINE GRAPE RED NOV 1 GL, NOV $4	Grape	201
1673015	WINE, GRAPE WH NOV 1 GL, NOV $4	Grape	202
1673020	WINE NOV 14%, NOV$4,NOV 1GL	Grape	204
1673025	WINE GRAPE NSPF NOV 1GL, NOV $4	Grape	205
1673030	WINE, GRAPE RED NOV 1 GL OV $4	Grape	206
1673040	WINE OV 14%, OV $4, NOV 1GL	Grape	210
1673045	WINE, GRAPE WHITE NOV 1GL OV $4	Grape	211
1673060	WINE, GRAPE NSPF NOV 1 GL OV $4	Grape	215
1673200	GRP WNE,NOV 14% ALHL OV 1 GL	Grape	217
1673400	MARSALA WNE OV 14% AL NOV1GL	Grape	217
1673520	SHERRY WINE NOT OVER 1 GAL	Grape	218
1673540	SHERRY WINE OVER 1 GAL	Grape	218
1673700	GRAPE WINE OV14% ALCHL NSPF	Grape	218
1674000	VERMOUTH IN CONT NOV 1 GAL	Grape	222
1674200	VERMOUTH IN CONT OV 1 GAL	Grape	223
1675000	FERMENTED ALCHL BEVRGS NSPF	Beverage	503
1675005	FERMNTD ALC BEV NSPF OV 14% ALC	Beverage	505
1675025	FER ALC BEV NSPF 7 TO 14% ALCH	Beverage	505
1675050	FERMNTD ALC BEV NSPF UN 7% ALCH	Beverage	505
1679000	IMITATIONS OF WINES	Beverage	505
1700100	LF TOBAC, UNSTM, 2 CTRY MIX	Tobacco	463
1700500	LF TOBAC, STEM, 2 CTRY MIXD	Tobacco	463
1701000	WRPPR TOB MIX OR NT, NT STEM	Tobacco	470
1701500	WRPPR TOB, MIX OR NOT, STEM	Tobacco	471
1702000	FILLER TOBACCO MIXED N STEMD	Tobacco	463

TSUSA commodity		Crop/End-Use	Page
1702500	TOBACCO OV35 PCT WRAPER STEM	Tobacco	463
1702800	CIG LEAF NT STEM, NOV 8.5IN	Tobacco	457
1703210	CIG LEAF NT STMD FLUE-CURED	Tobacco	457
1703230	CIG LEAF NOT STEMMED BURLEY	Tobacco	458
1703240	CIG LEAF NOT STEMMED, NSPF	Tobacco	459
1703500	TOBAC, NOV 35% WRAP, STEMMD	Tobacco	460
1703510	TOB STM FLU-CRD NOV35% WPR	Tobacco	461
1703520	TOB STMMD NSPF NOV 35% WPR	Tobacco	461
1704000	FILER TBCO LEAF N STMD NSPF	Tobacco	461
1704500	FILLER TOBACCO, STEMD, NSPF	Tobacco	462
1705000	TOBACCO STEMS, NOT CUT, ETC	Tobacco	469
1705500	TOBACCO STEMS,CUT,GROUND,ETC	Tobacco	470
1706020	CIGAR LEAF SCRAP TOBACCO	Tobacco	466
1706040	SCRAP TOBACCO NT CIGAR LEAF	Tobacco	467
1708050	TOB EXC SMOKNG, FLUE-CURED	Tobacco	463
1708070	TOBACCO, MFG OR NOT, NSPF	Tobacco	464
1750300	APRICOT AND PEACH KERNELS	Apricot	15
		Peach	343
1750600	CASTOR BEANS	Castor Bean	83
1750900	COPRA	Coconut Palm	129
1751500	COTTONSEED	Cotton	159
1751800	FLAXSEED, LINSEED	Flax	182
1752100	HEMPSEED	Hemp	230
1752400	KAPOK SEED	Kapok Tree	246
1752800	PALM-NUT KRNLS A PALM NUTS	Oil Palm	302
1753300	PERILLA SEED	Perilla	362
1753600	POPPY SEED	Opium Poppy	320
1753900	RAPESEED	Rape	396
1754200	RUBBER SEED	Rubber-Tree	417
1754500	SESAME SEED	Sesame	422
1755000	SOYBEANS	Soybean	427
1755100	SUNFLOWER SEED	Sunflower	444
1755400	TUNG NUTS	Tung	480
1755700	OIL BEARNG NUTS & SEED NSPF	Oil	600
1760000	BABASSU OIL	Babassu	22
1760100	CASTOR OIL, NOT OVER 20 CTS	Castor Bean	84
1761400	CASTOR OIL OV 20CT LOVIBOND	Castor Bean	84
1761500	CASTOR OIL OV 20 CT LB NSPF	Castor Bean	84
1761600	CORN OIL	Maize	270
1761720	COCONUT OIL, CRUDE	Coconut Palm	135
1761740	COCONUT OIL, REFINED	Coconut Palm	136
1761800	COTTONSEED OIL	Cotton	159
1762000	CROTON OIL	Croton	162
1762200	HEMPSEED OIL	Hemp	231
1762400	KAPOK OIL	Kapok Tree	246
1762600	LINSEED OR FLAXSEED OIL	Flax	182
1762800	OLIVE OIL, INEDIBLE	Olive	313
1762900	OLIVE OIL PKG UNDER 4O LBS	Olive	311
1763000	OLIVE OIL NOT UNDER 4O LBS	Olive	312
1763200	PALM-KERNEL OIL, INEDIBLE	Oil Palm	302
1763320	PALM KERNL OIL EDIBLE CRUDE	Oil Palm	301
1763340	PALM KRNL OIL,EDBLE,REFINED	Oil Palm	301
1763420	PALM OIL, CRUDE	Oil Palm	302
1763440	PALM OIL, REFINED	Oil Palm	303
1763800	PEANUT OIL	Peanut	346
1764000	PERILLA OIL	Perilla	362
1764200	POPPY SEED OIL	Opium Poppy	320
1764400	RAPESEED OIL INEDBL FOR MFR	Rape	397
1764500	RAPESEED OIL INEDIBLE, NSPF	Rape	397
1764600	RAPESEED OIL EDIBLE FOR MFR	Rape	396
1764700	RAPESEED OIL, EDIBLE, NSPF	Rape	396

TSUSA commodity		Crop/End-Use	Page
2022780	CDR EX W/RED D/W LBR, NSPF	Cedar	87
2023200	BALSA/TEAK LUMBER ROUGH	Balsa	22
		Teak	454
2023205	BALSA LUMBER, ROUGH	Balsa	23
2023215	TEAK LUMBER, ROUGH	Teak	454
2023300	BALSA/TEAK LBR DSD EX SIDNG	Balsa	23
		Teak	454
2023305	BALSA LUMBER DRESSD EXCL SIDING	Balsa	24
2023315	TEAK LUMBER DRESSED EXCL SIDING	Teak	454
2023420	LBR MAHOGNY RGH EXC SDG FLG	Mahogany	264
2023440	LBR,MAHOGANY DRSD EXC SDG,FLG	Mahogany	265
2023500	SPN CDR EBONY ETC LUMBR RGH	Cedar	87
		Ebony	172
		Lancewood	248
		Lignum Vitae	257
2023700	SPN CDR ETC LUMBER DRSD ETC	Cedar	88
		Ebony	172
		Lancewood	248
		Lignum Vitae	257
2023820	BOXWD, JAP MAPLE LBR, ROUGH	Boxwood	59
		Maple	274
		Oak	299
2023840	BOXWD, JAP MAP LBR, DRESSED	Boxwood	59
		Maple	274
		Oak	299
2024210	MAPLE LUMBER, NSPF, ROUGH	Maple	274
2024215	MAPLE LUMBER, NSPF, DRESSED	Maple	274
2024225	LUMBER, BIRCH, ROUGH	Birch	54
2024230	LUMBER, BIRCH, DRESSED	Birch	54
2024235	LUMBER, BEECH, ROUGH	Beech	51
2024245	BEECH LUMBER, DRESSED	Beech	51
2024250	OAK LUMBER, ROUGH	Oak	299
2024255	OAK LUMBER, DRESSED, WORKED	Oak	299
2024720	WOOD SIDNG, RED CEDR, RESAWN	Cedar	89
2024800	WD SIDING NSPF W. RED CEDAR	Cedar	89
2025600	HARDWOOD FLOORING, OAK STRP	Oak	298
2025820	HARDWOOD FLOORING, MAPLE	Beech	50
		Birch	53
		Maple	274
2026200	WOOD MOLDING, STANDARD, PINE	Pine	369
2200500	NAT CORK UNMFD A CORK WASTE	Cork Oak	155
2201000	CORK GRANLTD ETC NOV 6LB CFT	Cork Oak	155
2201500	CORK GRANLTD, ETC OV 6LB CFT	Cork Oak	155
2202000	CORK NA COMP N/ADV EX/CUT ETC	Cork Oak	155
2202500	VUL SHEETS, ETC OF CORK-RUB	Cork Oak	149
2203000	CORK INSULATION BLOCKS ETC	Cork Oak	150
2203100	CORK INSULATION, FITTNGS,ETC	Cork Oak	150
2203500	TAPER CORK STPRS, HLW O PERF	Cork Oak	150
2203600	CORK STOP N/HLW PER NOV 3/4	Cork Oak	150
2203700	CORK DISK N/HLW PER NOV 3/4	Cork Oak	151
2203900	CORK STOP N/HLW PERF OV3/4	Cork Oak	151
2204100	CORK DISK N/HLW PERF OV 3/4	Cork Oak	151
2204700	CORK STOPPERS NSPF N TAPERD	Cork Oak	152
2204800	CORK DISKS NES, NOT TAPERED	Cork Oak	152
2204900	CORK DSKS ETC NSPF CAN APTA	Cork Oak	153
2205000	CORK MANUFACTURES NSPF	Cork Oak	153
2220505	RATTAN STICKS 4 METERS LONG	Rattan	399
2220590	BAMBOO/RAT STICKS ROUGH/CUT	Bamboo	29
		Rattan	400
2221020	RATTAN WEBBING	Rattan	400
2221040	RATTAN EXCEPT WEBBING	Rattan	398

TSUSA commodity	Crop/End-Use	Page
2221500 BAMBOO SPLIT	Bamboo	30
2222000 WILLOW PREP FOR BSKT MAKERS	Willow	494
2222500 WILLOW,EX PRE F BASKET MAKER	Willow	495
2223000 WOV MTL BMBO RATN ETC F/BLDS	Bamboo	30
	Rattan	400
	Willow	495
2223400 WOV MATL,RAFFIA,F/BLINDS,ETC	Raffia Palm	395
2224000 BASKETS AND BAGS BAMBOO	Bamboo	25
2224100 BASKETS AND BAGS WILLOW	Willow	492
2224200 BASKTS A BAGS, RATTN, PLM LF	Raffia Palm	392
	Rattan	399
2400020 BIRCH VENR NT REINF OR BCKD	Birch	56
2400040 MAPLE VENR NT REINF OR BCKD	Maple	275
2401000 PLYWD, PLY SPANISH CDR FACE	Cedar	88
2401200 PLYWD, FACE PLY, PARA PINE	Pine	370
2401420 PLYWD BIRCH FACED SPEC DIMS	Birch	54
2401440 PLYWD BRCH FC NO FIN EXC DM	Birch	54
2401460 PLYWD BRCH FC CL FIN OV DIM	Birch	55
2401600 PLYWD, FACE PLY EU RED PINE	Pine	370
2401900 PLYWD, FACE PLY WALNUT	Walnut	484
2402320 PLYWD, FACE PLY SEN	Sen	422
2402340 PLYWOOD, FACE PLY MAHOGANY	Mahogany	266
2403000 WD-VENR PANEL SPANISH CEDAR	Cedar	89
2403200 WOOD-VNER PANEL PARANA PINE	Pine	370
2403400 WOOD-VNER PANEL BIRCH	Birch	56
2403600 WOOD-VNER PANEL EUR RED PINE	Pine	370
2405000 WD-VNER PANLS,1 SDE SPAN CDR	Cedar	89
2405200 WD-VNER PANLS,1 SDE PARA PIN	Pine	370
2405400 WD-VNER PANLS, 1 SIDE BIRCH	Birch	56
2405600 WD-VNER PANLS, 1 SIDE, EU RD	Pine	370
3001020 RAW COT ROUGH STPL UN 3V4 IN	Cotton	157
3001040 RAW COT NSPF STPL UN 1-1/8	Cotton	157
3001520 HAR COT ST 1-5/32 TO 1-3/8 INCH	Cotton	157
3001540 OTH COT ST 1-1/8 TO 1-3/8 INCH	Cotton	157
3001560 OT R COT ST 1-3/8 TO 1-11/16 IN	Cotton	157
3002000 RAW COT STP 1-11/16 IN OR MORE	Cotton	157
3003000 COTTON LINTERS WH BLCH OR PURF	Cotton	156
3004010 OT S WSTE CD STPS UN 1-3/16	Cotton	157
3004015 COT S WASTE CD ETC 1-3/16AOV	Cotton	158
3004025 COT COMB WASTE STP U 1-3/16	Cotton	158
3004030 COT S WASTE C OTH 1-3/16AOV	Cotton	158
3004035 COT S WASTE INCL LAP SL ROV	Cotton	158
3004060 COT WASTES, SOFT, NSPF	Cotton	158
3004070 COT HARD WASTE YARN & THRD WSTE	Cotton	158
3004500 COT WASTE ADV ETC UN 1-1/8	Cotton	158
3005000 COT WASTE ADV ETC 1-1/8 AOV	Cotton	159
3040200 ABACA RAW AND WASTES	Abaca	3
3040400 ABACA FIBERS PROCESSED ETC	Abaca	3
3040600 COIR RAW AND WASTES	Coconut Palm	136
3040800 CRIN VEGETAL RAW AND WASTES	European Fan Palm	175
3041000 FLAX, RAW	Flax	181
3041200 FLAX WASTE A ADV WASTE	Flax	181
3041400 FLAX PROCESSED NO CRD NO HCK	Flax	181
3041600 FLAX HACKLED	Flax	180
3041800 FLAX FIBERS, PROCESS, NSPF	Flax	181
3042000 HEMP RAW AND WASTES	Hemp	230
3042200 HEMP PROCESSED NO CRD NO HCK	Hemp	230
3042400 HEMP HACKLED	Hemp	230
3042600 HEMP FIBERS, PROCESS, NSPF	Hemp	230
3043220 JUTE BUTTS A WASTES	Jute	245
3043240 RAW JUTE FIBERS, NSPF	Jute	245

TSUSA commodity		Crop/End-Use	Page
3043400	JUTE SLIVER	Jute	245
3043600	JUTE FIB PROCESSED NOT SLIV	Jute	244
3043800	KAPOK, RAW AND WASTES	Kapok Tree	246
3044000	KAPOK FIBER PROCESSED	Kapok Tree	246
3044200	RAMIE RAW AND WASTES	Ramie	396
3044400	RAMIE FIBERS PROCESSED ETC	Ramie	396
3044600	SISAL A HENEQ RAW A WASTES	Henequen	231
		Sisal	425
3044800	SISAL A HENEQUEN FIB PROCESS	Henequen	231
		Sisal	425
3045000	SUNN, RAW AND WASTES	Sunn Hemp	445
3045200	SUNN FIBERS PROCESSED ETC	Sunn Hemp	445
3045600	OTH VEG FIB NSPF, RAW WASTE	Fiber	530
3045800	OT VEG FIB PROCES NSPF, ETC	Fiber	529
4012200	CREOSOTE OIL	Beech	51
4102440	ALIZARIN A INDIGO NATURAL	Indigo	242
		Madder	264
4105200	BENZALDEHYDE	Almond	6
4133200	COUMARIN	Tonka Bean	478
4134000	VANILLIN	Vanilla	482
4253000	MONSODIUM GLUTAMATE	Miscellaneous	552
4261200	LIME CITRATE	Lime	258
4267400	ARGOLS ETC U90% POT BITART	Miscellaneous	550
4350500	ALOES JALAP MATE ETC, CRUDE	Aloe	6
		Asafetida	19
		Buchu	62
		Cocculus Indicus	109
		Digitalis	171
		Ipecac	243
		Jalap	244
		Manna Ash	274
		Marsh Mallow	276
		Monkshood	278
4351000	ALOES,JALAP MANA,ETC ADVANCE	Aloe	7
		Asafetida	19
		Buchu	62
		Cocculus Indicus	109
		Digitalis	171
		Ipecac	243
		Jalap	244
		Manna Ash	274
		Marsh Mallow	276
		Monkshood	278
4353000	BARK CINCHONA ETC QUININE	Cinchona	101
4353500	BELLADONNA	Belladonna	53
4354000	COCA LEAVES	Coca	109
4354500	DIGITALIS (PURPUREA)	Digitalis	171
4355000	ERGOT	Rye	418
4355500	GENTIAN	Gentian	186
4356000	HENBANE	Henbane	231
4356500	NUX VOMICA	Strychnine Tree	437
4357000	OPIUM	Opium Poppy	319
4357200	POPPY STRAW EXTRACT	Opium Poppy	320
4357500	STRAMONIUM	Jimsonweed	244
4370000	BRUCINE AND ITS COMPOUNDS	Strychnine Tree	436
4370820	QUININE AND ITS SALTS	Cinchona	102
4370840	QUINIDINE AND ITS SALTS	Cinchona	102
4370860	CINCHONA BARK ALKALOID NSPF	Cinchona	101
4371200	ERGOTAMINE COMPOUNDS	Rye	418
4371300	NICOTINE AND COMPOUNDS	Tobacco	456
4371400	OPIUM ALKALOIDS	Opium Poppy	319

TSUSA commodity		Crop/End-Use	Page
4371600	STRYCHNINE AND SALT OF	Strychnine Tree	437
4371800	THEOBROMINE	Cocoa	129
4372040	THEOPHYLLINE A DERIVATIVES	Tea	453
4374880	CRUDE FICIN AND PAPAIN	Fig	177
		Papaya	332
4376400	MENTHOL	Peppermint	361
4376600	SANTONIN AND SALTS	Wormwood	495
4377200	THYMOL	Thyme	456
4391050	GINSENG ROOTS	Ginseng	191
4391070	PSYLLIUM SEED HUSKS	Psyllium	389
4393050	GINSENG IN ADVANCED FORM	Ginseng	191
4460510	GUTTA BALATA	Balata	22
4460520	GUTTA-PERCHA & GUTTAS, NSPF	Gutta-Percha	229
4460530	JELUTONG OR PONTIANAK	Jelutong	244
4460540	RUBBER MILK OR LATEX	Rubber-Tree	409
4460544	RIBBED SMOKED SHEETS GRDE 1	Rubber-Tree	410
4460548	RIBBED SMOKED SHEETS GRDE 2	Rubber-Tree	411
4460552	RIBBED SMOKED SHEETS GRDE 3	Rubber-Tree	411
4460556	RIBBED SMOKED SHEETS, NSPOF	Rubber-Tree	411
4460560	TECH SPECIFIED RUBBR GRDE 5	Rubber-Tree	412
4460564	TECH SPECIFIED RUBBR GRD CV	Rubber-Tree	412
4460568	TECH SPECIFIED RUBBR GRDE 1	Rubber-Tree	413
4460572	TECH SPECIFIED RUBBR GRD 10	Rubber-Tree	413
4460576	TECH SPECIFIED RUBBR GRD 20	Rubber-Tree	413
4460580	TECH SPECIFIED RUBBER NSPF	Rubber-Tree	414
4460584	NAT RUB N CONT FIL ETC NSPF	Rubber-Tree	415
4461000	NAT RUBBER CONT FILLERS ETC	Rubber-Tree	416
4461200	CHLORINATED NATURAL RUBBER	Rubber-Tree	417
4501000	FLAV EXT ETC NO ALCO, PILLS	Spice and Flavoring	627
4502010	PAPRIKA	Pepper	356
4502015	BLACK PEPPER	Pepper	350
4502025	SPICE OLEORESINS NSPF	Spice and Flavoring	627
4502040	OTH FLAV EXTR NO ALCO ETC	Spice and Flavoring	628
4503000	FLAV EXTR ETC NOT OV 20% ALC	Spice and Flavoring	632
4504000	FLAV EXTR ETC 20 TO 50% ALCH	Spice and Flavoring	634
4505000	FLAV EXTR ETC OV 50 PCT ALCO	Spice and Flavoring	634
4520200	ALMOND OIL BITTER	Almond	6
4520400	ANISE OIL	Anise	7
4520600	BERGAMOT OIL	Bergamot	53
4520800	CAMPHOR OIL	Camphor Tree	66
4521000	CARAWAY OIL	Caraway	69
4521200	CASSIA OIL	Cassia	82
4521400	CEDAR LEAF OIL	Cedar	86
4521600	CINNAMON OIL	Cinnamon	102
4521800	CITRONELLA OIL	Citronella Grass	105
4522000	CLOVE OIL	Clove	105
4522200	CORNMINT OIL & PEP OIL NSPF	Corn Mint	156
		Peppermint	362
4522400	EUCALYPTUS OIL	Eucalyptus	174
4522600	GERANIUM OIL	Geranium	186
4522800	GRAPEFRUIT OIL	Grapefruit	223
4523200	LAVENDER A SPIKE LAVENDR OIL	Lavender	249
4523400	LEMON OIL	Lemon	250
4523600	LEMON GRASS OIL	Lemongrass	253
4523800	LIME OIL	Lime	258
4524000	LIGNALOE OIL OR BOIS DE ROSE	Agalloch	3
		Rosewood	409
4524200	ORANGE FLOWER OR NEROLI OIL	Orange	321
4524400	ORANGE OIL	Orange	321
4524600	ORIGANUM OIL	Oregano	330
4524800	ORRIS OIL	Orris	331

TSUSA commodity		Crop/End-Use	Page
4525000	PALMAROSA OIL	Rosha Grass	409
4525200	PATCHOULI OIL	Patchouli	335
4525400	PEPERMT OIL OF MENT PIPRITA	Peppermint	362
4525600	PETTIGRAIN OIL	Bitter Orange	57
4525800	PINE NEEDLE OIL	Pine	369
4526000	ROSE OIL OR ATTAR OF ROSES	Rose	405
4526200	ROSEMARY OIL	Rosemary	408
4526400	SANDALWOOD OIL	Sandalwood	420
4526600	THYME OIL	Thyme	455
4526800	VETIVERT OIL	Vetiver	483
4527000	CANANGA OR YLANG YLANG OIL	Ylang-Ylang	496
4528005	CEDARWOOD	Cedar	89
4528010	CITRUS, NSPF	Essential Oil	526
4528020	NUTMEG OIL	Nutmeg	297
4528023	ONION AND GARLIC	Garlic	184
		Onion	314
4528025	PINE OIL	Pine	365
4528030	SASSOFRAS, OCOTEA CYMBARUM	Sassafras	421
4528035	SPEARMINT	Spearmint	429
4528042	OILS DIST OR ESSENT, NSPF	Essential Oil	526
4550400	PECTIN	Miscellaneous	553
4553000	VEG GLUE UNDER 4O CENTS LB	Miscellaneous	557
4553200	VEG GLUE NOT UN 4O CENTS LB	Miscellaneous	557
4602500	CITRAL NOV 10% ALC NOT MIXT	Lemongrass	253
4606000	MUSK IN GR OR PODS NOT MIXT	Musk Plant	293
4606500	RHODINOL NOT ARTIFICIAL MIXT	Geranium	186
4607000	SAFROL NOT IN ARTIFICIAL MIX	Sassafras	421
4607500	TERPINEOL NOT ARTIFICIAL MIX	Pine	371
4608010	CITRONELLOL	Citronella Grass	105
4611500	BAY RUM OR BAY WATER	Bay	38
4652500	SALTS FROM OILS, FATS NSPF	Coconut Palm	134
		Oil Palm	302
4653500	FATTY ACIDS SULPH COCONUT	Coconut Palm	134
		Oil Palm	302
4654500	FATTY ACHL SULPH COCONUT ETC	Coconut Palm	134
		Oil Palm	302
4656500	COCONUT PALM KERNEL A PM OIL	Coconut Palm	135
		Oil Palm	302
4662000	SOAP CONT CASTOR OIL	Castor Bean	84
4701600	LOGWOOD NOT CRUDE OR PROC	Logwood	262
4702300	CHESTNUT NOT CRUDE OR PROC	Chestnut	96
		Divi-divi	171
		Hemlock	230
4704000	GAMBIER	Gambier	183
4705030	QUEBRACHO WOOD	Quebracho	390
4705040	WATTLE	Wattle	487
4705500	MYROBALAN AND SUMAC	Myrobalan	295
		Sumac	443
4705740	QUEBRACHO NOT CRUDE OR PROC	Quebracho	390
4705760	WATTLE NOT CRUDE OR PROC	Wattle	488
4706000	VALONIA CRUDE OR PROCESD	Oak	300
4706500	VALONIA NOT CRUDE OR PROC	Oak	300
4902000	FATTY ACID FROM LINSEED OIL	Flax	182
4902200	FATTY ACIDS DRVD HMP KPK ETC	Hemp	230
		Kapok Tree	246
		Perilla	362
		Rape	396
		Sesame	422
		Sunflower	443
4902402	PALMETIC ACID	Miscellaneous	553
4902404	LAURIC ACID	Coconut Palm	137

TSUSA commodity		Crop/End-Use	Page
4902408	OTH FATTY ACIDS FR PALM OIL	Coconut Palm	133
		Oil Palm	302
4902410	FATTY ACIDS FR PALM OIL ETC	Coconut Palm	133
		Oil Palm	302
4902420	OTH FATTY ACIDS FR PALM OIL	Coconut Palm	133
		Oil Palm	302
4902650	FATTY ACIDS OF VEG ORIG ETC	Miscellaneous	550
4902670	FATTY ACID O VEG ORIG, NSPF	Miscellaneous	550
4904400	OTHER FATTY SALTS F LIN OIL	Flax	182
4904600	FATTY SALTS OF SESAME ETC	Hemp	231
		Kapok Tree	246
		Perilla	362
		Rape	396
		Sesame	422
		Sunflower	444
4904800	SALTS FROM COCONUT ETC	Coconut Palm	134
		Oil Palm	302
4905000	OTHER FATTY SALTS VEG ORIGIN	Miscellaneous	551
4909200	ESTERS FROM COCONUT ETC	Coconut Palm	134
		Oil Palm	302
4909400	OTHER FATTY ESTERS VEG ORIG	Miscellaneous	551
4930200	CUBE DERRIS TUBE ROOT CRUDE	Barbasco	34
		Derris	171
4930400	BARBASCO DERRIS TUBE ROOT AD	Barbasco	34
		Derris	171
4932000	NATURAL CAMPHOR CRUDE	Camphor Tree	66
4932100	NATURAL CAMPHOR ADVANCED	Camphor Tree	66
4934200	PREP CONTG 50% MONOSM GLUTAM	Miscellaneous	553
4935500	PYRETHRUM OR INSCT FLS CRUDE	Miscellaneous	554
4935600	PYRETHRUM INSECT FLOWERS ADV	Miscellaneous	555
4936600	LEVULOSE	Sweetener	641
4941000	VEGETABLE WAX CANDELILLA	Candelilla	67
4941200	VEGETABLE WAX CARNAUBA	Carnauba Palm	73
4941400	JAPAN WAX	Sumac	443
4941600	VEGETABLE WAX OURICURY	Ouricury Palm	332
4941800	VEGETABLE WAXES, NSPF	Miscellaneous	560
8350000	PLANTS ETC FOR USDA OR USBG	Miscellaneous	554
8670000	TEA FOR MFG OF CHEM PROD ETC	Miscellaneous	557
9225605	MUSHROOMS FZ, ARBITRARY NO.	Mushroom	283
9225609	STRAW MUSHROOMS NT FZ, ARB#	Mushroom	292
9225627	MUSHROM WH PREP NOV9OZ/ARB#	Mushroom	290
9225631	MUSHROOM SLICED NOV 9OZ/ARB#	Mushroom	290
9225637	MUSHRM NSPF PRP NOV9OZ,ARB#	Mushroom	290
9225643	MUSHROOM WH PREP OV 9OZ ARB#	Mushroom	291
9225647	MUSHROOM SL PREP OV 9OZ ARB#	Mushroom	291
9225653	MUSHRM NSPF PREP OV9OZ,ARB#	Mushroom	291